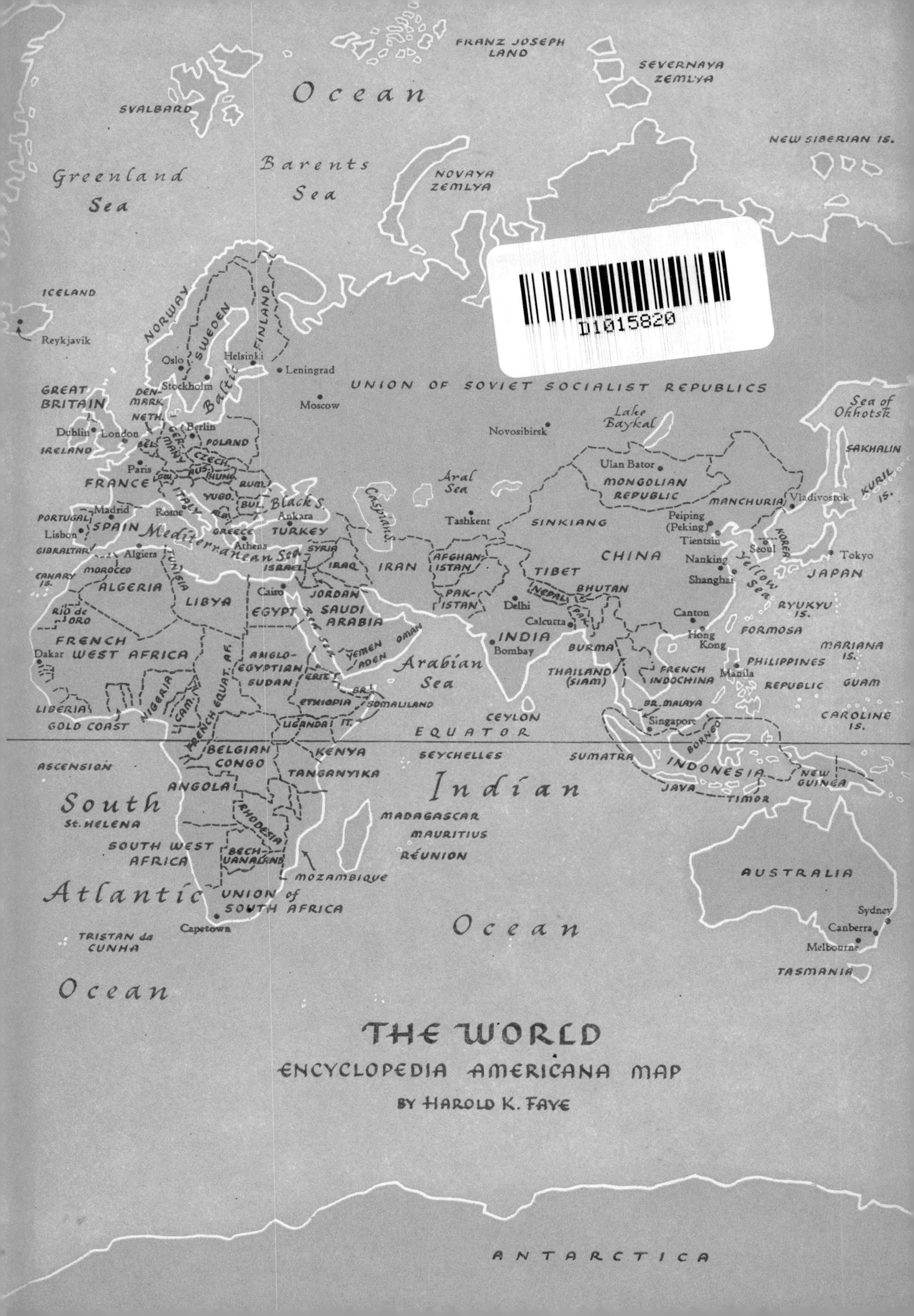

THE WORLD
ENCYCLOPEDIA AMERICANA MAP
BY HAROLD K. FAYE

The Encyclopedia AMERICANA

The International Reference Work

Complete in
Thirty Volumes

1829 1956

AMERICANA CORPORATION

New York • Chicago • Washington, D.C.

1956 EDITION

Printed in the U.S.A.

Library of Congress Catalog Card number: 56-5839

Printed and bound by
American Book–Stratford Press, Inc.
New York, U.S.A.

VOLUME XV

INDIA—JEFFERS

INDIA, Subcontinent of. The subcontinent of India contains the following political entities: Union, or Republic, of India (Bharat), Pakistan, Nepal, Bhutan, and the enclaves of French and Portuguese India. Its name comes from Greek into Latin and the languages of Europe, and means "Land of the (River) Indus." Indus, in turn, is a Greek adaptation of the old Persian and Avestan *hindu,* which is cognate to Sanskrit *sindhu,* or river, especially the River Indus.

The geography and economy of the subcontinent, its people, culture, and history, are discussed under the following headings:

For the area, population, government, and foreign policy of India and Pakistan, see INDIA, UNION OF; PAKISTAN.

1. THE LAND. India, as the term is here used, refers to that vast subcontinent which occupies more than 1,500,000 square miles of southern Asia. Triangular in shape, it extends from Iran, Afghanistan, and the Arabian Sea on the west to China, Burma, and the Bay of Bengal on the east. From its southern tip at Cape Comorin (latitude 8° N.) to the northern frontier of Kashmir (latitude 37° N.) the distance is approximately 2,000 miles; from Iran eastward to China the maximum distance is some 2,200 miles. Included within the territory are several political units. The two largest and most important, which together occupy approximately 95 per cent of the total area, are the states of India and Pakistan, newly formed in 1947.

Partly due to its size, but chiefly because of its isolation from the rest of Asia, India is generally referred to as a subcontinent. On all land frontiers it is surrounded by high barrier mountains. Not a single railroad crosses its borders. Roads and tracks are few in number and difficult to negotiate. Malaria-infested jungles and waterless deserts further impede contact between India and its neighbors.

To the north is the world's highest mountain system, the towering Himalaya. Composed of a series of ranges separated by profound valleys, the Himalaya stretch for 1,500 miles, from the gorge of the Indus on the west to the gorge of the Brahmaputra on the east. The chain has an average crestline elevation of 20,000 feet and contains many of the world's highest peaks—Mount Everest (29,141 feet), Kanchanjanga (Kinchinjunga, 28,146 feet), and Mount Godwin Austen (28,251 feet). Access across this barrier to the north is possible only during the short summer season via high passes. Where transverse valleys exist they are too deep and narrow to provide feasible routes to the interior.

Flanking the Himalaya on both west and east are north-south ranges which separate India from Iran and Burma. Though not as high as the Himalaya, the western mountains (the Sulaiman and Kirthar) are complex and generally difficult of access. Two important passes do afford passage through or around these ranges. Near the northern end of the Sulaiman is the celebrated Khyber which leads from India to Kabul, the capital of Afghanistan, and at the southern end of the Sulaiman, between this range and the Kirthar, is the Bolan gate, a broad opening which is the principal gateway to Quetta and other areas of Baluchistan. But beyond to the west, re-enforcing the barrier character of the region, is the Dasht-i-Kavir, or Great Salt Desert, of Iran. The Burmese ranges, on India's eastern frontier, are generally higher than the mountains of the west. Composed of a series of individual parallel folds oriented north and south, these Burmese ranges rise from deep, malaria-infested valleys to elevations in excess of 10,000 feet above sea level. Not a single east-west river breaks through the barrier and no easy crossing is available. Until World War II, when the Ledo and Burma roads were constructed, trails provided the only land routes between India and its eastern neighbors.

Although political frontiers penetrate the mountainous regions just described, the populous heart of India lies within the territory enclosed by the great arc of the mountain wall and by the seas and bays associated with the Indian Ocean. Within this area live about one fifth of the world's population. The census of 1941 showed a population of 389 millions. Estimates place the increase at 1.2 per cent, or nearly 5 million per year. In 1950 the population of the subcontinent was probably between 400 and 425 millions, making India one of the most densely peopled areas of the world.

Within the populous heart, however, the population is not evenly distributed. Densities vary from the almost empty Thar, or Indian, Desert region to upwards of 1,000 per square mile (of nonurban population) in eastern Bengal. Since India is predominantly dependent upon agriculture for its economic existence, land forms, climate, soil conditions, and other features of the natural environment are all-important in understanding the wide variations in population distribution.

Physiography and Geology.—South of the mountain wall, India is composed of two great physiographic divisions: the Hindustan or Indo-Gangetic plain, and peninsular India.

The Hindustan plain is one of the greatest stretches of flat alluvium in the world. Scarcely any variation in relief is present. Between the Jumna River at Delhi and the Bay of Bengal, 1,000 miles away, into which it eventually flows by way of the Ganges River, the drop in elevation is only 700 feet.

In ancient times, the present area of the Himalaya was covered by a great arm of the sea which extended westward to Europe. During Eocene, Miocene, and Pliocene times, the sea gradually disappeared and was replaced by the high Himalaya of today. Between the hills and mountains of the north and the resistant plateau of the south, a great oceanic deep was created. Here, since late Pliocene times, exceedingly fine-grained alluvial and aeolian materials of enormous depth have been accumulating. Borings have been made to 1,000 feet without encountering any variation in the size of the particles. Some authorities estimate that the same type of material extends downward to depths of 30,000 or 40,000 feet.

Although similar physiographically, the plain, in terms of population densities, historical pattern of settlement, economic activity, and climate, is really made up of two major parts. The dividing zone lies in the vicinity of Delhi, the historical gateway between east and west. It is here that the highlands of southern India and the hills and mountains of the north most nearly approach each other and the plain reaches its narrowest dimensions. West of Delhi population densities are only about one fifth what they are to the east; wheat takes predominance over rice as the principal cereal crop; and rainfall decreases markedly. West of Delhi the plain averages 300 to 400 miles in width; along the Ganges to the east it is generally less than 200 miles wide.

South of the plain is a complex region for which it is difficult to find an all-inclusive, descriptive term. For convenience the term "peninsular India" will be used for all of the territory south of the Hindustan plain. The region, however, is not all peninsular, since a sizable portion lies north of the embayed arms of the Indian Ocean and is definitely a part of the major land mass of Asia. In order to comprehend the broad outlines of the structure and geology of this vast area, it will be necessary to subdivide it into two major divisions: the coastal plains and the plateau.

The coastal plains of India occupy narrow belts between the arms of the Indian Ocean and the western and eastern edges of the plateau, known respectively as the Western and Eastern Ghats. South of Goa the western coastal area is known as the Malabar Coast. It is a densely populated alluvial plain hundreds of miles long. Lagoons and dune-covered bars separate the plain proper from the Arabian Sea on its seaward margin. The shallow character of the water, combined with the even nature of the coastline, precludes the formation of any good natural harbors. Cochin, the largest port and a center for trade in rubber, spices, coconuts, and rice, has an entirely artificial harbor. The eastern or Coromandel Coast is composed of alternating coastal plains, delta plains, and small remnant hills. Like the Malabar Coast, the Coromandel is densely populated and handicapped by the absence of good natural harbors. The chief port, Madras, like Cochin on the Malabar, has an artificial harbor.

The main portion of peninsular India is considered by geologists to be a remnant of the hypothetical continent Gondwana land, supposed to have extended through southern Africa to India. It is an area of long-continued geological stability and geologists cannot yet fully explain its origins and development. In broad outlines, it is a region of granite foundations over which there have been sedimentary deposits and lava flows. In several places basins and trenches have been formed by folding, faulting, and erosion of the surface. In general the plateau lies at elevations between 1,000 and 3,000 feet above sea level and slopes gently eastward from the Western Ghats to the Eastern Ghats. The Western Ghats have an average elevation of about 3,000 feet, while the Eastern Ghats average about one half that elevation. In the extreme south are the Nilgiri and Cardamon Hills. It is here that peninsular India attains its highest elevation in Mount Dodabetta (8,760 feet).

The nature of the plateau proper is best understood it it is divided into two major parts. By drawing a line from Banaras (Benares) to Goa, the plateau is divided into two areas which are strikingly different in character. East of this line is a region of hard crystalline rock covered with a thin layer of poor reddish soil. This region is further broken up into three massifs separated from each other by down-warped river valleys. These valleys (the Mahanadi and the Godavari) are, in general, fertile agricultural sections with dense population, whereas the massifs are areas of low productivity and sparse population. In fact, the northernmost of these massifs, the Chota Nagpur Plateau, is a wild, primitive, little-known country occupied largely by tribal groups. The Chota Nagpur Plateau does, however, contain India's chief coal deposit as well as other minerals and is the site of the works of the Tata Iron and Steel Company (Jamshedpur), one of the largest self-contained iron and steel plants in the world.

West of the Banaras-Goa line the plateau has been covered in many places with lava deposits. The southern half of this district is a rolling plains country interrupted by many small flat-topped hills. The soil is dark and fertile and cultivation is extensive. Unfortunately, much of this area is semiarid, but rainfall is generally sufficient for the growth of cotton, millet, and other drought-resistant crops. The northern portion of this part of peninsular India is composed of a series of hills, river trenches, and small plateaus which eventually terminate in the north-sloping Aravalli Hills. Perhaps the most important subregion of this portion of India is the Narbada River valley. This deeply eroded trench, some 600 miles long, forms the principal natural route between the west coast and the Ganges plain. It is a densely populated agricultural land with deep, fertile alluvial soil.

INDIA

Above: **The white marble Taj Mahal (begun in 1632) at Agra. It was built at the apogee of Mogul power in India by Shah Jahan as a tomb for his favorite wife, Mumtaz Mahall, and is considered by many to be the most beautiful building in the world.**

Herbert Mendelsohn from Shostal

Right: **The Birla Temple and reflecting pool, New Delhi.**

Victor F. Kayfetz from Shostal

Below: **At left, women carrying water from a well near Aurangabad in Hyderabad, southern India. At right, a wedding procession at Delhi.**

Cutler J. Coulson from Shostal

© Screen Traveler, from Gendreau

In Old Delhi, the courtyard of the Jami Masjid during prayers.

© Screen Traveler, from Gendreau

Pottery market at Ramnagar, in the state of Benares.

INDIA

Upper left: The Howrah Bridge, crossing the Hooghly River, and forming a means of communication between the industrial cities of Calcutta and Howrah. *Upper right:* Outdoor food sellers along Chandni Chok in Old Delhi, catering to the poorer classes who have no restaurants of their own and are forced to eat outside. *Center:* The wealthy residential section of Bombay, facing a picturesque beach on the Arabian Sea. *Below:* Outskirts of the village of Kullerie, in the Province of Sind, indicating the great need for improved living conditions, a problem facing the Indian leaders.

Photographs upper left, upper right, and below by Screen Traveler, from Gendreau; center by Black Star

INDIA

Top: Women salt workers at Mithapur, having their baskets loaded at the mine with natural salt to be refined at the mill.

Center: A betel nut vendor in the streets of Bombay, selling his hot mixture of betel nuts, betel leaves, and shell lime.

Below left: An example of overcrowded working conditions in this small shop in Calcutta where nine leatherworkers eat, sleep, and ply their trade.

Below right: A silver worker, still using crude, ancestral implements, yet producing intricate silver pieces, heats his charcoal fire, using his lungs as bellows.

Photographs top, center, and below right by Philip Gendreau, N. Y.; below left by Triangle Photo Service

INDIA

Above: **Carts and bullocks in Palitana decorated in silver in honor of a Jain woman who has fasted for six days.** ***Center left:*** **A Hindu priest praying in the streets of Bombay.** ***Center right:*** **A mother purifying her children in the sea during the festival of Shivatri, in which it is believed true devotion to Shiva, a Hindu god, can bring emancipation of the soul after death.** ***Below:*** **The Dasaswamedh Ghat, a bathing and landing place in Benares, along the Ganges River.**

Photographs by (1) Philip Gendreau, N. Y., (2) Triangle Photo Service, (3) European, (4) Screen Traveler, from Gendreau

INDIA

Examples of architecture in India. *Above:* A fortress built into the rock at Jodhpur. *Center left:* An inside court at Lallgarh Palace, with its many intricate, handcarved windows. From behind these windows women hidden forever from the view of man would secretly observe court visitors. *Center right:* The tower Kutb Minar, 238 feet high, built around 1200 A.D. by a maharaja for his wife to see the sacred river of Jumna, some distance away. *Below:* The ornately decorated Jain temple of Hathi Singh, at Ahmadabad, one of the most beautiful in India.

Photographs by (1) Screen Traveler, from Gendreau, (2, 4) Triangle Photo Service, (3) Black Star

INDIA

Left: A Maratha Hindu from Bombay State in western India. *Center:* An untouchable, the lowest caste in India, from Bombay. *Right:* A Sikh, one of a soldierly religious sect from the Punjab, northwestern India. The ornamental ring around his turban was formerly used as a weapon. Its edges razor sharp, it was hurled against the enemy like a boomerang.

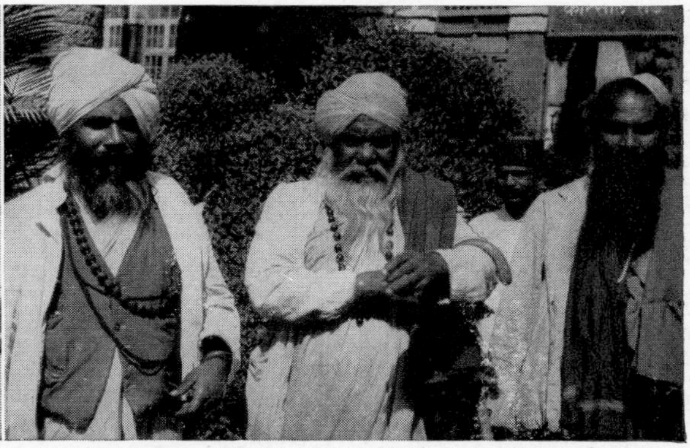

Left: Men carrying coconut offerings to the village god during a fire-walking festival. *Right:* A group of holy men or sadhus. The beads about their necks are prayer beads.

Left: Maratha woman carrying water near Bombay. These women learn from early childhood to carry almost anything on their heads. *Center:* A Hindu from Bengal wearing devotional marks on his forehead. This man is a Brahman, the highest and most cultured caste of the Hindu religion. *Right:* A wealthy Marwari bride from central India, wearing jewelry of gold and precious stones.

Photographs from (1, 3, 4, 6, 7) Black Star, (2) Philip Gendreau, N. Y., (5, 8) European

INDIA

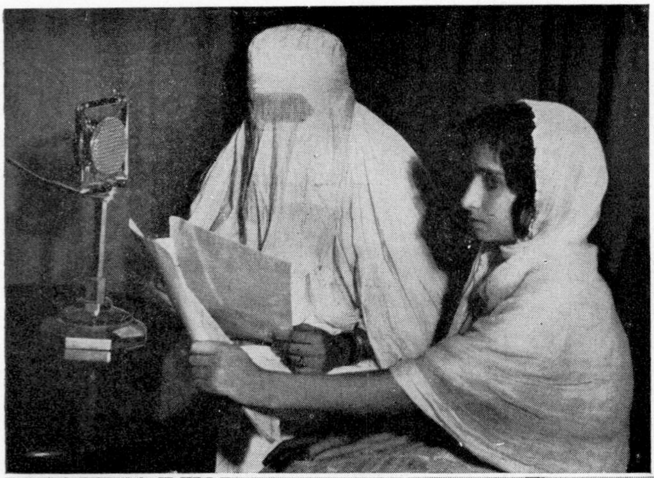

Left: Two Indian women in a broadcasting studio illustrate the dramatic contrast between the old and the new.

Below: A fine example of modern architecture: the Broadcasting House in New Delhi.

Photographs by (1) Triangle, (2, 3) Screen Traveler, from Gendreau

Above: The Moti Masjid, or Pearl Mosque, of Shah Jahan in the fort at Agra. The simple beauty of its proportions and its delicately ornate style executed in white marble make it one of India's architectural treasures.

INDIA, PAKISTAN AND CEYLON

BHUTAN
Total Population 300,000

Bumthang (cap.) F 3
Chomo Lhari (mt.) E 3
Paro Dzong E 3
Punakha F 3
Tongsa Dzong F 3

CEYLON
Total Population 6,657,339

Adam's Peak (mt.) D 7
Anuradhapura, 12,287 D 7
Badulla, 13,213 D 7
Batticaloa, 12,948 D 7
Colombo (cap.), 355,374 C 7
Dondra Head (prom.) D 7
Galle, 49,038 C 7
Jaffna, 62,922 D 7
Kalutara, 18,801 C 7
Kandy, 50,767 D 7
Kirigalpotta (mt.) D 7
Kurunegala, 13,510 D 7
Mannar, 5,190 D 7
Matara, 23,434 D 7
Moratuwa, 50,093 C 7
Negombo, 32,632 C 7
Nuwara Eliya, 9,840 D 7
Pidurutalagala (mt.) D 7
Puttalam, 7,764 C 7
Ratnapura, 12,367 C 7
Tangalla, 6,891 D 7
Trincomalee, 29,146 D 7

INDIA
Total Population 356,829,485

Abor (hills) F 3
Abu Road, 9,935 B 4
Adilabad, 11,128 C 5
Adoni, 35,431 C 5
Agartala, 17,693 F 4
Agra, 375,665 C 3
Ahmadabad, 788,333 B 4
Ahmadnagar, 70,418 B 5
Ahmedabad (Ahmadabad) 788,333 B 4
Ajanta, 3,560 C 4
Ajmer, 196,633 B 3
Ajmer (state), 693,372 B 3
Akola, 62,564 C 4
Alibag, 6,526 B 5
Aligarh, 141,618 C 3
Alipore, 46,332 E 2
Allahabad, 332,295 D 3
Alleppey, 116,278 C 7
Almora, 10,995 C 3
Alwar, 54,143 C 3
Amalner, 34,694 B 4
Ambala, 107,383 C 2
Ambikapur, 8,517 D 4
Amin Divi (isls.), 6,177 B 6
Amraoti, 61,971 C 4
Amreli, 25,485 B 4
Amritsar, 325,747 B 2
Anai Mudi (mt.) C 6
Anakapalle, 29,249 D 5
Anantapur, 21,482 C 6
Andaman (isls.), 21,316 F 6
Andaman and Nicobar Is. (terr.), 30,971 F 6
Andheri, 38,493 B 7
Andhra (state) C 5
Androth (isl.), 2.492 B 6
Arcot, 16,583 C 6
Arrah, 53,122 D 3
Aruppukkottai, 35,001 C 7
Asansol, 55,797 E 4
Assam (state), 9,043,707 F 3
Aurangabad, 66,725 C 5
Azamgarh, 24,307 D 3
Bagalkot, 24,521 C 5
Bahraich, 39,963 D 3
Baidyabati, 25,825 E 1
Balaghat, 11,482 D 4
Balasore, 19,405 E 4
Ballia, 23,520 D 3
Bally, 50,397 E 1
Balrampur, 35,461 D 3
Banaras, 355,777 D 3
Banas (river) C 3
Banda, 27,070 D 3
Bandar (Masulipatnam), 59,146 D 5
Bandra, 71,789 B 8
Bangalore, 778,977 C 6
Bankura, 46,617 E 4
Banswara, 12,772 B 4
Bareilly, 208,083 C 3
Barmer, 12,051 B 3
Barnagore, 54,451 E 1
Baroda, 211,407 B 4
Barrackpore, 59,717 E 1
Barsi, 36,870 C 5
Barwani, 12,569 B 4

† including suburbs

Basirhat, 26,348 E 4
Batala, 44,458 C 2
Beawar, 36,720 B 3
Belgaum, 75,482 B 5
Bellary, 56,148 C 5
Benares (Banaras), 355,777 D 3
Bengal, West (state), 24,810,308 E 4
Berhampore, 41,558 E 4
Berhampur, 43,536 D 5
Bettegiri (Gadag), 56,283 C 5
Bettiah, 30,309 D 3
Betwa (river) C 4
Bezwada (Vijayavada), 161,198 D 5
Bhadrakh, 19,550 E 4
Bhadreswar, 27,673 E 1
Bhagalpur, 114,530 E 4
Bhandara, 19,708 D 4
Bharatpur, 35,541 C 3
Bhatinda, 24,833 B 2
Bhatpara, 134,916 E 1
Bhavnagar, 137,951 B 4
Bhilsa, 14,472 C 4
Bhilwara, 15,169 B 3
Bhima (river) C 5
Bhimavaram, 21,049 D 5
Bhiwani, 43,921 C 3
Bhopal, 102,333 C 4
Bhopal (state), 836,474 C 4
Bhubaneshwar E 4
Bhuj, 26,331 A 4
Bhusaval, 36,352 C 4
Bidh, 15,222 C 5
Bihar, 54,551 E 3
Bihar (state), 40,225,947 D 4
Bijapur, 48,968 C 5
Bijnor, 27,900 C 3
Bikaner, 117,113 B 3
Bilaspur, 37,460 D 4
Bimlipatam, 9,914 D 5
Bina-Etawa, 8,979 C 4
Bobbili, 22,090 D 5
Bodinayakkanur, 28,435 C 7
Bombay, 2,839,270 B 8
Bombay (state), 35,956,150 B 4
Brahmaputra (river) F 3
Brijnagar, 11,549 C 4
Broach, 55,810 B 4
Budaun, 52,077 C 3
Budge-Budge, 32,394 D 2
Bundi, 20,846 C 3
Burdwan, 62,910 E 4
Burhanpur, 53,987 C 4
Calcutta, 2,548,677 E 2
Calicut, 158,724 C 6
Cambay, 34,941 B 4
Camorta (isl.) F 7
Cannanore, 34,649 B 6
Car Nicobar (isl.), 8,000 F 7
Cardamum (isl.) B 6
Cauvery (river) C 6
Cawnpore (Kanpur), 705,383 D 3
Chamba, 6,597 C 2
Chambal (river) C 3
Champdani, 31,833 E 1
Chanda, 35,730 C 5
Chandernagore, 47,785 E 1
Chandigarh C 2
Chapra, 55,142 E 3
Cherial (river) D 2
Cherrapunji F 3
Chetlat (isl.) B 6
Chhatarpur, 13,210 C 4
Chhindwara, 21,916 C 4
Chicacole, 22,249 D 5
Chidambaram, 26,212 D 6
Chikmagalur, 15,383 C 6
Chilka (lake) E 5
Chingleput, 17,829 D 6
Chinsura and Hooghly, 49,081 E 1
Chirala, 27,086 D 5
Chitaldroog, 14,528 C 6
Chittoor, 27,835 C 6
Churu, 28,269 B 3
Cocanada (Kakinada), 100,054 D 5
Cochin, 26,320 C 6
Coco (chanl.) F 6
Coimbatore, 197,755 C 6
Colaba (point) B 8
Colair (lake) D 5
Comorin (cape) C 7
Conjeeveram (Kanchipuram), 74,635 D 6
Cooch Behar, 16,000 E 3
Coondapur, 9,537 B 6
Coorg (state), 229,405 C 6
Cuddalore, 60,632 D 6
Cuddapah, 28,246 C 6
Cumbum, 22,177 C 5
Cutch (Kutch) (state), 567,606 A 4
Cuttack, 102,505 E 4
Dabhoi, 21,139 B 4

Daltonganj, 13,943 D 4
Damodar (river) E 4
Damoh, 26,795 C 4
Darbhanga, 69,203 E 3
Darjeeling, 25,873 E 3
Datia, 22,086 C 3
Davangere, 31,759 C 6
Deccan (reg.) C 6
Dehra Dun, 144,216 C 2
Delhi, 914,790 C 3
Delhi (state), 1,744,072 C 3
Deoghar, 19,792 E 4
Deoria, 15,198 D 3
Dewas, 22,949 C 4
Dhamtari, 14,071 D 4
Dhar, 22,015 B 4
Dharamsala, 9,653 C 2
Dharwar, 47,992 B 5
Dholpur, 21,311 C 3
Dhoraji, 37,647 B 4
Dhubri, 12,699 E 3
Dhulia, 54,406 B 4
Dibrugarh, 23,191 G 3
Dindigul, 56,275 C 6
Drug, 16,766 D 4
Dum Dum, 39,434 E 1
Duncan (passg.) F 6
Durgapur E 4
Dwarka, 10,876 A 4
Elephanta (isl.) B 8
Ellichpur, 31,475 C 4
Ellore (Eluru), 64,911 D 5
Eluru, 64,911 D 5
English Bazaar, 23,333 E 3
Ernakulam, 46,790 C 6
Erode, 39,483 C 6
Etawah, 53,114 C 3
Faizabad, 57,632 D 3
False (point), E 4
False Divi (point) D 5
Farrukhabad (Fatehgarh), 69,418 C 3
Fatehgarh, 69,418 C 3
Fatehpur, 23,253 B 3
Fatehpur, 27,436 D 3
Ferozepore, 82,502 B 2
Firozabad, 40,572 C 3
Fyzabad (Faizabad), 57,632 D 3
Gadag, 56,283 C 5
Ganges (river) E 3
Garden Reach, 109,160 E 2
Garulia, 20,150 E 1
Gauhati, 29,598 F 3
Gaya, 133,700 E 4
Ghat Kopar, 18,176 B 7
Ghats, Eastern (mt. range) D 5
Ghats, Western (mt. range) B 5
Ghazipur, 31,326 D 3
Giridih, 25,326 E 4
Goalpara, 7,793 F 3
Godavari (river) C 5
Godhra, 41,986 B 4
Gogra (river) D 3
Golconda (ruins) C 5
Gonda, 21,567 D 3
Gorakhpur, 132,436 D 3
Great (chanl.) F 7
Great Coco (isl.) F 6
Great Nicobar (isl.) F 7
Gulbarga, 77,191 C 5
Guna, 15,328 C 4
Guntur, 125,255 D 5
Gwalior, 34,488 C 3
Gwalior and Lashkar, 241,577 C 3
Hanamkonda, 133,130 C 5
Hardoi, 24,252 C 3
Hardwar, 40,823 C 3
Hassan, 14,596 C 6
Hathras, 46,994 C 3
Hazaribagh, 24,918 E 4
Himachal Pradesh (state), 1,109,466 C 2
Himalaya (mt. range) C 2
Hinganghat, 28,040 C 4
Hingoli, 14,601 C 5
Hissar, 28,618 C 3
Hooghly (river) E 2
Hooghly and Chinsura, 49,081 E 1
Hospet, 26,023 C 5
Howrah, 433,630 E 2
Hubli, 129,609 B 5
Hyderabad, 1,085,722 C 5
Hyderabad (state), 18,655,108 C 5
Ichchapuram, 11,159 E 5
Imphal, 99,716 F 4
Indian (Thar) (des.) B 3
Indore, 310,859 C 4
Indravati (river) D 5
Itarsi, 14,269 C 4
Jabalpur (Jubbulpore), 256,998 D 4
Jagdalpur, 11,304 D 5
Jaipur, 291,130 C 3
Jaisalmer, 7,340 B 3

Jalgaon, 48,596 C 4
Jalna, 48,423 C 4
Jalpaiguri, 27,766 E 3
Jamalpur, 39,401 E 4
Jamnagar, 104,419 A 4
Jamshedpur, 218,162 E 4
Jaora, 25,501 C 4
Jaunpur, 44,833 D 3
Jeypore, 12,504 D 5
Jhansi, 127,365 C 3
Jhunjhunu, 16,874 C 3
Jind, 14,909 C 3
Jodhpur, 180,717 B 3
Jorhat, 11,664 F 3
Jubbulpore, 256,998 D 4
Jullundur, 168,816 C 2
Jumna (river) D 3
Junagadh, 58,111 B 4
Kadayanallur, 29,652 C 7
Kakinada, 100,054 D 5
Kalyan, 31,356 B 5
Kamarhati, 42,545 E 1
Kamet (mt.) C 2
Kamptee, 26,930 C 4
Kanchipuram, 74,635 D 6
Kandla B 4
Kandakur, 10,396 C 5
Kanker, 5,173 D 4
Kannauj, 21,994 C 3
Kanpur, 705,383 D 3
Karad, 17,996 B 5
Karaikudi, 28,908 C 7
Karauli, 19,177 C 3
Karikal, 23,008 D 6
Karnal, 37,444 C 3
Karur, 27,575 C 6
Kasaragod, 11,566 B 6
Kasganj,, 28,465 C 3
Katihar, 26,326 E 3
Katni, 24,630 D 4
Kavaratti (isl.), 1,606 B 6
Keonjhargarh, 9,004 E 4
Khamgaon, 26,402 C 4
Khammam (Khammamett) 18,982 D 5
Khandwa, 38,493 C 4
Kharagpur, 129,636 E 4
Khasi (hills) F 3
Khurja, 35,376 C 3
Kirkee, 26,285 B 5
Kishangarh, 14,459 C 3
Kistna (river) C 5
Kohima, 3,507 F 3
Koil (Aligarh), 141,618 C 3
Kolar, 19,006 C 6
Kolar Gold Fields, 159,084 C 6
Kolhapur, 136,835 B 5
Konnagar and Rishra, 37,432 E 1
Kotah, 45,032 C 3
Kottayam, 33,364 C 7
Kovur, 10,601 D 6
Kozhikode (Calicut), 158,724 C 6
Krishnagar, 32,016 E 4
Kumbakonam, 67,008 C 6
Kurla, 39,066 B 8
Kurnool, 45,250 C 5
Kutch (gulf) A 4
Kutch (state), 567,606 A 4
Kutch, Rann of (lake) A 4
Laccadive (isls.), 18,393 B 6
Laful, F 7
Lansdowne, 6,174 C 3
Lashkar, 113,718 C 3
Lashkar and Gwalior, 241,577 C 3
Latur, 24,985 C 5
Ledo G 3
Little Andaman (isl.) F 6
Little Nicobar (isl.) F 7
Lucknow, 496,861 D 3
Ludhiana, 153,795 C 2
Lumding, 3,864 F 3
Lushai (hills) F 4
Madhya Bharat (state), 7,954,154 C 4
Madhya Pradesh (state), 21,247,533 C 4
Madras, 1,416,056 D 6
Madras (state) C 6
Madurai (Madura), 361,781 C 7
Mahabaleshvar, 5,090 B 5
Mahanadi (river) E 4
Mahbubnagar, 16,462 C 5
Mahe, 18,293 C 6
Mahim (bay) B 8
Mahuva, 22,058 B 4
Malabar (hill) A 8
Malad, 12,212 B 7
Malegaon, 39,924 B 4
Maler Kotla, 29,321 C 2
Malvan, 25,677 B 5
Mandla, 12,209 D 4
Mandsaur, 21,972 B 4
Mandvi, 28,750 A 4
Mangalore, 117,083 B 6

INDIA, PAKISTAN AND CEYLON

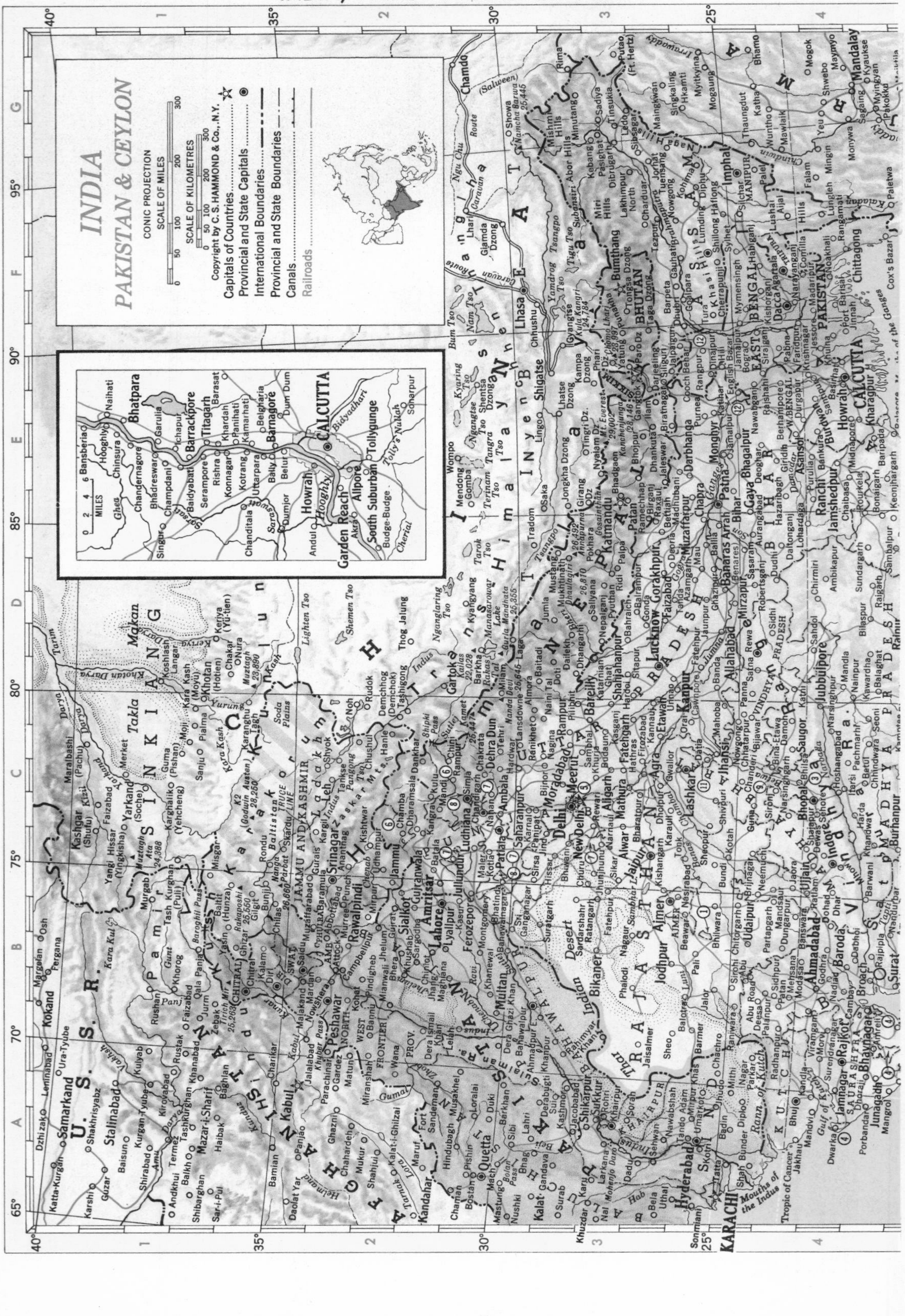

INDIA, PAKISTAN AND CEYLON

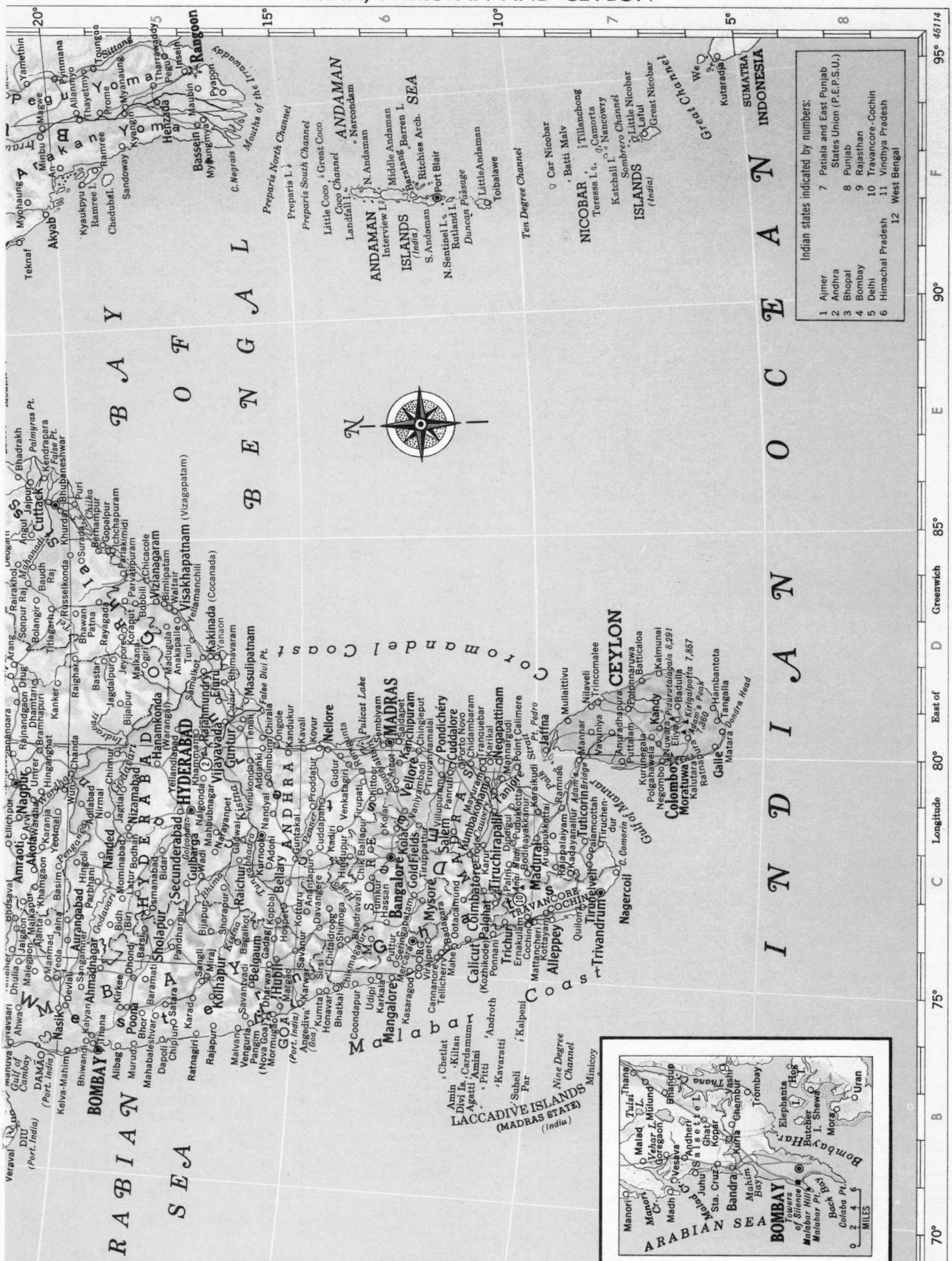

ARABIAN SEA
BAY OF BENGAL
INDIAN OCEAN
ANDAMAN SEA
CEYLON
HYDERABAD
MADRAS
BOMBAY
LACCADIVE ISLANDS (MADRAS STATE) (India)
ANDAMAN ISLANDS (India)
NICOBAR ISLANDS (India)
SUMATRA
INDONESIA
Coromandel Coast
Malabar Coast
Indian states indicated by numbers:
1 Ajmer
2 Andhra
3 Bhopal
4 Bombay
5 Delhi
6 Himachal Pradesh
7 Patiala and East Punjab States Union (P.E.P.S.U.)
8 Punjab
9 Rajasthan
10 Travancore-Cochin
11 Vindhya Pradesh
12 West Bengal
Longitude East of Greenwich
46114

INDIA, PAKISTAN AND CEYLON (Continued)

Mangrol, 18,818 .... A 4
Manipur (state), 577,635 .... F 4
Mannar (gulf) .... C 7
Mannargudi, 23,288 .... C 6
Manori .... A 7
Masulipatnam, 59,146 .... D 5
Mathura, 105,773 .... C 3
Mattancheri, 53,346 .... C 7
Mau, 29,357 .... D 3
Mayavaram (Mayuram), 32,670 .... D 6
Mayuram, 32,670 .... D 6
Meerut, 233,183 .... C 3
Mercara, 7,112 .... C 6
Mhow, 34,823 .... C 4
Middle Andaman (isl.) .... F 6
Midnapore, 43,171 .... E 4
Minicoy (isl.), 3,093 .... B 7
Miraj, 32,455 .... B 5
Miri (hills) .... F 3
Mirzapur, 70,944 .... D 4
Mishmi (hills) .... G 3
Monghyr, 63,150 .... E 3
Moradabad, 161,854 .... C 3
Morvi, 37,048 .... B 4
Murud, 8,436 .... B 5
Murwara (Katni), 24,630 .... D 4
Mutta (Mathura), 105,773 .... C 3
Muzaffarpur, 54,139 .... D 3
Mysore, 244,323 .... C 6
Mysore (state) .... C 6
Nadiad, 46,510 .... B 4
Naga (hills) .... F 3
Nagercoil, 51,657 .... C 7
Nagina, 26,077 .... C 3
Nagpur, 449,009 .... C 4
Naihati, 42,200 .... E 1
Naini Tal, 9,539 .... C 3
Nancowry (isl.) .... F 7
Nanda Devi (mt.) .... C 2
Nanded, 65,018 .... C 5
Nandurbar, 22,139 .... B 4
Nandyal, 25,886 .... C 5
Narbada (river) .... C 4
Narnaul, 23,063 .... C 3
Narsingpur, 12,908 .... C 4
Nasik, 55,524 .... B 5
Nasirabad, 17,804 .... B 3
Navanagar (Jamnagar), 104,419 .... A 4
Navsari, 35,445 .... B 4
Neemuch, 17,074 .... C 4
Negapattinam, 52,937 .... D 6
Nellore, 56,315 .... D 6
New Delhi (cap.), 276,314 .... C 3
Nicobar (isls.), 12,452 .... F 7
Nine Degree (chanl.) .... B 7
Nizamabad, 55,202 .... C 5
North Andaman (isl.) .... F 6
Nowgong, 12,972 .... F 3
Ongole, 21,184 .... C 5
Ootacamund, 29,850 .... C 6
Orai, 17,242 .... C 3
Orissa (state), 14,645,946 .... D 5
Osmanabad, 14,414 .... C 5
Palamcottah, 30,967 .... C 7
Palanpur, 21,643 .... B 4
Palghat, 55,160 .... C 6
Palk (str.) .... C 7
Palmyras (point) .... E 4
Palni, 24,706 .... C 6
Pandharpur, 33,329 .... C 5
Panihati, 27,410 .... E 1
Panipat, 37,837 .... C 3
Parlakimidi, 21,042 .... D 5
Parvatipuram, 19,456 .... D 5
Patan, 39,549 .... B 4
Patiala, 69,850 .... C 2
Patiala and East Punjab, States Union, (state), 3,493,685 .... C 2
Patna, 283,479 .... E 3
Penganga (river) .... C 5
Penner (river) .... C 6
Pilibhit, 44,709 .... C 3
Pondichery, 59,835 .... D 6
Ponnani, 17,838 .... C 6
Poona, 480,982 .... B 5
Porbandar, 48,493 .... A 4
Port Blair, 4,111 .... F 6
Preparis (isl.) .... F 6
Proddatur, 26,961 .... C 6
Pudukkottai, 34,188 .... C 6
Pulicat (lake) .... D 6
Punjab (state), 12,641,205 .... C 2
Puri, 41,055 .... E 5
Purulia, 30,445 .... E 4
Quilon, ... C 7
Raichur, 53,858 .... C 5
Raipur, 63,465 .... D 4
Rairakhol, 105,276 .... D 4
Rajahmundry, 105,276 .... D 5
Rajapalaiyam, 46,289 .... C 7
Rajasthan (state), 15,290,797 .... B 3
Rajkot, 132,069 .... B 4
Rajnandgaon, 19,039 .... D 4
Rajpipla, 15,855 .... B 4

† including suburbs

Rampur, 134,277 .... C 3
Ranchi, 106,849 .... E 4
Ratlam, 44,939 .... B 4
Ratnagiri, 17,904 .... B 5
Rewa, 26,008 .... D 4
Rewari, 30,673 .... C 3
Rishra and Konnagar, 37,432 .... E 1
Rourkela .... D 4
Saharanpur, 148,435 .... C 3
Saidapet, 41,347 .... D 6
Salem, 202,335 .... C 6
Salsette (isl.) .... B 7
Samalkot, 22,349 .... D 5
Sambalpur, 17,079 .... D 4
Sambhal, 53,887 .... C 3
Sambhar (lake) .... B 3
Sangli, 37,756 .... B 5
Santa Cruz .... B 8
Santipur, 29,892 .... E 4
Sardarshahr, 26,048 .... B 3
Sasaram, 27,201 .... D 4
Satara, 36,405 .... B 5
Satpura (mt. range) .... C 4
Saugor, 63,933 .... C 4
Saurashtra (state), 4,137,359 .... B 4
Savantvadi, 10,024 .... B 5
Secunderabad, 225,127 .... C 5
Sembiyam, 37,625 .... D 6
Serampore, 55,339 .... E 1
Seringapatam, 7,678 .... C 6
Shahjahanpur, 104,835 .... D 3
Sheopur, 8,378 .... C 3
Shillong, 38,192 .... F 3
Shimoga, 27,712 .... C 6
Sholapur, 266,050 .... C 5
Shorapur, 11,836 .... C 5
Sibsagar, 7,559 .... G 3
Sidhpur, 24,565 .... B 4
Sikar, 32,334 .... C 3
Siliguri, 10,487 .... E 3
Simla, 18,348 .... C 2
Sirohi, 9,501 .... B 3
Sironj, 13,906 .... C 4
Sitapur, 35,249 .... D 3
Sombrero (chanl.) .... F 7
Son (river) .... D 4
Sonpur Raj, 9,065 .... D 4
South Andaman (isl.) .... F 6
South Suburban, 104,055 .... E 2
Sri Ganganagar, 16,136 .... B 3
Subansiri (river) .... F 3
Surat, 223,182 .... B 4
Surendranagar, 21,622 .... B 4
Tanda, 26,128 .... D 3
Tanjore, 100,680 .... C 6
Tapti (river) .... C 4
Tehri .... C 2
Tellicherry, 36,320 .... B 6
Ten Degree (chanl.) .... F 7
Tenali, 40,639 .... D 5
Thana, 29,751 .... B 7
Thar (Indian) (des.) .... B 3
Tinnevelly (Tirunelveli), 60,676 .... C 7
Tiruchirapalli, 218,921 .... C 6
Tirunelveli, 60,676 .... C 7
Tiruppattur, 23,008 .... C 6
Tiruvannamalai, 33,575 .... C 6
Titagarh, 57,416 .... E 1
Tiobalawe .... F 6
Tollygunge, 149,817 .... E 2
Tollys Nullah (river) .... E 2
Tonk, 38,650 .... C 3
Towers of Silence .... A 8
Tranquebar, 11,111 .... D 6
Travancore-Cochin (state), 9,280,425 .... C 7
Trichinopoly (Tiruchirapalli), 218,921 .... C 6
Trichur, 57,524 .... C 6
Tripura (state), 639,029 .... F 4
Trivandrum, 186,931 .... C 7
Trombay .... B 8
Tuensang .... F 3
Tumkur, 21,893 .... C 6
Tungabhadra (river) .... C 5
Tuticorin, 75,614 .... C 7
Udaipur, 59,648 .... B 4
Ujjain, 129,817 .... C 4
Umrer, 19,361 .... C 4
Unao (Unnao), 20,107 .... D 3
Unnao, 20,107 .... D 3
Uttar Pradesh (state), 63,215,742 .... C 3
Uttarpara, 13,610 .... E 1
Vaniyambadi, 31,281 .... C 6
Vellore, 106,024 .... C 6
Vengurla, 21,663 .... B 5
Veraval, 30,275 .... B 4
Vijayavada, 161,198 .... D 5
Villupuram, 23,829 .... C 6
Vindhya (mt. range) .... C 4
Vindhya Pradesh (state), 3,574,690 .... D 4
Virajpet, 4,106 .... C 6
Viramgam, 27,834 .... B 4
Visakhapatnam, 108,042 .... D 5

Vizagapatam (Visakhapatnam), 108,042 .... D 5
Vizianagaram, 51,749 .... D 5
Wadhwan (Surendranagar), 21,622 .... B 4
Waltair, 133,130 .... D 5
Warangal (Hanamkonda), 133,130 .... D 5
Wardha, 28,359 .... C 4
West Bengal (state), 24,810,308 .... E 4
Wun, 12,225 .... C 4
Yanaon, 5,853 .... D 5
Yellamanchili, 9,054 .... D 5
Yellandlapad, 15,907 .... C 5
Yeotmal, 26,555 .... C 4

KASHMIR

Total Population 4,270,000

Anantnag, 11,985 .... C 2
Baltistan (region) .... C 1
Baltit .... B 1
Baramula, 12,724 .... B 2
Chilas .... B 1
Ghizar .... B 1
Gilgit, 4,671 .... B 1
Godwin Austen (K2) (mt.) .... C 1
Gurais .... C 2
Hunza (Baltit) .... B 1
Jammu, 50,379 .... C 2
K2 (Godwin Austen) (mt.) .... C 1
Karakorum (mt. range) .... C 1
Kargil .... C 2
Kishtwar, 3,235 .... C 2
Kunlun (mt. range) .... C 1
Ladakh (region) .... C 2
Leh, 3,372 .... C 2
Mirpur, 8,556 .... B 2
Muzaffarabad, 4,571 .... B 2
Nanga Parbat (mt.) .... B 1
Punch, 8,608 .... B 2
Rakaposhi (mt.) .... B 1
Rondu .... C 1
Shyok .... C 2
Skardu, 2,537 .... C 1
Soda Plains .... C 1
Srinagar (cap.), 207,787 .... C 2
Tankse .... C 2
Udhampur, 4,666 .... B 2
Yasin .... B 1
Zaskar (mts.) .... C 2

NEPAL

Total Population 6,283,649

Annapurna (mt.) .... D 3
Bhadgaon, 93,176 .... E 3
Bheri (river) .... D 3
Bhojpur .... E 3
Biratnagar .... E 3
Birganj .... E 3
Dailekh .... D 3
Dhankuta .... E 3
Dhaulagiri (mt.) .... D 3
Doti .... D 3
Everest (mt.) .... E 3
Gosainthan (mt.) .... E 3
Ilam .... E 3
Jumla .... D 3
Katmandu (cap.), 108,805 .... D 3
Mukhtinath .... D 3
Mustang .... D 3
Nepalganj .... D 3
Palpa .... D 3
Patan, 104,928 .... E 3
Pokhara .... D 3
Ramechhap .... E 3
Sallyana .... D 3

PAKISTAN

Total Population 75,843,000

Abbottabad, 27,602 .... B 2
Ahmadpur East, 20,404 .... B 3
Amb (state), 48,656 .... B 2
Bahawalpur, 41,646 .... B 3
Bahawalpur (state), 1,820,000 .... B 3
Baluchistan (prov.), 1,178,000 .... A 3
Bannu, 27,199 .... B 2
Barisal, 89,278 .... F 4
Beji (river) .... A 3
Bela, 3,905 .... A 3
Bengal, East (prov.), 42,119,000 .... E 4
Bogra, 24,996 .... E 4
Bolan (pass) .... A 3
Campbellpur, 17,671 .... B 2
Chenab (river) .... B 2
Chiniot, 39,042 .... B 2
Chitral .... B 1
Chitral (state), 107,000 .... B 1
Chittagong, †269,000 .... F 4
Comilla, 47,195 .... F 4

Coxs Bazar, 5,945 .... F 4
Dacca, †401,000 .... F 4
Dera Ghazi Khan, 35,909 .... B 3
Dera Ismail Khan, 41,613 .... B 2
Derabugti .... A 3
Dinajpur, 34,271 .... E 3
Dir .... B 1
Dir (state), 148,648 .... B 1
East Bengal (prov.), 42,119,000 .... E 4
Faridpur, 25,287 .... E 4
Fort Sandeman, 9,353 .... A 2
Gujranwala, 114,193 .... B 2
Gujrat, 46,971 .... B 2
Hab (river) .... A 3
Hindu Kush (mt. range) .... B 1
Hyderabad, 241,801 .... A 3
Indus (river) .... A 3
Jacobabad, 22,827 .... A 3
Jamalpur, 26,952 .... E 4
Jessore, 23,867 .... E 4
Jhang-Maghiana, 73,397 .... B 2
Jhelum, 38,567 .... B 2
Jhelum (river) .... B 2
Kalat, 2,463 .... A 3
Karachi (cap.), 1,006,416 .... A 4
Kasur, 63,086 .... B 2
Khairpur, 18,184 .... A 3
Khairpur (state), 320,000 .... A 3
Khanewal, 37,915 .... B 2
Khulna, 41,409 .... E 4
Khushab, 20,467 .... B 2
Khyber (pass) .... B 2
Kishorganj, 19,034 .... F 4
Kohat, 40,534 .... B 2
Kunar (river) .... B 1
Lahore, 849,333 .... B 2
Larkana, 33,247 .... A 3
Lyallpur, 179,127 .... B 2
Malakand .... B 2
Mardan, 48,827 .... B 2
Mianwali, 23,340 .... B 2
Mir means mountain, (Persian)
Mirpur Khas, 40,412 .... A 3
Mohenjo Daro (ruins) .... A 3
Montgomery, 50,185 .... B 2
Multan, 190,122 .... B 2
Mymensingh, 44,527 .... F 4
Nagar Parkar .... B 4
Narayanganj, 68,373 .... F 4
Nawabganj, 23,311 .... E 4
Nawabshah, 34,201 .... A 3
North West Frontier (prov.), 5,699,000 .... B 2
Nowshera, 23,114 .... B 2
Pabna, 31,924 .... E 4
Peshawar, 151,435 .... B 2
Phulra (state), 8,709 .... B 2
Pindigheb, 10,150 .... B 2
Port Jinnah .... E 4
Punjab (prov.), 18,814,000 .... B 2
Quetta, 83,892 .... A 2
Rajshahi, 39,662 .... E 4
Rangamati .... F 4
Rangpur, 30,501 .... E 3
Ravi (river) .... B 2
Rawalpindi, 236,877 .... B 2
Saidu .... B 2
Sargodha, 78,447 .... B 2
Sehwan, 3,827 .... A 3
Shikarpur, 45,335 .... A 3
Sialkot, 156,378 .... B 2
Sibi, 8,854 .... A 3
Sind (prov.), 4,619,000 .... A 3
Sirajganj, 37,545 .... E 4
Sui .... A 3
Sukkur, 77,026 .... A 3
Sulaiman (mt. range) .... A 3
Sutlej (river) .... B 3
Swat (state), 569,000 .... B 2
Sylhet, 32,773 .... F 4
Tando Adam, 21,260 .... A 3
Teknaf .... F 4
Tirich Mir (mt.) .... B 1
Wana .... A 2
Zhob (river) .... A 2

PORTUGUESE INDIA

Total Population 637,846

Angediva (isl.) .... B 6
Damão, 9,027 .... B 4
Damão (dist.), 69,005 .... B 4
Diu, 5,215 .... B 4
Diu (dist.), 21,138 .... B 4
Goa (dist.), 547,703 .... B 5
Margão, 17,933 .... B 5
Mormugão (Vasco da Gama), 14,140 .... B 5
Nova Goa (Pangim) (cap.), 31,950 .... B 5
Pangim (cap.), 31,950 .... B 5

SIKKIM

Total Population 137,725

Gangtok (cap.) .... E 3
Kanchenjunga (mt.) .... E 3

Climate.—Only the barest outlines of the unusual meteorological conditions which produce India's unique climatic conditions can be presented here, but a few generalizations will help in an understanding of India's climate.

Except for a small section of northwestern India, practically all of the subcontinent's rainfall results from a gigantic land-sea breeze, operating on a seasonal basis, known as the monsoon. In the period of low sun (winter in the middle latitudes or the cool season in India) winds are prevailingly from the northeast. In the period of high sun (summer in middle latitudes) winds are mainly from the southwest. The chief reason for reversal of wind direction is the difference in pressures which result from the differential heating of land and water at the various seasons of the year. In the period of high sun the land is rapidly heated, a low pressure is created, and air flows north and northeastward from the surrounding cooler seas to the land mass of India. This is the period of the southwest monsoon. During the period of low sun (the northeast monsoon) the land cools more quickly than the surrounding seas and air flows outward from India in a general southerly or southwesterly direction.

During and just preceding the period of the southwest monsoon the northward-moving air becomes saturated over the vast expanses of the Indian Ocean. When it strikes the elevated portions of the subcontinent it is suddenly lifted and cooled, and heavy precipitation results. Probably 85 per cent of all of India's rain comes at this period. The areas of heaviest precipitation are those sections where cooling is greatest and most sudden: along the Malabar Coast on the seaward slopes of the Western Ghats, and in Bengal where the air is lifted by the outliers of the Himalaya and the hills associated with the Burmese borderlands. On the slopes of the Western Ghats, rainfall of over 200 inches is not uncommon; on the hills of Cherrapunji, just north of the Ganges-Brahmaputra Delta, the average precipitation is 457 inches per year. Rainfall in the Ganges Valley decreases rapidly from eastern Bengal westward. In the delta country precipitation averages 60 to 80 inches per year; at Allahabad it is 40 inches; at Delhi, 25 inches; at Lahore, 21 inches. Above Delhi generally arid and semiarid conditions prevail in the lowlands. Most of the Punjab and all of the Thar Desert and Sind do not receive enough rainfall to support crop agriculture without irrigation, except along the Himalayan fringe and in portions of the northern Punjab. This last region has enough winter rainfall for a limited production of winter (ragi or raggee) crops, especially winter wheat.

The plateau of India is relatively dry. The air as it passes over the high edges of the plateau loses a major portion of its moisture. Moreover, in descending from the higher slopes to the lower level of the plateau, the air is warmed and its moisture-holding capacity is increased. Fairly heavy precipitation (generally over 40 inches) occurs in the northeast, where the winds sweep in from the Bay of Bengal toward the heart of India. Throughout the balance of the plateau, rainfall averages between 20 and 40 inches. During the southwest monsoon period, the southeast coast of India gets little rain. Because of the configuration of the country, the winds moving up the Bay of Bengal bypass this area. Winds from the west have lost most of their moisture on the windward side of the Western Ghats and on the Nilgiri and Cardamon Hills.

Climatic Regions.—The character of its wind system governs in large measure the seasonal distribution of India's precipitation. Topography controls to a marked degree the amount of rain occurring in any particular place. As a result, five major climatic regions can be recognized:

(1) The Malabar Coast and eastern Bengal areas have what is known as a tropical rainforest climate. Rainfall is heavy (generally over 100 inches) and is concentrated in the period of the southwest monsoon. But there is either some rainfall in other seasons of the year, or the soil is sufficiently moisture-retentive to support vegetation which requires constantly moist conditions. The rubber tree (*Hevea brasiliensis*), for example, which cannot withstand any extended period of drought, thrives in Malabar. Temperatures are constantly high, averaging well over 75°F. every month of the year.

(2) Most of the plateau and all of the middle and upper Ganges Valley have a tropical savanna climate. Rainfall is generally less here than in the tropical rainforest, averaging between 40 and 60 inches annually, but occasionally exceeding 100 inches. The principal difference between this climate and the tropical rainforest lies in the marked seasonal pattern of the rainfall. Except in the Madras district, practically all the rain falls during the southwest monsoon period. While seasonal temperature differences are somewhat more extreme than in the tropical rainforest, this difference is of far less importance than the contrast in the distribution of precipitation.

(3) Bordering the tropical savanna on the northwest and also forming a small pocket on the plateau, east of the central Malabar, are areas of tropical steppe. Temperature conditions are similar to those of the tropical savanna, but the rainfall is less (usually under 30 inches) and the rainy season is much shorter.

(4) Except for extreme northwest India, the balance of the country (the Thar Desert, Sind, portions of the Punjab, and Baluchistan) has essentially a low-latitude desert type of climate. Here rainfall is everywhere less than 10 inches per year. Temperatures express a somewhat greater seasonal and diurnal range than in the three preceding climates.

(5) In the extreme northwest is a region of middle-latitude steppe climate. Rainfall is scanty (generally under 20 inches per year), and there is a tendency toward a winter maximum. January temperature averages fall to 55°F. or lower and occasionally freezing temperatures may occur during the winter months. Aside from the mountain country, this is the only section of India not under a tropical regime.

Flora and Fauna.—In many parts of India, under the impact of long-continued intensive cultivation, the original vegetation cover has largely disappeared.

In the wetter eastern portion of the Himalaya, vegetation occurs in clearly defined altitudinal zones. From 5,000 to 9,000 feet evergreen oak forest prevails; from 9,000 to 12,000 feet temperate coniferous forests predominate; alpine vegetation is characteristic in the zone from 12,000 to 16,000 feet; and the permanent snow line comes in around 16,000 feet. In the western (drier) Himalaya, various types of temperate forest occupy the zone between 5,000 and 10,000 feet. In the drier areas, short grass and bushes are characteristic. The forested areas contain mixtures of broad-leaved oaks, needle-leaved pines, and deodars.

Along the southern edge of the eastern Himalaya (the sub-Himalayan zone) and in the Assam Valley along both sides of the Brahmaputra River, the characteristic vegetation is a tall, coarse swamp grass. Toward the west this gives way to shorter grass and to patches of thorn forest.

So much of the Hindustan plain is under intensive cultivation that only remnants of the original vegetal cover remain. Tidal swamp covers the seaward margins of the Ganges-Brahmaputra Delta. A brushwood jungle occupies portions of central Bengal, while west of Calcutta is a region of scrub jungle. In the middle and upper Ganges Valley there are patches of tropical deciduous and sal forest. Largely because of the low ground-water table, waste scrub is characteristic in the Punjab plains. Short grass and scrub forest are typical in most of the remaining areas of the western Hindustan plain.

Peninsular India has a wide variety of natural vegetation. Along the west coast and on the seaward flanks of the Western Ghats are many forested areas. Here dense evergreen tropical forests cover much of the highland country. Coconut palms are typical on the coastal dunes of Malabar. Along the Coromandel Coast mangrove swamps occur on the seaward edges of the large deltas. The slopes of the Eastern Ghats are covered with sal forest. On the plateau proper, tropical deciduous forest and grassland form the most typical vegetation. The forest cover predominates in the wetter areas, while grass and scrub occupy the drier portions.

The natural fauna of India, save for various types which might be classed as pests (wild hogs, rodents, snakes, insects, and the like) is confined largely to the less populous and more remote sections of the country. Here a considerable variety abounds. Among the large mammals, leopard, cheetah, tiger, wolf, bear, antelope, rhinoceros, and elephant are perhaps the most common. Of the cat family, the leopard is the most common and widespread, being found in all parts of India. The cheetah is found only in the Deccan, where it is trained to hunt antelope. The tiger, like the leopard, is found in all parts of India, but today it is seldom seen except in such remote and inaccessible places as the ill-drained, malaria-infested eastern sub-Himalayan zone, among the swamps of the Ganges-Brahmaputra Delta, and in the jungles of the plateau.

Wolves frequent the drier areas of the Hindustan plain and the plateau, where they are a constant menace to sheep raisers. The common black bear is found in many parts of India, but especially in the hilly and forested districts of the northern mountains. Another species, the Himalayan sun bear, also frequents the mountain country. This species is migratory in its habits, going into the high mountains during the summer rains and descending to lower elevations during the cool season.

Antelope are widely distributed but occur in greatest numbers in Gujarat and Orissa. Various species of deer are found in the forested areas of India, in the swamp country of lower Bengal and Assam, and in adjacent Tibet.

The most common type of rhinoceros found in India is the single-horn variety, found primarily in the Brahmaputra River valley. In the Sundarbans (Ganges-Brahmaputra Delta), a smaller species of the single-horn type is also common. Some two-horned rhinoceroses frequent the area in and around Chittagong. Elephants today are found only in remote hill sections. The area of greatest numbers is along the Assam-Burma border. They are also obtained from the jungle country of the plateau, especially in the hill country of the extreme south, notably in Mysore.

Among the pests, the wild hog and various rodents deserve special mention. These animals cause widespread damage in cultivated areas. One species of rat, the bandicoot, sometimes attains a size of two feet in length and a weight in excess of three pounds. It is responsible for great damage in the rice fields and gardens of India. Mosquitoes are an omnipresent health hazard in moist, ill-drained areas, as are flies in all sections of the country.

Mineral Resources.—Mineral production in India is very small, employing only about .1 per cent of the population, and yielding an annual per capita return of only about 25 cents. Undeveloped known resources, moreover, seem to give little promise of a prosperous future, especially when viewed in terms of the area and enormous population of the country. Additional supplies of minerals may yet be discovered, but the probability is low, to judge from the extensive geological surveys which were conducted under British direction. In many parts of India, too, the exploitation of low-grade mineral deposits is made possible only because of the availability of a very cheap labor supply.

India's principal mineral deposits are concentrated in three major areas: (1) in and on the edge of the Chota Nagpur Plateau (Bengal, Bihar, and Orissa); (2) in the Godavari Valley; and (3) in southern peninsular India (Madras, Mysore, and adjacent districts). In addition, there are small, widely scattered deposits.

Coal is one of India's chief mineral resources. Estimates of reserves range between 50 and 80 billion tons, much of it high-grade bituminous. Production averages between 25 and 30 million long tons per year, with the Chota Nagpur fields furnishing upwards of 90 per cent of the total. Other producing areas are in the Godavari and Mahanadi valleys. Iron ore is widely scattered in India and ranges in quality from low-grade lateritic ores of the plateau (30 per cent iron) to the rich hematite (60 per cent iron) in Chota Nagpur (Singhbhum district), where the Indians estimate reserves at 3,600,000,000 tons. A rich magnetite deposit is located in the Salem district of southern India, but no coal is available in the area and there are technological difficulties to be overcome before this ore can be profitably used. Iron ore production approximates 3,000,000 tons per year. India has important reserves of manganese, the largest deposits occurring in Madhya Pradesh (until 1950 known as Central Provinces and Berar), Bihar, and Orissa, and in Madras. Petroleum resources are very limited, though exploratory work indicates the possibility that extensive deposits may be located in Sind. There is a very limited production in the Punjab and Assam. Gold, valued at around $10,000,000 annually, is produced in the Kolar district of Mysore. Indian mica, most of which is muscovite, finds wide use in the electrical industry, where, because of its great purity, it is used for insulation. Annual production, valued around $5,000,000, accounts for three fourths of the world's high-grade sheet mica supply. India possesses only limited quantities of nonferrous metals. Small deposits of bauxite are widely scattered and limited supplies of copper and chromite are present, but there is a marked deficiency in tin, lead, and zinc.

Bibliography.—*The Imperial Gazetteer of India,* 2d ed., 26 vols., particularly vols. 1-4 (Oxford 1907–1909); Kenoyer, L. A., "Plant Life of British India," *Scientific Monthly,* January 1924; Kendrew, W. G., *The Climates of the Continents* (Oxford 1927); Sion, Jules, *Asie des Moussons,* vol. 2 (Paris 1929); Mukherjee, B. B., *An Economic and Commercial Geography of India* (Calcutta 1931); Brown, J. C., *India's Mineral Wealth* (London 1936); Champion, H. G., "A Preliminary Survey of the Forest Types of India and Burma," *Indian Forest Records,* vol. 1, no. 1 (Delhi 1936); India, Meteorological Department, *Memoirs* (Delhi 1876–1939); Wadia, D. N., *Geology of India,* 2d ed. (London 1939); Behre, C. H., Jr., "India's Mineral Wealth and Political Future," *Foreign Affairs,* October 1943; Lobeck, A. K., *Physiographic Diagram of Asia* (New York 1945); *The Indian and Pakistan Year Book and Who's Who* (Bombay, annually); U.S. Department of Commerce, *Foreign Commerce Yearbook* (Washington, annually); U.S. Department of the Interior, *Minerals Yearbook* (Washington, annually).

WILLIAM F. CHRISTIANS,
Associate Professor of Geography, University of Pennsylvania.

2. ECONOMIC DEVELOPMENT. The development of the rural economy of India may be divided into four major periods: that of the pre-British society (to 1793); the period in which new land systems were introduced (1793–1850); that of the spread of commercial agriculture (1850–1914); and the contemporary period (from 1914).

Pre-British Structure of Indian Society (to 1793).—The outstanding feature of the economy of India before the advent of British power was the self-subsisting and self-perpetuating character of its typical unit, the village. Most Indian villages came close to being little worlds unto themselves. The only outside authority which they acknowledged was that of some local princeling who in turn might be subordinate to a distant overlord, whether Hindu raja or Moslem nawab. The chief sign of submission to that authority was the payment each year of a share of the village crops, in some periods amounting to one sixth or less, and in others to as much as one third or even one half. As a general rule, the responsibility for making this payment, whether in produce or in money, was joint or collective, resting upon the whole village considered as a single unit.

Within the little world of the village, social and economic relationships were governed by customary patterns and conventions of immemorial antiquity. The cattle were tended and the soil was tilled by peasants whose fathers had been cultivators and whose sons would take their places when they came of age. In some parts of India a kind of rough equality was maintained by a periodic throwing together of all the lands of the village, followed by a fresh redistribution of the land among the cultivating peasants. Cloth for the garments of the peasants generally was spun and woven by families whose ancestors had been weavers long beyond the living memory of man. The other crafts were carried on by families which in effect were servants of the village. Their occupations passed on traditionally from father to son: the blacksmith, potter, and carpenter, who made and repaired the implements and utensils of the village; the silversmith, who made the village jewelry; and the oilseed presser. For their services these craftsmen received a regular stipend from the crops of the villagers. In some areas hereditary servants and slaves attached to peasant households performed both domestic and agricultural duties and received from their masters food, lodging, and clothing.

The village itself consumed most of the foodstuffs and other raw materials it produced. Its needs for handicrafts were satisfied by the families of craftsmen associated with the village. It was this tight union of agriculture and hand industry which made the village economically independent of the outside world except for a few necessities like salt and iron. The share of the village crops which went to the local magnate and moved on from him in a diminishing stream upward to the highest political overlord sustained the structure of government and provided subsistence for the urban population. As the local chiefs often constituted a rallying point against the center, some emperors and kings tried to weaken their power by collecting the land revenue without their participation. In their stead they created tax farmers or operated through subordinate revenue officials controlled by the imperial courts.

With the exception of the pilgrimage centers, India's towns and cities generally were little more than headquarters for the top political overlords or imperial courts. The industries which were carried on in these cities were of two classes: those which met the minimum wants of the urban population (clothing and shelter), and those which provided mainly luxury goods for the upper classes or implements of war for the army. Economically the cities had a one-way relation with the countryside, taking foodstuffs as tribute but supplying virtually no goods in return.

This was the structure of Indian society which, with regional variations, the British found between 1750 and 1850 as they conquered one part of India after another. The basic land relationships were rooted in century-old custom and usage rather than in any formal, elaborate set of statutes, legal cases, and court procedures about property. So long as the peasants turned over to the local potentate his customary tribute and rendered him the usual services, their right to till the soil and reap its fruits was taken for granted. Local rulers who repeatedly abused this right were considered oppressive; if they persisted, the peasantry fled to areas where the customs of the land were better respected. As land was still available for settlement and labor was not too cheap, local chiefs had to be careful lest they alienate the villagers.

There was nothing in India comparable to the highly developed forms of private property in land which were the rule in late 18th century England. There were no landlords and no tenants in the Western sense. The right to levy the land revenues was recognized to be the essence of political power. In effect, the supreme political authority was the supreme landlord.

The British conquest of India through the agency of the East India Company led to the most drastic changes in the Indian way of life of which we have record. The most fundamental of these changes was the disintegration of the older structure of the village community, partly as a result of new land systems introduced by the British, and partly as a result of the spread in the 19th century of commercial agriculture.

The Introduction of New Land Systems (1793–1850).—In making arrangements for collecting land revenue from the peasants in the areas of India which they conquered, the British were primarily concerned with securing the largest possible revenue. For it was basically from these sums that British conquest and consolidation in India were financed. Two major types of land revenue systems were devised, each of which shook the older structure of village life in India. In Bengal and adjacent areas, beginning in 1793, the British converted the tax farmers and revenue collectors into private landlords, granting them rights of private property in the land. This was done on condition that the new landlords would raise greatly enhanced revenues from the cultivating peasants and pass the bulk of these revenues on to the state. This land revenue system is known as the zamindari system (Hindustani *zamīndārī* from zamindar, *zamīndār,* or landholder, a word which more and more has taken on the connotation of landlord). In effect, the zamindari system in Bengal turned the village lands into the private property of the new landlords. The hereditary rights of the cultivators to the soil they tilled were virtually ignored; the British land arrangements left the village communities of Bengal in the power of the newly created landlords.

An entirely different land system was devised for large parts of Bombay and Madras, and later applied to areas in northeastern and northwestern India. Here the British, instead of creating private landlords, dealt directly with the individual peasants on the land, for thereby they hoped to be able to obtain more revenue than under the zamindari system. Each peasant was recognized as holding the particular plot or plots he occupied, but his right to the land depended upon annual payment in full of a heavy money rent to the state. Because it dealt directly with the peasant or ryot (*ra'īyat*), the new system was called the ryotwari (*ra'īyatwārī*) settlement. Whereas the zamindari system made the landlords masters of the village communities, the ryotwari system cut through the heart of the village communities by making separate arrangements between each peasant cultivator and the state.

These two systems, with a number of variants introduced in the course of the 19th century, were the dominant land systems of British India from 1793 to 1947. Under both of them, the old body of custom was submerged by the formidable apparatus of law courts, fees, lawyers, and formal procedures. For with the introduction of private property in land the purchase and sale of zamindars' holdings were explicitly sanctioned by law. All of this was too much not only for the humble peasants, but also for the new landlords. Most of the latter could not raise the heavy revenues required by the government and soon defaulted or sold out to merchants, speculators, and other sophisticated persons from the cities. These new landlords by purchase were interested only in the rents they could squeeze from the land; often they delegated the collection to middlemen who contracted to pay high sums annually. The latter in turn sublet to still other classes of middlemen, so that before long the unfortunate peasants of Bengal were supporting an impressive string of middlemen, speculators, and absentee landlords.

The ryotwari system also introduced some features of private property in land. The individual holders were registered and empowered to sell, lease, mortgage, or transfer their right to the use of the land. In contrast to the previous indigenous regimes, which had made more or less elastic demands upon the peasants, the British insisted rigorously upon prompt and complete payment of the stipulated sums. In cases of default livestock, household property, and personal effects might be attached, and the peasant might be evicted. The new land system thus made mobile both the land and the peasant, and left the way open for the growth in power of the moneylender and the absentee landlord.

Spread of Commercial Agriculture (1850–1914).—The older rural framework of India, weakened by the new land systems introduced between 1793 and 1850, was shattered by the spread of commercial agriculture between 1850 and 1914. Commercial agriculture—the production of cash crops for sale in distant towns or overseas markets, rather than for consumption within the village—grew rapidly because of a variety of conditions. One basic reason was the constantly recurring need of the peasants under the new land systems to find ways of getting money to meet the mounting demands upon them by the state and the landlords. Another basic reason for the rapid growth in the cultivation of cash crops was the fact that such a development was welcome to the British authorities in India, who did everything in their power to foster it. By the middle of the 19th century Britain itself had passed through the Industrial Revolution. British industries were then the greatest in the world, and they kept on expanding. British manufacturers clamored for raw materials and sought anxiously for good markets in which to dispose of their finished products. Under pressure from British merchants and manufacturers, India's coastal towns were linked with Britain in the 1840's by steamships and the interior of India was covered after the 1850's by the most elaborate railway network in Asia.

Once the railways were opened it became possible for the inland areas of India to produce for the world market. Wheat poured out of the Punjab, cotton out of Bombay, and jute out of Bengal. As commercial agriculture and money economy spread, the older practices associated with a subsistence economy declined. In some districts the peasants shifted over completely to industrial crops and had to buy their foodstuffs from dealers. Villagers sent to market the cereal reserves traditionally kept for poor years. They became less prepared to meet poor harvests. Years of successive drought in the 1870's and 1890's led to great famines and agrarian unrest.

To produce crops for distant markets the peasants required credit to tide them through the long period of turnover. They turned to the moneylender, who came to occupy a place of unprecedented importance. Although in pre-British times the local moneylender extended casual credit to meet occasional needs of the villagers, he occupied a subordinate place in the subsistence economy of the countryside. The new forms of landholding, land revenue systems, legal procedures, and commercial agriculture of the 19th century, however, opened up a golden age for the moneylender. The demand for his services became an inescapable part of the peasant's life; to the state the moneylender was of invaluable aid in converting the peasant's crops into cash and passing on the land revenue due to the government. The moneylender was encouraged to expand his activities by the fact that under the new order of things he could make a good and secure profit. If the peasants defaulted he could use the new legal procedures to attach their lands, livestock, and personal possessions. Furthermore, from the middle of the 19th century the price of land rose rapidly in value, thereby encouraging the moneylender to broaden his operations. He began to take over the peasants' land and rent it out. The moneylenders grew in number and in wealth.

The same railroads which carried away the commercial crops brought back machine-made industrial products to the villages. The village weavers and traditional handicraft servants had to compete in the second half of the 19th century with products like Lancashire cloth, which was then overrunning world markets. The village artisans no longer were sheltered by the friendly backwardness of the older village commune. Furthermore, the union of agriculture and hand industry which had been the basis of village life was disrupted. Under the impact of new forces the village could no longer remain the compact social and economic unit that it had been. The growing tendency was for each family to make ends meet as best it could. Deep in the interior of central India and in other areas difficult of access the handicrafts held on for a long time, and some still show strength. In the coastal zones and in the regions lying along the new railroads, however, the ancient village handicrafts declined. The village potter, tanner, dyer, oilman, and jeweler all faced strong competition from machine products, whether made in Britain or, after the close of the 19th century, in the new industrial centers that grew up in India. Since 1850 a dwindling proportion of the village artisans of the subcontinent have been able to subsist on what they have received for their services from the village. Millions of them have had to find other ways to gain a livelihood or to supplement their scanty earnings from the village. In most cases the only avenue open to them has been agriculture, and they have added steadily to the great pressure on the land which is one of the chief characteristics of contemporary Indian and Pakistani life.

Contemporary Rural Economy.—The outstanding characteristic of the Indian rural economy on the eve of the partition of the subcontinent in 1947 was the striking concentration of landed property. One or two million great magnates, large landlords, and moneylenders owned or controlled about one half of all the cultivated land. With few exceptions the members of these groups had no productive function. They did not farm their land with modern machinery nor did they apply fertilizers or concern themselves with the latest techniques of scientific cultivation. Instead, they stayed in the cities and leased out their property in tiny patches to peasants at high rentals. The income of the landlord and moneylender thus was drawn almost exclusively from rent and usury, and practically never from profits gained by growing crops on their own land. On a much smaller scale the same was true of some 3,000,000 petty landlords and rent receivers, chiefly city dwellers, who obtained some income from their minor properties.

Less than one quarter of the land was in the hands of some two or three million substantial peasant proprietors who actually tilled the soil. Except for this relatively small number of well-off peasants, India's working population on the land consisted of poor proprietors, poor tenants, and propertyless agricultural laborers. These three groups, totaling more than 100,000,000 working men and women, existed below what by 19th century standards would have been the barest minimum considered satisfactory. The level of debt was such that it exceeded in amount the total annual income of the small proprietor and tenant. A government handbook put out in 1938 by retired British officials noted tersely that "indebtedness, often amounting to insolvency, is the normal condition of a majority of Indian farmers."

Poor peasant proprietors and tenants are so dependent upon, and tributary to, the landlord-moneylender that their condition approaches that of servile or unfree labor. The clearest evidence for this is the character and extent of sharecropping. By the 1940's this accounted for one fifth of the sown area of Bengal and Bihar, one fourth of the United Provinces, one half of the Punjab, and large parts of southern India, Sind, and North-West Frontier Province. Half or more of the gross produce went to the landlord, who often as not provided neither seeds, implements, nor work animals.

At the bottom of the economic scale were 30,000,000 to 50,000,000 landless laborers. Since the 1870's they have increased more rapidly than any other significant part of India's population. The recruits to this class stemmed from peasants who had lost all their livestock and all their land to the landlord or moneylender. A striking number of them have come to serve in one or another form of unfree labor. Some were serfs who might be transferred from one master to another as the land changed hands. Others were bond servants who performed customary menial tasks for their masters.

Crop production methods have remained the time-honored ones dating back to pre-British times and passed on from generation to generation. There has been little or no impetus to technical progress because the benefits of improvements generally have been siphoned off by landlords, moneylenders, and middlemen. In most cases peasant holdings consisted of a number of fragments scattered among the various grades and types of land in the village. The basic unit of field production on large and small holdings alike has been a plot so tiny as to make modern methods irrelevant. In the Punjab two out of five peasants tilled units less than 2½ acres in size. In other provinces subdivision of holdings through inheritance proceeded so far that units of cultivation as small as 1/100 of an acre have been found. The only important examples of production on single great holdings have been the tea, coffee, and rubber plantations, originally founded and managed by British capital. But even here cultivation has been by old-fashioned hand methods and the working force has consisted of indentured or semifree labor.

Urban Economy.—One out of every seven Indians lives in a town with a population of 5,000 or more. The large cities which have sprung up or expanded since 1850 have functioned economically in a role supplementary to the needs of the British metropolitan economy. They have served as centers for handling the outward movement of raw materials and the inbound movement of manufactured goods from abroad. The factories which have come into existence in these cities either are devoted to consumers' goods and other light industries, or are workshops for maintaining transport services, particularly the railroads.

Indigenous enterprise made slow headway in 19th century India, partly because it came up against the power of the British mercantile houses. These houses had evolved a form of business enterprise peculiar to India: the managing agency. Under the managing agency system a single business organization runs the affairs of a dozen or more concerns operating in a number of different fields. The system arose when British merchant houses, like those which had pressed in the 1840's for the opening up of India, themselves later founded banks, opened coal mines, built jute factories, or started tea plantations. After 1850 the great British concerns played a predominant, almost quasi-monopolistic, role in the economic life of India. Indians desiring to enter fields in which British managing agencies already operated came to find it sound or advisable to place themselves under the protection of one or another of these houses. Throughout the 19th century would-be Indian captains of industry received little if any of the government help for infant industries which was so common in Europe and the United States. The first tariffs of even a moderately protective nature did not come into operation until the 1920's and up to 1947 the great British shipping lines were able to operate freely in the Indian coastwise trade.

The birth of modern industry in India has therefore been a prolonged and painful process. The total number of factory workers has never reached 1 per cent of the population, and since 1900 the urban craftsmen and other handicraft workers have declined not only in proportion to the rest of the population, but even in absolute numbers. It is the exceptionally slow rate of industrialization combined with the decline of handicrafts which explains the otherwise astounding fact that since 1900 India has become more and more of an agricultural country. In 1891 three persons out of five gained a living from the soil; by the 1930's the proportion was about three out of four.

There are two chief centers of modern industry in India: Calcutta with its environs, and Bombay and Ahmadabad (Ahmedabad) in western India. Heavy industry is concentrated in the Calcutta area. At Jamshedpur, 155 miles west of Calcutta, is the well-known works of the Tata Iron and Steel Company, which produces annually about 1,000,000 tons of finished steel. The coal mines which supply Tata's needs and most areas of India as well are concentrated around Asansol, about 120 miles northwest of Calcutta. They employ some 250,000 miners who turn out each year about 25,000,000 tons of coal. Near Asansol is the only other sizable steel works in India, that of the Steel Corporation of Bengal (SCOB), with a capacity roughly one third that of Tata.

The heart of Indian industry in and around Calcutta itself is the spinning of jute and its weaving into burlap. More than 100 jute and burlap mills employing close to 300,000 workmen stretch along both banks of the Hooghly River, which connects Calcutta with the Bay of Bengal. Calcutta's services as India's greatest rail hub and one of its two chief ports require a wide assortment of transport and engineering workshops and small metalworking plants, which together form the city's second largest industry. The mills and mines of the Calcutta-Asansol-Jamshedpur industrial complex employ altogether about 1,000,000 workmen.

The great industry of Bombay and of Ahmadabad 300 miles to the north of it is the spinning and weaving of cotton. Bombay has about 100 cotton mills employing more than 150,000 workmen, while Ahmadabad also has 100 mills but only about 100,000 workers. Whereas, however, Ahmadabad economically is only a cotton town, Bombay matches Calcutta as a great port and even exceeds it as a center of diversified light industries. In addition to the two great clusters of mills and shops in Calcutta and Bombay there are about a dozen smaller industrial centers of lesser rank such as Madras, Kanpur (formerly Cawnpore), and Bangalore. India's industrial position on the eve of war in 1939 may be summed up in three figures (at 1938–1939 prices), as follows: the value of capital invested in industrial plants was 6,750,000,000 rupees ($2,000,000,000); net annual output was worth 3,300,000,000 rupees ($1,000,000,000); and total factory employment was roughly 2,000,000 workers.

For India as a whole, the great bulk of the town dwellers are not factory workers but either hand artisans, unskilled laborers, or domestic servants. Estimates of the size of these three groups vary, but the total number of persons employed in them is at least 30,000,000. All three of these groups are employed by, or otherwise subordinate to and dependent upon, the urban middle classes. Large numbers of unskilled laborers are employed in construction and road building, and on docks and railways.

The bulk of the middle classes in the cities consists of petty traders, shopkeepers, middlemen, sweatshop owners, and small absentee landlords. From their families come lawyers, schoolteachers, and the lower ranks of government employees, such as clerks. For the middle classes generally, the struggle to make ends meet is a hard one, and only a small percentage of them achieve a moderate degree of comfort. In this more fortunate group fall the larger merchants and the successful lawyers, whose main practice is taken up with corporation law and suits about land.

Economic power and influence in the cities is tightly concentrated in the hands of a few thousand Indians who have successfully established themselves as industrialists and financiers. Perhaps even more striking than the concentration of control is the fact that most of the leading Indian businessmen have come from three tiny social groups: the Parsis (Parsees) of Bombay, the Marwaris of Rajputana, and the Jains of Gujarat.

Of the Parsis (see section on *Religion and Philosophy*) the most famous family is the Tatas. Despite the doubts of his countrymen and the scoffs of British engineers and government officials, Sir Jamsetji Tata (1839-1904), relying almost solely on his own resources, succeeded in founding the great Tata Iron and Steel Company. Besides textiles, iron, and steel, his descendants have large holdings in such basic industries as electric utilities, chemicals, machine tools, and airlines. The Tata interests comprise probably the most solid single Indian business group.

The chief Indian rivals of the Parsis have been the Marwaris, who originally were a group of moneylenders and merchants from Indian states in the interior of Rajputana. Quick to take advantage of the new economic opportunities presented in the second half of the 19th century, the Marwaris moved south to Ahmadabad and Bombay, and east to Kanpur and Calcutta. Along with the Parsis they were among the first to set up cotton textile mills. From these they expanded into every conceivable type of business in India. The wealthiest of the Marwari houses, that of the Birla brothers, has interests in cotton textiles, sugar mills, paper companies, cement plants, jute mills, insurance companies, newspapers, and weekly magazines.

Like the Marwaris, the Jains (see section on *Religion and Philosophy*) began their rise to prominence in the second half of the 19th century. In the cotton textile industry their holdings are second only to those of the Marwaris. The best known Jain concern is the house of Dalmia, which controls cement plants, airlines, sugar refineries, vegetable oil mills, daily papers, and periodicals.

Wealthy Moslems, whose income was derived chiefly from the land, did not attempt until quite late in the day to enter the fields of industry and banking. Up to 1947 not a single Moslem concern had holdings of dimensions comparable with those of the Parsis, Marwaris, or Jains. Of the substantial Moslem merchants and grain dealers, the best known was the Calcutta house of Ispahani, founded by immigrants from Persia.

The few great Indian houses have risen to their present position by dint of great effort in the face of many difficulties. Clashes among themselves and with their British competitors in India were frequent and severe in the opening decades of the 20th century. Since World War II, by which time the Indian houses may be considered to have arrived, all the established firms have tended to work together to prevent outsiders from intruding into their domain. In organization and structure the dominant Indian firms resemble the old British managing agency houses.

The war years from 1939 to 1945 brought unprecedented profits to the large mercantile and industrial firms. Prolonged and intense shortages of food and cloth prevailed for half a dozen years after 1942. Many textile manufacturers and food merchants took advantage of this to extract large prices from the consumers.

A 15-year program for national economic development jointly sponsored by representatives of the leading Indian business houses was put forward early in 1944. The Bombay plan, as it was called, proposed a great expansion of industry. It provided for a considerable degree of governmental planning and regulation of economic enterprise, so as to make the most rapid and efficient use of India's limited capital resources. At the time the Bombay proposals evoked much official and unofficial interest in planning, but developments since the end of the war were little influenced by blueprints of this sort. The postwar years were marked rather by a series of understandings between the great Indian houses and some of the largest manufacturing interests in Britain. Birla's, for example, reached agreement with the leading British firm of Nuffield's for the assembly, and for the manufacture later on, of automobiles in India. Tata's concluded an arrangement with the British cartel, Imperial Chemical Industries, Ltd., for the manufacture of dyes for the Indian textile industry. There were also negotiations in the direction of similar links with other important British and American concerns.

While carrying through these individual agreements, the Indian houses withdrew their earlier support of broad economic planning under governmental auspices. In the midst of the turmoil of the postwar years, culminating in the partition of India in 1947, the Indian houses campaigned for prompt abolition of wartime economic controls of prices and distribution. They also opposed measures to implement the plans which they themselves had previously drafted. With the establishment of the new Dominion of India in August 1947, Indian business attained both of its immediate objectives.

First, under its pressure, rationing and price control at the consumers' level were quickly ended. By the spring of 1948 prices had risen 50 per cent and more on many basic commodities, to the profit of Indian business and industry. This same price rise, however, was disastrous for the government of India, for India since World War II has been a food-importing area. The hasty ending of rationing and price control threw out of gear the country's delicately balanced food supply arrangements. To restore the balance, the government of India, in the winter of 1948–1949, had reluctantly to reimpose much of the rationing and price control it had previously terminated; and it had greatly to increase India's food imports. While these food costs were weighing heavily on the government of India, two other great costs were sapping the government's financial resources: the relief and rehabilitation of refugees from the great riots and migrations in the Punjab, consequent upon partition; and the financing of the clash with Pakistan over Kashmir, a heavy and steady drain after October 1947.

Second, in this setting, Indian business could persuade the government that broad economic planning would be beyond its strength. By 1949–1950, the bulk of the older plans had been abandoned, except for a number of multipurpose river control projects and a few other schemes.

Bibliography.—Comprehensive data on many aspects of the economy of India are given in the *Statistical Abstracts* published annually by the government of India. The chapter "India and Pakistan" in the symposium edited by Ralph Linton, *Most of the World* (New York 1949), furnishes a sketch of the broad lines of Indian economic development from the end of the 18th century to 1947. Kate Mitchell's *India Without Fable* (New York 1942) provides a brief account of economic problems in the 20th century. The classic description of modern industry is Daniel H. Buchanan's *Development of Capitalist Enterprise in India* (New York 1934). Many specialized books on India have been published by the Oxford University Press and its foreign affiliates; noteworthy among these are D. R. Gadgil, *Industrial Evolution of India* (Bombay 1944); B. C. Ghose, *Planning for India* (New York 1946); Dwarkanath Ghosh, *Pressure of Population and Economic Efficiency in India* (New York 1946); Hiryanappa Venkatasubbiah, *The Foreign Trade of India, 1900–1940* (New York 1946); M. L. Darling, *Punjab Peasant in Prosperity and Debt*, 4th ed. (London 1947); P. P. Pillai, ed., *Labour in South East Asia* (New York 1947). The best-known British work remains the study by Vera Anstey, *Economic Development of India* (London and New York 1936); it has a good bibliography of the older economic literature on the subject.

Daniel Thorner,
Research Assistant Professor of Economic History, University of Pennsylvania.

3. ANTHROPOLOGY AND SOCIOLOGY. This article offers an outline of Indic anthropology and sociology, within which a wealth of detail, impossible to cover here, may be incorporated. For this purpose, we will deal with five major topics: (1) the anthropological background of Indic history and existence; (2) the family in India and Pakistan; (3) the wealth and prestige system; (4) caste; and (5) the general nature of Indic society.

Anthropological Background.—The anthropological background of India and Pakistan may most conveniently be described under the four classical branches of anthropology: (1) archaeology; (2) physical anthropology; (3) linguistics; and (4) ethnology. In the last of these sections, we will touch briefly upon both the tribal areas and certain characteristics of the modern nations.

Archaeology.—Archaeological finds of southern and eastern Asia may be roughly dated relative to each other by the climatic rhythm of four pluvial, or wet and rainy, periods. These extend through the Pleistocene, and the earliest finds date from the second pluvial period in the Middle Pleistocene. The earliest Paleolithic artifacts of northwestern India are large, crude flakes called pre-Sohan (pre-Soan) from their stratigraphic position. There is, however, no apparent cultural continuity between these early finds and the Sohan core culture which begins later in the same period. They therefore stand alone without proven connections either in their homeland or in other areas.

The Punjab offers the clearest stratigraphy to date of any part of the subcontinent, and here two complexes, the Sohan and the Abbevilleo-Acheulean, developed independently through the second interpluvial and third pluvial periods. On the basis of existing data, these divergent cultures did not mix until the third interpluvial period, and after that Sohan continued alone through the remainder of the Pleistocene until the emergence of the highly developed Neolithic cultures of the Indus Valley sites under climatic conditions similar to those of the present day.

Sohan culture has affinities with the Far East. It is based upon choppers and chopping tools, and it now seems clear that it is to be regarded as a manifestation of a great complex of chopper-chopping-tool cultures found in southern and eastern Asia, including the Choukoutienian of China, the Anyathian of Burma, the Patjitanian of Java, and possibly the Tampanian of northern Malaya.

The Abbevilleo-Acheulean belongs to a hand-ax culture found also in the Middle East, Europe, and Africa. The region around Madras furnishes the closest approximation to stratigraphic sequence in southern India and the Madrasian belongs to this same Western hand-ax complex which, according to typology, has an extensive distribution in the peninsula. This culture has thus far not been found east of the Ganges. Since the classic western European sequence is absent from the Far East, it is clear that as early as the dawn of the Lower Paleolithic period, we have to deal with independent groups of core-tool cultures which have developed separately. They cover a span of perhaps 500,000 years. It is equally clear that both of these are represented in peninsular India.

In tracing the paths by which these divergent cultures reached the subcontinent, it is important to note that, although in the Late Cenozoic era Burma and northern India formed a continuous area with Villafranchian fauna, including *Equus*, *Elephas*, and *Bos*, as essentially an eastern extension of the upper Siwalik, direct connections between the two regions apparently ceased at the end of the Lower Pleistocene. Either the carriers of the Sohan complex came in before this break, a hypothesis for which there appears to be no evidence, or they had a choice of two routes: across the northern mountains or south of Burma. Both these routes from the east remain possibilities at the present time.

The path of direct contact with the west remained open, and it is small wonder that the great Indus Valley civilizations bear many elements in common with the high cultures of Mesopotamia and Egypt. Indeed, from the point of view of the Middle East, Mohenjo-daro and its related sites may be regarded as the farthest eastern extension of the Mesopotamian center. It would be unwise, however, to underestimate the local quality of many Indus traits. See also section on *Archaeology*.

Physical Anthropology.—No human skeletal remains have as yet been found in Pleistocene deposits in the subcontinent. Sinanthropus at Choukoutien, near Peking, and the Pithecanthropus finds of Java establish early forms of man for the Far East, but their relations to western evolutionary sequences remain unclear. The American anthropologist Earnest A. Hooton has posited the existence of an even distribution of physical types at the Pithecanthropus-Sinanthropus stage extending down the eastern half of Asia from Peking to Java and westward to northern India. Such a distribution is so far uncorroborated in its western extension and the most we can do at present is to leave the subcontinent in doubt between various eastern and western sequences of fossil man.

Homo sapiens, or modern man, belongs to the Upper Paleolithic, and there is a hiatus between fossil forms and modern variants of *Homo sapiens* which is often difficult to bridge. Three major modern races of man are commonly recognized: the Negroid, the white or Caucasoid, and the Mongoloid. In their larger distributions the descriptive distinctions among these three are fairly clear, but unfortunately numbers of living men can only with difficulty be forced into such a classificatory system. Two of these recalcitrant small groups have representatives in the southeastern parts of the subcontinent. The first includes the Negritos, who are clearly a pygmy Negroid type and are to be found with identical characteristics in central Africa, the Andaman Islands, and the Philippines; the second covers the Veddoid peoples of Ceylon. The latter have sometimes been associated with the aborigines of Australia to form an Australoid group, but any such association is highly hypothetical at best and leaves other groups like the Ainu of Japan unaccounted for. Although features of these two types occur, they are relatively infrequent and are seldom combined in any one individual. A true pygmy or Veddoid type is difficult to find at the present time either in peninsular India or Ceylon.

Pure Mongoloid physical types appear in the subcontinent mainly along the borders of Nepal and, whenever found, they can be identified as relatively recent immigrants from the northeast. In addition, a few Chinese have taken up residence in Indian cities. Numerous Caucasoid types, also mainly in the cities, can be traced directly to the recent historical conquests of the subcontinent by European nationals. The bulk of the population bears odd resemblances to both

Caucasoid and Negroid peoples: they are often dark skinned, with heavy, wavy black hair and black eyes; lips may or may not be full; noses are broad, or thin and high bridged; and the limbs are long in proportion to the trunk.

Migrations of Caucasoid peoples are known to have entered northern India via land routes from the west for at least 3,000 years. Armenoid characteristics are common, and a type similar to that of the strikingly tall and large-featured men of Afghanistan occurs throughout the northern regions. Blue eyes are not uncommon in the Punjab, and other physical features usually associated with Caucasoid types also occur. Aryan literature also makes it clear that early immigrants of light-skinned peoples found, and placed themselves as rulers over, an indigenous dark-skinned population. Following such data, some authorities place the peoples of the northern and western portions of the subcontinent with the Caucasoid racial group and describe the southern and eastern sections, including Bengal, as a mixture of Caucasoid and Negroid elements.

Numerous objections stand in the way of such a classification. It is certainly true that a band of dark-skinned peoples extends from Fiji across Melanesia, sweeps up to include India and reaches on to the African continent. The relations between the peoples of this great expanse, however, remain unclear and until more is known about the inheritance and origin of physical traits, and the prehistoric movements of people, they are not apt to be clarified. The population of the subcontinent is distinct enough to be named Hindu or Indic by some authors, forming a racial subclassification. More modern opinion tends to classify the dark-skinned Pacific Islands people as Mongoloid despite their color, and the most recent authorities, such as Alfred L. Kroeber, show no hesitation in placing all sections of the Indian subcontinent squarely within the Caucasoid or white race. Despite these classifications, the various evidences of relationship in physical type between the Indian subcontinent and the islands of the Pacific must not be lost sight of.

Linguistics.—Linguistic distributions in the subcontinent are dealt with in the section on *Languages,* and it remains in this section to note only that they suggest contacts to the east through the Munda (Kolarian) languages, ties through Indo-European tongues with the west, and an important Dravidian core, affiliations for which cannot be discovered outside peninsular India and Ceylon.

Ethnology.—We can pass directly, then, to ethnological evidence deriving from contemporary cultures. There is a rich anthropological literature on the so-called tribal areas of the peninsula. For a number of years certain peoples of these areas, such as the Toda of the Nilgiri Hills, were considered representative of some of the world's most ancient cultural heritages. It was usual to think of them retaining, because of their isolation, a mode of life truly primitive, superseded in more advanced areas by more highly civilized customs. They were regarded as handy living fossils through whom could be studied man's early cultural life. Such a view bears the unmistakable mark of 19th century thought, and it has not been validated by 20th century investigations. Although it is true that many ancient practices have been retained in India, especially among tribal groups, their isolation from the main currents of Indic life seems to have been greatly exaggerated. Simple as their ways may appear, they bear the general stamp of Indic society. In the simplest terms, the tribes are distinct because they are in various stages of being absorbed into Hinduism, and they are backward due to economic as well as to historic circumstances. A central belt of such tribes crosses the great plateau of Chota Nagpur with an extension north across the Santal Parganas to the Ganges River at Rajmahal. After a gap, this belt then includes the Nilgiris separating Travancore from the east coast. A western belt of tribes lives in the western hills of Aravalli and Malwa. And various land frontiers from Baluchistan to the eastern coasts of Bengal, isolated because of the nature of their terrain, are likewise occupied by tribal groups. On the whole, these peoples may be distinguished according to whether they are sedentary or semisedentary agriculturists or pastoralists, or depend for their livelihood upon food gathering in the remote forest tracts.

Wandering tribes are also to be found in most sections of the subcontinent. They live, literally, on the fringes of sedentary society, garnering their living from the great peninsular population. They owe their continued existence not only to their own ingenuity, but also to the great tolerance of the peninsular social system, which can find a place for any people either within its own structure or just outside of it. Such groups exist beyond the social pale, but they continue to exist.

A third group of tribes should also be mentioned. They are today predominantly followers of Islam and live through the fastnesses of the western mountains from Quetta to Afghanistan, the most widely known occurring along the northwest frontier. These people are neither backward nor primitive in any accepted sense. They owe their designation as tribes to their warlike independence, which has guaranteed them a measure of political separateness for unknown centuries.

Ethnological materials for the nontribal areas of India and Pakistan, for the great bulk of the village and city dwellers, are mainly conspicuous by their absence. In this respect, the situation in the subcontinent differs not at all from other of the so-called civilized portions of the globe. Some generalizations may, however, be useful for our present purposes.

The history of civilization is to a large extent the history of human inventions and of their cultural utilization. Many of the inventions upon which modern world society is based were apparently developed during the late Neolithic period. Some of these can be fairly accurately placed within the general area of the Middle East; others are more difficult to locate geographically. They include the domestication and utilization of certain animals, such as cattle, sheep, goats, and horses; the invention of the wheel, upon which both wheeled vehicles and engineering aids such as the pulley depend; stone architecture with the centralization of population in cities; and the art of writing. To these was added at a later date the use of metals for tools. India's contribution to world culture, especially in the area of intellectual pursuits, should never be underestimated. Quite apart from such fields, however, the simple fact that she shared in all the tangible traits we have listed demonstrates her close ties with the areas west of her peninsular boundaries during the Neolithic period.

The distributions of elements within another great human invention—agriculture—lend modern peninsular India a more complicated background. The evidence of agricultural crops and diet indicate that the subcontinent faced east as well as west. Whereas the northern sections are primarily grain-consuming areas like the Middle East and Europe, with the same staples of millet, wheat, and barley, the southern and eastern portions depend upon rice, and must be placed with southern China and the Pacific in the rice basket of the world. The pig, which also has an eastern distribution, is apparently old in the subcontinent; and yams, which are staple in many islands of the Pacific, play an important dietary role in southern parts of the peninsula.

Without our entering into greater detail, it becomes evident that ethnological materials support our earlier conclusions. From the beginning of man's cultural life to the present, peninsular India has served as a kind of hub for influences from both east and west. Ties with the Pacific Islands appear on many factual levels. And it should be further noted that, although we have not dealt equally with such factors, many elements of Indic life have been reworked into a unique pattern of their own.

Family.—In turning to a description of the family in peninsular India, we are faced again with the fact that its basic pattern has a wide distribution. The architectural unit, or compound, within which are separately housed several generations of persons, including members of the extended family such as brothers and nephews, extends from Africa through the Middle East to China. One supposes that, like other of the great human inventions, it dates from the Neolithic period. Our main concern here, however, is with the contemporary expressions of this familial complex as they occur in the subcontinent.

The Indic joint family system was legally recognized in Hinduism at least as early as the 11th century A.D., and may well have been developed in its present form long before that. It exists with only minor variations in most parts of the subcontinent today, and even the matrilineal systems of the Malabar Coast are incorporated within Hindu orthodoxy. The family is usually patrilineal, constituted of a number of related men—brothers, sons, grandsons, and cousins through the male line—and their wives. A female child remains within the joint family until marriage, when she enters the joint family of her husband. The affairs of the family, economic as well as social, are administered by the oldest able man, and the family regards itself as a single unit in both the production and consumption of economic goods. Distribution of privileges and property are theoretically divided evenly between the members of the family, but there is often considerable favoring of those persons who contribute most to family support or prestige. For its psychological significance, not less than its economic, it is important to note that a man may never be permanently alienated from his family by any act or series of acts. His position as a member of a family remains absolute. The same is true with only minor exceptions of a woman in her husband's family. After the birth of her children her security is as great as his.

Such a system immediately suggests monogamy, and the subcontinent is, indeed, essentially monogamous. In the north, plural wives are allowed only if the first wife is barren or becomes physically incapacitated and even in such circumstances are infrequent. Moslem law recognizes the legality of plural wives, but, except for certain overzealous—and well-to-do—individuals, the opportunities offered by the legal code are seldom realized. In any case, the earlier wife is not discarded. In the same way, divorce is legally recognized in both India and Pakistan today, but the incidence of divorce is phenomenally low. Marriage ordinarily occurs early, and it is for life.

The tribal areas differ most from recognized Indic society in their wide acceptance of brittle monogamy and of recognized premarital intercourse. Such customs seem clearly residuary and are suggestive of practices widespread in the more distant islands of the Pacific. They are largely limited to the southern and eastern portions of the subcontinent.

Marriage is certainly the most important event in the social existence of peninsular India. Mates are chosen early, and marriage arrangements are in the hands of the parents. Everywhere regulations regarding possible mates are strictly adhered to. The variety of these rules, however, is bewildering. Marriage seldom occurs across caste lines, but between some castes hypergamy, or reciprocal intermarriage, is usual. Degrees of relationship are also specified. The prohibited, or sapinda (Sanskrit *sapiṇda*), relationships in the north ordinarily include six or four degrees' removal through the paternal and maternal lines, respectively. South of the Narbada River, however, sapinda relations are just opposite to this, and the preferred marriage for a man is with the daughter of a maternal uncle, and the next best marriage is with the daughter of a paternal aunt. Cross-cousin marriage is also common in Bengal and has therefore a southern and eastern distribution. Certain groups, such as the Parsis, marry closely within the family. Villages in the Punjab are exogamous, irrespective of relationship, whereas many southern and eastern villages are practically endogamous. Castes, which are regularly endogamous, nevertheless contain subcastes, often called gotra, which are exogamous. So it goes. But the range of one's possible mates is always circumscribed by the family and social facts of one's birth. In the West, incest rules include only the close members of one's immediate family. In peninsular India, they are extended to include a large number of distantly related, or even unrelated, individuals, and there is a remarkable solidarity of family ties within these widely extended family groups. See also section on *Law*.

Wealth and Prestige System.—Peninsular India has known the greatest personal concentrations of wealth in the modern world. Family groups make constant efforts to accumulate reserves of land and jewelry, or both. Because of the general poverty few of these attempts may succeed, but it is still true that a few families, especially of ruling princes, have accumulated rights to extensive land revenues and vast quantities of nonproductive wealth such as gold and precious gems. The total range of per capita or, more accurately, of family wealth thus extends from dire need to fabulous luxury. Modern economic planning in India and Pakistan aims to correct this situation. In the meantime, the struggle for survival is often difficult enough. Nevertheless, it is constantly coupled with a struggle for relative wealth and position. Indeed, survival is often accomplished only by successful jockeying for positions which seem on the surface to be quite valueless. Once obtained, wealth and position are often perpetuated by various devices commonly present in class societies throughout the world.

It is important to note, however, that the value systems of the subcontinent, with few exceptions, emphasize nonmaterial successes such as wisdom, learning, orthodoxy, and prowess in fields ranging from athletics to the arts. In the traditional Hindu four stages of human life, ashrama (Sanskrit *āśrama*), the second is devoted to gaining a livelihood, the third to retirement in the forest from this struggle and to cultivation of the purer virtues, and the fourth to wandering asceticism. Without further elaborating the point, we may say that a wealthy man, or one of worldly position, is liable to be suspected automatically of dishonesty and blind self-interest. Such a judgment does not serve greatly to reduce the struggle for relative position, but it has tremendous effects upon recognized leadership and the prestige system. Men who devote themselves solely to wealth, the typical banyas (banias), are, at the same time, fawned upon and despised. Humble villagers, who are thought of as being outside the range of the most virulent struggles for material gain, often command considerable respect in the subcontinent, and in this they are to be sharply contrasted to the European peasant. Persons who receive a hearing in family, social, economic, or government affairs are most often those with other qualifications than wealth. But the truly great leader is the one who has the power of wealth, yet refuses to use it solely for his own ends, and who clearly demonstrates his right to recognition on some quite different count.

Caste.—The word caste has been used by a number of modern social theorists to refer to particular situations in various class societies. Wherever the position of individuals within a class is determined more or less rigidly by circumstances of birth, the class is often likened to a caste. Thus, it has become usual to speak of the position of Negro groups in the southern portions of the United States in terms of caste and class, stressing the fact that features of the Negro physical type set certain persons apart, from birth, from the more usual American class mobility. Caste thus becomes synonymous with a kind of frozen class system. Although such theorists make no reference to the Hindu caste system, the reader makes an easy transition from caste in their terms to the caste system. As a matter of fact, the association between certain caste practices and the evils of Western society is by no means new, and has had important repercussions upon Indian-Western relations from an early period. The abuses which occur within the system have long been obvious, and reform movements have been directed against them by Indian leaders from the 16th century to the present. But our immediate concern is for a fuller understanding of the caste system itself.

Though explicit in Hindu doctrine, caste is by no means a solely religious phenomenon. The caste system is at the core of life in Ceylon, India, and Pakistan whatever the religions of their citizens, and despite the fact that Ceylon, as primarily Buddhist, and Pakistan, as nationally Moslem, both hold religious doctrines antagonistic to much of caste practice. Other Buddhist and Moslem countries do not have caste. As the English anthropologist J. H. Hutton has said, caste is an exclusively Indic phenomenon.

According to Hindu tradition the castes originated in the four varna (Sanskrit *varṇa*), and knowledge of this tradition is widely circulated. It was explicitly formulated in the Vedic period. Furthermore, Vedic documentation has been accepted by scholars in support of the common belief that caste took its present form during the Aryan invasions of the Vedic period. Various social origins of caste have been suggested: that it was the device of a conquering people invented to keep a subjugated people under control and was further extended to maintain the power of the priesthood; that some form of caste arises when different racial stocks come together and is an expression of social inferiority and superiority; that the system develops naturally when differentiation of occupation becomes traditional; and that it arises from emphasis upon ritual purity. Some authors combine two or three of these hypotheses, and others could be mentioned. None of them can be fully satisfactory to the modern social scientist accustomed to dealing with the structural features of society. They all seem to be rationalizations after the fact.

Despite the multiplicity of caste theory, the descriptive materials on caste made by authors who have seen it in operation are amazingly uniform. Without our entering into the details of the system, an analysis of the descriptive data leads us to the conclusion that the caste system is founded upon three cultural conditions: (1) the explicit concept that the whole of society is made up of necessarily interacting parts; (2) the fact that social groups, however constituted, have autonomy over their own beliefs, their own customs, and their own practices and prejudices; and (3) the arrangement of groups into hierarchies according to which intergroup affairs are regulated. It is important to note that although castes are ranked in relation to each other, individuals are not ranked within castes. It is true that the individual's caste affiliation is determined by birth and may not be changed. But the relative position of castes may and does vary, and considerable effort has been expended in the past to raise the status of particular castes or to prevent the depression of other castes. With 2,718 castes reported in the census of 1931, there is a good deal of leeway for such action.

Recognition of the autonomy of castes in regard to their own affairs lends Hinduism its peculiar tolerance. Any group may make its own rules without interference from others, and in actuality these are often tolerated even when they interfere with smooth intergroup action. Castes on many levels in the hierarchy have often fought bitterly to protect their social, ritual, or occupational autonomy. They have even more often resorted to a flat refusal to change their practices under outside pressure. The influences of both Islam and modern Western society have been in the direction of weakening caste autonomy. Despite these influences, however, the structural aspects of caste are still strong in most of the subcontinent.

Nature of Indic Society.—The structure of a society is determined by the ways in which social groups are constituted and by the factors which knit these groups together. Whereas some world societies function through the interactions of groups defined in family terms, and others through the interplay of classes established on lines of relative wealth and position, the subcontinent embraces both of these. It further adds a third feature, caste, according to which social groups may be constituted on any basis at all but, once constituted, tend to be perpetuated. Caste in the subcontinent is not to be confused with class. The individual's caste is fixed, but although he may be hampered in his struggle by various factors inherent in his birth, his mobility in the class system of wealth and position and of personal prestige is not so fixed.

Not only, therefore, does the nature of Indic society reflect the general complexity of culture in peninsular India, but it points again to the varied sources from which it originated. The subcontinent is neither wholly of the East nor of the West. Yet nowhere does Indic culture demonstrate so clearly its genius for reworking foreign elements into its own pattern as in the intricacies of its social structure.

Bibliography.—Rivers, W. H. R., *The Todas* (London 1906); Risley, Sir H. H. *The People of India*, 2d ed. (Calcutta 1915); Hutton, J. H., *Caste in India: Its Nature, Function and Origin* (Cambridge, England, 1946); Smith, Marian W., "Village Notes from Bengal," *American Anthropologist*, vol. 48, pp. 574-92 (1946); Opler, Morris, and Singh, Rudra Datt, "Division of Labor in an Indian Village" in Coon, Carleton S., ed., *A Reader in General Anthropology* (New York 1948); Mandelbaum, David, "Family in India," *Southwestern Journal of Anthropology*, vol. 4, pp. 123-39 (1948); Smith, Marian W., "Kota Texts, A Review of the Primitive in Indic Folklore," *Journal of American Folklore*, vol. 61, no. 241, pp. 283-97 (1948); Mandelbaum, David, *Materials for a Bibliography of the Ethnology of India* (Berkeley, Calif., 1949); Movius, Hallam L., Jr., *Lower Palaeolithic Cultures of Southern and Eastern Asia* (Philadelphia 1949).

Supplementary Material: A great deal of valuable material is incorporated in various fictional or semipopular accounts such as Rudyard Kipling, *Kim* (London 1901); E. M. Forster, *A Passage to India* (London 1924); Penderel Moon, *Strangers in India* (New York 1945); and Hilda Wernher, and Huthi Singh, *The Land and the Well* (New York 1946).

Marian W. Smith,
Department of Anthropology, Columbia University.

4. LANGUAGES. The subcontinent of India, with a population comparable in numbers to that of Europe excluding Russia, presents a linguistic picture even more diversified. Four language families are represented there, of which two (Indo-European and Tibeto-Burman) are found outside of India. Two others (Dravidian; Munda) are unknown elsewhere. It also has several languages of few speakers each whose affiliations are dubious or unknown.

Indo-European.—Most of the inhabitants of the north of India—the Ganges, Indus, and Brahmaputra valleys, Rajputana, Gujarat, and the northern part of the Deccan—speak Indo-Aryan languages, a subfamily of the great Indo-European family, which occupies most of Europe. The history of Indo-Aryan speech falls into three periods: Old, Middle, and New.

Old Indo-Aryan.—This had several dialects, including the literary language Sanskrit (*saṃskṛta*). Old Indo-Aryan was introduced into India through the northwestern passes by invaders during the 2d millennium B.C. It underwent development in the course of time, and the oldest literary documents preserved already show traces of borrowing from a vernacular belonging to the next linguistic period as well as from Dravidian. Sanskrit is the classical language in which India's culture is couched, and all the other literary languages, whether Indo-European or Dravidian, contain many words borrowed from it and reflect its literary influence.

Middle Indo-Aryan.—Languages of this period are recorded in documents of various kinds; they are also called Prakrit (*prākṛta*). The inscriptions of the emperor Aśoka (3rd century B.C.) were written in a number of Prakrit dialects. The scriptures of southern (Hinayana) Buddhism are written in Pali (Pāli). The Jain sectarians wrote their scriptures in Ardha-Māgadhī and Jaina Māhārāṣṭrī. The old dramas are written partly in Sanskrit, partly in various Prakrits, and the Hindu grammarians describe these and still other Prakrits.

New Indo-Aryan.—The modern representatives of Indo-Aryan include a fairly large number of languages, most of them with many dialects which run into one another without well-marked boundaries. The languages of the Ganges Valley, from east to west, are as follows (the numbers of speakers are given in approximate figures according to the 1931 census of India before partition, the latest to publish an enumeration by language; about 1.5 per cent should be added for each year since then): Bengali (53 millions), Bihari (28 millions), Hindi, divided into Eastern and Western Hindi dialects (80 millions), Panjabi (16 millions). In western Punjab there is found a group of dialects called Lahnda (8.5 millions). In the southern part of the Indus Valley, Sindhi is spoken (4 millions). Rajputana is the home of a group of dialects called Rajasthani (14 millions). Gujarat is the home of Gujarati (11 millions). To the south are spoken Marathi in the west (21 millions) and Oriya in the east (11 millions). The Brahmaputra Valley is the home of Assamese (2 millions). Dialects called Pahari ("mountain dialects"; 2.75 millions) are spoken in the lower ranges of the Himalaya; Nepali is the most important. The northwestern part of the subcontinent has many tribes speaking Dardic languages and dialects; Kashmiri is the most important (1.5 millions).

The languages named, with but few exceptions, are, or have been, the vehicles of literary production. At present literatures thrive to a greater or lesser extent in Bengali, Assamese, Oriya, Panjabi, Gujarati, and Marathi. Hindi must not be omitted from this list, but is a special case. A Western Hindi dialect, originally spoken in the upper Gangetic Doab, that is, around Delhi and Mathura, became in the 12th and 13th centuries the speech of the soldiers and Hindu functionaries of Mogul administration at Delhi and Agra. Thence it spread to all centers of administration. When it was written, Arabic characters with the modifications used in Persia, were its alphabet. It became a literary language in the 16th century at Golconda in the Dravidian country. Later it received the name Urdu (from *zabān-i-urdū*, "language of the camp"); otherwise it is called Hindustani (language of Hindustan). As used today by Moslems, with loan words from Persian and Arabic and written in the Persian characters, it is called Urdu. As later cultivated by Hindus (as opposed to its first cultivation by Moslems) and written in the native north Indian Devanagari script, it is often called Hindi or High Hindi. This language during a number of centuries had the role of a lingua franca in north India through association with the Mogul administration and later the British administration. As Hindi, in its Devanagari written form, it is an official language of the Republic of India. As Urdu, written in Persian script, it is an official language of Pakistan.

Iranian.—Another Indo-European subfamily, Iranian, is represented in Pakistan by the Baluchi (Balochi) language, and by speakers of Pushtu (Pashto), who spill over from Afghanistan.

Dravidian.—The Dravidian family of languages is found only in India and Ceylon. It occupies all the peninsula south of the Indo-Aryan family and is second only to the latter in number of speakers. Four of the languages have old literatures, of which one, the Tamil, goes back to the beginning of the Christian era. The northern part of the Dravidian area is occupied by Kanarese (Kannaḍa), or Canarese, in the west (11 millions) and Telugu in the east as far south as the city of Madras (26 millions). In the Madras plains Tamil is spoken (20.5 millions). Malayalam is the language of the Malabar Coast (9 millions). Minor Dravidian languages are spoken by various small groups in the south—Tulu in Mangalore and the surrounding country on the Malabar Coast (650,000), Coorgi (Kodagu) in the Western Ghats (45,000), Toda (600) and Kota (1,000) in the Nilgiri Hills. In central India, within the Indo-Aryan area, there are several primitive tribes that speak Dravidian languages—Gondi with a number of divergent dialects (1,800,000), Kui (500,000), Kurukh (Oraon; 1 million), Malto (70,000), Kolami (28,000). Far to the northwest in Baluchistan (in Pakistan), the Brahui (200,000) speak a Dravidian language, in the midst of the Iranian Baluchi.

Munda.—The third most numerously represented family in India is Munda (Kolarian). Its speakers constitute economically primitive communities scattered throughout central India in the Indo-Aryan area. They number about 5 millions. Names of languages are Kherwari (including Santali, Mundari, and Bhumij), Kharia, Juang, Kurku, Sora (Saura; Savara), and Gadaba.

Tibeto-Burman.—The Tibeto-Burman language family, widespread in Tibet and Southeast Asia, is represented in India by several hundred languages, each with a small number of speakers, scattered along the Himalayan ranges (for example, Newari, spoken widely in Nepal) and in the hills of Assam (for example, the Naga dialects). The number of speakers is about 3 millions.

Other Languages.—Isolated languages are Khasi, spoken in Assam by 230,000 speakers; Burushaski, spoken in the Karakorum Range (20,000); and the languages of the Andaman and Nicobar Islands. (An Austroasiatic family, connecting the Munda languages, Khasi, and Nicobarese with some of the languages of Southeast Asia, has been postulated, but so far is hardly more than a guess.)

Select Bibliography.—Grierson, Sir George A., ed., *Linguistic Survey of India,* 11 vols. (Calcutta 1903–1928); Chatterji, S. K., *Languages and the Linguistic Problem,* Oxford Pamphlets on Indian Affairs, No. 11, 3d ed. (London 1945).

MURRAY B. EMENEAU,
Department of Classics, University of California, Berkeley.

5. LITERATURE.

The oldest and most important literature of India is that composed in Sanskrit. This is the classical verbalization of Hindu culture; all other literatures of India, with minor exceptions, are derived from it.

The Vedas.—The first period of Sanskrit literature is of uncertain chronology. It may have begun in the second half of the third millennium or the first half of the second millennium B.C. It ended in the first half of the first millennium B.C. There remains from this period a vast body of religious texts, called collectively the Vedas. The earliest of these texts are four ritual books, the *Saṃhitās* (or four Vedas). Their composition and editing undoubtedly occupied a long time, and the texts as they survive today show signs of much rehandling, and even of mishandling as the earliest forms of the language came to be archaic and in part unintelligible.

Of the four Vedas, the first is the Rig Veda (*Ṛgveda*), a hymnal containing 1,028 hymns in 10 books. The hymns were mainly composed for use in the morning and evening rituals connected with the household fire and the preparation of the soma drink; there are also wedding and funeral hymns. Traces of other interests also are found—dialogues between mythological and historical characters, riddles, and, of great importance for later developments in Hindu thought, attempts at explaining man's place in the universe and the origin of the universe. Much of this hymnology, though in verse, is unpoetic and unexciting. At times, however, the composers were visited by inspiration and real poetry resulted. We are often enough hampered in our appreciation of the Rig Veda by the extreme archaism of the language, which the Hindus of the post-Vedic times understood only with difficulty and which present day scholarship often labors over in vain. The stanzaic meters used in it reappear in classical Sanskrit verse in more highly developed forms. The type of composition associated with these meters is one in which each verse is almost always treated as a separate unit in subject as well as in meter; both Vedic and classical versification follows this model closely.

The Sāma Veda consists of a section of the Rig Vedic hymns with musical notations added.

The Atharva Veda, another large hymnal of 731 hymns, is chiefly a book of magic spells in verse. It also continues the Rig Vedic attempts at philosophy. Very little literary value is to be found in it.

The Yajur Veda texts are prayer books, giving both directions in prose for performing the rituals and the prose formulas and hymns to be uttered by the priests. There are in addition numerous discussions of the meaning of the rituals. These theological passages are of the same nature as the Brāhmaṇa texts that form the second major portion of the Vedic literature. In these, the rituals are discussed in all their symbolic and cosmic implications and a highly sophisticated ritualistic theory is developed. The Brāhmaṇas also present many mythological stories in explanation of the hymns and contain the crude beginnings of grammar, mathematics, and the other sciences, and further attempts at philosophy.

The last major section of the Vedas is the Upanishads (*Upaniṣad*). These advance the philosophic speculations begun in the Vedas and Brāhmaṇas, and in them we can see the main outlines of later Hindu philosophy and the germs of Buddhist and Jain doctrines as well.

The prose of the Vedas is simple in construction, probably close to colloquial usage; it abounds in repetition, both of words and of constructions, a quality permitting easy memorization, which was the method of transmission even after writing was introduced to India. At its best, this sort of prose may have an artless charm and a sinewy directness and energy, especially in narrative, but literary values other than these scarcely appear. Although it would be tempting to compare the Upanishads with Plato's Dialogues, it would be claiming too much for them. They have the same earnest impulse toward truth and, in addition, an urgency due to the composers' doctrine that knowledge of the truth will win the soul a blissful otherworldly existence. As literary productions, however, the Upanishads hardly rise above the level of other Vedic prose and, in fact, are at times cryptic, apparently depending upon further oral discussion for their elucidation.

The Grammarians.—During the last half millennium of the pre-Christian period and the first few centuries after Christ, there was much literary activity. The grammatical studies begun in the Brāhmaṇa period resulted in a number of phonetic texts whose object was to describe the correct pronunciation of the Vedas, since rituals would have been invalidated by incorrect pronunciation. The culmination of grammatical studies is seen in the great grammar by Pāṇini (5th or 4th century B.C.), and the two commentaries on it by Kātyāyana and Patañjali (probably 2d century B.C.). Pāṇini uses a prose style known as sutra (Sanskrit *sūtra*), developed from the earlier prose style but showing an extreme compression, so that much matter could be put into a short, easily memorized text. Both before and after him, the sutra is the form of many basic works on philosophy, law, ritual, and science. All these works required commentaries to make them intelligible. Patañjali shows an early type of clear and elegant prose commentary. Some later commentators developed a more highly elaborated and difficult prose style for this purpose. Still others wrote in simple verses of the epic type.

Buddhist and Jain Literature.—In this same period fall the beginnings of the Buddhist and Jain literatures. Both of them were first written in Middle Indo-Aryan languages. Buddhism came to use Pali; Jainism, Ardha-Māgadhī and Jaina Māhārāṣṭrī. Later on both were to cultivate Sanskrit in conscious competition with Hinduism. The early styles were not unlike the Brāhmaṇa prose; they seldom attained literary grace, perhaps even purposely eschewed it. The later styles, in Middle Indo-Aryan or in Sanskrit, came to strive, in a mild way, after the same literary values as those found in Hindu texts.

The Epics.—During all this period there must have been epic composition. The epics that have come down to us were perhaps not completely stabilized until some centuries later, but they took their general shape at this time. The folk epic *Mahābhārata* is the story of a great interclan war of succession in the Delhi region of the upper Ganges Valley; the *Rāmāyaṇa* is the story of Rāma and his war with the demons in Lanka (Ceylon) to recover his lost wife Sītā. Both epics drew to themselves much extraneous material. The *Mahābhārata* especially had so much story material and so many religious and legal treatises and other didactic matter inserted in it that it runs to approximately 100,000 couplets. It became in one sense another Veda or religious handbook, in another sense an encyclopedia of Hinduism, and its influence on Hindu literature, art, and thought continues down to the present day. One of its most important sections is the famous *Bhagavad Gītā,* or *Song of the Blessed Krishna* (*Kṛṣṇa*), a religio-ethical treatise that is one of the most widely used texts of Hinduism. The *Mahābhārata's* verses form generally a free-running narrative, which at times rises to respectable stylistic heights, marked by the same expansiveness that is familiar to the West in Homer. The didactic material is presented in verse of simple exposition, which, if it does not rise to lofty heights, yet at its best possesses earnestness and the grace of simplicity. These types of composition provide many models for later expository scientific texts and for the Purāṇas. In its final form, the *Mahābhārata* is said to have been recited by Vyāsa, a diaskeuast who heard it from earlier reciters. It is otherwise with the *Rāmāyaṇa,* whose 24,000 couplets purport to be the composition of one poet, Vālmīki. This poem shares the epic breadth of the *Mahābhārata.* Its style is somewhat more enriched than that of the *Mahābhārata,* with a greater abundance of figures of language and thought. Later literary criticism referred to Vālmīki as the Ādikavi, or first poet.

Kāvya, Or the Fully Developed Literary Style.—This period saw also a development of verse compositions with an even richer, more elaborate style than that of the *Rāmāyaṇa.* It came to be called *kāvya,* the work of the *kavi,* or poet. All the early works have vanished except those by the Buddhist poet Aśvaghoṣa (c.100 A.D.). His *Buddhacarita* (*Life of the Buddha*) and *Saundarananda* (*Poem About the Handsome Nanda,* one of the Buddha's disciples) are works of an early but already well-developed and fully conscious literary art. At the same time there was developed a dramatic literature of mingled prose and lyric verse. The verses are of *kāvya* type. The plays are the libretti of an operalike art form in mingled Sanskrit and Middle Indo-Aryan. Again, all early examples are lost; Aśvaghoṣa worked in this form, but we have only a few fragments of his productions.

The next period opens with the culminating figure of all Sanskrit literature—Kālidāsa. He almost certainly belongs to the great Gupta period (4th and 5th centuries A.D.), and perhaps he flourished in the early 5th century. Three *kāvya* works are certainly his—the *Raghuvaṃśa* (*Raghu's Lineage*), the *Kumārasaṃbhava* (*The War God's Birth*), and the *Meghadūta* (*The Cloud Messenger*); and three plays—*Shakuntala* (*Śakuntalā,* named for its heroine), *Vikramorvaśī* (*Urvaśī Won by Valor*), and *Mālavikāgnimitra* (*Mālavikā and Agnimitra,* the heroine and hero). The first named of each group is the best, in Hindu and in Western judgment, and they are the high points in Sanskrit literature. They are marked by a mature technical mastery of poetic form and figures of rhetoric, a skillful handling of situation and emotional suggestion, a classical restraint and perfection of outline. The themes are drawn predominantly from the old mythology or the epic; this is true of most of the later *kāvya* and drama. *Vikramorvaśī* depends on the Veda for its story; *Meghadūta* and *Mālavikāgnimitra* have romantic themes of the poet's own composition. Epic and romantic themes, along with the mythological, are the backbone of the later literature, with free invention less prominent than the use of stories already familiarly known.

For roughly a millennium after Kālidāsa, Sanskrit literature continued to be cultivated with some power and success. Imitative, weak productions were common also and continue down to the present day. The *kāvya* style, which culminated in poetic values in Kālidāsa's works, thereafter underwent development in a direction which is best characterized in a single word as intellectual. A highly self-conscious literary criticism grew up, one of its important traits being a minute dissection and classification of literary ornament, figures of speech. The *kāvya* came more and more to be composed in accordance with the rules of the textbooks of literary criticism. The figures of speech came increasingly to overlay the compositions, and in the end narrative and emotion were smothered by ornament. The poetical afflatus appeared again and again, and indeed was fully recognized in the theory, but if it did not operate within the rules of the textbooks, it had no chance of approval by the critics, who seem to have judged all by the rules and perhaps even to have been uncomfortable in the presence of poetical power that was unconventional and unadorned. Many of the *kāvyas* of this period show that their authors had no mean poetical gifts, but the methods of composition laid down and approved were never overthrown by a poetical revolution. Since Sanskrit was an unspoken language possibly already in Pāṇini's time, the wonder is not that no revolution took place, but that ambitious attempts at poetry continued as long as they did.

The literary critics rate as the greatest of *kāvyas* five works: the first two *kāvyas* of Kālidāsa already listed, Bhāravi's *Kirātārjunīya* (*Story of Kirāta and Arjuna*), an episode from the *Mahābhārata*, probably of the 6th century A.D.; Māgha's *Śiśupālavadha* (*Slaughter of Śiśupāla*), from the *Mahābhārata*, of the 7th century A.D.; and Śrīharṣa's *Naiṣadhacarita* (*Story of Nala*), taken from a famous interpolated story in the *Mahābhārata*, and written in the 12th century A.D. The last is an enormously ingenious example of *kāvya* at its most learned and least poetic. Several other works are rated highly. Bhaṭṭi's *Bhaṭṭikāvya* or *Rāvaṇavadha* (*Slaughter of Rāvaṇa*, 6th or 7th century A.D.) is based on the *Rāmāyaṇa* and deliberately illustrates the rules of poetic composition and of grammar. Kumāradāsa's *Jānakīharaṇa* (*Abduction of Sītā*; probably 8th century A.D.) is also based on the *Rāmāyaṇa*. Many other works have survived, most of them imitative and pedantic. Frequently, like Bhaṭṭi's work, they are constructed to show the author's competence in literary theory and in grammar rather than his real poetic ability. This pedantry could hardly have been avoided in a culture with such predominantly intellectualizing tendencies and interests as the Hindu; even Aśvaghoṣa and Kālidāsa are not entirely free from it.

Hindu taste took great pleasure in figures of speech comparable to Western puns. Kālidāsa seldom employed them, but they became much commoner later. The learned pedants of the period of decadence go on to triumphs of ingenuity by constructing works which punningly can be interpreted in two ways throughout. Saṃdhyākara Nandin (11th century) is probably the earliest to produce such a work, the *Rāmacarita* (*Life of Rāma*); in 220 verses he tells at the same time the story of the *Rāmāyaṇa* and the history of King Rāmapāla of Bengal. The device is used by various practitioners to tell at the same time the stories of the *Mahābhārata* and the *Rāmāyaṇa*, the stories of Rāma and Nala, the stories of the marriages of Shiva (Śiva) and Pārvatī and of Krishna and Rukmiṇī. One composer even succeeded in telling three stories at the same time, those of the *Rāmāyaṇa*, the *Mahābhārata*, and the *Bhāgavata Purāṇa*; he was Chidambara (Cidambara; 16th to 17th century), and the work is called *Rāghavapāṇḍavayādavīya* (*Story of Rāma, the Pāṇḍavas, and Kṛṣṇa*).

Kāvya methods were applied also to historical themes, which emerge from the treatment with little value as history or as poetry. Kalhaṇa's *Rājataraṃgiṇi* (*Stream of Kings*), on the Kashmir kings down to 1149 A.D., is the best. The Jain Hemacandra in 1163 A.D. wrote the *Kumārapālacarita*, which has as its object to tell of the reign of the Chalukya king Kumārapāla of Aṇhilvāḍa (Anhilwara; modern Patan) in Gujarat, and at the same time to illustrate the rules of Sanskrit and Prakrit grammar, in accordance with which its first 20 cantos are in Sanskrit and its last 8 in Prakrit.

Kālidāsa's *Meghadūta*, a lyric, idyllic poem describing the journey of a cloud sent by a traveler as messenger to his beloved wife, also set a model for numerous imitations, all of less value than their prototype.

Moralizing *sententiae* were drawn within the *kāvya* sphere by the obvious suitability of the stanzaic meters as a vehicle for a general sentiment and a brief example. The same form was used for verses on erotic and on religious subjects. Many poets practiced verse-by-verse composition of this type, on subjects drawn from all realms of Hindu experience. The verses were often collected in groups called *śataka* (hundred; cento), such as the three by Bhartrihari (Bhartṛhari, fl. first half of 7th century) on love, asceticism, and ethics; Amaru's on love; Bāṇa's (7th century) on the goddess Chaṇḍī (Caṇḍī); Mayūra's (early 7th century) on Sūrya, the sun god; and many others. Other collections, such as those on ethics attributed to Chanakya (Cāṇakya, 4th century), have no fixed number of verses. Many verses by different authors are preserved in anthologies, such as the *Kavīndravacanasamuccaya* (*Collection of Verses of Great Poets*, possibly prior to 1000 A.D.), Śrīdharadāsa's *Saduktikarṇāmṛta* (*Great Verses Which Are Nectar for the Ears*, 1205 A.D.), and numerous others. A famous early Buddhist collection of verses of this type is the *Dhammapada*, in Pali. Misplaced ingenuity results here also in works that can be read in two different ways. Rāmacandra in the 16th century wrote the *Rasikarañjana* (*Delight of Connoisseurs*), which is simultaneously an erotic poem and a eulogy of asceticism; it consists of 130 verses.

Kāvya compositions are not always in verse. The prose *kāvyas*, with their heavy encrustation of figures of speech, can go further than verse compositions in multiplying the ornaments, once the space limitations of stanzaic composition are removed. Subandhu (6th or 7th century) actually boasts of a pun in every syllable. The subjects of prose *kāvya* are usually nonmythical. Their narrative substratum is sometimes an invented story of the folk tale type, as in Bāṇa's *Kādambarī* (7th century A.D.), Subandhu's *Vāsavadattā*, and Daṇḍin's *Daśakumāracarita* (*Adventures of the Ten Princes*, 6th or 7th century A.D.). Bāṇa's *Harṣacarita* (*Life of Harṣa*) has to do with King Harsha (Harshavardhana). The history is so submerged in poetic fancies as to be extricable only with some difficulty, but the work is important for the pictures it gives of its times.

Folk tale, when collected and recorded, sometimes underwent a mild dressing up in the ornaments of *kāvya;* the stories themselves, however, usually remained the real center of interest. Somadeva's *Kathāsaritsāgara* (*Ocean of the Streams of Stories,* 11th century A.D.) is an enormous work in flowing, mildly decorated verses, with many shorter tales enclosed within the frame tale. It is a reworking, probably at some removes, of Guṇāḍhya's *Bṛhatkathā* (*Great Story*), which was in Paiśācī, one of the Prakrits; the loss of this early work is a serious one. Another reworking, closely allied to Somadeva's and near him in date, is Kṣemendra's *Bṛhatkathāmañjarī* (*Bouquet from the Great Story*), a dry, lifeless abstract with *kāvya* patches added at intervals. A third reworking, in a different line of transmission from the other two, is Budhasvāmin's *Bṛhatkathāślokasaṃgraha* (*Verse Abbreviation of the Great Story*), which has been recovered in a fragmentary form. Another famous collection of folk tales is the *Pañcatantra,* which has come down in a number of recensions with various names: *Tantrākhyāyika, Pañcākhyānaka, Hitopadeśa.* In the framework of the collection a teacher is represented as instructing young princes in the ways of political life by maxims illustrated by stories, which are usually animal fables. The work is a mixture of prose stories and verse maxims, with much of the *kāvya* in its verses. Another collection is the *Vetālapañcaviṃśati* (*Goblin's Twenty-five Tales*), each story of which leads up to a riddlelike problem which is solved by one of the characters in the frame story.

Both the Buddhist and the Jain literatures abound in folk tale collections. All the stories purport to be given for the sake of the morals that can be derived from them, but one suspects frequently that the monkish writers delighted in the stories for their own sakes. The Buddhist book of *Jātakas* (*Stories of the Buddha's Former Births*), containing over 500 tales, is the most famous of these collections. It dates, but in part only, from the pre-Christian period, and seems to have been finally composed in its present Pali form in the 5th century A.D. Another similar collection is found in the commentary on the *Dhammapada* (over 300 stories), slightly later than the *Jātakas.* Āryaśūra's *Jātakamālā* (*Garland of Jātakas;* 3d or 4th century A.D.) gives to a few stories a mixed verse and prose *kāvya* style that is almost lacking in the Pali stories. The commentaries to the Jain scriptures, in Prakrit and Sanskrit, record thousands of stories, usually in a bare narrative style with moralistic verses.

The *kāvya* style spread its influence far and wide. The lyric verses of the dramas are hardly to be separated from those of nondramatic composition and in fact are as little dramatic in character as are the arias of European opera. Important plays in the history of the Indian drama are *Mṛcchakaṭikā* (*Little Clay Cart,* prior to 6th century A.D.), by Shudraka (Śūdraka); *Priyadarśikā, Ratnāvalī,* and *Nāgānanda* by Harsha (Harṣa, probably King Harshavardhana, r. 606–647 A.D.; Viśākhadatta's *Mudrārākṣasa* (9th century A.D., or earlier); and Bhavabhūti's *Mālatīmādhava, Mahāvīracarita,* and *Uttararāmacarita* (probably 8th century A.D.). A group of 13 dramas of some excellence, which were discovered in 1910, have been attributed to Bhāsa, who was earlier than Kālidāsa, but the ascription is still uncertain. The most important of them is the *Svapnavāsavadattā* (*Vāsavadattā Seen in a Dream*). Many late dramas survive, most of them intended to be read rather than acted and of little literary or dramatic importance.

The work that is accepted as the latest of any importance in Sanskrit literature is Jayadeva's *Gītagovinda* (12th century A.D.). It is in a fully formed new genre—highly emotional and dramatic lyrics connected by transitional narrative and descriptive verses, all depicting an episode of Krishna's life in the spirit of highest devotion. It undoubtedly derived much from the contemporary vernacular literatures.

Prakrit Kāvya.—Prakrit poetry, that is, poetry in the Middle Indo-Aryan vernaculars, had appeared probably as soon as these vernaculars became differentiated from Sanskrit. It must, however, soon have fallen under the influence of the littérateurs dealing with Sanskrit poetry, for the earliest Prakrit poems that survive—Hāla's *Sattasaï* (*Seven Hundred Verses,* of the first half millennium A.D.), an anthology on love; and Pravarasena's *Setubandha* (*Rāma's Bridge,* 6th century A.D.), on a theme from the *Rāmāyaṇa*—are indistinguishable in style from Sanskrit poems on comparable subjects. The same is true of most late Jain poetry, whether in Sanskrit or in Prakrit.

Nonliterary Composition in Sanskrit.—During all this long period of literary activity, there was much other composition in Sanskrit, most of it without literary values. The philosophical and scientific works have been mentioned. The epic was continued in a jejune way by the 18 major and many minor Purāṇas (*Narratives of Old*). These contain primarily the mythology, cosmology, and ritual of classical Hinduism, but in addition much other material, so that some of them became veritable encyclopedias of Hinduism. The Tantra literature also is an exposition of certain religious cults.

North Indian Vernacular Literature.—Many of the modern vernaculars of north India have literatures of some age and standing. In general, they are dependent on the old traditions of Sanskrit literature. The epics and Purāṇas are translated or adapted frequently with some influence from the *kāvya* style. Writers of such works include Tulsī Dās (1532–1623), who composed a *Rāmāyaṇa* in the Awadhi dialect of the Eastern Hindi area; Lallūjī Lāl, author of *Prēmsāgar* (*Ocean of Love*), which is a prose rendering in High Hindi of the 10th book of the *Bhāgavata Purāṇa* (1804–1810); Jñāneśvar, who rendered the *Bhagavad Gītā* in Marathi verse about 1290; the translators into Bengali of the two epics, beginning in the 14th century; and others. The storybooks, such as the *Pañcatantra* and the *Vetālapañcaviṃśati,* have often been translated into Gujarati, Hindi, and other languages.

The religious and moralistic lyric, which begins in the Rig Veda and is an important strand in all Sanskrit literature thereafter, forms perhaps the richest element in the vernacular literature. It is noted for its fervor and intensity, and often possesses high stylistic qualities, both of the *kāvya* type and more untrammeled. Braj Bhākhā, a dialect of the Western Hindi area, became from the 15th century the accepted language in which to sing of Krishna in Hindustan; the poetess Mīra Bāī (fl. c. 1420) and the poet Bihārī Lāl (17th century) are only two of the famous names in this literature. Vidyāpati Ṭhākur (15th century) sang of Krishna in the Maithili dialect of Bihar. Kabīr (c. 1440–1518) composed in Hindi religious songs which embody a syncretism of Hindu and Moslem elements; Guru Nānak (c. 1469–1538), a pupil of Kabīr's, was the initiator of a line of teachers and religious poets whose compositions, mainly in Hindi, form the Granth Sahib, the sacred book of the Sikhs. In Bengali, Caṇḍīdās, a contemporary of Vidyāpati, sang of Krishna. In Kashmir the female ascetic Lallā (14th century) composed songs in honor of Shiva. The Maratha poets Nāmdev (1270–1350) and Tukārām (1608–1649) are only two of this area's many mystic singers.

The chivalric ballads in the local dialects of Rajputana (beginning in the 12th century) cannot be neglected even in a short sketch; they are a departure from the lines laid down in the older literature.

Dravidian Literature.—The literatures in the four great Dravidian languages of south India—Tamil, Telugu, Kanarese, and Malayalam—are, like those of the modern Indo-Aryan vernaculars, in general derivative from Sanskrit and predominantly religious. These literatures start earlier than those in the modern Indo-Aryan languages. Tamil has a proud literary history going back to the beginning of the Christian era, and its vast literature is second in importance only to that in Sanskrit. The earliest works preserved are a grammar, collections of sententious stanzas, and lyrics of devotion to the gods Shiva and Vishnu.

Foreign Influences.—Two important foreign influences have affected Indian literature. The Persian literature of the Mogul court was the direct progenitor of an important literature in Urdu or Hindustani (see section on *Languages*).

The influx of Western influences since the early 19th century had literary results as well as others. The vernaculars are now vehicles of such secular Western forms as the novel, essay, political speech, personal lyric, and drama of the European type. Much of the old mingles with the new; the proportion of each fluctuates with changing fashion. One literary world figure has already emerged in the person of the Bengali Rabindranath Tagore (1861–1941), whose poetry was recognized by the Nobel Prize for literature in 1913.

Select Bibliography.—Grierson, Sir George A., *The Popular Literature of Northern India*, London University, Bulletin of the School of Oriental Studies, vol. 1, part 3, pp. 87-122 (1920); Keith, A. B., *The Sanskrit Drama in Its Origin, Theory, and Practice* (Oxford 1924); id., *A History of Sanskrit Literature*, on the classical period, excluding the drama (Oxford 1928); Winternitz, Moriz, *A History of Indian Literature*, tr. by S. Ketkar and H. Kohn, vols. 1 and 2, including Vedic, epic, Buddhist, and Jain literature (Calcutta 1927–1933); Thomas, F. W., "Language and Early Literature," "Language and Literature," and Ghosh, J. C., "Vernacular Literatures," *The Legacy of India*, ed. by G. T. Garratt (Oxford 1937); Dasgupta, S. N., and De, S. K., *A History of Sanskrit Literature, Classical Period*, vol. 1, including *kāvya* and literary criticism (Calcutta 1947).

MURRAY B. EMENEAU,
Department of Classics, University of California, Berkeley.

6. DANCING, MUSIC, AND THE DRAMA. Dancing and the drama are closely related in the subcontinent of India. The very words for them indicate as much. The common Sanskrit verb meaning "dance" is *nṛt*, and a Prakrit (see section on *Languages*) representative of this is *naṭ*. The latter returns to Sanskrit as the base for deriving the common words indicating dramatic representation, pantomime, acting, and dancing. Accompanying the dance and drama is music, both instrumental and vocal. A drama, which contains plot, an abundance of lyric stanzas, music, and dancing—and that is the usual characteristic of the Sanskrit drama and of Indian drama generally—is commonly called nataka (Sanskrit *nāṭaka*). An actor or mime or dancer is *naṭa*. Dancing used in a drama in combination with the original plot is *nāṭya*. The dancing which is mere rhythm or graceful movement is *nṛtta;* that which is informed with aesthetic and intellectual content is *nṛtya*.

The Sanskrit treatises on aesthetics indicate that the purpose of a dance or a drama is to evoke aesthetic experience in the spectators. Art is not exercised merely to entertain the spectators or to permit the artist an opportunity of self-expression. The audience has a part and must be educated in appreciation. Aesthetic experience consists in finding in a work of art a particular quality or essence called rasa (flavor or taste), which is its fundamental feature or permanent mood. There are 9 of these—erotic, heroic, odious, furious, terrible, pathetic, wondrous, comic, and peaceful. In a work of art, as distinguished from a work without artistic quality, some one rasa must be dominant, though others may appear in a subordinate role. Besides these 9 basic moods there are 33 transient moods (joy, agitation, impatience, and others), which are ancillary to the basic mood. To produce the total desired artistic effect the author contributes plot and theme, and the dancer or actor utilizes gestures or other deliberate manifestations of feeling, as well as expressions of involuntary emotion, such as trembling or horripilation.

Dancing.—The classical Indian dance, being mimetic and meant to convey ideas and moods, is a language, and its principal means of expression is therefore gesture. Every bodily movement, however trifling, has significance as an exposition of thought, sharing that function with the vocal and the decorative (stage setting and the like) features of the performance. The dancer utilizes the limbs (defined as head, hands, armpits, sides, waist, feet, neck), the minor parts of the body (shoulders, shoulder blades, arms, back, stomach, thighs, calves, wrists, knees, elbows), and the features (eyes, eyelids, pupils, cheeks, nose, jaw, lips, teeth, tongue, chin, face); some works also mention other parts (heel, ankle, fingers, toes, palms). Every part of the body has many different uses, but the hands are the most important and may be used separately or jointly. The final number of combinations and permutations of parts of the body is almost unlimited, and the range and exactness of expression which can be attained are said by enthusiasts to equal those of speech.

Dancing has a wide and perhaps long usage in Indian religions. There are several small bronze female dancing figures from the Harappa period of the Early Indus civilizations (see section on *Archaeology*), which suggest that dancing then served a religious purpose. The Rig Veda mentions dancing, especially by the god Indra after he has slain his enemy Vritra (Vṛtra), or by the gods as a group; this dance is the activity of creating the universe. In certain Vedic ceremonies women engage in ritualistic dancing. The Buddhists and Jains show Indra as a divine dancer. Early Indian sculpture, like later sculpture and painting, has numerous representations of dancing in many different circumstances, often exhibiting poses with meaning identifiable from the later treatises. In Hinduism the dancer par excellence is the god Shiva (Śiva), who performed a dance after slaying a fierce dwarf demon, and the south Indian bronzes which show him as Nāṭarāja (King of Dancers), combining in the motions of his arms and feet all the activities of the cosmos, are among the finest products of Indian art.

There have been various schools of Indian dancing, of which the best known is that of Bharata, described in a text of perhaps the 3d century A.D., and illustrated by a long series of sculptures on a late 11th century gateway of the temple at Chidambaram in south India. Other texts of aesthetics and dancing were composed as recently as the 14th century. Another well-known school of dancing is that of Kathakali in Travancore, in which the story of the epic *Rāmāyaṇa* is enacted.

Besides these classical dances there are a number of varieties of folk dance in India, such as that done in Gujarat with jars in honor of Krishna, and the stave dance.

Music.—Indian music is melodic, not harmonic. The focus of interest is on singing; instrumental music is meant for accompaniment. There are many types of instruments but the commonest are drums (of many varieties) and the vina (*vīṇā*), or lute. In Indian music the octave has 7 tones. There are also 22 microtones, which do not divide the octave into equal divisions, but indicate degrees of difference from the tonic which the singer is using. In classical music the singer elects for his song a melody mold or mode called a *rāga* or *rāgiṇī,* of which there are traditionally 36, though more can be cited. The *rāga* consists of a tonic and certain selected microtones—a flat, a sharp, a very flat, and a very sharp, and sometimes one or two additional. Within the limits of these the singer extemporizes. In singing there is abundant use of variation and grace notes.

In the use of time Indian music employs a variety of bars. A bar may have a single beat but with three, four, five, seven, or nine units; or it may be a two-beat bar, but with each bar having a different number of units, or a four-beat bar. Cross rhythm may be used, the singer and the accompanist employing different times, which, however, have a common factor. The climax comes at the point when the two coincide.

The first musical literature of India is the Sāma Veda (see section on *Literature*), which gives information on the chants (*sāman*) used in the Vedic ritual. Later data appear in the *Bharatanāṭyaśāstra,* perhaps of the 3d century A.D., and in works from the 13th century on.

Drama.—The Indian drama is of obscure origin, but the Rig Veda contains a number of dialogue hymns which it has been suggested may have been recited dramatically or acted out. As we have noted, the words for actor and drama are ultimately derived from a base meaning "dance." Further, the Sanskrit drama may be interpreted as a series of lyrics dealing with the beauties of nature or personal emotions, which are connected by a slender thread of plot, and these are in fact the parts of the drama most highly appreciated by the Indian audiences. The inference is, therefore, that the dance and the song preceded the drama. That the drama has an origin in folk religious ritual is possibly inferable from the fact that the season for performing plays is particularly the spring, at the time of the festival of the god of love, and so drama appears in association with popular fertility cults. The classical Sanskrit drama is usually on a religious theme. In modern times folk plays are numerous, most of them dealing with the lives of Rāma or Krishna, who are incarnations of the god Vishnu. Another element contributing to the drama may be the puppet play, which seems to have existed in India by the 6th century B.C. or earlier and by some Western scholars is thought to have originated in India. The stage manager of the Sanskrit drama, who conventionally announces the subject of the play, is called *sūtradhāra* (string controller), and his assistant in old texts is called *sthāpaka* (arranger), both of which terms suggest the puppet play. The theory that the Greek drama may have influenced the Hindu is generally rejected today.

The Sanskrit drama is opened with a benediction (*nāndī*) spoken by the stage manager, followed by a prologue, whereupon the first actor is introduced. The play consists of acts in each of which the hero must appear; the act comes to an end when the stage is empty. An act usually does not extend over more than 24 hours. The action of a play is represented in prose, and the rasas most commonly depicted are the erotic and the heroic. The lyrics in the drama constitute the peak of Sanskrit poetic composition.

Different types of characters speak conventional dialects. Sanskrit is usually restricted to kings and other persons of high rank and Brahmans. Certain kinds of women (female ascetics, the chief queen, daughters of ministers, courtesans) are in theory permitted to use Sanskrit, but usually speak Prakrit, as do other women and men of lower rank. Within these groups there is further linguistic limitation; persons of one class use one sort of Prakrit, persons of another class use another. These Prakrits are stage, rather than genuine spoken, dialects.

There are several conventional characters. One is the *vidūṣaka,* a low-grade Brahman, speaking Prakrit instead of Sanskrit, who is the king's confidant, attendant, and go-between, gluttonous and stupid, and a comic figure. Another is the *viṭa,* friend of the king, a man about town. Another is the *śakāra* (one who pronounces *sh* for *s*), brother of one of the king's inferior wives, a rude, stupid, insolent, and often ridiculous upstart, whose mischief complicates the plot.

Bhāsa, the first of the important classical Indian dramatists, is of uncertain date, but earlier than Kālidāsa; the assignment of any surviving plays to him is controversial; Kālidāsa, who lived before and after 400 A.D., is the greatest Indian dramatist. He is noted above all for his *Shakuntala* (*Śakuntalā*), which dramatizes an episode of the epic *Mahābhārata* concerning King Dushyanta (Duṣyanta) and the nymph Shakuntala, whom the king discovers in a forest hermitage, weds, forgets by reason of a sage's curse, but finally remembers when he sees a ring he has left with her (this had been lost, swallowed by a fish, and found by a fisherman). Kālidāsa is also author of two other plays, *Mālavikāgnimitra* (*Mālavikā* and *Agnimitra,* the heroine and hero) and *Vikra-*

morvaśī (*Urvaśī Won by Valor,* a theme from the Veda). King Harsha (Harṣa), who ruled in northern India from 606 to 647 A.D., is the author of three plays which are sometimes suspected, but probably unjustly, of having been ghostwritten by the celebrated poet Bāṇa, who lived at his court. King Shudraka (Śūdraka), of uncertain date but probably not much later than Kālidāsa, wrote *Mṛcchakaṭikā* (*Little Clay Cart*), the story of the poor but honest Brahman Charudatta (Cārudatta) and the rich and noble courtesan Vasantasenā who loves him. It is an entertaining drama with a burlesque scene on the traditional and pedantic Indian science of thieving.

Bhavabhūti, who lived about 700 A.D. or later, is considered second only to Kālidāsa. He wrote three plays, the *Mahāvīracarita* (*Early Life of Rāma*), *Uttararāmacarita* (*Later Life of Rāma*), and *Mālatīmādhava* (the story of the heroine Mālatī and the hero Mādhava). Bhaṭṭa Nārāyaṇa, who probably lived before 800 A.D., is the author of the *Veṇīsaṃhāra* (*The Braiding of the Hair*), which is based upon an episode in the epic *Mahābhārata.* It tells the story of the wicked king Duḥśāsana who, after the Pāṇḍavas were defeated at dicing and had lost their common wife Draupadī, dragged her off by her unbraided hair. Bhīma, one of the Pāṇḍavas, swore some day to kill Duḥśāsana and did so. Thereupon, Draupadī's hair could be braided again. Viśākhadatta, who probably lived not later than 800 A.D., is the author of a historical play, without love interest, concerning the faithful minister Yaugandharāyaṇa, whom Chanakya (Cāṇakya), minister of Chandragupta Maurya, tried to win to his master.

Rājaśekhara, who lived about 900 A.D., wrote four plays, of which the best known is the *Karpūramañjarī* (*The Camphor Garland*), written entirely in Prakrit. Krishnamishra (Kṛṣṇamiśra, fl. c.1100 A.D.) is the author of *Prabodhacandrodaya* (*Rise of the Moon of Knowledge*), an allegory of virtues set in a Vishnu milieu.

A number of treatises exist on the drama; some others, which are not extant, are mentioned by the grammarian Pāṇini (fl. 5th or 4th century B.C.). Later authors of the 10th and 14th centuries divide the drama into 10 sorts of *rūpaka* (major types), and 18 *uparūpaka* (minor types).

Besides the Sanskrit plays, there exist today shadow plays and plays of many sorts in the vernaculars. Very popular are plays on themes of the Krishna cycle, composed in Braj Bhākhā (Braj Bhasha), a late literary language of Mathura; so, too, the Yātrā plays in Bengal, and the plays of the Rāma cycle. In such plays the stanzas may be fixed, but the actors may improvise fairly freely in the prose portions. The modern Indian stage and motion picture industry, though affected by Western technique, still exploits the religious and heroic legends of the epics and Purāṇas, heavily interspersed with song and dance.

Select Bibliography.—Ryder, A. W., tr., *The Little Clay Cart* (Cambridge, Mass., 1905); Fox-Strangways, A. H., *The Music of Hindostan* (Oxford 1914); Popley, H. A., *The Music of India* (New York 1921); Coomaraswamy, A. K., *The Dance of Śiva* (London 1924); Keith, A. B., *The Sanskrit Drama in Its Origin, Development, Theory, and Practice* (Oxford 1924); Coomaraswamy, A. K., tr., *The Mirror of Gesture* (New York 1936); Garratt, G. T., ed., *Legacy of India* (Oxford 1937); Daniélou, Alain, *Northern Indian Music,* vol. 1 (London 1949), vol. 2 in preparation; Ryder, A. W., tr., *Translations of Shakuntala, and Other Works* (New York, various dates).

W. NORMAN BROWN.

7. ARCHITECTURE. The earliest architectural remains in India are at the Indus Valley sites of the third millennium B.C. (see section on *Archaeology*). These contain an abundance of household architecture, but almost no monumental works except the so-called Great Bath. The latter is built of brick; it had an elaborate system of intake for the water, was surrounded by ancillary chambers with a puzzling passageway, and may have had a cult significance. It is not possible to relate this building to the development of Indian architecture in historic times.

For the period between the Indus civilizations and the time of the Mauryas (3d century B.C.) there is no information about Indian architecture. The Rig Veda and other Vedas speak of the fortified cities of the non-Aryans, and the same works and the Brāhmaṇas ancillary to them (see *Literature*) allude to buildings, pillars, doors, and other architectural elements but give no descriptions. Except for the great walls at Rajgaha (Rājagṛha) in Bihar, there are no archaeological discoveries from pre-Mauryan times to help reconstruct any monuments.

Buddhist, Hindu, and Jain Structures.—The Mauryan emperor Aśoka (r. c.274–237 B.C.) built an extensive palace with floors of wood, but using stone columns and other stone elements, the whole thought to be modeled on the palace of the Achaemenian kings at Persepolis. He erected stone pillars to carry his inscriptions, and set up stupas (Sanskrit *stūpa*), or memorial mounds, to honor the Buddha—the Buddhist texts credit him with 80,000 of these—and perhaps to honor the Jain saviors as well, if the claims of the Jain texts are to be accepted. No mound survives that can definitely be assigned to Aśoka's time as now standing, but that at Sanchi, which was remade and enlarged two centuries later and is hemispherical in shape, probably gives an idea of the appearance in his day. The early form was later displaced by a loftier type, having a high, straight barrel with a rounded top. Surrounding the mound was a stone railing which consisted of tall posts pierced for the insertion of horizontal rails, a clumsy type of structure for stone but practicable in wood. The railing had one or more gateways, torana (Sanskrit, *toraṇa*), which also reproduce wooden types, and they, and sometimes the railings also, were heavily ornamented. On top was an enclosed hallowed spot surmounted by an honorific parasol or a series of superimposed parasols.

In Aśoka's reign the practice of excavating caves in rock as religious shrines began. These caves reproduced wooden structures of an elaborate character, the product of a long evolution. Some of these caves are chaityas (*caitya*) or halls of worship, others viharas (*vihāra*), or residences for monks. The oldest is a chaitya of the Ājīvika sect in the Barabar Hills in Bihar. Slightly later is the Buddhist chaitya cave at Bhaja (early 2d century B.C.) in western India. A long room, barrel vaulted to the roof, was supported by sloping posts. At the rear was a stupa which the worshipers circumambulated. The entrance was a horseshoe-shaped arch, repeated in miniature as a windowlike decorative motif. In the oldest specimen, however, the door is a rectangle set in a wall framed by the arch and the decorative windows are missing. In a Buddhist chaitya hall at Karli (Karle), located near Bhaja but later than it by a century or more, the interior was provided with curved wooden beams like those of wooden structures. The cave monasteries of this period were plain, though their porches might carry decoration. Later viharas, besides having cells for monks, might also have stone benches, presumably for eating, and niches with images of the Buddha. Numerous cave temples were also excavated during the Gupta period and later, as in the series at Elura and Ajanta, both in western India. Private residences and palaces were still built of wood. Their types are exhibited in sculptures at Bharhut, Sanchi, and elsewhere.

By the end of the 4th century A.D., during the Gupta period (319–500), structural temples were built which still survive. A simple flat-roofed cell with a porch supported by pillars was a common type. In the 5th century such a temple may have a superstructure. Structural stone barrel-vaulted temples also appear in the 4th century, as in the Hindu temple at Chezarla in the northeastern part of Madras. The flat-roofed type of temple with a spire, sikhara (Sanskrit *śikhara*), over the shrine and a porch at the doorway appears in the 6th century, as in the Hindu temple at Aihole in southwestern India.

In medieval temple architecture there is a differentiation of types. In the north the sikhara type dominates. This has a porch, an anteroom, and a cell for the main image, over which last the tower rises as a square, rarely circular, element, with curved sides, corbeled inwards until the sides nearly meet. The spire consists of compressed stories, marked by dominating vertical lines, with an amalaka (Sanskrit *āmalaka,* a cushion-shaped crown resembling the myrobalan fruit) at the top, and a finial surmounted by a vase (*kalaśa*). Especially fine illustrations of subvarieties appear in the 10th to 12th centuries at Khajraho (central India) and at Bhubaneshwar (Bhuvaneshwar), in Orissa. Both the exterior and interior of the temple bear profuse ornamentation. The most elaborate are those of Gujarat and elsewhere in western India, whose type extended northwest through Rajputana to Delhi and Agra, and was used by both Hindus and Jains. Another type of temple, lower and more spread out, and with or without spires, appears in south India in the Hoyśala temples at Somnathpur (1268), Belur, and Halebid in Mysore State, and with spires and domes in western India in the Jain temples on Mount Girnar and on Mount Abu (13th century).

In south India another style was developing. This is illustrated in monolithic temples at Mamallapuram in the 7th century, and in structural examples of the 8th century at the same place (Shore Temple) and at Conjeeveram (Kanchipuram). Horizontal lines, formed by a series of rolling cornices, dominate in place of the vertical lines of the northern spire. The successive stories are decorated with pavilions or false windows (*kuḍu*), shaped like those of the early cave chaityas. The pillars are supported by lions. The summit of the roof is a square, circular, or polygonal dome, or a long barrel vault. One of the most remarkable of all Indian temples is the monolithic Kailāsanātha Temple of the late 8th century carved in the scarp at Elura. As time goes on the spire over the shrine (vimana; Sanskrit *vimāna*) becomes higher. The outer wall assumes more importance, because within it may be housed a great number of people. The entrance (*gopuram*) through the wall eventually becomes the dominating element of the temple complex and is copiously decorated. Pillared halls (*maṇḍapam*) are added and a tank.

Moslem Architecture.—The Moslems (in India the form Muslims is preferred) in India needed religious buildings differently planned from Hindu and Jain temples. Their mosques were meant for congregational worship, not individual. They also buried their honored dead in elaborate tombs, and cultivated civil architecture on a monumental scale. Distinctively Moslem architecture began in north India at about the beginning of the 13th century. The Moslems then used Hindu workmen and in building mosques adapted Hindu and Jain temple architecture by retaining parts of the forest of columns in the roofed and walled-in court surrounding the temple, but removing the temple itself, erecting a multiple-arched screen before the columns, and, generally, providing an unroofed courtyard before the screen. The ceiling of the covered part was vaulted, and the roof domed. Notable examples of such construction appear in the mosque called the Two-and-a-Half Day Hut (*aṛhāī din kā jhoṅprā*) at Ajmer (Ajmir) and the Quwwat-ul-Islām Mosque (begun in 1191) outside Delhi —beside the latter stands the Quṭb (Kutb) Minār (Tower of Victory), 238 feet high, of five stories, which was finally completed at a later time—and again at Cambay, in Gujarat.

Besides the developments at Delhi and nearby, many local Moslem styles arose during the 14th to 16th centuries. The most conspicuous were those in Ahmadabad (in Gujarat), Jaunpur (in Uttar Pradesh), Sasaram (in Bihar), Gaur (in Bengal), and Bijapur and Golconda (in the Deccan).

During the 16th and 17th centuries, Moslem architecture reached its peak under the Mogul (Mughal) emperors Akbar (r. 1556–1605), Jahāngīr (r. 1605–1627), and Shāh Jahān (r. 1628–1658). These rulers, admirers of Persian art, imported Persian architects. Their buildings retain many Indian elements, but all are blended with Iranian, especially in religious structures. Akbar's chief buildings were a tomb for his father, Emperor Humāyūn, outside Delhi; a palace fort of red sandstone at Agra; another at Lahore; and the red sandstone fort city at Fatehpur (Fathpur) Sikri, 23 miles from Agra. Under Jahāngīr, Akbar's tomb at Sikandra, outside Agra, was completed (1612–1613). In the gateway to the garden surrounding the tomb, the use of minarets was introduced. At Agra the remarkable white marble tomb of I'timād ud-Daulā, Jahāngīr's father-in-law, was completed at the inspiration of his daughter, Nūr Maḥall. Jahāngīr also had a mausoleum built for himself at Shahdara near Lahore.

Shāh Jahān built of marble rather than red sandstone, and is responsible for the many buildings in the Delhi fort, many others in the Agra fort, some others at Lahore, the great mosque, Jāmi' Masjid, at Delhi and similarly the Jāmi' Masjid of Agra. Above all other Indo-Moslem architecture is his Taj Mahal (Tāj Maḥall) at Agra, around a bend of the river from the fort and opposite it, which he built as a memorial to his beloved wife, Mumtāz Maḥall. Its great white dome is the dominating theme of Agra and the most distinguished symbol of Mogul rule. Shāh Jahān made use in his marble buildings of inlaid *pietra dura* ornament (previously employed in the tomb of I' timād ud-Daulā); and in many of his buildings he used foliated or cusped, instead of plain, arches. Shāh Jahān's was the golden age of the Moguls.

Under Aurangzeb (Aurangzīb, r. 1658–1707), last of the great Moguls, Indo-Moslem architecture declined; the most notable building of his period is the Jāmi' Masjid of Lahore. At this time also tombs erected in Sind, and some of the best Moslem buildings of the Deccan, such as the tomb of Sultan Muḥammad (d. 1656) at Bijapur, show Mogul influence upon local styles.

Under the British, European styles of architecture were introduced into India for government buildings and Indian styles were neglected. In the governmental buildings at New Delhi, erected in the 1920's under the supervision of a British architect, an effort was made to utilize Indian motifs of various periods.

Select Bibliography.—Fergusson, James, *The History of Indian and Eastern Architecture,* 2d ed., rev. by J. Burgess (London 1910); Coomaraswamy, A. K., *History of Indian and Indonesian Art* (New York 1927); Marshall, Sir John H., "Monuments," *Cambridge History of India* (New York): vol. 1 (1922), vol. 3 (1928); Brown, Percy, "Monuments," *Cambridge History of India,* vol. 4 (New York 1937); id., *Indian Architecture,* 2 vols. (Bombay 1942); Kramrisch, Stella, *The Hindu Temple,* 2 vols. (Calcutta 1946).

W. Norman Brown,
Professor of Sanskrit, University of Pennsylvania.

8. SCULPTURE AND PAINTING.

Sculpture.—Sculpture in historic India has been devoted to the uses of the intellectual life, and hence to religion. Because the ideas which it aims to clarify are abstract, it is symbolic and ordinarily lacks naturalism, especially in medieval and modern images, which may have more than the normal number of arms, or be hybrid forms, or exhibit unusual or forced poses. Nevertheless, when Indian sculptors have wished to portray a natural subject naturalistically, they have been able to do so.

In the Indus Valley culture of the 3d millennium B.C., there are both kinds of presentation. Skillful naturalistic art appears on the seals in figures of the bull, but some other animal figures, though realistic, are hybrid forms and symbolic. In dancing girl bronzes, the artist achieved litheness and rhythm in dealing with the human figure, but in the portrayal of a meditative god—if it is a god—with three faces, he may have aimed to symbolize some abstract conception.

In Aśoka's time, when the historic period of Indian sculpture commences, there is both naturalism and symbolism. Aśoka erected a number of columns to honor the law, as at Sarnath, where the Buddha preached his first sermon. On top of each was a capital ornamented with naturalistic animal figures. His artists could also treat the human figure with naturalness, as in the female chowry (*chauri* or fly whisk) bearer from Didarganj, near Patna. But in representing a *yakṣa* (yaksha or fertility deity) naturalism was not a goal, since the divinity did not actually have a human form. But the *yakṣa* did have power, which the human form was used to express. Stylistically, the latter sort of figure is primitive, being frontal—that is, preferring the face focus—and giving little attention to the lower part of the body. Other objects besides the human body could serve as symbols. Aśoka's column at Sarnath had at its top not the figure of the Buddha, but a wheel, the symbol of eternal and infinite truth, which the Buddha revealed.

Similarly, the Buddha's final nirvana (Sanskrit *nirvāṇa*)—we might say death—was symbolized by the stupa (Sanskrit *stūpa,* or memorial mound). So, too, the empty seat beneath the holy pipal tree where he got enlightenment (bodhi) was not used as an icon of the Buddha, but as an ocular reference to complete and saving knowledge become available to finite humanity. Under Mahayana Buddhism a Buddha figure was created.

Symbolism is also general in Jain and Hindu sculptures. The Jain *tīrthankaras* (saviors), being emancipated and therefore incorporeal souls, must be shown symbolically; hence they are represented as kings. Ideally, the creative artist in India, before portraying a deity, must realize the deity in the deity's highest, that is spiritual and suprasensuous, character. Afterwards he should think of the deity as transmuted into a lower, physical form, apprehensible by the senses, which then becomes the symbol to be used in his sculpture.

Following Aśoka's period, in the 2d century B.C., comes sculpture which remains flat but develops an angularity, as on the railing which once surrounded a stupa at Bharhut, and at Bhaja in the porch of the vihara (Sanskrit *vihāra*), or monk's residence. In the next century modeled three-dimensional work appears, as between 100 and 50 B.C. at Buddh (Bodh) Gaya, the historic site of the Buddha's enlightenment, on a railing ornamented with sculptured panels and posts. The classic period of early Indian sculpture is most abundantly illustrated at Sanchi (central India) in the carving on the torana (Sanskrit *toraṇas,* or gateways) around the great stupa, which date from about 50 B.C. to 75 A.D., with some of the work perhaps extending into the 2d century. The subjects come from the historical and legendary life of the Buddha, and the scenes exhibit town and country; court, village, and jungle; peace and war; heaven and earth. The Buddha himself is still represented aniconically, though gods and the Bodhisattva (that is, the Buddha in previous existences) have human form.

From about the beginning of the Christian era there was centered in the north at Mathura (Muttra) a school of sculpture executed in a mottled red sandstone, which supplied the entire northern region with its products. The characteristic Indian Buddha type develops in this school. A piece carved under the direction of a Friar Bala and discovered at Sarnath is dated in the third year of the reign of Kanishka (Kaniṣka) and is called a Bodhisattva (future Buddha) rather than a Buddha. It is a typical standing Buddha, with energy in the stance, gesture, and features, rather than repose and sweetness. The torso is finely modeled; the figure is round, though calculated for a frontal view. It was originally surmounted by a carved umbrella, now broken off, marked with lucky symbols. The seated Bodhisattva or Buddha type appears at about the same time. In an image from Katra (near Mathura) of the Buddha preaching, there appear the snail-shaped *uṣṇīṣa* (protuberance on the head) and the *ūrṇā* (curl of hair between the eyebrows). His seat is a lion throne—elsewhere it may be a lotus. A scalloped nimbus is behind him—in other figures this may be plain. The left hand rests on the thigh. In the later Kushana (Kuṣāṇa) Buddha type the robe is often over both shoulders, and more voluminously rendered than in the preceding period. In seated figures both feet are hidden; pedestals are often used. The head is covered with curls and the shaven head type disappears. This is the orthodox Indian type of Buddha, widely copied and developed, and carried to south India, Ceylon, and Southeast Asia. From these late Kushana times come numerous iconographic types of the Buddhist religion, illustrating nagas (Sanskrit *nāga,* or serpent), Bodhisattvas, *yakṣas* and *yakṣis* (male and female fertility divinities), and others. Jain iconography of this period uses similar types.

At the same time a somewhat similar development, chiefly Buddhist, was taking place in the Andhra country of northern Madras and at a few other places in the south. The material was white marble, and the period begins about 150 B.C. The most celebrated site of this school was at Amaravati, where there was a great stupa, now demolished. The legends illustrated there and at other sites involve abundant architectural detail, walled and moated cities, palaces, stupas, toranas, bodhi trees, and temples. The Amaravati sculpture is marked by a kind of nervous irritation, contrasting with the carelessness of contemporary Mathura; there is a wide range of emotions: wild transports of joy and violent outbursts of passion, ecstatic devotion.

In northwest India, in the Gandhara region, centered at Peshawar, from the 1st century B.C. until about 600 A.D., there existed a variety of sculpture, as of architecture, which was largely Hellenistic. Here another type of Buddha image, with Greek and Roman characteristics of repose, developed and spread to central Asia. Many scenes from the Buddha's historical and legendary life were also illustrated in the carved stone.

During the time of the imperial Guptas (319 to 500 A.D.), Indian sculpture attains its greatest elegance. The Buddha images of that period have the greatest finish and rhythm. The great Hindu revival of this period also brought a flowering of Hindu art, and pieces illustrating it are abundant.

Medieval India continued the Gupta tradition by elaborating the number of types and character of treatment. In eastern India a celebrated school flourished in Bengal and Bihar under the Pāla kings and later (8th to 12th centuries); it was used by both Buddhists and Hindus. In south India there are illustrated a wide variety of Hindu themes at many sites, as at Mamallapuram, south of Madras, in the 7th century; or in the cave temples of Elura (8th or 9th century), especially that known as the Kailāsanātha; or at Elephanta near Bombay. Other varieties are at Khajraho (10th and 11th centuries) in central India and at Bhubaneshwar (Bhuvaneshwar) and Konarak in Orissa, and on the Hoyśala temples in Mysore. Still later types appear in south India in the 16th century.

Bronze casting is preserved in historic India from Kushana times, and in the medieval period it was common in many parts of the country. The finest bronzes, as a group, come from south India. They represent chiefly deities and saints.

In a Moslem environment, sculpture is limited to floral and geometric design, often very intricate.

Painting.—The earliest surviving paintings in India come from Ajanta and were executed on the inner walls and ceilings of the Buddhist cave temples from the 2d century B.C. to the 6th century A.D. Some of the Ajanta paintings follow story themes; others are merely decorative animal and vegetation designs. They are emotionally rich and technically proficient, showing scenes of human relationships in settings of palace, home, and city. Slightly later (5th century) are the murals of Sigiriya in Ceylon and Sittanavasal (7th century) in Pudukkottai State in south India. Following them are other murals at Elura and Bagh, and still later are those from temples at various places in south India.

Indian painting is especially rich in miniatures, which for many centuries were used solely as illustration to manuscripts. The tiny panels on the manuscript folios show deities or narrative scenes. The oldest known specimens come from the end of the 10th century and were made in eastern India (Bihar, Bengal, Nepal) to illustrate Buddhist palm-leaf manuscripts. The best of this early eastern Indian school were done about the middle of the 12th century. This art is in the tradition of Ajanta painting and Pāla Buddhist sculpture. The style comes to an end in the 13th century. In western India (Gujarat) the Jains produced palm-leaf copies of their texts illustrated by paintings, of which the earliest known are dated at about 1100 A.D. This art has angularity of drawing and rashness of pose, and is peculiar in showing all but a very few figures with the face seen in a three-quarters view, the farther eye protruding beyond the cheek line into space. The finest examples of this early western Indian school were executed in the 14th century.

When paper came to India after the Moslem invasions, and came to be used as a material for book making at about 1400 A.D., books could be made of a different shape from the long narrow folios of palm leaves. More room was therefore available in 15th and 16th century paper manuscripts for the panels in which paintings were set. Most early western Indian painting of this time also was done under Jain auspices in Gujarat, but Hindus as well used this art, to illustrate both Vaishnava (Vaiṣṇava) and Shaiva (Śaiva) works. There exist also a few secular erotic works illustrated in this style at this time (15th century), conspicuously the *Vasanta Vilāsa* (*Sport of Springtime*). The palette of the early western Indian school is throughout its existence (12th to 16th centuries) simple, with a red, a blue, a yellow (or gold), a white, and a green.

Persian styles of miniature painting coming to India with the paper on which they were executed blended with the early western Indian school, and probably other local varieties of Indian painting, to produce the schools known as Rajput. This process becomes prominent in the 16th century, at about the end of which the Rajput schools begin to appear. A similar process took place in the Deccan at the same time. Though these paintings were meant to accompany text, like early western Indian manuscript illustrations, the amount of written material on a page might be slight. By the time the blending was complete and the schools well advanced, the painting had in many quarters come to outweigh the text. The Rajput paintings flourished in Hindu courts in Rajputana, Gujarat, and the Himalayan hill states. The themes were more often than not the loves of Krishna or the whole Krishna legend. Frequently such themes were used to illustrate the *rāgas* and *rāgiṇīs,* which are musical modes. Such types of painting were made until late in the 19th century.

Under the Moguls (Mughals), Persian miniature painting was introduced by Akbar and Jahāngīr into their courts at Delhi and Agra, where there arose a school which is known as the Mughal, blended of Persian and Indian, but with more of Persian and less of Indian than the Rajput styles. It has landscape and sky features of Persian art, with much of Persian drawing, coloring—the palette is much more extensive than that of the early western Indian style—and other characteristics, as of movement, and the high horizon in perspective. The subject matter is often portraiture or some historic episode.

Modern Indian schools associated with cultural nationalism draw a great deal from Ajanta, Rajput, and Mughal painting. Moslems are likely to favor Mughal and Persian style; Hindus develop old themes of their faith with influences from Ajanta and the Rajput schools. Some others are influenced by modern folk art.

Select Bibliography.—Gangoly, O. C., *South Indian Bronzes* (Calcutta 1915); Coomaraswamy, A. K., *Rajput Painting*, 2 vols. (New York 1916); Brown, Percy, *Indian Painting under the Mughals, A.D. 1550 to A.D. 1750* (Oxford 1924); Coomaraswamy, A. K., *History of Indian and Indonesian Art* (New York 1927); Bachhofer, Ludwig, *Early Indian Sculpture*, 2 vols. (New York 1929); Smith, V. A., *A History of Fine Art in India and Ceylon*, 2d ed., rev. by K. deB. Codrington (Oxford 1930); Brown, W. Norman, *Story of Kālaka* (Washington 1933); Kramrisch, Stella, *Indian Sculpture* (London 1933); id., *A Survey of Painting in the Deccan* (London 1937); Rowland, Benjamin, Jr., *The Wall-Paintings of India, Central Asia, and Ceylon* (Boston 1938).

W. NORMAN BROWN,
Professor of Sanskrit, University of Pennsylvania.

9. RELIGION AND PHILOSOPHY.

The 1941 census of India, which was taken before the country was divided into the two nations of India and Pakistan, reported the total population of about 389,000,000 to be divided by religion approximately as follows: Hindus, 254,900,000; Moslems (Muslims), 94,400,000; Christians, 6,300,000; Sikhs, 5,700,000; Jains, 1,500,000; Buddhists, 232,000; Parsis (Parsees, Zoroastrians), 115,000; Jews, 22,500; animists, 25,400,000; others, 410,000. Hindus were in a majority in all the great divisions of the country except the northwest (western Punjab, Kashmir, North-West Frontier Province, Sind, Baluchistan) and eastern Bengal, in which two areas Moslems were more numerous. Since partition, the latter regions, except for Kashmir, whose status was still in dispute in 1950, have constituted Pakistan, with national boundaries corresponding roughly, though not exactly, with the boundaries of Moslem religious preponderance. Pakistan includes regions which in 1941 had about 58,000,000 Moslems and 13,000,000 Hindus and animists.

Modern Hinduism and Brahmanism.—This is a total way of life, including social order, law, science, literature, and art. Incorporated in it is the body of Indo-Aryan religious thought and ritual cultivated by the learned class called Brahmans (Brāhmaṇas) and stemming from the Veda (see section on *Literature*), altered and expanded in post-Vedic times, and constituting the higher religion called Brahmanism. It is contrasted with a mass of belief subliterate in origin, some parts of which became associated with Brahmanic culture in ancient times, others intruding into the total scheme of Hinduism very lately, and the whole coming from all the various racial and cultural elements known to have existed in India. This is the lower religion or popular Hinduism.

Hinduism countenances every shade of theological belief, starting with the most naive form of animism, passing through polytheism and monotheism, to reach at the top a rigorous philosophical monism. It has no formal creed, no standardized cult practice, no controlling ecclesiastical organization. Its adherents usually ascribe incontrovertible authority to the Veda but refer to that ancient collection less frequently than to later texts. For theology and mythology they rely upon the two great Sanskrit epics, *Mahābhārata* and *Rāmāyaṇa*, and versions of them in modern vernaculars, such as that in Hindi by Tulsī Dās (1532–1623) of Banaras (Benares); the Purāṇas (also in Sanskrit), the most important of which were probably composed between the 6th and 13th centuries; and a class of texts called Māhātmya (usually recent works, generally in Sanskrit), which have limited geographical provenience and purvey edifying local religious legends. For cosmogony and cosmology they accept the statements of the Purāṇas. For religious law, they refer less to the oldest legal textbooks called Sūtras (thought to be of the first four centuries B.C.), which are closely attached to the Vedas, than to the later (2d-7th centuries A.D.) Shastras (Śāstras) (see section on *Law*). In cult practice they do not employ the old rites of the Vedic ritual texts but use an infinite variety of later-developed ceremonies.

To some Hindus all phenomenal existence is only relatively real—these are adherents to pure monism. Others may accept much simpler concepts. Probably the greatest number of those who are well read in the Hindu scriptures accept in some form, though often with considerable modification, the theory of the Purāṇas concerning the recurring dissolution (*pralaya*) of the universe and its recreation (*pratisarga*).

Conceptions of deity vary. On the medium and high intellectual levels Hindus are almost always adherents of sects or cults devoted to one of the great deities, Shiva (Śiva) and Vishnu (Viṣṇu), or to some lesser deity associated with one of them. Vishnu may be worshiped in his incarnations (avatars, Sanskrit *avatāra*), of which the two most popular are Rāma Chandra (hero of the *Rāmāyaṇa*) and Krishna (Kṛṣṇa). Shiva is often worshiped as the phallic symbol (linga), with which may be associated the female symbol (*yoni*) as the emblem of his wife, Pārvatī. Sectaries often wear distinguishing marks on their foreheads.

A variation of Hinduism is the Shākta (Śākta) cults, which promote adoration of the female principle or power called Shakti (*śakti*), represented as a goddess. As the creative and effective energy in the universe, this is considered by devotees to be more important than the male principle, represented in the god, which is otherwise only unrealized potentiality. This type of worship, also called Tantrism (its texts are known as tantra), is directed toward Devī (goddess), wife of Shiva, and otherwise known by many names such as Umā, Pārvatī, Durgā, Bhavānī, Kālī, and Ambikā.

On lower intellectual levels, chiefly among the illiterate portion of the population, Hindus may propitiate any of a large number of vegetation and fertility godlings, divinities of disease or misfortune, the village mother goddesses, ancestral spirits, the sun and moon. Trees, such as the variety of fig known as the pipal, and stones may be treated as sacred; also animals, such as the monkey, the peacock, the cobra, in some cases the tiger and the horse. Rivers, such as the Ganges, the Jumna (Yamunā), the Narbada or Nerbudda (Narmadā), the Godavari, the Kistna, the Cauvery or Kaveri may be holy; and so, too, mountains, such as the Himalaya and the Vindhyas. Astrology, divination, and the use of omens are common; the evil eye is feared.

On the highest intellectual level a Hindu seeks the one reality, whether conceived impersonally as Brahma (neuter) or theistically as Shiva or Vishnu.

Hinduism accepts as not requiring proof the joint doctrine of rebirth and works (karma). Every living creature, human or other, at the time of death is reborn in a different form, either higher or lower, whether as a human being, an animal, a heavenly creature, or a hell dweller. From that existence it will again be reborn, and so on endlessly. This round of rebirth is called the Sansara (*saṃsāra*). The precise form of each rebirth is always determined by the balancing, as in a mathematical equation, of the creature's deeds (karma) in previous existences. Escape from the cycle of rebirth constitutes salvation—*mokṣā,* mukti, nirvana (Sanskrit *nirvāṇa*) —and is in theory the ultimate goal of every living being, but is so difficult to attain that on the practical level the aim is almost invariably only to improve one's condition in the next existence. Rarely does anyone strive for more than a long life, perhaps lasting a few million or billion years, in the heaven of some god. Emphasis is laid upon having a guru (spiritual preceptor), who may be viewed as little less than God.

Places of worship range from the most primitive of wayside shrines, consisting of a stone set under a sacred tree and daubed with paint, symbolizing some form of divinity, to the most elaborate complex of structures constituting an enormous temple. The largest is at Srirangam in Madras, where the site, which is sacred to Vishnu, is enclosed by a wall about four miles in circumference. Certain cities are especially holy to Hindus, the most holy of all being Banaras on the Ganges. Hindus use images freely in their worship, as comprehensible symbols of a deity which has no form apprehensible by human senses. Worship may consist of offerings of flowers, fruit, grain, ghee (*ghī,* clarified butter), and money, and in some connections animal sacrifice. A worshiper may appeal to the deity directly or through the agency of a priest. Worship is usually individual, not congregational.

Religious authority vests in the Brahmans, who besides being custodians of the sacred learning constitute the priesthood. They officiate at religious ceremonies in homes or temples, and are other men's vicars in dealing with the deities. As astrologers they cast horoscopes, and then interpret them later throughout a person's life to determine auspicious and inauspicious moments and conditions for specific undertakings.

The social structure of Hinduism is embraced in the caste system. This separates mankind into many separate groups, each of which is designated by Occidentals as a caste. The word is a modification of the Portuguese noun *casta,* meaning "(pure) race, lineage," and is ultimately derived from the Latin adjective *castus* (pure); the Indian term means "group by birth" (jati, Sanskrit *jāti*). The various castes have different social precedence. At the top are the Brahmans, in traditional law constituting a highly privileged group, who have been the codifiers and formulators of the philosophy sanctioning the system, and the directors of the instrumentality for enforcing its rules. These constitute about 7 per cent of the total Hindu community. Caste is hereditary and it is not possible to transfer from the caste in which one is born to another. Neither can a non-Hindu individual ordinarily become a member of a Hindu caste, although under certain conditions a group of people can enter the Hindu system as a new caste.

The caste system prescribes strict regulations concerning marriage, which must usually be within the caste but outside the immediate family or clan; concerning eating, which is subject to taboos and complicated rules respecting the acceptance of food and drink from members of other castes; and concerning many other phases of human relationship. In its most extreme form the caste system has imposed onerous disabilities upon those lowest in the scale, known as Fifths, who are estimated at around 20 per cent of the Hindu community (49,000,000 according to the 1941 census). These perform the most degrading forms of work, such as scavenging. They have been held to pollute the higher castes through even proximity within some indicated distance and have been required to live in separate quarters in villages and towns or in separate villages. They have often been denied access to wells, roads, schools, and temples used by the higher castes, and have been forbidden by religious law to read or hear the recitation of the Hindu scriptures. In the 20th century these rules have been greatly eased.

In Hindu theory each caste has a separate social function or occupation, different from that of any other caste, but in practice the rule does not hold. The number of castes is impossible to determine, since the criteria are not sharply separated. Endogamous groups of more than 500 members each probably exceed 1,000 in number, but most of these are of only local provenience, with but a fraction of the total number appearing in any given area.

The castes are classified by the Hindus in five groups—in descending order of social worth. Brahmans (Brāhmaṇas, or spiritual leaders), Kshatriyas (Kṣatriyas; Rājanyas, or temporal rulers), and Vaisyas (Vaiśyas; commons—that is, merchant and artisan groups) are called twice born (*dvija*), because the boys in these three groups undergo a ceremony of initiation, whereupon ideally they enter upon their religious training. The two other groups are Sudras (Śūdras, or servants); and Panchamas (Sanskrit *pañcama;* fifths) or outcasts, also known eclectically as untouchables, exterior castes, scheduled castes, depressed castes, Paraiyas (pariahs), or, in Gandhi's term, Harijan (God's folk). The last two groups have no ceremony of initiation; most of them are descendants of lowly groups at one time or another granted a place by Indo-Aryan society and religion. The fivefold classification also breaks down, since a caste may in one census assign itself to one of these groups but in the next to the group higher. Every caste, no matter how low in the scale, always knows another which it considers lower.

Man's duty (dharma) is to satisfy his caste rules and fulfill his caste functions, to honor the gods, to observe the numerous ceremonies which ideally accompany every important aspect of life from conception to after death, and to perform miscellaneous good works, such as alms giving, the undertaking of vows and pilgrimages, often at specified times when great numbers of people gather in festivals, religious bathing, reverencing the Brahmans, and feeding the poor. Theoretically in India from the time of the texts known as Sūtras a man devoted most fully to religion, that is, especially a true Brahman, should divide his life into four periods or stages (ashrama, Sanskrit *āśrama*): (1) celibate studentship (*brahmacārin*); (2) householder (*gṛhasthd*), raising a family and fulfilling his worldly duties; (3) forest-dweller anchorite (*vānaprastha*), retiring with his wife to a remote place for religious duties and meditation; (4) wandering ascetic (*saṃnyāsin, bhikṣu*), having severed all ties with his family, living alone, subsisting on alms. This fourfold scheme is but rarely practiced today.

The center of ethics is ahimsa (*ahiṅsā*), the noninjury of living creatures, which Gandhi called nonviolence. The doctrine applies not only to mankind, but also to the animal world, varying in application toward the separate animal species but always demanding protection of the cow (male and female), which holds a position of peculiar sanctity in Hinduism.

Hinduism blends all its widely varying beliefs and practices into a whole by admitting, without explicit statement, that human capacities and powers are relative. It takes the position that men are not intellectually and spiritually equal. For this reason it is unrealistic to expect all human beings to believe alike, pursue the same goals, have identical behavior, attain the same spiritual heights. Absolute truth, that is, the knowledge of ultimate reality, can be achieved by only the rarest individual. Similarly, man's conduct is governed by rules that vary according to his spiritual and intellectual capacity. What is right for one man may be wrong for another. In this relative view of life lies the sanction for the social system of caste. A person is born to the status that suits his attainments in consequence of his deeds in previous existences; the functions of that status are those to be fulfilled.

Early Indus Civilizations.—Inferences concerning the religion of the prehistoric Early Indus civilizations (see section on *Archaeology*) are drawn from sculpture, pottery, figurines, seal designs, and other finds, especially of the Harappa period (c. 2500–1700 B.C.). No temples or indisputably religious edifices have been identified. The data give presumptive evidence for worship of a god who had characteristics similar to those of Shiva in historic times, for a cult of the Great Mother or Earth Goddess, and for phallic worship. Certain trees appear to have been sacred; including the pipal. In some representations trees have associated with them female figures which may be fertility divinities. Various animals appear to have had sanctity, including the tiger, elephant, buffalo, crocodile, rhinoceros, and mythical hybrid creatures. Symbols appear there which reappear in historic India with religious significance, among them the swastika. Small bronze dancing figures may indicate that religious dancing was practiced as in modern Hinduism.

Religion of the Vedas.—The religion of the Vedas, especially the Rig Veda (Book of Knowledge of Hymns; see section on *Literature*), derives in part from primitive Indo-European times, but its most prominent deities and ideas seem to come from some other source. It has a class of superhuman beings known as asura, some of whom, the Ādityas, are benevolent (Varuṇa, Mitra, Aryaman, Bhaga, Dakṣa [Daksha], Ansa), others of whom, called Dānavas, are malevolent, being demons (rakshas, Sanskrit *rakṣas*). The chief god (deva) of the Vedic pantheon, Indra, is also hard to associate with any Indo-European figure. Because of his pre-eminence he is often called the sole—that is, the supreme—god.

The central theme of Vedic mythology is the conflict between Indra, the champion of the gods and their king, and Vritra (Vṛtra, the encloser), chief of the Dānavas and personification of the hard covering within which were originally contained the elements needed for creation of the existent universe (the sat). Vritra is usually described as a serpent; Indra slew him with his weapon (vajra), or, as is often said, burst open his belly. Out flowed the waters (*āpas*), often described complimentarily as cows, to fill the celestial ocean. Marvelously, they were pregnant with the sun. The universe now had moisture, light, and warmth, and creation could take place. Order (rita, Sanskrit *ṛta*) was established and put under the administration of Varuṇa, and in due time man was created. Every creature—man or god—had a personal function (*vrata*) to fulfill as part of order. When he fulfilled it, he was living in accord with the sat, and so achieving his highest good.

The Vedic cult centered about the fire sacrifice, which was personified as Agni, god of the sacrifice and the divine priest. Offerings included animals, and ghee, but the most important was soma, an exhilarating drink pressed from some unknown plant, and also personified as the god Soma. This drink was especially dear to Indra. The fire ceremony, being elaborate, required a numerous and highly trained priesthood which became the source of the Brahman caste. In time the sacrifice came to be viewed as all powerful, operating as a kind of cosmic magic, which, when properly performed, could compel even the gods to the sacrificer's will.

The righteous dead went to the realm of the blessed, where lived Yama, the first man, to rejoice there with him and the gods. On the way they were protected from the demons by the two heavenly dogs, Śabala (brindled), and Śyāma (dark). The wicked, however, had no such protection, but, hobbled by their sins, were waylaid and overtaken by the demons and destroyed.

The private or household religion, covering personal matters such as love, disease, witchcraft, black magic, was provided for in the Atharva Veda (Book of Knowledge of Blessings and Curses).

In the late Rig Vedic period there are ventured various new explanations of the origin and operation of the universe. A kind of superdeism appears, centering around Prajāpati (Lord of Creatures). Or a world man, Puruṣa (Purusha, or Male), when sacrificed, provides the material of the universe. The sounds of the sacrifice, primordial and present, consisting of the crackling of the fire as the voice of Agni and the chants of the priests, are viewed as all controlling; this idea appears as the feminine deity Vāc (Voice). A strictly impersonal conception appears in Tad Ekam (Sole Principle, or neuter), from which all is evolved. These various speculations record the beginning of Indian philosophy.

Upanishads.—The Upanishads (*Upaniṣad*) extend the tentative Rig Vedic philosophical inquiries about the nature of the universe and also investigate the human psyche or soul. They do not develop these topics systematically, and the explanations offered in different Upanishads are not all mutually consistent. A frequent form of Upanishadic investigation concerns the four states of the soul: waking state, dreaming sleep, deep (dreamless) sleep, and the fourth state (*turīya*), indescribable in terms of the human senses, which is the final goal in man's search for the ultimate. Other passages teach that the soul is immanent in all creation, uniform in character, and the essential part of the individual. As described by the celebrated teacher Yājñavalkya, it is pure subject, distinct from all that is material, unknowable, capable of perceiving and of knowing all, yet unmatched by any second reality to perceive or know. All else but soul is only relatively real. Duality is in the final analysis false; ultimate truth lies only in a monistic conception of the universe. The identification of the human soul (atman, Sanskrit *ātman*) and the universal soul (brahman) on these terms is the supreme achievement of the Upanishads. Besides this monism, the Upanishads contain the view that both matter (prakriti; Sanskrit *prakṛti*) and soul (purusha, Sanskrit *puruṣa*) are real, being mutually exclusive and standing in complete contrast to each other.

In the Upanishads appear the first suggestions of the doctrine of rebirth (metempsychosis, transmigration of the soul) and retribution for one's deeds (karma) in succeeding existences. The Upanishads also speak of engaging in meditation with the aid of the technique known as yoga, described below.

In the great epic, the *Mahābhārata,* in one of its sections called the *Bhagavad Gītā* (*Song of the Blessed One*), which calls itself an Upanishad, Krishna, who is an incarnation of the god Vishnu, instructs Arjuna, leader of the army fighting for the right, and, though admitting the approach to self-realization through works and knowledge, emphasizes above all loving devotion (bhakti) to God.

Formal Philosophies.—In the period of approximately a thousand years from the time of the older Upanishads—that is, roughly, from around 500 B.C. to 500 A.D.—the six orthodox systems (darshana; Sanskrit *darśana,* meaning "viewing") of Indian philosophy were developed and given their classical form. These were less conflicting systems than complementary ways of viewing the universe. They provide the intellectual basis for Brahmanical Hinduism. In the order enumerated by the Hindus these systems are: (1) Pūrva (or Karma) Mīmāṅsā, "discussion of the first, or practical, part" of the Vedic religion; the formulation of its basic text is ascribed to Jaimini; (2) Uttara Mīmāṅsā, "discussion of the latter part" of the Vedic religion, often called Vedānta (end of the Veda); the formulation of its basic text is ascribed to Bādarāyaṇa; (3) Nyāya, "logical method," formulated in a text by Gautama (Gotama); (4) Vaiśeṣika, "differentiation," the philosophy of atomism, ascribed to Kaṇāda; (5) Sāṃkhya ("reason" or "enumeration"), which analyzes nature, and is ascribed to Kapila; (6) Yoga, which is primarily devoted to the technique of meditation, and is ascribed to Patañjali. This is the Hindu order; they are described here in another order, reflecting the relationship of ideas.

Pūrva Mīmāṅsā.—This system rationalizes Vedic fundamentalism, that is, the literal meaning and application of the Veda. It regards the Veda as authorless and self-revealed, and therefore authoritative. According to the Pūrva Mīmāṅsā, the world exists throughout eternity and is not subject to recurrent dissolution and recreation.

Sāṃkhya.—The Sāṃkhya system gets its name either from the application of reason to the analysis of the soul and nature or from the 25 principles or true entities (tattva) which it enumerates. The two basic contrasting entities are soul (purusha) and matter or nature (prakriti). Souls are infinite in number, and consist of pure intelligence. Each is independent, indivisible, unconditioned, incapable of change, immortal. It appears, however, to be bound to matter—prakriti, pradhana (Sanskrit *pradhāna*), avyakta. At the beginning of an eon, nature is in a state of rest, or inertia. It has three qualities (guna, Sanskrit *guṇa*) known respectively as goodness (sattva), passion (rajas), and darkness (tamas), which are in balance. But souls, because of their karma, begin to move; nature then stirs; the qualities fall out of equilibrium. From nature then evolve the other 23 principles. First is intelligence (buddhi); from this evolves the process or organ of individuation (ahankara; Sanskrit *ahaṃkāra,* "I-maker"). The latter differentiates itself cosmically and individually. Cosmically it produces the five subtle elements (*tanmātra*) of earth, water, fire, air, and ether, from which are produced the corresponding five gross elements (*mahābhūta*). These are the objects of sense. Individually, it produces the five senses (*buddhīndriya*) of hearing, touch, sight, taste, and smell, which make contact with the gross elements; also the mind; and also the five organs of action (*karmendriya*). This physiological psychology is common to Indian thought of all schools, with only minor variations. According to the Sāṃkhya, every individual has a subtle characteristic body (*liṅga deha*) consisting of intelligence, individuation, mind, and the ten organs of sensation and action. This is what transmigrates, being lodged in a gross body composed of the objects of sense. How soul has come to be associated with the subtle body is not made clear. Through knowledge the association may be terminated, and this separation constitutes salvation. The subtle body is dissolved and the soul exists in isolation. To obtain knowledge the best means is to pursue the technique of yoga.

Yoga.—This system of philosophy is an extension of the Sāṃkhya. It formulates systematically the techniques of meditation known as yoga, which means "harnessing" or "control" and refers to the control and suppression of the activities of the mind and the sense organs which are enumerated by the Sāṃkhya, so that these will not interfere with the soul in attaining self-realization.

The first stage of the Yoga technique is designed to cause the evolutes of intelligence (buddhi) to retract into intelligence, and this is accomplished by *kriyā yoga* (yoga of observances or physical acts) in five stages: (1) adoption of restraints (*yama*) from killing, lying, and other sins; (2) adoption of observances (*niyama*) of purity and other virtues; (3) use of posture (asana, Sanskrit *āsana*) suitable for meditation; (4) restraint of breath (*prāṇāyāma*); and (5) withdrawal of senses (*pratyāhāra*) from the objects of sense. Then comes the second main stage of Yoga, known as superior or royal yoga (*rāja yoga*) in three phases (*saṃyama*): (1)

concentration (dharana, Sanskrit *dhāraṇā*) of the intelligence (buddhi) on an object without wavering; (2) meditation (dhyana, Sanskrit *dhyāna*) as an uninterrupted mental state; and (3) trance (samadhi, Sanskrit *samādhi*), in which the individual is fully identified with the object of meditation.

Vaiśeṣika and Nyāya.—These were separate in origin but came to be combined in a common system. They both accept the idea characteristic of the Vaiśeṣika that the universe is composed of atoms (*aṇu, paramāṇu, kaṇa*), and both use a body of logic codified in the Nyāya. According to the Vaiśeṣika, the differences in the universe rise ultimately from the differences in the atoms. The idea of difference (*viśeṣa*) gives the system its name.

The Nyāya gives the rules of correct thinking. There are four ways of acquiring knowledge: (1) perception by the senses (*pratyakṣa*); (2) inference (*anumāna*); (3) analogy (*upamāna*); and (4) authority or credible testimony (*śabda*). Of these inference is the most important for acquiring philosophical knowledge. The Nyāya syllogism has five parts: (1) proposition; (2) cause; (3) illustration; (4) recapitulation of the cause, or application; and (5) conclusion. The standard example is of the mountain and the fire: (1) the mountain is on fire; (2) because it is smoking; (3) wherever there is smoke there is fire; (4) the mountain is smoking; (5) therefore it is on fire. Causation is considered to be material, or inhering, cause, which is invariable and primary for any given object; and effective, which is variable and secondary. Between these is sometimes considered to be a noninhering or formal cause. In a carpet, the threads are the material or inhering cause, the association of threads is the noninhering or formal cause, and the weaver's activities are the effective cause.

Uttara Mīmāṅsā or Vedānta.—This system is, more than any other, the lineal descendant of the philosophic speculations of the late Rig Veda and the Upanishads. A number of varying schools, however, claim the name of this system. Its basic textbook, by Bādarāyaṇa, composed possibly around the beginning of the Christian era, is called *Brahmasūtra* (treatise on Brahma), also *Vedāntasūtra, Uttaramīmāṅsāsūtra,* and *Śārīrakasūtra.* It consists of aphorisms, often no more than catchwords or mnemonic guides, in themselves unintelligible and meant to be accompanied by a commentary.

The celebrated Shankara (Śaṃkara), who lived around 800 A.D., is the author of the earliest surviving commentary on the *Brahmasūtra.* He taught unqualified monism (*advaitavāda,* doctrine of the nonsecond). His thinking starts with an examination of knowledge (vidya, Sanskrit *vidyā*). This is of two sorts: one is absolute (*nirguṇā,* without qualification); the other is relative (*saguṇa,* with qualifications). Shankara approaches the teaching of the Veda in the light of the higher knowledge. He refers to the passages of the Upanishads in which it is stated that Brahma (neuter), the supreme reality, is one only, without a second. This, other passages state, is identical with the individual reality. It cannot be described; all it is possible to say of it is that it is "not this, not this," that is, that it is nothing comprehensible to the senses and mind (using mind in the Hindu sense of the thinking organ, which is physical, as separate from the soul). It can be known only by itself, that is, by the soul in the individual, which is the universal soul. This knowledge is the higher, unqualified knowledge, coming from experience (*anubhava*), where subject and object become one, leading the individual to the realization "I am Brahma" (*ahaṃ brahmāsmi*). The world as we know it phenomenally is qualified being, which is to say, the absolute Brahma viewed by qualified knowledge or ignorance (avidya, Sanskrit *avidyā,* meaning "nonknowledge"), where maya (*māyā,* illusion or artificial construction) operates. This is Shankara's treatment of nature (prakriti). Brahma is existence (sat), consciousness (cit; chit), bliss (ananda, Sanskrit *ānanda*), completely self-sufficient. Men who live according to relative, qualified knowledge may, after death, go to the world of the fathers (as in the Veda) or the world of the gods or hell. But those who devote themselves to the higher, unqualified knowledge aim to carry knowledge up from stage to stage until it is complete and through experience one knows that he is Brahma. To this end the accepted method is yoga.

The most prominent of other Vedānta schools is that of Rāmānuja (probably fl. 12th century, in Conjeevaram in south India), for whom God is personal, is identified with Vishnu, and has internal differences. Souls and matter both are real. The goal of man is the union of his individual soul with God. The way to release is by devotion to Vishnu. His system is characterized as qualified monism (*viśiṣṭādvaita*).

Another school originating in south India is that of Mādhva (Madhava, probably 1197–1276), who was a dualist, recognizing the reality of God, souls, and matter. No two souls are alike. Still another is that of Vallabha (1475–1531), who was born in south India but preached in north India at Mathura, the center of the Krishna cult, and afterwards moved to Banaras. He called his view purified monism (*śuddhādvaita*). He rejected the idea of maya; the way to salvation is union of the human soul with the highest god (Brahma), who is personal as Krishna and is to be reached by devotion (bhakti). Another important cult centering on Krishna was that of Chaitanya (1485–1533) in Bengal. Still another sect calling itself Vedānta (advaita, monism) is that of Nīlakaṇṭha (14th century), who identified God with Shiva. The human soul is distinct from God, but its goal is to reach God, whereupon it diminishes, finally united with Him.

Some other sects have shown distinct Moslem influence. Of these one of the most important is that of Kabīr (c. 1440–1518), who came into contact with Sufism (Sufiism).

Reformed Hinduism.—Nineteenth century reform movements of Hinduism arose in part from the impact of Western ideas upon India. Among the most prominent of these is the Brāhma (or Brahmo) Samāj (or Samāja), a theistic nonidolatrous movement, using a congregational form of worship and favoring social reform, founded by Rām Mohan Rai (Rām Mohan Roy, 1772/1774–1833). This was later led by Debendra Nath Tagore (1817-1905), father of the poet Rabindranath Tagore, and Keshab Chandra Sen (Keshub Chunder Sen, 1838/1841–1884). Several other Samājas grew up under the influence of the Brāhma Samāj. Another important movement was the Ārya Samāj, founded by a Brahman named Dayānand (Dayananda) Sarasvatī (1824/1825–1883), who aimed to restore the religion and social institutions of the Veda (which he understood in his own peculiar fashion), to protect cows, to restore India's glorious past, and so to check the advance of Islam and Christianity. Still another was founded by Rāmakrishna Paramahaṅsa (born Gadādhar Chatterji or Chaṭṭopādhyāya, 1834/1836–1886), a Bengali Brahman, who taught that all religions lead to the same god and frequently experienced trance (samadhi). His favorite disciple, Vivekananda (born Narendra Nath Dutt, 1863–1902), spread the teachings of Rāmakrishna in the West, first at the Parliament of Religions in Chicago in 1893, and later in Europe. The Ramakrishna Society is active in social reform in India and in preaching in several Western countries.

Buddhism.—This religion is a heterodox Indian faith in that it does not recognize the authority of the Vedic scriptures. Its founder was Siddhārtha Gautama, commonly known by the honorific title of Buddha ("the enlightened one"), son of a petty ruler of a clan called Sākya or Shākya (*śākya*) at Kapilavastu in the northeast of the present Uttar Pradesh. Buddhist tradition places his death in 544 B.C., but modern scholarship sets his dates as 563–483 B.C. (or, alternatively, 558–478 B.C.). At the age of 29, he left home to follow the religious quest. For 6 years he wandered from teacher to teacher and engaged in ascetic practices, all to no avail, but at last, while seated in meditation under a pipal tree near the Ganges at Gaya in the region then called Magadha, he attained enlightenment, and spent the rest of his life preaching his doctrine. He founded an order of monks (vowed to avoid unchastity, theft, taking of life, falsehood) and later admitted an order of nuns, and recognized a lay congregation. He died at the age of 80.

The Buddha's teachings in their present form are all considerably later than the Buddha. The canon of the major division of Buddhism, which is known as Hinayana, is composed in Pali (see *Languages*), and was preserved in Ceylon (whence it went to Burma, Thailand, and Cambodia), where it was first put into written form in the 1st century A.D. (or possibly 1st century B.C.). It is known as the Tipiṭaka (Sanskrit Tripiṭaka, "Three Baskets") and is in three parts: (1) Vinaya Piṭaka, rules for monks; (2) Sutta Piṭaka, collection of discourses (*sutta*), that is, texts of psalms, stories, and other edifying material, in five sections; and (3) Abhidhamma Piṭaka, collection of works of the higher religion, bearing upon psychological questions. The Mahayana division of Buddhism, which became prominent at the time of King Kanishka, first used a Prakrit for its text; later it used Sanskrit and had a canon in Sanskrit, also called the Tripiṭaka, of which many works are preserved in India and Nepal, and others, now lost, exist in Chinese versions.

In the Pali canon the Buddha's basic doctrine is considered to be expressed in his first sermon, preached at Sarnath near Banaras. In this the Buddha accepts, without offering proof, the familiar Indian doctrine of the cycle of rebirth (Sansara) and karma (retribution in future existences for one's deeds), the whole constituting a process that is painful. His message was that escape from this situation comes by avoiding the two extremes of sensual indulgence and physical self-mortification and adopting the middle path. His basic theory is enunciated in the Four Noble Truths: (1) birth, old age, sickness, death, separation from what one wants, association with what one does not want—all are painful; (2) the pain rises from the desire for gratification of the passions and for existence or for the termination of existence; (3) the cessation of pain comes from complete extinction of this desire; and (4) the way to extinguish the desire is to follow the Noble Eightfold Path of right views, right resolve, right speech, right action, right living, right effort, right mindfulness, right concentration. In various other discourses the Buddha is represented as refusing to discuss controversial metaphysical problems concerning the duration of the world, the identity of the self and the body, and the existence of the saint after death. He gives as the psychological basis of his doctrine a chain of causation or dependent origination (Pali *paṭiccasamuppāda*) of 12 members, which starts with ignorance and ends with suffering.

The Buddha did not deny the reality of things of the world though he thought ill of them. Everything about the human being is a compound of the aggregates of being (Pali *khandha*), always in a state of change and therefore impermanent and painful. The only bliss is that of the immutable absolute, which the Buddha merely describes as the state of nirvana (Pali *nibbāna*, "blowing out"). The Buddha seems to have been vague on the subject of soul; the Pali texts specifically preach that there is no soul. The scriptures advocate meditation (*jhāna*, Sanskrit *dhyāna*), with the use of methods more or less similar to those of yoga. Ethics is centered on ahimsa and *metta* (loving kindness).

The Hinayana, as taught in the Theravāda school of the Pali canon, seems to have been dominant in India until about the beginning of the Christian era. After that the Mahayana grew to prominence. The principal Mahayana doctrines, as distinguished from those of the Hinayana, are: (1) doctrine of the Bodhisattvas (beings whose essence is true knowledge), who have attained the ability to become Buddhas but elect to remain in the universe so that they may make over their acquired merit to other beings; (2) doctrine of the Buddhas, innumerable supernatural beings distributed throughout time and space; (3) worship of images; and (4) idealistic metaphysics. This is the form of Buddhism which spread to central Asia, China, Tibet, Korea, Japan, and Java. The principal Indian schools of the Mahayana are (1) the Madhyamaka (or Mādhyamika), prominent from the 1st to 5th century A.D., whose best-known teachers were Aśvaghoṣa (c.100 A.D.) and Nāgārjuna (fl. 2d century A.D.); and (2) the Yogācāra (Vijñānavāda) school, prominent from about 500 to 1000 A.D., promulgated by the two brothers Asanga and Vasubandhu, who lived in the 5th century.

Jainism.—Like Buddhism, Jainism is a heterodox movement, whose historical records start in Magadha in the 6th-5th century B.C. It was promulgated by Vardhamāna Mahāvīra, son of a petty ruler. The Jains put the date of his death at 528 B.C., but modern scholarship sets it at 468 (or 487 or 477) B.C. Mahāvīra left home at the age of 30 to follow the religious life, and in the 13th year of vigorous asceticism won supreme knowledge. From then until his death 30 years later he preached in the area of Magadha and nearby. Though Mahāvīra is the founder of Jainism and established his own order, he seems to have been preceded 250 years earlier by a teacher called Pārshva or Pārshvanātha (Pārśvanātha), who had established an order requiring four vows of its followers: not to injure life, to be truthful, not to steal, to possess no property. The Jain texts tell of the union of this order with Mahāvīra's during Mahāvīra's lifetime. Mahāvīra added a fifth vow for his monks, which was that of chastity. Pārshva had allowed his followers two garments, but Mahāvīra, with a strict application of the prohibition against possessing property, permitted his monks none at all. Jain tradition indicates that the question of clothing for monks remained unsolved, and at about 300 B.C. the community split on the issue into two divisions: the Śvetāmbara (White-clothed) and the Digambara (Sky-clothed, that is, naked). The division was recognized in 79 (or 82) A.D.

All Jains believe that Pārshva and Mahāvīra were not the founders of the faith, but only the 23d and 24th in a series of teachers all of whom are called *tīrthankara* ("fordmaker," across the ocean of existence, and "founder of a church") or Jina; modern scholarship considers the first 22 to be entirely mythical. The word Jina is an epithet meaning "conqueror" (of the woes of life). From this is derived the religion's own term Jaina (follower, or doctrine, of the Jinas).

The Jain canon, which was written in the Ardha-Māgadhī language (see *Languages*) and transmitted by word of mouth, is said by the Digambaras to have been completely lost in the early 3d century B.C., at the time of a 12-year famine; the Śvetāmbaras claim that a portion of it was preserved. The oral tradition is said to have been put into writing in 454 A.D. The Digambara community lives mostly in Mysore; the Śvetāmbaras are located chiefly in Gujarat.

Jainism accepts the common Indian notions of rebirth and karma. Salvation consists of escape from the round of existence (Sansara). The universe experiences a continuous cycle of decline and improvement, descending and ascending like the hand moving around the face of a clock. We are now very near the bottom in the present cycle. The Jains acknowledge no universal god, though they have many lesser divinities or gods who are bound in the round of rebirth. The world is eternal and consists of six substances: souls, dharma (right), adharma (wrong), space, time, and particles of matter. Souls are innumerable and are of two sorts: the perfected (siddha), who are in Īṣatprāgbhāra at the summit of the universe, enjoying perfect happiness, incorporeal, invisible; and those bound by a subtle body of deeds (karma) to the present world, sullied by contact with nonsentient matter. Jainism carries the doctrine of noninjury (ahimsa) of living creatures to an extreme not otherwise paralleled in Indian religions.

Souls in the round of rebirth are considered by Jains to be of various sorts, depending upon the number of senses and certain other qualities which they possess, as follows: first, beings called *nigoda* with none of the senses; then, (1) beings with one sense, which is touch, and with body, respiration, and an allotted span of life; these include stones, clods, minerals, water bodies, fire bodies, and vegetables growing in the ground, such as potatoes, carrots, and beets, which the strictest Jains will not eat; (2) beings with two senses (touch, taste) and having, in addition to the qualities possessed by one-sensed beings, the power of speech; these include worms; most Jains start the practice of noninjury with this group; (3) beings with three senses (touch, taste, smell), which include ants, bugs, moths; (4) beings with four senses (touch, taste, smell, sight), which include wasps, scorpions, mosquitoes; and (5) beings with all five senses (adding hearing), which include hell dwellers, higher animals, human beings, dwellers in the various heavens—of this class some have the quality of mind.

Souls suffer bondage (*bandha*) to matter (*ajīva*) by karma, which is good (*puṇya*) or evil (*pāpa*). When all karma is finally destroyed, the soul attains salvation (*mokṣā*). . . .

The Jain lay community consists mostly of merchants. The Jains are in theory opposed to caste, but in practice they maintain close relations with Vaishnava merchant castes and intermarry with them.

Sikhism.—Sikhism is a reformed sect combining Hindu and Moslem elements, which was founded in the Punjab in the 15th century, and is centered today at Amritsar. It has drawn heavily upon the beliefs and practices of Islam. Its founder, Guru Nānak (c. 1469–1538), was familiar with Sufi (mystic Islamic) teachings; he preached monotheism, service to others, humility, self-restraint, and the mystical value of prayer. He abhorred idolatry, denied the validity of the Hindu caste system, setting up a common kitchen where all castes partook of the same food, and also opposed Moslem deistic theology.

Nānak was followed by nine other gurus. The new faith remained primarily a quietistic sect under the first five gurus, and acquired wealth. The sixth guru, Har Gobind (r. 1606–1645) rejected wealth and ease, and returned to the old simplicity, but adopted militarism and armed the community to resist both Moslem aggression and Hindu intolerance. The tenth and last guru, named Gobind (Govind) Singh (r. 1675–1708), in 1699 organized the military brotherhood into a band called Khālsā (Arabic Persian *khāliṣah,* "the pure"), whose members went through an initiation ceremony, took names ending in Singh (lion), abjured wine, the narcotic hemp, and tobacco, forbade the cutting of the hair (*keś*), imposed the carrying of a dagger (*kirpan*) and the wearing of drawers (*kach*), an iron bangle (*kartha*), and a comb (*kanga*). He was murdered in 1708. From the time of Har Gobind the Sikhs were in frequent conflict with the reigning Moslems. In the 19th century, Ranjīt Singh (1780–1839) established a Sikh kingdom in the Punjab and Sikh political power extended from the Sutlej River into Afghanistan. After the Sikh Wars the British annexed the Punjab in 1849 (see *History: 1707–1947*).

The Sikh scriptures consist of a book called Granth Sahib (Revered Book), which contains a great deal of prose and poetic material ascribed by Sikhs variously to Nānak, Kabīr, and other teachers. It is regarded as the sole voice of religious authority and is held in veneration by all sects of Sikhism.

Tribal Religions.—These are forms of animism or spirit worship practiced by economically backward preliterate people living in less desirable sections of the subcontinent. On contact with Hinduism, such a tribe is in time likely to become acculturated and acquire a place in the Hindu community as a low caste.

Islam.—For Islam in general see ISLAM; MOSLEM SECTS; for Moslem invasions and spread in India see section on *History: From the Earliest Times to 1707*. Islam in India has been chiefly Sunnite; Shi'ites are outnumbered 11 or

12 to 1. There are a number of Moslem sects in the subcontinent, of which one of the most interesting is the Ahmadiyah, founded by Mirza Ghulam Ahmad (1839–1908), who at the age of 40 became convinced that he had a divine mission, and in 1889, at the age of 50, announced that he had received a revelation, proclaimed himself as the Mahdi, the messiah of the Moslems, and the one destined to realize similar hopes for a new savior among Hindus, Christians, Buddhists, and Zoroastrians.

Christianity.—According to legend, Christianity was brought to India by the Apostle Thomas, and the legend may have some basis in fact. In any case, by the 4th or 5th century A.D. a Christian community of the Nestorian (Syrian) sect existed at Cochin in south India, where it still survives. In the year 1542, St. Francis Xavier arrived in India and spread Christianity by preaching; in 1560 the Inquisition was introduced. Protestant missions entered south India in the 17th century, and became vigorous in Bengal at the end of the 18th century. The greater part of the Indian Christian community is Roman Catholic and is found in south India.

Judaism.—Jews were settled on the west coast of south India by the 4th or 5th century A.D., and a very small community, divided three ways, still exists in Cochin. Most of India's 25,000 Jews, however, live in the large cities.

Parsiism.—This is the Indian form of Zoroastrianism. The Parsis (Persians) fled from Persia to India in the 8th century to avoid the Arabs and settled in Gujarat. In the 17th century many of them moved to Bombay where the greater part of their number now resides. They engage chiefly in commerce. See ZOROASTRIANISM.

Select Bibliography.—Bloomfield, Maurice, *The Atharvaveda* (Strassburg 1899); id., *The Religion of the Veda* (New York 1908); Macauliffe, M. A., *The Sikh Religion*, 6 vols. (Oxford 1909); Farquhar, J. N., *A Primer of Hinduism* (London 1912); id., *Modern Religious Movements in India* (New York 1915); Stevenson, M. S., *The Heart of Jainism* (London 1915); Avalon, Arthur (pseud. of Sir J. G. Woodroffe), *Principles of Tantra*, 2 vols. (London 1914–1916); Rhys Davids, T. W., *Buddhism, Its History and Literature*, 3d ed. (New York 1918); Farquhar, J. N., *An Outline of the Religious Literature of India* (London 1920); Eliot, C. N. E., *Hinduism and Buddhism*, 3 vols. (London 1921); Whitehead, Henry, *The Village Gods of South India*, 2d ed. (London 1921); Keith, A. B., *The Religion and Philosophy of the Veda and Upanishads*, 2 vols. (Cambridge, Mass., 1926); Rādhākrishnan, Sarvepalli, *Indian Philosophy*, 2 vols. (New York 1923–1927); Hume, R. E., *The Thirteen Principal Upanishads*, 2d ed., rev. (New York 1931); O'Malley, L. S. S., *Popular Hinduism* (New York 1935); Edgerton, Franklin, *The Bhagavad Gītā*, 2 vols. (Cambridge, Mass., 1944); Archer, J. C., *The Sikhs* (Princeton 1946); Mackay, E. J. H., *Early Indus Civilizations* (London 1948); Dasgupta, S. N., *A History of Indian Philosophy*, 4 vols., vol. 5 in preparation (Cambridge, England, 1922–1949).

W. NORMAN BROWN,
Professor of Sanskrit, University of Pennsylvania.

10. LAW. By Paragraph 18(3) of the Indian Independence Act (10 and 11 Geo. 6., Ch. 30) of July 18, 1947, in the two independent dominions of India and Pakistan then being created, the laws of British India and of the several parts thereof existing immediately before the appointed day, so far as applicable and with the necessary adaptations, were to continue as the law of each of the new dominions and the several parts thereof until other provision should be made by laws of the legislatures of the two dominions. On Nov. 26, 1949, the Constituent Assembly of India adopted a new constitution, which became formally effective on Jan. 26, 1950, and superseded the previous arrangement. In Pakistan a new constitution had not yet been drafted.

In undivided India personal law in matters of succession, marriage, divorce, adoption, gifts, and charitable endowments differed for Hindus and Moslems (Muslims), conforming in general principle to traditional law. In all other fields the statutory law applied to all persons irrespective of their religious faiths. Both systems of personal law claim divine origin and are interwoven with religion; both are based on custom and often originate from custom. But even personal law is suspended in certain agricultural tribes by customary law. A judicial decision on a customary practice is a binding authority.

Hindu Law.—In India, as in other countries of the Orient, law is an integral part of religion and ethics, and the books dealing with these subjects, called *Dharmaśāstras,* therefore offer us overwhelming data about religious purification and penance, prayer and sacrifice, prohibitions on food and drink, punishment in hell and rebirth, philosophy, eschatology, creation, funeral ceremonies and sacrifices to the dead, the study of the Vedas and asceticism, the manner of living and customs of Brahmans and kings, and other subjects which we do not generally expect to find treated in such books. Many of them say nothing at all about law proper, and only a few later compilations may be called purely juridical works.

According to the *Dharmaśāstras,* the Vedas (see section on *Literature*) should be regarded as the first and foremost source of ancient Indian law. In a narrow sense, the Vedas contain much data about sacrifices, penances, and prayers, as well as ethics, which are important for the history of customs, but they refer only occasionally to legal matters.

In the older books known as the *Dharmasūtras,* so far as they have been preserved, there are always found special sections on the law of inheritance, the law of government, legal procedure, and other features of law proper as it was taught and handed down traditionally in the oldest schools of the Brahmans.

The second stage of the legal literature is represented by the very numerous metrical works which have come down to the present time under the name of *Dharmaśāstra* or *Smṛti* (*Smriti*). They differ from the *Dharmasūtras,* which are composed partly or wholly in prose, in being written entirely in verse. Yet these works, to which the *Mānava Dharmaśāstra,* the most esteemed authority, belongs, appear partly to have originated out of older *Dharmasūtras* and are therefore at least connected with the Vedic literature.

The latest stage of Indian legal literature is formed by the commentaries and systematic works which have been developed from the *Dharmasūtras* and *Dharmaśāstras* since early medieval times. As the products of a new age, inspired by powerful princes and ministers, these extensive compilations gradually displaced the *Dharmasūtras* and *Dharmaśāstras* to the extent that at the time of the establishment of British rule in eastern India, the *Mitāksharā,* a law compendium of the 11th century, was the standard work in the greater part of India. For the historical study of Indian law, for which clarification of the beginnings is of particular importance, this very large group of works is indispensable, especially since they are helpful in understanding the original sources.

In addition to the traditions contained in the Vedas, *Dharmasūtras,* and *Dharmaśāstras,* the Brahmanical authors recognize as a third source of law the way of life and teachings of pious men, such as the *Sadācāra* and the *Śishṭāgama.* In connection with law proper, particular customs and manners of various countries, castes, and families are often emphasized as standard, though of course only so far as they are not opposed to the sacred law. The important position given in this respect to customary law is thoroughly in conformity with facts and renders it obligatory for those who deal with the history of law to search for traces and survivals of Indian customary law.

The most important sources of ancient Indian law are the *Āpastamba Dharmasūtra, Gautama Dharmasūtra, Vasishṭha Dharmasūtra, Vishnu Smṛti, Mānava Dharmaśāstra, Yājñavalkya Dharmaśāstra,* and *Nārada Smṛti.*

The number of authors and works on the *Dharmaśāstras* is legion. All of them were actuated by the most laudable motives of regulating Hindu society in all matters—civil, religious, and moral—and of securing for the members of that society happiness in this world and the next. They laid the greatest emphasis on the duties of every man as a member of the whole Hindu society and of the particular class to which he belonged, and very little emphasis on the privileges of men. They created great solidarity and cohesion among the several classes of Hindu society in India in spite of conflicting interests and inclinations and enabled that society to hold its own against foreign invaders.

Today Hindu law is applied to: (1) Hindus by birth and by religion, including those who after renouncing Hinduism have reverted to it; (2) illegitimate children both of whose parents are Hindus; (3) illegitimate children in cases in which the father is a Christian and the mother a Hindu, provided the children are brought up as Hindus; (4) sons of Hindu dancing girls of the Naik caste converted to Islam, in cases in which the sons are taken into the family of the Hindu grandparents and are brought up as Hindus; (5) Jains, Sikhs, Nambudri Brahmans.

Hindus are in theory divided into four major castes: Brahmans (Brāhmaṇas), Kshatriyas (Kṣatriyas), Vaisyas (Vaiśyas), and Sudras (Śūdras). Each of these is in turn subdivided into a number of subcastes, the latter being regarded by sociologists as the true castes. The first three of the major castes are *dvija,* or twice born. Through investiture with the sacred thread they have the right to study the Vedas and perform the samskara (Sanskrit *samskāra*), or sacraments. All of these rights except the samskara of marriage are denied to Sudras.

Today, as in ancient times, the main sources of Hindu law are found in: (1) *Śruti,* that is, divinely inspired works, including the mass of material known as the Veda; (2) the *Smṛti;* (3) customs which are based on lost or forgotten *Śruti* and *Smṛti;* and (4) judicial decisions.

The three principal *Smṛti* texts which are still considered sources of present day law are: (1) the Code of Manu (the *Mānava Dharmaśāstra*), compiled some time between 200 B.C. and 100 A.D.; (2) the Code of Yājñavalkya, written some time between 100 A.D. and 300 A.D. (the *Mitāksharā,* composed in the 11th century, is the leading commentary upon this code); and (3) the Code of Nārada, written some time between 100 B.C. and 400 A.D. In addition, there are more than 100 other *Dharmaśāstras* of greater or lesser importance.

The *Smṛti* texts do not agree with each other in all respects. The conflict between them gave rise to commentaries which often have been accepted as authoritative, even if they appear to scholars to proceed by wrong interpretation. Clear proof of usage outweighs the written text of the Hindu law.

In regard to succession and inheritance, there are in principle only two schools of law, the Mitākshara and the Dāyabhāga. (The latter is a digest of codes on division of inheritance, written between the 13th and 15th centuries A.D.) The difference between these two systems on the subject of inheritance arises from the fact that, while the doctrine of religious efficacy is the guiding system under the Dāyabhāga school, there is no such definite guiding principle under the Mitākshara school. Sometimes, consanguinity is regarded as the guiding principle; at others, religious efficacy. Succession to stridhana (Sanskrit *strīdhana*), or property held absolutely by a female, is governed by rules different from those which govern inheritance to the property of a male. The Mitākshara school recognizes two modes of devolution of property: survivorship and succession. The rule of survivorship applies to joint family property; the rules of succession apply to property held in absolute severalty by the last owner. The Dāyabhāga recognizes only one mode of devolution: succession. It does not recognize the rule of survivorship even in the case of joint family property. The reason for this is that, while every member of a Mitākshara joint family has only an undivided interest in the joint property, a member of a Dāyabhāga joint family holds his share in quasi severalty, so that it passes on his death to his heirs as if he were absolutelv seized thereof, and not to the surviving coparceners as under the Mitākshara law.

The joint family is a striking feature of Hindu society and Hindu law. A joint Hindu family consists of all males lineally descended from a common ancestor and includes their wives and unmarried daughters. A daughter ceases to be a member of her father's family on marriage and becomes a member of her husband's family. The joint and undivided Hindu family is ordinarily joint not only in estate, but also in food and worship. Hindu coparcenary is a much narrower body than the joint family. It includes only those persons who acquire by birth an interest in the joint or coparcenary property. The essence of a coparcenary under the Mitākshara law is unity of ownership. Joint family or coparcenary property is that in which every coparcener has a joint interest and a joint possession; it devolves by survivorship, not by succession, and is property in which the male issue of the coparceners acquire an interest by birth. (In some cases the widow takes a share equal to that of her husband or son.) Property acquired in business by members of a joint Hindu family through their joint labor and with the aid of the joint family property becomes joint family property, and where it has been acquired without the aid of joint family property the presumption is that it is the joint property of the joint acquirers. Generally speaking the normal state of every traditional Hindu family is joint, and in the absence of proof of division such is the legal presumption. All the legal rules applied according to Hindu law depend on whether the person to which the law is being applied belongs to a joint family or not. There are therefore separate rules on alienation, debts, partition, gifts, and other subjects which are applied differently to members of a joint family and to those who are not members of such a family.

A Hindu who is of sound mind and not a minor may dispose of his property by gift or by will for religious and charitable purposes, such as the establishment and worship of an idol, feeding Brahmans and the poor, performance of religious ceremonies, and the endowment of a university or a hospital. The moment the endowment is made, all rights pass from the dedicator. Where property is devoted absolutely to religious purposes, the possession and management of the property belongs in the case of a *devasthāna* (temple) to the manager of the temple, and in the case of a math (Sanskrit *maṭh*), or abode for students of religion, to the head of the math, who is called a mahant. Temple managers and mahants form a continuous representation of the property of the idol or of the math.

Marriage is a holy union for the performance of religious duties, not a contract. In principle, a Hindu may marry any number of wives, but a woman cannot marry another man while her husband is alive. Legislation in modern times has in some provinces and states changed this general rule. The historic practice has been that the parties to a marriage must both belong to the same major caste; otherwise the marriage is invalid. But a marriage between persons belonging to different subdivisions of the same caste is not invalid. For the purposes of marriage converts to Hinduism are regarded as Sudras. Therefore, the marriage of a Sudra with a Christian woman converted to Hinduism before marriage is treated as a marriage between two Sudras and is valid. A man cannot marry a woman of the same gotra or *pravara;* that is, he cannot marry a woman if his father and the woman's father are both descendants of a common ancestor in the male line. Similarly, a man and a woman cannot marry if they are sapinda (Sanskrit *sapiṇḍa*), or persons having a common ancestor within a prescribed degree. There are two schools of thought as to who are sapinda for marriage.

According to Hindu law, the wife is bound to live with her husband and to submit herself to his authority. The husband is bound to live with his wife and to maintain her. Divorce is not known in general Hindu law; a marriage creates an indissoluble tie between the husband and the wife. Judicial separation, however, is admissible.

Adoption is widely practiced and recognized in Hindu law. The objects of adoption are to secure spiritual benefits to the adopter and his ancestors, and to secure an heir and perpetuate the adopter's name. Adoption has the effect of transferring the adopted boy from his natural family into the adoptive family. In principle, it confers upon the adoptee the same rights and privileges in the family of the adopter as those of a legitimate son. On the other hand, the adopted son loses all the rights of a son in his natural family but does not sever the tie of blood between himself and the members of his natural family. For this reason he cannot marry in his natural family.

Bibliography.—Jones, Sir William, *Institutes of Hindu Law* (Calcutta and London 1796); Colebrooke, H. T., *A Digest of Hindu Law*, vols. 1-3 (Calcutta and London 1801); Jolly, Julius, *Outlines of an History of the Hindu Law of Partition, Inheritance and Adoption* (Calcutta 1885); West, Sir Raymond, and Bühler, J. G., *A Digest of the Hindu Law of Inheritance, Partition, and Adoption*, 4th ed. (Bombay 1921); Mayne, J. D., *A Treatise on Hindu Law and Usage*, 9th ed. (Madras 1922); Jolly, Julius, *Hindu Law and Custom* (Calcutta 1928); Jha, Ganganatha, *Hindu Law in Its Sources* (Allahabad 1930); Mulla, Sir D. F., *Principles of Hindu Law*, 9th ed. (Calcutta 1940); Kane, P. V., *History of Dharmaśāstra*, vols. 1-3 (Poona 1930–46); vol. 4 in preparation.

Moslem Law.—Moslem personal law has been applied in modern India to Moslems in some matters only, that is: (1) in those which have been expressly directed by the Legislative Assembly to be applied to Moslems, such as rules of succession and inheritance; and (2) to those which are applied to Moslems as a matter of justice, equity, and good conscience, such as the rules of the Moslem law of pre-emption. A Moslem is considered to be any person who professes that: (1) there is but One God, and (2) that Mohammed (Muḥammad) is His prophet.

Moslems are divided into two main divisions, namely the Sunnites and the Shi'ites. The Sunnites are in turn divided into four sects: the Hanafi, the Maliki, the Shafi'ites, and the Hanbalites. The Shi'ites are divided into three sects: the Ithna'ashariya, the Isma'ili, and the Zaydites. Moslem law applicable to each division or sect prevails for litigants of that division or sect. (See also MOSLEM SECTS.)

There are four sources of Moslem law: (1) the Koran (Qur'ān); (2) *ḥadīth,* that is, precepts, actions, and sayings of the Prophet Mohammed, not written down during his lifetime, but preserved by tradition and handed down by authorized persons; (3) *ijmā',* that is, consensus of Moslem scholars; and (4) *qiyās,* analogical deductions derived from a comparison of the first three sources when they do not apply to any particular case.

The whole estate of a Moslem who dies intestate, or so much of it as has not been disposed of by will, devolves on his heirs at the moment of his death. The heirs succeed to the estate as tenants in common in specific shares. Each heir is liable for the debts of the deceased to the extent only of a share of the debts proportionate to his share of the estate. There is no distinction of inheritance between movable and immovable property, or between ancestral and self-acquired property.

When the members of a Moslem family live in commensality, they do not form a joint family in the sense in which that term is used in Hindu law. There is not, as in Hindu law, any presumption that acquisitions by several members of a family living together are for the benefit of the family. If during the continuance of the family, however, properties are acquired in the name of the managing member of the family, and it is proved that they are possessed by all the members jointly, the presumption is that they are the properties of the family. If after the death of a Moslem his adult sons continue their father's business and retain his assets in the business, they are deemed to stand in a fiduciary relation to the other heirs of the deceased and to be liable to account as such for the profit made by them in the business. Similarly, members of a Moslem family carrying on business jointly do not constitute a joint family firm in the sense in which that expression is used in Hindu law.

In principle, every Moslem of sound mind and not a minor may dispose of his property by will (*waṣīyah*), which may be made either verbally or in writing. He cannot dispose of more than a third of the surplus of his estate after payment of funeral expenses and debts. Bequests in excess of the legal third cannot take effect unless the heirs consent thereto after the death of the testator. The Sunnites and the Shi'ites differ widely on other more detailed rules of succession.

An important feature of Moslem law is *waqf*, the permanent dedication by a person professing Islam of any property for any purpose recognized by Moslem law as religious, pious, or charitable. The moment the *waqf* is created, all rights of property pass out of the *wāqif*, or dedicator, and vest in the Almighty. The mutawalli (Arabic *mutawallī*), or superintendent of the religious beneficiary, has no right in the property belonging to the *waqf*. In principle, *waqf* property cannot be alienated and is not liable to attachment and sale in execution of a personal decree against the mutawalli, nor can the rents and profits derived from such property be seized by execution.

The right of *shuf'a*, or pre-emption, is a right which the owner of an immovable property possesses to acquire by purchase another immovable property which has been sold to another person. The right of pre-emption is recognized by custom among Hindus of some parts of India and is governed in principle by the rules of the Moslem law of pre-emption.

Marriage is a contract which has for its object the procreation and legalization of children. Every Moslem of sound mind who has attained puberty may enter into a contract of marriage. A Moslem may have as many as four wives at the same time, but it is not lawful for a Moslem woman to have more than one husband at a time. A Moslem male may contract a valid marriage not only with a Moslem woman, but also with a *kitābīya* (that is, a Jewess or a Christian), but not with an idolatress or a fire worshiper; a Moslem woman cannot contract a valid marriage except with a Moslem. She cannot contract a valid marriage even with a *kitābī* (Jew or Christian). If such a marriage is contracted, however, it is not void, but only irregular. The husband is bound to maintain his wife so long as she is faithful to him and obeys his reasonable orders. If he neglects or refuses to maintain her, the wife may sue him for maintenance. A woman after divorce, but not after the death of her husband, is entitled to maintenance during the period of iddat (Arabic *'iddah*), or the period during which a divorced or widowed woman must remain in seclusion and abstain from remarriage.

Dower or mahr is a sum of money or other property which the wife is entitled to receive from the husband in consideration of the marriage. If the amount of dower is not fixed, the wife is entitled to "proper" dower. The wife may refuse to live with her husband and admit him to sexual intercourse so long as the dower is not paid. The contract of marriage may be dissolved: (1) by the husband at his will, without the intervention of a court; (2) by mutual consent without the intervention of a court; and (3) by a judicial decree at the suit of the husband or wife. The wife is entitled to sue for a divorce on the grounds that her husband is impotent or that he has falsely charged her with adultery.

Bibliography.—Wilson, Sir R. K., *A Digest of Anglo-Muhammadan Law*, 6th ed. (Calcutta 1930); Fyzee, A. A. A., *An Introduction to the Study of Mahomedan Law* (London 1931); Mulla, Sir D. F., *Principles of Mahomedan Law*, 10th ed. (Calcutta 1933); Saksena, H. P., *Muslim Law as Administered in British India*, 2d ed. (Allahabad 1940); Tyabji, F. B., *Muhammadan Law*, 3d ed. (Bombay 1940); Fyzee, A. A. A., *Outlines of Muhammadan Law* (London 1950).

LUDWIK STERNBACH,
Honorary Professor of Ancient Indian Law and Dharmaśāstra, Bhāratīya Vidyā Bhavan, Bombay; Trusteeship Department, United Nations.

11. ARCHAEOLOGY. Stone Age.—Man's residence in the Indian subcontinent, as far as present evidence indicates, begins in Quaternary (Pleistocene) times. The earliest discovered remains are of Paleolithic flake tools from the Boulder Conglomerate stage at the close of the second interglaciation, found in the terraces of the Sohan (Soan) Valley among the upper Siwalik Hills in the Potwar area of the northwestern Punjab, Pakistan. Following this industry, known as pre-Sohan, is the Sohan (Early and Late) industry proper, which is found in a large area of the northwestern part of the subcontinent, and the Madras hand-ax industry, found at widely scattered sites in peninsular India with extensions into Rajputana and central India. Microlithic industries have been discovered from the extreme northwest to the tip of the peninsula and from Sind in the west to the coast of Orissa in the east. A proto-Neolithic industry has been identified in Kashmir and adjacent Punjab. Neolithic material has been recovered from sites in almost all major sections of the subcontinent, perhaps having been diffused from north to south.

Early Indus Civilizations.—The first remains of urban civilization in the Indian subcontinent appear at a number of sites in the Indus River system. At least four cultures have been discovered. The earliest of these is called Amri after the place where it was first identified, and is known from a poorly developed architecture, chert implements, shell, and a thin-walled painted pottery.

The second culture, discovered at Harappa and first described in print in 1924, is much the most frequently represented, endured for the longest period of time, was the most advanced, and has been well explored at Harappa, Mohenjo-daro, and Chanhu-daro. It was in contact with Sumer, Mesopotamia, as early as 2350 B.C., and possibly as late as the 17th century B.C. (or even a century or two later). It had well-constructed, fortified, and planned cities, chiefly of brick, provided with an excellent drainage system. Houses were usually separate and equipped with baths. It used copper and bronze extensively, and the people wore cotton clothing. They had jewelry of metal, shell, and pottery. Both cubical and tabular dice and many toys have been recovered. The thick-walled red Harappa wheel-made painted pottery has characteristic black painted decorations of foliage, animals, and geometric motifs. This culture had a system of writing, which appears abundantly on steatite stamp seals but has not been successfully deciphered. The cities were commercial, and appear to have dominated the surrounding country. In Baluchistan (both that in Pakistan and that in southern Iran) archaeological sites of the third millennium B.C. have been discovered along ancient trade routes leading to the West. A number of items of the Harappa culture reappear in later historic India and suggest that there was a continuous civilization during that time, though the connecting links have not been found. Who the people were who owned the Harappa culture is not known, though it is frequently suggested that they were Dravidians.

The third Early Indus civilization is known as the Jhukar. It was also well advanced, though less so than the Harappa, and it had cities built upon cities of the Harappa culture but of inferior architecture. Its polychrome painted pottery was different from that of the Harappa culture, and it had no writing. It appears to have belonged to a different people.

The last of the four early cultures is called the Jhangar, and is known only from a crude, handmade gray pottery with incised geometric designs. Its owners may have been nomads.

Rig Vedic Culture.—The next known period of civilization in India is that of the Rig Veda, but information about it is drawn exclusively from literary sources. No material remains have yet been identified. The people owning this culture had a language belonging to the Indo-European family and were closely related to the Iranians, forming with them a group called Indo-Iranian or Aryan. They are generally considered to have entered the Indian subcontinent through the passes of the northwest frontier at around 1500-1200 B.C. They kept herds, practiced agriculture, used metal, and perhaps had fortified settlements. They had chariots and may have introduced the horse into India. Wealth was measured in terms of cattle. Their chief weapon was the bow; they wore helmet and body armor. They gambled with *vibhīdaka* nuts for dice, raced horses, and had an intoxicating drink called sura (Sanskrit *surā*). Their society was patriarchal and divided into (1) Aryans, who were subdivided into Brahmans (Brāhmaṇas, or spiritual aristocracy), Kshatriyas (Kṣatriyas, or rulers and warriors), and Vaisyas (Vaiśyas, or commons); and (2) non-Aryans, who were Sudras (Śūdras, or serfs). Their religion (see section on *Religion and Philosophy*) seems to have been basically different from that of the Early Indus civilizations, and it is impossible to establish any relationship between the two cultures. The ruler of a tribe or clan was a king or raja (*rājan*); there was an assembly of the folk. By 1000 B.C., the Aryans had advanced over the Punjab, and, according to literary record, seem to have reached eastern Bihar and Bengal by 800 B.C. They may also by that time have got to central India from the Ganges Valley, and have gone down the Indus to the west of the Rajputana desert, crossed Kutch (Cutch), and arrived in Gujarat. No material archaeological data exist to reveal the details of this advance. Similarly, there is no material archaeological evidence to confirm the events narrated in the great epic, the *Mahābhārata*, concerning the war between the Pāṇḍavas and the Kauravas, traditionally later than the Vedic period.

Formation and Growth of Historic Indian Civilization.—The blending of the diverse elements which formed traditional historic Indian civilization took place during the 7th to 3d centuries B.C. For this period archaeological exploration has revealed much of topography, history, and social conditions to supplement literary data. During these centuries the Aryan Vedic civilization, as modified by contact with non-Aryans, established itself in north India. There are presumptive reasons for thinking that a Dravidian civilization also existed in south India at this time, but there is no conclusive archaeological evidence to support the theory. During these same centuries the Persian Empire often held as satrapies areas in Afghanistan, Baluchistan, and the Punjab through which business and cultural contacts were maintained between Persia and India, especially along the great trade routes which ran from Bihar across northern India to Bactria (Afghanistan) and beyond. During the same period there was ocean-borne commerce between western Indian seaports and the Persian Gulf and Red Sea.

In these same centuries the philosophic speculations of the Upanishads (*Upaniṣad*) were formulated, and the two heterodox religions of Buddhism and Jainism rose and had their first spread. The earliest known records of these faiths are literary, but in the 3d century B.C., the great emperor Aśoka (r. c.274–237 B.C.) of the Maurya dynasty, patron of Buddhism, who ruled a great empire from his capital Pāṭaliputra (modern Patna) in Magadha (part of modern Bihar), marked many sites sacred to that faith, as well as other sites, with commemorative inscribed columns. He also had edicts carved on rocks in many parts of his wide realm, somewhat in the manner of the Achaemenian kings of Persia.

The Aśokan inscriptions are not in Sanskrit, but in various spoken Prakrits (see section on LANGUAGES) of local provenience, and are written in two scripts. One of these, known as Kharoshthi (*kharoṣṭhī*), reading from right to left, is characteristic of Gandhara in the northwest; it is a form of a script which was in use in the Persian Empire at around 500 B.C., and was employed in India until about 450 A.D. The other script, known as Brahmi (*brāhmī*), reading from left to right, was employed throughout Aśoka's empire and appears to have been derived from a western Asiatic business script which was in use during the 7th-6th century B.C., though an unconvincing effort has also been made to derive it from the Harappa script. Brahmi is the source of all later native Indian scripts. The decipherment of these two scripts in the 19th century was basic to the study of Indian epigraphy and numismatics, and revolutionized knowledge of Indian history from the time of Aśoka to the Guptas (4th to 6th century A.D.).

As the period of formation of characteristic Indian civilization was coming to a close, the contact with Persian civilization, already mentioned, assumed a special form. In the old Persian Empire, following Alexander the Great's invasion (330 B.C.), there arose a blend of the Persian culture with the classical Greek and Roman, known as Hellenistic. This entered Bactria (Afghanistan) and northwestern India, where it was cultivated under a number of Indo-Greek kings, of whom the greatest was Menander, known to Indians as Milinda (c. 150 B.C.). When the Maurya dynasty collapsed (c. 185 B.C.), these kings pushed farther into India, taking with them the Hellenistic culture. After them, in the first century A.D., the Kushanas (Kuṣāṇa), a Central Asian people, came to India by way of Bactria, having been partly Hellenized on the way (see *History: From the Earliest Times to 1707*). Under these two sets of rulers, and their contemporaries and tributaries, both Hellenistic and native Indic civilizations existed side by side. It was thought in the 19th and early 20th century that India owed much of her historic culture to Hellenistic influence, but it now appears that India as a whole took very little from it that endured, except in astronomy, astrology, and medicine. In architecture and sculpture Hellenistic influence still exists in Kashmir, but elsewhere in modern India traces of it can be found only with patient search. Whatever India accepted from Hellenism in literature, art, and philosophy was thoroughly assimilated by the end of the 5th century A.D., when the Huns obliterated Hellenism in India.

During this period there was a notable development of urbanization and an increase of wealth with expansion of foreign commerce. Fairly large kingdoms existed by the time of the Buddha (563?-?483 B.C.); these were consolidated into an empire under Aśoka. Elaborate wooden houses are shown in the sculptures at Sanchi (1st century A.D.). Ownership of land vested in the state; peasants rented the use of it. The caste system in a rigid form had come into existence by the time of the legal works known as the Shastras (Śāstras, starting from about the 2d century A.D.), and the doctrine of pollution was marking the lowest or Fifths (Panchama; Sanskrit *pañcama*) off from the rest of the community. The administration of the state was well organized according to the Greek Megasthenes, who at about 300 B.C., visited the court of Chandragupta Maurya, grandfather of Aśoka. Further details of administration are given in the well-known *Arthaśāstra,* a work by Chanakya (Cāṇakya; also called Viṣṇugupta or Kauṭilya), Chandragupta Maurya's minister, which in its present form may be a reworking of as late a date as the 2d or 3d century A.D., but must contain a kernel of material from Mauryan times. The great flowering of Indian civilization was in the period of the Gupta dynasty, founded by Chandragupta I (r. c. 318/319-330 A.D.), and lasting to the 6th century, and continued culturally until the middle of the 7th century. At this time literature, science, sculpture, painting, the dance, the drama, and music assumed their classic forms, and the religion known as Brahmanical Hinduism, with Sanskrit as its literary vehicle, acquired the major features which persist to the present. Medieval Indian history may be considered to start after the close of the Gupta period.

Select Bibliography.—Barnett, L. D., *Antiquities of India* (New York 1914); *Cambridge History of India:* E. J. Rapson, ed., Vol. 1, *Ancient India* (New York 1922); Macdonell, A. A., *India's Past* (New York 1927); Masson-Oursel, Paul, Willman-Grabowska, Helena, and Stern, Philippe, *Ancient India and Indian Civilization,* tr. from the French by M. R. Dobie (London 1934); Cumming, Sir John G., ed., *Revealing India's Past* (London 1939); Krishnaswamy, V. D., "Stone Age India," *Ancient India,* no. 3, pp. 11-57 (Delhi 1947); Mackay, Ernest, *Early Indus Civilizations* (London 1948).

W. Norman Brown,
Professor of Sanskrit, University of Pennsylvania.

12. HISTORY: FROM THE EARLIEST TIMES TO 1707. The first exact date in Indian history is 326 B.C., the year in which Alexander the Great invaded India, but there is some reasonably sound historical information beginning with the 6th century B.C. (For the prehistory of the subcontinent see section on *Archaeology.*) The earliest Buddhist books describe northern India of the 7th and 6th centuries B.C. as divided into 4 great and 12 small kingdoms and a number of tribal republics. Since the Vedic period the center of political power had been moving eastward from the Punjab until, by the end of the 6th century, Magadha began to emerge as a great power.

Shortly before 500 B.C., King Darius I of Persia invaded and occupied northwestern India, which thereafter formed the 20th satrapy of the Persian Empire. It is not known how long this Persian occupation lasted or how much influence it had on the development of Indian civilization. When Alexander invaded India, he found no trace of Persian rule. Northwestern India was then divided into several small, independent states.

After conquering Persia, Bactria, and Afghanistan, Alexander reached the easternmost of the rivers of the Punjab, near Amritsar, northwest of Delhi. Here his troops mutinied and refused to go farther east. After organizing four satrapies in India and one in Afghanistan, three under Greek officers and two under Indians, he was forced to retreat. He had intended to hold his conquests permanently, for he had a dream of uniting East and West. If he had lived longer the whole history of India might have been different, but he died in Babylon in 323 B.C. By 317 all trace of Greek rule in India had disappeared, but Alexander had founded 8 or 10 cities in Bactria and the Oxus region, and there was Greek rule in Bactria for nearly 200 years (327–135 B.C.). More and more, however, the Bactrian Greeks were cut off from the west by the rise of the Parthian Empire, and more and more did they have to struggle against increasing pressure from Scythian tribes on the north and northeast.

The Mauryas (322?-c. 185 B.C.).—Shortly after Alexander's death, Chandragupta founded the Maurya dynasty. The Maurya empire—the first great empire of India, whose capital was at Patna (ancient Pāṭaliputra) in Magadha (modern Bihar)—reached its greatest extent under his grandson Aśoka, who ruled nearly all of India except the southern tip. For Chandragupta (322?–298 B.C.) and Aśoka (c. 274–237 B.C.) there is an unusual amount of definite historical information. For Bindusāra (298–c. 274 B.C.), the son of Chandragupta, there are only a trivial anecdote given by a Greek writer and a tradition recorded by the Tibetan historian Tāranātha that Bindusāra conquered the country between the eastern and western seas. The dominant political power in India has always been in the north. The Mauryas extended their political control over central India, and later the Moguls (Mughals) and the British ruled over central India and a large part of the south. None of the central or southern dynasties was ever able to occupy and control northern India.

The organization of Chandragupta's empire is better known than that of any other Indian king down to the time of Akbar. Much information has been preserved in a Greek book written by Megasthenes and in a Sanskrit text called the *Arthaśāstra.* About 302 B.C., Seleucus I Nikator, Greek ruler of western Asia, sent to the court of Chandragupta an ambassador named Megasthenes, who lived for several years at Pāṭaliputra and wrote, in Greek, a book giving a detailed account of the country and people. The book itself is not extant, but substantial fragments have been preserved in quotations by later writers. The *Arthaśāstra* gives us a glimpse of a world of thought and action utterly different from that which we get from the older religious Vedic literature. There are some minor discrepancies with Megasthenes, but very great agreement. The work is traditionally ascribed to Chanakya (Cāṇakya; Kauṭilya), Chandragupta's prime minister. The final redaction of the text in its present form may date from the beginning of the Christian era, but its essentials are corroborated by Megasthenes and may be taken as giving a fair picture of life and government in early Maurya times. The *Arthaśāstra* is probably the oldest extant work of secular Sanskrit literature and one of the most important works of Indian antiquity that have come down to us. It deals with government as regulating all matters of daily life, with practical worldly affairs, and with technical matters, economics, government, and politics rather than religion and philosophy.

In form, the government was an autocracy, tempered by reverence for the Brahmans, who were exempt from taxation and, as a general rule, from capital punishment except for treason. State was superior to church. There was some regard for the religious sanctity of the priesthood, but government was essentially free from priestly domination. There was a constant struggle for existence between kingdoms. In general, might was right. The spy system was highly organized, and the whole machinery of government seemed to depend on secret information as a safeguard against rival states, as a means of instigating revolutions in rival states, and as a means of maintaining a check on officials. Hence the frequent comparison of this book with Niccolò Machiavelli's *The Prince*. There is much on taxation (normally one sixth of the produce), on irrigation, on state control of butchers, liquor sellers, gamblers, and courtesans, on shipping by river and ocean, and on mining and metallurgy. Much attention was paid to meteorology, pastures and grazing grounds, and medicine, and to the taking of a regular census and the registration of travelers. The vigorous attitude toward life, and the efficient state organization of and control over innumerable practical details, surprises us after the almost exclusively religious texts of the Veda and the world-renouncing philosophy of the Upanishads. It is probable that a more energetic spirit was always present outside of Brahman religious and philosophical circles.

Aśoka, after waging one war in Kalinga, was converted to Buddhism and zealously proclaimed Buddhism in a number of inscriptions carved on rocks and inscribed on pillars in various parts of his great empire. The earliest inscriptions in India, they form one of the most remarkable series of public documents in world history. Aśoka preached the sanctity of animal life, the noninjury of any living creature, and the sin of the old Brahmanical animal sacrifices. He inculcated the virtues of truthfulness, of reverence for parents, elders, and teachers, of tolerance for the beliefs and practices of others, and of almsgiving. He emphasized inward piety rather than rituals and festivals. Officials were appointed who went through the country convening the people and preaching the Buddhist faith (dharma). Buddhist missions were sent abroad and to the far south of India. Aśoka was also a great builder of Buddhist stupas. He had roads constructed, and gardens for medicinal herbs planted. It has been suggested that his mildness and tolerance and his pacific tendencies in the midst of a turbulent world contributed to the rapid collapse of the Maurya empire after his death.

Northern India, 2d Century B.C.—4th Century A.D.—The Mauryas were succeeded at Pāṭaliputra by the Sungas (c. 185–73 B.C.) and the Kanvas (73–28 B.C.), who ruled over a much diminished empire. Under the Sungas there seems to have been a Brahmanical reaction to the Buddhism of Aśoka, and there are reasons for thinking that the period was of great importance in the development of secular Sanskrit literature.

After Aśoka's death the Maurya empire began to break up as the Bactrian Greeks pushed into India from the northwest and as central India became independent under the Andhra dynasty, which lasted from about 230 B.C. to about 225 A.D. For over 450 years the 30 kings of the Andhra dynasty ruled over the whole of the Deccan. This is the longest dynasty in Indian history. There are some inscriptions, but the history of the period is still obscure. It seems to have been an important period in the development of literature, art, architecture, and religion.

Early in the 2d century B.C. the Bactrian Greeks pushed over the Hindu Kush into the Kabul Valley and India. They won control of the whole of northwestern India and maintained themselves there until early in the 1st century, when they were overwhelmed by the coming of the Sakas and Kushans.

Some time between 170 and 165 B.C. a tribe called by the Chinese Yüeh-chi (Yuechi), which dwelled in eastern Turkestan and western Kansu, was attacked and defeated by the Hsiung-nu, who lived north of them in what is now known as Mongolia. The Yüeh-chi were probably Iranian; the Hsiung-nu were probably the ancestors ot the Huns. Defeated, the Yüeh-chi moved to the west, where they met the Iranian nomadic tribes called Sakas. These, driven out of their homeland by the Yüeh-chi, pushed off by the Bactrian Greeks, and blocked by the Parthians, moved southward through eastern Persia to Sakastan (modern Seistan). Many of these Sakas pushed eastward into India and then moved up the Indus Valley, through the Delhi gap, and down the Ganges Valley or the Indus Valley, across Kutch (Cutch), into Gujarat, and even into the northwestern part of the Deccan. We have coins and inscriptions of Saka kings from the 1st century A.D. until after 400 A.D. They rapidly became Hinduized.

The Yüeh-chi crossed the Oxus into Bactria and completely swept aside Greek rule there. For a century or more the Yüeh-chi, divided into five branches, dwelled in Bactria. At the end of the 1st century B.C. (or early in the 1st century A.D.) they were united by one king who belonged to the Kushan branch. Under the name Kushana (Kuṣāṇa), they pushed into India and founded an empire which covered most of northwestern India, Afghanistan, Bactria, and the western part of Turkestan. This empire lasted until about 220 A.D. The last of the Kushan kings bore an Indian name, a clear indication that the Kushans had gradually become Hinduized as had the Greeks and the Sakas.

The Gupta Empire, c.318–500 A.D.—Again there is a dark period in Indian history until the formation of the Gupta empire, founded by Chandragupta I about 318–319 A.D., and lasting to about 500 A.D. Its capital was Pāṭaliputra, where the Mauryas also had ruled. The Guptas ruled most of northern India, while the Deccan remained independent under various dynasties.

The 160 years covered by the reigns of the five great Gupta kings—Chandragupta I, Samudragupta, Chandragupta II, Kumāragupta I, and Skandagupta—were the golden age of Hinduism and classical Sanskrit literature. Literature, sculpture, painting, music, architecture, and science reached a high level of excellence. The country was rich and prosperous; the administration was tolerant and efficient. A series of important inscriptions makes it possible to reconstruct the history of the Gupta period with a fullness not possible since the time of Aśoka.

Much light is cast on the Gupta period by the account left by the Chinese pilgrim Fa-hsien, who came to India to visit the Buddhist holy places and to procure manuscripts. He left China in 399 A.D., traveled across central Asia, reached Magadha in 405, stayed there for six years, and returned to China by sea by way of Ceylon and Java, reaching home in 414.

By the time of the Guptas, Hinduism (see section on *Religion and Philosophy*) had become well established. The old sacrificial system of Brahmanism, with its emphasis on fire sacrifices and external ritualistic acts, had been replaced by temple and image worship. Sacrifice had been replaced by an attitude of worship and devotion (bhakti) to new gods or to gods who were of small importance in the Vedas—Vishnu, Shiva, Krishna, Rāma. Philosophical Brahmanism with its tendency to pantheism and monism continued as the higher theology and philosophy of Hinduism, aiming at salvation beyond that of the heavens of the personal gods. Popular Brahmanism was modified into the dharma of Hinduism, a traditional code of social customs.

At this time a new spirit had arisen in Buddhism which fundamentally changed its whole character. The old Buddhism of the Hinayana variety had been superseded by the Mahayana (see section on *Religion and Philosophy;* article on BUDDHA AND BUDDHISM). Mythology had begun to weave wonderful stories of the past lives of the Buddha when he was a Bodhisattva on his way to Buddhahood. The monks had begun to take up permanent residence in monasteries, to become lax in discipline or to plunge into metaphysical and logical speculation and scholastic wrangling. They lost their hold on the people and became merely monastic communities. Buddhism merged into the main stream of the popular religion, Hinduism.

By this time or somewhat earlier the Indians were using nine numerals with zero and place value. These were adopted by the Arabs in the 8th century and soon spread to western Europe, being called Arabic numerals only because they were transmitted to the West by the Arabs. Our numerals of the present day are very similar to those in Indian inscriptions of the 6th century.

India was not cut off from the rest of the world. We now know that the Indians were one of the greatest navigating and colonizing peoples of antiquity. From the first century of the Christian era, and probably from three or four centuries before that time, Indian culture had been spreading eastward to Indochina, from Burma to China, and through the islands from Sumatra and Java to Borneo and the Philippines. For more than a thousand years the whole of southeastern Asia was closely connected with India by trade and colonization. There were Indian colonies, Indian dynasties of kings, Indian architecture and art, Indian religions, and Indian codes of law and government in Southeast Asia. From the 9th to the 14th century Angkor in Cambodia was one of the most magnificent and flourishing cities in the world. Its civilization was largely Indian. The Buddhist stupa of Borobudur in Java is one of the most remarkable buildings of the ancient world. Indians traveled freely to Egypt and Arabia and there was a large amount of trade with Egypt (from the 3d century B.C.) and with the Roman Empire. Many Roman coins from the first two centuries A.D. have been found in southern India.

Northern India, 4th to 12th Centuries A.D.—The Gupta empire was destroyed by invasions of the White Huns during the latter part of the 5th century. These were probably Iranian and mixed tribes who were uprooted and shoved southward by the Huns as they moved westward toward Europe. They occupied northwestern India until about 528 A.D. The Indians describe them as fierce and cruel, and say that wherever they went their coming was marked by massacres and devastation.

Order was brought out of chaos by Harsha (Harṣa) of Kanauj (r. 606–647 A.D.) in a brilliant period of renaissance which did not survive his death. The Chinese pilgrim Hsüan-tsang (Yüan Chwang) gives an invaluable description of the India of Harsha's time. He started on his travels in 629, came across Central Asia, traveled over a large part of India, spending eight years in Harsha's dominions, and returned to China in 645 through Central Asia with a large collection of Buddhist manuscripts. The rest of his life was spent in correlating the results of his expedition and in translating Buddhist texts into Chinese.

The books of Hsüan-tsang, Fa-hsien, and other Chinese pilgrims, and of Megasthenes and other Greek visitors to India, are of great importance because there is practically no historical literature in Sanskrit. Scattered inscriptions, some genealogical lists, some semihistorical novels, dramas and epics which are so overlaid by romance that history is almost lost sight of, and a mass of highly romantic fables and stories make it impossible to reconstruct more than the bare bones of history except for a few periods where the narratives of more historically minded foreigners help to fill out the skeleton. In contrast to the Chinese and Greek travelers, none of the hundreds of Indians who traveled to Egypt, China, and the Far East have left records.

For over 500 years after Harsha the history of northern India is dominated by Rajput tribes who moved over the country and formed rapidly shifting kingdoms. Some of these tribes may have been descendants of old Hindu Kshatriyas (Kṣatriyas), but most of them seem to be tribes which came into India with the White Huns and became Hinduized.

Central and Southern India, 5th to 14th Centuries A.D.—Central India and southern India went their own way, little influenced by the happenings in the north. In the Deccan the most important kingdoms were those of the Western Chalukyas of Badami (550–753 A.D.), the Eastern Chalukyas of Vengi (7th to 12th centuries), the Rashtrakutas of Malkhed (753–973 A.D.), the Western Chalukyas of Kalyani (973–1190 A.D.), the Hoyśalas of Halebid in Mysore (1190–1327 A.D.), and the Yadavas of Deogiri (modern Daulatabad, 1190–1318 A.D.). In the south the earliest empire was that of the Pandyas. During the first three centuries of the Christian era a large literature grew up in Tamil, the language of the Pandya country. The Pandyas were succeeded by the Cholas, who also quickly absorbed the Cheras, another early dynasty.

The Pallava dynasty of Kanchi (Conjeeveram) played a large part in the history of south India, where it was the dominant power from the 5th to the 9th centuries, during the period between the two Chola empires. It has left many remarkable buildings. The Pallavas were succeeded by the great empire of the Cholas (907–1310 A.D.). Southern India was rich and prosperous because of foreign trade, especially with the Roman Empire. The influence of Brahmanism had already spread to the far south. By the 11th century all of southern India had become a part of the great Chola empire. All of these kingdoms in central India and the south were swept away by the great Moslem invasions of that region in the early 14th century, except for Vijayanagar (1336–1565 A.D.), the last great Hindu kingdom in India.

The Moslem Conquest, 8th to 14th Centuries.—After Mohammed's death in 632 A.D. the Arabs spread out of Arabia both westward and eastward. They conquered Mesopotamia and Persia in the 7th century and Sind in the beginning of the 8th century. Beginning about 1001 A.D., with Mahmud of Ghazni (971?–1030), there came a long series of Moslem plundering expeditions from Afghanistan into India, which gradually overcame Rajput resistance and occupied most of northern India.

In 1206 A.D., Delhi became the capital of a Moslem Indian empire which lasted until 1707 A.D. Gradually, Moslems occupied the greater part of central India (the Deccan) and much of southern India. In 1347, a rebellion established the Bahmanis at Gulbarga (1347–1526) as an independent Moslem power in central India. This empire eventually broke up into five parts, of which the most important were Bijapur, Golconda, and Ahmadnagar. These three were defeated and annexed by the great Moguls of Delhi, Shāh Jahān and Aurangzeb.

The result of the Moslem conquest was a great stagnation of Hindu literature, learning, and culture. Indian civilization had absorbed all the earlier invaders, but Hinduism has never been able to absorb Islam nor has Islam been able to suppress and absorb Hinduism. The two centuries of the Moslem conquest resulted in a great destruction of Indian art and architecture and of Hindu and Buddhist manuscripts, and in the virtual annihilation of the old Hindu nobility and ruling classes, except in the fastnesses of Rajputana. The five centuries of organized Moslem rule (1206–1707 A.D.) left little that was constructive except a remarkable Moslem art and architecture. The positive achievements of Islam in India must be left to Moslem historians. From the Hindu point of view the occupation was disastrous.

Moslem Rule, 1206–1707 A.D.—William H. Moreland, in *From Akbar to Aurangzeb* (p. 245, see *Bibliography*), describes the first half of the 17th century as a period in which the masses of the people were forced by the administrative system to live on the borderline of starvation or rebellion. Stanley Lane-Poole (*Mediaeval India*, pp. 422-23, see *Bibliography*) remarked that the most important effect of Moslem rule was the formation of a new vernacular, Urdu (see section on *Languages*), a new architecture and art, a few provinces still under Moslem rule, and a large Moslem minority which has formed a difficult element in the modern political situation of the subcontinent.

Between 1206 and 1526 there were 34 kings at Delhi. Eleven were deposed, assassinated, or killed in battle. It was a turbulent period of gradual consolidation of Moslem rule over northern India and its expansion into central India.

A more stable government began with the foundation by Baber (Babur, real name Zahir ud-Din Muhammad) in 1526 of the dynasty of the great Moguls, which lasted until 1707. Baber is one of the most romantic and attractive figures in Indian history and the author of delightful *Memoirs*. Descended from Tamerlane on his father's side and from Genghis Khan on his mother's side, he was king of Ferghana. Driven thence by his uncles he took possession of Kabul (1504) and started upon the conquest of India. He died in 1530. Humāyūn (r. 1530–1542; 1555–1556) succeeded his father but continually fought to retain his position in upper India and was finally defeated by Sher Shah (1542–1545), an Afghan chief. He became a homeless wanderer, and it was during this time that his son Akbar was born. Humāyūn found refuge in Persia, and in 1555 he was able to regain India.

The reigns of Akbar (1556–1605), Jahāngīr (1605–1627), Shāh Jahān (1628–1658), and Aurangzeb (Aurangzīb, 1658–1707) mark the high point of Moslem rule in India. The reign of Akbar, who was one of the greatest rulers of India, was marked by firmness and benevolence and by a policy of toleration and conciliation of Hindus. He organized a durable empire. He had an inquiring and receptive mind that tried to understand all creeds and doctrines; he went so far as to give up Islam and tried unsuccessfully to found a new eclectic religion. His administrative system is known in great detail through the encyclopedic work *Āīn-i Akbarī* (*Institutes of Akbar*), written by his close friend, confidential secretary, and adviser, Abu-l Fazl.

Jahāngīr and Shāh Jahān were much weaker men. The empire continued unimpaired under the impetus given by Akbar's organizing genius, and under the two rulers Moslem art and architecture reached its zenith in India. Jahāngīr was arbitrary and fitful, a patron of painting and architecture who considered that attention to administrative details was derogatory to royal dignity, and therein he was quite different from Akbar, who said that every minute spent in the comprehending of small things is a minute spent in the service of God. It was in the reign of Jahāngīr that the British first established themselves in India and sent their first embassy to the Mogul court. It has been said of Shāh Jahān that he was a strange compound of tenderness and cruelty, of justice and caprice, of refinement and brutality, of good sense and childishness. His health was finally undermined by drink and opium. The best-known building in India, the marvelous Taj Mahal, was erected by Shāh Jahān as the mausoleum of his favorite wife, Mumtāz Maḥall. Under Jahāngīr and Shāh Jahān there was a great increase of taxation to support extravagant nobles and luxurious courts and to pay for magnificent buildings. This was a crushing burden on agriculture and industry.

Aurangzeb was a stern puritan and religious bigot who persecuted Hindus and everywhere substituted Moslems for Hindus. He ate no animal food and drank only water. He allowed himself no self-indulgence in pleasures, fasted much, and tried to suppress singing and dancing. He knew the Koran by heart and spent much time in copying manuscripts. He was a man of the utmost physical and mental courage with a stern sense of justice, but he was respected rather than loved. Most of the latter half of his reign was spent in the Deccan waging long, fruitless wars against Bijapur, Golconda, and the Marathas, in an attempt to defeat the Shi'ites and set up an orthodox Mohammedanism in the south. His successors were feeble rulers, had short reigns, and spent much of their time in fratricidal wars. The great empire soon broke up into independent kingdoms.

Bibliography.—Lane-Poole, Stanley, *Mediaeval India* (New York 1903); Rhys Davids, T. W., *Buddhist India* (New York and London 1903); Watters, Thomas, *On Yuan Chwang's Travels in India* (London 1905); Shamasastry, Rudrapatha, *Kauṭilya's Arthaśāstra* (Bangalore 1915); Rawlinson, H. G., *Intercourse Between India and the Western World* (Cambridge, England, 1916); Smith, V. A., *Akbar, the Great Mogul* (London 1919); id., *The Oxford History of India* (Oxford 1919); Moreland, W. H., *India at the Death of Akbar* (London 1920); Smith, V. A., *Asoka,* 3d ed. (Oxford 1920); Leyden, John, and Erskine, William, tr., *The Memoirs of Babur,* ed. by Sir Lucas King (Oxford 1921); Giles, H. A., tr., *The Travels of Fa-hsien* (Cambridge, England, 1923); Moreland, W. H., *From Akbar to Aurangzeb* (London 1923); Smith, V. A., *Early History of India,* 4th ed. (Oxford 1924); Mukerji, Radhakumud, *Harsha* (Oxford 1926); Edwardes, S. M., and Garrett, H. L. O., *Mughal Rule in India* (Oxford 1930); Smith, V. A., *A History of Fine Art in India and Ceylon,* rev. by K. deB. Codrington, 2d ed. (Oxford 1930); Dodwell, H. H., ed., *The Cambridge Shorter History of India* (Cambridge, England, 1934); *The Cambridge History of India* (Cambridge, England): vol. 1 (1922), vol. 3 (1928), vol. 4 (1937); Rawlinson, H. G., *India: A Short Cultural History* (London and New York 1938).

WALTER E. CLARK,
Professor of Sanskrit, Harvard University.

13. HISTORY: 1707–1947. The 240 years between the death of the last great Mogul (Mughal) emperor, Aurangzeb (Aurangzīb, r. 1658–1707), and the inauguration of independent governments in India and Pakistan saw the European intrusion into the Indian subcontinent culminate in complete foreign conquest and then give way to a reassertion of power by Indian leaders determined to shape their countrymen's own destiny. These years may be conveniently divided into three periods. In the first, 1707–1815, European commercial penetration was supplemented by a military struggle between the British and French (assisted by their Indian allies) which left Britain unchallenged as mistress of India; in the second, 1815–1885, Britain built her Indian Empire; in the third, 1885–1947, a nationalist movement developed to whose leaders British power was finally surrendered, but not until many changes had been made in the Victorian bureaucratic regime and all efforts to preserve Indian political unity had failed.

British Conquest (1707–1815).—The progressive disintegration of Mogul central authority which characterized the early decades of the 18th century gave rise to struggles between Indian princes to which the European powers, already firmly entrenched in trading posts called factories, could not be indifferent. Doubtless, increased European commercial activity tending to turn the more important factories into fortified enclaves outside Indian control played its part in weakening the Mogul Empire. Nevertheless, the directors of East India trading enterprises in Europe did not embark willingly and deliberately upon the course of embroilment in Indian disputes from which the building of a British empire in India was to follow. Their chief concern was trade, at this period the purchase of India goods—that is, chiefly cotton and silk hand-woven cloth, raw silk, pepper, saltpeter, and sundry drugs—with the proceeds of cargoes of silver, base metals, and woolens exported from Europe. It was not without significance that the European powers which held almost entirely aloof from Indian disputes were the smaller trading nations—Portugal, the Netherlands, and Denmark. Britain and France were unable to do so primarily because of their involvement in wars with each other over European and American issues. The conditions under which Europeans lived and traded in 18th century India also helped to make it impossible for the subjects of the two foremost European powers to forget national rivalries in the pursuit of individual gain.

However much the directors of the British and French East India companies might wish to neutralize their shipping and their Indian factories from the consequences of war in Europe or in North America, they were defeated by the impossibility of confining the arena of Anglo-French naval conflict to the Atlantic and by the extensive opportunities open to their servants in India for the acquisition not only of wealth but of power. In the early 1740's the materials for empire building were already at hand. Internecine strife was clearly apparent in southeast India and latent elsewhere. Each contestant for Mogul administrative office or local lordship was eager to acquire European military skill and weapons in exchange for cash, credit, or grants of land. A few Europeans were aware of the possibilities of fashioning armies of European-officered Indian mercenary sepoys and Eurasian artillerymen. More Europeans were anxious to supplement profits from country trading within the Indian seas with profits from military and political activity. The arrival in India of the news that France and Britain, since 1741 *de facto* combatants in the War of the Austrian Succession on behalf of their respective allies, had at last officially declared war upon each other (March 1744), was but a spark to this tinder. Thenceforth, European initiative, enterprise, and greed, armed with powerful European weapons and assisted by Indian disunity and treachery, completed the destruction of the Mogul Empire and laid the foundations of British ascendancy.

The first theater of Anglo-French conflict in India lay in the southeast. Here, in a bewildering series of intrigues, the men on the spot supported their respective candidates for the subahship of the Deccan and the nawabship of the Carnatic. In the first phase the honors were distinctly with the French, not only because of Admiral Bertrand Mahé, comte de La Bourdonnais' capture of Madras (1746), which the diplomats restored to Britain in 1748 at the Treaty of Aix-la-Chapelle, but because of the skill of Marquis Joseph François Dupleix (governor general, 1742–1754) in buttressing his Indian allies' position and initiating in the Deccan the system of a French-officered subsidiary force paid with the revenues of lands especially assigned for the purpose. However, with young Robert Clive's renowned exploit in storming and holding Arcot (Aug. 31–Nov. 15, 1751) to relieve the pressure on the British-sponsored candidate for the nawabship in Trichinopoly, the tide began to turn against the French. Dupleix' dismissal (1754) by a government stung by serious military reverses, and under pressure from directors who had never approved Dupleix' policy, may be said to presage French failure in India. Nevertheless, to contemporaries the French in India appeared for many years afterwards to have the advantage of the British in military skill and in the arts of Indian diplomacy.

Far more significant for the future were the events which took place in Bengal upon the death of its nawab, Ali Vardi Khan, in April 1756. His young and dissolute successor, Siraj-(Suraj-) ud-Daula, perhaps prompted by a desire to prevent the Europeans from behaving in Bengal as they had in the south, rashly drove the British out of Calcutta and thus brought down upon himself the full force of a retaliatory expedition from Madras led by Clive. Bengal then lay exposed both to the exercise of European military skill marshaled by a "heaven-born general" and to the practice of the arts of fomenting treachery by an experienced coterie of Europeans and Indians. The recapture of Calcutta (1757), supplemented by a few months of intrigue, sufficed to undermine Siraj-ud-Daula's authority. Plassey, fought on June 23, 1757, was not so much a battle as the essential military climax of a carefully prepared coup d'état which ensured that future nawabs of Bengal would be mere puppets of the British. Despite its bizarre qualities as an engagement in which 2,000 sepoys and 1,000 Europeans defeated a vast Indian army honeycombed with treachery, Plassey may quite appropriately be regarded as the symbol and portent of European domination of India. The ease with which it laid open to conquest and spoliation one of the great Mogul viceroyalties invested it with glamour during the period of British rule. It came to epitomize the curiously complex web of European and Indian interests from which a new order in India was fashioned in the ensuing half century. In 1763, by the Treaty of Paris, French interests in India were reduced to Pondichéry (Pondicherry), Chandernagor, and a few other small posts.

By 1770 the outlines of the system on which British power was to rest in India began to be clearly discerned. In taking control, with the nominal consent of the almost powerless Mogul emperor at Delhi, of the revenue of Bengal, through the emperor's so-called grant of the dewanee (Hindustani *dīwānī*) in 1765, the British East India Company stood forth as a country power in its own right. Its advantages over other country powers in any contest for supremacy were three: its corporate immortality, its control of naval power, and its possession in Bombay and Madras of subsidiary bases of operations. Its disadvantages lay in its alien character and in the reluctance of its directors to sanction a policy of conquest and expansion.

For an understanding of the manner in which some hundreds of its servants were able in a few decades to secure it recognition as the most powerful of Indian princes, it is necessary to bear in mind the almost constant interaction of European and Indian events. In the London of the 1770's, the return of many a nabob with a fortune, and the prospect of avoiding the export of silver by purchasing homeward cargoes with the surplus revenue of Bengal, convinced both the government and the company that the Indian possessions were of immense and increasing benefit to the British nation. Henceforth, the company's affairs were subjected to ever-closer scrutiny and regulation by Parliament. No one doubted the chaotic and precarious state of the company's finances, but it was felt that, once the company's servants had been prevented from cheating their employer, Indian wealth would flow to Britain in an ever-broadening stream. In India, the newly arrived writers, factors, and military cadets were learning of the multifarious ways in which they could become wealthy as a consequence of the company's expanding political activities. Military campaigns, whether connected with the Anglo-French wars in Europe or not, gave opportunity for collusive supply contracts of many kinds. Assumption of governmental functions of any sort usually meant that a company's servant was in a position to bestow favors—for example, exemption from customs duties—for which the Indian mercantile community was willing to pay. Profits from such transactions could be reinvested directly or indirectly in ventures of various kinds, not the least of which were ever-expanding British country trading voyages in the Far Eastern seas.

It is against this background that the wars and annexations of the years 1765–1815 should be viewed. An era of frank spoliation under Clive gave way to a period of more subtle penetration under Warren Hastings (1772–1785). Of Hastings it may be said that his difficulties arose primarily from too great familiarity with Indian institutions and ways of life. To him, the company was an Indian power strengthening its influence vis-à-vis other Indian powers. By his opponents, India was seldom thought of apart from its place in British politics. Hastings infused with vigor an administrative machine still largely dependent on Indian personnel. He developed a subsidiary alliance system. Although he did not crush the power of the Moslem sultans of Mysore, Haidar (Hyder) Ali and Tipu (Tippoo) Sahib, in the First and Second Mysore Wars, he made the company's sword respected from Delhi to Cape Comorin. Fortunately for Hastings, the American War of Independence ended before France could follow up the naval victories which Admiral Pierre André de Suffren had won for her in the Indian seas. By the time Hastings left India, the bases of British economic and political dominance were firmly laid and all was ready for the march of British power.

A dramatic personal vendetta between Warren Hastings and Philip Francis had during the 1770's brought India more and more into the public eye in Britain. As a consequence of renewed financial embarrassments growing largely out of the American War of Independence, the affairs of the East India Company were drawn into the vortex of British politics in the early 1780's. The prospects of drastic reforms envisaged by Charles James Fox and his friends alarmed the most powerful among the India interests. After the direct intervention of King George III had caused the defeat of Fox's India bill in the House of Lords, the India interests helped greatly to consolidate William Pitt the Younger in power in 1784. Pitt's India act, which set the pattern of Indian government from 1784 to 1858, subjected the company's political activities to control by the state but left the company's patronage and commercial activities comparatively undisturbed. After the removal in 1786 of a clause requiring an investigation into the private fortunes of company servants upon their return to England, nearly every European intimately concerned with India was satisfied. British and foreign investors in the company were sure of their dividends. Europeans who had supplied the company in India with funds acquired in devious ways were certain that their bills of exchange on London would be paid. British and foreign agents concerned with remittances from India through non-British channels were sure that if the whole edifice of British power in India did not crumble, no law of the British Parliament could completely destroy their profits. Fixed salaries, supervision by governors no longer closely identified with the company's service, and other reforms were inevitable, but India could still offer attractive opportunities to enterprising Europeans.

To effect a policy of reform and meet the growing public criticism which was soon to culminate in Edmund Burke's orations against Hastings, the Pitt ministry chose as governor general the 1st Marquis Cornwallis, who was to redeem in India a reputation tarnished by the American disaster. Cornwallis, during the years 1786–1793, more than justified the government's choice. Personally incorruptible, he developed in Bengal an administrative policy which resulted in the efficient professional bureaucracy of the Victorian era. From his day dates the policy of Europeanizing all but the lesser ranks of the civil service which was to prevail throughout the next century. From his day, too, dates the beginning of the transformation of the company's Madras, Bombay, and Bengal armies into something more than mere mercenary forces without any tradition or *esprit de corps*. It was, however, 30 years before the pay and conditions of service in India were such that disaffection among the company's European military officers was not to be feared, and even longer before military efficiency ceased to be impaired by ill feeling between the company's army and the king's regiments stationed in India.

Lord Cornwallis' most lasting achievement, and the one which in the Indian mind has overshadowed all his efforts at reform, was the celebrated permanent revenue settlement in Bengal (1793). This arrangement, with which his name is always associated, though others both in India and Britain bore much of the responsibility for it, had the effect of making the Bengal zamindars not only landlords of the soil in the European sense, but landlords obligated to pay the government a fixed rent which could not be altered under the vastly changed circumstances of the next century.

Though a faithful adherent of the policy of no aggrandizement enjoined by both company and government, Cornwallis was drawn, largely through the complex machinations of European merchants and company servants, into a full-scale conflict with Tipu, sultan of Mysore (Third Mysore War, 1789–1792). In this contest, Cornwallis had the support of the two other strong country powers—the Marathas and the nizam of Hyderabad. Even after this war, which deprived Tipu of an immense treasure and half of his territory, there was some prospect that the company might be able to forego further territorial expansion. Many of the men most influential in directing policy sincerely wished the company to remain *primus inter pares*, holding the balance among the important country powers and acting, whenever necessary, in the name of a subservient and completely cowed Mogul emperor. The French Revolution, however, extinguished such hopes. Napoleon's Egyptian expedition of 1798 thrust India into the arena of world politics. In the person of the 1st Marquis Wellesley, governor general from 1798 to 1805, there came out to India a great proconsul who turned the company's ally, Nizam Ali, into a feudatory (1798); destroyed Tipu (Fourth Mysore War, 1799); took the first and most decisive steps in the conquest of the great Maratha chieftains; and paid no attention to the company's concern over its ever-mounting Indian rupee debt.

Meanwhile, British mercantile interests outside London, newly strengthened by the then imperfectly perceived consequences of the Industrial Revolution, were preparing for the final attack on the company's monopoly of the India trade. Although the true economic benefits to the British nation from the increasingly complex process of empire building in India at this period were in all probability of quite modest proportions, few contemporary Europeans doubted that they were enormous. Few of the merchants who so ably marshaled their influence in Parliament to open the trade with India to all British subjects in 1813 realized that the trade thus opened would soon differ profoundly from the India trade carried round the Cape of Good Hope since the days of Vasco da Gama. Nor did they realize that the new trade in which export of machine-made textiles and other consumers' goods was to be the dominant element would provide a far firmer base for empire than the old. Thus, as the company was ceasing to be a merchant in India and was concentrating its energies on the administration of its growing raj (Hindustani *rāj*), the machine had already begun the work of reducing India's old handicraft industries to a shadow of their former selves. India, for centuries a workshop for Europe, was about to fall completely under the domination of the new workshop of the world. Nowhere was the peace of 1815 more of a *Pax Britannica* than in the lands bordering the Indian Ocean.

British Raj, 1815–1885.—*Political and Military History.*—In considering the process by which the great bureaucratic Victorian Indian Empire was built, it is perhaps well to summarize the political and military history apart from other aspects of the story. After 1815 there was no turning back. As governor general succeeded governor general, the British color crept over the map—extinction of Maratha power under the 1st Marquis of Hastings (1813–1822) by 1820; conquest of Assam, Arakan, and Tenasserim (First Burmese War, 1824–1826), under Earl Amherst of Arakan (1823–1828); annexation of Coorg and strict control over many renowned and ancient Rajput houses under Lord William Cavendish Bentinck (1828–1835). With British power unchallenged from the Bay of Bengal to the eastern edge of the Indus Basin, it was only natural that the prospect of Russian expansion to the confines of India should begin to agitate more and more British minds.

In 1838 there were inaugurated profitless and unhappy policies which, in aiming to secure Afghanistan from Russian penetration, brought in their train defeats, military and diplomatic, which helped prepare the way for the Indian Mutiny of 1857. In brief, without sufficient attention to the slender potentialities of Russian policy or power in this region, without constant and unremitting adaptation to the ever-changing military situation among Pathan tribesmen and along the Perso-Afghan frontier, an attempt was made in the First Afghan War (1838–1842) to thrust British power beyond the Indus in support of Shah Shuja (r. 1803–1810; d. 1842), an unpopular Afghan chieftain. The war was, moreover, undertaken before the Sikh power in the Punjab was itself subdued (1845–1849), such was the measure of British confidence in the invincibility of the Anglo-Indian military machine under the administration of George Eden, earl of Auckland (1835–1841). There ensued the utter military defeat of 1842, when a faithful pony brought into Jalalabad the exhausted Dr. William Brydon as the sole survivor of an army of more than 4,000 troops and 12,000 camp followers which had sought safety by retreating through the passes from Kabul.

Although the conquest of Sind (1842–1844) and of the Punjab (1845–1849) were in a sense byproducts of Afghan disaster, neither these operations nor the marching of armies back and forth in southern Afghanistan could obliterate the consequences of the ill-starred First Afghan War. The spell of British invincibility was broken. Afghanistan was evacuated. The raj had lost face at a time when the Indian masses were becoming dimly conscious of the impact of such new forces as the nonofficial European merchant and plantation owner, the Christian missionary, the steamship, the telegraph, and the railway. Moreover, James Ramsay, 1st marquis of Dalhousie (1848–1856), a young and masterful administrator, pressed on in the 1850's with a policy of annexing the territories of Indian princes who were either without heirs or peculiarly impervious to admonitions of reform from the company's government. This policy culminated in 1856 in the annexation of Oudh, perhaps the worst governed of the premier states, but the one from whose domains most of the sepoys in the Bengal Army were recruited.

Upon Lord Dalhousie's successor, Earl Canning (1856–1862), the storm burst on May 10, 1857. Vexed as the problems of the origins of the Indian Mutiny (q.v.) are, there is no question but that the decisive factor was the widespread belief that the cartridges issued with the new Enfield rifles were greased with animal fats abhorrent to both Moslems (Muslims) and Hindus. Careful study of the first weeks of the mutiny shows no widespread conspiracy, concerted planning, or well-thought-out objectives. This does not mean, however, that various native princes and influential landlords did not join the movement for political motives or that it did not evoke vague stirrings of national consciousness among some of those chiefly concerned. Nevertheless, it was primarily a military revolt of one of the company's three armies. The Bombay and Madras armies were unaffected, as was most of the subcontinent outside the regions near Delhi in which the fighting took place.

The mutiny was suppressed with great severity in 1857–1859. The heroic, moving tales of the blowing up of the Delhi magazine, of the siege of Cawnpore (now Kanpur), and of the relief of Lucknow, on which Rudyard Kipling's generation was reared, form only the more colorful side of the story. The mutiny left a legacy of bitterness which persisted for at least a generation, but, even more important, wherever it may not have fostered hatred, it fostered the type of aloofness in the ruling race which the increasing number of Western-educated Indians most resented. In government the mutiny caused the dissolution of the East India Company and brought British efforts to modernize and reform the great Indian princely states to an abrupt and unnatural halt. The India Act of 1858 transferred all the East India Company's authority to the crown, and provided for the administration of India through a secretary of state for India in the British Cabinet.

With British dominance throughout the subcontinent assured after the suppression of the mutiny, the officials concerned with India's foreign policy became more preoccupied with the problem of the northwest frontier. Here the persuasiveness of the forward school and the belligerent imperialism of Benjamin Disraeli combined to produce a Second Afghan War (1878–1880) almost as inglorious as the first. The 1st Earl of Lytton (viceroy, 1876–1880), unable to readjust his Afghan policy quickly to Disraeli's diplomatic triumph over Russia at the Congress of Berlin, became involved in a war which did little to pacify the frontier, greatly increased the Indian debt, and left on the Afghan throne in Abd-er-Rahman (Abd-ur-Raman) Khan (r. 1880–1901), a chief who had every reason to prefer Russian to English influence.

Social and Economic Developments.—In Lord Lytton's day the men who staffed the great bureaucracy which had been built up during the two previous generations were of a somewhat different stamp from those who had served Lord Hastings. In 1815 the company's patronage system was still vigorous and a young man's hopes of an Indian career depended upon his connections. In the next 60 years there occurred a gradual extension of the Indian services beyond the coterie of families connected with East India interests in the 18th century. Among such families, varying social backgrounds had been represented—chiefly London merchant and shipping families, lesser country gentry, and younger sons of Scottish nonnoble houses—but by the early 19th century all were characterized by close association with India and Indians. Furloughs in those days were infrequent, keeping a European wife and children in India was a hazardous venture, and it was difficult to cut oneself off from Indian life. By 1880 all this was profoundly changed. The introduction of competitive examinations for the Indian services in 1853 tended to confine them to the best brains of the English university world, a world which can hardly be described as other than socially select. Improvements in communications and sanitation made it possible for nearly all British officials to keep British wives and children in India. Inevitably, the European station with its club grew up beside the military cantonment, its life divorced from the surrounding Indian world.

Improvement in communications led to the perfection of the bureaucracy. The most remote post office came into immediate contact with headquarters. A subordinate army of Indian clerks and messengers was available to copy and move the mountains of official papers which made the wheels of government revolve. At the top stood the viceroy, struggling desperately not to be buried under the ponderous files, and unquestionably the most hard-worked official in her majesty's dominions. Disraeli's action in 1877 in making Queen Victoria empress of India was criticized as out of keeping with British tradition, but it effectively symbolized the transformation which had taken place in Indian government since the days when the East India Company had a personality of its own.

In 1833 began the social and educational changes which were to lead to the first meeting of an Indian National Congress in 1885. This was the time when the effects of the Reform Bill of 1832 and the reform and free trade movements in Britain began to be felt in India. The company lost its monopoly of the China trade and became merely a vehicle for governing India, dominated largely by men who had served in India. The home government, however, was controlled by Whig politicians immersed in the Reform Bill struggle who had little experience of India. It was hardly extraordinary that they should stand for an ever-wider extension of Christian missionary enterprise and the introduction of an educational policy favoring the teaching of English and the dissemination of European rather than Oriental learning. Missionary policy had long been settled on the understanding that the government would continue its policy of neutrality with respect to all religions. Active controversy in the early 1830's concerned educational policy. The older generation of company servants, who knew something of the values of Indian learning both ancient and modern, were no match for the brilliant Thomas Babington Macaulay, future historian of the English Revolution of 1688. Macaulay, who came out to make his fortune as the new law member of the governor general's council in 1834, wrote in February 1835 the famous minute which was decisive in determining the English character of higher education in India.

With respect to elementary education, decisive action was not taken until 1854, when the dispatch of Sir Charles Wood (later 1st Viscount Halifax) declared that both English and vernacular languages should be used in diffusing European knowledge. The officials who drafted this dispatch, realizing the impossibility of securing enough persons qualified to teach English in the elementary schools, were inaugurating a policy of extensive government support to vernacular education for the masses. There had thus evolved by the postmutiny period the educational policy which was to become typical of modern India: stress on European learning, instruction in the vernacular at the elementary level, higher education on a British model, government grants-in-aid to all properly managed schools willing to accept government inspection, and equal treatment of each school accepting the conditions, irrespective of communal or other affiliations.

By 1885 civil and military government servants, businessmen, missionaries, and schoolmasters had built in India an empire very different from that over which the East India Company had presided. In 1815 the company's domain was still a country power, pre-eminent among country powers, and ruled by men whose outlook was often as much Indian as British. Most of these men believed in a policy of noninterference with Indian life and society and in limiting India's contacts with Europe to those arising from the commercial and administrative activities which ensured their own well-being. In 1885 India had become the greatest modern colony, a vast domain ruled by a *corps d'élite* sent out for that purpose by an alien European power.

Indian National Development, 1885–1947.— Although one or more Indian nationalist bodies met annually from 1885, the general history of India and the histories of Indian nationalist movements were not closely intertwined until after World War I. The Victorian bureaucratic machine moved ponderously on, hardly paying any heed to nationalist agitation except when moved to action by some overt act. Liberal-minded viceroys like George Frederick Robinson, 1st marquis of Ripon (1880–1884), were the exception, not the rule. The raj occupied itself with the perfection of antifamine programs, with army unification (1893), and with irrigation schemes. British rule was assumed to be permanent. The storm raised by Lord Ripon's attempt to deprive Europeans of their privilege of being tried always before European judges (Ilbert Bill) enjoined a continued policy of caution as far as indianization of the civil services was concerned. Nevertheless, indianization was begun on a modest scale, and was accepted as an inevitable goal of future policy. Before 1906, however, there was no serious consideration of extending self-government beyond very modest dimensions.

In the 1st Marquis Curzon of Kedleston (1899–1905), India received a proconsul of Wellesleyan stature exactly a century after Wellesley. Though not a century behind the times, Curzon was peculiarly blind to Indian sensibilities. His partition of Bengal into two provinces, made in the interests of bureaucratic efficiency, exasperated the rapidly increasing number of politically conscious Indians both within and outside Bengal. This action was perhaps the most important single factor which ushered in the period when peaceful nationalist agitation was occasionally embarrassed by the commission of political crimes of various sorts. It was greatly to the credit of the philosophic Liberal, Viscount Morley of Blackburn, who became secretary of state for India in 1905, that he did not allow himself to be diverted by sporadic acts of violence from his plans for drastic Indian political reform.

Lord Curzon's departure, hastened by his dispute with the 1st Earl Kitchener of Khartoum over the latter's proper functions as commander in chief in India (1902–1909), prepared the way for the first major step toward Indian self-government. The Morley-Minto reforms (Indian Councils Act) of 1909 introduced the elective principle for some seats in the governor general's Legislative Council and greatly increased the elective element in the provincial legislative councils. All this, however, was done on a basis of representing various communities, chambers of commerce, and other similar groups. In accordance with this principle, Moslems, who had sent a special deputation, led by the Aga Khan, to the viceroy, Gilbert Elliot-Murray-Kynynmound, 4th earl Minto (1905–1910), in 1906, received separate representation. This granting of separate electorates to minorities, though later vehemently criticized by Indian nationalists, was quite in keeping with the most advanced and liberal

British thought of the day with respect to broadening the base of Indian government. Nearly every Briton who studied the subject intimately at that time held that the British parliamentary system was entirely unsuited to Indian conditions. Not only was anything like universal suffrage for India regarded as unthinkable, but everyone assumed that the problem was to give the intellectuals and the propertied and influential segments of Indian communities a feeling that they had a share in the government of their country.

Consequently, by 1910 the autocratic nature of Indian government was hardly changed at all. The Morley-Minto reforms, however, did have the effect of causing many of the intellectual moderates prominent in nationalist bodies to feel that they had not labored in vain. Psychologically, the appointment of one distinguished Indian to the governor general's Executive Council, coupled with the association of many others in the high administrative and legislative spheres, marked a sharp break with the Victorian past. For this the Indian National Congress was largely responsible. It had met annually since 1885, when Allan Octavian Hume, a retired civil servant, and a few of his friends assembled about 100 people in Bombay with the benevolent acquiescence of the government. Year by year the organization had grown. Europeans, Parsis, and Moslems were prominent in it from its earliest years, but inevitably the majority of its members were Hindus, among whom lawyers from Calcutta and Bombay predominated. Its continued existence and the success it achieved in bringing pressure to bear upon the government caused Moslem religious leaders and landlords to realize how far the Moslem community had lagged behind the Hindu in producing an English-educated minority eligible for high government posts. The Moslem League was therefore formed in 1906.

The success of the great imperial durbar (*darbār*) of 1911, when the capital was moved to Delhi and the partition of Bengal was reversed, on the occasion of the coronation of King George V, was in itself a testimony to the strength of the British raj. All that nascent nationalism had accomplished was to associate with durbar government a handful of distinguished Indians, most of whom were out of sympathy with the National Congress. In Gopal Krishna Gokhale and Bal Gangadhar Tilak, Indian nationalism had produced its first great figures, the one a moderate, the other an extremist who was thought of as the inspiration of the increasing number of political assassinations. In 1913, however, the raj seemed more stable than ever and would doubtless have been capable of resisting change for many years had it not been for World War I.

World War I profoundly disturbed the placid currents of Indian political and administrative life. Not only did Indian troops fight in France and the Middle East, but the best of the British civil and military administrators were drawn away from India. Nationalists had a practical demonstration of the ability of Indian government to function without the accustomed quota of British personnel. When it appeared toward the end of the war that British officialdom was intent on returning to the old order of things, great resentment and frustration spread over India. Racial bitterness reached a climax with the Amritsar massacre of 1919, when Gen. Reginald Dyer ordered troops to fire on an unarmed mass meeting in an enclosure with only one very narrow exit. Nearly all politically conscious Indians felt that India's great efforts in the war had been betrayed, and that the Montagu-Chelmsford reforms (named for Edwin Montagu, secretary of state for India, and Frederic Thesiger, 1st viscount Chelmsford, viceroy 1916–1921), then being framed into the Government of India Act (1919), were very inadequate as an implementation of the solemn British wartime promise (Aug. 20, 1917) of ". . . the gradual development of self-governing institutions with a view to the progressive realization of responsible government in India as an integral part of the British Empire. . . ."

Nevertheless, the Montagu-Chelmsford reforms of 1919 definitely broke with the idea that India must follow some other path than that leading toward parliamentary self-government. The reasons for this change are complex, but it was a natural consequence of the attainment of a separate international position by the British self-governing Dominions during the war and at the peace conference. India, despite her juridically dependent status, could hardly be denied many of the privileges accorded to the Dominions, notably the privilege of signing the peace treaty separately and of becoming in her own right a separate member of the League of Nations. She was also accorded much more independence in fiscal policy than had been customary before the war. Moreover, the phrase "responsible government" used in the declaration of 1917 was, in view of its history in the Dominions, generally interpreted as meaning responsible cabinet government of the British parliamentary type.

The Montagu-Chelmsford reforms set the pattern which was to determine the actual administration of India from 1919 until the eve of independence. The central government at New Delhi underwent almost no change between 1919 and 1946; the system by which the British crown's paramountcy over Indian princely states was exercised changed slightly in form but not in substance. In the provinces, there was change: full autonomy on April 1, 1937 (when the Government of India Act of 1935 went into effect) replaced the partial autonomy granted in 1919, but World War II supervened so quickly that full provincial autonomy was to a large extent stillborn. In brief, what the Montagu-Chelmsford reforms did at the center was to set up a bicameral legislature—the upper house (Council of State) chosen by an electorate of approximately 80,000 and the lower (Legislative Assembly) by an electorate of approximately 1,000,000 (registration, about 5,000,000). Nominated members were still an important element in both houses; in choosing elected members communal electorates were used extensively. Legally, the executive remained authoritarian and bureaucratic, not responsible to the legislature and buttressed by extensive emergency powers. Practically, the central legislature was a fairly effective forum for the ventilation of grievances, accomplished much useful work, and, paradoxically, despite its powerlessness attracted some of the ablest Indian politicians, especially at times when nationalists were not boycotting the government and refusing to take their seats. In the provinces, the reforms introduced dyarchy—that is, the turning over of certain departments, such as those dealing with education and other "safe" subjects, to Indian ministers responsible to majorities in the lower houses of the provincial legislatures. Naturally, the system did not work well. The India Act of 1935 granted full provincial autonomy and expanded the provincial electorates to cover approximately 33,000,000 voters, but provincial governors retained ample emergency powers, including that of assuming full powers of administration in the event of political deadlock.

Within a decade after the end of World War I serious Hindu-Moslem differences in the nationalist movement began to appear. Among the causes for the disappearance of the earlier atmosphere of harmony, dating back to 1916 when the Congress had reluctantly acquiesced in the existence of Moslem electorates, must be listed the new revolutionary fervor imparted to the Congress movement by Mohandas K. Gandhi; the fiasco of the caliphate agitation (protest by Indian Moslems against the Treaty of Sèvres) of 1920–1922; Mohammed Ali Jinnah's emergence to leadership among the Moslems in contrast to Gandhi, as leader in the Congress; and increasing fear among Moslems of Hindu domination of any centralized parliamentary government. In his philosophical nonviolence, Gandhi developed a technique difficult for Moslems to understand and he further baffled Moslem nationalists by calling off a civil disobedience movement, because of outbreaks of violence (at Chauri Chaura), in 1922 when it seemed to be succeeding. At the time of the caliphate agitation, Mustafa Kemal (later Kemal Atatürk), by setting up a nonreligious Turkish state, and the moplas (moplahs, Moslem peasants of Malabar), by killing Hindus in southern India, greatly embarrassed the Moslems and Hindus who were attempting to mitigate the terms of the Treaty of Sèvres. As Gandhi developed the peculiar religious quality of his hold over the Indian masses, it was natural that Moslems, especially those of the more conservative and less revolutionary types, should turn to Jinnah or to other Moslem leaders.

The immediate occasion, however, of serious Hindu-Moslem rift was the Nehru report of the Indian National Congress of 1928, resulting from the challenge of British conservatives that Indians had many criticisms of the existing government but were never willing to draw a blueprint for a new one. Under the chairmanship of Pandit Motilal Nehru, a distinguished committee drew up a constitution for India on a dominion-status basis. Since it was not a federal constitution and made no concessions to Moslem susceptibilities, Moslem opinion was alienated. An all-India Moslem conference gathered at Delhi under the aegis of the Aga Khan. Representatives of the Moslem League, now solidly behind Jinnah, and of nearly all other Moslem organizations, proclaimed in 1929 the Moslem 14 points, which insisted on separate Moslem electorates, a federal government with residual powers in the provinces, a three-fourths majority rule in legislatures on all communal questions, and appropriate Moslem representation in both provincial and federal cabinets.

During the decade 1929–1939, the Moslem-Hindu rift steadily widened. Each of the great parties—the Congress and the Moslem League—perfected its organization under its own high command and gradually reduced to insignificance the smaller nationalist organizations, whether moderate, such as the liberals led by distinguished Indians who tried to find a compromise in a nonrevolutionary program, or extremists, such as the Hindu Mahasabha, which desired a Hindu raj. Henceforth the communal question was in the forefront of all Indo-British political discussion.

British officialdom, realizing the futility of a further approach through an all-British parliamentary commission, assembled the leading Indian princes and political leaders in London in 1930–1932 for three round-table conferences after publication of the report of the Simon Commission (named for Sir John Simon, later Viscount Simon). Gandhi, who had in the spring of 1930 dramatized the Congress struggle by a no-rent campaign and by a march to the sea against the government salt monopoly, was persuaded to make an appearance at the second conference. Nothing, however, could break the communal deadlock. Prime Minister Ramsay MacDonald found himself compelled, much against his will, to authorize a British communal award, allocating seats to the different Indian communities in the legislatures of the proposed new federal Indian constitution.

Six years of discussion (1929–1935) at last produced in the India Act of 1935 a new Indian constitution. Nothing, however, could get the federation, so laboriously worked out on paper, into being. The princes, at first willing to accede to the federation, shied off in such numbers that the federal part of the act remained a dead letter. The Congress Party, which had always inveighed against the scheme as being too heavily weighted in the princes' favor, was not loath to see it die. The Moslem League, with its fears of a Hindu raj, was also not displeased with the result. Thenceforth, the political struggle shifted to the provinces, where, under the act, full autonomy was to be tested for the first time. Following much searching of heart, the Congress Party decided upon a policy of accepting office in the provinces after receiving assurance that the governors' special powers would not be frequently or unreasonably used.

Soon after the act of 1935 went into effect (April 1, 1937), Congress ministries took office in 7 of the 11 provinces of British India, all of them Hindu-majority provinces except the North-West Frontier Province, where Khan Abdul Gaffar Khan, the Frontier Gandhi, and other Congress Moslems had built up a strong following. (Later a Congress ministry also took office in Assam.) During the ensuing two prewar years, the Moslem League accused the Congress of establishing Hindu tyrannies in the six Hindu-majority provinces (Madras, Bombay, United Provinces, Bihar, Orissa, Central Provinces) which denied Moslems their legitimate rights, especially in educational and cultural matters, and precluded the possibility of their ever wielding any political influence in these provinces. On its side, the Congress Party insisted that it did endeavor to give Moslem interests their due weight and that the Moslem League distorted every Moslem grievance for propaganda purposes.

World War II thus found the two great Indian communities more deeply divided than ever. The Congress Party proclaimed itself a noncommunal organization striving to achieve India's freedom through nonviolent revolution. The Moslem League frankly professed its communalism and sought support as the protector of 94 million Indian Moslems (1941 census) against the prospect of Hindu domination. Such was the situation when the Congress Party leaders ordered all the Congress ministries out of office in October 1939 on the ground that they could not participate in an imperialist war thrust upon India without her consent. This course naturally had the effect of placing the Moslem League in a stronger position than the Congress during the war. When much of Indian political life was necessarily suspended, whether or not wartime emergency measures were in force, Jinnah and other Moslem leaders were out of jail and free to develop for propaganda purposes the plan for a separate Moslem state called Pakistan, first suggested in 1933 by some Moslem students at Cambridge University. In 1940 the League adopted its famous resolution that "the areas in which the Moslems are numerically in a majority, as in the northwestern and eastern zones of India, should be grouped to constitute independent states in which the constituent units shall be autonomous and sovereign."

In March 1942, at a very dark period of the war, Prime Minister Winston Churchill's coalition government sent Sir Stafford Cripps to India with an offer which has since been the occasion of much controversy. Its main purpose was to gain the cooperation of both the Congress and the League with the existing government by transferring to Indians on a *de facto* basis all power save that of the command of military operations and by emphasizing dominion status with consequent option of secession from the British Commonwealth as the immediate postwar British program. Negotiations broke down mainly as a consequence of the difficulties inherent in the plan for ensuring effective British control of military operations. In the postwar part of the offer, however, the prospect of partition was hinted at in the provisions whereby dissatisfied provinces could stay out of the proposed union and form a union of their own on a dominion-status basis. The Congress Party therefore publicly condemned the offer for too great indulgence toward the Pakistan idea, while the Moslem League condemned it for precisely the contrary reason.

In the Quit-India campaign which followed the rejection of the Cripps offer, Gandhi, Jawaharlal Nehru (who had long been recognized as the nationalist figure next in importance to Gandhi), and all the other Congress leaders were arrested along with several thousands of their followers in August 1942. Each side accused the other of precipitate action; the viceroy, Victor Alexander Hope, 2d marquis of Linlithgow (1936–1943), insisted that widespread violence was planned, while Gandhi insisted that his arrest precipitated the violence. While Indian troops and resources made their contribution to victory and bureaucratic government prevailed not only in New Delhi but in most of the provinces, all political progress was at a standstill. Despite Gandhi's release on medical grounds in May 1944, the deadlock continued until, with the assurance of victory in Europe, more and more of the Congress leaders were freed in the first half of 1945. Gandhi's conversations with Jinnah in September 1944 had frustrated the hopes of those who believed that the two men could agree on some formula that would reconcile their differences on the Pakistan issue.

While the 1st Earl Wavell, viceroy from 1943 to 1947, was releasing political prisoners, planning to broaden the Executive Council, and preparing for the new elections scheduled for the winter of 1945–1946, the whole scene was changed by the overwhelming victory of the Labour Party in Britain in July 1945. The election tended to remove the Indian nationalists' reluctance to believe that Britain was really determined on a full transfer of power untinged by imperialism. Within 10 months, a conference attended by all political leaders was held at Simla in an unsuccessful effort to set up an interim national government (June 1945); new elections were held (November-December 1945); and a British Cabinet mission came out to India to form a plan of breaking the Congress-League impasse (March 1946).

The Cabinet mission's scheme, announced in a white paper on May 16, 1946, endeavored to keep India united while permitting Moslem-majority provinces to group themselves together with a great deal of autonomy. It set up a feasible procedure for the election of a Constituent Assembly by the 1,585 newly chosen (January-April 1946) members of the provincial legislatures, with 93 seats to be awarded to nominees of the princely states. Moreover, it gave assurance for the first time of Britain's readiness to abandon paramountcy over all the princely states. Neither Congress nor the Moslem League felt it wise to refrain from ultimate acceptance of the plan, but before the summer was out both parties were engaged in a dispute as to various points of interpretation. In September, Lord Wavell brought matters to a head by allowing a newly appointed Executive Council to function as an interim government led by Jawaharlal Nehru. This speedily caused the Moslem League leaders to review their decision and brought about an agreement to enter the government despite nonrecognition of the League's contention that it was the only body representing Indian Moslems. For a fleeting moment foreign observers thought a Hindu-Moslem accord would be reached, but it soon appeared that the government seldom if ever functioned normally. Ministers of the opposing groups seldom met face to face and most Cabinet business was done by correspondence. Moreover, the Moslem League let it be known that League members elected to the Constituent Assembly would not take their seats.

This situation remained virtually unaltered in December 1946 after Lord Wavell had succeeded in inducing Nehru and Jinnah to fly to London for conferences on the clarification of the Cabinet mission's plan. When such clarification had accomplished nothing in making the interim government workable, the British government decided (February 1947) to replace Lord Wavell with the 1st Earl Mountbatten of Burma and to announce that Britain would withdraw from India by June 1948 in any event, transferring power preferably to one government, but not hesitating to transfer it to more than one government if such action proved unavoidable. This fateful announcement caused intense political activity behind the scenes at both London and New Delhi. On June 3, 1947, came the announcement of the plan for the partition of India into two independent dominions—India and Pakistan. The Indian princely states, no longer under British suzerainty, would be left free to accede to either dominion or not, as they chose. Both the Congress and the Moslem League accepted the plan.

An Indian Independence Act was passed through the British Parliament with very little debate in July, and on the appointed day, Aug. 15, 1947, the British Indian Empire ceased to exist. In its stead, after great communal disturbances in the Punjab and Bengal, which took a toll of many thousands of casualties and involved the migration of at least 6 million people, there appeared two new nations, the one, India, covering most of peninsular India, since nearly all the princely states fell within its orbit; the other, Pakistan, with its 70,000,000 population (1947), the most populous Moslem state in the world, composed of two disparate blocs of territory—in the northwest, Baluchistan, Sind, the North-West Frontier Province, and the western Punjab up to a line drawn just east of Lahore; in the northeast, the Moslem-majority districts in eastern Bengal and the Sylhet district of Assam. Despite the continued membership of both countries in the Commonwealth of Nations, all politically conscious Indians hailed the end of the era of European rule which had so imperceptibly begun two centuries before. See also GREAT BRITAIN—*History;* biographies of major figures.

Bibliography.—Muir, Ramsay, *The Making of British India, 1756–1858* (New York 1915); Dodwell, H. H., ed., *Cambridge Shorter History of India* (New York 1934); Thompson, E. J., and Garrett, G. T., *The Rise and Fulfilment of British Rule in India* (London 1934); Andrews, C. F., and Mukerji, Girija, *The Rise and Growth of the Congress in India* (London 1938); Rawlinson, H. G., *India: A Cultural History* (New York 1938); Brailsford, H. N., *Subject India* (New York 1943); Moon, Penderel, *Strangers in India* (New York 1945); Moreland, W. H., and Chatterjee, A. C., *A Short History of India,* 2d ed. (New York 1945); Coupland, Sir Reginald, *India: A Restatement* (New York 1946); Majumdar, R. C., Raychaudhuri, H. C., and Datta, Kalikinkar, *An Advanced History of India* (New York 1946); Nehru, Jawaharlal, *The Discovery of India* (New York 1946); Smith, W. C., *Modern Islam in India,* rev. ed. (London 1947).

HOLDEN FURBER,
Associate Professor of History, University of Pennsylvania.

NOTE: The foregoing 13 articles on the subcontinent of India, as well as that on the Union of India, were prepared under the joint direction of the editors of *The Encyclopedia Americana* and Dr. W. Norman Brown, professor of Sanskrit at the University of Pennsylvania.

INDIA, French. See EAST INDIA COMPANIES; FRANCE—*Overseas Territories;* INDIA, UNION OF.

INDIA, Portuguese. See EAST INDIA COMPANIES; INDIA, SUBCONTINENT OF—*History.*

INDIA, Union of, one of the two dominions into which the former British Indian Empire was divided on Aug. 15, 1947. Its status was changed to that of a republic on Jan. 26, 1950, when a constitution, drawn up by an indirectly elected Constituent Assembly and adopted on Nov. 26, 1949, was formally introduced. The seat of government is at Delhi, which has a population (1941 census) of 521,849. The total area of the territory claimed by the Union of India is 1,221,880 square miles (the status of some of this area is disputed by Pakistan), and the population, as estimated in 1951, is 347,340,000, giving a density of 280 to the square mile. The country has a railroad system of about 33,984 miles. The principal ports are Calcutta (1941 population, including Howrah, 2,488,183), Bombay (1,489,883), Madras (777,481), and Cochin (26,320). The largest inland cities, with their 1941 populations, are Hyderabad (739,159), Ahmadabad (Ahmedabad, 591,267), and Kanpur (Cawnpore, 487,324).

The Union of India includes the following political divisions: (1) 9 states which until Aug. 15, 1947, constituted, in whole or in part, provinces of British India, and with which have been merged a number of minor princely states: Assam, Bihar, Bombay, Madhya Pradesh (formerly Central Provinces and Berar), Madras, Orissa, Punjab (East Punjab), Uttar Pradesh, and (West) Bengal (including Cooch-Behar); (2) 8 states formed of former major princely states or of unions of states: Hyderabad, Jammu and Kashmir (status disputed by Pakistan), Madhya Bharat, Mysore, Patiala and East Punjab States Union, Rajasthan, Saurashtra, and Travancore-Cochin; (3) 10 states of lesser size and rights formed of former lesser princely states or unions, or chief commissioner's provinces of British India: Ajmer (formerly Ajmer-Merwara), Bhopal, Bilaspur, Coorg, Delhi, Himachal Pradesh, Kutch (Cutch), Manipur, Tripura, and Vindhya Pradesh; and (4) the Andaman and Nicobar Islands.

The unit of currency is the rupee, divided into 16 annas; as of June 1950 it was valued at 21 cents in U.S. money. The flag has three horizontal stripes of equal width, the top saffron, the middle white, and the bottom dark green. In the center of the white stripe is Aśoka's wheel. The coat of arms, derived from a pillar erected by Aśoka at Sarnath near Banaras (Benares) also shows the wheel

Coat of Arms of India.

GOVERNMENT

Interim Period (Aug. 15, 1947—Jan. 26, 1950).—The Indian Independence Act, passed by the British Parliament in July 1947, provided for the setting up in India of two independent dominions—India and Pakistan—effective from Aug. 15, 1947, and announced that the paramountcy hitherto exercised by the British crown over the Indian princely states lapsed as of that date. When boundaries had been fixed, the Dominion of India consisted of: (1) six governors' provinces with boundaries unchanged—Madras, Bombay, Central Provinces and Berar, Uttar Pradesh, Bihar, and Orissa; (2) three governors' provinces formed as a consequence of dividing predominantly Moslem from predominantly non-Moslem areas—(East) Punjab, (West) Bengal, and Assam (without the Moslem-majority district of Sylhet); (3) areas administered directly by the central government through chief commissioners—Delhi, Ajmer-Merwara, Coorg, Panth Piploda, and the Andaman and Nicobar Islands; and (4) such princely states as acceded to the Dominion. By 1949 the process of accession within the orbit of India as distinct from

Pakistan could be said to be complete, the only unsettled issue being the future of Kashmir.

In form, the government of the Dominion of India resembled that of the other dominions of the Commonwealth of Nations. The governor general (1st Earl Mountbatten of Burma, until June 1948; Chakravarti Rajagopalachari, from June 1948 to formal application of the new constitution on Jan. 26, 1950) was appointed by the king on the advice of the Indian Cabinet led by Pandit Jawaharlal Nehru, which was responsible to a majority of the Constituent Assembly acting as an interim central legislature. In practice, all Indian politicians and officials realized that the situation was exceptional. Lord Mountbatten, in the first months of transition from the old order to the new, could not possibly confine his role entirely to that of a ceremonial head of state, nor could the Constituent Assembly, admittedly an interim body, possess all the attributes of a normally elected parliament.

The machinery set up by the British Parliament in the India Act of 1935 lay ready to hand for the purpose of effecting the transition to independence with a minimum of disturbance of administrative and legal functions. The Indian Independence Act gave an Indian executive the power to adapt the 1935 act to the new situation by the simple process of order in council. Pandit Nehru and his colleagues were thus able to bring to life the federal portion of the 1935 act, which had lain in abeyance, and to use the procedure for princely accession provided in that act as a framework within which to develop their own policy for the integration of former princely India with former British India. Consequently, the federal, provincial, and concurrent lists in the act of 1935 were the basis for determining which legislative subjects fell to the Constituent Assembly as an interim central legislature, which remained to the provincial legislatures of the nine governors' provinces; and which were shared between them.

The whole structure of provincial government, in which full responsible cabinet government had been inaugurated on April 1, 1937, remained virtually unimpaired. The provincial legislatures, newly elected in the winter of 1945–1946, continued as before; in cases in which a former historic province was partitioned, as in the Punjab, the members for the districts within the new India became the legislature of the new province. In a few cases, British officials were permitted to remain as governors for many months; in others, Indians were immediately appointed. Provincial legislatures were the popular base on which the new Dominion of India might be said to rest during the interim period. It was the members of these legislatures who elected the majority of the Constituent Assembly in which all *de facto* power actually resided. In February 1949, the Constituent Assembly contained 235 members so elected, plus 68 chosen by the governments of princely states, making a total of 303. The effect of all these measures was to give the leaders of the Indian Congress Party an administrative machine able to cope with the vast problems of partition without being unduly preoccupied with questions as to the constitutionality of its procedure or the legal validity of its acts.

By assigning the task of constitution making to a distinguished drafting committee, the Constituent Assembly during 1947–1948 was able to devote its almost undivided attention to its work as an interim legislature. Meanwhile, the new Dominion's Ministry of States and Home Affairs, under Nehru's second-in-command Sardar Vallabhbhai Patel, attacked the main problem which could simplify the work of constitution framing. Three methods were used to substitute for the jumble of more than 500 princely states which acceded to India (of the total of 562 in the subcontinent), a small group of administrative units comparable to governors' provinces and capable of becoming along with them the states of a new republic of India. Most of the smaller nonviable princely states were merged with adjacent provinces. These lost their administrative identity and their rulers accepted pensions on varying terms. Many middle-sized and large states were grouped into administrative unions, each of sufficient stature to be a state of the future republic. In these cases, new regimes based on responsible cabinet government were introduced; the chief prince became a rajpramukh, or the executive head of the union, and had a fixed privy purse; the other princes of the union retained a position of dignity within their own states but were virtual pensioners. In some instances it was planned to rotate the office of rajpramukh among a group of princes. The relationship of these new princely unions to the new government of India was governed by instruments of accession which gave the central government as much power over them as it exercised over the governors' provinces. Finally, a group of former Punjab hill states were merged into a union and placed directly under the central government; that is, they were put on an equal footing with such centrally administered areas as Delhi or Coorg and were not thought of as areas capable of possessing any states' rights within the future republic.

By 1949, when these processes were completed, there were only a handful of former princely states retaining separate administrative identities. Of these, Hyderabad and Kashmir were special cases. Hyderabad, the largest Indian state, refused to accede to either dominion and was the scene of disturbances which led to Indian military occupation in September 1948. In Kashmir, when the truce agreement between India and Pakistan took effect on Jan. 1, 1949, the capital, Srinagar, and adjacent regions recognized the authority of the government acting in the name of the maharaja, who had acceded to India in 1947; the western and northwestern portions of the region were under the so-called "Azad (Free) Kashmir" government sponsored and militarily supported by Pakistan. In December 1948, Mysore, Travancore, Bhopal, and Cochin were the only other major states left unaffected by the integration program of the Ministry of States and Home Affairs. In April 1949, Cochin was merged with Travancore and Bhopal's administration was taken over by the central government. The constituent units of the new Indian republic became the nine former governors' provinces plus a half dozen princely unions and three individual princely states: Hyderabad, Mysore, and Kashmir.

It was also decided in April 1949 that the new Indian republic would remain associated with the British Commonwealth. The Constituent Assembly approved the following declaration issued as a consequence of the meeting in London of the Commonwealth prime ministers:

> . . . The Government of India have informed the other Governments of the Commonwealth of the intention of

the Indian people that under the new constitution which is about to be adopted India shall become a sovereign independent republic. The government of India have, however, declared and affirmed India's desire to continue her full membership of the Commonwealth of Nations and her acceptance of the King as the symbol of the free association of its independent member nations and as such the Head of the Commonwealth.

The Governments of the other countries of the Commonwealth, the basis of whose membership of the Commonwealth is not hereby changed, accept and recognize India's continuing membership in accordance with the terms of this declaration.

Accordingly, the United Kingdom, Canada, Australia, New Zealand, South Africa, India, Pakistan, and Ceylon hereby declare that they remain united as free and equal members of the Commonwealth of Nations, freely cooperating in the pursuit of peace, liberty, and progress.

This meant, in effect, that India would continue to take her full share in intra-Commonwealth consultations with respect to defense, finance, and other economic and political matters and that her citizens would not be foreigners in other Commonwealth countries. Her position would differ from that of the others only in the republican form of government and absence of formal allegiance to the king as the sovereign in whose name all governmental acts are performed.

The Constituent Assembly, which began debate on the draft of a republican constitution in November 1948, completed discussion and amendment of the draft a year later. The new republican constitution took effect on Jan. 26, 1950, but the Constituent Assembly remained as an interim legislature until elections could be held throughout India on a basis of adult suffrage.

Constitution of the Republic of India.—*Form of Government.*—India is a sovereign democratic republic and a union of states. The term state is broadly defined: it is applied to all centrally administered areas except the Andaman and Nicobar Islands as well as to former governors' provinces of British India, former Indian princely states, and new unions of such princely states. Centrally administered areas, though called states, possess no states' rights whatever. The structure of the government is federal, but its spirit is unitary. The states which do possess any degree of states' rights have very limited powers as compared with the states composing such other federal unions as the United States of America, Canada, and Australia. As in Canada, residual power rests expressly in the central government. For the sake of clarity, the term state is not here used to refer to any centrally administered area.

Central Government.—Executive: All executive action is taken in the name of a president who is a ceremonial head of state acting on the advice of ministers responsible to a majority in the lower house of the central legislature. The president is a citizen over 35 years of age elected for a five-year term; he may be re-elected. He is chosen by an electoral college formed of the elected members of both houses of the central legislature and of the elected members of the legislatures of the states. Each member of the college casts a large number of votes, the exact number being determined by an elaborate method of calculation based on census figures for the population of each state. The problem of succession in the event of the president's death or disability is handled by the provision for a special presidential election within six months thereafter. A vice president, elected at a joint sitting of both houses of the central legislature, presides over the upper house; he acts as president only during the short interval prior to the special election. The provisions concerning the Cabinet introduce no novelty into the normally accepted conventions of the British cabinet system except for the provision of a professional attorney general, a portfolio obviously intended for an eminent lawyer whose tenure need not be affected by the vicissitudes of parliamentary politics.

Legislature: The central legislature consists of 750 members, 500 in a lower house called the House of the People, and 250 in an upper house called the Council of States. The 500 members of the House of the People are chosen by universal adult suffrage in such a way that there is not less than one member for every 750,000 persons, or more than one for every 500,000. The lower house is subject to dissolution in accordance with usual British practice; it is considered dissolved at the expiration of five years unless a proclamation of emergency is then in force. A Cabinet minister may not hold his post more than six months without a seat in either house. He may speak, but not vote, in the house of which he is not a member. Of the 250 members of the upper house, 12 are eminent citizens appointed by the president because of their achievements in literature, art, science, and other fields. The other members are elected by the elected members of the lower houses of the state legislatures according to a scheme based on population which restricts the princely states to less than 40 per cent of the seats. The upper house is not subject to dissolution, but the terms of the members are so arranged that one third expire every two years. Provisions for a joint sitting of both houses obviate the possibility of legislative deadlock.

Judiciary: There is one national judiciary depending on appointment by the central government and protected by the usual safeguards which ensure the independence of judges in Great Britain. Salaries cannot be reduced. Removal cannot be effected except by an address voted by two thirds of both houses of the central legislature on the grounds of proved misbehavior or incapacity. The Supreme Court of seven justices is the guardian and interpreter of the constitution. There is no limitation on the power of the central legislature to increase the number of Supreme Court justices.

State Governments.—Executive: In states formerly governors' provinces of British India, the governor is appointed by the president (that is, by the national Cabinet). The governor's dependence on the central government is designed to be close and intimate. He is not merely a ceremonial head of state who acts always on the advice of a state cabinet responsible to a majority of the lower house of the state legislature. There was to be such a cabinet, but the governor has power to reserve bills for the president's consideration and is given authority to act in his discretion to a considerable extent.

In states formerly Indian states or unions of such princely states, the prince serving as rajpramukh is executive head of the government of the state. Because of his hereditary position and the financial guarantees given to him by the terms of the relevant instrument of accession, his constitutional position is not precisely the same as that of a governor of a state which was formerly a governor's province of British India. Responsible cabinet government, however, is established in these states and their position vis-à-vis the central government was to be in nearly all respects the same as that of the former governors' provinces.

Legislature: The state legislative structure may be bicameral or unicameral. All state legislatures, with the concurrence of a majority of the central legislature, may decide to change from a bicameral to a unicameral system or vice versa. The powers exclusively within the state legislative sphere are limited to such matters as education, public order, and police. State legislatures would, however, exercise in practice many of the powers listed on the concurrent list of powers shared with the central legislature, such as criminal and civil procedure, marriage and divorce, probate, trusts, and contracts. It was expected that state legislatures deriving from the former legislative councils in certain princely states would exercise in practice greater powers than other legislatures.

Judiciary: There is no state judiciary.

Bill of Rights.—The list of fundamental rights enforceable in the courts is comprehensive and follows a United States, rather than a British, model. Its most significant provisions may be summarized as follows. No titles may be conferred. "No person shall be deprived of his life or personal liberty except according to procedure established by law." There are specific provisions against double jeopardy, *ex post facto* laws, and bearing witness against oneself. The prohibition of untouchability is absolute. No citizen on grounds only of religion, race, caste, or sex may be denied access to stores, hotels, restaurants, and places of public entertainment or to any well, tank, road, or place of public resort supported wholly or in part by public funds. Freedom of worship and equality of treatment of all religions by the state is provided for, but the state may regulate any "economic, financial, political, or other secular activity" associated with religious practice and may effect social welfare or reform by such measures as the opening of Hindu religious institutions of a public character to any class or section of Hindus. Citizens may assemble peaceably and without arms. The right of freedom of speech is qualified by the government's right to make any law relating to matter which "offends against decency or morality or which undermines the security of or tends to overthrow the state." The central legislature may by law prescribe the circumstances under which, and the class or classes of cases in which, a person may be detained for a period longer than three months under any law providing for preventive detention.

Citizenship.—The central legislature possesses full powers with respect to all matters concerning citizenship. Pending exercise of such powers, the following are citizens:

(1) Persons of Indian domicile born in India (or either of whose parents were born in India) or with five years' residence in India.

(2) Refugees from Pakistan who have entered India before July 19, 1948 and who have remained there and who were born in (or any of whose parents or grandparents were born in) the former British Indian Empire.

(3) Refugees from Pakistan who have entered India after July 19, 1948 and have registered with the authorities after six months' residence in India.

(4) Persons who were born in (or any of whose parents or grandparents were born in) the former British Indian Empire, but who are ordinarily residing abroad may be registered as citizens of India on application to the appropriate consular or diplomatic representative of India, but no person who has voluntarily acquired citizenship of a foreign state shall be a citizen of India, and no person who migrated to Pakistan after March 1, 1947 and remained there shall be a citizen of India.

Amendment.—The following matters are protected against hasty constitutional amendment: (1) the allocation of legislative powers between the Union and the states; (2) the representation of the states in the central legislature; and (3) the powers of the Supreme Court and the high courts. An amendment touching these matters must be ratified by one half of the states, as well as by the central legislature (a majority of the total membership in each house and a majority of at least two thirds of members present and voting being necessary for ratification). Amendments touching other matters may be effected by the central legislature voting as described above.

Emergency Provisions.—Faced with war or domestic violence (actual or potential), the president may issue a proclamation of emergency which enters into force at once but must be laid before the central legislature within two months. The central legislature may by resolution of both houses extend the period of emergency beyond the period of two months. While such a proclamation is in force, the central government may exert any degree of control over state governments, and the guarantees to individuals in the bill of rights may be largely suspended. If, upon receiving a report from a state governor or rajpramukh, the president is satisfied that the peace and tranquility of a state is threatened, he may proclaim an emergency in such state, whereupon he may virtually take over the state, suspend the legislature, and legislate for the state through the central legislature. Such a regime, if ratified within two months by the central legislature, and every six months thereafter, may continue for as long as three years. This provision is analogous to Section 93 of the British India Act of 1935, which empowered the British governor of a province, confronted by political deadlock or abstention which made government under the other provisions of the act impossible, to take over the administration of the province.

Policy Toward Minorities.—On May 12, 1949, the Minorities Committee of the Constituent Assembly rejected provisions which accorded, for a 10-year period, reserved seats in the lower houses of the central and state legislatures to scheduled tribes, scheduled castes, Moslems, Anglo-Indians, and Indian Christians (in Madras and Bombay only). The constitution, however, retained for a 10-year period provisions for reserved seats in the lower houses of the legislatures for certain scheduled tribes and scheduled castes (depressed classes, untouchables). Moreover, the scheduled tribes of primitive peoples, numbering approximately 10,000,000, retain their special status with adequate guarantees against exploitation. Authority was given to the president and the governors and rajpramukhs to nominate to the lower houses of the central and state legislatures a few representatives of the Anglo-Indian (Eurasian) community. Not more than two such representatives may sit in the central legislature.

Provisions Concerning Language.—According to Article 343, "The official language of the

Union shall be Hindi in Devanagari script" but ". . . for a period of fifteen years from the commencement of this Constitution, the English language shall continue to be used for all the official purposes of the Union for which it was being used immediately before such commencement." The central legislature may by law provide for the use, after 15 years, of English for such purposes as it may think fit. The president may, during the 15-year period, authorize the use of Hindi in addition to English for such official purposes as he thinks fit. After five years, the whole position with respect to language would be reviewed by a commission which would make recommendations to the president. The power to make other languages than English official languages of a state (for state purposes only) rests with the state legislature, and the president, if satisfied that a substantial portion of a state's population wish any language spoken by them to be recognized as an official language within that state, may require the official recognition of such language by the state government.

Directive Principles of State Policy.—A list of these principles is a unique feature of the constitution. They are simply admonitions and are not enforceable in the courts. The Cabinet is expected to bear them in mind in shaping its policy. These principles reflect the social philosophy of the Congress Party as it has developed under Nehru's leadership. Most notable perhaps is the emphasis on an "economic system which does not result in the concentration of wealth and means of production to the common detriment"; on the desirability of equal pay for equal work for both men and women; an old age, unemployment, and disability benefits; and on the desirability of fostering village panchayats (local assemblies). Also noteworthy is the setting up of free and compulsory education for all children under 14 years of age as a goal which should be reached within 10 years after the constitution comes into force.

Foreign Policy and Defense.—On more than one occasion since Aug. 15, 1947, the government of India defined its foreign policy as one of "aloofness from power blocs." Pandit Jawaharlal Nehru and his colleagues did not wish India to be thought of as aligned with the signatories of the North Atlantic Treaty. Nevertheless they desired to make India a bulwark against communism. With the eclipse of China, India stood in 1950 as the foremost Asiatic country, the natural leader of other Asiatic countries in the task of liquidating imperialism and colonialism. The great break with the past consisted in the direction of India's foreign policy from Delhi and not from London. Instead of being an adjunct of British policy, Indian policy was to be based on exclusively Indian considerations.

Among India's objectives in 1950 were: (1) the integration into India of Portuguese and French India; (2) the setting up of independent nationalist regimes in Southeast Asia; (3) the stabilization of such regimes, as in Burma; and (4) the protection of Indian minorities living outside India. None of these objectives were being sought in 1950 by aggressive, unilateral, or belligerent methods. The method for furthering the annexation of the tiny remnants of the Portuguese and French Indian empires to India was that of fostering plebiscites in these foreign enclaves and persuading the governments concerned to relinquish control. Should difficulties ensue, it was expected that India would advocate that the problem be considered by the United Nations. On June 19, 1949, Chandernagor voted overwhelmingly for union with India. The freedom of nationalist regimes in Southeast Asia was sought in 1947 and 1948 through Asian conferences held at Delhi and through vigorous advocacy of the nationalist cause in the Security Council and General Assembly of the United Nations. In 1948 and 1949, India consulted with the other interested Commonwealth countries on the means of helping the government of Burma to pacify that country. Through continuing membership in the Commonwealth, India expected to be in a better position to bring the utmost pressure to bear on the Union of South Africa with respect to South Africa's policy toward the Indian minority in the Union. In the United Nations since its inception, India has vehemently opposed South Africa both on the Indian minority issue and on the problem of the future government of the mandated territory of South West Africa.

In 1949 it was not clear whether failure to settle the Kashmir issue promptly and peacefully would overshadow all other issues confronting India and Pakistan. The furtherance of all India's foreign policy objectives and all plans for defense based on continuing membership in the Commonwealth depended upon the maintenance of peace between India and Pakistan. Were India to be obliged to undertake military expenditures on a scale comparable to that of the first year of the fighting in Kashmir, 1947–1948, the whole attention of the government would necessarily have to be given to preserving peace and stability in the Indian subcontinent. General relations between the two dominions improved during 1950, and in April a pact was signed on the treatment of minorities in their respective territories. Meanwhile the question of Kashmir remained under consideration by the United Nations.

India's defense plans in 1950 were based on continuing membership in the Commonwealth and on the maintenance of peace with Pakistan. Attention was concentrated on making the portion of the British Indian Army and Air Force allotted to India an ever more efficient military instrument staffed by wholly Indian personnel. The government decided in 1949 to increase the size of its small navy, but recognized that the substitution of Indian for British officers in the Indian Navy would require a much longer period of transition. Continuing Commonwealth membership was expected to give all the advantages of interchange of information and equipment which had characterized the period before independence. For subjects not treated in this article, and for information prior to Aug. 15, 1947, see INDIA, SUBCONTINENT OF.

HOLDEN FURBER,
Associate Professor of History, University of Pennsylvania.

INDIA INK, a black pigment, consisting commonly of lampblack, gelatin, and water. The usual basis is a finely divided solid carbon, mixed with a size to hold it in suspension when the ink is prepared for use by mixing with water. Originally made in China and Japan for writing and drawing, India ink is used in the West chiefly for black-and-white drawings.

INDIA RUBBER TREE, the name generally given to *Hevea brasiliensis,* which is indigenous to the region of the Amazon River and in the tributary areas of Peru, Bolivia, Ecuador, Colombia, and Venezuela. It is a large tree, of slow growth and long life, requiring low-lying, rich soil and abundant moisture. In Brazil it is found scattered wild through the tropical forest, but in Southeast Asia it is grown on plantations. See also RUBBER.

INDIAN AFFAIRS. Early in the history of the North American colonies it became clear that unrestricted individual dealings with the Indians could result only in confusion and conflict. Individual colonies passed ordinances requiring that the acquisition of Indian land be made by purchase with the concurrence of the governor or of the colonial assembly. This policy was expressed for all the English colonies in a royal proclamation issued Oct. 7, 1763, which declared that "the several nations or tribes of Indians—who live under our protection, should not be molested or disturbed in the possession of such parts of our dominion and territories as, not having been ceded to, or purchased by us, are reserved to them." Trading with the Indians was also early declared a government monopoly. Thus, a pattern of government concern for Indians and government dealings with Indians gradually was woven.

In 1775 the Continental Congress created a committee to deal with the Indians and to assure them of the continued friendship of the new nation to be. The Articles of Confederation conferred on Congress "the sole and exclusive right and power of . . . regulating the trade and managing all affairs with the Indians," and in 1779 the United States Congress adopted a resolution reading in part: ". . . no land (shall) be sold or ceded by any of the said Indians, either as individuals or as a nation, unless to the United States of America, or by the consent of Congress."

On Aug. 7, 1789, responsibility for Indian relations was transferred from a congressional committee to the secretary of war; on March 11, 1824, a Bureau of Indian Affairs was created within the War Department; on June 30, 1834, Congress passed the act which set forth the duties of the Bureau of Indian Affairs and forms the charter for much that is still done by it; and on March 3, 1849, the bureau was transferred to the civilian administration of the newly established Department of the Interior.

Purchase of Indian Lands.—The early policy of government purchase of Indian lands has been adhered to consistently, and it may be fairly said that 2.5 million of the approximately 3 million square miles of the United States have been bought from the Indians. While textbooks place great stress on the Louisiana Purchase and other similar transactions with such countries as Great Britain, France, Spain, Russia, and Mexico, the fact is that all the United States acquired in each of these transactions was the power to govern and to tax. Almost all the ceded territory that was not privately owned by Spanish, French, or Russian settlers was still owned by the Indians, and the property rights of all the inhabitants were safeguarded by the terms of the treaty of cession.

How much the United States paid for this land is a matter of conjecture, for in its land transactions with the Indians many treaties called for payment in land, goods, and services and for tax exemption of their reserved properties. Conservatively, these payments might be valued at more than $1,000,000,000. Moreover, many of the trade goods delivered by the whites, such as knives, firearms, and domestic animals, in their impact on primitive society gave the recipients a valuable technological superiority over other Indian tribes and over their environment which cannot be expressed in terms of money.

Treaties and Legislation.—The conquest and enslavement of new areas by more powerful invaders is part of the historic pattern of human relationships. Indians drove other Indians out of coveted territory when strong enough to do so; on each of the continents the various races and peoples have been continuously in movement, displacing one another as one gained in strength and the other weakened. The discovery, conquest, and settlement of the Americas was simply another chapter in this mass movement of peoples. In North America it differed in one essential aspect from past colonial experiences—early in the relations of the colonies with the Indians, it was established that free purchase and sale was to be the basis of dealings between the natives and the encroaching whites. This decision, however, did not prevent continuing quarrels between Indians and whites on the advancing frontier, a frontier which pushed forward more rapidly than the government was able to extend its authority. Repeatedly government commissions were called in to mediate between whites and Indians, and, while usually finding the whites at fault, the commissions were confronted by an accomplished fact, which remained to be legalized by some compromise not too favorable to the Indians or to the government's reputation for fair dealing.

The earlier theory that the United States government in negotiating with Indians was dealing with independent nations—a theory which led to 371 treaties with Indian tribes—was revoked in 1871 by an act of Congress which declared: "Hereafter no Indian nation or tribe shall be acknowledged or recognized as an independent tribe or power with whom the United States may contract by treaty." Thereafter all Indian legislation was dealt with by both houses of Congress. By 1950 there were on the statute books over 5,000 laws on Indian affairs.

This reservation of responsibility for Indian affairs to the national government has resulted in a proliferation of federal activities on their behalf. Congress legislates on such matters as the control of Indian resources, the determination of Indian tribal membership, the inheritance and distribution of property, jurisdiction over major crimes, and dozens of other municipal matters. Tax exemption of Indian lands, wisely demanded by Indian leaders as part of the purchase price for ceded lands, has made state and local governments reluctant to assume the financial burden of community services. The federal government therefore builds and operates schools and hospitals for Indians, builds and maintains roads and irrigation systems, manages forests and grazing lands, directs an agricultural extension service, and works with individual Indians and their leaders in the establishment of local self-government and in the development of Indian enterprises and reservation programs.

At various times new solutions for the Indian problem have been proposed, and many have been adopted. None have proved to be the immediate panaceas predicted by their supporters. The main reason for this has been that in most instances the decisions were made for the Indians, not with the Indians, and Indian resistance has served to defeat even the most well-intentioned proposals. It was at first thought that Indians might develop as dependent domestic nations, and the tribes were guaranteed their lands free from the interference of predatory whites and allowed to develop self-government. Since the frontiersmen disregarded the guaranteed rights of the Indians and the government did not entorce them, the project failed. On Feb. 8, 1887, the General Allotment Act was passed by Congress; it was designed to break up the larger reservations into smaller tracts, title to which would be given to individual Indians. It was assumed that individual ownership of property was the secret of American success and would therefore contribute to more rapid civilization and assimilation of the Indians. The restrictions on Indian lands were to continue for 25 years and then terminate. The Indians were then to receive clear title to their individual lands. Many tribes resisted the act, and most of the southwestern reservations were never allotted. In the northern areas where allotment was carried out, more than half of all Indian land was lost by the Indian allottee shortly after the relaxation of restrictions; the inheritance of allotments remaining in Indian ownership has resulted in their continuing subdivision between heirs until the inherited portions are too small for productive use.

During the 1890's general statutes were passed for the leasing of Indian lands to whites in the belief that this would increase their productive use and would stimulate Indians through emulation to better farm and grazing practices. This system also failed, because many Indians who preferred to operate their own lands were coerced into leasing. Deprived of their lands, they settled back to eke out an existence from the lease money.

Indian Reorganization Act of 1934.—The most recent attempt to move toward a solution of the Indian problem was the passage by Congress, on June 18, 1934, of the Indian Reorganization Act (IRA). In brief, this law repealed the allotment act and reimposed restrictions against alienation of Indian lands, to stop their loss; authorized the purchase for, or return to, Indian tribes of alienated lands; provided for sustained-yield operation of Indian forests; authorized the establishment of a revolving loan fund to make loans to individual Indians and Indian chartered corporations; authorized loans to Indians for advanced education; provided means of employing competent Indians in government service regardless of civil service restrictions; and provided the machinery for the organization of Indian tribes for self-government and the management of their own resources. For the first time, Indians were allowed the option of electing to operate under an act or to reject its terms. In 1934–1936, 258 tribal elections were held; 181 tribes, representing 129,750 Indians, voted to accept the act, while 77 tribes, enrolling 86,365 Indians, rejected it. Later amendments extended the operations of the IRA to Oklahoma and Alaska, where the process of tribal choice was not required. Whenever a group or village was ready to organize, it might do so.

The greatest gains under the IRA were: (1) the provision permitting tribes to organize as municipal corporations and to assume self-governing rights similar to those of the average American community and (2) the establishment of a loan fund with which to finance individual or group economic development. From the loan funds available from 1936 to 1948, the United States government loaned $13,809,000. The delinquency rate in repayments was less than 1 per cent—a better record than had been maintained by federal loan agencies serving non-Indians.

The Indian Service.—The majority of Indians are self-supporting, though at a relatively low economic level. Of the $48,850,589 appropriated for the operation of the Indian Service in 1949, only $1,550,941 was expended for direct relief. The remainder was spent for furnishing services authorized by Congress or required by treaty agreements. Of the total, $14,500,000 was spent on the operation of schools; $10,250,000, on health services and hospitals; and $11,500,000, on the construction and maintenance of irrigation projects, roads, schools, hospitals, and agency structures. The administration of these services in Washington and in the field cost about $4,000,000. In 1949 there were 7,496 full-time civil service employees engaged in Indian work, or about one for every 50 Indians; in the same year there was one federal, state, or local employee for every 24 non-Indians. In addition, the Indian Service, doing its own road work, irrigation, and building construction, had about 3,500 temporary employees. In the case of other government agencies, however, such employees would be working for contractors and would not be counted as government employees. If these temporary workers are added to regular employees, the ratio of employees to Indians was 1 to 30. The per capita cost of government services to Indians in 1949 was $111.21; the per capita cost of government services (other than military cost and debt retirement) for non-Indians was $200.

Education.—The school census of 1945 showed a total of 92,296 Indian children of school age. Of these, 31,927 were attending public day schools, 7,813 were in mission boarding schools, and 27,252 were in federal boarding and day schools. During World War II, 5,929 left the reservations with their parents and presumably enrolled in public schools, but there is no accurate record. A total of 19,375 were not in any school; of these, more than 15,000 were on the Navajo Reservation, where adequate school facilities were lacking. Between 1945 and 1950 places were made for about 4,500 Navajos in off-reservation federal boarding schools, and a school building program was undertaken on the reservation.

In 1949, the Indian Service operated 238 schools in the United States and 99 in Alaska. They ranged in size from one-room rural schools to consolidated 12-grade day schools enrolling 450 children. There were 17 nonreservation boarding schools in the United States and 3 in Alaska, and 66 reservation schools which operated boarding departments. Between 1928 and 1948 the number of Indian Service high schools had grown from 2 to 33; since the war the number of high school students has quadrupled. Federal Indian high schools are primarily vocational in program, preparing their graduates to make the best use of their native resources or training them for off-reservation employment. These schools are accredited in their home states, and about 20 per cent of their graduates go on to college or advanced vocational training. The Indian Service has never operated any schools of collegiate grade, but instead has encouraged high school graduates to attend regular colleges.

Resources.—From 1933 to 1948 the resources activities of the Indian Service more than tripled Indian income from agriculture, stock raising, forestry development, and mineral resources.

Health.—The Indian health service has greatly reduced the incidence of tuberculosis among the Indians, although in areas like the Navajo and Alaska, the death rate was still 10 times that of the white population in 1950. Applying the discovery by Dr. Fred Loe, an Indian Service physician, that sulfanilamide is a specific cure for trachoma, that disease has been eliminated on many reservations and greatly reduced on others. Infant mortality rates were still high in 1950, though the Indian birth rate remained so high that Indians were the most rapidly growing group in the general population.

The Health Branch of the Indian Service operates 64 hospitals in the continental United States and 7 in Alaska. In various clinics and through home visits, over 750,000 treatments are given annually, and more than 50,000 individuals receive hospital care.

As a result of a 10-year study in the United States and Alaska of the use of BCG (Bacillus of Calmette and Guérin) vaccination as a tuberculosis preventive, it was found that those who were vaccinated were much less likely to develop tuberculosis, and that among the vaccinated group there were 9 times fewer deaths from the disease. The Indian Service is therefore systematically administering BCG vaccination to children born in Indian Service hospitals and to children in Indian schools. In 1950 the Indian Service was building two tuberculosis hospitals in Alaska, at Sitka and Anchorage, supplying 500 new beds, in addition to approximately 200 beds in older institutions. There are Indian Service tuberculosis hospitals in Albuquerque, N. Mex.; Phoenix, Ariz., and Tacoma, Wash. The Indian Service has built tuberculosis wings for several public hospitals and contracts with their managements for the care of Indian patients. In 1950 additional tuberculosis hospitals were planned for the Navajo area.

Alaska Native Service.—The three native groups of Alaska are under the care of the Alaska Native Service, the title under which the Indian Service operates there. In 1949 the native population of Alaska consisted of about one third of the total, estimated at about 100,000. Indians occupy the interior valleys, and the southeast coastal littoral; Aleuts, the Aleutian Islands, Alaska Peninsula, and the south coast and islands almost to Yakutat; Eskimos, the coastal area, the river deltas, and most of the islands from Bristol Bay north and east to Demarcation Point on the Canadian border. Of the estimated 10,500 children of school age in 1950, 2,950 were attending Alaska territorial schools. About 5,200 were in federal day schools operating in native villages, on in the three boarding schools (of which two are high schools). There were about 600 pupils in mission schools. By 1950, however, no schools had been built in a number of native villages with a total of 1,750 children.

Many Alaskan villages have organized under the IRA, and have borrowed money to buy or build fish canneries, acquire and operate native stores, purchase boats and other fishing gear, and engage in other economic activities. A number of villages have greatly improved their economic status as a result of this development.

Indian Population and Development.—Despite the policy of removal by which the federal government attempted to move as many Indians as possible from the eastern and southern states and to resettle them west of the Mississippi, some Indians are still found in every state of the Union. Those Indians for whom the Bureau of Indian Affairs has a continuing responsibility are those with whom the government has had treaty relations, or for whom it has undertaken some legal responsibility. These live in 24 states (not including New York, where the basic responsibility for the Indians, by colonial treaties, lies with the state). There are more than 15,000 Indians, many of whom are recognized as such by their home states, who have no connection with the Indian Service; most of them live along the Atlantic seaboard and gulf coast. The 1945 census of the Office of Indian Affairs showed 392,000 Indians, compared with a low of 240,000 in 1900 and an estimated 800,000 in 1492.

Oklahoma has the greatest number of Indians, and Arizona is second; California, New Mexico, and South Dakota each have over 20,000. The Navajo is the largest tribe, with more than 65,000. The Sioux are next, followed closely by the Chippewa; both number 35,000 to 40,000.

While many Indian tribes were in 1950 fast moving toward the time when their affairs need no longer be supervised by the government, there were still many tribes which had received little attention in the past and had made little progress toward adapting their ways to modern economic demands. Thousands of individual Indians, however, are constantly taking their places on an equal footing with their white neighbors.

Inter-American Indian Affairs.—The First Inter-American Congress on Indian Affairs was held at Pátzcuaro, Mexico, April 14-24, 1937. Representatives of 19 American nations were present, Canada being the single abstainer among nations with an appreciable Indian population. The United States and Mexico took the leadership in seeking methods for raising the educational, health, and economic standards of the almost 30,000,000 Indians of North, Central, and South America. One of the important results of the congress was the establishment of an Inter-American Indian Institute, with headquarters in Mexico City. The convention authorizing this also provided for the establishment of national Indian institutes in the collaborating nations. Although the United States was quick to approve the convention, Congress, because of World War II, has not appropriated funds for a national Indian institute in the United States. The Second Inter-American Congress on Indian Affairs, held in June 1949, at Cusco, Peru, reviewed and amplified many positions taken at the first meeting.

Bibliography.—Leupp, F. E., *In Red Man's Land* (New York 1914); Schmeckebier, L. F., *The Office of Indian Affairs; Its History, Activities and Organization* (Baltimore 1927); Institute for Government Research, *The Problem of Indian Administration* (Baltimore 1928); Kinney, J. P., *Continent Lost—A Civilization Won* (Baltimore 1937); Cohen, F. S., *Handbook of Federal Indian Law* (Washington 1941); U.S. Bureau of Indian Affairs, information and tribal relations pamphlets (Washington 1948–); McNickle, D'Arcy, *They Came Here First* (Philadelphia 1949).

WILLARD W. BEATTY,
Chief, Branch of Education, Bureau of Indian Affairs.

INDIAN HEAD, Canada, town in Saskatchewan, 50 miles east of Regina. It has extensive grain interests, lumberyards, a home for aged men and an orphanage. Situated in a wheat-growing region, Indian Head also has grain elevators and flour mills. An agricultural experiment station and forestry school are maintained here by the Canadian government. Pop. (1946) 1,354.

INDIAN HEAD, the name of several mountains in the United States.

INDIAN HEAD, New Hampshire, a mountain and tourist settlement at the southern extremity of Franconia Notch, named from the mountain's close resemblance to an Indian profile. Its proximity to the famous Old Man of the Mountain attracts thousands of visitors each year.

INDIAN HEAD, New Jersey, the highest point of the Palisades, 550 feet in altitude; so called because it resembles somewhat the head of an Indian. It is situated in Bergen County, on the Hudson River opposite Hastings, N. Y.

INDIAN HEAD, New York, in the Catskill Mountains, 3,585 feet high. It is in Greene County.

INDIAN HEMP. A tough bast fiber employed in weaving, and in the making of nets by the American Indians. It is derived from the herb *Apocynum cannabinum,* and is sometimes known as Canada hemp.

INDIAN HUMPED CATTLE (known officially in the United States as BRAHMAN CATTLE, also ZEBU), a species of cattle (*Bos indicus*) distinguished by a high, fatty hump on the withers, by the prevalent ashy gray color, large drooping ears, enormous dewlap, and several structural peculiarities. They are the working cattle and draft animals all over India and eastward, more or less locally, to China. They are venerated by pious sects of Hindus, especially certain privileged bulls, called Brahmany bulls, which wander about the cities unmolested.

Because of their resistance to heat and certain diseases, they have been imported into the United States, where they have been crossed with Herefords, Aberdeen Angus, and Shorthorns; the latter cross producing the Santa Gertrudis breed.

Humped cattle are also known in Madagascar and in Ethiopia, and it has been suggested that the species were originally African. The Ethiopian form is a large animal with huge horns, called the sanga or galla ox.

INDIAN MUSIC. The music of the Indians of the United States and Canada was mainly a vocal art, although often accompanied by drums, rattles, flutes, whistles, and other instruments. In general the Indian did not conceive of music as a form of art; rather were his songs for a specific purpose: lullabies; work songs such as those sung by women grinding corn; traditional songs recalling the deeds of heroes; or most important of all, ceremonial songs and dances for such purposes as healing the sick, bringing rain, or arousing the warrior spirit. Inasmuch as ceremonial songs were means of communication with supernatural beings, their ownership was jealously guarded by tribes, clans, or even individuals; and since the supernatural forces addressed would not respond unless the ceremony were conducted in the prescribed manner, their exact rendering was carefully watched over. Being without a system of notation, the ability to learn a new song quickly and to retain it accurately was highly regarded among Indians.

Drums were universal. A single accented beat repeated endlessly had an almost hypnotic effect on the dancers as it was gradually increased in intensity, lighter beats being interpolated. Flutes were generally made of reeds; whistles, of bone, wood, or pottery. Rattles, usually considered sacred objects for use only in ritual, were made of innumerable substances; among them wood, tortoise shells, pods, and gourds.

Among the more highly civilized peoples of Mexico, northern Central America, and the Andean highlands, music was understandably more complex, although it adhered to much the same principles. Far more highly developed in modern times than that of other Indian peoples, it is now difficult to determine precisely how much of it is due to purely Indian sources and how much to Spanish influence.

Edward MacDowell, Charles Wakefield Cadman, Arthur Farwell, and Frederick Jacobi in the United States, Carlos Chávez in Mexico, and Heitor Villa-Lobos in Brazil are among the composers who have used Indian themes in their music.

Consult Burton, F. R., *American Primitive Music* (New York 1909); Densmore, F., *The American Indians and Their Music* (New York 1926).

INDIAN MUTINY, a revolt against the East India Company's rule of India, which broke out in 1857. British occupation of India had been largely aided by native troops called sepoys, who were enrolled under British officers in the service of the East India Company. At the close of the administration of James Ramsay, marquis of Dalhousie, in 1856, when the whole of India seemed to have been either reduced directly under British rule, or if retaining its native princes to have placed itself under British protection, the sepoy mutiny, a contingency for which the government ought not to have been altogether unprepared, occurred. Previous symptoms of disaffection had not been wanting. Mutiny had on several occasions broken out in the native army, in a way to indicate how easily, through causes which Europeans, from their defective sympathy with native thought and feeling, could not anticipate, these troops might be alienated; but, on the other hand, the general fidelity of the sepoys merited confidence, and this feeling prevailed over any grounds of suspicion which might have been formed from isolated occurrences.

The sepoys in Bengal were mostly either Mohammedans, or Hindus of the Brahmanical or military castes. The recent annexations had alarmed the native chiefs, while fanatical Hindus had been deeply offended by reforms, including the successive abolition of various rites of their worship. Two European regiments had been drafted off for the Crimean War, and had not been replaced. Others had been sent to Burma, and in the beginning of 1857 fresh regiments were dispatched to Persia, so that only eighteen regiments were left in all northern India, of which nine were in the Punjab. In Oudh, where, from its recent annexation, disaffection was rife, there was only one British regiment, and Delhi and Allahabad, the two chief arsenals, were guarded by native troops. To add to these favorable circumstances a Hindu devotee had prophesied the termination of British rule at 100 years after the Battle of Plassey (June 23, 1757).

What must have appeared to the British authorities as a slight enough incident was sufficient to give point and direction to a spirit of disaffection which so many circumstances tended to favor. At this time the Enfield rifle was introduced into the Bengal army. This rifle was loaded with a greased cartridge, the end of which required to be bitten off at the time of loading. By a natural inadvertence the authorities had neglected to consider how this seemingly trifling requirement might affect the easily excited sensitiveness of the Hindus in regard to caste, and this insignificant circumstance removed the last security, against a united movement of disloyalty among the native troops, by establishing a bond of sympathy between the Mohammedans and Hindus. A report got abroad that the cartridges were to be soaked in cow and pork fat. The prejudices of Hindus and Mohammendans were thus equally involved, and as this rumor rapidly spread, the excited imagination of the Sepoys conceived a conspiracy on the part of the government to convert them forcibly to Christianity, by compelling them to violate the laws of their own religion. When this grievance was explained it was at once removed, the manufacture of greased cartridges at Dumdum was stopped, and the men were instructed to grease them themselves with materials produced at the bazaars. Suspicion once aroused, however, was not to be allayed, and easily found a new object of contention. The paper of the new cartridges was glazed, and it was again alleged that grease was used in its manufacture. The spirit of disaffection became too deep-rooted for any measures of conciliation. Conferences among the disaffected gave rise to ambitious schemes and the original grievances became a pretext in the hands of unscrupulous leaders, whose excesses debarred them even from the plea of patriotism, to extirpate the British power in India. On 26 February the first overt act of mutiny took place at Berhampur, when a regiment refused to receive their cartridges. Another dangerous outbreak took place at Barrackpur on 29 March. The arrival of a British regiment from Burma and the disbandment of the disaffected regiments was thought to have ended the trouble, but it soon became evident that disaffection, which had only wanted an occasion, was spreading rapidly not only among the Sepoys, but among the Hindus generally. Another outbreak took place on 2 May, near Lucknow, when a regiment of cavalry were, by some oversight of the government's instructions, ordered to bite their cartridges. Sir Henry Lawrence succeeded by a show of force in disarming it. A more formidable outbreak occurred about the same time at Meerut, 35 miles northeast of Delhi, when the mutineers, with the assistance of the native inhabitants, indiscriminately massacred the Europeans and escaped to Delhi. The advance-guard of the mutineers reached Delhi on 11 May, and at once entered the city, where they were assisted by the king's servants in massacring the Europeans. The native troops cantoned outside the city in the meantime joined the main body of the mutineers, and assisted in massacring their European officers. About 50 Europeans sought refuge in the palace and placed themselves under the protection of the king, who had placed himself on the throne of the Moguls. These, after some days, were coolly murdered in an open court in presence of a general concourse of spectators, conspicuous among whom was Mirza Mogul, the king's eldest son, who had assumed the title of commander-in-chief. The magazine at Delhi had been blown up by its defenders; but the explosion was only partial, and most of its contents fell into the hands of the mutineers. European troops were now summoned from all quarters. Several regiments were detached from an expedition which was proceeding under Lord Elgin to China, and the Persian War having been concluded, the troops engaged there were immediately recalled. When intelligence of these events reached the Punjab, the mutinous spirit which prevailed among the large body of Hindustani troops there was promptly subdued by disarmament. The Sikhs, though the Punjab had been so recently annexed, continued faithful. But the revolt had spread rapidly elsewhere, and British authority was almost extinct, throughout the Bengal presidency. Everywhere the mutiny was attended with savage excesses — women were outraged, and Europeans, without distinction of age or sex, barbarously murdered. Sir Hugh Wheeler, at Cawnpore, was betrayed by Nana Sahib, maharajah of Bithur, who after offering aid, took the mutineers into his pay, and raising the Mahratta standard, besieged Cawnpore. The siege, or rather bombardment, lasted from 7–24 June, when a capitulation was agreed to, on a sworn promise of Nana Sahib to allow the garrison to retire to Allahabad. But as the embarkation was proceeding the boats were attacked by the Nana's troops and the men indiscriminately massacred. The women and children were for the meantime made prisoners. Sir Henry Lawrence was besieged in Lucknow, where he died on 4 July, from a wound received in a sortie.

Meanwhile mutineers had been converging on Delhi, and British reinforcements were hastening to the besieging camp on the ridge above the city. After protracted operations and repeated reinforcements on both sides, Delhi was taken by assault, 14–20 September. Sir Henry Havelock, who had been engaged in the Persian campaign, had arrived in Calcutta, and immediately set out for Allahabad, to commence operations for the relief of Lucknow and Cawnpore. While his force was victoriously advancing on Cawnpore, Nana Sahib on 15 July barbarously massacred his prisoners, consisting of 210 women and children. Havelock was succeeded in the command, at Lucknow, by Sir James Outram, who held it till relieved by Sir Colin Campbell, on 17 November. At first it was feared that the mutiny might extend to the Bombay and Madras presidencies, and from this cause and the occupation of the troops in Bengal, the mutineers had been left unchecked in Central India. At length columns organized in these presidencies entered Central India, and were united under Sir Hugh Rose. By the operations of these commanders the brave Rani of Jhansi, who died fighting at the head of her troops, was defeated, and Tantia Topi, whose military capacity had prolonged Nana Sahib's resistance, was captured and the mutiny was finally suppressed. The war was substantially closed by June 1858, although the complete pacification of Oudh was not effected till the end of the year. During the mutiny the Sikhs and Gurkhas remained loyal; and the bulk of the population was at least passively so. The suppression of the revolt was followed by a full amnesty to the rank and file who had not borne a hand in the massacre of Europeans, and by the transfer to the British government of the powers possessed by the East India Company. (See INDIA, EAST INDIA COMPANY). Consult the histories of the Mutiny, by Forrest (1904); Holmes, (1898); and Malleson (1878–80).

INDIAN OCEAN, that body of water which has Asia on the north, the East Indian Islands, Nicobar and the Andaman Islands, Australia and Tasmania on the east, Africa on the west, and the Antarctic continent on the south. The Cape of Good Hope and the southern extremity of Tasmania may be considered its extreme limits from east to west. Its length from north to south somewhat exceeds 6,500 miles, its breadth varies from 6,000 to 4,000 miles. Its gulfs are the Red Sea, the Gulf of Aden, the Persian Gulf, the Gulf of Oman, the Arabian Sea, the Bay of Bengal and the Great Australian Bight. Its islands are Ceylon, Madagascar, the Laccadives, Maldives, Socotra, Andamans, Nicobar, Mauritius, Bourbon, Kerguelen's Land, etc. The Ganges, Brahmaputra, Irrawaddy, Indus and Euphrates, empty into the Indian Ocean from Asia, and the Zambezi and Limpopo from Africa. The southeast tradewind blows between the 10th and 28th parallels of south latitude from April to October, after which date its limits are contracted; south of these are the northwest winds which prevail almost in the same latitude, in the Atlantic and Pacific. The monsoons are mainly in the north, from the continent of Asia to about latitude 8° S., and from the Mozambique Channel on the west to the western shores of Australia and the Sea of China. They blow for six months, changing about the equinoxes. North of the equator the northeast monsoon prevails from October to April, the southwest from April to October; while south of that the northwest monsoon blows while the northeast is blowing on the north side; and the southeast prevails during the time of the southwest monsoon north of the equator. In the hot season, likewise, when the southeast trade-wind recedes south, the northwest monsoon blows between the equator and the 12th south parallel. The hurricanes of this ocean usually range between lat. 9° and 35° S., extending from Madagascar to the Island of Timor. They usually come from the northeast, and travel southwest and south, returning again east. Their season is from December to April.

According to the most recent soundings the mean depth of the Indian Ocean is 2,300 fathoms, or somewhat greater than that of the Atlantic. The greatest depths are in the eastern part to the south of the equator, where it is estimated that there are fully 50,000 square miles with a depth of over 3,000 fathoms. The deepest sounding has been recorded off the southeast coast of Java, 20,340 feet. Over 13,000,000 square miles lie between the depths of 2,000 and 3,000 fathoms.

The area of land draining into the Indian Ocean is estimated at 6,813,600 square miles, and the rainfall on this land amounts to 4.379 cubic miles of water annually. The rivers flowing from the Asiatic continent are by far the most important, and they carry a vast amount of detritus into the Bay of Bengal and Arabian Sea, these forming immense deposits of blue mud. Along the African coasts, in depths from 100 to 1,000 fathoms, there are glauconitic sands and muds, and on these as well as other coasts, coral muds and sands, and blue and green muds in the shallower depths. In the deeper parts of the ocean, far from land, there are deposits of red clay, radiolarian-ooze, and globigerina-ooze. Toward the Antarctic continent the ocean bed is covered with a diatom-ooze.

The temperature of the surface waters varies much in different parts of the ocean, at different seasons, and under the influence of different winds. In tropical regions the temperature usually varies from 70° to 80° F., and the yearly range is 7° or 8° F. Off the Cape of Good Hope and Cape Guardafui, the annual range may be from 20° to 30° F. Sudden changes of temperature are often noticed off Cape Guardafui when the wind blows off shore.

The cold and deep water is thus drawn up along the coast to take the place of the warm surface water which is driven east by the wind

The temperature of the water at the bottom is very uniform and subject to little, if any, annual variation. In the Bay of Bengal and Arabian Sea temperatures of 33.7° F. and 34.2° F. have been recorded; these are only very slightly higher than those recorded by the Challenger in lat. 50° S. It is certain, therefore, that this deep cold water is slowly drawn into the Indian Ocean from the Anarctic to supply the place of the warm surface currents that are driven south by the winds.

The currents of the Indian Ocean are less constant than in the other oceans, being largely controlled by the monsoons. Some characteristic coral atolls and islands are found toward the central part, such as the great Maldive group, the Chagos, Diego Carcia, and the Cocos Islands. The tropical shores are generally skirted by fringing and barrier reefs which render navigation dangerous. Christmas Island is coral formation, while Saint Paul's, Mauritius, Rodriguez and others are of volcanic origin, and Madagascar, Ceylon, and Socotra, continental islands.

The Indian Ocean was little known to the ancients. The first Europeans who explored it seem to have been the Phœnicians, who in the 7th century B.C., held the thalassocracy, or marine domination, of the Mediterranean. Necho, an Egyptian monarch who flourished about 610 B.C., is reported by Herodotus to have sent some of his vessels, manned by Phœnicians, into the Indian Ocean, then known as the Erythræan Sea, to circumnavigate Africa. This they did, starting from the Arabian Gulf and regaining Europe by the Columns of Hercules. In the 6th century B.C. this sea was traversed by Hanno, a Phœnician admiral of Carthage. There is still extant his account of the voyage which is translated into Greek under the title 'Hanno's Voyage of Circumnavigation.' The Greek historian Arrian has given us an account of the coasting voyage of Nearchus, one of Alexander's generals, from the Indus to the mouth of the Tigris and Euphrates.

Hippalus, an Egyptian navigator who flourished about the beginning of the Christian era, was the first to observe the regular monsoons of the Indian Ocean, and to profit by them. In the 9th century the Arabs made frequent voyages across the Indian Ocean. In 1486 the Portuguese rounded the Cape of Good Hope, and in 1498 Vasco de Gama reached the coasts of India by the same route. In 1521 a ship of Magellan's squadron crossed the Indian Ocean in completing the first circumnavigation of the world, and has since been habitually traversed in a direct line between Arabia and Hindustan.

INDIAN OIL TREE. See BUTTER TREE.

INDIAN PAINT, the name of two American plants: (1) the golden seal (q.v.) or orange-root, which furnishes a yellow color; and (2) the bloodroot. See SANGUINARIA.

INDIAN AND PERSIAN LACQUER-WORK. See LACQUERS AND LACQUERWORK.

INDIAN PHYSIC, an American plant. See BOWMAN'S ROOT.

INDIAN PIPE, or **CORPSE-PLANT**, a smooth, waxy-looking, fleshy herb (*Monotropa uniflora*), of the family *Monotropaceæ*, widely distributed in dark, rich woods almost throughout North America and in eastern Asia. This plant is now classed with the saprophytes, which draw their sustenance from dead or decaying vegetable matter, roots, etc. From a matted mass of fibrous rootlets the white scaly stems rise to a height of perhaps eight inches, and bear solitary, nodding, white, inodorous flowers during the summer, followed by erect many-seeded fruits.

INDIAN RED, an impure oxid of iron, used as a pigment by painters. It was originally imported from India, but is now chiefly prepared by roasting ferrous sulphate. The sulphuric acid is expelled by the heat, and the red oxid of iron remains behind. It is very permanent, and the color varies from purplish to a yellowish red.

INDIAN RESERVATIONS. When the settlers from Europe came to realize that the Indians had human rights, and ought not to be enslaved or exterminated, the rule was generally adopted of confining the tribes to reservations, both for their own protection from unprincipled whites, and for the security of the white population. New York, Massachusetts, Connecticut, Rhode Island and other States enforced this policy in the colonial period and after independence, and the United States government has carried it out from an early date. Southern tribes east of the Mississippi were removed to the Indian Territory, which since 16 Nov. 1907 has become a part of the State of Oklahoma. Designated by solemn pledge of the National government as a permanent home for their race, there some of the tribes achieved a high degree of civilization, gained considerable wealth and merged into American citizenship. They are largely intermarried with whites, and to some extent with negroes, whom they formerly held as slaves. Other tribes, chiefly from the southwest, were gathered into the Indian Territory, but large Indian reservations, mainly of Sioux, are still maintained in the northwest, and altogether the various tribal reservations in the different States and Territories number over 100. The reservations are carefully guarded against intrusion by unscrupulous whites, and provision is made for the intellectual and physical welfare of the Indians, and for leading them to adopt civilized methods of self-support, instead of depending on the chase, which now offers only the most precarious returns, or on government aid, which, however, is not withdrawn under any circumstances while an Indian is in need of it. The sale of intoxicating liquor to Indians is severely punished when detected, but the law is frequently evaded. See CHEROKEE; CHICKASAW; CHOCTAW; CREEKS; INDIAN AFFAIRS; INDIANS, AMERICAN; SEMINOLE INDIANS.

INDIAN RIVER, a long lagoon in eastern Florida; separated from the Atlantic Ocean by a chain of narrow islands; extending about 120m. SE. from Volusia County to Saint Lucie Inlet in Martin County; and navigable as far north as Titusville to vessels of shallow draft. The river is from 300 feet to three miles wide and is in a famous citrus fruit, resort and fishing section.

INDIAN SCHOOLS, in the United States, are schools especially established either by private or denominational means or by the national government, for the education of children and youth of the Indian population of this county. For particulars concerning these schools see INDIAN AFFAIRS; INDIANS, EDUCATION OF THE.

INDIAN SHOT. See CANNA.

INDIAN SUMMER, the name given to a period of mild and pleasant weather which generally occurs toward the end of autumn. The term first made its appearance in the last decade of the 18th century. During the next decade the phrase was «second summer.» This indicates that the spell of weather known by this name was not generally noticed much before 1800. The term Indian summer became established about 20 years after its first appearance, which was in western Pennsylvania, and spread to New England by 1798, to New York by 1799, to Canada by 1821, and to England by 1830. The term, is, then, not an Americanism; to write in praise of Indian summer is now a literary convention of three continents.

It is by no means easy to account for the origin of the term. The principal characteristics of the season which it describes are haziness, smokiness, and high temperature. Some explanations of the origin of the term are (1) that the Indians predicted such spells of weather; (2) that the smokiness was produced by Indian fires; (3) that this was the last season of Indian attacks on the settlements of the whites; (4) that the season partook of the Indian character of deceptiveness; (5) that the name was given because one of the seasons of East India was similar in character. Horace Walpole used the term in 1778, not in reference to America, but in relation to weather in the tropics. «Squaw winter» was a name for the spell of cold weather preceding the Indian summer, and perhaps the key to the nomenclature is to be sought in this latter term. Analogous terms in use in England and Germany are: «Saint Martin's Summer,» «All Hallow Summer,» «Saint Luke's Summer,» «Old Woman's Summer.» Consult *Monthly Weather Review* (Vol. XXX, pp. 19–29; 69–79, Washington 1902).

INDIAN TERRITORY. See OKLAHOMA.

INDIAN TURNIP, a plant, *Arisæma triphyllum*, of the Arum family, known also as Jack-in-the-pulpit. It is one of the best known spring flowers of eastern North America, blossoming in April or May. The leaves are compound, each composed of three large entire leaflets; the "flower" really consists of a club-shaped spike of small greenish flowers surrounded by a large, hooded, corolla-like spathe, usually green striped with purple. In summer the flowers are succeeded by red berries. The root is a tuber, containing an acrid juice.

INDIAN or WILD TOBACCO, one of the North American lobelias (*Lobelia inflata*), also called asthma-weed and gagroot. Usually, its petals are blue, pale violet, or whitish.

INDIAN YELLOW, a color or dye that is yellowish red-yellow in hue and possesses high brilliance and high saturation; also used synonymously for cobalt yellow.

INDIANA, ĭn-dĭ-ăn'â, one of the East North Central states. It is bounded on the north by Lake Michigan and Michigan; on the east by Ohio; on the south by the north bank of the Ohio River, which divides it from Kentucky; and on the west by Illinois. The word Indiana means "land of the Indians."

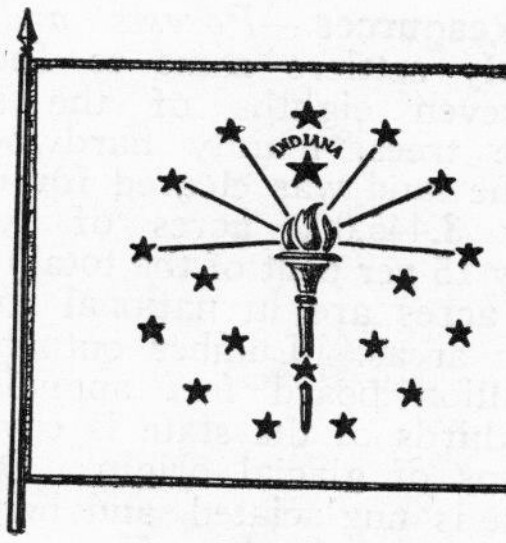

State flag.

Land area	36,205 square miles
Water area	86 square miles
Total area	36,291 square miles
Total, including Indiana's share of Lake Michigan	36,519 square miles
Latitude	37°47'—41°46' N.
Longitude	84°49'—88°4' W.
Altitude	316 feet to 1,240 feet
Population (1950)	3,934,224
Capital city—Indianapolis; Pop. (1950)	427,173
Admitted as a state	Dec. 11, 1816
Bird	Cardinal, adopted March 9, 1933
Flower	Zinnia, adopted March 3, 1931
Motto	The Crossroads of America
Nickname	Hoosier State
Song—*On the Banks of the Wabash, Far Away,*	adopted March 14, 1913
Tree	Tulip tree, adopted March 3, 1931

State seal.

Physical Characteristics. — *Topography.* — The terrain of Indiana is divided roughly into two types—flat or slightly rolling land in the central and northern sections of the state, and hilly country in the south, with the most rugged hills extending southward from Brown County to the Ohio River. There is little poor soil, but the most fertile is to be found in the central third of the state. The rugged terrain of southern Indiana contains numerous small-scale gorges and canyons. In Crawford County are two large caves, Wyandotte (q.v.) and Marengo, and mineral springs are located at French Lick and West Baden in Orange County.

Rivers and Lakes.—Four fifths of Indiana, in the center and southwest, is drained by the Wabash and its tributaries, the White, Eel, Mississinewa, and Tippecanoe rivers. The northeastern section is drained by the Maumee, which flows into Lake Erie at Toledo, Ohio; the extreme north by the St. Joseph and Kankakee; and the south by the Ohio River. None of the rivers flowing through Indiana are navigable commercially. The Department of Commerce reported that in 1939, 9,703,805 acres of land in occupied farms were included in drainage enterprises, of which 7,512,766 acres were planted. In all, 10,121,952 (in 1950, about 11,017,709) acres were in drainage enterprises, of which 9,424,503 were completely drained, and 534,496 were partially drained. There are approximately 1,000 lakes in northern Indiana. The largest is Lake Wawasee, in Kosciusko County, which covers 3,623 acres. Other large lakes, noted also as vacation resorts, are Maxinkuckee (Marshall County); Freeman (Carroll County); James (Steuben County), on which is located Pokagon State Park; Tippecanoe (Kosciusko County); and Shafer (White County).

Climate.—The climate of Indiana is mild, but there is considerable variation between the northern and southern extremities of the state. The average temperature for the entire state ranges from 31° F. in winter to 76° F. in summer. The annual mean is 53° for the entire state (49° for the north and 57° for the south). The growing season, or period between killing frosts, in central Indiana is 188 days. For the state as a whole, the average annual precipitation is 43 inches, ranging from 35 inches near Lake Michigan to 46 inches along the Ohio River.

Political Divisions.—*Cities.*—Of the 19 cities in Indiana with populations (1950) greater than 25,000, six—Indianapolis, Fort Wayne, South Bend, Evansville, Muncie, and Terre Haute—are centers of densely peopled areas classified by the census as metropolitan areas. Indianapolis, capital and largest city, is also one of the largest cities in the United States not located on navigable water. It is served by railroads and highways leading to all parts of the state and is an active commercial and industrial center. Its factories produce meat commodities, airplane engines, motor vehicle bodies, drugs, foundry and machine shop products, naval ordnance, printed material, electrical machinery, paper boxes, hosiery, clothing, canned goods, and paints and varnishes. Fort Wayne and South Bend, both in the northern part of the state, produce machinery and a wide variety of other products. Evansville, on the Ohio River, is the leading industrial center of southern Indiana, and produces refrigerators, automobile parts, furniture, and meat products. Terre Haute, in the west, is the center of the farming and mining area of the Wabash Valley.

The heavily industrialized cities of the Calumet region of northwestern Indiana—Gary, East

Chicago, Hammond, and Whiting—are included in the Chicago metropolitan area, and Clark and Floyd counties, in the Louisville (Ky.) area. The chief industry in the Calumet is iron and steel, and there is considerable shipping via Lake Erie. (See list of cities on back of the state map for population figures.)

Counties.—Indiana's 92 counties range in size from Ohio (87 square miles) to Allen (671 square miles) and in population from Ohio (4,223) to Marion (551,777). A list of counties and county seats follows:

County	County Seat	County	County Seat
Adams	Decatur	Madison	Anderson
Allen	Fort Wayne	Marion	Indianapolis
Bartholomew	Columbus	Marshall	Plymouth
Benton	Fowler	Martin	Shoals
Blackford	Hartford City	Miami	Peru
Boone	Lebanon	Monroe	Bloomington
Brown	Nashville	Montgomery	Crawfordsville
Carroll	Delphi	Morgan	Martinsville
Cass	Logansport	Newton	Kentland
Clark	Jeffersonville	Noble	Albion
Clay	Brazil	Ohio	Rising Sun
Clinton	Frankfort	Orange	Paoli
Crawford	English	Owen	Spencer
Daviess	Washington	Parke	Rockville
Dearborn	Lawrenceburg	Perry	Cannelton
Decatur	Greensburg	Pike	Petersburg
De Kalb	Auburn	Porter	Valparaiso
Delaware	Muncie	Posey	Mt. Vernon
Dubois	Jasper	Pulaski	Winamac
Elkhart	Goshen	Putnam	Greencastle
Fayette	Connersville	Randolph	Winchester
Floyd	New Albany	Ripley	Versailles
Fountain	Covington	Rush	Rushville
Franklin	Brookville	St. Joseph	South Bend
Fulton	Rochester	Scott	Scottsburg
Gibson	Princeton	Shelby	Shelbyville
Grant	Marion	Spencer	Rockport
Greene	Bloomfield	Starke	Knox
Hamilton	Noblesville	Steuben	Angola
Hancock	Greenfield	Sullivan	Sullivan
Harrison	Corydon	Switzerland	Vevay
Hendricks	Danville	Tippecanoe	Lafayette
Henry	New Castle	Tipton	Tipton
Howard	Kokomo	Union	Liberty
Huntington	Huntington	Vanderburgh	Evansville
Jackson	Brownstown	Vermillion	Newport
Jasper	Rensselaer	Vigo	Terre Haute
Jay	Portland	Wabash	Wabash
Jefferson	Madison	Warren	Williamsport
Jennings	Vernon	Warrick	Boonville
Johnson	Franklin	Washington	Salem
Knox	Vincennes	Wayne	Richmond
Kosciusko	Warsaw	Wells	Bluffton
Lagrange	Lagrange	White	Monticello
Lake	Crown Point	Whitley	Columbia City
La Porte	La Porte		
Lawrence	Bedford		

The People.—According to the 1950 federal census, 97.4 per cent (93 per cent white and 4.4 per cent Negro) of Indiana's population was native born. Of the 100,630 foreign-born residents, the predominant groups were immigrants from Germany (13,801), Poland (11,883), the British Isles (11,481), Hungary (6,703), Canada (6,179), Italy (5,508), Yugoslavia (5,009); and Scandinavia (3,909). Indiana's population in 1950 was 59.9 per cent urban, an increase of 4.8 per cent from 1940. From 1940 to 1950 the population of Indiana increased from 3,427,796 to 3,934,224, or 14.8 per cent, a greater percentage increase than for any other decade in the twentieth century. The center of the nation's population had been placed in Indiana since 1890 (in the 1940 census it was placed near Carlisle), but was shifted to Illinois in 1950.

Famous Men and Women.—Indiana men and women have attained fame and recognition in many fields. In statesmanship, they have included three secretaries of state—Walter Q. Gresham (near Lanesville, 1832–1895), John W. Foster (Pike County, 1836–1917), and John Hay (Salem, 1838–1905); a vice president, Thomas R. Marshall (North Manchester, 1854–1925); and Wendell L. Willkie (Elwood, 1892–1944), most expressive advocate of One World. Among Indiana's many authors are Lew Wallace (Brookville, 1827–1905), John James Piatt (Milton, 1835–1917), Edward Eggleston (Vevay, 1837–1902), Joaquin Miller (Liberty, 1839–1913), Maurice Thompson (Fairfield, 1844–1901), James Whitcomb Riley (Greenfield, 1849–1916), Charles Major (Indianapolis, 1856–1913), Annie Fellows Johnston (Evansville, 1863–1931), George Ade (Kentland, 1866–1944), George Barr McCutcheon (near La Fayette, 1866–1928), Meredith Nicholson (Crawfordsville, 1866–1947), Gene Stratton Porter (Wabash County, 1868–1924), William Vaughan Moody (Spencer, 1869–1910), Booth Tarkington (Indianapolis, 1869–1946), Theodore Dreiser (Terre Haute, 1871–1945), Charles A. Beard (Knightstown, 1874–1948), Mary R. Beard (Indianapolis, 1876–), Claude G. Bowers (Hamilton County, 1878–), Robert S. Lynd (New Albany, 1892–), Ernie Pyle (Dana, 1900–1945), and Ross Lockridge, Jr. (Bloomington, 1914–1948). Other famous Hoosiers are John S. Bobbs (1809–1870), of Indianapolis, first surgeon to operate for gallstones; James B. Eads (Lawrenceburg, 1820–1887), inventor of the diving bell; Eugene Debs (Terre Haute, 1855–1926), labor leader; Elwood Haynes (Portland, 1857–1925), inventor of the first successful clutch-driven automobile; Wilbur Wright (Millville, 1867–1912), pioneer in aviation; Eli Lilly (Indianapolis, 1885–), drug manufacturer; T. C. Steele (Owen County, 1847–1926), Otto Stark (Indianapolis, 1859–1926), and Wayman Adams (Muncie, 1883–), artists; and Paul Dresser (Terre Haute, 1858–1906), Cole Porter (Peru, 1893–), and Hoagy Carmichael (Bloomington 1899–), composers.

Natural Resources.—*Forests and Soils.*—When the early settlers came to Indiana, approximately seven eighths of the state was forested. The trees, mainly hardwoods, were cut down as the land was cleared for farms, and by 1945 only 3,445,000 acres of forest land (approximately 15 per cent of the total) remained. Some 725,640 acres are in national forests and land utilization areas. Lumber output approximates 200 million board feet annually. The northern two thirds of the state is covered with deep, rich loams of glacial origin. Only south central Indiana is unglaciated, and here the soil is thinner and less productive. Erosion has been a serious problem in some sections of the state, but since 1919, when the state conservation department was established, much has been done to reclaim eroded land.

Minerals and Power.—Coal is Indiana's leading mineral product, and there are more than 100 coal mines in the state. In 1952, Indiana mines produced 16,250,000 tons of coal valued at $65,650,000. The record for the greatest tonnage in the state's history was set in 1918, when 30,679,000 tons were mined. In 1944, the second most productive year, 27,962,000 tons were mined. Coal is obtained in 16 counties, but more than 75 per cent of the total production comes from the five counties of Vigo, Knox Pike, Sullivan, and Warrick. Strip pits normally yield about 58 per cent of the coal output.

Indiana limestone, known as the "nation's building stone," is quarried in Monroe, Lawrence, and Owen counties. During the construction era between World Wars I and II, limestone accounted annually for 67 to 87 per cent of all building stone, and of this total, Indiana furnished 86 to 97 per cent. Indiana limestone was the construction material used for the Rockefeller Center buildings in New York, the Pentagon and numerous other federal buildings in Washington, and many state capitols.

Indiana ranks among the leading states in the production of ceramics. Most of the clay is found in the west central part of the state. Brazil, seat of Clay County, describes itself as the "clay center of the world." Products made from Indiana clay include brick, tile, terra cotta, flower pots, conduits, jars, and vases. Another important resource is oil. Indiana produced 10,800,000 barrels of petroleum in 1950. The state is also an important producer of sand, gravel, and cement. Hydroelectric power accounts for only a small fraction of Indiana's power production, amounting in 1949 to 137,000,000 kilowatt hours out of a total of 11,227,000,000 kilowatt hours.

Parks and Preserves.—Indiana's state park system, one of the finest in the United States, is comprised of 15 parks with a total area of 42,464 acres. Acquired and developed to perpetuate typical scenery and geological formations as well as for recreational purposes, they are scattered from the sand dunes of Lake Michigan to the rugged hills and cliffs along the Ohio River. A total of more than 1,400,000 paid admissions to the parks in 1947 topped all records since the inception of the system in 1916 under direction of the late Col. Richard Lieber. The parks and their locations are as follows: Bass Lake, near Winona; Brown County, near Nashville; Clifty Falls, near Madison; Indiana Dunes, near Chesterton; Lincoln, containing the site of the cabin occupied by the Lincoln family during their stay in Indiana, near Lincoln City; McCormick's Creek, near Spencer; Mounds, which has the largest Indian earthwork in the state, Anderson; Muscatatuck, near North Vernon; Pokagon, near Angola; Shakamak, near Hymera; Spring Mill, which contains a reconstructed pioneer village, near Mitchell; Tippecanoe River, near Winamac; Turkey Run, near Marshall; Versailles, near Versailles, and Shades, the newest of the parks, near Waveland.

There are also 15 state forests with a total area of 87,210 acres, the equivalent of 2.4 acres for each square mile in the state. During the year ending June 30, 1946, a total of 3,373,585 forest tree seedlings was distributed at the cost of production to farmers and coal companies or used to reforest wastelands being acquired in the state forests. The 13 state fish hatcheries have 162 rearing ponds and 18 display ponds. During the year ending June 30, 1946, more than 4,644,000 plantings of fish from the state hatcheries were made in Indiana streams and lakes. In the same year, Indiana produced 117,441 game birds, game animals, and fur bearers at its four game preserves, which total 12,132 acres.

Other Points of Interest.—In addition to the state parks, there are 14 state memorials, which include the first state capitol at Corydon; the territorial capitol and the George Rogers Clark Memorial, both at Vincennes; the Tippecanoe battlefield memorial near La Fayette; Angel Mounds, the largest group of Indian mounds in the state, near Evansville; and the buildings of the Rappite colony, at New Harmony. In the city park at Rockport is a reconstructed Lincoln village. A large collection of material on Indiana history is housed in the state library in Indianapolis.

Production and Manufactures.—*Agriculture.*—Although Indiana is the 12th smallest state in area, its farm income is among the highest in the nation. In 1947, it exceeded $1,000,000,000 for the first time in the history of the state. According to the 1950 Census of Agriculture (preliminary figures) there were in Indiana 166,627 farms with a total acreage of 19,658,677. The average value of land and buildings was estimated at $16,550. In 1951, crops were harvested on more than 11,000,000 acres. As of Jan. 1, 1951, there were on Indiana farms an estimated 94,000 horses, 9,000 mules, 1,848,000 cattle, 472,000 sheep, and 4,934,000 hogs. Chickens numbered 19,609,000 on Jan. 1, 1950, not including commercial broilers.

The most valuable cash crop in the state is corn, of which an estimated 241,415,000 bushels were produced in 1951. The second crop, soybeans, totaled 36,448,000 bushels in 1951. In the production of each of these crops, Indiana normally ranks third among the states. Other leading crops include wheat, oats, tobacco, hay, red clover seed, popcorn, rye, apples, and peaches. The state ranks high in the production of tomatoes and is the nation's leading producer of peppermint and spearmint, raised in the rich muck soil of the northern part of the state. Other important muck crops are potatoes, celery, carrots, cabbages, and onions.

Industry.—Proximity to abundant sources of raw materials, a central location in one of the richest markets in the nation, and a network of rail, air, and highway facilities combine to make Indiana a leading industrial state. In 1950, Indiana ranked eighth in the value of its manufactured products, and in 1945 was seventh in the value of its war production contracts. The Indiana State Chamber of Commerce in its 1948 industrial directory listed 6,900 manufacturers and processors in 650 Indiana cities and towns. At least 400 of these firms, with a minimum of 37,000 new employees, represent industries established in the state after August 1945.

Virtually all important types of manufacturing processes are represented in the state. Leading in value are steel and other rolling mill products. Automobiles, automotive parts, petroleum, chemicals, furniture, glass, soap, refrigerators, agricultural machinery and implements, drugs, grain mill products, and clothing are other major industrial products. In 1948, there were in the state 761 steel production and fabrication plants, with an annual ingot capacity of more than 11,000,000 tons, representing 12 per cent of national capacity. Indiana ranks third in basic steel production, exceeded only by Pennsylvania and Ohio. The Calumet area of Lake County, center of most of Indiana's basic steel production, is one of the world's largest industrial concentrations. The Gary Steel Works of the Carnegie-Illinois Steel Corporation is the biggest steel plant in the world. Whiting, also in Lake County, has the largest oil refinery in the world.

On the basis of numerical units, lumber and millwork, with 259 plants in 104 communities, and the dairy industry, with 235 plants in 103 communities (1943), are other leading Hoosier industries. In another large industry, canning and packing, 148 canning companies operated 195 plants in 1946. These companies packed 15 fresh vegetable items valued in excess of $50,000,000. In addition, 10 companies dry-packed 13 items valued at $33,000,000, an increase in value of over 50 per cent since 1939.

According to United States Department of Labor statistics (1944), Indiana had the third best wartime record among the seven top industrial states in the percentage of man-hours lost through strikes, lockouts, and other work stoppages. In August 1945, Indiana labor and management leaders adopted the first state labor-management charter, calling for the settlement of all labor disputes by amicable means. Although this charter had no effect in law, the extent to which its spirit was adhered to is shown by the fact that, of the 308 intrastate labor dispute cases handled by Indiana Division of Labor in the 17-month period ending Nov. 1, 1947, only slightly more than one third involved strikes or lockouts. By that date, a total of 260 cases, involving 156,142 workers, had been resolved, with settlements pending on most of the others.

Transportation and Communications.—Indiana communities in all sections of the state are served by a modern, well-engineered highway system. Its network of paved roads includes such heavily-traveled federal highways as U. S. 40 (the old National Road) and U. S. 30 (Lincoln Highway), principal coast-to-coast routes; and U. S. 31 (Dixie Highway) and U. S. 41, two of the leading north-south routes. There are 10,430 miles of paved highways and city streets maintained by the state highway commission and 66,234 miles of roads under county supervision. The state has .27 miles of paved roads for every square mile of area. Compared with a national average of less than 40 per cent, 94.06 per cent of Indiana's highways are permanently surfaced with bituminous macadam, cement concrete, bituminous concrete, or brick. Less than 8 per cent (749 miles) of the state highway system has surfaces under 18 feet wide, while 2,674 miles range from 18 to 22 feet wide. Almost 70 per cent, or 7,007 miles, has surfaces 22 feet wide or wider, with 736 miles classified as superhighways of three or more lanes. All state expenditures for construction, maintenance, and repair of state highways are allocated from current motor vehicle license receipts and motor fuel tax collections.

All main railroad lines east of Chicago, and many vital north-south arteries, pass through Indiana. Indianapolis is the world's largest inland railroad center not on navigable water. Inside the state, railroads operate 6,954 miles of track, excluding double trackage and switches, and an additional 6,000 miles of second main line and tracks in sidings and yards. The first main line trackage is equivalent to one mile of rails for each five square miles of land area. (See state map for the names of the railroads serving Indiana.)

On Jan. 1, 1951, there were 148 commercially operated civil airports, including 34 municipal and 105 privately owned, in Indiana. There were three seaplane bases—at Evansville, Winona Lake, and Lake Tippecanoe—and four military airports. Indiana, strategically located on the principal north-south and east-west routes, was served in 1951 by eight regularly scheduled airlines: American, Chicago and Southern, Eastern, Trans World, United, Ozark, Delta, and Lake Central.

Through Lake Michigan on the north and the Ohio River on the south, Indiana has access to the Great Lakes and the inland waterway system. Gary and Indiana Harbor are the principal Lake Michigan ports in Indiana. Gary receives annually between 8 and 10 million tons of freight, and Indiana Harbor receives between 8.5 and 11 million and ships between 4 and 6 million tons. Indiana ports on the Ohio River are served by the American Barge Lines and Commercial Barge Lines.

Indiana is served by two units of the American Telephone and Telegraph Company—Indiana Bell Telephone Company and Illinois Bell Telephone Company—and several hundred independent telephone companies. The number of telephones in service in Indiana on Jan. 1, 1954, was estimated at 1,297,500, providing more than 30 telephones per 100 population.

Economic and Financial Factors.—As of Dec. 30, 1953, there were in Indiana 124 national banks with assets totaling $2,372,601,000, demand deposits of $1,658,048,000, and time deposits of $559,433,000. The state's 345 other banks, including trust companies, state banks, private banks, and mutual savings banks, held deposits of $1,684,913,000 and assets of $1,802,330,000. Indiana's state banks are forbidden to make speculative investments.

A constitutional provision which prevents the state from contracting any debts has helped establish state financing on a pay-as-you-go basis. Bonds issued by local units of government are limited by statute to 2 per cent of the assessed valuation of each local unit. Indiana general fund revenues, produced by state taxes, licenses, permits, charges, and fees, and excluding federal funds and collections, totaled $332,976,000 for the year ending June 30, 1952. Some 77.6 per cent of general revenue for the 1951–1952 fiscal period was derived from taxes. The principal types of taxes were the following: general sales and gross receipt taxes, yielding $126,746,000; a motor fuel tax of four cents a gallon ($46,840,000); alcoholic beverage taxes ($12,788,000); motor vehicle licenses ($25,302,000); and tobacco taxes ($13,-319,000), including a levy of three cents per package of cigarettes.

Per capita income in Indiana for 1952 was $1,685, representing a 240 per cent increase over the 1939 average of $495. Total income payments in 1952 were estimated at $6,917,000,000.

The 1951 assessed valuation of Indiana real estate, improvements, and personal property for taxation purposes was fixed at $5,214,593,147, in addition to which public utility property was assessed at $811,575,524.

Government.—The constitution of Indiana, the second in the history of the state, was adopted in 1851. It may be amended by a majority vote of each house in two consecutive legislatures, followed by a majority vote of the citizens voting upon the amendment. (By 1954 it had been amended 18 times.) There is no provision for the initiative or referendum except as authorized by specific statute, and even in such cases the vote is not binding on the succeeding General Assembly. State government is divided into three separate departments—executive, legislative, and judicial—as follows:

Executive.—The elective executive and administrative officers, with the length of their terms, are the governor and lieutenant governor, each four years; the secretary of state, auditor, treasurer, and state superintendent of public instruction, each two years; and the attorney general, clerk of the supreme and appellate courts, and reporter of the supreme and appellate courts, each four years. The governor is limited under the constitution to one four-year term in eight years. No limitation applies to the office of lieutenant governor. The secretary of state, auditor, and treasurer cannot serve more than four years in any six-year period. The governor appoints the heads of the state departments and is responsible for the preparation of the state budget. He may veto any measure enacted by the Indiana

Courtesy, Division of State Publicity, Indianapolis

The State Capitol, Indianapolis.

© A. F. Sozio from Gendreau

Lady Victory, portion of the Civil War Monument in the public square, Indianapolis.

© Gendreau

War Memorial, Indianapolis.

INDIANA

1950 Total Population 3,934,224

Abington (H5)........ 200
Adams (F6)........ 350
Adamsboro (E3)........ 150
Advance (D5)........ 413
Akron (E2)........ 946
Alamo (C5)........ 163
Albany (G4)........1,846
Albion ◉(G2)........1,341
Alert (F6)........ 110
Alexandria (F4)......5,147
Alfordsville (C7)........ 101
Algiers (C7)........ 102
Alquina (G5)........ 114
Altona (G2)........ 344
Ambia (C4)........ 356
Amboy (F3)........ 414
Americus (D3)........ 105
Amity (E6)........ 150
Amo (D5)........ 354
Anderson ◉(F4)....46,820
Anderson (riv.) (D8)
Andersonville (G5).. 250
Andrews (F3)........1,083
Angola ◉(G1)........5,081
Arba (H4)........ 84
Arcadia (E4)........1,073
Arcola (G2)........ 272
Argos (E2)........1,284
Arlington (F5)........ 430
Armstrong (B8)........ 155
Arthur (C8)........ 225
Ashboro (C6)........ 100
Ashley (G1)........ 680
Athens (E2)........ 105
Atlanta (E4)........ 613
Attica (C4)........3,862
Atwood (F2)........ 300
Auburn ◉(G2)........5,879
Augusta (C8)........ 117
Aurora (H6)........4,780
Austin (F7)........2,906
Avilla (G2)........ 669
Avoca (D7)........ 400
Azalia (F6)........ 100
Bainbridge (D5)........ 455
Banquo (F3)........ 105
Bargersville (E5)........ 413
Bass (lake) (D2)......
Batesville (G6)........3,194
Battle Ground (D3) 634
Bear Branch (G7)........ 120
Bedford ◉(E7)......12,562
Beech Grove (E5)....5,685
Bellmore (C5)........ 120
Belshaw (C2)........ 100
Bennetts Switch (E3)........ 120
Benton (F2)........ 225
Berne (H3)........2,277
Bethlehem (G7)........ 200
Beverly Shores (C1) 488
Bicknell (C7)........4,572
Big Blue (riv.) (F5)..
Bippus (F3)........ 200
Birdseye (D8)........ 354
Blackhawk (C6)........ 100
Blanford (B5)........ 750
Blocher (F7)........ 250
Bloomfield ◉(D6)...2,086
Blooming Grove (G5)........ 105
Bloomingdale (C5).. 434
Bloomington ◉ (D6)........28,163
Blountsville (G4)........ 229
Blue (riv.) (E8)........
Blue Ridge (F5)........ 100
Bluffton ◉(G3)......6,076
Boggstown (F5)........ 149
Boone Grove (C2)... 170
Boonville (C8)........5,092
Borden (F8)........ 426
Boston (H5)........ 257
Boswell (C3)........ 963
Bourbon (E2)........1,404
Bowling Green (D6) 235
Boyleston (E4)........ 110
Bradford (E8)........ 119
Brazil ◉(C5)........8,434
Bremen (E2)........2,664
Brems (D2)........ 112
Bridgeport (E5)........ 500
Bridgeton (C5)........ 350
Bright (H6)........ 275
Brighton (G1)........ 100
Brimfield (G2)........ 210
Bringhurst (E3)........ 253
Bristol (F1)........ 738
Bronson (Losantville) (G4) 247
Brook (C3)........ 915
Brooklyn (E5)........ 592
Brooksburg (G7)........ 132
Brookston (D3)........1,014
Brookville ◉(G6)....2,538
Browns Valley (D5) 125

◉ County Seat

Brownsburg (E5).....1,578
Brownstown ◉(F7).1,998
Brownsville (H5)........ 275
Bruceville (C7)........ 800
Brunswick (B2)........ 150
Brushy Prairie (G1). 100
Bryant (G3)........ 339
Buck Creek (D4)........ 279
Buckskin (C8)........ 250
Buffalo (D3)........ 135
Bunker Hill (B7)........ 500
Bunker Hill (E3)........ 659
Burdick (D1)........ 217
Burlington (E4)........ 600
Burnettsville (D3)........ 457
Burney (F6)........ 232
Burns City (D7)........ 242
Burr Oak (E2)........ 120
Burrows (E3)........ 350
Butler (H2)........1,914
Butlerville (F6)........ 306
Cadiz (G5)........ 222
Cagles Mill (res.) (D6)........
Cale (D7)........ 60
Cambridge City (G5)........2,559
Camden (D3)........ 600
Cammack (G4)........ 200
Campbellsburg (E7) 637
Canaan (G7)........ 270
Cannelburg (C7)........ 128
Cannelton ◉(D9).....2,027
Canton (E7)........ 125
Carbon (C5)........ 480
Carlisle (C7)........ 767
Carlos (G4)........ 120
Carmel (E5)........1,009
Cartersburg (E5)........ 260
Carthage (F5)........1,065
Cassville (E3)........ 100
Castleton (E5)........ 268
Cates (C4)........ 150
Cayuga (C5)........1,022
Cedar Grove (H6)........ 193
Cedar Lake (C2)......3,907
Cedarville (G2)........ 220
Celestine (D8)........ 120
Centenary (B5)........ 200
Center (E4)........ 275
Centerpoint (C6)........ 297
Centerton (E5)........ 125
Centerville (H5)........1,386
Chalmers (D3)........ 508
Chambersburg (E7) 200
Chandler (C8)........1,050
Charlestown (F8)......4,785
Charlottesville (F5). 400
Chester (H5)........ 102
Chesterfield (F4).....1,086
Chesterton (D1)........3,175
Chili (F3)........ 115
Chrisney (C8)........ 439
Churubusco (G2)....1,232
Cicero (E4)........1,021
Clarks Hill (D4)........ 493
Clarksburg (G6)........ 325
Clarksville (F5)........ 117
Clarksville (F8)........5,905
Clay City (C6)........1,068
Claypool (F2)........ 416
Clayton (D5)........ 598
Clear Creek (E6)........ 450
Clear Lake (H1)........ 151
Clear Springs (E7)... 205
Clermont (E5)........ 824
Clifford (F6)........ 232
Clifty (F6)........ 175
Clinton (C5)........6,462
Cloverdale (D5)........ 649
Cloverland (C6)........ 150
Clymers (E3)........ 150
Coal Bluff (C5)........ 128
Coal City (D6)........ 300
Coalmont (C6)........ 595
Coatesville (D5)........ 444
Coesse (G2)........ 150
Colburn (D3)........ 234
Colfax (D4)........ 725
Collegeville (C3)........ 600
Columbia City ◉ (G2)........4,745
Columbus ◉(E6)...18,370
Commiskey (F7)........ 100
Connersville ◉ (G5)........15,550
Converse (F3)........ 979
Cook (C2)........ 350
Correct (G7)........ 150
Cortland (F7)........ 102
Corunna (G2)........ 338
Cory (C6)........ 250
Corydon ◉(E8)........1,944
Cosperville (F1)........ 45
Cottage Grove (H5) 100
Covington ◉(C4)....2,235

Cowan (G4)........ 300
Crandall (E8)........ 149
Crane (D7)........2,000
Crawfordsville ◉ (D4)........12,851
Creston (C2)........ 110
Crisman (C1)........ 300
Crocker (C1)........ 150
Cromwell (F2)........ 449
Cross Plains (G7).... 150
Crothersville (F7)....1,276
Crown Point ◉(C2).5,839
Crumstown (E1)........ 200
Culver (E2)........1,563
Cumberland (F5)........ 550
Curtisville (F4)........ 122
Cutler (D4)........ 165
Cynthiana (B8)........ 591
Dale (D8)........ 850
Dana (C5)........ 854
Danville ◉(D5)........2,802
Darlington (D4)........ 711
Dayton (D4)........ 650
Decatur ◉(H3)........7,271
Decker (B7)........ 386
Deedsville (E3)........ 150
Deer Creek (E3)........ 120
Deerfield (H4)........ 100
Delaware (G6)........ 229
Delong (E2)........ 120
Delphi ◉(D3)........2,530
Demotte (C2)........ 700
Denham (D2)........ 150
Denver (E3)........ 528
Depauw (E8)........ 155
Deputy (F7)........ 250
Desoto (G4)........ 205
Dillsboro (G6)........ 681
Disko (E2)........ 150
Dover (H6)........ 100
Dover Hill (D7)........ 150
Dublin (G5)........ 993
Dubois (D8)........ 451
Duchemin (lake) (D1)........
Dugger (C6)........1,204
Dunkirk (G4)........3,048
Dunlap (F1)........1,154
Dunreith (G5)........ 196
Dyer (C1)........1,556
Eagletown (E4)........ 100
Earl Park (C3)........ 488
East Chicago (C1).54,263
East Enterprise (H7) 125
East Gary (C1)........5,635
East Germantown (Pershing) (G5)... 389
Eaton (G4)........1,598
Eckerty (D8)........ 180
Economy (G5)........ 285
Edgerton (H2)........ 112
Edgewood (F4)........ 796
Edinburg (E6)........3,283
Edwardsport (C7)........ 850
Edwardsville (F8)........ 120
Eel (riv.) (C6)........
Eel (riv.) (F3)........
Elberfeld (C8)........ 499
Elizabeth (F8)........ 211
Elizabethtown (F6). 323
Elkhart (F1)........35,556
Elkhart (riv.) (F1)....
Ellettsville (D6)........ 855
Elnora (C7)........ 849
Elwood (F4)........11,362
Eminence (D5)........ 175
English ◉(E8)........ 839
English Lake (D2)... 148
Epsom (C7)........ 125
Etna Green (E2)........ 444
Eugene (B5)........ 350
Evansville ◉(C9).128,636
Fair Oaks (C2)........ 200
Fairland (F5)........ 750
Fairmount (F4)........2,646
Fairview Park (C5). 902
Falmouth (G5)........ 200
Farmersburg (C6)..1,024
Farmland (G4)........ 943
Fawn (riv.) (G1)........
Ferdinand (D8)........1,252
Fillmore (D5)........ 375
Fishers (E5)........ 219
Fishersburg (F4)........ 130
Flat Rock (F6)........ 196
Flint (G1)........ 100
Flora (E3)........1,657
Florence (H7)........
Florida (F4)........ 100
Floyds Knobs (F8).. 455
Foraker (F1)........ 144
Forest (E4)........ 400
Fort Branch (B8).....1,944
Fort Ritner (E7)........ 150
Fort Wayne ◉ (G2)........133,607

Fortville (F5)........1,786
Fountain City (H5). 588
Fountaintown (F5).. 250
Fowler ◉(C3)........2,117
Fowlerton (F4)........ 292
Francesville (D3)........ 856
Francisco (B8)........ 606
Frankfort ◉(E4)....15,028
Franklin ◉(E6)........7,316
Frankton (F4)........1,047
Fredericksburg (E8) 211
Freedom (D6)........ 175
Freelandville (C7)........ 789
Freeman (lake) (D3)
Freetown (E7)........ 500
Fremont (H1)........ 947
French Lick (D7)....1,946
Friendship (G7)........ 130
Friendswood (E5)........ 115
Fritchton (C7)........ 125
Fulda (D8)........ 100
Fulton (E3)........ 366
Galena (F8)........ 207
Galveston (E3)........ 905
Garrett (G2)........4,291
Gary (C1)........133,911
Gas City (F4)........3,787
Gaston (G4)........ 729
Geist (res.) (F5)........
Geneva (H3)........ 999
Gentryville (C8)........ 234
Georgetown (F8)........ 449
Gessie (C4)........ 115
Glendale (C7)........ 150
Glenwood (G5)........ 412
Glezen (C8)........ 400
Goldsmith (E4)........ 242
Goodland (C3)........1,218
Goshen ◉(F1)........13,003
Gosport (D6)........ 672
Grabill (H2)........ 370
Grammer (F6)........ 125
Grand View (C9)........ 664
Granger (E1)........ 160
Grantsburg (E8)........ 90
Grasscreek (E3)........ 105
Graysville (B6)........ 100
Greencastle ◉(D5)..6,888
Greendale (H6)........2,018
Greenfield ◉(F5).....6,159
Greens Fork (H5)........ 413
Greensboro (G5)........ 241
Greensburg ◉(G6)..6,599
Greentown (E4)........1,160
Greenville (F8)........ 298
Greenwood (E5)......3,066
Griffin (B8)........ 249
Griffith (C1)........4,470
Grovertown (D2)........ 200
Guilford (H6)........ 300
Gwynneville (F5)........ 244
Hagerstown (G5).....1,694
Hall (E5)........ 125
Hamilton (H1)........ 376
Hamlet (D2)........ 659
Hammond (B1)......87,594
Hanna (D2)........ 450
Hanover (F7)........1,060
Hardinsburg (E8)........ 247
Harlan (H2)........ 500
Harmony (C5)........ 650
Harrodsburg (D6)........ 400
Hartford City◉(G4)7,253
Hartsville (F6)........ 340
Haubstadt (B8)........ 894
Hayden (F7)........ 200
Haysville (D8)........ 352
Hazleton (B8)........ 498
Hebron (C2)........1,010
Heilman (C8)........ 100
Helmer (G1)........ 110
Helmsburg (E6)........ 150
Heltonville (E7)........ 500
Hemlock (F4)........ 177
Herbst (F3)........ 250
Hibbard (E2)........ 100
Highland (B1)........5,878
Hillisburg (E4)........ 225
Hillsboro (C4)........ 526
Hillsdale (C5)........ 250
Hoagland (H3)........ 375
Hobart (C1)........10,244
Hobbieville (D6)........ 125
Hobbs (F4)........ 185
Holland (C8)........ 501
Holton (G6)........ 400
Home Corner (Vet's Adm. Hosp.) (F3) 3,950
Homer (F5)........ 150
Honey Creek (F4).. 125
Hope (F6)........1,215
Hortonville (E4)........ 125
Howe (G1)........ 576
Hudson (G1)........ 420
Hudsonville (C7)........ 76
Huntertown (G2)........ 500

Huntingburg (D8)...4,056
Huntington ◉(G3).15,079
Huntsville (F4)........ 265
Hymera (C6)........1,069
Idaville (D3)........ 500
Independence (C4).. 200
Indian Spgs. (D7).... 115
INDIANAPOLIS (E5)........427,173
Ingalls (F5)........ 666
Inglefield (B8)........ 100
Inwood (E2)........ 178
Ireland (C8)........ 325
Iroquois (riv.) (B3).
Jalapa (F3)........ 150
Jamestown (D5)........ 718
Jasonville (C6)........2,937
Jasper ◉(D8)........5,215
Jeffersonville ◉ (F8)........14,685
Jimtown (E1)........ 200
Johnson (B8)........ 250
Jolietville (E4)........ 125
Jonesboro (F4)........1,973
Jonesville (F6)........ 225
Kankakee (riv.) (C2)
Kempton (E4)........ 438
Kendallville (G2).....6,119
Kennard (G5)........ 485
Kent (F7)........ 123
Kentland ◉(C3)......1,633
Kersey (C2)........ 100
Kewanna (E2)........ 680
Keystone (G3)........ 225
Kimmell (F2)........ 300
Kingman (C5)........ 509
Kingsbury (D1)........ 281
Kingsford Hts. (D2) 1,104
Kirklin (E4)........ 734
Knightstown (F5)....2,486
Knightsville (C5)........ 678
Kniman (C2)........ 150
Knox ◉(D2)........3,034
Kokomo ◉(E4).....38,672
Koontz Lake (D2)..1,200
Kouts (C2)........ 718
Kurtz (E7)........ 225
La Crosse (D2)........ 618
La Fontaine (F3)........ 627
La Porte ◉(D1)......20,414
Ladoga (D5)........ 912
Lafayette ◉(D4)....35,568
Lagrange ◉(F1)......1,892
Lagro (F3)........ 545
Lake Bruce (E2)........ 100
Lake Cicott (D3)........ 128
Lakeland (D1)........2,172
Lakeville (E1)........ 736
Landess (F3)........ 135
Lanesville (E8)........ 314
Laotto (G2)........ 264
Lapaz (E2)........ 512
Lapel (F4)........1,389
Larwill (F2)........ 316
Laurel (G6)........ 680
Lawrence (E5)........1,951
Lawrenceburg ◉ (H6)........4,806
Lawrenceport (D7).. 125
Leavenworth (E8)........ 358
Lebanon ◉(D4)........7,631
Leesburg (F2)........ 428
Leipsic (E7)........ 150
Leiters Ford (E2)........ 250
Leo (G2)........ 385
Leopold (D8)........ 101
Leroy (C2)........ 350
Letts (F6)........ 208
Lewis (C6)........ 600
Lewisville (G5)........ 591
Lexington (F7)........ 350
Liberty ◉(H5)........1,730
Liberty Center (G3) 300
Liberty Mills (F2)........ 200
Ligonier (F2)........2,375
Lincoln (E3)........ 130
Lincolnville (F3)........ 200
Linden (D4)........ 590
Linton (C6)........5,973
Little (riv.) (G3)........
Little Elkhart (riv.) (F1)........
Little Vermilion (riv.) (B5)........
Little York (F7)........ 146
Livonia (E7)........ 185
Lizton (D5)........ 276
Logan (H6)........ 125
Logansport ◉(E3).21,031
London (F5)........ 135
Long Beach (D1)....1,103
Loogootee (D7)......2,424
Losantville (G4)........ 247
Lost (riv.) (D7)........
Lowell (C2)........1,621
Lucerne (E3)........ 200

INDIANA

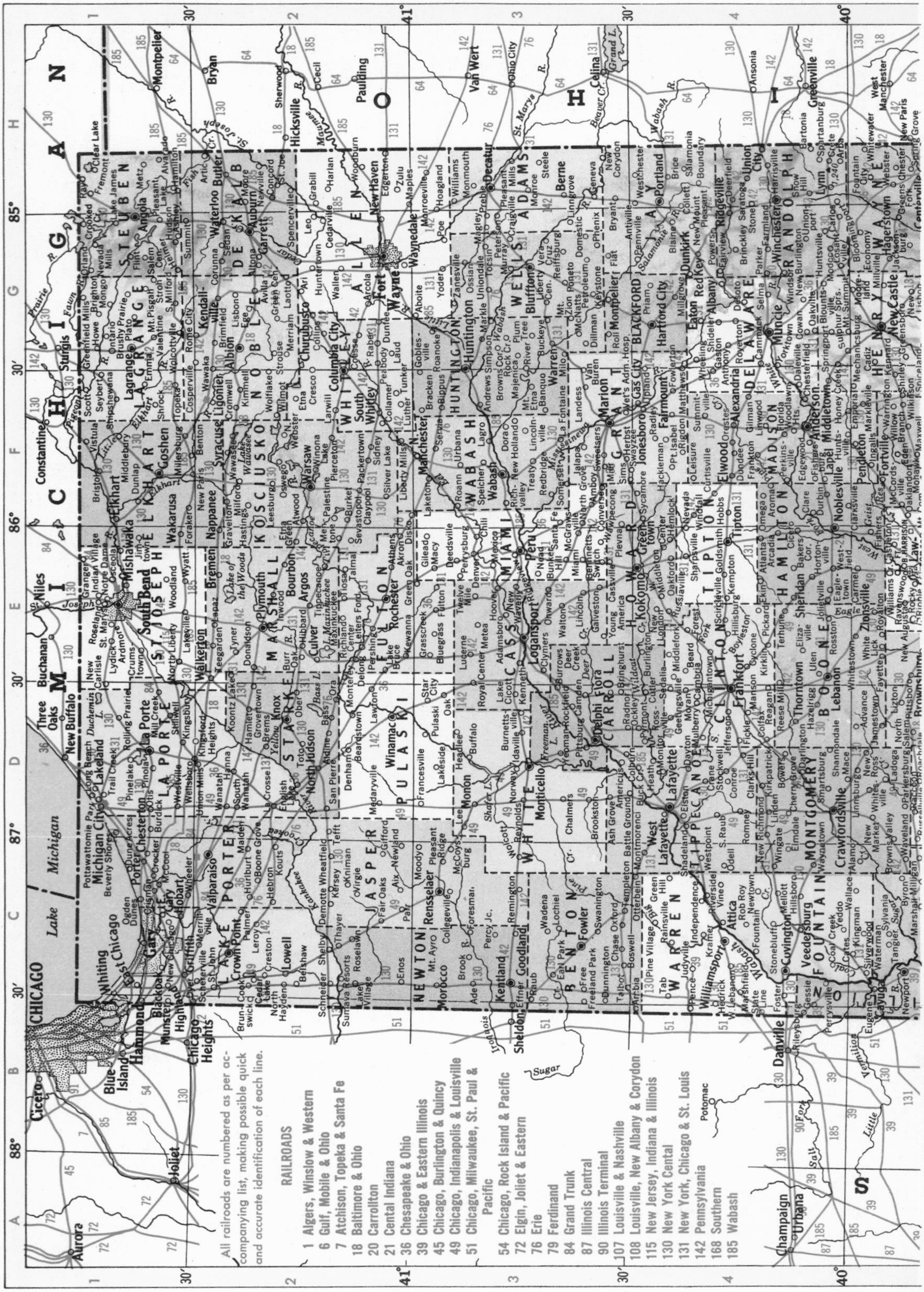
All railroads are numbered as per accompanying list, making possible quick and accurate identification of each line.
RAILROADS
1 Algers, Winslow & Western
6 Gulf, Mobile & Ohio
7 Atchison, Topeka & Santa Fe
18 Baltimore & Ohio
20 Carrollton
21 Cental Indiana
36 Chesapeake & Ohio
39 Chicago & Eastern Illinois
45 Chicago, Burlington & Quincy
49 Chicago, Indianapolis & Louisville
51 Chicago, Milwaukee, St. Paul & Pacific
54 Chicago, Rock Island & Pacific
72 Elgin, Joliet & Eastern
76 Erie
79 Ferdinand
84 Grand Trunk
87 Illinois Central
90 Illinois Terminal
107 Louisville & Nashville
108 Louisville, New Albany & Corydon
115 New Jersey, Indiana & Illinois
130 New York Central
131 New York, Chicago & St. Louis
142 Pennsylvania
168 Southern
185 Wabash

INDIANA

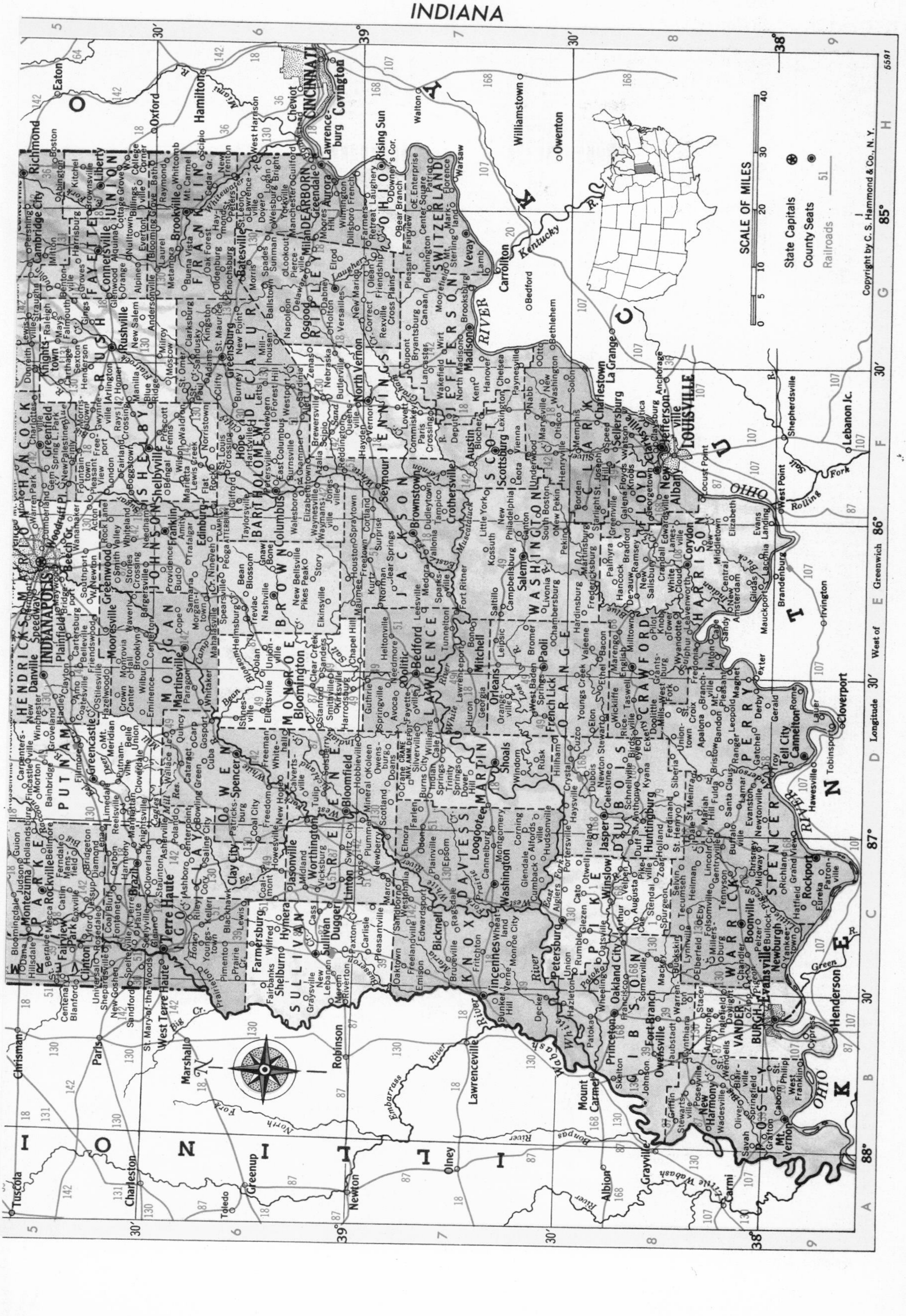

SCALE OF MILES
0 5 10 20 30 40
State Capitals
County Seats
Railroads
Copyright by C. S. Hammond & Co., N. Y.
5591
Longitude West of Greenwich
INDIANAPOLIS
LOUISVILLE
CINCINNATI
OHIO
KENTUCKY
ILLINOIS

INDIANA (Continued) — 1950 Total Population 3,934,224

Lydick (E1) 1,175
Lyford (C5) 368
Lynn (H4) 1,149
Lynnville (C8) 404
Lyons (C7) 695
Mackey (C8) 170
Macy (E3) 288
Madison ◉(G7) 7,506
Manilla (F5) 400
Maples (H2) 110
Marco (C7) 195
Marengo (E8) 801
Mariah Hill (D8)
Marietta (F6) 150
Marion ◉(F3) 30,081
Markland (G7) 200
Markle (G3) 733
Markleville (F5) 314
Marshall (C5) 326
Martinsburg (E8) 125
Martinsville ◉(D6) 5,991
Matthews (F4) 501
Mauckport (E8) 154
Maumee (riv.) (H2)
Maxinkuckee (lake) (E2)
Maxwell (F5) 285
Mays (G5) 200
Maywood (E5) 525
Mc Cool (C1) 250
Mc Cordsville (F5) 375
Mechanicsburg (G5) 250
Medaryville (D2) 833
Medora (E7) 627
Mellott (C4) 266
Memphis (F8) 380
Mentone (E2) 798
Merom (B6) 374
Merriam (G2) 110
Merrillville (C2) 1,400
Metamora (G6) 400
Metz (H1) 175
Mexico (E3) 521
Michigan (lake) (C1)
Michigan City (C1) 28,395
Michigantown (E4) 443
Middlebury (F1) 839
Middletown (F4) 1,731
Milan (G6) 1,014
Milford (F2) 952
Milford (Clifty) (F6) 175
Mill Creek (D1) 162
Millersburg (F1) 437
Millgrove (G4) 160
Millhousen (G6) 184
Milligan (C5) 100
Milltown (E8) 760
Millville (G5) 120
Milroy (G6) 800
Milton (G5) 752
Mishawaka (E1) 32,913
Mississinewa (riv.) (F3)
Mitchell (E7) 3,245
Modoc (G4) 275
Mohawk (F5) 150
Mongo (G1) 225
Monon (D3) 1,439
Monroe (H3) 428
Monroe City (C7) 453
Monroeville (H3) 1,150
Monrovia (E5) 375
Monterey (D2) 250
Montezuma (C5) 1,220
Montgomery (C7) 538
Monticello ◉(D3) 3,467
Montmorenci (D4) 235
Montpelier (G3) 1,826
Mooreland (G5) 497
Moores Hill (G6) 445
Mooresville (E5) 2,264
Moran (D4) 140
Morgantown (E6) 838
Morocco (C3) 1,141
Morris (G6) 500
Morristown (F5) 679
Mt. Ayr (C3) 222
Mt. Carmel (H6) 134
Mt. Comfort (F5) 115
Mt. Etna (F3) 171
Mt. Summit (G4) 295
Mt. Vernon ◉(B9) 6,150
Mulberry (D4) 950
Muncie ◉(G4) 58,479
Munster (B1) 4,753
Muscatatuck (riv.) (E7)
Nabb (F7) 110
Napoleon (G6) 350
Nappanee (F2) 3,393
Nashville ◉(E6) 526
Nebraska (F6) 104
Needham (E5) 110
Needmore (E7) 150
New Albany ◉(F8) 29,436
New Augusta (E5) 225

◉ County Seat

New Carlisle (E1) 983
New Castle ◉(G5) 18,271
New Chicago (C1) 921
New Corydon (H3) 105
New Goshen (B5) 600
New Harmony (B8) 1,360
New Haven (H2) 2,336
New Lebanon (C6) 125
New Lisbon (G5) 290
New London (E4) 210
New Marion (G6) 150
New Market (D5) 370
New Middletown (E8) 153
New Mount Pleasant (G4) 100
New Palestine (F5) 504
New Paris (F2) 985
New Pekin (F7) 543
New Point (G6) 322
New Providence (Borden) (F8) 426
New Richmond (D4) 391
New Ross (D5) 336
New Salem (G5) 206
New Salisbury (E8) 215
New Trenton (H6) 150
New Washington (F7) 750
New Waverly (E3) 190
Newberry (C7) 340
Newburgh (C9) 1,324
Newport ◉(C5) 660
Newtonville (D8) 123
Newtown (C4) 287
Nineveh (E6) 300
Noblesville ◉(F4) 6,567
Norman (E7) 110
N. Grove (F3) 126
N. Hayden (B2) 150
N. Judson (D2) 1,705
N. Liberty (E1) 1,165
N. Madison (G7) 715
N. Manchester (F3) 3,977
N. Salem (D5) 544
N. Vernon (F6) 3,488
N. Webster (F2) 487
Notre Dame (E1) 5,000
Oak (D3) 150
Oak Forest (G6) 120
Oakford (E4) 230
Oakland City (C8) 3,539
Oaklandon (E5) 346
Oaktown (C7) 763
Oakville (G4) 224
Oatsville (C8) 100
Ober (D2) 100
Ockley (D4) 140
Odell (C4) 210
Odon (C7) 1,177
Ogden Dunes (C1) 429
Ohio (riv.) (B9)
Oldenburg (G6) 591
Olean (G7) 225
Ontario (G1) 150
Onward (E3) 140
Oolitic (E7) 1,125
Ora (D2) 140
Orange (G5) 200
Orestes (F4) 482
Orland (G1) 386
Orleans (D7) 1,531
Osceola (E1) 1,091
Osgood (G6) 1,228
Ossian (G3) 761
Otisco (F7) 250
Otterbein (C4) 641
Otwell (C8) 400
Owensburg (D7) 400
Owensville (B8) 1,110
Oxford (C3) 888
Palmer (C2) 200
Palmyra (E8) 327
Paoli ◉(E7) 2,575
Paragon (D6) 463
Paris Crossing (F7) 132
Parker (G4) 915
Parkersburg (D5) 100
Parr (C2) 132
Patoka (B8) 626
Patoka (riv.) (C8)
Patricksburg (D6) 450
Patriot (H7) 315
Paxton (C6) 275
Pekin (E7) 553
Pence (C4) 122
Pendleton (F5) 2,082
Pennville (G4) 626
Perkinsville (F4) 250
Perrysville (C4) 462
Pershing (G5) 389
Peru ◉(E3) 13,308
Petersburg ◉(C7) 3,035
Pierceton (F2) 973
Pilot Knob (E8) 200
Pimento (C6) 125
Pine Village (C4) 311

Pinelake (D1) 250
Pittsboro (D5) 599
Pittsburg (D3) 350
Plainfield (E5) 2,585
Plainville (C7) 568
Pleasant Lake (H1) 500
Pleasant Mills (H3) 175
Pleasantville (C7) 200
Plymouth ◉(E2) 6,704
Poe (G3) 80
Poland (C6) 150
Poneto (G3) 244
Porter (C1) 1,458
Portland ◉(H4) 7,064
Poseyville (B8) 1,005
Prairie Creek (C6) 225
Preble (H3) 150
Princeton ◉(B8) 7,673
Providence (E6) 100
Pulaski (D3) 100
Putnamville (D5) 165
Pyrmont (D4) 100
Quincy (D6) 320
Radley (F4) 150
Radnor (D3) 110
Ragsdale (C7) 230
Rainsville (C4) 130
Raleigh (G5) 150
Ramsey (E8) 106
Raub (C3) 110
Ravenswood (E5) 498
Ray (H1) 175
Red Key (G4) 1,639
Reddington (F6) 220
Reese Mill (D4) 130
Remington (C3) 1,053
Rensselaer ◉(C3) 4,072
Reynolds (D3) 499
Richland (C9) 530
Richmond ◉(H5) 39,539
Richvalley (F3) 111
Ridgeville (G4) 950
Riley (C6) 251
Rising Sun ◉(H7) 1,930
Riverside (C4) 120
Roachdale (D5) 918
Roann (F3) 492
Roanoke (G3) 905
Rochester ◉(E2) 4,673
Rockfield (D3) 325
Rockport ◉(C9) 2,493
Rockville ◉(C5) 2,467
Rocky Ripple (E5) 528
Roll (G3) 150
Rolling Prairie (D1) 625
Rome City (G1) 1,303
Romney (D4) 500
Rosedale (C5) 673
Roseland (E1) 984
Rossville (D4) 739
Royal Center (E3) 876
Royerton (G4) 400
Rushville ◉(G5) 6,761
Russellville (D5) 361
Russiaville (E4) 1,025
St. Anthony (D8) 152
St. Bernice (C5) 1,200
St. Croix (D8) 100
St. Henry (D8) 183
St. Joe (H2) 479
St. John (C2) 684
St. Joseph (riv.) (E1)
St. Joseph (riv.) (H2)
St. Joseph Hill (F8) 200
St. Leon (H6) 288
St. Louis Crossing (F6) 150
St. Mary-of-the-Woods (B6) 1,300
St. Marys (riv.) (H3)
St. Meinrad (D8) 720
St. Paul (F6) 669
St. Peters (H6) 130
St. Philip (B9) 200
Salamonia (H4) 181
Salamonie (riv.) (G4)
Salem ◉(E7) 3,271
Saline City (C6) 115
Salt (riv.) (E6)
Saltillo (E7) 122
San Pierre (D2) 350
Sand (creek) (F6)
Sandborn (C7) 572
Sanders (E6) 200
Sandford (B5) 195
Sandusky (G6) 200
Saratoga (H4) 333
Sardinia (F6) 150
Savah (B8) 100
Schererville (C2) 1,457
Schneider (C2) 356
Schnellville (D8) 300
Scipio (F6) 200
Scircleville (E4) 181
Scott (F1) 100
Scottsburg ◉(F7) 2,953

Sedalia (E4) 180
Seelyville (C6) 898
Sellersburg (F8) 1,664
Selma (G4) 499
Servia (F3) 143
Sexton (G5) 80
Seymour (F7) 9,629
Shadeland (C4) 78
Shafer (lake) (D3)
Sharpsville (E4) 508
Shelburn (C6) 1,412
Shelby (C2) 519
Shelbyville ◉(F6) 11,734
Shepardsville (B5) 300
Sheridan (E4) 1,965
Shipshewana (F1) 277
Shirley (F5) 1,087
Shoals ◉(D7) 1,039
Sidney (F2) 168
Silver Lake (F2) 472
Sims (F3) 231
Smith Valley (E5) 150
Smithville (D6) 425
Solon (F7) 137
Solsberry (D6) 500
Somerset (F3) 255
Somerville (C8) 353
S. Bend ◉(E1) 115,911
S. Boston (F7) 125
S. Milford (G1) 350
S. Whitley (F2) 1,299
Southport (E5) 730
Sparksville (E7) 136
Spartanburg (H4) 200
Speed (F8) 1,000
Speedway (E5) 5,498
Spelterville (C5) 150
Spencer ◉(D6) 2,394
Spencerville (G2) 450
Spiceland (F5) 739
Spraytown (E6) 63
Spring Grove (H5) 333
Spring Lake Park (F5) 156
Springport (G4) 217
Springville (D7) 500
Spurgeon (C8) 327
Stanford (D6) 100
Star City (D3) 600
State Line (C4) 152
Staunton (C6) 487
Stendal (C8) 175
Stewartsville (B8) 240
Stilesville (D5) 330
Stinesville (D6) 355
Stockwell (D4) 632
Stonebluff (C4) 172
Straughn (G5) 345
Stroh (G1) 475
Sullivan ◉(C6) 5,423
Sulphur Spgs. (G4) 351
Sumava Resorts (C2) 125
Summitville (F4) 1,061
Sunman (G6) 358
Swanington (C3) 125
Swayzee (F4) 690
Sweetsers (F3) 535
Switz City (C6) 328
Syracuse (F2) 1,453
Talma (E2) 150
Tampico (F7) 150
Tangier (C5) 100
Taswell (D8) 110
Taylorsville (F6) 290
Tefft (D2) 140
Tell City (D9) 5,735
Templeton (C3) 143
Tennyson (C8) 409
Terhune (E4) 100
Terre Haute ◉(C6) 64,214
Thayer (C2) 250
Thorntown (D4) 1,380
Tiosa (E2) 125
Tippecanoe (E2) 400
Tippecanoe (riv.) (E2)
Tipton ◉(E4) 5,633
Tobinsport (D9) 205
Tocsin (G3) 175
Topeka (F1) 557
Toto (D2) 275
Trafalgar (E6) 439
Trail Creek (D1) 817
Treaty (F3) 90
Trinity Spgs. (D7) 150
Troy (D9) 537
Tunnelton (E7) 300
Twelve Mile (E3) 247
Tyner (E2) 250
Ulen (E4) 83
Underwood (F7) 328
Union (C8) 209
Union City (H4) 3,572
Union Mills (D2) 450
Uniondale (G3) 293

Unionville (E6) 475
Universal (C5) 479
Upland (F4) 1,565
Urbana (F3) 400
Utica (F8) 250
Valentine (G1) 110
Vallonia (E7) 510
Valparaiso ◉(C2) 12,028
Van Buren (F3) 815
Veedersburg (C4) 1,719
Velpen (C8) 197
Vera Cruz (G3) 143
Vernon ◉(F7) 480
Versailles ◉(G6) 886
Veterans Adm. Hospital (F3) 3,950
Vevay ◉(G7) 1,309
Vicksburg (C6) 390
Vincennes ◉(C7) 18,831
Vistula (F1) 100
Wabash ◉(F3) 10,621
Wabash (riv.) (B7)
Wakarusa (F1) 1,143
Waldron (F6) 700
Walkerton (E2) 2,102
Wallace (C5) 123
Wallen (G2) 120
Walton (E3) 837
Wanamaker (E5) 325
Wanatah (D2) 750
Warren (G3) 1,247
Warren Park (F5) 336
Warrenton (B8) 100
Warsaw ◉(F2) 6,625
Washington ◉(C7) 10,987
Waterloo (G2) 1,414
Watson (F8) 200
Waveland (D5) 553
Waverly (E5) 150
Wawaka (F2) 300
Wawasee (F2) 400
Wawasee (lake) (F2)
Waymansville (E6) 250
Waynetown (C4) 658
Webster (H5) 175
Weisburg (H6) 148
Wellsboro (D1) 170
West Baden Spgs. (D7) 1,047
W. College Corner (H5) 513
W. Harrison (H6) 308
W. Lafayette (D4) 11,873
W. Lebanon (C4) 642
W. Middleton (E4) 250
W. Terre Haute (B6) 3,357
Westfield (E4) 849
Westphalia (C7) 250
Westpoint (C4) 315
Westport (F6) 658
Westville (D1) 624
Wheatfield (C2) 496
Wheatland (C7) 735
Wheeler (C1) 400
Whitcomb (H6) 150
White (riv.) (B8)
White Pigeon (riv.) (G1)
Whiteland (E5) 465
Whitestown (E5) 550
Whitewater (H5) 104
Whitewater (riv.) (H6)
Whiting (C1) 9,669
Wilkinson (F5) 365
Williams (D7) 400
Williams Creek (E5) 288
Williamsport ◉(C4) 1,241
Wilmington (H6) 200
Wilmot (F2) 100
Winamac ◉(D2) 2,166
Winchester ◉(G4) 5,467
Windfall (F4) 963
Wingate (C4) 400
Winona Lake (F2) 1,366
Winslow (C8) 1,322
Wolcott (C3) 778
Wolcottville (G1) 672
Wolflake (F2) 250
Woodburn (H2) 540
Woodland (E1) 115
Woodruff Pl. (E5) 1,557
Woods (lake) (E2)
Worthington (C6) 1,627
Wyatt (E1) 250
Yankeetown (C9) 323
Yeddo (C4) 115
Yellow (riv.) (D2)
Yeoman (D3) 180
Yoder (G3) 200
Yorktown (G4) 1,109
Young America (E3) 250
Zanesville (G3) 300
Zionsville (E5) 1,536
Zulu (H2) 175

General Assembly, which may override that veto by a majority vote of both houses. A list of Indiana's governors follows.

Territorial

William H. Harrison		1800–1812
John Gibson		1812–1813
Thomas Posey		1813–1816

State

Jonathan Jennings	Democratic Republican	1816–1822
Ratliff Boon,	Democratic Republican (acting)	1822
William Hendricks	Democratic Republican	1822–1825
James B. Ray	Democratic Republican	1825–1831
Noah Noble	Whig	1831–1837
David Wallace	Whig	1837–1840
Samuel Bigger	Whig	1840–1843
James Whitcomb	Democrat	1843–1848
Paris C. Dunning	Democrat (acting)	1848–1849
Joseph A. Wright	Democrat	1849–1857
Ashbel P. Willard	Democrat	1857–1860
Abram A. Hammond	Democrat (acting)	1860–1861
Henry S. Lane	Republican	1861
Oliver P. Morton	Republican	1861–1867
Conrad Baker	Republican	1867–1873
Thomas A. Hendricks	Democrat	1873–1877
James D. Williams	Democrat	1877–1880
Isaac P. Gray	Democrat (acting)	1880–1881
Albert G. Porter	Republican	1881–1885
Isaac P. Gray	Democrat	1885–1889
Alvin P. Hovey	Republican	1889–1891
Ira J. Chase	Republican (acting)	1891–1893
Claude Matthews	Democrat	1893–1897
James A. Mount	Republican	1897–1901
Winfield T. Durbin	Republican	1901–1905
J. Frank Hanly	Republican	1905–1909
Thomas R. Marshall	Democrat	1909–1913
Samuel M. Ralston	Democrat	1913–1917
James P. Goodrich	Republican	1917–1921
Warren T. McCray	Republican	1921–1924
Emmett F. Branch	Republican (acting)	1924–1925
Ed Jackson	Republican	1925–1929
Harry G. Leslie	Republican	1929–1933
Paul V. McNutt	Democrat	1933–1937
M. Clifford Townsend	Democrat	1937–1941
Henry F. Schricker	Democrat	1941–1945
Ralph F. Gates	Republican	1945–1949
Henry F. Schricker	Democrat	1949–1953
George N. Craig	Republican	1953–

Legislature.—The Indiana General Assembly, which meets in regular session in odd-numbered years, consists of a Senate of 50 members elected for four-year terms, half of them every two years, and a House of Representatives of 100 members elected biennially. The length of regular sessions is limited to a maximum of 61 days. Special sessions called by the governor are limited to 40 days each.

Courts.—The highest court in the state is the supreme court, created by the constitution together with the circuit courts and justice of the peace courts. The five justices of the supreme court are elected on party tickets for six-year terms. The appellate court, created by the 1891 General Assembly to assist the supreme court, consists of six judges elected on party tickets for four-year terms. By legislative enactment, the state is divided into 82 judicial circuits, each with a circuit judge elected for six years with jurisdiction over civil and criminal cases. Ten of the circuits have two counties each; the remainder, one county each. Each judicial circuit elects a prosecuting attorney for a two-year term to handle criminal cases. Additional courts, created by the General Assembly to assist the circuit courts in the more populous counties, include superior courts in 14 counties; probate courts in Marion, St. Joseph, and Vanderburgh counties; criminal and juvenile courts in Marion and Lake counties; and a four-room municipal court in Marion county.

Suffrage and Elections.—General elections are held in November of each even-numbered year. Party primaries at which all officials except United States senators and elected state officials are nominated are held in May of the election year. Nominees for United States senator and the elective state offices are chosen at party conventions in May or June following the primaries. (There are no presidential preference primaries in Indiana.) Any citizen, 21 years of age or over, resident in the state for six months, in the county and township for 60 days, and in the district for 30 days, may vote in Indiana. Registration is permanent, and absentee voting is permitted. Both Australian paper ballots and voting machines are in use.

Local Government.—County constitutional officers are the clerk of the circuit court, auditor, and recorder, each elected for 4-year terms and limited to service of 8 years in any period of 12 years; and the treasurer, sheriff, coroner, and surveyor, each elected for 2 years, with the first two limited to service of 4 years in any period of 6 years. Other county officers are the board of county commissioners, composed of three members elected by districts and entrusted with control of county property; and a seven-man county council which passes on the county budget, sets the county tax rate, and authorizes county appropriations and bond issues. The county assessor, elected for a 4-year term, supervises the assessment of property for tax purposes. Each township has a trustee, elected for 4 years and limited to 8 years' service in any period of 12 years, who has jurisdiction over the public schools in his district. The township trustee sets the township budget, which must be approved by a township advisory board of three members elected for 4-year terms. Members of this advisory board, who must be resident property owners and voters, also set the township tax rate, approve contracts, and authorize bond issues.

The mayor-council form of city government is followed by all Indiana cities. The mayor and other administrative officers, councilmen, and the city judge are elected for 4-year terms.

Health and Welfare.—Between 1940 and 1947 mortality rates in Indiana decreased substantially. The crude death rate declined from 11.8 to 10.6 per 1,000 population. The maternal mortality rate of 2.9 deaths for every 1,000 live births in 1940 dropped to 1.2 deaths in 1947, a percentage decrease of 58.6. In the same period infant mortality rate fell from 41.9 deaths per 1,000 live births to 30.3, a decrease of 27.7 per cent. Tuberculosis deaths dropped from 40.2 to 29.4, and childhood communicable diseases (measles, scarlet fever, diphtheria, and whooping cough) from 4.6 to 2.4, per 100,000 population. The 1945 and 1947 sessions of the General Assembly passed several important public health acts. One reorganized the state board of health, clarified its responsibilities, and strengthened its power to promulgate rules and regulations necessary for the protection of public health. The board names the state health commissioner, who is the chief administrative official. Legislation also provided that a county and second-class cities within that county might combine to establish a full-time city-county health department, and that two to four adjoining counties might set up a combined, full-time health department. Under a decentralization program, the board of health operates five branch offices—in Valparaiso, Fort Wayne, Columbus, Washington, and Terre Haute.

One of the greatest forward steps in public health was the creation by the 1945 General Assembly of the Indiana Council for Mental Health. This council, with powers further strengthened by the 1947 General Assembly, supervises the various state institutions caring for the mentally ill. The council has authority to prescribe methods of psychiatric treatment, to set up standards of training for professional and nonprofessional hospital employees, and to organize mental hygiene clinics. Medical and psychiatric care take precedence over custodial care. The state institutions under the jurisdiction of the council are the Central State Hospital, Indianapolis; Logansport State Hospital, Logansport; Richmond State Hospital, Richmond; Evansville State Hospital, Evansville; and Madison State Hospital, Madison. all for the care of the mentally ill; the Fort Wayne State School in Fort Wayne and the Muscatatuck Colony at Butlerville, for the care and training of the feeble-minded; and the Indiana Village for Epileptics at New Castle.

Indiana's first statewide public welfare system was inaugurated in 1889, when the General Assembly established the Board of State Charities and Corrections and gave it broad powers of supervision and investigation. A 1936 special session of the General Assembly enacted the present welfare act and established a state program of public welfare conducted in cooperation with the federal Social Security Administration. Under this act the state Department of Public Welfare is responsible for the administration of assistance to aged and blind persons, aid to dependent children, eye treatment, and services for crippled children; the licensing and supervision of all children's institutions, child-placing agencies, nurseries, and boarding homes for children; the supervision of dependent and neglected children in foster homes and institutions; the supervision of parolees from the state's adult penal and correctional institutions; the inspection of county homes and county jails; and the licensing of nursing homes.

Administration of the public welfare program in Indiana rests with the state Board of Public Welfare, consisting of five members appointed by the governor. The administrator of the state Department of Public Welfare is also appointed by the governor. Under the welfare act, federal, state, and county governments cooperate in administering public welfare. A public welfare department in each county administers the program under the supervision of the state department.

Penal and correctional institutions for adult offenders are the Indiana State Prison and Indiana Hospital for the Criminally Insane, Michigan City; Indiana Reformatory, Pendleton; Indiana State Farm, Putnamville; and the Indiana Woman's Prison, Indianapolis. Institutions for juvenile offenders are the Indiana Girls' School, Clermont, and the Indiana Boys' School, Plainfield. Other state institutions are the Indiana State Sanatorium at Rockville and the Southern Indiana Tuberculosis Hospital at New Albany, for the care and treatment of tubercular patients; the Indiana State School for the Deaf and the Indiana School for the Blind, both at Indianapolis; the State Soldiers' Home, Lafayette; and the Soldiers' and Sailors' Children's Home, Knightstown.

Education.—Education has long occupied a prominent place in the thoughts and plans of Hoosiers. The Ordinance of 1787 creating the Northwest Territory stipulated that since religion, morality, and knowledge are "necessary to good government and the happiness of mankind, schools and the means of education shall forever be encouraged." The first state constitution (1816) further set forth that "it shall be the duty of the General Assembly, as soon as circumstances will permit, to provide by law for a general system of education, ascending in regular gradations from the township schools to State University, wherein tuition shall be gratis and equally open to all." The educational system envisioned under this farseeing provision was not, however, to be established for many years. The primary efforts of the first settlers were devoted to clearing forests, draining swamps, building log homes, and cutting roads.

Although a permissive educational system was established by the General Assembly, there was no efficient organization, and by the middle of the 19th century increasing numbers of people in the state began to realize that educational facilities had to be improved. The foundations of the present school system were laid by the constitution of 1851, which provided for a state superintendent of public instruction, and the General School Act of 1852, which established a state Board of Education and set forth an educational program. The successful fight for tax-supported schools "free and open" to all was led by Caleb Mills, Wabash College professor and president.

The duties of the state Department of Public Instruction include the administration of public elementary and secondary schools, school relief and inspection, teacher training and licensing, vocational education and rehabilitation, and school health and attendance. Public education expenditures in the 1951–1952 school year totaled $116,250,000, of which $51,144,000 was for higher institutions. The General Assembly in 1947 established new minimum levels for teachers' salaries, based on $2,400 for beginning teachers with four years of college training. By 1952–1953, salaries of Indiana's public school teachers had reached a $3,500 average. State aid annually provided to local school districts surpassed the $60 million level by 1952. Estimated enrollment in public elementary and secondary schools for 1952–1953 was 735,000 pupils, with about 25,000 classroom teachers.

Qualifications for Indiana teachers and school administrators include four years of college for a state teaching license, five years of college and five years of teaching experience for a life teaching license, and six years of college and five years of experience as an administrator or teacher for a city or county superintendent's license. Since 1897, Indiana has had a compulsory attendance law, with attendance through the 15th year now required. Indiana ranks high among the states in the number of township-consolidated schools in rural areas.

Indiana has four state-supported institutions of higher learning: Indiana University, Bloomington, with medical divisions and a law branch at Indianapolis and with centers scattered throughout the state; Purdue University, Lafayette; Indiana State Teachers College, Terre Haute; and Ball State Teachers College, Muncie. Funds expended for their operation and maintenance in the 1951–1952 fiscal year totaled $51,144,000. There are some two dozen other colleges and universities, in addition to numerous theological, art, and technical schools, and junior colleges. Enrollment in the autumn of 1953 totaled 59,459. Indiana University led in full-time enrollment (24,829 students), followed by Purdue University (11,014); Butler University, Indianapolis (5,648); the University of Notre Dame, South Bend (5,180); and Ball State (4,745).

Free public libraries in Indiana were instituted as part of the public school system adopted in 1852. By 1950, there were 240 public library systems serving 2,978,739 persons, as compared with 2,591,211 served in 1940. In 234 systems serving 2,945,180 persons in 1950, there were 928,474 registered borrowers, including 309,581 juveniles. The percentage of borrowers constituted over 31 per cent of the library-served population. Annual circulation totaled 15,821,188 in 237 systems, compared with 14,862,240 in 1946. The state's leading museum is the John Herron Art Institute in Indianapolis.

History.—In common with other regions throughout the Ohio and Mississippi valleys, the territory which now comprises the State of Indiana was once occupied by a prehistoric Indian people popularly called Mound Builders (q.v.). Their earthen forts and embankments, mounds, and village sites dating back to pre-Columbian times are found in about one third of Indiana's 92 counties. The most important of the Indian tribes in historic times was the Miami.

Indiana's recorded history began in the 17th century, when René Robert Cavelier, Sieur de La Salle (q.v.), became the first white man to explore the region. Following one of the two principal routes by which the early French explorers traveled from the Great Lakes to the Mississippi River, La Salle and a party of 28 men camped one night in December 1679 on the south bend of the St. Joseph River, en route from Lake Michigan to the Kankakee and Illinois rivers. La Salle returned to this area in the spring of 1681 and, as part of his plan to build a series of French forts from Lake Ontario to the mouth of the Mississippi for the protection of the western Indians and the fur trade against the Iroquois tribes, held conferences with the Miami and Illinois Indians under a great tree, later known as the Council Oak, at what is now South Bend. La Salle influenced the Indians to move into Illinois, but early in the 18th century the tribes began to return to Indiana, settling on the Maumee, Wabash, and White rivers. During that century Shawnee, Miami, Delaware, Potawatomi, Kickapoo, and other Indians roved the trackless wilds of Indiana.

In the first third of the 18th century the French established three forts and trading posts in the area. Fort Miami was erected at what is now Fort Wayne, and Fort Ouiatenon was built about 1720 on the Wabash River near the site of La Fayette. The most important and only permanent one of the three posts, however, was that established in 1731 or 1732 at Vincennes by François Marie Bissot, Sieur de Vincennes (q.v.), in whose honor it was named.

Relatively few French colonists had settled in Indiana by 1763, when the Treaty of Paris ended the French and Indian War with the cession to Great Britain of all lands east of the Mississippi. British soldiers were sent to garrison western posts, and the Indiana region came under jurisdiction of Henry Hamilton, the governor at Detroit.

Foreseeing the importance of the Old Northwest to the American cause in the Revolutionary War, George Rogers Clark (q.v.), with financial backing from Governor Patrick Henry of Virginia, recruited a small army which in the summer of 1778 captured Kaskaskia and took over Fort Sackville at Vincennes. Hamilton, coming down from Detroit, recaptured Fort Sackville in December 1778. Clark, who had remained at Kaskaskia, then headed eastward in February 1779 and, after pushing through the flooded lands along the Wabash, surprised Hamilton at Vincennes and forced his surrender in February 1779.

By the Treaty of Paris in 1783, Great Britain ceded the territory northwest of the Ohio River to the United States. Virginia relinquished her claims in 1784, and three years later the Congress of the Confederation enacted the Ordinance of 1787 for the Northwest Territory. In addition to providing for government of the territory and for its eventual admission into the union by states, the ordinance excluded slavery forever and guaranteed basic personal rights. In 1800 the Northwest Territory was divided into two parts, the territories of Indiana and Ohio, and William Henry Harrison became governor of Indiana Territory. (With the creation of Michigan Territory in 1805 and Illinois Territory in 1809, Indiana was reduced to its present limits.)

Meanwhile, beginning in the latter half of the 1780's and continuing for seven or eight years, hostilities between the Indians and the settlers grew in number and intensity. Under the leadership of the Miami chief Little Turtle, the Miami and other tribes united against the white men. After defeating militia, first under Gen. Josiah Harmar (1790) and then under Gen. Arthur St. Clair (1791), Little Turtle himself met defeat in 1794 in the Battle of Fallen Timbers (q.v.) at the hands of an army led by Gen. Anthony Wayne. By the Treaty of Greenville (q.v.) the following year, the Indians ceded a small strip along the eastern side of Indiana as well as most of Ohio to the whites. While more pioneers moved to Indiana, there was peace for almost 15 years between the whites and the Indians, and General Harrison was successful in obtaining the cession of most of southern Indiana and southern Illinois. Tecumseh, a Shawnee chief, then warned that further cessions would mean war and set about forming a confederation of Indian tribes. On Nov. 7, 1811, Harrison defeated the Indians in the Battle of Tippecanoe (q.v.) just north of where La Fayette now stands. This last major Indian battle in Indiana was followed in the fall of 1812 by the last big Indian massacre of whites, at Pigeon Roost in southern Indiana. (Subsequently, the Miami and other tribes sold the rest of their lands in Indiana and moved west of the Mississippi. By 1838, when the last of the Potawatomi left the state, only a few Miami remained.)

The close of the War of 1812 and the Indian wars which were a phase of it coincided with the end of Indiana's territorial era. A state constitution was drafted in June 1816 at Corydon, and Indiana was admitted to the Union as the 19th state on December 11 of that year. In 1813 the territorial capital had been moved from Vincennes to Corydon, which remained the state capital until 1825, when it was removed to the new town of Indianapolis.

As settlers swarmed into Indiana—by 1830 the state had a population of 343,031, and by 1840, 685,866—its development was marked by the flowering and failure of two attempts at communal colonization which attracted wide attention. The first began in 1815, when George Rapp, patriarchal leader of a group of people known as Rappites, and his followers came from Pennsylvania to establish on the Wabash a model community which they called Harmonie. All property was held in common. (See HARMONISTS.) In 1825, Rapp sold the community to Robert Owen (q.v.) of Scotland, who renamed it New Harmony. Owen and his followers continued the practice of common ownership of property, but dissension broke out. Acknowledging defeat, Owen left for England in May 1827. Although the communal experiment failed, New Harmony was the birthplace of such progressive movements as equal social and legal rights for women, the free school, and the free kindergarten.

River transportation, never very successful, was supplemented by winding roads hewed out of the forests. As farmers sought wider markets for their products, these became inadequate, and in the early 1830's the state, with borrowed funds, began the construction of several canals. The most important was the Indiana segment of the Wabash and Erie Canal, which was opened between La Fayette and Toledo in 1843. An internal improvement program embracing more than 1,000 miles of roads and canals was begun in 1836, but met with disaster because of extravagance, poor planning, and the panic of 1837. The heavy debt which burdened the young, struggling state as a result of attempting to underwrite these acute "growing pains" contributed in part to a provision of the 1851 constitution that prohibits the state from incurring indebtedness. Gradually, however, the state became more prosperous. Schools and colleges were built, and wood and brick houses replaced the earlier log cabins. Mines and quarries were active, and factories were constructed. In 1854, the Monon Railroad was completed between New Albany and Michigan City. In politics, Indiana remained Democratic until 1837, when a Whig was elected governor. After a short period of Whig popularity, the Democrats resumed control until 1860, when the first Republican governor was elected.

Many Indianans had come originally from the South, and some of them sympathized with the Confederacy when the Civil War broke out. The majority, however, loyally supported the Union, and under the energetic leadership of Governor Oliver P. Morton, Indiana supplied 208,000 men to the Union cause from a population of 1,350,248 (1860). Although there were no decisive battles on Indiana soil, there were some raids, the most daring being that of Gen. John Hunt Morgan, who in 1863 swept through Corydon, Salem, Dupont, and Versailles before being captured in Ohio. (See MORGAN'S RAID INTO INDIANA AND OHIO.) A hostile legislature elected in 1862 refused for two years to pass any appropriation bills, and Governor Morton was forced to borrow money on his own credit to finance military operations. More than 26,000 of Indiana's Civil War soldiers and sailors died in battle or from disease.

After the war new factories were built, and roads and railroads were constructed. Agriculture suffered from low crop prices, however, and many farmers and workingmen supported the Greenback and Populist movements. Conditions improved in the early years of the 20th century with the establishment of automobile factories in Indianapolis and iron and steel mills in the Calumet region. In World War I, Indiana furnished 146,332 men to the armed forces, of whom 3,354 died in service; also large quantities of war material and food. Agriculture enjoyed a boom during the war, but the farmers suffered severely from the postwar collapse in crop prices. Industry remained prosperous until 1929, however, and many new roads and other facilities were built during this period. Both industry and agriculture were hard hit by the depression, but by the late 1930's recovery was well under way, and in World War II Indiana farms and factories made an impressive contribution to the war effort. Over 400,000 Indiana men and women entered the armed services; more than 10,000 lost their lives.

Since 1860, Indiana political control has been fairly evenly divided between the two major parties. Through 1947 the state had had 14 Republican and 10 Democratic governors. In 1940, Wendell Willkie, native-son Republican presidential nominee, carried Indiana by a plurality of 25,403 votes. In that year, Republicans also won all state offices with the exception of the governorship, which went to the Democratic nominee, Henry F. Schricker. The Republicans also elected substantial majorities in each house of the General Assembly, as they also later did in 1950 and 1952. In 1944 and 1948, Thomas E. Dewey, and in 1952, Dwight D. Eisenhower, both Republicans, won Indiana's 13 electoral votes in their bids for the United States presidency.

Bibliography.—Levering, Julia Henderson, *Historic Indiana* (New York 1909); Nicholson, Meredith, *The Hoosiers* (New York and London 1915); Dunn, Jacob Piatt, *Indiana and Indianans* (Chicago and New York 1919); Esarey, Logan, *A History of Indiana from Its Exploration to 1850* (Fort Wayne 1924); Chambers, D. L., *Indiana, A Hoosier History* (Indianapolis 1933); Esarey, Logan, *A History of Indiana from 1850 to 1920* (Bloomington 1935); Sikes, Pressly S., *The State Government of Indiana* (Bloomington 1937); Carmony, Donald F., *Indiana* (New York 1941); Works Projects Administration, *Indiana: A Guide to the Hoosier State* (New York 1941); Indiana Economic Council, *Hoosiers at Work* (Indianapolis 1944); Carmony, Donald F., and Peckham, Howard H., *A Brief History of Indiana* (Indianapolis 1946); Indiana Department of Commerce and Public Relations, *Indiana—Your Logical Industrial Location* (Indianapolis 1946); Flick, Oka Stanton, *Indiana, the State and Its Government* (Chicago 1947); Banta, Richard E., ed., *Hoosier Caravan* (Bloomington, Ind., 1951).

PAUL M. ROSS,
Director, The Indianapolis Foundation.

INDIANA UNIVERSITY, the state university located at Bloomington. In accordance with a provision of the state constitution, the legislature passed an act in 1820 providing for the establishment of a state seminary, which was opened in 1824 under the name of Indiana Seminary; in 1827, it was raised to the dignity of a college, and in 1838 the name was changed to Indiana University. In 1867 the university was opened to women, and has since been coeducational in all its departments. The university is the head of the public school system of Indiana, and no tuition fee is charged; the government is by a board of trustees which reports biennially to the governor. Courses are offered in languages, science and history, graduates receiving the degree of A.B. or B.S. The degrees of Ph.D. and A.M. are given for graduate work. There are also schools of law and of medicine, and a biological experiment station on Winona Lake. A summer session is maintained.

INDIANAPOLIS, Ind., seat of Marion County, and state capital. Located in the center of the state and a focal point of industry, commerce, banking, and transportation, the city covers a flat terrain (altitude 739 feet) of about 55 square miles. The town of Woodruff Place is entirely within the city limits, but has never been annexed. The temperature of Indianapolis averages 21.7°F. in January; 86°F. in July. The business district lies in the heart of the city. Scattered about it are public buildings, the Union Station, and World War Memorial Plaza which covers five city blocks. In general, the residential section is on the north and east sides; the industrial, on the south and west. In 1950, Indianapolis had more than 125,600 residence units, over 57 per cent owner-occupied.

Industries.—In 1947, the Indianapolis metropolitan area had 944 industrial establishments producing almost $500,000,000 worth of goods and employing more than 73,000 production workers alone. Among the largest of the factories are those producing telephone sets, inner tubes, saws, engines, television sets, phonograph records, truck bodies, food products, and gloves. The city's stockyards, opened in 1877, cover 210 acres and are the largest east of Chicago. In 1950, 5,873 retail stores and 1,004 wholesale establishments served an estimated 1,337,700 people in 25 counties.

Transportation and Communication.—Seven railroad systems, 20 bus companies, 105 motor freight lines, and five airline companies served the city in 1950. The city had five radio stations, a television station, and three major daily newspapers with a total circulation (Sept. 30, 1949) of 458,021.

Government.—Indianapolis is governed by a mayor and a common council of nine members, all elected for four years. The mayor appoints the boards and department heads, and the council fixes their respective salaries. Members of the board of education are elected by popular vote.

Education.—The city's institutions of higher learning include Butler University, Indiana Central College, Marian College, Indiana University's schools of medicine, dentistry, and law; and extension schools of Indiana and Purdue universities. The city has both public and parochial high schools and elementary schools, as well as kindergartens and special schools, including state schools for the blind and deaf.

Cultural and Recreational Facilities.—In 1950, the Indianapolis Public Library had about 750,000 volumes and 97,015 registered borrowers; the Indiana State Library had 263,830 volumes, mostly nonfiction, including a collection in Braille and the largest existing collection of material about Indiana. Among the city's other facilities are the John Herron Art Institute (and Museum), the Arthur Jordan College of Music, and a children's museum. The city had 32 parks in 1950 covering 3,234 acres, and also 40 playgrounds. It had six city-owned and nine private golf courses, two midget auto racing tracks; American Association Baseball grounds; an arena for ice hockey matches and track for harness racing; and Butler Field House in which state-wide high school basketball tournaments are held annually. The Indianapolis Motor Speedway is the scene of the world-famous annual 500-mile auto race.

Other Points of Interest.—The city is the headquarters of the American Legion, the International Brotherhood of Teamsters, and 50 other nation-wide organizations. In the heart of the city is the Soldiers and Sailors Monument, completed in 1901 as the second highest monument in the United States (285 feet). In the city are more than 500 places of worship, representing all denominations.

History.—Almost four years after Indiana became a state, commissioners approved (June 7, 1820) a place at the confluence of Fall Creek and White River as the site for the state's capital. By Jan. 8, 1825, when the legislature first met in Indianapolis, the capital and county seat of newly-organized Marion County had 600 inhabitants, a brick courthouse, several taverns, a newspaper, and other evidences of growth, though it was not incorporated as a town until 1836. Meanwhile, in 1830, the National Road (later U.S. 40) was extended through the town. In 1847, Indianapolis was incorporated as a city (population, 8,091), and the Madison Railroad was completed giving it an outlet to the Ohio River. The city now began to develop rapidly as an industrial and marketing center, and a hub of the state's overland transportation system. In 1860, the population was 18,611; by 1870, it had risen to 48,244. Three developments of the 1880's and 1890's made for even more rapid expansion: the discovery near Indianapolis of cheap fuel (natural gas) for industry; an interurban trolley system; and the birth of the automobile industry. Census figures show the steady growth of the population: 105,436 in 1890; 233,650 in 1910; 364,161 in 1930; 427,173 in 1950, of which the great preponderance were native-born white.

Bibliography.—Dunn, A. W., *Civic Studies of Indianapolis* (Indianapolis 1907); Dunn, Jacob Piatt, *Greater Indianapolis* (Chicago 1910); Esarey, Logan, *History of Indiana*, vols. 3 and 4 (Dayton, O. 1924); Nolan, Jeanette Covert, *Hoosier City* (New York 1943); Murphy, M. E. and M., "Cities of America," *Saturday Evening Post*, Aug. 7, 1948.

RALPH F. ARMSTRONG,
Writer and Editor.

INDIANAPOLIS SYMPHONY ORCHESTRA, founded in 1930 as a cooperative organization. It was conducted by Ferdinand Schaeffer until 1936, when Fabien Sevitzky and Vladimir Bakaleinikoff were engaged as guest conductors. The orchestra was then reorganized on a permanent basis and financial management was put in the hands of the Indiana State Symphony Society. Sevitzky was appointed permanent conductor and has held the position since 1937. Eleven pairs of subscription concerts are given each season in the Murat Theatre as well as popular concerts and children's concerts.

INDIANOLA, city, Mississippi, county seat of Sunflower County; altitude 127.4 feet; on the Columbus and Greenville Railroad; 101 miles north of Jackson. Near the center of the fertile Yazoo-Mississippi delta area, it is an agricultural and trading center. Formerly called Indian Bayou, the name was changed (1886) to the present in honor of the Indian maid, Ola. It has mayor and council government. Pop. (1950) 4,369.

INDIANS, American. Christopher Columbus, sailing for the Indies, found instead the New World of the Western Hemisphere and called the native people Indians. This discovery, in 1492, and the centuries of exploration, conquest and settlement which followed revealed to the Europeans a world new in many ways. By the early 19th century the final contact between Europeans and a native group had taken place. Little by little, during recent years, the story of the American Indians and their ways of life in the past and present has been unfolded. But what would Columbus and his companions have seen if their's had been a bird's-eye view of the whole New World and its inhabitants?

By the 15th century the Indians were living in all parts of North, Central, and South America, from the Arctic Ocean to Tierra del Fuego and from the Atlantic Ocean to the Pacific. At that time the Indians probably numbered over thirteen million. Out of this total, about one million lived north of the Rio Grande, over three million lived in Middle America, and about 9 million lived in South America. To European eyes first seeing them, all American Indians looked much alike physically because of their hair and skin color. Actually, in other respects, there has always been some variation in physical type among the American Indians. In head shape, nose form, and bodily height the Indians would have revealed to the early discoverers their physical diversity.

The American Indian languages would have shown an even greater diversity to the Europeans. North and South America together contained more linguistic families than all the rest of the world. Forty different linguistic stocks were represented in North and Middle America and another 40 in South America. At the time of discovery the number of people speaking these different languages varied enormously. Some languages were spoken by only a few hundred people, while others were spoken by many people spread over large areas. A 15th century bird's-eye view of the New World would have shown an equally amazing variation in the way in which the Indians lived. In several parts of the New World, the European explorers found well-established, complex civilizations with a developed political, economic, religious, and artistic life. Between these peaks of development they found groups following different and simpler ways of life. They found groups living in settled towns and villages with an economy based on intensive farming, hunting or fishing. They also found people leading a simple nomadic life following wild game and gathering wild food. In some areas they found people living in substantial houses of stone or mudbrick near huge palaces, temples or fortresses. Elsewhere the dwellings were simple brush or skin shelters. The Europeans encountered complex, integrated state organizations with class stratification on the one hand and simple band organization on the other.

Sources of Information on the American Indian.—This glimpse of the diversity of physical type, language and way of life suggests a long and complex history for the American Indian prior to the 15th century. What is known of the time and place of origin of these Indians? What is known of the development of their ways of life and how do we find the answers to any of these questions? These topics have long been a favorite subject for speculation as well as for careful study. Most of the speculations about the origin and development of American Indian life have been based on completely superficial observations. Chance similarities between Egyptian civilization and the Maya Indians of Central America, for example, have lead some people to assume a close connection between these two groups. To make this connection practical some people have revived the legend of the lost continent of Atlantis. This same kind of speculation has lead to similar mistaken conclusions about other groups and other lost continents.

What are the careful and valid sources of information on these questions about the American Indians? Most of this information comes from studies made by anthropologists. They, with much help from historians, geologists, paleontologists, and specialists in other fields, have been piecing together the long story of the American Indians. From different specialists within the field of anthropology come the various parts of this story. The physical anthropologists study the skeletal material of the early Indians and the physical characteristics of the living Indians including blood-group affiliation which seems to have some racial significance. From the physical anthropologist comes our information about the racial affiliation of the American Indians. From the anthropologists who specialize in linguistic studies and who compare Indian languages and reconstruct the earlier types comes the story of the Indian languages. Other important sources of information are the anthropologists who specialize in archaeology and in ethnology. By careful excavation the archaeologist uncovers the remains of the prehistoric Indians. This includes skeletal remains, and such material evidence of pottery, houses, weapons and other equipment as survive. From this the archaeologist carefully reconstructs the early history of the Indians.

The ethnologist, by a study of historical documents and a comparison of living and recent Indian groups adds to the picture.

To complete their work in reconstructing the story of the American Indian, anthropologists receive the help of the paleontologists and geologists in establishing relative dates and time perspective. With the help of the botanists they have worked out the story of such an important native American plant as corn. And very valuable assistance has come from the work of radiation chemists in determining more specific dates for early prehistoric material. The methods and results of this work may still be subject to some modification, but they are now widely accepted. The findings are referred to as "Carbon 14" dates. New evidence is constantly being added to the study of the American Indian, and new interpretations of old evidence are sometimes necessary. But on the broad outlines and the major developments and time sequences in the story there is general agreement.

Peopling of the New World.—It seems certain that the American Indians did not originate in the New World but gradually migrated from Asia sometime after the end of the Ice Age. There is a variety of evidence to support this conclusion. To begin with, no archaeologist has found any human skeletal remains of an extremely early date or of a physical type significantly different from modern Indian types. Some tools, presumably man-made, have been found closely associated with extinct animal bones. But, unlike the situation in other parts of the world, the extinction of these animals was relatively recent in the New World. This absence of early human material is consistent with another line of evidence. Because there are no living anthropoid apes in the New World, and no fossil remains of extinct apes have been found, it seems most unlikely that early man could have evolved there.

Where, then, did the American Indian come from? In his most stable and most characteristic physical traits, the American Indian is like the Mongoloid stock found in most of Asia. They share blue-black color and straight, coarse quality of hair; generally dark skin color; and shovel-shaped incisor teeth. This does not, of course, equate the American Indian and the modern Chinese. It means, rather, that at some time in the past, a group of Mongoloid stock separated from the main group in Asia. After reaching the New World they probably had little or no contact with the main Mongoloid stock and developed certain characteristics of their own. The one New World group most similar to the Asiatic Mongoloids are the Eskimos. They, along with the tribes living in northeastern Asia, are classified as the Arctic Mongoloid race, a division of the Primary Mongoloid stock. All other New World aborigines are classified in the division of the composite Mongoloid stock called American Indian race.

The non-Mongoloid physical characteristics of the American Indians are the unspecialized ones which some authorities have classified as indicating an ancient "white" admixture to the predominantly Mongoloid base. Such a mixture might have occurred in some Indian groups before they left Asia, or they might represent a parental form like the modern whites or Mongoloids but less specialized than either of them. One important difference existed in the setting of the Asiatic and New World groups. The Asiatic Mongoloids were in touch with other racial strains, whereas those coming to the New World entered a free territory. One of the most interesting and puzzling differences between the Asiatic Mongoloids and the American Indians is that of blood group affiliation. The American Indian, in general, is very high in group O affiliation and very low in A, whereas O and A are of nearly equal frequency among the Mongoloids. It is possible that this variation occurred in the course of the original adaptation to the New World environment.

A matter which has received considerable attention in discussions of physical characteristics of American Indians is the apparent gradual change from an early, long-headed type to a later, round-headed type. A factor which makes it difficult to assess this difference is the practice of head deformation which was widespread in the New World, and which precludes the accurate measurement of many skeletal remains and living peoples. The question has been raised whether this change, if real, indicates additional migration into the New World or a local development. It should be noted that this same shift has been characteristic of peoples all over the world. Despite this possible variation in head shape, some regional differences in stature and in some minor physical characteristics, the American Indian shows relatively little physical variability. There is, in fact, less variation in the New World than in any comparable area of the Old World.

There is little doubt about the route which these early migrants took from Asia to North America. The two continents are close only at the Bering Strait, where they are about 60 miles apart. At an earlier time this distance was probably shorter, the crossing even easier. When the strait is frozen, it is possible even now to make the crossing on foot. It seems likely that groups of Asian hunters and fishermen, following the game, moved gradually across this area. Finding the climate and the food supply suitable they moved on, not knowing, of course, that they were entering a "new world." This process was repeated many times and the immigrants moved farther and farther south.

When could such migrations have taken place? They must have occurred at a time when climatic and glacial conditions were favorable. About eleven thousand years ago, at the close of the glacial period, the climate became mild enough to have permitted such migration. Earlier than that, glacial conditions would have been unfavorable. Archaeological excavations give no evidence of any human material of an antiquity greater than about ten thousand years. So, on the basis of all present evidence, the time of the first migration seems to have been between ten and eleven thousand years ago.

A peopling of the New World by any route other than the Bering Strait is highly unlikely for a number of reasons. South America is 2,000 miles from the nearest Pacific island. Chance voyages might have occurred over this route but it is most unlikely that a large group or repeated groups could reach the New World in this way. More important still is the evidence that the Pacific islands themselves were only recently settled, perhaps a few thousand years ago. So, despite all speculations about this route, it must be eliminated for these and other reasons.

Evidence of Earliest Culture.—The people who migrated into the New World were nomadic hunters, fishers, and food gatherers whose way of life was very simple. They brought with them from Asia a knowledge of the preparation and use of chipped stone tools, of projectiles propelled by spear throwers and perhaps shot from bows, the use of fire, and possibly the domesticated dog. The oldest archaeological evidence of an early culture in North America is named Folsom from the place of its first discovery in northeastern New Mexico. Similar material was found in other parts of the Western Plains; near Clovis, New Mexico; near Fort Collins in Colorado; and near Lipscomb, Texas. The projectile points found at these sites are of two kinds, the one rough and irregular and the other very finely chipped. Some of these projectile points were imbedded in bones of extinct bison, indicating that these are quite old even though so skillfully made. But, as has already been mentioned, association of man-made material with bones of extinct animals does not necessarily mean any great antiquity in the New World. The geological evidence for the age of the Folsom culture places it at the end of, or just after, the last glacial period. The Carbon 14 date for this terminal glacial stage is about 8500 B.C. which corresponds closely to the Carbon 14 date of 8000 B.C. for the Folsom material itself. A second kind of early culture, called Cochise from a site in southern Arizona, dates somewhat later in time than the Folsom material and differs greatly from it. The Folsom people were hunters, and left only scrapers, knives, and their unique projectile points. The Cochise people, on the other hand, left few scrapers and knives and no projectile points. They did leave many grinding tools (mortars, handstones, pestles, flat grinding-stones) indicating a seed-gathering economy. From these early cultures there is an unbroken sequence of sites extending to about twenty-five hundred years ago, almost to the beginning of pottery-making and agriculture.

We have seen that man first reached the New World about eleven thousand years ago. By about ten thousand years ago there was a hunting economy in the Western Plains, and, somewhat later, a gathering economy in the southern Arizona area. The seed-gathering Cochise culture persisted, with minor changes and additions right up to the time a few hundred years before Christ, when pottery-making, agriculture, and permanent houses were added, bringing in an era of great culture enrichment. The parallel period for the hunting people is less well-known but it seems possible that such a site as Ventana Cave in southern Arizona represents this period. The earliest layers in this cave contain material of a Folsomlike culture. On top of this there is material similar to the later stages of the Cochise culture. On top of this is a pottery-bearing layer dating from A.D. 1 to A.D. 1400 and on top of this is historic Indian material.

So far, we have been describing material only from the Southwestern United States. This area is well-known because its dry climate has preserved the early material and its lack of heavy vegetation facilitates archaeological discovery. There have been a few other scattered finds. Gypsum Cave in southern Nevada yielded artifacts indirectly associated with bones of extinct animals. The material is undoubtedly early but any exact dating is impossible. The same is true of cave material from southern Oregon, Big Bend sites in Texas, and caves near Salt Lake City. The Boylston fish-weir site in Boston, which may be four to five thousand years old, gives evidence of man in what is now the Eastern United States. Folsomlike points are found at the bottom of middens in the Eastern United States, left by hunting and gathering peoples. These middens date from 1000 to 3000 B.C.

At Tepexpan in the Valley of Mexico a human skeleton, elephant bones, and flake tools were found in one stratum. The evidence is not conclusive proof of early habitation of this site but it is promising.

Evidence from several parts of South America indicates that early migrants reached many parts of that continent, even distant Tierra del Fuego. The earliest archaeological evidence comes from three areas: the east Brazil highlands, the Andean highlands and southern Patagonia. In the caves of Lagoa Santa in the east Brazil highlands were found bones of extinct animals and human remains of a physical type different from the modern Indians. Here again, association with extinct animals does not necessarily indicate extreme age. The human skulls are, however, lower and longer than modern types. These same characteristics were found in skull material from another cave in the same region, and at Punin in highland Ecuador.

Other early campsites have been found in several parts of the Andes. In southern Patagonia cave sites at Palli Aike and Fell's yielded stratified remains from the time of the early hunters until the historic period. Material from shell middens in southern Tierra del Fuego and on the north coast of Chile indicate an early occupation by fishing groups. An estimation of the age of the Patagonian material, based on the rise of land level in relation to the sea, gives an age of eighteen hundred years for the earliest shell midden occupation. The Carbon 14 date for Indian hearths in Fell's Cave is eighty-five hundred years ago. From this we can conclude that the first migrants must have reached the South American continent considerably earlier.

The sites we have just described give us the picture of the earliest known New World cultural material. Dated by geological methods, they cover the period from roughly fifteen thousand years ago to five or six thousand years ago. In a few instances the record suggests connections with more recent material but on the whole there is still a gap in our information after about 5000 B.C. The next date which seems reasonable to assign to archaeological material falls somewhere around 1000 B.C. This is arrived at not by geological dating but from archaeological records. This record for many parts of North and South America runs back more or less consecutively from the present. The details of these sequences will be considered later. Suffice it to say here that on the basis of this material archaeologists estimate that the earliest development of the cultures in these sequences must have begun about two or three thousand years ago. This leaves us with a gap between the end of the earliest material, about 5000 B.C., and the onset of this new period about 1000 B.C. This interval will some day be filled in. We may find that our dating is at fault. Perhaps the dates of the older material are too early and the recent material too late, creating a false gap. Perhaps we will find more exact evidence for dating the extinction of the animal species found associated with the earliest human remains. Or, perhaps, additional archaeological discoveries will extend the recent record back in time, closing the gap from this end.

During this interval there must have been expansion of population, movements of people, and diffusion of culture traits within the New World. There may also have been some movement of people and of cultural material from Asia. We know this from the distribution of culture traits existing after the end of this gap. We find that certain simple elements of culture were almost universally distributed throughout the New World. These include: pressure flaking, grinding of stone, bone and horn, hafting of tools, firemaking, weaving or plaiting of baskets, mats, traps and weirs, projectile points used with either a spear thrower or a bow, the domesticated dog. Some of these traits are known from Folsom finds but others do not leave preservable remains to tell us how old they are. Because they are all traits characteristic of late Paleolithic and Mesolithic times in Europe and Asia, they may have been brought by migration or learned through contact across the Bering Strait. They may have reached the New World at one time or over a long period of time. Whatever their age or provenience they seem to be the common basis of the native New World cultures.

This set of material traits is nearly paralleled in distribution and presumptive age by another set consisting of social and religious institutions. Such traits leave, of course, no material remains but their wide distribution among historic Indian groups in both hemispheres suggests a long history. Such traits are: small hordes of kinsmen claiming the use of a tract of land; belief in magic and supernatural powers which are used sometimes for evil; crisis rites including ceremonies performed on such occasions as birth, puberty, death. These traits, like the set of material traits, may have reached the New World at one time or over a long period. Some may have been present by Folsom times or they may have reached the New World during the gap which followed the Folsom period and about which we know so little.

Areas of Indian Culture before the Conquest.—By the time the first Europeans reached the New World, the native people had spread across both continents. The hundreds of groups in which they lived fall into several areas of fairly uniform culture, and can be described and understood best in terms of these area settings. There are some differences of opinion among anthropologists as to the exact number of areas and the particular groupings in which the various tribes fall. But, on the whole, the disagreement concerns the smallest subdivisions within the subareas. It is generally accepted that the New World can be described in terms of ten large areas which can be divided at least once, giving twenty, or more, subareas.

The cultural areas into which the Indian tribes can be divided correspond closely to natural areas considered in ecological terms. This relation between cultural and natural areas does not imply that cultures are produced entirely by their environment. However, once established in an environment a culture tends to be stabilized and limited by that environment. Of the various aspects of environment (climate, terrain, altitude, fauna, vegetation) which affect culture, vegetation is perhaps the most important. There is a close correspondence between the cultural and vegetation areas in North and South America.

In North America there are six basic culture areas: Meso-American, Southwest, Intermediate (California and Intermountain), Northwest Coast, Eastern-Northern, and Arctic Coast. In South America there are four: Andean, Circum-Caribbean, Tropical Forest, and Marginal. Each of these areas is divisible into two or more subareas. The division of the New World into two continental areas creates a false impression of independent growth. Actually, the Meso-American and Andean areas together form a bicontinental core of development. By the 15th century when the Caucasians reached the New World, these two areas constituted a peak of development far ahead of any other areas in density of population, advancement of arts, political development and wealth. Archaeological evidence from these areas indicates that at the earliest known stages (some centuries before Christ), they were already far advanced. They were, in fact, already developed to a point which was never reached in many other areas.

This same circum-Isthmian region is the place of origin of native American cultivated plants. The most important of these, beans and maize could also be grown in more temperate latitudes. With the diffusion of these plants to areas outside their point of origin, it seems likely that other traits of culture would have spread. Some of the results of this occurrence will be seen in the following description of the culture areas. These will be given from the Andean and Meso-American areas outward for each of the two continents.

SOUTH AMERICAN CULTURE AREAS

Setting.—The South American continent is divisible into three major topographic zones: (1) the Andean region stretching along the Pacific Coast from Colombia to southern Chile; (2) the Tropical Forest area from the eastern slopes of the Andes across the valleys of the Amazon and the rivers of the Guianas, and including the eastern hill and coast area of Brazil; (3) the Tropical and Temperate Plains area stretching from Brazil to Tierra del Fuego. A fourth area, of interest as a cultural entity, is somewhat peripheral to continental South America. This is the Circum-Caribbean area which includes northern South America, all the West Indies, and Central America as far as the present Guatemalan border. The relation of this area to both the North and South American continents is complex and will be described in a later paragraph.

Race.—The South American Indians belong to the American Indian race which is a subdivision of the Mongoloid stock. The characteristics common to all South American Indians are straight, black hair, brown skin and brown eyes. On the basis of other physical characteristics they may be divided into four subtypes. The Indians of the Andean area are short of stature and brachycephalic (round-headed); the Indians living in the Tropical Forest area are short to medium in stature and mesocephalic (medium-headed); the Indians of the Matto Grosso, the Pampas, and Patagonia are tall and round-headed; the Indians of the highlands of Brazil, southern Chile and the Straits of Magellan are of medium to low stature and dolicocephalic (long-headed). The real significance of these differences in stature is not entirely clear. They may represent a difference in physical type, or they may be the result of differences in the kinds of food eaten by the various groups. With regard to head shape, evidence of dolicocephalic traits was found in the earliest archaeological sites in Ecuador and southern Brazil. This early evidence plus the presence of this long-headed type in the furthest part of the continent suggest that this may have been the characteristic type of the earliest inhabitants of South America. The round-headed type may have developed from the earlier type or, more probably, represents a later, separate migration.

Language.—The Indians of South America spoke about 250 languages, which are classified into some 40 linguistic stocks. At the time of discovery, the number of people speaking any of these different languages varied greatly; some were spoken by only a few hundred people living in a small area, others were spoken by many tribes spread over huge areas. In the Andean area, the principal linguistic families, from south to north, were the Araucanian, Aymara, Quechua, and the Chibcha which extended into Central America. Most of the Indians of the tropical forest spoke languages of the Arawak, Carib, Tupi, Pano, and Tucano families. Arawak and Carib extended into the West Indies. The Indians of the open country from Brazil to Tierra del Fuego spoke, for the most part, languages of the Gê, Guaycuru, Puelche, and Tehuelche families. Some of this linguistic distribution occurred rather late, perhaps a few hundred years before the conquest. The expansion of the Inca Empire, for example, was responsible for the wide distribution of Quechua and the suppression of local languages. The Incas, however, never succeeded in suppressing the Araucanian-speaking people of northern Chile who, today, speak that language. Other languages such as Arawak, Carib, and Tupi were spread by extensive migrations.

Prehistory.—The earliest migrants into South America were nomadic people who lived by hunting, fishing and gathering wild foods. They were not very different from their ancestors who had crossed the Bering Strait from Asia into the New World. Like those ancestors, the early migrants into South America had no knowledge of agriculture, metals, or pottery. Aside from such areas as the jungles of the Ecuadorian and Colombian coasts and of the Amazon, the extreme desert of northern Chile and the areas of the Argentine suitable only for the later herders and farmers, the South American continent provided extensive areas favorable for these early nomads. The highlands of the Andean mountains supplied the game and wild food suited to their needs. Because the main valleys of the Andes run north and south, a continuous southward migration was possible and doubtless accounted for the main flow of settlers. Some early groups also found suitable fishing sites along the Pacific coast. Others spread eastward from the Andean area into the east Brazil highlands, which also offered good hunting. Further country suitable for hunting and gathering wild foods was found in the Pampas and Patagonia, and on into Tierra del Fuego. Some of these hunting and gathering people were still living in the east Brazil highlands, the Pampas, Patagonia, and the Chilean archipelago at the time of the European conquest.

The earliest archaeological material from South America consists of two kinds: human skeletal material found associated with extinct fauna, and cultural remains found at campsites and fishing sites.

In 1835 about 800 caves in the Lagoa Santa area of the east Brazil highlands were explored by T. W. Lund, a Danish naturalist. The material from these caves consisted of bones of extinct fauna and some human skeletal material. The human material was especially interesting because it represented a physical type somewhat different from the modern Indians of that area. Material excavated from the Confins Cave in the same area corroborates the earlier discoveries. At Confins a human skeleton and parts of a fossil horse and of mastodon were found buried about two meters deep and sealed in by fallen debris. As has been mentioned in a previous paragraph, the exact age of extinction of New World fauna is uncertain but it does not necessarily imply great antiquity. In 1923 another fossilized human skull was found indirectly associated with extinct fauna in volcanic ash beds at Punin in the highland of Ecuador. The human skull material from these three areas, Lagoa Santa, Confins, and Punin are of a similar long, low type. Early campsites have been found in several places in the Andes. These contain stone tools such as points and scrapers. Two early cavesites, in southern Patagonia, Palli Aike and Fell's, (with a Carbon 14 age of eighty-five hundred years), contained stratified deposits of material ranging in age from the time of the early hunters up to the occupation by the historic Ona. Fishing sites have been excavated on the shores of southern Tierra del Fuego, the Chilean archipelago and the coasts of Chile and Peru. The oldest known shell midden age is about eighteen hundred years.

The story of the succeeding migrations and culture changes is still only incompletely known. Migrants probably continued to reach South America because the later physical type is short and round-headed. The one area from which we do have a fairly continuous history is the north coast of Peru. Evidence from buried villages indicates that the fishing people who lived here were raising cotton, beans, and gourds as early as 2000 B.C., although they did not make pottery or raise corn or manioc at that time. In this same area evidence is found of such subsequent developments as the making of pottery, domestication of the llama, cultivation of corn, manioc and other plants, the introduction of weaving, the use of metals, irrigation and the whole elaborate growth of art, architecture and a complex political organization.

Domestication of plants and of wild animals was of great importance in the development of New World cultures. With the possible exception of gourd and cotton, the domesticated plants of the New World are indigenous species, unrelated to plants of the Old World. Recent botanical investigations point to the conclusion that plants such as maize, sweet potatoes, peppers, peanuts, manioc and tobacco, which are each represented by a single species, are of South American origin. The lowland country, possibly the grassland of Paraguay and Bolivia seems a likely center of origin. Because maize became such an important crop in many parts of the New World, its domestication is of particular interest. It seems probable that maize is South American in origin because that is where the greatest number and most differentiated varieties of maize are found. Specifically, it seems probable that maize was developed from pod corn and that this development took place around Paraguay.

Other plants such as squash, beans, tomatoes, and cotton, which are represented by two or more species, may have been domesticated independently in South America and in Central America. Still other plants such as coca, the white potato, quinoa, and oca seem to be Andean in origin. Some of these plants achieved a wide distribution in the New World. But such an achievement would not have required any great span of time. Botanists consider that the whole process of domestication could have been completed in a few thousand years. We know that the Indians of the Peruvian coast, for example, had domesticated plants before they made pottery, probably about 2000 B.C. This would allow ample time beforehand for the process of domestication and time afterwards for the wide distribution of these plants.

The dog was the only domesticated animal known widely over South America. A few animals, such as the guinea pig and the llama and alpaca were domesticated in the Andean area. The guinea pig was known in many parts of the Andes but was not a very important animal. The llama and alpaca, probably domesticated at an early date from their wild relatives the guanaco and vicuña, were restricted to the high grasslands of the Central Andes and parts of northwestern Argentina. They were useful for transportation and as a source of wool, meat, hides, fertilizer, fuel and of bone for tools.

Cultures.—South American Indians can be grouped into four areas of native culture: (1) Andean, (2) Circum-Caribbean, (3) Tropical Forest, (4) Marginal.

Andean.—In terms of cultural development the Andean area consisted of three subareas, the central area of high culture flanked by the North and South Andean areas. The basic pattern common to the whole area at the time of the Spanish Conquest, was one of skillful farming which included the use of fertilizers and the building of irrigation ditches and elaborate agricultural terraces. Corn, beans, squash, potatoes, manioc, peanuts and peppers were the principal food crops. Cotton, coca and tobacco were also grown. The llama and alpaca served, in the central highlands, as pack animals and also as an important additional source of meat, and of wool and bone. Guinea pigs were widely raised for food.

The Andean farmers were also skillful craftsmen. They distinguished between two types of products, one for utilitarian purposes, and one, which was more elaborately and carefully made, for ceremonial or mortuary purposes. The pottery, weaving, and metal work showed many different styles at different times and places but was of a uniformly very high level of skill and beauty. The more skilled craft work was done by specialists, while the utilitarian wares were produced by each family. In contrast to most of the rest of South America the Andean people were sedentary and lived in centers of fairly dense population. Houses in the Central Andes were constructed of stone and adobe. In Colombia and Ecuador frame houses with thatched roofs were lined with stone or clay. The Auracanians in Chile built plank houses. In all these localities each household consisted of closely related families and a village was made up of several such households. Each village had its own chief and was usually also a religious unit. During long periods of their history these villages were united into larger political units. This development reached its height under the Inca who created a political empire extending from Ecuador to Chile.

The pattern of this Andean farmer culture was fairly uniform in the Central Andes over a long period of time. From extensive archaeological work in this area it is possible to reconstruct the development from very early beginnings to its greatest height under the Inca Empire shortly before the Spanish Conquest. In the Chicama and Viru valleys on the north coast of Peru there is evidence of an agricultural people who did not yet make pottery. This material dates from about 2000 B.C. and may well be the earliest New World culture which practised farming but lacked pottery. The subsequent cultural development had, of course, many local variations but was also marked by a surprising degree of uniformity. Three successive waves of cultural influence spread over most of the area. These are named Chavin, Tiahuanaco, and Inca, and may be dated respectively at about A.D. 1, 1000, and 1450. Each of these cultures is represented by stylistic differences in pottery, textiles, metalwork, and building construction.

The Incas, who were the last in this sequence, were originally a small tribe inhabiting Cuzco, a mountain valley in southern Peru. By means of a series of military victories, they conquered the tribes around them until they controlled an empire of six million subjects living in a territory which extended three thousand miles from Colombia to Central Chile. The Incas constituted the ruling class in their empire and established their capital at Cuzco. The characteristic enabling the Incas to build up and then maintain this huge empire was their ability to organize and administer. The state consisted of administrative units beginning with the empire itself and going down through the provinces and districts to the villages. The emperor was at the head of the officers administering these units and his power was absolute. He was, in fact, thought to rule by divine right because he was descended from the Sun, the chief Inca deity. All military and governmental officials were chosen from among the descendants of past emperors, concentrating the power in a small group.

When the Incas conquered a new tribe, much of the local culture was left undisturbed, but the group was incorporated into the empire and required to assume the cult of the sun. Quechua, the language of the Incas, was also the official language of the empire and replaced the local languages. The local leaders were absorbed into the administrative structure of the government. The farmland was divided into three parts for the support of the state, the Inca priesthood and the people. Everyone was required to work on these lands and also on public works such as roads. To insure loyalty and to spread their culture and the Quechua language, the Incas frequently transplanted thousands of people from one district to another. This was sometimes done to equalize population distribution and sometimes to minimize dissatisfaction. All aspects of their subjects' lives were rigidly controlled by the ruling Incas. There was a minimum of individual, personal liberty. However, all government officials were held responsible for the well-being of the people under them.

The communication necessary to maintain such an intricate administrative machinery was made possible by an elaborate system of roads. There were two roads stretching the length of the empire. One lay along the coast. The other, highland, road was paved with stones, ascended steep gradients by means of steps, and crossed rivers and gorges by means of suspension bridges up to 300 feet long. These two main arteries were connected by lateral roads which tied the whole kingdom together. Posthouses, storehouses, and inns were built at frequent intervals along these roads. The posthouses were only two or three miles apart so that a system of couriers could carry messages from one to the next. The storehouses and inns were, perhaps, fifteen miles apart and were for the convenience of official travelers as well as for the storage of food and arms. Another development which facilitated the administration of the empire was the Inca *quipu.* This was a counting device operated on a principle similar to that of the abacus. The *quipu* consisted of a thick cord from which hung knotted strings of different colors. The number and position of the knots represented numbers in a decimal system. The colors of the strings represented different kinds of objects. This device was used to keep statistical records of military, economic, and population matters. The Inca never developed any system of writing but the *quipu* enabled them to keep records of a limited variety.

Inca culture was really the culmination of developments which had been going on for a thousand years. Some of these reached new heights under the Incas who excelled in engineering and architectural skills. Besides the roads, which have already been mentioned, the Incas built elaborate systems of irrigation ditches and agricultural terraces. The ditches were sometimes cut through solid rock or carried along sheer cliffs on stone aqueducts. The stonefaced agricultural terraces covered entire slopes from the valley floor to the summit. The Incas also accomplished remarkable architectural feats. Their houses were simple stone or adobe structures with roofs of grass thatch. Their public buildings, on the other hand, were massive structures built with great skill. The construction was of huge dressed stones, laid without mortar and fitted with greatest exactness. These stones were sometimes cut into polygonal shapes and the edges were beveled. Among these buildings were palaces, temples and fortresses. The enormously imposing structures in the Cuzco area such as the fortress of Sacsahuaman, the temple at Ollantaytambo and some of the buildings at Machu Pichu date from the late Inca times and were the final examples of this development. The Incas were competent potters and weavers and did skillful work in metals, but they did not achieve such impressive results in these crafts as they did in the engineering and architecture. Their weaving and pottery were, in fact, less imaginative than were those of earlier periods.

When Francisco Pizzaro, leading the Spanish invaders, arrived in 1532 he was able to conquer the Inca Empire with surprising ease. This conquest was facilitated by a struggle which was taking place within the Inca dynasty. Pizarro capitalized on this state of civil war and, after the two Inca claimants to the throne were killed, he was able to take over control of the whole empire.

The Northern Andean subarea included Ecuador and highland Colombia. The people here were also sedentary farmers but their culture was in no way as highly developed as that of the Central Andes. Their greatest skill was in metal-working which was like that of the people of the Isthmus of Panama. The Chibcha at the northern extremity of this area had an elaborate political development with autocratic hereditary rulers.

The South Andean area included southernmost Peru, the north Chilean desert, a corner of northwest Argentina and a high, fertile stretch of Chile. The Calchaqui or Diaguite of northwest Argentina show some influence from the Tiahuanaco and Inca periods of the Central Andes. The Chiriguano came up from the area where Peru, the Chaco, and the Tropical Forest areas meet to challenge the Inca on their eastern border and were in turn influenced by Inca culture. The Araucanian farmers of central Chile seem to have been fairly independent of Inca influence and to have resisted, also, the Spaniards.

Circum-Caribbean.—The part of this area lying along northern South America, the Isthmus of Panama and up to the Guatemalan border was occupied by Chibcha-speaking peoples. The cultural development of these peoples was much less elaborate than in the areas to the north and south of them. The Chibcha were agriculturalists; they constructed irrigation systems and raised maize, potatoes, manioc, beans, and squashes. They also raised cotton and did fine weaving. Their houses were built of wattle and plaster, and they also built roads and suspension bridges. Their greatest handwork was of gold, in which they excelled, and which they traded as far away as the Maya, perhaps even beyond there to Mexico. The Chibcha lived in palisaded villages organized into a compact political system. Taxes or tribute were exacted in gold or cloth, and they also had markets and a kind of currency. Chibcha religion involved many sacrifices including human sacrifices to the sun. The religious leaders formed an organized priesthood with a leader. The fringes of this Isthmian culture extended into the highlands of Venezuela and, on the south, as far as the Inca area in Ecuador.

The island part of this Circum-Caribbean area was occupied by Arawak and Carib-speaking peoples. The orientation of their culture was toward the South American mainland. The earliest, pre-agricultural culture survived longest in western Cuba and the Bahamas. A Taino-speaking people, related to the Arawak in South America, overran this early population in most of the remaining islands. The place of highest development was in Puerto Rico and Haiti. Following the Taino came the Carib-speaking people, also from the South American mainland. And, lastly, the Spaniards arrived, and the native cultures disappeared so rapidly that our knowledge of them is very meagre.

Tropical Forest.—This area included the huge expanse of the Amazon Valley, the upper Orinoco, the valleys of the Guianas rivers and also the hill ranges and coast area of eastern Brazil. The river areas were true rain forest where travel was primarily by canoe, metal was completely absent and stone was very scarce. The hill and coast area was scrub forest. Food was actually fairly scant in this whole area so the people lived thinly scattered. Fish were an important source of food and they were caught in nets and traps, shot with arrows, or stupefied with poison. Hunting was done with bows and arrows and blowguns with poison darts. Practically all tribes farmed. The most important crop was cassava, although maize, squashes, beans, pineapples, and cotton were also raised. Manioc meal and tapioca were obtained from the cassava by means of graters, squeezers, and roasters, the poisonous juice being expelled by means of a most ingenious basketry press. One use of the cotton was in making hammocks, which seem to have been invented in this area. There was some pottery-making and weaving of cloth. Enormous dwellings housing a whole village of related families were made of thatch and supported on posts.

Although the dense vegetation and the tropical nature of this jungle area prevented the penetration of the aggressive Inca into it, the tropical forest tribes themselves moved about on the rivers quite easily and frequently. Most of their migrations were in search of new lands to farm. The wide scatter of different linguistic groups in this area reflects the frequency of migrations. Several villages speaking one dialect constituted a tribe but they had no formal organization. The villages were situated close to the rivers. Each had a chief and a council of male adults. Religious life was simple and medicine men carried out curing rites.

The thickness of the jungle vegetation has impeded archaeological investigation of the early history of much of this area. The Lagoa Santa and Confins caves in the east Brazil highlands have already been mentioned in connection with the discussion of early migrants. It is possible that the coastal shell middens will yield some information. On Marajo Island in the mouth of the Amazon River excellent, pre-Columbian pottery has been found. This pottery is modeled, incised and painted and certainly represents the finest workmanship of any kind east of the Andes.

Marginal Area.—The long area extending from the east Brazil highlands across the Chaco to the southern tip of South America was made up of two subareas. The southern part was occupied right up to the conquest by nomadic hunting tribes whose life was doubtless similar to that of the earliest nomadic hunters. In this area lived the Alacaluf and Yahgan Indians of the Chilean archipelago, and the Ona and Tehuelche of Patagonia. These four tribes are the most primitive in the New World and compare, in this respect, with the Australian natives and the Bushmen of South Africa. The Alacaluf and Yahgan Indians subsisted on the marine life of the archipelago, hunting seals and other sea mammals, gathering shellfish and fishing. The Ona and Tehuelche hunted land animals and gathered wild plants. Both groups had simple, portable skin shelters which they erected on stick frames. Their clothing consisted of capes, moccasins, and sometimes leggings which the Ona and Tehuelche made from guanaco skin while the Alacaluf and Yahgan used sealskins. All four tribes greased their bodies for protection against the cold, which was very severe. Both the mainland and the archipelago Indians had the simplest tools and utensils of bone, shell, stone and bark. The canoes of the Alacaluf and Yahgan were made of strips of beech bark sewn together and held in place by split saplings.

The middle part of this marginal area was the Chaco, an open plain where the Puelche, Querandi, and Charrua tribes lived. These tribes were fairly large and warlike. Their culture was not quite so simple as that of their more isolated neighbors to the south. They made some use of wood for utensils, ground seeds in stone mortars and, along the borders of this area, had acquired some pottery from their northern neighbors. Upon the arrival of Europeans and more particularly with the introduction of the horse into this area, these Indians readapted their culture and developed a life similar in many superficial respects to that of the Plains Indians of North America.

The Gê-speaking tribes are the northernmost group in the Marginal area and occupy the savanna and scrub country of east Brazil. Hunting, gathering, and fishing are important with the addition of some farming of sweet potatoes and yams. Their technology is also fairly simple although a few tribes make pottery. These tribes have, however, a rather complex social and ritual organization. Some of these Indians live in villages with a population of nearly three hundred. There is little or no intervillage organization. Each village is usually divided in halves for the regulation of marriage, performance of ceremonials and for competitive games. There are also ritual societies for the performance of ceremonials.

Very little is known of the prehistory of this whole Marginal area. Nothing has been found which would indicate any previous higher development. It is assumed that the simple culture in this area is a survival of the early cultural poverty.

NORTH AMERICAN CULTURE AREAS

Setting.—The North American continent includes a great range of topographic zones: Arctic, Mountain, Plains, Prairie, Woodland, Desert Plateau, and Jungle. In terms of native cultures, these topographic zones combine into six culture areas each of which may have several subareas: (1) the Meso-American area covering the region from central Honduras and El Salvador to northern Mexico; (2) the Southwestern area covering the desert and plateau regions of New Mexico and Arizona; (3) the Intermediate area including California and the intermountain region; (4) the Northwest coast area from Oregon north to Alaska; (5) the Arctic area; (6) the huge remaining area of Canada and the United States east of the Rocky Mountains constituting the Eastern-Northern area.

Race.—The Indians of North America, with the exception of the Eskimo, belong to the American Indian race which is a subdivision of the Mongoloid stock. The Eskimo are classified as Arctic Mongoloid because they show less admixture of non-Mongoloid stocks. Setting aside the Eskimo, the remaining North American Indians show some variation in head form and stature. The tribes of the Plains area are generally taller and more long-headed than, for example, the Indians of the Southwest and Meso-America. Here, as in South America, the differences in stature may be due to diet as well as to physical type.

Language.—There were 40 or more linguistic families in North America, some of which were spread over huge areas, others spoken by a few hundred people. The principal families, in terms of numbers and cultural importance, and the well-known tribes representing these families were: (1) Eskimo, spoken along the Arctic coast from Alaska to Greenland; (2) Athabascan, spoken by the Beaver, Dogrib, Yellow Knives, Carrier and others in the northwest interior of Canada and Alaska, by the Hupa, Kato and others in California and Oregon, and by the Navajo and Apache in Arizona and New Mexico; (3) Algonquian, spoken by the Arapaho, Cheyenne, and Blackfoot of the Plains area, by the Sauk and Fox, Cree, Menomini, Shawnee, Ojibway, Delaware, Kickapoo, Miami and others in the great expanse of eastern Canada, the area around and south of the Great Lakes, the New England and Middle Atlantic states area; (4) Iroquois, spoken by the Cherokee, Huron, Erie, Mohawk, and Seneca and others in the area of New York, Pennsylvania, Ohio, and adjacent territory; (5) Siouan, spoken by such Plains tribes as the Dakota, Assiniboin, Omaha, Osage, Hidatsa and Crow; (6) Muskhogean, spoken in the southeastern area by Choctaw, Chickasaw, Creek, Seminole, Natchez, and others; (7) Uto-Aztecan spoken by the Aztec, Seri, Yaqui, and others in Mexico, by the Hopi and Pima in the Southwest, and by the Ute, Comanche, Shoshone and others from Wyoming to southern California and across to Texas; (8) Maya, spoken in Guatemala and Yucatan, plus a small area further north in the Mexican State of Vera Cruz.

Prehistory.—The oldest evidence of North American prehistory was quite thoroughly described in earlier paragraphs. Here we will summarize such material as is necessary for our subsequent description of the native cultures which developed from this early base. The first migrants probably reached the North American continent about eleven thousand years ago fanning out slowly over the two New World continents wherever they found wild game, wild plants, and fish. The earliest known cultural materials in North America are from the Sandia Cave in New Mexico; the somewhat later Folsom people who were present in the Southwest by 8000 B.C., and of the Cochise people somewhat later still. Evidence of the persistence of the Cochise culture and the gradual addition to it of farming and pottery-making fill in the local, southern Arizona story up to the Christian era. At this point these early developments tie in with the known sequences of cultures which have been carried back from the historic period to the early years of the Christian era in Meso-America, the Southwest, and east of the Mississippi.

Cultures.—North America can be divided into six areas of native culture: (1) Meso-American, (2) Southwest, (3) Intermediate, (4) Northwest coast, (5) Arctic, and (6) Eastern-Northern.

Meso-American.—This area includes Mexico, except for its most northern part, British Honduras, Guatemala, and the adjacent parts of Honduras and El Salvador. For many years it was believed that the several cultures which reached a high degree of development in this area did so independently of each other and with only their most primitive phases in common. Recent archaeological work indicates that there was contact over practically all of this area during most of its history. Several culture patterns which were interrelated in origin became distinct, local developments from a common basis. These local developments will be considered from south to north.

The Maya people fall into two groups: the Lowland Maya lived in Yucatan, British Honduras, and the Peten district of Guatemala. They spoke Maya and such closely related dialects as Chol, Chorti, and Chontal. The Highland Maya occupied upland Guatemala and spoke the Quiche, Cakchiquel, and Mani dialects of Maya.

An erroneous early theory maintained that the Maya had domesticated maize and were the first American farmers. More recent botanical evidence indicates that maize is probably South American in origin. This information is of interest because it was assumed for many years that the elaborate Maya artistic and intellectual development went hand in hand with their skill as agriculturalists. Actually, plant domestication probably took place two thousand years before the great rise of Maya culture and several thousand miles further south.

The earliest period known for the Lowland Maya is called Formative and is based on pottery-types and other refuse-heap material from sites in the Peten district of Guatemala. During this period the basic Mayan astronomy, writing and mathematics were being developed. These intellectual achievements, the Maya calendar which is based on them, and the magnificent artistic expression reached their height during the classic period. The beginning of this period is set by the earliest known date of the Maya calendar—317 A.D. The calendar, based on centuries of astronomical observations and mathematical calculations, was exceedingly accurate. Calendrical inscriptions were used primarily to record ceremonial dates and are found inscribed on stone monuments in all parts of the Lowland Maya area. The Maya were also very skillful potters, lapidaries, sculptors, painters and architects, as is attested by the contents of tombs and by the buildings found in the Peten district and in Yucatan. They also built ball courts for the playing of a ritualistic game with a rubber ball. These skills were doubtless practiced by specialists. The average Mayan was a farmer living in a wood and thatch house near his field. Maize, beans, squash, pumpkins, sweet potatoes, avocados, and cacao were the food crops, while cotton and hemp were also raised. The farming technique required burning and slashing the jungle growth. New fields had to be cleared often because the jungle grass grew so luxuriantly in a field cleared of brush. The domesticated animals included turkeys, dogs, and bees. Wild pig and deer were hunted with blowgun, bow and arrow, poisoned darts or traps. The Maya lived in independent city-states each of which was a unit and had its own religious center. Each city-state was ruled by its priests.

The Maya classical period came to an end in the early 10th century. The late period, which followed, was characterized by a decline in Maya culture and the abandonment of their great cities in the Peten. They continued to occupy some of their cities in Yucatan where there was some local persistence of Maya culture but also a strong influence from the Toltec people of the Valley of Mexico on art styles and religious cults. Warfare among the city-states also developed. It was at the end of this period that the Spaniards arrived, conquering the Maya in 1540.

The Highland Maya never achieved the rich development of the Lowland group. They did have the calendar but their artistic development was not spectacular.

During the years in which Maya culture was growing and declining other developments were taking place to the northwest in the Valley of Mexico. These developments used to be described in the sequence Archaic, Toltec, and Aztec. Since the earlier 1930's this overly-simple sequence has been changed. The Archaic was clearly a well-developed pattern and so was renamed middle, leaving the term "early" for an, as yet, unidentified period. The subsequent periods are called Teotihuacan, Toltec, Chichimec, and Aztec.

The middle period is represented as gradually developing around the old Lake Texcoco which then was at a higher level. Farming, pottery-making and weaving were already practiced and the people lived in villages. They made large numbers of baked clay figurines, which evidently were of religious significance. Some middle period sites lie under a lava flow, leading a few people to assign a great antiquity to them. Geologists, however, do not agree. It seems much more likely that these sites fall somewhere between 350 B.C. and the year zero.

The Teotihuacan period overlapped at its early end with the middle. The fully developed Teotihuacan period was most impressive. The huge Pyramid of the Sun (700 feet at the base and over 200 feet high) dominates an enormous ceremonial center whose buildings are decorated with sculptures and murals. Teotihuacan culture seems to have reached its highest development about A.D. 500. The influence of the Teotihuacan style, probably spread by means of trade, has been traced to the coast, to the Monte Alban site in Oaxaca, to a site near Guatemala City, and to a classic Maya site in the Peten. It was once thought that the Toltec people had built Teotihuacan but, actually, they established their capital near Tula several centuries later. We have already noted their influence on the Maya of Yucatan. Some of the history from Toltec times on is known from records kept in picture writing. These records list kings' names and describe the defeats and victories of some of the cities from the ninth century to the Spanish Conquest. The Toltecs were displaced by the warlike Chichimecs from the north, and for some centuries there was warfare among the cities of the valley.

In the 13th century another invading tribe, the Aztecs, descended on the valley from the north. By 1324 they had established their capital at Tenochtitlan and, by gradually strengthening their position through alliances and conquests, finally dominated an empire extending to the Isthmus of Tehuantepec. Warfare was an important aspect of Aztec life and played a part in their religion, their social organization and their economy. All Aztec conquests were for the sake of obtaining tribute for their treasury and prisoners for sacrifices in their religious ceremonies. The Aztecs were primarily farmers raising maize, beans, squashes, sweet potatoes, tomatoes and chili peppers. They also raised cotton and maguey for the fibers. They had domesticated dogs and turkeys, caught fish with hooks, nets and weirs, and hunted deer and wild fowl with bow and arrow, spear thrower, nets and darts. In addition to weaving, the Aztec men did excellent work in wood, stone, masonry, metal and pottery. Some of these crafts were organized into hereditary guilds. The craftsmen traded their wares at markets or sold them for cotton cloth, cocoa beans or copper axe blades

Sioux Indian girl.

Blackfoot Indian boy: "Bear Medicine."

Cree Indian woman: "White Buffalo."

Cree Indian chief.

Portraits painted from life by Winold Reiss.

© Ewing Galloway

Two modern Cherokee Indians in their tribal costumes. Members of a famous tribe, they live in Oklahoma.

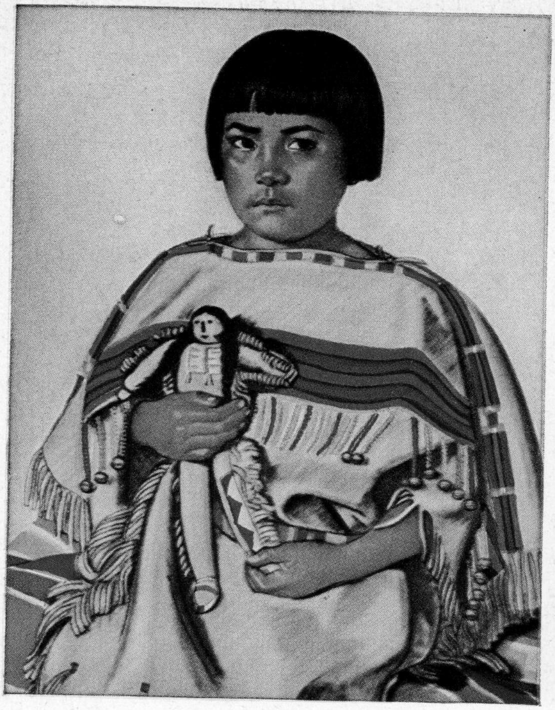

"Singing In The Clouds."

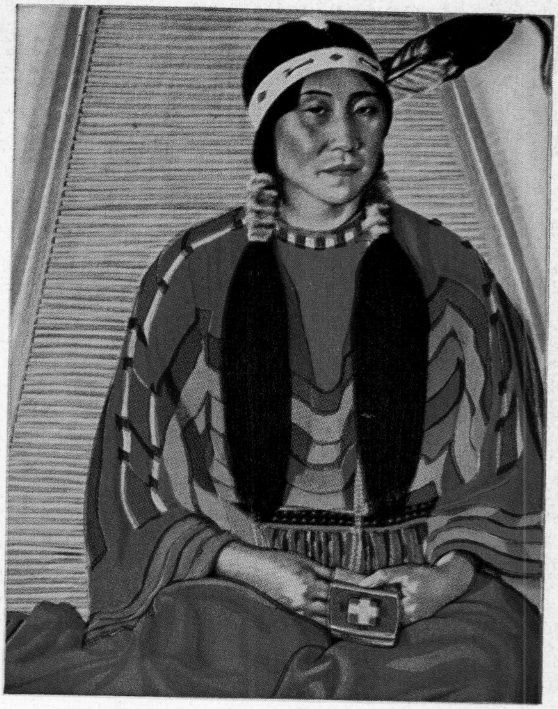

"Only Child."

"Plume."

"Big Face Chief."

Blackfeet Indians painted from life by Winold Reiss.

© Ewing Galloway

Left: Seminole Indian mother and child. *Right:* Two young members of the highly civilized Yakima tribe.

© Ewing Galloway

Mother and baby of the Navajo Indian tribe, in traditional dress. They are natives of Arizona.

Blood Indian girl: "Many Snake Woman."

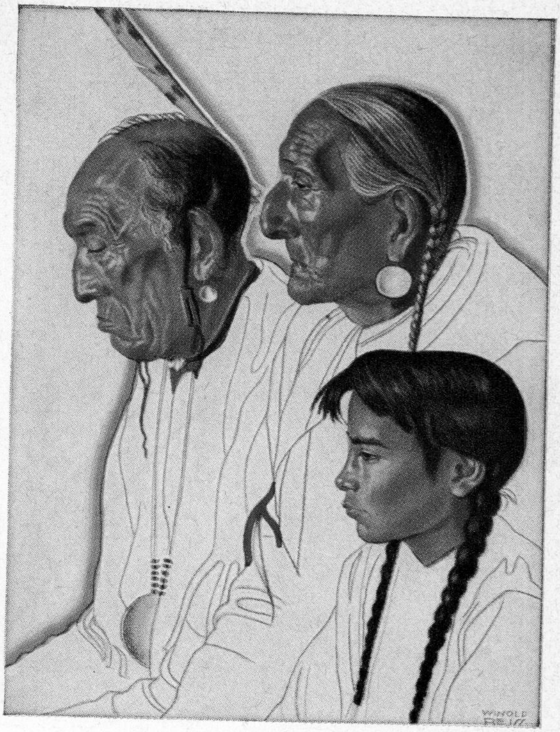

Three generations in a Cree Indian family.

A blind Paiute Indian.

Sioux Indian girl: "Rattling Day Woman."

Portraits painted from life by Winold Reiss.

Top: Two views of the Dakota sun dance painted by Short Bull, chief of the Oglala, a division of the Dakota, of the Sioux family.

Left: Ottawa Indian girls doing beadwork.

Above: Dakota shield, the chief figure of which bears a marked resemblance to the eagle of the Great Seal of the United States.

(Top and above) Courtesy American Museum of Natural History; (left) © Ewing Galloway

which were considered to be a kind of currency. All these wares were also carried long distances by itinerant merchants who traded them with other tribes. Their houses were of simple size and construction. They also built large earth pyramids, faced with sculptured masonry, which were bases for altars and temples. Their capital, Tenochtitlan, was on an island connected with the mainland by causeways and protected from attack by drawbridges.

Aztec society was divided intc four classes and was ruled by a king and his advisers, a council of representatives from the 20 clans which included the majority of the people. The king was also the war chief. The religious life of these people was conducted by priests, and consisted of a great many ceremonies pertaining to agriculture and warfare. The ceremonies were performed according to a ritualistic calendar which consisted of two hundred and sixty days divided into thirteen "months" of four "weeks" each, the week having five days. The Aztec also had a solar calendar of three hundred sixty-five days divided into eighteen "months" of twenty days each plus five supplementary days. Each division of both calendars had its own god who was considered to influence the events of that day. Before undertaking anything important, an Aztec always consulted the calendars to determine the appropriateness of the day. Another matter of interest in Aztec life was a game with religious and mystical importance played with a rubber ball in a large stone court.

In 1519 the Spanish soldiers landed at Vera Cruz with their leader Hernando Cortes. For two years the Aztecs succeeded in resisting them. Finally, Montezuma II (1480–1520) was imprisoned, hundreds of Aztecs were massacred, and the Spaniards, aided by reinforcements, conquered the Aztecs.

Outside these areas of highest development in Meso-America lay the Huastec, Totonac, and Olmec people of the Atlantic coast and lowland, the Zapotec of Oaxaca, and the Otomí and Tarascans to north and west of the Valley of Mexico. Of these, the most is known about the Zapotec, who seem to have had a distinctive culture touched by both Maya and Valley of Mexico influences. From a late period at the site of Monte Alban comes the famous gold jewelry made by the Mixtecs who conquered the Zapotecs.

To the north, across the rest of Mexico, lived Indian groups who had some characteristics of Meso-American culture but none of its highest developments. Farming was practiced in the western half and good pottery and some stone construction were made all over but neither the calendar nor picture writing were present. The archaeology of this area is not yet well known. It is, however, potentially very important because across it flowed the cultural influences which, we will presently see, reached the southwest from the high cultures of Meso-America.

Southwestern.—This area includes part of northern Mexico, all of New Mexico and Arizona, and the southern part of Colorado and Utah. Much of this area is very dry, with a rainfall of 10-15 inches a year. There are also high plateaus, mountains and mountain valleys, which receive 22-40 inches a year. The Southwestern area has been a particularly rich one for anthropological research. The country lends itself to archaeological reconnaissance and excavation because of its openness and its arid climate which affords excellent conditions for preservation. In addition, it is the first area for which any precise system of archaeological dating was developed. This technique, known as dendrochronology, is based on a comparison of the growth rings of trees. By a careful comparison of the rings on timbers and other wooden objects found in archaeological sites, with the rings on a master chart, dates for these sites are determined. This technique has carried dating back from the present to A.D. 11. As a result of these conditions, a fairly full story is known of the rich development of early cultures up to historic times. The main prehistoric Southwestern cultures were the Anasazi, the Hohokam, and the Mogollon. The Anasazi people (consisting of the early Basket Maker and their actual and cultural descendants, the Pueblo) lived on the plateau of northern Arizona and New Mexico. The Hohokam culture was parallel in time to the Anasazi, centered in the southern Arizona desert, and was ancestral to the present-day Pima and Papago of that area. The Mogollon culture centered in east central Arizona and west central New Mexico in mountainous country. It probably descended from the earlier Cochise culture.

The Anasazi culture sequence is made up of stages referred to as Basket Maker and Pueblo. It is not known just what preceded the Basket Makers. The earliest Basket Maker period dates from about 100–500 A.D. These people practiced agriculture but did not make pottery. As their name suggests, they wove many articles including baskets, bags, and sandals. They used the spear-thrower but did not have the bow and arrow. Their houses were temporary structures but they did line their food-storage pits with stone slabs which may have marked the historical beginning of their subsequent stone construction. A Modified Basket Maker period lasted from about 500–700. Turkeys had been domesticated and more varieties of maize introduced, and pottery-making was begun. Following this, the sequence of Pueblo development has been divided into five stages each a little richer and more complex than the one before. Pueblo I (700–900) had added the bow and arrow and cotton for cloth. Both were probably imports. Some masonry houses were built and a pottery decoration called corrugating was introduced. In the Pueblo II period (900–1050) rooms with common walls were built forming dwelling clusters so well-known for later years in this area. In Pueblo III (1050–1300) times, polychrome pottery decoration was begun. This was the period of the greatest development of masonry houses including such impressive and well-known sites as Mesa Verde and Chaco Canyon. Pottery-making and design also reached a high point in the Mimbres style. Pueblo IV (1300–1700) was a period of expansion and cultural development. By this time some of the present-day Pueblo towns were already occupied. It seems likely that the Pueblo ritual development, which was to become so elaborate, has its origin in this period. The Spaniards first reached the Southwest in 1540.

The villages of the historic Pueblo people, still lived in today, fall into three geographical groups: the Hopi (Walpi, Sichomovi, Hano [Tewa], Shipaulovi, Mishongnovi, Shungopovi, and Oraibi); Zuni (Zuni proper, Pescado, Nutria, and Oja Caliente); and the Rio Grande (Taos, Picuris, San Juan, Santa Clara, San

Ildefonso, Tesuque, Pojoaque, Nambe, Jemez, Pecos, Sandia, Isleta—all of which speak Tanoan languages; San Felipe, Cochiti, Santo Domingo, Santa Ana, Sia, Laguna, and Acoma—all speaking Keresan languages). Although there are differences among these three groups, they share such basic traits as dependence on maize and other cultivated foods; masonry construction; weaving on upright loom done by the men; cultivation of cotton; domestication of the turkey; common-wall houses; decorated pottery. These Pueblo people do some hunting including the deer and rabbit, and rabbitskin strips are woven into their clothing. They make basketry and do work in turquoise and metal which was unknown until introduced by the Spaniards. Pottery and such ceremonial paraphernalia as sand painted altars and masks are skillfully made and beautifully decorated.

Although differing still in detail, the Pueblo groups all have complex social groupings based on kinship relationships which are important in ceremonial and economic matters. Each village is also an independent unit which elects its own officers. The most elaborate flowering of Pueblo culture is in its ceremonial life. Ritualism is highly complex and includes elaborate masks, costumes, shrines, fetishes, dances and ritual acts. Many priests and religious societies are involved in carrying out the annual round of ceremonies some of the best-known of which are the Hopi snake dance, the numerous rain ceremonies and the masked dances of the kachinas.

Some of the initial stages and early development of this general pattern may be seen in the Pueblo IV period of the archaeological sequence. This same era saw the arrival of the Spaniards who first reached the Southwest in 1540 under the leadership of Coronado. The Indians were very hostile and because the Spaniards found no such treasure in this area as they had in Meso-America and Peru, it remained of interest to them primarily as a missionary field. It was not until 1598 that the Spanish succeeded in establishing a permanent occupancy. Even this was upset by the Pueblo Indians revolt in 1680, after which the Spaniards reestablished themselves by 1697. During this whole period from 1540–1697 a great dislocation of Pueblo populations took place and, whereas there had been seventy or more villages in 1540, by 1700 there were thirty or less. Despite prolonged contacts with the Spaniards and later with the Americans, the Pueblo Indians maintain their cultural identity and particularly their religious independence.

During the Pueblo IV period of Anasazi development, Athabascan-speaking people began coming down from the country to the north. These people had a hunting and gathering economy and, doubtless, a fairly simple cultural development. Some of these Athabascans, the present-day Apaches, moved south of the Pueblo area. Others, the Navajos (Navahos), settled near the Pueblo towns and learned such things as farming and weaving from the Pueblo people, although it should be noted that the Navajo women did the weaving instead of the men as among the Pueblos. The Navajos also took over a great many external aspects of Pueblo ceremonialism to which they gave their own meanings and emphasis. The Navajos may also have acquired the idea of clans, groups of relatives tracing their descent through either the male or female parent, from the Pueblos. The basic pattern of Navajo social grouping remained, however, the same. They continued to live in large, thinly-scattered family groups which differ completely from the compact Pueblo village group. They also continued to depend on hunting and, after the Spaniards introduced sheep into the Southwest, they developed a greater dependence on herding than did the Pueblos. Like the Pueblos, the Navajos learned to work in silver from the Spaniards.

Nowhere else in the New World were native cultures as undisturbed by the arrival of the Whites as in some parts of this Southwestern area. An amazing proportion of native Pueblo, Navajo and Apache culture was able to survive first Spanish and then American conquest. As a result, these groups have been a rich source of information about and insight into the life and culture of non-European people.

It seems probable that the Hohokam culture of southern Arizona was a development from the very early Cochise culture which was described in an earlier section. As for its subsequent growth, there are no tree rings dates for the desert area of this Hohokam culture, but crossties show that its development paralleled the Basket Maker-Pueblo in time. Hohokam culture is described in four stages. Agriculture and pottery-making were known in the earliest stage; the earliest projectile points were for bow and arrow; they had no masonry construction but did build dug-out ball courts in which a ritual game, known as far south as the Maya, was played. The Hohokam also had pyrite mirrors and copper bells similar to some known in Mexico. The Hohokam built irrigation ditches and their early houses were of post and brush construction. During their final developmental period the Hohokam were considerably influenced by contact with the Pueblo III and IV people, and they adopted such traits as common-wall houses of packed earth which they substituted for Pueblo masonry. When the Spaniards first reached southern Arizona in the early part of the 16th century, they found the Pima and Papago Indians living a life similar to but simpler than the classic Hohokam pattern. Their scattered house, built in pit-house style; canal irrigation; pottery made by paddle and anvil and painted red-on-buff; effigy vessels; and cultivation of cotton are so similar to the Hohokam culture as to suggest descent from that group.

The Mogollon culture, like the early Hohokam, was probably a development out of the later stages of the Cochise culture. In the earliest Mogollon period, about the beginning of the Christian era, agriculture was already practiced and pottery was made. Recent evidence indicates that these people began cultivating corn several centuries earlier, at a time before they made pottery. From the 1st to 11th centuries A.D. Mogollon culture showed a fairly uniform pattern with minor variations and developments. After about 1050 there is evidence of strong Anasazi influence either through contact or invasion. There is also evidence of Hohokam influence.

South and west of this core area of Southwestern cultural development are the Uto-Aztecan- and Yuman-speaking people of Southern California and Sonora. Their culture seems to be a simple version of the Hohokam type. In this group belong the Yaqui, Maya, Yuma and Mohave.

Intermediate.—This region, consisting of California and the intermountain area between the Rockies and the coastal mountains, was one of slow development and little change. The California portion of it includes the southern California desert, the broad valley and pine-covered mountains of central California and the densely forested northern part of the state. The earliest cultural material known from California comes from campsites along Lake Mojave (Mohave) and Pinto Basin in the southern California desert and at Borax Lake in central California. The same problem obscures the dating of all of these sites. On geological grounds their age might be the last pluvial period which ended about ten thousand years ago. Or, it may have been during a wet period which occurred about 1000 B.C. The later date seems more acceptable on archaeological grounds. California culture was quite similar to the pre-farming, pre-pottery culture of the Basket Maker people and remained so even until recent times. Because the food supply was ample and the climate was mild, the density of population was high even in the parts of California which had a nonagricultural economy. Cultural development remained on a fairly simple level with evidence of considerable local specialization.

The most extensive cultural subarea was in central California. Here subsistence was based on fishing, hunting and the gathering of wild seeds, particularly of acorns. Acorns formed the chief vegetable food and were made into bread by a complex process which eliminated their tannic acid. The houses of this area were simple brush or tule shelters, or lean-to structures made of poles. These people made no pottery but did make excellent baskets which were used for carrying water and food, for storage, and for cooking by the stone-heating method. Social and political organizations were rudimentary in this area. The religious development was very simple, consisting of a few ceremonies. Shamanism was quite important. An interesting characteristic of this area is the large number of languages spoken in a small area.

To the south of this central area the basic pattern did not change much except for the important addition of pottery-making, and a great increase in linguistic homogeneity. This was an area of a large group of Yuman- and Shoshonean-speaking peoples. North of the central area the contrast was more striking and resemblances to the Northwest Coast area appeared. Fishing was of major importance, a variety of sea foods was consumed along the coast and salmon was the major food along the interior rivers. The construction of plank houses, the use of wood and elkhorn for boxes and spoons, and also the increase in carving and decoration all suggest northern affiliations. The same was true of the more elaborate social organization characteristic of this subarea.

The Intermountain area consists of the Great Basin and the Columbia-Fraser Plateau regions. The Great Basin area, lying between the Rockies and the coastal ranges, was one of simple culture based on gathering wild foods. In this respect and also in basketry and house types, Great Basin culture resembled that of California. However, in terms of climate, vegetation and early development the Great Basin is closer to the Southwest. The seed-gathering, basket-making characteristics of the Great Basin are the same as those described for the Basket Maker people of the early period in the Southwestern area. Lovelock Cave in central Nevada had an Atlatl-culture similar to Basket Maker. Material similar to the early Pueblo periods has been found as far into the Great Basin area as the Utah-Idaho line and the Nevada-California boundary. At an early period California, the Great Basin and the Southwest had common characteristics. The Southwest area surged ahead to a very full development. California managed a few cultural achievements. The Great Basin succeeded only in preserving its simple, early level.

Indians of the Columbia-Fraser Plateau region lived by hunting, salmon fishing and gathering berries and roots, especially the camas. The abundant salmon supply allowed a fairly dense population to live in the dry Middle Columbia region. Archaeological evidence of early cultures is lacking. The material from more recent times suggests that the fairly simple culture known for the early historic times had already been in existence for several centuries or, perhaps, longer. Pottery was not made in this area, but basketry was well developed and bags, mats and clothing were woven of bark fiber. Clothing was also made of deerskin. The largest social unit in the Plateau was the village. A number of villages were grouped together through sharing common dialect and customs, but there was no political structure to tie them together into a tribe.

About the year 1720, actually before the beginning of the historic period in this area, the southern and eastern Plateau tribes were strongly influenced by the adoption of the horse and other culture traits from the Indians of the Plains to the east.

Northwest Coast Area.—The river mouth, coastal and island region stretching from Oregon to the Alaskan border forms the Northwest Coast area, one of the most distinctive in the New World. Life in this area centered around fishing in rivers, in bays and other protected salt water areas, and also in the open sea. Archaeological material is spotty for this area. However, from a comparative study of the recent cultures it seems likely that the people first lived on the rivers and later on the beaches. Finally some, especially in the north, took to the sea and the archipelagos. The tribes included in this area fall into three groups from north to south: (1) the Tlingit, Haida, Tsimshian; (2) Bella Coola, Kwakiutl; (3) Nootka, Quinault, Salish, Chinook, Tilamook, Yurok, Karok and Hupa. The most northerly groups showed the greatest cultural development. The Indians of this area were skillful and ingenious in their use of wood and in basketry and weaving. The Chilkat, a Tlingit tribe, wove blankets of goat hair by means of a warp suspended from a bar. All the tribes of this northern group built large dugout canoes and the houses of their winter villages were built of cedar timbers and split planks. They also made slat armor, boxes, and dishes of wood, and such ceremonial equipment as rattles and masks. They are, of course, renowned for their elaborately carved totem poles and house posts, covered with symbolic animal decorations. Their baskets were very well made. Pottery and metal-work were unknown. An interesting quality common to the techniques and style of decoration of all their work is its own force and its complete dissimilarity from anything around it or, for that matter, from anything in the New World.

The Northwest coast tribes also had a distinctive development of economic, social, and ritual organization. There was a great emphasis first on accumulating and then on distributing wealth in the form of food, dentalium-shell currency, slaves, and sheets of native copper. This distribution took place at huge feasts called potlatches which were given to celebrate important events in the life of the individual, such as naming, coming of age, marriage, assuming chiefly office, and death. This Northwest Coast culture is clearly different from anything else in the New World. It was, of course, too far from the Meso-American high culture area to have been influenced by it. A number of Northwest Coast traits show resemblances to traits known in Asia. Slat armor is known from as far away as eastern Asia. The emphasis on wealth as a basis for social status and the use of carved masks are suggestive of Indonesia and western Oceania.

Eskimo Area.—The Eskimos live on the long stretch of Arctic coast from southern Alaska, across the whole of northern Canada to Newfoundland and on the west coast of Greenland. Linguistically, this entire area is covered by one family, also called Eskimo. In physical characteristics the Eskimos differ somewhat from the American Indian proper. They represent a branch of the primary Mongoloid stock known as the Arctic Mongoloid. Archaeological work in the Eskimo area has established a sequence of cultural developments but, so far, has not succeeded in establishing any definite dates. The earliest material is possibly from around 400 A.D. or may be as old as 1 A.D. Relationships with northeastern Asia were strong in the early stages while some later developments were local. Eskimo culture represents a fascinating and remarkable adaptation to an extreme environment. The coastal Eskimos live, for the most part, by hunting seals, walruses and whales. Inland, the caribou are hunted for their meat and fur, both by coastal groups who move inland during the summer months and by a few Eskimo groups which spend the entire year in the caribou country. Other specialties are river salmon fishing in some delta areas and large whale hunting at Point Barrow. The Eskimo's equipment is made from the few materials available. The seal is not only a source of meat but also provides skin for clothing and boats as well as blubber for cooking and heating fuel. The Eskimos make two kinds of houses, both quite small and compact. The winter house is made of rocks and slabs of stone. The snowhouse, or igloo, used on trips, is made of blocks of ice which, because they spiral into a dome, support each other. The igloo serves as a permanent winter house in areas of extreme cold where blowhole fishing is done through the ice of the frozen bays. In most parts of the Arctic coast, wood is lacking or very scarce and is used only for sled runners and for thin boat frames. At the southern extremes of their territory the Eskimos use driftwood for building their houses. In some areas where wood is lacking whale ribs are used as roof supports. Eskimo boats are of two kinds. The kayak is a one-man hunting boat, decked over except for the hunter's seat. The umiak, which is open and larger, is used for transportation and for whaling. The Eskimos of the Aleutian Islands and the Pacific coast area lived in villages, but elsewhere they lived in scattered family groups. There were no tribal groups in the sense of a political organization but only in a geographical sense, indicating a group showing some cultural and linguistic uniformity.

Northern and Eastern Area.—The North American continent east of the Rocky Mountains and north of Mexico shows considerable environmental uniformity despite its great size and its wide range of latitude. Temperature range and precipitation are quite similar throughout the area. The whole eastern part is evenly covered with forest which to the west changes gradually to parkland and to the open grassland of the western plains. This environmental uniformity was reflected in a considerable degree of cultural uniformity. There were, of course, varying local adaptations, but during the pre-Caucasian period these did not reach any degree of intensification.

The prehistory of this area may, from present archaeological evidence, be seen as a sequence of four stages: Pre-pottery, Woodland, Hopewell, and Mississippian. Pre-pottery period sites are known from Massachusetts, New York State, the lower Ohio drainage, the Ozarks, the Mississippi delta, Florida, northern Texas and western Nebraska. These sites were also all pre-agricultural. The oldest of these sites are Clear Fork in Texas and Signal Butte in Nebraska. A date of 2000 B.C. is claimed for the latter. In any case, this eastern pre-pottery period extended back from the early centuries of the Christian era and may be as old as 3000 B.C. in some places. The Woodland period grew, largely, out of the pre-pottery period with the introduction of pottery-making and, perhaps somewhat later, maize agriculture. In some areas the Woodland culture persisted for a very long time while in other places local cultural developments grew out of it. Woodland pottery was cordmarked, a characteristic which can be traced northwestward to Asia and even resembles European Neolithic pottery. The implications of this resemblance are far from clear. The Woodland people also made smoking pipes, stone axes and chisels, and the so-called "banner stones" and "bird stones" of well-polished slate. Sites of this period are known from New England, Ohio, Illinois, Wisconsin, Kansas, Nebraska, and North Dakota.

Sites from the Hopewellian period are scattered along the Mississippi and its principal affluents, and also across the Gulf Coast to Florida. The highest accomplishments in eastern prehistoric art are from the Hopewell sites in southern Ohio. Particularly noteworthy are human and animal sculptures in stone, bone, and clay, elaborate curvilinear designs incised on pottery, large, finely chipped blades of obsidian and quartz crystal, and celts and elaborate ornaments of copper. It has been debated whether such Hopewellian traits as burial mounds, the accumulation of wealth, and the presence of chiefs were indications of importation or influence from Mexico. Because the greatest development occurred in Ohio, at the point farthest from Mexico, it seems likely that the Mexican influence was indirect.

The Mississippian period is known primarily from sites south of the Ohio River and east of the Mississippi plus some from Texas, Arkansas, and Oklahoma. Pottery from the later part of this period in Texas crossties with Pueblo pottery, giving a date of 1300–1450 A.D. During the Mississippi period mounds were built which served as the bases for temples. Very fine work was done in modeled and engraved pottery, and with shells and copper. The question of Mexican influence arises again here. Mexican motives may be found, especially in material from the southern states. There was, however, clearly a development from the Hopewell period.

Turning to later cultural conditions in the Northern and Eastern Area, some regional variations appear. In the Northern area of coniferous forest reaching across the continent from Newfoundland to Alaska, farming was impossible and the wild game was thinly scattered. As a result, the population was also thinly scattered and cultural development meagre. The caribou, which ranged clear across this area, was the major source of food and also supplied material for clothing and tents. Other traits characteristic of the area are: spruce and birchbark canoes; toboggans; babiche and bark fiber; the use of snares and nets; cooking with hot stones in baskets made of split spruce root. The tribes of this area camped along the rivers traveling by canoe in summer and on the ice in winter. They were independent of each other, having no tribal political systems. There was also little religious activity except for the prominence of shamanism. Hudson's Bay constitutes a dividing line within this area. The tribes to the east of it are the Algonquian-speaking Saulteaux, Cree, Montagnais, and Naskapi, all of whom share the basic pattern of this area. To the west of Hudson's Bay were the Dene whose culture was similar to the more easterly groups with the addition of some influences from the Eskimo on the one hand (kayak, some fishing implements), and from the Northwest coast tribes on the other hand (social classes based on wealth, clans, the potlatch, use of armor). In this area there is also salmon fishing and some use of planks for houses as well as the tipi and lean-to.

The next subarea within the Northern and Eastern Area is the Eastern Woodland Area which consists of three principal groups: (1) the Iroquoian tribes (Huron, Wyandot, Erie, Susquehanna, and the Six Nations); (2) the central Algonquin, lying west of the Iroquois and including the Ojibway, Ottawa, Menomini, Sauk, and Fox, Potawatomi, Peoria, Illinois, Kickapoo, Miami, Shawnee, and the Siouan Winnebago; (3) the eastern Algonquin including the Abnaki, Micmac, New England tribes, and the Delaware. Because so many of these tribes became extinct early in historic times, the details of their culture are not too well known but the following traits are characteristic: cultivation of maize, squashes and beans; the use of wild rice and maple sugar where available; hunting of deer, bear and buffalo; fishing on the lakes; some pottery cooking vessels; also vessels of wood and bark; splint basketry; a winter bark or mat-covered lodge and a summer rectangular bark house; the use of canoes, toboggans and snowshoes; skin clothing for men and women. The two eastern divisions were more intensive agriculturalists and made more use of pottery. The Iroquois did superior work in bone and in carving wooden masks. They also had a highly developed political organization, typical of an eastern pattern of confederacies which reached its final development in late pre-white times. The best-known of these confederacies was the Iroquois League of the Six Nations, which included the Mohawk, Oneida, Onondaga, Cayuga, Seneca, and Tuscarora. It seems certain that these large leagues developed out of a native pattern of small and unstable leagues. It also seems clear that the full development of these early leagues took place only after the pressure from white encroachment made a strong organization necessary and the acquisition of such Caucasian possessions as livestock and firearms produced a temporarily more stable economy.

The Southeastern subarea covers the region east from the Mississippi. It includes such tribes as the Natchez, Powhatan and Shawnee, all the Muskhogean groups (e.g., Choctaw, Chicasaw, and Creek), the Eastern Siouan (Ofo and Biloxi), and the Cherokee.

This was an area of intensive agriculture. Maize, pumpkins, melons, and tobacco were raised before White contact and fruit trees were quickly taken over from the Europeans. Dogs were the only pre-European domestic source of food but chickens, hogs, horses and cattle were quickly adopted. Deer, bear, bison, turkeys and other small game were hunted wherever available. The houses in this area were usually covered with thatch or bark, and sometimes had plaster walls reinforced with wickerwork; towns were fortified with palisades; clothing was made of deerskin, weaving was done with bark fiber and buffalo hair; fine mats were made of cane and some work was done with cornhusks; some special kinds of baskets such as the double basket and basket meal sieve were made; knives and darts were of cane; the blowgun was used; pottery was well made by the coil process with paddle decorations; there was no metal work or sculpture but some stone work. In some places temples, set on mounds, were used in sun worship; there were also elaborate rituals for planting and harvesting, and the political chiefs were considered to be under the sacred power of the Sun God. Strong confederacies were developed in this area, and there was a clan system and a society composed of chiefs and four classes of subjects.

The Plains subarea stretched from Texas to Saskatchewan and included the low plains or prairies on the east and the high plains along the foothills of the Rocky Mountains. It included such tribes as the Assiniboin, Arapaho, Blackfoot, Cheyenne, Comanche, Crow, Gros Ventre, Kiowa, Kiowa-Apache, Sarsi, and Teton-Dakota. The typical economy of the whole area was dependence on the buffalo and a limited use of roots and berries. There was a great development of work in skins, no basketry or pottery, and very little use of wood or stone. The typical dwelling was the conical skin tent or tipi. Social organization consisted of a simple band organization and a series of men's societies. The most important ceremonial observance was the Sun Dance but there were also minor ceremonial occasions. Within this general pattern were local variations. The tribes on the eastern border practiced agriculture, made some pottery and basketry, and performed agricultural ceremonies in place of the Sun Dance. They also had permanent houses covered with grass, bark or earth. The tribes on the western border depended more on deer and small game and less on the buffalo; they also made use of wild seeds and grains, and had brush and mat-covered shelters as well as tipis. They made good basketry but no pottery.

For the Plains area as a whole the period of florescence came with the introduction of the horse by the Spaniards in the 17th century. Before that, the farming tribes along the eastern border and some tribes in the foothills of the Rockies penetrated into the Plains but permanent occupation was sparse. Once the use of the horse had been mastered, the Indians could move into the Plains and exploit the buffalo more effectively. Some tribes, the Teton-Dakota and Cheyenne, for example, are known to have given up farming and taken to the life which developed into what is thought of as typical Plains culture. The final development was an elaboration of the basic pattern. Plains life centered around the buffalo which was the chief source of food, material for clothing, shelter, tools and medicines. The use of the horse enabled the Indians to capture enough buffalo to support them. The typical social group of the Plains was the band, several of which constituted the tribe. The bands of a tribe assembled at the beginning of summer to perform the Sun Dance, which was a tribal ceremony thought to ensure good hunting and the general welfare. There followed one or more tribal buffalo hunts, after which the bands dispersed and passed the remainder of the year separately. Since inter-tribal warfare was waged mainly in summer, the gathering of the bands in this season was also a measure of defense.

THE CONQUEST AND AFTER

The story of the American Indians after the time of the conquest is, for the most part, one of sudden and violent change which contrasts strongly with the slow, gradual centuries of pre-conquest development. Meso-America and South America were the first victims of the conquest. The arrival of Cortes in the Aztec capitol, Tenochtitlan, in 1520 and of Pizarro in the Inca capital in 1532 initiated the same series of struggles which ultimately took place over most of the New World. The balance was, to say the least, uneven. Numerical superiority was the only advantage on the Indians' side, and this was greatly outweighed by the firearms, armor, horses and training of the Spanish soldiers. The people who reached the New World in the period of Conquest were the soldiers, priests, fortune-seekers and colonists from several different European nations. They came from Spain, Portugal, Holland, France and England for a variety of reasons: for the sake of conquest, immediate exploitation, religious conversion or settlement. The variety of their purposes on the one hand, and, on the other, the varying nature of the Indian groups encountered, meant that the effect of the arrival of the white men differed, somewhat, from one area to another. The results depended on such factors as density of native population, suitability of the area for the new types of land use, and the susceptibility of the natives to the diseases introduced by their conquerors.

In the Marginal and Tropical Forest areas of South America, the Indians living along the coast and the navigable interior waterways were quickly absorbed or exterminated. In the less accessible parts of these areas, the natives first experienced an indirect contact with Spanish culture. They received new crops, domesticated animals and some tools and weapons before having actual contact with the whites. Among some tribes this lead to an improvement in their exploitive activities and an expansion of their native culture. With the added advantage of the horse for hunting and packing, the tribes of the Pampas and Patagonia could exploit larger areas. Later, after their first direct contact, whether the white settlers were missionaries or colonists, the natives were gathered into settlements where their native culture was quickly lost and the natives themselves were exposed to decimating epidemics. In the Circum-Caribbean area, the Indians of the Antilles and of the coast and lowland areas were exterminated or absorbed very rapidly by disease and enslavement. In the less accessible regions, such as the mountains, the native culture survived, but with a loss of such distinctive characteristics as its class system, organized warfare and special craft production.

In the Andean area, also, the native population suffered a great initial loss. At the time of the conquest in 1532 the Inca Empire (Andean region from northern Ecuador to northern Argentina and northern Chile) contained about four and a half million Indians. By 1571 this number was reduced by more than half, and by 1796 there were less than a million Indians in the area. After the wars of independence in the 19th century, the Indian poulation again increased until, today, in the old Inca area of highland Ecuador, Peru, and Bolivia, there are five and a half million Quechua-speaking people, and in the Lake Titicaca area, 500,000 Aymara-speaking people.

The population of this Andean area is today one of the two instances of very high proportion of Indian individuals in the New World. Except for Paraguay and the remote tropical forest of the upper Amazon, the populations of the other South American countries are largely white and mestizo with some Negroes and mulattoes in Brazil. During the years after the conquest, the Indian population of the Andean area tended to concentrate in the highlands, leaving the coastal section for the Spanish and mestizo population. This is quite apparent today in the contrast between the colorful and vigorous highland people and the somewhat somber and pallid coastal population. The native Andean crops and system of agriculture continued in use. The Spaniards did introduce barley and wheat but these were never widely accepted. The Indian methods of terracing and irrigating persisted, and the use of the Spanish wooden plow and of oxen as draft animals were introduced. The chief Spanish contribution to subsistence was their domesticated animals, the pig, chicken, burro, horse, cattle, sheep, and goats. These were added to the native use of the llama and alpaca. The introduction of Catholicism was so swift that by 1650 the Andean area was officially considered to be Christianized. The native religion was wiped out and only a few simple rites and ceremonies survived. Along with the loss of native religion went a great change in native craftsmanship. Ceremonial objects, which had constituted a large part of their craft output, were no longer needed. The native techniques persisted in the making of some utilitarian objects. The old belt looms are used as well as the European treadle loom. Sheep's wool is used as much as llama wool. Metalwork has all but disappeared but wooden bowls and woven baskets and mats are still made. The pottery is coarser than the pre-conquest ware and poorly decorated. It is made, for the most part, by the old techniques although the potter's wheel is now also used. Indian houses are made in much the same way as before but the large, public buildings were, of course, planned by Spanish architects. It is of interest to note in this connection that in the 1950 earthquake in the Cuzco area, the Spanish structures collapsed but the old Inca buildings survived. Most Indians of the Andean area continued to practice farming after the conquest, living in scattered, independent villages. Some are peon laborers on large haciendas, but many own their own land and live in communities which have many characteristics of native culture. In Peru and Bolivia there are 3,000 such communities of about 500 persons each. Every year, education and increased transportation facilities bring these rural areas into closer contact with the white, urban culture. Bilingualism is increasing, and gradually the native culture is being lost in the process of assimilation into the national culture.

In Meso-America the conquest began with the landing of Cortes and his soldiers at Vera Cruz in 1519. The Aztecs resisted bravely but in vain, and their emperor, Montezuma II, and thousands of their people were killed. Cortes than extended his conquest to Honduras and Guatemala. In Meso-America as in Peru a profound change resulting from the conquest was the imposition of the Spanish land-use pattern. This was a system of large estates worked by mass labor and was in complete contrast to the native system of communal lands allotted to individuals. Even in the case of such native empires as the Aztec and Maya (also the Inca in Peru), the trading and collecting of tribute which had brought widely scattered groups into contact had not done so at the expense of the local communities. In terms of items added to the native Meso-American culture, the Spanish introduced the burro, cultivation of wheat, sugar cane, coffee, potatoes and bananas. The use of money largely supplanted trade by barter. Iron tools, the plow and cart were added, and later the sewing machine, power corn grinder, and factory-woven cloth. In most communities pre-conquest deities and communal agricultural ceremonies were replaced by Catholic Church fiestas, and the cult of the saints replaced local and family deities. The native pattern in which religious and secular functions were combined has, of course, been replaced by one in which these functions are entirely separate.

The Indian population of Guatemala and Mexico has more than regained its aboriginal size. The estimated population for the two countries in 1500 is about three million people. In 1940 there were six million in Mexico and nearly two million in Guatemala. In proportion to the total populations of these two countries, 33 per cent of Mexico and 55 per cent of Guatemala is Indian. These figures are based on a definition of the word "Indian" in cultural rather than biological terms. That is, when natives have adopted the Spanish language, European clothing and other traits, they are no longer classified as Indians but as mestizos (mixed-bloods) even though they may be Indians racially. The proportion of individuals figured on the basis of Indian descent would be much higher than the proportions given. This classification of Indians on a cultural rather than racial basis reflects an attitude in which South and Meso-America differ from North America. In South and Meso-American countries a person is classed by his culture and not by his race. An Indian is a person with Indian culture; a Negro is a person with African culture, a white has white culture although not necessarily a white skin. This results in great racial and social fluidity. A person who is born an Indian, may, by education, by occupation and by acquisition of white modes of dress, speech and living, actually become a white. Also, two men who are brothers may be classed differently, one as an Indian, the other as a white. The vast majority of Indians, as well as of Negroes, in these countries still have their native cultural background which limits their ability to compete in the national, white culture. Nevertheless, the social fluidity allows individuals of special ability to achieve any status within the national culture. Indians and Negroes alike have made significant contributions as artists, doctors, lawyers, writers, and legislators. Another result of this fluidity is the emergence in some South and Meso-American countries of local cultures which are a blend of Indian and white elements. The cultures of such groups as the Guarani of Paraguay, the Ladino of Guatemala and the Criollo of Argentina are blends and although part of the national culture also preserve distinctive Indian characteristics.

A further fundamental difference in the post-conquest patterns in South and Meso-America as contrasted with North America, is that North America became urban and industrialized, whereas South and Meso-America have remained essentially agrarian and have retained to a considerable extent the pattern of large landholders with masses of native laborers. The present situation of the Indians under these circumstances is difficult. Those who have no land live in communities on the haciendas; those who have a little land may attempt to cling to community life and native patterns; and those who have enough land are able to produce a cash crop but still retain the old, local patterns of life. Whatever the Indian's situation, and whichever adjustment he may attempt to work out, the transitional phases are characterized by economic and cultural instability requiring special consideration to help him achieve a constructive and permanent solution.

It is of interest to notice that the areas of present-day concentration of Indian population were pre-conquest areas of population density. Nine-tenths of all American Indians live in the highland countries of Meso-America and South America which were early centers of high cultural development and dense population. The Spanish cultures added some new items to the content of these native cultures, but there was not a great disparity in the wealth of culture content and much enrichment also flowed from Indian to Spanish culture. Because, in these areas, neither culture completely engulfed the other, a blend emerged which could not have occurred under circumstances of great cultural disparity.

North of Mexico the pattern of settlement differed from that in Spanish America. The colonists arrived, on the whole, in family groups, settled and worked as families. In the eastern United States and Canada they found an area of low population density. Some of the Indian tribes of the eastern United States experienced a temporary period of expansion when, by indirect contact with the whites, they received some new plants and animals. But when contact became direct, the natives' tribal economy and the villages on which their social life was based were destroyed and it was not long before the Indians themselves were virtually extinct. The settlers wanted land and had little difficulty in conquering the Indians or pushing them westward until they reached the submarginal lands unsuited to white settlement.

It has been noted in an earlier section that the major development of the culture of the Plains Indians came as a result of their receiving the horse which had been brought to the New World by the Spaniards. This period lasted as long as the white man did not want the territory of the Plains Indians. After that came some of the bloodiest Indian wars and the establishment of the survivors on reservations. The tribes of the southwestern United States were in contact with Spanish civilization as early as the sixteenth century. Those tribes having a fairly advanced culture absorbed some Spanish elements and did not experience cultural disintegration. The Pueblo tribes of the Hopi mesas and of the Rio Grande Valley, and the Navajos and Apaches retained a large part of their aboriginal beliefs, practices, outlook and culture traits. Their ceremonial life is less influenced by missionary teachings and their social organization is less disrupted than is the case with any other New World groups. The Navajos have shown a remarkable increase in numbers. In less than a century they grew from 8,000 to 50,000; a higher rate of increase than that of the white population.

The characteristics of contact, conquest and reservation life are much the same for the Indians in Canada as in the United States. The exception is in the far north where a few partially assimilated tribes live. The largest group is the Eskimos who number about 36,000 (including those in Danish Greenland).

A dominant factor affecting Indians and Indian groups in North America has been the Anglo-American point of view about races and race segregation. This attitude, as we have already seen, was not held by Spanish and Portuguese people. In North America the races represented by the whites, Negroes and Indians have been, by tradition, socially segregated. Each of these groups contains within itself a wide range of occupational and social statuses and an Indian (or a Negro) may rise only within his own group. Because Indians have been physically separated on reservations their situation has been less obvious than that of the Negroes. It is, nevertheless, true that like the Negroes, they are classified on the basis of race and not, as in Spanish America, on a cultural basis.

It is estimated that in 1500, the Indian population of North America was about one million. Of these, about two hundred thirty thousand were in Canada and about seven hundred seventy thousand in the United States. The areas of greatest density were the Pueblo area of Arizona and New Mexico and a portion of central California. The only group which has made any marked increase is, as has been mentioned, the Navajos who increased from 8,000 to 50,000 in the last hundred years. The general Indian population has decreased. The estimates for 1940 give one hundred and eight thousand in Canada and three hundred ninety-five thousand for the United States.

The transformation of Indian life was not the only result of the meeting of European and Indian cultures. The white settlers were also influenced by the Indians and borrowed many useful things from them. This Indian influence has contributed much to the distinctive flavor which sets contemporary New World cultures apart from their parent cultures in Europe. The American Indian added new items to the world inventory of plants and domesticated animals. Among about forty unique plants are food plants such as maize, beans, melons, squash, pumpkins, tomatoes, avocadoes, white potatoes, chocolate, chili peppers, pineapple, papaya, and manioc (the source of tapioca); and other plants such as rubber, tobacco, chicle, quinine, and coca (the source of cocaine). Among the domesticated animals unique to the New World are the turkey, guinea pig, llama, and alpaca. A few prepared foods are also Indian in origin: maple syrup, tamales and pemmican. Another group of items made by the American Indians and taken over from them includes: the hammock, toboggan, parka, moccasin, dog-sled, canoe, the various ways of smoking tobacco (the pipe, cigar and cigarette), and also the use of snuff. The Indian has contributed richness and color to the literature of North America and of Spanish America.

Bibliography.—Hodge, F. W., ed., *Handbook of Indians North of Mexico,* Bureau of American Ethnology, Bulletin 30, 2 vols. (Washington 1907–10); Means, Philip Ainsworth, *Ancient Civilizations of the Andes* (New York 1931); Jenness, Diamond, *The Indians of Canada,* Bulletin 65, Department of Mines, National Museum of Canada (Ottawa 1932); Thompson, J. Eric, *Mexico Before Cortez* (New York 1933); Goddard, P. E., *The Indians of the Northwest Coast,* American Museum of Natural History, Handbook Series, No. 10 (New York 1934); Birket-Smith, Kaj, *The Eskimos* (New York 1935); Gann, Thomas and Thompson, J. Eric, *The History of the Maya* (New York 1935); Linton, Ralph, *The Study of Man* (New York 1936); Forde, D. Daryll, *Habitat, Economy and Society* (New York 1937); MacCurdy, G. G., ed., *Early Man* (Philadelphia and New York 1937); Wissler, Clark, *The American Indian* (New York 1938); Kroeber, A. L., "Cultural and Natural Areas of Native North America" in *American Archaeology and Ethnology,* vol. 38 (Berkeley, Calif. 1939); no one author, *The Maya and Their Neighbors,* ltd. ed. (New York 1940); Douglas, F. H., and D'Harnoncourt, R., *Indian Art of the United States, Museum of Modern Art* (New York 1941); Vaillant, George, *The Aztecs of Mexico* (New York 1941); Kelemen, Pal, *Medieval American Art* (New York 1943); Howells, W. W., *Mankind So Far* (New York 1944); Linton, Ralph, ed., *The Science of Man in the World Crisis* (New York 1945); Collier, John, *Indians of the Americas* (New York 1947); Steward, Julian, ed., *Handbook of South American Indians,* Bureau of American Ethnology, Bulletin 143, 6 vols. (Washington 1946–50); Benedict, Ruth, *Patterns of Culture* (New York 1946); Morley, Sylvanus G., *The Ancient Maya* (Stanford 1946); Martin, P. S., Quimby, G., and Collier, D., *Indians Before Columbus* (Chicago 1947); Bennett, W. C., ed., *A Reappraisal of Peruvian Archaeology,* Society for American Archaology, Memoirs No. 4 (Menasha, Wis., 1948); Kroeber, A. L., *Anthropology* (New York 1948); Bennett, W. C., and Bird, Junius, *Andean Culture History,* Handbook Series, No. 4, 3d ed. (Denver 1949); Wormington, H. M., *Ancient Man in North America,* Denver Museum of Natural History, Popular Series, No. 4, 3d ed. (Denver 1949); no one author, *Radiocarbon Dating,* Society for American Archaeology, Memoir No. 8 (Salt Lake City 1951); Tax, Sol, and others, *Heritage of Conquest* (Glencoe, Ill. 1952).

MALCOLM CARR COLLIER.

INDIANS, Education of the. Historic.—From the beginning the white man has assumed that the Indian was a pagan savage whose salvation lay in accepting the white man's way of life and the white man's religion. This point of view led to a disregard of the rights of the Indian wherever they conflicted with the desires of the white man. Ignoring the Indian's dependence on his "way of life" for his economic self support, the English along the Atlantic seaboard combined their educational undertakings with a destruction of the existing Indian way of life, apparently assuming that colonies of praying Indians were less dependent on hunting and fishing than their pagan former associates. John Eliot, who in 1646 initiated the education of Indians in Massachusetts, gathered his Indians into towns where he taught them the responsibilities of township government and the crafts of the white man, but with little evidence that these Indian communities ever became a real part of the economic fabric of colonial life. The Franciscans in California about a hundred years later (1769) encouraged the Indians who accepted the gospel to settle around the missions where they developed irrigation works and taught the Indians agriculture, cattle raising, and crafts useful to themselves and to their teachers.

That some of the white colonists were greatly concerned with the conversion and education of the Indians is evidenced by the work of Eliot and others. In addition to schools and churches built in the reported 14 towns of «praying Indians» of 1674, Harvard College, by its charter of 1650, Dartmouth College in 1769 (successor to Moor's Indian School) and the College of William and Mary in 1691, to mention three of the more prominent, were dedicated to the «education of Indian youth» and incidentally «English youth» also. Sharp practices between the whites and the Indians bred ill-will which flared out in fighting in which the Indian was frequently the defender rather than the aggressor. Ultimately the majority of whites were led to the conclusion that peaceful occupation of the eastern territory could best be achieved through the removal of the Indians, and regardless of the degree of culture acquired by individual Indians in these schools, most of the eastern tribes were uprooted and driven into the west, there again to find themselves in a losing encounter with the westbound whites.

Even in these earlier schools appeared the conflict in fundamental purpose which has persisted throughout the entire period of white relationship with Indians. There were those who believed that day schools in the Indian villages offered the most effective form of education for both children and adults. Others believed equally fervently that the best way to overcome the pagan and savage ways of the Indian was to remove him from contact with his family and friends and bring him up in the Christian atmosphere which could be provided by a remote boarding school. One finds repeatedly in the older records as well as in more recent statements the impression that young people introduced to the refinements, duties, and responsibilities of civilization could be counted upon to return to their own communities to serve as models in bringing their elders to an acceptance of the white man's way of life. Judged by results, this assumption appears to have been just as fallacious 250 years ago as it is today, for among Indians respect and leadership have been accorded to age rather than youth.

Theoretically the older schools laid stress upon instruction in husbandry, trades, and domestic arts. Many of them developed an «outing» system which placed partially-educated Indian girls and boys in suitable English-speaking homes where they received some small compensation, were permitted to attend the public schools, and where they received practical daily experience in farming or in a trade or in home craft through assisting the adults in the homes. Possibly the most significant of the more recent Indian boarding schools to emphasize the outing system was Carlisle, founded in 1879 by Captain, later General, Pratt, an officer in the United States Army who had become much interested in the welfare of Indians through his military activities in Indian Territory (now Oklahoma) and through having been charged with the care of a group of Indian prisoners sent to Florida as punishment for an uprising against the Federal Government. Captain Pratt became convinced that these Indians were capable of education and were warmly responsive to instruction from the white man. He obtained admission of some of these Indians to Hampton Institute, established about ten years earlier for the education of Negroes. Later he obtained from the Army the use of Carlisle Barracks in Pennsylvania, an abandoned army post where one of the more famous Indian schools was maintained until 1918.

For several years after the establishment of Carlisle the Federal Government made no large contribution toward its maintenance and operation as a school for Indians, much of the support during the early days coming from friends of Captain Pratt and from missionary societies. Pratt was successful in persuading the Quakers and the Pennsylvania Dutch of the surrounding area to accept his students on an outing basis thus exposing them to one of the best ways to acquire a fluent use of English and an acceptance of white standards. Many former Carlisle students never returned to their reservations. Many of them who did were at first completely submerged in tribal life and only as they matured and succeeded to positions of leadership within the tribal group were they able to influence their associates toward closer co-operation with the whites.

Despite the fact that the colonial governments, and after the Revolution the National Government, negotiated numerous treaties with Indian tribes by which the white man accepted responsibility for educating Indian children, it was not until 1819 that an appropriation of $10,000 was finally made. The following year the President was authorized to apply this sum annually in aid of societies and individuals engaged in the education of Indians. This led directly to the establishment of Indian schools by missionary bodies representing a number of the Protestant churches. Twenty-one such schools were listed in 1823; 38 in 1825. A majority of these schools were boarding schools, largely because the Indians were a roving people scattered over a wide territory from which they took their living by hunting, fishing, and occasionally by limited agricultural activity. About 1873 the Federal Government began to take increased interest in the establishment of Federal schools, and between 1880 and 1895 many of the larger Indian boarding schools were built, including among the more prominent Chemawa, Chilocco, Haskell, and Phoenix. During this same period criticism arose because of Federal support of denominational activity, and in 1901 Federal support for mission schools was completely withdrawn. However, many of the mission schools were maintained for tribes which possessed funds received from the Government in payment for lands ceded for white settlement, and these groups were persuaded to contribute from their tribal funds toward the maintenance of mission schools.

Statistics with regard to the number of Indian children enrolled in schools of various kinds are exceedingly unreliable, due to the fact that there is no accurate definition of what constitutes an Indian, census reports usually accepting the preference expressed by the individual, with the result that some people with small amounts of Indian blood are reported as Indians, while others with greater amounts of Indian blood report themselves as white. No accurate census has ever been made of the tribes living in more primitive conditions in the more inaccessible areas of the United States. It is estimated for example that there are approximately 45,000 Navajos scattered over their approximately 16,000,000 acres of semi-desert land, but no accurate count has ever been made. In 1926 it was reported that there were 84,553 Indian children of school age in the United States of whom 76,879 were eligible for school attendance. This did not include the total number of children attending the schools of the Five Civilized Tribes of Oklahoma. On the other hand in 1938 there are reported to be 83,913 children of school age, 82,622 of whom are eligible to attend school. The decrease is accounted for by the fact that this later report includes only children of one-quarter or more Indian blood, to whom Federal gratuity appropriations for the support of Indian schools are limited, for there has been a steady increase in the total Indian population during this same period.

Indian Day Schools.—Between 1926 and 1938 there occurred a resurgence in emphasis upon day schools, with a resultant decrease in the number of boarding schools from 77 to 45, and an increase in day schools from 131 to 211. This shift occurred because many persons concerned with Indian education believe that children can best be taught within their home environment. This change from the over-emphasis on boarding schools was also doubtlessly influenced by the survey of the Indian Service conducted by the Institute for Governmental Research at the instance of Secretary of the Interior, the Honorable Hubert Work, and reported on in February 1928. This survey outlined the type of community school recommended for development by the Indian Service and emphasized strongly the greater desirability of the day school and public school for Indian children. The increase in day schools could not have occurred had not more than $19,000,000 been expended during the decade on the construction of roads which penetrated into many of the more remote communities of the larger Indian reservations.

The new day schools have in most instances been erected in remote areas, far from white communities and in some instances among tribal groups who themselves do not form communities in the white sense. Among the Papagos and Navajos in Arizona, Indian homes are seasonal rather than permanent, families moving from one area to another as rainfall makes the grass suitable for grazing or small land areas suitable for agriculture. White persons, dependent as they are on ample supplies of potable water, little realize how deficient that necessity is in many parts of the Indian country. It is often necessary for Navajo Indians to transport domestic water as much as 15 miles from its source to their homes. An adequate variety of food, nourishing preparation of this food, cleanliness, and sanitation according to white man's standards, are therefore undreamed of and relatively impossible to achieve under such conditions. To be effective as an agency for instruction in better health practices, better sanitation, and better living, the Indian day school, in addition to other functions, has undertaken to supply some of these fundamental lacks. One of the first essentials in the modern day school plant is the development of an adequate water supply. Around this water supply has been developed a school structure which supplies: (1) the necessary number of classrooms to care for children in groups of approximately 30; (2) a kitchen for the preparation of a noon meal, for in many areas the family food supply is so irregular that many children are continuously malnourished; (3) a community room to be used as a lunch room at noon, as an auditorium by children and adults of the community, and as a work room equipped with sewing machines and other facilities for home making instruction and use by children and adults; (4) community shower baths where the children may be bathed at regular intervals and which may be used by the adults of the community; (5) a community laundry to which the women come to launder the family clothing; (6) a community shop where the men may bring their horses to be shod, their wagons to be repaired, or the lumber to build household furniture; (7) and quarters where the teacher and assistants may live. In many of the day schools the first teacher is a married man whose wife shares some of the responsibilities for community activities. In some areas she may be the housekeeper who prepares the noon meal and who supervises the adults in the use of home economics facilities. In most of the schools an Indian couple also is employed. The husband acts as bus driver, general mechanic and shop instructor, bringing the children to school from the more remote areas, keeping the plant in shape, and supervising children and adults in the use of the common handy tools. The wife often acts as housekeeper and as general community worker. Speaking both English and the native language these assistants play an important part in the modern educational program.

Around the school is frequently developed a school garden, irrigated in areas where this is necessary, which often becomes the nucleus for a community garden to furnish basic subsistence for the entire community. The school may also operate a milk goat herd, one or two dairy cows, poultry, or other live stock. The products of this activity contribute to the noon meal, but in an even greater degree the program trains the young people for similar responsibilities around their own homes. The school house is the centre for community meetings to discuss reservation civic problems; the school kitchen is the canning centre when it is time to preserve vegetables; the school garden is the experimental plot where new products are introduced, and new methods of agriculture tried out. The average day school today offers six years of instruction and compares favorably in academic achievement with the neighboring white public schools. In the more populous communities instruction through the ninth grade is included with emphasis on vocational instruction of value to the economy of the local community.

Total Federal Schools.—World War II disrupted many Indian communities, the young men joining the armed forces and many of the older men and women seeking war work. A number of Indian day schools closed. In 1946 the total number of Federal schools operating in continental United States was 242, of which 18 were nonreservation and 25 reservation boarding schools; 198 day schools, 8 of which operated small boarding units for remote high school pupils. Enrollment in the Federal schools was 15,476 day pupils, 13,798 boarders; mission and private schools, 7,464.

White children were also enrolled in 19 Indian Service schools. Public school enrollment was 31,927 Indian pupils of more than one quarter Indian blood for many of whom the federal government paid a subsidy to the local school districts.

In 1946 studies made on the Navajo Reservation revealed that there were in excess of 20,000 children of school age, for less than 5,000 of whom school facilities were available.

From 1884, when the first Federal schools were established, until March 16, 1931, when the education of natives was transferred to the Office of Indian Affairs, the Alaskan native schools were under the direction of the Office of Education. In 1945 the native population of Alaska, including Indians, Eskimos, and Aleuts, was estimated at 32,750, or a little over half the population of the Territory. With the exception of orphan homes erected after the great influenza epidemic of 1918, a majority of Alaskan schools have always been day schools operated in the native villages. In 1946 there were 113 day schools in an equal number of native villages, with an enrollment of 3,950, and three residential vocational high schools enrolling 421 students. The total number of natives enrolled in Federal schools was 4,371. During 1946, the Sitka Naval Base was transferred to the Indian Service for school and hospital purposes. Early in 1947 a 600-pupil vocational high school was opened there. An estimated 2,000 additional native students were enrolled in the Territorial schools which are operated primarily for whites. Approximately 1,500 children of school age were believed to be not enrolled in any school.

New Interest in Indian Culture.—Figures with regard to literacy or even with regard to the degree to which English has become the accepted language of Indian communities are no more accurate than population statistics. While English has been accepted as the major language by Indian groups in frequent contact with whites, more remote groups in all parts of the United States still persist in the use of the native languages, in many cases the older Indians speaking no English. There is increased interest upon the part of adult Indians in mastery of the English tongue, and many night classes have been established at their request.

The respect for Indian life and culture which led to the spread of the day school has fundamentally affected many other aspects of Indian education. The old prohibition against use of the native languages in school has been abandoned, and steps have been taken by the Indian Office to print readers in the vernacular as well as English for use in Indian schools for the larger tribal groups. It is believed that this will increase the racial pride of the Indian, develop and enrich his own culture, and thereby increase the probability that this culture may make substantial contribution to the greater American culture which surrounds it.

Increased emphasis is being placed on the preservation or revival of native Indian crafts as a means of improving economic conditions as markets for their products are found.

The right of Indians to maintain their native religions is recognized as equal to that of other minority groups, and Indian ceremonials, dances, and other native activities are being permitted. Indian music is being admitted to the schools, and native Indian games are being encouraged.

Indian High Schools.—On each of the large reservations where the Federal school system is maintained, there is a central high school. There is growing evidence that many of these high schools are beginning at last to fulfill the ideal frequently asserted, but not always very effectively realized, of vocational instruction contributing toward the economic self-sufficiency of their graduates. Typical of this development may be cited the Oglala Community High School, Pine Ridge, S. D., on the largest Sioux reservation, where the major economy is livestock. Here a land use program is the basis of the curriculum and the students operate a beef herd of about 300 registered cattle, an irrigated farm of approximately 250 acres, the girls being concerned with milk goats, poultry, and other small livestock, as well as the home-making work usually taught. Or the Wingate Vocational High School in the Navajo country where 18,000 acres of typical Navajo range land have been restored to normal carrying capacity through student application of conservation principles, where runoff water from flash floods is caught and stored in large reservoirs built by the students for the irrigation of forage and garden crops. This school also emphasizes improved quality in native crafts products, cooperating with an experimental laboratory in the improvement of native wool, developing native dyes, improving the quality of weaving in the native Navajo rug, and reviving and improving the quality of design in traditional Navajo silversmithing.

Higher Education for Indians.—Despite the fact that throughout the program of Indian education the emphasis is primarily vocational, increased encouragement has been given Indian students who wish to pursue advanced vocational or collegiate training. Under the loan provisions of the Indian Reorganization Act and other educational loan funds, approximately $25,000 a year has been loaned to Indian students for advanced education. Many students are pursuing professional courses which will permit them to enter the Indian Service after graduation, as teachers, clerks, and stenographers. By 1946 more than 2,600 Indians had benefited from such help. In 1946 more than 50 per cent of the employees of the Indian Service were Indians.

Indians in Public Schools.—Education of Indian children in public schools is no new thing. In colonial days a limited number of Indian children were permitted to attend school with white children. Under the Carlisle system, more than half the students enrolled were actually attending public school with the children of the families for whom they were working. In Oklahoma, Indian children have been accepted in public schools practically since statehood. In many states local school districts receive the same state apportionment on behalf of Indian children as for white children in attendance, regardless of payment of tuition by the Indian Service. However, the Indian Office contracts with three States for special services to Indian children because of handicaps of language, poverty, or health, and also contracts with 616 local school districts in various parts of the United States for the education of Indian children. The older graduates from many of these public elementary schools are permitted to enroll in non-reservation boarding schools when the need for vocational instruction is clear. Even if the public school, because of white contacts, offered the ideal environment for the education of Indian children the fact would not operate to reduce the number of Federally-operated Indian schools for many years, because most of them are maintained in non-taxpaying Indian areas where very few white people live, and the attendance necessarily is primarily Indian.

Curriculum.—The decade following 1928 saw an effort to develop a curriculum for Indian schools suited to the needs of each particular area—community gardens and milk goats in the day schools of the Sioux country; irrigated agriculture and cattle in the high schools; irrigated gardens and poultry in the Pima day schools; irrigated agriculture and cattle in the high schools; dry farming, irrigation, beef cattle and dairying in Oklahoma; agriculture for some, skilled trades for the others in southern California; to each according to his need.

Personnel.—Annually since 1936 the Indian Service has operated two or more summer schools for the in-service training of its educational personnel. Educational personnel in the Indian Service are Civil Service employees and gain their appointments through competitive examination. Since 1928 when the Indian Service was criticized for its lack of professional standards in the selection of teachers and its inadequate salaries, these standards have been raised. By 1939, elementary teachers in the Indian Service were required to be graduates of three or four-year teacher training institutions and high school teachers were required to have a college degree. Salaries have increased; elementary teachers enter the Service at $2,168 a year, high school teachers at $2,394; administrative positions start at $2,644 and range to $6,862.

Organization.—The program of Indian education is under the Education Division of the Bureau of Indian Affairs in the Department of the Interior, with headquarters in Washington. The Indian area of the United States is divided for educational supervision into five districts each headed by a district supervisor of Indian education. Cooperating with the Education Division at Washington and the area superintendents is a corps of special subject supervisors, making contact with the teachers in the individual schools. On a majority of Indian reservations Federal schools are under the immediate supervision of a reservation principal who is himself subordinate to the reservation superintendent in charge of the entire reservation program. An attempt is made to coordinate the work of the day schools with that of the reservation boarding high schools so that pupils are encouraged to complete the full 12 years of education.

WILLARD W. BEATTY,
Director of Education, Bureau of Indian Affairs.

INDICAN, a colorless substance chemically related to indigo, found in wood, in most plants yielding indigo-blue, and in human urine.

INDICATOR, in steam engineering, an instrument invented by James Watt, to record, graphically and automatically, the pressure in an engine cylinder at every point of the stroke. By means of the diagram that the indicator draws, it is possible to determine whether the valves of the engine are working correctly or not, and it is also possible to estimate the horse power that the engine is developing with considerable accuracy. Commercially, the steam-engine indicator may be had in many forms; but all are based on the same fundamental principle, which will be understood by reference to the diagram presented in Fig. 1. The paper upon which the indicator diagram is to be drawn is here supposed to be secured, flat, to a carriage which travels back and forth upon a track; the motion of the carriage corresponding precisely to the motion of the piston of the engine. In practice it would be inconvenient to have the carriage travel a distance equal to the whole stroke of the engine, and hence some form of reducing motion is used, so that the motion of the carriage may follow the motion of the engine piston accurately, but with materially reduced velocity. The indicator diagram is drawn by means of a pencil-point carried on the piston rod of a small steam cylinder which is situated below the carriage, and which opens freely into the cylinder of the engine from which the diagram is to be taken. The piston of the indicator is pressed downward by means of a spring whose strength is accurately known,

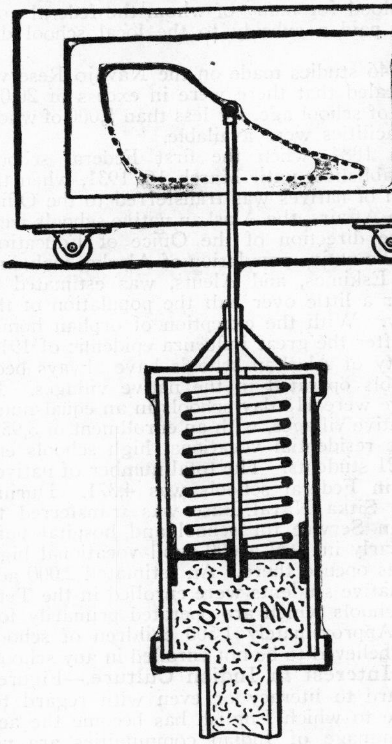

FIG. 1.

so that the increase of pressure corresponding to a rise of one inch in the position of the pencil-point is known. When the indicator is in operation, the pencil rises and falls proportionately to the pressure of the steam in the engine cylinder, and the carriage, with its attached paper, travels back and forth horizontally, at the same time, keeping pace precisely with the motion of the piston of the engine. Under these circumstances the pencil-point traces a diagram somewhat like that shown in the illustration. In practice, the paper upon which the diagram is drawn is usually wrapped about a cylindrical drum, which by rotating presents a new surface of paper for a new diagram. It follows the motion of the engine piston just as the carriage here shown.

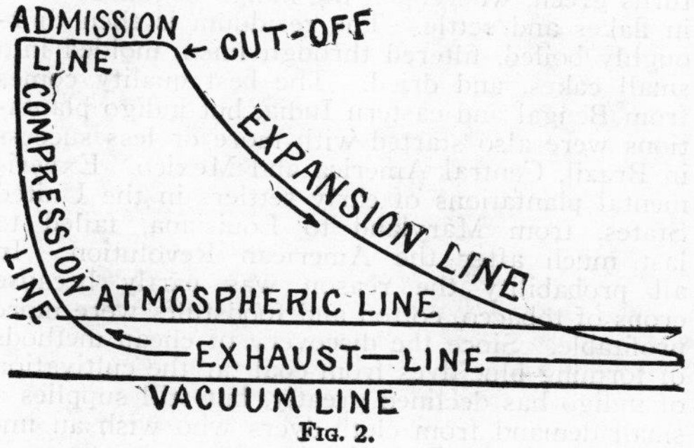

Fig. 2.

In Fig. 2 an enlarged view of an indicator card (or diagram) is given, together with the technical names of some of its more important parts. The arrows show the direction in which the pencil travels as the diagram is drawn. The "admission line" is the part that is drawn while the engine is in full communication with the boiler, and drawing steam from it. The angle marked "cut-off" corresponds to the instant at which the steam supply is cut off, and the expansion of the steam begins.

A considerable number of other mechanisms are termed indicators, as the stock-indicator, a receiving telegraph instrument that prints on an endless tape the figures, etc., of stock sales telegraphed; telegraph indicator, a telegraphic instrument having a vertical needle making indications on a dial, called also needle telegraph; circuit indicator, an upright galvanometer or the like for indicating the presence and character of an electric current; speed indicator, a gage having usually a dial and pointer for indicating visually the speed of a machine, etc.; track-indicator, a registering device for mounting on a railway car or locomotive to record the variations of the track from accurate level and alignment.

For detailed information concerning the steam-engine indicator and its uses, consult Pray, *Twenty Years with the Indicator;* Peabody, *The Steam Engine Indicator;* also, for less extended treatment, any good book on steam engineering.

INDICTION, a period or cycle of 15 years, believed to have been adopted from Egypt by Rome in the 4th century as a time basis for making property assessments. In the time of Athanasius it came into favor among ecclesiastical writers, and in the Middle Ages it was widely used in Europe. The Constantinian system reckoned indictions from Sept. 1, 312, while the Imperial (also known as Caesarean or Western) system began Sept. 24, 312. The Pontifical (also known as Papal or Roman) system adopted by the popes in the 9th century was based on the beginning date Jan. 1, 313, and after the 12th century was based on the birth of Christ. By subtracting 312 from any year A.D. and dividing the result by 15, the indiction may be found; or by using the birth of Christ as the beginning date, add 3 to the year and divide by 15, the quotient indicating the indiction and the remainder the specific year of that indiction. Thus, by these methods, the year 1950 corresponds to the third year of either the 109th or 130th Pontifical Indiction, depending on the beginning date used.

INDICTMENT, in-dīt′mĕnt, a formal, written accusation made by a legally convoked and sworn grand jury to the impaneling court, charging a person named or described therein with an act or omission in violation of the public law.

An indictment should be distinguished from a presentment (q.v.) which differs in that it is based on the jury's own knowledge and initiative rather than on evidence laid before it by the district attorney's office. An information (q.v.) serves the same purpose but is an accusation made by a district attorney in his official capacity, and has largely replaced the indictment as the accusation in misdemeanors (q.v.)—the less serious class of crimes—and in many states is also used in varying degrees for felony (q.v.) accusations.

This right to be confronted by a definite, combatable charge rather than a vague and variable one, is guaranteed by the Constitution in the 5th Amendment in all capital cases and those involving an "infamous" crime such being generally any felony, or any crime punishable by imprisonment in a state prison or for more than one year, etc.

As developed in the English common law and adopted in the United States, the indictment was extremely technical with great emphasis on words of art—that is, terms such as "traitorously" in indictments for treason, "feloniously" in felony cases, etc., which could be replaced by no other term no matter how synonymous appearing. The strictness of its construction led to a trial of technicalities rather than of truth since any error in describing a crime completely and in the language of the statutes, even in spelling or punctuation, or any failure in proof of any of the acts charged, could lead to the dismissal of the charge. The state was placed at great disadvantage thereby, and the modern rules have been considerably relaxed.

Nevertheless, the indictment remains a document that must be drawn with precision, although immaterial errors may be corrected during the trial. In addition to the formal particulars stating the court as having jurisdiction, etc., the indictment must identify the accused, the crime, and the time and place of its commission. The accused can be tried only on charges in the indictment, but a charge of first degree murder can be stated in five lines.

The deliberations of a grand jury are conducted in secret and its records can be made public only through a court order. Indictments are found only on a basis of evidence presented by a district attorney who must present such evidence as constitutes a *prima facie* case, showing, by documents or testimony of witnesses, all the essential elements of the crime. Naturally only such evidence is presented to the grand jury as is presumed will be available and admissible on the trial. Only the main points, however, are presented; and, without the details or procedure necessary in a trial, most indictments can be found "a true bill" or refused in a few minutes. The indictment is prepared by the district attorney and is likely to have been prepared even before the case is presented. If it is found valid, it is signed by the foreman and filed with the court, and a summons or warrant issued.

The accused does not appear before the grand jury to object to the issuing of the indictment since he is presumed innocent until the matters in the indictment are proved in a court trial where he can show the falsity, or the impossibility of proving the truth, of the charges. Where a crime has been committed by an unidentified person, an indictment can be issued against "John Doe" or "Jane Roe."

The laws of the 48 states exhibit substantial similarities in these matters, and the rules of federal criminal procedure in this regard have been deliberately framed to be a close approximation of the practice general to most states. A grand jury consists usually of from 16 to 23 persons of whom 12 (or, in some states, a majority of a quorum present) must vote in favor of issuing an indictment. If such a number do not find the charge reasonably likely of success, no action is taken unless an accused is already in custody, in which case specific notification must be made that no true bill was found. See also JURY.

INDIFFERENTISM, a system or state of indifference; specifically in metaphysics and ethics, the theory of a school of philosophers that the human will acts in utter indifference to all motives, and chooses merely as a judge decides. It is opposed to determinism. See also ETHICS; FREE WILL.

INDIGESTION. See DYSPEPSIA.

INDIGIRKA, ĭn′dĭ-gĭr′kȧ, a river of Siberia, in Yakutsk Autonomous Soviet Socialist Republic. It rises on the north slopes of Verkhoyansk Range and after a northerly course, estimated at 850 miles, through a frozen desert past a few villages, flows into the Arctic Ocean in latitude 71° N., and longitude 150° E. It is closed to navigation during the winter months.

INDIGO, ĭn′dĭ-gō, the name of a genus of plants and of the blue coloring matter obtained from them. The indigo plants are tall herbs of the pea family, forming the genus *Indigofera,* of which there are several color-yielding species in various warm parts of the world. The one yielding most of the commercial product and formerly extensively cultivated, is *I. tinctoria,* which is native to India, grows four to six feet high and has pinnate leaves. A West Indian species, *I. anil,* also yields indigo. The coloring matter is obtained largely from the leaves, and especially at the time of flowering when the crop is gathered by cutting down the plant and making immediate use of the green stems or foliage, or by drying them for subsequent treatment. This coloring matter is a chemical substance called *indican,* the glucoside of indoxyl, which is converted by oxidation into indigo. Until the discovery of the sea route to India the only blue vegetable dye available in Europe was that derived from the woad (q.v.), which was limited and costly; this dye-substance was therefore regarded as one of the most valuable of new commodities and a large capital was soon invested in its cultivation in India, Ceylon, China, and other regions, where a profitable industry continued until after the middle of the 19th century. The indigo is obtained by macerating the leaves and stems in vats for several hours. Fermentation begins and the water becomes clear yellow. It is then run off into a lower basin, where it is subjected to incessant agitation and gradually turns green, whereupon the indigo begins to form in flakes and settle. The residuum is then thoroughly boiled, filtered through linen, molded into small cakes, and dried. The best quality comes from Bengal and eastern India, but indigo plantations were also started with more or less success in Brazil, Central America and Mexico. Experimental plantations of early settlers in the United States, from Maryland to Louisiana, failed to last much after the American Revolution. In all probability the reason was partly because crops of tobacco, cotton and foodstuffs were more profitable. Since the discovery of cheap methods of forming blue dyes from coal tar the cultivation of indigo has declined greatly, but still supplies a small demand from cloth-dyers who wish an imperishable blue of certain tints.

The wild indigo of the United States is any of several species of a closely related genus *Baptisia,* which flourishes especially in the Southern and Eastern states. The best known is the yellow-flowered false indigo (*B. tinctoria*), or indigo brown, which has been used as the source of a blue dye and also to some extent as a domestic medicine.

Indigo Dyeing.—Before it can be employed in dyeing, indigo must be brought into solution; and as indigo itself is insoluble, it must be first transformed into a soluble substance so that it can penetrate the pores of the cloth, where it is subsequently again restored to the form of indigo. To bring the indigo into solution it is ground to a soft paste with water, after which it is thrown into vats along with ferrous sulphate, slaked lime and water. The ferrous sulphate reacts with the lime to form calcium sulphate and ferrous oxide, the latter being immediately oxidized at the expense of part of the oxygen of the indigo, which in its turn is reduced to a substance called indigo-white. This dissolves in the presence of excess of lime, and the fabric to be dyed is dipped into the vat after the liquid in it is clear. On removing the fabric the indigo-white which has penetrated its pores is reoxidized by the air to indigo-blue; and by repeating this treatment a shade of blue of any desired depth may be obtained. The dyed fabric is finally passed through dilute acid to remove any adhering lime or ferric oxide. Indigo appears to exist in the plant in the form of a glucoside known as "indican," which has the formula $C_{14}H_{17}NO_6.3H_2O$, and to be developed from this glucoside in the course of the fermentation by the action of special bacillus, which closely resembles the bacillus of pneumonia. Indigo is now made artifically, the production of synthetic indigo having shown a marked increase, along with other types of synthetic dyes, since

World War II. Artificial indigo blue (also known as indigotin) has the chemical formula $C_{16}H_{10}N_2O_2$ and appears to be identical with the natural product in every respect. Although used primarily for dyeing fabrics, indigo is used in the manufacture of certain printing inks and other products. See also DYEING.

INDIGO BIRD, a numerous and beautiful North American finch (*Passerina cyanea*), the male of which is dark greenish blue, while the female is grayish brown. They are migratory, but in summer spread over most of the United States, placing their neat nest and unspotted bluish eggs in garden bushes as well as in wild thickets. The male has one of the brightest and most persistent songs of any American bird, and he is easily habituated to captivity.

INDIGO SNAKE. See GOPHER SNAKE.

INDIRECT DAMAGES, claims for damages not directly inflicted by the illegal act complained of, but by other causes themselves due to that act. The great historical case is that of the United States claim for many hundreds of millions of dollars' worth of loss, resulting from Great Britain's bad faith or carelessness in letting the *Alabama,* the Confederate cruiser, escape from her ports to prey on our commerce. It was alleged that aside from the actual loss to our shipping and cargoes, we had been damaged to a far greater extent by the resultant effects, chiefly of three sorts: (1) The prolongation of the Civil War due to the encouragement given to the South and the straitening of the North. (2) The destruction of commercial lines and relations, which took long to recover after the war. (3) The raising of the rates of marine insurance. As these claims exceeded the cost of a war plus the indemnity we should have exacted if victorious, Great Britain refused to consider them; and the commission threw them out altogether as contrary to international law.

INDIRECT ELECTIONS. See ELECTIONS; ELECTORAL QUALIFICATIONS; CONGRESS.

INDIRECT EVIDENCE. See LEGAL TERMS.

INDIRECT TAXES. See DIRECT AND INDIRECT TAXES.

INDIUM, a shiny, ductile metallic element of a silver-white color, discovered by Ferdinand Reich and Theodor Richter through spectroscopic analysis during 1863 in the Freiberg arsenical ores. It is very rare. It is related to cadmium and zinc, and both are associated with it in nature; but it is found in many ores besides, although especially in zinc blende. This metal is obtained by heating the oxide with carbon and by other methods. It is soft, malleable and easily fusible. Its distinguishing property, however, and the characteristic which led to its discovery, is the indigo-blue line which all its compounds—so far as investigated—show in the spectroscope. The spectrum of indium exhibits two characteristic lines: one violet line *a,* and another blue line β; and besides these two fainter blue lines are visible if the burner in which the metal is volatilized be fed with hydrogen instead of coal gas. Its specific gravity is 7.1–7.4; its symbol In; and its atomic weight 114.8. It melts at 155°C. (=311°F.) and vaporizes above 1,450°C. Chemically, indium resembles aluminum and gallium, being chiefly trivalent. See also ATOMIC THEORY; CHEMISTRY; METALS; PERIODIC LAW.

INDIVIDUAL DIFFERENCES, Psychology of. In any science the primary interest is in the typical phenomena and general laws of the field. So it has been in psychology; but the interest of some investigators in subjecting the very differences between people to scientific treatment as phenomena in their own account has been powerfully supported by the modern interest in testing and classifying individual persons. Differential psychology, as it is also called, has come into its own with the demands of application in many practical areas.

Basic to all work in this field is the statistical concept of the normal curve of chance distribution (see Fig. 1, which is plotted from the expansion of the algebraic binomial $(x + y)^n$). It has been observed by other scientists and mathematicians that the laws of chance which govern the fall of a coin or a die obtain also for the occurrence of anatomical traits such as height or chest girth, and, as the psychologist Francis Galton found (see *Bibliography*), for the occurrence of mental traits of a great many kinds. Mathematically, the composite effect of innumerable factors operating independently upon a trait is to produce many occurrences of medium amounts of the trait with fewer and fewer cases of extremely high or extremely low amount, the gradation being represented not by a straight line but by a bell-shaped curve. Methodologically, then, we may expect to find most mental characteristics appearing in a great number of individuals in the proportions suggested by the curve; and clear departures from the curve then suggest the operation of some factor or factors that call for identification. The statistical and graphic methods with elaborations are useful in bringing out many aspects of individual differences: how a given John Doe resembles or differs from his group; how one group of people compares with another in their average score; how one group may have more scattered scores than another; how two mental abilities may or may not vary together.

Turning now from methodology to content and findings, we may limit our survey to two problems. *Male and female* differ, of course, anatomically especially after puberty. So far as intelligence is measurable, no reliable difference at all is found. Great differences in emotionality between man and woman are popularly assumed, but they have not been demonstrated experimentally—though available methods of measuring are far from adequate. In types of interests very great divergence is the rule, but here we deal with something that is certainly a product of social pressures and encouragements and hardly at all a matter of fundamental sex difference.

There is no basis for sorting human beings that is more commonly employed and more provocative of violence than that of *race.* Investigations of racial differences are peculiarly subject to errors that creep in from many sources aside from the unconscious biases of the examiners. For instance, to measure different races of people on American soil, or to apply to Polynesians or Mongolians tests that have been standardized in American schools, is to overlook serious conditions that may blanket out true

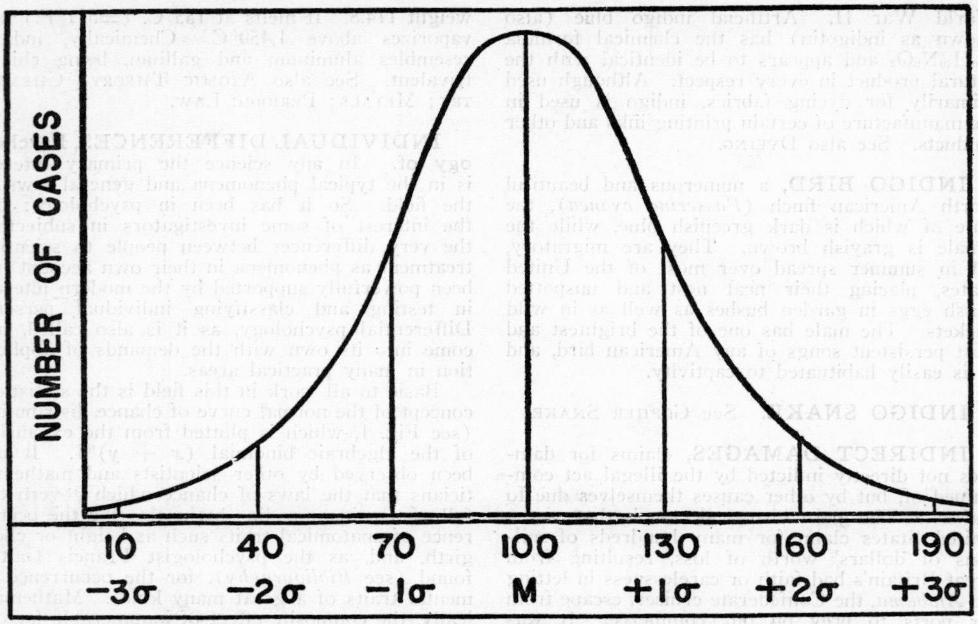

FREQUENCY CURVE WITH STANDARD DEVIATION AS A UNIT OF MEASURE ON THE BASE LINE
The mean score of the distribution is 100 points, the standard deviation is 30 points. Note the area of the curve (that is, the number of individual cases) comprehended by 1, 2, and 3 S.D.'s respectively, taken above and below the mean.

differences or may produce specious ones. Franz Boas' statement made in 1894 is as valid today: "The average faculty of the white race is found to the same degree in a large proportion of individuals of all other races." In this area as well as in other dimensions of variation, the sound rule is: so far as native traits are in question, what counts is not the group to which a person happens to belong; it is himself.

Some general conclusions that are much emphasized may be noted. The differences between individuals from the same group often exceed the differences between the means of different groups. Generally abilities go together, so that the individual who stands high in his population in one ability is somewhat more likely than not to stand high in another ability—popular opinion to the contrary notwithstanding. The effects of culture (that is, rearing, education, and social environment generally) are unquestionably very great in producing differences easily confused with native differences.

Bibliography.—Galton, F., *Inquiries into Human Faculty* (London 1883); Thorndike, E. L., *Educational Psychology*, vol. 3 (New York 1914); Schwesinger, G. C., *Heredity and Environment* (New York 1933); Freeman, F. S., *Individual Differences* (New York 1934); Anastasi, A., *Differential Psychology* (New York 1937).

JOHN FREDERICK DASHIELL,
Kenan Professor of Psychology, University of North Carolina.

INDIVIDUALISM, a regard for and emphasis of the individual. In the field of ethics, those doctrines which dwell upon individual welfare and are based upon the dictates of individual feeling. Under these views, it is taken for granted that if each indiivdual seeks his own highest welfare, social welfare will take care of itself. Individualism is opopsed to socialism and finds defense in the works of John Stuart Mill and Herbert Spencer. It becomes the duty of the state, under this conception, not to interfere with the individual except when it is necessary to preserve the opportunity for action. The function of the state is regarded as an artificial restraint, while individual initiative is a natural factor in evolution.

Bibliography.—La Monte, R. R., *Men versus the Man* (New York 1910); Hill, D. J., *Americanism; What It Is* (New York 1919); Wood, J. N., *Democracy and the Will to Power* (New York 1921); Blackmar, F. W., *Justifiable Individualism* (New York 1922); Hoover, H. C., *American Individualism* (Garden City, N.Y., 1922); Jordan, E., *Forms of Individuality* (Indianapolis 1927); Dewey, J., *Individualism Old and New* (New York 1930); Robertson, H. M., *Aspects of the Rise of Economic Individualism* (New York 1933).

INDIVIDUALITY, a separate and distinct existence. The fact that one thing may be distinguished from all others gives individuality its meaning. Whether the distinction is only relative or is absolute is disputed among philosophers. The problem arises out of the difficulty of thinking of any distinctive character of an individual, except its location in space or time, without using general concepts. With Plato, the universals alone were real. With Aristotle, reality was found in the concrete individual and the universal stood only for an abstraction. The same problem occurs in medieval times, in the discussion of the relation of God, Trinity and man, and in modern times in the question of the relation of the individual to society. For individuality in the zoölogical sense, consult Child, C. M., *Individuality in Organism* (Chicago 1915), and Huxley, Julian S. *The Individual in the Animal Kingdom* (Cambridge, Eng. 1911).

INDOCHINA, Associated States of. Formerly known as FRENCH INDOCHINA, the Associated States of Indochina occupy the eastern part of the Asian peninsula which extends south from Burma and China; the latter countries form their northern boundary; Thailand, the Gulf of Siam, and the South China Sea border them to the west, south, and east. Politically, the Associated States comprise the following three independent states, associated within the French Union under agreements ratified Feb. 2, 1950: Viet Nam, made up of the former protectorates of Tonkin, and Annam, and the former colony of Cochinchina; and the constitutional monarchies of Cambodia, and Laos. King Norodom Sihanouk, and King Sisavang Vong are chiefs of state respectively of Cambodia and Laos; Bao Dai, former emperor of Annam, is Viet Nam's chief of state—his residence is at Dalat (pop. 5,200, est. 1943). Saigon, which in 1887 became the administrative center for French Indochina and has juridically remained so (although in 1900 the governor general removed his residence to Hanoï), is the seat of the French commissioner general. It is also the administrative capital for Viet Nam and the seat of one of the three French high commissioners, and others, accredited to Laos and Cambodia, being stationed in the capitals of those states.

The aggregate area is 272,355 square miles (Viet Nam, 127,259 square miles; Cambodia, 53,668 square miles; Laos, 91,428 square miles). According to a 1952 estimate the population was 30,500,000, based on a 1951 estimate for Viet Nam of 25,000,000, a 1948 estimate for Cambodia of 3,748,000, and a 1950 estimate for Laos of 1,186,000. Saigon, the most populous city, combined in 1932 with the neighboring city of Cholon, has a population of 1,179,000 (1948 est.). Hanoï, capital of North Viet Nam (formerly Tonkin), is second in size with 237,146 (1948 est.). Phnom Penh (110,639, est. 1948) is the capital of Cambodia. The administrative capital of Laos is Vientiane (14,000, est. 1936); Luang Prabang (about 15,000), the ancient capital, is the royal residence.

Topography.—Indochina is essentially mountainous country. The Cordillera of Annam extends north and south across the entire length parallel with the eastern coast, forming plateaus and valleys flanked by the Cardamon Mountains in the west. Watering the central area, the Mekong, one of the longest rivers of southeast Asia, extends more than 1,900 miles from its source in China to its several outlets in the South China Sea. East of the Cordillera flows the Coi (Songkoi) or Red River, which, like the Mekong, is dissected at its mouth into numerous outlets. Frequent gorges and rapids limit the usefulness of these rivers. The Mekong is nevertheless a main artery of trade; at about the middle of its length it feeds Tonle Sap, a lake in western Cambodia, in which innumerable fish are taken annually when flood waters recede. Indochina's alternating dry and wet seasons are governed by the monsoons. There are wide variations in temperature corresponding with variations of latitude and altitude. Gales and typhoons occur during September in northern Annam.

The People.—Centuries of infiltration have produced a tangle of races. Annamese greatly predominate, there being about 23 millions of this group in the Viet Nam Republic. Khmer elements linger in Cambodia, representing a civilization which at its height in the 12th century built the great city of Angkor and the famous temple of Angkor Wat. Siamese racial influences also are apparent in central Indochina. The inhabitants of Laos have characteristics of the Thai peoples believed to have entered the peninsula in ancient times from Burma and China's Yunnan province and subjugated the aboriginal Khas ("savages"). Also of Chinese origin are Mois, primitive inhabitants of northern Laos. Subject to recurrent invasions, the Indochinese have remained essentially pacific, easy-going agriculturalists. The principal religion is Buddhism, interpreted as ancestor worship and combined, among the Annamese, with features of Taoism. Since 1930 some 2,000,000 adherents of Caodaism, in which elements are found of all the great religions, have formed a nationalist sect capable of controlling a considerable area of Cochinchina. A high level of craftsmanship is attained in native metal work, weaving, and the making of musical instruments. Primary schools number 4,428 and had some 549,343 pupils in 1951–1952. In the

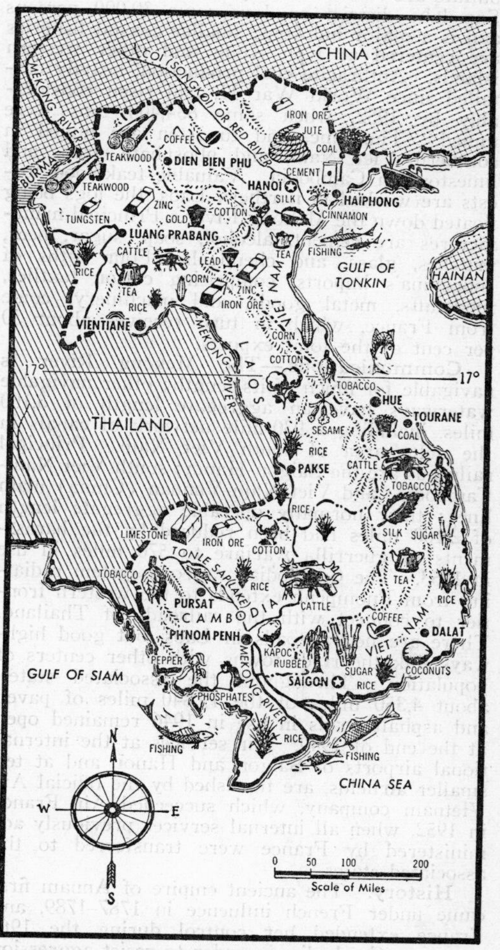

Indochina: Its principal products and resources.

larger cities there are also *lycées,* vocational schools, and colleges.

Production and Trade.—The fertility of the Mekong River valley enabled Indochina to become the second rice-producing country of the world, with an output exceeded only by Burma. Rice fields occupy some five-sixths of the cultivable land. Rubber production is next in importance as an export industry. Rice and rubber production have been maintained at a surprisingly high level on lands contested since 1946 between the associated states and the insurgent forces. Rice cultivation had advanced to an estimated output of about 13,100 million pounds in 1952–1953, while rubber production, principally in the Saigon region where some 25,000 workers are employed on French plantations, advanced 15 per cent from 1951 to 61,448 metric tons in 1952. Corn (maize) holds third place as an export crop. Cotton, pepper, and tobacco are grown in Cambodia; tea and coffee plantations are managed by the French in southern Viet Nam; cinnamon is a main crop of the Red River delta. Other agricultural products include kapok, coconuts, jute, sesame, vegetables, and citrus fruits. Several million cattle, pigs, horses, and buffalo are raised annually. Fishing in the Tonle Sap lake district employs some 30,000 persons and is a major industry; smaller coastal fisheries are centered at Koh Kong and other western islands. Anthracite coal production, heavily curtailed since World War II, had risen considerably by 1952, when some 834,400 tons were mined. Tin, zinc, and tungsten are mined in southern Viet Nam, and phosphate, iron, and limestone in Cambodia. Valuable teakwood forests are worked in northern Laos, the logs being floated down the Mekong River. Principal manufactures are cement, alcohol, soap, sugar, beer, matches, glass, and chemicals. Four fifths of Indochina's imports, comprising cotton textiles, foodstuffs, metal goods, and machinery, come from France, which in turn receives about 30 per cent of the total exports.

Communications.—The Mekong River is navigable for much of its length; other navigable waterways have an aggregate length of 3,100 miles, including a 930-mile network of canals in the delta area of south Viet Nam. Principal railroads are the Saigon-Hanoï; south Viet Nam-Cambodia; and Viet Nam-Yunnan (China) main lines; their normally operable aggregate length of 2,100 miles had been reduced by the harassments of guerrilla warfare to 570 miles in use in 1953. The Cambodian railroad system radiating from Pnompenh extends to the western frontier to connect with the railroads of Thailand. There are no railroads in Laos, but good highways link the river towns with other centers of population. Throughout the associated states, about 4,350 miles of the 19,840 miles of paved and asphalt roads in use in 1946 remained open at the end of 1949. Air services at the international airports of Saigon and Hanoï, and at ten smaller airfields, are furnished by the official Air Vietnam company, which succeeded Air France in 1952, when all internal services previously administered by France were transferred to the associated states.

History.—The ancient empire of Annam first came under French influence in 1787–1789, and France extended her control during the 19th century. Cambodia, in order to resist aggression from Siam (now Thailand), placed the kingdom under French protection in 1863; Cochinchina was added in 1867 as a colony in the French jurisdiction, and protectorates were later established over Tonkin (1882) and Annam (1884–1886). Laos was added as a fourth protectorate in 1893, and Kwangchowan acquired on 99-year lease from China in 1898. Following surrender of France to the Germans in 1940, Indochina gradually came under control of Japan, and the provinces of Battambang, Siemreap, and Sisophon were ceded to Siam. After Japan's defeat in 1945, however, and the restoration of French rule, the ceded provinces were recovered. Although consenting to incorporation of her protectorates in the Viet Nam Republic, organized by the Communist-led Viet Minh independence movement, France, which had recognized the new state March 6, 1946, refused to relinquish to it the colony of Cochinchina. A civil war followed. The rôle of Communist China, in furnishing matériel and leadership to the independence movement, so widened the issue as to give Indochina an importance hardly second to Korea in the global struggle.

The United States became involved as a principal supporter of the French-sponsored Bao Dai government. By early 1952 the Vietnamese forces totaled 215,000, to which Cambodia and Laos had each contributed seven battalions. Meanwhile on various dates during 1949 each of the associated states had become autonomous through bilateral agreements defining their relation to the French Union. Eleven million of Viet Nam's population were still within territory held by the Viet Minh insurgents in early 1954; a military decision seemed remote after seven years during which France had spent more than a billion dollars annually in the struggle, to which she had committed 22 per cent of officers of her regular army. The United States' contribution had risen steadily, and amounted by 1954 to about one third of the total cost of the war.

Main factors militating against the success of the French and associated forces in the struggle with the Viet Minh included: (1) lack of a strong nationalist sentiment in the new republic of Vietnam, reflected in small support for its new army, the largest constituent of the joint forces; (2) Vietnam's incompetent political leadership, Bao Dai setting the example of neglect of duty in spending much of his time on the French Riviera; (3) the ever increasing help given to the Viet Minh by China and Russia, in the form of generalship, troop training, munitions, and transport.

The military successes of the Viet Minh in Tonkin (North Vietnam) in the spring and summer of 1954, signalized by the capture of Dien Bien Phu on May 7, after a heroic 55-day defense by Brig. Gen. Christian de Castries, and the evacuation of a large part of the Red River delta area by French forces, induced France to negotiate with the Viet Minh at Geneva in July. On July 21, armistice agreements, drafted mainly by France's premier and foreign minister, Pierre Mendès-France, were signed, providing for the gradual yielding (in a 10-month period) of all Viet Nam north of the 17th parallel to Ho Chih Min's rebel government. Communist rule was thus assured for 77,000 square miles, while Bao Dai's domain was reduced to 50,000 square miles. Elections for a unified government, it was agreed, should be held within two years, and prisoners exchanged within 30 days. Indian, Polish and Canadian commissioners were appointed supervisers. See also FRANCE—*Government;* FRENCH UNION; CAMBODIA; LAOS; VIET NAM.

Bibliography.—Cordier, H., *Dictionnaire bibliographique des ouvrages relatifs à la Péninsule Indochinoise* (Paris 1932); Ennis, T. E., *French Policy and Developments in Indo-China* (Chicago 1936); Robequain, C., *The Economic Development of French Indo-China* (New York 1944); Gaudel, A., *L'Indochine française en face du Japon* (Saigon 1947); Levy, R., *L'Indochine et ses traités, 1946* (Paris 1947); Gourou, P., *Land Utilization in Indochina* (New York 1950); United States Department of State publication, Eastern Series 58, *Indochina* (Washington 1953).

INDO-CHINESE, generic name of the native population of Indochina, most of whom belong to the southern branch of the Mongol division of mankind, and speak monosyllabic toned languages of the Indo-Chinese linguistic family. See also LANGUAGES OF THE WORLD.

INDO-EUROPEAN LANGUAGES, the name invented by scholars to indicate a group of languages evidently related, that is, descending from one common ancestor-language, of which we possess no direct record. The name Indo-European is inexact in both its components, since not all languages of Europe belong to this family, nor is Indic the only Indo-European language outside of Europe. However, the other terms (Aryan, Aryo-European, Indo-Celtic, Indo-Germanic), although perhaps more correct, have not gained much foothold, at least in English-speaking countries.

The kinship of the Indo-European languages can still be seen quite clearly in some word classes such as the numerals, family names, and names for the parts of the body: English *three, mother, foot* are obviously identical with German *drei, mutter, fuss,* with Latin *trēs, māter, pēs* (*pedis*), Greek τρεῖς, μήτηρ (Doric μάτηρ), πούς (ποδός), Sanskrit *tráyas, mātā* (accusative *mātáram*), *pât* (accusative *pâdam*), and so on. Sometimes the identity is not quite apparent to the eye, or rather ear, of the layman, but becomes immediately clear when a few simple rules, deduced from other equations, are considered: thus the correspondence of the initial *f* of English *foot,* German *fuss* with the *p* of Latin *pēs,* Greek πούς, Sanskrit *pât,* is found also in many other words, such as English *father,* German *vater* (pronounced *fater*), Latin *pater,* Greek πατήρ, Sanskrit *pitâ* (accusative *pitáram*); English *fish,* German *fisch,* Latin *piscis.* On the other hand, Celtic loses initial *p* (English *f,* German *f*) and therefore *fish* is *iasc* (*a* is an epenthetic vowel) and *father, athir* in Old Irish.

From the study of the original Indo-European material, discovered with the help of such rules as Grimm's and Verner's laws (qq.v.), the original vocabulary and therefore the original culture and home of Indo-European people, before the separation, can be deduced. The Indo-Europeans had no words for tropical or even Mediterranean products, plants and animals, such as the laurel tree, the grapevine, the fig tree, the ape, the camel, the tiger, the donkey; but they had words for northern animals and plants, such as the bear, the wolf, the cow, the goat, the pig, the goose, the apple tree, the oak, the beech, the birch, the pine. Since they also had a name for snow, they obviously lived in a northern, cold climate; and this fact, as well as the names of some animals (especially the salmon) and plants points towards the eastern shores of the Baltic Sea (Latvia and Lithuania).

Their culture was very primitive, being in what we call the aëneolithic stage (late Stone Age with very little metal). They had a very modest form of agriculture including the plow, with some domesticated animals (pig, dog, goose, cow, goat, sheep; later the horse). They lived mostly by hunting and fishing. They had little acquaintance with navigation, very little industry, and almost no trade. They had of course no writing and counted no further than 100. All these conclusions are confirmed by the historical fact that in the whole Mediterranean and subtropical belt from Gibraltar to Calcutta, where ancient refined civilizations flourished, we see the Indo-Europeans arriving as northern barbarians, from the year 2000 B.C. on, destroying or assimilating previous native cultures (Minoan, Khattite, Babylonian, etc.) all belonging, it seems, to non-Indo-European peoples.

The Indo-European language was highly inflectional (English *boy: boys*), had vowel gradation (*gift, give, gave; song, sing, sang, sung*), distinguished sharply between the different parts of speech (especially noun and verb), had three genders (masculine, feminine and neuter or inanimate: English *he, she, it*), had a constant agreement between adjective, noun and pronoun, and a special predilection for anomaly and "suppletivism" (English *I am: you are: I was: I have been; I go: I went*). All of these characteristics, however, tend to disappear, more or less rapidly, in all Indo-European languages, and English is a very good example of it, having gone further away from the inflectional type than any other Indo-European language, with the possible exception of modern Persian. English has sharply reduced the endings (*I love, you love, we love, they love*), the vowel gradation (*love, I love, I loved, loved*), and the genders (that find now almost no formal expression except in some pronouns); the agreement between adjective and noun has disappeared entirely, and anomaly and suppletivism almost completely; and the distinction between the different parts of speech is weakening more every day, favored, of course, by the loss of the endings: *dance, loan, bomb, cut, want, will, love,* etc. are both nouns and verbs; in *I do not feel good,* or *hit him hard,* the difference between adjective and adverb is lost; in *I distinguish good and evil,* the distinction between noun and adjective is disappearing; *like* is in colloquial English a noun, a verb, an adjective, an adverb, a conjunction. A sentence like English *I danced once with my wife* or *I shall not loan the book to Peter* are examples of an agglutinative, not inflectional language (the words, *the, to, with, not* and *shall* cannot be used independently); *I see you are well,* or *I think we need money,* or *We love wine,* or *I give Peter what I want,* are sentences of an isolating language, for every word can be used in isolation (*we, love, what, wine, think, I, money*). The substitution, in colloquial American, of *good* for *well* (in the phrase *I feel good*), of *me* for *I* (it *is me*), of *loan* for *lend* and of *who* for *whom,* shows the trend of the language away from inflection. Sentences like *He saw the geese and the oxen running away* or *He went out of his father's house* show the remains of the inflectional type. See also LANGUAGES OF THE WORLD.

Bibliography.—Brugmann, K., *Elements of the Comparative Grammar of the Indo-Germanic Languages,* tr.

by J. Wright, 5 vols. (New York and Strasbourg 1888–95); Schrader, O., *Prehistoric Antiquities of the Aryan Peoples* (London 1890); Bender, H. H., *The Home of the Indo-Europeans* (Princeton 1922); Wright J., *An Elementary New English Grammar* (London-New York etc. 1924); Buck, C. D., *Comparative Grammar of Greek and Latin* (Chicago 1933); Prokosch, E., *A Comparative Germanic Grammar* (Philadelphia 1939); Buck, C. D., *A Dictionary of Selected Synonyms in the Principal Indo-European Languages* (Chicago 1949).

GIULIANO BONFANTE,
Princeton University.

INDO-IRANIAN LANGUAGES. See IRANIAN LANGUAGES AND LITERATURE.

INDONESIA, ĭn-dō-nē′zhȧ, **Republic of,** is a unitary state in southeast Asia comprising all of the archipelago formerly known as the Netherlands East Indies with the exception of Western New Guinea (Irian), the status of which remains in dispute. The chain of islands constituting Indonesia lie between the continents of Asia and Australia, straddling the equator, and separate the Indian Ocean from the Pacific. This archipelago, the largest in the world, consists of six main islands or island groups, and more than 3,000 smaller islands. The six main islands or

Coat of arms.

island groups comprise: Sumatra; Java; Lesser Sunda Islands (chiefly Bali, Lombok, Flores, Timor); Kalimantan (Indonesian Borneo); Sulawesi (or Celebes); and the Moluccas. Within the archipelago are British territories in north and west Borneo (North Borneo, Brunei, and Sarawak) and the Portuguese colony embracing the eastern half of Timor. The republic has a land area of nearly 600,000 square miles, and the population is estimated to number some 76,000,000.

The capital of Indonesia is Djakarta (Jakarta), on the northwest coast of Java; as capital of the Netherlands East Indies it was known as Batavia. Other large cities on Java include Surabaja (Surabaya), Bandung (Bandoeng), Djokjakarta (Jogjakarta), and Surakarta (Soerakarta). In Sumatra, Palembang, Medan, and Padang are the chief cities; and in the Lesser Sunda Islands, Den Pasar and Singaradja are the largest towns on Bali, Waingapu (Waingapoe) on Sumba (Soemba), Ruteng on Flores, and Kupang (Koepang) on the island of Timor. The principal towns of Kalimantan are Bandjarmasin (Bandjermasin) and Pontianak; of Sulawesi, Makassar and Menado (Manado); and of the Moluccas, Morotai and Ternate on Halmahera, Namlea on Buru (Boeroe), Ambon (Amboina) on the island of that name, Piru (Piroe) on Ceram, and Saumlakki on the Tanimbar Islands.

Geology.—In prehistoric times the western islands of Indonesia were part of the continent of Asia, while the eastern islands were joined to Australia. The waters of the ocean eventually rose, completely submerging the outer areas of both continents except for the upper portions of the mountains in those regions; and this chain of unsubmerged portions, now isolated from the continents, formed the Indonesian archipelago.

Topography.—The main tectonic features of Indonesia are: (1) the southern part of the Eurasian Shield, occupying the east coast of Sumatra, a narrow strip along the north coast of Java, the shallow Sunda shelf from which arise the islands of Banka, Biliton, the Riouw-Lingga Archipelago, Karimata Islands, etc.; (2) the Australian Shield, occupying the very shallow and flat Sahul shelf, the Aru Islands, and the greater part of the low lands of southern New Guinea. Between these two comparatively stable regions lies an unstable region of elongated and narrow mountain systems, separated from each other by deep sea channels. The mountain-forming forces are active in this middle region. A range of volcanoes traverses the archipelago from the northernmost point of Sumatra, along the west coast of that island in the Barisan Mountains, and along the south coast of Java in a chain having 22 eruptive points. In the intersection of these two lines, in the Strait of Sunda, lies Krakatoa, famous for its destructive eruption of August 1883. The range continues over the Lesser Sunda Islands to bend northward to the Banda Archipelago. A short second range is found in Halmahera and the adjacent islands. A third line begins in northern Sulawesi (Celebes) and connects over the Sangihe Islands with the volcanic range of Mindanao. The total number of volcanoes is 99.

Climate.—The climate is a tropical sea climate, uniform and monotonous, with abundant rainfall, light winds, high temperature, and high humidity. The proximity of the continents of Asia and Australia makes the archipelago into a monsoon region. The monsoon winds regulate rainfall, causing wet and dry seasons. The west monsoon, blowing in from India from November to March, brings heavy rains, causing torrents in the river valleys and inundations in the lowlands; during the dry season, from June to October, there is considerably less rain. However, since the archipelago extends over a distance of 3,000 miles, there is considerable variation in the time spans of the monsoons. Java, for example, has a minimum rainfall from May to August and a maximum during December, January, and February. Humidity is usually high, and the year-round rainfall is rather heavy. In Djakarta, the average annual rainfall is 80 inches; in Sumatra and Kalimantan, from 120 to 144 inches. The lowest temperature ever registered in Djakarta was 66°F., the highest was 96°F. (both in 1877); the mean temperature in the capital is 82°F.

Fauna and Flora.—The animal and plant life of Indonesia are characterized by both Asian and Australian influences. In the western islands are found elephant, tigers, wild boar, leopards, and rhinoceros; the orangutan is only to be found in Kalimantan and Sumatra. In the eastern part of Indonesia a great variety of marsupials is found. Among the smaller animals are sheep, goats, tapir, deer, wild pigs, squirrels, lemurs, bats, and flying foxes. Crocodiles abound in the rivers, and there are also pythons and lizards, one species of the latter attaining a growth of ten feet. Among the insects must be mentioned mosquitoes, white, black, and red ants, spiders, scorpions, and the remarkable walking leaf and walking branch. Annoying flies and leeches inhabit the forests. Countless varieties of birds include cockatoos, duck, kingfisher, parrots, pheasant, pigeon, peacock, and birds-of-paradise. Forests in the coastal regions are largely mangrove and nipa palm, giving way to tropical rain forests in the interior lowlands. In the higher areas, oak, chestnut, and rhododendron predominate, while the conifers prevail in the high mountain forests. The bamboo is found almost everywhere—one variety with a stalk 30 inches thick; and many flowers produce immense blooms. In the seas surrounding the islands are many types of fish, mollusks, crustaceans, sharks, and octopuses.

Minerals.—The most important are tin (on Banka, Biliton, and the west coast of Sumatra and Kalimantan), petroleum (northern and southern Sumatra, east Java, and east Kalimantan), bauxite (Riouw Archipelago), and coal. Gold and silver are found in moderate quantities on the large islands, where there are also small deposits of iron ore. Java has some manganese deposits, and restricted quantities of copper ore have been located. Diamonds are found only in southern Kalimantan. Other mineral deposits include asphalt, nickel, wolframite, platinum, and sulfur.

The People.—In Indonesia are many different physical types; and custom, dress, and folklore vary greatly in the various localities. The earliest Indonesian race was an admixture of five different stocks: Veddoid of Ceylon (a race intermediate between the Dravidians of India and the aborigines of Australia), African Negritoid, Australoid, Melanesian, and Papuan. The racial influence of the Veddas was by far the greatest. Several migrating waves subsequently passed over the islands. The short, stocky brown-skinned Proto-Malays surged on to the archipelago during the Neolithic Age, and at the same period the Mongols of Asia moved southward, overrunning the Malay Peninsula and gradually changing the physical characteristics of the Malays. Thus the Deutero-Malays who reached Indonesia in the Bronze Age had Mongol traits and possessed a higher cultural level than their predecessors. By the 11th century waves of migratory Indians had imparted a Buddhist flavor to the racial composition; and an even greater influence was exerted by the Moslems who subsequently arrived in Indonesia. The main ethnic groups on each of the six main islands or island groups are as follows: on Sumatra, Achinese, Coastal Malays, and Menangkabaus (all of the Deutero-Malay race), and Rejang Lampong and Bataks (Proto-Malays); on Java, Sundanese, Javanese, and Madurese (Deutero-Malays); on the Lesser Sunda Islands, Balinese (Deutero-Malays) and Alorese (Proto-Malays); on Kalimantan, Coastal Malays, Macassarese, and Buginese (Deutero-Malays), and Dajaks or Dayaks (Proto-Malays); on Sulawesi, Macassarese and Buginese (Deutero-Malays), and in the Moluccas, Alfurs, Papuas, and Ambonese (Proto-Malays).

Broadly speaking, the average contemporary Indonesian is light brown in color, and is short, slender, and frail of stature. His hair is black, ranging from completely straight to wavy; and the facial features are either sharply chiseled or Mongolian—the latter characterized by higher cheekbones and slightly slanted eyes. The emancipation of women began only in the 20th century. It was largely due to the efforts of Raden Adjeng Kartini (1879–1903), who was the first to initiate the abandonment of outmoded taboos against feminine education; her birthday, April 21, is marked as a public holiday in Indonesia. Women now have full equality with men, including the franchise and the right to conduct business and own property.

There are over 30 different languages, divided into 11 main groups, spoken in Indonesia, and some 250 recognizable dialects. Basically, the Indonesian language is a Malay tongue, and to this has been added Hindu and Arabic lingual contributions and a number of words borrowed from Sanskrit, Dutch, and other languages. The Malay language thus broadened has been designated the official language of the republic.

Religion.—About 90 per cent of the Indonesian population adhere to the Moslem faith. In many outlying districts, however, Islamic practice is plainly influenced by animism and local *adat* (customary law). The most important Moslem religious holiday is *Lebaran,* which occurs at the end of the Islamic fasting month; it symbolizes the purification and cleansing of the body and soul, and is an occasion for new clothes, festive foods, and greetings between friends and relatives.

The people of Bali and Lombok have remained completely Hindu in religion and culture; along with Buddhists, they make up an approximate 6 per cent of the population. Christianity was first introduced into Indonesia by the Portuguese, in the 16th century, and missionaries of several denominations have continued the work of proselytization; about 3½ per cent of the population are Christians. There are Christian communities on all the islands, the largest concentration being found in the Batak area of Sumatra.

Culture.—Since the beginning of the Christian era Indonesia has felt the impact of the Hindu, Moslem, and European cultures, each of which has left its imprint, in varying degrees, upon the indigenous social structure of the islands. The Hindu-Indonesian tradition in art which persisted until the beginning of the 20th century was highly stylized and stereotyped. It almost exclusively depicted scenes from the great Hindu epics, the *Ramayana* and *Mahabharata,* which illustrated the struggle between the forces of good and evil. Early paintings in water color on parchment leather are episodic in composition and represent an anonymous community art devoted entirely to Hindu religious beliefs and moral concepts. A few modern works in the traditional style by such contemporary Balinese artists as Tedjiwa and Gendjot reflect the influence of Western techniques introduced to Bali by European painters. In the years immediately preceding World War II young artists of Indonesia, aware of the static quality of the arts in their country, began to develop a genuine modern Indonesian art by adapting Western styles and techniques for the expression of their own cultural values.

Although the first Indonesian language novel was published in 1929 by Takdir Alisjahbana, cofounder of the monthly periodical, *Pudjangga Baru* (New Poet), the renaissance of Indonesian literature did not develop freely until after World War II. Outstanding contemporary poets and novelists, in addition to Takdir Alisjahbana, are Chairil Anwar, Asrul Sani, and Rivai Apin.

Dances and Plays.—Balinese and Javanese dances are the most popular of all those characteristic of Indonesia. The costumes of the performers are traditional, with gestures highly stylized and the faces of the dancers retaining an immutable and detached expression. Both Balinese and Javanese dances use the same leg technique (the turned-out thighs, legs, and feet typical of Hindu sculpture) and the same stylized movements of the hands. The music, called *gamelan,* is basically alike: the same five note scale and four-four rhythmic arrangement. Japanese court dances moved with a restrained dreamlike gravity. Other forms of the dance-drama are the mask plays, based on ancient Indonesian legends, and the *Langendriya,* cultivated only at the court of Surakarta; all the roles in the latter are sung and danced by women. The music of *gamelan* orchestras reflects the moods and actions of the dancers in harmony with the development of the story; such orchestras usually consist of light percussion instruments—mainly the drum (*kendang*) and gong—and string instruments—such as the *rebab* and zither. Drama forms include the *wayang* puppet plays, known in Indonesia since the 11th century and thematically based on Hindu epics; the *wayang polek,* three-dimensional wooden puppets usually depicting Moslem heroes; and the *wayang purwa,* two-dimensional shadow plays reflecting Hindu epics.

Crafts.—Unique handicrafts of Indonesia include the textile arts of *batik* and *ikat.* The former is a process of dyeing by the application of wax to those parts of the cloth not to be dyed; the latter is a more complicated textile process in which the threads are dyed before weaving to form the pattern. These textiles are used for garments for both men and women, and are used extensively for decorative purposes. Woodcarving is both decorative and religious in motive. Besides utilitarian objects like bowls and platters, the craft produces figures of ancient gods and legendary heroes. Wooden masks are also worn by the dancers in the dance-drama form of entertainment for the portrayal of character, either of the particular person represented or the nature of his disposition—cheerful, foolish, or evil. Much of both the old and modern Indonesian sculpture in wood represents characters of Hindu tradition and mythology; modern statues in wood, representing abstract ideas and modern concepts, are also carved. Silverwork is a highly developed craft in Java, Sumatra, and Bali. Jewelry and ornamental containers of very intricate design are wrought; and, in Sumatra, miniature houses and mosques in silver filigree. Other handicrafts include fiber weaving and basket work, especially in Sulawesi, Sumatra, and Kalimantan, sleeping mats, hats, baskets, and bags being made from rattan, palm leaves, and bamboo strips; beadwork is employed to decorate bags, belts, and ceremonial ornaments and garments; the handles and sheaths of daggers (*kris*) and swords are made in part of ivory and horn; and lamps, cooking utensils, and other utilitarian objects are made of brass.

Education.—Less than 5 per cent of the population was literate at the time Indonesia achieved its independence. Speedy introduction of general compulsory education was one of the first aims of the government of the republic, and within five years more than 10 million people had learned to read and write through the mass education program that was launched. A modern and complete educational system was to be established as soon as physical facilities and trained school teachers became available. Existing autonomous colleges were amalgamated immediately after World War II to constitute the University of Indonesia; its various faculties are located at Djakarta, Bandung, Bogor, Makassar, and Surabaja. The Gadjah Mada University, founded at Djokjakarta in 1946, was the first university to have an all-Indonesian faculty. Islam University, also founded at Djokjakarta in 1946, was the first modern university whose curriculum is based on Moslem culture and beliefs. Curricula in vocational training, social sciences, and literature are offered at the National Academy, established at Djakarta in 1949. The Pantja-Sila University, with schools of law, economics, and sociology, was opened in Padang, Sumatra, in 1951; and there are faculties of law and sociology at the Islamic Academy, opened at Medan, Sumatra, the same year. In Padang, there is also Sriwidjaja University; at Makassar, Sawerigading University; and at Bandung, Krisna Dwipajana University. The Economic Academy at Djakarta, financed jointly by the government and from private funds, provides advanced training in commerce and industry. At Djokjakarta is a Fine Arts Academy; and at Djakarta, an Academy of International Affairs.

Government.—Under the terms of the provisional constitution adopted in 1950, a president and vice president were elected by the House of Representatives; Achmed Soekarno became president, and Mohammed Hatta vice president. The unicameral legislative body is the House of Representatives. Pending elections, the 237 members were chosen on the basis of geographic, cultural, and political representation. With the setting up of the necessary electoral machinery, a Constituent Assembly will be elected to draft a permanent constitution. The dominant organ of government is a prime minister and cabinet responsible to the legislative body rather than to the president. Administratively, the republic is divided into ten provinces, each administered by a governor and a local house of representatives. The ten provinces (and their capitals) are as follows: West Java (Bandung); Central Java (Semarang); East Java (Surabaja); North Sumatra (Medan); Central Sumatra (Bukit Tinggi); South Sumatra (Palembang); Lesser Sunda Islands (Den Pasar); Moluccas (Ambon); Sulawesi (Makassar); and Kalimantan (Bandjarmasin).

Indonesia is a member of the United Nations, and it has diplomatic representation in many countries. In 1951 the republic complied with the United Nations embargo on the export of strategic materials to Communist China; and its representatives signed the Japanese Peace Treaty in San Francisco.

Agriculture and Livestock.—A fertile soil, abundant rainfall, and good tropical climate combine to give Indonesia immense agricultural possibilities. Large foreign-owned plantations have long concentrated on the mass growing of some

Above: Outdoor marketing in equatorial Bukittinggi, Sumatra, the Fort de Kock of the Dutch colonial era. *Below:* Roofed, gaily-painted native craft swarm the Moesi (Musi) River at Palembang, Sumatra.

INDONESIA

Top: Typical group of Indonesians in Jogjakarta, capital of the similarly named special district in Java. *Center row:* Ten-year-old Legong dancer of Bali; Balinese temple figure; Rice terraces in Java. *Bottom row:* Batak village in northern Sumatra; The Traffic and Irrigation Building in Bandoeng, a fine example of modern Javanese architecture.

Top photo by United Nations from Black Star. Two at left from Philip Gendreau, others by Screen Traveler from Gendreau.

INDONESIA

INDONESIA
LAMBERT AZIMUTHAL EQUAL-AREA PROJECTION
SCALE OF MILES
SCALE OF KILOMETRES
Capitals of Countries
International Boundaries
Railroads
Copyright by C.S. HAMMOND & CO., N.Y.
JAVA
SOUTH CHINA SEA
PACIFIC OCEAN
INDIAN OCEAN
JAVA SEA
CELEBES SEA
SULU SEA
BANDA SEA
FLORES SEA
ARAFURA SEA
TIMOR SEA
REPUBLIC OF THE PHILIPPINES
MALAYAN FEDERATION
NETH. NEW GUINEA (IRIAN)
TERR. OF NEW GUINEA
PAPUA
EASTERN NEW GUINEA
AUSTRALIA
EQUATOR

INDONESIA

INDONESIA

Adonara (isl.), 36,906 G 7
Alor (isl.), 68,029 G 7
Amboina, 17,334 H 6
Anambas (islands), 12,371 D 5
Arafura Sea J,K 8
Arnhemia B 5
Aru (islands), 18,176 K 7
Babar (isls.), 11,712 J 7
Bali (island), 1,074,924 F 7
Balikpapan, 29,843 F 6
Banda (islands), 13,036 H 6
Banda (sea) H 7
Bandjermasin, 150,219 E 6
Bandung, 765,084 H 2
Banggai (arch.), 49,836 G 6
Bangil, 20,236 K 2
Bangka (island), 230,000 D 6
Banjak (islands), 1,731 B 5
Banjuwangi, 25,185 L 2
Barisan (mts.) C 6
Barus, 9,615 B 5
Batang, 28,655 J 2
Batavia (Djakarta) (capital), 2,800,000 H 1
Batjan (islands), 14,543 H 6
Batu (islands), 12,619 B 6
Baturadja, 2,955 C 6
Baubau, 2,493 G 7
Bawean (island), 29,862 K 1
Belawan B 5
Belitung (Billiton) (isl.) 80,000 D 6
Bengkalis, 3,291 C 5
Bengkulu, 13,418 C 6
Billiton (island), 80,000 D 6
Bindjai, 9,176 B 5
Bintan (island), 25,895 D 5
Bintuhan, 1,918 C 6
Blitar, 27,846 K 2
Blora, 18,451 K 2
Bodjonegoro, 19,784 K 2
Bogor, 104,213 H 2
Bondowoso, 18,751 L 2
Bonthain, 6,711 F 7
Borneo (island) E 5
Brebes, 13,707 H 2
Buitenzorg (Borgor), 104,213 H 2
Bukittinggi, 14,657 B 6
Buru (island), 19,625 H 6
Butung (isl.), 106,730 G 6
Celebes (isl.), 5,500,000 G 6
Celebes (sea) G 5
Ceram (island) 95,636 H 6
Ceram (sea) H 6
Cheribon (Tjirebon), 54,079 H 2
Damar (isls.), 4,050 H 7
Dempo (mt.) C 6
Diamond (point) B 4
Djailolo H 5
Djakarta (capital), 2,800,000 H 1
Djambi, 22,071 C 6
Djatinegara H 2
Djember, 20,222 K 2
Djokjakarta, 294,985 J 2
Ende, 7,226 G 7
Flores (island), 494,851 G 7
Flores (sea) F, G 7
Fort de Kock (Bukittinggi), 14,657 B 6
Garut, 24,219 H 2
Gorontalo, 15,603 G 5
Gresik, 25,621 K 2
Gunongapi (isl.), 1,458 H 7
Gunungsitoli, 3,124 B 5
Halmahera (isl.), 83,822 H 5
Indonesia, 79,260,000
Indramaju, 21,190 H 2
Jakarta (Djakarta) (capital) 2,800,000 H 1
Java (island) D, E 7
Java (sea) D 6
Kahajan (river) E 6
Kai (islands), 50,648 J 7
Kalimantan (region) 3,000,000 E 5
Kandangan, 9,774 F 6
Kangean (islands), 40,743 F 7
Kapuas (river) D 6
Karakelong (isl.), 12,921 H 5
Karimata (arch.) D 6
Kawi (mt.) K 2
Kediri, 48,567 K 2
Kendari G 6
Kendawangan D 6
Ketapang (Borneo), 4,385 E 6
Ketapang (Madura) K 2
Kisar (isl.), 8,360 H 7
Kotaagung, 2,822 C 7
Kotabaharu E 6
Kotabaru, 3,756 F 6
Krakatau (isl.) C 7
Kraksaan, 4,738 K 2
Krui, 3,860 C 7
Kualakapuas, 8,682 E 6
Kualakurun E 6
Kuandang G 5
Kudus, 54,524 J 2
Kuningan H 2
Kupang, 7,171 G 8
Kur (island), 2,494 J 7
Kutaradja, 10,724 A 4
Kutoardjo, 11,496 J 2
Labuhan G 2
Lahat C 6
Lais C 6
Lamongan, 11,012 K 2
Langsa, 4,749 B 5
Laut (isl.), 20,723 F 6
Laut Ketji (isls.) F 7
Lawang K 2
Leuser (mt.) B 5
Lhoseumawe, 2,043 B 4
Lingga (arch.), 30,524 D 6
Lomblen (isl.), 47,245 G 7
Lombok (isl.), 701,290 F 7
Longiram F 5
Longnawan F 5
Lumadjang, 18,838 K 2
Luwuk G 6
Madiun, 41,872 J 2
Madjalengka, 8,596 H 2
Madjene F 6
Madura (island) K 2
Magelang, 52,944 J 2
Magetan, 15,152 K 2
Mahakam (river) F 6
Makassar, 250,000 F 7
Makassar (strait) F 6
Malacca (strait) C 5
Malang, 500,000 K 2
Malili G 6
Mamudju F 6
Manado, 50,000 G 5
Mangole (isl.), 3,598 H 6
Maras (mt.) D 6
Maros F 7
Martapura F 6
Masela (isls.), 2,151 H 7
Mataram F 7
Medan, 500,000 B 5
Meester Cornelis (Djatinegara) H 2
Menggala, 14,174 D 6
Mentawai (isl.), 18,149 B 6
Merak G 1
Meulaboh, 2,575 B 5
Modjokerto, 23,600 K 2
Molucca (isls.), 600,000 H 6
Molucca (sea) H 6
Morotai (isl.), 9,170 H 5
Muralabuh C 6
Müller (mts.) E 5
Muna (isl.), 108,719 G 7
Musi (river) C 6
Nangapinoh, 16,069 E 6
Natuna (isls.), 13,077 D 5
Nias (isl.), 187,199 B 5
Obi (island), 3,476 H 6
Ombai (strait) H 7
Padang, 108,728 B 6
Pajakumbuh, 5,914 C 6
Paleleh G 5
Palembang, 209,909 D 6
Pamekasan, 13,403 K 2
Pameungpeuk H 2
Pangkalanbrandan B 5
Pangkalpinang, 11,970 D 6
Pare, 22,388 K 2
Parepare, 6,273 F 6
Pariaman B 6
Pasangkaju F 6
Pasuruan, 36,973 K 2
Pati, 22,444 J 2
Pekalongan, 65,982 J 2
Pemalang, 29,249 J 2
Pematang Siantar, 15,328 B 5
Piru H 6
Ponorogo, 21,680 J 2
Pontianak, 45,196 D 6
Probolinggo, 37,009 K 2
Purbolinggo, 16,435 J 2
Purwakarta, 15,141 H 2
Purwokerto, 33,266 H 2
Purworedjo, 24,645 J 2
Raba, 6,781 F 7
Raja (mt.) E 6
Rambipudji K 2
Rangkasbitung G 2
Raung (mt.) L 2
Rembang, 13,791 K 2
Rengat, 1,949 C 6
Riouw (arch.), 77,149 D 5
Roti (isl.), 59,221 G 8
Salajar (isl.), 76,501 G 7
Salatiga, 24,274 J 2
Samarinda, 11,086 F 6
Sambas D 5
Sampit E 6
Sanana (isl.), 12,933 H 6
Sanggau E 5
Sangihe (isls.), 134,904 G 5
Sawahlunto, 15,146 C 6
Sawu (isls.), 33,622 G 8
Sawu (sea) G 7
Schwaner (mts.) E 6
Seaflower (strait) B 6
Sekadau E 6
Selatan (cape) E 6
Semarang, 500,452 J 2
Semeru (mt.) K 2
Serang, 11,163 G 1
Siak (river) C 5
Siau (isl.), 30,858 H 5
Siberut (isl.), 9,314 B 6
Siberut (strait) B 6
Sibolga, 10,765 B 5
Siborongborong, 3,076 B 5
Sidoardjo, 12,082 K 2
Simevlve (isl.), 19,302 A 5
Sindangbarang H 2
Singaradja, 12,345 F 7
Sintang, 4,474 E 5
Sipora (isl.), 3,892 B 6
Slamet (mt.) J 2
Solor (isl.), 14,761 G 7
Sorik Merapi (mt.) B 5
Sragen, 15,382 J 2
Subang, 10,539 H 2
Sukabumi, 34,191 G 2
Sukadana, 5,838 E 6
Sula (isls.), 20,137 H 6
Sumatra (isl.), 12,000,000 B 5
Sumba (isl.), 182,326 F 8
Sumbawa (str.), 314,843 F 7
Sumenep, 17,824 L 2
Sunda (strait) C 7
Surabaja, 847,843 K 2
Surakarta, 500,000 J 2
Takingeun, 1,411 B 5
Talaud (isls.), 23,825 H 5
Tambelan (isls.), 2,692 D 5
Tandjung F 6
Tandjungbalai, 6,823 C 5
Tandjungpandan, 15,708 D 6
Tandjungpinang, 5,789 C 5
Tandjungpriok H 1
Tandjungselor, 1,991 F 5
Tanimbar (isls.), 31,847 J 7
Tarakan, 11,589 F 5
Tarutung, 3,436 B 5
Tasikmalaja, 25,605 H 2
Tegal, 43,015 J 2
Telukbetung, 25,170 D 7
Ternate, 7,126 H 5
Tidore (isl.), 18,360 H 5
Timor (island) H 7
Timor (sea) H 7
Tjalang B 5
Tjepu, 21,861 J 2
Tjiandjur, 20,812 H 2
Tjilatjap, 28,309 H 2
Tjimahi, 21,994 H 2
Tjirebon, 54,079 H 2
Toba (lake) B 5
Togian (islands), 10,827 G 6
Tolitoli G 5
Tolo (gulf) G 6
Tomini (gulf) G 6
Tondano, 15,007 H 5
Trenggalek, 8,571 K 2
Tulungagung K 2
Waingapu, 2,127 G 7
Wangiwangi (isl.), 16,134 G 7
Watampone, 2,515 G 6
Wates, 7,784 J 2
We (island), 8,706 B 4
Weda H 5
Wonogiri J 2
Wonosobo, 10,710 J 2
Wowoni (isl.), 4,381 G 6

BRUNEI

Brunei (Br.), 40,657 E 5
Brunei (capital), 10,619 E 4

NETH. NEW GUINEA

Biak (isl.), 21,382 K 6
Carstensz (mt.) K 6
Dampier (strait) J 6
Demta L 6
Digoel (river) K 7
Fakfak J 6
Frederik Hendrik (isl.) K 7
Geelvink (bay) K 6
Hollandia (capital) K 6
Idenburg (river) K 6
Japen (isl.), 28,684 K 6
Mamberamo (river) K 6
Manokwari J 6
Merauke K 7
Misoöl (isl.), 2,018 J 6
Neth. New Guinea, 345,687 K 6
Noemfoor (isl.), 4,729 J 6
Orange (mt. range) K 6
Radja Ampat (isls.), 7,790 H 6
Salawati (isl.), 1,689 J 6
Sansapor J 6
Sarmi K 6
Schouten (isls.), 25,487 K 6
Seroei K 6
Snow (mts.) K 6
Soepiori (isl.), 4,105 K 6
Sorong J 6
Tanahmerah K 7
Valsch (cape) K 7
Vogelkop (pen.) J 6
Waibeem J 6
Waigeo (isl.), 2,840 J 5

NORTH BORNEO

Balambangan (island) F 4
Banggi (island) F 4
Beaufort, 1,576 F 4
Jesselton (capital), 11,704 F 4
Keningau, 301 F 4
Kinabalu (mt.) F 4
Kudat, 1,895 F 4
Labuan (island), 8,784 F 4
Labuk (bay) F 4
Lahad Datu, 811 F 5
North Borneo (state), 334,141 F 4
Papar, 1,772 F 4
Ranau, 252 F 4
Sandakan, 14,499 F 4
Sebatik (island) F 5
Semporna, 1,087 F 5
Tawau, 4,282 F 5
Victoria, 2,526 E 4
Weston, 835 F 4

PAPUA

Baniara C 7
Daru, 237 B 7
Fly (river) A 7
Kerema, 292 B 7
Louisiade (arch.), 10,384 D 8
Milne (bay) C 8
Papua (gulf) B 7
Port Moresby (cap.), 17,546 B 7
Samarai, 777 C 8
Torres (strait) A 7
Tróbriand (isls.), 9,134 C 7

PORT. TIMOR

Bobonaro, 467 H 7
Dili (capital), 1,795 H 7
Timor, 424,132 H 7
Vila Salazar, 400 H 7
Viqueque H 7

SARAWAK

Baram (pt.) E 5
Bintulu, 3,957 E 5
Iran (mts.) E 5
Kabong, 1,957 E 5
Kapit, 1,398 E 5
Kuching (capital), 37,954 E 5
Miri, 8,809 E 5
Mukah, 4,701 E 5
Rajang (river) E 5
Sarawak (Br.), 546,361 E 5
Sibu, 9,983 E 5
Simanggang E 5
Sirik (cape) E 5

TERR. OF NEW GUINEA

Bulolo, 1,689 B 7
Dampier (strait) C 7
Huon (gulf) C 7
Lae, 4,146 B 7
Madang, 1,550 B 7
New Britain (isl.), 90,000 C 7
Sepik (river) B 6
Wau, 1,865 B 7
Wewak, 879 B 6

of the export crops, and since establishment of the republic such crops are also being produced by increasing numbers of Indonesian farmers. Chief among the export crops are rubber, sugar, cinchona bark (yielding quinine, the specific for malaria), tea, coffee, oil palms, agave (hard cordage fibers), and cocoa. Other export crops include kapok (silky fibers from the seed of the silk-cotton tree), tobacco, copra (dried coconut meat), gutta percha, and spices (mainly black and white pepper, clove, nutmeg, and mace). Indonesia supplies about 60 per cent of the world's requirements of kapok, 90 per cent of cinchona bark, 85 per cent of the world's pepper, and 29 per cent of the world's copra. Rice, the main food of the people, is produced by the Indonesian farmers, and they also cultivate such food crops as corn, cassava (tapioca), coconut, sago (a food starch), peanuts, soybeans, fruit, and vegetables —particularly sweet potatoes, beans, and squash.

Cows and sheep are raised primarily for slaughter—rather than for dairying and wool production. In addition to cows, oxen and water buffalo are bred for use as draft animals. Horses are bred on the Lesser Sunda Islands, particularly on Timor and Flores; the Sandlewood breed of horse developed on the island of Sumba has a world-famous reputation.

Forestry and Fishing.—The dense forests covering most of the islands of the archipelago are rich in products of economic importance. Among the valuable woods are teak, sandalwood, ebony, and ironwood, and there are also bamboo, rattan (used for wicker products), mangrove bark (employed in the tanning of leather), indigo, and copal (a resin used in the manufacture of varnish and lacquer).

Fishing is an important industry, though not sufficient fish are secured to meet the domestic food needs. Tuna and many species of tropical fish abound in the seas surrounding Indonesia. There is a wholesale trade in fish on the west coast of Madura Strait, in the neighborhood of Surabaja, and at Bagan Si Api-Api, at the mouth of the Rokan River, on the east coast of Sumatra. Besides indigenous types, carp, herring, eel, and trout are plentiful in inland waters. Fish are also bred in the fresh, brackish, or salt waters of breeding ponds and in irrigated rice fields after harvesting of the paddy.

Industrial Production.—Serving the world market are the hat weaving industry near Djakarta and in the Priangan districts, which exports millions of hats annually; and the *batik* industry, which primarily supplies domestic requirements but also exports large quantities of *batik* cloth to British Malaya. Other industries supplying almost exclusively the domestic market are Indonesian straw cigarette factories, tile and roofing tile works, tanneries, and vegetable oil factories. Largely in the hands of Chinese are the rice mills, lime kilns, cement works, and furniture factories. Before World War II there were an auto assembling plant at Tandjong Priok, the harbor of Djakarta, and various engineering works, most of them near Surabaja. Automobile and bicycle tires were also made, and there were paper mills, soap factories, and glass-making plants. An industrial development program adopted by the republican government in 1950 envisaged plants for the manufacture of fertilizers, aluminum, plywood, tanning material, copra products, and textiles. Relatively little has been done to utilize the inland waterway system as a source of electric power. A large-scale hydroelectric development has been planned for Java's Bandung Plateau; and even more electric power will be obtained with the harnessing of the great rivers of Sumatra and Kalimantan.

External Trade.—In terms of monetary value, the principal export commodities are plantation rubber, crude oil and its products, copra, tin, tea, palm oil, tobacco, pepper, coffee, and kapok. Among other exports are areca nuts, cinchona bark, copal, damar, hard fibers, hides and skins, nutmeg, rattan, sugar, and tapioca products. The major components of Indonesia's imports consist of textiles, food and food products, and machinery. Other imports include fertilizers, automobiles, cement, and building materials.

Communications.—On the eve of World War II first class roads totaled some 43,700 miles in length, and the railroad system consisted of 4,611 miles of track. The most important rail line is that connecting the capital city of Djakarta with Surabaja, a distance of 550 miles. On all islands, and particularly in Sumatra and Kalimantan, the rivers serve as avenues of communication and transportation. There are steamship connections with Western Europe and with the Philippines, China, and Japan, and a considerable transshipment trade is also conducted through the British port of Singapore. Internal air services are supplied by Garuda Indonesian Airways, jointly owned by the government and Royal Dutch Airlines (KLM). Kemajoran Airport, outside Djakarta, is used by scheduled air services between Europe and Australia and the Orient.

History.—Both Hindu and Moslem empires had existed in Indonesia prior to the 16th century, when the Portuguese were the first traders to arrive from western Europe. They were ejected in 1565 from all parts of the archipelago except the eastern part of the island of Timor, but meanwhile Spanish and English traders had become active among the islands. The Dutch landed in west Java in 1596, and with the withdrawal of Spain a struggle for supremacy ensued between the English and Dutch. The Dutch East India Company was organized in 1602, and three years later Pieter Both was appointed first governor general of Netherlands Indies. In 1611 he moved his headquarters from Bantam to Djakarta; and the latter, renamed Batavia in 1619 during the governor generalship of Jan Pieterszoon (1618–1629), was henceforth the capital of the Netherlands Indies. The Dutch, in establishing a colonial system, came frequently into conflict with native rulers, and at the same time they repeatedly had armed affrays with their English rivals. In the middle of the 17th century English influence disappeared from the islands, and a century later the Dutch East India Company, unable to maintain its commercial monopoly and weakened by the cost of military operations against the sultanates, was forced into bankruptcy. The company was deprived of its charter in 1798 and direct control of the archipelago was taken over by the Batavia Republic—as the Netherlands was termed between 1795 and 1806. A number of important reforms were instituted during the rule of Herman Willem Daendels (q.v.) as governor general (1806–1811), and still more were put into effect successfully by Sir Thomas Stamford Raffles (q.v.) while the territories were occupied by the British (1811–1816). A treaty concluded in 1824 defined the respective spheres of the Dutch and British in the East Indies, and thereafter administration was slowly improved. At that period, however, Dutch administration did not extend over the whole of Java, Madura, and the Moluccas, where local sultans remained powerful, and elsewhere Dutch control was effective in only a few places—Padang and Palembang, in Sumatra; Pontianak, Sambas, and Bandjarmasin, in Kalimantan (Borneo); and Makassar and Minahasa, in Sulawesi (Celebes). A more liberal administrative policy was initiated in 1851, when Duymaer van Twist became governor general, but it was not until the early 20th century that the Indonesians were accorded any share in the local government. With conclusion in 1903 of a war against the Achinese which had commenced 30 years earlier, the Netherlands obtained undisputed sovereignty over the whole of the archipelago.

A movement for self-government was fostered by the Indonesian National Party, founded in 1927 by Achmed Soekarno, and it grew apace as the result of the economic depression of the 1930's. At the same period a group of Indonesian students in the Netherlands organized the Perhimpunan Indonesia (Indonesian Association) which, under the leadership of Mohammed Hatta, actively advocated the cause for Indonesian independence. Both these leaders and others were exiled by the government of the Netherlands Indies, and a petition by the People's Council for a self-governing Indonesia within the kingdom of the Netherlands was denied. This was the situation when Indonesia became one of the objectives of the Japanese in World War II. Small United States and British naval contingents attempted in vain to bolster Dutch defense of the archipelago, and after three months of heroic struggle against much larger forces the Netherlands Indies capitulated on March 8, 1942.

While the Japanese were exploiting the Indonesians with forced military and labor service, the Nationalist leaders returned from their Dutch-imposed exile; and on Aug. 17, 1945, two days after Japan surrendered, Soekarno, as president of a projected republic, issued the Indonesian Declaration of Independence. Six weeks later the British landed to accept the Japanese capitulation, and they were followed by Dutch officials who promptly refused to recognize the republican claims of *de facto* authority. After large-scale fighting had broken out, Lord Killearn, British special commissioner, arranged a truce and convened a conference between the Indonesians and the Dutch. This resulted in the Linggadjati Agreement, signed on Nov. 15, 1946, recognizing Indonesian sovereignty over Java and Sumatra; a federal United States of Indonesia was to be formed, and a Netherlands-Indonesian Union (the Netherlands, Surinam, Curaçao, and the United States of Indonesia) was to be created not later than Jan. 1, 1949.

Dutch-Indonesian conferences broke down completely on July 18, 1947, and fighting once more ensued. The United Nations Good Offices Committee succeeded in producing a cease fire and eventually the Renville Agreement, signed on Jan. 17, 1948, wherein the two parties reaffirmed their adherence to the proposed Federation and Union. Nevertheless, peace was not secured. In a surprise attack on Dec. 18, 1948, the Dutch captured Djokjakarta, the temporary republican capital, and seized Soekarno, Hatta, and other leaders. Yielding to proposals of the Security Council, the Dutch evacuated Djokjakarta in February 1949 and released the republican officials in July; and in August both parties agreed to a cease fire. As a result of a Round Table Conference convened at The Hague on Aug. 23, 1949, transfer of sovereignty from the Netherlands to the United States of Indonesia was proclaimed on Dec. 27, 1949; at the same time, there was created the Netherlands-Indonesian Union (a voluntary association between sovereign states), with the Dutch queen as symbolic head. The Republic of Indonesia was by far the most powerful of the 16 states composing the United States of Indonesia. The federated government functioned awkwardly, and within 12 months all 15 states voted to dissolve their respective governments and merge with the Republic of Indonesia. Thus, the unitary Republic of Indonesia was proclaimed on Aug. 17, 1950. Achmed Soekarno became the first president and Mohammed Hatta the vice president.

Bibliography.—Vandenbosch, Amry, *The Dutch East Indies* (Berkeley 1944); Honig, P., and Verdoorn, F., *Science and Scientists in the Netherlands Indies* (New York 1945); Vlekke, B. H. M., *The Story of the Dutch East Indies* (Cambridge, Mass. 1945); Kennedy, R., *Bibliography of Indonesian Peoples and Cultures* (New Haven 1946); Wehl, D., *The Birth of Indonesia* (London 1948); Gerbrandy, P. S., *Indonesia* (London 1950).

INDORSEMENT, *in law,* the act of writing or printing on the back of a written instrument, or that which is written or printed thereon. It is more particularly applied to the signature usually on the back of a negotiable instrument by which the title thereto is passed. Such signature must be that of the legal holder of the instrument, which must be delivered, or else be acquired by a bona fide holder, to make it valid.

INDRA, a Hindu deity especially worshiped in the Vedic period of the Hindu religion; it had great legendary popularity, also, in the Epic and Puranic periods. In old Vedic poetry he is represented as a mighty ruler of the bright firmament, and his principal feat is the conquest of the demon Vr'itra, a symbolical personification of the cloud which obstructs the clearness of the sky, and withholds the fructifying rain from the earth. See INDIA—*Religion;* VEDIC LITERATURE.

INDRE, ăɴ'dr', department, France, located in central France, once included in the old divisions of Berry, Orléanais, Marche, and Touraine. It has an area of 2,666 square miles; and is watered by the Indre, the Creuse, and the Vienne. The capital is Châteauroux; other important towns are Issoudun, Argenton, and Le Blanc. The department is chiefly agricultural, with some manufactures of textiles, leather, parchment, and iron. Pop. (1946) 252,075.

INDRE, river of France, 115 miles in length, rising in Creuse Department and entering the Loire 15 miles below Tours.

INDRE-ET-LOIRE, ăɴ'dr'-ā-lwär', department, France, formed out of the ancient provinces of Touraine, Poitou, and Anjou. The area is 2,377 square miles. Wine making is the chief industry. Tours is the capital. Pop. (1946) department, 349,685.

INDUCTION, *in logic,* that method of reasoning which establishes general laws or specific predictions of future, present or past facts on the basis of individual experiences. It is the type of argument by which, let us say, the law of universal gravitation is demonstrated on the basis of observations as to the mutual attraction of certain given bodies, or by which an insurance company is able to determine a safe price for future policies on the basis of past statistical tables, or by which the geologist may describe the history of a certain drainage system through his knowledge of the present status of the system and of the modifications taking place in the drainage systems of the present time. Induction differs from deduction not only in that it starts from particular facts rather than general laws, but also in that the propositions derived by an induction (not covering every single case of the law it sets out to establish) never even appear to have that apodictic certainty which we naturally attribute to the results of correct deduction from indisputable premises. An induced conclusion is only *probably* true; furthermore, if it is at all precise in its terms, it is in general only *approximately* true. The probable correctness of the successive digits of a decimal fraction obtained by inductive reasoning falls off with amazing rapidity. A number, the first nine digits of which are all but absolutely certain, may well have a highly probable 10th digit, a likely 11th and an absolutely worthless 12th.

Induction, then, is the probable and approximate demonstration of laws or predictions on the basis of concrete experiences. It is *not* what it has been considered by Hume and the other 18th century British empiricists: the formation of general ideas — i.e., universals — from mere particulars. In the first place, a universal is not a universal law, nor is a fact a particular. But furthermore, we do not form the notion of red by looking at this red thing and that, and abstracting from them their common quality, nor by associating with the image of one red thing all our past experiences of red objects. There are an endless number of attributes possessed by a group of things, and even exclusively possessed by this group. Redness can only be one of these. When we see the group we recognize redness either as the color quality they possess in common or as their simplest common attribute, or because redness is the property that most attracts our attention. In all these cases we must have a concomitant or antecedent consciousness of a universal — of color, simplicity or redness itself. The process described by the British empiricists simply does not exist, and every formation of a general notion from experience involves an existing awareness of general notions. That is, notwithstanding the contrary opinion of the nominalists, the general notions of qualities and relations which enter into the presentment of inductive laws are not mere mosaics of particular sense data. In a like manner, the inductive laws themselves are not mere mosaics of particular facts. A very common expression among inductive logicians, due to J. S. Mill, is «the uniformity of nature.» We are justified in proceeding from this fact and that fact and the other fact to the general law subsuming them all because nature is uniform. This principle of the uniformity of nature has two very different meanings. It may be little more than a tautology or it may be the cardinal law of natural science — or all science, for the matter of that. If the uniformity of nature means simply what it says, it means merely that two occurrences can never agree in all but one aspect and disagree in that one. Now, as even an approximately complete inventory of the aspects of an occurrence is never at our disposal, and since moreover the temporal and spatial position of an occurrence must be considered in enumerating its aspects, this law tells us, for all practical purposes, absolutely nothing. Nature might be perfectly uniform, even though the jumping of a flea should determine the motions of the planets; the establishment of astronomical laws, however, would be a somewhat difficult pursuit.

The uniformity of nature, as the scientist understands it, is much more than this. It could be called more appropriately the continuity of nature. Perhaps it is best to consider it in the form which it assumes in the Newtonian physics. In the Newtonian physics, the world is completely described when the density of the matter occupying each point of space at some instant is known, together with the magnitude and direction of its velocity. The investigations of physics consist then in determining the actual form of the relation between quantities representing time, space, local density, direction and magnitude of velocity. In the attempts to discover the function which the time forms of the remaining seven variables, one assumption is always made — that this function is in general (i.e., in the language of the mathematician except at a set of points of zero measure) what the mathematicians term *analytic*. One consequence of this is that the function is continuous — i.e., by making sufficiently small changes in the seven variables, we may make the difference of time that results smaller than any assigned quantity, and keep it smaller. Furthermore, if we take a large number of experimental determinations of the time and the other seven variables, it is possible to construct a unique function of the seven variables which will represent the time at each of these points and which, by simply increasing the number of experiments, may be made to differ from the function representing the actual course of phenomena by less than any assigned quantity over any desired period of time. Two things follow: first, sufficiently slight errors in the observations only mean slight errors in the law covering the observations; secondly, by increasing the number of observations, it is possible to render the maximum error in the law formulated to cover them less than any given value. These facts assure us that by taking a sufficient number of observations, and by exercising a sufficient amount of care in each observation, we may approximate as near to the truth as we desire. That the amount of labor in obtaining a reasonable approximation is not beyond all human powers is an article of faith which may be said to constitute a part of what we mean by the law of the uniformity of nature. Other important elements have to do with the spatial distribution of phenomena. Not only the very small, but also the very remote, is inaccessible to observation and measurement. The existence of a scientific physics depends on our ability to neglect the phenomena at sufficiently great astronomical distances. Similar propositions assuring us of the negligibility of that which is sufficiently difficult to observe are basal for other aspects of physical theory.

The law of the uniformity of nature in physics then involves something like the following aggregate of statements: (1) There is a single equation subsisting between the time, the density of matter at every point of space at the time, and the direction and magnitude of velocity at that point. (2) This equation is such that each of the unknowns involved is in general an analytic function of all the rest — that is, among other things, that sufficiently small changes in the other unknowns produce only slight changes therein. (3) The error as to the occurrences near us made by considering only those physical phenomena within a sphere of finite radius with ourselves at the centre ultimately decreases very fast as the radius of the sphere increases.

If these statements are taken together with rough estimates of the order of magnitude of the change that the changes of some of the physical phenomena mentioned in 2 and 3 entail in others, we have the barest outline of the law of the uniformity of nature as it is found in physics. This law is very far from being a tautology — it is not even obvious. Furthermore, it is specifically a law of physics, and has only been established since the time of Newton by inductive physical researches. Other disciplines, such as psychology, have related but different laws of uniformity. They all involve statements of the continuity of certain concrete phenomena. It appears, then, that induction demands antecedent universal propositions that are not identically true — *ex puris particularibus nil concluditur* is not confined to deduction. These synthetic propositions, a priori at least in part, go back and back until in the last analysis they are due simply to a general consonance between the human mind and the facts of nature. This consonance, which consists largely in a preference for continuity both on the part of the mind and of nature, is continually rendered more perfect by the attrition of our imaginings in the places where they disagree with our observations. The history of science consists in a gradual remodeling of each theory in the points where it is wrong, in a mathematical treatment of the errors of the last mathematical treatment. It will be seen that in the theory here developed the distinction between induction and deduction is not absolute, but is rather one of degree and attitude. The stages of an inductive research are: (1) the imagination of a theory to fit the facts; (2) the deduction of the consequences of the theory; (3) the verification of these consequences and the observation of their errors; (4) the imagination of a theory to account for the errors of the original theory or the formulation of a new theory avoiding these errors. The process runs through a regular never-ending cycle. Stages (1) and (2) are identically those of the mathematician in his purely deductive reasoning. Stages (3) and (4) may be paralleled in a mathematical research where the object is the formation of an algorithm which will subserve an especial end. The only difference is that the verification which the mathematician makes is complete, that of the physicist incomplete.

The importance given to continuity in this article may be expressed by saying that the chief inductive method of the scientist is what Mill calls the method of concomitant variations. Mill's canon for this method is: «Whatever phenomenon varies in any manner wherever another phenomenon varies in some particular manner, is either a cause or an effect of that phenomenon, or is connected with it through some fact of causation.»

It will be noted that Mill gives a causal interpretation to the method. It has always been the custom of the philosopher, and almost never the custom of the scientist, to interpret the laws of nature under the aspect of cause. A law of nature is simply a more or less precise formula to which occurrences conform. Sometimes, and only sometimes, the correlated phenomena will have a temporal order, and we may talk of antecedents and consequents. In such a case the antecedents may be called causes and the consequents effects. This implies no obscure effective force emanating from the cause and proceeding to the effect — Hume demolished that notion long ago. A causal interpretation of the universe, then, consists merely in selecting one especial type of inductive correlation and elevating it to the type of all induction whatever.

Causal language is particularly adapted to vague, ill-defined phenomena, about which we can assert little but their presence or absence. Accordingly Mill's remaining canons of induction deal with such phenomena. The method of agreement argues a causal relation between A and B when two trains of circumstances are known which begin in A, and have nothing else in common except their termination in B. The method of difference concludes that A causes B if a train of events is known which contains A and ends in B, while a train of events precisely similar except in that it does not contain A likewise fails to contain B. The joint method of agreement and difference is what its name would imply. The method of residues is that in which the unexplained parts of a nexus of events are linked up with one another. Not one of these methods is without grave dangers except in the hands of the scientist with a concrete knowledge of the field where he applies it. The artificial division of antecedent and consequent alike into a jig-saw puzzle of yes and no occurrences is vicious in the extreme.

Induction has been a method of human reasoning from time immemorial, and has especially characterized those centuries since Francis Bacon. Aristotle, who was the first to recognize induction as a scientific method, gave a very scant account of induction other than that by a complete enumeration of instances. Bacon followed him in this excessive restriction of inductive reasoning. The beginning of the 17th century marks a period when the progress of science had forced a consciousness of the inadequacy of the Aristotelian logic upon the world of learning. The accepted theory of deductive reasoning began to be supplemented in practice by a methodology, but no approximately adequate treatment of this methodology was developed until the middle of the 19th century. In 1840 Whewell (q.v.) published a work in which for the first time due credit was given to the function of imagining and speculation in inductive reasoning. Soon afterward Mill published his 'Logic,' in which he formulated the five methods of inductive research that have already been mentioned, and expressed the

theory, also mentioned above, that every induction is a syllogism with the uniformity of the nature as its major premise. Since the time of Mill the growth of inductive logic and methodology has been extremely rapid. (See LAW IN SCIENCE AND PHILOSOPHY; LOGIC; MILL, JOHN STUART). Consult Aristotle, 'Organon'; Bacon, F., 'Novum Organum'; Dorolle, M., 'Les Problèmes de l'Induction' (Paris 1926); Dubs, H. H., 'Rational Induction' (Chicago 1930); Lalande, A., 'Les Theories de l'Induction et l'Experimentation' (Paris 1929); Russell, B. A. W., 'Our Knowledge of the External World' (Chicago 1914); Whewell, W., 'Philosophy of the Inductive Sciences' (London 1840).

NORBERT WIENER,
Editorial Staff of The Americana.

INDUCTION, *in physical science,* the process by which a body having electrical or magnetic properties calls forth similar properties in a neighboring body without direct contact; in short, electrical influence. It is a familiar fact that an electrified or magnetized body causes electrical or magnetic disturbances in other bodies in its vicinity, when it is not in direct and visible connection with them, and this, in particular, illustrates the process known as induction. The word induction as employed by physicists occurs in combination with a number of other words, and involves, as well some other peculiar terminology, at which it may be not inadmissible to glance. Thus:

Statical or electrostatic induction is applied to the production of an electrical charge upon a body by the influence of another body which is charged with statical electricity. It can be shown by experiment that the inductive influence is transmitted through a non-conducting medium which may be considered as in a state of strain or tension. It is found, further, that the character of the medium determines the amount of induced electricity. The power of a non-conducting substance to transmit an influence of this kind, as compared with that of dry air, is known as its specific inductive capacity or dielectric capacity.

The principle of statical induction is involved in the electrophorus, in the Holtz and also in other influence or induction apparatus; and in the condenser, as in a Leyden jar, voltaic or electrodynamic induction, it is the production of an electric current, or rather an electric motive force, by the influence of an electric current. This latter is called self-induction when upon its own circuit; but mutual-induction, if it is the induction of a current upon another circuit. By current is here understood a definite quantity of electricity per second. When the current is induced by the action of a magnet, or when a magnetic condition is induced by an electric current, the result is alluded to as an example of electro-magnetic induction. Magnetic-induction is the production of magnetic properties in a magnetic substance, as in a soft-iron bar, by a near-by magnet, or by an electric current. Mutual induction is the reaction of two electric currents upon each other, a phenomenon due to the variations in distance between them. Peristaltic induction is applied by Thomson and others to mutual electrostatic induction between the wires of a multiple cable. Flow of induction across an element of surface in magnetism is the product of the surface of the element by the perpendicular component of induction.

Faraday disclosed the existence of the power and action of electric currents in neighboring conducting circuits to the world. His researches on induction, named by him «voltaic-electric induction,» were published in the 'Philosophical Transactions' during 1831–32. Joseph Henry, in 1832, observed that when contact was broken in a long galvanic circuit, a bright spark occurred, which did not appear, when the circuit was short. This was shown by Faraday, in 1834, to be due to the extra current induced by the various parts of the circuit in each other. Bachhoffner, and also Sturgeon, in 1837, demonstrated that superior action, in induction apparatus, of a bundle of iron wires to that of a solid bar of iron. Henry, in 1841, studied the inductive action of induced currents of different orders. De la Rive designed, in 1843, an electro-chemical condenser, consisting of a primary coil, which, by means of an extra current, could enable a single galvanic cell to decompose water. The same decomposition, however, had been effected by White in 1840. Ruhmkorff constructed, in 1850 or 1851, the first so-named «induction-coil,» the excellence of which was owing chiefly to the proper insulation of the secondary coil. Fizeau, in 1852, increased greatly the power of the coil by providing it with a condenser. This electrical instrument consists of two coils of wire wound one over the other upon a core consisting of bundles of iron wires. One of its circuits is called the primary circuit and the other the secondary circuit. These coils are employed for physiological purposes and also in connection with the telephone. But it is in connection with high-frequency electric currents for Röntgen ray work and wireless telegraphy that one finds the employment of the induction coil most often used at present. Of late years, coils of great power have been constructed, rivaling, if not exceeding, the most powerful electric machines in length and power of spark.

In considering induction, mention may be made to the interesting theory of Ampere. 'Ampere's theory' is applied to an electrodynamic theory proposed by Andre Marie Ampere. According to it, every molecule of a magnetic substance is supposed to be traversed by a closed electric current. Before magnetization the combined effect of these currents is zero. But by the magnetizing process they are supposed to be brought more or less fully into a parallel position. Then their resultant effect is said to be equivalent to a series of parallel currents traversing the exterior surface of the magnet in a plane perpendicular to its axis, and a certain definite direction, which, when the south pole is turned toward the observer, is that of the hands of a watch. These hypothetical currents are called Amperian currents. This theory is based upon the close analogy between a solenoid traversed by an electric current and a magnet. Ampere thus conceived that the magnetic action of the earth is the result of currents circulating within it, or at its surface, from east to west, in planes parallel to the magnetic equator.

The ultimate mechanism of induction is still somewhat obscure, but something has been learned of its general nature. In the early days **of physical science it was believed that bodies** can act upon one another even across spaces that are absolutely void, and at the present time it is sometimes convenient to assume them to act in this manner, in forming mathematical equations for the treatment of physical problems. It is no longer believed, however, that this is what actually happens in nature; the phenomena of electric and magnetic induction being now attributed to motions or stresses in the ether which transmits light. (See ETHER). Newton was of the opinion that induction is an ether-phenomenon, and in the first half of the 19th century Faraday may be said to have established the ether hypothesis upon a substantial experimental foundation. In later years Maxwell developed Faraday's conceptions mathematically, and added much more evidence that was partly theoretical and partly experimental; so that at the present time there are few or no physicists who doubt that induction is a manifestation of some form of activity in the light-bearing ether. Opinion is still divided, however, as to the precise nature of this activity. In fact, we cannot hope to gain any very precise information on this point until much more is known about the constitution of the ether itself.

The charging of a condenser is a phenomenon in electrostatic induction. If the condenser consists of two parallel plates (for example), of a given size and set at a constant distance from each other, and we charge it to a given potential, the quantity of electricity that must be put into it in order to charge it in this manner depends to a considerable extent upon the nature of the dielectric (or insulating material) which separates the plates. If the charge that is required when air is the dielectric is taken as unity, then with plate glass as a dielectric the charge will have to be 8.45 (according to Hopkinson), in order to bring the potential of the condenser up to the same value as before. If the space between the plates is filled with common turpentine, a charge 2.23 times as great as that required with air as the dielectric must be communicated to the condenser. It is evident, from these facts, and from others of the same nature, that electric induction depends, to a large extent at any rate, upon the nature of the medium which separates an electrified body from the other bodies upon which the inductive influence is felt. The constants that are given above are known as the «specific inductive capacities» of the dielectrics to which they refer.

Electrodynamic induction is the basis of practically all of the electrical machinery that has been found serviceable to man. The fundamental fact of electrodynamic induction may be stated as follows: If a closed electrical circuit, such as might be formed by joining the two ends of a copper wire, is placed in a magnetic field, then no current will be produced so long as the circuit is everywhere stationary, and the strength of the magnetic field remains everywhere invariable. If the intensity of the magnetic field is increased, a current of electricity will flow around the circuit while the intensity of the magnetism is changing, the intensity of the current being proportional to the rapidity with which the intensity of the magnetism varies. As soon as the magnetism again becomes constant, the current in the circuit ceases. If the intensity of the magnetic field be diminished instead of increased, a current will also be produced in the closed circuit, but it will be opposite in direction to that produced by increasing the magnetic field. Currents produced in this manner are called "induced currents." Instead of varying the magnetic field while the circuit is fixed in position, we may move the circuit about in the magnetic field. If the magnetic field is everywhere uniform in all respects, and the circuit is moved so as to always remain parallel to itself, then no induced current will be produced; but if the circuit is moved from a region where the magnetism is strong to one where it is weak, or vice-versa, a current will be induced in the circuit, just as if the circuit were kept stationary and the intensity of the magnetism varied. Induced currents are also produced when, instead of being translated from one region to another, the circuit is rotated in a magnetic field, in such a way that the number of lines of magnetic force passing through it is either increased or diminished. In the induction coil the intensity of the magnetic field is varied, while the circuit in which the induced current is to be produced is kept stationary. In dynamos, on the other hand, the magnetic field is maintained sensibly constant, while the circuit in which the induced current is to be produced is rotated or otherwise moved about.

A current moving in a closed circuit produces a magnetic field in the space above it, and this magnetic field, when it varies on account of the variation of the current that produces it, causes the production of induced currents in any closed circuit that may happen to be near. Let us conceive two closed circuits, A and B, to be situated near each other, and let there be a current produced by any means in the circuit A. So long as the current in A is constant, no current will be produced in B; but if the current in A is variable, an induced current will be observed in B, whose intensity depends upon the rate at which the current in A is varying, upon the resistance of the circuit B and also upon a certain numerical factor, whose value depends upon the sizes and shapes of the two circuits, upon their positions with respect to each other, and upon the nature of the medium (air, oil and whatever it may be) in which they are placed.

If a pair of circuits, A and B, are near each other, and A is carrying a constant current of intensity C_1, while B is carrying a constant current of intensity C_2, then the displacement of either circuit, relatively to the other, would cause induced currents to flow in both; and hence (in general) neither circuit can be moved without the energy of the system being affected. The difference between the energy of a pair of coils that are near together, and the energy of a similar pair of coils that are conveying identically the same currents but are infinitely remote from each other, is equal to MC_1C_2, where M is a numerical factor whose value depends upon the sizes and shapes of the two circuits, upon their relative positions and upon the medium in which they are placed. The factor M is called the «coefficient of mutual induction» of the pair of circuits.

The various parts of a single circuit act upon one another inductively, just as separate circuits do; and a circuit that is wound upon a spool, or otherwise coiled so that its parts come near together, possesses greater energy than the same circuit would have, if it was not so coiled.

This fact is expressed by saying that every circuit has a certain amount of «self-induction.» The energy that a circuit possesses in virtue of its self-induction is proportional to the square of the current that it is carrying, and to a certain numerical constant called the «coefficient of self-induction,» whose value depends upon the size and shape of the circuit, and upon the medium in which it is placed. Like the coefficient of mutual induction of a pair of circuits, the coefficient of self-induction of a single circuit can be computed, for certain simple cases, by methods given by Maxwell, in his 'Treatise on Electricity and Magnetism'; but in the general case the computation is exceedingly difficult, and altogether impracticable; so that the values of these coefficients for given circuits are usually determined experimentally, except when a very rough estimate will serve.

The general subject of induction is essentially mathematical in its character, and cannot be properly explained nor understood without the use of the calculus. Consult Nipher, 'Electricity and Magnetism'; Maxwell, 'Treatise on Electricity and Magnetism.' See also the articles ELECTRICITY and MAGNETISM, in this encyclopædia.

INDUCTION, Mathematical. Despite the age-long tyranny exercised by the Aristotelian logic — a tyranny having, at least in the domain of science, scarcely a match except in the case of Euclid's elements — the forms of thought, those diagrammatic representations of the orderliness of the reasoning processes, sustain to-day perhaps even greater interest than ever before (see SYMBOLIC LOGIC). The mathematician's interest in these forms is twofold, attaching to them both as norms for testing the validity of arguments and as constituting exceedingly subtle matter for mathematical investigation.

Of all argument forms, there is one which, viewed as the figure of the way in which the mind gains certainty that a specified property belonging but not immediately by definition to each element of a denumerable (see ASSEMBLAGE THEORY) assemblage of elements does so belong, enjoys the distinction of being at once perhaps the most fascinating, and, in its mathematical bearings, doubtless the most important, single form in modern logic. This form is that variously known as reasoning by recurrence, induction by connection (De Morgan), mathematical induction, complete induction, and Fermatian induction — so called by C. S. Peirce, according to whom this mode of proof was first employed by Fermat. Whether or not such priority is thus properly ascribed, it is certain that the argument form in question is unknown to the Aristotelian system, for this system allows apodictic certainty in case of deduction only, while it is the distinguishing mark of mathematical induction that it yields such certainty by the reverse process, a movement from the particular to the general, from the *finite* to the *infinite*. See ASSEMBLAGES, THEORY OF.

Of the various designations of this mode of argument, «mathematical induction» is undoubtedly the most appropriate, for, though one may not be able to agree with Poincaré (see *Bibliography* below) that the mode in question is *characteristic* of mathematics, it is peculiar to that science, being indeed, as he has called it, «mathematical reasoning par excellence.»

The nature of mathematical induction as it is ordinarily understood may be made clear by an example. Perhaps the simplest application of the method is found in the proof of the theorem:

$$(a)\quad 1+2+3+\ldots\ldots+n=\tfrac{1}{2}n(n+1)$$

where n denotes any positive integer whatever. Suppose it ascertained by observation or otherwise that

$$(1)\quad 1+2=\tfrac{1}{2}2(2+1),$$
$$(2)\quad 1+2+3=\tfrac{1}{2}3(3+1).$$

Facts (1) and (2) justify the *suspicion* that (a) may be a fact. The proof by mathematical induction that (a) is indeed true runs as follows: It is *assumed* that (a) is true for some definite but unspecified integer n. Then by adding $n+1$ to each member of the assumed equation, n having the same meaning as in the assumption, one finds that

$$(\beta)\quad 1+2+3+\ldots\ldots+n+\overline{n+1} = \tfrac{1}{2}(n+1)(n+2).$$

So it is seen that, if (a) *be* true for *some* integer n, it *is* true also for the *next* greater integer $n+1$. But by (2), (a) is true when n is 3; it is, therefore, true for $3+1$, or 4; therefore, for $4+1$, or 5. The argument is then usually closed by saying «and so on, hence (a) is true for any integer whatever,» or by an equivalent speech. The reader will recall that the binomial theorem, the Newtonian expansion of $(a+b)n$, where n is any positive integer, is justified in essentially the foregoing manner. Numerous other examples of propositions similarly established may be found in the better recent textbooks of algebra.

The nature and the rôle of the foregoing *et cetera*, «and so on,» demand consideration. Without it, the argument as stated seems obviously incomplete. But how is the *et cetera* to be logically justified? By reference to some axiom or principle of thought? If so, what? Or can the phrase be in some way dispensed with without damage to the argument?

Before attempting to answer them it may be well to show the inevitableness of the questions by a further analysis. Suppose it established, in regard to some property p (where, for example, p might signify the validity of the binomial theorem for some integral exponent): (1) that p belongs to the integer 1, that is, referring again to the mentioned example, the theorem is valid for the exponent 1; (2) that, *if* p belong to an integer n, it belongs to $n+1$. Propositions (1) and (2) furnish the means of generating, one after another, a sequence of syllogisms by which one proves first that p belongs to 2, then to 3, then to 4, and so on. Note that in order to ascertain by this analytic (syllogistic) method whether p belongs to a specified integer m, it is necessary to determine in advance the same question for each of the integers 2, 3, ..., $m-1$, in the order as written, a process requiring a number of syllogisms which is greater the greater the number m. Accordingly *this* method, of successive deductions, is not available for determining whether p belongs to each in the (infinite) *totality* of integers. Equally powerless to that end is experience (including observation), for this can take account of the individuals of a finite assemblage of objects at most. Either analysis or experience may avail if a sequence be finite, but if it be infinite both must fail. Not less vain is it to invoke finally the aid of induction as the term is understood and employed in the physical sciences, for this latter, resting upon a purely assumed order in the external universe, is confessedly *inductio imperfecta,* and, being such, can yield approximate certainty only.

Nevertheless, despite the inadequacy of the means mentioned, as soon as hypotheses (1) and (2) are admitted and the indicated sequence of deductions is *begun,* «the judgment imposes itself upon us with irresistible evidence» that p is a property of *all* the integers. Why? That is, how justify the «and so on»? It appears to be clear that the answer must be the adduction or invocation of an additional presupposition of formal thought, a presupposition whose formulation shall mark a conscious extension of the domain of logic by affirming as axiomatic that apodictic certainty can and does transcend every limited sequence of deductions or observations. Such presupposition, which may be called the axiom of infinity, is stated by Poincaré, in answer to the foregoing question, «why,» as follows: «It is the affirmation of the power of the mind which knows it is capable of conceiving the indefinite repetition of a same act as soon as this act is found to be once possible.» The act or operation, which cannot indeed be indefinitely repeated, but which by the axiom can be conceived as so repeated, is, in the present case, the construction of the syllogisms of the sequence above mentioned.

The *et cetera* in question is capable of justification without appealing, apparently at least, to the axiom of infinity, namely, by use of the so-called indirect method of proof, the method known as *reductio ad absurdum.* Thus let it be supposed that the argument sought to be indefinitely extended by means of the phrase «and so on» does not admit of indefinite extension along the ordered sequence of integers. There will, then, be a first integer, say $m+1$, for which the property p fails. As, by hypothesis, $m+1$ is the first integer for which p fails, p belongs to the preceding integer m; but since p belongs to m, it also belongs, by (2), to $m+1$. Hence the supposition that the argument does not admit of indefinite extension is false; and the conclusion is obvious. This procedure is convincing, but it is plainly less a natural completion than an «unindicated» fortification of the process it supplements. It is, besides, not entirely clear that the axiom of infinity is not surreptitiously subsumed by it.

By far the most penetrating investigation of the nature of mathematical induction was made originally by Richard Dedekind. (See *Bibliography* below). His procedure and result are, in brief, as follows: Let S denote a system of elements (things of any kind) such that there is a scheme of law ϕ of depiction by which S may be depicted upon itself, that is, a scheme by which each element e of S may be thought as corresponding to one and but one element e' of S and so that no two elements of S shall be thought as corresponding to a same element of S. The correspondent e' of e is called the picture or image of e. Every part of S (including S itself as a special case) thus depicted upon itself is named *chain under* ϕ. Denote by A an arbitrary part of S and by A_0 the assemblage of all the elements common to all the chains (in S) that contain A. It is obvious that, S and ϕ being given, there is one and but one A_0 for a given part A of S. A_0, which is easily seen to be itself a chain, is described as the *chain of A under* ϕ. Now let Σ denote an assemblage of elements. Dedekind proves the following

THEOREM.—*In order to prove that A_0 is part of Σ it is sufficient to prove:* (1) *that A is part of Σ; and* (2) *that, if an element A_0 belong to Σ, the image of that element belongs to Σ.*

Dedekind's proof, simplified, runs thus: Let $A_0 = A_1 + A_2$ where A_1 denotes the assemblage of all those elements of A_0 that belong to Σ. By (2), A_1 is a chain, and, by (1), contains A. Hence, by definition of A_0, A_2 has no element, whence $A_0 \equiv A_1$. Such is the beautiful and marvelously fundamental theorem which its author characterizes, perhaps a little extravagantly, as «the scientific basis» of mathematical induction. It is at any rate *a* basis, and by virtue of it, as shown below, proof by mathematical induction need have no recourse to an *et cetera* consisting of an endless sequence of syllogisms.

It will be instructive to apply Dedekind's theorem to the *completion* of the proof by mathematical induction of the binomial theorem.

$$(\alpha)\ (a+b)^n = a^n + na^{n-1}b + \ldots\ldots\ldots$$

for positive integral exponents. Let it be granted that

$$(\beta)\ (a+b)^1 = a + b,$$

and supposed it established in the usual way that (γ), if (α) be valid for some integer, as $n-1$, then it is so for the next, n. Denote by S the sequence of integers,

$$S \equiv 1, 2, 3, \ldots\ldots, n-1, n, \ldots\ldots,$$

by ϕ the scheme by which each number in S except 1 is the image of its predecessor, and let A be 1. Then A_0 is S identically. Let Σ denote the assemblage of positive integers for which (α) is valid. The reader will now observe that Dedekind's theorem enables one to prove by a *single* stroke, so to speak, that (α) is valid for all positive integers. For, by (β), (α) is valid for 1, that is, A is part of Σ and (1) is satisfied; and, as A_0, or 1_0, is S, it follows from ( ) that (2) is satisfied; γ hence S is part of Σ.

With the modern increasing interest in the philosophy of mathematics, mathematical induction has steadily gained in interest and acknowledged importance. Certain questions respecting its presuppositions and field await definite answers. It is agreed that every argument by mathematical induction is a mathematical argument, no matter what the subject-matter, but there is difference of opinion as to whether every mathematical argument is mathematical induction either in terms or in disguise. Were this converse true, mathematics (see MATHEMATICS) would be definable in terms of this mode of ratiocination. This and kindred questions are considered in the works cited below.

Bibliography.— Dedekind, 'Was Sind und Was Sollen die Zahlen' (also in English);

Poincaré, 'Sur la nature du raisonnement mathematique,' Revue de Méthaphysique e de Morale (Vol. II); Schröder, 'Algebra der Logik' (Vol. III); Russell, 'The Principles of Mathematics' (Vol. I); Keyser, 'Concerning the Axiom of Infinity and Mathematical Induction' (Bulletin of the American Mathematical Society, Vol. IX).

Cassius J. Keyser,
Adrain Professor Emeritus of Mathematics, Columbia University.

INDUCTION BALANCE, in physics, an apparatus designed for measuring and indicating the electrical conductivity of metals. It is based upon the principle of induction. The mere proximity of a metal, especially a metal that is a good conductor, will induce or draw magnetization as electrification from a charged wire, battery, etc. An induced current is always opposite in positivity to the near side of the charged source of current. In its most familiar form it consists essentially of four coils of fine wire, an electric battery, a circuit breaker and a telephone. Let the coils be designated, respectively, by the letters A, B, C and D; A being similar to B in all respects, and C being likewise similar to D. Coils A and B are placed in circuit with the battery, and coils C and D are placed in circuit with the telephone. The coils are disposed in pairs, A being placed near C, and B near D. If the current through A and B is rapidly interrupted, an induced current will, in general, flow through C and D, at each make and break; its presence being indicated by the sounds that it produces in the telephone that is in circuit with C and D. It is possible, however, to dispose the coils and their connections so that the current that A induces in C shall be sensibly equal and opposite to that which B induces in D. When the balance is perfect no sound will be heard in the telephone. If a piece of metal be now brought near the coil A, the intermittent current in A will induce currents in the mass of the piece of metal, and these, in turn, will act upon the coil C, producing induced currents in this coil which are not compensated by similar currents in D. The loss of balance will be at once indicated by the recurrence of sounds in the telephone; and in this way the metal fragment will betray its presence. The induction balance has been used successfully for locating bullets in the human body. The intensity of the sounds produced in the telephone depends not only upon the size and position of the disturbing piece of metal, but also upon its specific electrical resistance; and hence the balance may be used to compare the specific resistance of metals. When an induction balance is arranged for making measurements of electrical resistance it is usually termed an induction bridge.

INDUCTION COIL, one of the early electrical instruments, that simply illustrates the principle of induction, consisting of an iron core about which two wires are differently coiled: now used mainly for study, and in connection with high frequency currents, radiography and X-ray investigations. (See Induction). The essential features of the instrument are represented, diagrammatically, in the accompanying cut. A soft iron core is surrounded by two coils of wire, the finer one outside of the other. The outer coil is the one in which the high tension induced currents are produced; it is called the "secondary coil," and is not in direct electrical connection with any other part of the instrument. The inner coil, which is called the primary coil, is of coarse wire, wound close to the iron core, and is connected to a battery, so that when the current from the battery is flowing the primary coil causes the iron core to become magnetised. As is explained in the article Induction, no current is generated in the secondary coil, so long as the magnetism of the iron core remains constant; but whenever the magnetism of the core increases or diminishes, a current is produced in the secondary. A device called a "break" or "interrupter" is therefore provided, so that the magnetism of the iron core may be rapidly established and destroyed. The commonest form of interrupter is that indicated in the cut, which does not call for special explanation, since it is used in electric bells and other simple forms of electrical apparatus. The Wehnelt electrolytic interrupter is greatly in favor among physicists, however, and is now often used in connection with induction coils,

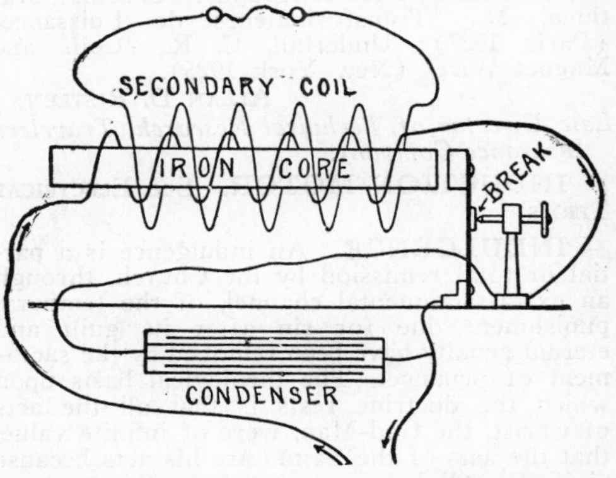

especially when they are to be run with the commercial current used for incandescent lighting, where the potential difference that is used is something over 100 volts. In the Wehnelt interrupter the primary coil on the iron core is made of a few turns of relatively thick copper wire, its purpose being solely to effect the magnetisation of the core; but the secondary coil, in which the induced currents are generated, is made of fine wire, and in order to multiply the inductive effect as far as possible, the secondary is made of great length, often containing many miles of wire. In the celebrated Spottiswoode coil the secondary contained no less than 280 miles of wire. The primary coil, being wound directly upon a soft iron core, commonly has a very considerable amount of self-induction, so that when the circuit is broken by the interrupter the current does not suddenly cease, but continues to flow across the interval at the break for an appreciable fraction of a second, as is readily seen by the strong sparking that occurs at the moment of interruption. In order to reduce the sparking as far as possible, a condenser of suitable capacity is provided, so that when the break is made in the circuit, the "after-current" due to the self-induction of the primary can discharge into the condenser, instead of passing across the break in the circuit and causing a spark. The condenser causes the interruption of the current in the primary coil to be much more sudden, and it materially increases the potential that is developed in the secondary coil, since this is proportional to the rate of variation of the magnetism of the core, and is much greater when the magnetism falls off abruptly than when it persists for an appreciable fraction of a second after the break has been made.

The induction coil was brought into something like its present form by Ruhmkorff, and is frequently known, in consequence, by his name. Improvements in the winding of the secondary coil were introduced by Ritchie of Boston about 1857. Ritchie's most important improvement consisted in disposing the secondary wire in sections, which were so related to one another that the risk of internal disruptive discharge through the coil itself might be reduced to a minimum. Induction coils are very generally used in studying the discharge of electricity through gases, for exciting X-ray tubes and in connection with the high potentials required in wireless telegraphy. Consult: Mathieu, M., 'Transformateurs de Puissance' (Paris 1927); Underhill, C. R., 'Coils and Magnet Wire' (New York 1925).

ALLAN D. RISTEEN,
Late Director of Technical Research, Travelers Insurance Company.

INDUCTION MOTOR. See ELECTRICAL TERMS.

INDULGENCE. An indulgence is a partial or total remission by the Church, through an extra-sacramental channel, of the temporal punishment due for sin after its guilt and eternal penalty have been removed by the sacrament of penance. The theological basis upon which the doctrine rests is that all the acts of Christ, the God-Man, were of infinite value, that the acts of the Saints are his acts because vivified by divine grace, and from this treasury of divine, supereminent merit the Church is able, so to speak, to pay the debt of temporal punishment for the repentant sinner.

Certain cardinal principles of Catholic life are requisite to obtain a correct idea of the Catholic doctrine of indulgences. Growth and adaptation have characterized the Christian organism from the Apostolic Council of Jerusalem to the Œcumenical Council of the Vatican. The development of doctrine, upon which such explicit emphasis was laid by the late Cardinal Newman, is of prime significance for the student who would institute a comparison between the teaching and practice of the Church in the matter of indulgences at the present day and during apostolic times. We may observe in passing that the principle of doctrinal development is in perfect harmony with the scientific spirit of the present age. Growth and adaptation are now believed to be distinguishing features of every living and progressive organism. We should not, therefore, expect to find the Catholic system of indulgences, in all its complex details, flourishing in the primitive Church. In harmony with the law of development, essential to every organization among men, we believe that the Church's "proud boast of *semper eadem*" is not defeated by calling attention to the richness, variety and flexibility of the outer forms of its polity and liturgy, or to the varying emphasis given to special dogmas in the course of its history, in response to the needs of particular eras. Unity in diversity is the Church's most appropriate motto. The doctrine and practice of indulgences, therefore, which obtain throughout the Catholic world at the present time must be sought for only in germ in Sacred Scripture and in the practice of the primitive Church, just as the bole, the branches and the foliage of an oak tree, "the monarch of the forest," existed potentially in the acorn from which it sprung.

Indulgences being the remission of the temporal punishment due to sin, the interpretation of the true character should start from the Christian idea of the nature and purpose of punishment. It is therefore strange that writers of all schools of opinion concerning indulgences should fail to correlate the two concepts. At the present day the conviction prevails almost universally among non-Catholic students of penology that punishment is exclusively disciplinary and correctional. No theory could be more alien to the spirit of the entire Old Testament or to the mind of the early Christian Fathers. The inflexible and rigorous justice of God making death the wages of sin appears in almost every page of the history of his covenant with Israel. The New Testament, founded on the atonement by Christ, only mitigates this view by impressing on the minds of men the possibility of vicarious satisfaction for their transgressions. But although Christ's atoning and vicarious sacrifice was all-sufficient in itself, or objectively considered, to satisfy the offended justice of his Heavenly Father, nevertheless the Christian economy of redemption demands each individual's co-operation at every stage in order to appropriate Christ's merits and make them subjective to himself. The opposite view (that is, the belief), that the creature has no active part in his sanctification and salvation, inclines toward Pantheism, robs good works and the Christian sacraments of genuine value, and differentiates the Lutheran from the Catholic position. According to Catholic teaching the guilt of sin is cleansed from the soul by the application of the merits of the precious blood of Christ through the instrumentality of the Sacraments, whose efficacy, in the case of adults, depends on the subjective disposition of the recipient. The eternal punishment due to sin disappears with the guilt to which it is annexed. But, besides having these supernatural and eternal relations and consequences, sin viewed even within the circumscribed limits of man's natural life on earth is an act of treason against God in His own kingdom involving forfeiture of all rights to life and all the good things with which God's providence has so bountifully enriched it. This temporal consequence of sin calls for a temporal reparation. The canonical penalties therefore imposed on the Church during the first centuries were intended to pay this temporal debt to the Divine justice, and were not merely disciplinary or correctional; and the sinner, in submitting to them, or in seeking mitigation from them through the intercession of the martyrs, recognized the necessity of his own personal act to satisfy the justice of God, either directly or vicariously by appropriating through the charity of the Church the superabundant merits of Christ and His Saints.

An indulgence granted to the living is an act of jurisdiction, or exercise by the Church of the power of the keys conferred on it in the well-known words of the Gospel of Saint Matthew: «And I will give to thee the keys of the Kingdom of Heaven, and whatever thou shalt bind on earth, it shall be bound in Heaven, and whatever thou shalt loose on earth, it shall be loosed in Heaven.» Every Church, in so far as it is a visible organization, claims in some degree a power of the keys, that is, the right to admit or exclude members — to determine fellowship. But the antithesis so emphatically expressed in the text between heaven and earth proves that the kingdom of heaven there spoken of is more comprehensive than the visible Church of Christ. It is proclaimed that the power of binding and loosing on earth bestowed upon the Apostles and their successors, is ratified in its every act by the supreme tribunal of God in the Church triumphant. In accordance with a well-known principle of Catholic exegesis, the best interpretation of a text of Sacred Scripture is furnished by the universal tradition of the Church from the age of the Apostles to the present time.

Saint Paul, in his epistles to the Corinthians, describes how he imposed punishment on the incestuous Corinthian and how he subsequently remitted it. The penalty was not merely an ecclesiastical censure of excommunication inflicted primarily for the purpose of safeguarding the flock of Christ. The Apostle expressly states that the chief motive which actuated him was anxiety for the individual salvation of the transgressor. Nor could it have been (as has been already shown) a mere disciplinary measure to impress upon the sinner the gravity of his crime or to test the sincerity of his repentance. Having no organic relation to confession, whether public or private, and no expressed or implied connection with perfect contrition, it was not a part of any conceivable Christian ordinance for the remission of the guilt and eternal punishment of sin. According to Catholic reasoning, it was therefore an exercise of the power of the keys by the Apostle to remit a temporal debt due to God for the offense; and since, according to universal Jewish and Christian belief, the Divine Justice rigorously demanded either direct or vicarious satisfaction, the Apostle could only concede that «indulgence» by appropriating to the individual sinner the superabundant merits of Christ and the Saints out of the treasury of the Church.

It will be observed that the Apostle of the Gentiles granted the first recorded indulgence in the form of an absolution. Indulgences usually took this form in the primitive Church. The early Fathers frequently refer to their being thus conceded by bishops on the presentation of a «Libellus Supplex» given to the penitent by some Christian martyr on the eve of suffering an heroic death for Christ. It is interesting to note that the present practice of never granting those favors except to persons who are in full communion with the Church, and who have received the Sacrament of Penance, was substantially insisted upon by Saint Cyprian. He demands that the martyrs should not grant «Libelli» except to persons who had abandoned their sinful career and given ample evidence of heartfelt contrition and sincere conversion. Indulgences in the first centuries of the Church having implied a diminution of the period of canonical punishment — the name by which this act of leniency was then known was φιλανθρωπία — (Consult Concilium Ancyra, can. 5; cf. Hefele, 'Conciliengeschichte'), such expressions as an indulgence of seven years and seven quarantines came into use. An indulgence of seven years means the condonation of as much of the temporal debt due to God for sin as canonical punishment extending over seven years would atone for. Likewise an indulgence of seven quarantines connotes a canonical punishment extending over seven Lents.

We find in the writings of Saint Augustine reference to the remission, in return for almsgiving, of temporal penalties imposed for minor ecclesiastical offenses. Thus there gradually grew up the custom of granting indulgences under the form of commutation. Under this form they were especially conspicuous during the period of the Crusades. Every person who confessed his sins in a sincere and contrite spirit, received Holy Communion and joined the Crusade for liberating the holy places from the infidels was declared to need no other penance. «*Iter illud pro omni Pœnitentia reputetur*» was one of the decrees of the Council of Clermont, held under Urban II in the year 1095. The system of commutation for almsgiving afforded opportunity for abuse, as was evident in the practice of «farming out» to laymen the collection of alms in return for indulgence. Thus, for example, in the case of the famous indulgence granted by Leo X, in 1517, to the Catholic faithful on condition that they would contribute to the completion of Saint Peter's basilica in Rome, the right of collecting the money was conferred, in the first instance, on Albert, bishop of Maintz, and then sold by him to an Augsburg banker. Circumstances like these gave occasion to the Protestant party to charge the Church with the «sale of indulgences.» Cardinal Pallavicini, the celebrated Jesuit historian of the Council of Trent, does not hesitate to say that if Leo X had been surrounded by able theologians and enlightened by their counsels he would have proceeded more cautiously in dispensing indulgences. However, it should in justice be recognized that the erection of Saint Peter's in Rome, the ancient capital of the Christian world, was an enterprise of the deepest interest to every member of the faithful. Together with the incidental abuses connected with commutations, other circumstances combined to inspire disaffection for the Holy See in the minds of European rulers and their dependents; and, as in the case of every revolution fed by prolonged and deeply-rooted discontent in the minds of those who control public opinion, a spark sufficed to start the conflagration. The life of Luther recently published by the Rev. Heinrich Denifle, O.P., and the abundant controversial literature which it has called forth from the ablest Protestant historians and theologians of Germany, have proved that the first Apostle of the Protestant Reformation was an epoch-maker by reason of conditions, not because he possessed in any high degree the qualities of the *Uebermensch.* Yet the nailing of his 95 thesis on the doors of the castle church of Wittenburg in protest against the indulgence granted by Leo X, and preached by Tetzel, subdelegate of Albert, bishop of Maintz, set all Europe aflame and destroyed the dogmatic unity of Catholic christendom.

Opposition to the doctrine of indulgences arose at different times, not because of their alleged novelty or repugnance to the religious sense of the Christian people, but because they did not always approve of the object for which alms were obtained by the preaching of indulgences, or because of the personal defects of those entrusted with their promulgation. It should be distinctly noted that these purposes were not always strictly religious. They were frequently philanthropic, such as the construction of bridges, the erection of hospitals, etc., and in such cases received the unqualified approval of princes and people. In order to comprehend the outburst which Luther was able to evoke against the indulgence granted by Leo X we must bear in mind, besides the questionable motives that are alleged to have partly inspired the action of that pontiff, also the bitter memories that tarried in the minds of European monarchs after their defeat on the question of investitures, and the death-blow dealt thereby to the feudal system. The entire antipathy aroused, for this and other reasons, against the Holy See in the time of Leo X found vent in the attack initiated by Luther on indulgences.

An indulgence may be acquired directly by the living and applied by them, with the consent of the Church, to the souls of the faithful departed. All Catholic theologians are unanimous in the opinion that an indulgence should not be granted without grave and substantial reasons, since the ordinary Christian economy demands that each individual should make personal reparation for the temporal debt due for his sins. Moreover, in order to participate fruitfully in an indulgence, certain conditions and dispositions are necessary on the part of the subject. He must be in the state of grace, have a genuine desire to gain the indulgence, and perform certain acts prescribed by the Holy See.

The application of indulgences to the dead is not a judicial act of the Church, whose jurisdiction is limited to the members of the militant or visible Church on earth. Remission of the temporal debt due to God for sin by the suffering members of Christ's mystical body in Purgatory is communicated to them by the Church by way of suffrage or supplication. In other words, she authorizes the living to join their petitions with hers that God may graciously accept the indulgences which they gain and in the measure in which they gain them, in behalf of the souls of the faithful departed. Indulgences are now dispensed partly by way of absolution and partly by way of commutation. The well-known distinction between partial and plenary indulgences should be understood in an objective sense. The degree in which any indulgence is actually gained or subjectively appropriated by the individual depends on his subjective disposition, according to the theological maxim: whatever is received is received according to the measure of the recipient. The most solemn of all plenary indulgences is that which is granted on the occasion of a jubilee such as that which was proclaimed for 1904 by His Holiness Pius X to mark the 50th anniversary of the definition of the Immaculate Conception by Pius IX.

THOMAS E. JUDGE, S.T.P.,
Formerly Professor of Mental and Moral Philosophy, Saint Patrick's College, Maynooth, Ireland; afterward Professor of Dogmatic Theology in The Saint Paul Seminary, Saint Paul, Minn.

INDULGENCE, Declaration of. See DECLARATION OF INDULGENCES.

INDULINES, dyestuffs, blue, bluish-red to black in shade. They were discovered in 1863 by J. Dale and H. Caro, and carry an English patent (No. 3307). They are formed by the interaction of para-amino azo compounds with primary monamines in the presence of a small quantity of mineral acid.

INDULT, a papal license, as when the Pope authorizes the bishop to grant certain relaxations during the Lenten fast required by physical necessity.

INDUNA, a word (Zulu-Bantu) signifying officer.

INDUS (Sanskrit, *Sindhu*), the chief stream of the northwest of India, and one of the great rivers of the world. It has a length of about 1,900 miles, and drains an area of more than 360,000 square miles. It arises in Tibet on the north of the Himalaya Mountains, nearly 100 miles northwest from the sources of the upper Brahmaputra (q.v.), on the north side of the mountain mass of Kailâs, 18,000 feet above sea-level. In the upper part of its course it takes a northwesterly direction along the northern foot of the main Himalayan range, enters the Kashmir territories, passes through Ladak, below the capital of which, Leh, it receives the Zanskar, farther on the Dras, after which it enters Baltistan. Here it receives, on the right, the Gilgit, from a glacier of the Karakoram, the largest tributary that joins it in the Himalayan regions, and takes the name of Indus or Sind. About 100 miles below this it takes a sudden bend toward the southwest, and after a course of about 180 miles more in this direction it leaves the loftier regions. At the British fortress of Attock in the Punjab — where it is crossed by a great railway bridge carrying the line to Peshawar — it is joined by the Kabul from Afghanistan, and here, 950 feet above the level of the sea, it is nearly 800 feet wide and from 30 to 60 feet deep according to the season. For the rest of its course (about 900 miles) it continues its southwesterly direction till it enters the Indian Ocean. At Kalabagh, 110 miles below Attock, it has a breadth of over 1,400 feet. Arriving in the low-lying country, its waters become charged with mud, and in the rainy season, and by the melting of the snow in the mountains, it overflows its banks. Near Mithankot it receives on the east the Panjnad, or united stream of the Five Rivers of the Punjab. Below the confluence it has a width of over 1,900 yards when the water is low. In Sind it gives off several extensive arms or canals, which are of great value for irrigation; and below Hyderabad it divides into a number of shifting mouths or estuaries, the most navigable of which is at present the Yatho mouth. The delta, formed by the enormous amount of alluvium brought down by the river, has a coast-line of about 130 miles, and the point or head of it at Tatta is 70 miles from the sea. The tide rises to this distance. The Indus loses much water from passing through dry and desert regions, and much is also drawn off for irrigation; accordingly it brings down much less water to the sea than the Ganges. Steamers of light draft ascend from Hyderabad to Multan. A railway ascends the valley of the Indus from the important port of Karachi to Peshawar.

INDUSTRIAL ACCIDENTS. See ACCIDENTS; MINE ACCIDENTS.

INDUSTRIAL ARBITRATION. See ARBITRATION, INDUSTRIAL.

INDUSTRIAL CHEMISTRY. See CHEMICAL INDUSTRIES.

INDUSTRIAL COMBINATIONS. See COMBINATIONS, INDUSTRIAL.

INDUSTRIAL AND COMMERCIAL LIBRARIES. See LIBRARIES—*Special Subject Library Services: Business.*

INDUSTRIAL CORPORATIONS. See CORPORATIONS, LEGAL.

INDUSTRIAL CRISES. See CRISES, ECONOMIC.

INDUSTRIAL DEMOCRACY. See DEMOCRACY.

INDUSTRIAL DESIGN. As used today "industrial design" is a very misleading term, largely because of the breadth of its scope. The word *industrial,* coming from *industry,* covers a wide field full of ramifications, while *design* has been subject to countless interpretations since the very beginnings of man. The artist, for example, and to a large extent, the layman, has always thought of design in terms of pattern and color—the decorative treatment of a surface. To the engineer, on the other hand, design means structure, with emphasis divided among function, materials, production techniques, and costs. Much of this confusion exists, no doubt, because few people, including those trained in the arts, sciences, and technology, understand or are willing to concede the meaning and whole nature of design. It is an altogether human tendency for each individual to interpret so broad a subject exclusively in terms of his own particular interest or training. Creative design is not merely decoration, nor is it merely structure; it is either or both. Like art, it cannot be defined restrictively, as if it were one single activity. Design is *any* skilled activity objectifying meaning and intention, conditioned and controlled by factors both tangible and intangible, and resulting in the solution of a contemporary human problem.

Design has its source in a concept, and to objectify this concept, organization and critical control of all conditioning factors are necessary. It is therefore a mistake to think that design is a solely inspirational activity. It calls for more than imagination to create. It requires a search for and collection of all available information, an understanding of all conditioning factors, a logical analysis and synthesis of all this information in terms of these conditioning factors, and finally, a specific organization and development. Thus it is true that design engineers working in industry (and there are thousands of them) might legitimately call themselves industrial designers. Yet to those who have closely followed the full development of design for industry and are best qualified to speak, it is the contribution of the artist-designer and not the engineer which fits into the current interpretation of the term "industrial design."

Industrial design, as it is recognized today, deals with the *appearance factor* of those products made *in mass by the machine.* Obviously, mass production cannot exist without mass acceptance. Experience teaches us emphatically that, whatever the reason, great numbers of people like the same things. That simple fact is the basis of successful mass production and mass distribution, for between mass production and mass distribution, or sales, lies the all-important essential of mass acceptance. Mass acceptance demands a fully developed design before the process of manufacturing begins—fully developed not only as it relates to human needs, function, materials, machine production techniques, and costs, but also in those aesthetic attributes controlling its appearance—distinction, timeliness, and, consequently, appeal. It is in this respect that industrial design differs vastly and essentially from handicraft design, which is, by its very nature, one of improvisation as the work progresses. Handicraft design concerns itself with limited production and is characterized by irregular and individual treatment, sometimes quite personal in nature, and therefore relatively high in cost. Industrial design, on the other hand, deals with vast multiple production, is characterized by precision and uniformity, and is consequently comparatively low in cost and impersonal in quality.

Here, then, for the first time in the history of the world is a new situation demanding additional study through new techniques, and additional talent—that of the artist-designer; for the design development must be perfected not merely to a point sufficient to carry an item through production, but also in those intangible qualities which create in the buying public the desire for possession. With the aesthetic limitations inevitable among engineers, production technicians, and workers on the one hand, and sales and advertising men on the other, there has arisen an urgent need for the artist-designer with an engineering, production, and merchandising viewpoint; one who can bring to the work of his technical and commercial associates the essential elements of timeliness, good taste, and aesthetic invention—all attributes of fine appearance and style which stimulate and achieve mass acceptance.

Obviously, however, fine appearance with all that it connotes cannot exist alone. This elusive and most important factor, though it calls for talent and imagination of a high order, can be solved only in relation to the other conditioning and controlling factors of creative design, namely: (1) environmental factors; (2) functional factors; (3) materials factors; (4) tools and tool processes factors; (5) economics factors. These factors condition all design, and have always conditioned it; they are not new. The handicraftsman encountered them, whether at the potter's wheel, bench, lathe, or loom; the architect or structural builder has always had them to contend with. Wherever the fine products of past ages have endured as vital records of their particular eras, it will be noted that this least tangible factor, fine appearance, has always been treated as an integral part of the design, not merely as decoration superimposed upon or applied to a completed structure.

As fine appearance cannot be divorced from the sum of influence of all the other conditioning factors of design, in like manner, design itself, like art, cannot be divorced from the sum of influence of human living. It is an integral part of man's daily life, not something to be brought out and considered on special occasions. All honest and vital design, again like art, grows out of and is related to a people's needs, environment, and a great many conditioning factors. The validity of this statement is apparent in a brief glance at any phase of artistic accomplishment in man's history, whether it be weapons, tools, ornaments, household utensils, furniture, architecture, or any one of a number of possible choices. For the purposes of this article, architecture has been chosen as an example, for the work of the structural builder, while only one section of the field, is yet enduring, monumental, more easily traced, and more widely known.

In a hot, dry, preservative climate, surrounded by an abundance of building materials and slave labor, the ancient Egyptians built low, massive temples and vast tombs, dignified, monumental, and characterized throughout by a feeling of permanence expressive of the Egyptian philosophy of immortality. These structures coincide entirely with what we might expect; they are altogether in keeping with the needs, materials, and methods of the people by whom they were built. (See EGYPTIAN ARCHITECTURE.)

A completely different set of circumstances existed in Greece. The Greeks were primarily a rational people. They were idealistic and imaginative, but their very idealism and imagination were tempered by the logic of pure reason. From an abundance of marble close at hand, they built temples of exceedingly fine proportions, small, simple, and completely adequate to their needs. An essentially well-balanced race, they were able, through keen discrimination, to select the essential and permanent, and discard the irrelevant, achieving restraint and moderation. (See GREEK ARCHITECTURE.)

The vast magnitude of their conquests presented an entirely new set of problems to be solved by the Roman people. By nature warlike and practical, as well as pleasure-loving, they had a genius for organization to which ample scope was given by the necessity for maintaining Roman order and civilization throughout their far-flung empire. Hence the Romans became notable for their magnificent and daring engineering feats, and especially for the development of the arch, making possible the spanning of great spaces. When they built naturally for some purely utilitarian purpose, the Romans built honestly, directly, and with great beauty and dignity. But they were an imitative people, and when they attempted to become «artistic» and sought to rival the Greeks of whose work they had not the slightest understanding, they failed. Here there was no aesthetic discipline, no spiritual restraint, only a desire for outward material display. (See under ARCHITECTURE; ITALY—*Art in Ancient Italy*.)

The art which we call Gothic was developed by the French in an age of great religious fervor, dominated temporally as well as spiritually by the Roman Catholic church, full of Christian symbolism and fraught with superstition. Its society was erected upon the great pyramidal structure of feudalism, wherein the centralized power of the Roman Empire was disintegrated, and baronial overlords harassed each other with private wars. To answer the needs of such an era a definite type of structural design arose—walled cities, great, impregnable castles, and, above all, the Gothic cathedral, of which every structural line expressed, functionally and aesthetically, the color, vigor, and daring of the medieval people. (See GOTHIC ARCHITECTURE.)

And so on, throughout history, vital creative design has expressed a specific purpose; it has been the people's answer to the problems presented them by their age and their locality. It has exploited those things which they had, and adapted itself to the lack of those things which they had not. Always it has remained consistent with certain rigid limitations, and the principles of design, combined with a sense of fitness and directness, have never varied. To be sure, a Greek temple is beautiful beyond the fact that it satisfied a specific need, because it embodies certain universal principles and attributes, but to appropriate its design for a bank or a library is as great an anachronism as to provide the city hall with a moat and a drawbridge. The great races of the past possessed no tricks or secrets; they simply solved their problems and fulfilled their needs by using the best means they had at hand. To go on forever copying the past, accepting the burdens and limitations of tradition, is to deny ourselves opportunities undreamed of before.

The age in which we live is incomparably broader than any preceding it. In the past man was greatly limited in the execution of his ideas by a lack of available materials. These materials may have existed elsewhere, but ancient man was compelled by the exigencies of contemporary transportation and commerce to carry out his ideas in materials close at hand, and, conversely, the lack or abundance of certain materials dictated his ideas, developed whole lines of reasoning, possibly whole philosophies of life. We of the present day are no longer limited to those materials which we happen to have around us. The exploitation of natural resources and the increase of commerce and transportation have made available to us materials from all corners of the earth. Ours is the age of science and invention, popularly known as the «power-tool age.» Conditions and life about us have completely changed; the horizons have widened; the tempo has quickened. New needs, new standards, new viewpoints have been created; a new civilization and a new art. (See BUILDING, IN THE UNITED STATES; CITY PLANNING.)

The handworkman in the days prior to the advent of the machine took a very personal attitude toward his work; his reputation as a master craftsman stood or fell by it. He must, of necessity, study and modify his designs, constantly setting a higher goal for himself. He took into consideration the function of that which he was designing, and the possibilities and limitations of his materials. Except in a very few instances, he used his tools honestly and directly. Within him was the inherent desire to create not only a good and useful article, but one pleasing to the senses of sight and touch. And such pleasure is not dependent upon chance; consciously or unconsciously there must be reason behind it, and this the good craftsman at his bench was able to supply. Thus, that which he created for use he also often endowed with those enduring qualities of art, and we see them treasured in our museums today.

All this the machine changed. It was rapid, impersonal, and performed its work with precision and uniformity. It was, in a word, efficient, and people became so preoccupied with this efficiency that they completely lost sight of the essential fact that the machine is merely another tool with which to work. It cannot think, plan, or modify; it merely accomplishes whatever mechanical function it is designed to accomplish, and nothing more. The creation of a work of art is not a matter of the tools employed, but of the human agency which employs them—of delicate perceptions, strong convictions, and the talent so to control the principles of design as to achieve those attributes of organization and unity. Thus with the introduction of the machine the skilled artisan and fine craftsman were pushed more and more into the background. Many products were turned out in vast quantities; vast numbers of people could enjoy things which even kings could not possess a century before. Inevitably, all sense of fine appearance and distinction disappeared; art was divorced from everyday living and relegated to the status of an occasional luxury. The creative faculty died out among the masses, and taste declined to the lowest level in centuries. The world was entering the first stage of its great industrial era—the pioneering stage.

To the pioneer the practical alone is of importance. The world is utilitarian to him, and only after these needs have been satisfied does he reach out after the finer things of life. Such a point was finally reached by the pioneers of industrialism, for there is a limit to mechanical efficiency. What one manufacturer can do, his competitor can duplicate. A highly standardized product is finally developed and the manufacturer must look for other qualities to exploit. Here appeal may assume tremendous importance; here the intangible factors may loom larger than the tangible; here, in a word, art enters industry, and here there is no limit.

The first approach, however, was a false one. Artists had been steeped in the traditional for too long a time to meet immediately the challenge of the machine. With the first realization of the appalling lack of fine appearance in machine-made products, there came an attempt to alleviate this ugliness by the addition of applied decoration borrowed from another age and an alien tradition. Such dishonest art, however, soon created a certain uneasiness in public opinion, and it was the advertising profession, ever on the alert for incipient trends, which first became conscious that the time was ripe for a change. With better merchandising and advertising methods it became evident that art was worth money in trade. Young artists were drafted into the advertising field, and there followed a tremendous development and exploitation of advertising design. Finally, by traveling in reverse, the point was reached which should have been the starting point—namely, the product itself. It became apparent that a great deal of time, money, and talent was being spent on visual presentation of many advertised products, of which the picture or rendering was stronger in appeal than the product itself. Finally it occurred to someone that a little of this talent put to work on the product might not only greatly improve it, but (which was of far more importance to this particular group) would facilitate its advertisement and sale. This was done, and thus was opened a new field, gigantic in scope, ranging from toothbrushes and tiny clocks to huge generators and transportation equipment. The motorcar manufacturers were perhaps the first to use the artist in the design development of their products, an innovation which demanded a certain courage, for while the artist has always been considered indispensable in the so-called art industries (such as furniture, jewelry, textiles, pottery, ceramics, and glassware), few executives in the general manufacturing field had, up to this time, given him any consideration. There has never been a great deal of sympathy between the artist and the manufacturer, nor is this difficult to understand, for neither has had any but a narrow conception of the whole nature of art and design. Now, however, the industrial executive has learned that art qualities are not to be found within picture frames only, but may be present in all products made by man. He has also learned that these qualities are universal and have universal appeal. Nor are they inconsistent with mechanical considerations; fine appearance and mechanical efficiency go hand in hand, each calling for closer co-ordination and relationship of parts, resulting in simplicity and greater economy. The difference between distinctive and fine-appearing products with a universal appeal, and those of mediocrity does not lie in the degree to which they are useful, nor yet, in most instances, in the quality of materials from which they are made; rather it is found in the measure of the artistic concept which created them and guided their production.

The opportunities opened up by the tremendous capacity of the machine with its parallel necessity of distribution, caused the intelligent creative artist to consider and study the whole nature of design. He discovered that all products made by mechanical methods and means were not necessarily unattractive, for here was beauty in abstract forms, beauty in sheer surfaces, beauty in precision and in the logic of good engineering. These forms with their hardness and austerity were not ugly—they were different, and grew out of their own era as logically as other forms represented their eras. He found that the modern engineer, like his Roman predecessor, often produces beauty when he does things with no other thought than function—carrying out his ideas directly, and with understanding and appreciation of materials and techniques. Furthermore, the artist came to realize that he, himself, is not so far removed from the engineer, for the engineer brings to his problem a sense of fitness, directness, simplicity, and economy—all factors with which the creative artist has always been more or less concerned. It is the artist's special province to bring, in addition, keen yet delicate perceptions, a fine sense of subtle relationships of form and color, balance, and unity. Finally he came to understand, as all creative artists in the past have understood, that although the principles and attributes controlling fine appearance are universal and unchanging, this factor can only be studied and solved in relation to the other conditioning factors, for all are interwoven and interactive, and these other factors are ever-changing. It might pay, therefore, to re-examine them more fully in the light of this new age of science, engineering, vast production, and distribution.

While it is necessary in discussing these controlling and conditioning factors to speak of them singly and in a certain order (for convenience' sake, in that order in which they were here earlier presented), it must be held in mind that in actual application they cannot be thought of or treated singly, separately, or in any particular order of importance. These factors are all equally important, related, and interwoven, and all of them must always be carried along together, never allowing any one or more to get out of control at the expense of another. A delicate balance must be maintained at all times. Only the competent artist-designer working in close co-operation with his technical and commercial associates can accomplish this end.

Environmental Factors.—The first conditioning factor to affect and govern creative design is that of environment. Our place in time and space conditions our needs and our ideas. We think and act as we do because of our environment. Our complex needs and ideas are quite different from those of our ancestors of a few generations ago, living, as they did, in an agricultural and handicraft age. Even in the present day, the needs, thoughts, and actions of some peoples are greatly different from ours because, geographically, they happen to be living in a primitive world many thousands of years removed from our scientific, mechanized, and commercial age. The continued stress on the word *creative* in speaking of design should be noted, for there are two kinds of design, one creative and contemporary, growing out of and related to our environment and needs; the other derivative, stemming from sources no longer related (or, at least, only remotely so) to our times. The creative artist or designer will always be marked by his sensitiveness of perception and readiness of response to the stimuli of his environment. This means that there can be no set formula for art or design. The most casual survey of the past will reveal the fact that down through the centuries, art has expressed many ideas, served many needs, and in so doing, has taken on many patterns and forms consistent with the different times, environments, and races. Whereas ideas grow out of and are related to human needs and environment, ideas alone are of no value until they are expressed—until they are organized and harnessed for work. This brings us to the second conditioning factor of design, that of function.

Functional Factors.—Function, in all products designed for usage, is of paramount importance, and in most instances, determines the form. It is obvious, for example, that a wheel must be round, not octagonal. But function alone does not necessarily produce beautiful form. Of late there has been much ado about the relationship of beauty to function—one school of thought holding out for purely functional forms. It is sufficient to say here that while the intelligent and competent designer's forms may not be always exclusively functional, he will always design to express function. This license often allows him to design a form of more interest and appeal than one which is purely functional. If all designed products were merely functional and nothing more, they would fail to win mass acceptance and would be bought only under necessity. The designer must co-ordinate and subordinate certain forms to the unified whole. Some form or part must be emphasized. While the forms may not always be functional, they should express function. A motorcar should express the dynamic quality it possesses, even while it stands at the curb. Here is a point where many industrial products fail; radio cabinets, for instance, are apt to take the form of anything from highboys or lowboys to some indefinable sort of cabinet expressive of nothing at all. The same is true of lighting fixtures (or rather, ornaments) which look like candles and furnish about as much illumination. The arbitrary alliance of an obsolete design with a new product is a negation of the whole meaning of design. One might reasonably expect an electric lighting fixture to function so as to provide a proper amount of illumination for a given purpose.

We have all seen many things which were functional yet lacked desirable aesthetic qualities. Let us come back to our wheel—an automobile wheel, to be specific. While it has remained fundamentally and functionally the same since the invention of the automobile, it has changed considerably in proportion and appearance in the past 20 years. It is a far cry from the long, spindly, wooden spokes, large diameter, and thin section to the smaller, better proportioned, and styled motorcar wheel of today. The same could be said of the motorcar body. The present body still seats the same number of people in the same location; access to the car is by the same means. In other words, the motorcar body of 20 years ago functioned in so far as seating accommodations are concerned, in about the same manner as the car of today—but what a change in body design. This is because of other factors which we shall discuss a little later. The point to be made here is: function is a conditioning factor of vital importance in design, but it does not necessarily make for fine appearance. On the other hand, in utilitarian products, fine appearance cannot exist in design without function. Transposed into concrete illustration, the finest appearing motorcar in the world, lacking means of access, or a motor, or some other functional part, cannot be considered a beautiful motorcar; it may be a beautiful assembly of materials and forms, but it will not be a motorcar. In like manner, a fine-appearing chair which is far too large or too small for the human frame and therefore not functioning as an object on which to sit comfortably, can scarcely be called a beautiful chair.

Materials Factors.—Before ideas can function or be expressed in this physical world of ours, they have to be made out of something concrete and tangible. The third conditioning factor, therefore, is that of materials. These, because of their inherent characteristics, have always exerted an influence and control over design—on its character, scale, texture, color, and so forth. All materials have certain inherent qualities, including that of beauty (or they have qualities, at least, capable of expressing beauty in the hands of the artist of discrimination and taste), which make them suitable for specific usage. We use or specify a certain material because of some one outstanding characteristic, such as the strength of steel, the lightness of aluminum, the transparency of glass, the plasticity of clay. We may find other favorable characteristics present, such as ease of workability, freedom from corrosion, attractiveness of finish, or low cost. However, along with the positive, or favorable, characteristics will come one or more negative or unfavorable ones which will immediately limit what can be done. For example, steel, as a design material, offers in the positive balance strength, rigidity, and a high modulus of elasticity. However, in the negative balance, as a limitation to be overcome, is the fact that steel is a corrosive material and must therefore be painted or plated.

From the production standpoint, the designer is concerned with a few of the outstanding characteristics of a material—its strength, weight, workability, and cost. From the standpoint of appearance and appeal, he is primarily interested in its color, texture, warmth or coolness, pattern (if any), possible applied finishes, honesty of usage, and character imprint of the tool or process. Within the past few years a number of new synthetic materials have been made available through research. Some of these materials possess unique inherent characteristics which make for utility and beauty. Great care must be taken, however, to avoid the natural tendency to supplant with new materials others superior in several characteristics for a given purpose, or to imitate others inferior in several characteristics for a given purpose. One material cannot take on the appearance of another without losing its own identity. Imitating another material may be an interesting technical feat, but commercially the practice is either pointless or deceptive. Such a procedure is bad economics and worse design.

Tools and Tool Processes Factors.—Materials in the raw accomplish nothing, so we must devise methods of working or fashioning them. Tools and tool processes, then, comprise the fourth conditioning factor and exert a realistic control over the nature of the design. Tools cannot think; they can do only what they are designed and built to do. If a product is to have beauty, distinction, integrity and authority, and still maintain the necessary balance of the other factors, notably cost, it must be so designed that the tools and processes naturally and honestly leave their imprint and character in the material. A sand-casting is pebbly in texture and needs a generous radius where two planes meet. A die-casting, on the other hand, is smooth and can have crisp edges and be thin in section. A plastic product, molded under pressure, may come from the mold completely finished; however, the process—the manner in which the material flows in the mold—will control the nature of the design. One could go to great lengths in citing the great variety of tools and processes used in fashioning many commonly used materials, but sufficient has been said to point out the stern disciplinary nature of the control of tools and tool processes over design.

Economics or Costs Factors.—We are living in an economic world, each of us facing economic problems every day. For that reason design control is immediately recognized by all—at least by all who remain solvent. When this economic control over design comes into action, it compels clearer, more far-reaching, as well as more ingenious and resourceful thinking and planning. Almost anything can be engineered and produced in this world if all regard for costs is ignored. Because of our colossal industrial setup, demanding large-scale production and distribution, one big problem today is how to hold design costs within the range which the mass market can stand, without sacrificing other equally important qualities, and so develop a product with a wide and ever-expanding market. It is axiomatic that good design is economic design. It would seem to follow then, that economic design (all other factors being considered) is good design; for economic design will be simple, direct, and honest; it will make wise use of materials, will take into consideration available manufacturing processes, and will take full advantage of the production setup.

Fine Appearance Factors.—Up to this point, most of the controls over design have been concrete and tangible; therefore no diversity of opinion exists concerning their importance. These factors cannot be avoided. There has never been any attempt to avoid them, even in the days of the handicraftsman. But fine appearance is less tangible, and is one quality concerning which every man offers an opinion. Fine appearance is no mysterious and occult quality to the trained artist. It depends upon the artist's taste, upon his concept, understanding, and manipulation of the principles of visual design. He applies these principles to the elements with which he has to work, whether these are lines, planes, solids, colors, or textures. He achieves the attributes of fine appearance: namely, an orderly and directed movement, relationship, balance, and unity.

There is something in our race history which causes us to prefer orderly movement to agitated movement; elements that are related, to those that are unrelated; elements that are balanced, to those that are unbalanced. In the final analysis, we unconsciously prefer those things whose elements have been so carefully studied and expertly organized as to maintain that delicate balance between variety and unity, with the proper amount of emphasis rightly placed and always under control. This the engineer, the technician, the skilled worker, the sales and advertising man have never been able to do. The contributions of the engineer and the technician, for example, are adequate from the standpoint of mass production, but totally inadequate from that of mass acceptance. The elements of taste, little understood in terms of conscious control, are the essence of all true art performance, and it is these which the properly trained and creative artist-designer brings to the problem—a timely style and distinction, together with those attributes of fine appearance which man has always unconsciously desired and accepted.

These very simple and (one would think) obvious essentials should be constantly in the mind of the designer and the producer alike. Neither designer nor producer should approach his work with autocratic delusions of his superiority over the other. They could come much more closely together, with far less lost motion and consequent economic waste, if each would keep in mind that together they are designing and producing for

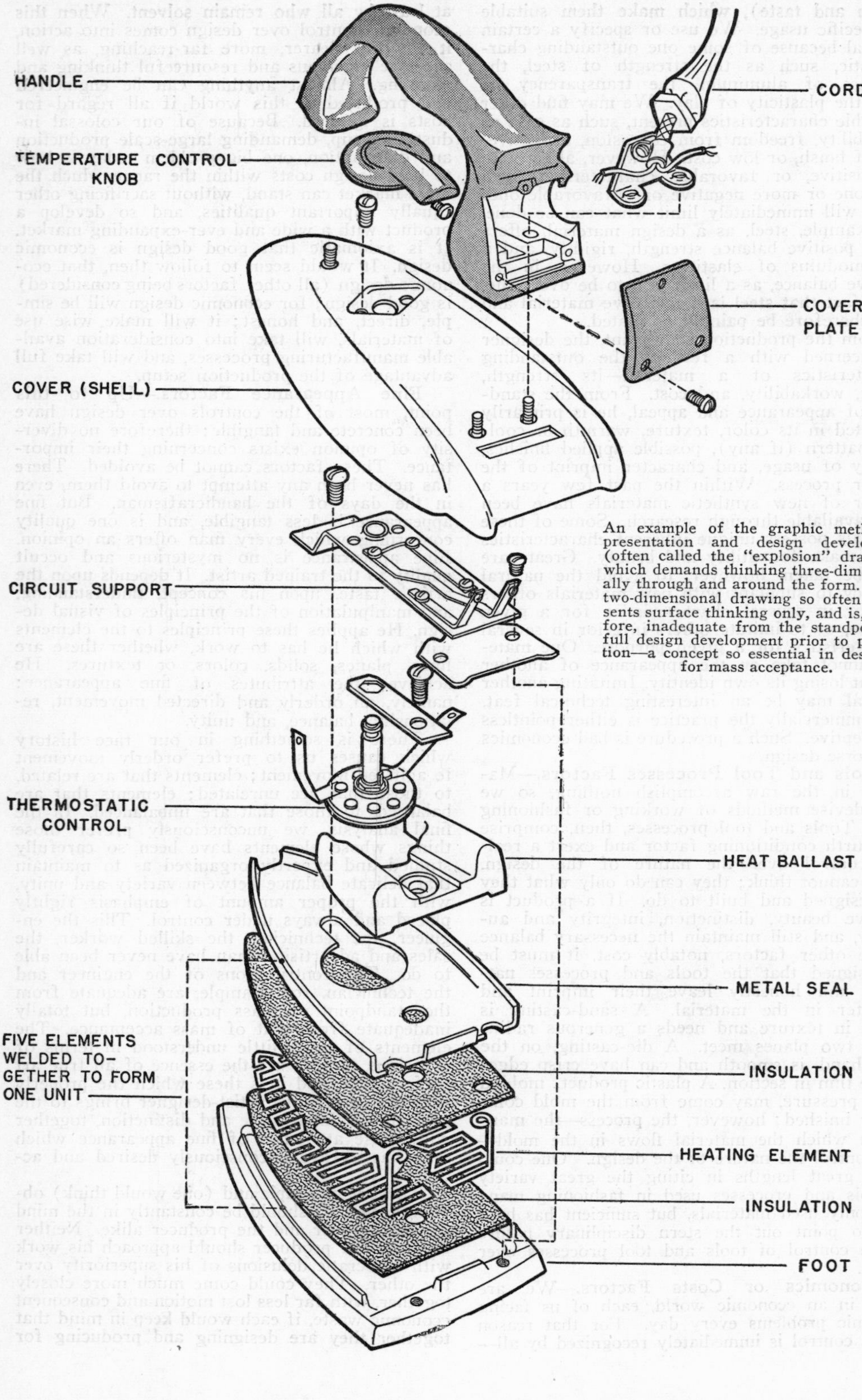

An example of the graphic method of presentation and design development often called the "explosion" drawing), which demands thinking three-dimensionally through and around the form. Mere two-dimensional drawing so often represents surface thinking only, and is, therefore, inadequate from the standpoint of full design development prior to production—a concept so essential in designing for mass acceptance.

the acceptance of a large and varied mass of consumers, for it cannot be too strongly stressed that mass production can exist only where there is mass acceptance. This problem did not face the handicraftsman of yesterday; he produced for himself or for a few consumers whose needs and likes he knew or could ascertain, whereas our present-day, large-scale producers are faced with the disquieting necessity of discovering in advance of production just what design is most likely to be needed and accepted by this large and scattered consumer-public.

It is reasonably apparent that our modern industries do know how to design for mass production. But so often they miss this equally important essential of designing for mass acceptance, simply because they fail to see the complete picture. Before a product can profitably achieve the widest mass acceptance, it must possess a delicate balance of three separate viewpoints—the manufacturer's, the retailer's, and the consumer's.

The manufacturer thinks mainly in terms of physics and chemistry, techniques and economics; the retailer, largely of turnover and makeup.

The consumer, while he is affected by the factors basically involved in manufacture, is not consciously concerned with either production or merchandising problems. Quality, usefulness, cost—these are of definite interest to him, yet his actual buying response is stimulated by the very factors which too many manufacturers consider so unimportant, and even whimsical, that they overlook them entirely, or ignore them. The consumer, to be specific, wants products that have all the factory can offer in quality and price. In addition to this he wants fine appearance, and if he does not find it he will not buy.

It becomes vitally important, therefore, that our mass production design problems be attacked by the proper methods—methods answering the needs not only of mass production (which have been pretty well solved), but also of this equally important and much more elusive problem of mass acceptance.

Methods of Creating Industrial Design.—There are three different methods of creating or developing a design: (1) graphic, (2) plastic, and (3) tectonic. The *graphic* method is entirely suitable to decorative and pictorial design for they are two-dimensional. However, this is the method almost universally used in three-dimensional design, and here it is not adequate unless the form is symmetrical or very simple and easy to comprehend. Speaking of simple forms, especially ones with subtle curves such as occur in ceramic and glassware, even the experienced designer can deceive himself if he limits himself solely to a graphic study. To be sure, the graphic method is quite suitable, even essential, for explaining crystallized ideas pertaining to three-dimensional form. But it must be noted that graphic presentation can only partially represent three-dimensional form; complete representation requires a number of different drawings or statements, and while these may be adequate from the standpoint of understanding the structure, imparting instructions, and devising means of production (as on a blueprint or working drawing), these planar or two-dimensional views are totally inadequate from the standpoint of complete visualization, flexible development, and the consequent evaluation (appreciation) of those formal qualities and attributes which make for fine appearance, appeal, and acceptance. One of the reasons so many industrial products are unsuccessful in appearance and appeal is that this essential has been ignored. It is therefore of vital importance to mass production industries to see the potentialities of, and to pursue a technique which will reveal the greatest number of tangible and intangible factors involved in the design. It is imperative that we adopt and use in conjunction with the graphic, the more adequate methods of complete design development—the *plastic* and *tectonic*—and avoid that method which provides but a single point of view, which is inevitably true of a graphic presentation.

Any product, article, or form that is plastic in quality in its entirety, or in part, must be developed by a plastic method in a plastic medium if it is to express fully the activating forces and principles of design, all essential if the form is to have fine appearance, distinction, and universal appeal, and escape the danger of becoming a mere paper, i.e., graphic or two-dimensional creation frozen into solid form. When we refer to a form as «plastic» (and here we are speaking of a quality and not a material) we mean that the negative volumes, that is, outside space or spaces, participate in and move with the positive volume or form. Possibly a simpler if more lengthy statement would refer to plastic form, for the most part, as that developing concavities and convexities, and therefore consisting of curving and twisting surfaces. The eye follows the directional and moving character a bending, curving, or twisting surface possesses, thereby participating in the sweep and flow of the form. A plastic form appears as an integral unit, as if poured in a mold—flexible, capable of being shaped and reshaped. Examples of plastic form are: sculpture, ceramic and glassware, motorcar bodies, a motor block, carburetor, vacuum cleaner, food mixer, electric iron, and telephone.

By tectonic form we mean a form composed of thin sections enclosing space. (Architectonic refers to architecture alone, and is tectonic.) In this instance, the eye does not participate in the form, but wanders about on the surface. To have strong directional movement the form has to be extreme in proportion or be modified through slight changes of form, changes of material, texture, or have grouped piercings or decoration. Typical tectonic forms are: buildings, furniture, cabinet work, boxes, packages, containers, and displays. Tectonic forms, unlike plastic ones, will appear fabricated—as, indeed, they always are, unless they are very small.

The industrial designer who approaches his job with competence and sincerity will proceed to make an exhaustive study of his problem, seeking all available information, which, in turn, must be analyzed and organized for later development. No man's judgment can be any better than the logical analysis of his information, and in the end it is the industrial designer's judgment, based upon a weighing of all factors, that will determine the success or failure of the problem. The industrial designer will collect his data from many sources and by various methods. Much will depend upon the nature of his position. If he is a member of a manufacturing company's staff of designers, practically all of his information about the problem at hand will come from discussions in conference with key representatives of such vitally concerned departments as engineering, sales, and works. In the larger companies additional and more highly specialized data may come from departments devoted to market analysis, engineering research, and sales promotion. If he is a free-lance designer, or a member of an independent design organization, he may be compelled to supplement what information he can get through his client with independent research. The designer on the staff of a large company, if he has, in addition to talent, mental breadth and sufficient emotional stamina to keep from becoming dulled by routine, can accomplish much, especially if he possesses the quality of leadership and can win the co-operation of his fellow workers. He has the tremendous advantage of being close to the problem in all of its complex ramifications. This the free-lance designer is never able to do, and, as a result, may attack the problem superficially or in an uneconomic way. On the other hand, the competent free-lance designer has the compensating advantage of possessing a fresh viewpoint—of not knowing too many ways a thing cannot be done. Being an outsider, he is free from internal pressures; his suggestions and ideas appear more authoritative; he is listened to.

In either case, with all available information analyzed, with all limitations known or foreseen, the industrial designer proceeds to *visualize* the possibilities. He "sees" emerging a certain form, capable of several different paths of development, depending upon the materials and manufacturing processes to be employed. He "pictures" the advantages of appropriate materials, the attractive qualities of a bit of textured surface serving as a foil for a smooth surface elsewhere, a bright trim here, a dramatic touch of color there. So it goes. This, in simple terms, is the first *creative* step in the industrial designer's job, and this he must be able to do.

Slowly his imaginative visions take form, usually first in two dimensions on paper, as the graphic method is rapid, inexpensive, and exceedingly expressive in the hands of a talented person. Sooner or later, however, he will be compelled to study it, wholly or in part, in three dimensions. If it is asymmetric and plastic in quality, he will use a plastic medium such as plasticene or clay. Typical examples of this type of design problem are: motorcar bodies or parts, sewing machine castings, electric or steam irons. Often the plastic studies are duplicated in plaster, as it is an excellent medium in which to study refinements of form and the play of light on a reflecting surface. Light and form are inseparable appearance factors in design, and herein lies the potentiality of not only beautiful and subtle variety but also appeal. In this procedure is the full development of the *aesthetic viewpoint* as contrasted with the *factory viewpoint* expressed in a purely technical working drawing. Here is the final development of *style,* and by style we mean creative expression of distinction and character, all growing out of and all related to usage, ultimate materials, and machine techniques. The style must spring from within the design; it dare not be imposed from without, like something extraneous. Should the design be tectonic in character and call for the careful proportionment and adjustment of several or many fabricated parts which cannot be adequately studied from one position, then it had best be developed in three dimensions through the use of cardboard, wood, sheet metal, sheet plastics, or other equally expressive materials. In either plastic or tectonic studies duplicates may be necessary in order to permit of variations and critical refinements; among these we can make rational analyses and comparisons. Such comparisons can be made only among tangible and concrete three-dimensional forms, never among drawings which only partially represent forms.

It might be well at this time to point out that the purpose of a thorough, three-dimensional study is not to make a model. Models are made from crystallized designs—from designs in their final form. Rather, the purpose is to keep the design in a fluid state, mobile and dynamic, never fixed or static, until it is carried as far as the conditioning factors and the designer's talents permit. It must be understood that the industrial designer himself may not actually make the plastic or tectonic studies in whole or in part; this may be delegated to a subordinate, or to another department, depending upon the size and type of design organization. He must, however, continually supervise the work and make the final decisions which represent his taste and judgment.

The design has now come through various stages of development; from an imaginative vision the designer has forged a concrete and significant realization. It has been influenced and shaped by many complex factors, some real and tangible, others intangible and psychological, though no less important, for each group of these factors is of equal value—all are interwoven and interactive. Intangible and psychological factors have never concerned the matter-of-fact type of mind, yet for mass acceptance these very factors may well be the ones that spell the difference between the commercial success or failure of a product.

Now, and not until now, the design is ready to be crystallized in the form of assembly and detail drawings—accurate, definite information, exact and unmistakable. Unfortunately all too many «factory-minded» designs begin and end with this working drawing, which, as pointed out before, is entirely inadequate for full development where mass acceptance is concerned. In many cases dramatic visualization of the design is necessary, and this is done by means of a rendering or picture of the design. However, this rendering should not be confused with, or taken for a real design study. While legitimate in that it permits of color, details, and accessories, and suggests or interprets finishes, and above all, saves time in presenting the visualization of an idea, it has, nevertheless, very definite limitations; the pretty picture does not solve a design problem from the manufacturing or mass *production* standpoint any more than the technical working drawing solves it from the appearance or mass *acceptance* standpoint. In some instances it may be necessary to carry the three-dimensional form to its logical conclusion, i.e., to fabricate an actual-size model of the crystallized design, true in form, color, and texture, to the as yet unmade manufactured product. Thus the cycle of design procedure is completed. It does not necessarily mean, however, that the industrial designer has finished his job. Many things can happen between the crystallization of the design and actual production. Factors which appeared clearly a few months before may have since become blurred; what appeared as known or fore-

Courtesy du Pont Company

Viscose tanks in a modern "Cellophane" plant.

INDUSTRIAL DESIGN

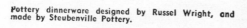

Pottery dinnerware designed by Russel Wright, and made by Steubenville Pottery.

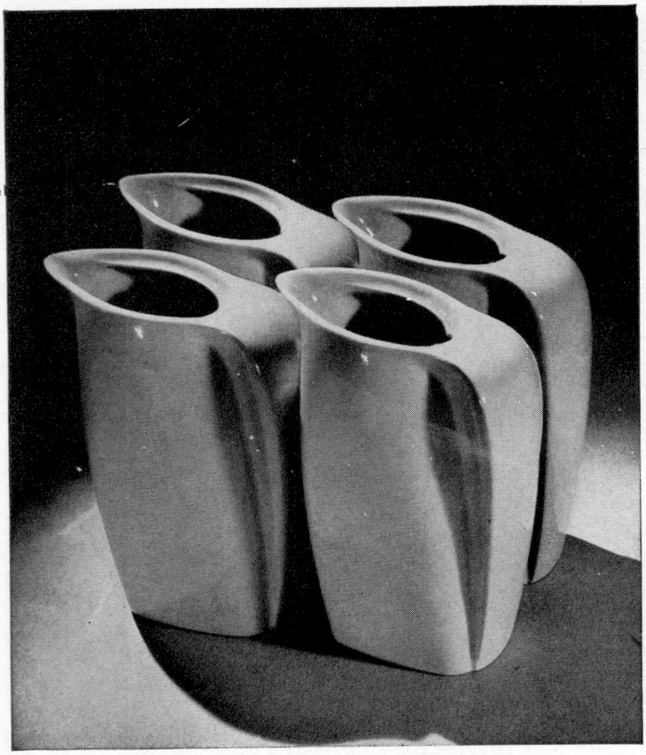

Mass production design for liquid containers to be used in refrigerator.

Three-dimensional design in plastic on the moldmaker's jolly.

Courtesy Pratt Institute

seen may have shifted with changed conditions. The designer has come a long way; he will not now forsake his contribution to a job to which many men have given their time, training, energy, and talent. And so he «follows through,» consulting and supervising, until the product leaves the assembly line, in fact until it reaches the hands of the consumer.

This procedure of designing and this attitude toward the job as a whole, starting with a study of the psychological and intangible factors, as well as those that are tangible and factual, and following through the various steps mentioned, costs money. It costs money for the very simple reason that it takes time, knowledge, experience, and talent to create, and all of these are worth money. But in the end—for sooner or later some study will have to be made—this method of designing for mass acceptance will be found to be economical in time and money, compared to the staggering cost of the wasteful and empirical bungling all too prevalent today in industry where mass acceptance design is involved. It is not easy to guarantee the success of a new design, but it has been amply proved that trained and careful study and procedure can vastly reduce the hazards which are inevitable where guesswork or prejudice dictate decisions.

Industrial design is not a science, yet, as compared to the fine arts, it borrows from science the realistic approach and the critical controls which have brought science to the heights it occupies today. Because of this, industrial design, properly practiced, is in a position to serve, with equal distinction, both art and industry.

DONALD R. DOHNER,
Industrial Designer and Head of Department of Industrial Design, Pratt Institute.

INDUSTRIAL DISTRIBUTION, as here used, refers to agencies and policies used by manufacturers in marketing goods. A full discussion of modern marketing methods would define the functions of the various institutions which serve all branches of commercial activity; then outline the practices used for distributing agricultural products, the methods used by manufacturers, and the organization and management of wholesale and retail trade. This all refers to the merchandising of movable commodities and takes no account of the interesting methods which have been devised for the sale of other goods, such as real estate, transportation, securities, professional services, entertainment, etc.

The Institutes of Trade.— In considering the manufacturer's problem specifically, it is worth while to begin with mention of the underlying institutes of trade. The first of these is the accepted system of weights and measures. Based in part upon legal enactment, and in part upon custom, the commercial measure is the unit to which price is usually attached. If it be in any degree vague, representative trading is discouraged and the cumbersome methods of lot inspection and of dickering and bargaining prevail. Modern trade is carried on with a system of weights and measures which is in part antiquated and in whole heterogeneous. The defects of the system have long stimulated reformers to work for a comprehensive and logical plan, such as the metric system appears to present. The trading community, however, is wedded to custom and is mindful of the inconvenience of the transitional period, of the capital invested in scales, containers, etc., and of the obsolescence which would overtake existing records if a change were made.

The System of Grades.— The second institute of trade is the system of grades, by which differences in quality are made definite and expressed. Without the foundation of legal enactment, which stabilizes our weights and measures, and with only so much public control as will prevent the grosser forms of fraud, the system of grades used in commerce is elastic. Old grades are continually being dropped and the names and definitions forgotten, while new grades with appropriate words or phases to designate them are introduced as advances in the manufacturing art require. The terminology of commercial grading is enormous: a book of large size is required to define the better-known kinds of textile fabrics. The legitimate terminology of grading is further overlaid by a vast variety of expressions used by traders either as a part of the game of trade puffery or as an endeavor to coin a trade name and get it introduced into the language as an indispensable trade term. Practically all of our systems of grades took their general form in an earlier day when few qualities were offered, and those were decidedly distinct from each other in physical properties. The need for a finer gradation of the quality scale has given rise to split grades or intermediate grades. In addition to these legitimate grades, the market has to cope with the skin grades of dishonest traders. Skin grades are qualities pitched so slightly below the recognized standard grades that while they may pass for what they are among traders and at an appropriate abatement of the standard-grade price they are expected to deceive consumers and sell at full prices to the general public.

Prices.— The third institute of commerce, and the most important, is price. A price is the exchange value of a commodity expressed in terms of money. The common expression is that price marks the equilibrium of demand and supply. The factors which determine price are not simply the primary supply of producers and the ultimate demand of consumers, but all those speculative activities of traders who, in anticipation of the future increase or decrease of supply or demand, alternately hold back goods from the market or throw reserves upon it. Since the manufacturing industry is reasonably stable in its productive capacity and the retail and wholesale industry likewise in its distributive capacity, and since the habits of consumers tend to remain reasonably constant over short periods of time, if left undisturbed by outside conditions, we must look elsewhere for the factors of change which are responsible for price fluctuations. Two of the chief causes of these fluctuations are changes in the weather, which influence the production of raw materials, and derangements in the credit mechanism of industry. These factors of change the manufacturer should learn to watch as barometers predicting future market movements.

The Market.— The fourth and final institute of commerce, to be here mentioned, is the market. A market is an assembly of traders actively engaged in trade, and so limited by location, by the class of articles dealt in and by the average size of sales that the action of any one trader promptly influences the action of others. From this interdependency of action there results the chief circumstance which characterizes a market, namely, that upon it a commodity has but one price at a given time. Discrepancies of price will of course result from imperfect competition, but a process of mutual value adjustment is the essence of market action. What is an efficient market? To answer this question it is necessary to recall that among the essential conditions for the efficient purchasing and selling of commodities there are required assortments to select from, protection for perishable articles, reliable measures of quantity and quality, transportation facilities, fair prices and flexible credit facilities. Assortments are judged by purchasers with reference to the market as a whole rather than as to the stock of any one firm. A city has the proper stocks only when its merchants go beyond the usual process of stocking what is called for, and make systematic study of the resources and requirements of the adjacent trade territory. Measurement of quality and quantity requires a variety of agencies, such as the grading rules and inspection service of produce exchanges. Efficient transportation is secured only in cities which plan comprehensive terminal facilities. Storage calls for special types of warehouses tied into the transportation system rather than, as is usually the case, operated as an annex to the buying and selling process. The formula for fair prices is to bring to bear upon each purchase and sale transaction all possible elements of supply and demand which are logically related to it. This means to bring the past and future supply of an article to bear upon the present price by warehousing. It calls for bringing diverse commodities to bear upon each other in so far as they are related, either in the productive sequence as raw materials and manufactured derivatives or as substitutes. The sequence can be drawn upon in the forward direction only where the converting (manufacturing) interests are active. The formula requires further that the price of the use of money for a period of time (which is interest) be brought to bear upon the probable fluctuations of the price of goods during that period. As the price of money for brief periods is chiefly the cost of appraising the security offered, those markets have the steadiest commodity prices where loanable capital is plentiful and where there exist the grading, measuring, storing, insuring, credit reporting and other facilities which make it safe to loan on stocks of merchandise. Finally, the prices of different markets should be brought to bear upon each other by an adequate system of reporting. From all of this it is evident that a market is a complex thing. A good market is rare. It does not just grow, as Topsy did. It is the result of intelligent joint effort on the part of its members.

The Manufacturer's Price Problems.— The manufacturer has his own characteristic relation to all of the institutes of commerce. It may perhaps be said that his chief commercial problems revolve around the subject of price. There are three of these problems which merit brief presentation. They are, first, the question of varying the price with the quantity sold; second, the effort to protect dealers' profits by charging different prices to different classes of buyers; third, the project of further protecting such profits by controlling the prices of resale or the prices charged by dealers when they sell to consumers.

Quantity Prices.— It has long been a custom of trade to give to trade buyers who purchase large quantities (case lots, car lots or entire output) a lower price than is accorded to the small buyer. This is justified as a rebate to the large buyer of a portion of the saving in agency expense, bookkeeping, collection expense, etc., which his large order involves for the manufacturer. Upon this saving rests one of the well-known types of economy of production on a large scale. To take advantage of it, a variety of trading organizations has been developed in the United States in recent decades. In the wholesale trade the great interstate jobbers have grown up to hunt for the larger orders, leaving intensive work with the small retailers to the local wholesalers. To equalize the competitive advantage the small wholesalers have, many of them, combined more or less loosely into buying groups pooling their orders in the hands of syndicate buyers. The syndicate buyer maintains buying offices in the larger markets. He either pools the orders sent to him by his patrons into large consolidated orders, or he peddles out large purchases which the financial embarrassments of manufacturers enable him to make at bargain prices. In the retail trade quantity prices have led to the growth of department stores which aim at local mass retail distribution. They have led, also, to the growth of mail order houses, which aim at national mass retail distribution. Finally they have led to the organization of chain store systems which aim to combine mass buying and local small-scale retail distribution. The retail institutions just mentioned not only work for quantity prices but to a considerable extent eliminate the jobber.

The result of the appearance of these quantity-buying, direct-purchasing institutions is that the regular trade — sometimes called "legitimate" — comprising the local wholesalers and the single-line and country-store retailers — has been awakened to hostility. This hostility has taken the form of expressions of opinion on the part of associations of wholesalers and retailers, and of more or less exclusive trading arrangements of the small retailers with those wholesale houses who do not sell to mail order houses and chain stores. It has also taken the form of discrimination against such manufacturer's goods as appear on the shelves of such stores. Inasmuch as the regular trade comprises the overwhelming majority of the merchandising business of the country, these hostile moves have been given respectful attention by the manufacturers. The answering policy of many manufacturers has been to charge one price to all trade buyers, regardless of the quantity purchased. This puts the small store upon an equality, in the first cost of merchandise, with its department store neighbor. Some manufacturers have adopted very elaborate policies for the protection of the small dealer, and have stimulated the antagonism of the small dealer against the large one, in order to pose as a friend and get the business.

It can be seen that excessive reductions of price for quantity tend to concentrate the buying function, as contrasted with the selling end of merchandising. By it buyer and salesman are forced apart. So the local store unit of the retail trade loses flexibility in assembling such stocks as the locality requires. Its stock, as illustrated by the chain-store stock, becomes standardized and a matter of safe staples chiefly. Quantity price operates to the disadvantage of the village and the sub-centres in the outskirts of cities. It is to the advantage of the large stores in down-town metropolitan districts. On the other hand the opposite policy of one price, regardless of quantity, prevents the large city from enjoying the advantage its mass of business entitles it to, and prevents the capable dealer who has built up a large business on merit from enjoying a portion of the advantage his large purchases give to those who supply him. It tends, therefore, to keep alive a large number of small, incompetent establishments based upon the principle of proximity to the consumer.

Classification of Customers.— The second price problem of the manufacturer, to which we have referred, has to do with the necessity of maintaining dealers' profits. Goods flow up hill in price, as water flows down hill. The difference between the price paid by a wholesaler and that paid by his customer who is a retailer is a spread, out of which must come the wholesaler's costs and profits. If a manufacturer sell to a retailer on the same terms as to the wholesaler who has been supplying him, it is obvious that the wholesaler cannot continue to patronize that manufacturer. If in a typical distributive chain we have manufacturer, commission merchant, wholesaler and retailer, there will normally be four price levels, each higher than the other, and each maintained at a certain spread with reference to the others by the normal operation of competition. Into this normal situation a disturbing influence has been introduced by the abnormal growth of certain retail and wholesale institutions, in response to the economy of quantity prices, and in response to superior managerial talent. These large institutions have very naturally tried to change their class as buyers and purchase on the same terms as institutions prior to them in the distributive chain. So we see everywhere retailers who advertise themselves "wholesalers and retailers," to facilitate an approach to manufacturers. It has been found difficult to frame a satisfactory definition of what a wholesaler is. Inasmuch as manufacturers are commonly admitted to buying privileges with other manufacturers and with wholesalers, all small shops and local repair men are anxious to be classed as manufacturers and to buy either from manufacturers' catalogues, or at least from the same traveling salesmen as serve the neighboring retailers. Hotels, likewise, are privileged buyers: therefore restaurants and boarding-houses put themselves forward as much as possible for the same privileges. Dealers and agents are usually advanced one class in the distributive chain: therefore an innumerable number of persons acquire agencies for the sale of wagons, automobiles, windmills and manufactured specialties, for the purpose of purchasing their private supplies at better advantage. Against this tendency to break down the classifications of trade merchants have been obliged to interpose an influence. This they have done by drawing up lists of classified buyers. Such lists are usually formed by the joint action of two trade associations and are promulgated to govern the conduct of the members with reference to the trade classes covered by the definitions.

Control of the Prices of Resale.—A third price problem has been forced upon manufacturers as a result of the intensity of competition between retailers. One of the modern tricks of retail selling is to offer one article or a few articles at a very low price, and feature the prices of these by advertising as "leaders." The psychology of the leader is that the customer will infer from the few low prices quoted that all prices in the store are equally moderate. In practice, the leader is supposed to bring the customer into the store where his cravings will be so intensified by the sight of merchandise that he not only purchases the leader, after which he came, but purchases a variety of other articles as well. These latter carry a good profit and recoup the loss on the leader, so that the result of the total transaction is a profit for the store. The best articles to choose as leaders are those branded or trade-marked articles which are known to be identical in whatever store they may be found. These will bring out in full force the price comparison, free from any possible argument that the quality may be better where the price is higher. When, therefore, a manufacturer builds up a reputation for uniform quality, and his goods become well known, his merchandise best serves the dealer as a leader. It might be concluded that if the dealer lowered the price he would simply sell more goods and so would confer a favor upon the manufacturer. The history of a leader is, however, that after it has served a temporary purpose of attracting attention, it is dropped. As it is impossible to at once restore normal prices for the article, the dealers who once featured it exclude it from stock, or if it have too well an established position with the consumer for this, relegate it to the background so that the losses on it will be as small as possible and push other things in preference to it. Distribution falls off, therefore, and the manufacturer is aroused to action. The action which manufacturers have taken has been along the line of endeavoring to dictate to wholesalers and retailers at what price they may sell, and to whom they may sell, and then to enforce these dictates by cutting off the supply of goods from those dealers who disobey orders. These efforts have brought manufacturers within the pale of the Federal laws which forbid contracts in restraint of trade. A considerable variety of devices has been invented by manufacturers in the endeavor to encumber the title to a movable chattel with restrictions, in connection with its sale, and without creating a bona-fide relation of principal and agent. These devices have been uniformly declared null and void by the United States Supreme Court.

EDWARD D. JONES,
Author of "Administration of Industrial Enterprises."

INDUSTRIAL EDUCATION. See EDUCATION, INDUSTRIAL.

INDUSTRIAL ENGINEERING, a science which has as its basic objective the provision of conditions which will permit the accomplishment of a given task in the least possible time, at the lowest total cost, with the least effort, and with the most satisfaction to the people who must do the work. It is the engineering approach applied to all factors including the human factor involved in the production and distribution of products or services.

Industrial engineering derives its name from the fact that it was first used by industry. Its initial use was largely confined to the factory. Although this continues to be its principal area of application, the industrial engineering approach was later found to be equally valuable in the office and in nonindustrial enterprises such as hospitals, hotels, libraries, and even in agriculture and in the home.

Because almost every activity of a business has its effect on the ultimate cost of the goods or services it produces, it is often difficult to make a clear distinction between industrial engineering and scientific management. In the period which immediately followed the development of scientific management by Fredrick W. Taylor at the beginning of the 20th century, industrial engineering in the language of the factory was considered to be nearly synonymous with time and motion study. With the passing of time, however, the industrial engineer found it desirable to include a consideration of more and more factors in his studies. His interest in quality, for example, led him into the field of quality control. Similarly he came to include among his specific interests such techniques, systems, and procedures as production control, budgets, standard costs, tool design, methods engineering, wage incentives, job evaluation, office procedures, and a host of others. As a background for his activities, he drew upon mechanical engineering, economics, sociology, psychology, philosophy, accountancy, and the like, welding the phases of these sciences which affected his activities into a new science.

It is quite difficult to differentiate between industrial engineering and management engineering. In popular usage, management engineering is considered to be a somewhat broader term including fields such as organization and administration which are not usually felt to be part of industrial engineering. The distinction is not clear cut, however, and the industrial engineer as he grows and broadens his experience is likely to find that he tends to call himself with increasing frequency a management engineer.

In 1943, the Work Standardization Committee of the Management Division of the American Society of Mechanical Engineers began a project of developing definitions for all terms used in the field of industrial engineering. In an attempt to define the limits of this field, the committee prepared the chart shown in slightly altered form by Fig. 1. This chart shows a number of the techniques and procedures which together make up industrial engineering. It will serve as a guide in the discussion which follows. The chart, however, by no means includes all of the techniques which are considered by one or more authorities as legitimately belonging to industrial engineering. Among the techniques and procedures which with some logic could be added to the chart are: production planning and control, inventory control, quality control, top management controls, plant location and construction, production line techniques, product design, office layout, storekeeping procedures, safety engineering, operator training, suggestion systems, and operations research. Even this list does not include everything in which the industrial engineer is interested.

Although the discussion which follows will confine itself largely to the areas shown on the chart, Fig. 1, which may be regarded as the hard core of industrial engineering, the essential broadness of the industrial engineering approach should be recognized. The history of the development of industrial engineering is one of constant growth and broadening. This is illustrated by the fact that in 1920, industrial engineering was taught in very few universities and then usually as a few unrelated elective courses tacked onto a mechanical engineering course. By 1950, 4-year university courses leading to the degree of Industrial Engineering, or B.S. in Industrial Engineering, were by no means uncommon.

Development of Industrial Engineering.— Fredrick W. Taylor, who is often referred to as the father of scientific management, also laid the foundations for much of what later came to be called industrial engineering. In 1882, Taylor was made the foreman of the machine shop of the Midvale Steel Company near Philadelphia, Pa. He soon recognized that the men whom he supervised were producing only a fraction of what they could produce. Since Taylor was responsible for the efficient operation of his department, this disturbed him, and he began to search for ways of increasing the productivity of his people. At length, he developed a procedure which he described at a meeting of the American Society of Mechanical Engineers in 1903 in a classic paper entitled "Shop Management."

Among other things, Taylor developed a system of time study and finally a formula for getting maximum production. His formula was: *The greatest production results when each worker is given a definite task to be performed in a definite time and in a definite manner.* Modern industrial engineering is based upon this formula, and although the procedures for accomplishing it have been increasingly expanded, developed, and refined with each passing year, the formula is still as fundamental for high productivity as it was when Taylor first advanced it.

In Taylor's time, the *definite task* was specified after a study of the job had determined the best operation sequence. The *definite time* was established by stop watch time study or from standard time data based on time study. The *definite manner*—that is, the method—was developed by painstaking experimentation and was recorded for the information of the worker and his foreman on an instruction card.

Taylor, stimulated in part at least by the work of Frank B. and Lillian M. Gilbreth in the field of motion study, recognized the importance of method. His accounts of pig iron handling, metal cutting, and the like are classic examples of early

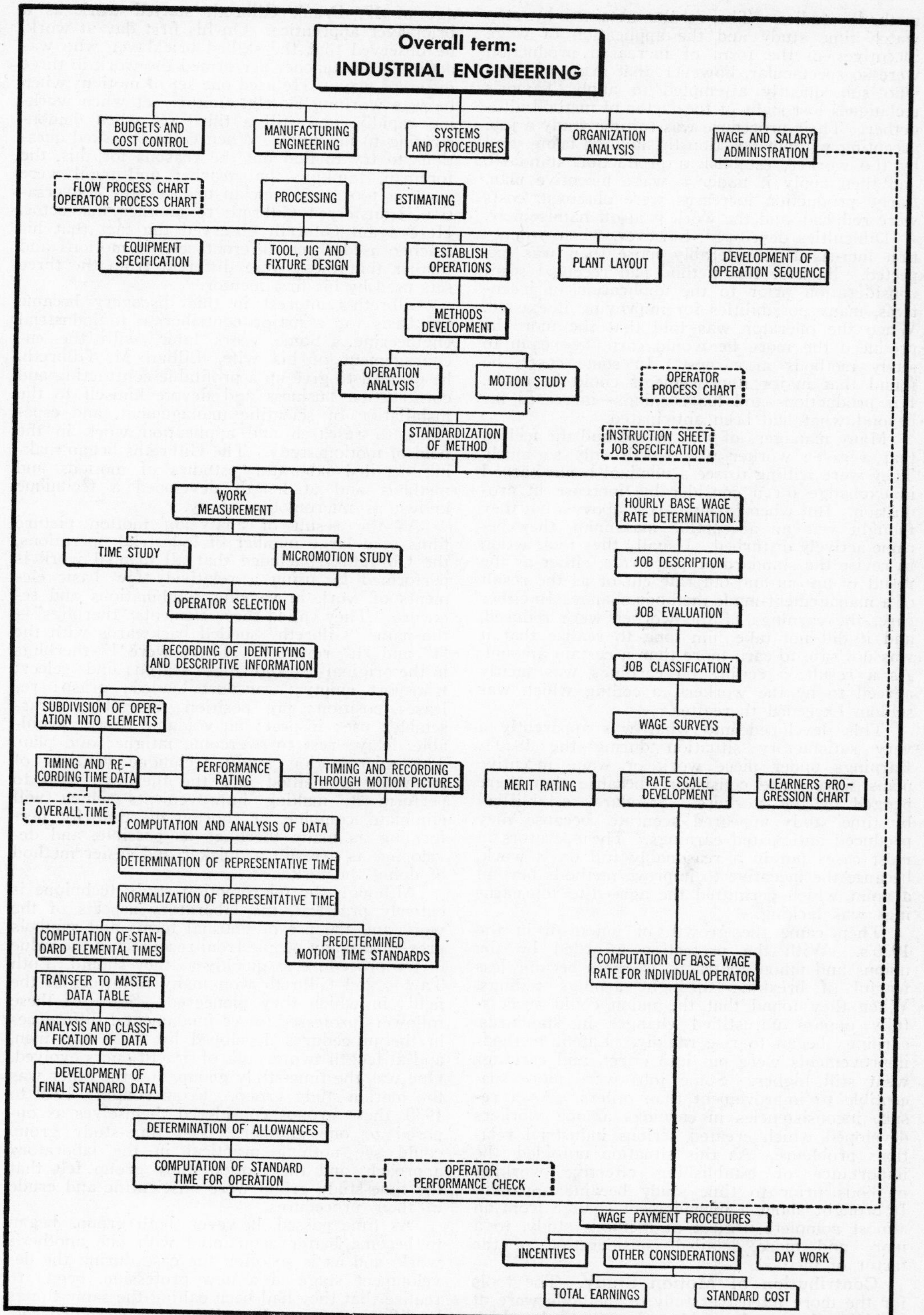

Fig. 1. Chart of techniques and procedures commonly included in industrial engineering.

methods studies. The results obtained by stop watch time study and the application of wage incentives in the form of increased production were so spectacular, however, that many of those who subsequently attempted to apply Taylor's techniques lost sight of the factor of method altogether. Their procedure was to time study a job, accepting without question the method being used by the worker, establish a production standard, and then apply it under a wage incentive plan. Large production increases were obtained, costs were reduced, and the work paid off handsomely.

Difficulties developed, however, when production increased considerably more than was expected. Because the method had received scant consideration prior to the application of incentives, many possibilities for improving it existed. When the operator was told that the more he produced the more he would earn, he began to study methods in earnest. In some cases, he found that major improvements could be made. His production—and his earnings—increased far beyond what had been anticipated.

Many managers of that period had the feeling that a given worker was worth only so much. They were willing to see a nominal bonus earned in exchange for a considerable increase in production. But when earnings rose above what they thought was an acceptable maximum, they became actively disturbed. Usually they took action to revise the standard or piece rate, either as the result of an out-and-out rate cut or as the result of a management-made methods change. In either case, the earnings of the worker were reduced, and it did not take him long to realize that it was not safe to earn more than a certain amount. As a result, a ceiling on earnings was tacitly agreed to by the workers, a ceiling which was seldom exceeded thereafter.

This developed into what was apparently a very satisfactory situation during the 1920's. Earnings under piece work or wage incentive plans were quite consistent—because they were pegged by the workers. Standards established by time study appeared accurate, because they produced anticipated earnings. The operators in most cases put in a reasonably full day's work, because the incentive to improve methods beyond a point which permitted the agreed-to top earnings was lacking.

Then came the growth of unionism in the 1930's. With the protection afforded by the unions and union contracts, workers became less fearful of breaking through earnings ceilings. When they found that the union could successfully oppose unjustified changes in standards, earnings began to rise rapidly. Latent methods improvements were put into effect, and earnings went still higher. Some jobs were more susceptible to improvement than others. As a result, inconsistencies in earnings among workers developed which created serious industrial relations problems. As this situation unfolded, the importance of establishing effective working methods prior to time study became apparent. It brought about a management change from an almost complete neglect of methods study, to a more and more detailed consideration of the factor of method.

Contribution of Motion Study.—The tools for the more intensive study of methods were at hand as the result of the pioneer work which had been done by Frank B. and Lillian M. Gilbreth in the field of motion study. In 1885 at the age of 17, Frank Gilbreth started work as a bricklayer apprentice. On his first day at work, he observed that the skilled bricklayer who was acting as his teacher performed the work in three different ways. He used one set of motions when he was working slowly, another set when working rapidly, and still a third set when demonstrating to his pupil. When Gilbreth asked questions to try to find out the reasons for this, the foreman, thinking that teacher and pupil were wasting too much time in unnecessary conversation, transferred Gilbreth to another instructor. Here again Gilbreth observed the fact that his teacher used three different sets of motions and further that these were different from the three sets used by his first mentor.

Gilbreth's interest in this discovery became the basis for a major contribution to industrial engineering. Some years later, with the encouragement of his wife, Lillian M. Gilbreth, he decided to give up a profitable contracting and construction business and devote himself to the installation of scientific management, and especially to research and application work in the field of motion study. The Gilbreths began making detailed laboratory studies of motions and methods and at length developed a technique known as micromotion study.

As the result of analyzing motion picture films of a large number of industrial operations, the Gilbreths concluded that all manual work is performed by using a relatively few basic elements of work in varying combinations and sequence. They called these elements "therbligs"—the name "Gilbreth" spelled backwards with the "t" and "h" reversed. There were 17 therbligs in the original list known as: search; find; select; transport empty; transport loaded; grasp; release; position; pre position; assemble; disassemble; use; inspect; unavoidable delay; avoidable delay; rest to overcome fatigue; and plan. The micromotion study technique consists of analyzing a method into the therbligs used to perform it, making improvements which will eliminate, combine, or shorten the time for performing as many therbligs as possible, and developing as a result a quicker and easier method of doing the task.

Although the micromotion study technique is entirely practical, the laboratory aspects of the work and the use of unusual terms and symbols prevented many people from recognizing the value of the procedure as quickly as they should. Both Taylor and Gilbreth won many followers in the fields in which they pioneered. Some of these followers professed to see fundamental differences in the procedures developed by these two men, and at length two groups of practitioners evolved. One was the time-study group, and the other was the motion-study group. From roughly 1910 to 1930, these groups considered themselves as opposed to one another. The time-study group could see nothing practical in the laboratory approach, and the motion-study group felt that the time-study group were unscientific and crude in their procedures.

As time passed, however, both groups began to become better acquainted with one another's work, and as is so often the case during the development stage of a new profession, began to realize that they had been calling the same things by different names. The differences were dropped, and the best features of both procedures were combined into an integrated procedure, which the author of this article and his associates in 1933 called for the first time as far as they know by the name "methods engineering."

The definition of methods engineering which they developed to explain this new term illustrates how the techniques which are the core of industrial engineering were beginning to form a logical pattern. According to this definition, "methods engineering is the technique that subjects each operation of a given piece of work to close analysis in order to eliminate every unnecessary operation and in order to approach the quickest and best method of performing each necessary operation; it includes the standardization of equipment, methods, and working conditions; it trains the operator to follow the standard method; when all this has been done, and not before, it determines by accurate measurement the number of standard hours in which an operator working with standard performance can do the job; finally it usually, although not necessarily, devises a plan for compensating labor which encourages the operator to attain or to surpass standard performance."

Major interest in methods improvement work began to develop in 1930. The United States of America was headed for the depths of the worst depression in its history. Business was almost at a standstill. A buyer's market existed, and competition was strictly on a price basis. Anything which would result in cost reductions was eagerly sought. Hence management was in a receptive mood for techniques which would improve methods. At this same time, the more advanced time study technicians were becoming aware of the incompleteness of their procedures as was pointed out above. Thus the time was ripe for the acceptance of methods study techniques.

In 1932, a book *Common Sense Applied to Motion and Time Study* by Allen H. Mogensen was published. This combined several articles by various men interested in methods study work with some of Mogensen's own experiences in what he presently began to call "work simplification" and gave one of the first coordinated presentations of the methods study practices which had been developed up to that point. Following this came an increasing number of other books, all stressing the importance of methods study. Among the more widely distributed books of this period were *Time and Motion Study and Formulas for Wage Incentives,* by Lowry, Maynard, and Stegemerten, 2d edition 1932, 3d edition 1940; *Motion and Time Study* by Ralph M. Barnes, 1937, 2d edition 1940; *Time Study for Cost Control* by Phil Carroll, Jr., 1938; *Applied Time and Motion Study* by Walter G. Holmes, 1938; and *Operation Analysis* by Maynard and Stegemerten, 1939.

The development of techniques of application of methods engineering and work simplification principles progressed rapidly from 1930 on. At the beginning of this period, the value of process charts, the questioning attitude, micromotion study, and the like as tools of methods improvement were fairly well recognized, but their application during a given methods study was likely to be unsystematic. Too many technicians tended to conduct their studies by concentrating on the correction of obvious inefficiencies, frequently overlooking greater possibilities for improvement. In effect, they often established efficient methods for doing unnecessary work.

Recognition of this caused the leaders in the field to develop a more systematic approach in the application of methods improvement techniques. The "operation analysis" procedure organized upon the principle of considering first things first was one example of this. It emphasized that there are nine major points or factors which should be considered for every operation studied. These, arranged in logical sequence, are as follows:

(1) Purpose of operation
(2) Relation of operation to other operations performed on the part
(3) Inspection requirements
(4) Material
(5) Material handling
(6) Workplace layout and tool equipment
(7) Common possibilities for methods improvement
(8) Working conditions
(9) Method

The "questioning attitude" tool—that is, deliberately asking why, where, when, what, who, and how about every detail of an operation—a tool used since the time of Taylor and Gilbreth, was expanded to include lists of practical questions to be applied to every step of operation analysis and even to every therblig.

These and similar developments helped to increase the effectiveness of methods improvement activities. The guiding principle of the industrial engineer became "with sufficient study, any method can be improved." Experience showed that this was literally true. The improvements were not always economically justified, but they were possible. Even after a job had been motion studied and improved, it often was possible to improve it still further as the result of more intensive study during which the problem was tackled afresh. A series of improvements could be made until the economics of the situation made further study unprofitable.

Methods improvement activities of this type resulted in many worthwhile economies and contributed importantly to increasing productivity wherever they were applied. They also introduced the problem of technological change and created tensions between management and the workers. The term "methods improvement" implies that an ineffective method is already in existence at the time the study is begun. The industrial engineer studies it, identifies unnecessary or ineffective motions, and by eliminating them improves the method. In effect, he corrects the mistakes which were made when the method was originally developed. His work is methods correction rather than methods engineering. Recognition of this fact led to the next important development in industrial engineering.

Predetermined Motion Time Standards.— It was repeatedly observed that human nature is such that it resists change. Thus when the industrial engineer sought to improve methods by changing old methods into better new methods, he frequently caused resistance or at least resentment on the part of the worker. His work which resulted in increased standards of living for society as a whole and hence was thoroughly desirable at the same time generated human relations problems which it would be better to avoid if possible. They could be avoided, however, only if methods were studied and improved before a job was put into production instead of after.

To do this, it became necessary to develop a somewhat different technique than time and motion study. What the industrial engineer needed, if he was to develop an effective method for doing a job before production started, was a procedure which would tell him how long it would take to perform any motion sequence he might be able to visualize without having first to train an operator to follow it and then to time it with a stop watch. The use of predetermined motion time standards proved to be the solution to this problem.

The idea of predetermined motion time standards had been attractive to industrial engineers from the very beginning. Taylor visualized a handbook in which the time for performing "every element in every trade" would be listed. Gilbreth spoke of a "range of time" in which each therblig could be performed.

The first practical attempt to develop predetermined motion time standards was made by A. B. Segur, a consulting engineer, prior to 1930. The results of his researches, however, were made available only to his clients so that his system of "motion time analysis" was imperfectly understood by the industrial engineering profession and its applications were limited. At the same time, the procedure when applied by properly trained engineers met with considerable success and helped to focus attention on the value of the predetermined motion time standard approach.

A somewhat similar procedure was developed by three industrial engineers of the Radio Corporation of America. An article by these three, "Motion Time Standards," by J. H. Quick, W. J. Shea, and R. E. Koehler, which appeared in the magazine, *Factory Management and Maintenance,* in 1945, gave a partial description of their procedure which they called the "Work Factor System." One of the major advantages which they pointed out for their system was that it eliminated the use of the stop watch in determining the time required to do manual work.

A third development in the field of predetermined motion time standards came as the direct result of seeking a solution to the human relations problem mentioned above. At the suggestion of the author, the Westinghouse Electric Corporation sponsored a study beginning in 1940 which led to the development of what is now called the "methods-time measurement procedure" or MTM. It was thought at first that it might be possible to develop a "methods formula" for various classes of work which would make it possible to establish an effective method without having to study an existing job. Accordingly an intensive study was made of sensitive drill-press work. When motion time data were at length compiled, it was found that they applied not only to sensitive drill-press work but to manual work of all kinds, because the same motions were used, as Gilbreth originally pointed out, "in varying combinations and sequence" throughout industry. The research was based on the therblig breakdown of micromotion study, although it was found necessary to redefine several of the basic elements in order to permit the exact measurement of time.

The procedure after several years of careful testing was described for the benefit of the industrial engineering profession in the book *Methods-Time Measurement* by Maynard, Stegemerten, and Schwab published in 1948. It attracted almost immediate attention because the need for such a procedure had long been clearly recognized. The magazine *Fortune* in its October 1949 issue published an article entitled "Timing a Fair Day's Work" which gave a popular explanation of the MTM procedure. The tables of predetermined motion time standards which they published to show how the procedure works are reproduced here as Fig. 2.

Industrial Engineering and the Worker.— From the very beginning, industrial workers took a keen interest in industrial engineering because it influenced nearly every phase of their industrial lives. The industrial engineer designed the methods and motion patterns they had to follow to do their work successfully. He trained them to use these methods or at least saw that they were properly trained. He influenced the conditions under which the work was done. He established the time which was allowed for doing the work and established the allowances given for rest, delays, and personal necessities. Finally he often influenced the amount which the worker earned through job evaluation and the application of wage incentives.

Since both industrial engineers and workers are human beings, it was inevitable that there would be a variety of relationships and attitudes among them ranging from complete distrust and hostility to full confidence and respect for one another's viewpoints. Thus it is impossible to say that "labor's attitude is thus and so" and have it be universally true. There has been a variety of attitudes from the beginning, some justified and some unjustified.

Speaking in terms of trends and recognizing that there are always many, many exceptions, it is probably safe to say that the early reactions of the workers to industrial engineering and scientific management were largely emotional. In spite of Taylor's assurances that scientific management resulted in a new emphasis on the importance of the individual workman, there was a tendency to fear it as a device which would reduce the worker to the status of a robot. The stop watch was looked upon as an inhuman mechanism designed to force workers to work at a pace which would quickly wear them out. This emotional attitude which was reflected in much of the management literature prior to 1920 finally caused the Congress of the United States of America to write into its appropriations bills for the Army and Navy in 1915 a clause prohibiting the use of the stop watch and the use of incentives in any Army or Navy installation. This ban persisted for 36 years.

It must be recognized that there was a certain justification for a distrust of industrial engineering. Inept or unscrupulous managements had demonstrated all too clearly that the stop watch could be used to the detriment of the worker. In a few instances, time studies were made secretly, standards were carelessly and inaccurately set, rates were cut when earnings reached a certain level, and the workers were unreasonably speeded up. The malpractices of a few managements damaged the reputation of industrial engineering out of all proportion to their numerical importance.

In addition, the period during and immediately following World War I witnessed the mushrooming into prominence of a number of self-styled "efficiency experts." Among them were a number of unqualified, untrained, unethical individuals who by misapplying a technique which they did not understand did much to damage the name of industrial engineering and to retard its application.

METHODS-TIME MEASUREMENT APPLICATION DATA

MEC FORM 204

R14B

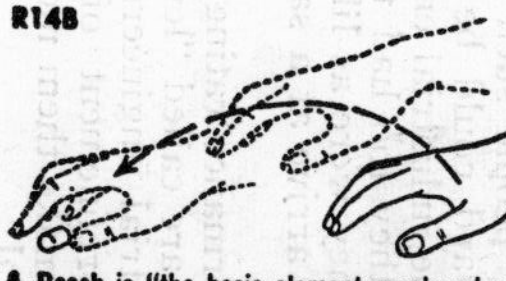

A Reach is "the basic element employed when the predominant purpose is to move the hand to a destination or general location." R14B is M.T.M. code for a Reach fourteen inches long, case B, taking 14.4 T.M.U.'s (Time Measurement Units) or .000144 hour.

M12C

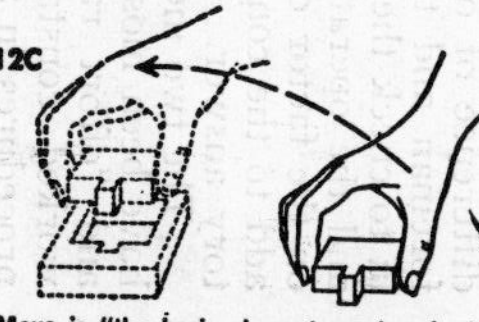

A Move is "the basic element employed when the predominant purpose is to transport an object to a destination." Case C moves are common on assembly operations. Skilled workers often develop faster Moves and Reaches involving "Hand in Motion." Weight factors have proved accurate.

T120°S

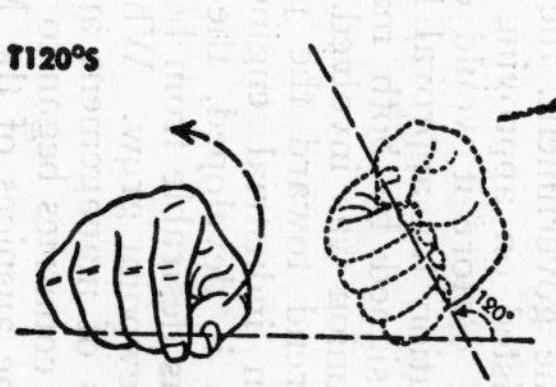

A Turn is "the motion employed to turn the hand either empty or loaded by a movement that rotates the hand, wrist, and forearm about the long axis of the forearm." The "Apply Pressure" motion is listed here because it was first observed in turning screws down tight.

TABLE I—REACH

Case	DESCRIPTION	Distance Moved Inches	A Std.	A Hand in Motion	A with C D or B	B Hand in Motion	C or D	E
A	Reach to object in fixed location, or to object in other hand or on which other hand rests.	1	1.8	1.3	2.1	1.5	3.6	1.7
		2	3.7	2.8	4.3	2.7	5.9	3.8
		3	5.0	3.8	5.9	3.6	7.3	5.3
		4	6.1	4.9	7.1	4.3	8.4	6.8
B	Reach to single object in location which may vary slightly from cycle to cycle.	5	6.5	5.3	7.8	5.0	9.4	7.4
		6	7.0	5.7	8.6	5.7	10.1	8.0
		7	7.4	6.1	9.3	6.5	10.8	8.7
		8	7.9	6.5	10.1	7.2	11.5	9.3
C	Reach to object in group.	9	8.3	6.9	10.8	7.9	12.2	9.9
		10	8.7	7.3	11.5	8.6	12.9	10.5
		[illegible]	9.6	8.1	[illegible]	10.1	14.2	11.8
D	Reach to very small object or where accurate grasp is required.	14	10.5	8.9	14.4	11.5	15.6	13.0
		[illegible]	11.4	9.7	15.8	12.9	17.0	14.2
		18	12.3	10.5	17.2	14.4	18.4	15.5
		20	13.1	11.3	18.6	15.8	19.8	16.7
E	Reach to indefinite location to get hand in position for body balance or next motion or out of way.	22	14.0	12.1	20.1	17.3	21.2	18.0
		24	14.9	12.9	21.5	18.8	22.5	19.2
		26	15.8	13.7	22.9	20.2	23.9	20.4
		28	16.7	14.5	24.4	21.7	25.3	21.7
		30	17.5	15.3	25.8	23.2	26.7	22.9

TABLE II—MOVE

Case	DESCRIPTION	Distance Moved Inches	A	B or E	C	D-B Hand in Motion	Multiplying Factor: Weight	Multiplying Factor: Factor
A	Move object against stop.	1	1.7	1.7	1.7	1.5	Up to 5#	1.00
		2	3.6	4.2	4.2	2.7		
		3	4.9	5.7	5.7	3.6		
		4	6.1	6.9	7.3	4.3	10#	1.03
B	Move object to approximate location.	5	7.3	8.0	8.7	5.0		
		6	8.1	8.9	9.7	5.7	15#	1.05
		7	8.9	9.7	10.8	6.5		
		8	9.7	10.6	11.8	7.2	20#	1.08
C	Move object to exact location.	9	10.5	11.5	12.7	7.9		
		[illegible]	11.3	12.2	[illegible]	8.6	25#	1.11
		12	12.9	13.4	15.2	10.0		
		[illegible]	14.4	14.6	[illegible]	11.4	30#	1.14
D	Toss object aside.	16	16.0	15.8	18.7	12.8		
		18	17.6	17.0	20.4	14.2	35#	1.16
		20	19.2	18.2	22.1	15.6		
E	Move object to indefinite location.	22	20.8	19.4	23.8	17.0	40#	1.19
		24	22.4	20.6	25.5	18.4		
		26	24.0	21.8	27.3	19.8	45#	1.22
		28	25.6	23.1	29.0	21.2		
		30	27.1	24.3	30.7	22.7	50#	1.25

TABLE III—TURN

Degrees Turned	Leveled T.M.U.	Degrees Turned	Leveled T.M.U.
30°	2.8	120°	6.8
45°	[illegible]	[illegible]	7.4
60°	4.1	150°	8.1
75°	4.8	165°	8.7
90°	5.4	180°	9.4
105°	6.1		

SMALL: No load or parts up to 2 pounds—Use table value.
MEDIUM: Loads from 2.1 to 10 pounds—Use 1.57 x table value.
LARGE: Loads from 10.1 to 35 pounds—Use 3.0 x table value.

APPLY PRESSURE 16.2 T.M.U.

TURN is a special case of REACH or MOVE. It is accomplished by a turning or torsional motion, during which the hand and wrist turn. When TURN is combined with a normal REACH or MOVE, determine time for TURN and REACH or MOVE from the tables and use the larger value.

TABLE IV—GRASP

Case	DESCRIPTION	Leveled T.M.U.
1a	Pick up Grasp—Small, medium, or large object by itself, easily grasped.	1.7
1b	Very small object or [illegible]	[illegible]
1c	Interference with Grasp on bottom and one side of object.	8.7
2	Regrasp	5.6
3	Transfer Grasp	5.6
4	Object jumbled with other objects so that Search and Select occur.	8.7
5	Contact, sliding or hook Grasp.	0

TABLE V—POSITION*

CLASS OF FIT		Easy to Handle: Symmetrical	Easy to Handle: Semi-Symm.	Easy to Handle: Non-Symm.	Difficult to Handle: Symmetrical	Difficult to Handle: Semi-Symm.	Difficult to Handle: Non-Symm.
1—Loose	No pressure required.	5.6	9.1	10.4	11.2	14.7	16.0
2—Close	Light pressure required.	16.2	19.7	[illegible]	21.8	25.3	26.6
3—Exact	Heavy pressure required.	43.0	46.5	47.8	48.6	52.1	53.4

SYMMETRICAL—Object can be positioned in an infinite number of ways about the axis which coincides with the direction of travel.

SEMI-SYMMETRICAL—Object can be positioned in several ways about the axis which coincides with the direction of travel.

NON-SYMMETRICAL—Object can be positioned in only one way about the axis which coincides with the direction of travel.

*Distance moved to engage—1" or less.

TABLE VI—DISENGAGE

CLASS OF FIT	Easy to Handle	Difficult to Handle
1—Loose Very slight effort—Blends with subsequent move.	4.0	5.7
2—Close Normal effort—Slight recoil.	7.5	11.8
3—Tight Considerable effort—Hand recoils markedly.	22.9	34.7

TABLE VII—RELEASE

Case	DESCRIPTION	Leveled Time T.M.U.
1	Normal Release performed by opening fingers as independent motion.	1.7
2	Contact Release.	0

TABLE VIII—BODY, LEG, AND FOOT MOTIONS

DESCRIPTION	Distance	Leveled Time T.M.U.
Foot Motion—Hinged at Ankle.	Up to 4"	8.5
For heavy pressure add.		19.6
Leg or Foreleg Motion.	Up to 6"	7.1
	Each add'l. inch	1.2
Sidestep—Case 1—Complete when leading leg contacts floor.	Less than 12"	Use Reach or Move Time
	12"	17.0
	Each add'l. inch	.6
Case 2—Lagging leg must contact floor before next motion can be made.	12"	34.1
	Each add'l. inch	1.1
Bend, Stoop, or Kneel on One Knee.		29.0
Arise.		31.9
Kneel on Floor—Both Knees.		69.4
Arise.		76.7
Sit.		34.7
Stand from Sitting Position.		43.4
Turn Body 45° to 90°—Case 1—Complete when leading leg contacts floor.		18.6
Case 2—Lagging leg must contact floor before next motion can be made.		37.2
Walk.	Per Foot	5.3

1 T.M.U. = .00001 hour = .0006 minute = .036 second

METHODS ENGINEERING COUNCIL
822 WOOD STREET PITTSBURGH 21, PA.

G1a

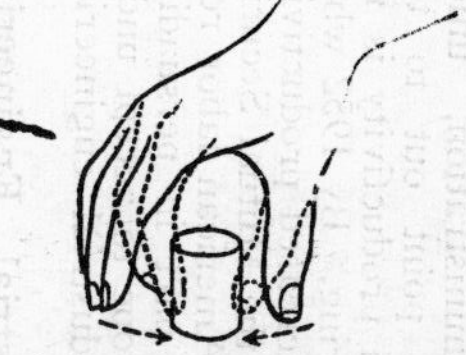

A Grasp is "the basic element employed when the predominant purpose is to secure sufficient control of one or more objects with the fingers or the hand to permit the performance of the next required basic element." Regrasp, first found by M.T.M., occurs when the hand shifts its grip.

P1NSE

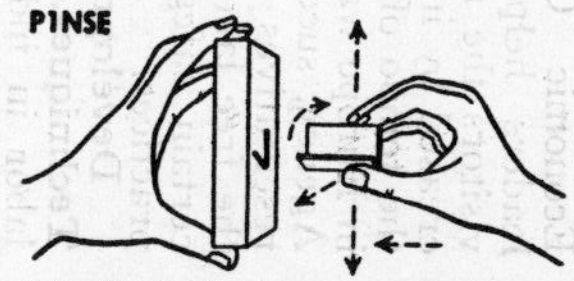

A Position is "the basic element employed to align, orient, and engage one object with another object where motions used are so minor they do not justify classification as other basic elements." Position shown is "Easy to Handle" because object is grasped close to point of engagement.

D2D

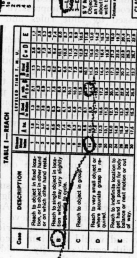

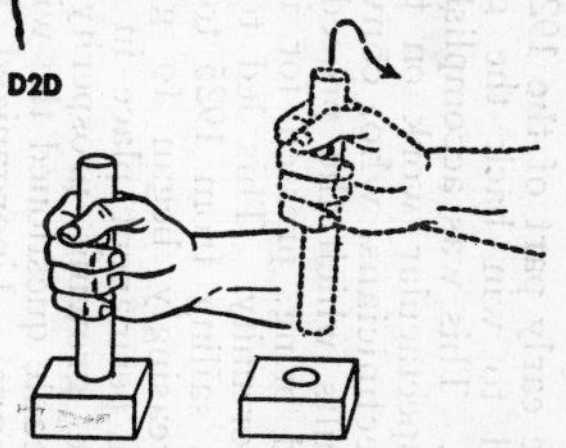

A Disengage is "the basic element employed to break the contact between one object and another, and it is characterized by an involuntary movement occasioned by the sudden ending of resistance." If the hand recoils more than five inches, the fit is considered to be "tight."

Adapted, with permission, from article on methods-time measurement by Perrin Stryker, *Fortune*, October 1949.

Hand studies based on drawings in *Methods-Time Measurement*, by H. B. Maynard, G. J. Stegemerten, and J. L. Schwab; McGraw-Hill Book Co., Inc.

FIG. 2. Simplified explanation of methods-time measurement procedure.

During the early part of the 1920's, industrial engineers had to win back the ground which had been lost. This was accomplished by sound, relatively unspectacular work on the part of a number of technicians, who, convinced of the beneficial results which the procedure, properly applied would bring, pressed for its application at every opportunity. This led to a period of fairly smooth sailing from 1925 to 1930. Management increasingly began to give industrial engineering a permanent place in the organization. In the growing prosperity of the late 1920's, few people questioned the wisdom of technological change. Unorganized labor in fact accepted it as a part of the normal development which was carrying the United States to an undreamed of level of material prosperity. The workers insisted that industrial engineering should be applied fairly and competently, but they raised little objection to any sound work which the industrial engineer wished to do.

In 1930, attitudes began to change again. The growing depression brought fears of unemployment. Suddenly security came to be the thing to be desired above all others. Instead of higher earnings—the factor which had gained acceptance for wage incentives up to that time—steady earnings seemed more important. With only a limited amount of work to be done, many workers began to feel that instead of doing it more quickly, making higher earnings temporarily, and then getting laid off, it was better to do the work more slowly so that it would last longer.

Shortly after 1933 under the encouragement given by the National Industrial Relations Act, unions began to grow in size and strength. In order to attract new members, it became expedient to attack management's activities, to produce grievances, real or imagined, and to promise the workers an immediate improvement in their lot if they would join the union. Industrial engineering lent itself well to attacks inspired by political considerations, and the popular union attitude was to oppose industrial engineering and related practices.

Management's answer to this was to attempt to "educate" its workers with respect to the purposes and fairness of industrial engineering. Courses in work simplification, time and motion study, and the like were held in which the participation of union representatives was invited. This trend fitted in well with labor's desire to have a greater say in the affairs of management. As they learned more about industrial engineering, they asked to have a part in the establishing of standards. They took a keen interest in all matters pertaining to wage incentives and began to have a great deal to say about plans currently in effect and new plans proposed by management. During World War II when wages were controlled by the government, the War Production Board insisted on approving all new wage incentive plans. Before it would consider a new plan, an application for approval had to be submitted jointly signed by both management and the union if a union was involved.

Thus the trend toward the participation of the workers in industrial engineering matters continued. As it developed, the acceptance of the procedure as desirable from both a social and an economic viewpoint grew. When after World War II groups of management and labor people from European countries began to visit the United States under the auspices of the Marshall Plan's Economic Cooperation Administration, union leaders helped management point out to the visitors the manner in which productivity is increased by industrial engineering. By 1952 when the tempo of the drive for increased productivity in Europe was stepped up by the Mutual Security Agency, successor to ECA, American labor representatives took a leading part in persuading the free labor unions of Europe to accept under certain safeguards sound industrial engineering practices.

Development of Industrial Engineering Techniques.—This keen interest on the part of labor in industrial engineering forced the constant improvement of industrial engineering procedures. For example, the most controversial step in the time study procedure is the one which involves "performance rating." The object of time study is to develop a time standard for doing a specified task which can be met by a qualified operator giving an average or normal performance. If the operator who is being time studied is working at the normal performance level, this is a simple matter. The time obtained from the study is the normal performance time and hence is the desired standard. But when the operator works at a pace which is slower or faster than normal performance, it is necessary to adjust the time values determined by time study to the normal level.

There have been a number of methods used for doing this. The earliest methods were purely mathematical. They called for adjusting the raw time study data by a series of elaborate computations until finally a calculated standard was obtained. The processes were impressive to those who are impressed by slide rules and mathematical computations, but they were for the most part meaningless as industrial engineers soon began to realize. The best of the mathematical procedures were based on the assumption that skilled operators performed each cycle of a repetitive operation in exactly the same time—or in other words were consistent in their performance times—which even casual observation showed was by no means the case. Other mathematical procedures did not have even this much logic behind them. They were all eventually discarded by industrial engineers in favor of procedures which require the time study observer to judge how well or how poorly the operator is working—known as performance rating.

Because performance rating is a subjective procedure involving the element of judgment, it often became a matter of controversy. An industrial engineer could sincerely believe that an operator was giving a below normal performance during a study and would rate him accordingly. The operator with equal sincerity could believe that he was giving a better than normal performance. There was no easy way of resolving this difference of opinion. Other people such as the foreman and the union steward could be called in to check the opinions of the industrial engineer and the operator, but since they too had to rely on the factor of judgment, they were as likely to add to the controversy as to arrive at a satisfactory answer.

The two methods of performance rating which have been most widely used are called "leveling" and "effort rating." Industrial engineers have worked constantly on the refinement of these procedures in an attempt to make them more objective and less controversial.

The leveling method of performance rating was developed in 1925 by Lowry, Maynard, and Stegemerten as an outgrowth of the book they were writing at that time on time and motion study. None of the then existing methods of arriving at standards representing average or normal performance seemed satisfactory to them when they attempted to describe them in their book. Therefore, they set aside their writing for a year and conducted a research study on performance rating.

The first step was to establish criteria for judging performance. The factors which were chosen after study and analysis as affecting performance most importantly were skill—or proficiency at following a given method; effort—or will to work; conditions—i.e., working conditions; and consistency. Skill and effort were seen to have the greatest effect. The range of useful skill and effort was divided into six classes: poor, fair, average, good, excellent, and super skill; and poor, fair, average, good, excellent, and excessive effort.

Each degree of skill and effort was next carefully defined. Average performance was considered to be the equivalent of the fair day's work which is to be received in exchange for a fair day's pay. It represented the effort level which could easily be maintained year in and year out by the physically normal operator without in any way requiring him to draw upon his reserves of energy. It was a pace which appeared somewhat slow when observed and which could be accelerated without too much difficulty under the encouragement of a wage incentive plan.

The operator considered to be giving an average performance with respect to skill was one qualified to do the job who had been at the work long enough to do it without undue hesitation, planning, or errors. He was not noticeably good at doing the job, but neither was he noticeably poor.

When all skill and effort levels had been carefully defined, the cooperation of approximately 175 time study engineers was obtained to determine by actual observation how much time was increased or decreased by performances below and above average. After a year of collecting data, the table shown by Fig. 3 was developed. The "leveling factors" added to 1.00 result in a multiplier which was used to adjust time data obtained during time study to the average performance level.

The effort rating procedure as it is most commonly used rates performance by judging speed of motions. The observed speed is compared with a mental concept of normal speed, and an adjustment factor is arrived at accordingly. If the observer believes that the operator is working 25 per cent faster than the normal pace, he multiplies the time data obtained from a time study of that operator by 1.25 to arrive at the normal time for doing the work.

Both of these procedures and the several variations which stem from them which have been used by industrial engineers required the use of judgment in rating observed performance. In order to improve the consistency with which industrial engineers rated performance, the Society for the Advancement of Management in 1943 set up a Committee on the Rating of Time Studies to study the problem of performance rating and to determine what could be done to improve existing procedures. The committee decided that

Skill			Effort		
+0.15	A1	Superskill	+0.13	A1	Excessive
+0.13	A2		+0.12	A2	
+0.11	B1	Excellent	+0.10	B1	Excellent
+0.08	B2		+0.08	B2	
+0.06	C1	Good	+0.05	C1	Good
+0.03	C2		+0.02	C2	
0.00	D	Average	0.00	D	Average
−0.05	E1	Fair	−0.04	E1	Fair
−0.10	E2		−0.08	E2	
−0.16	F1	Poor	−0.12	F1	Poor
−0.22	F2		−0.17	F2	
Conditions			**Consistency**		
+0.06	A	Ideal	+0.04	A	Perfect
+0.04	B	Excellent	+0.03	B	Excellent
+0.02	C	Good	+0.01	C	Good
0.00	D	Average	0.00	D	Average
−0.03	E	Fair	−0.02	E	Fair
−0.07	F	Poor	−0.04	F	Poor

FIG. 3. Leveling factors for performance rating.

rather than attempting to develop a new procedure, it could perform the greatest service by developing a set of standards against which any industrial engineer could check his own concept of normal and determine in general how he was rating performance in comparison with other industrial engineers.

Aided financially by industrial companies who appreciated the seriousness of the performance rating problem, the committee prepared a number of motion pictures of people working at various performance levels. They had these motion pictures rated under carefully controlled conditions by over 1,200 experienced time study engineers. Statistical treatment of the resulting data provided a series of bench marks against which any individual engineer could check his own concepts of performance levels. The motion picture films were made available for purchase by industrial companies to be used for training purposes. They proved to be an aid in improving the consistency with which a group of engineers judged performance and were used with good effect in developing a common concept of normal performance among industrial engineers, supervisors, and operators.

The effort to improve and refine industrial engineering techniques was by no means confined to the United States. In the field of performance rating, for example, important studies were made and reported upon in 1950 by engineers in Switzerland and France. In the field of predetermined motion time standards—where incidentally the problem of performance rating is largely eliminated—although the major developments came out of the United States, important contributions to the general fund of knowledge about motions and motion times were made in England, France, Holland, and Germany.

The fact that industrial engineering is used throughout the world presents a continuing problem in international standardization. Problems in terminology became so serious, for example, that in 1950 the International Committee on Scientific Management, CIOS, set up a subcommittee on the Standardization of Management

Terminology to begin work on eliminating what had been called "Management's Tower of Babel."

In the United States, similar activities were undertaken to bring a better degree of standardization and understanding to the industrial engineering field. The terminology project of the Work Standardization Committee of the American Society of Mechanical Engineers (ASME) has already been mentioned. This same society in 1941 established a Committee for the Standardization of Therbligs, Process Charts, and Their Symbols. Some idea of the difficulties of bringing about standardization in a vigorous and rapidly expanding field like industrial engineering may be gained from the fact that this committee worked six years, held innumerable meetings, and carried on lengthy correspondence with numerous industrial engineering authorities in the United States and Canada before it felt ready in 1947 to publish its first ASME Standard on *Operation and Flow Process Charts.*

Such activities, however, difficult as they are, have helped to develop the "universal language" which is so essential in scientific fields. The first page of the ASME Standard on *Operation and Flow Process Charts* illustrates how clear definitions and standardized symbols and terminology have sharpened this particular tool of industrial engineering. It reads as follows:

SECTION 1 PROCESS CHART

Definitions

1. *Process Chart.* A process chart is a graphic representation of events and information pertaining thereto occurring during a series of actions or operations.
2. *Operation Process Chart.* An operation process chart is a graphic representation of the points at which materials are introduced into the process and of the sequence of inspections and all operations except those involved in material handling. It includes information considered desirable for analysis such as time required and location.
3. *Flow Process Chart.* A flow process chart is a graphic representation of the sequence of all operations, transportations, inspections, delays, and storages occurring during a process or procedure, and includes information considered desirable for analysis such as time required and distance moved.
   (a) The material type presents the process in terms of the events which occur to the material.
   (b) The man type presents the process in terms of the activities of the man.

Process Charting Procedure

4. For analytical purposes and to aid in detecting and eliminating inefficiencies, it is convenient to classify the actions which occur during a given process into five classifications. These are known as operations, transportations, inspections, delays, and storages. The following definitions cover the meaning of these classifications under the majority of conditions which will be encountered in process charting work.

Activities Defined

5. *Operation.* An operation occurs when an object is intentionally changed in any of its physical or chemical characteristics, is assembled or disassembled from another object, or is arranged or prepared for another operation, transportation, inspection, or storage. An operation also occurs when information is given or received or when planning or calculating takes place.

6. *Transportation.* A transportation occurs when an object is moved from one place to another, except when such movements are a part of the operation or are caused by the operator at the work station during an operation or an inspection.

7. *Inspection.* An inspection occurs when an object is examined for identification or is verified for quality or quantity in any of its characteristics.

8. *Delay.* A delay occurs to an object when conditions, except those which intentionally change the physical or chemical characteristics of the object, do not permit or require immediate performance of the next planned action.

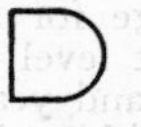

9. *Storage.* A storage occurs when an object is kept and protected against unauthorized removal, shown by inverted triangle.

10. *Combined Activity.* When it is desired to show activities performed either concurrently or by the same operator at the same work station, the symbols for those activities are combined, as shown by the circle placed within the square to represent a combined operation and inspection.

11. When unusual situations outside the range of the definitions are encountered, the intent of the definitions summarized in the following tabulation will enable the analyst to make the proper classifications.

Classification	*Predominant Result*
Operation	Produces or Accomplishes
Transportation	Moves
Inspection	Verifies
Delay	Interferes
Storage	Keeps

Wage Incentive Plans.—Frequent mention has been made of wage incentive plans because they have been an important part of industrial engineering activities since the time of Taylor. A review of the way in which wage incentive philosophies altered between 1900 and 1950 will help in understanding more clearly the changing, growing character of industrial engineering.

The period between 1900 and 1930 saw the reputation of industrial engineering sink to a low level as the result of rate cutting, the fumblings of the so-called "efficiency experts," and a variety of questionable practices on the part of some managements. It rose again as sound practitioners quietly demonstrated that industrial engineering properly applied could benefit everyone. The wage incentive installations of this period all had one feature in common. They were made largely as the result of unilateral decisions. If management decided to install an incentive plan, it selected the plan, established the standards, and started the plan in action at the time which best suited its own convenience. True, the more advanced managements endeavored to "sell" the plan to the workers, but the product was largely management's product designed without benefit of market research to see what the customer—that is, the worker—really wanted.

In doing the selling, the principal benefit which was offered was increased earnings. This fitted the philosophy of the times quite well. Rugged individualism was popular and everyone was interested in making more money for himself. So the money benefit was accepted, and the incentive which it provided caused the workers to pitch in and make even a poorly conceived wage incentive plan work reasonably well.

The depression of the 1930's intervened to make security seem more important than higher individual earnings. This period did not last long, but it had a profound effect on those who lived through it. Management's attitudes were shaped by the 1920's. They wanted to continue to make unilateral installations; they continued to rely on the appeal to the desire of the individual to make higher earnings in selling wage incentives to the workers. But the workers had changed their minds about the rightness of high individual earnings. They were even at that moment not quite sure that high productivity in general was socially desirable. So the stage was set for trouble as the unions began to grow, with enough tensions on both sides to cause many, many difficulties.

To overcome these difficulties, different solutions were tried. One which attracted a great deal of attention from 1934 to 1938 was in the automobile industry where the attempt was made to overcome the problems caused by direct incentives by going to measured day work. At the beginning of the change-over, the workers agreed that if they were paid the average earned rate they had received in the past they would continue to maintain their same output. They even agreed that the worker who did not keep up could be discharged. To management, this seemed to be the solution to many problems. Inconsistencies in earnings would immediately be eliminated. Because earnings were not tied directly to a standard, it was felt that the pressure would be taken off the industrial engineer and management for complete accuracy and that a better human relations situation would result.

But it did not work out that way. Human nature being what it is, little by little performance deteriorated. The burden of proof as to whether a given performance was acceptable was on management, and it became increasingly difficult to enforce high effort by disciplinary measures. The net result of measured day work, therefore, was a performance level which gradually fell toward the unmeasured day work level. Companies which were able to evaluate the results reported that production fell off by at least 25 per cent.

In spite of all of the problems involved, many companies continued to use and expand their use of wage incentives all through the difficult 1930's. They paid an increasing amount of attention to method, they strove for greater accuracy in setting standards, they gave guarantees which eliminated certain abuses of the past, and more and more they consulted with their workers on wage incentive problems, either voluntarily or as the result of union pressure. They demonstrated that wage incentives, properly and intelligently administered, still brought good results, and they paved the way for the next development which came at the beginning of World War II.

At that point, the need for greater production suddenly became apparent to nearly everyone. The make-work and slow-down attitudes born of the depression did not die immediately, but they were more or less pushed into the background for the duration. The War Production Board, desperate for more and more production, strongly advocated the use of wage incentives under certain conditions. The conditions were drawn up by men who understood wage incentive problems and served to create an understanding of sound wage incentive practices among a much larger segment of the industrial population than before.

As has been pointed out, in order to get approval for a new incentive plan, it was necessary to submit an application to the War Production Board signed by both management and the union if a union was involved. This meant that management could no longer take unilateral action. It was necessary to consult with the union about every detail of a proposed plan before the union would agree to go along. The industrial engineer was forced to develop his plans much more thoroughly than before; make accurate appraisals of the effect of the plan on production, earnings, and working conditions; and then by effective selling techniques in which the interests of the prospect were put above the interests of the salesman gain acceptance for his proposed course of action.

These wartime experiences helped to develop the industrial engineer to a state of greater effectiveness in the postwar period. He came to recognize clearly that his wage incentive plan had to be tailored to the needs and basic beliefs of the group who were to work on it. He had to become a human engineer as well as a technical engineer. But the net result was good. In addition to becoming a broader, more understanding man himself, his installations tended to receive greater acceptance from the workers. A big step forward toward more mature relations between workers and the industrial engineer had been taken.

Application of Industrial Engineering.—Industrial engineering procedures were first applied largely to highly repetitive work. It was entirely obvious that if a large number of identical parts had to be manufactured, it would pay to study and improve the methods by which they were produced, establish time standards, and introduce a wage incentive plan which would encourage high production through the payment of high earnings.

The early installations on highly repetitive work were so successful, however, that both management and the workers wanted them extended to less repetitive work. Management wanted the cost reductions which such installations bring. The workers on less repetitive work, seeing the higher earnings of those on the repetitive jobs, asked for the same opportunities to increase their pay.

For the industrial engineer, this situation

offered both an opportunity and a challenge. It offered an opportunity to extend the field of his service. At the same time, it presented a challenge to find better and quicker methods of doing his own work so that it would be economically justified. On low quantity work where only a few of a given part were produced, it obviously would be impractical to time study each operation in detail. The work would be completed long before the time studies could be worked up and the standards computed.

The solution to this problem was found in the development of standard data or time formulas. These are compilations of time study data obtained by time studying representative jobs in a given class of work, arranged so that they can be used for establishing standards for similar jobs which have not been time studied. Time formulas reduce the time required to establish a standard. The time required to make and work up a time study on repetitive work is commonly from 1 to 4 hours where the length of the operation cycle is fairly short, and may be much longer on larger work where one operation cycle may run as high as 100 hours. The time required to establish a standard from a time formula will in most cases range from 1 to 15 minutes.

The formula approach was suggested by Taylor, but industry was somewhat slow to use it. There were two reasons for this. On many classes of work, the derivation of a time formula is a fairly complex task. It is not easy for one who has no training in time formula work to understand how it is possible to develop a formula which will permit the establishing of accurate and consistent standards on an irregular activity such as, say, storeroom work. Therefore management was slow to authorize time formula derivation activities. The second obstacle was the length of time required to develop the time formula which on the average was about three months. It required considerable patience on the part of management and workers alike to wait while the engineer went through what seemed to be an endless series of studies and computations before the first standard could be set and incentive payment begun.

In spite of these obstacles, however, the use of standard data and time formulas spread, and standards and wage incentives were introduced on less and less repetitive work. With the coming of predetermined motion time standards, the time required to develop a time formula was sharply reduced, sometimes to as little as two weeks. This gave further impetus to the use of formulas. Applications spread from low quantity production work to such indirect labor operations as tool making, maintenance work, shipping and receiving, janitor work, and the like. The benefits to be derived from industrial engineering were found to be just as substantial on indirect labor operations as on direct labor operations.

Although industrial engineering has always been most widely used in factory work, it has been used for office work as well. It has also been applied with good results to distribution activities, particularly by the oil industry. Outside industry, industrial engineering applications have been made to all manner of activities where human labor is involved—in hospitals, homes, libraries, wholesale and retail establishments, and the like. Notable applications to agricultural work have been reported from Sweden, Hawaii, and the United States. By the end of the first half of the 20th century, it was evident to people in every country and in every walk of life that industrial engineering had much to contribute to the continuing raising of standards of living throughout the world.

Bibliography.—Maynard, H. B., and Stegemerten, G. J., *Operation Analysis* (New York 1939); Lowry, S. M., Maynard, H. B., and Stegemerten, G. J., *Time and Motion Study and Formulas for Wage Incentives* (New York 1940); Carroll, P., *Timestudy for Cost Control* (New York 1943); Louden, J. K., *Wage Incentives* (New York 1944); Presgrave, R., *The Dynamics of Time Study* (New York 1945); Taylor, F. W., *Scientific Management* (New York 1947); Maynard, H. B., Stegemerten, G. J., and Schwab, J. L., *Methods-Time Measurement* (New York 1948); Barnes, R. M., *Motion and Time Study* (New York 1949); Carroll, P., *How to Chart Time Study Data* (New York 1950); Gilbreth, L. M., *Quest of the One Best Way*, reprint (Bridgeport 1951).

Harold B. Maynard,
President, Methods Engineering Council, Pittsburgh, Pennsylvania.

INDUSTRIAL FATIGUE. Prior to World War I, even in highly industrialized countries like Great Britain and the United States, little thought was given to the problem of industrial fatigue, except by a few progressive manufacturers and scientific management experts. Wartime emergencies, however, led to governmental investigations. In Britain, the British Health of Munition Workers Committee, established in 1915, appointed a subcommittee to study effects of industrial fatigue; its *Memorandum* proved to be the first important study of the kind. In the United States, a subcommittee of the Council of National Defense in January 1918 published a similar report. It recommended various methods of reducing fatigue, as follows:

1. Adjusting Hours of Labor.—While it is obvious that the length of working day that avoids fatigue varies with different kinds of work and can be determined only by careful study, the tendency to increase hours and introduce overtime work has not always proved profitable. "A man can do more work in two hours than in one hour," say the committee, but "it does not necessarily follow that he can do more in twelve hours than in ten, or more in ten hours than in eight. In fact, whenever the work is of such duration that fatigue begins to be pronounced, it has been shown again and again that shortening the working-period actually increases the amount of work done."

2. Discouraging Overtime.—The committee's investigations seem to justify the discouragement of overtime on the ground that, if the ordinary day's work has been properly adjusted, it will stop just short of undue fatigue and the overwork necessitated by overtime will produce injurious results by diminishing the worker's efficiency, in lessening the output and increasing the amount of spoiled work.

3. Eliminating Sunday Work.—In advocating the elimination of Sunday work as a dangerous expedient, the committee's findings agree with the report of the British Health of Munition Workers Committee, who found that "seven days' labor only produces six days' output," and, they added, "the evidence before the committee has led them strongly to hold that if the maximum output is to be secured and maintained for any length of time, a weekly period of rest must be allowed."

4. Bad Effects of Night Work.—While the committee recognized the necessity of operating many factories on day and night shifts to increase the output of war supplies, they felt that in the long run night work will prove detrimental to the health of the workers, and they recommended a consideration of the plan to alternate day and night work, changing the shifts at intervals, say every other week. The report called attention to the fact that the British committee made a careful statistical study of the output under both systems and found that "where the same night-shift continues to be employed the total output is less than where there is an alternation of day- and night-work."

5. Rest Periods.—The introduction of rest- or recess-periods during the ordinary working hours has also been found effective in reducing fatigue and improving the quality of the output. In many plants all workers engaged intensively during the entire work-period are compelled to take two recesses, one in the morning and one in the afternoon. Such rest-periods are not optional but compulsory. The workers are forced to leave their machines and to move about and relax. In some cases a little food or a cup of tea or cocoa is provided.

6. Providing Seats.—The committee advised that, wherever possible, seats be provided in order that operatives may not have to stand all day; and suggested that, instead of being of uniform height, the "seats should be adjusted to the individual worker," and "where the worker's feet cannot reach the floor, foot-rests should be provided."

7. Value of Motion Studies.—The Committee also recognized the value of motion studies and the importance of the element of variety in the work performed, a conclusion that is in harmony with the theories of scientific management. In 1916, Richard A. Feiss, general manager of the Clothcraft Shops, Cleveland, Ohio, speaking before the American Public Health Association, declared that "speed in itself is not injurious. . . . There are conditions under which operating at half the best possible speed is more fatiguing and more injurious to the worker's health than operating at the best possible speed under proper conditions." This idea is also maintained by the committee, who advise that proper studies of motions be made with a view to the elimination of all awkward, unrhythmical and unnecessary motions, that the work may "be done with the least possible waste of energy and time." It also advocates the introduction of a little variety into work that must become monotonous through being the constant and rapid repetition of the same movement, and suggests that alternating processes might diminish the fatigue without diminishing the output.

8. Sanitation and Ventilation.—The committee found that fatigue diminishes and efficiency increases in keeping with the improvement of the sanitary conditions of the factory and the ventilation of the workroom. Excessive heat and humidity should be avoided as far as possible and the air should be kept in motion. Lighting facilities, the supply of drinking water, providing lunch-rooms and rest-rooms and the general sanitary condition of the toilets and wash-rooms, all play a part in the general plan for the elimination of fatigue. See INDUSTRIAL HYGIENE; INDUSTRIES, WELFARE WORK IN.

JOHN R. MEADER.

INDUSTRIAL FRUITS, those products of the soil which are sown and planted and upon reaching maturity are garnered or harvested, such as grain, vegetables and other crops. They are distinct from the natural fruits, such as trees, grass, etc., and are considered as personal and not real property. See GROWING CROPS, LEGAL STATUS OF.

INDUSTRIAL HOUSING IN THE UNITED STATES. Industrial housing is usually understood to mean housing of workers by employers. The growth of the copartnership movement in England and the strong advocacy of its introduction into the United States before World War I, and the federal government's own experiment in house building for wage earners during two world wars compel a broader definition. Industrial housing today is housing which contributes to industry, no matter by whom erected or managed.

Using the term in its older sense, however, industrial housing has a history in the United States which begins with the establishment of industries outside the home. The first American cotton mill was erected at the falls of the Pawtucket in 1790. Its successors in Rhode Island and Massachusetts were scattered along the streams that furnished their motive power. Compelled to plant the mills at a distance from established seaboard and commercial towns, the pioneer manufacturers were also compelled to build houses to shelter their employees. So began the New England mill villages, some of the earliest of which still remain along the little rivers that empty into Narragansett and neighboring bays.

The houses in these villages were well built, and even today, when sanitary conveniences and a public water supply have been added, most of them meet modern requirements. Moreover, they are far from unattractive with their grassy open spaces, their gardens and their fine old trees. It was necessary in the days of pioneer industry to build good houses, for the only available labor was the Yankee farmer's boys and girls who had been prejudiced against factory work by the tales brought from England of the horrors of industrial life. So the early industrial villages of America were designed to prove that their industrial life need not duplicate that of the Old World. Nor were the employers satisfied with the erection of good dwellings. They gave even greater care to the management of those dwellings. Especially were the dormitories or boarding houses of the girls and unmarried women kept under most careful supervision, and rules were enforced that would satisfy strict Puritan parents. Even the family dwellings were kept under a close supervision which limited considerably the freedom of the tenants.

In the early days, however, this regulation, which went far into the details of life, was accepted not only because it assured a good moral tone for the new communities whose inhabitants were mostly young people, but also because the employers or their chief representatives were a part of the community and shared its life democratically. The factory girls of the day became the manager's guests in the evening. This combination of democratic paternalism did not last, however. Even before the advent of coal and of immigrants from

Ireland and the continent of Europe the system had begun to break down. Employees became restive at having the same man both employer and landlord. The strict regulation which was necessary at the beginning became irksome as the villages developed into established communities.

The use of coal as a source of power caused some of these villages to develop into cities, Lawrence, Lowell, Pawtucket; it caused others to disappear, the owners finding it advisable to move to a place where railroad or water transportation was more accessible. When the villages grew into towns or the mills were moved to towns, the commercial builder appeared. To him the employees frequently turned with relief even when his houses were not so well built or cost more than those of the mill.

The mill owner also frequently welcomed this opportunity to drop the rôle of landlord. For there had been gradually developing a gulf between employer and employed. Though in the early days an owner often lived in Boston or Providence, the common traditions of a New England ancestry served to bridge this distance. But with the coming of the Irish with their different traditions and their different standards of living, the bond was weakened. When to the Irish succeeded Poles and Italians and even peoples of the Levant, the old democratic fellowship in the enterprise usually vanished entirely. The Lawrences of the new era became "pay envelope" cities, even the managers and heads of departments made their homes outside the mill communities. Then grew up the conception that the employer's concern in his employees ceased at the mill gates; cottages owned by the mill stood vacant or were turned into storerooms.

But this sharp cleavage of interests also proved impractical. With no community of interest there could be little or no mutual understanding, and labor troubles increased. Coincidently housing standards declined. The speculative builder, having no motive other than to secure the greatest amount possible for his property, developed the wooden three-deckers in place of the cottages and crowded them so close together that in some of the mill cities not only did gardens and yards disappear, but the windows of one house were practically boarded up by the walls of its neighbors, and what were once alleys became the thoroughfares giving access to solid lines of rear dwellings. The mill owners and their chief lieutenants, living far away from these conditions, persuaded that the matter was no concern of theirs, left the community without its natural leaders.

Then again the pendulum began to swing back toward its starting point. Compared with the suffocating, swarming, ill-regulated industrial towns and cities, the remaining old spacious mill villages had a new attraction. In some of them were the descendants of the original operatives. So new industrial villages were founded, some by employers who thought that in this way they would prevent labor troubles, some by men inspired by the more altruistic motive of rescuing their workers from intolerable living conditions. The spirit of the founders varied from the extreme paternalism of Pullman, which led to disillusion and failure, to the liberality of H. O. Nelson at Leclaire, which is still bearing fruit. This new group of industrial villages contains several which are notable for their beauty.

At the time the World War began not only was the number of industrial villages increasing rapidly, but discussion as to methods of financing and management were producing results that promised to do away with most of the dissatisfaction under the old régime. The old method of individual home ownership was falling into disuse and organized labor had definitely pronounced against it. Direct ownership of the employee's home by his employer had satisfied neither party. A first step away from this was taken by the incorporation of subsidiary companies so that the dwellings were no longer managed from the factory office. A further step had been taken in two or three instances by an adaptation of the English copartnership plan by which the tenants were gradually to become stockholders in the company that owns the houses. Then came America's entrance into the war.

During the years 1917–18 the United States government embarked upon a great experiment, the erection and management of wage-earners' dwellings. The signing of the armistice in November of the latter year left the experiment far from complete. One of the Federal agencies, the Emergency Fleet Corporation, had carried some of its developments to a point approximating physical completion, a small proportion of its dwellings were actually occupied. The other Federal agency, the United States Housing Corporation, handicapped by a later start, had not yet housed a single workingman's family. Neither agency had worked out a plan of management, though they had agreed for the time being not to sell any of their holdings. The Emergency Fleet Corporation controlled its properties through subsidiary corporations of the various shipbuilding companies through which it operated. The Housing Corporation owned its properties itself. The signing of the armistice led to some curtailment of the Fleet Corporation's housing developments, though in the main these were carried through, as shipbuilding did not cease with the war and the new dwellings were needed to hold the workers. The Housing Corporation, however, not only curtailed its projects, but wherever possible without too great loss, cancelled them entirely.

In spite of the failure to carry this great experiment to completion it exercised a considerable influence in various ways. First and most important it gave a notable impetus to the movement for government aid which before the war had been making only a slow and uncertain progress, Massachusetts being the only State in the Union which had committed itself, and it had done so only to the extent of $50,000 with which a small group of houses were built at Lowell. The war, however, demonstrated clearly both the vital importance of good housing to productive industry and the inability of private builders to meet the need. Second, it brought into the service of the wage-earner some of the leading architects, engineers and landscape designers of the country, who both because of lack of private work and the call of patriotism, for the first time turned their thoughts to the needs of men of small means.

The reverse side of the shield was financial. The need for the houses was urgent. Good planning, good designing, took little more time than no plan or design, perhaps rather less as they practically compelled an orderly procedure which prevented confusion and false starts. But speed forced into the background all thoughts of economy. The houses, with the exception of those in a few of the earlier developments, were good, but when completed their cost was high. This left a financial problem which cooled the ardor of many who otherwise would have been tempted to imitate the government's villages.

Yet the effect was notable, not alone in that these government-built villages have set a high standard by which to measure other industrial housing developments, but by breaking the taboo which had prevented government aid to housing in America, almost universal, though this long had been in other parts of the world.

In this article nothing has been said of the mining villages, which form a group by themselves. As with the pioneer industrial villages, the mining towns were of necessity built by the companies because they must be located with reference only to the mine. With them, however, there was the additional reason that their life was uncertain, depending upon the time it might take to exhaust the mine. This second reason also led to a policy of making these towns as cheap as possible, so they became a by-word for their squalor and ugliness. Yet before 1914 the new interest in industrial towns had affected them and great improvement had begun. See also CITY PLANNING; GARDEN CITIES.

Bibliography.— Meakin, Budgett, 'Model Factories and Villages' (Philadelphia); Taylor, Graham R., 'Satillite Cities' (New York 1915); 'Living Conditions for Employees' (in 'The Present Labor Situation,' The American Academy of Political and Social Science, 1917); 'Standards Set By the New Federal War Suburbs and War Cities' (American Civic Association, 1918); 'War Time Housing In America' (*National Municipal Review,* November 1918); 'The Houses of Providence' (a report, with notes on neighboring mill villages, 1916); Thomas, A. J., 'Industrial Housing' (Bayonne, N. J., 1925); and National Housing Assoc'n pamphlets.

JOHN IHLDER.
Executive Secretary, Philadelphia Housing Association.

INDUSTRIAL HYGIENE. The policy of providing healthful and comfortable working quarters for employees in commercial and manufacturing establishments has been developed within comparatively few years. Previously little thought was given to such matters and, in factories especially, operatives were crowded together in any kind of a shop that chance or a desire for economy might provide and the fact that many of these working places were both dismal and unsanitary had but little weight with the average employer.

To-day these conditions are changing so rapidly that poorly lighted, inadequately heated, improperly ventilated or otherwise unhealthful workshops are coming to be the rare exceptions to the rule. Instead, in the average shop, adequate toilet and washing facilities are now provided, problems of lighting and ventilation are solved by expert engineers, even such questions as the regulation of heat and humidity being given serious consideration, and every effort is made to see that the working conditions are such as not to impair the health and efficiency of the employee.

While the matter of hygienic and sanitary equipment has been fixed to a great extent in New York, New Jersey, Pennsylvania, Massachusetts and Wisconsin, where the legislatures have enacted laws setting a standard, not only for industry as a whole but, in many instances, for particular branches of industry, the improvements in these directions are in no sense confined to establishments that have been compelled by statute to adopt more modern methods. Even in communities that are unregulated by law or industrial code, similar improvements are constantly being made, for experience has so clearly demonstrated that these changes in working conditions quickly pay for themselves in the character of the service performed by the working force that even those employers who feel that they owe no such moral obligation to their employees have learned the lesson that proper hygienic and sanitary workshops make for greater and better production, and are

	Lavatories	Toilets	Drinking fountains	Lockers
Type	Individual	All porcelain; no wood	Bubbling type, arranged so lips do not touch metal.	Perforated metal, slanting top to prevent accumulation of refuse.
Located	In central building near lockers.	Substations near workers.	Where convenient to workers.	In central building.
Number	1 for 15 men	1 for 20 men	1 for 30 men	1 per man. If possible, one compartment for work and one for shop clothing.
Accessories	Hot and cold water, liquid soap, paper towels.	Automatic flush	....	Locked. Forced hot air ventilation to dry wet garments.
Plumbing	Open type, plain.			
Special features	Porcelain	Must have forced air ventilation.	In clean, light places.	It is advisable to arrange locker so that men coming off work at same time have every second or third locker to prevent crowding.
Note	Average time per man at washbasin 2½ minutes.	Compartments should not have doors as easier to keep clean.	....	If lockers are near washbasins a larger number can use both without waiting.

taking the steps necessary for the adoption of the methods that are everywhere proving so mutually advantageous.

In fact, these questions have assumed proportions of so great importance that, in several instances, employers' associations have conducted thorough surveys and adopted standards for the improvement of working conditions, even in communities unaffected by legislative statute. For example, the Welfare Managers' Group of the Detroit (Mich.) Executives' Club made a survey which included all of the important plants in that city, and, as a result, the preceding sanitary arrangements were suggested as necessary for the proper equipment of a manufacturing plant.

The committee also reported:

«The objections to paper towels, 'that we do not get our hands dry enough to prevent chapping,' can be done away with by a well-ventilated, warm dressing room, where the hands will dry while dressing. Where there are corners into which waste paper and refuse are thrown this can be largely eliminated by painting these corners white and lighting them well. One does not throw waste into clean corners. Tile floors should be laid in all wash-rooms, etc., where possible; otherwise, cement, well drained. Oily floors should be swept and scraped daily. Where cement floors are used, rubber pads for the men to stand on will help in increasing comfort and efficiency. All scrap metal should be kept clear of the workers.»

The Detroit committee also included «good lunch room and recreation facilities among our prophylactic treatment,» on the ground that properly prepared, carefully selected food and healthful recreation are important factors in the development of an effective hygienic and sanitary program.

In plants where workers are exposed to dangerous dusts or noxious fumes the installation of a lunch room is regarded as most essential, as all authorities agree that the cold luncheon eaten in the workroom, or in an unpleasant environment, must have a direct effect in reducing the physical fitness necessary to production. Where lunch rooms are not provided, it is advised that gas stoves or steam tables on which foods brought from home may be heated should be installed, and it is declared that even the policy of furnishing nothing more than milk, coffee, tea or soup at a nominal charge has invariably been found an economy to the employer. Where lunch room facilities are provided, however, care should be taken to see that the food served is of excellent quality, both in material and method of cooking, for otherwise it would be difficult to overcome the temptation to hurried eating, but it has generally been found that where food is selected for its nutritive value and is prepared with a view to ready digestion, satisfactory improvement in the health of the working force is noted, with a corresponding reduction of time lost through illness and intemperance.

While the part played by fresh air in the prevention of occupational disease is generally admitted, the vague character of the standards in vogue in different States has proved a great handicap to the manufacturer who is desirous of adopting the system best suited to the needs of his operatives. As Roach points out (*Industrial Management,* October 1917): «The terms 'adequate' and 'sufficient' have left him free to spend thousands of dollars on experiments, the results of which have too often given little of the protection to the health of the worker promised by irresponsible contractors.»

Expensive systems of air conditioning are naturally unnecessary in the ordinary workroom where nothing more than fresh air is needed, and they are rarely installed except where the process of manufacture requires absolutely dustless conditions or a stable degree of humidity. For ordinary purposes, draft deflectors placed at both top and bottom of windows afford satisfactory ventilation.

While plants with non-dusty processes often find this window equipment all that is necessary for ventilation, it is admitted that it cannot be depended upon where noxious vapors or excessive humidity have to be considered. The same objection can be made to so-called «natural draft» ventilators, which, while they often work satisfactorily when there is a sufficient breeze present, fail to accomplish their purpose on humid days when the noxious air lies close to the floor.

Where industrial dust or vapors must be removed from the air the adoption of the most approved dust exhaust system becomes necessary. In this connection Roach says:

«The usual and inexpert practice in building a dust exhaust system, such as is required for buffing, polishing or grinding wheels, is to proportion the main section pipe so that at all cross-sectional points it only equals the combined areas of the entering branch pipes; while the inlet of the exhauster used on such a system has an area that but equals the combined areas of all the branch pipes used on the system. For example, for 25 4-inch branch pipes the largest diameter of main pipe and exhauster would be 20 inches. A 50-inch exhauster would have an inlet 20 inches in diameter; if it were necessary to get a suction-head at each branch pipe sufficiently strong to displace 2 inches of water in a pressure gauge (commonly called a U-shaped tube) it would require an actual velocity of 4,000 lineal feet per minute in the branches, and it would be necessary for the exhauster to handle 8,720 cubic feet of air per minute. It would require approximately 16 horse power to obtain these results, which in itself is an important item.

«This kind of a system should no longer be permitted. Standards based on actual working tests and experience prove that efficiency requires for 25 4-inch pipes a main pipe with an area 20 per cent larger at all its cross-sectional points, than the combined areas of entering branch pipes. The inlet of the exhauster attached to the system must have an area 20 per cent larger than the combined areas of all the branch connections on the system. This kind of system would require a 55-inch exhauster having a main pipe 22 inches in diameter and, to obtain a suction sufficient to displace 2 inches of water in a U-shaped tube, the air in each branch pipe would be obliged to have a velocity of 4,000 lineal feet per minute. The exhauster would handle 8,720 cubic feet of air a minute and would take about 12 horse power to operate it.»

In many plants the hygienic and sanitary

control is in the hands of the industrial physician whose duties comprise a more or less close supervision over the physical condition of the operatives from the day they enter the employ of the company. Many concerns have adopted the policy of examining all applicants for employment before engaging them, with a view to determining the physical fitness of the man for the job which he is to be expected to perform; a smaller number of establishments insist upon periodic re-examination, in order that his physical defects may be detected as quickly as possible and he may be assisted in remedying them, while all employers who employ the physician have found that his services in accident prevention and general health supervision have proved of sufficient value to more than offset the cost of the service. So well established has this fact become that even plants that are too small to employ a permanent physician have established dispensaries, where they meet all requirements for first-aid through a plant nurse, the physician being called upon for examinations, or, when necessary, for more important services.

According to the report of the committee of the Detroit Executives' Club, a plant employing from 1,400 to 2,000 persons should devote three rooms to hospital purposes — a reception room, an examining room and a surgery or dressing room.

«The furniture needed in a reception room is enough chairs so that patients will not have to stand, and a stretcher. The examining room should have a rest cot, scales and other instrumental equipment, with two or more booths to facilitate examinations. The surgery room needs an operating table, an instrument case with necessary first-aid instruments, drugs and dressings, one or two pedestal wash basins and one waste can.»

So general has health supervision become in industry that the physicians engaged in such activities have organized an association, the Conference Board of Physicians in Industrial Practice, and it was in their behalf that Magnus W. Alexander, in August 1917, published his report on the «Cost of Health Supervision in Industry.»

The purpose of this report, as its compiler stated, was to inform employers of the actual cost of health supervision in the different industries. «To this end, the data were secured from plants engaged in many industries, in light, medium and heavy work, in comparatively safe as well as hazardous occupations, and in shops of various sizes and character, located in various parts of the United States. . . . The chief significance of these data, from a general viewpoint, is that it is possible to give such a large amount of medical and surgical service at a cost which averages only $2.21 per employee per year. . . . Where the average cost appears to be unusually high . . . the size and character of the medical staff is usually the determining factor. In some cases the cost is influenced greatly by the number of injuries treated in private or public hospitals, in others, by the amount of care given to all injuries, whether serious or slight, or by the extension of the service to include physical examination of all employees, treatment of sickness of employees at the plant and at home, and even by medical care of employees' families, or by a combination of all these features.»

Mr. Alexander concludes his report with the statement that «convincing proof of the economic value of health supervision in industry is afforded by the fact that it was found that no employer had abandoned the health supervision activities established in his plant. On the contrary, the prevailing tendency has been to invest even more money in extending the service.»

A summary of the report is as follows:

INDUSTRY	No. of establishments reporting	Total average number of employees	Total cases of all kinds	Total medical and surgical cost	Average annual cost per employee
Metal trades....	47	294,646	1,988,991	$541,771	$1 84
Rolling mills.....	7	49,317	358,574	137,047	2 78
Smelting and refining.........	1	1,270	2,832	6,932	5 46
Light and power.	7	24,921	49,046	92,601	3 72
Transportation...	5	35,795	81,591	69,633	1 95
Chemicals.......	6	10,572	78,744	34,797	3 29
Food...........	5	13,650	69,565	39,875	2 92
Rubber.........	5	27,462	234,069	76,089	2 77
Textiles.........	4	8,939	67,380	24,177	2 70
Paint...........	2	4,023	10,255	29,635	7 37
Leather.........	2	3,026	9,440	6,102	2 02
Publishing......	2	3,358	6,742	3,473	1 03
Coal mining.....	1	2,454	2,842	4,637	1 89
Gold mining.....	1	2,500	62,126	35,590	14 24
Coal and iron mining........	1	11,000	131,898	130,000	11 82
Miscellaneous....	3	2,611	11,019	6,126	2 35
	99	495,544	3,165,114	$1,238,485	$2 50

In several plants in this country, health supervision includes the care of the teeth and eyes, examinations being made by specialists in the employ of the firm; subsequent treatments usually being at the expense of the employee, though at greatly reduced rates.

The adoption of sanitary standards was the means taken to overcome the «sweat-shop» conditions that had operated so injuriously to several branches of the tailoring industry and, wherever there has been sufficient organization to adopt and enforce such regulations effective results have been reported. The standards adopted by the Joint Board of Sanitary Control in the cloak, suit and skirt industry of Greater New York forbid cellar shops and tend to prevent the establishment of workrooms under conditions that might prove injurious to health. They provide that shops located in buildings more than one story in height must have fire-escapes properly equipped with ladders to an adjoining building or with carefully adjusted full-length drop ladders. Where automatic sprinklers are not provided, there must be a sufficient number of chemical extinguishers or fire-buckets, and special caretakers should be appointed in each shop to see that the fire-buckets are kept filled and are ready for use in case of fire. No smoking is permitted in the workshops, doors must not be locked during working hours, signs marking exits and fire-escapes are to be conspicuously placed about the shop, fire-proof receptacles with tin lining and covers must be provided for rubbish, all openings and exits to fire-escapes must be left unobstructed by tables, machines, partitions or iron bars, and stairs are to be provided with secure handrails and safe treads.

Other regulations provide for adequate lighting, with sufficient window space and properly placed artificial lamps; for proper ventilation; and for the maintenance of sanitary conditions throughout the workshops, dressing rooms, and rest rooms.

Bibliography.—Clark, W. I., *Health Service in Industry* (New York 1922); Daiell, H. L., *First Aid and Medical Service in Industry* (New Brunswick, N. J., 1928); Dana, R. T., *The Human Machine in Industry* (New York 1927); Hackett, J. D., *Health Maintenance in Industry* (Chicago 1925); Hope, E. W., *Industrial Hygiene and Medicine* (New York 1923); Kober, G. M., *Industrial Health* (Philadelphia 1924); Lange, F. G., *Handbook of Safety and Accident Prevention* (New York 1926); New York State Research and Codes Bureau, *Industrial Hygiene Series* (Albany, N. Y.); Vernon, H. M., *Industrial Fatigue and Efficiency* (London 1921).

JOHN R. MEADER.

INDUSTRIAL INSURANCE. See INSURANCE, INDUSTRIAL.

INDUSTRIAL OR LABOR RELATIONS IN THE UNITED STATES. The terms "industrial relations" and "labor relations" are employed both as synonymous and contrasted expressions. In their broadest application, they are alternative terms which include the totality of economic, legal, social, political, and cultural relationships among men engaged in the production and distribution of goods and the performance of services. In this usage, they are applicable to agriculture and government service as well as to industry. And, historically, they include the relationships between master and indentured white servant, master and Negro chattel slave, and master craftsman and journeyman and apprentice of colonial times and the post-Revolutionary era up to the Civil War.

Generally, however, the terms are invested with a more restricted meaning. "Industrial relations" usually signifies the relationships between employer and wage worker which, with the rise of the factory system, large-scale modern industry, and the corporation after the Civil War, succeeded historically earlier relationships between master and servant and owner-manager and his few employees. The term is applied primarily to relations between management and labor in the manufacturing, extractive, transportation, communications, and distributive industries. In accordance with this usage, employer-employee relationships in other fields are commonly called labor relations; but the distinction is haphazard, for the two terms are also used interchangeably.

Considered in its more restricted meaning, "industrial relations" nevertheless includes a vast complex of diverse, varying, interacting, and interpenetrating relationships. Among essential aspects of industrial relations are wages and hours; labor and social legislation; vocational training; scientific management; inter-racial relationships; collective bargaining; the scope and power of employer organizations and combinations; the strength and status of trade unionism and the influence of the labor movement; labor-management disputes, and voluntary arbitration and government mediation and conciliation; strikes, the status of civil liberty, intervention by the state, and government seizure and operation of privately owned industry; and management and labor representation in government economic and industrial administrative bodies.

A Modus Vivendi Between Capital and Labor.—In their totality, these relations signify a *modus vivendi* between capital and labor whereby the production and distribution of goods and services are carried on under increasing governmental regulation. But it is a dynamic equilibrium which is the result of a long period of development and which, moreover, is in process of continual change.

The complex character of contemporary industrial relations stands in sharp contrast to the comparatively simple relationship which obtained between employers and employees during the early stages of the industrialization of the United States in the latter part of the 19th century. Basically, that relationship was an unwritten express or implied contract between the employer, who was increasingly a corporation, regarded at law as a juristic person, and the employee, who was invariably an individual. Payment of wages by the employer for work performed by the employee were the principal terms of the contract. Theoretically, employer and employee were equal parties, free to bargain for terms, and acquired equal rights and duties. Actually, however, the employer, because of superior economic strength over the individual employee—whose only marketable asset was his ability to work and who had no alternative but to work—possessed decisive bargaining advantages and dictated the terms of the contract, subject only to the loose and variable control of the competitive system. Owing to the relatively elementary state of industrial development, the rules governing work, formulated by the employer, were correspondingly simple.

Scientific Management.—Three basic factors profoundly modified the development of industrial relations to their present state. The first was the rapid technological revolution which made United States industry the most productive in the world. The development of vast enterprises employing first thousands, then tens of thousands, and, finally, hundreds of thousands of workers, made necessary complex codes of rules governing working conditions. Precision and smoothness are vital in the operation of mass-production industries. Economies made through division of labor and specialization are jeopardized by interruptions to the flow of work arising from absenteeism, tardiness, lack of discipline, and lack of efficient coordination on the part of management.

From these needs arose the theory and practice of scientific management. Originally, scientific management was limited in its basic aim to the achievement of increased productivity through improvement in the skill of the labor force and in the planning and coordinated operation of production. Subsequently, scientific management was extended to include the development of cooperation between capital and labor through cultivation of good will of both parties toward each other. Included in this sphere are establishment of fair standards of work; determination of appropriate, as well as effective, incentives for work, selection of personnel in accordance with the aptitude of workers for various positions and tasks; and a degree of cooperation between management and workers in the practical solution of these problems. Involved in this extension of scientific management are the application to industrial relationships of the principles of psychology and, in later years, of some tenets of psychiatric science. A further and important development of scientific management has been the cultivation, through public relations, of good will on the part of communities and consumers, both as an advantageous aid in the sale of products and services and as a practical application of a sense of social responsibility toward the public.

Trade Unionism.—The second factor in shaping the evolution of industrial relations was the development of the trade-union movement. For the arbitrary determination by the employer of the terms of the labor contract, the workers sought to substitute collective agreements between employers and workers organized in unions. Thereby labor expressed its desire for a higher standard of living and an improved status in United States society. And it sought to apply to industry the elementary principles of traditional American political democracy.

Its first efforts were confined to wages, hours, and measures to protect health and life while at work. These are still basic considerations in collective agreements, but they are now far from being the exclusive considerations. Gradually, as unions grew in size, strength, and influence and came to be accepted as socially necessary institutions performing valuable functions, the scope of labor's role increased and was reflected in collective agreements, which included, in addition to provisions relating to wages and hours, terms concerning sickness and death benefits, pensions, vacations, methods of employment, limitations on management's right to discharge workers, rules regulating work, and other matters.

Labor and Social Legislation.—Simultaneously, labor demanded of the state that it curb industrial autocracy and further the purposes of labor by the establishment of minimal standards, the provision of various benefits designed to afford workers a measure of security against the uncertainties inherent in the modern industrial system, and the creation of specific labor rights and immunities. Through collective agreements and legislative enactments, the powers and rights of management were limited and the position of labor improved.

Labor-Management Cooperation.—Although unions had been recognized by the courts since the 1840's as lawful combinations, their legal status was long undefined by statute and they had no standing before the courts as parties in suits over the enforcement of contracts. They were strongly resisted by employers. The history of this phase of labor relations is in large part a record of conflict which frequently culminated in violence and often in bloodshed. With the passage of time, however, management learned to accept unionism as a permanent feature of industrial relations and to cooperate with it; while organized labor, once established and relatively secure in its acceptance, tended, for its part, to demonstrate a sober sense of responsibility with respect to its obligations to management and the preservation and enhancement of the national economy. Progressively greater emphasis was placed by both sides on conciliation and arbitration than on lockouts and strikes as means of solving disputes, and some industries in which conflict had been frequent, experienced as much as a quarter of a century of industrial peace.

The Government in Industrial Relations.—A profound change in the role of government was the third basic factor in determining the course of industrial relations. In the prevailing views and attitudes of the latter part of the 19th, and the early years of the 20th, century, the regulation of industrial relations, as of economic relationships generally, was excluded from the functions of government. The regulation of industrial relations was held to be the concern of industry and labor. Only when they dramatically affected the public interest, as in the serious disturbance of public order in large-scale strike violence, were industrial relations considered a proper concern of government.

However, as the growing economy of the United States became increasingly complex, and vast corporate enterprises, in pursuit of their private interests, vitally affected the public welfare, the need for regulation of economic processes by the government became pressing. Participation by the government in industrial relations, following the economic crisis of 1929, formed an important part of the measures undertaken by the federal government under President Franklin D. Roosevelt to cope with the depression.

The essential features of the new policy with respect to industrial relations, which was intended to promote industrial peace, were statutory affirmation of the right of labor to organize, to bargain collectively, and to strike; prohibition of interference with these rights on the part of employers; and establishment of agencies for the mediation, conciliation, arbitration, and administrative disposition of disputes between management and labor. Sweeping regulatory powers over economic relationships, including industrial relations, were vested in the president during World War II. After the war, governmental participation in industrial relations was extended by Congress. By the terms of the Labor Management Relations Act of 1947 (the so-called Taft-Hartley Act), unions achieved definite legal status as parties to contracts; the rights of employers in industrial relations were redefined more favorably, and the rights of labor were partly restricted; and the scope of governmental intervention in strike situations was enlarged.

The Labor Contract.—In its basic legal aspect, the capital-labor relationship is a contract in which the contracting parties are the employer and employee. As shown above, the emergence of the labor contract marks the outcome of efforts to preserve individual bargaining as the exclusive or paramount mode of defining the employment relationship, and of counterefforts to introduce controls over the bargaining process intended to offset the disadvantage of labor.

The upshot has been the development of labor and social legislation and collective bargaining. Statutes and administrative enactments and judicial decisions made thereunder greatly restrict the freedom of the parties in bargaining by establishing minimum limits for the terms which enter into labor contracts, determining conditions under which labor contracts are negotiated, providing for the disposition of labor-management disputes, and restricting the right, primarily of employers, but also to some extent of employees, to enter into and to terminate labor contracts at will.

Collective-bargaining agreements are similar in effect. Formerly, they were not regarded as contracts and were not enforceable at law. Later, the common-law development of union rights crystallized a judicial tendency to recognize collective agreements as contracts. By provisions of the Labor Management Relations Act of 1947 they were made binding contracts, enforceable through suits by and against unions.

In form, the labor contract continues to be an agreement between employer and individual employee. In substance, it is increasingly, as the scope of collective agreements and social legislation is enlarged, a means of effecting a relationship, the characteristics of which are predetermined by agreement and can be altered subsequently by further agreement.

See also FACTORY SYSTEM; FACTORY MANAGEMENT; INDUSTRIAL ORGANIZATION AND ADMINISTRATION; SCIENTIFIC MANAGEMENT; ACCIDENTS—*Occupational Accidents;* INDUSTRIAL FATIGUE; INDUSTRIAL HYGIENE; LABOR TURNOVER; VOCATIONAL EDUCATION; VOCATIONAL GUIDANCE; TRADE SCHOOLS; CRISES, ECONOMIC; UNEMPLOYMENT; LABOR LEGISLATION; SOCIAL LEGISLATION; WORKMEN'S COMPENSATION; COMBINATION, INDUSTRIAL; EMPLOYERS' ASSOCIATIONS; DEMOCRACY—*Democracy as a Form of Industry*; EMPLOYEE REPRESENTATION; LABOR OR TRADE UNIONS; LABOR MOVEMENT IN AMERICA; STRIKES AND LOCKOUTS; ARBITRATION, INDUSTRIAL.

Bibliography.—The descriptive, statistical, analytical, and historical literature on industrial relations is stupendous and is constantly growing. However, an authoritative comprehensive work on the subject has not been written. General historical background material is contained in Charles and Mary Beard, *Rise of American Civilization*, 3 vols. (New York 1929–1939); Louis Hacker, *Triumph of American Capitalism* (New York 1940); John R. Commons and associates, *History of Labor in the United States*, 4 vols. (New York 1918–1935).

Discussions of important phases of industrial relations will be found in Frederick W. Taylor, *Scientific Management* (New York 1947); Franklin E. Folts, *Introduction to Industrial Management* (New York 1949); Ralph M. Barnes, *Motion and Time Study Problems and Projects* (New York 1949); Thomas W. Harrell, *Industrial Psychology* (New York 1949); William S. Hopkins, *Labor in the American Economy* (New York 1948); Benjamin M. Selekman, *Problems in Labor Relations* (New York 1950); John T. Dunlop, *Collective Bargaining: Principles and Cases* (Chicago 1949); Charles Gregory, *Labor and the Law*, rev. ed. (New York 1949); Harry A. Millis, *From the Wagner Act to Taft-Hartley* (Chicago 1950); Sterling Spero and Abram Harris, *The Black Worker* (New York 1931); Horace R. Cayton and George S. Mitchell, *Black Workers and the New Unions* (Chapel Hill 1939); J. B. S. Hardman and M. F. Neufeld, eds., *The House of Labor* (New York 1951).

Valuable data will also be found in U.S. Senate Commission on Industrial Relations, *Final Report and Testimony Submitted to Congress; Annual Report, Bulletin*, and other publications of the U.S. Department of Labor; *Historical Statistics of the United States, 1789–1941*, the annual *Statistical Abstract of the United States*, and *Monthly Report on the Labor Force*, all published by U.S. Department of Commerce, Bureau of the Census; *Studies and Reports* and *Industry and Labor*, publications of the International Labour Office; *Annals* of the American Academy of Political and Social Science; and the publications of the Twentieth Century Fund and the National Industrial Conference Board.

THOMAS STAMM.

INDUSTRIAL ORGANIZATION AND ADMINISTRATION. In the early years of American business, administrative control was a matter of private or family-owned organizations of the simplest sort. The first large undertakings requiring corporate form and a scheme of formal financing were the toll roads, canal companies, and the railroads. The chief factor which caused an increase in the size of businesses during the half-century 1840–1890 was the invention of machinery. The large-scale operation which machinery and the use of mechanical sources of power suggest has been realized because of the enormous domestic market, the ample capital available, the freedom of the country from tradition and the existence of a spirit of daring. By the decade 1895–1905, these experiments had sufficiently developed the technical aspects of manufacturing that engineers could boldly plan groups of specialized plants under united control. In the meantime, the accountants had learned how to keep untangled the most heterogeneous affairs; and the distributive or marketing machinery was devised for handling the entire domestic market in a single campaign. Since the possible economies from the elimination of competition were very large, there occurred the so-called "trust movement," which resulted in the consolidation of many hundreds of individual plants into a small number of great consolidated corporations. In the process of putting these enterprises together, and of operating them, the art of corporation financing, and its underlying technique of accounting, have achieved a forced growth.

Overlapping this period in part, but operating most intensively from 1910 to 1914, there occurred the movement known as "scientific management." Broadly speaking the purport of this movement is that a group of engineers applied the precise and systematic methods of investigation and calculation recognized in the engineering sciences to the study of shop processes, and that by so doing they uncovered astonishing inefficiencies and were able to recommend a system of functionalization of shop executives and a policy of standardization upon the best methods which systematic study should discover. Scientific management is an effort to apply the scientific method to a certain portion of the shop practice. It met with determined opposition because it did not adequately apply the knowledge and spirit of the times in its handling of the wage earner. A further account of this movement may be found under the heading SCIENTIFIC MANAGEMENT. At the present time the interest of business executives in the evolution of new methods centers in "human engineering." There has been an accumulation of knowledge concerning hygiene and public medicine, the causes of fatigue and accidents, and the wastes of the hiring-and-firing methods in vogue, which demands application. It is realized that men should be carefully chosen for their work and given special training for it. Organized labor has enforced the idea upon the public mind that the laborer should have a voice in determining the conditions in which he works. And finally there are new ideals of the "square deal" and of service which are making their way among the more advanced employers.

Departments of Business Administration.—The ordinary functions of business administration fall into four classes: (1) financing—in charge of the chief officers, working in close relations to the board of directors; (2) manufacturing—in charge of a general manager or superintendent, directing a corps of foremen in the shops; (3) selling—under the direction of a sales manager, with district agents and salesmen; (4) personnel relations—in charge of an employment manager or superintendent of personnel.

Financial Organization and Management.—If the inauguration of a business takes the usual course of large modern enterprises, there will first appear upon the scene a promoter who discovers undeveloped properties or poorly-managed concerns, forms a plan for their development, secures options upon them and puts his project before capitalists. Capital may be represented by a syndicate manager, who acts for a group of banks and large private investors in investigating the projects presented. If a project be found meritorious, its financing will be taken over on conditions which ensure adequate control of the subsequent operations of development. A corporation will then be formed which, under its charter powers, elects officers, enters into contracts, issues securities, receives funds, secures plant and equipment and otherwise prepares to do business.

The liabilities of a business corporation may be briefly listed as bonds, short-term notes, preferred stock, common stock, commercial paper and open accounts. The bonds of manufacturing enterprises (unless the business of certain public utilities be included therewith) should represent but a small fraction of the total capital, for the reason that the earnings of such businesses have, in the past, been subject to violent fluctuations. Preferred stocks are a business man's risk. They may be described as intermediate in security between bonds and common stocks. They will, in many cases, represent the cash and property contributed to the business by the group of interests connected with its organization and development. Common stocks receive dividends only after interest on the bonds and dividends on the preferred stock have been paid. There is no margin of safety to protect them. Their hazard is not so much the correctness of the process of valuing assets as it is the skill of the management in earning income. They are an appropriate investment only for men of means who are intimately associated with industrial management.

The financial authorities of a business are responsible to allot the funds raised from the issue of securities as advantageously as possible to the various requirements. A portion will go into buildings and equipment and other relatively permanent forms. This may be designated as fixed capital. Another portion must be reserved for raw materials, finished stock, pay roll and credit advances to customers. This is circulating capital. Fixed capital loses value slowly as a result of wear and tear. Circulating capital changes its form of investment rapidly. A balance in the bank last week may have been paid out as wages and be now represented by goods in the warehouse. Next week, if the goods are sold, it may take the form of a credit advance to a customer.

As fixed capital is relatively enduring, a large amount of funds should not be put into such a form until it is certain that the enterprise is to be of a permanent nature. Fixed capital may be of various degrees of specialization. The more specialized the form the more difficult it is to sell, and the more its selling price depends upon the hazard of a single set of market conditions. The degree to which it is proper to specialize capital is a function of the conference felt in the soundness of the project. The utilization of fixed capital is a process requiring the continuous supplying of circulating capital. Materials and labor must be provided to support the process of production. A plant is valueless when not in motion. To keep it under headway money must be constantly poured into it in amounts which in the average case may equal the total capital of the business annually. It is a somewhat common error of business finance to place an unduly large proportion of the assets in fixed form. The homely caution of Poor Richard may well be remembered, "It is easier to build two chimneys than maintain one in fuel." The financial organization of a private business connects with the general financial machinery of the country through the company's published reports, through the certified public accountant who vouches for the report he signs and through the general banking system. It is further connected by the investment bankers who purchase the securities after investigation and sell them to the investing public, by the stock exchanges which exert some slight control over the probity of the methods of the corporations whose securities they admit to listing privileges, by State commissions which are rapidly taking over the functions of authorizing security issue and by the general machinery of law. See Industrial Distribution.

Administration of Manufacturing Processes. The highest authority in a business, on matters pertaining to productive processes, may be known as the general superintendent or works manager. In the initial stages of the business this officer will have the leading influence in determining the location of plants, the layout and character of buildings and the selection of machinery. When preliminary plans result in the construction of a mechanical automaton, and it becomes necessary to add men and materials and to indicate methods of production, in order that the enterprise can become a going concern, the general superintendent will take on a much expanded range of responsibilities. He will be expected to keep the physical equipment and productive processes up to standard and to employ an adequate force of foremen, laborers and skilled men of the various crafts. He will control the progress of work in relation to the demands of the sales department by a schedule and a system of orders, which control all productive labor and the use of material. The design of articles and the accuracy of manufacture is effected through a designing department and a system of inspectors. As a means of improvement he will use time studies and motion studies. The information thus accumulated he will embody in standards, which will be promulgated as the prescribed methods. The ideal is standardization, which is such an effective control of performance that every case conforms to the rule laid down. These prescribed methods will be communicated by general or standing orders and by shop orders. In a business of any size, orders should be written. The standing orders, when gathered together, will compose a "book of rules." The shop orders will be supplemented by instruction cards, to convey precise information as to the materials to be used, the machine or tool to employ, the process to select, the time the task should take, the machine adjustments, etc., etc. A particular instruction card will be prepared in advance for each task, and will be issued from the planning room, for the workman's convenience, each time the job is given out.

The planning room is the chief service aid of the superintendent and the foreman on technical matters. It may, in a typical instance, contain a routing or order-of-work clerk in charge of the planning board, an instruction card clerk, a clerk in charge of time slips and cost records; and it will probably serve also as headquarters for the engineer who calculates the proper speed of machinery, and the time study man who studies manual operations.

From the foregoing statement of duties it can be seen that the general superintendent has a very wide range of responsibilities. To be able to function efficiently, in the face of the enormous evolution of science and technique which has taken place in recent years, he should confine himself to general supervision, entrusting details to a staff of specialists. There has grown up in the best-managed businesses a number of service departments or staff aids for the express purpose of relieving the general superintendent. Such are the tool room, the stores department, the engineering department, the designing and drafting room, the inspection department and the planning room. Usually also the cost department and the employment department will be answerable to him. To a considerable degree the difference in efficiency of manufacturing enterprises depends upon the ability of the superintendent to comprehend the functions of service departments, and his success in organizing about him a staff of specialists who relieve him and his foremen. An executive blockade exists in many businesses because the general superintendent and foremen are overloaded. The remedy is to apply the principal of specialization and division of labor in administration, as it is applied among the craftsmen and common laborers in the shops.

Administration of Personnel Relations.— Within the last 15 years, the attention of business executives has been increasingly drawn to the problem of employment management, or as it is sometimes called, «human engineering.» For years the demand of labor organizations, and the waste and violence of strikes, have made the «labor problem» synonymous with a class contest over the sharing of the product. Recently, the relation between employer and employee has begun to take on a different character. It has been found that a great many things can be done which will benefit both. A field of harmonious policies has opened itself. The labor problem begins to appear to be a matter of the careful selection of men for their work, the provision of comfortable working conditions, the prevention of accidents, the safe-guarding of health, the careful setting of wages on the basis of an honest study of all the facts, including the cost of living, and a variety of activities which develop interest in work, loyalty to a common cause, and the mutual welfare. Experience has proved that these problems can best be handled by having a separate department of the business, which can devote itself to them; and by putting in charge of this department a first-class executive. The movement to install such officers is a resultant of progress in accounting, staff organization, functional foremanizing, vocational guidance, industrial training, the new wage systems, safety first, hygiene and medical aid, and the use of the committee system of shop management. The functions of the employment department are, for the most part, not new in industry. They are now being gathered together under one authority so that they may be handled in a more expert manner, that they may be harmonized into a consistent policy, and that they may be made the definite responsibility of competent officers. Among the causes which are responsible for the attention now being given to personnel supervision is the extension of cost accounting to the factors which influence labor efficiency. The cost of labor turnover is being calculated. The cost of accidents, of sickness, of absenteeism, of improperly placed men and of strikes is being studied. The employment manager is, in one sense, a labor-cost accountant. The organization of an employment department does not involve an increase in the cost of doing business. On the contrary, it means an economy, by reason of a reduction in the number of persons to be trained, a saving of foremen's energy, a reduction in accidents and a gradual increase in the average skill and experience of employees. Proper employment conditions attract superior workmen, and generate a co-operative spirit; this affects favorably the rate of production, the waste of stock and the quality of output. See LABOR TURNOVER.

The employment manager is necessary to apply the art of mental testing and vocational guidance in ascertaining the fitness of prospective employees. He best can direct industrial training to provide the talent which the employment records show to be most needed. He knows the process of establishing fair base rates of wages, of working out wage scales, of checking minimum rates against the local cost of living, and of planning simple and specific production bonuses. The employment manager has come in with safety first, because it has been found that three-fourths of the accidents are due to the carelessness or ignorance of the working force. His department works along the lines of hygiene, sanitation, medical aid, canteens and health education, to cut down accidents, reduce fatigue and cure antagonism of mind. Employment supervision represents a movement in the direction of the democratic shop, in which a voice is given to labor in determining the working conditions. It is a means of applying that conception of truth and service which has revolutionized selling and advertising. As the customer is «sold» goods — that is to say is thoroughly convinced and satisfied — so a workman is «sold» his job. The latter has to be satisfied as to the task, the working conditions, the wages and the general policies, before he becomes a genuine employee.

The employment manager is coming in as a new staff man to relieve general executives. Staff or service departments are already familiar in the form of accounting departments, statistical departments and the like. This principle of staff service is now being carried over into the field of human engineering. General executives are demanding well-chosen men, men who are free from accidents and in sound health, men satisfied with their pay, and men so treated that they form a permanent and contented force, ready to co-operate loyally in the general plans of the enterprise. Of all the standardized agencies a service department can furnish to a general executive, the greatest is a first-class man. In a somewhat analogous way the employment manager represents a step in specializing the work of the foremen. His coming makes the foreman less of a jack of all trades, just as the coming of the tool room, the stock room and the designing department did. Under the new system, the foreman can no longer sell jobs, or protect pets, or cover up his own incompetence by discharging a man. When the foreman becomes accustomed to the new system he finds it a great relief. He gets a more even and dependable run of men than he could provide for himself, and he is free to become an expert in shop processes. See EMPLOYMENT MANAGER; EMPLOYMENT MANAGEMENT.

EDWARD D. JONES,
Professor of Business Administration, University of Michigan; Author of 'Administration of Industrial Enterprises,' etc.

INDUSTRIAL ORGANIZATIONS, Foreign. See LABOR DEPARTMENTS, FOREIGN; LABOR LEGISLATION, FOREIGN; LABOR, INTERNATIONAL OFFICE OF.

INDUSTRIAL PEACE, Experiments in. The desire to find a common ground of understanding between capital and labor with a view to reducing the enormous financial wastage resulting from needless labor strikes is the purpose back of every experiment in industrial peace that has been inaugurated during the past 20 years. The first efforts in this direction assumed the form of some type of profit-sharing, the idea being that the prospect of sharing in the profits of the employer would appeal to the self-interests of the workers and so inspire more loyal and efficient service. Theoretically, the idea appealed to many practical men, and various developments of the profit-sharing scheme have since been carried out. The failure of many of these projects has not had a permanently discouraging effect upon those who favor some such form of co-operative business effort, chiefly because of the fact that, in at least a majority of cases, the lack of success can be traced to local causes which proved stronger than the principles involved. Thus, the attempts of employers to use the profit-sharing ideal for advertising purposes or as a means of evading appeals for increases in wages, have invariably proved disastrous. At the same time, some of the largest concerns in the country have adopted this form of rewarding their employees, and with such satisfactory results that it is still in force. One reason why the number of failures charged against the profit-sharing idea is so great is that so many schemes that cannot properly be called profit-sharing have been classified under this designation. Thus, numerous forms of co-operative effort, including plans for participation in stock ownership through instalment purchase, bonus systems, pension schemes, and various projects of a welfare character have erroneously been classed as «profit-sharing.»

The term «profit-sharing» was first defined by the International Co-operative Congress, which was held in Paris, in 1889, and was stated to be «an agreement freely entered into by which the employees receive a share, fixed in advance, of the profits,» while the term «agreement,» as used in this connection, was defined to cover «not only agreements binding in law but as including also cases where the agreement is only a moral obligation.» The term «profit» was defined as «the actual net balance or gain realized by the operations of the undertaking»; «a share» as «a sum paid to the employees out of the profits,» such share to be «dependent upon the amount of the profits» and «not indeterminate,» or, in other words, «it must not be a share which an employer fixes, at the end of some period, at his absolute discretion, as distinguished from a prearranged basis,» while the proportion of the total working force of a concern that must share in the benefits before real profit-sharing conditions can be established was declared to be «not less than 75 per cent.» Making allowance for certain elasticities in interpreting this definition, necessitated by typically American conditions, the United States Bureau of Labor Statistics (Bulletin 208) reports that it found 60 genuine profit-sharing plans in operation in the United States. Of these, seven were established prior to 1900 while 29 have come into existence since 1911 and 21, or about one-third of the number, in the three years between 1914 and 1916. More than three-fifths of the concerns operating on a strict profit-sharing basis were located in three States, New York, Massachusetts and Ohio. Since the publication of this report, the number of plants adopting some form of genuine profit-sharing has been considerably augmented and advocates of this method of securing closer co-operation between employer and employee believe that the next government report will show more favorable conditions, not only in an increased rate of distribution but in other results more definitely indicative of the general practicability of the plan.

The National Association of Corporation Schools reported, in November 1918, that a recent survey of profit-sharing schemes showed that 39 plans had been abandoned, 10 because of labor troubles and strikes; seven because the employees were dissatisfied; five because the employers found that they operated unsatisfactorily; five because of failure under diminution of profits; four on account of lack of appreciation on the part of employees; two because of changes in business management, and one because the employees sold out their stock on a war market. The reasons for eight abandonments was not stated.

The Corporation School Bulletin states (November 1918) that while it is difficult to eliminate all the obstacles enumerated, they may be gotten around, and «in this,» it continues, «we are making some progress through careful study of the operating conditions and of the factors and fundamentals underlying each particular business. We are learning through our mistakes. Workmen are being classified and consideration is being given to what is just and fair to each class of employees. The reward is being fixed in proportion to certain definite desired accomplishments, in regard to output, the cost of production and other factors the value of which to the firm concerned can be figured. In consequence it will be possible to determine just what the share of each class of employee should be in producing the desired results and to reward accordingly — a decision which, in its turn, must lead to the reward of individuals in each class in proportion to the individual results obtained by workmen, foremen, superintendents, salesmen and managers, together with a greater confidence on the part of both employers and employed in the intrinsic justice of the movement itself.»

A comparatively recent development of the profit-sharing ideal is in operation in Louisville, Ky., where, in addition to paying employees as good compensation as would be paid for the same class of work in any other industry, all workers receive a division of the total net profits, 50 per cent being placed to the credit of the regular surplus or reserve fund from which dividends for the stockholders are declared, while the remaining 50 per cent is divided in three equal parts: One-third being allotted to the executives, one-third to the manufacturing and recording division and one-third to the sales division. In distributing the allotment to the workers and clerical force, the weekly or monthly wage of the individual is used as a basis for calculation, the assumption being that a man who is paid a weekly wage of $25 is of more value than the man who received $18 a week, and, therefore, is entitled to a proportionately greater share in the profits. This is, perhaps, one of the simplest and most generous forms of profit-sharing reported. From this 50 per cent participation plan the rate of distribution ranges down to about 2 per cent of the earnings of the employee.

The Rockefeller plan for the maintenance of industrial peace developed as the result of the serious labor troubles which were encountered by the Colorado Fuel and Iron Company, in 1913. To prevent a repetition of these disturbances, John D. Rockefeller, Jr., representing the Rockefeller interests, the largest stockholders in the company, visited the mines, quarries, steel works, timber properties and other activities of the corporation, and, after familiarizing himself with actual conditions, with the assistance of the company's sociological department, drafted a plan for a form of industrial democracy that has operated so successfully that a similar system of workers' representation was provided for the employees of the Standard Oil Company, in March 1918. The unique feature of the Rockefeller plan is that it provides the machinery through which grievances and suggestions as to working conditions may be brought to the attention of the proper executives. While this is a matter that can more easily be arranged in smaller concerns, it represents one of the most serious problems with which large corporations have to deal, and Mr. Rockefeller is the authority for the statement that this method of meeting this difficulty has operated satisfactorily to the operatives as well as to the officers of the company. Under this plan, employees are given representation through delegates elected by secret ballot, and these representatives are not only empowered to settle with the officers of the company any grievances which may arise from time to time, but also participate in the regulation of all matter of welfare through joint committees on industrial co-operation and conciliation; safety and accidents; sanitation, health and housing, recreation and education. Regular district conferences between the employees' representatives and the company's officers are held, and it is guaranteed that, on these occasions, all matters of concern to the workers shall be discussed. The plan provides elaborate machinery by which the rights of an employee who has a grievance may be properly safeguarded, means being arranged through which disputes that cannot be settled otherwise may be taken as far as the president of the company, if necessary. The discharge of employees is also arranged under agreement with the employees' representative and can be only for causes previously agreed upon and posted where each worker may become familiar with the conditions. These include:

(1) Violation of the law; (2) Violation of prescribed safety rules and regulations; (3) Insubordination or use of profane or abusive language; (4) Absence from duty without notice except for sickness or other causes beyond the operative's control; (5) Harboring disease that may endanger the health of others; (6) Changing working places without orders or prowling around the works from assigned places; (7) Falsifying or refusing to testify in investigations of accidents or for false statements at time of application or physical examination; (8) Neglect or carelessness resulting in damage to railroad equipment; (9) Robbing railroad journal boxes of waste; (10) Wilful neglect in care or use of company's property; (11) Obtaining material on fraudulent orders.

The results of the operations of this plan are reported by Mr. Rockefeller (in 1918) to be as follows:

(1) Uninterrupted operation of plants and increased output; (2) Improved working and living conditions; (3) Frequent and close contact between employees and officers; (4) Elimination of grievances as a disturbing factor; (5) Good-will developed to a high degree; (6) The creation of a community spirit.

Mr. Rockefeller also declares that the «representatives of the men in the camps and mills have assured me that all grievances nave been adjusted to the satisfaction of the employees, are in process of adjustment or the employees have been convinced that their grievances were not well founded. The representatives have expressed their own unqualified endorsement, approval and appreciation of the plan, which attitude, they say, is that very generally of the rank and file of the men, who constantly value the plan more highly as they understand its working better.»

The application of this plan of co-operation to the Eagle (New Jersey) works of the Standard Oil Company occurred in 1918. At an election held on 27 March, 14 delegates were elected to represent the employees and the first meeting between these representatives and the officers of the company was held on 1 April. At the election, 92.2 per cent of the total number of wage-earners voted.

As in the West, the operation of the plan in Bayonne, N. J., is supposed to guarantee to each worker full justice and protection in all his rights. Future wage adjustments will be made in joint conference between the representatives of the workers and the company's officials, while discharges and suspensions are permitted only under similar conditions as those which exist in the Colorado Fuel and Iron Company, and any employee who feels that he has been unjustly treated or who thinks he is subjected to unfair conditions may through his elected representative appeal to the general superintendent, or even to higher officials of the company.

The so-called profit-sharing plan of the Ford plants has been in operation since 12 Jan. 1914 and has proved successful, not only by increasing the stability of the working forces but also by bringing about a marked improvement in the morale of the organization. At the time this plan was adopted, it was widely announced that Henry Ford had established a minimum wage of $5 per day, but this statement was not strictly true as participation in the new rate of wage was confined to those who, in the opinion of Mr. Ford, were capable of using it «within limitations.» The actual minimum wage, at the beginning of 1914, was fixed at 34 cents per hour. To those who could comply with the conditions imposed by the Ford plan, additional remuneration in the form of a share of profits was paid, the minimum share of 28½ cents per hour bringing the minimum earnings to 62½ cents per hour, or the widely-advertised $5 per day. The employees considered as possible participants in the profit sharing were classified in three groups: 1. All married men living with and taking good care of their families. 2. All single men, over 22, of proven thrifty habits. 3. Men under 22 years of age, and women, who were the sole support of some next of kin or blood relative. These restrictions were established because, as John R. Lee, one of the executives of the Ford Company, has stated: «it was clearly foreseen that $5 a day in the hands of some men would work a tremendous handicap along the path of rectitude and right living and would make of them a menace to society. So it was established at start that no man was to receive the money who could not use it advisedly and conservatively; also, that when a man seemed to qualify under the plan and later developed weaknesses that it was within the province of the company to take away his share of the profits until such time as he could rehabilitate himself.»

To assure each operative just treatment under the new wage scheme, a large corps of specially trained investigators was employed to carry out the follow-up work upon which continuance in the profit sharing necessarily depended, and so successfully has the plan operated that, by the spring of 1916, about 90 per cent of the entire force were receiving their share of the profits. This naturally means that there has been a great improvement in the personnel of the organization. Thrifty habits have been developed; intemperance has largely ceased to be a considerable factor; domestic conditions have materially improved, while the increase in physical attributes is shown, not only in the reduction of the number of absentees but also in the productive achievements of the workers.

The concern that has most recently adopted a plan designed to afford employees a share in management is the Bethlehem Steel Corporation, and the idea is to be put in operation in all of the subsidiary companies, including several of the large shipbuilding corporations of this country. The principles of representation adopted by the company will, it is hoped, give all employees a voice in regard to the conditions under which they labor and provide an orderly and expeditious procedure for the prevention and adjustment of any future differences, as well as to anticipate the problem of continuous employment.

The plan provides that employee's representation shall be on the following basis: Plants employing under 1,500 persons, one representative for each 100 employees; where 1,500 to 10,000 persons are employed, one representative for each 200 employees; when plants employ more than 10,000 persons, one representative to each 300 employees. Representatives are elected for a term of one year and shall be deemed to have vacated office upon severing connections with the company. Any employee who has been on the payroll for not less than six months, who has reached his majority and is either an American citizen or has secured first papers is entitled for election as representative, while employment by the company for 60 days gives an operative the right to vote on questions of representation. The company appoints a management's representative whose duty it is to keep the management in touch with the representatives.

As in the Standard Oil plan, most of the detailed work of the organization is performed through various committees, which include: Rules; Ways and Means; Safety and Accident Prevention; Practice, Methods and Economy; Employees' Transportation; Wages, Piece Work, Bonus and Tonnage Schedules; Employment and Working Conditions; Health and Works Sanitation; Education and Publications; Pensions and Relief; Athletics and Recreation, and Continuous Employment and Condition of Industry.

The company by agreement guarantees that a representative shall be free to discharge his duties in an independent manner, without fear that his standing with the management will be affected by any action taken by him in his official capacity, and, to assure such independence of action, he is given permission to take a question of alleged discrimination against him on this account to any superior officer, to the president of the company, and, failing relief, to the State Department of Labor or to the secretary of labor of the United States.

Grievances which may occur in the future are to be handled by means of the machinery provided for this purpose. For example, where an employee is unable to adjust any matter with the foreman of the works where he is employed, it may be taken, either by the employee himself or, if he prefers, by his representative: (1) to the superintendent of the department; (2) with the management's representative, and (3) with one of the superior officers of the company, who will endeavor to effect a settlement, or who may, with the approval of all parties concerned, refer the question to the proper joint committee, consisting of the committee of employees' representatives with the addition of the same number of company's representatives, named by the management. If this method fails to effect adjustment within a reasonable time, the matter may be referred to the general joint committee on appeals, and if this settlement proves unsatisfactory, the president of the company shall be notified, and the question in dispute may thus be referred to an arbitrator, or arbitrators, to be determined by the nature of the controversy.

Another experiment in industrial peace through democracy in management was started in the Middle West in June 1914, and, as reported by the United States Department of Labor, the plan has proved so effective that all such questions as wage bargaining, hours of labor, discipline, discharges and adjustment of all grievances have now been put upon a collective basis.

Under this plan, all phases of management in which the employees are directly interested are handled through three separate bodies, known respectively as the senate, the cabinet and the house of representatives. The senate and cabinet represent the interests of the firm, while the members of the house of representatives are elected from among those employees of the company who have been in continuous service for at least six months, the election being by popular vote, in the ratio of one representative for every 15 employees, with the exception that a department having less than 15 operatives is given a representative.

Both the senate and the house of representatives have the power to initiate a proposition that is of interest to the employees, and may discuss and act upon all matters affecting their welfare. In case of disagreement in the actions of these two bodies, the matter is referred to a joint conference committee composed of an equal number of members from each body, and the results of their deliberations are finally submitted to the cabinet — composed of members of the executive board of the firm — for approval.

Much of the detailed business of the industrial congress is transacted by joint standing committees, including the betterment committee, which hears all complaints and adjusts grievances, the welfare committee, which deals with questions affecting the health and comfort of the workers, and the wage committee, the functions of which are: (1) To recommend and pass upon general changes in wages; (2) to suggest and pass upon minimum and maximum rates to be paid for the various operations according to skill involved, length of service and steadiness in attendance; (3) to sit with the planning board of the company for the purpose of passing upon individual increases in wages, and (4) to receive complaints of individuals to whom increases were denied. See ARBITRATION, INDUSTRIAL; PROFIT SHARING.

JOHN R. MEADER.

INDUSTRIAL RELATIONS COMMISSION. A commission created by act of Congress 23 Aug. 1912, for the purpose of inquiring into the general condition of labor in the principal industries of the United States, including agriculture, and especially in those industries which are carried on in corporate forms; into existing relations between employers and employees; into the effect of industrial conditions on public welfare and into the rights and powers of the community to deal therewith; into conditions of sanitation and safety of employees; into the growth of associations of employers and of wage earners; into the extent and result of methods of collective bargaining; into any methods which have been tried in any state or in foreign countries for maintaining mutually satisfactory relations between employees and employers; into the methods of mediation and conciliation; into the scope, methods and resources of existing bureaus of labor, and into possible ways of increasing their usefulness; into the question of smuggling or other illegal entry of Asiatics into the United States or its insular possessions, and of the methods by which such Asiatics are gaining admission, and to report to Congress recommendations for remedying existing difficulties. The commission consisted of nine members, including three employers of labor, three representatives of labor organizations and three representatives of the public at large. It separated its work into two large division: (1) public hearings; (2) research and investigations; and published valuable reports. Its final report was presented at the first session of the 64th Congress. It expired in August 1915.

INDUSTRIAL REPUBLIC. See INDUSTRIAL PEACE, EXPERIMENTS IN.

INDUSTRIAL REVOLUTION, The. Down to the middle of the 18th century few mechanical inventions had been made and people were still using the appliances in use at the time of the Pharaohs. The people of western Europe continued to till their fields with crude implements, harvest their grain with a sickle and thresh it with a flail, weave their cloth on hand looms, and saw and plane their boards by hand as their forefathers had done for 3,000 years. Means of transportation and communication had shown similar stagnation. As an illustration of the backwardness of invention we may take the textile industry, which was carried on in every home. From the days of Penelope in the time of Homer down to 1760 only three improvements had been made in the method of making cloth, and only one of these introduced any considerable change. The first was in the process of fulling the cloth: instead of throwing it into a brook and having it trod into the mud by the bare feet of children it was now fulled by means of a water fuller run by water power. A second really significant change was made in the 15th century. It was the substitution of the spinning wheel for the distaff and spindle; but while the spinner could spin much more rapidly, she was still unable to spin more than one thread at a time. The third change was the "fly-shuttle," invented by John Kay in 1738, by which the weaver could manipulate his loom more rapidly and easily.

Industrial Revolution in England.— Suddenly, however, a series of inventions was made in England, beginning about 1760, which completely revolutionized the existing methods of industry and introduced a new industrial era. Greater and more far-reaching mechanical changes occurred in the next few decades than in all the world's history before. Machinery was substituted for hand tools, the factory system supplanted the domestic system of home works, and industry gradually assumed the shape that is familiar to us. This series of changes is known as the Industrial Revolution, a name first applied by Arnold Toynbee about 1880, but which is now in general use.

Just why the Industrial Revolution should have occurred at the time when it did, or why it should have taken place in England rather than on the Continent, are difficult questions to answer. Necessity seems to have preceded invention in this case as generally, for the need of improved mechanical appliances was keenly felt in England, France, Germany, Switzerland and other countries, and considerable progress had been made in the physical and chemical sciences. England took the lead in industry for several reasons. In the first place she possessed the most important raw materials either at home (wool, coal and iron) or in her colonies (sugar, iron, cotton, dye and other woods). All of these were of such a character that they could best be worked up in quantity; there was therefore a demand for machinery for this purpose in England. Her insular position and the consequent ease of waterway communication — which was the quickest and cheapest — gave her command of larger markets than any of the continental countries. The political situation in England was such as to ensure domestic tranquillity and the security of property rights, which were essential to the development of manufactures. In this connection might be mentioned also the breaking down of the restraints of the guild system and the development of a good system of patent law. Capital was already accumulating in England, much of it won from the colonies by trade, there was a sufficient supply of skilled labor, and under the domestic system there had grown up a class of middlemen or enterprisers who could conduct business on a large scale. The conditions were ripe in England for a rapid industrial development, and when a series of technical improvements was made after the middle of the 18th century, adjustments in organization quickly followed.

The first important inventions occurred in the textile industry. Under the domestic system, where the processes of spinning and weaving were both carried on by hand, a principal difficulty had been to provide enough yarn, as it required the work of from 5 to 10 spinners, each spinning a single thread, to keep one weaver occupied. In 1767 James Hargreaves invented a machine known as the jenny, which operated eight spindles instead of one; this number was later raised to 80. The following year Richard Arkwright patented a machine in which the threads passed through two sets of rollers, of which the second pair was driven at a higher speed and thus drew out the wool or cotton into thread. This roller machine was known as the water frame because it was operated by water power. It had, however, one drawback, in that it did not twist the fibre tightly enough to make fine thread. But this difficulty was met in 1779 by Samuel Crompton, who combined the best features of the two earlier machines into one, which because of its hybrid origin was named the «mule.» As a result of these improvements in spinning machinery the traditional relations between the spinners and the weavers was reversed and more yarn could be produced than the hand looms could weave into cloth. In 1784 Dr. Edward Cartwright turned his attention to the construction of a power loom, which he succeeded in perfecting some three years later. Other improvements were made in the processes of printing and bleaching the cloth, but it remained for an American, Eli Whitney, to complete the series of improvements by his invention of the cotton gin in 1792. Whereas only a pound of cotton could be cleaned of its seeds in a day by hand, with the aid of the gin a man could clean 300. Unlimited cheap raw material was thus assured cotton manufacturers. The effects of these inventions upon the textile industry were revolutionary.

But in order that the new inventions might be made serviceable and machinery utilized to the utmost, it was necessary that it be driven by some non-human power. Indeed it cannot be too strongly emphasized that the vital feature in the Industrial Revolution lay in the substitution of power for human muscles. As long as man was confined to the use of hand tools his powers of production were strictly limited by the number of human hands available for this purpose, but as soon as machinery was invented and was driven by non-human power, there was no limit placed upon his powers of production through physical limitations. It depended now upon his ability to make the machines and to develop the power. Windmills were well known, but were unsatisfactory for this purpose, and at first water power was resorted to. But not until the steam engine was perfected did man have a really efficient instrument for this purpose. With this invention mankind entered upon an entirely new phase of development, and one that opens new vistas for the future.

The expansive power of steam was known to the ancient Greeks, but not until the 18th century was it put to practical use. In 1705 Newcomen constructed a practicable engine for pumping water out of the mines, and it was while repairing one of these crude affairs that James Watt in 1769 invented the improvements that made it a modern machine. It was now made adaptable for driving spinning machines, power looms and other mechanical devices. Its first use, however, was for pumping water, which had previously been a great menace, out of the coal mines, and hoisting the coal to the surface. This gave a great impetus to coal mining, which was further hastened by the invention of the safety lamp. The art of smelting iron by coal was made available about 1750, and in 1784 Corte discovered the process of «puddling.» Other improvements were made in the blast, the substitution of rollers for the hammer, and in appliances for handling heavy castings. These changes reacted powerfully on the iron industry and the manufacture of machinery, as the new processes made iron stronger and at the same time more malleable and easily worked up. There was now no limit to the supply of strong and powerful machines, for which the demand seemed unceasing.

Results.— The effects of the Industrial Revolution were momentous and far-reaching, and resulted in a veritable social revolution. The most striking result was the great increase of productive power of a society equipped with these new appliances. Unfortunately, however, the benefits of this increase in output and wealth were very unequally distributed; the landlord and the capitalist class profited greatly, but the mass of the wage-earners gained little if any by the new inventions. Indeed for a while it seemed as if they suffered only loss, for the use of machinery permitted the use of the labor of women and children on a large scale and rendered valueless the painfully acquired skill of the former hand workers. A second result was the destruction of the domestic system of production and the substitution therefor of the factory system. Under the former system industry had been carried on within the home by the domestic artisan, who generally owned his tools. Now, however, the new machines were much too expensive to be owned by a cottage workman, and it was moreover impossible to operate them in the home, as they were driven by power. It became necessary to bring both machines and workmen together in factories, where the building, the machinery and the materials were owned by the capitalist enterprisers. This brought about a sharp distinction between the two classes of workers involved, the capitalists on the one hand and the wage-workers on the other. Due to the need of capital in order to undertake manufacturing under the new conditions, the worker became more dependent upon the capitalist for employment. These facts brought to the front questions of labor and capital, which have become increasingly important as time has passed. See FACTORY SYSTEM.

Industrial Revolution in the United States. — The term Industrial Revolution has usually been applied to the sudden and remarkable series of changes that occurred in industry in England between 1760 and 1790, though it took another generation for them to work themselves out. The old domestic system of industry was completely transformed and a revolution wrought in the economic and social life of the people. It is interesting to raise the question whether other countries have experienced similar changes and whether we can apply the term to other periods than that just mentioned. The nearest approach to an industrial revolution in the United States probably occurred in the 30-year period beginning with 1808, when a series of political and industrial events led the people to develop manufacturing by the factory system in addition to agriculture and commerce. This did not lead to any revolutionary changes as in England, since there had never been any widespread development of the domestic system of manufactures before this time. The transfer from one system to the other was therefore accomplished without any painful readjustment or suffering. A similar industrial transformation from agricultural to manufacturing conditions occurred in France between about 1820 and 1850, and in Germany after 1870.

What has been regarded as a presage of a coming industrial revolution in the United States has found expression in recent experiences in the South, where local campaigns against the existing type of factory management have been in evidence. The upheaval has been under the auspices, at least, of the American Federation of Labor. In the later part of the 19th century, mills were few and the mill workers were anxiously dependent on retaining the chance to work, whatever the cost of toil and long hours. With the very large increase in the number of plants in the South, work has become more secure and the worker has begun to question the fairness of the share he is required to take. As matters stand, the manufacturer in the South profits by a labor differential of about 15 per cent. However, the movement for reform has so far been rather for an increase of wages, and that a modest one, than for any substantial reduction in either the hours or the arduousness of the labor. See GREAT BRITAIN-INDUSTRIAL REVOLUTION; HISTORY, MODERN.

Bibliography.—Darvall, F. O., 'Popular Disturbances and Public Order in Regency England (New York 1934); Beard, C. A., 'The Industrial Revolution' (London 1902); Bowden, W., 'The Industrial Revolution' (New York 1928); Mitchell, B., 'The Industrial Revolution in the South' (Baltimore 1930); Schmiedeler, E., 'The Industrial Revolution and the Home' (Washington 1927).

ERNEST L. BOGART,
Professor of Economics, University of Illinois.

INDUSTRIAL SCHOOLS, an English term variously applied; sometimes synonymous with the so-called Ragged Schools, in which mechanical arts are taught; sometimes designating ordinary elementary schools in which agriculture, domestic science or some other industrial art is taught during a portion of the school day. The term is becoming obsolete, having fallen into disfavor because of its application to reformatories.

INDUSTRIAL SERVICE. See INDUSTRIES, WELFARE WORK IN.

INDUSTRIAL TERMS. The following list embraces many of the important terms that are used technically in the several commercial industries. Such terms as are usually regarded as self-explanatory, as well as those that have no general application, have been omitted. Those that are of more than ordinary importance will be found defined more fully under their appropriate heading.

ABB.— In wool-sorting the quality of the wool is denoted by the terms: "fine abb," and "coarse abb."

ACIERAGE.— In engraving, the deposition of a very thin layer of steel on the face of an engraved copper plate, to increase its durability under the stress of printing.

ANNEALING.— The process of treating substances by heat to remove their brittleness and yet make them tough and inclined to be elastic.

ANTICHLOR.— A term used in bleaching to denote the method employed to remove or neutralize the injurious effects of the free chlorine left in some bleached materials.

ARCH.— When a portion of a lode is left standing, in mining, because it is too poor to work or is needed as a support, it is called an "arch."

ASHLARING.— In carpentry, the placing of upright studs to form vertical walls of a room constructed under the slopes of a peaked roof.

ASTERISM.—A term in printing denoting the three asterisks sometimes placed before a sentence to call attention to it.

ATTEMPERATION.— Regulating the temperature of the beer-worts in brewing.

ATTENUATION.— The decrease in density of the beer-worts in brewing is termed "attenuation."

AUTOGENOUS SOLDERING.— Joining pieces of the same metal by fusing them together by a melting heat applied at the juncture.

AVIVAGE.— A process for clearing and brightening the colors in dyeing.

BACK.— (a) In metal-mining, the portion of the lode that lies between the level and the one next above it; (b) in coal-mining, the inner end of a heading where work is being conducted; (c) the thickest and best hides are termed "backs" in the leather trade.

BACK-CASING.— A wall of dry brick sunken through sand or gravel in mining.

BACKLASH.— In coal-mining, the backward suction after an explosion of firedamp.

BACK-STAY.— In printing, the leather strap used to check the carriage of the press; in lathes, a support to prevent the work from springing away from the cutting tool.

BALK.— When a bed of coal suddenly thins out it is termed a "balk."

BALLOONING.— In spinning, the bellying outward of the thread while it is being wound on the bobbin.

Band.— A layer of rock that is interstratified with coal.

Barney.— A small car used in mining to push the mine-car up a slope; the pit from which it runs is termed the "barney-pit."

Barrel-work.— Pieces of native copper too small to be handled as mass-copper, but large enough to be shipped in barrels.

Bastard.— (a) An impure brown sugar made from the refuse of previous boilings; (b) the large mold into which the sugar is drained is also called a "bastard;" (c) in printing, any type whose face is out of proportion to the size of its body is termed "bastard" type.

Bastard Flatting.— In painting, the "egg-shell" semi-gloss surface produced by using three times as much turpentine as oil in the paint mixing.

Bating.— The process of steeping hides and skins to render them soft and fit for tanning.

Battery.— The timber structure that is used to prevent coal from sliding down a shute.

Bay.— In mining, an open space for waste in a long-wall working.

Beaming.— (a) Winding the warp-yarn on a loom in the manufacture of cloth; (b) working hides with a slicker over a beam in the leather trade.

Beater.— (a) A machine used in cotton manufacturing to open and clean the cotton before it passes to the carder; (b) a knife used for breaking flax or hemp; (c) the batten of the loom used for weaving.

Beaumontage.— The filling material used to stop small holes in wood or metal work; in the first instance made of varnish thickened with chalk and resin, in the case of iron, with a mixture of iron filings and sal ammoniac.

Benching.— A term applied to the process used in getting the coal after it is holed.

Black-liquor.— A crude acetate of iron used, in dyeing, as a mordant.

Bleed.— (a) In bookbinding, to trim the margin too closely; (b) in dyeing, extracting the coloring matter.

Bleu-de-roi.— The term used to denote the cobalt-blue color in European porcelain.

Blick.— The iridescence appearing on gold and silver at the end of the refining process.

Blooming.— Clouding of a varnished surface usually through the absorption of moisture.

Blue-cap.— In mining, the bluish or brownish halo which, when it appears around the flame of the safety lamp, indicates a dangerous quantity of fire-damp, is termed the "blue-cap."

Boards.— The hard paper-stock inserted between the printed sheets in a press to remove an indentation of impression; often called "press-boards."

Bone.— The term used to define the slaty portions in a coal mine.

Bonnet.— The shield used to protect a mine shaft from substance which might otherwise fall into it.

Border.— The rim fixed about the bed-plate used in milling to prevent the meal from falling off before it reaches the proper opening.

Bossing.— The working of lead sheets into hollow forms by pressure, without cutting and soldering.

Box Calf.— Chrome-tanned calf-skins, which bear square markings due to rolling the skins lengthwise and from side to side while still damp.

Boxing In.— In printing, the enclosing of special reading matter with a frame of rule.

Branning.— A term that is applied both to the process of steeping cloth before or after it is dyed, and to the steeping of skins before tanning.

Brood.— The term applied in mining to all heterogeneous mixtures found with copper or tin ore.

Brush.— An instrument constructed of several small trees, like the birch, and used by farmers instead of a harrow in covering grain, or small seed after sowing.

Buck.— The breaking of ore into small pieces for jigging.

Buddle.— In mining, to wash ore free from earthy matter the water is run over an inclined hutch which is termed a "buddle."

Bulling-bar.— In mining, the bar used to ram clay fillings into open cracks before blasting.

Bully-head.—The name by which the sledge-hammer used by miners is popularly known.

Bultow.— In the fishing industry, the practice of stringing many hooks on one line, used in fishing for cod off the Banks.

Bunchy.— Used in mining to denote that the ore is irregularly distributed through the lode in small masses, or "pockets."

Bundle.— (a) In paper-making, 2 reams of printing, or brown paper; (b) in spinning, 20 hanks, or 6,000 yards of linen yarn.

Buntons.— The timbers put across a mining shaft to divide it into compartments.

Butt.— A hide of sole leather in which the belly and shoulders have been cut off.

Cade.— A term of measurement in the fishing trade, denoting either 500 herrings, or 1,000 sprats.

Cage-seat.— The framework at the bottom of a shaft, so arranged as to reduce the jar when the cage drops upon it.

Calf.— A term applied to a bookbinding in calf-skin. This binding is of several grades: Divinity calf, a dark-brown binding, with blind stamping and no gilding; half-calf, in which the backs and corners only are of calf-skin; mottled calf, a calf binding of pale color in which the decorations have been made by the sprinkling of acid; smooth calf, or plain, undecorative leather; tree calf, a bright, brown calf binding stained by acid to imitate the trunk and branches of a tree.

Camber.— In building, the amount of curvature upward given a horizontal beam; for cast iron $\frac{3}{4}$ inch for each 10 feet of span; for steel, $\frac{1}{2}$ inch for the same span.

Cancels.— In printing, the pages of a book which have been reprinted because of error in copy or type. They are marked usually by an asterisk in the bottom margin of the page.

Canch.— A term used to denote that part of a floor or roof of a gangway that is removed to equalize the grade because of a fault, or break in the strata.

Cant Brick.— A brick cut at any angle other than a right angle.

Cannel.— A form of weaving that produces a corded or rep tissue.

Cap.— A term denoting certain sizes and shapes in paper: Double cap, 17 x 28 inches; exchange cap, a fine quality paper, used in printing bills of exchange; flat cap, or full cap, 14 x 17 inches; foolscap, usually 12 x 15 inches; legal, or pot cap, 13 x 16 inches, etc.

Carcase.— In building, the rough structure of a building (or a ship) before finishing work is begun.

Carding.— The disentangling of wool, cotton or other fibres with a card, preparatory to spinning. See Combing.

Carriage.— In building, the inclined timber structure which supports the staircase.

Carrot.— In the fur trade, to dress a pelt to preserve it from insects.

Carrots.— Rolls of tobacco after they have been so prepared that they require only to be ground and sifted to be made into snuff.

Case.— (a) A shallow wooden tray, the partitions making the small boxes in which the various characters of type required by printers are kept in order for the use of compositors. (b) A book cover that has been made separately from the book for which it is intended.

Case-hardening.— Producing a thin surface layer of steel upon soft iron articles by heating them to cherry-redness in contact with charcoal or other carbon.

Casse-paper.— The wrinkled, broken, or otherwise imperfect paper rejected by the trade.

Cassette.— The utensil in which chinaware is baked; sometimes called the "coffin."

Cast.— (a) The water used in the preparation of beer. The quantity that is first placed in the mash-tub is termed the "first cast;" that which is subsequently added, the "second cast," "third cast," etc. (b) In bee culture, an after swarm led by a maiden queen.

Catchword.— In printing, the setting of the first word of the following page at the lower right-hand corner of the page form — found only in old books.

Catgut.— Strips cut from the specially treated intestines of sheep and horses.

Certosina Work.— A term used to denote the inlay of certain light materials — like ivory or satinwood — upon dark woods like walnut.

Chase.— In printing, a square, open framework of iron into which the type forms are fastened to facilitate moving and working on the press.

Chase Mortise.— In building, a mortise with one side on a bevel to allow the easier entrance of the tenon.

Chemical Pulp.— Wood pulp in which the fibres have been separated by chemical process instead of by mechanical means.

Chilled Castings.— Iron castings with hardened surface produced by casting in metal molds which conduct away quickly the heat of the molten iron.

Chop.— (a) In milling the product of the first crushing of the wheat; (b) also used to denote the brand and quality of tea imported from China, as "first chop," etc.

Chrome Leather.— Leather tanned with chromium salts instead of vegetable tanning agents.

Cissing.— In painting, the appearance of small dull spots in a varnished surface due to underlying oil or grease.

Clearcole.— A coating of glue size and chalk laid upon plaster walls before painting them.

Clicker.— The workman who cuts the uppers and soles for boots and shoes.

Clog.— The short pieces of timber used in mines to prop the roof.

Closing-machine.— (a) A machine that sews heavy cloth or leather with a lockstitch, alike on both sides; (b) apparatus used in rope-making to twist the already made strands into rope.

Cobbing.— In mining, a process of breaking the ore that the better parts may be sorted out.

Cockle.— (a) A large stove used in the making of porcelain, to dry the biscuit-ware after its glazing preparatory to burning; (b) the kiln used for drying hops.

COLD BEND.— In iron specifications, the angle at which iron bars or plates break when bent cold.

COLOR.— (a) In gold mining, the particles of gold that are shown when auriferous sand is washed out; (b) in printing, the evenness of distribution of ink in an impression.

COMBING.— In spinning, the removal of short fibres from the carded textile before it is spun.

COMMERCIAL.— A term used to denote the shape and size of paper: Commercial letter, 11 x 17 inches; unfolded commercial letter, small, 10½ x 16½ inches; commercial note, 8 x 10 inches, unfolded.

COMPANIONSHIP.— In printing, a number of compositors employed in setting up a quantity of copy under the direction of one leader.

COMPOST.— A mixture of various manuring substances used by agriculturists in fertilizing land.

CONCENTRATOR.— A machine used, chiefly in mining in the United States, to separate the ore from the rock with which it was associated in the lode.

CONDITIONING.— In spinning, the dampening of cotton fibre to restore its natural percentage of moisture before spinning.

COP.— The cylindrical form in which cotton yarn is built up when spun on the mule. There are three sizes: Pin cop, bastard cop and twist cop. Woolen cop is of conical form.

CORD.— (a) In fancy weaving, the interval between two vertical lines of the design is termed a "cord;" (b) the same term is used in bookbinding when a book is tied firmly between two boards to assure its drying smoothly. The term "Maitland cord" is used in weaving to denote the cord which extends along the wooden shafts of leaves to which the heddles are secured.

CORDING.— The term denoting the arrangement of the treadles in a loom by which they are made to move in such clusters and time as the production of the pattern may necessitate.

CORE-PIECE.— The yarn running through the centre of a rope to assure its solidity.

CORNER.— The triangular tool used in bookbinding to decorate the corners of a book.

COUCH.— (a) The operation, in brewing, of spreading the steeped grain upon the floor to convert it into malt; (b) in paper-making, the act of removing the paper from the mold upon which it has been formed that it may be placed upon the felt.

COUCH ROLL.— In paper making, a felt-covered roll which squeezes out the surplus water from the sheet of wet pulp as it leaves the wire.

COUNTER-LODE.— A term used in mining to denote a lode running in such a direction in relation to the main lodes that it crosses or intersects them.

COUNTS.— In spinning, the relative diameter of threads, as measured by the weight of a stated length. Single thread counts in cotton are the number of hanks of 840 yards in 1 pound: That is, a 20-cotton thread is 20 hanks to the pound. In worsted, the basis is 560 hanks to the pound. In wool, it is the number of one-yard skeins in 1 dram.

COURSING.— The method of regulating the ventilation of a mine by conducting the air through various doors, stopings, etc.

CRABBING.— In woolen manufacture, a treatment of the cloth with live steam through a perforated roll; the object being to prevent subsequent wrinkling.

CRADLE.— (a) A movable hanging scaffold used by painters and builders, supported from above, and operated by ropes and pulleys; (b) in mining, a rocking tray for washing out placer gold.

CRAM.— In weaving, a warp that has more than two threads in each split of the reed.

CRAWLING.— In painting, the wrinkling of varnish, due to too heavy a coat or a sudden rise in temperature while the varnish is drying.

CRAZING.— In the pottery industry, when the glaze separates from the body and forms blisters.

CREASER.— A tool used in bookbinding to define the width of the bands of a book, and to fix the position of the lines on the backs and sides.

CREASING.— A course of tiles projecting on each side of a wall at the top, to prevent the soaking in of water falling upon it.

CREEP.— If the pillars of a mine are not sufficiently large, or the roof is not fully supported the pressure of the superincumbent strata sometimes causes a bulging or rising of the under-clay. Collieries have been entirely destroyed by "creep."

CREEPING.— The movement backward of a rubber tire when it is too loose on the rim.

CRIZZLING.— In glass manufacture, a blemish of the surface due to using cold tools upon it while in the plastic state.

CROP.— An untrimmed hide, struck for sole-leather, is termed a "crop," or "crop-hide" in the trade.

CROPPED.— In binding signifies that the margins of the pages have been trimmed too close.

CROPPING.— In cloth making, a machine process for shearing the nap of cloth.

CRUP BUTT.— In leather work, the oily part of a horsehide which covers the loin of animal, used especially for the uppers of hunting and fishing boots.

CRUTCH OR CRUTCHER.— A term used in soap-making to denote the perforated instrument with which the various ingredients are kept mixed while cooling.

CULLET.— In glass manufacture, clean waste and broken glass from previous meltings and castings added to a raw batch to initiate the fusion.

CURE.— In leather making, the substance used to prevent decomposition in raw hides and skins. The commonest cures are salt, arsenic, boracic acid and some of the coal-tar carbolic products.

CUT.— The block upon which a picture is engraved and from which it is impressed in printing.

CUTTER.— Usually applied, in mining, to a joint or crack which crosses a better defined system of cracks in the same rock.

DABBER.— The use of the "dabber" by printers has largely ceased since the introduction of the ink roller, but the same term is now applied to instruments used by etchers and stereotypers. The former is used to ink the surface of engraved blocks or plates; the latter to dab the back of the damp paper used in the papier-mache process of stereotyping, in order that it may be driven into the interstices of the type.

DABBING.— The term applied to the process in stone-working by which the surface of the stone is covered with small indentations, after having been made uniform.

DAM.— The term applied to the underground wall frequently constructed to hold back water, air or gas.

DAMPING.— A process used in bleaching to add a certain amount of moisture to a fabric, after it has been starched, that it may be properly finished.

DANDY.— The running-out fire for the melting of pig-iron in tin-plate manufacturing.

DANDY-ROLL.— The wire-gauze cylinder beneath which the web of water-pulp is passed in paper-making to drain it partially of water and impress the watermark.

DASH-POT.— A controlling device for checking sudden movements in mechanisms, consisting of a cylinder filled with oil or water in which moves a loosely fitted piston.

DASH-WHEEL.— The partially submerged wheel used in cotton manufacturing to wash and rinse calico in the piece.

DEAD GROUND.— In mining, those parts of the vein which do not contain ore.

DEAD MELTING.— In foundry practice, heating metal to a temperature considerably higher than its melting point.

DECK.— Used in mining to denote the loading or unloading of cars upon the cage.

DECKLE-STRAP.— The contrivance used in paper-making to define the width of the sheet by regulating the flow of pulp.

DELE.— A term used in proofreading to direct the compositor or printer to remove a letter, word or phrase.

DEMY.— A standard size in paper sheets. Printing demy is 22½ x 17½ inches; writing demy, 20 x 15½ inches; drawing demy, 22 x 17 inches.

DENTELLE.— In bookbinding, a style of finishing with delicate lace-like tracery in gilt.

DEPTH OF FOCUS.— The capacity of a lens (q. v.) to focus on one plane images of objects located at widely differing distances from the lens. This capacity is enhanced by the use of smaller stops.

DERBY FLOAT.— In plastering, a tool for smoothing freshly laid plaster. It consists of a longish board with a peg handle near each end. See FLOAT.

DEVIL.— (a) An errand-boy employed in a printing-office; (b) a plumber's fire-pot for heating solder and lead.

DIP CRANK.— A crank formed by bending a rod to crank form instead of building it up from separate pieces, or cutting it from a forging.

DIPPING.— A process in ceramics by which a coarse clay body is coated with fine enamel by being plunged into the liquid which constitutes the coating.

DISCHARGE.— In dyeing, the process by which white patterns are produced on colored grounds by a chemical bleaching or release of the color.

DISCOVERY CLAIM.— In mining law, the portion of ground held by reason of the first discovery of its mineral deposits.

DISHED.— The form given to wheels or discs where the centre is in a hollow as compared with the plane of the rim.

DISTRIBUTE.— A term used in printing for the process of returning dead matter (type no longer required) to the cases; "thrown-in" is another term used to define this process.

DOCTOR.— (a) A term in wine-making, used to indicate that the character of the wine has been changed by the addition of another liquor; (b) to alter any commodity for purpose of deception.

DOFF.— A term that has several distinctions in the textile manufacture: (a) The process of stripping the cotton or wool from the cards preparatory to spinning; (b) the act of mending broken threads; (c) the removal of full bobbins to give place to the empty ones.

DOLLY.— (a) A soft polishing mop rotated at high speed for putting the final surface on metal work to be plated; (b) in mining, a heavy tool, sometimes of wood for crushing soft materials.

DONGOLA.— As applied to leathers, skins which have been tanned by both the vegetable and mineral tanning agents successively.

Dossil.— The roll of cloth used to clean the ink from an engraved plate prior to printing.

Double.— A term used to denote the size and quality of paper: Double medium, a printing paper, 24 x 38 in.; double royal, a printing paper, 26 x 40 in.; double demy, 35 x 22½ in.; double imperial, 44 x 30 in.

Double-dyeing.— A method of dyeing mixed goods by which the wool and cotton are dyed separately with colors that have no affinity for the other fibre.

Double-milled.— A term applied to denote that cloth has been fulled twice to make it finer in quality.

Doubler.— (a) A machine for doubling and drawing silk; (b) a still made to intercept and redistil the vapors of distillation; (c) a felting placed between the fabric and the press before printing.

Downcast.— A term used to denote the system of ventilation used in mining, the shaft down which the air passes into the mine being called the "down-cast."

Draft.— In weaving, a chart or plan showing the cording of a loom or the arrangement of the heddles.

Drag.— (a) A light iron-rod tool with a tapering spiral end, used by miners in cleaning out bore-holes before introducing the blasting charge; (b) the device that guides wood to the saw in saw-milling; (c) also applied in printing to denote the thickened impression on one side of the letters produced by the scraping of the sheet on the type.

Draw.— In cotton spinning, the extent of the outward and inward run of a mule carriage, usually 63 or 64 inches. The speed of the mule is designated by the number of draws per minute.

Drawing-paper.— A term used commercially to describe a variety of stout papers manufactured expressly for use in drawing. The regular sizes are as follows: Cap, 13 x 16 in.; demy, 15½ x 18½ in.; medium, 18 x 22 in.; royal, 19 x 24 in.; superroyal, 19 x 27 in.; imperial, 21¼ x 29 in.; elephant, 22¾ x 27¾ in.; columbier, 23 x 33¾ in.; atlas, 26 x 33 in.; theorem, 28 x 34 in.; double elephant, 26 x 40 in.; antiquarian, 31 x 52 in.; emperor, 40 x 60 in., Uncle Sam, 48 x 120 in.

Drawing Rolls.— Rolls used in spinning machinery set in successive pairs, each of which turns more rapidly than any previous pair, the sliver (q.v.) passing through them in succession.

Draw-boy.— Formerly the weaver's assistant; now, a mechanical device used in drawing the heddles to form the pattern of the cloth to be woven. The machine upon which this figure-weaving is done is known as the "draw loom."

Drawn.— A term denoting the method of freeing substances from all particles of iron and steel by use of a magnet.

Dresser.— (a) The workman employed in type-foundries to remove all defects from the types in preparing them for sale; (b) the tool, or machine employed to cut and dress the furrows on a millstone; (c) a mallet used by plumbers for flattening sheet-lead; (d) one of the picks used in mining.

Drift.— A term used in mining to describe the nearly horizontal passage ways frequently excavated in working a mine; sometimes called a "drive."

Drill.— (a) In agriculture, when a field is not sown broadcast, but in rows, it is said to be in "drills"; (b) also the machine for sewing in this way.

Drift-joint.— When two sheets of metal used in roofing have been joined without soldering by a step-down, so that the joint forms a water-conductor the arrangement is known as a "drip-joint."

Drop-bar.— A term applied to the bar or roller on a printing-press that regulates the passage of the paper sheets to impression.

Drop-finger.— In some cylinder printing-presses the rods that are employed to hold the sheets in place until they can be seized by the grippers are termed the "drop-fingers."

Dropper.— A term used in mining to denote a branch or spur that connects with the main lode but does not materially enrich it.

Dropping.— A term used to denote a defect in the product of the glassmaker. It is caused by the accidental dropping of crude glass or furnace lining into the molten glass in the melting vessel.

Drop-roller.— Used in printing to denote the roller that drops at specified intervals to supply the printing ink for distribution on the ink table.

Droving and Striping.— A process in stone-cutting by which the shallow parallel grooves are made along the length of the rough-hewn stone.

Drunken Saw.—A "wobbling" circular saw set off at right angle on its arbor, used for cutting a groove in timber, the width of the groove being governed by the aberrance from a right angle.

Drying-off.— A term denoting the process by which an amalgam of gold is evaporated.

Drying-plates.— Used in brewing to denote the series of frames in the malt kiln. They are placed one over the other, and, being covered with woven wire, the hot air ascends through them in such manner as to dry the malt.

Dummy.— In plumbing, a wooden rod having a lump of lead at the end, used for ramming out dents in lead pipe.

Dump.— Used in printing to denote the act of removing types from the stick to place them on a galley.

Dung-bath.— In some processes of dyeing and calico-printing the cloth is subjected to a "dung-bath," composed of warm water, animal's dung, etc., for the purpose of removing the superfluous mordant.

Easing.— In weaving gauze, the motion by which the tension of the warp is slackened during the formation of the cross-sheds.

Egg-shell.— A term used commercially to denote the thinnest and most translucent of china or porcelain.

Egg-shell Finish.— See Bastard Flatting.

Elbow-plate.— In paper-making, the cutter of the rag-cutting machine when bent to an angle in the middle.

Electroplating.— The process of coating articles with silver or other metal by means of electrolysis.

Electrotyping.— The process of making plate copies of any engraved or molded surface by means of electrical deposition.

Ensilage.— An agricultural term used to denote the process of preserving fodder, etc., in a green state by storing the materials under pressure in silos or in pits dug in the ground.

Entasis.— The slight convexity in the upright outline of a pillar or column; more pronounced in Roman architecture than in Greek types.

Face.— In coal-mining, the working, or portion of the seam that is being mined.

Fascet.— A rod, or basket of wire used in carrying the bottle from the mold to the leer in glass-manufacture.

Fat-color.— Paint which has been long mixed and has become thickened and greasy.

Fat Liquor.— In leather manufacture, an emulsion of fish or other oils with soap, and, usually yolks of eggs, used as a dressing for skins.

Fat-Work.— In printing, when copy is particularly profitable to the compositor owing to the fact that it has much open space that may be filled with quads, or that in other ways favors rapid execution, is termed fat-work. To beat, or ink "fat" in printing means that a form of type has been given an excess of ink.

Feeding.— In printing, a term denoting the method of placing the sheets of paper in such position that they are ready to meet the requirements of the press.

Feints.— The first products of distillation which come over from a pot-still when making whisky.

Fettling.— The operation of removing fins, etc., from castings.

Figging.— In soap making, a spotty appearance of the soap due to undissolved specks of potasium stearate; considered a mark of excellence. It is simulated by the addition to common soaps of flecks of clay or talc.

Filature.— In silk-culture, a reel by which the silk is drawn from the cocoons. Also used as to the quality of the raw silk marketed on these reels.

Fillet.—(a) In weaving, a strip of card-clothing; (b) in dairying, a perforated curb used to confine the cheese-curds; (c) a wheel-shaped tool used in bookbinding to impress a gilt line, or decoration upon the covers of books; (d) in printing, a rule fixed with lines that may be used as a border.

Filling.— (a) The term by which the woof or weft thread of a woven fabric is known; (b) in soap making, the treatment through which the soap is made to carry an excess of water or other adulterant.

Filling Can.— In rope-making, the can in which the sliver is condensed and wound after coming from the doublers.

Fine-drawing.— The term applied to the finishing process in cloth manufacture. By exposing the cloth to a strong light all the minute holes due to breaks are discovered so that they may be repaired with a needle by the introduction of sound yarns in the place of those that have proved defective.

Fining-Roller.— A cylindrical sieve of wire cloth used in paper-making to retain the coarse fibres and knots so that they cannot pass through with the finely ground stuff.

Fire-gilding.— A process of gilding by the application of an amalgam from which the mercury is afterward driven by the heat of a muffle, leaving a fine film of gold.

Fixing Bath.— (a) In tanning, the catechu-bath is followed by another known as the "fixing" bath. It consists of water sufficient to cover the skins, acidified with nitric acid, modified with a little glycerine; (b) in photography the chemical bath used to dissolve from an exposed plate the silver salts not changed by the action of light.

Flashing.— (a) A strip of sheet lead, zinc, or copper used to make a watertight joint between a roof and the chimney passing through it, or in the valleys formed by angular intersections in a roof; (b) in glass manufacture, the laying upon glass of a thin coating of glass of another color.

Flatting.— In painting, the laying of a coat of paint with a dead surface.

Flesher.— The tool used in leather manufacture for the purpose of fleshing hides, that is, removing adhering flesh or fat.

FLIGHT.— The series of steps between a floor and a landing.

FLITCH.— The piece of wood or metal added to a beam to strengthen it. The beam is thence termed a flitched beam.

FLOAT.— (a) The flat metal tool used by masons for smoothing the surface of fresh plaster; (b) in weaving, the passage of the shuttle crosswise above or below the threads but without intersecting them.

FLONG.— The combination of moist tissue paper and paste used in stereotyping by the papier-mache process to form the mold or matrix from composed types or engraved surfaces.

FLOOR.— In brewing, each steeping is known as a "floor" or "piece."

FLOORING.— Used in brewing to denote the operation of spreading the grain on the malt-floor, that it may be kept at an even temperature, to check germination.

FLOW.— A term used in ceramics to denote the flux that is used to make the colors run and blend in firing.

FLUE WORK.— In pipe organs, those "stops" which produce their tones by the vibration of air columns, and not by reeds. They include the "principal," "flute," and "stopped" groups.

FLUFFING.— In leather manufacture, the process of smoothing a leather surface on an emery wheel.

FLURRY.— A term used in calico printing to denote the condition of frothiness which is sometimes developed by the colors during the process of printing.

FLY.— (a) One of the arms of a spinning-frame which revolves around the bobbin to twist the yarn as it is wound upon it; (b) in cotton and wool spinning, the term applied to the fibre collecting on the carding rolls; (c) in weaving, a shuttle with wheels driven through the shed by a jerk; (d) in printing, the mechanism which receives and delivers the separate sheets as they are printed on the press; (e) in piano-making, the hinged board with which the keys are covered when not in use; (f) in clocks, the fan which controls the speed of the striking train.

FLY-NUT.— A nut with wings by which it may be turned with the fingers.

FOLIO.— While the word "folio" is used to denote the size of a book it is also applied as a descriptive term for several sizes of paper, each of which is designated by a specific name: Pot folio, 7½ x 12½ in.; foolscap folio, about 8 x 12½in.; flat-cap folio, 8½ x 14 in.; crown or post folio, 9½ x 15 in.; demy folio, 10½ x 16 in.; medium folio, 12 x 19 in.; royal folio, 12½ x 20 in.; superroyal folio, 14 x 22 in.; imperial folio, 16 x 22 in.; elephant folio, 14 x 23 in.; atlas folio, 16½ x 26 in.; columbier folio, 17½ x 24 in.; double elephant folio, 20 x 27 in.; antiquarian folio, 26½ x 31 in.

FOOLSCAP.— A term applied to a writing paper varying in size from 12 x 15 to 12½ x 16 inches. The term was derived from the water-mark, a fool's cap, which formerly appeared upon all the papers that bore this name.

FOOTLINE.— A term used in printing to denote the last line of a page of type. It is usually left blank, although it sometimes contains the number of the page or the signature on the sheets.

FOOTS.— The impure residues left after the refining of oils, fats, waxes, and greases.

FORMAT.— In printing, the plan of the page form of a book; as folio, octavo, etc.

FORWARDER.— A term used in bookbinding to designate the workman whose duty it is to receive the sewed book, put on its back, cover, etc., and prepare it for the finisher.

FRIZING.— In leather manufacture, the removing of a very thin layer from the grain (hair) surface of a skin.

FULL-FACED.— A term used in printing to describe a type with the thick lines that make it print extremely black.

FURNITURE.— The term "furniture" in printing denotes the pieces of wood or metal that are placed around the pages of type, not only to keep them the necessary distance apart but to assist in fastening them securely in the chases. When the furniture has been systematically cut into various standard lengths and widths, so that they may be easily combined, the pieces are known as "labor-saving furniture."

FUSTAIN.— The term applied to a short twilled cotton fabric, usually a cloth having a short pile, like corduroy, velveteen, etc.

GAGING-THREAD.— In weaving, a thread introduced temporarily to stop the weft-thread at a specified point.

GALLEY.— An oblong, shallow tray, now usually made of brass, but sometimes of wood, used in printing by compositors as a place to deposit the type they have set. Galleys in which the type may be locked are known as proof-galleys. Standing galleys are inclined frames fitted with cleats on which the type galleys rest. A proof taken from types being held on galleys is termed a "galley-proof."

GASSING.— In textile manufacture, the process of singeing off loose fibres and fluff from thread by passing it through a gas flame.

GATHERING.— (a) In glass-making, the method of coiling the molten glass on the end of an iron tube preparatory to the work of blowing; (b) in book-binding, the collecting of the printed and folded sheets in their proper consecutive order.

GIGGERING.— A process in bookbinding by which the burnished lines are laid by a sliding or rubbing movement, upon covers decorated in antique fashion.

GIGGING.— The process of finishing cloth by drawing the loose ends of wool in a fabric to the surface to form a nap. After the work of napping is completed the fabric is ready to be finished by shearing.

GILLING.— A term denoting a process for making all fibres level and even in the manufacture of woolen yarns or worsted.

GINGERBREAD-WORK.— A phrase used, somewhat as a term of contempt, in describing the fanciful shapes of the ornate wood-work and carvings seen in the ornamentation of houses, furniture, etc.

GLAIR.— In book-binding, a foundation applied where gilding is to be laid, made of whipped white of egg and a very little vinegar.

GLANCE.— A term used in mining to designate those ores in which a peculiar lustre and color indicates that they are of metalliferous combination.

GLORY HOLE.— A small furnance used to reheat glass in process of manufacture.

GLOSSING.— A term denoting the operation of twisting the hanks of silk, in silk-manufacture, after they have been dyed and dried. This process is sometimes termed "stringing."

GLYPTOGRAPH.— An engraving or carving on a precious stone.

GOODS.— The raw oils, fats and greases employed in soap making.

GOTHIC.— A term used by American printers to describe a style of square-cut printing-type very similar in appearance to the old Roman mural letter. In England this title is given to a boldface antique type.

GRAINING.— In leather manufactures, the impressing of skins with a fictitious grain or surface, to imitate more valued leathers.

GRAIN TIN.— Tin of the finest quality produced in this form by striking it a sudden blow when it is heated to near its melting point. Being brittle at this temperature, pure tin falls into a mass of grains.

GRATING.— In spectroscopy, a surface ruled with very fine lines, 5,000 to 40,000 to the inch; if on glass, it is called a Transmission Grating; if on metal, a Reflection Grating.

GRAVEL.— Used in brewing to denote the appearance of the beer when yeast-cells are floating about in it in the form of fine "gravel."

GRAY PIG.— Pig iron which shows a dark gray crystalline fracture, due to its content of graphitic carbon; as distinguished from white pig, which is a definite carbide of iron.

GRAY SOUR.— In cotton bleaching the dilute hydrochloric acid bath, employed to dissolve out the lime soaps formed in the lime boiling.

GRIZZLE.— A brick which has been slack-burned but is hard enough to hold its shape.

GRIZZLIES.— An arrangment in the mine sluice to receive and cast aside all the large stones brought down by the current during the process of washing the auriferous gravel.

GUARDS.— In book-binding, the narrow strips of paper bound in with the leaves at the back of the book to allow for pasting in material, as in a scrap-book.

GULLET.— The hollows between the teeth of a circular saw The filing out of these hollows as the teeth wear down is called gulleting.

HACKLING.— In flax-manufacture "hackling" is the process of preparing the flax for spinning by the removal of all foreign substances and smoothing and equalizing all the lengths of fibre.

HALF-BOUND.— A style of binding for books in which the backs and corners are of leather; as half-calf, half-morocco.

HALF PLATE.— In photography a standard size of glass plate, measuring 4¾ by 6½ inches.

HALF-TONE.— A term used to designate a photographic process in which a screen made either of netting or ruled glass, is interposed between the lens and the sensitized plate, and from the image thus produced, a positive image is made upon the prepared metal plate. This is etched into relief by the use of acids.

HALL-MARK.— A term used industrially to designate any official stamp that has been placed upon an object of trade to denote genuineness.

HARD-CURED.— A term used in the fishing industry to designate that the fish specified has been cured by being thoroughly dried in the sun after salting, a process by which all the moisture has been evaporated.

HARDENING.— A process used in hat manufacturing, by which the bodies of the hats are rubbed and pressed hard for the purpose of felting the material as well as to diminish the size and render them more dense. A hardening-kiln is a kiln in which the transfer printing process in pottery is completed: The pottery being relieved from all superfluous oils by exposure to a low heat.

HARNESS.— The term applied to the apparatus in a loom by the operation of which the warp-threads are shifted alternately to form the shed.

HESSIAN.— A coarse cloth made of a combination of hemp, and jute and used for bagging is known as "Hessian" by the trade.
HIGH-PROOF.— Commercially all highly rectified spirits are termed "high-proof."
HOGGING.— The curvature upward of a beam between its ends — the reverse of sagging.
HOLLANDER.— In paper making, a special type of machine for beating up rag pulp.
HOLLANDS.— A term which, while formerly applied only to linens imported from the Netherlands, is now used to designate the glazed and unglazed linen cloths that are made in many places. "Brown Hollands" is a cloth that maintains much of the original color of the retted flax-fibre, it having been subjected to but little bleaching or boiling.
HONEYCOMBING.— In cloth-manufacture, a term applied to designate a thin fabric in which the stitches, running diagonally across the material, have been drawn tight in such a manner that the spaces between them are puffed or in relief.
HOP-JACK.— A term applied to a vat with a false bottom used in brewing. It is so arranged that it retains the solid substances in the mash-tubs, but allows the wort to flow away after it has been boiled and the hops have been added.
HOPPER.— Used, in milling, to denote the inverted-cone-shaped trough through which the grain passes on its way to the shaking-shoe.
HORSE-POWER.— A term used as a unit of measurement in every industry in which power machinery is used. Although several values are assigned to this unit the prevailing value, both in America and England, is Watt's horse-power, which places it at 33,000 foot-pounds of work per minute, or 7,460 megaergs per second about three-quarters of the actual power of a horse. Indicated horse-power, commonly abbreviated I. H. P., is the actual work performed by the motive power, as calculated from the indicator diagram of cylinder pressures.
HOST.— In plant industry, an animal or plant which sustains the existence of a parasite.
HOT METAL.— In smithing, metal which is at forging or welding heat.
HOT SHORT.— Applied to iron which contains so much sulphur as to be brittle when hot. Also called "Red Short."
HOUSING.— In carpentry, a joint in which the whole dimensional body of one piece of lumber is let into another piece; as with the treads and risers in a staircase.
IMPOSITION.— The act of laying pages of type, etc., upon a smooth stone slab to secure them in the chases and prepare them for the press.
INDENTION.— A term used in printing to denote that a certain amount of blank space has been left before the line, or a specified number of lines of type. An indenting of every line after the first, with an increasing blank constantly shortening on both sides is termed "diamond" indention. An indenting of every line except the first, that being of full width and so overhanging the others, is termed "hanging" indention.
INFUSION.— A term used in brewing to denote the process of preparing the mash by treating the bruised malt with water at a temperature of from 70° to 75°.
INVERSION.— The alteration of dextrorotatory cane sugar into laevorotatory fruit sugar through the action of dilute acid. The product is termed "invert sugar."
JAPANNING.— The process of coating the surface of metal, wood, etc., with varnish which is immediately hardened by exposure to high temperature.
JIGGER.— (a) In mining, a mechanical appliance for sorting ore; (b) in pottery, the vertical lathe on which is made flat ware, like plates and saucers.
JOLLEY.— In pottery, a machine used in the manufacture of cups, jugs, and other hollow ware.
JUMPER.— In mining, a heavy hand-drill resembling a crow-bar, having a chisel edge, and operated by jumping it up-and-down in the drill hole, either by hand or machinery.
KERFING.— (a) The process of preparing wood for bending without breaking by making a series of small cuts in it with a sawing-machine; (b) in cloth-manufacture, the process of removing the wool by passing it through a shearing-machine.
KETTLESTITCH.— In book-binding, the chainstitching at the head and tail of a book, holding the sections firmly together previous to binding.
KIP LEATHER.— Leather made from the skins of young cattle raised in India.
KIPPERING.— In the fish trade, the process of curing fish by cleansing them, dressing them with pepper and salt, and curing them, either by drying them in the open air, or, artificially, by subjecting them to the smoke of some prepared substances.
KNOP YARN.— In textile manufacture, a kind of yarn which has been twisted in such a way as to form knops or bulging spots.
LACQUER.— A form of varnish made with an evaporable solvent; drying by evaporation and not by oxidation and resinification as do true varnishes.
LAGGING.— The non-conducting material with which boilers and steam pipes are covered to prevent waste of heat. The term is also applied to the operation of applying such covering.
LAMINATED WORK.— In carpentry, the beams or ribs built up from thin layers fastened together.
LAP.— In woolen manufacture, the fleece as it is delivered by the condenser.
LARRYING.— Bedding the inside bricks of a thick wall in thin mortar.
LAW CALF.— In book-binding, the calfskin commonly employed in binding law books. As a rule it is not dyed, and has a whitish appearance.
LAYER.— The vat in which hides are left to lie for six to ten months in a strong solution of tannin, towards the end of the tanning process.
LAYING.— The term is applied to two distinct stages in rope-making: (1) the twisting of three or more yarns to form a strand; (2) the twisting of three strands to form a rope. The machine that performs this operation is termed a "laying machine," the wooden cone placed between the strands to prevent a slack twist is termed a "laying-top."
LINE.— In linen manufacture, the best part of the flax fibre after hackling. If the roots and tips of the stems are cut off, it is more valuable, and is called "cut line."
LINGOES.— Lead weights varying from 12 to 20 pounds, steadying the harness in silk looms.
LOCK NUT.— A thin auxiliary nut screwed down upon an ordinary nut to prevent its loosening.
LOUVER.— A ventilating opening built like a Venetian blind, but with the slats not movable. It excludes rain, but admits air freely.
LUTE.— The refractory cementing material used to fill joints and cracks in high temperature furnaces.
MACERATION.— The softening of substances by soaking them in a fermenting liquid of a warmish temperature.
MACKLED.— In printing, the effect on a printed sheet which has dragged on the inked type at the moment of impression.
MANIFOLDING.— A term used in business circles to denote the process of making several impressions of a single letter or document by one operation, as by means of a manifolding-machine, or by the use of carbon paper.
MASH.— Used in brewing and distilling to describe the mixture of ground grain that has been infused in warm water.
MELLOWING.— In tanning, the aging of the tanning liquors through fermentation. The term is applied also to a similar process which goes on in harsh leathers, when dampened and laid in a pile.
MERCERIZING.— Treatment of cotton cloth with a cold solution of caustic soda while stretched taut, the soda being dissolved away by acid before the tension is released. The cloth becomes stronger, takes dye more readily, and acquires a silky lustre.
MILLING.— (a) The process of manufacturing cereals into flour or meal. There are two methods of milling: (1) low milling in which the grain is ground but once before being bolted, and (2) high milling, in which it is ground repeatedly; (b) in pottery, the operation of grinding and mixing the slip; (c) the process resorted to in tanning to open and soften the pores of hides; (d) in cloth manufacture, the process of felting cloth to thicken it; (e) the machining of metals with revolving cutters; also the corrugating of the rims of discs, coins, etc.
MOROCCO.— In book-binding, a fine quality of tanned goat-skin.
MUFFLER.— An arched oven-like furnace in which crucibles are heated without direct exposure to the flames.
MULE.— In spinning, a reciprocating machine which draws and twists the thread when moving in one direction, and winds it on spindles on the return.
NIGGER.— In soap making, the dirty, watery layer which settles in the soap pans during the manufacture of filled soaps.
NIPPLE.— A short piece of pipe having a right-hand thread cut its entire length on the outside surface.
NOBLING.— The squeezing and hammering of a mass of spongy iron from a puddling furnace, to weld it into solid metal.
NOILS.— Small masses of clustered wool fibres removed from wool fleece by the combing machines.
PADDLING.— A method of tanning light skins in a vat in which a revolving paddle keeps liquor and skins in constant motion.
PANNING.— In placer mining, the gentle rotary shaking of a mass of gravel and water in a miner's pan so as to facilitate the settlement of the gold particles to the bottom. The fine sand and float with some of the water is allowed to slop over during the panning.
PASTE WASH.— In book-binding, a dilution of paste with water, used as a surface on which to lay the glair (q.v.) previous to gilding.
PATINA.— The delicate green incrustation which gathers on the surface of copper and bronzes after long exposure to the air. The finest patina is formed on those bronzes in which tin is in large proportion, and little or no zinc. It is imitated by immersing bronze in acetic acid.

Picking.— In weaving, the throwing of the shuttle by the picker, or driver.

Piece-goods.— The trade name for fabrics that have been woven in lengths suitable for retail sale by linear measure.

Pig.— (a) In glass manufacture, the grooved iron support for the blowpipes or working rods at the mouth of the glass furnace; (b) the form in which newly melted iron or other metal is cast for marketing.

Pitting.— A defect in varnish work showing tiny holes scattered over the surface, due to varnishing upon a damp or greasy surface.

Place Bricks.— Soft bricks of use only for interior walls where they will be covered with plaster.

Plus Thread.— A thread cut on a bulge of a bolt or rod which has been made thicker where the thread is located, so that the diameter of the substance of the rod is not reduced by the depth of the thread.

Pocket.— In mining, a cavity containing a mass of ore which is not connected in any way with a vein or lode.

Point.— The unit of measurement in types, each point being about one seventy-second of an inch. The various types in use in the United States and their relative sizes in " points " are as follows: Excelsior, 3 points; brilliant, 3½; semi-brevier, 4; diamond, 4½; pearl, 5; agate, 5½; non-pareil, 6; minion, 7; brevier, 8; bourgeois, 9; long primer, 10; small pica, 11; pica, 12; English, 14; two-line brevier, 16; great primer, 18; paragon, 20; two-line small pica, 22; two-line pica, 24; two-line English, 28; four-line brevier 32; three-line pica, 36; double paragon, 40; four-line small pica, 44, and four-line pica, 48 points.

Pointing.— In masonry, a neat finishing of joints between bricks or stones; accomplished by scraping out the rough edges of the original mortar and filling in carefully with a finer grade of mortar, which is often colored.

Poling.— In metallurgy, the reduction of copper oxide in molten blister copper, by the inserting into the liquid metal a pole of green wood. If too much wood is used the copper is said to be overpoled; if too little wood, it is underpoled.

Ponty.— In glass manufacture, an iron rod tapered for part of its length, used in working molten glass. In some localities it is called a " working iron."

Porgie.— The raw material, largely menhaden, and much of it offal, from which fish oil is extracted.

Porter.— In metal working, a bar attached to a fagot of rods or a forging, by which it is held and guided during the process of hammering.

Pot Arch.— In glass manufacture, a small furnace in which the glass pots or crucibles are fired before being used in the melting furnace.

Potsher.— In paper manufacture, a machine for breaking and bleaching pulp.

Pot Metal.— An alloy of copper and lead, with sometimes small additions of zinc and tin, used as a cheap substitute for brass.

Priming.— (a) The first coat of paint applied upon new work as a foundation for the subsequent coats. It is rich in oil, and has enough white lead to make a firm attachment; (b) the technical name for the foaming or frothing of water in a steam boiler, caused by greasy or dirty water, or by forcing the fire.

Proof Bar.— In metallurgy, a rod of steel laid with a charge in a cementation furnace, and withdrawn at intervals to give evidence of the degree of progress of the operation.

Proof Spirit.— That grade of dilute alcohol or alcoholic liquor which contains 50 per cent by weight of absolute alcohol. A larger percentage is " overproof," a smaller, " underproof."

Puddling.— (a) In metallurgy, the conversion of pig iron into malleable iron by burning out the carbon, sulphur and phosphorus in association with free atmospheric air; (b) the stopping of leaks and crevices in a reservoir with a " puddle " of clay with a little water.

Pugging.— The rough plaster or slag wool filling placed between the beams of a floor as a deadener of sound.

Pug Mill.— In brick making, the mill in which the ingredients are mixed together. Also used as to a cement mixer.

Quarter-plate.— A term used in photography to denote the size of a plate. Thus, a quarter-plate measures 3¼ x 4¼ in.; a half-plate, 4¼ x 6½ in.; a whole plate, 6½ x 8½ in.

Quenched Steel.— Steel which has been hardened to an extreme degree by plunging it when red hot into cold water.

Quicklime.— Lime fresh from the kiln which has not absorbed moisture from the air and become air-slaked.

Quincunx.— A method of setting a group of fruit trees so that four of them stand at the corners of a rectangle and the fifth at the intersection of its diagonals.

Rabbling.— The stirring process in puddling iron, effected with a bar with a hooked flat end, called a rabble.

Racing.— A sudden increase in speed of an engine when released from its load; as when the propeller of a steamship is lifted from the water by wave motion in stormy weather.

Racking.— In liquor making, the aging of the liquor by allowing it to flow in small streams or a very thin sheet from one vessel to another, thus exposing it to the air.

Rag Bolt.— An iron bolt with barbs or an enlarged end for embedding in masonry so it cannot be withdrawn.

Raglet.— The groove cut in a wall into which the flashing (q.v.) is imbedded.

Raising.— In woolen manufacture, the operation of drawing out a nap of fibre on the cloth by means of teazles; as in beavers, meltons, and pilot-cloth, and in blankets.

Rectify.— To redistil, as in making whisky, which is said to be rectified when it has been twice distilled.

Red Short.— See Hot Short.

Reducing Furnace.— A furnace in which the metallic elements are separated from their ores; as in a blast furnace.

Reedy.— In weaving, a streaky appearance due to the threads of the warp rolling in the splits of the reed.

Reef.— In mining, the outcrop of a vein of ore.

Regenerating Furnace.— A furnace in which the heat of the waste gases is used to heat the incoming air-blast. Where gas is used for fuel this also is heated by the hot waste.

Register.— In printing, the accurate adjustment of type and paper so that the second page of a leaf is printed exactly on the back of the first page imprint.

Rendering.— The first coat of plaster laid on a brick wall.

Retting.—The treatment of flax by soaking it in water in which certain bacteria carry on a fermentation which releases the fibres.

Roan.— A tanned and dyed sheepskin used in book-binding. It resembles Morocco, but is cheaper and not so durable.

Roasting.— The process of heating certain ores to a temperature lower than the reducing point. It secures oxidation and the elimination of sulphur, and thus simplifies the subsequent reduction.

Roving.— In textile manufacture, the tape-like band of sliver after preliminary twisting, and previous to spinning.

Rumble.— A revolving cylinder in which small castings are placed so that they may be cleaned of adhering sand and mould by chafing against each other.

Russia.— In book-binding, a leather made of the skins of young cattle treated on the flesh side after tanning with the oil of birch, from which it acquires its characteristic odor. Cheaper grades are made of goat or sheep skins.

Rust Joint.— A joint made in iron piping by filling the gap with a mixture of iron filings and sal ammoniac, which in a short time forms a compact hard and waterproof mass.

Safety Plug.— A plug of fusible metal set into the shell of a boiler, and which melts when the rising pressure raises the temperature to the danger point, allowing the steam to blow off.

Salt a Mine, To.— A swindling operation by which a mine is made to seem more valuable than it really is by the surreptitious introduction of ores obtained elsewhere.

Screed.— A narrow strip of plaster laid accurately to the required surface, and used after hardening as a guide for the floats.

Setting.— In leather manufacture, the smoothing and stretching of a hide until all creases and wrinkles are obliterated.

Seven Pound Lead.— In plumbing, sheet lead of such thickness that one square foot weighs seven pounds.

Skiver.— In book-binding, the thin grain split of sheepskin used for cheap leather bindings.

Shells.— Those parts of the lay in weaving in the grooves of which the reed fits. They are of two classes and are termed " upper " and " under " shells.

Sliver.— The textile fibres gathered into a tape-like strand preliminary to roving and spinning.

Smudge.— In plumbing, a mixture of lampblack with other substances, smeared over a piece of work to prevent the solder from taking hold where it is not wanted.

Soaking.— In metallurgy, cooling slowly a freshly cast ingot of steel in a soaking-pit — a hole in the ground fitted with brick chambers to receive the ingot and allow its heat to escape gradually

Sod Oils.— The oils obtained by pressing skins which have been curried with cod, whale, or olive oils. When refined, sod oils are highly esteemed for watches and other delicate machinery.

Souple.— Silk fibre from which about half of its natural gum has been removed, rendering it lighter in weight and softer in feel.

Souring.— In leather making, the treatment of leather with weak organic acids, to remove stains and bleach the surfaces preparatory to dyeing.

Spinning.— In metal working, the formation of round hollow ware by pressing sheet metal into a mold revolving on a lathe.

Split.— A skin which has been split into two layers parallel with its surface; usually effected by a cutting machine.

Stove Screw.— A bevel-headed screw with the thread cut close up to the head; used particularly for holding parts of stoves together.

Striker.— A pronged lever set astride a driving belt for shifting it on or off the driving pulley

Stripping.— The tearing or breaking off of the threads of a screw or the cogs of a gear-wheel.

Suint.— The natural grease of sheep's wool. When refined, it is called lanoline.

Sump.— In mining, an excavation below the level of the mine floor, in which water collects.

Tacky.— The condition of the surface of paint or varnish before it is quite dry, so that it is slightly sticky when touched gently with the dry finger.

Tap.— In pipe-fitting, the tool which cuts internal or female threads. The tap first used in this operation is slightly tapered, and is called the "taper tap."

Tempering.— In pottery, the mixing and working of the clay into proper condition for molding.

Tooling.— In book-binding, the ornamentation of a book cover by pressing lines into it with heated tools. They are "blind lines" if without gilt. A book so ornamented is said to be tooled.

Torching.— The coat of plaster applied on the under side of a roof of tiles laid on battens.

Tossing.— In metallurgy, the oxidation of impurities in melted tin by lifting the metal in ladles and pouring it slowly back from a height, thus exposing it to the air.

Touter.— Industrially, a person who makes it his business to solicit trade for a shop.

Tow.— The short and twisted fibres of flax separated out in the process of combing. It is carded and spun into coarse rope yarns.

Trebles.— Sheet iron of gauges 25 to 27 in the Birmingham wire scale.

Tree Calf.— In book-binding, a brown calf which has been stained and squeezed to produce a conventional tree-like pattern on its surface.

Tup.— The principal mass of iron in a steam hammer head to which is attached the steel face piece.

Tuyere.— The nozzle through which the air-blast enters a blast furnace.

Union.— In textile manufacture, a cloth in which the warp is of one kind of fibre, and the weft of another.

Valley.—The V-shaped hollow between two intersecting roof surfaces.

Vamping.— In leather making, the undue swelling of a hide during the liming process.

Venice Turpentine.— An oleo-resin obtained from the sap of the larch. It dries very slowly and with considerable body.

Waling.— The horizontal pieces which support the planking at the sides of a trench.

Wall.— Used in mining to denote the surfaces of the rock between which the ore is inclosed. If the vein is inclined at such an angle that the ore is over the miner's head it is termed a "hanging" wall; if it is beneath him it is called a "foot" wall.

Warble.— In leather manufacture, a small hole in the hide pierced by the bot-fly.

Warp.— (a) In agriculture, the operation of fertilizing a poor piece of land by artificial inundation from waters which have large quantities of earthy matter; (b) in weaving the threads that extend lengthwise in a loom. The roller upon which the threads are wound is termed the "warp-beam"; the machine which treats them with size before they are wound is the "warp-dresser," while the machine which draws the warp threads through the dye beck is termed the "warp-dyer."

Wash.—Used in mining to denote the process of separating the ore from earthy and other matter by the employment of water. The fermented wort from which the spirit is extracted in distilling is also termed the "wash."

Water Gas.— A fuel-gas produced by blowing steam over a bed of red-hot coals. It carries about 40 per cent of carbon monoxide, and is a deadly and quick poison. It is sometimes used for illuminating with Welsbach mantles, and is sometimes carburetted so as to give the ordinary yellow gas-flame. Its use in house lighting is forbidden in many communities.

Weft or Woof.— In weaving, the thread which is carried by the shuttle, and is laid transversely to the warp.

Winning.— The work of developing a mine preparatory to the work of mining is termed "winning."

Wiped Joint.— In plumbing, a joint made to connect two ends of lead pipe which abut each other. One end is slightly expanded so the the other will set into it, and the joint is then encased in plastic solder, which is shaped by continually wiping it with a cloth until it has set.

Working Iron.— See Ponty.

INDUSTRIAL VOCATIONAL TRAINING. See Education, Industrial.

INDUSTRIAL WORKERS. Education and Training of. Industrial education is that form of education, whether given in a school, a factory or elsewhere, the controlling purpose of which is to train for wage-earning, or to advance the power of wage-earning in the trades and industries. It must be considered from the standpoint of education as well as of industry. Education is the fitting of the individual to take his place and do his part in the life of his community and his time. Industrial education is, then, the fitting of those who are in industry effectively to serve and to achieve in and through their field of activity. There are 9,000,000 wage-earners in the factories of the United States, supporting directly and indirectly including themselves upward of 30,000,000 people. They are working in 275,791 factories. Their educational and economic development are of utmost consequence from whatever standpoint it is viewed. The joy of life, if not its purpose, is service, self-expression, achievement. The daily task may be easy or difficult. If it is simple, that is no reason for allowing the worker to do it poorly. If he can be taught to do it with proficiency in a week or a month, not to say a year, without loss of wages meantime, he has as great right and need of this brief training as a professional man to the 10 or 12 years of additional training which the public rejoices to give him without charge after the period at which the working boy leaves school.

Great as have been the faults of Germany, she so thoroughly developed the industrial intelligence of her workers as to surprise the world. Sixty-five per cent of the men in the topmost places in her industries, in both the managerial and technical fields, came from the ranks of her working boys, who quit the regular schools at from 12 to 14 years of age, but by industrial education, which interpreted their daily tasks and made clear the ways of advancement, in apprenticeship and continuation schools (wherein education is «continued» after leaving the common schools), these boys, as men, surpassed most of the graduates of her higher technical institutions in the attainment of high industrial positions.

Joy in work comes from mastery of work. We like to do what we can do well. We dislike to do what we fail to understand or do poorly. The dislike of work of many who labor is due in great measure to the state's neglect educationally in not teaching the mastery and the dignity of labor. «The latest gospel in this world is, know thy work and do it. All true work is sacred; and in all true work, were it but true hand labor, there is something divine.» (Carlisle). It is the inherent right of every person to be taught to express himself effectively and happily in some field of the world's work, small or large, and by mastery therein to serve himself and society to best advantage. Never taught one thing only that he may rest with that, but so that through the mastery of one thing and the learning of another, he may rise to the limit of his abilities. However much a nation develops its natural resources, it is economically blind if it fails fully to develop its human values, which are the one natural resource which gives value to all others, and the only one that increases with use. The economic value of the human efficiencies of the working people of the United States is estimated at more than $200,000,000,000, or five times the value of all other natural resources combined. The spiritual values, the happiness and self-respect, that come of developed efficiency are incalculable. It is for these and other considerations that each community in the

United States spends upon public education about one-third of all its tax receipts, making a national total of about $650,000,000 annually, aside from an investment of more than a billion dollars in school plants, and both items rapidly increasing. But all this is apparently with the college as the aim, although only 3 per cent of the people take the college course. About $5,000 of public funds are spent upon anyone who fits himself for a profession, but scarcely a dollar especially to fit in his occupation any one of the 96 per cent of the people outside the professions.

Education is a state function. Whatever is done must be by the several communities under the requirement and supervision of the state. Most states require attendance at the public school of all children from the 7th to the 16th year, with, however, the important provision that after the 14th year any child may secure, if he wishes, a working certificate permitting him to leave school forever, with the further provision, in some States that he has completed the sixth grade of the common school, and in other States simply that he is able to read and write the English language acceptably, this latter provision often being carelessly regarded.

Only one child in 30 graduates from the high school; only one in five enters the high school; only one in three finishes the high school; and only half the children who enter school finish the 6th grade. By the end of the 6th grade children have learned little or nothing of fractions, nothing of decimals, only a little local geography and nothing of the rights and obligations of citizenship and the social order. Investigation indicates that the great majority of that half of all American children who leave school by the 6th grade and the 14th year of age are not compelled to by financial circumstances. They leave because they have reached the period of adolescence, at which time the will and the creative faculties assert themselves and nature impels them to «do things,» unconsciously to imitate Him who in the six days made the world. This impulse is especially compelling with concrete- or hand-minded children. Those who continue in school are mostly the imaginative children to whom the world of books is often very real.

The mind of man is said to be «hand-made.» Through the hand the race has learned a great part of all it knows. Work must be interpreted and made an instrument of education for the vast number who apparently will be educated, if at all, only in and through the life of labor. Legislation might compel these workers to remain in the common schools away from labor and income for a short period longer, often without advantage, sometimes to their hurt, and never to their adequate education, as education must be made available throughout the better years of life.

It is coming to be generally realized that each state must, following the best practice of the countries of Europe, set up and foster, financially and otherwise, educational facilities for the effective advancement of the millions of wage earners in the industries and elsewhere, with their daily needs and experiences as the centre of interest in their educational activities. The foremost industrial nations of Europe by apprenticeship and otherwise have for generations so trained their industrial wage earners. It is commonly conceded that Germany took the lead in the year 1885 in a series of legislative provisions which in the following years have developed a system of industrial education as effective for her wage-earners as are the provisions common to all countries for professional training. She finally came to require in great sections of that empire that every working child under 16, and in the best practice under 18, shall be released by the employer for from 8 to 12 hours per week during working hours, while fresh and vigorous, for training in his occupation or in a better one if need be.

We speak of «blind-alley» and hopeless jobs as the lot of our working children. Germany discovered that there is no such thing as a «blind-alley» job; that there is no job but may lead to high accomplishment under intelligent direction. Consequently 85 per cent of American working children are in «blind-alley» jobs, from which their elders see no way out, while in Munich 85 per cent of the working children are trained in connection with their work in ways that lead readily to high places.

France, Switzerland, Denmark and other nations have legislated in effect like Germany but less extensively. England, impressed by the Continental practice, and especially by German methods and success, planned so to legislate in 1914 but was deterred by the World War. She paused, however, at the height of the conflict, on 8 Aug. 1918 to enact educational measures requiring every child to attend the regular schools from the 5th to the 14th year of age and empowering local authorities to increase the compulsory period until the 15th year. Compulsory day continuation schools must be established for all young persons, unless they are being otherwise educated, up to the age of 16, and after 1925 up to the age of 18. The minimum number of hours of attendance per year at continuation schools shall be 280 and after 1925 shall be 320. Thus England, formerly the most backward of the great European nations in vocational training, takes an advanced position, far ahead of the United States.

Of all these nations, Germany failed to require the teaching of citizenship, of the rights, duties and obligations of the worker as a member of society. In 1903 her greatest authority, Dr. Kerschensteiner, lamented that her industrial schools «did not contain a single subject of instruction which serves any other purpose than the acquisition of technical skill and knowledge, or the promotion of trade efficiency.» Since that time, a poor beginning was made in this training but in a way regretted by many of her own leaders in that it did little more than inculcate a false exaltation of her ruling classes and a blind obedience in all others. What we sow, we reap. To fail to educate in efficiency is to suffer inestimable economic loss. Not to teach the duties and obligations of citizenship, is to endanger the democracy of the world.

In the United States in the last 15 years the legislatures of several States have enacted permissive legislation authorizing local boards of education to require the attendance of all working children under 16 upon part-time or continuation schools, but in all these States only one city, Boston, had the courage to act in 1916, with New York city following later in a less extensive way.

State legislation which merely authorizes a local community to require the attendance of its working children upon continuation schools is therefore shown to be inadequate and virtually useless. It is a shirking of legislative responsibility as respects the lives of working children. If the State as such will not safeguard its children, single communities will not.

In 1911 Wisconsin required that every working child in cities of 5,000 population or more attend continuation school for four hours a week until 16 years of age for eight months annually, which provision was later extended to eight hours per week for 10 months until 17 years of age. This legislation proved entirely practicable. It was readily accepted by employers and all others as of high social and economic advantage and is evidence that any State can thus serve its working people. In 1915 Pennsylvania required that every working child under 16, in whatever occupation, attend continuation school for eight hours weekly during working hours. All-day trade schools have proved ineffective as a means of general industrial education. They were tried and generally abandoned in Continental Europe long ago. Working people either cannot or will not attend such schools and forego income and the experiences and hopes that lie in the field of labor for the years required for training in such schools. From 1880 to 1910 there was much agitation for the establishment of these schools in the United States. In those 30 years, however, only 13 such schools were established with a total attendance of less than 2,000 students, being not more for the whole country than should receive industrial training in the average manufacturing city of 50,000 people. The training in these schools is so general in character as to lack immediate interest and not to fit for the specific tasks their graduates enter upon. The cost to the public averages from $150 to $200 per pupil per year. There are 2,000,000 working children under 16 in the United States in industry, agriculture and commerce and more than 5,000,000 under 18. All these children have equal right and need of training in their occupations. There are 30,000,000 older wage-earners to whom the opportunity for training for advancement should be open, many of whom would avail themselves of it. In a single typical industrial city, Milwaukee, it was estimated that a relatively small number of superior wage-earners in her industries in 1910 were sending $80,000 annually to correspondence schools for such industrial training as they could so secure. It was then that Wisconsin provided that her wage-earners should have education in their occupations in continuation schools directly adapted to their circumstances even as her university provides for those who are more fortunately circumstanced. Said the Pennsylvania superintendent of schools, "to educate all children who need it, through any such all-day, all-week schools as have been developed yet, would bankrupt any State." And the loss in wages to the learners would be as great as the cost to the State. The correlation of instruction in continuation schools with the work in the factory makes both work and school educational.

The cost of superior continuation school training in Europe is about $25 per pupil year. It sometimes costs less in the United States because it is not yet of the European quality. The increased interest and efficiency of the workers in the factory should equal or exceed this cost. Because of this increase in efficiency in the factory many great manufacturing institutions in the United States introduced training departments at their own expense during the war period for the training of new workers and the up-grading of old employees, spending in several instances as much as $50 per learner. By this expenditure the employer secured a more contented worker, reduced labor turnover greatly and reduced the wastage of materials. Since the war many of these establishments are continuing these training departments and other manufacturers are introducing them as an essential means of development for the vast production of peace times.

Among the essential provisions for industrial training for all who need it may be noted: First. It must be part-time or continuation, therefore, not requiring the worker to abstain from work and income. Second. Attendance must be made compulsory by the State for all working children under 16, or better 18, during working hours and readily available to all older persons through life at their option so that any worker may continually uplift himself by securing at all times whatever instruction he needs to qualify for the next step forward. Compulsion in the matter of school attendance of young children is only the recognition of the right of the child and the duty of the State, and this recognition expressed in terms of agreement and action. Wherever tried it finds ready acceptance. Third. Industrial schools, and equally those for agriculture and commerce, must be under the control and direction of special State and community boards whose personnel is directly representative of industry and labor. The leading nations of Europe after trial of all other methods insist upon this practical direction and place this education in the Department of Commerce or Labor and not in the department of general education. Only those with life-long and successful experience in industry can know when industrial education is truly industrial and make it so. Wisconsin accepted this principle in establishing a State Board of Vocational Education consisting of three employers, three wage-earners and the State superintendent of schools, the latter being the link between the general and the industrial schools. She also provided that the general board of education in each city appoint a board of vocational education consisting of two representative employers, two wage-earners and the city superintendent of schools, with full authority, subject only to the State board of vocational education. The Federal government, upon advice of the leading organizations of wage-earners, employers and others accepted this principle in making the Federal board of vocational education consist of the Secretaries of Labor, Agriculture and Commerce and one lay representative each, from labor, agriculture and commerce. This Federal board is advisory to

State boards of vocational education and distributes Federal aid in amounts increasing annually until 1925 and thereafter when it aggregates $7,000,000, being $3,000,000 each for industry and for agriculture and $1,000,000 for the training of teachers, but limited in each case to not more than one-half the total spent by a State for these purposes. In Massachusetts and Connecticut a limited number of industrial schools have been highly developed under the supervision of the general State Board. This Board, however, is composed principally of, and in industrial matters dominated by the judgment of, especially qualified manufacturers. In American States where academic school influences control in the direction of industrial education, as formerly in Europe, this education is remote, impractical, lacking in «production» sense and ineffective. Fourth. Training in industrial schools must be upon production, i.e., the making of real things for commercial use in the same manner as they are produced in factories. In Massachusetts it is required that industrial schools «shall conduct a productive shop which conforms in all desirable factors with commercial standards. The work on which pupils are trained shall be planned and perfected with reference to its commercial value and shall be judged by commercial standards.» «The most effective shop work is that done on a commercial basis for an outside customer. Work done to fill pupils' orders is least satisfactory.» «The general atmosphere, system, standard, practice and administration of the school shall be that of a good industrial shop.»

It has been objected to this method that it commercializes education and takes bread out of the wage-earners' mouths by supplying the market from public institutions. The value of school products, however, is inconsequential, being about one-third of the salaries of the teachers who are taken out of industry, or from one-fifth to one-tenth of what these teachers would produce were they left in industry as wage-earners. The leaders of labor support this position in all communities where it has been well worked out. Fifth. Teachers of processes and operations must have had extensive practice and successful experience in factories. They should have that developed «sixth sense» common to the professions, indicating thorough appreciation and understanding of the intricacies and methods of the production. Only the related academic instruction may be given by instructors whose shop experience has been less extensive. Sixth. Every trade must be taught, that of the baker, jeweler, barber, tin-smith, potter, watchmaker, decorator — every trade requiring developed skill — and not the four or five trades only that are commonly taught in old-time trade schools. In Munich there are some 60 schools teaching 50 trades, besides 15 schools for the least intelligent workers who must follow the unskilled trades. These workers are taught to keep personal accounts, how best to use their slender incomes and the fundamentals of citizenship. Seventh. Instruction must be directly correlated with the daily tasks and experience of the learner. Boys and men learning the butcher's trade must be taught to cut all kinds of meat and figure on shrinkage, waste, etc. A butcher shop cannot be in a public school. Consequently a local commercial shop must be used. A large city can have a commercially operated bakery in its industrial school. Smaller communities can readily arrange to use for a few of the dull hours of the day the facilities of a local baker, he giving the practical instruction and advising concerning the related instruction.

Instruction in citizenship should make much of local institutions, social and industrial, as a point of contact.

Mathematics and English should in each case be taught in terms of the learner's occupation.

The following brief excerpt from Industrial Continuation Courses are illustrative:

(a) From a course for boys from 14 to 18 in a school in a tannery;

Monday — Review of Chrome re-tan and Combination tannage:

I. Chrome re-tan.
  1. Solution for re-tan.
    a. 2 per cent tannoline to 100 lb. leather.
    b. Run in drum two hours.
    c. Horsed five hours.
  2. Purpose.
    a. To tan green spots.
    b. To make leather firm and solid.

II. Combination 10 hours.
  1. Cossack only has combination tannage.
  2. Chrome re-tanned first.
  3. Horsed 10 hours instead of five hours.
  4. Solution.
    a. Extracts used are quebracho, hemlock, spruce, gambier.
    b. About 100 lb. extract to 1000 lb. leather.
    c. Run in drum five hours.
  5. Horsed 10 hours.

Tuesday — Lecture of Foreman of Stuffing Department.

I. Definition of stuffing.
II. Purpose of stuffing.
III. Kinds of leather and processes.
  1. Hemlock tannage.

* * *

(b) From outline course in painting

Painting: Sample exhibit from outline course.

8. Filler.
  a. Silex.
9. Wax.
  a.
10. Water paints.
  a. Kalsomine.
  b. Whiting.
  c. Chalk.
  d. Lime.
  e. Colors and binders.
11. Supplies.
  a. Pumice.
  b. Patten stone.
  c. Curled hair.
  d. Sand paper.
  e. Steel wool.
  f. Sponges.
  g. Chamois.
  h. Cheese cloth.
  i. Muslin.
  j. Cotton waste.
  k. Burlap.

C. Color study.
  1. Pigments and colors.
    a. Primary.
    b. Secondary.
    c. Intermediate.
    d. Complimentary.
  2. Quality of color.
    a. Value of tone.
    b. Degree of light which color reflects.
    c. Tints and shades.
    d. Intensity.
  3. Color analysis.
    a. As to hue, value and intensity.
    b. To enable individual to qualities indicated above.
  4. Color harmony.

D. Design.
  1. Shape.
  2. Harmony of proportion.
  3. Rhythm or interrelation.

E. Commercial practice.
  1. Reading plans and specifications.
  2. Methods of buying.
  3. Preventing waste and losses.
  4. Forms for doing business.
  5. Building codes.
  6. Laws relating to
    a. Contracts.
    b. Liens.
    c. Bonds.
    d. Insurance.

• • •

(c) Civil government. Tentative outline of suggestive nature common to all students.

I. HOME.
 A. Purpose.
  Social, civil, educational.
 B. Organization.
  1. Father.
  2. Mother.
  3. Children.
  4. Relatives.
 C. Operation.
  1. House.
  2. Facilities.
   a. gas.
   b. water.
   c. light.
   d. food.
   e. heat.
 D. Maintenance.
  Source of:
  1. Occupations:
   a. Father.
   b. Mother.
   c. Brother.
   d. Sister.
   e. Relatives.
 E. History.

* * *

II. INDUSTRY. (Select prominent industry in locality).
 A. Purpose.
  1. To the individual.
   a. Provides occupations through which to develop ability and opportunity for service.
   b. Provides income.
  2. To the community.
   Production.
 B. Organization.
  1. Directors or owner.
  2. General manager.
  3. Superintendent.
  4. Foreman.
  5. Assistant foreman.
  6. Other employees.

* * *

 5. Regulation of industry.
  a. Hours of labor.
  b. Wages.
  c. Insurance.
   Accident.
   Sickness.
   Old age.
  d. Education.
   Part-time — day.
   Apprenticeship.
   Evening schools.
   Dull-season schools.

* * *

III. THE INDUSTRIAL REVOLUTION.
 A. The primitive family as the industrial unit.
 B. Combinations of families.
 C. Development of specialization in industry.
 D. Concentration in cities for
  1. Power.
   a. Water.
   b. Steam.
   c. Electricity.
   d. Gas.
  2. Shipping facilities.
   a. Water.
   b. Railroads.
 (Note: Trace out the industrial development of your locality along these lines).
 E. Effects upon the community.
  1. Home life.
  2. Employment of
   a. Men.
   b. Women.
   c. Children.
  3. Wages.
   a. Day work.
   b. Piece work.
   c. Bonus.
   d. Profit sharing.
   e. Co-operation.

* * *

IV. COMMUNITY MANAGEMENT. (City, state and nation. Work out first for your city according to outline, and then for state and nation).
 A. Purpose.
  1. Discussion — bring opinions from homes.
 B. Organization.
  1. Mayor-council system.
  2. Commission system.
   Commission manager or council manager system.
  3. Departments.
   a. Justice.
   b. Education.
   c. Public works.
   d. Fire.
   e. Police.
   f. Charity.
  4. Operation.
   a. City Hall.
   b. Schools.

IV. COMMUNITY MANAGEMENT — Cont'd.
   c. Streets.
   d. Parks.
   e. Play-grounds.
   f. Fire houses.
   g. Jails.
   h. Hospitals.
  5. Maintenance.
   a. Taxation.
    Land.
    Improvements.
    Personal property.
    Poll tax.
    Corporation tax.
    Income tax.
    Inheritance tax.
    Liquor.
    Tobacco.
   b. Licenses.
    Occupations.
    Privileges.
    Ownership (automobiles, dogs, etc.).
 C. History.
  Develop history of above topics in your locality.
 D. Maintenance.
  1. Labor.
   a. Kinds (to be obtained by children from particular industries studied).
   b. Rates of payment.
   c. Opportunity for advancement.
   d. Quality of — skilled or unskilled.
   e. Supply of and demand for.
   f. Annual pay-roll.
  2. Product.
   a. Nature.
   b. Amount by physical units.
   c. Market.
   d. Value.
   e. Total sales per annum.
  3. Overhead — Expenses, such as light, heat, interest, insurance, rent, depreciation, nonproductive labor, etc.
 E. History of.
  1. Location.
  2. Establishment.
  3. Development.
 (Note: Apply foregoing outline under II to several local industries).

Eighth. Most of this training for working children must be given in public schools and a large part of it for older workers. Schools or training departments must, however, be set up in factories under State supervision for that great part of the 9,000,000 factory workers who do not need or will not take an extended course in training in the industrial schools.

The development of industrial training departments in factories for the quick intensive fitting of new workers to their tasks and the upgrading of more experienced workers has been one of the interesting experiences of the great war. Such training departments are also known as vestibule schools. France and England found these factory training departments a war necessity for replacing enlisted, skilled men by women and for developing in old employees the high technical skill required in war production. The French Ministry of Munitions early in the war required every manufacturer employing 300 workers or more to install these training departments. The British Ministry of Munitions in many of its contracts for war supplies required this of her manufacturers. In the United States the Council of National Defense through its section on industrial training assisted manufacturers in their development of training departments in the earlier months of the war. The United States Training Service, established in August 1918, then became the Federal agency in this field. Since the armistice so many factories are using this method as to give promise of a great improvement in American productive methods and of happier and greater production by the wage-earners. It is estimated that 25 per cent increase in production is secured through factory training departments. Of the 9,000,000 industrial workers, nearly one-half are in 3,000 factories; 1,613,000 are in 833 factories of 1,000 or more employees each. See EDUCATION, INDUSTRIAL.

Bibliography.—Bowman, C. A., 'Graphic Aids in Occupational Analysis for Guidance and Teaching' (Milwaukee 1924); Brewer, J. M., 'Case Studies in Educational and Vocational Guidance' (Boston 1926); Eaton, T. H., 'Education and Vocations' (New York 1926); Hall, H. S., 'Trade Training in School and Plant' (New York 1930); Keller, F. J. and Viteles, M. S., 'Vocational Guidance Throughout the World' (New York 1937).

H. E. MILES.
Chief of Training, United States Training Service, Washington, D. C.

INDUSTRIAL WORKERS OF THE WORLD, or I. W. W., a labor organization of revolutionary character, with tenets similar to those of the Syndicalists. The strike of the Western Federation of Miners at Colorado in 1903 brought to a head the grievances of labor and its need for new centralization. A conference of labor leaders was held at Chicago in 1904, which resulted in a general convention of labor delegates a few months later at which the leading principles of such an organization were outlined. Another convention took place in 1906. The many factions which constituted the labor revolutionists fought for supremacy, and several schisms widened and separated the groups. The «revolutionaries» opposed the «reactionaries»; the «political» and «industrial» socialists could not agree; and the local trade-unionists were pitted against the believers in one all-embracing union of workers. A fourth convention produced the final preamble which may be briefly outlined by some of its leading principles: «The working-class and the employing class have nothing in common. Between these two classes a struggle must go on until the workers of the world organize as a class, take possession of the earth and the machinery of production and abolish the wage system.» «It is the historic mission of the working class to do away with capitalism.» «An injury to one is an injury to all.» The organization differs from syndicalism in that it proposes to build up, after the pattern of capitalistic organization, but on revolutionary lines, a tremendous and all powerful organization of all workers. It does not desire to remodel existing trade unions, but to establish a new and broader organization. It has no use for mediation, conciliation or arbitration, and considers no contract binding on employees. To strike whenever they can inconvenience employers most is the fixed policy of the members. They renounce sabotage but endorse the general strike and all forms of direct action.

The I. W. W. directs about 500 recruiting stations and has five national administrations in Hawaii, Australia, New Zealand, Great Britain and South Africa respectively. They made tremendous efforts to reach the agricultural laborers. They have trained strike leaders and propagandists throughout the country who have been conspicuous in notorious campaigns.

At the convention held on 20 Nov. 1916 a pertinent war declaration was adopted. «We condemn all wars and for the prevention of such we proclaim anti-militaristic propaganda in time of peace, thus promoting solidarity among the workers of the entire world; and in times of war, the general strike in all industries.» The unpatriotic efforts of the I. W. W. in this latter direction after the United States entered the war in 1917 were suppressed by the government. The circulation of the official organ in the United States, *Industrial Solidarity* (weekly) in 1928 was 228,650 copies. Other papers, mostly weeklies—one daily—are printed at various places in this country in Finnish, Spanish, Hungarian, Italian, and Czecho-slovakian.

The I. W. W. claimed, 1912–14, over 70,000 members; in 1925, 36,000; in 1926, 30,000. Anti-syndicalist laws passed by the States since 1918–19 caused the removal of the sabotage clause in the I. W. W. constitution but convictions for advocation of destruction of property continued for a period of some years. San Quentin Prison in 1926 held 66 I. W. W.'s with one to ten year sentences. Such repressive measures acting just when a bright industrial era is upon us, have served to take the heart out of the movement. Its members are now split in two, those of the Pacific Coast differing in theory and policy. This form of Syndicalism in the United States seems no longer tenable. See SYNDICALISM.

Bibliography.—Brissenden, P. F., 'The I. W. W.; a Study of American Syndicalism' (New York 1920); Ebert, J., 'The I. W. W. in Theory and Practice' (Chicago 1922); Hanson, Ole, 'Americanism versus Bolshevism' (Garden City, N. Y. 1920); Haywood, W. D., 'Bill Haywood's Book' (an autobiography, New York 1929); Irwin, W. H., 'How Red is America?' (New York 1927); Mereto, J. J., 'The Red Conspiracy' (New York 1920); Saposs, D. J., 'Left Wing Unionism' (New York 1926); Savage, M. D., 'Industrial Unionism in America' (1922).

INDUSTRIALISM, a term of somewhat vague significance, employed in different senses by different writers. With some it is a type of social organization; with others it means our present system in which industry predominates as militarism did in past centuries. According to Spencer it is a theoretically possible form of society purely industrial in all its activities. The last is the sense mostly frequently attacked by preachers, pseudo-reformers and others.

INDUSTRIES, Welfare Work in. An interesting and valuable feature of modern industrial life is the attention given by many employers to the safety, comfort and health of workers. The new impetus in this field takes its origin not only from philanthropic and paternalistic motives, but from the demands of modern business for scientific management and industrial efficiency. In addition to reform legislation making many such measures effective, an increasing number of employers have found it expedient to adopt various methods for safeguarding and protecting their employees. The result has been manifest not only in the improvement of the immediate working environment and the creation of numerous safety devices, but in the provision for lunch and rest rooms; recreation facilities, rest periods in monotonous work; medical inspection and attention which includes all arrangements from simple first aid to elaborate hospitals, factory physicians, sanitariums, home care by nurses; social organization and education of workers; housing facilities; insurance, pension, etc. A welfare secretary is often employed whose duties consist in caring for the general personal interest of the employees, and in addition, the engaging and readjusting of labor, the meeting of complaints and solving the problem of discipline. The principle of the entire work is the most economic use of the energy available by the right adjustment between the worker and the machine and the adaptation of both to the general work. The result from the employer's point of view has been a marked increase of output because of the lessening of fatigue, the adjusting of the «man to the job» and the heightening of interest on the part of the employed. Studies of the labor problems have established the necessity of such measures for efficiency. (See LABOR LEGISLATION IN THE UNITED STATES). Consult Proud, E. D., 'Welfare Work' (1916); Cadbury, E., 'Experiments in Industrial Organization' (London 1912); Hoxie, R. F., 'Scientific Management and Labor' (New York 1915); Whitney, A. L., 'Rest and Recreation Rooms and Rest Periods for Employees' (monthly review of United States Bureau of Labor Statistics, Vol. V. October 1917, No. 4); id. 'Medical, Surgical and Hospital Treatment for Employees' (id. September 1917, pp. 59–67); Goldmark, Josephine, 'Fatigue and Efficiency' (1912); Lee, John, 'The Principles of Industrial Welfare' (London 1924); Kelly, E. T., ed. 'Welfare Work in Industry' (London 1925); Boettiger, Louise A., 'Employee Welfare Work' (New York 1923).

INDY, an'de', Paul Marie Théodore Vincent d', French composer: b. Paris, 1851. His early instruction on the piano was received from his mother under whose tutelage he mastered the instrument before his 14th year. Subsequently he studied under Diémer, Lavignac, Marmontel and César Franck. He served in the army during the war with Germany in 1870–71. He entered the Conservatory of Paris after the war and in 1873 was a member of the organ class. He was choirmaster for the Société des Concerts du Châtelet; made manager of the National Musical Society (1885); its president in (1900); inspector of music, Paris schools and managed several choral societies; a founder of the Schola Cantorum (1896); conducted his own works with the Boston Symphony Orchestra (1906). Wrote the operas 'Fervaal' (1897) and 'L'Etranger' (1903). Excels as a composer of instrumental music. Wrote 'Jean Hunyade,' 'La Forêt enchantée' and 'Wallenstein,' symphonic poems; orchestral suites, 'Le chant de la cloche,' some chamber music, choruses, piano and organ pieces. 'Poème des rivages,' suite symphonique (1922); 'La Legende de Saint Christophe; drama sacre' (1919). He published biographies of César Franck (1906) and Beethoven (1910). With Sérieyx he wrote 'Cours de composition musicale' (3 vols., 1902–12). Consult Borgex, L., 'Vincent d'Indy' (Paris 1913); Sérieyx, A., 'Vincent d'Indy' (ib. 1914); Coeuroy, A., 'La musique française moderne' (Paris 1922); Saint-Saëns, C., 'The Ideas of M. Vincent d'Indy' (*Musical Times*, London, 1920). D. 1931.

INEBRIETY. See ALCOHOLISM.

INERTIA, in physics, denotes the mechanical continuance, or persistence, of energy in existence. The German language has two words for our word «inertia.» An explanation of these should serve as an illustration of the way in which inertia is used in a dual sense by English-speaking physicists. *Beharrung,* the better of the two German terms, because it is a positive expression, has been defined above. The other German word is *Trägheit,*— a literal German translation of what we commonly mean by inertia. But there are some experimental as well as theoretical considerations which reveal that whenever one understands by inertia the non-appearance of new energy, or motion, or activity,— and this is the meaning of *Trägheit* — one does so by laying all the emphasis on a merely negative characteristic of inertia. A gentleman of Vienna, J. Popper, alluded while conversing with Prof. Ernst Mach, a distinguished physicist, to an interesting parallelism subsisting between the meaning of inertia as used in physics and the meaning of heredity as employed by biologists. Mach's version of Popper's remarks was given in an inaugural address delivered on assuming the rectorate of the University of Prague, from which we quote as follows: «Take a body in motion; the body retains the velocity acquired in (or *inherited* from) the interval of time just preceding, except it be changed in the next moment by an accelerating force. In the case of the body in motion the change of velocity (abänderung) was looked upon as a matter of course, while the discovery of inertia (or persistence) created great surprise; in Darwin's case, on the contrary, the heredity (or persistence) was taken for granted, while the principle of variation (abänderung) appeared novel.» From this is revealed the notion of continuity or persistence underlying both the idea of heredity and the idea of inertia. Inertia thus places emphasis on the idea that so long as nothing interferes to bring about change everything in nature will remain as it is. The law of inertia indeed explains itself. Wherever we meet with it, it need not be accounted for. An explanation becomes necessary only when inertia appears to be lacking.

The term is thus used to denote the law of the material world that all bodies are absolutely passive or indifferent to a state of rest or motion, and would continue forever at rest, or persevere forever in the same uniform rectilinear motion, unless disturbed by the action of some extrinsic force. Even in ancient times thinkers attributed to matter a certain inaptitude, reluctance or renitency to motion. But that a body in motion required the operation of an extrinsic cause (potential or actual) to bring it to rest was first discovered by Galileo. He was led to this discovery through his examination of the principle of the height of ascent. Kepler, conceiving the disposition of a body to maintain its motion as indicating an exertion of power, prefixed *vis;* and the compound expression *vis* inertia («force of inertia») though less accurate than inertia merely, has been nevertheless generally retained. Huygens, upon whose shoulders the mantle of Galileo fell, formed a sharper conception than the latter had of the law of inertia. He achieved this by generalizing the principle respecting the heights of ascent, a principle laid under contribution by Galileo. Christian Huygens writes: "If gravity did not exist, nor atmosphere obstruct, the motions of bodies, a body would keep up forever the motion once impressed upon it, with equable velocity in a straight line." It may be mentioned in passing, that the principle respecting the heights of ascent employed by Huygens in this connection, is identical with the principle of excluded perpetual motion. Sir Isaac Newton showed that if the property of inertia is possessed to an equal degree by two different substances these substances will have equal heaviness or weight. So it appears that that part of the principle of inertia involving continuance in rest if undisturbed was known even to the ancients, and by them attributed to a certain repugnance of matter to motion. It was thus reserved for Galileo to show that the remaining portion of the principle was equally true and general.

The word inertia occurs in compounds, namely, as in moment of inertia. The moment of inertia of a body or a system of bodies upon or round an axis is the *sum* of the products obtained by multiplying each element of mass by the square of its distance from the axis. But with regard to a plane or point, the moment of inertia is the *sum* of the elements of mass each multiplied by the square of its distance from the given plane or point. There are other compounds, and phrases, in which the word inertia conveys a specific meaning. All, like the above, are defined in the better works on physics.

We gain our first conception of inertia by the attempts that we make to move bodies that are at rest, or to stop those that are in motion. As to the underlying notion of continuity inherent in the idea of inertia, we can hardly say more, philosophically speaking, than that nothing in the known world is inconsistent with the hypothesis that all changes are really continuous. Indeed if the self-evident belief in permanence or continuity had not existed, the same laws which are now formulated in terms of this belief might just as well have been formulated without it. Even if bodies are suspended freely, so that fractional forces are negligible, we find that their state of rest or motion cannot be modified without the exercise of a certain amount of muscular force; and by abstracting our own personality in the case, we gradually come to the conception of inertia as a physical property inherent in all bodies. Inertia has been popularly described as a "passive resistance" to change of motion; but this expression is objectionable because it is entirely inaccurate. Freely suspended bodies (that is, bodies that are free from frictional force) cannot be said to "resist" forces that are applied to them. On the contrary, they yield instantly to the smallest force; but a small force, when exerted upon a given body, for a given length of time, does not produce as great a change of motion as would be produced by a large force acting upon the same body for the same length of time. The conception of inertia shades insensibly into that of mass; the mass of a given body being proportional (by definition) to the velocity that is communicated to the body by a force of standard intensity, acting upon it for a standard length of time. See also MASS; MATTER; MOLECULAR THEORY.

INES DE CASTRO. See CASTRO, INÉS, OR INEZ, DE.

INFALLIBILITY, exemption from the possibility of error. The word is used as applied to arguments, statements, reasoning, or the formation of judgments, and does not include impeccability or exemption from the error of sin. The infallibility of the Roman Catholic Church means that "the Church can neither deceive nor be deceived in matters of faith or morals." Also, she is limited to the definition of truths as revealed by Christ and contained in Scripture and tradition. The seat of infallibility rests in the pope as successor to St. Peter (Matt. 16:18), and in the bishops in communion with the See of Rome, whether dispersed or united in a general council. In the acts of the Vatican Council held in Rome in 1869–1870, during the pontificate of Pius IX, the following is the text defining the nature of the infallibility of the pope: "the Roman Pontiff, when he speaks ex cathedra—that is, when in the exercise of his office as pastor and teacher of all Christians he defines, by virtue of his supreme Apostolic authority, a doctrine of faith or morals to be held by the whole Church—is, by reason of the Divine assistance promised to him in blessed Peter, possessed of that infallibility with which the Divine Redeemer wished His Church to be endowed in defining doctrines of faith and morals; and consequently that such definitions of the Roman Pontiff are irreformable of their own nature (ex sese) and not by reason of the Church's consent." The Greek Orthodox Church, the Church of England, and the Protestant Episcopal Church believe that infallibility resides in the universal church in accordance with Christ's promise of the Spirit that should guide His followers unto all truth (John 14:16).

Consult Toner, P. J., "Infallibility" in *The Catholic Encyclopedia* (New York 1910–1918); Butler, Dom Cuthbert, *The Vatican Council*, 2 vols. (London 1930).

INFAMY and INFAMOUS CRIMES, in common law the first means disqualification from giving legal evidence as a result of having committed the second, the theory being that a person capable of such crimes is incapable of speaking the truth. Both in Great Britain and generally in the United States this disqualification has been abolished by statute, and previous convictions for crime have been considered to affect a person's credibility without impairing his legal capacity to give evidence. Infamous crimes are strictly those which entailed punishments. The fifth amendment to the federal Constitution speaks of "capital or otherwise infamous crime" and we read in Nathan Dane's *General Abridgement and Digest of American Law,* vol. 2, pp. 567–570: "Punishments clearly infamous are death, gallows, pillory, branding, whipping, confinement to hard labor and cropping." Infamous punishments include imprisonment in state prison or penitentiary with or without hard labor, and crimes which entail such punishments are undoubtedly to be considered infamous crimes, in the sense implied in the fifth amendment to the Constitution.

INFANCY. The term infancy is usually used as covering the first 12 months of life. As growth is a continuing process such an arbitrary chronological definition is not satisfactory. Infants 12 months of age vary considerably in their physical development and in what they can and cannot do. By custom age is dated from the time of birth. The actual age, however, is the time that has elapsed since the time of conception. Thus at birth one infant may be anywhere from two months younger to a half month older than another baby born at term. While this may make little difference later on in life, it may make a striking difference in his rate of development during the first twelve months. A better conception of infancy is to consider it as the period beginning at birth and ending with the development of independent locomotion. Before an infant can walk everything must be brought to him. With the development of walking he starts out to explore and investigate the world in which he lives, and to which he must learn to adjust himself. Thus the "babe-in-arms" conception of the term infancy, whether it ends at 10 months of age or 14 or 15 months, is preferable.

No other period of life reflects the results of the developments in science which have taken place in the last half century more than the period of infancy. In 1900 over 15 out of every 100 infants born alive failed to survive the period of infancy. In 1950 this figure had fallen to a little over three. In addition a marked decrease has taken place in the amount of sickness. The average infant of today is larger, weighs more, and is stronger and sturdier than the infant of a comparable age 50 years ago. This has resulted from many factors. Advances in the medical sciences play a most important part, but in addition there are such factors as pure milk and water supplies, better housing, and a nationwide campaign of education in the care of the infant that started about 1910. While this campaign in its early days had of necessity to do with such material things as feeding, clothing, and bathing, which carried with it a certain amount of rigidity and dogmatic directives, there has been a shift in recent years to get away from rigidity, and considering only the physical side of health and development. It is well expressed in the title of a book by C. A. and M. M. Aldrich, which has become something of a slogan of the present day attitude toward infancy, *Babies are Human Beings* (New York 1945). Infants, like adults, are individuals, and have differences in their likes and dislikes, emotional stability, and their wants and needs. Above all it is recognized that they must have love and affection, and human relationships as well as material care. More and more it is being realized that the character and kind of care that is received in infancy has a definite influence not only on the physical development and health of the older child and adult, which has long been accepted as a fact, but on the emotional and psychologic development of the individual. These vitally affect his future happiness, relationships with others to whom he must adjust, and the niche in life he must carve out for himself.

Heredity and Environment.—The development which takes place during infancy is governed by both heredity and environment. Identical twins, which result from the splitting of a single ovum, will be very much alike in their physical characteristics and emotional reactions even if they are separated early in infancy and reared apart. Non-identical twins, which result from the fertilization of two ova at the same time, often show a marked difference in size, weight, and physical characteristics, and in their emotional reactions, even if reared together and fed exactly the same. On the other hand the environment plays an important part in the development during infancy. Intelligence is a hereditary endowment but whether or not this intelligence is developed to the fullest extent depends on the environment. The frequency and severity of diseases greatly affect the development of the infant. While a few diseases are hereditary in nature, they are mostly uncommon and of little importance, when compared with the number of diseases acquired from the environment. Since the tremendous growth that takes place during infancy is its most striking physical characteristic, it naturally follows that the adequacy of the diet, an environmental factor, will greatly influence this physical growth. Thus both heredity and environment are of importance to the child as he passes through infancy. As to which is the most important is a fatuous argument.

Physical Growth.—At no other period of life is the velocity of growth in any way comparable to that of infancy. An infant of average weight at birth will double its weight in approximately five months, and by 12 months the birth weight will be tripled. This is a gain of 200 per cent. The gain during the second year is only around 25 per cent of the weight at the end of the first year. A small premature infant (one of five and one-half pounds or less at birth) grows with an even greater velocity, but is almost always below the weight of an average full term infant at a given age. At birth the average weight of a full term infant is around seven and one-quarter pounds. Boys average a little more than girls, and for certain races the average birth weight is less. The birth weight is governed chiefly by the length of intrauterine life, but the diet and health of the mother during pregnancy play a part and there is a distinct genetic influence on weight and size. At birth the head is larger in circumference than the chest but by the end of infancy the two are approximately the same. The legs are relatively short in proportion to the rest of the body. The fastest growing bone in infancy is the lower jaw. This accounts for the rapid change in looks, and why an infant at birth may have a facial resemblance to one member of the family and in a few months may look more like another. Normal infants vary so much in size and weight at different age levels in infancy that it is impossible to state what a given baby should weigh. All that can be said is that it is so much above or below the mean or average at that age. An infant weighing 12 pounds when four months of age may be as normal and as well developed as another weighing 16 pounds. It is simply that one is below and the other above the average or mean weight for four months.

Motor Development.—More important than the actual size and weight measurements is the matter of the motor development. What is important is what a baby *does* at the progressive age levels of infancy. The pattern of motor development in infancy is a cephalo-caudal pattern —one that starts at the brain level and gradually progresses downward. Thus at birth some of the special senses, as sight and hearing, are present but there is no control of the head, arms, or legs. By four weeks an average full term normal infant will be able to hold his head up momentarily, and at an eight-week level will be able not only to hold up the head but when prone will raise his head from the table. By this time he is beginning to hold objects placed in the hand and makes efforts to put them in the mouth. By six months control of the back muscles is established and the infant can sit erect. By eight months he can use his arms for finer controlled motions as transferring objects from one hand to the other, but is just beginning to obtain control of the legs by pulling up and crawling. Final control of the legs for walking does not come until around a year of age. All this time the special senses which were present at birth have been steadily progressing. Words are learned through hearing and the development of speech, and names and words are associated with objects. While a baby has sight at birth, fused vision using both eyes does not develop until two months, but by three months sight and sound are associated. This rapid and early development of the special senses is necessary as it is through their use that the infant learns. By observing the age at which certain things are done in infancy, norms have been worked out with which comparisons can be made for the individual infant. These are referred to as "developmental diagnoses." They must be used with caution. A baby prematurely born will usually be found at a lower chronological level if a comparison is made by dating the age from the day of birth. Further it by no means holds that an individual who shows rapid development in infancy will be intellectually superior later in life. Infants who spend infancy in an institution are nearly always behind infants reared in a home where they receive love and attention. Illness in infancy may cause developmental delay. It is only when there is a decided general delay of development of practically all of the motor functions that a suspicion of low mental capacity is justified.

Dentition.—The deciduous or first set of teeth start to appear during infancy, but dentition is not completed until the age of two to two and one-half years. The first teeth to erupt are usually the lower central incisors between six and seven months of age. The time of eruption may vary considerably and variations of two months either way from this figure are not unusual in normal infants. Seemingly the time of eruption is governed to a considerable extent by genetic factors, and early and later teething "runs in families." On the other hand the quality of this first set of teeth depends to a large extent on the diet and health of the mother during pregnancy. It is extremely rare for teething to cause any trouble to a normal healthy infant. What is more important as regards dentition in infancy is that during the period of deciduous teething the permanent teeth are being formed, although they do not erupt until about the sixth year. Hence the diet of the infant is of great importance in determining the quality of the permanent teeth which must last for many years. The diet in infancy must be adequate in calcium (obtained almost entirely from milk) and other minerals, and in certain vitamins (particularly D) if the teeth of the older child and adult are to be good and not poor.

Emotional Development.—Emotional reactions are limited at birth but develop and change rapidly during infancy. Infants show marked differences in the degree and extent of their emotional reactions which determine their personality. Thus one will be active, irritable, and respond rapidly to stimuli, while another will be slow, placid, and content. One will cry excessively on the slightest discomfort, while others are so stolid they will respond very little to pain. In the early weeks of infancy the chief emotional reaction is one of displeasure, expressed by crying, from stimulation produced by some discomfort, as when the infant is hungry or wet. Some infants even in the first few weeks cry from loneliness, while others will express displeasure if they are disturbed. Displeasure reactions expressed by crying continue throughout infancy, but the stimuli change at different levels of development. At four or five months when the infant has learned to grasp objects he will cry if they are removed. At about the same time he will express displeasure if given foods he does not like. By eight months fear develops and the baby may cry if greeted by a stranger or placed on a strange bed. At the nine-month level infants may show jealousy by crying if the mother attends to another child. On the other hand there is little response showing an emotion of pleasure in the early weeks of infancy. It is not until the sixth week that the average infant begins to show an occasional smile from some stimulation which causes pleasure. At a three-month level pleasure may be shown by grunts or squeals when preparation is made for feeding. At six or seven months the infant will selectively reach for and enjoy certain objects. The stimuli which produce pleasure reactions increase rapidly from this time on as finer motor functions and coordination develops. Play activities develop which give pleasure reactions. It is questionable whether shyness develops in infancy and what is looked upon as shyness is probably a fear emotion. Affection is present in late infancy as shown by the preference for certain siblings. The emotions of modesty, shame, blushing, and guilt are not present but develop later. While in normal infants the various emotional responses to stimuli appear at fairly constant developmental levels, there is a marked difference in the degree and extent of the emotional response. There is nothing like the similarity that occurs in physical growth at the various levels of development. Infants have definite personalities.

Nutrition and Feeding in Infancy.—It is almost universally stated that the breast milk of the mother is the best food for an infant. While this is ordinarily true, as it is the natural milk for the species, modern methods of artificial feeding have so improved in recent years that it is impossible to detect any advantage in the physical growth and development of breast-fed over bottle-fed infants. Breast feeding after five or six months may be harmful unless supplemental foods are added. The value of breast milk is quite dependent on the diet of the mother. For many years it has been known that an infant on the breast or on the bottle might develop certain diseases due to the lack of certain substances in the milk which were called "accessory food substances." In 1911 the term "vitamin" was coined to designate these substances, and two in particular are of great importance in infancy. One, vitamin C, found in citrus fruits, was necessary to prevent a bleeding disease called scurvy, and the second, vitamin D, had to do with the deposition in the bones of calcium from the milk, or otherwise softening of the bones developed which brought about such conditions as "bow legs." One of the chief reasons for the earlier insistence on breast feeding was that infants who were fed cow's milk were prone to develop and die of diarrheal diseases. Breast milk is sterile and hence it became recognized that any form of substitute food—chiefly cow's milk—must be sterilized. But sterilization destroyed certain of these accessory food substances. With the isolation of the various vitamins it became possible to sterilize the cow's milk, and add the vitamins which are necessary for healthy normal growth, either from their natural sources, or synthetically prepared by chemical methods. Thus a rational satisfactory basis for artificial feeding was established which in recent years has quite changed the entire picture of feeding in infancy and led to the lowering of the death rate mentioned above. Both breast and cow's milk are deficient in certain minerals such as iron to meet the infant's requirements after five or six months. Hence supplemental foods as vegetables, egg yolk, and cereals are introduced earlier in the diet in infancy than they were formerly. While these usually are not essential before five or six months for their food value, it has been found that if started earlier, by the third or fourth month, the infant would take them readily and would not go on a "strike" as so often occurred when they were not introduced until the infant was eight months old, as was the custom up to a few years ago. Thus the most important reason for the introduction of supplemental foods early in infancy is psychologic rather than nutritional. The total food needs of a young infant expressed in calories is relatively very great. A young infant requires around 50 calories per pound of body weight per day, compared with from 20 to 25 per pound of body weight for an adult weighing 150 pounds. Today an artificial diet for an infant is so constructed that it meets his total energy requirements, contains sufficient protein and minerals to meet growth needs, and contains an adequate amount of vitamins. The result is that from a physical standpoint artificially fed infants are equal to those breast fed. Aside from the simplicity and cheapness of breast feeding which makes it desirable, a most important reason for breast feeding is the mother-child relationship it develops which reacts to the infant's benefit. In the last 10 years there has been another change in infant feeding practice based on the conception of the infant as an individual and a human being, and not just as a young growing animal to be fed and cared for. In the past the total requirements of the infant for maintenance and growth were calculated, and the total amount divided into equal portions to be given at fixed intervals. At present there is a tendency to let the infant take the amount he wants whenever in one way or another he expresses a demand for food. There is a decided variation in this demand in early infancy, but after a few weeks or months the infant usually works out a pattern that is satisfactory both to the infant and to the parents. This so-called "self demand" schedule works out very well for most infants, and is an example of doing away with "rigidity" in infancy, and of regarding each infant as an individual.

BORDEN S. VEEDER, M.D.,
Professor of Clinical Pediatrics, Washington University School of Medicine.

INFANT, *in law.* By the common law persons come to majority at the age of 21 years, until which time they are called in law *infants,* but by common usage in the United States the word minor prevails. This rule is practically universal, by statute, for males, but many states fix the age at 18 years for females. Some states make all people adults when they marry. Infants cannot, in general, bind themselves by contracts, as they are supposed not to have sufficient discretion and ability for this purpose. But this is their privilege, and their contracts are accordingly held in general not to be void, but only voidable at their election; and they may elect to avoid their contracts in relation to personal property either after or during their minority, except such as they may have entered into for necessaries suited to their condition in life. They cannot confirm any contracts so as to be bound by them until their majority. Contracts affecting realty are usually held not to be avoidable by infants until after their majority. Infants may possess property, but it must be under the management and control of a guardian. They have not the right of citizens as to voting and discharging other political functions. But in regard to crimes and punishments, and trespasses and private wrongs, their conduct is regulated by the same laws as that of the other members of the community, in case of their being of sufficient age and discretion to understand their duties and obligations. And for this purpose no general limit can be assigned, as some children are much more intelligent than others of the same age; and it will again depend, in some degree, upon the nature of the offense committed, or the wrong done, whether a child of any given age can be considered legally guilty of it, since some offenses and wrongs can be more easily understood to be such than others. The law, in general, has a tender regard for youth, and does not permit them to be convicted and punished for offenses and trespasses unless it appears clearly that they have sufficient knowledge and discretion to distinguish them to be such. There are exceptions to the incapacities of minors as to contracting, and these exceptions are made for their benefit. Thus an infant not sufficiently furnished with necessary clothes, food, lodging, medical services, or instruction by his parent or guardian, and not being under the immediate superintendence of the parent or guardian, may make a valid contract which may be enforced against him. However, an infant who has contracted for and received necessaries is liable for their reasonable value only, and not necessarily for the agreed price. Infants require the consent of parents or guardians to marry. The jurisdiction in respect to infants is generally vested in either probate or orphans' courts. These courts appoint guardians to take charge of the property of infants, and, in case of the decease of the father, to take charge of their persons; but during the life of the father he ordinarily has the guardianship and control of the persons of his children until they are 21 years of age.

Sir William Blackstone thus treats the subject *infant:* "Infants have various privileges, and various disabilities; but their very disabilities are privileges, in order to secure them from hurting themselves by their own improvident acts. An infant cannot be sued but under the protection and joining the name of his guardian, for he is to defend him against all attacks as well by law as otherwise; but he may sue either by his guardian, or by his prochein ami, or alone for wages in the county courts. In criminal cases an infant of the age of 14 years may be capitally punished, but under the age of seven he cannot. The period between 7 and 14 is subject to much uncertainty; for the infant shall, generally speaking, be judged *prima facie* innocent; yet if he was *doli capax*, and could discern between good and evil at the time of the offense committed, he may be convicted, and undergo judgment and execution of death, though he has not attained to years of puberty or discretion.»

INFANT JESUS, Daughters of the Congregation of the, is an order in the Roman Catholic Church. It owes its origin to Anna Maroni, a native of Lucca, who having come to Rome entirely destitute, succeeded by her industry in securing a competency. In more advanced years, her charitable feelings prompted her to establish an institution where poor girls should be instructed in such work as would enable them to earn a livelihood. The clergy approved of her plan, and afforded her much assistance, and it was finally established as a regular institution. In 1673 Pope Clement X acknowledged the existence of the society, gave it bylaws, and endowed it with sundry privileges, under the appellation of Daughters of the Infant Jesus. The number of the Daughters allotted to each convent was fixed at 33, in commemoration of the number of years Jesus lived upon earth. The novitiate lasts three years; the sisters make vows of poverty, chastity and obedience. Such as may wish to leave the convent are allowed to do so before taking the vows, but in that case, they are to leave to the convent all they brought to it at their admission. Prayers and fasts are strictly enforced. The regular habit of the order consists of a wide, dark brown dress, and a white hood.

INFANT MORTALITY. See VITAL STATISTICS.

INFANT SCHOOL. See EDUCATION; FROEBEL; KINDERGARTEN.

INFANTE, José Miguel, Chilean statesman: b. Santiago de Chile, 1778; d. 1844. He took part in the War of Independence in 1810 and subsequently served as president of the Junta. 1817 he was dispatched as special envoy to Argentina. He always acted from pure and disinterested motives, refusing public office whenever he felt that conditions were safe without him, and opposing the granting of arbitrary authority to individuals. He founded *El Valdiviano Federal* in 1821 and remained its editor until his death. Many progressive measures were sponsored by him, notably the emancipation of the slaves and the founding of the Chilean educational system. He was offered the post of chief justice of the Supreme Court in 1843 but declined to serve.

INFANTE, former Spanish title of all princes of the blood royal with the exception of the heir to the throne, who was styled *El Principe de las Asturias.* The title was also bestowed on consorts of royal princesses and was used similarly in Portugal before that country became a republic.

INFANTICIDE, the murder of a child born alive, is a crime of frequent occurrence. The main cause of the crime is shame, induced by a dread of the social disgrace attaching to mothers of illegitimate children; though in many instances infanticide has been the result of violence produced by puerperal insanity. The morbid disposition to kill the newly born has also been observed in certain of the lower animals. The sanctity of human life, from its beginning to its close, is a maxim of modern civilization, and the law treats as a murderer whoever wilfully terminates it at any stage. According to the law of England every woman who employs means to procure criminal abortion is guilty of felony, and liable to penal servitude for life, or not less than three years; and severe penalties are inflicted on those who aid women to procure miscarriage. The concealment of birth is a misdemeanor, and may be punished with imprisonment for two years. In the United States, when a child's death is occasioned by an illegal act, such act is considered either murder or manslaughter according to the circumstances. The crime, however, is rarely punished, and in large cities many cases occur each year which are never reported to the authorities.

Infanticide was prevalent in Greece and Rome. In modern times many barbarous peoples are guilty of wholesale child-murder. Among some of the Pacific Islanders and aboriginal Australians there is a great destruction of infant life. The Hindus used to destroy female children without compunction. In China infanticide is said to be very common. See also ABORTION.

INFANTILE PARALYSIS. See POLIOMYELITIS.

INFANTRY, troops that fight on foot, using small arms, machine guns, bayonets, antitank rocket launchers (bazookas), cannon up to more than 4 inches in caliber, mortars up to more than 3 inches in caliber, hand grenades, flamethrowers, explosive charges, and tanks. Modern infantry is capable of offensive and defensive combat on all kinds of ground against hostile ground troops including tanks; and it moves to the combat area on foot, or by train, ship (amphibious troops), armored vehicles (armored infantry), airplanes (parachute or glider infantry). In combat, infantry seldom fights alone but is usually supported by artillery and sometimes by aviation, chemical and antiaircraft units, and naval gunfire.

Infantry has formed the main fighting element of armies since ancient Greece and Rome, with the exception of a period from shortly after the time of Charlemagne until the beginning of the 15th century during which troops on horse (cavalry) were considered the most powerful forces in battle. But even during this period important battles, notably Crécy (1346) and Poitiers (1356), saw infantry gain the day over mounted forces.

Armament.—Until World War I, infantry was generally armed homogeneously throughout each regiment or similar unit; the infantry of 1914 was equipped with the military rifle. Trench combat, however, brought out the need for a number of special weapons to increase the fire power of infantry, and still others were added during World War II.

Notwithstanding this powerful armament, infantry is not considered capable of meeting strong opposition without the aid of other arms such as artillery. Combat troops of all fighting arms are consequently organized with service troops in large units called infantry divisions.

Organization.—The United States Army has two kinds of infantry divisions, the airborne and the normal infantry division. The infantry division as established just after World War II (but undoubtedly susceptible of further change with new developments in weapons) contained some 16,000 officers and enlisted men, about 10,700 of which (67 per cent) comprised three regiments of infantry. These were armed with approximately 3,300 caliber .30 carbines and semiautomatic rifles; 175 caliber .30 automatic rifles and light machine guns; and with 33 caliber .50 machine guns; 118 2.36 inch antitank rocket launchers (bazookas); 27 57-millimeter (mm.) antitank guns; 27 60-mm. mortars; 18 81-mm. mortars; 18 75-mm. guns; 9 heavy tanks each carrying one 90-mm. gun, and 9 heavy tanks, carrying 105-mm. howitzers. The supporting units were four battalions of field artillery, three containing a total of 48 105-mm. howitzers; and one with 16 155-mm. howitzers. The division also contained one battalion each of engineer and medical troops and one company each of signal, ordinance, quartermaster, and military police troops, and one troop (company) of reconnaissance armored cavalry.

The airborne division contained a total of about 13,600 and was similarly organized except that two of the three infantry regiments were parachute infantry, numbering some 2,500, and the other, glider infantry numbering some 3,000; and that the supporting weapons were lighter and somewhat fewer.

In both types of infantry divisions all weapons too heavy to be carried readily for long distances by a single soldier are usually transported on motor carriers, towed by trucks, or moved on self-propelled mounts with tracks like tanks. To an infantry division, for purposes of combat, may be added supporting units of tanks, tank destroyers, additional field artillery and antiaircraft, chemical, and engineer units. A division has its own airplanes for reconnaissance purposes. An armored (tank) division contains three battalions of roughly 1,000 infantry each, which move in armored trucks.

After the close of World War II, a United States infantry regiment consisted of a headquarters and headquarters company, a service company, a cannon company, an antitank company, and three infantry battalions each of five companies (one headquarters company, three rifle companies each of 7 officers and 235 men, and one heavy weapons company of 7 officers and 188 men). In the regimental headquarters company are clerical, communications, intelligence, reconnaissance, and antitank mine troops. The service company contains a regimental headquarters platoon and a transportation platoon operating some 70 motor vehicles. The cannon and antitank companies contain the larger supporting weapons of the regiment.

All armies of World War II contained large amounts of infantry. The Russian and the German armies each had several hundred divisions and the British, Japanese, and Chinese armies somewhat less. The United States Army had 89 divisions, 5 of which were airborne, 16 armored, and 78 normal infantry divisions. The six Marine Corps divisions were essentially infantry divisions; each had three marine infantry regiments and supporting units similar in make up to those of the army divisions.

The importance of infantry in World War II is evident from these facts: In the United States Army, infantry sustained over 70 per cent of all air and ground troops casualties, yet formed less than 20 per cent of the army. It sustained 90 per cent of all casualties among the United States ground combat forces.

Tactics.—The possible tactical tasks of an infantry unit are numerous. A given infantry battalion, for example, before an attack by a large force of which it is a part, may be an advance guard for its regiment preventing a too sudden contact with the enemy, or part of a flank or rear guard protecting the whole force from a possible hostile attack from a side or from the rear. During an attack, it may be one of the leading elements; or it may be in the reserve of a regiment or some larger unit, perhaps entering the battle later. In defensive combat it may occupy an outpost placed out from the main defenses to warn of the enemy's approach in force and delay his advance; or it may occupy a sector of the main defenses or form part of a reserve. Between battles, the battalion may move in motors to a point distant from the main force, there to observe the enemy and send warning of his movements. Again, in a retirement, the battalion may have the difficult task of helping to block the enemy's attempts to pursue the main force; or it may simply be itself part of the main force marching away from the enemy. There are also such special battle tasks as leading the crossing of a river or a landing on a hostile shore against a defending enemy, defending the line of a river or beach against attack, or moving by airplane, and landing by parachute or plane to attack a distant and vital objective.

All of these things the infantry usually accomplishes with the aid of artillery, and, in many situations, tanks, aviation, or chemical units. It then follows that infantry tactics, from the viewpoint of commanders of armies and the larger units of an army, are in general the tactics of the whole force. Infantry regiments and smaller units, however, may be said to use distinct infantry tactics which can best be illustrated by a description of what leading infantry units do in an attack and in a defense.

A planned and coordinated attack by an army seldom begins without a period of preliminary fighting during which the force "gains contact" with the opposing force. An attack may then be ordered by the commander to be made from a given area in a certain direction, the leading troops to cross a given line at a given hour on a given day. Infantry, in approaching its line of departure to attack, leaves the roads as soon as it comes within possible range of the enemy's artillery and advances across country, moving in small columns of 40 or 50 men with 100 yards or more between them. The line of departure is usually the last hill, ridge, or other cover from fire, before the leading troops may come under the fire of hostile riflemen or machine gunners. Behind the line of departure, the troops usually halt and make last-minute preparations for the attack. Heavy machine guns, mortars, and other supporting weapons are placed in positions behind or near the line of departure from which they will be able to fire generally over the heads of the attacking troops. Shortly before the leading rifle units move to cross the line of departure and begin the attack, the supporting weapons may open a heavy preparation fire on the main hostile defenses. There may also be a bombing attack on the enemy's positions. The leading infantry units then move to the line of departure and, fully deployed, begin their attack. If tanks are assisting them, the tanks may move forward first to be allowed shortly by the infantry, or the infantry may have to help the tanks get forward by first destroying or capturing the enemy's antitank weapons.

In beginning and continuing their advance from the line of departure, infantry rifle units avoid all appearance of moving in lines of men. They move rather in small columns or groups with some space between men. Each battalion advances, keeping in a zone of action designated beforehand, and all units keep direction by compass or landmarks. Each small group advancing uses the ground to the best advantage for cover, by keeping away from exposed ground; or if such ground has to be traversed, by crossing it in quick dashes, a few men at a time.

Until enemy small arms and other fire becomes heavy, there is little or no fire by the attacking infantry, although supporting fires continue. But as soon as hostile fire becomes intense, the attacking troops begin to return it. From this point on, the attack consists mainly of maneuver and fire by small units. The fire of the riflemen and light machine gunners in the leading units is not a general blast directed toward the enemy and covering his whole front. They fire at targets indicated by movements of enemy soldiers or the smoke or sound of their weapons, thus to gain fire superiority; that is, to reduce the accuracy and quantity of the enemy's fire through the effect of the combined fires of infantry and artillery, and sometimes of aviation and chemical troops, against him.

In each small infantry unit, during this phase of an attack, a few riflemen attempt to work forward along the ground, using every hump, depression, or tree for cover, while others keep up a heavy aimed fire. At any lull in the enemy's fire, the whole unit advances by short rushes from one covered point to the next. Light machine gunners continue to direct their fire through gaps between rifle units ahead of them, attempting always to gain ground from which they can fire obliquely across the front of adjacent units not as far advanced as they are.

It may be that a given infantry unit will find its zone of action mainly consisting of open, level ground much exposed to enemy fire. Here, it may prove impossible without special measures to gain fire superiority and advance. A more intense support from artillery and supporting infantry weapons may be enough, though often in World War I it was not. Smoke shells fired by artillery or chemical troops may be used to help the attackers across such ground. These completely blind the aim of hostile infantry and reduce the effectiveness of rifle fire by as much as 90 per cent. Air bombing assistance may also be provided to help infantry at such times but is often not available.

A third method of overcoming heavy hostile resistance is founded on a basic operation of infantry in modern offensive combat. In every attack, each unit keeps working forward without regard to the progress of the units on its right and left, and no attempt is made to keep the attack on a line. The only limitation is that successful units must not push so far ahead of others that they lose all contact. Since each attacking unit is distributed in considerable depth (a regiment, for example, is a mile or more deep), this means that a unit can advance ahead of adjacent units at least its full depth before it has gone too far to receive assistance from its neighbors and is thereby in danger of its being cut off and surrounded by the enemy. These tactics, first used on a large scale by the German Army in the great spring drive of March 1918, and then called soft-spot, or infiltration tactics, take full advantage of the uneven progress of attacking units. The units that do succeed in gaining ground often find themseves abreast and even beyond the areas of hostile resistance that are holding up their less successful neighbors. Consequently, men of supporting units advancing close behind the leading elements of an unchecked unit can usually find positions from which they can open fire to the flank, and sometimes from the rear, upon the enemy resistances checking an adjacent unit. This subjects these resistances simultaneously to (1) heavy fire from the front by the checked unit, and (2) intense machine-gun fire from a side or from the rear. To these fires are often added (3) increased fires from supporting artillery guns, infantry mortars and heavy machine guns, and sometimes from aviation. The additional supporting fires can often be obtained merely by shifting part of the supporting fires that have been helping a successful unit.

Once a stubborn, hostile resistance holding up a unit is reduced, that unit can again advance and does so to occupy the area of the hostile resistance and further continue its advance. It is sometimes the case that such units find a weakened enemy ahead and can in turn give help to adjacent units which earlier aided them. Thus modern infantry offensive tactics consist largely of a shouldering forward first by one leading unit and then another, wherever the enemy's resistance proves to be least. Indeed, it is almost a rule that commanders use their reserves (about one third of each unit, regardless of its size, is kept some distance in rear of the leading attack elements as a reserve for later use), not to help the units that find it hardest to advance, but to help those that make the best progress. The failure to do this, and the continued, stubborn, senseless attempts to storm the strongest enemy positions instead of exploiting gains made against weakness—this, combined with the mistaken beliefs that massed artillery can blast through hostile resistance and that infantry must advance erect and in lines—cost millions of lives from 1914 to 1918. An infantry attack against stout resistance will always cost lives. It has no chance whatever of success, other than minor gains, unless economy of life is attained through efficient use of maneuver and supporting fires as generally used in World War II.

Once infantry comes close to a still active hostile resistance, an assault may be necessary across the last few yards of ground. These are usually spontaneous rushes begun by a small unit whose leader sees a chance for quick success. An assault stands small chance of success over a greater distance than about 150 feet. Often, however, hostile resistances, receiving heavy fire from more than one direction, will indicate surrender, or will retreat, before an assault is made. Supporting fires must, of course, be lifted to other targets when attacking troops come close to the areas where shells or bombs are falling. Smoke fires are likewise stopped in time to allow the smoke to thin out as attacking units near it. Once leading units gain their designated objective, they help less successful units to reach it; and when it is fully gained, a new attack may then begin on the next objective.

Defensive Tactics.—Infantry defensive tactics are based on a thorough organization of the ground and the means of defense. A commander, in other words, studies the ground he is to defend and the ground over which the enemy must advance to reach it, and then fits his units and their particular weapons to the ground. This assumes that he will have some time to prepare for an attack and if his security measures are sound, he almost always will. For there will be outpost or other covering troops stationed well out to all sides to warn of a hostile approaching force and to delay that approach. Reconnaissance aircraft may also give warning. Consequently, a given infantry unit may have a number of hours, or even many days, to prepare against a hostile attack.

In carrying out these preparations an infantry commander does not distribute his troops evenly across the sector or around the perimeter his unit is to defend. Instead, he picks out the small areas within his whole area which, defended by groups consisting of riflemen and light machine gunners, will be hardest for the enemy to approach and capture. He finds the positions in his area from which is supporting weapons can best cover with fire the ground an attacking enemy must cross to reach his area. Indeed, so important are heavy machine guns in a defense that he may establish them first as a framework, and then place his riflemen and light machine-gun troops, and his other supporting weapons.

Nor are the heavy machine-gun and rifle and light machine-gun positions established on a general defense line. The result is, rather, an irregular checkerboard of defense in which, let us say, the red squares of the checkerboard, much reduced in size, represent the ground actually occupied by troops, and the black squares represent the ground covered only by the defensive fires of troops. Thus the only front line in a modern infantry defense is an irregular imaginary line tangent to the foremost of the small areas actually occupied by troops. Thus, too, all defensive areas have depth as well as width. The division of the front of any unit between the smaller units composing it depends largely on the ground. As a consequence one forward battalion may have one third of the front—the hardest third to defend—and the other forward battalion the two thirds easiest to defend, and the third (reserve) battalion will be in position to support either.

The fires of the foremost light and heavy machine guns are usually arranged so that they cross each other (interlock) across the general front. The riflemen defend generally by fire to their front. To the fires of the rifles and machine guns are added those of the infantry mortars and infantry and artillery guns in support. These weapons can cover only a certain fraction of the ground to their front with fire at one time. Accordingly, the commander makes a flexible plan through which artillery or mortar fire can be placed on several at a time of many different areas to his front—wherever they are needed most when the enemy attacks. The areas where fire is wanted are then indicated by signal, by telephone or radio message, or by messenger. The commander places his supporting antitank weapons to protect by their fire all favorable routes of approach for tanks toward the position.

Once the plan of defense is determined all defending troops dig in. The degree of intrenchment depends on the time available for digging. As much as possible is done. Hence, defensive works may be anything from simple individual protective holes to a Maginot Line. Barbed wire may be strung in front of the defended areas and intricately woven across the whole front. Tank traps and antitank barriers and mines are also installed.

As the enemy attacks, he meets stronger and stronger defensive fires until their full devastating blast is centered on his leading troops. But if he uses smoke, or there is heavy fog, or it is night, then main reliance must be placed on machine guns fixed by day to sweep areas to the front. And this fire is fully effective only on level ground. Persistent gases may also be used to drench areas through which the enemy must pass to attack, tanks can be used to augment the other fires, and tanks and troops both can be thrown in counterattack against the enemy, disorganized by the defensive fires, to defeat and drive him back.

The infantry of other armies has similar organization and tactics. Infantry will probably have two important missions in possible future wars: (1) to constitute airborne invading forces to follow up atomic bomb attacks; and (2) to form the forces to resist such invasion. See also ARTILLERY; GUNS, LAND; MILITARY SCIENCE; TACTICS; TANK.

JOSEPH I. GREENE,
Colonel, United States Army, Retired, Editor, "The Infantry Journal."

INFECTION, the introduction of disease-producing microorganisms in the body. Infection may result in a number of different ways. Microorganisms may be introduced by means of direct injury. When a person falls and cuts the hand, the bacteria of pus production or of tetanus may be so introduced, and blood poisoning or tetanus may develop. Many infections come by means of the intestinal tract. Thus typhoid is commonly obtained from milk or drinking water. The intestinal worms, tapeworm, roundworm, are contracted in this manner, and a number of other parasites, particularly the trichina, may come from infected food taken into the alimentary canal. Infection may also occur by means of the air passages. The bacillus of tuberculosis is most often taken into the body in this way, and finding suitable soil, it causes the development of the dread disease. The bubonic plague is frequently contracted through the disease germ entering the air passages. At the present time it is deemed not unlikely that a number of infectious diseases, notably influenza, diphtheria, scarlet fever, measles, whooping cough, are contracted through the respiratory tract by infection with the exciting cause. Occasionally direct contact seems necessary for infection, as in gonorrhea and syphilis. In malaria, and probably in yellow fever, the active agent that causes the disease is introduced into the body by the bite of an insect, the mosquito. In malaria one particular genus (*Anopheles*) serves as an intermediate host in the developmental history of the parasite, in a manner analogous to the history of the development of a number of the intestinal worms. It is not unlikely that a large number of diseases may be disseminated by the bites of insects of one kind or another. In all the infectious diseases the element of a real, live, and active contagion should never be overlooked. Infectious diseases do not spring out of nothing. There must be some sort of contact in order that a person become infected. A most important part of the treatment of all infectious diseases is the protection of other people by proper care of all one's own excretions during sickness. The doctrine so frequently taught by some that sickness is ignorance is an important half-truth. But for the ignorance of people concerning the proper care of those afflicted with infectious diseases with reference to the protection of others, measles, diphtheria, scarlet fever, whooping-cough, typhoid fever, consumption, and a number of other maladies would be entirely eradicated from civilized communities.

INFERENCE, the mental process of deriving a new judgment from certain premises or assumptions. It is a familiar fact that the mind passes naturally from given facts to more or less assured conclusions based upon them, as when we expect that rain will follow a change in the appearance of the sky. When such mental transitions become explicit so as to be susceptible of being arranged as a series of propositions, we have inference. Inference is more or less experimental, and therefore subject to test by certain rules with regard to its correctness. See DEDUCTION; FALLACY; INDUCTION.

INFERNO. See DIVINE COMEDY, THE.

INFIDEL, in modern parlance, one who deliberately rejects the Christian faith after obtaining knowledge of it. In former times a man might be an infidel who had never heard of Christianity. *Infidelis* in ecclesiastical language means «unbelieving,» and is applied to unevangelized heathen as well as doubters and apostates. Thus in the Roman Catholic Church a bishop *in partibus infidelium* merely means a bishop whose diocese is set in heathen countries.

INFINITE SERIES. See SERIES.

INFINITESIMAL CALCULUS. See CALCULUS, INFINITESIMAL.

INFINITIVE, the indefinite mode in which the verb is represented without a subject. As the verb expresses an action, or a state, it generally belongs to a subject whose action or state is expressed; but if we wish to express the mere idea of this action or state we use the infinitive, which, therefore, in many languages is employed without further chance as a substantive — for instance, in Greek and German — only preceded by the neuter article; but as the verb expresses an action or state under certain conditions of time, the infinitive can also express the action or state in the present, past, or future, though these conditions are not expressed in all languages by peculiar forms. Some languages express it by some grammatical contrivance, as is the case in English, where it is denoted by *to* prefixed to the general uninflected form of the verb, as *to love* = Latin *amare; to have loved* = Latin *amavisse.* The infinitive may be regarded as the point of transition from a verb to a substantive, and is often used as the subject of a proposition.

INFINITY, a notion which has assumed the most varied forms, characterized by few common characteristics except the transcendence of our customary notions of boundedness and limit. The chief types of infinitude which come to the attention of the mathematician and philosopher are cardinal infinitude, ordinal infinitude, the infinity of measurement, the ∞ of algebra, the infinite regions of geometry and the infinite of metaphysics.

Cardinal infinitude pertains to assemblages and only to assemblages. An assemblage is finite if it can be exhausted by taking member after member from it. It is what is called reflexive if it can be paired off in a one-one manner with a class derived from it by the removal of one term. Whether all non-finite classes are reflexive is not known, as all supposed demonstrations of this statement rest in the insecure basis of Zermdo's axiom. (See ASSEMBLAGES, GENERAL THEORY OF). The set of all classes which can be paired off in a one-one manner with a given class or assemblage is known as a cardinal number. The cardinal numbers of reflective classes are known as transfinite cardinal numbers. Reflective classes are perfectly definite and bounded, though their manner of limitation is not susceptible of being based on an enumeration, as is the case with finite classes.

Ordinal infinitude is a property of well-ordered series. A series is an order which establishes a definite and unique precedence between any two terms which it concerns, and which is such that if it makes a precede b and b precede c, it makes a precede c. A series is well ordered if every series generated by an operation included in its ordering operation has a first term. A well ordered series is infinite if it contains a cardinally infinite number of terms. Two well ordered series are ordinarily similar if their terms can be put in a one-one correspondence in such a manner that corresponding terms always bear the same relation of precedence or succession to corresponding terms. An ordinal number is the set of all well ordered series similar to a given series. It is transfinite or infinite if it is the number of an infinite series.

Infinitude enters into a system of measurement in two different ways: as infinitude of subdivision and as infinitude of distance. A scale of measurement is a system of entities such that every pair has a corresponding real number, which is regarded as the distance separating the members of the pair. The infinite divisibility of a distance is the fact that the distance can be regarded as the sum of a chain of distances stretching from one point to the other, and of as small a magnitude as may be desired. This is preconditioned by the fact that between every two real numbers there lies another real number. The infinite extent of a system of measurement consists in the fact that starting from any point it is possible to find another point removed from it by a distance of arbitrarily great magnitude.

Strictly speaking, the symbol ∞ has no meaning except in some such context as $f(\infty)$. $f(\infty)$ is an abbreviation for the limit of $f(x)$ as $|x|$ increases without limit, and is only significant when $f(x) - f(x')$ can be made arbitrarily small if $|x|$ and $|x'|$ are only chosen larger than some number A. $f(\infty)$ may also be written $\lim_{x=\infty} f(x)$. $f(+\infty)$ or $\lim_{x=+\infty} f(x)$ means the limit of $f(a+ib)$ where a and b are real and a increases through positive values without limit. $f(-\infty)$ and $\lim_{x=-\infty} f(x)$ have the analogous meaning. $f(+\infty)$ and $f(-\infty)$ may exist when $f(\infty)$ is meaningless.

In ordinary Euclidean geometry parallel pairs of lines and intersecting pairs of lines exhibit many important analogies. The convenient expression of these is rendered possible only by the adjunction to the ordinary points, lines and planes of certain entities, called points, lines and planes at infinity. The method of this adjunction differs in the several mathematical disciplines, for it is dictated by considerations rather of convenience than of logical necessity. In solid projective geometry (q.v.) the adjoined points form a plane cutting every ordinary line or space in one point. This enables the universal law to be formulated, that every two lines intersect in one point, and only in one point. In the theory of the functions of a complex variable (q.v.), on the other hand, it is much more convenient to regard the entire infinite region as a single point, lying on every line.

The infinite of philosophy, corrupted though it is with much undigested and misunderstood mathematics, contains a motive of its own. It is that which lacks external relation, not merely in so far as it is of a spatial, temporal or numerical character, but in any manner at all.

The idea of the infinite is as old as the Ionian philosophy, when Anaximander (610 B.C.) declared that the one in the many, the basis of being in Nature, was *το ἄπειρον*, the infinite. The reality of infinitude has been the source of much controversy, and the tendency of many modern philosophers is to deny it, for there is unquestionably a difficulty in the entrance of the unrelated into the cognitive relation. The discursive nature of knowledge makes us bring every object into a context. This difficulty of finding a context for the infinite is the basis of those antinomies of Kant (q.v.) which concern it. «An infinite number,» says Bosanquet, «would be a number which is no particular number, for every particular number is finite. It follows from this that infinite number is unreal.» On the other hand F. H. Bradley states the contrary, in the clearest terms, «We may be asked whether Nature is finite, or infinite. . . . if Nature is infinite, we have the absurdity of a something which exists; and still does not exist. For actual existence is, obviously, all finite. But, on the other hand, if Nature is finite, then Nature must have an end, and this again is impossible. For a limit of extension must be relative to an extension beyond. And to fall back on empty space will not help us at all. For this (itself a mere absurdity) repeats the dilemma in an aggravated form. But we cannot escape the conclusion that Nature is infinite. And this will be true not of our physical system alone, but of every other extended world that can possibly exist. . . . Every physical world is, essentially and necessarily, infinite.»

It seems as if Aristotle had a clearer and more logical view of infinity, *το ἄπειρον* than many moderns such as Bosanquet. He says, *λεῖπεται οὐν δυνάμει εἰναι το ἄπειρον.* He means of course, that, with regard to finite human intelligence, the infinite remains unrealized, although logically it could be realized, and of course, when we speak of infinite time, or infinite creative change in nature, we speak of something which potentially exists, but is only gradually becoming actual. In other words, we can transcend whatever relations we choose, so long as we do not transcend Relation.

Professor Royce of Harvard has undertaken the task of vindicating the concept of the actual Infinite against the charge of self-contradiction. He is controverting Mr. F. H. Bradley of Oxford, who while he admits «we cannot escape the conclusion that Nature is infinite,» expresses also his belief that such an assertion is a contradiction in terms. Professor Royce attempts to accomplish this vindication by proving the following theses:

1. The true Infinite, both in multitude and in organization, although in one sense endless, and so incapable in that sense of being completely grasped, is in another, and precise sense, something perfectly determinate. Nor is it a mere monotonous repetition of the same, over and over. Each of its determinations has individuality, uniqueness and novelty about its own nature.

2. This determinateness is a character which, indeed, includes and involves the endlessness of an infinite series; but the mere endlessness of the series is not its primary character, but simply a negatively stated result of the self-representative character of the whole system.

3. The endlessness of the series means that by no merely successive process of counting, in God or in man, is its wholeness ever exhausted.

4. In consequence, the whole endless series, in so far as it is a reality, must be present, as a determinate order, but also all at once, to the absolute experience. It is the process of successive counting, as such, that remains, to the end, incomplete, so as to imply that its own possibilities are not yet realized. Hence, the recurrent processes of thought reveal eternal truth about the infinite constitution of real Being,— their everlastingly pursued Other; but themselves,— as mere processes in time — they are not that Other. The true Other is, therefore, that self-representative system of which they are at once portions, imitations and expressions.

5. The Reality is such a self-represented and infinite system. And herein lies the basis of its very union, within itself of the one and the many. For the one purpose of self-representation demands an infinite multiplicity to express it; while no multiplicity is reducible to unity except through processes involving self-representation.

6. Nevertheless, the Real is exclusive as well as inclusive. On the side of its thought the Absolute does conceive a barely possible infinity.

other than the real infinity, a possible world, whose characters, as universal characters, are present to the Absolute, and are known by virtue of the fact the Absolute thinks.

The Royceian theory of the infinite is based on the analogy of cardinal infinitude, and presupposes that there is such a thing as a complete universe. Certain paradoxes discovered by Russell and Burali-Forti tell very strongly against the existence of a complete unity embracing all lesser unities. Royce's work possesses value rather as an account of the potential infinity of a universe capable of indefinite enlargement than as a description of a given, complete infinite. Furthermore, it is clear that systems of much less extent than the Royceian infinite may possess the self-reflecting property of cardinal infinity. (See ASSEMBLAGES, GENERAL THEORY OF). Consult Bosanquet, B., 'Logic' (2d ed., Oxford 1911); Bobzano, 'Paradoxien des Unendlichen' (Leipzig 1851); Bradley, 'Appearance and Reality' (2d ed., New York 1902); Cohn, J., 'Geschichte des Unendlichkeitsproblem in abendländischen Denken bis Kant' (Leipzig 1896); Fullerton, G. S., 'The Conception of the Infinite and the Solution of the Mathematical Antinomies' (Philadelphia 1887); Keyser, C. J., 'The New Infinite' (New Haven, Conn. 1915); Kowalewski, G. W. H., 'Die Klassischen Probleme der Analysis des Unendlichen' (Leipzig 1921); Ritter, W. E., 'The Probable Infinity of Nature and Life' (Boston 1918); Small, L. L., 'Elements of the Theory of Infinite Processes' (1923).

NORBERT WIENER,
Editorial Staff of The Americana.

INFLAMMATION, a term long used to indicate the phenomena that follow mechanical, chemical or physical injuries to living tissues. These changes have been described for centuries as rubor (redness), calor (heat), dolor (pain) and tumor (swelling), which are the phenomena particularly seen on surface inflammations. At the present time the idea is becoming fixed that inflammation is a conservative process, the phenomena attending nature's effort to rid the tissue of harmful substances. In the normal process of repair of an injury there are changes which closely resemble the milder types of inflammation; but when to a mechanical, chemical or physical injury there is added a growth of micro-organisms, the reply on the part of the body-cells differs from the ordinary repair of injury. The changes witnessed depend upon the strength and kind of invading micro-organism and the particular tissue invaded. The first change is *hyperæmia*, a suffusion of the part with blood from capillary dilatation; following this the liquid part of the blood, the serum, is poured out into the tissues and offers its resisting powers to the poisonous substance. If these measures be insufficient, the white blood-cells called phagocytes congregate in the tissues, destroying the invading organisms, by actually consuming them and neutralizing their toxic products. During this struggle there is more or less death of the cells, called «degeneration»; large masses «slough»; the remnants of the cells and the phagocytes killed form the thick fluid called pus. When an inflammation goes on to the formation of pus, it is spoken of as *purulent* or *suppurative*. Certain poisons cause a peculiar reaction on the part of the tissues, characterized by the formation of new tissue that is unable to carry on the function of the part. This tissue is the same as the connective tissues, and the process is called *productive inflammation*. The poisons that continue to act for a long time are particularly apt to cause this reaction, and the inflammation is called *chronic* because of its permanency. Catarrhal inflammations are these same processes when they occur in mucous membranes; the appearance of these catarrhs, however, is different, owing to the peculiar structure of mucous membrane and to the fact of the epithelial covering offering excellent resistance to invasion. When death of cells occurs they can readily be cast off. Croupous inflammation is the term used to describe those in which there is considerable destruction of the superficial layers of the mucous membrane, which, with the fibrin of the blood, forms a coating or «false membrane» on the surface. Granulation tissue (q.v.) is the name applied to the tissue formed during the repair of an injury. Names are given to certain types of inflammation having a characteristic appearance to the naked eye, but microscopically there is nothing absolutely distinctive in these except their arrangement. Particular examples of these are tubercular and syphilitic inflammations.

The majority of the diseases of the body that we recognize as entities are due to inflammation in some tissue or organ, but the picture depends on the various changes in the functions of different parts of the body. The kind and virulence of the generated poison, together with the reaction on the part of the body-tissues, makes the complete picture that we seek to recognize. The treatment of inflammation is, in large part, the practice of medicine and surgery. Efforts to help the tissues combat against invasion are made with more success as knowledge is gathered of the peculiar invading forces and the natural modes of defense. It is not that we wish to combat the inflammation *per se*, but rather to make it unnecessary by helping it to a successful issue. The actual destruction of the bacteria by drugs introduced into the body is of little use, for they would be apt to cause as much destruction of the body-cells as of the invading cells; but their toxines, which cause the actual damage, we are learning to neutralize by the administration of artificially prepared antitoxins, and by placing the body and its special tissues under the most favorable conditions for developing its natural forces of resistance.

In exposed parts of the body, where antiseptics may be applied, the toxic germs may be killed, and various measures that change the blood-supply may be advantageous. Where death of tissue takes place, nature may require help in its removal. It has long been the rule to evacuate pus wherever it is formed, unless its escape from the tissues is easy.

The treatment of chronic inflammation is entirely different, as this is a process where actual structure is changed beyond repair in many instances. The all-important question is whether the tissue can carry on its proper functions; for if it can, the body need not suffer. The inflammatory process is arrested in its progress by the removal of the irritating cause, by improving the blood-supply of the part and the vitality of the body generally. These constitute the measures in general applied for the cure of chronic inflammations, it being understood that the endeavor is to place the tissues in such a condition that they may carry on their functions for the good of the whole organism; and the failure of these measures shows either that they are at fault or that the tissue-change has gone too far. See also BRONCHITIS; MENINGITIS; NOSE AND THROAT, DISEASES OF.

INFLATION AND DEFLATION.

—These terms are used respectively to describe the divergence of price levels from a conceived normal level. If the value or purchasing-power of money shows a persistent tendency to decline in terms of goods, the phenomenon is designated "inflation," and is marked by rising prices; the reverse, "deflation," is marked by falling prices. Thus inflation and deflation are manifestations of changes in the relation of money to goods.

Corrective Price Adjustments.—The terms are not used to describe "spotty" changes affecting particular commodities. In the *absence of controls*, such changes are occurring constantly within the price structure, overall levels remaining substantially unchanged. They may be only temporary, tending to restore the previous equilibrium between demand and supply; or they may be more permanent if the price change does not set in motion forces that tend to re-establish the former ratio between money and such commodities. Generally speaking, recurring fluctuations, such as above described, are attributable to the inability of producers and traders—for one reason or another—to anticipate demand or supply, or both, with precision. However, assuming no restraining or augmenting influence, forces are set in motion which tend to restore the former equilibrium within the limits of the time required to make adjustments. Be that as it may, it should be said that instances of changes such as the above, whether temporary or more or less permanent, should be described simply as corrective.

Throughout this article. the reader should bear in mind the increasing pressures both of an external and internal character, which operate to restrain, or even to prevent, the interplay of forces operating in an economy subject to free competition. It can scarcely be said that the prices of the products of industry and agriculture, or the wages paid to labor, or the rates charged by the utilities for service, or the interest paid to banks, or indeed the output of industry and agriculture, are determined in all such areas solely by free competition.

This does not mean that our excursions into the theory of inflation and deflation, or our study of the repercussions of one or the other upon the economy, are carried out in a predetermined vacuum. It means rather that we are operating in a frame of reference where the forces of competition are "under wraps"—controlled competition, it has been called. Within the limits prescribed, there is still feverish competition for credit among the same industries and different industries; the same for labor; the same for the products of agriculture. There is furthermore competition in service among like industries, and throughout all industries, for the buyer's dollar. There is competition among railroads, and highway and water and air carriers; and among natural-gas and coal producers, even though the charges of each are subject to government regulation. Without attempting to pursue this diversion further, it may be safely asserted that while competition as a direct regulator has received "body-blows" both internally and externally, it remains a factor in the overall economy, leaving the broad principles herein set forth in connection with the subject of this article, quite valid, although subject to modifying conditions to which reference will subsequently be made in the practical illustrations of the phenomena.

Inflation—Causes and Effects.—The term, inflation, stripped of refinements, simply means a decline in the value of money in terms of goods and services; hence more money is required to purchase a given amount. The phenomenon arises when purchasing-power in the hands of the people expands more rapidly than the things that money buys. Of course the same result would follow if the tempo of purchases and sales were accelerated without any increase in the volume of money or bank credit. The essential conditions are dynamic purchasing, coupled with comparative scarcity of goods.

If the quantity of things which people buy expands as rapidly as the means of payment, prices remain unchanged. The equation of exchange remains the same. This follows because purchasing-power—either through increased volume of currency or bank credit (or both), or by the increased velocity of one or the other (or both)—moves in harmony with increased supply.

The Inflationary Spiral.—The persistence of an upward price trend fosters further advances so long as prices obtained by producers and traders yield satisfactory profits. Buyers bid against each other for supplies which are relatively limited. They are subject to an urge to exchange money, the purchasing power of which is constantly declining, into goods, thereby gaining possession of something which will continue to increase in value as long as the price trend surges forward.

Velocity of circulation and bank credit, or deposit currency, are important factors in the consideration of price movements. Velocity concerns the rate of turn-over of money or bank credit. The doubling of this rate is practically equivalent to a corresponding increase in money, and hence in purchasing power. Therefore, high velocity of circulation, without an equivalent expansion in the volume of goods and services, reacts to raise prices.

In the process of adjusting means of payment to business activity, bank credit plays a decisive role. Indeed the larger part of "deposit" currency arises from the loans and discounts of commercial banks. During "booms," the volume of such loans expands under the stimulus of increased profit prospects. The deposits arising from such loans are distributed through the use of bank checks. Since depositors do not ordinarily demand cash in excess of a fraction of their deposits, the commercial bank holds currently large balances which are available for the further expansion of loans. Such balances are conserved by the system of clearing checks among banks through the clearing house, the system being projected to the nation through the instrumentalities of the Federal Reserve system. The economy of cash assets is realized by daily transfers of net balances, due other banks, to the appropriate clearing agency which effects the distribution among the creditor banks.

Thus, the customary policy of depositors in

carrying balances (whether arising from loans and discounts, or checks, or actual cash), together with the economies realized through the clearance of checks as above described, enables the commercial bank to safeguard depositors by keeping in cash only a fraction of its demand deposit liabilities. The mechanism multiplies the ability of banks to expand bank credit, and through it, to expand purchasing power—a great factor in sustaining and promoting inflation; but a factor that is balanced when goods are forthcoming to absorb such credit.

In the United States the banking mechanism, under the Federal Reserve Act, provides further means of expanding purchasing power and thus increasing the inflationary potential. Commercial paper and certain other assets held as collateral enable American banks to replenish their loanable funds at the hands of the Federal Reserve bank of their respective districts. They may secure direct loans on such assets or they may rediscount eligible commercial paper. The reserve banks may in turn replenish their supplies of federal reserve notes through application to the Secretary of the Treasury and by the deposit of such paper (commercial paper and government bonds) as security for such advances. (A gold certificate reserve of 25 per cent must also be submitted.) Thus, in the United States, currency- and bank-credit-expansion go hand-in-hand, the effects of such expansion being enhanced by increased velocity during periods of rising prices.

An acute stage is reached in the national economy when persistently rising prices fail to stimulate further increase in production. The British economist, the late John Maynard Keynes, had this in mind when he stated: "When a further increase in the quantity of effective demand produces no further increase in output and entirely spends itself on an increase in the cost-unit fully proportionate to the increase in effective demand, we have reached a condition which might be appropriately designated as one of true inflation" (*The General Theory of Employment, Interest and Money,* p. 303, New York 1936). This technical statement may be paraphrased as follows: So long as output responds to rising prices, the prospect is favorable for production to overtake effective demand. However, when producers are either unable or unwilling to assume the additional capital and operating expenses necessary further to expand output, the additional prices paid serve only to increase costs without increasing output.

Other authorities content themselves with the statement that inflation is indicated when the ratio of price progression persistently exceeds that of output. Be that as it may, the crisis has been reached when a sufficient sector of the lower income group withdraws from the market to render the maintenance of production at prevailing prices untenable. At this juncture the break in prices is precipitated by pressure on producers and traders to liquidate their holdings in order to meet contracts for loans, wages and supplies.

Deficit Financing and Inflation.—Governments frequently resort to deficit financing emergencies to procure bank credit to supplement funds arising from taxation. To the extent that such credit does not give rise to a corresponding increase in the production of consumer goods, the result is inflationary. Business loans procured at a bank for current expenses anticipate the production of marketable goods, the sale of which provides funds for the liquidation of the loans. Government bank loans, on the other hand, when used to finance an expensive war, expend themselves on implements of war, not on consumable goods that command a market. At the same time, such loans find their way into the incomes of the people, greatly augmenting their purchasing power in the face of a dearth in the normal supply of consumer goods. As the gap widens with the progress of hostilities, prices move progressively upward if not subject to drastic control. Of course if the gap should be narrowed or obliterated by taxation or by loans made to the government out of the people's savings, the inflationary trend would be restrained. It has, however, generally been found impracticable or inexpedient to finance modern wars largely by taxation, or out of savings. As a result, nations involved in a major war, where the national integrity is at stake, customarily exact such revenues from taxation as may be deemed feasible, providing the remainder from bank credit or currency expansion, or both.

Deflation—Causes and Effects.—The above procedure in reverse is described as deflation. Its effects are likewise cumulative. When prices reach levels that cannot be sustained by lower income groups, the volume of purchasers left in the market is insufficient to support prevailing price levels. The trend may be accelerated by such phenomena as buyers' strikes, and the pressure on the part of those encumbered with inventories to turn them into cash. This pressure permeates the whole economy, inducing buyers to cling to their money awaiting still lower prices; and sellers to divest themselves of marketable goods before prices go lower. The movement to liquidate may approach the panic stage under the compulsion to meet obligations incurred under higher price conditions. The sequel is depression and stagnation.

The trend downward may be cushioned by various devices designed to restore confidence. Modern governments have resorted to such expedients as government spending for public works, relief expenditures often based on deficit financing, reduction of discount rates, easing requirements for currency issues, guaranteeing loans, absorption of surpluses, curtailment of production, devaluation of the currency, and purchase of government bonds in the open market. These and numerous other techniques are, of course, designed to increase purchasing-power in order to reverse the downward trend of prices. (There is diversity of opinion among economists as to the salutary effects, in the long run, of some of these expedients.)

War Financing and Inflation.—Historically, inflation and deflation have usually been associated with wars and their aftermath. In American experience, all the major inflations have accompanied or followed wars that were important enough to constitute a strain on the economy. It is significant that prices reached their peak at the *conclusion* of the War of 1812 and the Civil War (1861–1865), but the peak was not reached in the great wars of the 20th century until several years after conclusion of hostilities. There are reasons for this difference that will be noted. The War of 1812, while not costly, was financed largely by the United States government through bond issues which were sold at a 40 per cent discount, with the depreciated paper of state banks constituting the larger part of the currency in circulation. Meanwhile, the blockading of American ports not only destroyed the market for the most important American export product, cotton; it also cut off imports of manufactured products from England. These facts were largely responsible for spiraling prices in the United States during the war (1812–1815).

The American Civil War was financed on both sides largely by irredeemable paper money. The federal Government, after an initial issue of $150,000,000 bonds carrying 7.3 per cent interest, adopted United States notes ("greenbacks") and Treasury notes (specified issues) as the media for meeting all obligations of the Treasury. At the beginning of the war in 1861, the volume of money in circulation was $435 million; at its close (1865), $714 million, the larger part of which was United States notes. By the close of the war, wholesale prices had more than doubled. Deflation then set in and continued until gold redemption was restored in 1878. The downward trend of prices was associated with the freezing of the volume of greenbacks outstanding, the rapid expansion of industry and agriculture after the war, and the persistent effort of the Treasury to restore the gold standard at the prewar ratio. The new National Bank notes were not in sufficient volume to fill the gap.

When the Spanish-American War was precipitated in 1898, the country was emerging from a depression. Prices had dropped to the lowest levels in the century, the trend being upward when the war broke. The cost of the war was met by a light inheritance tax and $200,000,000 bond issue. In the rapidly growing economy, the burden was scarcely perceptible. With the exception of several dips of short duration, the general trend of prices continued upward through World War I. The close of the 19th century and the first years of the 20th were associated with corporate development and consolidation; the emergence of the United States as a colonial power; expansion of international trade; rapid growth of manufacturing; the revival of agriculture after the decline following the Civil War; the resumption of foreign investments in the United States following renewed commitments to the gold standard in 1897; the discovery of great gold resources—these and other similar factors are considered as responsible for the persistent upward trend of prices rather than any inflationary influence stemming from the Spanish-American War.

The two great wars in which the United States has been engaged during the present century were financed in considerable part by taxation and the sale of savings bonds. A significant part, however, was financed by bank credit, a procedure regarded as highly inflationary. The net monetary cost of World War I is estimated at $34.5 billion. One third of this cost was covered by taxation, the balance by the sale of bonds to the public, to the commercial banks, and to the Federal Reserve banks. The earlier intention to attract purchases of "Liberty" bonds was somewhat vitiated by a campaign to encourage people to finance such purchases through loans procured from the commercial banks.

During the war, there had been a great expansion in American industrial and agricultural output. Under governmental stimulus, wheat acreage expanded more than 50 per cent; actual production, 38 per cent. The expansion of the staple crops, livestock and poultry, was also significant. Exports of such products to our armed forces and allies rose to unprecedented proportion. Land values for the country rose 70 per cent, doubling in the grain belt. Industry likewise expanded.

The inflation and deflation followed the typical pattern: there was a great expansion of buying power but a contraction of goods available for domestic consumption. The increased buying power was directly attributable to the expansion of bank credit and money in circulation. Loans, discounts, and investments of all commercial banks more than doubled. The Federal Reserve banks made liberal credit advances to the member banks, fortified as they were by their ability to procure all the currency required to support our expanded economy. Money in circulation increased more than 76 per cent; per hour wages, 215 per cent; savings deposits nearly doubled.

The above expansion of bank credit and money meant an expansion in buying power. Meanwhile, supplies of consumer goods could not keep pace. Solomon Fabricant, on the basis of carefully compiled data from official sources, declared there was even a slight decline in the output of all manufacturing industries during the war years (*The Output of Manufacturing Industries,* p. 44, National Bureau of Economic Research). Agricultural output above normal, was absorbed by exports to our troops and allies. Such exports, together with vast supplies of arms, ammunition, guns, artillery, etc., represented so much withdrawn from the domestic market, leaving a great gap between buying power in the hands of the people and goods available for domestic purchase. The result: Inflation! More money for less goods!

When the war was over and all controls removed, the upward trend of prices was accelerated. The break came in May 1920, at a point where wholesale prices were double prewar prices. The drop was precipitate. Farm prices were hardest hit. Having no alternative to meet mortgage payments on land and machinery bought at inflated prices, farmers continued to cultivate the war acreage. By mid–1922, the prices of farm products had dropped about 80 per cent below the average for 1919–1920. Although industrial prices had recovered by the close of 1922, agricultural prices generally followed a downward trend. In 1933, they were below the levels of 1914.

The total direct money cost of World War II to the United States is estimated at $330 billion. The sources of revenue were as follows: 45.6 per cent from taxation; 54.4 per cent from borrowing from commercial banks and the public. The banks absorbed about 45 per cent of the war bonds issued; and non-bank investors about 55 per cent. An effort was made to attract public investments out of savings and current income. An unknown but considerable amount, however, was financed through the commercial banks, thus adding to the inflation potential associated with the Treasury's procurement of deposit credit on the security of bonds taken by the banks. Since the use of bank credit in such large volume (nearly $90 billion) was an important factor contributing to the inflation, the record must be sketched.

The backbone of the bank-credit structure of the country resides in the Federal Reserve System. The 12 Federal Reserve banks extend credit to the member banks against acceptable

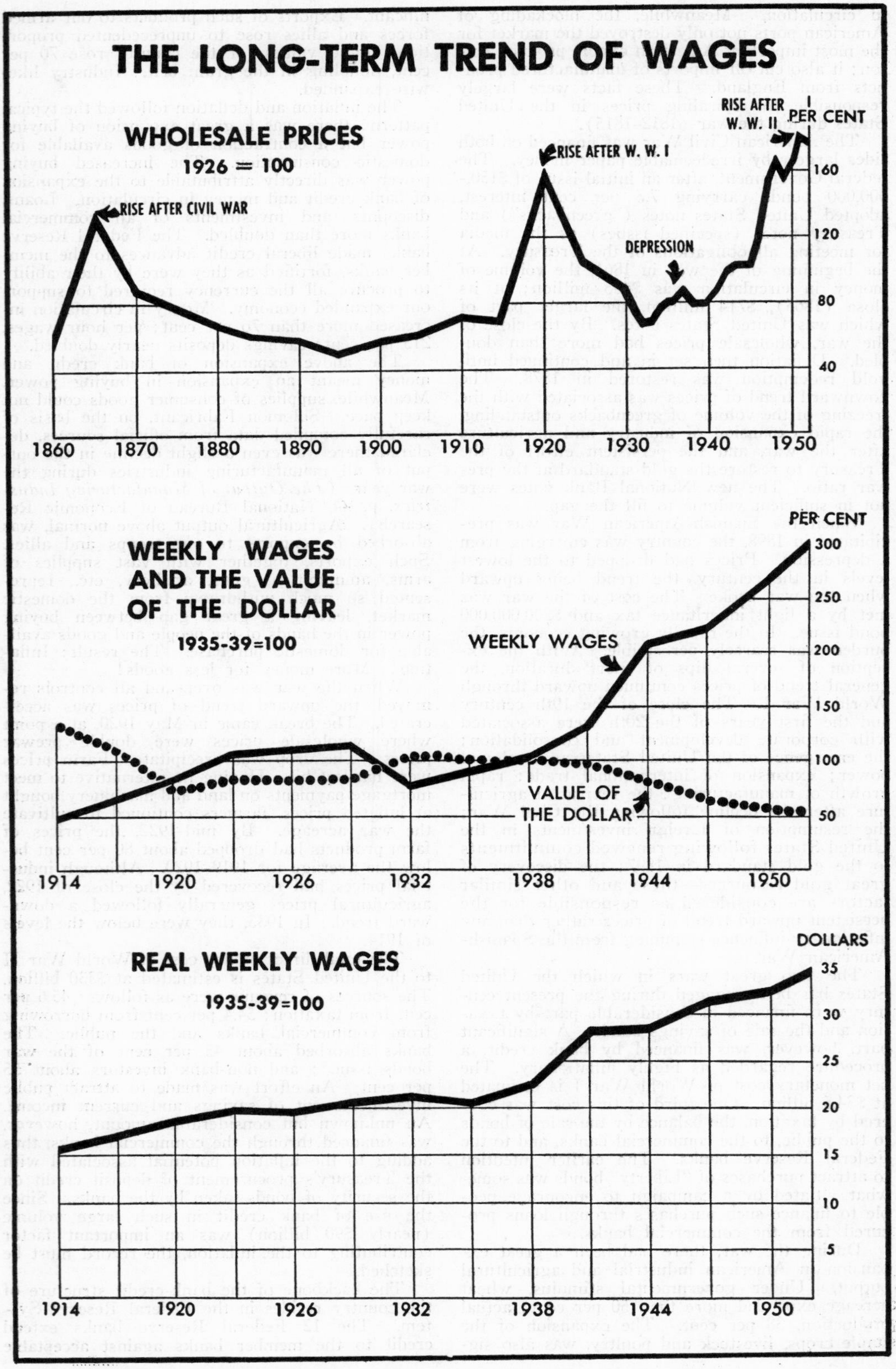
THE LONG-TERM TREND OF WAGES
WHOLESALE PRICES
1926 = 100
RISE AFTER CIVIL WAR
RISE AFTER W. W. I
RISE AFTER W. W. II
PER CENT
DEPRESSION
160
120
80
40
1860
1870
1880
1890
1900
1910
1920
1930
1940
1950
WEEKLY WAGES AND THE VALUE OF THE DOLLAR
1935-39=100
PER CENT
300
250
200
150
100
50
WEEKLY WAGES
VALUE OF THE DOLLAR
1914
1920
1926
1932
1938
1944
1950
REAL WEEKLY WAGES
1935-39=100
DOLLARS
35
30
25
20
15
10
5
1914
1920
1926
1932
1938
1944
1950

assets deposited by the latter, and they also supply Federal Reserve notes (currency) to meet the claims of member-bank borrowers for cash. Member banks may submit government bonds or any other acceptable assets, in their application for loans; or they may offer eligible commercial paper for rediscount. The credit extended is entered to the account of the appropriate member bank, and may be drawn upon by the latter to meet its own obligations to other banks, or to supplement its currency in order to meet over-the-counter demands for cash.

The ability on the part of the reserve bank to expand credit, is limited only by its capacity to issue Federal Reserve notes to member banks. The ample supply of collateral, required by the Treasury as security for such notes (government securities, gold certificates, and some eligible paper), in the portfolios of the reserve banks, was

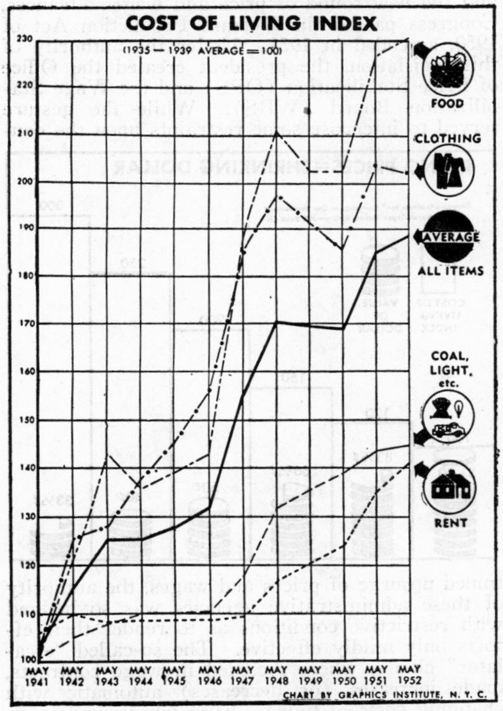

adequate for almost any conceivable demand on the part of the member banks for cash. Holdings of government securities during the war expanded from $2.8 billion to $20 billion; gold certificates in the hands of the Federal Reserve agent averaged considerably in excess of $18 billions.

After setting aside about $4 billion, to cover the legal requirements for a 25 per cent reserve against the reserve deposits of member banks, there remained approximately $14 billion to cover the minimum of the same percentage against Federal Reserve notes issued by the reserve banks. With ample government securities available for the balance of the collateral required, the central banks at no time were called upon to strain their note issue capacity. During the war, money in circulation expanded from $7.5 billion to $28.5 billion at its close, $24.4 billion of which were Federal Reserve notes.

The commercial banks showed a similar expansion in loans, demand deposits—and the holding of government bonds. Total loans and investments rose from $50.8 billion to $140.2 billion. Demand deposits expanded from $32.5 billion to $105.9, an increase of 226 per cent. A large part of these holdings gave rise to demand deposits—to the credit of the United States Treasury. Nongovernment loans increased more than 50 per cent, a part of this adding to the inflationary potential since it represented funds borrowed by depositors with which to purchase government bonds. The expansion of demand deposits—to the account of the government was augmented by the reduction of the reserve requirements of member banks in central reserve cities, and the war amendment exempting all member banks from carrying reserves against deposits arising from war loans, or paying the insurance assessments against such deposits.

The expansion of bank credit and currency above described was reflected in increased incomes in the hands of the people. The total national income increased from $70.8 billion in 1939 to $161 billion at the close of 1945. Factory payrolls expanded 193 per cent. Absolute wages practically doubled, but the volume of goods available for purchase did not expand in a ratio anywhere nearly comparable to that which characterized the increase in money incomes. Before noting the trend of prices, an attempt must be made to present a cross-section of the "goods" side of the equation of exchange.

In 1940, the physical volume of manufactured goods, expressed in index numbers, is placed at 125 (1935–1939 = 100). At the close of the war the index stood at 203.

In terms of dollars, the total national product increased from $97 billion in 1940 to $197.3 billion in 1945. During this period, the war effort absorbed 40 per cent of the total national product. Indeed in 1943 and 1944, the war effort required about 43 per cent of the national product (average $82.5 billion per year). After deductions for taxes, depreciation, etc., the disposable incomes of individuals for 1940 and 1945 were $73 and $138 billion respectively. If it be assumed that 40 per cent of the volume of industrial production in 1945 was taken by the war effort, the volume remaining for consumer purchase was only about 22 per cent above that for 1940; but purchasing power in dollars was about twice that of the prewar year. The pressure of dollars upon the dearth of goods gave rise to inflation. Doubtless it would have been greater had it not been for such devices as absorption of buying power by heavy taxes and the sale of savings bonds; price control; rigid limitations on consumption credit; and a net increase in the total output available for domestic consumption.

In spite of the above restraining influence, the gap between buying power and goods could not be completely bridged. Wholesale prices rose more than 35 per cent; the cost of living, 28 per cent. Following the war, with the unprecedented accumulation of savings in the hands of the public, and the five-year period of short-supply, the situation was ripe for further price increases. The virtual withdrawal of government controls by mid-1946 was the signal for the price trend to become more dynamic.

Overall industrial production from 1945 to 1951 inclusive expanded 8.3 per cent. For the same period the wholesale commodity index advanced 67 per cent above that for 1945 and personal incomes, 46 per cent. The significant fact, of course, is that production was falling far short of the pace set by expanded buying power. It was a sellers' market, while the manufacturing industries sought feverishly to meet the insistent demand for more goods, and to remove all ration and price controls, and restrictions on installment credit, restrictions on wages. The backlog of bonds in the hands of the commercial banks provided adequate basis for the continuance of credit—now geared to the domestic production machinery.

High war profits left many industries in a position to expand from within, plowing back earnings in the conversion of war plants to the domestic demand that for some years could not be satiated. Prices of industrial products mounted. Under the device of parities, the prices of agricultural products surged forward. Under the pressure of advancing costs of living and postwar strengthening of trade union organization, wages followed and often surpassed increases in living costs—but not for long as the inflationary spiral moved in high gear. Higher wages and prices followed. The Congressional election in 1946 and the National, in 1948, made it difficult to enact a comprehensive system of controls. The country had become tired of them.

Bank loans that had reached unprecedented heights during the war, expanded from $26 billion at the close of 1945 to $38, $43, and $52 billion at the close of 1947, '49 and '50 respectively; advancing to $55 billion June 30, 1951, and $58 billion at the close of the year added to the stimulus. Money in circulation expanded consistently though moderately until the close of 1947, when a slight decline set in. Consumer credit, with the removal of restraints, standing at $2.3 billion at the close of 1945 had advanced to $13.5 billion six years later. Total personal income rose from $160.7 billion in 1945, to $251 billion at the close of 1951. In spite of mounting buying at inflated prices, personal savings advanced from $1.6 billion at the close of 1945 to $17.2 billion December 31, 1951.

All price indexes reflect the resurgence of buying power after the war. It will suffice to indicate a few. The all-commodity price index had moved 65 per cent above the average for 1945 by February 1952; the cost of living, 46 per cent.

There were signs that the inflation had about run its course when the defense program was resumed with the threat of Russian aggression. The launching of the Marshall Plan, followed by the organization of the North Atlantic Pact, and then the war in Korea gave impetus to the trend. The leveling off of wholesale prices which had started in 1948, and had dropped about 5 per cent in 1949 surged far beyond the war peak in 1951—again, the resumption of war expenditures and the curtailment of the output of goods for domestic consumption intervened. Government expenditures for defense rose progressively every quarter after the opening of hostilities in Korea. By the fourth quarter of 1951 they were at an annual rate of $44 billion, which is a little short of half the most costly year of the war.

As the inflation mounted, there were widespread demands for the resumption of controls. Marriner S. Eccles, formerly chairman of the Board of Governors of the Federal Reserve System, supported by Thomas B. McCabe, his successor, declared before the Senate Banking and Currency Committee, July 1948, that a serious crisis faced the country. He thought the President's proposals were inadequate to meet it. The inflation, he said, had gone so far that even drastic measures could do little more than halt its progress. He opposed the income tax reduction of 1948, the postwar abolition of the excess profits tax and the control of installment credit, the continued support of agricultural prices at inflated levels, the further expansion of bank credit and currency. He recommended rigid control of bank credit and the restoration of other controls that had been abandoned.

President Truman, in his mid-year (1948) economic report, took substantially the same position save for his opposition to Eccles' insistence that the government should discontinue supporting agricultural prices at inflated levels.

Following the outbreak of hostilities in Korea, and the new round of price and wages advances, Congress passed the Defense Production Act of 1950, amended in 1951. Under the authority of this legislation, the president created the Office of Price Stabilization (OPS) and the Wage Stabilization Board (WBS). While the gesture served to interpose some restraints upon the con-

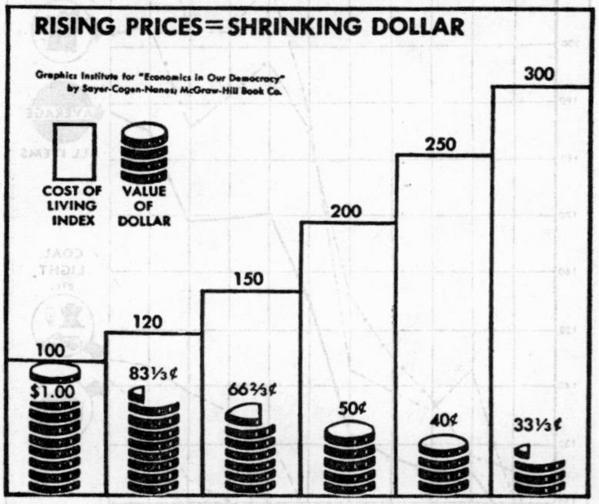

tinued upsurge of prices and wages, the authority of these administrative agencies was so hedged with restrictive conditions as to render their efforts only mildly effective. The so-called "escalator" clause, where included in wage contracts, made increases (or decreases) automatic with changing costs of living. Even where wage contracts did not contain the clause, the WSB was inclined to open contracts for renegotiation under pressure of the rising cost of living.

By the same token, industry generally was permitted to raise prices when a showing could be made that wage increases could not otherwise be absorbed. Such concessions gave rise to wage increases to offset rising prices, then to increased prices to offset rising costs, and then increased wages. This is in the pattern of the typical inflationary spiral. The OPS was further limited in its power to "hold the line" by the provision exempting products of agriculture from price ceilings "below 90 per centum of the price received (by grade) by producers on May 15, 1951, as determined by the Secretary of Agriculture."

Meanwhile the secretary of agriculture retained his authority under previous legislation to fix "parities," which conditioned generally the authority of the OPS. The wholesale prices of specific commodities are subject to price ceilings fixed by the Secretary of Agriculture. It may be said that the price and wages structures in both agriculture and industry are subject to the *escalator* principle, the reciprocal compensating features operating to stimulate inflation. As to whether the principle can be applied when costs of living and production costs move sharply downward remains to be seen. There have been only a few such changes, and they were not significant.

The Federal Government and Price Trends.—The analysis of price trends, characterizing the major wars and their aftermath, brings into focus the great changes that have taken place in the relation of government to the economy of the people; and also changes in the methods of financing such expenditures. These considerations are pertinent to price movements, and they are related to the ability of the economy to make its accommodations to recurring imbalances arising, on the one hand, from shortages in consumer goods and high volume of purchasing power, and on the other, from "surpluses" of goods and depressed purchasing power. Governments now generally intervene to cushion the shock of such contingencies. Of course the effects of such intervention may be quite different for different industries. Even an industry which may be outside restraining or accelerating measures becomes conscious of the reaction of any influence the effect of which is to change the pace of any major factor in the economy. Illustrations from American experience will serve to demonstrate the far-reaching repercussions of governmental action bearing upon one or more sections of the economy.

Beginning with the great depression of the 1930's, the federal government has followed the policy of supporting the prices of agricultural products. Although the procedure has gone through several changes since its inception, the object has been to limit the volume of output in order to raise prices, thus attempting to counteract the operation of so-called economic forces that were driving agriculture into bankruptcy.

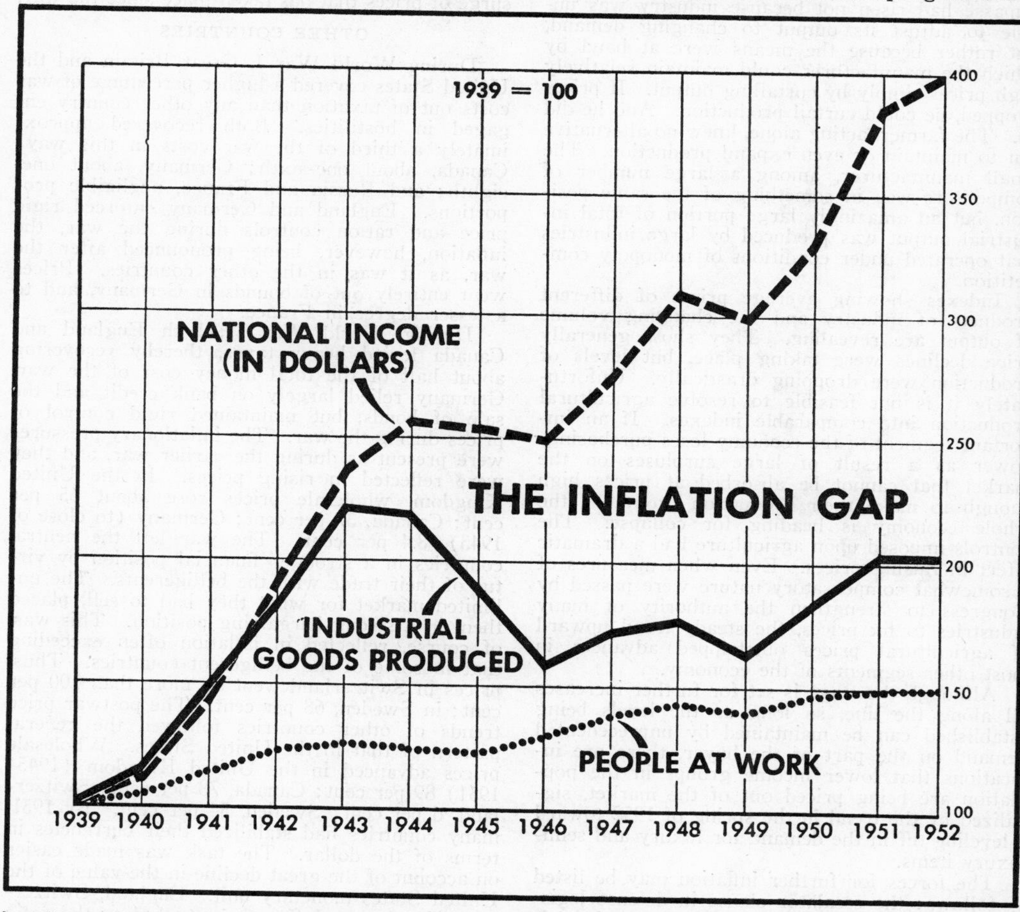

The devaluation of the dollar, the Agricultural Adjustment Administration (AAA), the relief payments, the liberalization of credit, were all designed to reverse the trend of prices, especially farm prices. Of course the National Industrial Recovery Administration (NIRA) undertook to limit the output of manufacturing for the same purpose, and also to improve the bargaining position of labor. When the NIRA was held to be unconstitutional, the crop control program (modified to meet the strictures imposed by the courts—its effectiveness unimpaired) came into full force and effect. Although governmental authority for limitation of the output of industry had been withdrawn, the repercussions of the farm-control program operated to increase the cost to the manufacturer of all supplies from the land that constituted his raw material; and, of course, the policy served to increase the cost of living, and hence wages.

In devising the original control programs to limit the output of both the great segments of the economy, little attention was given to the fact that prices of manufactured goods had not fallen to the low levels which characterized the products of the farm. Indeed the NIRA, while in effect, served to perpetuate the difference between agricultural and industrial prices. The impassé had risen not because industry was unable to adjust its output to changing demand, but rather because the means were at hand by which the manufacturer could maintain relatively high prices simply by curtailing output. If prices dropped, he could curtail production. And he did so. The farmer, acting alone, knew no alternative but to maintain or even expand production. The small manufacturer, among a large number of competitors was in something of the same position, but an amazingly large portion of total industrial output was produced by large industries that operated under conditions of monopoly competition.

Indexes showing average prices of different products of industry and the changing volume of output are revealing. They show generally price declines were taking place, but levels of production were dropping drastically. Unfortunately it is not feasible to resolve agricultural production into comparable indexes. If an important segment of the economy loses purchasing-power as a result of large surpluses on the market that cannot be absorbed at prices high enough to make their production profitable, the whole economy is heading for collapse. The controls imposed upon agriculture had a dramatic effect in raising prices. Even when measures of a somewhat compensatory nature were passed by Congress to strengthen the authority of many industries to fix prices, the steady trend upward of agricultural prices outstripped advances in most other segments of the economy.

Although the stage is set for further increases all along the line, so long as the levels being established can be maintained by unprecedented demand on the part of the buyer, there are indications that lower income groups in the population are being priced out of the market, signalized by the trend in the spring of 1952 toward a leveling off in the demand for luxury and semi-luxury items.

The forces for further inflation may be listed as follows: the escalator clause in defense legislation by which the prices of manufactured products and the wages of labor may advance to compensate for rising prices; the parity provision under which the government enters the market to absorb agricultural prices if they fall below parity (a sort of escalator clause for agriculture which reflects rising prices of things the farmer buys in rising prices for his own products); the Miller-Tydings and the Robinson-Patman acts which strengthen the hand of industry to protect prices of certain products from competition; the suspension of installment-credit controls in May 1952, and of Regulation X (restricting real-estate credit) in September 1952; the defense program and the Atlantic Pact are also important factors.

There are some restraining influences and they are probably operating to stabilize prices at somewhere near current levels. The total increase in production; the operation of defense mobilization agencies in checking, somewhat, advances in prices and wages; the imposition of heavy income, excess profits, and corporate taxes; slight increases in the reserve requirements of member banks; and the 1952 arrangement between the Federal Reserve Board and the Treasury by which the latter concedes to the former a stronger hand in the control of the interest rate. These retarding influences working together are potent. They may be expected to counter, if they cannot fully restrain, the upward surge of prices that has taken place since the war.

OTHER COUNTRIES

During World War I, Great Britain and the United States covered a higher percentage of war costs out of taxation than any other country engaged in hostilities. Both recovered approximately a third of the war costs in this way; Canada, about one-sixth; Germany, about one-eighth; and Russia and France, negligible proportions. England and Germany enforced rigid price and ration controls during the war, the inflation, however, being pronounced after the war, as it was in the other countries. Prices went entirely out of bounds in Germany, and to a lesser degree in France.

During World War II, both England and Canada levied heavy taxes, thereby recovering about half of the total money cost of the war. Germany relied largely on bank credit and the sale of bonds, but maintained rigid control of prices during the war. The inflationary pressures were present as during the earlier war, and they were reflected in rising prices. In the United Kingdom, wholesale prices rose about 65 per cent; Canada, 37 per cent; Germany (to close of 1943), 8.4 per cent. The war left the neutral countries in a stronger financial position by virtue of their trade with the belligerents. The unlimited market for what they had to sell, placed them in a strong bargaining position. This was, of course, reflected in inflation often exceeding that in some of the belligerent countries. Thus, prices in Switzerland went up more than 100 per cent; in Sweden, 68 per cent. The postwar price trends of other countries followed the general pattern of that in the United States. Wholesale prices advanced in the United Kingdom (1945–1951) 89 per cent; Canada, 78 per cent; Switzerland, 6 per cent; Sweden, 54 per cent. By 1951, many countries had stabilized their currencies in terms of the dollar. The task was made easier on account of the great decline in the value of the United States monetary unit. England, Switzerland, Sweden, and Canada, returned to the ratio prevailing in 1939. However, the Canadian dollar, reacting to heavy capital movements from the United States and mounting inflation in the latter, attained a premium in terms of the United States dollar in the spring of 1952. Germany, Belgium, and a number of other countries, fixed somewhat lower ratios. The French franc was stabilized in 1950 but at a ratio to the dollar far below that prevailing before the war.

Bibliography.—American Academy of Political and Social Sciences, *Proceedings,* vol. 9, No. 1 (New York 1920); Cassel, G., *Money and Foreign Exchange After 1914* (New York 1923); Keynes, J. M., *Monetary Reform* (New York 1924); *League of Nations, Commercial Policy in the Interwar Period* (Geneva 1924); Hawtrey, R. G., *Monetary Reconstruction,* 2d ed. (London 1926); League of Nations, *The Course and Phases of the World Economic Depression* (Geneva 1931); Wright, P. G., *Inflation and After* (Charlotte, N. C., 1934); Robbins, L. C., *The Great Depression* (London 1935); Willis, H. P., and Chapman, J. M., *Economics of Inflation* (New York 1935); Keynes, J. M., *The General Theory of Employment, Interest and Money* (New York 1936); Mills, F. C., *Prices and Recession Recovery* (New York 1936); Keynes, J. M., *How to Pay for the War* (New York 1941); Early, J. S., *British Wartime Price Administration and Price Movements* (Washington 1942); Fellner, W. J., *A Treatise on War Inflation* (Berkeley, Calif., 1942); League of Nations, *Statistical Yearbook of the League of Nations* (Geneva 1942–44); League of Nations, *World Economic Survey* (Geneva 1942–44); League of Nations, *Economic Stability in the Postwar World* (Geneva 1945); Board of Governors of the Federal Reserve System, *Federal Reserve Bulletin*, monthly (1946–51); Chandler, L. V., *Inflation in the United States, 1940–48* (New York 1951); also *Statistical Abstract of the United States*, published annually, by Department of Commerce Washington, D.C.

THOMAS A. KIBLER,
Professor of Economics, Ohio State University.

INFLECTION (Latin, *inflexio*, a bending), that process in grammar which modifies words when placed in relation to other words in a sentence; the act or process of varying the form of words, as by altering the endings or suffixes, so as to express grammatical relationship. It was primarily called bending, evidently because the word was bent to a new shade of meaning. It includes both declining and conjugation, and it is interesting to note that declining also carries out this same idea of bending down the word. In the grammatical term "case," from the Latin *cado*, to fall, there is also the same idea of falling away. Hence, it is well to regard inflection, in grammar, as the allowing of a word to fall away in a different manner to express some relationship.

We say "I love," "he loves," "I am loved" and sometimes "thou lovest." In each case the fundamental idea of love is the same, but the ending on inflection is bent to agree and harmonize with the noun.

In the case of nouns, pronouns and adjectives, we call this process *declension*, and this term was once also used for verbs, but has been displaced by *conjugation*. Nouns and their adjectives should agree in gender, number, person, and case.

In primitive speech it is obvious that men talked largely by nouns, mainly of one syllable, for the most common things are thus named, viz.: eye, ear, arm, leg, nose, knee, axe, bow, box, tree, hole, sun, moon, etc. Then came longer nouns, as house, elbow, throat, breast, arrow, etc. Then came words of action, the verbs. Qualifying words followed, now known as adjectives and adverbs. Then came joining words, the conjunctions, prepositions and articles. The next step in the development of language was obviously the showing of relationship. As expressions of gender, came "he," "she" and "it"; adding s came to show the plural in most cases; the person, as present or objective, was suggested by "I" and "you"; the case is illustrated by "thou" (nominative), "thine" (possessive), and "thee" (objective).

To conjugate means primarily to join in couples or pairs, but it has been extended in meaning "to state the principal parts of a verb." Conjugation is a connected process of giving the entire series of inflections of a verb, that is, all its forms in person, number, mode, tense and voice. Many conjugations seem tedious and unnecessarily prolix, but other languages may be more difficult in this respect, as Arabic, in which verbs have 15 conjugations, in theory if not always in practice. In English the common auxiliary verbs am, do, have, shall, will, may, can, asserting respectively existence, action, possession, obligation, volition, liberty, power, assume the function of inflections and are themselves inflected to denote past time. In French the same inflectional law exists, the connection between the auxiliary and the root being closer than in English. *Aimer-ai*, I have to love, that is, I shall love, is compounded of the infinitive *aimer*, to love, and *ai*, I have, the first person present indicative of *avoir*. The same is the case in Italian and Spanish.

Pronominal and predicative roots are combined to form one word in the Semitic and Aryan tongues, which are therefore called inflectional, a process impossible in monosyllabic languages like the Chinese or in languages of the agglutinate order like those of the Turanian family. The Semitic and Aryan families of languages, which admit of phonetic corruption both in root and the terminations, are called organic or amalgamating languages. The pronominal termination varies according to the person or number. Thus the Sanskrit *mi, si, ti*, the endings of the three persons singular of the present of the verb, are perhaps from the personal pronouns *ma, sva, ta* and the persons of the plural indicate the plural number by the form of the pronominal affixes. The plural of masculine and feminine Greek and Latin nouns of the third declension is probably a contraction of the duplication of *sa*, the pronoun of the third person. See also GRAMMAR.

INFLORESCENCE, INFRUCTESCENCE, botanical terms referring respectively to methods of flowering and fruit-bearing. The flowering shoot frequently bears only a solitary, either axillary or terminal flower. In many cases, however, the metamorphosis of the generative region, which results in the production of flowers, has led to the formation of a special system of fertile shoots termed an inflorescence or, after the fruit is formed, an infructescence. (See FLOWERS; FRUIT.) Such inflorescences are wanting or ill developed among the gymnosperms, while in the angiosperms they are often well differentiated, constituting unities of a higher order. The modifications exhibited by the fertile shoots of such an inflorescence are due, partly to a difference in their mode of branching, partly to the reduction or the metamorphosis of their leaves. These changes are the result of an adaption to pollination, in the endeavor to aggregate and at the same time render the flowers more conspicuous by the reduction of the foliage-leaves. Sometimes the whole system of fertile shoots is converted into an attractive apparatus, as in the *Araceae*, where the axis and the subtending leaf of the inflorescence have assumed the function, usually exercised by the perianth, of enticing insects.

The solitary flower excepted, the principal types of inflorescence are called *racemose, cymose*, and *mixed*. Representative of the racemose are the lily of the valley (raceme) and the cherry (corymb); of the cymose, the phlox (cyme); and of mixed type, the form called thyrsus in which the main axis is racemose, while secondary and later axes are cymose. Another mixed type is the verticillaster in which nearly sessile cymes in pairs surround the axis.

INFLUENZA, an acute epidemic infectious and contagious disease, sometimes becoming pandemic. It is characterized by an inflammation of the mucous membrane of the respiratory tract and the disease is accompanied by a train of symptoms such as headache, backache, sudden onset of fever, and not infrequently by serious lung complications, among them pleurisy, pneumonia, middle-ear infection, and neuritis. Influenza is often referred to as grippe or flu and it is no newcomer in medicine, having a long and devastating history in the annals of mankind. Pandemics have occurred and have been recorded as early as the year 1510. It has always been noted that an epidemic is composed of three distinct waves as the disease sweeps over the world. These waves are observed as being separated by many months, the second wave generally being the most serious. Pandemics or worldwide occurrences of influenza have been recorded in 1781, 1832, 1847, 1889, and 1918. In each of these instances the disease became epidemic in a definite area. Although the infectious agent is not definitely known, it is quite probably a filtrable virus which is commonly associated with *Hemophilus influenzae,* a small nonmotile bacillus referred to as the *Pfeiffer bacillus* from Richard F. J. Pfeiffer who described it in 1892. A number of other bacilli are also found in patients who are examined during epidemics in various parts of the world, but it is impossible to state that all are identical. Sporadic cases of influenza may be encountered at any time but epidemics are commonest in winter. The disease attacks individuals at any age but is most prevalent between 10 and 40 years. An attack may confer some immunity upon the individual but recurrences are frequent. Uncomplicated influenza is only rarely a cause of death, but in severe and rapidly fatal cases the patient may be overwhelmed and perish before the clinical signs of pneumonia are apparent. In all fatal cases changes are present in the lungs. Usually bronchopneumonia is present with extensive involvement of several lobes. Within the small bronchi is a widespread purulent exudate with necrosis of the wall of the bronchus. In many patients who develop pneumonia the pneumococcus is found in the lung exudate. Effusions into the pleural cavity are common and edema of the lung is by no means rare. Outside the lung area many lesions also occur but these are not characteristic. Involvement of the pericardial cavity, hemorrhage from the intestine, and nephritis all have been observed in complicated cases.

The incubation stage of the disease is short, from one to three days. The onset is sudden, especially in the epidemic type, and is marked in general by a true chill and a rise in temperature to 102°F. or even to 104°F. The respiration is increased and the pulse rate also but not in proportion to the increase in temperature. Nosebleed may be present. Practically all patients have respiratory symptoms such as running at the nose, laryngitis, and bronchitis with expectoration. The patient seems dull and apathetic. Simple, uncomplicated cases usually show improvement within 24 hours, and the temperature reaches normal within two or three days. When a typical case is encountered, especially during an epidemic, the diagnosis is easily made. There are seldom any after effects. Severe forms without complications present the same train of symptoms but to an exaggerated degree. The chill is more severe, the pain in the limbs worse, and the prostration extreme. The temperature may be as high as 105°F. Cough is racking, pain in the chest agonizing, and there may be nausea and vomiting. The patient looks extremely ill and often remains prostrated, with continuous fever, for as long as 10 days before convalescence begins. If the fever remains high after 10 days a complication is probably present. In about 10 per cent of the cases of influenza the pneumonic type is present, the signs appearing on the third or fourth day. The pneumonia may be bronchial or lobar in type, the former being more common. With the appearance of pneumonia the patient becomes more toxic and cyanosis is present. Occasionally a severe and rapidly fatal pneumonia is observed in which the patient is *in extremis* within 24 hours and dies within another day. Such cases were frequent during the epidemic of 1918. In the pneumonic cases where actual pneumonia is present the mortality may be from 20 to 60 per cent.

The complications of influenza are many. A chronic bronchitis may develop lasting for many months and incapacitating the patient. Empyema is somewhat common in some epidemics. Small pulmonary abscesses may develop. Occasionally a pneumothorax is observed due to rupture of an abscess which communicates with a bronchus through the pleura. Gangrene and necrosis of the lung is an occasional and serious complication. Pulmonary tuberculosis has been known to follow a severe attack of influenza and cerebrospinal meningitis has been reported. A host of nervous symptoms may follow, and some clinicians regard the nervous manifestations as second in importance to those concerned with lung involvement. Neuralgias, neuritis, herpes zoster (shingles), optic neuritis, and involvement of the cranial nerves are possibilities as complications. The heart is seldom seriously damaged in consequence of an attack of influenza. Heart symptoms, however, are frequently encountered. The diagnosis of influenza is not difficult during an epidemic and is based on the acute onset with chills, fever, and aching of the limbs accompanied by cough. The tongue is coated, the mucous membrane of the nose is intensely red but without excessive discharge, while the throat as a rule is only slightly reddened. Mild cases may not be well defined. Common colds are sometimes difficult to separate from influenza, but it should be emphasized that a cold begins generally with premonitory symptoms of malaise, snuffles, sore throat, and hoarseness, while influenza comes on with great abruptness and immediate prostration. Influenza may be confused with typhoid and paratyphoid fevers, pulmonary tuberculosis, and, in the early stages, before the rash becomes apparent, with measles. Occasionally meningitis, dengue, smallpox, and undulant fever may be mistaken for it.

The outlook in uncomplicated cases, especially if pneumonic symptoms are absent, is extremely good except in the aged and those in manifestly poor general condition. The mortality varies greatly in different epidemics, ranging from 10 to 50 per cent. Death without lung involvement seldom occurs but in the presence of a lung complication the prognosis will have to be altered. In the septic, fulminating type, death may take place within 48 hours from hemorrhage and lung edema. Increase in cyanosis, a dusky color, with greatly increased respiratory rate are bad signs.

Convalescence from influenza is often slow, and even if the attack lasts but a few days, several weeks may elapse before the patient is entirely recovered. The symptoms are usually those of extreme weakness and fatigue, with dizziness, poor appetite, and lack of desire to get about.

Prevention of influenza is of considerable importance. Persons in good health should not associate with those having the disease. Epidemics have been known to start from a single individual, so contagious is the malady. Especially should one avoid contact with secretions from the eyes, nose, and mouth of an infected person. All such secretions from persons ill with influenza should be burned and linen, dishes, and similar items in use by a patient should be sterilized. In some instances schools will have to be closed, and public meetings prohibited during epidemics. Strict isolation and quarantine are to be insisted upon as with any contagious disease. Drugs are of little value in prevention and antiseptic sprays are not to be depended upon. Face masks, when worn by trained individuals, are of use. Vaccines are of uncertain value. An immune serum has been produced, but the role of immune sera in the protection of humans is still in the experimental stage. The same may be said of the use of influenza virus although extensive research along these lines is in progress. The treatment of influenza is not specific since no drug is known that will control its course. Prompt recognition of the disease with proper management of the individual case is of vital importance. Bed rest should be insisted on at once, and the patient should be kept in bed until the temperature has been normal for 24 hours. Fresh air and a high carbohydrate diet, with liquids only, for the first day are to be recommended. The fluid intake should be three to four quarts daily. High fever, severe headache, and a troublesome cough will require symptomatic treatment. The use of barbiturates or even opium may be necessary. In severe toxemia, blood transfusions or saline infusions may be used. Vaccines are of little use in the average case. Complications are treated as they arise. Penicillin may be of benefit in certain cases.

Consult Cecil, R. L., *A Textbook of Medicine* (Philadelphia 1944); Yater, Wallace M., *Fundamentals of Internal Medicine* (New York 1944); *Cyclopedia of Medicine, Surgery, and Specialties,* "Influenza," vol. 7 (Philadelphia 1949).

HAROLD WELLINGTON JONES, M.D.

INFORMATION, a proceeding for some offense, usually against the government, differing from an indictment in not being found by a grand jury. It is usually brought by an authorized public official and is in use in the United States and England. The use of the information in the United States is restricted to misdemeanors in criminal cases, and it is allowed in certain civil cases, as to bring a person into court who has assumed the duties of a civil office to show by what authority he so acts, or to arraign a corporation for failing to observe the provision of its charter, etc. In England information in criminal cases is brought by the attorney general or solicitor general, but not for treason, misprision of treason or felonies. However, it is rarely used there except for aggravated offenses, such as sedition, or crimes that are pernicious, as attempting to bribe public officials. In the United States, in some jurisdictions, violations or attempted violations of the revenue laws are proceeded upon by information. The term is also applied to the written sworn statement made, as before a committing magistrate, prior to the issuance of a summons or complaint.

INFORMER, a person who sues for a penalty against those who have infringed any law or penal statute. To encourage the apprehending of certain felons, guilty of offenses not so much criminal as bordering on criminality, many English statutes, from 1692 downward, granted rewards to such as should prosecute to conviction. The penalty in whole or in part inflicted in the case of a successful conviction and immunity from certain troublesome parish offices were the inducement held out to informers. In many cases this practice has been resorted to in modern statutes. But the institution of a crown prosecutor in England and of prosecuting attorneys in the United States has nullified the importance of informers to a great extent.

INFRALAPSARIANISM, in soteriology (which deals with salvation as effected by Jesus Christ), the theological tenet and practice of those Calvinists who maintain the dogma of absolute divine decrees of election and approbation and consider the decree of election as contemplating the apostasy as a past event, and the elect as being at the time of election in a fallen and guilty state. Infralapsarianism is really synonymous with sublapsarianism, and is opposed to supralapsarianism. Sublapsarianism conveys the general idea of having been "done after the time of the fall of man"; and this is the meaning, considered etymologically, of intralapsarianism also. The Infralapsarians suppose that God in predestinating had respect to man, not merely as a fallen being, but specifically as either also redeemed through union with Christ, or as condemned through final impenitence. This, it need scarcely be said, amounts to an assertion that God decrees men to suffer His wrath on the ground of their foreseen guilt. This is the ultra-Calvinism of the Gomarist school. And it is consciously or unconsciously, implicitly or explicitly, presupposed—that an all-loving God somewhere in His Word appears as Creator of men simply with the sovereign purpose of then damning them eternally! It assumes likewise that believers are elected on the ground of foreseen faith and obedience, whereas the finally impenitent are predestinated to perdition by a damnatory decree on the grounds of their foreseen impenitency. This rigid Christianity refers the eternal election of men and their reprobation by God to His foreseeing, rather than His positively decreeing, that all men would fall in Adam, and thus would deserve reprobation; and thus the election of grace becomes conceived as simply a remedy for existing evil. Out of the entire mass of mankind thus fallen, God in his sovereign grace freely elects a certain number to life; and by virtue of the same electing act. He in an equal exercise of His sovereignty leaves others, nonelect, to the death which their sins deserve. Some, calling themselves Preteritionists, hold a modified doctrine. These reject the dogma that God has determined in the exercise of His authority to elect any, but to blessing. Yet they nevertheless contend for the decree of preterition, in virtue of which God has determined to pass by those who are not saved. Can it be necessary more than to allude to the gross fatalism so obviously inherent in all these dogmas? Here the Bible takes on the aspect of a gloomy epic, terrible and grand as the elder 'Edda,' a book to plunge man into melancholy; the prophets thunder out doleful menaces; men burden their minds with the pitiless doctrines of Calvin. Fancy, if you can, the effects of such ideas on solitary and morose minds! An anthropomorphic superstition pervades them all. Admitting for a moment that God decrees anything at all (which, seriously, is to look upon him as Zeus, or even as a human legislator, making enactments) — might one not logically adopt the principle that He decrees in respect of what He does, but not in respect of what He does not do; and conclude that He decreed, by an absolute decree, to save the saved, but did not decree not to save the lost? And, obiter dicta, in all fatalism, whether (said to be) Christian, Mohammedan, Hellenic, Old Norse, Roman or Teutonic, whether Materialistic, Socialistic, Individualistic or Intellectualistic — and all are *variations* on a single theme — there is involved a fictitious idea both of causation and of necessity. Man's will is free. And it is no more logical — and this all determinists do, whether openly or tacitly — to presuppose that prevision creates the future, than to presuppose that memory creates the past.

INFRINGEMENT, a breach or violation of an agreement or right, especially the infraction of the copyright, patent rights or trademark of another. The usual method of procedure for the injured party is to secure an injunction restraining the infringement and to enter an action for the damages sustained. See COPYRIGHT; PATENTS, etc.

INFUNDIBULUM. See PITUITARY BODY.

INFUSION, in pharmacy, an aqueous solution of a medicinal substance obtained by treating with water, usually without the aid of boiling. The water may be either hot or cold, varying with the object to be obtained. According to the directions of the United States Pharmacopœia, infusions are generally prepared by pouring boiling water upon the drug and macerating in a tightly closed vessel until the liquid cools. The active principles are in this manner extracted more rapidly and, as a rule, in much larger portions than if the solution is colder. Heat is not advisable if the active principles are volatile. If an infusion is desired of a greater degree of concentration than that obtained by the process of maceration, it is frequently prepared by percolation, in which operation the drug is sliced or broken up into small fragments, packed in a percolator, and the water, either hot or cold, is passed through. Infusions are sometimes made with the aid of other liquids than water, but this is the exception rather than the rule. Infusions do not keep well, and therefore they should be made extemporaneously and in small quantities. In household medicine, infusions are very widely employed. These may be made at home or made by the pharmacist. It is essential to remember that if they are made in hot weather in large quantities they must be sterilized.

Infusion of saline solution into the blood-vessels is a very important procedure in medicine. It is employed largely in the treatment of shock and in severe hemorrhage, especially following operations of childbirth. The solution that is used is known as a normal salt-solution and consists of about one teaspoonful of common salt to a pint of water. This solution should be boiled carefully for one-half to three-quarters of an hour, the amount of evaporating water being made up as the boiling proceeds, and after being made it should be kept in large bottles provided with cotton plugs for stoppers. In severe cases of hemorrhage, infusion has often saved life, as it provides a body of fluid on which the heart and blood-vessels can act. The salt-solution is usually introduced into one of the large veins of the arm at a temperature of one to two degrees above that of the body temperature. See BLOOD TRANSFUSION.

INFUSORIA, protozoa or organisms of the primary division of the animal kingdom, consisting of single cell or groups of cells, of the classes *Flagellata* and *Ciliata,* so-called from propagating and abounding in infusions of organic matter. While the term, first used in 1763, is now restricted to the ciliate protozoans, it often includes the flagellate protozoans as well. The latter are represented by the monads. These are exceedingly minute, round or pear-shaped animals, which move by one or two lash-like processes called flagella. They contain a nucleus and contractile vesicles. Some of them are fixed by a stalk, and are provided with a collar, as in *Codosiga,* out of which the flagellum projects. One of the simplest monads (*Heteromita*) is obtained by placing a cod's head in water at a temperature of about 70° F. In a few days the water will swarm with these monads. The young germs will live in boiling water, but perish at a temperature of from 212° to 268° F., while the adults are destroyed at 142° F.

In the ciliata infusoria the body is more or less flattened and covered with cilia (*Paramecium,* etc.). They have on the under side of the body a slightly defined mouth (or cytostome), which is permanently open, and the food is swept into it by the action of the cilia around it. The mouth leads into a funnel-shaped throat or cytopharynx, which ends in the protoplasm of the body. The food-particles swept into this throat and pressed into the protoplasm form a small enlargement which finally sinks farther in forming the «food vacuole,» which, by the flow of the protoplasm, is carried about the body, while the digestible portions are absorbed and the waste matter is cast out at a fixed point,— a sort of vent (cytopyge). The fresh-water forms have contractile vesicles, and in certain species the animal possesses so-called stinging rods (trichocysts), which are very minute and are placed vertically to the surface of the cortex; by some students they are supposed to be tactile rather than stinging structures. What correspond to the muscular fibres of the higher animals cause the quick convulsive movements observed in these creatures. Two important organs are present in all ciliate infusoria, that is the nuclei. The larger nucleus (macronucleus) is an oval, rod-like or spiral body, which appears to control the processes of feeding and motion. The other nucleus (micronucleus) is much smaller and is concerned with reproduction. Reproduction occurs usually by self-division, and more rarely the infusorians contract into a ball and divide into spores, which grow to become adults. The periods of fission are at times interrupted by the process of conjugation, which only differs from sexual reproduction in the fact that two individual infusorians meet and fuse together and then separate, the result being a process of fertilization which leads to a complete new formation of the nucleus, and thus to a new organization of the animal.

The more specialized infusoria are *Stentor* and *Vorticella*. The former is large enough to be seen without a lens. It is purplish, and under the microscope shows itself to be a beautiful creature. It is trumpet-shaped, with a spiral tract of thicker cilia around the mouth-end. The most highly organized infusoria are the bell-animalcules (*carchesium,* etc.), which are compound bell-shaped forms, forming colonies with forked branched stalks. The nucleus is sausage-shaped, and near it is the micronucleus. They form a white mass like mold on the stems and leaves of aquatic plants. Some of the infusoria are parasitic in the digestive and circulatory organs of the higher animals. For a more detailed and illustrated account, consult, W. Saville-Kent's ‹Manual of the Infusoria, including a description of all known flagellate, ciliate and tentaculiferous protozoa, British and foreign, and an account of the organization and affinities of the sponges› (London 1880–82).

Bibliography.—Bennett, J. H., ‹On the atmospheric germ theory and origin of infusoria› (Edinburgh 1868); Ehrenberg, C. G., ‹Verbreitung und Einfluss des mikroskopischen Lebens in Süd und Nord-Amerika› (Berlin 1843); Estabrook, A. H., ‹Effect of Chemicals on the Growth of Paramecium› (Baltimore 1910); Fulton, J. F., Jr., ‹Trichodina Pediculus; and a New Closely Related Species› (Boston 1923); Jennings, H. S., ‹Behavior of the Lower Organisms› (New York 1923); Lepsi, I., ‹Studii Faunistice Morfologice si Fiziologice asupra Infusoriilor din România› (Bucharest 1927); Lund, E. J., ‹The Relations of Bursaria to Food› (Baltimore 1914); Roux, J., ‹Faune Infusorienne des Eaux Stagnantes des Environs de Genève› (Geneva 1901).

INFUSORIAL EARTH, a term often but incorrectly applied to diatomaceous earth. See DIATOMS.

INGALLS, in'gâlz, **James Monroe,** American soldier: b. Sutton, Vt., 25 Jan. 1837. He served in the Civil War, participating in the Atlanta campaign, and remained in the South during the Reconstruction period until 1871. In the following year he was graduated at the Artillery School, Fort Monroe, Va. In 1882 he founded the department of ballistics at the United States Artillery School, Fort Monroe, and was principal instructor there until the school suspended operations in April 1898, on the outbreak of war with Spain. He was retired from the army 25 Jan. 1901 and was advanced to the rank of colonel, retired, by act of 23 April 1904. He wrote on professional topics for encyclopedias and in the *Journal of United States Artillery* and the volumes ‹Exterior Ballistics› (1883; 1885; 1886); ‹Ballistic Machines› (1885); ‹Handbook of Problems in Exterior Ballistics› (1890; 1901); ‹Interior Ballistics› (1894; 1911); ‹Ballistic Tables› (1891; 1900); ‹Ballistics for the Instruction of Artillery Gunners› (1893). He died at Stamford, Conn., 23 Feb. 1927.

INGALLS, John James, American lawyer: b. Middleton, Mass., 29 Dec. 1833; d. Las Vegas, N. Mex., 16 Aug. 1900. He was graduated from Williams College in 1855, and was admited to the bar in 1857. In 1858 he moved to Kansas and established a law practice there, first in Sumner, and in 1860 in Atchison. In 1859 he was a delegate to the First Constitutional Convention. He was secretary of the territorial council in 1860, and of the State senate in 1861, and in 1862 was elected a member of the senate. During the Civil War he acted as judge-advocate of the Kansas militia (1863–65) and for three years edited the Atchison *Champion.* In 1873 he became a Republican member of the United States Senate, and was re-elected in 1879 and 1885. Charges that bribery had been practised in connection with his election in 1879 were made in and investigated by both the Kansas house of representatives and the United States Senate. They were found to be partially true, but Senator Ingalls himself was entirely exonerated and the claim to his seat was fully sustained. He was president pro tem. of the Senate from 1887–91. In 1891 he was again a candidate for senator, but was defeated by the Farmers' Alliance. During his service in the Senate he was known as one of its most eloquent members. From that time till his death he devoted himself chiefly to lecturing and writing. His writings were published by Conelley, W. E., ed., ‹A Collection of the Writings of J. J. Ingalls› (Kansas City 1902). Consult Inman, H., ‹J. J. Ingalls› (in ‹Distinguished American Lawyers,› H. W. Scott, ed., p. 457, New York 1891); Kansas Bribery Investigation Committee, ‹Report of the Special Committee of the Kansas House of Representatives, etc.› (Topeka 1879); Taft, G. S., ‹Compilation of Senate Election Cases› (49th Congress, 1st Session, Senate Misc. Doc., No. 47, Washington 1885).

INGALLS, Melville Ezra, American railroad president: b. Harrison, Me., 6 Sept. 1842; d. 11 July 1914. He was educated at Bowdoin and at Harvard. He practised law successively at Gray, Me., and at Boston, Mass. In 1867 he was elected to the senate of Massachusetts. Becoming interested in railroads he was, in 1870, president of the Indianapolis, Cincinnati and Lafayette Railroad and in the following year was appointed its receiver. After effecting a thorough reorganization he added other roads which together are known as the «Big Four,» the Cleveland, Cincinnati, Chicago and Saint Louis Railroad. He was chairman of the system until 1912 when he retired. He was also for many years executive head of the Chesapeake and Ohio Railway Company and in 1905 was chosen president of the National Civic Federation.

INGALLS, Rufus, American soldier: b. Denmark, Me., 23 Aug. 1820; d. New York city, 15 Jan. 1893. He was graduated from West Point in 1843, fought in the Mexican War and was brevetted first lieutenant for gallant and meritorious conduct. In 1854–55 was a member of Steptoe's expedition to the Northwest. At the outbreak of the Civil War he defended Fort Pickens, Fla., then became quartermaster of the Army of the Potomac, and was present at many of the important engagements, was twice brevetted for gallant and meritorious conduct, and at the close of the war had attained the rank of major-general. In 1867 he became successively quartermaster of the military division of the Atlantic, Pacific and the Missouri, quartermaster-general of the United States army, and brigadier-general in 1882 and was retired in 1883.

INGE, ĭnj, **William Ralph,** English clergyman and author: b. Crayke, Yorkshire, England, 6 June 1860. He was educated at Eton and at Kings College, Cambridge, where he won many honors. He was assistant master at Eton, 1884–88. At the same time, 1886–88, he was Fellow of Kings College. In 1889–1904 he became Fellow and tutor of Hertford College, Oxford. He was vicar of All Saints, Ennismere Gardens, London, 1905–07, Margaret professor of divinity, Cambridge 1907–11, and 1911–34 dean of Saint Paul's, London. He was select preacher at Oxford 1893–95, 1903–05, 1920–21; at Cambridge in 1901, 1906 and 1910–12–13–20. In 1899 he delivered the Bampton Lectures, and in 1906 he delivered the Paddock Lectures in New York City. In 1915 he was lecturer at Sion College. In 1902 he was examining chaplain for the bishop of Lichfield. He delivered the Lyman Beecher Lectures at Yale University in 1925. His works include several on mysticism in which subject he is an authority. His more recent works include: 'Personal Religion and the Life of Devotion' (1924); 'The Platonic Tradition' (1926); 'Lay Thoughts of a Dean' (1926); 'England' (The Modern World; Vol. 7, London 1926); 'Science and Ultimate Truth' (1916); 'The Church in the World' (1927); 'Assessments and Anticipations' (1929); 'Christian Ethics and Modern Problems' (1930); and some school books.

INGELOW, ĭn'jĕ-lō, **Jean,** English poet and novelist: b. Boston, Lincolnshire, 17 March 1820; d. Kensington, London, 20 July 1897. Her first published work appeared anonymously in 1850 under the title 'Rhyming Chronicle of Incidents and Feelings.' It was followed by 'Allerton and Dreux: or the War of Opinion' (2 vols., 1851), a story, and 'Tales of Orris' (1860); but not till the publication of 'Poems,' in 1863, did Miss Ingelow become famous. This volume won the enthusiastic praise of critics and the instant approval of the public, and by 1879 had passed through 23 editions. The most widely appreciated poems in it are 'The High Tide on the Coast of Lincolnshire'; 'Songs of Seven'; 'Divided'; and 'Supper at the Mill.' Later volumes were 'Studies for Stories' (1864); 'Stories told to a Child' (1865); 'Poor Mat' (1866); 'A Sister's Bye-Hours' (1868); 'Mopsa the Fairy' (1869); 'Off the Skelligs' (4 vols., 1872), her first long story; 'The Little Wonder Horn' (1872), a new series of stories told to a child; 'Fated to be Free' (3 vols., 1881); 'Sarah de Berenger' (3 vols., 1879); 'Don John' (3 vols., 1881); and 'John Jerome' (1886). A second volume of verse, 'A Story of Doom and Other Poems,' appeared in 1867 and a third volume, 'Monitions of the Unseen' in 1885. Collections of her poems were published as 'The Poetical Works of Jean Ingelow' (New York 1894; London 1898). Her works have been even more popular in America than in her native country. She was at her best as a writer of children's stories, even though her popularity during her life was based chiefly on her poetry. The latter contains some few very excellent pieces, but the bulk of it has not stood the test of time. In her own days, however, she was greatly admired for her songs, and many of her poems, indeed, have considerable lyrical merit. Consult Anon., 'Some Recollections of Jean Ingelow and her Early Friends' (London 1901); Stuart, G. B., 'Personal Recollections of Jean Ingelow' (in *Lippincott's Monthly Magazine,* Vol. LXXVII, p. 306, Philadelphia 1906).

INGEMANN, ĭng'ĕ-man, **Bernhard Severin,** Danish poet and novelist: b. Torkildstrup, on the island of Falster, 28 May 1789; d. Sorö, 24 Feb. 1862. He was educated at the University of Copenhagen, and it was while a student there that he published his first 'Poems' (1811–12), of a dreamy, melancholy nature, showing the influence of German romanticism, and displaying the unhealthy state of his body and mind. In 1814 he published a long allegorical poem, 'The Black Knights,' which showed a marked advance. The next six works which he produced were plays, the tragedy 'Blanca,' brought out in 1815, being the most popular and successful, though 'The Miraculous Child Reinald' (1816) was undoubtedly the best. 'The Subterranean Ones, a Story of Bornholm,' his first prose work, was written in 1817, and the following year he started on a tour of the Continent, returning in 1819. On his return he wrote his 'Stories and Miraculous Tales,' which was published in 1819, followed in 1820 by two volumes of poems, 'The Travel Lyre,' and in 1821 by a comedy, 'Magnetism in a Barber's Shop,' which, however, was unsuccessful, and thereafter he confined himself to prose work. In 1822 he accepted the chair of Danish language and literature at the Academy of Sorö, and then began his voluminous writings on historical subjects, his novels probably being inspired and copied from the Waverly novels, by Scott. The subjects and characters were taken from Danish history, and, while they were to a great extent inaccurate, were possessed of such strong nationality that they became of great interest. Among these historical romances were 'Valdemar the Victorious' (1826); 'Erik Menved's Childhood' (1828); 'King Erik and the Outlaws' (1833); 'Prince Otto of Denmark and His Time' (1835); 'Queen Margaret' (1836); 'Holger Danske' (1837). From 1837–39 he wrote a collection of 'Evening and Morning Songs,' which became very popular on account of their great beauty of religious expression. From this time until his death his writings were mainly religious and the last of his works, 'The Apple of Gold,' was published in 1856. A number of his works have been translated into English and many of them into German. His collected works in 41 volumes were published in Copenhagen (1843–65). He left an autobiography which was edited by Galskjöt (1862). His correspondence was published in 1879, edited by V. Heise, and his letters to Grundtvig were edited by S. Grundtvig (1882). Consult Brandes, G., 'Essays' (Copenhagen 1889); Nörregaard, J., 'B. S. Ingemanns Digterstilling og Digterværd' (Copenhagen 1886); Petersen, R., 'Mindeskrift over B. S. Ingemann' (Copenhagen 1889); Schwanenflügel, H., 'Ingemanns Liv og Digtning' (Copenhagen 1886).

INGENHOUSZ, ĭng'ĕn-hous', **Jan,** Dutch physician and scientist: b. Breda, Holland, 8 Dec. 1730; d. Bowood, the seat of the Marquis of Lansdowne, England, 7 Sept. 1799. He studied medicine at Louvain, Leyden, Paris and Edinburgh, and after practising in his own country for several years removed to London in 1764 or 1765. In 1769 he was appointed aulic councillor and body physician to the Austrian Empress, Marie Theresa, and to Joseph II, introducing vaccination against smallpox in Vienna. After serving for nine years in that capacity he returned to London, where he began his scientific researches, later becoming a fellow of the Royal Society, and publishing in its 'Philosophical Transactions' several treatises and essays. From 1780–89 he again resided in Vienna, devoting himself chiefly to experiments in chemistry, physics and botany. From 1789–99 he lived in England. His works include 'Experiments on Vegetables, Discovering Their Great Power of Purifying the Common Air in Sunshine, but Injuring it in the Shade, or at Night' (London 1779; Leipzig 1780; Paris 1787–89); 'Respiration of Plants' (Vienna 1786); 'Miscellanea Physico-Medica' (Scherer, J. A., ed., Vienna 1795); 'Essay in the Food of Plants and the Renovation of Soils' (London 1796). Collections of his scientific papers were published in German (Vienna 1785) and in French (2 vols., Paris 1785–89). Dr. Ingenhousz is credited with being the discoverer of carbonic acid, assimilation of plants, and he also invented the plate electrical machine. Consult Weisner, J., 'Jan Ingen-Housz' (Vienna 1905).

INGERSOLL, ing'gēr-sŏl, **Charles Jared,** American statesman, lawyer and author; son of Jared Ingersoll (q.v.): b. Philadelphia, 3 Oct. 1782; d. there, 14 May 1862. After finishing his collegiate course he studied law, was admitted to practice, traveled in Europe and became attached to the American embassy to France. In 1812 he was elected to Congress, taking his seat in May 1813. In 1815 he was appointed United States district attorney for Pennsylvania, an office which he held until 1829. Shortly after he was elected to the legislature of Pennsylvania. He was a member of Congress 1841–47 as representative of one of the districts of which the county of Philadelphia was then composed. He was the author of the poem 'Chiomara' (1800), of the tragedy 'Edwy and Elgwia' produced in Philadelphia (1808), of 'Julian' (1831); and of 'Inchiquin — the Jesuit's Letters on American Literature and Politics' (1810); 'Historical Sketch of the Second War between the United States and Great Britain' (4 vols., 1845–52), etc. Consult Meigs, W. W., 'Charles Jared Ingersoll' (Philadelphia 1898).

INGERSOLL. Ernest. American naturalist: b. Monroe, Mich., March 13, 1852; **d.** Brattleboro, Vt., Nov. 13, 1946. He attended Oberlin College and the Museum of Comparative Zoology of Harvard University, where he was a pupil of Agassiz, and in 1874 and 1877 was connected as naturalist with the Hayden survey. He was also an expert on the United States Fish Commission, and later became known as a popular writer and lecturer on scientific subjects. In 1901 he was lecturer in zoology at the University of Chicago. Among his works are 'Nests and Eggs of North American Birds' (1880–81); 'Oyster Industries of the United States' (1881); 'Knocking 'Round the Rockies' (1883); 'Country Cousins' (1884); 'The Crest of the Continent' (1884); 'Down East Latch-Strings' (1887); 'Wild Neighbors' (1897); 'The Book of the Ocean' (1898); 'Nature's Calendar' (1900); 'Wild Life of Orchard and Field' (1902); 'The Life of Animals' (1906); 'Zoology'; 'Birds in Legend, Fable and Folklore' (1923); 'Dragons and Dragon Lore' (1928); and several juvenile tales —'The Ice Queen,' etc. After 1899 he conducted the department of natural history in the weekly edition of the *Montreal Star.*

INGERSOLL, Jared, American politician: b. Milford, Conn., 1722: d. 1781. Upon the passage of the Stamp Act he was appointed, in 1765, a stamp agent in Connecticut and accepted the post by the advice of Franklin. This subjected him to the personal abuse and insults from which all colonial stamp agents suffered, and finally he was forced to resign; later, in 1770, becoming an admiralty judge. He was the author of a pamphlet called 'The Stamp Act' (1776).

INGERSOLL, Jared, American lawyer: b. Connecticut 1750; d. Philadelphia, 21 Oct. 1822. Having been graduated at Yale College in 1766, he went to London, was entered of the Middle Temple and passed five years in the study of law. The American Revolution breaking out while he was still in London, he espoused the cause of the colonies, although the son of a Loyalist. He went from London to Paris, where he remained for 18 months, making the acquaintance of Franklin. Returning home, he took up his residence in Philadelphia, where he won almost immediately a prominent position as a lawyer. In 1787 he was chosen one of the representatives of Pennsylvania in the convention which framed the United States Constitution. Twice attorney-general of the State, he was United States district attorney for Pennsylvania, presiding judge of Philadelphia County District Court and in 1812 the Federal candidate for Vice-President of the United States.

INGERSOLL, Leonard Rose, American educator: b. New York, 1 June 1880. He was graduated at Colorado College in 1902 and received the degree of D.Ph. at the University of Wisconsin in 1905. In 1905–08 he was instructor, in 1908–10 assistant professor, and 1910–25 associate professor of physics at the University of Wisconsin and professor since 1925. He is a Fellow of the American Association for the Advancement of Science; member of the American Physical Society. He has invented the glarimeter for measuring gloss of paper (adopted as standard government test in 1925). With O. J. Zobel he published 'An Introduction to the Mathematical Theory of Heat Conduction' (1913). He has contributed many articles to scientific journals, chiefly on subjects connected with the electro-magnetic theory of light.

INGERSOLL, Robert Green, American lawyer, lecturer and author: b. Dresden, N. Y., 11 Aug. 1833; d. Dobb's Ferry, N. Y., 21 July 1899. He received a common school education in various towns in Ohio and Illinois where his father, a minister, held charges and was admitted to the bar at Mount Vernon, Ill., in 1854. He soon became prominent in the courts and in Democratic politics. In the Civil War he recruited the 11th Illinois Cavalry and entered the army as its colonel. He was in the battle of Shiloh and saw considerable fighting in Tennessee. On Dec. 18, 1862, while trying with a force of 600 men to intercept a Confederate raiding party, he was captured by a force of 10,000 men but was soon paroled and given command of a camp in Saint Louis. Soon afterward he resigned. After the war he became a Republican, and was made attorney general of Illinois in 1867. He was a delegate to the Republican National Convention in 1876 and placed in nomination for president, James G. Blaine, whom he termed "the plumed knight." His nominating speech gave him national reputation as an orator, and he afterwards lectured frequently, always before immense crowds. He was an agnostic and in his lectures attacked the Bible and the beliefs of the Christian religion. He was prominent in politics for several years, and had he not given such frequent expression to his agnostic views he would doubtless have been honored with high offices, though, to judge from his refusal of two or three diplomatic posts, he was far from eager for office. He took up his permanent residence in New York City in 1885 and practised law there till his death, being one of the most successful trial lawyers of his times. His lectures on theological subjects formed for many years the basis of extensive and frequently violent discussion and attacks. His most famous lectures include: *Some Mistakes of Moses; The Family; The Liberty of Man, Woman and Child; The Gods;* and *Ghosts.*

His publications include: *Lectures Complete* (1886); *Prose Poems and Selections* (1888); *Famous Speeches* (1906); and *Political Speeches* (1914). A complete collection of his works was published in 12 volumes (New York 1900).

Bibliography.—Dement, R. S. *Ingersoll, Beecher and Dogma* (Chicago 1878); McClure, J. B., ed., *Mistakes of Ingersoll*, etc. (Chicago 1879); Curtiss, S. I., *Ingersoll and Moses* (Chicago 1880); Brann, H. A., *The Age of Unreason* (New York 1881); Lambert, L. A., *Notes on Ingersoll* (Buffalo 1883); Duganne, A. J. H., *Injuresoul; A Satire for Science* (New York 1884); Hubbard, Elbert "Ingersoll" in *Little Journeys to the Homes of Eminent Orators*, vol. 13, p. 23 (East Aurora, N. Y., 1903); Goldwaite, V., *The Philosophy of Ingersoll* (San Francisco 1906); Kittredge, H. E., *Ingersoll; a Biographical Appreciation* (New York 1911); Gorham, C. T., *Robert G. Ingersoll* (London 1921).

INGERSOLL, Royal Rodney, American naval officer: b. Niles, Mich., Dec. 4, 1847; d. La Porte, Ind., Apr. 21, 1931. Graduated at the United States Naval Academy, he received several promotions, attaining the rank of rear admiral in 1908. He retired the following year. As an active naval officer he served in all parts of the world. During the war with Spain he commanded the *Supply* and in 1905 was in command of the *Maryland.* He was member of the General Board of the Navy at the time of his retirement. On July 7, 1917 he was again placed on duty in the Bureau of Ordnance. He had published *Text-Book of Ordnance and Gunnery* (1887); *Exterior Ballistics* (1891); *Elastic Strength of Guns* (1891).

INGERSOLL, Canada, town in Oxford County, Ontario, on the Thames River and the Canadian National Railway, 19 miles northeast of London. It is the marketing center for a rich grain and fruit-producing section, and has an important trade in lumber, grain, cheese and general country produce. It manufactures furniture, condensed milk, tools, automobile parts, furnaces, brooms, paper products, and fertilizers. The town has natural gas and electric power. Pop. (1941) 5,782.

INGHAM, ĭng'ăm, **Benjamin,** English evangelistic leader: b. Ossett, Yorkshire, June 11, 1712; d. Aberford, 1772. He received his education at Batley School and at Queen's College, Oxford, where he graduated B.A. in 1734. In 1735 he was ordained, and, becoming associated with John and Charles Wesley, went with them to Georgia, remaining two years. In 1738 he went with John Wesley on a visit to the Moravians in Germany and became so strongly attached to their doctrines that he broke with the Wesleys and founded in Yorkshire several congregations of what were known as "Moravian Methodists," but more commonly as "Inghamites." He endeavored to unite in this organization the chief doctrines of the Moravians and Methodists, and so successful was he as bishop or general overseer that in a few years there were 84 of these congregations in England. He moved to Aberford about the time of his marriage with a daughter of the Earl of Huntingdon in 1741 and succeeded in converting the whole surrounding neighborhood to his faith. In 1760, however, the greater part of his followers deserted him after he adopted many of the mystical views of Robert Sandeman (q.v.). Only about 13 of the Inghamite churches followed him into the Sandemanian sect. The rest were absorbed by other sects, especially by the Methodists. He wrote *A Discourse on the Faith and Hope of the Gospel* (Leeds 1763).

Consult Tyerman, L., *The Oxford Methodists* (London 1873).

INGHAM, Charles Cromwell, American painter: b. Dublin, Ireland, 1796; d. New York Dec. 10, 1863. He was a pupil of William Cunning at the Dublin Academy, came to New York in 1817, was there a founder of the National Academy of Design (1826), and its vice-president in 1845–1850. He painted many portraits and miniatures of beautiful women and children, as well as of prominent men; amongst the latter are to be mentioned portraits of De Witt Clinton and Lafayette. His works include *Day Dream; The White Plume; The Flower Girl; The Death of Cleopatra.*

INGLE, Richard, English sea captain of the 17th century. When the civil war arose in England Ingle was engaged in the tobacco trade in Maryland. He espoused the cause of the Parliament against Charles I and in 1645 expelled Governor Calvert from Maryland. The latter, however, gathered forces and again took possession of the province late in 1646. During the 20 months of his rule Ingle committed many outrages and plundered several of the inhabitants. Charges were made against him in England, where he defended himself on the ground that he had acted from religious motives and had plundered only "papists." When the proprietary government was restored in 1646, Ingle was not included in the general amnesty granted to the other rebels. On Nov. 14, 1653, he petitioned for a share of prize money, and thereafter disappears from history.

Consult Ingle, Edward, *Capt. Richard Ingle, the Maryland Pirate and Rebel, 1642–1653* (Baltimore 1884).

INGLEBY, ĭng′g'l-bĭ, **Clement Mansfield,** English writer and Shakespearean critic: b. Edgbaston, near Birmingham, Oct. 29, 1823; d. Ilford, Essex, Sept. 26, 1886. He was educated at Trinity College, Cambridge University, receiving his B.A. degree in 1847 and his M.A. in 1850. He practiced law with his father, a well-known Birmingham solicitor, until 1859, when he moved to Ilford, near London, and devoted himself to writing on metaphysical and literary subjects. His best-known works are his Shakespearean studies, among which are *The Shakespeare Fabrication* (1859) and *A Complete View of the Shakespeare Controversy* (1861), both on the literary forgeries of John Payne Collier (q.v.); *Centurie of Prayse* (1874); *The Still Lion* (1874), republished as *Shakespeare Hermeneutics* (1875); *Shakespeare: The Man and the Book* (1877–1881); and an edition of *Cymbeline* (1886). He also wrote *Outlines of Theoretical Logic* (1856) and *Introduction to Metaphysic* (1864–1869).

INGLEFIELD, Sir **Edward Augustus,** British naval officer and explorer: b. Cheltenham, March 27, 1820; d. London, Sept. 5, 1894. He studied at the Royal Naval College, Portsmouth, from 1832 to 1834, when he went to sea. In 1840 he participated in naval operations off the coast of Syria, and then served in the West Indies. In 1845 he was promoted to the rank of commander. He commanded the yacht *Isabella* on a cruise to Smith Sound in 1852 in search of Sir John Franklin (q.v.). On his return to England, he published an account of this cruise, *A Summer Search for Sir John Franklin* (1853), and was made a fellow of the Royal Society and awarded the gold medal of the Royal Geographical Society. As commander of the *Phoenix,* he made two more trips to the Arctic: one in 1853 to relieve Sir Edward Belcher, and one in 1854 in which he rescued part of the Belcher expedition and made a last attempt to find Franklin. He fought in the Black Sea during the Crimean War. In 1869 he was promoted to the rank of rear admiral. He served as second in command in the Mediterranean from 1872 to 1875, when he became a vice admiral. He was commander in chief in the North Atlantic in 1878–1879. He was knighted in 1877, and two years later was promoted to the rank of admiral. He retired in 1888. Inglefield invented the anchor known by his name and the hydraulic steering gear.

INGLEWOOD, city, California, situated in Los Angeles County, at an altitude of 115 feet, 10 miles southwest of downtown Los Angeles, of which it is a residential suburb. It is served by the Atchison, Topeka and Santa Fe and the Pacific Electric railroads; the Los Angeles International Airport is nearby. The city has chinchilla farms, oil refineries, and plants producing airplanes, machinery, metal products, pottery, plastics, and furniture. Founded in 1873 by Daniel Freeman, Inglewood was laid out in 1887 and incorporated in 1908. It is governed by a mayor and council. Pop. (1950) 46,185.

INGLIS, ĭng′g'lz, **Charles,** British prelate: b. County Donegal, Ireland, 1734; d. Halifax, Nova Scotia, Feb. 26, 1816. Educated in Ireland, he went to Pennsylvania in 1755 and for three years taught school at Lancaster. In 1758 he went to England, where he was ordained in the Church of England. In 1759 he was assigned to a missionary post in Dover, Del., where he remained until 1765, when he became assistant to the rector of Trinity Church, New York City. He became known for his advocacy of the establishment of an American episcopacy and for his work on behalf of the conversion of the Indians. He received an honorary M.A. degree from King's College (now Columbia University) in 1767, and about three years later became one of its governors. In 1770 he received an honorary M.A. degree from Oxford University, and in 1778 an honorary D.D. A stout Loyalist, he refused to omit from the service at Trinity prayers for the king and the royal family, and after the occupation of New York City by George Washington in 1776, he retired for a time to Flushing, Long Island. Returning to New York City in 1777, he became rector of Trinity. When the British evacuated the city in 1783, he went at first to Halifax, Nova Scotia, and then to England, where, in 1787, he was consecrated bishop of Nova Scotia, the first colonial bishop of the Church of England. He went to the colony soon thereafter, was made a member of its council in 1809, and remained there until his death.

His son, John Inglis (b. New York City, 1777; d. London, England, Oct. 27, 1850), was also a clergyman. He was educated at King's College, Windsor, Nova Scotia; became a deacon in 1801; and assisted his father until 1816, when he went to England. In 1839 he was consecrated third Anglican bishop of Nova Scotia. Inglis was a benefactor of King's College, and he opposed the Anglican test required as a condition for entrance to that institution.

Sir John Eardley Wilmot Inglis (b. Nova Scotia, Nov. 15, 1814; d. Hamburg, Germany, Sept. 27, 1862), son of the preceding, was a soldier. His entire career was passed in the British 32d Foot Infantry, which he joined in 1833. He served in Canada during the insurrection of 1837, and in the Punjab in 1848–1849. He was in command of his regiment at the outbreak of the Indian Mutiny in 1857. Inglis is celebrated chiefly for his brave defense of Lucknow, whose garrison he commanded from July 2 to Sept. 26, 1857. For his services he was knighted and promoted to major general.

INGOLDSBY LEGENDS, The, a collection of tales, mostly in verse and nearly all humorous, by the Rev. Richard Harris Barham (q.v.), whose pseudonym was Thomas Ingoldsby. They appeared in *Bentley's Miscellany* in 1837–1840, and were collected in book form in 1840, with a second and third series in 1847. The literary sources of the tales are extremely varied, ranging from saints' legends, medieval chroncles, and Kentish traditions to Jean de La Fontaine's *Contes,* Johann Wolfgang von Goethe's *Zauberlehrling,* and Friedrich de La Motte-Fouqué's *Undine,* so that they offer the richest mixture of witchcraft, ghosts, magic, and demonology, with legal, genealogical, heraldic, ecclesiastical, and gastronomic history and anachronisms. Its careful technique in the details of narrative and description is in the tradition of Sterne; and its rollicking masculine fun is the peculiarly English fun of a by-gone day of roast-beef, puddings, and ale, a hierarchical social order, and a gentlemanly acquaintance with the classics. Its defects are the often flippant handling of themes essentially serious; the rarity of its genuine wit or humor — their place being generally occupied by fun and volubility; its employment of digression beyond the point where digression ceases to amuse and begins to bore; and its outworn insularity and prejudices. These penalties it pays for smacking so racily of its time and its land; Ingoldsby takes the gauge of early Victorian England relaxing over the nuts and wine; yet, all deductions made, does it so excellently well as to make itself the permanent model of its *genre*. Various editions are illustrated by Cruikshank, and by Leech and Tenniel. Early issues are now in request. Consult 'The Life and Letters of the Rev. Richard Harris Barham,' by his son, R. H. D. Barham (London 1870).

Samuel Lee Wolff.

INGOLSTADT, Bavaria, town situated at the confluence of the Danube and the Schutter, 52 miles north of Munich. It contains an ancient ducal palace, now used as an arsenal, old university buildings, theatre, a Gothic Frauenkirche, a Franciscan convent and nunnery, ammunition works, a school of military engineering, gun powder works, cloth factories and breweries. It was a royal villa in the 9th century and received its charter as a town before 1255. In 1539 it was fortified. It suffered severely in the wars incident to the Reformation; was ceded to Austria in 1743 and in 1800 was taken by the French and its fortifications were dismantled. Since 1870 it has ranked as a fortress of the first-class and improved defensive works have since been erected. Pop. 26,630. Consult Gerstner 'Geschichte der Stadt Ingolstadt' (Munich 1853).

INGOT, a small bar of metal formed by casting it in molds. The term is chiefly applied to the bars of gold and silver intended for coining, although both iron and steel are molded into ingots.

INGRAHAM, ĭng'grạ-ạm, **Duncan Nathaniel,** American naval officer: b. Charleston, S. C., 6 Dec. 1802; d. there, 16 Oct. 1891. He entered the navy as midshipman in 1812, served during the War of 1812 and in the Mexican War before Vera Cruz and Tampico, and became a captain in 1855. While in command of the sloop-of-war *Saint Louis* he arrived at Smyrna 22 June 1853, and under instructions from the American Minister at Constantinople, took action in the case of the illegal arrest by order of the Austrian Consul, of Martin Koszta, an American citizen of Hungarian birth, which assumed considerable international importance. (See Koszta Affair). After his return he acted for more than four years as chief of the bureau of ordnance and hydrography of the navy department. In 1860 he resigned from the United States Navy, entered the Confederate service and became a commodore, serving as chief of ordnance at Richmond, Va., and as naval commander at Charleston, S. C.

INGRAM, ĭn'grăm, **Arthur Foley Winnington,** Anglican bishop: b. 26 Jan. 1858, Worcestershire, England. He was educated at Marlborough College and Keble College, Oxford. He was private tutor 1881–84; curate of Shrewsbury 1884–85; private chaplain to the bishop of Litchfield 1885–89; chaplain to the archbishop of York and to the bishop of Saint Albans and head of Oxford House, Bethnal Green 1889; rural dean of Spitalfields, 1896; canon of Saint Paul's, London, 1897–1901 and bishop of Stepney for the same period. From 1901 he was dean of the Chapels Royal and bishop of London. He had a wide reputation as a preacher. He was author of 'Work in Great Cities' (1895); 'The Men Who Crucify Christ' (1896); 'Christ and His Friends' (1897); 'Banners of the Christian Faith' (1899); 'The Gospel in Action' (1906); 'Early English Colonies' (1908); 'Joy in God' (1910); 'Secrets of Strength' (1911); 'Attractiveness of Goodness' (1913); 'Church in Time of War' (1916); 'Gospel of the Miraculous' (1916); 'Day of God' (1916); 'Under the Dome' (1916); 'Call of the Father' (1917); 'Potter and the Clay' (1917); 'Rays of Dawn' (1918); 'Victory and After, (1919); 'Spirit of Peace' (1921); 'Re-Building the Walls' (1922); 'The Spirit of Jesus' (1925); 'The Sword of Goliath' (1926); 'Some World Problems' (1927). He died at Upton-on-Severn, Worcestershire, 26 May 1946.

INGRAM, John Kells, English educator: b. County Donegal, Ireland, 7 July 1823; d. Dublin, 1 May 1907. Educated at Trinity College, Dublin, he became professor of oratory and English literature there (1852), Regius professor of Greek (1866), and librarian (1879). He was vice-provost of the college and president of the Royal Irish Academy. His 'History of Political Economy' in the 'Encyclopedia Britannica' (9th ed.), was separately published (1888) and widely translated. He further wrote 'A History of Slavery and Serfdom' (1895); 'Sonnets and other Poems' (1900); 'Human Nature and Morals according to Auguste Comte' (1901), etc.

INGRASSIA, Giovanni Filippo, Sicilian physician: b. Palermo, 1510; d. there, 6 Nov. 1580. He studied at the University of Padua, where he received the degree of doctor in medicine in 1537. He taught with great success in Naples. He made several important anatomical discoveries. In 1563 he was named first doctor of Sicily by Philip II of Spain, and during the pestilence which devastated Palermo in 1575 he acquired the lasting esteem of its citizens by his work in suppressing the plague. He was granted a pension of 3,000 gold crowns. His more important works are 'Jatropologia, liber quo multa adversus barbaros medicos disputantur' (1558); 'De tumoribus præter naturam' (1553); 'Ragionamento sopra l'infermitā epidemica del 1558' (1560); 'Methodus curandi pestiferum contagium' (1583); 'In Galenum librum de ossibus doctissima et expertissima Commentaria' (1603). Consult Eloy 'Dictionnaire historique de la Médicine.'

INGRES, Jean Dominique Auguste, zhŏṅ dō-mē-nēk ō-güst ăṅg-r, French historical painter: b. Montauban, Aug. 29, 1780; d. Paris, Jan. 14, 1867. He studied art in Paris under Jacques Louis David, reputedly founder of the French classical school of painting, and in 1801 won the Prix de Rome for his *Achilles Receiving the Messenger of Agamemnon.* From 1806 until 1820 he resided in Rome, making an exhaustive study of Raphael and the old masters and there producing some of his finest paintings. For the next four years he was in Florence, and in 1824 he returned to Paris, where he spent ten years painting and teaching. In 1834 he went back to Rome as director of the Académie de France in succession to Horace Vernet; and from 1841 until his death he again worked in Paris. All his life he remained a pronounced uncompromising adherent of the classical school of painting, and for this was at times excessively attacked. Although his drawing, usually unimpeachable, was often superb, his coloring was weak, thin, and cold. In 1855 he was made a grand officer of the Legion of Honor, and in 1862 he was named a senator. His works are numerous, and comprise generally serious historical and classical subjects. Many of his paintings are in the Louvre, on the ceiling of one of the apartments of which is painted his *Apotheosis of Homer,* a magnificent epic. Others at the Louvre include portraits of Mme. and Mlle. Rivière and of M. Bochet; *Grande Odalisque; Bertinainé;* portrait of Cherubine; *Jeanne d'Arc; La Source; Oedipus and the Sphinx;* and *Grande Baigneuse.* Among other well known pictures were portraits of Napoleon I (Liége Museum) and Mme. d'Haussonville (Château Coppet); *Jupiter and Thetis* (Aix Museum); *Romulus Vainqueur d'Acron* (École des Beaux Arts, Paris); *Martyrdom of Saint Symphorien* (Autin Cathedral); *Stratonice* (Chantilly Museum); *Christ and the Doctors* (Montauban Museum); and *Vow of Louis XIII* (Montauban Cathedral). Consult Blanc, C., *Ingres, sa Vie et ses Ouvrages* (Paris 1870); Mommeja, J., *Collection Ingres au Musée de Montauban* (Paris 1905); Lapauze, H., *Ingres, sa Vie et son Oeuvre* (Paris 1911). See also PAINTING—*Romanticism and Classicism.*

INHALATION, in medicine, a mode of applying remedies directly to the respiratory tract. Either steam alone, steam charged with drug vapors, or drugs finely subdivided in sprays, are breathed into the air passages as deeply as possible. This method of medication is useful only in relieving inflammations of the upper air passages and possibly the trachea and larger bronchi. The air in the smaller bronchi is not changed by breathing, but by the diffusion of gases, so that substances in aerial suspension are deposited on the surface before reaching the smaller divisions of the bronchial tubes. Steam does not penetrate far, but is cooled, and deposits moisture as far as the trachea. The old-fashioned croup kettle and many devices for carrying out the same idea are used for the first stages of laryngitis. Many substances, such as tincture of benzoin, are added to the boiling water, but render it no more efficacious. Instead of conducting the steam directly to the mouth and nose by a funnel or tube, it may be well to place the patient in a simply enclosed tent, formed of bedclothes, and to allow the steam to charge the confined air. This method is particularly advisable for infants and older children.

INHAMBANE, ĭn-yăm-bä'nĕ, Mozambique, seaport at the mouth of the Inhambane River, 248 miles northeast of Lourenço Marques, capital of a district of the same name. It was first occupied by the Portuguese in the 16th century. Sugar and coconut products constitute the principal products of the district. By agreement with the government of the Union of South Africa, many thousands of the inhabitants of the district are employed each year in the goldfields of the Witwatersrand. Inhambane district, 21,000 square miles in area, has a population of 437,519. The population of the seaport is 11,349.

INHERITANCE, as an easily comprehended term, is the acquisition of either real or personal property by will or intestacy on the death of a former owner. In both American and English jurisprudence, inheritance is a term restricted to the passing of real property by descent, or devise, while personal property devolves or descends to distributees. See DESCENT IN LAW; HEIR; INTESTACY.

INHERITANCE TAX. Broadly speaking, the term inheritance tax as used in the United States includes all taxes imposed upon property of a decedent at the time of his death (whether distribution be made by devise, bequest, or inheritance) and, in some cases, on property given away by the decedent before his death. The term is indiscriminately applied to what are known as transfer taxes, succession duties, death, probate, legacy, and estate taxes. Such taxes are imposed by the laws of the United States and by the laws of most states. These estate taxes are usually imposed on the estate of a decedent over the amount of allowed exemptions. Inheritance or succession taxes are imposed on the transfer or the right to receive such inheritance. The payment of such taxes by the estate or by a legatee depends upon the terms of the will of the decedent and the law of the state where the will is probated.

Three Federal inheritance tax laws, all of an emergency nature, preceded the enactment in 1916 of the Federal estate tax law. In anticipation of war with France, Congress passed the Stamp Act of 1797, which placed a tax upon legacies and shares of personal estates in excess of $50. The rates were low, and exemptions were made in favor of the nearest of kin. This tax was repealed in 1802. In 1862, during the American Civil War, a legacy tax was imposed on the distribution of personal property, and stamp taxes were imposed on the probate of wills and letters of administration. The rates on legacies were graduated from ¾ of 1 per cent to 5 per cent, according to the degree of kinship. These duties were slightly increased in 1864, and to them was added a succession tax on real estate. The law was not strictly enforced and the taxes were repealed in 1870, the total yield therefrom having amounted to less than $15,000,000. The income tax law of 1894, which the Supreme Court of the United States declared unconstitutional, included as income property acquired by gift or by inheritance. Again in 1898, during the Spanish-American War, duties were imposed on legacies and distributive shares of personal property. The rates were graduated. On amounts between $10,000 and $25,000 the tax ranged from ¾ of

1 per cent to 5 per cent; on larger amounts, the tax progressively increased to a maximum of 15 per cent on shares in excess of $1,000,000. The total yield from the tax, which was repealed in 1902, was $22,500,000. In 1935 President Franklin D. Roosevelt recommended to Congress the imposition of Federal inheritance taxes, in addition to existing estate taxes, on very large inheritances, but the bill failed of passage.

The United States Internal Revenue Code imposes a Federal estate tax at graduated rates on estates of decedents whose taxable assets are over $60,000. Life insurance is generally included as an asset. Under the 1948 Revenue Act the rates of such taxes graduate from 3 per cent on the net taxable estate over $60,000 to 61 per cent on taxable amounts over $50,000,000. This revenue act allows as a deduction from the taxable estate an amount received by the surviving spouse up to one half of the adjusted gross estate. The revenue collections from the Federal estate tax for the year 1948 yielded $822,392,626.85. There is no inheritance tax for the state of New York. The tax is a transfer tax upon the assets received by a person from the estate of a decedent, and depends upon the degree of relationship of the legatee or distributee unless the will provides to the contrary. This transfer tax does not apply to estates of persons who died after Sept. 1, 1930. The tax imposed upon estates is now known as the estate tax, and its provisions are enumerated in the laws of the State of New York. The revenue for the state from this tax for the fiscal year ending March 1, 1948, yielded $34,392,625.85.

In Great Britain (England, Scotland, and Wales), the existing death duties in 1949 were three: the estate duty; legacy duty; and succession duty. An Anglo-American Convention aimed at avoiding the double taxation of estates was ratified by the British and United States governments on July 25, 1946. It does not apply to legacy or succession duties. The death duties in Great Britain on estates of persons dying after April 10, 1946, were greatly increased due to the world wars. The rates of such taxes graduate from 1 per cent on £2,000 to 75 per cent on £2,000,000 and over.

The tax laws of the various states of the United States allow certain exemptions in computing such taxes, based upon the amount of property received by certain next of kin. The laws of each state must be examined to determine the amount of such exemptions and the rates of tax.

INHIBITION, in legal jurisprudence, is a prohibition which the law makes or a judge ordains. It has no specific reference today, but was relevant in the ecclesiastical law in the jurisdiction of English church government.

In England, inhibition is a writ from a higher to a lower court, as an ecclesiastical court in England, forbidding further proceedings; also, in English law, a command, as from a bishop, to a minister to cease performing ministerial functions. In Scots law, inhibition is an order restraining an heir from contracting debts affecting injuriously the rights of others in the heritable property. It is sometimes used also in Scots law in the sense of an order secured by a husband forbidding the giving of credit by another to his wife. It was formerly used in English law as synonymous with writ of prohibition.

INIA, a genus of toothed cetaceans similar to dolphins, but placed on structural grounds in the allied family *Platanistidae,* with the fresh-water dolphins of the Ganges and the La Plata. The single species (*I. groffrensis*) is called bouto and tucuxi, and is found in some of the upper tributaries of the Amazon, and in the lakes near the Cordilleras. It measures about eight feet in length, and has a long cylindrical snout with stiff hairs, and a very slight dorsal fin. It feeds chiefly on fish, and is hunted for the sake of its oil.

IÑIGUEZ. See GARCIA IÑIGUEZ.

INITIAL DIP. See DIP.

INITIATIVE, in political science, is a correlative term of the referendum and recall, a method of government employed by mass voters in the United States to secure more direct participation in legislation without the intervention of the legislature. The initiative and the referendum as a principle of American law was established at the beginning of the republic. The initiative, an introductory step, is started by a petition for the enactment of measures by popular vote, either introducing legislation or requiring the voters' ratification of laws first passed by the legislative bodies. Its prototype was the constitutional convention and the state conventions, followed by cities, townships and school districts, especially in New England. In 1898 the state of South Dakota became the first state to promote such procedure, and many states followed that example. The movement gained headway rapidly because the opinion prevailed in many sections that state legislatures were no longer representative of the people but were dominated by political rings and moneyed interests. While the referendum (q.v.) is effective in killing pernicious legislation and acts as a preventive to the enactment of such laws, the initiative affords a remedy for the legislatures' indifference to public needs and its persistent refusal to pass legislation urgently required, because of opposition by a corrupting lobby or hidden influence. The initiative and referendum for city ordinances is authorized in many commission-governed cities. It has taken a place beside direct primaries, the presidential preference primary, the recall of elective officials, and the short ballot as an effective means of enforcing popular will; but the initiative is somewhat difficult and cumbersome, and its judicious use is yet to be demonstrated, having been cautiously employed and sparingly used. The state of Oregon has been foremost in its use, and nearly 50 per cent of its laws submitted since 1902 have been ratified.

The Federated Republic of Switzerland, since its establishment at the beginning of the 19th century, has successfully tried and effected the initiative, referendum, and recall.

INJALBERT, ăn-zhăl-bâr′, **Jean Antoine,** French sculptor: b. Béziers, 1845; d. 1933. He studied sculpture under Augustin Alexandre Dumont, and in 1874 won the Prix de Rome for his *Douleur d'Orphée.* In 1877 he exhibited at the Salon a huge bas relief *La Tentation,* and in the following year a *Christ en Croix,* now in the Rheims Museum. Injalbert had the gift of imparting life to his work and a wonderfully rich imagination. His *Titan* surmounts a great fountain at Béziers. His *Hippomène* is in the Luxembourg. Other works are *L'Hérault, l'Orb, le Lez,* in the vestibule of the prefecture of Montpellier, the two groups of *Enfants aux lions* also in Montpellier, the façade of the theatre of Béziers; figures on the Pont Mirabeau of Paris; the Moliere monument at Pézenas; the *Fronton du Petit Palais* at the Paris Exposition, 1900; and the *Kriegerdenkmal in Cabrières* (Vaucluse), 1921.

INJECTOR, a mechanism for feeding water into a steam boiler while it is in operation, through the force of its own steam. The action of this device is based on that principle of hydrodynamics by which the velocity of a moving body of water or other liquid may be transmuted into pressure, and vice-versa, by proper arrangements of conduits and apertures.

In the injector a jet of steam, issuing from the boiler at a velocity of from 1,500 to 3,500 feet per second (depending upon the boiler pressure), is passed through a conical nozzle, indicated in the diagram by the letter A, from which it passes into another cone-shaped tube B. The open space O around the cone A is connected freely with the water-supply pipe D. This space may be filled with water by gravity from a reservoir above its level; or the action of the injector may be so arranged that through the exhausting of the air in B and O by the jet of steam a vacuum is produced and water may be thus "sucked" up from a well below, if the lift is not more than 15 to 18 feet. The rush of steam through the conical "combining tube" B drags along with it a conical shell of water lying next the walls of B and encasing a cone-shaped body of steam in its center. As the

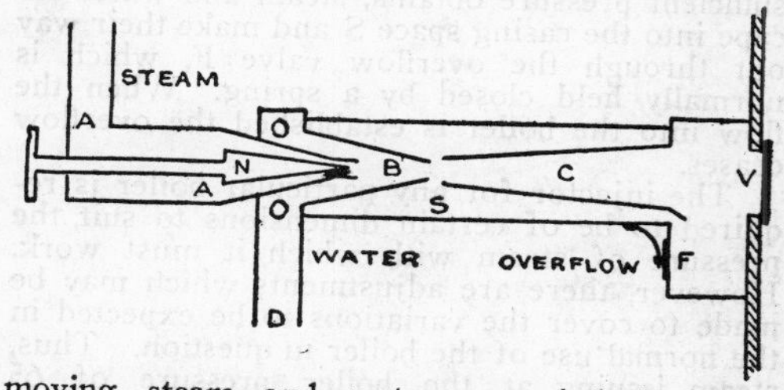

moving steam and water are choked at the apex of B, the steam is compressed, in part condensed and in part absorbed by the water, which takes up its velocity to a large degree and rushes into the apex of the conical tube C. Here the flare of the cone is in the opposite direction and as the column of water moves forward into this tube its velocity lessens as the tube grows larger, and is resolved into pressure, which presently becomes greater than the steam pressure in the boiler by which the

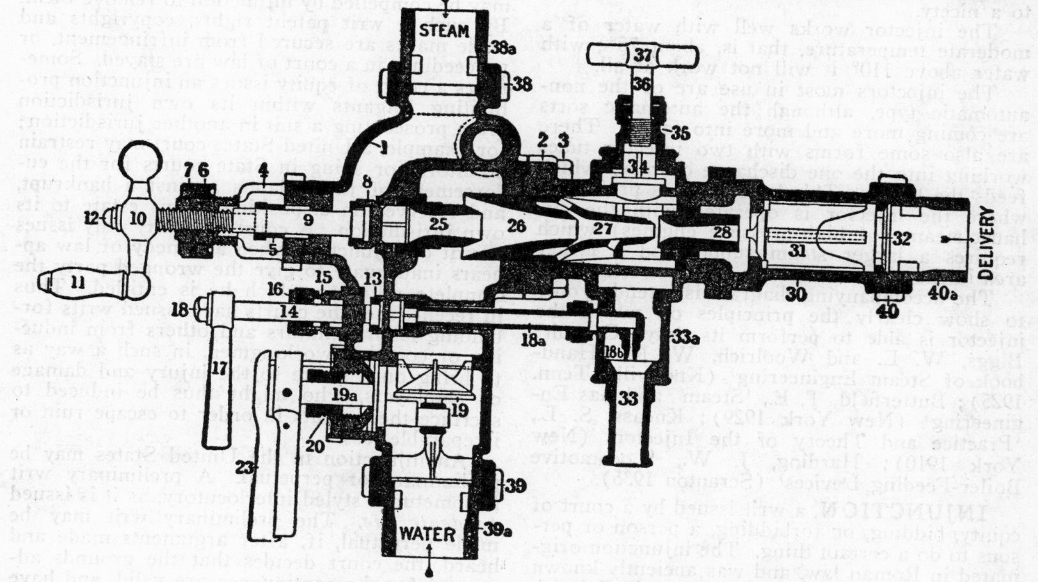

MONITOR INJECTOR WITH NAMES OF PARTS.

1. Body (back part)
2. Body (front part)
3. Body Screw
4. Yoke
5. Yoke Gland
6. Yoke Packing Nut
7. Yoke Lock Nut
8. Steam Valve Disc and Nut
9. Steam Valve Spindle
10. Steam Valve Handle
11. Steam Valve Rubber Handle
12. Steam Valve Top Nut
13. Jet Valve Disc and Nut
14. Jet Valve Spindle
15. Jet Valve Bonnet and Nut
16. Jet Valve Gland
17. Jet Valve Lever Handle
18. Jet Valve Top Nut
18a. Jet Tube
18b. Lifting Nozzle
19. Water Valve
19a. Eccentric Spindle
20. Water Valve Bonnet
23. Water Valve Lever Handle
25. Steam Nozzle
26. Intermediate Nozzle
27. Condensing Nozzle
28. Delivery Nozzle
30. Line Check
31. Line Check Valve
32. Stop Ring
33. Overflow Nozzle
33a. Overflow Chamber with Nut
34. Heater Cock Check
35. Heater Cock Bonnet and Nut
36. Heater Cock Spindle
37. Heater Cock T Handle
38. Coupling Nut, Steam End
38a. Tail Piece, Steam End
39. Coupling Nut, Water End
39a. Tail Piece, Water End
40. Coupling Nut, Delivery End
40a. Tail Piece, Delivery End

check valve V is kept closed. The valve V then opens and permits the water in C to flow through. At this instant the varying pressures throughout the injector come to an equilibrium, based on the condition of that pressure at which the water flows freely from the injector into the boiler — and that condition continues indefinitely as long as the steam pressure in the boiler remains uniform. Previous to the establishing of the steady flow, that is, before sufficient pressure obtains, steam and water escape into the casing space S and make their way out through the overflow valve F, which is normally held closed by a spring. When the flow into the boiler is established the overflow ceases.

The injector for any particular boiler is required to be of certain dimensions to suit the pressure of steam with which it must work. However, there are adjustments which may be made to cover the variations to be expected in the normal use of the boiler in question. Thus, steam issuing at the boiler pressure of 65 pounds may be made by the proper configuration of the conical tubes of the injector to exert a pressure of 90 pounds at the check valve into the boiler. While this pressure is too high for the feeding in of a normal supply of water — that required to replace the water which the boiler evaporates into steam from hour to hour — the pressure in the injector may be modified to a degree by the needle valve N in the steam supply pipe, and the discharge of the injector into the boiler regulated to a nicety.

The injector works well with water of a moderate temperature, that is, about 75°; with water above 110° it will not work at all.

The injectors most in use are of the non-automatic type, although the automatic sorts are coming more and more into favor. There are also some forms with two injector tubes working into the one discharge chamber which feeds the boiler. This latter type is preferable where the injector is operated with the exhaust steam (of high-pressure engines) which requires a larger steam supply and a larger area in the steam orifices to do the work.

The accompanying diagram is intended only to show clearly the principles on which the injector is able to perform its duty. Consult: Biggs, W. E. and Woolrich, W. R., 'Handbook of Steam Engineering' (Knoxville, Tenn. 1925); Butterfield, T. E., 'Steam and Gas Engineering' (New York 1929); Kneass, S. L., 'Practice and Theory of the Injector' (New York 1910); Harding, J. W., 'Locomotive Boiler-Feeding Devices' (Scranton 1935).

INJUNCTION, a writ issued by a court of equity, bidding, or forbidding, a person or persons to do a certain thing. The injunction originated in Roman law, and was anciently known as an interdict, a name it still bears in Scottish practice. It was introduced as a remedy for some of the abuses of common law, and as a preventive, when evasion of common law provisions seemed possible. It is to-day one of the most potent of the legal remedies of an equitable character which stand on the statute books.

There are three main divisions in the purposes for which a writ of injunction is issued. A writ may be prohibitive, protective, or restorative. In the first place it may forbid the commission of certain acts of a civil nature which are charged with injustice. Second, it may be so framed as to protect such civil rights of an individual or a corporation as seem to be threatened. Third, it may order the restitution or restoration of such rights as have unlawfully been taken away from an individual or a corporation. These characters of the writ have been clearly expounded by Blackstone, as follows:

«This writ may be had to stay proceedings at law, whatever stage they may have reached; to restrain alienations of property *pendente lite*, and tenants for life and others having limited interest from committing waste. It may be granted to restrain the negotiation of bills of exchange, the sailing of a ship, the transfer of stock, or the alienation of a specific chattel, to prohibit assignees from making a dividend, to prevent parties from removing out of the jurisdiction, or from marrying, or having any intercourse, which the court disapproves of, with a ward. The infringement of a copyright or a patent frequently calls for the exercise of this beneficial process; which may also be had to restrain the fraudulent use of trade marks, or of the names, labels, or other indiciæ of the makers or vendors of goods and merchandise, and in a large class of cases, far too numerous to be mentioned here.»

The first two kinds of injunction are most commonly used, and a familiar example of the prohibitory writ is that which orders the abatement of a nuisance. A railroad which lays tracks without first gaining the right of way may be compelled by injunction to remove them. By such a writ patent rights, copyrights and trade marks are secured from infringement, or proceedings in a court of law are stayed. Sometimes a court of equity issues an injunction prohibiting litigants within its own jurisdiction from prosecuting a suit in another jurisdiction; for example, a United States court may restrain creditors for suing in State courts for the enforcement of their claims against a bankrupt, and reserve the disposition of his estate to its own jurisdiction. A court of equity only issues a writ of injunction when a remedy of law appears inadequate to give the wronged party the complete relief to which he is entitled. Thus in recent cases the courts have issued writs forbidding labor agitators and others from inducing or coercing workingmen, in such a way as to bring on a strike to the injury and damage of employers, who might thus be induced to sacrifice their rights in order to escape ruin or irreparable loss.

An injunction in the United States may be preliminary or perpetual. A preliminary writ is sometimes styled interlocutory, as it is issued *pendente lite*. The preliminary writ may be made perpetual, if, after arguments made and heard, the court decides that the grounds advanced for the continuance are valid, and have been so proved by evidence. Failure to obey an injunction is punishable as a contempt of court (q.v.). Consult: Academy of Political Science, New York; 'Fact-Finding in Labor Disputes' (New York 1928); Frankfurter, F. and Greene, N., 'The Labor Injunction' (New York 1930); Frey, J. P., 'The Labor Injunction' (New York 1922); Kerr, W. W., 'A Treatise on the Law and Practice of Injunctions' (London 1914); 'U. S. Judiciary Committee' 'Hearings on Senate Bill 1482' (1928).

INJUNCTION, Government by. See GOVERNMENT BY INJUNCTION.

INJUNCTION, Theatrical, a term applied to a mandate issued by a court of equity, to compel or prevent the performance of some act for which money damages would not properly compensate the injured party. Relief by injunction in matters pertaining to theatricals is probably more frequently sought than in any other business or profession, and precedents in law established in this class of cases have become of considerable importance. At first, courts of this country and England refused to grant injunctions against actors for the purpose of compelling them to perform their contracts, a learned justice saying: «The court could not regard as law the old adage that 'a bird that can sing and will not sing must be made to sing.'» But latterly, when the service of an actor became recognized and it was made to appear clearly that an actor or singer, by intelligence, education and other artistic accomplishments and talents, was of extreme importance to one who had invested money in the production of a play or opera it was held that a court of equity would by injunction enforce a covenant in a contract. But this has simply gone to the extent of compelling a fulfilment of the contract, or forcing the artist to remain idle during its term. The services of every actor will not be enjoined. He must actually possess some exceptional merit, so that his services may be termed special, unique and extraordinary, and it must be shown they cannot be fulfilled by any other person without injury to the employer. In the case of Lumley *v.* Wagner, the courts of England enjoined Johanna Wagner, a prominent prima donna of the early 50's from appearing at Covent Garden Opera House, London, in violation of her contract with Lumley; and then for the first time the British courts asserted their authority over contracts of actors, and granted an injunction forbidding her rendering professional services for any but her original employer.

In the United States, the Federal courts recognized the right of a manager to have the exclusive services of his employee, and in McCall *v.* Braham an injunction was granted which prevented Lillian Russell from violating her contract. In the State courts, the case of Augustin Daly *v.* Fanny Morant Smith (49 How. Pr. 150), Superior Court Justice Freedman also appreciated the fact that the ancient rule had been abrogated and the modern one compelling actors to live up to their agreements, as other individuals, was there enforced. The contract must unquestionably be fair. The rights of both parties to it must be equal. In other words, if the contract gives the manager the right to terminate it by giving notice before the expiration of the contract, a like right of termination must also be given the actor; and as stated before, the actor's services must be special, unique and extraordinary. In this latter connection, it seems uncertain where to draw the line. In the case of Carter *v.* Ferguson the court refused to grant an injunction to Mrs. Leslie Carter against William J. Ferguson, an actor, saying that his services were not so special and unique as to warrant a court of equity's interference. In Charles Hoyt *v.* Loie Fuller, the court granted an injunction against the dancer, holding that a serpentine dance in the performance of which she became famous, warranted the court's interference by injunction. In George Edwardes, the London manager, *v.* Cissie Fitzgerald, the New York Supreme Court granted an injunction against Miss Fitzgerald, on the theory that a certain wink of her eye used in a play was of special merit, and a drawing card. In Harris *v.* Sparks, an injunction was granted against John Sparks, the Irish comedian, the ground being that his portrayal of an Irish character was special, unique and extraordinary. While in the still later case of Shubert Brothers *v.* Aimee Angeles, imitations given by the performer were considered so special, unique and extraordinary as to warrant the granting of an injunction. Each case, however, must be determined by its own peculiar circumstances. In the Harrison Grey Fiske *v.* Tyrone Power case, the court refused to grant an injunction against Tyrone Power, although his ability as an actor was exploited in the newspapers, on the ground that his services were not so special, unique and extraordinary as to justify an injunction. But in guarding the rights of an actor, the courts will see that no advantage has been taken of him by the manager, and that the manager for whom he is to perform is of such financial responsibility as to insure the salary of the actor. In the case of Rice *v.* D'Arville, Edward E. Rice, the theatrical manager, sought to restrain Camille D'Arville from performing for others; but on the defense that Rice was insolvent and indebted to her on a previous contract, Justice Oliver Wendell Holmes, then of the Massachusetts Supreme Court, would not compel her to perform for Rice.

Injunctions in the theatrical profession are not confined to actors and actresses, but are often invoked to prevent the piracy of a play or the use of a name. Where a play or a scene from a play has been copyrighted, the Federal courts alone have jurisdiction of the matter, and will by injunction prevent anybody from performing or producing it as their own. When there has been no copyright the common law protects the work, as well as its title; and the use of a similar name, or a name which is apt to deceive the public into the belief that it is the one already used by an author, will likewise be enjoined. An instance is the case of Charles Frohman *v.* Arthur Fraser, where the use of the title «Sherlock Holmes» was enjoined, this name having been adopted by William Gillette as the title of a play, notwithstanding the name had been used by A. Conan Doyle as the title of his novel. In that case the court held that Mr. Gillette having first used the name in connection with a theatrical production was entitled to all emoluments arising from it. Notwithstanding the numerous attempts to avoid the principles of law applicable to this class of cases, it matters not whether it is the actor who is involved or the theatrical manager, the American courts are humane, equitable, just and careful, and invariably zealously guard the interests of those engaged in the theatrical profession, as well as those engaged in any commercial business. See INJUNCTION; GOVERNMENT BY INJUNCTION; COURT; EQUITY; CHANCERY; CONTEMPT; LAW, etc.

INJURIES, Industrial. See ACCIDENTS, CAUSES AND PREVENTION OF; WORKMEN'S COMPENSATION.

INJURY, in law, an act by which the rights of another person or of the state are violated and for which the party whose rights are so invaded may institute action for damages against the perpetrator. Wrongs called *damna absque injuria* are those acts while injuring another do not permit the latter the right to enter an action, there being no remedy for such acts. See also CRIME; CRIMINAL LAW; EQUITY; TORT.

INK, a colored liquid used for writing; also a liquid or paste used for printing. Of the many varieties of ink the oldest known is India or China ink which is thought to have been used in China as early as 1200 B.C. Usually marketed in dry cakes or sticks, India ink is made of lampblack or ivory black mixed with glue or a gum. Its rich blackness and permanence are distinctive qualities. Sepia, extracted from the squid, octopus or cuttlefish, was used as an ink in ancient times. Nutgall ink, made of nutgalls and copperas (green vitriol), seems to have been known as early as the 2d century A.D. It is essentially the standard black ink of commerce today; however, the tannic acid constituent is now generally supplied by some other substance than nutgalls.

The following are some of the more important kinds of inks:

Aniline.—An aniline dye solution in a volatile solvent or dilute gum, used for printing in bright colors, or at high speeds.

Cancelling.—Suspension of lampblack in oil, used for stamp pads.

Copying.—An iron-tannic acid ink.

Diamond.—Mixture of barium sulfate and hydrofluoric acid used for writing on glass.

Fugitive.—When treated with water, or bleaching chemicals, it disappears; used for printing bank checks.

Invisible, Secret, or Sympathetic.—Normally invisible, such inks (there are many varieties) become visible when the writing is exposed to heat, light, water, or particular chemicals.

Printing.—There are three types: (1) pigment suspension in a mineral oil, or in a drying oil; (2) aniline; and (3) a warm molten resinous pigment for high-speed printing.

Bibliography.—Ruxton, P., "Printing Inks," vol. 12, *Typographic Library* (Washington, D.C., 1928); Wolfe, H. J., *The Manufacture of Printing and Lithographic Inks* (New York 1935); The International Printing Ink Association, *Three Monographs on Color* (New York 1935); Mitchell, C. A., *Ink* (London 1937).

INK DRAWING. See ART DRAWING.

INKBERRY or **WINTERBERRY,** an evergreen shrub (*Ilex glabra*) of the holly family native to the Atlantic coast from Massachusetts to Florida, also to Alabama and Mississippi. Its slender and flexible stems are two to four feet high and its leaves, about an inch in length, are lanceolate, of leathery texture, and present a shining upper surface. It bears small, very black berries which are valued for decoration. Formerly its bark and leaves were used medicinally, especially for fevers.

INKERMAN, ĭng'kẽr-män, village, USSR, on the site of a ruined town in the Crimea, at the head of the harbor of Sebastopol, at the mouth of the Chernaya River. It gives its name to the sanguinary battle fought on the heights overlooking the town, on Nov. 5, 1854, when the Russians unexpectedly attacking the British camp were repulsed with great slaughter on both sides. In World War II it was captured by the Germans on June 28, 1942.

INLAYING is the art of producing an ornamental surface by inserting varicolored forms and substances and reducing the whole to a smooth uniform condition, but with a pattern formed by the contrasting material introduced. Its essential difference from mosaic work (q.v.) is that mosaic is mainly made up of very small surfaces, while inlaid work is additional to a surface, as of ivory on wood, already existing, to add to its beauty. Various kinds of metal or wood, or pearl and ivory, are employed in this process, which is now applied chiefly to the production of ornamental articles of furniture. When wood of one color is inlaid with others of different colors, as in ornamental devices in flooring, it is generally called parquetry, the various pieces of wood being usually disposed in regular geometrical figures. Marquetry is simply the French term for inlaying. The art of inlaying iron or steel with other metals, as gold or silver, is called damascening. Boulle (or buhl) and riesener work, once highly prized, have lost much of their celebrity. The former is named from Charles André Boulle, an Italian cabinetmaker to Louis XIV, and the latter from Jean Henri Riesener, a Franco-German cabinetmaker to Louis XVI. Boulle for the most part inlaid brass on tortoiseshell, Riesener a dark wood on a tulip-wood ground. The usual instrument for cutting out veeners for inlaying is a fine saw, mounted in a bow or arched handle, and worked in short quick movements. Three or four veneers are sometimes cut simultaneously in this way. Inlaying with stone, a Florentine specialty, is called *pietra dura,* and differs from mosaic in having the holes not cut through the ground, which is commonly of black marble, but only to a regulated depth.

INMAN, Henry, American artist: b. Utica, N. Y., Oct. 28, 1801; d. New York, N. Y., Jan. 17, 1846. From early boyhood he manifested a taste for art, and in 1814 John W. Jarvis, the portrait painter, offered to receive him as a pupil, and he was bound an apprentice for seven years. After completing his apprenticeship he devoted himself to portrait painting. In 1832 he married and settled at Mount Holly, near Philadelphia. He was a founder of the National Academy of Design and one of its vice-presidents. Among his most characteristic portraits are those of Chief Justice John Marshall, Marquis de Lafayette, William Penn, Martin Van Buren, Fitz-Greene Halleck, John J. Audubon, DeWitt Clinton, Clara Barton, and Bishop William White. Many of his portraits are in public buildings in New York, Albany, and Philadelphia. He also painted landscape and genre scenes. His portrait of the poet William Wordsworth, made while he was in England in 1844–1845 and now at the University of Pennsylvania, is one of his best known.

INN, a river of Europe which issues from a lake at the foot of the Piz Longhino in the Rhaetian Alps, at an altitude of about 8,000 feet, forms a series of small lakes, the best known of which is that of Saint Moritz, then flows northeast through the deep and narrow valley of the Engadine, in the Swiss canton of the Grisons, enters the Tyrol at Martinsbruck, passes Innsbruck, Hall, and Kufstein, and shortly after enters Bavaria. At Mühldorf it turns east till it receives the Salza, where it begins to form the boundary between Ostmark and Bavaria, and joins the right bank of the Danube at Passau, after a course of over 300 miles. On account of its rapid current it is of little importance as a navigable river, but it is used extensively to bring timber rafts down to the Danube from the well-wooded mountain regions of its upper section. Consult Greiuz, R., 'Von Innsbruck nach Kufstein Eine Wanderung durch das Unterinntal' (Stuttgart 1902).

INN AND INNKEEPER. In Great Britain inns are houses where travelers are furnished, for the profit of the provider, with food and lodging, and may be set up without license by any person, provided he refrains from selling excisable liquors, which, of course, require a license. Hotels, public-houses, taverns, victualing-houses and coffee-houses are all inns when the keepers of them make it their business to furnish travelers with food and lodging; otherwise they are not. In the United States the equivalents of inns are the road-houses, hotels in cities and taverns in rural districts. See HOTEL; HOTELS IN AMERICA; TAVERNS.

INNATE IDEAS, in epistemology and in metaphysics, are ideas as of right, wrong, freedom, immortality, and of God, supposed by some to inhere in the mind, in which case they are opposed to acquired ideas, and synonymous with inborn or inherited ideas. But innate has also another meaning. Not infrequently it is understood as synonymous with natural, essential, necessary, abstract, pure, a priori, transcendental, or with universal. In the sense of inborn, innate conveys a notion of something temporal. At the outset of this article, it may be admitted, without hesitation, that no inborn ideas exist at all. But likewise, it must be granted that innate ideas, as synonymous with the Kantian a priori, as of God, etc., not only exist, but they have both objective validity and are among the most certain cognitions grasped by the mind of man. For the formal sciences, pure mathematics, logic and pure natural science, are not inborn or inherited, but yet are most certainly a priori, and therefore innate in one (the legitimate second sense) of the word. The term innate as applied to ideas was not, as some say, first employed by the philosopher Descartes. Long before his works appeared, innate, as applied apparently to inborn ideas, was in common use in England, and it is to be found in a poem of Sir John Davis, published four years before Descartes was born. The title of this poem tells us expressly that there are innate ideas in the soul. Then with the taunting question put to Descartes the question of innate ideas enters modern philosophy. The prevailing misapprehension with respect to the doctrine usually ascribed to this philosopher can only be accounted for by supposing that the opinions of Descartes have been more frequently judged from glosses of his nominal followers than from his own works. Among those who seem to have misunderstood Descartes was the lively but superficial philosopher Voltaire. As Descartes not only has been misunderstood by Voltaire, but also by a number of others, it may not be amiss to quote him (as the passage in which his elucidation of his conception occurs is very rare), and let the reader judge for himself.

«When I said that the idea of God is *innate* in us, I never meant more than this, that Nature has endowed us with a faculty by which we may know God; but I have never either said or thought that such ideas had an actual existence, or even that they were species distinct from the faculty of thinking. I will even go further, and assert that nobody has kept at a greater distance than myself from all this trash of scholastic entities, in so much that I could not help smiling when I read of the numerous arguments which Regius has so industriously collected to show that infants have no actual knowledge of God while they remain as yet unborn. Although the idea of God is so imprinted on our minds, that every person has within himself the faculty of knowing God, it does not follow that there may not have been various individuals who have passed through life without making this idea a distinct object of apprehension, and in truth, they who think they have an idea of a plurality of Gods, have no idea of God whatever.» ('Cortesii, Epist.,' Pars. I, Epist. xcix). For Voltaire's misrepresentation of this idea of Descartes the reader may turn to Voltaire's «Letter 13,» in his 'Letters on the English Nation.' A number of Dutch divines whose opinions differed widely from those of Descartes, found it convenient to shelter their solemn nonsense under his established name. No doubt some of Voltaire's strictures might have found an application there. It is probable too, as Hume says, that no more was meant by those who denied innate ideas than that all ideas were copies of our impressions. Dr. Cudworth, who felt that there are some ideas of the mind not stamped upon it from sensible objects without, and therefore which arise from the innate vigor and activity of the mind, enumerates a rather complete group of such innate ideas. He divides them as follows into two groups: (1) Ideas of wisdom, folly, prudence, imprudence, knowledge, ignorance, verity, falsity, virtue, vice, honesty, dishonesty, justice, injustice, volition, cognition, «nay,» he says «of sense itself» as a species of cognition, and which is not perceptible as an idea by any sense. (2) Ideas of cause, effect, means, end, order, proportion, similitude, dissimilitude, equality, inequality, aptitude, inaptitude, symmetry, asymmetry, whole, part, genus, species, and the like.

Perhaps no word in philosophy has been responsible for more confusion than the word idea. In Plato what in logic is called an universal, that is the common nature which thought recognizes in different particular things. Nowadays it sometimes means an opinion, sometimes mental images and sometimes it appears merely as an element in a paraphrasis as in «have an idea of.»

Some of the greatest names in European philosophy are associated with the discussion of the question of innate ideas. Besides those already mentioned are Newton, Clark, Malebranche, Lord Shaftesbury, Hobbes, Locke,

Hume, Leibnitz, Cousin and Kant. What the followers of Cousin term universal, necessary and absolute, those of Descartes designate as innate ideas. The difference between the philosophers is more verbal than real. Hobbes, indeed, in his zeal against Descartes, appears to have been not conscious of the fact that his conception of time as the mere «phantasm of before and after notion,» along with the reason he gave for so saying, makes him approach more nearly the adherents of inborn ideas than even his opponent Descartes. In this respect the late Herbert Spencer, who seems puzzled by his very natural possession of abstract ideas approaches Hobbes very nearly. At bottom, however, no essential difference between the real sentiments of the more important disputants, as Locke and Descartes existed at all. Modern psychology has set the question at rest. The genesis of ideas is as follows: A sensory experience, with many other impressions like it, is realized in consciousness, and a sentient being has a sensation. Sensations become, in time, percepts. Many percepts of the same kind become concepts or ideas. From concepts abstractions are drawn. And among such abstractions our ideas of freedom, immortality, and even of God, are to be numbered. In other words, «nihil est in intellectu, quod non fuerit in sensu,— there is nought in knowledge, that was not born of the spirit.»

INNER LIGHT, The, or INWARD LIGHT. A doctrine especially emphasized by the Quakers. The teaching is that within every soul there is a revelation of God. There is a revelation of God in Nature, there is a revelation of God in the Bible, but there is also the Inner Light revealing God. It may be only a seed and may not come to perfection, for its call may be denied. It differs from the Methodist doctrine of the witness of the Spirit in that it is recognized as always residing in the heart, while the witness of the Spirit comes from without through experience. It differs from the conscience, because its function is not to determine the difference between right and wrong but to illume the soul and make it aware of the presence of God. Consult Barclay, Robert, 'An Apology for the true Christian Divinity'; Bradford, A. H., 'The Inward Light.'

INNER MONGOLIA. See MONGOLIA.

INNER RHODES, or INNERRHODEN. See APPENZELL.

INNES, ĭn'ĕs, **Alexander Taylor,** Scottish jurist: b. Tain, Ross and Cromarty, Scotland, 18 Dec. 1833; d. Edinburgh, 27 Jan. 1912. He was educated at Edinburgh University, and was admitted to the Scottish bar in 1870. He was an authority on Scottish Church law and wrote 'The Law of Creeds in Scotland' (1867, and brought down to date in 1902); 'Church and State: A Historical Handbook' (1890); 'Studies in Scottish History' (1892); 'The Trial of Jesus Christ' (1899); 'Scottish Churches and the Crisis of 1907.'

INNES, Cosmo, Scottish lawyer and antiquary: b. Durris, 9 Sept. 1798; d. Killin, 31 July 1874. He received his education at the Edinburgh High School and at Glasgow and Oxford universities. In 1822 he passed as a Scottish advocate, became sheriff of Moray in 1840, and subsequently was appointed clerk to the Second Division of the Court of Session. In 1846 he was elected to the chair of history in the University of Edinburgh. He is best known, however, as the author of 'Scotland in the Middle Ages' (1860); 'Sketches of Early Scotch History' (1861) and volume I of 'Acts of the Scottish Parliament.' He published also a volume of lectures on 'Legal Antiquities' (1872), and was the author of several memoirs, including one of Dean Ramsay. Consult the memoir by his daughter, Mrs. Hill Burton (1874).

INNES, Thomas, Scottish historian: b. Drumgask, Aberdeenshire, 1662; d. Paris, 28 Jan. 1744. At 15 he was sent to Paris, where he studied at the College of Navarre and the Scots College, of which latter body his eldest brother was principal after 1682. Thomas received priest's orders in 1692, and after three years of mission work at Inveraven, Banffshire (1698–1701), returned to Paris, and became prefect of studies in the Scots College. To pursue his researches he paid a visit or two to England and Scotland; and Wodrow, who saw him at Edinburgh in 1724, describes him as «a monkish, bookish person, who meddles with nothing but literature.» Withal, he was a staunch Jacobite, but no Ultramontane, and is said to have been tainted with Jansenism. He may justly be looked on as the precursor of Niebuhr and Niebuhr's successors; for his 'Critical Essay on the Ancient Inhabitants of Scotland' (2 vols. 1729) is much the earliest of all scientific histories. It was meant for an introduction to a 'Civil and Ecclesiastical History of Scotland,' one volume of which, coming down to Columba's death, he prepared for the press, while another, bringing down the narrative to 831, was left incomplete. Both were edited for the Spalding Club by Grub (Aberdeen 1853). The aim of the whole work was «to counteract the inventions of former historians (Hector Boice), and to go to the bottom of the dark contrivances of factious men (George Buchanan) against the sovereignty of our kings»; and though he thus wrote with a purpose, his honesty and acumen were such that the work retains a permanent value. Consult 'Memoir' by Grub; Chambers' 'Biographical Dictionary of Eminent Scotsmen' (Glasgow 1837); 'Dictionary of National Biography' (Vol. XXIX, London 1892); Forbes. 'An Account of the Familie of Innes' (compiled 1698; first printed, Aberdeen 1864).

INNESS, George, American painter: b. Newburg, N. Y., 1 May 1825; d. Bridge of Allan, Scotland, 3 Aug. 1894. His art education began in boyhood and when 16 years of age he learned map engraving. He first attempted nature sketching in 1843, when he showed such promise that he was admitted into the studio of Regis Gignoux, New York; but soon opened a studio for himself and through the liberality of a patron was enabled to visit Europe. After spending 15 months in Italy and one year (1850) in France he finally made his home at Eagleswood, near Perth Amboy, N. J. He was looked upon as the first among American landscape painters, and was not only a clever and imaginative interpreter of the scenery among which he lived, but a man of intellect, a thoughtful yet bold theorist on art subjects and an incisive critic. He had a keen appreciation of American scenery, and the sky and atmosphere of the eastern States were sympathetically portrayed with an earnestness that recalls the sentiment of the Fontainebleau-Barbizon school. His early paintings are distinguished by conscientious care for detail, vivid perception of color, and the panoramic breadth of a bold and unconventional originality. After 1878 his style had ripened, and his technique grew simpler and less highly elaborated. He was willing to sacrifice all cleverness of touch in handling detail for the sake of portraying the emotion, or transitory effect of light and cloud in a landscape, the perturbation of storm or wind, the pageant of sunset, or the magic calm of a moonlight scene. In such productions his command of color was very remarkable. His pictures are much prized by connoisseurs, and when offered for sale command high prices. Five of them are in the Metropolitan Museum of Art, New York. Among the finest are 'Under the Greenwood'; 'Close of a Stormy Day'; 'Pine Groves of Barberini Villa'; 'An Autumn Morning'; 'Autumn Gold'; 'The Edge of the Forest'; 'Passing Storm'; 'Moonrise'; 'Winter Morning, Montclair, New Jersey.' Consult Caffin, C. H., 'American Masters of Painting' (New York 1902); Daingerfield, E., 'George Inness, The Man and his art' (New York 1911), and 'Fifty Paintings by George Inness' (New York 1913); Trumble, A., 'George Inness, a Memorial' (New York 1895).

INNESS, George, Jr., American painter: b. Paris, France, 5 Jan. 1854; d. Cragsmoore, N. J., 27 July 1926. He was the son of George Inness (q.v.), landscape painter, whose pupil he was at Rome in 1870–74, and of Bonnat at Paris in 1875. He began to exhibit at the National Academy in 1877, and became a member of the National Academy of Design in 1899. In 1899 he obtained a gold medal at the Paris Solon. He was forcible, and skilful in color. His work includes landscapes and animal subjects. Among his pictures are 'The Pride of the Dairy' (1878); 'Pasture at Chemung'; 'A Mild Day' (1887); 'Morning on the River' (1902) and work in the *Century Magazine* with which he was connected from 1913 till his death. He wrote 'The Life, Art and Letters of George Inness' (1917).

INNISFAIL, or Isle of Destiny, the name frequently applied to Ireland by the bards and sometimes also by Anglo-Irish writers.

INNISKILLING. See ENNISKILLEN.

INNOCENT, the name of 13 popes, as follows:

INNOCENT I, Saint: b. Albano; d. 12 March 417. He succeeded Anastasius I as bishop of Rome in 402. He supported Saint Chrysostom (q.v.) when the latter was driven from his see of Constantinople through the machinations of the Empress Eudoxia. Rome was pillaged by Alaric in 410, during his pontificate. He is commemorated by the Roman Catholic Church on 28 July. His correspondence is edited in Migne, 'Patrologia Latina' (Vol. XX).

INNOCENT II (GREGORIO DE' PAPI, or PAPARESCHI): b. Rome; d. 23 Sept. 1143. He was elected Pope in 1130 by a part of the cardinals, while the others elected Peter of Leon, who took the name of Anacletus. Innocent fled to France, where he was acknowledged by the Council of Etampes, by Louis VI, and soon after by Henry II of England; also by the Emperor Lothaire, who conducted him in 1133 to Rome, where he occupied the Lateran, while Anacletus occupied the Castle of Crescentius, the church of Saint Peter, and a large part of the city and maintained himself against Innocent until his death in 1138. He held the second Ecumenical Council in the Lateran, which condemned Arnold of Brescia and his heresy, declared all the decrees of Anacletus null, and excommunicated Roger of Sicily, who had supported the latter. Roger, however, obliged Innocent to acknowledge him as king, absolve him from excommunication, and invest him and his heirs with Apulia, Calabria and Capua. His letters are published in Migne, 'Patrologia Latina' (Vol. CLXXIX, Paris 1844–64).

INNOCENT III (GIOVANNI LOTHARIO CONTI): b. Anagni, Italy, 1161; d. Perugia, Italy, 16 July 1216. On the death of Celestine III (1198) he was unanimously elected at the age of 37. Innocent, in the vigor of manhood, endowed by nature with all the talents of a ruler, possessed of an erudition uncommon at that time, and favored by circumstances, was better qualified than any of his predecessors to elevate the Papal power. By his clemency and prudence he gained over the inhabitants of Rome, obliged the imperial prefect to take the oath of allegiance to him, and directed his attention to every quarter where he believed that a papal claim of property or of feudal rights existed. He concluded treaties with many cities of Tuscany for the mutual protection of their liberties and those of the Church, and soon obtained possession of the ecclesiastical states in their widest extent. He excommunicated Philip Augustus, king of France; laid the kingdom under an interdict in 1200 because Philip had repudiated his wife Ingeburga, and obliged the king to submit. He was still more decided in his treatment of John, king of England, who refused to confirm the election of Stephen Langton as archbishop of Canterbury. Innocent laid the kingdom under an interdict, and in 1212 formally deposed him. John was finally obliged to submit, resigned his territories to Rome, and received them as a papal fief from Innocent. All Christendom acknowledged the Pope's spiritual sovereignty; two Crusades were undertaken at his order, and his influence extended even to Constantinople. Innocent was one of the greatest popes and rulers. It has been said of his rule, as of that of Gregory VII, whom he most resembles, that in those times the power of the Pope was salutary as a bond of union for Europe, in which the still firmer bond of a common civilization and knowledge did not, as at present, exist. In 1215 he held a council, the fourth Lateran and twelfth general which passed the decree making confession and communion obligatory at Paschal time. Frederick II was acknowledged as German emperor, and the Franciscan and Dominican orders were confirmed. His correspondence is in Migne (Vol. CXIV–CXVIII). Consult Von Hurter, 'Geschichte des Papstes Innocenz III und seiner Zeitgenossen' (4 vols., 3d ed., Hamburg 1841–43); Luchaire, 'Innocent III' (Paris 1904–08); Mann, 'Lives of the

Popes in the Early Middle Ages' (London 1914).

INNOCENT IV (Senibaldi di Fieschi): b. Genoa; d. Naples, 7 Dec. 1254. He was Pope from 1243–54 and was perpetually at feud with the German emperor Frederick and his successors. They came to terms in 1244, but these were misinterpreted and Frederick set out to capture Innocent. The Pope fled to Lyons where he called a general council to decide the issue (1245). It was not until after Frederick's death that Innocent was able to return to Rome (1253). Conrad IV, Frederick's successor, continued the strife, for which he was excommunicated in 1254. He died a few weeks later, and his cause was espoused by Manfred, his natural son, who, placing himself at the head of Moorish troops, defeated the Papal army in December of that year. Innocent survived this defeat by five days. He published a commentary on the Decretals of Gregory IX, first printed at Strassburg (1477). Consult Weber, 'Der Kampf Zwischen Papst Innocent IV und Kaiser Frederick II' (Berlin 1900).

INNOCENT V (Pietro Idi Tarentasia): b. Savoy, 1225; d. Rome, 22 June 1276. He was of the Dominican Order, taught at Paris, and became Archbishop of Lyons (1271). Shortly afterward he became Cardinal. His pontificate lasted only from 20 January to 22 June of the year 1276. The struggle between the Guelphs and Ghibellines occupied his short reign, as well as efforts to reclaim the Eastern Church for Rome. Innocent V published commentaries on the Bible and on the sentences of Peter Lombard. Consult Gregorovius, F., 'History of the City of Rome in the Middle Ages' (Vol. VI, London 1898); Pastor, L., 'History of the Popes' (Vol. I, London 1906); and Carboni, 'De Innocentio V, Romano Pontifice' (Rome 1894).

INNOCENT VI (Etienne d'Albert): b. Mons, France; d. 12 Sept. 1362. His pontificate extended from 1352 to 1362, and during this period the Papal residence was at Avignon. He was a man of great learning, and encouraged education and literature. Petrarch lived at his court for a time. Consult bibliography under Innocent V, above, and Pastor, L., 'Innocent VI et Blanche de Bourbon, lettres du pape' (ed. by Daumet, Paris 1901).

INNOCENT VII (Cosmo de' Migliorati): b. Sulmona, Abruzzi, Italy, 1366; d. Rome, 6 Nov. 1406. He was Pope from 1404 till his death, but was opposed by the antipope, Benedict XIII, who held his court at Avignon. Consult Gregorovius, F., 'History of the City of Rome in the Middle Ages' (Vol. VI, London 1898).

INNOCENT VIII (Giovanni Battista Cibo): b. Genoa, 1432; d. 25 July 1492. He was descended from a noble family of Genoa. Paul II made him Bishop of Savona, and he was appointed cardinal by Sixtus IV. He became Pope in 1484 and was for some time at war with Ferdinand of Naples and held the sultan Bajazet's brother Zelim a prisoner. He showed marked favoritism to the various members of his family. He made his natural son, who had been born to him before he began his ecclesiastical career, ruler of several towns near Rome, and married him to the daughter of Lorenzo de'Medici. For this favor on the part of the Medicis, he made the 14-year-old Giovanni de'Medici a cardinal. Consult Serdonati, 'Vita e fatti d'Innocenzo VIII' (Milan 1829).

INNOCENT IX (Giovanni Antonio Facchinetti): b. Bologna, Italy, 1519; d. 30 Dec. 1591. He studied law, and later was appointed bishop by Pius IV. After the Council of Trent, he became nuncio at Venice, which post he held for six years. Under Gregory XIII, he was cardinal, and was well favored by this pope's successors. He occupied the papal chair only from the 29th of October preceding his death. He published a number of works on philosophy and politics.

INNOCENT X (Giovanni Battista Pamfili): b. Rome, 7 May 1574; d. 6 Jan. 1655. In 1629 he was elevated to the cardinalate and became Pope in 1644. Under him the temporal and spiritual power of the papacy was greatly increased. In 1651 he condemned the Treaty of Westphalia and he formally condemned Jansenism in 1653. Consult Ciampi, 'Innocenzo X Pamfili e la sua corte' (Rome 1878); Hergenröther, 'Katholische Kirche und christlicher Staat' (Freiburg 1872).

INNOCENT XI (Benedetto Odescalchi): b. Como, Italy, 1611; d. 12 Aug. 1689. He served in his youth as a soldier in Germany and Poland, took orders later and rose through many important posts, became cardinal in 1645, and was elected Pope in 1676, on the death of Clement X. He was eminent for his probity and austerity; zealously opposed nepotism and simony, and restrained luxury and excess. He condemned the New Testament of Mons and several other Jansenistic works. He also anathematized sixty-five propositions drawn from the works of modern Causists and condemned Molinos and the Quietists. He determined to abolish the right of asylum exercised in Rome by foreign ambassadors; but Louis XIV would not yield to so just a claim, occupied Avignon, and imprisoned the papal nuncio in France; in consequence of which the authority of the Pope received a severe blow by the IV Propositiones Cleri Gallicani in 1682. These disputes were highly favorable to the English Revolution, as it induced the Pope in 1689 to unite with the allies against James II, in order to lower the influence of Louis XIV. Consult Gérin, 'Le pape Innocent XI et la révocation de l'Edit de Nantes' (in *Revue des questions historiques*, Paris 1878); id., 'Innocent XI et la révolution anglaise de 1688' (Paris 1876); Immich, 'Papst Innocenz XI' (Berlin 1900); Bryce, 'Holy Roman Empire' (New York 1911).

INNOCENT XII: b. Naples, 13 March 1615; d. 27 Sept. 1700. He became archbishop of Naples, a cardinal in 1681 and Pope in 1692. During his pontificate Louis XIV and the French bishops revoked the declaration of the French clergy, and submitted to the judgment of the Holy See in the matters in dispute during the pontificate of Innocent XI. Consult von Ranke, Leopold, 'History of the Popes' (Vol. II, London 1908).

INNOCENT XIII (Michelangelo Conti): b. Rome, 15 May 1655; d. 7 March 1724. In 1695 he was made archbishop of Tarsus, and became a cardinal in 1707. He was also made bishop of Viterbo in 1712 and succeeded Clement XI in the papal chair in 1721.

INNOCENTS, Feast of Holy, variously styled Innocent's Day and Childermas, a festival generally observed on the 28th, but in the Eastern Church on 29 December, in commemoration of the massacre of the children at Bethlehem, "from two years old and under," by the order of Herod, with the purpose of destroying among them the infant Saviour. The Church of England at the Reformation retained it in its ritual among its anniversary festivals. Saint Cyprian refers to these children as martyrs, as does Saint Augustine with still greater explicitness. It is to them that the hymn of Prudentius, 'Salvete Flores Martyrum,' is addressed.

INNOCENTS ABROAD, The, a famous book of travels, by Samuel L. Clemens ("Mark Twain"). In a vein of highly original humor this widely-read book records a pleasure excursion to Europe, the Holy Land, and Egypt, in the sixties. Descriptions of real events and the peoples and lands visited are enlivened by more or less fictitious dialogue and adventures.

INNOMINATE ARTERY. See AORTA.

INNOMINATE BONE. See PELVIS.

INNS OF CHANCERY. Originally buildings or building groups in London set aside as residences for the clerks of the chancery courts. They were 10 in number but have long since ceased to exist as public offices, being now merely incorporated societies. See CHANCERY.

INNS OF COURT are certain societies in London exclusively invested with the right to call to the bar in England. The colleges of the English professors and students of common law are called inns, the old English word for the houses of noblemen, bishops and others of extraordinary note being of the same signification as the French *hôtel*. Societies of lawyers, which before the Conquest held their chief abodes for study in ecclesiastical houses, began to be collected into permanent residences soon after the Court of Common Pleas was directed to be held in a fixed place,— a stipulation which occurs in the great charters both of King John and Henry III. In these houses exercises were performed, lectures read and degrees conferred. The Inns of Court are each self-governing and all have equal privileges, and they are officered by benchers — members of standing at the bar — and stewards, and possess the power of disbarring members in case of serious misdemeanor. The inns have extensive ranges of buildings with suites of chambers generally occupied by barristers. Each inn maintains a chapel, the Inner and Middle Temple having the joint use of the Temple Church. The four inns of court are: the Inner Temple and Middle Temple (formerly the dwelling of the Knights Templars, and purchased by some professors of law more than three centuries since); Lincoln's Inn and Gray's Inn (anciently belonging to the earls of Lincoln and Gray). King's Inn, Dublin, the legal school in the Irish capital, and the Faculty of Advocates in Edinburgh, the Scottish law incorporation, perform analogous functions with the English inns of court in their respective countries.

INNSBRUCK, ĭns'brook, or **INNSPRUCK** (from ancient name ŒNIPONTUM; locally called SCHPRUCK), town and capital of the Tyrol, beautifully situated at an elevation of 1,880 feet. 59 miles south of Munich, on the banks of the Inn, near its confluence with the Sill, and almost in the centre of the valley of the Inn (Innthal), the sides of which are enclosed by mountains several miles distant, but so lofty (7,000 to 8,500 feet) as apparently almost to overhang the town. It consists of the town proper, situated on the right bank of the river, and of five suburbs. It is for the most part well built. The houses are generally of a limestone breccia and from four to five stories high, and built in the Italian style. The buildings most deserving of notice are the Hofkirche, containing the tomb of the Emperor Maximilian I, one of the most splendid monuments of the kind in Europe, though he himself is not interred in it; and the tomb of Hofer; the church of Saint James, with a painting by Lucas Cranach; the Jesuit church, considered the handsomest in the town; the Capuchin church, with good paintings; the new palace, built by Maria Theresa, a very extensive edifice, with gardens which stretch along the side of the Inn and form an excellent promenade; the old palace, in which the archdukes of Tyrol and several of the German emperors used to reside; the university, founded in 1677 and re-established in 1826, well endowed, provided with a great library of 260,000 volumes, botanical garden and cabinet of natural history and attended by about 1,300 students; a gymnasium and several other important educational establishments; and the museum, called Ferdinandeum, rich in all the productions both of art and nature within the limits of the Tyrol. The manufactures include woolen, silk and cotton tissues, gloves, mosaics, glass, etc. As the capital of the Tyrol, Innsbruck is the place of assemblage for its states and the seat of superior appeal, civil and criminal courts and of many important public offices. Many of the spots in the immediate vicinity have become memorable for the noble exploits which the Tyrolese peasantry performed in the War of Independence. Pop. 56,380, and mainly composed of German-speaking Roman Catholics.

INNUENDO, ĭn'ū-ĕn'dō, in law, an interpretation of words held to be injurious; specifically, in an action for libel or slander, an averment by the plaintiff that written or spoken words of the defendant, though apparently not actionable, are in reality defamatory. This clause is used in a declaration to explain the meaning of words only when they are ambiguous in meaning or application. If not justified by preceding averments, it may be rejected as superfluous. See LIBEL; SLANDER.

INNUITS, ĭn'ū-ĭts. See ESKIMOS.

INO, daughter of Cadmus and Harmonia, second wife of Athamas (q.v.), king of Bœotia, who drew upon herself the anger of Hera by nursing Dionysus, the son by Zeus of her sister Semele. In order to favor her own children she projected the murder of her stepchildren, Phryxus and Helle, who saved themselves by flight. Hera, still more highly incensed, made Athamas, the husband of Ino, mad, and he dashed Learchus, his eldest son by Ino, against a rock. Ino fled with her youngest son, Melicertes, and threw herself with him into the sea. Ino and Melicertes were made sea deities at the prayer of Dionysus. Ino was worshiped under the name of Leucothea. There are a number of variations of this legend. It formed the basis of lost tragedies by Æschylus, Sophocles and Euripides, as well as by other Greek and Roman writers. Consult Gruppe, O., 'Griechische Mythologie und Religionsgeschichte' (2 vols., Munich 1906); Preller, L., 'Griechische Mythologie' (2 vols., 4th ed., 1887).

INOCARPUS, ī-nō-kär′pŭs, a genus of leguminous plants, having unifoliolate leaves and yellow flowers in axillary spikes. *I. edulis* is the South Sea chestnut, native of Tahiti. It is a large tree, with luxuriant foliage, the delicate evergreen leaves being six inches or more in length. It furnishes seeds or nuts much valued in the South Sea Islands, the inhabitants gathering them while green and mashing them for food.

INOCULATION. See INFECTION; VACCINATION.

INOFFICIOUS TESTAMENT, a testament under which no provision is made by the testator for his issue and in which no reason is assigned for the omission. In nearly all jurisdictions such a testament is considered void. See HEIR; SUCCESSION; TESTAMENT.

INOSIT ($C_6H_{12}O_6$), from Greek *is, inos,* a nerve, a muscle), a saccharine substance found in the muscular tissues of the heart, as well as liver, brain, kidneys, etc. It appears both in health and, to an abnormal amount, in disease. It exists also in a number of plants, such as foxglove, potato, kidney-bean, acacia, asparagus, cabbage. See GLUCOSE.

INOUYE, ē′nō-oo′yā′, **Kaoru**, MARQUIS, famous Japanese statesman: b. 1835; d. Tokio, 1 Sept. 1915. As a young man he was violently opposed to the intrusion of foreigners at the time when Japan first sanctioned the building of foreign legations in Tokio. Together with his friend Ito, afterward Prince Ito, he set fire to the newly-built British legation as a protest. A secret visit to England in 1864, however, completely changed the ideas of Inouye and Ito. It was forbidden then for Japanese to leave their country, hence visits to foreign lands had to be carried out surreptitiously. The enlarged views which Inouye and Ito took back home brought them into collision with their countrymen and led to a murderous attack on the former. The new ideas spread, however; the great clans of Satsuma, Tosa and Choshu rallied to the cause of national regeneration. Inouye was one of the most prominent leaders in the great reform movement that culminated with extraordinary rapidity in the revolution of 1867 and brought Japan at a bound from a condition of Oriental mediævalism into the front rank of nations. Bows and arrows were still used in the army. In 1870 Inouye became Vice-Minister of Finance in the Okuma administration, his first official appointment. Down to 1898, when he retired from public life, he had held the portfolios of Foreign Affairs, Home Affairs, Finance, Agriculture and Commerce. In every department he displayed resourcefulness, courage and energy, gaining a reputation as a great statesman and a builder of modern Japan. In 1894, after the Japanese had driven the Chinese out of Korea, Inouye was sent to Seoul to reorganize the Korean administration and to superintend the introduction of much-needed reforms. At the outbreak of the Russo-Japanese War Inouye, though in retirement, was commanded by the emperor to attend all important councils and to advise the Minister of Finance. He was created a count in 1884 and marquis in 1907. See JAPAN.

INOWRAZLAU, e′no-vrats′laf, Poland, town of the province of Posen, 20 miles southwest of Thorn. It contains a gymnasium, Kurhaus and a mediæval church. Its industrial establishments comprise iron works, sugar refineries, flouring mills, brick yards, salt works, etc. It has also a large trade in the agricultural products of the district of which it is the centre. Pop. 24,600.

INQUEST, *in law*, a formal legal inquiry into special matters, as a death, lunacy, an undefended lawsuit or the like; also, the jury making such inquiry. The term had its origin in remote antiquity. It has been in use in England for various purposes for many centuries. It was used not only for official investigation into judicial matters but administrative matters as well.

One of its most important functions, today, both in American and in English law, is to investigate deaths under certain circumstances, as in prison, where violence is suspected, etc. The inquest is usually in charge of an officer known as the coroner, but sometimes it is conducted by a medical inspector, as in some jurisdictions in the United States. The evidence at inquests is taken under oath, after the jury has viewed the body. Often medical experts are called in and a post-mortem examination made of the body. If the verdict of the jury in attendance finds any person guilty of homicide, he is committed to prison to await trial. See CORONER.

Another function of the inquest is to determine whether the government is the lawful owner of lands or goods by forfeiture or lands by escheat. This proceeding is known as «inquest of office» or «office found.» In the United States generally this proceeding is held by a commissioner, or similar official, under the direction usually of the Attorney-General. Still another function of the inquest is to determine, under the direction of the sheriff of a county and a jury, the amount of damages due from a defendant to a plaintiff in cases in which the defendant failed to appear or answer and judgment was by default. The procedure is also common in cases of garnishment, replevin and attachment to decide who is entitled to the property in dispute.

INQUILINE, ĭn′kwĭ-lĭn, a term applied in zoology to animals which live as tenants within the nests or homes of other animals. The use of the term is almost entirely confined to entomology and then often restricted to the cases in which the rightful and the intruding tenants are closely related. Similar cases among other animals are commonly designated as commensalism (q.v.), but these and similar terms are used rather loosely. Examples of the inquiline relation occur among the termites, ants and bees, but are known especially among the gall-flies (*Cynipidæ*); indeed, one entire division, comprising more than 500 species. is named

Inquilinae, because of the predominance of this mode of life. These insects differ but little in structure from the true gall-flies, but they lack the power to produce galls and consequently deposit their eggs within those of other species. They infest certain species of galls, as those of the blackberry and some oak-galls, in large numbers and sometimes more than one kind occur in a single gall.

INQUISITION, The. In ancient Roman Law, and in the Papal Canon Law which grew up from it, two forms of criminal procedure were recognised, the Accusatorial and Inquisitorial. The former is familiar to us all; a definite prosecutor called into court a definite defendant, and sought to prove his case by ordinary forms of testimony and pleading. The second, however, needs explanation. Under this procedure, a great part was played by *fama;* that is, by *report,* not in the loose sense of "common rumour," but as the testimony of two or three knowledgeable and trustworthy witnesses. When such a *fama* reached the ears of judicial authorities, then the man was *infamatus* (or *diffamatus*) of the offenses in question. The judge then became his accuser: "You are *diffamatus* of such and such an offence: therefore you must appear before me and clear yourself on oath, and if possible by the oath also of a specified number of competent witnesses." Thus an inquiry (*Inquisitio*) is set up; and, whereas under *Accusatio* the burden of proof would have rested upon the prosecutor, it is now laid upon the defendant. To grasp this clearly is to understand, from the very first, why the medieval Inquisition never struck full root in England, where the Common Law was a natural growth of English life, "broadening down from precedent to precedent."

It was equally natural that inquisitorial procedure came to be generally and intimately associated with questions of religious belief.

Here again, we cannot understand the Middle Ages so long as we ignore the eschatology of that period: men's current convictions in the matter of Heaven and Hell. During more than a thousand years, the orthodox belief was one of almost inconceivable severity. Hell was conceived as a place of torment infinite in duration, and indescribable in its horror. Moreover, it was assumed that the great majority of mankind were destined to this eternal torment. St. Thomas Aquinas, quite as a matter of course, contrasts the "few" of the saved with the "multitude" of damned. St. Bernardino (d. 1444), from whom as a Franciscan we might expect special human sympathy, even taught that the Harmony of the Universe necessarily demanded this contrast; that the Music of the Spheres would have been imperfect but for the bass part supplied by the howling of the guilty multitude.

These ideas had reigned from time immemorial, and the most unforgivable of all delinquencies was deathbed impenitence: *Extra Ecclesiam nulla salus.* In such an atmosphere as this, the most horrible social crime was that which dragged down to Hell not only the heretic himself, but perhaps thousands of perverts with him. Therefore Pope Innocent III, in 1199, formally condemned heresy as the most unpardonable of treasons, "since it is far more grievous to sin against the eternal than against an earthly Majesty." This memorable decree laid the foundation of the Inquisition as an institution unprecedented in world history. It was upon this basis that St. Thomas Aquinas bent his genius to build the theory which his faithful followers have held down to the present day. "If false coiners or other felons are justly committed to death without delay by worldly princes, much more may heretics, from the moment that they are convicted, be not only excommunicated, but slain justly out of hand." (*Summa Theologica,* 2ª 2ªᵉ, *Quest.* xi, art. iii).

The Roman Church—*Ecclesia Romana* as it was commonly called in the Middle Ages—claimed then, and has never since renounced, the philosophical title of *Societas Perfecta:* a state in its own right, with powers of legislation over all its subjects and the sanction of punishment over the disobedient, even to the extreme penalty of death. It claims that its subjects are all men or women who have received Christian baptism, whether deliberately or as infants at the font.

For the claims of the state in matters of conscience, see Bishop Creighton in his *Persecution and Tolerance* (1895). The early Christians had differed much from each other; nearly a hundred sects developed in the first hundred years. In some cases there were mortal enmities; in others we find remarkable tolerance, as when Justin Martyr, the earliest surviving apologist (160 A.D.) condemns only those who reject the faith with contumely, and honors with the title of Christian such pagan philosophers as Socrates and Heraclitus, since they lived for the truth, and Christ is Truth. In a later generation (200 A.D.) Tertullian gloated over the hell-pains awaiting pagan torturers, in a passage rendered notorious by Gibbon and Lecky; but this was when the unpopular sect had been embittered by persecutions. Presently, the tables were reversed, and Christianity was victorious under Constantine I.

In the great domestic quarrel provoked by Arius (325 A.D.), the emperor finally sided with the majority of bishops. He banished the heresiarch, commanded under pain of death that all his books should be surrendered, and sent him into exile with the two bishops who still maintained his cause. From that time forward the state made itself responsible for government in the church. Heretical priests were punished. Paganism was condemned as a *superstitio,* and the pagan temples were disestablished and plundered with even greater thoroughness than Henry VIII showed in the England of 1530.

In 381, the Emperor Theodosius set his seal to a series of enactments which punished heresy. In 385, the heretic Priscillian was executed by the Emperor Maximus, despite the protests of St. Martin of Tours. A generation later St. Augustine, who at first had pleaded for tolerance of the Donatists, emphatically revoked this in course of time, appealing to what seemed practical experience, since confiscation of property and other similar penalties are efficacious in calling men's attention to the orthodox faith. A generation later (438) Theodosius II published his celebrated *Code* of Roman Law, in which, *inter alia,* are severe laws against pagans and heretics, thus giving the Church the status of a *Societas Perfecta,* with legislative and punitive powers.

There was now a lull in religious manslaughter; Europe was too troubled, and too barbarous, for any important anti-clerical movement to come into collision with the hierarchy. But, all this while, there was gradual infiltration of organised heresy from the East. The Manichaean creed had just enough in common with Christianity to be a dangerous rival. St. Augustine himself had been a Manichaean in early life, and had found the heretics formidable enemies in his African bishopric. The gloom of the Dark Ages (6th to 11th century) from which very few intimate social records have survived, doubtless hides much underground nonconformity. But when we come to that religious and intellectual revival which deserves to be called the Renaissance of the 11th century, we suddenly find heresy very much alive. The chronicler, Ralph Glaber, a Cluniac monk, tells us how, around the fateful year 1000, "it seemed as if the world shook itself and cast off its hoary age, and clad itself everywhere in a white robe of Churches." Yet this light fell upon a barbarous world.

"It is horrible to relate what corruptions then prevailed among men." There were plagues and famine and cannibalism among the multitude; and in the Church itself, Glaber stigmatises the debaucheries of one pope (Benedict IX) as "too horrible to relate," while he accuses the whole clergy as demoralized by greed, and infected from the head with the mortal sin of simony. In such a world as this he describes four pestilent outbreaks of heresy in the most civilized parts of Western Europe; and from this time forward the chain is complete, down to the Renaissance and Reformation. We find four fairly definite periods: Lynch Law, Civil War, Episcopal Inquisition, and Papal Inquisition.

The "white robe of Churches" came in a period of Lynch Law. The lay authorities, as a whole, were definitely hostile to the innovators, and the multitude could be raised against them. Here and there, a bishop or priest can be found more merciful than the mob, but this is very rare, and we may apply the legal maxim: *Fecit qui profuit* (He did the deed who profited by it). For to the clergy this was a matter of life and death. Religious changes involve social revolution, and heresy threatens violence and plunder. The totalitarian claims of Rome, while on one hand they gave her increased power, rendered her otherwise vulnerable in many directions. Thus, during the 11th century, both sides mobilized their forces, and, by 1100, all tended to civil war. It was a time of rapid advance in the arts of peace and civilization. The monastic orders grew apace; the hierarchy and the feudal nobility were better organized and disciplined, and it became increasingly impossible to drift onwards on a system of Lynch Law and guerrilla warfare. Orthodoxy and Heterodoxy mobilized their respective forces; until, at last, in the 12th century, came civil war on a great scale.

On the eve of this explosion, we have a most significant sidelight from the Rhineland, which shared with northern Italy and southern France the credit of greatest advance in civilization. This is an exchange of letters between Erwin, Prior of Steinbach near Cologne, and Bernard, who stands beside St. Francis among the greatest of canonized saints. He was learned, eloquent almost beyond all of his age, and fearless in his dealings with popes and princes: Pope Eugenius III had been one of his pupils. About 1130 A.D. he had made a special missionary journey among the heretics of southern France, the land of the Troubadours. Here the saint, confessedly, met with little success. Erwin now wrote describing his own difficulties with organized heresy in the Rhineland. The folk described by Erwin answer to those Beghards, Béguins, Béguines who, after long hesitation on the verge of revolt, finally plunged or were thrust into the abyss, and were in the 13th century identified or confused by Bernard Gui with "spiritual" Franciscans. Here, under Erwin's pen, they appear far more nearly akin to the later Vaudois. The good prior found them attractive; and therein lay the difficulty. Their lives seemed blameless; and these unbelievers boldly challenged the multitude of believers with Christ's criterion: "By their fruits ye shall know them."

That was a mystery for St. Bernard also; he had often deplored that his Church set a bad moral example; she was preyed upon by a cancer, and the remedies seemed only to make her worse. He was constrained now to admit the apparent regularity of these men's lives, and even their frequent semblance of piety. The heretic "is pale with fastings; he eats no bread of idleness; he works with his hands for his livelihood, where then is the fox?" It lies in their contempt of Church authority: they "give holy things to the dogs." They are "a vile and rustic crew, unlettered and altogether unwarlike." Even their righteousness is but as filthy rags: "they do indeed abstain, but they abstain heretically." These words are typical of the spirit which inspired orthodoxy in those days.

St. Bernard is often quoted as an apostle of tolerance, in something like the modern sense; men quote his words: "Faith is a matter of persuasion, not of force." But we must read on for a few lines and we shall find how in his succeeding words he very plainly appeals for the punishment of persistent heretics. (In *Cant. sermo* LXIV. c. 12.) The hierarchy was puzzled; popes and councils had no clear-cut policy. It is not until 1209 that we find a council definitely basing itself upon the plain claim of "Death for the Heretics" as a maxim both of Canon Law and of State Law. Thenceforward, this lies at the very foundation of medieval European society. Meanwhile, things were steadily drifting towards civil war, which broke out in 1195.

Southern France, Languedoc, was more advanced even than the Rhineland. It had a social system far older than the North. It was less warlike, more mercantile, more luxurious, and less papalistic. Jews flourished there, and society was strikingly tolerant of religious differences. In consequence, it had become a favorable ground for the spread of Manichaean doctrines which had filtered in from the East. Recent scholars have doubted whether these Provençal heretics held the creed with Eastern exactness, but there is no doubt of their main features. They held a dualism, an equilibrium between good and evil, God and Satan, which shall endure until the end of all things. Meanwhile, there is perpetual conflict between Light and Darkness, Mind and Matter. The flesh is evil; therefore, true religion is strictly ascetic. Sexual commerce is sinful, even in matrimony. Diet must be vegetarian, rejecting even eggs and everything that has had life, with an illogical exception for fish. Those strict rules, however, were binding only upon the *perfecti*: the multitude, *credentes*, seem in practice to have differed little more from orthodoxy than did the Quakers of the first generations. The whole sect called themselves *Cathari*, "the Pure." They had a hierarchy of their own, with rites and sacraments partly imitated, perhaps, from the Church, but more probably derived from those same sources of Imperial Rome from which the priesthood had borrowed so freely. They reprobated bloodshed and swearing and set up against the Catholic extreme unction a ceremony which pushed to extremes that fundamental repudiation of the flesh. It was called *Endura*, a religious suicide by starvation or a wet napkin spread over the face on the deathbed.

Jules Michelet (followed by H. C. Lea and Abbé E. Vacandard) judges that it would have been disastrous to civilization if the *Cathari* had conquered in the civil war of Languedoc. But was there any valid reason to anticipate such a victory? The *Endura* itself it not immeasurably more barbarous than some forms of asceticism which orthodoxy has admired; and there is no probability that these *Perfecti* would have destroyed throughout Europe the immemorial institution of marriage, and would have thus involved wholesale race-suicide, as even such a moderate churchman as Vacandard argues. Is it credible that, if St. Bernard had been consistent in leaving the decision to "persuasion, not arms" any more would have been done to depopulate the world than had been already done by a thousand years of monastic celibacy? Swearing, again, is often cited as a crucial point. The structure of medieval society, it is argued, was fundamentally feudal: its elaborate network of legal and customary obligations reposed upon the multiple oaths of fealty, taken publicly on the Gospels, at every turn. But would European culture actually have been wrecked by the obligation to find gradually some firmer basis?

Great churchmen of the Middle Ages complained constantly that this flood of oaths debased the moral currency. No doubt the heretical tenets implied social as well as religious revolution; but it is quite mistaken to represent the men as mere anarchists. Abbé Vacandard condemns severely those modern apologists who press this argument, in flat contradiction with the records. He writes: "As a matter of fact, the Inquisition did not condemn merely those heresies which caused social upheaval, but all heresies as such." In fact, he points out, men were often prosecuted after their death—even 20 or 30 years later. Why should Inquisitors take all this trouble with men whom God had already judged, and who could do no further harm to society? Because, as Vacandard points out, this "almost incredible frequency of prosecutions against the dead" went to fill the coffers of the Inquisition.

The Inquisitor Eymeric, one of our best original authorities, confesses with brutal frankness that the Inquisition of the day (1360) languishes because nearly all the wealthy heretics have been condemned, and this Holy Institution must live upon its scanty pickings from the poor. Thus Catharism and Waldensianism on the Continent, like Lollardy in England, were driven underground. Those three heresies by this time were hammered into some similarity by common sufferings of persecution.

The Waldensians, or Vaudois, were a sort of Bible-Christians founded about 1180 by Peter Waldo, a rich merchant of Lyons, who gave his money to the poor and embarked upon a missionary career founded upon the translation and popular exposition of Scripture in the native tongue. He began as peaceably as John Wesley, but was driven to separation from this totalitarian world which had no room for rival religious organizations. One of Macaulay's most often-quoted sayings is only superficially true—that Rome, unlike other churches, has succeeded in utilizing religious enthusiasm and keeping the mystic within her bosom. Darwin, when he lived in a country of fir-woods, wondered that the meadows were not full of self-sown firs. It was only by degrees that he realized that thousands of such seedlings were all the time around him, remorselessly cropped by the cattle or the mowers before they had grown recognizable. Microscopic observation of the Middle Ages shows us a similar process among the seedlings of religious nonconformity. The heretics were often, as St. Bernard describes them, obscure and unwarlike. They showed that astounding tenacity of memory which has often been observed in illiterate folk. More than one Inquisitor testifies to their enormous superiority in this field over the parish clergy. Sacconi writes in about 1250: "I have heard and seen a certain ignorant rustic who recited Job, word for word, and many who knew perfectly the whole New Testament." He contrasts this with the "negligence of Catholic teachers." These men, therefore, were most formidable antagonists in an age when books were so few and dear that a Bible cost more than the whole yearly income of an ordinary parish priest.

Bernard Gui (1300) warns Inquisitors that "it is not expedient to dispute concerning the Faith against such astute heretics in the presence of layfolk." St. Louis, in many ways a most noble character, warned his knights against disputing with an unbeliever; let him rather "thrust his sword into the man's belly, as far as it will go." In about 1230, a certain weaver at Toulouse would say publicly: "lords, hear me! I am no heretic, for I have a wife, and lie with her and beget children, and I eat flesh and lie and swear, and am a faithful Christian." In 1247, another Toulousan, Pierre Garcias, burst out: "If I could lay hold on that god who, out of a thousand men whom he had made, should save one and doom all the rest, I would tear and rend him tooth and nail as a traitor, and would count him as a false traitor and spit in his face."

When the civil war was thoroughly kindled there was little to choose between the combatants in frenzy of conviction or brutality of methods. The Catholics at one moment tore out their prisoners' eyes and cut off their noses, claiming just right of reprisals. When the Catharist city of Béziers was stormed (1209) by Simon de Montfort's Crusaders, Innocent's cardinal legate reported to the pope that "our men, sparing neither rank nor sex nor age, slew about 20,000 souls" and pillaged the whole city. The contemporary papal chronicle puts it more tersely: "almost all were slain." Innocent, without a word to hint that his Crusaders had done more than their strict duty, wrote now to congratulate them on the remission of past sins and the accession of worldly wealth which they will have earned through their obedience to the vicar of Christ.

It is sometimes urged that the procedure of the Inquisition is not unique: that each separate item can be paralleled from elsewhere. Even though this were true, it would not exonerate the inventors of this particular compound; gunpowder has its own peculiar character and peculiar effects even though sulphur, charcoal, and saltpetre, taken separately, behave very differently. But the excuse itself is fundamentally false. It is contradicted by the best of contemporary lawyers, Bernard Gui, whose *Inquisitor's Manual* has been published, in its most important section, by Messrs.

Champion of Paris at a popular price, with French translation. Bernard writes clearly that *Multa sunt specialia* in Inquisitorial procedure. He specifies a concrete instance: whereas other courts demanded a minimum of two witnesses against the suspect, the Inquisition often acted upon a single testimony. Its main characteristics were, briefly, as follows:

(1) The fundamental bias has already been described, the man was *defamatus,* and bore the burden of proving his innocence.

(2) His judges were purely ecclesiastical, and therefore prejudiced against him: the civil power strove vainly to secure even the right of consulting the documents.

(3) The procedure was secret.

(4) As a rule, the names of witnesses were also concealed; they might be partial or even infamous persons, yet the suspect had no chance of challenging them but at random.

(5) In fact, infamous persons were explicitly admitted to testify though in other courts their testimony was altogether refused.

(6) So, again, children were admitted to testify adversely, whereas neither the infamous person nor the child might speak in defence.

(7) Advocates were at first allowed, but if the person was proved guilty, the advocate had to share his punishment; this was so shamelessly exploited that, finally, even the pretense of advocates for the defense was abandoned.

(8) It was equally hopeless to rely upon favorable witnesses; for they were pretty sure to get into trouble as abettors of heresy.

(9) Torture might be inflicted not only on the suspect, but also upon any witnesses whom it was hoped to enlist for the prosecution.

(10) This had, in practice, no legal limits. It was indeed forbidden to *repeat* torture; but the man who had been racked on Monday might be racked again on Tuesday under the excuse of *continuation.*

(11) A very small nonconformity might be magnified into a deadly crime.

(12) The medieval Inquisitor pushed in where the pagan of ancient Rome had disdained to tread. When Trajan commissioned Pliny to persecute, he forbade the seeking-out of secret Christians. Yet the medieval heretic had no such immunity. Every man was bound in strict conscience to spy upon and denounce his neighbor.

(13) There were other rigors, of which the result is that an acquittal, pure and simple, is almost unheard of in these records. Very seldom was there less punishment than the yellow Crosses of Infamy, about a foot long, to be worn night and day upon every garment but the shirt, which held the victim up to the mockery of the multitude.

In Bernard Gui's *Register* (between 1249 and 1258), among 200 suspects, there is not a single acquittal. In his whole lifetime he convicted 930, of whom 42 were burned. Of the rest, 307 were condemned to prison; and all 930 were liable to total confiscation of their goods.

A word must be added concerning those two items, prison and confiscation. The former was frequently used as a most serviceable weapon in the war of nerves. "Confess, or you shall go to prison," was generally effective with men who knew very well what sort of dungeon this was. As to confiscation, it will be seen how far this went to supply the sinews of war.

One most important point must be noted because it is so frequently alleged by apologists. The Church, it is argued, explicitly repudiates the shedding of blood; she only condemned the heretic as a theological question undoubtedly within her competence. Then she handed on the condemned man to the civil power, "the Secular Arm." The latter, however, had no option but to burn him. Any magistrate who refused would himself be liable to be burned alive. So the hierarchy could preach *"Ecclesia abhorret a sanguine."* "Let us call it a legal fiction," writes Abbé Vacandard apologetically. Most people probably will give it a more invidious name.

Here then, was a lethal weapon, an invention as elaborate and as devastating in its own way, as gunpowder. It was inevitable that despotism should seize upon it as a ready tool. Even its spectacular sides, its cross of infamy and campaigns of blood and flame, were not so deeply operative as the leaden pressure, ubiquitous and unrelaxing of centuries of tyranny. History shows us this, in the rule of the Arian anti-Catholic invaders of Africa, and in the far milder, but still very regrettable, rule of Elizabeth in England and in Ireland.

From the year 1239 onwards, most Europeans lived under a terror which was not less harmful for being so often unconscious. England, it is true, with her greater political freedom than the Continent, suffered only twice from the Inquisition proper. In 1311, Philippe-le-Bel of France, with Pope Clement V as his uneasy partner, used it as a tool for disreputable political ends: the destruction and pillage of the Templars. The unscrupulous use of torture in France, produced a series of confessions which nobody believes now, and which, indeed, were often revoked by the victims themselves outside the torture-chamber. In England, no cogent evidence could be found, because the English courts permitted no torture. Therefore Clement approached Edward II with a bribe and a threat: Obey, and we give you plenary absolution for past sins; disobey, and you fall under excommunication. Edward yielded "out of reverence for the Holy See," and enough evidence was scraped together to justify the desired confiscation and pillage. During Mary's reign, again, the Inquisition was revived in England for a few months.

There are three other outstanding instances of the Inquisition used as a political weapon in the Middle Ages. In 1318, Pope John XXII let it loose upon the "Spiritual" Franciscans, so that his Inquisitors condemned and burned, as impenitent heretics, four men whose recorded offenses amounted only to this, that they clung obstinately to the primitive simplicity of Franciscan garb and manners, even in face of the pope and the Franciscan officialdom of that day. Again, in 1430, Joan of Arc was condemned for witchcraft (her real crime being her noble patriotism) by a judge who was a tool of the English conquerors. It was not until our own days that she was formally sainted by her own church. Once more, in 1498, the friar Savonarola was burned for his political and social opposition to the Medici family and the notorious Pope Alexander VI. He was put seven times to torture with slender results. "It would be easy," writes Abbé Vacandard, "to cite many instances of the same kind, especially in Spain."

The Inquisition in Spain.—Medieval Spain was almost equally divided between three religions —Christian, Moslem and Hebrew. Paradoxically, this led on the whole to tolerance, since none of the three saw any proximate chance of "liquidating" completely the other two. There were occasional resorts to formal Inquisitorial methods, and sometimes anti-Semitic explosions even on an extensive scale, and the Moslem population formed standing political difficulties; but these were mostly dealt with on the *solvitur ambulando* principle. Jews and Moslems arrived at some of the highest positions in State and even in Church; and on all hands the quiet infiltration was enormous. This very fact of Semitic ascendancy largely motivated the great anti-Semitic movement of the 15th century, in which many thousands of Moslems and Jews had no choice but between "conversion" and death, and where St. Vincent Ferrer, for instance, is recorded by his partisans to have baptized four thousand in a single day. Hence came a dizzy multiplication of "New Christians" (*conversos,* popularly labeled *Marranos,* swine) who dominated the laboring and professional classes of Spain. Pogroms became frequent; and here, as elsewhere at earlier dates, the Inquisition substituted some sort of legal regularity for mere lynch-law.

Queen Isabella of Castile, "The Catholic," obtained the formal foundation of the Inquisition from Pope Sixtus IV. It began operations in 1480; her husband, "Ferdinand the Catholic," joined her whole-heartedly; and gradually the institution struck root throughout the peninsula. Sixtus did indeed send another bull severely criticizing its methods; but his objections were ignored. The two sovereigns, from the first, used it as the foundation of their political despotism. Thenceforward, from century to century until 1834, it was the most characteristic of Spanish institutions.

Its methods were medieval, "writ large." Church and State were here in complete fundamental accord; kings and popes might quarrel over details, but those were the quarrels of lovers. An able Roman Catholic writes very truly: "No church could be more arrogantly national than the Spanish, fenced around as it was with exemptions, royal, episcopal, monastic. But none was ever more Catholic. It bred neither heresy nor schism." Confiscations, beyond even the medieval scale, ensured enormous revenues which supported both royal splendor and the Roman religion to an extent never surpassed in history. In the 16th century, when Spain gathered also immense revenues in bullion from the New World, she bade fair to dominate Europe. That was her Golden Age in literature and art, the age of Cervantes and Velasquez. But this was at the cost of a royal and aristocratic extravagence, of an unabashed financial corruption, and of a burden upon the working classes, which have seldom been equaled for so long and on so large a scale.

Inquisitorial statistics have often been handled in irresponsible fashion; in most cases of wide divergence it is safe to take the lower figures. At the first *Auto de Fé* (Seville, 1481), six persons (men and women) were burned. Within the next eight months, 292 more were burned, 98 imprisoned for life; many more were torn from their graves in order to justify confiscation of their property. Under Tomás de Torquemada (q.v.) the tempo rose considerably. He was appointed Grand Inquisitor in 1483, making this institution "the first act of United Spain." Under Philip II (1569) the principles of the Inquisition were transplanted to Mexico, where 879 trials took place in the next quarter of a century. Meanwhile, the revolt of the Low Countries, costing a murderous war before Belgium was brought to heel and Holland finally severed from Spain, must be put down mainly to the score of the Inquisition. In Portugal a little later (1651–1673) the records show 184 burned alive, 59 burned in effigy with confiscation, and 4,793 penanced. As many as 1,500 "penitents" were paraded on one single occasion.

Within those postulates of Spanish political thought, it was only logical to carry out persecutions or deportations of Jews and Moors, sometimes piecemeal or again on an enormous scale. The Jews were banished by law in 1492, from which time onwards the country was filled with Jewish *Marranos.* Those who remained constantly fed the *Autos de Fé,* while those who escaped enriched the commercial and cultural life of other countries: everywhere they founded respected communities, as in Amsterdam, Hamburg, London and New York. The Moriscos, on the other hand, finally added to their minor and continual political sufferings one of the most picturesque tragedies of all time, the mass-deportation of the whole Moorish population, insofar as such completeness was fully possible, between 1609 and 1615. The few who remained were strictly forbidden all use of their ancient language and customs. National life was thus impoverished by the loss of its most laborious factor. By a strange irony of history, the most recent victory of physical force in Spain was won by an orthodox general (Francisco Franco) commanding an enormous proportion of Moorish soldiers, and foreign mercenaries.

The 18th century showed gradual decay of the Inquisition, but only in proportion to the decay of the whole country, which is calculated to have lost 50 per cent of its population since the days of Ferdinand and Isabella. In 1808 Napoleon abolished it, and its resurrection lasted only until 1834. But there remained an incalculable debt for past errors and crimes. The Comte de Montalembert, a fervent Catholic, contrasted the racial virtues of Spain with her political and social decadence in 1800: "She has fallen from gulf to gulf, from despot to despot, from favorite to favorite."

Modern apologists avoid dealing with the reluctant confessions of many among the most eminent Roman Catholic historians. Cardinal Richelieu, a realistic statesman who shrank from few deeds that his policy demanded, described the expulsion of the Moriscos, in his *Memoirs,* as "the boldest and most barbarous counsel recorded in the history of all preceding ages." Montalembert wrote "I grant indeed that the Inquisition in Spain destroyed Protestantism in its germ; but I defy anyone to prove that it has not given it throughout Europe the support of public opinion and the sympathies of outraged humanity. It has created in both worlds inexhaustable nourishment for impiety, and for the hatred and discredit of Catholicism." Lord Acton, his contemporary and a far greater historian, was even more emphatic. "The Inquisition is peculiarly the weapon and peculiarly the work of the Popes . . . . No other institution, no doctrine, no ceremony is so distinctly the individual creation of the Papacy, except the Dispensing Power. . . . It was the negation not only of religious liberty, which is the mainspring of civil, but equally of civil liberty, because a government armed with the machinery of the Inquisition is necessarily absolute."

Bibliography.—Very valuable, as enabling readers to study the documentary evidence at first hand, are (1) Bernard Gui's *Manuale Inquisitorum* (Latin of important pages with French translation, Champion 1926–27) and (2) Msgr. J. M. Vidal's *Tribunal de l'Inquisition de Pamiers* (Toulouse 1906). The best handy volume is Abbé E. Vacandard's *L'Inquisition*, valuable for the views of a learned Roman Catholic priest, who acknowledges his obligations to Lea, but criticizes him sometimes freely (tr. New York 1908). Equally useful and more comprehensive is A. S. Turberville's *Medieval Heresy and the Inquisition* (London 1920). By far the most comprehensive and valuable (despite serious lapses and shortcomings) is H. C. Lea's *History of the Inquisition*, 8 vols. (New York 1922). For Spain see C. Roth's *Spanish Inquisition* (London 1927). See also G. G. Coulton's *Inquisition and Liberty* (London 1938).

GEORGE GORDON COULTON,
Author of "Five Centuries of Religion"; formerly Lecturer in Ecclesiastical History, Trinity College, Cambridge.

INQUISITIVE WOMEN (LE DONNE CURIOSE), an opera in three acts by Ermanno Wolf-Ferrari (libretto adapted by Luigi Sugana from a Goldoni comedy) first produced in Munich in 1903. The first dramatic work of the composer to secure more than local notice, this opera, or "musical comedy," as he terms it, quickly achieved world-wide success by reason of its vivacity and delicate charm. Of German and Italian parentage, Wolf-Ferrari is an eclectic. The artistic lineage of *Le Donne Curiose* is plainly traceable to Mozart, though both *Meistersinger* and *Falstaff* influences are apparent. The orchestra, effectively used, is relatively a small one and in some respects the treatment harks back to an earlier day, when leading motives were less known. The music is distinguished by lyric simplicity and rhythmical variety. The prevailing character is improvisational, well adapted to the slight tale of harmless intrigue which it accompanies. There are several easily recognized numbers—the trios in the first act, the quartet in the second, Rosaura's love soliloquy and the succeeding pages of almost Mozartean simplicity, the prelude to the last act, the barcarolle chorus and the final ensemble. There is no great emotional intensity, nor intellectual depth, but means and end are fitted in a thoroughly artistic and satisfying way.

LEWIS M. ISAACS.

INSANE, Institutional Care of the, in the United States. Previous to the 19th century there was, practically speaking, no such thing as care of the psychotic and no hospitals in which to care for them. The mentally ill were either permitted to roam at large, to subsist on begging and other charities, or indifferently confined with paupers in poorhouses or with criminals in prisons, or perhaps more frequently were cared for as best they could be by their people at home. This latter type of care was often not much better than the care that they received in prisons and in poorhouses because their folks were equally ignorant of how to minister to them.

Previous to the beginning of the 19th century there are recorded here and there laws addressed to the problem of the care of the psychotic. In 1676 a law of Massachusetts delegated the care of the person and the estate of the dependent psychotic to the selectmen. In 1798 a law was passed in the same State which provided for the commitment to the house of correction of lunatics who were "furiously mad." In 1811 the Massachusetts General Hospital was incorporated and the McLean Hospital established and subsequently opened in 1818. As early as 1650 in Rhode Island we find the Puritan, Roger Williams, making an urgent appeal on behalf of Mrs. Wilson, urging provision for her, whom he describes as a distracted woman. In 1725 a law was passed permitting inland towns to build houses of correction for vagrants and also for "mad persons." In 1742 the care of all the psychotic and imbeciles was given to the town council with power to appoint guardians for their estates. In 1828 the Dexter Hospital was opened and in 1847 the "Butler Asylum for the Insane." Similar records of legislation are found in a number of the other States, more particularly States along the Atlantic Coast. The earliest action in this country providing for the special care of the psychotic in specially constructed hospitals was taken by the "Religious Society of Friends" in 1709 and this action resulted in the foundation of the Pennsylvania Hospital in 1751. A portion of this hospital was set apart for the psychotic and the first patients were admitted in 1752. The first State hospital, however, for the exclusive care of the psychotic was established in Virginia and is now known as the Eastern State Hospital, at Williamsburg, Va. It was incorporated in 1768 under the name of the "Public Hospital for Persons of Insane and Disordered Minds" and its first patients were admitted in 1773. In 1806 an authorization to a hospital in the city of New York was granted to erect additions and provide suitable apartments for maniacs adapted to the various forms and degrees of psychosis. Other important dates in the early part of the 19th century were the opening of an institution for the care of the psychotic at Frankfort, Pa., by the Society of Friends in 1817, the founding of the Hartford Retreat, in Hartford, Conn., in 1824, the opening of the South Carolina State Hospital for the Insane in 1824, of the Eastern State Hospital at Lexington, Ky., in 1824, of the Western State Hospital at Staunton, Va., in 1828, of one of the buildings of the Blockley Almshouse for the dependent insane in Philadelphia from 1830 to 1834, the Maryland State Hospital for the Insane in 1832, and the New Hampshire State Hospital for the Insane at Concord in 1842.

From this period on the erection of State hospitals went rapidly forward in the different States of the Union. The first law for the creation of a State hospital in New York was passed in 1842. The Utica State Hospital was opened approximately in 1850. The creation of this hospital, as of many others, was largely the work of Dorothea Lynde Dix (1802–87) whose broad philanthropy extended over many States of the Union and in Europe as far as Istanbul. It was through her efforts that institutions were erected in Massachusetts, Pennsylvania, New Jersey, Rhode Island, North Carolina and the District of Columbia. Some 32 institutions in this country owe their existence, in whole or in part, according to her biographers, to her efforts.

These laws and the founding of these hospitals as above noted show the origin sporadically of those activities which were addressed toward the more humane and intelligent care of the psychotic. From the beginning of the 19th century on these activities became more numerous and the demands for better care gradually increased. For the most part, however, throughout the first half of the century and during a considerable period of the latter half, the psychotic were cared for in a desultory and unintelligent way, largely by local communities, more especially in the various county houses throughout the States. This county house care of the psychotic placed them on a social par with the paupers, and it not infrequently became a matter of pride to see how cheaply the county could care for these unfortunates. Not only was this true, but the mentally sick patients in the almshouses received practically no medical attention whatever, except as they might be visited occasionally by the physician who was employed to look after the almshouse patients and who almost always was a practitioner in a nearby town and only spent a brief period at intervals at the almshouse or came out on emergencies when requested. He practically never had any experience or any special knowledge of mental illnesses and did little more than look after the physical condition of his patients, generally in a very crude way. The quarters where the mental cases were kept were usually presided over by persons who had no idea of the nature of their problems, were ignorant, often cruel and unsympathetic, so that the lot of these poor people was indeed miserable. They were practically prisoners shut out from all intercourse with their fellows, confined in quarters that were often filthy, dark, unsanitary and unhygienic in every particular, dominated by ignorant and not infrequently cruel caretakers, cheaply fed and clothed, with no medical supervision worthy of the name, and without any effort being made in any direction to bring about an improvement or to effect a cure. The most important move toward the latter part of the century which was made for the better and more humane, more intelligent and scientific care of the mentally ill, was the movement inaugurated in many of the States for State care, namely, provision by the State of public hospitals for the psychotic, with the consequent removal from the almshouses of this class of patients and transferring them to the State hospitals.

This was the only solution of the neglect and inefficiency of the county care system. The most fundamental defect of the county care system was that the county was too small a political unit to undertake the problem. It had not enough money to properly equip an institution nor did it have a sufficiently broad vision to secure the services of persons competent to handle the problem. All these matters were changed in the State hospitals. The state hospital was well built, well equipped and for the most part well officered, and the improvement in the care of the psychotic as a result was very great.

In the first period of State hospital care the main effort was to get away from the abuses of the county system and was directed toward humane and philanthropic efforts. The dealing with the mentally ill patients as though they were sick and trying to effect a cure was as a matter of fact in the minds of the early hospital superintendents, but did not prevent them in many instances from making the mistake of creating enormous asylums for the so-called chronic psychotic and setting apart single institutions for the care and treatment of the acute cases, thus making out of the asylums places where all hope was lost for those who entered, and overcrowding and overworking the acute reception hospitals beyond their capacity. For many years, for example, the Utica State Hospital at Utica, N. Y., was reserved for the acute cases of the State, while other institutions, as they were built, were reserved for the chronic, incurable class. The next movement was to make out of all of the State institutions hospitals in the real sense of that word, places where the patients would be dealt with as actually ill and an effort made to cure them. The first efforts in this direction were crude, consisting largely in endeavors to treat the patients as patients were treated in general hospitals by keeping them in bed, making observations upon their general physical condition, taking their pulse, temperature, respirations, examining urine, the internal organs, etc., and treating the physical disease which might be found as a result of such examination. This movement did much toward getting better surroundings for the patients, it was contemporaneous with the establishment of training schools for nurses in the State institutions, and its general result was a vast improvement in the quality of care.

Throughout this latter period the hospitals had more or less actively been engaged in a study of the problems of mental disease with a view to discovering their scientific bearings. These researches led to the definite establishment in connection with well-organized State institutions of scientific departments, usually consisting of a laboratory for clinical pathology, and generally also a laboratory for research in pathology. In these laboratories the autopsy material was studied with a view to discovering the correlation between the mental symptoms of the patient and the changes that were found to have occurred in the brain.

Beginning with the latter portion of the 19th century the several States began to appreciate the great extent of the economic problem that was involved in the care and treatment of the psychotic in their large public hospitals, and there began to be a more or less consistently directed attitude of study of these problems together with a study of methods of administration and control which would look toward higher efficiency and greater economy. The result has been that in most of the States where there are several institutions for the care of the psychotic that these institutions are controlled by a central body, a lunacy commission or a board of control, usually appointed by the governor. Sometimes these boards of control have still larger powers and include all of the charitable institutions. The details differ in the different States, but central control is the thing aimed at. Along with this central control the scientific departments of the institutions increase in importance and in some instances, as in New York, Massachusetts, Illinois, there are central research departments for all of the hospitals.

The changes in the outlook for the care of the psychotic largely as a result of all this scientific work have been very great. Interest no longer centers in the autopsy room in attempts to correlate pathological findings and mental symptoms. The interest now is in the living patient and the scientific institutions have elaborated their departments of clinical pathology for the purpose of studying the processes that are going on in the living patient, while psychological investigations are becoming much more in vogue with the development of definite interests in psychotherapeutics.

The large housing problem which confronts the several States is still dealt with by the State hospitals, none of which are longer considered, however, as institutions for the chronic psychotic. All of the hospitals are equipped for taking care of all varieties of illness, mental and physical, acute and chronic. It is recognized, however, that in large centers of population there should be easy access to wards where mental illness could be intelligently handled. The result has been the creation of psychopathic wards or institutions in a number of cities: Albany, N. Y., Boston, Ann Arbor, Mich., Baltimore. These institutions care for the great stream of mental cases which come from large urban populations and which ordinarily would be distributed in other wards of the city hospital. For example, the alcoholic wards of Bellevue hospital are under the immediate charge of the psychiatrist in charge of the psychopathic pavilion. Thus are the problems of general medicine and psychiatry coming to be considered together and their respective specialists are coming to be of mutual assistance.

As mental disease has come to be considered more and more a matter of defective psychological adjustment and methods of psychotherapy have been more and more applied, the hospitals have reached out into the communities which they serve and through the intermediation of dispensaries and social workers have endeavored to extend aid to these communities and also endeavored to assist the discharged patients in rehabilitating themselves in the community. The State hospital, therefore, has come in the past hundred years from a condition in which it was merely a place to confine «mad» persons, to be a center for education in matters pertaining to mental illness and for the rehabilitation of failures and defects in adjustment for the community in which it is located.

As outlined, the problem of the care of the psychotic has been gradually evolving as it became progressively larger, first a matter for villages and townships, and for counties, and finally a matter for individual State hospitals, receiving patients from a certain number of counties, then a matter for the State as a whole, governing its several State hospitals by a central board. Beyond that there has never been any recognized statutory central control. The superintendents of all of the institutions for the care of the psychotic have been organized into a medical society which has now been in existence since 1844, originally known as the Association of Medical Superintendents of American Institutions for the Insane. Since 1893 it has been known as the American Medico-Psychological Association. This association has been the clearing-house to which was brought all institutional problems and has served most eminently in the work of the care of the psychotic in several States of the Union. This until recently has been the only agency which in any way correlated the work of the several institutions throughout the country. In 1909, however, there was organized the National Committee for Mental Hygiene under the stimulus and as a result of the unceasing efforts of Mr. Clifford W. Beers. Mr. Beers had himself had a serious attack of mental illness in the course of which he had been a patient in more than one institution. As a result of his experience he felt convinced of the need of an organization which was independent either of political influence or financial or other personal consideration which would help various hospitals to deal with their problems to better advantage. As always happens in large problems the individual elements of which are dispersed over a wide territory, many of the institutions and some of the States remained very backward in their care of the psychotic. There were no members in their hospitals of the central organization, The American Medico-Psychological Association. As some of the State institutions were as badly off as had been the county asylums, it became the function of the National Committee to endeavor to improve these bad spots throughout the country and in doing so it took an attitude of helpfulness rather than one of criticism and as a result almost always found that defects in methods were due to ignorance, many primitively conducted institutions really believing that they were giving the best possible service that medical science could suggest. Such institutions were quick to avail themselves of the help of the National Committee and a great deal of improvement throughout the country has resulted from its activities. This has been the work of the National Committee until the beginning of the European War, when it turned its attention practically entirely to war work. The great importance, however, which the conduct of this war of necessity attached to mental problems will result in great benefit to this particular department of medicine.

WILLIAM A. WHITE.

Revised by SMITH ELY JELLIFFE, *Consulting Neurologist.*

INSANE, Statistics of. Statistical data relating to the insane in the United States are found principally in federal census bulletins, reports of state departments charged with the supervision of the insane, reports of individual state hospitals, and special studies. In 1904, 1910, 1923, and 1933 the federal Census Bureau issued special statistical volumes relating to the insane and feeble-minded. Prior to 1904, the data concerning the insane were made a part of the general decennial census report. Beginning with 1850 and continuing to 1890, an attempt was made at each decennial census of the population to secure a complete enumeration of the insane by inserting a question relative to insanity in the general population schedule. The results down to 1880 were unsatisfactory, as it is generally believed that only a small portion of the people suffering from mental disorders was enumerated as insane. At the 10th census, 1880, the returns of the enumerators were supplemented by special reports from physicians. The latter reported about 17 per cent of the total number of insane enumerated in that year. In taking the census of 1890, no attempt was made to secure supplemental data from physicians. Consequently, the number of insane enumerated in that year did not show an increase commensurate with the growth of the population. In the census of 1900 and of 1910 the question relating to the insane was omitted from the general population schedule. In 1904 a census of the insane in institutions was taken by special enumerators appointed for such purpose. A similar census was taken in 1910 and 1923. Beginning with 1926 the Census Bureau has made an annual census of patients in hospitals for mental disease. These yearly enumerations have been much less elaborate than the comprehensive census of 1923. In 1933, however, the census included several items that had not been covered in previous annual censuses.

These various enumerations of mental patients, although in part incomplete, give a general view of the increase in mental disease in the United States since 1850. The following tabulation shows the total insane enumerated in the censuses prior to 1904, and the patients resident in mental hospitals enumerated in later censuses, together with the number per 100,000 of population in each census year.

Year of census	Total insane enumerated	
	Number	Per 100,000 population
1938*	444,949	343.0
1934*	389,500	308.8
1923*	267,617	245.0
1910*	187,791	204.2
1904*	150,151	183.6
1890	106,485	170.0
1880	91,959	183.3
1870†	37,432	97.1
1860†	24,042	76.5
1850†	15,610	67.3

* No enumeration of insane outside of institutions.
† Enumeration believed to have been seriously deficient.

The data given in the foregoing table show a steady increase of patients in institutions in the United States from 1850 to 1938. Explanations of the increase include the rise in the average age of the population, the disproportionate growth in urban population, the general upward trend in the use of hospitals, the longer life of patients which results in their accumulation in hospitals, and many other factors. All of these explanations have a degree of validity, but together they do not fully account for the large increase in the rate of mental disease. A closer study of the matter reveals the fact that the principal increases in mental disorders are found in the arteriosclerotic, alcoholic and dementia praecox groups. Arteriosclerosis is apparently increasing more rapidly than the population is aging. The rate of alcoholic mental disease is closely correlated with the rate of over-indulgence in alcoholic beverages. As the cause of dementia praecox is not fully known, its increase cannot be adequately explained.

Although there is a deplorable accumulation of mental patients in hospitals, counteracting influences are at work. These in time should reverse the present trend and ultimately reduce the patient population of mental hospitals.

Mental Patients in the Several States.—Owing to various factors, such as institutional provision for the insane, distribution of urban and rural population, the composition of the population with respect to age, nativity and race, marked differences in the ratios of the insane to the general population are found in the various states. The following table shows the insane in institutions in the United States by divisions and states in 1938 and 1923, together with the number per 100,000 of general population in each of the two years.

RESIDENT PATIENTS IN HOSPITALS FOR MENTAL DISEASE IN THE UNITED STATES BY DIVISIONS AND STATES, 1 JAN. 1938 AND 1 JAN. 1923

Divisions and States	Number		Rate per 100,000 of general population	
	1 Jan. 1938	1 Jan. 1923	1 Jan. 1938	1 Jan. 1923
United States	444,949	267,617	343.0	245.0
New England	40,605	26,876	470.1	352.7
Maine	2,614	1,864	303.6	240.6
New Hampshire	2,043	1,399	398.2	313.5
Vermont	1,803	1,277	468.3	362.3
Massachusetts	23,948	15,869	538.5	399.0
Rhode Island	2,619	1,630	384.6	262.8
Connecticut	7,578	4,837	433.0	333.8
Middle Atlantic	120,744	70,535	438.3	306.4
New York	70,605	40.986	543.9	382.6
New Jersey	16,665	8,864	382.0	267.4
Pennsylvania	33,474	20,685	328.1	230.0
East North Central	89,380	56,881	345.0	255.0
Ohio	20,646	13,163	306.4	218.8
Indiana	9,556	6,595	274.0	220.6
Illinois	31,471	19,061	398.7	284.4
Michigan	15,885	8,971	327.1	230.7
Wisconsin	11,822	9,091	403.8	335.6
West North Central	42,906	31,355	309.7	245.4
Minnesota	10,396	6,691	391.3	271.2
Iowa	8,553	6,902	334.5	281.7
Missouri	11,800	8,806	294.1	256.5
North Dakota	1,848	1,269	261.0	190.9
South Dakota	1,610	1,297	232.7	199.5
Nebraska	3,907	2,988	286.4	225.8
Kansas	4,792	3,402	256.8	190.1
South Atlantic	51,728	28,637	298.0	198.1
Delaware	1,117	518	426.3	226.9
Maryland	8,416	4,719	500.4	316.8
District of Columbia	5,574	3,931	873.7	898.4
Virginia	9,423	5,129	345.9	216.1
West Virginia	3,827	2,134	204.2	139.8
North Carolina	6,644	3,692	189.1	139.3
South Carolina	4,068	2,414	215.8	139.8
Georgia	8,445	4,150	272.7	139.7
Florida	4,214	1,950	250.2	190.4
East South Central	23,902	13,450	221.5	149.1
Kentucky	6,637	4,708	225.7	192.2
Tennessee	5,877	3,407	201.7	143.3
Alabama	6,783	2,718	233.0	113.1
Mississippi	4,605	2,617	227.5	146.2
West South Central	30,628	14,936	236.5	140.7
Arkansas	4,943	2,121	239.7	118.0
Louisiana	5,947	3,322	278.8	181.0
Oklahoma	6,898	2,895	269.7	136.3
Texas	12,840	6,598	207.3	135.7
Mountain	10,965	6,471	288.6	184.0
Montana	1,859	1,438	344.9	242.3
Idaho	903	609	182.1	132.6
Wyoming	993	426	422.6	205.9
Colorado	4,284	2,147	398.9	220.0
New Mexico	756	392	179.1	106.3
Arizona	843	554	204.6	150.7
Utah	1,008	700	193.8	149.3
Nevada	319	205	312.7	264.8
Pacific	34,091	18,476	383.8	312.1
Washington	6,769	3,815	407.0	270.2
Oregon	5,219	2,666	506.2	328.4
California	22,103	11,995	357.1	324.4

It is seen that the number and rate of mental patients in institutions increased in every state from 1923 to 1938. In the District of Columbia the number increased but the rate declined, due probably to the great influx of government employes in Washington. The states having the highest rates of patients under treatment in 1938 were: Massachusetts, 538.5; New York, 543.9; Oregon, 506.2; and Maryland, 500.4. The states having the lowest rates were: New Mexico, 179.1; Idaho, 182.1; North Carolina, 189.1; and Utah, 193.8. The states that have large cities and that early established hospitals for mental patients, as a rule, have the highest rates of patients under treatment.

Insane in Foreign Countries.—Available statistics of the insane in foreign countries are very unsatisfactory. The classifications of mental disorders in the various nationalities are dissimilar, and wide variations exist in the provision made for the care of the mentally afflicted. In some cases the insane are enumerated with the feeble-minded and epileptic, and the number of the separate classes is not given.

On account of neuroses arising from the stresses of army life, it is believed that mental disorders have greatly increased in the belligerent countries of Europe since 1914, but the conversion of hospitals for the insane into military hospitals and lack of funds for the construction of additional institutions have reduced the number of civil insane in institutions in some of these countries. Current statistics of the insane in the European countries are therefore misleading.

In an accompanying table are given data compiled from official reports relative to patients in hospitals for mental disease in various countries in the years specified. The marked variation in rates shown in the table is due in part to differences in hospital provision for the insane in the several countries, in part to actual differences in the prevalence of mental disease among racial groups, and in part to unlike classifications whereby certain countries include mental defectives and epileptics among the insane.

In the United States and several other countries, the number of resident patients has been lessened in recent years by the use of systems of parole and family care. These systems vary widely in their operation, but their common objective is to place in the community under supervision patients who are no longer in need of hospital care and treatment. If patients so placed improve or recover, they are discharged when it is deemed safe and practicable to do so. The accompanying table relates only to patients resident in hospitals. In most countries data relating to community cases are not available.

PATIENTS IN HOSPITALS FOR MENTAL DISEASE IN CERTAIN COUNTRIES WITH RATES PER 100,000 OF GENERAL POPULATION

Country	Year	Resident patients	Rate per 100,000 of population
Australia	1936	28,550	374.0
Austria	1935	13,605	202.7
Canada	1939	42,687	295.4
England and Wales	1939	123,903	310.1
Finland	1938	9,147	236.7
Germany	1936	139,198	206.8
Italy	1937	91,760	209.0
Japan	1935	83,365	120.4
New Zealand	1937	7,797	481.8
Norway	1937	5,946	204.6
Poland	1937	15,931	46.0
Scotland	1939	19,550	392.0
Sweden	1934	18,742	302.3
Switzerland	1935	14,790	360.7
United States	1938	444,949	343.0

Sex and Marital Condition of Mental Patients.—The rate of incidence of mental disease is higher among males than among females. The difference is due principally to the higher rate of syphilitic and alcoholic disorders and dementia praecox among males. Manic-depressive psychoses, however, are more prevalent among females.

Of the 332,517 patients resident in state hospitals for the insane in the United States on 1 Jan. 1934, 174,196 were males and 158,321, females. Of the 69,368 first admissions to such hospitals in 1933, 41,029 were males and 28,339, females. The rates of first admissions per 100,000 of general population of same sex were 66.0 and 46.7, respectively. Similar disparities are shown by previous census bulletins and also by official reports of other countries.

With respect to marital condition of mental patients the two sexes differ widely. The following table shows rates by marital condition computed from the census of first admissions taken in 1933.

FIRST ADMISSIONS TO STATE HOSPITALS BY MARITAL CONDITION AND SEX, 1933

Marital Condition	Number per 100,000 population of same sex and marital condition		Per cent distribution		Per cent distribution of population in 1930	
	Male	Female	Male	Female	Male	Female
Total	66.0	46.7	100.0	100.0	100.0	100.0
Single	48.1	25.1	39.0	25.8	34.1	26.4
Married	69.8	54.1	44.8	50.0	60.0	61.1
Widowed	205.5	112.0	10.1	18.7	4.6	11.1
Divorced	....	....	4.5	4.6	1.1	1.3
Unknown	....	....	1.6	.9	.2	.1

*15 years of age and upwards.

It is noted that the percentage of single persons among male patients is much higher than among female. Conversely, the females have the higher percentages of married and widowed. The percentage of the married among patients of both sexes is lower than that among the general population 15 years of age or over. Those forms of mental disease that occur in early life are clearly a deterrent to marriage.

Age of Mental Patients.—Mental disease is rare among children, and comparatively few cases occur in the second decade of life. Thereafter, the rate increases with advancing age and becomes very high among persons 65 years of age and upwards. The latest available data pertaining to rates of first admissions to state hospitals by age and sex are given in the following table:

FIRST ADMISSIONS TO STATE HOSPITALS BY AGE AND SEX, 1933

Age	Number		Number per 100,000 population of same age and sex	
	Male	Female	Male	Female
All ages	41,029	28,339	66.0	46.7
Under 15 years	285	199	1.6	1.1
15 to 19 years	1,709	1,255	29.7	21.7
20 to 24 years	3,376	2,296	63.3	41.5
25 to 29 years	3,529	2,665	72.6	53.6
30 to 34 years	3,937	2,898	86.3	63.6
35 to 39 years	4,057	3,011	86.7	66.5
40 to 44 years	4,011	2,850	97.0	74.0
45 to 49 years	3,879	2,674	105.6	79.3
50 to 54 years	3,340	2,205	106.7	77.5
55 to 59 years	2,723	1,707	112.2	76.9
60 to 64 years	2,490	1,584	128.3	87.5
65 to 69 years	2,165	1,346	152.7	99.5
70 to 74 years	2,010	1,312	202.7	136.9
75 to 79 years	1,552	998	283.4	178.6
80 to 84 years	846	622	336.9	219.4
85 and over	324	353	276.8	227.6
Unknown	796	364	....	....

Causes of Mental Disease.—Causes of mental diseases are multiple rather than single. Several factors may operate together to cause the onset of a psychosis. Alcohol has always been a prominent factor in the causation of mental disease; its influence which declined in the United States from 1917 to 1921, has since increased. Syphilis is the primary cause in all cases of general paresis and of psychoses with cerebral syphilis. Opium and its derivatives, cocaine and other habit-forming drugs, cause psychoses in comparatively few cases. Arteriosclerosis, by reducing the blood supply to important parts of the brain, renders this organ unable to perform its natural functions and thus causes various forms of mental disorder. Blows on the head cause insanity in a similar way by injuring brain tissues. Fevers and exhausting physical diseases often give rise to mental disease. Other causes are mental, such as fear, joy, anger, grief, or anxiety.

Abnormal mental make-up in either the temperamental or intellectual sphere is a predisposing cause of mental illness in many cases. The abnormal mind gives way to unusual stress which the normal mind is able to withstand. When stress is prolonged or of extraordinary severity, as in army life, even the most stable mind may give way.

The following table shows the relative prominence of the principal definite causes among males and females as reported by the New York State hospitals:

Causes of Mental Disorders Among First Admissions to the Civil New York State Hospitals for the Insane, 1939

Causes	Number of cases*			Per cent		
	Males	Females	Total	Males	Females	Total
Alcohol	1,018	212	1,230	14.7	3.5	9.4
Syphilis	881	328	1,209	12.7	5.3	9.3
Drugs	29	37	66	0.4	0.6	0.5
Abnormal make-up	3,906	3,793	7,699	56.4	61.8	58.9
Injury to head	165	31	196	2.4	0.5	1.5
Physical illness	622	1,094	1,716	9.0	17.8	13.1
Senility	737	992	1,729	10.6	16.2	13.2
Arteriosclerosis	1,584	1,332	2,916	22.9	21.7	22.3
Epilepsy	130	108	238	1.9	1.8	1.8
Death in family	57	187	244	0.8	3.0	1.9
Loss of employment or financial loss	284	289	573	4.1	4.7	4.4
Disappointment in love	85	247	332	1.2	4.0	2.5
Pregnancy	...	30	30	..	0.5	..
Childbirth	...	73	73	..	1.2	..
Other specified causes	222	389	711	3.2	6.3	5.4
Unascertained	596	510	1,106	8.6	8.3	8.5
Total first admissions	6,929	6,139	13,068	...	...	...

* As each case reported was enumerated, the number of causes exceeds the number of patients.

Classification of Mental Patients.—The first nation-wide census of the insane in the United States with reference to psychoses of mental diseases was taken in 1922. Difficulty was experienced by some institutions in making a complete classification of patients, notably by those that had not used the classification prior to the time of taking the census. Later censuses have been on a more uniform basis.

In the table given below a comparison is made between the results of the federal census of first admissions to mental hospitals in 1922 and in 1938. Notable increases are seen in the alcoholic, arteriosclerotic, and involutional groups. There is also a marked increase in the group «without psychosis» which consists of mental defectives, epileptics, drug addicts and alcoholics not insane, and psychopaths. The figures denote a growing tendency to use the mental hospitals for all types of psychiatric disorders.

The marked increase in first admissions to mental hospitals shown by this table indicates that mental disease has become a major health problem.

Mental Disorders of First Admissions to Hospitals for Mental Disease in the United States, 1938 and 1922

Mental Disorders	Year ended 31 Dec. 1938		Year ended 31 Dec. 1922	
	Number	Per cent	Number	Per cent
General paresis	7,816	7.1	6,294	8.8
With other syphilis of central nervous system	1,496	1.4	893	1.2
With epidemic encephalitis	332	0.3	643*	0.9
With other infectious diseases	456	0.4		
Alcoholic	4,913	4.5	2,693	3.8
Due to drugs or other exogenous poisons	628	0.6	615	0.9
Traumatic	621	0.6	229	0.3
With cerebral arteriosclerosis	11,977	10.9	3,438	4.8
With other disturbances of circulation	719	0.7	....	..
With convulsive disorders	1,942	1.8	1,813	2.5
Senile	8,566	7.8	6,845	9.5
Involutional	3,844	3.5	1,803	2.5
Due to other metabolic, etc. diseases	1,338	1.2	2,226	[illegible].1
Due to new growth	173	0.2	61	0.1
With organic changes of nervous system	895	0.8	97	0.1
Psychoneuroses	4,226	3.8	2,777	3.9
Manic-depressive	12,239	11.1	11,393	15.9
Dementia praecox	21,223	19.3	15,526	21.7
Paranoia and paranoid conditions	1,857	1.7	1,881	2.6
With psychopathic personality	1,206	1.1	914	1.3
With mental deficiency	3,054	2.8	1,899	2.6
Undiagnosed	3,824	3.5	4,194	5.9
Without psychosis	16,744	15.2	5,157	7.2
Unclassified	....	....	285	0.4
Total	110,089	100.0	71,676	100.0

* Not separately classified in 1922.

Movement for Uniform Statistics of Mental Disorders.—As previously pointed out, statistics of the insane until recent years dealt principally with the number enumerated in various states and countries without regard to the kinds of mental disease with which they were afflicted. In fact, the absence of a generally accepted classification prior to 1917 prevented the collection of national statistics of mental diseases. The first bureau of statistics for the study of mental diseases was established in 1908 by the New York State Commission in Lunacy (now the State Department of Mental Hygiene). The commission adopted a uniform classification of mental diseases for use in its 13 state hospitals, and required the medical officers of each hospital to submit to the commission's statistician a statistical card report concerning each case admitted, readmitted, discharged or deceased. From such cards yearly statistical reports have been prepared and published, and the cards have been filed according to identification number and psychosis. The department now has a file of uniform cards of about 250,000 first admissions—the largest collection of systematic data concerning mental diseases in the world. By combining the cards received from all the hospitals for a series of years, the bureau is able to make intensive studies of the separate mental diseases.

The success of New York's pioneer work led the American Medico-Psychological Association (now the American Psychiatric Association) to undertake a movement for uniform statistics of the insane throughout the United States. At the meeting of the association held in Niagara Falls in June 1913, a special committee was appointed to devise ways and means of securing uniform statistical reports from institutions for the insane. This committee, after prolonged conferences, submitted its final report to the association at the annual meeting held in New York in May 1917. The report recommended the adoption of a new classification of mental diseases and submitted outlines of 18 statistical tables for use in the annual reports of institutions for the insane. The committee stated that «the lack of uniformity in hospital reports at the present time makes it absolutely impossible to collect comparative statistics concerning mental diseases in different states and countries, and extremely difficult to secure comparative data relative to the movement of patients, administration and cost of maintenance and additions»; and that the «importance and need of such uniform data have been repeatedly emphasized by officers of the association, by statisticians of the United States Census Bureau, by editors of psychiatric journals and by administrative officers in various states.» «Such data,» the committee adds, «should serve as the basis for constructive work in raising the standard of care of the insane, as a guide for preventive effort, and as an aid in the progress of psychiatry.» The report of the committee was unanimously adopted, and a standing committee on statistics was appointed to secure the adoption of the new classification and statistical system by federal and state authorities. In February 1918, such standing committee affiliated with the National Committee for Mental Hygiene which had received a special gift for statistical work.

Through the co-operative work of the two organizations, a uniform system of statistics of mental diseases was put into operation in nearly all the state hospitals for the insane in the United States during the summer of 1918. The classification and statistical system has since been adopted in Canada and Peru and in part in Scotland.

The association's classification of mental disorders, which was revised at its annual meeting in 1934, consists of 22 groups of principal psychoses, some of which are subdivided into more or less distinct types. The classification is not regarded as final, but will be revised from time to time to keep pace with the progress of psychiatry.

At the second International Congress on Mental Hygiene, which was held in Paris in 1937, the matter of uniform statistics of mental disorders was thoroughly discussed and a resolution was passed providing for the appointment of an International Committee on Nomenclature and Statistics of Mental Disorders. See also Hospital, Psychopathic; Insane, Institutional Care of the, in the United States; Mental Diseases; Mental Patients, Family Care of.

Bibliography.—Census reports: Insane and Feeble-minded in Institutions, 1904 and 1910; Patients in Hospitals for Mental Disease, 1923, 1933 and 1938; Annual reports of New York State Department of Mental Hygiene, 1910–1940.

Horatio M. Pollock,
Director, Mental Hygiene Statistics, State of New York.

INSANE ASYLUMS, Cottage System or Village Plan. A form of construction for insane asylums and charitable institutions, in which large buildings are replaced by detached cottages. The cottages vary in size from those which will accommodate six to a dozen patients to larger ones which will accommodate 20 or more. They are usually constructed either in groups or along streets and avenues as a village. In the former, the several groups are given up to a particular industry as a farm group, where the patients are employed at farming, and others, as the garden, the brick yard, shop industries, etc., all of these being a part of one institution on a single large estate. In the village plan the institution is laid off in streets and avenues, and has the appearance of an ordinary village, each cottage having a flower garden in front, shade trees, etc. In either plan, there is conveniently located near the center of the plant an administration building, a hospital for the sick and those requiring special care, a bakery, a laundry and other utility buildings. The cottages may be constructed of wood or other material, and the cost of construction is small as compared with the old plan of asylum construction. It is, besides, more homelike, more convenient for administration and permits of indefinite expansion. Some of the best-known institutions constructed on this plan are Alt-Scherbitz near Leipzig; Gabersee near Munich, Germany; the Saint Lawrence State Hospital at Ogdensburg, N. Y., and the Craig Colony for Epileptics at Sonyea, N. Y. See also Mental Patients, Family Care of.

INSANITY. This is a purely legal term. Its use as a medical term should cease as it leads to interminable confusion and defeats the ends of justice. The confusion is very old, however, and will take time to eradicate. Insanity then simply represents certain legal situations which by reason of one or another disease, chiefly involving the brain, render the individual responsible or not responsible for a criminal act, an act of contract making or of making a will. If, according to the evidence adduced before a properly constituted legal tribunal, it is decided that the individual's acts in question were not responsible, or he did not have contract capacity, or he did not possess testamentary capacity, because of some disease, injury or defect of the brain, then the individual in question has thrust upon him a legal status—insane. It is necessary to insist upon the purely legal character of the situation—because the tests for responsibility for contract capacity, for testamentary capacity vary with every jurisdiction. Thus a man may be insane in New York and sane in New Jersey, or vice-versa. Thus it must come about that **the word insane—insanity, etc., must be con-**

fined purely to its legal usage — or better abolished entirely.

The confusion arose in the days of the Roman law, and law is such a conservative instrument it is hard to eradicate old conceptions. In Roman days all brain diseases were lumped into one. The Romans despised Greek subtleties, they said, just as most stupid people despise their superiors in intelligence. The Greeks had separated various brain diseases and gave them different names. They were really a scientific people. But the Romans had a passion for organization. They lumped all of these very diverse diseases and called them «*Insania.*» To them insania was *a* brain disease. What are really different brain diseases, they called «forms of insanity.» This is a false and nonsensical concept and leads to much mischief in our present law court practice. Thus in New York State the legal test for responsibility is whether the individual knows the nature and quality of an act and knows whether it is wrong. There are a number of very severe and chronic mental illnesses which totally destroy an individual's responsibility, but such individuals may still retain this purely intellectual test. New York State would electrocute such seriously sick individuals and commit an act of gross injustice. In New Jersey — another feature is added to this test — namely, the capacity to resist an impulse, and in other States other tests. The whole test business is largely a farce, and is founded on the totally erroneous idea in the minds of law givers that there is such a disease as «insanity» and that it has different «forms.» There is no such thing as a disease «insanity» — and there are no forms of it, just as there is no disease called «cough.» One may cough from dust, from gas, from tuberculosis, from bronchitis, from cancer of the larynx, to warn a friend or to hide a confusion. Certainly dust, gas, tuberculosis, bronchitis, cancer, warning and hiding are not *a* disease. So an individual may have a brain tumor, he may have a meningitis, a syphilis of the brain, tuberculosis of the brain, thyroid poisoning, a paranoia, a dementia precox or any of a hundred different and dissimilar diseases, and as a result of such a disease he may commit an antisocial act, which if resulting from the disease caused him not to know the nature and the quality of the act, not know it was wrong, or knowing these things even, may have believed himself commanded by God to do the deed, then, varying with the State's legal definition, he becomes legally insane. He acquires a purely legal status. He has not got any insanity. There is no such disease. He may have one of the diseases just enumerated, which causes him to acquire a legal status. See Psychiatry; Mental Diseases.

INSANITY, in the legal sense, such a degree of mental unsoundness as to call for the restraint of the person afflicted or to justify the authorities in depriving him of the management of his property and affairs. An insane person comes in contact with the law (1) when he suffers from such unsoundness of mind that it is necessary for his own or the public welfare that his liberty be restricted; (2) when he is incapable of managing himself or his affairs, or of directing their management; and (3) when a plea of insanity is entered on his behalf in answer to a criminal charge. Insanity in a legal sense includes only questions of life or property, competency and responsibility, and ability to transact the affairs of life. According to the law of the United States, the modern view is that whether a person is or is not insane is in every case a question of fact. The courts are quite liberal in attempting to sustain wills of persons who are not wholly insane. If a person has sufficient understanding to comprehend the nature of the testamentary act, knows the nature of his property and shows clearly that he could decide why he wanted his property to go to the beneficiaries named, his will is usually received and probated. An insane person is responsible for his torts. He is criminally responsible for his actions, unless from defective mental power or from mental disease he cannot understand the nature of his acts, or does not know that his act is wrong, or is unable to control his conduct — unless, in the last case, his want of control arises from his own fault. An insane person must sue or defend an action through his guardian *ad litem.* A person confined against his will as insane is entitled to a writ of *habeas corpus* and a judicial inquiry as to the legality of his detention.

INSCRIPTIONS. The term inscriptions comprises, in its widest sense, all words or word-signs engraved (or painted) on relatively durable materials such as natural cliffs, wrought stone, baked clay, metal or even wood. For reasons of practical convenience, however, certain sorts of inscriptions are grouped apart; for example, legends on coins and the lettering on painted vases. The etymological sense of inscription (Latin *inscriptio,* «in-scratching») is not to be taken so strictly as to exclude raised lettering. The rôle of inscriptions in modern times accords in general with the ancient use, but is much less extended. Then, copies of official and religious documents were frequently promulgated in the form of inscriptions, a usage that no longer survives, though commemorative and titular inscriptions are still plentifully employed. In general, inscriptions serve one of two purposes: (1) they constitute a record, and the material containing them is wrought for the express purpose of receiving the inscription (example, known from literature only, Moses' stones tables that held the decalogue); (2) the object on which the inscription is engraved fulfils a purpose of its own, while the lettering indicates the name, nature, purpose, maker or owner of the material object (commemorative column, mirror, ring, etc.). To these may be added another class, (3) the incidental inscription, a notice or entry upon an object not prepared to receive it.

Inscriptions furnish materials of value to students in many fields. To the historian — and we must understand history to be the life-record of the nation and its citizens — they supply evidence of great value, all the more valuable because nearly always contemporaneous with the facts recorded. The incidental as well as the formal record may bear testimony. An example of this sort has been found on the leg of a colossal statue at Abusimbel in Nubia, whereon Greek mercenaries who had ascended the Nile under the leadership of Psammetichus — more probably the second (594–589 B.C.) than the first (654–617) of that name — traced a brief notice of their expedition. The incidental inscription is particularly apt to furnish details valuable for social history. To the archæologist inscriptions of the second class furnish testimony of value for topography (witness the fragments of the marble *Forma Urbis,* an ancient inscribed plan of the chief buildings of Rome) and for the precise identification of statues and other works of art. The discovery of inscriptions is among the express tasks of the excavating archæologist, who thus supplies the raw material, so to speak, for the historian or philologian. To the philologian inscriptions yield the key to the history of writing and, if his interests lie in the comparative and historical study of words, give him a fuller knowledge of their form. To the philologian of literary interests, inscriptions yield a knowledge of historical fact or of vocabulary that may lead to a correct interpretation of a difficult literary passage. For example, the Greek historian, Thucydides, records (6.54) an altar inscription set up by Peisistratus (527–510 B.C.), which, he says, was still «in clear evidence,» but «in dim letters.» The identical inscription was found in 1877, with lettering perfectly distinct, and the literary interpretation of «dim» had to be revised and brought into accord with the facts. Meantime, the archæologists had learned that red or blue paint was employed to bring out more clearly the lettering of Greek inscriptions, and it was easy to infer that not the incision but the coloring of this inscription was dim in the time of Thucydides. Inscriptions previously known from literary works have for the philologian the added value of yielding testimony concerning the reliability of the manuscript tradition. Thus the best manuscript of Thucydides is of the 10th century A.D. and, as the last in a long chain of copies, must have been exposed to a great deal of corruption in transmission. The fact that a treaty recorded by the historian (5.47) corresponds almost exactly with the (fragmentary) inscription recording the alliance is reassuring for the MS. tradition. The *littérateur,* even, may be concerned with material furnished by inscriptions. One of the most considerable fragments of the poet Simonides, for example, has reached us in a copy on stone of an epitaph (epigram) in honor of the Megarians who fell in the Persian War. Some literatures have survived only as inscriptions.

It is safe to declare that inscriptions are as widely diffused as the art of writing. Even a primitive picture, if painted to convey a message, would constitute an inscription. Hieroglyphics (conventionalized picture writing) constitute the most primitive type of writing, and inscriptions of this sort, in the Maya language, are found in Yucatan. Though probably not earlier than the discovery of America, these represent, as regards writing, the same stage of culture as the hieroglyphics of Egypt (4700 B.C.). Chinese inscriptions — the Chinese being a highly conventionalized hieroglyphic script — of 1200 B.C. are also extant. The Mayan (and Aztec) system is still very imperfectly understood. Egyptian hieroglyphics were likewise long undeciphered, but in 1822 the Rosetta Stone (q.v.), a trilingual in Greek, demotic Egyptian, and hieroglyphics whereon the names Ptolemy and Cleopatra were of frequent occurrence, furnished a clue to the hieroglyphics which had been conventionalized, through a syllabary, to a pure phonetic system. —— This means, to invent an instance, that a picture (symbol) representing motion [= (to) go] comes to be used for the syllable *go* in a proper name like Goshen (this step was taken by Aztec hieroglyphics), or in a word like gopher: and that in the last stage the syllable sign *go* reduces to the letter *g.* —— The decipherment and interpretation of Egyptian inscription belongs to the science called Egyptology. See EGYPT.

The cuneiform script, invented by the Acadians of Chaldæa, found its way to the Semites of Babylonia and Assyria. This was a syllabary, developed from an earlier pictorial system, and such it remained in those countries, where not only small objects like seals and cylinders, but whole libraries of clay tablets (reaching back into the 4th millennium B.C.), have been found. These tablets contain genuine literary works as well as the documents and announcements commonly included under the term inscriptions. The University of Pennsylvania is in possession of some 35,000 cuneiform documents, a collection particularly rich in fourth and second millennium records, and outnumbered only by the British Museum and the Louvre collections. The Tell-el-Amarna Letters are historically among the most noteworthy cuneiform inscriptions. Found by an Egyptian peasant woman in 1887, the collection is now split up between the Berlin and British museums, though a part remains in Egypt. These tablets contain a correspondence between three kings of Egypt (15th century B.C.) and the rulers of Babylonia, Assyria, Armenia, the states of Asia Minor, Syria and Palestine. Of transcendent importance for the early political history of western Asia, this correspondence is also accounted to confirm the validity of the Hebrew Scriptures as an historical record. It is noteworthy for the history of culture that the petty chief of every town could command the services of a scribe able to write a letter in Assyrian — the common correspondence language, it would seem, of all those countries. The science of Semitic Cuneiform belongs to Assyriology (q.v.).

Fortunately the Assyrian syllabary, after being borrowed by the Medic Aryans, was converted into an alphabetic system. King Darius (521 B.C.) caused an Old Persian (Protomedic) inscription of 413 lines, averaging 6 feet each, with versions in Neo-babylonian and Neo-elamitic, to be inscribed on the Great Rock of Behistun, at a height of 400–500 feet. The same script had been observed on another short inscription found at Persepolis, which evidently contained proper names chiefly. As early as 1802 Grotefend allocated the names Darius, Xerxes and Hystaspes to certain script groups in these brief formulæ, and correctly isolated nine of the 13 symbols concerned. In course of time the entire Protomedic cuneiform alphabet was identified and subsequently the more complex Semitic syllabaries were worked out, resulting in the decipherment of the older cuneiform. In the Behistun inscription Darius, following precedents of Assyrian kings, summed up the history of his accession and reign. Copied in 1844 by Mr. H. C. Rawlinson, it has been carefully inspected again (1903) by the American scholar, Mr. A. V. W. Jackson.

Farther west, the Phœnicians, also Semitic, developed, perhaps from Egyptian hieroglyphics, a true alphabet, out of which sprang, on the one hand, the scripts used by the Hebrews, Arabs, Persians and Hindus, and on the other the Greek (and Roman) type. The most notable early inscription in alphabetic Semitic is the Moabite Stone (q.v.) (9th century B.C.), which recounts the victory of Mesha, king of Moab, over Israel. The language used differs but slightly from that of the Hebrew Scriptures, of the historical validity of which the Moabite Stone, like the Tell-el-Amarna Letters, is held to be in general confirmatory. [For facsimile, transcript and translation consult Hastings' 'Dictionary of the Bible' (III, p. 405 seq.)]. Phœnician-Greek bilinguals from Cyprus, belonging to the 4th century B.C., are extant; also Phœnician-Cypriote, which furnished the key to the Cypriote syllabary. Punic inscriptions proper are chiefly of the dedicatory sort, and relatively late, all after the Greek period. Aramaic dockets on Assyrian contract tablets (8th century B.C.) form another instance of early alphabetic Semitic.

India also has its inscriptions. The oldest (250 B.C.) and most interesting are the religious edicts of King Piyadassi, known as the Asoka Edicts, which are engraved on rocks and pillars. They inculcate the religion and morals adopted by this king after his conversion to Buddhism. These inscriptions, in two unknown alphabets (Karosthī and Brahmī), were deciphered chiefly by James Prinsep, who, in the winter of 1837–38, single-handed, unraveled the Brahmī script. He guessed that in certain brief Brahmī inscriptions, plainly of a votive character, a frequently recurring final group of letters must stand for the notion «gift» and be equivalent, if the language was Sanskritic, to *dānam*. He further surmised that the consonant preceding *dānam* must be the genitive (possessive) sign — *s*. He thus isolated the three consonants *s, d, n,* and, with this start, soon identified the entire alphabet.

Greek and Roman inscriptions have been more studied and are accordingly more systematized for study than any others. The ancient Greeks were themselves conscious of the importance of inscriptions. Herodotus used them as sources, and Thucydides and Xenophon quoted them. Decrees are sparingly mentioned by Isocrates, but freely quoted by Demosthenes, who probably made use of the papyrus originals from the department of archives, not all decrees being promulgated on stone. Euripides alludes to the custom of inscribing formal compacts on tripods and dedicating them in temples. Greek antiquaries and scholars even made collections of inscriptions and Polemon (300 B.C.), who was neither the first nor the last of these collectors, owing to his zeal as an inscription hunter, got the nickname of *stèlokopas,* «tablet-picker.» Roman writers also — Cicero, Livy, Pliny the Elder, Suetonius — occasionally mentioned inscriptions of historical interest. Varro, the antiquary, and the lexicographer, Verrius Flaccus, commented on the diction of inscriptions; while Polybius the Greek historian of Rome, actually cited inscriptions, making a fuller use of them than Livy. But no interest in collecting inscriptions, comparable to the Greek interest, ever developed among the Romans. From the Revival of Learning on, scholars were not lacking to show an interest in classical inscriptions, but the modern impulse may be said to have had its point of departure in the first quarter of the 19th century when the Prussian Academy, under the promptings of August Boeckh, inaugurated the great collection known as the 'Corpus Inscriptionum Græcarum' (4 vols., 1825–56), which contained nearly 10,000 numbers. But fresh inscriptions are ever coming to light — *dies diem docet* — and in 1891 the number was estimated at 50,000. There has been a steady increase ever since. Excavations are now pursued in Greece and Grecian countries with a diligence and at an outlay never before known.

Bibliography.—The general reader may consult to advantage Roberts, E. S., *Introduction to Greek Epigraphy* (London 1887); Dittenberger, W., *Sylloge Inscriptionum Graecarum* (4 vols. London 1924); Scheil, V., *Ancient Persian Inscriptions of the Achaemenides Founded Sousa* (London 1927); Boyer, A. M. and others, *Kharosthī Inscriptions Discovered by Sir Aurel Stein In Chinese Turkestan* (London 1930); Rushforth, G. M., *Latin Historical Inscriptions Illustrating the History of the Early Empires,* 2nd edition (London 1930); Kent, R. G., *Recently Published Old Persian Inscriptions* (Phila. 1931); Gelb, I. J., *Hittite Hieroglyphs* (Chicago 1942); Hayes, W., *C. Ostroka and Name Stones from the Tomb of Sen-Mut (no. 71) at Thebes* (New York 1942).

EDWIN WHITFIELD FAY,
Late Professor of Latin, University of Texas.

INSECT POWDER. See INSECTICIDE.

INSECTA. See INSECTS.

INSECTICIDE, ĭn-sek'tĭ-sīd, defined by the Congress of the United States (36 Stat. 331) as "any substance or mixture of substances intended to be used for preventing, destroying, repelling, or mitigating any insects which may infest vegetation, man or other animals, or households, or be present in any environment whatsoever."

World War II enormously stimulated research to find synthetic substitutes for pyrethrum, rotenone, and nicotine, supplies of which fell far short of demand. The best known of these synthetics is DDT (dichloro-diphenyl-trichloroethane). Developed in Switzerland in 1939 and brought to the United States in 1942, it was used by both allied and axis military forces to combat lice (carrier of typhus), mosquitoes (carrier of malaria), flies, and bedbugs. Of the present production of more than 3,000,000 pounds per month, the greater part goes into the preparation of agricultural dusts and solutions for combating the codling moth, Japanese beetle, pink bollworm, gypsy moth, white-fringed beetle, potato insects, and many other pests. Benzene hexachloride, $C_6H_6Cl_6$, called 666 by the British, exists as several isomers, of which the gamma isomer is by far the most toxic. Known in England as Gammexane, the gamma isomer is now manufactured in the United States. It is more toxic than DDT to the housefly and is effective against several insects resistant to DDT, for example, the boll weevil.

The methoxy analog of DDT, 1-trichloro-2,

2-bis (p-methoxyphenyl) ethane, and 1,1-dichloro-2,2-bis (*p*-chlorophenyl) ethane, called DDD or TDE, both of which are less toxic than DDT to mammals, are being manufactured on a considerable scale. A nonchlorinated product, hexaethyl tetraphosphate, introduced in Germany as a substitute for nicotine has given good results in small field trials against aphids, mites, and caterpillars and is now produced in the United States. The insect repellent adopted by the United States Army and referred to as 6-2-2 (dimethyl phthalate, Indalone, and 2-ethyl-1,3-Hexanediol) is now released for civilian use. The United States Navy's newest repellent NMRI-448 (70 per cent 2-phenylcyclohexanol and 30 per cent 2-cyclohexylcyclohexanol, by volume) is also being offered for sale.

The principal insecticides and the consumption of each in 1944 are shown in Table 1. The retail value of all insecticides sold in the United States is not less than $100,000,000 annually.

ESTIMATED CONSUMPTION OF THE PRINCIPAL INSECTICIDES AND FUNGICIDES IN THE UNITED STATES DURING 1944

Item	Quantity (Pounds)
Arsenicals:	
Lead arsenate	85,595,000
Calcium arsenate	36,059,000
Paris green	1,875,000
Fluorine compounds:	
Cryolite	15,500,000
Sodium fluoride	4,000,000
Sodium fluosilicate	3,000,000
Fumigants:	
Calcium cyanide	1,500,000
Carbon disulphide	5,000,000
Carbon tetrachloride	6,000,000
Chloropicrin	750,000
D-D mixture (1,2-dichloropropane and 1,3-dichloropropylene)	400,000
Dichloroethyl ether	500,000
Ethylene dichloride	6,000,000
Hydrocyanic acid (liquid)	3,000,000
Methyl bromide	530,000
Naphthalene	25,350,000
Paradichlorobenzene	11,500,000
Sodium cyanide	500,000
Fungicides:	
Copper chemicals (basis $CuSO_4.5H_2O$)	117,000,000
Sulphur	200,000,000
Plant insecticides:	
Pyrethrum (1945 figure)	12,597,000
Nicotine (100 per cent basis)	1,197,000
Rotenone plants (derris, cube, timbo, 5 per cent basis)	3,500,000
Petroleum oils	250,000,000
Phenothiazine	3,500,000

Of the inorganic insecticides the most important are the arsenicals. Acid lead arsenate, made by combining litharge and arsenic acid, is the principal material relied upon by apple growers to combat the codling moth, which otherwise might spoil the annual crop of 100 million bushels of apples. Lead arsenate is also used on a large scale for the control of the gypsy and brown tail moths on elm and other shade trees in New England, for combating the Japanese beetle, and for many other purposes. Calcium arsenate is used largely in dusting cotton plants for the control of the boll weevil. Sodium arsenite is the most widely used poison in grasshopper baits. It is also used in large quantities as a weed killer and against the Mormon cricket. White arsenic is also used in grasshopper baits. Paris green is used to a considerable extent by home gardeners and also by commercial growers of potatoes. Paris green is sometimes mixed with calcium arsenate to increase its toxicity to the cotton leaf worm, and mixed with sulphur it is effective against some of the hemipterous insects that infest cotton. This is a striking example of control of sucking insects by a poison formerly regarded as useful only against chewing insects. Magnesium arsenate was at one time used against the Mexican bean beetle, but it has now been largely replaced by derris or cube. Manganese arsenate, a brown powder, was brought out for use on tobacco and was also extensively tried for the control of the codling moth but is now little used. Antimony, an element closely related to arsenic, is used in the form of tartar emetic dissolved in sweetened water for combating certain species of thrips. Certain compounds of fluorine find extensive use as insecticides. Sodium fluoride is an excellent roach powder and is also effective against lice on chickens. Sodium fluosilicate may be used in place of arsenic in poison baits for grasshoppers and the European earwig, and it is also effective against roaches. The more soluble fluosilicates, such as those of zinc, magnesium, and ammonium, are used in aqueous solution to moth-proof woolen goods, as are also the fluosilicates of ethylenediamine and certain other organic bases. Cryolite (sodium fluoaluminate) has proved effective for the control of codling moth larvae in the Pacific Northwest, and large quantities are consumed for this purpose. It has also been applied to tobacco and other crops for the control of chewing insects. Yellow phosphorus, in the form of a paste containing 1 or 2 per cent of this element, is very effective against rodents and the American roach. Mercuric chloride, although dangerous to man, has been used in ant poisons and for destroying thrips on gladiolus bulbs and for the cabbage maggot and angle worms. Mercurous chloride is also useful for the control of the cabbage maggot. Copper in the form of the basic sulphate present in bordeaux mixture has some repellent value against flea beetles and is a specific for leafhoppers on potatoes and beans, but its principal use is as a fungicide on potatoes and apples. Elemental sulphur is a valuable insecticide and fungicide. Large quantities are used in the form of a fine dust to which a small amount of calcium phosphate, magnesium carbonate, or other conditioner is usually added to prevent caking and insure free flowing through a dusting machine. These dusts are applied to combat the citrus thrips in California, fleahoppers on cotton, and the potato leafhopper on beans, as well as spider mites. Powdered sulphur is also mixed with derris, pyrethrum, Paris green, and other materials for use against many species of insects. Wettable sulphurs, prepared by grinding sulphur with a gum and sodium silicate or with certain wetting agents, are similarly used as sprays. Lime-sulphur solution is used against scale insects on fruit trees and the potato psyllid, and also as a fungicide. The consumption of this material for the control of scale insects has declined, being replaced in part by oil emulsions.

One of the most striking developments in the last 10 years has been the great increase in the use of organic insecticides. Those of natural origin include tobacco, pyrethrum, derris, cube, quassia, and hellebore. The insecticidal principle in tobacco is nicotine, and about 1 million pounds of this alkaloid, largely as an aqueous solution of the sulphate, are consumed annually in the United States. When mixed with soap this solution is very effective against many sucking insects, particularly aphids. When vaporized by dropping on a steam pipe or other heated surface or by burning tobacco or absorbent paper impregnated with tobacco extract, nicotine is highly effective against many greenhouse insects. Vaporized nicotine has also been successfully used against the pea aphid, a long canopy being dragged over the pea vines to confine the vapor. Nicotine dusts, usually with hydrated lime as a carrier, also find wide application. When nicotine sulphate is added to an aqueous suspension of bentonite (a kind of zeolite), nicotine bentonite is formed. This compound appears to be the most successful substitute for lead arsenate yet developed for codling moth control. Pyrethrum flowers, a species of chrysanthemum, are grown largely in Japan, although Kenya Colony, Africa, produces a superior grade and is rapidly forging to the front in production. As many as 20 million pounds of pyrethrum have been imported in a single year. Pyrethrum powder mixed with talc or other diluent is used against cabbage caterpillars and many other agricultural insects. Its principal use, however, is in the manufacture of sprays for combating household insects. These sprays are usually made by incorporating the active principles, called pyrethrins I and II, from about one pound of flowers in one gallon of a highly refined kerosine. Derris and cube roots are imported from the East Indies and South America, respectively. These roots contain rotenone as well as other active principles. The high potency of rotenone against insects is realized from the fact that rotenone is 15 times as toxic as nicotine to the bean aphid and 30 times as toxic as lead arsenate when fed to silkworms. More than 3 million pounds of these roots are now imported annually for the preparation of dusts and extracts. The dusts, made by mixing the pulverized roots with clay or talc, are used to combat cabbage caterpillars, the Mexican bean beetle, the pea aphid, the pea weevil, and some other insects. The powdered roots may also be suspended in water and used as sprays. The extracts are often mixed with pyrethrum extracts or certain synthetics for incorporation in household fly sprays. An American plant, the devil's shoestring, also contains rotenone in its roots, and it may be possible to produce this valuable insecticide in this country. Hellebore is used to a limited extent as a mild stomach poison, particularly against currant worms. The use of quassia as an insecticide is limited largely to the control of aphids on hops. A large number of plants yield essential oils, and many of these, such as the oil of citronella, are mosquito repellents. Geraniol, a constituent of Java citronella oil, is used to lure Japanese beetles to traps. Pine tar oil, produced by the destructive distillation of longleaf pine, is a valuable repellent to protect animals against the screwworm fly. Of all organic compounds, the hydrocarbons found in various petroleums are used on the largest scale. For application on growing plants they must be carefully refined to remove the greater portion of the unsaturated compounds. These oils, emulsified in water with soap or other emulsifying agent, have to a considerable extent replaced lime-sulphur solution for the control of scale insects on fruit trees. The lower boiling fraction, such as kerosine, is used as a vehicle for extracts of pyrethrum or derris or various synthetics to make household fly sprays.

Many materials are used as fumigants. The oldest is sulphur dioxide, which is highly effective against bedbugs and other household insects, but is now seldom used because of its corrosive and bleaching action. Carbon disulphide has been extensively used to kill weevils in grain, but on account of the fire and explosion hazard less dangerous materials have been put on the market. Among these are chloropicrin, ethylene dichloride, propylene dichloride, methyl bromide, and a mixture of ethylene oxide and carbon dioxide. These materials are relatively free from fire hazard and have come into large-scale use for the fumigation of all sorts of stored products. The ethylene oxide-carbon dioxide mixture is used in the National Archives Building in Washington, D. C., to destroy insects attacking books and manuscripts. It is also widely used to kill insect life in packaged cereals, dried fruits, nuts, and tobacco, and to destroy molds in spices. Hydrocyanic acid is extensively employed for the fumigation of all sorts of buildings and ships, as well as of citrus trees in California. The last operation is performed under tents at night to lessen the injurious action of the cyanide upon the trees. Formerly prepared by adding potassium cyanide to dilute sulphuric acid, hydrocyanic acid is now manufactured and marketed on a large scale as a liquid in cylinders. Sodium cyanide has replaced potassium cyanide where the old pot method of evolution is still used. Other ways of applying hydrocyanic acid are the scattering of calcium cyanide, which on contact with moist air readily yields hydrocyanic acid gas, and the distribution of disks of absorbent diatomaceous earth impregnated with the acid.

Other organic insecticidal materials include soaps, which are effective against aphids but are more commonly used with other more potent materials such as nicotine, and also to emulsify oils in water. The neutral oils from coal tar have a limited use as dormant sprays, but are too injurious to plant life to be applied during the growing season. Naphthalene is used in the manufacture of moth balls and is also valuable as a soil fumigant against wireworms. Paradichlorobenzene is used to combat clothes moths and the peach borer. Coal-tar creosote is the principal wood preservative for impregnating telephone poles, fence posts, and railroad ties and has had a large use in constructing chinch bug barriers and for proofing timbers against termites. Sticky fly papers are made from castor oil and rosin, and the latter is also used in making soaps. Rosin residue, a tacky material remaining after the distillation of rosin, is a valuable adhesive for use with derris powder. Beta-naphthol is used in corrugated-paper bands which are placed around the trunks of apple trees to trap and poison codling moth larvae; metaldehyde has shown surprising efficacy in the control of slugs, and diphenylamine is recommended for application to wounds on domestic animals to protect them against screwworms (blowfly larvae). Of the newer synthetic materials that have appeared on the market in ever-increasing number in the last decade, some of the most widely used are butyl carbitol thiocyanate, an ingredient of fly sprays; tetramethylthiuram disulphide, a repellent for the Japanese beetle; various derivatives of cyclohexylamine, effective as contact insecticides; 4, 6-dinitro-ortho-cyclohexylphenol, which has been found especially toxic to the red spider in California citrus groves; and phenothiazine and xanthone, which in preliminary tests have shown considerable promise for the control of codling moth larvae.

Recent useful information on insecticides, as well as on the more than 6,000 species of injurious insects against which insecticides are employed, will be found in the publications of the Bureau of Entomology and Plant Quarantine of the United States Department of Agriculture. Various state agricultural experiment stations also issue information on this subject. See also under Agricultural Chemistry; Fungicide.

Bibliography.—Martin, Hubert, 'The Scientific Principles of Plant Protection, with Special Reference to Chemical Control' (2nd ed., Edward Arnold & Co., London 1936); Metcalf, C. L. and Flint, W. P., 'Destructive and Useful Insects, Their Habits and Control' (2nd ed., McGraw-Hill, New York and London 1939); Shepard, Harold H., 'The Chemistry and Toxicology of Insecticides' (Burgess Publishing Co., 426 So. Sixth St., Minneapolis 1939).

R. C. Roark,
In Charge, Insecticide Investigations, Bureau of Entomology and Plant Quarantine, U. S. Department of Agriculture.

INSECTIVORA, an order of mammals, all of small size, usually five-toed, more or less plantigrade, and as a rule possessing clavicles. "The snout is generally long, and is often prolonged into a small proboscis. There is a tendency for the teeth to be of a generalized type and their number is often the typical mammalian 44. Moreover, trituberculate teeth, which are certainly of an ancient form, are common." These teeth are adapted to feed on worms and insects alone. Many other evidences go to show that the type is a very old one, and Beddard thinks it may have survived because of the small size, imitative adaptiveness and nocturnal habits. Woodward speaks of the group as probably the little-altered survivors of some of the most primitive placental mammals, agreeing with the *Credonta* in their low type of brain. Most of the families may be traced back to the upper Eocene. The order falls into two divisions, (1) True Insectivores, including the hedgehogs (*Erinaceidæ*), squirrel-shrews (*Tupaiidæ*), tanrecs (*Centetidæ*), otter-shrews (*Potamagalidæ*), hutias (*Solenodontidæ*), golden moles (*Chrysochloridæ*), elephant-shrews (*Macroscelidæ*), aquatic moles (*Talpidæ*), shrews (*Soricidæ*); and (2) Dermaptera, embracing only the colugos (*Galeopithecidæ*). See Hedgehog; Mole, etc.

INSECTIVOROUS PLANTS, a collective name for plants that entrap insects and other small animals, feeding on the captures by a process of true digestion, or absorbing the results of decomposition. The best known is the Venus' fly-trap (*Dionæa muscipula*) of the order Droseraceæ. It is a native of the peat bogs of the Carolinas. The halves of the leat blade are movable on the mid-rib, and furnished on each margin with teeth. On each half of the blade are three sensitive hairs, and the whole surface is thickly set with digestive glands. Immediately an insect touches one of these hairs the blades close, the teeth interlock, the glands exude their digestive juice on the insect, and the products are absorbed. In the common sundew (*Drosera rotundifolia*) the same result is obtained by means of stalked glands, which also function as tentacles, bending over to secure the prey; and in the butterwort (*Pinguicula vulgaris*) the margins of the leaf are the agents of capture, while the digestive juice is excreted by stalked and sessile glands on the leaf blade. *Aldrovandia vesiculosa,* an aquatic plant of southern and central Europe, has leaves which function like those of Venus' fly-trap. Drosophyllum lusitanicum, a native of Portugal and northwestern Africa, has stalked glands as well as sessile, but they do not bend over to confine prey. Their viscid secretion acts as a digestive ferment as well as a means of capture. Bladder-wort (*Utricularia*) is a floating plant common in lakes and pools. The traps or bladders, found on the submerged branches, are modified leaf organs, and present a general resemblance to the commonest prey water-fleas. The trap is entered by a door, which opens inward, but not outward, so that escape is impossible. The products of decomposition are absorbed by the cross-shaped cells lining the inner surface of the bladder. In the pitcher plants compound leaves are modified into pitcher-like receptacles, sometimes with a lid, as in the common *Sarracenia purpurea* and the southern *S. flava,* both growing in bogs. The attractions for insects are bright colors, and glands secreting nectar. Beneath the sweet bait is a slippery surface, affording insecure foothold, and insects pitching thereon fall into the secretion at the bottom. In the Old World genera Nepenthes and Cephalotus there appears to be a true digestive process; in the group of which the American genus Sarracenia is the only type, the products of decomposition are absorbed, and in the genus Dischidia, from India and Australia, pitchers store water for use by the plant. Consult Darwin, 'Insectivorous Plants.' See Carnivorous Plants.

INSECTS (Lat. Insecta), a class of the phylum Arthropoda (Gr. *arthros,* joint + *pous,* foot), or animals in which the feet are jointed, and all but the most primitive and a relatively small number of specialized forms are capable of flight. They are also commonly known among students of zoology as Hexapoda because all insects have six legs in the adult stage; the few that do not have this number have vestiges of them. In the four-footed butterflies, the first pair of legs is very greatly reduced in size, while in the legless mayflies, all the legs are reduced but none are functional. The closest living relatives of the insects are the Arachnida, or spiders and their relatives, which have four pairs of legs; the Crustacea represented by the crabs, shrimps, and related forms, which normally have five pairs of legs; and the more primitive forms, the Chilopoda (centipedes), with one pair of legs on each of the body segments, and the Diplopoda (millepedes), with two pairs of legs on each body segment.

The insects are the most numerous of all the animals. It is estimated that more than 700,000 different kinds have already been described, and

INSECTS

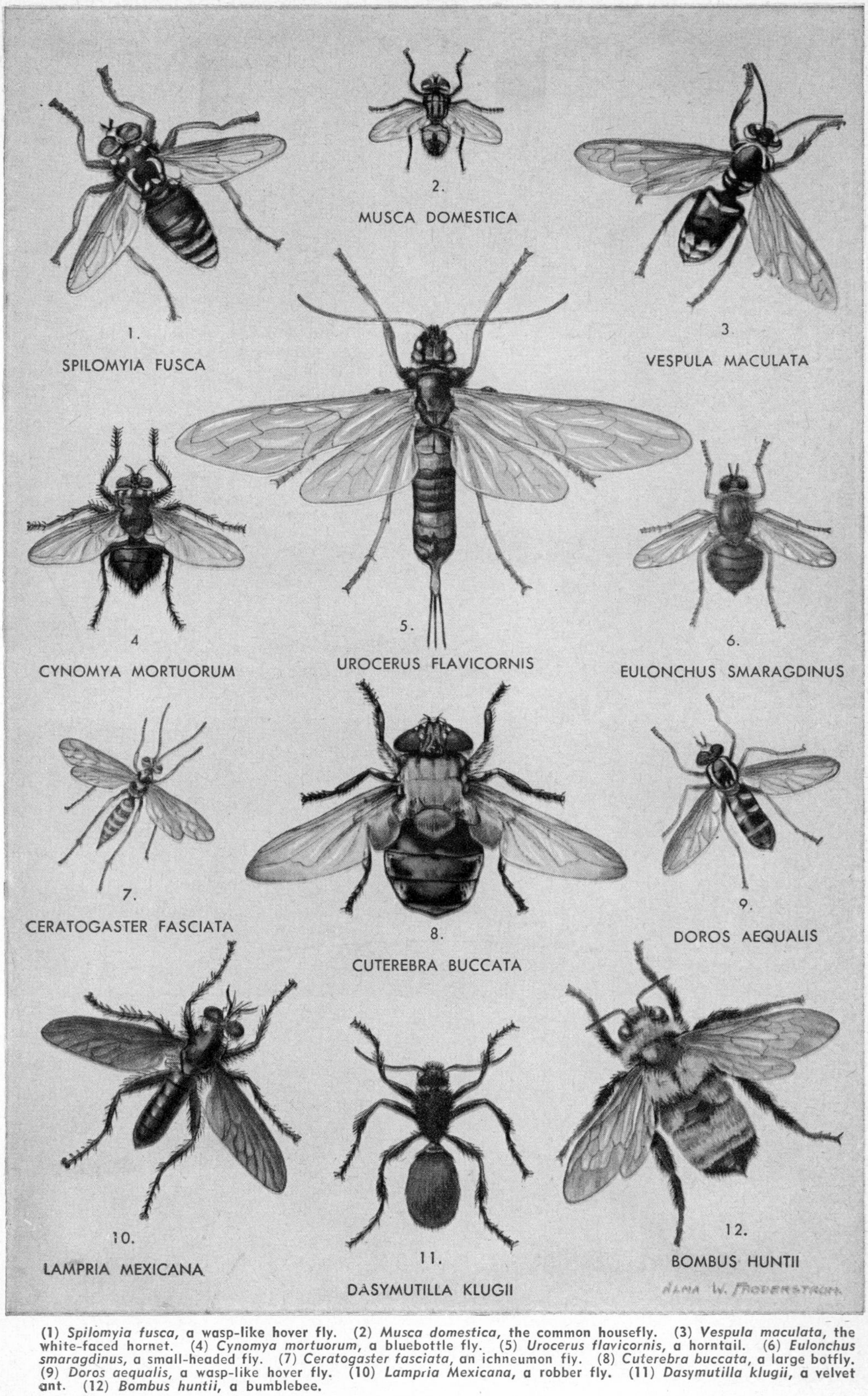

(1) ***Spilomyia fusca*****, a wasp-like hover fly. (2)** ***Musca domestica*****, the common housefly. (3)** ***Vespula maculata*****, the white-faced hornet. (4)** ***Cynomya mortuorum*****, a bluebottle fly. (5)** ***Urocerus flavicornis*****, a horntail. (6)** ***Eulonchus smaragdinus*****, a small-headed fly. (7)** ***Ceratogaster fasciata*****, an ichneumon fly. (8)** ***Cuterebra buccata*****, a large botfly. (9)** ***Doros aequalis*****, a wasp-like hover fly. (10)** ***Lampria Mexicana*****, a robber fly. (11)** ***Dasymutilla klugii*****, a velvet ant. (12)** ***Bombus huntii*****, a bumblebee.**

INSECTS

Conchuela, *"Chlorochroa ligata"* (Say)

Praying Mantis, feeding on grasshopper.

Spined Predaceous Bug, *"Podisus maculiventris"* (Say)

Girdled Cicada, *"Tibicen cinctifera"* (Uhl.)

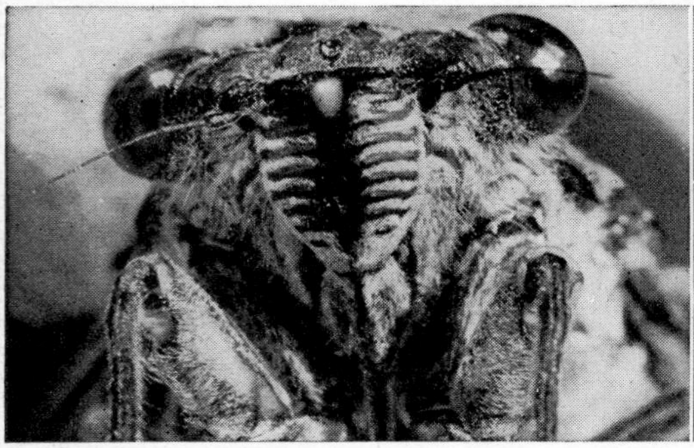

Cicada, *"Cacama crepitans"* (Van D.)

Grasshopper.

Black Pine Sawyer, *"Monochamus scutellatus"* (Say)

Oil Beetle, *"Meloe proscarabaeus"* (L.)

thousands more are being described each year. On the basis of new kinds found in collections made in regions where there has been little collecting, it is estimated that the total number of different kinds of insects will exceed 6,000,000 when all are discovered. The best known groups are the butterflies and some families of beetles, but even in these, relatively little is known about their biology. Of the large orders, least is known about the flies, wasps, and parasitic Hymenoptera.

CHARACTERISTICS OF INSECTS

Like all other invertebrate animals, the skeleton of the insect is on the outside. This consists of a hard outer covering made rigid by the impregnation of chitin (q.v.). The insect's body is divided into three sections: the head, composed of 6 fused segments; the thorax, of 3 segments; and the abdomen, of 10 to 12 segments; but the number may appear to be fewer owing to fusion of some of them.

Head.—The head consists of a capsule containing the brain, eyes, antennae, and mouth parts, the posterior part of the head having an opening (*foramen magnum*) leading to the neck and thence to the thorax and abdomen. The segments composing the head have become so fused that there is no sign of segmentation. The mouth parts consist of an upper lip or labrum, a pair of opposed or lateral jaws or mandibles, a second lateral pair of jaws, called maxillae, and the lower lip, consisting of a lower pair of fused organs, termed the labium. In biting insects, a palpus is present on both the maxillae and the labium; in sucking insects, they are absent; and in the flies, only the maxillary palpi are present. The mouth parts may be variously modified, according to the habit of the insect. In the sucking insects, they fit together to form a tube, the labium forming the main sheath, the mandibles and maxillae being serrate or saw-toothed at the tips to allow penetration of hard surfaces in order to obtain food. In many flies the mouth parts are adapted for lapping and are broadened at the tip.

There are two types of eyes: compound and simple. The compound eyes are formed of a number of facets or ommatidia, and are what are generally called "the eyes." The eyes are situated on each side of the head and are usually brownish in color. The facets are hexagonal in shape and vary in number from as few as eight in some flies to as many as 25,000 in some beetles. Each facet is an eye in itself, but despite the large number, the sight of most insects is poor. The dragonflies, some of which have as many as 20,000 ommatidia, have the best sight. However, the image formed is not clear and the eyes apparently register movement rather than the outline of objects within the range of the insect's vision. In many insects, and particularly in the predaceous, diurnal forms like the assassin flies, there is an area of enlarged facets which definitely increase the vision of the insect, since it has been observed that insects flying below or above the sight range of the enlarged facets are ignored; in some, the enlarged facets are near the middle of the eye, but they are often toward the top. The simple eyes, or ocelli, are usually three in number, arranged in a triangle between the compound eyes toward the top of the head. It is believed that the ocelli merely differentiate between light and darkness. The ocelli are often entirely absent or only two may be present, the anterior one having disappeared, or all may be reduced in size and efficiency. In many of the horseflies (Tabanidae) the ocelli are absent; hence the compound eyes must distinguish light, since these are all diurnal, bloodsucking insects.

The antennae of insects, of which there are two situated generally on the front of the head between the eyes, are extremely variable in size and shape. In some forms they are very elongate and may be composed of from 2 to more than 60 segments; they are absent in the Protura, the most primitive of living insects. They are of simple form in the primitive insects, tapering (setaceous) from base to tip. Other forms are filiform, or of almost equal thickness throughout; moniliform, the segments being more or less globular or beadlike; serrate or saw-toothed, the segments being prolonged to give a saw-toothed appearance to the organ; pectinate, or comblike, a portion of the segment being greatly produced on one side, usually the lower; clavate, or clubbed, the segments increasing in width from near the base toward the apex; capitate, or abruptly clubbed, the apical segments being enlarged, the intermediate ones, narrow; and lamellate, in which several apical segments are modified so as to have a leaflike or foliate appearance, or plumose, or featherlike, as in many moths. In many insects having short antennae, there are normally three segments, the remaining segments being represented by a style or bristle situated at the tip (See HEMIPTERA and DIPTERA). However, in many Diptera the style is replaced by a dorsal or terminal arista: when dorsal, it is always called arista; but when terminal, it is termed style when thick, and arista when hair-like. The arista is subject to many modifications: it may be bristle-like, jointed, or apparently jointed, only at the base, lamellate, plumose, clavate, and so on; in the flies it is always present in the Cyclorrhapha, or muscoids, except in the family Cryptochaetidae, the larvae of which are predaceous upon scale insects.

The full functions of the antennae have not been determined, but they are of a sensory nature and are chiefly responsible for the sense of smell; thus in those forms that do not depend upon sight for this purpose, they serve to guide the insect to its food supply. It also seems certain that the antennae convey to the nervous system, and thence to the wings and legs, impulses concerning wind direction and velocity; thus the insect is enabled to ordinate its wing beats and utilize its hind legs as a rudder to compensate for the pressure produced by air currents. The sensation transmitted by the antennae is received through sensory pits, as well as through sensory hairs of various sizes, including those on the arista. Obvious sensory pits may vary from one to several hundreds, but the thin membranes between the joints may play an important part in the reception and transmission of external impulses.

Thorax.—The thorax consists of three fused segments, each bearing a pair of legs. The anterior section is known as the prothorax, the middle section as the mesothorax, and the posterior segment as the metathorax. The wings are borne on the latter two sections, and are operated by powerful muscles: they are double-layered sacs of the body wall and contain nerves, tracheae, and blood. In their development from small pads in the newly emerged adult, blood is pumped into them and they slowly expand. After development, most of the blood returns to the body, the wings harden, and the veins of the wings remain as hollow supporting structures. The important parts of the legs are the coxa, the basal segment which articulates with the body, the trochanter, femur, tibia, and tarsus. The tarsus, or foot, usually consists of five segments, but in many of the orders, the number is fewer, usually three or two; the last segment normally ends in a pair of claws. In the flies, which have only one pair of wings, there is a pair of organs situated on the metanotum behind and below the wings, known as halteres or balancers. These serve to balance the fly during flight, and if one or both are removed, the insect is incapable of organized flight.

Abdomen.—The abdomen is composed of 10 or 11 segments, but no more than three may be obvious, the others being fused, reduced, or modified to form the external genital organs. In some insects there is a pair of cerci, jointed appendages at the end of the abdomen; in others, such as the silverfish, there are three long appendages. In immature forms, both the abdomen and thorax may possess gills and other appendages.

Nervous System.—The nervous system consists of a nerve chord extending the length of the body, on the lower side, with varying numbers of nerve ganglia, the greatest number being present in the primitive forms. The brain, located in the head, is the largest of the ganglia, strong branches radiating from it to the eyes, ocelli, antennae, and mouth parts. The heart is a rather simple tube lying in the upper part of the body: its pulsations pump the blood from front to rear. There is no venal system, the blood flowing freely through the body cavity and being purified by oxygen provided by the tracheal system.

Digestive System.—The chief parts of the digestive tract are the pharynx, esophagus, crop, stomach, colon, and rectal arc: the gastric caecae and Malpighian tubules are important accessory parts. The main reproductive organs are the ovaries, oviduct, vagina, and egg guide in the female, the latter opening to the ovipositor and a spermatheca, in which the sperm is stored in the female. In the male there is a pair of testes and lateral ducts, which unite to form the ejaculatory duct; there may also be accessory glands.

Respiratory System.—This system is of a simple nature, consisting of a series of tracheae through which oxygen is carried to all parts of the body, the blood being purified by contact with the oxygen. The external openings are called pores or spiracles. Carbon dioxide is removed by the respiratory system.

Sensory System.—The sense of hearing in insects is apparently keen, but it is evidently tuned to a higher pitch than that of humans; insects can hear sounds that are quite inaudible to the human ear. Male mosquitoes are attracted by the noise made by the females, while in other insects the females are attracted by sounds made by the male. This is true of the crickets, katydids, and the cicadas. Few insects have obvious ears, but "ears" are present in the legs of grasshoppers. For the most part, sound is heard through sensory pits or are audible through vibrations transmitted by sensory hairs. The cockroaches and other insects have membranous areas on the tarsi which probably serve for both hearing and smelling.

The sense of smell is very highly developed in some insects. Male moths have been attracted from distances of well over a mile by the discharges of freshly hatched females. Dung beetles, flies, and other insects appear almost instantly on fresh dung or dead animals in order to feed and lay their eggs. Many insects feed upon only certain kinds of plants, and while it is not known how they recognize them, it seems likely that odor is the chief factor.

Food.—The food of insects consists of practically all kinds of vegetable and other matter, either dead or alive, but on the whole, plant life and other insects provide the chief diet. The ants are among the most general feeders, having adapted themselves to innumerable diversified habitats. One kind or another of them feeds on fats and oils, starches, sweets, meat, other insects and fungi, the leaf-cutting ants raising their own fungi in subterranean chambers and often traveling a mile or more in order to obtain suitable fungus-growing material. Many kinds, such as the mosquito and horsefly (qq.v.), feed on the blood of both warm-blooded and cold-blooded animals. The mosquito may also suck the juices of plants, as do most of the true bugs. Many flies (see FLESHFLY and BLOWFLY) and beetles (see ROVE BEETLES) live upon dead animal matter and aid in purifying the air by disposing of putrefying matter. Carcasses may be seething masses of the larvae of many kinds of insect life, and the carcass of as large an animal as a horse or a cow may be entirely stripped of flesh within a week or two. Other insects, such as the skin beetles, obtain substenance from the drying bones and from the liquids that have seeped into the ground. The botflies (q.v.) and some blowflies are parasites of warm-blooded animals, living internally, either in the flesh or in the digestive tract. The most important of the insects are those that are parasitic on other insects. They may be either internal or external parasites, and may attack all stages. Many Hymenoptera are parasites of the eggs of other insects. An enormous number of flies and wasps are parasitic, chiefly upon Lepidoptera and Coleoptera, and it is these hordes that are chiefly responsible for keeping nature in balance. Predaceous insects do their part and are to be found among most of the orders, but they are scarcely as valuable as the parasites because they show less discrimination in the selection of their prey: the Chinese preying mantis may, at times, be a pest because it kills honey bees, and a few large predaceous flies have the same habit. Because a great many kinds of insects, particularly Hymenoptera, Diptera, and Lepidoptera, feed on pollen and nectar which is obtained from flowers, they are of the utmost importance in pollination, and many kinds of plants cannot reproduce without them. The chief pollinators of red clover are the bumble bees, and it was impossible to grow this crop in New Zealand until the bees were introduced. The honey sacs of some tropical plants are so deeply seated that they can be reached only by the long "tongues" of certain hawk moths (q.v.), and certain thrips are essential for the production of a large crop of cacao beans: other thrips are pests of the plant. Edible figs (*Ficus carica*) are possible because of the existence of *Blastophaga psenes*, a tiny hymenopteron that can exist only in the presence of the figs. There are two or three other kinds of edible figs but they are of minor commercial importance, and there are a number of other small Hymenoptera closely related to *B. psenes* that pollinate other varieties of figs. The food habits of many insects are not known. There are butterflies and true flies that live in the nests of ants, and probably injure their host in some way, since the larvae are protected against them. Other insects, that is, *Cremastocheilus* (Coleoptera), may be enemies of the ants but are welcomed in their nests because they produce sweet secretions. Few insects store food, but this is common practice among the ants, bees, and wasps. In most cases, food is stored for the purpose of feeding the young, as with the solitary bees and wasps. In some cases the adults may feed upon the stored food in case of emergency, but the honey ants and the honey bees provide food for themselves in order ot carry them over the winter. That this is an old habit is attested by the fact that other insects prey upon them by feeding upon the stored food.

Social Habits.—The social habits of insects are chiefly confined to the Hymenoptera and the termites. These have developed the highest communal organization, as demonstrated by the existence of various castes or classes adapted for doing certain types of work. While five or six different castes may be present in a termite's nest, there may be 29 different types of individuals in a single ant nest. Only three are found in the nest of the honey bee: the queen, drone, and worker. The queen may lay an enormous number of eggs, more than a million in the case of certain species of termites. The social habit carries with it a long-time continuation of the existence of the colony, and the feeding and protecting of the young. The social bees and wasps have developed stinging organs in order to protect their young; ants both bite and sting, while termites have developed fighting castes. In temperate regions, where there is a lack of food in the winter, insects, such as the yellow jacket (q.v.) which feeds upon nectar, pollen, and other insects, survive only as queens or reproductive females, the workers and males dying off with the advent of cold weather, each queen establishing a new colony in the spring. Other insects, such as the ambrosia beetle (see WOOD-BORING BEETLES) and the flat bug, are more or less social, adults and immature stages living together. Ambrosia beetles carry fungus spores on their bodies from their birthplace to their new home, and their offspring feed on the fungus growing in the tunnels. The larvae of many moths and butterflies are gregarious, since they cluster together to feed or rest. The American tent and other caterpillars build tents in which to rest or feed, and the larvae of the io moth are often gregarious until they reach maturity. The caterpillars of the mourning cloak and many other butterflies have similar habits, as do those of many sawflies.

Flight.—Insects were the first flying animals, and among them are to be found the speediest creatures in the world. Some of the botflies, the hawk moths, and dragonflies are the fastest of the insects. Most adult insects have four wings, but the Diptera have only two. In many of those having four wings, the Lepidoptera and Hymenoptera, the front and hind wings are hooked together during flight. In the Coleoptera, the front wings are used to cover and protect the abdomen, and are held more or less upright during flight. The hawk moths and some damsel flies are able to fly backwards a short way, while hover flies can move sideways for short distances. The only insects that are known to fly before they are mature are the Ephemeridae or mayflies. In this order the subimagoes emerge from the mature nymphs. In these, the wings are dusky, and it is not until they have shed their skins that the wings become glassy.

Because of lack of use, or need, many kinds of insects have lost their wings. Ants and termites use them only for nuptial flights, after which they are discarded. Many kinds of beetles and flies are unable to fly because the flight wings are reduced or absent. In the flightless beetles, the wing covers are usually firmly united; the bedbug and flies of the family Nycteribiidae (bat parasites), the females of some moths, and many phorid flies living in the nests of ants and termites are wingless. Other insects have the wings reduced in size and are unable to fly. The females of the silkworm, the gypsy moth, and others have fully developed wings, but are incapable of flight.

Migration.—A common phenomenon among insects is migration. The best known of the migrants is the monarch butterfly (*Danaus archippus*). In North America, the adults migrate from their northern breeding grounds to the southern United States and Mexico, adults returning north in the spring. It is not known whether the same individuals return north, but it is known that the northern migrants do not live through the summer. During their southward migration, the butterflies congregate in great numbers on certain trees or shrubs in order to spend the night, the same resting places being used year after year. In the south they have the same habit of congregating at night, and in the Pacific Grove region of California, it is unlawful to disturb or capture the resting butterflies. Some of the large dragonflies migrate south in the autumn, but little is known about them, and it is not known whether there is a northern migration in the spring.

The migratory movements of butterflies, particularly those belonging to the family Pieridae, have been observed in many parts of the world, but in none of these has an annual movement in a definite direction been clearly demonstrated. Migration in many cases, such as among grasshoppers, chinch bugs, and army worms, is caused by the failure of food supply, resulting in a concerted movement in search of food. The hordes thus gathered together are often so large as to destroy all green things in their path.

Mimicry.—Among insects mimicry is common. Many kinds of flies are similarly colored to bees and wasps, fly in very much the same manner, and act in the same way when captured, even going through the motion of stinging, while buzzing loudly. Some bugs bear a close resemblance to ants of the same region, while some butterflies resemble others that are apparently distasteful to birds. Most of the clearwing moths (Aegeriidae) look like wasps, as do most tropical members of the family Zygaenidae.

Life History.—Insects are divided into two groups, depending upon the changes which take place during development. In the group of which the grasshopper is an example the newly hatched insect bears a close resemblance to the adult, whether the latter be winged or not; there is an *incomplete metamorphosis* or change of form. In the second group, such as flies, butterflies, and bees, there is no close resemblance between larva and adult, and a complete metamorphosis takes place.

Complete metamorphosis indicates the presence of egg, larva, pupa, and adult, but the egg may be eliminated by the production of living young, a condition found in many flies, and particularly evident in the flesh flies of the genus *Sarcophaga*. The development of eggs occurs among most insects, and even when larvae are born alive, they have usually hatched from eggs in the ovaries of the female, but reproduction can take place in other ways. In some sarcophagids, the female, which normally deposits living maggots on suitable food, may also lay eggs, if the food supply is abundant and the eggs have not hatched within her body. In some Muscidae, the larvae may develop within the mother's body until as much as half grown; in the tsetse flies, the larvae are practically mature, and the same is true of the Pupipara, the bird and bat parasites of the order Diptera.

The egg hatches into a larva which may be variously known as a grub, maggot, worm, wireworm, caterpillar, or some other name, depending upon locality. This is the active growing stage of all insects having a complete metamorphosis, and the only stage during which the insect grows. When fully mature, the larva transforms into a pupa. The larva of each kind of insect has certain characters by which it can be distinguished from that of any other kind of insect. Sometimes, as with the Lepidoptera, the differences are very great, but in the maggots of flies and Hymenoptera, they may be slight.

The pupa is the stage in which the transformation from larva to adult takes place. As a general rule, the larval skin is cast off, but in some flies it remains as a protective cover for the pupa itself: in such cases, it is called puparium. The pupa is entirely different in appearance from the larva, and may or may not show external indications of the appendages of the prospective adult insect. It may or may not be protected by a covering (cocoon) produced by the larva. Cocoons vary in size, shape, and consistency. They may be composed wholly of silk or may consist of the larval hairs, or leaves, or debris, fastened together with silken strands. Many larvae form a smooth cell in the ground or in wood, in which they transform to pupae. The pupa of butterflies is known as a chrysalid or chrysalis, except in the very rare cases where they construct cocoons.

The adult insect emerging from the pupa has no resemblance to the larva or the pupa; there has been a complete change in appearance between each stage.

In the incomplete metamorphosis, as exemplified by the true bugs and the grasshoppers, the newly hatched animal has much the appearance of the adult, and the change to the adult form is gradual. They lay eggs, and the emerging insect is known as a nymph. The nymph sheds its skin at periodic intervals, a slight change in appearance taking place each time. Eventually wing pads (in those forms having wings as adults) appear, and usually after one or two more molts the wings are fully developed and the insects are mature.

Reproduction.—Parthenogenesis, or reproduction without males, is a fairly common phenomenon among insects. Many sawflies, weevils, and aphids are known only from the female sex, and have probably existed for millions of years without males being developed. In the aphids, males are usually developed, in temperate regions, in the fall, the spring, and summer—generations being composed entirely of females; but the same species of aphid that produces males in the north, may exist without them in warm regions. In the honeybee, parthenogenesis may develop among the workers, which are females in which the sex organs are undeveloped, but in this case, the eggs laid always produce drones, or males.

Paedogenesis is one of the strangest phenomena of nature. It occurs in Cecidomyidae, or gallflies, of the genus *Miastor,* and also in the European genus *Oligarces*. In the females, large eggs develop in the ovaries and the hatching larvae devour the body of the mother and shortly thereafter each larva gives birth to from 7 to 30 daughter larvae. This may continue for several generations, but some sexual forms usually develop during each generation.

Polyembryony occurs in a few parasitic Hymenoptera. It results from division taking place within the egg, and several to many larvae emerging from a single egg.

CLASSIFICATION OF INSECTS

The classification of insects into their various orders is not particularly difficult, even though several systems of classification are in use and the number of recognized orders is variable, depending upon the authority consulted. In general, the tendency is to increase the number of orders, families, and genera, and it seems unlikely that any classification acceptable to all students of the class will be developed within many decades. However, E. O. Essig's *College Entomology* (1942) gives a generally accepted and conservative classification, dividing the class into two subclasses, the second subclass being divided into two divisions, with a total of 33 orders.

Subclass Apterygota.—The subclass Apterygota includes primitive insects in which wings have never developed, and in which there is no marked difference in appearance between the newly hatched individual and the adult. This group is often classified as insects undergoing development without metamorphosis; all of them have biting mouth parts retracted within the head. This subclass includes the following orders:

Protura (the proturans): with 9 to 12 abdominal segments and without antennae.

Thysanura (bristletails or silverfish): with long antennae and three "tails."

Aptera (campodeids): with long antennae and with parallel-sided abdomen bearing only two "tails."

Collembola (springtails or snowfleas): with 4 to 6 segments in the antennae, and the abdomen frequently provided with an organ enabling it to leap into the air.

Subclass Pterygota.—The subclass Pterygota includes forms with the mouth parts of various types, either biting, lapping or sucking, either winged or descended from winged forms. They may have a complete or incomplete metamorphosis, and are divided into two divisions on this basis.

I Division Exopterygota.—the orders placed under the division Exopterygota, in which there is incomplete metamorphosis, are:

Orthoptera: with biting mouth parts, many segmented antennae; a distinct ovipositor in the female, and stridulating organs; the hind legs usually developed for leaping. The order, as restricted (the three following orders are frequently included), contains the grasshoppers, locusts, katydids, crickets, tree crickets, and mole crickets. In the grasshoppers, locusts, and katydids, the wings of the adults are laterally appressed to the abdomen, which is more or less laterally compressed. In the crickets, the wings are dorsal and appressed to the dorsal surface of the abdomen.

Grylloblattodea: with biting mouth parts, long antennae, no simple eyes, 5 segments in the tarsi and no wings. They are more closely related to the Orthoptera than to the Aptera, to which they show a superficial resemblance. They have a length of more than one inch.

Blattaria (the roaches, or cockroaches): The antennae are long, the legs all adapted for running. The wings are folded over the back; cerci are present. Eggs are contained in a capsule which is usually carried by the female until or near the time of hatching; sometimes the eggs are retained in the ovaries until they hatch.

Phasmida: The walkingsticks have biting mouth parts and are phytophagous. The antennae, legs, and abdomen are long, and the flight wings, if developed, are folded beneath short wing covers. The eggs are large and are dropped to the ground, where they may remain for a few weeks or for more than a year before hatching.

Mantodea (the Mantids): The preying or praying mantids are usually more robust than the phasmids. They have biting mouth parts but are predaceous on other animals. The eggs are laid in masses and covered by a protective secretion. Most are winged in the adult stage.

Dermaptera: The earwigs have been included with the Orthoptera. They have a pair of forceps or pincers at the end of the abdomen, biting mouth parts, and are phytophagous, predaceous, or scavengers. The females of many kinds protect their eggs and young, attacking any intruders. They are incapable of inflicting serious wounds, and "enter ears," if at all, merely for the purpose of hiding.

Diploglossata: with antennae elongate, biting mouth parts, wings absent, eyes atrophied, abdomen with a pair of long, unsegmented cerci. The sides of the body are almost parallel. This is the smallest order of insects, only two species being known up to 1946. They are found only on African rats.

Plecoptera: The stoneflies or salmonflies have biting mouth parts, long antennae, parallel-sided abdomen with a pair of cerci, wings with numerous cross veins, the wings held flat over the body when at rest. The larvae are aquatic and have gills. More than 1,300 different kinds have been described.

Isoptera: The white ants or termites have many-segmented antennae, biting mouth parts and four or five segmented tarsi. They are phytophagous and live on both dead and living wood, the roots of plants, and in fruits resting upon the ground. They are social insects and have several castes. They are used as food in tropical regions.

Zoraptera: A very small order with long, moniliform antennae and two segments in the tarsi; they may or may not have wings, have biting mouth parts and incomplete metamorphosis. They are social insects and frequently live in the nests of termites.

Embioptera: A small order of small, slender insects, in which the females lack wings and the males may have them; the antennae are filiform, the thorax almost as long as the abdomen, the legs short, and with three tarsal segments, the first segment of the front tarsi containing silk glands. They build silken webs in which they live.

Corrodentia: The psocids, book lice, or bark lice are small, winged or wingless, with biting mouth parts and incomplete metamorphosis. The head is large and the prothorax small. Usually there are two pairs of wings; the venation is simple. The antennae are usually long and filiform.

Mallophaga: The biting lice are found chiefly on birds, but some attack mammals. They have biting mouth parts and feed on hair, feathers, and epidermal scales. Almost all are small and all are wingless. The antennae are composed of three to five segments. The tarsi consist of one or two segments, usually with one or two claws, but these may be absent. The metamorphosis is incomplete.

Anoplura: The sucking lice are wingless and are parasites of mammals and have an incomplete metamorphosis, the thorax is partly fused, and the tarsi have one segment and one claw which is usually adapted for grasping hair.

Ephemerida: The mayflies are small to medium-sized, soft-bodied insects. The antennae are small; the mouth parts vestigial; the eyes are large, with facets of different sizes. The cerci are long and segmented; the wings have many cross veins. The nymphs are aquatic and breathe through gills. The order is sometimes called Ephemeroptera.

Odonata: The dragonflies and damselflies have two pairs of wings of rather similar shape. The antennae are small, and the eyes large. The thorax is moderately heavy, and the abdomen long and narrow. The labium is large—especially in the nymphs—and hinged, and is used, together with the legs, in capturing and holding prey. The nymphs are aquatic and breathe through gills. The metamorphosis is incomplete, the adult emerging from the full-grown nymph, which crawls from the water; both stages are predaceous.

Thysanoptera: The thrips are all small, easily recognized insects when mature. The wings are feathered, having long hairs in front and behind. The mouth parts are modified for chafing or sucking, the antennae with six to nine segments. Metamorphosis is incomplete. Many are wingless as adults. Most are phytophagous but some are predaceous.

Hemiptera: The true bugs have two pairs of wings, but these may be absent or reduced in size; they are held flat over the body when at rest, and the basal half or more of the front pair is coriaceous; the apical part, membranous. They have sucking mouth parts, usually short antennae with four or five segments, the tarsi with one to three segments. They are phytophagous, predaceous or parasitic on warm-blooded animals. The metamorphosis is incomplete.

In the suborder Homoptera the clearwing bugs include the cicadas, tree hoppers, leaf hoppers, scale insects, plant lice and others. They have sucking mouth parts, short or long antennae, and two or three segments in the tarsi; four wings are present; only one pair in male coccids. All are phytophagous, but some will suck blood upon occasion. They are often placed as a distinct order; the wings are usually held roof-like over the abdomen. The metamorphosis is incomplete.

II Division Endopterygota.—The Endopterygota, the second division, includes orders in which

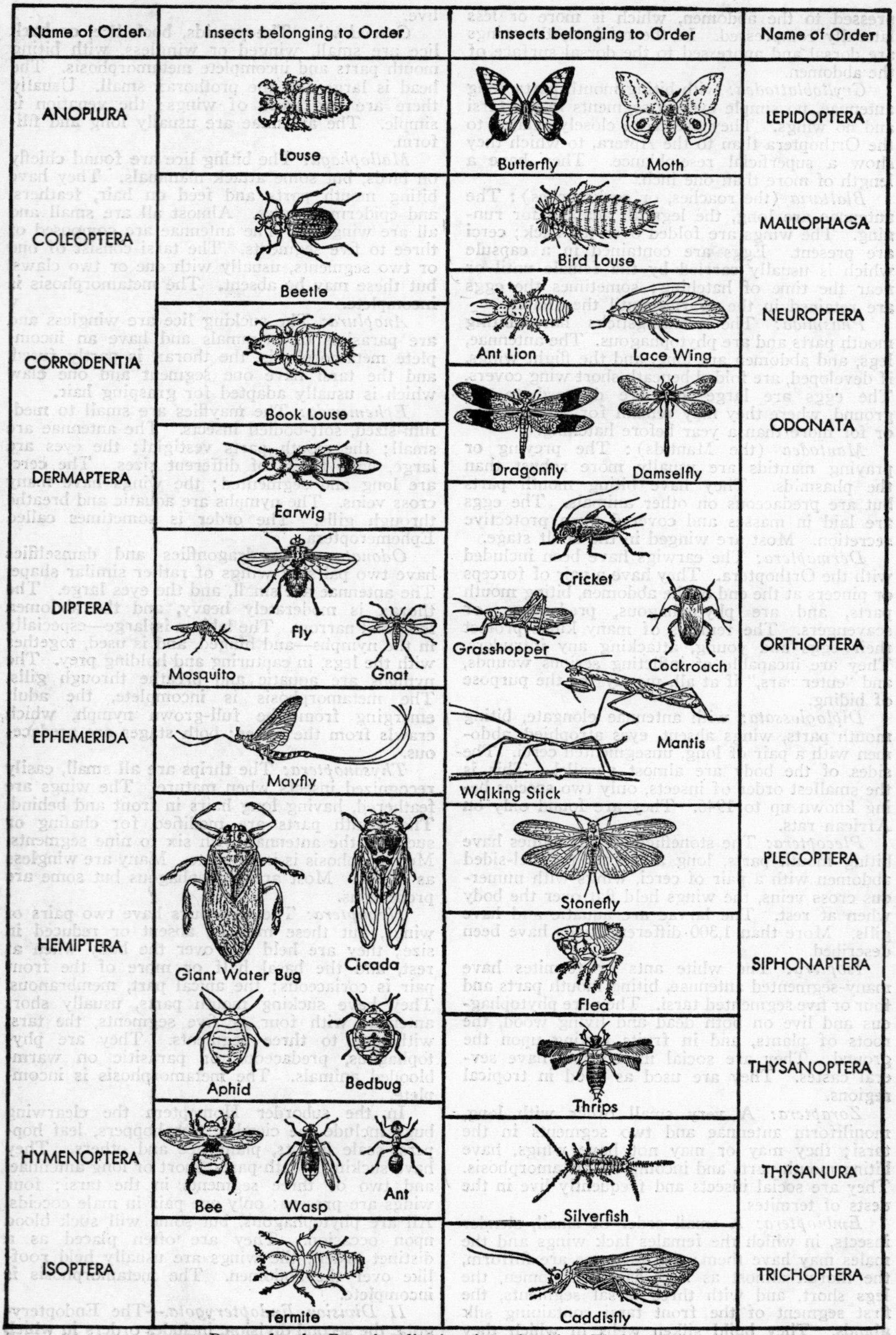

Name of Order
Insects belonging to Order
Insects belonging to Order
Name of Order
ANOPLURA
Louse
LEPIDOPTERA
Butterfly
Moth
COLEOPTERA
Beetle
MALLOPHAGA
Bird Louse
CORRODENTIA
Book Louse
NEUROPTERA
Ant Lion
Lace Wing
DERMAPTERA
Earwig
ODONATA
Dragonfly
Damselfly
DIPTERA
Fly
Mosquito
Gnat
ORTHOPTERA
Cricket
Grasshopper
Cockroach
Mantis
Walking Stick
EPHEMERIDA
Mayfly
HEMIPTERA
Giant Water Bug
Cicada
Aphid
Bedbug
PLECOPTERA
Stonefly
SIPHONAPTERA
Flea
THYSANOPTERA
Thrips
HYMENOPTERA
Bee
Wasp
Ant
THYSANURA
Silverfish
ISOPTERA
Termite
TRICHOPTERA
Caddisfly

Drawn for the *Encyclopedia Americana* by Alma Froderstrom.

there is a complete metamorphosis, a pupal stage being present.

Megaloptera: The dobsonflies or fishflies have long, many-jointed antennae, biting mouth parts, five segmented tarsi, and numerous cross veins in the wings. The larvae are aquatic, but crawl from the water to pupate. The nymphs of the dobson flies are called hellgramites and toe biters.

Neuroptera: The nerve-winged insects or lacewings are a group of diverse forms with varied habits. They have biting mouth parts; long or short antennae. The wings are held rooflike over the body and have many cross veins. The larvae vary extremely in habits. The aphis lions and ant lions are well known members of the order. At one time, almost all the insects with numerous cross veins in the wings were included here.

Raphidiodea: The snakeflies have somewhat the appearance of mantids: the head is large, the antennae long, the wings have numerous veins and cross veins, and the prothorax is elongate and necklike. The larvae are mostly arboreal. They have usually been included in the Neuropetra.

Mecoptera: The scorpionflies have the mouth parts situated on a produced snout; the antennae and legs are long. The wings are of similar shape and have fairly numerous cross veins. The larvae are caterpillar-like, with or without prolegs. The adults are carnivorous or saprophagous, and somewhat resemble crane flies in life.

Trichoptera: The caddiceflies have biting mouth parts, long antennae, hairs on wings and body, and very few cross veins in the wings. The larvae are aquatic or semiaquatic, and most of them build cases or nests. They are sometimes referred to as "aquatic moths," and the separation from the lepidoptera is not easy where the most primitive moths are concerned.

Lepidoptera: The butterflies and moths are readily recognized by the presence of scales on the wings. Their antennae are long, but varied in shape. They have sucking mouth parts, but these may be reduced and functionless. The larvae are caterpillars, and are generally phytophagous; a few are predaceous, while some live on animal products. The adults live on nectar and pollen.

Coleoptera: The sheath-winged insects include the beetles and weevils. The front wings are coriacious and form a protecting cover for the hind wings and abdomen. The antennae are variable and all have biting mouth parts. The habits of adults and larvae are extremely variable.

Strepsiptera: The twisted-winged insects or stylops are a peculiar order, the larvae being parasitic on bees and wasps, and causing a deformation. Only the males have wings, which are folded under the small wingcovers. Distribution from one host to another occurs during the larval stage.

Hymenoptera: The bees, wasps, ants, ichneumons, and sawflies are a diverse group with extremely diversified habits. The mouth parts are either biting or sucking, the antennae are elongate, the wings with relatively few veins, and the hind pair smaller than the front pair, though hooked to them in flight. They are solitary or social. The larvae of the sawflies resemble caterpillars, those of others are legless grubs.

Diptera: The flies have only one pair of wings with few cross veins. They have a pair of balancers or halteres toward the back part of the thorax. The antennae, wing venation, and habits are extremely variable. They are of great economic importance.

Siphonaptera: The fleas are wingless, blood-sucking insects and all are parasitic on warm-blooded animals. They are laterally compressed, and their hind legs are adapted for leaping. The larvae are wormlike and live on fats and oils in cracks in floors and in the soil. They carry diseases and some kinds burrow under the skin. See also ENTOMOLOGY, ECONOMIC; FLOWERS AND INSECTS; separate articles on the various orders and insects.

Bibliography.—Ferris, G. F., *The Principles of Systematic Entomology* (Palo Alto 1928); Metcalf, C. L., and Flint, W., *Destructive and Useful Insects: Their Habits and Control* (New York 1928); Cheeseman, Evelyn, *Hunting Insects in the South Seas* (London 1932); Imms, A. D., *A General Textbook of Entomology* (New York 1934); Comstock, J. H., *An Introduction to Entomology* (Ithaca 1940); Essig, E. O., *College Entomology* (New York 1942); Herms, W. B., *Medical Entomology* (New York 1943); Matheson, R., *Entomology for Introductory Courses* (Ithaca 1944); Curran, C. H., *Insects of the Pacific World* (New York 1946).

CHARLES HOWARD CURRAN,
Curator, Department of Insects and Spiders, American Museum of Natural History.

INSIGNIA OF RANK, Military and Naval.—In common use in all armies of the world today are the uniforms and the insignia of rank. The uniform distinguishes a military man from a civilian. The insignia of rank distinguish one grade of military man from another.

The adoption of the military uniform in the 17th century and the adoption of the badge of rank in the 18th century meant two important changes in military history. The modern professional army had become respectable and rationalized.

During the Middle Ages, the art of war was the property of the aristocratic classes. The fighting man was distinguished by his armor and his equipment. The knight was a specialist in fighting, and his battles were fought in small numbers with little organization. With the battles of Crécy and Agincourt, the specialist with his armor and horse was displaced by larger armies of men on foot carrying longbows and later, muskets. By the 16th century the professional army had come into its own. It was no longer an aristocratic organization. The soldiers were taken from the rabble of the countryside. They were badly paid and ill-treated, and they were despised by the civilian population. A 17th century sign would read: "Beggars, thieves, prostitutes, and soldiers not allowed."[1] Such was the position of the soldier at the beginning of the 17th century: without uniform, without insignia, considered one of the lowest classes of society.

During the Thirty Years War (1618–1648), the uniform was brought into use for the first time. Louis XIV's household troops were distinguished from others by the uniform that they wore. Soon military leaders saw the advantages of this innovation. It brought better morale. It gave a new distinction to the fighting man that had formerly been but a member of the rabble. By the end of the century the professional army had been made respectable, and the uniform was in use as the symbol of this respectability.

In the 18th century the badge of rank came into use. It was part of the long movement of

[1] See R. R. Palmer, "Frederick the Great" in *Makers of Modern Strategy,* edited by E. M. Earle (Princeton 1944).

rationalization of the art of war. Military leaders in the 17th and 18th centuries realized the importance of organization and planning in modern military action. Distinction of rank was necessary for this, and the insignia of rank was needed for this distinction. With the introduction of mass armies during the French Revolution, organization and planning became even more important. The uniform was needed to identify the great numbers of conscript troops. The insignia of rank were needed to symbolize the organization that converted them from a mob into an effective fighting machine. The specialization coming with modern scientific warfare has increased the number of insignia and the number of uniforms.

Today, the various governments prescribe the required uniforms and insignia for their fighting forces. To wear the wrong or unauthorized insignia or uniform is a criminal offense, and the military regulations specify in minute detail the description and requirements of military costume.

The various insignia of rank worn today in some of the minor as well as the major military forces of the world are as follows:

ARGENTINA

Army.—The insignia of rank of officers of the army is worn on shoulder straps of service uniforms and overcoats and on the cuffs of the full dress as follows:

General of the Army: Two gold wheat sprigs below three gold rhomboids on red disks.
Major General: Same, but two gold rhomboids.
Brigadier General: Same, but one gold rhomboid.
Colonel: Three gold suns on disks of color depending on branch.
Lieutenant Colonel: Same, but two gold suns.
Major: Same with one gold sun.
Captain: Three serrate-edged silver disks.
First Lieutenant: Same but with two disks.
Lieutenant: One silver and one gold disk.
Sublieutenant: One silver disk.

The cap insignia consists of the coat of arms surrounded by a wreath with a rosette above of sky-blue and white.

The distinguishing colors of the arm or service is as follows: cavalry, madder red; infantry, green; engineers, black; artillery and general officers, scarlet; health department, dark red; justice, electric blue; clergy, violet; administrative, brown.

Aviators wear a blue-gray uniform and an insignia on breast consisting of two wings with the national emblem, enclosed in wreath, in center.

Navy.—The insignia of rank of officers of the navy is worn on the cuffs of blue service and dress uniforms and on shoulder marks of other uniforms. It is identical to that of the British Navy except that a lieutenant (junior grade) has one and one half stripes, an ensign one stripe, and a midshipman one half stripe. Officers of the Engineer Corps wear sky-blue velvet between stripes; Paymaster Corps, white velvet; surgeons, red velvet. Aviators wear an insignia on breast consisting of two wings with national emblem, superimposed on anchor enclosed in circle of national colors, in center.

Officers of the Marine Corps wear a distinctive insignia consisting of an anchor on two crossed cannon with the national emblem superimposed thereon.

Air Force.—The sleeve insignia of officers of the air force (*Aeronáutica*) is as follows:

Brigadier General: A gold stripe 1 cm. wide and 25 cm. long; superimposed in the center a lozenge, one of its vertices bent beneath the stripe; three other gold stripes of equal width and length set below; a fifth broad gold stripe (38 mm.). Stripes are separated by 5 mm. spaces.
Brigadier Major: Same as brigadier general, but only two stripes of 1 cm. width.
Brigadier: Like brigadier general but one stripe only.
Commodore: Like brigadier general, but three middle stripes are 3 mm. wide and fifth stripe is 3 cm. wide.
Vice Commodore: Like commodore, but with only two 3 mm. stripes.
Commandant: Like commodore but with one stripe.
Captain: Like brigadier general but with four stripes, the three lower of 3 mm. width.
First Lieutenant: Like captain but with two narrow stripes.
Lieutenant: Like captain, but only one narrow stripe.
Ensign: One 1 cm. gold stripe with lozenge.

BELGIUM

Army.—The insignia of rank of officers of the army, embroidered or metal, are gold stars, and gold wide or narrow bars, worn on a patch on the lapels and on shoulder straps of service dress and coat. The wide bars are straight on the service dress, curved on overcoat and raincoat.

Lieutenant General: Three gold stars in triangle above two wide gold bars and below double lightning design (foudres) on lapel patch—three gold stars on the shoulder straps.
Major General: Two gold stars above two wide gold bars and below double lightning design on lapel patch—two gold stars on the shoulder straps.
Colonel: Three gold stars in triangle above one wide gold bar. Eventually a single lightning design (demi-foudres) will be worn by holders of General Staff Brevet. This applies to the army and the air force from the rank of colonel to captain inclusively.
Lieutenant Colonel: Two gold stars above one wide gold bar.
Major: One gold star above one wide gold bar.
Captain Commandant: Three gold stars below one narrow gold bar.
Captain: Three gold stars.
First Lieutenant: Two gold stars.
Second Lieutenant: One gold star.

Lapel patches of different color and different piping indicate the branch of service or corps. The patches on overcoats and raincoats are of the same material as the garment.

The color of the cap band for generals is amaranth; for colonels, scarlet; for all other ranks, khaki. The cap insignia consists of double or single lightning device, royal crown, or regimental device.

Navy.—The insignia of rank of the navy is identical with that of the British Navy. Commodore is the highest rank.

Air Force.—The insignia of rank of officers of the air force is worn on the sleeves of service uniforms and on the shoulder straps of overcoats, raincoats and battledress.

Lieutenant General: Two wide below three narrow black trimmed blue stripes.
Major General: Two wide below two narrow stripes.
Colonel: One wide below three narrow stripes.
Lieutenant Colonel: One wide below two narrow stripes.
Major: One wide below one narrow stripe.
Captain Commandant: Three narrow stripes, the top stripe having a loop.
Captain: Three narrow stripes.
First Lieutenant: Two narrow stripes.
Second Lieutenant: One narrow stripe.

General officers wear on lapel patch the double lightning design; General Staff Brevet holders, a single lightning design.

The cap is similar to the British R.A.F. but with Belgian wings surrounded by double laurels (officers) below the royal crown. For warrant officers and noncommissioned officers, the same with single laurel.

BRAZIL

Army.—The insignia of rank of officers of the Brazilian Army is worn on shoulder straps as follows:

Marshal: A round disk with the southern constellation enclosed in a larger disk of small stars all superimposed upon a star, surrounded by a wreath. Below are three wreaths.
General of Division: The same with two wreaths.
Brigadier General: The same with one wreath.
Colonel: Three disks and stars as described for marshal, but instead of being surrounded by a wreath, it is superimposed on a yellow-red representation of the sun.
Lieutenant Colonel: The same with upper star without the superimposed sun.
Major: The same with only the lower star superimposed on sun.
Captain: Three disks and stars without the sun.
First Lieutenant: The same with two stars.
Second Lieutenant: The same with one star.
Candidate Officer: One plain star.

The arm or service insignia is worn on either side of the lapel of the coat.

The cap device is the same as the disk described for a marshal's insignia of rank.

Navy.—The insignia of rank of officers of the navy is worn on the cuffs of sleeves of blue service and dress uniforms and on shoulder marks of other uniforms. That worn on the sleeves and on the shoulder marks of officers below the rank of captain is identical with that worn by officers of the Argentine Navy, except that there is no loop above a midshipman's stripe. Insignia of rank on shoulder marks for officers of flag rank and captain is as follows:

Admiral: Gold shoulder mark with silver foul anchor above a triangle of three silver stars. The upper star has superimposed on it a white circle with five small stars within a laurel branch on each side.
Vice Admiral: The same except that all stars are plain and the laurel is omitted.
Rear Admiral: The same with two plain stars.
Captain: A silver foul anchor above the four gold stripes.

Officers, other than those of the line, Engineer Corps and Construction Corps, wear corps device instead of the loop above the stripes.

The corps device of the Marine Corps is a gold fouled anchor superimposed on crossed rifles.

CANADA

Army.—The insignia of the rank of officers of the army is the same as that of the British Army as follows:

Field Marshal: Crossed batons on a wreath of laurel, with crown above.
General: Crossed sword and baton, with crown and star above.
Lieutenant General: Crossed sword and baton with crown above.
Major General: Crossed sword and baton with star above.
Brigadier: Crown above three stars, two lower stars side by side.
Colonel: Crown and two stars below.
Lieutenant Colonel: Crown and one star below.
Major: Crown.
Captain: Three stars.
Lieutenant: Two stars.
Second Lieutenant: One star.

Badges of rank for officers are worn on both shoulder straps of the battledress blouse, service dress jacket, summer dress jacket, greatcoat, British warm coat and the shirt when worn without a jacket.

Insignia of rank of warrant officers and noncommissioned officers is as follows:

Warrant Officer Class I: Canadian coat of arms.
Class II: Crown in wreath.

Noncommissioned Officers:

Squadron Quartermaster Sergeant: Three chevrons and crown.
Battery Quartermaster Sergeant: Three chevrons and crown.
Company Quartermaster Sergeant: Three chevrons and crown.
Staff Sergeant: Three chevrons and crown.
Sergeant: Three chevrons.
Corporal or Bombardier: Two chevrons.

Badges of rank for warrant officers Class I and Class II are worn on the forearm of both sleeves, of the battledress blouse, service dress jacket, summer dress jacket, and greatcoats. On other garments, including working clothing, they are worn on the right only. Badges of rank for noncommissioned officers are worn with the point of the chevron downward. They are worn on both sleeves of the battledress blouse, summer dress jacket and greatcoat. On other garments, excepting waterpoof coats, but including working clothing, on the arm only.

The lance appointment of a trooper, gunner, sapper, signalman, driver, private, guardsman, fusilier, rifleman or craftsman, is shown by badges worn wtih the point of chevron downward on the uniform as follows:

Lance Bombardier: One chevron.
Lance Corporal: One chevron.

It is worn on both sleeves of the battledress blouse, summer dress jacket and greatcoat. On other garments, excepting waterproof coat, but including working clothing, on the right arm only.

Corps or unit are shown by a cap badge worn on the military headdress as follows:

Field Marshal: The royal crest with crossed batons within a laurel wreath.
General Officers: The royal crest with crossed sword and baton within a laurel wreath.
Brigadiers and Colonels: The royal crest.

Personnel of each corps wear a corps metal cap badge except that personnel of units of the Royal Canadian Armoured Corps, Royal Canadian Infantry Corps, and Canadian Officers' Training Corps wear a unit or contingent metal cap badge.

Gorget patches are worn on the collar of certain garments by personnel of the Canadian Army as follows:

Field marshals, general officers, brigadiers and colonels wear the appropriate gorget patch on the collar of the service dress, summer dress jacket and battledress blouse.

Officers and warrant officers Class I of the Active Force wear a corps collar badge except in the case of units of the Royal Canadian Armoured Corps and Royal Canadian Infantry Corps. They may wear a unit collar badge. Corps and unit collar badges are worn on service dress and summer dress jackets only.

Warrant officers Class II, NCO's and men wear corps or unit collar badges of the approved design on the summer dress jacket by personnel of the Active Force, in accordance with regimental custom.

Navy.—The insignia of rank of officers of the Canadian Navy is similar to that of the British Navy and is denoted by the same number and width of stripes (except flag officers) on the shoulder straps of other uniforms.

The word "Canada" appears on all buttons, and "Canada" on the shoulders.

The branch to which the officer belongs is denoted by different colors between the stripes (executive—plain, supply—white, engineering—purple, electrical—green, medical—red, constructor—grey, instructor—blue, ordnance—royal blue, special branch—light green.)

The uniform of chief petty officers, petty officers and men is similar to that of the British Navy. Buttons show the word "Canada," and "Canada" appears on the shoulders of all uniforms. The men wear a cap ribbon which reads "HMCS" followed by the ship's name. Substantive rate below chief petty officer is denoted by badge worn on the left arm and branch or trade insignia is worn on right arm.

Officers and men above the rate of petty officer, 1st class, also wear a khaki uniform similar to the United States Navy but with the above mentioned insignia.

Air Force.—The insignia of rank of the Royal Canadian Air Force is the same as that of the Royal Air Force and is a light blue braid of varying widths. It is worn on the shoulder of the greatcoat, raincoat, and working jacket, and on the sleeve of the tunic. The letters "R.C.A.F." instead of "R.A.F." are worn on the wings, which are on the left breast of the tunic, and also on the buttons of the uniform.

Warrant officers are of two classes: warrant officer, Class I, wearing the royal arms; warrant officer, Class II, wearing the crown. Noncommissioned officers are of three classes: flight sergeant, three chevrons with crown above; sergeant, three chevrons; corporal, two chevrons.

CHINA

Army.—The insignia of rank of the Chinese Nationalist Army was changed in May 1946 and now conforms in a general way to that of the United States Army. The following insignia are worn on the shoulder straps:

Special Ranking General: Five gold stars fastened together in a circle.
General of the Army: Four gold stars fastened together in a square.
General: Three gold stars fastened together in a triangle.
Lieutenant General: Two gold stars.
Major General: One gold star.
Colonel: Three gold plum flowers (Chinese national flower) in a triangle.
Lieutenant Colonel: Two gold plum flowers.
Major: One gold plum flower.
Captain: Three silver bars.
First Lieutenant: Two silver bars.
Second Lieutenant: One silver bar.
Warrant Officer: One silver square.

The insignia signifying the branch of service (corps device) in most corps are the same as those of the United States Army. The corps devices (gold) are as follows: artillery, cannon on wheels; cavalry, crossed swords; infantry, crossed rifles; signal, crossed flags; quartermaster, wheel; engineers, castle; staff, crossed batons; military police, crossed pistols; tank, tank. For officers below the rank of general, the corps device is worn on the left side of the collar. On the right side is worn a gold plum flower. Officers of general rank wear no corps device but wear the plum flower on both sides of the collar. General officers wear on sleeves a piping of red; field officers, yellow; company officers, blue.

The rating insignia for noncommissioned officers are the same as those for similar ratings in the United States Army.

Air Force.—In the air corps the insignia of rank is worn on the outer part of lower sleeves as follows (all bars are of gold):

General: Three narrow bars above two wide bars.
Lieutenant General: Two narrow bars above two wide bars.
Major General: One narrow bar above two wide bars.
Colonel: Three narrow bars above one wide bar.
Lieutenant Colonel: Two narrow bars above one wide bar.
Major: One narrow bar above one wide bar.
Captain: Three narrow bars.
First Lieutenant: Two narrow bars.
Second Lieutenant: One narrow bar.

A gold eagle is worn above the sleeve stripes.

All flying officers wear a winged three-bladed propeller on each side of the collar. All non-flying officers wear a winged two-bladed propeller with wheel in the center.

Navy.—As in the United States Navy, the rank of officers of the navy is denoted by the number and width of stripes of gold lace on the sleeves of the blue service and dress uniforms and on the shoulder marks of other uniforms:

Admiral of the Fleet: One broad stripe with four medium stripes above.
Admiral: One broad stripe with three medium stripes above.

Vice Admiral: One broad stripe with two medium stripes above.
Rear Admiral: One broad stripe with one medium stripe above.
Commodore: One broad stripe.
Captain: Four medium stripes.
Commander: Three medium stripes.
Lieutenant Commander: Two medium stripes with one narrow stripe above.
Lieutenant: Two medium stripes.
Junior Lieutenant: One narrow stripe above one medium stripe.
Sublieutenant: One medium stripe.

Above the gold stripes all line and engineer officers wear a circle of wheat. On the shoulder marks, the insignia of rank are as follows:

Admiral of the fleet, vice admiral, rear admiral, commodore: shoulder marks completely covered with gold lace, with silver sun enclosed in blue circle above silver crossed anchors and with four, three, two, one, and no silver star below respectively.

Captain, commander, and lieutenant commander: shoulder marks covered with two wide gold lace stripes, with one silver sun enclosed in blue circle above silver anchor and three, two, and one silver star respectively.

Lieutenant, junior lieutenant, and sublieutenant: shoulder marks covered with three narrow gold stripes, with silver sun enclosed in blue circle above three, two, and one silver star respectively.

Staff corps officers wear, between stripes, color of branch of service.

DENMARK

Army.—The insignia of rank of the officers of the army is worn on the shoulder marks. For dress uniforms the shoulder marks of officers of the rank of general, colonel and lieutenant colonel are pear shaped, for all other officers rectangular shaped. For generals they are interwoven in gold; for all other ranks, the color of the arm or service. For field service uniforms, the shoulder marks for all ranks are rectangular in shape with gold button at the top and bordered with braid. The rank is designated as follows:

General, Lieutenant General, and Major General: Three, two, and one large silver star.
Colonel, Lieutenant Colonel, and Major: Three, two, and one medium-sized star respectively.
Captain, First Lieutenant, and Second Lieutenant: Three, two, and one small star respectively.

For service uniforms, the stars are of gold; for dress uniforms, silver.

Warrant officers (*officiant grippin*) wear buttons in place of stars.

Navy.—The insignia of rank of officers of the navy is worn on the sleeves of blue service and dress uniforms; also on shoulder marks or epaulets. Naval officer ranks are designated as follows:

Admiral: Three large stripes with one medium stripe above.
Vice Admiral: Two large stripes with one medium stripe above and below.
Rear Admiral: One large stripe with one medium stripe above and two medium stripes below.
Commodore: Four medium stripes.
Captain: Three medium stripes and one narrow stripe between top two stripes.
Commander: Three medium stripes.
Lieutenant Commander: Two medium with one narrow stripe between.
Lieutenant: Two medium stripes.
Sublieutenant: One medium stripe.

All officers of the line of executive branch wear a loop above the top stripe. Nonexecutive officers wear the corps device over the stripes instead of the loop.

The cap insignia consists of gold anchor placed on the national "cocada" and surmounted by gold oak leaves and crown above.

Aviators of the army wear wings with two crossed guns and one cannon between, and a crown above, all in gold.

Aviators of the navy wear wings with anchor between and crown above.

FRANCE

Army.—The insignia of rank of officers and warrant officers of the French Army, formerly worn on sleeves of blue uniforms, are now worn (since 1944) on the shoulders and on the headdress. On the shoulder straps the insignia for general officers are as follows:

Marshal of France: Seven silver stars.
General of Army: Five silver stars.
General of Army Corps: Four silver stars.
General of Division: Three silver stars.
General of Brigade: Two silver stars.

For officers below the rank of general in the infantry, artillery, engineers, health service and certain cavalry units (Spahis), the insignia is as follows:

Colonel: Five gold stripes, the upper two separated from lower three.
Lieutenant Colonel: Five stripes (three gold and two silver or inversely, depending on corps). the upper two separated from lower three.
Major: Four gold stripes, the upper one separated from lower three.
Captain: Three gold stripes.
Lieutenant: Two gold stripes.
Second Lieutenant: One gold stripe.

Officers of the cavalry, Quartermaster Corps, military police and Chasseurs Alpins wear stripes of silver in place of gold, and gold in place of silver. The same insignia is worn on caps. General officers wear under the star insignia rows of oak leaves. Marshal of France has three; generals, except general of brigade, two; and general of brigade, one. Other officers wear the same number and kind of stripes on cap as stripes on shoulder straps. Chief of warrant officers wears one stripe of the same color as the officers of the corps but with red thread in center. Warrant officers wear a stripe similar to the officers of the corps but of the opposite metal, that is, silver when the officer's is gold, with red thread in center. All other noncommissioned officers wear chevrons on the left sleeve as follows: master sergeant, three chevrons, gold or silver, depending on corps; sergeant, one chevron, gold or silver; chief corporal, three chevrons (one gold or silver, two in wool); corporal, two woolen chevrons. The private (first class) is distinguished from a simple private by a single woolen chevron.

The arm or service is indicated by the color patches on the kepis (caps) and on the left sleeves, as follows:

Branch of Service	Color of Kepi	Color of Collar Patch
Infantry	Dark blue, red top	Khaki
Cavalry	Black, red top	Black
Artillery	Black	Red
Engineers	Black	Black velvet
Quartermaster Corps	Dark blue, red top	Light blue
Medical Corps	Dark red velvet	Dark red velvet
Veterinary Corps	Crimson	Crimson
Pharmacist	Green	Green
Military Police	Black, blue top	Black
Spahis	Light blue	Light blue
Chasseurs d'Afrique	Light blue, red top	Light blue
Chasseurs Alpins	Black, light blue top	Black

Air Corps.—The insignia of rank for the air corps is the same as that of the army of equal rank with the exception that stripes are worn around sleeves instead of on shoulder straps. On the caps (above the stripes or rows of laurel leaves and below the stars of general officers) are worn two wings, gold for all officers and noncommissioned officers including sergeant; lower ranks, orange.

Navy.—The insignia of rank of officers of the French Navy is worn on the sleeves of the blue uniform and on the shoulder marks of other uniforms. On the sleeve the insignia is as follows:

Admiral: Five silver stars.
Vice Admiral (in command of forces): Four silver stars.
Vice Admiral: Three silver stars.
Rear Admiral: Two silver stars.
Captain: Five gold stripes (the upper two separated from lower three).
Commander: Five stripes, three gold, two silver (the upper separated from lower three).
Lieutenant Commander: Four gold stripes (the upper one separated from lower three).
Lieutenant: Three gold stripes.
Lieutenant (junior grade): Two gold stripes.
Ensign: One gold stripe.
Midshipman: One broken blue and gold stripe.

The insignia on the shoulder marks are identical with those on the sleeves with the addition of a gold foul anchor above the stars or stripes. The commissioned enlisted corps (up to and including commander) wear the same insignia but distinguished by a vertical patch on top of the stripes and no anchor is worn on the shoulder marks. The line, administrative, and commissioned enlisted corps wear no corps color on the sleeves or shoulder marks. Other corps wear the corps color as the background on the shoulder marks and the sleeve stripes. Corps flag officers wear a narrow patch of corps color, with three gold buttons sewed along the sleeve seam. Administrators and civil engineers wear silver stripes in place of gold and gold where line officers wear silver.

On blue uniforms, officers of the army, air force, and navy also wear a gold shoulder (epaulet) strap, fore and aft, with gold embroidery on top. General and flag officers are distinguished from senior officers by wearing a wider strap. Junior officers wear straps the same width as those of senior officers but with less embroidery. Warrant and noncommissioned officers, except corporals, wear straps of gold without embroidery, but with red thread interwoven in center. Corporals and privates wear none.

ITALY

Army.—The insignia of rank of officers of the army is worn on the shoulder straps of all uniforms. All officers and enlisted personnel of all services except flag officers, who have a gold star, wear a silver star on either side of collar. The color and design of the collar patch show to which branch of the service and to which regiment they belong. The insignia of rank, worn on the shoulder straps, is as follows:

Lieutenant General: Three gold stars on shoulder mark of silver braid.
Major General: The same with two gold stars.
Brigadier General: The same with one gold star.
Colonel: Three gold stars on shoulder mark with gold braid edging.
Lieutenant Colonel: The same with two gold stars.
Major: The same with one gold star.
Captain: Three gold stars on shoulder mark without edging.
First Lieutenant: The same with two gold stars.
Second Lieutenant: The same with one gold star.

Officers of rank of general wear on cap chin straps of interwoven silver braid; officers of field rank wear chin straps of interwoven gold braid. Officers of lower ranks wear chin straps of plain gold braid.

Navy.—The insignia of rank of officers of the navy is worn on the outer cuffs of the sleeves of blue service and dress uniforms and overcoats and on the shoulder marks of white uniforms and is indicated by the width and number of gold stripes. The upper stripe forms a loop above.

Admiral, Vice Admiral, Rear Admiral: Three, two, and one medium gold stripe respectively above Greek frieze design.
Captain, Commander, Lieutenant Commander: One broad stripe below three, two, and one medium stripe respectively.
First Lieutenant: Three medium stripes with a small gold baton below.
Lieutenant, Lieutenant (junior grade), Ensign: Three, two, and one medium stripe respectively.

Noncommissioned officers, 1st, 2d, and 3d class, three, two, and one medium gold stripe with interwoven blue threads respectively.

The corps insignia instead of loop is worn above.

The shoulder mark of officers of flag rank is covered with gold braid with anchor above three, two, and one star respectively.

Officers of branches of the service other than the line or executive branch wear colors between the stripes as follows:

Ordnance constructors, yellow brown; naval constructors and engineers, dark purple; medical officers, blue; paymasters, red; chemists, green; harbor masters, gray green.

The cap insignia for officers of the line consists of an anchor enclosed in wreath of oak leaves and surmounted by a tower, all in gold. Officers of other corps wear the corps insignia instead of the anchor.

Air Force.—The insignia of rank of officers of the air force is identical with that of officers of the navy, and is as follows:

Lieutenant General, Major General, Brigadier General: Three, two, and one medium gold stripe respectively, above gold Greek frieze design.
Colonel, Lieutenant Colonel, Major: One broad stripe with three, two, and one medium stripe above respectively, all in gold.

Captain, First Lieutenant, Second Lieutenant: Three, two, and one medium stripe respectively.

A diamond shape instead of loop is worn above top stripe by all ranks. The insignia of rank is worn on the outer cuffs of sleeves of all uniforms except the white uniforms and field service uniforms. On the latter two uniforms the insignia is worn on shoulder marks with gold wings above. On the former, a gold bordered shoulder strap enclosing gold wings is also worn. The cap insignia consists of an eagle enclosed in wreath of oak leaves, all of gold.

NETHERLANDS

Army.—The insignia of rank of officers of the Royal Netherlands Army, worn on the lapels of the coat, is as follows:

Lieutenant General: Four silver stars.
Major General: Two silver and two gold stars.
Colonel: Three silver stars with horizontal gold stripe above.
Lieutenant Colonel: The same with two silver stars.
Major: The same with one silver star.
Captain: Three silver stars.
First Lieutenant: Two silver stars.
Second Lieutenant: One silver star.
Warrant Officer: One silver button.

Chaplains wear a cross above the insignia. The arm or the service is indicated on the shoulder strap as follows: infantry, a horn; cavalry, two crossed swords; artillery, two crossed guns; engineers, a helmet; general staff, a star.

The cap insignia consists of a golden cockade with orange center.

Navy.—The rank of officers of the Royal Netherlands Navy is denoted by the number and width of stripes of gold lace on the sleeves of the blue service and dress uniforms (with stars above for officers of flag rank), and on the shoulder marks of other uniforms. A loop is worn above the top stripe.

Admiral: One broad gold stripe below one medium gold stripe with four silver stars above.
Vice Admiral: The same with three silver stars.
Rear Admiral: The same with two silver stars.
Captain: Four medium gold stripes.
Commander: Three medium gold stripes.
Lieutenant Commander: Two medium gold stripes with one narrow gold stripe between.
Lieutenant: Two medium gold stripes.
Ensign: One medium gold stripe.
Chaplain: Two medium gold stripes below one medium light blue stripe. On the shoulder mark above the stripes is a cross enclosed in sprays of oak leaves, all in gold.

The various corps are distinguished by means of insignia worn on the cap emblem, buttons, and lapels of the blue uniforms. Corps insignia, except for chaplains, do not appear on the shoulder marks. Corps insignia is as follows: line, gold anchor below gold crown; engineers, gold torch on crossed gold arrows below gold crown; medical, gold caduceus below gold crown; aviation, gold six-cylinder motor on gold two-bladed propeller below gold crown. The cap insignia is the same except that the distinguishing insignia is enclosed in sprays of gold oak leaves.

NORWAY

Army.—A new uniform with new insignia is at present under consideration for the Royal Norwegian Army and Air Force. The present insignia of rank is worn on the shoulder straps of overcoats and on the collars of service uniforms as follows:

General, Lieutenant General, Major General: Three, two, and one large silver star on shoulder strap of gold braid and on gold collar patch respectively.
Colonel, Lieutenant Colonel, Major: Three, two, and one silver star on shoulder strap and on coat lapel with silver stripe around the strap and along part of the edge of collar.
Captain, Lieutenant, Second Lieutenant: Three, two, and one silver star on shoulder strap and coat collar.

Badges for various arms of service, similar in shape to United States decorations and medal ribbons, are worn on battledress as follows: infantry, red; artillery, red and blue; engineers, blue and red; signals, blue and white; intelligence, green; quartermaster, yellow; transport, yellow and blue; ordnance, red, blue, and red. Noncommissioned officers wear chevrons (point up) as follows: staff sergeant, three chevrons over crown; sergeant, three chevrons; corporal, two; vice corporal, one.

Navy.—The insignia of rank of officers of the Norwegian Navy is the same as that of the British Navy with the following exceptions. The highest rank is that of admiral. An admiral wears a medium stripe below the broad stripe besides the three medium stripes above. Also vice admirals and rear admirals have a medium stripe below the broad one. A commodore wears three stripes over a semibroad stripe. Midshipmen, third class, wear three stars; second class, two stars; first class, one star. Chief petty officers and petty officers wear two or one gold chevron; conscripted petty officers, one red chevron. Enlisted ratings, 1st class, wear three diagonal stripes and anchor; leading seamen and stokers, one red chevron and anchor.

Commissioned officers of the executive branch have the "curl" or loop, as in the British Navy, above the stripes, while those of the Naval Reserve have a triangular loop. Other branches of the service, other than the executive, have the same number and width of stripes but with color between stripes as follows: engineers, purple; surgeons, red; paymasters, white; technical and special branches, green.

Air Force.—The air force wear insignia of rank identical with that of the army. The insignia is worn on the shoulder straps of the battledress and on the top coat. Colonels, lieutenant colonels, and majors wear a braid across the strap and nearest to the outer side with stars (or star) as on the army shoulder strap.

On the service coat the insignia is worn on the collar as in the army.

PORTUGAL

Army.—The insignia of rank of officers of the army is denoted by the number and width of stripes of gold lace on the sleeves. Officers of general rank wear stars above.

General: One wide stripe below a narrow stripe with three stars above.
Brigadier General: The same with two stars above.
Colonel: Three narrow stripes above one medium stripe.

Lieutenant Colonel: Two narrow stripes above one medium stripe.
Major: One narrow stripe above one medium stripe.
Captain: Three narrow stripes.
First Lieutenant: Two narrow stripes.
Second Lieutenant: One narrow stripe.

The arm or service is indicated as follows: cavalry, two crossed swords; infantry, two crossed guns; artillery, two crossed cannon; engineers, medieval fort.

Navy.—The insignia of rank of officers of the navy are denoted by the number and width of stripes of gold lace on the sleeves of blue service and dress uniforms and by the same number and width of stripes (except flag officers) on the shoulder marks of other uniforms; a loop is worn above the upper stripe of line officers. Gold buttons are worn above and below the stripes on the sleeves.

Admiral: One broad and one medium stripe with four gold stars below; four gold stars below silver anchor on shoulder marks bordered with gold oak leaves.
Vice Admiral: The same with three gold stars.
Rear Admiral: The same with three silver stars.
Captain: Three narrow stripes above one medium stripe.
Commander: Two narrow stripes above one medium stripe.
Lieutenant Commander: One narrow stripe above one medium stripe.
Lieutenant: Three narrow stripes.
Ensign: One narrow stripe.

Officers, other than those of the line, are distinguished by the corps cap insignia and the corps color used as a background for the rank stripes on sleeves and shoulder marks as follows: doctors, red; construction engineers, dark green; engineers, mechanical and engine construction, purple; administration, blue; commissioned enlisted corps, brown.

The cap insignia consists of a silver anchor enclosed in oval of gold enclosed in two sprigs of oak leaves and coat of arms above.

UNION OF SOVIET SOCIALIST REPUBLICS

Army.—In 1941 the Soviet Army uniforms and insignia of rank were changed. The insignia of rank are worn on shoulder marks as follows:

Marshal of the Soviet Union: One large silver star below silver national coat of arms on a gold braid-covered shoulder mark with red borders.
Chief Marshal: One silver star within two silver branches of laurel tied at bottom and below the corps insignia.
Marshal: Large silver star below the corps insignia.
General: Four silver stars below the corps insignia.
Colonel General: Three silver stars below the corps insignia.
Lieutenant General: Two silver stars below the corps insignia.
Major General: One silver star below the corps insignia.

Shoulder marks of all line officers of general rank are of interwoven gold lace with a border of red for all corps except air force (light blue), and engineers (raspberry). Shoulder marks of staff officers are of silver lace with gold stars.

Colonel: Three silver stars below the corps insignia.
Lieutenant Colonel: Two silver stars below the corps insignia.
Major: One silver star below the corps insignia.

Shoulder marks of above officers of field rank are of gold lace with two longitudinal stripes and border of color of corps, arm, or service.

Captain: Four silver stars, one above three in triangle, below corps insignia.
Senior Lieutenant: Three silver stars, below corps insignia.
Lieutenant: Two silver stars, below corps insignia.
Junior Lieutenant: One silver star, below corps insignia.

Shoulder marks of above company officers are of gold lace with one longitudinal stripe and border of color of corps.

Infantry officers do not wear corps device above insignia of rank.

Shoulder marks of brown instead of gold are worn on field uniforms.

The insignia and colors denoting arm or service (corps device) are as follows:

Armored: Gold tank—red.
Infantry: Gold crossed guns within circle—raspberry.
Cavalry: Gold crossed swords within horseshoe—dark blue.
Artillery: Gold crossed cannon—red.
Engineer: Gold crossed hammer and wrench—black.
Chemical: Two acetylene tanks crossed with receptacle in center (all in gold)—black.
Medical Corps: Serpent around urn (gold)—red.
Veterinary Corps: Same in silver.
Air: Gold winged propeller—light blue.
Intendance: Gold star, sickle and hammer—red.

Enlisted personnel wear shoulder marks of color or arm or service, as follows:

Master Sergeant: Broad horizontal gold stripe with narrow vertical stripe below with corps insignia.
Staff Sergeant: Broad gold stripe with corps insignia below.
Sergeant: Three narrow horizontal gold stripes with corps insignia below.
Corporal: Two narrow horizontal gold stripes with corps insignia below.
Private, 1st Class: One narrow silver stripe with corps insignia below.
Private: Without stripes.

With field uniforms the shoulder marks are brown with stripes of red or brown.

The cap device consists of a five-pointed red star on which the national emblem of crossed hammer and sickle is inscribed.

On dress uniform general officers wear three gold patches on cuff of sleeve; field officers, two; company officers, one.

Navy.—Line officers and line engineering officers wear on all blue uniforms, except overcoats, insignia of rank on the cuffs of the sleeves and also on shoulder marks. Officers of other corps wear the insignia of rank only on the shoulder marks. On white uniforms and overcoats, shoulder marks only are worn by all officers. Line and line engineering officers are also the only ones having navy titles. Officers of all other corps have army titles.

The insignia of rank worn on sleeves of line and line engineering officers consists of horizontal gold bars (instead of stripes around sleeve), the number and width for officers of flag rank being identical with the stripes of United States naval officers of the same rank. The insignia of rank of officers of lower grades is as follows:

Captain, 1st grade: One broad bar.
Captain, 2d grade: Four medium bars.
Captain, 3d grade: Three medium bars.
Captain Lieutenant: One narrow above two medium bars.
Senior Lieutenant: Two medium bars.
Lieutenant: One narrow above one medium bar.
Junior Lieutenant: One medium bar.

Above the gold bars is worn a gold star. Officers of flag rank wear a large gold star with gold hammer and sickle in center; other officers a small gold star.

The insignia of rank on shoulder marks for all line and line engineering officers is as follows:

Admiral of the Fleet, Admiral, Vice Admiral, Rear Admiral: Shoulder marks completely covered with interwoven gold lace, with one large, three, two, and one small gold star with anchor in red center respectively.

Captain, 1st grade; Captain, 2d grade; Captain, 3d grade: Shoulder marks covered with one wide and two narrow gold lace stripes with three, two, and one silver star respectively.

Captain Lieutenant, Senior Lieutenant, Lieutenant, Junior Lieutenant: Shoulder marks covered with two wide gold lace stripes with four, three, two, and one silver star respectively.

The insignia of rank shown on shoulder marks of other corps are distinguished by difference in color of braid, stars and piping; and in some corps, by the addition of the following corps device worn above the stars: line engineers, crossed hammer and monkey wrench (gold for flag rank, silver for other ranks); medical, snake wound around urn (silver); legal, shield superimposed on two crossed swords (gold).

Everyone, men as well as officers, wears shoulder marks. The shoulder marks of warrant officers have one wide longitudinal gold stripe; chief petty officers, one wide latitudinal gold stripe; petty officers, 1st class, three medium latitudinal gold stripes; petty officers, 2d class, two; leading seamen, one; seamen, none.

UNITED KINGDOM

Army.—The insignia of rank of the British Army is worn on the shoulder straps of the service coat, overcoat, and field jacket of commissioned officers:

Field Marshal: Crossed red batons within a golden laurel wreath, surmounted by a crown of gold with red inlay.
General: A gold crossed sword and baton with a four-cornered star above surmounted by a crown of gold with red inlay.
Lieutenant General: A gold crossed sword and baton surmounted by a crown of gold with red inlay.
Major General: A gold crossed sword and baton with a four-cornered gold star above.
Brigadier General: Three four-cornered gold stars surmounted by a crown of gold with red inlay.
Colonel: Two four-cornered gold stars vertically spaced, surmounted by a crown of gold with red inlay.
Lieutenant Colonel: One four-cornered gold star surmounted by a crown of gold with red inlay.
Major: A crown of gold with red inlay.
Captain: Three four-cornered gold stars, vertically spaced.
First Lieutenant: Two four-cornered gold stars, vertically spaced.
Second Lieutenant: One four-cornered gold star.

All of the above insignia are sometimes worn in dull bronze.

Red collar or gorget patches are worn by all officers of staff rank. Those of brigadier general and above wear a red collar patch with a gold stripe of laurel leaf design through the center. Those of the rank of colonel wear a colored collar or gorget patch with a stripe of black braid through the center. Gorget patches are worn in different colors according to the branch: Royal Engineer Service, blue (bright); education, blue (pale); General Staff and Ordnance, red (scarlet); medical, cherry; veterinary, maroon; chaplain, purple; dental, green; pay, yellow.

The ranks of colonel and above are distinguished by a colored band around the cap. The cap device for field marshal consists of two crossed red batons superimposed on two branches of gold laurel leaves tied at the bottom, surmounted by a crown in gold and red with multicolored jewels in crown and golden lion on top; general officers, crossed sword and baton superimposed on wreath, all in gold and surmounted by a crown with lion above; all other officers, regimental or other badge. The cap visor of field marshal is covered with gold; general, one row of gold.

Corps, departmental, or regimental badges are worn on the lapels of the tunic.

Warrant officers, noncommissioned officers, and enlisted men wear rank and appointment badges on both forearms. Tradesmen and instructors' badges are worn below rank badges by warrant officers. Noncommissioned officers wear chevrons (point downward) on both upper sleeves with regimental and corps badges on or above: lance corporal, or lance bombardier, one chevron; corporal or bombardier, two; sergeant, three; color sergeant and corporal of horse, staff sergeant, three chevrons and crown.

Royal Air Force.—The rank of officers of the Royal Air Force is denoted by the number and width of stripes of black and blue braid (gold on full dress) on the cuffs of the sleeves of all uniforms except the winter greatcoat. On the latter uniform, shoulder marks with the same insignia designation are worn.

Marshal of the R.A.F.: One broad and four medium stripes.
Air Chief Marshal: One broad and three medium stripes.
Air Marshal: One broad and two medium stripes.
Air Vice Marshal: One broad and one medium stripe.
Air Commodore: One broad stripe.
Group Captain: Four medium stripes.
Wing Commander: Three medium stripes.
Squadron Leader: Two medium and one narrow stripe.

Flight Lieutenant: Two medium stripes.
Flying Officer: One medium stripe.
Pilot Officer: One narrow stripe.

The cap device of marshal consists of two bunches of gold laurel leaves tied at bottom with gold flying eagle superimposed, the top of wreath enclosing crown with lion above; other officers, a flying eagle above four laurel leaves tied at bottom surmounted by a crown, all in gold, with color in crown. Corps or departmental badges are worn on the lapels of the tunic.

Warrant officers, noncommissioned officers, and enlisted men wear rank and appointment badges on both forearms. Noncommissioned officers wear chevrons (point downward) on both upper sleeves with corps badges above; corporal, two chevrons; sergeant and flight sergeant, three chevrons.

Navy.—The insignia of rank of officers of the British Royal Navy, except commodore (1st class), is similar to that of the United States Navy, and is denoted by the number and width of stripes on the sleeves of the blue service and dress uniforms and by the same number and width of stripes (except flag officers) on the shoulder marks of other uniforms.

Admiral of the Fleet: On sleeve, one broad stripe and four medium stripes above; gold lace-covered shoulder mark, with crossed batons within a laurel wreath and royal cipher above, surmounted by a crown.
Admiral: One broad stripe with three medium stripes above; gold lace-covered shoulder mark with three eight-pointed silver stars and crossed sword and baton above, surmounted by a crown.
Vice Admiral: One broad stripe with two medium stripes above; gold lace-covered shoulder mark, with two silver stars vertically and crossed sword and baton above, surmounted by a crown.
Rear Admiral: One broad stripe with one medium stripe above; gold lace-covered shoulder mark, with large silver star and crossed sword and baton above, surmounted by a crown.
Commodore, 1st class: One broad stripe with one medium stripe above; gold lace-covered shoulder mark, with silver foul anchor and two silver stars horizontally above, surmounted by a crown.
Commodore, 2d class: One broad stripe.
Captain: Four medium stripes.
Commander: Three medium stripes.
Lieutenant Commander: Two medium and one narrow stripe.
Lieutenant: Two medium stripes.
Sublieutenant: One medium stripe.
Midshipman: White collar patch with brass button and white loop below.
Warrant Officer: One narrow stripe.

All officers wear a curl above the stripes instead of a star as worn in the United States Navy. Corps officers (as opposed to line or executive officers) are distinguished by colors which appear between the rank stripes on sleeves and shoulder marks: Ordnance Corps, dark blue; Engineers Corps, purple; electrical engineer, green; shipwright and naval constructor, silver gray; medical, scarlet; dental, orange; ward master, purple; supply and secretariat, white; instructor and schoolmaster, light blue; special branch (RNVR only), dark green.

Officers of the Royal Navy, Royal Naval Reserve, and Royal Navy Volunteer Reserve are differentiated only by the form of their rank stripes.

The cap insignia of commissioned officers consists of a silver foul anchor within two branches of gold laurel leaves, tied at bottom, and surmounted by a golden crown with red inlay and multicolored jewels.

The caps of captains and commanders have a single row of gold laurel leaves on the visors. The cap visors of flag officers have two rows of gold laurel leaves.

UNITED STATES

Army.—The cap insignia of officers and enlisted men is the United States coat of arms, the former in cut-out form, the latter on a disk. The cap insignia for warrant officers and United States Military Academy cadets is the same as the insignia worn by them on their coat lapels.

Shoulder insignia worn on service coat, overcoat, and field jacket of officers and warrant officers is as follows:

General of the Army: Five silver stars, fastened together in a circle, worn below the coat of arms of the United States, in gold color with shield and crest of enamel.
General: Four silver stars.
Lieutenant General: Three silver stars.
Major General: Two silver stars.
Brigadier General: One silver star.
Colonel: One silver spread eagle.
Lieutenant Colonel: One silver oak leaf.
Major: One gold oak leaf.
Captain: Two silver bars.
First Lieutenant: One silver bar.
Second Lieutenant: One gold bar.
Chief Warrant Officer: One gold bar with rounded edges, having a brown enameled top and longitudinal center of gold.
Warrant Officer (junior grade): One gold bar with rounded edges, having a brown enameled top and a latitudinal center of gold.
Contract Surgeon: One silver bar.

When the shirt is worn without the service coat, general officers of the line wear insignia of rank on both sides of the collar. All other officers and warrant officers wear the insignia of rank on the right side of the collar. On the left side, the insignia indicating arm, service, or bureau is worn.

Insignia of rank is worn by officers and warrant officers on the left side of the garrison cap and on the front of the steel helmet.

Warrant officers, Army Mine Planter Service, wear their insignia of rank on the sleeves of jackets:

Master: Four bands of brown braid with brown foul anchor above.
Chief Engineer: Same as master, substituting three-bladed propeller for anchor.
First Mate: Same as master with three bands instead of four.
Assistant Engineer: Same as chief engineer with three bands instead of four.
Second Mate: Same as first mate with two bands instead of three.
Second Assistant Engineer: Same as assistant engineer with two bands instead of three.

Chevrons to denote the grade of enlisted men are worn on the outer upper half of both sleeves of all coats, the field jacket, the shirt when worn without a coat, and of work clothing. *Master sergeant* (*1st grade*) wears three chevrons above three arcs. *First sergeant* (*1st grade*) wears three chevrons above three arcs with a hollow lozenge between the lower chevron and the upper arc. This is an occupational title appropriate to a first grade position of such special importance in the noncommissioned officer corps that distinctive insignia of grade is provided. *Sergeant 1st class* (*second grade*) wears three chevrons above two arcs. *Sergeant* (*third grade*) wears three chevrons above one arc. *Corporal* (*4th grade*) wears two chevrons. *Private, first class* (*5th grade*) wears one chevron. The occupational title of *sergeant major* applies to the appropriate individuals at regimental and battalion levels. Combat insignia is of gold color background with dark blue color chevrons, arcs and lozenge. Noncombat insignia is of dark blue color background with gold color chevrons, arc and lozenge. The former is worn by combat personnel, the latter by noncombat personnel.

All officers wear on the collar and lapel of the service coat the letters "U.S." and, centered below, the insignia indicating the arm, service, or bureau. Warrant officers wear the insignia of warrant officers in lieu of arm or service insignia. Enlisted men wear a gold colored disk insignia on each side of collar with the letters "U.S.," and on each lapel a disk insignia of arm, service, or bureau.

The insignia for collar and lapel of coat for general of the armies of the United States, chief of staff, former chiefs of staff, and full generals may be such as they may prescribe.

Each arm, service, and bureau has a distinctive insignia worn on both lapels of coat as follows:

Adjutant General's Department: Enameled red, white, and blue shield.
Air Corps: Pair of wings with vertical silver propeller.
Armor: Side view of tank.
Aide to General: Shield surmounted by an eagle. Stars in chief indicate grade of general whom the aide serves.
Cavalry: Two crossed sabers.
Chaplain: Christian, silver Latin cross; Jewish, silver Mosaic tablet with Roman numerals surmounted by the Star of David.
Chemical Corps: Benzine ring superimposed in the center of crossed retorts.
Corps of Engineers: Triple turret castle.
Artillery: Two crossed field guns.
Finance Department: Diamond.
General Staff Corps: United States coat of arms on silver star.
Infantry: Two crossed muskets.
Inspector General's Department: Sword and fasces crossed and wreathed with inscription *Droit et Avant.*
Judge Advocate General's Department: Sword and pen crossed and superimposed on two bunches of laurel leaves tied at bottom.
Medical Department, Medical Corps: A caduceus; other corps, a caduceus with letters to denote various corps superimposed.
Military Intelligence Reserve: Eared shield bearing a circle within which is a sphinx in profile couchant.
Military Police: Two crossed pistols.
National Guard Bureau: Two crossed fasces superimposed on an eagle.
Staff and Administration Reserve: Coat of arms of the United States within a ring.
Ordnance Department: Shell and flame.
Permanent Professors, Masters of the Sword and Civilian Instructors of the United States Military Academy: Coat of arms of the United States Military Academy consisting of the shield of the United States bearing helmet of Pallas over a Greek sword and surmounted by an eagle displayed with scroll and motto.
Quartermaster's Corps: Sword and key crossed on wheel surmounted by flying eagle, felloe of wheel set with 13 stars.
Signal Corps: Torch superimposed on two signal flags crossed.
Special Services: Three tilting lances superimposed upon a green enamel wreath, two in saltire and one in pale, of gold color metal.
Transportation Corps: Ship's steering wheel, superimposed thereon a shield charged with winged car wheel on a rail.
Warrant Officers: An eagle rising with wings displayed standing on a bundle of two arrows, all enclosed in a wreath.
Women's Army Corps (WAC): Head of Pallas Athene. When assigned to an arm or service, the insignia of that arm or service is worn in lieu of the Pallas Athene.

Most of the arm, service, or bureau insignia for enlisted men have counterparts among the insignia for officers. Army Mine Planter Service has the same device as that of the artillery with the addition of a mine case in lower angle.

Distinctive colors or two-colored combinations are worn to distinguish the arms, services, and bureaus. They are worn as ornamentation and trouser stripes of dress uniforms and on cord-edge braid, hat cords and distinctive insignia, as follows:

Adjutant General's Department: Dark blue and scarlet.
Air Corps: Ultramarine blue and golden orange.
Armor: Green and white.
Cavalry: Yellow.
Chaplain: Black.
Chemical Corps: Cobalt blue and golden yellow.
Corps of Engineers: Scarlet and white.
Artillery: Scarlet.
Finance Department: Silver gray and golden yellow.
Infantry: Light blue.
Inspector General's Department: Dark blue and light blue.
Judge Advocate General's Department: Dark blue and white.
Medical Department: Maroon and white.
Military Intelligence Reserve: Golden yellow and purple.
Military Police: Yellow and green.
National Guard Bureau: Dark blue.
Ordnance Department: Crimson and yellow.
Permanent Professors, U.S. Military Academy: Scarlet and silver gray.
Quartermaster's Corps: Buff.
Signal Corps: Orange and white.
Special Services: Emerald green and silver gray.
Staff Administrative Reserve: Green.
Transportation Corps: Brick red and golden-yellow.
Warrant Officers: Brown.
Women's Army Corps (WAC): Old gold and moss-tone green.

General officers' hats and caps usually have

gold cords; other officers' including WAC's, gold and black; warrant officers, silver and black.

Navy.—The rank of officers of the United States Navy and Naval Reserve is denoted by the number and width of stripes of gold lace on the sleeves of the blue service and dress uniforms. On overcoats, the stripes are black mohair.

Fleet Admiral: One two-inch stripe, with four one-half inch stripes above.
Admiral: One two-inch stripe with three one-half inch stripes above.
Vice Admiral: One two-inch stripe with two one-half inch stripes above.
Rear Admiral: One two-inch stripe with one one-half inch stripe above.
Commodore: One two-inch stripe.
Captain: Four one-half inch stripes.
Commander: Three one-half inch stripes.
Lieutenant Commander: Two one-half inch stripes with one one-fourth inch stripe between.
Lieutenant: Two one-half inch stripes.
Lieutenant (junior grade): One one-half inch stripe with one one-fourth inch stripe above.
Ensign: One one-half inch stripe.
Aviation Cadet: While student, star without a stripe on shoulder marks.
Midshipmen: One-eighth inch gold stripe denoting classes: 1st class, one horizontal stripe; 2d class, two diagonal stripes; 3d class, one diagonal stripe; 4th class, without stripe.
Chief Warrant Officer: One one-half inch broken blue and gold stripe.
Warrant Officer: One one-fourth inch broken blue and gold stripe.
Navy Nurse: The same number of stripes for the insignia of rank as male officers, but without the star or corps insignia.
Woman Commissioned Officer and Warrant Officer: The same number and size of stripes as a male officer of similar rank. A corps device of the same color is worn above stripes.

The insignia of rank worn on the shoulder marks by all commissioned officers, up to and including captain, and by all warrant officers and midshipmen, is the same as that worn on the sleeves. The shoulder marks of flag officers are covered with gold lace and have the following insignia:

Fleet Admiral: A silver foul anchor above five silver stars fastened together in a circle.
Admiral: A silver foul anchor above four silver stars.
Vice Admiral: A silver foul anchor above three silver stars.
Rear Admiral: A silver foul anchor above two silver stars.
Commodore: A silver foul anchor surcharged with a silver star.

Staff officers of flag rank wear corps device superimposed on anchor.

In addition to the insignia of rank indicated by the number and size of the stripes, officers of the several corps wear above the stripes (except on overcoat sleeves) the following corps insignia:

Line Officer: Gold star.
Medical Officers: A silver acorn embroidered upon a gold spread oak leaf.
Dental Officers: A gold spread oak leaf with a silver acorn on either side of stem.
Supply Officers: A gold sprig of three oak leaves and three acorns.
Civil Engineers: Two crossed sprigs, each of two gold live oak leaves and a silver acorn.
Chaplains: Christian, a gold Latin cross; Jewish, gold Mosaic tablet with Roman numerals surmounted by the Star of David.
Leader and Assistant Leader, U.S. Navy Band and officer in charge, U.S. Navy School of Music: A gold lyre.
Hospital Corps: A gold caduceus.
Medical Corps Service: A gold spread oak leaf with a twig.
Medical Service Corps: Spread oak leaf embroidered in gold, with twig below the stem and attached thereto.
Chief Warrant Officers and Warrant Officers, Hospital Corps: Gold caduceus.
Navy Nurse Corps: Gold spread oak leaf.
Chief Boatswains and Boatswains: Two gold-crossed foul anchors.
Chief Gunners and Gunners: Flaming spherical gold shell.
Chief Machinists and Machinists: Three-bladed gold propeller.
Chief Carpenters and Carpenters: Gold carpenter's square.
Chief Pay Clerks and Pay Clerks: Similar device as for the supply corps, but without the acorn.
Chief Electricians and Electricians: Gold globe.
Chief Radio Electricians and Radio Electricians: Four gold zigzag rays of lightning or a spark.
Chief Aerographers and Aerographers: Gold-winged sphere with arrow.
Chief Photographers and Photographers: Gold camera.
Chief Torpedomen and Torpedomen: Gold torpedo.
Chief Ship's Clerks and Ship's Clerks: Two gold-crossed quills.

When summer working uniform is worn without the coat, a miniature metal pin-on rank device similar to that worn by army officers is worn on the collar of the khaki or slate-gray shirt. Officers of the line wear rank designations on both sides of the collar; officers of the staff corps wear them only on the right side and on the left the corps device. Chief warrant officers wear their corps devices in silver, warrant officers in gold on each side of the collar of the shirt. Women commissioned officers and warrant officers wear the insignia of rank and corps device in same manner as male officers.

The cap device for all commissioned officers consists of a silver shield superimposed on two crossed gold foul anchors and surmounted by a silver spread eagle. The cap visors of captains and commanders have a single row of gold oak leaves. The cap visors of flag officers have two rows of gold oak leaves. The cap device of warrant officers consists of two crossed gold foul anchors; of a midshipman, gold foul anchor mounted upright; and of chief petty officers, gold foul anchor with "USN," surcharged thereon, mounted upright. On garrison caps, commissioned officers wear the insignia of rank on the right side of the cap and the cap device on the left side. Chief warrant officers wear the corps device (in silver) on the right side, and their cap device on the left side. Warrant officers wear their gold corps devices on both sides of the cap. Chief petty officers, chief cooks, and chief stewards wear their miniature cap device on the left side.

The rating badges of chief petty officers and petty officers are worn on the left sleeves between the shoulder and elbow. Rating badges consist of an eagle, chevrons and specialty marks, the rating or class of petty officer being indicated by the number of chevrons, the particular branch by the specialty marks.

Specialty marks are worn as part of the rating badge of chief petty officers and petty officers and without rating badges in certain other nonpetty officer ratings.

Marine Corps.—The insignia of rank of commissioned officers of the Marine Corps correspond with the relative rank of commissioned officers of the army and is worn in the same position on the shoulder straps. General is the highest rank held in the Marine Corps. Commissioned warrant officers wear a gold bar with a wide red enameled stripe in center; warrant officers, a gold bar with narrow red enameled stripe in center; and second leader marine band, a silver lyre. Rank insignia is also worn on both sides of collar of shirt. The Marine Corps cap ornament for officers and enlisted men consists of a half globe showing the Western Hemisphere intersected by a foul anchor and surmounted by an eagle with wings extended. For officers' dress it is in silver and gold; officers' service, bronze; enlisted men's dress, gold; enlisted men's service, bronze. This ornament, without rope, is also worn on garrison caps and on each side of the collar of service and dress uniforms of officers and enlisted men. Aides-de-camp wear a shield of the United States surmounted by a gold eagle with a star or stars to indicate rank of the general whom the aide is serving. For service uniforms the insignia are in dull bronze and worn on the lapels of coat.

The ratings of noncommissioned officers and privates 1st class are indicated by chevrons worn on both sleeves of blouse and overcoat and on khaki shirt between elbow and shoulder. Privates 1st class wear one chevron; corporal, two chevrons; sergeant, three chevrons; staff sergeant, three chevrons, the lower one joined by an arc; technical sergeant, same as staff sergeant with two arcs; master sergeant, same as staff sergeant with three arcs.

Air Force.—The cap insignia for officers and warrant officers is the same as that of officers of the army, but it is made of oxidized silver. The visor of the cap worn by general officers and colonels is black broadcloth embroidered with lightning, cloud, and dart pattern in aluminum wire. The cap insignia for airmen is the United States coat of arms, convex, pierced with a beveled ring, but made of oxidized silver.

Rank insignia for officers and warrant officers is identical with that of the army and is worn on the shoulder loop of service coat, jacket, and overcoat in the same manner. When the shirt is worn without the coat, officers and warrant officers wear the insignia of rank on both sides of the collar. Rank insignia for officers and warrant officers and distinctive insignia for airmen is worn on the left side of the garrison cap.

All Air Force military personnel wear identifying Air Force insignia as follows: cap insignia on the front center of service cap; all officers, "U.S." on both sides of the coat and jacket collar; all airmen, "U.S." in circle on right side of coat and jacket collar, Air Force wing and propeller in circle on left side; shoulder sleeve insignia on coat, jacket, or shirt sleeve near shoulder; wartime patch of unit in which the individual served during the combat period is optionally worn; appropriate aide-de-camp insignia are worn on the lapels of coat or jacket; chevrons to denote the grade of enlisted men are worn centered outward on each sleeve, midway between elbow and shoulder; master sergeant and first sergeant wear three chevrons, inverted, centered on a pierced star, and three wing-type arcs inverted beneath star; technical sergeant wears three chevrons, inverted, centered on a pierced star, and two wing-typed arcs inverted beneath star; staff sergeant wears three chevrons, inverted, centered on a pierced star, and one wing-type arc inverted beneath star; sergeant, corporal, and private 1st class wear three chevrons, two chevrons, and one chevron, respectively, inverted, centered on a pierced star.

Air Force buttons on uniforms contain the Great Seal of the Department of the Air Force in clear relief against a horizontally-lined background and are made of oxidized silver. The winter uniform is of a distinctive slate-blue; the summer uniform is sun tan.

Coast Guard.—The insignia of rank of the Coast Guard is identical with that of the navy for corresponding grades. Gold lace stripes are worn by all commissioned and warrant officers upon the sleeves of blue uniforms and on the shoulder marks of the white and khaki unfiorms and overcoats. For chief warrant officers and warrant officers, the sleeve stripes and stripes on shoulder marks are broken, alternating blue and gold. The number and width of stripes, representing the various ranks, are the same as those of the navy. Admiral is the highest rank held in the Coast Guard.

Instead of the star above the stripes, line officers wear the Coast Guard shield. On the shoulder marks of officers of flag rank, the shield is superimposed on the anchor.

There are no medical corps officers in the Coast Guard. In time of war they are supplied by the navy; in time of peace, by the Public Health Service.

The various chief warrant officers and warrant officers of the Coast Guard are the same as those of the navy. Their distinguishing devices are the same with the exception that the shield is worn between the corps device and the stripes.

The cap device of commissioned officers and chief warrant officers consists of a horizontal silver foul anchor being held by gold spread eagle with silver shield superimposed thereon. The cap device of warrant officers consists of silver shield surmounting two crossed gold foul anchors. The cap device of chief petty officers consists of vertical gold anchor with chain with silver shield superimposed thereon.

JOEL WILLIAM BUNKLEY,
Rear Admiral, United States Navy (Retired), author of "Military and Naval Recognition Book."

INSKIP, John Swanel, American clergyman, evangelist and editor: b. Huntingdon, England, on Aug. 10, 1816; d. Ocean Grove, N. J., March 7, 1884. He was brought to America in 1820, the family settling first at Wilmington, Del., and then in Chester County, Pa. In 1836 he entered the Methodist Episcopal ministry and was pastor of churches in Pennsylvania, New York, and Ohio. Until his death he edited *The Christian Standard and Home Journal* of Philadelphia. He was an evangelist of unusual ability. In 1881–1882 he took an extended evangelistic tour, conducting meetings in England, India and Australia, traveling in the year 31,000 miles, conducting over 500 public services, and witnessing over 5,000 conversions. He wrote more than 160 columns of editorial matter for his paper on the trip and conducted an extensive correspondence besides. He was the author of *Methodism: Explained and Defended* (1851); *Songs of Triumph* (1882).

Consult McDonald, William, *Life of John S. Inskip* (Boston 1885).

INSOLATION, ĭn-sō-lā'shŭn, heating by direct exposure to the sun's rays. In geology it has significance in the process of weathering by heating and cooling of rock surfaces with resulting expansion and contraction and shattering of the rock mass. See also EXFOLIATION.

INSOLVENCY, ĭn-sŏl'vĕn-sĭ. In a popular sense the word insolvency applies only to persons without property or means sufficient to satisfy their creditors. The legal definition embraces all who are unable to pay their debts at maturity in the ordinary course of business, even though they may possess assets exceeding their liabilities. A failure to meet overdue obligations renders a person liable to proceedings against him in a court of insolvency, in which his assets may be taken into the possession of the officers, marshaled and distributed to his creditors. Should there be an amount in excess of what is required to pay the creditors and the expenses of administration, the balance so remaining is the property of the debtor. From a very early period in the history of civil government, laws have existed providing for proceedings by creditors against insolvent debtors, by which the debtor's property could be taken from his possession, to be held by another as a trust fund to be applied to the payment of his just debts. In case of an insufficient amount to pay all debts in full, provisions are usually made for a *pro rata* distribution. These laws have generally provided for classes of preferred debts, payments of which were to be made in full, even though such payments exhausted the entire assets. Preferred claims commonly included all claims of the government or state, and often claims for labor to a limited amount, and claims for the necessaries of life. Provisions are usually made for the exemption of certain articles to the use of the debtor, not to be included in the assets. The Constitution of the United States provides that Congress may establish uniform laws on the subject of bankruptcy throughout all the states, and the first act upon that subject was passed in 1800, since which time there has been some Federal bankruptcy law, with brief interregnums. A uniform national law upon the subject now exists. The first act of Congress upon this subject provided for proceedings by the creditors only, but in 1841 an amendment provided for voluntary proceedings by the debtor, by which he could surrender his property and obtain a discharge from all of his debts, provided he had been guilty of no fraud. In the absence of a national law on the subject of insolvency, the states all have authority to enact and enforce laws upon that subject. The federal act now provides for voluntary proceedings by the debtor, as well as proceedings against him by the creditors, with provisions for his discharge. The various state acts have usually contained such provisions. The federal act during its continuance suspends all State insolvency laws covering the same ground. See also BANKRUPTCY LAWS.

INSOMNIA, ĭn-sŏm'nĭ-ȧ, a disordered condition of the body characterized by sleeplessness. It may be due to toxic condition, mental or physical exhaustion, or other causes. The usual treatment is directed to removing the cause. Hot baths, hot food, applying heat to the soles of the feet are also applied with considerable success in many cases. See also SLEEP.

INSPECTOR, or INSPECTOR GENERAL, in military affairs, terms of somewhat vague significance. There are inspectors general of cavalry, infantry, artillery, engineers, aviation, militia and volunteers, whose duties are really those which their names infer — viz., the periodical inspection of the several corps of their respective arms, and the pointing out of deficiencies, the corps being under command, however, of its own officers, and not of the inspector general. The inspectors general of musketry and gunnery instruction are charged with the direct superintendence and ordering of such instruction throughout the army. In the medical department the inspectors general of hospitals constitute the highest grade of surgeons.

INSPIRATION, ĭn-spĭ-rā'shŭn, in theology, the communication by the Holy Spirit, to writers and speakers, of a portion of the knowledge and feeling of God, in such fashion that they can be communicated to other men; especially used in relation to the Bible. On the fact of inspiration rests all attribution of divinity to the sacred writings above any others; but theories of its method and extent have necessarily changed with the advance of critical knowledge. They have never had an authoritative pronouncement even from the Catholic Church which allows liberty of judgment on this; the Bible not holding the supreme place there as in Protestant bodies, and the latter being too divided for a credal statement on this point, by the very causes which call for one. All theories rest not only on the necessary implication of divine character in the Bible, but on two specific passages: 2 Timothy 3:16; "All Scripture is given by the inspiration of God, and is profitable for doctrine" (Revised Version, "Every Scripture inspired of God is also profitable for teaching," which does not relinquish the claim of inspiration); and 2 Peter 1:21, "Holy men of God spake as they were moved by the Holy Ghost" (Revised essentially the same). The Scriptures were the Old Testament.

The early Church did not generally dwell on theories of inspiration, regarding it as a passive "ecstasy" in which divine truth was communicated but rarely going on to its effects on the inspired writings of the methods which produced them. Origen, however, the great builder of doctrinal framework, formulated an exact theory of "plenary" or entire inspiration, which preserved the writers from all faults of memory, and left no iota either incorrect or superfluous in Scripture. But others held that all believers were inspired in different degrees; as this made all believers infallible interpreters of the Scriptures, the perilous nature of such a doctrine led to the opposite one, that there was an inspired official depositary of interpretation as well as an inspired canon of writings. The mediæval schoolmen evolved the theory that there were two kinds of inspiration in the Scriptures: direct, found where moral and doctrinal truths are directly taught; and indirect, in historical passages, whence ethical truths can only be derived by allegorical interpretation.

Regarding inspiration not as a purpose but a method, there are three explanations within the limits of orthodox Christianity: the «plenary» or verbal, the dynamic, and what may be termed the «irradiant» theories. The remaining one, which makes the inspiration only that common to all human beings — who are part of the divine mind — and having no part in any special revelation, is really not a theory of inspiration at all, as it holds that there is none; that all things are parts of the world's evolution, and the sacred writers and the Bible were evolved like the rest, though the latter is the greatest moral product of the world, and to be reverenced in the moral rank as we reverence the greatest writers and thinkers in theirs.

In the early uncritical ages of the Protestant churches, the universal and obvious theory of inspiration was the plenary. The original text of the Bible was dictated word for word by the Holy Spirit, the writers being merely penmen, or media on whom were impressed certain phrases, which must not be varied on peril of distorting the divine revelation. The words of Scripture thus transmitted are God's words, to each reader as if spoken directly to him by the Deity, and no matter to what subject they relate, be it doctrine or history, the origin of man or the duty of man. That there are different styles, corresponding to different writers, means only that God has accommodated his expressions to their natures, for his own utilities. Hence the least particle in the Scriptures is surcharged with meaning, and if anything seems in conflict with science, history, or other portions of the Bible, it arises from corruption of text, bad translation or other change from the actual revealed language. This is the only theory with perfect logical continuity; unhappily it can only be maintained, in face of the increasing body of knowledge of texts, facts and natural ethics, by those willing to abnegate their own right of criticism wholly in favor of their own infallible interpretation. Indeed, the chief argument for the latter is that the divine purpose would be defeated, if its intention in giving the revelation were made null by the misunderstanding of fallible human faculties.

The dynamic theory is the first step outside this bulwark enforced by the impossibility of maintaining verbal inspiration and relegates the divine agency to an indirect function. In place of its dictating the exact phraseology and the precise facts, the writers are so filled with divine force that for all purposes of conveying the essential divine purpose, that of showing the truths of sin and danger and the path of salvation, they are a portion of the divine and incapable of error. Under this theory the writers are left a free hand, according to their own limitations and those of their age, in dealing with narrative facts or their own guesses at them; but are guided explicitly in all matters of faith and morals. In order to be received, the revelation had to be accommodated to the mental conditions of different ages; and men of each received guidance from God to present it so that it was true in relation to them, and remained so for all ages under all conditions. The warrant of the Bible is its incomparable and superhuman system of ethics, and its proof of divine origin is that evident superiority to all human devices.

The «irradiant» theory is a recent one, and a step farther from the old claim of entire divinity. In this view the record as such has no divinity, nor infallibility of any kind. There is a divine revelation, but it acts by generating moral ideas in certain great selected men, and which, once generated, are left to fight their way and take their chance like the other useful ideas of the world, and undergo disbelief and mutilation, with the certainty that according to God's purpose truth will prevail at last. The proof of divinity in Christianity lies in the fact that its moral truths are the greatest in the world, and were original with it.

Another theory is based on evolution, in this both revelation and inspiration are dispensed with, and there is retained only that enlightenment which comes with all development through environment and the laws of variation. In human progress lies the real divine revelation. The Bible is a purely human book, but the greatest of all books, and as such should retain its place as the foundation of our religious structure.

Bibliography.— Briggs, ‹The Bible, the Church, and Reason› (New York 1892); Delitzsch, ‹De Inspiratione Scripturae Sacrae quid Statuerint Patres Apostolici et Apologetae Secundi Sæculi› (Leipzig 1872); Dodds, ‹The Bible: Its Origin and Nature› (New York 1905); De Witt, ‹What is Inspiration?› (ib. 1893); Gibson, ‹Inspiration and Authority of Holy Scripture› (ib. 1912); Ladd, ‹Doctrine of Sacred Scripture› (2 vols., ib. 1883); Orr, James, ‹Revelation and Inspiration› (ib. 1910); Raymond, G. L., ‹Psychology of Inspiration› (ib. 1908); Rohnert, ‹Die Inspiration der heiligen Schrift und ihre Bestreiter› (Leipzig 1889); Row, ‹Inspiration: Its Mode and Extent› (London 1864); Sanday, ‹Inspiration› (ib. 1893); Schultz, ‹Old Testament Theology› (Edinburgh 1892); Seeberg, ‹Revelation and Inspiration› (New York 1909); Simon, ‹The Bible an Outgrowth of Theocratic Life› Edinburgh 1886).

INSTALLATION, the act of giving possession of an office, rank or order with the accustomed ceremonies, applied especially to the ministerial or pastoral office in the church. The term is now generally used for a formal introduction to any office.

INSTERBURG, Prussia, town in the province of East Prussia, at the confluence of the Angerapp and Inster, 57 miles east of Königsberg. The town church is famed for its wood carvings. Other churches are three Evangelical, one Roman Catholic and a synagogue. Its industrial establishments include iron foundries, flax-spinning mills, machine shops, cement works, leather works, etc. It has a good trade in cereals, flax, vegetables, lumber, etc., and horse-breeding is extensively carried on. The town was founded in the 14th century by the Knights of the Teutonic Order. In 1583 it received civic privileges and thereafter grew apace. It was besieged by the Swedes in 1679. A fire nearly destroyed it in 1690 and a pestilence decimated its population in 1710. Pop. 31,627. Consult Töws, 'Urkunden zur Geschichte des Hauptamts Insterburg' (Insterburg 1895–97).

INSTINCT. Every organism is born with a number of tendencies to behave in certain specific ways when confronted with stimuli to which they are adequate. These tendencies not only increase in number and complexity as we pass from the protozoa to the primates, but also vary similarly within a single organism. The amœba inherits three simple reactions; tendencies to move toward certain stimuli, to turn away from others and to engulf still others for food. Man, at the other extreme, has innumerable innate dispositions, and they vary in complexity, as, for example, tendencies to cough and to sneeze, to fear and to become angry, to associate with his kind and to think to a conclusion. All these tendencies are instinctive, and instinct may be defined as «the general name for these innate tendencies» (Titchener), or as a «congenital mode of behavior dependent upon inherited dispositions within the lower brain centres» (Morgan), or again as «a combination of congenital responses unfolding serially under appropriate stimulation» (Watson). Despite differences in emphasis and systematic treatment these three definitions are in agreement as regards essentials, and all three ultimately refer instinct to the nervous system. It is a mistake, therefore, to suppose, as is popularly supposed, that instinct is a faculty provided by Providence to direct the actions of animals and opposed to the faculty of reason furnished for the guidance of man. Such a view purports to explain but, in fact, explains nothing, and it overlooks the fact that man probably has more instincts than the lower animals. If, then, an instinct is a tendency which in the final analysis belongs to the nervous system, then it follows that we must go to biology, particularly physiology, for a detailed description. Nevertheless, instinct has also a psychological aspect, instinctive acts are accompanied by mental processes, and some mental patterns have as their physiological correlates certain instinctive tendencies. Much needless controversy has arisen through a confusion of the biological and psychological points of view, and confusion can only be avoided by considering the two aspects separately.

Biology.— The biologists have as yet done little more than to clear the ground for future work; the detailed study of instincts is yet to come. Furthermore, no classification of instincts has thus far found general acceptance. Instinct may, however, be roughly marked off from the physiological reflex on the one hand and from habit on the other. The former, of which the knee-jerk, heart-beat and eye-wink will serve as examples, is as a rule confined to a single group of muscles whereas instinct usually involves the entire organism. Habit is a tendency which is acquired during the lifetime of the organism. We cannot, of course, push these distinctions too far; there is no sharp line of demarkation between reflexes and instincts, and not only are many habits based upon instinctive tendencies but many instincts are not perfected at their first appearance. The results of the experimental investigations may be summarized as follows: (1) Not all instincts make their first appearance at birth; in the vertebrates, at least, new tendencies appear at different stages of growth particularly between birth and puberty. In white rats, for example, the instinctive act of «face washing» does not appear until the 12th day, play about the 15th day and sexual activities about the 65th day; the monkey does not as a rule begin to walk before the third week, to make characteristic vocal sounds before the ninth week and the sexual instincts do not appear until the end of the first year. (2) We have seen that instincts are not always perfected when they make their first appearance. When this is the case, it sometimes happens that the characteristic act of a species may be modified or even completely inhibited by subsequent experience. Baltimore orioles reared in captivity and in isolation developed a song quite different from the usual song of their kind; English sparrows reared with canaries gave up the chirp of the sparrow for the peep of the canary; the tendency of a pike to strike at a minnow was completely inhibited after successively bumping against a glass plate inserted in the aquarium and in front of the minnow. (3) The less selective instincts like rest, sleep and play are extraordinarily persistent although in the human organism they may repeatedly find new forms of expression; others, however, which seem to be conditioned upon the bodily state of the organism as, for example, the various instincts of the mother in caring for her young, may wane and fade out. (4) Yerkes has found that some instincts like savageness, wildness and timidity in rats, and the direction of whirl in the dancing mouse are hereditary traits.

Psychology.—We turn to the psychological aspect of instinct. Here, although even less is definitely known than on the biological side, three problems stand out in bold relief. We have to investigate the mental processes that are present in the instinctive act (the action consciousness), to describe other mental states which are conditioned upon instinctive tendencies, and to work out the relation of instinct to meaningful experience. As regards the first, work on the human organism seems to show that the instinctive is of the same type as the sensori-motor act, i.e., the perception of the object touches off the reaction, there is necessarily no conscious representation of the determination to act or of the action's end. We have no reason to suppose, therefore, that, for instance, the wren is in the least aware of what it is doing or why it is doing it when it builds its nest. This does not mean, however, that, accompanying the instinctive act, there is no psychological experience. On the contrary we may safely assume that even in the lowest forms of animal life some sort of sensory experience releases the disposition and to an extent determines the subsequent course of the action. Secondly, psychologists are agreed that, particularly in the case of the grosser emotions, the emotive is an instinctive consciousness, and the psychology of the emotions is, therefore, in a sense a psychology of instincts. In fear, for example, the vaso-constriction, the rapid heart-beat, the spasmodic respiration, the glandular secretions are touched off by instinctive tendencies, and the correlated patterns of organic sensations and feelings form the core of the mental experience. Aside from this general statement little is established as regards either a detailed description of the emotions or of their number and variety. It is, perhaps, because of their instinctive basis that psychology has found it difficult to bring the emotive instincts under experimental control. Finally, the more we learn about instinctive tendencies the more apparent it becomes that the situations from which they proceed are meaningful, but we need not suppose that the organism is necessarily aware of the meaning. The chick in the egg feels (we may only guess as to its nature) a vague discomfort, and the complicated reaction by which it makes its egress from the shell is released. How this particular tendency to react thus to this particular situation originated is a question which cannot be answered until biology has given us a satisfactory theory of the origin and transmission of instincts.

Bibliography.—Allen, A. H. B., 'Pleasure and Instinct; A Study in the Psychology of Human Action' (London 1930); Babson, R. W., 'Instincts and Emotions: Should They Be Suppressed or Harnessed?' (New York 1927); Bernard, L. L., 'Instinct; a Study in Social Philosophy' (New York 1924); Cook, P., 'Instinct in the Cell and Organism' (Alhambra, Calif., 1926); Diblee, G. B., 'Instinct and Intuition' (London 1935); Fabre, J. H. C., 'The Wonders of Instinct' (London 1918); Garnett, A. C., 'Instinct and Personality' (London 1928); Hingston, R. W. G., 'Problems of Instinct and Intelligence' (London 1928); Morgan, C. L., 'Instinct and Experience' (New York 1912); Tead, O., 'Instincts in Industry' (1918); Trotter, W., 'Instincts of the Herd' (1919). HARRY P. WELD.

INSTITUTE OF FRANCE, The, official name for a group of learned societies in France, having for object the fostering of some branch in art, literature, science or philosophy. At present it consists of five sections, the official names of which are: (1) L'Académie Française; (2) L'Académie des Inscriptions et Belles Lettres; (3) L'Académie des Beaux Arts; (4) L'Académie des Sciences; (5) L'Académie des Sciences Morales et Politiques. The creation of the Institute of France was decided on by the Conventior in the Constitution of the year III (1795); Section 298 of that Constitutional Law reads as follows: «There is, for the Republic, a national Institute entrusted with the care of collecting all discoveries, and furthering the progress of arts and sciences.» The Charter of Foundation, however, admitted only three sections: (1) «Sciences Physiques et Mathématiques; (2) Sciences Morales et Politiques; (3) Littérature et Beaux Arts,» avoiding the denomination of Academy, which was considered as reactionary by the new-born republic. Among the 144 members of the Institute, 66 belonged to the first section, which, at that time, was deemed the most important of the three. One-third of the members were appointed by a decision of the Directory; these first 48 members chose themselves a new contingent of 48; and finally these 96 elected the third and last contingent, also of 48 members. The Directory granted to each of these an annuity of 1,500 francs ($300) which was then deemed sufficient to keep a man above the poverty line. To-day, although it is no longer deemed sufficient, as every visitor to Paris must know, this annuity has not been raised, although Napoleon wished to increase it to 5,000 francs; in fact, it amounts only to 1,200 francs, as 300 francs are deducted every year in order to create a fund which is redistributed, under the form of *jetons de présence* (attendance fees), to the members who attend the sittings of their respective academies. The Institute of France was introduced to the public in the *Salle des Cariatides,* of the Louvre, which was splendidly decorated for the ceremony, which took place on the 15th *Germinal of the year IV* (4 April 1796) and was attended in great solemnity by the State Ministers, the Diplomatic Corps and a magnificent crowd; from the speeches which were delivered, from the grandiose ceremony of inauguration, «the impression was created,» said M. Raymond Poincaré, in his address, on the Commemoration Day of the Centenary of the Institute (in 1895), «that a great thing had been achieved, and public homage was paid to the Unity of Sciences by a rejuvenated nation.» In 1805 Napoleon, who, as First Consul, had already given a special costume to the members of the Institute, decided that the latter should have their own palace; the Institute was therefore transferred to the palace which faces the Louvre over the Pont-des-Arts, and which bears the name of Palais de l'Institut. Its library (which must not be mistaken for the Bibliothèque Mazarine, in another portion of the same building), consists of 500,000 volumes. The name Academy which had been suppressed by the convention was revived by Louis XVIII in 1816; since 1870, the five of them meet together every year in a solemn public assembly, on the 25th of October. On that occasion some of the prizes granted by the Institute are delivered to the winners. In its present condition, the Institute has 231 ordinary members (*membres titulaires*) to whom must be added 296 correspondents; some of the latter are foreigners, and we may mention among the Americans who are *Associés* or *Correspondents de l'Institut:* Edward Charles Pickering, Simon Flexner, George Birkhoff, Albert F. Blakeslee, William Bowie, L. E. Dickson, R. A. Milikan, H. N. Russell, Frank Schlesinger, Selmar Waksman, Whitney Warren, John D. Rockefeller, Welles Bosworth, W. Delano, William Morris Davis, Albert A. Michelson, James Mark Baldwin, Charles William Eliot. The most important of all the prizes which are given by the Institute is the Prix Osiris (triennial), which amounts to 100,000 francs. This prize was established by Baron Osiris. The *Prix Osiris* was granted in 1903 to Dr. Roux in consideration of his researches on *serums* and transferred immediately by him to the Institut Pasteur of which he was the director; in 1906 the prize was awarded to M. Albert Sorel in consideration of his historical researches. Many other prizes have been offered to the Institute by rich individuals: the oldest of these liberalities was made as far back as 1819 when Baron de Montyon bequeathed an annuity of 37,000 francs for the purpose of rewarding «the most virtuous actions and the books which may best further the progress of morality.» In 1886 the

Château de Chantilly with its very valuable library (Musée Condé), was given to the Institute by the Duc d'Aumale: in 1897 the Château de Langeais, one of the finest types of French architecture, was given by M. Jules Siegfried; in 1906 the private house of M. Thiers, first president of the 3d Republic, was bequeathed by Mlle. Dosne, his niece; in 1900 M. Jean Debrousse bequeathed 1,000,000 francs "to be used by the Institute as it will deem most proper." Many other donations and legacies have been made to the Institute and to each of the five Académies. Every year numerous prizes for hundreds of thousands of francs are distributed to men of letters, artists, men and women in difficult circumstances, etc., so that the Institute acquires further prestige every year. To be "Membre de l'Institut" is a great honor, of which Napoleon himself was very proud; the foreign correspondents may be struck off the list when the Institute considers that they have failed in any particular circumstance: the most prominent case of such elimination was that of the German professors who, at the beginning of World War I, tried, in their *Address to the Civilized World* to justify the invasion of Belgium. Among the German correspondents who were struck off the list, we may mention Herren Wilmowitz-Moellendorf, Darpfeld, Harnack, de Groot, Karl Robert, Wundt Riehl, Liebermann, Adolf von Baeyer, Felix Klein, and Emil Fischer.

Bibliography.—Institut de France, *L'Institut de France* (Paris 1889); Franqueville, A. C. F. de, *Le premier siècle de l'Institut de France,* 2 vols., (Paris 1895); *L'Institut de France,* ed. by Laurens, 2 vols. (Paris 1907–08); Derrouch, A., *L'Institut de France* (Paris 1938).

Let us now examine each of the five Académies.

I. The Académie Française (such was the original name), was founded by Cardinal de Richelieu, minister of Louis XIII, in 1635. A few years before, the poet Antoine Godeau and his cousin Conrart, secretary to the king, used to meet every week at the latter's house which was situated at the corner of Rue Saint Martin and Rue des Vieilles-Etuves, with a few distinguished friends of literary taste. When Richelieu, in 1635, inquired of these gentlemen whether "they would not like to be formed into a company under the authority of the state," they could not but accept such direct invitation. Richelieu understood from the beginning the important part which the new-born Academy could play in the development, unification and purification of the French language; and his ambition, among others, was that French should acquire the same perfection, importance, and power of domination as Latin and Greek. As early as 1634, that is to say one year before it was officially constituted, the Academy decided to prepare a *le Dictionnaire de la langue française;* the first edition of which was published in 1694. Since that time seven revised editions have been published; the second in 1718, the third in 1740, the fourth in 1762; the fifth, under the convention which had first suppressed it; the sixth and the seventh in 1835 and 1877. The eighth edition began to appear in 1929. When Richelieu died in 1642, the Academy chose, as patron, Chancelier Pierre Séguier, who invited the members to hold their weekly meetings in his own private hotel. But, when Séguier died, the Academy did not seek a patron among state ministers, or great personages who might perhaps become an obstacle to its independence; it applied directly to the king himself, believing, which was right enough, that the king as a patron would remain a stranger to all coteries and petty intrigues which were more or less favored by ministers. In fact under the protection of Louis XIV, during 42 years, the Academy enjoyed great freedom, independence, and even privileges such as a right to two invitations at all official festivities at the court, the right of appeal direct to the king without the medium of his state ministers. Besides, it was invited by Louis XIV to make its permanent abode in the Louvre, the king's own palace, from which it was removed only in 1793 by the convention. The rooms occupied by the Academy were situated on the ground-floor, and are at present part of the French Sculpture Gallery (Salles du Puget and Salle des Coustou). Toward 1693, when La Bruyère was elected, the Académie Française was composed of a most brilliant Pleiad of writers, who greatly cooperated in making the reign of Louis XIV one of the most glorious and in giving to the history of French literature an unparalleled splendor; if indeed Corneille and Colbert were dead there were still Bossuet, Fléchier, Fénelon, Racine, La Fontaine, Boileau, Perrault, Fontenelle. The next generation of Academicians was not so brilliant: the "Grande Seigneurs," great dignitaries and other personages of high station, finally considered that certain seats in the Academy belonged to them or their caste as a sort of birthday right: three dukes de Coislin, for instance, were Academicians; even today the "parti des ducs" still exists under the "Coupole"; it means that the old aristocracy is always represented in that ancient institution, but it is right to say that members of the nobility are elected as much on account of their literary achievements as of their aristocratic origin. During the 18th century, however, some men of great literary fame belonged to the Academy; among them we must mention d'Alembert who wrote the celebrated preface to the *Encyclopédie;* he was one of the most appreciated men in Europe. Frederick II, king of Prussia, wanted him to live in Berlin and, for that purpose, offered him the presidency of his own academy; Catherine, empress of Russia, wanted him to educate her son; fortunately he refused these kingly and imperial offers in order to devote himself to the great cause of emancipation which was more or less outlined in the *Encyclopédie* and which was to triumph in 1789 and the following revolutions. Voltaire, Duclos, Condorcet were also members of the Academy. During the second half of the 18th century the whole of Europe turned its attention to that Institution; all the monarchs and princes who came to Paris (the king of Denmark, the king of Sweden, the king of Prussia, the Imperial Russian crown prince, etc.), made a point to attend at least one of its meetings. On June 28, 1917, at the reception of M. Alfred Capus, General Pershing was solemnly entertained at the Palais de l'Institut. Although the great French Revolution had been prepared by some of the most distinguished members of the Academy, the latter was finally considered by the convention as a reactionary institution smacking too much of the *ancien régime* and ancient prerogatives. It was suppressed in 1793. It revived when the Institut de France was created in 1795, under another name as the Classe de langue et littérature françaises. In 1816, however, Louis XVIII restored it to its former name of

Académie Française which has been retained ever since. About the same time (1819), Baron de Montyon left by testament to the Academy an annuity of 37,000 francs which is distributed every year in the form of two prizes (*prix Montyon destiné aux ouvrages les plus utiles aux mœurs;* and *prix de vertu, fondation Montyon*). Since that time many prizes have been instituted by the Academy, thanks to the numerous gifts, donations and legacies which have steadily increased its financial power. The following list of prizes, although incomplete, distributed by the Academy, will give an idea of its social and literary importance:

Prize	Francs	
Montyon	37,000	yearly
Souriau	1,000	"
Marie Lasne	1,800	"
de Sussy	8,000	"
Camille Favre	13,500	"
Lelevain	1,500	"
Emile Robin	1,000	"
Lange	6,500	"
Buisson	3,500	"
Louise Varat-Larousse	4,500	"
Savourat-Thénard	5,500	"
Pérou	1,000	"
Bausa-Gessiomme	2,500	triennial
Agemoglu	1,900	yearly
Rigot	3,200	"
Jules Favre	1,000	"
Passemard	1,000	"
Anonymous	1,000	"
Anonymous	4,500	biennial
Peyrard-Beaumanoir	3,000	yearly
Broquette-Gonin	12,000	"
Alexandre Broquette-Gonin	8,000	"
Tremblay	1,000	biennial
Bigot	6,000	"
Baron and Baronne Léopold Davillier	6,000	yearly
Argut	4,000	"
Cavelan	6,000	"

All these prizes are generally awarded, according to the wishes of their founders, to such persons, male or female, as live an exceptionally virtuous and laborious life, and are considered as having reached a high level of family, social or moral perfection. Nearly all prizes are awarded annually: the following conditions are required of the competitors; the action eventually to be rewarded must have been continued into the last two previous years. A detailed memorandum, with approved certificates, signed by local authorities, and giving full information concerning the competitor's eventual right to a prize, must be sent to the *Chef du Secrétariat de l'Institut.* Such memorandum must not be signed nor sent by the competitor himself. The latter's name, Christian name and place of residence must be placed at the head of the memorandum. The number of academicians is 40. Whenever one of the seats becomes vacant, the Academy elects another member to take the place of the deceased. The new member is formally admitted into the «illustre compagnie» at a solemn and pompous meeting; on such occasion each «immortel» wears his green uniform, cocked hat and sword; there is a restricted number of seats for the public; in fact it is very difficult to get admission; as a rule the audience is of an extremely select and aristocratic character. The reception consists essentially in the exchange of two speeches, rather lengthy, between one member of the academy and the «récipiendaire,» the latter devoting his remarks to the virtues, talents and achievements of his predecessor, whilst in his own *discours,* the other party never forgets to impress upon the new member that the academy has secured immortality for his name, if not his literary works; in a harmless, humorous and half innocent manner, he unloads upon the newcomer a number of appropriate remarks in which the audience takes a great delight. The following is a list of the members of the academy living at the beginning of the year 1939:

Gabriel Hanotaux	A. Chaumeix
Henri Lavedan	M. Weygand
Maurice Donnay	P. Benoit
Marcel Prevost	A. Bonnart
Henri Bergson	F. Mauriac
Alfred Baudrillart	F. d'Esperey
Henri Bordeaux	L. Berard
Louis Chevrillon	Duc de Broglie
Georges Goyau	A. Bellessort
Edouard Estaunie	C. Farrere
Georges Lecomte	L. Gillet
Emile Picard	G. Duhamel
A. de Caumont	E. Jalouy
F. de La Force	J. de Pardoidony
Louis Bertrand	L. Lacaza
Paul Valery	Greute
A. Hermant	J. de Lacratdh
E. Mâle	C. Maussor
L. Madelin	A. Maurois
M. Paléologue	J. Tharaud
Marshal Pétain	

II. The Académie des Inscriptions et Belles-Lettres was created by Colbert in 1663. It was known first under the name of La Petite Academie, then of L'Académie des Médailles, then of L'Académie Royale des Inscriptions et Médailles in 1701, and finally under its present name since 1716. It was temporarily suppressed by the Revolution and revived when the Institut de France was created in 1795. The Académie des Inscriptions is interested mainly in historical studies and investigations concerning numismatics, all sorts of ancient documents and inscriptions, living and dead languages. Every year it distributes many prizes to the students and writers whose historical researches appear to be useful. The prix Gobert (10,000 francs yearly), for instance, is intended to reward «the most learned and exhaustive research concerning French history.» More than 80,000 francs are offered in prizes every year by the Academy for similar works and researches. The Académie consists of 40 members.

III. The Académie des Sciences was also created by Colbert under Louis XIV, in 1666. The meetings were held first in the King's library and, from 1699 to 1793, in the Louvre. There are 78 members. Today the sections, which fall into two groups—the Mathematical Sciences and the Physical Sciences, are as follows: geometry, mechanics, astronomy, geography and navigation, general physics; chemistry, mineralogy, botany, rural economics, anatomy and zoology, medicine and surgery. For two years, 1793 to 1795, it was suppressed. The Academy of Science offers many annual prizes ranging between 1,000 to 100,000 francs. One prize (Prix Pierre Guzman) of 100,000 francs will be awarded to any one who will discover the means of communicating with a star other than the planet Mars, that is to say, who will make a sign to a star and receive an answer to that sign. Another prize of 100,000 francs will be awarded to the person who will discover the means of curing Asiatic cholera.

IV. L'Académie des Beaux-Arts was created in 1648 by a famous artist, Charles Le Brun, under the patronage of M. de Charmois, an influential courtier, under the name of

Académie Royale de Peinture et de Sculpture. The 12 initial members of that company opened a school (École du Modèle); later on, in 1656, the king invited them to hold their meetings in the Louvre where they remained until their academy was temporarily suppressed by the Convention. In 1666 the Académie de France à Rome, a school where French artists completed their studies, was created by the Académie Royale de Peinture et de Sculpture with the co-operation of Colbert. That school is located at present in the Villa Médicis; the École des Beaux-Arts, in Paris, is under the control of the Académie des Beaux-Arts. There are 40 members, some Associates and Correspondants. The sections are: architecture, painting, sculpture, engraving, and music-composition. Numerous prizes are awarded every year to artists, students, etc. . . . in order to encourage the progress of fine arts and, at the same time, to guide public opinion which is sometimes slow in recognizing the merits of artists.

V. L'Académie des Sciences Morales et Politiques was created under the name of Classe des Sciences Morales et Politiques in 1795, as one of the sections of the Institute. It was suppressed quietly in 1803 by Napoleon who did not give any reason for his decision. It may be that the inquisitive spirit and criticisms of that Institution on political matters, social and religious controversies did not please a despotic sovereign; nobody, however, has been able to discover any proper justification of such sudden suppression. It was restored under its present name by Louis-Philippe, in 1832, when it joined the four other academies in the Palais de l'Institut. It is divided into five sections: (1) Philosophy, (2) Morals, (3) Legislation and Jurisprudence, (4) Political Economy, Statistics and Finance, (5) Histoire et Géographie. The number of Academicians is 40. Some important prizes are awarded every year, some of them amounting to 10,000, 12,000 and 15,000 francs; the prix François Joseph Audiffred (15,000 francs), was awarded, in 1917, to Cardinal Mercier, the great unconquerable Belgian prelate who has deserved universal admiration. The list of these prizes increases steadily from year to year, thanks to the generosity of rich individuals. Anybody interested in the prizes awarded by the Institut de France may have full particulars regarding the conditions, the subjects proposed, etc., by applying to the Secrétaire Perpétuel of any one of the five academies. The Institute publishes also every year a booklet giving the names of all the members and correspondences of each academy, under the title of 'Annuaire de l'Institut.'

Henri de Montfort,
Chef du Secrétariat de l'Institut.

INSTITUTE OF SOCIAL SERVICE, American. See Social Service.

INSTITUTES OF THE CHRISTIAN RELIGION, The ('Christianæ Religionis Institutio'), by which John Calvin laid the foundations of Calvinism, stands unique among books that have had immediate, deep, wide, and lasting influence on Christian thought and life not alone for the author's youth, the comparative brevity of the theological studies that preceded it, and the speed at which it was completed, but also for the fulness with which the system it presents was elaborated at the work's first appearance in 1536. For though revised and extended, more logically and inclusively presented, in the edition of 1539, still further revised in 1543 and 1550, and reaching its final form only in 1559, it shows throughout no sign of change of position, still less of retraction. Begun in 1534 when Calvin was barely 25, the book was practically completed when in August, 1535, Calvin addressed the remarkable letter to King Francis I, with which it opens. As this letter shows, the Institutes were composed, or at least completed, to meet a present necessity, to correct an aspersion on his fellow reformers. The French king, wishing to suppress the Reformation at home yet unwilling to alienate the reforming princes of Germany, had sought to confound the teachings of the French reformers with the attacks of Anabaptists on civil authority. «My reasons for publishing the Institutes,» Calvin wrote in 1557, «were first that I might vindicate from unjust affront my brethren whose death was precious in the sight of the Lord, and next that some sorrow and anxiety should move foreign people, since the same sufferings threaten many.» Therefore he wrote in Latin, but he proceeded immediately to translate his work into French, and in both forms it gained quickly wide circulation.

«The hinges on which our controversy turns,» says Calvin in his letter to the king, «are that the Church may exist without any apparent form» and that its marks are «pure preaching of the word of God and rightful administration of the sacraments.» If such preaching bring disorder, the blame is not with it but with Satan. The 'Institutes,' in this first form, follow the traditional arrangement, observed also in Luther's short catechism of 1529, and fall into six chapters. The first three, dealing with Law, Faith, and Prayer, and, in the main, the fourth, treating of the sacraments of Baptism and the Lord's Supper, are expository. The last two were of necessity more controversial, for they dealt with «False Sacraments,» namely Confirmation, Penance, Unction, Orders, and Matrimony, and with Christian Liberty, Ecclesiastical Power, and Civil Administration. The controversial tone, even here, is, however, less pronounced than in later revisions, and what are commonly regarded as the distinctive features of Calvinism are less emphasized.

The 'Institutes' in this first form were not merely a logical and felicitous exposition of Reformation doctrine; they proved the inspiration to a new form of Christian life. Their debt to Luther in the treatment of Faith and Sacraments, to Martin Bucer in what is said of Divine Will and Predestination, and to the later scholastics for teaching involving unsuspected implications of freedom in the relation of Church and State, has been clearly traced. Yet the 'Institutes' were justly felt to be as a new voice, and before the year was out there was demand for a second edition. This came in 1539, amplifying especially the treatment of the Fall of Man, of Election, and of Reprobation, as well as that of the Authority of Scripture. It showed also a more irenic temper toward Luther in the section on the Lord's Supper. The edition of 1559, claiming to be «almost a new work» is in fact a complete recasting of the old 'Institutes' into four books and 80 chapters, on the basis of the Apostles' Creed. In this form the work was translated into French and Dutch in 1560, into English in 1561, into German in 1572, into Spanish in 1597. Seven other editions and four abridgments appeared in English before the end of the 16th century. A judicious summary of the teachings of the 'Institutes' is to be found in W. Walker's 'John Calvin,' pp. 409–429. No book of its century showed such power to spread ideas and to unify the strivings for reform. That cardinal period in Christian development found in this book the most logical, clear, characteristic presentation of what reformers prized as truth, and, though its teachings are nowhere held to-day in their fulness, the place of the 'Institutes' as a Christian classic is secure.

Very important in their apparently unrealized implications were the teachings of the 'Institutes' on civil government. They counted it the function of an ideal state to see that no «offenses against religion break out or be disseminated.» It was, indeed, a duty to submit to rulers negligent in this regard; but «if they command anything against God, let us not,» says Calvin, «pay the least regard to it nor be moved by all the dignity which they possess as civil magistrates» ('Institutes,' IV, xx, 32). With the example of church officers responsible to the congregations they served, such teaching could not fail to stimulate the movement toward individual liberty and democratic freedom.

Changes from the teaching of the 'Institutes' among those who most cherish Calvin's memory are notable in the matter of church discipline and in regard to the duty of civic rulers to guard the purity of the church. Changes are seen also in the doctrine of the Scripture, of election, reprobation and human depravity. This is natural. The appeal of the 'Institutes' was to the intellect, and these very changes are in large part the result of the vigorous thinking which the 'Institutes' demanded and of which they were so eminent an exemplar. The standard edition of the 'Institutio' is in Calvin's Works, edited by Baum, Cunitz and others (59 vols., Brunswick, 1863–1900); the last volume has a full bibliography. Translations by H. Beveridge (3 vols., Edinburgh, 1845–46) and others. See Rayburn, H. Y., 'John Calvin, his Life and Works' (New York 1914); Penning, L., 'Life and Times of John Calvin' (New York 1912); Walker, W., 'John Calvin' (New York 1906).

BENJAMIN W. WELLS.

INSTITUTES OF ORATORY, The ('De institutione oratoria'), of Quintilian, composed after his retirement from active life, took more than two years to write (89–91), but was withheld for a few years until the urging of his friends compelled its publication, the circumstances of which are given in a foreword addressed to his publisher, the bookseller Trypho. The work itself, consisting of 12 books and dealing with the whole education of the future orator, was dedicated to Vitorius Marcellus (the same to whom Statius addressed the fourth book of his 'Silvae'), whose son Geta showed talent. Quintilian probably also had in mind his own elder son. He repeatedly attacks the ordinary handbooks of rhetoric, while his own theory is based on his own experience and the best views of different authorities, especially Dionysius of Halicarnassus, Cæcilius, Chrysippus, Cicero (upon whom his exposition is mainly founded and from whom he seldom differs and then only with reluctance), Cornuficius and Celsus. Quintilian insists that the orator must be of good moral character as well as versed in rhetorical accomplishments. His illustrations are drawn mainly from the classical writers and he attacks the style of his own day, at the same time warning the pupils also against the early writers. Especially interesting is the 10th book, which treats of literary criticism as regards the Latin and Greek prose writers and poets useful to the orator. The chief manuscripts of the 'Institutiones' date from the 10th and 11th centuries. A large and annotated edition is that of G. L. Spalding (Vols. I–IV, Leipzig 1798–1816), C. G. Zumpt (Vol. V, 1829) and E. Bonnell (Vol. VI, containing lexicon and indices, 1834), but the pincipal edition is that of C. Halm (Leipzig 1868), revised by F. Meister (Prague 1886–87). Book X has been separately edited by J. E. B. Mayor (pt. I, London 1872), E. Bonnell and F. Meister (5th ed., Berlin 1882), G. T. A. Krüger and G. Krüger (3d ed., Leipzig 1888) and W. Peterson (Oxford 1891). The 'Institutiones' have been translated several times into several of the continental languages and an English translation by J. S. Watson (2 vols., London 1902–03), with notes based on Spalding, appears in the 'Bohn Classical Library'.

HERBERT F. WRIGHT.

INSTITUTIONAL CARE OF THE INSANE. See INSANE, INSTITUTIONAL CARE OF.

INSTITUTIONAL CHURCH, a noncredal organization of Christians, to supplement the regular church methods and ministrations — preaching, prayer-meetings, Sunday school, and pastoral visitations — by helpful social work in the community. The moving spirit is the same as in the Y. M. C. A., University Settlement, Salvation Army, Rescue Missions, Christian Endeavor societies, etc.; but «with the emphasis on Church, not Institution.» The prime object is to reannex to the church the functions which other bodies have been compelled to fill by its neglect of its duty; and strengthen it by gathering potential Christian elements which under the old system do not come to it, as well as by combining in itself all the claims to public gratitude and interest now shared between the purely ecclesiastical and the purely social institutions, or the halfway houses like the Y. M. C. A. It differs from the latter in not merely furnishing a religious atmosphere which may lead to church membership, but enrolling members at once in a real church of Christian work by absorbing the secular features of the other; in a word, to do, without vows or uniforms, what the Catholic Church has always done with its charitable functions — make them an integral portion of the church organization. Hence, it is not by itself a church in the sense of the Roman Catholic or the Methodist Church, but in a broad sense a description of any church which adds educational or social work; in general use, a title of any which throws into this work its predominant vitality. Free pews are an essential accompaniment, as the social aristocracy fostered by rented pews contradicts the basal democratic principle of institutional work; hence it is sometimes called Free Church, but preferably Open Church. The present name originated with President Tucker of Dartmouth College, who applied it to Berkeley Temple, Boston.

The movement started chiefly with the High Church element in England, modeled on the Catholic idea; it flourished for two generations in that country before reaching the United States, about 1880. Now a large number of churches — Episcopal, Congregational and Baptist in the forefront, but also Methodist, Presbyterian, Unitarian — have adopted the idea with increasing vigor, besides the work of this class always performed by the brotherhoods and sisterhoods of the Roman Catholic Church. One of the earliest of these was Plymouth Church of Indianapolis, inspired by the memory of Mr. Beecher. Notable among others are the Saint Bartholomew, Saint George, Saint Paul and Judson Memorial of New York, and the Tabernacle of Jersey City; Berkeley Temple, Parker Memorial, and Ruggles Street Baptist of Boston; Grace and Bethany of Philadelphia; Ninth Street of Cincinnati, Pilgrim of Cleveland; Plymouth Tabernacle of Detroit; People's of Saint Paul; and the Denver Tabernacle. In 1894 the Open and Institutional Church League was organized in New York; it held several conventions in Eastern cities (1895–1901), and for three years published the 'Open Church' as its organ, but has practically lapsed, being merged in the 'National Federation of Churches and Christian Workers.' The total of its work, however, is not shown by its nominal membership; the same spirit has infected outside churches, and their methods are being more and more adopted as a general basis of work.

The platform of the League stated that it aimed to save all men by «abolishing, so far as possible, the distinction between the religious and the secular»; by «open church doors for every day and all the day, free seats, a plurality of Christian workers, the personal activity of all church members, a ministry to all the community through educational, reformatory and philanthropic channels, to the end that men may be won to Christ and his service, that the Church may be brought back to the simplicity and comprehensiveness of its primitive life.» It is not correct to say, as is often done, that its methods are purely secular: its *additional* methods beyond the regular religious ones are so, for the very reason it exists. These involve a thorough organization for social and philanthropic work; but the religious features are sedulously conserved and carefully fitted to the work, the spirit of worship being cherished and made the centre of inspiration. The service generally ends in the communion; there is congregational singing of both hymns and chants, led by a highly trained choir, and often responsive readings; the whole with the sermon are intended to be brief, varied, and attractive. Sunday schools are carefully attended to; prayer meetings given new features; in summer there are open-air meetings; and other Christian associations, endeavor societies, brotherhoods, etc., are encouraged. The officers and workers of the church are given active special duties, such as pastoral visiting, reception and welcome of strangers, canvassing for the various activities of the church; and there are not only subpastors, but deaconesses, sisters and nurses. The purely secular side embraces all departments of culture, physical, intellectual and moral, as well as direct charities.

INSTITUTO BUTANTAN, (The Institute of the Government Health Department of São Paulo, Brazil), founded in 1899 by Vital Brazil—prominent in developing serum therapy against animal poisons. Present director: Eduardo Vaz. Its museum contains a huge collection of snakes, spiders, scorpions and other poisonous animals. Live snakes are kept in the park in specially constructed pits. The laboratories are dedicated to research work on public health problems, on the classification of poisonous animals and the study of their venom, besides producing vaccines against the more common tropical diseases such as dysentery, typhoid fever, smallpox, typhus, and sera for the treatment of diphtheria, tetanus, gas gangrene, and the bites from poisonous snakes, spiders and scorpions. A recently opened chemotherapeutical department prepares anti-leprosy drugs. The library, specialized in ophidic literature, publishes annually the *Memorias do Instituto Butantan.* The park and museum are open to the public and form a very popular tourist center.

INSTITUTO HISTORICO E GEOGRAPHICO BRAZILEIRO (Brazilian Historical and Geographical Institution), a Brazilian society devoted to the advancement of historical and geographical knowledge, founded at Rio de Janeiro in 1839. Under its auspices and with its aid many historic documents relating to the early history of Brazil have been printed and thus made available to historical students throughout the world. The society publishes many such documents, also accounts of geographical explorations, etc., in its periodical *A Revista Trimensal.*

INSTRUMENT, *in law,* a written document evidencing an agreement or acknowledging a claim, as a deed, grant or will. The term has been held to mean also, in its widest sense, any written document, as a statute or record, but scarcely to apply to accounts, memoranda, or ordinary letters.

INSTRUMENT OF GOVERNMENT, the written constitution under which Oliver Cromwell governed Great Britain and Ireland from 16 Dec. 1653 to May 1657. It consisted of 42 articles, and vested the legislative power in the hands of «one person and the people assembled in parliament.» The executive power was placed in the hands of Cromwell as Lord Protector of the Commonwealth; his office was made elective and he was to be assisted as executive by a council of state of from 13 to 21 members. Councilors were appointed for life. A new parliament was to be called every third year, and a parliament could not be dissolved in less than five months except at its own request. There were 460 members in the single chamber — 400 for England and Wales and 30 each for Ireland and Scotland. The distribution of seats was altered. A property qualification of £200 was placed on voters,

Roman Catholics and those who had opposed Parliament during the Rebellion were disfranchised. This constitution contained several elements of weakness and its downfall was assured as soon as it dared assert its independence of or opposed the lord protector.

Consult Gardiner, Samuel Rawson, *Constitutional Documents* (Oxford 1889); and Jenks, Edward, *Constitutional Experiments* (London 1891).

INSTRUMENTAL MUSIC. See MUSIC; MUSICAL INSTRUMENTS; ORCHESTRA MUSIC.

INSTRUMENTALISM, in philosophy, a system, akin to pragmatism, according to which thought is considered an organic function, the object of which is to maintain the even tenor of experience, restoring the latter when it is interrupted or confronted by a special situation. See EPISTEMOLOGY; PRAGMATISM.

INSTRUMENTATION, in music, the arranging of music for a combined number of instruments. The nature and character of the musical ideas must determine whether the instrumentation shall be simple or artistic, and perhaps complex; the latter being the case when some of the instruments take a more prominent part than others. For both purposes, a thorough knowledge of every instrument in the orchestra is absolutely necessary, as without this instrumentation becomes only a deafening mass of sounds. The stringed instruments, from their nature, in most cases, form the principal parts of a score, around which the other instruments move, without depriving them of their importance. The wind instruments represent, more or less, a subordinate chorus, which may again be divided into two kinds: the wood instrument and the brass, which, with the stringed instruments, give three essentially different choral effects, that may be mixed together in endless variety. A knowledge of the art of instrumentation is acquired only by great experience; at the same time much may be learned by consulting the best works on the subject such as Berlioz, Louis Hector, *Traité d' Instrumentation;* Gassner, Ferdinand Simon, *Partiturkenntniss.*"

INSTRUMENTATION. The drive for mass production in industry initiated by World War II stimulated the drive for the development and use of instrumental methods of chemical analysis. The trend has been along three distinct lines: (1) Application of recent electronic developments toward the manufacture of commercial instruments to measure well-known physical properties with a precision and rapidity hitherto unattainable; (2) the automatizing of single- and multiple-unit operations either to record automatically specific physical characteristics or both to record and control as in the case of temperature regulation or by actuating valves for introduction of reactants; (3) the development of new techniques, notably ultramicroscopical and radioactive tracer methods.

Most notable developments have been in the spectrophotometric field, both in emission and absorption spectroscopy, and cover almost the entire range of measurable electromagnetic radiations. Although well-known since the time of Robert Wilhelm Bunsen, the science of emission spectroscopy has not been extensively applied to routine industrial control problems until the last decade. During this time the spectrograph has developed from a relatively simple light-resolving instrument, useful for qualitative work but of relatively minor importance for quantitative estimations, to a complex electronic device which permits the rapid (one to two minutes) precise estimation of multiple constituents. This has been particularly useful in the metallurgical field for the rapid testing of minor constituents in aluminum, magnesium, steel, and other alloys. A typical example is the Quantometer, a grating-type instrument, which not only resolves the spectrum excited by an aluminum spark, but which simultaneously measures the relative intensities of specific lines for as many as sixteen elements which are usually present in relatively small amounts. By previous calibration, the intensities of the specific lines actuate counters so that the actual percentage of each of the elements may be directly read from the instrument as soon as the spark discharge (30 to 120 seconds) stops. Thus, the analytical control work for a melt of aluminum which used to require days of painstaking wet chemical analyses is accomplished in a matter of minutes. Such a development could not have been accomplished except for the development of highly sensitive and stable electrical components. These are essential for a consistent power supply, as well as for the measurement of the low level light intensities involved.

By the use of quartz optics and photocells sensitive to low levels of ultraviolet radiations, highly precise and rapid quantitative absorption work is now possible in the ultraviolet region of the spectrum (notably from 2100 to 3500 Å). The Beckman DU model spectrophotometer has given great impetus to this field by making generally available an instrument which is stable and relatively easy to operate and which permits either absorbancy or per cent transmission measurements at highly monochromatic wavelengths with great rapidity and with a precision of one per cent. Thus, it is now possible to use ultraviolet absorption bands of substances not only for identification purposes, but also for highly precise quantitative measurements. This technique has been of particular value in the field of organic chemicals, notably in the fields of pharmaceuticals and dyestuffs.

A recently marketed double-cell instrument which uses photomultipliers and which automatically scans the entire ultra-violet (U.V.) region, comparing a sample in solution against a solvent blank, now enables the chemist to chart accurately the U.V. spectrum of a compound in a matter of two to ten minutes depending upon the detail desired. In such an instrument the slit width is automatically controlled simultaneously with the wavelength drive so as to obtain maximum resolution and optimum sensitivity at each wave length. For such instruments, hydrogen discharge lamps serve as continuous energy sources.

In the visible region of the spectrum many precise and direct reading photoelectric spectrophotometers are available including filter type, replica grating, and glass prism-type instruments. The filter type are the simplest in construction; because of their ruggedness and relatively low cost, they are used most widely for routine control work. These instruments have largely replaced the visual-type colorimeters which were so very dependent upon the individual operator's eyesight and personality.

The availability of commercial instruments applicable to the infrared region of the spectrum now permits this region to be used widely. Relatively simple single-purpose instruments are in common use for controlling gas streams or for measuring the change in concentration of a single component. For general survey work over large portions of this region of the spectrum, instruments with sodium chloride prisms, lenses, and cell windows are being widely used in the 1.5 to 15.0 micron region. Other optics, such as potassium bromide and silver iodide, have extended the useful region up to 25.0 microns. These instruments are now widely used for the characterization of compounds—the infrared spectrum of each substance being sufficiently complex so as to be likened to a "fingerprint" of the substance. The ability specifically to identify definite groups within the molecule, namely nitrate groups, sulphonate groups, and others such as C — O — C, C = C, C = O, free O — H, N — H, is making this technique of particular value to synthetic organic chemists. In the petroleum field, distillate composition is being rapidly controlled by absorbency measurements at different wavelengths, each more or less specific for a definite component, followed by calculations involving the solving of simultaneous equations so as to yield quantitative data for each constituent. The simultaneous determination of four component systems is commonplace, and as many as eleven and twelve component systems may be resolved in this fashion. This development has been made possible by the availability of electronic computors since the manual solution of simultaneous equations involving four, five, six, and more unknowns would be economically impossible because of the man-hours of calculations required.

For routine survey use in the infrared region, both single- and double-beam instruments are commercially available. Either Nernst glowers or globar elements are used for energy sources with bolometers or thermocouples being used as pickups. Since direct currents of very low energy levels are involved, suitable precise measurement has been a problem. A common practice in use is to employ a beam chopper in the light path so as to convert the direct current to a pulsating current which may then be handled like alternating current for amplification. A recent innovation permits direct transmission readings in a single-beam instrument. In this instrument a solvent blank is initially scanned, the slit width being automatically adjusted to give 100 per cent transmission over the region being investigated. The necessary slit-width settings are automatically recorded on a wire recorder, and when a sample is then placed in the path, the wire recorder continuously adjusts the slit width so that it becomes possible to obtain a differential absorbency curve (of sample versus solvent). Some of the advantages of such a system include measurement of the sample in the same cell as the blank and the lack of necessity of having two perfectly balanced beams. Such an instrument is, of course, dependent upon its electrical stability between runs and its sensitivity to line voltage fluctuations.

The development of sensitive flame photometers permits rapid determinations of potassium, sodium, lithium, and other elements by atomizing the sample into a hot gas flame and measurement of the intensity of specific lines energized therein. Sensitivities down to 0.1 parts per million by this technique are now commonplace.

The two major war products, radar and atomic energy, have introduced radical changes in the laboratory. The atomic energy project, of course, is now making available to the chemist radioactive elements which were never available before and which can be used for "tracer" techniques. A whole new field of instrumentation has been introduced for these "tracer" studies by the construction of rapid and sensitive Geiger-Müller counters, scaling, and recording units.

In fields other than the photometric, progress has been also outstanding. The really first new developments in the construction of an analytical balance in 50 years have resulted in a direct reading balance which operates under constant load, and thus constant sensitivity, and enables direct weighing of substances with a sensitivity of 1/20 of a milligram (total load 200 grams).

The glass electrode is now universally used both for the measurement of pH and for the automatic control of acidity. New glasses have permitted the manufacture of sturdy, heavy-walled and sensitive electrodes applicable over a wide temperature range and useful at high pH values.

Automatic titration assemblies are now readily available which carry out either electromotive force type titrations (acid-base, oxidation-reduction, and precipitation type reactants) or polarization type ("dead stop") titrations automatically. In these instruments a measured sample is added to a suitable titration vessel, the instrument is set for the desired endpoint, and the titrant is then automatically added until this endpoint is reached.

The use of the polarographic technique is being advanced along two lines. Recording instruments (either pen and ink or photographic) are now available which automatically trace a polarographic curve, using the dropping mercury electrode, over any desired voltage range. On the other hand, the rotating platinum electrode is being used for amperometric titrations at fixed voltages. With the advent of standardized diffusion current constants, it is necessary that the rate of flow of mercury, *m*, from the dropping mercury electrode be known precisely. For this purpose an automatic mercury-measurer is now available.

High-frequency induction-type furnaces have been introduced, primarily for the determination of carbon and sulphur in steels. In these furnaces the power consumption is relatively low since it is only in use during the actual combustion of the sample. High-frequency oscillator circuits have also been introduced to carry out electrodeless titrations. Primary applications have been to halogen titrations.

The mass spectrograph is being commercially utilized primarily for the analysis of multicomponent hydrocarbon mixtures although its original use for the separation and measurement of mass isotopes continues.

The field of extraction is now playing a very important part in the separation of closely related rather complex substances. This has made itself felt by a host of workers in the field of countercurrent distribution studies wherein a solute is permitted to come to equilibrium between two immiscible solvents. As a result, rather complex mechanisms have been devised to permit continuous stage countercurrent distribution studies by automatic robots.

In the field of gas analysis many specific physical measurements are being utilized for automatic control. A magneto-acoustical system is in commercial use for the detection of a few hundredths of a per cent of oxygen. Interferometric methods are in use for the analysis of nitrogen-argon mixtures. Manometric methods for many gases permit automatic recording of the pressure involved. A very sensitive differential manometer which can detect differences as low as 0.000001 atmosphere over a range of 1 mm. of mercury to 1 atmosphere depends on the principle of the aneroid barometer. The measurement depends upon the motion between a pair of nesting diaphragms which are soldered together to form a very thin capsule containing the gas or vapor. One diaphragm remains stationary and the second is attached to a displacement gage with the four resistance wires serving as a Wheatstone bridge.

Viscosity measurements of liquids are now largely based on measurement of the torque exerted on a rotating stirrer. A wide range of viscosities may be measured by using different sized or shaped spindles, paddles, or disks, together with various strength torque springs. This procedure lends itself to automatic recording.

Electrical titration methods are generally limited in their use by the nature and sensitivity of the electrodes used. Recently, the introduction of high-frequency oscillator titration circuits has permitted titrations without any electrodes being immersed in the titration cell. Three factors govern the characteristics of an oscillator which includes a liquid or solution in its tank circuit. These factors include the circuit constants of the oscillator, the volume of the solution and its location in the circuit, and the conductance of the solution as affected by its ionic or dipole concentration. The changes in conductance during a titration cause variation in such loading and thereby permit the course of a titration to be precisely followed without electrodes being actually immersed within the solution. This new method of analysis thus utilizes the energy absorption from a high frequency field as the basis of a new conductometric method of analysis. Wide use of this technique is being made in the determination of chlorides in water, especially as related to the petroleum field. It will undoubtedly be applied to other fields and other types of titrations as chemists become familiar with the principles.

H. A. FREDIANI,
Merck and Company, Inc.

INSTRUMENTS, Engineering. See ENGINEERING INSTRUMENTS.

INSTRUMENTS, Musical. See MUSICAL INSTRUMENTS.

INSUBRES, a Celtic people of northern Italy. In the 4th century B.C. they settled in the region between the Alps and the Apennines. They were frequently at war with the Romans after 222 B.C., and in 194 their capital Mediolanum (Milan) was taken and they were finally brought under the yoke of Rome.

Consult Holder, A., *Altkeltischer Sprachschatz,* vol. 2 (1904).

INSULAR CASES, a series of legislative problems created by the "accretion" to the United States of insular possessions following the Spanish American War in 1898. They arose over Pres. William McKinley's recommendation in his message on the convening of the 56th Congress, Dec. 3, 1899, that "legislation should be enacted establishing a civil government in Puerto Rico," and involved the status of the citizens of our insular possessions and the constitutionality of an intra-national revenue tax. The Foraker Act, April 11, 1900, defined the relation of the island to the United States, by placing it on a status outside of the Constitution and also outlined a scheme for the government of dependencies that obligated the nation to a new and united policy. This gave rise to the Insular Cases which debated the question of the right to demand duty for commercial articles imported into the United States from Puerto Rico. On appeal the Supreme Court decided that the insular possessions were obtained under the clause regulating the making of treaties, and "that the power to acquire territory by treaty implies not only the power to govern such territory, but to prescribe upon what terms the United States will receive its inhabitants, and what their status shall be."

INSULATION. From the generation of electricity to the use of electricity, the two fundamental materials required (not including magnetic materials) are conductors and insulators, the one being as important as the other. Electrically speaking, all material may be divided into two general classes, conductors and insulators, depending upon their relative resistance to the flow of electricity. Conducting materials must have low resistance; and insulating materials, high resistance. Insulating material is required where mechanical contact is made by the conducting material. From an economic standpoint, conducting material is limited to copper and aluminum, but for insulating purposes many materials are available.

Insulation resistance is the resistance of the material to the passage of current. It is proportional to the thickness of the material (if the material is homogeneous), and inversely proportional to the area. Insulation resistance is measured in ohms, or in megohms (1 megohm = 1,000,000 ohms).

Dielectric strength is the strength against breakdown under electric stress. It is usually expressed in terms of the voltage per unit thickness (usually volts per mil) at which the insulation fails or becomes punctured. It does not vary with area, but increases when the thickness increases.

The output rating of a piece of electrical equipment is limited by the temperature its insulation can withstand without excessive deterioration. Common types of organic insulation, such as cotton, silk, linen, and paper, rarely permit a rated temperature rise greater than 55°C. (131°F.) over an ambient temperature of 40°C. (104°F.). Where higher temperatures are unavoidable, asbestos can be used if the attendant space factor is not prohibitive, and if the low tensile and dielectric strengths are not of great importance. Mica had been employed extensively, but its lack of mechanical strength and its high cost have imposed certain limitations on its use. The maximum operating temperature of electrical apparatus is now limited only by the qualities of the impregnant used.

Electrical Insulating Material.—The selection of insulating material depends upon several factors, such as low power factor, high dielectric and mechanical strength, flexibility, and resistance to heat, abrasion, moisture, and deterioration. Porcelain is a good insulator which possesses practically all the foregoing characteristics except flexibility. Rubber, on the other hand, is flexible but will not stand heat or abrasion. The most widely used insulating products are combinations of several materials, such as mica, paper, and varnish. Paper, for example furnishes the base upon which mica is fastened by means of varnish; the combination possesses good dielectric strength, flexibility, and resistance to moisture.

CLASSIFICATION OF INSULATING MATERIALS

Thermal Classification.—Insulating materials are divided in this category into four classes: Class O, Class A, Class B, and Class C, which are thus defined by American Institute of Electrical Engineers standards.

Class O.—This insulation consists of cotton, silk, paper, and similar organic materials not impregnated with, nor immersed in, oil. The temperature limitation is 85° C. (185° F.).

Class A.—This group includes cotton, silk, paper, and similar organic materials impregnated with, or immersed in, oil; also enamel as applied to conductors. The temperature limitation is 125° C. (270° F.).

Class B.—This category includes inorganic materials, such as mica and asbestos, in built-up form combined with binding substances. If Class A material is used in small quantities in combination, for structural purposes only, the combined material may be considered as Class B, provided that the electrical and mechanical properties of the insulated winding are not impaired by the application of the temperature permitted for Class B material. Temperature limitation is 145° C. (293° F.).

Class C.—This insulation consists of inorganic materials, such as pure mica, porcelain, slate, glass, and quartz. There are as yet no stated temperature limits for these materials.

Physical Classification.—Insulation materials are physically classified as solids, liquids, plastics, varnishes and lacquers, and gases.

Solids.—In the group of solids there are: *natural solids* such as marble, slate, asbestos, quartz, mica, lava, soapstone, Alsifilm (bentonite); *vitreous solids* such as, glass, porcelain, and Mycalex (inorganic thermoplastic); the *fibrous* (treated and untreated) organic solids, including asbestos, cellophane, cotton, glass yarn, hemp, linen, nylon, paper, rayon, silk, and wood; and the *lastics,* which include buna, gutta-percha, koroseal, natural rubber, neoprene, thiokol, and ethylene polysulphide.

Liquids.—Among liquids used as insulation are *natural oils,* such as linseed, tung, pine, and castor, which are used in insulating varnishes, or in binders for built-up insulation; *mineral oil* (transformer and switch); *varnishes; synthetic liquids* (chlorinated derivatives of the benzenoid hydrocarbons) such as Pyranol, Inerteen and Dykanol "A," all of which are fireproof. Solvents are not used as insulation directly, but insulating varnishes and compounds include amyl and butyl acetates, acetone, alcohols, benzene, benzine, carbon tetrachloride, naphtha, petroleum, toluene, and turpentine.

Plastic Materials.—Several types of plastic materials are used for electrical insulation. The *gums or natural plastics* include asphaltic, coumarone-indene, fossil, shellac, and vegetable (applied as liquids, melted, dissolved, or in liquid suspension). *Cold-molded plastics* include portland cement and filler, calcium silicate and filler—both impregnated with resins or asphalts; *waxes* used are beeswax, mineral, and paraffin. Two types of *synthetic resins* are used for insulation—the molded and laminated plastics, such as acrylic, alkyd, casein, meleic, phenolic, resorcinol, formaldehyde, rubber, urea, formaldehyde and urea furfural, vinyl copolymers; and the cellulose compounds (therma plastics), such as cellulose acetate, cellulose acetobutyrate, ethyl, cellulose, and nitrocellulose.

Varnishes and Lacquers.—Insulating materials of this type are manufactured from natural gums and oils, and from synthetic resins. There are also hybrids, spirit varnishes, wire enamel, and solvent varnishes.

Gases.—Among insulating gases used in electrical insulation are air, carbon dioxide (CO_2), nitrogen (N_2), hydrogen (H_2), and rare gases such as helium, xenian, argon and krypton.

The properties and general characteristics of some of the insulating materials mentioned above are given in Table 1.

MATERIALS AND THEIR USES

A brief description of some of the best known insulating materials and of the way in which they are used is given in the following paragraphs.

Glass.—One of the oldest substances used for insulating purposes is glass. While the principal application of glass insulation has been for rigid insulators, recent developments have made it available in fabricated, flexible form.

Porcelain.—Like glass, porcelain is an excellent rigid insulator, but is not available in flexible form. Its principal use is for buildings, high voltage insulators, cleats, and bodies of wiring devices. Porcelain possesses high dielectric and fair mechanical strength, and is resistant to heat, moisture, and deterioration, but its lack of flexibility greatly restricts its use. Next to glass and cotton, it is the oldest of all insulating materials.

Slate.—This material is especially suitable for use wherever rigid insulating support is required for mounting switches and for control equipment. Slate, obtainable without metallic veins, has high insulation resistance and sufficient dielectric strength for all medium-voltage service, it cannot carbonize; thus in case of "flashovers," or electrical breakdown, it prevents short-circuiting. Slate is also resistant to heat, moisture, chemical fumes, and oils. In the early days of the industry, slate was used for switchboard panels. While it is still used for this purpose in limited quantities, substitutes are taking its place.

Marble.—This decorative material was once used for switchboards, especially in locations exposed to the public view. Its insulating characteristics are about the same as those of slate.

Mica.—Widely used as insulation is mica, an anhydrous silicate of aluminum and potash, or sodium, mined in the form of large laminated crystals. It is readily split into thin, tough, parallel-sided laminae, or flakes, with thicknesses as thin as 0.0008 mm. It has high insulation qualities and will withstand high temperatures. In its natural state, mica is impure, lacks flexibility, and has excessive surface leakage. Therefore the laminae are separated according to purity, and

TABLE 1—PROPERTIES OF INSULATING MATERIALS

Material	NEMA Temp. Class	Description	General Application	Usual Thickness	Dielect. Breakdown Volts per Mil
Cotton Tape	O, A		Coil finishing	0.005 to 0.015	20
Asbestos Tape	B		Coil finishing	0.007 to 0.015	20 to 70
Glass Tape	B		Coil finishing	0.003 to 0.015	96
Mica Tape	B	Built-up mica on paper or cloth	Armature coil winding	0.005 to 0.010	600 to 700
Kraft Paper	O, A	Tough brown paper	Layer insulation and wrappers	0.003 to 0.005	60 to 150
Glassine Paper	O, A	Glossy-hard translucent	Layer insulation	0.001 to 0.002	200
Varnished Paper	A	Varnish-treated paper	Layer insulation	0.002 to 0.005	900
Fish Paper	O, A	Extra-tough heavy paper	Pads, outer layer insulation	0.004 to 0.015	200
Asbestos Paper	B	Paper made of asbestos fibers	Layer insulation	0.010 to 0.025	20 to 200
Fish Paper and Mica	B	"Sandwich" of two materials	Wrapper insulation	0.010 to 0.020	400
Varnished Cambric	A	Varnish-treated cloth	Layer insulation and wrappers	0.007 to 0.010	1000
Varnished Silk	A	Fexible varnish-treated silk	Layer insulation and wrappers	0.002 to 0.004	1000
Flexible Mica	B	Built-up mica with flexible resinous binder	Terminal insulation and wrappers	0.010 to 0.060	500 to 600
Vulcanized Fiber	O, A	Chemically converted paper. Sheets and tubes.	Motor insulation and arcing resistance	0.005 to 2.000	50 to 350[1]
Phenolic Laminated Plastic	A, B	Fabric or paper-reinforced resinous sheets, tubes and molded shapes.	Severe service insulation	0.015 to 8.000	75 to 750[1]
Cotton Yarn	O, A	Multiple and ribbons	Wire covering, coil insulation	0.0020 to 0.010	90
Silk Yarn	O, A	Multiple and ribbons	Wire covering	0.0007 to 0.010	140
Glass Yarn	B	Multiple and ribbons	Wire covering	0.0007 to 0.010	200
Enamel	A	Film on wire	Wire covering	0.0001 to 0.0012	500

[1] Depending upon thickness (inversely proportional).

are cemented together to form flexible plates of any thickness.

The two kinds of mica most generally used for insulating purposes are: (1) Muscovite, usually called white or India mica, and (2) phologophite, generally called amber mica. White mica withstands temperatures up to 500° C.; and amber mica, up to 800° C.

Mica, probably the most valuable insulating material in general use, has the following characteristics: (1) high insulation resistance; (2) high dielectric strength; (3) High mechanical strength; (4) Good flexibility; (5) low moisture absorption; (6) Comparatively good heat conductivity; (7) Low deterioration from heat; (8) Excellent resistance to acid; (9) A specific inductive capacity, or dielectric constant, from 4 to 8; (10) Low dielectric loss or power factor (2 to 5 per cent).

Thin paper or cloth backing for mica, with a bond of shellac, asphalt, or synthetic resins, make possible flexible mica in the form of tape, coil wrappers, and tubes. For hot or cold molding, white mica may be bonded with a thermoplastic material. Mica can be used in conjunction with other insulating materials, such as fish paper, rope paper, or kraft paper, for sheet insulation, or for special purposes.

Asbestos.—When used for insulation purposes, asbestos generally takes the form of paper or paper tape, asbestos millboard, or asbestos lumber, and in such forms it may contain from 10 to 20 per cent of wood pulp and glue, which give it strength. Chrysotile asbestos can be spun and made into asbestos cloth or cloth tape, which usually contains about 14 per cent cotton. Selected long-fiber material is made into 100 per cent asbestos twine.

While asbestos is a very poor electrical insulator, it is excellent for absorbing insulating compounds. When dry and properly treated, is valuable for high temperature insulation, and for the dissipation of corona in high-voltage apparatus. It is also one of the few fabrics that cannot be destroyed by termites. Flexible cords used with domestic heating appliances, such as flat irons, have an asbestos covering between the rubber insulation over the conductors and the outer braid. This construction makes the cord fire resisting.

Fibreglas.—This electrical insulating material is woven from two kinds of yarn: continuous filament, and staple fiber. Continuous filaments, or fibers, are produced by mechanical drawing of the molten glass into fibers of great length (measured in miles); they have a general resemblance to natural silk or rayon in the manner in which they are later processed. Staple fibers are produced by steam drawing of molten glass into fibers varying from 8 to 14 inches in length, which have a general resemblance to cotton or worsted fibers.

Both fibers are inorganic, incombustible, durable, nonabsorbent, and relatively nonhygroscopic —properties commonly associated with the glass from which the fibers were made. In addition they are resilient, extremely flexible and have extraordinary unit tensile strength, exceeding that of the strongest piano wire—properties peculiar to glass in the form of fine fibers.

Fibreglas cloth is used as a base in the fabrication of varnished cloth, or cambric, and as a backing for mica. It is available in full cloth width, or cut into narrow tapes. A complete line of Fibreglas-mica cloths and tapes is also available.

Fibreglas also serves as a base for material of laminated products, available in a variety of thicknesses which can be machined or formed into intricate shapes as required. All Fibreglas products are used for electrical insulation in the same manner as any standard textile product.

Fibreglas electrical textiles successfully withstand temperatures in excess of 1,000° F. without impairment of their electrical properties, and they withstand temperatures in the neighborhood of 650° F. before losing their original flexibility and resiliency.

Individual glass fibers are relatively nonhygroscopic and nonabsorbent—properties of major importance in many electrical applications. Fibreglas electrical insulation is resistant to external abrasion, and to attack by moisture, acids, oils, and most corrosive vapors. The high insulation resistance (the ability to resist the flow of current through or over the surface of an insulating material) of Fibreglas impregnated tapes is substantially in excess of that of cotton or asbestos materials of similar character.

Because Fibreglas electrical yarns and tapes combine high temperature resistance, exceptional electrical properties, and great tensile strength, they permit the design of many types of electrical equipment in which the amount of insulation material used is substantially reduced.

Cotton.—Like all other organic materials, cotton is not adapted to the high-temperature applications which inorganic materials satisfactorily withstand. However, cotton is widely used for electrical insulating purposes in various forms of fabrics. Such fabrics are usually processed with different varnishes, gums, or compounds. Some of these composite materials have highly valuable insulating properties.

Untreated materials are used to a great extent for oil-type transformer insulation. They are thoroughly dry when immersed in the oil, which rapidly impregnates all fibers, resulting in an insulating material acquiring excellent physical properties from the cotton and dielectric strength from the oil.

The fundamental Class A materials are treated, or "pretreated" fabrics, of which there are numerous varieties. The two kinds in most common use are tan-linseed oil, or tung oil varnish-treated cloths; and black varnish, and asphaltum or bitumen compound treated cloths.

When tested in sheet form between two-inch circular electrodes, the instantaneous breakdown voltage of the tan-varnished cloth will usually be not less than 1,000 volts per mil; of the black cloth, 1,200 volts per mil.

Silk.—The insulating properties of silk are about the same as those of cotton. Because of its strength and smooth finish, silk is used principally to insulate magnet wire. Its cost is higher than that of cotton, and it is not generally used, except where space is an important factor, silk materials being thinner than cotton.

Adhesive or Friction Tape.—This cotton fabric insulating material is treated with a viscous rubber or bitumen compound; it is not often used as insulation for electrical apparatus, except in coil end connections of low-voltage induction motors, where it is completely covered with varnish or shellac. When fresh and in good condition, it may possess a dielectric strength of about 100 volts per mil, but it deteriorates rapidly when exposed to air.

Insulating Paper and Pressboard.—These materials are used extensively for insulating purposes in some types of electrical equipment such as transformers, circuit breakers, motors, and generators. However, for such insulating purposes, special papers not subject to rapid deterioration are required. These papers are made from pure cotton rag, Manila fiber, and purified chemical wood pulp.

Insulating papers vary from thin tissues to "fish" papers, thick pressboard, and Fullerboard types. Untreated paper has a tendency to absorb moisture, and has little insulating value where moisture may penetrate, but when impregnated with varnish, oils, or compounds, its high dielectric strength, high insulation resistance, and other valuable insulating properties are maintained.

Paper is used for the insulation of magnet wires and high-voltage cables, and is often used in combination with other insulating materials, such as mica, in making insulating tapes.

Insulating papers for wire are made in three general types, known as Standard, Flexrope, and Super Flexrope. The differences in the three grades lie in the quality of softness, Standard being the most hydrated and therefore the hardest. All three types have a 100 per cent rope content. Other grades contain varying percentages of rope, the remainder of the material used being sulphate wood pulp or cotton fiber. Power-cable insulation is made of 100 per cent Manila fiber, or of 100 per cent sulphate wood pulp, and is not stocked in mixtures of these materials. Some grades are tinted in various colors for identification purposes.

Uses of Insulating Papers.—

(1) Insulation of magnet wire, enameled or bare, both in combination with cotton insulation, or alone.

(2) Insulation for transformer coil wire-dry or liquid-filled types—flat, square, or round.

(3) Lamp-cord insulation, to replace cotton and prevent corrosion of copper by rubber, also to permit easy stripping of insulation.

(4) Insulation of telephone wires in lead-covered cable: (a) as insulation of individual wires, (b) as core wrapping, where paper jackets the cable as a whole rather than individual wires.

(5) Insulation of high-voltage cables.

(6) Insulation of battery cables, automotive wire, and service-entrance cable.

(7) Mica-tape paper.

(8) Capacitor paper.

Motor slot and miscellaneous insulation is available in thin sheets, or in rolls of high-density press paper made of cotton, mixtures of cotton and purified chemical wood pulp, and 100 per cent Manila fiber.

Formex.—Known by its trade name, this modern development in insulation consists of a round magnet wire, the insulation of which is provided by a layer of high-grade paper, bonded or cemented over a very high quality enameled wire. It possesses more than 50 per cent greater dielectric strength than other insulated wires. The over-all size of the insulated conductor is smaller than that of conventional insulation. It therefore enters slots easier, permitting the use of more copper in a given slot area.

Varnishes.—A liquid form of insulation applied to tape, mica, and other materials to give additional electrical protection, and also to give added protection from moisture, oil, and dirt.

In the early days of the electrical industry, shellac and other gum solutions were the only materials available for electrical insulation. Shellac was soon found to be unsatisfactory for many reasons, prominent among which were: (1) brittleness, which caused cracking and flaking off; (2) permeability, which resulted in electrical breakdown in the presence of moisture; and (3) thermoplasticity, which caused the dried film to flow when subjected to heat.

Later, combinations of pitches, asphalts, and gums with drying oils were made available in a wide variety of grades to meet the ever-changing demands of the electrical industry. Also, it has often been found possible to blend two insulating varnishes having different characteristics to produce a third varnish having characteristics not found in either of the two. Instead of the narrow choice available in the early days of the industry, modern electrical men have a choice of clear and black varnishes, air-drying and baking varnishes, finishing varnishes, oil-proof enamels in various colors, synthetic gum-base varnishes, and many others.

Raw Materials Used.—The chief raw materials used in the manufacture of insulating varnishes may be listed as follows:

Oils: tung oil, linseed oil, soybean oil, oiticica oil, perilla oil, castor oil, and fish oil.

Gums: (natural) rosin, copal, congo, kauri.

Gums: (synthetic) phenol formaldehyde, glyceryl phthalate, maleic, ester, polyvinyl, coumarone, araclor, urea formaldehyde.

Asphalts: gilsonite, manjak, grahamite, Trinidad, and petroleum residues.

Pitches: vegetable, coal tar, animal, and marine.

Driers: lead, cobalt, manganese, zinc, and vanadium are used in conventional varnishes as resinates, linoleates or tungates. The naphthanates of lead, cobalt, manganese, and zinc are used in most synthetic gum-base varnishes.

Thinners.—Benzine (VM & P naphtha, a petroleum derivative), mineral spirits, denatured alcohol, coal tar solvents.

The petroleum solvents are preferred for baking varnishes. Coal tar solvents are sometimes used, but these should not be used when the varnish is to be applied directly over enameled wire. Some of the synthetic gum-base varnishes require a special solvent, in which case it is best to procure this article directly from the varnish manufacturer. If the wrong solvent is used, the solid content of the varnish may be thrown out of solution, the drying retarded, or the finish impaired.

Removing Moisture.—All cotton, silk, and paper covered wires absorb and retain a certain amount of moisture. When units wound with these types of wires are to be treated with insulating varnish, the moisture must be removed and replaced with varnish. If allowed to remain, this moisture would eventually damage the insulation and cause electrical breakdown.

To remove the moisture, it is necessary to preheat the unit to a temperature preferably above the boiling point of water. A temperature of 240° F. is usually regarded as standard. The length of time that units should be preheated depends on the size of the unit and the depth of the winding. A minimum of two hours should be allowed. Any air remaining inside the windings will be expanded considerably, as it will be at a temperature of 240° F. On immersion in the varnish, this air will cool and contract, thus drawing additional varnish into the windings. The heat imparted by preheating also tends to drive off solvents from inside the windings, and helps to insure an even bake throughout.

Uses for Insulating Varnishes.—There are many uses for the various types of insulating varnishes that are on the market.

Baking Varnishes.—These varnishes should be used, when possible, for new coils and windings, as they give much greater flexibility. Because they dry more thoroughly, there is less danger of solvents being trapped. Some air-drying varnishes will "skin" in the can, so on voids they will "surface seal" and trap solvents unless great care is used. There are times when the dimensions of the unit to be varnished are such that adequate oven space is not available for baking. In this case a carefully selected air-drying varnish may be used. This type of varnish must be carefully applied. If a heavy coat is required, several thin coats are better than one thick coat, and each coat should be allowed to dry thoroughly before applying the next. A baking varnish is also preferable in repair work, although an air-drying varnish may be used; but it must be remembered that the life, flexibility, and resistance to oils, alkalies, and acids, will not equal that of a baking varnish.

Air-Drying Varnishes.—Widely used as finishing varnishes, for extra protection, are air-drying varnishes. An air-drying varnish such as Synthite No. 924, applied over an oilproof varnish, affords a greater protection against alkalies. Air-drying varnishes are also used a great deal in emergency rush work.

Finishing or Spirit Varnishes.—These varnishes are used chiefly for preventive maintenance work. A periodic coat of spirit varnish will fill cracks and seal defects that occur in the original insulation. A finishing varnish is often applied over a nonoilproof air-drying varnish, thus giving it an oilproof surface.

Oilproof Enamels.—This enamel is generally used on commutator end bars, V-rings, and string bands to prevent any creepage of oil from the bearings to the windings. There are two types in general use, the quick-drying alcohol solvent grades, and the slow-drying flexible grades. The latter has greater flexibility, and is used on coils where expansion and contraction prohibit the use of any varnish giving a brittle surface.

Synthetic Gum-Base Varnishes.—These varnishes serve many purposes. Some produce a hard finish which holds the wires in one solid mass, thus preventing any movement of the wires in the slots of a high-speed armature, and eliminating internal short circuits, or throwout. A varnish of this type may be used in deep coils while they are being wound; a coat is applied with a brush to each layer, and when it is baked, no wet varnish is trapped in the coil, as occurs in the use of conventional baking varnishes.

Other grades are so formulated that a second coat may be applied after the first coat has been baked for a short period; the oil is dipped, drained, and baked for one hour, then a second coat is applied, and finally a full bake is given. This method saves time and money. Many of these varnishes also afford exceptionally good protection against chemical corrosion, and some provide very high dielectric strength.

Insulating Compounds.—This type of material falls into three main classifications:

Impregnating Compounds.—While chiefly used to fill voids in certain types of coils, particularly when the voids are too large to be filled successfully with varnish, these compounds are also applicable where an extremely heavy coating is required over the winding of a coil. Although these compounds can be applied by dipping, they are often applied by the vacuum-and-pressure-impregnating process.

Filling Compounds.—One type of these compounds is used to fill in between coils and containers, for example in certain types of transformers, such as radio and neon sign transformers.

Other types are used for cable splices, potheads, and bifurcating boxes. Still other types are designed for filling countersunk screwheads, and for other such purposes, in switchboards and panels.

Stator Compounds.—These compounds differ from the two foregoing classifications in that they are supplied in a semifluid state, and are either air dried or baked. They are applied to the exposed ends of stator coils with a trowel, or putty knife, to provide a solid, impervious seal. If the implement with which they are applied is repeatedly dipped in benzine, a smooth finish will result. Certain types of stator compounds are furnished at a consistency that allows them to be applied with a brush.

Plastics.—Since the invention of Bakelite in 1909, plastics have played an important part in electrical insulation. Plastics are used in practically all electrical devices, and have given the designer and user of such equipment many advantages over older insulating materials. Plastics provide not only insulation, but also a means for supporting or mounting electrical devices, in which capacity they take the place of wood, slate, porcelain, marble, and other materials formerly used. There are many plastics available having desirable characteristics for insulation. They are as well established as solid insulation, and give great promise for the insulation and protection of wires and cables. The more important plastics are listed in Table 2.

TABLE 2—SYNTHETIC MATERIALS WITH PROMISING CHARACTERISTICS AS ALTERNATIVES TO RUBBER FOR WIRES AND CABLES FOR INSULATION

Material	Chemical Type	Remarks
Buna S	Butadiene Polymer	Vulcanizable. Rubber-like. Copolymer with styrene. Extrudable.
Butyl Rubber	Hydrocarbon Polymer	Vulcanizable. Extrudable.
Ethyl Cellulose	Cellulose Derivative	Thermoplastic. Extrudable.
Hycar EP	Butadiene Polymer	Vulcanizable. Rubber-like. Copolymer. Extrudable or calendered strips.
Polythene	Ethylene Polymer	Thermoplastic. Extrudable.
Polystyrene-Rubber	Styrene Polymer with Rubber	Mix with rubber and vulcanize. Extrudable.
Saran	Vinylidene Chloride Polymer	Thermoplastic. Applicable as threads or tapes.
Styron	Styrene Polymer	Thermoplastic. Not extrudable. Threads or tapes.
Tenite II	Cellulose Derivative	Thermoplastic. Extrudable. Cellulose-acetate-butyrate.
Vistanex	Isobutylene Polymer	Not vulcanizable. Rubber-like. Mixed with resins or rubber. Extrudable.
	For Jacket or Covering	
Chemigum	Butadiene Polymer	Vulcanizable. Rubber-like. Copolymer. Extrudable or calendered strips.
Hycar OR	Butadiene Polymer	Vulcanizable. Rubber-like. Copolymer. Extrudable or calendered strips.
Perbunan	Butadiene Polymer	Vulcanizable. Rubber-like. Copolymer with acrylonitrols. Extrudable or calendered strips.
Thiokol	Organic Polysulfides	Both thermoplastic and vulcanizable types. Extrudable.
	For Insulation or Jacket	
Koroseal	Plasticized Vinyl Chloride Polymer	Thermoplastic. Extrudable.
Neoprene	Chloroprene Polymer	Vulcanizable. Rubber-like. Extrudable or calendered strips. Several types.
Vinylite	Plasticized Vinyl Chloride Polymer	Thermoplastic. Extrudable. Copolymer with vinylacetate.

A very important plastic insulating material known as the *silicon resins* offer great possibilities for electrical insulation. They are well adapted to this use, and superior to all other insulating materials where thermal aging or excessive moisture are encountered. Silicons are used primarily as a varnish or binder. The use of silicon resins will make it possible to operate electrical machinery, such as motors and generators, at higher temperatures than ever before, and will accordingly reduce their size for a given output.

Laminated Insulating Materials.—This large group of materials forms an essential and important part of all electrical equipment. In the group are many different grades and types, but they are all related because they employ the same or similar ingredients combined in a different manner.

Each of the materials is made of a filler (or base) and a binder. The fillers used are cotton, glass fibers, asbestos fabrics, paper, and mica flakes. The binders are numerous types of synthetic resins, varnishes, shellacs, and gelatinizing chemical compounds, such as zinc chloride. There are many different types within these classes of fillers and binders which permit almost unlimited selection for controlling the properties of laminated products.

Laminated insulating materials are produced in sheet, rod, and tube form. An unlimited variety of insulating parts for electrical equipment can be fabricated from these basic forms by machining, forming, and punching methods. The outstanding characteristics which account for the widespread use of this class of insulating materials are: dielectric strength, power factor, water resistance, mechanical strength, light weight, and toughness. Other desirable properties, such as resistance to chemicals, vibration-damping capacity, and the low coefficient of friction, are responsible for many other uses of these materials, in which electrical insulation is not a primary requirement.

Vulcanized fiber is made by laminating sheets of rag paper treated with zinc-chloride solution to form a homogeneous mass by gelatinizing and interlocking the cellulose fibers. Removal of the zinc chloride, by bleaching and drying, produces a dense, homogeneous material which has many uses in the electrical industry. This material possesses hardness and denseness, which enable it to resist abrasion; high mechanical strength; toughness to withstand shock loads; and high dielectric strength under normal atmospheric conditions. Moreover, it is easily machined.

The dielectric strength of fiber may be reduced as much as 75 per cent after prolonged exposure to humid atmosphere. Under no circumstances should it be used as an insulating material where even occasional immersion in water is likely to occur.

Fish paper insulation is an exceedingly tough insulating paper developed primarily as an insulation for armature slots and field coils. Extra strong fibers are used, and the chemical treatment, which is somewhat different from that used in the manufacture of vulcanized fiber, insures those qualities which are most essential in an insulating paper. Such insulation is made in sheet and continuous rolls, or in ribbon rolls for automatic machines. It is furnished in a natural dark gray color only. In manufacturing electrical equipment, fish paper insulation is used in armature wedges, slot insulation, attachment plugs, brush backs, brush-holder bushings, bushings, casings for enclosed fuses, commutator rings, insulation for armature and field coils, ignition cable tubes, panel boards, push buttons, switch bars, arc chutes, interpole barriers, rail and trolley insulation, and grommets.

Fiber may also be treated during the process of manufacture with special water-proofing resin. Fiber thus treated possesses characteristics which qualify it for many uses in the electrical industry. It is hard, and will resist abrasion; it is dense, tough, and strong; it has high dielectric strength; it has good arc resistance, but not so much as has untreated fiber; it is easily machined; and it resists moisture better than does untreated fiber.

Laminated insulation in tubular form, which is widely used, is made by impregnating special kraft paper with resin and shellac mixtures, and by subsequently heating it under pressure. Such tubes are more resistant to arcing than most synthetic resinous laminated materials, and they possess excellent dielectric properties. These tubes are used for bus insulation, cable joints, wall bushings, supports, transformer tank linings, motor and generator brush holders, collector rings, coil supports, and for other such purposes.

Insulation for Transformers and Circuit Breakers.—Insulation used for transformers and circuit breakers is usually made up in sheets of layer insulation, for small spaces, and for encircling the entire core in transformers. Most insulation of this sort consists of new cotton cuttings and purified chemical wood pulp, and is made up in the following three grades: (1) 100 per cent cotton rag; (2) 75 per cent cotton rag, 25 per cent purified chemical wood pulp; and (3) 50 per cent cotton rag, 50 per cent purified chemical wood pulp.

Commutator Insulation.—Either white or amber mica is used for commutator insulation. However, if white mica is used for commutator segments, it is necessary to undercut the segment, as the copper bars wear faster than the mica, thus causing a rough surface and a pitting of the bars. To offset this disadvantage, white mica plate is usually less expensive than amber. Amber mica, however, is sufficiently soft to afford even wear with the copper bars, and for this reason undercutting is not usually necessary.

Consult Miner, D. F., *Insulation of Electrical Apparatus* (New York 1941).

E. S. LINCOLN,
Consulting Engineer.

INSULIN, one of the class of substances called hormones, which have the peculiar function of exciting action in some other organ of the body, at a greater or less distance. The duty of the hormone insulin is to regulate the metamorphosis of sugar (glucose) into fat. In the absence or insufficiency of insulin, the excess of sugar is found to be forced into the urine, and also is deposited in the muscular tissue of the heart, and the diseased condition known as diabetes results. Insulin is a product of those parts of the pancreas known as the islets of Langerhans, from their discoverer, and was isolated first by Dr. F. G. Banting, of the University of Toronto, and thus made available as a remedial agent in the treatment of diabetic conditions. As the insulin must become a part of the blood stream to accomplish its function, the present treatment is by way of hypodermic injection, administered by a physician. Efforts are being made to devise some insulin-carrying substance which can make its way into the blood stream when taken by the mouth, as are other medicines. Chemically, insulin is a proteose substance, with the formula, $C_{90}H_{150}O_{24}N_{22}S_2$. See also DIABETES MELLITUS; MEDICINE, RECENT PROGRESS IN.

INSURANCE. The act whereby for a consideration, the *premium,* one party, the *insurer,* binds himself in a contract, the *policy,* to indemnify or guarantee another, the *insured,* against loss through the happening of a specified contingency, the *risk.* The device of insurance is one of the important safeguards developed for eliminating or reducing loss to the individual arising from certain kinds of risk. Moreover, in providing protection against potential loss, it performs a social function even if no loss occurs, this function serving notably in circumstances where credit is used. Reduction or prevention of loss also is an objective to which the activities of the insurance business increasingly are directed.

Risk may be defined as the chance of loss (though the word is used commonly also to refer to the subject of the risk); hazard, as the cause or source of the loss. Risks are estimated according to the expectation of loss and may be classified with respect to their nature into (1) *physical risks,* depending on age, health, condition, location, structure, occupancy, and exposure; and (2) *moral risks,* arising from such mental conditions as motivate dishonesty, negligence, and insanity. Hazards may be (1) common to all in a community, as price changes, wars, and windstorms; or (2) restricted to individuals, as occurrences causing loss or injury to one's self or property, or causing loss or injury to another or his property.

Except in self-insurance, the basis of insurance is the pooling of risks by the transfer of individual risks to a group. The insuring group, or carrier, may be an association, a corporation, or a government. In order to continue its function, it must collect funds sufficient to pay losses and expenses. To do this successfully the aggregate of risks so transferred must be large in numbers and widely spread. The method of weighing the risk and fixing the premium is based upon the *law of large numbers* as used to apply the *theory of probabilities.* This law is derived from the observation that the larger the number of instances taken, the closer the result approximates the theoretical probability. In certain lines of insurance the nature of the risks permits the calculation of elaborate and precise tables.

With respect to the kind of subject matter

PERCENTAGE DISTRIBUTION OF ASSETS, INSURANCE COMPANIES IN THE UNITED STATES
(Dec. 31, 1946)

	Life companies[1] (mutual and stock legal reserve) percentages	Fire and marine companies[2] (stock and mutual) percentages	Casualty and surety companies[2] (stock and mutual) percentages
Bonds	73.4	43.4	59.6
United States government	44.9	35.3	51.6
Canadian and other foreign government	2.6	1.7	0.9
State and political division	1.3	2.6	2.8
Railroad	6.1	1.9	1.7
Public utility	11.6	1.1	1.6
Industrial and miscellaneous	6.9	0.8	1.0
Stocks	2.6	37.5	19.0
Railroad	0.2	2.2	1.1
Public utility	0.7	4.8	3.0
Bank and insurance	(3)	12.8	5.4
Industrial and miscellaneous	1.7	17.7	9.5
Mortgage loans	14.9	0.7	0.9
Policy loans and premium notes	3.9	0.0	0.0
Agents' balances	(3)	4.9	7.6
Real estate	1.5	1.4	1.0
Cash	1.5	10.5	10.2
Miscellaneous assets	2.2	1.6	1.3
Total	100.0	100.0	100.0

(1) Based on data of the Life Insurance Association of America for 49 legal reserve companies holding over 90 per cent of the total admitted assets of all such companies.
(2) Based on data from *The Spectator*.
(3) Not segregated.

insured, insurance may be divided broadly into: (1) *personal insurance*, including life, disability, and social insurance; and (2) *property insurance*, including fire, marine, casualty, liability, and fidelity insurance, and suretyship. In point of priority, the practice of marine insurance long preceded insurance against fire and upon lives. In our modern conception of the term it existed among Italian traders before the year 1400, and was introduced by them to London. There the organization of underwriters at Lloyd's began to operate shortly after 1688. In America, marine insurance has been available since the early 1700's. Though life insurance policies were issued in England in the latter part of the 16th century, such insurance did not become common until after 1700. The first corporation for insuring lives in America was the Presbyterian Ministers' Fund, chartered in 1759, but the real growth of life insurance in the United States did not come until after 1850. Fire insurance dates from the great fire of London of 1666, and in the following century a number of companies were organized in America to write this type of coverage. The various lines of casualty insurance are of more recent origin, the youngest important one being aviation insurance. In this, Lloyd's wrote the first policy in London in 1912, and their underwriting agency in America was the first there, ten years later.

In the United States in 1946 there were approximately 380 legal reserve life insurance companies, and more than 450 fraternal and assessment associations; in addition, about 260 banks were handling savings bank life insurance in Massachusetts, New York, and Connecticut, where this kind of insurance is permitted. Operating in the fire and marine field were approximately 415 stock companies, 225 important mutual companies, about 1,000 smaller mutuals, and a few over 30 reciprocals, interinsurance exchanges, and American Lloyds organizations. Writing casualty and surety business were approximately 230 stock and 160 mutual companies of importance with 60 smaller mutuals. In this branch of insurance were also 45 reciprocals, interinsurance exchanges, and American Lloyds organizations, over 100 assessment accident and health associations, and about 115 hospital service associations.

Apart from these private enterprises, various governments and governmental agencies in the United States engage in a fairly wide range of insurance, quasi-insurance, and pension plans. State and local activities include workmen's compensation funds, public property insurance funds, a small state life insurance fund (Wisconsin), hail insurance in three states (North Dakota, Montana, and Colorado), and a large number of pension systems for teachers, firemen, and other public employees. The operations of the federal government in this general field are broad. There are pension funds for war veterans and federal employees, an unemployment insurance plan, a system for retirement and unemployment benefits for railroad employees, indemnification plans for bank and building loan accounts, and crop insurance. The Social Security Act was passed in 1935, and under its amendment of 1939 the system of old-age and survivors insurance was inaugurated. The government's first plan of life insurance for members of the armed forces, the United States Life Insurance, was instituted during World War I, and in 1940 the National Service Life Insurance was provided for those in World War II. In the latter war, the government also sponsored the War Damage Corporation in writing policies of protection against enemy attack.

Supervision and regulation of insurance companies were administered exclusively by the several states until 1944, when the United States Supreme Court held that the business of insurance is commerce and that, when its activities cross state boundaries, it is interstate commerce and thus subject to regulation by Congress under the commerce clause of the federal Constitution.

As a business institution, insurance obviously performs important services in American economic and social life. Its scope may be appreciated from the following data. On Dec. 31, 1946, the total assets held for the benefit of policyholders by all legal reserve life insurance companies in the United States were estimated to be over 48 billion dollars; those of the stock and mutual fire and marine companies, over 4 billion dollars; and those of the stock and mutual casualty companies, over 3 billion dollars. On the same date, the life insurance companies carried insurance in force of over 173 billion dollars. The coverages written by the fire, marine, casualty, and surety companies, by their very nature do not yield readily estimates of the total liabilities assumed. In 1946 all private insurance carriers combined paid to policyholders and beneficiaries a total of more than 4 and two thirds billion dollars.

Investments comprising the assets of American insurance companies are a cross section of the economic life of the nation. They are widely diversified not only as to kind, maturity, industry, and company, but geographically as well, within the United States and Canada. This diversification has meant not only greater safety for policyholders, but has served the useful purpose of bringing to many sections of the country a more adequate supply of capital than would be available locally. Two aspects of investment placement may have special mention: The first is the record of the insurance companies in purchasing United States government bonds to help finance World War II; this was particularly notable in the case of the life insurance companies as may be seen from the fact that in 1941 the portfolios of 49 of the largest of them held less than 6 and one-half billion dollars of such securities, while at the close of 1946 the total in this class was above 21 billion dollars. The second is the increasing interest developed during the past decade in housing-unit projects; though this tendency was initiated by the larger companies, there is evidence that the smaller ones also are entering the field.

In the preceding table is shown the percentage distribution of the composite assets of American insurance companies, divided according to type. Obviously, the portfolio of an individual company will not conform exactly to these averages.

For details of the principal insurance systems and topics relating to insurance, see articles under their respective titles.

WOODHULL HAY,
Educational Editor, "The Weekly Underwriter."

INSURANCE, Accident. See ACCIDENT INSURANCE.

INSURANCE, Automobile. See AUTOMOBILE INSURANCE.

INSURANCE, Aviation. See AVIATION INSURANCE.

INSURANCE, Burglary. See BURGLARY INSURANCE.

INSURANCE, Credit. Credit insurance is designed to alleviate the business difficulties resulting from bad debt losses by shifting some of the burden or risk to an insurance company. Though the idea of insuring open credit accounts was introduced in the United States in 1837, it was not till 1889 that this type of coverage actually began to be written, the first policy being issued by the United States Credit System Insurance Company. At various times after that year other credit insurance companies were formed and a number of casualty insurers also entered this field, but in 1945 virtually the entire direct underwriting was in the hands of two companies, the London Guarantee and Accident Company, Ltd., and the American Credit Indemnity Company of New York. This latter company, incorporated in 1893 and acquired in 1936 by the Commercial Credit Company, Baltimore, Md., for many years has occupied the predominant position in the business with the major part of the premium volume. In 1945 reinsurance was being written by four of the leading companies in the casualty reinsurance line.

Credit insurance is available only to manufacturers and wholesalers, not to retailers. In this area of business operations, bad debt losses are severe owing to the common practice of extending credit; they run annually into hundreds of millions of dollars, reaching figures usually much higher than total losses from fire. Credit insurance guarantees indemnity for losses up to amounts specified in the policy sustained through the insolvency of the debtors in excess of the insured's normal bad debt losses as shown by his record or as agreed upon with the insuring company. This normal loss is excluded because it is regular and predictable and because the function of insurance is not predicated on such a certainty; moreover, it properly can be taken care of as one of the costs of doing business, chargeable to sales or treated as any other expense. Probably because bad debt losses in the United States have risen sharply after wars and in periods of financial depression, the originators of credit insurance evidently regarded it as protection only against abnormal credit losses occurring during business crises or through some catastrophe, such as fire, flood, tornado, or crop failure; but its usefulness has proved to be considerably broader, for the experience of the insurers has shown that abnormal debt losses result from a wide variety of causes, both internal and external in all lines of business regardless of general or local economic conditions. Indeed, statistical analyses over a number of years reveal that a far greater percentage of failure losses has been caused by personal reasons, such as incompetence, inexperience, or lack of capital, than by outside influences. Thus credit insurance essentially is an all-risk contract, for it does not specify that the bad debt loss must be caused by any particular hazard. The fact of insolvency is sufficient.

There are 10 basic forms of policies falling into two broad groups: (1) general or blanket coverage policies; and (2) specific coverage policies. The first applies to the risk of abnormal loss on the total volume of the insured's business; the second to single accounts or a specified group of accounts. Except as will be noted later, the main provisions of both groups of policies are similar.

First, provision is made for the aggregate limit of the policy coverage and for the separate coverage limit for each of the insured's customers. These latter limits are based on the highest amount of credit that would be owing at one time by any debtor of a given rating as shown in the standard mercantile rating books.

Second, the normal loss expectancy is fixed after an analysis of the risk. This sum is calculated at a specific rate on gross sales, less allowances and returns, and deducted from the total of all losses, but provision is made for a stipulated minimum. The rate may vary from less than $\frac{1}{20}$ of 1 per cent to as high as 2 per cent.

Third, the insured is required to participate in each loss by deducting a specified percentage from the net loss on any particular debtor. In preferred risk classifications this rate is 10 per cent and it may be increased to 25 per cent or more for very hazardous risks. This coinsurance clause is essential to sound credit underwriting, for every sale contemplates a profit to the insured; and furthermore, it tends to prevent an undue credit expansion and means a reduction in premium cost.

Fourth, insolvency is not restricted in credit insurance policies to a legal definition of the term. It has been broadened to include 12 conditions, varying from formal bankruptcy proceedings to abscondence, insanity, or death in case of a sole debtor. Furthermore, even without the happening of insolvency as provided above, most of the policy forms permit the insured to file an account before it is past due for a specified period, usually 90 days, in which case the insurance company deems that the insolvency of the debtor has occurred, and the loss is admitted as if an actual insolvency existed.

Specific coverage policies are available in three main forms. In one a single account is covered with the usual coinsurance but no normal loss deduction. The second guarantees debt losses above a specified amount, which is borne by the insured; it requires no coinsurance. The third, a group coverage, fixes the amount for each named customer and bases the premium on the amount of actual shipments; it carries a coinsurance but no normal loss clause.

Within the limits of the policy provisions, credit insurance protects accounts receivable as an asset and, through it, protects the insured's working capital and possibly also his net profits. To the extent of such protection it is possible to use accounts receivable more readily as collateral for bank loans. The insurance company makes payment to the insured before the money otherwise could be collected, and in this manner provides needed working capital. Finally, the credit insurance policy, through its coverage provisions, tends to serve as a conservative guide for the extension of credit.

Woodhull Hay,
Educational Editor, "The Weekly Underwriter."

INSURANCE, Crop. See Crop Insurance.

INSURANCE, Fidelity. See Fidelity Insurance.

INSURANCE, Fire. See Fire Insurance.

INSURANCE, Fraternal. In the general field of life insurance the type known as fraternal insurance refers to that system of mutual protection provided on the cooperative plan to members of societies organized in a wide variety of ways but having in common certain characteristic purposes in addition to offering the benefits of life insurance. These purposes are designed to engender fellowship and benevolent helpfulness through activities social, moral, religious, educational, and patriotic. The spirit of fraternalism is of venerable origin; as a trait in human nature it may be traced to remote antiquity. In ancient Greece and Rome there were societies whose members, bound by congenial ties, in simple ways provided mutual self-help in times of illness or death. Similar benevolences were practiced in western Europe during the Middle Ages; and in England, with the growth of manufacture and trade, guilds, formed for mutual protection in various crafts or religious groups, granted aid, in one form or another to needy members. After the period of the Reformation, which saw the disappearance of the guilds in England, the fraternal benefits they had provided through contributions to a common fund were assumed by a new kind of cooperative association, the British friendly societies. As the principle of insurance was clearly recognized in their operations along with their social features, and as they made attempts to collect adequate sums to meet the benefits promised to members, they are regarded as the direct ancestor of American fraternal societies. Because in the early days their actuarial practices were not on a sound basis, many of these friendly societies were unable to survive the increasing average age of their members; in the 19th century, however, with corrective legislation and supervision by Parliament, they were put on a sound financial basis and are now solvent and successful. See Friendly Society.

In the United States, though a few fraternal benefit societies were organized prior to 1868, it was in that year that the system of fraternal insurance as a national institution had its beginnings, the credit being given to John Jordan Upchurch, a railway shop foreman in Pennsylvania, who founded the first lodge of the Ancient Order of United Workmen. By incorporating with insurance benefits elements of brotherhood, mutual self-help, and ritualistic forms of procedure at meetings, he stamped the pattern for the development of fraternalism in America. Many other societies were formed in succeeding years, but they were so imbued with the spirit of equality that, like their prototypes in England, they passed through troublous times financially because of their failure to solve the underlying problem of fixing adequate rates to create reserves to meet the increasing cost as members advanced in age. At first equal sums from each member were collected at the time of each death, then assessments were made at regular intervals; later still the concession was made to grade these amounts according to age. Step by step the societies went forward through experimentation, and in 1886 they took the initiative of inviting state supervision, which opened the way for regulatory state laws for fraternal insurance. The use of scientifically determined rates was begun in the early years of the 20th century, though judged by later standards they did not prove satisfactory. By 1946, standard mortality tables had been adopted by virtually all the societies, more than 77 per cent of them employing the *American Experience Table of Mortality,* the one commonly used by the legal reserve, or commercial, life insurance companies; but the interest rates assumed by the fraternals for reserve purposes have not been as conservative as those used in reserves of the life companies. In effect, the great majority of the fraternal benefit societies now are writing many of the forms of life insurance coverage developed by the old-line life companies—notably whole life, 20-payment life, endowment and juvenile insurance, with provisions for nonforfeiture rights, such as loan and cash surrender values, paid-up insurance and extended term insurance, with modifications to meet their particular needs. In addition, many of the societies offer term insurance, whole life with disability and old age insurance, or disability, sickness, and accident insurance. The current legal reserve certificates thus have been modernized and are adaptable to the basic requirements of life insurance protection, as, for example, educational funds, family protection, mortgage redemption, old age, and optional modes of settlement at death or other maturity.

On a sound economic basis fraternalism in America has prospered. The societies weathered the severe years of the depression, 1932 and 1933. According to reports gathered by *The Fraternal Monitor,* on Jan. 1, 1946, there were over 200 fraternal benefit societies in the United States and Canada with a membership of 9,021,719 in 95,857 lodges; they had assets of $1,789,756,463 and carried insurance to the total of $7,422,244,990. The amounts of the certificates in most of the societies range from a minimum of $100 to $500 to a maximum of $1,000 to $10,000, the average amount written being over $1,000.

Designed originally for the benefit of the workingman, the societies in the 20th century liberalized this conception so as to attract persons in many different walks of life. It may be noted in this connection that President Harry S. Truman became a fraternalist in 1913, and that former President Franklin D. Roosevelt at the time of his death had been a member for 12 years. Memberships as a rule are selective, that is, are formed from specialized groups with some mutual bond of interest, such as ancestral nationality (this group comprising about one half of all of the societies and representing more than 20 nationalities), occupation, religion or sex; some admit both men and women, while others are open to all persons in the community. A few of the names will illustrate this principle: Danish Brotherhood in America; La Société des Artisans Canadiens-Français; Order of Scottish Clans; Slovene National Benefit Society; Police and Firemen's Insurance Association; Mutual Beneficial Association of Pennsylvania Railroad Employees; United States Letter Carriers' Mutual Benefit Association; Baptist Life Association; Free Sons of Israel; Lutheran Brotherhood; Polish Roman Catholic Union of America; United Russian Orthodox Brotherhood of America; Woman's Benefit Association.

Distinctive Features.—Fraternal benefit societies are distinguished on the one hand from those organizations, such as the Free and Accepted Masons, the Benevolent and Protective Order of Elks, and intramural company associations, which, though engaging in activities for aiding or for relieving distress of their members, do not provide life insurance; and on the other hand from the life insurance companies, whether stock or mutual, organized for this specific purpose. Referring to the latter distinction, there are a number of underlying differences between the two systems. Some arise from the nature of the contracts employed and others from the structure and purposes of the organizations. In the first class it is observed that the life companies issue what is known as a closed contract, commonly called a policy, whereas the contract of the fraternal societies, called a certificate, is an open contract. The point of this difference lies in the fact that none of the terms of the policy can be changed by the insurance company without the consent of the insured, whereas, in the case of the certificate, the society may do so. To illustrate: should the reserve of a fraternal become impaired, the governing body may levy an assessment to cure the deficiency, and it is not necessary in such case to resort to a court proceeding; effectuating such an adjustment entails a campaign of education among the members to convince them of the necessity of their acceptance. Moreover, virtually all of the states require that the certificate be an open contract in order to carry out the original concept of a mutual insurance undertaking. Another difference arising from the nature of the contract is that the policy establishes simply a contractual relationship between the company and its insured providing life insurance benefits, whereas membership in a fraternal society entitles the member to share in a great variety of privileges in addition to the life insurance benefits.

In the second class of differences above referred to are certain features, implanted early in the fraternal system and now specified by statute in most of the states as essential requirements. First, a fraternal benefit society must be organized without capital stock and carried on solely for the mutual benefit of its members and their beneficiaries, but not for profit. With respect to the stock life insurance company the difference is apparent. This difference is less obvious in the case of a mutual company, which also is operated for the benefit of its policyholders. Like the mutuals, many fraternals in fact have made substantial returns when their financial condition justified such action. In 1945, for example, again on the authority of *The Fraternal Monitor,* 97 societies returned $8,354,413 to their members in the form of refunds, dividends, and waiver of payments. Another distinguishing feature of the fraternal society is that it has a lodge system with ritualistic form of work. Lodges may be found in virtually every city and town in the United States. Especially in small or rural communities they serve as an important club, but everywhere they provide a forum for developing democratic practices of self-organization and parliamentary procedure, and a medium for social, fraternal, charitable, and patriotic activities. The incorporation of ritualism in both initiation and routine ceremony dates from the time of the founder, Upchurch, and its influence in teaching the cardinal virtues through symbolism and imagery well justifies its continuance. Furthermore, the lodge system, by affording membership in a particular lodge, provides local organized contact among fraternalists that contributes materially to the realization that they are engaged in a mutual undertaking, for the meetings are held at stated times and the discussions inculcate a common interest in the affairs not only of the lodge, but of the society. The third item in this class of differences is that a fraternal society has a representative form of government. Not only do the members of a lodge elect their own officers but they elect from their own number representatives to go to a state or district convention, which in turn chooses representatives to the national governing body; in some societies the delegates to the latter are sent directly from the lodges. Voting by proxy is not permitted. This governing body, called frequently the Supreme Lodge, meets variously from one to four years and exercises control of the affairs of the society, making and mending its constitution and bylaws, establishing new lodges, and determining the terms of the certificates the society wishes to write. To provide for management in the intervals between these meetings, the governing body elects a board of trustees or directors, and officers. The expenses of management are provided by sums separately collected from the members, though in some societies the premium rates are adjusted to meet these ends, and by law the mortuary and expense funds must be kept separate. A large number of the societies since 1914 have expanded their facilities for learning and practicing the democratic forms of government by organizing juvenile lodges where boys and girls before reaching the age of adult membership, usually fixed at 16, are admitted as insurance members and taught the ways of good citizenship. According to *The Fraternal Monitor,* on Jan. 1, 1946, the 159 societies having juvenile departments had an enrollment of 1,353,260 juvenile members with an insurance of $742,571,347.

An understanding of fraternal insurance is inseparable from a comprehension that always consciously present in purpose and action is the supporting system of mutual benevolences which has dominated fraternalism from its inception. Though certain forms of activity have been developed with more emphasis in some societies and lodges than in others, cooperative help is a practice common to all fraternals and is regarded as a primary obligation. Reference already has been made to lodge activities that engender a spirit of fellowship, teach respect for moral principles, and offer opportunities for self-discipline and self-government, prerequisites to good citizenship. To illustrate the breadth of the scope, a few others may be mentioned. In way of direct charities, funds are collected for temporary and permanent care of the aged and disabled, the sick and the orphaned among the members; 24 societies reported in 1945 to the National Fraternal Congress that they were maintaining 7 hospitals and 16 homes at various places throughout the country. In addition, help is given to their needy in emergencies, such as advancing payments and dues, providing rent, food and clothing, and supplying free nurse and hospital service. To these welfare objectives may be added a wide range of social and recreational functions, including entertainments, musicals, and sports contests, organized in the lodges to promote fellowship and develop talent.

National Fraternal Congress. — Organized in 1886, the most influential instrumentality in the development of fraternalism is the National Fraternal Congress of America. In 1945 its 105 societies represented 82 per cent of the total fraternal membership in the United States and Canada. Supported by 36 auxiliary state and regional congresses and three associations—actuarial, managers,' and law—it is the representative body of the fraternal system, cooperating with the National Association of Insurance Commissioners and sending envoys to national meetings of the life companies. It has fostered practices of safety and permanence, and proposed constructive legislation. Among the forward steps actively sponsored by the congress are the enactment of uniform laws to define fraternal benefit societies, the creation of adequate reserves and the adoption by the societies of sound mortality tables, whole family protection and juvenile insurance. Beginning as early as 1944 and continuing in 1945 and 1946, many conferences were held by committees of the congress and the National Association of Insurance Commissioners to work out a suitable uniform fraternal code for enactment in all the states; a spirit of cooperation prevailed, considerable progress was made, and the conferences were to be continued. Among the matters discussed were the organization of new societies, the licensing of agents, limitations on the designation of beneficiaries and nonmedical business.

Of the many activities of the National Fraternal Congress there are two that may be noted specially because they illustrate the purpose to maintain the service of fraternalism in America as a sound instrument of insurance protection. The first is that through the Fraternal Field Managers' Association, the congress instituted in 1937, after careful preparation, a course of study designed to equip their field workers with adequate knowledge of the principles of life insurance and to train them in valid methods of explaining these principles and of devising proper life insurance programs to meet particular needs. To this end a comprehensive training book was published, and plans were made to reward those who successfully passed a set examination by granting them the designation of fraternal insurance counselor. With a public that is becoming better informed on life insurance, this educational program, by increasing the competence of the life underwriter, is a step toward according him professional status in the community as an adviser on an economic matter of personal and family importance. The second activity referred to is the adoption of a progressive public relations program with institutional literature. In 1943–1944 it published 50,000 copies of *Fraternal Insurance Protection in America* and distributed copies of six articles for use in the society journals. There were 171 fraternal society journals listed in 1946 by *The Fraternal Monitor.*

A similarly representative organization in Canada is the Canadian Fraternal Association, which is separate from, though not competitive with, the National Fraternal Congress. It is composed of 20 societies operating in Canada, and many societies are members of both organizations.

WOODHULL HAY,
Educational Editor, "The Weekly Underwriter."

INSURANCE, GROUP. See GROUP INSURANCE.

INSURANCE, GUARANTY. See GUARANTY INSURANCE.

INSURANCE, HEALTH. See HEALTH INSURANCE.

INSURANCE, Industrial. Industrial life insurance may be defined in general terms as family life insurance, conducted principally for the purpose of providing individual life insurance for those who can afford only small sums and must pay for it by weekly or monthly payments usually collected at the home. Some of the legal definitions are as follows:

United States—New York State:

"The term *industrial life insurance,* as used in this chapter, shall mean that form of life insurance, either

(1) under which the premiums are payable weekly, or

(2) under which the premiums are payable monthly or oftener, but less often than weekly, if the face amount of insurance provided in any such policy is less than one thousand dollars and if the words 'industrial policy' are printed upon the policy as a part of the descriptive matter." (New York State Insurance Law—§ 201.)

Canada—Province of Ontario:

"*Industrial contract* means a contract of life insurance for an amount not exceeding $2,000, exclusive of any benefit, surplus, profit, dividend or bonus also payable under the contract, and which provides for payment of premiums at fortnightly or shorter intervals, or, if the premiums are usually collected at the home of the insured, at monthly intervals." (The Insurance Act R.S.O. 1937, chap. 256, 1, 29.)

Most of the other provinces in Canada have a similar definition.

Great Britain:

"*Industrial assurance* in Great Britain is defined by statute as a business of effecting assurances upon human life, the premiums in respect to which are received by collectors who make visits at the homes of the policyholders for that purpose, the premiums being payable at intervals of less than two months."

The above quotation from an article entitled "The Progress of Industrial Assurance in Great Britain since the London Congress of 1927" by F. H. Spratling, in the *Transactions of the Tenth International Congress of Actuaries,* gives the essence of the definition of industrial assurance included in the Industrial Assurance Act of 1923.

While in scientific principles industrial life insurance does not differ from ordinary life insurance, in practice it has certain distinctive features. The amounts of insurance per policy are generally smaller than in ordinary insurance, averaging in the United States somewhat more than $250 per policy. The premiums, instead of being payable directly to the home office of the insurance company, are usually received by agents at the home of the insured. The premiums are usually payable at short intervals, such as weekly or monthly, and correspond in a general way to the frequency of payment of wages in the class of population being insured. Very often the amount of premium to be paid is taken as the unit, the amount of insurance varying for different plans and ages. The amounts of insurance are based upon mortality tables reflecting the experience on industrial insurance, or in some countries upon population mortality tables. Such tables generally reflect the higher mortality experienced on industrial as compared with ordinary insurance. With a few exceptions, the insurance can be taken out on all members of the family from birth to age 65 or over, without distinction as to sex. The age used in determining the benefit or premium is usually the age next birthday rather than nearest birthday. In the majority of countries other than the United States and Canada, industrial insurance is also characterized by an initial period of limited benefits, varying from six months to three years. During this period the amount of death benefit payable on all policies effected without a medical examination is usually limited to the return of premiums paid or to a fraction of the face amount of insurance, unless death occurs from accident, or in some cases, from certain other specified causes. The contracts themselves and their provisions are kept as simple as possible in order that they may be practical in application and easily understood by the policyholders.

History.—For its origin, industrial insurance can point to the guilds of the Middle Ages whose place was taken in England, after the Reformation, by friendly societies and burial clubs. These were voluntary associations which met periodically, collecting dues, which were the same for all ages, and undertaking to bury members out of the fund so paid in. Their management was usually poor and the benefits uncertain. The first company to transact industrial life insurance, the Industrial and General, was founded in England in 1849. An offshoot, called the British Industry Life Insurance Company, was formed in 1852, and two years later, in 1854, the Prudential Assurance Company, which had been in existence six years as an ordinary company, began writing industrial business. This company soon absorbed the British Industry Life Insurance Company and became the largest writer of industrial insurance in England, which position it still occupies. The steady growth of industrial insurance in Great Britain is indicated by the following table:

INDUSTRIAL INSURANCE IN GREAT BRITAIN*

Year	Number of policies in force	Insurance in force
1893	13,324,778	£128,064,110
1903	23,810,937	234,220,274
1913	37,556,248	428,690,925
1923	51,493,663	715,603,343
1933	66,595,929	1,088,769,588
1943	81,257,093	1,488,871,116

* Excluding business done by friendly societies.

There are in Great Britain a number of organizations transacting industrial insurance known as friendly or collecting societies which are very probably the direct descendants of the old friendly societies or burial clubs formed after the Reformation. (See FRIENDLY SOCIETY.) Most of these organizations are very small and, prior to the passage of the Industrial Assurance Act of 1923, were subject to little government supervision. At the end of 1938, 149 societies reported 24,475,000 industrial policies in force. The amount of insurance per policy averaged slightly less than on policies of the regular industrial offices.

The progress of industrial insurance in England attracted attention in America, and about 1870 there were in existence a few societies similar to the friendly societies of England. One of these, the Hildise Bund, collected dues weekly and paid a part of them to the Metropolitan Life Insurance Company to be credited toward quarterly premiums on policies issued by the company on the lives of the members of the bund. In 1875 a small corporation in Newark, N.J., known as the Widows' and Orphans' Friendly Society, changed its name to the Prudential Friendly Society, later The Prudential Insurance Company of America, and in November began the business of industrial insurance on the lines of the English Prudential Company after which it was named. Four years later, in 1879, the Metropolitan Life Insurance Company of New York and the John Hancock Mutual Life Insurance Company of Boston, companies which had been previously writing ordinary insurance, entered the industrial field. Almost three fourths of the total industrial insurance in force at the end of 1944 in the United States was in these three companies. The following table (*Spectator Year Book,* 1945) shows the rapid growth of the business in the United States:

INDUSTRIAL INSURANCE IN UNITED STATES COMPANIES

Year	Number of companies	Number of policies in force	Insurance in force
1877........	1	11,226	$ 1,030,655
1884........	3	1,076,422	108,451,099
1894........	12	6,847,892	802,016,133
1904........	18	15,671,107	2,135,594,314
1914........	27	31,134,303	4,170,971,777
1924........	53	68,073,589	11,309,136,316
1934........	65	82,579,393	17,650,708,523
1944........	97	100,364,759	27,047,642,610

The foregoing table does not include the data of some of the small companies. Some of them issue policies which combine industrial life insurance with health and accident benefits, collecting a weekly premium for the combined benefits.

In the United States, industrial life insurance was for many years sold almost exclusively on a weekly premium basis. Ordinary insurance was offered with premiums payable once, twice, or four times yearly. In the middle 1920's, however, monthly premium insurance was introduced by a number of companies. Because of the expense involved, companies writing only ordinary insurance placed limitations on the minimum monthly premium they would accept, usually specifying $10 as the minimum. Companies writing both ordinary and industrial policies were able to issue monthly premium policies for much smaller amounts by collecting and accounting for premiums in the same manner as for industrial policies. One of the three largest of these companies issues monthly premium policies for the smaller amounts, in general $500 or less, as industrial contracts, and for the larger amounts as ordinary contracts. The other two issue all of their monthly premium policies as ordinary contracts. The cost of the monthly premium policies, which is about the same whether they are issued as industrial or ordinary, is less than that of weekly premium policies, because of the less frequent payment of premiums and larger amounts of insurance involved.

Industrial insurance was introduced into Canada in 1881 and has grown rapidly, the larger portion being divided among two United States companies, a Canadian company, and an Australian company. The Canadian business in force in 1944 amounted to 4,101,179 policies, insuring $1,256,868,575.

Industrial insurance was introduced in Australia in 1884. Due to the character of the country it did not flourish as in America or England but nevertheless showed a steady growth. In 1937 there were more than two and one-quarter million policies in force assuring £99,544,000.

In New Zealand, the government started the business of industrial insurance as early as 1875 but discontinued it shortly thereafter. In 1881 the government revived the work of the industrial branch of its Insurance Department, but finally abandoned the business in 1887. Since that time industrial insurance has been transacted by private companies, which in 1940 had 460,650 policies and £22,621,000 of insurance in force.

(NOTE. — Industrial insurance in European countries is described in the next few paragraphs from the most recent information available. It should be noted, however, that such information refers in general to dates prior to the beginning of World War II, and consequently may not be representative of the present status of industrial insurance in the countries that were involved in the conflict.)

In Germany, industrial insurance suffered from the conditions following World War I more than ordinary insurance. However, the industrial business rallied after stabilization of the currency and, during the depression, it suffered considerably less than the ordinary business. At the end of 1938 there were in force 20,466,868 industrial policies insuring 6,886,390 thousand reichsmarks. In Germany, as on the Continent generally, endowment plans of industrial insurance have been especially popular, affording as they do a convenient, safe and practical means of saving.

In France, one company which was founded in 1858 wrote a number of "small assurances." The failure of this company in 1902 and of other similar ventures resulted in the loss of public confidence in industrial insurance until just before World War I, when new companies began specializing in this business. Progress was arrested during that war, in 1920 there being only three companies writing industrial insurance exclusively, although other companies wrote a few industrial policies along with their ordinary business. Thereafter the growth was resumed and at the end of 1932, 13 companies had 525,000 policies in force insuring 3,200 millions of francs. At the end of 1945, the largest French company, which writes more than one third of the entire amount issued in France, had about 740,000 industrial policies in force insuring about 7,500 million francs.

Industrial insurance attained a rapid growth in Belgium. In 1927 there were 20 companies, including 6 cooperative ventures, in addition to the State Caisse d'Assurances transacting this kind of business. At the end of 1938 there was about 2,600 million francs of industrial insurance in force.

Industrial insurance was introduced into Denmark in 1896, all premiums being on a weekly basis. At the end of 1925 there were in Danish companies 526,453 policies in force insuring 239,983,513 kroner, the number of policies being equal to about one sixth of the total population. In Norway, industrial insurance was first issued in 1903, there being three companies doing this business by the end of 1926. At that time there were 155,474 policies for 124,313,667 kroner in force. In Sweden, the first company to issue industrial insurance was founded in 1899. The business had increased so that the four companies active in 1925 had over one billion kroner in force at the end of that year.

In Switzerland, industrial insurance had been introduced prior to 1900 and at the end of 1943 there were 1,067,854 policies in force insuring 1,688,268,771 francs. In Italy, a National Insurance Institution which was started in 1925, issued such industrial insurance as has been written. At the end of 1938 there were in force in the institution 2,577,000 policies for over 17,370 million lire.

Among the other countries, Holland has a large number of small industrial policies in force, insuring 1,120 million guilders at the end of 1941. For the Union of South Africa, there were 251,439 policies for £6,486,000 of insurance in force at the end of 1939. Other countries that have transacted industrial business on a limited scale include Rumania, Brazil, Mexico, and Finland.

Policy Contracts.—Industrial insurance is transacted on both the life and the endowment plans but not in general on the term plan. A popular life plan is that on which premiums cease at an advanced age, for example at 70 or 75. Another is that on which premiums are payable for only 20 years. Endowment insurance is issued for various terms, the most popular being 20 years. Long-term endowments maturing at a specified advanced age are also issued. Since 1939 the law of New York State has not permitted the issuance of industrial life insurance policies on the endowment plan to residents of that state, and the three largest United States companies no longer issue 20-year endowment policies on a weekly premium basis. In the past, various plans involving special features have been issued, but the current tendency in industrial insurance is to limit it to a few basically simple and easily understood plans of insurance. In almost all policies issued at the so-called "juvenile" ages (under 10) the amount of insurance payable at death increases with the attained age of the insured, until a maximum amount payable is reached, which then remains level throughout the subsequent duration of the policy.

In the United States, the legal minimum standard for industrial reserves generally has been the *American Experience Table of Mortality.* Most companies, however, use the *Standard Industrial Table,* or the new 1941 *Standard Industrial Table,* both of which are more stringent bases, in their valuations. Until recently, the rate of interest assumed in valuation was generally 3½ per cent, but many companies are now using a lower rate.

Although in general, industrial insurance is issued only on standard lives at standard premium rates, a few companies in the United States and several in Europe issue industrial insurance on a substandard basis to lives that do not measure up to the qualifications for standard insurance either because of medical impairments, occupations, or for other reasons.

A very large proportion of industrial business is issued on a nonmedical basis. Medical examinations are usually given only in certain instances, such as when they are required by law, when the amount of insurance applied for is relatively large, when an agent, through lack of experience, is not qualified to appraise the risk correctly, or when there is some indication of an impairment.

Policy Provisions.—The provisions of the policies of industrial insurance do not differ in principle from the provisions of policies of ordinary insurance. They are usually incontestable after one or two years and free from restrictions as to residence and travel. They include a grace period for payment of premiums, which in the United States is usually either four weeks or one month. In case of lapse for nonpayment of premiums, nonforfeiture values in the form of extended term insurance for a limited period or reduced paid-up insurance can be obtained provided the policy has been in force for a certain minimum period. In the policies currently issued by the large United States companies, the minimum period of premium payments for nonforfeiture extended term insurance is only 13 or 26 weeks. Cash values are also available after a minimum duration of premium payments, which is 3 years in the large United States companies. A provision for revival upon satisfactory evidence of insurability, if premiums are not in arrears beyond a specified period, is also usually included.

Because of the nature of the business, industrial policies have several provisions not found in ordinary policies, among which the following, as applicable to policies issued in the United States and Canada, might be mentioned:

Facility of Payment Clause.—Because of the small amounts of the policies and of the fact that payments under industrial policies are often made to persons who are in urgent need of the funds, it is important that the companies be able to make settlement promptly and with the smallest possible expense and trouble to the payee. It often happens that at the time of death, the beneficiary named in such policies has separated from the family or no longer retains the status that existed at the time of the purchase of the insurance; yet necessary changes in the policy may not have been made. In order to permit the companies to make prompt settlements, there is usually found in the industrial policy a so-called Facility of Payment Clause. In the form used currently in the policies of the larger companies, the Facility of Payment Clause permits the company to make the payment under industrial policies to any relative by blood or connection by marriage of the insured appearing to the company to be equitably entitled to such payment, if claim is not made by the named beneficiary within a stated period of time after the death of the insured, that is, 30 or 60 days, or if the named beneficiary is the estate of the insured, or dies before the insured, or is not legally qualified to give a valid release.

The Health Clause.—In most companies the application for industrial insurance is not attached to the policy and made a part of the contract, hence the statements included therein with respect to the health of the insured and other factors affecting his insurability are not generally available for use by the company as evidence in case of misrepresentation by the insured. For this reason industrial policies issued by most companies contain a clause limiting the liability on the policy within the contestable period, ordinarily to a return of premiums, if facts of major importance with respect to such things as the health and previous medical history of the insured are not made known to the company and endorsed by the company on the policy.

At least one large company, however, does not include such a clause in its industrial policies currently issued, since a copy of the application is attached to and made part of all such policies.

Additional Accidental Death Benefit.—Most industrial policies include a provision for the payment, in addition to the regular death benefit, of an accidental death benefit equal to the face amount of the policy if death occurs by accidental means. In contrast to the practice in ordinary insurance, there is usually no specific additional premium for this benefit. The benefit is generally limited to deaths which occur between certain ages and is at times modified for accidental deaths while engaging in certain unusually hazardous occupations.

Limited Disability Benefit.—Industrial insurance often includes a limited disability benefit for which no specific additional premium is charged. In the large companies the benefit consists of the payment of a lump sum and the waiver of future premiums, and is paid only in the event of blindness or loss of limbs.

Refund on Account of Direct Payment of Premiums.—The weekly premium industrial policies of the large companies and a few smaller companies contain a clause which provides for a refund of a stated percentage of the premiums paid (usually 10 per cent), provided such premiums are paid continuously for one year, in person or by mail, directly to the company at one of its offices, thereby saving the expense of collection by an agent.

Option of Acceptance.—Most industrial policies include an option to surrender within two or three weeks of the issue of the policy, if the terms of the policy are not satisfactory, or if its conditions are not accepted and agreed to. If this option is exercised, all premiums paid are returned to the premium payer.

Certain options granted ordinary policyholders are not included in industrial contracts because they would be of little use with small amounts of insurance and would involve disproportionate expense. For example, the provisions for policy loans and for settlement in the form of income over a period of years or for life would not be practical for such small policies.

Dividends.—A large portion of industrial insurance is eligible to participate in the surplus earnings of the companies. The three companies in the United States having the largest volume of industrial insurance in force are all mutual. The small average size of the policies involved and hence the small amounts of money represented by each unit of surplus distributed, known as a dividend, make it impractical to allow a choice on the part of the policyholder as to the method by which he will receive this dividend. It is therefore customary for each individual company to have a uniform method of distributing dividends which is applicable to all or to a large group of industrial policies. The two most popular methods in use in the United States and Canada are to allow the dividend as a credit toward premiums or toward the purchase of paid-up additional insurance payable on the same terms as the original contract. In the United States and Canada, these dividends are normally apportioned annually. In Great Britain, although most of the companies are stock companies, a portion of the profits, usually determined according to the charter of the company, is distributed to industrial policyholders. This distribution usually takes place annually and is generally in the form of additions to the amounts of insurance payable either on the same terms as the original contract or only in the event of a claim during a certain period. Various other forms of dividends to industrial policyholders, such as dividends to shorten the premium-paying period or to bring closer the maturity date of the policy, a refund of a certain number of premiums upon termination of the policy, and special cash dividends payable upon death, maturity, or surrender are also in use.

Mortality.—The lower income groups, for whom industrial insurance is intended, experience higher death rates than persons in better circumstances. In order not to exclude a substantial proportion of these groups, a greater degree of mortality risk is accepted at standard premium rates for industrial than for ordinary insurance. Persons in certain occupations, for instance, who would be charged a higher than standard premium rate for ordinary insurance, are granted industrial insurance at standard rates. Consequently, the mortality among industrial policyholders is considerably higher than that among those insured under ordinary contracts, and in the United States and some other countries has been slightly above that of the general population.

The higher rates of mortality among industrial risks are illustrated in the following table which compares the number of deaths per thousand exposures at each of several specified ages according to (1) the *United States Life Table* for white male lives compiled by the United States Bureau of the Census from census returns for the continental United States, covering the deaths reported in the years 1929, 1930 and 1931; (2) a table representing modern experience on ordinary policies, excluding the first five years of insurance, prepared by a committee of the National Association of Insurance Commissioners (U.S.) appointed to study the need for a new mortality table and other related topics. This table (Table Z of the report of the committee) is based on the experience under ordinary policies of the principal American life insurance companies during the years 1925–1934; and (3) death rates based on the experience of the Metropolitan Life Insurance Company during the years 1929–1931 on white male lives insured under its weekly premium industrial policies. Although the rates shown are not in all respects strictly comparable, they afford a rough comparison of the mortality of the general population, of ordinary policyholders and of industrial policyholders during the period to which they refer. Rates for white male lives are used for the general population and for industrial policyholders in order to be more nearly comparable with the ordinary experience shown, which is composed predominantly of white male lives.

DEATHS PER 1,000

Age	U.S. Life Table, 1930 White Males	Modern * Ordinary Experience (1925–1934)	Metropolitan Industrial Experience White Males (1929–1931)
20	3.2	2.2	3.1
25	3.7	2.4	3.9
30	4.1	2.5	4.7
35	5.1	3.2	6.2
40	6.8	4.5	8.8
45	9.3	6.9	12.3
50	12.8	10.1	17.8
55	18.2	15.4	24.7
60	26.4	23.4	35.0
65	38.7	35.6	50.6

* Table Z of the report of the Committee to Study the Need for a New Mortality Table—National Association of Insurance Commissioners (U.S.).

Industrial mortality has shown a notable improvement in recent years. This improvement has been greater for industrial mortality than for the other classes. At the present time (1946), the mortality of industrial policyholders is still considerably in excess of that of ordinary policyholders, but very likely is not materially different from that of the general population.

Expense.—From its very nature, industrial insurance costs more to transact than ordinary. Industrial premiums are payable more frequently, necessitating additional servicing, and the average industrial policy is much smaller. For a given amount of insurance (or premium), it is therefore necessary to handle many more industrial than ordinary transactions. Despite this fact, the difference in expense charges between the two branches is not great. A comparison in one of the large United States companies found that the average expense charge on its weekly premium industrial policies exceeded that on its monthly premium ordinary policies by about 13 per cent of the weekly premiums. This higher expense charge can be reduced to about 3 per cent if the industrial premiums are paid directly to one of the company's offices, thereby receiving the refund of 10 per cent of the premiums granted under the terms of its weekly premium policies.

The ratio of expense to premium income on industrial business has shown a remarkable decrease since the business was inaugurated. The introduction of small monthly premium policies and of the 10 per cent refund for direct payment of weekly premiums has resulted in important savings to policyholders. On weekly premium insurance serviced by the agent at the policyholder's home, the companies have made continuous advances in their efforts to handle this insurance at the lowest possible cost, through improvements in accounting methods and in the efficiency with which the business is conducted. As a result, the expense rate of conducting the business is now far below that of what it was in the early 1920's.

In countries other than the United States, progress has also been made in reducing the expense of industrial insurance. The expense rate on small policies for which the premiums are received at the policyholders' homes is about the same in the largest company in Great Britain as in the largest United States companies.

Field Organization.—One of the distinctive features of industrial insurance is that the premiums, instead of being payable directly to the home office of the insurance company, are usually called for by agents at the home of the insured. This characteristic limits the territory over which a company can efficiently operate to the larger towns and cities and requires a very different type of field organization from that of a purely ordinary company. The following description applies specifically to industrial insurance in the United States but in most details is typical of such insurance throughout the world.

The territory over which the company operates is divided into various areas or districts. Each district, which may be a part of a large city or the whole of a small city together with the surrounding cities and towns, contains a unit of the field organization consisting of a manager or superintendent, usually with several assistants, and a number of agents, varying from a few to 50 or more. Each agent is assigned to a specific subdivision of the business of the district, termed a debit. He is expected to receive premiums and perform all necessary services to policyholders embraced in his debit, and writes new industrial policies chiefly on persons residing within the territory assigned to him. Generally the agent solicits ordinary insurance also.

Because of the fact that the agent must spend much of his time in collecting premiums and in serving the policyholders on his debit, the method of compensation of such agents differs materially from that of agents of purely ordinary companies. Compensation for industrial business consists in general of two or more parts: a service commission which is usually based on the amount of premiums collected; a compensation for new business, which may be a percentage of the first-year premiums collected on policies secured by the agent, or may be based upon the actual increase in business accomplished by the agent; and in some companies a conservation commission is also paid, the amount of which is determined in general by the relative persistency of the business entrusted to the agent's care. In some European countries, however, compensation for new business is based more on the ordinary method of paying a commission upon the issuance of a policy. The commission is often modified or delayed in order not to incur the loss involved in complete payment of commission on a policy which lapses shortly after issue.

Persistency.—Economic conditions have a very important influence on the lapse rate of life insurance. During times when unemployment and curtailed incomes are prevalent, the number of policyholders who are forced to interrupt premium payments or to surrender their policies for much-needed cash is greater than in normal times. The reverse is true when economic conditions are unusually favorable. In 1941, a year in which economic conditions were neither extremely favorable or unfavorable, one large American company experienced a lapse rate of 5.4 per cent on its weekly premium policies. Since each of its agents services about 1,000 weekly premium policies, this lapse rate represents the lapse of one policy per agent per week. This company has also reported an analysis made of all the premiums paid on the policies that terminated in 1941. This analysis indicated that 31.5 per cent of the premiums had been paid on policies which became death claims, 21.6 per cent on policies that matured as endowments, 44.1 per cent on policies that were surrendered for cash (having been in force for an average period of 15 years), 2.5 per cent on policies that expired at the end of the period of nonforfeiture paid-up term insurance, and 0.3 per cent on policies on which premium payments were discontinued very shortly after they were issued so that the policy was not entitled to a nonforfeiture value.

The companies continually try to keep terminations at a minimum consistent with the welfare of policyholders. To this end, considerable effort is made to conserve insurance against contemplated lapse, by pointing out to the policyholder the advantages of maintaining existing insurance in force if at all possible. As a fundamental preventive of lapse, the companies discourage in every conceivable way the writing of business which is not likely to continue. The compensation of agents is usually determined in a manner calculated to discourage their presenting applications where the business does not seem likely to persist. Agents are constantly reminded of the futility of issuing business which cannot be expected to continue in force. Often the compensation of managers or superintendents is dependent in some manner on lapse rates, especially of the recent issues of their districts, thus producing an incentive for the managers to do everything possible to encourage writing only that business which will persist.

Insurance of Children.—The insurance of children, particularly in English-speaking countries, is an important feature of industrial insurance. It received its start in the early years of the Prudential Assurance Company in Great Britain and since that time has grown rapidly. It has been the subject of considerable discussion and legislation. In England the law for many years has permitted the insurance of children within certain statutory limits.

In America the practice of insuring children dates back to the beginning of industrial insurance. In 1892 New York State adopted a law specifically permitting insurance on the lives of minors when taken out by a person liable for the support of the minor, with certain restrictions as to amount. Certain other states and Canadian provinces soon followed the example of New York.

Considerable opposition to child insurance was encountered at first, but most of this was founded on conjecture rather than fact, and proposed legislation forbidding the insurance of children repeatedly failed of passage. Colorado was the only state which adopted a law forbidding this type of insurance, and this statute has since been repealed. The writing of industrial insurance on the lives of children has been so conducted and has so successfully fulfilled its purposes that agitation for its prohibition has virtually ceased.

The restrictions on the amounts of insurance which could be carried on the lives of minors according to state and provincial laws have been modified from time to time. Insurance is now permitted from birth in all provinces of Canada and in all states in the United States. The restrictions on the amounts of insurance on the lives of persons over age 10 in Canada and over age 14½ in the United States have been entirely removed. In the United States, only New York limits the amounts of insurance on the lives of children under age 14½.

The insurance of children has not been developed in such large degree in non-English-speaking countries. In those countries where it is permitted, children's insurances are usually written on the endowment plan with small death benefits, sometimes only a return of premium, provided.

The present legal limits of industrial insurance on the life of a child, applicable under varying conditions in the various jurisdictions, are as given in the following table:

Age next birthday	Canada (Ontario, etc.)	Great Britain	Age nearest birthday	New York State
1	$ 100	£ 6	0	$ 100
2	200	6	1	200
3	300	6	2	300
4	400	10	3–9	400
5	500	10	10	1100
6	600	10	11	1200
7	700	15	12	1300
8	800	15	13	1400
9	900	15	14	1500
10	1000	15		

Underwriting.—An important development in industrial insurance has been the increasing emphasis placed by the companies on fitting the insurance to the family's needs and circumstances. Through the instruction and training of agents and through the establishment of underwriting regulations, the companies have encouraged sound family insurance programs.

Care is taken to ensure that families will not attempt to buy more insurance than they can afford to maintain. Proper distribution of insurance within the family group, with primary consideration given to the insurance needs of the wage earner, is also stressed. Efforts are made to sell the insurance which, in amount and in frequency of premium payment, best fits the family's circumstances. Weekly premium insurance is sold only for small amounts, generally $500 or less, and less expensive monthly premium insurance is recommended when larger amounts of insurance are desired and when the family can conveniently pay its premiums by the month.

These and other steps taken by the companies in establishing sound insurance programs, and in adjusting these programs in harmony with changing family circumstances, have done much to assist policyholders in obtaining the greatest possible benefit from their premium money.

Health and Welfare Work.—Companies transacting industrial life insurance have an unusual opportunity to do effective health and welfare work through the agents who call regularly at millions of homes. This opportunity has not been overlooked by the companies in the United States, for they have taken an active part for many years in the various branches of health work. Chief among their activities have been the dissemination of health literature and the offering, by some companies, of visiting nursing service to their industrial policyholders without extra charge. Cooperation with municipal, state and provincial health departments, schools and private agencies, as well as the projects undertaken by the companies themselves, have been important factors in the promotion of general public health work in the United States and Canada.

One of the largest United States companies has specialized to an unusual degree in health and welfare work over the past third of a century. It distributes pamphlets and leaflets and maintains a visiting nurse service for its industrial policyholders. In 1945, alone, 31,000,000 pamphlets were given out and 1,600,000 nursing visits made. In cooperating with community agencies, its activities cover such fields as home economics, health education in schools, educational motion pictures and exhibits, safety campaigns, and health surveys of various communities. It publishes studies of the mortality of its policyholders, as an aid to public health, and has conducted extensive community health demonstrations and sickness surveys and in numerous ways has contributed to the support of movements for the improvement of health.

Some British companies maintain nursing services and issue health literature, while at least one company, in connection with its mortality and sickness statistics, makes health surveys and cooperates with public health agencies. In Australia, two companies at least have entered upon health work, including nursing service for industrial policyholders. In Sweden, the industrial companies have done much to help those suffering from tuberculosis, while at least one company has started a program of health education.

Special Concessions.—Industrial insurance companies, particularly in the United States and Great Britain, have allowed their policyholders a great many special concessions not provided by the policy. In case of default for nonpayment of premiums, the provisions for revival are often modified in practice. For example, in many cases the requirement of satisfactory evidence of insurability is waived if premiums are in arrears for only a short period.

Industrial policies issued in the United States many years ago generally contained no provision for cash surrender values. Later it became customary to provide such values after premiums had been paid for 10 years. However, during the economic depression of the 1930's in particular, some companies made concessions to policyholders in extreme need by allowing a cash surrender value on policies which contained no provision therefor, or on other policies at an earlier date than that specified in the contract. Some companies have extended this latter concession, to grant cash surrender values on any policy without requirement of extreme need, after the minimum period of premium payments specified in the cash surrender provision of the latest policy form (three years in the case of the larger companies). In certain cases changes from one plan to another, sometimes involving a cash payment to the policyholder, are permitted. A number of companies likewise permit industrial insurance to be changed to ordinary insurance when the circumstances of the insured make such a change desirable and the insured can meet the conditions of insurability required for ordinary insurance. These change privileges are of great assistance to many policyholders in adjusting their insurance programs to their current means.

Some of the companies have increased the amounts of insurance on policies issued many years ago to bring the benefits up to, or partly up to, the level of those in policies issued at later dates. In addition, some of the companies have granted "dividends" on old whole life policies to make them paid-up at age 70 or 75 in line with current issues. The additional accidental death benefit and disability or "loss of eyesight or limbs" benefit have not always been provided for in industrial policies in the United States. At the time these provisions were added to newly issued policies, many companies also made the provisions retroactive to all policies previously issued which were in force at that time.

Prior to 1915 most industrial policies in the United States were nonparticipating by their terms. In 1897, however, one of the largest companies voluntarily declared dividends—or "bonuses," as they were subsequently called. These voluntary dividends were continued each year, with important additions from time to time, and the company paid or credited to the holders of nonparticipating industrial policies during the years 1897–1915 over $49,000,000 in its various forms of bonuses. Another large company similarly paid or credited a substantial sum while a stock company. Both of these companies became mutual companies in 1915.

The companies issuing industrial insurance constantly endeavor to improve their policy contracts, give added benefits, remove restrictions, and be as liberal in their relations with policyholders as sound principles of management and current conditions will permit. In most cases new advantages are extended retroactively to those who had bought their policies before the new features were adopted. Most of the special concessions described above are instances of this effort to bring all policies up to date so that all policyholders, old and new, may be provided with the utmost possible protection and service.

Bibliography.—*Transactions of the Eighth International Congress of Actuaries,* vol. 1 (1927) and *Transactions of the Tenth International Congress of Actuaries,* vol. 2 (1934) contain several papers describing industrial insurance in various countries. Literature dealing primarily with American industrial insurance includes: Kineke, F. D., "Some Aspects of Modern Industrial Insurance," *Record of the American Institute of Actuaries,* vol. 21, p. 23 (1932); Huebner, S. S., *Life Insurance,* chap. 23 (New York 1935); Kineke, F. D., "A New Industrial Policy," *Record of the American Institute of Actuaries,* vol. 26, p. 28 (1937); Magee, J. H., *Life Insurance,* chap. 23 (Chicago 1939); Davis, M. E., *Industrial Life Insurance in the United States* (New York 1944); Maclean, J. B., *Life Insurance,* chap. 16 (New York 1945).

Leroy A. Lincoln,
President, Metropolitan Life Insurance Company.

INSURANCE, LIABILITY. See Liability Insurance.

INSURANCE, Life. Life insurance is a system of insurance that does one or a combination of two things: it provides for the payment of a stipulated amount of money (1) upon the death of the person insured; or (2) at a stated time, if the person insured is still living.

The insurance agreement is contained in a written contract called a *policy.* There are at least two parties to this contract: one party, the company offering the insurance, is called the *insurer,* or simply *the company;* the other party, the person whose life is to be insured, is called the *insured* (in some policies, the *assured*).

There is a third party to the life insurance agreement when the insurance is applied for by someone other than the person whose life is to be insured. For example: a father might insure the life of a minor child; or a corporation might want insurance on the life of a key employee; the father or the corporation would then become the third party and would be called the *policyholder* (or *policyowner*). However, in most instances there are only two parties to the contract, and the insured is also the policyholder.

The money consideration paid to the company as compensation for life insurance is called the *premium.*

The person or persons named to receive any payments under the policy upon the death of the insured is called the *beneficiary.* Unless otherwise agreed, the policyholder will have retained certain specified rights, such as: surrendering the policy for its cash value; making policy loans; exchanging for another type of policy; assigning the policy as collateral; changing the beneficiary. Policyholders should *read their policies,* and ask the company to explain any points that are not entirely clear.

Life insurance policies are subject to the general law of contracts and also to specific state laws which apply only to life insurance contracts; in addition to containing all provisions that are standard in similar policies issued to insurers of the same age, each policy must cover the following essentials:

(1) Name and age of the insured.
(2) The amount of insurance and when and how it is to be payable (at death, at the end of a period of years, at a given age; in one sum, in installments, etc.).
(3) The date of the policy.
(4) The beneficiary.
(5) The amount of the premium; when and for how long payable.
(6) Extra features, if any (such as disability and accidental death benefits), and the premium to be paid for them.
(7) Any special amendments (such as extra premiums required for occupational hazards, or the physical condition of the insured).
(8) Any other provisions not found in similar policies issued to insureds of the same age.

There are three broad classifications of life insurance: ordinary; industrial; group. *Ordinary* life insurance is by far the largest and oldest classification of the three. Usually, policies are issued in units of $1,000 or more; medical examinations are required in most instances; all premiums are figured on an annual basis, but may be paid (at a small extra cost) semiannually, quarterly, or (in many companies) monthly. *Industrial* life insurance differs from ordinary in that: insurance is issued in amounts under $1,000 (usually $500 or less), the exact amount being determined by the premium unit, as 10 cents or 25 cents weekly; medical examinations are seldom required; premiums, payable on a weekly or monthly basis, are normally collected in the home by an agent of the company. (See also INSURANCE, INDUSTRIAL.) *Group* life insurance is made available, usually to the employees of one employer, under a master policy. Group life insurance will be described in more detail later in this article. Of the total of all life insurance in force in the United States, Dec. 31, 1946: about 67 per cent was ordinary; 17 per cent industrial; 16 per cent group.

Historical Background.—Life insurance is not a new idea. There is a record of a policy being issued June 18, 1583, in the Royal Exchange, London, England, to one William Gibbons; and studies of the number of people that will die in a given year (the basis for determining the cost of life insurance) were published as early as 1592 (London Bills of Mortality). This was the period when it became a fairly common practice for private businessmen, called *underwriters*, to insure a ship captain against death or capture by pirates during a voyage. The premium charged for this protection is believed to have averaged about 5 per cent; the insurance was for short periods only (normally the duration of the voyage); and the beneficiary was usually the shipowner or merchant who employed the captain.

In 1699 the Society for the Assurance of Widows and Orphans was organized; this is believed to have been the first life insurance association to be established independently of any business or financial organization. The Amicable Society for a Perpetual Assurance Office, founded in 1706, issued advertising that was prophetic of many modern uses for life insurance. This society's policies were recommended as a means of: providing at least some money for the families of those "whose income is usually subject to be determined or lessened at their respective deaths"; setting up survivorship annuities for husbands and wives; creating legacies for servants and other dependents; and furnishing collateral for loans that might not be repaid if the borrower died.

The first company to issue policies for stated amounts with premiums based on the age of the insured and the period for which the insurance was granted, commenced operations in 1762 as the Society for Equitable Assurances on Lives and Survivorships; known today as the Equitable Assurance Society of London, it is now (1947) the oldest life insurance company in the world that does not restrict its business to a single class of policyholders.

In 1759, the Presbyterian synods in New York and Philadelphia set up a corporation that is believed to have been the first life insurance company in the United States. Described as a Corporation for the Relief of Poor and Distressed Presbyterian Ministers and the Poor and Distressed Widows and Children of Presbyterian Ministers, the Presbyterian Ministers' Fund in 1947 was almost 200 years old. Having survived every crisis in the history of the United States, this company is a convincing example of the stability of life insurance.

In 1794, the Insurance Company of North America became the first business corporation to sell life insurance in America. However, the company issued only six policies in five years and discontinued its life insurance business in 1804.

Life insurance got an actual foothold in the United States in 1842, when the Mutual Life Insurance Company of New York was chartered;

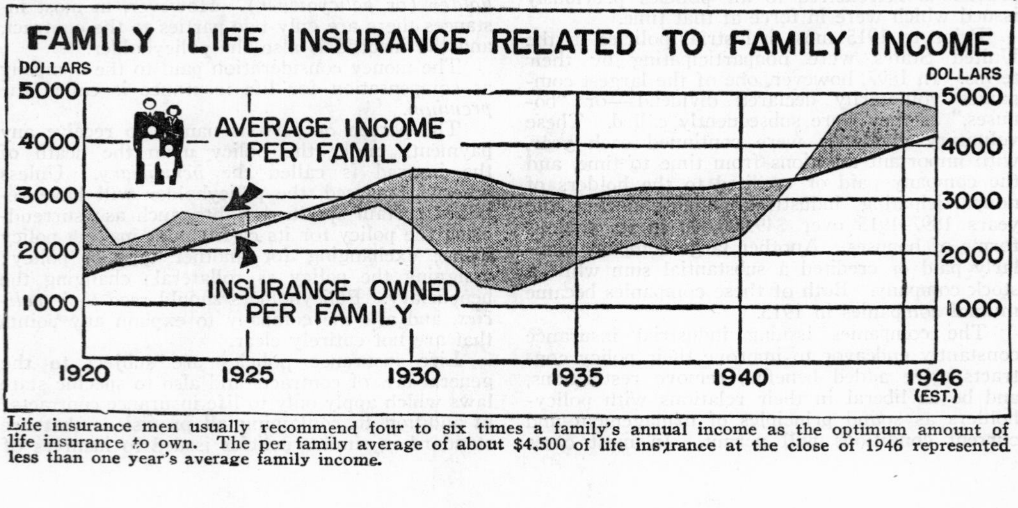

Life insurance men usually recommend four to six times a family's annual income as the optimum amount of life insurance to own. The per family average of about $4,500 of life insurance at the close of 1946 represented less than one year's average family income.

its first policy was issued Feb. 1, 1843. The New England Mutual Life Insurance Company of Boston had been granted a charter in 1835; but this company did not actually begin business until 1844. By 1860, 30 life insurance companies had been organized; however, only 8 were still operating in 1869.

Until after the Civil War, most United States life insurance was sold for burial fund purposes. Policies contained no loan or cash values; premiums had to be paid on or before the due date or the insurance was forefeited, together with everything paid in up to that time; there were also many cramping restrictions on occupation and travel. It was in this period that life insurance became known as a "die to win" proposition; this conviction was firmly held by many people, long after it ceased to have any foundation in fact. There was a real need for life insurance, or it probably could not have survived its early growing pains.

The years from 1860 to 1900 brought a number of important liberalizations and improvements in life insurance policies and in the operation of the business; but it was also a time when exploitation by unscrupulous financial operators made it difficult for even the best managed companies to hold public confidence and respect.

This stage in the development of life insurance ended with the so-called Armstrong investigation of the business, conducted in 1905 for the New York State legislature by Charles Evans Hughes. The investigation resulted in a number of changes in insurance laws, in New York and throughout the United States; it also marked the beginning of a period during which life insurance has become an important factor in the economic structure of the nation, and to the financial security of its families. A comparison of the relative growth of life insurance in force and of growth in population illustrates what happened during the period 1900–1946: since 1900, total life insurance in the United States has increased to more than 20 times the 1900 volume, while the population has increased only about 85 per cent.

In the United States on Dec. 31, 1946, more than 73 million persons were insured for a total amount in excess of $174 billion; this was a per-family average of about $4,500. Death benefit payments during 1946 amounted to approximately $1,280 million; and payments to living policyholders totaled another $1,520 million. To guarantee future payments to policyholders and their beneficiaries, at the end of 1946 United States life insurance companies had set aside $42 billion in policy reserves; at the same time, total assets of these companies amounted to an estimated $48,500 million.

Legal Reserve and Level Premium.—All of the $174 billion of life insurance in force in the United States (Dec. 31, 1946) was issued by so-called *legal reserve* companies, offering *level premium* life insurance. They are called legal reserve companies because they set up and invest policy reserves as required by laws of the various states where they are licensed. These reserves are set aside for the payment of future benefits to policyholders and beneficiaries. In addition to specifying the amounts to be set aside in policy reserves, the investment of these funds is limited, by law, to certain types of securities and property.

There are three types of legal reserve life insurance companies: mutual, stock and mixed.

Mutual companies are owned by the policyholders and controlled through a board of directors or trustees; there are no stockholders.

COMPARATIVE YEARLY COST OF LEVEL PREMIUM AND RENEWABLE TERM LIFE INSURANCE BOUGHT AT AGE 20

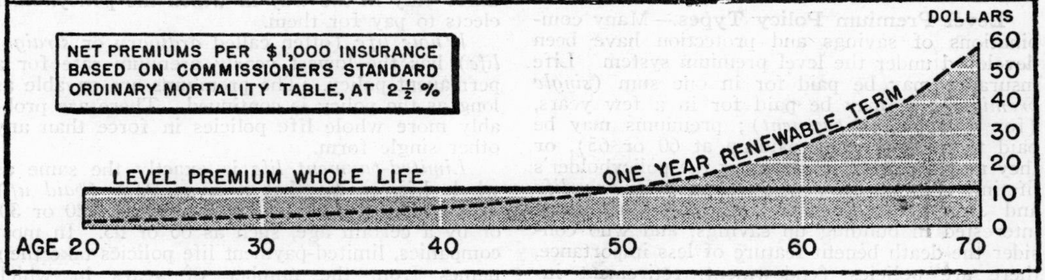

Any savings that result from operating economies, fewer death claims than were allowed for, or interest earned in excess of requirements, go into surplus. Part of this surplus is distributed to policyholders in policy dividends; part is held as an extra reserve to take care of unforeseen contingencies (epidemics, such as the influenza scourge that swept the world in 1918; financial panics of national proportions, and so on).

Stock companies are owned and controlled by stockholders, who furnish their capital as security, over and above premiums, for the payment of death benefits and other policy obligations. Any savings made are regarded as profits and belong to the stockholders. Before the payment of stockholder dividends, a surplus is built up for the extra protection of policyholders; because of the capital structure, this surplus can be smaller than that maintained by mutual companies.

Mixed companies are stock companies which make provision for the payment of dividends to policyholders. In some instances, a limit is placed on the amount of profit which may be paid to stockholders. The difference between total savings and stockholders' profits goes into surplus for distribution on much the same basis as in mutual companies.

Mutual companies are often called *participating* companies, and stock companies *nonparticipating*. The stock companies' method of offsetting policyholder dividends allowed by mutual companies is to fix a lower gross premium on their policies. The bulk of all life insurance in force in the United States (1947) is in mutual companies.

The accompanying chart illustrating the basis of level premium life insurance was prepared by the Institute of Life Insurance (New York, N. Y.) for use in its documentary motion picture, *The Search for Security.* In a booklet describing this film, the institute states:

> Everybody knows that as people get older their chance of dying increases. If the amount one had to pay for a life insurance policy each year covered only the risk of death in that particular year, the rate would increase year by year, every year a man lived. The actual cost of protection at 70 years of age would be almost 17 times what it was at 30.
>
> Thus, while a man is young and the probability of death is rather remote, the cost would be low. But, approaching the end of his productive years and with the probability of death greatly increased, the cost would become too great for him to pay. The situation obviously limited the usefulness of life insurance.
>
> To solve the problem, a plan called the *level premium* was conceived. Under this plan, the premium for any policy is based on the age of the person when his policy is written, and it never increases. In the early years of his policy a man pays more than the actual cost of his protection. But in the later years, he pays less than the actual cost of protection at the older ages. Thus the cost is averaged out. The extra money that he pays in the early years is used to build up a reserve fund which is invested, and, together with interest earnings, is used to help meet the higher cost of his protection when he is older and the risk is greater.

Level Premium Policy Types.—Many combinations of savings and protection have been developed under the level premium system. Life insurance may be paid for in one sum (*single premium*); it may be paid for in a few years, (for example, *20-payment*); premiums may be paid to a given age (paid-up at 60 or 65), or they may be stretched out over the policyholder's lifetime (*whole life,* also called *ordinary life* and *straight life*). For those who are most interested in building up savings, and who consider the death benefit feature of less importance, there are policies (endowment, retirement income) to fit almost any goal they may have set.

However, regardless of its particular provisions, every policy issued must stand on its own legs and offer the same value to every member of the group that buys it; all level premium policies are developed from the same basic calculations. In life insurance, as in most other things of lasting value, the policyholder gets exactly what he pays for; this is essentially what happens: at any one age, the larger the premium for each $1,000 of death benefit, the larger the amount of money available to the policyholder during his lifetime. The only question of comparative values in the policies of a single company is: Which policy best fits the policyholder's particular requirements?

There are three principal types of level premium policies: term; life; endowment.

(1) *Term* policies are issued for a limited number of years; they are payable only in the event of the insured's death during the term period; and they contain no savings feature. They are level premium policies, however, in the sense that the premium charged does not increase during the term of years for which the policy is issued (1, 5, 10, etc.). Many term policies may be renewed for an additional period; if this is done, they take the increased premium for the attained age of the insured. Most term policies may be converted (exchanged) for a regular life or endowment policy.

The most frequently used term policies are written for 5, 7, or 10 years; 15- and even 20-year plans are offered by many companies. From the insurance company's standpoint, term policies can be issued for any desired number of years; but over the longer periods the higher cost is not apt to be attractive.

Term policies are seldom to be recommended for anything more than temporary protection. They are sometimes used: (a) to protect a loan on other life insurance; (b) to cover the amount of a mortgage or other indebtedness that will be retired in a few years; (c) as an option on some form of permanent insurance. For example, a young attorney, married and just starting to build a practice, would need life insurance, but he might not have enough income to be able to pay for the kind and amount of life insurance he wants. Term insurance can be used to provide the needed death protection for a few years and, through the conversion or exchange privilege included in most term policies, it would also protect him against becoming uninsurable.

(2) *Life* policies are available in several forms; all pay the insurance money at death; all contain substantial savings features, building up loan values that can be drawn on in emergency and cash values that may be converted into a retirement income in later years; life policy forms differ only in the way in which the policyholder elects to pay for them.

Whole life (often called *ordinary* or *straight life*) has the lowest yearly premium rate for a permanent policy. The premiums are payable as long as the policy is continued. There are probably more whole life policies in force than any other single form.

Limited-payment life is exactly the same as whole life, except that it is paid for (*paid up*) in a specified number of years, usually 20 or 30, or by a certain age, such as 60 or 65. In most companies, limited-payment life policies take their names from the number of years in which premiums are payable—*15-payment* life, and so on. These policies are popular with people who want to get their life insurance paid for during their most productive years. Premiums for each $1,000 are larger than for whole life at the same age (because of the shorter premium-paying period), but the savings features are proportionately increased. Because of the extra emphasis on savings, many younger policyholders buy these policies, especially *20-payment* life, as a compromise between whole life and one of the endowment forms.

(3) *Endowment* policies are really insured savings plans. They provide a means of accumulating a stated amount of money in an agreed number of years, called the *endowment period.* If the insured lives and makes the specified number of premium payments, the sum insured is paid to him, in one sum or in regular income payments starting at the end of the endowment period; if he dies in the meantime, the sum insured is paid to the beneficiary, just as it would be under one of the life plans. There is a wide range of endowment policies and, as with the life policies, they are similar except for the number of years in which premiums are payable. The most-used endowment forms are probably the *20-year endowment* and *endowment at age 60* or *65.*

Retirement income endowments are similar in most respects to regular endowment policies; but they are adjusted to pay a specific life income at the end of the endowment period. These policies are usually sold in units of $10 per month income at maturity for each $1,000 of insurance.

Most retirement income policies mature at age 60 or 65, but they are offered by some companies for age 50, 55, and in some instances for maturity at age 70.

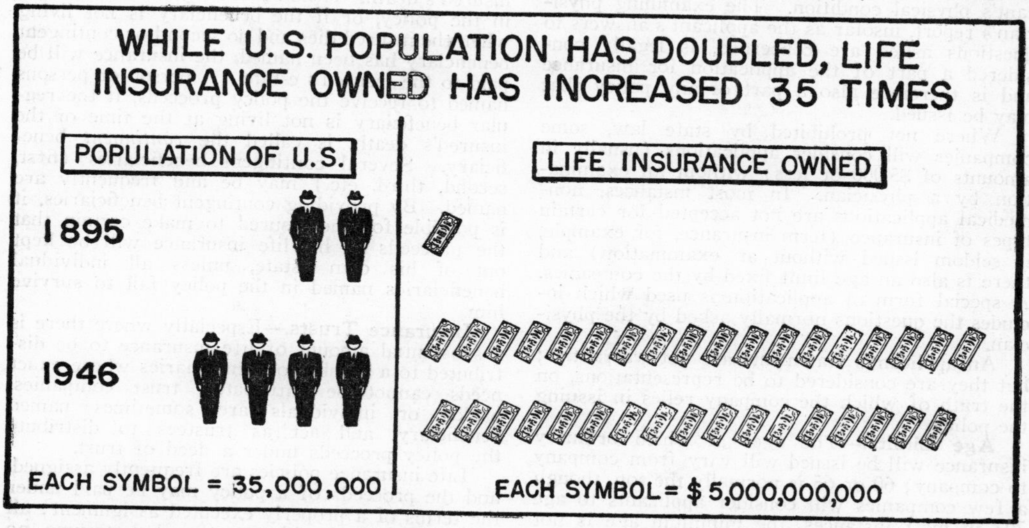

Miscellaneous Policies.—Term insurance is combined with life policies (usually whole life) to produce a number of special purpose plans.

Modified life is a policy offered by a number of companies with a reduced premium for the first few years (either three or five, as a rule); at the end of this initial period, the premium increases to an amount more than the original whole or ordinary life premium would have been, but less than the premium for new whole or ordinary life at the older age.

Some companies write life insurance on two or more lives in single policies, called *joint* or partnership policies. They contain the provisions found in regular policies on a similar plan (whole life, limited-payment life, endowment), except that the death of any one of the persons insured matures the policy. These policies are sometimes used to insure business partners, and for joint insurance on the lives of husbands and wives; but there are two reasons why they are seldom recommended: (1) the survivors are left without insurance; (2) joint insurance offers less attractive cash and other surrender values than separate policies.

Family income is a life policy (usually whole life) which, at the insured's death, pays the beneficiary an income of $10 per month for each $1,000 of insurance. This income is continued for a specified number of years, called the family income period; at the end of that time the sum insured is paid. The family income period varies; in most instances it is set at 20 years from the original date of the policy. For example: if the insured died, say seven years after the policy was purchased, the income would be paid to his beneficiary for 13 years; but if he died 20 or more years after the policy was purchased, there would be no family income period, and the sum insured would be payable at once.

Family income policies are designed to help solve the problem of the man with a limited income and a growing family to provide for. Theoretically at least, his need for life insurance will be greatest during the years when his children are still of school age; this is the reason for providing an income for 20 years (10- and 15-year plans are also available) from the date of the policy, in the event of death during that period. Because the monthly income is normally $10 for each $1,000 of insurance, it is usually possible to conserve the sum insured for a few years without working a hardship on the family. In this way, the policyholder can be sure his widow will have at least some money left after the children are grown.

Types of Policies Purchased.—In June of 1944, the Life Insurance Agency Management Association made a study of the types of ordinary policies purchased from 50 companies during that month. It was considered that this sample was a fair indication of policy preferences at that time:

	Per cent
Whole life	22
Limited-payment life	36
Modified life	5
Endowment	21
Retirement income	7
Term insurance	4
Family income and miscellaneous	5

Application and Examination.—Life insurance companies base their premium calculations on the probability of survival from year to year of normally healthy people with average background, occupation and habits, called *standard risks.* Men and women who, because of a dangerous occupation, unfavorable physical condition or family history, or for any other reason, cannot be considered average people, are known as *substandard risks.* As a rule, substandard risks are not eligible for life insurance at the same premiums offered standard risks. For that reason, it is important that the company know, at the outset, whether the person applying for life insurance is, or is likely to become, a substandard risk.

The person to be insured is asked to complete and sign an *application* covering simple but essential information; this application becomes a part of any insurance policy issued. A physical examination of the applicant is also required for most ordinary life insurance. The examining physician's report covers: (1) the applicant's answers to questions asked by the physician; (2) the physician's statements concerning the applicant's physical condition. The examining physician's report, insofar as the applicant's answers to questions asked are concerned, is legally considered a part of the application for insurance and is therefore also a part of any policy that may be issued.

Where not prohibited by state law, some companies will consider applications (usually in amounts of $5,000 or less) without an examination by a physician. In most instances, nonmedical applications are not accepted for certain types of insurance (term insurance, for example, is seldom issued without an examination) and there is also an age limit fixed by the companies. A special form of application is used which includes the questions normally asked by the physician.

An applicant's statements are not warranties; but they are considered to be representations, on the truth of which the company relies in issuing the policy.

Age Limits.—The ages at which ordinary insurance will be issued will vary from company to company; 60 or 65 is normally the top, though a few companies will consider applicants to age 70; in most instances, the minimum age is not less than 10 years.

Juvenile Insurance.—Many companies issue special ordinary policies, called *juvenile insurance*, below age 10; some will consider children at birth; others at one or two years of age. Most juvenile policies contain all cash, loan, paid-up insurance, and extended insurance values found in similar policies issued to adults. Juvenile policy forms available nearly always include whole life, limited-payment life, and at least some of the endowment forms.

Generally, the full amount of a juvenile policy is not available as a death benefit until some fixed age (usually age 5).

A number of companies offer juvenile insurance with the added provision that, in the event of the death or total and permanent disability of the person paying the premiums (usually a parent), further premiums will be waived by the company until a specified age (usually 21) when, presumably, the child will be able to make the payments. The extra charge for this waiver of premium provision is relatively small, but the person on whose life the waiver is based must be able to qualify for life insurance.

Important Policy Provisions.—While there are many different policies, and a still larger number of descriptive names given to relatively similar policies, owing to state laws their standard provisions are reasonably uniform.

Insured's Age.—It is important that the insured's correct age appear in the application for insurance. The age determines the premium; and in many policies which mature or become paid up at stated ages such as 60 or 65, the age also determines the number of years during which premiums are to be paid. For life insurance purposes, the insured's age is his *nearest* age. Companies usually accept the insured's simple statement of age at the time the policy is issued; but satisfactory proof of age should be furnished to the company so that no question can arise after death. Every company will accept proof of age (birth certificate, etc.) during the lifetime of the insured.

Beneficiary.—The original beneficiary named in the policy may be any person or persons who would suffer an economic loss as a result of the insured's death. If no beneficiary has been named in the policy, or if the beneficiary is not living when the insured dies and no second or contingent beneficiary has been named, the insurance will be paid to the insured's estate. A person or persons named to receive the policy proceeds, if the regular beneficiary is not living at the time of the insured's death, is called the *contingent* beneficiary. Several contingent beneficiaries (first, second, third, etc.) may be and frequently are named. By providing contingent beneficiaries, it is possible for the insured to make certain that the proceeds of his life insurance will be kept out of his own estate, unless all individual beneficiaries named in the policy fail to survive him.

Insurance Trusts.—Especially where there is a substantial amount of life insurance to be distributed to a number of beneficiaries whose exact needs cannot be anticipated, trust companies, banks, or individuals are sometimes named beneficiary, and act as trustees to distribute the policy proceeds under a deed of trust.

Life insurance policies are frequently assigned, and the proceeds of a policy may be paid under the terms of a properly executed assignment; all companies permit this practice, but assume no liability for the validity of any assignment.

Premium.—The premium is the money consideration for which the company agrees to carry out the terms of the policy. Premiums may be paid once a year (all ordinary premium calculations assume that they will be paid annually, in advance); or, at the policyholder's option and subject to an additional charge, they may be paid semiannually, quarterly, or, in many companies, monthly. These fractional payments are frequently called (sometimes in the policy itself) the premium; but it is well to bear in mind that the actual premium is the annual premium; on this account, many policies provide that any portion of the current annual premium which is unpaid at the insured's death will be deducted from any settlement due under the policy. Most companies will not issue an ordinary policy calling for a premium less than some minimum amount (often $10).

After the first premium has been paid, the payment of any subsequent premium (or semiannual, quarterly or monthly installment) may be made within one month after it is due; during these so-called *days of grace* the policy remains in full force. In the event of death during this grace period, the premium due and unpaid will usually be deducted from any payment due the beneficiary. Some companies specify that the grace period is "one month of not less than 30 days"; other policies specify 30 days; and still others, 31 days.

A policy is said to *lapse* and the company's liability ceases (except for the nonforfeiture values explained later in this article) if any premium or installment of a premium is not paid before the end of the grace period.

A lapsed policy may be *reinstated* by: (1) furnishing satisfactory evidence that the insured still meets the company's rules of insurability;

and (2) the payment of all arrears in premiums due, with interest (usually 6 per cent or less) to the date of reinstatement. Many companies put a limit, normally a stated number of years, on the time during which a lapsed policy may be reinstated; others will consider reinstatement at any time. But in all cases, evidence of insurability must be satisfactory to the company.

Disability benefits are seldom a part of the policy itself; in most instances these benefits are covered in a supplementary agreement for which an extra premium is charged, and which is attached to and made a part of the policy.

The disability provision in widest use is called a *waiver of premium;* it provides that if the insured becomes totally disabled before a stated age, usually 60, and if the disability is presumed to be permanent, any premium becoming due while the disability exists will be waived. Premiums waived will not be charged against any settlement due either the insured or the beneficiary. If the insured recovers, then premiums must be paid from the date of recovery on.

Some companies issue disability benefits which, in addition to waiving premiums, pay the insured an income while he is totally disabled. The income provided varies between $5 and $10 per month for each $1,000 of insurance, depending on individual company practice.

Definitions of what constitutes total and permanent disability vary somewhat with the different companies, as do premiums charged for this type of protection; however, many companies define a total disability as one which prevents the insured from performing the duties of any gainful occupation; and in the absence of prior proof, total disability which lasts six consecutive months is presumed to be permanent until recovery. The premium charged for disability protection is an extra premium and does not add to the savings features in the policy. Most disability protection ceases at 60 or 65, though it may be discontinued by the insured at any time.

Double indemnity is also an extra benefit requiring an additional premium that does not add to the nonforfeiture values in the policy. The double indemnity supplementary contract provides for the payment of an additional amount equal to the amount of insurance specified in the policy, if death results solely from accidental means, before a specified age (in most cases 65 or 70) and usually within 90 days of the date of the accident.

Dividends.—A policy dividend is the share allotted to an individual policy in that portion of the company's surplus that is set aside for distribution to its policyholders. Surplus is built up from three sources: (1) The actual amount paid in death claims seldom equals the amount allowed for in calculating premiums; this saving goes into surplus. (2) Policy reserves required to pay future death claims are accumulated at a fixed rate of interest; if the invested reserves earn more than this interest requirement, the excess goes into surplus. (3) In addition to the amount required for current death claims and the reserve for future claims, most life and endowment insurance premiums contain an added allowance for expenses, called *loading;* if the company spends less than this allowance, the difference goes into surplus.

As explained in describing the nature of mutual life insurance companies, only a portion of a company's surplus is paid out in policy dividends; part of each year's savings is held as an additional reserve against future contingencies.

Most policies provide that policy dividends may be: (1) paid to the policyholder in cash; (2) used to reduce current premiums; (3) left with the company to accumulate at not less than the rate of interest specified in the policy (any accumulated dividends and interest will be paid in addition to any other benefits in the policy, and these accumulations may be withdrawn by the policyholder at any time); (4) used to increase the amount of insurance by purchasing fully paid-for additions to the policy. The amount of the additions will be whatever the dividend will purchase at the single-premium rate for the insured's attained age. In a life policy, these dividend additions are paid, in addition to the insurance, at death; in an endowment policy they are payable at the end of the endowment period or at prior death. This option is particularly valuable to the insured who becomes uninsurable for any reason after purchasing his policy; it yields the maximum increase in death protection.

All dividend-paying policies provide that when the policyholder fails to make a selection, one of the options will be automatic; many companies name (4) as the automatic option.

Dividends Are Not Guaranteed.—In most states, life insurance companies and their representatives are prohibited by law from estimating, beyond the current year, the amount that will be paid in future policy dividends. They are, however, permitted to illustrate what will result if the current scale of dividends is maintained.

It is the practice of some companies to allow policy dividends at the end of the first year the policy is in force; others, at the end of the first year, provided the second year's premium is paid; still others make their first policy dividend payments at the end of the second or a later year.

Nonforfeiture Values.—Loans against policy reserves were first granted in about 1848. In 1853, policy valuation tables representing some nine years' work by Elizur Wright of Boston, were published. As a direct result of Wright's campaigning for adequate reserves on all policies and a square deal for all policyholders who might be forced by circumstances to discontinue their life insurance, the Massachusetts legislature passed a bill in 1858 requiring all companies doing business in that state to grant surrender values in the form of extended term insurance. In 1879, New York passed a nonforfeiture law granting fully paid-up insurance on lapsed policies. By 1900 nearly all legal reserve policies contained tables of cash surrender, loan and other so-called nonforfeiture values.

All life and endowment policies, with the exception of term insurance, provide that, if the policyholder fails to pay premiums or voluntarily surrenders the policy, the policyholder may receive a cash surrender value specified in the policy. Instead of taking cash, the policyholder can have a fully paid-up policy for whatever amount of insurance the cash value will purchase at the single-premium rate for the insured's attained age. If a life policy was surrendered, the paid-up insurance will be a life policy, payable at death; if an endowment policy was surrendered, the paid-up policy will be an endowment maturing at the same time the original policy would have matured. The policyholder may pass up both cash and paid-up insurance and elect to have the insurance kept in force, as term insurance, for whatever number of years and days the cash value will pay for at the single-premium term insurance rate. Most companies allow these values after two or three annual premiums have been paid.

Policy loans are granted in amounts not greater than the existing cash value, at a rate of interest stipulated in the policy. The policyholder's failure to repay either principal or interest on a policy loan does not terminate the policy until they exceed the existing cash value. Existing loans and unpaid interest are, of course, deducted from any payments due under the policy; they reduce the amount of paid-up insurance, and the amount for which, as well as the number of years and days, the policy could be extended as term insurance.

Incontestability.—All policies are incontestable after they have been in force for either one or two years (depending on state laws and company practice). The company's right to contest payment of a claim during the first year or two is a necessary safeguard; otherwise, unscrupulous persons about to take up some extrahazardous occupation, or who might be suffering from a probably fatal disease not likely to be discovered by the examining physician, could get and keep insurance to which they were not entitled. If the company can prove, during the contestable period, that deliberate misstatements were made in the application for insurance, then, under certain circumstances, the policy can be voided. But the burden of proof is always on the company. Nearly all policies contain a provision excluding the payment of any insurance in the event of suicide during the contestable period.

Income Options.—Insurance money due the beneficiary or the policyholder may, of course, be drawn in one sum. But in most policies, several payment plans, frequently called *income settlement options,* are available.

Interest Only Option.—Under this option the insurance money is held by the company and interest (at not less than a rate specified in the policy) is paid for an agreed number of years, or during the lifetime of a beneficiary or beneficiaries; at the end of this specified period, the insurance will be paid in one sum as directed in the policy. The interest option can be arranged flexibly (for example, the beneficiary can be permitted to withdraw all or part of the insurance money, at will, or up to stated amounts during any one year), or it can be made literally interest *only* for a desired number of years.

Installments of a Fixed Amount.—This option provides for the payment of a fixed amount, annually or at more frequent intervals, as long as the insurance money plus the company's stated rate of interest will last. For example, the policyholder who feels that his beneficiary must have a minimum of $150 a month could select the fixed amount option and, by providing enough life insurance, continue the income for the length of time it will be needed.

Installments for a Fixed Time.—This option is identical to (2), except that the number of months or years during which the income is to be paid is the determining factor. Under (2), the amount of insurance money available sets the *length of time* during which the income will be paid; under (3), the policyholder says that his beneficiary must have an income for a fixed length of time, and the amount of insurance money available determines the *size of the income* that can be paid.

Installments for Life.—Under this option the beneficiary receives an income, usually monthly, for life. Technically, the insurance company uses the insurance money to purchase an immediate life annuity at the attained age of the beneficiary; therefore, the older the beneficiary, the larger the income that can be paid for each $1,000 available.

The type of policy (life, endowment, term) has nothing to do with the income options; they are affected only by the *proceeds* of the policy. After a policy matures (at death or the end of an endowment period) or when it is surrendered for the cash value, there is a certain amount of money available; the various settlement options were designed solely to aid the policyholder or beneficiary in making the best possible distribution of that money.

Normally, any option may be selected by either the policyholder or the beneficiary. Usually, the policyholder may change his directions about settlement as often as he likes *while the policy is still in force.* After the insured's death, the beneficiary may select one of the income options instead of taking the insurance money in cash, but cannot, as a rule, make any change in an income settlement arrangement previously made by the policyholder. Nor can the insured or beneficiary decide to take an income settlement after accepting the insurance money in cash.

Annuities.—There are many forms of annuity. In general, they are contracts that provide for the payment, by the company issuing the annuity, of stipulated amounts of money at regular intervals (monthly, quarterly, semiannually, annually). It is usually provided that these payments will be continued for the lifetime of the person, called the *annuitant,* on whose life the annuity is based. However, an annuity may be written to provide a stated number of payments instead of a life income.

Essentially, an annuity is life insurance in reverse. A life insurance policyholder (with a whole or ordinary life policy) agrees to pay the life insurance company a fixed premium as long as he lives; at his death, the insurance company agrees to pay the insurance money to his beneficiary. The policyholder may pay only one premium, or he may live to pay many, but death terminates the policy; there are no further premiums to pay. A man buys life insurance because he might not live long enough to accumulate, in any other way, the minimum amount of money he wants his dependents to have. On the other hand, an annuitant (buying an immediate life annuity with no refund provision) deposits a sum of money with a life insurance company, then receives an income as long as he lives. He may receive only one payment, or he may live to receive a great deal more than he deposited, but death terminates the annuity; there are no further income payments made by the company. A man buys an annuity because he might outlive his ability to earn and wants to be sure of an income as long as he lives.

Annuities may be divided into two main classes: (1) *immediate* annuities; (2) *deferred* annuities. The full money consideration for an immediate annuity is paid to the company in one sum; the income starts immediately. The consideration for a deferred annuity is deposited in one sum, or it may be paid in installments; the

income starts at some specified time in the future.

There are three principal types of immediate annuity: (a) *Life annuity*—the income is paid for the lifetime of the annuitant. There is no refund of any part of the money deposited by the annuitant, even though he might die on the day after the annuity became effective; nor can the annuity be surrendered for any cash value during the lifetime of the annuitant. (b) *Refund life annuity*—similar to a life annuity, except that if the annuitant dies before receiving as much in income payments as the original amount deposited with the company, the income payments will be continued until the company has paid back the full amount of the original deposit. (c) *Cash refund life annuity*—similar to a refund life annuity, except that any difference due at the death of the annuitant will be paid in one sum. Cash refund annuities may also be surrendered for a stipulated cash value during the lifetime of the annuitant.

Joint and survivor annuities are similar to the plans just described, except that the contract is based on more than one life (usually two) and the income is continued until the last annuitant dies.

An *annuity certain* is a contract under which an income will be paid at stated intervals for a fixed length of time. The income from an annuity certain is not dependent on any person's living or dying. When the proceeds of a life or endowment policy are paid as income for a fixed number of years, say 10, that is an annuity certain.

The income return to the annuitant, per $1,000 of the original deposit made with the company, will be largest under the nonrefund plan; slightly less under the refund plan; and still less if the cash refund plan is selected.

Deferred annuities pay the annuity income commencing at the end of a stated number of years from the date of the contract. Most deferred annuities are written on some variation of the cash refund basis; they usually provide for the refund of all deposits in the event of death before the annuity income commences, and the refund of any excess of deposits over income received, if death occurs after the income commences.

Annuity deposits and the amount of income to be paid are calculated from a mortality table, much as in the case of life and endowment insurance. However, as experience has shown that annuitants live longer than people without guaranteed incomes, allowance is made for this factor. The fact that women, particularly in the older age groups, live longer average lives than men is also taken into consideration.

Annuity proposals are usually quoted in two ways: (1) the amount of annuity income to be paid for a given deposit, usually $1,000 on an immediate annuity basis and $100 annually on a deferred basis; and (2) the amount of deposit required to produce a stated income, say $10 a month or $100 a year.

Annuities have been sold extensively in England and throughout Europe for many generations; but their wide use in the United States did not begin until after World War I. The Institute of Life Insurance estimated that at the end of 1946, United States life insurance companies held over $6,500 million that had been set aside by the owners of 2,965,500 annuity policies, calling for the payment of present or deferred annual income to the annuitants of $932 million. This amount of $932 million in annual income was 46 per cent larger than the comparable figure for 1940 and 106 per cent over that for 1935. The total number of annuities owned at the close of 1946 was 62 per cent greater than in 1940, and was 191 per cent larger than the number in force in 1935.

Group Life Insurance.—First offered in 1911, group life insurance usually covers a number of people (50 or more) who are employees of a common employer, or members of an organization such as a trade union. In all states not prohibiting nonmedical life insurance, group insurance is normally written without medical examination. In some states, an abbreviated form of examination is made to comply with the law. In most instances, however, the only evidence of insurability required is that the person to be insured shall be actively employed at the time the policy goes into effect.

A master contract is issued to the employer or organization putting the plan into effect; each person insured receives a certificate giving the amount of insurance, the name of the beneficiary, and stating the insured person's right to buy an ordinary type of life or endowment policy, in the event of termination of employment.

Some group policies are paid for by the employer, but in most instances the cost is shared. A common practice is for the insured person to pay 60 cents per $1,000 of insurance per month, regardless of age, and for the employer to pay the balance of the cost for the entire group insured. Group premiums are based on special one-year term rates; this means that the premium for each insured person goes up each year. However, in practice the total premium for the group insured tends to remain level or increase slowly; people who die or terminate their employment in the group are usually replaced by younger persons, and the average age of the group tends to remain fairly constant.

The amount of insurance available to each person is determined by a formula stated in the master policy; often this is equivalent to one year's salary or earnings.

By the end of 1946, 14 million American workers in 40,000 firms and organizations were protected by group life insurance. The total protection in force under these plans was about $28 billion, an average of approximately $2,000 for each person insured. This figure of $28 billion was twice the total in force in 1938 and nearly three times the 1934 total.

An important social contribution of group life insurance is that it enables some people to secure life insurance protection who would not otherwise be eligible, because of poor health or for other reasons.

A variation of the group plan is used to insure certain classes of borrowers during the period when loans are being repaid.

In addition to group life insurance, there are several other types of protection provided by employer-employee groups today, including such coverages as hospitalization, accident, illness, medical and surgical expense, and retirement annuities. See also separate article GROUP INSURANCES.

Salary Savings Insurance.—Sometimes called salary allotment or salary budget, salary savings insurance is the name for a method of buying individual life insurance. It is not a special kind of life insurance. The basis of the salary savings plan is simply an agreement whereby an employer will deduct life insurance premiums from an employee's salary and remit them to the life insurance company. Usually these deductions are made monthly, and are for whatever amount the employee authorizes from time to time.

The salary savings plan is attractive to many employers because it encourages their employees to save money and because it puts them on an equal footing with larger buyers of life insurance, insofar as monthly premium payment privileges are concerned. Many workers who, under other circumstances, would be likely to own no life insurance other than industrial or group, can through the salary savings plan put considerably more money into savings and protection. Some employers have so far endorsed the salary savings idea as to make a contribution toward the cost of whatever insurance their employees bought under the plan.

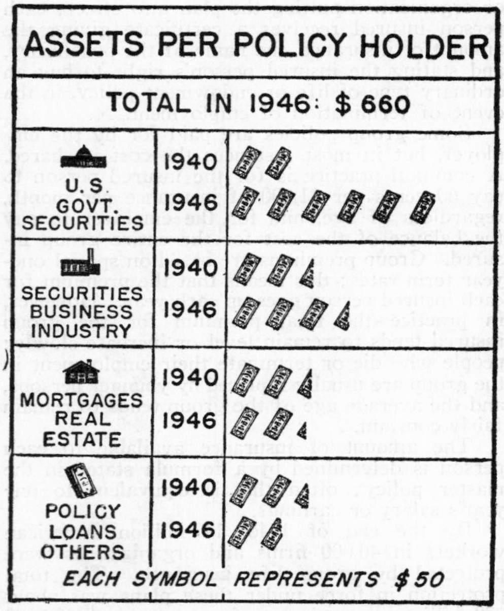

Principal Uses for Life Insurance.—There are probably as many different uses for life insurance as there are human problems involving a need for money at some future time.

Common Uses.—The six most common uses are:

(1) A clean-up fund for burial and debt payment purposes. Policies are usually payable in one sum; sometimes to the estate, but most frequently to the widow or some other named beneficiary who would normally want to be responsible for the policyholder's debts. The average clean-up fund is $1,000 to $5,000. Money for the cancellation of a home mortgage is sometimes listed under the clean-up fund head.

(2) A readjustment fund for the family of a man who dies. Sometimes this is a lump sum of $1,000 or more; often it is in the form of an income of $100 or more a month for from one to five years (depending on the policyholder's circumstances and the family's living standard). The purpose of this fund is to give the family a chance for gradual adjustment to whatever permanent reduction in living standards may be necessary.

(3) An income during the time when young children are growing up: usually an income large enough to pay for necessities for the widow and children until the latter are old enough to be self-supporting. Where this minimum cannot be provided, a smaller income is sometimes arranged for the same number of years to supplement whatever the widow is able to earn.

(4) An educational fund: usually enough life insurance to pay a monthly income which will cover all or at least a portion of living expenses and tuition during college years. Educational funds are sometimes built up through endowment policies on the lives of the children to be educated.

(5) A life income for widows. Even when it is not possible to provide a substantial income, policies are often set aside to guarantee a small

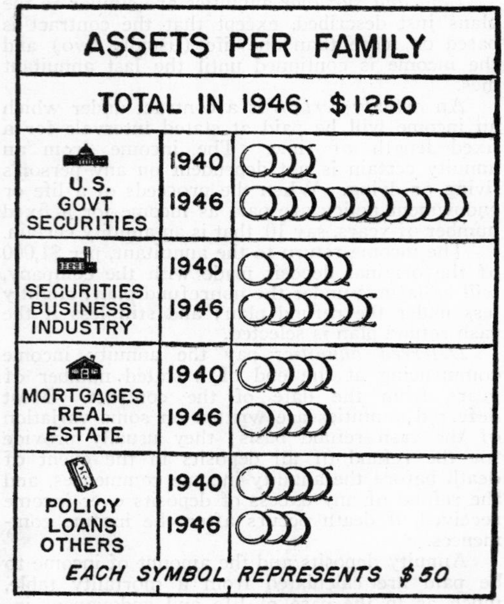

amount. The theory is that a widow with, say $30 a month that she cannot lose or outlive, will be better off and ultimately more independent than one with $100 a month for five or ten years, or with an equivalent amount in cash.

(6) A retirement or old age income for the policyholder. A retirement income is often provided by surrendering other policies, such as readjustment and family income, after the need for that protection has been outlived, and taking the cash surrender values in the form of a life income. This privilege is one of the most valuable and least understood byproducts of the average policyholder's life insurance.

Special Uses.—There are a number of special uses for life insurance. The best known are: (1) business insurance; and (2) estate and inheritance tax insurance.

Business insurance: The principal forms of business insurance are:

(a) *Partnership insurance*—usually written on the lives of the partner-owners of a business or professional firm and tied up with an agreement specifying that the policy proceeds, in the event of the death of a partner, will be used to buy or help buy his interest from his heirs.

(b) *Stock retirement insurance*—usually written on the lives of stockholders in close corporations under an agreement which, in principle, is much the same as that used in partnership insurance. The purpose behind both partnership and stock retirement insurance is to keep the business in the hands of active owners and, at the same time, provide that the heirs of a partner or stockholder will receive a fair cash price for their interest.

(c) *Key-man insurance*—insurance on the life of an individual whose death will mean a money loss to a business. Key-man insurance is sometimes called *brain insurance* and is probably what most people are thinking of when they refer to business insurance. Key-man policies are often assigned to banks, or other creditors, as additional collateral for loans made to the business.

(d) *Sole-proprietor insurance*—usually written on the life of the sole or predominant owner of a business. When used for the protection of the owner's family, it is actually personal insurance; when taken out or assigned for the protection of creditors, it becomes key-man insurance used for credit or collateral purposes; when it is made payable to an employee or employees to enable them to purchase and carry on the business, this form of business protection closely resembles partnership insurance.

Estate and inheritance tax insurance: In a broad sense, this is life insurance for clean-up purposes; however, the amounts involved are large enough and the requirements sufficiently specialized to warrant a separate classification. The purpose for which most life insurance is purchased is to create an estate, or at least to add to the policyholder's estate. The purpose of estate and inheritance tax insurance is to conserve estates already created. This latter purpose is also concerned with several possible drains on an estate other than the taxes to which it is liable.

Administration expenses may and often do reach substantial totals. Securities sold at the wrong time (a frequent necessity when wealthy men and women die without enough life insurance to cover the immediate cash needs of the estate) sometimes bring losses that add up to more than all other estate settlement expenses combined.

Bequest insurance: The use of life insurance for specific bequests, usually to charitable or educational institutions, increased considerably during the years following World War I. A less pretentious but individually important use for life insurance is the earmarking of special policies to provide birthday, Christmas, and other anniversary remembrances.

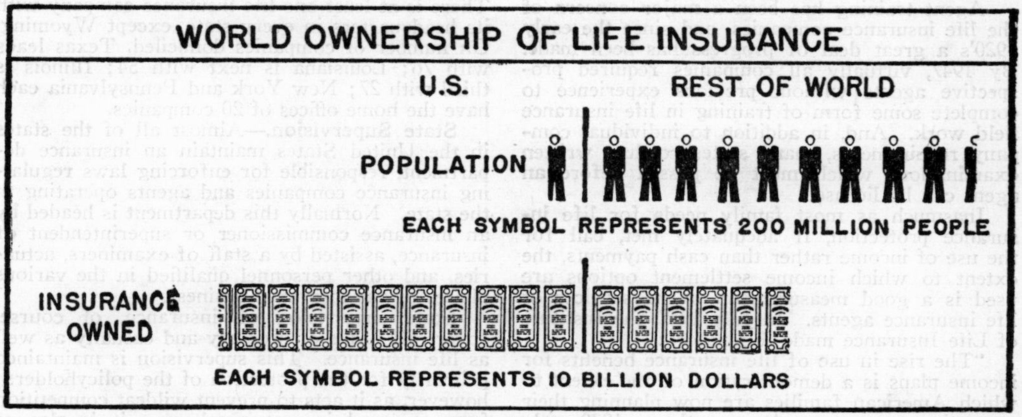

(Year 1938)

Services of the Agent.—The bulk of all legal reserve life insurance is sold by agents (life underwriters) representing the companies. Life insurance offers one of the few (and in many instances the only) practical means by which the average man can create a substantial estate for his family, and at the same time make a secure, workable provision for his own old age. In a very real sense, life insurance is a cooperative venture for the general good of all of the people. It follows, logically and inevitably, that the successful life insurance agent, who is the contact man between the institution of life insurance and its policyholders, must work for the common good of the business and the policyholder.

Fortunately, in the life insurance business, virtue is not its own and only reward. Life insurance agents are paid, largely in direct proportion to the results of their work: (1) for the sale of new insurance; and (2) for keeping that insurance in force. The life insurance man who sells the kind and amount of life insurance and annuities that best fit his prospect's immediate and probable future circumstances and needs accomplishes two objectives: he reduces the difficulty of keeping his business in force; and he builds prestige in the eyes of his policyholders and is recommended by them to their friends and associates. All of which reduces to a simple two-point code of working ethics, quoted here from *The Life Agent's Qualification Handbook* (Rough Notes Co., Inc.), and closely adhered to by a majority of all established life insurance agents:

"1. Make no recommendation to any prospect or policyholder which you would not yourself adopt, if your circumstances and his were identical.

"2. Give full consideration to the life insurance he already owns in making any proposal of new insurance."

The services of a trained life insurance agent are concerned more with explaining than they are with selling life insurance. The principal uses for life insurance are not especially complex, but seeing to it that all life insurance bought fits into a well-defined pattern, based on the policyholder's individual requirements, calls for the services of a life insurance agent who is thoroughly grounded in his business.

Agent training has been a major concern of the life insurance companies, and since the early 1920's a great deal of progress has been made. By 1947, virtually all companies required prospective agents without previous experience to complete some form of training in life insurance field work. And, in addition to individual company requirements, many states conduct written examinations which must be passed before an agent can be licensed.

Inasmuch as most family needs for life insurance protection, if adequately met, call for the use of income rather than cash payments, the extent to which income settlement options are used is a good measurement of the services of life insurance agents. In July 1947, the Institute of Life Insurance made this report:

"The rise in use of life insurance benefits for income plans is a demonstration of the extent to which American families are now planning their protection programs. As recently as 1930, only 10 per cent of the then smaller benefit payments were used for income plans and in 1920 the figure was only about 5 per cent. In 1946, 44 per cent (about $586 million) of life insurance benefits available were used to set up continuing income plans." The institute also estimated that at the close of 1946 a total of $3,800 million of life insurance benefit payments were being held for income distribution. The institute stated that the life insurance agents of the country had "made a major contribution to this orderly planning of family financial programs."

Life Insurance Personnel.—At the end of 1946 it was estimated by the Life Insurance Agency Management Association that the life insurance business in the United States employed 297,700 people. That figure represented an increase of about 50,000 over total life insurance employment in the years just before World War II. Agents and agency managers accounted for 170,500; there were 32,800 field office cashiers and clerks; company home offices employed the remaining 94,400.

On Dec. 31, 1946, there were 509 legal reserve life insurance companies in the United States; this was an increase of 46 in the number of these companies doing business one year previously and 214 more than there were in 1918. There is at least one life insurance company with its headquarters in every state, except Wyoming. On number of companies domiciled, Texas leads with 76; Louisiana is next with 54; Illinois is third with 27; New York and Pennsylvania each have the home offices of 20 companies.

State Supervision.—Almost all of the states in the United States maintain an insurance department, responsible for enforcing laws regulating insurance companies and agents operating in the state. Normally this department is headed by an insurance commissioner or superintendent of insurance, assisted by a staff of examiners, actuaries, and other personnel qualified in the various phases of the insurance business.

State supervision of insurance, of course, covers all forms of property and casualty as well as life insurance. This supervision is maintained primarily for the protection of the policyholders; however, as it acts to prevent wildcat competition from unsound insurance schemes, it is also of direct value to the companies and agents.

The costs of maintaining state supervision are met with a small fraction of the premium and other taxes paid by the companies to the various states in which they operate.

Income of the Life Insurance Companies.—In 1946, the total income of United States life insurance companies amounted to nearly $8 billion. This income was from two principal sources: (1) premium payments from policyholders; and (2) earnings from investments bought with the money the companies set aside for future payments to policyholders and beneficiaries. In effect, each dollar of the $8 billion was made up of 79 cents in premiums and 21 cents of investment income.

Life insurance companies dispose of their income in three main channels: (1) death benefit payments and payments to living policyholders, including policy dividends, account for 41 cents

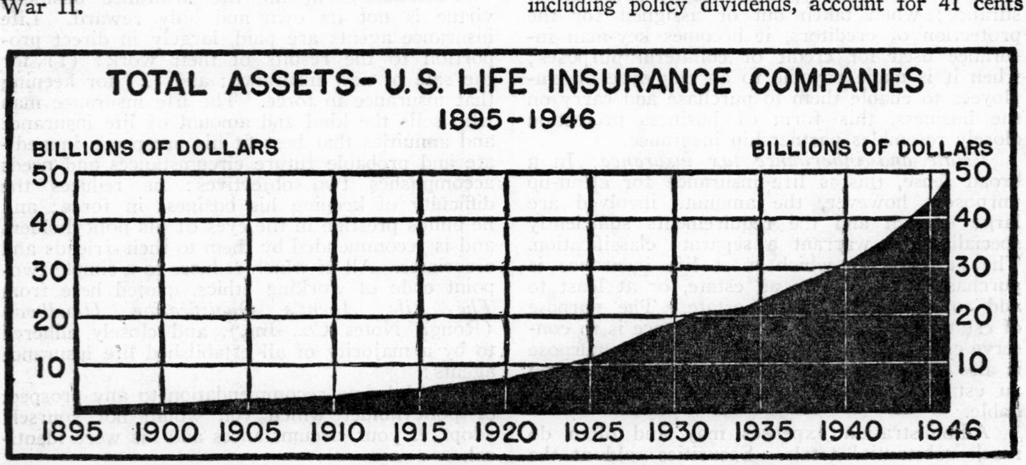

Total assets of 48 billion dollars at the close of 1946 consisted of: 42 billion dollars set aside, as required by law, for the payment of future death claims and other policy benefits; 6 billion dollars in funds held for income payments to beneficiaries, current policyholder dividends, other payments to policyholders and beneficiaries, and as surplus for the extra protection of policyholders.

of the 1946 average income dollar; (2) 42 cents was earmarked as a reserve to guarantee future payments as they come due and put into the best investments available; (3) it takes 170,000 agents and about 128,000 other personnel to take care of the 175 million separate life insurance policies in force. There are also taxes and other expenses. These field and home office costs of doing business account for the remaining 17 cents of the income dollar.

For every 79 cents policyholders paid in premiums during 1946, they or their families received 83 cents in present payments or future credits set aside as reserve.

Investments of the Life Insurance Companies.—On Dec. 31, 1946, United States life insurance companies had policy reserves of approximately $42 billion and total admitted assets of just over $48 billion. The rate of growth of life insurance is evident in the fact that total assets at the end of 1946 were more than $15 billion above the total for 1941.

Life insurance investments play an important part in financing the various segments of the American economy.

The breakdown of the 1946 portfolio shows that United States government bonds totaled $21,500 million, up $1 billion during the year. The 1946 figure was a new high, but the increase over the previous year was the smallest since 1940, reflecting the lessened call for federal financing following the end of the war. As a result, more life insurance funds were available for meeting general financing needs.

Total industrial and miscellaneous bonds owned increased over $1 billion in 1946 to $3,100 million. Public utility bonds owned stood at $5,400 million, an increase of $200 million. Railroad bonds totaled $2,700 million, a decrease of $300 million from the 1945 total. Stocks owned rose $100 million to $1,100 million, twice the 1941 figure. Mortgages increased over $350 million to a total of $7 billion.

Life insurance investments are well diversified geographically. At the start of 1946, the Institute of Life Insurance reported total investments in the North Central states amounted to $11,391 million; those in the Southern states totaled $10,150 million; Middle Atlantic, $9,393 million; New England, $2,163 million; Mountain, $1,149 million; Pacific, $3,115 million.

The total of policy loans outstanding at the end of 1946 was about $1,860 million; this compares with a total at the end of 1940 of $3,091 million and the peak total in 1932 of $3,806 million. Commenting on the policy loan situation early in 1947, the Institute of Life Insurance stated: "Life insurance policyholders not only have a record amount of life insurance protection in force, but they have outstanding against it the smallest percentage of policy cash values withdrawn as loans since the turn of the century. Today, less than 1/20 of policy cash values has been borrowed by the policyholders; at the start of the war, they had borrowed 1/10 of these values and 10 years ago the ratio was about 1/6. Through extensive repayments in the war years, as well as sharp reduction in new borrowing, the policyholders have materially enhanced the protection under their policies. Their life insurance is in a stronger position today than at any time in the past."

1947 Changes.—By January 1, 1948, legal reserve life insurance companies having more than 95 per cent of all level premium life insurance in the United States had completely revised their policies to conform with new state laws that became effective on that date. These laws require the use of an up-to-date mortality table, and a new method of figuring cash values. At the same time, most of the companies adopted a 2¼ per cent or 2½ per cent interest rate for the calculation of premiums and values for all new policies issued. These rate adjustments and other changes did not affect any life insurance already in force; they applied only to new life insurance issued after the changes were made.

The new mortality table is the *Commissioners 1941 Standard Ordinary Table,* usually known as the C.S.O. table (a similar table is in use by companies issuing industrial insurance). The C.S.O. table is based on the actual experience of life insurance companies, covering the years 1930 to 1940. Mortality rates are lower than in the *American Experience Table* the companies have been using for many years: much

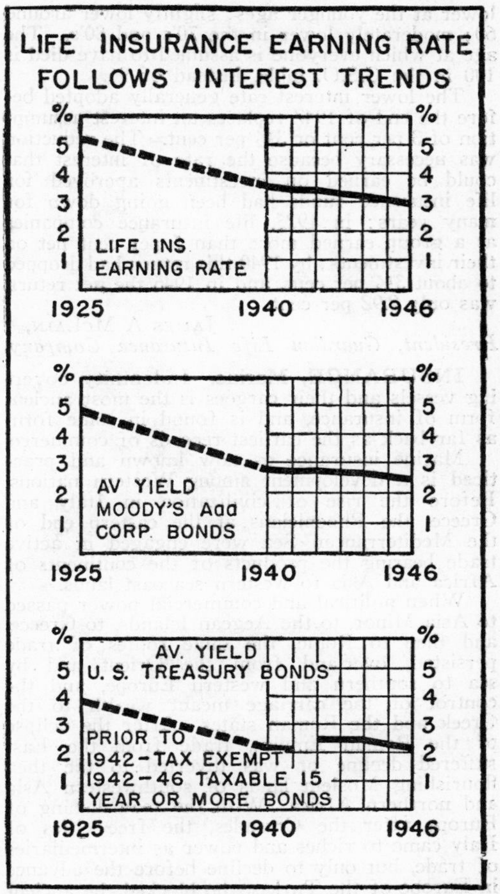

Net interest earnings in excess of 5 per cent in 1925 operated to reduce the cost of life insurance to policyholders and increased the amount of incomes paid to beneficiaries and annuitants. By 1946, net interest earnings had dropped to 2.92 per cent. This trend, coupled with materially increased expenses in all operating departments of the business, has increased the cost of life insurance and reduced or eliminated extra interest dividends to beneficiaries and annuitants.

lower at the younger ages; slightly lower around 60; moderately lower in the 70's and 80's. The age at which everyone is assumed to have died is 100 in the C.S.O. table, instead of 96.

The lower interest rate generally adopted before the end of 1947 replaces an interest assumption of 3 per cent or 3½ per cent. The reduction was necessary because the rate of interest that could be earned on investments approved for life insurance funds had been going down for many years: in 1925, life insurance companies as a group earned more than 5 per cent net on their investments; by 1940 this return had dropped to about 3½ per cent, and in 1946 the net return was only 2.92 per cent.

JAMES A MCLAIN,
President, Guardian Life Insurance Company.

INSURANCE, Marine. Indemnity covering vessels and their cargoes is the most ancient form of insurance, and is found in some form as far back as the earliest records of commerce.

Marine insurance as now known and practiced is a development among Western nations. Before the rise of civilization in Italy and Greece, the Phoenicians at the eastern end of the Mediterranean Sea were engaged in active trade bearing the products of the continents of Africa and Asia to western seacoast lands.

When political and commercial power passed to Asia Minor, to the Aegean Islands, to Greece, and then to Rome, the same routes of trade persisted, overland from the Orient and by sea to southern and western Europe, and the control of the carriage meant wealth to the Greek and the Roman states. After the eclipse of the Roman Empire, trade from the East suffered decline or was diverted to the then flourishing Moslem lands of southwestern Asia and northern Africa. With the reawakening of Europe after the Crusades, the free cities of Italy came to riches and power as intermediaries of trade, but only to decline before the advance in Europe of the Turks, who blocked the ancient caravan routes and thus forced the eyes of mariners westward, bringing about the discovery of the American continents. Thus also was sea traffic widened and the centers of trade and wealth shifted step by step from the Mediterranean to Spain and Portugal, the Low Countries, and the northwestern coast of Europe.

There is no doubt that water-borne commerce was protected against the perils of the sea from very early times, as traces of some form of indemnity are found in the sea regulations of Greece and Rome, as well as in the Code of Justinian and in the port ordinances of the Italian free cities. Only in recent centuries has insurance come to such importance as to fall under general public regulations; hence the scarcity of records of the simple business arrangement that sufficed earlier.

In place of the modern procedure of insurance on a ship and cargo for a sum paid over by the insured, the ancient practice was more like a silent partnership on the side of the insurer; for instance, the Roman patricians who shunned open relations with trade were wont to loan money privately on sea ventures at the good rate of 10 per cent, on the condition of repayment if the voyage was safely accomplished, but of no return whatever if ship and cargo were lost. The principal owner, being the mariner, had the larger interest in the success of the venture, and thus the silent partner had a fair chance of profit.

In contrast with this narrow sharing of the hazard, modern marine insurance, like all other insurance, rests on a wide distribution of loss, and the basic premium or cost is determined from the average of loss gathered from experience for each type of vessel and class of voyage, and is modified by the immediate considerations and circumstances of the time, such as season of the year and state of war.

For over two centuries the business of marine insurance has centered in Lloyd's of London. In 1871, Lloyd's was first incorporated as an exchange for the regulation of marine underwriting after the manner of other commercial exchanges. As far back as the 17th century seafarers were wont to gather in the coffee houses near the London docks to fraternize and transact their business. One, Edward Lloyd, kept such a house and shrewdly catered to his clients by affording facilities and supplying intelligence as to shipping and mariners. In the course of time he contrived to have news from all over the world drift his way and then to establish sources of information in all the leading ports.

The first simple plan of Lloyd's was for a mariner to post a slip recording his vessel, cargo and prospective voyage, and those who signed up—perhaps to the number of 50 or 100 for £50 and upward, whatever each was willing to assume on the risk—were the underwriters. More than any other branch of insurance, marine business depends on entire honor between all parties and a well-developed judgment as to shipping, trade, times, and seasons. Marine underwriting judgment depends fundamentally on marine information, which Lloyd's has aimed to supply most completely. Its several publications give particulars as to vessels and mariners and fullest intelligence as to their location and fortunes at sea. In the 18th century, the procedure of effecting marine insurance above described gradually gave way to the practice whereby business is placed largely by agents or brokers, and as they present their papers an underwriter, representing himself or a company, must be ready at short notice to decide for or against participation. There is no opportunity for particular inspection of risks. The rating of the vessel, according to age and build, and the standing of the owners and the mariner are his main reliance.

Since the first quarter of the 18th century, British joint stock companies have competed with Lloyd's and now transact the larger part of the marine business done in Great Britain, and the two together carry the bulk of the world's marine insurance. The stock companies depend on Lloyd's for the intelligence essential to their operations. By means of the cables, a great deal of insurance flows into London from all over the world, owing to the advantages possessed and cleverly used by the London underwriters in the way of worldwide banking and trade facilities, as well as marine intelligence. In fact, London marine underwriting has achieved a clear monopoly, so that it can afford to underbid competitors to secure patronage.

American marine insurance began in colonial times with personal, private underwriting at the several Atlantic ports, much on the early plan of Lloyd's. Under the rigid laws of the mother country, the larger traffic was confined to English bottoms, which always loyally carried English insurance, but a lively coastwise and West India trade existed in America up to the American Revolution, and men of means were to be found in every port, able and willing to finance and underwrite adventures on the sea, as such trade was profitable enough to yield an ample return for all concerned.

The hostilities conducted during the War of Independence increased the hazard of traffic by sea sufficiently to cut off the form of private insurance that was in practice, but the opportunities for privateering more than compensated the extra risk for the bolder American mariners. As commerce began to revive under the new national life inspired by the adoption of the Constitution in 1789, the demands of a world trade that opened to American shipping with its unlimited supply of shipbuilding timber, called for an amount of security that could be met only by organized capital. Attempts to copy London Lloyd's at several times failed. The long seaboard, the lack of communication, and the separate interests of the states did not afford the unity of action needed to promote success.

Hardly was American marine insurance thus started in a larger way, when the Napoleonic wars brought it disaster. During the winter of 1793–1794 about 600 American vessels were seized and detained in British ports, lest the mariners should supply the enemy French with necessities. It took the better part of a year, and sometimes years, to get news and to make settlements, and the companies waited long years for a settlement of their consequent claims against government. This vexatious state of affairs continued in spite of protest and threat of war, and the War of 1812 brought no better security to American shipping. Between 1803 and 1812 nearly 1,600 American vessels were captured by British, French, and other European powers.

The American marine made a slow recovery after the settlement of European peace in 1815, but from 1830 to 1860 enjoyed a large growth. This was the era of the clipper ships, when the American sails and sailors outsped all competitors. Vessels left American ports in numbers even for the Far East. Importing firms owned their craft and sent their representatives to dispose of the cargo and to buy for the return trip the silks, tea, coffee, spices and other products of China, Japan, and India. The voyage took many months. Insurance rates were necessarily high, but the business was uniformly placed with American companies and marine business prospered with the prosperity of the importer.

The Civil War demoralized a large American overseas trade and American marine insurance shared the disaster. The national energies were called home and such traffic as still ventured forth was liable to fall victim to Confederate raiders that were fitted out in Europe. While the conflict was on between North and South, the change from wood to iron construction and from sail to steam power went on apace. When American trade was able to look out again upon the sea, after the close of the war, British shipping everywhere had the advantage in speed and capacity, and Lloyd's of London clinched the situation by means of its power to make ratings, to supply quick intelligence, and to afford political and financial backing to its clients.

These advantages possessed and used by British marine insurance companies were demonstrated after 1870 when they began to establish American branches. They were able to enter the states to do business under easier conditions than domestic companies enjoyed, and by vigorous rate cutting made such inroads that many of the latter were compelled to abandon the field. (C.M.)

During World Wars I and II a renewed impetus was given marine insurance in the American market, which includes both American companies and foreign admitted companies. Though this market continues to grow as the United States becomes more prominent in international finance and trade, and though it has become a potent factor especially where trade to or from the country is involved, London still (in 1946) is the world center for insurance. American insurance has not yet developed the worldwide character of English insurance. This is due in part to the youth of the American market in comparison with London, and in part to the fact that the United States has relatively few possessions or interests beyond the limits of continental North America; moreover, through centuries English government, shipping, banking, and insurance have operated in close conjunction, to the benefit of all.

Following the lead of the London market, the Board of Underwriters of New York, organized in 1820, established agents throughout the world to survey losses, furnish local information, and in general to assist individuals holding policies issued by subscribing companies to the board. The American Institute of Marine Underwriters, established in 1898, also provides a close link with similar institutions in other world markets, particularly London; through this medium, standard clauses have been drawn and action taken on matters vital to the best interests of marine insurance.

An important part of marine insurance is reinsurance, which allows companies to spread large liabilities so that in the event of a catastrophe no one company's position is jeopardized. Formerly, the domestic market had few facilities of this nature and relied almost entirely on London. By the time of writing this article (March 1946) reinsurance by companies in the American market was on a larger scale than ever before and, in addition, this market had formed many reinsurance arrangements. In particular, the American Marine Insurance Syndicates provide a sharing arrangement under which the risks on high-valued hulls, fleets of vessels and builder's risks can be spread over the market with mutual advantage. (T.M.T.)

On cargo, reinsurance exchanges have been set up for shipments of commodities of high value and large volume, such as, to mention a few, cotton, burlap, and export automobiles. The outstanding example of a reinsurance arrangement in this market was the formation in 1939 of the American Cargo War Risk Reinsurance Exchange, which reinsured virtually all of the cargo war risks written in the United States during World War II and reimbursed the companies for the very considerable war claims paid in the course of the conflict. The London market was used by the exchange only for reinsurance on large lines or particularly hazardous risks. The functioning of this reinsurance exchange, making it possible for the American underwriters to meet the full needs of American merchants even during the height of submarine sinkings in 1942, contributed substantially to strengthening the American market and making it self-sustaining and, together with other developments, is impressive evidence that this market is maturing. (W.H.)

War Risks.—Originally, marine insurance held acts of war to be an integral part of the perils of the sea against which marine property was to be protected. Shortly after the Napoleonic wars, however, war risks began to be viewed independently; and now they are so treated through issuance of a war policy as a distinct and separate, self-sustaining document, at least in the American market. When there is peace and no threat of war, war risk insurance is little in demand; on the other hand, during times of international conflict or threats of international conflicts, war risk may become a much more hazardous peril for marine underwriters. Accordingly the marine policy excludes the risks of war by a warranty known as the F. C. & S. warranty (free of capture and seizure).

Coverage in a war policy is mainly against the physical risks of war, such as mines, torpedoes, attack by air, capture by the enemy, and similar perils; but it is not complete insurance. For example, it excludes claims based on loss of, or frustration of, the insured voyage or adventure caused by arrest, restraints, or detainments; it excludes also commandeering, pre-emption, requisition, or nationalization by the government of the country to or from which the goods are insured.

During World Wars I and II, when the Allied nations controlled the sea and seizure of any merchandise intended for their enemies was practically inevitable, the policy further excluded capture and seizure by the British and their allies, including the United States after the latter's entry in those wars.

In the first of these conflicts the principal war risk hazard was submarine attack, though considerable damage was done by raiders, as the *Emden* and the *Wolf*, and by mines. In the second, raiders were virtually nonexistent insofar as important damage was concerned, whereas the German submarines again caused great destruction especially in the early part of 1942. In addition, a new peril arose in the form of attack from the air, which developed great magnitude in and around the British Isles and on the run to Murmansk.

While most war risk losses are caused patently by torpedoes, mines, capture by the enemy or air attack, borderline cases exist where it is not always easy to determine whether a particular loss falls within the marine or war risk policy. Such cases are relatively few in number but often present important issues for decision. A controversy may spring, for example, from different interpretations of the exclusion in the F. C. & S. clause of claims arising as a consequence of hostilities or warlike operations. The incidents of a convoy may be cited to illustrate the difficulties involved. With large groups of vessels with armed escorts, sailing without lights, zigzagging, navigating waters from which channel markings have been removed, the dangers of stranding and of collision are greatly increased. Two merchant ships collide, or a merchant ship collides with a war vessel; a merchantman sinks while ramming what was supposed to be a submarine but which proved to be something else. Casualties of various kinds are bound to occur and many of them squarely raise the issue as to which of the policies carries the burden of liability for the loss. Where a war vessel is involved, the nature of her operations at the time is critical; thus, destroyers patrolling in search of enemy submarines, or warships convoying merchantmen, are engaged in warlike operations, whereas a warship proceeding to port to have her boilers overhauled might be held to be an exception.

A leading case involving this type of controversy was that of the *Coxwold.* In this proceeding the British House of Lords handed down a decision (in 1942) that was at variance with the intention of the London underwriters, in that the court declared this case was a war peril, whereas the underwriters had intended an occurrence of this kind to come under the marine policy. As a result of this decision, the English underwriters specifically took under the marine cover certain losses from wartime conditions, principally cases of stranding and collision, which the courts had held were war losses. In addition, they included losses due to collision between merchant and war vessels, which for many years had been treated as war losses.

The American market, however, took the opposite position. This was done largely because in the country's domestic economy the marine insurance business was a factor in the Office of Price Administration's price structure of essential commodities. With the end of the war, this consideration no longer was a factor, and the American underwriters revised their F. C. & S. clause to correspond with that of the London market.

Another source of controversy derives from application of the principle that it rests upon the assured to prove that the loss or damage he is claiming for has been proximately due to a peril insured against. Questions involving this principle arise chiefly when vessels disappear at sea. If there is no direct evidence to settle the point whether the loss was due to a marine risk or to a war risk, resort must be had to the balance of probabilities. This rule was illustrated in the case of the British ship *Inveramsay* posted as missing in World War I. Noting that German submarines were known to have been actively engaged in the waters where she had last been reported, the Court of Appeal (in 1920) held that to attribute the ship's disappearance to hostile torpedoes was not mere surmise but a legitimate inference. As the policy in suit contained the F. C. & S. warranty, no right of recovery was allowed.

When in June 1939, it became apparent to American underwriters that war in Europe was almost inevitable, some 150 marine insurance companies formed the American Cargo War Risk Reinsurance Exchange in order to meet the eventual needs of the insuring public. Under this plan all the war risk insurance written by the individual members was reinsured in the exchange, each company taking an agreed percentage. There thus was made available an adequate marine insurance market for all the requirements of American commerce, even during the disastrous year of 1942 when war risk losses paid exceeded by several times the premium volume of a normal peacetime year's business. The London market was used for reinsurance only on large lines or especially hazardous risks. Lines of $3,000,000 and $4,000,000 on one vessel were fairly common, one being over $7,000,000.

In the summer of 1942 the American government in the interests of the national economy began to offer war insurance at noncompensatory rates on imports of cost-of-living commodities, and the American underwriters acted as agents of the War Shipping Administration in the issuing of war risk open policies, and in the handling of declarations and claims. The commercial market, however, continued to write the bulk of war risk insurance on export shipments and on imports of luxury and other nonessential commodities. As the submarine menace decreased, the commercial rates gradually were lowered to those charged by the War Shipping Administration and the business returned to the commercial market. On July 1, 1945, the War Shipping Administration withdrew officially from insuring war risks on cargo.

War risk insurance continued to be written after the cessation of hostilities in 1945 because of the existence of floating and uncharted mines. This protection was necessary because of experience after World War I, when as late as 1922 vessels were sunk by these destructive vestiges of war. (E.R.K.)

T.M.T. T. M. Torrey,
Insurance Company of North America.
W.H. Woodhull Hay,
Educational Editor, "The Weekly Underwriter."
E.R.K. Edward R. King,
American Institute of Marine Insurance.
C.M. Charles Maar,
Insurance Department, State of New York.

INSURANCE, Science and Economics of. Insurance forms an integral element of modern social and commercial life. So completely is the service of insurance interwoven with modern economic affairs that it is difficult even to conceive of a progressive society that would long carry on without its benefits. This usefulness becomes the more evident the more its practices and results are appraised, in relation to individual and national well-being.

As a highly developed mechanism, insurance is a more or less exact science which utilizes other branches of science in its successful operation; and as the most satisfactory institution so far conceived for minimizing the social cost of risk, it is also an important branch of economics and, therefore, one of the social sciences. Any plan of insurance is, fundamentally, simply a means of spreading over many individuals a possible monetary loss too severe to be carried with ease by any one person. The scientific basis underlying the insurance principle is the same in all its branches, that is, the law of large numbers, from which has been developed that branch of mathematics known as the theory of probabilities. Accurate and precise observations of a fairly large and homogeneous mass of facts are important phases of the scientific process, and constant testing of the resulting conclusions against subsequent experience is also an essential element. Fairly exact calculations may be made of the risks involved in any insurable contingency; the financial equivalents necessary to meet them may then be calculated. In practice, of course, numerous other factors must be taken into account, including compound interest, and operating expenses.

The recognition of insurance as a science dates back several hundred years. Numerous observers in the late 1600's and early 1700's added their contributions, and in 1747 Corbyn Morris published his classical *Essay Toward Illustrating the Science of Insurance.* In present day practice, the various branches of insurance differ materially in the degree to which scientific computations are utilized — the practice being most universal in the life insurance field but less evident perhaps in some newer fields of insurance where sparsity of data, the character of the contingency insured against, or other factors may make exact analysis less practicable.

Application of scientific principles to insurance had its inception in the field of life contingencies, and the pioneering accomplishments of actuaries earned the institution an early and well-merited reputation among scientific men. But substantial progress through scientific procedure has been made in many other types of insurance company activity, particularly in the 20th century. In life insurance, for example, medical investigation and rating, classification of occupational and other hazards, and the formulation of life and health conservation standards all have made great strides at the hands of insurance organizations. In the fire and casualty insurance fields, rate making is carried out to a large degree on scientific bases that involve recognition and classification of occupancy, structural, exposure, and many other factors. Several branches of the insurance industry have attained eminence in the application of scientific principles and procedures to inspection and other loss-prevention activities, including testing of mechanical and electrical appliances.

Furthermore, the American insurance industry has made extensive use of, and has contributed to the advancement of knowledge in, the so-called practical or applied phases of economic science—including investment, interest-rate, and general statistical analyses, scientific studies of insurance markets, and perfecting of accounting standards and procedures. The practice of employing full-time economic experts is growing, in part encouraged by the increasing complexity of the economic environment; while investment analysts are now found in all American insurance companies of significance.

All such scientific activities by insurance companies—whether actuarial, underwriting, investment, medical or legal research, sales research, or other—have as their goal not only improvement of the product sold, and of the service rendered to policyholders, but a smooth and efficient functioning of the insurance industry as an integral part of national economic life.

As a branch of economics, insurance is receiving widespread attention in American colleges and universities. Many of these institutions have prescribed a general course in insurance principles as a part of the requirements for all students of business administration. Specialized training in insurance is likewise offered in a number of the well-known institutions such as the University of Pennsylvania and Columbia University in the East, Ohio State University and Indiana University in the Middle West, the University of Texas in the South, and the University of California in the West. Figures made available in 1940 for the academic year 1938–1939 revealed a total of 584 insurance courses offered by 235 American colleges and universities; 99 of these institutions offered instruction in two or more main fields of insurance. Specialization in insurance was possible for undergraduates at 16 schools, and for graduate students in 7 schools. Approximately one half of all these insurance courses were set up after 1930. (C.L.P.)

In addition to these facilities in institutions of higher learning, opportunities for insurance study and training are offered in a wide variety of schools and courses throughout the United States, maintained or sponsored directly or indirectly by the industry itself—by companies, associations, societies, or affiliated study groups. A notable school of this kind is conducted by the Insurance Society of New York which offers courses in all branches of insurance; in 1946 it had an enrollment of more than 1,000 students. Other organizations foster education by providing outlines and texts for study and by encouraging scholarship through awarding certificates, fellowships, or professional designations to persons successfully passing their examinations. Among these are the Insurance Institute of America, the Life Office Management Association Institute, the American College of Life Underwriters, and the American Institute for Property and Liability Underwriters. The outstanding academic society in the field of insurance education is the American Association of University Teachers of Insurance, an affiliate of the American Economic Association.

Within the industry the tradition of exact analysis early developed in Great Britain and Germany has been ably carried on in the United States and Canada. A number of professional societies have been formed for research and deliberation: the highly esteemed Actuarial Society of America, the American Institute of Actuaries, and the Casualty Actuarial Society; in the field of law, the Association of Life Insurance Counsel, the International Association of Insurance Counsel, the Federation of Insurance Counsel, and the Section of Insurance Law of the American Bar Association; in economics, the Insurance Economics Society of America. Furthermore, numerous associations composed of company or individual membership have permanent staffs of technical and research specialists, and most of the larger companies retain their own scientific and economic advisers. The deliberations and reports of the National Association of Insurance Commissioners are of the highest value in the field of legislation and administration. Noteworthy also is the cooperation of the Chamber of Commerce of the United States of America, through its Department Committee for Insurance. Also contributions have been made by governmental and other technicians in the field of social insurance, for example, those of the Bureau of Research and Statistics of the Social Security Board.

As insurance broadens it functions and interests to meet the requirements of an expanding national economy, so the activities of research and education are directed into channels best selected to serve it. While great attention is given to the various types of company organization, policy contracts, coverages and the operational techniques, the underlying problems of theory and policy are being studied by practitioners qualified as specialists in their fields. The place of risk in an economy, the scientific principles determining the uses and kinds of insurance for particular risks or income groups, and the extent to which insurance is economically desirable are among such subjects. Economic factors and business cycles are analyzed. Intensive surveys are made of the investment policies and operations of insurance companies, and the results compared with those of other financial institutions; and the relation of all such financial activities to economic developments in general is observed and interpreted. Problems of great magnitude and intricacy arise from the exercise by government of its power in insurance. These revolve chiefly about regulation and taxation, and are multiplied by the diversity of legislation in the several states. A new factor was introduced in 1944 by a decision of the United States Supreme Court that insurance is commerce and thus in its interstate activities subject to regulation by the paramount power of Congress, followed in the succeeding year by the exercise of this power by Congress expressing its intent with respect to the regulation of the business of insurance. The situation thus created required a re-examination of the supervisory system developed by the states and consideration of remedial legislation to bring that system into coordination with the congressional policy. These problems and their solutions, involving the fundamental relationship between government and insurance and the established principle that insurance is charged with a public interest, are receiving most careful study from scientific as well as practical aspects.

Bibliography.—General: Mowbray, A. H., *Insurance,* 2d ed. (New York 1937); Ackerman, S. B., *Insurance,* rev. pr. (New York 1939); Magee, J. H., *General Insurance,* rev. ed. (Chicago 1942); Michelbacher, G. F., *Casualty Insurance Principles,* 2d ed. (New York 1942); Kulp, C. A., *Casualty Insurance,* rev. ed. (New York 1942); Maclean, J. B., *Life Insurance,* 6th ed. (New York 1945).

Economic Theory and Functions: Willett, A. H., *The Economic Theory of Risk and Insurance* (New York 1901); Hoffman, F. L., *Insurance Science and Economics* (New York 1911); Hardy, C. O., *Risk and Risk Bearing,* rev. ed. (Chicago 1931); Betterley, P. D., *Buying Insurance* (New York 1936); Manes, A., *Insurance* (New York 1938); Huebner, S. S., *The Economics of Life Insurance,* rev. ed. (New York 1944); *Annals,* American Academy of Political and Social Science; *Journal,* Insurance Institute of London; annual *Proceedings* of the Life Insurance Association of America and of the American Life Convention; hearings and monographs of the Temporary National Economic Committee (1939–41).

Special Phases: Sawyer, E. W., *Insurance as Interstate Commerce* (New York 1945); reading lists issued by the three actuarial societies above named.

Current developments are reviewed in yearbooks, annual reports of insurance commissioners, and proceedings of various insurance organizations; in *The Insurance Almanac,* an annual of insurance facts; and in periodicals as *The Weekly Underwriter, The Spectator, The Eastern Underwriter, Insurance Advocate,* and *Best's Insurance News,* New York; *The National Underwriter* and the *Journal of American Insurance,* Chicago; *The Insurance Field,* Louisville, Ky. (W.H.)

C.L.P. Corliss L. Parry.
W.H. Woodhull Hay.

INSURANCE, Workmen's Compensation. See Workmen's Compensation.

INSURANCE LAW. The term *insurance law* embraces that part of the common and statutory law which prescribes and defines the rights and duties of insurers when acting as such, and the correlative rights and duties of those who deal with them.

Insurance law in the United States shares the history and characteristics of the American legal system of which it is but a part. The common law system of developing a body of law through the medium of judicial precedents, and the idea of a statutory law enacted by a constitutional legislature, became and have remained the primary features of the American legal system.

Under the common law system of the United States, the courts in deciding cases which come before them do not turn to a supposedly all-embracing code of laws for the rule of decision, but in theory make their decisions in accordance with the established customs of fair dealing as found by the courts. This case or decisional law, which is in the form of judicial opinions, is called the *common law.* The common law is continually evolving as the courts apply it to new and varying situations.

While most of the principles of law applied by the courts in the disposition of insurance cases are but general principles of law, equally applicable to all similar transactions, the courts have formulated out of those features of insurance which distinguish it from other commercial transactions, a fairly sizable number of legal principles which are peculiar to insurance. It is this body of law which may properly be classified as the *common law of insurance.* The insurance cases which reach the courts represent an exceedingly small fraction of the total number of insurance transactions which are completed daily.

The statutory law of the United States is the law enacted by the legislatures of the 48 states and by Congress. Beginning in the 1850's *statutory insurance law* took form through legislation by the various states so that now no state is without laws affecting insurance or without administrative authority for their enforcement. Though each state passed laws that it deemed advisable for its own jurisdiction, there exists sufficient uniformity among them to enable large insurers to do business without great inconvenience in any state it wishes to enter.

Most of these statutes pertain to such matters as taxation, policy provisions and details of organization, operation, maintenance of reserve funds, and reports to administrative officials. The ever-widening scope of statutory insurance law has led to codification by many of the state legislatures. These developments, together with the peculiar intricacies springing from the relationship between the statutory and the common law of insurance, have justified the classification of insurance law as a separate branch of law recognized as such in legal literature and in law schools.

Power in the states to enact statutes affecting insurance was confirmed in 1868 by the United States Supreme Court. Though Congress during the succeeding 77 years passed no laws expressly regulating the business of insurance with the exception of those it enacted as legislation for the District of Columbia, its power to do so was brought for the first time in 1944 before the Supreme Court for determination. In deciding the issue, the court held that insurance as now conducted is commerce, and that when its activities cross state lines it is interstate commerce and as such subject to regulation by Congress under the commerce clause of the federal Constitution.

This decision had an immediate effect upon the operation of statutory law: with respect to existing federal acts regulating interstate commerce, it made these applicable to insurance insofar as insurance was interstate in character and to the extent that such acts were applicable to the business of insurance; and it rendered invalid all state statutes that were in conflict with such acts.

In the following year Congress specifically exercised its power to regulate insurance by enacting the statute known as Public Law 15, thus inaugurating a new and different period in the development of insurance law in the United States. See also INSURANCE SUPERVISION.

Bibliography.—COMPREHENSIVE WORKS: Cooley, R. W., *Briefs on the Law of Insurance,* 8 vols. (Kansas City, Mo., 1927–32); Couch, G. J., *Cyclopedia of Insurance Law,* 9 vols. (New York 1929–31) with *Cumulative Supplement,* 3 vols. (New York 1945); Appleman, J. A., *Insurance Law and Practice,* 19 vols. already published (Kansas City, Mo. 1941–46).

GENERAL: Vance, W. R., *Handbook of the Law of Insurance* (St. Paul 1930); Long, R. H., *Richards on the Law of Insurance,* 4th ed. (New York 1932); Cady, E. W., *The Law of Insurance* (New York 1934); Patterson, E. W., *Essentials of Insurance Law* (New York 1935); Laverty, F. J., *Insurance Law of Canada,* 2d ed. (Toronto 1936); Sawyer, E. W., *Insurance as Interstate Commerce* (New York 1945).

WOODHULL HAY,
Educational Editor, "The Weekly Underwriter."

INSURANCE PATROLS, also known as fire patrols, protective departments, and salvage corps, are organizations maintained (1946) in 11 of the larger cities by fire insurance companies doing business in those cities. Although these organizations are supported by the insurance business, they are closely associated with the local fire departments and operate under the control of the fire chief at time of fire.

The object of these patrols is to protect property from damage due to water and smoke at time of fire, and to protect property against additional loss from the elements following a fire. The apparatus, of a type similar to fire department apparatus, carries waterproof covers and other appliances for protecting buildings and contents from damage. They operate mostly in business districts, and are available upon call by the fire department in other sections of the city. These companies respond to fire alarms with the municipal fire department.

This service, by organizations separate from the regularly established fire departments, was created as early as 1840 during the period when municipal fire departments were mainly volunteer and not highly trained. Such organizations have operated in as many as 21 of the largest cities in the United States, but after 1913 no new insurance patrols were established, and a number were discontinued as the municipal fire departments assumed the responsibility for salvage service. With the advance in the science of fire fighting, improvement in fire prevention methods and building construction, the need for separate insurance patrols was materially reduced. Approximately 74 per cent of the regularly organized municipal fire departments carry salvage equipment and appliances, and perform salvage as a part of their regular fire fighting operations.

INSURANCE SUPERVISION. Public interest in the sound conduct of the insurance business was recognized from an early period in the United States. Insurance was regarded as a matter to be regulated locally by the several states, and beginning with the case of *Paul* v. *Virginia* in 1868 this view was fostered and augmented by decisions of the United States Supreme Court for more than 75 years, leading to the generally accepted doctrine that the business of insurance was not subject to federal laws. On June 5, 1944, the Supreme Court decided in the case of *United States* v. *South-Eastern Underwriters Association et al.* that the business of insurance is commerce and that when its activities cross state boundaries, it is interstate commerce and thus subject to regulation by Congress under the commerce clause of the federal Constitution. On that day the regulation of insurance entered a distinctly new and different period of development.

During the prior period, a considerable body of state law and departmental regulations was created to supervise the business of insurance. In every state there is either an officer charged solely with this duty, or some officer who has this responsibility in connection with others. Each state fixes its own conditions upon which insurance companies may operate, and the supervising official has a rather wide discretion in determining whether or not they are entitled to be licensed or should have their licenses revoked.

At the outset, insurance supervision was concerned chiefly with regulations for filing financial statements and simple tests for solvency. With the growth of the business, however, and the development of new types of coverage and policy forms, the scope of supervision expanded and the number of laws increased. This legislation ranges from laws requiring certain standard provisions or prohibiting other provisions, to those prescribing the exact form of policy or requiring the approval of a form by the supervising official before it may be issued.

Taxation and deposits constitute important subjects of state legislation, and many of the states have enacted retaliatory or reciprocal laws for the benefit of companies domiciled in their own jurisdictions. In a number of states associations of property insurers or similar organizations are allowed to prepare uniform rates for use by their members, and in some of these instances the supervising officials are given power to approve the rates so established.

Laws of the various states vary widely as to the licensing of agents and brokers; in certain states the requirements are little more than mere form, while in others the applicants have to pass successfully written examinations set by the supervisory authority. Most of the states have what are known as resident agent laws, which provide that policies must be secured through licensed agents residing in the state.

In matters of finance through statutes and regulations, provisions are made for the form and content of annual statements, for prescribing the general types of securities in which company funds may be invested, and for periodic examinations of each company's fiscal affairs. At an early date (1858) Massachusetts enacted a law requiring life insurance companies to maintain scientifically calculated reserves against their contracts to assure their continued solvency, thus inaugurating the legal reserve system of life insurance.

A highly influential body in bringing about uniformity in legislation and administration in the several states is the National Association of Insurance Commissioners. It holds annual meetings, consults with representatives of the industry, and proposes uniform codes, laws, and forms for state adoption.

Such, in general outline, was the system of insurance supervision that had been developed at the time of the Supreme Court decision referred to previously. The immediate legal effect of that adjudication was that the power of Congress to regulate the interstate business of insurance became paramount and that state statutes in conflict with existing federal statutes applicable to the interstate conduct of insurance were to that extent invalid. There were then a number of such federal statutes which, while general in character, were, or might be held to be, applicable to insurance, notably the Sherman Act (1890) and certain other laws against discrimination and unfair competition, and two labor relations laws: the National Labor Relations Act (1935) and the Fair Labor Standards Act (1938).

Uncertainties arose as to the validity of state tax laws as well as of state regulatory provisions, and as to the effect upon the business of insurance of the immediate applicability of the federal antitrust acts. In March 1945, therefore, Congress undertook to stabilize the situation by enacting a statute known as Public Law 15, which expressed its policy in respect to the regulation of the business of insurance. Its general purpose was to remove existing doubts as to the right of the states to regulate and tax the business of insurance and to secure more adequate regulation of such business. To accomplish this purpose, the act provided that the application to insurance of the antitrust laws and certain related statutes, but not of the labor relations laws, should be suspended till Jan. 1, 1948, excepting the provisions in the Sherman Act against agreements to boycott, coerce or intimidate; and that after that date these laws again should be applicable to the business of insurance "to the extent that such business is not regulated by state law." As to other acts of Congress it provided that they should not invalidate or supersede state laws regulating or taxing the business of insurance unless such acts specifically related to such business. Declaring that "the continued regulation and taxation by the several states of the business of insurance is in the public interest," Congress thus invited collaboration by the states in defined areas in the future regulation of insurance and allowed an interval of approximately two sessions of the state legislatures for them to adjust themselves to its expressed supervisory policy, the intent of which appeared to be that insurance must remain a free competitive enterprise.

Under the leadership of the National Association of Insurance Commissioners in cooperation with the All-Industry Committee, a representative group of insurance executives and qualified attorneys from the chief policy bodies in the industry, numerous conferences have been held to formulate and procure the adoption of legislation that would be reasonably uniform throughout the states and at the same time adequate to meet the requirements set forth in Public Law 15. Much of this remedial legislation is needed before the beginning of 1948, when the period of suspension as provided in that law expires, and many problems of an underlying nature justifying fuller consideration may not be resolved till after that date, but in the large view the Supreme Court decision in 1944 stands high as a marker on the long road of insurance supervision. See also INSURANCE LAW.

WOODHULL HAY,
Educational Editor, "The Weekly Underwriter."

INSURANCE TERMS. Words of precise meaning used to define insurance contracts, or used in connection with such contracts:

Abandonment.—In ocean marine insurance, the exercise by the insured of his right, in the event of constructive total loss, of relinquishing to the insurer the salvage in order to establish a claim for total loss.

Abordage.—In ocean marine insurance, the obligation of the insurer of a ship damaged by another ship through collision on the open sea to indemnify the insured for the loss, with right of recovery at civil law against the party causing the damage.

Acceptance.—In general, the validating act to an insurance contract by the insurer in agreeing to accept for a specified premium a risk offered for insurance. In ocean marine insurance the act of the insurer that perfects the rights of the insured in the recovery of his loss when he has offered abandonment.

Accident Insurance.—Indemnifies for bodily injury or death caused by accident, including loss of time from occupation, and hospital, nurse, surgical and medical expenses.

Accounts Receivable Insurance.—Indemnifies for loss through inability to collect accounts because of damage to, or destruction of, records.

Actuary.—In insurance, the official in an insurance company whose function is to make the mathematical calculations necessary to maintain the business on a sound financial basis; these include the valuation of contingent liabilities, the computation of risks, the construction of premiums, and the determination of various items as reserves, loss ratios, dividends, and nonforfeiture values.

Agreement.—In insurance, a contract written or oral between the insurer and the insured made before the issuance of the policy. It embodies an understanding on essential provisions.

Agricultural Insurance.—See term *Crop Insurance.*

Aircraft Hull Insurance.—Indemnifies for loss or damage to aircraft or parts thereof arising from all risks or specified perils.

Aircraft Liability Insurance.—Covers legal liability of owner or operator of aircraft for bodily injury, death, or property damage arising from ownership, maintenance, or use of aircraft covered by the policy.

Aircraft or Vehicle Property Damage Insurance.—Indemnifies for damage to property resulting from collision with, and caused by, aircraft or objects falling therefrom, or other vehicle, not owned by insured.

Aircraft Personal Accident Insurance. — Indemnifies passengers or pilots for bodily injury or death caused by aircraft accident.

Airmeet Liability Coverage.—Special form of aircraft liability insurance, providing coverage for airmeets.

Airport Liability Coverage.—Special form of aircraft liability insurance, providing coverage for airport owners and operators.

All Risks Coverage.—Insures against all risks of loss or damage directly arising from any external cause; certain forms specify exclusions.

American Experience Table of Mortality.—Shows number of people dying each year by age groups; used by life insurance companies in fixing premium rates.

Annuity Policy.—Provides income to one or more persons for life or for a specified period. Different forms are available to meet particular needs; with the exception of the *annuity certain,* which continues for a specified time regardless of any contingency, annuity payments are contingent on the happening of some agreed event, as the first death of a number of beneficiaries in a *joint life annuity,* or the last death of a number of beneficiaries in a *last survivor annuity.* Payments are made at fixed intervals.

Assessment.—In ocean marine insurance, the contribution apportioned among the various interests in general average. In mutual insurance companies, a call upon premium notes given by members as a substitute for the investment of paid-up stock.

Assessment Insurance.—A form of life insurance written by certain fraternal societies or associations wherein the premium payments are not fixed in the policies but determined by the insuring organizations as the needs to meet claims require.

Assigned Accounts Bond.—Guarantees that borrower will apply to reduction of loan collections from accounts receivable pledged as collateral.

Automatic Coverage.—Operates to include change in subject matter insured or its location without notice to insuring company.

Automobile Insurance-Damage to One's Own Car.—Indemnifies owner for loss or damage to his automobile or its contents.

Automobile Liability Insurance.—Covers legal liability for bodily injury, death or property damage arising from ownership, use, or maintenance of any automobile covered by the policy.

Automobile Nonownership Liability Coverage.—Extension of coverage of automobile liability insurance to include legal liability of insured arising from use by his employees in his business of automobiles not owned by him.

Average Clause.—See term *Coinsurance or Average Clause.*

Aviation Insurance.—A class of insurance comprising aircraft hull, aircraft liability, and aircraft personal accident insurance.

Bail Bond.—Assures appearance of arrested person or payment by surety of penalty.

Bailee's Customers' Floater. — Provides coverage for laundries, dyers, cleaners, tailors against loss or damage to customers' property during processing on premises, or in transit.

Bailee's Liability Insurance.—Covers legal liability of custodian of goods of others for loss or damage by named perils, excluding those of improper processing.

Bankers Blanket Bond.—Provides coverage for financial institutions against loss arising from dishonesty of employees, burglary, inside or outside robbery, and also from forgery if this additional coverage is purchased.

Barratry.—In ocean marine insurance the willful commission of any unlawful or fraudulent act or breach of duty in the management of a ship or its cargo to the injury of the owner and without his consent.

Bid Bond.—Guarantees that bidder on contract will undertake contract if it is awarded to him.

Binder.—Form protecting insured till policy is issued, and subject to policy's conditions.

Blanket Policy or Form.—Covers several properties or risks in one instrument.

Blanket Position Bond.—A fidelity bond covering all employees insured, each separately for uniform amount, new or substituted employees being automatically covered.

Boiler and Machinery Insurance.—A class of insurance comprising a number of liability and direct damage coverages against loss, damage, bodily injury, or death caused by boiler or machinery accidents.

Brokers Blanket Bond.—Provides coverage for securities brokers similar to that of bankers blanket bond.

Burglary Insurance.—See term *Residence and Outside Theft Insurance.*

Business Interruption Insurance.—Indemnifies for operating expenses continuing, and profits not earned, during period when business is interrupted by risk insured against.

Capital Sum.—Amount or portion thereof payable in accident insurance policy upon specified disability caused by accident.

Cargo Insurance.—Covers merchandise during ocean transportation together with shore and inland risks incidental thereto.

Cash Surrender Value.—Amount receivable by life insurance policyholder when he cancels his policy or permits it to lapse; it is an optional nonforfeiture value.

Casualty.—A term frequently used in insurance as a synonym for accident.

Casualty Insurance.—A general class of insurance embracing those forms that indemnify insured for certain kinds of losses caused by accident to his own person or property, and those that cover his legal liability to others for bodily injury, death, or property damage.

Coinsurance or Average Clause.—In partial losses, provides that insured bear deficiency when he carries less insurance than a specified percentage of total value.

Collision Insurance.—In automobile insurance, indemnifies owner for damage to his automobile caused by collision with stationary or moving object. Collision coverage is provided also in other types of insurance.

as aircraft or vehicle damage, aircraft hull, ocean marine, and elevator insurance.

Comprehensive Automobile Liability Policy.—Covers legal liability of insured arising from any hazard involved in maintenance, operation, or use of any automobile regardless of ownership.

Comprehensive Dishonesty, Disappearance, and Destruction Policy.—Combines coverages of primary commercial blanket bond, the two forms of money and securities policies, securities insurance policy (for lessees of safe deposit boxes), and depositors' forgery bond; usually all or any combination of these coverages may be selected.

Comprehensive General-Automobile Liability Policy.—Combines coverages of comprehensive automobile liability and comprehensive public liability policies.

Comprehensive Liability Insurance.—A class of insurance embracing those forms that on a broad basis cover legal liability of insured for any hazard not excluded.

Comprehensive Personal Liability Policy.—Broad form of coverage for individual's legal liability for bodily injury or death; includes sports and residence coverages and embraces acts of insured's wife and minor children.

Comprehensive Public Liability Policy.—Covers legal liability of insured for bodily injury or death sustained by persons not in his employ, except liability arising from maintenance, operation or use of automobiles.

Compulsory Insurance.—Refers to those forms of insurance that are required by statute in certain jurisdictions, as automobile liability, workmen's compensation, social old age and unemployment insurance.

Consequential Damage Coverage.—By endorsement on direct damage policy, indemnifies for indirect loss arising from accident to an insured object on premises, as from fire, explosion, or breakdown.

Constructive Total Loss.—May be established when cost of recovering and repairing damaged property would be commercially unprofitable.

Contract Bond.—Guarantees that party to a contract, commonly for construction or engineering work, will faithfully perform its terms.

Contractors' Public Liability Policy.—Covers legal liability of insured for bodily injury or death arising from his contract operations, including the existence of tools and equipment left or abandoned at place of work.

Contractual Liability Policy.—Protects insured against liability of others, which he has assumed, for bodily injury or death.

Court or Judicial Bond.—Assures to litigant in court pursuit of remedy, or protection to his adversary; there are many types and their forms are prescribed by law.

Coverage.—Denotes the protection promised against the risks specified in an insurance contract.

Credit Insurance.—Guarantees payment to insured of bad debt losses in excess of specified amount, with special provisions for coinsurance on certain classes of risks.

Crop Insurance.—Indemnifies for loss or damage to crops arising from a variety of causes, as hail, drought, frost, floods, and disease.

Custodians Bond.—Guarantees that custodian will retain possession of property pledged as collateral by borrower till loan is repaid, with partial withdrawals authorized by lender.

Customs Bond.—Guarantees payment of duty and taxes on entry into United States of property from foreign source.

Deductible Clause.—As applied to insurance, specifies amount in excess of which the insured may recover in claim for loss.

Deferred Insurance.—A form in which the liability of the insurer does not begin until a specified future date.

Depositors' and Commercial Forgery Bond.—Provides coverage of depositors' forgery bond and also coverage against 75 per cent of insured's pecuniary loss through forgery or alteration of negotiable instruments received for goods delivered or services rendered.

Depositors' Forgery Bond.—See term *Forgery Bond.*

Depreciation Insurance.—Provides indemnity for loss measured by the difference between value of building less depreciation and cost of replacing a building of like character.

Deviation.—In ocean marine insurance, the voluntary departure of a vessel, without necessity or reasonable cause, from the usual course of the voyage for which she was insured; such a departure is held to be a breach of an implied warranty by the insured and terminates the liability of the insurer. On the same reasoning any unusual or unnecessary delay releases the insurer from all risks.

Disability Insurance.—A general class of insurance embracing those forms, as accident, and health insurance, that indemnify for loss through disability as distinguished from death.

Discovery Bond.—A fidelity bond covering losses discovered during life of bond though occurring previously.

Dog Liability Coverage.—See terms *Residence, Farm Liability Insurance; Comprehensive Personal Liability Policy.*

Double Indemnity Provision.—In life, accident, and health insurance, provides double the amount payable, if death or specified disability is caused through specified accidents.

Double Insurance.—Exists when two or more policies cover the same interest of the same insured against the same risks in proportions exceeding the sum necessary to provide complete protection. The insured may sue upon all the policies although he may obtain but one satisfaction.

Elective Indemnity Provision.—In an accident insurance policy, this provision grants option to insured to choose with respect to specified disabilities between receving scheduled amounts at once or in weekly payments.

Elevator Insurance.—In various forms, provides coverage for legal liability of insured for bodily injury, death, or property damage arising from existence or use of elevator or equipment, and provides indemnity to him for damage to his own property through collision of elevator or object carried thereon with another object.

Employers' Liability Insurance.—Covers legal liability of employer for bodily injury or death to employees; restricted to employees not under workmen's compensation laws.

Endowment Insurance.—Provides for payment of policy amount at end of specified period, as 10 or 20 years, or at age 55, 60, or 65.

Errors and Omissions Insurance.—Provides coverage for financial institutions with loans on mortgaged property as collateral, against loss arising from inadequate insurance on such property resulting through error.

Excess Commercial Blanket Form.—Provides fidelity coverage in excess of primary coverage on schedule or blanket forms.

Excess Indemnity Endorsement.—On blanket position bond, provides fidelity coverage against loss caused by employees in any positions selected in excess of primary coverage.

Expense Loading.—Portion of premium calculated to meet insured's share of the operating expenses of the insuring company.

Extended Coverage Endorsement.—Extends fire insurance coverage to include windstorm, hail, explosion, riot, aircraft, motor vehicle, and smoke damage.

Extended Term Insurance.—Provides coverage to life insurance policyholder in policy amount for such period as would be purchased by the cash surrender amount used as single premium payment; it is an optional nonforfeiture value and usually operates automatically if holder does not select a different nonforfeiture value.

Extra Expense Insurance.—Provides funds to insured for additional expense required to maintain operations interrupted by fire.

Fidelity Bond.—Indemnifies employer for loss of property, owned by him or in his custody, through dishonesty of his employees.

Fiduciary or Probate Bond.—Guarantees faithful performance of court orders, and of official duties, as collection, safekeeping, distribution, and accounting, by official, as executor, administrator, trustee, receiver, appointed by court to administer estate funds.

Fine Arts Floater.—Indemnifies for loss or damage to scheduled objects of art, in named or any location, arising from all risks with exceptions, and from named perils.

Fire Insurance.—Indemnifies for stated term for loss or damage to specified property by fire.

Floater Policy, or Floater.—Covers mobile property not easily insured by specific forms because it changes value or location; in ocean marine insurance, covers cargo on any ships of approved lines.

Forfeiture Bond.—Type of bond that grants to obligee right to demand payment of full penalty for any infraction of bond conditions.

Forgery Bond.—Indemnifies for loss through forgery or alteration of negotiable instruments. There are many forms, as for depositors, financial institutions, and securities houses.

Fraternal Insurance.—A class of life insurance providing mutual protection, on the cooperative plan, to their members by noncapital stock societies. Such societies aim also to engender fellowship and benevolent helpfulness through activities of a lodge system.

Freights Insurance.—Covers freight as cargo, if at risk of cargo owners; covers voyage freight or charter hire for account of vessel owner.

Fur Floater.—Indemnifies individuals for loss or damage to furs and fur garments in any location arising from all risks with specified exclusions.

Furrier's Customers Floater.—Provides coverage for furrier against loss or damage to fur or fur-trimmed garments left for storage, alteration or repair.

Garage Liability Insurance.—Covers legal liability of garage owner arising from ownership, maintenance, or use of any automobile in insured's premises, and such liability arising from ownership, maintenance, occupation, or use of the insured premises.

Garment Contractor's Floater.—Provides coverage for manufacturer of clothing against named perils on premises of his contractors and their subcontractors, and against transit risks.

General Average.—In ocean marine insurance, a loss caused or extraordinary expense incurred by voluntary and successful act to avert common peril, requiring contribution by all insureds to indemnify interests affected by such loss or extraordinary expense.

General Average Bond.—Guarantees that owner of goods subject to general average will pay his proportionate contribution when ascertained; it is given to obtain immediate release of such goods.

Glass Insurance.—Indemnifies for loss through breakage from any cause except fire, and for damage through acids or chemicals, to various kinds of glass, including lettering and frames.

Group Annuity Policy.—Provides income to employees for life after retirement age.

Group Insurance.—Provides blanket coverage for a number of persons associated in a unit, as common employment or organization.

Hangar Keepers' Liability Coverage.—Special form of aircraft liability insurance, providing coverage for owners or operators of aircraft hangars.

Health Insurance.—Indemnifies for loss of time from occupation through sickness, and for hospital, nurse, and surgical expenses, and in one form also for medical expense; written only in combination with accident insurance.

Hospitalization Insurance. — Indemnifies for hospital and related charges incurred through accident or disease.

Hull Insurance.—See terms *Vessels, Hull Insurance; Aircraft Hull Insurance.*

Identification Indemnity Provision.—In accident insurance policy, undertakes to pay expense of notifying insured's relatives and putting him in their care, with limit usually of $100, if by reason of injury he is unable to communicate with them.

Indemnity Bond to Sheriff.—Type of court bond protecting sheriff against loss for wrongful attachment or sale of property.

Industrial Life Insurance.—Provides coverage similar to that of ordinary life insurance but not in so many forms and usually with earlier age of maturity; the amounts of insurance, determined by the age of the insured at the time of issuance of policy and by the amount of his premiums, are small, averaging less than $300, and the premiums are payable weekly or monthly.

Inland Marine Insurance.—A class of insurance embracing those forms that indemnify for loss or damage through sundry perils to various kinds of mobile property in transit.

Installment Floater.—Provides coverage for vendor, or vendor and vendee, against loss through transportation and fire hazards to property purchased by installments when title remains in vendor. This coverage may be extended also to other hazards.

Installments for Life Option.—Provides that upon the maturity of a life insurance policy a stated amount will be paid monthly, quarterly, semiannually, or annually for the life of beneficiary, or for a specified period to beneficiary and other specified persons.

Insurable Interest.—Exists when beneficiary has reason to desire continuance of life of insured person or property and would suffer economic loss by death or destruction of, or injury or damage to, such subject matter.

Insurance.—The act whereby for a consideration (the *premium*), one party (the *insurer*) binds himself in a contract (the *policy*) to indemnify or guarantee another (the *insured*) against loss through the happening of a specified contingency (the *risk*). Insurance may be classified (1) on the basis of the kind of subject matter insured, as *personal insurance,* including life, disability, and social insurance, or as *property insurance,* including fire, marine, casualty, liability, and fidelity insurance, and suretyship; and (2) with respect to the nature of the risk insured against, as involving *physical risks,* depending on location, structure, occupancy, and exposure, or *moral risks,* arising from such mental conditions as motivate dishonesty, negligence, and insanity.

Interest Option.—Provides that interest at stated rate on amount due on life insurance policy at maturity will be paid monthly, quarterly, semiannually, or annually to beneficiary. The principal sum by agreement is withdrawable or payable to other specified persons on the happening of a specified contingency.

Internal Revenue Bond.—Guarantees payment of taxes and compliance with regulations on certain products within the United States, as alcohol, spirits, beer, wine, gasoline, tobacco.

Joint Life Insurance.—A form of life insurance which is payable upon the first death of those named as the insured; it is written with various terms to meet individual needs and may be made payable to the survivor or survivors or to a third-party beneficiary.

Judicial Bond.—See term *Court or Judicial Bond.*

Leasehold Interest Insurance.—Provides coverage for holder of long lease if, when cancelled by lessor on happening of a peril, as fire, its rental is less than current rentals.

Liability Floater.—Covers legal liability of carrier to shipper or consignee for loss or damage to property transported.

Liability Insurance.—A class of insurance embracing those forms that cover legal liability of insured to others for bodily injury, death, or property damage; called also third-party insurance.

License Bond.—Guarantees compliance with law and regulations by persons engaged in certain enterprises that affect the public interest, as electricians, milk dealers, auctioneers, and amusement park operators.

Life Insurance.—See terms *Ordinary Life Insurance; Industrial Life Insurance.*

Limited Installment Option.—Provides that amount due on life insurance policy at maturity with interest will be paid monthly, quarterly, semiannually, or annually to beneficiary for a specified period or in specified amounts till the total is exhausted.

Limited Payment Life Insurance.—Provides coverage similar to that of ordinary life insurance, but premiums are due for specified period only, as for 10, 20, or 30 years.

Loss.—In insurance, the amount of diminution or destruction of the values of, or the amount of the charge upon, the insured by the direct consequence of the operation of the risk covered, according to the values specified in the policy; it constitutes a basis for a claim against the insurer.

Lost Instrument Bond.—Protects issuer of duplicate lost valuable paper against loss through reappearance of original.

Manufacturers' Public Liability Insurance. — Covers legal liability of insured for bodily injury or death arising from his business operations, including installing and servicing off premises.

Marine Liability Insurance.—Covers legal liability of insured to third parties for loss, damage, or expense arising from ownership, use, maintenance, repair or construction of any craft or instrumentality in use in ocean transportation, including liability for bodily injury, illness, or death.

Money and Securities Policies.—One form, *premises all risks* policy, provides coverage against loss of money and securities on premises caused by destruction, disappearance, or wrongful abstraction thereof, and damages to premises caused by robbery or burglary; another form, *messenger all risks* policy, provides coverage against loss of money and securities outside premises in transit by custodian, caused by destruction, disappearance, or wrongful abstraction thereof. Both forms exclude losses caused by dishonest employees, voluntary surrender of the property, or forgery.

Name Schedule Bond.—A fidelity bond covering employees listed, each for a fixed amount.

National Service Life Insurance.—Offered by the federal government with special provisions as to amounts of protection and terms of payment to men and women in the armed forces during wartime, the extra hazard of military service being assumed as a national risk.

Nation-Wide Definition and Interpretation of the Insuring Powers of Marine and Transportation Underwriters.—Statement approved by National Association of Insurance Commissioners, 1933, to clarify in certain respects the state insurance laws with reference to overlapping insuring powers of insurers, and to coverages involving misapprehension among fire, marine, and casualty insurers. It enumerates (1) conditions under which marine and/or transportation policies may cover imports, exports, domestic shipments, and personal property floater risks; and (2) conditions under which such policies shall not cover property.

Nonconcurrency.—Arises when terms of policies are not alike as to items covered, interests insured, or distribution clauses.

Nonforfeiture Provisions.—State benefits available to life insurance policyholders upon lapse of policy for nonpayment of premium; they are (1) cash surrender value, (2) paid-up insurance, and (3) extended term insurance. The third usually is automatically operative unless holder selects one of the other two.

Ocean Marine Insurance.—Covers vessels, cargoes and freights chiefly against sea perils (sinking, stranding, and collision), and incidental shore and inland risks.

Old Age Insurance.—A class of insurance embracing those forms—individual, group, or social—designed to provide financial security for aged persons.

Open Policy.—One in which the value of the subject matter insured has not been fixed but has been left to be determined in case of loss, or one in which the risk or subject matter insured is not fixed but is covered by insurer as reported by insured.

Optional Settlements.—Ways in which a life insurance policyholder or his beneficiary may elect to have applied the amount payable on the policy at maturity in lieu of one immediate cash payment; they are (1) interest option, (2) limited installment option, and (3) installments for life option.

Ordinary Life Insurance.—Provides coverage for life of insured; if he lives to age 96 the policy amount is paid to him in cash on that anniversary date.

Outage Insurance.—By endorsement on boiler and machinery insurance policy, indemnifies for increased cost of maintaining business without the damaged object.

Overinsurance.—Exists when insurance is written in an amount larger than is justified by the risk. It may occur, for example, in life, fire, or accident and health insurance.

Owners', Landlords', and Tenants' Public Liability Insurance.—Covers legal liability for bodily injury or death arising from ownership, maintenance, occupation, or use of insured premises.

Owners' and Contractors' Protective Liability Insurance.—Covers legal liability of owner or general contractor for bodily injury or death through acts respectively of his contractor or subcontractor.

Owners' Protective Contract Bond.—Guarantees owner that construction contract will be performed faithfully and that labor and material-men will be paid.

Paid-Up Insurance.—Amount of coverage available to life insurance policyholder upon and after he cancels his policy or permits it to lapse, without further premium payments; it is an optional nonforfeiture value and may not be less than the cash surrender value.

Parcel Post Insurance.—Indemnifies shipper for loss through all risks of package, insured or uninsured, registered or unregistered, in custody of Post Office Department till arrival at addressee's premises. There is a reporting form for monthly reports by larger shippers, and a coupon form, 100 to 1,000 coupons, for smaller shippers.

Partial Disability.—In accident insurance, injury that prevents insured from performing one or more important duties of his occupation.

Participating Insurance.—Refunds to insureds a portion of premiums, representing earnings by insuring company through excess interest received on investments, favorable mortality experience and savings in expenses. In nonparticipating insurance such earnings are anticipated in the premium rates, and company profits benefit the stockholders.

Particular Average.—In ocean marine insurance, loss of, or damage to, a particular interest (ship, cargo or freight) which is not general average.

Partnership Insurance.—May be written (1) insuring each partner for the amount of his capital, which is thus safeguarded for the use of the firm upon the death of the insured; or (2) insuring the partners in a joint life policy wherein upon the first death the amount is payable to the survivors and the insurance expires.

Pension Trust.—Provides income to employees for life after retirement age, premiums being contributed by employer and/or employees; separate policies usually are issued, though blanket policies also are written.

Permit Bond.—Guarantees compliance with law and regulations by persons operating on or under public property or in the air.

Personal Effects Floater.—Provides coverage for insured and family against all risks, with exceptions, of loss or damage to personal effects, as those of a tourist, with exclusions, in any location.

Personal Jewelry-Fur Floater.—Provides coverage for insured and family against all risks, with exceptions, of loss or damage to scheduled jewelry and furs in any location.

Personal Liability Insurance.—See term *Comprehensive Personal Liability Policy.*

Personal Property Floater.—Covers all personal property, with specified exceptions, of insured and family, wherever located, against all risks of loss or damage, with exclusions in certain cases.

Position Schedule Bond.—A fidelity bond covering positions listed for a fixed amount.

Power Interruption Insurance.—Indemnifies for consequential loss or spoilage arising from accident in public utility equipment causing interruption of service.

Primary Commercial Blanket Bond.—A fidelity bond providing coverage similar to that of blanket position bond, but differing in that it specifies amount available for any single loss rather than separate amounts for each employee.

Principal Sum.—Amount or portion thereof payable in accident insurance policy upon death or specified disability caused by accident.

Pro Rata Premium.—Charged when insurer cancels policy, or when insured cancels one policy and takes another with same insurer.

Probate Bond.—See term *Fiduciary or Probate Bond.*

Processing Floater.—Provides coverage for processor of goods, as cotton, silk and wool, against named perils on premises, and transit risks.

Products Public Liability Insurance.—Covers legal liability of insured for bodily injury or death through use, consumption, or existence of his product after he relinquishes it.

Professional Liability Insurance.—Covers legal liability of persons, as physicians, surgeons, dentists, and druggists, for bodily injury or death caused by malpractice, errors or mistakes of insured or his nurses or clerks.

Profits and Commissions Insurance.—Indemnifies manufacturer or middleman for loss of earned profits or commissions through damage to finished goods resulting from named peril.

Prospective Restoration Clause.—After discovery of loss on fidelity bond, restores face amount for losses subsequently occurring.

Public Liability Insurance.—A class of insurance embracing those forms that cover legal liability for bodily injury, death or property damage, except liability arising from maintenance, operation or use of automobiles. The common forms are: manufacturers' and contractors' liability; owners', landlords', and tenants' liability; elevator liability; owners' and contractors' protective liability; products liability; and contractual liability.

Public Official Bond.—For federal, state and local governments, guarantees faithful performance of official duties by public officials, and safekeeping and accounting of public funds. The form of bond usually is fixed by law.

Reduced Rate Average Clause.—See term *Coinsurance or Average Clause.*

Reinstatement. — Refers to reinstatement of policy amount after loss, or in life insurance to reinstatement of policy after lapsation.

Reinsurance.—A contract by which an insurance company procures a third party, commonly an insurance company, to insure it against loss or liability by reason of a policy it has written.

Rent, Rental Value Insurance.—Indemnifies owner-occupant when forced to evacuate premises as a result of fire for cost of rent in other premises during period of rehabilitation, or landlord for loss of normal rental income during enforced evacuation of tenants from a similar cause.

Reporting Form or Policy.—Covers fluctuating properties or risks, premium being based on periodic reports by insured.

Representation.—As applied to insurance, distinguished from warranty. See term *Warranty.*

Reserve.—In life insurance, portion of premium set aside and invested by insuring company to build up fund to meet future death claims.

Residence, Farm Liability Insurance.—A division of owners', landlords' and tenants' public liability insurance, includes garages and outbuildings, and injuries from pets on premises. Coverage for acts of dog off premises may be added by endorsement.

Residence and Outside Theft Insurance.—Indemnifies insured and entire family including guests and servants within premises for loss of property caused by burglary, robbery, theft, or larceny. Outside coverage without charge (except in New York City counties of Bronx, Kings, New York, and Queens) also is included except on guests.

Retroactive Restoration Clause.—After discovery of loss on fidelity bond, restores face amount for losses subsequently discovered.

Reversionary Interest.—Refers to benefits payable to a named beneficiary upon death of insured; while this term has general and wide application, specific policies, such as reversionary annuities, and deferred survivorship annuities, otherwise known as continuous installment policies, provide for payment of income benefits to a named beneficiary at death of the insured.

Rider.—A printed agreement attached to an insurance policy.

Scheduled Property Floater.—Provides coverage against loss or damage to a variety of named items of mobile property in any location, arising from specified or all risks.

Securities Insurance Policy (for Lessees of Safe Deposit Boxes).—Provides coverage against loss caused by destruction, disappearance, or wrongful removal of securities in, or from, leased safe deposit boxes. It excludes losses caused by dishonest employees or authorized representatives of the insured, or by voluntary surrender of the property by them or by the insured.

Securities Policy.—Provides coverage for financial institutions and brokerage houses against specified losses caused by defective securities. This coverage commonly is incorporated in bankers and brokers blanket bonds.

Settlement Options.—See term *Optional Settlements.*

Short Rate Premium.—Charged for less than one year, or when policy is cancelled by insured without reinsuring in same insurer.

Single Premium Life Insurance.—Provides coverage similar to that of ordinary life insurance, with total premium obligation paid in one amount.

Social Insurance.—A general class of insurance embracing those forms designed to protect wage earners and their dependents, as workmen's compensation, old age, unemployment, accident and health insurance.

Specific Policy or Form.—Covers at a specific location against hazards insured.

Sports Liability Insurance.—Covers legal liability of insured for bodily injury or death arising from his activity in athletic sport or game, except professional activity.

Superseded Suretyship Rider.—Endorsement on new fidelity bond, providing continuous coverage with replaced bond.

Supplemental Contract or Deposit Receipt.—Is in effect a receipt issued by a life insurance company to a claimant under a life insurance policy for funds held for the claimant's benefit under settlement options, (1) interest, (2) life annuity, 10, 15, or 20 years certain, (3) payment of principal and interest over a specified period of years, or (4) a specified income for as long as the proceeds will last.

Supply Bond.—Guarantees that supplier of goods will perform terms of his contract.

Suretyship.—An undertaking by one party (the *surety*) guaranteeing performance by another party (the *principal*) of an obligation with a third party (the *obligee*).

Surrender Value.—See term *Cash Surrender Value.*

Teachers' Liability Insurance.—Covers legal liability of teachers and faculty members for bodily injury or death arising from personal acts in connection with their profession.

Term Insurance.—Provides coverage for a specified period, the policy amount being payable if insured dies during the period.

Third-Party Insurance.—See term *Liability Insurance.*

Time Policy.—In ocean marine insurance, provides coverage for vessel or cargo or both for a specified period of time.

Title Insurance. — Indemnifies real estate owner or mortgagee for loss arising from defective title, or encumbrances.

Tontine Policy.—Provides that at the end of a specified period the surplus fund shall be distributed among those in their class who have kept their policies in force, the lapsing members of each class forfeiting their rights and receiving nothing and the reserve values of their lapsed policies being credited to the surplus fund.

Total Disability.—In accident insurance, injury that prevents insured from performing any and every duty of his occupation.

Total Loss.—In ocean marine insurance, a total loss occurs when the subject matter is entirely destroyed or so damaged that it is of no use or value to the insured, or when the insured is deprived entirely of his property; see term *Constructive Total Loss.* In fire insurance, a total loss occurs when the subject matter loses the essential character of the property insured; complete physical destruction usually is not required by the term, provided the remaining portion, though unburned, cannot profitably be utilized.

Transportation Insurance.—A general class of insurance embracing those forms that indemnify for losses arising from transportation risks. In inland marine insurance, it is the basic form of in-transit coverage with many optional endorsements or riders for specific coverages.

Underwriter.—In insurance, one who appraises and selects risks submitted for insurance; by extension, commonly one who solicits insurance business and submits it to insurance company for acceptance.

Unearned Premium Endorsement.—Indemnifies for loss of portion of paid premium caused by reduction of policy amount through loss.

Unemployment Insurance.—A class of insurance embracing those forms designed to provide relief for wage earners and their dependents during periods of unemployment.

Unknown Hazards.—A hazard within the scope of the coverage but the existence of which with respect to the individual risk is unknown.

Use and Occupancy Insurance.—See term *Business Interruption Insurance.*

Valued Policy.—States within the instrument itself the amount to be paid in case of loss, thus avoiding determination of such amount after loss by appraisal or adjustment.

Vessels, Hull Insurance.—Covers ocean-going vessels, yachts, barges, and tugs on annual basis or for specific voyages.

Voyage Policy—In ocean marine insurance, provides coverage for vessel or cargo or both from one designated port to another; more than one voyage may be covered in one policy.

Wager Policy.—In insurance, one in which the insured has no insurable interest in the subject matter insured; being considered generally as a form of gambling, such a policy is not valid except where the validity of a wager may be recognized. In ocean marine insurance, agreements, often called "honor agreements," may be written where the interest of the insured is difficult or impossible to prove.

Warehouse Bond.—Guarantees validity of receipt given for property by warehouseman, or payment of duty and taxes, and compliance with regulations, on property received by warehouseman.

Warranty.—As applied to insurance, a statement or engagement by insured which if not true or fulfilled voids the insurance contract. It is distinguished from a representation, which is an inducement and need be only substantially true or fulfilled.

Workmen's Compensation Insurance.—Assumes obligation of insured under workmen's compensation laws and covers his legal liability for bodily injury or death to employees whose employment does not fall within such laws.

WOODHULL HAY,
Educational Editor, "The Weekly Underwriter."

INSURRECTION, the act of rising against governmental authorities, active opposition to the power of the state. In the United States, power to suppress insurrections by employing the militia is given to Congress by the Constitution, Art. I, Sec. 8, Clause 15. In 1792 and 1807 acts were passed giving the president power to call forth the militia when notified by an associate justice of the Supreme Court or a district judge that the execution of the laws is obstructed, and on application of a legislature or a governor, when the legislature could not be convened, and to employ also the land and naval forces of the United States. The Whisky Insurrection (q.v.) was directed against the federal authority and the president employed force to suppress it on notification by the federal judge. During the Buckshot War (q.v.), in 1838, between the Whigs and Democrats in Pennsylvania, the governor of that state asked for assistance, but it was refused. The governor of Rhode Island made a similar application during the Dorr Rebellion (q.v.) and the regulars were held ready for action, but their aid proved unnecessary. These last two cases came under Art. IV, Sec. 4, of the federal Constitution, which provides "that the United States shall protect" each state on application of the legislature, or of the executive, against domestic violence.

When the Civil War began the president was obliged to take prompt steps in calling out the militia, though no application had been made to him as required by the acts of 1792 and 1795. His action was justified by Art. II, Sec. 3, of the Constitution, providing that "he shall take care that the laws be faithfully executed," but Congress on Aug. 6, 1861 formally validated and made legal all of President Lincoln's previous acts, proclamations and orders. The Force Bill (q.v.) of 20 April 1871 gave the President special power to use military force in certain contingencies. In the South during the reconstruction period, and in the North, during strike riots, Federal troops have been used.

INTAGLIO, a method of cutting a stone or gem by which the design is cut or hollowed out — not raised, as in a cameo. In art, the term means the opposite of relief, denoting the representation of a subject by hollowing out a gem or other substance; so that an impression from the engraving has the appearance of a bas-relief. Intaglio letters have been effectively used in printing in recent years, and much of the effectiveness of colored printing is due in large measure to a process or processes closely akin to intaglio.

INTEGRAL CALCULUS, a branch of infinitesimal calculus, treating of the methods of deducing relations between *finite* values of variables from given relations between contemporaneous infinitesimal elements of those variables. It is thus the inverse of the differential calculus. Its object is to discover the primitive function from which a given differential coefficient has been derived. This primitive function is called the integral of the proposed differential coefficient, and is obtained by the application of the different principles established in finding differential coefficients and by various transformations. To illustrate — with the integral calculus one may discover the relations connecting finite values of variables, as x and y, from the relation connecting their differentials, as dx and dy. Integral calculus is thus the doctrine of the limit of the sum of infinitesimals of which the number increases, while the magnitude decreases, both without limit, yet according to some law. The more proper concern of the integral calculus is besides the finding and discussion of integrals, with such matters as the theory of spherical harmonics, the theory of residuation, and parts of the theory of functions. The sign of integration is «$\int$,» which is a form derived from the old or long «*s*.» It is the initial of the word «sum,» and came into use owing to the conception that integration is the process of summing an infinite series of infinitesimals. Before even the notation of the differential calculus and its rules were discovered by Gottfried Wilhelm von Leibnitz (1646–1716), he had invented the notation and had found some of the rules of the integral calculus. Leibnitz first used the now well-known sign «$\int$» or long «*s*» as short for the «sum of» when considering the sum of an infinity of infinitesimals as is done in the method of indivisibles. Leibnitz himself attributed all his mathematical discoveries to his improvements in notation; and the fact that we still use and appreciate Leibnitz's «$\int$» (and one must add his «*d*») even though our views as to the principles are very different from those of his school, is perhaps the best testimony to the question of notation. The integral calculus may be distinguished from the differential calculus by another feature than inversion; namely, by the greater importance in it of imaginaries. The integral calculus is frequently called the indirect or inverse method of fluxions, the analytic processes by which a function may be found such that being differentiated it shall produce the given differential. By writers on «fluxions» this function is called the «fluent» or the flowing quantity. By writers on the infinitesimal calculus it is called the integral of the proposed differential. The origin and constitution of quantities is called «fluxions» in the scheme of Sir Isaac Newton (1642–1727), because conceived to express the manner of generation of quantities by the motion of other quantities. In the scheme of Leibnitz the language employed is «infinitesimals» or «differences»; because they are conceived to express the constant addition of one indefinitely small quantity to another. In the scheme of Newton, or «fluxions,» the finding of the sum of all differences is called the «inverse» or the «indirect method.» It is thus that this method of obtaining the quantity generated is identical with the method of finding the «fluents.» And this same method in the language of Leibnitz is called «integration» or the finding of the «integrals.» The two systems are therefore in no respect whatever different except in their origin and in their language; their rules, principles, applications and results are for all practical purposes the same. In Newton's system an «$\int$» or f is used to express the «fluent.»

To find the integral of a differential is to integrate that differential, and this process by which this integral is found is called integration. With the integral calculus a mathematician endeavors to transform the given expressions into others which are differentials of known functions, and thus deduce formulas which may be applied to all similar forms. The number of such formulas is said to be unlimited. The collection of Meyer Hirsch is a well arranged and though originally published long ago at Berlin is still useful.

Sir Isaac Newton (1642–1727) undoubtedly arrived at the principles and practice of a method equivalent to the infinitesimal calculus generally much earlier than Leibnitz, and, like Roberval, his conceptions were obtained from the dynamics of Galileo. He considered curves to be described by moving points. An «arc» thus became the «fluent» of the velocity of the point with which it is supposed to be described. Newton's notation (it must be admitted) for the «inverse method of fluxions» was far clumsier, even, and far inferior to Leibnitz's «$\int$,» the long «*s*.» And it was owing to the long acrimonious dispute between Newton and Leibnitz, mixed up with insinuations anent what is sometimes mistakenly called «patriotism,» that for considerably more than a century British mathematicians failed to perceive the great superiority of the «notation» of Leibnitz. In fact it was not until the beginning of the 19th century that there was formed, at Cambridge, a society to introduce and spread the use of Leibnitz's notation among British mathematicians.

«It may be said» (we quote Sophus Lie) «that the conceptions of differential quotient and *integral*, which in their origin certainly go back to Archimedes, were introduced into modern science by the investigations of Kepler, Descartes, Cavalieri, Fermat and Wallace. . . . The capital discovery that differentiation and integration are *inverse* operations belongs to Newton and Leibnitz» (in *Leipziger Berichte* XLVII, 1895, Math.-phys. Classe, p. 53). And indeed in the opinion of one who has contributed much to the advancement of American mathematics as well as of Britain (indeed, of the world!), J. J. Sylvester, "it seems to be expected of every pilgrim up the slopes of the mathematical Parnassus, that he will at some point or other of his journey sit down and invent a definite integral or two toward the increase of the common stock." (See CALCULUS, INFINITESIMAL and consult his 'Notes to the Meditation of Poncellet's Theorem,' Mathematical Papers, Vol II, p. 214). Consult also Archimedes of Syracuse 'On Method'; with an introduction by David Eugene Smith and an English translation by Lydia G. Robinson (Chicago); Cavalieri, 'Geometria Indivisibilium' (1635); Cheyne, 'Fluxionum Methodus Inversa' (1703); Condorcet, 'Du Calcul Integral' (1765); Craig, 'De Calculo Fluentium' (1718); Descartes, 'Letters,' 'Geometry,' etc. (1637); Euler, 'Institutiones Calculi Integralis' (3 vols., Saint Petersburg 1768–70); Fermat, 'Opera Varia Mathematica' (1679); Hymer's 'Intégral Calculus' (1844); Kepler, 'Nova Stereometria Doliorum Vinariorum' (1615); La Place, 'L'Usage du Calcul aux Differénces Partielles,' (1777); Leibnitz, 'Quadrature of the Circle' (1682) and 'Nova Methodus pro Maximis et Minimis itemque Tangentibus' (1684); Newton, 'De Analysi per Æquationes Numero Terminorum Infinitas' (1669 and 1712); 'Principia' (1687); and 'The Method of Fluxions' (1736); Picard, E., 'Traité d'Analyse,' 4 vols. (1891).

Among recent works are: Berg, E. J., 'Heavisides Operational Calculus' (New York 1929); Bush, V., 'Operational Circuit Analysis' (New York 1929); Carson, J. R., 'Electric Circuit Theory and the Operational Calculus' (New York 1926); Fine, H. B., 'Calculus' (New York 1927); Forsyth, A. R., 'Calculus of Variations' (Cambridge 1927); Granville, W. A., 'Elements of the Differential and Integral Calculus' (Boston 1929); Griffin, F. L., 'Mathematical Analysis' (Boston 1936); Haefner, P., 'Einfuehrung in die Differential und Integralrechnung' (Stuttgart 1912); Hunter, W., 'Groundwork of Calculus' (London 1929); Jeffreys, H., 'Operational Methods in Mathematical Physics' (Cambridge 1927); Koestler, W. and M. Tramer, 'Differential, und Integralrechnung' (Berlin 1913); Miles, E. J. and J. S. Mikesh, 'Calculus' (New York 1930); Kestelman, H., 'Modern Theories of Integration' (New York 1937); Michell, J. H., and Belz, M. H., 'Elements of Mathematical Analysis' (New York 1937).

INTEGRAL EQUATIONS. An integral equation is an equation connecting two variables, an independent variable x, and a dependent variable u, in which u occurs (in at least one term) under the sign of integration. An example of such an equation is

$$(1)\ f(x) = g(x)u(x) + \int_a^b K(x, t)u(t)\,dt,$$

in which $f(x)$ and $g(x)$ are given functions of x, $K(x, t)$ is a given function of x and t, and a, b are known functions of x, one or both of which may be constant. The above equation is called *linear*, since u enters to the first degree only. It is *homogeneous* when $f(x)$ is identically zero. It is the most general form of linear equation. The fundamental problem connected with eq. (1) is to solve *it* for the unknown u; that is, to express u as a known function of x.

The theory of integral equations is the most recent development of importance in the domain of pure mathematics. The foundation for a general theory of such equations was laid by Volterra in several papers published in Italian scientific journals in 1896. Since then this new field has developed with great rapidity and already has an extensive literature. In spite of this rapid growth the magnitude and difficulties of the problem in its general form are such that only the simplest cases have been worked out with any degree of completeness. These cases group themselves under the following four types:

I. Volterra's equation of the 1st kind:

$$f(x) = \int_0^x K(x, t)u(t)\,dt;$$

II. Volterra's equation of the 2d kind:

$$f(x) = u(x) + \lambda\int_0^x K(x, t)u(t)\,dt;$$

III. Fredholm's equation of the 1st kind:

$$f(x) = \int_0^1 K(x, t)u(t)\,dt;$$

IV. Fredholm's equation of the 2d kind:

$$f(x) = u(x) + \lambda\int_0^1 K(x, t)u(t)\,dt.$$

The function $K(x, t)$ is called the *kernel* of the given equation (It., nucleo; Fr., noyau; Ger., Kern); λ is an arbitrary constant.

These types include the equations that naturally present themselves in connection with other branches of mathematics or in the solution of physical problems. It was, in fact, from such sources that integral equations began to claim the attention of mathematicians and to press for a systematic investigation. The first attempt to solve an integral equation occurs in a memoir by Abel, published in 1823 in connection with the following mechanical problem: To determine the arc of a curve situated in a vertical plane such that a heavy particle starting at rest from the highest point P of the arc and moving by the attraction of gravity along the curve to its lowest point O, shall make the descent in a time $f(h)$ which is required to be a given function of the vertical altitude h between O and P. This problem leads to the integral equation

$$\sqrt{2g}\,f(h) = \int_0^h \frac{u(y)\,dy}{\sqrt{h-y}}$$

in which $2g$ is the acceleration due to gravity, approximately 32, and $u(y)$ is the unknown function $\sqrt{1+\left(\frac{dx}{dy}\right)^2}$, x and y being the rectangular coördinates of a variable point on the required curve. It will be observed that Abel's equation is of Type I, with $K(h, y) = \frac{1}{\sqrt{h-y}}$. Abel found the solution of this equation to be

$$u(y) = \frac{\sqrt{2g}}{\pi}\frac{d}{dy}\int_0^y \frac{f(h)\,dh}{\sqrt{y-h}}.$$

The simplest case is that in which $f(h)$ is constant. This is the celebrated problem of the tautochrone, which may be stated as follows: To find an arc of a curve such that a heavy particle descending along it under the action of gravity shall arrive at the lowest point in the same time, from whatever point of the curve the point begins to fall. This solution readily leads, in this case, to an inverted cycloid with its vertex at the lowest point.

Niels Abel was the first to perceive the essential character of integral equations and to make some effort to develop a method for their solution. He applied his ideas to the more general equation.

$$f(x) = \int_0^x \frac{u(t)\,dt}{(x-t)^a}, 0 < a < 1,$$

for which he obtained a solution by the aid of infinite series. This method is not regarded, however, as satisfactory and cannot therefore be considered as affording a basis for a general theory. In the interval between Abel's first paper and Vito Volterra's fundamental work, several writers had occasion to solve integral equations in connection with problems of mathematical physics. Joseph Liouville (1832), who was the next after Abel to consider this subject, and who apparently was unaware of the work of his predecessor, was led to Abel's equation in connection with various physical problems. He introduced the method of successive substitutions which has recently been made applicable to much more difficult equations. The first attempt to solve an equation of the Fredholm type was by Carl Neumann (1877) in his method for the solution of Peter G. L. Dirichlet's problem. This consists in developing $u(x)$ in increasing powers of λ. But Neumann's development, while converging in the case of Dirichlet's problem, does not converge in the general case. Neumann's method was applied with success, however, by Volterra to the general equation of Type II. In a brilliant memoir published by the Swedish mathematician Erik Fredholm, in 1903, a general method for solving equations of types III and IV was given, thus completing, at least in outline, the theory for linear equations.

While integral equations have found their greatest usefulness in the field of applied mathematics, they are of importance also in connection with other lines of pure mathematics, such as Theory of Functions, Calculus of Variations and Differential Equations. In the first of these, mention has already been made of the fundamental problem of Dirichlet: To determine the values of a harmonic function within a region bounded by a closed curve, given the value of the function at every point of the boundary. It is with differential equations, however, that this subject has the closest contact. In many cases a single integral equation is the equivalent of a differential equation together with certain auxiliary equations of condition. Liouville, in 1837, solved a differential equation by means of an integral equation in order to express the desired solution in the form of a series which should converge with sufficient rapidity. In dealing with equations containing more than one independent variable, the integral equation has this advantage over the corresponding partial differential equation, in that the extension from one variable to several variables offers no appreciable increase in difficulty in the former case, while the difficulty is seriously augmented in the latter case. There has also been developed a theory of integro-differential equations which involve not only the unknown function $u(x)$ but its derivatives as well. These are likewise of importance in physical problems.

For a detailed exposition of the theory of integral equations, consult: Ballantyne, J., *The Integral Calculus—New Methods and Theorems* (Boston 1919); Buhl, A., *Les Théories Einsteinennes et les Principes du Calcul Intégral* (Paris 1922).

J. I. HUTCHINSON,
Late Professor of Mathematics, Cornell University.

INTEGRAPHS. See INTEGRATORS.

INTEGRATORS and **INTEGRAPHS**, instruments for ascertaining the area, moments and moments of inertia relative to any axis of any figure by tracing its outline. They facilitate finding displacement, moments of stability and inertia, center of gravity, etc., of ships; the tensile strength, resistance and safe load of beams, girders, cables and the contents of embankments, cuts, etc.

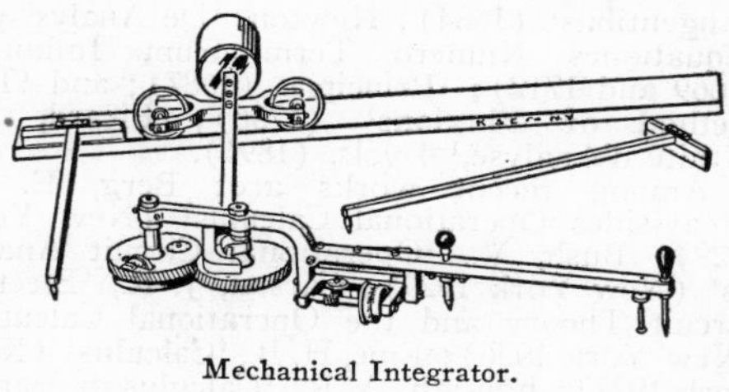

Mechanical Integrator.

The readings of the integrator multiplied by the constants of the instrument give area, and moment, and with some instruments, moment of inertia. From point readings of the integrator, the integral curve can be computed and plotted, while the integraph draws the integral curve as the operator traces the outline of the original figure. The ordinate of the integral curve multiplied by the constant of the integraph gives the area of the original figure. By tracing the integral curve and proceeding in the same manner, the moment of the original figure is obtained. Continued repetitions of the operation give the moment of inertia and moments of the 4th, 5th, etc. order. These instruments are of great value in shipbuilding and various kinds of construction.

INTELLECT, in philosophy and in psychology, the thinking principle of a mental constitution. The word is derived from the Latin *intellectus,* discernment by the senses, from *intellegere* or *intelligere; intellectus—a,—um* is derived from *inter* between and *legere* to gather, or to collect, or to choose; and thus conveys the general idea of "that which has power to choose between." In modern psychology intellect is the designation of the whole cognitive power as distinguished from feeling, sensation, volition and conation.

INTELLECTUALISM, in philosophy, theories which emphasize the intellect as contrasted with the affective and volitional aspects of consciousness. In philosophy it applies, for example, to Herbart's doctrine of presentations, in which cognitive experiences are made primary in the explanation of mind. The historical antithesis between sensation and intellect gives the term intellectualism to theories which find the ultimate nature of reality in some form of thought or reason. By some reality is reduced to intellectual relations. In æsthetics the view of intellectualism regards the ideas suggested by an object as the important factors in beauty. Recent philosophic thought, however, is departing from the crass intellectualism of even a few years ago. Bergson is the greatest figure who has opposed intellectualism in our day.

INTELLIGENCE. See INTELLECT.

INTELLIGENCE IN ANIMALS. See ANIMAL, MIND IN THE BRUTE.

INTENSITY OF SENSATION. Every sensation has at least four attributes: Quality, clearness, duration and intensity. No one of these can be further defined than to say it is an aspect of immediate experience. By intensity of sensation, therefore, is meant that aspect of experience which, for example, we ascribe to tones as loud or faint, to colors as bright or dull, to pressures as heavy or light, to tastes and smells as strong or weak. It is important to distinguish between intensity of a sensation and intensity of stimulus. The latter is physical, and is always measurable by some physical unit; the physical intensity of tones, for example, may be measured by amount of physical energy, weights by number of grams or ounces, lights by so much candle power, etc.

Intensity of sensation is partially conditioned upon intensity of stimulus. There are stimuli, however, which do not give rise to sensation; some tones are too faint to be heard, some weights too light to be felt, some solutions too weak to arouse taste, etc. We have then, as a first problem, to determine the intensity of stimulus which will just produce a sensation. Such a determination, to be valid, must be made under rigorously controlled conditions; the possibilities of error on the part of the observer are so numerous that the same type of methodical procedure is as necessary for its determination as for the just noticeable difference. (See DISCRIMINATION, SENSIBLE). The magnitude representing the stimulus which just arouses a sensation is known as the stimulus-limen, or RL. This may be defined as that stimulus which, in 50 per cent of a large number of observations, is reported as «present,» while in the remaining 50 per cent it is reported as «not present.» It is a calculated value; and like the DL, it is an ideal, a most probable value.

We may, nevertheless, think of the RL as a point somewhere on the scale of stimulus-intensity. The lower limit of this scale is zero intensity and it is, therefore, below the RL; the upper limit is infinity, since theoretically we may gradually increase the energy of a tonal vibration, add candle power to candle power, pile gram upon gram without end. The intensity of sensation which corresponds to the RL is, on the other hand, the zero point of the scale of sensation-intensities; theoretically, the upper limit of this scale is again infinity; but practically it is subject to the capacity of the sense-organ.

We have seen that the unit of the stimulus scale is some physical unit like the gram or candle-power. What now is the unit of the sensation scale? The answer to this question is fundamental to the larger problem of mental measurement. Until the middle of the last century philosophers had said that mental measurement was impossible because there was no unit of measurement in terms of sensation itself. Nevertheless, the astronomers had already divided the stars into six magnitudes, and it has since been found that the difference in intensity between a star of the first and one of the second magnitude is approximately equal to that between stars of the second and third, third and fourth, fourth and fifth and fifth and sixth. Each magnitude is, then, a point on a scale, the points are equi-distant as measured by differences in intensity, and the difference between any two contingous points may be taken as the unit of the scale. We may say, therefore, that the difference between stars of the first and sixth magnitude is five times the difference between the first and second magnitudes. Such a unit, which we may call a supra-liminal difference, is, of course, an arbitrary one, but it has proved to be adequate to the measurement of intensity in nearly if not all sense departments. A unit which gives less direct measurements but which has a greater range of applicability, because its magnitude is expressed in terms of the stimulus, is the just noticeable difference or the DL. We cannot assume off hand, to be sure, that all least differences are equal, that least steps at various parts of the scale are equal steps, but the experimental evidence is, on the whole, favorable to this assumption.

What now, it may be asked, is the relation between the two scales, the one of stimulus differences, the other of intensity differences? Do equal differences in intensity of sensation correspond with equal differences of intensity of stimulus? In seeking the answer to this problem we may employ either of our two units of sensation. We have only to determine the physical intensity of every point on the supraliminal scale, and then see whether the physical differences are or are not equal to the sensation differences; or, employing the other unit, to take a number of DL's from some portion of the scale and then compare the differences between their magnitudes. Since these magnitudes are expressed in terms of the stimulus, the relation of their differences will furnish an immediate answer to our question.

We find, whichever unit we employ, that the two scales do not correspond point for point, that equal differences in intensity of sensation correspond rather with *relatively* equal differences in the intensity of stimulus. Let us suppose, for example, that the points on the sensation scale form an arithmetical series like 1, 2, 3, 4, etc., then the points on the stimulus scale to which these will correspond will form a geometrical series like 2, 4, 8, 16, etc., or like 3, 9, 27, 81, etc.; the exponent of the geometrical series varies with the sense department — for noise it is 4/3, for light 101/100. This law, which is known as Weber's Law (q.v.), explains many phenomena of everyday life which, however, are so common that they often fail to excite our notice. The relation of black print to the white page seems always the same, yet the intensity of sunlight changes with every hour of the day; the painter is able to simulate a natural scene, yet he cannot begin to reproduce the actual intensities of light and shadow by means of his pigments; the same musical composition may be rendered by orchestra and again by piano without loss of dynamic effect, yet the intensity of the former is much greater than that of the piano. All these result from the fact that the sense impressions depend not upon their absolute but upon their relative likeness. Consult: Adrian, E. D., 'The Basis of Sensation' (New York 1928); Myers, C. S., 'Textbook of Experimental Psychology' (London 1910); Pradines, M., 'Philosophie de la Sensation' (Paris 1928); Stopford, J. S. B., 'Sensation and the Sensory Pathway' (London 1930); Roberts, H. A., 'Sensations As If—' (New York 1937); Titchener, E. B., 'Experimental Psychology,' 3 vols. (New York 1927); Troland, L. T., 'The Mystery of Mind' (New York 1926); Valentine, C. W., 'Introduction to Experimental Psychology' (London 1926); Watt, H. J., 'The Sensory Basis and Structure of Knowledge' (1925).

Harry P. Weld,
Assistant Professor of Psychology, Cornell University.

INTENT, Common, a law term: in the rules of legal construction, the natural sense given to words. It is the rule that when words are used which will bear a natural sense and an artificial one, or one to be made out by argument or inference, the natural sense shall prevail. It is simply the rule of construction and not of addition. Common intent cannot add to a sentence words which have been omitted. (2 H. Blackst. 530). In pleading, certainty is required; but certainty to a common intent is sufficient; that is to say, what upon reasonable construction may be called certain, without recurring to possible facts. (Co. Litt. 203-a, Dougl. 163).

INTENT, INTENTION or INTENDMENT, in criminal law and in the law of evidence: the purpose; formulated design; a resolve to do or forbear a particular act; aim; determination; end; object,—which a person may have. It is not synonymous with motive, attempt, or, as some think, with promise. In its literal sense, the stretching of the mind or will toward a particular object.

To render an act criminal or wrongful, intent must exist. And with this intent must be combined a wrongful act, mere intent is not punishable. And generally, perhaps always, intent and act must concur in point of time. But wrongful intent may render criminal an act otherwise lawful.

Intent is in a certain sense essential to the commission of a crime, and in some classes of cases it is necessary to show moral turpitude, but there is a class of cases where purposely doing a thing prohibited by statute may amount to an offense though the act does not involve moral wrong. When shippers pay a rate when under honest belief that it is the lawful rate when it is not, we have an instance of this.

Some jurists incline to a somewhat James-like (see Intent in psychology) interpretation of Intent, even in law. Intent «is the exercise of intelligent will, the mind being fully aware of the nature and consequences of the act which is about to be done, and with such knowledge, and with full liberty of action, willing and electing to do it.» Among such interpretations see Burrills (Circ. Ev. 284, and notes). To accept this method, however, appears to mean the acceptance of «Intent» in what at the beginning of this article is called the «literal sense» rather than the «legal.»

A wrong done to the person or property of another is punishable at law without consideration of the intentions of the person committing the violence or trespass. But when an engagement has been made by person, or a written disposition of property executed, the intention of the person making the engagement or signing the deed is fair matter for legal inquiry. In this connection a subsequent stipulation by word of mouth is not competent to nullify or modify the terms of a written engagement. Intent also forms an important part in suits for defamation, fraud and negligence. Negligence must have intent to make it criminal, so must defamation and fraud and malicious mischief. Consult Thayer, 'Preliminary Treatise on Evidence' (1898); Black, 'Construction and Interpretation of Laws' (1896); Hardcastle, 'Rules which govern the Construction and Effect of Statutory Law' (1900).

INTENT, or INTENT OF CONSCIOUSNESS, in psychology is virtually identical with the goal of conscious endeavor at a specific moment in time. In German the word *meinen* is probably the nearest equivalent to our word Intent, though either *Sagenwollen,* or the phrase *in Sinne haben* might answer the purpose equally as well. French psychology employs «intention»; Italian, «intento.» Modern English «Intent» may also be compared with M.E. the Fr. and O.F. «entent,» attention, purpose. All these words, except those of German psychology mentioned above, are in ultimate origin from the Latin word «intentum,» or «intensum,» the past participle of the Latin verb «intendere,» meaning «to intend,» «to extend,» «to stretch out.»

The psychologist James employs «intent» in a manner peculiar to his system of psychology, to designate what intelligent consciousness «means or intends.» As stated it is not usually employed in this sense by psychologists. Its usual sense is implied in the definition given at the beginning of this article, and this is a sense which marks a certain point of view from which one may regard an «object.» It is almost a law, that in any conscious process having unity of interest there must also exist a corresponding unity of object. This is shown by Baldwin. Exceptions are rather apparent than real. Partial presentations, of course, come before consciousness as appearances, but as appearances, always of one and the same total object, which consciousness is endeavoring to know in its completeness. If our interest be merely attainment of knowledge, fuller, more definite, or more vivid, the object, as it becomes more perfectly known, is identical with the object as previously less perfectly known. For it is, says Baldwin, what the mind consciously means or intends. While one's attention is constantly employed upon an object, the end pursued becomes progressively defined in the process of its achievement. And in so far as such an object remains indefinite, or partially developed in consciousness, it is an intent. The result of a concrete mental determination, that state in which any specific process in consciousness issues and completes itself, is known as «End-state» (the German *Enzu-stand,* the French *etat final,* and the Italian *stato finale*).

Bradley employs «content» in a sense analogous to that in which intent is understood under the definition of it given at the head of this article. Content in this sense, however, is peculiar to Bradley. For as ordinarily applied, content (of consciousness) means all special modifications of conscious experience, whatever may be their nature, and not merely objects of consciousness. Pleasure or pain are thus part of the content of consciousness, but neither are always an object or an intent of consciousness.

Intent is the consciousness, obiterdicta, of the general nature of the end-state, and is mental progress toward an ideal we have successive stages of intent.

INTERCALARY («called or proclaimed between»), the day added to February in leap-year, also the month or days occasionally inserted in the calendar to make it correspond with the solar year. In botany, the term is applied to the growth of the cell-wall when a new deposition takes place in such a manner that an interposed piece of cell-wall from time to time appears. See CALENDAR.

INTERCESSION, Doctrine of, a theological tenet founded on the Scriptural representation of Christ, who having made the redemption an accomplished fact on earth ascended to plead with his heavenly Father for the sinners redeemed by the shedding of His blood. We are not to suppose that God needs to be interceded with in the sense that he is reluctant to pardon sinners, or that he becomes more disposed to do so through the pleading of Christ. Since it is evident from the whole tenor of the New Testament, as well as from a multitude of special passages, that the sacrifice of Christ on Calvary for the reconciling of sinners unto God was itself the offering of God's own love to the world (John iii, 16–17), we must regard the intercessory work of Christ rather as illustrating the eternal holiness of God and the changeless love of the Saviour, and as intended to keep continually in view the sacrifice of atoning grace whose tender mercy it develops. This doctrine is common alike to Catholics and Protestants. Catholics, however, believe that the Blessed Virgin and the saints intercede indirectly through the Saviour, who alone has the ear of the King of the universe. Mohammed is regarded as a powerful intercessor by his followers.

INTERCHANGEABLE PARTS, of industrial or military implements, are the key to all the vast expansion of modern manufacturing. Without these, only a small fraction of it, and consequently of new population human or animal, agriculture, engineering and industrial civilization in general, could have come into being. A glance at its implications will show that this seemingly extravagant proposition is sober fact.

The principle of interchangeability affects production in two ways: through the original manufacturing, and through repairing. In manufacture it makes possible the turning out, in separate departments, in vast masses at full speed, in exact shape for immediate assembling, of all the individual parts used in great numbers in complicated machines, from the screws of a watch to the rivets of a giant steamship. Without this, the different parts would require an army of fitters to make them work with each other, and indefinitely more time for assembling, hence a much diminished production and higher expense. In repair, if every replaced part of a watch or sewing-machine, a gun or a reaper, had to be individually filed or hammered or reforged into adjustment, the delay and expense would greatly decrease the articles' use and the work done by their means; and for military service, repair would involve so much remanufacturing on the field as to make modern warfare quite impracticable. Now, reflecting that the multiplication of men is conditioned by that of goods and employment, of food by farms and transportation, of the latter by engineering, and so on, the conclusion above is easily substantiated.

Owing to mechanical niceties to be explained later, the principle did not attain much close accuracy in use till toward the middle of the last century; and as might be expected, was first developed in making firearms, where masses of lives were involved and the highest of stakes to be won. The Springfield, Mass., armory was the first to bring it to a high grade of embodiment. Somewhat later, the Waltham Watch Company applied it, under much more difficult conditions, to the minute, sometimes almost microscopic, parts of its watches. The constant effort of all large implement manufacturing for many years has been toward perfecting its application; and its success largely gauges the increased use of machinery in place of men, and of mechanical utilities.

The first requisite is obviously that each part shall come within very small limits of variation, neither stick nor «shuck»; the one stopping or slacking movement and increasing frictional wear and heat, the other making movement ineffective and irregular and breakages likely. Or if, say, a fuse, its cavity must hold pretty closely the same amount of explosive to determine time and goal. Hence the standards of accuracy and craftsmanship must be kept very high; in the long run it is most economical if worth attempting at all. Any saving on expense by slighting severe requirements is more than sunk on increased cost in assembling, to say nothing of rejected work and impaired reputation.

While every step must help to ensure this uniformity, it must be frankly accepted that there is a certainty of some error in each; and the proper course is not to attempt eliminating it wholly — an impossible task, and beyond a certain limit costing more than it is worth,— but to determine the limits up to which it is neglectible, and hold it within them. Constant accurate measurement for those limits is therefore the basic need; and the limits themselves depend on the class of work and closeness of adjustment required. Thus, if a piece is to be one inch in a given dimension, with an ordinary steel scale we are sure of it within about 1/100 inch; with a micrometer, about 1/4000; on a measuring machine, about 1/100,000. The latter is not available in most small establishments; and when the standard of accuracy must be held high, the best means of guarding against discrepancies from independent measurements is by the establishment of a model. All measurements are then comparative instead of direct, and correct within much smaller limits of error. If this be neglected, its lack will be a constant hindrance to the high standard requisite in all the better classes of implements; and no other system so economical and reliable has yet been devised within the general reach. An example is the 36-inch bronze bar in government archives as a legal standard of length. Drawings of each part for general shop reference should also be provided, with all dimensions and tolerances clearly shown.

Next must be established the allowable deviations from the model. These are controlled mainly by two factors: first, the proper functioning of the whole,—thus the largest shaft must always assemble into the smallest bearing; second, how small a variation can be maintained in manufacture. This done, means of testing the accordance of the parts with these standards must be furnished; namely, gauges representing the largest and smallest permissible size for each important dimension. An inspection organization should be carefully trained to use these, and throw out any piece not conforming to them, to save further labor on it or mischief in assembling, and prevent more of its sort being made. Such a service can retrench much useless expense; in fact, if in any large plant it does not save far more than its cost in a year, something is very wrong.

But further uniformities than size, which gauges and drawings concern solely, are called for. Physical characteristics must conform also. This is effected by specifications dealing itemwise with strength, hardness and finish, composition of materials, and vital points to be watched most closely in course of making; and prescribing both frequency of tests (enough to establish sure accuracy) and manner of manufacture, also in detail any special treatment contingently called for, as heat treatment of steel.

Equipment to obtain results simply and inexpensively is a business necessity. It must be carefully suited to the special requirements of the product, as a type of appliance very satisfactory in one class of manufacturing may be quite unfit for another.

These steps are indispensable for interchangeability. The model should remain fixed till a new or improved design is devised. The tolerances are subject to some experimental change, but should be put on a fixed basis at the earliest feasible moment; and never altered to suit inaccuracies in manufacturing methods or other temporary convenience, as the ultimate loss outweighs the saving. The specifications of course change with new methods or materials. All these are so essentially interwoven that slighting any one makes the rest unsure, and every change should be carefully considered as to affecting the whole system. A well-balanced whole will give far more efficient results than one with some elements much in advance of the others.

The Model.— This affords for all dimensions a direct comparison against a physical standard, the most uniform method available with the usual measuring equipment. The whole object will be to reproduce it in quantity as closely as possible, and such reproduction should be carefully kept in mind in developing it. To aid in this, no operations on it should be performed by hand tools (as a file), because such cuts are hardest and costliest to reproduce. All cuts should be machining cuts.

But its development consists of far more than merely producing a piece of work as a standard for other production. Every cut taken should be governed, where possible, by some profile plate, size block, angle plate, form tool or master plate that will be available later for construction of the manufacturing equipment. This will eliminate much of the necessity for several independent settings to reproduce the same sizes or shapes, ensure much greater uniformity throughout, and in the long run prove a real economy. Every step must be considered as to how it affects not only the model itself, but the reproduction of these same sizes, profiles and locations in the working tools and equipment.

To make the model, as often done, an independent unit merely for comparison of measurements, is a wasteful economy far overbalanced by increased expense of making the necessary tools. The more intricate the model, the greater the economy in liberal use of master plates, templets and all other useful special equipment. It should be very carefully kept, not handled or hit, and used only in cases of question and for verifying tools and gauges as needed. It must not be confused with the experimental models; the work is assumed to be past the experimental stage. This ultimate standard is in a class by itself, and must be done by skilled craftsmen of the highest type. At present the manufacturers of firearms are the leaders in this branch.

The Tolerances, or Allowed Variations.—Several factors are involved in establishing these. First, they must never be so great as to injure the operation of the mechanism; yet since expense of manufacturing increases very fast with severity of requirements, economy demands as large a tolerance as consistent with proper functioning. Second, those on one piece must not overlap the sizes fixed for companion parts. The extreme sizes must be compared with each other; so that, for example, the largest pin will always enter the smallest hole, the smallest never be too loose in the largest hole. Third, it must always be kept in mind that the only dimension on any part controllable within close limits is the distance between where it is supported and the surface being machined by the cutting tool. Thus the method of holding the work determines the correct locations of the dimensions; or, vice-versa, those locations determine the holding points for machining. Fourth, the accuracy of the machining facilities available determine the actual possibilities of closeness, and hence should be carefully considered in the original design. The actual extent of tolerances will be a matter of experiment or experience. The same care should be exercised, and the same factors considered, in altering a tolerance as in establishing it.

The Drawings.— These have been used since very early times, and in many cases today are the only standards; models not being in universal use. Even with models, they are always an invaluable aid for shop reference; while since the invention of cheap duplicating processes such as blue-prints, photostats, etc., their frequent use is actively encouraged. They mostly show each part in detail, give all required dimensions and usually the tolerances. Great care must be exercised in placing the dimensions on them. These should be shown between the points intended to hold certain relations to each other. In no case should the location of any point be given with limits from more than one point in the same straight line; otherwise the tolerances will be misleading, as it is impossible to control the variation between more than two such points at once. Wherever possible, a working point or surface should be established in each plane, and all points located from this only; much expense and confusion will be eliminated. Whenever the drawing itself does not give sufficient information, notes should be added.

The Gauges are measuring instruments of fixed dimensions; and where tolerances are established, show two sizes, maximum and minimum, differing by the smallest amount attainable in practice. For example, the gauge for the size of a hole would consist of two cylinders, the smaller just entering the hole and the larger not. The wear on gauges is considerable, and they should be frequently and carefully inspected; preferably by comparison of measurements with a duplicate set of master gauges, themselves carefully checked against the model, and standards of the allowable variations from it. Their design depends upon their purpose. Wherever possible, they should admit of ready repair or correction. It is often possible so to construct them that the parts which control the gauging sizes will receive no wear, thus keeping the maintenance cost very low and insuring the duplication of the original sizes.

Owing to the inevitable factor of error above noted, it is impossible to make any two gauges exactly alike; and to make them within 1/100,000 inch of each other would cost a hundred times as much as within 1/10,000. With this variation, however slight, and with work going through several successive inspections, much difficulty will be met unless proper precautions are taken. No matter how closely several sets of gauges are made to each other, after very short use a variation develops, due to difference in amount of wear and in methods of handling them. When working to gauges, the work will always follow the gauges. The setting of a tool is not changed, a tap or a reamer is not replaced, as long as the work passes the gauges used. So if they wear excessively and are not set right, the work gets farther and farther away from its original standard, and discovery is perhaps made by loss and discredit. The following practice, if strictly adhered to, will almost eliminate these difficulties, and reduce the entire problem to whether the combination of operator, machine and tools is suitable to produce duplicate work:

First, a set of master gauges, duplicates to the working gauges, and checked closely to whatever standard is used. These must under no circumstances be employed to gauge a piece of work; only as standards to check the working gauges.

Second, a positive limit of error for gauges, governed by the tolerance on the given part and the cost of the gauge; all to be inside the total tolerance allowed on the part. For example, a maximum plug gauge could be smaller but never larger than the master, a minimum larger but never smaller.

Third, the sets of gauges should be sorted into groups, according to requirements of inspection. Assuming a shop inspection and a final inspection, three groups would be needed; one for the operators, one for shop inspectors, one for final inspectors. Again assuming that the final inspectors will use two sets constantly, the shop inspectors three, and the operators four, nine sets will be in use at the same time. All gauges should be graded according to size; the two of each type closest to the masters will be sent to the final inspectors; the next three, varying a little more inside the limits, to the shop inspectors; the last four, with the greatest but still allowable variation, to the operators. Each operator should hold his work to the gauges furnished him, regardless of any variance from those of other operators.

Fourth, all gauges in use should be checked periodically against the masters, and discarded, repaired, or regraded according to condition, regardless of which job they were returned from. The frequency of this will be determined by practice, as a capable gauge man will soon determine how many pieces a gauge will measure in given hands without losing its size. Some can be used only on a few hundred pieces before wearing appreciably, others will measure several thousand. Work manufactured continuously needs a duplicate outfit. All gauges of any one type, or the duplicates of any one master, to be used during the same period, should be checked at the same time, to permit of proper grading and comparison.

Fifth, all persons who use the gauges should be carefully instructed and trained in their use. A gauge is an expensive and comparatively delicate instrument, and a careless operator can spoil one on the first piece he gauges; or a foreman with one in his drawer can ruin it by knocking around or mishandling. The final inspectors should set the standard of handling and use, and instruct all others as far as possible to use them likewise.

Work must be held to slightly closer tolerances than the maximum allowable, since it is impossible to work to a maximum without sometimes exceeding it; so the operator has the gauges allowing the smallest working tolerances, as his normally receive the greatest amount of wear.

The Specifications.—Only on very simple or familiar mechanisms do the drawings, gauges, etc., give sufficient information for intelligent manufacture. Specifications should form an integral part of the equipment. As said above, they should explain clearly and definitely the requirements and desired results, character and composition of materials, the chief functioning points and sizes, class of workmanship demanded, and any unusual manufacturing methods required; with the character and method of inspection. In fact, any information of value in the process should find here a permanent record. If any requirements are unimportant, and economy is the main factor, that fact should be stated also. These specifications may be incorporated on the drawings, if desirable and they are simple; otherwise be kept as an independent record, and revised to keep abreast of current practice. They are as yet a rarity in general establishments, but their value and help are becoming more widely acknowledged. The best examples are in government supplies, as munitions.

The Manufacturing Equipment consists of the tools, jigs, fixtures and machines required. A jig or fixture is a device for holding a piece in proper position while some machining operation is performed upon it. Each operation usually needs a special jig. Its general type or design depends entirely upon the part to be wrought. One factor, however, remains constant, and must always be kept in mind for satisfactory results; the locating points for any operation should always be those from which the machined surface is dimensioned. A strict observance of this fundamental principle will eliminate many manufacturing difficulties.

If a model has been suitably developed, many size blocks, master plates and other valuable accessories will be available, that will not only ensure greater accuracy in the equipment and a corresponding uniformity in the product, but greatly decreased expense in equipment costs. In any event, if a model is available, all equipment should be carefully tested to it before being forwarded to the production departments.

The Production, a general mechanical business, need not be dealt with here; the next step is

The Inspection.— This department has the responsibility, and should have the power, of maintaining the standards of accuracy and quality. It should be entirely independent of the production department, whose duties are incompatible with its own, and too often held and performed as hostile. It must be provided with all needful testing and checking apparatus; and its duty is to see that all work is up to the mark before passing from machine to machine, or department to department. Its detailed duties depend upon the nature of the product; but in any case its personnel should be individuals of good judgment, intimately acquainted with the requirements, and well trained in the use of the testing facilities.

The Assembling furnishes final proof whether due attention has been paid to the factors of size; unhappily, the test for quality of material mostly lies in use, and detection of neglect comes too late. If the parts may be assembled without fitting or further machining, and the mechanism performs its functions properly, it is conclusive evidence that the dimensions have been kept true. On the other hand, if fitting or other modifications are necessary, it is equally conclusive proof that some vital factor has been overlooked, and investigation to locate and correct the trouble should follow. In truly interchangeable work, no machining will be performed in the assembling room.

Interchangeable manufacturing requires many types of skilled workmen. As operations are simplified, the needed skill becomes less; but a corresponding increase is required in preparation work and supervision. The basic principles remain fixed, but their application must be modified to suit particular factors of product, class of equipment available and type of workmen employed.

EARLE BUCKINGHAM,
Associate Member, American Society Mechanical Engineers.

INTERCOASTAL, or INTRACOASTAL CANAL, as it was later called, the title officially given to the inland waterway under construction along the Atlantic coast. The same title is used popularly for the inland waterway in process of construction along the shores of the States bordering on the Gulf of Mexico, extending from the Mississippi River to the Rio Grande, and in fact a recognized part of the Mississippi system.

The Intracoastal Canal, or Waterway, may be said to have had its beginning with the Chesapeake and Delaware Canal, on which work was started in 1824. It was opened to navigation in 1829. Of the total cost, about $2,500,000, the United States Government contributed $450,000, and the States of Maryland, Pennsylvania and Delaware also assumed a share, the remainder being raised by the sale of stock. In its earliest days this canal was of very modest proportions both in width and depth. Later it was enlarged and deepened to 9 feet, and three locks introduced. In 1921 the Government bought this canal and gave it a bottom width of 90 feet and a depth at medium low water of 12 feet.

The «Delaware and Raritan Canal» has been looked upon as a second link in the Atlantic intracoastal waterways. Its former route of 44 miles has been reduced to 34 miles by Government surveyors, and this new route has received their approval, but up to 1 May 1931 the necessary appropriation had not been made. This canal would reduce the time of water transportation between New York and Philadelphia from 20 hours to 8 hours, and its completion to a depth of 12 feet would afford an inside route from Boston to Norfolk for more than 60 per cent of the traffic now borne by ocean-going vessels.

From Norfolk to Beaufort the existing channels are approximately 12 feet deep for 100 miles of the 128-mile distance—by way of the Albemarle and Chesapeake Canal, owned by the United States Government. From Beaufort to Florida, the inside route is far from complete. In 1930 the work was proceeding vigorously, with four dredges at work. This section is due to be finished to a depth of 12 feet by 1933, as far as Cape Fear River, 92 miles from Beaufort. Southward from the Cape Fear River the surveyed route is via Georgetown and Charleston, to the Saint Johns River, and by way of this river to Miami. For miles, the existing inland channels north and south of Charleston are but three feet in depth. Although many years must elapse before the 12-foot channel reaches Florida, citizens of that State look forward to a branch canal crossing the northern part of Florida and connecting with the Gulf of Mexico. Of the 237 miles across the State, 105 miles would lie through existing channels of the Saint Johns River. However, 15 locks would be required and the cost is estimated at $16,500,000.

Of the section of the inland waterway under canalization between the Mississippi River and the Rio Grande, along the Gulf coasts of

Louisiana and Texas, and which unfortunately is also called (locally) the Intracoastal Canal, gratifying progress is to be recorded. During 1930, active work was being carried on along 120 miles of the Louisiana coast. On two sections, namely, from the Vermilion River to the Mermentau River (45.3 miles), and from the Mermentau to the Calcasieu (36.5 miles), nine dredges were in operation, and this part of the canal is to be completed by the end of 1931. From Portsmouth, or Palacios Point on Matagorda Bay, to Corpus Christi (96.1 miles), the canal will follow shallow waters, in which some dredging must be done. No work is needed on the section from Calcasieu to Port Arthur, as here the canal will follow a natural waterway 30 feet deep, for 50 miles. At the close of 1930, a stretch of 28 miles, from Morgan City to the Vermilion River, was all that remained along the Louisiana coast to complete the waterway to the Texas line, via the Plaquemine route. From Morgan City to Weeks Bayou the canal follows existing waterways.

The purpose of the canal is three-fold—transportation, irrigation and reclamation; the last, vital. In the marsh areas of southern Louisiana are many so-called islands with fertile strips of higher land in the marsh; these are served by the waterway and railroad construction is impracticable. In some sections of Louisiana the local community has contributed to the cost and in all sections the right of way, 300 feet in width, is furnished without cost to the United States. With the completion of the canal the whole region will be vastly benefited.

INTERCOLLEGIATE ATHLETICS. See EDUCATIONAL ATHLETICS.

INTERCOLONIAL CONTROVERSIES. See BOUNDARIES OF THE UNITED STATES.

INTERCOLONIAL RAILWAY. This railway and the Prince Edward Island Railway are owned and operated by the government of Canada as part of the government railways. They are under the charge of the Department of Railways and Canals, which is presided over by the Minister of Railways and Canals, who is a cabinet minister. The intercolonial extends through the provinces of Quebec, New Brunswick and Nova Scotia, connecting the cities of Montreal and Quebec with the cities of Saint John, Halifax and Sidney on the Atlantic Coast. Its length, including branches, is 1,562 miles.

The history of the Intercolonial is interesting, but there is space here for only a brief outline. The construction of a railway from the Atlantic Ocean to the Saint Lawrence River at Quebec, through the British provinces, was proposed in 1832. An exploratory survey from Point Levis, opposite Quebec, to Saint Andrews on the Bay of Fundy, was made, with the assistance of the British government, in 1836, and a practicable route was found, but nothing further was done at that time because of representations from the United States government that part of the surveys were in territory claimed by the State of Maine. Other explorations were subsequently made until 1846, when the Royal Engineers, under instructions from the British government, commenced the survey of several routes from Halifax to Quebec. These surveys were completed in 1848, and the route recommended by the engineers was, generally speaking, that adopted when the Intercolonial was constructed many years afterward. The surveys showed that there were several routes by which such a railway could be constructed, but the provinces considered that the work was too great and costly for their unaided resources; under these circumstances the greater project was laid aside for a time and each of the provinces in its own way, and independently of the others, turned its attention to the construction of railways which were destined afterward to form parts of the Intercolonial.

The province of Canada in 1849 passed an act affording assistance to railway companies by guaranteeing their bonds, and the Halifax and Quebec Railway was particularly mentioned in this act. In 1852 the Grand Trunk Railway Company was incorporated and subsidized. Another company was also incorporated and subsidized, in the same year, to build a railway from opposite Quebec to Trois Pistoles. This company was amalgamated with the Grand Trunk Railway Company, and the latter built the line from Point Levis, opposite Quebec, to Rivière du Loup, 126 miles, which was opened in 1860. The company did not build as far eastward as Trois Pistoles.

The province of New Brunswick in 1853 also commenced railway construction, and built, as a government work, a line from Saint John to Point du Chene on the Gulf of Saint Lawrence, 108 miles. It was opened in 1860, and was called the European and North American Railway. By 1870 this railway had been extended eastward and completed to the boundary of Nova Scotia. It was opened in December of that year.

In June 1854 the province of Nova Scotia began construction of the Nova Scotia Railway, which was opened from Halifax to Truro (61 miles) in December 1858, together with a branch line to Windsor (32 miles). An extension of this railway from Truro to Pictou, on the Gulf of Saint Lawrence (52 miles) was opened in May 1867.

On 1 July 1867, the provinces of Canada, Nova Scotia and New Brunswick were, by an act of the Parliament of Great Britain, united into a confederation called the Dominion of Canada. Under that act the railways owned by the individual provinces became the property of the Dominion. By this act also provision was made for an intercolonial railway connecting the Saint Lawrence River with Halifax, and for a line connecting Truro with Rivière du Loup. This division, opened 9 November 1872, formed the connection between the Nova Scotia Railway and the European and North American Railway. These three railways totaling 370 miles, were, on the same date, consolidated into the Intercolonial Railway.

In 1911, the line from Ferrona Junction to Sunny Brae, Nova Scotia (13 miles), was purchased, and in 1914 the New Brunswick and Prince Edward Island Railway (36 miles) began to be operated in connection with the Intercolonial. In 1915, the Saint John and Quebec Railway, from Gagetown to Centerville, in New Brunswick (105 miles) was added. After

1914, the Intercolonial Railway of New Brunswick became part of this system. In 1918 the Canadian Northern Board was appointed to operate and manage all Canadian Government Railways; and in 1922 this board was succeeded by the New National Railway Board.

As an entity, the Intercolonial Railway has now disappeared and the lines and property which comprised that company are now operated as part of the Eastern Lines group of the Canadian National Railways. The operated mileage comprised within this group—which includes all lines east of the «gateways» Levis and Diamond Junction, Quebec within the borders of Canada—was 3,388.22, on 31 December 1930. The operating revenues for the Eastern Lines in the year 1930 amounted to $28,598,553.45 and the operating expenses were $33,028,515.65, showing a net deficit from railway operations for the year of $4,429,962.20. This deficit was due largely to preferential rates granted the people along these lines and in contiguous territory by the Canadian Government to enable industries of the maritime provinces to compete on an equal basis with those of Central Canada in the Western and Central Canada markets. For this reason the operational figures do not present a true picture of railroad operating efficiency, as the deficit would disappear if the rates on the Eastern Lines were the same as those prevailing on the rest of the system. The preferential rates apply also to those lines of the Canadian Pacific east of the points cited above, and they apply generally on traffic originating within the maritime provinces and passing through and beyond these gateways. The legislation introducing these preferential rates is known as «The Maritime Freight Rates Act» and it was passed by the Parliament of Canada in July 1927. The lines formerly known as the Intercolonial Railway traverse Canada's «Atlantic Provinces,» a region noted for its picturesque scenery, and now studded with summer resorts, with several sections particularly attractive to fishermen.

INTERCOLUMNIATION (from Lat. *inter,* between, *columna,* column), in classical architecture, refers to the clear space between two columns of a peristylos, or system of roof-supporting columns, though sometimes it means the distance measured at the lower parts of shafts, between their centres, and referred to in terms of diameter of a column at its base. A Roman architect and engineer, Vitruvius, a contemporary of Augustus, enumerates five varieties of intercolumniation, assigning by means of the foregoing scale of measurement, definite proportions to each. They are as follows:

1. Pycnostylos (Gr. πυκνος, «thick,» and στυλος, column, implying thick arrangement), in which the spacing equals one diameter and a half. 2. Systylos (Gr. συν, with, and στυλος, column, that is, with columns harmoniously arranged), where columns are two diameters apart. 3. Eustylos (Gr. ευ, well, and στυλος column, as the derivation implies, a style preferred, and meaning with columns a due distance apart). Some authorities say the proportion was two diameters and a quarter; others, two diameters and a half. 4. Diastylos (Gr. δια, through, and στυλος column, implying columns wide apart), in which the space between the columns consisted of three, or even, according to some authorities, of four diameters. 5. Aræostylos (Gr. ἀραιος, wide, and στυλος, column, implying columns sparsely ranged), that style in which the distance between the columns used is four and sometimes five diameters,—the former distance being however that to which the name is in strict usage applied. It is suited only to the Tuscan order, and the span is possible only when the epistylium or architrave is of wood. A sixth arrangement is also known, the Aræosystylos (Gr. αραιος, wide, συν, with, στυλος, column), in which the intercolumniations are alternately systylos and aræostylos. This way of building places four columns in a space equal to eight diameters and a half. The central intercolumniation is equal to three diameters and a half, and the others on each side only half a diameter, so that coupled columns are introduced.

In the ruined remains of fine architecture which have survived down to the present time, ancient intercolumniation rarely if ever illustrates the Vitruvian dimensions, which therefore have, by some authorities, been regarded as arbitrary. He appears to have spoken only of Roman forms, or only of those of the Greek style, with which he became acquainted through such reports about Hellenic temples, as he had among his authorities. In the Doric examples, such as the Parthenon and the temple of Diana Propylæa at Eleusis, the proportion is said to be one and one-quarter (1¼) diameters. Temples of the Ionic and Corinthian order resemble each other. The proportions in these are, on the whole, greater; they average about two diameters. But it would be a mistake to overlook in this connection the relative proportion of height to diameter in a column, and to disregard the width of the peristyle. In one temple of the Ionic order, that of Apollo Smintheus, in Asia Minor, the peristyle is of double width, and the intercolumniation is just one and one-half diameters. To the ancients, the eustylos was the most correct as well as the most beautiful arrangement; and the author of 'De Architectura' preferred this proportion to that of any of the others, declaring it at one and the same time the strongest and the most convenient. Consult Vitruvius, 'De Architectura' (trans. by Morgan, Prof. Morris H., as 'Vitruvius: the Ten Books on Architecture' (Cambridge, Mass., 1915).

INTERDICT, an ecclesiastical decree which forbids the performance of certain acts of public worship. When an interdict was laid upon a town, district or country, all the churches were closed, the bells were silent, the sacraments, except infant baptism and extreme unction (and sometimes even these), were withheld, the rites of burial were not performed and all the public ceremonies of religion were suspended. Interdicts may be general, as applied to a country or city; particular, as applied to a parish or diocese; personal, as applied to a person, or some class of persons. The bishops seem to have anciently exercised the right of publishing interdicts; for in 870 Hincmar, bishop of Laon in France, issued one against a parish in his diocese. One of the earliest censures of this sort on record was imposed upon the city of Rouen in the 6th century on account of the murder of the Archbishop Pretextatus by order of Queen Fredegonda. In 997 Gregory V laid the kingdom of France under an interdict because King Robert had married his cousin, and the king was abandoned by most of his court. The same penalty was inflicted upon the kingdom of England under Stephen (1147) by Eugenius III, under John (1207) by Innocent III, under Henry VIII (1535) with little effect by Paul III and under Elizabeth (1587) by Sixtus V. Adrian IV laid Rome under an interdict for the purpose of compelling the Romans to drive out Arnold of Brescia. Gregory IX made use of the same instrument of compulsion in his quarrel with the Emperor Frederic II. During the Middle Ages the interdict was a powerful engine of attack for the popes in their contests with sovereigns, as the popular dread of its effects was so great that kings were often forced by rebellions to submit to almost any conditions in order that it might be taken off. From the time of the Reformation general and local interdicts have become rare. When Paul V laid Venice under an interdict in 1606, the churches were not closed, and only a minority of the bishops submitted to it.

INTERDICT, in Scottish law, an order issued by the Court of Session to stay or prohibit a person from an act presumed to be illegal or wrongful. It is similar to the injunction in English and American procedure. Consult Erskine, John, ‹Institute of the Law of Scotland› (Edinburgh 1773; new ed., 1898).

INTERDICTION, in Scottish law, a process for protection from imposition of persons of imbecile minds. It is similar in process and effect to the American commission in lunacy. In Louisiana and Quebec the practice is similar to that of Scotland, these states having derived their legal system from the Roman law.

INTERESSE TERMINI, in law, the interest held by a lessee after the grant of the lease and before his actual entry. This interest has been held alienable at common law, and upon the death of the lessee it goes to his executors. Such an interest at common law, however, required an actual entry by the lessee to create an estate in him, but if the interest has been created by a conveyance under the Statute of Uses, the estate vests in the lessee at once without actual entry by him.

INTEREST («it concerns» — the party in issue—originally an award of damages, later used to evade the anti-interest laws), a charge for the use of money, by custom computed annually, on a basis of so many out of each 100 units loaned; but without diminishing the capital. It is possible to pay interest without loss, because, under conditions now general, the borrowed money can be employed in productive industry, from which a return equal to or greater than the interest can be obtained; or because comfort, prestige, or moral advantages of many kinds are derivable, justifying the expenditure when enough is left. Such borrowing is now useful on the whole, because civilization has ingrained a self-restraint in the masses which makes them in most cases manage money soberly and prudently. But in the early ages this was not so, except in a few developed commercial cities: Babylon carried on business by interest loans, and even bottomry bonds on shipping; Tyre probably did so; the great Athenian commerce was built up entirely by it, as Demosthenes explicitly says, but the mass of people were not fit to have the use of money, had no remunerative employment for it, and borrowed it only to use in self-indulgence, or in desperation because any rate was a choice of evils. There was little property to pledge, and the security was mostly the debtor's person; foreclosure meant selling him for a slave, and the grievance which called for Solon's legislation was the debt-slavery of a large section of the citizens. Hence arose a violent prejudice against the system altogether, as immoral in itself; the law of Moses prohibited it between Jew and Jew; Aristotle says it is essentially immoral, because money cannot breed money (this in the age of Athenian commerce), and never was meant for any such use; the Christian Church inherited the reprobation from the Jewish, and for many centuries forbade its members to take «usury» (money for the use of money, that is, interest at any percentage), and the secular laws were correspondent. In England interest did not become legal till the time of Henry VIII, but had been actually practised for many generations, by legal fictions of partnership or breach of contract, etc.; previously it was in the hands of the Jews — who were so indispensable as financial agents that a Jew who was converted to Christianity had all his property confiscated — and later of the Lombards. The first English permissive statutes fixed 10 per cent as the legal limit that might be charged; early in the 17th century it was set at 5. No serious doubt of the power of governments to regulate the current rate of interest obtainable was entertained till Bentham wrote his ‹Defence of Usury› in 1786, proving that the laws could not possibly have any effect; because if the legal rate fixed was equal to or greater than the current rate it could not work any change in it; and if less, holders of money would not lend without obtaining their price plus an insurance for the risk of legal punishment. The doctrine was violently disliked, and has not even yet overcome the determination of the mass to show their dislike of usury by statute, or their belief that they can affect rates; but in a few American States of late years the anti-usury laws have been abolished. Of course a legal rate is always provided in default of contract.

Interest is not a natural right, but a matter of law or contract. The holder of a note payable without stipulation of interest cannot claim any until the note has become due and remains unpaid; thenceforward it draws money at the legal rate. The United States pays no interest on its debts, except where bonds are issued specifying it.

The legal and contract rates of interest in the various States and Territories of the United States are as follows (figures representing rate per cent): Alabama legal rate 8, contract rate 8; Alaska legal rate 8, contract rate 12; Arkansas legal rate 6 to 10, contract rate 0 to 10; Arizona legal rate 6, contract rate 10; California legal rate 7, contract rate 12; Colorado, legal rate 8, contract rate 12; Connecticut, legal rate 6, contract rate 12; Delaware, legal rate 6, contract rate 6; District of

Columbia, legal rate 6, contract rate 8; Florida, legal rate 8, contract rate 10; Georgia, legal rate 7, contract rate 8; Hawaii, legal rate 8, contract rate 12; Idaho, legal rate 7, contract rate 10; Illinois, legal rate 5, contract rate 7; Indiana, legal rate 6, contract rate 8; Iowa, legal rate 6, contract rate 8; Kansas, legal rate 6, contract rate 6; Kentucky, legal rate 6, contract rate 6; Louisiana, legal rate 5, contract rate 8; Maine, legal rate 6, contract rate unlimited; Maryland, legal rate 6, contract rate 6; Massachusetts, legal rate 6, contract rate unlimited; Michigan, legal rate 5, contract rate 7; Minnesota, legal rate 6, contract rate 8; Mississippi, legal rate 6, contract rate 8; Missouri, legal rate 6, contract rate 8; Montana, legal rate 8, contract rate 10; Nebraska, legal rate 7, contract rate 10; Nevada, legal rate 7, contract rate 12; New Hampshire, legal rate 6, contract rate unlimited; New Jersey, legal rate 6, contract rate 6; New Mexico, legal rate 10, contract rate 12; New York, legal rate 6, contract rate 6, any rate on call loans of $5,000 and up; North Carolina, legal rate 6, contract rate 6; North Dakota, legal rate 6, contract rate 10; Ohio, legal rate 6, contract rate 8; Oklahoma, legal rate 6, contract rate 10; Oregon, legal rate 6, contract rate 10; Pennsylvania, legal rate 6, contract rate 6; Philippine Islands no fixed rate; Porto Rico, legal rate 6, contract rate 12; Rhode Island, legal rate 6, contract rate unlimited; South Carolina, legal rate 7, contract rate 8; South Dakota, legal rate 7, contract rate 12; Tennessee, legal rate 6, contract rate 6; Texas, legal rate 6, contract rate 10; Utah, legal rate 8, contract rate 12; Vermont, legal rate 6, contract rate 6; Virginia, legal rate 6, contract rate 6; Washington, legal rate 6, contract rate 12; West Virginia, legal rate 6, contract rate 6; Wisconsin legal rate 6, contract rate 10; Wyoming, legal rate 8, contract rate 12.

These rates result from tradition. A few States have made recent attempts to keep down the contract rate of interest to the rate that is actually current in the community; in the others, unspecified debts bear 6 to 8 per cent interest while the current rate is 5. As to the contract interest, 13 States forbid anything beyond the legal rate; while two — New York and Pennsylvania — allow any contract rate on «call loans» over $5,000.

The theories of interest, like most economic principles, are much disputed by economists. The chief theories are those of «abstinence,» holding interest to be a reward of abstinence from using up the capital in enjoyment (a variant of this regards it as a result of the general appreciation of the present above the future); of «productivity,» holding it to be the return for production by capital in the same way that wages are a return for production by labor; the combination of the two, regarding the return as fixed by supply and demand, the latter depending on productivity and the former on abstinence; and the «monopoly» theory, which considers it a toll levied on the product of labor by the capitalists who control the means of production.

INTEREST, as employed in psychology and pedagogy, is a term conveying at least two or three distinct ideas. The word also, in the vulgar sense, applies loosely to what is meant by personal advantage; as, for example, it is «to a man's interest» to obtain this or that. Etymologically, interest conveys the idea of a condition of being concerned about, or having a share in anything, in which sense also we find it used as a legal term. Perhaps its most definite meaning is that of the psychological law of interest, the law or principle that those elements of a past experience the most effective for recall are those which at the time of the experience received the greatest share of attention or aroused the highest degree of interest. Thus the great French psychologist, T. Ribot, uses the term. He remarks that «the influence of emotional states must be stated as a principle, but not as an exclusive cause. It is summed up in what Shadworth Hodgson has called the Law of Interest.» ('Psychology of the Emotions'). The word interest, derived from the Latin *interesse,* literally «to go between,» to make a difference, to concern, to be of importance, yielded in the course of a long evolution all the meanings of interest, both legal and psychological, as used in English.

Psychologically, interest may be broadly defined as the «consciousness which accompanies mental tendencies of any sort, so far as they terminate upon mental objects or stimulate to construction of them.» (Baldwin). It is also from another point of view a phase of feeling, an intellectual feeling. It is always manifested by voluntary attention. Its opposite is the feeling of alienation and repulsion that accompanies a presentation of matter that is foreign to the experience of a student, or other person. By attention one understands the «conscious activity of the mind.» Thus psychologically, interest and attention are closely allied *events.* Baldwin remarks that interest may be considered either as a stimulus or as a result of voluntary attention. Perhaps it is more precise to say that interest and attention are the subjective and objective aspects, respectively, of the same mental activity. This amounts to saying that the effective assimilation of new material into the course of experience is interest when viewed from the standpoint of the mental affections,— the emotion and personal attitude that accompany it. It is attention when viewed as the active outgoing of mental habits in grasping and in mastering the subject matter before one. All views of the relation subsisting between interest and attention acknowledge, at least, the intimate connection of the two; and it is precisely this connection which becomes significant in pedagogy. Like attention, interest as a state of the mind depends upon the proper balance of the old and new in experience. Neither interest nor mental activity appears to be the conditions of attention. Interest is either a general name for the subjective conditions of attention when ascribed to the object or it is used to designate a mood which accompanies all attention. Mental activity is really also bodily activity — a mass of sensations that comes from the contraction of muscles in different parts of the body. The contractions result from motor innervations which accompany attention. The interest of curiosity, the desire to know, may be defined as a primary form of interest, as distinguished from custom and habit and preference. Baldwin regards the former as being more of the nature of a stimulation to the intellectual function; the latter he regards as the resultant of a frequent performance of the function. This latter aspect, he tells us, is that which also underlies the popular use of the term in the plural, "interests" meaning one's prevailing and permanent disposition.

Where the material is almost entirely novel, there is an excess of stimulation if there is interest at all. The responsive power of the mind under such conditions is not infrequently overwhelmed and confused, and as a result we have sometimes discouragement or aversion. These truths have their importance for pedagogy, as well as for the psychologist. As a feeling we may well remind ourselves that interest is the feeling that something, the object of the feeling, concerns one. As the word aversion implies, on the other hand, there is in it a strong tendency of the mind to turn away and devote itself to a more congenial and rewarding object than the one which should concern it. Even when this tendency is overcome in part, it means divided, and consequently wasted, energy, as compared with unified, whole-hearted activity, where interest is naturally and directly sustained. On the other hand, what is thoroughly familiar denotes the mastered, the habitual. This state of affairs awakens tendencies that work automatically and mechanically. If there is also a new factor about which habits may play, these habitual tendencies will furnish a foundation for intense and concentrated interest. But, it is a matter of common knowledge, if there is no stimulation beyond that evoking the established habits, the result will be ennui, monotony, routine; the effect is that of walking in a treadmill where nothing new is achieved. A certain degree of difficulty, a certain amount of obstacle to overcome, enough to set the problem of a readjustment of habit, is necessary for sustained interest. The self must be allowed to proceed with thoroughly awakened powers; and this is impossible without a challenging difficulty. The fact just stated throws light upon the relation between desire, or interest, and effort, and helps to place the relation of the doctrine of interest to that of discipline. The doctrine itself is in pedagogy a sort of expression for a number of different motives. As long as a child lives in the mere present he is absorbed in his immediate concerns only. All his powers are directed and discharged upon the immediately present stimulus. There are for the child few if any ends, or conceived results, to be reached, after an intervening time, through the controlled adaptation of conditions as means. And whenever there is an end it usually lies in such a near future that but little thought has to be given to the management of the intermediate conditions. The state of immediate interest characterizes the play activities. In this sense only can one look upon interest as a form of amusement, a stimulus through the play-instinct to induce intellectual effort. When, however, more remote ends are to be reached by consistent and sustained maintenance of a series of acts that of themselves lack immediate interest, but that are of interest because of their importance for the remoter end in view, we have mediate interest. Mediate interest being dependent on an idea, a purpose, a conscious aim, involves an intellectual interest in a way in which the emotional element accompanying direct absorption does not. The mediate interest is dependent upon the persistence of an idea, a conscious aim—and this involves the thought of the bearing of the immediately present upon the attainment of this end. Control of the activity and the source of interest, reside in what is conceived—a thing always physically absent when it is a thing and not in perception when non-physical. The remoteness of the end in time means of course the increase in the number of difficulties to be dealt with, one after another. Therefore we may be certain that the seriousness, the depth of the interest of the self in its objective—its aim—is continually confronted with tests. Under these conditions, while physical effort will go to the means for reaching the end, the moral and the intellectual effort will be directed to sustaining the idea of a purpose in such force as to give it motive power. All the elements of apparent conflict of interest and effort, with immediate attractiveness, immediate agreeableness, immediate pleasurableness, on the side of interest, while serious and important values are all on the side of effort—is what disturbs some well-meaning educators. Hence the situation has been completely misinterpreted in theories of education, with respect to both its moral and other higher implications. In this way interest has been regarded by some as inherently unworthy, objectionable as a factor; some appear to assume that it operates only as a temptation away from the objectively important. Identified thus with the attractive and swerving power of the immediately pleasurable and placed over against what reason shows to be really worth while, it has been the source of much misery to both pupil and teacher. Its logic is bad; and its results are worse. Logically, it implies that the objectively valuable end is totally devoid of interest, so that sheer effort of the will has to be relied upon as the sole motive for keeping the self in its right course—for keeping it struggling against the seductions of interest. The previous analysis it is to be hoped will reveal the fault of this conception. For in truth what sustains effort is not sheer appeal to will power, but interest in an end, an interest, both indirect, intelligent, and at times, even moral, as distinguished from that which is immediate, purely personal, emotional, sensuous. We do not mean to imply that some ends should be immoral; it is intended above to take cognizance of the fact that there is a realm of the morally indifferent. The genuine educational need is therefore not to eliminate interest, but to foster indirect interest, the interest that is not immediate but mediate. Yet it would be well to remember that immediate interest also has its claims: it remains a fundamental trait of all aesthetic and artistic life. In either case whenever a pupil becomes intensely and sincerely interested in an end which reflection holds up, the sense of separation between means and end tends to disappear from consciousness.

Bibliography.—Engle, J. S., *Analytic Interest Psychology* (Baltimore 1904); Lange, K., *Apperception* (Boston 1905); Sullivan, E. H., *Attitude in Relation to Learning* (Princeton 1927); Fryer, D., *Measurement of Interests in Relation to Human Adjustment* (New York 1931); Thorndike, E. L., *Psychology of Wants, Interests, and Attitudes* (New York 1935); Strong, E. K., *Vocational Interests of Men and Women* (Stanford, Calif., 1943).

INTERFERENCE, *in physics,* a name applied to the mutual action of "waves" of any kind upon one another—a phenomenon by which, under certain conditions, the vibrations and their effects are increased, diminished, or neutralized.

As a word, interference was formed on the false analogy of such words as "difference"; it was derived from *interfere,* which in turn came from the Latin *ferire,* to strike, and conveying the idea of a horse striking one foot or ankle against an opposite foot or ankle while moving along. Thomas Young in *Philosophical Transactions* (1801) first introduced the term and the idea underlying it into optical studies, when he employed it in his Bakerian lecture on the *Theory of Light and Colours.* Since Young's time, the idea of interference has been extended so as to describe any kind of coming together of waves or vibrations, whether those of snow, sand, water, light, sound, heat, or electricity—in short, wherever the wave motions collide. Interference may be observed when two different trains of waves come together upon the surface of water or any other liquid. Where the crest of a wave belonging to one system coincides with the crest of a wave of the other system, the elevation of the water surface is equal to the sum of the heights that the separate waves would have if each existed in the same place alone. When a crest of one of the waves coincides with the trough of another, the disturbance of the water surface is reduced, and the elevation (or depression) which results is equal to the difference between the elevation of one of the component waves and the depression of the other one.

The kinds of interference that are of the greatest practical importance in physics are those which occur among sound waves or among waves of light. The phenomena in these cases are ultimately of the same general sort as those observed upon the surface of water. A familiar result of the interference of sound waves is the production of "beats" when two or more trains of waves, having but slightly different wavelength, come together while the two are moving in nearly the same direction. This phenomenon is exhaustively treated in Hermann L. F. von Helmholtz's *Sensations of Tone* (1875), and is also discussed in all of the better works on physics.

The more familiar of the interference phenomena that are afforded by light may be observed in connection with soap bubbles and with very thin plates of transparent solids. Light, upon striking the soap bubble or the thin plate, is reflected toward the eye from both surfaces; and the trains of light waves that reach the eye from these two sources, since they have a slight difference of phase (which varies, moreover, from point to point of the bubble or the plate), interfere with one another so as to produce effects that are often very beautiful and striking. A soap bubble, when viewed by monochromatic light, often appears to be covered with dark lines due to the fact that at the points that appear dark, the two trains of light waves, coming respectively from the inner and outer surfaces of the soap bubble, nearly or completely neutralize each other. When the bubble is viewed by white light, we do not commonly see the dark lines, their places being taken by bands of color. This is because the different colors that compose white light have different wavelengths, so that at any given point in the bubble only a portion of the colors are destroyed by interference, leaving the remaining constituents of the white light to produce their full chromatic effect upon the eye. See also WAVES AND WAVE MOTION.

Consult Anderson, J. A., *The Wave-length in Astronomical Interferometer Measurements* (Chicago 1922); Barus, C., *Displacement Interferometry Applied to Acoustics and to Gravitation,* 3 vols. (Washington 1925); Fabry, C. E., *Les Applications des Interférences Lumineuses* (Paris 1923); Michelson, A. A., *Studies in Optics* (Chicago 1927).

INTERFEROMETER, ĭn-tẽr-fẽr-ŏm'ē-tẽr, an instrument which utilizes interference patterns of light waves in measuring the thickness of a thin film, or which can be used to determine the length of light waves. The interferometer developed by Albert Michelson has been used to determine the diameter of stars; another type in use today was developed by Fabry and Perót in France.

INTERIM, in the history of the Reformation, the name of several compromises forced on the German Protestants by edicts of Charles V, especially that of 1548, regulating religious and ecclesiastical matters "in the meantime," until they could be decided by a general council. The *Ratisbon Interim* was drawn up in 1541 by a commission which included Johann Eck, Martin Bucer, Julius von Pflug, John Gropper, Johannes Pistorius, and Melanchthon (Philipp Schwarzerd). Many doctrinal points were smoothed over, but the differences in regard to the ecclesiastical power and the sacraments were too great to be reconciled. By the Protestants in general, the whole movement was looked on as a scheme to entrap them into a formal return to the Roman Catholic Church. In 1548 at Augsburg, the emperor appointed Johannes Agricola, Michael Helding, and Pflug to prepare a new interim. This *Augsburg Interim* conceded to the Reformers communion in both kinds, and the marriage of priests. Great opposition developed in North Germany and the pact was revoked in 1552. Elector Maurice of Saxony secured the adoption of the *Leipzig Interim* in 1548, according to which the Protestant creed remained intact, with an admixture of the old ceremonial; the papal and episcopal powers were also recognized to a limited extent.

INTERIOR, Department of the. An executive branch of the United States government, whose secretary is a member of the president's Cabinet, this department was established March 3, 1849, as the Home Department with the Indian Office and General Land Office as its major activities. Today the department has become increasingly responsible for the development and conservation of the vast resources of land, water, and minerals that have been the foundation of the country's dynamic expanding economy. It has been called "a department of the West" because its first half-century was devoted to the development of the vast Western territory, including the providing of land grants to railroads and colleges for the extension of transportation and education. It has also been called the "mother of departments" since three government Cabinet agencies—the departments of Agriculture, Labor, and Commerce—had their beginnings in the Department of the Interior.

As the agency of the federal government responsible for assuring adequate supplies of energy for an expanding economy, the department conducts programs for the development and wise use of vital energy sources, including hydroelectric power, petroleum, natural gas, coal, and synthetic fuels. It supervises programs of exploration, research, and development to meet the vast industrial demands for mineral raw materials. It promotes activities to assure the progressive development and conservation of land and water resources to meet growing needs. It is also concerned with programs in human relations essential to the assimilation of Indian and Alaskan native populations.

By 1951 the Interior Department was responsible for the supervision, care, and improvement of more than 572 million acres of land, including 310 million acres located in the Territory of Alaska. The Bureau of Land Management supervised 471.5 million acres; the Bureau of Indian Affairs, 59.5 million; the National Park Service, 22.9 million; the Fish and Wildlife Service, 12.3 million; and the Bureau of Reclamation, 5.7 million. As a result of United States Supreme Court decisions, the department also had jurisdiction over an estimated 569.8 million acres in the submerged continental shelf.

The department maps the physical features of the land; locates mineral deposits; assists in their development and efficient production; investigates surface and ground water supplies; develops irrigation and hydroelectric projects in the 17 Western states; provides research and market information on food and game fish; encourages the conservation of wild game birds and animals; preserves the natural beauty of park areas, national monuments, and historical sites; administers Indian tribal resources and aids in the social, economic, and cultural advancement of Indians; provides health and educational facilities for more than 400,000 Indian and native citizens in the United States and Alaska; and coordinates the activities of federal agencies in the territorial areas of Alaska, Hawaii, Puerto Rico, Virgin Islands, Guam, American Samoa, and the Trust Territory of the Pacific Islands.

The department administers the Connally "Hot Oil" law which controls the interstate and foreign shipment of oil produced in violation of state conservation laws; serves as advisor to other government agencies on matters pertaining to oil and gas; and markets the electric power produced by flood-control dams erected by the Corps of Engineers.

Under the Defense Production Act of 1950, the department was made responsible for assuring that the country's fundamental resource base was adequately expanded to assure the attainment of the objectives of the national defense program. The resources under the jurisdiction of the secretary of the interior include electric power, petroleum, natural and manufactured gas, coal, coke and coal byproducts, minerals, and fisheries. To handle these defense responsibilities the department established the Petroleum Administration for Defense, the Defense Minerals Administration, the Defense Electric Power Administration, the Defense Solid Fuels Administration, and the Defense Fisheries Administration.

The duties and responsibilities of the secretary and undersecretary of the interior are shared by four assistant secretaries covering natural resource and adminstrative fields. The assistant secretary for mineral resources is responsible for the Division of Oil and Gas, Division of Geography, Bureau of Mines, and the Geological Survey. The assistant secretary for public land management coordinates the activities of the Office of Land Utilization, Office of Territories, Bureau of Land Management, National Park Service, Fish and Wildlife Service, and the Bureau of Indian Affairs. The assistant secretary for water and power development supervises the work of the Division of Water and Power, Bureau of Reclamation, Bonneville Power Administration, Southwestern Power Administration, and the Southeastern Power Administration. The administrative assistant secretary is responsible for the Division of Budget and Finance, Division of Property Management, Division of Management Research, Division of Personnel Management, and the Division of Administrative Services.

W. J. DOUGHERTY,
Director of Information, Department of the Interior.

INTERIOR DECORATION. Under the general designation of interior decoration are included all the various applications of the decorative art (q.v.) to the adornment of the interiors of buildings. The subject comprises *monumental* interior decoration, which is largely architectural and has to do with the decorative treatment of the floors, walls, and ceilings of important buildings; and *domestic* interior decoration, which has to do with the furnishings as well as the architectural treatment of rooms and halls in private residences. The decoration of hotels and clubs occupies a position intermediate between the two divisions. In the first division we are concerned chiefly with the architectural design of the interior. In the second division these architectural elements are less conspicuous. The fundamental principles of art are the same in both divisions, but the applications are widely different.

Monumental Interior Decoration; Methods and Resources.—In order to make the interior of a great building—as a hall, church or theater—decoratively pleasing, the artist may employ the resources of pure form or of color, or of both together, as is most often the case. Any-one who has seen the interior of Grant's Tomb in New York realizes that its decoration is wholly one of form—of architectural features and paneling, executed for the most part in white plaster. At the other extreme is the Sistine Chapel of the Vatican in Rome—an interior almost absolutely devoid of architectural embellishment, made glorious by the decorative painting of its walls and ceilings by the greatest artists of the Renaissance. But in general, form and color are combined, as in the great basilica of Saint Peter; in the superb Camera della Segnatura by Raphael in the Vatican; or, to cite a more modern example, in the gorgeous staircase hall of the Opera in Paris. One element in our judgment of the two systems, however, must inevitably be that of the more sustained, varied, and intellectual interest inspired by noble mural paintings as compared with richness of architectural detail. The content of mere architectural detail is soon apprehended, owing to its dependence on repetition of similar forms, and its novelty of interest is therefore soon exhausted. See also MURAL PAINTING; DECORATIVE ART.

The resources of interior decoration of a monumental character are, then, first of all architectural forms or (collectively) *membering;* secondly, carving and sculpture; thirdly, the use of fine or semiprecious materials of rich natural color, such as marble, porphyry, onyx, highly polished woods and the like; fourthly, the applied arts of inlay and mosaic and the kindred art of stained glass; and fifthly, mural painting, which includes the painting of ceilings and vaults and ranges from the simplest harmonies of flat coloring on the various surfaces, through all varieties of painted ornament to the highest forms of allegorical, symbolic and historic painting. To these resources should be added the decorative treatment of the accessories and fixed furniture of the building, such as grilles and gates and railings in metal, pulpits, choir-screens and sedilia in stone and marble and wood, and other like essential features of the interior equipment. All these resources may be called into service in a single interior to produce almost overwhelming effects of richness and splendor, as in the original state of the church of the Divine Wisdom (Hagia Sophia, now a museum of Byzantine art) at Constantinople, built in the 6th century; contemporary descriptions of this interior, in prose and in verse, exhaust the resources of language in the effort to portray the glories of that marvelous edifice. The interior of the Camera della Segnatura at Rome, mentioned above; of the cathedral of Sienna; of Saint Mark's at Venice; of the Taj Mahal (q.v.) at Agra (India) and of some of the Mogul palaces of that country; of certain halls in the Alhambra at Granada (Spain); of the staircase hall and *foyer* of the Opera at Paris; of the Panthéon and parts of the Hôtel de Ville of that city; of the Public Library at Boston, Mass., and of the Congressional Library at Washington, D. C., illustrate in varying ways and degrees such combinations of architecture and the applied arts respectively in mediæval, Reniassance and modern times.

Historical Survey; Pre-classic Decoration. — Certain caves in France and Spain have preserved to us the remarkable efforts of primitive man to adorn these interiors with paintings of animals. (See ABORIGINAL ART). These date back probably to an antiquity of at least 25,000 years. Then follows a hiatus of many millenniums preceding the earliest extant Egyptian interiors of tombs and temples, with which historic art in interior decoration may be said to begin. In the temples the solemnity of pillared hypostyle halls and of the sanctuaries was relieved and enriched by pictures and bands of hieroglyphics, cut into the stone in outline or carved in low relief, and painted in brilliant colors. The pictures represent gods and kings, sacrifices and sacred vultures, with conventional ornament executed in the same way. The walls of the tombs were adorned with scenes from real life, sometimes painted on plaster, sometimes cut in low relief on the stone (Tomb of Perneb in the Metropolitan Museum, New York). As ancient as some of these Egyptian works are the remarkable paintings of walls in Crete, especially at Knossos; while somewhat later in date (9th to 6th century B.C.) are the decorations in the palaces of the Assyrian kings. Low relief pictures on alabaster or limestone slabs formed a high wainscot in the halls of these palaces; above were probably borders in encaustic tile and tapestries or other hangings. In places even the pavements were of alabaster carved with ornaments in low relief.

The Classic Period.—Of the Greek interiors almost nothing has survived to our time; all the «restorations» shown in books and models are conjectural. We know from literary sources that mural painting was practised; the Stoa Poikile at Athens was a public colonnade whose wall behind the columns was covered with such paintings. At Olympia there was found a beautiful fragment of decorative pavement executed in hard stucco in black and white. Since color was freely used on the exteriors of temples it is probable that the interior columns and walls were painted and the wooden ceilings richly painted and gilded, perhaps paneled somewhat like the stone ceilings of the exterior colonnade or pteroma.

It was the Romans who, of all antique peoples, developed interior decoration to its greatest splendor by recourse to new methods and materials and processes. The Roman decorative system was that of a dress or sheathing or facing of fine material applied to a massive core-construction of coarser materials, such as rubble, concrete or brick. This was faced with stucco, or sheathed with marble and adorned with columns, niches, recessed arches, moldings, entablatures and panels, for which provision was made in the more massive primary construction. Columns were of polished granite, porphyry or marble; capitals and entablatures were richly carved; there was much ornament of stucco molded in relief and brilliantly painted, and ceilings and vaults were deeply paneled, with rich ornaments in relief painted and in parts gilded. The lower parts of the walls were wainscoted with precious marbles, and the floors were of marble in patterns of various colors or in mosaic of *opus Grecanicum.* (See MOSAIC). The vastness of the Roman interiors of temples, baths and basilicas unemcumbered by columns, and the majesty of their lofty vaulted ceilings, produced effects of internal grandeur never before dreamed of, which were greatly enhanced by the splendor of the materials employed. The Pantheon remains to-day a marvelous example of this splendor, though deprived of the former enrichments of its majestic paneled dome. The brilliant wall paintings of Pompeii (q.v.), the Pompeiian and Roman painted reliefs in stucco, and many Roman mosaic floors, preserve for us examples of Roman interior decoration of a less monumental sort.

The Mediæval Styles.— With the fall of Rome, the leadership in the arts passed to Constantinople, where the Byzantine style rapidly developed in the 6th century to its culmination in Hagia Sophia, the church of the Divine Wisdom. It was pre-eminently a style of interior decoration, not of external splendor. Deriving from Roman precedents the system of massive vaulted construction with surface facing of marble sheathing and applied decoration, it introduced two new and transcendently important elements — the dome on pendentives and the use of pictorial and ornamental mosaic in brilliant colors on a gold ground, to cover all vaulted surfaces. Fine surface-incised carving was used sparingly and effectively, but the main effect was of rich and harmoniously-blended colors upon every visible surface. Fresco-painting (see FRESCO) was employed in some cases instead of mosaic on walls and vaults, at least in the later churches. The

Courtesy Museum of Fine Arts, Boston

Georgian room, Newland, Gloucestershire, England. The house was built in 1748.

Courtesy W. & J. Sloane

A contemporary country living room.

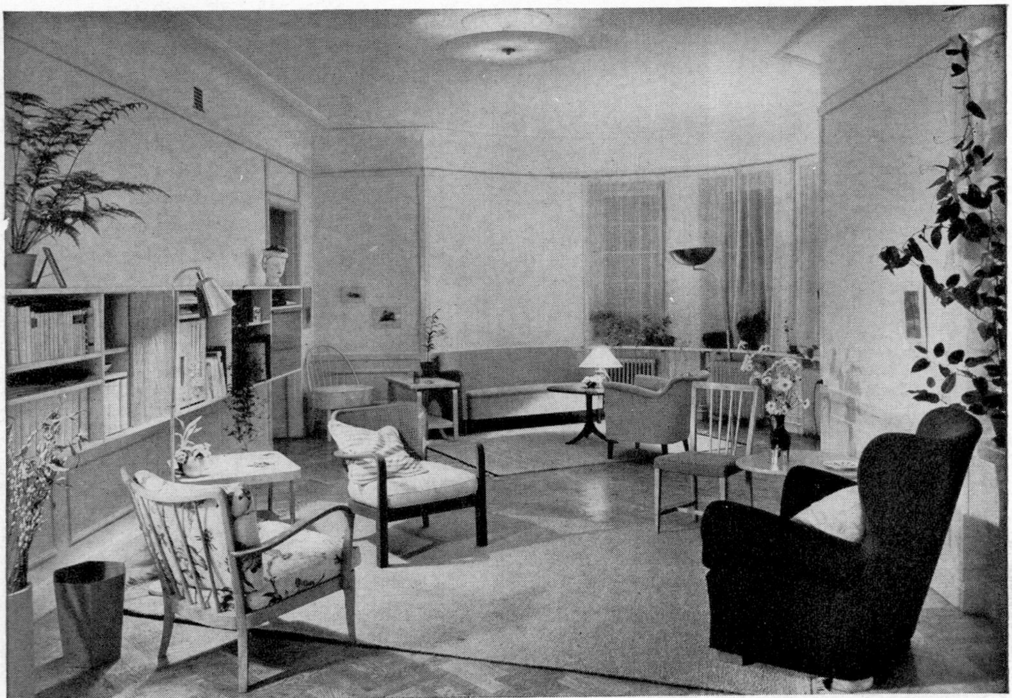

Courtesy The American-Swedish News Exchange, Inc.

A modern Swedish interior. Light colors in the rugs, upholstery, woodwork, and walls, contribute to a general impression of cheer and spaciousness in the room. Note also the many green or flowering plants.

Courtesy W. & J. Sloane

A well-designed living room. Patterned slipcovers and draperies enliven the handsome but somber furniture.

This modern dinette ensemble is made of solid birch wood.
Courtesy Heywood-Wakefield Company

A modern bedroom ensemble.

INTERIOR DECORATION

Courtesy (1) and (3) W. & J. Sloane; (2) Kohler Company

Top: Today's kitchens are colorful and attractive as well as functional. _Left:_ The current trend in bathroom designing is to make every inch count. Note the ample storage space here. _Above:_ Accessories, such as this beautiful Wedgwood lamp, are useful additions in the interior decoration of many types of rooms.

Byzantine mosaic-workers and other artists found wide employment in Italy, and when in 1047 the Venetians set about the reconstruction of the church of Saint Mark, it was built upon the model of the church of the Apostles at Constantinople, largely by artificers from that city. Though much smaller than Hagia Sophia, and though some of its mosaics are of a much later age than the 11th century, it is to-day one of the richest and most splendid interiors in the world. Of much earlier date are the two basilicas of San Apollinare at Ravenna (6th century) with fine mosaics, those of San Apollinare Nuovo being particularly impressive. The baptistery of the Orthodox and the domical church of San Vitale at Ravenna also offer striking examples of Byzantine interior decoration in marble and mosaic.

The Romanesque period in western Europe, from the 8th to the mid-12th century, produced little of importance in interior decoration except in Venice as just noted, and in Sicily where a blending of Oriental and Byzantine influences has left to the world a number of remarkably beautiful and impressive interiors in churches and chapels at Palermo and in the neighboring cathedral of Monreale. The pavements of these are patterned in colored marble, the walls wainscoted with marble crested with Arabic patterns, the walls and domes and apses glow with impressive symbolic pictures in mosaic, and the timber ceilings were painted in brilliant colors The baptistery of Florence (10th century) and the neighboring church of San Miniato are exceptions to the general rule of severity of interior effect of the Romanesque architecture.

For the remarkable styles of interior decoration of the Arabs, Moors and other Mohammedan peoples — styles in which pictorial representation and sculpture were excluded by religious prejudice and geometric and conventional ornament in brilliant colors in plaster, tiles and inlay developed to their utmost splendor during the Middle Ages, see MOHAMMEDAN ART.

With the development of Gothic architecture, first in France, later in northern and central Europe, and finally in Italy, wholly new resources were brought to the service of interior decoration. Structural forms were multiplied and enriched, to enhance the decorative effect of the lofty vaulted naves and aisles. To the splendor of clustered shafts, grouped moldings, carved capitals, molded vaulting-ribs and intricate traceries were added symbolic sculptures and grotesques, and color was introduced in the blazing glory of the stained glass windows. To a limited extent also painting was resorted to in certain parts of the architecture and even of the sculpture, an decorative pavement-tiles in browns, blacks, dark reds and yellows were used with discretion on the floors of choirs and chapels; but the chief color effects were in the windows, whose brilliant hues tended to kill the soberer tones of painted walls and moldings. Mosaic and marble were not favored outside of Italy, and the vaults were seldom painted at all. The English interiors, less lofty and majestic than the French, were on the other hand far richer in decoration, with multiplied complexities of shafting in black Purbeck marble, finer and more numerous moldings, and, above all, magnificent vaults in complex patterns of vault-ribs. In Italy, in contrast with western and northern Europe, the mediæval builders of the Gothic period depended upon color rather than architectural membering for interior effect. They often painted both the walls and the vaults; splendid inlays of black, red and white marble adorned the floors; mosaic was frequently applied to restricted places or features, and the fixed furniture was of great decorative magnificence. Stained glass, however, was not much used; the Italian windows were small and far apart, and offered no such field for blazing transparent color as the clear stories and aisle windows of the North. The 14th century witnessed the culmination of this Italian mediæval art, above all in Florence, Assisi, Padua and Sienna. The mural paintings of the chapels and cloisters of Santa Croce and Santa Maria Novella at Florence, and the works of Giotto and his followers in Florence, Assisi and Padua are unsurpassed for pure decorative propriety and richness. (See GIOTTO; MURAL PAINTING). The «Upper» and «Lower» church of San Francesco at Assisi offers the most complete and perfect example of consummate interior decoration effected solely by the brush of the painter without any aid from architectural embellishments, to be found anywhere, with the sole exception of the Sistine Chapel of the Vatican at Rome.

Renaissance Decoration.— The Renaissance ushered in a new age and a new spirit in art. Not only were the fine arts thenceforward no longer confined almost exclusively to the service of the Church, but they were also transformed by two influences — a new and enthusiastic study of nature in all its aspects, leading to a new realism previously unsought; and a new inspiration from the arts and culture of antiquity. There was great increase of private luxury, and a marvelous broadening of the scope of painting and sculpture as well as architecture. Palaces were made as splendid as churches, and churches were adorned with new splendors in marble, stucco, painting and gilding. The dome became the dominant internal feature in church design, and often received a specially rich decoration of paneling and painting or mosaic. Delicate relief-ornamentation in stucco was combined with color, after ancient Roman models. Mural painting reached its highest development. Ceilings, whether vaulted or horizontal, were treated with especial magnificence, with rich paneling or painting or both combined. Rome especially abounds in splendid examples of this consummate art of the 16th century, as in the Loggie (arcades) of the Vatican, the Camere or Stanze (apartments) of that palace, the Villa Madama, and of course the incomparable Sistine Chapel. The vaults and dome of Saint Peter's and many other ceilings are noteworthy; while in Venice the walls and ceilings of the hall of the Great Council and of many other superb rooms display the master works of Titian, Tintoretto, Paul Veronese, Palma the Younger and others of the Venetian masters of oil painting. (See article PAINTING). With the close of the 16th century and throughout the 17th, decorative art declined — not in splendor but in taste. The love of display, the toleration of sham, the abuse of stucco, of gilding and of strong-colored marbles, and the introduction of theatrical and attitudinizing sculpture, led to great extravagance and excesses of effect, destructive of real dignity and solemnity. Much of the interior decoration in Saint Peter's and nearly all that in the Jesuit churches of the 17th and 18th centuries, both in and out of Italy, is of this meretricious character. In Germany this «Baroque» style of interior decoration was especially riotous and uncontrolled by architectural propriety, though often amazingly clever and effective. In France the Renaissance style, introduced by Italian artists at first, ran a somewhat similar course, but never reached the extremes of artistic extravagance noted in Italy and Germany. Church interiors were much more severe, more sparing in applied decoration, and retained much more of structural expression and truthfulness. French palace decoration received under Louis XIV and XV a peculiar progressive development, making much use of white and gold, and of delicate though increasingly fantastic and capricious detail, as will be later noted. Under Louis XVI and under Napoleon («First Empire») the tendency toward fantastic originality of detail was reversed, and interior decoration became more and more classic, restrained and finally severe

The 19th century witnessed the almost total eclipse of true and sincere work in interior decoration, as in all the arts, for at least the first half of its course. Under Napoleon III («Second Empire») there began in France a notable revival of all the arts, and, partly through French influence, this revival gradually made its appearance in other countries. The progress of archæology, the development of machine-manufacture, the immense expansion of commerce and industry, all tended, however, to lead artists astray and to hamper the development of original creation. On the other hand, the multiplication of schools of art and of museums and the growth of wealth and taste have given the arts a new stimulus and new opportunities. Among notable interiors of the last century in Europe may be mentioned in London the Houses of Parliament and the mosaics of Saint Paul's Cathedral, in Paris, the stair hall and foyer of the Opera, the stair hall and Salle des Fêtes of the Hôtel de Ville, and the mural paintings in the Panthéon. Examples in the United States will be noted later.

Present-Day Monumental Interior Decoration.— Outside of the United States, which form the subject of a separate section of this article, interior decoration has followed the general movement of modern art since 1900. As to style, two distinct currents are observable; one conservative and classic, tending to the revival or imitation and development of old-time traditions; the other, revolutionary and romantic, seeking new forms and methods of expression and striving to break away from tradition. These currents are equally discernible in architectural decoration and in decorative painting, and appear in the interior decoration of all the European countries in varying degrees. The decorators of the first group are subdivided broadly into the classicists and the mediævalists, according as they seek to reproduce the decorative effects of Greek or Roman types on the one hand or of Byzantine, Romanesque or Gothic art on the other. The multiplication of books, prints and photographs of historic art, the ease of modern travel and the greatly increased mechanical and material resources of our time have made such revival and imitation perfectly practicable and even rational. The practice in the best work is not to copy, but to design upon the basis of a thorough mastery of the principles and methods of the historic styles. The decorators of the second group, while they must of necessity start with something of the knowledge and experience accumulated by the centuries, consciously strive to avoid any suggestion of the forms, combinations and types of the past, and to devise in their place new and original media and forms of artistic expression. The movement of which their efforts are the result began in Paris near the end of the last century, and made a sensational appeal to the world-public in the great exhibition of 1900. It has been variously called «Art Nouveau» (New Art), «Moderne Kunst» (Modern Art) and «The Secession,» and has been carried to the furthest extremes in Germany and Austria, especially in Bohemia. But its most notable productions have been rather in domestic interiors and the minor arts than in monumental interiors, and these for the most part in hotels, restaurants, theatres and other places of amusement rather than in churches and the more stately works of interior design.

Modern ecclesiastical interior decoration has generally followed, more or less closely, the traditional styles of the past; either the Gothic (or less frequently the Byzantine or the Romanesque), or the Italian Renaissance. Mural painting is less often depended upon than architectural enrichment and conventional ornament, the richest decoration being bestowed upon the chancel or choir or «Sanctuary» of the church.

A. D. F. HAMLIN.

Domestic Interior Decoration.—Many people who have a great interest in furniture and decorations of the various periods are timid about trying to apply their knowledge to the decorating of their own homes. Yet decoration is one of the simplest of all arts. After the few guiding laws are learned, practice in applying them will bring rich reward in original, interesting, and individual rooms.

A home that expresses the personalities of those who dwell within is far more interesting than a home that is correct in every detail of line, form, and color, but that has no soul. The wise professional decorator knows this and works closely with her client in order to avoid a stereotyped house. A decorator is often an economy. In all the larger cities there are decorators with their own shops or decorators who are on the staffs of the department stores. They charge a percentage on what they buy, and because they are able to buy at wholesale prices, the only charge is often just what anyone would be forced to pay for a retail purchase. Therefore, it is often wise to take advantage of their trained skill and experience. Where a decorator is not available and the amateur wishes to try his own hand, the following rules will be of use: The first thing that must be considered is the prevailing style of decoration to be used. Naturally, this is determined by the architecture of the house. If an apartment is to be decorated, the style of the background will obtrude itself less, but will be felt in such details as fireplaces, door frames and windows. It is not difficult to recognize differences in architecture, but comparisons with standard reference books or charts of architectural types will dispel any doubts as to the actual type. Knowing the architectural type determines pretty well what styles of decoration you can or cannot use. Naturally, with informal architecture and provincial styles, the decoration must also be informal. With the more formal types, formal decoration should prevail. For simplicity, the following groups have been arranged:

If you have a house of tropical architecture, either derived from the Spanish or Italian types, or placed in Florida or California; made of stucco or adobe; roofed with tiles or slate; with casement windows set in wood frames or leadings, you will use—

Floors of broad oak planks, tile, marble or linoleum, or rubber tile to imitate marble. You may use oriental rugs or simple Indian rugs.

Walls will be of rough plaster, plain, painted or stenciled, hung with tapestry, velvet or brocade panels bound with dull gold braid; or with old mirrors and religious paintings framed in heavy architectural mouldings.

Furniture will be of Spanish or Italian types; Early English Oak; the simpler and heavier French Provincial pieces; the Spanish Mission or Californian oak; or the painted Tyrolean or Swiss; or the painted Pennsylvania Dutch Early American pieces.

Draperies will be of velvet brocade; of heavy linen, block-printed in simple patterns; or of heavy cotton and rayon weaves, hung in heavy simple folds directly to the floor from rods of iron or wood.

Upholstery will be of leather, plain or tooled in gold; of velvet or of brocade.

Accessories are lamps of heavy pottery with parchment shades; wrought iron chandelier and candelabra; candle-sticks of carved and gilded wood; polished brass and copper.

Colors used will be ruby and wine red, deep blue, purple and gold, the richness of jewel colors set off by neutral color walls and heavy dark furniture.

If you have a house of the Tudor style, with stucco and half timbering; a cottage in the «Cotswold» style, with a shingled roof laid like thatch; an early American house in either the Cape Cod or the salt-box style; or if you have a Norman type farmhouse with whitewashed bricks and tiled roof, you will use—

Floors of broad oaken planks, of tiles, of slate, or painted floors. Rugs may be oriental, or hand woven or hand-hooked rag rugs. Needle-work rugs are enjoying a new vogue for this type of decorating.

Walls will be rough plaster; pine paneled with simple treatment; or random width feather-edged boards fitted together perpendicularly; or walls entirely covered in wall-paper; partly paneled with wall-paper; or painted in flat color.

Furniture will be any of the pieces from the following styles; Early English Oak; simpler walnut pieces in the William and Mary styles; French Provincial; Early American maple or pine or the Painted Peasant furniture.

Draperies will be of printed linen, of chintz, either plain or printed, glazed or unglazed. Ginghams or plaid; cottons, striped, look especially well. Curtains will be hung straight from a valance or may be tied back. The windows on the Tudor or the French Provincial house are apt to be casement windows, while those of the Early American type houses will be «double hung,» with sashes that raise. In any case, the panes are small, adding decorative value of their own, so that the sheer glass curtain is sometimes omitted. If privacy is desired they can be shirred on a half way rod in the French style, or hung straight in the English style, or ruffled and tied back in the American style.

Accessories are of pewter, brass or copper; or wrought iron; all of these materials being used in lamps, wall bracket lights or chandeliers. Pottery lamps are also used and china should be of the simple potter type or of delft patterns. Prints, colored engravings or simple paintings may be hung on the walls, with samplers being particularly appropriate. Mirrors are small and framed in simple, heavy mouldings.

If you have a house in the Georgian or Colonial style, either brick or white painted wood with formal mouldings showing Grecian ornament, with Palladian windows, or tall windows with larger panes of glass, with an imposing formality showing throughout; or if you have a house adapted from the formal French architecture you will use—

Floors of narrow oak boards laid plain or in parquet patterns; of marble or of rubber tile or linoleum in formal patterns, or carpeting extending to the walls; or Oriental or Chinese rugs.

Walls will be paneled in natural pine or painted paneling; paneled up to the chair rail and papered above in formal pictorial papers, in scenic or floral designs, or in patterns adapted from the hand painted Chinese designs of trees, flowers and birds against a silver ground; or in very formal interiors, covered with brocade all over or in panels. If painted plastered walls are used they should be smooth, and may be used with a stenciled border or a walnut border.

Furniture will be of Eighteenth century designs, either French or English, made of walnut or mahogany, or of painted pine with the surface designs showing Baroque swirls or Chinese designs. Lacquer or japanning is used on cabinets. Fine inlay and veneering is very beautiful and combines many woods. There are many highboys, lowboys, commodes, cabinets, tea-tables, and china cabinets. Furniture comes in pairs to lend more formality. Sofas and settees, armchairs, side chairs, stools, all show needlework or tapestry upholstery. Card tables have tops of needlework. Use any pieces of Queen Anne, Chippendale, or Louis XV or XVI style.

Draperies will be of chintz or printed linen; of damask or brocade, patterns in large designs using flowers and garlands; or of heavy satin. They will hang straight to the floor from under a heavy shaped and stiffened cornice of fabric or of wood, or they will loop back over brass or crystal arms of fabric «tie-backs.» Glass curtains should be silk gauze or ninon. Venetian blinds look well in these formal rooms.

Upholstery will be of needlework, tapestry, brocade, velvet, leather, and, in the less formal interiors, of chintz and printed linen.

Accessories will be lamps of fine china or of Chinese jade and semi-precious materials carved into figures; of Chinese porcelain figurines, of Staffordshire figures; wall brackets will be of carved and gilded wood; of brass, with or without crystal drops; chandelier of crystal or of Waterford glass with branched arms for many candles; gilt bronze clocks and accessories in the French style, a rich formality in many fine accessories.

Colors will show a wider range, but soft colors look particularly well with mahogany. Old rose, sapphire blue, dull gold and soft greens are particularly popular.

If you have a house that is very formal in style, showing the influence of the Greek Revival, using brick walls, plain or painted; or of wood; or perhaps a city house of marble, you must keep your interior very formal and use only furniture that shows the same influence. There are many styles to choose from, inspired by the work of such famous designers as Adam, Sheraton, Hepplewhite; or the French Empire designers, Percier and Fontaine; or the styles of the later English Regency, or the American Federal designers, Duncan Phyfe or Samuel McIntyre.

Floors will be hard wood, either plain or parquet; or of marble, rubber tile or linoleum, laid in formal classical patterns showing borders of Greek fret or anthemion. Carpets may be used extending to walls, and are more often patterned than plain. Rugs should be of Aubusson type in classical designs or the simpler of the Chinese rugs may be used.

Furniture will be of mahogany, of satinwood, of birch or ebony, and may be mounted with gold ornaments showing wreath, garland, swag, or sphinx; or painted. Caning is used on the seats of the chairs. Furniture is lighter in proportion, using fewer curves, more straight lines, particularly in the legs.

Draperies are of satin, damask or brocade; and in the less formal rooms of toile de jouet printed in classical designs, showing Grecian figures, wreaths and garlands. The valance of the less formal styles gives way to intricate swags looped over poles, showing color contrast in the linings and the fringe edgings. Side drapes fold back and forth in the formal manner to show contrasting color in the linings and are occasionally of an entirely different material from that used in the swag at the top of the window.

Upholstery is of satin, damask, brocade; of leather, or of zebra or leopard fur. Velvet and chintz are used occasionally.

Accessories are lamps of gilt bronze, marble and crystal; of classical figures in marble and terra cotta. Shades are of parchment, of silk or of tôle painted with classical borders. Mirrors are larger and are often set into the wall with a heavy frame. Paintings are portraits or scenes in oil, or engravings richly framed in gold.

Colors are very sophisticated in type and consist of strong contrasts, such as black and white, gold with sharp purple, saffron, turquoise, jade, magenta and such unusual tones. This style is so formal in character that it is often used in rooms of semi-public character such as restaurants, reception rooms in hotels, or supper rooms. It combines very well with furniture of the so-called Modern Classic style and is therefore very popular for use in city apartments.

Most of the modern furniture that is being shown in the shops is designed to combine well with one or more of the traditional styles. The Swedish modern is excellent with furniture of the provincial types, and may be used with the French Provincial pieces or in the Georgian interiors. Discretion must be shown in combining any furniture to see that similar proportions are maintained. Pieces that are out of proportion throw the whole room out of scale. In the above groupings, proportions are generally similar, but *every period and style produce both light and heavy pieces.*

Because rooms are smaller now than they have been in the past, certain styles are out of fashion favor. The style of Louis XIV is seldom used, and English Oak has been out of style. The latter is now being stripped of its dark finish and bleached to a light tone that makes it look new and attractive. Victorian furniture, too, has been out of style, but the decorators have discovered that the simpler pieces can be bleached, painted and reupholstered to make them very attractive in our present day interiors. Interest has revived in the Southern interiors of Civil War days, and furniture designers are adding these styles to the variety that they present to the public.

After considering style, and proportion, the next important thing to consider is suitability to purpose and practicality of use. Certain types of furniture seem very feminine because of their delicacy of detail and proportion, and because of the curved lines used. Naturally, they would not be used in a man's bedroom or in the game room, but would be used in a woman's bedroom, in a dressing room, or possibly in a formal reception room or a breakfast room. Similarly the furniture of heavier proportions and bolder, stronger detail is more suitable for men, for offices, smoking rooms, or libraries. Because furniture of the 18th century falls between these two styles, is neither too curved or dainty, or too bold in detail, it has maintained its top rank as far as sales volume is concerned for many years. It is more popular with men and women than the more formal classical styles, although, thanks to the assistance given by modern classic, these sell well in cities, and represent more sophisticated taste.

Color is very important in decoration. We all have favorite colors, and we all have colors that we violently dislike. Certain colors cause no mental reaction at all; we are indifferent to them. Therefore color must be considered very carefully. A room that is to be lived in, that cannot be repainted in a month or two, must have careful thought before the color is chosen. Violent contrasts are exciting and amusing when first done. The effect gained is stimulating, but when lived in day after day can be too stimulating; can cause quarrels, and quick temper. A room that must be lived in should show the favorite colors of those who are to inhabit it, but in a restful, harmonious manner. Soft, neutral backgrounds help, for many colors can be used in smaller areas. For instance, against a gray or a tan wall, (or against walls that are sufficiently grayed shades of any color) you can combine three or four apparently unrelated colors with great success. For instance, suppose you paint the wall a pinkish gray, hang vivid blue draperies at the window, use mahogany furniture with upholstery in rose and green tones, you will have a restful and attractive living room, but a room that avoids monotony. Timid decorators might use several shades of one color, for this is restful, but unless spiked by a note of vivid contrast, is very boring.

As for textures and patterns, a safe rule to follow is not to combine more than three different types in one room. Upholstery could show two different patterns with a plain rug. With a patterned rug, plain upholstery should be used, but one could be shiny and one dull, or have surface interest in weave.

For a time white walls enjoyed a tremendous vogue. They made the room appear larger, and were introduced by a famous designer who understood gradation of value and contrast of texture so well that she could combine a white rug, white upholstery and white accessories without monotony. Handled by less expert hands this would lack the sparkle that dusty pastel colors would achieve against the same walls. Colored ceilings and colored floors look well with white walls and are a welcome change but should never be used unless the ceiling is high.

Dull, dark walls have had a recent vogue, but make a room appear smaller and therefore should be handled with care. Brilliant color and large areas of light furniture or upholstery must be used with such walls to avoid lugubrious effect.

Some of the modern decorators have felt that painting all four walls the same color, or the same value of a color was monotonous and have changed color on the various walls. Some rooms have been decorated with three white walls, and one colored wall interrupted by white draperies. Painted panels of a different color often add prominence to an interesting piece of furniture or line a niche behind a bed. When the wall is papered, it can be broken by such painted panels, or by one painted wall, with great success.

Color laws require an understanding of the relation of colors in order to achieve attractive harmonies. It is therefore necessary to understand the balance of color.

Draw a circle and divide it six times evenly. At the points thus found, starting at the top and working clockwise, write yellow, orange, red, purple, blue and green. These colors are known as the primary and secondary colors, and are the most vivid of all colors when used in their full intensity. Bright red is the brightest of all; blue, next; while yellow is light, but bright; and green comes next. Because purple is dark and heavy it never becomes as strong as any of the others, but may be brightened somewhat by adding white. Now mark off between the colors the intermediate colors, that are called by the hyphenated names of their neighbors; yellow-orange; red-orange, red-purple, blue-purple, blue-green, and yellow-green.

Before proceeding further, it is necessary to know that all colors with blue in them are cool colors, and should not be used in rooms with a northern exposure. Colors that have red in them are warm colors, and should be used carefully or not at all, in rooms with sunlight. Of course, if a very sunny effect is desired, yellow should be used, and a room that has too much light, and seems too «glary» can use dull, softened purples on the walls.

The warm colors are called advancing colors and the cool colors are called receding colors. Therefore, never use warm colors on the walls of rooms that should appear large, but use instead such colors as blue-green, green or blue.

In combining colors, this color circle will be of great help. Pastel tints of a color, or greyed values of a color combined with that color in its fuller intensity, achieve a restful effect and should only be used in a bedroom. Even then it is better if relieved by small flashes of other colors in accessories. The three near neighbors on the color circle are called analogous colors, and also achieve a restful effect. By varying the tones of these colors, and by varying the intensity, or textures, a more interesting effect can be gained. In a room with a pale yellow wall-paper, draperies of plaid in tones of orange are used. A dull orange yellow rug is on the floor. Obviously with maple furniture this would be very uninteresting, but with mahogany furniture it would achieve more interest. The colors that are directly opposite each other on the color circle provide the most contrast, and are called complementary colors. These should be used only in a room where gayety and stimulation are desired. A sun-porch with an orange tile floor and soft blue walls, for instance, combining both these colors in gay chintz at the windows; or a game room that uses green and red; or a breakfast room or kitchen in yellow-green and red-purple.

An interesting effect may be had by combining the analogous scheme with the complementary, using only one complementary to add spice to the otherwise restrained related colors. For instance, in a living room that used dull red-orange draperies, with soft pigskin colored upholstery (yellow-orange), the accessories should be in vivid blue. The furniture in brown would be a greyed shade of red-orange and the rug could be either a dull blue or a soft rust shade.

For gayety, an easy harmony to handle is the triad. Three colors that are equidistant on the color circle are used together. Thus a room could have coral draperies (tinted red-orange) against pale yellow-green walls, with a dull purple or «egg-plant» carpet.

One of the easiest harmonies to use is «unrelated colors used with sufficiently large areas of neutral color.» This means that many colors in varying intensities may be used in a room that has walls that are white, grey or tan; or in a room that has a black rug. Of course, care should be used to arrange the colors so that they do not «fight»; so that the values are correct, and so that areas are not too large. Suppose, for an example, we have an Empire room with a black and white marble-ized floor. Using sulphur yellow draperies, and vivid green-blue upholstery would be most effective; or in a room with pinky beige walls use a plum colored rug (dull red-purple), turquoise blue draperies (tinted blue-green) with lime yellow lining (tinted green-yellow). This would be unusual and interesting and because of the softness of the wall color would be satisfactory.

The hardest color scheme to use is the neutralized harmony. In this scheme all colors used have a tone of one color, and it takes a great deal of experience or experimentation to achieve harmony without discord. Starting with blue as the neutralizing agent, use a grey-blue wall, a rug of egg-plant (blue-purple), draperies of turquoise, and upholstery of dull red that has a purple cast.

After learning how to combine colors, the psychology of color must be considered. Certain colors are depressing, such as the cool colors in dull, dark or greyed values. Other colors are stimulating such as the warm colors in practically all their values. Some people have violent color likes and dislikes and these should always be considered in decorating. Care should be taken to make a room a proper background for the person or persons who are to occupy it. Color becomingness should be considered. A pale blonde will look best in a room that is soft in value, rather than vivid and obtrusive in color. A vivid person, likewise, can "wear" a vivid room becomingly, but may wish to have a dull, dark room to better display her charms. Children like bright colors. Their rooms should use them, but in small, rather than large areas. People who are inclined to be melancholy will find that yellow and all the shades through to red are best for them to live with, while a person of a violent temper should never have much red around to excite it. Green and red in large areas should be avoided in a dining-room, as they are too stimulating in effect, and cause indigestion.

After learning all the laws of decorating, all the things that go to make up a pleasant interior, it is necessary to "shake well and add a little seasoning." One of the most successful of our present day decorators, in lecturing to a class, said that she always counted on having a slightly discordant note in every room in order to gain accent. This is a splendid idea, but only when handled by an expert. The home decorating magazines are full of hints on decorating. Many of the rooms shown are very lovely. Others are thoroughly mediocre. Much knowledge can be gained by a careful analysis of these pictures. Originality is one of the most necessary things next to good taste. If you can gain these two things, and stamp the room with your personality, or with the personality of the people who are to inhabit it, you are a successful interior decorator.

Bibliography.—Adler, H., *The New Interior* (New York 1916); Eberlein, H. D., and others, *The Practical Book of Interior Decoration* (Philadelphia 1919); De Wolfe, E., *House in Good Taste* (New York (1920); Burbank, E., *Be Your Own Decorator* (New York 1922); Jakway, J. B., *Principles of Interior Decoration* (New York 1922); Fales, W., *A Simple Course in Home Decorating* (Boston 1923); Northend, M. H., *The Small House; Its Possibilities* (New York 1923); Frohne, H. W., and others, *Color Schemes for the Home and Model Interiors* (Philadelphia 1924); Gilman, R., *Great Styles of Interior Architecture* (New York 1924); Gloag, J., *Color and Comfort in Decoration* (New York 1924); Kelly, A. A., *The Expert Interior Decorator* (New York 1924); Seal, E. D., *Furnishing the Little House* (New York 1924); Clute, E., *The Treatment of Interiors* (New York 1926); Ionides, B., *Color and Interior Decoration* (New York 1926); McClelland, N. V., *Practical Book of Interior Decoration Wall-Treatments* (Philadelphia 1926); Frankl, P. T., *New Dimensions* (New York 1928); Koues, H., *On Decorating the House* (New York 1928); Palmer, L., *Your House* (Boston 1928); Post, E., *The Personality of a House* (New York 1933); Ionides, B., *Colour in Everyday Rooms* (New York 1934); Rutt, A. H., *Home Furnishing* (New York 1935); Stewart, R., and Gerald, J., *Home Decoration* (Toronto 1935); Fales, W., *What's New in Home Decorating* (London 1936); Burris-Meyer, E., *Decorating Livable Homes* (New York 1937); Miller, J. D., *Interior Decoration* (London 1937); Patmore, D., *Decorating for the Small Home* (New York 1937); Whiton, S., *Elements of Interior Decoration* (Philadelphia 1937); Knauff, C. G. B., *Refurnishing the Home* (New York 1938); Draper, D. T., *Decorating Is Fun* (New York 1939); Maas, C., *Common Sense in Home Decoration* (New York 1939); Miller, G., *Decoratively Speaking* (New York 1939); Ford, J., and K. M., *Design of Modern Interiors* (New York 1942); Lord, J., and others, *Text Book on Painting and Decorating* (Toronto 1946); Rockow, H. M. K., and J., *Creative Home Decorating* (New York 1946); Dutton, R., *English Interior, 1500 to 1900* (London 1948); Lee, R. W., and Bolender, L. T., *Fashions in Furnishings* (New York 1948); Patmore, D., *Decoration for the Small Home* (London 1948); Lewis, E. H., *Furnishing on a Budget* (1948); Stephenson, J. B., and Lowrie, C. E., *How to Choose, Decorate and Repair Your House* (New York 1948); Carpenter, N. A., *Modernising the Home* (Melbourne, Australia, 1949); Clifford, C. R., *Period Furnishings* (New York 1947); Ketcham, H., *How to Use Color and Decorating Designs in the Home* (New York 1949); Matthew, W. P., *Home Decorating* (New York 1949); Ogg, E., *Decorating the Small Apartment* (1949); Parry, J. P., *A.B.C. of Home Decoration* (London 1949); Pearce, W. J., *Painting and Decorating* (1949); Williams, H. L., and O. K., *How to Furnish Old American Houses* (New York 1949); Aronson, J., *Book of Furniture and Decoration*, new ed. (New York 1950); Brandt, M. K., *Decorate Your Home for Better Living* (New York 1950).

KAY HARDY,
Director, The American School of Design.

INTERJECTION, a word thrown in, to express some sudden emotion or passion; an exclamation such as ah! alas! ouch! d—n! They are hardly considered parts of speech and never form grammatical parts of a sentence; they seem more akin to the sounds uttered by the lower animals than to articulate language.

INTERLAKEN, ĭn'tẽr-lä-kĕn, or ĭn-tẽr-lä'kĕn (meaning "between the lakes"), commune, Switzerland, in Bern canton; 26 miles southeast of the town of Bern. It is beautifully situated near the left bank of the Aare River in the valley of Boedeli, between the lakes of Thun and Brienz. It contains a beautiful old castle and numerous hotels and is the starting point for many tourist excursions into the surrounding Alps. Pop. (1941) 4,059.

INTERNAL-COMBUSTION ENGINE. The internal-combustion engine is a heat engine in which the fuel is burned (that is, united with oxygen) within the confining space of the engine itself. This burning process releases large amounts of energy, which are transformed into work through the mechanism of the engine.

This type of power plant thus differs from the steam engine, which uses what might be called an external-combustion process because its fuel is burned apart from the engine (and under a boiler to convert the water in the boiler into steam, which then flows to the engine to expand and do work).

In general, it cannot be said that the internal- or the external-combustion process is inherently more efficient. The most efficient heat cycle known to man (the Carnot) adds all of the heat to the working substance at the highest possible temperature and rejects all it rejects, at the lowest possible temperature. From this standpoint, the internal-combustion engine has the advantage on the high-temperature side, while the external-combustion or vapor cycle does better on the low-temperature side.

The highest temperatures reached in the cycles used in internal-combustion engines can be much higher than those practicable in the cycles of the steam engine or even the mercury-steam system, since, with the latter processes, the heat must be transferred through the metal walls of the chamber in which the fuel is burned to the working substance. This, in turn, limits the upper temperature to the maximum that the walls can stand.

On the low-temperature side, however, the steam or vapor cycle expands to and rejects heat at a considerably lower temperature than is possible with the internal-combustion engine.

Thus, as a practical matter, a complete analysis may be required to determine which type of engine would be more efficient in a specific case.

In general, the internal-combustion engine has

become the means of propulsion in the transportation field, with the exception of locomotives and large ships. Even here, in recent years, the internal-combustion engine (the Diesel, in particular) has become quite popular, for it offers the advantage of light weight, clean operation.

In stationary applications, size of unit and local factors often determine the choice between the use of steam and Diesel engines. Diesel power plants have a distinct economic advantage over steam engines when the size of the plant is small, 100 to 150 horsepower (hp.). However, there are many Diesel-engine plants much larger than this. If process steam is not needed in large quantities, Diesel plants of 2,000 to 5,000 hp. are often desirable. Internal-combustion engines are particularly appropriate for seasonal industries, because of the small standby losses with these engines during the shutdown periods. Also, because of these small standby losses, Diesels are often used as standby units in steam power stations, for they are flexible and will quickly pick up the load.

History.—The first experimental internal-combustion engine was made by a Dutch astronomer, Christian Huygens, who, in 1680, applied a principle advanced by Jean de Hautefeuille in 1678 for drawing water. This principle was based on the fact that the explosion of a small amount of gunpowder in a closed chamber provided with escape valves would create a vacuum when the gases of combustion cooled. Huygens, using a cylinder containing a piston, was thus able to move it by the external atmospheric pressure.

The first commercially practical internal-combustion engine was built by a French engineer, Jean Joseph Étienne Lenoir, in 1860. It used illuminating gas as fuel. Two years later another French scientist, Alphonse Beau de Rochas, enunciated the principles of the four-stroke cycle, but Nikolaus August Otto built the first successful engine operating on this principle (1876). This engine also burned illuminating gas, but with increased efficiency because of compressing it before ignition. Otto secured an American patent in 1877 on the engine illustrated in Fig. 1. The Otto cycle has continued to be the familiar designation for all explosion or constant-volume engines.

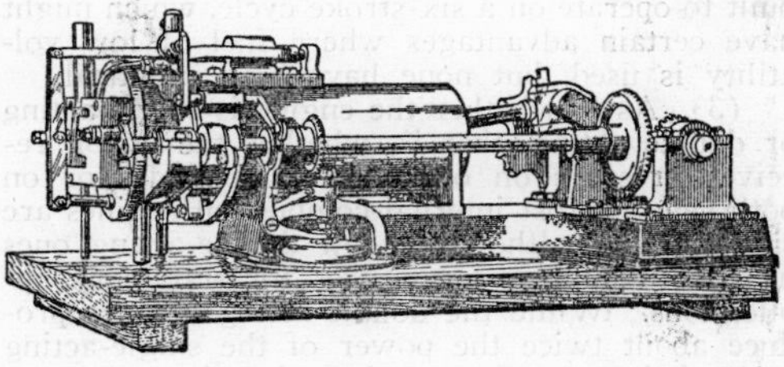

FIG. 1. Model of engine on which Otto secured his American patent in 1877. Now in Smithsonian Institution.

The advantages of compressing the charge before igniting it were probably discovered by an Englishman, William Barnett. At least he was the first to cover the principle in a patent, which was issued to him in 1838. Barnett also pioneered the two-stroke-cycle idea, but Dugald Clerk, a Scottish engineer, did the most in its early development—to circumvent Otto's patents.

In 1892 Rudolf Diesel, a German, conceived the idea of igniting the fuel by injecting it into air that, by compression, had been heated to a point where its temperature would start combustion. Since then his name has been identified with the combustion or constant-pressure type of engine, as distinguished from the Otto or explosion type.

Diesel's work was entirely with relatively large, slow-speed engines, but since his death (1913), high-speed Diesels have been developed. These engines employ a modification of the Diesel cycle.

Contemporaneously with Otto's work in Germany, a Boston engineer, George Brayton, designed an engine (Fig. 2) to burn gasoline. One of his engines was exhibited at the Philadelphia Centennial Exposition in 1876.

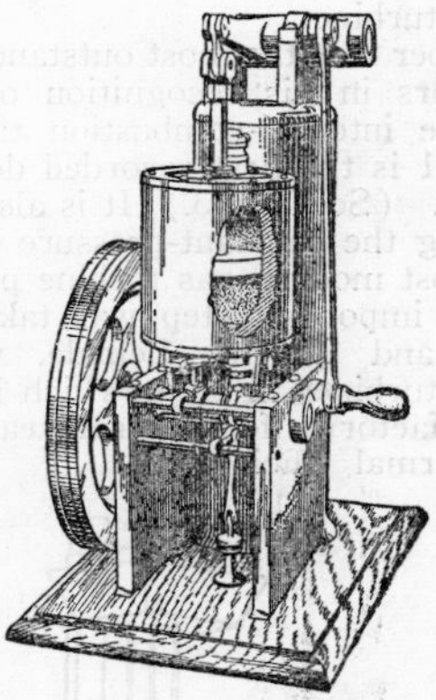

FIG. 2. Patent model of Brayton engine. Also in Smithsonian Institution.

The means of igniting the combustible mixture passed through several stages before higher speeds and, hence, lighter engines could be made available for vehicles and boats. Otto used a flame to touch off the gas, and the best speed he could get was 150 to 200 revolutions per minute (rpm.). One of his workmen, Gottlieb Daimler, set up his own shop and developed what became known as hot-tube ignition. By regulating the heat of the tube, he could control the point at which ignition took place. He succeeded in attaining 800 to 1,000 rpm. speeds high enough to make the automobile practicable. This was in 1883 and gas was still the fuel.

Attention was then turned to the development of carburetors by which gasoline could be atomized or vaporized to substitute it for gas as a fuel, making the use of internal-combustion engines possible in portable applications. Daimler in Germany and Fernand Forest in France both accomplished this in 1885. Daimler had the better engine but Forest the better carburetor.

Atomization of the liquid fuel, that is, breaking it up into minute particles and mixing them with air (to supply the oxygen) to form the combustible mixture, is the function of carburetors. Daimler approximated this by forcing air through the liquid fuel, and the entrained particles, by contact with the hot tube, were gasified before igniting. Forest sprayed the fuel into a stream of air, on the principle of perfume atomizers or insecticide sprayers. Later, an associate of Daimler's, Wilhelm Maybach, invented the float-feed carburetor, which has become the accepted form.

Karl Benz, another German, taking Daimler's engine and Forest's carburetor, installed them in a tricycle, adding electric ignition. In 1885 he built the first gasoline automobile, which quickly became and still is the largest field of application of internal-combustion engines. (See AUTOMOBILE—*Automobile Engine.*)

Gas Turbines.—The principle of the turbine has been known for a long time. About 100 A.D., Hero, the Alexandrian philosopher, built a reaction turbine, which converted steam pressure into mechanical power.

This invention, as well as Giovanni Branca's steam jet-operated turbine of 1629, was the inspiration for later inventors in their attempts to substitute combustion products for steam as a more convenient method of power generation by means of a turbine.

John Barber was the most outstanding of these early inventors in his recognition of the possibilities of the internal-combustion turbine. His patent of 1791 is the first recorded description of a gas turbine. (See Fig. 3.) It is also significant in anticipating the constant-pressure cycle, which is used in most modern gas turbine power plants.

The next important step was taken by René Armengaud and Charles Lemale, who started building gas turbines in 1894, which it is claimed worked satisfactorily for several years, although at a low thermal efficiency.

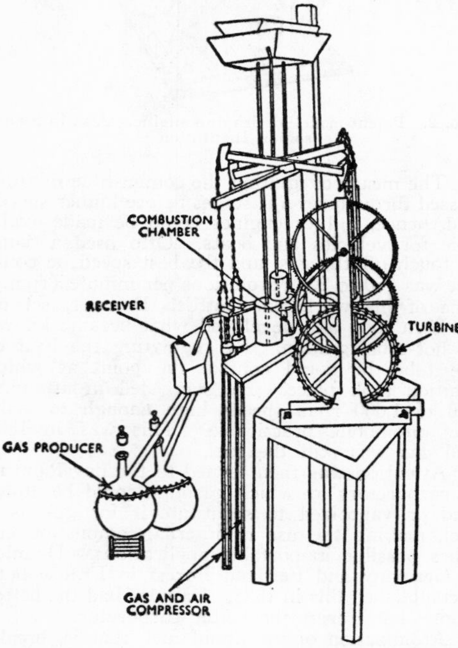

From *Modern Gas Turbines,* Arthur W. Judge, Chapman & Hall, Ltd., London, 1947.

FIG. 3. Gas turbine patented in 1791 by John Barber.

By the beginning of the 20th century many other turbines were in the process of being built, such as the Stolze air turbine and the Holzwarth constant-volume gas turbine.

Other work was being done by Charles Gordon Curtis, who was granted a United States patent for a gas turbine in 1895, and Dr. Sanford A. Moss, who, in 1902, was operating a de Laval turbine with the aid of combustion products.

In 1903 the General Electric Company commenced research that was directed toward the development of the exhaust-driven supercharger for aircraft engines.

Although engineers of many countries were working on the problem, the British Frank Whittle is credited with having devised the first practical solution to the problem of aircraft propulsion by thermal jet reaction using a gas turbine-compressor unit. His original patent was dated 1930 although it was not until 1944 that an aircraft employing his ideas was actually flown by the British Royal Air Force and the United States Air Force.

Meanwhile, several German firms had been doing important research: Junkers, Heinkel-Hirth, and BMW (Bavarian Motor Works). Out of this work came the development of a jet engine that was installed in an HE-178 (Heinkel-Hirth). It flew in August 1939—the first jet-propelled aircraft to fly.

Classification.—The principal types of internal-combustion engines are:

(1). Gasoline engines.
(2). Diesel engines.
(3). Gas engines.
(4). Gas turbines and the various types of engines employing the principle of the jet.

The first three of these are what are called reciprocating engines, that is, power is transformed into work by the reciprocating action of a piston. Piston engines come in all sizes from the tiny model airplane engine to such large units as the 8,000-hp. Nordberg Diesel engine, as shown in Fig. 4.

Reciprocating internal-combustion engines have been classified in many ways, such as:

(1). According to the ideal cycle that should be used as a standard of comparison with the real engine. The principal ideal cycles are the Otto and the Diesel.

(2). According to the number of strokes of the piston necessary to complete one power cycle: the four-stroke cycle and the two-stroke cycle. (These designations are often abbreviated to four-cycle and two-cycle and to four-stroke and two-stroke. The latter phrases are preferable.) A few highly experimental engines have also been built to operate on a six-stroke cycle, which might have certain advantages where fuel of low volatility is used, but none have been practical.

(3). As to whether the engine is single acting or double acting, that is, whether the piston receives pressure on only one of its sides or on both sides. Most internal-combustion engines are single acting, although a few double-acting ones have been built in large sizes for stationary applications. While the double-acting engines produce about twice the power of the single-acting ones of the same bore and stroke, there are mechanical difficulties in design that limit the use of this type.

(4). According to the fuel used: gas, gasoline, or fuel oil.

(5). According to use: automotive, marine, stationary, or portable.

(6). As to the arrangement, position, and number of cylinders. The axes of the cylinders may be vertical (Fig. 5), horizontal, or inclined (Fig. 6). The cylinders of multicylinder engines may also be arranged side by side or they may be end to end (with pistons opposed, as shown in

Fig. 7); they may be radial, as in many aircraft engines (Figs. 8 and 9), or they may be inclined in banks, as in the V-type of engine (Fig. 6).

There are other variable characteristics that are often pertinent to the description of a given engine; for example, the method of governing, the method of introducing fuel into the combustion space, and the arrangement of the valves.

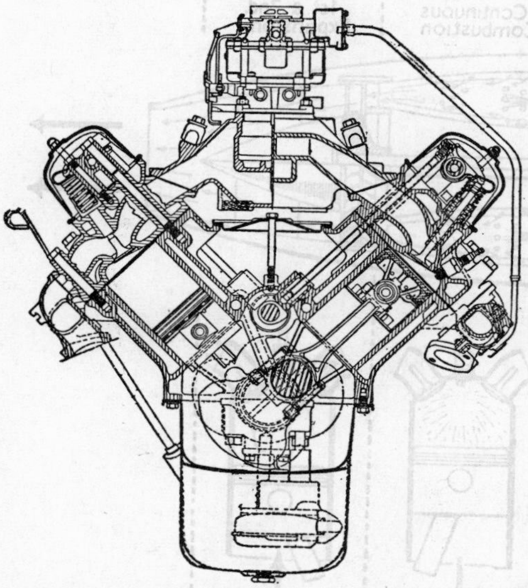

Fig. 6. Transverse section of Studebaker V-8 engine.

During recent years considerable progress has been made in the design and application of gas turbines employing internal combustion for stationary use and for locomotive, marine, automotive, and aircraft propulsion purposes.

These gas turbines can be classified as follows:

(1). Constant-pressure turbine, in which the turbine wheel is actuated continuously by the products of combustion admitted from the combustion chamber. (Actually, pressure does vary under load changes, so a better name would be continuous-combustion turbine.)

(2). Explosion or intermittent-combustion turbine operating according to the constant-volume-cycle method. (An example is the German Holzwarth gas turbine.)

(3). Open-combustion-chamber turbine, in which heat is supplied while both pressure and volume are changing. (The Karavodine turbine built in 1908 is an example.)

No further mention will be made of the latter two types, as they are little used today. The constant-pressure type has pretty well taken over, being used in aircraft, as well as most other turbine power plants.

Aircraft engines of the nonreciprocating type all employ the principle of jet propulsion. The types that have been developed so far are:

(1). Turbojet.

(2). Turboprop. (Although most of the power output from this engine is generated as propeller thrust, roughly 20 per cent is pure jet thrust.)

(3). Ramjet or athodyd (*ae*ro-*th*erm*o*-*dy*namic *d*uct).

(4). Rocket engine.

(5). Pulsejet or flying bomb (V-1).

Only the first two of these always employ a gas turbine as an integral part of the design.

(For further information about aircraft power plants, see AERONAUTICS—*3. Aircraft Propulsion Systems;* ROCKET; JET PROPULSION.

Another type of engine is the compound power plant. Basically, it consists of a reciprocating engine plus some means—generally a turbine—for extracting energy from the exhaust gas and converting it into power.

All present-day versions also include a supercharger to increase the pressure of the air being fed to the reciprocating engine.

On one type of compounding, the turbosupercharged engine, the piston engine delivers all the shaft power, the turbine merely developing enough power to drive the supercharger. (See section *Supercharging.*)

In some cases, both piston engine and turbine contribute shaft power. For example, on the compounded, 18-cylinder Wright Cyclone aircraft engine, turbine power in excess of supercharger demands is fed to the engine crankshaft through a system of gears.

In other designs such as the free-piston gas generator plus turbine, the piston engine powers the compressor only, and the turbine supplies all the shaft power.

The Cycle.—The processes that take place in regular sequence in any internal-combustion engine are as follows: (1) induction, (2) compression, (3) combustion and expansion, and (4) exhaust. When an engine goes through this series of processes once, a cycle is said to have been performed.

Although there are many types of cycles, the ones in greatest use today are (1) the Otto cycle, in which the fuel is burned at essentially constant volume (used mainly in gasoline engines); (2) the Diesel cycle, in which the fuel is burned at constant pressure (used in low-speed Diesel engines); and (3) a modified Diesel cycle, in which the first portion of the fuel is burned at approximately constant volume and the last portion at nearly constant pressure (used in high-speed Diesel engines).

The constant-volume and constant-pressure processes were originally developed for reciprocating engines, but modifications of them are also used in gas turbine units.

In fact, although gas turbine units and reciprocating engines are quite different mechanically, the series of operations is basically the same for both power plants, as shown in Fig. 10. The only real difference is that, in the turbine unit employing constant-pressure combustion, power is produced continuously, whereas in the reciprocating engine it is produced intermittently. (In the constant-volume-combustion turbine, power is, in the same manner, produced intermittently.)

The operation of the reciprocating engine shown here (a four-stroke Otto-cycle engine) is as follows: on the first downward stroke of the piston, a mixture of fuel and air enters the cylinder around the open inlet valve. When the piston reaches the bottom of its stroke, the inlet valve closes so that on the return upward stroke the charge is compressed. When the piston reaches approximately the uppermost point of travel (top dead center), the charge is ignited by the spark. Then the expansion of the gases resulting from combustion forces the piston downward again for the power stroke. Finally, the second upward stroke of the piston drives the burned gases out of the cylinder around the open exhaust valve.

The gas turbine unit shown in Fig. 10 is an aircraft turbojet engine with a multistage axial compressor and a single-stage turbine. Air enters the front of the unit and is compressed by

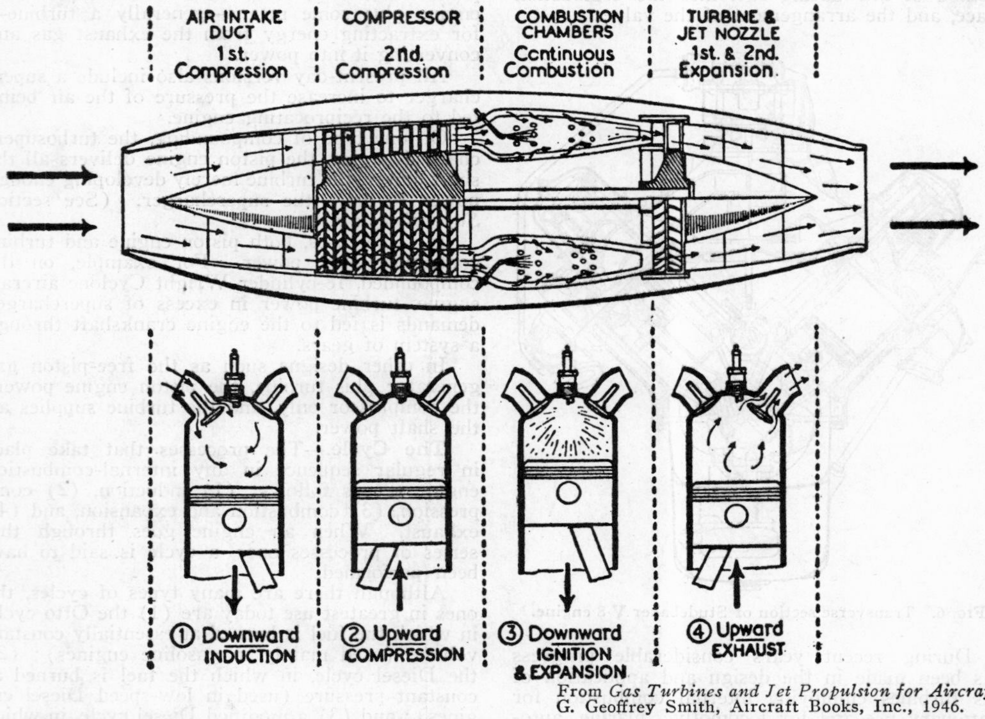

From *Gas Turbines and Jet Propulsion for Aircraft,* G. Geoffrey Smith, Aircraft Books, Inc., 1946.

FIG. 10. Comparison of rotating and reciprocating power units. In lower series of diagrams, the four intermittent strokes of a reciprocating engine are approximately aligned with the four continuous functions of turbine-jet unit.

degrees as it passes through the several stages of the compressor. From here it enters the combustion chambers into which kerosine is sprayed and burned continuously. The tremendous heat released by the combustion of the fuel expands the gases but, as the chambers have open ends (in contrast to the closed cylinder of a piston engine), there is no rise in pressure (since the turbine unit employs the constant-pressure process).

By reason of the rapid expansion, the heated gases force their way at increased velocity through the only exit from the chambers, namely, between the guide vanes in the stator ring of the turbine. These vanes direct the flow to the approximate angle of attack for the blades of the turbine, causing the turbine wheel to rotate possibly at 8,000 to 16,000 rpm. In this manner, power is developed to drive the compressor fixed at the front end of the shaft.

After the gases have passed through the turbine they escape through the rear of the unit. This mass of gases being projected rearward at high velocity produces a force that drives the airplane forward.

Although most reciprocating gasoline engines operate on the four-stroke cycle, that is, one cycle is completed in four strokes of the piston or two revolutions of the crankshaft, the outboard motor is an example of a two-stroke-cycle gasoline engine.

As shown in Fig. 11, the same events take place with the exception that they are accomplished in only two strokes of the piston or one revolution of the crankshaft since the piston is not used to expel the exhaust gases and suck in the fresh charge. Instead, while the piston is at the bottom of its stroke, the fresh charge is injected under a slight pressure so that it sweeps

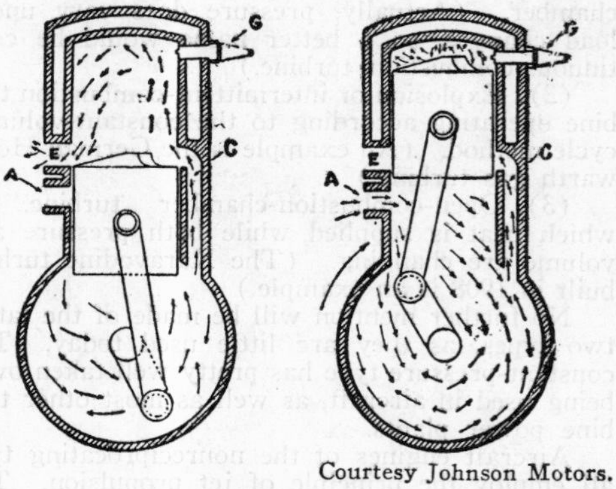

Courtesy Johnson Motors.

FIG. 11. Events in 2-stroke-cycle engine with crankcase scavenging—left: down stroke—power; right: up stroke—compression; between strokes—exhaust and intake.

A—Intake port to crankcase
C—Transfer passage
E—Exhaust port
G—Spark plug

out the spent gases. A deflector on top of the piston, as shown in Fig. 11, directs the incoming

Courtesy Prof. C. F. Taylor, M.I.T.

Fig. 4. Comparison of 8,000-horsepower Nordberg Diesel engine with 1/7-horsepower Arden model airplane engine.

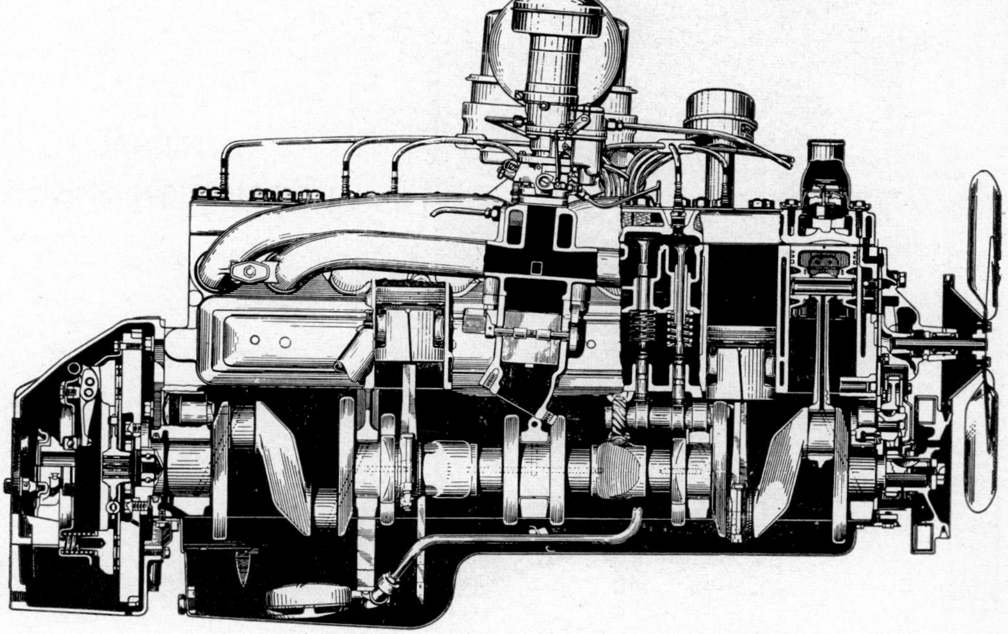

Fig. 5. Cutaway side view of Packard straight-eight engine.

Fig. 7. Continental 6-cylinder opposed aircraft engine.

INTERNAL COMBUSTION ENGINE

Fig. 8. Pratt & Whitney 9-cylinder Wasp engine model R-1340.

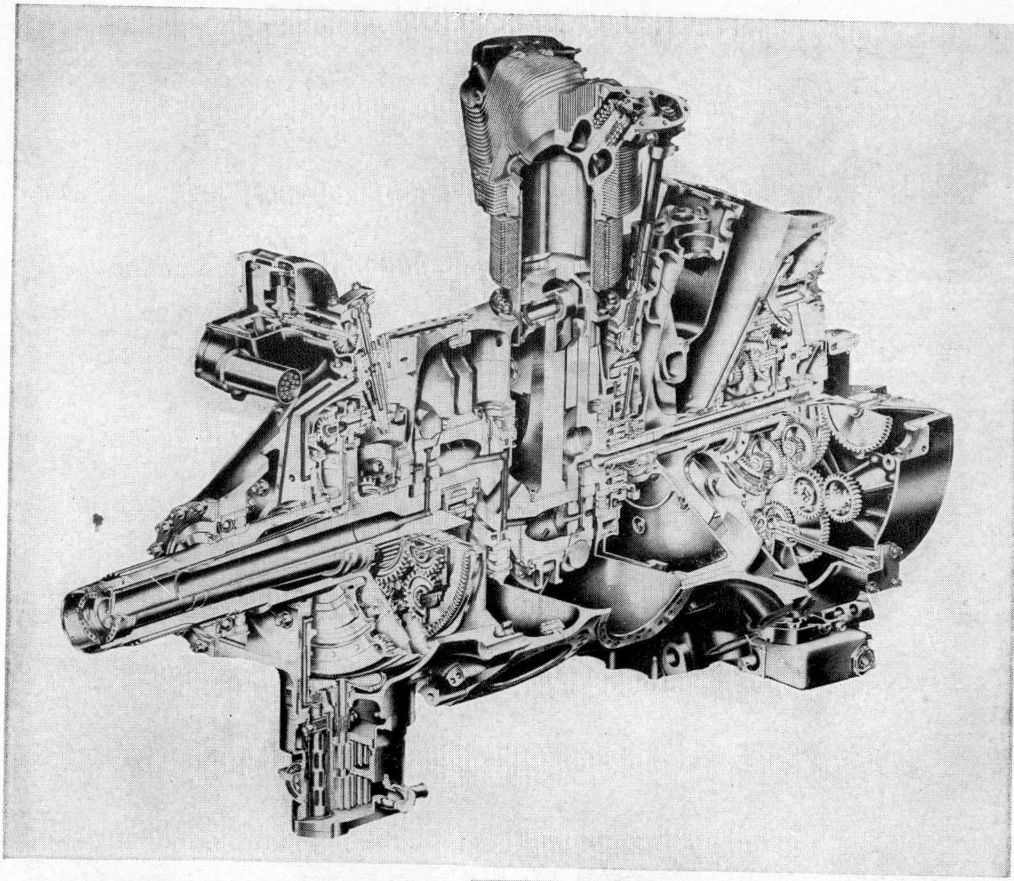

Fig. 9. Cutaway view of Wright 18-cylinder cyclone engine model 18 BA.

INTERNAL COMBUSTION ENGINE

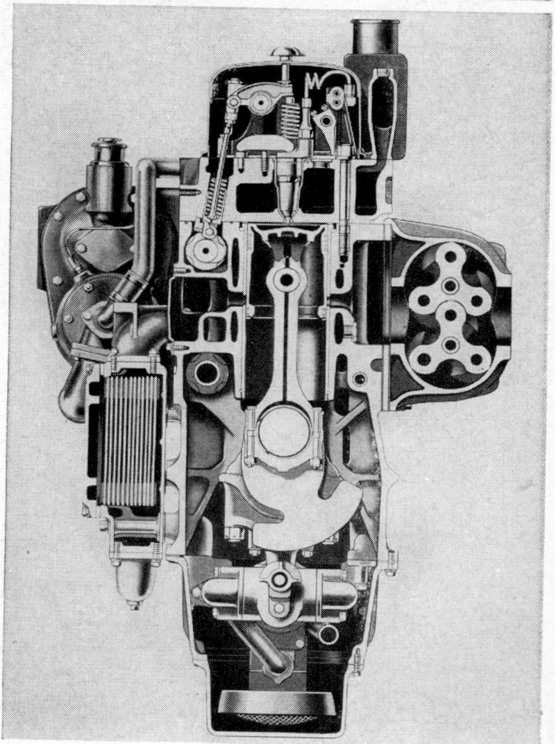

Fig. 23. Cross-section of Allis-Chalmers Diesel engine for tractor operation, showing open combustion chamber.

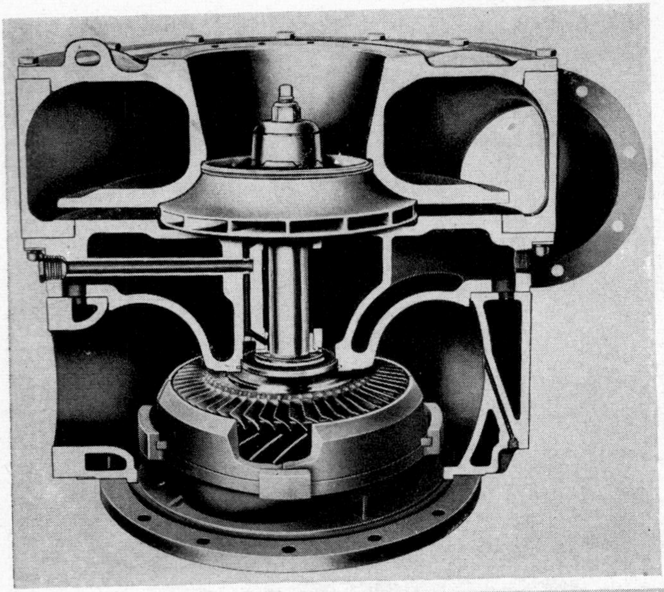

Fig. 31. Elliott turbosupercharger for Diesel engine (based on Büchi system).

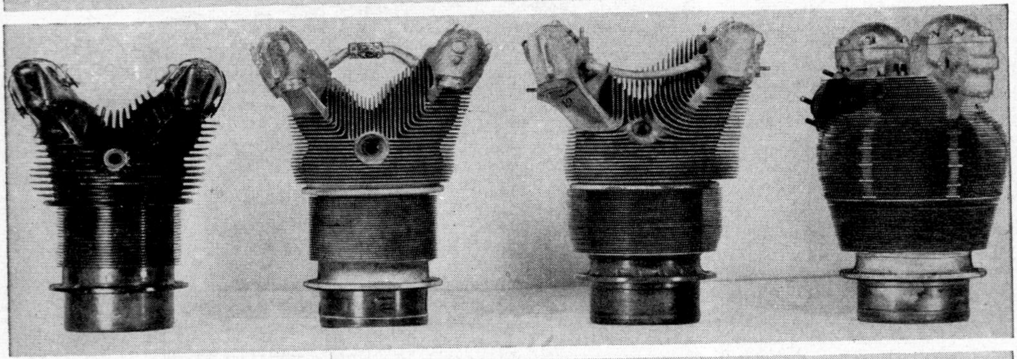

Fig. 35. Changes in cylinder design of typical aircraft engine during 19 years.
Courtesy Society of Automotive Engineers

Fig. 39. Ingersoll-Rand gas-engine-driven compressor unit.

charge toward the top of the cylinder to do this.

The cycle starts with the piston at its outer dead-center position and the cylinder filling with combustible mixture at about atmospheric pressure, coming through passage *C* from the crankcase and driving before it the spent gases from the previous power stroke. These are escaping through the exhaust port *E*. As soon as the piston starts to move upward, it closes ports *C* and *E* and the charge begins to be compressed. As the piston continues to move upward, it reaches a point where port *A* is uncovered, allowing a new charge to be drawn into the crankcase. At the top of the stroke, ignition takes place from spark plug *G*, burning the mixture, which expands and forces the piston downward for the power stroke. During this stroke the fresh charge in the crankcase is compressed slightly, so that when port *C* is again open to the combustion chamber, this charge will be able to flow in and displace the burned gases.

Since the four-stroke engine has only one power stroke for two revolutions, while the two-stroke engine has one for each revolution, it would seem that a two-stroke engine should develop twice the power of a four-stroke engine of the same size, running at the same speed. Actually, the two-stroke engine is able to develop only some 70 to 90 per cent more than a four-stroke engine of the same size or displacement because of:

(1). Poorer scavenging.

(2). A smaller weight of combustible mixture in a given size of cylinder.

(3). A greater loss of unburned fuel.

(4). A small power consumption in compressing the air that scavenges the cylinder.

(5). The loss of pressure by early exhaust.

In engines employing the Diesel cycle, air alone is drawn into the cylinder and compressed to about 500 pounds per square inch (psi). This compression raises the air temperature to the point where, as soon as fuel is injected, combustion occurs, without the help of a spark. The burning takes place at nearly constant volume.

In the modified Diesel cycle, fuel injection is started early enough so that part of the fuel burns at constant volume and the balance at constant pressure.

Engines operating on this modified cycle have compression ratios higher than are customary with the Otto cycle but lower than the usual Diesel compression ratios. This necessitates the use of glow plugs, hot bulbs, or similar devices to facilitate starting.

The two-stroke cycle is more suited to the Diesel cycle than to the Otto and is thus more widely used in engines employing this cycle. There is no fuel in the intake charge of air, which is used to scavenge the cylinder, and thus an excess wastes no fuel. As in all Diesels, the fuel is not injected until after the compression of the air.

Gas Turbines.—In its simplest form, a gas turbine power plant consists of:

(1). A rotary compressor unit.

(2). A combustor.

(3). A turbine.

The compressor and turbine are mounted as a single rotating unit. After the power plant has been started by an auxiliary power source such as an electric motor or a piston engine, some of the power developed by the turbine is used to drive the compressor. Thus, the output of the turbine power plant is the difference between the turbine power and the power required to drive the compressor; it is obvious, therefore, that the efficiency with which the compressor delivers air is of paramount importance.

Three main types of compressors are in use today: the centrifugal, the axial, and a positive-displacement type called the Lysholm.

The compressed air flows from the compressor to the combustor where it unites with the fuel, generally kerosine, which is injected through nozzles so as to atomize it and thus give more complete combustion. A high-voltage spark is used to initiate combustion, after which the spark is cut off because of the continuous nature of the combustion process in a turbine engine.

The turbine itself consists of a shaft to which are attached the blades against which the high-velocity, high-temperature gases impinge to develop power. A high efficiency and suitability for high-temperature operation are essential requirements of turbine materials. In fact, the major developments that made possible the commercial use of the internal-combustion turbine were in metals that retain substantial strength at temperatures of 1,200°F. and higher, and in more efficient compressors.

The speed with which the gases pass through the turbine creates special problems of erosion. Also, the materials used must not be prone to "creep" or grow with cyclic variations of temperature (that is, repeated heating and cooling in service).

Recent work has proved, for example, that ceramics and a combination of ceramics and metal called a ceramel have excellent possibilities because they can withstand the high temperatures.

To achieve higher efficiencies than are possible with the simple gas turbine unit, the three basic components may be used in multiple and in various arrangements. They are also often augmented by other components such as the regenerator (to recover waste heat and transfer it to a point where the temperature is lower and the pressure higher) and the intercooler (to remove heat from the working medium between stages of compression).

Compared with the reciprocating aircraft engine, the turbine unit has lower specific weight, adaptability to much higher speeds, and the upper limits of thrust capacity of a single unit are much greater. On the other hand, at present it has considerably higher fuel consumption and it is not adaptable to low-speed, light planes. Turboprop units do, however, extend the range of gas turbine units to lower-speed applications and have improved fuel consumption.

Compared with the Diesel, for example, as applied to locomotives, simple gas turbines use less space, are lighter, and presumably would require less maintenance. Their chief disadvantage is a poorer fuel economy. Also, the output of the gas turbine is more seriously affected by adverse atmospheric conditions of temperature and altitude than is the Diesel.

In heavy-duty stationary and marine applications, space-consuming heat-recovery devices and the like, which must be used in order to approach Diesel efficiencies, wipe out the basic space and simplicity advantages.

Although further developments may permit favorable comparisons with the steam plant, at present the comparison is unfavorable to the gas turbine. The long-time reliability of the steam plant has not yet been demonstrated by the turbine. The compressors are far larger than the corresponding feed-water pumps. The plant capacity is more sensitive to deterioration of turbine and compressor efficiency. Thus far, the single-unit capacity of the gas turbine is also considerably short of that for large steam-turbine installations.

The discussion of turbine elements given earlier should make it clear that mechanically the gas turbine unit is quite different from the reciprocating engine. There are no pistons, valves, or ignition apparatus (save for two ignition plugs to start combustion of the fuel). After starting, no warming up period is necessary, as bearings are few; there are no metal-to-metal sliding surfaces; consequently, only a simple lubrication system is needed.

Compared with piston engines, turbine units are also:

(1). Less critical regarding type of fuel. High heat value, not antiknock rating, is the criterion.

(2). Virtually vibrationless because of the exclusive use of rotating components. There is also an absence of mechanical noise, and exhaust noise is greatly reduced.

(3). Self-cooled by airflow, so that no radiator or projecting air scoops are required.

A size, weight, and fuel comparison of the Boeing-502 gas turbine with various reciprocat-

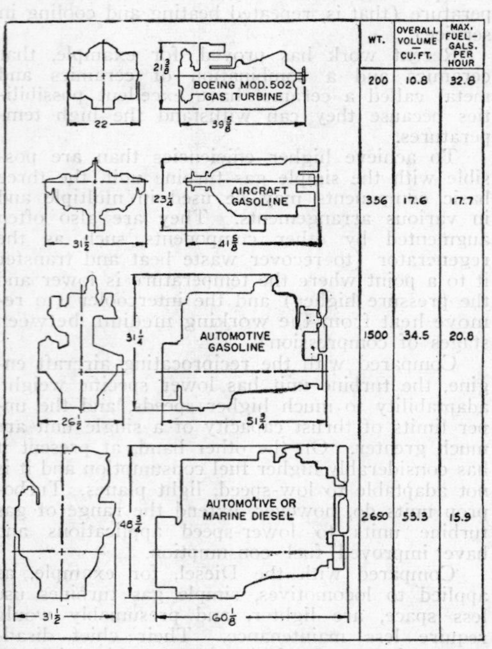

FIG. 12. Comparison of gas turbine and piston engines of equal rating.

ing engines is shown in Fig. 12. The Boeing-502 is an experimental gas turbine designed for ground vehicles such as trucks. It develops a maximum of 175 hp.

The rest of this article will be concerned mainly with reciprocating engines. For further information about gas turbines see JET PROPULSION; AERONAUTICS—*3. Aircraft Propulsion Systems.*

Indicator Cards.—The events that occur in any reciprocating engine may conveniently be pictured by a graph with pressure plotted along the vertical distance (ordinate) and actual volume in the combustion space as the horizontal distance (abscissa). These plots are called indicator diagrams or cards.

Various types of indicators have been developed that give an accurate plot of this pressure-volume relationship for an engine in actual operation. For a low-speed engine the mechanism of this indicator can be relatively simple, as shown in Fig. 13.

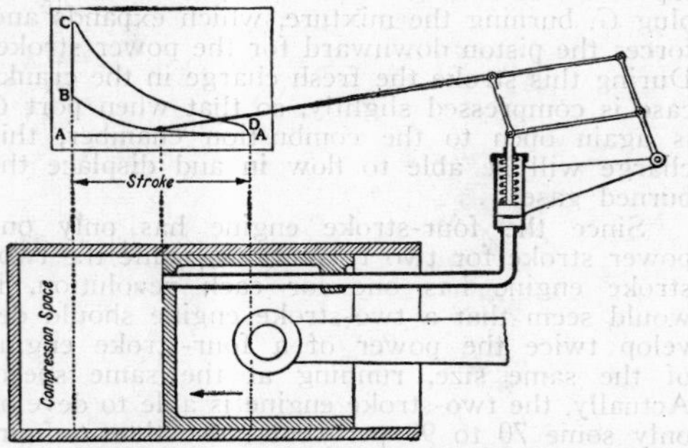

From *High-Speed Combustion Engines,* P. M. Heldt.

FIG. 13. Schematic diagram of indicator for recording cylinder pressure changes in low-speed engine.

This device is unsuited for high-speed engines, however, because of the inertia effects of its moving parts and the pencil friction, which are excessive at high speeds. Other mechanical indicators, as well as optical and electrical indicators, are available that avoid these errors for high-speed work.

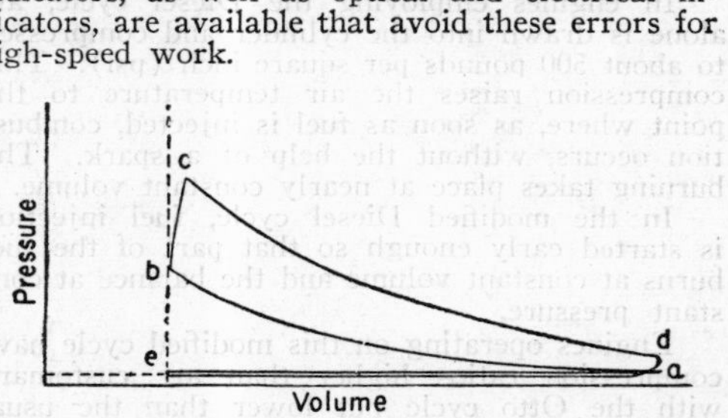

FIG. 14. Pressure-volume diagram of Otto or explosion engine cycle.

A typical indicator card for an engine operating on the Otto cycle is shown in Fig. 14. Point *e* represents the conditions at the start of the cycle. After the piston has completed the exhaust stroke, the pressure in the cylinder is slightly above atmospheric, and the piston is at top dead center, that is, the volume in the combustion chamber is at its minimum. The intake valve then opens, and the piston moves down the cylinder until bottom dead center is reached. This is represented by point *a*, which shows that the volume in the cylinder is at its maximum. At this point the intake valve closes, and the piston starts to move back on the compression stroke. This is represented by the line *a-b*, which shows how the volume decreases and the pressure increases to the point *b*. At this point ignition occurs, causing combustion of the gases, which in turn causes a rise in pressure to point *c*.

Although in the ideal Otto cycle the line *b-c* would be vertical, it can be seen that in actual practice there is a slight increase in volume because the piston has begun to move outward again, even during the short time when combustion is taking place. Line *c-d* represents the expansion or power stroke, when the piston is being forced down the cylinder by the expanding gases. At point *d* the exhaust valve opens, the pressure quickly drops to practically atmospheric, as the exhaust stroke takes place along *d-e*.

The indicator card for a Diesel engine is shown in Fig. 15. Here it can be seen that the compression stroke *a-b* compresses the charge to the maximum pressure occurring in the cycle. At point *b* fuel is injected and essentially constant-pressure ignition takes place along line *b-c*. Then the expansion or power stroke occurs along line *c-d*.

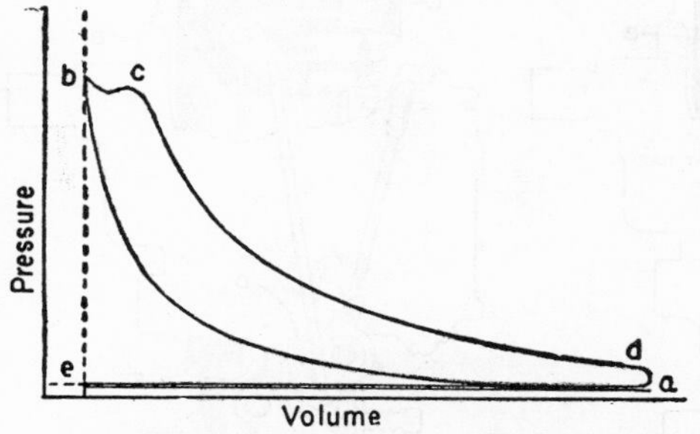

FIG. 15. Pressure-volume diagram of Diesel or combustion engine cycle.

Briefly, the main differences between the events that occur in the Otto-cycle engine and the Diesel-cycle engine are:

(1). The Otto has approximately constant-volume combustion; the Diesel, approximately constant-pressure combustion.

(2). The Otto charge is not compressed to as high a degree as the Diesel. For this reason it requires an ignition system to provide a spark, whereas the Diesel is self-igniting.

(3). Because of the lower pressure, the fuel can be injected before compression in the Otto engine, whereas in the Diesel it cannot be injected until after compression and at the point when ignition is to start.

Air-Fuel Mixture in Otto Engines.—Theoretically, 15 pounds of air must be mixed with each pound of gasoline in order to supply just enough oxygen to complete the combustion of the fuel. In actual practice, however, it is seldom that this exact ratio of air to fuel is used. For maximum economy, such as is desired for normal operation, more air must be supplied (usually about 16 to 17 pounds of air per pound of fuel). Otherwise, combustion will be incomplete and some of the fuel wasted, that is, it will pass through the engine unburned or partially burned.

There are several reasons why this extra air is needed: (1) A thoroughly homogeneous mixture of air and gasoline cannot be obtained in the very short time available, so that all the fuel particles can react with all the oxygen particles. (2) In a multicylinder engine, it is practically impossible to get an absolutely uniform distribution of fuel to all the various cylinders; some cylinders always receive richer mixtures (that is, containing a higher proportion of fuel) than others. (3) The dilution of the mixture by the exhaust products left in the clearance space reduces the probability that all the fuel particles will react with oxygen particles.

When the air/fuel ratio is increased above 16 to 17, the efficiency begins to drop off. When the ratio gets above 18, that is, the mixture becomes too lean, the drop in efficiency and loss of power become quite rapid. Finally a point is reached where combustion does not occur at all.

On the other hand, greater power is obtained (although at the expense of efficiency) with a richer mixture than 15/1. Greatest power (such as is needed for quick acceleration and maximum speed up grades) is obtained with air/fuel ratios of 12 to 13.

Thus we see that the setting of the carburetor for maximum power is quite different from that for maximum efficiency. Moreover, for smooth idling of the engine, the mixture must be even richer, 11.2 being a typical figure. This very rich mixture is needed at idling speeds for two reasons: (1) because the pressure in the manifold system is below atmospheric, thus inducing a leakage of air, which dilutes the mixture, and (2) because the amount of fresh mixture entering the cylinder is small, so that there is a relatively large degree of dilution of the charge by the burned gases remaining in the cylinder.

The modern carburetor is designed to provide approximately these various air/fuel ratios: an economical mixture for the usual operating conditions, richer mixtures when the demand is for greater power, and an especially rich mixture for idling.

Carburetors.—The carburetor is used in engines employing the Otto cycle. Its function is to break up the gasoline into tiny particles and mix it with the proper amount of air to give efficient combustion.

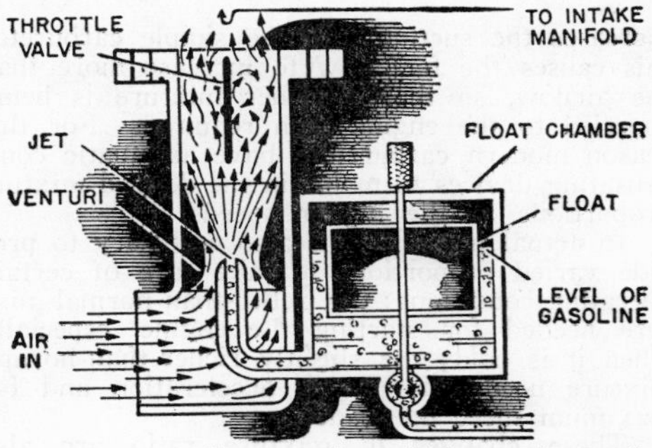

Courtesy General Motors Corporation.

FIG. 16. Carburetor in its simplest form.

A simple carburetor of the float type is shown in Fig. 16. Gasoline is forced by the fuel pump into the float chamber shown at the right. The float, so called because it floats in the gasoline, acts to close the fuel intake valve when the gasoline reaches the proper level.

The suction stroke of the engine piston induces a flow of air into the carburetor, as shown at the left. This air passes through a narrowed section called the venturi. The purpose of the venturi is to speed up the flow of air so as to cause a decrease in air pressure to slightly below atmospheric at its narrowest section, known as the throat.

Located at the throat is the jet or discharge nozzle, as shown in Fig. 16. Since the pressure in the float chamber is at atmospheric and that at the jet is slightly below atmospheric, gasoline is pushed through the jet and into the air stream. As the fuel leaves the jet it is atomized or broken up into small drops.

The greater the difference between atmospheric pressure and the pressure at the throat, the more gasoline flows into the air stream. If the jet and venturi are properly proportioned, there is an automatic action that results in greater fuel flow when the airflow becomes greater. When the throttle valve is opened wider, more air as well as more fuel is pulled in, so the proportions (the mixture ratio) remain roughly the same.

Actually, opening the throttle usually increases the speed of the engine, which in turn increases the suction. In the simple carburetor this causes the fuel flow to increase more than the airflow, so that a richer mixture is being supplied to the engine than required. For this reason modern carburetors have automatic compensating devices to maintain the desired mixture proportions at the higher speeds.

In actual practice it is also necessary to provide varied proportions to take care of certain operating conditions: the richer-than-normal mixture needed for starting the engine, especially when it is cold; the slightly richer-than-normal mixture needed for quick acceleration and for maximum speed up grades.

These changes in mixture ratio are also effected automatically in carburetors built today. For example, at least two jets or fuel passages are provided from the float chamber to the venturi, one for idling and low-speed operation, the other for higher speeds or harder pulling. There are also various other auxiliary devices built into the carburetor, mostly to change the fuel/air ratio or to take care of some special condition.

One of these devices is the choke valve. It looks much like the throttle valve but it is located in the air intake passage of the carburetor. When it is partly closed, a high vacuum is formed beneath it. More fuel and less air are pulled in, giving the much richer mixture needed to start the engine.

On most modern cars the choke valve is controlled automatically, that is, the driver has no control over it. As shown in Fig. 17-I, when the engine is cold, a thermostatic spring B in a casing connected by a pipe with the exhaust header holds the choke A nearly closed. Acting against the thermostat is a piston C in a cylinder connected by a pipe with the intake manifold. After the engine starts and a vacuum is created in the intake manifold, the piston opens the choke part way (Fig. 17-II), and as soon as the exhaust gases heat the thermostat, it relaxes its tension and the choke opens completely (Fig. 17-III). Usually, there is a device connected with the automatic choke (in this case the fast-idle cam D acting against throttle stop screw E) that holds the throttle partly opened so that the engine operates at faster than idling speed while the engine is warming up.

The simple carburetor shown in Fig. 16 is of the up-draft type, that is, the air enters the carburetor at the bottom and leaves it at the top.

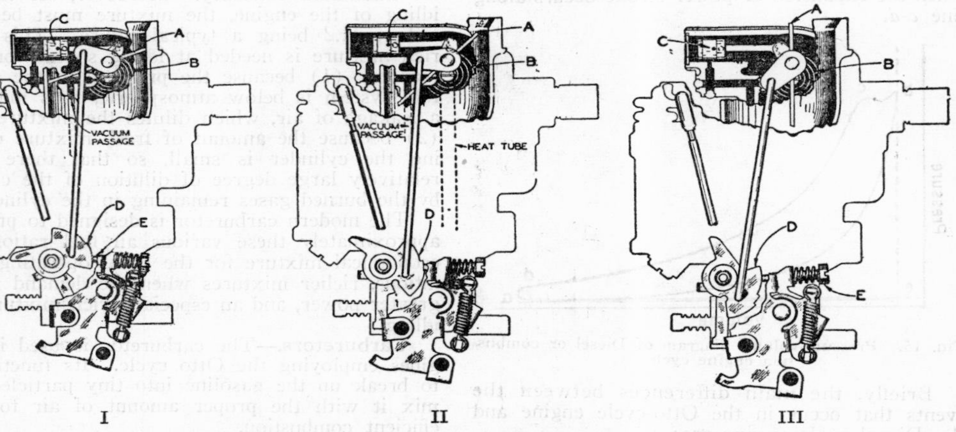

FIG. 17. Three positions of automatic choke in Stromberg carburetor.

Today, on most vehicles at least, carburetors are of the down-draft type—the air enters at the top and leaves at the bottom.

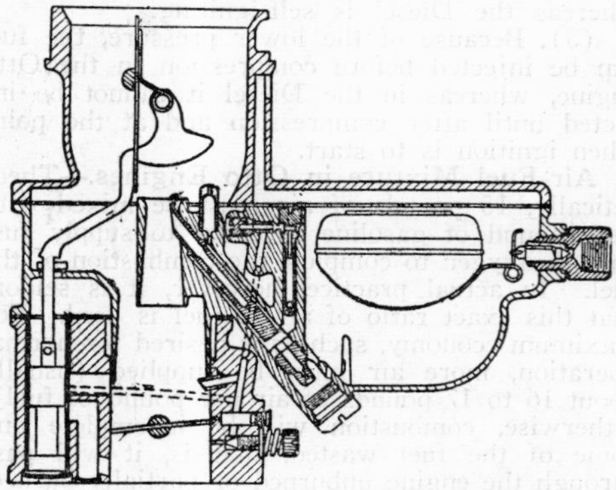

From *High-Speed Combustion Engines*, P. M. Heldt.

FIG. 18. Stromberg down-draft carburetor.

The down-draft carburetor (Fig. 18) permits a manifold of larger cross-section because the fuel flows down into the manifold instead of being lifted up into it. The location of the carburetor above the engine makes it more accessible for inspection, adjustment, and repair, and the air entering the carburetor is cooler.

For aircraft use, the float-chamber carburetor is rapidly being replaced by the newer pressure type because the latter overcomes two of the limitations of the float carburetor when applied to airplanes: (1) its limited operation with respect to attitude, that is, angular tilt, and (2) its icing tendency. The pressure carburetor derives its name from the fact that fuel pressure is constantly maintained at the discharge nozzle as long as the engine is operating.

Direct fuel injection is, however, promising to replace both types of carburetors for aircraft engines because it provides improved power and fuel economy, as well as ice-free operation. The injection equipment consists of small pumps which are designed to force a metered amount of gasoline into each cylinder or the intake manifold adjacent to each cylinder. The idea is similar to that of injectors used on Diesel engines (see next section).

Fuel Injection for Diesel Engines.—The heart of the Diesel engine is its fuel injection system. Its purpose is to force a small amount of fuel (broken up into finely divided particles) into the highly compressed, high-temperature air in the cylinder just before the piston reaches the top of its compression stroke.

There are two methods of injecting fuel into the combustion chamber: air injection and airless injection (also called mechanical injection and solid injection).

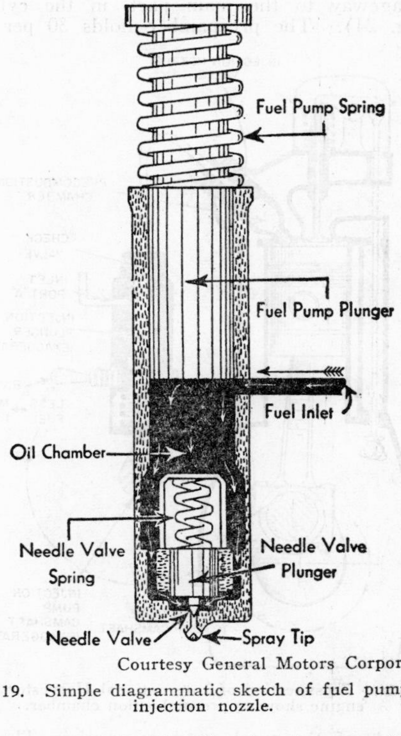

Courtesy General Motors Corporation.

FIG. 19. Simple diagrammatic sketch of fuel pump and injection nozzle.

With air injection, the fuel is sprayed into the cylinder by means of highly compressed air. This method is little used, however, because it requires a compressor, which adds mechanical complexity and weight and consumes up to 10 per cent of the brake horsepower.

Today, therefore, the airless injection method predominates. There are many variations of this type, such as the unit pump injection system (Fig. 19) and the common-rail system.

In any solid injection system, it is necessary to have a pump that will force the fuel into the cylinder against the compression pressure of 500 or 600 psi. The volume of liquid to be injected is very small, and it must be injected at a very high velocity in order that it may be thoroughly atomized and yet be capable of penetrating through the whole volume of air. The jet must be so disposed and directed that a stream of liquid is not likely to impinge on the cylinder wall or piston, where rapid carbonization would occur.

With the unit injector, the pump and nozzle are combined in one unit, the whole mechanism being fitted in the cylinder head. It is operated by a rocker arm controlled by the same camshaft that operates the valves. The pump itself consists of a plunger fitting closely in a cylinder. There are also means for varying the amount of fuel it pumps in one stroke. The plunger builds up pressure on the small amount of liquid in the cylinder until the pressure is great enough to open a spring-loaded check valve. This may be as high as 20,000 psi. When it opens, the fuel is forced into the cylinder through a number of very small holes in the nozzle, shooting a fine spray in all directions.

Controlling the amount of fuel pumped by the injectors speeds up or slows down the engine, just as does opening or closing the throttle of a gasoline engine.

In the common-rail system, a constant pressure is maintained in the fuel discharge line, and the discharge to the cylinder is controlled by the lift, timing, and duration of opening of the fuel valve. One or more pumps are used to furnish fuel under high pressure to one pipe or reservoir having branches to all the cylinders.

Combustion Chambers.—The combustion chamber is the space in the engine where burning of the fuel occurs. In the Diesel engine,

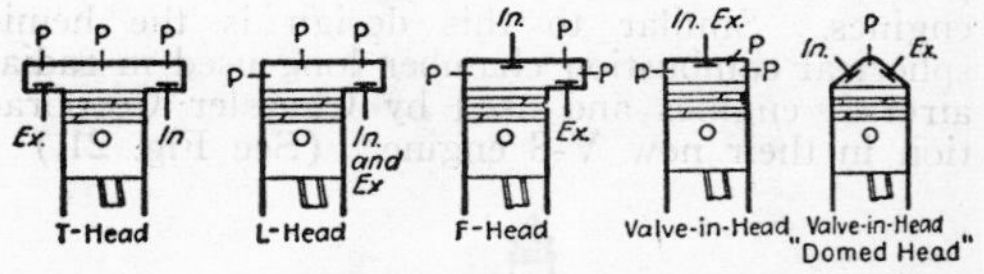

From *Mechanical Engineers' Handbook*, 5th edition, edited by L. S. Marks, 1951, McGraw-Hill Book Co., Inc.

FIG. 20. Combustion-chamber shapes and valve locations (*P* indicates possible spark-plug location).

since the fuel is injected after the air has entered the chamber, it is also the space where the fuel and air are mixed before and during the burning.

The combustion chamber must be designed most carefully since upon it depends in large measure how well combustion occurs, that is, how quickly, how completely, how smoothly, and whether with or without knocking.

In general, combustion chambers of four-stroke spark-ignition engines are classified according to valve arrangement and the degree of turbulence that is induced in the chamber during the burning process.

Common types of nonturbulent chambers include the T-head, L-head, F-head, valve-in-head, and domed-head designs. (See Fig. 20.)

The T-head is practically obsolete because it

does not permit the use of high compression ratios and requires two camshafts.

The L-head design, much used in the automotive field, has a more compact combustion chamber, permitting higher compression ratios, and requires only one camshaft; it is, however, restricted in valve size by the center-to-center distance between cylinders in a multicylinder engine.

The F-head permits large valves, requires one rocker arm mechanism for the inlet valve, has a slightly more compact combustion chamber, and permits a slightly higher compression ratio than the L-head design.

The valve-in-head design has a very compact combustion chamber, but it is restricted in valve size. It permits higher compression ratios than the foregoing designs, but it requires either rocker arms and pushrods or an overhead camshaft mechanism.

The domed-head is a modification of the valve-in-head design that permits large valves,

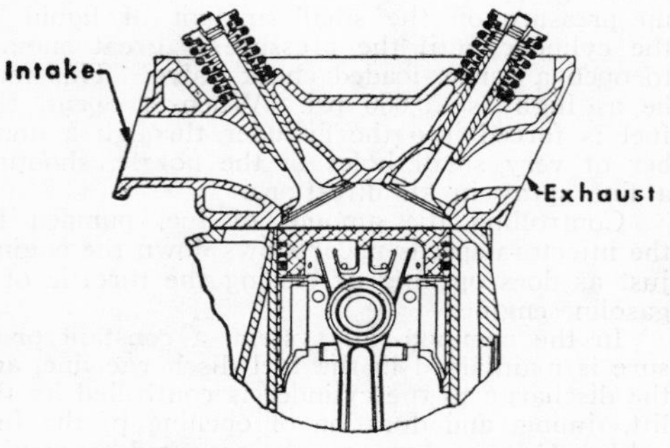

Fig. 21. Cross-section through hemispherical combustion chamber of Chrysler V-8 engine.

has the most compact combustion chamber, and permits the highest compression ratio. It requires an overhead camshaft or otherwise complicated valve mechanism for cylinder in-line engines. Similar to this design is the hemispherical combustion chamber long used in radial aircraft engines and used by Chrysler Corporation in their new V-8 engine. (See Fig. 21.)

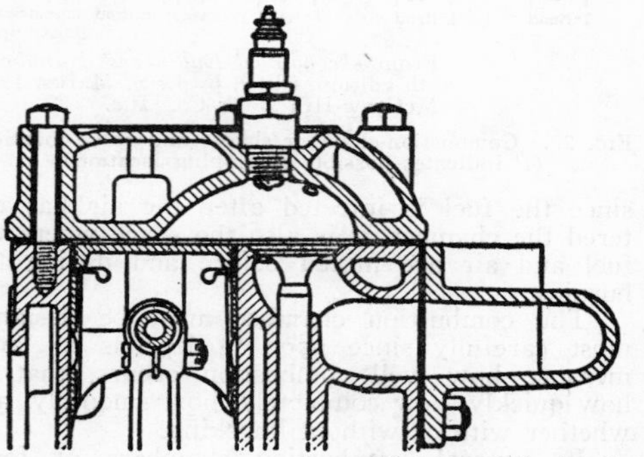

From *High-Speed Combustion Engines,* P. M. Heldt.

Fig. 22. Turbulence type of combustion chamber developed by Ricardo.

Sir Harry Ricardo, an English engineer, introduced high turbulence into combustion-chamber design by lowering part of the cylinder head (see Fig. 22) so that the piston closely approaches this part at the top of its stroke. The charge is forced out of this thin space, greatly agitating the entire mixture and resulting in a faster, more complete combustion.

Most four-stroke-cycle compression-ignition engines have valve-in-head construction. The classification of these engines according to combustion-chamber design is based upon the method of controlling the combustion process:

(1). Open combustion chamber.
(2). Precombustion chamber.
(3). Ante- or divided-combustion chamber.
(4). Air-cell combustion chamber.

In the open combustion chamber the fuel is injected under high pressure directly into the clearance space or chamber between the piston and the cylinder head. (See Fig. 23.)

The piston head is usually shaped to fit the fuel spray, and air swirl moves the unsprayed air into the fuel spray. Air swirl is accomplished by intake port design, by shrouding the intake valve, or in the two-stroke engine, by using tangential intake ports. High turbulence is obtained by having the piston approach part of the cylinder head very closely, thus forcing the gases out of the small clearances and agitating the mixture. The open chamber gives highest efficiency and easiest cold starting with the lowest compression pressure.

The precombustion chamber is much used in this country. It is a small chamber located in the cylinder head and connected by a small passageway to the main part, in the cylinder (Fig. 24). The prechamber holds 30 per cent

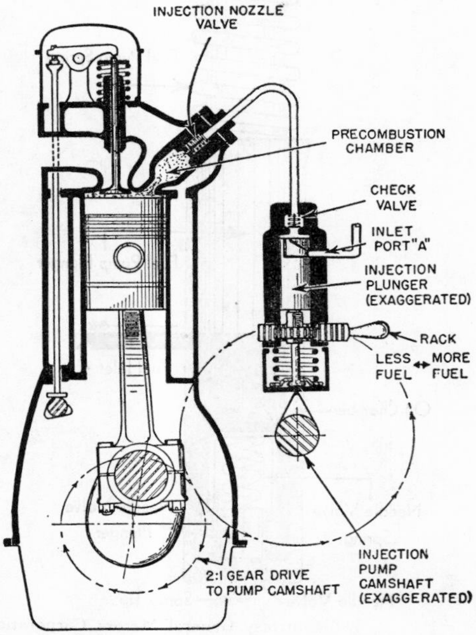

Fig. 24. Cross-section of International Harvester Diesel engine showing precombustion chamber.

or less of the total combustion air. The fuel is injected into the small chamber, and except under light loads, partial combustion occurs and discharges the burning mixture into the main combustion space, creating turbulence, mixing the fuel and air, and producing vigorous burning. This type of combustion chamber produces a smooth combustion process, but it has fairly high fluid friction and heat transfer losses.

Ante- or divided-combustion chambers are modifications of the precombustion chamber, having a major chamber in the cylinder head and the major chamber at a position near the connecting passage and may be directed at the air cell. Little, if any, fuel enters the air cell, which discharges its air into the partly burned mixture during the expansion stroke. This results in a

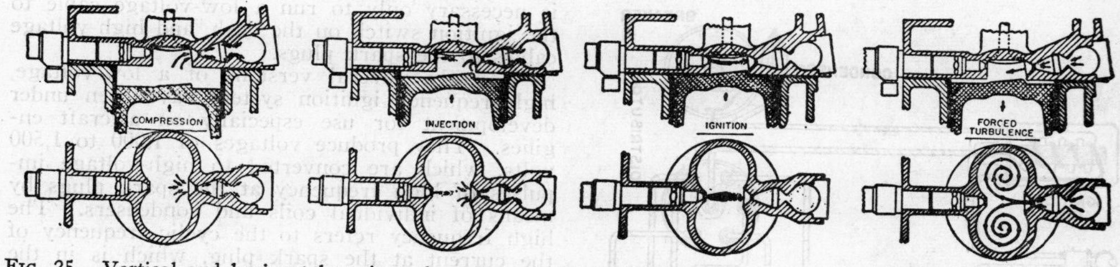

Fig. 25. Vertical and horizontal sections through combustion chamber and air cells of Buda Lanova engine showing actions at four periods indicated.

usually only a small clearance space between the piston and the cylinder head. The passageway between the two chambers is considerably larger than that in the precombustion-chamber type. Close piston clearances produce high turbulence in the ante-chamber and promote rapid combustion.

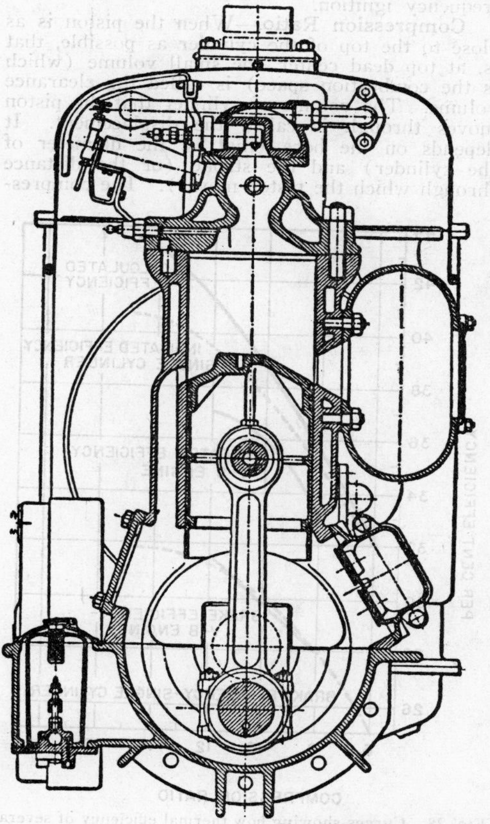

From *High-Speed Diesel Engines,* P. M. Heldt.

Fig. 26. Avance hot-bulb tractor engine.

Air-cell combustion chambers are also divided into two parts with a restricted connecting passage. (See Fig. 25.) Fuel is injected into late but smooth combustion process, which is less efficient than with combustion nearer the top-center position.

Ignition.—The type of ignition used on fuel-injection engines depends on the degree of compression reached, as follows:

(1). Low-compression engines (6 to 10 compression ratio) require some external heat application to a tube, bulb, or plate, at least for starting (called surface ignition). After operating temperatures have been reached a sufficiently high temperature is maintained at the tube, bulb, or plate to ignite the fuel. (See Fig. 26.)

(2). Medium-compression engines (10 to 14 compression ratio) require some form of ignition, such as an electric spark or electric hot wire, for starting. The spark is sometimes still used even after operating temperatures have been reached.

(3). The high-compression engine (14 to 16 compression ratio) is the true Diesel. It uses a compression pressure of about 500 psi. It requires no means other than compression for igniting the fuel.

In the gasoline engine it is necessary to supply a spark to start the burning of the fuel-air mixture after it has been compressed by the upward stroke of the piston.

A spark plug (or sometimes two of them) fits into the wall of the combustion chamber. It has two wires or electrodes, which extend slightly into the chamber and are separated from each other by a narrow gap. High-voltage electricity is led to the spark plug so that it jumps the gap from one electrode to the other at the proper instant. This causes a spark, which starts combustion.

There are two general systems of electric ignition in use today:

(1). Battery ignition, widely used in passenger cars, trucks, and buses.

(2). Magneto ignition, as used on most aircraft engines, as well as farm tractors and outboard marine engines.

A typical battery ignition system is shown diagrammatically in Fig. 27.

There are two circuits in the electrical system, that is, two complete paths around which the electricity flows. These are the primary or low-voltage circuit and the secondary or high-voltage circuit.

The low-voltage circuit (6 volts on passenger cars in this country, 12 volts on European cars) is as follows: the current flows from the battery (one terminal of which is grounded to a metal part of the car) through the ammeter, ignition switch, the heavy or primary winding of the coil (several hundred turns of wire of comparatively large diameter) to the ignition points of the

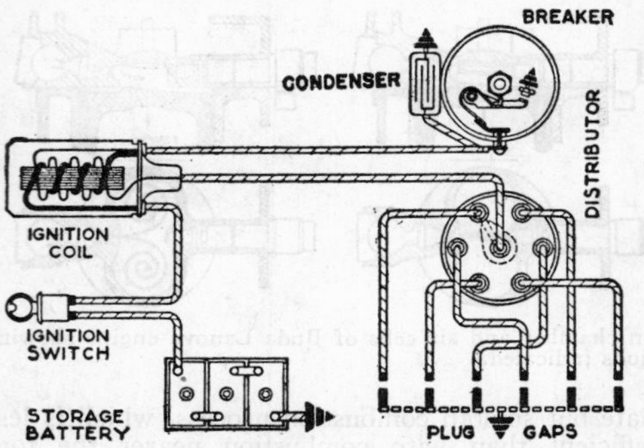

Courtesy Delco-Remy Division.

FIG. 27. Simplified battery ignition circuit diagram.

breaker. Here the circuit is completed by grounding. A condenser is also attached to the primary circuit, the other end being grounded.

The secondary circuit starts from ground in the secondary winding of the coil (which consists of 10,000 to 20,000 windings of fine wire) and passes through a heavily insulated wire into the center of the distributor cap. A contact carries the current to the rotor, which, as it revolves, distributes the current to the six segments (as shown in Fig. 27), which in turn send it to the spark plugs through the connecting wires. (About 10,000 volts is needed to make a spark jump a gap of 0.025 to 0.040 inch in an engine in operation.) After the current jumps the spark-plug gap, igniting the fuel mixture, it is grounded.

As long as an electric circuit is flowing steadily in the primary circuit, no current flows in the secondary. If that circuit is suddenly broken, however, a momentary high voltage is set up in the secondary circuit. This may be as much as 20,000 volts.

This operation is accomplished by means of the breaker in the primary circuit, which cuts this circuit often enough to send a high voltage to each spark plug each time it needs to be fired. It consists of a pair of contacts, which are opened and closed rapidly by a cam having as many points as there are cylinders. The cam is operated by the engine so that the contacts open near the top of the compression stroke of each piston. Thus, the primary circuit is continually being broken thereby sending a series of high-voltage surges through the secondary circuit.

A condenser is incorporated in the breaker case to help give a quick, clean electrical break and to get a good spark in the combustion chamber.

The function of the distributor is to get the high-voltage current generated in the secondary coil to the proper spark plug at the proper time.

Although the breaker and the distributor have been discussed as if they were two separate units, in an automobile they are combined in one unit. The same shaft drives the distributor rotor and the cam that opens the breaker contacts.

A magneto ignition system has all the parts of the battery ignition system and in addition, a generator for producing alternating current impulses directly in the primary winding of what is, in effect, a spark coil.

An advantage of the magneto is its self-contained character. All of the elements of the system are in one compact unit from which it is necessary only to run a low-voltage cable to the ignition switch on the dash, and high-voltage cables to the spark plugs.

Recently, several versions of a low-voltage, high-frequency ignition system have been under development for use especially on aircraft engines. They produce voltages of 1,000 to 1,500 volts, which are converted to high-voltage impulses of high frequency at the spark plugs by means of individual coils and condensers. The high frequency refers to the cyclic frequency of the current at the spark plug, which is in the neighborhood of one million cycles per second, or over 100 times the frequency of the conventional system.

Such a system reduces the problems encountered with high voltages in the spark-plug leads and seems to be effective in avoiding the normal results of plug fouling. Greatly reduced spark-plug erosion is also attributed to the high-frequency ignition.

Compression Ratio.—When the piston is as close to the top of the cylinder as possible, that is, at top dead center, the small volume (which is the combustion space) is called the clearance volume. The volume of cylinder that the piston moves through is called the displacement. It depends on the bore (that is, the diameter of the cylinder) and the stroke (or the distance through which the piston moves). The compres-

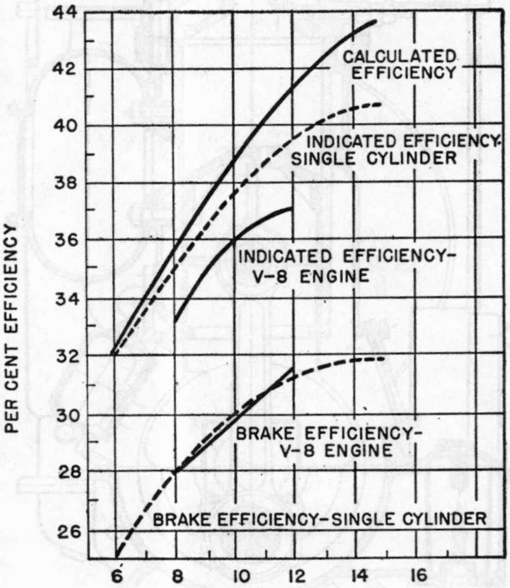

FIG. 28. Curves showing how thermal efficiency of several types of engines varies with compression ratio.

sion ratio is defined as the piston displacement plus the clearance volume (which is the total volume when the piston is at bottom dead center) divided by the clearance volume. The compression ratio of an engine is very important, because when it is changed, other factors affecting the performance and efficiency of the engine also change. (See Fig. 28.) An increase in compression ratio, for example:

(1). Increases the compression pressure.
(2). Increases the compression temperature.
(3). Decreases the dilution with exhaust products.

At a particular compression ratio, the ideal Otto cycle is more efficient than the Diesel. In actual practice, however, Diesel engines are generally more efficient than Otto-cycle engines because the former can operate at higher compression ratios. If the compression ratio is too high (for a particular fuel) in an Otto engine, a phenomenon called detonation or knock will occur.

Detonation.—The automotive and petroleum industries spend millions of dollars a year on the study of detonation, and still there is not perfect agreement among engineers as to just what it is and what to do about it.

Briefly, it may be explained as follows: When the mixture is ignited, combustion starts at the spark and spreads through the combustion chamber behind what is called the flame front. As the temperature of the burned gases rises, they expand and compress the unburned gases. If the compression ratio of the engine is too high, the unburned gases are compressed to the point where they get so hot that spontaneous combustion begins at some point remote from the spark. There is a rapid increase in pressure at this point, which results in violent, vibrating pressure waves. The audible evidence is a metallic click or knock when these waves strike the wall of the combustion chamber. Excessive detonation is accompanied by severe pressures, which may eventually damage the engine. In addition there is a small loss of power when detonation occurs. However, since the engine is operating at close to maximum thermal efficiency when detonation is incipient, maximum efficiency is often obtained when there is a slight detonation or "ping."

It should be noted that compression ratio is not the sole determining factor affecting detonation. For this reason, especially in recent years, a number of developments have been made that have permitted compression ratios to be increased without detonation. These include:

(1). Special substances (called antiknock agents), that can be added to a fuel to help it to resist detonation, such as tetraethyl lead and triptane.

(2). Redesign of the shape of the combustion chamber to reduce detonation.

(3). Increasing the rate at which heat is carried away from the combustion space by the use of thinner sections in the head, by the use of materials of higher heat conductivity, such as aluminum alloy and bronze for the head, and by improving the conductance of heat from the top of the piston.

(4). Reducing the number of local hot spots in the combustion space by better finishing, which removes small projections that may become red hot and cause spontaneous ignition, and by more efficient cooling of various parts near or in the combustion chamber, such as the spark plug and the valve seats.

Octane Rating.—The antiknock properties of gasoline are measured by a concept called octane number: the higher the octane number, the less the tendency of a gasoline to knock. The octane rating of a fuel is obtained by supplying the fuel to a standard test engine and comparing its knocking property with that of a reference fuel of known octane number. The reference fuel is a mixture of iso-octane (which has high antiknock properties) and heptane (which has very poor antiknock qualities). If a fuel being tested has the same knocking characteristics as, for example, a mixture of 70 per cent iso-octane and 30 per cent heptane, it is said to have an octane number of 70. By this method of rating, pure iso-octane would have a rating of 100.

Recently, fuels have been developed with better knocking properties than iso-octane and therefore with antiknock ratings of greater than 100. These fuels, which are particularly for aircraft use, are rated by a new system, called performance number. For example, the performance number of triptane plus 4 cc. tetraethyl lead per gallon is 360. This means that in a supercharged engine it is capable of giving 3.6 times as much power as iso-octane.

In general, engines of 6.5 compression ratio require a fuel of about 75 octane to give nonknocking performance.

It has been estimated that a fuel of about 100 octane used in an engine with a 12.5 compression ratio will give some 35 per cent more mileage in an automobile. It should be noted that for an engine to benefit from high-octane fuel, it must be designed for it.

Recently, much interest has been aroused by the addition of what are called mechanical octane numbers to an engine. This term was devised to define the variation in octane requirements among engines of the same compression ratio. Anything we do to an engine that allows it to operate without knock on fuels of lower octane rating increases the mechanical octane number of the engine. For example, the elimination of internal hot spots or lowering the temperature of the exhaust valve would allow the achievement of a good many mechanical octane numbers.

Cetane Number.—Analogous to octane number for gasoline is the cetane number of fuel oils. This number is a measure of the speed with which the fuel ignites, that is, the time lag between the beginning of injection and the rapid pressure rise due to combustion. If the cetane number of a fuel is too low for a particular engine, rough running will result, especially at high speeds. Fuels of high cetane number give smooth combustion and provide easy starting. The lower the engine speed, the less important the cetane number.

Cetane is a fuel with a high ignitability. It is mixed with alpha methylnaphthalene, which has a low ignitability, to form a reference fuel. If the fuel being tested has the same ignitability (measured by the ignition lag) as a mixture of, for example, 60 per cent cetane and 40 per cent alpha methylnaphthalene, it is said to have a cetane number of 60.

In general, cetane numbers of fuel oils range from 30 for large, slow Diesel engines to as high as 60 for high-speed engines.

Corresponding to antiknock agents for gasoline there are certain ignition accelerators that may be added to Diesel fuels in the proportions of 1 to 5 per cent (which is higher than the corresponding percentage of tetraethyl lead used in gasoline). These substances, such as ethyl nitrate and amyl nitrate, reduce the delay period and so tend to reduce "Diesel knock." Unfortunately, they also add to the cost.

Supercharging.—Supercharging is often used to retain the sea-level power (or as close to it as practicable) of engines operating at altitude. It is also used, in certain cases, to increase the output of land and marine engines, especially Diesels.

Quite simply, supercharging is a method of increasing the density of the air being supplied to the engine by some sort of compressor. In other words, by compressing the air to a density greater than atmospheric, we are able to get more of it into the cylinders, thus providing greater power without increasing the size of the engine and without having to run it at undesirably high speeds.

The supercharger consists of an air compressor and some means of driving it. The compressor may be of any type—reciprocating, rotary, positive displacement, centrifugal, or axial flow.

Supercharging is particularly important for aircraft engines because (1) at high altitudes the power of an unsupercharged engine falls off drastically (for example, an unsupercharged engine of 1,000 hp. at sea level would produce only 500 hp. at 18,000 feet) and (2) it is possible to produce a marked improvement in sea-level performance of an engine without seriously affecting its life or dependability.

Although both positive-displacement and centrifugal compressors have been used for aircraft, the centrifugal is rapidly taking over the field.

Two types of centrifugal superchargers are used in this service:

(1) Gear-driven type.
(2) Exhaust-driven turbosuperchargers.

The first is driven by a train of gears from the crankshaft, and the second by a gas turbine, which in turn is driven by the exhaust gases.

The exhaust-driven supercharger has the greater flexibility, and the compressor power is furnished nearly free because the operation of a supercharger on the exhaust subtracts but little from the net power of the engine. It utilizes part of the exhaust energy, which would otherwise be wasted. (See Fig. 29.)

It does, however, involve exhaust piping problems and overheating difficulties in manifolds, turbine blades, and other parts subjected to high temperatures.

The gear-driven supercharger is frequently built with two-speed drives, or with two-stage compressors (two separate compressors in series), or both, to provide greater flexibility, range, and efficiency for all conditions of altitude and flight.

Except for high-speed engines, such as are used on racing cars, supercharging is not common on automobiles because, if the engine is already operating at optimum compression ratio with the available fuel, the addition of supercharging would cause detonation. To eliminate the detonation it would be necessary to lower the compression ratio, enrich the mixture, or increase the octane number of the fuel.

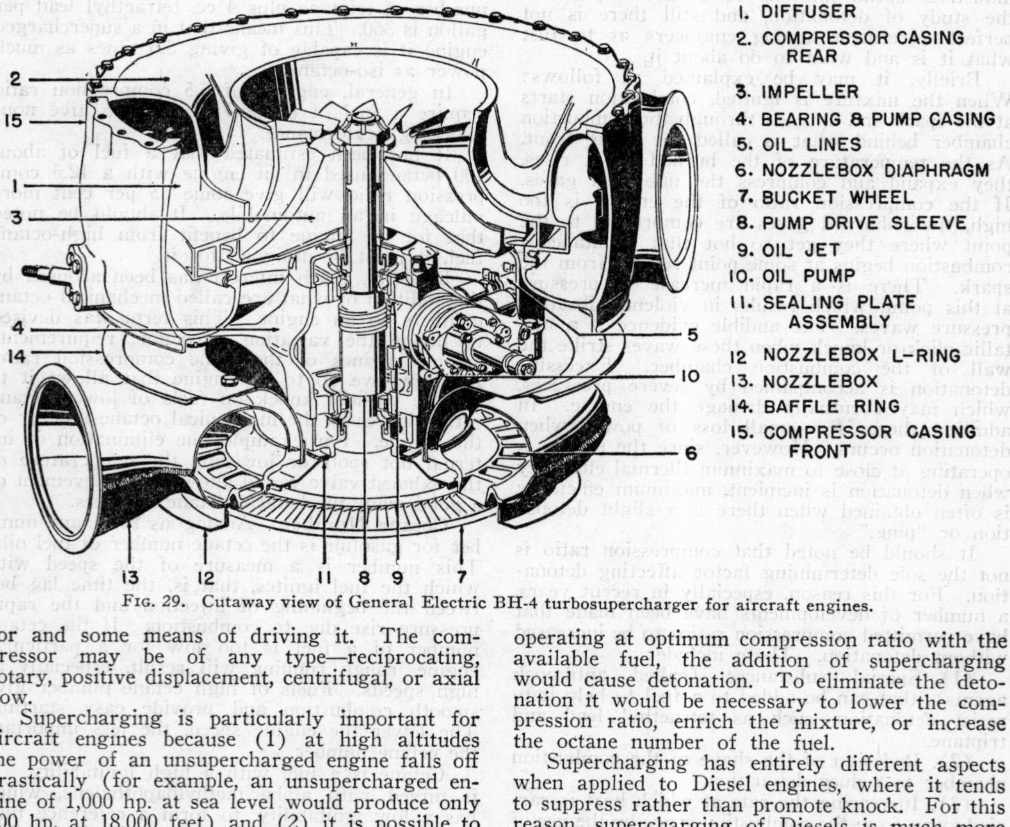

FIG. 29. Cutaway view of General Electric BH-4 turbosupercharger for aircraft engines.

Supercharging has entirely different aspects when applied to Diesel engines, where it tends to suppress rather than promote knock. For this reason, supercharging of Diesels is much more common.

Probably the most used methods of supercharging Diesels are by means of the Roots-type blower and the centrifugal blower.

The Roots blower (Fig. 30) consists of two rotors inside a housing. Each rotor has two, three, or four lobes, which fit together like gear teeth as the two rotors are driven from the engine crankshaft. Air is drawn in and carried around the outer side of the rotors to the outlet and into an air chamber, which entirely surrounds the lower part of the cylinders. This compartment of air under pressure is fed to the cylinders.

Although these blowers are somewhat expensive to build, they have been very popular because they give trouble-free service for long periods and, except for a characteristic whine at highest speeds, are quiet running.

The centrifugal type is inexpensive and requires no attention beyond bearing lubrication. A particularly popular application of the centrifugal compressor is in the Büchi system for supercharging Diesels. (See Fig. 31.) An exhaust gas-driven turbine is used to drive the compressor that supplies the air to the engine.

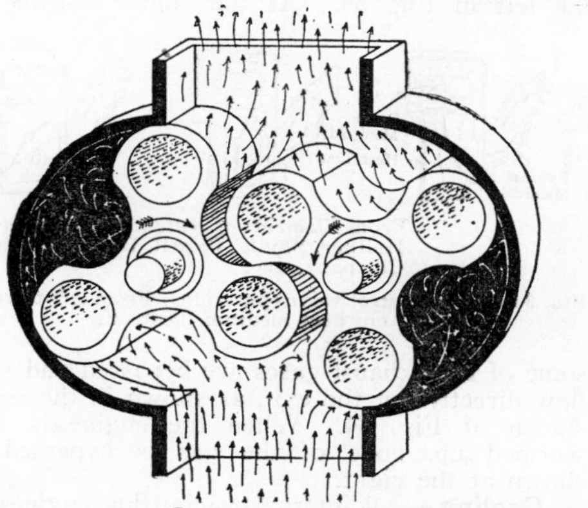

Courtesy General Motors Corporation.

FIG. 30. Roots blower.

The Büchi turbosupercharger increases the weight of a four-stroke Diesel only 1 to 2 per cent but raises its output by as much as 50 per cent. It has even been claimed that for a given maximum power output, a Diesel fitted with a Büchi unit is actually cheaper in first cost than an unsupercharged engine. Its specific fuel consumption (pounds of fuel per brake horsepower-hour) is at least as low as that of the unsupercharged engine, over a wide range of load.

Valves and Mechanism.—In the operation of the internal-combustion engine a fresh charge of air, or mixture of fuel and air (depending on whether it is a Diesel or Otto engine) must flow into, and be trapped in, the cylinder at the proper time during each cycle. A short time later the products of combustion must be allowed to flow out of the cylinder.

The first requisite of valves is that they allow the engine to breathe freely, that is, the resistance to flow through the valve opening should be minimum so that there is little difference in pressure between the cylinder and the surrounding atmosphere. When the valves are closed they must seal the combustion space tightly, or loss of compression will result.

The mechanism must open and close the valve at the proper times as well as giving it the desired lift. The demand for quiet operation has brought forth designs that seat the valves with practically no noise.

The most common valve is the poppet, which consist of a head and stem. The head was originally a flat disk to which the stem was attached. The temperature of the exhaust-valve head will run somewhere between 900° and 1400°F., depending on the conditions of operation. In fact one series of tests showed that under full-load conditions the exhaust valve may reach 1475°F. —a cherry red. At such temperatures the stress in the valve head may cause its deformation. This has led more or less to the development of the tulip valve. This design makes possible a good streamlining of the head into the stem without adding excessive weight. Hollow valve stems are used to reduce weight. The hollow stem is sometimes filled with sodium (which melts at valve-stem temperatures and is an excellent conductor) so that it carries the heat from the head along the valve stem. The effect of sodium cooling on exhaust valve temperature is shown in Fig. 32.

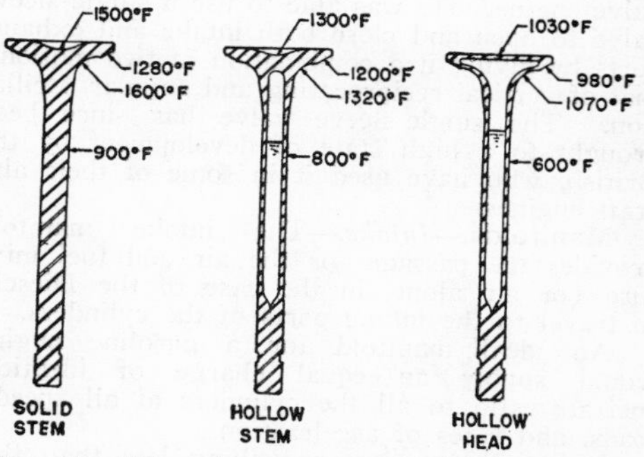

FIG. 32. Effect of sodium cooling on exhaust valve temperature.

Sleeve Valves.—The double-sleeve valve was invented by Charles Y. Knight in 1905. He applied it to an engine that was called the "silent Knight" because its operation was so quiet. This was due to the reduction in valve noises. Other advantages of the sleeve valve include the elimination of valve grinding and minimum leakage. Their chief disadvantage was the difficulty in providing satisfactory lubrication. Failures in lubrication occasionally caused the sleeves to stick, which often wrecked the engine.

The valve consists of two concentric sleeves (Fig. 33) located between the piston and the

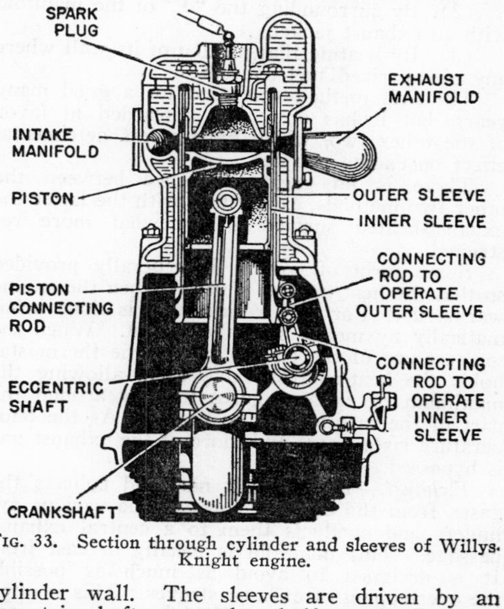

FIG. 33. Section through cylinder and sleeves of Willys-Knight engine.

cylinder wall. The sleeves are driven by an eccentric shaft operated at half speed. Ports in the two sleeves and in the cylinder wall form the intake and exhaust openings. The upper ends of the sleeves slide back and forth between the cylinder head and the wall.

The motion of each sleeve is dependent on the eccentricity or stroke of the sleeve, the length of the small connecting rod, and the relation between the eccentric shaft center and the line of motion of the upper end of the connecting rod. The outer sleeve is driven by a longer connecting rod; thus, it has a slightly different motion from that of the inner sleeve.

In 1910 Peter Burt patented a single-sleeve-valve engine. He was able to use a single-sleeve valve to open and close both intake and exhaust ports by giving it a combination of two motions, that of vertical reciprocating and angular oscillation. The single-sleeve valve has since been brought to a high state of development by the British, who have used it in some of their aircraft engines.

Manifolds.—*Intake.*—The intake manifold provides the passage for the air and fuel mixture (or air alone, in the case of the Diesel) to travel to the intake ports of the cylinders.

An ideal manifold for a gasoline engine would supply an equal charge of identical fuel/air ratio to all the cylinders at all speeds, loads, and rates of acceleration.

In actual practice, something less than this is attained, for various reasons. For one thing, less than half the gasoline is actually vaporized by the carburetor, the rest being in the form of fuel particles ranging from a fine mist to particles of appreciable size. Thus, a manifold that distributes the air equally among the various cylinders will not necessarily distribute the fuel equally, for the inertia effect of the fuel particles is considerably greater than that of air molecules.

To get the fuel properly vaporized heat from the exhaust gases is supplied by one of the following methods:

(1). By preheating the air before it enters the carburetor.

(2). By surrounding the "T" of the manifold with an exhaust jacket.

(3). By heating that portion of its wall where any unvaporized fuel collects.

The first method was used for a good many years, but it has now been discarded in favor of the other two, which have a less detrimental effect on engine power.

There is no great difference between the other two methods, except that with the latter the exhaust-heated surface is somewhat more restricted.

Some form of control is generally provided so that the heat may be shut off when the engine warms up. For best results this is done automatically by means of a thermostat. When the temperature of the engine is low, the thermostat holds the heat-control valve open, allowing the maximum of exhaust gases to flow around the part of the manifold to be heated. As the temperature rises, more and more of the exhaust gas is bypassed.

Exhaust.—The exhaust manifold collects the gases from the exhaust ports of the various cylinders and conducts them to a central exhaust passage. This manifold is usually of cast iron. It is designed to avoid as much as possible the overlapping of exhaust strokes. This is often done by dividing the manifold into two or more branches so that no two cylinders will exhaust into the same branch at the same time.

If the exhaust gases are used to heat the intake charge, the center portion of the exhaust manifold may be connected to the intake manifold through a heat trap and exhaust damper, as shown in Fig. 34. The damper is controlled thermostatically to deflect the hot gases upward and around the intake manifold when the temperature of the engine is below a predetermined value. This heat control is automatic. When the engine is cold, all the exhaust gases are bypassed around the intake manifold, as shown at the left in Fig. 34. As the engine warms up,

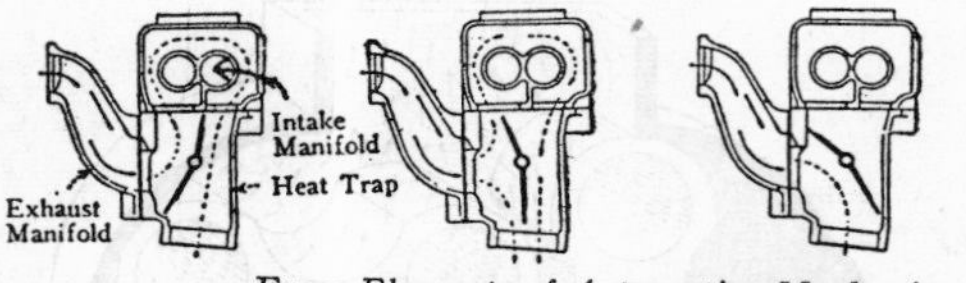

From *Elements of Automotive Mechanics,* Heitner, Shidle, Bissell, D. Van Nostrand Company, Inc.

FIG. 34. Heat control valve operation. From left to right: heat on, heat medium, heat off.

some of the exhaust gases are bypassed and some flow directly out the exit, as shown in the center sketch of Fig. 34. When the engine is fully warmed up, none of the gas is bypassed, as shown at the right.

Cooling.—All internal-combustion engines require some means of cooling. Very roughly, one third of the energy of the fuel is transformed into mechanical energy and one third is removed with the exhaust gases. The remaining third must be transferred through the cylinder walls and head and carried off by some cooling medium circulating over the exterior surfaces.

Air-cooling has been most popular in the aircraft and motorcycle fields. Although much used when the automobile industry was in its infancy, it has lost its popularity here, the last air-cooled passenger-car engine in this country being the Franklin, the manufacture of which was discontinued in the early 1930's.

When air is used as the coolant, the outer surfaces of the cylinders and heads are cast with fins and flanges to give more heat-dissipating surface. (See Fig. 35). For most motorcycle and aircraft engines, the speed of the vehicle provides sufficient movement of air around the fins to give the necessary cooling. In certain applications, however, it may be necessary to increase the circulation of the air around the fins by means of blowers. For greater effectiveness, the cylinders may be surrounded with casings of sheet metal or cowling to form ducts through which a more positive circulation of air may be maintained, especially with the aid of the blower.

When liquid cooling is used, the cylinders and heads are jacketed by casting them with cored passages through which the cooling liquid is circulated.

The circulation of the liquid may be by:

(1). Thermosiphon effect.

(2). Pump.

The thermosiphon principle, used only on a few tractors and road vehicles, depends on the fact that heated water expands and therefore tends to rise. The cooling system is so arranged that this tendency is used to effect the circulation of the water through the system.

Generally, the circulation of the cooling water or other liquid is accomplished in more positive fashion by means of a small centrifugal pump.

For stationary and marine applications where

an abundance of cooling water is available, the heated water is wasted and replaced by cold water. On vehicles and liquid-cooled aircraft engines, however, the water is used repeatedly, being cooled between its courses through the jackets in an air-cooled radiator that forms part of the cooling system.

In addition to a pump, most modern liquid-cooled systems employ a thermostat, which prevents the water in the engine jacket from circulating through the radiator until its temperature has reached a point suitable for efficient engine operation.

Instead of keeping the cold water from circulating through the radiator, some vehicles have thermostatically controlled radiator shutters. The thermostat acts to close the shutters thus keeping the air from the radiators when the jacket water is below a predetermined temperature.

Because the temperature of a cooling system open to the atmosphere is limited by the boiling point of its liquid (212°F. for water and considerably lower if an alcohol is used as the antifreeze), pressure systems have been devised. To date, these have generally been limited to 4 to 8 psi above atmospheric pressure. In this range, each pound per square inch that the pressure is raised above atmospheric raises the boiling point of water about 3 degrees, so a radiator operated at 4 psi attains a cooling capacity increase of 10 per cent. A special pressure cap, designed to relieve the pressure when it reaches the value for which it has been set, must be used. It must also relieve the vacuum that forms in the system when the steam therein condenses after the engine has been shut down.

Evaporative cooling systems employing a hopper are often used on small stationary engines. The hopper is a large open water tank to which make-up water is added as evaporation takes place. Other evaporative systems employ a radiator, which is not open to the atmosphere, but becomes a condenser of steam. The condensate can then be pumped back into the water jacket.

Lubrication.—The distribution of oil to the bearings in an engine can be accomplished in several ways. In early engines, and even now in some stationary engines, oil is fed to each bearing from an individual supply. Usually a gravity sight-feed oiler is used for each cylinder, main bearing, and crankpin bearing, which makes use of a "wiper" action to get the oil from the oiler outlet.

Next came the mechanical oiler, which delivers the oil under pressure from a common supply to each bearing by means of individual plungers and oil lines. The quantity for each bearing is metered according to the need for lubricant. Some bearings on large stationary engines are oiled with ring oilers, which dip into a small sump and carry the oil up to the shaft.

The automotive engine usually has a self-contained oiling system in which the oil is continuously recirculated. The lower part of the crankcase provides the sump or reservoir for the oil supply. There are several systems for supplying the oil to the moving surfaces.

In the splash system (Fig. 36) the lower ends of the connecting rods have dippers, which travel through oil troughs at the bottom of the stroke and splash the oil over the lower cylinder surfaces as well as the crankcase surfaces. The piston spreads the oil over the upper cylinder surfaces while ducts or channels lead the oil to the crankshaft and camshaft bearings. The lower connecting-rod bearings have oil forced in through an oil hole in the lower half during the time the rod dips into the oil.

The main disadvantage of this system is the lack of positive circulation to the bearings, which limits the bearing loading and quantity of oil circulated. Also, the bearings are not cooled appreciably by the oil.

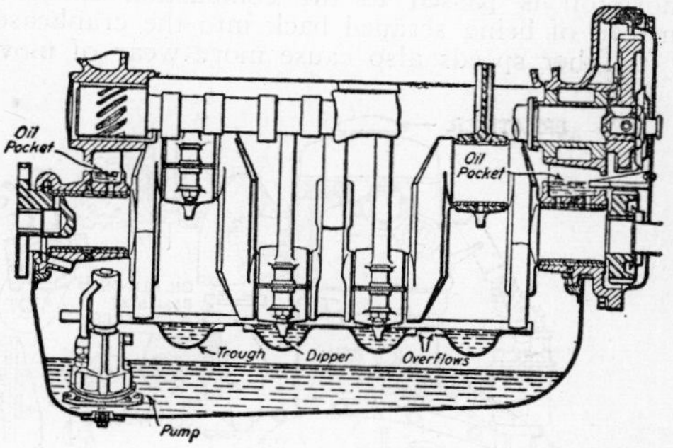

From *High-Speed Combustion Engines*, P. M. Heldt.

FIG. 36. Diagram of splash system of lubrication.

The forced-feed system (Fig. 37), which supplies the oil under pressure, has now practically replaced the splash system for automotive engines. The oil flows through a strainer and into the suction line of a gear pump, which is usually located in a sump in the bottom of the crankcase. The pump forces the oil directly to the crankshaft main bearings. From here it is forced through holes drilled in the crankshaft to the lower connecting-rod bearings. From these bearings the oil is forced through holes drilled in the connecting rods to the wristpins.

Leads from the main bearings deliver oil to the camshaft bearings. Even in the full-pressure system, the oil from the ends of the connecting-rod bearings is thrown up to lubricate the lower part of the cylinder walls. The piston then spreads it over the rest of the wall.

The forced-feed system is favored because of the positive introduction of oil to the bearings and the cooling effect of the large quantities of oil that can be circulated over a bearing.

Various combinations of splash and forced-feed lubrication systems have also been developed.

Airplane engines must operate satisfactorily in any position. For this reason they generally use what is called the dry-sump system. That is, very little oil is retained in the crankcase sump. The oil is scavenged by a pump and delivered to a main oil tank placed in any convenient position. This necessitates the use of at least two pumps: one for scavenging the crankcase and the other for feeding the oil back to the main bearings and other parts of the engine.

There are three ways in which oil can be consumed in an engine in good condition:

(1). Burned in the combustion chamber.

(2). Leakage where the crankshaft or other shafts protrude from the crankcase.

(3). Loss of oil mist or vapor from the breather.

Engine speed is the most important factor affecting oil consumption. As engine speed increases the oil temperature rises, reducing the oil viscosity. This causes more oil to flow through the crankpin bearings, which in turn causes more oil to be sprayed on the cylinder walls. At high speeds the rings do not follow the cylinder wall as closely as at low speeds. They tend to act something like surf boards, riding on the film of oil. Under this condition more oil is passed to the combustion chamber instead of being scraped back into the crankcase.

Higher speeds also cause more wear of moving parts, which then have larger clearances for oil to flow out of.

In general, the condition of the cylinder bores, pistons, rings, and the various clearances between these parts have more to do with oil consumption than do the characteristics of the lubricant used.

The development of oil control rings has done more to control the oil passed to the combustion chamber than any other factor. However, a good oil control ring that gives satisfactory oil consumption at high speeds is apt to cause insufficient lubrication and excessive wear at low speeds. The best compromise seems to be excessive oil consumption at high speeds.

In some small two-stroke engines, as used in marine service, the lubricating oil is mixed with the fuel and fed directly to the cylinder walls, where the gasoline evaporates from it into the combustion space.

Engine Vibration and Mechanical Balance.—In general, there are two forms of motion in a reciprocating engine that may give rise to vibration:

(1). Rotary.
(2). Reciprocating.

Mechanical balance of an engine is attained when the moving parts (both rotating and reciprocating) are arranged so that they counterbalance in operation, thereby minimizing vibration.

Rotating parts are balanced mechanically by bringing them into static and dynamic balance.

A rotating part is in static balance if, when its bearing sections are placed on parallel knife edges, set in a horizontal plane, the part remains in any position to which it is rotated.

Such a part is not necessarily in running or dynamic balance. That is, it is possible to have the center of gravity of the part lie on its axis of rotation (thus giving static balance) and still not have the weight balanced along the axis, so that the part wobbles endwise when it is rotated at high speed.

The crankshaft and flywheel are the principal rotating parts to be balanced mechanically.

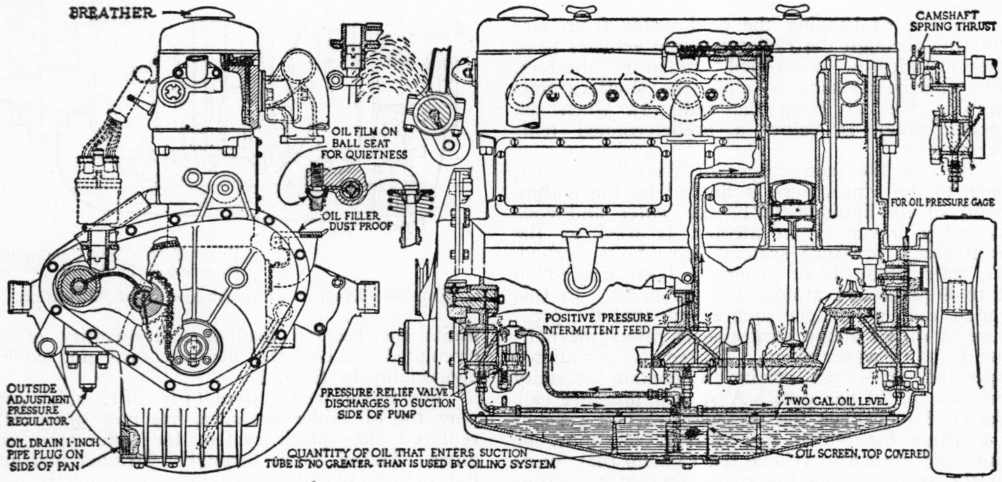

From *High-Speed Combustion Engines*, P. M. Heldt.

FIG. 37. Forced-feed system of lubrication.

Bringing the reciprocating parts into mechanical balance is much more complicated than for rotating parts.

The weight of the piston and connecting rods moving one way and then the other produces considerable vibration. The crankshaft is subjected to shocks in bringing these parts to a stop at each end of each stroke. These shocks are called "primary inertia forces." They are increased in intensity by the gas pressure on the piston at the end of the cycle.

In a well-built engine, all pistons and all connecting rods are the same weight within close limits, and the flywheel and crankshaft assembly is balanced dynamically. By such practices much of the vibration is minimized.

There are, however, certain types of vibration that still must be eliminated or at least minimized in every engine. For instance, there is torsional vibration of the crankshaft, which is caused by a slight winding and unwinding of the crankshaft resulting from the application and release of the power impulses on the crankthrows of the crankshaft.

Every crankshaft has an inherent natural frequency of vibration. If the frequency of the torsional vibration should correspond to the natural frequency of the crankshaft (be in resonance), the vibration would become excessive and the crankshaft might break. Speeds at which resonance occur are called "critical speeds."

A number of methods are used to minimize torsional vibration. One is to design the crankshaft so that its basic or highest critical speed is above the maximum speed of the engine, and to damp out the torsional vibration that occurs at lower speeds by special means or by natural bearing friction. Most 6- and 8-cylinder automotive engines depend on torsional vibration dampers because of the relatively long crankshafts and high speeds of these engines. One type, called a "harmonic balancer," is provided with an inertia weight that is set in motion by the torsional vibration but, because its motion is out of phase with or opposed to that of the crankshaft, it tends to neutralize the vibration of the crankshaft or damp it out.

Another type of vibration is caused by the torque reaction of the connecting rods on the cylinder block as they push against the crankpins to cause rotary motion of the crankshaft. The torque reaction of the connecting-rod impulses tends to rotate the cylinder block in a direction opposite to that of the crankshaft. These reactions tend to vibrate the cylinder block. In most instances this vibration is minimized by increasing the number of cylinders and by mounting the engine on rubber.

Power and Its Measurement.—Engines of all kinds are rated in horsepower, which is a measure of the rate at which they can do work. The term horsepower is used in different ways, for instance: (1) Indicated horsepower is the power developed inside the cylinder by the expansion of the gases. It can be obtained by measuring the area of the indicator card. (2) Brake horsepower is the power the engine actually delivers. It can be measured by means of such equipment as the Prony brake, fluid friction dynamometer, electrical dynamometer, and the transmission dynamometer.

The difference between the indicated horsepower and the brake horsepower is called the friction horsepower. It represents the horsepower lost because of the friction of the moving parts.

There is another commonly used—if more or less fictitious—horsepower called the AMA rating (known in England as the RAC rating and often erroneously called the SAE horsepower). It is much used for taxation purposes. The formula for calculating this horsepower is $D^2N/2.5$, where D is the diameter or bore of the cylinder in inches and N is the number of cylinders. This simplified formula is based on three assumptions:

(1). A mean effective pressure of 90 psi.
(2). A mechanical efficiency of 75 per cent.
(3). A piston speed of 1,000 feet per minute.

At the time when the Royal Automobile Club of England developed this formula, it represented fair average values for automobile engines, but in modern engines they are very much exceeded. Mean effective pressures of 120 to 130 psi are regularly obtained. Efficiency is up to 85 per cent or more. Piston speeds can be over 2,000 feet per minute. Thus, a good modern engine may actually develop a brake horsepower of three or more times its AMA rating.

Efficiencies and Their Measurement.—The engineer uses various types of efficiency to describe how well his engine is operating. For instance, he uses the expression "thermal efficiency," which is simply output divided by input. If the output is the net work as obtained from an indicator diagram and the input is the energy contained in the fuel, the ratio is the indicated thermal efficiency. If the output is the brake work, as measured, for example, by a Prony brake, then the brake thermal efficiency is obtained.

The thermal efficiency is governed chiefly by the range of temperatures through which the working fluid, be it gas or steam, passes on its way through the engine. This range is greater for internal-combustion engines than for steam engines, hence the former are inherently capable of higher thermal efficiencies, that is, they are capable of converting into work a higher percentage of the total heat of the fuel than are steam engines.

Then there is engine efficiency, which is the actual thermal efficiency divided by the thermal efficiency of the corresponding ideal cycle (that is, the ideal Otto cycle for gasoline engines and the ideal Diesel cycle for Diesels). If, for example, the brake thermal efficiency is divided by the thermal efficiency of the ideal cycle, then the result is the brake engine efficiency. The brake engine efficiency indicates the magnitude of the losses occurring within the cylinder, such as those due to fluid friction, incomplete combustion, and mechanical friction.

Also of great importance is the mechanical efficiency, which is the brake work divided by the indicated work, or the brake horsepower divided by the indicated horsepower.

Performance Data.—Fig. 38 shows curves that indicate the kind of performance obtained from a gasoline engine on a dynamometer test.

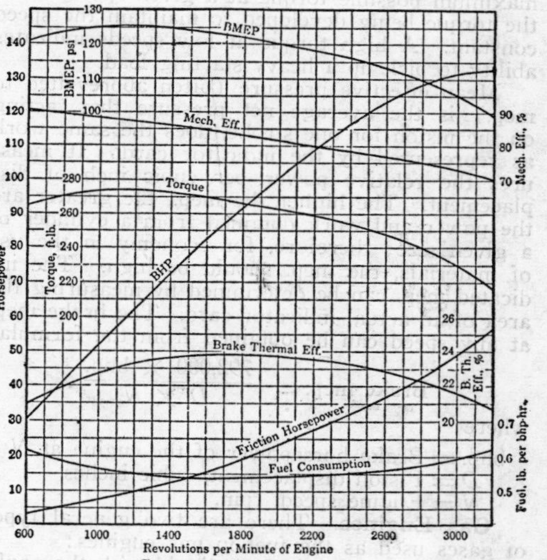

Courtesy Continental Motors Corporation.

FIG. 38. Typical performance curves for automobile engine of 6.37 compression ratio, operated on 75-octane gasoline with wide-open throttle (engine speed of 1600 rpm corresponds to car speed of 30 to 35 miles per hour).

This graph is for a 4-inch diameter by 4 ⅜-inch stroke engine with a compression ratio of 6.37, operated on 75-octane fuel. The test was run with wide-open throttle. The economy at a particular speed is not as good with a partially closed throttle as when it is wide open. An engine speed of 1,600 rpm. corresponds to a car speed of 30 to 35 miles per hour, the exact value depending on the rear-axle gear ratio.

Brake horsepower output increases to a peak, in this case at about 3,200 rpm. (apparently). At higher speeds, the output would decrease. A value read from this curve at any particular speed is the horsepower delivered with wide-open throttle and the engine warmed up. In the ordinary operation of an automobile, it is seldom that the throttle is wide open for any length of time.

Friction horsepower is determined by driving the engine with the dynamometer and noting the consumption of power. Thus, this power includes that necessary to pump the gases into and out of the cylinders. It goes up rapidly at high speeds. At maximum speed, it may be about half the brake output of the engine.

It is to be noted that mechanical efficiency drops off as speed increases. This is due to the rise in friction horsepower at the higher speeds.

Since the fuel consumption is related directly to the brake thermal efficiency, as the curve for brake thermal efficiency rises (to a maximum at about 1,800 rpm.) the fuel consumption decreases. Over a fairly wide range both these curves vary little, a desirable characteristic. At very high speeds, however, the brake thermal efficiency drops off rapidly, causing the fuel consumption to rise steeply (not shown in Fig. 38). Thus, not only does the power necessary to drive a car at high speeds increase very rapidly (about as the cube of the speed), but the efficiency of the engine falls off.

Torque is significant for an automobile engine because the acceleration or pickup of the car depends on the available torque, which is the maximum possible torque at a given speed minus the torque being developed to maintain the speed constant. A high torque at low speeds indicates ability to pick up a heavy starting load.

Mean effective pressure (often abbreviated to mep.) is the average net pressure that, acting on the piston for one stroke, does the same work as represented by the indicator card. It measures the relative power per cubic inch of displacement. The higher the mep., the greater are the power and work obtained from a cylinder of a given size; therefore, for economy in the use of materials, the mep. should be high. The indicated mep. can be determined by measuring the area of an actual indicator card. The brake mep. at any speed can be obtained from the formula:

$$\text{Brake mep.} = \frac{792{,}000 \times \text{bhp.}}{D \times N}$$

where:

bhp. = Brake horsepower of the engine at N
D = Piston displacement, cubic inches
N = Engine speed, rpm.

Gas Engines.—There are two general types of gases used as the fuel in gas engines:

(1). Those that become liquid with the application of only a moderate degree of pressure.

(2). Those that remain gases until compressed under very high pressures at very low temperatures.

The first classification includes such fuels as propane and butane, which are designated liquefied petroleum gases, or LPG for short.

LPG is used to some extent as a fuel for trucks and buses. If it is used in engines designed to burn gasoline, certain changes must be made, such as the use of a pressurized fuel tank, the addition of a converter (which is a combination pressure regulator and vaporizer), and a special carburetor.

The use of LPG as a fuel for automotive vehicles is limited, however, by several factors, such as: the high degree of explosiveness of the fuel (it is more easily exploded than gasoline), the need for engines of high compression ratio to take advantage of the high antiknock rating of the fuel, and its relatively high cost.

Purely gaseous fuels are used only in stationary engines because the engine must be near its fuel source. It is impossible to carry even highly compressed gases in a quantity great enough to permit any considerable range of action to a vehicle.

Gas is used as a fuel only when there are available cheap natural or byproduct gases in adequate quantities. Thus, outside the natural gas regions, the most extensive application is in connection with blast furnace plants, in which large quantities of combustible gases are produced as a byproduct. Here they can be used to operate blowing engines that furnish air to the furnaces and to drive generators to supply electricity for the plant and neighboring communities.

Fig. 39 shows an example of a gas engine driving a compressor.

Most gas engines operate on the Otto cycle, although dual-fuel engines have also been built that operate on the Diesel cycle and run on either

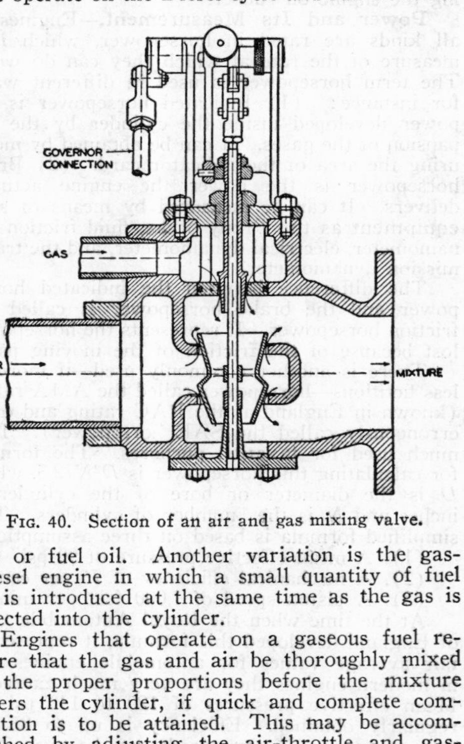

FIG. 40. Section of an air and gas mixing valve.

gas or fuel oil. Another variation is the gas-Diesel engine in which a small quantity of fuel oil is introduced at the same time as the gas is injected into the cylinder.

Engines that operate on a gaseous fuel require that the gas and air be thoroughly mixed in the proper proportions before the mixture enters the cylinder, if quick and complete combustion is to be attained. This may be accomplished by adjusting the air-throttle and gas-throttle valves for the proper gas/air ratio and directing their streams to meet at right angles to assure good mixing, as shown in Fig. 40. This gas mixing valve takes the place of the carburetor.

Bibliography.—Boyer, G. C., *Diesel and Gas Engine Power Plants* (New York 1943); Heitner, J., Shidle, N. G., and Bissell, T. A., *Elements of Automotive Mechanics* (New York 1943); Smith, G. G., *Gas Turbines and Jet Propulsion for Aircraft* (New York 1946); Heldt, P. M., *High-Speed Diesel Engines* (Nyack, N. Y., 1947); Judge, A. W., *Modern Gas Turbines* (London 1947); *Principles of Automotive Vehicles* and *Fundamentals of Diesel Engines* (Superintendent of Documents, Washington, D.C., 1947); Faires, V. M., *Theory and Practice of Heat Engines* (New York 1948); Heldt, P. M., *High-Speed Combustion Engines* (Nyack, N. Y., 1948); Anderson, J. W., *Diesel Engines* (New York 1949); Chatfield,

C. H., and others, *Airplane and Its Engine* (New York 1949); Frazee, I. A., and others, *Automotive Fundamentals* (Chicago 1949); Newton, K., and Steeds, W., *Motor Vehicle* (London 1950); Lichty, L. C., *Internal-Combustion Engines* (New York 1951).

ELEANOR ALLEN,
Managing Editor, "SAE Quarterly Transactions," Technical Editor, "SAE Journal."

INTERNAL REVENUE SYSTEM. The system of taxation in the United States, which goes by this name, was the outgrowth of necessity and of the administrative genius of Alexander Hamilton. Today its sphere covers the revenue of the United States collected from income taxes, the chief sources of which are individual, corporation, estate and trust taxes; also duties on imports, taxes on alcohol, tobacco; postage, and the consumption or excise tax on manufactures and sales. A commissioner of internal revenue, under the secretary of the treasury, has the general superintendence of all matters relating to the collection of internal revenue, and prescribes regulations therefor. The law of Sept. 2, 1789, creating the Treasury Department, had been drawn by Alexander Hamilton, and with such precision and comprehensiveness that but few changes have since been made in its substance or language. The young secretary considered it to be the duty of the new national government to assume the obligations incurred by the states in the prosecution of the War of Independence. Notwithstanding the void in the federal treasury and the straitened finances of the country at large, he had prevailed on Congress, after a bitter struggle, to become responsible for the payment of about $24,500,000 of debt, which the states were unable to meet and had practically repudiated. The new government itself was little better off. The revenues from customs were inadequate; the nation was poor and imports were small. Hamilton's suggestion was to place an excise on domestic distilled spirits. Though there was as yet no formal differentiation of political parties, the antagonism between the broad and strict constructionists of the Constitution was already manifesting itself. The design of the secretary to exercise within the states, as well as at ports of entry, the taxing powers which he believed to reside in the federal government, met with strong resistence from the Anti-Federalists, who regarded the project as unwarrantably intrusive into the domestic affairs of the states. Moreover, the opposition obtained the support of powerful business interests and of a considerable body of public opinion. There were about 100 distilleries in Massachusetts alone, most of them in Boston, where West Indian molasses (exchanged by Yankee traders for their exports of fish and lumber) was converted into New England rum. In the West and South whisky was made from grain at hundreds of stills in commercial quantities. Rum and whisky were articles of general consumption. The first bill introduced in Congress in 1790 was defeated; but before the end of the session, by the act of March 3, 1791, Hamilton had secured a measure imposing a tax on distilled spirits, graduated from 11 to 30 cents per gallon, according to alcoholic content and the origin of the raw material, domestic or foreign. Although the impost weighed more heavily on rum, made from imported molasses, than on whisky made from home-grown corn, the demonstrations against it became particularly violent in the Allegheny and Cumberland mountain regions. In September 1791 a revenue officer was tarred and feathered in western Pennsylvania, as a defiance of the government. The incipiency, progress and suppression of the Whisky Rebellion (q.v.) it is not proposed here to discuss. Suffice it to say that, when it collapsed in September 1794, it left the right of the federal government to levy excise on domestic products and within the States firmly established. The right to tax whisky was never thereafter questioned, except by the "moonshiners" of the Appalachian highlands, whose conflict with the "revenuers" has continued to this day.

Having obtained recognition for the principle, Secretary Hamilton proceeded to give it wider application. An excise laid in 1794 on carriages used for pleasure or ostentation was assailed as unconstitutional; but the Supreme Court (*Hylton v. U.S.*, 3 Dallas, 171) sustained the act. The objection that the tax, being direct, should have been apportioned among the states according to population, evoked from the court the remark that the only taxes it could conceive to be direct were head taxes and land taxes. In 1794 also laws were passed imposing excise taxes for selling at retail foreign wines and liquors: an excise of 8 cents a pound was laid on snuff; an internal revenue duty of 2 cents a pound was laid on sugar refined in this country, also a tax on sales by auction. By the law of July 6, 1797, "stamped vellum, parchment or paper" was required to be used for a great variety of legal documents and negotiable instruments. In these several laws the internal revenue system, as it ultimately took form, was broadly outlined. All of these enactments were repealed, however, on April 6, 1802, little more than a month after the inauguration of Jefferson as president and the ouster of the Federalists. The revenue derived from internal taxes in the few years they were actually collected amounted to $6,325,000, besides which about $700,000 though assessed remained unpaid at the time of the repeal. The financial necessities of the government, occasioned by the War of 1812, compelled recourse once more to forms of taxation other than customs dues. Nearly all the excises of Hamilton's internal revenue system were reimposed in 1813 and, for the first time, home industries other than the distilleries and snuff factories were taxed. There was a new tax on carriages, now including harness; on boots and leather, beer, candles, caps and hats, parasols and umbrellas, paper, playing cards, and saddles and bridles; also on watches, jewelry, gold, silver and plated ware. Stamped paper was required for bonds, bills, notes and other commercial instruments. Here are all the incidences of taxation, which have become characteristic of the internal revenue system; but its mainstays, then as later, were the whisky and tobacco taxes. After the war they were all repealed and, thenceforward, until 1861, the ordinary revenues of the federal government were derived exclusively from the customs.

The act of Aug. 5, 1861 was primarily intended to (temporarily) increase duties on imports; though it also imposed a direct tax of $20,000,000, to be assessed on land and collected for the government by the states. The law of July 1, 1862, however, which is entitled: "An act to provide internal revenue for the support of the government and to pay interest on the public debt," was a conscious effort to establish a new system of federal taxation. It created the Office of Commissioner of Internal Revenue in the Treasury Department and provided for an organization of collectors and inspectors, which has been maintained substantially as first organized up to the present time. The tax on whisky was fixed by the Internal Revenue Law, as the act was called, at only 20 cents per proof gallon, probably following the precedent of the law of 1813; but this tax was increased by three successive enactments in 1864, first to 60 cents, then to $1.50 and, finally, to $2 per gallon, where it remained until 1868. The newly developed oil industry received marked attention, for quite as heavy a tax was placed on illuminating and lubricating mineral oils (20 cents per gallon) as was originally placed on whisky; moreover, refiners of oil were subjected to all the provisions applicable to distillers of spirits with respect to special (license) taxes, bonds, returns, assessments and removals to and withdrawals from warehouses. All other illuminants then in common use, such as gas and candles, were likewise taxed, but this accorded with the general policy of the act to obtain revenue from everything in sight. It taxed bar, hoop and sheet iron, steel, wire, wood screws and cut nails; locomotives and marine engines and boilers; brass tubing and lead pipe, textile fabrics, clothing and trimmings, felt hats, silk hats and bonnets, hides, leather and factorymade shoes, hoopskirts, diamonds, jewelry, watches, and gooseberry wine; also sugar, ground spices, chocolate and dry mustard. The products of domestic agriculture, cotton excepted, went free and farmers were unlicensed; but special, or license, taxes were placed on practically all other occupations. The butcher, the baker and candlestick maker (this is a literal truth) had to pay, and so did doctor and lawyer. The stamp taxes were expected to yield $20,000,000 a year, but they produced twice that amount. All legal documents, all kinds of commercial instruments, including checks and receipts, bonds, insurance policies, conveyances and mortgages had to be stamped; and, if unstamped, the law declared them void and forbade them being placed on record or used as evidence. The law also imposed dues on successions and legacies, and a tax of from 3 to 5 per cent, graduated to their amount, on incomes. Most of these were, and were so intended to be, war taxes. Reductions began to be made in 1866 by the first Congress that met after the restoration of peace. Many of them were abolished in 1867 and 1868 and practically all of them, including the tax on incomes (but excluding the stamp taxes and the excises on whisky, tobacco and beer) were lifted by the law of July 14, 1870.

The Internal Revenue Act and its successful enforcement had demonstrated the wide scope of the taxing powers of the federal government. Its right to levy tax on incomes was not successfully assailed until 1894, when the United States Supreme Court declared the Income Tax Law passed that year to be unconstitutional. Most of the stamp dues were abolished in 1872, the longest to continue being those on checks, toilet articles, patent medicines and playing cards. The taxes on whisky, beer, manufactured tobacco and cigars became the enduring features of the federal system of internal taxation; and they were the most productive. The largest amount collected under the Internal Revenue Law of 1862 in any year was in 1866, before any of the war taxes had been abolished, when $310,000,000 was turned into the Treasury from this source. The total collections in the 30 years following 1864, when the original act of 1862 obtained its final form, amounted to approximately $4,550,000,000, of which two thirds was derived from whisky, beer and tobacco. By the act of July 13, 1866, stamps were first required to be affixed to beer kegs as evidence of payment of the tax on the contents. The result was so satisfactory, in this particular, that two years later tax-paid stamps were required to be affixed to the original packages of distilled spirits when taken out of bond, and to each box or other container of cigars and manufactured tobacco before the goods left the factory where they were made. As a substitute for, or as an additional check on, the elaborate systems of accounting employed to prevent frauds on the revenue, the tax-paid stamp has abundantly proved its usefulness. Its efficiency came into question in 1875, when the "Whisky Ring" trials disclosed a jugglery with distillers' and rectifiers' stamps (which are not tax-paid but merely certify the contents of the packages) whereby the government had been defrauded of many millions. The success of the frauds was due, however, to the corruption of revenue officers as well as to defects in the stamp laws. Since the introduction of new checks, suggested by the experience with the "Whisky Ring," there have been no serious losses in the collections. This is remarkable in view of the fact that the tax on distilled spirits, $1.10 per gallon, was about four times the first cost of the product. In 1950 the tax on distilled spirits was $9.00 per proof gallon which is now about twenty-seven times the first tax cost of the product.

The only important excise taxes in the United States at the beginning of the century were customs duties and excises on alcohol and tobacco. In 1902, these accounted for 97 per cent of federal tax receipts. In 1919, they produced only one fourth of federal tax income. In 1933–1934, they produced more than one half of federal tax receipts.

Since the beginning of World War II these taxes have increased enormously, principally the result of federal budgetary requirements, the manufactures excise tax reaching a high of 20 per cent on so-called luxuries as jewelry, furs, cosmetics, luggage, handbags, and sundry articles. As a consequence, the increase in excise tax has given rise to a demand of organized employees for higher salaries and wages.

The significance of excise taxes can be rightly understood only when they are viewed as a part of the whole system of taxation. (See also INCOME TAXES.)

Internal revenue from alcohol excise tax for fiscal years ending June 30 were as follows: 1948, $2,255,326,754; 1949, $2,210,607,168; 1950, $2,219,-202,085; from tobacco excise tax: 1948, $1,300,-280,153; 1949, $1,321,874,769; 1950, $1,328,464,-346: from manufacturers excise (sales taxes): 1948, $1,649,234,053; 1949, $1,771,532,723; 1950, $38,957,131,769.

The grand totals of internal revenue income from all sources were as follows: 1947, $39,108,-385,742; 1948, $41,864,542,295; 1949, $40,463,-125,019; 1950, $42,504,798,200.

STEPHEN PFEIL,
Revised by HUGH L. NEHRING,
Attorney-at-law.

INTERNAL RHYME, in poetry, rhyme within a line, as distinguished from end rhyme, the rhyming of the last syllables of lines. Coleridge in *The Rime of the Ancient Mariner* often employs internal rhymes, as "We were the first that ever burst into that silent sea," and "The Wedding-Guest he beat his breast," likewise Poe in *The Raven*—"Ah, distinctly, I remember it was in the bleak December."

INTERNAL SECURITY ACT, The, an act of the United States Congress, also known as the McCarran Act, passed, over the president's veto, on Sept. 23, 1950. Its purpose is the control of subversive activities in the United States. It does not make membership in Communist organizations unlawful but prohibits and penalizes certain acts, such as conspiring to establish totalitarian dictatorship in the United States, transmitting without authorization, if an employee of the United States, "classified" information to a foreign country or Communist organization, etc. Communist organizations must register the names of their officers with the attorney general yearly and if a *communist-action* organization—the act differentiates on this and certain other points between *communist-action* and *communist-front* organizations—of their members also. They must file yearly financial statements and must identify the communistic origin of material they distribute by mail and their radio and television programs. Their members may not use American passports, may not hold non-elective positions under the United States, and if they belong to a *communist-action* organization, may not work in a defense facility. The act strengthens provisions against espionage and sabotage and extends to ten years the time limit for prosecution. The act authorizes the president under specified circumstances to proclaim the existence of an *Internal Security Emergency* during which persons "reasonably" suspected of being subversives, may be placed in detention.

The act provides for the exclusion of aliens who are, or once were, members of any totalitarian party or its affiliates—Communist, Fascist, Nazi, Falangist, and so forth. (An amendment adopted in March, 1951, has exempted from exclusion certain minor groups.) It broadens and makes more severe the deportation provisions applicable to them. It denies naturalization to aliens who within ten years of their application for American citizenship belonged to any totalitarian group and revokes the citizenship of those who within five years after naturalization join such a group. The act requires aliens seeking naturalization—irrespective of their political beliefs and with a few exceptions—to be able not only to speak English as was formerly required, but also to read and write it and to promise under oath to bear arms in behalf of the United States if asked to do so.

MARIAN SCHIBSBY,
Formerly Associate Director, Common Council for American Unity.

INTERNATIONAL, or INTERNATIONALE. The origin of the famous International Association of Workingmen was largely due to a group of political exiles. In 1836, a number of German exiles at Paris banded themselves together as a secret society, *The League of the Just,* with communistic principles. Becoming involved in the Paris rising of 1839 they moved their headquarters to London, where they met with workingmen from Northern Europe whose native tongue also was German. The original basis of the *League* had been a kind of sentimental communism, as expressed by their motto, "all men are brethren." Gathering their intellectual inspiration from Karl Marx, they adopted his doctrine that economic conditions control the entire social structure, and that therefore the main thing in a social revolution was a change in economic conditions. The group of exiles put themselves into communication with Marx, which led to a congress being held in London in 1847 when a reorganization took place and the party adopted the name of the Communist League. Its leaders commissioned Marx and Engels to expound the principles of the league in a manifesto which appeared shortly before the "February Revolution" of 1848 broke out in Paris.

The "all men are brethren" motto was discarded and replaced by the slogan, "Proletarians of all lands, unite!" In May 1849 Marx had been acquitted of high treason and expelled from Prussia; after a brief sojourn in Paris he moved to London and settled there for the rest of his life. Meanwhile, the Communist Manifesto (q.v.) had been translated into most European languages and become virtually the Socialist revolutionaries' creed.

It was the second International Exhibition of London in 1862 which furnished the occasion, curiously enough, for the founding of the International Association of Workingmen; still more remarkable was the fact that a purely capitalistic enterprise should have provided the necessary material. At that time the English workman was considered to be unequaled in the world, and it occurred to certain French manufacturers and newspapers that it would be a useful plan to send a delegation of workingmen to London during the exhibition period to study British methods. German capitalists fell in with the idea. Thus, besides businessmen from all parts of Europe, a large number of foreign workers, artisans or craftsmen, were assembled in London in 1862. What was not on the agenda, however, was the presence of Karl Marx in London. He quickly realized what this assemblage of workers might mean and promptly utilized every opportunity that offered to disseminate his own doctrines among the visitors, especially his conviction that the workers of the world should unite. The seeds fell on fertile soil, and two years later, on Sept. 28, 1864, a great meeting of workingmen of all nations was held at St. Martin's Hall, London, under the presidency of Professor E. S. Beesly, the English historian and positivist. Marx was the chief inspirer of the movement; he was assisted by Mazzini's secretary, Major Wolff—a circumstance from which arose the statement that Mazzini was the founder of the International. As a matter of fact Mazzini mistrusted the whole affair and soon withdrew from it. A provisional committee was appointed to draw upon the statutes of the association; these were to be submitted to a Universal Congress proposed to be held the next year at Brussels. There were 50 delegates in the committee, in which England, France, Germany, Switzerland, Italy, Poland and other countries were represented. There was no secrecy about their procedure; it was by the widest publicity that they hoped to spread their propaganda, the headquarters of which was fixed in London.

Thus was born the International Workingmen's Association. According to John Spargo's biography of Marx, the International was to speed the day when, "like slavery and feudal serfdom," wage labor would be replaced by associated free labor. To attain this objective, "the working class must . . . acquire political power, the mastery of the State, and use it to obtain possession of the socially necessary means of production. To acquire this political power they must first of all unite, must take an interest in international politics, watch the diplomacy of their governments closely, and uphold the simple rules of morality in the relations of private persons and of nations." At first the new association made little progress. The first congress was not held until 1866, at Geneva; after the second congress, Lausanne, 1867, it spread rapidly and acquired an influence which alarmed the French government; the third congress came at Brussels in 1868 and the fourth at Basel, Switzerland, in 1869. On the last of these occasions a number of anarchists attended, headed by Bakunin (q.v.), the Russian anarchist, to whom the doctrines of Marx seemed too tame to produce useful results. The International was at the zenith of its power in 1870. In 1872 its congress at The Hague became a battlefield of clashing factions and conflicting ideas; it virtually perished in that struggle. According to E. de Laveleye ('Socialism of To-day') the majority of the delegates were nevertheless bourgeois; but, in reality, the sentiment of revolt against the aristocratic direction of the more intelligent members always persisted, and it fastened principally upon Karl Marx, the true founder of the International, and the only political brain that it contained. But to keep in existence a vast association embracing very numerous groups of different nationalities, and influenced sometimes by divergent currents of ideas, to make use of publicity as the sole means of propaganda, and yet to escape the repressive laws of different states, was evidently no easy task. It could hardly have lived on after the only man capable of directing it had been ostracized. Personal jealousies contributed their share to the fall of the International. The final congress of the First International was held at Philadelphia in 1874; it was attended by less than a dozen men, who formally dissolved the organization. The headquarters of the General Council had been removed from London to New York in 1872, and the dissolution was a consequence of its dissociation from the European labor field, in the midst of which it had flourished.

The international movement among workers fell into abeyance from the early seventies until 1889, in which year the Second International was born at Paris, and its headquarters established in Brussels in 1890. The principal force in the new concern was represented by the German-Social Democratic Party and militarism was the main object of its attacks. Almost entirely political in character—as distinct from the economic aspect—it demanded the abolition of standing armies and the creation of international arbitration tribunals; it was laid down, not unreasonably, that as the people have to fight the wars and to pay the cost, they should also have a voice in determining the vital questions of peace and war. These demands were reaffirmed in Brussels in 1891, at London in 1896 and at Paris in 1900. At the last-named congress Jean Jaurès declared that the organization of international peace and brotherhood was the most important question before the gathering. The policy toward militarism came up again, and the meeting declared against all appropriations for army and navy.

The Second International met again in 1904, at Amsterdam, during the Russo-Japanese War, when fraternal greetings were sent to the proletariat of both countries and the Socialists and workers of all lands were called upon to oppose with all their might the continuance of war. Tremendous enthusiasm was aroused when delegates from Russia and Japan clasped hands and declared that they entertained no animosity against each other.

Stuttgart was the scene of the next International congress, in 1907, when the question of wars and their prevention was again discussed. A resolution was finally passed in which war in general was attributed to competition from markets, militarism, national prejudices and the desire to weaken the growing power of the working class. Juarès and Bebel vigorously advocated a general strike as the most effective weapon to prevent the outbreak of war. A similar measure had been adopted in a resolution by the French Socialist congress earlier in the same year; the Stuttgart assembly, however, being strongly German in element, reflected the German fear of the disrupting influence of the general strike plank and it was finally resolved that the general strike might be used as a *possible* method of averting war, though not an indispensable one. Militarism again loomed large at the next congress, Copenhagen, 1910. Europe had recently passed through an anxious period, and another (1911) was shortly to follow. War was in the air; the Old World was rushing on towards the abyss and far seeing men of all shades united in strenuous efforts to avert the international disaster they feared was approaching. The Stuttgart program was revived and the congress again demanded the Socialist representatives should refuse the means for armament and advocated disarmament, arbitration of international disputes, the abolition of secret diplomacy and a guarantee of all nations against military attack or suppression by force. A special congress of the Second International was convened at Basel on 24–25 Nov. 1912 to discuss the Balkan situation, which threatened to set Europe in flames. This was the last meeting before the World War; in it the working classes of all lands were again urged to use the means which promised to be most efficacious in preventing war; and, in the event of war, to exert themselves to the uttermost to bring it to a speedy conclusion. With prophetic vision the congress declared that if the Balkan imbroglio were allowed to spread, it "would become the most frightful danger to civilization and the workers."

In the light of what was destined to happen only 20 months later—in July, 1914—it is interesting to record the solemn admonition of the Basel congress to the Socialists of Austria-Hungary and environs: they were urged "to prevent any attack of the Austrian Monarchy upon Serbia." As all the world now knows, it was exactly an attack upon Serbia which precipitated World War I. The Second International was revived after that conflict ended, supporting socialism throughout the world but excluding Communists from its ranks. With headquarters in London, it adopted the statutes of the Labor and Socialist International (the "L.S.I."), which sought to attain its objectives by reason rather than by force.

Meanwhile, the Third, or Communist, International (known generally by the abbreviated term of "Comintern") was born in Moscow, March 2-6, 1919. It espoused the ideals of Karl Marx and the principles of the First International, but had no organic connection with the government of the Soviet Union. Nevertheless the manifesto issued by the first conference was composed by such Russian Communist leaders as Nikolai Lenin and Leon Trotsky (qq.v.), who saw in their government the nearest approach to a fulfillment of their own ideals. At the congress held in 1922 the Comintern was declared by its spokesmen to be "the revolutionary international of the working classes," and it boldly proclaimed that it stood "squarely for the overthrow of capitalism and the establishment of the workers' and farmers' government throughout the world." It advocated the Soviet form of organization and the dictatorship of the proletariat. The most outstanding achievement of the sixth congress, in 1928, was adoption of the "Program of the Communist International," in which a declaration was made of the intent to carry out the teachings of Marx, with the ultimate aim of world communism. The seventh and last congress was held in 1935. On May 15, 1943, in the midst of World War II, the executive committee of the Comintern announced its dissolution, and Communist parties in all countries were asked to ratify this step. In 1947 a new international Communist organization was created under the designation of Communist Information Bureau, popularly known as Cominform (q.v.).

INTERNATIONAL ARBITRATION. See ARBITRATION, INTERNATIONAL.

INTERNATIONAL BOUNDARY TRIBUNAL. See ALASKA BOUNDARY COMMISSION.

INTERNATIONAL COURT OF JUSTICE, judicial organ of the United Nations, frequently referred to as the WORLD COURT. This instrument for building up a body of international law was successor to the Permanent Court of International Justice (q.v.), which had been created by the League of Nations and with the latter was discarded as outcome of World War II. The statute of the new World Court, which formed part of the Charter of the United Nations adopted on Oct. 24, 1945 (see UNITED NATIONS), differed in few respects from that of the old Permanent Court of International Justice. Since the court is open only to the states "parties to the present statute," it necessarily excluded those nations unacceptable for membership in the United Nations; while the judges, whose numbers remained at 15, were elected by the United Nations General Assembly and Security Council, each voting independently of the other, no distinction was made between permanent and nonpermanent members of the latter body; and whereas the earlier court met once a year only, for a stipulated term, the new organ was in permanent session. Yet another difference between the two bodies was the relationship of the United States to them; whereas that country had declined to join the League of Nations and to subscribe to the protocol of the Permanent Court of International Justice (though accorded a seat on the latter body), she had become a signatory to the Charter of The United Nations and thereby a full member of the International Court of Justice.

On Feb. 6, 1946, at the first sessions of the United Nations General Assembly and Security Council, in London, a bench of 15 jurists to sit on the new World Court was elected, 5 members for a full nine-year term, and 5 each for ten and five years respectively. The representative of the United States was Green Haywood Hackworth, hitherto legal adviser to the State Department, and the other 14 judges came from Belgium, Brazil, Canada, Chile, China, Egypt, El Salvador, France, Great Britain, Mexico, Norway, Poland, the Soviet Union, and Yugoslavia. The salaries of the judges were fixed at 44,000 Dutch guilders a year, with a special allowance of 15,000 guilders for the president of the court and up to a maximum of 10,000 guilders for the vice-president. The first meeting of the International Court of Justice was held in April 1946, at The Hague, seat of its predecessor; the members elected as its president José Gustavo Guerrero, of El Salvador, who had occupied the like office with the Permanent Court of International Justice from 1937 until its demise in October 1945.

INTERNATIONAL DATE LINE. The imaginary line at which dates change, being made later by one day by those who cross the line from east to west and earlier by one day by those crossing it from west to east. It is a somewhat irregular line drawn through the Pacific Ocean in a general northerly and southerly direction and separating the islands of the Pacific Ocean in such a manner that all those lying to the east of it carry the same date as the Americas, while all those on the west of it carry the same date as Japan and Australia.

INTERNATIONAL EDUCATION. In broad usage, the term "international education" comprises all types of educational relations among nations. The phrase "educational relations" in this case includes informational and cultural as well as strictly educational contacts. In this connection it is noteworthy that in the United States the use of the word "cultural," as applied to international relations, is apparently being superseded by the use of the word "educational," which has a more definite meaning for most Americans.*

In narrow usage, the term "international education" refers principally to international cooperation or association in educational undertakings, particularly in the exchange of students, teachers, and educational materials. Used in this sense, the term would not include purely informational or propaganda programs and other activities not strictly educational.

Origin.—Internationalism in education may

* This evolution was reflected in the abolition of the Division of Cultural Relations of the United States Department of State in January 1944, and the transfer of its functions to other offices then established within the department. These functions were later inherited by the offices of Educational Exchange and International Information.

be traced to the universities of ancient Greece, where teachers and students gathered from many lands. In his *University Life in Ancient Athens,* W. W. Capes stated that the student body was generally composed of men of different religious beliefs, from various nations. Many clubs were formed of men of the same nationality banded together for social reasons.

J. W. H. Walden, in his study of *The Universities of Ancient Greece,* recorded that the great library at Alexandria in Egypt, which was international in character, reportedly contained 700,000 volumes in the middle of the 1st century B.C.; while at the same time the library of Pergamum, a rival center of research used by various nationalities, numbered 200,000 volumes. At Alexandria, the learning, philosophy, and religion of East and West met under the patronage of the early Ptolemies. Later Rome took over, in large measure, the treasures of the Greek libraries and continued the fostering of education on an international scale.

Developments to 1900.—In his authoritative article on international education in the *Encyclopedia of Educational Research,* W. W. Brickman draws attention to the important role played by Christianity in the early development of international education. He points out that throughout its formative years and during the medieval period, Christianity engaged in missionary teaching across all frontiers and served as an international force toward educational unity.

Like the ancient Athenian universities, the medieval universities of Europe drew their students from many nationalities. From a study of the history of the University of Paris, Gabriel Compayré reached the conclusion that there the scholars and masters first grouped themselves according to their natural affinities of race, and later according to the similarity of their studies.

In the great medieval universities, enormous numbers of persons assembled, comprising scholars of all ages, conditions, and nationalities. Since the universal language of instruction in the medieval universities was Latin, and since the writings of the Greeks and Romans dominated university teaching, there was marked international uniformity in learning. The universities continued to be centers of internationalism in education until the emergence of national, state-controlled educational systems in the 19th century. Since then, educational theories and practices advanced in any one nation have been continually studied in others.

The development of the printing process by Germans of the Rhine Valley during the Renaissance came at a time when enthusiasm for knowledge had spread outside the universities. Printing made possible the exchange, on a large scale, of knowledge among the nations.

During the 19th century, various international movements contributed to the development of the international perspective in education. In his scholarly work entitled *The Schools and International Understanding,* Spencer Stoker recounts the growing interest in internationalism, in the atmosphere of which a desire for international intellectual cooperation was evident, particularly during the latter half of the century.

Developments after 1900.—Outstanding developments in international education in the 20th century have been: the arrangements for international scholarships such as those provided by the will of Cecil John Rhodes, and more recently by the Fulbright Act of the United States Congress; the promotion of the teaching of international goodwill; and the establishment of important new organizations and institutions concerned with international educational relations, particularly the exchange of students.

The Rhodes Scholarships.—Cecil John Rhodes, British statesman who died in 1902, left a will bequeathing about £2,000,000 for the foundation of perpetual scholarships at Oxford University to be held by students from the more important British colonies and from the United States. A codicil to the will gave an insight into Rhodes' views concerning the value of education in promoting understanding and peace among nations. Rhodes expressed in the will his desire to encourage and foster an appreciation of the advantages which he believed would "result from the union of the English-speaking peoples throughout the world."

Of over 1,100 American Rhodes scholars who have been selected since the inauguration of the scholarships in 1904, practically all have returned to the United States to live. In his book on *The American Rhodes Scholarships,* published in 1946, Frank Aydelotte attributed to Rhodes scholars an international point of view and a conception of the kinship of the English-speaking nations of the world.

The Institute of International Education.—Prior to World War II, the Institute of International Education, a nonprofit organization with headquarters in New York, had developed programs for the exchange of students between the United States and Germany, Austria, France, Italy, Switzerland, Czechoslovakia, Hungary, Brazil, and Chile. Since the war, the institute has arranged student exchanges with a number of other countries.

Shortly after the institute was founded in 1919, its officials appealed to the American colleges and universities for scholarships to be given to well-chosen foreign students for study in American institutions of higher education. The appeal met with a generous response. The institute then applied to the governments of European countries for scholarships to enable American college graduates to study in their universities, these being government institutions. Those governments which had been impressed by the accomplishments of the United States in World War I and were eager to win the friendship of the new young giant in international affairs gladly matched the scholarships provided by American sources. By 1939, when World War II began, the institute had exchanged more than 5,000 students on scholarships between institutions of higher education in the United States and in foreign countries. Within the limits of its resources, the institute has realized to an appreciable extent its objective to remove misunderstandings between the American and foreign peoples by the use of educational agencies and to build goodwill in its place.

The China Institute in America.—In 1901, the United States claimed reparations of $25,000,000 from China for losses sustained in that country during the Boxer Rebellion. In his annual message to Congress on Dec. 3, 1907, President Theodore Roosevelt stated that it was "the first intention" of the United States government to release China "from its legal liability for all payments in excess of the sum which would prove to be necessary for actual indemnity to the United States and its citizens." In this connection, the president suggested that the United States aid Chinese education, especially by promoting the education of Chinese youths in America.

By authority of joint resolutions of Congress approved May 25, 1908, and May 21, 1924, a total of over $18,000,000 of the indemnity was remitted to China specifically to be used for educational purposes. The Chinese government placed the remitted funds in a trust, administered since 1925 by the China Foundation for the Promotion of Education and Culture, for the education of Chinese youths in China and in the United States, and for other educational purposes including the establishment of libraries and museums. The China Institute in America, created by the foundation in 1930, has promoted the exchange of professors and students, the extension of knowledge of Chinese culture, and assistance to teachers, students, editors and authors in the United States. As a result of the remission of the Boxer indemnity for educational purposes, China has obtained American-trained leaders in various phases of national life and friendly relations between China and the United States have been furthered.

The China Institute also administers the Yünnan provincial government scholarships and the Chinese Ministry of Education fellowships for study in the United States, and the Chinese government scholarships for American veterans of the China theater to study in China.

Other Organizations.—Private organizations which carry on the exchange of persons with other nations for educational purposes are numerous, particularly in the United States.

A representative example of the many binational organizations is the American-Scandinavian Foundation in America, which has counterparts in Sweden, Norway, Iceland, and Denmark. In normal years, the foundation maintains annually about 100 Scandinavian graduate students in American universities and an average of 25 United States students in Scandinavian institutions, together with over 150 trainees in American banks, hospitals, and industrial firms.

In the field of international education, activities of American business firms cover broad areas geographically and functionally. These areas include: (1) technical training offered by American companies to foreign nationals, who are actual or potential employees; (2) the program of the International Training Administration, in which American business firms cooperate with the United States government and many foreign governments; (3) educational services of American concerns in foreign countries.

Technical training for non-United States personnel may be offered in the United States or in the country where the company operates. Although the training programs are conducted primarily in the interests of the companies concerned, the long-range educational gains accruing to other countries are readily apparent.

Examples of other American organizations and institutions furthering some phase of international education (principally the education of foreign students in the United States) are: the International Institute of Teachers College, Columbia University; the American Association of University Women; the American Chemical Society; and scores of individual colleges and universities.

Outstanding among organizations established in other countries and concerned with some element of international education have been the Universitaire de Hautes Études Internationales (Geneva, 1927), the Deutsche Pädagogische Auslandsstelle (1929), and the Bureau International d'Éducation (Geneva, 1925, reorganized in 1929 as an intergovernmental institution).

Before World War II, three international Conferences on Examinations sponsored by the Carnegie Foundation for the Advancement of Teaching and by the International Institute of Teachers College, Columbia University, drew educators from many countries into collaboration in educational pursuits.

United States Government Participation.—The government of the United States has engaged in several types of activities in the field of international education. These may be listed as follows: (1) the bilateral relations entered into by the United States government under its own coordinated, national program of educational and cultural cooperation with other countries, particularly in Latin America; (2) the international educational relations participated in by the federal government as a member of or contributor to several international organizations, such as the Pan American Union; (3) the relations with defeated nations under the program for their reeducation in the ways of democracy.

The basic policy of the United States government in this field has been to foster mutual understanding, appreciation, and respect. Actions by Congress and by several presidents have contributed to the evolution and implementation of this policy.

For a number of years the educational and cultural relations with foreign countries have constituted one phase of the foreign policy of the United States. Since a few years prior to World War II, the government of the United States, like the governments of a number of other countries, great and small, has placed increasing emphasis on activities in this field.

Activities of the national, bilateral program of the United States government in educational exchange with other nations have been authorized by acts of Congress establishing the functions of the various agencies participating, and by acts specifically providing for certain phases of the program. Activities have included the exchange of special information and materials; the interchange of specialists, professors, and students; and cooperative educational programs.

Through membership in the International Bureau of American Republics and in the Pan American Union which developed from it, the United States has participated in inter-American educational exchanges since 1906.

During and since World War II, the government of the United States has collaborated with the governments of other Allied nations in establishing and promoting the activities of the United Nations Educational, Scientific and Cultural Organization (UNESCO), and in efforts to reconstruct the educational systems of war-devastated countries and re-educate the defeated nations formerly under totalitarian governments.

The Fulbright and Smith-Mundt Acts.—On Aug. 1, 1946, President Harry S. Truman signed the Fulbright Act providing that some of the currencies and credits of other countries acquired by the United States through the sale of surplus property abroad might be used for educational exchanges. The act established a Board of Foreign Scholarships which selects persons to receive awards and supervises the educational activities undertaken. The Department of State administers the program. The Smith-Mundt Act of January 1948, likewise administered by the Department of State, prescribes in broad terms the specifications for a major program of international information and educational exchanges.

UNESCO.—During World War II an important new page was turned in the story of the development of international education. In November 1945, delegates from the United States and 43 other countries, meeting in London, drafted a permanent constitution for the United Nations Educational, Scientific and Cultural Organization. The constitution came into force when adopted by the governments of over 20 nations within the following year. The preamble warns that the peace will fail unless founded "upon the intellectual and moral solidarity of mankind." The charter provides for detailed activities of the organization in fulfilling the general functions of: (1) collaborating in the advancement of mutual understanding of peoples; (2) giving fresh impulse to popular education and to the spread of culture; and (3) maintaining, increasing, and diffusing knowledge. The first UNESCO General Conference was held in Paris in November and December 1946.

A joint resolution approving United States membership in UNESCO passed both houses of Congress in 1946 and was approved by President Truman on July 30 of that year. The resolution authorized the establishment of a national commission to serve as a bridge between UNESCO and the government and private voluntary groups in the United States.

Re-education and Educational Reconstruction.—Two major problems in international educational relations emerged from World War II, namely: (1) the reconstruction of the educational systems of the war-devastated countries; and (2) the re-education of the defeated nations in the ways of democracy.

The Commission for International Educational Reconstruction, established in 1946, grew out of a series of conferences called by the American Council on Education to consider the critical problems of education in the war-devastated countries. The commission has endeavored to stimulate and coordinate American voluntary efforts on behalf of education in the war-torn lands.

Before the close of World War II, interested agencies of the governments of the United States and certain allied countries cooperated in formulating policies for the re-education of the Axis nations. The plans called for the suppression of extreme nationalistic teachings and the furtherance of instruction in democratic ideals.

The overall re-education policy recognized that the reorientation of the Axis nations toward a democratic way of life was primarily an educational task requiring international cooperation.

Bibliography.—Hundreds of books, pamphlets and articles dealing with various phases of international education have been published. The following selected list includes some of the larger works most readily available in libraries and book stores. Numerous additional references may be found under the heading "International Education" in the *Education Index* since 1932.

Faries, J. C., *The Rise of Internationalism* (New York 1915); Institute of International Education, *Annual Report of the Director* (New York 1920–); Capes, W. W., *University Life in Ancient Athens* (New York 1922); Prescott, D. A., *Education and International Relations* (Cambridge, Mass., 1930); Harley, J. E., *International Understanding, Agencies Educating for a New World* (Stanford University 1931); Stoker, Spencer, *The Schools and International Understanding* (Chapel Hill, N. C., 1933); Gray, G. W., *Education on an International Scale* (New York 1941); Educational Policies Commission, *Education and the People's Peace* (Washington 1943); Hemleben, S. J., *Plans for World Peace through Six Centuries* (Chicago 1943); Carr, W. G., ed., "International Frontiers in Education," *The Annals* (American Academy of Political and Social Science, September 1944); Institute of International Education, *The Institute of International Education, 1919–1944* (New York 1944); Kandel, I. L., ed., *Post-War Educational Reconstruction in the United Nations* (New York 1944); Carr, W. G., *Only by Understanding, Education and International Organization* (New York 1945); Kandel, I. L., *United States Activities in International Cultural Relations* (Washington 1945); Quattlebaum, C. A., *Educational and Cultural Phases of U.S. Foreign Policy* (Washington 1946); Quattlebaum, C. A., *Educational and Cultural Relations of the United States with Foreign Countries* (Washington 1947); Brickman, W. W., "International Education," *Encyclopedia of Educational Research* (New York 1949).

CHARLES A. QUATTLEBAUM,
Education Analyst to Congress, Legislative Reference Service, The Library of Congress.

INTERNATIONAL EMERGENCY FOOD COUNCIL, an intergovernmental organization established in 1946 to formulate recommendations for allocation to various countries of food and auxiliary materials in short supply. It assumed and expanded the functions of the wartime Combined Food Board of which the United States, Great Britain and Canada were members. In the spring of 1946 the board was subject to widespread criticism for its inability to cope with the growing food crisis; it was also accused of giving preferential treatment to certain countries. The United Nations Relief and Rehabilitation Administration sharply censured it for its inadequacies in March 1946. Two months later a special meeting of the U.N. Food and Agricultural Administration (FAO) was convened, attended by delegates of 21 nations able to make contributions to alleviate the threatened famine conditions. The conferees recommended establishment of the International Emergency Food Council. This council functioned through commodity committees responsible for preparing and obtaining agreement on allocations recommendations. Twelve committees operated in the spring of 1947, each handling a particular commodity, as sugar, meat, rice, and so forth. Dr. Dennis A. FitzGerald was secretary general of the council and his staff was appointed by the FAO. Considering the greatly improved world conditions of the following summer and passing of the crisis, the council on Nov. 11, 1947, voted its own dissolution, the FAO to take over its functions when a majority of member nations had ratified the vote. However, it continued operations into 1948. Though becoming a committee of the FAO, it retained its separate identity until finally dissolved early in 1949, its functions assumed by other FAO agencies.

INTERNATIONAL FALLS, city, Minnesota, county seat of Koochiching County; 135 miles northwest of Duluth; on the south bank of the Rainy River which here forms the American-Canadian international boundary, separating Minnesota from Ontario; served by the Northern Pacific Railroad. A bridge connects it with Fort Frances, Ont. A port of entry, it has a customs house and is a station of the U.S. International Border Patrol. The center of a truck farming and dairying region, the chief agricultural products are clover, alfalfa seed, potatoes, and vegetables. Town manufactures include newsprint, paper products, insulite, and butter. Founded in 1881 by Alexander Baker, it was incorporated as a village in 1901 and as a city in 1910. Mayor and council government. Pop. (1950) 6,261.

INTERNATIONAL LABOUR ORGANIZATION (ILO). The International Labour Organization was established at the Paris Peace Conference in 1919 on the basis of proposals made by the conference's Commission on International Labour Legislation under the chairmanship of Samuel Gompers, president of the American Federation of Labour. Its constitution forms Part XIII of the Treaty of Versailles of June 28, 1919, and is also incorporated in the treaties of St. Germain, Neuilly, and Trianon.

The original members of the organization were the 29 signatories of the Treaty of Peace, who became members of the League of Nations, and 13 states which were invited to accede to the Covenant of the League. Eighteen states subsequently admitted to membership in the League also became members, and four states became members otherwise than by virtue of their League membership. The United States, which joined the organization Aug. 20, 1934, falls in the latter category. Several newly independent states have recently been admitted to membership, and on Jan. 1, 1951, 62 states were members.

The organization comprises the International Labour Conference, the International Labour Office, and the governing body. The conference, which held its first session in Washington in 1919, meets, usually annually, at the call of the governing body. Among its principal functions is the formulation of standards of working and living conditions which are incorporated in recommendations and conventions. The governments of member states are required to bring recommendations to the attention of their competent national authorities with a view to legislative or other action to implement them, and to report on the action taken. A convention must be ratified by a stipulated number of states before it comes into force. If a member state ratifies a convention, its decision to do so must be reported, and an annual report furnished on how it is applying it. Ninety-eight conventions and 88 recommendations had been adopted as of 1950, and the conventions had received a total of 1,200 ratifications. Among the subjects dealt with by the recommendations and conventions are hours of work, paid vacations, the protection of women and children, prevention and compensation of industrial accidents, social insurance, colonial labor, and seamen's conditions. The 1944 conference extended the mandate of the organization by authorizing it to "examine and consider all international economic and financial policies and measures" in the light of their effect on human welfare, and declared that "in discharging the tasks entrusted to it," the organization, "having considered all relevant economic and financial factors, may include in its decisions and recommendations any provisions which it considers appropriate." An extraconstitutional conference held in New York in 1941 agreed that the organization should contribute to the establishment of a peace based on social justice.

The structure of the conference is tripartite, each national delegation consisting of two government delegates, one delegate representing management and one representing labor. Each delegate may be accompanied by advisers. A two-thirds vote is required for the adoption of recommendations and conventions.

The governing body is composed of 32 members. Eight of the seats are held by the states of chief industrial importance, 8 by governments elected by the other states, 8 by persons elected by the workers at the conference, and 8 by persons elected by the employers. Elections are normally held every three years. The body functions as an executive council of the organization, fixes the agenda of the conference, supervises the work of the International Labour Office, and frames the organization's budget.

The International Labour Office is the permanent secretariat of the organization. It is headed by a director who is appointed by the governing body and who in turn appoints the staff. The office prepares reports for the consideration of the conference and the governing body, and collects and distributes information on industrial and labor subjects. Its publications include the monthly *International Labour Review*, the quarterly *Industrial Safety Survey*, the *Year-Book of Labour Statistics*, the bimonthly *Legislative Series*, and studies and reports on economic and social subjects. Publication is usually in the English, French, and Spanish languages. The officials of the office are recruited from the member countries, and are under obligation not to seek or receive instructions from any authority external to the organization. Technical assistance from office experts is available to the member states in the framing of legislation and regulations.

CAMPBELL BALLANTYNE,
Information Officer, International Labour Office.

INTERNATIONAL LANGUAGE, general term applied in modern times to artificial languages designed for facilitating intercourse between peoples whose national languages or mother speeches differ one from the other. These artificial languages aim toward facility of acquirement through general rules which admit of no exception although some are little less complicated than English for example. In this encyclopedia the principal artificial languages are treated under their own headings, as Esperanto, Volapük, Ro. Over 100 have been devised. Their chief characteristics consist in phonetic spelling, simplicity and regularity of syntax, forms, and word derivation, and freedom from idiomatic phrases. Of the natural international languages, Latin, French and English are dominant in the respective fields of scholarship, diplomacy, and trade.

INTERNATIONAL LAW. In a decision of 1927 the Permanent Court of International Justice ruled: "International law governs relations between independent States."

Before Hugo Grotius (1583–1645) there were many who wrote upon matters relating to international affairs. Among these are the well-known names of Victoria (1480–1575), Ayala (1548–1584), Suarez (1548–1617) and Gentilis (1552–1608). The great work of Grotius, *De jure belli ac pacis* (1625), formulated and clarified much of what is now called international law. From this foundation Grotius gained the title of "Father of International Law." His work influenced the leaders in international affairs almost immediately and the important Treaty of Westphalia at the end of the Thirty Years' War, 1648, embodied ideas of this great master. To Grotius all writers acknowledged their indebtedness.

From the days of Grotius different schools began to develop. One school, sometimes called the «naturalists,» particularly followed the natural law theories, theories in their harmony or agreement with the inherent forces of the universe. Another school, the «Positivists» looked particularly to customs and treaties for the sources of international law. Aside from those who were commentators upon the work of Grotius, the main contributions were from writers upon special topics, such as the writings of Bynkershoek (1673–1743). The systematic work of Vattel (1714–67) had wide circulation in Europe and in America as did that of the American, Henry Wheaton (1785–1848). With the increase in the number of court decisions involving principles of international law, there has arisen a clearer definition of the field of international law and a recognition of its binding character.

Treaties, particularly since the Treaty of Westphalia of 1648, have embodied international law. Where the same clause occurs in a large number of treaties or when a large number of states are parties to one treaty the principle or principles tend to be generally accepted as law. Such was the case in regard to some parts of the Treaty of Utrecht of 1713 which were repeated in other treaties of the 18th century. The doctrine of the balance of power in Europe as a basis of peace, clearly set forth in this treaty, was accepted as a fundamental principle in the diplomatic negotiations in Europe for many years. According to Talleyrand a hundred years later in 1813 the balance of power was «a combination of the neutral rights and interests of the Powers, by means of which, Europe aims at securing the following objects:

«1. That no single Power, nor any union of Powers shall have mastery in Europe.

«2. That no single Power nor union of Powers shall be able to infringe the actual possession and recognized rights of any other Power.

«3. That it shall no longer be necessary, in order to maintain the established state of affairs, to live in a state of imminent or actual war, and that the proposed combination shall secure the peace and repose of Europe against the efforts of a disturber by diminishing his chances of success.»

If all that had at times been hoped for from the acceptance of this doctrine of balance of power had been realized, law in international relations would have developed much more rapidly.

Another principle that has been embodied in many treaties following the Treaty of Utrecht was in its brief form «free ships make free goods» and there was also coupled with it the principle that «enemy ships make enemy goods.» This was a step in advance of earlier practice, particularly of the 17th century, which did not acknowledge that innocent enemy goods under a neutral flag were free from capture. A hundred years later Napoleon claimed that these doctrines of the Treaty of Utrecht had «become through their adoption in subsequent treaties, the common law of nations.»

Progress has, however, been made in international law as in other law and in general there has been a tendency to free commerce from restraints. In respect to the treatment of goods upon the sea, the United States which had in the late 18th century but recently come into the family of nations as the first member from outside of Europe, endeavored to obtain complete exemption from capture of innocent private property even if belonging to enemy persons. This principle was even embodied in certain treaties made by the United States, but it did not receive general approval.

While the precedents of the long negotiations leading to the Treaty of Westphalia of 1648 established some clear lines of diplomatic practice, there were many points upon which disputes were common. The disputes sometimes led to personal encounters. As the diplomatic agent was regarded as embodying in the foreign state the dignity of the state which he represented, he endeavored to obtain for himself the place of greatest prominence. He strove for the highest place at the table, the chair at the right of the sovereign on ceremonial occasions, and by fair means or foul to gain precedence. Bribery of officials was common and some of the books of the early 18th century explain the principles of its use. The rivalry of states became at length so keen that it seemed desirable to lay down laws for the precedence of diplomatic agents. The Congress of Vienna of 1815 embodied a conventional agreement which with an addition at the Congress of Aix-la-Chapelle in 1818 established the grade of diplomatic representatives as follows:

1. Ambassadors, legates and nuncios.
2. Envoys and ministers.
3. Ministers resident.
4. Chargés-d'affaires.

This fixing of the grades removed friction that had long existed, as states were expected to exchange representatives of equal rank. The United States did not, however, send abroad agents of the grade of ambassadors until the Act of Congress of 1 March 1893 authorized such action on the part of the President.

As freedom of action was essential for the performance of the functions of the diplomatic agent, the principle of inviolability was extended not merely to the person of the diplomat but to his suite, family and hôtel or official residence with all the personnel and equipment which might be necessary or reasonably convenient for the proper performance of his functions. He was also entitled to certain honors, such as salutes according to his grade. His prerogatives, if an ambassador, extended to the right to ride in a coach with six horses and outriders and to remain covered in the presence of the sovereign if the sovereign did not remove his hat. Other grades were entitled to lesser marks of respect. The establishing of these rules removed the causes of many earlier contests over rank and dignities and enabled the diplomatic agents to live in harmony and transact the business of the state, receiving the honors not as personal but as for the states which they represented. Each state in sending its representative and in determining his grade determined his rank at the court to which he was accredited. Minor differences have arisen, but for the most part the controversies as to rank which were common before 1815 have come to an end.

Other problems which were once perplexing in international relations, as for instance, the regulation and later the suppression of the slave trade have likewise disappeared.

Some problems have taken new form as the use of private vessels in the time of war after the abolition of privateering. New problems have arisen, as in the regulation of the use of the air. To meet these changes the international law development of the 19th and 20th centuries has tended to become more and more conventional.

The conventional international agreements were at first generally incidental to some other international act as in the agreement fixing the grades of diplomatic agents. The same was true of the Declaration of Paris of 1856 in which it was stated that the plenipotentiaries who signed the Treaty of Paris «considering that maritime law had long been the subject of deplorable disputes . . . cannot better respond to the intentions by which their governments are animated than by seeking to introduce into international relations fixed principles, in this respect.» They accordingly made «the following solemn declaration:

"1. Privateering is and remains abolished.
"2. The neutral flag covers enemy's goods, with the exception of contraband of war.
"3. Neutral goods, with the exception of contraband of war, are not liable to capture under the enemy's flag.
"4. Blockades, in order to be binding, must be effective—that is to say, must be maintained by force sufficient really to prevent access to the coast of the enemy."

The United States and several other powers did not adhere to this declaration, though its principles were generally recognized. The United States wished in 1856 to go farther and as in earlier and later days, to secure the general exemption from capture of private property at sea.

Agreements reached by states assembled for the purpose of formulating what may be called international law gradually became common. It would seem but natural that the destruction of life without advantage to any state would be an early matter of attention as a subject for a formulated international agreement. Yet the first international agreement relating to this matter to receive general assent was concluded in 1864, and known as the Geneva Convention for the Amelioration of the Condition of Wounded in Armies in the Field. The representatives of 12 European states announced in the preamble their purpose to be to mitigate «the evils inseparable from war, to suppress useless severities, and to ameliorate the condition of soldiers wounded on the field of battle» It was a long time for the world to wait for such legislation. This Geneva Convention of 1864, which provided for the immunity of the hospital corps, was not immediately ratified, however. The United States did not adhere to this convention till 1882, and this was the only international agreement of general scope and relating to war to which even the United States became a party before the end of the 19th century.

The Conference of Saint Petersburg followed in 1868 and was attended by representatives from 17 European states, and these agreed upon the Declaration of Saint Petersburg, which denounced among the signatories «the employment by their military or naval troops of any projectile of a weight below 400 grammes, which is either explosive or charged with fulminating or inflammable substances.»

The Geneva Convention of 1864 and the Declaration of Saint Petersburg of 1868 related particularly to a state of war. Soon other matter became increasingly the subject of international conferences, and before the end of the 19th century, general conventional agreements had been made and signed by a large number of states acting together upon such matters as an «International Bureau of Weights and Measures» (Metric System), 1875; «International Protection of Industrial Property,» 1883; «Protection of Submarine Cables» (in time of peace), 1884; «Exchange of Official Documents, Scientific and Literary Publications,» 1886; «Repression of African Slave Trade,» 1890; «Formation of an International Union for the Publication of Customs Tariff,» 1890; and «Regulations of Importation of Spirituous Liquors into Certain Regions of Africa,» 1899. Such international agreements became a part of the written law of nations, but covered only a very small part of the entire field of international relations in peace and war.

There was developing toward the end of the 19th century a belief that by agreement among the states of the world a basis of conventional law could be reached which would do much to alleviate possible friction and even to avoid war. The extent to which this belief was realizable was to be put to the test. While the United States and Spain were still at war, at the diplomatic reception of 12 Aug. 1898, at Saint Petersburg, Count Mouravieff, Russian Imperial Minister of Foreign Affairs, delivered to the representatives of the Powers a communication from His Majesty the Czar. While the nature of the document gave rise to surprise, its character and source demanded immediate attention. Mentioning the competition in development of means of international combat and the effect of this competition upon the states of the world, he proposed an international conference, saying that:

"To put an end to these increasing armaments, and to find means for avoiding the calamities which menace the entire world, that is the supreme duty which lies upon all nations."

The United States replied that:

"Though war with Spain renders it impracticable for us to consider the present reduction of our armaments, which even now are doubtless far below the measure which principal European powers would be willing to adopt, the President cordially concurs in the spirit of the proposal of His Imperial Majesty."

On 11 Jan. 1899 another circular was presented to the Powers containing a tentative program. This program suggested agreement upon (1) limitation of armaments; (2) restrictions upon new methods of warfare; (3) prohibition of firing from balloons; (4) prohibition of submarines and rams; (5) adaptation of principles of Geneva Convention of 1864 to naval warfare; (6) neutralization for vessels saving those overboard after battles at sea; (7) revision of rules of war on land; and (8) acceptance of principles of mediation and arbitration with a view to preventing armed conflicts. Of these eight topics suggested, seven look to furthering peace by limitations upon the conduct of war, and the last topic suggests a quasi-legal method of furthering the movement toward peace.

Following the suggestion of the Czar, representatives of 26 Powers met on 20 May 1899, in the House in the Wood at The Hague, and remained in session a little more than two months. This is known as the First Hague Peace Conference. The Conference drew up three conventions, three declarations, one resolution, and six wishes: Conventions: (1) for the pacific settlement of international disputes by means of good offices and mediation, commissions of inquiry and arbitration; (2) regarding the laws and customs of war on land; (3) adaptation of Geneva Convention of 1864 to maritime warfare. Declarations: (1) prohibiting the discharge of projectiles from balloons; (2) the use of projectiles for the diffusion of deleterious or asphyxiating gases; (3) the use of expanding bullets. Resolution affirming the desirability of the restriction of military budgets. Wishes for further consideration of various matters upon which the Conference had not reached agreement. The last topic upon the program suggested by the Czar had become the first convention of the First Hague Conference, or the furtherance of the aim of peace by means quasi-legal in character assumed a foremost place in the results of these deliberations at The Hague; and the first item in the program, the attainment of international peace through the restriction of the means by which each nation had hitherto maintained its rights, viz., effective armament, became the subject of a resolution and a wish. The Conference asserted its confidence in the law as the method for settling international disputes.

Following this conference of 1899 there was a wider interest in the possibility of law for the world. While the Russo-Japanese War of 1904–05 was still in progress, a request was made by those interested that President Roosevelt call another conference. He had already taken the first steps toward such action when advised that the Czar of Russia desired to call the conference and at the close of the Russo-Japanese war the Czar carried out the plan. It was now fully admitted that the work of the First Hague Conference of 1899 had been of great value for the world.

Eight years later, in 1907, a Second Hague Conference further elaborated and formulated conventional agreements, and to this Conference representatives of 44 of the states of the world came, giving ample evidence of the tendency to accept the principle of international legislation. Some of the conventional agreements have been tested in the course of years. The court established for the settlement of international disputes attained a recognized standing. Cases affecting all parts of the world have already been decided and the awards accepted. The Second Hague Conference extended the scope of the law. Among its propositions which have not been adopted as yet into the law of nations was that to establish an international prize court. This proposition was generally approved in principle though a satisfactory method of selection of judges was not devised. To supplement this prize court convention an attempt was made by 10 maritime nations in 1908–09 at the International Naval Conference at London to formulate the laws which the court should apply. The Declaration of London of 1909 embodied the labors of this Conference. This Declaration has not been ratified though the provisions of the Declaration have often been cited in courts and in negotiations. It is not merely in these broad national matters that the formulation of the law has progressed, but in recent years many such matters as the following have become subject of general international agreements: literary and artistic copyrights, 1902; sanitary measures, 1903; white slavery, 1904; potent drugs, 1906.

Rights, persons and property, and jurisdiction on land and sea earlier had received attention; in more recent years the use of the air has been the subject of international regulation, as in the conventions of 1906 and 1912. To the last of these conventions the representatives of about 40 non-American political unities affixed their signatures, many of the larger states allowing here, as in some other conventions, participation in the formulation of the law to the divisions of which the state entity was composed. The legislation thus rested upon a broader base than in many conventions of earlier years.

In the application of the law for nations the progress has been exceedingly rapid. Cases which have defied the best efforts of diplomacy for generations, as the North Atlantic Fisheries dispute, have been settled by due process of law in a few weeks. Cases which might have resulted in long and disastrous international contention have been resolved in the light of law. Where recourse to legal settlement of disputes was in earlier times the last resort, it has become the first, and not merely the parties to the controversy may begin the action, but third parties may of right suggest or even try to bring the parties to submit the case to the decision of the court.

It requires only a review of the conventions since 1899 to show how rapid is the formulation of the law for nations. These international laws, in addition to many private matters, cover the pacific settlement of international disputes, limitation of the employment of force in the collection of contract debts, laws for war on land, rights and duties of neutral powers and persons in war on land, status of enemy merchant ships at the outbreak of hostilities, the transformation of merchant ships into warships, the laying of automatic contact submarine mines, bombardment by naval forces in time of war, care of sick and wounded in time of war, rights and duties of hospital ships, exercise of right of capture in maritime war, prohibition of discharge of projectiles from balloons, rights and duties of neutral powers in time of war.

Not merely had the law developed and become somewhat widely the subject of formal international acceptance, but many of the conventions embodying the law had been put to severe tests. Probably few more serious tests could be imagined than that which one part of the convention for the Pacific Settlement of International Disputes received in 1904 during the Russo-Japanese War. In this convention there had been placed a section providing for a sort of international grand jury called a Commission of Inquiry to investigate the facts in case of a dispute between nations when agreement to resort to such a procedure could be reached. On the night of 21 Oct. 1904, a division of the Russian fleet under Admiral Rozhdestvensky, on its way from the Baltic Sea to the Far East, while passing through the

North Sea near the Dogger Banks, fired on the British fishing fleet. The fishermen suffered the loss of one trawler, five were damaged and two men were killed and six wounded. Great Britain was an ally of Japan and the sympathy in the British Isles was generally with the Japanese. When the news of this disaster spread, the demand for action was urgent upon the British government. Orders were issued by the Admiralty to the Mediterranean, Channel and Home fleets, and the British Foreign Office announced on 25 October that it had made known to Russia «that the situation is one which in the opinion of His Majesty's Government does not admit of delay.» The same day the Czar in a message to the King said «he would take steps to afford complete satisfaction as soon as the circumstances of the case were cleared up.» On the following day the Russian fleet arrived at Vigo and reported that the reason for the firing was the presence of Japanese torpedo boats among the fishing vessels. This the fishermen denied. The demand in England for war had a little time to subside and fortunately the method for honorable submission of such a dispute existed in the Convention of 1899, to which Great Britain and Russia were parties, and it was agreed to submit the dispute to a Commission of Inquiry. The commission was composed of admirals from the American, Austrian, French, British and Russian navies. The report of the commissioners was adverse to the Russian contentions and the incident was closed by the immediate payment of £65,000 to Great Britain. Thus a dispute which might have been regarded as an ample cause for war was by peaceful methods settled promptly and honorably.

This provision for commissions of inquiry was elaborated in 1907, that it might, if occasion arose, become even more serviceable.

Another Convention of 1899 prohibited the discharge of projectiles or explosives from balloons for a period of five years. While this period expired during the Russo-Japanese War, both Russia and Japan continued to observe the spirit of the prohibition. The most powerful states were unwilling to renew this convention in 1907, but there was an increasing interest in the problems of the use of the air in time of peace and in time of war.

Conferences on aerial navigation were frequent in the 20th century. Rules of aerial highway and regulations for aircraft and operators were adopted.

The use of radio led to the agreements as to stations at The Hague in 1907, and during the World War the use of the air became a matter of capital concern both for neutrals and belligerents. The Convention for the Regulation of Aerial Navigation, 1919, recognized the exclusive sovereignty of the state in «the air space above its territory.» Other conventions followed and the use of the radio for the dissemination of propaganda as well as for ordinary news service gave rise to new problems. The international law of the air now covers a large field of agreements among states.

The rules for war on land were also tested and further changes were found necessary in 1907.

Not merely was there made in 1899 provision for a commission of inquiry but also for a court of arbitration. It was thought for a time that this court would never function. It remained for two American republics to first test the court of arbitration. In 1902 the United States and Mexico took before the court its first case.

This was the case of the Pious Fund of the Californias, which had been in dispute from the annexation of Upper California in 1848 by the United States. An arbitral award in 1875 had granted to the United States claimants 21 years' interest on one-half the fund which had originally been given to the missionaries for their work in the Californias. The interest for subsequent years had not been paid and it was claimed by the Catholic Church of California. The contention of the United States was upheld by the arbitrators and the protracted dispute was at an end.

Other cases came to The Hague Court after this first award and it soon became customary for states to request that in case of dispute «the matter be referred to The Hague.»

The next case related to the preferential treatment for the powers which had blockaded Venezuelan ports in order to enforce the payment of debts due their citizens. Here not two but ten states were involved, representing Europe, North America and South America. This case was quickly followed by one in which Germany, Great Britain and France appeared against Japan in the matter of the perpetual leases in that country, thus introducing Asia also before the court. Another case involving Asiatic interests was the case of the right of the Muscat Dhows to fly the French flag, which was a subject of difference between Great Britain and France.

These four cases were before the court at The Hague between 1902 and 1905. In 1907, at the Second Hague Conference, the convention relating to the court was amended and extended to meet the needs which experience had demonstrated.

The first case under the revised convention was settled in 1909, the Casabianca case, which had brought France and Germany to the verge of war. The same year the controversy over the maritime boundary between Norway and Sweden was adjusted.

In 1910 the court attempted to settle the disput between the United States and Great Britain over the North Atlantic Fisheries. This dispute had continued in varying forms for about 100 years. Diplomatic negotiations had failed many times. Within a few weeks a decision accepted by both parties was reached by the court.

Questions of national honor and fundamental rights were considered in such cases as the case of Savarkar in 1910, the case of the *Manouba* and of the *Carthage* in 1913, and varicur aspects of financial claims in those of the Orinoco Steamship Company in 1910 and the interest on Russian indemnities in 1912. In June 1914, The Hague Court made an award settling the land boundaries in the island of Timor.

The range of cases settled by the court is accordingly very wide. The frequency of resort to the court was rapidly increasing before the World War. Interests involving the Americas, Europe, Asia, Africa and the area near Australia had been considered. Seventeen of the 44 states represented at the Second Hague Conference had appeared at least once and some six times before the court at The Hague. The awards of the court had in every instance been accepted in good faith and observed.

The decision in the *Zamora* case before the judicial committee of the English Privy Council on April 7, 1916, showed that the only sound basis for international relations is respect for international law. This case and many prize cases during the First World War showed respect for law even in time of war.

The Treaty of Versailles in the preamble stated as one of its objectives: "the firm establishment of the understandings of international law as the actual rule of conduct among Governments." To this end Article 14 of the Covenant of the League of Nations provided for the "establishment of a Permanent Court of International Justice." This court was formally opened at The Hague on Feb. 15, 1922, and according to the statute of the court was to "be in addition to the court of Arbitration organized by the Conventions of The Hague of 1899 and 1907, and to the special Tribunals of Arbitration."

The first advisory opinion of the Permanent Court of International Justice was handed down on July 31, 1922, and the first judgment on Aug. 17, 1922. From that time on cases before the court multiplied, and states not members of the League were entitled to bring cases to the court as well as members of the League. The judges were chosen as representing "the main forms of civilization and the principal legal systems of the world." Provisions were often introduced in later treaties for bringing before the court disputes between the parties to the treaties. The decisions and opinions of the court on many matters have already built up an increasing body of international law based upon action of this Court of International Justice. See also ARBITRATION, INTERNATIONAL; ARMED NEUTRALITY; BLOCKADE; DECLARATION OF LONDON; DECLARATION OF WAR; MERCHANT VESSELS, NEUTRAL, RIGHTS OF; NEUTRALITY.

Bibliography.—United States Department of State, *Papers Relating to Foreign Affairs* (Washington, n.d.); Grotius, Hugo, *De Jure belli ac pacis* (1625; English tr., Washington 1913); Hyde, C. C., *International Law, Chiefly as Interpreted and Applied by the United States,* 2 vols. (Cambridge, Mass., 1922); Bynkershoek, C. van, *De domino maris* (1703; English tr., Washington 1923); Hall, W. E., *Treatise on International Law,* 8th ed. (New York 1925); Cobbett, Pitt, *Cases on International Law,* 5th ed. (London 1931); Spaight, J. M., *Air Power and War Rights,* 2d ed. (Toronto 1933); Hudson, M. O., *A Treatise on the Permanent Court of International Justice* (New York 1934); Brierly, J. L., *The Law of Nations,* 2d ed. (Toronto 1936); Wheaton, H., *Elements of International Law* (New York 1937).

GEORGE GRAFTON WILSON,
Professor Emeritus of International Law, Harvard University.

INTERNATIONAL LAW, Changes in. Two world wars and the continuous activity of governments in the fields of international organization, legislation, and adjudication have greatly effected the development of international law since 1914. Changed though it may be, international law has survived recent cataclysms as it has survived earlier ones, although the present crisis has probably been more serious than any which the world has witnessed since the 17th century.

The outstanding factors influencing international relations during the past century have been, on the one hand, the rise of nationalism, consequent upon more extended literacy, democracy and centralization of national political and economic authority; and on the other hand, the development of internationalism, consequent upon inventions which have expedited world communication, travel and transport, increased international trade, and developed international organization in fields of science, the arts, business, labor, agriculture, communication, humanitarianism, public administration, political relations and many others. In 1894, the distinguished French publicist Bonfils wrote: "Public international law proposes to reach a compromise between two actions contrary in fact, that of the principle of autonomy of states, and that of the notion of the cosmopolitan society. Neither of these two principles ought to supplant the other, nor to be put completely to its practical application." (*Manuel de droit international public,* Paris, 1894, 6th ed., Fauchille, 1912, section 24, p. 10). These two tendencies have each been exaggerated by the factors referred to and as a result the task of international law in compromising them has become more difficult. That difficulty has been reflected in the rapid oscillation between wars of extreme violence and institutional constructions of extraordinary scope which have characterized international life since 1914.

Nationalism, nurtured in 19th century ideas of liberalism, was effected by protectionist pressures of business, by socialistic pressures of labor, by imperialistic pressures of politics, by militaristic necessities in waging war, and by the defensive urge to acquire invulnerability from blockades after the First World War. As a result, nationalism developed among the politically less experienced populations into fascism, naziism or communism, creating totalitarian states with control of government, economy, religion and opinion centralized in irresponsible dictators intent on continually expanding the sovereignty, self-sufficiency, military power and living space of the national group. Nationalism of this form, equipped with such modern devices as the airplane, the submarine, heavy mobile artillery, machine guns, conscription, propaganda and controlled economy has given war a totalitarian character, regimenting the population and subjecting civilians to hardships unparalleled in history. Whether the atom bomb will reinforce this tendency or—by the very magnitude of its threat—will revolutionize the world order, remains to be seen.

The totalitarian states in their early history avowed new concepts of international law. While the conceptual repudiation of established international law by Fascist, Nazi and Communist governments has tended to decline, in proportion as these governments entered into relations with others and were confronted with the need to solve international problems, yet in practice these states have shown an extreme propensity to neglect the rules of international law especially those designed to ameliorate war. Other states have also departed from established law, partly in retaliation and partly in adapting themselves to changed technical and political conditions.

While it cannot be said that the rules, accepted by custom and by the great lawmaking conventions of the 19th and early 20th centuries, have ceased to be binding, their application has been modified in practice. Among such practices may be noted belligerent (1) internment of enemy civilians, (2) bombardments, (3) destruction of merchant vessels, (4) proclamation of war zones, (5) controls of neutral commerce, and (6) utilization of neutral territory. Neutrals have also resorted to new practices, such as, (7) renunciation of trading privileges, and (8) proclamation of peace zones on the high seas.

1. While in the past, enemy civilians were sometimes expelled from belligerent territories, they were usually allowed to remain unmolested or given a period of grace in which to wind up their affairs and leave. Since the First World War, however, enemy civilians have been interned and treated substantially as prisoners of war by most belligerents. Persons liable to military service have been taken from neutral vessels on the high seas and made prisoners of war. In short, civilians formerly of little military importance are now regarded as a military asset to their country, if not on the front line then as workers in military production, and they have been treated accordingly by the enemy.

2. Bombardments by land artillery were formerly confined to the armed forces or to defended towns, though in naval war the right of bombarding military objectives on land was recognized. Aviation has opened new fields to bombardment, and while in principle, bombardment for terrorization of civilian populations is considered illegitimate, it has occurred especially in the Spanish Civil War and all theaters of the Second World War. Bombardment of military objectives from the air was recognized as legitimate in the Draft Articles of 1923, prepared by experts in pursuance of a Washington conference resolution. Since railroad centers, docks and factories in densely populated communities may come under this designation, and since the aim of bombers, driven up several miles by antiaircraft defences, cannot be very accurate, the risk to civilians is very great, even if the law is observed. The threat of aerial bombardment has undoubtedly increased the diplomatic power of a government, suspected of ruthlessness, and equipped with a considerable air force. With increasing range, speed and capacity of aircraft; development of rockets; and augmentation of the power of bombs, culminating in the atom bomb, defenses against the bombing of civilians and industries in any part of the world have been reduced to the fear of retaliation. This condition has turned attention away from the effort to control war and toward the effort to prevent war.

3. In the conduct of commercial warfare the sinking of prizes has always been considered an exceptional act permitted only in case of necessity, after the passengers and crew have been placed in safety. The submarine, incapable of sparing prize crews and vulnerable to attack by defensive armaments on merchant vessels, has proved unable to engage in commercial warfare under these rules. An unratified convention of the Washington Conference of 1922 declared that, as a consequence, submarines could not engage in commercial war. A generally ratified provision of the London Naval Treaty of 1930 reiterated the old rule about safety of passengers and crew. Nevertheless, both belligerents, though parties to this convention, engaged in submarine sinkings in the war of 1939–45.

4. The principle of freedom of the seas has meant for over two centuries that in time of war merchant shipping is free to utilize all sea areas, beyond the three-mile limit, subject only to acknowledge belligerent rights of visit and search, and capture for carriage of contraband, breach of blockade, unneutral service, or enemy character, subject since 1856 to the rule that free ships make free goods. In wars since 1914, however, belligerents have mined vast areas of the sea and proclaimed zones where, on account of mines, submarines or destroyers, navigation was unsafe. Though neutrals at first protested, they have in a measure acquiesced in such actions and have, in some cases, forbidden their ships to enter zones deemed dangerous. Thus, the American Neutrality Act of 1939 authorized the president to proclaim barred zones, and under it he proclaimed the waters surrounding the British Isles, including the North Sea, such a zone. The act was repealed Nov. 17, 1941. A disposition to tolerate encroachments upon freedom of the seas has been manifested among jurists, as indicated by the Harvard Research in International Law, which permits a belligerent to establish blockade zones extending 50 miles from the enemy's coast. (Articles 1 (e), 69.)

5. Belligerent extensions of contraband lists, broad applications of the rule of continuous voyage and ultimate destination, and resort to retaliatory measures rendering all trade, direct or indirect, to or from the enemy liable to capture have seriously impaired earlier neutral rights of trade even with other neutrals. But going beyond this, belligerents have insisted on a deflection of neutral ships to ports for search and have withheld bunker coal facilities from neutral vessels and blacklisted neutral firms, barring them from trade with the belligerent's nationals, if they would not stop trading with the enemy. While neutrals at first protested, they have in a large measure acquiesced and, in some cases, have embargoed their own trade in certain commodities with belligerents. Jurists have manifested a certain tolerance for such practices. The Harvard Research in International Law suggested abandonment of the old rules in respect to contraband, and substitution therefor of an elaborate system of certification of vessels with consent of the belligerents, all uncertified vessels being liable to a high degree of belligerent contorl. (Articles 61, 63.)

6. The inviolability of neutral territory from belligerent operations has been a fundamental rule, though Japan and Russia fought their war in 1904 in Chinese territory. Germany began the war of 1914 with an invasion of neutralized Belgium. Russia in 1939 insisted on bases in Estonia, Latvia and Finland, and when the latter resisted the demand, began military operations in Finnish territory. Belligerent airplanes frequently cruised over Dutch and Belgian territory before these states were attacked by Germany in 1940. Neutrals in the vicinity of belligerent operations lost all confidence that their territory would be respected.

7. Aware that efforts to defend their trading rights might lead them into war, neutrals have, to an increasing degree, shown an inclination voluntarily to abandon the exercise of these rights. During the First World War many European neutrals prohibited the trade of their na-

tionals with belligerents in many commodities, and by the Act of 1939 the United States prohibited American ships from trading with belligerents or traveling through proclaimed zones in the theater of hostilities. This act also required transfer of titles to all goods shipped from the United States to belligerents in whatever vessels they went. Other neutrals have made similar self-denying ordinances.

8. Neutrals have in the past insisted that hostilities must not occur in their territorial waters. They have even objected to hovering by belligerent war vessels outside of these waters. Going far beyond this, the American countries in the Declaration of Panama, in October 1939, warned belligerents not to engage in hostile acts in a zone 300 miles or more around the American continents except Canada. This warning was not observed by belligerents, particularly in the *Graf Spee* incident, and the American countries considered possible procedures for making it effective before the Japanese attack at Pearl Harbor involved them in the war. The difficulty of assuming responsibility for actually preventing hostilities in so vast an area has been recognized.

These changes have in practice tended to blur the distinction between civilians and combatants, and to limit the rights of neutrals, thus extending the range of military action. But even more significant has been the blurring of the distinctions between war and peace, and between belligerents and neutrals. From the ending of the Napoleonic Wars to the beginning of the First World War, wars were limited in time, area and methods. They began and ended at determinable times and included definite belligerents. The III Hague Conventions (1907) required that war be begun only by a declaration or an ultimatum with a time limit. There were, it is true, numerous interventions, insurrections, and pacifications, not rising to the dignity of war, but sometimes involving considerable casualties. They were, however, usually conducted by great powers against small or backward peoples, and did not cause serious international disturbance. They were considered police operations, in contrast to war, which was regarded as a duel in which the belligerents were equal and must be treated impartially by neutrals.

The extraordinary rise of internationalism, and the extraordinary destructiveness of totalitarian war has, however, shaken the moral, economic and political foundations of this concept of war as a legitimate and institutionalized procedure. The League of Nations Covenant went far toward abolishing war in the legal sense. "Resort to war" in violation of the covenant was declared illegal and rendered the aggressor liable to economic sanctions by all members of the League. These members were at the same time bound to assist the victim of aggression (Article 16). Thus the essential feature of war in the legal sense, jural equality of the belligerents and the jural impartiality of the neutrals, was eliminated in case it was begun in breach of the covenant. While the covenant left gaps through which legitimate war might creep, these were blocked by the Pact of Paris, signed in 1928 and subsequently ratified by nearly all the states of the world. Parties to this instrument "condemn recourse to war for the solution of international controversies, and renounce it as an instrument of national policy in their relations with one another." Furthermore, they "agree that the settlement or solution of all disputes or conflicts of whatever nature or of whatever origin they may be, which may arise among them, shall never be sought except by pacific means."

The parties to these instruments proceeded to develop procedures for determining the aggressor and for imposing sanctions. A state engaged in hostilities, which refused to accept an armistice or other conservatory measures proposed by the consulting states, was considered an aggressor. Sanctions included moral denunciation, acceptance of the "Stimson doctrine" that the aggressor should not be recognized as acquiring any legal titles by his illegal action, and economic embargoes. Certain sanctions were applied in the Chaco and Manchurian hostilities, but more elaborate sanctions were applied in the Ethiopian expedition inaugurated by Italy in 1935.

While the application of these new principles was not successful in preventing war or in thwarting aggression, the opinion continued, and was given renewed emphasis in the Declaration by United Nations of 1942 and the United Nations Charter of 1945, that the international duel is incompatible with modern civilization, and that it may be both immoral and impolitic to treat the aggressor and his victim alike. The prestige of neutrality in the old sense has, therefore, been greatly weakened.

Aggressively inclined states have reacted to the same opinion by manifesting a disinclination to acknowledge that they are engaging in war. They have sought to represent their military activities as policing expeditions like the interventions and pacifications of the earlier period. In the hostilities from 1920–40 there were no declarations of war except in the Chaco affair and in the wars against Germany in 1939. The United States proclaimed neutrality only in the latter and in the Ethiopian hostilities of 1935. The hostilities in Spain, in the Far East and in Finland, though the first two each involved more loss of life than did the American Civil War, were not recognized as war in the legal sense. Nonbelligerents, even if they did not apply sanctions, wished to hold themselves free to do so. The League recommended discriminatory action, not only in the Ethiopian hostilities but also in the Chaco, Far Eastern, and Finnish hostilities. The United States government through the Export-Import Bank made loans to China and to Finland, gave destroyers to Britain, and aided the Allies by lend-lease, all of which would have been incompatible with the international law of neutrality.

Thus war, instead of being a status, which arises from the decision of the state which declares it, or which begins hostilities with warlike intent, and which thrusts the status of belligerency or neutrality upon other states whether they wish it or not, has become a status which exists only insofar as the states of the world recognize it. If they choose to recognize the hostilities, not as war but as aggression, and to discriminate in favor of the victim, they are free to do so under the covenant, the pact, and other antiwar treaties. They are obliged to do so under the United Nations Charter.

The consequence, therefore, of the intensification both of war *de facto* and of efforts to prevent such war, has been a tendency for war *de jure* to disappear. The distinction between states of war and peace, between war and hostilities short of war, between belligerency and neutrality, have all become less precise, as have the rules defining belligerent and neutral rights.

The decade of juristic optimism and of organized internationalism following the First World War was characterized by a distinct lack of interest among jurists in the laws of war and neutrality and an extraordinary increase of juristic interest in the development of the international law of peace, especially the law defining procedures of international adjudication, legislation and administration and the law regulating international co-operation in matters of communication and transit, administration of mandated territories, protection of minorities, the trade in opium and narcotic drugs, slavery and the slave trade, conservation of the resources of the sea, etc. The Permanent Court of International Justice, the International Labor Organization and the League of Nations operated efficiently and, until the outbreak of the Second World War, with increasing prestige in the nonpolitical fields. Throughout this period, however, it was realized that these achievements were endangered by the continued insistence of states upon the free exercise of their military, political and economic sovereignty. Efforts were accordingly made by international conferences to bring about military and economic disarmament and to require the submission of all international disputes to some form of pacific settlement. These efforts, while achieving some successes in the Washington Disarmament Treaties of 1922 and the considerable ratification of the optional clause of the Permanent Court of International Justice and the General Act of Pacific Settlement were not adequate. Movements for economic self-sufficiency following the failure of the economic conference of 1927, contributed to the great depression of 1929, and to the rise of international tensions. Hostilities were renewed in 1931 with the Japanese invasion of Manchuria and they rapidly spread, through Italian, German, Soviet and further Japanese aggressions, to Ethiopia, Spain, China, Albania, Czechoslovakia, Poland, France, Britain, the Dominions, the Baltic States and Finland, carrying in their wake a reduction of international co-operation, a decline in international confidence, a weakening of the League of Nations and the Pact of Paris, a diverting of the energy of all states to military preparedness, or to war itself.

It seems to be clear that international law cannot, without important changes, maintain order in a world in which both nationalism and internationalism have reached the intensity and organization which they have in the 20th century. Sovereignty of the national state must be limited by appropriate laws and institutions, especially in the military, political and economic fields, if international co-operation for the welfare of mankind is to develop. The alternative appears to be a further isolation of national cultures and economies and a general diminution of the standards of living. The anarchy which results from extreme claims of sovereignty, and the wars which result from this anarchy, are incompatible with the progress of civilization in a rapidly shrinking world. The important development of the science and practice of international law, the increasing number of individuals, organizations and journals devoted to the subject since the organization of the League of Nations and the Permanent Court of International Justice in 1920, suggests that international law will not disappear. The grave problems of sanctions and of legislation, of collective security and of peaceful change, were not solved by the League of Nations, but the need to solve them became greater than ever. It is now clear that the victors in the First World War made a serious error in attempting to curb the military and political sovereignty of states while retaining their economic sovereignty which might be exercised to deprive the states, more dependent upon external markets and sources of raw materials, of the requirements of life, particularly when those curbs, such as arbitration, antiwar and disarmament obligations, were not supported by adequate enforcement arrangements. The motives of revenge, stimulated by a sense of economic insecurity, augmented by the depression, contributed to the exaggerated nationalism among the dissatisfied states which led to aggression.

Modern conditions of interdependence and rapid technological change placed new burdens upon international law. It must develop legislative procedures to adapt state power to the needs of the community of nations, parallel with its development of executive procedures to prevent violation of the law. The difficulties of these problems, however, cannot be minimized. Normal reliance upon coercing states as such, was rejected by the makers of the United States Constitution and did not work under the League of Nations Covenant. Powerful states resent coercion and their nationally minded populations, cleave closer to the aggressor government when external sanctions are imposed against it. Furthermore, the states applying sanctions suffer inconveniences and dangers and are apt to be hampered by a public opinion opposed to visiting hardships upon that section of the aggressor state's population innocent of wrongdoing.

No less difficult has been the problem of peaceful change. Even federations have not often transferred territory from one member state to another. Article XIX of the League of Nations Covenant which envisaged changes of territory and of inapplicable treaties, as an offset to the guarantee of the territorial status quo by Article X has not been successfully applied. President Wilson's draft article from which these two clauses of the covenant developed contemplated a closer relationship between them. In his thought, the territorial guarantee was to be subject to an international right of eminent domain, exercised by the League of Nations, and involving compensation to the states deprived of rights. He suggested: "The contracting powers unite in guaranteeing to each other political independence and territorial integrity; but it is understood between them that such territorial readjustments, if any, as may in the future become necessary by reasons of changes in present racial conditions and aspirations or present social and political relationships, pursuant to the principle of self-determination and also such territorial readjustments, as may in the judgment of three-fourths of the delegates (at the assembly) be demanded by the welfare and manifest interest of the peoples concerned, may be effected, if agreeable to those peoples; and that territorial changes may in equity involve material compensation. The contracting powers accept without reservation the principle that the peace of the world is superior in importance to every question of political, jurisdictional boundaries."

Such a procedure may be useful but it seems probable that a legislative authority which will gradually reduce the military and economic importance of boundaries may prove more practicable than such an authority to change the boundaries themselves. With freedom of interstate commerce and with the prohibition of interstate war, it has not been necessary to change boundaries of the states in the United States. Experience under the Articles of Confederation, as in the modern family of nations, suggests that forces of interdependence cannot function if sovereignty can erect tariff walls and prepare for military aggression without limitation. International law must assure freedom of trade and communication and security from military invasion across all frontiers as well as a moderate protection of the civil rights of individuals, especially the freedom of opinion and the press. Only with the latter can the world be protected from the intense nationalism which may be produced by the propaganda devices now available when counterpropagandas are barred.

Before the First World War certain weaknesses in international law had been recognized, particularly (1) the lack of a legal interest of third states in the observance of international law when their own immediate interests were not involved, (2) the emphasis on international rights rather than international responsibilities, (3) the lack of a legal obligation of states to accept external judgments in their controversies, and (4) the lack of an international organization to represent the general interest in law observance, to provide for impartial adjudication of disputes, and to enforce responsibilities under international law. It was hoped that the peace ending the First World War would remedy these deficiencies.

Thus, with respect to the legal interest of states, Elihu Root said in 1915: "If the law of nations is to be binding, if the decisions of tribunals charged with the application of that law to international controversies are to be respected, there must be a change in theory, and violations of the law of such character as to threaten the peace and order of the community of nations must be deemed to be a violation of the right of every civilized nation to have the law maintained and a legal injury to every nation. . . . Wherever in the world the laws which should protect the independence of nations, the inviolability of their territory, the lives and property of their citizens, are violated, all other nations have a right to protest against the breaking down of the law. Such a protest would not be an interference in the quarrels of others. It would be an assertion of the protesting nation's own right against the injury done to it by the destruction of the law upon which it relies for its peace and security." ("The Outlook for International Law," *Proceedings* of the American Society of International Law, 1915.)

With respect to international responsibilities the present writer wrote in 1919: "Thus, though international law must continue to aim at preserving the independence and autonomy of states, it must assume that its own preservation is more important. It follows that international law can no longer be conceived by text writers as a series of deductions from an assumed 'fundamental right of states to exist.' The responsibility of states to assure the existence of the law will have to be conceived as even more fundamental. . . . States cannot survive where sovereignty can override the law. As the price of existence, states must accept definite responsibilities for maintenance of law." ("Effects of the League of Nations Covenant," *American Political Science Review,* November 1919.)

With respect to the right of self-judgment and the need of international organization, John Bassett Moore wrote in 1915: "If states do not succeed (in gaining redress for injuries by amicable modes) it is laid down that we may try inamicable methods, ranging all the way from retorsion to retaliation, embargo, commercial nonintercourse, severance of diplomatic relations, and display of force, to reprisals, which are acts of war, and to war itself, which is in its physical aspect merely general reprisals. Nevertheless, if actual force be employed, there is always the danger of forceful resistance, ending in war; and in that event we may have the incongruous result that the aggressor, without submitting to the examination of any tribunal the justice of his cause, may, in the exercise of the 'rights of war,' conquer or destroy the injured power which he has by his own wrong driven to become his adversary. This principle, which I conceive to be the capital defect of international law at the present day, is perhaps to be explained as the survival of the superstitions that preserved in municipal law for so many centuries the process of trial by battle. However this may be, it is flagrantly at variance with all conceptions of human right, and can be effectually got rid of only through further organization. It is in this respect, as I have intimated, that international law differs from municipal law—not in its essence or its obligation, but in the method of its declaration and administration. Within the state we have an organization for the making, declaration and enforcement of law, whereas, as between nations, we are obliged to a great extent to rely upon their voluntary concurrence or co-operation. In other words, we lack in the international sphere that organization which gives to the administration of law within the state a certain security. This defect it is the business of nations to supply by forming among themselves an appropriate organization. The essential features of such an organization would be somewhat as follows: (1) it would set law above violence: by providing suitable and efficacious means and agencies for the enforcement of law; and by making the use of force illegal, except in support of a duly ascertained legal right, or in self-defence . . . , (2) it would provide a more efficient means than now exists for the making and declaration of law . . . , (3) it would provide more fully than has heretofore been done for the investigation and determination of disputes by means of tribunals, possessing advisory or judicial powers, as the case might be. . . . Occasional disturbances such as these (domestic insurrections) should by no means lessen our estimate of the importance of organization for the maintenance of law, either international or internal. They should on the contrary serve to emphasize not only the necessity of organization, but also the importance of extending its scope and increasing its efficiency." ("Law and

Organization," *American Political Science Review,* February 1915.)

The new institutions established after the First World War sought to effect all of these changes but they did not achieve either justice or order in the world. There is a growing opinion that the task cannot be fulfilled unless international law develops into a federal law operating directly on individuals.

Certain steps in this direction have been taken, as for instance, the right of petition accorded to the minorities and to the inhabitants of mandated territories, and the increasing tendency of jurists to treat individuals as subjects of international law, a tendency which has gained some support from the practice of arbitral tribunals in adjudicating claims of aliens against the state of residence. Though formally such claims are presented by the state of which the injured individual is a national, in fact the individual is often recognized by the tribunal as the real party at interest.

These tendencies have received greater impetus in the declaration by the United Nations during the Second World War and the charter of their organization established in 1945. These declarations emphasized the freedoms of the individual rather than the rights of states, and organizations in the fields of relief and rehabilitation, food and agriculture, aviation and telecommunication, trade and finance, and sciences, education, and culture were established to serve human needs directly as did the International Labor Organization which continued from the earlier period. The United Nations Charter, while founded on the principle of the sovereign equality of members and the obligation of members to settle disputes peacefully, to refrain from the threat or use of force in their relations, and to assist the United Nations in preventing aggression (Art. 2), was declared to be the work of "we the peoples of the United Nations." Furthermore, among its primary tasks is the promotion of "universal respect for, and observance of, human rights and fundamental freedom of all without distinction as to race, sex, language or religion."

A practical exemplification of the direct relationship of the individual to the world community was exhibited in the charter for the trial of major war criminals concluded among the United Nations in August 1945. This charter defined crimes against the peace, war crimes, and crimes against humanity for which there should be individual responsibility irrespective of the official position or governmental authorization of the defendant. The International Military Tribunal established at Nürnberg in accordance with this charter tried 21 Nazi officials indicted for one or more of these offenses and a similar tribunal in Tokyo tried the principal Japanese officials responsible for the Far Eastern War.

Although the entry of the organized world community into the field of protecting certain individual rights and of punishing certain individual crimes is an important move in the direction of world federalism, a considerable opinion appears to be convinced, particularly since the explosion of the atom bomb in August 1945, that more rapid progress in this direction is necessary.

International law will doubtless continue to balance the principle of national sovereignty against the principle of world union; but the rapid strides of science and technology in eliminating distances, augmenting powers of destructive aggression, and reducing powers of defense have created a state of mind prepared to shift the center of equilibrium in the direction of world unity. This has led to institutions and legal principles designed to augment the relative authority of the world community. The sentiment of nationality and the tradition of sovereignty remain, however, as active forces. The governments, particularly of great states, hesitate to relinquish their prerogatives. Consequently the problem of establishing an international law able to maintain the world in dynamic stability will not be easily solved.

The difficulty has become accentuated because of the developing opposition between two halves of the world led respectively by the Soviet Union and the United States. The Soviet Union has opposed the evolution of the United Nations in the direction of world govment; has freely used the veto in the Security Council, thus hampering the work of that organization; and has curtailed trade and communication across the iron curtain which separates it and its satellites from the rest of the world. The Western Powers have persevered in their efforts to build the United Nations and its specialized agencies into instruments for rehabilitating war-shattered economies, for promoting human welfare, and for developing a sense of world solidarity. Under their leadership, the United Nations has accomplished much in the field of international economic and social relations, but relatively little in the field of international security. It has not been able, because of Soviet opposition, to achieve a world regulation of atomic energy or agreements upon limitation of armament. It has, however, declared a Universal Bill of Human Rights and has opened a Convention on Genocide for ratification. It has also recognized that action by states in suppressing colonial revolts or discriminating against minorities in such a way as to threaten international peace and security is not within the domestic jurisdiction of the state, but is subject to the United Nations. The United Nations has also assumed competence to bring about important political changes, as in the partition of Palestine. It has established an International Law Commission, instructed to develop and codify the law concerning the rights and duties of states and international crimes. In most of this activity, the Soviet government and its satellites have played either an obstructive or a reluctantly acquiescent role. The Western Powers have, therefore, been forced to recognize that the United Nations, so long as it lacks the capacity to make decisions because of the veto, and lacks the material forces which were intended to be, but have not been, placed at its disposal, cannot assure security. Consequently, they have utilized the freedom, recognized in Article 51 of the Charter, to create regional arrangements for collective self-defense. Treaties for this purpose were signed by the American powers at Rio de Janeiro in 1947 and by five Western European powers at Brussels in 1948. An arrangement among all the North Atlantic Powers, or even among all United Nations members that want to join, has been projected as a practical means for eliminating the veto and assuring common action against aggression by states desiring an orderly world.

It remains to be seen whether, from the

power rivalries, of states, of regional arrangements, and of general international organizations, a more stable condition of affairs will develop in the shrinking world within which the new international law, forbidding aggression and protecting human rights, can be maintained by suitable institutions.

Bibliography.—Garner, J. W., *International Law and the World War*, 2 vols. (London 1920); Oppenheim, L., *The Future of International Law* (London 1921); Nippold, Otfried, *The Development of International Law After the World War* (London 1923); Politis, Nicholas, *The New Aspects of International Law* (Washington 1928); Wright, Quincy, *The Future of Neutrality, International Conciliation* (New York 1928); id., *Research in International Law Since the War* (Washington 1930); Fischer, Sir John W., *International Change and International Peace* (Oxford 1932); Hudson, M. O., *Progress in International Organization* (Stanford 1932); Lauterpacht, H., *The Function of Law in the International Community* (Oxford 1933); Fischer, Sir John W., *Some Aspects of the Covenant of the League of Nations* (Oxford 1934); Lauterpacht, H., *The Development of International Law by the Permanent Court of International Justice* (London 1934); Hudson, M. O., *By Pacific Means* (New Haven 1935); Taracouzio, T. A., *The Soviet Union and International Law* (New York 1935); Zimmern, Sir Alfred, *The League of Nations and the Rule of Law, 1918–1935* (London 1936); Dunn, F. S., *Peaceful Change* (New York 1937); Eagleton, Clyde, *Analysis of the Problem of War* (New York 1937); Wright, Quincy, *A Study of War* (Chicago 1942); Carnegie Endowment for International Peace, *The International Law of the Future* (Washington 1944); Lauterpacht, H., *An International Bill of the Rights of Man* (New York 1945); Jessup, Philip, *A Modern Law of Nations* (New York 1948).

QUINCY WRIGHT,
Professor of International Law, University of Chicago.

INTERNATIONAL MEDIATION AND ARBITRATION. See ARBITRATION, INDUSTRIAL; LABOR LEGISLATION, FOREIGN.

INTERNATIONAL ORDER OF JOB'S DAUGHTERS, a society of girls between the ages of 13 and 20, relatives of Master Masons and meeting in "bethels" (places of worship), each supervised by a guardian council of, or women related to, Master Masons. The society fosters education, maintaining an educational loan fund, and character building through moral and spiritual development, by teaching a greater reverence for God and the Holy Scriptures, loyalty to flag and country, and deeper respect for parents and elders. Founded at Omaha, Nebr., in 1920, the society has bethels throughout the United States controlled by State Grand Councils and a Supreme Guardian Council.

INTERNATIONAL PEACE CONFERENCE. See HAGUE COURT, THE.

INTERNATIONAL SOCIETY OF CHRISTIAN ENDEAVOR, a religious society for young people, organized Feb. 2, 1881, in Williston Congregational Church, Portland, Me., by Reverend Francis E. Clark. Its several branches in the United States include the Junior, Intermediate, and Mothers' branches.

The constitution has been printed in more than 60 different languages. The movement is interdenominational and international, with more than 80,000 societies in more than 80 denominations and 60 nations. Aggregate membership in 1954 was about 3,000,000.

The World's Union of Christian Endeavor has held conventions all over the world. The International Society of Christian Endeavor takes in North American societies. Its headquarters are at Columbus, Ohio. *The Christian Endeavor World,* issued monthly and also founded by the Reverend Francis E. Clark, is its international organ.

INTERNATIONAL TELECOMMUNICATION UNION, The (ITU), an international body whose chief purpose is "to maintain and extend international cooperation for the improvement and rational use of telecommunication." Formed in 1932, at Madrid, it replaced the International Telegraph Union, established at Paris, 1865. Its structure consists of a plenipotentiary conference, administrative conferences, and several permanent organs: an administrative council, a general secretariat, the International Frequency Registration Board (IFRB), the International Telegraph Consultative Committee (CCIT), the International Telephone Consultative Committee (CCIF), and the International Radio Consultative Committee (CCIR). The seat of the union in 1954 was Geneva, Switzerland.

INTERNATIONAL TELEPHONE AND TELEGRAPH CORPORATION, an American holding, service and management company, with head offices in New York, organized to develop all branches of electric communications. Subsidiary companies are in most principal cities of the world. It holds a two thirds stock interest in the American Cable and Radio Corporation, which controls All America Cables and Radio, Inc.; Commercial Cable Company; and Mackay Radio and Telegraph Company, Inc.

INTERNATIONAL UNIONS FOR THE PROTECTION OF PROPERTY. (1) International Union for the Protection of Industrial Property, founded at Paris, Mar. 20, 1883, and having a permanent organization, the International Bureau for the Protection of Industrial Property, at Bern, Switzerland. The Union functions under the terms of the International Convention for the Protection of Industrial Property, signed at Paris in 1883, and revised at Brussels in 1900; at Washington, 1911; at The Hague, 1925; and at London, 1934. There are 40 member nations, including the United States. Comprehended within the International Union and occupying the same office at Bern are three restricted unions. These are: the Limited Union for the Repression of False Marks of Origin, established by the Special Agreement of Madrid in 1891, with a membership of 21 nations; the Limited Union for the International Registration of Manufacture and Trade-Marks, also founded at Madrid on the same date and by a similar special agreement, with 19 members; and the Limited Union for the International Registration of Industrial Designs or Models, founded by the Special Agreement of The Hague, in 1925, with 10 members.

(2) **International Union for the Protection of Literary and Artistic Works,** founded at Bern, Switzerland, Sept. 9, 1886. Its functioning organization, the International Bureau for the Protection of Literary and Artistic Works, is closely associated and collaborates with the International Convention for the Protection of Industrial Property; together they are called the United International Bureaus for the Protection of Intellectual Property. The charter of the International Union for the Protection of Literary and Artistic Works is the Convention of Bern, dated Sept. 9, 1886. It was revised at Ber-

lin in 1908; at Rome in 1928, and at Brussels on June 26, 1948.

The United International Bureaus publish four monthly reviews in French. These are *La propriété industrielle, Le droit d'auteur, Les marques internationales,* and *Les dessins et modèles internationaux.* They also conduct two international registration services, one for manufacture and trade-marks and the other for industrial designs and models. The bureaus give advice and consultations, prepare the agenda for meetings considering revisions of the diverse conventions, and publish information concerning national legislation for the protection of intellectual property.

A similar arrangement for the international registration of trade-marks among Western Hemisphere nations was initiated by the Pan American Convention of Buenos Aires, 1910, revised at Santiago in 1923. See also COPYRIGHT; PATENTS; TRADE-MARKS.

INTERPELLATION, *in law,* the act of demanding an official explanation of a member of the government, as in France and some other European countries. It is used more frequently in Italy and France than elsewhere. After due notice, any member of the particular legislative body may interpellate the ministry, and this often results in a general debate. Frequently a ministry resigns as a result of an interpellation. The right of permitting or refusing an interpellation rests with the legislative body, not with the ministry. An interpellation is followed usually by a vote of confidence or of want of confidence in the government.

INTERPLEADER, *in law,* a procedure by which a person having goods, money, or the like in his possession may have the ownership thereof judicially determined in case of dispute between two or more claimants. Usually such a suit is brought in equity. It is called "multiplepoinding" in Scots law. One seeking this remedy must show that two or more persons claim against him the same thing, obligation, or the like; that he is not in collusion with any of such parties; that he has no beneficial interest in the subject matter of the suit; that he cannot decide without danger of prejudice to his rights who is the rightful claimant, and must show that he is willing to meet his obligation to the lawful owner. It is of importance in modern practice, both in Great Britain and in the United States, in the relations involving bailor and bailee, landlord and tenant, common carrier and shipper, tax collector and landowner, agent or consignee, and principal or consignor, sheriff and party claiming goods levied upon.

INTERPRETATION, *in law,* the art of determining the meaning of a speaker, or a writer, or of the parties to a written instrument, as a contract, deed, or the like. Courts of equity, in their interpretation and construction of instruments, follow the same rules as courts of law. The terms interpretation and construction, while frequently used interchangeably by some writers, should be differentiated according to others. In interpretation, they contend, the court decides simply the meaning of words and sentences, whereas in construction the court decides what is their legal effect. Interpretation is merely logical reasoning, while construction is legal reasoning, these writers insist. The two terms, nevertheless, in practice at least, are generally used with identical meaning. The rules for interpretation vary to some extent with the particular class of instrument in dispute. For instance, wills are liberally construed, as the testator is not presumed to know the legal signification of all the terms he employs, but is held to use such in their popular meaning. On the other hand, a deed is generally construed strictly and against the maker when there is ambiguity. A contract must not be strictly nor liberally construed, but the intention must be drawn in the light of surrounding circumstances, as customs of the place or time, social conditions, and the like. Statutes abrogating the common law, as well as penal statutes, must be strictly construed. The same rule is applied to statutes affecting private rights. On the other hand, statutes designed to prevent fraud are liberally construed, and statutes must generally not be construed so as to operate retrospectively.

Some general rules of interpretation are as follows:

(1) The meaning of a word, clause, or other part of an instrument must be construed in the light of the whole instrument. Such disputed part may have its ordinary meaning entirely changed by this rule. (2) The meaning of the maker of an instrument is to be taken from what is therein contained and also from what may be fairly implied by custom or the like. (3) Due weight must be given to the construction placed upon the instrument by the parties themselves. (4) Words are to be taken in their ordinary meaning unless the writing or the attending circumstances indicate a contrary intention. (5) Where two interpretations are possible, that is to be preferred which is fair and reasonable. (6) Usually ambiguous language is to be construed against the maker of a private writing, as a contract or a deed.

In addition to the foregoing list, which is not complete, a large number of special rules have been framed to fit particular cases.

INTERPRETATION OF DREAMS, The (in German *Die Traumdeutung*), a book by Sigmund Freud (1900; translated by A. A. Brill, 1913) which has become a fundamental part of modern psychiatric therapy. It interprets the mind as an interfunctional unit of the Ego (the conscious, rational faculty), the Super-Ego (the Censor, or moral faculty), and the Id (the unconscious, irrational faculty). In presenting dozens of actual dream analyses, Freud demonstrates that dreams are neither meaningless nor prophetic, but are intelligible psychic productions. All dreams are symbolic fulfillments of wishes and desires suppressed by the Super-Ego. Freud notes three fundamental dream mechanisms: (1) Condensation, the fusing of various elements in the Id for economical transference to the Ego; (2) Displacement, the transferring of psychic importance and stress from the true objects in the Id to apparently trivial objects in the manifest dream; and (3) Dramatization, the embodiment of abstract ideas or emotions in visual terms. All of these processes also serve to disguise the expression of the suppressed wish from the Super-Ego. Since there is no standard, universal symbolism in dreams, the dream-analysis depends upon the dreamer's free-association of the manifest dream-content in terms of his own life experience. The forgetting of dreams is the belated activity of the aroused Super-Ego.

INTERSTATE COMMERCE. See COMMERCE, INTERSTATE.

INTERSTATE COMMERCE LEGISLATION. See COMMERCE, INTERSTATE.

INTERSTATE CONTROVERSIES. See UNITED STATES—*Area and Boundaries.*

INTERVAL, in music, is the distance or difference of pitch, arithmetically expressed, between any two tones of a given scale. Occidental nations, including those of the Americas, employ the diatonic scale (see SCALE), an octave comprising five tones and seven semitones, named after the first seven letters of the alphabet. The affix of a flat or sharp before a note denotes its quality but does not affect its name, and the eighth note, being in unison, commences a new octave. Taking the scale in the key of C major the various intervals are: minor second = E–F or B–C; grave major second = C–D, F–G, A–B; grave minor third = D–F; minor third = E–G, A–C, B–D; major third = C–E, F–A or G–B; perfect fourth = C–F, D–G, E–A, G–C′, or B–E′; acute fourth = A–D′; acute augmented fourth = B–F; grave diminished fifth = B–F′; grave fifth = D–A; perfect fifth = C–G, E–B, F–C′, G–D′, A–E; minor sixth = E–C′, A–F′, B–G′; major sixth = C–A, D–B, G–E′; acute major sixth = F–D′; grave minor seventh = D–C′, G–F′, B–A′; minor seventh = E–D′, A–G; seventh = C–B, F–C′; octave = C–C′, D–D′, and so on. By taking various notes of the diatonic scale as starting points and measuring known intervals from these, we arrive at intermediate notes of the scale, of which the following are examples: C♯ minor third below E; D♯ minor second below E; E♭ minor third above C; A♭ minor sixth above C; B♭ minor seventh above C; B♯ 3 major third above C. The difference of pitch between C and C♯ or between D and D♯ is called a semitone, and an interval increased or diminished by a semitone is said to be augmented or diminished. This applies especially to the interval of a fourth or a fifth, which with the octave are said to be perfect, because any augmentation or diminution mars their consonance. The major sixth or third may, however, be diminished to a "minor" sixth or third without destroying the consonance; and the term "minor" is also applied to the diminished second or seventh. Intervals confined within the octave are simple, when they exceed it compound; the octave beginning a new series, the ninth is the octave of the second, and so forth.

INTERVENTION refers in international law to the dictatorial interference by a state in the internal affairs of another state or in the relations between two other states. It is formally forbidden by a number of treaties, especially among American states, and has been described as illegal in essence and to be justified only by its success.

Intervention is distinguished from mediation, or the offering of advice by a state after a request by other states, and from representations or protests which concern the demanding state's own interests or rights. It is also sometimes distinguished from interposition, or forcible action by one state in the territory of another to protect its nationals, and from defensive action to prevent an immediately threatened aggression. It may take the form of either military or diplomatic action; but diplomatic intervention implies resort to force if the demands are not complied with.

The motive of intervention is political, rather than legal. The United States has, in pursuance of policies related to the Monroe Doctrine (q.v.), intervened in Caribbean republics —in Cuba to establish the independence of that state, and in others to maintain order and international obligations. It has been party to treaties which permitted intervention in Cuba, Santo Domingo, Haiti, and Panama, although these treaties were subsequently terminated in connection with the "good neighbor" policy.

Great powers have frequently intervened, sometimes collectively, to prevent a state from getting so powerful as to disturb the balance of power. A system of international relations based on an equilibrium of power can hardly avoid occasional interventions of this kind. Intervention to stop gross inhumanities against minorities or dependent peoples have also occurred, and have been considered justifiable if the purpose was genuinely humanitarian. Often such interventions have veiled political purposes.

The League of Nations Covenant declared that "the League shall take any action that may be deemed wise and effectual to safeguard the peace of nations," and the United Nations Charter gives the Security Council "primary responsibility for the maintenance of international peace and security." Action authorized in pursuance of these provisions has sometimes been called "collective intervention," and is undoubtedly legal if in pursuance of the authority given the organization by its members.

The problem of preventing circumstances from arising which will induce states to intervene in the affairs of others is the major problem of international law and international organization, and can hardly be solved without in some degree subjecting the sovereignty of states to the world order. Nations continue reluctant, however, to surrender their sovereignty in this manner.

Consult Harcourt, Sir William G. G. V. V., *Letters by Historicus on Some Questions of International Law* (London 1863); Stowell, Ellery C., *Intervention in International Law* (Washington 1921); Fenwick, Charles G., *International Law*, 3d ed., pp. 228-248 (New York 1948).

QUINCY WRIGHT,
Professor of International Law, University of Chicago.

INTESTACY, the legal state of a person dying without having disposed of his property by last will and testament. In Britain, formerly, intestacy did not affect real estate, which was disposed of in accordance with the rule of descent. Legislation, which became effective there on Jan. 1, 1926, provided that both real and personal property shall devolve in the same way. The effect of intestacy in the United States varies in accordance with the laws of inheritance fixed by each of the states. Intestacy may be complete, as when a valid will is not left by the dead proprietor; or partial when the extant will only provides for the distribution of part of the property where a testator failed to make a residuary clause. In these cases the property passes to the heirs or next of kin of the decedent in accordance with the laws of the place where the property is.

The distribution under intestacy by the statutes of the various states of the United States may vary, but as an example in a common situation when a deceased is survived by husband or wife and children, one third of his estate is apportioned to the surviving husband or wife, and the remaining two thirds is divided equally among the children. Should there be a predeceased child with three grandchildren, such grandchildren would take the share of the predeceased child per stirpes, that is, a distribution by representation.

Actually, the law of the state makes the will of the decedent in cases of intestacy. The necessary steps for the administration of the property of an intestate is begun by filing a petition for letters of administration, obtaining jurisdiction of the necessary parties, and the issuance of the letters by the surrogate. There being no executor, the surrogate appoints an administrator, usually a person interested in the protection and conservation of the property. The surrogate may require the administrator to file a bond for the faithful performance of his duties. Usually those most closely related to the deceased are entitled to receive letters of administration in preference to one who is not so closely related. See DESCENT AND DISTRIBUTION; HEIR; INHERITANCE.

INTESTINE, BOWEL, or GUT. In man and the higher animals, that portion of the alimentary tube or canal lying between the stomach and the anus. The human bowel is divided into a small and a large intestine, the two parts varying in structure, movement, and function. The small intestine originates at the pyloric end of the stomach, and its first 8 to 10 inches form the duodenum. This section is divided into several [usually four] different portions and lies deeply within the upper abdominal cavity, embracing the head of the pancreas. Some 4 inches below the pylorus, is situated the opening of the common duct of the gall bladder and the pancreas through which bile and pancreatic juice are discharged into the intestine. At its end, the duodenum merges with the jejunum, the name applied to the upper two fifths of the small intestine, the lower three fifths being known as the ileum. Differences in gross structure of these two portions of the small intestine are not marked immediately, and only in its lower or terminal end does the ileum show distinct characteristics and definite changes. In general the jejunum is to be found in the left and upper portion of the peritoneal cavity, and has thicker walls than the thinner ileum, which occupies the lower portion of the belly cavity. The lumen of the small intestine, from the duodenum down, gradually becomes less, so that at the cecum its diameter is but little more than an inch as contrasted with nearly two and one half inches in the duodenum. The ileum is inserted at a point several inches above the lower limit of the cecum, which is the actual beginning of the large intestine. The cecum itself is a blind pouch lying in the lower right portion of the abdominal cavity, from which it continues upward as the ascending colon as far as the under surface of the liver. There it becomes the transverse colon. At its lower and posterior portion the cecum gives off a functionless organ well known to fame, the vermiform appendix (see APPENDICITIS). From its beginning near the liver and gall bladder, the transverse colon passes across the peritoneal cavity, within the folds of the great omentum and beneath the lower border of the stomach, to the region of the spleen, where it turns downward at the splenic flexure, continuing its course as the descending colon. As it descends it becomes curved, somewhat like the letter S, forming the sigmoid flexure, the beginning of the rectum. The latter passes over the brim of the bony pelvis deep into the pelvic fossa, ending at its outlet, the anus (see COLON; RECTUM). The small intestine is usually about 23 feet in length, the large bowel being about 5 feet. In anatomical structure both portions of the alimentary canal have four coats, known from within out as the mucous, the submucous, the muscular, and the serous or peritoneal. The muscular layers contain both longitudinal and encircling fibers which by their contractions accomplish the movement known as peristalsis. In the small intestine, which is concerned largely with absorption of nutrient material, the result of digestive processes, the mucous membrane is thrown up into permanent folds or rugae, each extending more than halfway around the inside of the bowel, the result being that a large area is provided for absorptive processes. The inner surface is provided with minute, fingerlike projections called villi, each having a large absorbing vessel in the center. At the bases of the villi are tubular and branching glands [of Brunner and Lieberkuhn] that penetrate deep into the mucous membrane. Scattered irregularly over the surface are small collections of lymphoid tissue [the so-called solitary follicles]. In the ileum these follicles form collections known as Peyer's patches, and it is these which are attacked in typhoid fever, being the site of ulcers and occasional perforations. The muscular coat of the bowel already mentioned consists of two layers: an inner one, running about the circumference of the intestine; and an outer one, or longitudinal layer. The large bowel or colon has neither folds nor villi, its absorbing power being mainly for water. It is not as movable as the small intestine since it is fixed to the posterior wall of the peritoneal cavity except in the transverse portion, which has considerable mobility. The entire bowel is well supplied with a network of blood vessels contained within the mesentery or supporting peritoneal fold, by which it is attached to the posterior wall of the abdominal cavity. It has also a complicated nerve supply governing its secretory function and peristaltic action (see PHYSIOLOGY).

Diseases of the Intestine.—Intestinal diseases should be considered as including all disturbances referable to any part of the small or large bowel, from duodenum to anus. The general and all-inclusive term for these maladies, or at least most of them, is intestinal dysfunction. Interference with normal function of the intestine does not mean necessarily the existence of any structural change in the organs involved. Many manifestations, such as constipation, diarrhea, distention, abdominal pain, and so on, may be of reflex origin and may show no evidence of actual pathology. For this reason, intestinal indigestion, intestinal stasis, dyspepsia, and the like must be considered as vague terms which fail to describe a particular disease. Any classification of intestinal diseases of a medical or nonoperative nature will include constipation, diarrhea, intestinal neuroses, melenema, fatty stools (steatorrhea), food poisoning (ptomaines, botulism), ulcerative colitis, diverticulitis, and perhaps regional ileitis, to mention some of the more important. Some of these medical conditions may become of surgical interest in certain cases.

The occurrence of intestinal parasites does not of itself constitute a disease but merely an infestation of the intestinal tract which may cause symptoms. Among surgical conditions affecting the intestine may be listed appendicitis, intestinal obstruction, tuberculosis, and malignant tumors. Regional ileitis is also of surgical importance. Gastric and duodenal ulcers [peptic ulcer], duodenitis, and hemorrhoids should be regarded as pertaining to pathologic conditions of the stomach and anus, respectively, rather than to the intestine itself (see STOMACH; ANUS; HEMORRHOIDS).

Constipation.—This is a functional disorder, and does not constitute a true disease, since it is caused by some disturbance of the regulatory mechanism of the bowel. It may be acute or chronic, and the portion of the bowel involved is usually the colon and especially the rectum, and not the small intestine. Among many conditions responsible. any or all of which may be present, may be mentioned insufficient fluid intake, improper diet, lack of exercise, careless and irregular bowel habits, and the abuse of laxatives (see CONSTIPATION).

Diarrhea.—This is the reverse of constipation, and is not a disease but a symptom. The acute variety may be the result of infection involving the intestinal tract, such as food poisoning, bacillary dysentery, amebic dysentery, ulceration of the colon, infestation by intestinal parasites which cause irritation, and the like. It may arise also from ingestion of irritative metals, such as arsenic, lead, and mercury. The cause of the chronic form is often obscure and difficult to determine and must be sought for among a host of diseases, including ulceration of the colon from tuberculosis, bacillary dysentery, pernicious anemia, leukemia, sprue, hyperthyroidism, and malignant disease of the colon although the last is usually associated with constipation. The underlying cause must be ascertained before effective treatment can be instituted.

Neurosis as Cause of Intestinal Disorder.—Neuroses, manifested by bowel dysfunction, are extremely common. They are often disposed of by such terms as indigestion, spastic colitis, mucous colitis, and irritable colon. Many persons afflicted with a neurosis, who are really not at all ill, become "bowel conscious," fretting over the mildest of symptoms and examining each stool with meticulous care and anxiety. Frequently such persons regard mucous, a constituent of normal colons, as indicating the presence of disease, and it is difficult to wean them from this belief. In spite of the chronicity of most neuroses and the complaints of those having bowel symptoms, the lack of interference with the general health of those affected, together with the fact that no blood, pus, or parasites are observed in the stools, furnish strong evidence against the presence of any actual disease.

Melenema.—This is a general term to indicate the passage of blood from the anus, and is not in itself a disease. The symptom may be discovered by accident, is often unaccompanied by pain, and is not noted in many cases since the individual may not see his bowel movement. If the passage of blood be considerable it will cause a feeling of uneasiness and perhaps of faintness. In any event, the symptom is to be regarded with seriousness. Unless the loss of blood can be established by examination as coming from hemorrhoidal veins at the anus (piles), the cause should be searched for until it can be ascertained with certainty. The commonest sources of bleeding outside of hemorrhoids are anal fissure, rectal ulcer, and malignant tumor of the colon and rectum. Occasionally blood will issue from portal obstruction in the liver or from ruptured hemorrhoidal vessels high in the colon as a result of far advanced arteriosclerosis. Blood arising from the stomach, duodenum, and biliary passage is generally dark in appearance, due to partial decomposition in its passage through the digestive tract (so-called tarry stools).

Colitis.—Inflammation of the colon, of any degree of seriousness other than that arising from causes already mentioned, is generally chronic. In course of time the colon becomes congested and its mucous surface eroded. In advanced cases these eroded areas or ulcers show deep craters, and the diseased areas may coalesce to form a single large ulcer. Eventually the bowel becomes indurated and inelastic, with a considerably narrowed lumen. Symptoms may persist for years, with gradual decline in health and marked loss of weight. The disease is not particularly common, and is confined largely to elderly people. Another disease seen in this age group is diverticulosis [dilatation of the colon in certain areas] and its companion diverticulitis. The latter may become serious, and may necessitate surgical intervention if an abscess forms or if the area becomes the seat of malignant tumor.

Regional Ileitis.—This is a nonspecific, granulomatous, inflammatory disease involving the terminal ileum. Although it had been recognized many years before, the disease was first described adequately in 1932. At first thought to be rare, it is now regarded as fairly common. No single bacterial, virus, or chemical agency can be assigned as a cause. The disease resembles tuberculosis of the bowel and also certain forms of dysentery. While localized generally in a small section of the ileum, several feet of small bowel may become involved after several years, the process even extending to the jejunum. It is frequently complicated with other intestinal diseases and with intestinal fistula. It has been mistaken for acute appendicitis. The symptoms are abdominal pain, distention, failure of digestion, and loss of weight, together with recurring attacks resembling intestinal obstruction. After a considerable period of months or years the segment of intestine affected loses its elasticity and becomes cicatrized and inelastic, so that it is practically functionless. The diagnosis is suggested by the symptoms, and especially by the presence of an abdominal fistula which refuses to heal. It is confirmed by X-ray findings. The treatment is not always successful. Medical treatment is directed usually to diet, which must be such that the damaged bowel will absorb it with the least irritation possible, and to the administration of chemical foods by mouth or by injection into the circulation if nourishment cannot be borne by the usual channels. Surgical treatment may involve resection of the diseased intestine in part, or anastomosis of the intestine so as to bypass the diseased segment, allowing the intestinal contents to pass through healthy intestine and leaving the diseased loop in situ.

Acute Appendicitis.—This is a bacterial infection often followed by suppuration (perforation) of the vermiform appendix (see APPENDICITIS).

Intestinal Obstruction.—This is an extremely acute intra-abdominal calamity of the utmost gravity. Its causes are manifold, including constriction of the bowel from pressure (such as bands of tissue which compress it), hernia (in which a loop of small intestine is held prisoner by the hernial ring so that it cannot escape into the abdominal cavity), intussusception (the telescoping of one loop of bowel into another; seen most often in infants), narrowing of the lumen of the bowel from any cause (as malignant disease or the action of caustics), impaction of feces, pressure of huge collections of gallstones, foreign bodies lodged in the intestines, and masses of intestinal worms. Still other causes, often most difficult of diagnosis, are thrombosis and embolism of a vessel supplying a segment of intestine and resulting in localized intestinal gangrene from failure of the blood supply. Any obstruction of the small bowel, whether from pressure, circulatory failure, or of mechanical or static origin, will result in an alarming train of symptoms. There is severe abdominal pain, vomiting (after several hours), which in late stages becomes fecal, abdominal distention without relief through bowel movements or the passage of gas, and mounting toxemia and prostration. If unrelieved by surgery within a short time of onset, the patient succumbs. The object of surgical intervention is to relieve the obstruction wherever it is found and to aid the paralyzed bowel to regain its tone and function. The toxic obstruction following operations (especially where peritonitis is present [ileus] in which the small intestine is paralyzed), is susceptible of relief through the use of lavage, using a special nasal rubber catheter running to the duodenum, maintained in place in connection with a negative pressure apparatus which keeps the stomach empty until the paralyzed bowel begins to function. Chronic intestinal obstruction involves usually the large intestine. If caused by foreign bodies or impacted feces, it is often relieved by simple measures. If the foreign body cannot be removed thus, or if a tumor be present, appropriate surgical intervention is indicated, according to the nature of the case.

Malignant Disease of the Intestine.—This is confined almost entirely to the colon and rectum. There are comparatively few tumors of the intestinal tract which are nonmalignant. Most new growths of the bowel are carcinomatous or adenocarcinomatous. A favorite site is the sigmoid colon, with the rectum next in order of frequency. Fortunately for the success of surgery, most tumors of the colon can be diagnosed and attacked before metastasis has occurred to other parts of the body. However, not all cancers transfer cells late instead of early, and operative interference should never be delayed unduly. The most favorable time is when the diagnosis is made and the surgeon indicates he is ready. The symptoms of intestinal cancer are often unnoticed or given only slight attention by the patient, since they are apt to be general. Thus gradually increasing and obstinate constipation is the rule. There is gradual but steady loss of weight, increasing pallor and failure of strength, not to be accounted for by the everyday life of the patient. Anemia develops and then cachexia, the latter becoming so noticeable that acquaintances will remark it. Sometimes, but by no means always, a tumor can be felt through the abdominal wall. Occasionally, blood will be seen in the bowel movements. Diagnosis can be made usually by rectal or simoidoscopic examinations, supplemented by X-ray studies. The course of the disease is a few years at most unless resection of the diseased bowel can be done, with removal of the tumor and providing for end to end anastomosis; or if that is impossible and the anus must be removed with the diseased rectum, an artificial anus. If the operation can be completed before transference of malignant tumor cells to other locations has occurred, a complete cure is generally possible.

Bibliography.—Gray's *Anatomy, Descriptive and Surgical,* 29th ed.; Morris' *Human Anatomy,* 10th ed. (Philadelphia 1942); Yater, Wallace M., *Fundamentals of Internal Medicine,* 3d ed. (New York 1944); Christopher, Frederick, *Textbook of Surgery,* 4th ed. (Philadelphia 1945); Orr, Thomas G., *Operations in General Surgery* (Philadelphia 1945); Grant's *Atlas of Anatomy,* 2d ed. (Baltimore 1947); Piersol, George M., ed., *Cyclopedia of Medicine and Surgery* (Philadelphia 1948).

HAROLD WELLINGTON JONES, M.D.
Former Director, Army Medical Library; Editor, "Blakiston's New Gould Medical Dictionary."

INTIMIDATION. See CORRUPT PRACTICES ACTS.

INTONING, the practice of delivering prayers in the recitative form. Intoning differs little from chanting: in the latter case the cadence is more developed, the divisions more rhythmical, and the music in continuous harmony. In intoning the greater part of the prayer is recited on one note and then sung by several voices in unison, the closing words of the sentence being sung to the proximate notes of the scale and in harmony.

INTOXICATION (literally poisoning, commonly restricted to poisoning by means of alcohol, for a discussion of which latter see ALCOHOLISM). Intoxication in the sense of poisoning may result from poisons having their origin outside of the human body (exogenous poisoning), or from poisons which may be developed within the body itself (endogenous poisoning, or autointoxication). Some of the most important problems connected with the infectious diseases concern themselves with the study of the intoxications that result from the formation of toxins by specific bacteria distributed throughout the human body during the course of a disease. From the same point of view many of the most complicated intoxications result from variations in the normal metabolism of the body. Thus, in diabetes mellitus (q.v.) there is developed an acid intoxication (diabetic coma), which is due to the inability of the body properly to neutralize by its alkaline salts the excessive amounts of acid produced as a result of the perverted metabolism of this disease. Similarly, in Bright's disease a type of intoxication (uremic poisoning) results from failure of the kidneys to eliminate poisonous products from the human body.

INTRENCHMENT, in fortification, any work, consisting of not less than a parapet and a ditch, which fortifies a post against the attack of an enemy. As a means of prolonging the defense in a regular work of permanent fortification, intrenchments are made in various parts, to which the defenders successively retire when driven in from forward works. Bastions are ordinarily intrenched at the gorge by a breastwork and ditch, forming either a re-entering angle or a small front of fortification. An army in the field often strengthens its position by intrenchments, as by a continual line of parapet and ditch, or by a line with intervals, consisting of detached works of more or less pretension flanking each other. The war in Europe, which began in 1914, was marked by an unprecedented system of intrenchment, with shelters, dugouts, barbed wire obstacles. See FORTIFICATIONS; WAR, EUROPEAN.

INTRODUCED SPECIES. A long catalogue might be made of species of animals and plants which have been transferred by accident or design from their native country or locality to other regions. Sometimes, as in the case of salmon in New Zealand, rabbits in Australia, the European house sparrow in America and elsewhere, or Western fishes in Eastern waters, this is done by design; but in the great majority of cases the introduction is accidental and unwelcome, as in the case of the hundred and more species of injurious insects brought into the United States from foreign lands (or the fewer sent abroad from here), and the very many species of "weeds" naturalized on our and other shores. Such introductions are in the main accidental, the eggs or seeds or grown individuals passing from one region to another in ships or railway trains, or cargoes or discharged ballast; so many plants have been introduced by the latter means that botanists class the group of alien weeds as "ballast plants." See also IMMIGRATION, ANIMAL AND VEGETAL.

INTROIT, in-trō'ĭt (from the Latin *introire,* to go into, to enter). An antiphon and psalm sung by the choir at the beginning of the Mass. The text of the antiphon, or introit proper, varies with the days of the ecclesiastical year, but is almost always drawn from Holy Scripture. From the opening words of these introits many Sundays derive the names by which they are popularly known, such as Laetare, Gaudete, or Quasimodo Sunday. Originally the introit was in the form of an entire psalm, preceded by an antiphon, but now it has been shortened so that only one verse of the psalm is sung, followed by the *Gloria Patri* and a repetition of the antiphon. Other names for the introit are *ingressa* (Ambrosian); *praelegere* (Gallican); *and officium* (Mozarabic).

INTROSPECTION, a method of observing and analyzing one's own mental states and processes, his thoughts and feelings. Suppose that one has a mental picture of yesterday's scene or has a feeling of impatience: if he notes this awareness and subjects it to examination, he is introspecting. This had been the psychological method par excellence until the last two or three decades. Two theoretical challenges of the validity of the method were recognized and met. One was that the very turning of a person's attention upon his feelings and train of ideas is likely to interfere with the natural flow of such processes. Another was that in the very act of attending intellectually to a present state of mind, he inevitably changes its very character. To both challenges the answer was that introspecting properly includes much retrospecting, much recalling of the immediate past; and so the particular character of the just-recalled is not essentially altered.

To use the introspective method requires long training. One error of the untrained is that he often confuses what he knows about the external source of stimulation with the description of his sensory experience as such; that is, he may be thinking too much about the coated papers he is looking at and too little about the colorful experiences he is having, just as colors.

Techniques became highly refined in the Wilhelm Wundt tradition. States of awareness were formally broken down into what were held to be their component elements. The perceptive awareness of an architectural column—to employ an example—might be analyzed first into two sensory modalities, the visual and the muscle-sense. These were further identified as possessing particular attributes of quality, intensity, duration, extensity. The visual appearance of the left-hand side might be of brighter hue, the views obtained by right and by left eye might vary in their exact spatial extent, the slight muscular strains as the observer shifts his regard from column to background and back again might become noticeable enough as he attends to them, and numerous other sensory characters might be brought out in this way. In addition, the experience as a whole might be toned agreeably, this agreeableness being of moderate intensity and diffused. From such an example it is seen that the traditional use of introspection was oriented toward analysis primarily.

An expanded method of introspection was that adopted by Oswald Külpe and his followers by which they reported their totality of experiences of the moment; and they were apparently rewarded by the discovery of other kinds of awareness than those admitted by the orthodox schools, including thought processes that went on consciously but without any imagery.

Although it has been used in a different historical context, the term "phenomenological" has much in common with "introspective." Consistently with the etymology of the word *phenomenon,* which means "appearance," *phenomenology* is the study of immediate experience at its face value and purely descriptively. The term has been adopted by several psychological and philosophical schools, which take their various departures from an attempt at "pure experience," "immediate experience." In this generic sense, phenomenology may be thought of as including the more specialized introspection.

The length of the training and the unusual character of the methods led the behaviorists to charge that the introspective procedure was esoteric. And at all events, contemporary psychologists ordinarily employ a person's introspections as strictly ancillary to the objective observing of his behavior. See also THOUGHT.

Bibliography.—Sully, J., *The Human Mind* (London 1892); Ladd, J. T., *Psychology, Descriptive and Explanatory* (New York 1894); Stout, G. F., *Manual of Psychology* (New York 1899); Boring, E. G., *History of Experimental Psychology* (New York 1929).

JOHN FREDERICK DASHIELL,
Kenan Professor of Psychology, University of North Carolina.

INTROVERSION, a term in psychology describing a mental state characterized by withdrawal of interest from the outer world and its concentration upon the inner self and one's own thoughts. The introvert thinks only or chiefly about himself or his own needs. Within himself in his own world of fantasy he finds satisfactory responses to the objects and situations of his environment. C. J. Jung introduced the term "introversion" which Freud stated had for original meaning "the turning aside of the 'libido' from the possibilities of actual satisfaction" to fantasy. But in its general use the term has a somewhat broader meaning. The introvert type of individual focuses his mental activity upon himself, centering his thoughts on his own personality. The introvert and the extrovert type (also introduced by Jung) in their extremes are considered opposites. The extrovert expresses his feelings in external action to satisfy a condition or conflict within his personality which he is unwilling or unable to face. Introverts are readily recognized by their indifference or slight response to things happening about them, by their preference for solitude, by a shy retiredness, and especially by an excessive tendency to day dreaming. Extreme introversion is found in various psychopathic conditions such as dementia praecox. The introvert is not necessarily neurotic, but adverse environmental conditions may spur him on to an escape from reality and the adoption of a fantasy personality, whether of Caesar, Napoleon or other world figure of dominating character. Some psychologists believe that in their extreme forms these opposite types are inborn; while others think that the original state of the individual lies between the two opposites and that environmental factors determine toward which he will turn. Still others believe that both heredity and environment combine as causative factors.

INTRUSION. See VOLCANISM; GEOLOGY.

INTUBATION, the introduction of a tube into an orifice or an organ, as the larynx, to keep it open. Specially designed tubes for such a purpose are sometimes used in cases of croup, and diphtheritic obstruction, as a substitute for tracheotomy.

INTUITION, *in philosophy,* immediate knowledge, attained without deliberation or reasoning, as opposed to empirical knowledge which is built up by experience. The term has wide use in connection with intuitional systems of ethics which set forth conscience as a function which gives direct recognition of right and wrong, either in a choice between two acts, or between two principles of action. In the theory of knowledge, intuition is the immediate apprehension of truth, whether that be sensory truth or necessary forms of thought, or ultimate knowledge of the nature of God.

INTUITIONISM, a term used to designate loosely a wide range of philosophic theories in metaphysics, ethics and aesthetics, among which the common feature is an insistence upon the existence of direct, immediate apprehension of truth, beauty or right, without any necessary dependence upon experience. In general such philosophic tendencies are set over against empirical theories. The latter have generally carried the day in modern philosophy; in so far at least as concerns the recognized necessity for the action of experience in order to give solid foundation for belief, opinion and theory of every kind. In modern literature the term has its most important bearing in ethical affairs. See EMPIRICISM; EPISTEMOLOGY.

INTUSSUSCEPTION, the reception of one part within another, as of a sword in a sheath; as applied to the bowels, it expresses the slipping of one portion of the intestines into and constriction of another. It is a rather common form of intestinal obstruction, especially in infants, among whom over 25 per cent of all cases occur. It is fatal unless removed by surgical operation. In plant physiology, the term signifies the growth of a cell wall by taking up new matter throughout, instead of laying it on by opposition.

INULIN, a substance resembling starch, but intermediate in nature between that body and the gums. It occurs in the roots of elecampane, dandelion and certain other plants, and also in the Jerusalem artichoke and the common potato. When pure it is a tasteless white powder consisting of spherical particles. Its chemical formula is probably a multiple of $C_6H_{10}O_5$ though $C_{72}H_{124}O_{62}$ has been suggested. It is insoluble in alcohol and but slightly soluble in cold water, although it is very hygroscopic. It dissolves freely in hot water. It melts at 320° F., becoming thereby converted into a different substance known as "pyro-inulin." It is not fermentable and does not reduce Fehling's solution. Iodine renders it brown or yellow. Other names by which inulin is known are dahlin (q.v.), alantin, and sinistrin.

INUNDATIONS, floods caused usually by the overflow of a river or by the ocean, sometimes by the giving way of a dam or other barrier. Since the dawn of history no century and scarcely any large country have been free from floods. The region of the Nile in Egypt, and of the Hwang Ho, or Yellow River, in China, have suffered most from this cause; and the Nile stands alone as at once a terribly destructive and a beneficial agent, for its overflows have not only irrigated the surrounding dry country, but greatly enriched it by spreading over it the fertilizing sediment collected and conveyed in the stream. Sanitary science has greatly reduced the danger of pestilence that always follows a great flood, and that formerly was often as destructive of human life as the floods themselves.

The following are some of the most noted inundations of record: 245, the sea swept over Lincolnshire, England, and submerged thousands of acres; 353, a flood in Cheshire, England, destroyed 3,000 lives and a great number of cattle; 738, an overflow of the Clyde drowned 400 families in Glasgow; 1014, a number of seaport towns in England and the Netherlands were destroyed; 1100, the coast of Kent, England, was deluged and the Goodwin Sands bank formed by the sea; 1108, Flanders was submerged by the sea and the town and harbor of Ostend completely covered; 1134, a large part of Flanders was again submerged; 1164, a considerable part of the coast of Friesland was swallowed up; 1170, many miles of country in the northern part of Holland were engulfed with great loss of life; 1219, the breaking of the dykes along the Zuyder Zee caused great destruction of life and property; 1277, 44 villages in Holland were destroyed; 1282, 72 towns and villages in Holland were submerged and 100,000 persons drowned; 1287, another breaking of the dykes caused a loss of 80,000 lives; 1362, 30 villages on the coast of Nordstrand were destroyed; 1377, 50 miles of territory and 72 villages in Holland were swept away and the course of the Maas and Rhine rivers changed; 1421, by the breaking of the dyke at Dort 10,000 people in the town and 100,000 in the vicinity were drowned; 1530, a general failure of the dykes caused an overflow of the low lands and a loss of life estimated at 400,000, and of property in proportion; 1570, Antwerp, Bruges, Hamburg, Rotterdam and Amsterdam were submerged and 30,000 inhabitants drowned; 1617, 50,000 persons were drowned in a flood in Catalonia, Spain; 1634, a flood swept away several villages on the Nordland coast of Denmark, and drowned 11,000 people and 66,300 cattle and 10,800 people and 90,000 cattle were drowned at Hamburg, Bremen and Oldenburg; 1717, the «Christmas» flood along the entire north coast and in England totally destroyed 5,000 dwellings, and 3,500 partially; 1787, mountain torrents drowned 2,000 persons in Navarre, France; 1811, 24 villages near Presburg and nearly all their inhabitants were swept away by an overflow of the Danube; 1813, large provinces of Austria and Poland were flooded and many lives lost (6,000 in Silesia, and 4,000 in Poland), and 2,000 Turkish soldiers on an island near Widdin were drowned by a sudden overflow of the Danube 1816, the overflow of the Vistula River laid 119 German villages under water, and caused great loss of life and property; 1829, the same river broke through the dyke at Dantzig, drowned a large number of people and destroyed 4,000 dwellings and 10,000 cattle; 1830, an overflow of the Danube at Vienna flooded the homes of 50,000 inhabitants; 1833, 10,000 horses were swept away, and 1,000 persons drowned in Canton alone during the great October flood; 1840, a rising of the Saone river, France, and the bursting of its banks, caused 60,000 acres to be submerged and many houses destroyed in Lyons, Avignon, La Guillotière, Voise, Marseilles and Nismes; 1846, by the Loire flooding the centre and southwest of France, $20,000,000 damage was sustained; 1849, 160 squares and 1,600 buildings were flooded in New Orleans; 1852, the Hoang-Ho, in China, burst its banks, cut a new bed into the Gulf of Pechili and wrought tremendous losses; 1855, Hamburg was half submerged and suffered enormous property damage; 1861, Bengal, India, suffered great loss of life and property by a deluge in its most fertile districts, and famine and pestilence followed; 1866, the north of England was visited extensively by floods; 1870, Rome, Italy, suffered great loss; 1874, the bursting of a badly constructed dam caused the destruction of several villages in the valley of Mill River, Mass., and loss of 144 lives; 1876, destructive flood occurred in France and Holland; 1882, many persons were drowned and much property destroyed by overflows in the Mississippi and Ohio valleys; 1887, the Hoang-Ho, China, broke its banks, deserted its natural bed, spread over a thickly populated plain, cut an entirely new road to the sea, washed away 300 villages, and submerged the lands around 300 more between Cheng-Chou and Chung-mon, submerged more than 1,500 villages south of Kaifeng, rendered 2,000,000 people homeless and caused a loss of life estimated from 1,500,000 to 7,000,000; 1889 (31 May), the giving way of the Stony Creek dam in the Conemaugh Valley, Pa., caused the total destruction of the city of Johnstown and several neighboring towns, and caused a loss of about 5,000 lives and more than $20,000,000 of property. The same year was marked by very disastrous floods in China and Japan. In 1890, the levees of the Mississippi gave way in many places, and the waters flooded large areas of land in Mississippi and Louisiana. The worst crevasse was caused by the giving way of the Morgansea, near Bayou Sara. In 1903 there was a great rising of the Kansas, Missouri, Mississippi and Des Moines rivers; several large cities, including Kansas City, Des Moines and Topeka, were inundated, the loss of life was over 300, and of property about $10,000,000. In the same year Paterson, N. J., and the entire Passaic Valley were flooded, about $3,000,000 damage being done in Paterson. In 1912 the Mississippi flooded 15,000 square miles and cost $45,000,000. The Ohio in 1913 cost 400 lives and $180,000,000 and almost destroyed Dayton. In 1921 a flood in Pueblo, Colo., cost 500 lives and $25,000,000. In April-May 1927 floods in the Mississippi Valley left 700,000 persons homeless, about 600,000 almost destitute; inundated 14,000,000 acres, and caused property damage in excess of $300,000,000. Floods in 12 States in March 1936 caused 171 deaths, property damage estimated at $500,000,000, and rendered 500,000 homeless. They were extremely severe in New England and Western Pennsylvania, especially in Pittsburgh.

INVALIDES, Hôtel des, an establishment in Paris where wounded veterans of France are cared for at the public cost. Its foundation dates from 1671, under Louis XIV; at first it was a place of retirement for the aged servants of court favorites as well as for invalided soldiers, but this abuse was ended by St. Germain in the reign of Louis XV. With its high gilded dome, under which are the tombs of Napoleon, Turenne, Vauban, Jerome and Joseph Bonaparte, and Marshal MacMahon, it is one of the most conspicuous monuments of Paris. The buildings, which cover about 30 acres, were begun in 1671 and completed in 1675. They furnish accommodation for 6,000 inmates. The façade of this last structure is 660 feet in length. It stands about 600 yards back from the Seine, facing the Esplanade des Invalides, a fine open place about 900 feet wide, containing several rows of trees and extending to the river opposite the Champs Elysées. In 1789 the private property of the institution was alienated and it has since been supported from the public revenue. The body of Napoleon rests in the crypt of the dome.

INVAR, an alloy of nickel and steel with exceedingly small coefficient of heat expansion, only one-twenty-fifth that of steel. It is used for measuring-rods in geodetic work, for pendulums and other purposes where liability to heat expansion vitiates accurate work. It contains 36 per cent of nickel. The name is a condensation of the word invariable. See Clock and Geodesy.

INVARIANTS AND COVARIANTS.

1. These terms were introduced and are still ordinarily employed, in connection with a special mathematical theory, namely, the theory of the linear transformation of algebraic forms developed by Cayley and Sylvester during the middle third of the 19th century. The central idea, however, is a very general one, which has been applied in recent years to almost all branches of mathematics. It deserves, in fact, to be ranked with such fundamental concepts as function and group. We therefore divide our sketch into three parts as follows: (1) The general concept of invariant; (2) the theory of algebraic forms, or invariants in the narrow sense; (3) other invariant theories.

The General Concept.

2. The suggestion for the formation of the concept comes from the familiar observation, at the bottom of all science and philosophy, that, while the world about us is in a continual state of change, there are yet certain aspects or properties which are unaltered. To find the permanent in the changing is the most general statement of the problem of invariants. Abstractly, the idea may be explained more definitely as follows: Consider a set of objects or elements O of any conceivable kind, finite or infinite in number; and a set of operations or transformations T, each of which interchanges the objects in a definite manner. Then a property of an object O is said to be *invariant*, provided it holds for all the objects obtained from the given O by the transformations T. Similarly, any relation between a number of O's which holds for the transformed O's is said to be an invariant relation, that is, an invariant relation of the given objects with respect to the given transformation.

The idea of *covariant* involves nothing essentially new. An object $\bar{O}$ is said to be a covariant of a given number of objects O_1, O_2, etc., provided $\bar{O}$ is invariantly related to $O_1, O_2, \ldots$. In this case, if any one of the transformations T converts $\bar{O}$ into $\bar{O}'$, O_1 into O_1', O_2 into O_2', etc., then the relations connecting $\bar{O}'$ with O_1, O_2, etc., are the same as those connecting $\bar{O}$ with O_1, O_2, etc.

3. The idea is best illustrated by examples from geometry. Consider a number of points $P_1, P_2, \ldots$, connected with a solid body. When the body is displaced, its points take new positions, P_1', P_2', ... Many such positions are possible, since the displacement may be made in an endless number of ways. But in every case, of course, the distance between P_1' and P_2' is the same as that between P_1 and P_2. That is, distances between points are invariant with respect to rigid displacement.

Suppose next that the solid carrying the points is not only displaced but is magnified (or diminished) according to any scale. (We may, for example, picture such a change as produced by subjecting the homogeneous solid to a higher or lower temperature). The solid is then converted into one of different size but of the same shape, that is, a similar solid. Distances are changed in the same ratio. Hence $P_1'P_2'/P_2'P_3' = P_1P_2/P_2P_3$. That is, the ratio of any two distances is invariant with respect to similitude transformations.

4. In both examples, points on a straight line are converted into points on a straight line. Collinearity is then a relation which is invariant with respect to displacements and similitude transformations. A more general type of transformation for which this is true is the homographic or projective transformation. We consider, for simplicity, only the case of figures drawn in a plane M. From a fixed point (termed the centre of projection) outside of M draw lines to the various points of M until they intersect a second plane M'. Thus, every point P in M is associated with a definite point P' in M'. The operation of passing from a figure in M to the corresponding figure in M' is termed projection. Concretely, we may think of the centre of projection as a source of light and the figure in M' as the shadow of that in M.*

If we consider three points P_1, P_2, P_3 on a straight line in M, they are converted, by projection, into points P_1', P_2', P_3' on a straight line in M'. But in general the distances and also the ratios of distances will differ. In fact, three points have no invariant, since they may be converted into three points at arbitrarily assigned distances by a suitable projection. If, however, we take four points (on a straight line) it may be shown that, for any projection,

$$\frac{P_1P_3}{P_3P_2} : \frac{P_1P_4}{P_4P_2} = \frac{P_1'P_3'}{P_3'P_2'} : \frac{P_1'P_4'}{P_4'P_2'}.$$

In each member of this equation we have a combination of the distances between four points which is termed their cross ratio (anharmonic ratio). Hence the cross ratio of four collinear points is invariant with respect to projective transformation.

5. Let the figures considere' be all the ellipses of a plane. With respect to displacement an ellipse has two invariants, the major and the minor axis. With respect to similitude transformation, there is one invariant, the ratio of the axes, or what is essentially the same, the eccentricity. Finally, in the projective theory there are no invariants, since one ellipse may be converted into any other (and even into any proper conic).

In this connection we may illustrate the notion of a covariant. The centre of an ellipse is a covariant with respect to displacement and magnification, but not with respect to projection. For if the plane containing an ellipse E and its centre C is displaced or magnified, so that ellipse E is converted into another ellipse E' and the point C is converted into a point C', then C' is necessarily the centre of E'; while under projection this is not the case. A similar result holds for the centre of gravity of any figure, plane or solid.

6. Another well-known type of transformation is that known as inversion. Take a fixed circle F with centre C and radius r, and suppose that any point P of the plane is converted into the point P' situated on the line CP, so that $CP \cdot CP' = r^2$. The points P, P' are then said to be inverse with respect to the circle F. By the inverse of a curve is meant the locus of the points inverse to the points of the curve. The collinear relation of points is no longer invariant, for a straight line (not passing through C) is converted into a circle. An arbitrary

* It is however necessary to include the ideal shadow formed by producing the rays away from M.

circle is converted into a circle, but the centre of the circle is not a covariant point. The most important property of the transformation is this: the angle at which any two curves intersect is equal to the angle at which the inverse curves intersect. Angles are invariant with respect to geometric inversion.

7. We pass now to a few simple examples of the general definition in No. 2, in which the objects and transformations are analytic instead of geometric.

Let the objects O be functions of any number of variables, and let the operations T performed on these functions be the permutation of the variables involved. A function written down at random, for example x^2+2yz, changes its form when say x and y are interchanged. There are exceptional functions, like $x^2+y^2+z^2$ and $xy+yz+xz$, which are not altered by interchanging the variables in any way, and are termed symmetric. The symmetric functions are invariant with respect to permutation of the variables.

In the differential calculus it is shown that the exponential function e^x has the property of being its own derivative. The only functions which are invariant with respect to the process of differentiation are in fact those of the form ae^x, where a is a constant. It is obvious that if the first derivative is equal to the original function, all the higher derivatives will also be equal to the function.

The trigonometric functions have a period of 2π or 360°. Such a function $f(x)$ is unaltered in value when x is replaced by $x+2\pi$. It is obvious that the double application of the operation, that is, the replacing of x by $x+4\pi$, will also leave $f(x)$ invariant. The periodic character thus involves the invariance of the function with respect to all the operations $(x, x+2k\pi)$ (this denotes the replacing of x by $x+2k\pi$), where k is any integer. We note here that if one of these operations, say that of adding $2k'\pi$ to the angle, is followed by another, say that of adding $2k''\pi$, the result is the same as the single operation of adding $2(k'+k'')\pi$, which is a member of the set. The set of operations thus possesses the essential property of a group.

8. In general, if an invariant is found with respect to certain operations, T_1, T_2, ..., the invariance also holds for all combinations of these operations. Adding these combinations to the original operations, a set is finally obtained with the group property; this is then termed the group generated by the given operations.

Thus, in connection with No. 6, since angles are unaltered by inversion with respect to any circle, it follows that they are unaltered by successive inversion with respect to a number of circles. The inversions themselves do not constitute a group; but the totality of combinations is the important group of circular transformations which are expressed analytically by the linear transformations of a complex variable and of its conjugate.

9. The general problem of the mathematical theory of invariants may now be restated as follows: Given any group of transformations, and any set of configurations (mathematical objects) which are converted into one another by these transformations, to find the properties of the configurations which remain unaltered. There are thus as many types of invariant theories as there are types of groups and types of configurations. The distinction according to groups is the more fundamental.

10. The relation between the concepts invariant and group is thus very intimate. Suppose that instead of assigning transformations and seeking invariants, the question is inverted: Given a property or a function, find the transformations which leave it invariant.

Thus, if space is to be deformed so as to leave the distance between every pair of points unaltered, the deformation must be simply a displacement. The totality of displacements forms a group; for if one displacement is followed by a second, the effect is the same as that due to a single displacement. In general the totality of transformations defined by one or more invariants is a group. Many groups are defined in this way.

11. In connection with any group this question may be asked: Given two configurations, is it possible to convert the one into the other by a transformation belonging to the assigned group? If this is the case, the configurations are said to be *equivalent* with respect to the group.

Thus, two figures are equivalent with respect to the displacement group when they are congruent; they are equivalent with respect to the similitude group when they are similar. The study of equivalence with respect to the projective group is the main object of projective geometry; its systematic analytic treatment depends upon the theory of algebraic forms considered below.

The importance of the notion of equivalence depends upon the fact that equivalent configurations necessarily have the same invariant functions and properties. Thus in studying the projective properties of (proper) conics, it is sufficient to consider the case of a circle. The circle may thus be taken as the *type* or *canonical form* of the class of conics.

The Theory of Algebraic Forms.

12. This part of modern algebra deals with the invariants of algebraic forms with respect to the group of linear transformations. It has been variously termed the theory of forms, the algebra of quantics, the algebra of linear transformations, the linear or projective invariant theory. Traces of the idea may be found in papers by Lagrange, Gauss and Cauchy; and simple results on quadric forms were given by G. Boole (1841); but the construction of the systematic theory begins with the memoirs of A. Cayley (1845–) and J. J. Sylvester* (1851–). The recent developments are due mainly to German and Italian mathematicians.

13. The objects considered are algebraic forms. A *form* or *quantic* is a rational integral homogeneous function of any number of variables. Forms are classified according to the number of variables and the degree in which they are involved. A *binary* form involves two variables; a *ternary,* three; a *quaternary,* four; in the general case of p variables the adjective p-ary is employed. The degree in which the variables enter is termed the *order* of the form;

*Most of the technical terms employed (including invariant, covariant, form) are due to Sylvester, who gloried in the title of "The Mathematical Adam."

we denote it in general by n. If n is one, the form is linear; if two, quadric (or quadratic); if three, cubic; if four, quartic (biquadratic); etc.

Thus the binary cubic form is

$$ax^3+bx^2y+cxy^2+dy^3,$$

where x, y are the variables and a, b, c, d the coefficients. It is usual, however, to distinguish the variables and the coefficients by subscripts, a notation which has the advantage of generality and symmetry; also binomial coefficients are introduced. Thus the above form is written

$$a_0x_1^3+3a_1x_1^2x_2+3a_2x_1x_2^2+a_3x_2^3.$$

The ternary quadric is

$$a_{11}x_1^2+a_{22}x_2^2+a_{33}x_3^2+2a_{23}x_2x_3+2a_{13}x_1x_3+2a_{12}x_1x_2.$$

The general binary form is

$$(1) \quad a_0x_1^n+\frac{n}{1}x_1^{n-1}x_2 + \frac{n(n-1)}{1\cdot 2}x_1^{n-2}x_2^2+\ldots+a_nx_2^n.$$

14. The group employed consists of the totality of linear transformations of the variables. A linear transformation from the original variables $x_1. x_2, \ldots x$ to the new variables $X_1, X_2, \ldots X_p$ is defined by p equations of the first degree, as follows:

$$x_1=l_{11}X_1+l_{12}X_2+\ldots+l_{1p}X_p,$$
$$x_2=l_{21}X_1+l_{22}X_2+\ldots+l_{2p}X_p,$$
$$\ldots\ldots\ldots\ldots\ldots\ldots$$
$$x_p=l_{p1}X_1+l_{p2}X_2+\ldots+l_{pp}X_p.$$

The determinant

$$\Delta=|l_{ij}|,$$

whose elements are the p^2 coefficients in these equations, is termed the *modulus* of the transformation. It is assumed that Δ does not vanish; for in the latter case the X's cannot be expressed in terms of the x's, that is, the transformation is not reversible.

We shall deal mainly with binary variables and then employ the simpler notation

$$(2) \quad x_1=l_1X_1+m_1X_2, \quad x_2=l_2X_1+m_2X_2.$$

The modulus is $\Delta=l_1m_2-l_2m_1$.

15. When a linear transformation is carried out on a form, the latter is converted into a form of the same order containing the new variables. The coefficients of this transformed quantic depend of course upon the transformation employed. Thus if in the quadric

$$f\equiv a_0x_1^2+2a_1x_1x_2+a_2x_2^2$$

we make the substitution (2), the result is a new quadric,

$$F\equiv A_0X_1^2+2A_1X_1X_2+A_2X_2^2,$$

where

$$A_0=l_1^2a_0+2l_1l_2a_1+l_2^2a_2,$$
$$A_1=l_1m_1a_0+(l_1m_2+l_2m_1)a_1+l_2m_2a_2,$$
$$A_2=m_1^2a_0+2m_1m_2a_1+m_2^2a_2.$$

It is easy to verify that

$$A_0A_2-A_1^2=(l_1m_2-l_2m_1)^2(a_0a_2-a_1^2).$$

According to the general definition in No. 2, the function $a_0a_2-a_1^2$ is not an invariant function, since it is not equal to $A_0A_2-A_1^2$; but the relation $a_0a_2-a_1^2=0$ is invariant, since its fulfilment necessitates $A_0A_2-A_1^2=0$. This is sometimes expressed by saying that the function is a *relative* invariant.

It is usual, however, to modify somewhat the general definition as follows: A function of the coefficients of a quantic is said to have the invariant property when it is equal to the same function of the coefficients of the transformed quantic, except for a factor depending only upon the coefficients of the linear transformation. Thus if $\phi(a)$ is such a function, where a denotes the coefficients collectively, and if A denotes the coefficients in the new form, then

$$(3) \quad \phi(A)=M\phi(a),$$

where M depends only on the transformation coefficients.

All such functions can be expressed in terms of rational integral functions with the same property. These are termed simply invariants. Thus an *invariant* is a rational integral function of the coefficients with the property expressed by (3).

16. A *covariant* of a quantic differs from an invariant only in that it involves both the coefficients and the variables. Its defining property is expressed by

$$(3') \quad \phi(A, X)=M\phi(a, x).$$

Thus the binary cubic

$$a_0x_1^3+3a_1x_1^2x_2+3a_2x_1x_2^2+a_3x_2^3$$

has the covariant

$$(a_0a_2-a_1^2)x_1^2+(a_0a_3-a_1a_2)x_1x_2+(a_1a_3-a_2^2)x_2^2;$$

for when the cubic is linearly transformed, it is found that the corresponding expression

$$(A_0A_2-A_1^2)X_1^2+(A_0A_3-A_1A_2)X_1X_2 + (A_1A_3-A_2^2)X_2^2,$$

built from the new coefficients and variables, reduces to the original expression multiplied by $(l_1m_2-l_2m_1)^2$.

17. Invariants and covariants are collectively termed concomitants or, more simply, *comitants*. We give now a few of their important general properties.

A comitant is homogeneous in the coefficients (a) and in the variables (x). Its dimension in the former is termed its degree (d); its dimension in the latter, its order (m). For an invariant, of course, $m=0$.

The factor M produced by the linear transformation is for every comitant an entire power of the modulus Δ. Hence

$$(4) \quad \phi(A, X)=\Delta^w\phi(a, x).$$

The exponent w is termed the *weight* of the comitant.

The proof of the first theorem depends on the use of linear transformations of the special type $x_1=\rho X_1$, $x_2=\rho X_2$; that of the second theorem depends on the group property of linear transformations and the fact that Δ is not factorable.

18. The weight w, order m, and degree d of any comitant of a binary n-ic are connected by the relation

$$2w=nd-m.$$

This holds in the example given in No. 16, where $n=3$, $m=2$, $d=2$, $w=2$.

Taking $m=0$ and n odd, we have the corollary. A binary form of odd order cannot have an invariant of odd degree.

When n is even, so is m. Hence a binary form of even order cannot have a covariant of odd order.

19. The preceding definitions and theorems may readily be extended to *simultaneous* comi-

tants, that is, invariants and covariants of two or more forms.

20. An important process for the formation of simultaneous comitants depends on this principle: If in an invariant $\phi(a_0, a_1, \ldots a_n)$ of a single form f, we substitute $a_0 + \kappa b_0$ for a_0, $a_1 + \kappa b_1$, for a_1, etc., and expand the result according to powers of κ, the first term is the original invariant $\phi(a)$, the coefficient of κ^d is the corresponding invariant $\phi(b)$ of a form g with coefficients $b_0, b_1, \ldots b_n$, and the remaining coefficients are simultaneous in variants of f and g.

For example, when this principle is applied to the invariant $a_0a_2 - a_1^2$ of a quadric $f = a_0x_1^2 + 2a_1x_1x_2 + a_2x_2^2$, we have

$$(a_0 + \kappa b_0)(a_2 + \kappa b_2) - (a_1 + \kappa b_1)^2$$
$$= a_0a_2 - a_1^2 + \kappa(a_0b_2 - 2a_1b_1 + a_2b_0) + \kappa^2(b_0b_2 - b_1^2).$$

It follows that $a_0b_2 - 2a_1b_1 + a_2b_0$ is a simultaneous invariant of f and $g = b_0x_1^2 + 2b_1x_1x_2 + b_2x_2^2$.

The coefficient of the first power of κ, by Taylor's theorem, is

$$b_0\frac{\partial\phi}{\partial a_0} + b_1\frac{\partial\phi}{\partial a_1} + \ldots + b_n\frac{\partial\phi}{\partial a_n}.$$

Hence if the operation $b_0\dfrac{\partial}{\partial a_0} + b_1\dfrac{\partial}{\partial a_1} + \ldots + b_n\dfrac{\partial}{\partial a_n}$ is applied to an invariant of a single form, the result is an invariant of two forms. The operation is known as the *Aronhold process.*

21. In the domain of simultaneous comitants the distinction between invariants and covariants may be said to disappear. All the covariants of a form f may be obtained from the simultaneous invariants of f and a linear form $u_1x_1 + u_2x_2$ by the substitution of x_2 for u_1 and $-x_1$ for u_2.

22. *Geometric Interpretation.*— If a binary form f of nth order is equated to zero, the resulting equation, by the fundamental theorem of algebra, determines n values of the ratio $x_1 : x_2$. Taking $x_1 : x_2$ as homogeneous coordinates of a point on a straight line, we thus obtain a definite set of n points corresponding to the form f. Conversely, if a set of n points is given, the form f is determined (except for a numerical factor).

Linear transformation of x_1, x_2 has the same effect upon the points of the line as the projection of the given line upon a second followed by the displacement of the second line upon the first. Hence an invariant of f equated to zero represents a projective relation between the corresponding n points, that is, a relation not altered by the process of projection. Similarly, a covariant of order m represents a set of m points projectively related to points defined by f.

Thus, the vanishing of the invariant $a_0a_2 - a_1^2$ of a quadric form means that the two root points coincide. Again, the vanishing of $a_0b_2 - 2a_1b_1 + a_2b_0$, derived in No. 21, means that the pairs of points represented by the two quadrics are situated harmonically.

The interpretation often suggests the invariant character of complicated algebraic functions. For example, the *resultant* of two equations, $f = 0$, $g = 0$ (that is, the expression which vanishes when and only when the equations have a common root), is a simultaneous **invariant of f and g. The condition that the equation $f = 0$ shall have equal roots leads to** an invariant termed the *discriminant* of f.

23. *Absolute Invariants.*— By considering fractional instead of integral functions of the coefficients, it is possible to obtain *absolute invariants,* that is, functions which are unaltered by linear transformation. The factor M in (3) is then unity. An absolute invariant is necessarily the ratio of two (relative) invariants having the same weight. We give an example in connection with the form of fourth order. Here there are two invariants I and J with weights 3 and 2 respectively. Linear transformation affects them as follows: $I' = \Delta^3 I$, $J' = \Delta^2 J$. Hence $I'^3/J'^2 = I^3/J^2$. That is, I^3/J^2 is an absolute invariant.

Geometrically, every absolute invariant of any number of forms is expressible in terms of cross ratios of the corresponding points.

24. *The Symbolic Notation.*— The most powerful method for attacking the general problem of our subject, the determination of all the comitants of any number of forms and their interrelations, is the so-called *symbolic* method. The origin of the method is to be found in Cayley's hyperdeterminants (1845), but the symbolic notation itself is due to Aronhold (1859). The general theory was developed by Clebsch and Gordan (1870–).

A binary form of nth order is represented by the nth power of a linear form,

$$f = (\alpha_1x_1 + \alpha_2x_2)^n.$$

Here the α's are merely symbols which have a real meaning only in the combinations

$$\alpha_1^n = a_0,\ \alpha_1^{n-1}\alpha_2 = a_1,\ \alpha_1^{n-2}\alpha_2^2 = a_2, \ldots, \alpha_2^n = a_n.$$

The Roman letters denote real coefficients and the Greek letters symbolic coefficients. The latter were termed *umbrae* (shadows of quantities) by Sylvester.

A combination of α's of dimension $< n$ has no real meaning. On the other hand, if the dimension is a multiple of n, there are several corresponding real quantities. Thus $\alpha_1^{2n-2}\alpha_2^2$ represents both a_0a_2 and a_1^2. This ambiguity is removed by introducing several equivalent sets of umbral quantities, each entering in precisely the nth dimension. We abbreviate by writing $\alpha_1x_1 + \alpha_2x_2 = \alpha_x$, $\beta_1x_1 + \beta_2x_2 = \beta_x$, etc. The given form is then

$$f = \alpha_x^n = \beta_x^n = \gamma_x^n, \text{ etc.}$$

The fundamental theorem is as follows: Every comitant of binary forms f is expressible symbolically as a combination of determinants of the type $(\alpha\beta) = \alpha_1\beta_2 - \alpha_2\beta_1$ and linear factors of the type $\alpha_x = \alpha_1x_1 + \alpha_2x_2$. In the case of invariants, only the determinants are involved. Conversely, all combinations of these two types (in which each set of symbols is involved in the proper dimension) represent comitants.*

Thus the quadric $f = \alpha_x^2 = \beta_x^2$ has the invariant $(\alpha\beta)^2$. Expanding, we have

$$(\alpha_1\beta_2 - \alpha_2\beta_1)^2 = \alpha_1^2\beta_2^2 - 2\alpha_1\alpha_2\beta_1\beta_2 + \alpha_2^2\beta_1^2$$
$$= a_0a_2 - 2a_1a_1 + a_2a_0,$$

which is simply twice the discriminant $a_0a_2 - a_1^2$.

25. *Transvectants.*—Among the comitants of two forms, $f = \alpha_x^n$, $g = \beta_x^m$ (here α and β are

* Sylvester observed certain formal analogies between this symbolism and that employed in chemistry, and developed a so-called chemico-algebraic theory. Consult Grace and Young, 'Algebra of Invariants,' (Cambridge 1903, p. 366).

non-equivalent symbols), those represented by $(\alpha\beta)^{\kappa} a_x^{n-\kappa} \beta_x^{m-\kappa}$ are of special importance, since they are of the first degree in each set of coefficients. They are termed the *transvectants* of f and g and are denoted by $(f, g)^{\kappa}$, Gordan has shown that all comitants may be derived by the repeated application of the process of transvection.

The first transvectant of two forms is termed their *Jacobian;* its non-symbolic value is $\frac{\partial f}{\partial x_1}\frac{\partial g}{\partial x_2} - \frac{\partial f}{\partial x_2}\frac{\partial g}{\partial x_1}$. The transvectant $(f, f)_2$ is termed the *Hessian* of f; its non-symbolic value is $\frac{\partial^2 f}{\partial x_1^2}\frac{\partial^2 f}{\partial x_2^2} - \left(\frac{\partial^2 f}{\partial x_1 \partial x_2}\right)^2$.

26. *Complete Systems.*—In general, a set of forms has an infinite number of comitants. Thus any entire power of a comitant, or a product of powers of two comitants, is also a comitant. It is evident, however, that there cannot exist an infinite number of algebraically independent comitants, since all are functions of a finite number of coefficients and variables. The following result is fundamental in the systematic theory: For a given set of forms there exists a finite number of comitants such that every comitant of the forms is a rational integral function of the selected comitants. The latter constitute the *complete system* of the given forms.

The proof was first given by Gordan (1870) by means of the symbolic method. It has since been simplified and generalized by numerous investigators—in particular, Hilbert.

27. We now give the complete systems for the forms of order 1, 2, 3, 4:

Linear form. No invariant; the only covariant is the given form $f = a_x$.

Quadric form. One invariant (the discriminant) $D = (\alpha\beta)^2$; one covariant $f = a_x^2$.

Cubic form. The only invariant is the discriminant $R = (\alpha\beta)^2(\alpha\gamma)(\beta\delta)(\gamma\delta)^2$; in addition to $f = a_x^3$, there are two covariants, $H = (\alpha\beta)^2 a_x \beta_x$ (the Hessian of f) and $Q = (\alpha\beta)^2(\alpha\gamma)\beta_x\gamma_x^2$ (the Jacobian of f and H).

Quartic form. Two invariants, $I = (\alpha\beta)^4$, $J = (\alpha\beta)^2(\beta\gamma)^2(\gamma\alpha)^2$; three covariants, the given form $f = a_x^4$, its Hessian $H = (\alpha\beta)^2 a_x^2 \beta_x^2$, and the Jacobian of f and H, namely, $T = (\alpha\beta)^2(\alpha\gamma) a_x \beta_x^2 \gamma_x^3$.

Every invariant of the quartic form is thus a rational integral function of I and J; every comitant is a rational integral function of I, J, f, H, T.

28. The systems given are *irreducible;* that is, no member of a system can be expressed as a rational integral function of the other members of the system.

Complete irreducible systems have been calculated for single forms up to the order 10 and for pairs of forms up to the order 4. The system of the quintic contains 23 members.

While the finiteness of the system is assured, no general formula for the exact number of irreducible comitants is known.

29. *Ternary Forms.*—Many of the results stated for the binary case apply with little change to ultrabinary forms. There are, however, certain aspects of the general theory which are disguised when only the binary case is studied.

Consider a ternary form $f(x_1, x_2, x_3)$ of nth order. (The symbolic representation is a_x^n, where $a_x = a_1x_1 + a_2x_2 + a_3x_3$). If x_1, x_2, x_3 are taken as the homogeneous co-ordinates of a point in a plane, the equation $f = 0$ defines a curve of nth order. The vanishing of an invariant denotes a projective property of the curve. A covariant defines a curve which is projectively related to the original curve.

The principle of duality suggests the introduction of line co-ordinates u_1, u_2, u_3. When the x's undergo a linear transformation, the u's undergo another linear transformation, which is said to be *contragredient* to the first. A function involving the u's and having the invariant property is termed a *contravariant* of f. Geometrically it represents a curve considered as the envelope of its tangent lines. A *mixed* comitant is one involving both point co-ordinates and line co-ordinates; geometrically it defines a so-called *connex.*

The complete system of the ternary quadric $f = a_x^2$ consists of the covariant f, the invariant $D = (\alpha\beta\gamma)^2$, the contravariant $F = (\alpha\beta u)^2$, and the so-called identical form u_x. Here $(\alpha\beta\gamma)$ represents a determinant of third order $(\alpha_1\beta_2\gamma_3)$. Geometrically, $f = 0$ represents a conic considered as a point locus, $F = 0$ represents the same conic regarded as line envelope, and $D = 0$ denotes that the conic degenerates to a pair of straight lines.

30. *Quaternary Forms.*—Here the essentially new feature is that in addition to point co-ordinates (x_1, x_2, x_3, x_4) and the dual plane co-ordinates (u_1, u_2, u_3, u_4), it is necessary to consider line co-ordinates $(p_{12}, p_{13}, p_{14}, p_{34}, p_{42}, p_{23})$. Comitants may contain, besides the coefficients of the given form, any combination of these types of variables. Little advance has yet been made in the complete treatment of even the simpler cases.

31. Gordon's method for proving the existence of a complete system applies only to binary forms. The proof for forms of any kind (including multiple forms containing two or more sets of variables) was first given by Hilbert (1890). The basis of his method is the following theorem, which has many important applications:

In any assemblage containing an infinite number of forms it is possible to select a finite number of members $F_1, F_2, \ldots, F_r$ so that every member can be written $F = P_1F_1 + P_2F_2 + \ldots + P_rF_r$, where the P's are forms not belonging necessarily to the given assemblage.

Other Invariant Theories.

32. *Special Linear Transformations.*—Forms have been treated with respect to linear transformations of special type. Thus the transformations $x_1 = aX_1 + \beta$, $y_1 = aY_1$ lead to the so-called *seminvariants* of binary forms.

Again, the formulas for passing from one system of rectangular co-ordinates to another,

$$(5) \qquad x = X\cos\theta - Y\sin\theta + h, \quad y = X\sin\theta + Y\cos\theta + k,$$

constitute a special linear group. Invariants with respect to this group are termed Cartesian or metric or orthogonal. In the case of the conic $ax^2 + bxy + cy^2 + dx + ey + f = 0$, there are three such invariants, $a + c$, $b^2 - 4ac$, and the discriminant. The latter is the only one which is invariant in the projective theory.

If $a+c=0$, the conic is a rectangular hyperbola; if $b^2-4ac=0$, it is a parabola.

For any number of variables the linear transformations which leave a given quadric form unchanged constitute a type of group which arises in many applications (line and circle geometries, geometry on a quadric surface, etc.).

33. The general method of finding the invariants of any continuous group involving a finite number of parameters is due to Sophus Lie. An r parameter group is generated by r independent infinitesimal transformations; these determine a set of r partial differential equations whose solutions are the invariant functions.

34. A *differential invariant* is one that contains the derivatives of the variables. Thus for the group (5) the expression $\frac{y''}{(1+y'^2)^{\frac{3}{2}}}$ is a differential invariant. It represents in fact the curvature of an arbitrary curve at a point; this is obviously independent of the system of axes to which the curve is referred.

35. Special theories of invariants have been constructed in connection with *differential equations.* Thus an ordinary linear equation,

$$\frac{d^ny}{dx^n}+p_1(x)\frac{d^{n-1}y}{dx^{n-1}}+\ldots+p_n(x)=0,$$

is converted into an equation of the same kind by the substitution $x=\phi(X)$, $y=Y\psi(X)$. The totality of substitutions here forms an infinite continuous group, since ϕ and ψ are arbitrary functions. By an invariant of the equation is meant a function of the coefficients $p_1, p_2 \cdot$ and their derivatives, which retains its value (except perhaps for a factor depending on the transformation) when formed from the coefficients of the new equation.

36. *Differential Forms.*— In the theory of surfaces the distance between two consecutive points of the surface is given by the formula

$$ds^2=E(u,v)du^2+2F(u,v)\ du\ dv+G(u,v)dv^2.$$

The second member is a binary quadratic differential form. Such forms possess a theory of invariants with respect to arbitrary change of variables. Any change is expressed by $u=\phi(U,V)$, $v=\psi(U,V)$, where ϕ, ψ are arbitrary functions. The simplest example of an invariant is the expression, depending on E, F, G and their partial derivatives, which represents the Gaussian curvature.

37. *Arithmetical Theory of Forms.*— In this theory, inaugurated by Gauss, the coefficients and variables involved are supposed to be whole numbers. Attention has been confined mainly to the binary quadratic $ax^2+2bxy+cy^2$. The transformations are defined by $x=\alpha X+\beta Y$ $y=\gamma X+\delta Y$, where the coefficients $\alpha, \beta, \gamma, \delta$ are integers such that $\alpha\delta-\beta\gamma \neq 0$. In this case then, the group is discontinuous.

38. *Automorphic Functions.*— Such discontinuous groups arise also in the theory of functions. Thus in No. 7 it was seen that the trigonometric functions are unaltered by the substitutions $x=X+2k\pi$. Similarly, a doubly periodic function (of a complex variable) is invariant with respect to $z=Z+k_1w_1+k_2w_2$, where w_1, w_2 are the given periods and k_1, k_2 are arbitrary integers. The modular function is invariant with respect to the linear group $z=(\alpha Z+\beta)/(\gamma Z+\delta)$, where $\alpha, \beta, \gamma, \delta$ are integers such hat $\alpha\delta-\beta\gamma=1$. The problem of finding all functions which admit an infinite discontinuous group of linear transformations is one of the most important in recent investigation. Such functions are termed *automorphic.* They have been classified by Poincaré into Fuchsian and Kleinian according as the defining group involves real or complex coefficients.

Bibliography.—*Andoyer,* ‘Théorie des forms’ (Paris 1898); Boole, *Cambridge Journal of Mathematics* (Vol. III, 1841); Cayley, ‘Memoirs upon Quantics’ (1854–78), Collected Papers, Cambridge; Clebsch, ‘Théorie der binären algebraischen Formen’ (Leipzig 1872); Clebsch-Lindemann, ‘Vorlesungen über Geometrie’ (Vol. I, Leipzig 1875, new edition 1907); Elliott, ‘Algebra of Quantics’ (Oxford 1895); Gordan, ‘Vorlesungen über Invariantentheorie’ (2 vols., Leipzig 1885–87); Grace and Young, ‘Algebra of Invariants’ (Cambridge 1903); Hilbert ‘Mathematische Annalen’ (Vol. XXX, 1890); Meyer, ‘Bericht über die Fortschritte der projectiven Invariantentheorie, Berichte Deutsche Mathematiker-Vereinigung’ (Vol. I, 1892); Salmon, ‘Lessons introductory to the Modern Higher Algebra’ (Dublin, 1st ed., 1859, 4th ed., 1885); Study, ‘Methoden zur Theorie der ternären Formen’ (Leipzig 1889); Sylvester, ‘Calculus of Forms’ (1852–54), Collected Papers (Cambridge 1903).

EDWARD KASNER,

Professor in Mathematics, Columbia University.

INVASION, the entry into a country by a public enemy. As early as 1795 Congress provided by law for protection against the invasion of the United States by any foreign nation or Indian tribe. The act made it lawful whenever there should be an invasion, or imminent danger of one, for the President to call out such number of the militia of the State or States convenient to the place of invasion as he might think necessary to repel it. This, strengthened in some respects by amendments, has been in force ever since. An invasion has usually all the elements of war, and the invaders may be dealt with as persons at war with the country invaded, in accordance with usages of warfare without the declaration of war by Congress. The Supreme Court of the United States has decided that a State is invaded when there is a domestic rebellion within its territory, and that the same rules of law may be enforced as in the case of an invasion by external foes. This decision practically abolishes all distinction between invasion and insurrection, and the same rules which furnish a remedy for invasion can be applied in the suppression of an insurrection or local rebellion. In case the State militia is not sufficiently strong, or not easily available, the standing troops of the United States may be ordered out by the President, if indeed it be necessary to call upon the State troops before resorting to the regular troops of the United States. It is not necessary that actual armed violence shall be resorted to in order to constitute insurrection. Any combination of persons too powerful to be suppressed by the ordinary course of judicial proceedings is tantamount to insurrection, and warrants the use of the effective measures provided for by law for its suppression.

INVENTIONS. An invention is recognized to be any new or useful mechanical contrivance or article, method, discovery, composition of matter, or system not previously known or used, or any improvement on any known machine, art, method or system. Below is given in chronological order a list of important inventions and discoveries beginning with the 16th century, with the title of the invention, the year it was made, the name of the inventor and his nationality:

LIST OF PRINCIPAL INVENTIONS AND DISCOVERIES

Date	Invention or discovery	Inventor	Nationality
3d Cent. B.C.	Compound pulley and water screw	Archimedes	Greek
105 A.D.	Paper	Ts' ai Lun	Chinese
c.1450	Printing from movable type	Johann Gutenberg	German
1560-1603	Electricity and magnetism	William Gilbert	English
c.1581	Isochronism of the pendulum	Galileo Galilei	Italian
1589	Knitting machine	William Lee	English
1590	Compound microscope	Zacharias Janssen	Dutch
1593	Thermometer	Galileo Galilei	Italian
1609	Telescope (refracting)	Galileo Galilei	Italian
1620	Screw printing press	William J. Blaeu (Blaeuw)	Dutch
1621	Iron furnace (use of coke in smelting)	Dud Dudley	English
1630	Use of steam	David Ramseye	English
1630	Kepler's astronomical telescope	Constructed by Christopher Schriener	German
1636	Micrometer	William Gascoigne	English
c.1640	Mezzotint engraving	Ludwig von Siegen	German
1640	Bay Psalm Book, first book published in the American colonies	Printed by Stephen Daye	American
1642	Adding machine	Blaise Pascal	French
1643	Barometer	Evangelista Torricelli	Italian
1654	Air pump	Otto von Guericke	German
1656	Pendulum clock	Christian Huygens (Huyghens)	Dutch
1668	Telescope (reflecting)	Sir Isaac Newton	English
1669	Phosphorus	Hennig Brand (Brandt)	German
1671	Multiplying machine	G. W. von Leibnitz	German
1681	Machine for generating electricity	Otto von Guericke	German
1690	First steam engine with a piston	Denis Papin	French
1696	Discovery of difference between electric conductors and insulators	Stephen Gray	English
1698	First practical application of steam power for mechanical purpose	Thomas Savery	English
1700	Three-wheeled carriage propelled by steam	Richard Cugnot	French
1704	*Boston News Letter*, first newspaper in America	John Campbell	American
1705	First atmospheric pressure steam engine	Thomas Newcomen	English
1708	First to produce electric spark	Dr. J. Wall	English
1709-11	Piano and hammer action for piano	Bartollomeo Cristofori	Italian
1714	Typewriter	Henry Mill	English
1714	First use of mercury in thermometer	G. D. Fahrenheit	German
1717	Diving bell	Edmund Halley	English
1718	Electrometer (pith-ball)	John Cantor	English
1725	Stereotyping	William Ged	Scottish
1726	Gridiron pendulum	John Harrison	English
1727	Electrical plate glass machine	Martin de Planta	French
1729	First electric signal sent along a wire	Stephen Gray	English
1733	Flying shuttle	John Kay	English
1733-39	First to discover that electricity is of two kinds—positive and negative	Charles de Cisternay Du Fay	French
1740	Steel crucible process	Robert Huntsmand	English
1746	Leyden jar	John Bevis	English
1749	Marine chronometer	John Harrison	English
1752	Lightning rod experiments	Benjamin Franklin	American
1754	Heliometer	John Dollond	English
1756	Hydraulic cement	John Smeaton	English
1758	Achromatic lens	John Dollond	English
1760	Lightning conductor	Benjamin Franklin	American
1763-69	First motor-driven road carriage	Joseph Cugnot	French
1765	Steam engine (condensing)	James Watt	Scottish
1767	Spinning jenny	John Hargreaves	English
1769	Throttle spinning machine	Richard Arkwright	English
1769	Steam engine	James Watt	Scottish
1776	Submarine boat ("Bushnell's turtle")	David Bushnell	American
1777	Circular wood saw	Samuel Miller	English
1779	Spinning machine-mule jenny	Samuel Compton	English
1779	Discovery of elements uranium, titanium, zirconium	Martin Heinrich Klaproth	German
1780	Steel pen	Samuel Harrison	English
1780	Bifocal lens	Benjamin Franklin	American
1781	Compound steam engine	Jonathan C. Hornblower	English
1781	Double-acting steam engine	James Watt	Scottish
1783	Gas balloon	Joseph E. and Étienne M. Montgolfier	French
1783-84	Puddling iron furnace	Henry Cort	English
1784	Plow, with cast iron mold board, and wrought and cast iron shares	James Small	Scottish
1784	Embossed printing for the blind	Valentin Haüy	French
c.1784	Shrapnel shell	Henry Shrapnel	English
1785-88	First true water-tube boiler	James Rumsey	American
1785	Power loom	Edmund Cartwright	English
1785	Parachute	Francois Blanchard	French
1786	Threshing machine	Andrew Meikle	Scottish
1786	Nailmaking machine	Ezekiel Reed	American
1786-87	First steamboat trial in U.S.	John Fitch	American
1788	Drum threshing machine	Andrew Meikle	Scottish
1789	First motor driven road vehicle in America	Oliver Evans	American
1790	Machine for printing on linen	William Nicholson	English
1790	Machine for stitching; forerunner of sewing machine	Thomas Saint	English
c.1790	Machine for cutting nails	Jacob Perkins	American
1790-91	Soda from salt	Nicolas LeBlanc	French

LIST OF PRINCIPAL INVENTIONS AND DISCOVERIES—*Continued*

Date	Invention or discovery	Inventor	Nationality
1792	Gas used as an illuminant	William Murdoch	Scottish
1793-94	Cotton gin	Eli Whitney	American
1795	Hydraulic press	Joseph Bramah	English
1796	Lithography	Aloys Senefelder	Bohemian
1797	Cast iron plow	Charles Newbold	American
1797	Carding machine (improved)	Amos Whittemore	American
1800	Electric battery	Alessandro Volta	Italian
1800	High pressure steam engine	Richard Trevithick Oliver Evans (independently)	English American
1800	Discovered exhilarating effect of nitrous oxide when inhaled (anaesthesia)	Sir Humphry Davy	English
1801	Jacquard machine for figured-weaving	Joseph Marie Jacquard	French
1802	Photographic experiments	Thomas Wedgewood and Sir Humphry Davy	English
1802	Application of twin screw propellers in steam navigation	William Symmington	English
1803-04	Discovery of osmium and iridium	Smithson Tennant	English
1804	Rocket	Sir William Congreve	English
1804	Screw propeller	John C. Stevens	American
1804	Steam locomotive on rails	Richard Trevithick	English
1804-05	Canning of food	Nicolas Appert	French
1805	Life preserver	John Edwards	English
1805	Electroplating process	Luigi Brugnatelli	Italian
1807	Wood mortising machine	Marc I. Brunel	French
1807	Improved paper making machine	Henry and Sealy Fourdrinier with Bryan Donkin	English English
1807	Gas meter (wet)	S. Clegg	English
1807	Steamboat navigation on the Hudson River (the *Clermont*)	Robert Fulton	American
1808-10	Polarization of light	Étienne Louis Malus	French
1808	Barium, strontium and calcium metallic magnesium first prepared	Sir Humphry Davy	English
1808	Voltaic arc	Sir Humphry Davy	English
1808	First steamboat to make a trip to sea, (*Phoenix*)	John Stevens	American
1809	Law of combining volumes	J. L. Gay-Lussac	French
1810-11	Breech-loading rifle	John M. Hall	American
1810	Homeopathy introduced	Samuel Hahnemann	German
1811	Printing press (Steam)	Friedrich König	German
1812	Storage battery	J. B. Ritter	German
1814	First locomotive in Scotland	George Stephenson	English
1814	Percussion cap	Joshua Shaw	American
1815	Miner's safety lamp	Sir Humphry Davy	English
1815	Gas meter (dry)	S. Clegg	English
1815-19	Stethoscope	Réne T. H. Laënnec	French
1816	Knitting machine, circular	Marc I. Brunel	French
1816	Kaleidoscope	Sir David Brewster	English
1816	"Columbian" printing press	George E. Clymer	American
1817	Paper machine (cylinder)	Thomas Gilpen	American
1819	Cast iron plow (modern shape)	Jethro Wood	American
1819	Galvanometer	J. S. Schweigger	German
1819	Electromagnetism discovered	Henry C. Oersted	German
1820	Quinine	P. J. Pelletier and J. B. Caventou	French
1820	Hygrometer	John F. Daniell	English
1820	Calculating machine	Charles Babbage	English
1821	Theory of electro-dynamics first propounded	André Ampère	French
1822	Multicolor printing	Peter Force	American
1822	Discovery of thermoelectricity	T. J. Seebeck	German
1822	Power platen printing press	Daniel Treadwell	American
1822	Conversion of electric current into mechanical motion	Michael Faraday	English
1822	Early type setting machine (automatic)	William Church	American
1823	Liquefaction and solidification of gas	Michael Faraday	English
1823	Silicon	J. J. Berzelius	Swedish
1824	Portland cement	Joseph Aspdin	English
c.1824	Proved law to which all heat engines are subject	Nicholas Leonard S'Carnot	French
1824	Pinmaking machine	L. W. Wright	American
1825	First successful steam locomotive	George Stephenson	English
1825	Electromagnet	William Sturgeon	English
1826	Electrical spur wheel	Peter Barlow	English
1827	Muzzle-loading needle gun	Johann N. von Dreyse	German
1827	Law of electrical resistance	George S. Ohm	German
1827	Law of galvanic circuits	George S. Ohm	German
1827	Differential for road vehicles	Onésiphore Pecqueur	French
1827	Isolation of aluminum	Friedrich Wöhler	German
1827	Friction matches	John Walker	English
1827	Turbine (hydraulic)	Benôit Fourneyron	French
1828	Prism for polarized light	William Nicol	English
1828	Hot-air blast for iron furnaces	J. B. Neilson	Scottish
1829	Thermoelectric needle for determining internal bodily temperatures	Antoine C. Becquerel	French
1829	First steam locomotive to operate on a railroad in the U.S. (*Stourbridge Lion*)	Built in England for United States	English
1829	First American typewriting machine	W. A. Burt	American
1829	Braille Printing	Louis Braille	French
1830	Sewing machine	Barthelemy Thimonnier	French
1831	Flanged rail	Robert L. Stevens	American
1831	Electricity generated from magnetism	Michael Faraday Joseph Henry	English
1831	Chloroform	Samuel Guthrie	Scottish
1832	Locomotive *Old Ironsides*	Matthias W. Baldwin	American
1832	First conception of electric telegraph	Samuel F. B. Morse	American
1833	Adoption of steam whistle for locomotives	George Stephenson	English
1833	Gas meter (dry)	James Bogardus	American
1833-34	Reaper	Cyrus H. McCormick and Obed Hussey	American
1834	Discovery of aniline in coal tar	Friedlieb F. Runge	German
1834	Ice machine (compressor system)	Jacob Perkins	American
1835	Revolver	Samuel Colt	American
1836	First working model of telegraph	Samuel F. B. Morse	American
1836	Electric battery (Daniell's cell)	John F. Daniell	English
1836	Phosphorus matches manufactured in United States	Alonzo Dwight Phillips	American

LIST OF PRINCIPAL INVENTIONS AND DISCOVERIES—*Continued*

Date	Invention or discovery	Inventor	Nationality
1836-41	Introduction of screw propeller on commercial vessel	John Ericsson	Swedish
1837	Electric telegraph for sending messages patented	Sir Charles Wheatstone	English
1837	Electromagnet used in place of permanent magnet in dynamo	Charles G. Page	American
1838	First stereoscope	Sir Charles Wheatstone	English
1838	Steam hammer	James Nasmyth	Scottish
1838	Babbitt metal	Isaac Babbitt	American
1839	Photography (Daguerreotype)	Joseph N. Niepce, Louis Daguerre	French
1839	Ozone	Christian F. Schönbein	German
1839	First boat electrically propelled	M. H. Jacobi	German
1840-44	Telegraph perfected. First message sent 1844	Samuel F. B. Morse	American
1840	Making photo-prints from paper negatives	William Henry Fox Talbot	English
1840	Photographic portraits (Daguerreotype process)	Samuel F. B. Morse	American
1842	Ether as an anaesthetic	Crawford W. Long	American
1843	Typewriting machine patented	Charles Thurber	American
1844	Vulcanized rubber	Charles Goodyear	American
1844	The use of nitrous oxide gas as an anaesthetic	Dr. Horace Wells	American
1844	The electric arc light (gas retort carbon in a vacuum)	J. B. Foucault	French
1845	Automatic adjustment of electric arc light carbons	Thomas Wright	English
1845	Pneumatic tire	Robert W. Thompson	English
1846	Sewing machine (improved)	Elias Howe	American
1846	Guncotton	Christian F. Schönbein	German
1847	Regenerative steam engine	Sir William Siemens	German-English
1847	Rotary printing press	Richard M. Hoe	American
c.1847	Nitroglycerine	Ascanio Sobero	Italian
1847	Chloroform in surgery	Sir James Y. Simpson	Scottish
1848	Current generated by a dynamo used to excite its magnet	Jacob Brett	English
1849	Corliss engine	George H. Corliss	American
1849	Turbine, hydraulic	James B. Francis	American
1849	Watch making machinery, first factory-made watches	Aaron L. Dennison	American
1850	Mercerized cotton	John Mercer	English
1850-51	Electric locomotive	Charles G. Page	American
1851	Gordon printing press	George P. Gordon	American
1851	Refrigerating machine	John Gorrie	American
1851	Opthalmoscope	Hermann L. F. von Helmholtz	German
1851	Photography (collodion process)	Scott Archer	English
1852	Reticulated screen for half-tone photographic printing (instantaneous photography)	William H. F. Talbot	English
1852	Gyroscope	Jean B. Léon Foucault	French
1852	Airship	Henri Giffard	French
1853	Condensed milk	Gail Borden	American
1853	Laws of magneto-electric induction	Michael Faraday	English
1853	Duplex telegraph	Wilhelm J. Gintl	Austrian
1853	Laws of electrostatics	Michael Faraday	English
1853	Electrolysis	Michael Faraday	English
1854	Four-motion feed for sewing machines	Allen B. Wilson	American
1854	Magazine firearm	Horace Smith and Daniel Baird Wesson	American
1854	Dynamo-electric machine; (drum wound armature)	Werner von Siemens	German
1855	Safety matches	J. E. Lundstrom	Swedish
1855	Rubber dental plate	Charles Goodyear, Jr.	American
1855	Gas burner (Bunsen burner)	Robert Wilhelm Bunsen	German
1856	Aniline dyes	Sir William H. Perkin	English
1856	Printing machine for the blind (contains elements of the present typewriting machine)	Alfred E. Beach	American
1856	Furnace (improved regenerative)	Sir William Siemens	German
1856-57	Bessemer steel	William Kelly Sir Henry Bessemer	American English
1857	Electric fire-alarm telegraph	William F. Channing and Moses G. Farmer	American
1857	Shoe-sewing machine	Lyman R. Blake for George McKay	American
1858	Refrigerator	Ferdinand P. E. Carre	
1858	Feed injector for boilers	Henri Giffard	French
1858	Cable car	E. A. Gardner	American
1859	"Harrison steam boiler"	Joseph Harrison	American
1859-60	Prism spectroscope	Gustav R. Kirchhoff Robert W. Bunsen	German German
1859-60	Gas Engine (first practical internal combustion engine)	Jean Joseph Étienne Lenoir	French
1860	Cylinder lock	Linus Yale	American
1860	Linoleum	Frederick Walton	English
1860	Storage or secondary battery	Gaston Planté	French
1860	Electric lamp (carbonfilament)	Joseph W. Swan	English
1861	First described publicly an electrical telephone	Johann Philipp Reis	German
1861	Passenger elevator (steam)	Elisha G. Otis	American
1861	Motion picture projector	Coleman Sellers	American
1861	Electric furnace	Sir William Siemens	German
1862	Revolving turret for floating battery	Theodore Timby	American
c.1862	Smokeless powder	Johann F. E. Schultze	Prussian
1862	Gatling gun	Richard J. Gatling	American
1862-63	Sleeping car	T. T. Woodruff	American
1863	Railway block signals	Ashbel Welch	American
1863	Soda (from salt, ammonia and CO_2)	Ernest Solvay	Belgian
1864	Sleeping car (with folding upper berth)	George M. Pullman	American
1865	Bicycle	Pierre Lallement	French
1866	Dynamite	Alfred B. Nobel	Swedish
1866	Open-hearth steel process	Sir William Siemens	German
1866	Torpedo (self-propelled)	Robert Whitehead	English
1866	The Atlantic cable laid	Cyrus W. Field	American
1867	Dynamo electric machine	Sir William Siemens	German

LIST OF PRINCIPAL INVENTIONS AND DISCOVERIES—*Continued*

Date	Invention or discovery	Inventor	Nationality
1867	Dynamo electric machine	Sir Charles Wheatstone Henry Wilde (separately)	English English
1867	Reinforced concrete	Joseph Monier	French
1867-68	First practical typewriting machine	Christopher L. Sholes Carlos Glidden Samuel W. Soulé	American American American
1868	Automatic car coupler	Eli Hamilton Janney	American
1869	Antiseptic surgery	Sir Joseph Lister	English
1869	Railway air brake	George Westinghouse, Jr.	American
1870	Celluloid	John Wesley and Isaiah Hyatt	American
1870	Mowing machine with differential gear	Rudolf Eickemeyer	American
1871	Compressed air rock drill	S. Ingersoll	American
1871	The Goodyear welt shoe-sewing machine	Charles Goodyear	American
1871	Photographic gelatine bromide emulsion (basis of present rapid photography)	R. L. Maddox	English
1872	Dynamo-electric machine	Zenobe T. Gramme	Belgian
1873	Initial steps in color photography	Hermann W. Vogel	German
1873	Theory that light is an electrical phenomenon	James C. Maxwell	English
1873	Telegraph (quadruplex system)	Thomas A. Edison	American
1875	Electric searchlight	Henry Wilde	English
1875	Railway refrigerator car	G. F. Swift Co.	American
1876	First satisfactory web perfecting printing press	Andrew Campbell	American
1876	Telephone	Alexander Graham Bell	American
1876	Four-cycle gas engine (Otto motor)	Nikolaus August Otto	German
1876	Electric candle	Paul Jablochkov	Russian
1877	Glider	Otto Lilienthal	German
1877	Loose-contact telephone transmitter or microphone	Émile Berliner	American
1877	Phonograph	Thomas A. Edison	American
1878	Automatic grain binder	John F. Appleby	American
1878	Electric arc lighting	Charles F. Brush	American
1879	Cathode-ray tube	Sir William Crookes	English
1879	Cash register	James Ritty	American
1879	Incandescent light	Thomas A. Edison Sir Joseph Swann (independently)	American English
1880	Typhoid bacillus isolated	Karl J. Eberth and Robert Koch	German
1880	Evaporated milk	John B. Meyenberg	American
1881	Color photography	Frederick E. Ives	American
1882	Tuberculosis bacillus isolated	Robert Koch	German
1882	Hydrophobia bacillus isolated	Louis Pasteur	French
1883	Cholera bacillus isolated	Robert Koch	German
1883-84	Diphtheria bacillus isolated	Edwin Klebs F. A. J. Löffler	German German
1884	Motor car	Karl Benz	German
1884	Bicycle (modern type)	James Starley	English
1884	Bacillus of tetanus	Arthur Nicolaier	German
1884	Fountain pen perfected	Lewis E. Waterman	American
1884	Antipyrine	Ludwig Knorr	American
1884	Photographic roll films	William H. Walker	American
1884	Linotype	Ottmar Mergenthaler	German-American
1884	Artificial silk	Count Hilaire B. de Chardonnet	French
1884	Steam turbine (reaction type)	Sir Charles A. Parsons	English
1884	Manganese steel	Robert Hadfield	English
1885	Bordeaux mixture	Alexis Millardet	French
1885	Maxim recoil operated machine gun	Sir Hiram S. Maxim	American
1885	Automobile engine, (2-stroke)	Karl Benz	German
1885	Graphophone and dictaphone	Charles S. Tainter	American
1885	Gas mantle	Carl von Welsbach	Austrian
1886	Halftone engraving process	Frederick Eugene Ives	American
1887	Daimler engine for automobile	Gottlieb Daimler	German
1887	Gramophone	Émile Berliner	American
1887	Photography, roll-film	Hannibal Goodwin	American
1887	Monotype	Talbert Lanston	American
1887	Hertzian waves	Heinrich Hertz	German
1888	Recording adding machine	William Burroughs	American
1888	Pneumatic tire (developed independently)	John B. Dunlop	Irish
1888	Trolley car (practical system)	Frank J. Sprague	American
1888	"Kodak"	George Eastman	American
1888	Process for hardening the surface of steel ("Harvey Process")	Hayward A. Harvey	American
1888	System of polyphase electric current	Nikola Tesla	American
1889	Steam turbine (impulse type)	Carl G. P. de Laval	French
1892	Acetylene gas	Thomas L. Wilson	American
1892	Diesel engine	Rudolf Diesel	German
1892	Wireglass	Frank Shuman	American
1892	Viscose	Charles Frederick Cross E. J. Bevan	English English
1892	Electric motor (alternating current)	Nikola Tesla	American
1892	Vacuum bottle	James Dewar	English
1892	Coherer (for detecting "wireless" waves)	E. Branly	French
1893	Motion pictures (kinetoscope)	Thomas A. Edison	American
1894	Motion pictures (phantascope)	Charles F. Jenkins	American
1894	Color photography (ruled screen process)	John Joly	Irish
1895	Principle of the modern motion picture projector	Thomas Armat	American
1895	X-rays	Wilhelm K. von Roentgen	German
1895	Photoelectric cells	Julius Elster Hans F. Geitel	German German
1895	Gasoline automobile in United States	George Baldwin Selden	American
1895	Wireless telegraphy	Guglielmo Marconi	Italian
1896	Foundation laid of science of radio-activity i.e., emanation of penetrating rays from luminescent bodies	Henri Becquerel	French
1896	Phenomena known as Zeeman effect	Pieter Zeeman Hendrik A. Lorentz	Dutch Dutch
1897	Thermit process	Hans Goldschmidt	German
1897	Nernst Lamp (electric incandescent lamp)	Walther Nernst	German
1898	Submarine boat (first successful)	John P. Holland	American
1898	Photographic paper, sensitized	George Baekeland	American

LIST OF PRINCIPAL INVENTIONS AND DISCOVERIES—*Continued*

Date	Invention or discovery	Inventor	Nationality
1898	Radium discovered	Madam Marja S. Curie	French
1899	High speed steels	Frederick W. Taylor Maunsel White	American American
1900	Pupin coil which extended range of long-distance telephone	Michael I. Pupin	American
1900	Cellophane	J. E. Brandenberger	French
1900	Caterpillar tractor	Benjamin Holt	American
1900-01	Airship (rigid type)	Ferdinand von Zeppelin Alberto Santos-Dumont (independently)	German Brazilian
1901	Automobile mower	Deering Harvester Co.	American
1901	Took patent for synchronizing a motion picture projector with phonograph, first conceived by George W. Brown	Léon E. Gaumont	French
1902	Hydrogenation (catalytic)	Paul Sabatier	
1903?	Nickel storage battery	Thomas A. Edison	American
1903	Airplane	Wright Brothers (Orville and Wilbur)	American
1904	Electron tube (practical)	Sir John A. Fleming	English
1904	Photo transmission by wireless	Arthur Korn	German
1904	Automatic acceleration of railway motors	George Westinghouse	American
1905	Gyroscopic compass	Elmer A. Sperry	American
1905–16	Theory of relativity	Albert Einstein	German
1907	Three-electrode vacuum tube	Lee De Forest	American
1907	Plastic (Bakelite)	Leo H. Baekeland	American
1907	Color photography (Autochrome process)	Auguste and Louis J. Lumière	French
1909?	Maxim silencer for firearms	Hiram P. Maxim	American
1910?	Electric lamp (ductile tungsten filament)	William D. Coolidge	American
1911	Air conditioning	Willis H. Carrier	American
1911	Hydroplane	Glenn H. Curtiss	American
1911	Air-cooled gun	Isaac N. Lewis	American
1912	Flying boat (seaplane)	Glenn H. Curtiss	American
1912	Optophone	Edmund E. Fournier d'Albe	English
1912	Audion	Lee De Forest	American
1913	Electric light (gas filled tungsten)	Irving Langmuir	American
1913	Radio receiver (heterodyne)	Reginald A. Fessenden	Canadian
1913	Electron tube improvements	Irving Langmuir	American
1913	Radio receiver (cascade tuning)	Ernst F. W. Alexanderson	Swedish-American
1913	Talking motion pictures	Thomas A. Edison	American
1914	Liquefaction of coal (for producing gasoline)	Friedrich Bergius	German
1914?	Radio transmitter (triode modulation)	Ernst F. W. Alexanderson	Swedish-American
1914	Tank (military)	Gen. Ernest D. Swinton	English
1915?	Radio tube oscillator	Lee De Forest	American
1916?	X-ray tube	William D. Coolidge	American
1917	Submarine detector	Max Mason	American
1918	Protactinium discovered	Lise Meitner Otto Hahn	Austrian German
1919	First experiment in which the energy of an atomic nucleus was released	Ernest Rutherford	English
1920?	Development of classical quantum theory of atomic structure (Bohr theory)	Niels Bohr	Danish
1920?	Wilson cloud chamber	Charles T. R. Wilson	Scottish
1922?	Insulin (isolation)	Sir Frederick G. Banting Charles H. Best	Canadian Canadian
1923	Arc tube	Ernst F. W. Alexanderson	Swedish-American
1923	Iconoscope	Vladimir Zworykin	Russian-American
1925–26	Television	John L. Baird Charles F. Jenkins (independently)	Scottish American
1925	Phototelegraphy	Bell Telephone Laboratories	American
c.1926	Compton effect (change in wave length of scattered X-ray)	Arthur H. Compton	American
1926	Rocket (first liquid fuel)	Dr. Robert H. Goddard	American
1928	Autogiro	Juan de la Cierva	Spanish
1928	Electronic pickup tube (image dissector)	Philo Farnsworth	American
1928	Penicillin	Sir Alexander Fleming	English
1930?	Neoprene (based on discoveries by Julius A. Nieuwland)	Wallace H. Carothers	American
1930?	Discovery of heavy hydrogen	Harold Urey	American
1931	Cyclotron	Ernest O. Lawrence	American
1933?	Radio (wide-band frequency modulator)	Edwin H. Armstrong	American
1934?	Garand rifle	John C. Garand	American
1935?	Kendall's compound E (forerunner of cortisone)	Edward C. Kendall	American
1935	Radiolocator (Radar)	Sir Robert A. W. Watt	Scottish
1935	Prontosil (forerunner of sulfanilimide)	Gerhard Domagk	German
1935?	First pulse radars designed	Sir Robert A. W. Watt U.S. Army Signal Corps Laboratory British National Physical Laboratory	Scottish American English
1935	Cortisone	Edward C. Kendall and co-workers, Mayo Clinic	American
1937	Nylon	Wallace H. Carothers	American
1937?	Jet propulsion	Frank Whittle	English
1937?	Transuranium synthesized (element 93)	Enrico Fermi	Italian
1938	Fission of uranium	Lise Meitner Otto Hahn Fritz Strassman	Austrian German German
1939?	Dynamo (electric machine modulator)	Ernst F. W. Alexanderson	Swedish-American
1940?	Carried forward Sir Alexander Fleming's discovery of penicillin	Ernest B. Chain Sir Howard W. Florey	English English
1943?	Streptomycin	Selman A. Waksman	American
1943?	Bacitracin	Balbina Johnson Frank L. Meleney	American American
1945	Atomic bomb	World famous scientists under the direction of J.R. Oppenheimer	
1949	Acth	Armour Research Laboratories	American

INVENTORY, a detailed written schedule or list of chattels, goods, merchandise, debts, credits, lands, tenements, etc., made either for commercial purposes, or for legal proceedings, such as bankruptcy. It began in Roman law, under which the heir, on filing an inventory of the decedent's estate, was not liable for the latter's indebtedness beyond the sum which descended to him. In nearly all modern legal systems executors and administrators are obliged to make an inventory of the property in their charge in order to secure it to the persons entitled to it. Guardians and curators in some jurisdictions are obliged to file inventories of the estates held in trust by them for their wards.

INVERARAY, ĭn-vẽr-âr'ĭ, Scotland, royal and municipal burgh, capital of Argyllshire, situated on Loch Fyne, at the mouth of the Aray, 40 miles northwest of Glasgow. The town contains an obelisk in memory of the Campbells who were hanged here without trial in 1685, an ancient market cross and a church. Herring fishing is the principal industry. It became a burgh in 1472 and was made a royal burgh in 1648. Inveraray Castle nearby is the seat of the dukes of Argyll. Pop. (1940) 455.

INVERCARGILL, ĭn-vẽr-kär'gĭl, New Zealand, city, situated on New River, South Island, some 17 miles inland and 110 southwest of Dunedin. Owing to its proximity to Foveaux Strait, the town enjoys considerable maritime prestige. It has three outlying towns on the Bluff, called North Invercargill, South Invercargill and East Invercargill. It is situated in a rich agricultural district, has manufactures of woolens and flour and saw mills. Pop. including suburbs (1941 est.) 26,400.

INVERCHAPEL, Baron (Sir Archibald Clark Kerr), British diplomat: b. London, March 17, 1882; d. Greenock, Scotland, July 5, 1951. Educated by private tutors, he entered the diplomatic service in 1906. After four years in the Berlin embassy, where he attained the rank of third secretary, he was transferred to Buenos Aires in 1910 and a year later to Washington. His appointment in 1913 as British secretary to the British and American Claims Arbitration Tribunal took him to Rome. Four months after the outbreak of World War I he was gazetted to the legation at Teheran and by 1916 had full charge of the legation's commercial affairs. In November of that year he persuaded the Foreign Office to allow him to enlist and, a member of one of the proudest old Scottish families, served as a private in the Scots Guards for the remainder of the war. After hostilities ended he resumed his career with appointment as British agent at Tangier. In December of the latter year he became minister to Guatemala, from which he transferred to Santiago, Chile, in 1928. From 1931 to 1935 he represented His Majesty's government in Sweden, and during the succeeding three years was ambassador to Iraq at Baghdad. His assignment as ambassador to China in 1938 proved the confidence of the Foreign Office in his skill as a negotiator; for it occurred at a time when Japan was attempting the conquest of China, and Britain, faced by imminent war with Germany for which she was utterly unprepared, realized the danger of becoming embroiled in another war in the Orient. Kerr's activities were consistently pro-Chinese, yet he was forced to follow conciliatory tactics with Japan. In 1941, at Chungking, his home was destroyed and the British embassy badly damaged by Japanese bombing. In January 1942, appointed ambassador to Moscow, he succeeded Sir Stafford Cripps, and the following month left for his new post. He attended the Yalta Conference in February 1945 and the Big Three Foreign Ministers meeting at Moscow in October. Ordered to Java in January 1946 to endeavor to find a solution to the Netherlands-Indonesian dispute, in the same month he was appointed ambassador at Washington. After conferences with Indonesian Premier Sjahrir and Governor General van Mook he returned to London. Knighted in 1935, he became a baron in January 1946 and in April took the title Baron Inverchapel of Loch Eck, Argyllshire. On June 5 Lord Inverchapel presented his ambassadorial credentials to President Truman. He was succeeded by Oliver Shewell Franks on Feb. 12, 1948.

INVERNESS, ĭn-vẽr-nĕs', Canada, town of Inverness County, Nova Scotia, on the Canadian National Railway and on the Gulf Shore, 150 miles from Sydney, amid picturesque scenery. It has a fine bathing beach, and is a coal-mining center. Gypsum and fire clay are found nearby. Pop. (1940 est.) 2,975.

INVERNESS, Scotland, a royal, municipal, police burgh, capital of the county of Inverness-shire (q.v.) and chief town of the Highlands, situated at the mouth of the river Ness. It is on the Highland Railway, 109 miles west-northwest of Aberdeen. Its setting is picturesque, among cultivated fields and woodlands framed with mountains and hills. Inverness is a very ancient town, and was one of the Pictish capitals. It has a quite modern appearance with wide streets, beautiful suburbs and fine villas. The first charters of Inverness as a burgh were granted by King William the Lion. In 1411 the town was burned by Donald, lord of the Isles, on his way to the Battle of Harlow and in 1427 a parliament was held here by James I. In High Street stands the famous town cross and the Clach-na-cuddin, an ancient stone. In the same street are the town hall and the exchange. The town contains the Raining's School, a royal academy, Saint Andrew's Cathedral, a public library, infirmary, asylum and observatory. The industrial establishments comprise shipyards, woolen factories, foundries, tanneries, soap works, railway shops, saw mills, thread mills, etc. There is a considerable coasting trade. Pop. (1940 est.) 22,583.

INVERNESS-SHIRE, Scotland, the largest county of the kingdom, includes Badenoch, Glenroy, and the valley of the Spey on the east, Lochaber on the south, Glenelg, Glen Garry, Arisaig, Moydart and Frazers County on the west, Glen Urquhart and Glen Morriston toward the center. It includes also Strathglass on the north; and several of the western islands, viz., Skye, Harris, North and South Uist, and Barra, Eigg, etc. The mainland portion is bounded on the east by Aberdeen, Banff, Moray, and Nairn, west by the Atlantic and Ross, north by Ross and Cromarty and south by Perth and Argyll. Its area is 4,211 square miles, of which more than two thirds consist of barren heath. The wildest and most mountainous portion is toward the west, comprising a tract 70 miles in extent, designated the "Rough Bounds." The most extensive moss in Great Britain lies on the south of Badenoch, where, in the naturally formed wooded islands, large herds of deer find a refuge. The natural pines occupy a larger space than in any other county of Britain. Some mountains attain considerable height. Ben Nevis is 4,406 feet above sea-level and Cairngorm is over 4,000. The geological formation is various; but primary rocks consisting of gneiss, mica-slate, granite, porphyry, and trap rocks prevail. The most fertile soil of the county rests on the red sandstone in the valley of the Aird, and between the county town and Beauly. There are several lakes, as Loch Ness, Loch Lochy, Loch Laggan, Loch Ericht, etc. The principal rivers are the Spey, Lochy, Beauly, Findhorn, Nairn, Ness, Garry, Morriston and the Foyers. The land belongs to about 80 or 90 proprietors. The battle which decided the fate of the Stuarts was fought April 16, 1746, on Culloden Moor, a few miles from Inverness. The Gaelic language is spoken generally. Inverness is the only town. Pop. (1940 est.) 81,000.

In the literature concerning Scottish legend and history Inverness-shire occupies a considerable place; to the story of the Bruce and to the romance of 1745 it affords background. In Sir Walter Scott's poetry, *The Lord of the Isles,* and in his prose, *Legend of Montrose,* may be specially noted, while his diary of a yachting tour has much about the island parts of the country. These same islands inspired the famous anonymous poem, *From the Lone Shieling,* and much about them and the mainland will be found in Dr. Samuel Johnson's *A Journey to the Western Highlands of Scotland.* Robert Burns' associations are recorded in his song on *The Lovely Lass of Inverness.*

INVERSION, a change of order whereby the first becomes last and the last first. (1) In rhetoric, a reversal of the natural order of words for the sake of euphony, emphasis or the like; also the turning of one's own argument against him by an opponent in discussion. (2) In chemistry, a change in molecular structure which is usually induced by fermentation or by heating with a dilute acid, as in the case of starch, sugar, etc. Thus starch and dextrine are changed into glucose, cane sugar into invert sugar, and maltose into glucose. (3) In geology, the overturning or folding over of strata by igneous agency, so that the order of their succession seems reversed. (4) In mathematics, the operation of changing the order of the terms, so that the antecedent shall take the place of the consequent and the reverse, in both couplets. Thus, from the proportion $a : b :: c : d$, we have, by inversion, $b : a :: d : c$. (5) In music, the transposition of certain phrases having a common root. (*a*) The change of a chord by making one of the inner notes act as a bass note, by which means as many inversions can be made as there are actual notes in the chord, not counting the root, the harmony in such inversions remaining the same, though the order of component parts is changed; (*b*) alteration of intervals by making that which was the upper note the lower, and the reverse, the inversion of an interval within the octave being readily found in the difference between the figure 9 and the interval known; (*c*) the alteration of a subject produced by inverting the intervals of which it consists.

INVERTASE, or INVERTIN, an enzyme occurring in many fungi, notably in certain yeasts (for example, the saccharomyces), and also in the seed-plants. It transforms cane-sugar into a mixture of dextrose and levulose; this mixture being called invert-sugar because it turns the plane of polarized light to the left, while the cane-sugar from which it is obtained turns it to the right. According to some writers, a yeast cannot invert cane-sugar except by secreting invertase; but *Monilia candida* effects the inversion, and yet produces no invertase. In this case the action is probably due to some other enzyme, hitherto unidentified. Invertase probably plays a very important part in vegetable chemistry. Like other enzymes, it can apparently perform an unlimited amount of chemical work, without sensible diminution of its own substance. Invertase is most active at a temperature of from 120° to 140°F., and in a slightly acid medium. It has been isolated in the form of a powder. See FERMENTATION.

INVERTEBRATES, a collective term for those divisions or phyla of the animal kingdom that lack a vertebral column (backbone) or the forerunner of the backbone, the notochord, used to contrast with the highest phylum of the animal kingdom, the Chordata, that possess either a vertebral column (the vertebrates) or a notochord or both. The distinction between invertebrates without an internal skeleton of cartilage or bone and the vertebrates with such a skeleton was first recognized by Jean Baptiste Lamarck about 1800, but many years elapsed before certain groups of animals without such a skeleton were recognized as possessing a notochord and hence were alligned with the vertebrates to make the phylum Chordata. The name Invertebrata is not used as a taxonomic category because the invertebrates comprise some 20 phyla, each of which is coordinate with the phylum Chordata, and because these phyla show no close relationship to each other, but the term "invertebrates" is in constant use among zoologists in the collective sense mentioned.

INVESTIGATION, Criminal. Criminal investigation is today a field, separate and distinct, with its own specialized methods and techniques. The vital importance of crime to the national life, during the past quarter century, has necessitated the development of investigative techniques which could make available evidence to identify the guilty and to exonerate the falsely accused.

The field of criminal investigation in America has been shaped by the democratic tradition of the nation. The law enforcement officer, in investigating crimes, must locate evidence which can be introduced in a court of law. He must conquer the criminal by superior investigative ability and techniques, operating at all times within the realm of the law. The rights of every individual, even of the criminal himself, must be scrupulously observed. The peace officer's powers are limited, defined and continually scrutinized by the courts.

The judicial system of the United States, likewise, has affected the techniques of modern day criminal investigations. The law enforcement officer is the investigator, not the prosecutor. He does not, on his own initiative, authorize or decline prosecution, express recommendations or make evaluations. This duty belongs to the prosecutor who, if the case goes to trial, will present in court the evidence secured by the investigator. The investigating officer, of course, may testify in court—not concerning his personal opinions or feelings, but the facts as determined through his inquiries. These requirements demand that the criminal investigation be impartial and objective, the facts obtained without color or bias.

Criminal investigation, of course, is a separate field only in reference to the development of specialized standards and a professional code of conduct. In reality, the investigation of crime is closely related to, and dependent on, many fields of human endeavor. The criminal, in preying on society, touches many phases of life. He is, unfortunately, universal in nature, appearing, in some shape or form, in practically every profession or occupation. Law enforcement, in order to meet his challenge, must combat him on his own ground. If the thief, for example, has utilized an acetylene torch in a burglary, law enforcement must familiarize itself with acetylene torches—this process might provide valuable clues. Or in other instances the investigating officer might be required to learn something about the manufacture and packaging of shoes, the mining of copper, the manufacture of steel, the building of model trains. Wherever the criminal operates, law enforcement too must operate—and draw fully upon the knowledge and technical know-how of the component elements of society.

Science.—In its many ramifications, science has become an integral part of criminal investigative work. Metallurgy, toxicology, serology, firearms identification, hairs and fibers, petrography, document examination, spectrography: these facets of science are rendering yeoman service, day after day, to criminal investigators. A scrap of paper, a broken lead pencil, a chip of paint, a tangled thread—these items, under the enlightening glow of science, may reveal the clue which will solve the case. Science gives precision, objectivity and perspective to the peace officer.

The FBI Laboratory, for example, examines each year thousands of pieces of evidence for America's law enforcement agencies. The Laboratory, which is equipped with the latest scientific instruments, is staffed with highly trained technicians, each an expert in his particular field. Science today is highly specialized. For law enforcement to benefit, directly and indirectly, from every aspect of science, expert technicians must be used. Specimens range from bicycles to baby carriages, specks of dirt to fraudulent checks, a rusty firearm to a poison pill. The entire sweep of scientific knowledge, a sweep which each year is becoming greater, is being brought to bear in behalf of the scientific investigator.

The impact of science upon criminal investigations may be illustrated by citing a few specific examples:

The analysis of body fluids (serology) is an important adjunct of the investigation of crimes, such as murder, assault and hit-and-run accidents. The most frequent examination of this type is to determine the presence of blood. If blood is confirmed, additional tests are run to ascertain whether the blood is human or animal. If animal, the type of animal can be determined through the use of sera prepared in the FBI Laboratory. On the other hand, if the blood is human, the technician can determine the blood group of the person from whom the blood came. A suspect may claim, in reference to stains on his clothes, that they are bloodstains of a dog or some other animal or that they came from his own blood, resulting from a nosebleed or an injury. These chemical analyses, though not providing a positive means of identification, help substantiate or disprove alibis advanced by the suspects.

Another application is in the field of petrography, which includes the study of crystalline substances, soils, and minerals. The Laboratory expert, through the use of the petrographic microscope, which utilizes polarized light, is able to examine soil samples, identify their contents, and compare them with other samples obtained at the scene of the crime or elsewhere in the course of the investigation. The examination of dirt adhering to a suspect's shoes or in his trouser cuffs may be helpful in disproving or verifying an account of his whereabouts at a particular time, or in furnishing circumstantial evidence indicating that the suspect had been at the scene of a crime. Likewise, examination of a suspect's or victim's clothing may reveal the presence of mineral matter or industrial dust, which, upon analysis, may furnish data regarding his occupation or environment.

Science has enabled the criminal investigator, for example, to make dyes, which are associated with many objects of everyday life, such as clothing, plastics, wood, and inks into firm and dependable allies. The FBI Laboratory analyzes dyes by means of a spectrophotometer. This instrument, which allows the various colors of the spectrum to pass, one at a time, through the dye, which has been placed in solution, records in graph form the special characteristics of the dye. These graphs serve as ready references to identify dyes submitted in the future to the Laboratory.

In still another aspect of criminal investigation, that is, the analysis of documents, science has come to the aid of the law enforcement officer. The altering, forging and illicit issuance of checks represent today a major problem for every police department in the nation. The FBI Laboratory is able, through various chemical and mechanical devices, to identify a great percentage of the fraudulent checks which are submitted. Ultraviolet light brings forth erasures. Latent fingerprints can be developed, and through the operation of the National Fraudulent Check File numerous professional confidence men can be identified. This file, which contains many thousands of fraudulent checks, is composed of a number of sections. Checks are filed according to the method of preparation, for example, by handwriting, hand printing, and mechanical methods of preparation, such as typewriting and checkwriting. Each fraudulent check received is searched through the appropriate section of this file. If an identification is made the submitting agency will be furnished not only with background information about the individual involved, but also, if available, his arrest record and photograph. In many instances the subject is already in custody, and the contributor will then be informed as to the individual's location. If the fraudulent check cannot be identified, a photographic copy is placed in the file for comparison with other checks subsequently submitted for examination.

The National Fraudulent Check File is illustrative of the role which standard comparison files today play in criminal investigative work. These files contain specimens of known standards which are used for comparison with unknown material submitted. Time after time, through these comparisons, identifications are effected. The FBI Laboratory, for instance, maintains such files, among others, as the Rubber Stamp File, Paper Watermark File, National Automotive Paint File, Shoe Print File, and Tire Tread File.

In the Tire Tread File the FBI Laboratory has attempted to keep currently on hand the blueprint specifications of tread and side-wall designs produced by tire manufacturers throughout the country. An investigating officer who finds what appears to be a significant tire tread at the scene of a crime can photograph it, make a sketch drawn to scale, and then make a plaster cast of it. When these are sent to the FBI Laboratory, examiners can frequently identify the tread as a particular brand and give the contributor valuable investigative information as to the size, brand, manufacturer and distributor of the tire which made the questionable tread. The identification can be made more readily from a good plaster cast than from photographs or sketches; and a good photograph is, of course, better than a sketch. The FBI's Tire Tread File also contains retread and recap designs currently in use. Although any design may be reproduced in recap or retread work, it is still frequently possible in the Laboratory to tell whether a print was made by a recapped or retreaded tire. Moreover, many retreading and recapping companies develop original designs, some of which are peculiar to certain localities and readily identifiable.

Science admittedly has greatly affected criminal investigations. However, the significance of science must be gauged, not in the past, but in the future. In the years ahead science, with ever increasing speed and accuracy, will tear away the shrouds of darkness, doubt and uncertainty. The unsolved case of today will become, with the aid of science, the solved case of tomorrow. The law enforcement officer, to keep abreast of the criminal, must constantly utilize the latest developments of science.

The FBI Laboratory, in this connection, is carrying on research programs designed to elicit new scientific applications and techniques. The latest scientific equipment is being brought to bear on investigative work. For example, the assistance rendered to scientific crime detection by the FBI Laboratory has recently been immeasurably increased through the operation of the electron microscope. This instrument, which has ten times the magnification of a high power light microscope, has enabled the FBI Laboratory to make examinations of evidence which previously had been impossible.

The electron microscope embodies an entirely new approach in the field of magnification. The use of light waves and glass lenses, necessary requirements of the ordinary microscope, are eliminated in favor of electrons, operating in a vacuum and passing through magnetic lenses. This process enables the FBI Laboratory to obtain magnifications of approximately 22,000 times, which may be increased, by use of photographic enlargements, to 100,000 times. The examiner, thereby, is capable of making a more detailed and exhaustive analysis.

The FBI Laboratory is able through the electron microscope, not only to examine more closely and extensively specimens of evidence but, by means of an electron diffraction attachment, to determine the identity of very minute unknown substances submitted for examination. The diffraction attachment creates a diffraction pattern, similar in appearance to a series of concentric circles, which, when studied, reveals the nature of the substance in question. This feature of the electron microscope will make available to law enforcement officers investigative clues previously inaccessible to them.

The electron microscope is symbolic of what science can do for law enforcement. This instrument, though only in its infancy as applied to criminal investigations, offers unlimited possibilities.

Fingerprints.—For many years fingerprints have played an invaluable role in criminal investigative work. Man for centuries has utilized various systems of identification, such as branding, tattooing, distinctive clothing, photography and body measurement (Bertillon system). These systems, without exception, have not produced completely desirable results. Only fingerprinting, of all the methods of identification, has proved to be both infallible and feasible.

The science of fingerprinting for identification purposes is based upon distinctive ridge outlines which appear on the bulb on the inside of the end joint of the fingers and thumbs. These ridges have a definite contour and appear in several general pattern types, each with general and specific variation of not only the pattern but also the size and thickness of the ridges and the size and spacing of the pores. The outlines of these ridges appear most clearly when inked impressions are taken upon paper, so that the ridges are black against a white background, caused by the failure of the ink to fill the depressions between the ridges. Impressions may also be made with blood, dirt or the greasy substance emitted by the sweat glands through the ducts or pores which constitute their outlets. The background or medium may be paper, glass, porcelain, wood, wax, putty, silverware, or any smooth, nonporous material.

Criminal identification by means of fingerprints is one of the most potent factors in obtaining the apprehension of fugitives who might otherwise escape arrest and continue their criminal activities indefinitely. The peace officer is enabled not only to locate dangerous and badly wanted criminals, but to secure complete and accurate information about a prisoner's previous criminal history and to solve cases which previously had baffled the best investigative techniques.

The FBI's Identification Division, founded in 1924, possesses the largest collection of fingerprints in the world. At present over 114,000,000 fingerprint cards are on file. They are divided into the criminal and noncriminal files. The criminal files contain roughly 19,000,000 sets of prints, representing over eight million individuals. The non-criminal, or civil identification files, account for more than 80 per cent of the fingerprints. They contain the fingerprints of members of the armed forces, government employees, individuals who were fingerprinted while applying for jobs in defense plants during World War II, and persons who voluntarily have had their fingerprints recorded as a permanent means of identification. This latter group includes private citizens, club members, Boy Scouts, and others interested in the science of fingerprinting.

The Identification Division of the FBI has

steadily increased in size and effectiveness over the years. In 1924, at the time of its founding, the Identification Division consisted of 810,188 fingerprint cards. These cards represented a consolidation of the fingerprint collections of the National Bureau of Criminal Identification, sponsored by the International Association of Chiefs of Police, and the Leavenworth Penitentiary Bureau. In its first year of existence, the Identification Division received and handled 104,660 fingerprint cards, a daily average of less than five hundred. By the end of the 1942 fiscal year, fingerprint cards were coming in at the rate of over 114,000 a day and the total number on hand rocketed to nearly 43,000,000. The peak year for the Identification Division was 1943, when a total of 28,733,286 fingerprint cards was received. This great avalanche of cards resulted from the wartime activities of the nation. In the 1949 fiscal year, a total of 3,508,480 cards, or a daily average of 13,867, was received.

The effectiveness of the Identification Division has increased with the volume. In the 1925 fiscal year, when less than a million prints were on file and fewer than five hundred records a day were being received, 22.4 per cent of all arrest fingerprint cards received were identified. In 1949, with over 112,000,000 prints on file, this percentage had risen to 73.68.

Fingerprints, day after day, are performing feats of accomplishment for the peace officer. A set of fingerprints received by the Identification Division in the morning may result in the apprehension of a fugitive before nightfall. In February 1950, for example, the Identification Division identified 841 fugitives and maintained notices in its files on a total of 82,893 wanted persons.

The Identification Division serves as a national clearinghouse for fingerprints in the United States. In addition, through the international exchange of fingerprints criminals who have fled across national boundaries can be identified and located. The FBI in the 1949 fiscal year maintained an exchange service with 79 foreign countries and territorial possessions. A total of 13,975 fingerprint records were exchanged. The FBI succeeded in identifying, with previous records, 23.89 per cent of the fingerprint cards received from outside the country. Approximately eleven (10.75) per cent of those transmitted from this country were identified by the recipients with records previously on file.

Fingerprints serve, in addition to their criminal functions, many humanitarian purposes. For example, they aid in the location of missing persons, frequently absent from their homes for many years; the identification of amnesia victims; identification of mutilated bodies of servicemen killed in action and unidentifiable by any other means; the determination of the identities of victims, otherwise unidentifiable, of airplane crashes, railroad wrecks, or disasters by fire, explosion and accident.

Personnel Training.—Criminal investigations, in the final analysis, depend upon the men who perform them. The latest scientific equipment can be available, the most complete system of records in operation, but unless the employees in every position—administrator, supervisor, investigating officer—possess technical know-how and training, the quality of investigations will be low. The training of the criminal investigator, in present day law enforcement, is an item of the most extreme importance.

Law enforcement, unlike that of 25 years ago, is today a profession which must handle many complicated and involved problems. The peace officer often is required, with but a few seconds' notice, to conduct a crime scene search, perhaps at the site of a murder, the hideout of a bank robber, or at the locale of an extortion payoff. He must be able to handle, with dispatch and precision, the problem at hand. The evidence, an hour, even ten minutes later, may be moved or destroyed. Witnesses will have disappeared. The law enforcement officer must possess thorough training in criminal investigative techniques, training which he can apply instantly and efficiently.

Trained law enforcement personnel is vital, not only for the solution of criminal cases, but for the protection of the general public. The peace officer, among many other things, must be meticulously schooled in the use and maintenance of firearms. He carries a hand weapon. This gun, in untrained hands, can wreak terrific damage on innocent individuals. The law enforcement officer must know safety precautions, the correct way to shoot the weapon, where and in what cases to fire. Indiscriminate and irresponsible gunfire by law enforcement is indefensible. The trained officer will use the weapon, and other features of law enforcement, with a very minimum of risk, for the protection of society.

Every efficient, up-to-date law enforcement agency will have, in some form or other, personnel training programs. New recruits must be taught the rudiments of law enforcement; experienced officers must keep abreast of new developments. Training classes enable the group to share and benefit by the experiences of others; to learn the proper methods of handling scientific equipment; to know in what ways other law enforcement agencies and officers can assist. The successful criminal investigator blends individual initiative and skill with group knowledge and technical know-how.

The FBI, for example, conducts a 14-week training school for new Agents. These men, before they are assigned to actual investigative work in the field, learn the correct techniques and methods of operation: firearms, crime scene searches, fingerprints, laboratory work, mechanics of arrest, report writing. They are given both classroom instruction and practical demonstration work. The training classes are designed to equip them to meet the actual problems which they will encounter in investigative cases. When these Agents leave the school, however, their training does not stop. Approximately every two years they return to Washington, D. C., for a two-week refresher course, where they are acquainted with the most recent developments in law enforcement work. In between these in-service training classes the Agents are given training at regular intervals in their offices of assignment.

The FBI, through the FBI National Academy, has attempted to assist in the training of local police officers. This school, founded in 1935, is designed to train selected peace officers to be police instructors and executives. These men are given a twelve-week training course, which includes instruction in such subjects as traffic control, police organization and administration, investigative techniques, firearms, the operation of police laboratories, and fingerprints. The final two weeks are devoted to specialized topics which afford the individual officer an opportunity to study particular fields most applicable to his department. There is no charge for the training by the FBI. The student must pay only for his travel and personal living expenses while in Washington, D. C.

In addition, the FBI, in 1949, participated in 2,509 local police training schools. These schools provide, on a local basis, training of the type offered in the National Academy to law enforcement officers throughout the nation. The initiative in setting up schools is taken by the local agencies and the FBI participates only upon specific request. Normally most of the instruction is given by FBI Agents and FBI National Academy graduates.

To perfect a new technique of criminal investigation is not enough. This information must be transmitted to the rank and file of law enforcement. The success of criminal investigations is dependent on the investigating peace officer making science, fingerprints, and other techniques work for him. And to accomplish this, to translate theoretical knowledge into practical application, is the work and responsibility of the training program.

Each criminal case presents different problems. The key of solution in one case, perhaps fingerprints, document examination, firearms identification, spectrographic analysis, will not necessarily solve another case. Crimes may appear, from original observation, to be identical, but, almost invariably, intensive investigation will reveal that they are different, usually much different. The same criminal, or gang, specializing in a particular type of violation, will approach the problem differently, leave different clues, make dissimilar getaways. A murder, to the criminal investigator, is not a murder to be investigated like all other murders. The officer, drawing from general principles of investigative procedure, must, in each instance, apply the key which appears most likely to solve the case.

The criminal investigator has today at his disposal powerful weapons of crime detection. Each day his abilities, through development of new techniques, are being increased. But in the final analysis the esprit de corps of the investigator, the will to do the job, is the most potent tool in the hands of law enforcement. The very best tools, handled by the half-hearted officer, become rusty and dull. The alert investigator, even with inadequate equipment, can do good work. Capable personnel supplied with adequate working tools—this is the only way the quality of criminal investigations can be maintained at a consistently high level.

J. Edgar Hoover,
Director, Federal Bureau of Investigation.

INVESTITURE, the act of investment implying the right to give possession of an office, honor, benefice or manor. In the mediaeval or feudal law, it was the open delivery of a feud or a right to lands and hereditaments, by a lord to his vassal, thus, by external proof, affording evidence of proprietorship. To use the words of Blackstone, "Investitures, in their original rise, were probably intended to demonstrate, in conquered countries, the actual possession of the lord, and that he did not grant a bare litigious right, but a peaceable and firm possession. At a time when writing was seldom practised, a mere oral gift, at a distance from the spot that was given, was not likely to be long or accurately retained in the memory of by-standers, who were very little interested in the grant." For this reason investiture was performed by the presentation of some symbol to the person invested, as a branch of a tree, etc. In the primitive church, after the election of a bishop, and his consecration, the early Christian emperors claimed a right of confirmation. Charlemagne is said to have introduced this practice, and to have invested the newly consecrated bishop by placing a ring and crozier in his hands.

The custom, however, existed, nor does it appear to have been objected to or opposed during the lapse of two centuries from his reign. The disorderly state of Italy, which succeeded the death of Charlemagne, frequently interrupted the exercise of this right by the Carlovingians; but even so late as 1047, when the empire had passed to another line, Henry III received an explicit admission of his prerogative, and repeatedly used it. The investiture in the lesser sees followed as a matter of course. Alexander II issued a decree against lay investiture in general, which was revived by Gregory VII (Hildebrand), who, having succeeded in annulling the prerogative of the emperors to nominate or confirm popes, sought to disjoin entirely the ecclesiastical from the civil rule. It was not, however, until the papacy of Calixtus II, in 1122, that the question was terminated, as it appears, materially to the advantage of the Holy See. In France, even under the papacy of Hildebrand, the right of investiture does not appear to have been made a subject of open quarrel. In spite of the protests of the Holy See, the kings exercised the power, but at length relinquished the presentation of the ring and crozier, and contented themselves with conferring investiture by a written instrument, or orally, upon which they were left in peaceable possession of the power. But in England Paschal II was engaged in a contest little less fierce than that which he maintained with the emperor. Anselm, the primate, refused to do homage to Henry I for his see. The king seems to have asserted an unqualified right of investiture, which the pope, who was appealed to, as unqualifiedly denied. After a protracted struggle, and continued threats of excommunication, the controversy ended in England, as it did afterward in Germany, by compromise. Paschal offered to concede the objections against homage provided Henry would forego the ceremony of investiture. To this he agreed (1107).

INVESTMENT BANKERS ASSOCIATION. See Banks and Banking—*Bankers' Associations in the United States.*

INVESTMENT BANKS AND BANKING. See Banks and Banking—*Investment Banking.*

INVINCIBLES, an Irish secret society of 1882, an off-shoot of the Fenians (q.v.). One of the objects of the Invincibles was to "remove" or assassinate government officers or others who might incur the displeasure of the association or its leaders. On May 6, 1882 the society succeeded in "removing" Lord Frederick Cavendish, who had just arrived from England as Secretary for Ireland, and Thomas A. Burke, the under-secretary, in the Phoenix Park at Dublin. The plot was directed against the latter, and the former, attempting to protect his friend, shared his fate. On Feb. 20, 1883, 20 persons charged with complicity in the murders were brought to trial; 5 were condemned to death, and the others received prison sentences. The chief witness for the prosecution, who revealed all the secrets of his fellow conspirators, was James Carey. He was shot dead on board ship near Natal, on July 29, 1883, by Patrick O'Donnell, who was subsequently tried and executed for his crime.

INVISIBLE GLASS. See GLASS, NON-REFLECTING; GLASS, VARIETIES OF—*Invisible Glass.*

INVISIBLE IMPORTS AND EXPORTS, a term applied to items appearing in a country's balance of trade that are not actual merchandise. Such items include tourist expenditures, immigrant remittances, shipping dues, and interest on investments.

INVOICE, a list or bill of goods; a detailed statement of merchandise in stock or to be shipped. An invoice often accompanies a shipment of goods along with the bill of lading from the consignor to the consignee. It is not a document of title or a contract of sale, and it has no value in law other than as a memorandum. When goods are shipped to foreign countries, consular invoices must frequently be signed by the consul of the country of destination.

INVOLUCRE, in seed plants, is a group of bracts surrounding flowers in their unexpanded state, and occupying a place on the floral axis beneath them after their expansion. The bracts forming an involucre are generally grouped in a whorl. The cups of such nuts as the acorn and the hazelnut may also be regarded as involucres.

INVOLUTION, in mathematics, is the raising of a quantity to any assigned power. It is the inverse of evolution, in which the root of a quantity is extracted. See also ALGEBRA; ARITHMETIC; ASSEMBLAGES, GENERAL THEORY OF; CALCULUS, THE INFINITESIMAL.

IO, ī'ō, *in Greek mythology,* was a priestess of Hera at Argos. According to most accounts she was the daughter of the river god Inachus. Zeus fell in love with her and, to protect her from the jealousy of Hera, changed her into a beautiful white heifer. Hera was not deceived, however, and she sent a gadfly to torment Io and thus persecuted her through many lands. The wanderings of Io were a favorite subject in Greek poetry and painting. Finally, Io reached Egypt, where Zeus restored her to her former condition and fathered her son, Epaphus, ancestor of Danaus. Io has often been associated with Isis in Egypt.

In astronomy, Io is the traditional name applied to the innermost satellite of Jupiter (Satellite I), which was discovered by Galileo Galilei in 1610.

IOANNINA, yô-ä'nyê-ä (formerly JANINA or JANNINA; YANINA or YANNINA), city, Greece, capital of the Department of Ioannina, situated in Epirus, on Lake Ioannina, approximately 200 miles northwest of Athens. The commercial center of an area producing grain, fruit, and wine, the city has long been celebrated for its silk manufactures. It is the seat of a metropolitan of the Greek Orthodox Church, and it has an airport. There are a number of Byzantine churches and the ruins of an ancient fort known as the Iron Castle.

Founded in Byzantine times, Ioannina was seized by the Normans under Robert Guiscard in 1081, but reverted to imperial control shortly thereafter. In 1204, Michael Angelus Comnenus (Michael I) made it the capital of the despotate of Epirus, but the city was recaptured by imperial forces in 1262. In 1431 it was taken by the Turks. From 1788 to 1822 it was the seat of Ali Pasha, the Lion of Janina. After the First Balkan War, in 1913, it was annexed to Greece. Ioannina was heavily damaged during World War II. Pop. (1951) 32,268.

IODINE, ī'ō-dīn, a nonmetallic element analogous in its general properties to chlorine and bromine. Its chemical symbol is I; its atomic number, 53; and its atomic weight, 126.92. Iodine was discovered in 1811 by Bernard Courtois (q.v.), in the mother liquors of kelp that had been used for the production of sodium carbonate, occurring in combination with sodium and magnesium. It is still obtained from the ashes of certain seaweeds (particularly on the coasts of Japan and Brittany), but about 80 per cent of the world's commercial supply is obtained in the course of purifying *caliche,* or Chile saltpeter, which is found in immense beds in the northern part of Chile. In the process large quantities of iodine are permitted to escape, so that about 97 per cent is wasted. Iodine is also produced commercially from the brackish waters flowing from oilwells, particularly in southern California, Italy, and Indonesia. In California iodine is profitably produced by treatment with nitrous acid, the iodine being expelled from its salty compounds in the form of gas. The gas is captured in activated charcoal, from which it is released in a vacuum and subsequently solidified by pressure.

With hydrogen, iodine forms the important compound HI, known as hydriodic acid. With metals, it forms binary compounds called iodides, which may also be regarded as salts of hydriodic acid. Of these the most important is potassium iodide, KI, which is used extensively in medicine. It is prepared by dissolving iodine in a solution of caustic potash, evaporating it to dryness and then igniting. This salt is very soluble and crystallizes in cubes. The iodides of ammonia, sodium, strontium, and zinc are used to a more limited extent.

Iodoform, a yellow crystalline powder with a peculiar characteristic odor when warmed, is much used in surgical dressings. Its formula is CHI_3, and its chemical structure and properties are analogous to those of chloroform. Iodoform may be prepared by dissolving iodine in an alcoholic solution of caustic potash. The iodoform thus produced separates as a precipitate. In Germany it is prepared to some extent by the electrolysis of a similar solution.

Iodine and its compounds are to some extent used in photography, and to a greater extent in synthetic chemistry, for the preparation of coal tar colors and other substances.

Iodine forms two important oxyacids, which are known respectively as iodic acid, HIO_3, and periodic acid, HIO_4+2H_2O. These are analogous, in their chemical deportment, to chloric and perchloric acids. It also forms the interesting chlorides IO and ICl_3.

Free iodine combines with starch to form a remarkable deep blue compound, whose production is a well-known test for the presence, in a given substance, of either starch or free iodine. To detect the presence of iodine in a solution, a few drops of thin, clear starch paste are added to the solution to be tested (which should be cold), and hydrochloric acid is added until the reaction is acid. A couple of drops of a concentrated solution of potassium nitrite are then added, when the dark blue color of iodide of starch will instantly be produced, if iodine is present. This test may readily be modified so as to serve for the detection of starch. The reaction is not given by dextrin, nor by other isomers of starch.

Of recent years iodine has found a comparatively large use as an ingredient in prepared feeds for stock, particularly those herds in the interior of the country, its use showing a decided improvement in rate of growth and general health. See also HYDRIODIC ACID; IODINE IN MEDICINE.

IODINE AND IODIDES IN MEDICINE. Iodine and its iodides — especially those of sodium and potassium — have been used in medicine since the Chinese are supposed to have introduced them, 2000 B.C. or earlier. The exact method of action of the iodides is not clear, but it would seem that iodine, being a normal constituent of the human body, is a very essential element in normal metabolism. It is found in comparatively large quantities in the thyroid gland, which is known to exercise a very important action in the general body-metabolism, and it is probably by means of the stimulation of the general metabolism of the body that the iodides manifest their beneficial action. The iodides are freely absorbed from watery solutions by mucous membranes throughout the body, particularly in the stomach and intestine. They are taken up into the blood, pass through the tissues, stimulating the lymph-flow, and are excreted in the urine in the form of salts. The iodides are likely to irritate the digestive system. Iodine itself possesses a local irritant action. It is soon converted into the iodides when taken internally, and causes similar internal changes.

When the iodides are taken in large doses, or even in small doses for a long time, a form of chronic poisoning known as iodism results. In this the chief symptoms, found in the air-passages, consist of a catarrh, especially of the nose, with profuse watery secretion, sneezing and sometimes bronchitis. There is usually swelling and irritation of the throat and tonsils, and salivation. Nausea and gastric discomforts are common, and skin-eruptions are frequent. There is usually loss of weight, and if the iodide has been taken for a very long period a condition of cachexia, characterized by a great loss of flesh, weakness, depression and restlessness, may result. The chief use of the iodides in medicine is in the treatment of tertiary syphilis, on which it has a specific effect. It is also useful in actinomycosis, metal poisoning, high arterial tension, arteriosclerosis, aortic aneurism, colloid goitre and rheumatic affections. It is also very useful in the various joint-pains of a chronic character, usually known as chronic rheumatism. Iodine is valuable in the treatment of those diseases known to result from thyroid insufficiency, notably in myxœdema (q.v.), and in cretinism, its allied form in children; also as a stimulant for the respiratory and nasal passage, in chronic bronchitis, asthma and dry nasal catarrh. See also STRATEGIC and CRITICAL MINERAL SUPPLIES.

IODOFORM. Tri-iodomethane, CHI_3, was discovered by Serullas in 1822. It is formed by the interaction of ethyl alcohol and iodine in the presence of caustic alkalis. Acetone, acetaldehyde and many other compounds may also yield varying quantities of iodoform when treated with iodine and caustic alkalis or carbonates. Iodoform has also been obtained from derivatives of acetylene; and of late years it has been formed from ammonium iodide in the presence of potassium hypoiodite, potassium carbonate and ammonia.

On a commercial scale iodoform is prepared by the addition of iodine to an aqueous solution of sodium carbonate in the presence of ethyl alcohol. The temperature of the reaction mixture is maintained at 70°–80° C. The main portion of the iodine is converted into iodoform, which being insoluble forms a yellow precipitate. The remainder of the iodine dissolves in the reaction mixture as sodium iodide. From the latter the iodine is recovered by the use of chlorine, and converted into iodoform with an additional quantity of sodium carbonate and alcohol. A repetition of this process will increase the yield of iodoform. In this method acetone may be substituted for ethyl alcohol, and potassium carbonate for sodium carbonate.

A second process, extensively employed at the present time, consists in the electrolysis of a water solution of potassium iodide, alcohol or acetone, and an alkaline hydroxide or carbonate, at a temperature of 65° C.

Iodoform crystallizes in lemon-yellow plates. It has a persistent unpleasant odor, melts at 119° C. and dissolves in absolute alcohol, ether, carbon bisulphide and other solvents. With alcoholic potash it yields potassium formate and potassium iodide. In the presence of arsenious acid and sodium hydroxide it is converted into methylene iodide, and with phosphorus pentachloride it yields chloroform. With dry silver nitrate iodoform forms an explosive mixture.

Iodoform was first employed in the treatment of wounds in 1880. When brought in contact with wounds or sores it acts as a good antiseptic and promotes healing. The action is probably due to the liberation of iodine and other products at the temperature of the body. It is extensively used in the treatment of scrofula, goitre, cancer and in syphilitic and tuberculous ulcerations. When iodoform is taken in large doses into the system, it may produce symptoms of poisoning, nausea and vomiting, headache, sleepiness, hallucinations and even death.

The objectionable odor of iodoform has been masked by combining it with a variety of substances such as volatile oil of camphor, balsam of Peru and paraformaldehyde. A number of good iodoform substitutes have been prepared. Some of these are related to iodoform both in composition and in their mode of decomposition. Iodoformin, for example, is a compound of iodoform and hexamethylenetetramine; it liberates iodoform when it is used as a surgical dressing. Iodol (tetraiodopyrrol) and Aristol (dithymoldiodide) are also more or less related to iodoform. Among other substitutes for iodoform may be mentioned europhen, vioform, xeroform, noviform, loretin, and Airol.

V. S. Babasinian,
Late Professor of Chemistry, Lehigh University.

IODYRITE or **IODARGYRITE**, a native iodide of silver (AgI), containing 46 per cent silver. Greenish or yellowish in color, it occurs in Nevada and New Mexico.

IOLA, ī-ō′lȧ, city, Kansas, seat of Allen County, situated on the Neosho River, at an altitude of 960 feet, 109 miles south-southwest of Kansas City. It is served by the Atchison, Topeka and Santa Fe, the Missouri-Kansas-Texas, and the Missouri Pacific railroads, and has a municipal airport. In a productive grain and dairy farming district, Iola has creameries and milk condensing plants, as well as industrial establishments producing bricks and cement, clothing, and food products. The city is the seat of Iola Junior College. Riverside Park, where the Allen County Fair and Southeastern Kansas Exposition is held annually, has facilities for outdoor sports. The public library contains collections of state history and of works by Kansans. Laid out in 1859, Iola became a county seat in 1865 and was incorporated in 1870. It has the commission form of government. Pop. (1950) 7,094.

IOLANTHE, ī-ō-lăn′thē (in full Iolanthe, or the Peer and the Peri), a comic opera in two acts, with text by W. S. Gilbert and music by Sir Arthur Sullivan. It was originally produced at the Savoy Theatre in London on Nov. 25, 1882, and a year later at the Standard Theatre in New York. The plot is concerned with the richly humorous contrast between the world of fairies, in which Iolanthe has disgraced herself by marrying a mortal, and the world of British peers, which receives the brunt of many of Gilbert's wittiest sallies. The complications are centered around Strephon, Iolanthe's son, and Phyllis, his sweetheart, who objects to his attentions to his fairy mother, believing her to be a rival.

IOLCUS, ī-ŏl′kŭs, ancient city, Greece, situated in Thessaly, probably northeast of the modern Volos. It is celebrated as the home of Jason and as the place from which the Argonauts departed.

IOLITE (also known as Dichroite or Cordierite), a natural silicate of magnesium and aluminum, of uncertain formula. It contains a small amount of calcium and some iron. Iolite crystallizes in the orthorhombic system, in the form of short columns of a hexagonal tendency. It is blue in color, but shows different tints under different lights. Its hardness is 7 to 7.5, and its specific gravity, 2.6 to 2.66. Iolite is found in Connecticut and New Hampshire, several countries of northern Europe, Brazil, Ceylon, and elsewhere. It is sometimes used as a gem stone. Deep blue iolite is known as lynx sapphire; light blue iolite, as water sapphire.

ION, ī′ŏn, Greek dramatist and poet: b. Chios, c.490 B.C.; d. before 421 B.C. As a young man, he went to Athens, where he made the acquaintance of the leading men of the time, including Cimon, Pericles, Themistocles, Aeschylus, Sophocles, and possibly Socrates. He wrote a number of tragedies, of which only fragments survive, as well as poems, a history of the founding of Chios, and memoirs. He was known for his polished style, and he was included by the Alexandrians in their list of canonic poets.

Consult Nauck, August, *Tragicorum Graecorum Fragmenta*, 2d ed. (Leipzig 1889).

IONA, ī-ō′nȧ, island, Scotland, one of the Inner Hebrides, situated in Argyll, 1.25 miles west of the southwest end of Mull, from which it is separated by Iona Sound. Approximately 3 miles long and 1.5 miles wide, the island has a total area of 3.5 square miles. About one third is under cultivation, chiefly to grains and potatoes, and the remainder consists of hill pastures, rocks, and shell beaches. The island has no trees.

Iona is rich in historical associations. It was here that St. Columba (q.v.) came about 563 to establish a monastery that became a center of the Celtic Church. Missionaries were sent out from the island, and pilgrims came from many lands. In the 8th and 9th centuries the island was raided by Norsemen, and the monastery was burned down. It was restored in the 11th century by St. Margaret, consort of Malcolm III of Scotland. She is said to have built St. Oran's Chapel, the oldest remaining building on the island, about 1080. A new Benedictine monastery was founded in 1203; it was dismantled in 1561, but the Cathedral of St. Mary, dating mainly from the late 15th and early 16th centuries and later restored, survives. The Iona Community, a religious brotherhood founded in 1938, has undertaken the restoration of the monastery. Other points of interest on the island include the Iona Cross, possibly of the 9th or 10th century; and St. Oran's Cemetery, where 48 kings of Scotland, 4 kings of Ireland, and 8 kings of Norway and Denmark are said to have been buried.

IONIA, ī-ō′nĭ-ȧ, ancient district, Asia Minor. Comprising that part of the coastal area inhabited by Ionian Greeks, as well as the islands of Samos and Chios, it extended along the Aegean Sea for about 90 miles, from near the mouth of the Hermus (modern Gediz) River to the Halicarnassus Peninsula, and inland for 20 to 30 miles. According to traditional accounts, Greek colonists from Attica settled there about 1000 B.C. They founded a league of 12 cities—Phocaea, Ephesus, Miletus, Clazomenae, Erythae, Teos, Lebedos, Colophon, Priene, Myus, Chios, and Samos—to which Smyrna (modern İzmir) was added later. The district grew wealthy on commerce and agriculture, and it made notable contributions to Greek culture, including a school of philosophy, an architectural order, a musical mode, and many writers. Ionia was made tributary to Lydia by Croesus (r. 560–546 B.C.), and, about 547 B.C., to Persia. Except for a period of partial independence from 479 to 387 B.C., it remained under Persian domination until 334 B.C., when it was conquered by Alexander the Great. In Roman times it was part of the province of Asia.

IONIA, city, Michigan, seat of Ionia County, situated on the Grand River, at an altitude of 650 feet, 33 miles east of Grand Rapids. It is served by the Grand Trunk and the Chesapeake & Ohio railroads. The trading center for an area producing wheat, apples, and livestock, Ionia has flour mills and meat packing plants, as well as factories producing furniture, pottery, machinery, edged tools, automobile parts, tile, and clothing. There are local library and hospital facilities. The city is the seat of the Michigan State Reformatory and Ionia State Hospital. Settled in 1833, Ionia was incorporated as a village in 1865 and as a city in 1873. Its charter was revised in 1897 and 1924. It is governed by a mayor and council. Pop. (1950) 6,412.

IONIAN ISLANDS, island group, Greece, situated in the Ionian Sea, off the southwest coast of Albania and the west and south coasts of the Greek mainland. The principal islands, seven in number, are, from north to south, Corfu (Kérkyra), Paxos (Paxoi), Leukas (Lefkás; Santa Maura), Ithaca (Ithákē), Cephalonia (Kephallēnía), Zante (Zakynthos), and Cerigo (Kýthēra). Except for Cerigo and its dependent islets, which are included administratively in Attica, they are divided for purposes of local government among the four nomes (departments) of Corfu, Leukas, Cephalonia, and Zante, with a total area of 751 square miles. All of the islands are mountainous, and they do not have enough arable land to produce sufficient grain to be self-supporting. The climate is comparatively warm, and rainfall averages about 50 inches a year. The principal crops are grapes, olives, and currants, and these, together with wine and olive oil, are shipped to the mainland and to foreign countries. Industry is generally undeveloped.

The islands often figure in the history of ancient Greece, but singly, not collectively. Corfu and Cephalonia were seized by Robert Guiscard in 1081. Venice acquired Corfu in 1386, and the island remained under Venetian control until 1797. The other islands were also dependencies of Venice for varying periods from the 15th century on. In 1797 they were ceded to France under the Treaty of Campoformio, but they were taken by Russia in 1798–1799, and from 1800 to 1807 they formed the Septinsular Republic under Russian occupation and Turkish protection. The islands were again ceded to France under the Treaty of Tilsit (1807). In 1815 they became a British protectorate, called the United States of the Ionian Islands. Great Britain ceded the islands to Greece in 1864. Pop. (1951) including Cerigo, 238,413.

IONIAN MODE. See Mode.

IONIAN PHILOSOPHY is the name given to the early Greek hylozoism and henism of the thinkers of the Ionian school of philosophers. Since the term hylozoism is apt to be misleading and the term henism to be misunderstood, they require explanation. In the first place, hylozoism is not synonymous with materialism. To some, of course, it suggests theories that deny the separate reality of life and spirit. And, indeed, in the days of Thales (q.v.), the first Ionian thinker, and even much later, the distinction between matter and spirit was not keenly felt, much less formulated in such a way that it could be either definitely affirmed or denied. But the uncreated, indestructible reality with which Ionian thought concerns itself was a body, or even matter, if we choose to call it matter. It was not matter, however, in the sense in which matter is opposed to spirit. Hylozoism thus is characteristic of any system which explains all life, whether physical or mental, as ultimately derivable and derived from animated matter. Ionian hylozoism consisted chiefly in an inquiry after the first principle or element, regarded as animated, out of which the sense-perceptible world is constructed. Thus Thales, Anaximander, Anaximenes, Heraclitus, Anaxagoras, and other Ionian thinkers, because they followed one general tendency, possess, intellectually considered, another common characteristic. In thought they are henistic. By henism is understood those philosophic efforts to subsume everything under one general notion, be it motion, or matter, or spirit, or matter in motion, or evolution, or an unknown substratum, like the Kantian "thing-in-itself" and the Spencerian "unknowable." Henism is, briefly, one-notion, single-idea philosophy. All Ionian philosophers asked: From what did the world come? The growing body of thought which may be traced through successive representatives of the Ionian school is always that which concerns a primary substance. The astronomical and other theories are, in the main, peculiar only to the individual thinkers of the school. Greek philosophy thus began as it ended, with the search for what was abiding in the flux of things.

Philosophy arose in Greece as elsewhere in the attempt to discover the laws of outward phenomena, and the origin and successive stages of the world's development. The earlier thinkers stand in closer relation to the previous religious or mythical views; they seek to substitute an intelligible hypothesis, based on real things, for the myths of the poets. Even the myths, which described the generation of the gods and the origination of worlds, however, implied at least a view of a single, connected world-process, and of an inclusion of all in the universe within that process. Sky, earth, sea, days, seasons—in short, all detached phenomena—were given unity and relation even in the Greek poets, in such beings as Gaea (earth) and Ouranos (heaven) and similar deities. Thus, closely in touch as were the earlier Ionian thinkers with the Olympian religion, with its deities of the sky and the ocean, their task was to substitute for such personifications actual, concrete substances, a work they sought to complete through closer contact with nature. All sought to explain the material universe as given in sensory experience. The chief aim was to secure an answer to the inquiry: What is the one original element, if indeed it is only one, or what are the original elements, if more than one, of which the universe consists? The philosophers found ready to hand in the mythic cycles the conception that the world was one. From what did it come? Their answers were usually given in terms of matter, movement, and force. Concerned mainly with the ontological or metaphysical problem, the thought of the Ionian thinkers was in its chief characteristics cosmological. The other problems of the philosopher—epistemological, logical, ethical, and aesthetical—receive but passing note, if any. The characteristic work which distinguishes the speculations of this school is the endeavor to refer all sensible things back to one original principle in nature. And as their efforts began with a search for laws, so were those efforts rewarded by the earliest conception of what became the most fruitful idea evolved in the whole body of Ionian thought, namely, the notion of «rational law» or *logos*, and «justice» (δικη), which controls a world process and regulates allotted changes. When the regular course of nature was first realized by members of the Ionian School no better word for it could be found than «δικη.» It is the same metaphor which still lives on in our expression «natural law.» Here we see the decree of Zeus, the destroyer of the gods, the social and religious law of justice, becoming the central conception for viewing the physical process, an achievement which could not dispose of all those implications, like for example fatalism, which cling to the modern term law even in the science of to-day. A law of changes gave a union of the «one» and the «many» to the thought of some of these early thinkers. All the members of the school were one in method and in aim. The one great principle which underlies all Ionian thought, though it is first put into words by Parmenides, is that «nothing comes into being out of nothing and nothing passes away into nothing.» Their acute penetration into the philosophical problem is testified by the fact that they attempted to recover not only the beginning of all things, but the eternal ground of all things for thought. And it is true that important beginnings of a theory of evolution are to be found in the speculations of the earliest Grecian school of philosophy.

«Nothing is born of nothing» (Parmenides of the Eleatic School). From what then did the existing world come? In the history of the Ionian School (q.v.) two principal ways of viewing nature, a dynamical and a mechanical way, present themselves at its very beginning and proceed side by side to its very close. The dynamical theorist proceeds on the supposition of a living energy which in its development spontaneously undergoes continuous alteration both of form and quality and consequently considers all generation in nature as explicable by successive transmutations of energy. The mechanist, on the other hand, rejects all generation in the proper sense of the word and all alteration of the qualities and forms in nature, and accounts for all appearances by certain changes in the outer relations of space. Here a theorist proceeds, therefore, on the assumption of certain permanent material elements, which change place in obedience to motion, either originally inherent or extrinsically impressed; and thus it is a theoretical explanation of the world which if carried out in all its implications will lead to the conclusion that all apparent generation of natural forms and qualities is educed by the various combinations into which material elements of originally distinct forms mutually enter. The two theories rest on views directly opposed to each other. With the exceptions of Anaxagoras, Anaximander and Archelaus, the Ionian hylozoists all show an inclination to adopt the dynamical explanation of the world. By all, excepting the three philosophers named, *nature* is regarded as naively animated, alive, and its successive changes as so many spontaneous developments of life. And by them it was accepted as a principle that a single elementary substance passes through a series of transformations, by means of expansions, condensations and other modifications considered as processes of life. Thus those who admitted one rather than a plurality of elements were obliged to endow it with a principle of vitality to account for existing variety. They thus adopt dynamism, a rather crude form of henism. Archelaus, Anaximander and Anaxagoras, on the contrary, believed in a plurality of elements, two or more, and considered mechanical interaction of these as sufficient to account for the existing state of things. What is the original element, if only one, or, what are the original elements, if more than one, of which the universe consists. Two periods can likewise be distinguished in the development of the reply to this question owing to its reformulation and the manner in which different thinkers in the school approached it. Prior to the advent of Heraclitus attempts were made to find a material substance of which all things consist. What were the materials out of which all things arose and into which they will again return? What is the substratum of things seen? Thales, Anaximenes, Diogenes and other dynamists as well agree in regarding the universe as the result of a single principle, element or power. All sensible things are modifications of this principle, real only in reference to their ultimate ground, a substance of which all things consist. After the time of Heraclitus the question became: How did the sensible world become what it is? Of what nature is the motive force? Here the germs of a more philosophic doctrine is apparent. Heraclitus, indeed, retains the simplicity of an original element, his «fire,» but it is apparent that this fire is only a sensible symbol, used only to present more vividly to the mind the idea of an energy of a vital principle, the ground of all outward appearances. He with his principle of universal flux gave thinking a new turn and proceeded to explain everything in terms of force and motion, or dynamic energy. It would indeed be a mistake to regard philosophers of the Ionian school as materialists. They distinguish between law operating in the external world and the apprehension of phenomena; and vaguely also between subjective and objective. But we meet with thinkers of the mechanistic tendency. Anaxagoras and Anaximander agree in this respect, that they consider the world to be made up of numberless small particles of different kinds and various shapes by the change in whose relative position all phenomena are to be accounted for. This hypothesis is combined by Anaxagoras with the Supreme Reason, author of all that is regular and harmonious in the disposition of the particles or elementary atoms. Out of what did the existing world proceed? Thales, the first Ionian philosopher, answered out of water, which Anaximander denied and replied that the ground of all being is the boundless, the infinite or the all-embracing. Pherecydes of Syra believed that the primal substratum of all things was earth; but both Anaximenes and Diogenes contended that the existing state of things proceeded out of air. Heraclitus said the original element was fire; Anaxagoras, however, that the world came into being through the motor energy of intelligence; while Archelaus, the teacher of Socrates, believed that primordially the elements were two in number, fire and water, sense-perceptible symbols of heat and cold which can be felt but not seen. And to Hermotimus, whose existence, however, some deny, deeming him mythical, others credit the original formulation of the doctrine of the supreme regulative intelligence, an idea which he is said to have taught his pupil Anaxagoras.

Aristotle believed that the view of Thales had its origin in the observation that all that *grows* appears to have its nourishment in moisture and the observation that *germination* seems to owe its existence to the presence of water. Aristotle adds further that Thales maintained the world to be full of gods and that all motion indicated their presence and the presence of souls. Thales believed that behind infinite multiplicity there was unity. This unity he symbolized with water. Anaximander sought for the primal substance of all things; and postulated an entity intermediate between air and fire on one hand; between earth and water on the other. This entity he called the infinite. To him all differences being finite, these differences have emerged out of the infinite. This infinite has been always and will remain throughout all eternity. Change, growth and decay are explained on the principle of compensation. All things proceeded out of the infinite. All will at some time return to it. According to all appearances, Anaximander's «infinite» is equivalent to the «chaos» of other philosophers and of the myths. «Nous,» according to him, is the most pure and subtle of all things. It has all knowledge about all things and also infinite power. Anaximander's theory is thus only one step from pure theism. With him the work of the eternal begins with a kind of providence, not with creation. He did not allow that objects had taken their shape through the accidental or through blind fate. They received their form through the agency of a shaping spirit or Nous, infinite, or boundless, self-potent and unmixed with anything else. The infinite always preserved its unity; its parts alone underwent changes. Thus he tells us that there are an infinite number of worlds, a product of infinity, and that corruption proceeds from separation. Anaximenes made the first principle of things to consist in air, an entity considered as infinite, and possessed of perpetual motion. All things proceeded from this air; all are definite and circumscribed; and divine power resided in air and agitated it. Coldness and moisture, heat and motion rendered this substance visible. Likewise they gave air forms, according to the different degrees of condensation. All elements thus proceed from heat and cold. Diogenes contradicted the pluralism of Heraclitus and claimed that all things were at bottom the same, or interaction he claimed would be impossible. The substrate confirming the opinion of Anaximenes, he declared, was air; and gave it out that the attributes of this substrate were infinity, eternity and intelligence. This intelligence alone, according to Diogenes, would produce unaided the orderly arrangement which is observable in nature; and it is likewise the foundation of human mentality, which originates simply by inhalation. Anaxagoras may be considered the first who clearly and broadly distinguished between mind and matter. By isolating reason from all else, by representing it as motor-energy of the Cosmos, in popularizing the terms which suggested personality and will, Anaxagoras gave an impetus to ideas which were the starting point of Aristotelian philosophy in Greece and in Europe at large. Before Anaxagoras no one can be said to have postulated clearly a creative intelligence. In nature this thinker imagined that there are as many kinds of principles as there are species of compound bodies. He was the first to superadd mind to matter, opening his work with the pleasing language: «All things were confused. Then came mind and disposed them in order.» Heraclitus felt that charge is the essential fact of experience. That this is, what it is, in virtue of its perpetually changing relations. Fire, symbol of the primary substance, is that out of which all came, into which again all will return. It is a divine, rational process, the harmony which constitutes the universe. Here follows the doctrine of immortality. The individual, like the phenomena of sense, comes out of the infinite and is again merged in it. While we live our souls are dead within us. When we die our souls are restored to life. For then they approach most nearly to perfection when least differentiated from the elemental fire. This is at once the assertion and the denial of self — resembling a fundamental principle in Buddhism. See GREEK PHILOSOPHY; PHILOSOPHY; PHILOSOPHY, HISTORY OF.

IONIAN SCHOOL, at times called also the Ionian Sect, was the oldest among the ancient schools of Greek philosophy. It originated in Asia Minor under Thales of Miletos, about 600 years before the beginning of the Christian era. Diogenes Laërtius places the birth of Thales during the 35th Olympiad, that is, between 640 B.C. and 636 B.C.; and the philosopher died, according to Apollodorus, in his 78th year, but according to Sosicrates, in his 90th year. The other most famous exponents of Ionian thought after the advent of Thales of Miletos were Anaximander of Miletos, Pherecydes of Syra, Anaximenes of Miletos, Heraclitus of Ephesus, Diogenes of Apollonia and Anaxagoras and Hermotinius of Clazomenæ. It is a most interesting fact in the history of Greek thought that its birth took place not in Greece but in its colonies on the eastern shores of the Ægean Sea. The first name in the list, not alone of Ionian, but indeed of European, thought, is Thales. From Asia Minor the *spirit* of Ionian philosophy passed into Greece, at first under Anaxagoras, then afterward under Archelaus, the master of Socrates. The interval between Thales and Archelaus amounted to a period of not less than 150 years. Thus Athens, taught from Ionia, became in turn the headquarters of philosophy and the parent of the most celebrated Greek schools. The labors of the Ionian School cleared the way for all those schools which at a later period undertook to explain the physical world and served at once as a model and as a starting point for Leucippus, Democritus, Empedocles, Aristotle and Epicurus. In truth most of the schools which arose in Greece from the time of Thales to the time of the great thinker Socrates — roughly speaking during the period between 600 B.C. and 400 B.C. — and constituted the first philosophic period, were in some sort so many offshoots of the Ionian School. Pythagoras, born at Samos, became the pupil of Pherecydes; Xenophenes, the founder of the Eleatic School, was a native of the Ionian city of Colophon; Abdera, the birthplace of Leucippus and Democritus and the seat of the school which they founded, was a colony from Phocæa; and besides, Democritus was the pupil of Anaxagoras. In the course of its development, the Ionian School was contemporary with other Greek schools, among which the Abderitan and Eleatic schools and the systems of Empedocles and Pythagoras were the most important.

The Ionian Philosophy (q.v.), notwithstanding the celebrity of its first professors, most of whom are named above, soon failed in classical Grecian schools and in Greece never afterward recovered its ancient reputation and authority. This was owing to the suspicion of impiety under which it lay in Athens; to the early growth of new branches from the Socratic stock; and to the rise and spread and vigor of the Eleatic and the Epicurean mode of thought. Ionian philosophy thus disappeared in antiquity for the first time owing to the dual opposition of sullen, unlearned bigotry and the incisive critique it received at the hands of its more profound rivals, like, for example, the Socratic Philosophy.

History has preserved the record of numerous attempts that have been made to form a rational conception of the whole world of phenomena and to recognize in the universe the action of one sole active force by which matter is penetrated, transformed and animated. These attempts are traced in classical antiquity in those treatises on the *principles of things* which emanated from the Ionian School and in which all the phenomena of nature were subjected to hazardous speculations based upon a small number of observations. By degrees, as the influence of great historical events has favored the development of every branch of science supported by observation, that ardor has cooled which formerly led men to seek the essential nature and connection of things in purely rational principles. In recent times the mathematical portion of natural philosophy has been remarkably and admirably enlarged. The method and the instrument (analysis) have been simultaneously perfected. That which has been acquired by means so different by the ingenious application of atomic suppositions, by the more general and intricate study of phenomena and by the improved construction of new apparatus — is now the common property of mankind.

Thales and the earlier members of the school stand in closer relation to the previous mythic and religious cosmologists than the later members. And they seek to substitute intelligible hypothesis, based on real things or events, for the myths of the poets. The first attempt to disenthrall the philosophic intellect from the all-personifying religious faith and to constitute a method of interpreting nature distinct from the untaught inspiration of inferior minds is to be found in Thales in the 6th century before the Christian era. It is to Thales and to a small number of other independent Greek thinkers that philosophy owes the substitution of an impersonal nature for the personified cosmos, conceived as the proper object of study. The Greek word, φυσις, denoting nature and its derivatives *physics* and *physiology,* unknown in the sense which Thales understood it to Homer and Hesiod, as well as the word *kosmos* to denote the mundane system, first appears in these philosophers' speculations. But it must be allowed that the distinction between personal and impersonal was not strongly felt in antiquity and it is a mistake to lay overmuch stress upon it. It seems rather that the real advance made by the scientific men of Miletos was that they left off telling mere tales. They gave up the hopeless task of describing what was where as yet there was nothing and asked instead what all things really are now. The great epistemological principle which underlies all their thinking, though it is first put into words by Parmenides, is that *nothing comes into being out of nothing and nothing passes away into nothing.* See GREEK PHILOSOPHY; IONIAN PHILOSOPHY.

IONIAN SEA, that part of the Mediterranean Sea communicating with the Adriatic Sea or Gulf of Venice by the Strait of Otranto, and having Greece and part of Albania on the east, Sicily and part of southern Italy on the west. This sea, divided from the Adriatic Sea by a submarine ridge rising in the Strait of Otranto, has a shoal or submarine ridge, already referred to by Strabo, which joins Sicily and Tunis, as the true geological boundary of its basin on the west. Over this shoal the waters of the Mediterranean do not rise much more than 100 fathoms, a narrow flood connecting two divisions of the main sea. Its greatest breadth is between Cape Passero in Sicily and Cape Matapan in the Morea, which is about 400 miles. This waste of water washes all the shores of the Ionian Islands excepting those of Cerigo. From the more elevated spots in one of these historic islands the prospects are magnificent. From the high places in Corfu the view takes in two seas, and in clear weather one may discover the faint line of the Italian coast, near the city of Otranto, more than 70 miles away.

Dry cold winds passing over the snows upon the Albanian hills and those of Greece impart to the islands and the surrounding Ionian Sea a chill more piercing-cold than is common even in regions more to the north. The sirocco of southeast wind blows over the sea and its isles during 126½ days annually.

The deepest points in the whole stretch of the Mediterranean waters have been found to lie beneath the surface of the Ionian Sea. Near its centre, say about 36° N. and 18° W. of Greenwich, soundings reveal 2,170 fathoms of water. Then due south of the land of the Morea there is an abrupt fall, in about 36° N., and the greatest depth beneath the surface of the whole watery surface of the Mediterranean is found to lie. The Gulf of Taranto and Squillace, washing the shores of Italy, and the Gulf of Arta, Patros and Arcadia on the coasts of Greece, are among the more important inlets of the Ionian Sea. And the Gulf of Patros is connected with the waters of the historic Gulf of Lepanto. The ebb and flow of tides so marked at Venice are on the whole little perceptible on the shores of the Ionian Sea. In some places it does not rise an inch.

The origin of the Roman designation, Ionium Mare, is very doubtful. The term is found first in the works of the poet Aeschylus, who died 456 B.C., though exactly what meaning he attaches to it cannot be clearly ascertained. By this poet, and the ancients generally, the name is usually derived from the "sore-wasting" wanderings of Io, daughter of Inarchus, the river-god of Argos, and its first king. But it is more probable that the sea obtained its name from the Ionian colonies which settled the island of Cephallenia in the Ionian Sea, along with other islands off the coasts of Greece in the same locality. According to Theopompus, Strabo tells us, the name "Ionian" itself was derived from an ancient chieftain's name, Ionius, a native of ancient Issa, now Lissa, a small island in the Adriatic Sea.

IONIC DIALECT. See GREEK LANGUAGE.

IONIC ORDER, a style of architecture, so named from the district of Ionia, in ancient Greece, where it originated. Its most marked difference from other orders is seen in the capital of the column, in which spiral ornaments or volutes predominate. From the Doric it also differs in providing a base for the column. A dentil band on the cornice is also proper to the Ionic, in which it was first employed. These Ionic peculiarities appear to be of Eastern origin, probably Assyrian, as is indicated by the employment of the honeysuckle ornament so frequently met with there. Excellent examples of this style are the temple of Fortune at Rome, that of Minerva Polias and that of Erechtheus in Athens.

IONIC THEORY, another name for the Arrhenius Electrolytic Dissociation Theory. For further discussion of this theory the reader is referred to the articles on ARRHENIUS; ELECTROLYSIS; SOLUTIONS.

IONIZATION. See ELECTROLYSIS; ELECTRON THEORY; SOLUTION.

IONOSPHERICS, that branch of science which is concerned with the study of the ionosphere, or outer layer of the atmosphere overlying the stratosphere. Ionosphere derives its name from the existence of a large number of electrified ions, presumably produced chiefly by the ultraviolet radiation from the sun, and constituting the ionized layers of atmosphere. The ionosphere consists of at least three ionized layers differentiated from each other by a change in the ionic concentration and electron density. The uppermost of these layers is the so-called F layer, the discovery of which has been generally attributed to E. V. Appleton. This layer forms a reflecting shell from which radio waves of the higher frequencies are turned back to earth, thus making long distance communication by radio possible. In the daytime the F layer splits into two layers, the upper of which is designated F_2 and the lower of which is F_1.

Below the F layers there exists the E layer which turns back the radio waves of broadcast frequencies (550–1500 kilocycles). This layer was originally postulated by Arthur E. Kennelly in 1902 and gave us our first conception of the existence of an ionosphere. Six months later it was independently announced by Oliver Heaviside (1850–1925) of England. In honor of the discoverers, the E layer is frequently referred to as the Kennelly-Heaviside layer.

Below the E layer there is evidence of the existence of a lower ionized shell of the earth's atmosphere from which radio waves of very low frequency are reflected.

The science of ionospherics is intimately related to that branch of radio engineering which is concerned with the propagation, transmission, and reception of radio waves through the medium of the upper layers of the atmosphere. The problems of the production and decomposition of the ionized layers and of the absorption and reflection of radio waves by reason of their existence, form the principal subject matter with which the science of ionospherics is concerned.

HARLAN T. STETSON,
Cosmic Terrestrial Research, Massachusetts Institute of Technology.

IONTOPHORESIS. See ELECTROTHERAPEUTICS.

IORGA, yor'gȧ, **Nicolae,** Rumanian historian: b. Botoshani, 1871. He received his education at Iashi, Paris, Berlin and Leipzig and became professor of history at the University of Bucharest in 1894. He was elected member of the Rumanian Academy in 1910. He took an active interest in politics and was soon made leader of the National Democrats. His works include 'Philippe de Mezières et la croisade au XIVe siècle' (1896); 'Notes et extraits pour servir à l'histoire des croisades' (1899–1902); 'Geschichte der Rúmänen' (1905); 'History of the Byzantine Empire' (1907); 'Geschichte des Osmanischen Reiches' (5 vols., 1907–13); 'History of Rumanian Literature in the 18th Century' (1901); 'History of Rumanian Literature in the 19th Century' (1902–09).

IOS, ī'ŏs, an island in the Aegean Sea, one of the Cyclades, said to have been the birthplace of Homer. According to the ancients his mother was born here, and the poet's grave was likewise located here. It is situated about 13 miles south of Naxos. The principal occupations are the cultivation of cotton, olives, wine and cattle raising. Pop. about 2,000.

I O U, a written acknowledgment of debt, usually made in this form: "To A. B I O U Ten Dollars.—C. D. May 12, 1946." In Great Britain when the name of the creditor is stated, such a document is evidence of a debt of the amount stated due to him by the person whose signature it bears. It is not treated as a promissory note, for the reason that it contains no promise to pay. In the absence of the name of the creditor the document is *prima facie* evidence of such a debt being due to the holder of the document. It is not negotiable. The letters I O U are of course used instead of the words "I owe you" on account of the similarity of sound. In the United States it has been declared negotiable by the decisions of some courts, and it can everywhere be sued upon as an account stated without proof of the origin of the debt.

IOWA, ī'ō-wȧ, lies between the Mississippi River on the east and the Missouri and Big Sioux rivers on the west. It is bounded by Minnesota on the north, by Wisconsin and Illinois on the east, by Missouri on the south, and by Nebraska and South Dakota on the west. The name Iowa was taken from the Iowa River, which in turn took its designation from a tribe of Indians known as the Ioways. The meaning of the Indian word *Iowa* is not definitely known, the explanations including "beautiful land," "this is the place," "sleepy or drowsy ones," and "gray snow."

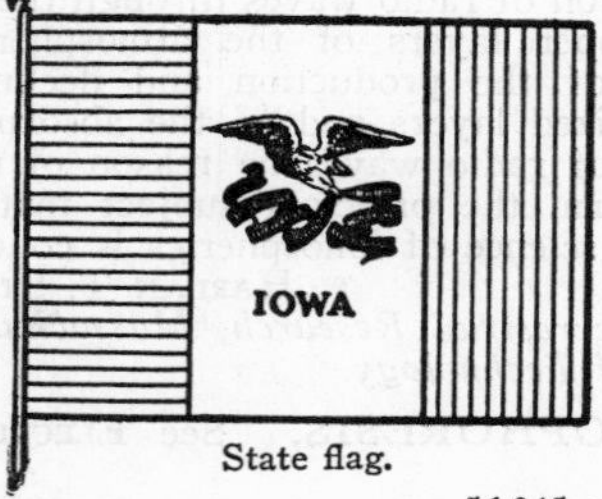

State flag.

Land area	56,045 square miles
Water area	245 square miles
Total area	56,290 square miles
Latitude	40°36'—43°30' N.
Longtiude	89°5'—96°31' W.
Altitude	477 feet to 1,670 feet above sea level
Population (1950)	2,621,073
Capital city—Des Moines; Pop. (1950)	177,965
Admitted as a state	Dec. 28, 1846
Bird	Eastern goldfinch, adopted March 29, 1933
Flower	Wild rose, adopted May 7, 1897
Motto	Our Liberties We Prize and Our Rights We Will Maintain
Nickname	Hawkeye State
Song	*Iowa,* adopted March 20, 1911
Tree	No official tree

Physical Characteristics.—*Topography.*—The surface of Iowa is, in general, a plain which slopes to the southeast. The highest point in the state is Ocheyedan Mound, in Osceola County, with an altitude of 1,670 feet; the lowest point is at Keokuk, a little over 477 feet above sea level. The mean elevation of Iowa is approximately 1,100 feet and some two thirds of the area is between 800 and 1,400 feet above sea level.

Rivers and Lakes.—The watershed runs from the northwest corner of the state to the southeast, about two thirds of the total area draining into the Mississippi River by way of the Upper Iowa, Turkey, Maquoketa, Wapsipinicon, Cedar, Iowa, Skunk, and Des Moines rivers. The southwestern third of the state drains into the Missouri through such streams as the Floyd, Little Sioux, Boyer, and Nishnabotna rivers. The Mississippi shoreline is approximately 312 miles long, while the Missouri River bounds Iowa for some 200 miles. The major ports on the Mississippi are Dubuque, Clinton, Davenport (Rock Island), Muscatine, Burlington, and Keokuk. Sioux City and Council Bluffs are the main ports on the Missouri.

Glaciers once covered the greater part of the surface of Iowa and the glacial drift formed a number of relatively small lakes in the northwest. Some 73 natural lakes are listed in Iowa, Clear Lake, Spirit Lake, and Lake Okoboji being the largest. The total area of these lakes, including the numerous oxbow lakes along the Mississippi, is 43,432 acres. There are 17 artificial lakes supervised by the State Conservation Commission.

Climate.—Since Iowa lies in the center of a great continental land area stretching from the Arctic Ocean to the Gulf of Mexico, there are great variations in temperature, occasionally as much as 50 degrees in a day. The average temperature for January for the years 1873 to 1946 was 18.8° F. The lowest reading was —47° F. on Jan. 12, 1912. The average temperature of July during the same period was 74.6° F., the maximum being 118° recorded at one point on July 20, 1934. The average temperature throughout the years from 1873 to 1946 was 48.1° F. The rainfall in Iowa varies from year to year but is usually sufficient for growing crops. The average precipitation for 1873 to 1945 was 31.66 inches. The maximum recorded was 58.8 inches in 1902 and the minimum was 12.11 inches in 1910. Since 1892 snowfall has averaged a little more than 30 inches a year. The growing season varies, the average being 158 days. The variations in temperature in the central area give rise to winds and storms, moving in great circles across the land. Occasionally a tornado in summer and a blizzard in winter are destructive but usually the winds are moderate, bringing moisture or refreshment.

Political Divisions.—*Cities.*—Municipalities are corporate units with governmental powers. They have only the authority specifically granted to them by law. Four cities are still operating under their old special charters—Davenport, Muscatine, Wapello, and Camanche. Other cities, such as Sioux City, Cedar Rapids, Ottumwa, Burlington, Fort Dodge, and Keokuk, are governed by commissions; others, including Des Moines, Council Bluffs, and Iowa City, under city-manager plans; and others, under the general framework of a mayor and council. Cities with a population over 15,000 are first-class cities, those with a population over 2,000 and under 15,000 are second-class cities, and all the others are towns. (See list of cities on back of state map for populations.)

There are still townships in Iowa but almost all authority has been transferred to larger units. Justices of the peace are the only officials elected by townships and often no one is even a candidate.

Counties.—There are 99 counties in Iowa, ranging in area from Dickinson with 382 square miles, to Kossuth with 979 square miles. A list of the counties and their county seats follows:

County	County Seat	County	County Seat
Adair	Greenfield	Bremer	Waverly
Adams	Corning	Buchanan	Independence
Allamakee	Waukon	Buena Vista	Storm Lake
Appanoose	Centerville	Butler	Allison
Audubon	Audubon	Calhoun	Rockwell City
Benton	Vinton	Carroll	Carroll
Black Hawk	Waterloo	Cass	Atlantic
Boone	Boone	Cedar	Tipton

IOWA

Iowa is a leading agricultural state. *Above:* Iowa's hog-producing record continues to set new highs. *Right:* The threshing of wheat during harvest time. *Below:* The mechanized weeding and cutting of corn flourish over the state's flat terrain.

(1) Courtesy Iowa Development Commission; (2) © photo by Burton Holmes, from Ewing Galloway; (3) © Gendreau

Left: State Capitol Building, Des Moines. Below: Airview of Cedar Rapids. The city's civic center is uniquely located on Municipal Island in the channel of the Cedar River. On the island are City Hall, the Municipal Auditorium, the Chamber of Commerce Building, the Linn County Court House, and the county jail.

Left: Iowa Development Commission, Des Moines

Below: Cedar Rapids Chamber of Commerce.

Right: The fine old administration building of the State University of Iowa. Before 1846, this Iowa City structure housed the last assembly of the territorial government. It later served as the state's first capitol. Below: Central city, Des Moines. The court house is in the foreground.

Right: Photograph by Charles Phelps Cushing, New York

Below: Des Moines Chamber of Comerce

IOWA

1950 Total Population 2,621,073

Ackley (G3)............1,608
Ackworth (G6)........ 95
Adair (D6)............ 827
Adel ◉(E5)............1,799
Afton (E6)............ 936
Agency (J7)............ 525
Ainsworth (K6)........ 396
Akron (A3)............1,251
Albert City (C3)...... 736
Albia ◉(H6)............4,838
Albion (H4)............ 492
Alburnett (K4)........ 254
Alden (G4)............ 829
Alexander (G3)........ 278
Algona ◉(E2)............5,415
Alleman (F5)............ 108
Allerton (G7)............ 761
Allison ◉(H3)............ 771
Alpha (K3)............ 122
Alta (C3)............1,348
Alta Vista (J2)........ 312
Alton (A3)............1,038
Altoona (G5)............ 763
Alvord (A2)............ 263
Amber (L4)............ 115
Ames (F4)............22,898
Anamosa ◉(L4)........3,910
Anderson (B7)........ 120
Andrew (M4)............ 280
Angus (E5)............ 150
Anita (D6)............1,112
Ankeny (F5)............1,229
Anthon (B4)............ 770
Aplington (H3)........ 702
Arcadia (C4)............ 425
Archer (B2)............ 167
Aredale (H3)............ 204
Arion (B5)............ 220
Arispe (E7)............ 110
Arlington (K3)........ 661
Armstrong (D2)........ 943
Arnolds Park (C2)...1,078
Arthur (C4)............ 243
Ashton (B2)............ 588
Aspinwall (C5)........ 107
Atalissa (L5)............ 204
Athelstan (D7)........ 115
Atkins (K4)............ 387
Atlantic ◉(D6)........6,480
Auburn (D4)............ 350
Audubon ◉(D5)......2,808
Aurelia (C3)............ 807
Aurora (K3)............ 225
Austinville (H3)........ 130
Avery (H6)............ 175
Avoca (C6)............1,595
Ayrshire (D2)............ 334
Badger (E3)............ 301
Bagley (E5)............ 922
Baldwin (M4)............ 208
Bancroft (E2)............ 901
Barnes City (H6)........ 326
Barnum (E3)............ 193
Bartlett (B7)............ 88
Bassett (J2)............ 125
Batavia (J7)............ 524
Battle Creek (B4)..... 873
Baxter (G5)............ 618
Bayard (D5)............ 634
Beacon (H6)............ 371
Beaconsfield (E7)..... 104
Beaman (H4)............ 191
Beaver (E4)............ 114
Bedford ◉(D7)........2,000
Beech (G6)............ 106
Belle Plaine (J5).......3,056
Bellevue (M4)........1,932
Belmond (F3)........2,169
Beloit (A2)............ 90
Bennett (L5)............ 357
Benton (E7)............ 128
Bernard (M4)............ 149
Bertram (K5)............ 128
Berwick (G5)............ 113
Bettendorf (N5)........5,132
Big Rock (M5)........ 106
Big Sioux (riv.) (A3)
Birmingham (K7)........ 643
Blairsburg (F4)........ 257
Blairstown (J5)........ 523
Blakesburg (H7)........ 401
Blanchard (C7)........ 214
Blencoe (A5)............ 328
Blockton (D7)............ 407
Bloomfield ◉(J7)......2,688
Blue Grass (M5)........ 337
Bode (E3)............ 492
Bonaparte (K7)........ 642
Bondurant (G5)........ 328
Boone ◉(F4)..........12,164
Bouton (E5)............ 159
Boxholm (E4)............ 304
Boyden (B2)............ 541
Boyer (riv.) (B5)...........
Braddyville (D7)..... 249
Bradgate (E3)............ 188

◉ County Seat

Brandon (K4)............ 319
Brayton (D5)............ 239
Breda (C4)............ 506
Bridgewater (D6)..... 296
Brighton (K6)............ 705
Bristow (H3)............ 313
Britt (F2)............1,908
Bronson (A4)............ 295
Brooklyn (J5)............1,323
Brooks (D7)............ 180
Brunsville (A3)............ 112
Buckeye (G4)............ 192
Buffalo (M6)............ 695
Buffalo Center (F2) 1,087
Bunch (H7)............ 103
Burlington ◉(L7)...30,613
Burnside (E4)............ 105
Burroak (K2)............ 250
Burt (E2)............ 572
Bussey (H6)............ 633
Calamus (M5)............ 381
California (B5)............ 125
Callender (E4)............ 387
Calmar (K2)............ 937
Calumet (B3)............ 250
Camanche (N5)........1,212
Cambria (G7)............ 125
Cambridge (G5)............ 573
Cantril (J7)............ 353
Carbon (D6)............ 282
Carlisle (G6)............ 903
Carnarvon (C4)............ 115
Carpenter (H2)............ 165
Carroll ◉(D4)..........6,231
Carson (C6)............ 596
Carter Lake (B6).....1,183
Cascade (L4)............1,299
Casey (D5)............ 703
Castalia (K2)............ 221
Castana (B4)............ 265
Castle Hill (J3)............ 425
Cedar (H6)............ 110
Cedar (riv.) (K4).....
Cedar Falls (H3)...14,334
Cedar Hts. (H3).......
Cedar Rapids ◉ (K5)............72,296
Center Junction (L4) 153
Center Point (K4)..... 987
Centerville ◉(H7)....7,625
Central City (K4)..... 965
Chapin (G3)............ 200
Chariton ◉(G6)........5,320
Chariton (riv.) (G7).
Charles City◉(H2) 10,309
Charlotte (M5)............ 427
Charter Oak (C4)..... 710
Chelsea (J5)............ 482
Cherokee ◉(B3)........7,705
Chester (J2)............ 226
Chillicothe (J6)............ 196
Churdan (D4)............ 593
Cincinnati (G7)............ 703
Clare (E3)............ 179
Clarence (M5)............ 791
Clarinda ◉(C7)........5,086
Clarion ◉(F3)............3,150
Clarksville (H3)........1,210
Clay Works (E4)........ 175
Clayton (L3)............ 136
Clear (lake) (G2).......
Clear Lake (G2)......4,977
Clearfield (D7)............ 547
Cleghorn (B3)............ 246
Clemons (G4)............ 202
Clermont (K3)............ 625
Climbing Hill (B4).. 140
Clinton ◉(N5)........30,379
Clio (G7)............ 162
Clive (F5)............ 250
Clover Hills (F5)...... 408
Clutier (J4)............ 302
Coalville (E4)............ 350
Coggon (L4)............ 604
Coin (C7)............ 407
Colesburg (L3)............ 326
Colfax (G5)............2,279
College Spgs. (C7).... 368
Collins (G5)............ 432
Colo (G4)............ 538
Columbus City (L6) 350
Columbus Jct. (L6).1,123
Colwell (H2)............ 122
Commerce (F5)............ 152
Conesville (L6)............ 252
Conrad (H4)............ 649
Conroy (J5)............ 200
Conway (D7)............ 168
Coon Rapids (D5)...1,676
Coralville (K5)............ 977
Coralville (res.) (K5) ....
Corning ◉(D7)..........2,104
Correctionville (B4). 992
Corwith (F3)............ 480
Corydon ◉(G7).......1,870

Coulter (G3)............ 271
Council Bluffs ◉ (B6)............45,429
Craig (A3)............ 142
Crawfordsville (K6). 286
Cresco ◉(J2)............3,638
Creston ◉(E6)............8,317
Cromwell (E6)............ 147
Crystal Lake (F2).... 286
Cumberland (D6)..... 493
Cummings (F6)........ 131
Curlew (D3)............ 151
Cushing (B4)............ 248
Cylinder (D2)............ 143
Dakota City ◉(E3). 637
Dallas (G6)............ 421
Dallas Center (E5).. 944
Dana (E4)............ 184
Danbury (B4)............ 601
Danville (L7)............ 450
Davenport ◉(M5).74,549
Davis City (F7)........ 432
Dawson (E5)............ 286
Dayton (E4)............ 793
De Soto (E5)............ 280
De Witt (N5)............2,644
Decatur (F7)............ 196
Decorah ◉(K2)........6,060
Dedham (D5)............ 360
Deep River (J5)....... 379
Defiance (C5)............ 368
Delaware (L4)............ 192
Delhi (L4)............ 383
Delmar (M4)............ 415
Deloit (C4)............ 235
Delta (J6)............ 562
Denison ◉(C4)........4,554
Denmark (L7)............ 300
Denver (J3)............ 635
Derby (G7)............ 194
DES MOINES (F5)............177,965
Des Moines (riv.) (J7) ....
Dewar (J3)............ 150
Dexter (E5)............ 643
Diagonal (E7)............ 472
Dickens (C2)............ 311
Dike (H4)............ 517
Dixon (M5)............ 208
Donnellson (K7)........ 589
Doon (A2)............ 517
Douds (K7)............ 425
Dougherty (G3)........ 212
Dow City (B5)............ 524
Downey (L5)............ 126
Dows (F3)............ 948
Drakesville (J7)........ 222
Dubuque ◉(M3)....49,671
Dumont (H3)............ 718
Duncombe (E4)............ 378
Dundee (L3)............ 176
Dunkerton (J3)............ 409
Dunlap (B5)............1,409
Durant (M5)............1,075
Dyersville (L3)........2,416
Dysart (J4)............1,089
Eagle Grove (F3)....4,176
Earlham (E6)............ 771
Earling (C5)............ 341
Earlville (L4)............ 661
Early (C4)............ 742
East Nishnabotna (riv.) (C6) ....
East Peru (F6)............ 204
Eddyville (H6)............ 941
Edgewood (L3)............ 696
Effigy Mounds Nat'l Mon. (L2) ....
Elberon (J4)............ 225
Eldon (J7)............1,457
Eldora ◉(G4)............3,107
Eldridge (M5)............ 376
Elgin (K3)............ 642
Elk Horn (C5)............ 566
Elkader ◉(L3)............1,584
Elkhart (F5)............ 222
Elliott (C6)............ 482
Ellston (E7)............ 158
Ellsworth (F4)............ 439
Elma (J2)............ 731
Elvira (N5)............ 210
Elwood (M4)............ 125
Ely (K5)............ 155
Emerson (C6)............ 556
Emmetsburg ◉(D2).3,760
Epworth (M4)............ 536
Essex (C7)............ 763
Estherville ◉(D2)......6,719
Evansdale (J4)............3,571
Everly (C2)............ 547
Exira (D5)............1,129
Exline (H7)............ 342
Fairbank (K3)............ 653
Fairfax (K5)............ 335
Fairfield ◉(J6)........7,299

Fairport (M6)............ 150
Farley (L4)............ 745
Farlin (E4)............ 85
Farmersburg (L3)..... 263
Farmington (K7)..... 899
Farnhamville (D4)... 399
Farragut (C7)............ 495
Farson (J6)............ 100
Fayette (K3)............1,469
Fenton (E2)............ 446
Ferguson (H5)............ 178
Fernald (G4)............ 100
Fertile (G2)............ 397
Festina (K2)............ 160
Floris (J7)............ 215
Floyd (H2)............ 440
Floyd (riv.) (A3).....
Fonda (D3)............1,120
Fontanelle (E6)............ 812
Forest City ◉(F2)....2,766
Fort Atkinson (J2)... 273
Fort Dodge ◉(E3).25,115
Fort Madison ◉ (L7)............14,954
Fostoria (C2)............ 147
Franklin (L7)............ 146
Frankville (K2)............ 169
Fraser (E4)............ 219
Fredericksburg (J3) 701
Frederika (J3)............ 210
Fredonia (L6)............ 133
Fremont (H6)............ 471
Fruitland (L6)............ 150
Galt (F3)............ 117
Galva (C3)............ 492
Garber (L3)............ 153
Garden City (G4)..... 150
Garden Grove (F7). 417
Garnavillo (L3)............ 581
Garner ◉(F2)............1,696
Garrison (J4)............ 457
Garwin (H4)............ 518
Geneva (G3)............ 242
George (B2)............1,210
Gibson (J6)............ 101
Gifford (G4)............ 118
Gilbert (F4)............ 297
Gilbertville (J4)........ 399
Gillett Grove (C2).... 150
Gilman (H5)............ 508
Gilmore City (D3).. 746
Gladbrook (H4)............ 862
Glenwood ◉(B6).....4,664
Glidden (D4)............ 996
Goldfield (F3)............ 665
Goodell (F3)............ 242
Gooselake (N5)............ 148
Gowrie (E4)............1,052
Graettinger (D2).....1,016
Grafton (G2)............ 278
Grand Jct. (E4).......1,036
Grand Mound (M5) 526
Grand River (F7).... 350
Grandview (L6)....., 311
Granger (F5)............ 300
Grant (C6)............ 237
Grant Center (A4)..
Granville (B3)............ 350
Gravity (D7)............ 369
Gray (D5)............ 183
Greeley (L3)............ 360
Green Island (N4)... 120
Green Mountain (H4) 199
Greene (H3)............1,347
Greenfield ◉(D6)....2,102
Greenville (C3)............ 173
Grimes (F5)............ 582
Grinnell (H5)............6,828
Griswold (C6)............1,149
Grundy Center ◉ (H4)............2,135
Gruver (D2)............ 135
Guernsey (J5)............ 113
Guthrie Center ◉ (D5)............2,042
Guttenberg (L3)........1,912
Halbur (D4)............ 235
Hamburg (B7)............2,086
Hamilton (H6)............ 245
Hamlin (D5)............ 200
Hampton ◉(G3)......4,432
Hancock (C6)............ 264
Hanlontown (G2)....... 257
Hansell (G3)............ 190
Harcourt (E4)............ 303
Hardy (E3)............ 139
Harlan ◉(C5)............3,915
Harper (J6)............ 182
Harpers Ferry (L2). 252
Harris (C2)............ 319
Hartford (G6)............ 221
Hartley (C2)............1,611
Hartwick (J5)............ 107
Harvey (H6)............ 346
Hastings (C6)............ 308
Havelock (D3)............ 307

Hawarden (A2)........2,625
Hawkeye (J3)............ 511
Hayesville (J6)............ 137
Hayfield (F2)............ 200
Hazelton (K3)............ 550
Hedrick (J6)............ 733
Henderson (B6)......, 208
Herndon (E5)............ 100
High (K5)............ 130
Highland Center (J6) 85
Hills (K5)............ 248
Hillsboro (K7)............ 253
Hinton (A3)............ 345
Hiteman (H6)............ 250
Holland (H4)............ 221
Holstein (B4)............1,336
Holy Cross (L3)........ 139
Homestead (K5)....... 150
Hopkinton (L4)............ 731
Hornick (A4)............ 310
Hospers (B2)............ 604
Hubbard (G4)............ 836
Hudson (H4)............ 613
Hull (A2)............1,127
Humboldt (E3)........3,219
Humeston (G7)............ 750
Huxley (F5)............ 422
Ida Grove ◉(B4).....2,202
Imogene (C7)............ 274
Independence ◉ (K4)............4,865
Indianola ◉(F6).......5,145
Inwood (A2)............ 644
Ionia (J2)............ 301
Iowa (riv.) (H4).......
Iowa City ◉(L5)...27,212
Iowa Falls (G3)......4,900
Ira (G5)............ 103
Ireton (A3)............ 573
Irvington (E3)............ 110
Irwin (C5)............ 381
Jackson Jct. (K2).... 107
Jamaica (E5)............ 303
Janesville (J3)............ 445
Jefferson ◉(E4).......4,326
Jerome (G7)............ 130
Jesup (J4)............1,158
Jewell (F4)............ 973
Johnston (F5)............ 750
Joice (G2)............ 244
Jolley (D4)............ 195
Kalo (E4)............ 150
Kalona (K6)............ 947
Kamrar (F4)............ 261
Kanawha (F3)............ 747
Kellerton (E7)............ 483
Kelley (F5)............ 244
Kellogg (H5)............ 670
Kensett (G2)............ 424
Kent (E7)............ 169
Keokuk ◉(L8)........16,144
Keosauqua ◉(J7).....1,101
Keota (K6)............1,145
Kesley (H3)............ 125
Keswick (J6)............ 276
Keystone (J5)............ 438
Killduff (H5)............ 145
Kimballton (D5)........ 428
Kingsley (A3)............1,098
Kingston (L7)............ 150
Kinross (J6)............ 105
Kirkman (C5)............ 131
Kirkville (H6)............ 213
Kiron (C4)............ 255
Klemme (F3)............ 555
Knierim (D4)............ 133
Knoxville ◉(G6).....7,625
La Moille (G4)............ 151
La Motte (M4)............ 280
La Porte City (J4)....1,770
Lacona (G6)............ 430
Ladora (J5)............ 273
Lake City (D4)........2,308
Lake Mills (F2)........1,560
Lake Park (C2)............ 924
Lake View (C4)........1,158
Lakeside (C3)............ 219
Lakota (E2)............ 443
Lamoni (F7)............2,196
Lamont (K3)............ 574
Lanesboro (D4)............ 280
Lansing (L2)............1,536
Lanyon (E4)............ 120
Larchwood (A2)............ 415
Larrabee (B3)............ 158
Latimer (G3)............ 434
Laurel (H5)............ 257
Laurens (D3)............1,556
Lawler (J2)............ 539
Lawton (A4)............ 254
Le Claire (N5)........1,124
Le Grand (H5)............ 393
Le Mars ◉(A3)........5,844
Le Roy (F7)............ 91
Ledyard (E2)............ 327
Lehigh (E4)............ 881

IOWA

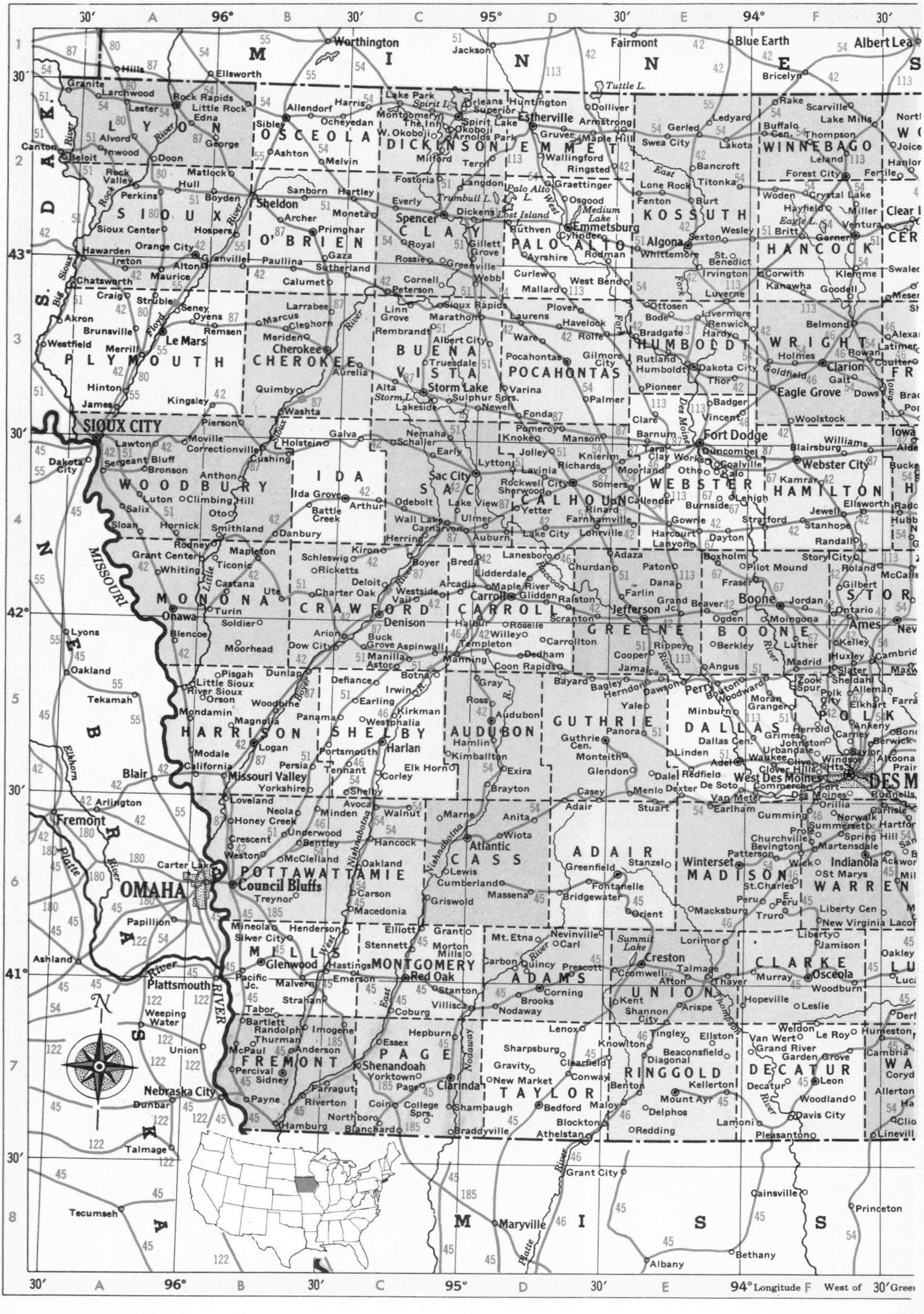

MINNESOTA
Worthington
Jackson
Fairmont
Blue Earth
Albert Lea
S. DAKOTA
NEBRASKA
MISSOURI
LYON
OSCEOLA
DICKINSON
EMMET
KOSSUTH
WINNEBAGO
SIOUX
O'BRIEN
CLAY
PALO ALTO
HANCOCK
PLYMOUTH
CHEROKEE
BUENA VISTA
POCAHONTAS
HUMBOLDT
WRIGHT
WOODBURY
IDA
SAC
CALHOUN
WEBSTER
HAMILTON
MONONA
CRAWFORD
CARROLL
GREENE
BOONE
STORY
HARRISON
SHELBY
AUDUBON
GUTHRIE
DALLAS
POLK
POTTAWATTAMIE
CASS
ADAIR
MADISON
WARREN
MILLS
MONTGOMERY
ADAMS
UNION
CLARKE
FREMONT
PAGE
TAYLOR
RINGGOLD
DECATUR
SIOUX CITY
OMAHA
Council Bluffs
Fort Dodge
Des Moines
West Des Moines
Ames
Le Mars
Storm Lake
Spencer
Estherville
Emmetsburg
Algona
Denison
Carroll
Atlantic
Red Oak
Shenandoah
Clarinda
Creston
Osceola
Boone
Jefferson
Harlan
Missouri Valley
Nebraska City
Plattsmouth
Fremont
Blair
Maryville
MISSOURI RIVER
Longitude West of Green
96°
95°
94°
43°
42°
41°
30′
A
B
C
D
E
F
1
2
3
4
5
6
7
8

IOWA

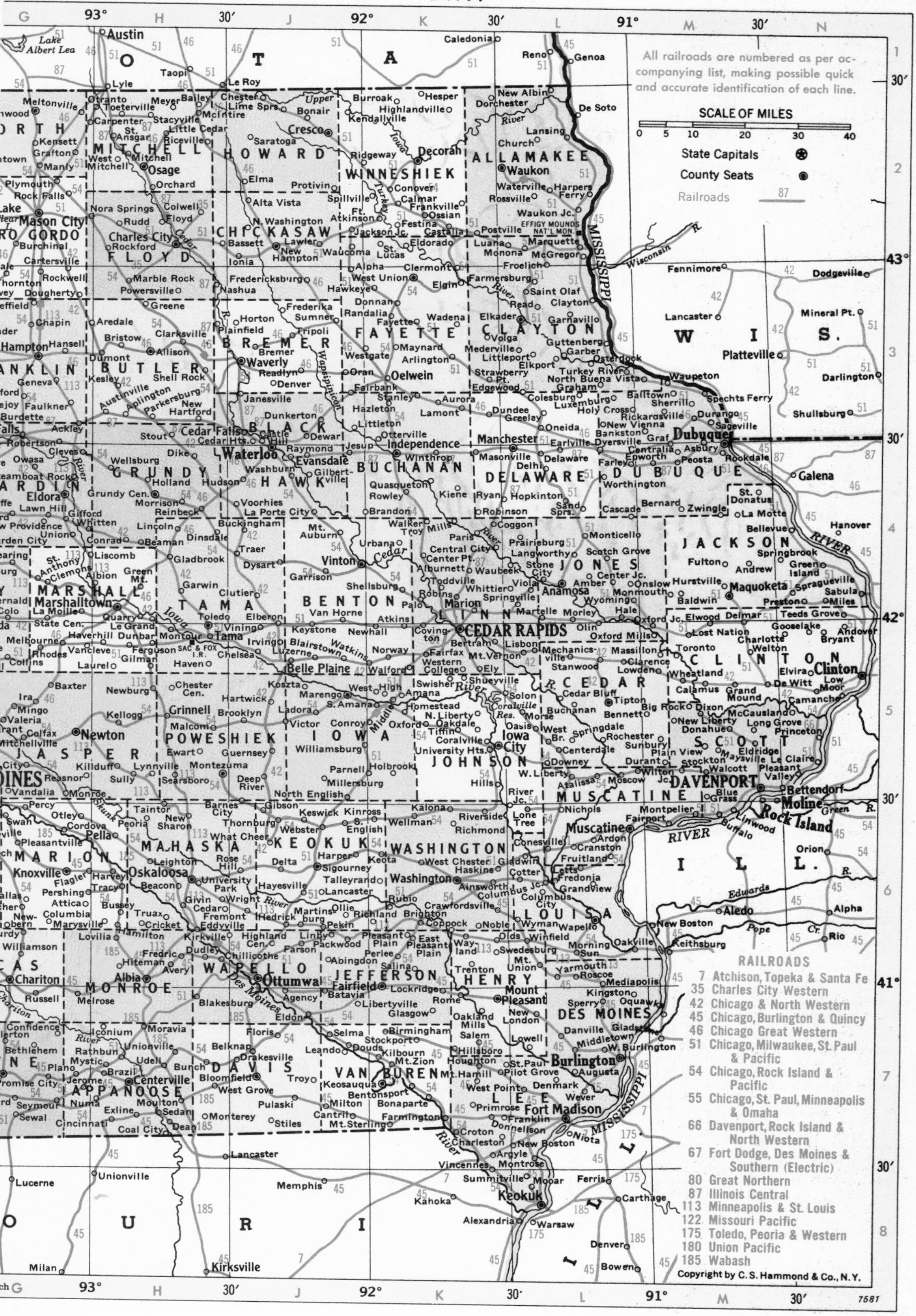
All railroads are numbered as per accompanying list, making possible quick and accurate identification of each line.
SCALE OF MILES
0 5 10 20 30 40
State Capitals
County Seats
Railroads 87
RAILROADS
7 Atchison, Topeka & Santa Fe
35 Charles City Western
42 Chicago & North Western
45 Chicago, Burlington & Quincy
46 Chicago Great Western
51 Chicago, Milwaukee, St. Paul & Pacific
54 Chicago, Rock Island & Pacific
55 Chicago, St. Paul, Minneapolis & Omaha
66 Davenport, Rock Island & North Western
67 Fort Dodge, Des Moines & Southern (Electric)
80 Great Northern
87 Illinois Central
113 Minneapolis & St. Louis
122 Missouri Pacific
175 Toledo, Peoria & Western
180 Union Pacific
185 Wabash
Copyright by C. S. Hammond & Co., N.Y.
7581
93° 30′ 92° 30′ 91° 30′
43° 42° 41°
MITCHELL
HOWARD
WINNESHIEK
ALLAMAKEE
FLOYD
CHICKASAW
FAYETTE
CLAYTON
BUTLER
BREMER
BLACK HAWK
BUCHANAN
DELAWARE
DUBUQUE
GRUNDY
MARSHALL
TAMA
BENTON
LINN
JONES
JACKSON
CLINTON
CEDAR
SCOTT
JASPER
POWESHIEK
IOWA
JOHNSON
MUSCATINE
MARION
MAHASKA
KEOKUK
WASHINGTON
LOUISA
MONROE
WAPELLO
JEFFERSON
HENRY
DES MOINES
APPANOOSE
DAVIS
VAN BUREN
LEE
MINNESOTA
WIS.
ILL.
MISSOURI
MISSISSIPPI RIVER
Austin
Decorah
Waukon
Cresco
Osage
Mason City
Charles City
Waverly
Waterloo
Cedar Falls
Independence
Manchester
Dubuque
Marshalltown
Toledo
Vinton
CEDAR RAPIDS
Marion
Anamosa
Maquoketa
Clinton
Tipton
DAVENPORT
Bettendorf
Moline
Rock Island
Iowa City
Muscatine
Newton
Grinnell
Montezuma
Marengo
Oskaloosa
Knoxville
Pella
Sigourney
Washington
Wapello
Ottumwa
Fairfield
Mount Pleasant
Burlington
Fort Madison
Keokuk
Albia
Chariton
Centerville
Bloomfield
Keosauqua
Galena
Platteville
Kirksville
Memphis

Leighton (H6) 118
Leland (F2) 209
Lenox (D7) 1,171
Leon ◉(F7) 2,139
Lester (A2) 217
Letts (L6) 404
Lewis (C6) 511
Liberty Center (F6). 110
Libertyville (K7) 311
Lidderdale (D4) 180
Lime Springs (J2) 551
Lincoln (H4) 194
Linden (E5) 290
Lineville (G7) 482
Linn Grove (C3) 320
Lisbon (L5) 952
Liscomb (H4) 278
Little Rock (B2) 533
Little Sioux (B5) 349
Little Sioux (riv.) (B3)
Littleport (L3) 139
Livermore (E3) 615
Lockridge (K7) 233
Logan ◉(B5) 1,550
Lohrville (D4) 698
Lone Rock (E2) 188
Lone Tree (L6) 639
Long Grove (M5) 156
Lorimor (E6) 505
Lost Nation (M5) 557
Lovilia (H6) 619
Low Moor (N5) 279
Lowden (M5) 642
Luana (K2) 220
Lucas (G6) 420
Luther (F5) 131
Luton (A4) 154
Luverne (E3) 553
Luxemburg (L3) 120
Luzerne (J5) 186
Lynnville (H5) 406
Lytton (D4) 373
Macedonia (C6) 298
Macksburg (E6) 220
Madrid (F5) 1,829
Magnolia (B5) 207
Malcom (H5) 406
Mallard (D3) 399
Malvern (B7) 1,263
Manchester ◉(L3) 3,987
Manilla (C5) 1,035
Manly (G2) 1,473
Manning (C5) 1,801
Manson (D3) 1,622
Maple River (D4) 120
Mapleton (B4) 1,857
Maquoketa ◉(M4) 4,307
Marathon (C3) 565
Marble Rock (H3) 470
Marcus (B3) 1,263
Marengo ◉(J5) 2,151
Marion (K4) 5,916
Marne (C6) 214
Marquette (L2) 641
Marshalltown ◉ (G4) 19,821
Martelle (L4) 228
Martensdale (F6) 161
Martinsburg (J6) 219
Marysville (G6) 165
Mason City ◉(G2) 27,980
Masonville (K4) 133
Massena (D6) 459
Matlock (A2) 104
Maurice (A3) 256
Maxwell (G5) 802
Maynard (K3) 455
Mc Callsburg (G4) 290
Mc Causland (M5) 150
Mc Clelland (B6) 159
Mc Gregor (L2) 1,138
Mc Intire (H2) 300
Mechanicsville (L5). 850
Mediapolis (L6) 834
Melbourne (G5) 510
Melcher (G6) 898
Melrose (G7) 310
Melvin (B2) 325
Menlo (E5) 421
Meriden (B3) 164
Merrill (A3) 605
Meservey (G3) 297
Middletown (L7) 229
Miles (N4) 344
Milford (C2) 1,375
Millersburg (J5) 200
Millerton (G7) 140
Milo (G6) 525
Milton (J7) 719
Minburn (E5) 353
Minden (C6) 328
Mineola (B6) 145
Mingo (G5) 227
Mississippi (riv.) (L7)
Missouri (riv.) (A4)
◉ County Seat

Missouri Valley (B5) 3,546
Mitchell (H2) 168
Mitchellville (G5) 906
Modale (B5) 283
Moingona (F4) 150
Mondamin (B5) 489
Monmouth (M4) 198
Monona (L2) 1,346
Monroe (G5) 1,108
Montezuma ◉(H5) 1,460
Montgomery (C2) 150
Monticello (L4) 2,888
Montour (H5) 380
Montpelier (M6) 200
Montrose (L7) 643
Mooar (L8) 235
Moorhead (B5) 392
Moorland (E4) 248
Moran (F5) 150
Moravia (H7) 652
Morley (L4) 157
Morning Sun (L6) 939
Morrison (H4) 169
Moscow (L5) 195
Moulton (H7) 985
Mt. Auburn (J4) 216
Mt. Ayr ◉(E7) 1,793
Mt. Etna (D6) 90
Mt. Pleasant ◉(L7) 5,843
Mt. Sterling (J7) 144
Mt. Union (L6) 167
Mt. Vernon (K5) 2,320
Moville (A4) 964
Murray (F6) 767
Muscatine ◉(L6) 19,041
Mystic (H7) 1,233
Nashua (J3) 1,609
Nemaha (C3) 184
Neola (B6) 839
Nevada ◉(G5) 3,763
New Albin (L2) 568
New Boston (L7) 116
New Hampton ◉ (J2) 3,323
New Hartford (H3) 584
New Liberty (M5) 126
New London (L7) 1,510
New Market (D7) 573
New Providence (G4) 212
New Sharon (H6) 1,089
New Vienna (L3) 204
New Virginia (F6) 342
Newburg (H5) 105
Newell (D3) 884
Newhall (K5) 366
Newton ◉(H5) 11,723
Nichols (L6) 348
Nodaway (D7) 233
Nodaway (riv.) (D7)
Nora Springs (H2) 1,257
N. Buena Vista (L3) 148
N. English (J5) 853
N. Liberty (K5) 309
N. Washington (J2). 159
Northboro (C7) 167
Northwood ◉(G2) 1,767
Norwalk (F6) 435
Norway (K5) 441
Numa (G7) 248
Oakdale (K5) 650
Oakland (C6) 1,296
Oakville (L6) 360
Ocheyedan (B2) 700
Odebolt (C4) 1,279
Oelwein (K3) 7,858
Ogden (E4) 1,486
Okoboji (C2) 336
Olds (K6) 187
Olin (L5) 626
Ollie (J6) 298
Onawa ◉(A4) 3,498
Onslow (M4) 244
Ontario (F4) 140
Oran (J3) 110
Orange City ◉(A2) 2,166
Orchard (H2) 114
Orient (E6) 427
Orleans (C2) 317
Osage ◉(H2) 3,436
Osceola ◉(F6) 3,422
Oskaloosa ◉(H6) 11,124
Ossian (K2) 804
Otho (E4) 403
Otley (G6) 177
Oto (B4) 302
Ottosen (E3) 127
Ottumwa ◉(J6) 33,631
Owasa (G4) 100
Oxford (K5) 543
Oxford Jct. (M4) 663
Oxford Mills (L5) 103
Oyens (A3) 95
Pacific Jct. (B6) 550
Packwood (J6) 211
Palmer (D3) 296

Palo (K4) 285
Panama (B5) 230
Panora (E5) 1,062
Parkersburg (H3) 1,300
Parnell (J5) 206
Paton (E4) 404
Patterson (F6) 133
Paullina (B3) 1,289
Pella (H6) 4,427
Peoria (H6) 150
Percival (B7) 250
Perry (E5) 6,174
Pershing (G6) 300
Persia (B5) 373
Peru (F6) 250
Peterson (C3) 589
Pierson (B3) 453
Pilot Mound (F4) 246
Pisgah (B5) 327
Plainfield (J3) 387
Platte (riv.) (D8)
Pleasant Plain (K6). 148
Pleasant Valley (N5). 500
Pleasanton (F7) 130
Pleasantville (G6) 893
Plover (D3) 243
Plymouth (G2) 395
Pocahontas ◉(D3) 1,949
Polk City (F5) 336
Pomeroy (D3) 868
Popejoy (G3) 201
Portsmouth (C5) 299
Postville (K2) 1,343
Prairie City (G5) 834
Prairieburg (L4) 210
Prescott (D6) 372
Preston (N4) 684
Primghar ◉(B2) 1,152
Princeton (N5) 495
Promise City (G7) 218
Protivin (J2) 283
Pulaski (J7) 381
Quarry (H4) 204
Quasqueton (K4) 374
Quimby (B3) 398
Raccoon (riv.) (D4).
Radcliffe (G4) 638
Rake (F2) 351
Ralston (D4) 166
Randalia (K3) 132
Randall (F4) 202
Randolph (B7) 295
Rathbun (H7) 229
Raymond (J4) 260
Readlyn (J3) 468
Reasnor (G5) 227
Red Oak ◉(C6) 6,526
Redding (E7) 200
Redfield (E5) 892
Reinbeck (H4) 1,460
Rembrandt (C3) 296
Remsen (B3) 1,280
Renwick (E3) 474
Rhodes (G5) 369
Riceville (H2) 962
Richland (K6) 591
Richmond (K6) 140
Ricketts (B4) 166
Ridgeway (K2) 307
Ringsted (D2) 578
Rippey (E5) 354
River Sioux (B5) 135
Riverside (K6) 631
Riverton (B7) 472
Robins (K4) 272
Rock (riv.) (A2)
Rock Falls (G2) 139
Rock Rapids ◉(A2) 2,640
Rock Valley (A2) 1,581
Rockford (H2) 979
Rockwell (G3) 753
Rockwell City ◉ (D4) 2,333
Rodman (D2) 123
Rodney (A4) 127
Roland (F4) 687
Rolfe (D3) 997
Rome (K7) 134
Rookdale (M4) 132
Rose Hill (J6) 243
Rowan (F3) 304
Rowley (K4) 249
Royal (C2) 495
Rudd (H2) 398
Runnells (G5) 307
Russell (G7) 566
Ruthven (D2) 868
Rutland (E3) 225
Ryan (K4) 362
Sabula (N4) 888
Sac and Fox Ind. Res. (H5)
Sac City ◉(C4) 3,170
Sageville (M3) 118
St. Ansgar (H2) 981
St. Anthony (G4) 175

St. Benedict (E2) 135
St. Charles (F6) 319
St. Donatus (M4) 100
St. Lucas (K2) 158
St. Olaf (L3) 158
St. Paul (L7) 113
Salem (K7) 473
Salix (A4) 337
Sanborn (B2) 1,337
Sandyville (G6) 92
Saylor (F5) 100
Scarville (F2) 105
Schaller (C4) 841
Schleswig (B4) 751
Scranton (D4) 891
Searsboro (H5) 183
Selma (J7) 175
Seney (A3) 82
Sergeant Bluff (A4) 569
Sewal (G7) 100
Seymour (G7) 1,223
Shambaugh (D7) 251
Shannon City (E7) 171
Sharpsburg (D7) 147
Sheffield (G3) 1,163
Shelby (C5) 592
Sheldahl (F5) 211
Sheldon (B2) 4,001
Shell Rock (H3) 1,013
Shellsburg (K4) 632
Shenandoah (C7) 6,938
Sherrill (M3) 162
Sibley ◉(B2) 2,559
Sidney ◉(B7) 1,132
Sigourney ◉(J6) 2,343
Silver City (B6) 311
Sioux Center (A2) 1,860
Sioux City ◉(A3) 83,991
Sioux Rapids (C3) 1,010
Skunk (riv.) (H6)
Slater (F5) 583
Sloan (A4) 654
Smithland (B4) 373
Soldier (B5) 323
Solon (L5) 527
Somers (E4) 217
S. Amana (J5) 185
S. English (J6) 248
Spencer ◉(C2) 7,446
Spillville (J2) 363
Spirit (lake) (C2)
Spirit Lake ◉(C2) 2,467
Spragueville (N4) 115
Spring Hill (F6) 86
Springbrook (N4) 109
Springville (L4) 680
Stacyville (H2) 544
Stanhope (F4) 420
Stanley (K3) 158
Stanton (C7) 570
Stanwood (L5) 547
State Center (G5) 1,040
Steamboat Rock (G4) 395
Stockport (K7) 346
Stockton (M5) 165
Stone City (L4) 200
Storm (lake) (C3)
Storm Lake ◉(C3) 6,954
Story City (F4) 1,545
Stout (H3) 135
Strahan (B7) 100
Stratford (F4) 673
Strawberry Point (K3) 1,247
Struble (A3) 91
Stuart (E6) 1,500
Sully (H5) 452
Sulphur Spgs. (C3). 90
Summitville (K8) 86
Sumner (J3) 1,911
Sunbury (M5) 100
Superior (D2) 240
Sutherland (B3) 835
Swaledale (G3) 205
Swan (G6) 194
Swea City (E2) 869
Swedesburg (L6) 104
Swisher (K5) 205
Tabor (B7) 869
Tama (H5) 2,930
Templeton (D5) 385
Tennant (C5) 95
Terril (C2) 425
Thayer (E6) 152
Thompson (F2) 698
Thompson (riv.) (E7)
Thor (E3) 271
Thornburg (J6) 138
Thornton (G3) 441
Thurman (B7) 284
Tiffin (K5) 256
Tingley (E7) 333
Tipton ◉(L5) 2,633
Titonka (E2) 589
Toddville (K4) 200

Toledo ◉(H4) 2,106
Toronto (M5) 165
Traer (J4) 1,627
Trenton (K6) 104
Treynor (B6) 247
Tripoli (J3) 1,124
Troy (J7) 103
Truesdale (C3) 158
Truro (F6) 354
Turin (B4) 160
Turkey (riv.) (K2)
Underwood (B6) 278
Union (G4) 490
Unionville (H7) 204
University Hts. (K5) 446
University Park (H6) 457
Upper Iowa (riv.) (K2)
Urbana (K4) 414
Urbandale (F5) 1,777
Ute (B4) 563
Vail (C4) 532
Van Horne (J4) 511
Van Meter (E5) 364
Van Wert (F7) 318
Varina (D3) 144
Ventura (F2) 300
Victor (J5) 741
Villisca (C7) 1,838
Vincent (E3) 193
Vinton ◉(J4) 4,307
Volga (L3) 423
Wadena (K3) 316
Walcott (M5) 480
Walford (K5) 165
Walker (K4) 549
Wall Lake (C4) 753
Wallingford (D2) 229
Walnut (C6) 888
Wapello ◉(L6) 1,755
Wapsipinicon (riv.) (J3)
Washburn (J4) 132
Washington ◉(K6) 5,902
Washta (B3) 403
Waterloo ◉(J4) 65,198
Waterville (L2) 199
Watkins (J5) 130
Waubeek (K4) 120
Waucoma (J2) 385
Waukee (F5) 501
Waukon ◉(L2) 3,158
Waverly ◉(J3) 5,124
Wayland (K6) 600
Webb (D3) 235
Webster (J6) 136
Webster City ◉(F4) 7,611
Weldon (F7) 229
Wellman (K6) 1,071
Wellsburg (H4) 744
Wesley (E2) 509
W. Bend (D3) 772
W. Branch (L5) 769
W. Burlington (L7) 1,614
W. Chester (K6) 218
W. Des Moines (F5) 5,615
W. Liberty (L5) 1,866
W. Mitchell (H2) 112
W. Nishnabotna (riv.) (C6)
W. Okoboji (C2) 158
W. Point (K7) 662
W. Union ◉(K3) 2,141
Westfield (A3) 172
Westgate (K3) 226
Westphalia (C5) 160
Westside (C4) 393
Wever (L7) 100
What Cheer (J6) 1,119
Wheatland (M5) 568
Whiting (A4) 663
Whittemore (E2) 678
Whitten (H4) 174
Whittier (K4) 134
Williams (F3) 519
Williamsburg (J5) 1,183
Williamson (G6) 294
Wilton Jct. (M5) 1,446
Winfield (L6) 888
Windsor Hts. (F5) 1,414
Winterset ◉(E6) 3,570
Winthrop (K4) 604
Wiota (D6) 227
Woden (F2) 272
Woodbine (B5) 1,304
Woodburn (F7) 255
Woodward (F5) 908
Woolstock (F3) 255
Worthington (L4) 337
Wright (J6) 125
Wyoming (L4) 724
Yale (E5) 293
Yarmouth (L6) 160
Yorktown (C7) 146
Zearing (G4) 514
Zwingle (M4) 132

County	County Seat	County	County Seat
Cerro Gordo	Mason City	Lucas	Chariton
Cherokee	Cherokee	Lyon	Rock Rapids
Chickasaw	New Hampton	Madison	Winterset
Clarke	Osceola	Mahaska	Oskaloosa
Clay	Spencer	Marion	Knoxville
Clayton	Elkader	Marshall	Marshalltown
Clinton	Clinton	Mills	Glenwood
Crawford	Denison	Mitchell	Osage
Dallas	Adel	Monona	Onawa
Davis	Bloomfield	Monroe	Albia
Decatur	Leon	Montgomery	Red Oak
Delaware	Manchester	Muscatine	Muscatine
Des Moines	Burlington	O'Brien	Primghar
Dickinson	Spirit Lake	Osceola	Sibley
Dubuque	Dubuque	Page	Clarinda
Emmet	Estherville	Palo Alto	Emmetsburg
Fayette	West Union	Plymouth	Le Mars
Floyd	Charles City	Pocahontas	Pocahontas
Franklin	Hampton	Polk	Des Moines
Fremont	Sidney	Pottawattamie	Council Bluffs
Greene	Jefferson	Poweshiek	Montezuma
Grundy	Grundy Center	Ringgold	Mount Ayr
Guthrie	Guthrie Center	Sac	Sac City
Hamilton	Webster City	Scott	Davenport
Hancock	Garner	Shelby	Harlan
Hardin	Eldora	Sioux	Orange City
Harrison	Logan	Story	Nevada
Henry	Mt. Pleasant	Tama	Toledo
Howard	Cresco	Taylor	Bedford
Humboldt	Dakota City	Union	Creston
Ida	Ida Grove	Van Buren	Keosauqua
Iowa	Marengo	Wapello	Ottumwa
Jackson	Maquoketa	Warren	Indianola
Jasper	Newton	Washington	Washington
Jefferson	Fairfield	Wayne	Corydon
Johnson	Iowa City	Webster	Fort Dodge
Jones	Anamosa	Winnebago	Forest City
Keokuk	Sigourney	Winneshiek	Decorah
Kossuth	Algona	Woodbury	Sioux City
Lee	Keokuk Fort Madison	Worth	Northwood
Linn	Cedar Rapids	Wright	Clarion
Louisa	Wapello		

The People.—The oldest known inhabitants of Iowa were the mound builders, believed to be ancestors of the Indians. The northeast section of the state had, at one time, hundreds of mounds—conical, linear, and effigy—made by these Iowans of prehistoric ages. Some mounds are found in other areas. A few cave dwellings have been found.

When white men came into Iowa in 1673 they found red-skinned people living in the area. Most important among the tribes were the Ioways (who gave the name to the state), the Otoes, Missouris, and the Sioux. As white settlement moved westward, the Sac or Sauk and Fox, the Winnebago, and the Potawatomi moved, or were moved, into Iowaland.

These Indians lived in a tribal state, not owning land individually, but making claim to certain districts as hunting grounds. By 1851 all the Indian tribes had ceded their claims to Iowaland to the government of the United States, but in the 1850's a small contingent of Sac and Fox Indians came back to Iowa and bought some land. The Iowa General Assembly gave them permission to remain and today some 400 Indians, mostly Foxes, live on the 3,300 acres of land they have purchased in Tama County. They prefer to be called Mesquakies.

The white settlers who came into Iowa in the 1830's were chiefly pioneers from the east or south. Some families stopped for longer or shorter periods in Ohio, Indiana, or Illinois. Some came from the south by way of Missouri and Kentucky. Beginning in the decade of the 1840's, Iowa began to attract immigrants direct from Europe, largely from the northern European countries. Of the 261,650 foreign-born residents of Iowa in 1880, 33.7 per cent were from the German Empire, 12.4 from Great Britain, 16.8 from Ireland, 17.6 from Norway, Sweden, and Denmark, 4 from Bohemia, 8 from British America, and 1.8 from Holland. The 1950 census reported that of 84,582 foreign-born residents, 22,774 were from Germany, 20,236 from Scandinavia (Denmark, 7,625; Sweden, 7,080; Norway, 5,531); 6,078 from the Netherlands; 6,320 from Great Britain, including Northern Ireland; 3,819 from Czechoslovakia; and 4,122 from Canada. In 1840, there were 172 free Negroes and 16 slaves in Iowa Territory. In 1880, there were 9,516 Negroes in Iowa and in 1950, 19,692 Negroes, 1,084 American Indians, and 751 other nonwhites. Iowa has always been predominantly rural. In 1950, 1,250,938 persons were classified as urban dwellers and constituted 47.7 per cent of the total population, while 1,370,135 persons lived in rural areas.

Famous Men and Women.—Among the many people of note, native born in Iowa, are: Herbert Clark Hoover (West Branch, 1874–) 30th president of the United States; Henry Agard Wallace (Adair County, 1888–) former vice president of the United States; Harry Lloyd Hopkins (Sioux City, 1890–1946) public official and administrator; E. T. Meredith (Avoca, 1876–1928) secretary of agriculture; William D. Leahy (Hampton, 1875–) naval officer; William Frederick Cody, known as Buffalo Bill (Scott County, 1846–1917) scout and showman; William (Billy) Ashley Sunday (Ames, 1863–1935) evangelist; and Newell Dwight Hillis (Magnolia, 1858–1929) Congregational clergyman.

Iowa is well represented in the field of literature by: Thomas Beer (Council Bluffs, 1889–1940) author; Ellis Parker Butler (Muscatine, 1869–1937) humorist, author of *Pigs is Pigs;* Marquis William Childs (Clinton, 1903–) journalist; George Cram Cook (Davenport, 1873–1924) novelist, playwright, and dramatic director; Paul Hamilton Engle (Cedar Rapids, 1908–) poet; Carl Van Vechten (Cedar Rapids, 1880–) writer; Bess Streeter Aldrich (Cedar Falls, 1881–) writer; Susan Glaspell (Davenport, 1882–1948) novelist, awarded Pulitzer Prize for novel, *Alison's House;* James Norman Hall (Colfax, 1887–1951) writer, co-author of many novels with Charles B. Nordhoff, *Mutiny on the Bounty* and *High Barbaree* being two of them; Harry Hansen (Davenport, 1884–) editor and war correspondent; Josephine Frey Herbst (Sioux City, 1897–) writer; Emerson Hough (Newton, 1857–1923) writer, known as advocate of the preservation of wild life and national parks; MacKinlay Kantor (Webster City, 1904–) writer; Honoré Willsie Morrow (Ottumwa, 1880?–1940) novelist; James Floyd Stevens (Monroe County, 1892–) writer, famous for his Paul Bunyan stories; Ruth Suckow (Hawarden, 1892–) writer; Margaret Wilson (Traer, 1882–) novelist, awarded Pulitzer Prize for her novel, *The Able McLaughlins;* and Phil (Philip Duffield) Stong (Keosauqua, 1899–) writer.

A few of the people famous in music, painting, and sculpture are: Sherry Edmundson Fry (Creston 1879–) sculptor; Nellie Verne Walker (Red Oak, 1874–) sculptor; Abastenia St. Leger Eberle (Webster City, 1878–1942) sculptor, exhibited in leading cities of America and Europe; Grant Wood (Anamosa, 1892–1942) painter and sculptor; and Clarence Eugene Whitehill (Marengo, 1871–1932) operatic baritone.

Natural Resources.—The greatest physical

asset of Iowa is its deep, fertile soil. In the northwest and north central sections, including almost two thirds of the state, the soil consists largely of glacial deposits—pulverized limestone, clay, sand, and gravel—mixed with the remains of vegetation to make a top soil of rich black loam. Large boulders, brought down from the north by the glaciers, are found in this area. In the south and southwest and along the Missouri River, an area equal to about one fourth of the state is covered by a soil called loess, derived from fine particles of clay and lime brought in by the wind in the form of dust. Along many of the rivers are flood plains covered by rich alluvial deposits. Such areas may be flooded if the rainfall is unusually heavy.

In prehistoric days the area of Iowa was thickly covered with grass, shrubs, or trees, and rains washed little soil away, but intensive cultivation of fields, especially those on the hillsides, has resulted in serious erosion and great loss of the valuable top soil of Iowa farms. Contour plowing and planting, rotation of crops, grass where gullies are likely to develop, and trees planted in strategic places are being used to retard this erosion. Flood control by means of dams is being considered.

About 95.5 per cent of the land surface of Iowa is included in farms and it is estimated that one fourth of all grade-A land in the United States is in Iowa.

Flora.—When white men first came to the Iowa area they found the surface of the prairies covered with luxuriant grasses, wild berries, and flowers of many kinds. Along the rivers and in scattered areas were forests of oak, ash, hickory, basswood, cottonwood, walnut, maple, and elm, covering about 18 per cent of the area. The red cedar, the only evergreen tree native in Iowa, gave the name to the Cedar River. Only a few areas in Iowa still have the native grasses, shrubs, and flowers, for most of the state's surface has been plowed many times. Timber still covers an estimated 2,245,000 acres of the state, chiefly in the northeast.

Fauna.—The early settlers found Iowa a land full of game—birds and animals—with fish in the rivers and lakes. Wild game included prairie chickens, deer, wild pigeons, quail, grouse, ducks, wild turkeys, rabbits, and squirrels, all used for food, and wolves, beaver, and smaller animals hunted for pelts and furs. Buffalo were found in Iowa but not in great numbers. Most of these animals have largely disappeared although there are still some deer, rabbits, squirrels, and game birds. The ringneck pheasant has been imported into Iowa and is now a major game bird. Smaller birds which either live in Iowa or migrate through the state include the robin, meadow lark, blue jay, cardinal, blackbird, junco, thrush, sparrow, goldfinch, woodpecker, and crow. The wild pigeon, once seen in great flocks which were said to darken the sky, has disappeared. Hawks and owls are the chief predatory birds. Instead of wild animals and birds, Iowa now produces horses, cattle, hogs, sheep, chickens, ducks, and turkeys.

Minerals.—Coal in southern and central Iowa, gypsum in northwestern Iowa, and clay and stone in scattered areas, are the mineral resources. In early days some lead was mined in the northeast around Dubuque.

Water Power.—The smaller streams once furnished water power for over 700 small mills. Water power is no longer so extensively used, although in recent years, electric utilities have hydroelectrically produced about 17 per cent of Iowa's total electrical energy output.

The rivers of Iowa, especially those draining the northeastern section, have large potential water power, only part of which has been developed. The great dam at Keokuk on the Mississippi is the largest source of power in Iowa. Interior cities having considerable water power available are Ottumwa, Maquoketa, Delhi, Cedar Rapids, Iowa Falls, Decorah, Mitchell, and Independence. The Des Moines and Iowa-Cedar rivers are estimated to have large water power possibilities. Continued construction of the Missouri River Basin Project will affect Iowa.

Parks, Reservations, and Preserves.—Iowans have planned to reserve some of the state's area for community recreation and maintain 88 state parks with an area of almost 30,000 acres. Of forested areas, about 20,000 acres are state and federal forest preserves. The parks, forest preserves, lakes, and monuments under the supervision of the State Conservation Commission are visited each year by over four million persons. The state parks and forest preserves are game refuges and most game animals and many birds are protected by law at certain seasons, if not throughout the year. The Effigy Mounds National Monument in Allamakee County, a tract of over 1,000 acres on which are located many historic works of the ancient mound builders, was established on Oct. 25, 1949, and was transferred to the National Park Service.

The Sac and Fox Indian lands, on the banks of the Iowa River, cover about 3,300 acres. Although this tract of land is known as the Tama Reservation, it is not a reservation, since the government did not reserve it for the Indians. It was bought by them.

Production and Manufactures.—*Agriculture and Animal Industry.*—Because of the rich soil, sufficient rainfall, and a reasonably long growing season, agriculture is the main industry in Iowa. In 1950 there were 203,159 farms as compared with 213,318 in 1940, and the total area in these farms was 34,264,639 acres, approximately 95.5 per cent of the total land area. In April 1950, 790,424 persons lived on farms, about 3.4 persons per farm, indicating that Iowa farms are family projects. The average Iowa farm in 1950 totaled 168.7 acres and was valued at $27,566 for its land and buildings. Owners farmed 48.8 per cent of the farm land in 1945 and tenants operated 51.2 per cent. Farm lands and buildings were assessed at $1,679,844,771 in 1945, the land alone having a valuation of $1,425,348,295. Land has usually been assessed at approximately 60 per cent of its market or actual value, so the market value of this Iowa land would be approximately $2,375,580,500. Iowa farm mortgages totaled $606,612,000 on Jan. 1, 1945, $116,785,000 less than in 1942, and $960,420,000 less than it was in 1924. Government payments to farmers for 1950 totaled $10,920,000.

The census of 1950 reported that 184,760 farms had electricity and that 166,343 had telephones. The activities of the Rural Electrification Administration and cooperative associations greatly increased the use of electricity in rural areas, and by mid-1950, 91 per cent of Iowa's farm homes were using electricity and 82 per cent had telephones. Farm machinery has come to be a large investment on most Iowa farms.

In 1940 the census takers reported that farm machinery was valued at $242,047,000, the highest in the United States. In 1945 the value of machinery was estimated at $354,263,259. Farmers in 1950 owned 228,097 automobiles, 240,941 tractors, and 62,375 motor trucks.

Some idea of the agricultural production in Iowa is indicated by the following tables compiled from the 1950 Census of Agriculture:

LIVESTOCK ON IOWA FARMS APRIL 1, 1950

	Farms reporting	Number	Valuation
Horses and colts [1]	98,304	247,770	$ 10,695,080
Mules [2]	4,119	8,820	456,284
Cattle and calves	182,558	4,539,670	583,388,924
Hogs and pigs	170,501	10,716,220	251,388,499
Sheep and lambs	23,304	898,409	16,665,152
Chickens [3]	173,726	26,508,420	26,858,644
Turkeys [3]	1,018	72,523	345,335

[1] Including ponies. [2] Including mule colts. [3] Four months old and over.

MARKETED LIVESTOCK AND LIVESTOCK PRODUCTS, 1949

	Number	Value
Cattle	2,055,879	$412,607,202
Calves	650,536	55,357,344
Whole milk (pounds)	1,082,733,207	38,079,722
Cream (pounds of butterfat)	123,726,253	78,326,082
Hogs and pigs	14,297,684	587,482,147
Sheep and lambs	873,428	16,844,313
Horses and mules	39,374	1,801,886
Chickens	22,220,744	21,813,354
Chicken eggs (dozens)	231,264,105	84,101,839

PRODUCTION AND VALUE OF CROPS, 1949 [1]

	Harvested acres	Harvested production	Harvested value
Corn (bu.)	10,847,806 [2]	503,589,858 [2]	$ 668,359,560 [3]
Oats (bu.)	6,084,870 [4]	232,591,455 [4]	146,900,689
Soybeans (bu.)	1,312,467 [5]	29,596,245	63,873,256
Alfalfa hay (tons)	1,055,922	2,226,503	49,960,848
Clover or timothy hay (tons)	1,710,184	2,286,665	38,171,935
Winter wheat (bu.)	354,154	6,621,333	12,182,109
Flaxseed (bu.)	109,810	1,505,329	5,384,169
Red clover seed (bu.)	249,883	185,242	4,632,323
Vegetables sold	31,623	......	2,594,824
All crops harvested	.....	......	1,020,793,130
All crops sold	.....	......	320,308,808

[1] Figures in table are for total acreage, production, and value, including value of products sold, unless otherwise indicated. [2] Harvested for grain. [3] Value of corn harvested for all purposes. [4] Oats threshed or combined. [5] Includes some acreage not harvested.

Fisheries.—Since Iowa is an inland state, fishing is limited to the rivers and the few small lakes. In 1943–1944, 1,085 commercial fishing licenses were issued in Iowa and these fishermen took 4,234,701 pounds of fish from the Mississippi River and 110,990 pounds from the Missouri. The most common fish caught for sale in Iowa are carp, buffalo, catfish, bullheads, gar, northern pike, suckers, sheepshead, dogfish, sand sturgeon, and quillback.

During the biennium 1942–1944, a total of 130,202,775 young fish were distributed by the state conservation commission to the lakes and streams of Iowa.

The state conservation commission also has charge of rescuing fish left stranded by floods and various conditions due to the operation of the locks in the Mississippi. For the biennium 1942–1944 this work in the Mississippi River included the salvage of 5,218,726 fish. Floods in inland rivers in 1944 made the rescue of stranded fish important and for the 1942–1944 biennium 20,977,333 fish were taken from oxbow lakes and flooded areas and returned to the waters of the rivers.

Forest and Forest Products.—Iowa has little in the way of a lumber industry, although woodworking industries of various kinds are important. In 1940, Iowa produced only 10 million board feet of lumber.

Minerals and Mining.—Iowa is not rich in minerals. In the early days deposits of lead in the vicinity of Dubuque attracted settlers but these deposits have been exhausted. Bituminous coal is the most valuable mineral and underlies about 13,000 square miles in some 20 counties in south central and southwestern Iowa. In 1917 a record 8,965,830 tons of coal were mined in Iowa and brought $21,096,408. Since then, coal production has decreased and in 1944, Iowa produced only 2,690,000 tons, slightly more than one fourth of the 1917 total, but the value was $9,496,000. In 1949, coal production had fallen to 1,724,484 tons. Cement is first in value among minerals processed in the state. It is made by mixing powdered limestone with clay or shale. In 1949, Iowa produced 6,655,208 barrels of cement, valued at $14,602,554. Iowa ranks third among the states in the production of gypsum, deposits of which cover some 25 square miles in the vicinity of Fort Dodge. In 1949, Iowa produced 858,464 tons of gypsum valued at $2,188,002. Among other mineral products in 1949 there were 6,831,190 tons of stone valued at $8,663,201, 7,978,229 tons of sand and gravel worth $4,446,661, and clay products valued at $628,674.

Manufactures.—Most Iowa manufacturing is centered about the processing of food and the production of nonelectrical machinery. Meat, dairy products, canned goods, dried eggs, cereals, and bakery goods are the principal processed foods. In 1950 there were 146,332 manufacturing employees in Iowa, who received wages totaling $448,052,000. The total value added by manufacture was $925,762,000. The great majority of Iowa plants employ fewer than 50 persons, and Des Moines and Waterloo are among the chief industrial cities. Among the state's nationally known products, other than its meat and creamery products, are washing machines manufactured at Newton, fountain pens, at Fort Madison, cereals prepared in Cedar Rapids, at the largest cereal mill in the world, and gypsum products produced at Fort Dodge.

PRINCIPAL INDUSTRIES, 1950

	All employees [1]	Value added by manufacture [2]
Food and kindred products	53,088	$299,068,000
Nonelectrical machinery	36,327	229,352,000
Chemicals and allied products	4,440	71,399,000
Printing and publishing	9,881	67,553,000
Fabricated metal products	5,539	38,787,000
Stone, clay, and glass products	4,559	37,713,000
Primary metals	4,658	27,539,000
Rubber products	3,018	21,648,000

[1] Average number for 1950. [2] Value of products less cost of materials, supplies, fuel, electric energy, and contract work.

During World War II, many workers migrated to cities where war industries offered high wages. Some workers were employed in war plants at such places in Iowa as Burlington and Ankeny, but others went to out-of-state industrial centers, thereby contributing to an estimated decrease in Iowa's population. Whereas in 1942, 56,480 men and 21,412 women had been employed in 341 Iowa manufacturing plants, by 1944, factory employment had declined slightly to 51,409 men and 24,782 women. After World War II, manufacturing employment climbed beyond its previous levels to 61,683 men and 22,244 women in 1946, and following the Korean War, reached a high of 159,732 workers who, in 1952, were paid $594,970,000 in wages, approximately $3,800 per employee.

Transportation and Communications.—In Iowa's early history, transportation was overland on foot, on horseback, and by ox-drawn wagons, or by river in canoes, pirogues, bateaus, flatboats, keelboats, barges, and, beginning in the 1820's, steamboats. Traffic was generally by river in a north or south direction, but just before the Civil War, railroads began to lay tracks across Iowa, and the flow of traffic assumed an increasingly east to west direction. As a consequence of the competition provided by the railroads, river traffic waned until the 20th century, when the federal government undertook to provide a nine-foot channel in the Mississippi River and built locks and dams at key places. As a result, barges came to be used more frequently, particularly for the transport of coal, oil, and machinery northward on the Mississippi and to haul grain southward. By the 1950's, barges were carrying millions of tones of freight to or past Iowa ports, most of it northbound.

Railroad tracks were constructed in Iowa as early as 1855 and roadbeds were soon built to extend north and south as well as east and west. By 1952, Iowa stood fourth among the states in railroad mileage, with the claim that no town in the state was more than 12 miles from a railroad. Excluding some 400 miles of electric interurban lines, Iowa's railroads were operating 8,577 line miles in 1952. In a representative year (1941), Iowa's railroads carried 374,410,091 tons of freight and 83,648,603 passengers.

Airways also came to be an important transportation factor in Iowa life. United Air Lines serves Des Moines, Cedar Rapids, Muscatine, and Iowa City; Braniff Airways has flights to Sioux City, Fort Dodge, Mason City, Waterloo, Des Moines, Ottumwa, Dubuque, Clinton, and Burlington; and Ozark Air Lines serves Burlington, Muscatine, and Keokuk. By the start of 1953, Iowa had 33 commercial and 58 municipal airfields included in its total of 156 fields.

Automobiles entered Iowa in the 20th century and, with motor trucks and buses, became an important mode of transportation as soon as hard-surfaced roads were built. Iowa's roads, for the most part, were laid out on section lines, so that most farms were easily accessible. Of the more than 100,000 miles of public rural roads in Iowa, almost 9,000 are classified as primary roads under the supervision of the State Highway Commission, while more than 90,000 miles comprise local and county trunk roads which are largely under the supervision of county boards of supervisors. By 1952, more than 6,000 miles of Iowa's rural highways were surfaced with high-type materials such as concrete, cement, and asphalt; over 65,000 miles had such surfacing as gravel, stone, and slag; and about 30,000 miles were unsurfaced. Iowa levies a five-cent tax on each gallon of gasoline, and revenue from this tax, from motor vehicle registration fees, from a use tax imposed on the sale of new motor vehicles, and from 10 per cent of all general sales tax receipts, is used to build and maintain highways.

The importance of motor transportation in Iowa is suggested by the fact that in 1951 there were 1,100,191 motor vehicles registered in the state, including 895,948 passenger cars and taxis and 191,931 trucks and buses. Bus lines annually carry more than 20 million passengers, and there are over 100 each of interstate and intrastate motor freight lines serving Iowa.

Telegraph lines were extended into Iowa in 1848. A tax report for 1944 indicated telegraph mileage as having grown to 10,124,353, with the valuation of telegraph properties assessed at $8,348,880.70. Telephone lines were introduced about 30 years after the telegraph. By 1951, telephone carriers with annual operating revenues exceeding $100,000 had put into operation 1,447,000 miles of wire in cables and 160,000 miles of aerial wire, and were handling, on a yearly basis, 892,900,000 local and 24,812,000 toll calls originating from their installations. As of Jan. 1, 1954, there were 184,100 business and 705,500 residential telephones in Iowa.

Commercial broadcast stations active in 1953 included 49 AM and 16 FM radio stations and two television outlets. Newspapers in 1952 included 44 dailies with a circulation of 1,360,564, and 408 weeklies with a circulation of 631,412.

Economic and Financial Factors.—*Banks.*—Iowa has a dual system of banks—state and federal. As of Dec. 31, 1953, there were 96 national and 516 state banks in Iowa. National banks reported deposits of $859,182,000 and total assets of $921,335,000; state-chartered banks reported deposits totaling $1,695,849,000 and assets of $1,833,168,000. The fiscal growth of state banks is indicated by the expansion of demand and time deposits and other financial indicators. Demand deposits in state banks were $300,865,450 in 1941, $918,672,462 in 1946, and, at the end of 1953, $1,226,094,000. Time deposits totaled $182,471,902 in 1941, $348,939,342 in 1946, and $469,750,000 at the end of 1953. Loans outstanding climbed from $259,410,000 in 1941 and $250,794,254 in 1946 to $678,035,000 on Dec. 31, 1953. There are also in the state several private banks, 89 savings and loan associations, 216 credit unions, and numerous small-loan companies.

Finance.—The expenses of local governments in Iowa—school districts, counties, and municipalities—are financed largely by a mill levy on property, amounting to an average of $51.09 per $1,000 in 1952. The valuation of all property in 1952 (less exemptions) on which taxes were collectible in 1953 was $4,370,606,375, including real property with a valuation of $3,196,674,993. Property taxes collected in the fiscal year 1950–1951 approximated $185 million.

Expenditures by the state government in the 1951–1952 fiscal year amounted to $290,902,000, including $87,968,000 for roads and highways, $54,405,000 for education, $39,576,000 for public welfare, and $17,151,000 for health and hospitals. The state has no long-term debt except that incurred in connection with the financing of bonds for bonuses to World War II veterans.

Personal Income.—Per capita income of

Iowans, which stood at $546 in 1929 and then dropped to $248 in 1932, rose to $468 in 1939, to $1,109 in 1945, and to $1,545 in 1952.

Insurance.—One of the most important business activities in Iowa is insurance. There are 16 local life insurance companies operating in the state and numerous domestic fraternal beneficiary associations, fire insurance companies, casualty companies, and branch offices of national insurance firms. Life insurance policies in force in Iowa in 1952 amounted to $3,987,000,000, representing an average of about $4,500 per family.

Taxation.—The state government secures most of its income from various types of licensing (yielding $34,286,401.72 in the 1952–1953 fiscal year); from general sales and use taxes, and from such taxes as those on individual and corporate income.

IOWA TAX AND LICENSE REVENUE

Type of tax or license	1951–1952	1952–1953
Total tax and license revenue	*$168,244,000*	*$169,353,000*
General sales and use tax	59,289,000	60,413,000
Motor vehicle licenses	32,550,000	33,910,000
Motor fuel tax	31,620,000	31,449,000
Individual income tax	19,703,000	18,214,000
Cigarette tax	5,022,000	5,107,000
Insurance premiums tax	4,446,000	4,810,000
Death and gift taxes	3,939,000	4,625,000
Beer tax	3,094,000	3,129,000
Corporate income tax	2,884,000	2,312,000
Occupational and business licenses	1,290,000	1,306,000
Vehicle operators' licenses	1,292,000	1,179,000
Hunting and fishing licenses	1,088,000	1,057,000
Corporation fees	236,000	267,000
Property taxes	127,000	133,000
Alcoholic beverage licenses	85,000	76,000
Chain store licenses	32,000	32,000

Iowa derives additional revenue from liquor store profits and from the federal government. Receipts from the latter totaled $41,745,000 in 1951–1952, including $19,342,000 for public welfare, $4,259,000 for education, and $10,327,000 for highways. Local governments contribute minor amounts to the state, principally toward public health and welfare.

Government.—*Executive.*—Iowa has the usual form of state government, with a governor who is elected by the voters for a two-year term and who serves at the head of the executive department. In addition, voters elect the lieutenant governor, secretary of state, auditor, attorney general, treasurer, and secretary of agriculture for two-year terms, and commerce commissioners for four-year terms. The superintendent of public instruction was formerly elected, but effective Jan. 1, 1955, was made appointive by the Board of Education.

The governor appoints many officials and boards, usually with the approval of the Senate. Among those officials named by the governor are the adjutant general, comptroller, superintendent of banking, the industrial commissioner, and the commissioners of highways, health, taxation, insurance, welfare, conservation, and labor. Board and commissions appointed by the governor include the boards of education, control, parole, and social welfare, and the liquor control, highway, conservation, employment security, and tax commissions.

A list of the state's governors follows:

TERRITORIAL

Robert Lucas		1838–1841
John Chambers		1841–1845
James Clark		1845–1846

STATE

Ansel Briggs	Democrat	1846–1850
Stephen Hempstead	"	1850–1854
James Wilson Grimes	Whig and Free Soil Democrat	1854–1858
Ralph P. Lowe	Republican	1858–1860
Samuel J. Kirkwood	"	1860–1864
William M. Stone	"	1864–1868
Samuel Merrill	"	1868–1872
Cyrus C. Carpenter	"	1872–1876
Samuel J. Kirkwood	"	1876–1877
Joshua G. Newbold	"	1877–1878
John H. Gear	"	1878–1882
Buren R. Sherman	"	1882–1886
William Larrabee	"	1886–1890
Horace Boies	Democrat	1890–1894
Frank Darr Jackson	Republican	1894–1896
Francis M. Drake	"	1896–1898
Leslie M. Shaw	"	1898–1902
Albert B. Cummins	"	1902–1908
Warren Garst	"	1908–1909
Beryl F. Carroll	"	1909–1913
George W. Clarke	"	1913–1917
William L. Harding	"	1917–1921
Nathan E. Kendall	"	1921–1925
John Hammill	"	1925–1929
Daniel W. Turner	"	1929–1933
Clyde L. Herring	Democrat	1933–1937
Nelson G. Kraschel	"	1937–1939
George A. Wilson	Republican	1939–1943
Bourke B. Hickenlooper	"	1943–1945
Robert D. Blue	"	1945–1949
William S. Beardsley	"	1949–

Legislature.—The General Assembly of Iowa comprises a Senate and a House of Representatives. Their duties and powers are prescribed by a constitution adopted in 1857, with a number of subsequent amendments. The General Assembly begins its regular biennial sessions on the second Monday in January of odd-numbered years. The Senate has 50 members, elected by districts for four years, approximately half being chosen at each election. The lieutenant governor presides over the Senate. The House of Representatives is composed of 108 members elected for two years. Each of the 99 counties elects one representative and each of the nine most populous counties elects an additional representative. Regular sessions usually last three months. The governor may veto acts passed by the assembly, but legislation may be repassed over his veto by a two thirds majority vote. The state legislators receive a salary of $2,000 per biennial session.

Courts.—The state's Supreme Court has nine justices elected for six-year terms, one third being elected at each biennial election. The state is divided into 18 judicial districts, and district court sessions are held at the county seat of each county. Each district elects at least two district judges. Some districts have three, four, or five judges, and one has six, making a total of 70. Cedar Rapids, Iowa Falls, Keokuk, and Oelwein have superior courts, and other towns and cities have municipal courts.

Elections.—General elections in Iowa are held on the first Tuesday after the first Monday of November in even-numbered years. Candidates are nominated at primary elections held on the first Monday of June preceding the general elections. All voting is secret, and voting machines are extensively used. Primary elections are "closed," and a voter must ask for the party ballot he prefers and cannot vote for any primary candidate of another party. The constitution does not provide for the initiative, and the referendum is used only on state constitutional amendments, on certain types of proposed bond issues, and in a few other cases.

Local Government.—Local government is divided between the counties and municipalities, both of which are created by the General Assembly. Finances of local governmental units are strictly regulated by state laws and are supervised by the state auditor. County administration is by a board of supervisors, an auditor, sheriff, clerk of the court, recorder, and treasurer, all elected by the voters for two years. The auditor serves as assessor, with a deputy in charge of the work. A superintendent of schools is elected by an elective county board of education. The supervisors are the policy determining agency and they levy the property taxes within the limits set by the General Assembly.

Social Welfare.—The first state institution in Iowa was the penitentiary established at Fort Madison in 1839. A second penal institution, known as the State Reformatory for Men, was opened at Anamosa in 1876 and the State Reformatory for Women was established at Rockwell City in 1918. A training school for boys at Eldora and a training school for girls at Mitchellville complete the penal institutions. A state board of control supervises the institutions for the care of criminals, delinquents, defectives, and some classes of dependents. The board is composed of three full-time persons appointed by the governor for 6-year terms. The board of control also has charge of the Iowa Soldiers' Home at Marshalltown, the Iowa Soldiers' Orphans' Home at Davenport, and the State Juvenile Home at Toledo.

A state department of social welfare, headed by a board of social welfare of three members appointed by the governor, supervises state relief activities, aid to the blind and to dependent children, old age assistance, and child welfare. It works with the federal social welfare agencies and with the county agencies. County relief and welfare work may be carried on by a county board of social welfare in charge of all such work, or, if the supervisors prefer, the board of supervisors administers relief and the county board of social welfare has charge of other social welfare work. Beginning in 1946, Iowa put into effect a retirement system for all public employees, who may retire at age 65. The employee contributes a per cent of his wages.

Education.—*Public Education.*—Iowa education has moved steadily from schools operated by individuals, societies, or churches toward an educational system financed by taxation and controlled by the state. In the beginning, even elementary schools were privately operated or, at least, were supported by rates paid by the parents. The school law of 1858 fixed the policy of free public elementary schools and about 20 years later free public high schools largely took the place of private academies. School attendance is required for at least 24 weeks for children between 7 and 16 years of age, and school boards may require attendance for the entire term.

The public schools are managed by local boards of directors elected by the voters in the district. They are, however, regulated by state law, with certain requirements as to term of school, curriculum, expenditures, and certification and pay of teachers. Local boards, however, have wide powers. They are supervised by a county superintendent of schools chosen by a board of five members—four elected by districts in the county and one at large—and by a state superintendent of public instruction who is appointed by the nine-member State Board of Education.

Teachers' certificates are granted by the state board of educational examiners composed of the superintendent of public instruction and the following persons appointed by the governor: one of the presidents of the three state institutions of higher learning, a president of one of the privately endowed colleges, a county superintendent of schools, and a city superintendent of schools. The law does not guarantee the tenure of teachers, although there is a provision requiring notification of discontinuance by a certain date.

Many schools maintain commercial and industrial departments and some schools have special rooms for abnormal and handicapped children. The state also maintains schools for the blind and the deaf under the board of education, and the feebleminded under the board of control.

Iowa has three institutions of higher education —the State University of Iowa (q.v.) at Iowa City (1847), the Iowa State College of Agriculture and Mechanic Arts at Ames (1858), and the Iowa State Teachers College at Cedar Falls (1876). These institutions are under the jurisdiction of the State Board of Education, which is appointed by the governor. There are also 15 district and county junior colleges.

Private Education.—Most Iowa communities have parochial schools maintained by the Roman Catholic churches and there are a few other church and private elementary and high schools. Attendance at such schools, if they comply with the requirements made by the laws of Iowa, satisfies the legal requirement as to school attendance and graduates of such high schools are admitted to colleges which accredit them. The state, however, makes no contribution to their support.

There were private colleges in Iowa at an early day, chiefly those sponsored by various churches. Many of these have been discontinued or have become junior colleges, but the list still includes the following: Iowa Wesleyan College at Mt. Pleasant, the oldest college in Iowa; Grinnell College at Grinnell; Cornell College at Mt. Vernon; Drake University at Des Moines; Coe College at Cedar Rapids; Morningside College at Sioux City; Simpson College at Indianola; Luther College at Decorah; Loras College at Dubuque; St. Ambrose College and Marycrest College at Davenport; William Penn College at Oskaloosa; Central College at Pella; and Upper Iowa University at Fayette.

Educational Level.—Iowa has always had a low illiteracy rate, about one half of one per cent. The census of 1950 indicated that only 9,050 of 1,539,185 persons over 25 years of age had not attended school. Some 51,405 others had completed fewer than five grades; 439,305 had finished eighth grade; 372,870 had been graduated from high school; 126,980 had attended college up to three years; and 77,575 had attended higher institutions for four or more years. The median number of school years completed was 9.8 (whites, 9.9; nonwhites, 8.6; males, 9.0; females, 10.7); the national average was 9.3.

Libraries.—The state of Iowa maintains a traveling library at Des Moines to assist small libraries and furnish books to communities having no library facilities. Free public libraries in Iowa are maintained largely by taxation. The state department of history and archives at Des Moines maintains a library, a museum, and an archives department and publishes *The Annals of Iowa.* The state historical society at Iowa

City has a library of some 90,000 volumes and publishes *The Palimpsest,* a monthly magazine, and *The Iowa Journal of History and Politics,* a quarterly, as well as books on Iowa history. Publications are distributed to all public libraries free of charge.

Religion.—Religion has always been an important part of Iowa life. The religious census taken in 1936, the last taken by the government, stated that Iowa had 1,086,989 church members. Of these 294,833 were members of the Roman Catholic Church, 204,047 were Methodists, and 61,682 were Lutherans. Iowa was twentieth among the states in number of churches and eighteenth in number of church members.

History.—The written history of Iowa goes back to June 25, 1673, when two French explorers, Louis Jolliet (or Joliet) and Père Jacques Marquette, landed near the mouth of the Iowa River on their way down the Mississippi. The French claimed the area and named it Louisiana. It was an imperial province but, in 1762, France ceded the area west of the Mississippi to Spain and Spain held sovereignty over it until 1800 when Napoleon compelled Spain to return it to France.

During the Spanish regime three grants of land were made in what is now Iowa. The first of these was a grant of some 189 square miles in the vicinity of Dubuque to Julien Dubuque in 1796. Dubuque, a French-Canadian, had come to the site of present-day Dubuque in 1788 and secured permission from the Indians to mine lead. He died in 1810 and the settlement disappeared. Grants were made in 1800 to Basil Giard, a Frenchman, and in 1799 to Louis Honoré Tesson, a French-Canadian.

In 1803, Napoleon sold western Louisiana, which included Iowa, to the United States and in 1804, President Jefferson sent Captains Meriwether Lewis and William Clark up the Missouri River to explore it. Sergeant Charles Floyd died near the present site of Sioux City and was the first white man buried in Iowa soil. In 1805, Lieut. Zebulon M. Pike made a trip up the Mississippi River.

About 1830 white settlers began to infiltrate into Iowaland, but were driven out, except in the Half-breed Tract (donated to half-breed persons in 1824), until after the Black Hawk War of 1832. In the treaty which followed, the Indians were compelled to cede a tract of land, about 50 miles wide, west of the Mississippi. White settlers soon pushed into the cession and, after June 30, 1833, they were permitted to remain although the land was not for sale. Again in 1836 and 1837 the Sac and Fox made smaller cessions and in 1842 they agreed to give up all their lands in Iowa in 1845. The Winnebago, moved into northeastern Iowa from Wisconsin, were compelled to cede their lands in 1846, the Potawatomi surrendered their claim to land in the southwest the same year. The Sioux gave up their claims in 1851, but a small outlaw band returned in 1857 to commit the Spirit Lake massacre. About the same time a small peaceful band of Sac and Fox returned to central Iowa and bought a small tract of land in Tama County.

The Iowa area was attached to the territories of Indiana, Louisiana, and Missouri, but after Missouri became a state in 1821, Iowaland was left without civil government until 1834 when it was attached to Michigan Territory. In 1836 it was made a part of the Territory of Wisconsin and on June 12, 1838, the Territory of Iowa, including also Minnesota and parts of North and South Dakota, was established, the name being suggested by a small guide book published in 1836 by Albert M. Lea. Iowa was admitted as a state on Dec. 28, 1846.

The first settlers took up claims on unsurveyed lands and organized claim associations to protect claim owners. The early towns included Dubuque, Peru, Davenport, Fort Madison (where a fort had been built in 1808), and Burlington. Burlington was made the temporary capital of Wisconsin Territory in 1837 and became the first capital of the Territory of Iowa. Iowa City was laid out in 1839 as the permanent capital, but in 1857 the capital was moved to Des Moines.

The population of Iowa grew rapidly during the first years. In 1836 it was 10,531, in 1838 it was 23,242, in 1840 it was 43,112, and by 1850, Iowa had 192,212 inhabitants.

During the early years the United States had supervision of all Indian land and built a number of forts in Iowa to maintain order. These were Fort Madison, 1808–1813, Fort Des Moines (No. 1) at the mouth of the Des Moines, 1834–1837, Fort Atkinson, 1840–1849, Fort Des Moines (No. 2), 1843–1846, and Fort Clarke (Fort Dodge), 1850–1853. Fort Des Moines (No. 3) was established in 1901 and Camp Dodge in 1907.

The establishment of civilian agencies kept pace with the population. The first school was opened near the site of the town of Montrose in 1830 with Berryman Jennings as teacher. The oldest college in Iowa is Iowa Wesleyan, founded in 1842. The Methodists built the first church in Iowa, a long building, at Dubuque in 1834. The famous "Little Brown Church" was completed in 1864. The first newspaper was established at Dubuque in 1836. The first telegraph line was used in Iowa in 1848 and the first railroad—from Davenport to Iowa City—was completed by Jan. 1, 1856. Aided by land grants, four railroads were completed across Iowa from east to west soon after the close of the Civil War. The first telephone line in Iowa was constructed in 1877 and the first automobiles were brought into the state about 1900. Airplanes came in about a decade later and radio ten years after that.

Before the Civil War, Iowa was Democratic in politics, but James W. Grimes, elected governor as a Whig in 1856, was a founder of the Republican Party and Iowa has had a Republican governor ever since, except in 1890–1894 and 1933–1939.

From earliest times, Iowans have figured conspicuously in the military operations of their country. In 1780, Jean Marie Cardinal, then living at the lead mines at the site of Dubuque, was killed while resisting a British attack on St. Louis. During the Mexican War a Mormon battalion was enlisted at Council Bluffs. Guthrie, Harden, Mills, Page, Ringgold, Taylor, and Worth counties were named for heroes in the Mexican War and Buena Vista and Cerro Gordo for battles. Four Iowans served as major generals in the Civil War and the state furnished 48 regiments of infantry, nine regiments of cavalry, and four batteries of artillery, about 80,000 men, losing some 12,000 of them. In the Spanish-American War, Iowa furnished four regiments of infantry, two batteries of artillery, a signal corps unit, and a company of colored soldiers. One Iowa regiment, the 51st Infantry, saw service in the Philippines. The 3d Iowa Regiment of the National Guard was included in the Rainbow Division in World War I, during which more than 113,000 Iowans served in the armed forces, of whom over 2,000 were fatalities. In World War II, Iowa contributed about 265,000 men and women and lost 8,234. The first Women's Army Corps (WAC) training camp established was located at Fort Des Moines, and navy fliers were trained at Iowa City and Ottumwa.

After World War II, major political developments included approval by the voters in 1948 of a soldiers bonus, enactment in 1949 of a 20-year, billion-dollar highway program, and creation in 1951 of a Budget and Financial Control Committee and of a Division of Personnel.

In April 1952, the Missouri and Mississippi rivers caused the greatest flood damage to property in the history of the state.

Bibliography.—Gue, Benjamin F., *History of Iowa,* 4 vols. (New York 1903); Cole, Cyrenus, *History of the People of Iowa* (Cedar Rapids 1921); Mahan, Bruce E., and Gallaher, Ruth A., *Stories of Iowa for Boys and Girls* (New York 1929); Federal Writers Project, *Iowa: A Guide to the Hawkeye State* (New York 1938); Briggs, John E., *Iowa Old and New* (Chicago 1939); Cole, Cyrenus, *Iowa Through the Years* (Iowa City 1940); Petersen, William J., *Story of Iowa,* 4 vols. (New York 1952); id., *Iowa History Reference Guide* (Iowa City 1952); *The Iowa Journal of History and Politics* (issued quarterly; Iowa City 1903–); *The Palimpsest* (issued monthly; Iowa City 1920–).

Ruth A. Gallaher,
Former Associate Editor, The State Historical Society of Iowa.

IOWA, State University of, an educational institution forming an integral part of the public school system of the state, situated at Iowa City. It was established in 1847, receiving control of lands given by the federal government. The university is controlled by the Iowa State Board of Education, appointed by the governor of the state, subject to confirmation by the Senate. Its work is organized in the following divisions: division of teaching and research, comprising the colleges of liberal arts, engineering, law, education, commerce, the graduate college, and the summer session, which offer courses leading to the degrees of B.A., B.S., LL.B., J.D., B.S.C., and the professional engineering degrees, in addition to M.A., M.S., and Ph.D.; division of health sciences and services, comprising the colleges of medicine, dentistry, and pharmacy, together with the university hospitals, the psychopathic hospital, the state bacteriological laboratory, and the hospital school for severely handicapped children, with courses leading to professional degrees; the extension division, including a bureau of public affairs and a bureau of visual instruction, as well as a radio station; the child welfare research station, and the school of religion. The library, which lost 25,000 volumes by fire in 1897, now has more than 725,000 volumes. The university issues a series of publications under the title *Studies,* which cover a wide educational field: child welfare, education, engineering, humanistic studies, natural history, Spanish language, business, and aims and progress of research. The extension division conducts correspondence courses, makes motion pictures, and provides the public schools of Iowa with visual aids and many practical bulletins on a variety of subjects. For the 1950–1951 academic year the university enrolled 9,125 full-time students (6,724 men and 2,401 women) and its faculty comprised 674 full-time teachers. Endowment totaled $1,438,715.

IOWA CITY, Iowa, city and Johnson County seat; alt. 685 feet; on the Iowa River, and on the Chicago, Rock Island and Pacific; and the Cedar Rapids and Iowa City (electric) railroads, 121 miles east of Des Moines; has a municipal airport, with airline service. The surrounding territory is principally agricultural. There are no factories in the city. It is the seat of the State University of Iowa; see Iowa, State University of. The university campus is divided, by the river, into east and west sections. The university has notable collections of books, manuscripts, paintings, and statuary. Its library, museum, fine arts building and dramatic art building are open to the public, and the university hospital serves the city. Iowa City was the first capital of the state, and the old Capitol is used as an administration building by the university. In the Civil War years the old county fair grounds were used as an army camp. The state music festival is held here annually, in the spring. Other annual events are the university's Homecoming Day in the fall, when alumni revisit the campus, and Governor's Day, in the spring. The site for the capital was platted in 1839; the municipality was incorporated as a city in 1853. In 1857 Iowa City ceased to be the capital, and Des Moines was selected as its successor, as being nearer the population center of the state. The city has a city-manager form of government. Pop. (1950) 27,212.

IOWA FALLS, Iowa, city in Hardin County; alt. 1,107 feet; on the Iowa River; 49 miles east of Fort Dodge; on the Chicago, Rock Island and Pacific; Illinois Central; and Chicago and North Western railroads. Local industry centers upon the packing and shipping of dairy and poultry products, feed milling, and machine shops. Ellsworth Junior College is located here. Iowa Falls was known successively as Rocksylvania and White's Mill, prior to its incorporation in 1856. Pop. (1950) 4,900.

IOWA RIVER, in the state of Iowa, rises in Hancock County, near the Minnesota state line and flows southeast into the Mississippi River, north of Burlington. It is 300 miles long, and is navigable to Iowa City, 80 miles from its mouth.

IOWA STATE COLLEGE OF AGRICULTURE AND MECHANIC ARTS, founded in 1859, opened in 1869, and located at Ames, Iowa. It offers graduate and undergraduate courses in agriculture, engineering, home economics, industrial science, and veterinary medicine. Its campus and farms cover over 1,300 acres, and its grounds, buildings, and equipment are valued at approximately $24 million. Endowment funds in 1950–1951 amounted to $1,385,000. For the regular 1950–1951 academic year enrollment totaled 6,846, including 5,159 men and 1,687 women, and the faculty included 815 full-time teachers. The library contains more than 420,000 bound volumes. Iowa State College is supported in part by appropriations received from the United States government under the Morrill acts.

IOWAS, a Siouan tribe formerly living in Minnesota, Iowa, and Missouri, but now in Kansas and Oklahoma. J. O. Dorsey reported (1883) their tradition that they were originally "a part of the Winnebago nation."

IPECAC, ĭp′ē-kăk, or **IPECACUANHA**, ĭp-ē-kăk-ū-ăn′ȧ, a South American plant of the order *Rubiaceae* variously called by botanists *Cephaëlis ipecacuanha* and *Psychotria ipecacuanha.* The plant, which is found mainly in moist shady forests in Brazil, is a creeping herb or subshrub with mostly bare stems, only the extremities producing leaves. The small white blossoms, which are borne in heads with long stalks, are followed by dark purple berries. The rather fleshy more or less divided roots were in medicinal repute among the South American Indians, and gradually found their way into European medicine under the name "ipecacuanha." They have been considered emetic, nauseant, diaphoretic and expectorant, and in large doses are poisonous. They appear in commerce in various grades (gray, brown and red), which are dependent mainly upon the season at which they are gathered, the way they are dried, the age of the plants, and other factors. The chief supplies are collected during January, February and March by the Indians. Another species, *C. acuminata,* is found in Venezuela, Panama and Nicaragua.

Owing to the slow growth of the plant and the low price the roots command, ipecac is not cultivated commercially; it has, however, been successfully grown in various parts of the world. It is a constituent of Dover's powder. The roots of several other plants are substituted for those of true ipecac among the best known being those of *Tylophora asthmatica* and *Sarcostemma glaucum* (Venezuelan ipecac), both of the natural order *Asclepiadaceae.* Other species of *Psychotria* and certain species of *Richardsonia* are similarly but unofficially employed.

Wild or American ipecac (*Gillenia stipulacea*) of the rose family, is a common plant in the southeastern United States and as far north as western New York. It is a perennial herb about three feet tall, bearing paniculate corymbs of white or pale rose colored flowers. It is hardy, of simplest culture and being graceful is frequently planted for ornament in flower borders where the soil is of good quality.

IPHICRATES, ī-fĭk′rȧ-tēz, Athenian commander: b. about 415 B.C.; d. Thrace, about 353 B.C. Raising himself to eminence from humble origins, he made his name as the initiator of improvements in Greek arms and was the first to show the effectiveness of light armed troops, called *peltasts.* In the Corinthian War he commanded a company of peltasts which nearly annihilated a battalion of hoplites, and in 386 became a mercenary commander in Thrace, and later in Syria against the Egyptian kings.

Returning to Athens in 373, Iphicrates relieved Corcyra, besieged by the Lacedaemonians, but failed to prevent Epaminondas from invading the Peloponnese. In 367–364 he unsuccessfully led the Athenian forces attempting to regain Amphipolis, retired to Thrace, but later commanded the Athenian fleet at Ambata (355) with his son Menestheus. After this battle an attempt to impeach him for having refused to engage the enemy during a storm resulted in his acquittal.

Consult Xenophon, *Hellenica;* Plutarch's *Lives: Agesilaus, 22.*

IPHIGENIA, ĭf-ĭ-jē-nī′ȧ, in Greek legend, a daughter of Agamemnon and Clytemnestra (according to some accounts, an illegitimate daughter of Theseus and Helen). For some reason Agamemnon was obliged by Artemis (Diana) to sacrifice his daughter, and the Greeks, on their way to Troy, were detained by the goddess at Aulis until the sacrifice was made. On the advice of the high priest Calchas, she was brought to Aulis, and under the pretense that she was to be married to Achilles, was led to the altar. But in the moment when the priest was about to give the deathblow, Iphigenia disappeared, and in her stead a beautiful hind was substituted whose blood gushed out on the altar. Artemis had relented and conveyed her in a cloud to Tauris, where she became the priestess to the goddess.

At Tauris in conformance with the law of the country, she was obliged to sacrifice every Greek who landed there. Thus were the circumstances when her brother Orestes was advised by the oracle to take away with him the Taurian image of Artemis in order to free himself from the guilt of his mother's murder (see CLYTEMNESTRA). Upon his arrival at Tauris, Iphigenia eventually recognizes him as her brother, and the two contrive a means of escape and carry off the image, but not without the divine assistance of Athene.

The story is first told in the *Cypria,* a Greek poem describing the events preceding the *Iliad,* and is also depicted on vases, sarcophagi, and wall paintings. The two episodes in the story were dramatized by Euripides, whose *Iphigenia in Aulis* and *Iphigenia in Tauris* are the most common source for the legend. Among the many later works based on the Iphigenia story, the most notable on the Aulis episode are those of Racine and Gluck (see IPHIGÉNIE EN AULIDE); on the Tauris episode, those of Goethe and Gluck (see IPHIGENIE AUF TAURIS; IPHIGÉNIE EN TAURIDE).

IPHIGENIE AUF TAURIS, ĭf-ĭ-gā′nĭ-ē ouf tou′rĭs, a tragedy in verse by Johann Wolfgang von Goethe, originally written in prose in 1779 and performed by members of the court of Karl August in Weimar with Goethe playing the part of Orestes. It was not put into verse until 1786 during Goethe's first trip to Italy, and on Jan. 6, 1787 he wrote of its completion to friends in Germany.

Goethe derived his plot from the drama of Euripides but his treatment of the material, although directly inspired by the Greek original, deviates essentially from it. Iphigenia persuades Thoas, the king of Tauris, to cease the cruel custom of sacrificing Greek strangers, and he, in love with the priestess, offers her marriage. On her refusal the king is irritated and orders the human sacrifices recommenced. Orestes and Pylades, arriving at the temple, would have been the first victims, but upon recognition of her brother Iphigenia devises an escape which the noble simplicity of her nature prevents her from carrying out, since it involves the betrayal of Thoas. She openly tells the king the whole story and requests her release with her brother and his friend—a request which is granted.

By his superb rendering of the character of Iphigenia and his replacing of the Euripidean *deus ex machina* with the moral resources of a human being, Goethe has expressed the problem of human destiny in modern terms, and man's strife and renunciation imposed by the will of the goddess becomes the striving of man toward understanding and truth within a framework of human necessity.

IPHIGENIE EN AULIDE, ē-fē-zhā-nē′ äN-nō-lēd′, the name of a verse tragedy in 5 acts by Jean Jacques Racine and an opera in 3 acts by Christoph Willibald Gluck. Racine's drama was first presented at court in 1674 and to the public in the following year. Coming after such oriental subjects as *Bajazet* and *Mithridates, Iphigénie en Aulide* was a return to the classical world of *Andromache* (1667) and has been ranked among the author's best works. The plot follows the Euripidean drama (see IPHIGENIA), with one notable exception. Racine introduced the character of Eriphile, a captive of Achilles who accompanies Iphigenia to the Greek camp, and having fallen in love with Achilles, warns the Greeks of her rival's attempt to flee on hearing her fate. Iphigenia is prepared for her death when Calchas announces that Eriphile fulfills the requirements of the sacrifice and is put to death in the place of Iphigenia.

Gluck's opera *Iphigénie en Aulide* was first produced in Paris in 1774 (see GLUCK; OPERA—*Gluck*) on a libretto by the Marquis Du Rollet. It also follows the general outlines of Euripides' tragedy, with an altered denouement. Achilles tries to save Iphigenia from the sacrifice but she, not wishing to see the hero disgraced, resolves to die. Just as the sacrifice is about to take place, Achilles is prepared to rescue Iphigenia by force of arms, but the goddess Artemis interposes, declaring herself appeased and the opera ends with Iphigenia and Achilles momentarily united before the latter leaves for Troy.

An arrangement of Gluck's *Iphigénie en Aulide* was made by Wagner and performed in Dresden in 1847. For Gluck's other opera based on the Iphigenia legend see IPHIGÉNIE EN TAURIDE. Other operas on the Aulis events of the legend were composed by Antonio Caldara (1718); Karl Heinrich Graun (1748); and Luigi Cherubini (1788).

IPHIGENIE EN TAURIDE, ē-fē-zhā-nē′ äN tō-rēd′, an opera in 4 acts by Christoph Willibald Gluck, with a text by Nicolas François Guillard, first performed in Paris in 1779. In the operatic "war" between Gluck and the Italian composer, Niccolo Piccini, both composers were commissioned to write an opera on this subject and Gluck's, produced first, established his position as the leading opera composer in Paris.

The plot is substantially that of the original legend with minor variations (see IPHIGENIA). At the end, Pylades escapes and returns just as the Taurian king is about to sacrifice both brother and sister, stabs the king, and the three of them sail away in safety. Among the several other composers who set this story to music are André Campra (1704); Tommaso Traeta (1763); and Baldassare Galuppi (1768).

IPPOLITOV-IVANOV, ĭp-pŭ-lyē′tôf-ĭ-vä′-nôf, **Mikhail Mikhailovich,** Russian composer: b. Gatchina, near St. Petersburg, Nov. 19, 1859; d. Moscow, Jan. 28, 1935. In 1881, to avoid confusing his real name, Ivanov, with a music critic of the same name, he added his mother's name to his own. A student of Rimski-Korsakov in St. Petersburg he made his debut there as a composer and conductor in 1883, and for ten years at Tiflis in the Caucasus he directed the music school, conducted at the Imperial Theater, and studied Georgian folk music, whose influence on his musical style has linked him with the Russian National School. After 1893 he taught and composed in Moscow. Ippolitov-Ivanov's compositions include the operas *Ruth* (1887), *Azra* (1890), *Ole from Nordland* (1916), and the completion of Musorgski's opera *Marriage* (1931); one symphony (1907); many orchestral pieces, of which the *Caucasian Sketches* is the most popular; and works for chamber and vocal groups. Complying with the spirit of the Soviet regime, he also composed a revolutionary opera *The Last Barricade* (1933–1934) and several songs and marches, some of which were used by the Red Army. He was the author of *The Science of the Formation and Resolution of Chords* (1897, in Russian) and *Fifty Years of Russian Music in My Memories* (1934; in English, *Musical Mercury,* New York, 1937).

IPSEN, ĭp′s′n, **Ernest Ludvig,** lo͝oth′vēg, American portrait painter: b. Malden, Mass., Sept. 5, 1869; d. Miami, Fla., Nov. 2, 1951. He studied at the Boston Museum of Fine Arts and the Royal Academy at Copenhagen, and is known for the many portraits of famous persons which hang in galleries and educational institutions throughout this country. Since 1923 a member of the National Academy, he won the Lippincott prize for his *Mr. Lauth and Bottles* at the Pennsylvania Academy of Fine Arts exhibition in 1936, and many other awards. Among his portraits are those of Elihu Root, Dr. Henry van Dyke, Chief Justice William Howard Taft, and General Robert E. Lee.

IPSWICH, ĭps′wĭch, city, Australia, in Stanley County, Queensland, on the Bremer River, 20 miles west-southwest of Brisbane. It is located in a thriving agricultural region, also favored with extensive coal deposits. It has iron foundries, woolen mills, and lumber yards. Pop. (1947) 26,218.

IPSWICH, county borough, England, a river port in Suffolk, on the Orwell River at its confluence with the Gipping, 10 miles northwest of Harwich and 68 miles northeast of London. The older parts of the town have narrow crooked streets, some of the old houses of which are ornamented with curious carved work. It contains numerous churches and benevolent institutions, a town hall, art museum, mechanics' institute, corn exchange and an ancient mansion of the Tudors. Of its educational establishments the principal is the grammar school founded by Cardinal Wolsey and endowed by Queen Elizabeth.

The Saxon Gyppeswyk, Ipswich was also a Roman settlement, remains of which still exist. It was pillaged by the Danes in 991 and again in 1000. The modern city is a large industrial center, manufacturing railway supplies, agricultural implements, electrical equipment, nonferrous metals, feed cakes, and sugar. Pop. (1951) 104,788.

IPSWICH, town, Massachusetts, in Essex County, 28 miles northeast of Boston on the Ipswich River, state highways, and the Boston and Maine Railroad. Altitude 30 feet. Ipswich's major industry was the manufacture of hosiery until 1927, when the mills were closed and their machinery sold to Russia. Several minor industries now occupy the mill buildings. Ipswich is a popular summer resort and famous for its shellfisheries and Crane's Beach for swimming.

Among the landmarks of the town are the Whipple House (1640), the South Church (1748), and the John Heard House (late 18th century).

The town was settled as Aggawam in 1633 by John Winthrop and a group of 12 pioneers. In the following year, its name was changed to Ipswich (after Ipswich, England) by resolution of the Massachusetts General Court. As early as 1634 it had a meeting house. Ipswich was one of the Massachusetts towns which offered stubborn resistance to the arbitrary taxation introduced under Governor Andros and a number of its citizens were punished for this action. The Rebellion Tablet marks the spot where the townsfolk gathered to protest the governor's oppression nearly 100 years before the Revolution. The township includes Ipswich village (pop. 4,952) and since 1951 has been governed by a city manager. Pop. (1950) 6,895.

IQUIQUE, ē-kē'kä, city, Chile, a seaport and capital of the province of Tarapacá on the edge of the Atacama Desert, 900 miles north of Santiago. Served by railroads and an airport, it is a trading and manufacturing center with petroleum and sugar refineries, cement factories, and fish-canning plants. Nitrates are mined and shipped from nearby deposits.

Founded in the 16th century, the city was almost entirely destroyed by earthquakes in 1868 and again in 1877. In 1879 it was taken by Chile from Peru. Pop. (1949 est.) 35,985.

IQUITOS, ē-kē'tōs, city, Peru, a riverport and capital of the province of Maynas and the department of Loreto on the upper Amazon, near the mouth of the Nanay River, 1,268 miles northeast of Lima by overland route. Altitude 350 feet. Ocean-going vessels drawing 14 feet ascend the Amazon to this point and the river is navigable for lesser craft for 425 miles further up. It has regular steamship connection with Belém, Brazil, via Manaos, connecting there with steamers for the United States and Europe. There are also frequent sailings for all places on the larger tributaries of the Amazon, and small launches keep in touch with small settlements, some of them 400 miles from the Amazon.

Iquitos is the trade center for the entire area of Peru lying east of the Andes. For this great and fertile region it is the place of export, the principal articles being rubber, tobacco, cotton, timber, ivory nuts, balata, and others. The city has machine shops, sawmills, ship yards, cotton gins, factories making straw hats, and soaps (from cottonseed oil), and distilleries producing rum from sugar cane juice.

In the territory surrounding the city, which is largely agricultural, the crops are chiefly of cotton, corn, tobacco and rice. Cattle are raised and there is some export of raw hides. From the forests come large quantities of rubber, balata, chicle and timber. Some clearings made in the forests have been turned into promising banana plantations. Iquitos dates from 1863 when a Peruvian settlement was founded here on the site of a fishing village. Pop. (1946 est.) 36,213.

IRADE, ē-rä'dĕ, a Turkish decree or command of the former Sultans. It was directed to the grand vizier, and he made it public.

IRAN, ē-rän'; Anglicized ī-răn', ĭ-, (1) the name of an extensive highland area in western Asia comprising about 1,000,000 square miles, mostly in Persia-Iran, Afghanistan, and Baluchistan. See IRAN, PLATEAU OF. (2) The name officially adopted in 1935 by the modern kingdom of PERSIA, covering about 628,000 square miles approximately between the Caspian Sea and the Persian Gulf, north and south, and Afghanistan and Iraq, east and west. Pop. (1951 est.) 20,000,000. For geography and political and social history, see PERSIA-IRAN. For cultural history, see PERSIAN ART; PERSIAN LITERATURE; PERSIAN MYTHOLOGY; IRANIAN LANGUAGES AND LITERATURE.

IRAN, Plateau of, a great tableland in western Asia, stretching from the plain of the Tigris in the west to the valley of the Indus in the east, and from the Caspian Sea and the Turanian desert in the north to the Persian Gulf and the Indian Ocean in the south. This vast region includes Persia-Iran, Afghanistan, Baluchistan, part of Iraq, and some of the border lands of India. The population forms the Iranian branch of the Aryan race. In the Pehlevi inscriptions of the famous Sassanid ruler, Shapur I (A.D. 242–72) the country is called Aïran, i.e., the land of the Aryan, in distinction from Aneran, land of the non-Aryan; the latter since the days of Firdusi is termed Turan.

The extremes of climate over this wide area were just as pronounced in ancient as in modern times. As witness the modern Persian saying: *Irân hêfte klimat dâred,* i.e., Iran has seven climates. Along the Persian Gulf in the districts of Bushire and Khorramshahr, it is very hot, in the Elburz range intensely cold. Very diversified also have always been its characteristics and features. However, both in the remote past and in more recent times the region of Iran, though a rather ill-defined unit, has been of enormous influence, not only geographically and ethnologically, but in its bearing on history, in the diffusion of the Indo-Germanic idioms. Topographically considered the immense area is surrounded on all sides by high mountain ranges, these aiding materially in keeping out invaders and preserving within the enclosed territory a homogeneity of language and customs. Thus, despite the numberless vicissitudes undergone by the Iranian stock during immemorial ages, all the accounts that have come down to us seem to agree in ascribing to the people of this area a set of traditional habits and customs as well as a physical makeup which tally in the main with those still observable in the Persians of today.

The earlier travelers and authors, notably Eratosthenes and Strabo, limited the appellation of Ariana (or Iran, Eran) to its southeastern portion, excluding Persia proper, Media and Bactria. Pliny confounds in his description Ariana with Aria, Areia, i.e., the district of Herat in Afghanistan. But Strabo admits that many writers gave to Ariana a more extended meaning, comprising the Persians, Medes, Bakhtrians and Sogdians, as they all spoke the same language, with slight dialectic variations.

The whole enormous area, of which the Persia of today with its 628,000 square miles is but about one-third, is rather poorly watered, lacks adequate rainfall in large sections of it, and presents vast stretches of salt-impregnated wholly arid and barren land. The great desert domain, in fact, extends right across the high plateau, going from a northwesterly in a southeasterly direction, and dividing the fertile provinces of the whole into two groups. This desert is continuous from the southern base of the Elburz Mountains (overlooking in the north the Caspian) to the arid ranges of Makran, bordering on the Persian Gulf. It is about 800 miles in length, but varying greatly in width. The indigenous name for this desert is Dasht-i-Lut, and of it the saline swamps and the salt area are known as the Dasht-i-Kavir.

From the foregoing it may easily be seen that in productiveness, too, the Iranian plateau varies enormously. It is believed to be the original home of the peach, the melon, the cucumber, the cherry and the rose, the wheat plant and the poplar. In general, on its territory grow the trees, the fruits and the cereals of the temperate and of the subtropical zones. There are districts, such as, for example, Masanderân and Gilan provinces, and the region of Shiraz and Shushtar where the yield is enormous. Wherever the rainfall is abundant, such as along the shores of the Caspian and parts of the southwest, and where woods are still remaining and rivers are flowing in a permanent bed, there is also fertility, and wherever these conditions do not subsist the contrary prevails. Some districts, like those of Bushire and Jask in the south and around the entire shore of the Caspian Sea, have plenty of rain. The plateau of Iran, however, suffers unavoidably in its prosperity from the almost total absence of large and navigable rivers.

The population of Iran—using the term in the widest sense—seems to have been much greater in antiquity than at the present time. Undoubtedly incessant warfare, deforestation and a deficient system of tilling the soil practiced for thousands of years and pursued down to our own days, as well as unwise administration and laws, are largely responsible for this.

In historical times Iran (Eran) and Fars (Persia, *Farsistân*) were for long periods almost identical. This refers not merely to the exploits and religion of its people, but also to their art, science, language and literature.

Consult Gutschmid, H. von, *Geschichte Irans von Alexander dem Grossen an* (Tubingen 1888); Niedermayer, Oskar von, *Die Binnenbecken des Iranischen Hochlandes* (Munich 1920); Gabriel, Alfons, "The Southern Lut and Iranian Baluchistan," *Geographical Journal,* 92:193-210, London, 1938.

IRANIAN, a name applied to racial groups of people speaking the Iranian stock of languages. In historic times the Iranians appear on the shores of the Oxus and of the rivers of upper Sogdiana, and thence spread southwest through Balkh and Badakshan. It is probable that in the flourishing ages of the Persian empire the Iranic races were spread much farther, to the Kura River and even beyond. Colonies of Iranians were to be found in the Crimea and mingled with the Thracians. It is thus established that the Iranians were in ancient times the connecting link between the Aryan races of Asia and of Europe. At an early period the Iranians and the Indians probably formed but a single group of races. In antiquity the chief components of the Iranic peoples were the Medes and Persians, as well as the inhabitants of those provinces designated as Ariana; but beside them there were also the ancient nomadic hordes of Iranic stock, the Daha or Dahans, who afterward mingled with the Turanians that occupied the steppes of Turkestan as far as the Sarmatians and Scythians of the present south of Russia. That the latter, though, were conscious of their Aryan and Iranian descent is proved by the names borne by the Scythian (Scolot) kings, such as Ariantas and Ariapithes, Greek settlers on the Euxile (Black Sea) early became acquainted with the Scythians. Herodotus (5th century B.C.) notes two classes which had abandoned nomadic life; two Hellenized tribes and a farming class that raised grain for export.

In our day, under the head of Iranians, may be classed the Persians and the Parsis, scattered throughout Persia and India; the Tadjiks, who speak Persian and follow agriculture or commerce, in Afghanistan, Baluchistan and Turkestan; then the Kurds and Lures, the Afghans, the Ossetians in the Caucasus, the Tais in the region of Baku, the Goorans in Kurdistan, the Galtchas and Pathans on the Pamir plateau and, perhaps, the Armenians. All these populations and tribes stand on very different levels of culture and are also greatly distinguished physically from each other, owing to admixture of foreign elements—such as the Uzbeks and Sarts in Central Asia, influencing the Tadjiks; the Dravidas doing the same with the Baluchis, and the Semitic neighbors in the West playing a similar part. Generally speaking, the Iranians are dolichocephalous and swart, while the Ossetians and Galtchas are brachycephalous and fair.

The system of religious worship developed by the Iranians started, of course, with that of the Aryans as a whole. With the latter they shared the myths of Ahura, Mithras, the dragon-slayer Verethreghna (Indra), Apam—Napat (lightning); they believed in the divine afflatus brought about by *soma* and its preparation; in the injunction to "good thoughts and good works," imposed alike by the Iranian Avesta and the Indian Veda; in the supreme order of the world, controlling men and gods alike, in fire-worship, sun-worship, the sacrificial and purifying flame. And in spite of later rites, many hoary sagas and legends have survived, such as that of a fearful battle waged by the sun-god against a terrific serpent; that of the first man, Yama, who now rules in the nether world; that of the "Glorious One" (Husrava, Chosroes), who meets death at the hands of his unknown father (compare the saga of Hildebrand and Hadubrand, the Sakuntala, the Kalevala) and others which antedate historic times. It is certain that the Gathas (ancient psalms) were extant as early as the 13th or 14th century before our era.

Zoroastrianism, in the form in which it became the dominant creed of the Iranians, made wise use of the old gods and of the early heroes, transfusing them into efficient helpers of the All-Ruler, Ahura Mazda (Ormuzd). In the reign of the legendary King Gushtasp, the patron of Zerdusht (Zoroaster), a period antedating the prevalence of his dogma in Media, in 714 B.C., by several centuries, this prophet and sole founder of one of the purest creeds of the East, attains to power as a teacher. The substance of his tenets was that in this world there are two groups of powers confronting each other in a war without cessation—the powers of Good, of Light, of Creative Strength, of Life, of Truth, and the powers of Evil, of Darkness, Destruction, Death, Deceit. The "great Wisdom," Mazda, with his servants, the "Undying Holy Ones," and a great host of subordinate angels and helpers, is forever facing, battling with, conquering the Evil Spirit (Angra Mainyu, Ahriman) and his tools. The latter are slightly altered reincarnations of the old Iranian gods, now discarded and cursed as "Evil Workers." Zoroaster asks each man to ponder and choose his position with regard to the fundamental problems of life and religion. From his teachings sprang a priesthood, the Magians, entrusted with the task of administering to the needs of the believers. Zoroastrianism was still strong in the early part of the Christian era, and under the Sassanids, about 220 A.D., there came a revival. This we see from a polemic against the Christians (Armenians) during the reign of Yezdegerd II, about 450 A.D., the details of which have been preserved by the Armenian historian, Elishe. The creed of Zoroaster, however, toppled and fell, an easy prey to Islam during the early caliphate in the 7th century. Iran, it is true, for the larger part embraced Shiah, and thus became the inveterate foe of the Sunnite Arabs and Turks; but it nevertheless became Moslem, fanatically so, and buried its ancient national faith forever. The modern Iranians have, however, retained the chief marks of their fathers—a great suppleness of mind, a joyous, lively temperament, a taste for and skill in poetry, the arts and artcraft, an extraordinary politeness and suavity of manners.

Bibliography.—Darmesteter, James, *Etudes Iraniennes* (2 vols., Paris 1883); Geiger, Lazarus, *Grundriss der iranischen Philologie* (in Geiger and Kuhn's *Zeitschrift*, Strassburg 1902); Tomaschek, X. F., *Centralasiatische Studien* (Vienna 1880).

IRANIAN LANGUAGES AND LITERATURE. These may be interpreted under two categories as follows: (1) the dead and living languages of Iran which are related to the family of languages sometimes called Aryan and often Indo-European; (2) the dead and living languages of Iran which are non-Indo-Iranian such as Semitic, Turanian-Altaic, or primitive Caucasian.

Aryan Languages.—There is a widely accepted theory that the Aryan family of languages were originally fairly closely unified as early as the third millennium B.C. The home of these Aryan languages has not been clearly defined, but most authorities indicate the plausibility of regions lying west of the Caspian Sea extending as far west as central Europe. In the main branches, such as Sanskrit, Persian, Greek, Latin, German, and Slavic, there are striking similarities in the words for snow, certain trees, horse, cow, wolf, silver, gold; for the family relationships, such as mother, father, brother, daughter; and in hundreds of other words for useful objects—but no common word for sea. Some time late in the third millennium the Aryan primitive unity seems to have broken up. As the peoples using these languages migrated, separate evolutionary trends took place, while borrowings from the peoples whom they conquered contributed to the changes. By about 2000 B.C. there were two rather clearly defined groups: the western Indo-Germanic group and the eastern Indo-Iranian. The key word used in distinguishing these two subdivisions is the word for "hundred": *"centum"* in Latin and *"satem"* in Sanskrit. The *centum* group largely settled in Europe, but small communities migrated to the East, such as the Tocharian group which established itself in central Asia. The *satem* group includes the Slavic of eastern Europe, the Iranian, and the Sanskrit of India.

The migrations which carried the Indo-Iranian languages to Iran and India seem to fit best into the period between 2000 and 1500 B.C. As they wandered around seeking living space, the Aryan tribes drove the primitive inhabitants into hilly or difficult regions and appropriated the better lands for themselves. It was probably in this period that the earliest Gâthas were composed. These poems were not reduced to writing until later ages; passed down by oral tradition for centuries before being recorded, they thus represent the oldest Iranian linguistic tradition. The Gâthas came to form a part of the collection called the Rig-Veda. Dating back to the middle of the second millennium B.C., the Rig-Veda represents a compilation of centuries of ritualistic hymns. It was not reduced to written form until the 3d century B.C.

About the 12th century B.C. several wandering Aryan-speaking tribes invaded the plateau of Iran. In 835 B.C. the Assyrian king, Shalmaneser III, met the spearhead of these invaders called the Medes (Mad or Mat). They later settled in northwestern Iran. Whether they reduced their language to writing is yet unknown. Rock-cut tombs assigned to the period and supposed to belong to Median aristocracy are without inscriptions. The only surviving terms are names of persons and objects imbedded in documents of a later age. Following them came the Pars, who had settled in southwestern Iran by the middle of the next century. A smaller group, the Khuz, penetrated the plains near the Persian Gulf. The Carmanians, the Sakas, and others settled in central or eastern Iran. These all called themselves Aryans and spoke related tongues. They eventually gave their names to such locations as Hamadan (Hang Mat-an), Fars, Khuzistan, Kerman, and Seistan. Still others occupied eastern Afghanistan, where they established Pashto (Pushtu), which has become the official language of that country since 1936.

It is worthy of note that the Achaemenian kings, who boasted that they were Aryans, adopted or borrowed from the Medes the title "King of Kings of the Aryan Tribes." This word in old Persian is "Eranshahr" and it indicates the probability that each one of the tribes had its own king, and that the distinguishing factor between an Iranian and a non-Iranian was his tribal membership and his language, which could be distinguished from any non-Aryan group surviving under the Aryan political federation. The name of Iran, therefore, goes back at least to the 6th century B.C. as the official name of the country, or the political federation which ruled it. Within the group known as Eranshahr, hegemony shifted from tribe to tribe, first from the Mad of the northwest to the Pars of the southwest. After the Hellenic period, the Parthians (Parth or Parti) of the northeast revived Eranshahr (c.250 B.C.–226 A.D.), following which it reverted to the Pars again (Sassanian dynasty 226–641 A.D.).

The Aryan dialects formed into the Zend, spoken in the south and east (Bactria), and the Avestan, which has been identified by several authorities as the survival of Median, the language of the northern regions. Earliest records of the Zend are found in the famous inscription of Darius I at Behistun (Bisitun) dating to 520 B.C. It consisted of an alphabet of 36 signs. The teachings of Zoroaster, genuine or attributed to him, were collected later in a combination known as the Zend-Avesta. Additional inscriptions are known near Hamadan, and in 1936 a wealth of material was discovered in the royal Achaemenian palaces at Persepolis and on the "Kaabeh of Zoroaster" at Naksh-i-Rustam. The language is closely related to Sanskrit.

Alexander the Great allowed most of this literature to be destroyed and Greek was substituted as the official language during the four centuries of Arsacian rule (c.250 B.C.–226 A.D.). These kings considered themselves philhellenes and suppressed official expression in Iranian terms. But with the outburst of Iranian nationalism fostered by the Sassanian dynasty (226–641 A.D.), the Old Persian, which had always been the language of the people, reappeared in Pahlavi or Middle Persian. One of the main documents is the great inscription found at Paikuli (dated about 293 A.D.). There were dialects such as the Middle Parthian in the north, Middle Sogdian in the northeast (which had a revival in the 9th century A.D.), and Middle Sacian in the east.

The Arab conquest of 641 imposed Arabic upon Iran, except where heretical groups persisted in preservation of the old literature in secret. A colony of Persians who refused to accept Islam migrated to India, taking their religious books with them and thus preserved a mass of literature which probably would have been lost in Iran. These Parsis still utilize the Zend or Pahlavi for their ritualistic devotions. The great counter-reaction to Arabic swept in during the 10th century. At the court of Mahmud (d. 1030) in Ghazni, poets vied in a renaissance of Persian. The most famous of Persian patriots, Firdausi, composed the *Book of Kings* (*Shah Nameh*) in pure Persian, carefully screening out Arabic words, and thereby established the style for Modern Persian (1010). It differed slightly from its parent speech, becoming greatly simplified. Final consonants were weakened; the noun retained only two cases, the nominative and the objective; vestiges of the definite article were kept; the verb showed similar simplification, there being only two main parts, rather closely related. Tense relations were indicated by the addition of prefixes and auxiliary verbs (to be, to have). Person was indicated by suffixes.

Although the Seljuk Turks invaded Iran in 1040 they borrowed the culture of Iran. Modern Persian increased in popularity. Travelogues, such as Nasir-i-Khosrau's *Safar-Nama,* later the *Siyasat-Nama,* a treatise on government by the celebrated Nizam-al Mulk, and various studies in geography made their appearance. This was also the age of Omar Khayyam and the *Rubaiyat.* An excellent translation of Al-Tabari's *Annals* was made in pure Persian. During the Crusades, Fars took the lead in cultural prominence, developing such outstanding poets as Saadi (13th century) and Hafiz (14th century). Coupled with Jalal-ud-din Rumi (1207-1273), the mystic, and Jami (d. 1492), these four and a number of lesser lights raised Persian to a pinnacle whence its influence flowed eastward to the Mogul court in India, Persian becoming the court language of Agra, while westward it was considered a sign of culture in Stamboul (now Istanbul) to be able to read or to write Persian.

The religious influence of Islam, with its preference for Arabic as a divinely revealed eternal tongue, weighed heavily on Persian literature. Arabic was a sign of erudition, wherefore writers too frequently rivaled each other in their effort to use Arabic words, phrases, and idioms. During the 18th and early 19th centuries, Persian became little more than a vehicle for connecting Arabic words. Many compound words appeared—half-Arabic, half-Persian. After 1852, with the appearance of Nasr-ed-Din Shah (1848–1890) of the Kajar dynasty (Turkish) official efforts to simplify Persian appeared. This tendency was accelerated by groups of students who went abroad, especially by a group in Berlin who, after the turn of the 20th century, published *Iranshahr* and other literary magazines of excellent taste. The rise of Iranian nationalism under the vigorous rule of Riza Shah Pahlavi (1925–1941) witnessed a continuing revolt against Arabic culture and an effort to restore Persian to its former glory. An academy was established in Teheran. Its function was to purify Persian from foreign words. Long lists of Persian and Arabic words were issued monthly, the former to be introduced through schools, the press, and the platform, while the latter were strictly prohibited. Unfortunately, the bulk of literature appearing consisted of translations from French and English originals, much of it worthless trash. Yet much original material also saw the light. This trend came to a sudden end on Aug. 25, 1941, when foreign troops invaded Iran; Riza Shah Pahlavi abdicated Sept. 16 and fled, and the academy practically ceased to function.

Aside from the official Persian imposed upon the country by the Teheran government's effort at cultural unification, many Iranian branch languages are alive in peripheral regions. Generally, they have remained purer and more archaic because of their isolation. Around the southern shores of the Caspian, in the provinces of Gilan and Mazanderan, the common speech is called Gilak or Talishi. It is reminiscent of the Persian of Saadi and is spoken by nearly a half million people, but has no significant literature. Some authorities consider it the purest Iranic now extant. In eastern Afghanistan, Pashto is being revived as the official language, although Modern Persian has been the vehicle of communication for centuries. In western Iran several languages are discernible. Kurdish is the language of some 3,500,000 people stretching into Iraq, Syria, and Turkey. From the known traces of the ancient Median language, it is suggested that it has been one of the chief elements in the formation of Kurdish. However, so variegated are the Kurdish dialects that some are incomprehensible to Kurds of a distant region. The Mukri dialect is conceded to be the purest. It has developed only a small literature. Probably most voluminous in literary production has been the Sorani dialect of Kermanji (Kurdish), which centers around Sulaimaniya in Iraq. On the periphery, Kurdish has mixed with foreign tongues to form the Zaza in eastern Anatolia (around Siirt) and the Laki near Kermanshah in the south. A courageous effort to use the Latin script has been made by Kurdish leaders in exile in Damascus. The three centers of agitation for development of Kurdish as a means of education are at Saujbulagh (Iran), Sulaimaniya (Iraq) and Damascus (Syria). In Turkey the central government is making extreme efforts to eradicate Kurdish culture and to impose the Turkish. This movement is complicated by strong political overtones. In Iran also printing of Kurdish literature is prohibited. During the brief Kurdish Republic of Mahabad (1946), the modern name for Saujbulagh, there was a flurry of Kurdish literary production encouraged by the donation of a printing press by the Soviet Union, but inasmuch as this material was politically separatist, it was condemned to destruction upon collapse of the regime. Farther south are found the Lurs, whose speech betrays early Iranic origins. West of Isfahan are the Bakhtiari tribesmen, whose speech is reminiscent of old Persian. In the southeast are Baluchi, remnants of age-old Iranian settlers, whose dialect differs from their neighbors. Isolated in the northwest Caucasus are a few thousand Ossetians, descendents of the Alans, whose mountain home has protected them from loss of an Iranian speech, though separated in time and space. Nestled in high valleys, small pockets of vestigial Iranian communities are to be found whose speech sounds medieval. In 1938 Miss Ann K. Lambton published *Three Persian Dialects,* which illustrates this phenomenon. These archaic local dialects have no literature. Best known is the Tati, a survival of Pahlavi, used in Azerbaijan and near Kazvin.

Armenian remains a puzzle. At first glance, it appears to be an Iranian offshoot because of the thousands of loan-words found in common usage. These words are traceable to the Parthian period (c.250 B.C.–226 A.D.). The consensus is that Armenian actually goes back to an independent branch of Indo-European, millennia older, which fused with Caucasian forms; then because of the intimate political association in Pers-Armenia during the Parthian and Sassanian periods (c.250 B.C–641 A.D.), Armenian took on an added load of Middle Persian terms. It first was reduced to writing in the 5th century A.D. in the monumental translation of the Bible into the classic (*gerapar*) form. Islands of Armenian communities, each using a distinctive dialect, have survived in parts of Iran, but their cultural association has been tied closely to the mother country of Armenia, where a voluminous literature has been produced. In peripheral regions Armenians have borrowed Turkish or Persian loanwords heavily from their neighbors and, in some cases, lost their mother tongue completely. The educated Armenians speak Eastern or "Russian" Armenian, which differs from "Turkish" or Anatolian Armenian.

Non-Iranian Languages.—Iran has been the home of many non-Iranian languages. The earliest recorded language of Iran was Elamite (third millenium B.C.) with its center at Susa. While records have been scant, one column of the famous Behistun inscription is in Elamite. In 1936 fresh finds of tablets were made at Persepolis. As far as can be determined, Elamite was not related to the Indo-European family.

About the 18th century B.C., there appeared the Kassite Empire. The Kassites or Cossaens left little but a series of names, but these indicate no Indo-European associations.

Following the 9th century B.C., Assyrian kings made repeated raids into western Iran. After the disappearance of the Assyrian Empire, the cultural heritage lived on and, during Christian times, the Eastern Aramaic dialect, called Syriac, became the language of the Nestorian Church, which had several thousand members in northwestern Iran. Numerous religious documents in this branch of the Semitic languages have been preserved. Known in the 8th and 9th centuries as the Peshitta, it is the ritualistic language of the Nestorian Church. Because of World War I, the Assyrian community was scattered and its literature has almost disappeared in Iran.

Another of the dead languages used in Iran as an official language was the Babylonian, employed by the Achaemenid kings (550–330 B.C.). It was the third form in the trilingual inscription at Behistun and is found elsewhere in ancient rock carvings.

In 641 A.D., the Arabs invaded Iran and established Arabic as the written tongue. Iranians did not speak Arabic except in southwest Iran, where tribesmen related to the Arabs of Iraq carried their speech with them. (Vigorous efforts were made by Riza Shah Pahlavi, 1925–1941 to force a substitution of Persian, but the program was only slightly successful).

The records of the 7th century indicate that Turkish elements were intruding into northeast Iran at that time. Under the middle Abbasid caliphs, Turks were hired as mercenaries to fight the many battles of the caliphs, resulting in the establishment of numerous Turkish-speaking garrisons throughout the Eastern Caliphate. By 1050 the trickle of Turkish migrants became a flood. They settled throughout the north of Iran, and in Anatolia, setting up Seljuk military fiefs, which established Turkish all the way from the Gobi Desert to the Aegean Sea. The Turkic dialects in Iran, principally the Azari, remain today as the mother tongue of most of the people of Khurasan and Azerbaijan as well as of the Qashgayi tribes in the south. It has had little literary influence, however, though the dominant ruling dynasties of Iran for 700 years have been Turkish-speaking families from the north. This Turkic dialect in Khurasan resembles the speech of the Turkoman tribes of southern Russia and northern Afghanistan. In Azerbaijan, it is more akin to the Turkish of Erzurum. It has borrowed more Persian and considerably less Arabic than the Turkish of Anatolia (Osmanli Turkish). In recent years, the Turkish Republic has sought to revive Turkish words to replace Arabic or Persian loan words and in the small literature of Azari poetry was discovered a rich source of archaic but untainted Turkish. An agglutinized language, it boasts one of the most regular grammars of any language in the world. There is but one principal part to the verb, and syllables representing the tenses, voices, and persons are added to the root in regular order. It is therefore rich in flexibility, expressibility, and clarity. The Soviet Union has adapted it to use with a Russian alphabet, although the Arabic script is also used. In 1944, with the appearance of a Soviet-inspired autonomous revolution in Azerbaijan, this "Azari" Turki was made the official language of the province, but the permanence of such a practice will depend upon political developments in the future.

Bibliography.—Bartholomae, C., *Grundriss der iranische Philologie* (Strassburg 1901); Browne, Edward G., *A Literary History of Persia,* 2 vols. (London 1902); Sapir, Edward, *The History and Varieties of Human Speech* (Washington 1902); Bartholomae, C., *Zur Kentnis der Mittle-Iranische Mundarten,* 5 vols. (Heidelberg 1916–1923); Sapir, Edward, *Language, an Introduction to the Study of Speech* (New York 1921); Browne, Edward G., *History of Persian Literature in Modern Times* (London 1925); Bloomfield, Leonard, *Language* (New York 1933); Gray, Louis H., *Foundations of Language* (New York 1939).

EDWIN M. WRIGHT,
Office of Near Eastern and African Affairs, Department of State, Washington. D.C.

IRAPUATO, ē'ra-pwa'to, Mexico, town in the State of Guanajuato, 32 miles from Guanajuato, on the Mexican National Railway. It has convents and churches of the Spanish colonial period. The country about is fertile under irrigation and strawberries, fruits and maize are grown profitably. Pop. (1940) 32,377.

IRAQ, Asia, better known to the Western World as Mesopotamia (i.e., Land between Two Rivers), is bounded on the north by Turkey, on the east by Iran, on the west by Syria, Trans-Jordan and Saudi Arabia, and on the south by Saudi Arabia, Kuwait, and the Persian Gulf. It has a very ancient civilization which goes back to the years preceding 4000 B.C. Around 630 A.D. the Arabs conquered the country and have occupied it uninterruptedly. In 750 A.D. Iraq became the center of the great Arab Empire and Baghdad (q.v.) was built to be the capital. During the reign of Harun-al-Rashid (c. 786–809 A.D. q.v.) Iraq reached the zenith of its material and intellectual achievements. In 1638 Sultan Murod Khan IV, Ottoman ruler, conquered and subjugated the country and it remained part of the Ottoman Empire until World War I. The mandate for Iraq as an independent state (under the peace treaty with Turkey) was entrusted to Great Britain. Its sovereignty was recognized in a treaty signed by Iraq and Great Britain in 1930 and with Iraq's admission to the League of Nations in 1932 the mandate was terminated. Iraq declared war on the Axis on Jan. 17, 1943, and is a member of the United Nations.

The area of Iraq is 143,000 square miles, two thirds of which are plains with an altitude of from fifty to four hundred feet. The rest is mountainous. The population (1945) numbers approximately 5,000,000 racially composed of 75 per cent Arabs, 18 per cent Kurds, and the remaining 7 per cent Turks, Assyrians, Sabians, and Yazidis. Jews number around 100,000 and Christians 90,000. Islam is the prevailing religion: 55 per cent of the population belong to the Shiah sect and the remainder are Sunnis. Arabic is the official language, with Kurdish semiofficial in provinces where Kurds form the majority.

Iraq is a constitutional hereditary monarchy with Feisal II as its king. Emir Feisal, third son of the Grand Sherif of Mecca, then king of Hejaz, was chosen king by referendum. On his death (Sept. 9, 1933) he was succeeded by his son, Ghazi (born March 21, 1912). King Ghazi was killed in an automobile accident on April 3, 1939 and was succeeded on the throne by his son Feisal (born May 2, 1935). Prince Abdul Illah, King Feisal II's maternal uncle, was named regent and in 1943 became prince apparent to the Iraqi throne. In Iraq, youths attain their majority at eighteen; King Feisal II will accordingly assume his prerogatives on May 2, 1953.

Iraq has a written, rigid contitution providing a bicameral legislature. A constituent assembly meeting in Baghdad in 1924 passed an organic law and an electoral law for the election of deputies to the Chamber of Deputies. Deputies are elected by secret indirect balloting on the basis of one deputy for every 20,000 inhabitants. Voting is confined to Iraqi male citizens over 21 years of age. Members are elected every four years, unless the king chooses to dissolve the Chamber before the expiration of its term. The number of deputies in office varies proportionately with the increase or decrease of the population: in 1946 there were 120. The Senate is composed of not more than one fourth of the number of deputi s. Members are appointed by the king for eight-year terms of office. An amendment to the constitution is voted by both houses meeting in joint session; if the proposed amendment received a majority of votes cast, the existing Chamber of Deputies is dissolved and a new one elected. A joint session again considers the amendement; if approved, it is incorporated in the constitution.

The prime minister is appointed by the king. He selects a Cabinet of not less than six and not more than ten members who are acceptable to the legislature. No minister can remain in office unless he is appointed to the Senate or elected deputy within six months of the nomination to the Cabinet posts. The Cabinet must resign if it fails to enjoy the confidence of the king.

Iraq has a unitary, centralized government. Administratively the country is divided into 14 liwas (provinces). The governor (mutessarif) as administrative head of the province is responsible to the minister of interior. He is appointed or dismissed by the decision of the Council of Ministers with the approval of the king. The liwa is further divided into quadas (districts) and is governed by a quammagem (district administrator) who is answerable in all his activities to the mutessarif. The naheih, (subdistrict) smallest administration unit, is administered by a local official called mudir naheih.

Public security is maintained by a police force under the governor's authority, but technically under the direction of the director general of police. Military service is compulsory. All men between the ages of 19 and 25 are subject to military service; those having college degrees are trained as reserve officers. The Military College, Staff College, Aeronautic School and army technical schools provide officers for the army. The Iraqi Army numbers around 50,000 strong and is composed of all branches of modern army units with air and naval units attached to it.

Education in Iraq is free but not compulsory and is controlled by the ministry of education. The educational system of Iraq provides six years of primary education and five years of secondary schooling, to be followed by higher education. In the primary school great attention is paid to rural education, and schools have been opened among the tribes throughout the country. In the secondary schools the curriculum for girls emphasizes child care and domestic sciences. The courses for boys are divided into three branches, scientific, literary, and commercial. Besides the free government schools there are private denominational, secular, and foreign schools for boys and girls. All schools are subject to inspection by the ministry of education and receive grants in aid. There are also professional schools and colleges which are controlled by the ministry of education and other ministries, according to their speciality. Thus there are the Law College, the Medical College, the Nursing and Midwifery School, the School of Pharmacy, the Engineering College, the Staff College, the Aeronautic School, the Police College, the Invalid Schools, Prisons Schools, and College of

Theology. Iraq also maintains a considerable number of scholarship students abroad.

There are two different court systems in Iraq; one is civil and the other religious. Civil courts are identical with those of western European countries: they include the Court of Peace, Criminal Court, Civil Court of First Instance, Court of Appeal, and the Court of Cassation. The religious courts deal, in accordance with Koranic laws, with inheritance, and according to the tenets of each of the other religions with marriage and divorce.

Baghdad, the capital, is the largest city of Iraq with a population exceeding 600,000. Situated on the Tigris River, approximately in the geographical center of the country, it is an important trade, communication, and industrial center. It also has great tourist interest, for in addition to the beautiful scenery along the Tigris bordered by date trees, Baghdad possesses numerous mosques and ancient buildings of rich, historic value. The amendment to the Constitution adopted in January 1943 declares that the seat of government may be transferred temporarily from Baghdad to any other center in the country as might be necessitated by an emergency situation.

Mosul, Iraq's second largest town, has a population of 160,000. Situated also on the Tigris, about 280 miles north of Baghdad, it is likewise an important commercial and communication center. Basrah, the chief port of Iraq, with a population of about 85,000 is situated on Shatt-al-Arab, approximately 80 miles from the sea. The port is large and equipped with all modern facilities to load and unload cargo ships. Kirkuk, about 150 miles northeast of Baghdad, is an important town in the Iraqin oil wells district. It is from this area that the long pipelines begin which cross the desert and terminate in two ports on the Mediterranean—Haifa and Tripoli. Iraq has 1,200 miles of railway connecting the main important cities from south to north and from east to west. The interior lines are the meter gauge and the Baghdad-Europe lines are of the standard gauge. Rivers have great importance in Iraq as arteries of communication. The Tigris is navigable throughout the year. From Basrah to Baghdad, a distance of nearly 550 miles, large steamers can be utilized, but from Baghdad to Mosul in the north only small river craft can navigate. The Euphrates is also navigable the year round, but here, too, only small river craft can be used. Three of the most important airports in the Near East are located in Iraq, namely, the Habaniah, Baghdad, and Basrah airports. These are equipped with the most modern facilities for air traffic from the west to the east and vice versa. There are 4,000 miles of all-weather motor traffic roads connecting most of the towns and all the districts and provinces. A web of motor car roads connects Iraq with the neighboring countries. Bridges over the Tigris and Euphrates and their tributaries connect the major highways. The greatest bridges in the country are those bearing the names of the three late Kings: Feisal, Ali, and Ghazi.

Iraq is one of the most important agricultural countries in the Middle East. Endowed with exceptional climatic conditions and topography it grows a large variety of crops, the most important being wheat, barley, sesame, dates, maize, corn, cotton, timber, and rice. With these products Iraq could supply the need of the entire country for all seasons, especially in view of the high fertility of the soil, the rainfall and rivers, which supply sufficient water for permanent cultivation. Stock breeding is an important and widespread rural industry, especially that of sheep, cattle, water buffalo, camels, and the famous Arabian horse. For agricultural development the Iraqis have made considerable use of the two great rivers, the Euphrates and the Tigris, by conducting a network of canals and building dams, dikes, barrages, and regulators. Iraq is rich in minerals too. Petroleum is the most abundant and valuable of its raw materials and is found in all parts of the country. The four companies which have acquired oil concessions in Iraq are the Iraqi Petroleum Company, Basra Petroleum Company, the Mosul Petroleum Company, and the Khanagen and Rafidden Company. They are shareholding concerns and, with one exception, export their products. Khanagen and Rafidden Company is primarily a local consumption enterprise conducted to supply the needs of the country. The Government receives royalties from these companies, plus four shillings in gold (80 cents) for each ton produced. Schemes for doubling the production of these oil companies are being worked out and it is expected that a new pipeline connecting Iraq with the Mediterranean will be laid in the near future. Other minerals are tar (the production of which is more than sufficient for the country's requirements) sulphur, coal, salt, iron, lead, and copper.

The geographical situation of Iraq as a center of communication between the East and West allows it to play a dominant part in the trade of that region. The main imported commodities are cotton, silk, and woolen textile goods, machinery, motor cars, sugar, metals, and timber. The exported goods are wheat, dates, barley, corn, licorice, wool, cotton, hides, sheep, goats, horses, and cattle.

Many government clinics and dispensaries have been opened in various provinces and the standard of health has greatly improved since the end of World War I. Malaria is the commonest disease in Iraq and the government is taking steps to combat it wherever it is rampant. Mobile dispensaries have been organized by the government to go out into the desert and extend medical aid to the tribes. The water system has also been greatly improved.

Iraq has several banks. Of the six main banks, three are foreign and three national. In each instance the "home office" is in Baghdad and branches are located in various towns and districts. The medium of exchange is the national dinar, which is equivalent to an English pound sterling or, at the present rate of exchange, $4.05. The dinar is divided into 1,000 parts, each called a fils. Currency notes are issued to the value of from 250 fils to 100 dinars. For lesser sums there are different coins varying in amount from 100 to 200 fils.

Iraq's budget in 1946 amounted to 23,000,000 dinars or approximately $93,000,000. Sources of revenue are mainly derived from direct and indirect taxes, i.e., tax on incomes having a maximum of 33 per cent profit, tax on holdings and lands, petrol royalties, and customs duties. Expenditures are chiefly for education, health, defense, social services, and irrigation. Iraq has no public debt, but enjoys a credit with Great Britain totaling 85,000,000 dinars, or about $350,000,000. The government has floated loans in order to introduce constructive reforms in the agricultural and industrial fields of the country.

The Iraqi government has instituted a special department for antiquities and archaeology. Many archaeological expeditions have visited Iraq since the early 19th century, and important excavations in different parts of the country have been undertaken. Famous among them were the discoveries in Babylon, Nineveh, Ur, Kish, and other ancient towns. The Department of Antiquities has taken special interest in the excavating works, and is developing a museum similar to those of the Western World.

The flag of Iraq is black, white, green, and red with two white stars on the red field.

OMAR ABU KHADRA,
The Arab Office, Washington, D.C.

Bibliography.—Foster, H. A., *The Making of Modern Iraq: A Product of World Forces* (Norman, Okla., 1935); East and West Association, *What to Read about Iran, Iraq, and Afghanistan* (New York 1942); Lloyd, Seton, *Twin Rivers: A Brief History of Iraq from the Earliest Times*, 2d ed. (Oxford 1947); Gamble, F. H., *Economic and Commercial Conditions in Iraq* (London 1949).

IRAZU, ē-rä-sōō, volcano, Costa Rica, in the center of the republic near the city of Cartago, 11,200 feet above sea level. Vapor clouds arise continually from the crater. The volcano was active in 1841 and again in 1910, doing great damage to Cartago.

IRBIT, ĭr-byēt′, town, Soviet Russia, in the Sverdlovsk Region, Russian Soviet Federated Socialist Republic, 110 miles northeast of Sverdlovsk. There are chemical and metallurgical works, and peat and brick plants, and spirits, beer, and leather products are also manufactured. The town is located on one of the early main roads in Siberia, and a trade fair was held here annually from 1643 until the outbreak of World War I; the fair was reinstituted in 1921, but was discontinued in 1930. Pop. about 12,000.

IREDELL, James, American jurist: b. Lewes, Sussex, England, Oct. 5, 1751; d. Edenton, N. C., Oct. 20, 1799. He migrated in 1767 to North Carolina, and in 1774 he was appointed collector of customs at Edenton. In 1775 he was admitted to practice law, and during 1777-1778 he served as judge of the state superior court. He was attorney general of North Carolina from 1779 to 1781, and in 1787 he became a member of the Council of State. At the constitutional ratification convention in 1788 he supported adoption of the federal Constitution. He was appointed sole commissioner to collect and revise the acts of previous assemblies; "Iredell's Revisal" was published in 1791. From 1790 until his death he served as an associate justice of the United States Supreme Court. He was the father of James Iredell, 1788–1853 (q.v.).

IREDELL, James, American politician: b. Edenton, N. C., Nov. 2, 1788; d. there, April 13, 1853. He was the son of James Iredell, 1751–1799 (q.v.). After graduating at Princeton in 1806 he studied law and was admitted to the North Carolina bar. In the War of 1812 he raised and commanded a company of volunteers. He practiced law in Raleigh, N. C., and from 1816 was frequently a member of the state legislature. During 1827–1828 he was governor of North Carolina, and from 1828 until 1831 he served as a United States senator. In 1833 he was appointed one of three commissioners to collect and revise all the statutes in force in North Carolina.

IRELAND, John, American prelate: b. Burnchurch, County Kilkenny, Ireland, Sept. 11, 1838; d. St. Paul, Minn., Sept. 25, 1918. In 1849 he migrated to the United States with his parents, who settled in St. Paul in 1853. He was sent to France to study theology at the seminaries of Meximieux and Hyères, and following his return to St. Paul in 1861 he was ordained in the Roman Catholic priesthood. In 1862–1863, during the early stages of the American Civil War, he served as a chaplain in the Union Army. He was appointed rector of the cathedral at St. Paul in 1867, and in 1875 he became coadjutor bishop. In 1884 he was made bishop, and in 1888 he was consecrated the first archbishop of St. Paul. He was influential in securing the founding of Catholic University, Washington, D.C., in 1889.

IRELAND, William Henry, English literary forger: b. London, 1777; d. there, April 17, 1835. He imposed spurious Shakespearian manuscripts upon his father, Samuel Ireland, a bookseller and engraver, who was a Shakespeare enthusiast, and also upon other men of letters. These documents included a transcript of *King Lear*, extracts from *Hamlet*, and the pseudo-Shakespearian plays *Vortigern and Rowena* and *Henry II*. *Vortigern* was purchased by Richard Brinsley Sheridan and produced by him in 1796 at Drury Lane, where it proved to be a complete failure. The forgeries were detected by Edmund (Edmond) Malone (q.v.), and Ireland acknowledged the fraud in his *Authentic Account of the Shakespearian Manuscripts* (1796); in his *Confessions* (1805) he gave a more detailed account of his forgeries, removing the suspicion that his father may have been an accomplice. *Vortigern* and *Henry II* were published in 1799, and *Vortigern* again in 1832. He also wrote several original romances, ballads, and narrative verse. Ireland's career formed the basis of a novel by James Payn, *The Talk of the Town* (1885). His father's correspondence concerning the forgeries, as well as some of the specimens of the latter, are in the manuscript division of the British Museum. R. W. Lowe's *Bibliographical Account of Theatrical Literature* (London 1888) contains some of the numerous pamphlets published at the time of the discovery of the forgeries.

IRELAND. The island, separated from England on the east by the Irish Sea and St. George's Channel, covers 31,840 square miles, of which 26,602 square miles are in Eire (Republic of Ireland) and 5,238 square miles in Northern Ireland. (See IRELAND, REPUBLIC OF; NORTHERN IRELAND.) It is divided into 32 counties, formed gradually from the 11th to the 16th centuries. These counties are by tradition grouped into four provinces as follows—LEINSTER PROVINCE: Carlow, Dublin, Kildare, Kilkenny, Leix or Laoighis (formerly Queen's County), Longford, Louth, Meath, Offaly (formerly King's County), Westmeath, Wexford, Wicklow; MUNSTER PROVINCE: Clare, Cork, Kerry, Limerick, Tipperary, Waterford; CONNACHT (or CONNAUGHT) PROVINCE:

Galway, Leitrim, Mayo, Roscommon, Sligo. ULSTER PROVINCE includes three counties of Eire—Cavan, Donegal, and Monaghan—and the six that form Northern Ireland—Antrim, Armagh, Down, Fermanagh, Londonderry (or Derry) and Tyrone. Confusion is caused by the fact that the word "Eire" is the Irish for Ireland and may, with equal validity, designate the entire island or the 26 southern counties; while "Northern Ireland" is often referred to as "Ulster" though it consists only of six out of the nine counties within that province.

Topography.—Most Irish views include mountains as at least a distant background in the landscape, and it is the variety of scene that gives the country its scenic attraction. There are no mountains of great height, and the loftiest, Carrauntoohill (Carrantual), 3,414 feet, is in the Reeks of Kerry (Macgillicuddy's Reeks): but in several of the major mountain ranges deep valleys, heath-covered moorlands, and occasional lakes combine to give an impression of rugged grandeur. Nowhere is this more vividly seen than in the extreme west of Connacht, where the Twelve Bens (misnamed Pins) of Bunnabeola in Connemara rise to over 2,000 feet above many square miles of peat bogs on ground only 100-200 feet above sea level. In Achill Island, similar sharp hills over 2,000 feet high rise precipitously from the sea itself; and Slieve League, in the extreme southwest of Donegal, is equally impressive. Several of the mountainous parts of Ireland, visited most by tourists, are close to the sea. In Donegal, western Connacht, and Kerry, mountain ranges are penetrated by long marine inlets, varied in form but everywhere making a scene of great beauty. In the east, the major range is the Leinster chain, which extends for 70 miles southwestwards from Dublin, parallel to the coast: this range has various local names, such as the Dublin Mountains (near the city), the Wicklow Mountains (in the county of the same name), and the Blackstairs Range. The highest peak is Lugnaquilla, 3,039 feet, and there are several fine valleys such as Glendalough, as well as highlying moors of wide extent. The Mournes are a sharp range in County Down, which rise to 2,796 feet in Slieve Donard direct from sea level: the range has some remarkable deep valleys. North of Belfast, there is an upland, the Antrim plateau, mostly 1,000-1,500 feet high but intersected by several valleys known here as "glens" and separated from the sea only by a very narrow lowland traversed by the Antrim coast road. Less spectacular but interesting plateaus are formed of Carboniferous rocks in the Castlecomer upland (between the Barrow and Nore rivers), the uplands on either side of the lower Shannon (parts of counties Cork, Limerick, and Kerry, and those to the west of County Clare), and a group of uplands in County Sligo and adjacent counties. These plateaus are mainly 1,000-2,000 feet high and include among their strata some of coal measure age, though most of these are unproductive and only in Castlecomer is there any mining of significance.

Physical maps reveal at once that the uplands of Ireland have two marked trends. In the extreme south, the hills run east-west, finally reaching the Atlantic in a series of peninsulas: elsewhere, however, the hills run from northeast to southwest, as in the Leinster chain, the Slieve Bloom, and other ranges in the southern half of Ireland, in the Mourne Mountains, and in the sharp-peaked ridges of the northwest. Around the mountains there are lowlands, covering in all more than three quarters of the whole island. The greater part of these lowlands is floored by Carboniferous rocks, but some are developed on earlier strata, and their variety of surface form is due to a complex glaciological history. Almost the whole area of Ireland was covered by ice at some phase in the Quaternary Ice Age, and drifts of varying thickness, some very shallow but others as much as 200 feet deep, occur over large areas: in the lowlands north and south of Galway Bay, however, drifts are absent and remarkable expanses of bare limestone are seen, some devoid of vegetation, but others with low-growing hazels and occasional ash trees. A major effect of the glaciation was the disorganization of the drainage, for peat bogs were formed widely in the Central Lowland and lakes filled hollows, of which some had been ground out by the ice and others lie between various glacial deposits. And not the least remarkable feature is a belt of drumlins (see *Geology,* below) occurring mainly in a band of country 50 miles wide from the Ards Peninsula (south of Belfast Lough) westward to Clew Bay, County Mayo, with extensions through the Erne Valley to Donegal Bay. They are also numerous in the Bann Valley.

Coastlines are varied in form. In the east there are rocky shores and cliffs, some of which have splendid exposures of glacial drift. Wexford Harbour, Dublin Bay, Carlingford Lough, Strangford Lough, and Belfast Lough are the major inlets; at various points along the coast there are sand dunes. The south coast has several long inlets—two of which form the harbors of Waterford and Cork: much of the coast has cliffs some 200 feet high, broken by numerous estuaries and coves. In the west, there is some magnificent coast scenery. Western Cork and Kerry consist of peninsulas with hills, some of which terminate in high cliffs, and islands add variety to the scene. The long estuary of the Shannon is tidal to Limerick, 50 miles from the open sea. County Clare has some fine cliffs, notably the Cliffs of Moher, which have a vertical drop of 600 feet. Limestones in north Clare and in the Aran Islands are exposed in horizontal slabs, seared by weathering into pavements. In Galway Bay, there is a marked contrast between the limestones to the south and the ancient metamorphic rocks to the north; and in the west there are numerous islands. This scenic type is continued northwards to Clew Bay, where the drumlins, at the western extremity of their great spread across Ireland, appear as a multitude of islands. Quartzites, highly resistant metamorphic rocks, form massive precipices almost 2,000 feet high in Achill Island and in the southwest of County Donegal; but otherwise the coasts of this area are varied in form, though including numerous cliffs. Four long inlets of County Donegal—Lough Foyle, Lough Swilly, Mulroy Bay, and Sheep Haven—add to the variety of an intricate coastline. As a whole, the coasts of Ireland are remarkable for their scenery and variety.

Hydrography.—Rivers have complicated courses in Ireland, due to an involved geological history and the deposition of large quantities of glacial drift. A puzzling feature is that certain rivers flow over the Central Lowland in courses almost level, and then fall rapidly to sea level in their last few miles. The Shannon, for example, falls 100 feet in the last 16 miles from Lough Derg to the tidal level at Limerick, and there is a similar fall at Ballyshannon, on the Erne: both these falls have now been used for hydro-electric stations. Several other rivers, such as the Liffey, the Barrow, and the Nore, flow through gorges for many miles before they reach the sea.

The Shannon, the longest river in the British Isles, rises in the Carboniferous uplands near Sligo Bay, falls steeply to Lough Allen (164 feet), and then flows gently across the lowland; it passes through several lakes, of which the two largest are Lough Ree and Lough Derg. Its three major tributaries, the Suck, Inny, and Brosna, are similar slow-flowing lowland rivers. The Erne, which flows to Donegal Bay, is a river draining an intricate drumlin country marked by numerous lakes, of which the two largest are upper and lower Lough Erne. In the north, the Foyle-Strule river system consists of one main stream and several tributaries; the Bann rises on the north side of the Mourne Mountains, and flows northward, including in its course Lough Neagh (150 square miles), the largest lake in the British Isles. The Boyne and its tributary the Blackwater drain eastern parts of the Central Lowland, and the Liffey rises in the Leinster chain and winds round the west side of these mountains to reach the sea at Dublin. Only one river, the Slaney, cuts through the Leinster chain.

The rivers of the south and southeast have courses of great interest. The streams flowing to Waterford Harbour—the Barrow, Nore, and Suir—pass through peat bogs on wide lowlands in their upper courses, but entrench themselves in gorges as much as 100 feet deep nearer the sea. From a point near Clonmel, the Suir has an west-east course, a feature seen also in rivers still farther south—the Blackwater, its tributary the Bride, the Lee and (another river) Bride at Cork, the Bandon, and numerous smaller streams. All these rivers flow in valleys between the east-west chains of mountains to which reference has already been made: the Blackwater and the Lee turn south and reach the sea in striking estuaries. Most of the remaining rivers are short and insignificant.

As a whole the rivers of Ireland have great interest for the physical geographer: in the Central Lowland they are sluggish, slow-moving streams bordered in places by extensive peat bogs, but in the lower reaches they are swifter-moving, pleasant stretches of water. Few visitors trouble to explore these valleys, but the Foyle, the Boyne in County Meath, the "three sisters" (Barrow, Nore, and Suir) which unite in Waterford Harbour, the Blackwater, and, to quote Edmund Spenser, "the spacious Shenan (Shannon) spreading like a sea," all have their distinct beauty.

Geology.—The oldest areas of Ireland are the pre-Cambrian masses, comparable to those of the Scottish Highlands, in the northwest (counties of Donegal, Londonderry, and Tyrone) and in the west of the Connacht Province (western Mayo and western Galway). Within these areas, there are varied rocks, including gneisses, schists, granites, and quartzites; and it is the last of these that form some of the striking hills, including some sharp conical peaks such as Errigal in County Donegal, Nephin in County Mayo, the Twelve Bens (or Pins) of Connemara, and the Maamturk Mountains, both in County Galway. As a whole, these areas of ancient rocks include both mountains and lowlands in a complex intermixture, and additional topographic variety is given by the marine inlets and fragmented coastlines.

Caledonian mountains, formed by earth movements in Silurian and Devonian times (over 300 million years ago), include the ranges of County Donegal and County Derry, where the hills have a clearly-marked northeast-southwest line: seen especially in the Sperrins, in Donegal it is accentuated by the existence of deep valleys between each range. In County Sligo, the Ox Mountains have the same northeast-southwest trend, but it is less clear in County Mayo and County Galway. On the east side the hills from the south of Belfast Lough inland almost to the Shannon have the same trend, but there are few sharp ranges except for the Mourne Mountains of County Down, where granites of a late date (Tertiary) formed a line of hills having the same Caledonian northeast-southwest line. In the southeast, the Caledonian movement was accompanied by an uprising of granite, and the Leinster chain (parts of which are also known as the Wicklow Hills, the Blackstairs Mountains, and Mount Leinster) consists of a vast anticlinal arch: after many millennia of erosion, the granites have been exposed in the center and the Silurian and older rocks left on either side. The Caledonian ranges have numerous peaks over 2,000 feet, and in County Wicklow, Lugnaquilla, as has been noted, is 3,039 feet high: the northeast-southwest line is a major feature in the physical geography of Ireland, not only in the west but in the east, particularly in the Leinster chain, which is broken as a range by only one river, the Slaney.

After the mountain-building storms, a period of slow accumulation followed in which Devonian and Carboniferous strata were laid down. Some of the Devonian beds, known as Old Red sandstones, were later to offer great resistance to erosion, greater in fact than either the older Silurian and Ordovician beds or the newer Carboniferous strata. A further mountain-building period, the Armorican, followed in Carboniferous and Permian times, and some remarkable mountain ranges were formed in consequence. Of these, the clearest are the long east-west lines of hills which extend from County Waterford to the peninsulas of Kerry: in these ranges the highest ground is formed of the Old Red sandstones—mentioned above as strongly resistant to erosion. In these ranges there are some high peaks, including Carrauntoohill (Carrantual), 3,414 feet, the highest point in Ireland, and Galtymore, 3,018 feet. Where the Old Red sandstones have been removed by erosion, upland basins exist, floored by older Silurian and Ordovician rocks: the Comeragh Mountains formed of Old Red sandstone, for example, rise as a craggy range above such an upland basin. In the valleys, Carboniferous limestones are exposed. In the extreme south, the Old Red sandstones exist in ridges, 600-800 feet high.

South of a line drawn from Dungarvan to Dingle Bay, the Armorican ranges are continuous from east to west except for a few gorge-like stretches of river valley, notably that of the Blackwater from Cappoquin to Youghal. Many of the rivers flow in west-east valleys for the greater part of their course; and the Blackwater is an excellent example. North of the Dungarvan-Dingle Bay line, the ranges are isolated from one another by extensive lowlands: these include the Slievenaman Range, the Comeraghs, the Knockmealdowns, the Galtee Mountains and the magnificent ranges of the Dingle peninsula. In structure these ranges are similar to those farther south, but the intermingling of lowlands makes them even more impressive in appearance. Everywhere the east-west line prevails, and is as marked a feature of Irish topography as the northeast-southwest line of the Caledonian folds.

In one long and variously named series of hills, extending from the neighborhood of Limerick, where it is called the Slieve Felim, to the Slieve Bloom, near Maryborough, Armorican ranges of similar structure to those farther south are aligned from northeast to southwest—that is, parallel with the Caledonian chains. Grenville Cole suggested that these Armorican mountains have been folded over previously-existing Caledonian chains.

Carboniferous rocks cover over half the area of Ireland. There is a full range of strata: over most of the country, Carboniferous limestones occur, and all the younger strata have been removed, but three plateaus of coal measures, millstone grits, and upper limestones remain. Of these, the first is the Castlecomer—Slieve Ardagh plateau; the second, the Munster "coalfield" extending from Killarney to Galway Bay; and the third, the plateaus extending from County Sligo to County Monaghan. Although coal measures form part of these plateaus, they contain very little coal. The Castlecomer—Slieve Ardagh area has limited resources of anthracite, but in the so-called Munster coalfield, the seams are thin, heavily faulted, and almost valueless. There is a small coalfield in the third plateau area, in the Arigna district beside Lough Allen. As elements in the landscape of Ireland, these plateaus are of no particular attraction: but they have long even skylines of considerable interest. The Castlecomer plateau is some 1,000 feet high and the Slieve Ardagh (separated from Castlecomer by the Nore Valley) reaches similar altitudes. The Munster plateau is divided into two by the Shannon, and on the south has long even skylines, 1,000-1,200 feet high, rising to over 1,400 feet; in County Clare, hills of similar height exist. The Sligo-Monaghan plateaus are divided into a number of parts by deep valleys, above which they rise to 1,500-2,000 feet.

The Central Lowland of Ireland is floored almost entirely by Carboniferous limestone: much of it is 200-400 feet high. It extends from the shores of County Dublin across the country to Galway Bay and Clew Bay. Everywhere except in a belt of lowland extending north and south from Galway Bay, these limestones are covered with glacial drifts: this driftless area includes some remarkable limestone pavements.

In the northeast the Triassic, Liassic, and Cretaceous beds were laid down, but they are exposed at the surface only in a few places, notably the Lagan Valley. Elsewhere they are covered with basalts, poured out in Tertiary times in a series of flows 15-20 feet thick and covering in all some 1,500 square miles. From the Antrim coast road to the north of Belfast, it is possible to see the Cretaceous chalks, Liassic clays, red Triassic marls, and sandstones beneath the cover of basalts: blocks of basalt have slipped from the escarpment over the underlying strata. This northeastern area consists of plateaus and wide lowlands: the edge of the plateau is clearly seen in Cave Hill and Divis, immediately to the west of Belfast and in the plateau of County Antrim farther north, but in the lower Bann Valley basalts underlie lowlands. The most spectacular outcrop of the basalts is the Giant's Causeway, County Antrim, where hexagonal basalts are exposed on the coast: here it is possible to walk for several miles beside a remarkable series of cliffs, which have a lower layer of regular, hexagonal columns and an upper layer of thin irregular prisms molded into fantastic shapes and called by such names as the Giant's Organ.

The last—and in many ways the most important—phase in the geological history of Ireland was its glaciation. Two main icesheets left limestone-bearing drift over large parts of the Central Lowland: in the northeast the drifts are derived partly from Scottish sources and also include some basalt and chalks of local origin. There were also various mountain glaciations, some of small extent but leaving (for example, in the Comeraghs and the Reeks of Kerry) a number of wonderful corrie basins. Other mountain glaciations were larger: those of the Wicklow Mountains, for example, carried ice far from the center of the hills, and an even greater icesheet which covered the mountains of Kerry and western Cork extended to the eastern limit of County Cork; the drifts are largely sand and gravel. A few small areas of Ireland were apparently never covered by ice, but almost everywhere else the soils and surface drainage are affected by the glaciation.

Glaciation has affected the physical geography of Ireland in various ways. In parts of the west, notably in Connemara (the area west of Galway), the ice apparently removed the soil and left bare rock surfaces—much as it did in parts of Canada or of Finland—but over most of the lowland there is an accumulation of drift, molded into drumlins in a wide belt of country extending from Belfast Lough and the neighborhood of Dundalk westwards to Donegal, Sligo, and Clew bays; and there are also isolated swarms in the lower Bann Valley, various lowlands of north and west Donegal, and, far to the south, in Bantry Bay. Drumlins, it has been estimated, cover one eighth of the surface of Ireland: some are of considerable size, even as much as a mile long, but many are 400-500 yards long and half as broad. These "little hills" are generally 50-100 feet high—but only a few of them have been penetrated by cuttings and some may have a rock core. Normally the true "drumlin" is thought to consist entirely of drift, but many hills that look like drumlins may be due to the deposition of drift on a rock surface.

As the last icesheet decayed, vast quantities of water were liberated and the surface drainage of the country was restored. Meltwaters formed some remarkable channels in and around various uplands: in the Wicklow Mountains, for example, there are over 100 meltwater channels, some quite small but others hundreds of feet deep though now occupied only by small "misfit" streams. In this case ice on either side of the mountains prevented the escape of meltwater to the east or west, and so channels were cut in a north-south direction, parallel to the trend of the mountains. And the channels of other ranges, such as the Mournes, the Carlingfords, and the Sperrins, are almost as spectacular. It is, however, the eskers of the lowlands that have excited the greatest curiosity. These are long sinuous ridges standing at least 20-30 feet above the surrounding countryside; they exist in east-west and in north-south lines across the central lowland. Their origin has been ascribed to deposition of gravel and sand in streams beneath the icesheet, to the formation of deltas in standing water at the margin of an icesheet, and to various other causes. They are interesting features of the Irish central lowland; in some places they are surrounded by peat bogs.

Soils.—As yet, there has been comparatively little soil analysis in Ireland, though the importance of this subject in an agricultural country was recognized as long ago as 1907, when J. R. Kilroe published his *Soil Geology of Ireland.* He showed that most of the Irish soils originate from drifts and were varied in quality, here sandy and there clayed: where drifts did not occur, some of the older rocks, such as quartzites, certain granites, and shales, weathered into infertile soils left uncultivated, though the patches of drift upon them were used for farmland. Equally, some of the bare limestone country of County Clare and County Galway is valueless for agriculture, but where these limestones have weathered into soil, a nutritive herbage develops which forms admirable pasture for sheep and cattle.

Study of drainage will provide one key to the qualities of Irish soils. Over most of the country, rainfalls are high (see below) and therefore soils retentive of moisture, such as clays, are frequently waterlogged, especially in low-lying areas. On a slope with good natural drainage, even a heavy clay soil will be suited to cultivation: in a depression, it may be a marsh, thickly covered with reeds and even wild iris but having a certain value as a pasture. Such soils are markedly acid, and therefore the fertilizers used include lime and various phosphates, partly in order to give some alkaline content. Lighter soils, such as sands, are less frequent in Ireland, though they include the famous Curragh area near Kildare, an open sheepwalk on glacial sands covering nine square miles. The eskers of the lowland normally consist of gravels and sands, generally of such low fertility that they are left uncultivated as lines of heath or woodland: but light soils are comparatively rare and the prevalence of clayey drift, containing some lime, may partly explain why so large an area of farmland is left as pasture.

Clearing of the lowland bogs of Ireland has been regarded for more than a century as one way of adding vast tracts of agricultural land for the use of the farming community. The lowland bogs vary in size from a few square yards to many square miles: the largest single expanse is the Bog of Allen, near Kildare and Edenderry. It is thought that lowland bogs develop on a fen in areas of impeded drainage, that after the Ice Age large areas between the drifts were covered with water, and that here, in time, marshy fens developed. Under the conditions of heavy rainfall, decaying vegetation was built up into a peat bog, spongy in texture, with acid water permeating the steadily increasing layers of vegetable matter. These conditions have prevailed from about 750 B.C. (the sub-Atlantic period), when the climate became moister than in the previous climatic phase (the sub-Boreal period, about 2500–750 B.C.): in this earlier period the fens developed and trees grew so plentifully that they are frequently seen when bogs are cleared. Advocates of bog clearing to provide new farmland on the underlying fen soils perhaps forget that under the present climatic conditions they would need a highly elaborate drainage to provide rich fields for crops, though cleared bogs are commonly used for potato growing and some good yields are obtained.

Climate.—What is generally called the "West Maritime" type of climate is excellently developed in Ireland. Lying to the west of Britain, it is traversed by numerous depressions from the Atlantic, all of a rain-bearing character. Cold anticyclones of continental origin in winter are less frequent than in Britain, and warm anticyclones of tropical origin are less marked in summer than in the south of England. As a whole, the climate may be described as "mild, moist, and changeable"; extreme cold, long frosts, heavy snows in winter and scorching days in summer are regarded as exceptions to the normal routine, in which one season grades imperceptibly into the next with rain as the only common element through the year. Late frosts and snows have been recorded in May, as in Britain; and every year contains some exceptional weather conditions.

Averages of temperature show a clear difference in winter between the west and east of Ireland. The mean monthly temperatures for winter in the west are 44°-45°F. (December to March), but slightly less in County Donegal, and in the east 41°-43°F. (November to March). The south coast is similar to the west, and the northwest to the east. On all the coasts, the temperatures are slightly higher than those inland at this season, and warm soft breezes, not infrequently accompanied by mist and rain, are characteristic. In summer, the isotherms show a steady decrease of temperature from south to north, from 60°-61°F. in Cork to 57°F. on the coasts of County Donegal. The evergreen quality of vegetation in the west is thought to be due to the lack of any marked check to plant growth through either cold or lack of rain: the arbutus, for example, a Mediterranean plant, is a low shrub in its own home but a tree in Ireland.

Rainfall in Ireland is, by general consent, excessive, and some four fifths of the country has 30-50 inches, whereas a similar proportion of England has 20-30 inches. Only some 500 square miles, in County Dublin and County Meath, has less than 30 inches, and in the mountains there are annual averages of 50-100 inches. Relief rain figures prominently in the west, and the highest falls, 90-100 inches, are recorded from Kerry, western Mayo, and western Galway (for example, Gap of Dunloe, Killarney, 94 inches). There are also heavy falls at some of the western lowland stations near the mountains, such as Garinish Island, Bantry, County Cork, 70 inches, and Kenmare, 65 inches. The number of rain days (that is, when more than 0.01 inch falls within 24 hours) is high everywhere, and varies from 175 in the extreme southeast to 200-250 on the west coast, and even more in the western mountains: at Cahersiveen, County Kerry, the rainfall of 56 inches falls on 252 days and in 834 hours, twice as many as in London. In the west, there is a marked winter maximum of rainfall; but in the east, a more even distribution. Dublin has its highest monthly fall in August, due to occasional thunderstorms or very heavy depression rains.

Westerly winds predominate in Ireland, though

IRELAND

Along the road skirting one of the beautiful lakes of Killarney.

© Gendreau

O'Connell Bridge, Dublin.

IRELAND

The famous, timeworn Cross of Cashel (8th century), County Tipperary.

The Round Tower on the rock of Cashel, near Tipperary.

© Gendreau

The ruins of Ross Castle, Kerry County.

IRELAND

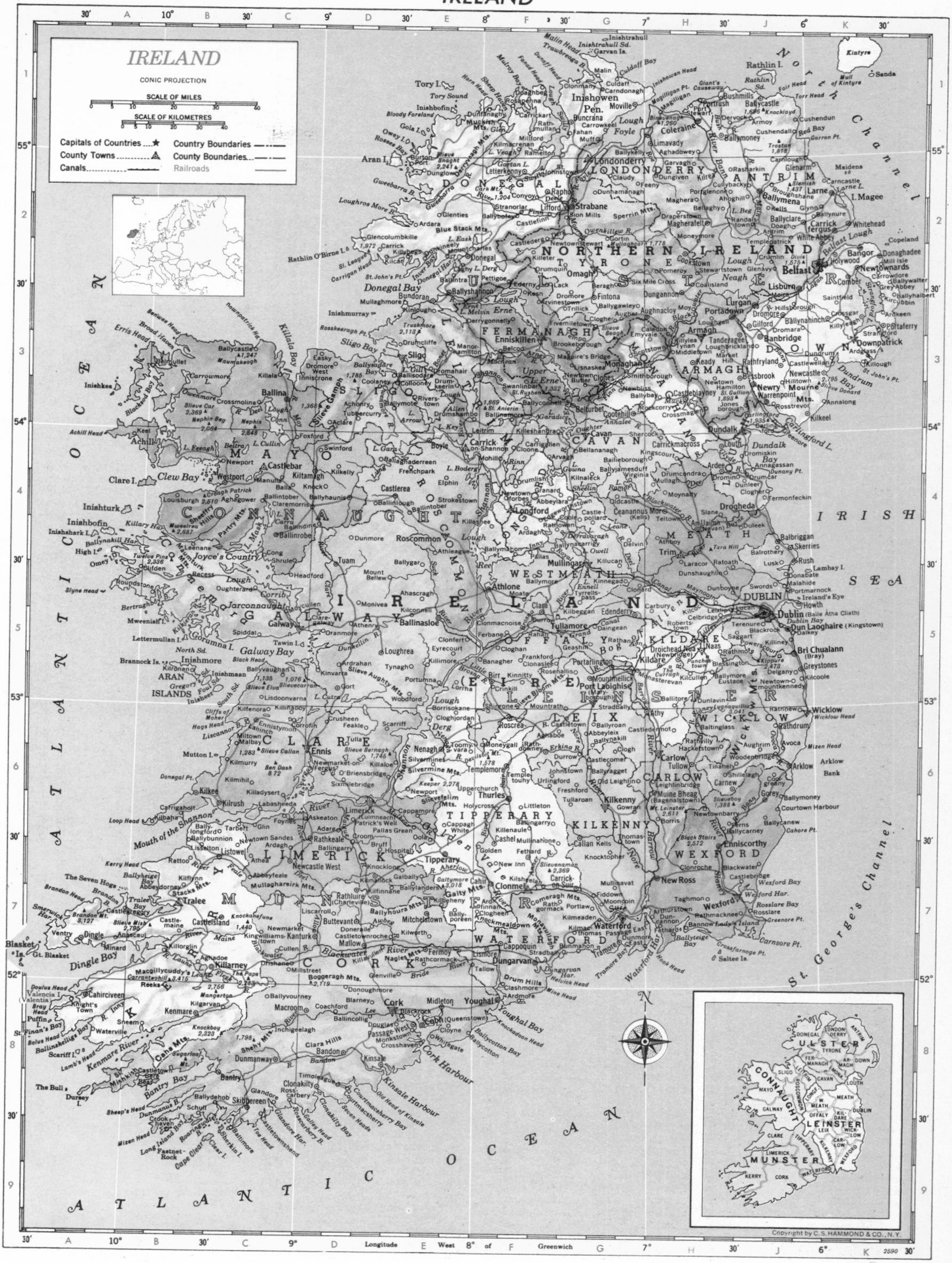

IRELAND
CONIC PROJECTION
SCALE OF MILES
SCALE OF KILOMETRES
Capitals of Countries
County Towns
Canals
Country Boundaries
County Boundaries
Railroads
NORTHERN IRELAND
IRELAND (EIRE)
ULSTER
CONNAUGHT
LEINSTER
MUNSTER
DONEGAL
LONDONDERRY
ANTRIM
TYRONE
FERMANAGH
ARMAGH
DOWN
MONAGHAN
CAVAN
SLIGO
LEITRIM
MAYO
ROSCOMMON
LONGFORD
GALWAY
WESTMEATH
MEATH
LOUTH
DUBLIN
KILDARE
OFFALY
LEIX
WICKLOW
CARLOW
WEXFORD
KILKENNY
TIPPERARY
CLARE
LIMERICK
KERRY
CORK
WATERFORD
ATLANTIC OCEAN
North Channel
IRISH SEA
St. George's Channel
Belfast
Dublin (Baile Átha Cliath)
Dun Laoghaire (Kingstown)
Longitude West of Greenwich
Copyright by C. S. HAMMOND & CO., N. Y.

IRELAND

Abbeyfeale, 1,162 C 7
Abbeyleix, 633 G 6
Achill (isl.) A 4
Adare, 459 D 6
Ahascragh, 226 E 5
Allen (lake) E 3
Allen, Bog of (marsh) H 5
An Uaimh (Navan), 4,271 H 4
Anascaul, 202 B 7
Aran (isl.), 1,304 D 2
Aran (isls.), 1,768 B 5
Ardara, 423 E 2
Ardee, 2,489 H 4
Ardfinnan, 413 F 7
Arklow, 5,203 J 6
Arvagh, 413 F 4
Askeaton, 564 D 6
Athboy, 418 H 4
Athea, 227 C 7
Athenry, 1,181 D 5
Athlone, 9,015 F 5
Athy, 3,752 H 6
Aughrim, 351 J 6
Baile Átha Cliath (Dublin), (cap.), 522,183 K 5
Bailieborough, 741 G 4
Balbriggan, 2,920 J 4
Ballaghaderreen, 1,359 E 4
Ballina, 6,220 C 3
Ballinamore, 723 F 3
Ballinasloe, 5,596 E 5
Ballincollig, 371 D 8
Ballindine, 235 C 4
Ballingarry, 309 D 7
Ballinlough, 252 D 4
Ballinrobe, 1,185 C 4
Ballintra, 268 E 2
Ballybay, 974 G 3
Ballybofey, 781 F 2
Ballybunnion, 956 B 7
Ballycastle C 3
Ballyconnell, 282 F 3
Ballycotton, 346 F 8
Ballydehob, 297 C 8
Ballygar, 282 E 4
Ballyhaunis, 1,057 D 4
Ballyjamesduff, 667 G 4
Ballylanders E 7
Ballylongford, 447 B 6
Ballymahon, 634 F 4
Ballymore Eustace, 340 J 5
Ballymote, 779 D 3
Ballynakill, 287 G 6
Ballyporeen, 285 E 7
Ballyragget, 430 G 6
Ballyshannon, 2,813 E 3
Baltimore, 169 C 9
Baltinglass, 840 H 6
Banagher, 701 F 5
Bandon, 2,527 D 8
Bantry, 2,319 C 8
Barrow (river) H 7
Bear (isl.), 534 B 8
Bellananagh, 313 G 4
Belmullet, 676 B 3
Belturbet, 1,152 G 3
Birr, 3,285 F 5
Blarney, 874 D 8
Blessington, 449 J 5
Borris, 484 H 6
Borrisokane, 595 E 6
Boyle, 1,934 E 4
Boyne (river) J 4
Brandon (mt.) A 7
Bray Head (prom.) A 8
Bri Chualann (Bray), 12,062 K 5
Bruff, 586 D 7
Buncrana, 3,039 G 1
Bundoran, 1,680 E 3
Buttevant, 769 D 7
Cahir, 1,589 F 7
Cahirciveen, 1,687 A 8
Callan, 1,506 G 7
Cappagh White, 315 E 6
Cappamore, 559 E 6
Cappoquin, 826 F 7
Carlingford, 500 J 3
Carlow (county), 34,162 H 6
Carlow, 7,667 H 6
Carndonagh, 633 G 1
Carnew, 392 H 6
Carnsore (point) J 7
Carrantuohill (mt.) B 7
Carrickmacross, 2,045 H 4
Carrick-on-Shannon, 1,492 F 4
Carrick-on-Suir, 4,757 F 7
Cashel, 2,829 F 7
Castlebar, 5,288 C 4
Castleblayney, 2,173 H 3
Castlecomer, 722 G 6
Castledermot, 449 H 6
Castlefinn, 330 F 2
Castlegregory, 260 A 7
Castleisland, 1,491 B 7
Castlepollard, 495 G 4
Castlerea, 1,198 D 4
Castletown, 246 G 6
Castletown Bere, 654 B 8
Castletownroche, 425 D 7
Cavan (county), 66,377 G 4
Cavan, 3,555 G 3
Ceanannus Mor (Kells), 2,125 G 4
Celbridge, 567 H 5
Clara, 1,684 F 5
Clare (county), 81,329 D 6
Clare (isl.), 401 A 4
Claremorris, 1,063 C 4
Clear (isl.), 500 C 9
Clew (bay) B 4
Clifden, 905 B 5
Clogheen, 505 F 7
Clogher, 552 J 4
Clonakilty, 2,742 D 8
Clonaslee, 231 F 5
Clones, 2,455 G 3
Clonmel, 10,471 F 7
Cloughjordan, 462 E 6
Cloyne, 620 E 8
Cobh (Queenstown), 5,711 E 8
Collooney, 364 E 3
Conn (lake) C 3
Connaught (prov.), 471,978 B 4
Connemara (dist.) B 5
Convoy, 627 F 2
Cootehill, 1,489 G 3
Cork (county), 341,284 D 7
Cork, 74,567 E 8
Corrib (lake) C 5
Corrofin, 230 C 6
Courtmacsherry, 213 D 8
Crinkill, 307 F 5
Croom, 822 D 6
Crosshaven, 848 E 8
Crossmolina, 707 C 3
Daingean, 660 G 5
Delgany, 206 J 5
Derg (lake) E 6
Dingle, 1,545 A 7
Donabate, 261 J 5
Donegal (county), 131,530 F 2
Donegal (bay) D 3
Donegal, 1,131 F 2
Doneraile, 775 D 7
Douglas, 1,818 D 8
Drogheda, 16,779 J 4
Droichead Nua (Newbridge) 3,007 H 5
Dromahair, 262 E 3
Drumlish, 195 F 4
Drumshambo, 515 E 3
Dublin (county), 693,022 J 5
Dublin (Baile Átha Cliath), (cap.), 522,183 K 5
Duleek, 329 J 4
Dun Laoghaire (Kingstown), 47,920 K 5
Dunboyne, 334 H 5
Duncannon, 201 H 7
Dundalk, 19,678 H 3
Dunfanaghy, 382 F 1
Dungarvan, 5,423 F 7
Dungloe, 581 E 2
Dunkineely, 250 E 2
Dunlavin, 408 H 5
Dunleer, 394 J 4
Dunmanway, 1,439 C 8
Dunmore, 530 D 4
Dunmore East, 302 G 7
Dunshaughlin, 169 H 5
Durrow, 425 G 6
Edenderry, 2,596 G 5
Edgeworthstown, 514 G 4
Elphin, 537 E 4
Emyvale, 204 H 3
Ennell (lake) G 5
Ennis, 6,097 D 6
Enniscorthy, 5,948 J 7
Ennistymon, 1,124 C 6
Erne (river) E 3
Erne (lake) F 3
Erris Head (prom.) A 3
Eyrecourt, 291 E 5
Ferbane, 272 F 5
Fergus (river) D 6
Fermoy, 4,017 E 7
Ferns, 441 J 6
Fethard, 984 F 7
Finn (river) F 2
Foxford, 773 C 4
Foyle (inlet) G 1
Foynes, 636 C 6
Frankford, 507 F 5
Frenchpark, 201 E 4
Freshford, 491 G 6
Galty (mts.) E 7
Galway (county), 160,204 D 5
Galway, 21,316 C 5
Galway (bay) C 5
Glenties, 665 E 2
Glin, 584 C 6
Golden Vale (plain) E 7
Gorey, 2,889 J 6
Gort, 1,008 D 5
Gorumna (isl.), 1,909 B 5
Gowran, 317 G 6
Granard, 1,150 F 4
Grand (canal) G 5
Greystones, 1,633 K 5
Hacketstown, 518 H 6
Headford, 412 C 5
Hospital, 633 E 7
Howth K 5
Inishmore (isl.) B 5
Inishowen (pen.) G 1
Inniscrone, 488 C 3
Johnstown, 248 G 6
Joyce's Country (dist.) B 4
Kanturk, 1,632 D 7
Kenmare, 907 B 8
Kerry (county), 126,644 B 7
Kilbeggan, 717 G 5
Kilcock, 670 H 5
Kilcoole, 413 K 5
Kilcullen, 655 H 5
Kildare (county), 66,437 H 5
Kildare, 2,286 H 5
Kilfinnane, 724 D 7
Kilkee, 1,677 B 6
Kilkenny (county), 65,235 G 6
Kilkenny, 10,572 G 6
Killadysert, 315 C 6
Killala, 337 C 3
Killaloe, 901 D 6
Killarney, 6,298 C 7
Killenaule, 471 F 6
Killeshandra, 432 F 3
Killorglin, 718 B 7
Killybegs, 886 E 2
Kilmacthomas, 388 G 7
Kilmallock, 1,117 D 7
Kilmihil, 208 C 6
Kilnaleck, 241 G 4
Kilronan, 271 B 5
Kilrush, 3,154 C 6
Kiltamagh, 970 C 4
Kilworth, 256 E 7
Kingscourt, 548 H 4
Kinnegad, 319 G 5
Kinsale, 1,930 D 8
Kinvarra, 323 D 5
Knight's Town, 199 A 8
Lahinch, 313 C 6
Laracor H 4
Leane (lake) B 7
Lee (river) D 8
Leighlinbridge, 326 H 6
Leinster (prov.), 1,334,754 F 5
Leinster (mt.) H 6
Leitrim (county), 41,209 E 3
Leix (county), 48,430 G 6
Leixlip, 504 H 5
Letterkenny, 3,004 F 2
Liffey (river) H 5
Lifford, 484 F 2
Limerick (county), 141,239 D 7
Limerick (Luimneach), 50,820 D 6
Lisdoonvarna, 332 C 5
Lismore, 1,089 F 7
Listowel, 3,149 C 7
Longford (county), 34,553 F 4
Longford, 3,845 F 4
Loop Head (prom.) A 6
Loughrea, 2,847 E 5
Louisburgh, 268 B 4
Louth (county), 68,771 J 4
Lucan, 728 J 5
Lugnaquillia (mt.) J 5
Luimneach (Limerick), 50,820 D 6
Lusk, 431 J 4
Macroom, 2,277 C 8
Malahide, 2,030 J 5
Mallow, 5,583 D 7
Manorhamilton, 833 E 3
Mask (lake) C 4
Maynooth, 581 H 5
Mayo (county), 141,867 C 4
Meath (county), 66,337 H 4
Midleton, 2,828 E 8
Millford, 318 F 1
Millstreet, 922 D 7
Miltown Malbay, 668 C 6
Mitchelstown, 2,148 E 7
Moate, 1,274 F 5
Mohill, 848 F 4
Monaghan (county), 55,345 H 3
Monaghan, 4,723 G 3
Monasterevan, 415 H 5
Moneygall, 280 F 6
Mooncoin, 243 G 7
Mount Bellew, 276 D 5
Mountcharles, 338 E 2
Mountmellick, 2,501 G 5
Mountrath, 972 F 5
Moville, 969 G 1
Moy (river) C 3
Muine Bheag (Bagenalstown) 1,874 H 6
Mullinahone, 315 F 7
Mullingar, 5,643 G 4
Munster (prov.), 898,861 C 7
Mweelrea (mt.) B 4
Naas, 3,731 H 5
Nenagh, 4,420 E 6
New Ross, 4,903 H 7
Newbliss, 205 G 3
Newcastle West, 2,632 D 7
Newmarket, 797 C 7
Newmarket-on-Fergus, 574 D 6
Newport, 491 E 6
Newport, 370 C 4
Newtown Sandes, 245 C 6
Newtownbarry, 726 H 6
Newtownforbes, 420 F 4
Newtownmountkennedy, 468 J 5
Nore (river) G 7
Offaly (county), 52,544 F 5
Oldcastle, 619 G 4
Oola, 325 E 6
Oranmore D 5
Oughterard, 433 C 5
Passage East, 354 G 7
Passage West, 2,658 E 8
Pettigo, 243 F 2
Port Laoighise (Maryborough), 3,304 G 5
Portarlington, 2,246 G 5
Portlaw, 925 G 7
Portmarnock, 324 J 5
Portumna, 871 E 5
Queenstown (Cobh), 5,711 E 8
Ramelton, 777 F 1
Raphoe, 803 F 2
Rathangan, 432 G 5
Rathdowney, 730 F 6
Rathdrum, 1,284 J 6
Rathkeale, 1,480 D 7
Rathluire (Charleville), 1,582 D 7
Rathmore, 288 J 5
Rathmullen, 408 F 1
Rathnew, 341 J 6
Ratoath, 228 H 4
Ree (lake) F 5
Roscommon (county), 68,102 E 4
Roscommon, 2,013 E 4
Roscrea, 2,988 F 6
Rosscarbery, 311 C 8
Rosslare, 308 J 7
Royal (canal) G 4
Rush, 1,925 J 4
Saggart, 267 J 5
Saint George's (channel) K 7
Saint Johnstown, 268 F 2
Scarriff, 340 E 6
Schull, 316 B 8
Shannon (river) B 6
Sheelin (lake) G 4
Shercock, 223 G 4
Shinrone, 406 F 5
Sixmilebridge, 398 D 6
Skerries, 2,457 J 4
Skibbereen, 2,341 C 8
Slaney (river) H 7
Slieve Snaght (mt.) E 2
Slievenaman, (mt.) F 7
Sligo (county), 60,513 D 3
Sligo, 13,529 E 3
Sneem, 302 B 8
Stradbally, 750 G 5
Stranorlar, 493 F 2
Strokestown, 618 E 4
Suir (river) G 7
Swanlinbar, 342 F 3
Swilly (inlet) F 1
Swinford, 1,195 D 4
Swords, 1,136 J 5
Taghmon, 383 H 7
Tallow, 716 F 7
Tara (hill) H 4
Tarbert, 320 C 6
Templemore, 1,964 F 6
Thomastown, 718 G 7
Thurles, 6,276 F 6
Timoleague, 249 D 8
Tinahely, 256 H 6
Tipperary (county), 133,313 F 6
Tipperary, 5,148 E 7
Toomyvara, 247 E 6
Tory (isl.), 257 E 1
Tralee, 11,045 B 7
Tramore, 2,825 G 7
Trim, 1,309 H 4
Tuam, 4,010 D 4
Tubbercurry, 882 D 3
Tulla, 424 D 6
Tullamore, 6,165 G 5
Tullow, 1,739 H 6
Tyrrellspass, 213 G 5
Ulster (prov.), 1,623,994 E 2
Urlingford, 453 F 6
Valencia (Valentia) (isl.), 1,015 A 8
Virginia, 297 G 4
Waterford (county), 75,061 F 7
Waterford, 28,691 G 7
Waterville, 223 A 8
Westmeath (county), 54,463 G 5
Westport, 3,104 C 4
Wexford (county), 90,032 H 7
Wexford, 11,979 H 7
Whitegate, 248 E 8
Wicklow (county), 62,590 J 6
Wicklow, 3,326 K 6
Youghal, 4,752 F 8

naturally a country subject to so many depressions has winds from all quarters: but at most stations for which detailed records exist, nearly two thirds of the winds come from some direction between south and northwest. Winds of gale force average 40 a year on the west coast, and several winds of more than 90 miles per hour have been recorded. On Jan. 30, 1925, a train was blown off a viaduct in County Donegal and most of the passengers killed or injured. The light railways take special precautions against gales; for example, the West Clare Railway authorities ballast the carriages with concrete when the winds reach 60 miles per hour, and traffic ceases when the winds reach 80 miles per hour.

The climate has a direct effect on the vegetation, described below. It cannot be too strongly stressed that the figures used in this section are averages and that the weather varies considerably from one season to another. For Queen's University, Belfast, figures for 79 years (1861–1939) are available: the average rainfall was 34.9 inches, but this occurred in only two years, though most years had within 15 per cent of the average. A few, however, had as much as 25 per cent more or less than the average, and it seems that a period of dry years is followed by a period of wet years.

Flora and Fauna.—Ireland is poorer in flora than Britain: it is estimated to have only two thirds as many species of plants as its neighbor, due to the fact that Ireland was separated from Britain before Britain was separated from continental Europe. Much of the Irish flora must have survived the Ice Age either on the ice-free strips within the country or on unglaciated areas now submerged. There are some species of American origin, which are presumed to have reached Ireland and Greenland, and others are of Mediterranean origin: these are found largely but not exclusively, on the west coasts, in some places intermingled with one another and in others among plants of European origin.

The American species include an orchid (*Spiranthes stricta*), found in damp meadows and in the Bann Valley, and a rush (*Juncus macer*) which has been discovered in County Wicklow and also in the extreme southwest. None of the American species is conspicuous, and more interest lies in the consideration of Mediterranean plants, which include the arbutus (see above) growing into a tree, various ericas (heaths), and various saxifrages. The wealth and variety of saxifrages in the west of Ireland has attracted many botanists: one, *Saxifraga spathularis,* which grows in Portugal, northern Spain, and the Pyrenees, is luxuriantly developed in mountain areas of Kerry, Cork, Galway, and Mayo. Alpine plants have a poor range of species, and although the mountains have wide heathery moorlands, there is no continuous area of land at a sufficient altitude to possess an arctic-alpine vegetation similar to that of the English Lake District, Snowdonia (North Wales), or the Scottish Highlands. Alpines are more frequent in the north than the south, though in Ireland, as in the west of Scotland, they occur at all altitudes down to sea level. In all probability, the remarkable spread of alpine plants in the west is due to indirect climatic influence: the restriction of tree growth by seawinds has left land available for other plants. Consequently, there are some strange mixtures of plants in the west, notably in the Burren of County Clare, which has the alpine species *Dryas octopetala* and *Gentiana verna* mingled with the Mediterranean maidenhair fern (*Adiantum capillus-veneris*): the latter is found in sheltered hollows and cracks in the limestone pavement. The restriction of vegetation to ground species characteristic of the west coast is a feature shared by the similar coasts of Scotland and Norway.

Only a short distance from the coast, in sheltered places, luxuriant tree growth is seen, notably in the Killarney Valley, which has rich woods in which trees are covered with ferns and mosses, and the ground flora forms a dense mat of vegetation. In exposed places the phenomenon of wind-shearing is seen: a grove of trees will have low growth on the west and higher growth on the east, and single trees will have their buds killed on the west side. In these circumstances, it is difficult to establish a treeline in terms of altitude, for on the west coast the treeline is at sea level, at 600-800 feet in Kerry, and in the east, for example in the Wicklow Mountains, it is at 1,200 feet or more, in some sheltered valleys.

At the present time, Ireland has a mere 2½ per cent of its area in woodland, less than any other European country except Iceland, but before the woods were cleared for agricultural expansion and other purposes, a large part of the land was covered with forest, though the bogs are naturally treeless. Nevertheless, Ireland has a wooded appearance, as numerous single trees are planted in hedgerows or as small sheltering woods near farmlands. The oak is the dominant tree in most woods, along with birch, or ash (this especially on limestone soils), hazel, rowan, and many more: in damp places, alders and willows are found. Hazel scrub is developed in profusion on the limestones near Galway Bay, away from the west coast. There are only two native conifers, the juniper and the yew, but various pines and larches have seeded themselves plentifully and even invaded some of the country's oakwoods and birchwoods: other introduced trees, such as the sycamore, have also spread by seeding. and in the rich moist woods of the Killarney area rhododendrons have run wild. Even the exotic bamboo will grow luxuriantly in sheltered places in the south of Ireland: the National Botanic Gardens at Glasnevin, Dublin, have a remarkable collection of trees drawn from various parts of the world.

The fauna, like the flora, has fewer species than Britain, but it includes some species with a likeness to those of Scandinavian and Arctic regions, and others with Mediterranean affinities. Of the mammals, the fox, the badger, the otter, the stoat are all abundant, but the weasel and the polecat do not exist. Wolves were exterminated by the 18th century. Hedgehogs abound, but there are no moles, and Irish visitors to Britain are puzzled by the molehills of many pastures. There are fewer types of bats in Ireland. The Irish hare is the varying hare of the Scottish highlands and various alpine and northern regions of continental Europe, but it does not normally change its coat to whiteness in winter in Ireland.

Of the birds, there are fewer species, but many sea birds exist in vast numbers on the cliffs, especially on the west coast; these include gulls and dippers. Certain birds of prey, such as the peregrine falcon, nest on seacliffs and mountains throughout the country, and the golden eagle nests in the remoter parts of Mayo and Donegal. But a number of familiar English birds, such as the nightingale, the reed warbler, and the tawny owl, are quite unknown in Ireland: the magpie, said to have arrived in a small flock in 1684, has spread widely through the country.

The brown lizard is the only native reptile, and the absence of snakes (said by legend to have been banished by St. Patrick) is well known. The common frog is abundant, but only a single species of the three British newts is found. Some of the invertebrates show Mediterranean affinities, notably a spotted slug found in western Kerry and western Cork. A snail, *Helix pisana,* is found in the east and in Britain only in south Wales and Cornwall; it also occurs in southern France and along the Mediterranean shores. Researches on the fauna raise the same fascinating problems of origin that are raised in considering the flora: clearly there is a complex relationship between the two.

Bibliography.—Cole, G. A. J., *Ireland the Outpost* (London 1919); Cole, G. A. J., and Hallissy, T., *Handbook of the Geology of Ireland* (London 1924); Fitzgerald, W., *Historical Geography of Early Ireland* (London 1925); Praeger, R. L., *The Botanist in Ireland* (Dublin 1934); id., *The Way That I Went* (London and Dublin 1937), popular but informative; Evans, E. E., *Irish Heritage* (Dundalk 1942); Freeman, T. W., *Ireland: Its Physical, Historical, Social and Economic Geography* (London 1950).

There are also sections on Ireland in works dealing with the British Isles, especially: Mackinder, H. J., *Britain and the British Seas* (Oxford 1907); Herbertson, A. J., and Howarth, O. J. R., ed., *Oxford Survey of the British Empire,* vol. 1 (Oxford 1914); Stamp, L. D., and Beaver, S. H., *The British Isles,* 2d ed. (New York 1937); Demangeon, A., *Les Isles Britanniques* (trans. by E. D. Laborde, London 1939; Paris 1927).

T. W. Freeman,
Reader in Economic Geography, University of Manchester.

HISTORY TO 1601 A.D.

Irish literature contains stories of the occupation of the island by various peoples—Nemedians, Fomorians, Firbolgs, Tuatha De Danann, Milesians—in succession. The last-named people, called in Irish the *Clanna Miled,* has been identified generally in modern times with the Celts, who brought to Ireland a Celtic language or languages and Celtic civilization about the middle of the first millennium B.C. Ireland marked the western limit to a great movement of expansion which carried the Celts from a homeland somewhere in central Europe to Asia Minor, Spain, the Low Countries, France, and England. Beyond Galway lay the Atlantic breakers and the boundless waste of ocean on which frail barques ventured at their peril.

A glimpse of Ireland at the dawn of history is afforded by tales of the Cú Chulainn or Ulster literary cycle. The personages whose doings this cycle records would have lived about the beginning of the Christian era. By that time the island had been parceled out among five major kings, a division that was to last until the Middle Ages, when Meath would lose its ancient status and Ulster, Leinster, Munster, and Connacht become the four Irish provinces. The Finn cycle of Irish literature, which belongs perhaps to the 3d century A.D., shows no appreciable change in the Irish political situation, though it does indicate changes in civilization. Struggles for power between the five kings led to the predominance of the Meath dynasty in the northern half of Ireland (Leth Cuinn) and to the predominance of the Munster dynasty in the southern half of Ireland (Leth Moga). Finally, at a date before 400 A.D., the Meath dynasts established their claim to suzerainty over the whole of Ireland and to the corresponding title Ri Erend (King of Ireland). Their chief fortress was on the hill of Tara, which thus became fixed in tradition as the capital, the home of the high-king, the symbol of national unity, the focus of national aspirations.

The first high-king of whom the historian can speak with certainty is Niall of the Nine Hostages, undoubtedly one of the greatest Irishmen who ever lived. Three of his sons won for themselves a new kingdom in northwestern Ulster; other sons were settled in strong positions in the large midland region between the Shannon and the Irish Sea. Two of his brothers were successively kings of Connacht. His son, Loeguire, was high-king when St. Patrick came as a missionary to Ireland (the traditional date is 432 A.D.). Niall's direct descendants, the Ui Neill, held the kingship of Ireland without a break from 482 to 1002. From 732 onwards this highest honor in the land went alternately to the Ui Neill of Ulster and the Ui Neill of the midlands. From Niall, too, descended the best-beloved of native Irish saints, Columba of Iona, or Colmcille, the princely families of O'Neill, ODonnell, MacLoughlin, O Maelsechlainn, and a host of lesser families who form no small part of the population of Ireland in modern times.

Within a short time after the introduction of Christianity Ireland enjoyed a period of bloom in the realms of religion, learning, and art, to such an extent that the country could be called "The Island of Saints and Scholars." In the political order there was no comparable advance. From the beginning of the 6th century to the beginning of the 9th century society remained essentially unchanged. Individual liberty was highly prized; so also, the liberty of the family within the local state; the liberty of the small rural state within the small local kingdom; the liberty of the small local kingdom within the five larger kingdoms; the liberty of these (Ulster, Meath, Leinster, Munster, Connacht) in their relations with the king of Ireland. Though the high-king's prestige was immense, his political power outside his own patrimony was generally restricted: it depended much on personal distinction and, in the ultimate analysis, on the size of his army and the capacity which he showed when he led it into the field.

Norse Invaders.—In 795 Ireland was attacked for the first time by a dangerous foreign enemy. He came from the pagan and barbarian north (chiefly, it would seem, from Norway rather than from Denmark or Sweden) and continued his depredations for more than two centuries. This is the Norse Era in Irish history (795–1014). In the art of seamanship the Northmen then had no equals in Europe, outside of Byzantium, and they used their one accomplishment to win riches and power at the expense of other peoples. From 795 to 837 Ireland was thrown into turmoil by their raids. They came in fleets, sometimes large, sometimes small, landed suddenly in a bay or creek, despoiled the countryside (especially the peaceful monastic settlements), and returned with booty to the safety of their ships before the local state could gather its army in self-defense. In 837 they took permanent possession of a strip of land near the Liffey mouth. This is the origin of the town and later city of Dublin. Now and afterwards the Irish kings showed more eagerness to use the Norse as foils in the game of politics than to drive them once for all from the country. An unfortunate campaign, in which Munster was defeated by the high-king and grievously weakened led to the foundation of the two Norse towns, Waterford and Limerick, in the south of Ireland about 920. The presence of the Northmen at Limerick led to a fierce local reaction. Surrounding the new settlers was a little state called Dal Chais. The energetic dynasts of this people waged relentless war on the intruders, building up in the process an army which in time became strong enough not merely to subdue the foreigners but to secure for its commander the kingship of Munster. Brian Boramha (Brian; Brian Boru), second Munster king of the Dalcassian line, deposed the Ui Neill monarch, Malachy II, in 1002, and took his place as king of Ireland. In a famous battle fought at Clontarf, near Dublin, in 1014, Brian was opposed not only by Irish malcontents but by the Norse of Dublin assisted by a formidable force of Norse auxiliaries from abroad. Brian's victory, won at the cost of his own life, broke forever the power of the Northmen in Ireland. In the next generation they accepted the Christian faith, after which they lived on in their own towns, under the immediate rule of their own leaders but subject to Irish kings.

Political Ferment.—An unhappy consequence of Brian Boramha's intrusion into the high-kingship was confusion at his death. On the one hand his son and successor in Munster was unable to take his brilliant father's place as king of Ireland; on the other hand, the tradition of Ui Neill succession was shattered beyond repair. Thus it happened that for half a century (1022–1072) the throne of Ireland remained empty. The principle was maintained that supreme political authority in the country should be represented by a high-king, but there was no ruler strong enough to merit recognition as such. Strife increased, not only between state and state, but also within various states and even within dynasties, a development whose deepest roots lay in the Irish system of succession to kingship. When a vacancy occurred it was filled by election. The prince chosen was one of a group, all of whom had rights that were theoretically equal. Disappointed candidates were all too prone to remain in a state of permanent conspiracy against the more fortunate rival who had been elected. This weakness in the Irish constitution had inevitably been intensified by the disintegration due to the Norse invasions.

Donnchad, son of Brian Boramha, was the chief ruler in the Ireland of his day, but his power was meager outside of Munster. Deposed by his nephew Toirdelbach in 1064, he journeyed as a pilgrim to Rome; and at his death he was buried there in the church of San Stefano Rotondo. By 1072 the prestige of Toirdelbach O'Brien had increased to the point when he could lay claim to the kingship of Ireland, but that goal was never reached during the 14 years of life that remained to him.

A greater man than Toirdelbach was his son, King Muirchertach O'Brien. He was an enthusiastic supporter of the movement for reform inaugurated by Pope Gregory VII. One of his daughters married a son of King Magnus of Norway; another daughter traveled to England to become the wife of a powerful Norman lord. Muirchertach exchanged letters with St. Anselm of Canterbury, who addressed him as "glorious King of Ireland." The title, however, was never quite justified by Muirchertach's achievement, for away in the north, near Derry, sat a king, Domnall Mac Lochlainn, whose opposition he was unable to overcome.

Muirchertach O'Brien died in 1119, leaving his inheritance to nephews of lesser caliber. Mac Lochlainn died soon afterwards, and the chief place on the stage of Irish politics passed to the king of Connacht, Toirdelbach O'Connor. He used naval power with some effect in the Shannon River and along the Atlantic seaboard. He also built bridges at strategic points and erected fortresses of the new type, called castles, which the Norman conquerors had multiplied in England. O'Connor's success was for a time remarkable, but the promise of his early years was not fulfilled, and long before his death in 1153 his failure to reduce the other Irish states to submission was painfully evident. His successor as chief claimant to the kingship of Ireland was Muirchertach Mac Lochlainn, grandson of the Domnall mentioned above. By 1161 his ambition seemed to be realized but fortune soon deserted him, and in 1166 he lost both throne and life. The way was then open for Ruaidri O'Connor, son of Toirdelbach, to win recognition as king of Ireland. In that capacity he presided over the great national assembly at Tailtiu in Meath in 1168. The days of struggle for the high-kingship seemed to be over and the throne of Ireland firmly in the keeping of the royal house of Connacht.

Anglo-Norman Penetration.—Peace, however, was a gift which the people of Ireland were not destined to enjoy. O'Connor, in the first major action of his rule as high-king, expelled Diarmaid Mac Murchadha from the kingship of Leinster. The deposed ruler crossed the Irish Sea and sought help from Henry II of England. Henry had already contemplated the conquest of Ireland, for we have it on the word of John of Salisbury that in 1154 he had sought sanction for the step from the English-born Pope Adrian IV. Thus the appeal of Mac Murchadha provided a happy excuse for the furtherance of his policy. The English king espoused enthusiastically the exile's cause. Small contingents of Norman knights were sent to Ireland with Mac Murchadha, but were easily defeated by the high-king. Then, in August 1170, came an army of picked men under a redoubtable leader, Richard de Clare, 2d earl of Pembroke, better known as Strongbow. O'Connor and his troops found themselves confronted by a situation with which they were unable to cope: the Norman knights were clad in armor from head to foot; they carried long lances and fought from horseback; and they were assisted by archers armed with longbow and crossbow. Moreover, they had the rigid discipline of professional soldiers, and they were skilled in erecting fortifications which the Irish lacked instruments to reduce. In a word, the Normans were incomparably superior to the Irish of the day in military organization.

The inevitable result followed. Waterford fell, and also Dublin. When Mac Murchadha died, Strongbow, who had married his daughter, claimed the succession to Leinster. O'Connor besieged Dublin, but without success. Henry II himself arrived in Ireland in October 1171, and stayed until Easter 1172. O'Connor and the Irish princes submitted to the Norman king on the understanding that this would save them from the depredations of the barons. But in this they were mistaken; large areas of Irish land were parceled out to the nominees of the crown. After three years of warfare a treaty was signed at Windsor between O'Connor and Henry II, but its terms were violated by Henry and the Norman lords, and the struggle continued.

For over a century the tide of fortune favored the Norman invaders, who carved out for themselves principalities in all parts of Ireland. Henry II sent his son, Prince John, to govern the conquered island in 1185. When John became king of England he built a strong castle at Dublin and arranged to have the country administered by a central government. An attempt was made to fill the bishoprics and higher offices of the Church with Anglo-Norman prelates. The 13th century saw not only the conquest of Connacht but the rise to eminence of the two great Fitzgerald families of Kildare and Desmond and the families of De Burgh (Burke) and Butler.

By 1300 Norman power had passed its peak and an Irish recovery had begun. After the victory of Bannockburn (June 1314), Robert Bruce got in touch with the Irish princes and encouraged their efforts to form a national league. His brother, Edward Bruce, was crowned king of Ireland on May Day, 1316, but in a battle near Dundalk (October 1318), Bruce was killed and the Norman colony saved. During the long campaign English organization weakened and the Irish began to advance steadily in every portion of the island.

Assimilation of the Normans.—Remarkable in the 14th century is the extent to which the Normans became assimilated. In the case of the great lords the change was partial, for though they adopted Irish civilization, they did not renounce their allegiance to the English crown. By 1366 the colony had become so "degenerate" that Lionel, son of Edward III, was sent from England to provide a remedy. The "Statutes of Kilkenny" which he promulgated sought to preserve the English way of life in that part of Ireland which the colonists still controlled. The Statutes were a dead letter, and before the century ended the government in Dublin was compelled to pay "black rent" to Mac Murchadha of Leinster to restrain him from attacking the capital. Visits of Richard II in 1394 and again in 1399 ended in utter failure.

In the 15th century the picture remains essentially the same. During this period the Fitzgeralds in Desmond and Kildare reached the zenith of their power. Gerald, the "Great Earl" of Kildare (1477–1513), held the office of deputy (viceroy) for 30 years and ruled Ireland like a king. But the old order was changing with the accession to the throne of England of highly autocratic Tudor sovereigns.

Tudor Period.—Gerald, son of "the Great Earl," and himself 9th earl of Kildare, was appointed lord deputy by Henry VIII. Wolsey, however, hated the Fitzgeralds and was resolved to bring about their downfall. Kildare survived unscathed until 1533. Summoned to London then to answer charges, he named his son, "Silken Thomas," deputy in his stead. A report soon reached Ireland that the earl had been executed. Thomas immediately rebelled. In the campaign which followed he was defeated and forced to surrender; and he and his five uncles were beheaded in the Tower of London in 1537. With them the house of Kildare, as an independent force in Irish politics, came to an end.

The break of Henry VIII with Pope Clement VII had of necessity repercussions in Ireland. Henry had carried through the Irish Parliament acts that gave him complete control of ecclesiastical affairs. All monasteries were suppressed, save such as for the moment lay outside the reach of Henry's arm. Tudor power in the political field was now overwhelming, and the Irish princes tried to counteract it by securing aid from Henry II of France, but the negotiations came to nothing.

Queen Mary Tudor initiated the policy of expelling native Irish from their holdings and introducing in their stead planters from England. The idea appealed also to her successor, Elizabeth, and was applied by her with effect in Munster towards the end of her reign, when a favorable opportunity offered.

Elizabeth's policy in Ireland, like that of Henry VIII, was based on two main principles: complete control of the whole country by means of government officials operating from Dublin, and complete uniformity in religion. This meant constant warfare, since the Irish were prepared to fight to the death for their freedom and for their Catholic faith. In Ulster, where the old Irish population had been least disturbed, the opposition was strongest. Shane O'Neill ruled the northern province for years like a king. When not at peace with Elizabeth and her deputies he fought them with considerable success. His own overbearing rule was, however, resented by Ulster chiefs and in a quarrel with the MacDonnells of Antrim he was slain in 1567.

Soon afterwards a confederacy of Irishmen was formed under the leadership of the Desmond nobleman, James Fitzmaurice Fitzgerald. The Irish princes and lords, hamstrung in their effort to make war by the lack of guns and ammunition, appealed to Philip II of Spain for help. Philip dallied, as always. The religious issue was now uppermost and the papal court, no less than the court of the Spanish king, was interested in the result. Small expeditions were fitted out and sent to Ireland, but they were annihilated by the English commanders. Sir James was killed (1579). Gerald Fitzgerald, the 15th earl of Desmond, lacked energy and ability as a leader. So the movement collapsed; Desmond was beheaded (1583) and his great estates in Munster divided into plots and disposed of to English planters.

Within a few years, however, resistance was renewed on a national scale. The leaders were Hugh O'Neill, earl of Tyrone (since 1585) and Hugh O'Donnell of Tyrconnell or Donegal. O'Neill had been taken to England as a boy and educated in English ways. O'Donnell had twice been captured and twice escaped from Dublin Castle; with his second and successful bid for freedom, on Christmas Eve 1591, the Nine Years' War may be said to begin.

Nine Years' War.—Not only did all attacks on the north by English armies fail, but in 1598 O'Neill won an important victory over the English commander, Marshal Bagenal, at the Yellow Ford, near Armagh. The result was a great increase of enthusiasm and a gathering of forces from all Ireland under O'Neill's standard. Elizabeth was alarmed. A new army of immense size was collected and sent to Ireland under the command of Robert Devereux, 2d earl of Essex, but it achieved nothing and the campaign ended in a truce and the drafting by O'Neill of conditions under which he was willing to make peace. These were rejected by Elizabeth; and Essex, after a foolish revolt, lost his head. His place was taken by Lord Mountjoy, who adopted the ruthless policy of burning all crops and all food and so reducing the people to submission by famine rather than by arms. O'Neill had appealed to Spain for help, above all for artillery, without which his army could not maintain itself in the field. Philip III at last (September 1601) sent a small contingent of men and arms, but it landed at Kinsale in the south, where it could give only the minimum of assistance to O'Neill. Soon the Spaniards were shut in by the English fleet at the harbor mouth and by Mountjoy's army on the land side round the walls. O'Neill and O'Donnell marched from the north to the Spaniards' relief. It was decided, against O'Neill's better judgment, to undertake a general assault on the English lines. This took place on Dec. 23, 1601, and completely miscarried. The Battle of Kinsale proved to be a defeat from which O'Neill and O'Donnell were unable to recover. They were compelled to sue for peace and to accept the conditions which the English were willing to offer.

JOHN RYAN, S. J.

HISTORY FROM 1601 TO 1800

The Battle of Kinsale proved to be decisive: the prospect of an independent Irish nation, based on the old Gaelic order, was quickly to disappear. Hugh O'Neill held out in Ulster until 1603, when he made his submission to the lord deputy, Mountjoy, only to find that Queen Elizabeth had died a week before. With the new king, James I, O'Neill had been on friendly terms: had he delayed his submission, he might at least have been spared some indignities. Mountjoy, however, was not vindictive, and with James disposed to leniency the reign opened promisingly enough for Ireland. The promise was not maintained. Alarmed by the Gunpowder Plot (q.v.) and unable to stem the anti-popery tide in England, James had little power, even had he the will, to prevent measures against the Irish Catholics. Those measures soon extended beyond the enactment of laws enjoining conformity with the Established Church. Under the lord deputyship of Sir Arthur Chichester (1604–1614) the ground was prepared for the Penal Laws under which Irish Catholics were to labor for more than two centuries. Catholics were *ipso facto* suspected rebels; and from this uncongenial atmosphere O'Neill, O'Donnell, and others of the "Old Irish" decided to take refuge in exile. "The Flight of the Earls" in 1607 symbolized the collapse of the Old Irish society; and it was made the excuse for the most comprehensive confiscation and resettlement of land that had yet been effected. Half a million acres in Ulster were distributed to settlers from across the channel, mainly Presbyterians from the Scottish Lowlands. The natives, though not expelled outright, found themselves left in possession only of land that was too poor in quality to be an attraction to the newcomers.

To confirm all the measures taken in the early part of his reign, James called a parliament in Dublin in 1613. With some skill, this assembly was "packed" to ensure a Protestant majority. The loyalty of the minority of Catholic representatives was not in question, but it was determined that they should have no opportunity to make use of the occasion to attack the Penal Laws. They were nevertheless strong enough, if not to secure a much greater degree of toleration, at least to ensure that no further steps were taken against them, and in 1615, James, finding that little was to be obtained from the parliament, ordered its dissolution.

In the last years of James's reign Ireland was tranquil, and comparatively prosperous; and the accession of Charles I, who had married a Catholic and was himself "High Church," gave promise of still brighter days to come. Charles, however, regarded Ireland throughout his reign primarily as a potential source of revenue, to be obtained if necessary by double-dealing. Concessions to the Catholics were offered for cash; the money was paid over, but the Graces (as these concessions were termed) were never given statutory effect. No real departure, in fact, was made from the Irish policy of James until, in 1632, Thomas Wentworth arrived as lord deputy, determined to make Ireland a source both of wealth and of strength to the crown. Roman Catholic and Protestant were played off, one against the other, to keep them occupied while Wentworth strove to restore the royal prerogatives and powers—and the revenues attached to them—that had fallen into the hands of local magnates. Many of his reforms were salutary, but they brought him the undying hatred of the monopolists—men such as Richard Boyle, earl of Cork who as a young man had arrived in Ireland a penniless adventurer and risen to be the greatest power in the land. Wentworth, made earl of Strafford in 1640, had been recalled in 1639 to deal with Charles's increasing difficulties at home; and it was largely the evidence of the men he had angered in Ireland that helped, two years later, to bring him to the block.

Insurrection.—In the meantime, the government of Ireland had fallen into the hands of supporters of the Puritan Parliament of England, whose actions helped to precipitate a rebellion in 1641 in which the natives rose and massacred the Ulster settlers. The insurrection was an outburst against repression, rather than a calculated nationalist uprising; and the issues were confused by the fact that Charles, who originally attempted to put down the rebels, was soon in need of their assistance against his Parliamentary foes. The Irish Catholics formed a confederacy, calling back from the continent the exiles Owen Roe O'Neill and Gen. Thomas Preston to lead their forces. Owen, a nephew of Hugh O'Neill, was the natural leader of the Old Irish stock; Preston, of the Catholic Old English. In addition there was the Anglican James Butler, marquis of Ormonde, Charles's lord lieutenant in Ireland, at the head of the Royalist forces. Ormonde, at first ordered to put down the rebels, was soon required by Charles to come to terms with them, to secure their help against the Parliamentary forces. Between these groups divisions were inevitable, serious enough to enable the Parliamentary forces, numerically far weaker, to survive. Not even Owen Roe's resounding victory at Benburb in 1646 succeeded in dislodging them, and antagonism between the Royalists and the Catholics paved the way both for Charles's final defeat and for Oliver Cromwell's subjugation of Ireland. Cromwell arrived in Ireland in 1649, promptly avenging the deaths of the Ulster settlers in his massacres of the inhabitants of Drogheda and Wexford. The combination of terrorism and military skill led to the collapse of the rebellion, though it was not finally stamped out until 1652.

Cromwellian Regime.—"Cromwell's Curse" was not to be forgotten or forgiven in Ireland. Not only were the Irish defeated in the field; all their estates east of the Shannon were forfeited. Over half of the land to the east of the river was confiscated and redistributed in a resettlement by contrast with which the Plantation of Ulster 40 years earlier was unsystematic and naïve. Some 30,000 Irish soldiers were allowed to go into exile in the service of continental powers, and thousands of commoners were sent to virtual slavery in the West Indies. The power of the Old English in Ireland went the way of the power of the Old Irish: henceforth for generations the new English element dominated the country's life. A union with Britain was enacted in 1653, providing for Irish representation in the English Parliament; and only the short duration of Cromwellian rule prevented Ireland from effective anglicization.

The Restoration in 1660 did not entirely redress the balance, as Charles II was unwilling to risk unpopularity by concessions to the Irish Catholics. The Irish Parliament was restored, but Catholics were no longer allowed to take seats in it. Although some of the Catholic lands were regained by their former owners, the Protestant "ascendancy" remained firmly established, and such toleration as the Catholics were able to obtain in practice was only on sufferance. The Anglican Church alone was officially recognized. Again, a period of peace under the able rule of Ormonde, who was lord lieutenant for the greater part of the reign, brought a revival in prosperity; and at Charles II's death in 1685 the country was in a fair way to recovery from the chaos of the 1640's. But the brief rule of his successor, James II, brought with it disaster. The appointment of a Catholic, Richard Talbot, earl of Tyrconnell, as commander in chief and then as lord deputy, led to a revival of the hopes that had given rise to the Catholic Confederacy. Some political power was restored to Catholic hands, and when William of Orange drove James from England in 1688, the Irish gave James their loyalty as the legitimate king. James had no sympathy with Irish national aspirations, but he saw in these loyal subjects a weapon which he could use to procure his restoration. Louis XIV of France thought to use the Irish in pursuance of his wider aims, and in 1689 he dispatched James in a French fleet to Kinsale. Once again, the divided and sometimes conflicting motives of the Irish helped to paralyze their effort. The greater experience and skill of William's forces led to the crushing defeat of the Irish at the Battle of the Boyne in 1690, and the following year, the last of their commanders, Patrick Sarsfield, surrendered at Limerick and was allowed to depart with most of his men to fight for France, as the "Wild Geese," on continental fields.

Penal Laws Maintained.—If the settlement made by William III was less repressive than Cromwell's, the reason was that there was not so much to repress. In the event, however, the new reign bore more heavily on the Irish because the Penal Laws were not relaxed, as they had been on similar occasions under the Stuarts, as soon as a state of emergency no longer existed. The Penal Laws remained, and were actually intensified, although this was a flagrant breach of the treaty made at Limerick. Under them, the Catholics sank into the condition of helots. Legally designated "Papists," they found the doors to the acquisition of land, to education, and to administrative posts closed to them. Their decline was facilitated by the introduction of the potato, which provided a food upon which peasant families could live on the minimum of land, assisting the Catholic peasantry to sink into a squalor and misery as abject as was to be found anywhere in Europe.

The Protestant "ascendancy," however, soon found themselves unable to profit from the subjection of their fellow countrymen. Even if the Irish Parliament had not been in effect manipulated by the English executive, it was in any case severely restricted in its competence. Ireland was to all intents subject to British rule. In commerce, this was particularly galling. The industry of the country was virtually annihilated by English legislation at the behest of English traders, jealous of potential rivals; and only linen, among Irish manufactures, continued to enjoy prosperity.

Under Queen Anne the Penal Laws became yet more rigorous; for example, a gavelkind (land tenure) act was passed ruling that land owned by Catholics must be divided up amongst all the owners' heirs, unless the eldest should become a convert to the Established Church, in which case all the property would be his. The Irish had not brought this further burden upon themselves, crushed and dispirited as they were. It was their misfortune that the Stuart pretenders to the British throne continued to act as a threat to the safety of the House of Orange, and then of the Hanoverian dynasty, giving repression its justification.

The first half of the 18th century would be black indeed, were it not illuminated for a brief spell by the genius of Jonathan Swift. He appeared on the scene at a time when his country's commerce was nearly extinguished, its religion vindictively penalized, and its government in alien hands. The viceroys rarely felt it necessary even to visit the country under their charge, and the land was ruled by lords justices, who transacted such routine business as was required with the help of a Parliament well "packed" with placemen—the "undertakers," as they came to be called. Most of the lucrative posts went to Englishmen. In 1719 the Declaratory Act finally removed what little substance of Irish legislative independence remained, affirming the right of the English Parliament to bind Ireland in its acts; and only the shadow—the corrupt Irish Parliament—remained. So confident were the English of their strength in Ireland that a project put forward in 1722 that would have led to a debasement of the Irish coinage for the profit of William Wood, a protégé of one of George I's former mistresses, was casually accepted. In his *Drapier's Letters,* Dean Swift, a Protestant, unleashed all the resources of his devastating invective against "Wood's halfpence." The effect was electrifying. For the first time, the Protestants were united for the Irish cause in a national issue. They roused themselves to such good purpose that the coins never made their appearance, and the English had hastily to dispatch a viceroy of some ability, Lord Carteret, to the scene.

Now that there was so little to fear from the Catholics, crushed as they were beneath the

Penal Laws, Irish Protestant nationalism began sporadically to assert itself against the irritations and humiliations of alien rule. Thus it came about that, although the Stuart rising of 1745 had little impact upon Ireland, before the turn of the half century Charles Lucas, by his political pamphlets, had gone some way towards reviving the popular feeling that *Drapier's Letters* had aroused in Dublin. A section of the Irish Parliament, too, was bestirring itself to make a demand for greater control of the national finances, and in 1753 the Commons actually threw out a money bill that had been sent over from England. Pensions and titles were hurriedly distributed to win over the dissidents. For a few years an uneasy quiet was restored; but during the viceroyalty of Lord Townshend the system of government by "undertakers" received further shocks. Townshend arrived in 1767; the following year an act was passed limiting the duration of parliaments to eight years, and in 1769 the Commons again rejected an English money bill.

Patriot Movement.—This time the attempt to bring the Irish Parliament under control was less successful. A new generation of Irish Protestants was springing up, including such men as Henry Grattan and Henry Flood, who had strong links with the Whig reformers in Britain. A Patriot Party began to grow, demanding an Irish Parliament emptied of "undertakers," with power to control the country's finance and commerce. The American War of Independence came fortuitously to their assistance. Anxious for Irish help, which was freely given, the British government felt it expedient to make certain trade concessions to Ireland, and to conciliate the Catholics, in case they should be tempted to join forces with the Patriots. Relief acts removed some of the worst of the Penal Laws. But the vital step was taken when the offer of the Patriot Party to raise a volunteer force for the defense of Ireland, against a threatened French invasion, was accepted. The Volunteers, a predominantly Protestant body led by the duke of Leinster in the south and the earl of Charlemont in the north, became first a fashionable and then a formidable force; and when their moral support was ranged behind the Patriots in their campaign to secure reform, the British government had to be told that the movement had become too strong to be resisted. The disasters in America had driven Lord North from office in Britain; and the new Whig government sent the duke of Portland to Ireland as lord lieutenant, prepared to concede parliamentary independence. The Declaratory Act was repealed, and in May 1782 Ireland, in Grattan's words, became a nation.

Or so it seemed, to judge by the popular rejoicing. But very quickly, certain weaknesses in the new constitution were revealed. Legislative independence might have been established in theory, but the practical limitations to effective self-government remained formidable. The lord lieutenant and his secretaries of state, in whose hands lay the executive power, were English nominees. Had the legislature been more representative and independent it could, by withholding supplies, have bound the executive to its will; but the majority of the seats in the Commons were controlled by a few powerful landowners, whose adhesion to the executive proved to be easily purchasable by pensions and promises of titles, honors, and awards. The judiciary were likewise dependent upon "the Castle"—the seat in Dublin of the Irish executive—for their advancement.

Party Strife.—No sooner had independence been gained than the Patriot Party suffered from a split which materially lessened its chance to reform the constitution that it had just won. Flood and Grattan quarreled, giving the Castle the opportunity to consolidate its hold upon the Commons; the Volunteer movement lost its impetus, and the Patriots their power. By 1784 the Irish Commons were scarcely less under the executive's thumb than they had been earlier in the century.

The venality of Parliament did not, however, prevent the enactment of commercial regulations that did much to revive Irish prosperity. The Corn Law brought in by the Irish chancellor of the exchequer, John Foster, was to make Ireland one of England's chief granaries for the next half a century. In 1785 the agreement of William Pitt, who had become prime minister in Britain, was obtained to some commercial propositions that would, if carried, have put the two countries on almost equal trading terms. The propositions passed through the Irish Parliament, but English commercial interests, their fear of Irish competition aroused, procured such substantial amendments that the bill became unacceptable to the Irish legislature, and had to be withdrawn. That so much British opposition had been aroused was, however, in itself a tribute to the growing commercial vitality of the Irish nation that characterized the period.

The government's hold over the legislature was not shaken until 1789, when the possibility that the Prince of Wales, whose Whig sympathies were well known, might become regent during George III's madness, induced many members to join Grattan in supporting the prince's claims. But the king recovered his sanity; the Castle restored its majority by a lavish creation of peerages and pensions; and the rekindled hopes of the Patriots were again quenched. Thereafter the feeling began to grow in Ireland, fostered by the success of the revolutionaries in France, that constitutional changes could only be won, as they had been in 1782, by threat of force. In 1791 Wolfe Tone founded the Society of United Irishmen in Belfast, where the nucleus of the organization was provided by the northern dissenters, still sufferers to only a less degree than Catholics under the Penal Laws. The society spread rapidly over the country, mainly among the Protestant middle class. At the same time, the Catholic movement showed signs of revival. A deputation that laid its grievances before George III in London was received with sufficient royal favor to secure a further measure of relief, giving Catholics the vote, subject to a property qualification. They were, however, still excluded from the Parliament.

Their success encouraged the United Irishmen to press more strongly for electoral reform. The government, alarmed at hints that force might be used if peaceable methods failed, prosecuted Hamilton Rowan and others of the society's leaders in 1794. The movement was driven underground, losing its more law-abiding elements, and gradually taking on the characteristics of a conspiracy.

Rebellion.—The last chance that the electoral problem might be settled peaceably was lost when

Lord Fitzwilliam was recalled in 1795 from the viceroyalty that he had held for only a few weeks. He had come determined to carry a measure of Catholic emancipation, and had made a beginning by removing from office some of the ultra-Protestant officeholders who had installed themselves after 1782. They had powerful friends in Britain who succeeded in alarming Pitt; Fitzwilliam was replaced by Lord Camden, and the "ultras" were restored. The new lord lieutenant resolved to meet the growing revolutionary threat with coercion. A severe Insurrection Act was followed in 1796 by the suspension of habeas corpus. The United Irishmen, in their turn, were driven to more extreme measures, and in the same year two comparatively new recruits to the movement from the ranks of the aristocracy, Lord Edward Fitzgerald and Arthur O'Connor, went to the continent to seek French assistance. Wolfe Tone, who had left Ireland earlier, was before them; and he succeeded in persuading the French to send a fleet with an expeditionary force to Ireland. He himself was on one of the ships that reached Bantry Bay at Christmas, 1796, but appalling weather prevented disembarkation of the troops, and the chance was lost.

The threatened invasion made the Castle intensify the campaign of coercion. The military were given almost unlimited license to use torture, flogging, and execution to exterminate the rebel movement. Grattan and his followers, who had clung to the hope of constitutional reform, left public life in disgust, and the United Irishmen, in loose association with the Defenders, a Catholic peasant movement, laid plans for insurrection with or without French aid. The United Ireland movement, however, was riddled with spies and informers, who reported its every step to the Castle; and before the date fixed for the outbreak, every prominent leader had been captured or killed. Nevertheless, the rebellion broke out in the spring of 1798. It was disorganized and ill led, doomed to failure from the start; only in the southeast did the rebels achieve even momentary success, and within a month the rising had been suppressed. A French force that arrived too late to be of any help was quickly rounded up; Tone was captured at sea; Fitzgerald had been killed trying to escape arrest; and the other leaders were prepared to secure their lives by relating in full the movement's history in a formal confession.

Union.—The rebellion confirmed the British government in a view with which Pitt had been toying for many years: that only in a union of the two countries could their mutual safety be secured against internal and external enemies. Early in 1799 the union was proposed in the Irish Parliament. The motion was defeated. The rebuff only made the Castle the more determined. The Catholics were won over with the promise of emancipation; the Protestants were reassured by the argument that Catholics could never be more than an impotent minority in the British Parliament at Westminster. Such propaganda still proving insufficient, large-scale purchase was resorted to. Lord Castlereagh was employed systematically and cynically to buy out enough opponents of the measure with places, pensions, and titles, to insure a majority. In 1800, in spite of a last eloquent appeal from Grattan, the Irish Parliament signed its own death warrant by passing the Act of Union; and the nation that he had helped to create relinquished, for over a century, its nationhood.

BRIAN INGLIS.

HISTORY FROM 1800 TO 1922

Although the Act of Union in 1800 extinguished the Irish Parliament and transferred all legislative power to London, there had been hopes of relief from the oppression which had been exerted for years by the Protestant "ascendancy" in Ireland. William Pitt had gained much Catholic support for the Union by promising that it would be at once followed by the admission of Catholics to Parliament. Catholics had been entitled to vote in the Irish elections since 1793, and it was assumed that they would soon elect Catholic members and assert their rights. But George III vetoed Catholic emancipation, and Irish questions were left entirely in the hands of the ascendancy executive in Dublin Castle. An insurrection in Dublin headed by Robert Emmet in 1803 was easily suppressed; and the following years brought a steady decline of Irish industry and trade.

Such protection of Irish interests as had been provided by the Irish Parliament was now withdrawn. Dublin ceased to be the center of social and political life, and even those landowners who continued to sit in Parliament now attended in London instead of Dublin. Many more left Ireland entirely and became absentee landlords, exacting all that they could in rents, through middlemen who found during the Napoleonic wars that it was most profitable to divide estates into small holdings, at extortionate rents which could be paid while agricultural prices were high. This increase of small holdings, combined with complete neglect by the landlords to make any improvements, produced an appalling standard of living and of housing. Young laborers could become tenants of a few acres and build a wretched hovel, equal to anything that could be got later in life; and they married in great numbers, so that the population grew with abnormal rapidity for the next 40 years.

While poverty increased among the people, a new Catholic middle class was slowly arising since the relaxation of the anti-Catholic laws. They had been excluded for generations from owning land, or even from practicing certain trades, and all the professions. But many of them had become prosperous through trade with France and other countries, and their sons could now become lawyers or doctors, though they could not enter public life.

Catholic Emancipation.—The new generation found a leader in the Catholic barrister, Daniel O'Connell, who devised means of conducting an agitation for Catholic rights within the law. By insisting on the right to petition Parliament, and by using the courts as a platform when he defended in political prosecutions, he aroused such a formidable agitation that in 1815 he could have won the admission of Catholics to Parliament, if he had accepted the proposed British veto on the appointment of Irish bishops. But he refused all such terms, and allowed the agitation to subside until 1823, when he founded the Catholic Association on a broad democratic basis, with a vast membership subscribing a penny a month. All Catholic Ireland supported his popular agitation, and in 1828 he was elected for County Clare as a Catholic candidate who would not take his seat until the oath against the Catholic religion was abolished. The duke of Wellington, British prime minister, feared civil war, and in 1829, by threatening resignation, he compelled George IV to sign the Catholic Emancipation Act.

Catholics could now be elected to the British Parliament, but the Protestant ascendancy still owned most of the land and its wealth, and had a complete monopoly of power. But experience showed that without a national legislature, there was no hope of economic and social reforms. O'Connell abandoned his legal career to become the leader of a national movement for repeal of the Act of Union. His attempts to continue political agitation on the former lines were suppressed by the Whig ministry which was elected in 1831 to carry parliamentary reform in Britain, and for ten years O'Connell gave the Whigs a chance to fulfill their promises to improve Irish conditions. But in 1840 he decided to revive the popular agitation, by his old method of collecting small subscriptions from the people.

After a discouraging start, he found new support from a group of young men who founded the *Nation* newspaper in October 1842. They were led by Charles Gavan Duffy and Thomas Davis, who preached national recovery by promoting economic and cultural as well as political life. With their help, in 1843, a series of "monster meetings" was organized all over Ireland to demand repeal of the Union. The climax was to be a vast rally at Clontarf in October; but the government blocked all the approaches with troops and artillery, and O'Connell had to cancel the meeting. Soon afterwards he and all the prominent leaders were prosecuted for seditious conspiracy and imprisoned.

Potato Famine.—An appeal against their sentence succeeded unexpectedly, but when O'Connell came out of prison his health and his nerve were broken. The young men became impatient of his appeals for caution, and conflict had already arisen between him and the Young Ireland Party before Davis died suddenly in September 1845. Duffy then gathered a group of still younger men around the *Nation* newspaper, and the events which followed drove them to revolutionary policies. The population had increased very rapidly to 8¼ millions by 1845, and the standard of living was so low that a large proportion subsisted almost entirely on potatoes. In 1845 the potato blight, of which both the cause and the remedy were still unknown, reached Ireland, and produced a famine which became devastating when the potato crop was again ruined in 1846 and 1847. Fully half a million people died directly from starvation or from typhus and cholera. Millions more were barely kept alive by soup kitchens and the most meager relief, provided largely by private sources, much of it coming from America. A vast exodus by emigration began, and the roads were crowded with refugees heading for the ports to escape to Britain or the United States.

Young Ireland Rebellion.—O'Connell was slowly dying with softening of the brain, and he died at Genoa in May 1847. The Young Irelanders had already seceded from his Repeal Party, and they were appealing for organized resistance to prevent the export of food from Ireland, which only paid the landlords' rents. The bloodless revolution in Paris in January 1848, which replaced Louis Philippe by a French republic, had encouraged Young Ireland with hopes of similar success in Ireland after the harvest. John Mitchel, a young Ulster Protestant, became the chief advocate of armed rebellion, and the government passed a Treason Felony Act under which he was convicted and deported. The military garrison was greatly increased, and the plans for a rising were forestalled by orders to arrest all the leaders. William Smith O'Brien and all those who were not yet arrested vainly attempted a rising in County Tipperary in June 1848. He, Thomas Francis Meagher, and others were sentenced to death for high treason, and next year they were deported to join Mitchel as convicts in Tasmania.

Fenians.—Many of the Young Irelanders escaped to America or to France, and in the following years, devoted themselves to organizing Irish resistance overseas. The Fenian Brotherhood was formed as a secret society in the United States in 1858. It soon extended widely in Great Britain and Ireland, while its central direction remained in America. A fierce hatred of Britain resulted from the vast emigration which began with the great famine; and as the Irish population in America steadily increased, it became a powerful factor in foreign relations. In 1851 the Irish population had declined to 6½ millions, and it had lost 800,000 more by 1861. In Britain and in Ireland the Fenians provoked widespread alarm by acts of violence and political agitation; but another attempted rising in 1867 was easily put down.

Pressure from overseas and the fear of continued Fenian activities compelled the British Parliament to consider practical reforms. William Ewart Gladstone became leader of the Liberal Party in 1867, and as prime minister soon announced that he would disestablish (sunder the state connection of) the Protestant Church in Ireland, which still exacted tithes from an overwhelmingly Catholic people. He carried disestablishment in 1869, and in 1870 also secured passage of an Irish Land Act which conceded the tenant's right to security of tenure, so long as he could pay his rent, and to compensation for improvements. But emigration, chiefly to America, continued to drain away the most active young men and women for many years. The population fell steadily until 1921, when it was around 4,350,000. It became increasingly evident that only a national legislature could organize recovery.

Home Rule Movement.—In 1870 the Home Rule League was founded by an eminent Protestant lawyer, Isaac Butt, who had previously been a leading opponent of O'Connell's agitation for repeal of the Act of Union. Its demand for a subordinate parliament in Ireland was inspired neither by the sanguine nationalism of Young Ireland nor the bitter Fenian hatred of England; but it met with no success until a young Irish landlord, Charles Stewart Parnell, joined Butt's party and began to obstruct all parliamentary business. His unflinching and ruthless defiance in the British Parliament soon attracted other young members, and in 1878 he was elected leader of the Irish Nationalist Party. Butt and his earlier colleagues were soon displaced by such ardent young nationalists as T. M. Healy, William O'Brien, John Redmond, and John Dillon.

While Parnell produced chaos in the House of Commons by systematic obstructions, a new movement for land reform in Ireland had been started by Michael Davitt. The son of an evicted tenant, he had been imprisoned as a Fenian convict in England. In 1879, after his release, he founded the Land League in the poorest districts of Ireland, to demand fair rents and fixity of tenure. On lines similar to the new trade unionism, he organized the small tenant farmers to resist evictions and refuse payment of exorbitant rents. A means of agitation which could not be prevented as illegal was found in "boycotting" all landlords who became involved in disputes with the Land League, which many of them opposed by threatening to evict those who joined it.

Parnell joined forces with Davitt's Land League and quickly galvanized the whole country by combining the agitations for Home Rule and for land reforms. He sought to obtain a "balance of power" at Westminster by forming a compact party of some 80 members pledged to support any English party which conceded their demands. Gladstone soon yielded to this pressure by carrying his Land Act of 1881, which set up fair rent courts. Parnell was imprisoned for obstructing operation of the act, but was soon released, while both English parties (Liberals and Conservatives) made overtures about introducing a Home Rule bill. Gladstone split the Liberal Party by proclaiming Home Rule as his policy, and his first Home Rule bill, in 1886, was defeated in the Commons.

Support in Britain for Irish Home Rule had grown widely when Parnell's political career was suddenly wrecked in 1890 by his becoming involved in the divorce suit brought by his parliamentary colleague Capt. William Henry O'Shea. Gladstone then announced that he could not continue his alliance with Parnell, and the Irish Catholic bishops also demanded his resignation, but Parnell would make no concession. A bitter split developed, and only a small minority of Parnellites retained their seats. Parnell fought his opponents with fierce energy but died from exhaustion in 1891. Deprived of his leadership, the nationalist agitation made no progress. Gladstone made a second attempt with his Home Rule bill of 1893, but it was rejected by the House of Lords. Not until 1900 was the Irish Nationalist Party reunited, when John Dillon, who had led the anti-Parnellite majority, agreed to serve under Redmond.

Land Reform.—Years of Conservative government had killed all hopes of gaining Home Rule, when Arthur James Balfour, on becoming leader of the House of Commons in 1895, adopted a new Tory policy of introducing constructive reforms. Local government by elected councils was conceded; administrative departments were created to develop the western counties and to promote agriculture and technical instruction. And in 1903 the Irish Land Purchase Act induced the landlords to sell their estates on favorable terms to the state, which enabled the tenants to buy their farms by terminable annuities. But the drain of emigration continued, and economic progress was stagnant. The agitation for Home Rule lost the driving force that it had derived from being linked with the agitation for land reforms, which were now attained. Redmond's reunited Nationalist Party at Westminster could offer no more than a resumption of Parnell's tactics of independent opposition at Westminster.

A new generation turned from politics to revive the nationalist idealism of Young Ireland. Douglas Hyde and Eoin MacNeill founded the Gaelic League to preserve and revive the Irish language. There was a similar movement to promote Irish industries. Sir Horace Plunkett began to organize agricultural cooperative societies. Hopes of a Home Rule measure revived when the Liberals won a large majority in the House of Commons in 1903. But disgust with the failure of Liberal promises produced the rise of the Sinn Fein movement, led by Arthur Griffith, which demanded total withdrawal of the Irish members from Westminster, and an intensive reconstruction at home. The prospect changed when Redmond gained the balance of power in British politics, after David Lloyd George's radical budget of 1909 was thrown out by the House of Lords. Redmond promised full Irish support if the Liberals would introduce Home Rule. After the Lords' veto had been abolished in 1911 by the Parliament Act, the third Home Rule bill was introduced in 1912.

Ulster Opposition.—The Conservatives then adopted new methods under Andrew Bonar Law's leadership. They organized violent resistance to Home Rule in Ulster, where they had for years had a compact Unionist majority in the eastern counties around Belfast. In a reckless political campaign, all the leading Tory politicians encouraged the Ulster Unionist leader, Sir Edward Carson, in organizing a provisional government in Belfast. They exploited openly the anti-Irish sympathies of most officers in the British army, which produced a mutiny in March 1914, when the cavalry officers at the Curragh (a military training camp in southern Ireland) resigned their commissions rather than move into Ulster. The younger nationalists formed a national force of Irish Volunteers to assert their rights. Both forces obtained arms in defiance of government prohibitions, and civil war seemed imminent.

The sudden declaration of war against Germany in August 1914, compelled Prime Minister Herbert Asquith to postpone implementation of the Home Rule Act, passed in September, in order to placate the Conservative opposition and restore national unity. Redmond had a sincere reverence for the British Empire as a federation of self-governing Dominions, and he gave his immediate support to Asquith. He asked the government to leave the defense of Ireland jointly to the Irish and the Ulster Volunteers, and undertook to raise divisions of Irish recruits for active service. But the anti-Irish influences at the War Office under Lord Kitchener prevailed. A strong reaction in Ireland set in against Redmond's recruiting appeals, while nationalist meetings and propaganda were suppressed by the government.

Easter Rebellion, 1916.—Meanwhile the Fenian organization had decided to provoke an armed rising in Ireland while Britain was involved in a European war. Its small and secret membership grew as political repression increased. On Easter Monday, 1916, a sudden rising by less than 2,000 men in Dublin, under the leadership of Patrick Pearse and James Connolly, seized the General Post Office and other buildings and proclaimed an Irish republic. They held out for six days while British forces devastated much of the city. Most of the leaders were sentenced to death, and several thousand political suspects were imprisoned or deported to Eng-

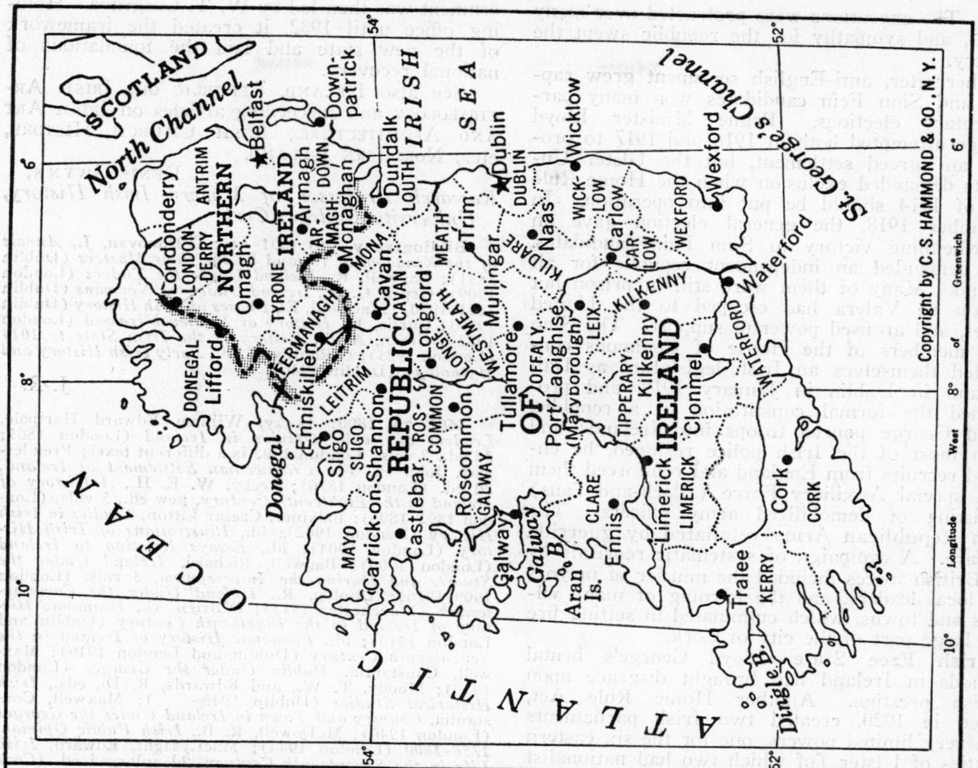

Ireland: The Republic and Northern Ireland.

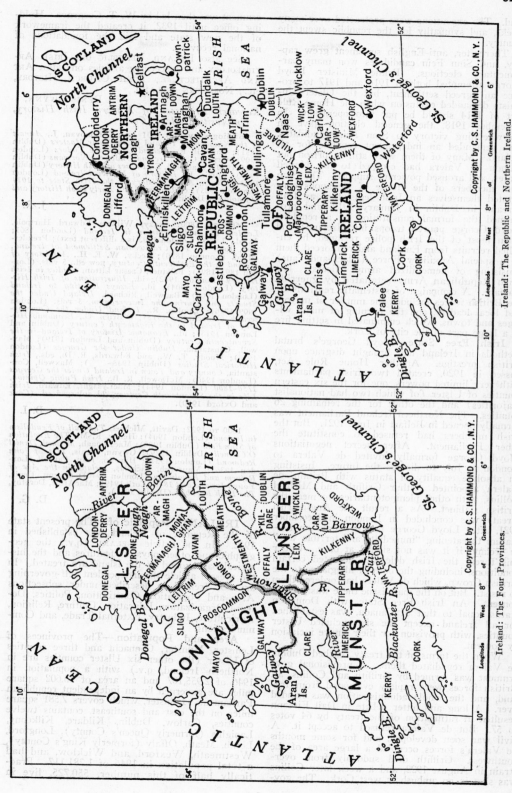

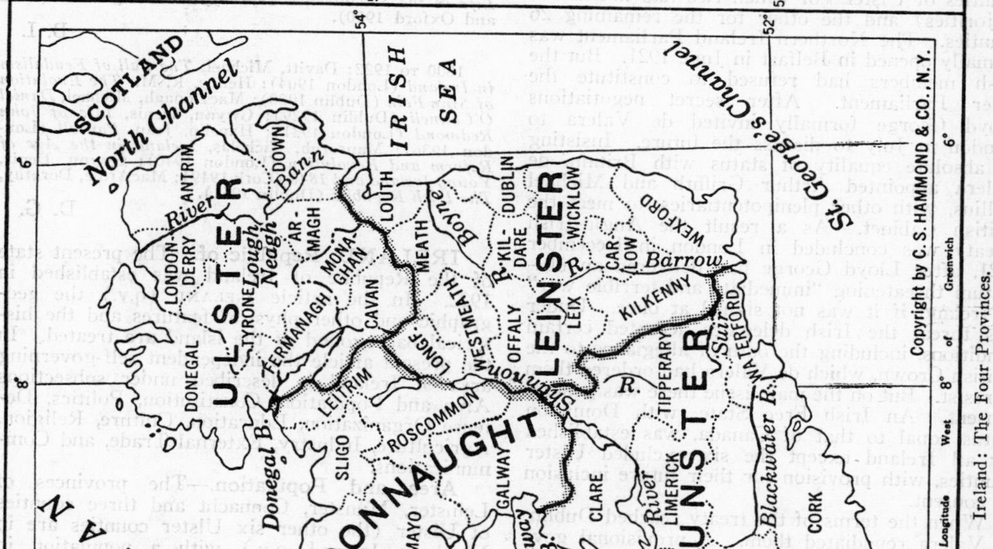

Ireland: The Four Provinces.

land. The executions were protracted over many weeks, and sympathy for the republic swept the country.

Thereafter, anti-English sentiment grew rapidly, and Sinn Fein candidates won many parliamentary elections. Prime Minister Lloyd George attempted both in 1916 and 1917 to produce an agreed settlement, but the Ulster Unionists demanded exclusion when the Home Rule Act of 1914 should be put into operation. In December 1918, the general election gave an overwhelming victory to Sinn Fein candidates, who demanded an independent republic for all Ireland. Many of them were still in prison but Eamon de Valera had escaped to the United States, and aroused powerful support. The Sinn Fein members of the House of Commons constituted themselves an Irish legislature as Dail Eireann in Dublin in January 1919, and proclaimed the formal constitution of a republic. Lloyd George poured troops into Ireland; and when most of the Irish police resigned, he enrolled recruits from England and reinforced them by a special Auxiliary Force (Black-and-Tans) consisting of demobilized army officers. The Irish Republican Army retaliated by guerrilla warfare. A campaign of systematic reprisals by the British forces included the murder of mayors and local leaders, and the burning of many villages and towns, which culminated in setting fire to a large part of the city of Cork.

Irish Free State.—Lloyd George's brutal methods in Ireland had brought disgrace upon British prestige. Another Home Rule Act, passed in 1920, created two Irish parliaments with very limited powers, one for the six eastern counties of Ulster (of which two had nationalist majorities) and the other for the remaining 26 counties. The Northern Ireland Parliament was formally opened in Belfast in June 1921. But the Irish members had refused to constitute the other Parliament. After secret negotiations Lloyd George formally invited de Valera to London in July to discuss the future. Insisting on absolute equality of status with Britain, de Valera appointed Arthur Griffith and Michael Collins, with other plenipotentiaries, to meet the British Cabinet. As a result the Anglo-Irish Treaty was concluded in London in December 1921, after Lloyd George had delivered an ultimatum threatening "immediate and terrible war" in Ireland if it was not signed at once. Under this threat the Irish delegates accepted certain conditions, including the oath of allegiance to the British Crown, which de Valera had ordered them to resist. But on the main issue there was general consent. An Irish Free State, with Dominion status equal to that of Canada, was established for all Ireland except the six excluded Ulster counties, with provision for their future inclusion by consent.

When the terms of the treaty reached Dublin, de Valera repudiated them. A provisional government was formed by Griffith and Collins, all British forces were rapidly evacuated from Ireland, and the whole administration was handed over. A long and bitter debate in Dail Eireann resulted in ratification of the treaty by 64 votes to 57. But de Valera refused to accept it. A civil war soon developed, and for some months de Valera's forces occupied a large area of the southwest. Griffith died suddenly from overstrain in August 1922, and a week later Collins was shot in an ambush in west Cork. The government was then led by W. T. Cosgrave. Holding office until 1932, it created the framework of the new state and laid the foundations of national recovery.

See also IRELAND, REPUBLIC OF; IRISH ARCHAEOLOGY and succeeding articles on IRISH ART AND ARCHITECTURE; IRISH CHURCH HISTORY, etc.; NORTHERN IRELAND.

DENIS GWYNN,
Research Professor of Modern Irish History, University College, Cork.

Bibliography.—TO 1601 A.D.: O'Donovan, J., *Annals of the Kingdom of Ireland by the Four Masters* (Dublin 1851); Bagwell, R., *Ireland Under the Tudors* (London 1909); Orpen, G. H., *Ireland Under the Normans* (Dublin 1911–1920); MacNeill, E., *Phases of Irish History* (Dublin 1919); Curtis, E., *History of Medieval Ireland* (London 1923); Green, A. S., *History of the Irish State to 1014* (London 1925); O'Rahilly, T. F., *Early Irish History and Mythology* (Dublin 1946).

J. R.

1601 TO 1800: Lecky, William Edward Hartpole, *Leaders of Public Opinion in Ireland* (London 1861; 3d ed., 2 vols., London 1903 is a different text); Prendergast, John P., *The Cromwellian Settlement of Ireland*, 2d ed. (London 1870); Lecky, W. E. H., *A History of Ireland in the Eighteenth Century*, new ed., 5 vols. (London 1892–1896); Falkiner, Caesar Litton, *Studies in Irish History* (London 1902); id., *Illustrations of Irish History* (London 1904); id., *Essays Relating to Ireland* (London 1909); Bagwell, Richard, *Ireland Under the Stuarts and During the Interregnum*, 3 vols. (London 1909–1916); Dunlop, R., *Ireland Under the Commonwealth* (Manchester 1913); O'Brien, G., *Economic History of Ireland in the Eighteenth Century* (Dublin and London 1918); id., *Economic History of Ireland in the Seventeenth Century* (Dublin and London 1919); Maxwell, Constantia, *Dublin Under the Georges* (London 1936); Moody, T. W., and Edwards, R. D., eds., *Irish Historical Studies* (Dublin 1938–); Maxwell, Constantia, *Country and Town in Ireland Under the Georges* (London 1940); McDowell, R. B., *Irish Public Opinion, 1750–1800* (London 1944); MacLysaght, Edward, *Irish Life in the Seventeenth Century*, 2d enlarged ed. (Cork and Oxford 1950).

B. I.

1800 TO 1922: Davitt, Michael, *The Fall of Feudalism in Ireland* (London 1904); Henry, R. M., *The Evolution of Sinn Fein* (Dublin 1920); MacDonagh, Michael, *Daniel O'Connell* (Dublin 1929); Gwynn, Denis, *Life of John Redmond* (London 1931); Hanslip, Joan, *Parnell* (London 1936); Mansergh, Nicholas, *Ireland in the Age of Reform and Revolution* (London 1940); Gwynn, Denis, *Young Ireland and 1848* (Cork 1949); MacArdle, Dorothy, *The Irish Republic* (Dublin 1951).

D. G.

IRELAND, Republic of. The present state of the Republic of Ireland was established in 1922. In the article IRELAND (q.v.) the geographic and other physical features and the historical background of the island are treated. In the present article the independent self-governing area of Ireland is described under subsections Area and Population, Constitution, Politics, Defense Organization, Education, Culture, Religion, Agriculture, Industry, External Trade, and Communications.

Area and Population.—The provinces of Leinster, Munster, Connacht and three counties of Ulster (the other six Ulster counties are in Northern Ireland, q.v.) with a population in 1946 of 2,955,107 and an area of 26,602 square miles are governed by an independent republican Parliament. Leinster, which covers 7,581 square miles on the east and southeast, contains twelve counties, Carlow, Dublin, Kildare, Kilkenny, Laoighis (formerly Queen's County), Longford, Louth, Meath, Offaly (formerly King's County), Westmeath, Wexford, and Wicklow, and had a total population in 1946 of 1,281,117. Practically half of this number, 550,725, live in the capital city, Dublin, and its suburbs. The density of population in the rural areas is mainly between 60 and 120 per square mile. The principal towns, after the metropolis, are Dundalk (population 18,562), Drogheda (population 15,715), Wexford (population 12,296), and Kilkenny (population 10,291). Munster, in the southwest, is 9,317 square miles in area and is divided into counties Clare, Cork, Kerry, Limerick, Tipperary, and Waterford. Its population, 917,306, is spread at much the same density as in Leinster in the rural areas of Limerick, north Cork, and Waterford. In the other counties the density is higher, particularly in Kerry, in some parts of which it is between 200 and 300 persons per square mile. The largest city is Cork (population 89,877), on the south coast, which has a good harbor. The cities of Waterford (population 28,269) and Limerick (population 42,970) are the other main population centers in the province. Galway, Leitrim, Mayo, Roscommon, and Sligo, the five counties of Connacht, cover 6,611 square miles of mainly rugged land in the West. The population totaled 492,797 in 1946. Despite the poverty of the soil the density of the rural population is great, a few districts along the seaboard having between 300 and 400 persons per square mile. In south Mayo the population density per square mile is between 200 and 300, while in the rest of the province it ranges between 100 and 200. The principal urban centers are Galway (population 20,370) and Sligo (population 12,920). The three counties of Ulster under the jurisdiction of the Republic of Ireland are Donegal, the most northerly county in the island, Cavan, and Monaghan. Their area is 3,093 square miles and population was 263,887 in 1946. The population density of these counties, except west Donegal, is between 100 and 200 per square mile. In the coastal districts on the west it is higher, being over 400 per square mile in some parts. There are no large urban centers, as the centers of trade for these areas lie mainly in Northern Ireland. While the south, west, and most of the east limits of the republic are the sea coast, on the northeast there is a land frontier 240 miles long through Ulster. Donegal, which lies alongside this boundary, has but a tenuous land connection five miles long with the rest of the republic. In general, the natural increase in population of the country is offset by emigration, which is mainly to Great Britain. Under native government the emigration rate has declined considerably.

Constitution.—The republic is governed under the constitution passed by plebiscite in 1937. The national Parliament consists of the president and two houses—Dail Eireann (House of Representatives) and Seanad Eireann (Senate). The president is elected by the direct vote of the people, and holds office for seven years. On the advice of the head of the government he summons and dissolves Dail Eireann, and he appoints the prime minister (Taoiseach) on the nomination of Dail Eireann. The supreme command of the defense forces is vested in the president, who is aided and advised in carrying out his functions by a Council of State. The representative house of Parliament consists of 147 members elected by adult suffrage under a system of proportional representation. The Senate has 60 members, 11 of whom are nominated by the Taoiseach, 6 are elected by the universities, and the remaining 43 are elected on a vocational basis which allots representatives to cultural, industrial, labor, agricultural, and administrative interests. The Senate has no power to veto legislative proposals, and is allowed a maximum of 90 days to consider and amend bills sent to it by the Dail.

The executive power of the state is exercised by the government, which is responsible to Dail Eireann and may consist of not less than seven and not more than 15 members. The prime minister nominates the members of the government, who are appointed by the president after being approved by the Dail. Each member of the government has charge of a department of state and is the minister responsible to the Parliament for that department. The departments are finance, agriculture, external affairs, justice, local government, education, lands, industry and commerce, posts and telegraphs, defense, and health and social welfare.

The constitution setting out the organization of government states the fundamental civil rights of the citizens and makes provision for the protection of the personal liberty, freedom of conscience, and free expression of opinion of the citizens. No amendment of the constitution can be made except with the approval of the people given at a referendum, and any legislation passed by the Parliament which infringes the constitution is invalid. The courts of justice may be called on to act as an independent arbiter to decide whether a statute is repugnant to the constitution or otherwise. The courts of justice consist of a Supreme Court, a High Court, a Court of Criminal Appeal, a Central Criminal Court, a Circuit Court, and a District Court. The judges are independent in the exercise of their functions, but administrative functions in connection with the organization of the courts are carried out by the minister for justice, who has the responsibility for the enforcement of law. He controls the police force, which does not carry firearms.

Politics.—Fianna Fail, led by Eamon de Valera (who was in 1938 president of the Assembly of the League of Nations), was in 1951 the largest political party in Dail Eireann, having almost one half of the seats. Against this party, which held office from 1932 to 1948, was an alignment of smaller parties. Of these, Fine Gael is the largest; its principal figures are Richard Mulcahy and John A. Costello (who was Taoiseach from 1948 to 1951). William Norton is the leader of the Labour Party, which is rather small as organized workers tend to vote for other parties. Its main strength is in rural rather than urban areas. Clann na Talmhan, a party which is almost completely confined to Connacht, is led by Joseph Blowick; it is interested mainly in the problems of small holders in the west. A small party led by Sean MacBride (minister for external affairs in 1948–1951) entered the political arena in 1948 and helped to defeat de Valera. This party, Clann na Poblachta, suffered an eclipse in the 1951 general election. Independent deputies maintain the balance of power between Fianna Fail and the other parties, and the election of a government depends frequently on their support. Differences in policy between the parties are slight. There is unanimous opposition to the continuance of partition, the severance of the six Ulster counties from the jurisdiction of the Irish Parliament. Partition conditions foreign policy, on which there is also unanimity. While being anti-Communist, all parties have decided on a policy of neutrality in the event of war. As long as partition is maintained by Britain the Irish government will not enter into a military alliance with the anti-Communist countries. The government felt that to join the Atlantic Pact, one clause of which guaranteed existing frontiers, would mean the recognition of the border as permanent. All parties are pledged to a scheme of social welfare, the extension of health services, and the provisions of adequate housing. The actual differences between the parties arise more from personalities and past history. There are Irish ambassadors in the United States of America, Spain, the Vatican, Great Britain, France, Canada, and Australia, and Irish representatives also in Switzerland, Portugal, Norway and Sweden, Netherlands, Lebanon and Syria, Italy, Germany, Belgium, and Argentina. These countries have diplomatic representatives in Ireland. In international affairs, Ireland actively participates in the Organization for European Economic Cooperation and advocates closer European collaboration. Representatives of the republic attend the Council of Europe at Strasbourg, and the minister for external affairs is a member of that body's Committee of Ministers.

Defense Organization.—The Irish army had a strength of only 6,000 in December 1950. The Fianna Fail Party maintained that a permanent establishment of 12,500 is essential to form a well trained nucleus in the event of war. According to Fine Gael, 8,000 would be sufficient and as much as could be armed. As the republic is outside the Atlantic Pact, it finds great difficulty in obtaining military equipment. Besides the army, there is a small air corps and an Irish Naval Service whose main function is to patrol territorial waters and protect the fishing. The volunteer reserve, which undergoes annual training in camp, was 36,000 strong in 1950, about one fifth of its wartime strength. Recruitment to the defense forces is voluntary.

Education.—The constitution acknowledges the right and duty of parents to provide for the education of their children, and the state provides free primary or elementary education, which is compulsory up to the age of 14. The Department of Education pays grants to colleges for the training of teachers of all religious denominations, and it pays the teachers of primary schools. Secondary schools are under private control but are subject to examination by the department, which lays down the curriculum and gives grants on a capitation basis to the upkeep of the schools and pays the greater part of the teachers' salaries. Vocational schools, controlled by the local authorities and maintained partly out of local rates (taxes) and partly from grants from the central fund, are established in all the cities, the principal towns, and some rural areas. They provide technical training for apprentices to trades. University education is given at the three constituent colleges of the National University of Ireland—at Dublin, Cork, and Galway—and at the University of Dublin (Trinity College). The number of university students is over 7,000 each year.

Culture.—The teaching of the Irish language has a special place in Irish education. It is an essential part of the courses in primary and secondary schools, and it has a special place in university education. In many schools, all the subjects, except English, are taught through the medium of Irish. This is because it is a policy laid down by all political parties to foster the native language, which declined considerably in the last 100 years of English rule and is now the everyday language of only some districts in the south and west. In the Institute for Advanced Studies, the government established schools of research in cosmic physics, higher mathematics, and Celtic studies; and the National Museum, National Library, and National Gallery, supported by the government, collect objects, books, manuscripts, and paintings of cultural and artistic value. Subventions are paid to cultural bodies—such as the Abbey Theatre and learned societies—and a scheme to coordinate artistic and cultural work under a director of fine arts was undertaken in 1951. (See also separate articles on CELTIC LANGUAGES; CELTIC PEOPLES; GAELIC LITERATURE; IRISH ARCHAEOLOGY; IRISH ART AND ARCHITECTURE; IRISH LITERARY REVIVAL; IRISH LITERATURE IN THE ENGLISH LANGUAGE; IRISH MUSIC.)

Religion.—The vast majority of the inhabitants of the republic are Roman Catholics—in fact, 94.3 per cent in 1946. The minority consisted of 4.2 per cent Protestant Episcopalians and less than 1 per cent Presbyterians. The Roman Catholic population is increasing since 1926, but the other religions are declining. The census for 1946 showed, however, an increase in the number of infants of the Protestant religions, but the birth rate among Roman Catholics is consistently higher than that among the other religions. Protestants are much fewer in the provinces of Munster and Connacht than in Leinster, but they are most numerous in the three Ulster counties. They are stronger in urban than in rural areas. All the churches are organized on an all-Ireland basis; both the Roman Catholic and Episcopalian primatial sees are at Armagh, in Northern Ireland. The constitution guarantees freedom of religion, and religious differences are not the lines of political division. Each political party has members of all religious persuasions, and various members of the government have been Protestants, as was the first president under the 1937 Constitution, Dr. Douglas Hyde. The most important of the minor religious groups in 1946 were the 8,355 Methodists and the 3,907 Jews. Practically all the Jews were in Dublin city, where they have a flourishing community. The Society of Friends is a small body numerically but plays an important part in commercial life. See also IRISH CHURCH HISTORY.

Agriculture.—Farming is the largest single industry in the country, and practically one half of the workers are employed directly on the land. Three quarters of those engaged in agriculture are farmers and their families, while the paid agricultural employees are but one quarter of those in the industry. The size of farms may reasonably be divided into three groups—subsistence holdings under 30 acres, medium farms between 30 and 100 acres, and large farms over 100 acres. The smallest group predominate in Connacht and the three Ulster counties, while the medium farms are more usual in the other provinces. The largest holdings, which are most common on the rich grasslands of the limestone central plain, play an important part as fattening lands in the country's cattle export trade. More typical, however, of Irish agriculture is mixed farming, in which tillage provides mainly for the feeding of livestock with perhaps some barley, wheat, and sugar beet for sale. The farmers' main business is the breeding and rearing of livestock, principally cattle. Pigs are reared mainly on the small farms, on which poultry rearing is also a usual side line; there are few specialized poultry farms. Sheep are reared on the uplands and brought to the lowlands for fattening. Dairying predominates in Munster, where the cooperative movement, owing its origin at the end of the 19th century to Sir Horace Plunkett, inspired the establishment of creameries. Fishing is but of local importance and gives little employment. Before World War II the total agricultural output was absorbed almost equally into three channels—consumption on the farms, the home market, and the export trade. Between 1939 and 1945 the export trade consumed only one fifth of the output, but in the postwar years this increased to practically the prewar position. During the war the country had to produce to meet the needs of the home population. Much more wheat was grown and, like other countries, the farmlands were not adequately fertilized. To provide food for the home market, a system of compulsory tillage was introduced. As a result, at the end of the war in 1945 the soil was depleted and agricultural output had fallen. In 1949 a ten-year scheme of land rehabilitation was initiated by the Irish government for the improvement of farms. Drainage is the main part of the project, which plans to reclaim 4.5 million acres of nonproductive or underproductive land. The Department of Agriculture gives credit facilities to enable farmers to purchase fertilizers. This work received aid mainly by loans from the United States under the European Recovery Program.

Industry.—Ireland's poverty in mineral deposits and its political domination by England in the 19th century are among the reasons why it had little industrial development. In the republic, however, since the foundation of the state efforts have been made to produce power in the country instead of depending on imported coal. The Shannon hydroelectric station, constructed between 1925 and 1929, initiated modern power development; 40 per cent of the Shannon supply is used for industrial purposes, and the demand for electricity led to further hydroelectric development on the rivers Liffey, Erne, and Lee. Electricity is made available throughout the country, and is applied to agriculture under a rural scheme organized by the Electricity Supply Board, a state company which controls electrical development. Modern mechanical methods are used by another state company, the Turf Board, which is helping to replace imported fuel by producing peat from Irish bogs. The virtual collapse in the supply of imported fuel during World War II caused greater dependence on peat than ever before, and in the years after the war a plant was erected to use peat for the generation of electricity. The first peat-fired generating station was established at Portarlington, in County Laoighis, on the bog which extends across the central plain of Ireland. Industry expanded after 1922 and continues to develop. In 1950, one fifth of the working population was engaged in industry, as against one tenth in 1926. Government planning achieved a scattering of industry, and many small towns were revitalized by the location of new factories in them. There is a social as well as an economic aspect in the policy of industrial development, in that it brings employment to rural towns and helps to keep the population rural while reducing dependence on foreign suppliers for products which can be produced in the country. A number of industries depend for their raw material on agriculture. Bacon factories and meat-canning plants are scattered throughout the state. Sugar-beet processing is carried on at Carlow, Thurles, Mallow, and Tuam and these practically supply all the home needs in sugar. Beverages are manufactured mainly from barley, and by far the largest brewery is that of Guinness, located in Dublin.

A third of the agricultural machinery used by farmers is made in the country. Leather and clothing manufacture rapidly expanded under native government. Light industries dependent for raw materials on foreign imports—such as the making of aluminum utensils, enamelware, electric bulbs, and electrical equipment—were set up to supply the home market. This rapid expansion of industry was carried out despite the lack in the initial stages of skilled labor, and the result was felt during World War II, when the republic suffered much less from wartime shortages than might have been expected had the industries not been established. The establishment of cement factories has provided material for a drive initiated by the state to provide adequate housing. In 1926, 27.2 per cent of the population was badly housed, but by 1946 this was reduced to 16.8 per cent.

External Trade.—Agricultural products are the mainstay of the export trade of the republic. Live cattle are roughly one third of the total annual exports. Eggs, meat, beer, stout, and Irish whisky are other substantial items of export. The traditional customer for these is Britain, which purchases three quarters of the total exports. This position is kept up by trade agreements, which guarantee to the republic prices on a long-term basis and commits Britain to supplying certain quantities of coal and raw materials in return. These guaranteed prices are usually tied to those paid to the English farmer, and increases to home producers in Britain benefit Irish farmers. In return, the republic is committed to send most of its exportable surplus of foodstuffs to Britain. One eighth of the total exports of the republic go to Northern Ireland, and about one half of that to other European countries. Exports to the United States of America are negligible. The principal Irish imports are machinery and electrical goods, textiles, coal, vehicles and parts, maize (corn), mineral oils, fats, and motor spirit. Consumption goods are less than one third of the imports, while the rest is made up of materials for industry and agriculture and other capital development. More than one half of the republic's imports are from Britain and, despite its small size, the republic ranks about fifth among Britain's customers. Imports from the United States of America are second in importance, and are slightly greater than those from the continent of Europe. There is a substantial deficit between the value of exports and imports, which is met largely by invisible income. The most important item of invisible income derives from tourist traffic, which is encouraged by the government. Tourist receipts are a tribute to the charms of Ireland as a holiday resort and also to the abundance and variety of food available at moderate cost. British visitors in the years after World War II took advantage of the nearness of Ireland to escape the austerity imposed on them in England, while the international reputation of the beauty spots of Wicklow, Connemara, and Killarney, and the abundant fishing, shooting, and hunting facilities, attracted many. Another source of invisible income is interest on external assets. In 1920 the republic had substantial investments in Britain, and these were increased during World War II, when there was a reduction in imports. After 1945 some of these investments were repatriated to cover capital development in Ireland and to meet the deficiency between income and expenditure—which was due to the purchase of machinery. One of the difficulties of Irish trade is the disparity between dollar expenditure and dollar earnings. In the years between the first and second world wars this did not create any problem, due to the convertibility of sterling into dollars. The development of the dollar-earning potentialities of the tourist trade helped, after 1945, to meet Ireland's dollar deficit.

Communications.—The rail, road, and canal transport services in the greater part of the republic are nationalized, being operated by Coras Iompair Eireann. The roads are maintained by local county councils, aided by grants from the government; they are the basis of the Irish communications system. The nationalization of transport was essential to coordinate the three main services and to avoid the financial collapse of the railways. One of the major problems created by the partition of Ireland is in transport, as the Great Northern Railway has road and rail services on both sides of the border. The area served by this company, which is not nationalized, covers the north of Leinster and the Ulster counties, and is the link between Belfast, in Northern Ireland, and Dublin. The canals, which date from the 18th century, link Dublin to the Shannon and to the Barrow; they carry an appreciable amount of heavy goods, mainly fuel and agricultural produce. The railways carry much heavy freight as well as passengers; their financial position, however, is insecure, and many branch lines are closed as uneconomic. To help to maintain essential supplies during World War II, the government set up Irish Shipping Limited; it created a merchant fleet which was expanded in the postwar years. In air communications the republic has an important position, being on the western fringe of Europe. The customs-free airport at Shannon is an international air station and provides excellent facilities for the Atlantic air routes. A national air service is operated by Aer Lingus Teoranta, which operates direct services from Dublin Airport to Paris, Amsterdam, London, Liverpool, Glasgow, and Manchester. The Department of Posts and Telegraphs operates the telephonic service; there are automatic exchanges in the large cities. It also controls the radio service, which is paid for by the licensing of receivers; broadcasting is carried on from studios in Dublin and Cork on two medium wave lengths.

THOMAS P. O'NEILL,
National Library of Ireland.

HISTORY

The Irish Free State, antecedent to the Republic of Ireland, was established on Jan. 15, 1922, as outcome of the Anglo-Irish Treaty of Dec. 6, 1921, which gave Ireland the status of a British dominion. The meetings of Irish and English representatives in the negotiations leading to the treaty were largely brought about and inspired by Sir John and Lady Lavery in that great portrait painter's studio in London. Six of Ulster's counties, however, which had accepted Home Rule in 1920, chose to remain part of the United Kingdom as Northern Ireland (q.v.). After long dispute, an agreement made on Dec. 3, 1925, fixed the boundary between the Irish Free State and Northern Ireland.

The year 1922 brought civil war in the Irish Free State, for that country was bitterly divided on the issue of accepting the treaty of 1921. On January 7 the Dail (Parliament) ratified the treaty by 64 votes to 57 and on the 14th, meeting as the Southern Parliament of Ireland, again ratified it. Meanwhile, on January 9 Eamon de Valera left the Dail, while Arthur Griffith as president and Michael Collins as premier prepared to implement the treaty according to their signed word. The text of the Irish Free State Constitution was published on June 15th. Elections for the Dail held the following day resulted in a majority for the new constitution of 58 members to 36. After the elections, there was a battle in Dublin for the Four Courts (the courts of justice) between the government forces and republican rebels, at the end of which the priceless records of Ireland went up in smoke. On July 6, de Valera declared civil war, accusing the provisional government of military dictatorship supported by British "big guns." The civil chaos overwhelmed Griffith's sensitive soul and he died August 12 mourned even by his opponents; William Cosgrave succeeded him as president of the Dail. The country suffered another loss on August 22 when Collins was killed in an ambush. The civil war continued until the end of May 1923. In August, the general election returned only 44 Republicans out of 153, for the people required peace even at the cost of accepting the treaty. De Valera refused from prison to take the oath of allegiance to Britain, a prerequisite to entering the Dail. Among the many schemes introduced by Cosgrave at this period were the sugar-beet industry and the Shannon Electrical Supply—"sweetness and light" in the words of Swift.

The Imperial Conference of 1926 in London led to the Statute of Westminster, which placed the dominions on an equal footing with Britain. In March, de Valera, putting aside Sinn Fein, formed the new Party of Fianna Fail (Warriors of Destiny). He finally took the oath of allegiance (no doubt under the Euripidean sense—"the tongue hath sworn but not the mind") and entered the Dail on July 9, 1927. Yet another leader was lost the following day, when Kevin O'Higgins, Cosgrave's leading minister, was assassinated. He had been in close communication with the British Cabinet on a scheme of Irish dominion unity. With O'Higgins passed any possibility of Ulster becoming a political part of Ireland for a generation. A Public Safety Act then passed widened the scope of treasonable acts.

By 1932 Fianna Fail had penetrated the country, at a general election winning 72 seats to 56 by Cumann na nGaedheal, Cosgrave's party; Independents and Labour held 24 seats. In July de Valera commenced an economic war against Great Britain, Ireland's chief customer, with results dubious to the economy of both countries. On Jan. 4, 1933, a further general election gave de Valera 77 seats to Cosgrave's 48, and others 17.

On May 3 the oath of allegiance to Britain was abolished. In 1934 an important pact was made based on Irish cattle exports and coal imports from Britain, Ireland's main exchange always being meat for the product of the mines.

In 1936 the Constitutional Amendment Act removed the king from all internal authority in Ireland, and the office of governor general (held by James MacNeill in succession to Timothy Healy) was abolished. At the same time, by the External Relations Act the king's name was restored for use in external affairs, but subject to the orders of the Executive Council.

General elections on July 1, 1937, gave de Valera 69 against 48 Fine Gael, Labour 13, and Independents 8. On that date, also, a new constitution was approved by plebiscite; it went into operation on Dec. 29, 1937. In place of Irish Free State, the name Ireland (in Gaelic *Eire*) was restored; the constitution assumed the inclusion of Northern Ireland within the nation's territorial limits. De Valera made an agreement with Neville Chamberlain, British prime minister, on April 25, 1938, for the return of the ports of Cobh, Berehaven (Bearhaven), and Lough Swilly to Irish control. In June, de Valera obtained an overall majority, and Douglas Hyde, founder of the Gaelic League, was installed as president. As a result of the report of the Banking Commission, Irish currency remained tied to sterling. A Treason Act was passed in March 1939 because of the bombing campaign by the Irish Republican Army (then a revolutionary group) in Britain, and in April summary arrest and trial was declared for state offenses; the I.R.A. was outlawed on June 23. When World War II began in September, Ireland declared neutrality; it also objected in 1942 to the use of bases in Northern Ireland by United States forces. Though the government remained neutral, a large number of Irish volunteers from southern Ireland passed into the British services. The Irish names in the honor and casualty lists did much to mitigate the adverse effects of Ireland's neutrality in the British mind. The Shamrock Club, in London, preserved the names of 10,000 "neutrals in uniform."

In 1945 Sean T. O'Kelly was elected president of Ireland. During his presidency de Valera lost and then regained power. Under a coalition, on Dec. 2, 1948, the External Relations Act of 1936 was repealed by the Republic of Ireland Act, and thus the last link with the British Empire was broken. The Republic of Ireland was proclaimed on April 18, 1949.

The Irish Free State had been an active member of the League of Nations (de Valera served as president of the Council in 1932, and of the Assembly in 1938), but the republic was thrice denied membership in the United Nations by the veto of the Soviet Union. Nevertheless, Ireland was a member of six of the specialized agencies of the United Nations and also of the Organization for European Economic Cooperation, and in 1949 it became one of the sponsors of the Council of Europe. However, the republic refused to join the North Atlantic Treaty Organization, declaring that while it was in full sympathy with its aims it could not cooperate therein while the partition issue remained outstanding.

At the general elections of Feb. 4, 1948, de Valera's Fianna Fail Party had been placed in a minority by a coalition of parties under John Costello (Fine Gael, Clann na Poblachta, Clann na Talmhan, and Labour). The new foreign minister, Sean MacBride, took the extreme but logical view of Irish Republicanism, and expounded it personally in Britain, France, and the United States. However, his party (Clann na Poblachta) was overwhelmingly defeated at the elections of May 30, 1951, and de Valera, without an overall majority, took office. His Fianna Fail Party won 69 seats, against 78 for all other parties. De Valera, surviving all recent history, continued to urge the ending of partition by "friendly approach" to Northern Ireland and the British government. Meantime, the vital questions of Irish life remained at the mercy of successive and bitterly divided factions on the issues of farming, fisheries, and forestry. Under the coalition, James Dillon advanced agriculture, and new efforts were made to replant a treeless island. Rural life was rapidly declining, owing to emigration of the youth to towns at home and abroad; Dublin had collected one sixth of the population of the whole republic. The youth (particularly the female) were leaving Ireland at every opportunity to work in Britain. To popularize rural life, the Muintir na Tire, a social, nonpolitical organization, was working efficiently under Father John M. Hayes. The census of April 8, 1951, showed that the population was still under three millions (provisional figure: 2,958,878).

Bibliography.—Ireland, Tom, *Ireland Past and Present* (New York 1942); de Valera, E., *Peace and War: Speeches . . . 1932–1938* (Dublin 1944); id., *Ireland's Stand: Speeches . . . 1939–1945* (ibid. 1946); MacManus, M. J., *Eamon de Valera: A Biography*, 4th ed. (Dublin 1948); O'Faolain, S., *The Irish* (London 1948); Shearman, H., *Anglo-Irish Relations* (London 1948); O'Neill, D., *The Partition of Ireland: How and Why it Was Accomplished*, 3d ed. (Dublin 1949); White, T. De Vere, *Kevin O'Higgins* (London 1949); Curtis, E., *History of Ireland*, 6th ed., rev. (New York 1951).

See also IRELAND; IRISH ARCHAEOLOGY, and succeeding articles on IRISH ART AND ARCHITECTURE, IRISH CHURCH HISTORY, etc.

SHANE LESLIE,
Baronet of Glaslough, County Monaghan

IRELAND ISLAND, one of the Bermuda Islands. See BERMUDA.

IRENAEUS, ī-rē-nē'ŭs, **Saint,** Christian prelate, a father of the Greek Church: b. about 130; d. unknown. He was reared in Asia Minor, where he was a pupil of Polycarp, and became apostle of the Gauls. In 177 he was bishop of Lyon. According to tradition, he suffered martyrdom in the persecution under Emperor Septimius Severus.

IRENE, ī-rē'nē, the name of three empresses of the Eastern Roman (Byzantine) Empire.

(1) IRENE (752–803), an Athenian by birth, was married in 769 to Leo IV, and following his death in 780 she became regent during the minority of their son, Constantine VI. Zealous for the re-establishment of image worship, she summoned a church council at Nicaea in 787 which decreed the restoration of images to the churches and defined the veneration due to them. When Constantine was proclaimed sole ruler in 790 she was forced to abdicate, but her title of empress was confirmed in 792. For five years she plotted to regain power, and in 797 she caused her son to be seized and put to death. Thereafter she was sole ruler until 802 when, the patricians having repudiated her in favor of Nicephorus, her minis-

ter of finance, she was dethroned. She was exiled to Lesbos, where she died the next year.

(2) IRENE DUCAS (1066?–?1120) was the wife of Emperor Alexius I Comnenus. After her husband's death in 1118 she conspired with her daughter, Anna Comnena (1083–?1148), to place the latter's husband, Nicephorus Bryennius, upon the throne instead of her own son, John II Comnenus. When the plot failed she and her daughter retired to a convent.

(3) IRENE (d. 1161) became, in 1146, the first wife of Emperor Manuel I Comnenus. The marriage had been arranged by her brother-in-law, Holy Roman Emperor Conrad III.

IRENE, ī-rēn′, **Sister,** Roman Catholic religious: b. London, England, May 12, 1823; d. New York City, Aug. 14, 1896. Originally named Catherine Fitzgibbon, in childhood she moved to the United States, and in January 1850 she joined the community of the Sisters of Charity, at Mount Saint Vincent, taking the name of Mary Irene. She became sister superior of Saint Peter's School, Barclay Street, New York City, in 1856, and in 1869 she founded, and became director of, the city's first home for deserted children, later known as the New York Foundling Hospital. She continued to head the institution until her death, and also founded the Seton Hospital for Incurables at Spuyten Duyvil.

IRETON, ĭr′tĕn, **Henry,** English parliamentary commander and regicide: b. Attenborough, Nottinghamshire, 1611; d. Limerick, Ireland, Nov. 26, 1651. He was graduated at Trinity College, Oxford, and in 1629 took up the study of law at the Middle Temple. With outbreak of the civil war he joined the Parliamentarians, fighting at Edgehill in 1642 and Gainsborough in 1643, and in 1645 commanding the cavalry on the left wing of Oliver Cromwell's army at the Battle of Naseby; he was wounded and captured, but made his escape. In 1646 he married Cromwell's daughter, Bridget. From 1645 he was a member of Parliament, taking a prominent part in the negotiations which made that body subservient to the army. He helped frame the ordinances for the trial of Charles I, was one of the king's judges, and signed the death warrant. In 1649 he accompanied Cromwell to Ireland as second in command, and the next year was left by him in that island as lord deputy. He captured Carlow, Waterford, and Duncannon in 1650, and Limerick shortly before his death. Buried in Westminster Abbey, after the Restoration in 1660 his body was taken up, suspended from the gallows with that of Cromwell, and buried in the same pit.

IRGIZ, ĭr-gēz′, river, Soviet Central Asia, in the west central part of the Kazakh Soviet Socialist Republic, 270 miles in length. It rises in the southeastern slopes of the Ural Mountains, and flows in a southeasterly direction to enter Lake Chelkar Tengiz (northeast of Lake Aral). The small town of Irgiz, on the river of that name, lies 220 miles southeast of Aktyubinsk; several caravan routes converge here. Another Irgiz River, 300 miles long, is a tributary of the Volga, which it joins opposite Volsk after a westerly course through the Kuibyshev Region.

IRIARTE, Tomás de, Spanish poet: b. Orotava (Tenerife, Canary Islands), Sept. 18, 1750; d. Madrid, Sept. 17, 1791. He was a nephew of Juan de Iriarte (q.v.) and was educated under the direction of his elder brother, Fray Juan Tomas de Iriarte, and later in Madrid with his uncle. At the age of 17 he wrote a drama (in verse), *Hacer que hacemos,* and at this early age he began translating dramas from French for the theaters of the city. So successful was he at this work that some of his original dramas were produced. On the death of his uncle in 1771, he succeeded him as official translator in the office of the secretary of state; and five years later he was appointed archivist to the supreme war council. In 1787 his works were published in six volumes in Madrid. A goodly part of his energies was taken up in quarrels with the critics of the day and with some of his literary contemporaries, the most notable of which was Juan Pablo Forner (1756–1797), who in turn, lashed him without pity, and sometimes without reason. Through the intrigues of his enemies Iriarte was summoned before the Inquisition in 1786, on the charge of propagating French heretical doctrines. But he was able to satisfy the ecclesiastical authorities as to his orthodoxy. Iriarte did much translation and wrote poems and dramas, and attempted other forms of literary work, but his fame today rests on his fables in verse, which are counted by far the best of their kind in Spanish. Their excellence is due not so much to the poetic talent of the author, which was not very great, as to the interesting form in which the fables are thrown, the ingenuity of many of them, their simplicity, vivacity, grace, and appearance of naturalness supported by fertility of invention. These *Fables* became immensely popular, and were translated into most of the languages of Europe. Perhaps the interest in them in Spain was increased by the belief that, under the guise of fable, Iriarte was holding up to ridicule many of his literary detractors.

IRIARTE, or YRIARTE, Y OROPESA, ē-ryär′tā ē ō-rō-pā′sä, **Juan de,** Spanish poet: b. Orotava, Tenerife, Canary Islands, Dec. 15, 1702; d. Madrid Aug. 23, 1771. He was the nephew of Tomas de Iriarte (q.v.). Educated in the College of Louis the Great, in Paris, he went to Madrid in 1724, where he became clerk in the Royal Library (1729) and ultimately librarian (1732). Owing to his linguistic ability he was appointed official translator to the secretary of state (1742); and the following year he was elected a member of the Academia Española. He composed hundreds of epigrams and sonnets, and also poems in Latin. Besides a Greek paleography, he published a notable catalog of the Greek manuscripts in the Royal Library.

IRIARTEA, ĭr-ĭ-är′tē-ȧ, a genus of palms, all South American, marked by smooth, tall stems and pinnate leaves with somewhat triangular leaflets. The best-known species is the pashuiba palm (*I. exorrhiza*), which has aerial roots. The wood is very hard.

IRIDACEAE, ī-rĭ-dā′sē-ē, in botany, a natural order of endogenous plants, mostly herbaceous, though a few are somewhat shrubby. They usually have either rootstocks or corms. The leaves generally are sword-shaped, in two rows and equitant. The perianth is six-partite and often very beautiful, in some regular, in others irregular. There are three stamens, with the anthers bearing outward. The fruit is a three-celled, three-valved capsule. The family (the iris family) yields about 900 species in 60 widely distributed genera throughout the temperate and tropical zones. Some are hardy perennials, others for early summer growing, and there are a few hothouse varieties. Iris, gladiolus, and crocus are familiar examples of the order. Saffron and orrisroot are the principal economic products.

IRIDESCENCE, ĭr-ĭ-dĕs′ĕns, the intermingling and interchange of the spectrum colors on surfaces. Typical surfaces which produce iridescence are those of soap bubbles or mother-of-pearl. The iridescence is produced by the minute irregularities of the surface which, in reflecting white light, split it up into its constituent colors by the phenomenon of interference. The word comes from the Greek *iris,* meaning rainbow.

IRIDESCENT GLASS. See GLASS.

IRIDION (Polish *Irydyon*). The dismemberment of Poland, still more, the disastrous Polish revolution of 1830, had bred the sentiment of national hatred against the oppressors, but Count Zygmunt Krasiński (q.v.), in all his poetry, cautioned his people against hate as an expression of patriotism and preached inner perfection as a means of obtaining the highest good for his country. His work, *Iridion,* which appeared in Paris in 1836, is a poem-drama of exquisite beauty, based on Krasiński's reading of Montesquieu, Gibbon, and Niebuhr. In this poem he wished to give a picture of the fall of pagan Rome and the triumph of Christianity, and tried to show that it was not Greek hatred, but Christian humility, that renovated the Roman world. In the days of the domination and corruption of the Caesars, Iridion, who is represented as of Greek ancestry, sought vengeance against the Rome that had betrayed Athens and throttled Corinth. His mother was a priestess of Odin, and after her death he gave his sister to Heliogabalus, so that she might unsettle the emperor's mind. Iridion, as prefect of the Pretorians, urges Heliogabalus to conspire against Rome. The African Massinissa, versed in magic, persuades him to arm the Christians. Iridion, in the Catacombs, falls in love with a Christian maiden, who thinks that he will bring about the millennium. But just as he appears to be victorious, the bishop of Rome denounces his militancy. He returns to the northern gods of his mother. Heliogabalus and his sister perish. Massinissa tauntingly tells Iridion that Christ will some day rule over Rome, and puts him into a lethargic sleep. He does not awaken until 1835 in the north, but he now loves Christ's cross and has abandoned all ideas of revenge. *Iridion* was translated from the German and French by Martha Walker Cook, in *The Undivine Comedy and other Poems, by the Anonymous Poet of Poland, Count Sigismund Krasińsky* (Philadelphia 1875).

LEO WIENER.

IRIDIUM, ī-rĭd′ĭ-ŭm, a metallic element resembling platinum in its general properties, and occurring in nature in the metallic form, alloyed, usually, with platinum and osmium. It is found in the Soviet Union, South America, and Tasmania. Iridium was first definitely identified, in 1804, by Smithson Tennant, who found it in the residue left after dissolving platinum from its ore with aqua regia; in the residue was also found osmium, generally in alloy as irodosmine (q.v.). Separation of iridium from other metals which are included in the platinum group is difficult; for the usual processes employed, the more extended works on metallurgy and the chemistry of the metals must be consulted. Iridium is frequently obtained in the form of a spongy gray mass, or a gray powder; but by heating either of these to whiteness, and subjecting them to compression, the metal may be brought into the form of a compact, lustrous mass resembling steel. In this form it is harder than iron, and somewhat malleable when hot, though brittle when cold. At ordinary temperatures it has a specific gravity of about 22.4, being among the heaviest substances known. Its specific heat is about 0.0323 at ordinary temperatures, and its coefficient of linear expansion (Fahrenheit) is about 0.0000039. Its melting point is very high, the estimates given by various authorities ranging from 3,600°F. to 4,500°F. Compact iridium, after being strongly heated, is insoluble in all acids, and is not affected by air or moisture. The metal has the symbol Ir. and an atomic weight of 193.1 if O = 16. It forms numerous salts.

IRIDOSMINE, ī-rĭ-dŏz′mĭn, a natural alloy of iridium and osmium in varying proportions, is a hard, slightly malleable mineral, crystallizing in hexagonal prisms. It usually contains some platinum, and, frequently, other metals of the platinum group. While found with deposits of platinum in the Ural Mountains, and in small quantities elsewhere, its chief source is in placer deposits in southwestern Tasmania, discovered in 1925. No primary source for these placers has yet been found. This compound metal is silvery white and resists attack of all known acids, and hence is of great value in chemical and electrical industries. The Tasmanian metal is found in grains of such size and quality as to be immediately available for nibs of gold pens.

IRIGA, ē-rē′gä, town, Philippine Islands, in Camarines Sur Province, Luzon, 22 miles by rail southeast of Naga (formerly Nueva Caceres). Northeast of the town is an extinct volcano, of the same name, 4,023 feet above sea level. The town, the largest in the province, is located in a fertile agricultural region. Pop. (1939) 31,005.

IRIGOYEN, ē-rē-gō′yän, **Hipolito,** Argentine lawyer and statesman: b. Buenos Aires, 1850; d. there, July 3, 1933. He was of Basque ancestry. Following the revolution of 1890, in which he took an active part, he became leader of the Radical Party, opposed to the wealthy landowners. In 1916, with adoption of the secret ballot, he was elected president of the republic. He undertook a program of labor reforms, and opposed his country's entry into World War I in 1917. With expiry of his term in 1922 he retired from the presidency, being succeeded by Marcelo Torcuato de Alvear, likewise a member of the Radical Party. He was reelected president in 1928 for a six-year term, but disorders broke out in September 1930 and he was driven from the presidency by the Conservatives, led by José Francisco Uriburu. Released after a brief imprisonment on a warship, he became reconciled with Alvear, who was exiled in 1931. The two were suspected of instigating the unsuccessful revolt of 1932.

IRIS, ī'rĭs, in Greek mythology, daughter of Thaumas and Electra, sister of the Harpies, the fleet golden-winged messenger and servant of the Olympian gods, especially of Zeus and Hera. Iris was originally the personification of the rainbow, though she does not appear in the Homeric poems as the goddess of the rainbow. She is sometimes represented as a beautiful virgin with wings and a variegated dress, with a rainbow above her, or a cloud on her head exhibiting all the colors of the rainbow. Iris is the name of a planetoid.

IRIS. See EYE.

IRIS FAMILY, a family of monocotyledonous herbs, mostly perennials with tubers, corms, or rhizomes, and usually with an acrid flavor. About 800 species belonging to more than 50 genera have been described from temperate and tropical climates, mostly from South Africa and tropical America. They are characterized by two rows of leaves, the outer of which fit over and protect the inner (equitant); regular or irregular perfect flowers which are frequently handsome; perianth six-parted, the other floral organs in threes; and many-seeded, three-celled fruits (capsules). Some species have been used as food in countries where they are native; others furnish rootstocks which are used for making perfumes, especially orris; some few have been employed to a limited extent in medicine but the species most widely popular are cultivated for ornamental purposes. Of these last the most important genera are *Iris* (fleur-de-lis), *Gladiolus, Freesia, Crocus, Tigridia, Tritonia, Sisyrinchium, Ixia* and *Belamcanda*, elsewhere described.

The plants of the genus *Iris* constitute one of the chief ornaments of the northern regions of the globe, and usually grow in wet places, bearing flowers of various colors, but the prevailing tint is blue. The common wild iris or flag (*I. pseudacorus*), common in Europe and also found in the eastern United States, has yellow flowers of large size and long swordlike leaves. The gladdon or stinking iris (*I. foetidissima*) is a British species, with bluish flowers. The favorite garden sorts are mainly florists' varieties of the two species *I. germanica* (the German or bearded isis) and *I. laevigata* (the Japanese iris), and their hybrids with other types. Also used in gardens are *I. xiphioides* (the English iris); *I. persica* (Persian iris); and *I. susiana* (Chalcedonian iris). The roots of *I. florentina* supply the orris root of the drugstores. Several wild species are found in the United States.

IRISH ARCHAEOLOGY. Prehistoric and ancient remains in Ireland are noteworthy for three outstanding features: the importance of the Bronze Age; the great flowering of Early Christian art; and the wealth of field monuments to be seen throughout the country. The Bronze Age in Ireland is notable not only for the large amount of material—bronze, gold, burial pottery, and other objects, but also because of the influence exercised by Ireland on other areas. The Early Christian period saw the development of artistic endeavor which reached its zenith in the 8th century, was interrupted by the Viking invasions, but was ultimately enriched by them in the acquisition of new motifs so that a splendid renaissance resulted in the 11th and 12th centuries. While much of this is the domain of the art historian it is also that of the archaeologist, whose methods enable style sequence to be fitted to a chronological framework, and whose excavations help to provide fixed dating points and also yield a picture of the everyday life. The field monuments of all types and periods—megalithic (great stone) tombs, burial mounds, open or defended habitation sites, monastic remains—are to be found in remarkable profusion, and excavations of these are yielding profitable results. Methodical excavations in Ireland on an adequate scale were rare prior to the 1930's. In 1932 a five-year program was initiated by the Harvard Archaeological Mission to Ireland, and from 1934 onwards Irish archaeologists were able to excavate important sites with the aid of state grants. These activities have resulted in a changed picture of several periods and aspects of Irish archaeology, but an immense amount remains to be done—on whole classes of monuments in some cases, and to fill the gaps in our knowledge of others.

Mesolithic Period.—Attempts to indicate a Palaeolithic occupation of Ireland must be regarded as disproved or dismissed for lack of proof. Kilgreany cave, claimed by the Bristol Spelaeological Society in 1928 to show Palaeolithic habitation, was re-excavated by the Harvard Mission in 1934, and the earliest evidence of human activity there was found to be Neolithic. Implements of limestone found on the Sligo coast and held to be Palaeolithic (Mousterian) led to a prolonged controversy, but those found *in situ* were not implements, and those which are admitted to have been humanly manufactured were not *in situ* and are therefore of doubtful date. Geologically, Palaeolithic occupation of Ireland is not impossible, as clear evidence of mild interglacial periods has been found. One of the difficulties of the recognition of Palaeolithic industries is the limitation of abundant flint supply to the northeastern corner of the country, and industries of other materials are less easy to recognize.

Some of the large flint implements from the northeast have also been claimed to be Palaeolithic, but are now established as belonging to the Mesolithic cultures—which are the earliest definite evidence of a colonization of Ireland. These cultures, associated with the postglacial transgression of the sea which resulted in the 25-foot Raised Beach, have been divided into two phases, Larnian I and Larnian II (named from the site at Larne, County Antrim), and are regarded as being in large measure derived from the Upper Palaeolithic (Creswellian) of Britain. The Larnian is mainly represented around the coast of Antrim and Down, but work since 1946 has shown that it extended much further south—to the coast of Louth and Dublin.

Neolithic.—The vast quantities of flint implements which are the remains of the Larnian culture represent a food-gathering people, and their economy persists in certain manifestations of the Neolithic—though essentially the latter marks the introduction of agriculture and the keeping of domestic animals. On the River Bann, hearths sealed in the diatomite clay are believed to be associated with fishing and the drying of fish, and have yielded Neolithic pottery and pointed flint implements (Bann flakes) which are the development of flints of the preceding Larnian cultures. Similarly, the settlements on the sandhills presumably represent seasonal activities, and in them have been found Neolithic pottery (and also later material). A more settled economy is attested by the discovery of Neolithic habitation sites at Lough Gur, County Limerick. The first of these sites was discovered in 1939, and a series of excavations was conducted on them during the 1940's. The importance of the Lough Gur evidence is the finding there of Neolithic (and Bronze Age) houses—round and rectangular in plan. The inhabitants depended largely for their sustenance on cattle-raising and to some extent on small scale agriculture. A remarkable site at Lyles Hill, near Belfast, consists of a bank enclosing an area of more than 12 acres, at the center of which is a cairn (mound of stones) covering a cist grave. The bank and the layer under the cairn contained immense quantities of Neolithic pottery sherds. The Neolithic period saw the introduction of the custom of building megalithic tombs. These tombs are of various classes in Ireland and, on the available evidence, the earliest type appears to be the so-called "horned cairn," in many examples of which pottery and other grave furniture (leaf-shaped flint arrowheads) of Neolithic type have been found. These graves consist essentially of long galleries of upright stones originally roofed with slabs and divided into a series of compartments by pairs of jamb stones. The front of the tomb is distinguished by a crescentic façade, sometimes of imposing proportions. The burials are usually by cremation. These tombs are found in the northern half of the country; their distribution extends from Carlingford Lough, on the east coast, to County Sligo, on the west. Related to othem are more elaborate structures ("lobster-claw cairns"), found in Sligo, Mayo, and Donegal, on the northwest. They consist of an open circular or oval court surrounded by uprights and a series of segmented galleries which are entered from the court.

Other Neolithic burials of nonmegalithic type include burials (cremated and inhumed) in stone cists, with or without mounds, and in ring-barrows (very low mounds with surrounding ditch and bank).

The pottery gives some indication of cultural connections—with the British Neolithic A (Windmill Hill), which is part of the western group of European ceramics, and with the Neolithic B culture, whose roots are in the Baltic area. The Windmill Hill type of pottery in Ireland is much more widespread than is the Neolithic B, but shows such local developments as heavy and exaggerated rims with ornament. As well as these round-based vessels, a heavy, coarse, flat-based ware occurs which has affinities with the "grooved" ware of Britain (as at Scara Brae, in Scotland) and perhaps ultimately with the Horgen ware of Switzerland and the French (Seine-Oise-Marne) gallery graves. This pottery lasts on into Bronze Age times and provides one of the roots from which the cinerary urn develops.

Bronze Age.—The Bronze Age in Ireland began soon after 2000 B.C., and the preceding Neolithic appears to have provided a short introduction (perhaps of only a few centuries duration) which overlapped with the Bronze Age. In the Neolithic, however, the foundations for the succeeding culture were laid, and the same sites (for example, those at Lough Gur) continued to be inhabited. Ireland's importance in the Bronze Age was doubtless due as much to the development of the farming economy introduced in Neolithic times (and for which so much of the land was eminently suitable) as to the mineral deposits which the primitive metallurgists exploited. Gold was obtained from the Wicklow area, and possibly elsewhere. Copper mines which were worked in ancient times are known in Waterford, Cork, and Kerry. It is uncertain how much of this ancient working is genuinely prehistoric, but some of the mines (Mount Gabriel, County Cork) show significant similarity with the Bronze Age mines of the Austrian Tyrol.

In the Early Bronze Age Ireland produced certain metal types which are either Irish developments or distinctive variants of those known elsewhere and, because of their distinctiveness, these can be traced outside of the country, thus giving evidence of the role of Ireland in the general development of early metal-working. Among the Irish exports are flat axes (at first of copper, then of bronze, some with characteristic ornament), halberds (blades which are mounted at right angles to the shaft), gold lunulae (crescentic neck ornaments), and gold disks (so-called "sun disks"). The export routes of these commodities, or perhaps the routes followed by craftsmen, can be traced across Britain and to northern and western Europe, on the evidence of objects which are either actual exports or local copies.

The vigorous Irish Early Bronze Age was an amalgam of developments from the Neolithic together with influences from different sources. The beaker folk (known from their special type of pottery vessels), who spread through Europe from the Iberian peninsula, were formerly thought to have had little influence in Ireland. Since the 1930's, however, their pottery has been found in many megalithic tombs of the gallery grave class, in the sandhills, and in the Lough Gur area in considerable quantity—on habitation, burial, and ritual sites. The beakers belong in part to the international type (with S—profile), in part to the special type (A—beakers) developed in Britain.

Gold lunulae found in the Iberian Peninsula are a backwash along a route which brought many influences to Ireland—the origin of the lunula, the idea of the halberd, flint javelin heads polished on both faces. The splendid "passage graves" (megalithic tombs consisting of a chamber reached by a long passage—the whole covered by a great mound) provide the most spectacular result of Iberian influence. Some examples are of enormous size—Newgrange, Dowth, and Knowth, on the Boyne, cover each an acre in area. They tend to group in cemeteries: on the Boyne, County Meath; at Loughcrew, County Meath; at Carrowkeel, in County Sligo; and in a simplified form at Carrowmore in the latter county. Usually placed on hilltops, these tombs are impressive monuments. Some evidence (pottery) is available for their beginnings in the Neolithic, but they belong in the main to the Bronze Age. A feature of the Irish passage graves is the art (magico-religious carvings) on the building stones of such tomb groups (Boyne, Loughcrew, and elsewhere). This art has affinities in Malta, in the southwest of Spain, and even in the Canary Islands; the carvings at Newgrange are paralleled by those in Gavrinis, Brittany. Other rock scribings, not in tombs but on rock surfaces (mainly in the southwest of Ireland), indicate further connections with Iberia, in this case with Galicia—possibly due to the arrival of early metal-workers from that area.

Gallery graves different in structure from the horned cairns are of two types—the one typical of the northern part of Ireland, the other, very numerous, of the south. Both are dated to the Early Bronze Age by the beaker and other pottery found in them. Independent in origin, but influenced by the ornament of the beakers, is the "food vessel," so-called because it frequently occurs with burials of unburnt bodies (laid on the side with flexed limbs) and was intended to contain food for the journey to the next life. In its variety of form and ornament the food vessel is an index of the many sources of influence and inspiration which were combined in the Early Bronze Age culture of Ireland. The food vessel is used also with, or to contain, cremated burials; and later, in an enlarged form, it becomes an urn in function and type.

Other structures which may contain burials but which are primarily ritualistic in purpose are the stone circles and related monuments. Though not as impressive as the British "henges" (Stonehenge, Woodhenge, and others) they are varied and numerous in Ireland. Because of their ritual use, lack of finds makes them difficult to date, but one at Grange, near Lough Gur (possibly the finest, consisting of a ring of great uprights placed inside an earthen bank), is securely dated to Early Bronze Age times. A large enclosure with standing stone and grave at the center, surrounded by bank and fosse, at Furness, County Kildare, is similarly dated.

Middle Bronze.—The Middle Bronze Age is a continuation and development of the Early Bronze Age. Known metal forms persist or evolve—the knife-dagger grows into the large dagger and the rapier. A rapier found at Lissan, County Derry, 30 inches in length, is one of the most graceful examples of prehistoric bronze casting. The bronze flat axe is now provided with side flanges and stop ridges, and becomes the "palstave." Native type spearheads with loops for attachment to the shaft are influenced by the Continental riveted type, and hybrid forms result. Work in bar gold tends to replace the products of sheet gold of earlier times, and twisted gold torques are used as neck ornaments or perhaps, in the case of the great examples found in Tara, as waist ornaments.

Late Bronze.—The Late Bronze Age, which began sometime after 1000 B.C., is characterized by a great increase in the amount and variety of the equipment. The quantity of bronze and gold of Late Bronze Age date in museums is very large, and hoards (associated finds of objects) are a feature of this period. The new metal types—leaf-shaped swords, socketed axes, trumpets, buckets, cauldrons, gold gorgets (neck ornaments), and many others—are not a development of Middle Bronze Age examples, but represent new cultural influences from different sources. How far these are the result of actual invasion, and how far it is justifiable to connect them with the introduction of the Celtic language, are matters of speculation and controversy. The numerous innovations, however, did not cause Ireland to lose her initiative. Some of the gold ornaments are peculiar to the country, others, and some of the bronzes, are distinctive native adaptations of Continental prototypes. The bronze cauldrons exemplify this; magnificent specimens of craftsmanship, they are translations into metal of pottery vessels—the Greek *dinos.* They are part of the evidence that Ireland received impulses not only from the northern and western continent but also along the old Mediterranean-Atlantic route.

In the Late Bronze Age there was also cultural continuity from the earlier period. If, as seems likely, the grouping of urn burials in flat cemeteries owes its origin to the Continental urnfield cultures, the parallel development of cairns with numerous graves (multiple-cist cairns) must be ascribed to a development from the megalithic tombs. A group of urn burials found in a "ring fort" at Cush, County Limerick, is of importance for the dating of such forts, of which there are thousands in Ireland. Usually circular enclosures (known in Irish as *rath, lios,* etc.), with one or more banks and ditches, they provided protection for the habitations built within them. The Cush example had been deserted as a habitation site before the burials were inserted in it. It therefore predated the Late Bronze Age burials, and we have hints on other sites of even earlier beginnings for this class of structure. Accompanying many of these forts, and sometimes built independently of them, are souterrains—underground structures which served as places of refuge and for storage. Crannogs (artificial islands in bogs and marshes), built for the protection of their inhabitants, originated in lakeside settlements in Neolithic times. A small example at Rathjordan, County Limerick, belongs to the Early Bronze Age, and a larger specimen at Knockalappa, County Clare, is dated to the Late Bronze Age—Early Iron Age transition.

Early Iron Age.—Several factors make the Early Iron Age the most unsatisfactory period in Irish archaeology. The time of its introduction is difficult to define because of the vigor of the overlapping Late Bronze Age; at Knockalappa, for instance, pottery similar to British Iron Age A accompanied Bronze Age equipment—the leaf-shaped sword, gouge, and sunflower pin. The absence of a Roman invasion means that the Iron Age is regarded as extending to the 5th century, but without precise chronological fixed points. Yet this period is important historically because it is reflected in the great saga literature (the Cú Chulainn and the Finn Cycles), and it is the time when the notable early historical sites achieved importance. But none of these sites—Tara, Cruachain, Emain, Tlachtga, to name but a few—has been yet excavated. Their investigation should shed much light on an obscure phase.

The 1st century B.C. and the 1st century A.D. see the establishment in Ireland of an Iron Age culture definite in character though limited in distribution and comparatively meager in the amount of material available. The crannog at Lisnacrogher, County Antrim (unfortunately, not scientifically excavated), yielded amongst other objects sword scabbards with curvilinear ornament related to the Iron Age B culture of Britain and ultimately to the La Tène of the Continent. The ornament on the scabbards, in common with much of the contemporary Irish Iron Age material, finds its source of inspiration in Britain—particularly North Britain. The development in Ireland is, however, distinctive, and several types are not paralleled outside the country. The outline of the objects and the ornament they bear show a taste for curved forms (in Continental origin, a geometric treatment of vegetal designs)

IRISH ARCHAEOLOGY

Gold lunula belonging to the Early Bronze Age.

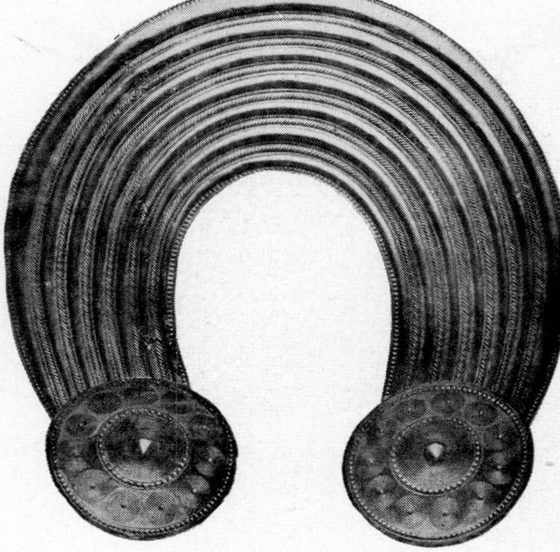

Gold gorget. Late Bronze Age.

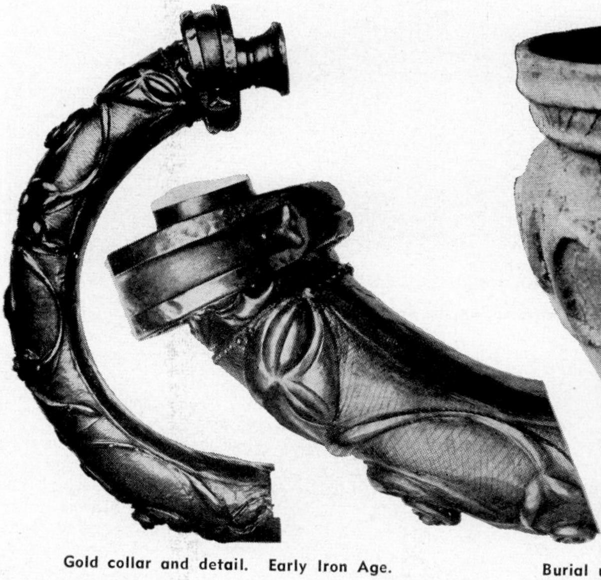

Gold collar and detail. Early Iron Age.

Burial urn of "encrusted urn" type. Late Bronze Age.

Ornamented stone, an example of megalithic art, excavated in 1950.

Photographs (top and center) © National Museum, Dublin; (bottom) courtesy Seán P. Ó Ríordáin

IRISH ARCHAEOLOGY

Bronze cauldron discovered at Castlederg. Late Bronze Age.

"Food vessel," a well-ornamented specimen, found with burial, 1950. Middle Bronze Age.

View of one of the burial mounds, unexcavated, on the Boyne River. Probably Bronze Age.

St. Kevin's Church and round tower, Early Christian monastic ruins, in the Vale of Glendalough.

Photo (top left) © National Museum, Dublin; (bottom) courtesy Irish Tourist Association; (others) courtesy Seán P. Ó Ríordáin

which later plays so important a part in Irish art development. Brooches, pins, trumpet ends, horse bits of bronze, and inscribed bone flakes (these last found in a passage-grave at Louchcrew), all bear this ornament. Related motives are to be found on stone—at Killycluggin, County Cavan, Castlestrange, County Roscommon, and Turoe, County Galway—on monuments for which direct Continental prototypes (Brittany) must be sought.

Roman Influence.—Though Ireland lay outside the sphere of Roman conquest, the Roman domination of Britain was bound to have influences on the neighboring island—as did also, in some measure, the extension of Roman power to the shores of Gaul. Roman objects are of sporadic occurrence in Ireland and probably arrived in various ways—by barter, in the possession of refugees from Roman power, and by loot. They belong mainly to two groups. The one, late 1st and early 2nd century A.D., probably reflects unsettled conditions consequent on the imposition of Roman rule in Britain; with these Roman objects native British products were introduced—as in the find of Lambay Island, County Dublin. The second group, of the late 4th and early 5th century, came in as loot brought by Irish raiders who descended on Roman territory when the imperial power was breaking; the objects thus acquired (silver plate, ingots, and coins) were of less importance than were the incidental contacts which resulted in the acquisition of techniques that were added to the repertoire of the native craftsmen. During the Roman period in Britain the Irish artists continued to develop the curvilinear ornament of La Tène ancestry, and applied it now to splendid *repoussé* work in bronze and gold—on gold collars (as from Broighter, County Derry, and Clonmacnoise, County Offaly), on enigmatical bronze disks, and, in a delicate form of cast ornament, on cone-shaped horns from crowns or helmets. But by the end of the Roman period they added millefiori work (the use of multicolored glass rods), niello, and filigree.

The great bank and ditch known as the "Black Pig's Dyke," which runs between County Armagh and County Donegal, is said to have been inspired by the Roman Wall across Britain, though it could hardly have been successfully manned in a military sense and it must have been no more than a precaution against cattle raiding. Great hill-forts, which are a feature of the pre-Roman Iron Age in Britain, are rare in Ireland, but this form of defensive structure occurs in a modified form on some of the royal sites (Tara, Emain, Ailenn) and elsewhere. One, excavated in 1949, at Freestone Hill, County Kilkenny, is dated to the 4th century. Meanwhile, many ring-forts and crannogs must have been in occupation at this time, and also at least a proportion of the numerous promontory forts which are found on the coast. Some examples excavated in County Cork during 1949–1950 did not yield datable finds but showed structural features similar to those in Cornish and Breton promontory forts.

Early Christian Period.—The term "Early Christian" is used for the period from the introduction of Christianity in the 5th century to the late 12th century. The stressing of the *Christian* aspect is justified by the fundamental changes which the Christian faith brought about in the pattern of life and consequently in the archaeological record.

Forts, crannogs, and houses similar to those of pre-Christian times continued to be built and occupied. However, as well as the secular sites, remains from this period include churches (or church sites, where scant remains or tradition mark the places from which wooden or even stone buildings have vanished), monasteries, great and small (and their accompanying memorials—grave slabs, inscribed pillar-stones, crosses), as well as round towers (built largely as refuges from Viking raids) and the dwelling cells of the monks. The monasteries were in some cases modeled on the secular forts—with enclosing bank or wall. What astonishes is their prodigious number—not all datable, and certainly not all of contemporary foundation; but it is clear that already, in the 5th century, ecclesiastical establishments began to be built plentifully throughout the land, and in the 6th the foundation of the great monasteries began—with that of St. Enda of Aran as the first example. Little remains of the buildings of the most famous monasteries, but a site like that on the Great Skellig (off the coast of Kerry)—little more than a bare rock in the ocean—indicates the essentials of the early monasteries. Being in a treeless spot, the buildings were entirely of stone. Small churches and a collection of beehive cells are a reflex of the type of monasticism—eremitical, ascetic to an extreme degree—which produced a multiplicity of buildings instead of the single building of Continental monasticism as established by the Benedictines.

The curvilinear art of the Iron Age survives on pins (hand-pins), brooches (so-called latchets), and other minor objects, frequently now with the addition of enamel. But it is Christianized by its use on the monastic sites—on stones with ornament alone, or ornament combined with crosses of various forms. The designs develop in complexity, new motifs such as interlacing and figure representation are added, and the magnificent high crosses of stone result—mainly with geometric ornament in the 8th century, with scripture subjects in the 9th and 10th, and again with ornamental carvings in the 11th and 12th. The illumination of manuscripts of the Gospels gave a new medium for the artists of the monasteries. Examples are the books of Durrow (7th century), Lindisfarne (early 8th), and Kells, the greatest (early 9th). Lindisfarne is but one of the foundations which resulted from Irish missionary activity in Britain and the Continent. The minute complexity of the illuminators' work reacts on the metal workers and enamelers who originally inspired it, and such treasures as the *Ardagh Chalice* and the *Tara Brooch* are achieved.

Viking Influences.—Relics of the Viking invasions which began in the late 8th century are strangely limited—one large cemetery at Dublin, and sporadic finds through the country. The loot of the raiders carried back to Norway—ornaments, reliquaries, church lamps—is important archaeologically because it is found in dated contexts—mainly in graves of the 9th century—and fills many of the gaps in the Irish record. Irish motifs influenced Scandinavian art and, notwithstanding the shock of the invasion, Irish craftsmen continued to work. The high crosses were still carved, metalwork continued, though the great 8th century overshadows the two that follow and make it difficult to recognize their products. Paradoxically, it is not until after the breaking of the Viking power at Clontarf that the Irish artist accepted northern motifs and incorporated them in his repertoire, blending them, however, in a manner which was distinctly his own.

Meanwhile church building had developed. The use of mortar (perhaps introduced in the 7th century) made larger structures possible; the roof, formerly of dry-stone corbels, was elaborated, and ornament was used on doors, chancel arches, and windows. But even the beautiful Romanesque churches, with interesting variety of ornament, are small buildings not comparable to those of the Continent. The coming of the Cistercian builders of great abbeys, in the early 12th century, is the herald of the end of the era.

Bibliography.—Coffey, G., *The Bronze Age in Ireland* (Dublin 1913); Macalister, R. A. S., *Archaeology of Ireland*, 1st ed. (London 1928); Ryan, J., *Irish Monasticism, Origin and Early Development* (Dublin 1931); Movius, H. L., Jr., *The Irish Stone Age* (Cambridge 1942); O Riordain, S. P., *Antiquities of the Irish Countryside* (Cork 1943); Henry, F., *Irish Art in the Early Christian Period* (London 1947); Childe, V. G., *Prehistoric Communities of the British Isles* (London 1949). Full bibliographies in Mahr, A., "New Aspects and Problems in Irish Prehistory" in *Proceedings of the Prehistoric Society*, 3 (1937), and O Riordain, S. P., "Prehistory in Ireland, 1937–1946," in *ibid.*, 12 (1946).

Seán P. Ó. Ríordáin,
Professor of Archaeology, University College, Dublin.

IRISH ART AND ARCHITECTURE.

Ireland's position as an art and architectural country is conditioned by the fact that it is situated at the extreme northwest angle of Europe, far from the center of eastern Mediterranean civilization and thus destined to receive its art impulses at long remove. Insularity retarded invasion in bulk and then insured long periods of incubation so that at well-defined moments the elaborated ideas flowed back into Europe, as for example: the gold trade of the second millennium B.C.; the medieval missionary movement (650 A.D. onwards); or the late 18th century leavening of European literature into Romanticism through Celtic, specifically the Ossianic, epic. The antique Irish ringed cross, revived by 19th-century patriotism, became popular in many places as a memorial of the valorous dead from 1914 onwards.

Iberian explorers of 2,000 B.C. or so opened up the country when they discovered gold in quantity in the streams of the Wicklow Hills just south of Dublin, establishing a tradition of gold-work which was maintained up to the Anglo-Norman Conquest of the 12th century. Late Celtic settlers coming mainly by way of northern Britain from Europe about 250 B.C. onwards brought in the first developed ornamental style, a style destined to reach new heights in the Christian era from 450 A.D.: it continued logically with Norse admixture till the Conquest, a long drawn-out business which destroyed the native development without creating new styles. However, within the core of the English settlement around Dublin in the 18th century a new nationalism developed, enriching the country economically and making Dublin one of the art cities of Europe. After an awkward pause in the middle of the 19th century this renewed itself until fused with Gaelicism and, influenced by native epic, a new art urge appeared; Ireland, which tends to develop along normal European lines, is still individualistic and not entirely uninfluenced by American attitudes.

Dublin remains the art capital and possesses the principal art school (National College of Art), housed indifferently but staffed by a brilliant group of art professors which includes leading painters like Seán Keating, president of the Hibernian Academy, and Maurice MacGonigal, its curator. The Hibernian Academy, founded in 1820 in succession to the Society of Artists, aims to include in its membership established painters; it holds an annual exhibition available to the public for a month. Adjoining the college is the National Gallery, opened in 1854, regarded as one of the best of the smaller European galleries, a position due to its second director, Henry F. Doyle (1869–1892).

In the same area are the National Library, with a large print collection, and the National Museum, which includes valuable archaeological and decorative art collections offering a wide selection of exhibits to the craftsman desiring foreign models or seeking to emulate the masterpieces of the Celtic and medieval periods in Ireland.

Dublin has also a good gallery of modern painting (Charlemont House), due ultimately to Sir Hugh Lane (drowned in the *Titanic* disaster in 1912) which was intended to house a large collection of modern French masters; owing to a faulty will, these have been retained in London. Belfast, capital of Northern Ireland, has a good combined museum and gallery and an awakening art school; other provincial Irish towns since 1930 have been founding the nuclei of museums and galleries, the permanence and eventual value of which cannot yet be assessed. An Art Act intended to forward organization and development became law in 1951.

Additional annual art functions like the Oireachtas Art Exhibition and the Living Art Exhibition give scope to numerous artists having different objectives, while the art centers of the Dublin Painters (7 Stephen's Green) and the Waddington and Dawson galleries, are rarely free of special exhibitions which sometimes include works by noted foreign painters and sculptors, including extremists of various kinds.

Iberian Art.—To the early Iberian settlers and gold seekers in Ireland coming from Spain and Portugal by way of western France and Brittany the first flashes of a definitive art may be attributed, finding its expression in the decorative or symbolic treatment of many of the great stones and flags which form their chamber-and-passage tombs. These are chiefly situated in the Boyne Valley (an Irish "Valley of the Kings") and the adjacent Loughcrew Hills, all in the ancient central kingdom of Meath. It is a residual art long removed from the original representations of goddesses and the like. The same general age, just after 2000 B.C., produced a more systematic style, geometrical in character, applied to gold crescentic neck-ornament, bronze axes, and earthenware. Throughout the Bronze Age proper, decoration of a related character is the sole evidence of artistic expression, borne out by superb series of gold ornaments, gradually becoming more sophisticated as the age advanced; the heavy gold collars of the close of the period reproduce leather armor, bronze neck-guard and shield details, evidence of a new art influence involving northwest Central Europe.

Early Celtic Art.—With the coming of Marnian Celts a more elaborate and still more abstract decorative style was introduced linking Ireland through northern Britain with northeastern France and Switzerland, where the style achieved a name, La Tène, a noted site on the Lake of Neuchâtel. It became the leading Irish style for centuries, playing a notable part in the efflorescence of culture between 750 and 1050 A.D. and strongly influencing modern Irish ideas. It is in essentials the Greek palmette reduced to graceful groups of spirals or scrolls ending in or uniting lobes, either flat or in relief; these latter may meet to form "trumpet ends" or lens-forms disposed throughout the ornament. The classical monument of this art, which may date 250 B.C., is the western Irish *Turoe Stone,* a low rounded pillar over which is cast, like a chasuble, two fields of ornament finished at the end with a Wall-of-Troy or simple fret ornament; it is sculptured in low relief carving, the field being pocked to give emphasis to the pattern, and the whole may have been covered with a thin plating of gold for which treatment there is both literary and archaeological evidence in connection with other cult objects. In the main, however, the art is preserved or recorded as the main decoration of metal wares, brooches, scabbards, chariot- and house-fittings, mirrors, and the like. Certain unexplained bronze disks in which stylized human faces are worked out in embossed La Tène ornament, and a cylindrical gold torque of great magnificence found on the shore of Lough Foyle, Northern Ireland, are notable masterpieces of the metalworker's art. Actual sculptures in the round exist, but they share the continental Celtic sculptor's lack of appreciation for style and anatomy.

Christian Period.—The succeeding epoch, 250–550 A.D., one of political disturbance, is rather arid of art achievement, but with the coming of Christianity in the 5th century and the growth of flourishing monasteries this condition was gradually replaced by a fine flowering of a native art inspiration, the materials selected helping to mark out the periods of the development; that of the great illuminated manuscripts, that of the tall, free-standing high-crosses and that of the metal shrines, all of course overlapping in one way or another. A faded Celtic ornamental style so-called Ultimate La Tène, occurs in bronzes, etc., and, reaching into the earliest mss., foreshadows the astonishing revival of Celticism of the succeeding age.

Illumination.—Irish illumination as such is incomprehensible apart from the missions sent forth by St. Columba (Columcille) of Derry, who died in 597 A.D., dominating northern England and much of Scotland. In the former area, surviving Celtic ornament might be found alongside animal scrolls introduced by the Angles and other Germanic tribes. Rich Byzantine manuscripts were introduced from Italy by St. Augustine of Canterbury, in 596, and by Benedict Biscop of Wearmouth and Jarrow, in northern England, about 675. The Irish style came therefore to be compact of Celtic, Germanic, and Byzantine motives in an essentially Byzantine framework. The three principal monuments of this distinctive and impressive art are the *Book of Durrow* (County Kildare), the *Book of Lindisfarne* (off the English northwest coast, a monastery founded for St. Aidan and a party of Irish monks by St. Oswald, Anglian king of Northumbria), and the *Book of Kells* (County Meath); all three books belonged to abbeys under the influence of Iona (off the southwest Scottish coast) and, of course, the Columban Rule. It can be presumed that the three works date to about 700–775,* and many other manuscripts bear the same imprimatur of Celticism—for example, the St. Gall Gospels, in Switzerland. *Lindisfarne,* by reason of its delicacy of treatment, is nearest the supposed model; *Durrow,* in its relative simplicity, appears as a "try-out"; while *Kells,* despite the grave stylization of the portrait element, is, by its wealth of coloring, the extraordinary fineness of its interlacement, its luxuriant fancy, and the numerous small and quite irrelevant colored drawings, the outstanding work of the group and epoch. The *Codex Amiatinus,* in the Laurentian Library at Florence, is reasonably regarded as best illustrating the original foreign exemplar or exemplars. The book-contents, apart from text, are mainly pages given up to portraits of Christ, the Virgin, the Evangelists, the Symbols of the Evangelists, the Christ sign in Greek (XP) which is the tour de force of these manuscripts, and columnar arcades enclosing the Eusebian canons (gospel cross references); some pages are all ornament: such pages may now be regarded as originating in earlier book-cover and colophon-page designs, the East Mediterranean source of which is already known. Despite the seeming disorder of the decoration—spirals, interlacements, and frets—a rigorous panel arrangement dominates, and the presence of the Byzantine mosaicist and marbleworker in spirit is unmistakable. A special tribute has to be paid to the fine naturalistic birds which characterize *Lindisfarne.*

Sculptured Crosses.—Peace essential for such prolonged and delicate labors disappeared with the Viking raids, about 850 onwards, on the Irish and British coasts, especially those about the North Channel. Irish genius now expressed itself in superb high-crosses which are in effect the projection of manuscript ideas in stone, even as to form, namely, a combination of the Greek and Latin crosses with the normally surrounding circle of the former set squarely at the junction of the arms of the cross. Their main date is perhaps 800–950 A.D., with an extension to the 12th for some atypical varieties. Byzantine inspiration furnished northern Britain with two tall stone crosses, those of Bewcastle and Ruthwell, which provided the general idea for the intense Irish development; they clearly derive from the *Cross of Constantine* at Jerusalem, adjusted to an Anglo-Saxon carved-timber tradition. Columban influence stands behind the movement. Kells (County Meath) has thus a number of exemplars and Durrow has one notable cross, but the finest examples are those of Monasterboice (County Louth) and Clonmacnoise (County Offaly). Armagh can be taken as the center point of the whole northern series. An early group at Ahenny (County Carlow) is notable for its almost wholly ornamental character; and in one the wedge-shaped foot, as if pared for fitting to its pyramidal base, indicates that these lofty monuments derive in part from a long line of carved timber monuments of which no exemplar survives. The leading groups, scripture-crosses as they were called, show numerous panels illustrating parallel scenes from the Old and New Testaments but with free use of purely decorative items derived from the manuscripts. Often the cap is of house-form and illustrates not only contemporary architecture but shrines of the house type. The importance of these crosses in the history of European sculpture is the essential theme of the works on the subject by Arthur Kingsley Porter (1883–1933).

* These dates are controversial. See IRISH ARCHAEOLOGY—*Early Christian Period.*

Art Metalwork.—Celtic craftsmanship which left a permanent tradition of fine metalwork behind it was strengthened by the importation of workers with a new style by St. Patrick and other missioners. The typically Irish penannular brooch, a long pin with a large ring and a derivative of the Roman buckle, occupies an important place in this phase of Irish art history; in due course the ring and head were flatted and the terminals formerly turned back, then flatted, and finally unified, providing three main surfaces which came to be decorated in the richest manner possible but in a style closely related to that of the illuminated manuscripts and the high-crosses. The high peak of this series is the *Tara Brooch,* found on the east coast of Louth; an attached silver chain of fine wire mesh shows that it was one of a pair. This gem of western European art is made the recipient of numerous techniques; gilding, niello, chasing, enameling, and jewel-cutting, the last mentioned, small human heads of garnet(?) at the hinge joining the chain to the ring. This ring is a near parallel in design to the ring of the principal Irish high-cross (Monasterboice), evidence of interinfluence. The second primary jewel of the same epoch is the *Ardagh Chalice* (County Limerick) a ministral two-handled chalice with deep bowl, a very short stem, and a domical base with flatted foot; the handles, highly ornate in character and having close relation with brooch details, are embellished with red and deep blue enamel bosses. A typical manuscript band of ornament, gold panels separated by enamel bosses, surrounds the cup; underneath this are the names of the Apostles (including Paul), emblematic of the Last Supper, Christ being represented by ornamental medallions of gold spirals in a Greek cross setting on either side of the cup. The interior of the base, which could be observed when lifted up by the priest, is a crystal surrounded by several zones of gold paneling set off with amber (now largely missing). The piece is rightly regarded as the outstanding jewel of its kind for the age. The writer dates these two ornaments on the basis of accumulated techniques to about 950–1000, but a date two centuries earlier is often mentioned; and a similar diversity of view may arise regarding the latest jewel added to this short series—a reliquary belt composed of hinged and curved sections with paneled ornaments, the *Moylaugh Belt* (County Galway), a late discovery: some of the ornaments simulate high-cross heads of a type usually assigned to the 11th century, for example, that of Drumcliffe, County Sligo.

Eleventh- and 12th-century metalwork is illustrated by a number of elaborate book-shrines, bell-shrines, house-shrines, and crozier-shrines, mostly of a high standard of workmanship but signalized by the intrusion of Viking ornament and a progressive coarsening of detail. *St. Patrick's Bell* (5th century) and its silver shrine (about 1100 A.D.) constitute outstanding Irish insignia. The latter is a tabernacle form, the front decorated with panels of coarse gold spirals in a book-cover setout; the back is a perforated silver panel with swastika motive, based on Continental transennae, or shrine-panels in carved stone, a constant feature of Irish metal shrines; the narrow sides are filled with a coarse wire scrolling, and have rings for suspension. This epoch ends with two notable monuments: the ark-shaped processional *Shrine of St. Manchan* (Boher, County Offaly), having an elaborate array of stylized figures, the saint, and his community; and the processional *Cross of Cong* (County Galway), a shrine made for a portion of the True Cross. The general design of the latter is that of the *Constantine Cross,* with scalloped sides, the front being filled with gilt panels of animal-style interlacement and a crystal at the center. The very tall high-cross of Tuam, which is decorated in a low-relief interlacement in the same style, brings the main Irish development to a logical close. Shortly after these objects were made the Anglo-Norman conquest of Ireland began (1169) and a long period of artistic chaos ensued.

Pre-Conquest Architecture.—The architecture of the pre-Conquest period is divided between two very different modes based respectively on wicker construction and stone corbelled work, assimilated as to style to timber forms now no longer existing. Western Ireland, because of its treeless character and the effective recourse to dry-stone walling, is remarkable for a series of ancient fortifications. The chief examples of these are the remote hill forts of Staigue (County Kerry) and Aileach (County Derry), and the elaborate promontory forts of the Aran Islands, notably that of Dun Aonghusa, all belonging to the Celtic epoch. Even in the beginning of the metal age, well-built tombs with entrance passage and corbel-built chamber characterize the Boyne Valley and other cemeteries. Details of wicker construction are preserved in the Celtic romances, and advert to both circular and rectangular structures. It is the corner-post and gable elements of the latter which contribute leading features to the first stone churches (these often of very limited size). The circular form continued in earliest Christian times as clochain, or beehive cells, for hermits dwelling along the west coast—for example, the laura on Skellig Michael, County Kerry.

From these, an oblong oratory type evolved, still corbelled (such as that at Gallerus, County Kerry). Soon small oratories with erect walls appear (Mac Dara's, County Galway), but the corbelled tradition continued in roof construction right up to the climax of Irish pre-Conquest building, as in Cormac's Chapel. This is a unique Romanesque gem of the 12th century, replete with twin square towers (implying Rhenish influences), recessed entrance, and tympanum, and a free use of arcades with painted designs within for surface decoration. The features of this insular development are: battered (sloping) walls, the batter lessening as time advanced, sloping door and window jambs parallel to the wall batter, corner antae (piers) on the east and west walls, and projecting square moldings on the gables, the latter details being pictures in stone of features in contemporary timber construction; the gable was topped with a winged finial, itself a timber derivative. Doors were mainly square-headed, with a relieving slab above, usually bearing the Christ sign (Greek cross) or, as at Maghera (County Derry), a sculptured Crucifixion in the style of the high-crosses. From 1000 A.D. onwards, normal arched doors, often deeply recessed with zigzag and human-head ornament, and even interlaced designs thinly sculptured, become common: Killeshin, County Carlow, is a fine example. Chancel arches were similarly treated. The evolution of plan was equally deliberate, the small oratory becoming the sanctuary in a two-piece plan of which the nave was perhaps three times its area (as at Rahan, County Offaly). No transepts figure in this development, and square apses, where they occur, as in the next epoch, are the rule.

The principal centers for examples of these types are the monastic settlements of Clonmacnoise (County Offaly) and Glendalough (County Wicklow). Columba's House at Kells (County Meath) illustrates the growth of the clochan or beehive cells through much straining to be the upper chamber or priest's room over a tiny oratory. With the assaults of the Vikings, from the 9th century onward, monasteries were more carefully defended. Thence evolved the tall round-tower, so characteristic of the Irish countryside, consisting of a cylindrical tower with conical stone roof; the door was pitched high above the ground, and string courses carried five or six floors, lighted by slit windows, often four in number, at the top. Their Irish name, *cloig-theach,* indicates that they were regarded as belfries, but they also served as refuges and treasuries. Their period is between 900 and 1050. The finest example, with external string courses, is that of Ardmore (County Waterford). That at Glendalough gives centrality to an extensive monastic settlement. As in other structures, the towers are slightly battered (inclined), that at Ardmore especially so.

Later Developments.—With the introduction of the Cistercian Order by St. Malachy, straight from Clairvaux, France, an end was brought to the traditional modes of the Irish monastery, and with it the native tradition in building. His establishment at Mellifont, in the Boyne Valley, was built in a Late Romanesque manner in 1142, it was followed by others still building when the Anglo-Norman Conquest began. The following centuries are therefore full of building activities. Cathedrals, abbeys, and the like are effectively provincial versions of English and French work, tending in the 15th century to evolve into a subordinate national style; the main feature was a square-tower crowning the transept crossing and the old square apse. Christ Church Cathedral, Dublin, bears ample evidence of its relation to churches of Somersetshire, England, itself not a strong building center. The suppression of the abbeys in the 16th century left them without successors for a long time to come. Notable remains survive at Holy Cross, County Tipperary, and Cong, County Galway. Military architecture began in 1170 A.D. with the erection over a wide area of eastern Ireland of timber castles surmounting high motes (eminences) and surrounded by baileys (outer walls) and palisades at ground level; it ended with stoutly built stone castles, shadows in plan and general character of Anglo-Norman building in England. The "frontier" citadel of Trim, County Meath, is a good example of military architecture. Abbeys were often castellated, and the frequent presence of battlement motives in quite late church building no doubt re-echoes this earlier age of strife.

With the year 1700 and the absence of any serious threat of an Irish recovery, nationalism came to roost in the English Pale itself and a movement of city embellishment appeared especially in Dublin. By the end of the century numerous public buildings of neoclassic design had sprung up at artistically strategic points in the city complex, mostly associated with the architect James Gandon: Parliament House, the Four Courts Buildings, the Custom House, King's Inns, and later, in the early 19th century, the General Post Office. The interspaces were filled with good Georgian mansions, many of which boasted superb ceilings and fireplaces. Houses like those of the earl of Charlemont and the duke of Leinster, in neo-Palladian style adjoining fine squares, helped to complete the Dublin architectural scene around 1750. The style, which had many rural triumphs also (like the seat of the Connollys at Castletown and that of the Leinster family at Carton, both in County Kildare, residences of palatial design, extent, and even contents), had sufficient validity to bear translation to colonial America. This further variety of the style is epitomized in the White House, itself built during 1792–1800 by the Irish architect, James Hoban of Kilkenny; the structure has many points in common with Leinster House and the President's House (formerly Viceregal Lodge), Dublin. Hoban had done much fine work in Carolina before being discovered by Washington, indicating that this fine flowering of American civilization, its Colonial Palladian, can, like much else, have a strong Irish backing. Sculptors now emerged, such as Edward Smith, John Henry Foley, and John Hogan, mostly trained in the Roman school of the time; they began to fill a long vacant gap in Irish art history. A mere handful of wood carvings, some in polychrome and a few recumbent figures of Anglo-Norman grandees, are all that unite the present age with that of the high-crosses in the line of distinguished sculpture.

In the new economic recovery, largely stimulated by the example of the American colonists, the decorative arts began to flourish. Glassmakers from Stourbridge, in England, established in Waterford, at the end of the 18th century, a factory which produced in generous quantity many finely cut forms of domestic glassware, chandeliers, decanters, footed salvers, and the notable salad-bowl forms beloved of collectors. A tapestry school begun near Dublin in the time of Charles II promised remarkable achievements but failed to hold its ground. In Galway, silver almost maintained the traditional link with the past, but in general Irish silver attuned itself to English and French design. An assay office in Dublin ensured high standards not only in metal but technique, and Irish silver is not unreasonably cherished by the collector. The noted *de Burgo-O'Malley Gothic Chalice,* probably made in Galway, indicates that despite unsettled conditions fine aesthetic achievements were possible even in the 15th century.

Minor Arts.—The minor decorative arts like furniture and textiles benefited enormously by the changed conditions: much of the former survives, but owing to the lack of house accounts and illustrated sales lists the art is largely anonymous. On the other hand, the close interest taken by the Dublin Society in linen and cotton print design has left us ample records of the textile industry, though surviving examples, topical or classical figurings for the most part, are very rare. The period of flowering was between 1730 and 1830. Neocolonialism even turned to the native harp and its rich musical tradition; while a personified Hibernia, already on silverwork from 1731 and now a rival to Britannia herself, often became the badge not only of Irish workmanship but of high quality also.

Irish lace (and crochet), because of its international *réclame* and mature excellence, is often regarded as an old traditional art. In effect, however, it is a 19th-century inspiration which struck surprisingly deep roots, and in a relatively short time it came to equal, if not excel, the products of Brussels and Valenciennes; Limerick and Carrickmacross are the two centers especially associated with the art. While still of interest to the connoisseur, the lacemaking movement has practically disappeared, the victim of a change in fashions.

Ceramics lagged far behind Continental standards. Nevertheless the 18th-century Delamain factory at Dublin held much promise, and the 19th century Beleek factory (County Fermanagh), through its imaginative designs and its unusual mother-of-pearl luster, attracts some tastes and is of interest to American collectors.

Modern Epoch.—The short-lived efflorescence of the latter half of the 18th and early 19th century ended with the Great Famine of 1847. A new trend upwards, terminating in the present republic, then appeared; it was bound up, however, with a reversion to the antique Gaelic background, with its superb epic literature and art. So, from 1890 onwards, there was achieved a new mastery of the Irish consciousness affecting industry, drama, music, and literature. Already a few meritorious painters, like James Barry of Cork (q.v.), a rival of Joshua Reynolds, had demonstrated Irish possibilities. The new wealth of late 18th-century Ireland had given work for many competent portrait painters, later to come, like English painters of the time, under the virile influence of the American painter, Benjamin West (q.v.), president of the Royal Academy, in London. In London at that period was also another American, Gilbert Charles Stuart (q.v.), who, before returning to the United States, dwelt in Dublin and there produced many pictures, including some of the patriotic notabilities of the Irish Parliament; this service was parallel to that which he afterwards rendered the founders of the new republic of the West. The extent to which the Irish painter Nathaniel Hone (1718–1784) may have contributed to the style of these brilliant American painters in the direction of a natural and vital portrayal emancipated from classical and English social conventionalism cannot be overemphasized. Some of the latter's best work is in miniatures, a category in which Charles Robertson (1760–1821) and the more prosaic John Comerford (1770–1782) of Kilkenny also deserve honorable record. The groups just mentioned emphasize the strong forces linking national and artistic growth; however, little divided the artists of this short-lived renaissance in tone from the contemporary English movement, and this is true, of course, of the first painters of free America.

The French movements of the 19th century left Ireland untouched to any serious extent, though the habit of looking to Italy remained constant. The brothers Mulvany, both academic painters, appeared to be on the verge of discovery with their studies of peasant life. Again, the depiction of movement, especially animal movement (which still remains a weak point in Irish painting), received an adequate and, for 19th-century Europe, new inspiration from Michael Angelo Hayes (1820–1877), an interpreter of British military events and Irish genre subjects. Some of his pictures engraved by Rudolph Ackermann (1820–1877), of Düsseldorf and London, acquired wide popularity. James Arthur O'Connor (1792–1841), with his romantic and often moonlit German and Irish landscapes, was, however, no substitute for a Théodore Rousseau or a John Constable—though of sufficient merit to obtain a kind of revival in Ireland about 1940. Daniel Maclise (1806–1870) was certainly a competent painter and of large ideas, though modern taste shows the same disregard for his drama-influenced creations as for those of Lawrence Alma-Tadema: his *Marriage of Strongbow and Eva* (Norman conqueror and daughter of a Leinster king) was long the *pièce de résistance* of the National Gallery of Ireland. We can be thankful, however, for his sympathetic portraits of Thomas Moore, the Irish poet of the early 19th century, and of the English novelists Charles Dickens and Harrison Ainsworth. Ireland became the home of the young English painter, George Chinnery (1774–1825), whose Irish portraits make such a striking contrast to his gracious and much-sought-after portrayals of Chinese and Indian life; he may be quoted as indicating the continuing art life of the Irish capital and its power of attracting genius.

Eventually the appearance at the turn of the century of Walter F. Osborne and Nathaniel Hone, noted landscape painters taught by European experience, indicated lines appropriate to a school not then likely to possess an extensive clientele at home. The great portrait painter, William Orpen, an Irish "Gilbert Stuart," was able to bestride both Ireland and Britain with his lightsome and easy portraiture of interesting personalities. Patrick Tuohy, many of whose paintings are in New York, where he tragically died, might easily have excelled him despite his grimmer handling of reality. Sir John Lavery, a competent society painter whose canvases have enriched the municipal galleries in Dublin and Belfast, and who painted mostly in London, never achieved an Irish vernacular despite valued depictions of Sir Roger Casement and other notable men of the revolution. Irish taste seems to demand a slight cartooning approach, and this is strongly visible in the early work of Jack Yeats, brother of William Butler Yeats, the distinguished poet, in his studies of western peasant life; his later work is indicative of a personality of extraordinary fantasy and dynamic color skill. His popularity and perhaps his status are adumbrated by the fact that a first-day of an exhibition of his works, 21 in all, saw 16 of them sold at a total of £6,000 (Oct. 8, 1951).

The developed Irish school now took shape in the persons of Seán Keating, Seán O'Sullivan, Leo Whelan, and Maurice MacGonigal, influenced by, but by no means following too closely, current European modes: Spain rather than France or Italy attracted them, a throwback to early Iberian sympathies perhaps. The west Irish scene occupied the patternist painter, Paul Henry, while more routine landscape painters like Frank McKelvey and J. Humbert Craig chose the north Irish scene, the former in his later humor clearly deriving some inspiration from the great Corot. The fairy and mythic element found interpretation in the light works of AE (George Russell), the poet, who left no successors: the dream atmosphere of Lady Glenavy's, Patrick Hennessy's, and Cecil Salkeld's studies, the last influenced by Hilaire Degas, is entirely personal to these artists. In Northern Ireland, the distinguished humanist painter, William Connor, has reduced large numbers of agricultural and indus trial types to the sympathetic expression of his able canvases. In sculpture there is less to be said: Oliver Sheppard, a robust modeler, has left many pieces which shadow forth ancient epic. Albert Power, most typical Irish sculptor, was a good portraitist and a sympathetic interpreter of children: his fish sculptures in Irish green marbles are special to him. It is usual to swell the tale by including the Irish-Americans, Jerome Connor and Andrew O'Connor, who at an advanced stage in their career resumed their artistic citizenship: both are well known in the United States and are well represented in Irish collections. Augustus Saint-Gaudens (1848–1907), born in Dublin of Franco-Irish parentage and founder of the modern American school of sculpture, can hardly be added to this group. He is, however, represented in the city of his birth by the strongly designed statue in bronze of the Irish tribune, Charles Stewart Parnell (1846–1891), with its striking triangular obelisk.

It is a sign of vitality that a junior school is making its way sunwards: men more sympathetic to the European trend like Fergus Ryan, an urban painter, and Louis Le Brocquy, who has become the *fauve* of a group of which the Northern Irish painter, Daniel O'Neill, may become the leading light. Junior sculptors are Lawrence Campbell, Peter Grant, Miss Hilary Hearne, and Gabriel Hayes, of whom Miss Hearne is the sole modernist, a student of pure form. Rosamond Praeger is a sensitive creator of child studies.

A parallel growth of "Celtic" art marks this new phase and has given us superb *Book of Kells* work, that of Art O Mornachain, and the precious pieces of the metalworker's art by Miss Mia Cranwill—some of them now in San Francisco Cathedral. Medieval Irish art also invaded the goldsmiths' atelier, producing "Celtic" ideas of ornament and even reproductions and adaptations. Enameling, never logically developed in Ireland, found a new expression in the work of Oswald Reeves, mostly subsidiary to metal pieces, but the art failed to maintain itself, in spite of some fine achievements. Greater emphasis may be laid on stained glass of this epoch, whether it be the Romanesque masterpieces of An Tur Gloine (The Glass Tower), the Gothic-Celtic creations of the Clarke Studios, or the frank Renaissance work of Messrs. Earley's workshops, often reminiscent of the glass in Prague Cathedral. Several art guilds—like the Cuala Industries, a Yeatsian foundation, and the notable Dun Emer Guild, noted for superb carpets and embroideries employing pure Celtic design—gave shape and direction to a movement whose outlines have tended in later times to become blurred.

A promising movement to revive Irish Romanesque traditions in architecture naturally accompanied the uprisal, but save for the Honan Hostel chapel, at Cork, and the parish church at Spiddal (County Galway) the movement, especially associated with the name of William A. Scott, has not been intense. The fine Byzantine interior of University College Church, Dublin, has a more magnificent successor in the basilican cathedral of Mullingar, County Westmeath. Romanesque taste, however, survived though in later times contenting itself with Italian hill-country and Spanish-American models and suggestions. The fine 19th-century revival of Gothic produced Killarney Cathedral by A. W. Pugin, founder of the style; the superb twin-towered primatial cathedral in Armagh (architect, J. McCarthy), the old ecclesiastical capital where St. Patrick established his primitive church buildings in the 5th century, and St. Peter's Church (architect, George C. Ashlin) of the Vincentians, in Dublin.

Bibliography.—Medieval Art: Illumination, Sculpture, and Metalwork: Stokes, Margaret, *Early Christian Art in Ireland*, rev. ed. (Dublin 1911); Porter, A. K., *The Crosses and Culture of Ireland* (New Haven 1931); Mahr, A., and Raftery, Joseph, *Christian Art in Ancient Ireland*, 2 vols. (Dublin 1932, 1941); Gogan, L. S., *The Ardagh Chalice: Ireland's Holy Grail* (Dublin 1932); Henry, Françoise, *La sculpture irlandaise pendant les premiers siècles de l'ère Chrétienne*, 2 vols. (Paris 1933); Micheli, G. L., *L'enluminure du haut moyen âge et les influences irlandaises* (Brussels 1939); Sexton, Eric H. L., *A descriptive and bibliographical list of Irish figure sculptures of the Early Christian period, with a critical assessment of their significance* (Portland, Me., 1946); Henry, Françoise, *Irish Art in the early Christian period* (London 1947); Masai, F., *Essai sur les origines de la Miniature dite irlandaise* (Brussels 1947); on this see *Acta Archaeologica* (Copenhagen 1947); Codex Cenannensis, *Book of Kells*, 3 vols. (Bern 1950).

Architecture: Georgian Society, *Records of domestic architecture and decoration in Dublin* (Dublin 1909–1913); Champneys, A. C., *Irish ecclesiastical architecture, with some notice of similar or related work in England, Scotland, and elsewhere* (London 1910); Sadleir, T. U., and Dickinson, P. L., *Georgian Mansions in Ireland, with some account of the evolution of Georgian architecture and decoration* (Dublin 1915); Harvey, John, *A study in environment* (London 1950); Leask, H. J., *Irish Castles and Castellated Houses* (Dundalk 1950).

Later Art: Strickland, W. G., *A Dictionary of Irish Artists*, 2 vols. (Dublin 1913); Desnaroux, Hélène, *L'oeuvre du sculpteur O'Connor* (Paris 1927); Konody, P. J., and Dark, S., *Sir William Orpen, Artist and Man* (London 1932); Elmes, Rosalind M., *Catalogue of engraved Irish portraits* (Dublin 1938); Bodkin, T., *Twelve Irish Artists* (Dublin 1940); Lavery, Sir John, *The Life of a Painter* (London 1940); Elmes, R. M., *Catalogue of Irish Topographical Prints and Original Drawings* (Dublin 1943); Conor, W., *The Irish Scene* (Belfast 1944); MacGreevy, T., *Jack B. Yeats: An Appreciation and an Interpretation* (Dublin 1945); Henry, P., *An Irish Portrait* (London 1951); Kernoff, H., *Woodcuts* (Dublin 1951); O'Brien, D., *Miniatures of the 18th and 19th Centuries* (London 1951).

Liam S. Gogan,
Keeper of Art and Industrial Division, former Deputy Keeper of Irish Antiquities Division, National Museum of Ireland.

IRISH CHURCH HISTORY. The opening date in Irish ecclesiastical history is 431, when Palladius was sent by Pope Celestine I "as their first bishop to the Irish who believed in Christ." By that time the conversion of Gaul was complete and the conversion of Britain far advanced, so that the extension of the Christian faith to Ireland was to be expected. Palladius was not the person through whom this work was destined to be accomplished. It is likely that he died before this task was well begun, for the traditional date of the coming of his successor to Ireland is 432. This Patricius (Patrick) was a Briton of respectable ancestry who had been taken prisoner by Irish raiders at the age of 16 and sold as a slave to a master in County Antrim. After six years he had managed to escape. Soon he felt within himself the stirrings of a missionary vocation. He studied in Gaul as well as in his native Britain, was possibly for a time a monk at Lerins, in the Mediterranean near Cannes, was certainly a cleric attached to some church like Auxerre before the "desire of his soul" could be realized, and he set foot in Ireland at the head of a band of British and Gallic missionaries.

St. Patrick found Ireland almost wholly a pagan country; he left it at his death predominantly a Christian land. This is the evidence of the *Confession*, a short spiritual autobiography penned by him in the evening of his days. It is the evidence also of Irish records. which begin to take reliable shape precisely at this period. St. Patrick is thus the Apostle of Ireland, and has been honored as such with a devotion for which there are few parallels from the middle of the 5th century down to the present time.

It is obvious that the Apostle would seek to reproduce in Ireland the church organization which he knew so well in Britain and Gaul. In the way of this, however, there were obstacles which it was difficult to overcome. Chief among these was the lack of cities; of places, in other words, where episcopal sees would normally be fixed. Some deviation from the Continental model thus became inevitable. Another peculiarity, which began to appear in St. Patrick's lifetime and gathered momentum, in extraordinary fashion, about the year 520, was the popularity of the monastic ideal. Before the 6th century ended Ireland was dotted with monasteries and smaller religious houses. Most of these were ruled by abbots, who were priests, not bishops. The result was an increase in the prestige of the abbatial position to a point far beyond what St. Patrick had ever foreseen. Abbots came to represent the highest power in the ecclesiastical order, though never equated in dignity with bishops, who in "honour-price" continued to rank with kings.

Saints and Scholars.—The Golden Age of the Irish Church—relatively short, as all periods of unwonted prosperity are wont to be—may be placed within the years 620–740. High idealism and strict observance within the monasteries resulted in profound peace. The monks held themselves aloof, with astonishing success, from the ambitions, jealousies, and quarrels of the secular states. To outside observers Ireland looked an *Insula Sanctorum*—Island of Saints. Thanks again to the ancient Celtic heritage of education, it was taken for granted that the monks should be no less learned than the poets, brehons, and chroniclers of native tradition. Hence every monastery had its school. Classical literature was introduced and cultivated. The works of the fathers and writers of the church were studied. Irish *literati* became skilled in the writing of Latin prose and verse. Thus the *Insula Sanctorum* became at the same time an *Insula Doctorum*—Island of Scholars.

Missionary Efforts.—Before the 7th century ended the monks had begun to carry Irish sanctity and Irish scholarship abroad. St. Columba (Columcille) of Derry settled in Iona in 563, and from that conveniently situated missionary center sent heralds of the Christian faith to the greater part of what is now Scotland. The Irish mold given to the Scottish Church was retained to the 12th century. In 635 missionaries were sent from Iona to Northumbria, where their work was remarkably successful. Irish missionaries labored, too, in East Anglia, Mercia, and even in Wessex, so that their share in the conversion of England to Christianity is very considerable. Owing to disputes about the paschal date, the close connection between Iona and Northumbria was broken in 664, but Irish influence continued, especially in the monasteries, where the alliance between asceticism and learning was maintained. Beyond the English Channel, in Continental Europe, St. Columban of Luxeuil was a zealous reformer as well as an enthusiastic monk. To the impulse given by his three original foundations in Burgundy, about 50 monasteries in the Frankish kingdom traced their origin. He was famous also as a preacher of penance. His last foundation was at Bobbio, in northern Italy, a monastery that was to rank as a leading center of culture in Europe in the early Middle Ages. Irish saints and missionaries were to be found also in the eastern Frankish empire. St. Kilian (Cillian) was martyred at Würzburg; and St. Vergil of Salzburg (died 784), active as an abbot, bishop, and evangelist, was yet more renowned as a scholar. We know that he taught the sphericity of the earth and the existence of antipodes. In the 9th century, when the great tide of religious fervor was on the ebb, Ireland was still sending forth teachers to the Continent. Two of these, Sedulius the Irishman (Scottus) and John the Irishman (Johannes Scottus or Scotus, or Eriugena) have left names of distinction, the former as a poet and grammarian, the latter as a Neo-Platonist philosopher and theologian.

Church Decline and Revival.—About the middle of the 8th century monastic Ireland entered on a period of decline. The movement was accentuated by the confusion due to chronic raids (795–837), followed by more sustained attacks and partial settlement on the coast (Dublin, Waterford; and Limerick, in the Shannon estuary) on the part of the Northmen. These singled out monasteries and churches for destruction, in the first place because they were pagans, hostile to Christianity, in the second place because they were freebooters, who found the monasteries rich in artistic and other treasure. As the monasteries were also unprotected, they were easy and rewarding to despoil. The simple fact is that the chief occupations of the Norse during two centuries were robbery, arson, and murder. It is obvious that the losses, religious, cultural, moral, caused directly by them were immense; what cannot definitely be assessed is the indirect damage, due to the impossibility of normal progress, in the three spheres just mentioned, which their presence in the country occasioned. Unfavorable conditions in Rome and in the church generally at this time must also be taken into account. In Ireland, as elsewhere, the encroachment of the secular princes steadily increased. Armagh itself, the primatial see, fell into the hands of a local sept, and was ruled by members of it who did not trouble to receive ecclesiastical orders from 957 to 1105. The enslavement of the church was complete.

Hardly had Hildebrand, the energetic Pope St. Gregory VII, died, when the reaction which he sponsored spread to Ireland. By the end of the 11th century it had gathered strength. Another 50 years, and reform on the widest scale was an accomplished fact. Important dates are 1101, when Cashel, the old capital of Munster, was bestowed as a gift upon the church and soon afterwards constituted a metropolitan see; 1106, when the Abbot of Armagh was consecrated bishop and the usurpation by laymen ended; 1111, when a synod held at Rathbresail, under the presidency of a papal legate, divided the country into territorial dioceses ruled by bishops; and 1152, when a synod at Kells, presided over by a cardinal sent for the purpose from Rome, completed the work of reorganization, so that it has never since required substantial alteration. Meanwhile, in 1148, the most distinguished of the reforming prelates, St. Malachy of Armagh, had died at Clairvaux. The old Irish monasteries, with their lands, had become the hereditary possession of lay lords to an extent that made their return to their original status impracticable. They were therefore abandoned and a new monastic system, that of the Cistercians, similar to theirs in spirit, was introduced in their stead.

Assimilation of the Normans.—The Anglo-Normans invaded Ireland in 1169, and after 80 years of constant fighting they were masters of about two thirds of the country. Early in the 14th century the tide had turned and the Irish princes were winning back more and more of their ancestral lands. In the course of time the Norman lords became largely assimilated, so that it could be said of them that they were *Hibernicis ipsis Hiberniores*—more Irish than the Irish themselves. As there was no difference in faith between the Irish and the Normans, the problems which the church had to face were purely political. In general, the clergy of the two races may be said to have gone their separate ways. The great medieval religious orders flourished—Cistercians, Premonstratensians, Canons Regular, Knights Hospitaller of St. John of Jerusalem, Trinitarians, Franciscans, Dominicans, Carmelites, Hermits of St. Augustine, and Canonesses of St. Augustine. Where the writ of the English king ran he tried to control appointments to bishoprics. Attempts to exclude the members of one race from entering a community predominantly of the other race were condemned as unchristian by the popes. It is remarkable that throughout the whole medieval period no university was founded in Ireland: those who wished to secure an intellectual information of superior quality had to go abroad to find it.

Reformation Era.—When Henry VII mounted the throne of England in 1485 the power of the crown in Ireland was almost nominal. In the course of the half century that followed it became very real. Thus when Henry VIII declared himself supreme head of the church in his realms in 1534, the repercussions in Ireland were immediate. An archbishop who would carry out every royal wish was appointed to the see of Dublin by the king. All religious houses were suppressed. There was not, for the time being, any serious opposition: the local lords were ready to share in the monastic plunder; the prelates were induced to strain their consciences rather than die in what they took to be a passing quarrel; the mass of the people were bewildered and but dimly aware of the issue. The scene was transformed, however, under Edward VI, when the First Book of Common Prayer was introduced. No ability or violence on the part of the king's deputy and servants could get this Protestant liturgy accepted. Hence Queen Mary Tudor found no Protestants in Ireland to persecute. Her successor, Queen Elizabeth, again renounced the jurisdiction of the pope in matters spiritual, reintroduced the Book of Common Prayer, abolished the Mass, enjoined attendance at Protestant worship on Sundays and holy days under penalty of fine. For a decade or so after her accession the law last mentioned was but sporadically enforced.

With the excommunication of Elizabeth by Pope Pius V in 1570 quasi toleration ceased. The religious situation in Ireland was now abundantly clear: on the one side was the bulk of the Irish nation—Gaelic, Norman, settlers of English race and tongue in the medieval towns—immovable in loyalty to the inherited Catholic faith; on the other side was the governmental group, in number a small minority but possessed of the whole machinery of state and determined to use it to make Protestantism the sole religion of the country. In the revolts of the next 30 years, that of Lord Baltinglas in Wicklow, that of the Desmonds in Munster, that of O'Neill and O'Donnell which spread to all Ireland, religion was never the sole but it was always a primary issue.

A peaceful solution was not found. The might of arms, confirmed by the victory at Kinsale (1601), enabled the English deputy and officials to take over the churches, cathedrals, ecclesiastical property of all kinds, and bestow them on their own nominees, who thus became in Ireland the counterpart and the projection of the Protestant Established Church in England. A university, exclusively Protestant in its constitution, was founded in Dublin by Queen Elizabeth in 1591. Into this church, however, and its university, the people refused to come. Appointments to the various sees were made by the popes, as formerly; and Catholic clergy, whatever the obstacles, continued to minister to their flocks. When persecution became active they went underground; when persecution relaxed they built modest chapels in laneways and remote places. To solve the problem of education, colleges for Irish students were opened abroad, at Salamanca, Louvain, Antwerp, Bordeaux, Compostella, Lisbon, and Rome.

Confederation of Kilkenny.—With the accession of Charles I came a small measure of relief. The king, refused supplies by his Parliament, was prepared to sell some concessions or "Graces" to the Irish Catholics for money. But persecution was soon renewed and was continued under Strafford. Growing discontent led to open revolt among the Catholics of Ireland in 1641. By the summer of 1642 the insurgents, who had set up legislative and executive machinery (the Confederation of Kilkenny) held the whole country with the exception of a few of the larger towns. Soon afterwards Charles I and his Parliament were at war. The Confederation was quite ready to lend aid to the king on the two conditions of complete religious toleration and a free and independent Irish Parliament. Pope Innocent X sent a nuncio, Rinuccini, archbishop of Fermo, to be his representative with the Confederation. Negotiations with the king and with his deputy in Ireland brought disunity into the Confederate councils, and the insurrection was already a failure when Charles I was beheaded and Rinuccini left Ireland for Italy. A month later (March 1649), Oliver Cromwell arrived in Dublin with a powerful Parliamentary army to begin a campaign that was to result in the annihilation of Irish resistance.

Protestant Ascendancy.—For the defeated Catholics there was no mercy. The "Cromwellian settlement" deprived them of all their lands in three out of the four provinces. Any men of mark whose lives were spared were ordered to transport themselves to Connacht, the poor province between the Shannon and the Atlantic seaboard. Soldiers and adventurers from England were settled on the confiscated lands. All Catholics were expelled from the towns and their places taken by Protestant burghers. In the sequel, the planters remained a relatively small minority but they possessed nearly all the good land, and with it the wealth of the nation, while the Catholics, despite predominance in numbers, were treated as an inferior class, tolerated only because they could serve the new owners.

Even after the Restoration of Charles II

(1660), the position of the Catholics in Ireland improved but little. Very few of those who had suffered for Charles I recovered their property. The Catholic population generally was miserably poor; priests were fined, imprisoned, and persecuted. Towards the end of the reign the "Popish Plot," invented by Titus Oates, brought about the imprisonment of many Catholic bishops and the hanging at Tyburn, London, on the evidence of perjured informers, of the primate and archbishop of Armagh, Oliver Plunkett (1681).

James II sought to place Catholics and Protestants on an equal footing, as well in Ireland as in Britain. When James lost the throne of Britain he found support in Ireland, where he landed in March 1689. A parliament, summoned by him to meet in Dublin, enacted that there should be complete religious toleration. The campaign which followed ended in his defeat and in the Treaty of Limerick (October 1691), one article of which guaranteed to the Catholics of Ireland such privileges "as they did enjoy in the reign of King Charles II." But this article was destined to remain a dead letter.

Penal Laws.—The 18th century, for the Catholics of Ireland, was the period of the Penal Laws. Catholics were excluded from the professions and from the more lucrative forms of trade; they could not become magistrates nor grand jurors, nor members of a town corporation. All ecclesiastical dignitaries were ordered to leave the country. Catholics were not allowed to have schools; and if educated abroad and ordained priests, were not permitted to return. After the death of George I (1727) these laws were less rigidly enforced. During the reign of George II it became clear that the Catholic Church could not be eliminated, and a mild movement for the repeal of the Penal Laws could be initiated (The Catholic Committee, 1757). Relaxations began in 1771, and Catholic relief bills were passed in 1778, 1782, 1792, and 1793.

Emancipation.—Before the Act of Union (of the kingdoms of Great Britain and Ireland) was passed in 1800, William Pitt, the English prime minister, let it be understood that the Catholics would be freed from their disabilities before the law, virtually at once. But King George III was so violently opposed to the suggestion that nothing could be done. The question was revived in 1805. Soon afterwards the Catholics of Ireland received a new and eminently capable leader in the person of Daniel O'Connell. Against the proposal that in reward for the granting of emancipation the British government should have a veto on the appointment of Irish Catholic bishops he set his face resolutely. When Catholic Emancipation was finally granted by the Duke of Wellington's government in 1829, its value was not diminished by any such condition. After 1829 Catholics in Ireland were free in legal theory; but their social status was still low, their proportion of the national wealth negligible, their educational facilities meager, their general condition backward and condemned to remain so for decades to come.

Protestantism Divided.—While the clergy and laity of native Irish race, the Anglo-Normans, and the old English merchants of the towns refused to accept the supremacy in matters spiritual of the English sovereigns, and the doctrines of the Reformers, the contrary was true of the officials and other new settlers of English race, and of some of the highly Anglicized families in Dublin and its neighborhood. Protestantism in Ireland at the death of Queen Elizabeth was represented by this small group. Hugh O'Neill, earl of Tyrone, and Rory O'Donnell, earl of Tyrconnell (Tyrconnel), harassed beyond endurance by the Dublin government, fled to the Continent in 1607. They were immediately proclaimed outlaws, and their patrimony, with that of all their followers, was declared forfeit to the crown. Thus immense tracts of land, including almost all of the counties of Donegal, Derry, Tyrone, Fermanagh, Cavan, and Armagh, were at the disposal of King James; Antrim and Down were afterwards added. James I proceeded to plant all these lands with English and Scottish settlers. This policy was carried into effect. Among the colonists the Scots were more numerous than the English. Though the teaching in Trinity College, Dublin, from its foundation, had been Calvinistic in tone, and the Established (state-supported) Church in Ireland was far more Calvinistic in spirit than its counterpart in England, the English and Scottish colonists failed to agree, so that Protestantism in Ireland faced the future in two divisions—Protestants with episcopacy and Protestants without episcopacy (Presbyterians).

The Irish insurrection of 1641 brought heavy losses to the Protestant Episcopal Church. Cromwell's settlement favored the Puritans, who were the predominant element in the new class of landowners. Charles II did something to restore the balance; the Protestant Episcopal Church was again established and richly endowed, but "Acts of Uniformity" failed to compel the Presbyterians to accept its system. They went their own way as Nonconformists (dissenters).

Once James II had been defeated, the Protestant Episcopal Church was restored by William and Mary to its position of pre-eminence. All the lords and commoners who increased the severity of the Penal Code belonged to it. Hence not only the Catholics, who formed four fifths of the population, were penalized, but also Presbyterians, who refused to receive the Sacrament according to the usage of the Established Church, were disqualified from holding positions of honor and trust under the crown. George Berkeley and Jonathan Swift are the two prelates of greatest distinction during the 18th century. At the union of the kingdoms in 1800 the Established Church of Ireland was united with that of England.

Disestablishment.—After emancipation, the Protestant Episcopal Church continued to levy tithes on an extensive scale for its own upkeep from Protestants and Catholics alike. The impost was naturally resented by the Catholics and led to conflicts called the "tithe war." A solution that proved to be satisfactory was found in 1838. Meanwhile the anomalous position of the Established Church in Ireland had been brought to the notice of the Parliament in Westminster. No steps were then taken; but the census of 1861, which showed that the number of Catholics in Ireland was 4,505,265, while Protestant Episcopalians numbered 693,357, Presbyterians 523,291, Methodists and other dissenters 76,661, opened the way to an unanswerable claim for disestablishment (severance of the relationship to the state). This was carried through by Gladstone in 1869. By the Irish Church Act of that year the Protestant Episcopal Church of Ireland was disestablished and disendowed, but given at the same time complete freedom to provide for its own future and liberally compensated for the pecuniary losses which the change involved. Legislative and administrative power resides since 1870 in a general synod consisting of the two archbishops and 12 bishops, and a house of representatives elected from the clergy and the laity. In the six counties of Northern Ireland still attached to Britain, the Protestant Episcopal Church continues to exert great influence. In the 26 counties, which in 1921 became Saorstat Eireann (the Irish Free State), and in 1949 the Republic of Ireland, it retains its university (Trinity College) and its two cathedrals in Dublin; it is also facilitated by the Ministry of Education, and is protected by express "recognition" in the constitution.

The affairs of the Presbyterian Church are regulated by a general assembly, presided over by a moderator who is elected annually. It has (1951) 580 ministers, 567 congregations, and 510 manses. Like the Protestant Episcopal Church, the Methodists, the Society of Friends, and the Jews, it is recognized as a religious body that merits protection in the constitution of the Republic of Ireland.

Constitutional Status of Catholic Church.—In that constitution the Roman Catholic Church receives special recognition "as a guardian of the Faith professed by the great majority of the citizens." It is governed, under the pope, by four archbishops (one of whom, the archbishop of Armagh, primate of all Ireland, is generally a cardinal) and 23 bishops. A central theological university (St. Patrick's College, Maynooth) and the three colleges of the National University of Ireland (founded 1910) at Dublin, Cork, and Galway, supply its needs in the sphere of higher education. Its missionary activity in lands of English tongue and, more recently, in Africa and the East, is very extensive.

In the Republic of Ireland, statistics give (1951) 2,786,033 Catholics (94.3 per cent); 124,829 Protestant Episcopalians; 23,870 Presbyterians, 8,355 Methodists, and 3,907 Jews. In the six counties of Northern Ireland there are 428,290 Catholics (33.5 per cent), 390,931 Presbyterians, 345,474 Protestant Episcopalians, and 55,135 Methodists.

See also IRISH SCHOOLS AND SCHOOLMEN OF THE MIDDLE AGES.

Bibliography.—Bury, J. B., *Life of St. Patrick* (London 1905); Kenney, J. F., *The Sources for the Early History of Ireland* (New York 1929); Ronan, M., *The Reformation in Dublin* (London 1930); Ryan, J., *Irish Monasticism* (Dublin 1931); Gougaud, L., *Christianity in Celtic Lands* (London 1932); Henry, F., *La Sculpture Irlandaise, pendant les douze premiers siècles de l'ère chrétien* (Paris 1933); Phillips, W. Alison, *History of the Church of Ireland* (Oxford 1933); Edwards, R. D., *Church and State in Tudor Ireland* (London 1935); Gwynn, A., *The Medieval Province of Armagh* (Dundalk 1946).

JOHN RYAN, S.J.

IRISH DRAMA. See IRISH LITERARY REVIVAL; IRISH LITERATURE IN THE ENGLISH LANGUAGE.

IRISH ELK. See FALLOW DEER.

IRISH FREE STATE. See IRELAND, REPUBLIC OF—*History*.

IRISH LANGUAGE. See CELTIC LANGUAGES; GAELIC LITERATURE.

IRISH LITERARY REVIVAL is the name customarily used to denote the literary activity in Ireland during the first half of the 20th century. Sometimes it is spoken of as the Celtic renaissance, a wider and looser term.

Background and Beginnings.—The Irish literary revival took place during the life span of William Butler Yeats (1865–1939), the Irish poet, and it would not be completely untrue to say that his work constituted most of what is spoken of as the Irish literary revival. The reasons for a renaissance taking place at one particular time more than at any other are rarely valid, because this presupposes that every renaissance must have a precise and scientific explanation. What really seemed to have happened at the time of the Irish literary rebirth was that Ireland, during a period of utter despair, suddenly found herself with an important poet in the family. The betrayal of Charles Stewart Parnell (q.v.), the uncrowned king of Ireland, crushed Ireland politically, and for the moment it seemed as if there was nothing Irishmen could do except look into their own hearts. For about 10 years after the death of Parnell in 1891 there was a lull in Irish politics, and it so happened that Yeats, a major poet, was beginning his career at this time and was able to take advantage of the silence to lay the foundation for his work later on. Without Yeats there would have been no literary revival. It is just that simple; but there were situations and influences, both political and emotional, which helped him in his work, and those are things that may be explained logically. To understand their significance, however, it is necessary to know something of the background of Irish literary and political history.

Since about 1170, the year the Anglo-Normans invaded Ireland, the population of the country has been divided into two classes: those who speak English and those who speak Gaelic. The English speakers became the ruling class and are referred to as the Anglo-Irish. England was generally regarded by the Anglo-Irish as the mother country and, to them, English literature was the only literature. It was to this class that George Farquhar, Oliver Goldsmith, Richard Brinsley Sheridan, Jonathan Swift, Oscar Wilde, and others belonged. The Gaelic speakers, though a majority, were regarded by the Anglo-Irish as mere natives, and although they produced a considerable literature in the Gaelic language, it remained virtually unknown to the Anglo-Irish until the middle of the 19th century. The Anglo-Irish writers were content to write in the English tradition because they were not aware of any other one in which they could write. The result was that though they did very fine work, there is little about it that can be considered distinctively Irish. Whether or not this was a defect is a question that does not concern us here; but there is no denial that their work was good, despite what some consider its un-Irish flavor.

Discovery of the Gaelic Tradition.—During the early years of the 19th century, hints that there was a Gaelic tradition began to filter into Anglo-Irish writing, and Thomas Moore's *Irish Melodies* (1804–1834), though written for an English public, were perhaps the first revelation of a distinctly Irish spirit in Anglo-Irish writing. Jeremiah Callanan (1795–1829) also caught something of the Irish spirit, and his verse shows the influence of the cadences of Gaelic versification. Neither Moore nor Callanan, however, was completely aware of the Gaelic tradition.

Towards the middle of the century a few curious professors discovered Gaelic literature and undertook to translate many of the Gaelic sagas as a kind of scholarly exercise. In 1840, for instance, the Irish Archaeological Society was founded for the purpose of preserving Gaelic manuscripts and for their translation into English. The interest shown in Gaelic Ireland by this society was purely academic; its patrons were mostly members of the British aristocracy, and had they been able to foresee that their society was laying the foundations of what has since been regarded as a nationalistic literature, it is doubtful that they would have continued with their work. Other societies were formed later: the Celtic Society in 1845 and the Ossianic Society in 1853. These societies did good work and gave employment to at least three important scholars, John O'Donovan (1809–1861), Eugene O'Curry (1796–1862), and Standish Hayes O'Grady (1832–1915). These scholars translated most of the ancient Irish sagas and poems and published the result of their work in the journals of the societies. Many German scholars joined in the philological aspect of the work, the most notable being Johann Kaspar Zeuss, Rudolf Thurneysen, and Kuno Meyer. In 1853 Zeuss published a Gaelic grammar, *Grammatica Celtica.*

Men of creative genius such as James Clarence Mangan (1803–1849), Sir Samuel Ferguson (1810–1886), and Standish O'Grady (1846–1928) were excited by the discoveries of the scholars, they having been educated to believe that there was no literature outside of English literature. Immediately they began to rewrite the stories and poems of Gaelic Ireland in romantic fashion. Mangan and Ferguson were interested mostly in the poems, and some of their interpretive translations are among the finest poems in Anglo-Irish literature. Thomas Osborne Davis, Charles Gavan Duffy, John Mitchel, and a few other nationalistic politicians and journalists saw in the discoveries something they could use to further their political cause, and they wrote about it in their newspapers and preached it from their platforms.

But it was Standish O'Grady's translations of the sagas and his *History of Ireland* (1878) that had the greatest influence. O'Grady, believing in the sacredness of ancient tradition, saw that it would be disastrous to allow Ireland's past to be hidden away in scholarly publications. He decided to rewrite the stories in popular fashion. This he did brilliantly, not only in his *History of Ireland,* but also in *Cuculain and His Contemporaries* (1880) and other books.

Influence of Yeats.—All this happened at a peculiarly fortunate moment. Victorian literature was running its course, was becoming cliché and barren, and the Anglo-Irish writers were delightfully shocked when they found a new well of inspiration in Gaelic tradition. It was at this precise moment that Yeats was born. Yeats belonged to the Anglo-Irish class, and consequently did not understand a word of the Gaelic language. But his imagination was fired by O'Grady's translations, and on many occasions he acknowledged his indebtedness to him. George Russell (AE), in an introduction to the works of O'Grady (Dublin 1919), spoke not only for himself but for all the writers of the Irish literary revival when he wrote:

> When I close my eyes and brood in memory over the books which most profoundly affected me I find none excited my imagination more than Standish O'Grady's epical narrative of *Cuculain* . . . With reference to Ireland, I was, at the time I read, like many others who were bereaved of the history of their race. I was a man who, through some accident, had lost his memory of his past, who could recall no more than a few months of a new life, and could not say to what songs his cradle had been rocked and what mother had nursed him, who were the playmates of childhood, or by what woods and streams he had wandered. When I read O'Grady I was as such a man who suddenly feels ancient memories rushing at him, and who knows he was born in a royal house, that he had mixed with the mighty of heaven and had the very noblest for his companions. It was the memory of race which rose up within me as I read, and I felt excited as one who learns he is among the children of kings. That is what O'Grady did for me and for many who were my contemporaries. . . . In O'Grady's writings the submerged river of national culture rose up again a shining torrent, and I realised as I bathed in that stream that the greatest evil one nation could inflict on another was to cut off from it the story of the national soul.

Having made this great discovery, Anglo-Irish writers were fired with interest in Irish literature and in the spirit that pervaded it. Many looked for guidance as to how they might make the best use of their discovery, and Yeats was fortunately there to direct the form it should take. Yeats perceived that Gaelic-speaking Ireland rarely read anything, but was always willing to listen, whether it be to a political speech or to a sermon. From his awareness of this fact rose the idea of founding a theater which would be truly representative of the real Ireland so ignored by his class. He would establish a poetic theater.

Having decided that a theater was what was needed, Yeats set about preparing the country for it. He felt that the Irish mind was too long enslaved and that a literary revival would not be possible until national pride was reawakened in the Irish people. He at once became a vigorous nationalist and developed a deep personal regard for John O'Leary, the Fenian leader. He also met Maud Gonne, a violent nationalist, fell in love with her, and for her wrote *The Countess Cathleen* (1892).

Literary Societies.—It seemed to Yeats that Ireland was not quite ready to receive him, so he moved to London, where he drifted for a time into the circle of the Aesthetes. O'Leary and his other friends, fearing that he was in danger of selling his soul for an empty aestheticism, begged him to return. He did not do so immediately, and in 1891, with two other Anglo-Irish writers, Thomas William Rolleston and John Todhunter, founded the Irish Literary Society in London. This society attracted to it most of the other Anglo-Irish writers who were living in London, including Katharine Tynan, Alice Milligan, William Larminie, and Stopford Brooke. All of these writers were extremely minor, but they were almost carried into significance by the influence of Yeats and the romanticism created by O'Grady and the rest. In the same year Yeats went over to Dublin and established there a similar society, The National Literary Society. John O'Leary was its first president, and its members included Douglas Hyde, George Sigerson, and Standish O'Grady.

Gaelic League.—The purpose of these societies was to give an opportunity to a new generation of critics and writers to denounce the propagandist verse and prose that had gone by the name of Irish literature and to substitute for it certain neglected Irish writers such as Sir Samuel Ferguson. Standish O'Grady, and James Clarence

Mangan. The society had no political affiliations. From this society sprang the Gaelic League, founded in 1894 by Douglas Hyde (q.v.). Hyde's idea was to revive the Gaelic language, which was then dying, as the spoken language of the whole country. Yeats did not think it worth his own while to learn the Gaelic language, but he supported the Gaelic League (before it became a propaganda machine) because he considered it an effective means of awakening the Irish people to a consciousness of their history and tradition. Douglas Hyde, though mostly a pamphleteer in favor of the Gaelic language, did some writing that had a significance for the Irish literary revival. His *Love Songs of Connacht* (1894), translations from the Gaelic, helped to set the mood for writers of the revival movement. His *Literary History of Ireland* (1899) was also a valuable contribution.

Irish Literary Theatre.—The literary societies of London and Dublin created an audience for Yeats and his ideas. In 1889 Yeats published *The Wanderings of Oisin,* and during the 1890's he was writing the lyrics which formed the volume, *The Wind Among the Reeds.* In 1893 he published a collection of fairy lore which he entitled *The Celtic Twilight.* The following year he had his poetic play, *The Land of Heart's Desire,* produced in London.

But despite his success in London, Yeats could see that only in Ireland could he do the things he wished to accomplish; so, with the help of George Moore, the novelist, and Edward Martyn, a wealthy Irish landlord and minor playwright, he went to Dublin and produced his own play, *The Countess Cathleen* and Martyn's *The Heather Field* at the Antient Concert Rooms in 1899. To Yeats' amazement his play was received with boos and hoots because some saw in it a theological heresy. When he recovered from the surprise, Yeats accepted the insults as the traditional greetings for a messiah, and, from then on, always treated the mob, whether it be English, Irish, or American, with violent disdain.

He named his dramatic company The Irish Literary Theatre, and was back in Dublin the following year with another series of plays. After producing the third series of plays in Dublin, in 1901, he rid himself of George Moore and Edward Martyn and associated himself closely with Lady Augusta Gregory, a friend of his from Coole, in the west of Ireland. Yeats had not given up the idea of founding a poetic theater in Ireland, and in 1902 he had another play which he had written, *Cathleen Ni Houlihan,* produced by a group of actors led by the Fay brothers, Willie and Frank. He formed another society, the Irish Dramatic Company, consisting of himself, Lady Gregory, the Fay brothers, and John Millington Synge, an Irish writer whom he had discovered in a Paris garret. It was Yeats' ability to discover genius that made an Irish literary revival possible.

Synge and Lady Gregory.—When Synge returned from Paris, on Yeats' urging, he first went to live among the gypsies in Wicklow and, later, among the inhabitants of the Aran Islands, off the west coast of Ireland. The peasants on the Aran Islands spoke the Gaelic language but also knew a little English. Synge quickly absorbed the life of these primitive people and wrote plays about them. *Riders to the Sea* is a one-act tragedy about an island woman who has lost all her sons to the sea; while Irish, it has many of the elements of Greek tragedy. *In the Shadow of the Glen* was disliked because Synge tells of an unfaithful Irish wife. *The Playboy of the Western World* raised an even bigger storm. In this play Synge tells how the peasants in a village in the remote west of Ireland hide a young fellow (the Playboy), who claimed that he was fleeing from the police because he had killed his Da (father) with a blow of a loy (long, narrow spade). This was too much for an Irish patriotic audience, and they rioted at the first performance because they considered the play an insult to Irish character by suggesting that these peasants would condone a murder. This, they claimed, was not the kind of play that should be put on by a theater that claimed to be national. Yeats' policy, however, was not to give the public what they liked but rather what he thought was good for them, so he called in the police and continued the play under heavy guard. This was the final insult from the point of view of Irish patriots, and they avoided Yeats and his plays in the future. Yeats, however, had a decided plan of action and he carried on, despite all opposition, to give Ireland a literature worthy of her tradition. Synge died in 1909, his death being a great loss to the Irish literary revival.

Lady Gregory (1859–1932), too, began to write plays under Yeats' influence and direction. She is best known for her comedies, *Spreading the News, Hyacinth Halvey, The Rising of the Moon,* and many others. She also translated many plays from the French and was interested in the folklore of Ireland. Hence her books *Cuchulain of Muirthemne* (1902), *Poets and Dreamers* (1903), *Gods and Fighting Men* (1904), *A Book of Saints and Wonders* (1906). Lady Gregory wrote her plays in dialect, and the language of the Irish literary revival is sometimes referred to as the Kiltartan dialect, a name taken from the parish where Lady Gregory lived.

Abbey Theatre.—In 1904 Miss Annie Elizabeth Fredricka Horniman, a wealthy English lady, presented Yeats with a small theater in Abbey Street, Dublin, named the Abbey Theatre. From 1904 onwards the Abbey Theatre was the center around which the literary revival in Ireland moved. Now that he had a theater of his own, Yeats put into effect his theories and ideals. First of all it would be a poetic theater where the imaginative mind of Ireland would find expression. It was to be a place almost as sacred as a church, and those who come there must not expect vulgar entertainment but must come rather to listen to a poet explain his vision. Above all, there was to be no place in it for politics, because politics presuppose defense and argument, and a continual apology makes the mind barren and kills intellectual innocence. He wanted the plays performed there to be literature and to have style. Furthermore, the English language, according to Yeats, had worn itself out during Victorian times, and his theater needed a language that was fresh. The Gaelic language would be acceptable, but none of the literary revivalists knew that language. The language Yeats finally adopted was the dialect of English spoken by the peasants from the west of Ireland. Although these peasants spoke English, they thought first in Gaelic, and the result was a fresh and unspoiled language with personality. This is the language used in the plays of Synge and Lady Gregory. As found in the plays, it is not completely authentic, but it has a quaint, unreal, dreamy flavor; hence the slightly derogatory term sometimes applied to this movement—the Celtic mist.

Yeats also had fixed principles on acting, which was to be statuesque and unobtrusive—as fitting for a drama which was to be poetic and ritualistic. Yeats disliked a large audience in his theater, and the plays frequently infuriated those who came, especially when it was thought that the ideas expressed ran counter to popular national sentiment. Sometimes it appeared to the politicians that Yeats was an enemy of Ireland, but he refused to be dictated to and followed his own ideals to the end. The result of this policy was that he established a literature of the highest integrity and which expressed the Irish spirit and tradition.

Sean O'Casey.—Yeats discovered not only Synge but also another major dramatist—Sean O'Casey. O'Casey was born in the poverty-stricken slums of Dublin. He received little formal education, but he read widely and attended the Abbey Theatre whenever he could afford the entrance price of sixpence. He submitted a play to the Abbey, but it was rejected with some encouraging remarks. The next play he sent in, *The Shadow of a Gunman* (1923), was accepted and was an immediate success. Like all his early plays, this one was centered around the Dublin slum-dwellers. It is realistic, but is lifted to an imaginative level; it is also extremely amusing. Then followed his greatest play, *Juno and the Paycock* (1924), also about life in the slums of Dublin. The characterization is brilliant. Lady Gregory said that the play reminded her of Tolstoy, and other critics have described it as the greatest play since *Hamlet*. O'Casey's next play, *The Plough and the Stars* (1926), caused a riot in the theater because some oversensitive patriots thought it an attack on Irishmen who fought during the Easter Rising of 1916. The dialogue in these early plays by O'Casey is the most authentic Irish dialect of all the plays of the Irish literary revival. Shortly after the production of *The Plough and the Stars* O'Casey went to live in London, and though he subsequently wrote many plays they can hardly be said to belong in spirit to the Irish revival.

Other Dramatists.—Yeats was also responsible for the discovery of many other dramatists, of whom Lennox Robinson and T. C. Murray are the most important. Murray is best known for his plays *Birthright* (1910) and *Maurice Harte* (1912), which treated of Irish peasant life in a lyrical fashion. Robinson wrote many plays, but is best known for *The Far-off Hills* (1928), *Drama at Innis* (1933), and *Church Street* (1934). Robinson wrote realistically of the broken-down Anglo-Irish aristocracy. Other plays worth mentioning as belonging to this period would be St. John Ervine's *Mixed Marriage* (1910), and Paul Vincent Carroll's *Shadow and Substance* (1937). This play by Carroll was the last play of any consequence performed at the Abbey Theatre before the death of Yeats and the ultimate collapse of the Abbey as a theater of integrity.

Yeats the Poet.—Yeats was not a great dramatist and, though he wrote plays that were memorable, he will be remembered primarily as a poet. His early verse is strongly influenced in subject by pre-Christian Ireland and in form by the aesthetic and symbolistic movements in England and France. This is especially true of his early collection of poems, *Poems* (1895), and *Wind Among the Reeds* (1899). In his later verse he outgrew his "Celtic twilight" mood as in *The Wild Swans at Coole* (1917); there we find him stretching for a more eternal subject. *The Tower* (1927) and *The Winding Stair* (1929) contain much of his best and most vigorous poetry. Yeats also wrote *The Celtic Twilight* (1893), a collection of folk stories.

George Bernard Shaw.—While Yeats was carrying on a literary revival in Ireland, Bernard Shaw (1856–1950) was engaged on one of his own in England. Although he did not write in the "Celtic twilight" tradition, he undoubtedly must be regarded as a major figure in the Irish literary revival. He was an intellectual as opposed to an imaginative writer, and his clear views and pungent satire acted as an antidote to those writers who frequently drifted out of the Celtic mist into a Celtic fog. He was born in Dublin, and all through his life that city remained his emotional home. He was employed as a clerk in a realtor's office for a short while, but retired from it and went to London to make his way as a writer. His early years in London were difficult, and although he wrote five novels he could not find a publisher for them. He was a successful music critic for a while. Then he became interested in play writing and discovered there one of his greatest talents. For over 50 years thereafter he wrote plays of all types—histories, comedies, sketches, farces. He ignored conventional plots, and many of his plays might be described as brilliant conversational pieces. Some of his best known plays are: *Candida* (1895), *John Bull's Other Island* (1904), *The Doctor's Dilemma* (1906), *Pygmalion* (1912), *Saint Joan* (1923), the last considered by many to be his best play. A large number of his plays were produced at the Abbey Theatre in Dublin despite the fact that Yeats disliked plays that were not founded on a poetic idea. Shaw wrote brilliantly on every topic, and was an entire Irish literary revival in himself.

George W. Russell and Others.—Even in Ireland, Yeats was not the only influence though he was by far the greatest. George W(illiam) Russell (1867–1935), better known as AE (AEon), though not a great poet, gathered around him many writers of talent. He was a mystic, economist, painter, and essayist as well as a poet. He was born in County Armagh but moved to Dublin at an early age, and was a student of the Metropolitan School of Art before he was 13 years old. There he met Yeats, and through him became interested in theosophy. His *Homeward: Songs by the Way* (1894) attracted wide attention. In 1897 he joined the Irish Agricultural Organization Society, and in 1906 became editor of *The Irish Homestead,* journal of that society; in 1923 *The Irish Homestead* amalgamated with *The Irish Statesman,* with Russell remaining as editor. *The Irish Statesman* was unique as a magazine in that it was read by intellectuals in most countries, as well as by Irish farmers. AE attracted to his magazine all the best writers, and all of them felt honored when their writings appeared in it. AE's home in the Dublin suburbs was the meeting place of most of the writers associated with the Irish literary revival.

AE had a religion all his own, which some wit described as AEtheism: it was a mixture of

Irish mythology and Hindu philosophy. He sought in the Irish mythology for hints of an ancestral lore identical with that of the Eastern sages. This mystical religion influenced his contemporaries, and contributed to the "Celtic mist." AE expounded his religious philosophy in *The Candle of Vision* (1918), and his political idealism in *The Interpreters* (1920). His collected poems were published in 1913, but he wrote much that was of interest later on, especially *The House of the Titans and Other Poems* (1934). Perhaps because he was a lesser genius than Yeats, he was easier to approach and therefore had a greater influence, more personal if less profound than Yeats'.

Minor writers of the movement who gathered under AE's cloak were, Alice Milligan, Eva Gore Booth, Padraic Colum, Ella Young, and Seumas O'Sullivan. Although these minor writers may have failed as poets of consequence, they served as a necessary backdrop for the literary revival. Of the minor writers, Francis Ledwidge (1891–1917), showed most promise, but his career was cut short when he was killed in action in Flanders; his two books of poems, *Songs of the Field* (1915) and *Songs of Peace* (1916), had a magic quality and in form were heavily influenced by the Gaelic poetic mode.

Before *The Irish Statesman* became defunct in 1930, AE introduced in its pages poets who, if they did not belong to the Irish literary revival proper, at least developed from that stream and initiated a secondary revival in Irish poetry and letters. Frank O'Connor (born in 1901), though now known only as a story-teller, began as a poet in *The Irish Statesman.* Frederick Robert Higgins (1896–1941) was another; he came from Meath, Ledwidge's county, and his verse has much in common with that of Ledwidge. He wrote of the fields in a lyrical fashion, but his verse lacks intensity and that inner sincerity which is essential to poetry. *Dark Breed* appeared in 1927, *Arable Holdings* in 1933, and *The Gap of Brightness* in 1940. Higgins was managing director of the Abbey Theatre for a while before he died.

Patrick Kavanagh (born in 1904) also began as a poet in *The Irish Statesman,* but after the death of AE he disentangled himself from those influences associated with it and wrote freshly and originally about the Irish countryside; of his books of verse, *A Soul for Sale* (1947) is the most significant. He is also the author of *The Green Fool* (1938), a prose work which is a mixture of autobiography and fiction. *Tarry Flynn* (1949) is a novel on the frustration in Irish country life; the romanticism of the Celtic twilight is cast aside for a less charming but more sincere approach.

Prose Writers.—Although poetry and drama predominated during the Irish literary revival, the prose writing of the period is also significant. The novelists, like the playwrights, broke away from the 19th-century tradition, which usually displayed the Irishman as a wild, screaming lunatic who carried a clay pipe in his hat and a shilellagh in his hand.

George Moore (1852–1933) was the most important prose writer of the early years of the movement. He was born in Mayo, but lived for many years in Paris and in London. He was deeply influenced by Gustave Flaubert and Honoré de Balzac, and is a brilliant stylist. He wrote many realistic novels, the most notable being *Esther Waters* (1894). He has been called the first realistic novelist since Daniel Defoe. In 1900 he assumed a nationalistic pose and returned to Ireland, but his nationalism was too flamboyantly insincere and only caused embarrassment to those supporting what they cryptically called "the cause" (meaning the cause for Irish political independence). Yeats described Moore as "preposterous and ungovernable." While in Ireland, Moore wrote a series of short stories of Irish life which were published under the title *The Untilled Field* (1903); they were translated into the Gaelic language also. Moore's greatest contribution to the Irish literary revival was his trilogy, *Ave* (1911), *Salve* (1912), and *Vale* (1914). These books give a fascinating and slightly comic account of the Irish literary revival and of all those associated with it; they are brilliantly satiric, and should be read by anyone interested in knowing more of the Irish literary activity. Moore was a mocker and a blasphemer, and he laughed to the very end. On his instructions, his body was cremated and the ashes deposited in a hole on the top of a mountain on his estate in the west of Ireland. AE preached a panygeric on that occasion in which he pointed out that Moore "loved the land if he did not love the nation."

James Stephens (1882–1950) began writing as a poet, but he suddenly achieved fame as a prose writer in 1912 with the publication of *The Crock of Gold.* This book is unique and difficult to label. It is a brilliant fantasy, resembles a novel in form, and has an Irish background; it has been universally recognized for a long time as a classic. Some of his other books of prose are *The Charwoman's Daughter* (1912) and *The Demi-Gods* (1914). It has been remarked that his prose is closer to poetry than much of his verse. John Millington Synge, the playwright, wrote two volumes of travel-sketches, *The Aran Islands* (1907) and *In Wicklow, West Kerry and Connemara* (1910) which are interesting for their style and for their description of Irish life. Edith Anna OEnone Somerville and Martin Ross (Violet Florence Martin) collaborated in a book entitled *Experiences of an Irish R.M.* (1899) which is considered by some to be very amusing.

Seumas O'Kelly wrote a number of plays, including the very sentimental *The Shuiler's Child* (1909), but his best work is the short story, *The Weaver's Grave* (1920), which describes the peculiar fear of the Irish peasant that he might, in error, be buried in someone else's grave. Daniel Corkery (born in 1878) wrote some good realistic, though quiet, stories of Irish country life, including *The Threshold of Quiet* (1917) and *The Wager and Other Short Stories* (1950); he is also the author of *The Hidden Ireland* (1925), a study of Gaelic Ireland in the 18th century. Lord Dunsany (born in 1878) is worth mentioning for his fantasies: *The Gods of Pegana* (1905), *Time and the Gods* (1906), *The Sword of Welleran* (1908), *Dreamer's Tales* (1910), and many others. His fantasies, however, lack the high imaginative qualities of those by James Stephens. Flann O'Brien (1911–) is the author of a notable fantasy, *At Swim-two-birds* (1939).

Joyce.—James Joyce (1882–1941), though he disavowed any connection with the Irish literary revival, is nevertheless generally regarded as a distinct part of it.

But I must not accounted be
One of that mumming company

he wrote of Yeats and the Abbey Theatre. He was born in Dublin and attended the Jesuit college of Clongowes Wood. In 1907 he published a little book of lyrics entitled *Chamber Music.* Seven years later *Dubliners,* a book of short stories about Dublin life, was published. It showed that its author had a sharp perception for the nuances of Dublin dialect, which he used with skill. The cold style was learned from Gustave Flaubert, and it was particularly suited to his Thomistic temperament. *A Portrait of the Artist as a Young Man* which followed in 1916 is also about Dublin life, but is slightly scholastic in tone. Joyce, unable to make a living in Dublin, went abroad and lived in Trieste and Paris while he worked on a new book, *Ulysses* (1922). This was a novel of Dublin life, and though it is extremely long, the action takes place all in one day. Joyce employed in this novel a new technique which has been described as "the stream of consciousness." By this is meant that he records the conscious and subconscious thoughts of his characters and allows them to weave in and out of the story in what might appear to be a disorder. This new method of novel writing caused a sensation and it was much discussed in intellectual societies in Paris and America. The book is still banned in many countries for its alleged obscenity. The hero of *Ulysses* is Leopold Bloom, a Jew, and Joyce intended that he represent the human race. The dialogue is realistic and alive. *Finnegans Wake* (1939) is even more obscure than *Ulysses.* It is highly praised by those who profess to understand it, and by others it is condemned as the ravings of a sick mind. Joyce had no successful imitators, and AE said of him that he was a cistern and not a fountain.

Novelists.—Liam O'Flaherty, Peadar O'Donnell, and Frank O'Connor are all realists. Liam O'Flaherty was born on the west coast of Ireland. His early short stories describing the life lived in that area have both freshness and vigor; his realism is always touched with a lyricism which lifts his stories to an imaginative plane. He is the author of many novels and books of short stories, including *Thy Neighbour's Wife* (1924), a novel; *Spring Sowing* (1926), stories; *The Informer* (1926), a novel; *Famine* (1937); *Short Stories of Liam O'Flaherty* (1937); and *Two Lovely Beasts* (1948). He also wrote short stories in the Gaelic language. Peadar O'Donnell was born in Donegal, among the Gaelic-speaking peasants of that area. His novels, which portray the life of the poverty-stricken peasants struggling to survive, include *Islanders* (1925), *Adrigoole* (1928), *The Knife* (1930), and *On the Edge of the Stream* (1934). He had a passion for justice, and this caused him to devote much of his time to humanitarian work on behalf of the Donegal migrant laborers.

Frank O'Connor was born in Cork about the year 1901. He fought in the struggle for Irish political freedom in the early 1920's, and his first book of stories, *Guests of the Nation* (1931), told of his experience as a rebel. He came under the patronage of AE, who brought him to Dublin and arranged a job for him as librarian. Most of his early work, which is full of vitality, appeared first in *The Irish Statesman.* In 1932 he published his first novel, *The Saint and Mary Kate.* Those that followed included *The Wild Bird's Nest* (1932), *Bones of Contention* (1936), and *Selected Short Stories* (1946). He wrote two plays while he was a director of the Abbey Theatre and translated many poems from the Gaelic, including Merriman's *The Midnight Court.* The scene of most of his stories is laid in Cork. His early stories are his best work.

The autobiography in four volumes of Sean O'Casey, the playwright, is an important contribution to Irish prose writings: *I Knock at the Door* (1939), *Pictures in the Hallway* (1942), *Drums under the Windows* (1945), and *Inisfallen, Fare Thee Well* (1949). Of the four volumes the first, which is probably the best, describes O'Casey's childhood and the Dublin life of the time; the style is vigorous and the point of view clear. *Drums under the Windows* is unfortunately influenced to its detriment by the style of James Joyce. *Inisfallen, Fare Thee Well* discusses, among other things, his own relation to the Irish literary revival.

Essayists.—The essay form was widely cultivated during the period under review. Almost every Irish writer wrote essays. Yeats is probably the most important essayist, because he was the most important writer. Many of his early essays appeared in *Bealtaine* and *Samhain,* the periodicals issued by the Irish Literary Theatre. Many of his books of prose consist of essays—such as *The Cutting of an Agate* (1912), *The Trembling of the Veil* (1922), and *Dramatis Personae* (1936). Yeats was a brilliant essayist, and though he had a clear style, he concentrated more on saying something than on the means of saying it.

AE also wrote essays of a high order of merit, most of them appearing in *The Irish Statesman.* The essays of Shaw on every conceivable topic are so well known that it would serve no purpose to discuss them here. George Moore wrote many delightful essays on literature, art, and music. While they are noted more for their style than for their content, there are critical comments and ideas in them that have more than passing value. John Eglinton (William Kirkpatrick Magee) concentrated on the essay form alone; the fact that he was a close friend of Moore is sufficient to indicate that his attitude was sceptical, detached, and ironical. Eglinton set himself the task "to introduce new unassailable ideals of nationality, to sink the wells of thought beneath the barren surface of tradition, and to bring Ireland into political and spiritual unity." Although a definite part of the Irish literary revival, he had, like Moore, little sympathy with it. He is a fine stylist, and Yeats described his writings as full of "orchestral harmonies." However, he had little to say that was original, and he took his stand in favor of cosmopolitanism in literature rather than nationalism. He came from the north of Ireland, and perhaps this had some influence on his point of view. His books include: *Two Essays on the Remnant* (1896), *Pebbles from the Brook* (1901), and *Anglo-Irish Essays* (1917). Ernest Augustus Boyd was an essayist and critic. Two of his books are important: *Ireland's Literary Renaissance* (1916) and *The Contemporary Drama of Ireland* (1918).

Ballads.—Ballad writing was popular during the period, and many of the ballads, written anonymously, will remain permanently in Irish literature. Some of the ballad writers whose names we know are: Alfred Perceval Graves, author of *Father O'Flynn,* Patrick Joseph McCall, who wrote *Irish Fireside Songs,* and Francis Arthur Fahy, author of *The Ould Plaid Shawl.*

Bibliography.—O'Grady, Standish, *Early Bardic Literature* (1879); Zimmer, H., *The Irish Elements in Mediaeval Culture* (1891); Duffy, Sir C. G., Sigerson, G., and Hyde, D., *The Revival of Irish Literature,* addresses (1894); Hyde, D., *A Literary History of Ireland* (1899); Yeats, W. B., *Synge and the Ireland of his Time* (1911); Brown, S. J., *A Guide to Books on Ireland* (1912); O'Donoghue, D. J., *The Poets of Ireland* (1912); Gregory, Lady I. A., *Our Irish Theatre* (1914); Yeats, W. B., *Reveries over Childhood and Youth* (1915); Boyd, E. A., *Ireland's Literary Renaissance* (1916, with bibliographical appendix); Figgis, D., *AE—George W. Russell* (1916); MacDonagh, T., *Literature in Ireland* (1916); DeBlacam, A. S., *Gaelic Literature Surveyed* (1929); Malone, A. E., *The Irish Drama* (1929); Corkery, D., *Synge and the Anglo-Irish Literature: A Study* (1931); Yeats, W. B., *Dramatis Personae* (1936); Hone, J. M., *W. B. Yeats* (1943); Kavanagh, P., *The Story of the Abbey Theatre* (1950).

PETER KAVANAGH,
Author of "The Irish Theatre" and "The Story of the Abbey Theatre."

IRISH LITERATURE IN THE ENGLISH LANGUAGE. This phrase is used to indicate the writing of those persons who, though born in Ireland, wrote exclusively in the English language and, generally speaking, directed their writing toward an English public.

Until the mid-19th century the majority of the Irish people spoke only Gaelic, and only a very small, but important, minority spoke English. The first contingent of Anglo-Norman invaders entered Ireland in 1169; the towns were quickly seized by the Strangers (as they were called), and an English-speaking colony was established. Strengthened by succeeding expeditions in 1170 and 1171, the English-speakers became the ruling class and generally were disliked by the native Irish. After some generations the early English settlers became more Irish than the Irish—as one writer put it; and they, in turn, resented all subsequent invasions by the English. However, they always regarded England as the mother country, in much the same manner as the Irish-Americans regard Ireland. Until early in the 20th century the English-speakers never really amalgamated with the native Irish or Natives (as they called them); consequently reference is usually made to them as the Anglo-Irish.

Extreme Irish nationalists sometimes speak disparagingly of the Anglo-Irish and accuse them of being un-Irish. This is a narrow view based on the false notion that only those who speak flatteringly of a country can justly claim to be its citizens. In fact, it was precisely because the Anglo-Irish were not encumbered with a false sentiment for Ireland that they wrote so well and added so much luster to Irish literature. They wrote, it is true, for an English public, but, because they were Irish and living in Ireland, they necessarily must have had Irish emotions. Anglo-Irish writers could not escape, even if they had so wished, the Irish color and attitude. But even if no Irish attitude were obvious in their writing, there would be nothing requiring apology. What really mattered is that they wrote well.

The contribution to English literature by Irish writers using the English language is greater than one may assume from a casual glance. Immediately the names of the best Irish writers come to mind—Jonathan Swift, Oliver Goldsmith, Richard Brinsley Sheridan, Oscar Wilde, Bernard Shaw—but there are many others whose writing has added vigor to what is called English literature. It is possible to exclude the Brontës (whose father was Irish) and William Congreve (who spent the most impressionable years of his life in Ireland) and yet to have a very impressive list. There is no branch of English literature which Irish writers have not invaded and at times have dominated. It is said sometimes that Irish literature in English began with Swift (1667–1745), but the inaccuracy of this statement is demonstrated by St. John Seymour in his book *Anglo-Irish Literature, 1200–1582.* There he quotes a poem entitled *The Land of Cokaygne* (written in the last half of the 13th century) in which the friars of Kildare are satirized because they appear to have made, in dumb show, theatrical representations of some of the incidents in the Bible. So quick were the Anglo-Irish to adopt the drama, and so great is their accomplishment in this branch of literature alone, that it may be best to discuss first their contributions to drama.

DRAMA

Beginnings of the Drama Form.—The earliest reference to a dramatic entertainment occurring in Ireland is in a document consisting of 17 constitutions of a Dublin provincial council which Archbishop Thomas Minot held at Kilkenny in 1366. According to the seventh constitution, which is entitled *Constitucio ne mercata in ecclesiis vel earum acris seu cimiteriis teneantur, nec negociaciones seculares exerceantur,* priests are ordered to forbid "such theatrical games and frivolous spectacles, by which the churches are dishonored; and the aforesaid priest must warn them, under suspension, and order them in future to abstain from such acts and to cease from them under pain of greater excommunication."

It is clear from this canon that in Ireland at that early period plays of some kind were acted both in the churches and in the cemeteries. We know that it was customary in both England and France at the same period for plays to be acted inside churches, and that ecclesiastical authorities legislated against the practice. In Marsh's Library, Dublin, is a copy of a religious processional, written in the 14th century and owned in the 15th century by the Church of St. John the Evangelist, Dublin. It is the usual type of processional, describing the coming of the three Marys to the tomb of Christ, but written as a play. There is, however, no conclusive evidence that it was performed in Ireland. Again, *The Pride of Life* (1343), of which the manuscript was discovered in Dublin, is the earliest known morality play in the English language. The texts of two other religious plays of an early period, *The Play of the Sacrament* and *Abraham's Sacrifice,* are preserved in Trinity College Library, Dublin. It is most likely that these plays were performed in Ireland.

That medieval pageants were popular in Dublin during the 15th century is attested by the *Chain Book of the City of Dublin,* which gives an exact account of the pageant held in 1498. But the first really important dramatic performance in Ireland occurred at Kilkenny on Aug. 20, 1553, when two plays, still extant, written by John Bale (1495–1563), the Protestant bishop of Ossory, were acted at the Market Cross. With some truth Bale may be described as the father of Anglo-Irish drama, although he was an Englishman by birth and by breeding. He was a prolific writer of moralities, all of which are violently anti-Catholic. His best-known play is entitled *Kynge Johan* (written before 1548). Bale's importance to Irish dramatic development may easily be underestimated because of his brief stay in Ireland—less than a year. Since he introduced to Ireland plays of some topical significance, it may be claimed that these plays had an influence on Irish dramatic literature.

Early Playwrights.—Ireland's first public theater was built by John Ogilby (1600–1676), a Scot, in Werburgh Street, Dublin, some time between 1634 and 1638; and James Shirley (1596–1666), the English dramatic poet, was invited to Dublin to write plays specially for the new theater. Shirley chose an Irish theme for one of his plays, *St. Patrick for Ireland.* This play treats the story of St. Patrick's conversion of the Druids; John Eglinton says of it that "it enables us, far better than a good many of the acknowledged sources of the period, to realise how the Anglo-Irish felt towards their country on the eve of the rebellion." Shirley really set the standard for Anglo-Irish drama, and very soon Anglo-Irish writers were following his example. Ireland gave four playwrights to English literature before 1660: Sir John Denham (1615–1669), Richard Flecknoe (d. 1678), Henry Burnell (fl. 1641), and Henry Burkhead (fl. 1645). It is doubtful whether Denham should be claimed as an Anglo-Irish writer for, as an English historian recorded, "before the Foggy Air of that Climate could influence or adulterate his Mind, he was brought from thence." Flecknoe, who wrote many plays, was a very bad poet, and is mentioned with contempt by Pope in the second line of the *Dunciad.* Burnell, it is claimed, was pro-Irish, but his one surviving play, *Landgartha,* shows no trace of it. Henry Burkhead's *A Tragedy of Cola's Furie or Lirenda's Miserie* treats of the insurrection of 1641 from the Irish point of view. During the 17th century the Jesuits produced Latin plays in Ireland.

Irish Dramatists.—After the Restoration (1660) Anglo-Irish writers took a very active interest in the English stage. Roger Boyle, earl of Orrery (1621–1679), was the first to introduce the heroic play to England. Thomas Southerne (1660–1746) was highly regarded as a playwright; in his *Oroonoko,* a very popular play, he attempts to expose the evils of the slave traffic.

George Farquhar (1678–1707), though hardly equal to the Irish-educated William Congreve (1670–1729), was scarcely less significant than he. Farquhar's plays were less refined than Congreve's, but they were more human. There is a Rabelaisian gaiety about them which, if not typically Irish, is certainly not English. Farquhar's is real critical comedy. He disliked pretense, and in his plays he took great pleasure in exposing the conventional affectations and deceits of certain ranks of society and, especially, of the English army officer. Farquhar anticipated the modern domestic drama. He set an example for his contemporaries, who unfortunately were not great enough to profit by it. His best-known plays are *The Recruiting Officer* and *The Beaux's Stratagem.*

Another Anglo-Irish playwright of the period was Susanna Centlivre (1667–1723). She is best known for her plays, *The Busy Body* and *The Wonder!* Although she was not a great dramatist, William Hazlitt thought highly of her. "Her plays," he wrote, "have a provoking spirit and volatile salt in them which will preserve them from decay. *The Wonder!* and *The Busy Body* are properly comedies of intrigue. Their interest depends chiefly on the intricate involution and artful denouement of the plot, which has a strong tincture of mischief in it, and the wit is seasoned by the archness of the humour and sly allusion to the most delicate points."

Although Richard Steele (1672–1729) is remembered only as an essayist, his plays were at least a minor addition to English dramatic literature; their weakness lay in his sentimentalism. *The Funeral* is the most readable among them; the passage in which he satirizes the undertaker is quite amusing. Hazlitt thought little of Steele as a dramatist, and characterized his plays as "rather homilies in dialogue, in which a number of very pretty ladies and gentlemen discuss the fashionable topics of gaming, of dueling, of seduction, of scandal, etc., with a sickly sensibility that shows as little hearty aversion to vice as sincere attachment to virtue." Steele's *The Conscious Lovers* was a popular success.

Other Anglo-Irish dramatists of this period were Owen Swiney (b. 1680), Samuel Madden (1686–1765), William Philips (d. 1734), Charles Coffey (d. 1745), Michael Clancy (d. 1760), Charles Molloy (d. 1767), and Henry Brooke (1703–1783).

18th-Century Playwrights.—Oliver Goldsmith (1728–1774) and Richard Brinsley Sheridan (1751–1816) are undoubtedly the best-known dramatists who wrote in English during the 18th century. Both were Irishmen. Goldsmith contributed to every major phase of English literature; he was a poet, a novelist, a dramatist, and an essayist. As Samuel Johnson (1709–1784), to whose circle he belonged, said of him, "he touched nothing that he did not adorn." He wrote two plays, *The Good Natur'd Man* and *She Stoops to Conquer;* he is also the author of a farce called *The Grumbler.* It would not be difficult, if one so wished, to indicate the Irish influence in Goldsmith's writing, especially in *She Stoops to Conquer,* whose boisterous good humor and ridicule of the sentimentalism characterizing the contemporary comedy of tears are undoubtedly facets of the Irish temperament. *She Stoops to Conquer* could have been written only by an Irishman; it is full of that reckless, devil-may-care spirit peculiar to the Irish. Goldsmith, while essentially Irish, does not exhibit intentionally the characteristics which lead to stage Irishism, but passively allows his Irish nature and spirit to express themselves.

Sheridan, like Goldsmith, is so universally known for his contribution to English literature, that it is unnecessary to discuss his work at any great length here. His *The Rivals* and *The School for Scandal* are still acted and enjoyed. Although he did not equal Farquhar for imagery of language or Congreve for style, Sheridan is nonetheless a dramatist of power. In one thing at least he excelled Congreve and Farquhar—he held the follies of his age up to delightful ridicule. The equal of *The Rivals* and *The School for Scandal* as pieces of satirical comment on the mannerisms of middle-class society have never been written before or since. Leigh Hunt describes him as "a Shakespeare without a heart"; and Hazlitt said of him that "among the comic writers of the last century he shines like Hesperus among the lesser lights." Like most Irish writers, he spent most of his life in England and wrote for an English public.

Arthur Murphy (1727–1805), author of 21 plays and frequently compared by scholars with Sheridan, was a member of Johnson's circle. His best-known play is *The Grecian Daughter.* Essentially a sentimentalist, Murphy tried to write in the true comic vein and, because he attempted the compromise, he failed as a writer. His plays, however, are significant in the history of Anglo-Irish drama.

Hugh Kelly (1739–1777), a great friend of the English actor David Garrick (1717–1779), is the author of *False Delicacy,* a sentimental play which was a great popular success. Kelly was very conscious of Ireland, and wrote *The School for Wives* "in defence of Law and Irishmen." He attempts the Irish idiom, but the result is neither authentic nor artistic.

John O'Keeffe (1747–1833), the popular writer of ballad-opera, romantic comedy, and farce, was born in Dublin. He is the author of at least 77 dramatic pieces, many of which are still remembered. Hazlitt says of O'Keeffe: "He might well be called our English Molière . . . In light, careless laughter, and pleasant exaggerations of the humorous, we have had no one equal to him. There is no labour or contrivance in his scenes, but the drollery of his subject seems to strike irresistibly upon his fancy, and run away with his discretion as it does with ours." His best dramatic piece is *The Agreeable Surprise.* O'Keeffe wrote many interesting songs, of which *Amo, Amas, I Love a Lass* became very popular.

Other Ango-Irish dramatists of the late 18th century were: Charles Macklin (1697?–1797); Paul Hiffernan (1719–1777), Francis Gentleman (1728–1784), Isaac Bickerstaffe (1735–1812), Robert Jephson (1736–1803), Frederick Pilon (1750–1788), Leonard MacNally (1752–1820), infamous in Irish history as an informer, William Preston (1753–1807), Walley Chamberlaine Oulton (1770–1820), Isaac Jackman (fl. 1777), William Macready (fl. 1780), and Andrew Franklin (fl. 1785).

Irish Dramatists of the 18th Century.—In the 19th century, Irish writers still dominated English dramatic literature. This is not to claim for them that they were great dramatists for, as is well known, the English drama degenerated in that century. Dion Boucicault (1820–1890) was a prominent writer of melodramas. He had a sentimental love of Ireland but, being Anglo-Irish, he was not completely aware of the Gaelic tradition. Consequently the characters in his plays are little better than the stage Irishmen of older plays—slightly better dressed and less wild. Yet, despite his obvious weakness as a playwright, he was superior to most of his contemporaries. His faults were those of his generation—a love of splendor and of melodrama. *The Colleen Bawn* is still remembered and frequently produced. Boucicault spent some time in the United States, and his play, *The Octoroon* (1859), exhibits a picture of life in the southern United States.

James Kenney (1780–1849) was also a prolific playwright, for he wrote upward of 50 plays. He was so popular that Byron, in his *English Bards and Scotch Reviewers,* makes a slighting attack on him:

> Yet what avails their vain attempts to please,
> While British critics suffer scenes like these; . . .
> While Kenney's "World"—ah, where is Kenney's wit?—
> Tires the sad gallery, lulls the listless pit.

James Sheridan Knowles (1784–1862) was considered by some of the best critics to be "the first tragic writer of the age." While that is an overstatement, it may be true to say that he was the author of the best acting plays of the period. *Virginius* is considered his best play—and the character of Virginius was William Charles Macready's most popular portrayal.

Other Anglo-Irish dramatists of the 19th century were: Andrew Cherry (1762–1812), John Till Allingham (fl. 1799–1810), Samuel Lover (1799–1868), Joseph Stirling Coyne (1803–1838), and George Francis Armstrong (1845–1906).

Oscar Wilde (1856–1900) is one of the best known of all the Anglo-Irish playwrights. Although he lived at a period when a new romantic movement in Anglo-Irish literature was being formed, his plays belong to the 18th-century tradition. His mother was nationalistic and had given her son two very Irish middle names, Fingal O'Flahertie, but he ignored Ireland and wrote entirely for a wider public. Wilde's plays belong to the "manners" tradition, and all the characters protrayed by him are taken from upper-class English life. He moved in that society and wrote only about the life which he knew intimately. His best-known play is *The Importance of Being Earnest.* Wilde's weakness as a dramatist, according to William Archer, is that "he treated the art of the dramatist with contemptuous insincerity." He was so in love with style that he put up more than his subject matter could carry. But, for all that, Wilde was a fine dramatist and, as Frank Harris predicted, "he will live with Congreve and Sheridan as the wittiest and most humorous of all our playwrights." If any Irish influence is to be found, it must be sought in the subtle psyche which hovers between the lines, but his contribution to English dramatic literature is no less because of that. Oscar Wilde's plays were the final flowering of the old tradition, for after Wilde's death another Anglo-Irishman, W. B. Yeats (1865–1939), gave English drama a new turn and a new inspiration (see also IRISH LITERARY REVIVAL).

PROSE

To give an idea of the Irish contribution to English prose, one conveniently, if quite arbitrarily, may divide the writers into five general classifications: (1) those who went to live permanently in England, either through economic necessity or because they believed that their roots were there; (2) those who interpreted and explained Ireland to a foreign audience; (3) those who pictured Ireland as a savage and turbulent country and those who added a journalistic touch; (4) those who wrote popular "thrillers"; (5) those who wrote about Ireland out of their own experience.

Authors Domiciled in England.—The only link with Ireland of the writers in the first category lies in the fact that their Irish temperament showed through their work, even though they made no attempt to portray Irish life. To this category belong Jonathan Swift, Richard Steele, Laurence Sterne, Oliver Goldsmith, and many others. Swift was the greatest of them all. He was the dean of St. Patrick's (Protestant) Cathedral, Dublin. Swift wrote, not for an Irish or an English public, but for himself and for humanity. He was not bound by a narrow nationalism when he wrote his *Drapier's Letters* demanding justice for Ireland; he was fighting for a principle and not for a nation. Every nation may claim Swift, just as all may claim Shakespeare. As H. L. Mencken has shown, Swift had the true universal approach—he began by attacking the Irish as a race of Yahoos, then proceeded to assail the English, and ended by condemning the whole human race. As if to make his judgment on humanity emphatic, he ended his own life in a blaze of insanity. He hated ignorance and stupidity, and he lashed that which he destested with a savage satire. This is certainly one facet of the Irish character.

Swift, no doubt, would ridicule any claim that he was an Irish writer, but he would deny even more indignantly that he was an English one. He had a rebellious and intellectual mind, which diverted Anglo-Irish writers from that sentimental approach to Ireland which damned a considerable portion of 19th-century Irish literature. The liberal attitude, bordering on revolution, of such Anglo-Irish writers as Henry Grattan (1746–1820) and Edmund Burke (1729–1797) must be attributed in a great measure to Swift's influence. If Swift had a contempt for the Yahoos in Ireland, he had also an equal contempt for the Yahoos in every other country. He made Anglo-Irish writers conscious of their individuality, and established for them a tradition which, if not Irish, was just as certainly not English. It is for this reason that he frequently is called the father of Anglo-Irish writing.

Richard Steele, already mentioned as a dramatist, also belongs to this classification, although his sentimentality occasionally compels him to acknowledge his Irish lineage. Steele is recognized with Addison as the writer who did most to establish the essay as a special literary form. *The Tatler,* founded by him in 1709, was the precursor of the modern newspaper. Yet, despite his sentimentality, he must have inherited much of the rebelliousness which is so much a part of Swift. In 1710 he lost his government position because of a satire which he had written, and later he was expelled from Parliament on the charge of seditious libel.

Laurence Sterne left Ireland in his boyhood for England, and later indulged in European travel for his health. Many regard his *Sentimental Journey* (1768) and his novel *Tristram Shandy* (1760) as obscene. *Tristram Shandy* was denounced by Dr. Johnson, Oliver Goldsmith, Horace Walpole, and others, on moral and literary grounds. Some claim that Sterne represents a definite facet of Irish character, though most Irishmen would deny it.

Oliver Goldsmith is easy to recognize as an Irishman, if only because of his casual attitude to life. It is said that he was so sentimentally charitable that he often gave away money which he himself badly needed. Goldsmith has been described as "an inspired idiot," but unjustly so. His foolishness was assumed to guard his integrity—a very Irish trait. Goldsmith's contribution to the development of the essay is considerable, and his *The Vicar of Wakefield* (1766) is a polished novel, though it was written long before the novel-form was completely developed. His writing has charm, a quality which some ascribe wholly to his racial heritage. Goldsmith achieved greatness.

Other creative writers of prose belonging to this classification were: Roger Boyle (1621–1679), who wrote a long romance entitled *Parthenissa,* Richard Head (1637–1686), Mary Davys (fl. 1756), Henry Brooke (1703–1783), Richard Griffith (d. 1788), William Chaigneau (1709–1781), Charles Johnstone (1719–1800), Frances Sheridan (1724–1766), Elizabeth Ryves (1750–1797), James White (d. 1799), John Corry (fl. 1825), Adelaide O'Keeffe (1776–1855), Thomas Moore (1779–1852), Lady Morgan (1783–1859), James Sheridan Knowles (1784–1862), the Countess of Blessington (1789–1849), and Elizabeth Hardy (1794–1854).

Interpreters of Ireland to Others.—To the second classification (those writers who attempted to explain Ireland to foreigners) belong Maria Edgeworth (1767–1849), Charles Lever (1806–1872), Samuel Lover (1797–1868), William Hamilton Maxwell (1792–1850), and some others. Maria Edgeworth was by far the best writer of this group, but this distinction does not mean that she was a writer of the first importance. She was, indeed, a minor writer, because her range of vision was narrow and because her knowledge of the common people of Ireland was derived merely from casual observation of the peasants on her father's estate. She wrote about Ireland as truthfully as she knew how, and her novels at least give a good picture of the "Big House" and all that it entailed in Ireland. In literature, *Castle Rackrent* (1800) marks the first appearance of an Irish peasantry drawn truthfully instead of their customary misrepresentation as uncouth creatures suffering from semilunacy. Edgeworth portrayed the life of the Irish governing classes and of the rising middle class.

Charles Lever, in dedicating his novel, *Jack Hinton the Guardsman,* stated: "I have no presumptious expectation of elucidating the mysteries or of solving the difficulties of Irish character, but with the less ambitious object of exhibiting some of their peculiar features, some of their moods of mirth and melancholy, I have ventured in these sketches." Actually Lever elucidated only his own incompetence as a novelist of Irish or any other life. His intention was probably good, but his achievement was meager. In *Harry Lorrequer,* and in his other novels, he catches nothing of the real Irish spirit, and succeeds only in portraying the stage Irishman of older days. Lever's novels are now forgotten, but for a time Lever was the most popular novelist of his day. He is interesting now only as a phenomenon representing the misguided attitude of the less intelligent Anglo-Irish toward their country.

Samuel Lover, though his intention was the same as Lever's, achieved more because of his poetic mind. His best-known novel, *Handy Andy* (1824), is, of course, stage Irish, but the opening chapter is so funny (in a farcical way) that it almost lifts it above mediocrity. The character represented by Handy Andy is an Irish peasant who is constantly making idiotic blunders. The novel was so popular that the word Handy Andy has found its way into the dictionaries.

Depicters of a Tumultuous Ireland.—The writers placed in the third category (those who pictured Ireland as a savage, turbulent country) differ from those in the second class only in degree. The mood in the novels of Maria Edgeworth and Charles Lever was calm. The Irish peasant may have been a blundering idiot, but he was not dangerous. In the novels of the Banims and of Gerald Griffin, however, he is pictured as a savage person with turbulent passions. John Banim (1798–1842) has been described as the Walter Scott of Ireland, because he wished to do for Ireland what the Waverley novels had done for the Scottish people. So in 1823, with the collaboration of his brother Michael (1796–1874), he began the project of *Tales of the O'Hara Family*. The first series of stories was very popular, and further series were issued until the death of John, whose portrayal of the Irish peasant was utterly false and lacked humor. Although Michael Banim wrote the best story of the series, *Crohoore of the Billhook,* he did not write any more after his brother's death.

The novels of Gerald Griffin (1803–1840) were of the same type as those of the Banim brothers, and of no higher quality. In 1828 appeared his *Tales of the Munster Festivals,* written while he stayed with his brother in Kerry. They were so well received that Griffin began a full-length novel, *The Collegians,* which he finished (1829) in London. The Irish revolutionaries of 1848 accepted *The Collegians* as an outstanding novel of Irish life. This is no tribute to their literary judgment, because the novel is melodramatic and false, not only to Irish life but even to nature. The misfortune of Griffin was that he thought that he was writing seriously of Ireland, when he peopled his novel with villains of the deepest dye and heroes of the highest integrity. If *The Collegians* is read today, it is because of its comic appeal. Dion Boucicault turned the story into a highly successful melodrama, *The Colleen Bawn.*

Other Anglo-Irish writers who fit into this category (however awkwardly) were: Sir Martin Archer Shee (1769–1850), Edward Mangin (1772–1852), George Croly (1780–1860), Robert Bell (1800–1867), Miles Gerald Keon (1821–1875), and Kathleen O'Meara (1839–1888).

Writers of Emotional Fiction.—In the fourth classification (those who wrote "thrillers"), Charles Robert Maturin (1782–1824) and Joseph Sheridan Le Fanu (1814–1873) are the most important. While the novels of Maturin, who wrote of the supernatural, had little merit in themselves, they had a great influence on the rising romantic school of France; and even on Sir Walter Scott, who not only reviewed and praised *Montorio* but also imitated *The Milesian Chief* in his own *The Bride of Lammermoor.*

Le Fanu was Ireland's best writer of "thrillers." While other writers in this medium were content to place the scene of their stories in lands where the impossible might be accepted as probable, Le Fanu was more precise and gave definite time, place, and environment to his subject. Le Fanu's stories are highly melodramatic, eerie in the extreme, and reminiscent of the stories of Edgar Allan Poe. They are still very readable. His best novels are *Uncle Silas* and *In a Glass Darkly.*

Other Anglo-Irish writers who may be mentioned here were: Regina M. Roche (1764–1845); Harriet L. Martin (1809–1891); Lady Lytton (1802–1882), author of *Cheveley, or The Man of Honour* (1839), a novel in which she made her husband the villain; Marmion W. Savage (1803–1872); Mayne Reid (1818–1883); (Bartholomew) Elliot Warburton (1810–1852); and Sir George Tomkyns Chesney (1830–1895).

Delineators from Personal Knowledge.—William Carleton (1794–1869) is not only the best writer within the fifth classification (writers about Ireland as they knew it), but possibly the best Irish novelist. Carleton was a Gaelic-speaking peasant and therefore not properly an Anglo-Irishman. No one before or since his time has written so faithfully, so simply, so powerfully, and so well of the Irish peasant. Carleton was born in Ulster, the most historic part of Ireland. He was conscious of Ireland's tradition for the simple reason that he was conscious of himself. He did not write romantically of the country, because poverty at home made him aware of Ireland as it really was. Moreover, he wrote in an authentic Irish idiom, of which the dialogue in the plays of the Irish literary renaissance is only a pale shadow. Carleton's *Traits and Stories of the Irish Peasantry* are brilliantly realistic and are a better picture of the Ireland before the Famine (1845–1850) than anything which may be read in a history book. One of his most admirable characteristics is that he never shrinks before emotion, while at the same time he avoids sentimentality. Probably Carleton's best story is *Dennis O'Shaughnessy Goes to Maynooth.* He wrote many novels, but these are of less interest than his short stories. He turned Protestant that he might receive the patronage of the wealthy, but despite this fact he represented Catholic Ireland more accurately than any other writer. Carleton's stories are not popular, because they are written in a difficult dialect of English.

Other writers who attempted to write about Ireland sympathetically were: Anna M. Hall (1800–1881), Charles J. Kickham (1826–1882), Emily Lawless (1845–1913). None of them, however, rose above the mediocre.

The writers for *The Nation* newspaper, founded in 1842 by Thomas Osborne Davis (1814–1845) and Charles Gavan Duffy (1816–1903), are worthy of mention. Here was the first deliberate attempt to found a school of Irish literature in the English language. Most of the writers for *The Nation* were Anglo-Irish Protestants; and all were extremists who believed in revolution and who rejected, as un-Irish, literature which did not obviously breathe the Irish spirit. The greatest of the writers belonging to this group was John Mitchel (1815–1875). He was, of course, a revolutionary, was transported to Australia as a felon, escaped to the United States, fought for the South in the American Civil War, and edited (1864–1865) the New York *Daily News.* Mitchel's *Jail Journal* is the bible of revolutionary Ireland. It describes his travels to Van Diemen's Land (Tasmania), and its theme is that only through revolution can there be hope of freedom. There are some fine descriptive passages in the book, which is still fresh, even though the ideals for which he fought have largely been achieved.

Thomas D'Arcy Magee (1825–1868) merits mention here for his *History of Ireland,* which often is more creative than factual. He escaped from Ireland in 1848 and became editor for a time of the Boston *Pilot* which was edited later by another escaped rebel, John Boyle O'Reilly (1844–1890).

Lady Wilde (1826–1896) contributed under the name "Speranza" to *The Nation;* she was very nationalistic, and wrote *Ancient Cures, Charms, and Usages of Ireland* (1890) and similar works. She was the mother of Oscar Wilde (q.v.), who, it must not be forgotten, was a brilliant writer of prose. He wrote some delightful fairy tales but is best known as a prose writer for *The Picture of Dorian Gray* (1891).

Irish writers also contributed extensively to English literature as historians, philosophers, orators, scholars, and journalists. (For Irish prose writers after 1900, see IRISH LITERARY REVIVAL.)

POETRY

Almost every writer thus far mentioned wrote also in verse. Swift was a not inconsiderable poet, as his *Stella's Birthday* and other poems adequately demonstrate. Goldsmith is well known as a poet of importance, and his *The Traveller* and *The Deserted Village* have a permanent place in English poetry. Richard Brinsley Sheridan wrote some pleasant songs, which may be found scattered throughout his plays. John O'Keeffe, another playwright, wrote some romantic songs, which are not entirely forgotten.

Nahum Tate (1652–1715) and Nicholas Brady (1659–1726) published in 1696 their joint metrical *New Version of the Psalms of David.* Tate, though elected to the position of poet laureate, added little to the glory of Irish literature, for he was regarded by Pope and other writers of authority as possibly the worst poet who ever held that position.

19th-Century Poets.—It was not until the 19th century, however, that Irish poets, becoming conscious of Ireland and her tradition, wrote best. In Ireland, 1798 was a year of revolution, when many Anglo-Irishmen associated themselves definitely on the Irish side against Britain. As has been shown, they knew little of Gaelic-speaking Ireland until then, but the spirit of nationalism was abroad, and they quickly sensed the importance of uniting themselves completely with every facet of Irish life. First came Charlotte Brooks (1750–1803) with her series of translations, *The Reliques of Irish Poetry* (1789). Then followed Jeremiah Joseph Callanan (1795–1829) and Edward Walsh (1805–1850), who in their translations from the Gaelic reproduced faithfully the wavering rhythm of the Gaelic verse-form. Callanan's best known translation, *The Outlaw of Lough Lene,* begins:

Oh, many a day I have made good ale in the glen,
That came not of stream or malt—like the brewing of men.
My bed was the ground; my roof, the greenwood above,
And the wealth that I sought, one far kind glance from my love.

But the real link between the Anglo-Irish and Gaelic-speaking Ireland was through music, and it was provided by the *Irish Melodies,* composed between 1807 and 1834 by Thomas Moore (1779–1852). For a century Moore was regarded as Ireland's national poet, but it must be admitted that his reputation was based partly on his brilliance in the world of society. His songs were just sufficiently Irish in a polite way to make them attractive to an English audience. For this reason his influence in England was great and, without question, he contributed much to establish the idea in the English mind that the Irish were not a race of barbarians. More important still, he gave courage and inspiration to Irish writers. Moore's verse is essentially too superficial and facile to have been a major influence, but it was just the thing at that time to establish the idea of a dignified Ireland with long traditions. Moore knew little of Ireland's history, but he was captivated by the Irish melodies of the 17th and 18th centuries, and he succeeded in putting appropriate words to them which, in a peculiar way, expressed something of Ireland's national spirit and aspiration. He came closest to the true poetic spirit in his *Avenging and Bright* and *At the Mid Hour of Night.* Occasionally he achieved the Gaelic cadence. Moore's weakness is derived from the fact that he was not sufficiently close to the source of Gaelic inspiration.

Verse in "The Nation."—*The Nation,* and the spirit of violent nationalism which it propagated, brought into existence a whole school of verse writers. Men with a talent for writing verses, and many others who had none at all, thought it their duty to express their nationalistic emotions and political ideas in verse. The result of this was that much of the verse of the *Nation* school is too didactic and rhetorical to warrant its classification as poetry. Thomas Osborne Davis (1814–1845) is the best representative of this group. His *My Land* is probably his best piece, but *A Nation Once Again* was his most popular song, and for a long time it was accepted as Ireland's unofficial national anthem. John Kells Ingram (1823–1907), a professor in Trinity College, contributed a rousing song—*Who Fears to Speak of Ninety-Eight?*—to *The Nation.* It was so great a success as a battle cry that the author's conscience disturbed him and he later disclaimed authorship. Another good song writer was John Keegan Casey (1846–1870), who is best remembered for his rebel song, *The Rising of the Moon.* Ireland's greatest ballad, *The Wearing of the Green,* and that other stirring song, *The Shan van Vocht,* belong to an earlier period; no one knows who wrote them. Two other famous Irish ballads, *The Croppy Boy* and *Johnny, I Hardly Knew Ye,* are also anonymous.

James Clarence Mangan (1803–1849), Ireland's most intense poet, also contributed to *The Nation.* However, it cannot be said that he properly belonged to that school of writers. Mangan was a distressed spirit and not a propagandist. His free translations from Gaelic are among the best poems written by Irishmen in English. His *O'Hussey's Ode to the Maguire* has great power, and his *Dark Rosaleen* and *The Woman of Three Cows* are far superior to their Gaelic originals. Probably his best original poem is *The Nameless One.* It is autobiographical and full of passion:

Roll forth, my song, like the rushing river,
That sweeps along to the mighty sea;
God will inspire me while I deliver
My soul to thee! . . .

Go on to tell how, with genius wasted,
Betrayed in friendship, befooled in love,
With spirit shipwrecked, and young hopes blasted,
He still, still strove. . . .

There is little doubt that Mangan was Ireland's greatest poet. Students of Mangan should not miss reading John Mitchel's excellent essay on him, which is included in an edition of Mangan's collected poems.

As translators from Gaelic, Sir Samuel Ferguson (1810–1886), for his *Cashel of Munster,* and Thomas William Rolleston (1857–1920), for his *Clonmacnoise,* should be mentioned. Other Irish poets of some account are: William Drennan (1754–1820), Richard A. Millikin (1767–1815), Charles Wolfe (1791–1823), William Carleton (1794–1869), Samuel Lover (1797–1868), Aubrey Thomas de Vere (1814–1902), William Allingham (1824–1889), Timothy Daniel Sullivan (1827–1914), John Todhunter (1839–1916), John Boyle O'Reilly (1844–1890), Emily Lawless (1845–1913), and Alfred Perceval Graves (1846–1931).

Oscar Wilde resembled Goldsmith in that he succeeded brilliantly in almost every form of literature. His *Hélas!* is a sonnet of great strength, and his *The Ballad of Reading Gaol,* written while he was in jail, holds a permanent place in English poetic literature.

(For the contribution of Irish poets to English literature after 1900 see IRISH LITERARY REVIVAL.)

Bibliography.—Webb, A. J., *A Compendium of Irish Biography* (Dublin 1878); McCarthy, J. H., and others, eds., *Irish Literature,* 10 vols. (Philadelphia 1904); Read, C. A., and Hinkson, K. T., eds., *The Cabinet of Irish Literature,* new ed., 4 vols. (London 1905); O'Donoghue, D. J., *The Poets of Ireland* (Dublin 1912); Crone, John S., *A Concise Dictionary of Irish Biography* (London 1928); Seymour, St. John D., *Anglo-Irish Literature, 1200–1582* (Cambridge 1929); Gwynn, S. L., *Irish Literature and Drama in the English Language* (London 1936); Kavanagh, Peter, *The Irish Theatre,* contains an extensive bibliography (Tralee, Ire., 1946).

PETER KAVANAGH,
Author of "The Irish Theatre" and "The Story of the Abbey Theatre."

IRISH MOSS. See CARRAGEEN.

IRISH MUSIC. From references in early medieval manuscripts it is clear that music played an important role in the life of the ancient Irish. Music-making is mentioned in connection with banquets and ceremonious occasions, warfare, and the casting of spells; and harpers figure in many of the legends. The chief instruments in use in the earliest period were the five- or six-stringed quadrangular harp (as represented on the stone cross at Castledermot, County Kildare), the *tympan* and the *fidil* (stringed instruments played with a bow), and the *píopaí* (bagpipe), which was the instrument of the humble folk. Military instruments were the *corn* (horn) and *stoc* and *sturgan* (two types of trumpet). The triangular harp, of which representations are found from the 11th century on, seems to have been introduced into Ireland by the Norse invaders. In its Irish form it was not strung with hide or horsehair but with metal—iron, silver, or bronze; it ranged in size from the small *ocht-tedach* (an eight-stringed instrument used to accompany singing and hung from the girdle) to the larger and more resonant *clairseách,* of which the earliest example extant is the so-called Brian Boru harp (having 30 strings and dating from about the 13th century), which is now in the library of Trinity College, Dublin.

Church Music.—Some evidence exists to show that the ecclesiastical chant was brought to Ireland in the 5th century by St. Patrick himself; but, contrary to the general belief, the chant sung in Ireland was not Roman but Gallican—as practised in Gaul up to the 8th century. Roman chant does not seem to have been introduced into Ireland until the period of the Norman invasion —with the advent of English and continental orders. Though great schools of learning flourished in Ireland from the 6th to the 10th century, and Irish monks were active missionaries all over western Europe, there is little evidence to support the assertions made by Grattan Flood and others concerning their contributions to the development of western church music; the term "Irish Anglo-Saxon" neume-type, coined by no less an authority than Peter Wagner, is fanciful as far as the Irish element in this neume-type is concerned. The earliest known instance of music notation in an Irish manuscript occurs in the 11th-century Drummond Missal, in which the chant of parts of the mass is indicated by means of neumes—characters of a notation which is the progenitor of our present-day system of music notation. But the Drummond Missal is a Roman missal adapted to local uses, and none of the chants mentioned so frequently in medieval Irish literature have so far come to light.

Whereas, on the Continent, polyphonic music gradually evolved during the early medieval period in the monasteries and churches, in Ireland, the Norman conquest, the clash between the native traditions and those of the invaders, and above all the wars, plantations, and persecutions of the succeeding centuries, combined to deny to church music a normal course of development. The surviving musico-liturgical manuscripts embody a tradition derived from the English, Anglo-Norman, or Continental houses which became established in Ireland from the 12th century.

Harp Music.—Throughout the medieval period, however, the native tradition of music, especially of harp-playing, continued to flourish. Writers such as Giraldus Cambrensis in the 12th century, Dante in the 13th, and Galileo in the 16th pay tribute to the excellence of Irish harp-playing, and numerous masters of the instrument are mentioned in the annals. At the courts of the princes and chieftains, poems composed by the *file* or *bard* were recited or chanted by a *reacaire,* to the accompaniment of an *oirfeadach* (harper). The professional harper ranked, according to the Brehon Laws, as a *bo-aire* (non-noble rent-paying freeman with property), and was the only musician entitled to "honor price"—an additional fine payable by reason of his rank in the event of injury.

Unfortunately we have little information as to the nature of the music played by the harpers. The long panegyrical poems recited or sung in the halls of the nobility were so complex in meter that they could not have lent themselves to a musical setting in our sense of the word. It is possible that the main part of the verse was chanted in a monotone, punctuated with cadential melodic inflections in the manner of psalmody, and supported by chords on the harp. Such a method of performance is described as surviving in Mayo as late as the 18th century. As regards the harp music itself, a 17th-century Welsh manscript in the British Museum (Add. MS. 14905), transcribed from an earlier manuscript and purporting to contain early medieval Welsh harp music, may give some inkling as to its style, since the Welsh and Irish traditions of harp-playing were closely related. Arnold Dolmetsch has deciphered the tablature in which the manuscript is written, and parts of the transcription have been performed and recorded, revealing a style quite unlike that of any music hitherto known; primarily harmonic in its texture, it embraces curious chord-formations and conveys a remote, other-worldly atmosphere by means of methods which seem decidedly impressionistic. However, many aspects of this manuscript are still problematical, and our factual knowledge of

Irish harp-playing is limited to some technical points. The wires, plucked by the harper's long, crooked nails, produced a sweet and tinkling tone very different from the more robust tone produced by gut strings. Owing to the excessive vibration, each string had to be damped before the next was plucked, involving a technique so exacting in the case of fast-moving passages that unless the player started at an early age there was little hope of his becoming proficient. Chords were played downwards, not upwards as today, and there seems to have been much doubling of the melodic line in octaves. In general, the style of playing was fluent, delicate, and highly-ornamented.

Decline of the Harp.—Throughout the wars of the 14th and 15th centuries, and the plantations of the 16th century, the harpers continued to practice their art; and though penal enactments against harpers and rhymers were made intermittently for over three centuries—from the passing of the Statute of Kilkenny in 1367 to the reign of William of Orange—such measures (savagely carried out) were primarily directed against the strolling entertainers, who were often politically active, and not against the harpers patronized by the nobility. After the Battle of Kinsale (1601), however, with the final passing of the old Gaelic order, harp-playing began to decline. The families which had patronized the harpers were for the most part outlawed and their estates confiscated, the planters who immediately succeeded them were no supporters of native art, and harp-playing, from being a privileged calling, fell to being a humble one. In the heyday of medieval minstrelsy, poet, singer or declaimer, and harper were three specialists who combined in the performance of poetry, but now these offices were merged in the one individual. At the same time the esoteric bardic poetry and harp music, unintelligible to the *nouveau riche* as to the simpler folk to whom the harpers had now to turn for support, gave way to popular verse and tuneful music in the folk style. Such music had, of course, coexisted with the earlier bardic art, but from now on it was to become the main vehicle of expression.

Carolan.—With the comparative tranquillity which followed the Treaty of Limerick (1691), conditions became more favorable for the pursuit of music, and the rural gentry, including the few native families who had not been dispossessed, began to cultivate European as well as native music. During this period lived the last and greatest of the poet-harpers, Turlogh Carolan (1670–1738), who composed many hundreds of songs, chiefly in honor of his patrons, both Irish and Anglo-Irish, whose houses he visited in the course of his travels. The songs, named after the patrons to whom they were addressed, were sung by the blind poet-composer to an accompaniment on his harp. Gay, humorous, or elegiac, they show great versatility, some being in the traditional style and based on gapped scale-forms, others clearly revealing the influence of contemporary Italian music—such as Carolan would have heard in the drawing-rooms of his patrons. An edition of some of Carolan's songs was published in Dublin by John and William Neale about 1720—the earliest surviving example of music printing in Ireland.[1]

[1] A monumental work on Carolan by Donal O'Sullivan, *Carolan, his Life and Times*, including an edition of some 200 of his songs, remains unpublished for lack of funds.

The harpers who succeeded Carolan were executants only; they continued to dwindle in numbers, and were mostly in straitened circumstances. If changed social conditions were responsible for the fate of the harpers, the decline of the harp itself, which had been so popular an instrument for amateur music-making in the previous century, is explained by the difficulty of its technique as compared with that of keyboard instruments; as well as by the fact that, being a diatonic instrument, it could not cope with the ever-widening range of modulation and of chromaticism during this period—such as was readily available on the harpsichord, the violin, and (when it appeared towards the latter part of the 18th century) the piano.

Belfast Harp Festival.—Before the last vestiges of the harp tradition had died away, an attempt was made to preserve them by the organization of harp festivals—at Granard from 1781 to 1785, and at Belfast in 1792. At the latter festival Edward Bunting, a Belfast organist, noted down the tunes played by the harpers, and these notes were later drawn on for his three-volume *Ancient Music of Ireland,* the first important collection of traditional music. Unfortunately Bunting's method of notation was a primitive one. In the case of songs, since he knew no Irish, the words were not noted with the tune. In the case of harpers' airs, no distinction was drawn between what was sung and what was played, and the reproductions of traditional harp music in his 1840 volume consist almost entirely of elaborate piano arrangements constructed out of purely melodic jottings made many years earlier. Despite its shortcomings, however, Bunting's collection was a notable work for its time, and has remained the chief source of what little information we possess with regard to harp-playing in Ireland.

Folk Song Tradition.—At the end of the 18th century the tradition of folk song was still fully alive throughout the country. Countless airs were in circulation and new poems continually written for the more well-known airs. While Irish remained the language of the vast majority of the people this tradition was able to hold its own, even against the rise of the English ballad—for popular English songs such as those of Charles Dibdin (q.v.) began to have a vogue in Ireland at the turn of the century. But with the suppression of the Irish language in the schools and its gradual abandonment as the vernacular in the second half of the 19th century, the tradition of folk song commenced to suffer the fate which had already befallen the harp music.

Moore's "Melodies."—From 1808 to 1834 the *Irish Melodies* of Thomas Moore (q.v.) appeared serially in ten volumes—melodies from the Bunting and Holden collections to which the poet wedded his admirable lyrics. The *Melodies* achieved an immense popularity, and were instrumental in making Irish songs known to the townsfolk, to whom traditional singing was a closed book, and known in England and abroad. Were it not for Moore's *Melodies,* on the general abandonment of the Irish language the majority of the people would have lost all touch with their own music. But the *Melodies,* elegant, nostalgic, and sentimental, were far removed from the elemental beauty of traditional singing in Irish, which continued to decline in all but the remoter districts.

Folk Song Collections.—Fortunately, a number of collectors throughout the 19th century worked to place on record what remained of this rich store of song, chief among them William Forde, and John Edward Pigot (whose collections have remained for the most part in manuscript), George Petrie, and Patrick Weston Joyce. The transcription of folk song, however, particularly of that free, unmeasured style so usual with Irish traditional singers, can only be partially successful; for such limited methods of notation as the rank and file of collectors use are inadequate to reproduce the irregular meter, the subtle rhythmic nuances, and the peculiarities of intonation due to the survival of other scale-forms, which are so essential a part of the tradition. The early collectors were too often ignorant of the mode-systems underlying the airs, so that foreign key-signatures and accidentals, and even changes adopted to make the airs "conformable to the laws of harmony" have to a certain extent become incorporated in the corpus of traditional music as taken down in the collections. Careful and scholarly methods, such as those adopted by Martin Freeman in his Ballyvourney Collection (*Journal of the Irish Folk Song Society,* vol. 6), were rarely in evidence. The ideal method of preserving folk song is, of course, by means of recording plus transcription, and this method has been adopted by the Irish Folklore Commission, which houses among its collection of some 3,000 folk songs a large number of ediphone recordings.

Taken all in all, the preserved corpus of Irish folk music is generally believed to be the finest and most varied produced by any nation. Song airs—plaintive, lilting, rugged, or wild and sweeping—shapely narrative airs, religious songs, lullabies, occupation songs, drinking and martial songs, are all to be found, showing the widest range of tonality and the simplest, symmetrical structures as well as chain-structures of the most intricate kind. Incredible as it may seem, there is no specific reference to dancing in early Irish literature, and the dance music—reels, jigs, hornpipes and "set" dances—is of relatively modern origin.

Clash of Traditions—Anglo-Irish Music.—Irish folk music, unlike that of nations whose music followed a normal course of development, has never been properly assimilated into a broader tradition of art music, due to the chasm—political, social, and religious—which existed for centuries between the spontaneous song in the vernacular which was the natural expression of the Irish people, and the purely English tradition of music-making in the towns.

Ever since the Norman invasion a musical culture had begun to develop in the Pale (the English settlement around Dublin), and other centers of English or Anglo-Norman influence, which had few points of contact with the music of the native Irish. Most of the records are ecclesiastical, and manuscripts such as the 14th-century psalter of Christ Church show the Anglo-Norman tradition of Christ Church and St. Patrick's Cathedrals in Dublin. There seems to have been little creative activity, however, and certainly no counterpart to the school of polyphony which flourished in England from the 15th to the 17th centuries.

Secular music in the towns also seems to have followed an English pattern. It is significant that six of the *Cantilenae* for festivals and other occasions written in the 14th century by Richard Ledrede, bishop of Ossory, for the use of the vicars choral of Kilkenny Cathedral were directed to be sung to English tunes, and two to French tunes. In Kilkenny, as elsewhere, ordinances were issued forbidding Englishmen to speak Irish, and the music as well as the language of the "wilde Irishrie" would have fallen equally under the ban.

The vicissitudes of Anglo-Irish church music may be understood, in face of the wars of the 14th century, the lax and confused state of religious organization in the 15th, and the wholesale confiscation of monasteries in the 16th. Superimposed on the old conflict between native and foreign religious establishments was now the new conflict which arose with the Reformation. After the Reformation English organists and vicars choral were frequently imported, and two noted madrigal writers of the English school were appointed organists at Christ Church Cathedral, Dublin—John Fermer, who held this post from 1596 to 1599, and Thomas Bateson, who held it from 1608 to his death in 1630. During the Cromwellian period church music was suppressed and organs removed or destroyed, and in some of the cathedrals the services were reduced to those of a mere parish church.

Music in Dublin.—Towards the end of the 17th century, after the turmoil of the Jacobite wars had subsided, conditions became more stable, and Anglo-Irish music entered on a period of prosperity which was to lead to Dublin becoming one of the most musically active cities in Europe. A large number of musical societies came into being, among them the Hibernian Catch Club (the oldest body of its kind still in existence), while concerts for charitable purposes, "benefit" concerts, and performances of ballad opera became the vogue. Crow Street Music Hall was built by the Dublin Academy of Music in 1730 "for the practice of Italian musick," and the New Musick Hall, in Fishamble Street, was opened in October 1741. Here George Frederick Handel gave the first of his series of Dublin concerts on December 23 of the same year, and on April 8, 1742, he gave the first public performance of the *Messiah,* amid unprecedented scenes of enthusiasm. Handel's visit was followed by that of Thomas Augustine Arne, who between 1742 and 1744 produced his masque *Comus* and his opera *Rosamund,* and gave the first performances of his oratorio *The Death of Abel* and his serenata *Masque of Alfred* at the Theatre Royal, in Smock Alley.

The eminent violinist Francesco Geminiani had been teaching in Dublin and giving concerts there from 1733 to 1740. His pupil, Matthew Dubourg, led the viceroy's band from 1728 to 1765, and had the privilege of assisting at the first performance of the *Messiah* and at Handel's other Dublin performances. In 1764 Garrett Colley Wellesley, 1st earl of Mornington (father of the duke of Wellington), a composer of church music and of glees, was appointed to the newly-created chair of music in Dublin University.

In the latter part of the 18th century Dublin could boast ten music shops (some of them firms of music publishers), eight harpsichord and piano manufacturers, three firms of instrument makers, and two firms of organ builders. Members of the Anglo-Irish aristocracy formed orchestras and cultivated chamber music, and the patronage of music as a social art was at its zenith. Creative activity was not lacking, the chief composers being Lord Mornington and Philip Cogan.

19th-Century Music.—With the passing of the Act of Union in 1800 and the abolition of the Irish Parliament, Dublin lost must of its significance as a focal center of political and social life, and the patronage of music by the nobility began to wane. In the 18th century Dublin had not only been a hub of musical activity but had attracted eminent musicians from England and the Continent. In the 19th, the chief names to be recorded are those of Irishmen who lived and worked abroad, such as John Field (1782–1837), Dublin-born pianist and composer of nocturnes and piano concertos, who was the first Irishman to gain an international reputation as a composer; Michael William Balfe (1808–1870), also born in Dublin, composer of *The Bohemian Girl;* William Vincent Wallace (1813–1865), born in Waterford, composer of *Maritana* and *Lurline;* and a number of minor figures such as Thomas Simpson Cooke, William Rook, and George Alexander Osborne.

At the same time, a new consolidation of music in Dublin set in with the founding of a series of societies devoted to the regular performance of the orchestral and choral repertory. The earliest of these was the Sons of Handel, founded by Francis Robinson in 1810. This was followed by the Antient Concerts Society, founded by Joseph Robinson, son of Francis, which lasted from 1834 to 1863. At the International Exhibition, Dublin, of 1851 Joseph Robinson assembled a choir and orchestra of no less than 1,000 performers, while in 1856 another society, the Philharmonic, gave the first performance in Ireland of Beethoven's *Choral Symphony.* Later, Joseph Robinson founded the Dublin Musical Society, which gave regular performances from 1876 to 1902 with a chorus and orchestra of about 350. Towards the end of the century the chief figures in the musical life of Dublin were Sir Robert Prescott Stewart (1825–1894), organist at St. Patrick's Cathedral and for a time at Christ Church, and professor of music at Dublin University, who was a prolific composer of organ and church music, and Michele Esposito (1855–1929), an Italian who was appointed professor of piano at the Royal Irish Academy of Music in 1882. Esposito founded the Dublin Orchestral Society, conducting its concerts from 1899 to 1914, and as conductor, composer, pianist, and teacher he dominated music in Dublin for nearly half a century.

In Belfast, the Philharmonic Society, founded in 1874, has been the main source of concert activity, and the society's chorus and orchestra (conducted by Sir Robert Stewart from 1877 to 1890, and from 1913 to 1950 by E. Godfrey Brown) has continued to give an unbroken series of subscription concerts, at some of which major works by composers such as Edward Elgar, Granville Bantock, John Ireland, and Ralph Vaughan Williams have been conducted by the composers themselves.

Stanford, Harty, Moeran.—Sir Robert Stewart's pupil, Charles Villiers Stanford (b. Dublin, 1852; d. London, 1924), and Esposito's pupil, Hamilton Harty (b. County Antrim, 1880; d. London, 1941), proved to be the two most eminent Irish musicians of their time, though both, like their fellow composers earlier in the century, left Ireland at an early age and took up residence in England. Both were knighted for their services to music. Stanford's large output and his work as teacher of a whole generation of English composers belong to the achievements of the English school, but in his editions of *Moore's Irish Melodies* and of the *Petrie Collection of Irish Music,* and in such works as the *Irish Symphony* and the five *Irish Rhapsodies,* he paid tribute to the folk song of his native country. Harty was one of the greatest conductors of his age. As a composer his work is distinguished more for its orchestral virtuosity than for its intrinsic worth, but his tone-poem *With the Wild Geese* and the *Irish Symphony* still survive in the repertoire.

The tradition of Stanford and Harty has to a certain extent been carried on in the work of Ernest John Moeran (1894–1950), a composer of Irish extraction, whose chief works, the *Symphony in G Minor* and the *Violin Concerto,* owe much to the inspiration of Irish folk song and of the landscape and sea coast of County Kerry, where both works were for the most part conceived and written.

Modern Developments.—Due chiefly to the country's checkered history, the general organization of music in Ireland is much behind that of other countries. After World War I the main advances were due to the development of broadcasting. Radio Eireann supports a symphony orchestra of 65 players which gives symphony concerts twice a week in the Phoenix Hall, Dublin, and the broadcasting programs, which are relayed by stations at Athlone, Dublin, and Cork, provide the main source of music for the Irish public. The British Broadcasting Corporation, Belfast, has been an important factor in the revival of music in Northern Ireland, though its symphony orchestra was disbanded on the outbreak of World War II. Apart from broadcasting, recitals by artists of international reputation are given weekly during the season by the Royal Dublin Society. New standards in opera have been achieved by the Dublin Grand Opera Society, which holds two seasons annually, and has brought the casts of the Paris Opera Comique and the Hamburg State Opera to Dublin. The chief music festivals are the Feis Ceoil, a general festival music, and the *Oireachtas,* a festival of Irish music and of the Irish language and literature, both founded in Dublin in 1897; they are the prototypes of the network of music festivals and *feiseanna* held annually throughout the country, particularly in Northern Ireland. Chairs of music exist in Dublin University, the National University of Ireland (at the university colleges in Dublin and Cork), and the Queen's University, Belfast. Dublin has four schools of music (two public and two private) and Cork has one, but Belfast is without any. Concert activity in Dublin is severely handicapped by the lack of a concert hall, but Belfast has its fine Ulster Hall, and Cork its City Assembly Hall. The large music section of the Library of Trinity College, Dublin (Dublin University) is rich in manuscripts, and there is a noteworthy collection of harps, bagpipes, and Dublin-made harpsichords and pianos in the National Museum of Ireland.

The chief names in the modern musical annals of Dublin have been those of Count John McCormack (1884–1945), celebrated tenor; Vincent O'Brien (d. 1946), organist of the Pro-Cathedral; Fritz Brase (d. 1940), founder of the Irish Army School of Music and (1927–1936) conductor of the Dublin Philharmonic Society; and John F. Larchet, professor of music at University College, Dublin. The foremost authority on Irish folk music is Donal O'Sullivan, director of Irish folk song studies at University College, Dublin. Modern Irish composers include Herbert Hughes (d. 1937), E. Norman Hay (d. 1943), and Carl Hardebeck (d. 1946), the pioneer of the Irish folk song revival; John F. Larchet, Frederick May, Arthur Duff, Brian Boydell, Eamonn O Gallchobhair and Reamonn O Frighil. Conductors include Michael Bowles, music director and conductor, Radio Eireann (1941–1948), and J. M. Doyle, conductor of the Dublin Grand Opera Society and director of the Irish Army School of Music.

Bibliography.—Bunting, Edward, *The Ancient Music of Ireland*, vols. 1 and 2 (London 1796, 1809), vol. 3 (Dublin 1840); Petrie, George, *The Petrie Collection of the Ancient Music of Ireland* (Dublin 1855); O'Curry, E., *On the Manners and Customs of the Ancient Irish*, 3 vols. (London 1873); Armstrong, R. B., *The Irish and the Highland Harps* (Edinburgh 1904); *The Journal of the Irish Folk Song Society* (London 1904–1939) includes the *Bunting Collection of Irish Folk Music and Songs*, edited by Donal O'Sullivan (vols. 22-29); Flood, Grattan W. H., *A History of Irish Music*, 2d ed. (Dublin 1906); Joyce, P. W., *Old Irish Music and Songs* (Dublin 1909); Fox, Charlotte Milligan, *Annals of the Irish Harpers* (London 1911); Fleischmann, Aloys, ed., *Music in Ireland* (Cork 1952).

ALOYS FLEISCHMANN,
University College, Cork.

IRISH SCHOOLS AND SCHOOLMEN OF THE MIDDLE AGES. The Irish monastic schools, dating from the 5th century, were celebrated all over Europe; the lay schools, though playing an important part in spreading learning at home, were not so well known. These two classes of schools were quite distinct all through the literary history of Ireland, and, without interfering with one another, worked contemporaneously. By the 7th century Irish missionaries were scattered all over Europe, and for more than two centuries Ireland maintained her glorious position. Then, in the 9th century, came the invasions by the Northmen, who spread destruction among the Irish schools and monasteries. As Ireland was a group of petty kings, her recovery was quicker than might have been expected. Towards the close of the 11th century, according to St. Malachy and St. Bernard, the old Irish monastic and missionary spirit had become dimmed, chiefly by the Norse invasions. These two saints apparently agreed on the introduction of the reformed Benedictines into Ireland. The Irish postulants, sent to Clairvaux to be trained under the eye of St. Bernard, returned to Ireland as professed monks in 1142 and laid the foundation of Mellifont; within ten years Mellifont founded seven new abbeys. Before the Anglo-Norman invasion of 1170, there were 12 Cistercian monasteries in Ireland, five of which had been founded from England and Wales.

The Anglo-Norman invasion, with the political division of the country between the native Irish and the "adventurers," brought about a division among the new religious foundations into Irish and English houses. The Dominicans were the first of the friars who came to Ireland, and their first house was in Dublin (1224), the center of the Anglo-Norman government. Yet, they soon had Irish foundations—Athenry, founded by Myler Bermingham (1241); Cashel, founded by David McKelly, archbishop of Cashel (1245); and Carlingford, founded by Richard de Burgh (1305). The Franciscan Province was established in Ireland about 1231, but its early houses were established chiefly at the seaports, where English influence was strong. Within 15 years (before 1256) Irish houses stood at Cashel, Nenagh, Limerick, Multifernan, and New Ross. Between 1285 and 1325 the cleavage between Irish and English houses (Franciscan and Dominican) went on apace, so that (1325) the Franciscans definitely divided their houses. Nenagh, County Tipperary, became the custodian of the Irish friars, with Athlone, Ennis, Clare-Galway, Galway, Armagh, Cavan, and Killeigh as their sister houses. English influence was gradually shrinking, and the Irish houses consequently were adding to their numbers.

Religious Schools and Writers.—These are so numerous that space can be provided for only the most important. One of the earliest writers was Congan, abbot of Cistercian Suir Abbey (about 1150), who wrote the *Acts of Malachy* (archbishop of Armagh), *Epistles to St. Bernard*, and the *Acts of St. Bernard*. It was by his persuasion that St. Bernard undertook to write the Life of St. Malachy. Marian O'Gorman, abbot of Knock Abbey, County Louth (1171), wrote the supplement of the famous *Martyrology* of Aengus of Tallaght. John Duns Scotus (13th-14th centuries), the "Subtle Doctor" and Franciscan, has had his life and works edited by Luke Wadding, the celebrated Irish Franciscan, in 12 volumes (1639). Experts, however, are not agreed about the country of his birth, Ireland, Scotland, or England, or even about the year of his birth or of his death. Of the writers of the Cistercian Order, we can mention only a few principal ones. Matthew O'Heney, of Holy Cross Abbey, County Tipperary, afterwards archbishop of Cashel (1192–1206) and papal legate (1194), wrote, among other works (since lost), a *Life of St. Cuthbert, Bishop of Lindisfarne*, and several *Epistles to Pope Celestine III*. Henry Crump, doctor of divinity and professor at Oxford (1390), belonged to the Abbey of Baltinglass, County Wicklow (1382), and was a prominent opponent of John Wycliffe (Wiclif), English religious reformer. Donchadh O'Daly, abbot of Boyle, County Roscommon (d. 1250), "was an eminent bard, and in the hymneal species, was superior to all the poets of his time." Felix O'Dullany, of Jerpoint Abbey, County Kilkenny, governed the diocese of Ossory, 1178–1202, endowed the abbey, and was buried in a tomb on the north side of the hign altar—where many miracles are said to have been wrought. Maurice MacGibbon, abbot of the Cistercian monastery of Nenay (Maigue), Limerick (founded in 1148 from Mellifont), was appointed archbishop of Cashel in 1567; he had a strenuous time in Elizabeth's reign, and escaped to Oporto, Portugal, where he died in 1578.

The 15th century saw an enormous production of Irish annals, chronicles, and philosophical and theological treatises. John of Ireland (c.1460), a Dominican friar, published a *Manipulus Florum*, a "Collection of the best flowers out of all the Sacred Writers, proper for all subjects." One Malachy O'Lachnayn, a secular priest of Killaloe, wrote an *Antiquum Missale* consisting of psalms, offices, and lives of saints, in Gothic character and illuminated (MS. in Trinity College, Dublin). In the 16th century the *Whole Philosphy of John Scotus* was published by Maurice O'Fihely, a Franciscan and archbishop of Tuam, who also published a *Dictionary to Holy Scriptures* (Venice 1603). A James Walsh, an Irishman who became a divinity student at Oxford, translated into English the writings on Ireland of the celebrated Giraldus Cambrensis (Giraldus or Gerald de Barri Cambrensis). Writers on philosophy and commentators on St. Thomas's writings continued in the 16th century. The latest was Edmund Tanner, bishop of Cork (1574–1579), who was the author of *Dissertations on the Summa of St. Thomas.*

Annals.—These are the materials for a real history of Ireland. The principal ones now remaining in the Gaelic language are those of *Tighernach, Ulster, Loch Cé, Inisfallen, Boyle, Connacht, Donegal,* and the *Chronicon Scotorum.* Those of *Clonmacnois* are lost in the Gaelic version, but a translation into English is extant (1627). Besides these, we have in Latin those of Multifernam, Grace, and Clyn. Tighernach died in 1088, but his *Annals* have been continued down to 1407. His compilation is a remarkable instance of the great learning and devotion to scholarly pursuits of the Irish laymen of the 10th and 11th centuries, and affords evidence of a cultivation and diffusion of literature which, at so early a period, would do honor to the history of any country. Fragments of these *Annals* are in the Bodleian and Trinity College, Dublin, libraries; they were edited by Whitley Stokes (1830–1909) in the *Revue Celtique,* vol. 16. In order of time, the next compilation of ecclesiastical and general historical records, is that of Inisfallen, about the year 1215; the monastery in Loch Lein (Killarney) dates from the 6th century, so that the compilation may have been begun about the 10th century. These *Annals* were reproduced in facsimile from the original manuscript (Rawlinson B. 503, in the Bodleian Library, Oxford) by the Royal Irish Academy, Dublin, in 1933. The *Annals of Boyle,* part in Irish and part in Latin, begin with the Creation and reach down to 1253; the Cistercian monastery at Boyle was founded quite near the ancient Irish monastery. The *Annals of Ulster* gathered the abundant materials that had accumulated since Tighernach's time down to 1498, the date of the death of the compiler, MacManus; W. M. Hennessy edited in four volumes, Irish and English (1887–1901), the manuscripts in Trinity College, Dublin, the Bodleian Library, Oxford, and the British Museum. *The Annals of Loch Cé,* near Boyle, County Roscommon, are known as a continuation of the *Annals of Tighernach;* the manuscript in Trinity College, Dublin, was edited and translated by W. M. Hennessy (London 1871). The *Annals of Connacht* begin with the year 1224 and end in 1562, but the years 1394–1397 are missing; the only copies extant are in Trinity College, Dublin, and the Royal Irish Academy. They are probably a fragment of the *Annals of the O'Duigenans of Kilronan,* County Roscommon. Of the history of the *Chronicon Scotorum,* by the celebrated Duald MacFirbis, little is known; three copies are extant—one in Trinity College, Dublin, and two in the Royal Irish Academy. MacFirbis was the last of a long line of lay historians and chroniclers of Tireragh, County Sligo. The compilation, which includes the period between 375 and 1135 A.D. and is one of the most authentic collections, is from more ancient annals (ed., W. M. Hennessy, London 1866). The only known copy of the so-called *Annals of Clonmacnois* is an English translation of the year 1627, in the quaint style of the Elizabethan period. It seems to be a faithful rendering of the original Irish version, and comes down to the year 1408. It was translated into English in 1627 by Conell Mageoghagan (ed., D. Murphy, Dublin, 1896).

The Annals of the Kingdom of Ireland by the Four Masters are the most important of all in point of interest and historical value. Michael O'Clery, the chief of the Four Masters, and inspirer of the great national literary work, was born near Ballyshannon, County Donegal, in 1580, of a family of hereditary scholars, lay and ecclesiastical; he probably was educated by the Franciscans there, and became a member of the order. In 1627 he visited the various Irish religious houses and other repositories of ancient Irish manuscripts and laboriously copied all the important tracts dealing with the ecclesiastical and civil history of the country. The work begins with the Deluge, Anno Mundi, 2242, and ends in 1616 A.D. It covers about 4,500 years of a nation's history in 1,100 quarto pages. No perfect copy of the autograph is known to exist. Trinity College, Dublin, has a portion from 1335 to 1603, and T.C.D. has a portion from 1170 (imperfect) to 1616 (ed. J. O'Donovan, Dublin 1851). Surviving Gaelic literature amounts in volume to many times that of classical Rome, and was an important factor in European literary history.

We can deal only briefly with the Latin *Annals of Ireland.* We know the name and station of some of the writers, and approximately their date. *Clyn's Annals* were written by John Clyn, a Franciscan friar in the convent of that order in Kilkenny; in 1336 he was guardian of a Franciscan house founded by James, earl of Ormonde, in his earldom of Carrick. His description of the plague of 1348 is simple and pathetic, and the concluding lines of his *Annals* are also pathetic: "I leave parchment for continuing the work, if haply any man survive." He died the next year. From the Scottish invasion of 1315 to the plague of 1348 may be considered the period of *Clyn's Annals.* (See *Annals of Ireland* by John Clyn and Thady Dowling, with *Annals of Ross,* edited by R. Butler, Irish Archaeological Society, Dublin, 1849). The *Annales Hiberniae* were compiled about 1537–1539, probably by James Grace, who is said to have belonged to the Priory of St. John, in Kilkenny; they begin at 1074 and end at 1370 (the manuscript, in Trinity College, was published by the Irish Archaeological Society, Dublin, 1842). For an account of the enormous output of literature and chronicles by Irish scholars it must suffice to refer the reader to Eugene O'Curry's *Lectures on the Manuscript Materials of Ancient Irish History* (1860). The authors of most of the other Anglo-Irish Annals are unknown; they express no personal feeling and record events almost mechanically. A brief list of the Annals will suffice: *Clonenagh* in Laoighis; *Cong,* of the 10th century, an account of Irish families, kings, and Irish saints; *Mellifont,* 1142–1500; *Multifernan,* West Meath, Franciscan Monastery, 1245–1274; *Nenagh,* County Tipperary, Franciscan, 1336–1370; *Duiske,* County Kilkenny, Cistercian Monastery, written in 1512 and continued to the suppression of the monasteries about 1540.

Lay Schools.—Nearly all the professional physicians, lawyers (brehons), poets, builders, and historians were laymen. A large proportion of the men chronicled in the Irish Annals during the whole period of Ireland's literary pre-eminence, as distinguished in art and general literature, were laymen. The old schools taught by Christian ollaves or doctors—laymen—the representatives of the druid teachers of ancient times, still held their ground. There were several classes of these schools. In the bardic schools were taught poetry, history, and general Irish literature. Some were for law and some for other special professions. Edmund Campion, in 1571, saw schools for law and medicine where "they speake Latine like a vulgar tongue, whereat they begin as children and hold on sixteene or twenty yeares." The position of the bards was well established in the earliest tradition of the Irish polity. In the Anglo-Norman period, after the invasion of 1170, the Normans built monasteries where education was given as in the English monasteries, but the Irish chieftains continued their private schools of law, medicine, poetry, and history, and their output of Gaelic literature. Those schools were hereditary, passing from father to son, and lived on wherever independence was retained or where the invaders were assimilated. The later bardic schools of poetry date from about the 13th to the middle of the 17th century; they produced a plentiful supply of manuscript material, but very little has been published. The time is not yet ripe for a proportioned survey of it. One of its most remarkable features is that it deals with a continuous Irish historical present; the same manner of life, the same mode of thought, were apparent in the 18th as in the 8th century—the Gaelic Catholic civilization. Every chieftain had an annalist or bard in his school of poetry and history; we have a long list of the chief bardic families. The greater chiefs had each, severally, a law school, and we know the names of the great lawyers for the interpretation of the ancient Brehon law. The training course for a lawyer lasted 20 years. Each chief had a doctor hereditary in the family, and again we have the names. These schools were supported by grants of lands from the Irish chiefs.

A few words about the English policy in education in Ireland will not be out of place. In 1320 Pope Clement V made an effort to erect a *Studium Generale* in Dublin as a center of higher studies for the whole of Ireland. The project was doomed to failure from the start, as the pope did not realize Irish conditions and that a university in Dublin would be confined almost exclusively to the English settlers. In the Tudor period (from 1485) the shadow of impending change fell upon the Irish schools, yet at this time the O'Clerys of Donegal (the family of the principal member of the "Four Masters"—the Annalists) kept three schools—for literature, history, and poetry. During the Reformation period, Henry VIII tried in 1537 to set up an English school in Dublin as "the Irish language kept many of his Irish subjects savage and wild," but the scheme ultimately failed as funds were not available. Yet, in 1540 Henry suppressed three religious houses: the Convent of the Canonesses of St. Augustine of Grace Dieu (north County Dublin), founded in 1190 for the education of the young ladies of the Pale in the English tongue; the Cistercian Abbey of St. Mary's; and the Cathedral Chapter of Holy Trinity (Dublin), where the boys of the Pale were educated. The lord deputy and council of Ireland had recommended in vain that they be spared, as there were no other schools to take their place. The confiscation of Irish and Anglo-Norman Catholic schools went on apace. In the reign of James I a few schools in the Irish-speaking districts managed to continue, especially in Galway, where a flourishing academy for classics and general education was kept by the celebrated John Lynch, afterwards bishop of Killala. In 1615 James' commissioners visited the school, which they found full of scholars from all parts of Ireland and "highly efficient," yet they ordered it to be closed. In spite of the penal laws many schools struggled to exist, but ended up as "hedge schools."

Medical Schools.—In the pre-Christian period in Ireland the Druids ranked next in importance to the kings. They were priest-physicians and teachers. In the early Christian or monastic period medicine was taught and practiced by the monks in their schools. The great libraries of Britain and the Continent contain numerous manuscripts that show that the monks were diligent students of medicine. As early as the 6th century the Irish monks had established on the Continent *Hospitalia Scothorum* (Irish Hospitals). Medicine and surgery were carefully studied in Ireland from the very earliest times. The kings and the great Irish families had physicians attached to their households whose office was, as in other professions, hereditary. In the 10th century the physicians, like the rest of the community, took family names: there are abundant notices in Irish writings of the household hereditary physicians of most of the leading chiefs. The stipend usually consisted of a tract of land and a residence, free of rent and tribute, together with certain allowances. The Irish medical manuscripts were written on vellum. The members of each medical family had generally their own special book, which was handed down from father to son. Other books were copied from time to time, so that the chief medical families had libraries containing the medical knowledge then available. The oldest medical manuscript in Ireland appears to be one copied in 1352. The manuscripts between the 13th and 18th centuries, preserved in the libraries of Dublin, London, and Oxford, form a collection of medical literature in the Irish language which is probably the largest in existence in any one tongue. There are 80 medical manuscripts in the Royal Irish Academy, Dublin, some of which have been published.

The physics and psychology of Aristotle were the foundation on which the medical physicians raised the structure of their study of the pathology of body and mind. Further, the school system of the scholastics was taken over *in toto* by the medical schools and, as the formal logic of the schools was adopted in the disputations and writings of the medical faculties, the study of scholastic logic was an essential part of the medical discipline. This new medical learning was introduced into Ireland in the 14th and 15th centuries. The Irish doctors took over as a whole the medical system and tradition of their continental brethren. This explains the presence in Irish medical manuscripts of philosophic treatises that were considered by the continental doctors necessary to the scientific study of medicine. There are Gaelic versions of the standard textbooks, and it is known that some of the Irish medical men had studied medicine outside Ireland. The number of extant Irish texts is considerable, but the study of this medico-philosophical literature has been almost entirely neglected up to the present time. There are manuscripts of the type in Trinity College, Dublin; British Museum; National Library, Dublin; National Library, Scotland; Bodleian Library, Oxford; University of Edinburgh; and the Royal Irish Academy. Under James I these hereditary practitioners were stripped of their holdings and followed their liege lords to foreign lands; many of them never returned to their native land but gained fame abroad.

Art Schools.—In the 5th century St. Patrick kept in his household artists in several mediums. The pastoral staff was of wood and of small size —practically a walking stick with an ornamental case. Its manufacture seems to have formed a regular branch of Irish monastic art. We still preserve beautiful specimens of these richly adorned staffs—such as that of Clonmacnois (in the National Museum, Dublin) and that of Lismore (in the Castle). Two processional crosses, that of Cong (National Museum) and that of Clogher (at Monaghan), were of oak covered with bronze designs, enamels, filigree work, and precious stones, and date from the 12th century. The two-handled chalice of Ardagh (National Museum), of about the 8th-10th century, was composed of gold, silver, bronze, lead, enamel, glass, amber, and mica. The relic shrines, preserved, are similarly precious. Some of the leather satchels for carrying those shrines around are also preserved. The Irish artists nowhere displayed more manual dexterity, ingenuity, and invention than in the art of copying and adorning religious manuscripts; they are the fairest specimens of caligraphy and illumination now extant. We need only mention the celebrated *Book of Kells* (8th century). As to church building, the two finest monuments of Irish Romanesque style are the Cathedral of Clonfert (County Galway) and Cormac's Chapel, on the Rock of Cashel (County Tipperary). The latter marks the zenith of the Hiberno-Romanesque style (1134). In artistic iconographic stone-carving of monumental high crosses, Ireland was especially rich; about 55 still remain from the 8th-10th centuries. In the 10th and following centuries Celtic crosses attained a high degree of beauty and wealth of ornament. In music, the Irish teachers continued their art in spite of the Danish invasion. In 1185, Giraldus Cambrensis, the famous Anglo-Norman writer on Ireland, stated that Irish music had "a singular charm, quick and lively, and withal sweet and blithe in tone." He mentioned especially the harp, that was probably used in the monasteries as part of the ritual. He stated that "the bishops, abbots, and saints of Ireland were wont to carry their harps with them on their journeys, and that the sounds they drew from them were a source of pious delight." Again, he stated that the Irish harpists "are incomparably more skilful than those of any other nation I have ever seen." For centuries after the time of Giraldus, music continued to be cultivated uninterruptedly in the Irish schools, and there was an unbroken succession of great professional harpists which continued to the 17th century, and after.

Bibliography.—De Visch, C., *Bibliotheca Scriptorum*, O. Cist (Cologne 1655); Ware, James, *Bishops* (Dublin 1745); id., *Writers* (Dublin 1745); Burke, Thomas, *Hibernia Dominicana* (Cologne 1762); Archdall, Mervyn, *Monasticon Hibernicum* (Dublin 1786), ed. by Moran (Dublin 1873–1876); O'Curry, Eugene, *Lectures on the MS. Materials for Ancient Irish History* (Dublin 1861); Dimock, J. F., ed., *Giraldi Cambrensis Tipographia Hibernica* (London 1867); O'Curry, Eugene, *Manners and Customs of Ancient Irish People* (London 1873); Healy, John, *Irish Ancient Schools and Scholars* (Dublin 1890); Hyde, Douglas, *Literary History of Ireland* (London 1899); Stuart, James, *City of Armagh*, ed. by Ambrose Coleman (Dublin 1900); O'Heyne, John L., *Irish Dominicana*, ed. by Ambrose Coleman (Dundalk 1902); Joyce, P. W., *Social History of Ancient Ireland* (London 1903); Bergin, Osborne, *Journal Ivernian Society*, vol. 5 (1913); Corcoran, Timothy, *State Policy in Irish Education* (Dublin 1916); Molony, Michael, *Irish Ethno-Botany* (Dublin 1919); Fitzmaurice, E. B., and Little, A. G., *Franciscan Province of Ireland* (Manchester 1920); Lawlor, H. J., *St. Bernard's Life of St. Malachy* (London 1920); Nicholson, William, *Irish Historical Library* (Dublin 1724; Manchester 1920); Ronan, Myles V., *Reformation in Dublin, 1536–1558* (London 1926); Blacam, Hugh de, *Gaelic Literature Surveyed* (Dublin 1929); Ronan, Myles V., *Reformation Under Elizabeth, 1558–1580* (London 1930); Ryan, John, *Irish Monasticism* (Dublin 1931); Gougaud, Louis, *Christianity in Celtic Lands* (London 1932); Shaw, Francis, *Medieval Medico-Philosophical Treatises in the Irish Language* (*Feil-Scribhinn Eoin Mhic Neill*) (Dublin 1940).

MYLES V. RONAN,
Parish Priest; Member, Royal Irish Academy; Fellow, Royal Historical Society.

IRISH SEA, the body of water between England on the east and Ireland on the west. It is connected with the Atlantic Ocean on the north by the North Channel, and on the south by Saint George's Channel. The north shore of Wales and the southwest shore of Scotland are washed by this sea It is almost circular in form, about 140 miles north and south, and the same east and west. Morecambe Bay is the largest arm of the sea on the coast of England; and on the west coast, Dublin and Dundalk bays are the most important. The Isle of Man lies in the center of the sea. The ancients termed the Irish Sea *Oceanus Hibernicus*.

IRITIS, ī-rī'tis, inflammation of the iris of the eye. There are several types of the disease, depending upon the cause. Rheumatism and syphilis frequently result in plastic iritis, and the contraction of a fibrinous exudation deforms the iris. In spongy iritis, a fibrinous coagulum takes place in the anterior chamber of the eye. Catamenialis iritis may occur at menstrual periods.

IRKUTSK, ĭr-kōōtsk', city, Soviet Russia, capital of the Irkutsk Region, in the southern part of Asiatic Russia, on the right bank of the Angara River 45 miles from the southwest shore of Lake Baikal. Prior to the Revolution of October 1917, it was the residence of the governor general of eastern Siberia and the seat of an archbishopric of the Greek Orthodox Church. A great fire in 1879 destroyed many important buildings, including the library and museum of the Siberian section of the Russian Geographical Society. There are a university, founded in 1918, and several colleges. Varied manufactures include machinery for the Lena gold fields. The city was founded in 1652 as a center for trade in fur and skins with Siberia, and commerce with China increased its importance. John Ledyard (q.v.), the American traveler, described Irkutsk as a settlement of some 2,000 houses; he was arrested there on Feb. 24, 1788, on the instructions of Empress Catherine II (Catherine the Great). Between 1918 and 1921 the city was the scene of much disturbance. A Czechoslovak force fighting on behalf of the Allies occupied it on July 8, 1918; it was soon lost to the Bolsheviks, but was recaptured on August 17. Admiral Aleksandr Vasilievich Kolchak, counterrevolutionary leader, retreated to Irkutsk after the fall of Omsk in 1919; here he was forced to resign on Jan. 4, 1920, and on February 7 he was captured and shot by the Bolsheviks. Pop. (1939) 243,380.

IRNERIUS, ĭr-nēr'ĭ-ŭs, or **WARNERIUS,** or **GUARNERIUS,** Italian jurist: b. Bologna, 1050?; d. ?1130. Regarded as an authority on the Justinian Code, he wrote *Summa Codicis*, the first systematic treatise on Roman law.

IRON, Ralph, the pen name of Olive Schreiner (q.v.).

IRON.—The following 12 articles in this section describe the chemical element *iron* and its properties; methods of manufacture, mining, and handling. For the convenience of the reader and for quick reference the heading of each article is listed below together with its number in the series:

1. Chemical Element Iron and Its Properties	
2. Older Processes 3. Cast Iron 4. Pig Iron 5. Wrought Iron 6. Malleable Iron	Manufacture
7. Origin of Iron Ores 8. Districts of the United States 9. Iron Ore Supplies 10. Mining and Handling	Iron Ores
11. Iron and Steel, Metallography of	
12. Iron and Steel Industry in the United States	

1. CHEMICAL ELEMENT IRON AND ITS PROPERTIES.—The term iron has such a variety of applications in referring to the many alloys of which iron is a base, that it is difficult for the average person to use the term correctly. Iron has been known from prehistoric times. Molding records, decaying monuments, fabulous legends, and sibylline traditions have been examined, but no one has found out how man discovered the utility of iron, or how man first learned the art of extracting the metal from its ores. The name iron undoubtedly was applied to this metal after man had discovered how to extract or separate it from its ores, and the name for iron differed in every language. The term *ayas* in Sanskrit was shared in common with copper by the Latin and Teutonic languages—Latin, *oes;* Gothic, *aiz.* Apparently the term *ayas* finally assumed the special meaning of iron, being derived from the older name of copper. The Gothic *eisarn* (iron) is considered by J. and W. Grimm as a derivative form of *aiz. Eisarn* is changed in Old High-German to *îsarn,* later to *isan,* the Modern German, *eisen,* while the Anglo-Saxon *îsern* leads to *iren* and iron. In its true sense, the term iron refers to the absolutely pure form of the metallic element iron. As iron has never been produced in the chemically pure form, pure iron is merely a metallurgical curiosity. There are several methods of producing forms of iron which are nearly pure and are available commercially. These commercial forms of nearly pure iron are available to the research scientist, enabling him to carry on many different tests in an effort to determine the mechanical, physical, and chemical properties of nearly pure iron. The following account of the characteristics of nearly pure iron are based upon the results of this research. All references are to the various forms of commercially pure iron and not to the many alloys of which iron is the basic element, such as iron casting, pig iron, malleable iron, etc. These forms of iron contain large percentages of carbon and other elements; they are highly alloyed ferrous products which differ chemically and physically from the commercial forms of nearly pure iron.

The early history of iron is inextricably tied up with mythology, religion, and folk lore. The first iron to be used by primitive man was unquestionably meteoric iron (essentially an alloy of iron and nickel) which, aside from having potentialities as a tool or weapon, possessed two characteristics that impelled those primitive people to worship it. First was the desire of the people to have as a fetish some object of supernatural origin to be the abode of a spirit and thereby give to its possessor power over such a deity. Second, this fetish object must be readily transportable so that in times of stress or danger early man could have a god that was close at hand. Meteoric iron, a heaven-sent material, was an ideal fetish, because it undoubtedly came from the sky, and as a celestial visitor it was a suitable home for the spirit.

Biblical references to iron are a measure of its antiquity. There are 90 references to this metal in the Old Testament, but only 7 in the New, tending to indicate that after the birth of Christ, iron had become so common that it no longer merited unusual consideration.

Production of Iron.—With perhaps the exception of the meteoric source and a very few portions of the earth's crust, metallic iron is found in chemical combination with other elements, principally as an oxide, mechanically mixed with certain amounts of earthy matter (chiefly sand or clay), and occurring in deposits known as ore. The operation of reducing the ore to a metallic iron is known as *smelting.* The extraction of iron from some of its ores (smelting) is easily carried out, as it is only necessary to mix ores with charcoal and create a brisk fire to cause the metal to separate. If the ores are pure, the metal itself will be relatively pure and require very little if any refining. Iron produced by this process results in a pasty and unfused mass which is easily worked under the hammer and may be wrought into useful forms.

Ores.—Iron ores, from which the metal may be extracted, occur in large deposits in every continent of the globe; however, smelting operations can be carried on only in localities where iron, fuel, and flux can be assembled at moderate transportation costs. The only important varieties of ore are hematite (Fe_2O_3), magnetite (Fe_3O_4), limonite (hydrated Fe_2O_3), and siderite ($FeCO_3$).

Reduced Iron.—The oldest and most widespread commercial method of extraction is by reduction of iron oxide. Such oxides may be concentrated magnetite ore, with byproducts such as mill scale or partially oxidized iron scrap borings, turnings, etc. Reduction is accomplished at temperatures between 900° C. and 1090° C. in an atmosphere rich in carbon monoxide or pure hydrogen. Nearly pure iron has been produced by numerous processes involving the use of crushed ore and removal of the oxygen from the iron by use of carbonaceous or reducing conditions. This method is not new, as primitive man produced iron in this manner. Iron produced by the reduction process is often referred to as a sponge iron, from its spongelike character. Sponge iron has been almost exclusively used as a melting stock for electric furnaces as a raw material or base for the production of high grade steels. It is also a raw material for the production of an iron powder or iron in a finely divided state. Such iron powder may be used in the fabrication of iron or iron alloy parts by the technique of powder metallurgy, whereby iron powder or alloyed iron powders are cold pressed in steel dies to the shape desired. This cold-pressed shape is then heated, sintering the pressed powder together to form a solid resembling a cast or forged part.

Carbonyl Iron.—A very pure form of commercial iron may be produced by allowing carbon monoxide gas to pass over sponge iron at suitable temperatures and pressures, forming an iron carbonyl which is liquid at room temperature. The iron carbonyl decomposes to form again both the metal and carbon monoxide at higher temperatures and atmospheric pressure. Iron produced from iron carbonyl is nearly pure, containing less than 0.0007 per cent carbon and less than 0.01 per cent oxygen. Other elements may not be present in quantities that can be determined. The relative purity of this form of iron makes it ideally suited for the manufacture of magnetic cores. In the powder form it is also used in the field of powder metallurgy.

Electrolytic Iron.—Electrolytic iron, prepared by electrolytic deposition, is as pure a form of iron as may be obtained by any method. There are two processes used for making iron by the electrolytic process. In one, the anode consisting of metallic iron is arranged so that the electric current flows from the iron anode, which furnished the iron, through an electrolyte composed of ferrous chloride ($FeCl_2$) and then to a revolving rod or sheet which forms the cathode. The pure iron is deposited on the cathode in the form of a tube or sheet and can later be stripped from it. In another process, iron is deposited from a solution obtained by leaching iron sulphide ore. A graphite anode permits the current to enter the solution. This is the only known commercial method of producing iron from sulphide ore. Electrolytic iron, when deposited by the usual methods, is brittle, owing to the hydrogen present in the iron. In this brittle form it can easily be broken and made into a powder iron. By heating the deposited electrolytic iron to a red heat (annealing), the hydrogen is driven off, and the iron becomes ductile, the ductility increasing with the temperature of annealing or by repeating the operation. Electrolytic iron may be used in the powder form for the powder metallurgy fabrication field, or remelted and cast into useful forms, or cast into blanks or ingots for rolling or forging. As a raw material it may be used as a base for the manufacture of high-grade ferrous alloys.

COMPOSITION OF ELECTROLYTIC IRON

	Per Cent
Carbon	0.006
Phosphorus	0.005
Sulphur	0.004
Silicon	0.005
Total impurities	.020

Ingot Iron.—Ingot iron is the product of the basic open hearth furnace, the careful manipulation of which produces a commercially pure iron. Only carefully selected raw materials are used in order to keep the iron as free from impurities as possible. The practice used in melting and refining is about the same as for ordinary steel practice with the basic open-hearth process; however, during refining, further purification is carried out by adding a very pure ore to the heat in order to oxidize the small amounts of silicon, manganese, and carbon left in the bath. The molten metal is then degassified, tapped into ladles, and then cast into ingot molds, forming cast ingot iron. Ingot iron is also known as open hearth iron. It is used in sheet metal and plate work, such as roofing, pipe, and tanks, as a base for vitreous enameling, and in electrical work, since its electrical resistance is low, owing to its purity.

A TYPICAL ANALYSIS OF INGOT IRON

	Per Cent
Carbon	0.012
Manganese	0.017
Phosphorus	0.005
Sulphur	0.025
Silicon	0.002
Total impurities	0.061

Physical Properties of Iron.—As the structure and properties of iron are greatly influenced by the kind and amount of impurities present in the different forms produced by the various commercial methods, it should be appreciated that the following discussion concerning the nature of iron and its behavior is based on information made available from research carried out with the various forms. Complete agreement as to the exact values for the various properties and characteristics is not to be expected. The following physical properties are averages of many different tests made by different specialists on the available commercial forms of pure iron:

PHYSICAL CONSTANTS OF IRON

Chemical Symbol	Fe
Atomic No.	26
Atomic Weight	55.85
Density, g./cm.³ at 20° C. (68° F.)	7.87
Density, lb./in.³ at 68° F. (20° C.)	0.284
Atomic Volume, cm.³/g. Atom	7.1
Melting Point, ° C.	1,535
Boiling Point, ° C. (760 mm. Pressure)	3,000
Specific Heat, cal./g./° C. at room temperature (Equals Btu./lb./° F. at room temperature)	0.1075
Latent Heat of Fusion, cal./g.	65
Latent Heat of Fusion, Btu./lb.	117
Linear Coefficient of Thermal Expansion /° F. at Room Temperature. × 10⁻⁶	6.6
Linear Coefficient of Thermal Expansion /° C. at Room Temperature. × 10⁻⁶	11.9
Thermal Conductivity, cal./cm.²/cm./° C./sec. at Room Temperature	0.19
Electrical Resistivity, Microhm—cm.	9.8
Modulus of Elasticity (Tension), lb. per sq. in. × 10⁶	30

Nuclear Structure.—The nucleus of the iron atom consists of 26 protons and 30 neutrons equal in number to the atomic weight of iron (56). The proton is the basic constituent of atomic nuclei having a positive charge. The nucleus of the iron atom, therefore, carries a 26-fold positive charge and is surrounded by enough electrons (26) (unit of negative electricity), to make the atom electrically neutral. The ratio of the weight of the iron atom (56) to the number of neutrons (30) is 0.536. This quantity is an indication of the nuclear stability which is quite large for iron.

Arrangement of Electrons.—The 26 outer electrons are believed to be distributed on 4 shells as follows: the inner K-shell 2, L-shell 8, M-shell 14, and the outer N-shell 2.

Crystallographic Properties.—Iron is found to crystallize in the cubic system with the possibility of existing in two different arrangements of the atoms; body-centered cubic for alpha, beta, and delta iron, and face-centered cubic arrangement for gamma iron. The body-centered cubic arrangement of atoms consists of 9 atoms, 8 atoms of which form the 8 corners of a cube, with the 9th atom located at the center of each unit cube. The face-centered cubic arrangement consists of 14 atoms, 6 of these being placed in the center of each of the 6 cube faces.

Transformation Points.—Iron, upon solidification and during subsequent cooling to room temperature, undergoes polymorphic changes or alterations in crystal structure. The changes that occur during cooling from the temperature of solidification to room temperature reverse themselves upon heating. The temperatures at which these polymorphic changes occur have been called "critical temperatures," and are designated by the notation A2—A3—A4. Upon heating, the changes occur at 770° C. for the A2 transformation, 910° C. for the A3, and 1390° C. for A4. Below the A2 transformation temperature (770° C.) iron exists in the alpha, body-centered form, between A2 and A3 in the beta, body-centered form, between A3 and A4 in the gamma, face-centered form, and between A4 transformation and the beginning of melting, in the delta, body-centered form. These polymorphic changes are influenced by changes in pressure at a constant temperature just as the changes in melting and boiling are affected by changing pressures. The properties of one polymorphic form of iron will differ from those of another form. For example, gamma iron can dissolve up to 1.7 per cent carbon, whereas alpha iron can dissolve only 0.03 per cent carbon. These remarkable polymorphic changes that occur during heating and cooling of iron account, in no small measure, for the importance of iron as the "master metal," and contribute largely to the heat treatment effects obtained in the operation of hardening of steels.

Electrical Properties.—The most predominant electronic property of metals is electrical conductivity. The explanation of this property is based on the conception that electrons are furnished the iron, through an electrolyte comfree to move throughout the atomic space-lattice at definite energy levels while holding the positive atomic nuclei together. This freedom of movement of electrons provides a means by which a stream of electricity may be conducted through a crystal by the application of an external potential which accelerates the electrons and causes them to flow in the direction of the positive side of the applied potential. Electrical resistance arises from any condition which tends to hinder this transfer and flow of electrons. The electrical resistance of iron is greatly influenced by impurities and by previous thermal and mechanical treatment, so that the reported values for iron are often discordant. A value of 9.8 microhm—cm. at 20° C. is considered by H. E. Cleaves and J. G. Thompson to be the best approximation for the resistivity of iron. The electrical resistivity of iron, like other metals, changes with temperature. Cold deformation of the iron crystals increases the resistivity.

Magnetic Properties.—Nearly pure iron is a most important magnetic substance and is capable of being magnetized very highly when surrounded by a solenoid of wire conveying an electrical current, the iron forming a solecore. Magnetization persists only while the current is flowing, for upon cessation of the current, iron retains a negligible amount of magnetism. It is this property of temporary magnetization that makes iron a valuable material for cores of electric magnets or solecores, the action of which plays such an important part in telephone, telegraph, relays and instruments of all kinds. It is also used in the manufacture of magnetic chucks, clutches, and separators of all kinds. The magnetic properties of iron, like the electrical properties, are sensitive to small changes in treatment and amount of impurities. A continual decrease in magnetic properties occurs when heating iron until the A2 transformation 770° C. takes place, at which point iron loses its magnetic properties, becoming nonmagnetic; however, it regains its magnetic possibilities upon cooling again. The temperature at which this loss of magnetism occurs is known as the *Curie Temperature,* one of the most interesting phenomena exhibited by the metal iron.

Mechanical Properties of Iron.—Commercially pure iron is a relatively soft, ductile metal which cannot be hardened by any heat treatments such as are applied to steels. Owing to its high ductility, it can be formed cold by drawing, rolling, stamping, or bending. Any cold forging or forming is accompanied by an increase in hardness and strength. Impurities and alloying elements such as carbon greatly alter the mechanical properties of iron. The element carbon, more than any other constituent, affects the properties of iron, and changes iron to steel. The following indicates the mechanical properties that can be expected from ingot iron which has been annealed to produce a dead soft condition:

Tensile strength in lbs. per sq. in.	38,000
Yield strength in lbs. per sq. in.	19,000
Ductility as measured by percentage elongation in 2 in.	43 to 48
Per cent reduction of area	70 to 77
Hardness as measured by the Brinell Hardness Test	67 Brinell

The mechanical properties of iron may be increased by cold deformation or cold work-hardening. The tensile strength of ingot iron may be increased to approximately 100,000 lbs. per sq. in., with the Brinell hardness increased to approximately 220 Brinell, by subjecting it to severe cold working. Cold working is the only practical way in which the mechanical properties of commercially pure iron may be changed, as this metal is not susceptible to hardening by heating and quenching as is the case with such iron-carbon alloys as steel. The only heat treatment that is carried out with commercially pure iron is that of annealing after cold work-hardening. Annealing may be done by heating the cold work-hardened iron to a temperature range from 650° C. to 750° C. followed by cooling to room temperature. This treatment will restore the original soft, ductile condition of the iron.

Corrosion of Iron.—The metal iron is silverlike in color, and when freshly polished or burnished acquires a bright metallic luster. Iron under ordinary conditions at room temperature in air tends to rust. The tendency of iron to corrode in air is its most unfortunate property. The fact that the structure of iron, unless protected, tends to disintegrate into a red powder causes us to spend millions of dollars annually to avoid destruction of objects of iron. But the process of rusting, although familiar, is not simple. It is not merely the union of oxygen with iron to form the oxide Fe_2O_3. The rust is a hydrated oxide of varying composition, to which we may assign the formula $3Fe_2O_3.n H_2O$. Pure iron tends to rust slowly; the greater the amount of some impurities present, the more rapidly the process takes place. Furthermore, iron does not rust in the absence of water; even if water is in contact with it, the process is not particularly rapid if that liquid is pure. Aqueous solutions of electrolytes cause the action to go on with great rapidity, as anyone can observe by watching the conduct of iron in contact with sea water. The protection of iron from rusting involves merely the formation over the surface of a film which is impervious either to air, or to water, or to both. To attain this end, the metal is coated with zinc, tin, terne metal or vitreous enamel; or the film of magnetic oxide, formed while the iron is cooling (after hot rolling), may be left on the iron.

Polished iron, when heated above room temperature in air or steam, will oxidize by the formation of layers of iron oxide with an aggregate composition intermediate between FeO and Fe_3O_4. Thin oxide films forming between a temperature range of 190° C. and 375° C. furnish the so-called *tempering colors* used by the old-time workmen in tempering steel. The thickness of oxide film is comparable with the wave length of light, and the films furnish a series of interference tints with the dominant color altering as the film thickens. The colors vary from a pale yellow at 190° C. through blue to a gray color at 375° C. As the layers of oxide get thicker, a dark, smooth film is formed, until at a high temperature (1000° C.) a blistering effect occurs. When iron has been exposed to a temperature around 700° C., the smooth, surface film of oxides will offer good resistance to subsequent rusting at room temperature.

Oxides of Iron.—There are three definite oxides formed from the combination of iron and oxygen: iron monoxide, or ferrous oxide, FeO; ferrosic oxide, Fe_3O_4; and ferric oxide, Fe_2O_3. Ferrous oxide, FeO, may be prepared in a number of ways, many of which involve some form of oxidation of iron at some elevated temperature between 200° C. and 700° C. When prepared by gaseous reduction, FeO is a black powder. Ferric oxide, Fe_2O_3, occurs in the native form as hematite (ore), and if prepared artificially, ferric oxide is the end product of the oxidation of iron, of its lower oxides, or hydroxides, and many of its salts. Ferrosic oxide, Fe_3O_4, is a black, magnetic oxide which occurs in nature as the mineral magnetite, one form of which is termed *lodestone.* Fe_3O_4 may be prepared, artificially, by oxidizing iron at a high temperature, either in air or in steam, or by heating carbonate of iron to 350° C., in a current of carbon dioxide.

Although the compounds of iron are of far less importance than the metal and its alloys, there are numerous essential industrial processes in which compounds of iron are employed. The compound salts of iron belong to two classes: the ferrous compounds, and the ferric compounds. The former are generally green in color, which may be changed rather readily to the ferric salts by oxidizing agents, and even tend to undergo that change spontaneously when exposed to air. Ferric compounds are usually red or yellow in color and are stable in air, although they may be changed by energetic reducing agents to the ferrous varieties.

Ferrous Salts.—The most common ferrous salt is the sulphate $FeSO_4.7H_2O$, sometimes called *green vitriol,* or *copperas.* It is obtained in large quantities as a byproduct in the process of galvanizing or tinning of iron and steel to remove scale. The metallic surface to be coated is cleaned by dipping the metal into a bath of sulphuric acid. The action of the acid on the scale produces most of the sulphate, and the superficial attack of the metal produces the remainder. The sulphate accumulates in the bath from which it may be obtained by crystallization. It is a green crystalline salt which tends, upon storage, not only to effloresce, but to oxidize to the brown, basic ferric sulphate. It is used in the manufacture of inks, in dyeing, as a disinfectant, and in water filtration.

Ferric Compounds.—Ferric chloride, $FeCl_3.6H_2O$, is a yellow salt, which gives, by hydrolysis, an acid reaction when dissolved in water. In an alcoholic solution, tincture of iron, it is used as a medicine. Ferric oxide, Fe_2O_3, is much used as a cheap but effective red pigment (Venetian red), and, in another form, as the most expensive rouge. Its color varies with its purity and fineness.

Iron salts have long been used in inks. A common variety is that made by mixing a solution of ferrous salt with tannic acid. Ferrous tannate is soluble and nearly colorless, and the ink is given bluish color by addition of a dye.

Complex Cyanides of Iron.—A yellow crystalline salt, potassium ferrocyanide, $K_4Fe(CN)_6.3H_2O$, is obtained from heating nitrogenous organic matter, potassium carbonate, and iron together, and then leaching the fused mass with water. By the action of strong oxidizing agents, such as chlorine, upon solutions of potassium ferrocyanide, a red salt, potassium ferricyanide, $K_3Fe(CN)_6$, is obtained. Prussian blue, $Fe_4(Fe(CN)_6)_3$ may be prepared by such treatment of potassium ferrocyanide, and has considerable use as a pigment and in laundry bluing.

Bibliography.—Tiemann, Hugh P., *Iron and Steel* (New York 1933); American Society for Metals, *Metals Handbook* (Cleveland 1939); Bray, John L., *Ferrous Production Metallurgy* (New York 1942); Wulff, John, *Powder Metallurgy* (Cleveland 1942); Johnson, Carl G., *Metallurgy* (Chicago 1945); Cleaves, H. B., and Thompson, J. G., *The Metal—Iron* (New York 1946).

CARL G. JOHNSON,
Professor of Mechanical Engineering, Worcester Polytechnic Institute.

2. OLDER PROCESSES AND DIRECT REDUCTION (SPONGE IRON).—

"Older processes" and "direct reduction" are treated together, because from the earliest times until about 1350 A.D. all the iron made in the world was produced by the direct reduction of iron from iron ore in a single step or process.

Coal being unknown, charcoal was the universal metallurgical fuel of ancient man, and iron ore was directly reduced to metal by local smiths in small, charcoal forge fires in the countries bordering on the eastern shores of the

Mediterranean Sea nearly a thousand years before the Periclean age in Greece. Many different names were given to the product of this direct process, one among others being the term "sponge iron."

One of the earliest references to the term "sponge" in connection with iron, is that of the Roman historian, Diodorus Siculus, of the 4th century B.C., who mentions the production on the island of Elba of pieces of iron "resembling great sponges" by the melting of pieces of iron stone (iron ore) in special furnaces. The burning charcoal in these furnaces not only furnished the required temperature, but, as we now know, also served as the reducing agent needed to combine with the oxygen of the ore.

The term "sponge" was appropriate to the product obtained by heating iron ore in a charcoal fire, as the resulting porous, spongy mass of partly reduced iron mixed with melted ore and gangue looked very much like a large black sponge. The ore itself, due to its impurities (gangue), had a lower melting point than the metallic iron, and the porous, spongy appearance of the lumps or sponges pried from the bottom of a charcoal forge fire resulted from the fact that some of the unreduced ore and mineral impurities melted together, forming a slag which ran out leaving holes in an unmelted network of solid, freshly reduced metallic iron.

Earliest Production of Iron.—The first intentional production of iron probably occurred about 1500 B.C. in the area between the Black and Caspian seas, on the southern slope of the Caucasus Mountains. By 1350 B.C. the art of iron smelting had spread from this area throughout Mesopotamia, Palestine, and Egypt, and soon thereafter to the entire Mediterranean World.

Up until the middle of the 14th century, when the first iron smelting furnaces which were large enough and supplied with a sufficiently powerful air blast to be capable of producing molten or "pig" iron came into use in Europe, all metallic iron made by man was produced by the direct process, that is, sponge iron made directly from ore.

Naturally occurring forms of iron oxide (iron ore) are always more or less contaminated with foreign mineral matter, which taken together as a whole are called gangue. The gangue in iron ore is usually made up of siliceous or clayey matter, with the addition at times of some lime-bearing minerals. The object of all iron producers is to reduce the iron oxide part of the iron ore to metallic iron and separate it from the gangue. In the early direct processes, the charcoal forge fire was not hot enough to melt the reduced iron, which consequently remained solid; it was hot enough, however, to melt some of the unreduced iron ore and gangue. This mixture of gangue and unreduced ore, which had a very much lower melting point, was known as cinder, and most of it ran out from the lower part of the fire at the side or bottom of the hearth. The product was a porous lump (loupe) of soft reduced iron; it always contained some entrapped cinder, which was largely eliminated by reheating the loupe to a high forging temperature in a second forge fire and then hammering the metal, at first gently all over to consolidate it, and then more vigorously to pound the molten cinder out of the hot, malleable mass. Several reheatings were usually required.

In the blast furnace, the separation of the metal from the slag or cinder is accomplished much more simply, as the temperature is high enough to melt the iron as well as the gangue. The metal, being heavier and not mixing with the molten slag, collects in a layer at the bottom of the blast furnace from which it can easily be tapped off separately from the lighter slag.

The Earliest Iron Furnace.—The earliest iron-producing furnace was probably a simple vertical hole a few feet deep, dug in the steep clay bank of an open hillside. The hole was uncovered at the top and had a draft hole located at the bottom to face the prevailing wind, furnishing the "blast" for burning the charcoal. It was soon learned, however, that a stronger blast than that obtainable in this way was necessary for effective operation, and hand or foot operated bellows were used to furnish it. It is said that, even before the advent of the Iron Age, bellows had been developed in Egypt for melting copper and bronze and precious metals in clay pots or crucibles by blasting charcoal piled around them with air to make the charcoal burn faster.

To obtain a temperature high enough to melt iron in a shaft furnace, charcoal must be burned with a forced draft or blast. The early bellows were neither large nor powerful enough to do this. Instead, every country developed its own variation of the charcoal forge and made iron by direct reduction of the ore without melting. All of these forges worked on the same principle of adding iron ore to a charcoal fire blown by a forced draft of air usually supplied by bellows.

Medieval Forges.—An English adaptation of the direct process was carried out for several centuries in the Wealdon Forest near London in forges known as bloomery hearths. These consisted of circular mounds built up of alternate layers of charcoal and ore and covered with clay. When a mound was completed, it was blasted with air until the charcoal was burned out. The cinder melted and was tapped off to one side. After the mound had partly cooled down, it was broken open, and a mass of three to four hundred pounds of reduced sponge iron was removed from the bottom.

In a commoner European variation of this process a smaller batch of ore was treated in a charcoal fire on an open brick or stone hearth, the charcoal being similarly blown with a bellows, usually through a hole in the rear wall of the hearth. Charcoal and ore were fed to the fire for several hours, either in alternate layers, or as a mixture, depending on the local practice, until a 50- to 75-pound lump or loupe of reduced iron formed in the lower part of the burning charcoal. After pokers had been used to pry it out, it was picked up by tongs, still white hot and dripping with cinder, and carried to an anvil to be hammered together into a rough bar or bloom as previously described. After reheating and hammering or forging, in order to remove as much cinder as possible, these early sponge iron blooms were fashioned into finished bars not greatly different in appearance, chemical composition or physical properties from present-day wrought iron bars which are made from pig iron either in the old-fashioned puddle furnace or by the modern Aston process.

A well-known early forge of this type was used for centuries on the island of Corsica, becoming known as the Corsican forge. A still commoner type, known as the Catalan forge, was used throughout Europe; it is supposed to have originated in Catalonia, Spain. There were many other local variations of this same charcoal hearth process in different parts of the ancient and medieval world. In the United States, modern types of the Catalan forge with water-cooled hearth side plates, power-driven blower engines, preheated air blast and stacks to carry away the smoke and waste gases were still in operation as late as 1901. This was probably the last of the Catalan forges, but even as late as 1945, in parts of Africa, India, and China, small amounts of iron were still made locally in tiny blast furnaces, a few feet high, fed with ore and charcoal and blown by hand-worked bellows or hollow-log, piston air pumps.

Advent of Blast Furnace.—By the 17th century, the blast furnace process introduced two centuries earlier had already showed its superiority as a producer of iron over the earlier charcoal forge or bloomery processes owing to its much greater productive capacity. This was true even though the pig iron it produced still had to be further refined in "finery" forges to make wrought iron, and the two stages together required more fuel. The blast furnace continued to be the pre-eminent producer of iron from iron ore, neither the older charcoal hearth and bloomery forge processes nor the more modern direct reduction sponge iron processes having at any time accounted for more than a very small fraction of the total iron produced. In modern times over 99 per cent of the world's production of metallic iron is reduced from its ores in blast furnaces.

Modern Definition of Sponge Iron.—Since the early 1920's the term sponge iron has come to mean not only directly reduced sponge iron in the historical sense, but almost any kind of iron or steel made directly from ore, with the exception of pig iron made in a blast furnace. Technically, sponge iron is usually defined as iron ore or oxide reduced to metal without fusion; that is, a direct ore reduction or sponge iron process is one in which solid particles of metallic iron are obtained directly from solid particles of ore without any melting of either the ore or the iron.

Theoretical Advantages of Direct Reduction Processes.—Despite the almost universal acceptance of the blast furnace for smelting iron from its ores, interest in the possibility of producing iron direct from the ore never died out; renewed interest was particularly apparent in the 1920's and again in the early 1940's. Different direct reduction or sponge iron processes have been proposed over the years, and hundreds of patents have been issued on them throughout the world. A considerable number of them have progressed past the paper stage and have been actually tried out experimentally. This continuing attempt on the part of technical men in many different countries to develop an economical direct or sponge iron process has been due to the fundamental theoretical advantages of direct production. These are: first, the simplicity of producing a finished product from the ore in a single step; and second, the lower fuel requirement of the single step process, particularly if advantage is taken of carrying it out at low temperature with a gaseous reducing agent. Iron oxide is rapidly reduced to iron by carbon monoxide at temperatures between 1800° and 2000° F. and at temperatures as low as 1000° F. by hydrogen. This contrasts with temperatures of well over 3000° F. which occur in normal blast furnace practice.

The theoretical heat requirement for the gaseous reduction of ore to metal without melting, in the solid state, is also much lower than when the reduction takes place by contact with hot carbon. This fact is well known from blast furnace operation. A smoothly running blast furnace operating with low fuel consumption is recognized as one in which the ore has been nearly completely reduced to sponge iron by the gases in the upper part or shaft of the furnace, before it has reached the lower, incandescent melting zone in the hearth. If the low temperature, gaseous reduction or sponge iron reaction in the shaft of the blast furnace is incomplete for any reason, the unreduced portion of the ore must be reduced by hot carbon in the hearth, thus increasing the fuel consumption of the furnace. It may be said, therefore, that efficient sponge iron formation is necessary for good blast furnace practice.

Commercial Sponge Iron Processes.—Outside of the very limited iron powder field, only two direct reduction or sponge iron processes are known to be in commercial production, and both are in Sweden. The older, the so-called Sieurin process, has been in operation at Hoganas, Sweden, since about 1910. A very pure ore containing 71 per cent iron is packed in tall clay pots in alternate layers with fine coal and burnt lime. The pots are stacked in a ceramic-type kiln fired with producer gas made from low-grade coal and heated to a temperature of from 1800° to 2000° F. for a period of several days. After cooling, the pots are opened and the loosely consolidated round cakes of sponge iron are removed and compressed to a specific gravity of about 5. The product contains over 95 per cent iron and is used by steel makers, particularly in Sweden, for the production of the higher grades of cutlery, tool and gun steels.

The other commercial Swedish process is known as the Wiberg process. First proposed in 1918, a 2-ton per day commercial unit was placed in operation at Sodafors in Sweden in 1930 after considerable preliminary experimental and development work. Its capacity has subsequently been enlarged. In this process, pure magnetite concentrates are first sintered into lumps and then charged into a low shaft furnace through which hot carbon monoxide gas is passed. The hot gas reduces the ore. The spent gas, containing the carbon dioxide formed by the reduction reaction, is withdrawn from the upper side of the furnace and circulated through hot coke in a separate unit to reduce the carbon dioxide again to monoxide. The coke is kept hot electrically, and the revivified spent gas, after passing through it, is returned to the furnace to reduce more ore. About a fourth of the gas is burned in the upper portion of the furnace to preheat the ore.

In 1943, the Wiberg process produced between 7,000 and 8,000 tons of iron per year, while the Hoganas plant was said to be producing about 15,000 tons.

In the early 1930's, the Germans developed a Norwegian adaptation of the Wiberg process, called the Norsk-Staal process, which they operated for a number of years on high-grade, imported Swedish ore. It was reported to be technically successful and to have produced up to 30,000 tons of sponge iron per year, but its costs were too high to permit it to compete with the ordinary methods of steel production.

Another German direct process using a high-temperature rotary kiln is known as the Krupp-Renn process. This was developed to treat lean, high silica ores. The ore was fed, mixed with coal into one end of the kiln, and heated high enough to reduce and melt both iron and gangue. The result was a mixture of globules of iron, suspended in a viscous mass of gangue which was granulated by running it into water. This was subsequently crushed and the iron separated by magnetic means. Some slag stuck to the iron, so that the magnetic separation was not perfect, and the product had to be treated further.

Rotary Kiln Processes.—A number of rotary kiln sponge iron processes have been tried in the United States. The United States Bureau of Mines did a great deal of work on the reduction of iron in rotary kilns in the 1920's. The United States Steel Corporation tried out a process using three rotary kilns in sequence (one each for heating, reduction, and cooling) known as the Hornsey-Wills process, in the middle 1920's at Lorain, Ohio. In 1945, the Bureau of Mines placed in operation at Laramie, Wyoming, a large experimental rotary kiln which had a design capacity of 50 tons per day. The rotary kiln processes have had trouble producing a high-grade product due to contamination of the sponge iron by the gangue in the ore and the ash and sulphur in the coal usually used as a reducing agent.

A few other direct reduction processes have attained more or less prominence in the technical press since 1930. W. H. Smith of Detroit, Michigan, was active in the development of a process about 1930 which was carried out in vertical retorts through which a mixture of ore and carbonaceous reducing material descended slowly. The retorts were externally heated, the ore attaining a temperature between 1600 and 2000° F. Its capacity was limited by the necessity of transferring the entire heat requirement for reduction through the walls of the retorts. The inventor died before the process was commercialized. In 1943–1944 the Bureau of Mines experimented with a plant in Texas designed by Julian Madaras, using natural gas as the reducing agent. The natural gas was first partially converted into carbon monoxide and hydrogen by heating it with steam to give it more reducing power. The Madaras process was a batch process designed to reduce lump ore by passing hot reducing gases under pressure through it at approximately 1800° F. The pressure on the gas was varied between 35 and 65 pounds per square inch to aid the penetration of the reducing gas into the ore. Twelve-inch lumps of ore were approximately 85 per cent reduced after about 16 hours in the reducing chamber.

Still another process was one developed by G. H. S. Anderson in the 1920's, units of which were said to have operated successfully in Japan in the 1930's. In this process a mixed layer of ore and coal was spread on a large revolving circular hearth and heated from above by closed muffle flues. In this way, the oxidizing combustion gases used to supply the heat required for reduction were prevented from coming into direct contact with the ore being reduced.

Another process known as the Brassert-Cape process was tried out during World War II in a commercial size plant at Warren, Ohio, designed to produce 100 tons of sponge iron per day. This process utilized the hydrogen content of hot coke oven gas as the reducing agent and was distinguished from other previous or contemporary processes by its much lower operating temperature, between 1100° and 1250° F. instead of 1600-2000° F. At this low temperature only the hydrogen in the coke oven gas reacted with the ore. The reducing unit was a 12-hearth Herreshoff furnace. Magnetite concentrates, the size of coarse sand, were fed into the top of the furnace and moved slowly downward by revolving rabble arms over each of the 12 hearths, as hot coke oven gas passed upward countercurrently. The gas was cleaned after passing through the furnace and returned to the steel mill for use as fuel. The plant attained only about one third of its designed capacity and was no longer operated after the war emergency was over, although its product was used successfully in the production of a number of trial heats of electric furnace steel.

Requisites for Successful Sponge Iron Process.—To be successful, a sponge iron process must produce a high-grade product, one containing a minimum of undesirable impurities. Nearly everything except metallic iron constitutes an undesirable impurity. Because direct reduction without melting offers little opportunity for eliminating gangue from the ore, a high-grade ore or ore concentrate must be used as raw material, lower-grade ores being left to the blast furnace. Since the development of new wet magnetic concentrating methods in the 1930's, iron ore concentrates of much higher purity than ever before have become available. American reserves of magnetic iron ore suitable for concentration are also known to be much greater than was formerly believed to be the case. These two factors are so favorable to sponge iron production that they lead one to predict that development of the direct production of metallic iron from its ores without fusion will be continued in the United States until a commercially successful process is achieved.

Bibliography.—Beck, Ludwig, *Geschichte des Eisens,* 5 vols. (Berlin 1891); Swank, James Moore, *History of Iron Manufacture in All Ages* (Philadelphia 1892); Peters, Richard, Jr., *Two Centuries of Iron Smelting in Pennsylvania* (Chester, Pa. 1921); Straker, Ernest, *Wealdon Iron* (London 1931); Boylston, H. M., *Introduction to the Metallurgy of Iron and Steel* (New York 1936); Sisco, Frank T., *Modern Metallurgy for Engineers* (New York 1941).

CHARLES F. RAMSEYER,
Assistant to the President, H. A. Brassert & Company.

3. CAST IRON.—Gray cast iron (synonym: gray iron) is the most widely used of all cast materials. The term "gray iron" is derived from the characteristic gray fracture, as opposed to the lighter colored fractures of most steels. The presence of the dark graphite flakes in gray iron is responsible for its unusual fracture color or shade. Gray cast iron castings range in size from heavy machinery parts weighing well over 100,000 pounds to small castings such as piston rings weighing but a few ounces. This material finds wide usage because it combines useful engineering or service characteristics with ease and economy in overall production. Large users include the automotive industry (major casting tonnage, cylinder blocks), municipalities (gas and water piping), machinery builders, agricultural implement manufacturers, chemical and oil industries, building and furnishing industries, railroads, steamships, and so on, down to the cast iron skillet in the kitchen. In all these fields it has been challenged by other materials—the skillet is made also in aluminum and in steel. Competitive challenges have been met by improved classes of gray iron. In some cases other materials have proved superior, while in many cases gray iron has supplanted other materials.

Foundries where iron castings are made are found in nearly all cities where the population is 50,000 or over. There are about 2,880 iron foundries in the United States. Their capacities vary from small shops melting perhaps 10 tons per day, to large establishments whose daily melt may exceed 250 tons. The total melting capacity of the iron foundry industry is about 26 million tons per year, castings production about 17 million tons.

Beside iron castings, other metals and alloys such as steel, aluminum, magnesium, brasses, bronzes and others are made in cast as well as in wrought form. The casting industry is in total the fifth largest of all manufacturing industries.

The metal industries (cast and wrought) have developed tremendously since the advent of the Industrial Revolution. Manufacture, agriculture, transportation, and communication have grown concurrently with developments in metals and in their applications. Thus the material aspects of social development are connected in marked degree to developments and progress in the metals industry.

Although archaeologists have found that ornamental iron castings were made by the Chinese about 500 B.C., it was not until the 14th century that commercial iron castings were made in Europe. Their first large-scale usage was for cannon balls, initiated at Menningen, Germany, in 1388. The first casting made in the United States was a cooking kettle, made at Lynn, Mass. in 1642. The industry soon spread among the colonies. Most early castings were intended for domestic use, such as cooking ware, stove parts, pumps, and the like. Metal used was pig iron (itself essentially a gray iron) direct from the blast furnaces. The cupola, in which most gray iron is melted today, was developed in commercial form by an Englishman, John Wilkinson, in 1794. The first cupola in America was one built in Pennsylvania about 1820.

Like steel, gray iron is an alloy or series of alloys containing various percentages of iron, carbon, and other elements. As distinguished from steel, gray iron has a high total carbon content and low ductility. The greater proportion of the carbon in gray iron is in the form of graphite.

Defined technically, cast irons are alloys of iron and carbon containing so much carbon that as cast they are not appreciably malleable. Usually from 1.7 to 4.5 per cent carbon is present, and, in most cases, an appreciable percentage of silicon. All cast irons are eutectiferous alloys, and are classified commercially as follows: (1) pig iron (blast furnace product, see article 4, *Pig Iron*); (2) white cast iron (a hard not graphitized product); (3) malleable cast iron (see article 6, *Malleable Iron*); (4) gray cast iron.

Gray cast irons as cast have combined (cementitic or carbide) carbon not in excess of an eutectoid percentage (usually approximately 0.8 per cent carbon). The usual total carbon percentage is in the range 2.70 to 3.60 per cent. Percentages of graphitic or free carbon may range from about 1.90 to possibly 3.50 per cent.

All gray irons contain considerable percentages of silicon, usually in the range 1.0 to 2.8 per cent. They also contain appreciable percentages of manganese and phosphorus, and small percentages of sulphur.

A considerable tonnage of gray iron, called alloy iron or alloyed gray iron has elements such as nickel, chromium, copper, molybdenum, etc., added to enhance or modify its mechanical and manufacturing properties.

"Semisteel" is a term which has been used for gray irons of actual or supposed better mechanical properties than the average gray irons. Material sold under such a name does not have the ductility and high impact characteristics of steel—it is true gray iron. In better informed engineering circles the term "semisteel" is obsolete. A wide variety of strength classes is available under gray iron specifications. The engineer wisely and safely prescribes the strength class required, and is not misled by misnomers, such as semisteel and various trade names which sometimes imply that a true gray iron product is something else.

Usual gray irons are magnetic, and of ferritic base. Some very highly alloyed irons, called austenitic irons, are practically nonmagnetic and have markedly enhanced resistance to numerous corrosive fluids.

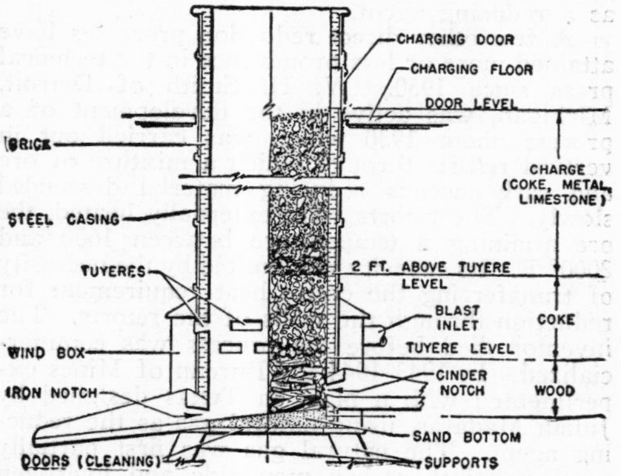

FIG. 1. Vertical section through cupola furnace for producing gray iron.

MANUFACTURE

Melting Practice.—*Gray Iron (Cupola Practice).*—The major portion of the gray iron produced in this country is melted in the cupola furnace. The cupola is a vertical, cylindrical type of furnace consisting of a steel shell lined with fire brick (Fig. 1). The furnace is charged through a charging door which is located 15-20 feet above the bottom plate. At the lower end of the furnace is the wind box, or air chamber, as shown in the diagram. Air enters the cupola through the tuyeres. The cupola is a simple and an economical melting unit because the fuel and the metal are in intimate contact with each other.

Fuel, metal, and flux are charged through the charging door of the cupola. Coke is charged first and the initial charge is known as the bed charge. Iron is then charged upon the coke. Alternate layers or charges of coke and iron are introduced into the cupola. Where flux is used it is charged on the coke. The coke bed is ignited by means of kindling wood or an oil torch. The bed charge of coke usually extends from 28-50 inches above the top of the tuyeres.

The charge of iron depends upon the capacity of the cupola. The cupola sizes are referred to as the inside diameter of the lining of the cupola. Cupola sizes may range from 18 inches in diameter to over 100 inches. The size used for ordinary commercial practice varies from 42-84 inches in diameter. The rated capacities on these sizes are from 5-25 tons of metal melted per hour.

The quantity of coke used depends upon the quantity of metal charged. The bed charge is a definite height above the tuyeres. Consequently, this portion of the coke goes in by volume instead of by weight. The succeeding charges of coke are in direct proportion to the metal charged. This proportion varies from one part of coke to 7-12 parts of iron.

The metal charged into the cupola consists of gray iron scrap and pig iron. Steel scrap is also used where strength of the finished casting is important as steel scrap increases the strength by modifying the composition of the iron. The proportions of gray iron scrap, pig iron, and steel scrap are governed by the type of casting. It is customary to find considerable difference in mixture of metal used, even among foundries making the same class of work.

Limestone is used as a flux in cupola operation. The purpose of the flux is to form a slag with the dirt, impurities in the metal, and the coke ash. Fluorspar (calcium fluoride) is sometimes used as a fluxing agent in combination with the limestone. The purpose of the fluorspar is to thin the slag and also to aid in the removal of sulphur, although correct proportions of limestone will ensure a fluid slag and some sulphur removal. Various forms of soda ash are used as fluxes, particularly in the ladle. Proper slagging improves the quality of the iron.

The air is introduced into the cupola through the tuyeres. Usually, the introduced air is at room temperature, but preheated air (hot blast) is also used. The volume of air introduced is important and governs the melting rate of the cupola. The air is used in the combustion of the coke, which in turn melts the iron. Under ordinary conditions the blast pressure will vary from 8-20 ounces per square inch, depending on the cupola height, number of charges, and character of charged stock. Some of the larger production foundries have increased blast pressures to 30 ounces per square inch, in order to obtain greater capacity from the cupola.

Devices are available which permit control of the weight of air entering the cupola. This method is more accurate from the standpoint of control than is the measurement of the air volume.

The metal mixture entering the cupola is governed by the composition of the metal desired for the finished castings. Pig iron is the base of the charge. Charges are seldom made up entirely of scrap. Since the pig iron is of known composition, the greater the amount of pig iron and the smaller the amount of purchased scrap, the more uniform is the composition of the resulting castings. For high-grade castings such as automobile cylinders, the percentage of pig iron is about 35-45 per cent of the charge, while for castings such as sash weights practically no pig iron is used.

Electric Furnace Melting.—There has been a steady increase in the utilization of electric furnace melting for cast iron. This is particularly true in the production of special cast irons. The electric furnace lends itself to a high degree of control in respect to composition and temperature. In some cases, large quantities of scrap, such as borings, can be utilized and a good grade of casting produced. The lower cost of scrap metals for the electric furnaces helps to compensate for the excess melting cost as compared to the cupola.

Two types of electric furnace are in general use: (1) three-phase direct arc; (2) single phase indirect arc of the rocking type. Good results are reported from both types of furnaces.

In some cases the electric furnace is used for the entire melting process while in other cases a duplex method is used. In the duplex method all or part of the charge is melted in the cupola and the molten metal is refined and superheated in the electric furnace. Additions of alloys and steel may be made to the metal in the electric furnace. For steady production the duplex method is usually more economical, owing to the low melting cost in the cupola.

Air Furnace Melting.—The air furnace is used to a limited extent in the production of gray iron castings. This is a hearth type of furnace, in which a refractory wall (fire bridge) near one end separates the hearth from the combustion chamber (fireplace), and a refractory wall (flue bridge) separates the hearth from the stack (flue) near the other end; a removable type of roof permits the charging of large pieces of scrap; flames from the burning fuel (coal, fuel oil, or gas) sweep across the hearth and leave through the stack. The air furnace is frequently used for the higher strength cast irons, because it lends itself to accurate control of composition, and higher pouring temperatures are obtained than with the cupola.

Molding.—A mold is a form or cavity in a refractory material, into which molten metal is poured. The shape of the cavity determines the final shape of the poured metal after cooling. Molds are made by using a pattern whose shape is essentially that of the desired casting. A refractory (such as molding sand) is packed around the pattern. The pattern is then withdrawn, leaving its imprint or shape as a cavity in the refractory. Suitable orifices (known as gates) are provided to permit entry of the molten metal into the cavity or shape.

A majority of gray iron castings is made in so-called green sand molds in which the sand is not baked before molding. The usual refractory is molding sand. This often is a natural product characterized by a silica grain base, the grains being coated by clay which occurs in natural molding sand deposits. When slightly moistened such molding sand has considerable coherence, and maintains its shape when pressed or rammed into place. It also is permeable to gases generated when molten metal is poured into the mold.

The molding operation usually employs a two-part flask, or container for the sand and pattern, because of necessity of removal of the pattern from the sand, to leave the imprint desired.

When the casting to be made is not a solid design (such as a solid cylinder) but contains an opening through it (as a cylindrical bushing) or is a metal shell (such as a valve body), refractory cores corresponding to the inner dimensions

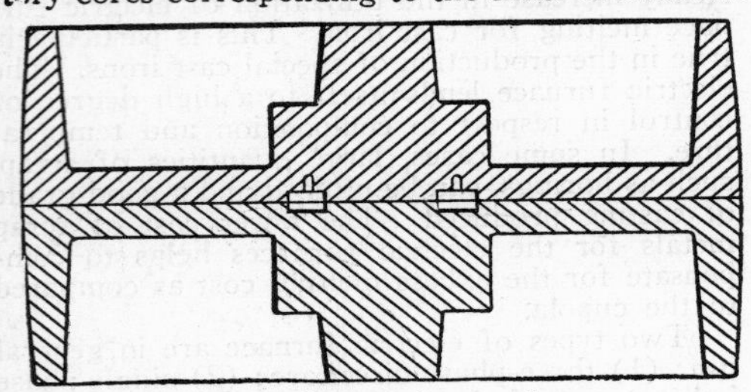

FIG. 2. Pattern for a pulley.

of the casting are placed in the mold cavity. The molten metal flows into the space between the mold cavity and the core, and when solidified has the desired shape and wall thickness.

A simple method of making a mold is shown in Fig. 2. These illustrations show, in cross section, (1) pattern for a pulley, which pattern it will be noted is split into two parts. (2)

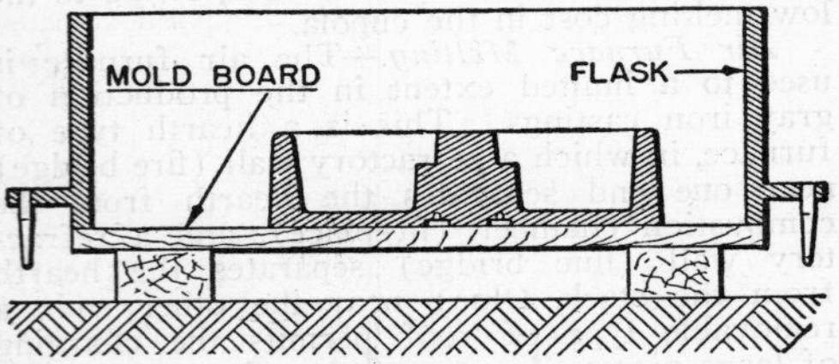

FIG. 3. The drag or lower half of pattern shown in Fig. 2.

(Fig. 3) shows one half of the pattern, the drag or lower half. This is placed on a mold board, on which also rests the flask or container for the refractory molding sand. When the sand is placed therein and rammed about the pattern, the drag (lower half) is rolled over. This will be recognized as the bottom part in (3) (Fig. 4) shown with sand as dotted shading. This illustration shows the cope (or top

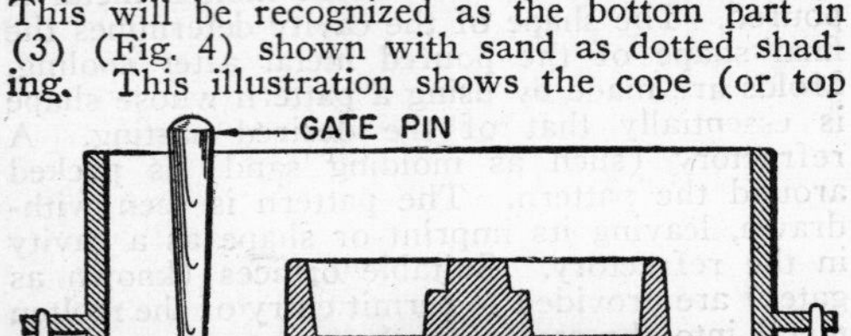

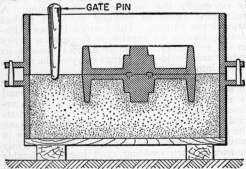

FIG. 4. The drag rolled over, after ramming of sand about the pattern.

half) of the pattern and flask in place, with a gate pin (a portion of the pattern) to make an orifice to receive the molten metal. (4) (Fig. 5) shows the assembled mold, after the pattern has been withdrawn, and a central core placed to make the opening in the hub of the pulley. Molten metal is poured into the opening, upper left, flows downward, then transversely through a "runner" (which has been cut into the drag) and so into the cavity, whose shape is that of the

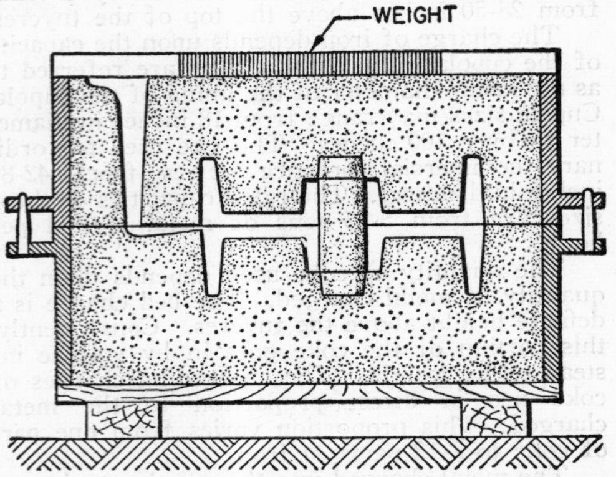

FIG. 5. Assembled mold after pattern is withdrawn and a central core inserted.

pulley to be made. (The white or unshaded areas in Fig. 5 represent the metal sections.)

After the metal has solidified, the mold is "shaken out" and the casting removed. The "runner" is broken or cut off, and the core broken or punched out. The casting is cleaned from adhering molding sand, usually by shot or sand blasting. It then is ready for machining and other finishing operations.

Molding is an ancient art. Only in relatively recent times have scientific approaches and extensive mechanization of the operation been used. Demand for huge numbers of castings of a given design has resulted in development of largely automatic molding operations. Patterns and gating systems often are mounted on plates. The molder places a half flask on the plate. Sand from a hopper fills the flask. Pressure is exerted on the sand by an automatic device (such as a pressure plate) compacting it around the pattern and in the half flask. The pressure plate is lifted automatically. A vibratory or other device slightly loosens the pattern from the sand, then lifts the half flask (with its design imprinted by the pattern). The molder places the half flask on a conveyer. While one molder is making the upper or cope part, another may be making the drag or bottom part of the mold. If a cored job, a coresetter places the cores in position (print pattern extensions, into which projections on the cores are placed, are provided for locating and anchoring the cores). The cope halves are placed on the drag halves. When the mold halves are weighted or clamped (to keep the pressure of the molten metal from lifting the copes) the molds are ready for pouring. Ladles of molten metal are transported from the melting furnaces to the molds, and these last then are "poured off," or filled.

The handling of materials is an involved engineering problem in modern production foundries. Machinery has to a great degree supplanted the shovel and wheelbarrow, and the hand carried ladles of molten metal.

The molten metal flows from the spout of the cupola into a ladle, which is picked up by a crane or by monorail systems and mechanically transported to the pouring floors. The molds to be filled are on a conveyer line. When metal poured into them has solidified, the conveyer takes molds (and castings) to a "shakeout" station, where sand and cores are separated from the castings. The sand is largely recoverable and is carried to mixing machines where it is "tempered" (proper moisture content restored) and rebonding material ; incorporated. From thence it goes to hoppers or storage tanks. From these it is delivered again to the molders for re-use. All these operations are under technical control. Magnetic separators have taken out any metal particles. Bonding materials (such as clays, bentonite, etc.) and moisture have been added on the basis of laboratory tests which ascertain the amounts needed; mixing machines and screens break up all sand lumps, aerate and cool the sand, and place it in best physical condition for re-use.

The castings and attached gating systems are separated mechanically or manually. The gating systems (called returns) are conveyed back to the furnaces for remelting. The castings are cleaned, usually by mechanical means, such as "blasting." In blasting, a high-pressure stream of hard metal shot or coarse silica sand, or even water, quickly cleans the castings of adhering molding sand, so that they can be more readily machined.

The cylinder block of an automobile is a good example of a gray iron casting made by production methods. Such blocks are extensively cored, to provide the water jacket and cylinder bores. Examination of a broken block in a junk dealer's yard and a visit to a local foundry will prove highly informative to the interested reader.

Although the larger percentage of high-production castings is made by "green sand" molding, substantial tonnages are made by other methods. In "dry sand" molding, the refractory (natural or synthetic sand with supplementary binders) is rammed (packed into the mold, around the pattern) while moist. After withdrawal of the pattern the flask halves are dried in an oven. Cores then are placed, flask halves closed, and molds poured. Such molds avoid problems of moisture generated during pouring (as in green sand molding). The molds are stronger and better able to withstand the erosive effects of flowing molten metal and its pressure effects. As used for fairly large castings, dry sand molds allow casting of more complicated shapes.

Among methods used for producing very large castings, pit molding is typical. Instead of using a drag (bottom part of a flask) an excavation (or "pit") is made in the foundry floor. The pattern is placed therein and sand with special binder suitably packed around it. A cope flask is rammed and the pattern or pattern parts are removed from cope and drag. Such molds usually have a bonding material (such as a molasses, dextrin, or starch compound) sprayed or swabbed on the surfaces. The mold surface is skin dried by means of a torch or other heating device. Cores are placed and the mold closed (cope placed on drag).

Since pit molding is not a highly repetitive operation, a high degree of craftsmanship is required. Loam molding also is a specialized art. Loam molds may be used for large concentric castings such as large kettles, cylinders, ring gears, etc. Instead of using full patterns, the general contours are made by use of sweeps (templates or boards having a beveled edge), and some sections made by use of skeleton and part patterns. The backing is made of brickwork, faced with a special loam sand. Faces of loam molds (and cores) are skin dried.

A considerable tonnage of cast iron pipe is made by centrifugal casting or "spinning." A cylindrical metal mold mounted nearly horizontally and faced with suitable refractory is employed. No cores are used. Metal is run into the mold, and the mold rotated rapidly. This throws and holds the molten metal against the inner surface of the mold, until solidified. The shell thickness of the pipe is controlled by the amount of metal run into the mold.

In die casting, molten metal is forced under pressure into a metal die (mold) and pressure is maintained until the metal has solidified. This method is more often used with low melting temperature nonferrous alloys than with gray iron. However, some small, intricate and highly repetitive designs have been made in gray iron. A major problem is obtaining a refractory which protects the metal die (permanent mold) from the deleterious effects of the molten metal.

The ancient "lost wax" process (as described in the *Autobiography of Benvenuti Cellini*) has been revived in what is called precision casting. The method is similar to that used by dentists in making the gold portions of a bridge. This process is rarely used for gray iron.

About 1920 molding was a highly empirical art, demanding great skill and ingenuity. Science and engineering have substituted controlled methods for much of the skill, and mechanical devices for much of the old strong-back labor.

Gray iron is a very satisfactory alloy to cast. It possesses excellent fluidity, so that intricate designs can be run. Its shrinkage (liquid) and contraction (solid) are lower than most metals. Thus it is relatively easy to get sound castings to quite close dimensions.

Metallurgical studies of solidification characteristics and control through directional solidification have promoted more logical designs and indicated the most effective ways to feed for shrinkage (that is to provide reservoirs, called risers, of molten metal which can flow into the casting during its solidification and natural contraction period and thus compensate for the contraction, which last might otherwise leave voids or "shrinkage cavities").

The most widely used refractory for molding is natural molding sand. Such natural product varies considerably. In the old days "feel" and experience were the only guides—sometimes sorry ones. Today foundries test their sands for bond (strength), permeability (ability to allow gases to escape), moisture, and grain fineness. Standards are set and technical control exercised. The desired properties are attained by the use of synthetic additions and by blending. Other refractories than molding sands have been used, for example cement. Oils (used in cores) and other binders and surface coating agencies have been studied, and means devised for testing and controlling, by laboratory methods, many of the procedures that formerly were largely empirical. Numerous and effective as these advances have been, the foundryman and metallurgist are constantly engaged in seeking further improvements in both quality and economy.

Design and Section Size.—From the viewpoint of producing internally sound castings and relatively complicated shapes, gray iron is an excellent casting alloy. These good casting characteristics are due to its relatively low shrinkage and contraction, and to its high fluidity. However, it is highly desirable that sections of the casting are so proportioned that the sections most distant from the point or points where the casting is to be fed will solidify first, with solidification progressing toward the heads or risers, where the hottest fluid metal is located. "Progressive solidification" is highly helpful in the production of sound castings, and for this reason the design should, insofar as is possible, approach uniformity in section size. Then the

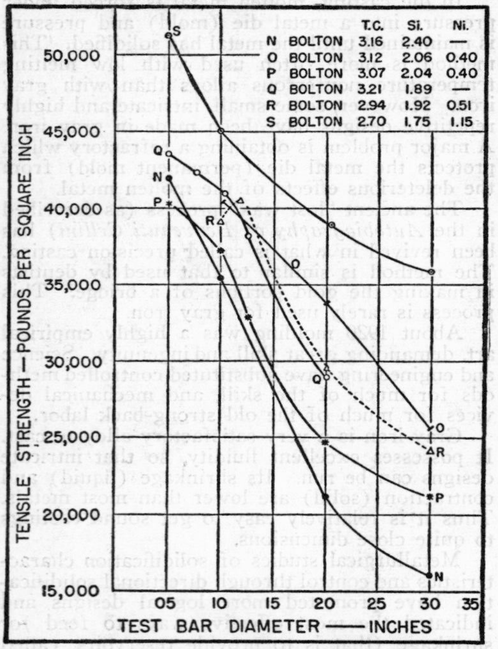

FIG. 6. Showing the relationship between tensile strength and diameter of gray iron test bar.

pouring temperatures and speeds, the arrangement of gates and risers and other controllable factors can be employed to best advantage. While designs are not limited to simple and uniform sections, the artifices that must be employed to achieve success with poor designs, from a foundry viewpoint, always add to the cost of production. In a given foundry, all types of castings made do not possess the same section size, the weights of different designs vary, and it is at times necessary to provide different section sizes in the same casting design.

In a given gray iron composition, the strength varies according to the section size into which it is cast. Gray irons are more sensitive to differences in cooling rates than most alloys. Sections of heavy castings cool more slowly than lighter ones.

Fig. 6 illustrates this effect, as determined from tests on test bars of various sizes. In all cases strength drops as bar size increases. However, the amount and degree of loss in strength is much less in the case of low carbon, alloyed, high-strength iron (top curve) than it is for the somewhat higher carbon, higher silicon metal (bottom curve). The metallurgist and designer must select suitable material not only by strength prescription, but also by the strength desired or needed in a given section. Referring again to Fig. 6, if 35,000 pounds per square inch is required, iron represented by the bottom curve is suitable only for sections represented by a test bar which is one inch in diameter. For sections that cool as slowly as the 3-inch test bar, iron possessing the characteristics shown by the top curve must be employed.

PRINCIPLES OF CONTROL OF PROPERTIES

In the case of pure metals, such as copper, lead, and silver, there is but one structural component—the crystals or grains of the pure metal. Often the possibilities of modifying mechanical properties, such as strength and hardness, are relatively limited. In cast form, some variations in grain size can be effected by differences in cooling rate, as by casting in sand (slower cooling) or into metal molds (faster cooling). Working (and especially cold working) may be used to achieve internally stressed conditions which can considerably augment strength and hardness. However, few casting designs are adaptable to further forming by deformation or working.

Many alloys have two or more structural components. Alterations in the amounts and distribution of the components can be employed to effect marked changes in mechanical properties. Such alterations can be made by variations in composition, by heat treatments, and by other means.

Gray iron is essentially an alloy of iron and carbon. The other elements present are useful in that they affect the iron and carbon structural components.

The matrix, or base metal structure of gray iron, somewhat resembles that of steel. However,

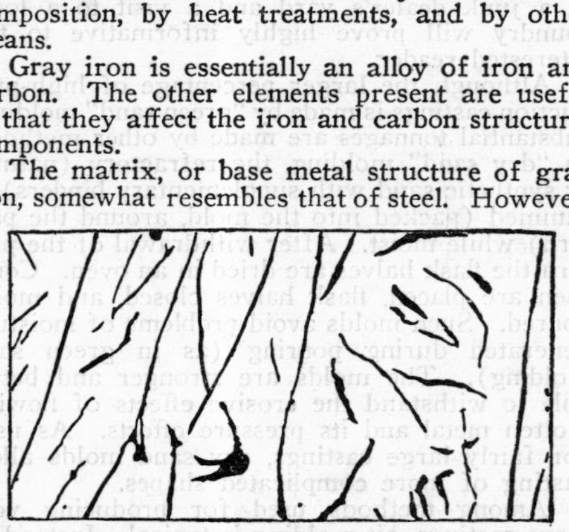

FIG. 7. Coarse graphite flakes in "open" gray iron.

gray iron contains graphite flakes. These flakes are without strength and break up the continuity of the matrix. It is the presence of graphite flakes that makes gray iron an alloy of low ductility. They also impart the characteristic dark gray fracture color, add greatly to machinability (as compared to steel) and (because they expand when the metal is at high temperature and rather plastic) lessen the contraction characteristics and enable sharper mold impressions when formed.

FIG. 8. Fine graphite flakes in "close-grained" gray iron.

A piece of gray iron, polished, and examined under the microscope, appears as shown in Figs. 7 and 8. Fig. 7 shows coarse flakes, characteristic of weak and so-called open grain iron, Fig. 8 shows smaller and evenly distributed flakes, characteristic of strong and close-grained iron.

To a great degree the foundry metallurgist controls the properties of the iron by controlling the amount, size, and distribution of these flakes. Also, he takes into consideration the matrix, particularly in respect to combined carbon (found in the lamellar structure known as pearlite), and a phosphorus-rich component known as steadite (in gray iron, largely a binary eutectic of iron and phosphorus). Factors influencing the properties of gray iron are: (1) chemical composition; (2) structural and mechanical make-up of the melting charge; (3) melting process; (4) thermal and mechanical history—furnace spout to cooled casting; (5) subsequent heat treatment; (6) design and workmanship. With factors 2, 3, 4, 5, and 6 constant, the properties depend upon composition. However, various foundries employing different methods may produce considerably different results with the same composition, or, conversely, the same result with diverse compositions.

Chemical control is exercised largely through the elements carbon (total) and silicon and, to lesser degree, through manganese, phosphorus, and sulphur. Alloying elements such as nickel, copper, molybdenum, chromium and others may be employed to modify or augment the results attainable by the preceding elements. Special modifying agencies, known as inoculants, may be employed in small percentages. Among these are silicides (such as calcium silicide), graphitic carbon, and various complex additions containing one or more of the following elements: vanadium, titanium, nickel, chromium, aluminum, etc.

The furnace charge contains various percentages of pig iron, gray iron returns (gates and risers), scrap castings, and usually some steel scrap. These influence the metal not only according to their composition, but also according to their size and shape. Light pieces behave differently than heavy ones during the melting, probably because of the differences in areas exposed to combustion gases.

The operation of the cupola, in respect to the amounts of coke (and its character), the weight of iron charged, the amount of air used, slagging practices and other factors distinctly influence the mechanical characteristics of irons of given chemical composition. Likewise, iron melted in the electric furnace differs from iron of like composition made in the cupola.

Temperatures attained during melting have marked influence on the properties of the metal, as does the temperature at which the metal enters the mold. Gray iron is materially influenced by the rate at which it is cooled from the molten state to temperatures somewhat below the eutectoid (about 1100° F.). The size of section, the thermal conductivity of the mold and other factors alter the microstructure and the mechanical properties of the metal.

Influence of Carbon.—An increase in total carbon content (other factors equal) increases graphitic carbon content, with a consequent decrease in strength, a slight decrease in indentation hardness and appreciable improvement in machinability. Over the usual commercial total carbon range, an increase also promotes greater fluidity, and a decrease in shrinkage and contraction characteristics. The modern trend is toward lower carbon and higher silicon irons. Some of the disadvantages of lower carbon are offset by the action of silicon, and a better engineering product is attained.

Influence of Silicon.—Silicon is a graphitizing element, useful in controlling the relative proportions of combined and graphitic carbon. Irons with a very low silicon content do not graphitize as cast. All the carbon then occurs as an extremely hard brittle component—iron carbide, or "cementite" or "chill." Such metal is known as white iron. It is practically unmachinable and has few direct uses.

In the production of gray iron sufficient silicon is incorporated to avoid formation of white or mottled (partially white) iron. If low strength (maximum graphite) is desired, a high silicon content with fairly high carbon is employed. If in an attempt to get maximum strength, the silicon is decreased too much, white or chilled spots and unsatisfactory machining and engineering properties are incurred.

Besides decreasing the stability of iron carbide (thus acting as a graphitizer), silicon lowers the percentage of carbon required for the eutectic. This effect modifies the graphite distribution in irons of like carbon but dissimilar silicon contents. It is easier, in cupola melting, to keep the total carbon content lower in presence of high silicon.

In commercial gray irons, the silicon content rarely is allowed to exceed 3.0 per cent. Probably 90 per cent of the tonnage of gray iron castings has silicon contents within the range 1.75 per cent to 2.75 per cent. Certain special cast metals used for their high resistance to acid corrosion have silicon contents about 13 to 17 per cent and carbon under 1.0 per cent. These alloys are not gray irons. Graphite is absent. They are somewhat difficult to machine, and have relatively low shock resistance. Some alloys with lower silicon content (7 or 8 per cent) containing nickel and chromium also, are used for heat resisting parts, such as grates.

Influence of Manganese.—The manganese content of most commercial gray irons is within the range 0.40 to 0.90 per cent. Manganese combines readily with sulphur in gray irons, forming a relatively harmless inclusion, manganese sulphide. Changes in manganese content within this percentage range do not have very marked effects.

Influence of Sulphur.—In the presence of sufficient manganese (0.40 to 0.90 per cent) sulphur up to 0.10 per cent, or perhaps more, is without appreciable deleterious effect on gray iron.

Influence of Phosphorus.—Phosphorus contents of most commercial gray irons are within the range of 0.15 to 0.90 per cent. Phosphorus is found in a separate structural component known as steadite. One part of phosphorus plus nine parts iron form about ten parts steadite by volume. Steadite itself is rather hard and brittle. Its melting point is low, about 1800° F. Up to perhaps 0.30 or 0.40 per cent phosphorus, this element is without very marked effect on gray iron. At over about 0.50 per cent phosphorus content there is enough steadite so that this component forms nearly continuous grain boundaries, producing a cellular or network structure in the matrix. This net work (other factors being equal) lowers the deflection (ability to bend without fracture) and impact characteristics of the iron. It affects the strength but little. Higher phosphorus also promotes fluidity. However, this effect sometimes is accompanied by a greater tendency toward shrinkage effects, hence greater attention to design and gating is needed. Under some conditions machinability is somewhat impaired. Conversely, abrasive wear resistance may be somewhat improved.

Influence of Alloys.—Since 1925 usage of so-called "alloys" or alloying elements in gray iron has grown rather rapidly. Among the more commonly used are nickel, copper, chromium, and molybdenum. In commercial gray irons these elements are useful both in helping in the control of graphitization characteristics and in strengthening or otherwise modifying the matrix structure. In high percentages (18 per cent or higher "alloy" content) new types of cast irons, the austenitic cast irons, have become available. These are relatively nonmagnetic and have a useful range of resistance to various acid and caustic corrosives.

It was estimated that in 1945 between 10 and 20 per cent of gray irons contained appreciable percentages of added alloys. In 1930 it was estimated that only about 2 per cent had such additions.

Alloying elements may be classified in two general groups—those which promote graphitization and those which restrain it by lessening the tendency of iron carbide to graphitize. The former group lessens tendency toward formation of "chill," the latter to promote the formation of chill or tendency toward hard white iron.

The metallurgist commences his control of the mechanical properties of gray iron by first regulating the total carbon content by raw materials mixture, melting process, etc. The other elements (normal and alloying) are used to control the amounts of graphitic and combined carbon, their distribution, etc.

Silicon is a powerful graphitizer. If sufficient amounts are used to ensure freedom from chill in light, rapidly cooled sections, excessive graphitization and coarse grain are likely in heavy and more slowly cooled sections of the same casting. Such nonuniformity in structure is accompanied by undesirable nonuniformity in mechanical properties. If the silicon content should be reduced to a point where proper structure is attained in the heavy sections, the lighter sections may be found chilled, hard, unmachinable, and brittle. By use of supplementary alloying elements of mildly graphitizing type such as nickel or copper, and keeping silicon down to amounts suitable for the heavier sections, chill is avoided in the light sections. The net result is greater structural and mechanical uniformity throughout all sections. It is fortunate that these mild graphitizers (such as nickel and copper) have relatively much less graphitizing effect in heavy sections. Furthermore, they tend to harden and strengthen the matrix in these heavy sections.

Chromium is a powerful carbide-stabilizing element. When heavy sectioned castings and light sectioned ones are to be poured from the same molten iron mixture, the silicon content is made suitable for the light sectioned castings, Metal going to the heavier ones has some chromium added. This offsets the action of silicon, which otherwise would be excessive for the purpose. In many cases it is found desirable to use complex alloy additions, for example nickel-chromium, copper-chromium, nickel-chromium-molybdenum and others, so balanced as to attain combinations of structure and properties less easily attainable by simple procedures.

Molybdenum is a mild carbide stabilizer. Suitable additions afford one of the simpler methods of increasing strength without the marked danger of encountering chill, incurred by use of more powerful carbide stabilizers. Molybdenum tends toward the production of a finer grained, stronger matrix structure. When it is used, a slight upward revision of silicon content, or the addition of a mild graphitizer (such as nickel or copper) is the usual practice.

The best foundry practice includes suitable manipulation of carbon and silicon practice first, to get the best combination of these for the purpose involved. Alloys and alloying elements are used to supplement only when necessary. Reduction of total carbon content is in itself very potent toward promoting uniformity of strength, particularly throughout medium and heavy sections. If the iron is properly processed and the normal elements are in correct balance, alloys and alloying elements, if necessary, can then be used most effectively and economically.

Controls Other Than Composition.—*Inoculation.*—It has been discovered that various substances and admixtures added to the molten iron shortly before pouring may considerably modify its structural and mechanical properties. Such substances are called "inoculants." Calcium silicide was probably the first used inoculant. Other silicon-containing substances, such as nickel-silicon and ferrosilicon, are used. Various complex alloys which may contain vanadium, nickel, chromium, copper, titanium, aluminum, molybdenum, etc., in various proportions, and even graphitic carbon have been employed. Inoculants are added in quite small amounts. Their action is different and in some respects more potent than that of additions of alloys and alloying elements previously discussed. Inoculants can and are being used in numerous cases to lessen tendency toward chill, or hard spots. In this respect they act as graphitizers. Under some conditions (especially on external surfaces) some gray irons may tend toward production of extremely fine graphite flakes in a soft or ferritic matrix. In such cases inoculants often have been found useful to produce a normal sized graphitic structure and a desirable pearlitic matrix. (These effects are not necessarily paradoxical.) If molten inoculated iron is allowed to stand for a long period, the effects of the inoculant gradually disappear. It is thought that inoculants act as nuclei for the formation of graphite flakes.

Superheating.—High melting temperature has marked effects on the properties of gray iron. In the case of irons of fairly high carbon content, high melting temperatures (usually in the range 2850° F. to 3000° F.) tend to retard slightly normal graphitization tendencies and to bring about finer grain and increased strength. Section sensitivity is decreased. Ordinary cupola melting temperatures are lower than the superheating range. Therefore, when superheat is desired electric furnaces are often used. Since the costs of electric melting are high, the usual practice is to melt the iron in the cupola, and transfer the molten metal to an electric furnace for superheating.

Heat Treatment.—Heat treatments of gray iron are undertaken for one of two purposes: (1) alteration of structure and mechanical properties, or (2) relief of internal stresses as set up in the casting process.

If a gray iron is heated above the eutectoid transformation range (for example to about 1550° F.), the ferrite (alpha iron) changes to gamma iron. The gamma iron is capable of dissolving the combined carbon of the pearlite, forming a solid solution known as austenite. If the metal is quenched (cooled rapidly), the austenite has not time enough to revert to the normal or pearlitic condition when passing through and below the eutectoid transformation range. A transition product, usually martensite, is formed. Martensite is hard and brittle. Its formation results in lowered strength. If, however, the metal is tempered or drawn (heated back to a moderately elevated temperature, say 750° F.), the brittle martensite is decomposed and intermediate structural products formed. The net result is an increase in strength and hardness. In irons of suitable composition the tensile strength increase may be about 40 per cent above the original value.

Oil is a commonly used quenching medium. The use of alloys and fairly low total carbon contents are desirable in irons to be heat treated. Because it is nonductile, quenching of gray iron is best confined to simple shapes.

Conversely, for machining purposes, it may be desirable to soften the iron. This is accomplished by annealing. The castings are heated to the temperature range 1500° to 1600° F., and cooled slowly therefrom. Under properly controlled conditions all the combined carbon is converted to graphite. The metal structure then consists wholly of a ferrite matrix and graphite flakes. It is soft (usually around 120-130 Brinell hardness number) and highly machinable. Annealing treatments result in loss of strength, a reduction of about 20 per cent from the original cast strength being usual.

Relief from internal stresses may be accomplished by heating for suitable periods to about 900° F. or slightly above. As a casting cools it contracts, and since cooling rates are not uniform, due to variations in section size, certain portions will contract more rapidly than others. Expansion and contraction effects are also set up by structural changes in the transformation range. These effects set up internal stresses which may seriously weaken castings of complicated design. Although reheating (stress-relief) at about 900° F. does not produce structural changes, the metal does become more plastic, and thus the internal stresses are eliminated by plastic flow.

Various other heat treatments are used occasionally on gray irons. Among these are flame hardening (surface quenching), isothermal quenching, induction hardening, and nitriding (a case treatment). The principles involved are essentially similar to those employed for steels.

PHYSICAL PROPERTIES

The attributes or characteristics which a substance possesses are termed its physical properties.

Density.—The specific gravity of gray irons varies from about 6.95 for weak, coarse grained irons to about 7.35 for irons in the 30,000-40,000 pounds per square inch strength classes. Some of the high strength, low carbon alloyed irons have densities of about 7.5. That of white cast iron is about 7.7. (The specific gravity of cast steel is somewhat higher, about 7.80.)

A specific gravity of 7.7 is about 487 pounds per cubic foot, or 0.29 pound per cubic inch. A specific gravity of 7.0 is about 437 pounds per cubic foot or 0.26 pound per cubic inch.

Gray iron thus is appreciably lighter (per unit volume) than steel. The major reason is the presence of graphite flakes (specific gravity about 2.25) in gray iron.

Melting and Freezing Temperature Ranges.—Unlike pure metals, gray iron does not melt, or freeze, at some single temperature. Each of the structural components: eutectic, primary austenite, and steadite (phosphorus rich component) melts, or conversely, freezes, at a different temperature or temperature range.

The initial freezing point (above which the metal is completely liquid) may be as high as about 2450° F. for low carbon iron. As the carbon (and silicon) content is increased, the initial point (liquidus) becomes lower, reaching, in irons of eutectic composition, about 2100° F.

The final solidification or solidus temperature (or, conversely, the point above which all low phosphorus cast irons start to become liquid) is just above 2100° F.

The phosphorus-rich component steadite remains fluid until a temperature of below 1800° F. is reached.

Specific Heat.—Specific heat is the heat (expressed in Btu. or in calories) required to raise the temperature of a unit mass one degree (° F. in case of Btu., ° C. in case of calories). The specific heat of a high carbon iron at different temperatures is shown in Fig. 9. The specific

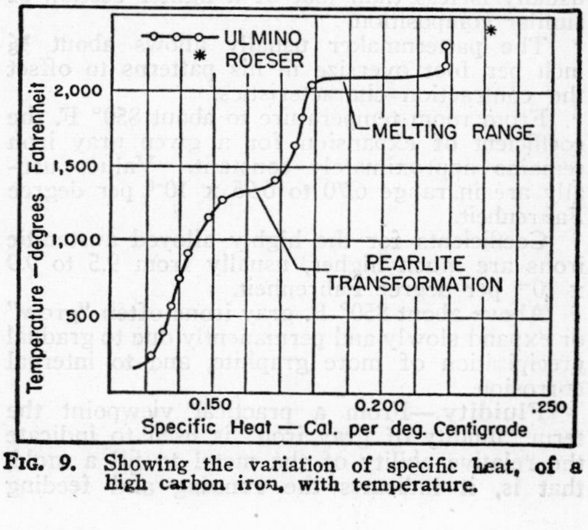

FIG. 9. Showing the variation of specific heat, of a high carbon iron, with temperature.

heat increases with increase in temperature. There is an abrupt increase when entering the pearlitic transformation range, where alpha iron (ferrite) changes to gamma iron (austenite). There is a large increase where the metal changes from solid to liquid. The heat of fusion is about 47 calories per gram.

Contraction.—The qualitative relationships of temperature and of contraction characteristics are shown in Fig. 10.

Coefficient of volume shrinkage in liquid state is about 0.006 per cent per degree Fahrenheit (0.011 per degree Centigrade). The volume change during solidification may be as low as 1.6 per cent for a high carbon, high silicon gray iron composition to as high as 5.8 per cent in a low carbon, low silicon white iron composition. The lower carbon gray irons, showing relatively high contraction, liquid to solid, must be well fed with fluid metal if "shrinkage cavity" defects are to be avoided.

The solid contraction of gray iron is lower when graphite content is high, that is, high car-

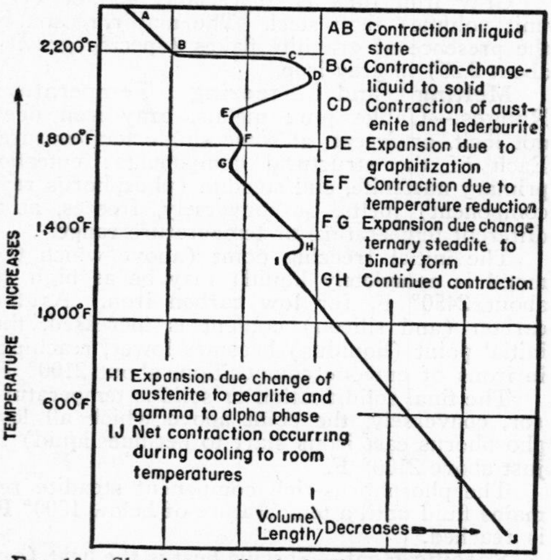

FIG. 10. Showing qualitatively the contraction and expansion of gray iron at various temperatures.

bon, high silicon irons show lower solid contraction. The solid contraction of a heavy section usually is less than that of a lighter section of similar composition.

The patternmaker usually allows about ⅛ inch per foot oversize in his patterns to offset the contraction characteristics.

From room temperature to about 850° F. the coefficient of expansion for a given gray iron remains approximately constant. Values usually are in range 6.70 to 6.95 x 10^{-6} per degree Fahrenheit.

Coefficients for the highly alloyed austenitic irons are much higher, usually from 9.5 to 9.9 x 10^{-6} per degree Fahrenheit.

Above about 850° F. gray irons often "grow" or expand slowly and permanently due to gradual precipitation of more graphite, and to internal corrosion.

Fluidity.—From a practical viewpoint the term "fluidity of gray iron" is used to indicate the relative ability of the metal to fill a mold, that is, it indicates the running and feeding qualities of the metal. In this sense, fluidity increases directly with increase in temperature of the molten metal, with increase in the percentage of total carbon plus 0.3 x percentage silicon, and with increase in phosphorus content. These latter (increase in carbon plus 0.3 silicon, and increase in phosphorus) act indirectly, in that they lower the final solidification temperatures.

Surface Tension.—Surface tension (dynes per square centimeter) in an iron 3.22 per cent carbon, 2.76 per cent silicon and 0.49 per cent phosphorus was found to be 936 at 2313° F., and 914 at 2404° F. (This compares with 1,018 for gold at 2050° F. and 1,178 for copper at 2100° F.).

Thermal Conductivity.—The usual range of thermal conductivity of gray iron extends from 0.100 to 0.140 calorie per square centimeter per second per centimeter per ° C.

Thermal conductivity decreases with an increase in temperature and with an increase in flake graphite (accompanied by an increase in total carbon). However, a reduction in combined carbon in a given iron (as by annealing) is effective in increasing thermal conductivity despite an increase in graphite content. (The conductivity of iron carbide is quite low.)

The thermal conductivity of gray iron is lower than that of steel, and markedly lower than that of nonferrous alloys. However, its excellent castability in thin sections (which expose large areas to dissipate heat) and low cost make it suitable for applications such as radiators, stoves, cooking ware, glass molds, drying equipment, and brake drums.

Corrosion.—Gray iron is more resistant than carbon and low alloy steels to many types of corrosion. Although in moist atmospheres it forms a rust coating rather readily, continued rust penetration and consequent disintegration usually is quite slow in comparison to steel, perhaps because the underlying graphite flakes form a protective (and adherent) coating.

In water pipe, cast iron has given splendid life. In soil pipe it usually lasts much longer than steel pipe.

Although different classes of gray iron do not vary much in resistance to a given water or soil condition, different waters and different soils vary quite widely in their corrosive effects. For example, some mine waters contain small percentages of sulphuric acid, others contain copper salts. In these and similar cases specially alloyed metals are required to resist the corrosive effects.

As is the case with all common metals, corrosion resistance of gray iron is impaired when stray electric currents are encountered (as in cities). Many crude oils and refinery products are relatively noncorrosive toward gray iron. High sulphur oils containing moisture, and some of the salt crudes are rather corrosive toward gray iron and steel. Gray irons are usefully resistant to most natural and artificial gases.

Although gray iron is resistant to strong sulphuric acid (60° Bé. to 66° Bé.), it is attacked rapidly by more dilute sulphuric acid. Hot fuming sulphuric acid (oleum) attacks and disintegrates gray iron. Gray iron is fairly resistant to cold concentrated phosphoric and nitric acids, but impurities such as hydrofluoric acid and chlorides materially impair its resistance. Dilute phosphoric and nitric acids attack gray iron quite rapidly. It is not resistant to hydrochloric (muriatic) acid in any concentration.

Gray iron is resistant to many alkaline and caustic solutions, for example: sodium hydroxide, lye, soda ash, ammonia, etc. It is not embrittled by exposure to strong, hot caustics. Where some slight coloration (due to solution of traces of iron) is not objectionable, gray iron has proved very useful in alkaline fluids, as used in manufacture of glass, sodium silicate, soap, viscose rayon, paper, dyestuffs, textiles, treatment of petroleum, etc. In general, fine close grained irons (as in the 30,000-40,000 pounds per square inch tensile classes) are more resistant to corrosives than are the lower strength, more open grained types.

With but few exceptions, the usage of small amounts of alloy elements is of little or no benefit toward enhancement of the corrosion resistance of gray irons.

Increases in temperature of corrosive fluids usually increase their corrosive effects. Gray irons are frequently used at elevated temperatures. At quite high temperatures (850° to 900° F. and over), ordinary gray irons are subject to "growth," a type of internal disintegration produced by extreme graphitization and considerable internal corrosion. Above about 1100° F. gray irons usually scale rather rapidly, particularly where combustion gases contain corrosives such as oxides of sulphur.

Several types of special cast irons have been developed to resist various types of corrosives. Prominent among these are the austenitic gray irons known commercially as "Ni Resist" and "Causul Metal." These are manufactured to several compositions, embraced within the following range: nickel 14 to 30, copper 4 to 7, chromium 0.5 to 3.5, molybdenum to 1.0 per cent. Some of these are quite usefully resistant to sulphuric acid, over the total range, dilute to concentrated. (They are not resistant to hot oleum.) They are resistant to the less severe types of hydrochloric (muriatic) acid conditions and to some phosphoric acids. Nitric acid attacks them severely. They have fair resistance to some organic acids, such as acetic, oleic, stearic, red oils, etc. Types containing 18 per cent or more nickel (with or without other alloys) are nearly immune to the corrosive effects of alkalies and caustics, weak or strong. However, they are subject to stress—corrosion is strong, hot caustics. If stresses are kept below about 10,000 pounds per square inch, they can be used safely with boiling concentrated caustics.

While not immune to rust, they form rust slowly, and do not disintegrate by rusting. They are resistant to scaling at elevated temperatures and are not subject to growth. In many services austenitic irons are economical substitutes for some of the high alloy stainless steels.

High silicon irons (usually about 15 per cent silicon) are resistant toward many acids, exceptions being hydrofluoric acid and hot concentrated hydrochloric (muriatic) acid. They are useful for conditions where free "wet" chlorine is encountered, and are unusual in that they have good resistance to solutions containing copper salts. The high silicon irons have the disadvantage of being hard and brittle. Thus they are costly to manufacture, and their fragility necessitates that they be handled carefully in installation and usage.

The high chromium irons (usually 24 to 35 per cent chromium) are resistant toward many corrosives, including nitric acids (except fuming) and solutions containing free chlorine. They are nearly rust immune and highly resistant to scaling. They are attacked by strong caustics.

Corrosive conditions vary so widely that specific recommendations should be made only after study of the particular case. This discussion should be used only as a general guide.

Electrical Properties.—Resistance of gray iron to passage of electrical current is higher than that of ordinary carbon steel. Gray iron is not a good current conductor. Increase in flake graphitic content may be expected to increase resistivity. Silicon increase has a similar effect, and so does increase of nickel.

Treatments which produce the nodular form graphite (as in malleable cast iron) tend to decrease resistivity. Commercial gray irons usually have specific resistance (microhms—centimeter) within the range 50-110. Gray iron resistance grids find some uses where fairly high current is involved. Its resistance is relatively high and its thermal dissipation characteristics are good.

Magnetic Properties.—Gray iron (ferrite-pearlite matrix) is magnetic. The highly alloyed austenitic cast irons are but slightly magnetic. Increase in magnetic induction and permeability and decrease in coercive force are attained when the metal is low in combined carbon. Such a material also has low hysteresis loss. An increase in the graphitic carbon content in flake form does not affect the hysteresis loss, but inhibits attainment of high magnetic induction. Lack of structural continuity (because of graphite flakes) causes small demagnetizing forces. This limits retentivity and unsuits the metal for usage in semipermanent magnets. Because of its relatively low permeability and inability to carry as high flux densities as rolled steel, gray iron is of limited use for magnetic applications in electrical machinery. It is used for frame members where flux densities are low, and inexpensive yet complicated shapes are needed.

Mechanical Properties.—The physical properties which concern the mechanical utilization of the material are further classified as mechanical properties. Useful mechanical properties of a material depend largely upon its strength, namely ability to resist forces. Strength may be manifested by resistance to flexure (property of rigidity) and to permanent deformation (property of plasticity). The term "strength" also contemplates resistance to local destruction (as by fracture or breakage) and to more general disintegration (as in wear).

In the case of gray iron the potential strength properties are inherent in the matrix, or continuous structure. The matrix contains many weak graphite flakes. The amount, size, shape and distribution of these may have more influence on strength than the matrix structure itself. Thus, to get a high strength iron, it is necessary to provide a strong matrix, and also to control the graphite so that the latter is least effective in breaking up matrix continuity.

Mechanical loadings can be grouped as (1) "static" (slow rate of loading) and (2) "dynamic" (rapid or nearly instantaneous loading). Gray irons are particularly useful where static loadings are contemplated. Since they do not possess much ductility and are not appreciably plastic, dynamic loads of high intensity may cause rupture. This does not mean that gray iron is a brittle material. It has quite a useful range of toughness. Furthermore, it is not sensitive to "notch effects," and also possesses marked "damping" capacity. The latter minimizes the danger of load build-up through synchronous effects, which sometimes adversely affect more ductile metals.

When cast iron is stressed, the resultant strain consists of both elastic and plastic deformation. The true tensile properties of gray iron are not shown fully in the ordinary tensile test. The breaking load or ultimate strength is determined, also the relative rigidity. To determine the possible elastic rigidity and the plastic deformation, repeated loading tests must be employed.

Owing to difficulty in establishing the time elastic modulus in routine testing, this characteristic, in gray irons, usually is expressed as relative modulus at 25 per cent of ultimate tensile strength. This is determined by the slope from 0-0 of a line passing through the strain exhibited at 25 per cent of ultimate tensile strength. Relative moduli of elasticity so determined may be as low as 12,000,000 pounds per square inch for weak soft irons to possibly 28,000,000 for the very highest strength irons whose tensile strengths approach 100,000 pounds per square inch.

Deformation in gray irons has been shown to consist of both elastic and plastic components. It is known that ductile materials such as steel, if loaded for long periods, will fail at stresses much below the tensile strength as determined in short time testing. Test specimens "neck down" and lose maximum total load carrying ability. Cast iron in tension does not neck down or deform much in cross section, even at the breaking load. "Creep tests" are used to determine the maximum loads which can be sustained over long periods of time. In such tests the specimens are loaded to predetermined stress intensities and remain so loaded for long periods of time—about 1,000 hours or more. If continued extension of a specimen is observed, the material is said to creep or flow under the load. If no extension is observed, the material is considered to be within its limiting creep strength.

Such tests indicate that (at room temperatures, and probably up to 650° F. or slightly above) the long-time strength of gray iron approaches the test value determined by the ordinary short-time test, and that yield strength and tensile strength are practically the same, once "set" (permanent deformation) is removed.

Tensile strength is important from viewpoints of engineering design and of manufacturing economy. Tensile strength is a variable used in most engineering formulae. It thus influences size of sections necessary for the required design. With stronger iron, lighter sections often can be used. On the other hand, stronger irons usually are somewhat more expensive to machine, and also may require more costly foundry procedures. The designer thus must balance the various economic factors of weight and other production expenses.

Modern practice classifies engineering gray irons according to minimum tensile strength. This classification is given in the table above, an excerpt from the American Society for Testing Materials, Specification A-48-41.

As shown, classes from 20,000 to 60,000 pounds per square inch are available under that

Class	Tensile Strength Minimum, pounds per square inch
No. 20	20,000
No. 25	25,000
No. 30	30,000
No. 35	35,000
No. 40	40,000
No. 50	50,000
No. 60	60,000

specification. The bulk of commercial gray irons is found in the classes from 25,000 to 50,000 pounds per square inch minimum tensile strength. However, irons above 70,000 pounds per square inch minimum tensile strength are obtainable by special processes, compositions, and treatments. Any iron found testing below 20,000 pounds per square inch tensile strength suggests the likelihood of unsoundness, due to bad design, to improper selection of composition, to poor foundry practice, or to a combination of these.

Usage of gray iron in unfired pressure vessels is restricted to a maximum of 450° F. by various codes. Within this limitation there is no perceptible change in strength; in fact, no published tests have indicated any deterioration up to 700° F., and perhaps appreciably higher in the case of the stronger classes of gray iron. For this reason the American Society for Testing Materials provides a specification (A 278) covering classes suitable for usage to 650° F.

Transverse Strength.—The transverse test is widely used for foundry control and specifications. In this test, the test bar is supported on knife edges and broken by a load applied midway between these supports. The distance between supports is the span. Deflection at the center is measured. Usually the ultimate load in pounds and the ultimate deflection in inches are reported. Since the load and deflection depend on the span and size of the section, as well as the material, the sizes of test bars and span are specified.

The deflection at the moment of breaking gives some measure of ductility. As tested on the conventional transverse bar of 1.2 inches diameter over 18 inches span, deflections on various irons may run from 0.15 to 0.35 inch. The higher strength irons usually show somewhat lower deflections than the soft ferritic irons. High phosphorus lowers deflection values. At a given strength level, higher deflection may indicate tougher iron.

Compression Strength.—Cast iron is much stronger in compression than in tension. On a series of tests covering many types of cast iron the compression strength ranged from 65,000 to 160,000 pounds per square inch. The ratio of compression strength to tensile strength varies from about 4.5-1 for the weaker irons to 2.5-1 for the stronger irons.

Shear Strength.—This property is rather closely proportional to tensile strength. The tensile strength (pounds per square inch) plus 9,000 pounds per square inch approximates the shear strength, in pounds per square inch. (This relationship is for regular gray irons. It would not hold for high phosphorus irons, mottled irons, or chilled irons.)

Torsional Strength.—The ratio of torsional strength (modulus of rupture in torsion) to tensile strength usually is within the range 1.2 to 1.4. The torsional strength is higher than the tensile strength, and increases with increase in

tensile strength.

Hardness.—The Brinell hardness test is a useful one for gray iron castings. The Rockwell test is also used, employing the *B* scale and the steel ball. In the "as cast" condition, commercial (nonalloy) gray iron castings will range from 130-210 Brinell hardness. The alloy cast irons will run higher and heat-treated irons may run over 600 Brinell hardness. Ordinary white irons will range from 321-534 Brinell while alloy white irons may run as high as 700.

Although the trend of indentation hardness is to increase with increase in tensile strength, the ratio of hardness to tensile strength is not constant. One property cannot be safely predicted from the other. The relationship of Brinell hardness to compressive strength is fairly constant. Compressive strength often can be approximated by multiplying Brinell hardness number by 750, up to values of about 200 Brinell hardness number.

Brinell number is a general indicator of machinability, but is not an accurate measure of that property.

Wear.—The term *wear* has generic rather than specific significance. Wear signifies a gradual eating away or dissolution of a structure resulting from the action of mechanically applied agents. Often mechanical wear and deterioration by corrosion act concurrently. The wearing agent may be a fluid (gas or liquid) or a solid.

With a perfect lubricant film there can be no wear. Wear occurs when there is no lubricant, or when the lubricant film breaks down, or when the lubricant is imperfect and a carrier of wearing agents (abrasives).

In the case of metal to metal wear (no lubricant), gray cast iron reveals a high degree of usefulness. Its highly heterogeneous structure effectively inhibits seizure and galling. It not only wears well on itself, but also with many other alloys. It has a tendency to cut much softer alloys, but usually works well with alloys as hard or harder than itself. This property of gray iron is among those responsible for its extensive use in machine tools, where heavy pressures and imperfect lubrication occur, and in automobile cylinders, where temperature and partial lubricant breakdown are factors. An example of metal to metal wear is in automobile brake drums. Gray iron, with its graphitic structure, is more free from the tendency toward seizure than the nongraphitic ferrous alloys.

The properties in gray cast iron which are associated with a low rate of wear are pearlitic matrix, suitable hardness, and high strength. Other things being equal, an iron with a pearlitic matrix will resist wear better than one containing free ferrite.

Heat treatment or special alloy additions which produce martensite, and other hard matrices improve wear resistance. Usually some increase in resistance to metal to metal wear may be expected from such increased hardness. However, the major gain is from increased resistance to abrasive action (sand or grit, etc.). Localized heat treatment (flame hardening) has proved useful.

White cast irons are relatively resistant to abrasion. Some of the alloyed hard white irons not only are resistant to abrasive influences but also have good resistance to galling and seizure.

Because there are many types of wear it is practically impossible to set up any laboratory test which will give an adequate measure of the wear resistance of a material in service. However, laboratory tests have been of value in helping to develop better materials for resisting wear. Some of the conclusions from laboratory tests are as follows: (1) wear resistance increases with matrix hardness; (2) with increasing combined carbon content, the resistance to wear of gray irons increases rapidly up to 0.60 per cent combined carbon and then slightly up to 0.85 per cent; (3) increasing silicon content decreases resistance to wear.

Machinability.—Machinability ranges of cast irons are wide. Cast irons may be made to suit many conditions, remembering that ease in machining is usually inversely proportional to the strength of the casting. Machinability of metals has been variously determined with reference to: (1) tool life, (2) type of finish obtained, (3) power required.

The composition, structure, and physical properties of cast iron extend over a wide range. Dependent upon these factors, cast iron varies from one of the most readily machinable to the most unmachinable of ferrous materials. At one extreme of this range we have completely annealed permanent mold cast iron, which is the most readily machinable; at the other extreme is white or chilled cast iron and iron hardened by heat treatment. Annealed permanent mold cast iron possesses excellent machinability because the structure consists of iron containing no combined carbon and broken up by a high percentage of finely divided free carbon flakes, together with freedom from burned-in sand at the surface. Chilled or white iron is extremely difficult to machine because its structure is composed chiefly of hard iron carbide in both pearlitic and massive form, unbroken by any flakes of free carbon.

When nickel with low silicon and chromium content is used, it permits machining irons of considerably higher hardness than could be machined without the use of nickel. The reason for the ability to machine irons of 225-250 Brinell in alloy compositions is that no massive carbides exist in the matrix. As soon as plain cast iron exceeds a hardness of about 220 Brinell, it usually contains hard carbides, especially at the edges and corners of light castings.

Chromium is a carbide former, and if as much as 0.25 per cent is added to plain cast iron which is already at the limit of machinability, the iron may become difficult to machine. Care should therefore be taken in adding chromium, where machinability is a factor. However, on many soft irons, as much as 0.50 per cent chromium may be added with little effect on machinability.

The high chromium irons (35 per cent chromium), although white irons, structurally are softer and more readily machinable than other white irons.

The austenitic gray irons have approximately the same machinability as regular gray irons of equivalent tensile strength. However, the austenitic irons are subject to surface work hardening when surface distortion without proper metal removal is incurred. Improperly sharpened tools and rubbing action by tools or by chips should be avoided.

The high silicon (15 per cent) cast irons are quite difficult to machine, and grinding is usually employed. The newer carbide tools have possibilities.

Molybdenum is frequently used as an alloy addition in cast iron to obtain increased strength and wear resistance. Where molybdenum is used to increase hardness and strength without the formation of carbides, machinability will usually be inversely proportional to the hardness and strength produced.

The surface condition of iron castings is most important in determining machinability. Frequently castings are condemned as unmachinable when the metal itself is quite machinable, but difficulty is caused by the presence of burned-in sand on the casting. Where burned-in sand is present, any attempt to make light surface cuts will cause rapid failure of the tool. A sufficient depth of cut must be made to ensure the point of the tool being well below the surface of the casting.

The character of the surface finish obtainable in machining cast iron is dependent upon the size of the graphite flakes and the total amount of the graphite. A high total carbon, high silicon cast iron with large graphite flakes will show a pitted surface when machined due to tearing out of particles of metal between the graphite flakes. Rough cuts taken on coarse grained cast iron will exaggerate the pitted appearance by tearing out small particles of iron. The lower carbon irons will give a much better appearance when machined.

Newer types of tool materials, such as the tungsten carbides and newer machine tool designs permit rates of metal removal in some operations which were not attainable with older tool materials and with older type machine tools. The newer carbide tools are more resistant to the abrasive action of small carbide particles, to the hard phosphorus-rich component steadite, and to burned-in sand. Usually the resistance of cast irons does not produce high tool pressures. It is not prone to seize and crater on tool faces. In many cases newer tools and newer machines permit faster machining of many types of cast iron.

Dynamic Strength.—Metals are often used under rapidly repeated or alternated loadings. To the layman such loadings often are referred to as vibratory stresses. The engineer calls ultimate resistance to such stresses fatigue strength or endurance limit. As with other metals the endurance limit of gray cast iron is less than its ultimate tensile strength.

Deterioration in fatigue is progressive in nature, much more gradual than failure in tension of a ductile material. Under a sufficiently large number of restressings, incipient fractures are started in small flaws, since the latter promote increased localized stress intensity (the start of cracks) and the gradual progress of fracture from these points. In ductile materials, fracture in tension tests is preceded by perceptible elongation and reduction of cross sectional area. In these same materials fatigue may be sudden, as the repetitions of stress result in sudden brittle-acting failure, with no stretch or elongation to give warning of impending fracture, with the exception of possible visible cracks.

It is said (incorrectly) that the steel has crystallized, because of this brittle fracture. It was always crystalline, and the alternating stresses, not the crystallinity of the material, caused the characteristic fracture.

The endurance limit of gray iron in completely reversed cycles of bending stress varies from about 40 to 55 per cent of its tensile strength. (This is also about the same proportional relationship found in case of steels.) Thus a stronger gray iron can be expected to have a higher endurance limit than a weaker iron. This is also true of alternating torsion stresses and of alternate tension-compression stresses.

Some ductile metals, for example some types of steel, are very sensitive to notches and other surface discontinuities. When these exist, the material may fail in fatigue (endurance) at quite low stresses. Fortunately many gray irons, especially the lower strength classes are much less affected by notches and other surface discontinuities.

As is the case with most metals, corrosive effects may lower the endurance limits of gray irons.

The effects of elevated temperature are quite similar on both tensile strength and endurance limits. Up to about 800° F. these properties are changed little from their room temperature values.

Damping: Gray iron is effective in damping or absorbing vibratory impulses. This property (damping) is measured by the length of time it takes for a vibrational impulse to die out. A hard steel tuning fork has low damping capacity. If struck it will continue to vibrate audibly for some seconds, and inaudibly for some longer time. If the fork were made of lead, it would sound dead when struck. Lead has very high damping capacity. Gray iron is intermediate in this characteristic. Imposed oscillations are more rapidly dampened in cast iron than in steel.

Damping capacity is a significant factor in choice of materials for machines which encounter vibrational impulses during operation. If such impulses synchronize, the amplitude of vibration may become very great, and result in failure or breakage. In all cases vibrations mean loss of useful power, and interfere with accuracy in alignments. Designers have learned to take good advantage of gray iron's relatively good damping capacity.

Impact: Gray iron is not employed where high resistance to impact or shock is a requirement. It does, however, possess a surprisingly wide range of usefulness where mild shock resistance is required. Automotive pistons are a familiar example. Lately, even in large Diesel engines, gray iron crankshafts have proved quite adequate.

There is no exact relationship between shock resistance and tensile strength. Stronger irons, particularly the lower carbon varieties, usually are the more shock resistant. Of two irons alike in strength, the one with more ductility, or with greater deflection in the transverse test may be expected to have the greater shock or impact resistance. High phosphorus content tends to lower shock resistance.

JOHN W. BOLTON,
The Lunkemheimer Co.

4. PIG IRON.—Pig iron is the crude, commercial, metallic product of an iron blast furnace and is the basis of the whole iron and steel industry. Practically all forms of iron and steel products in existence originally came from pig iron, which in turn was smelted from natural iron ores or from iron-bearing byproducts; meteoric iron (usually museum exhibits) and "direct reduction" iron, often in the form of "powdered iron," and as Swedish "sponge iron," are the commercial exceptions, in very small tonnages. The name "pig iron" was applied first to solid pig iron because it was cast in a sand pig bed where the molten iron ran through a long groove or trough and thence into many smaller groves at right angles, so that it looked like a litter of pigs nursing at the side of the mother sow. When the iron solidified, the long piece became the "sow" and the offshoots became the "pigs" that had been molded in the sand "pig bed." When cast iron molds, or "chill beds," replaced the sand pig bed (which had to be made up after each cast), the names sow and pigs followed the solid pig iron. When the iron from the furnace was poured into a pig machine, there were no longer any sows and all the pig iron became "iron in pigs." Pig beds are becoming obsolete, but pig iron is the commercial and technical name given to this important metal whether it is in its liquid or in its solid form. Iron in pigs is the name given by the United States Tariff Commission to solid pig iron; "hot metal," or "direct metal" is the name given by iron and steel men to the molten metal as it is conveyed from the blast furnace to the steel mill or to the foundry for "direct castings."

Contrary to the decision once announced by the United States Tariff Commission, "that molten iron is not an article of commerce," much molten iron is carried on standard railroads, over rivers, between different towns and companies, as well as between various departments of the same steel company. Metallurgically there is no reason why hot metal could not be transported across the boundary lines of adjoining countries, such as across the St. Mary's River from the Canadian "Soo," or across the Rio Grande at Piedras Negras, Texas, into Mexico. Hot metal is delivered directly from "merchant" blast furnaces to large foundries, making such heavy castings as ingot molds or cast iron pipe.

A "merchant" blast furnace is one that makes pig iron for foundries and sells it on the open market; a "steel plant" or "captive" blast furnace produces steel-making pig iron, usually basic or Bessemer iron.

Where smaller castings are made in large quantities, like engine blocks for automobiles, it is sometimes the practice to pour the hot metal from the blast furnace into a hot metal mixer. Usually molten scrap (cast iron and steel) from a cupola is mixed with the hot metal from the mixer, and the two streams of molten metal flow into a receiver that is continually kept at the right temperature for pouring into the molds. The analysis of the molten metal in the receiver is controlled by mixing the right amounts of hot metal from the mixer and from the cupola.

There are many grades of pig iron classified chiefly by the chemical analysis, especially the phosphorus content, partly by the subsequent use, and also by the blast furnace fuel used in its production. The General Technical Committee of the American Iron and Steel Institute has selected 14 grades of pig iron listed below as representing compositions of proven merit and in extensive use for a wide variety of purposes. Such irons are called standard grades of pig iron.

It is recognized that compositions other than those listed in the tables of irons may be produced and will at times be required for specialized uses. Irons so specified are termed nonstandard irons.

For convenient reference, standard grades of pig iron listed herein are designated by the use of prefix letters, suffix letters, and numerals. A prefix letter is used which designates grades in order of increasing phosphorus content, as follows:

	Designation	Phosphorus content
LP	Low-phosphorus	0.035 per cent, maximum
LPi	Intermediate low-phosphorus	0.036 to 0.075 per cent
Bes	Bessemer	0.076 to 0.100 per cent
M	Malleable	0.101 to 0.300 per cent
B	Basic—Northern	0.400 per cent, maximum
Fl	Foundry—Northern low-phosphorus	0.300 to 0.500 per cent
Fh	Foundry—Northern high-phosphorus	0.501 to 0.700 per cent
Fs	Foundry—Southern	0.700 to 0.900 per cent
Bs	Basic—Southern	0.700 to 0.900 per cent
Cn	Charcoal iron—Northern	0.100 to 0.200 per cent
C1	Charcoal iron—Southern	0.035 per cent, maximum
C2	Charcoal iron—Southern	0.100 to 0.200 per cent
C3	Charcoal iron—Southern	0.400 to 0.700 per cent
S	Silvery	0.300 per cent, maximum

Silicon and manganese contents are designated by a six-number system in which the first three numerals designate the average silicon content; the average manganese content is similarly indicated by the last three numerals. For example, in LP 113088, LP denotes phosphorus content of 0.035 maximum; 113 denotes silicon content of 1.00 to 1.25 per cent; and 088 denotes manganese content of 0.76 to 1.00 per cent.

The four preceding paragraphs are quoted from pages 3 and 4 of Section 1 of *Steel Products Manual Pig Iron and Ferroalloys;* then there follow 31 pages, with 15 tables of the intricate variations of pig iron that can be made in a blast furnace, having different combinations of the four chief elements, silicon, sulphur, phosphorus, and manganese. The ferroalloys commonly made in a blast furnace are spiegeleisen, ferromanganese, ferrosilicon, and ferrophosphorus. Other ferroalloys with commercial grades are ferrosilicon, silicomanganese, ferrochromium, ferrovanadium, ferrotungsten, ferromolybdenum, and ferrotitanium.

All of the above pig irons, made with coke, are sold and graded on chemical analysis; grading and selling by "fracture" is obsolete. Charcoal pig iron was sold and graded on "fracture" for the past 300 years in the United States, but now there are no more charcoal blast furnaces in the latter country that make sand-cast pig iron; the only charcoal blast furnace left uses a pig casting machine and the iron is sold on analysis. This makes obsolete the 15 grades of charcoal pig iron that prevailed up to World War II.

The market price of charcoal pig iron has always been higher than that of any other grade, beginning with quotations of anthracite and charcoal pig iron in Philadelphia in May 1842. (For about 200 years previously there had been nothing but charcoal pig iron made in this country; in 1946, only coke pig iron and charcoal pig iron were made.) The premium on charcoal pig iron for about 20 years previous to World War II averaged $7 per ton above similar grades of coke pig iron; this premium was doubled during the war, owing to the scarcity of charcoal pig iron.

Actual market prices of pig iron will not be given here; they can be found in such trade journals as *The Iron Age* and *Steel.* There are silicon differentials, not to exceed 50 cents per ton for each 0.25 per cent silicon content above the base grade, which is 1.75-2.25 per cent.

In some iron ores, especially those imported from the shores and islands of the Mediterranean, there are small amounts of metals that give trouble in smelting, such as zinc, lead, and arsenic; the zinc and lead do not go into the pig iron, but arsenic does and gives trouble in the subsequent steel. Small amounts of vanadium, nickel, and copper in the iron ores go into the pig iron with beneficial results.

Blast Furnace.—The iron blast furnace (see illus.) is the largest of metallurgical furnaces. In principle, it is one of the simplest means of separating a metal from its oxides and producing a commercial product. In practice, it is a complicated apparatus for handling large tonnages of solid materials, tremendous volumes of cold and hot atmospheric air and still larger volumes of hot gases, for furnishing the room in which a multiplicity of chemical reactions and physical changes can take place at the same time, and for providing a hearth, or crucible, where the molten metallic and nonmetallic products can be received, separated and drawn off, separately, at stated intervals. The blast furnace itself is a vertical series of steel-clad cylinders lined with refractories, through which a continual flow of solids is descending from top to bottom, meeting a continual flow of hot gases ascending from bottom to top, and then outside. Down through this gigantic heat exchanger, which sometimes is 105 feet high from the iron notch to the top, passes a column of several thousand tons of ore, coke, and limestone in 24 hours, all of which is gasified or liquefied by the time it reaches the hearth of the furnace. Up this vertical furnace is blown a hurricane of hot gas that began with 60,000 to 90,000 cubic feet of atmospheric air per minute. Here is one of the paradoxes of blast furnace practice. A big modern blast furnace has a cubical capacity of 35,000 to 45,000 cubic feet; in operation, it is filled up to the stock line with solid iron ore, coke and limestone, and yet a volume of air blast equal to twice its cubical contents is blown into it every minute. Thus there is a descending column of cold solids, getting hotter every minute, meeting an ascending column of hot gases, getting cooler every minute. In addition to the physical phenomena of the exchange of heat, the working of gravity, the calcining of limestone, the roasting of ore, and the diffusion of gases, there are chemical actions and reactions of reduction, oxidation, solution, carbon impregnation, slag formation, sulphur absorption and sulphur removal, and, incidentally and only for a short interval, the formation of the sponge iron which quickly absorbs carbon and becomes the more fusible pig iron, the final product of the iron blast furnace.

Previous to World War I there was no rule for determining the capacity of an iron blast furnace, and 600 tons of pig iron per 24 hours was about the maximum production. In October 1920, the Southern Ohio Pig Iron & Coke Association, after two years of work by a special committee, announced a rule for calculating the capacity of a blast furnace, as follows: "Regardless of grade of pig iron produced, blast furnaces of modern construction should burn about the same amount of fuel daily under same operating conditions. For each grade of pig iron the tonnage which can be produced will depend upon the quality of fuel used, yield of ore mixture and blast temperature. The tonnage of coke which can be burned in a unit of time has a certain ratio to the working volume of the furnace. The working volume is taken as volume from center line of tuyeres to two feet below bell when closed . . . It has been found that, with good practice, 60 pounds of coke can be burnt each 24 hours per cubic foot working volume . . . It is necessary to adopt a base coke, a base theoretical yield ore mixture, and a base hot blast temperature and then make allowances for variations as encountered."

The analysis of the base coke referred to is as follows:

	Per cent	
Fixed carbon	89	
Sulphur	1	(maximum)
Ash	9 to 10	
Volatile	1 to 2	

The structure of the coke is tough, but not dense or fragile, and free from breeze.

By the year 1930 the output of a standard sized blast furnace was 1,000 tons of pig iron per 24 hours; during World War II, it was 1,500 tons, with a few actually making 1,700 tons at times, with a maximum for a day of 1,976 tons.

The main parts of a blast furnace are: (1) the hearth or crucible where the molten iron and slag collect; (2) the tuyere zone where the air blast enters and combustion takes place; (3) the bosh or zone of fusion; (4) the shaft with its upper and lower zones of reduction and its exchange of heat from ascending hot gases to the descending column of solid raw materials; (5) and the top with its receiving hopper, double bells and hoppers, revolving top, downcomer arches for the escaping gases, and uptakes and bleeders to relieve any sudden extra gas pressure inside the furnace. In order to get the optimum results as to tonnage, all of these parts must have the proper dimensions, angles, and locations. These are called the lines of the furnace.

All these sections of the furnace are encased in steel plates, of strength and thickness requisite for the demands of the expansion from heat and pressures inside the furnace. Each section is lined with firebrick and other refractories, suitable for the demands of that section, such as: excessive temperatures and the chemical and physical action of large quantities of molten iron and slag in the hearth; intense heat and evolution of hot gases in the bosh; the wear of the slowly descending solid materials and the abrasive action of the rapidly ascending, dust-laden, hot gases in the shaft; and the wear from impact of the cold raw materials that are dropped off the big charging bell at the top of the furnace, and where there is danger from the chemical, as well as the physical, action of the swiftly moving hot gases. In order to protect these several kinds of refractory linings, and to extend the life of the whole lining of the furnace, many devices are used, mostly hollow water-cooled iron, or copper, plates or castings. Naturally, the hearth needs the greatest protection, because at times it will contain several hundred tons of molten iron, and slag, at maximum temperatures of slag approximately 2800° F.

Besides using the highest grade of firebrick, burned at high temperatures in the brick kiln and machine-ground to exact size, sometimes in the larger furnaces a layer of sillimanite is spread across the hearth between the courses of the bottom blocks (firebrick 18" by 9" by 6"). Between the firebrick solid bottom, the firebrick side walls, and the heavy steel hearth jacket, there are placed cast iron, water-cooled, vertical hearth plates extending the total height of the jacket. At the tuyere zone there are the copper water-cooled tuyere coolers and also many copper (generally called "bronze") bosh plates above, below and between the tuyere coolers. The bosh walls are protected on the outside by heavy steel bosh bands, or else enclosed entirely by a steel bosh jacket; in either case there are several rows of copper ("bronze") bosh plates, through which flows a constant stream of water. The shaft of the furnace, extending from the mantel to the top platform, has a steel shell outside the brick lining. Between the brick and the steel there is usually some packing that acts as insulation and also as an expansion joint. The brick lining of the shaft, mostly of inwall brick, is sometimes protected by cooling plates of either copper or of water-cooled cast iron plates. The firebrick at the top of the furnace consists of very hard, dense brick, generally protected at the stock line, and for several feet below, by some sort of armor, either of steel or cast iron.

The waste gas ("top gas," or blast furnace gas) from the top of the furnace, amounting in volume as it passes out of the furnace to about 30 per cent more than the volume of atmospheric air blown into the furnace, goes through one or more downcomers extending downward from the top of the furnace to the dustcatcher, where the heavier particles of the flue dust are removed from the hot (250°-450° F.) dry gas, and thence to some form of gas washer, scrubbers and dryers. The final gas is cleaner than the air we breathe, the dust being reduced from about 10 grains per cubic foot down to less than 0.01 grain of dust per cubic foot.

The cleaned blast furnace gas of about 90-105 Btu. per cubic foot is used for heating the hot blast stoves (20 to 25 per cent) under boilers, underfiring of coke ovens, in gas engines, and sometimes at integrated steel plants it takes the place of producer gas for soaking pits, and reheating furnaces.

Hot Blast Stoves.—The air blast from the blowing engines is heated to a temperature as high as 1600° to 1800° F. in a regenerative hot blast stove made of firebrick checkerwork incased in steel sheets 20 to 25 feet in diameter and 85 to 105 feet high, in which the cleaned waste gas from the furnace has been burning for two hours or more. There must be the right balance of heating surface and brick volume so that the heat from combustion of the gas can be stored up and then given out again to the air blast which flows through the checkerwork in the opposite direction from the hot gas. Usually two, or more, stoves are being heated while one or two stoves are "on the furnace." A three-pass stove will have its individual stack, as seen in the photograph; two-pass stoves have one large draft stack in common.

Hot Metal Ladles.—The hot metal ladles mentioned above are of two general types. One is the upright, short-pour ladle car of 50 to 100 tons capacity on a heavy, underslung, steel frame mounted on two standard railroad trucks. A motor for tilting the ladle is mounted on the frame. The other is the Pollock mixer-type, hot metal ladle car of 100 to 200 tons capacity, as shown in the illustration herewith which can be completely enclosed for safe transportation over standard railroad tracks for considerable distances. Both types of ladles are lined with special ladle brick or with silica "firestone."

Hot Metal Mixers.—At steel plants and at large foundries, the hot metal from successive casts of one or more blast furnaces is poured from the hot metal ladles into a hot metal mixer which is a big, steel encased container mounted on trunnions, with a thick firebrick lining, kept hot by a gas or oil flame, and tilted for pouring into the transfer ladles with the same big hook and overhead crane as is used for handling the hot metal ladles. The large, mixer-type, hot metal ladles can be poured directly into the transfer ladles that are used to fill the open hearth steel-making furnaces.

Blast Furnace Practice.—The efficiency of the modern iron blast furnace depends on the time and the regularity of the "through-put" of the raw materials that are charged into the top of the furnace through the revolving top and through the double bell and hopper, and down into the furnace itself. The revolving top distributes the materials regularly onto the "big bell" which is a conical, steel casting suspended by a bell rod connected to the bell beam in such a way that the bell travels vertically downward to deliver the stock (ore, coke, limestone, and scrap) into the furnace, and then travels upward to seat itself tightly on the beveled edge of the big hopper so as to prevent the escape of the blast furnace gas. The little bell is then lowered so that the stock in the little hopper drops onto the big bell. The little bell and hopper are revolved by a mechanism that causes the delivery of the stock onto the big bell in such a predetermined way that the "charges" are delivered evenly around the periphery of the stock line, first a charge of coke and then a charge of ore and limestone, and any scrap that is charged into the furnace. This device is the McKee revolving top. During World War II, these big charging bells reached enormous sizes, some being 15½ feet in diameter and weighing 45,000 pounds.

The raw materials are taken from the ground level to the top of the furnace in the skip cars running on the tracks of a double skip hoist, generally electrically operated, as shown in the photograph. The coke is filled into the skip cars from the coke bins without weighing; all ores and limestone are carefully weighed in a scale car before being dumped into the skip cars.

It is the responsibility of the blast furnace superintendent to see that just the right volume of coke is charged into the furnace during the right intervals of time, that the right weights of iron ore and of limestone follow each charge of coke, and that the right volume of air blast is heated to the right temperature and blown regularly each minute into the furnace at the tuyeres at the right blast pressures.

Because the blast furnacemen of the United States, operating men, executives and engineers, had developed during the period between the two world wars a blast furnace practice that accomplished wonderful results as to big tonnages and operating economies, there grew up what is called "American blast furnace practice." The American designs of blast furnace plants, and the methods for their operation have been spread all over the world, so that by the end of World

War II the big 1,500-1,700 ton furnaces were making pig iron in Russia and India and other countries as well as in the United States. Much of this progress was due to the free exchange of ideas and experiences of the operating men in such groups as the Southern Ohio Pig Iron & Coke Association (now defunct), The Eastern States Blast Furnace and Coke Oven Association, the Blast Furnace and Coke Association of the Chicago District, and the Iron and Steel Division of the American Institute of Mining and Metallurgical Engineers.

Raw Materials.—The essential raw materials for the production of pig iron are iron ore, fuel, flux, and the air blast. A few places in the world have all these in close proximity, notably the Birmingham District of Alabama. Usually, one or more ingredients are transported long distances by rail and water, as in the case of the Lake Superior iron ores which go hundreds of miles to the blast furnaces using the famous Pittsburgh seam of coal for their coke. The assembling costs of the raw materials is a vital factor in the cost of the pig iron.

Iron Ores.—The iron ores commonly used in the iron blast furnace are the oxides of iron: ferric (Fe_2O_3) and magnetic (Fe_3O_4). These are more abundant than any other iron-bearing minerals. The ferric oxide, usually called hematite, often occurs in various forms of hydrates, or combinations of Fe_2O_3 with fixed proportions of "combined water" (H_2O). The Brown Ores of the South and the Southwest, especially in Alabama and East Texas, are hydrated oxides of iron. The percentage of iron (Fe) that must be in an iron-bearing mineral before it can be classed as a merchantable iron ore varies greatly from 25 per cent to 70 per cent, depending on its capability of being beneficiated before charging into the blast furnace, and on the character of the "gangue" of the iron mineral, that is, the nonmetallic elements that are combined with the iron either chemically or mechanically. The gangue of some iron ores, especially certain ores in Red Mountain, in the Birmingham District of Alabama, contain enough lime and magnesia to flux all the silica and alumina in the gangue of that ore, and even a little left over to flux a part of the ash in the coke. These are called "self-fluxing" ores, and, although the iron content is low, they are very desirable. The ore from Muscoda No. 4 mine is such an ore, with the following analysis: Fe, 35.57 per cent; SiO_2, 12.38 per cent; Al_2O_3, 3.45 per cent; CaO, 17.38 per cent; MgO, 0.56 per cent in the dried sample. The natural ores and minerals of iron are as follows:

Name	Classification	Formula	Fe content (per cent)	Sometimes called
Hematite	Ferric oxide (hexagonal)	Fe_2O_3	70.0	Red ore
Magnetite	Magnetic oxide (octahedral)	Fe_3O_4	72.4	Black oxide
Martite	Ferric oxide	Fe_2O_3	70.0	
Limonite	Hydroxide	$2Fe_2O_3.3H_2O$	59.8	Brown ore
Turgite	Hydroxide	$2Fe_2O_3.H_2O$	66.2	
Goethite	Hydroxide	$Fe_2O_3.H_2O$	62.9	
Siderite	Carbonate	$FeCO_3$	48.2	Spathic iron
Franklinite	Oxides	$(Fe, Mn, Zn)O.(Fe, Mn)_2O_3$	21.0	Franklin ore
Ilmenite	Oxides	$(FeTi)_2O_3$	variable	Titaniferous magnetite
Chromite	Oxides	$FeCrO_3$	variable	Black sands
Wolframite	Oxides	$(FeO.MnO)WO_3$	variable	
Pyrite	Sulphide	FeS_2	46.7	Iron pyrites
Pyrrhotite	Sulphide	Fe_6S_7	variable	Magnetic pyrites
Chalcopyrite	Copper-iron sulphide	$CuFeS_2$	30.4	Copper pyrites
Marcasite	Sulphide	FeS_2	46.7	White iron pyrites

The iron ores that are compounded with other metals, especially the sulphide ores, must be treated in some way to separate the iron as far as possible from the other ingredients, usually by roasting, before they can be charged into the blast furnace. Besides the natural iron ores mentioned above, there are several iron-bearing byproducts containing enough iron to make it profitable to smelt them in the iron blast furnace. These are:

(1) Blue Billy, the iron oxide residue from roasting sulphide ores; (2) flute dust, the fine dust carried out of the top of the blast furnace, and recovered in the gas cleaning equipment; (3) roll scale, the rich iron oxide obtained while rolling steel in the steel mills; (4) mill cinder, the rich iron slag from the puddling process for making wrought iron; (5) slag, from the open hearth furnaces, Bessemer converters and Spiegel furnaces; (6) borings, turnings, crop ends, stove plate, slag scrap, miscellaneous small iron and steel scrap.

At integrated steel plants (an integrated steel plant includes byproduct coke ovens, blast furnaces, open hearth furnaces or Bessemer converters, and rolling mills) it is usual to send a part, or all, of the open hearth slag to the blast furnaces so as to utilize the fluxing value of the excess lime and magnesia and recover most of the manganese and iron. An ordinary open hearth slag will have 10-16 per cent Fe; 4-7 per cent Mn; 43-48 per cent CaO; 6-8 per cent MgO; 12-20 per cent SiO_2; 2-8 per cent Al_2O_3; 1.50-2.35 per cent P; 0.16-0.22 per cent S. Open hearth furnaces producing ingot iron make a slag much higher in iron and lower in lime. The slag from blast furnaces making spiegel contains enough manganese (about 12 per cent) to make it desirable to smelt with iron ores that are deficient in manganese, such as the Eastern magnetites.

Fuels.—Practically all the pig iron in the world is made with coke, either beehive coke or byproduct coke. The only other fuel in the United States is charcoal. Even in the electric furnace process for making pig iron, solid fuel of either coke or charcoal must be used. Charcoal is the blast furnace fuel used in Brazil. It was the only fuel used in the United States for the first 200 years, up to the use of anthracite in 1840. Anthracite predominated from 1855 to 1875; beehive coke from 1875 to 1919; and byproduct coke from 1919 on. The peak tonnage of charcoal pig iron in the United States was reached in 1890 (628,145 gross tons), with 135 active charcoal blast furnaces, and the production has steadily decreased ever since, with only one charcoal furnace in blast at the end of World War II, and one being built. Anthracite ceased to be a regular blast furnace fuel during World War I. It has been used intermittently, mixed with coke, during coke shortages. It is being used in Italy and Russia. Small amounts of certain kinds of bituminous coals (No. 1 Sharon seam in Ohio) that are noncoking are still used for certain special grades of pig iron, mixed with coke, in the United States, and in Scotland.

In the manufacture of beehive coke from bituminous coking coals, all of the volatile byproducts are wasted in the black smoke that arises from the beehive ovens that predominated in the coke industry up to World War I and became almost extinct just previous to World War II. The demand for coke then became so great that many new beehive coke ovens were built in many parts of the country where coking coals were available. Since a part of the coal itself is burned to furnish the heat for the coking process, the yield of coke in the beehive oven is only 62 to 66 per cent, depending on the amount of volatile matter in the coal.

Byproduct coke was first used in the chemical industry where a dense lumpy coke was desired and where the byproducts required complicated chemical processes and costly equipment. The introduction of byproduct coke as a blast furnace fuel proceeded rather slowly, but when prejudice and inexperience were overcome by hearty cooperation of the coke oven men and the blast furnacemen, the great advantage of conserving the volatiles so as to reduce the cost of the coke was recognized, and byproduct coke became the almost universal blast furnace fuel wherever coking coals were available.

The yield of coke in byproduct coke ovens is considerably higher than in beehive ovens, but it is still dependent on the percentages of ash and volatile matter in the coal. A good coal would yield about 1,400 pounds of coke per ton (2,000 pounds) of coal; 100 pounds of coke breeze; 10 gallons of coal tar; 2.8 gallons of motor benzol; 24 pounds of ammonium sulphate; 6,500 cubic feet surplus gas. A good blast furnace coke has about 2 per cent moisture; 89 to 92 per cent fixed carbon; 1.50 to 2.00 per cent volatile matter; 4.50 to 7.00 per cent ash; and not over 0.60 per cent sulphur; coke with over 1.0 per cent sulphur is not standard and is usually subject to a reduction in price. All byproduct coke is screened and sized, the smaller sizes being sold for domestic coke; the size for blast furnace coke varies according to conditions of the supply and the vagaries of blast furnace operators; usually it is coke that passes through screens having openings or mesh 4 inches to 3 inches and remains on screens of 1¼ inches to 1 inch mesh. Blast furnace coke should be tough, not dense or fragile, and free from breeze.

Flux.—The smelting of iron ores requires a flux stone, either an almost pure limestone (calcium carbonate, $CaCO_3$) or a dolomite—a double carbonate of calcium and magnesium $(Ca,Mg)CO_3$. Lime (CaO) is essential for the formation of CaS, calcium sulphide, the very stable compound which removes the sulphur that otherwise would combine with the iron and make an undesirable high-sulphur pig iron. Some magnesia (MgO) is always desirable in a flux stone as it tends to lower the melting temperature of very basic slags. Too much magnesia simply increases the bulk of slag beyond the optimum volume. The ash of the blast furnace fuel and the gangue of the iron ores (the earthy ingredients of the blast furnace "burden") combine with the lime and magnesia and go into the slag. The decrease of efficiency of the fluxing value of the stone will be approximately double the amount of silica and alumina contained in the flux stone.

Slag.—The control of the composition of the slag is of prime importance to the blast furnace superintendent, because the smooth running of the furnace and the quality of the pig iron depend upon it. The temperature of the molten slag (above 2700° F. in making basic iron), which is always higher than that of the molten pig iron (2450° to 2700°), determines the critical temperature of the hearth above which only certain necessary operations of the process can be carried out. (J. E. Johnson, Jr., "The Physical Action of the Blast Furnace," *Transactions, American Institute of Mining and Metallurgical Engineers,* vol. 36, p. 472, 1906.)

The character of the slag is the determining factor in the "personality" of the pig iron, especially as to the controllable limits of silicon, sulphur, and to a certain extent the manganese; it also controls the proportions of combined and graphitic carbons in the pig iron, but not the total carbon.

There are various methods for slag disposal, such as running molten slag direct to dry slag pits alongside the blast furnace, direct to a granulating pit, filled with water, alongside the furnace. It may also run directly into cinder ladles ("slag pots") which are hauled away by a locomotive to dry slag pits at a distance from the furnace, or furnaces, or used for fills along a river bank or in low land. (See article 5, *"Wrought Iron"* for another use of molten slag.) Several types of cinder ladles are shown in the illustration alongside the cast house wall.

The uses of slag have been increasing greatly since the days when unsightly "slag dumps" were seen near every blast furnace of the 19th century. These dumps are now being reclaimed for making fireproof aggregate, roofing material, or mineral wool. Granulated slag is used for making portland cement by grinding to a slurry, mixing with limestone, and burning in a rotary cement kiln; it is also used for insulating packing, railroad fills, and "making ground" in low lands. Air-dried, solid slag is crushed, screened to different sizes, and sold for making roads, railroad ballast, concrete, and roofing material. Mineral wool is made direct by blowing a jet of steam into the molten slag as it runs from the furnace, or after the solid slag has been melted, in an ordinary cupola with coke. Such mineral wool is so white that it is called "slag wool," and is made into "bats," or pads, and used for insulation in buildings and refrigerators. "Loose wool" is the slag wool in small balls about the size of marbles that can be blown by compressed air inside the walls and roofs of dwellings to insulate them from cold and from hot weather.

In some cities the building code specifies

blast furnace slag as aggregate for reinforced concrete above certain heights; limestone aggregate cannot stand the heat like the slag.

Air Blast.—Of all the materials used in the blast furnace for making a ton of pig iron, the weight of the atmospheric air blown in through the tuyeres for the combustion of the coke is the greatest, as is shown by the following table:

Iron ore—52 per cent Fe.	4,047 lbs.	—1,807 gross tons
Coke—8 per cent ash....	1,900 lbs.	—0.848 gross tons
Limestone—3 per cent SiO_2	1,000 lbs.	—0.446 gross tons
Solid materials	6,947 lbs.	—3.101 gross tons
Air blast	7,942 lbs.	—3.545 gross tons
Total materials	14,889 lbs.	—6.646 gross tons

Totals per 2,240 pounds pig iron

Generally the air blast comes directly from the atmosphere outside the blowing engine house through pipes to the hoods over the intake valves of the air cylinders of the blowing engines, which may be vertical or horizontal reciprocating engines driven by steam, gas, or electricity. Again, they may be turbo blowers of up to 90,000 cubic feet of air per minute and up to 30 pounds pressure. As far back as the end of the 18th century, the British ironmasters were trying to improve the quality of the air blast when they discovered that their blast furnaces did not make as much pig iron in the hot summer months as in the colder winter months. They overlooked the fact that it is the *weight* of oxygen in the air blast that controls the weight of fuel burned at the tuyeres of the blast furnace, and that the hot air of the summer weighed less per cubic foot than the cooler air in the winter months. Paradoxically, and with due respect to those early researchers, the greatest tonnage of pig iron yet made in a day, a week, and a month was by No. 2 Edgar Thomson blast furnace at Braddock, Pa., in the month of July 1945 (1,976 tons, 12,189 tons, and 50,590 net tons respectively). At the end of another century, James Gayley and David Baker, brilliant and courageous blast furnacemen, experimented on the reduction of the moisture in the air blast. Gayley went so far as to freeze out all the moisture possible by refrigeration with ammonia machines, and patented and operated the Gayley dry-blast process which startled the steel industry with its amazing economies and big tonnages. As blast furnace practice was studied more and more by technical men, it was found that a certain amount of moisture in the blast was essential for the optimum catalytic action of the hydrogen that was dissociated in the tuyere zone. Therefore, there must be a certain amount of moisture in the air blast at all times, and if this certain amount (not less than about three grains of moisture per cubic foot of blast) can be kept constant by air conditioning apparatus, then there will be more regular operation of the furnace and a lower amount of coke per ton of pig iron.

The enriching of the percentage of oxygen in the air blast by removing a part of the nitrogen or by adding oxygen has not yet become standard practice, because no one has yet demonstrated that it would make more or cheaper pig iron. The inert nitrogen of the atmospheric air blast acts as the carrier of the surplus heat of the hearth upward through the descending column of solids which must be brought from the outdoor temperature to the white heat in front of the tuyeres. However, it is not only possible, but most probable, that a reasonable increase in the percentage of oxygen in the air blast would help to give a higher blast temperature, a lower coke consumption per ton of pig, and increased tonnage, all of which would be debited by the cost of producing the impure oxygen.

Beneficiation of the Raw Materials.—Very few, if any, of the iron ores are charged into the blast furnace just as they come from the mine. Some of the preparation, or beneficiation, may be simply the screening out and crushing of the lumps so as to have the ore more nearly all of the same screen size. In some cases the beneficiation is very elaborate, including crushing, fine grinding, magnetic concentration, tabling, flotation, and sintering. In cases of excessive moisture, iron ores are put through dryers to remove some of the excess water, thus increasing the iron content and decreasing the freight to destination. Iron carbonate ores are roasted, either in rotary or stationary kilns, for removal of most of the carbonic acid gas and making the ore into the richer hematite. Some carbonate ores contain enough iron sulphide so that the ore can be crushed fine and the sulphur used for fuel in a sintering machine. The abundant magnetic iron ores of New York, New Jersey, and Pennsylvania, some of them running as low as 30 per cent in iron, are crushed and ground fine and put through magnetic concentrators that remove most of the gangue and produce a rich magnetic iron ore that is too fine to be put into a blast furnace and must be agglomerated in a sintering machine. It has been found that the famous red ores of Alabama will have to be crushed to smaller sizes than was customary when both the ore and the coke were very cheap in the Birmingham District. In crushing and screening the red ore, much fines are produced and these must be sintered before charging into the blast furnace. Some fine ores are nodulized in a rotary kiln, and some few are biquetted, but sinter gives the best results in the blast furnace. The washing of iron ores which are mixed with clay and sand removes this worthless material and in some cases also removes excess moisture. This is done in "log washers."

Sintering Plant.—Here shown is the exterior of one of the largest of the new sintering plants erected by the United States government during World War II, from a photograph of the Greenawalt sintering plant at Tahawus, N. Y., built for, and operated by, the National Lead Company. The estimated annual capacity is 630,000 net tons of sintered magnetic iron concentrates from the titaniferous iron ore of the famous MacIntyre mine at Sanford Lake; the ilmenite (oxide of titanium) is first removed from the ore. This plant is dust-proof.

Statistics.—The production of pig iron in the United States began in the little charcoal blast furnace in Saugus, Mass., built in 1645. Nothing but charcoal pig iron was made in the United States until 1840 when anthracite was first used. James M. Swank, in his classic, *The Manufacture of Iron in All Ages* (1892), says, "No tabulated statistics of the production of iron in our Colonial history are extant, and the materials for such a compilation appear to be entirely wanting." The census report of 1810 shows 153 blast furnaces and a production of 53,908 tons of cast iron made. Beginning with the year 1810 and continuing to 1933, a chart showing the annual pig iron production in the

United States according to the fuel used (charcoal, anthracite, raw coal, coke) was published in *The Iron Age* of Nov. 29, 1934 (page 20 et seq.). In comparing statistics of pig iron production, care must be taken as to the number of pounds in a "ton," whether 2,240 or 2,000 pounds.

The American Iron and Steel Institute, New York, has been the authority on pig iron tonnage or production since the days of the American Iron and Steel Association.

The total capacity of the 225 active iron blast furnaces of the United States reached the peak of 66,256,810 net tons in 1945.

Bibliography.—American Iron and Steel Institute, *Yearbook; Transactions, American Institute of Mining and Metallurgical Engineers;* Forsythe, R., *The Blast Furnace and the Manufacture of Pig Iron* (New York 1908); rev. ed. by Meissner, C., and Mohr, J. A. (New York 1922); Morgan, J. J., *Blast Furnace Practice* (London 1910); Johnson, J. E., Jr., *Blast Furnace Construction in America* (New York 1917); id., *The Principles, Operations, and Products of the Blast Furnace* (New York 1918); Clements, F., *Blast Furnace Practice,* 2 vols. (London 1929); Sweetser, R. H., *Blast Furnace Practice* (New York 1938).

RALPH H. SWEETSER,
Consultant Engineer, Blast Furnace Practice.

5. WROUGHT IRON.—In 1934, the Committee A-2 on Wrought Iron of the American Society for Testing Materials defined wrought iron as follows: "A ferrous material aggregated from a solidifying mass of pasty particles of highly refined metallic iron with which, without subsequent fusion, is incorporated a minutely and uniformly distributed quantity of slag."

This definition is based upon metallurgical characteristics and is an amplification of the significance of the title, namely, a malleable ferrous material which may be shaped by a forging or related plastic deformation method. Prior to the development of modern steel-making processes—the Bessemer in 1855 and the open hearth or Siemens-Martin between 1862 and 1868—close metallurgical distinctions were not necessary, since wrought iron was virtually the sole ferrous metal adaptable to a forging operation.

Consideration of wrought iron as an entity involves first, the historical aspect, and second, its place in the more recent and contemporary industrial picture.

History and Development.—The origin of wrought iron may be taken as coincident with the earliest record of ferrous products. The limitations of primitive methods of manufacture undoubtedly resulted in a material conforming to the general characteristics of what we now classify as wrought iron.

Iron has been known from prehistoric times. It is frequently mentioned in Egyptian literature, and some samples in the British Museum are believed to date from 3733 B.C. Iron instruments, tools, and weapons were used in Greece in 1400 B.C. and in Assyria and Italy in 1100 B.C. History records their use in central and western Europe in 1000 B.C., and in Styria and Carinthia before the Christian era. The noted Pillar of Delhi is usually assumed to date from 400 A.D. The use of iron was general in Europe in the Roman Empire, and heat treatment of weapons and tools was then practiced.

The Catalan forge, originated about 1293 A.D. by the iron workers of Catalonia in Spain, represented a major advance in the manufacture of wrought iron direct from the ore. This was a hearth type of furnace consisting of a crucible in which the mixture of ore and fuel was placed. The air blast, produced by means of a trompe or water blower, entered the furnace through tuyeres (nozzles) near the bottom. The efficiency of the Catalan forge, which is said to have produced about 140 pounds of wrought iron in five hours, was considerably higher than that of earlier furnaces. It was in use in the American colonies.

The American bloomery, an offspring of the Catalan forge, represented the highest development of the hearth type of furnace. The hearth was rectangular in shape, with water-cooled metal sides, and was surmounted by a chimney for carrying off the waste gases. A forced hot blast was used, the bellows being driven by a water wheel or steam engine. As in all other direct processes, charcoal was used as a fuel. The bloomery was used in the United States as late as 1901.

Although direct processes for wrought iron production have been abandoned almost completely by the most advanced nations, they are still used by primitive peoples in some parts of the world. In all of these methods through the ages, the reduction of the ore produced an iron with a relatively low metalloid content, a pasty mass at the temperatures attainable. At the same time the gangue of the ore—silica, and other earthy oxides—formed a fluid slag in combination with some of the iron oxide. The product was a weldable sponge or ball intermingled with some of the slag. This was wrought or forged to a bloom for subsequent fabrication. Aside from the relative primitiveness of method in apparatus, manpower and efficiency, it was necessary to use high purity ore and fuel. There was no control of product through secondary reactions which are characteristic of more modern methods of making iron and steel with quantity output of specification grades from large-scale sources of ore and fuel. In the contemporary era, sporadic attempts along the line of direct reduction are faced with the same limitations of control and flexibility, plus economic and engineering factors in competition with today's two-step practice in the manufacture of iron and steel.

About 1350 in central Europe, a revolutionary transition in the iron industry was instituted. The apparatus developed was known as a *stuckofen* and was the progenitor of the modern blast furnace. The development was the result of efforts to reduce the fuel consumption and cost of manufacture by increasing the size and height of the furnace with a shaft type of furnace. There was no thought of a changed product, but the alterations of customary conditions, the somewhat higher temperatures, and the longer and more intimate contact of the charcoal fuel and reducing gases with the metallic iron resulted in a fluid product akin to today's cast or pig iron. Compared with wrought iron, it had a lower melting point, higher fluidity, and was relatively hard and brittle with a granular structure, unlike the fibrous wrought iron. It was of little direct use until the art of casting was developed, but the furnace in the succeeding centuries came into its major role for the production of the pig iron so important in our modern iron and steel processes.

Throughout the ages, man's greatest need has been for a ferrous product of a malleable, ductile type, which could be formed by plastic deformation, hot or cold, and having a relatively high degree of ductility. With limited use for the cast or pig iron of the *stuckofen* and its offspring, inventive effort was concentrated upon refining the product to the condition of the wrought iron in general demand. An attempt was made to reduce the metalloid content of cast iron (carbon 2-4 per cent, silicon 1-2 per cent) together with manganese and phosphorus, to the characteristics of the forgeable product with metalloid content of the base metal a few hundredths of 1 per cent in each case—notably, in the light of modern metallurgical knowledge, by the virtual elimination of the alloyed carbon.

Charcoal hearths, of which the Walloon, Lancashire, and South Wales are characteristic names, are modifications of the direct reduction hearths. In these forges, known as "fineries," the pig iron was melted with charcoal fuel under the oxidizing influence of a blast issuing from a single or double tuyere. The metal, relieved of its oxidizable metalloids, trickled to the bottom of the hearth and solidified to a spongy mass with slag impregnation and was removed as a wrought iron bloom. These furnaces have been used to produce a so-called charcoal or knobbled iron from iron or steel scrap as a starting metal.

General inefficiency of prevailing equipment and methods and, more particularly, the heavy drain upon timber reserves because of the necessity of charcoal for fuel were a serious handicap to the development of the iron industry. Some relief came in 1730–1735 with Darby's use of coke made from England's abundant coal.

The divorcement from charcoal became complete with the invention, by Henry Cort in England in 1784, of a method which has continued to the present era and is known as the "puddling process." This marked an important epoch in the metallurgy of iron. To make the use of more impure but cheaper fuel possible, Cort proposed to conduct the refining of the pig iron in the hearth of a reverberatory furnace, out of contact with the fuel itself and its contaminating influences. The fuel was burned in a separate firebox, the substance to be treated coming in contact only with the flame and gases resulting from the combustion of the fuel. Cort's hearth was sand-lined, and the process came under the name of "dry puddling." The siliceous hearth caused a heavy waste of iron. Marked improvement came with the introduction of an iron oxide bottom by Joseph Hall in England in 1830. This was the inception of the "wet puddling" or "pig boiling" process. It has remained as the puddling process substantially without change to the present and, prior to the entry of the Bessemer and open hearth processes, it was the bulwark upon which war, industry, and the needs of construction rested.

Puddling.—The puddling furnace is a simple, reverberatory, coal-fired furnace, sometimes with a waste heat boiler in the stack. In the Pittsburgh district, the single furnace was used with a charge of about 600 pounds. It was manned by two puddlers. In the eastern United States, double furnaces were the rule. These were really two single furnaces, back to back, with the walls removed to make a single hearth with one stack. The charge of 1,200 to 1,300 pounds was worked by four men, two on each side. The furnaces had a cinder (iron oxide) bottom, and were lined with plastic iron ore. The charge was cold pig iron and required about one and three-quarter hours for completion of the heat. Five heats constituted a turn with a man-turn output of about 1,400 to 1,500 pounds. The fuel requirement with a long flame, bituminous coal was 2,600 to 2,800 pounds per gross ton of product. The furnace temperature was about 2600° F. After the pig iron had become molten, some iron oxide in the form of mill scale was added to the bath. This caused progressive elimination of the undesired metalloids—silicon, carbon, manganese (almost completely), and phosphorus and sulphur to some degree—depending upon operating conditions. The oxides of silicon, manganese, and phosphorus combined with iron oxide from the scale and from the "fettle" (lining) to form a fluid slag of highly basic nature, essentially about 80 to 85 per cent iron oxide and 10 to 15 per cent silica, with small amounts of the oxides of manganese, phosphorus, and aluminum. The carbon, last to be removed, came off as a gas, bubbling through the liquid bath as the so-called "boil." In the final stages of lessened intensity of the boil, the iron "came to mature" and "grained." This was the completion of refining to virtually pure iron, with a melting point considerably above the operating temperature of the furnace and the progressive solidification of the refined metal. Throughout the reaction period and particularly during the boil, the heat was rabbled with long bars through the side door of the furnace, to aid in disintegration of the mass and permit thorough exposure to the refining influences.

The final spongy metallic mass in the liquid slag was compacted into two or three "puddle balls" which were removed from the furnace with tongs, squeezed to a cylindrical bloom, then rolled on the initial heat to rough, rectangular muck bars. In these operations, surplus slag was ejected, and the characteristic fiber of wrought iron was produced by a threadlike elongation of the slag filaments in the metal matrix. For most commodities, the muck bar was sheared to appropriate short lengths, piled, heated to welding, and rolled to desired "single refined" sections. For some commodities, piling and rolling were repeated to obtain greater reductions, finer slag distribution and higher resultant ductility in the product thence classed as "double refined" iron.

Mechanical Puddling.—Prior to the advent of the age of steel, marked by the introduction of the Bessemer and open hearth processes, some attempts were made to attach mechanically operated rabbles to the puddling furnace to reduce the arduous labor. Also much effort was expended on mechanical puddling, with machines to carry out the entire operation. A conspicuous example in America was the Danks furnace of 1870. Steelmaking was expected to put puddling and wrought iron into oblivion, and efforts for improvement in manufacture waned. Persistent recognition of the merit of wrought iron in certain services, notably against corrosion and fatigue stresses, gave it impetus in spite of limitations in manufacture, and caused a revival of interest in mechanical puddling.

In general, the methods have employed furnaces of a rotary or oscillatory type, with focu-

of attention upon obtaining agitation of the charge in simulation of the manual effort of the puddler. Failures have been caused by inconsistencies in quality of material produced, difficulties of maintenance of equipment, and comparative manufacturing costs unattractive for capital investment. The names of James P. Roe, W. C. Ely, Ford and Henry D. Hibbard have been associated with these methods, some of which reached commercial scales of production.

The revolving furnaces have had their most successful application in "bushelling," that is, heating iron or steel scrap to form a ball which is squeezed and rolled into muck bar for so-called "common iron," a product somewhat below quality grade.

Modern Practice.—An outstanding operation for the production of wrought iron is that of the A. M. Byers Company in the Pittsburgh district. It was the result of a careful study of the metallurgical features of wrought iron, followed by long experimental effort to reproduce the quality characteristics in a controlled and economical manner. The integral steps involved: (1) refining a pig metal charge to a low metalloid content—Bessemer, open hearth or electric steel processes; (2) production of and melting the desired slag, done without difficulty in modified standard furnaces from iron oxide and silica ingredients; (3) disintegration and solidification of the metal and incorporation therein of the desired slag: the crux of the process; (4) compacting the composite mass and squeezing out surplus slag. The result is a product conforming in all respects to characteristics of quality wrought iron. The existing plant began operations in 1930. With the present lack of a blast furnace for supplying direct metal, pig iron of standard Bessemer grade is melted in cupolas. Desulphurization is effectively accomplished with soda ash or caustic soda in the cupola transfer ladle, so that a sulphur content below 0.03, or even lower if desirable, is regularly obtained. This molten pig metal is full blown in 10-ton acid Bessemer vessels to a carbon content of about 0.06 per cent, with silicon and manganese virtually nil.

Shotting.—The required slag conforms to quality wrought iron standards and is melted in a battery of powdered, coal-fired, rotary furnaces. These have replaced the former tilting, open hearth type furnaces. The slag ingredients are roll scale, iron ore, and sand. The molten slag is teemed in the batches required from time to time for the make-up needs of the operation. "Shotting" is the key operation. The blown metal is poured in a steady stream at a rate of one ton per minute into a deep bath of molten slag in large, unlined ladles carried by cars on a circular transfer track. With ample volume of slag at a temperature manitained well below the freezing point of the refined metal, continuous solidification of the metal takes place. Accompanying this is the liberation of all of its dissolved gases with sufficient force to disintegrate the metal and produce a spongy ball of iron, impregnated with the liquid slag. In modern practice the general size of bloom is three to four tons, produced on an approximate 15-minute heat cycle. At appropriate stations the large surplus of slag is decanted into another ladle, and the sponge ball is dumped into a squeezing press. There it is compacted, at welding heat, into a rectangular bloom which, after reheating, is rolled on a standard blooming mill to billets or slabs. The heat exchange in the shotting operation permits immediate re-use of the decanted slag, with melting only for make-up requirements. The output of modern plant is from 800 to 1,000 tons per day. Most of the product, such as skelp, plate, etc., is rolled from solid sections, in marked contrast to the older wrought iron practice of building muck bar piles. Stay bolts, engine bolts, and locomotive forgings of double refined quality are still rolled from heavy slab piles. The process is under complete control in each of the integral steps and in the chemical and metallurgical characteristics of the materials and product. The wrought iron produced meets all specification requirements and finds outlets as welded pipe, sheets, plates, bars, and forging stock.

Wrought iron finds product applications because of inherent properties of ductility, ease of working and welding, and superior resistance to customary services involving corrosion, shock or fatigue conditions. Mechanized production broadens its horizon if quality standards are maintained.

Bibliography.—Turner, T., *Metallurgy of Iron* (London 1908); Aston, J., "The Problem of Wrought Iron Manufacture and a New Process for its Manufacture," *Yearbook,* American Iron and Steel Institute (New York 1925); Dechant, F. H., "The Ely Process of Mechanical Puddling for the Production of Wrought Iron," *Yearbook,* American Iron and Steel Institute (New York 1925); Roe, J. P., "The Roe Puddling Machine," *Yearbook,* American Iron and Steel Institute (New York 1925); Aston, J., "Trend of Development in the Wrought Iron Industry," *Papers, American Institute of Mining and Metallurgical Engineers,* vol. 1 (New York 1926); id., "A New Development in Wrought Iron Manufacture," *Transactions, American Institute of Mining and Metallurgical Engineers,* vol. 84 (New York 1929); Rickard, T. A., *Man and Metals,* 2 vols. (New York 1932); Aston, J., "Wrought Iron in Today's Industrial Picture," *Transactions, American Institute of Mining and Metallurgical Engineers,* vol. 116 (New York 1935); Aston, J., and Story, E. B., *Wrought Iron, Its Manufacture, Characteristics and Applications* (Pittsburgh 1939); Camp, J. M., and Francis, C. B., *Making, Shaping and Treating of Steel* (Pittsburgh 1940).

JAMES ASTON,
Consulting Metallurgist, A. M. Byers Company.

6. MALLEABLE IRON.—Malleable iron (malleable cast iron or American malleable cast iron) is a ductile cast metal produced by the heat treatment of a graphite-free cast iron.

History.—Cast iron is easy to produce in any required form by pouring liquid metal into a suitable mold and letting it freeze, but it is without ductility. Wrought iron and steel possess ductility but originally had to be forged to shape. Malleable iron was invented to combine the two properties at a time when steel castings were unknown.

The absence of ductility in cast iron is due to the presence of a relatively large amount of carbon, from 2 per cent to 4 per cent of the metal. This may be present in either or both of two forms: graphite and cementite. The former is the element carbon and in the gray cast irons is present in flakes, resembling crumpled pieces of paper or tin foil. Once present, nothing short of melting can be done to overcome its embrittling effect on the metal.

Being in flakes, the graphite interrupts the continuity of the metal much more than does an equal amount of graphite in the nodular form found in malleable.

Cementite is an iron carbon compound having three atoms of the former to one of the latter and represented by the symbol of Fe_3C. Its extreme hardness and brittleness account for these properties in white cast iron. This effect can be overcome by heat-treatment.

Two processes have been invented to convert white cast iron, not containing any graphite which would permanently impair ductility, into malleable iron which is reasonably ductile.

The process first discovered in Europe removes the carbon from the metal, reasonably completely. This is accomplished by holding the castings a sufficient time, dependent on their thickness, at temperatures in the neighborhood of 1800° F., while packed in iron ore. The ore furnishes oxygen which combines with the carbon to form carbon monoxide which escapes as a gas. The reaction:

$$\underset{\text{Ore}}{Fe_2O_3} + \underset{\text{Cementite}}{3\,Fe_3C} = \underset{\text{Iron}}{11\,Fe} + \underset{\text{Gas}}{3CO}$$

represents its principle and not its complete sequence of steps. The inventor of the process is no longer known, but it was described by the French physicist René Antoine Ferchault de Réaumur in 1722 without pretense of originality. Such malleable iron is called "white-heart" from the color of its fracture and is still an important article of manufacture in Europe.

On July 4, 1826, Seth Boyden of Newark, N. J. found that he could make a metal which he described in his diary as "dark in color and tougher than any I have yet seen." Since he worked before the days of metallography, he did not know that he was working on a new metallurgical principle, namely, the spontaneous dissociation of iron carbide at temperatures well below the freezing point.

$$\underset{\text{Cementite}}{Fe_3C} = \underset{\text{Iron}}{3\,Fe} + \underset{\text{Graphite}}{C}$$

The flaky graphite of gray iron attains its form while crystallizing at a temperature near the freezing point of the alloy where the soft and plastic metallic matrix exercises little or no restraint on its growth into thin platelike forms. In Boyden's process the temperature is low enough to make the graphite grow in more compact and nearly equiaxed masses called "temper carbon." The product is called "black-heart" malleable and is invariably used in the United States.

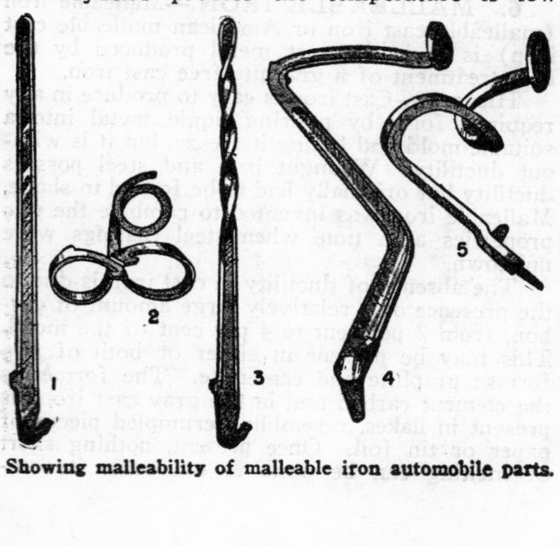

Showing malleability of malleable iron automobile parts.

Some antiquarian evidence has been offered that black-heart malleable was made in Scandinavia in the 14th century, but the proof is not convincing enough to overcome all doubt.

In modern practice the two processes are not completely separable. The decarburization of the white-heart process is usually accompanied by some graphitization, and the graphitizing reaction in the black-heart process involves some incidental decarburization.

Uses.—In the United States malleable castings are used preponderantly in automotive parts because of their great ease of machining along with strength and ductility. For similar reasons, they are also used very extensively as pipe fittings. Other important uses are in agricultural implements, railway track and trolley parts, certain types of chain belts, and a great multitude of minor applications. The maximum production at the peak of each of the two world wars was approximately at the rate of 1,000,000 tons per year, exclusive of pipe fittings.

Methods of Manufacture.—In its early experimental stages the white cast iron for malleablizing was produced by melting in crucibles. Rather soon the reverberatory furnace came into use in America for melting the white cast iron. These furnaces grew in size from capacities of 500 or 1,000 pounds to capacities of about 40 tons. Reverberatory furnaces were originally hand fired with coal, but now the use of either pulverized coal or oil mixed with air in suitable burners is practically universal.

To the makers of white-heart malleable, high carbon and sulphur content is not particularly objectionable since the former is to be burned out anyway and the latter retards graphitization, and they have adopted the cupola as a measure of economy. The cupola has also commended itself to the makers of pipe fittings as an economical way to produce sound and leakproof castings.

For automotive, railway, and other uses, lower carbons are desired than the cupola can produce, because the more temper carbon nodules that exist in an object, the weaker it will be. To combine the economy of cupola melting with the convenience it offers of producing a continuous supply of metal, the practice of feeding a reverberatory furnace not with solid iron but with liquid cupola iron and of taking off a steady stream of liquid metal has been adopted.

An alternative is to reduce the carbon and otherwise to adjust the composition of cupola metal in electric furnaces. To these two "duplexing" processes may be added a technique, now discontinued, of mixing cupola metal and liquid Bessemer steel in an electric furnace in a "triplexing" operation.

The white iron castings are then heat-treated. For the white heart process this is almost invariably done by packing them in a mixture of hematite ore, which has been previously used, and some new ore to make up for the oxygen expended during these previous uses. The containers are white cast iron pots or boxes. These are heated to approximately 1800° F. and maintained at this temperature for the requisite time which, for example, may be from 6 to 10 days.

The time to decarburize a casting completely is approximately proportional to the square of its thickness. This introduces difficulties when castings of various thicknesses are annealed together, for after the carbon is completely gone, oxidation of the iron must be feared. The matter becomes still worse when a single casting varies greatly in cross section. Attempts were made in 1945 to decarburize in a muffle through which a gas of suitable composition is caused to flow. It is possible to select compositions which will oxidize carbon but not iron, and to produce them by the incomplete burning of coal gas.

The black-heart process requires no chemically active packing since the reaction does not involve any outside agency. Graphitization goes on simultaneously at all points in a casting. Its rate is determined primarily by the rate of diffusion of carbon in iron, which varies with the temperature, and by the number of nodules which can be formed, being a function of grain structure. Both may depend on chemical compositions. Heat treatments represent a holding at 1700° to 1800° F., followed by slow cooling to below the critical point (usually about 1300° F.) and sometimes a subsequent holding of that temperature.

According to the composition, the quality requirements, the size of the annealing furnace charge, and the type of furnace, heat treatments vary widely in time. An overall time of about 24 hours is claimed, although it is unusual; 32 to 44 hours may be encountered; 65 hours is quite common, but muffle furnaces of large capacity may require 6 to 8 days. Since to anneal rapidly, small charges and highly mechanized furnaces are required, there is some incompatibility of low cost and fast times.

The simplest furnaces are similar to those used in the white-heart process: the large brick chambers into which stacks of pots containing castings are set, and into which flame passes from pulverized coal, oil or gas burners. For rapid handling, the bottom of the furnace may be a flat-topped car on which the pots stand. Cars can be pulled out and pushed into a cooler furnace without losing much of the heat contained in the furnace structure.

In continuous kilns, cars loaded with pots pass down a long tunnel, fired at intervals, so that as the charge passes through, it remains at each temperature the desired time. Large castings are often not packed in pots but placed in muffles of firebrick or silicon carbide to protect them from the flame. The muffle is then heated from the outside. In view of the long heat treatments, some means of protecting the castings from too oxidizing gases is necessary.

Chemical Composition.—The composition of the hard iron for conversion into black-heart malleable depends upon many factors. Carbon is adjusted from considerations of strength and may be from 2 per cent to 3 per cent. Silicon is desirable as it accelerates graphitization in annealing, but if too high, will cause "primary" or flaky graphite to form during freezing, and thus ruin the product. Small castings may have more silicon than large ones, since primary graphitization is greater with slow freezing. Silicon may be as high as 1.65 per cent under very favorable circumstances, and as low as 0.90 per cent for many large castings. Manganese is usually adjusted to three times the sulphur and the latter accepted as produced according to the melting process.

Phosphorus is found in amounts ranging from 0.08 per cent to 0.20 per cent. It strengthens the metal, but a combination of high phosphorus and silicon predisposes the metal to intergranular brittleness under impact. This can be overcome by quenching from 1250° F., but brittleness at sub-zero temperatures will remain.

High carbon and phosphorus make it easier to cast small sections, but the former reduces strength and elongation. Silicon, up to that amount which causes graphitization during freezing, is advantageous because it makes for faster annealing.

The only alloys useful in improving the properties of malleable iron are copper and molybdenum. Small amounts of copper increase the resistance to acid corrosion. Larger amounts, up to 1.50 per cent, increase the strength, especially of high-carbon iron. Copper slightly accelerates the graphitizing rate and is therefore often used in connection with molybdenum, a slight retarder, since both increase the strength of malleable iron.

In white-heart malleable, carbon and silicon control are not so important, provided only that primary graphitization is avoided. Either manganese is kept much lower or sulphur is kept higher than in black-heart. Manganese usually does not exceed the sulphur. Phosphorus is generally kept lower in white-heart than in black-heart, usually below 0.10 per cent.

Mechanical Properties. — Specifications adopted in 1939 by the American Society for Testing Materials for black-heart cupola malleable iron require a tensile strength of 40,000 pounds per square inch, a yield point of 30,000 pounds per square inch, and an elongation of 5 per cent. The same society's specifications, adopted in 1933, and reaffirmed in 1944, provide for two grades. One has a required tensile strength of 50,000 pounds per square inch, a yield point of 32,500 pounds per square inch, and an elongation of 10 per cent; the other, a tensile strength of 53,000 pounds per square inch, a yield strength of 35,000 pounds per square inch, and an elongation of 18 per cent. These properties are inseparably related to a particular form and size of test specimen prescribed and identical for all three specifications.

The grade of lower strength and elongation is the more machinable, and the impact resistance of the two last-named grades is about equal. Malleable iron has very high magnetic permeability and is well suited to magnetic circuits using direct current. Like all unlaminated cores, its eddy current loss is relatively high. Alone among the commercial forms of iron, black-heart malleable's elongation changes directly and not inversely with tensile strength. Its machinability is better than that of any ferrous material of similar ductility.

The mechanical properties of white-heart malleable are described by British specifications adopted in 1927. Round specimens 0.564 inch in diameter are required to have a tensile strength 44,800 pounds per square inch and an elongation of 5 per cent in 2 inches. A bar 1 inch by ⅜ inch in cross section is required to bend 45° around a mandrel of 1-inch radius.

Pearlitic Malleable.—This is a term chosen with insufficient respect for the exact meaning of terms. It is used to designate malleable iron purposely containing combined carbon, whether this is present as pearlite or in some other metallographic form. These materials are produced by one of three types of processes. Starting with white cast iron identical with that used for black-heart malleable, the annealing cycle may be shortened, particularly near the critical points, in order to leave the desired amount and form of combined carbon. Alternatively, chemical elements retarding the graphitizing process, such as manganese, molybdenum or chromium, may be added to the white molten cast iron as required, in order to produce the desired result, after a normal annealing cycle or a modified one. Lastly, malleable iron may be heated above the critical point, to 1480° F., for example, where graphite will redissolve very quickly in an amount determined by the temperature. The material is then cooled in such a manner as to produce the desired structure.

Since innumerable combinations of techniques are available, it is not unnatural that the properties of these so-called pearlitic malleables will vary widely. All are stronger, less ductile, less machinable, and harder than malleable. All of them are also of higher electrical resistivity and lower magnetic permeability. The ductility which can be had for a given strength depends very largely on the properties of the original, completely annealed malleable in those pearlitic malleables which are produced by reheat-treating that product.

Three quite important types of microstructure are found in the matrix of pearlitic malleable. This matrix, in which the temper carbon is imbedded, consists of two metallic constituents: carbon-free iron or ferrite, and iron carbide or cementite. The form of the latter is greatly variable. In some pearlitic malleable the carbide is somewhat uniformly dispersed through the ferrite. In another type the graphite nodules are surrounded by "bull's eyes" of carbide-free ferrite, the remainder of the structure consisting of a somewhat uniform dispersion of carbide in ferrite. In the third type, the matrix consists of ferrite grains, separated by a network of carbide dispersed in ferrite.

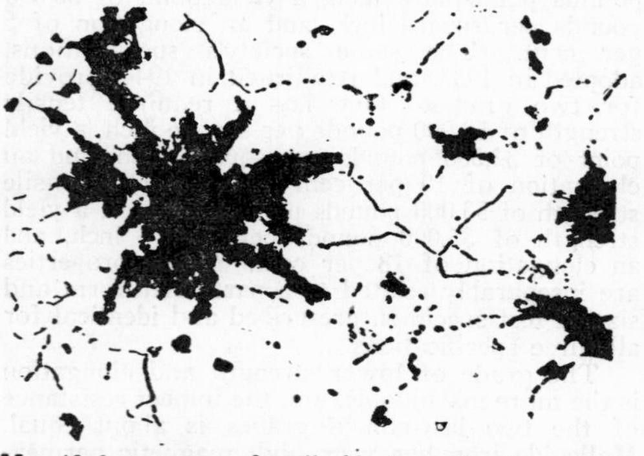

Magnified structure of malleable iron, showing nodular carbon.

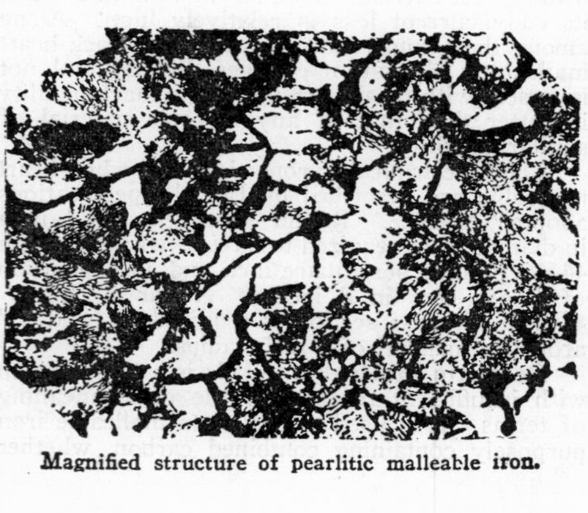

Magnified structure of pearlitic malleable iron.

As these patterns change, the resulting properties also change greatly. Pearlitic malleables may have ultimate strengths of over 100,000 pounds per square inch with very low elongation, 1 per cent or 2 per cent, for instance. At the other extreme is the correlation of strength and elongation found in ordinary black-heart malleable.

There are no analogues to these pearlitic malleables among the white-heart malleables. If decarburization is there incomplete, the centers of heavy sections are pearlite, in extreme cases interspersed with massive carbides. This condition, however, is not desired and is not tolerated in sections which are to be subject to severe usage.

Welding Malleable.—Since black-heart malleable reverts to pearlitic malleable on heating above the critical point, welding processes are limited to procedures involving either the use of very low melting electrodes, which frequently lack strength, or to the use of subsequent, accurately controlled, heat-treatments to undo the effects of reheating in welding. Completely decarbonized, white-heart malleable can be welded in the forge fire or by any of the methods applicable to low-carbon steels.

Graphitizable Steel.—Since about 1937, alloys which are sufficiently low in carbon as to be properly classified as steel and high enough in silicon to graphitize readily have come into use. Their composition may be about 1 per cent carbon and 1.25 per cent silicon. They are most frequently used in modifications analogous to the pearlitic malleables and find their principal application in automotive construction.

Bibliography.—Schwartz, H. A., *American Malleable Cast Iron* (Cleveland 1922); Schüz, Emil, and Stotz, R., *Der Temperguss* (Berlin 1930); "Symposium on Malleable Casting," *Transactions of the American Foundrymen's Association,* vol. 39 (Chicago 1932); Leroyer, M., *La Malléable* (Paris 1936); "Symposium on Pearlitic Malleable," *Book of American Society for Testing Materials Standards, 1936* (Philadelphia 1936); "Symposium on Graphitization of White Cast Iron," *Transactions of the American Foundrymen's Association, 1942,* vol. 50 (Chicago 1943); "Symposium on Malleable Iron Melting," *Transactions of the American Foundrymen's Association, Sept. 1943—June 1944,* vol. 51 (Chicago 1944); Malleable Founders' Society, *American Malleable Iron, a Handbook* (Cleveland 1944).

H. A. Schwartz,
Manager of Research, National Malleable and Steel Castings Company.

7. ORIGIN OF IRON ORES.—Iron ores are defined as those parts of the earth's crust from which iron can be extracted at a profit. Most of the common red and brown colors in rocks and soils are caused by the presence of iron oxides, but in only a few places can the materials be profitably mined. Many factors tend to determine whether or not an iron-bearing rock is ore. Chief among these factors are the size of the deposits, the composition, texture, and structure of the ores, the proximity to transportation, and a situation where mining costs can be kept low. Large amounts of coking coal are required in iron smelting, and iron ore can be transported to coal-mining centers cheaper than coal can be carried to the iron ore mines. For this reason the largest iron and steel centers are in coal-producing areas such as western Pennsylvania and the valley of the Ruhr River, while Brazil and like countries, although they possess tremendous reserves of high-grade hematite and magnetite, have very little coking coal and produce iron ore chiefly for export. High-grade ores near the fuel supplies are sought first, and as they become depleted, imported ores compete with lower-grade and poorer-quality ores near the furnaces.

Iron Formation.—The largest quantity of high-grade iron ores in the United States is found in the Lake Superior region in Minnesota, Michigan, and Wisconsin. Rocks similar to those from which the ores were derived are found around the ore bodies. These rocks were probably laid down on the floor of the ocean, and consist chiefly of alternating layers one-quarter inch to two inches thick of iron carbonate and silica, with subordinate amounts of iron silicates. The best ores are soft, nearly pure red and brown iron oxides from which the silica has been leached and the carbon dioxide removed from the iron carbonate. Some geologists think that as the region was elevated above the sea, the "iron formation," as the iron carbonate and silica are known, was exposed to weathering for long periods of time. The silica was removed, the iron carbonate was decomposed, and the residual material is the iron ore as we know it today. Other geologists do not agree with the hypothesis of weathering. They point out that the Lake Superior region is traversed by many dikes of a dark green, igneous rock. The intrusions of such rocks are supposed to be accompanied by very large quantities of warm waters. These waters would decompose the iron formation and leach the silica more readily than cold atmospheric waters. The ore bodies would then be the residual material after such leaching had taken place. Iron formation, consisting of layers of quartz and an iron mineral such as iron carbonate, hematite, or magnetite is widely distributed; the Lake Superior region, Labrador, Brazil, Venezuela, Scandinavia, Africa, India, and Western Australia all possess tremendous tonnages, running into the billions. From their layered character and distribution, iron formations are thought to have been deposited in the ocean, although similar rocks are nowhere known to be forming now. The ultimate source of such tremendous amounts of iron in the ocean is difficult to account for, but it may have been added from the interior of the earth at times of volcanic activity, or the iron formations may be chemical precipitates which received their iron from deeply weathered land masses.

Clinton Ores.—Other types of iron ores are also formed beneath the sea. The Clinton iron ores are found in scattered areas from New York to the Birmingham district in Alabama where they reach their maximum development. There are four common types of Clinton ores, all of which are generally bright red in color and contain considerable calcium carbonate. The first type is "flaxseed" ore, which contains small, flat hematite grains, with numerous fragments of fossils changed to hematite. The second type is called oolitic ore. This consists of small ellipsoids of hematite, one or two millimeters in diameter, in a calcium carbonate matrix. The individual ellipsoids are made up of hematite that has grown around small cores of sand. The third type of ore is "fossil ore" and contains many fragments of fossils coated with or altered to hematite. The fourth type is sandstone ore, in which each grain of sand is coated with hematite and the whole cemented into a solid mass by hematite and calcium carbonate. The view is generally held that the Clinton ores were formed by direct sedimentation; the iron was contributed slowly into shallow marine basins and gradually was deposited around and altered to a limited extent the limy materials on the bottom of the sea. Along the outcrops of the Clinton ore beds the calcium carbonate is leached, and the ores are soft and rich (40-50 per cent iron). In depth, below the zone in which weathering is active, the ores are hard and contain less iron (35-40 per cent iron) and more calcium carbonate than near the surface. Most ores of this type contain phosphorus in appreciable amounts Oolitic ores are known in many other areas: the so-called minettes of Luxembourg and Lorraine the Wabana ores of Newfoundland, and the ores in the Yorkshire district of the British Isles being outstanding examples. These ores are not always red, but may as commonly be gray, brown, greenish, or yellow. They are believed to be of shallow marine origin and vary widely in composition.

Salzgitter Ores.—The well-known Salzgitter ores of central Germany are also thought to be of marine origin. The beds, up to 100 feet thick or exceptionally thicker, contain smooth, brown, limonitic nodules, generally half an inch or less in longest dimension, which are scattered through a claylike matrix. Siderite (iron carbonate) or black band ores were formerly of considerable importance, both in Europe and the United States, but they have been largely superseded by other types of ores. These ores in places are associated with coal beds and are thought to have been deposited in shallow bogs or marshes along the coasts.

Magmatic Segregation Deposits.—Many iron ores are associated with rocks that at one time have been molten (igneous rocks). As these molten rocks cool, the minerals in them crystallize, some more rapidly than others. The minerals, which include magnetite and titaniferous magnetite, settle to the bottom of the molten mass and locally they form layers which are now rich enough to mine. Some of the deposits in the Adirondacks and in the Ural Mountains are thought to have been formed in this manner. They are called magmatic segregation deposits. The well-known deposits of Kiruna and Gellivare in Sweden are considered to be magnetite which settled out of a molten rock and was then injected into its present position.

Contact or Igneous Metamorphic Deposits.—Molten igneous rocks are at times accompanied by large quantities of fluids which contain, among other constituents, appreciable amounts of iron. As the molten materials cooled, the fluids released from them tended to work into and through the enclosing solid rocks.

Where the iron-bearing fluids encountered favorable chemical and physical conditions, iron, principally as magnetite, hematite, and in sulphides, was deposited along with other minerals, such as garnet. Deposits formed in this way are generally found near the contacts between igneous rocks and the rocks which have been intruded, thus being called contact or igneous metamorphic deposits. Deposits of this type are widely distributed and have yielded much good ore. Characteristic examples are the Iron Springs deposits in Utah and the Cornwall deposit in Pennsylvania. Where the fluids associated with molten rocks traverse iron formation such as that in the Lake Superior region, the iron may be dissolved, transported, and reprecipitated in amounts that can profitably be mined. This ore is known simply as replacement ore, meaning that it has taken the place of former rocks which have been dissolved and removed. The deposits at Steep Rock Lake in southwestern Ontario are generally considered to be of this type.

Laterites.—In Cuba and in many other places in the tropics, residual mantles of iron-rich soil called laterites are found, and locally they have been mined. Laterites ordinarily consist of iron oxide pellets one-half inch or less in diameter, scattered through dark red to yellow, iron-rich soil. They are thought to be the residual materials left after long continued weathering, in warm climates, of limestone and the dark green iron-rich igneous rocks such as serpentine and peridotite. Laterites are porous, bulky ores that contain much water and generally have about 40 per cent iron, though exceptional ores contain about 45 per cent iron. Because of their low grade, laterites are not highly desirable for the export trade, but with the depletion of high-grade ores in the Lake Superior region it is possible that the laterites may become an important source of ore to the United States. Laterites are favorably situated for cheap mining and contain many millions of tons in reserve.

Limonite.—Limonite is one of the most widely distributed and best known of the iron minerals. It ranges considerably in color from the common reddish brown of rust through the yellows and browns of the ochers, siennas and umbers used in pigments. Limonite is deposited by many springs where they emerged from their orifices, and it accumulates as "bog ore" in many swampy and marshy places. Limonite is carried in solution with carbon dioxide, with humic acids, and with sulphuric acid formed by the oxidation of pyrite. It is readily precipitated by the loss of CO_2 or by the neutralization of the acid; it forms thin iridescent films on quiet water, and many times these films have been mistaken for oil. The bog ores are seldom high-grade, as they are everywhere mixed with sand and clay and are generally high in phosphorus.

Brown Ore.—The brown iron ores of the eastern United States, such as the Scotia deposit in Pennnsylvania, have many points of resemblance to bog ores and may have been formed originally in shallow water. As known today, the ores consist of irregular lumps of hard sandy limonite in a yellow or brownish soil, from which they must be washed. The washed ores are low-grade. Other brown iron ores, such as those of Cartersville, Georgia, are fine grained mixtures of limonite and clay, left in pockets on the rough surfaces of the rock at the base of the zone of weathering.

Black Sand.—Another well-known type of iron-bearing deposit that has been of little economic value is the black sands of river bars and beaches. The most abundant mineral in these sands is probably magnetite, although hematite and ilmenite are common. The black sands are heavier than most other sands and tend to be concentrated in shallow pockets and near the bottoms of beaches and bars.

Pyrite.—Residues left after the removal of sulphur from pyrite are readily sold as iron ore. Material of this type is imported along the eastern seabord of the United States and is sold by many sulphuric acid plants.

Low-grade Ores.—As high-grade ores near the smelting centers are gradually depleted, lower-grade ores and ores with small amounts of objectionable but removable impurities are sought. These ores can generally be charged directly into furnaces, but this is a bad practice, as it results in a lower yield per furnace and much larger quantities of slag. As a result, beneficiation and concentration methods are used to improve the character and grade of the ores. Open pit ores are preferred to underground ores as they are cheaper to mine and require a smaller original capital investment. In the Lake Superior region, particularly in the western Mesabi range, soft decomposed ores, from which insufficient silica has been leached to permit them to be shipped directly to the smelters, are mined as wash ores. These wash ores, where cheaply available, are mined and flushed through a screen, where the coarse silica and the unwanted fine materials are removed. In the United States large tonnages of iron-bearing material that can be cheaply mined and concentrated by jigging, magnetic separation, and high density methods, are being developed in several places. These ores must generally be crushed, concentrated, and then sintered before use. Dust and fine grained particles must be kept at a minimum since in a furnace they blow out through the stack, tend to clog the flues quickly, and to clinker and cake in the charge. Sintered ores are much desired, as from any one deposit the sintered product is generally uniform in character and permits smelting with a minimum of changes in the furnace charge. Sintered ores are also of hard, porous character and are generally of good grade, containing a minimum of volatiles and sulphur.

Taconite.—On the eastern Mesabi range in Minnesota the iron formation is cut off on the east by a basic igneous rock called the Duluth gabbro. Near this igneous mass, and east of the main producing deposits, the iron formation is greatly indurated. It is extremely resistant to weathering and forms bold hills that stand well above the surrounding terrain. The average grade of the east Mesabi iron formation (called taconite) is about 30-35 per cent iron in the form of hematite and magnetite, and the reserves are measured in billions of tons. Much money has been spent and is still being spent in an attempt to devise a process whereby this marginal material could be utilized. The hardness has so far proved to be the main difficulty; the rock is expensive in the amounts of both drill steel and dynamite required to break it, and the crushing charges before concentration are prohibitive. This hematite-magnetite-quartz rock would be of tremendous commercial value if the cost of mining and concentration could be lowered, or if the price of iron should be increased. Elsewhere in the Lake Superior region considerable experimental work is being done on those parts of the iron formation that contain iron carbonate. The iron carbonate is soft and is easily weathered; it does not stand out like the east Mesabi taconites, and hence its quantity and distribution are but poorly known. Other countries, less fortunately situated than the United States in reserves of iron ore, have used materials that in the United States would not even be considered marginal ore. For example, during World War II Germany depended to a great extent on Salzgitter ores, which average less than 30 per cent iron.

Difficulties from Impurities.—Impurities in iron ores that cause the most difficulties under American practices are sulphur, phosphorus, and titanium, though many other metallic and nonmetallic constituents are objectionable. Sulphur is commonly in the form of pyrite or marcasite (FeS_2), although other sulphide minerals are at times encountered, and in some mines gypsum ($CaSO_4$) causes difficulties. The sulphur can be largely removed by sintering or roasting, adding to the cost of smelting. Phosphorus is difficult to remove, and most of it goes into the iron, making it brittle. Basic Bessemer converters (Thomas process) are used in most European iron mills, and pig iron high in phosphorus is required in this process. The best of the high-phosphorus ores come from Sweden. The phosphorus is concentrated by the converter process, in a high-lime slag, which is then crushed and sold as fertilizer. Titanium makes a sticky slag and adds to the cost of smelting, although experiments suggest that ores containing several per cent of titanium may be used in the future, if necessary. This should result in a great enlargement of the iron ore reserves in the United States, as many known deposits of titaniferous magnetites have not been used. It is possible that part of the smelting costs will be borne by the titanium, which may be recovered from the ores or slags by a chemical process and used in making titanium paint.

Benefits from Impurities.—On the other hand, certain impurities in ores are of aid in smelting or are recovered as byproducts. Certain self-fluxing ores contain iron, lime, and silica in nearly the correct proportion needed for smelting, and alumina and silica are required in certain special purpose ores. Many efforts have been made to form alloys by direct smelting of ores that contain minor amounts of the alloying material, such as nickel. These efforts are ordinarily unsuccessful because of the great difficulty in obtaining the exact amounts of the alloying material needed and the exclusion of unwanted substances. Metallurgists much prefer to add nickel, for example, to iron rather than to smelt directly an iron-nickel ore. Much of the laterite in eastern Cuba contains small amounts of nickel and chromium, and efforts have been made to smelt the material directly. At Nicaro, in eastern Cuba, nickel is being recovered from the laterites, but the iron and chromium are being discarded. Manganese is used in iron ore smelting to remove undesired substances from the melt and is called a scavenger. Certain iron ores such as those of the Cuyuna range in Minnesota and the Siegerland deposits of Germany contain a few per cent of manganese. These ores are much desired and command premium prices. Minor amounts of copper are found in many magnetites of contact or igneous metamorphic types and in magmatic segregation deposits. This copper is seldom recovered and generally goes into the iron. At the Cornwall district in Pennsylvania the magnetite ores contain recoverable amounts of iron pyrite, chalcopyrite (copper iron sulphide), and cobalt. These byproducts add appreciably to the value of the ore, and the cobalt particularly is a resource of one of the scarce mineral commodities in the United States. Minor amounts of vanadium are found in many iron ore deposits, although vanadium is rare or absent in the Lake Superior deposits. Vanadium appears to be most commonly associated with, though not confined to, the titaniferous magnetites. Vanadium was not recovered from iron ores in the United States prior to 1941, but during World War II, Germany depended entirely on vanadium recovered from Swedish and low-grade German ores that contained from 0.03-0.20 per cent vanadium. Minor amounts and traces of little-known and little-used elements, such as indium and thallium, are found in deposits of iron ores, and it is possible that they may be recovered in the future.

CHARLES F. PARK, JR.
Department of Geology, Stanford University.

8. IRON ORE DISTRICTS OF THE UNITED STATES.—During the early days of the United States, the iron ore industry was centered along the eastern seaboard, and such iron ores as were needed were mined in the Eastern states. In 1854, the first shipments of iron ore were made from the Lake Superior region, and almost since its discovery this region has dominated the iron ore production of the country. Lower-grade and higher-cost deposits were forced to close, and many of the districts that were profitably operated during the early days of the United States were abandoned. A few deposits, situated close to supplies of coking coals, or because of special properties of their ores, remained in operation. During World War II, the abnormally large demands for iron ores and the impending exhaustion of some of the high-grade deposits of the Lake Superior region caused an unprecedented search for deposits of possible ores. Many old districts were explored, a few were revived, and a few previously unworked properties were developed.

The total crude iron ore mined in the United States, according to statistics published by the United States Bureau of Mines, was 111,020,145 long tons in 1944; 119,674,980 long tons in 1943; and 126,527,150 long tons in 1942. About one third of the mined ore was shipped to beneficiation plants, and two thirds were sent directly to iron and steel furnaces. During 1943 the Lake Superior region yielded 85 per cent of the total United States production, and in 1944, 84 per cent of the production.

Lake Superior Region.—The districts in the Lake Superior region are known as ranges, because the hard iron formation generally stands up as low hills and ridges above the surrounding country. There are six principal ranges: the Mesabi, Cuyuna, and Vermilion ranges in Minnesota; the Penokee-Gogebic range in Wisconsin and Michigan; and the Marquette and Menominee ranges in Michigan. Several other ranges such as the Baraboo and Gunflint, and minor districts such as Republic and Amasa, contain iron formation and have contributed small amounts of ore.

LAKE AND RAIL SHIPMENTS OF LAKE SUPERIOR IRON ORE IN LONG TONS, BY RANGES

Range	1944	1943	1942	1941	1940
Mesabi	62,509,212	64,906,280	70,280,087	59,772,543	45,667,677
Vermilion	1,538,560	1,779,014	1,924,877	1,847,094	1,547,469
Cuyuna	2,586,264	3,065,555	3,035,532	2,441,042	1,734,176
Total Minnesota	66,586,264	69,971,276	75,299,667	64,060,726	48,949,322
Gogebic	5,604,354	5,486,918	6,237,894	6,301,379	5,975,727
Marquette	4,790,177	5,601,418	6,540,731	6,254,391	5,920,463
Menominee	4,876,210	4,902,556	4,930,434	4,131,363	3,103,334
Total Michigan-Wisconsin	15,270,741	15,990,892	17,709,059	16,687,133	14,999,524
Total U. S. ranges	81,857,005	85,962,168	93,008,726	80,747,859	63,948,846
Total Canadian ranges	498,635	450,973	486,666	462,747	361,394

LONG TONS OF VARIOUS ORES SHIPPED BY LAKE

Grade	1944	1943	1942	1941	1940
Bessemer	16,864,758	18,563,195	19,231,564	17,253,399	12,885,181
Non-Bessemer	60,111,928	61,188,377	68,169,690	58,487,895	47,428,154
Manganiferous	2,318,820	2,713,147	2,509,870	2,195,379	1,797,342
Siliceous	540,740	656,440	776,762	921,884	608,632
Aluminiferous	31,991	—	—	—	
Total United States ranges	79,868,237	83,121,159	90,687,886	78,858,557	62,719,309

AVERAGE ANALYSES OF ORES SHIPPED FROM UNITED STATES RANGES DURING 1944

Grade	Percentage of Iron	Percentage of Phosphorus	Percentage of Silica	Percentage of Manganese	Percentage of Moisture
Bessemer	54.18	.038	8.63	.35	9.43
Low-phosphorus non-Bessemer	51.56	.071	8.04	.66	11.03
High-phosphorus non-Bessemer	51.37	.429	7.25	.30	9.48
Manganiferous	43.21	.208	9.93	5.70	11.67
Siliceous	37.10	.041	42.72	.09	2.85
Aluminiferous	48.43	.062	7.86	.34	15.78
Combined grades	51.72	.088	8.42	.74	11.02

Two other well-known productive deposits of the Lake Superior region, the Michipicoten range and the Steep Rock district, are in Canada. The production statistics in the above tables were taken from data published by the Lake Superior Iron Ore Association.

By far the most productive iron ore mine in the United States, if not in the world, is the Hull-Rust-Burt-Sellers on the Mesabi range. This open pit yielded 18,593,172 long tons of usable ore in 1944, and 19,421,349 long tons in 1943. In 1942, the year of maximum production, this open pit yielded about 21,535,000 long tons of ore. The second most productive mine in the Lake Superior region in 1944 was the Rouchleau Moose, also on the Mesabi range, which yielded 4,391,157 long tons of ore. During 1944 there were 19 mines in the Lake Superior region, each of which produced over 1,000,000 long tons. The following table shows the production of the Lake Superior region at 10-year intervals, beginning in 1890:

Year	Long tons
1890	9,011,000
1900	19,102,000
1910	43,440,000
1916 (maximum production during World War I)	66,672,000
1920	50,417,000
1930	47,185,000
1932 (depression year)	3,589,000
1940	63,948,000
1942 (maximum production during World War II)	93,008,726
1945	75,714,750

Clinton Ores.—The Clinton iron ores have been prospected and locally mined from New York to Alabama, but in general the ore beds are too narrow and too low in grade to be of commercial interest. The deposits reach their maximum development at Birmingham, Alabama, which is the second largest iron-ore producing district in the United States. The ores at Birmingham are in part self-fluxing, as they contain from about 5 per cent to 20 per cent CaO. They are conveniently situated near large supplies of coking coals. In 1944 the Birmingham area produced 6,432,122 long tons of ore, and in 1943 yielded 7,469,440 long tons. Most of the ore is bright red hematite, though about 243,336 long tons of brown ore were produced near Birmingham in 1944. Clinton iron ores are also mined in eastern Tennessee, although the deposits generally are narrow and are of little economic value.

Eastern Brown Ores.—The brown iron ores of the Eastern states have been mined extensively in the past from Vermont southward through Massachusetts, Connecticut, southeastern New York, New Jersey, Pennsylvania, Maryland, Virginia, West Virginia, North Carolina, Tennessee, and Georgia into Alabama. During World War II many of these deposits were examined and sampled. A few are still operated, though the total output is small, and much of it is used in the manufacture of paints. Similar brown iron ores are known in southwestern Kentucky.

Magnetite Deposits.—The magnetite deposits of the Eastern states form a resource of increasing value. From 1938 through World War II, several deposits in the Adirondack Mountains of New York were opened. Some of these deposits, like the Clifton, mine direct shipping ores; others such as the deposits in the Mineville district, the Benson mine and the Chateaugay mine, require concentration of the ores. The titaniferous magnetite at Tahawus, New York is being mined for its titanium content, and the magnetite is stored, as the titanium is higher than furnace practice will permit. Other magnetite deposits in northeastern and southeastern New York are operated, and the Scrub Oaks mine in northern New Jersey was a steady producer during World War II. During 1944, New Jersey produced 1,087,948 tons of magnetite, of which about 384,000 tons were direct-shipping lump ore. The Cornwall mine in eastern Pennsylvania is one of the best-known iron mines in the East and has been a steady producer for many years. Scattered magnetite deposits are known in Virginia, North Carolina, and South Carolina; these deposits so far have proved to be small and of little economic value. Extensive reserves of eastern magnetites are known, and it is expected that they will assume a position of increasing importance as the higher-grade Lake Superior ores are exhausted.

Black Band Ores.—During the early days of the United States, considerable attention was paid to the so-called black band or iron carbonate ores of Kentucky, Ohio, Pennsylvania, and West Virginia. These districts have been idle for many years and, barring unforeseen developments, will probably remain idle.

Missouri and Arkansas.—Two types of deposits have been productive in Missouri and Arkansas—first, the filled-sink deposits of west-central Missouri, southeastern Missouri and northeastern Arkansas; and second, the hematite-magnetite ores of Iron Mountain, Missouri. The filled-sink deposits are brown residual ores of good grade. They are much sought but have been largely depleted. During 1944 and 1945 the Iron Mountain deposit, which had been idle for many years and was considered to be exhausted, was opened by underground developments, and a concentration plant was erected.

Wisconsin and Iowa.—Brown ores have been explored at Waukon in northeastern Iowa and at Spring Valley in west-central Wisconsin. Red oolitic hematites similar to those of the Clinton ores are found in the Iron Ridge district of southeastern Wisconsin.

Texas.—Large high-grade deposits of brown iron ores are known in eastern Texas. These deposits were developed considerably during World War II and in 1944 yielded about 275,000 long tons of ore. The Llano district of central Texas contains deposits of magnetite which have been mined.

Western Deposits.—The iron ore deposits of the Rocky Mountain and Pacific Coast states have been developed in areas tributary to the western coking-coal producing centers, particularly, Pueblo, Colorado, and Provo, Utah. The principal ore supply for the Pueblo furnaces has come from the Hartville district in Wyoming, where specular hematite is mined. Other deposits in Wyoming include the hematites of the Seminole and Rawlins districts, and the large tonnages of noncommercial, titaniferous magnetites at Iron Mountain. Small deposits of brown ores are known in the southeastern part of the state.

Colorado.—Numerous deposits of magnetite, hematite, and brown iron ores are known in Colorado but they are, without exception, of small commercial value. Several, such as the Caribou and Grape Creek deposits, contain titaniferous magnetites; others contain sulphur and phosphorus in prohibitive amounts. In New Mexico the magnetite deposits at Fierro have been productive, and considerable effort has been made to develop other deposits such as those on Chupadera Mesa in the central part of the state.

Arizona and Nevada.—Numerous deposits of hematite and magnetite, and a few of brown ores, have been prospected in Arizona and Nevada, but none of them has been developed extensively. Many of the deposits have been inadequately explored, and it is possible that large ore bodies may be developed.

Iron Springs District.—The Iron Springs district in southwestern Utah has been mined at sporadic intervals since 1874. The high-grade magnetite ores have been shipped for the most part to the iron furnaces at Provo, Utah, although during World War II a considerable proportion of the ore went to Pueblo, Colorado, and some went to the blast furnaces at Fontana, California. This district contains large reserves of good ore and is conveniently situated near the Utah coal fields. During 1943, Utah produced 922,959 long tons of magnetite and in 1944 produced 1,542,281 long tons. It is expected that the Iron Springs district will continue to furnish a major part of the ores used in western smelters. Other deposits of magnetite, hematite, and brown ores are known in Utah, but they appear to be small and inconsequential.

California.—California contains about 50 well-known deposits of iron ores scattered throughout the state. Magnetite deposits predominate, but hematite and brown ore bodies are known. Very few of the deposits have been developed commercially; many of them have been prospected, however, and some, such as the Eagle Mountains district, contain reserves of millions of tons of high-grade ore. Some deposits contain prohibitive amounts of deleterious material such as sulphur or phosphorus; others such as Iron Mountain and Kingston Mountains are said to be superficial in extent and to contain tonnages too small to permit profitable mining. During World War II, the Vulcan district in San Bernardino County was developed, and considerable tonnages of ore were sent to the furnaces at Fontana. In 1944, California produced 809,196 long tons of iron ore and in 1943 produced 783,826 long tons. During 1944, 95,929 tons of ore were mined near Redding and were used as ballast in ships.

Northwestern States.—The iron ore districts of the Northwestern states have yielded a very small part of the nation's production. The deposits for the most part are small, low-grade, or inaccessible. In Oregon, efforts have been made to develop the brown iron ores at Scappoose, near Portland. In Washington, some magnetite has been mined for ballast at Buckhorn Mountain in the northeastern part of the state, and in other districts of northeastern Washington small amounts of iron ore have been mined and used locally in the cement industry. The Iron Mountain deposit in Idaho has been partly explored, and several other deposits of hematite and magnetite are known in the state, although undeveloped. In central Montana, the Sheep Creek brown ores and the magnetite-hematite deposits in the vicinity of Wolf Creek have been explored. In the Black Hills of South Dakota, small quantites of soft iron ores were mined for use in the paint industry.

CHARLES F. PARK, JR.,
Department of Geology, Stanford University.

9. IRON ORE SUPPLIES.—Deposits of iron ores are widely distributed throughout the world and have been known since the early days of man. Many of the largest deposits are still poorly explored, principally because of their remoteness from transportation and the lack of nearby supplies of coking coals. A list of the countries that contain deposits of iron ores or potential ores would include the names of most of the larger countries of the world and many of the smaller ones. The number of countries in which deposits have been exploited on a large scale is much shorter. During the stimulus of World War II, some favorably situated iron ore deposits were worked at capacity; others, such as those of Cuba and South America, which are dependent on foreign countries for their market, were practically idle because of lack of shipping facilities.

North and Central America.—The United States produces more iron ore than any other country in the world, although its potential high-grade ore reserves are far less than those of several other countries. In North America, outside of the United States, large amounts of ore have been produced from the high phosphorus oolitic hematite at the Wabana mine, in Newfoundland. This ore, because of its high phosphorus content, is shipped largely to Europe. The Michipicoten range in the Lake Superior region of Canada has operated steadily for years, and in 1944–1945 the Steep Rock deposits in the Atikokan range were developed. Several deposits of hematite and magnetite are known in British Columbia but have been of small economic value. Large quantities of potential high-grade iron ores are known in central Labrador, but production has been retarded because of the inaccessibility of the country. Several magnetite-hematite deposits are known in Mexico, but they are small and remote. Probably the best-known deposits are at Cerro de Mercado, north of Durango, which yield an average of about 140,000 tons a year. Other magnetite and hematite deposits, such as are at Las Truchas, Michoacan, Mexico, are known in western Mexico and in Central America, particularly in Nicaragua and Honduras. The hematite ore bodies at Daiquiri, near the southern coast of eastern Cuba, continue to produce a few thousand tons of ore yearly, although the deposits are considered to be largely exhausted. The laterite deposits of Cuba, and to a lesser extent of Puerto Rico and Haiti, constitute a tremendous reserve of potential low-grade ore. Efforts have been made to mine the laterites at Mayari, in northeastern Cuba, but they have been of questionable success.

South America.—Probably the largest and richest iron ore deposits in the world are in the State of Minas Gerais, Brazil about 325 miles inland from the ports of Victoria and Santa Cruz, north of Rio de Janeiro. The well-known deposit at Itabira is the most accessible to the coast, but efforts have been made to develop several of the other ore bodies. The ores carry 55-69 per cent iron and are very low in phosphorus and sulphur. Brazil contains no adequate deposits of coking coal, so that most of the iron ore produced is for the export trade. In 1944, Brazil exported about 206,000 metric tons, and in 1943, about 323,000 metric tons. Other very large deposits of potential iron ore in Brazil are in the State of Mato Grosso, near Corumbá on the Rio Paraná. These deposits are extremely remote from any large iron-smelting centers and are undeveloped. High-grade hematite-magnetite ores (60-68 per cent iron) are found in the Sierra de Imataca, along the lower stretches of the Orinoco River in Venezuela. Small amounts of these ores have been shipped to the United States, but the river is navigated with difficulty, and enough efficient work has not been done on the deposits to evaluate them properly. Iron ores are known at many places along the western slope of the Andes range. Efforts were made in Peru during 1944–1945 to develop the Marcona deposit. In Chile the Tofo deposit has been a steady producer for many years. The ore at El Tofo is high-grade hematite with martite that contains about 58 per cent iron, and, because of the convenient location of the deposit on tidewater, the ore can be profitably shipped to the eastern United States. In addition to the high-grade deposits of South America, large tonnages of laterites are reported to exist in Dutch and British Guiana, in Peru, and in Uruguay.

Europe.—Large reserves of iron ores are known in Europe, but in general the ores are lower in grade than ores elsewhere in the world. In the British Isles the oolitic Jurassic ores of Northamptonshire, Cleveland, Lincolnshire, Leicestershire, Oxfordshire, and Kent-Dover and the carbonate black band and clay band ores of South Wales average less than 30 per cent iron. These constitute the principal sources of ores in the British Isles, although the higher-grade hematites of Cumberland and Lancashire are also mined. The minette ores of Luxembourg and Lorraine have been among the most productive deposits in Europe. These ores are oolitic, grayish or yellowish in color, high in phosphorus, and contain an average of about 35 per cent iron. During 1944, France produced 9,265,290 metric tons of ore, and in 1943 produced 16,879,160 metric tons of ore. This ore was mostly from minettes, but magnetite and hematite were produced in Normandy and Brittany. The principal Spanish ores are mined near Bilbao in northern Spain and are exported in normal times to England and Germany. Small amounts of ore are also produced in the Sierra Menera, Sierra Morena, and in other districts along the south coast. The average Spanish ores contain from 45-58 per cent iron. Germany has no large supplies of iron ore within its own boundaries, and depends largely upon imports for its supplies. In the late 1930's, the low-grade Salzgitter and Peine ores were developed, and Germany depended upon these deposits for a large part of its iron ore supply during World War II. These ores average less than 30 per cent iron and contain appreciable phosphorus and about 0.08 per cent vanadium, which may be recovered from the slag. The Siegerland carbonate ores of the east Rhine are much sought as they contain several per cent of manganese.

Other commercial deposits are in the Lahn-

Dill, Thuringia, and Weser districts, and in Württemberg and Bavaria. Small deposits of iron ores are known in Czechoslovakia, and it is estimated that the State of Slovakia produced about a million tons in 1942. Italy produces very little iron ore, but has founded an iron industry on limited supplies of ore, supplemented by the use of pyritic residues. Some ore is obtained from the island of Elba. At Eisenerz in Styria, Austria, a famous deposit of siderite has been mined for many years. Deposits of iron ores that are generally small or of inferior grade are known elsewhere in the Balkans—Greece, Albania, Bulgaria, and Poland. The classic Banat magnetite district, formerly in Hungary, is now in Rumania and Yugoslavia. Small amounts of iron ores are annually produced in Switzerland and Portugal. Some of the richest and best-known iron ores of Europe are those of Sweden. The magnetic ores at Kiruna, in the extreme northern part of the country, are among the largest deposits of this type in the world. Most of the ore contains a high percentage of phosphorus and is smelted to produce iron for the Thomas process. The Loussavaara mine near Kiruna contains similar high-grade magnetites and is known because of the unusually high phosphorus content of its ores. A short distance south of Kiruna, in southern Lapland, is found another large magnetite ore body at Gellivare. This deposit is similar to that at Kiruna but locally contains pyrite (FeS_2), chalcopyrite ($CuFeS_2$), fluorite (CaF_2), and other minerals. In central Sweden high-phosphorus magnetites and low-phosphorus hematites are found. Other celebrated magnetite deposits of Sweden are at Persberg, Långban, Nordmark, Norberg, and Dannemora. The Taberg Mountain district in southern Sweden contains large deposits of titaniferous magnetite which have 6-7 per cent titanic dioxide. Another large titanic iron mass is found at Routivare in northern Sweden. Sweden lacks an adequate supply of coking coal, though it has made efforts to use hydroelectric power in smelting. Most of the ore mined is shipped in normal times to England and Germany. Norway contains several large iron ore deposits, somewhat similar to those of Sweden, but of lower grade. The so-called dry or siliceous ores of Norway and Sweden are found at many places but are particularly well developed in northern Norway in South Varanger near the Finnish frontier. Similar magnetite-hematite ores that are distinctly of sedimentary origin are found at Naeverhaugen and Dunderland, also in northern Norway. Many of the Norwegian ores require concentration and sintering before charging in the furnaces. An unusually large body of titaniferous hematite is developed at Egersund, Norway. The iron ore deposits of Russia are widely distributed, but the best-known and most extensively developed deposits are in the European part of the country. Krivoi Rog in South Russia contains large tonnages of hematitic ore that carry 45-60 per cent iron. Another very large deposit of brown ores is on the Kertch Peninsula in the Crimea. This ore commonly contains about 35-40 per cent iron, a few per cent of manganese, and is high in phosphorus and sulphur. The Kertch ores are generally fine-grained and sandy. The Ural Mountains contain several productive districts: Gora Magnitnaja, Tagil, Bakal, and Komarov. The ores are principally magnetites and brown ores.

Asia and the Pacific Islands.—Magnetite and siderite are found in large deposits in the Altai Mountains in Siberia, and several other little-known but large deposits have been reported in Siberia. Magnetite has been reported on the Pacific coast near Saint Olga Bay. Japan proper contains only small amounts of iron ores. The principal deposit is at the Kamaishi mine. Other deposits have been operated by the Japanese in Korea and in Manchuria. The Fengtien Province of Manchuria contains large reserves of low-grade, banded hermatite and magnetite, that average about 30-35 per cent iron. Many scattered deposits have been reported in China; probably the best known are the magnetites along the Yangtze River. Low-grade oolitic ores are found at Hsuan-Lung, northwest of Peking. Extensive laterite deposits are found in the Philippine Islands, particularly in Surigao in Mindanao, and unknown quantites of hematite and magnetite have also been reported from several places in the archipelago. Small deposits of iron ores are worked in Indo-China, Borneo, and the Malay States. India contains some of the largest iron ore resources in the world. The banded deposits northwest of Calcutta in southeastern India are similar to those of the Lake Superior region and support an expanding iron and steel industry at Tatanagar. Iron ores are mined in South Australia and to a much less extent in New South Wales, Queensland, and Tasmania. High-grade deposits are reported at Yampi Sound on the northern coast of Western Australia. New Zealand has extensive reserves of black sands, much of which are said to contain appreciable amounts of titanium. Southeastern Borneo, New Caledonia, and the central part of the Celebes are said to contain tremendous amounts of laterite and several magnetite ore bodies are known in the Dutch East Indies. Small ore deposits are worked in Arabia and Turkey.

Africa.—A good grade of hematite is mined in North Africa in Algeria, Tunisia, and Morocco, solely for the export trade, principally to Germany and England. Large reserves of fair ore, partly titaniferous, are known in the Union of South Africa, particularly in the Transvaal near Pretoria. Many iron ore deposits, including very large reserves of laterites, are known throughout Africa, but little has been done to develop them commercially. Some of the best-known are in Sierra Leone, Liberia, Belgian Congo, Nigeria, Togoland, Rhodesia, French Guinea, and Madagascar.

Reserves of the World.—The total known reserves of iron ore in the world are tremendous; they were estimated in 1946 to include about 45 billion long tons of ores of all grades. In addition, there are estimated to be about 160 billion tons of potential ore.

Bibliography.—Eleventh International Geological Congress, *The Iron-Ore Resources of the World* (Stockholm 1911); Van Hise, C. R., and Leith, C. K., *The Geology of the Lake Superior Region,* U. S. Geological Survey Monograph 52 (Washington 1911); Cayeaus, L., *Les Minerais de fer Colitiques de France* (Paris 1922); Wagner, P. A., *The Iron Deposits of the Union of South Africa,* Memoir 26, Geological Survey of South Africa (Washington 1928); Leith, C. K., *The World's Iron Ore Supply,* (World Engineering Congress, Tokyo 1929); Gruner, J. W., "Hydrothermal Oxidation and Leaching Experi-

WORLD PRODUCTION OF IRON ORE DURING 1937 IN METRIC TONS BY COUNTRIES PRODUCING IN EXCESS OF 200,000 TONS

Country	1937 Production	Per cent of Total Production	Principal Mining Method
North America			
United States	73,250,649	34.55	Open pit and underground
Newfoundland	1,635,554	.77	Underground
Cuba	496,258	.23	Open pit
South America			
Chile	1,489,637	.70	Open pit
Brazil	209,715	.10	Open pit
Europe			
France	37,839,000	17.85	Underground
USSR	26,000,000	12.26	Open pit and underground
Sweden	14,952,549	7.05	Open pit and underground
Great Britain	14,443,146	6.81	Open pit and underground
Germany	9,575,234	4.52	Underground and open pit
Luxembourg	7,766,254	3.66	Underground
Austria	1,884,694	.89	Open pit
Czechoslovakia	1,836,495	.87	Underground
Spain	1,269,742	.60	Open pit and underground
Norway	1,008,225	.48	Open pit
Italy	997,805	.47	Open pit
Poland	780,152	.37	Open pit and underground
Yugoslavia	629,172	.30	Open pit
Greece	300,498	.14	Underground
Hungary	290,044	.14	Open pit
Belgium	265,540	.13	Underground
Asia			
India, British	2,883,548	1.36	Open pit
Malay States	1,688,155	.80	Open pit
Philippine Islands	601,190	.28	Open pit
Korea	207,500	.10	Open pit
Africa			
Algeria	2,427,230	1.14	Open pit
Morocco, French and Spanish	1,491,601	.70	Open pit
Tunisia	943,763	.45	Open pit
Sierra Leone	644,160	.30	Open pit
Union of South Africa	461,796	.22	Open pit
Oceania			
Australia	1,900,983	.90	Open pit
All Others	1,829,711	.86	Open pit and underground
Total	212,000,000	100.00	

Ref. United States Bureau of Mines *Yearbook*, 1941, pp. 569–70.
In the United States all iron ore is handled on a gross ton (2,240 pound) basis. In Europe a metric ton of 2,204.6 pounds is used.

ments; Their Bearing on the Origin of Lake Superior Hematite-Limonite Ores," *Economic Geology* November 1930; Lindgren, W., *Mineral Deposits* (New York 1933); Dunn, J. A., "The Strategic Significance of the Distribution of the World's Mineral Wealth," *Transactions*, Mineral and Geological Institute of India, vol. 33 (1936); The Lake Superior Iron Ore Association, *Lake Superior Iron Ores* (Cleveland 1938); Hart, Charles, "Known Iron Ore Resources of the World and Their Significance," *Iron and Steel Engineer*, May 1939; Mikami, H. M., "World Iron-Ore Map," *Economic Geology*, November 1944.

CHARLES F. PARK, JR.,
Department of Geology, Stanford University.

10. MINING AND HANDLING OF IRON ORE.—The geographical locations where the world's iron ore mines have been developed are largely controlled by the cost of assembling raw materials for the steel industry. Because the value of iron ore and coking coal is low in relation to weight, the cost of transportation restricts the distance such materials can be moved economically. As a rule, it is cheaper to move ore to fuel than fuel to ore. Low-priced coking coal has been the dominant factor influencing the location of iron and steel industries. The cost of iron delivered at the consuming center and the quality of ore determine the value of iron ore, and the grades marketed vary greatly for different localities.

PRINCIPAL IRON ORE PRODUCING DISTRICTS IN THE UNITED STATES

District	1937 Production in Gross Tons	Per cent of Total	1942 Production in Gross Tons	Per cent of Total	Per cent Iron Average Grade Shipped, 1942
Lake Superior	61,657,635	85.52	91,064,194	86.30	52.02
Southeastern	6,351,053	8.81	9,165,462	8.68	37.12
Northeastern	3,145,177	4.36	3,119,506	2.96	61.01
Western	939,683	1.31	1,534,022	1.45	51.44
All Others			643,011	.61	63.74
Total	72,093,548	100.00	105,526,195	100.00	51.08

1937 figures represent a high rate of production during a peacetime year. 1942 represents peak wartime production. Principal producing states are: Lake Superior district (Minnesota, Michigan, Wisconsin); Southeastern district (Alabama, Georgia); Northeastern district (New York, New Jersey, Pennsylvania); Western district (Wyoming, Utah, California, New Mexico and Missouri).

PRODUCING COUNTRIES

The foregoing table lists the production of iron ore by countries producing in excess 200,000 metric tons during 1937, the year of greatest iron ore production prior to World War II:

During 1937, eighteen countries produced in excess of 1,000,000 gross tons each of iron ore, but only seven of these exceeded 5,000,000 tons. The relative importance of these seven producers and their relation to principal importing and exporting countries is portrayed on the preceding chart.

The extensive iron ore exports of France and Sweden move to Europe's steel plants located close to coal. The movement of the iron ores of French Lorraine to the coal fields of the Ruhr and Saar valleys as well as to Belgium and Luxembourg is paralleled in America by the shipments of Lake Superior district iron ores to the coal districts of Pennsylvania, Ohio, Indiana and Illinois. In the latter case there are no international barriers to impede this commerce, and American enterprise has developed the greatest steel producing and manufacturing region in the world.

Grades of Ore Shipped in the United States. The chemical and physical properties of iron ores vary greatly. The presence or absence of desirable elements or objectionable impurities and the physical make-up of ores, as well as their iron content, determine their value at consuming centers.

Phosphorus, sulphur, and silica are the chief impurities found in American ores. When phorphorus is less than .045 per cent, the ores are classed as Bessemer grade. The quantity of permissible phosphorus and silica varies with furnace practices, but usually silica in excess of 8 per cent produces too much slag and is undesirable. Lime, magnesia and, at times, alumina are beneficial as fluxes. Manganese is especially desirable, and if it exceeds 5 per cent, the ore is called manganiferous iron ore and is not classed as iron ore. Manganiferous iron ores come largely from the Lake Superior district where the Cuyuna range in Minnesota is the principal producer.

Generally, ores high in iron content are preferred, and lower-grade ores in most districts are concentrated to improve their quality. Local conditions determine the grades used.

In marketing iron ores, analyses of iron refer to the quantity of metallic iron in the ores as shipped and not to dry analyses made after drying samples at 212° F. to eliminate moisture. Lake Superior ore shipments average more than 10 per cent moisture.

In the Lake Superior district, where freight to market is a major item of cost, the average grade of ore shipped is about 51.5 per cent iron; material containing up to 35 per cent iron is not ore and is called iron formation. Some day much of this material will be concentrated into a high-grade marketable product.

In contrast, in the southeastern district tributary to Birmingham, Alabama, where iron, coal and limestone occur close together, the ores used, which contain lime and are partly self-fluxing, average only about 36 per cent iron.

Northeastern district shipments from New York, New Jersey, and Pennsylvania average more than 61 per cent iron. Most of this material is a magnetic concentrate or sintered concentrate, produced from low-grade magnetic material containing from 25 per cent to 50 per cent iron as mined. Concentration of such material is necessary in order to yield a high-grade product marketable at consuming centers in competition with Lake Superior or imported ores.

The grades of Western ores as shipped range from about 51 per cent iron for Utah ores to about 55 per cent for California ores.

Lake Superior District.—The Lake Superior district is the greatest iron mining region in the world. It includes the mining localities or ranges tributary to Lake Superior navigation in Minnesota, Wisconsin, and Michigan, and also in Ontario, Canada. These ranges have been developed as follows:

Most of the ore produced in the Lake Superior district moves nearly a thousand miles to market. This is possible because of large-scale, economical operations and cheap water transportation. The average rail haul of ore from mines to Upper Lake ports is about 75 miles. The lake haul is about 750 miles with an additional rail distance of about 150 miles to inland furnaces.

The shipping season is geared to Great Lakes navigation and lasts about seven months each year, depending on weather conditions. Underground mines operate on a 12-month basis and stockpile their winter production. In the open pits stripping operations continue during the freeze-up period, thereby spreading employment and utilizing equipment.

Mining.—There is a wide variety of iron min-

DEVELOPMENT OF RANGES, LAKE SUPERIOR DISTRICT

(Gross Tons)

Range Name	Location	First Shipped	1942 Shipments	Per cent of Total	Total Shipments Including 1944	Per cent of Total
Marquette	Michigan	1854	6,540,731	7.00	230,124,450	10.46
Menominee	Michigan	1872	4,930,434	5.27	208,088,388	9.46
Gogebic	Michigan-Wisconsin	1884	6,237,894	6.67	245,187,669	11.14
Vermilion	Minnesota	1884	1,924,877	2.06	75,770,532	3.44
Mesabi	Minnesota	1892	70,280,087	75.17	1,378,117,290	62.65
Michipicoten	Ontario, Canada	1900	486,666	.52	5,885,746	.27
Moose Mountain	Ontario, Canada	1908	—	—	404,874	.02
Cuyuna	Minnesota	1911	3,035,532	3.25	52,563,951	2.40
Atikokan	Ontario, Canada	1944	—	—	16,552	.00
All Others	Wisconsin-Minnesota		59,171	.06	3,502,543	.16
Total United States Ranges			93,008,726	99.48	2,193,354,823	99.71
Total Canadian Ranges			486,666	.52	6,307,172	.29
Grand Total			93,495,392	100.00	2,199,661,995	100.00

ing methods in use, depending on the shape, size, and location of ore bodies and on the character of the ore and the surrounding rocks. Some ore bodies are close to the surface as on the Mesabi range, and others extend to considerable depths which, on the Gogebic range, exceed 3,000 feet below the surface. Some ores are low grade and require beneficiation before shipment, and others consist of nearly pure iron oxides containing 70 per cent iron.

The mining methods used are those giving greatest safety with maximum efficiency. Where ore bodies dip steeply with small surface exposure, or extend to great depths, underground mining methods are necessary. If the ore is close to the surface with relatively large areas of outcrop, open-pit methods are employed.

In underground mines, top slicing and caving methods are used extensively, especially where the ores are soft. In hard ores, open stope methods are employed, as on the Marquette range. At other places, cut and fill and variations of open stope methods are used.

Mechanization of underground operations is well developed, and innovations are continually being tried out. Because of the great weight or high specific gravity of iron ores in comparison to equivalent volumes of other ores as mined, the equipment used in iron mines is usually of sturdier construction than is generally employed in other mining operations. Machines drill the ore and, after it is blasted, it is moved with mechanical scrapers or loaders to reach shaker conveyors, conveyor belts or electric rail haulage, or a combination of these methods of transportation, to shafts where it is hoisted to the surface and loaded into railway cars or placed on stockpiles.

Open pit mining has its greatest development on the Mesabi range and is described under that heading.

Mesabi Range.—During 1942, 70,280,087 gross tons of iron ore were shipped from the Mesabi range. Production came from 78 open pits and 9 underground mines. This array of operations is condensed into a length of 80 miles and offers an opportunity to view, almost side by side, a wide range in the methods of handling ore.

The largest ore bodies in the Lake Superior district occur on the Mesabi range in iron formation which has a gentle dip and most of the ore is within 600 feet of the surface. The ore bodies consist of iron oxides formed by oxidation of various iron minerals and by solution and removal of silica from the iron formation, leaving a characteristic soft, porous ore easy to drill and blast. Previous to mining operations, most of the ore was covered with glacial clays, sands and gravels which ranged from a few feet to 250 feet in thickness. Part of the ore lies beneath a capping of iron formation overlaid by drift. Where the cost of removing overburden is not excessive, an open pit method is used. The quantity of stripping removed to uncover an ore body during development and operation of an open pit may exceed the tonnage of ore produced. The material stripped consists of glacial drift, iron formation, and lean ores which are segregated into separate dumps to facilitate possible future utilization. The dumps which have accumulated during the development and shipment of more than a billion tons of open pit ore from the Mesabi range form prominent landmarks near major operations.

Nearly all of the ore in the open pits requires drilling and blasting before it can be handled by power shovels. Standard mobile churn drilling rigs are used for this purpose. In other regions where the ore is harder, closer drilling is required to break the ore, but otherwise the mining methods are essentially the same.

In the open pits the choice of equipment (locomotive haulage, truck or conveyor belt, or a combination of these) and power (steam, electricity, or Diesel) varies with the operation.

Starting in the middle 1930's, locomotive haulage has given way to trucking and belt conveyor installations, and steam locomotives used in the larger pits are being replaced with Diesel electric units, first introduced during 1940.

Power shovels, which previous to 1922 used steam power and operated from railway tracks, have been replaced with smaller, more mobile, and quicker acting electric or Diesel shovels mounted on caterpillar treads.

The evolution in operating methods is illustrated by the changes which have occurred at the Albany mine near Hibbing, Minn. This property is one-half mile long and one-quarter mile wide and its ore body extends onto adjacent property having separate ownership where it is mined by different interests. The Albany mine was opened up in 1902 as a milling pit. The overburden of glacial drift was stripped by steam shovel. An inclined shaft was sunk to the bottom of the ore body from which a system of development drifts (tunnels) extended underneath the ore to be mined. Vertical openings called raises extended from these drifts to surface through the ore. The surface ore was "milled" or shovelled into these raises and drawn off into cars which were hauled by mules to the inclined shaft, and the ore hoisted to the surface. In 1913 the limits of the pit were extended and a narrow gauge railway system was installed. This was changed to a standard gauge railway system in 1924, and the ore was then hauled to the surface by steam locomotives. By 1939, six switchbacks were required to reach the bottom of the pit and much ore was tied up in track benches. A truck haulage system was substituted during 1939, thereby releasing additional ore for mining and obtaining operating economies.

Ore from the property west of the Albany mine, which is part of the same ore body and open pit is handled by trucks which load onto a conveyor belt, carrying the ore from the pit to railway ore cars on the surface.

There is considerable variation in the arrangement of conveyor belts in different pits. At one mine the belt extends from a railway loading pocket on the surface through an underground incline to beneath the ore body. Raises extend from underground feeder belts to the pit bottom with ore delivered to the raises by trucks. At other properties, conveyor belts extend in part through pit walls or are built entirely in the open from pit bottom to railway pockets on the surface.

Several large open pits developed to supply wartime ore requirements use standard railway equipment, but in general the smaller operations use truck or conveyor belt haulage.

The most spectacular mining operation on the Mesabi range is the Hull-Rust-Mahoning open pit at Hibbing. The ore body, parts of which are separately owned and operated, covers an area of 1,200 acres and is more than 3 miles long with a width ranging up to one-half mile and a depth of about 450 feet. Waste material removed between 1895 and 1945 exceeded 270,000,000 gross tons with ore shipments totaling 383,000,000 gross tons. During the war period, from 1941 through 1945 inclusive, more than 110,000,000 tons of ore were shipped, and each year's shipments exceeded 20,000,000 tons, or, more than 20 per cent of all the iron ore mined from the United States during this period. Haulage of ore mined in the main pit is mostly by rail and during 1944, 40 locomotives were used, of which 13 were steam and 27 were Diesel-electric. Twenty-six power shovels operated, 20 of which were electric and 6 were Diesel, varying in size from 1.5-8 cubic yard dipper capacity. Parts of the ore body have been bottomed, and trucking, called "scramming," was used to deliver ore from power shovels and clean-up jobs to railway cars in the pit. Haulage from several subordinate parts of the eastern end of the main pit was by truck, conveyor belt, and, in one case, a shaft which had ore delivered to it from a conveyor belt serviced by trucks on the pit floor.

When rail haulage is used in the open pits, the ore loaded may go directly into railway ore cars for delivery to shipping ports, or it may require crushing or concentrating by milling methods before shipment. Direct shipping ore is sampled in 5- or 10-car lots as it leaves the mines. Ores requiring crushing, screening, or concentrating are sampled before and after treatment.

Crushing and Screening. Often crushing and screening, or screening alone, is necessary to improve the physical structure of ores as well as to effect some concentration. Lumpy, hard, siliceous material is locally found with good ore, and this lean material can be removed from screens while softer, richer ore breaks to finer sizes and passes through the screens. Products from crushing and screening plants are not classified as concentrates.

Concentration.—Large tonnages of iron-rich material in the iron formation contain too much silica to be used directly in the blast furnace, and such material requires concentration to a purer form. Some lean ores, especially on the western Mesabi range, contain fine, unleached silica grains which can be washed away with a stream of water. These ores are called "wash ores." In other places the silica is in coarser consolidated pieces attached to iron oxides and requires crushing before removal by gravity or other concentration processes. Certain portions of iron formation contain large quantities of finely disseminated and banded magnetite which can be concentrated magnetically after fine grinding. Other portions of iron formation with iron in the ferric state can be roasted to make the iron magnetic, after which magnetic concentration is possible. Various methods of concentration are necessary, depending on the nature of the material to be beneficiated.

The wash ores were the first to be concentrated on the Mesabi range, and the first shipment of concentrates amounting to 9,816 gross tons was made in 1907. Since then, jig, high density or "sink and float," and magnetic concentrates, have been processed. From 1907 until 1945, about 208,000,000 gross tons of concentrates were shipped from Minnesota. This material, by displacing direct shipping ores of richer grade, has conserved the latter for future use. Since 1907 the ratio of concentrates to ore shipments has increased from .03 per cent to more than 22 per cent, and the ratio of total concentrates to total shipments for the period 1907 to 1945 is about 14 per cent. During the war years of 1942–1945, nearly 45 beneficiation plants on the Mesabi range and 5 on the Cuyuna range were in operation, and each year these plants shipped a total of more than 15,000,000 tons of concentrates. The rated capacity of these plants is much larger than this.

An accompanying photograph shows a concentrating plant on the western Mesabi range. This plant, completed in 1910, had shipped more than 55,000,000 tons of concentrates by 1945, and the flow sheet was improved many times during this period.

Metallurgical research by many mining companies and other organizations has been greatly expanded in recent years in order to improve the structure and grade of iron ores now being used, as well as to make commercial ore products from lower-grade iron formation. Enormous quantities of such material containing 30 per cent or more iron are present in the Lake Superior district. However, the low value of iron ore requires extremely low-cost concentration processes. The price received for the iron contained in iron ore after it is transported down the Great Lakes is slightly less than one-half cent per pound, of which transportation costs amount to about one-quarter cent per pound of contained iron. There is not much margin for concentration and other expenses, and economic handling on a large scale is required for all operations from mine to furnace.

At the consuming centers, Lake Superior concentrates are in direct competition with Northeastern district concentrates and imported ores. Also the pig iron processed from iron ores in the blast furnaces is in competition with purchased scrap iron for making steel. The importance of scrap iron and the fact that more than 45 per cent of all American steel is now made from scrap were emphasized by the scrap drives during World War II. The increasing use of scrap iron by displacing iron ores is a very important factor in the iron ore trade.

Grading of Ore.—Iron ore shipments from the Lake Superior district are carefully graded to meet strict specifications of the iron trade, and each cargo shipment conforms closely to some guaranteed content of iron, phosphorus, silica, and manganese.

A typical shipment of Mesabi range ore is handled as follows: loaded railway cars from the mine crushing plant or concentrator are sampled in 5- or 10-car lots before being delivered to railway company assembly yards near the mines; there they are grouped into trains of various lengths and hauled by heavy steam locomotives to classification yards near the docks. En route from mine to classification yards the ore cars pass over track scales which record automatically the gross weight of each car. While the ore is in transit, the previously taken samples are analyzed for iron, phosphorus, silica, manganese, and moisture; the ore grader, using these results, determines how the ores should be mixed to yield a cargo of specified grade. Instructions are relayed to the yardmaster at the classifying yards, and, upon arrival of the ore trains, the cars are regrouped according to the desired "block" or group of dock pockets for a designated boat. Ore for a single cargo may be sorted from different trains and come from different mines. Additional mixing is sometimes obtained by dumping ore from several cars into the same ore pocket, and such ores are thoroughly mixed as they flow into the boats.

In some districts, domestic and foreign, where ore shipments vary in grade as received at the furnace, bedding plants similar to those used in the copper industry are used to provide a uniform furnace feed. Blending is controlled by stocking bridges with belt conveyor feed and a traveling reversing discharge which builds stockpiles in long piles composed of many successive layers of ore. A reclaiming machine spans each stockpile and takes cross-section cuts which include a portion of each layer of the stockpile. Conveyor belts then carry the ore from bedding plants to furnaces.

Transportation: Railway equipment, docks, and ore boats in the Lake Superior district are specially designed for large-scale, efficient and rapid ore handling. All railway ore cars are of steel hopper type, 24 feet long, which dump into alternate pockets on high level, pocket type ore loading docks where 12-foot pockets correspond with 12- or 24-foot spacing of boat hatches. Capacity of ore cars is 50 or 75 gross tons; dock pockets hold 250-400 tons each; and ore boats carry loads ranging up to 18,000 tons. The central portion of these vessels is cargo space, with crew quarters, engines, and fuel grouped together in bow and stern.

At upper lake ports, ore from the ore docks flows by gravity from ore pockets through long steel spouts into the holds of the boats, and the loading time of a boat is about 4 hours. The record loading time for a cargo of 12,817 tons is 16.5 minutes. Unloading at lower lake ports is done rapidly by means of huge clamshell buckets of 9-ton capacity or by means of giant electrically driven Hulett unloaders with maximum bucket capacities of 20 tons. There are about 300 ore boats in service with a carrying capacity per trip of nearly 3,000,000 gross tons. An ore boat can make a round trip in about a week unless coal is carried on the return voyage, in which event the round trip may take as much as 10 days. Ore from lower lake ports goes either directly to consuming furnaces or to stockpiles at the docks.

Ranges in Ontario, Canada.—The Atikokan and Michipicoten ranges in Ontario, Canada, occur within the Lake Superior district and their production is shipped via Lake Superior. Much of this ore is consigned to furnaces in the United States.

The first ore shipment from the Atikokan range was made during 1944 after a large river was diverted and a lake pumped out to uncover ore which lay beneath 50-150 feet of water and considerable mud, clay, and gravel. This development, now an open pit power shovel and trucking operation, will eventually require underground mining methods. The ore is shipped by rail about 140 miles eastward to Port Arthur on Lake Superior where a high level, pocket-type dock was completed during 1945.

The Michipicoten range ore is mostly an iron carbonate. After mining, which includes openpit as well as underground operations, the ore is crushed and roasted to drive off carbon dioxide. This calcined product is then sintered and shipped by rail to a Michipicoten harbor. Port facilities include a 12,000-ton loading bin with a conveyor belt system for loading ore boats.

Southeastern District.—Iron mining in the southeastern district is centered around Birmingham, Alabama, where the advantage of the coexistence of iron ore, coal, and limestone offsets the lower quality of the ores used.

The ores near Birmingham, called Clinton ores, are red hematites of bedded sedimentary origin, and they dip about 20° from the horizontal but flatten to around 10° in depth. Mining, which started in open pits in soft leached ore, is now mostly confined to underground operations in hard ore. Inclined shafts called slopes follow down just beneath the ore seams, and in some places these haulage ways extend for a mile or more down the dip. Levels extend out from the slopes, and the ore is mined in open stopes excavated working places where pillars are left to support the roof or hanging wall. After drilling and blasting, the ore is scraped with mechanical loaders into ore cars and transported by rail to loading pockets at the main slopes. The ore flows into skip cars, and, after being hoisted to the surface, it is crushed, screened, and sized before being shipped to nearby furnaces. The ores as mined average 35-37 per cent iron, with 0.2-0.4 per cent phosphorus, and in large part they contain enough lime to be selffluxing.

Some Clinton ore is mined on a smaller scale in northeastern Alabama, Georgia, Tennessee, and Virginia.

In addition, brown ores, consisting principally of limonite associated with clay, sand, and gravel, are mined in open pits. These ores require washing and screening before shipment. The largest production of this type of ore comes from the Russellville area of northwestern Alabama, with additional shipments from Kentucky and Tennessee.

Northeastern District.—The Northeastern district includes producing mines in New York, New Jersey, and Pennsylvania. The ore consists of magnetite in various amounts associated with ancient banded rocks. In several places the iron occurs as nonmagnetic hematite or martite as well as magnetite. Impurities include phosphorus, sulphur, titanium, and silica. Some of the ore is rich enough for direct shipment as premium lump ore, but most of it, as mined, ranges from 25 to about 50 per cent iron and requires concentration. Concentration plants in service at the end of the war had a rated annual production capacity in excess of 5,000,000 gross tons of concentrate which should average better than 60 per cent iron.

New York.—Mining operations are now centered in the Adirondack area of northeastern New York, where the entire iron mining practice has been renovated and expanded since 1937.

Underground mines are located near Port Henry and Lyon Mountain where the magnetite ore horizon dips at variable angles. Inclined shafts extend downward, usually just beneath the ore. Where the ore horizon is steep enough for the ore to run by gravity, shrinkage stopes (an overhead mining method where sufficient broken ore is left in the stope to provide wall support and act as a working platform) are used. Where the ore lies flatter, the ore is mined in open stopes, and mechanical scrapers

IRON

Courtesy The William B. Pollock Company

Modern blast furnace.

IRON

Left: Primitive method.
Center left: Ancient method.
Center right: 14th century Catalan forge.
Bottom left: Puddling process, 18th century.
Bottom right: Early 20th century puddling process.

Historical development of the manufacture of wrought iron.

Courtesy A. M. Byers Company

Pouring excess slag from the ladle, leaving a white-hot sponge ball of iron.

Dumping the 7,000-pound sponge ball onto the platform of the 900-ton press, which will squeeze it into a wrought iron bloom.

Modern sintering plant.

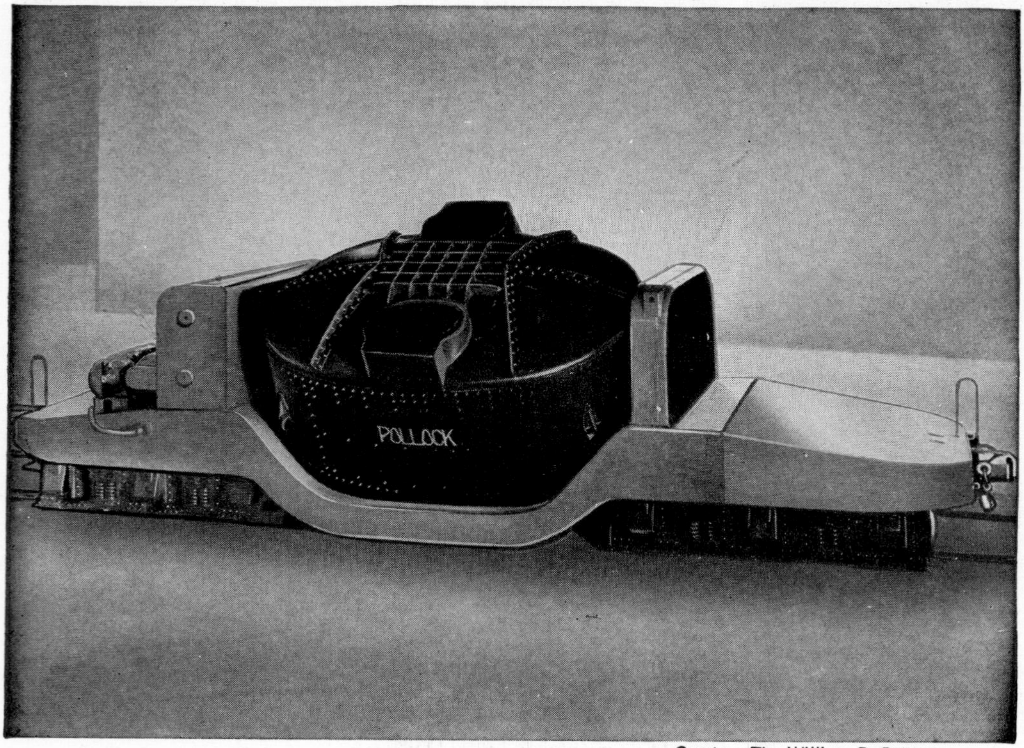

Courtesy The William B. Pollock Company

Mixer type of hot metal ladle.

IRON

Courtesy A. M. Byers Company

Melting of pig iron in cupola furnaces.

IRON

Courtesy A. M. Byers Company

Top: Melting of slag in a tilting open hearth.

Bottom left: Refining of molten iron in a Bessemer converter. Bottom right: Pouring the molten refined iron into liquid slag.

IRON

Courtesy Oliver Iron Mining Company

Top: Spruce open pit and underground iron mine, Eveleth, Mesabi Range, Minn. Headframe to shaft of underground mine in background. Power shovel-trucking operation in foreground.

Bottom: Looking west into Hull-Rust-Mahoning open pit iron mine, Hibbing, Mesabi Range, Minn.

Courtesy Oliver Iron Mining Company

Top: Conveyor belt hauling iron ore from Gross Marble Mine, near Marble, Minn.
Bottom: Trout Lake iron ore concentrator, Coleraine, Mesabi Range, Minn. More than 55,000,000 gross tons of wash ore concentrates have been shipped from this plant.

IRON

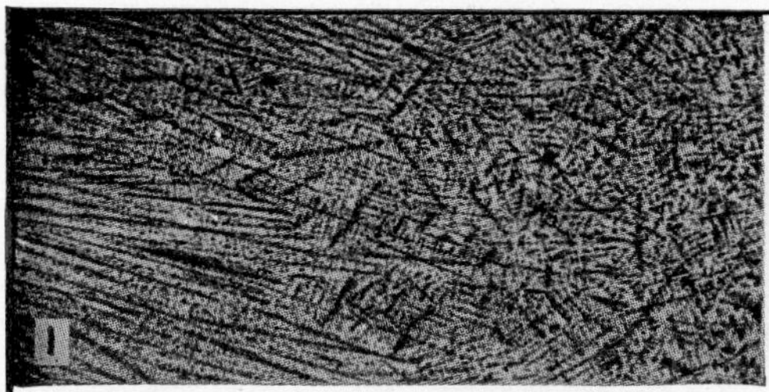

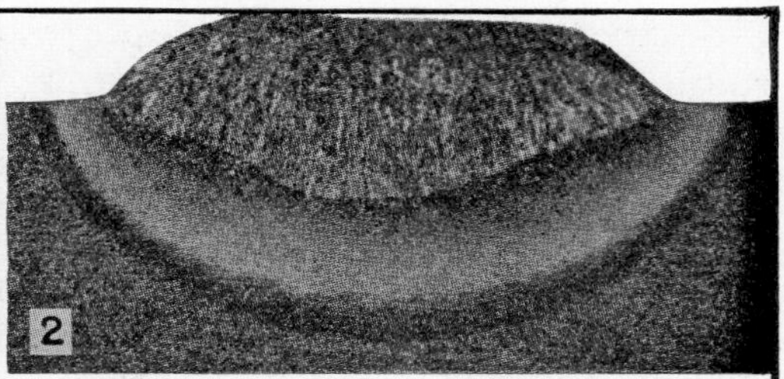

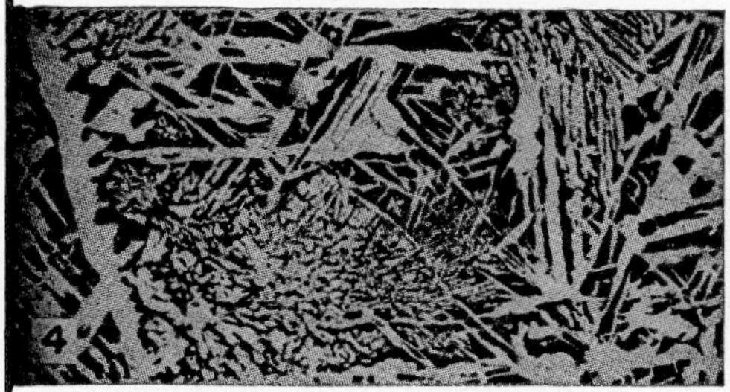

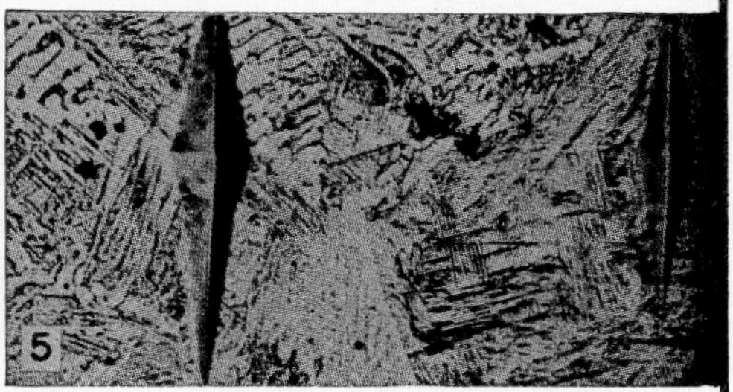

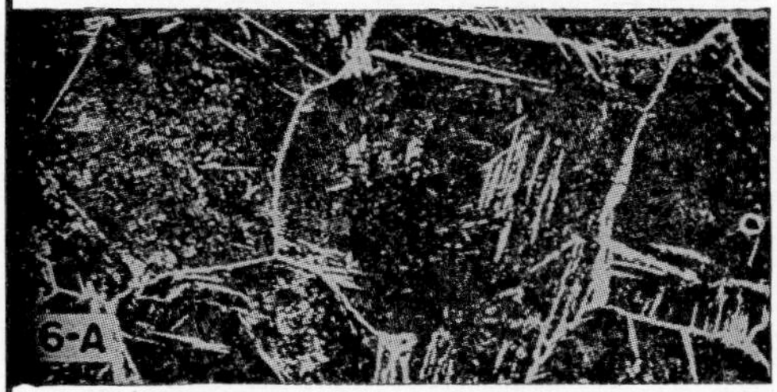

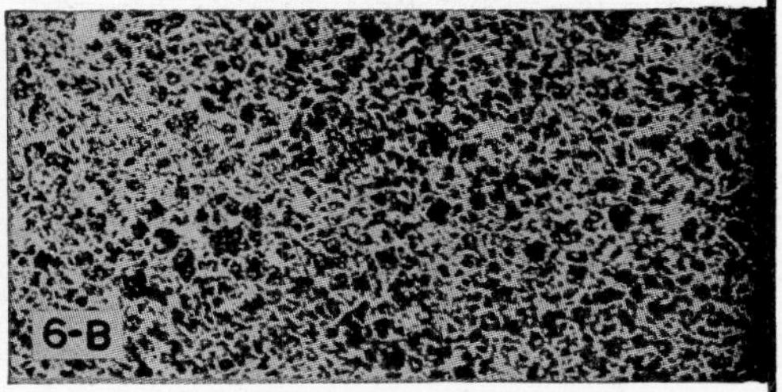

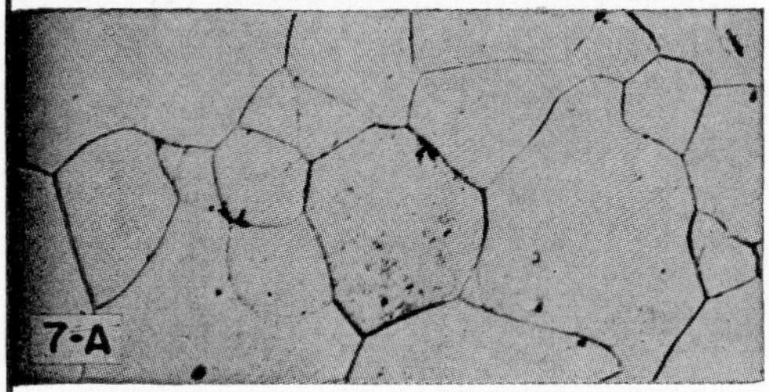

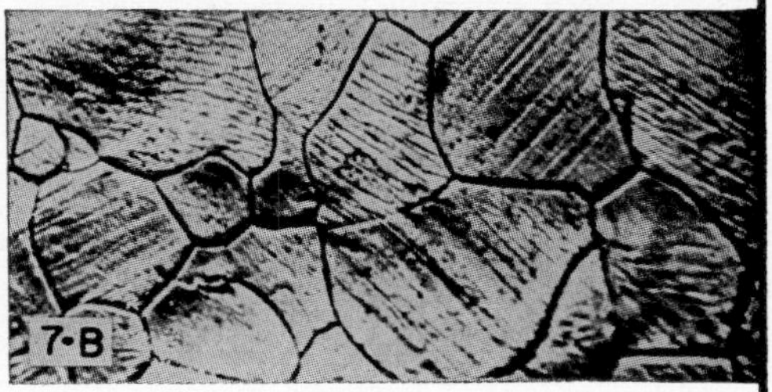

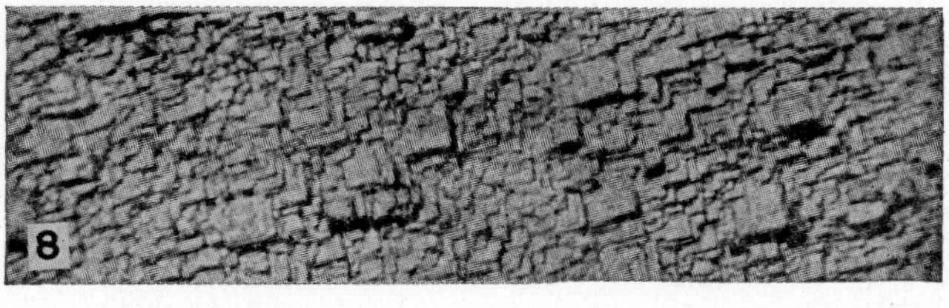

1. Pine tree crystals in steel casting X3.
2. Structure of electric-arc weld in steel plate X4.
4. Typical structure of cast steel X40. Same specimen as in Fig. 1.
5. Variation in structure and hardness in region of weld X400. Same specimen as in Fig. 2.

6-A, B. Coarse- and fine-grained types of steel X100.

7-A. Typical structure of iron X500.
B. The same spot as A, after cold working.

8. Cubical crystallites revealed in slowly cooled iron X900.

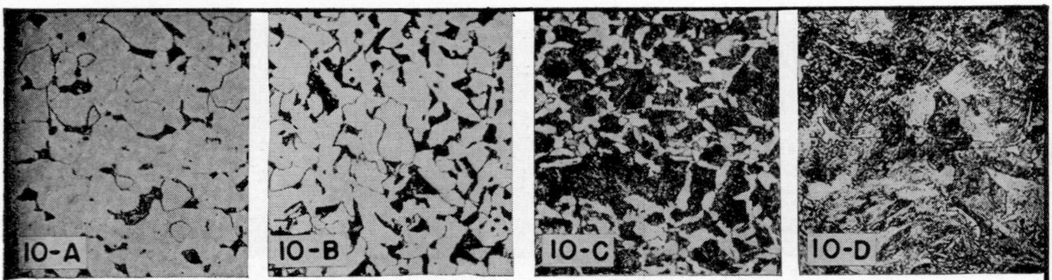

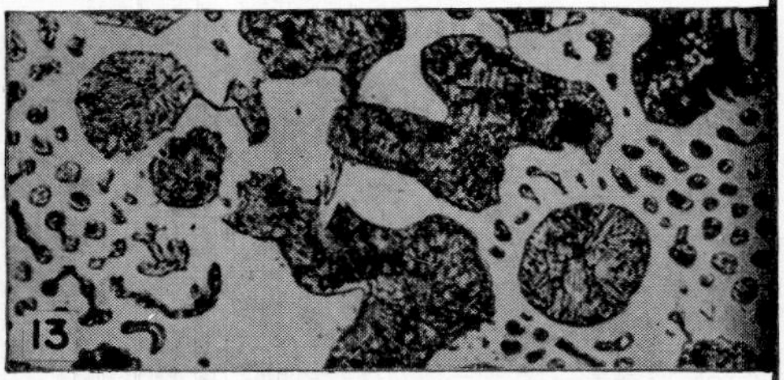

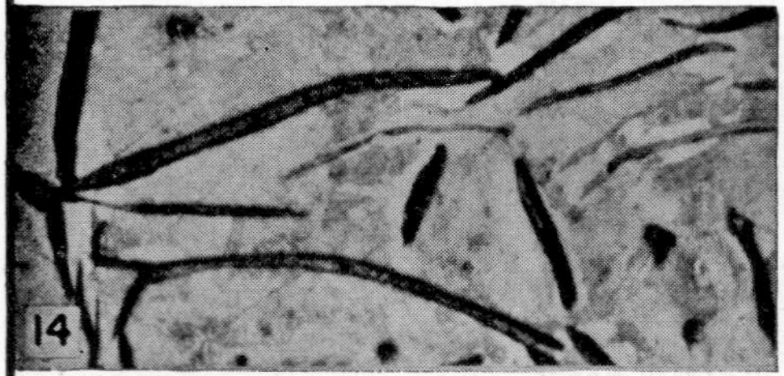

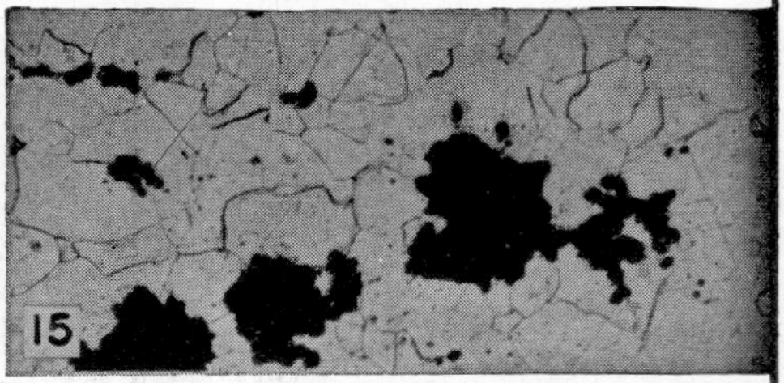

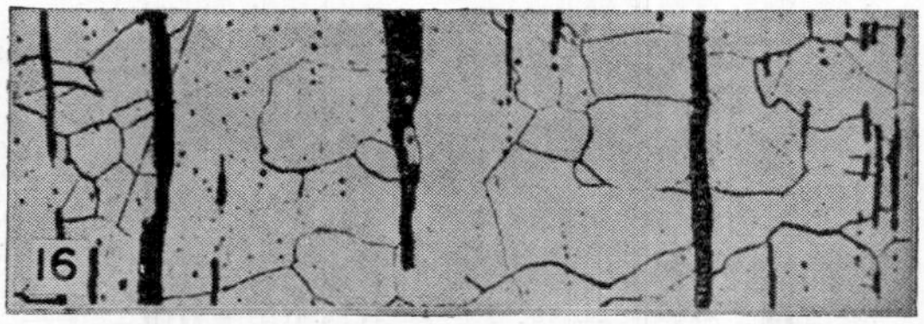

10. Relative amounts of ferrite and pearlite in slowly cooled steels of increasing carbon content up to 0.8 per cent carbon, X100. The ferrite is light and the pearlite is the dark constituent. *A,* 0.11 per cent carbon; mainly ferrite with some pearlite. *B,* 0.20 per cent carbon; less ferrite than *A* and more pearlite. *C,* 0.46 per cent carbon; there is now more pearlite than ferrite. *D,* 0.80 per cent carbon; substantially all pearlite.

11. Structures of 1.20 per cent carbon steel X500. *A,* pearlite with cementite grain boundaries. *B,* ferrite groundmass with cementite globules.

12. Structure of quench-hardened steel X500. This acicular or needlelike structure which forms in quench-hardened steel is called "martensite."

13. Structure of white cast iron X500. The white areas are massive cementite, the dark areas are pearlite.

14. Structure of gray cast iron X100. The large black plates are flakes of graphite; the groundmass is composed of pearlite and some ferrite.

15. Structure of malleable cast iron X100. The black patches are graphite nests; the groundmass is ferrite.

16. Structure of wrought iron X100. The matrix is ferrite. The dark parallel streaks are slag.

IRON

Courtesy Oliver Iron Mining Company

Top: Ore boat about to be loaded at a Lake Superior type ore dock. Spouts not yet lowered into hatchway of empty vessel. Note ore cars on dock.

Bottom: Ore classification yard near a Lake Superior port, where ore cars of various grades are regrouped to make cargo shipments of uniform specified grades.

IRON

Ore boat riding low in water and carrying more than 18,000 gross tons of iron ore, being unloaded by Hulett unloaders at a Lake Erie port.

move it into ore cars on tramming levels where it is hauled by storage battery locomotives to the inclined hoisting shafts. The ores, as mined, range from 25-50 per cent iron, which is increased by magnetic concentration to better than 63 per cent iron. Concentrates are sintered before shipment to produce a suitable agglomerate for furnace charging.

Open pit and, in part, underground mining methods are employed in the western Adirondacks at two properties developed during World War II. Magnetic sintered concentrates containing in excess of 62 per cent iron are concentrated from crude ores ranging from 25-42 per cent iron. At one property sulphur in the form of pyrrhotite is concentrated with the magnetite, but this sulphur is eliminated by roasting during the sintering operation.

New Jersey.—Iron mining in New Jersey is now mostly in the Mount Hope-Dover area where the crude ore usually ranges from 25-50 per cent iron. Some of the ore contains more than 60 per cent iron and is shipped as premium lump. The magnetite-rich ore zones or lenses dip steeply and also trend or pitch northeastward in depth. Shafts either follow the dip of the ore bodies or are vertical with crosscuts driven to reach the ore. Mining is by shrinkage stoping. Magnetic concentration raises the shipping grade of ore to 60 per cent or more in iron content. In one case where some hematite occurs with the magnetite, the hematite is recovered on vibrating tables after magnetic separation of the magnetite.

Pennsylvania.—Principal iron ore production in Pennsylvania comes from a combined open pit and underground operation near Cornwall. The crude ore contains about 35-45 per cent iron, 0.1-0.6 per cent phosphorus, 0.5-2.0 per cent sulphur and 0.2-1.0 per cent copper.

The ore body pitches or extends downward at about 30°, and the upper portion of it is mined as an open pit which is nearly a mile long, 1,000 feet wide and 600 feet deep. The open pit ore is churn-drilled and blasted in benches ahead of power shovels which load into trucks. These dump into an inclined skip which delivers ore to a crushing plant from which it is transported by rail to the concentrator.

Open stope, shrinkage stope, and block caving (described under *Western District* below) mining methods are used underground, and ore is hauled in tram cars to an inclined shaft for hoisting to surface.

The ore requires crushing and fine grinding, after which magnetic concentration, jigging, and tabling are necessary to yield a magnetic concentrate containing more than 55 per cent iron. This concentrate is sintered before shipment. Copper is recovered as a byproduct during concentration.

Western District.—Most western iron ores are magnetites, or mixtures of hematite and magnetite, mined by open pit methods.

Wyoming.—Hematite associated with iron formation of Lake Superior type is mined by underground methods near Sunrise, Wyoming. This ore body was originally mined as an open pit, but all mining is now underground where block caving is used very successfully. After extensive development of a level, the ore to be caved is undercut and the weight of the overlying rocks crushes the ore. It is then drawn off through chutes into mine cars. This mining method requires careful supervision of the manner of drawing, in order to prevent dilution of the ore with waste rock. The Sunrise ore is shipped by rail to Pueblo, Colorado.

Utah.—The ore bodies being mined in Utah have very little overburden and are well suited for mining by open pit methods. The first Utah iron mines were developed with tunnels driven into hillsides beneath the ore. The tunels were connected to open pits or "glory holes" by vertical openings. The ore was milled to these openings and trammed on tunnel levels to railway shipping pockets. All mining is now by open pit methods at Iron Mountain, where the ore is loaded by electric power shovels into trucks which dump into a crushing and screening plant from which the ore flows by gravity into railway cars for shipment to furnaces near Provo, Utah.

During World War II, other open pit operations at Iron Mountain and Iron Springs shipped ore to Pueblo, Colorado and Fontana, California.

California and New Mexico.—Open pit mines in California and near Hanover in New Mexico use power-shovel, trucking operations.

Missouri.—Principal production of iron ore in Missouri comes from Iron Mountain where mining started in an open pit; it is now an underground operation. The ore is concentrated by jigging and tabling, and the product, containing about 55 per cent iron, is shipped to Granite City, Illinois.

Numerous small brown ore pits, mostly in southeastern Missouri, produce ore as market conditions warrant.

Texas.—Open pit mining of northeastern Texas brown iron ores started during World War II. The crude ore contains about 27-42 per cent iron which is concentrated to about 53 per cent iron. Peacetime mining operations depend largely on local consumption.

FOREIGN COUNTRIES

The only countries, other than the United States, which have adequate coking coal reserves together with iron ore supplies, domestic or imported, to support major iron and steel industries, are: (1) Russia; (2) France with Germany; (3) Great Britain; (4) and possibly India and Australia. Major sources of iron ore used by these countries are reviewed below.

Russia.—The principal iron mines of Russia are located near Krivoi Rog in the Ukraine and at Magnitogorsk in the Ural Mountains. The Krivoi Rog area produces about 60 per cent of Russia's iron ore from underground mines where sublevel stoping or caving methods are used to mine lens-shaped ore bodies more than 2,000 feet long and equally deep. The ore averages about 57 per cent iron, 8 per cent silica, and 0.05 per cent phosphorus, and, together with coal from the Donets Basin, forms the nucleus of an important iron and steel industry.

The Magnitogorsk ore ranges from 45-60 per cent iron and is mined by open pit methods. This ore is shipped eastward by rail nearly 1,500 miles to the Kuznetsk steel plant in the Kuzbas Basin coal fields, and coal is carried on the return trip to a steel plant near Magnitogorsk. These steel plants played an important part in Russia's war effort after the Ukraine was overrun by the Germans during 1941.

France.—France's production of iron ore is usually second only to that of the United States.

The steel industry of France is concentrated in the Lorraine Basin of northeastern France where large deposits of minette iron ore of sedimentary origin occur. Minor quantities of ore extend into nearby Luxembourg and Belgium. The minnette ores resemble the Clinton ores of the Birmingham district in America and, as mined, most of the ore averages about 30 per cent iron, 0.7-0.9 per cent phosphorus, 12-20 per cent lime, and 5-10 per cent silica. Some siliceous phases contain from 12-25 per cent silica. The ore beds are flat-lying and are mined underground from vertical shafts. A retreating room and pillar mining method is used, and pillars are left to support the surface. Mechanical loaders, conveyor belts, and shaker conveyors are used in some of the mines.

Minette ores are exported to the coal fields of the Ruhr and Saar valleys as well as to Belgium and Luxembourg, and coal is imported from these areas for the French iron and steel industry.

Germany.—Previous to 1918, while Germany controlled Lorraine, the minette ores supplied most of Germany's iron ore requirements. With the loss of Lorraine after World War I, domestic iron ore deposits were developed which contain only about 30 per cent iron with 25 per cent silica. These lean ore bodies were mined chiefly by underground methods, with shafts ranging to 2,000 feet in depth. Production supplied only about 13 per cent of Germany's metallic iron requirements, and she was forced to import ores, chiefly from France and Sweden.

Sweden.—The major Swedish iron production is from the Kirunavaara open pit in northern Sweden or Lapland, where ore is loaded by electric power shovels into mine cars for delivery to a crusher in the pit and transported in 35-ton bottom dump cars. These are hauled by electric locomotives to Lulea on the Baltic or to Narvik, Norway for export. The ore docks at Narvik and Lulea resemble Lake Superior type docks, without storage pockets.

Other deposits in Lapland and near Grangesberg in southern Sweden are mined underground by shrinkage stoping method; these ores are crushed and concentrated to yield a high-grade, low-phosphorus product. Southern ores shipped from the port of Oxelösund are loaded on steamers either by grab buckets of 17-ton capacity or by conveyor belts.

Export ore contains about 60-62 per cent iron and 0.15-2.76 per cent phosphorus and, previous to World War II, was shipped principally to Germany and Great Britain.

Great Britain.—The iron mines in Great Britain are located chiefly in the Middlesborough, Northampton, Leicester, Frodingham, and Cleveland mining districts. The ore occurs in flat-lying sedimentary beds which are mined largely in open pits. A maximum 85 feet of cover is removed to expose ore ranging from 6-30 feet in thickness. Overburden is stripped by power shovel, chain bucket excavators, or by dragline. The ores contain only about 30 per cent iron and 0.3-0.7 per cent phosphorus. Lime and silica vary for different deposits, and bedding plants similar to those used in America are in use at some furnaces to provide a uniform furnace feed. It is necessary to import ores of better grade for use in the British iron and steel industry.

Newfoundland.—High phosphorus, Wabana ores mined from Bell Island, Newfoundland, are exported to Europe as well as being used at furnaces in Nova Scotia, Canada. These deposits are close to American markets, but American practice has not been designed to use these high-phosphorus ores.

The Wabana ores, of sedimentary origin, occur in several beds interbedded with other sediments which dip away from Belle Island beneath the ocean bottom. Inclined double shafts follow down the dip of the beds, and mining of the ore has progressed from two to three miles beyond the shoreline at depths of 1,600 feet below sea level, equivalent to 1,300 feet below sea bottom. A room and pillar mining method is used, and from 40-50 per cent of the ore is left as pillars. Mechanical loaders, scrapers, and power shovels are used underground to load cars. The ore is crushed on the surface and moved two miles to shipping port. The shipping grade of ore averages about 51 per cent iron, 11.5 per cent silica, and 0.92 per cent phosphorus.

Other Countries.—Iron mining in other parts of the world is mostly by open pit methods. There is a wide range in the extent of mechanization of mining operations in foreign countries. In the open pit at Kirunavaara, Sweden, power shovels and mine cars are of American make, and this mining operation compares favorably with the best American practice. In contrast, in densely populated India where labor is cheap, iron ore is carried in baskets by natives from open cut working faces to railway cars.

Bibliography.—New York, Western, and Company, *Engineering and Mining Journal* (New York 1866–); *Transactions, American Institute of Mining and Metallurgical Engineers,* published annually (New York 1871–); American Iron and Steel Institute, *Annual Statistical Report* (New York 1913–); Eckel, E. C., *Iron Ores; Their Occurrence, Valuation, and Control* (New York 1914); Mines Experiment Station, *Mining Directories of Minnesota* (Minneapolis 1922–); Lake Superior Iron Ore Association, *Analyses,* published annually (Cleveland 1926); U. S. Bureau of Mines, *The Iron and Steel Industries of Europe,* Economic Paper 19 (Washington 1929); id., *Minerals Yearbook,* published annually (Washington 1933); Works Projects Administration, *National Research Project on Iron Mining* (Washington 1937); The Lake Superior Iron Ore Association, *Lake Superior Iron Ores* (Cleveland 1938); Camp, J. M., and Francis, C. B., *Making, Shaping and Treating of Steel* (Pittsburgh 1940).

R. H. B. Jones,
Chief Geologist, Oliver Iron Mining Company.

11. IRON AND STEEL, Metallography of.—Metallography deals with the crystal structure of metals and alloys, with the effect of the composition and treatment of the alloy on the structure, and, in turn, with the way the structure affects the properties. Metals are made up of crystals similar in appearance to the crystals in a polished piece of granite. Metal crystals may be very soft and ductile or they may be very hard and brittle; they may be very coarse or very fine. The properties of an alloy may depend as much on the size, shape, and distribution of its various crystals as on the composition. The crystal structures of iron and steel are of remarkable variety, enabling metallographic study to reveal a surprising amount of information about the composition and treatment of any particular specimen. These structures suggest how defects present may be eliminated, how desired qualities may be attained, and how new or improved alloys may be produced. Metallography is one of the most important means of production-control, inspection, and research of iron and steel.

Visual Examination.—Significant structural features in iron and steel articles are frequently large enough to be observed with the unaided eye. For example, the fracture of a broken specimen may indicate whether the structure is coarse or fine, uniform or heterogeneous. The more usual procedure preparatory to visual examination is to etch deeply a section cut through the specimen with a hot solution containing one volume of water to one volume of concentrated hydrochloric acid for about 15 minutes. The etched surface will then clearly reveal the degree of fineness and uniformity of the structure, the rolling direction of a rolled article, the presence of porosity and unsoundness in a casting and cracks.

Figs. 1 and 2 illustrate typical structures of deep etched steel as they appear when viewed with the unaided eye or as magnified somewhat with a hand lens. Fig. 1 shows the dendritic or pine tree crystals which form in cast steel. The elongated crystals at the left are at the surface of the casting and the crystals at the right, of uniform diameter in all directions, are at the interior of the casting. Fig. 2 shows a section through an electric-arc weld on a steel plate. The humped region at the top is the fused-in metal from the melted electrode; directly underneath are various layers of the plate in which the structure was changed by the welding heat; beneath is the unchanged structure of the plate.

An interesting example of visual examination is the detection of cracks in steel by means of magnetic powder. The steel specimen is magnetized and fine magnetic powder is sprinkled over the surface, or the specimen is immersed in kerosene in which the magnetic powder is suspended. The magnetic powder will gather at any crack that may be present in the magnetized specimen, bridging the crack and thus making it clearly visible.

Microscopic Examination.—For revealing the finer details of the structure of iron and steel, the microscope must be used. In most cases the crystalline constituents are of such a size that their significant features can be revealed at the moderate magnification of X100. Frequently a higher magnification such as X500 is necessary. The limit of useful magnification of the optical miscroscope is about X2000. The newly invented electron microscope has been applied to the study of metals. In this way magnifications as high as X20,000 and higher have been attained. On a still finer scale, the positions of the atoms in the unit cells or lattices of which crystals are composed can be determined by X-ray diffraction analysis. In iron these unit cells are of the cubic type. At temperatures below 1670° F. for pure iron, the lattice is *body* centered cubic, known as *alpha,* or alpha iron, an iron atom being present at each corner of the cube and in the center of the cube. On heating pure iron above 1670°, the lattice changes to *face* centered cubic, known as *gamma,* or gamma iron, an iron atom being present at each corner of the cube and in the center of each face of the cube. At 2552° F., the lattice again changes to *body* centered cubic, known as *delta* or delta iron. The two types of cubic lattice in iron are illustrated in Fig. 3. Alpha iron can dissolve up to 0.035 per cent carbon and larger amounts of other alloying elements, and the resulting solid solution is called *ferrite;* gamma iron can dissolve up to 1.7 per cent carbon and varying amounts of other alloying elements, and the resulting solid solution is called *austenite.* The amount of the elements dissolved in the alpha iron and gamma iron depends upon the maximum temperature attained and the time during which the iron is at this temperature. The amount of the elements retained in the dissolved state in the solid iron depends upon the cooling rate from the maximum temperature, any subsequent reheating and cooling, and the preferential effect of one element upon the solubility in iron of the other elements. The length of a side of the body centered unit cube of iron (as illustrated in Fig. 3) is approximately 1/100 of a millionth of an inch.

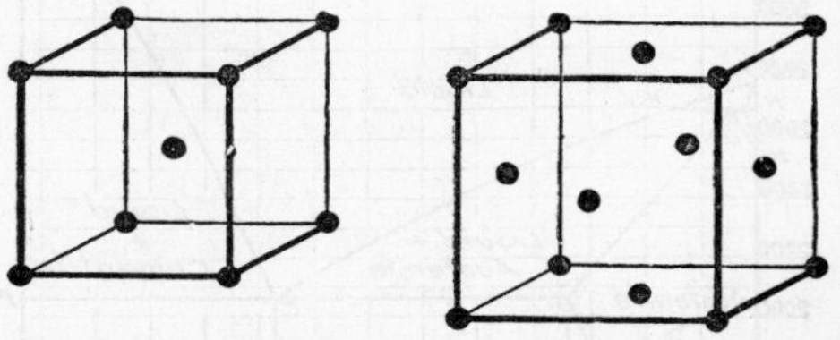

Fig. 3. Constitutional diagram of iron and iron carbide.

Before a specimen can be examined under the microscope the surface to be viewed must be properly prepared. The usual method is to grind and polish a section cut through the specimen. The polished surface of the specimen must usually also be etched to reveal the crystal structure fully. Metals are opaque so that you cannot see through them by transmitted light as in the case of some minerals; they have to be observed by reflected light. In grinding and polishing, a convenient sized specimen having one side about ½ square inch in area is first ground on a coarse emery wheel, then on finer emery papers, and finally polished with polishing cloth mounted on a wheel. In this final stage a very fine abrasive like alumina suspended in water is applied to the polishing cloth. The polishing action should be a cutting action as much as possible, and also should be mild, so as not to flow and smear metal over the surface. Many structural features may be observed in the as-polished condition, but usually the specimen is also etched. Light etching as with 2 per cent nitric acid in alcohol for about 15 seconds is usually sufficient. After etching, the specimen must be rinsed, washed in alcohol, and carefully dried. Metallography is a fine art, and beautiful results can be obtained when the structures are properly revealed.

Figs. 4 and 5 show the structures, as magnified by the microscope, of the same specimens as are illustrated in Figs. 1 and 2 without appreciable magnification. Fig. 4 shows the coarse, angular type of structure which may appear in steel in the as-cast state. Fig. 5 illustrates the structures at the weld of Fig. 2. In Fig. 5 the fused-in metal of the weld is at the left and the first layer beneath the fused-in metal, il lustrated in Fig. 2, is at the right. The dark, vertical, diamond-shaped impressions in Fig. 5 were made for testing the hardness, the smaller the impression produced by the test load, the greater the increase in hardness. The fused-in metal at the left of Fig. 5 is softer (larger impression); the metal at the layer at the right is harder (smaller impression).

Fig. 6 illustrates coarse- and fine-grained structures in steel. Specimens *A* and *B* were steels of similar composition heated in the same way for 8 hours at 1700° F. in a carburizing compound, consisting mainly of powdered coke. Steel *A* became coarse; steel *B* remained fine. The fine-grained type of steel can be produced by adding to the molten steel about 2 pounds of aluminum per ton of steel. The fine-grained type

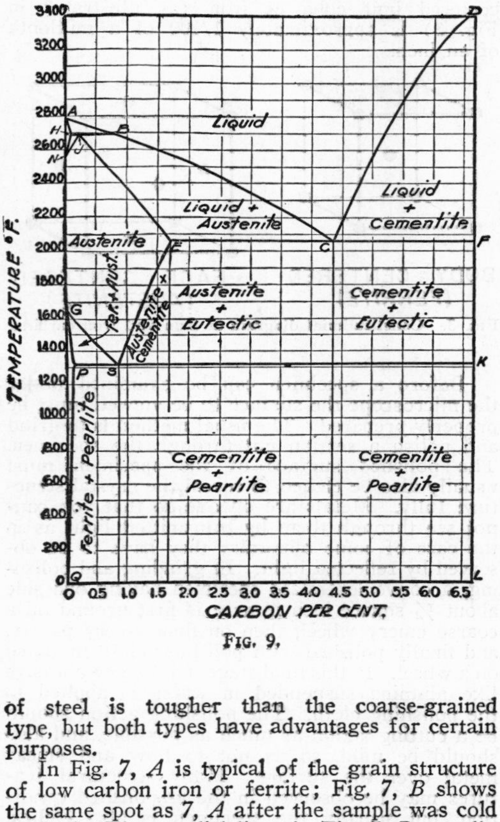

Fig. 9.

of steel is tougher than the coarse-grained type, but both types have advantages for certain purposes.

In Fig. 7, *A* is typical of the grain structure of low carbon iron or ferrite; Fig. 7, *B* shows the same spot as 7, *A* after the sample was cold worked. The parallel lines in Fig. 7, *B* are slip lines which formed as a result of the cold working. The effect of cold work is to harden the iron. With proper technique the cubic crystal habit of ferrite grains may be revealed. This is illustrated in Fig. 8.

Constitution of Iron Carbon Alloys.—Low carbon iron, steel, and cast iron all belong to the series of alloys of iron and carbon. One of the best ways of indicating fundamental differences among these alloys is the constitution diagram of the iron-carbon alloys. In Fig. 9 may be seen the whole series of alloys of iron and carbon; from carbon-free iron at the left, to alloys containing 6.7 per cent carbon at the right. The effect of temperature on these alloys from 0° F. to above their melting point is also indicated.

Steels are the most important iron-carbon alloys. The steels range in carbon content from about 0.1 per cent carbon to about 1.5 per cent carbon. Beyond this carbon content, from about 2 per cent carbon to about 4.5 per cent carbon, are the alloys known as the cast irons.

It may be seen in the diagram of Fig. 9 that as the carbon content of the alloys goes up, the solidification temperature goes down. Thus pure iron completely solidifies at the very high temperature of about 2800° F. But steels completely solidify at lower temperatures, as indicated by the boundary line *JE*. Above the line *JE* some "liquid" is present along with the "solid austenite," whereas below the line *JE*, only solid austenite is present. At the point *E* an alloy of 1.7 per cent carbon completely solidifies at about 2100° F. All alloys higher than this in carbon (including the cast irons) completely solidify at about 2100° F., along the line *ECF*. The composition at the point *C* on this line is the alloy of iron and carbon with the lowest melting point. This is called the eutectic composition, the word *eutectic* signifying lowest melting point. The cast irons are close to the eutectic in composition, and their consequent low melting point is one of the main reasons why cast irons are used. The cast irons are much more easily melted than the low-carbon steels; they can be made very fluid and, therefore, make good castings.

Carbon is the hardening constituent in steel. In slowly cooled steel, carbon is present as a hard, iron-carbon compound (iron carbide) called *cementite*. In steels with less than about 0.8 per cent carbon, the carbon is incorporated in the constituent called *pearlite*, which consists of alternate lamellae of ferrite and cementite. In slowly cooled steels with less than 0.8 per cent carbon, the constituents present are ferrite and pearlite as indicated in Fig. 9 in the region below the line *PS*. In slowly cooled steels containing more than 0.8 per cent carbon, ferrite is no longer present; in these alloys, the carbon up to 0.8 per cent carbon is present as the cementite lamellae in pearlite; the rest of the carbon forms cementite boundaries about the pearlite grains.

As indicated in Fig. 10, low-carbon steel consists mainly of ferrite with some pearlite. The ferrite is the light constituent and the pearlite, the dark constituent. As the carbon content increases, the amount of pearlite increases and the amount of ferrite decreases. In slowly cooled steel with about 0.8 per cent carbon, the structure consists entirely of pearlite. Obviously, pearlite has a composition of approximately 0.8 per cent carbon.

In slowly cooled steels which have a carbon content greater than that of pearlite, cementite (iron carbide) forms boundaries about the grains of pearlite. This is illustrated in Fig. 11, *A*. These rather thin cementite boundaries (the cementite is light colored) may be seen in about the center of Fig. 11, *A*, where several boundaries join. Fig. 11, *A* also illustrates the details of the structure of pearlite. The alternate lamellae in pearlite produce a fingerprint pattern which is easily recognized when viewed at the proper magnification. In Fig. 11, *A*, in which the fingerprint structure is clearly visible, the magnification is X500. In Fig. 10, at X100, the magnification is too low to resolve the fingerprint pattern of the pearlite.

The steel of Fig. 11, *B* has about the same carbon content as Fig. 11, *A*. By a special heat treatment the cementite (iron carbide) was coalesced into globules to form "spheroidized cementite." The structure consists of a ferrite groundmass containing the cementite globules. A steel having such a structure is considerably softer than a steel of the same composition in which the structure consists of pearlite and cementite boundaries as in Fig. 11, *A*.

Hardening of Steel.—Many steels for engineering structures are used in the slowly cooled (air-cooled) condition, and these steels owe much of their hardness and strength to the presence of pearlite, as has been indicated above. However, a much higher order of hardness is obtainable if the steel is cooled very rapidly from above its critical temperature, instead of being allowed to cool slowly. Such rapid cooling from above the critical temperature, as by quenching the hot steel in cold water, is what is meant by "hardening." Reference to Fig. 9 of the iron-carbon constitution diagram will be helpful in explaining what takes place in the quench hardening of steel.

As previously described, iron exists in two forms, as ferrite below the critical temperature and as austenite above the critical temperature. The critical temperatures are indicated by the lines *PSK* and *GSK* in Fig. 9. Above the line *GSK* the iron is present as austenite; below the line *PSK* it is present as ferrite; between *PS* and *GS* there is a mixture of ferrite and austenite, as indicated by the arrow in the diagram. Hardening can occur mainly because the austenitic form of iron can hold a large amount of carbon in solution, whereas ferrite can hold only a minute amount of carbon in solution. It is indicated in Fig. 9 that austenite can hold as much as 1.7 per cent carbon in solution whereas ferrite can hold only about 0.035 per cent. If a steel is cooled slowly from above the critical temperature, the carbon can separate when the critical temperature is traversed, and the austenite changes to ferrite and cementite. But when the steel is very rapidly cooled through the critical temperature, there is not time enough for the cementite to separate. The austenite transforms to ferrite but the cementite does not separate. The bulk of the cementite is, therefore, retained in the ferrite in supersaturated solution, although some of the cementite precipitates as an extremely fine (submicroscopic) dispersion. The extreme hardness of quench-hardened steel may be attributed to the supersaturated solution and fine dispersion of the cementite in the ferrite.

Fig. 12 shows the acicular or needlelike constituent which forms in steel when hardened by quenching from above the critical temperature. This constituent is called *martensite.* Martensite is extremely hard and it is the structure desired in steel for metal-cutting tools, files, and cutlery. Extreme hardness generally denotes brittleness. Thus as-quenched martensite may be too brittle. Quench-hardened steel can be made tougher and less brittle by heating it somewhat after quenching. Such heating is called tempering. The higher the tempering temperature, the softer and less brittle and the tougher is the steel. The quenched and tempered structure is, therefore, the commonly sought structure in heat-treated steel. The tempering temperature is determined by the hardness required in the finished article. For extreme hardness the tempering temperature may be about 400° F.; for great toughness the tempering temperature may be as high as 1200° F. During tempering the cementite separates from the martensite. At the higher tempering temperatures the cementite coalesces into particles large enough to be resolved in the microscope. After tempering at about 1200° F., the cementite appears as the good-sized globules of spheroidized cementite illustrated in Fig. 11, *B*.

Effect of Alloying Elements.—A word may be said about the effect of the alloying elements in steel, such as nickel, chromium, molybdenum, vanadium, and others. The alloying elements may be present in solution in the ferrite, and some of them may also be combined with carbon and one another to form carbides. In this way they may exert a considerable strengthening effect. However, the main effect of the alloying elements is in slowing down the rate at which austenite transforms to ferrite and cementite during cooling through the critical temperature region. As a result, instead of requiring extremely fast cooling from above the critical temperature to produce martensite as in plain carbon steel, very much slower cooling from above the critical temperature is sufficient to produce martensite in alloy steel.

The importance of this will be clear from the following example. A 1-inch diameter bar of plain carbon steel, which is heated to a temperature above the critical temperature and then immediately quenched in cold water, will cool rapidly enough to form martensite, only at the surface. Martensite will be formed only to a depth of about 1/8 inch. In the interior of the plain carbon steel bar the rate of cooling even in cold water will be too slow to form martensite. On the other hand, in a 1-inch bar of alloy steel similarly quenched or even more slowly cooled, as by quenching in oil, the martensite will form throughout the bar. Accordingly, the main effect of the alloying elements is to make possible very deep hardening of large sections, and likewise the attainment in large sections of the desired quenched-and-tempered tough structures. In thin sections, as in wire, just as high strength and toughness can be obtained with plain carbon steel as with many alloy steels.

Cast Iron.—The place of the cast irons in the iron-carbon constitution diagram of Fig. 9 has already been discussed. In these high carbon alloys the carbon may be present as cementite or as graphite.

Cast iron in which all of the carbon is present as cementite is called white cast iron. It contains about 3 per cent carbon and about 0.5 per cent silicon. The structure of white cast iron is illustrated in Fig. 13. The large white areas are massive cementite and the dark areas are pearlite. Because so much of the very hard constituent cementite is present, white cast iron is extremely hard and brittle. It is used for such purposes as grinding balls in ball mills and chilled rolls for rolling metal.

In gray cast iron most of the carbon is present as flakes of graphite. The structure of gray cast iron is illustrated in Fig. 14. For the carbon to be present in the form of graphite instead of cementite, the alloy must contain a good deal of silicon, which promotes graphitization. Ordinary gray cast iron contains about 3.5 per cent carbon and about 1.75 per cent silicon. The groundmass structure of gray cast iron is pearlite and ferrite and is hence quite tough. However, this groundmass structure is broken up by the graphite flakes so that gray cast iron is brittle. Yet, gray cast iron castings find many applications, for example, in automotive cylinder blocks and pistons, stoves, radiators, etc. The graphite in gray cast iron improves its machinability.

Another variety of cast iron is called malleable iron, the structure of which is illustrated in Fig. 15. Malleable cast iron contains about 2.5 per cent carbon and about 1.25 per cent silicon. The silicon content is low enough for the alloy to solidify as white cast iron. There is enough silicon present, however, to promote graphitization in the subsequent heating or annealing process to which this type of casting is subjected. This "malleableizing" annealing is done in two stages, first, heating at about 1600° F. to graphitize the massive cementite, and second, heating at about 1325° F. to graphitize the last remnants of pearlitic cementite. In malleable iron, the graphite which forms during the malleablizing annealing is present as rounded nests (Fig. 15) instead of as elongated sharp flakes as in gray cast iron (Fig. 14). Because of this and also because the matrix of malleable iron is entirely composed of soft ferrite, malleable iron has considerable toughness and is not brittle like gray cast iron.

Wrought Iron.—Unlike cast iron, which is a high carbon cast material, wrought iron is a low-carbon forged or rolled material. Wrought iron is substantially carbon free. It is distinguished by the fact that during its manufacture slag is incorporated into its structure. The elongated slag streaks in a wrought iron bar are illustrated in Fig. 16. These slag streaks impart a "fibrousness" to the structure.

Bibliography.—Rosenhain, W., *Introduction to the Study of Physical Metallurgy* (New York 1935); Epstein, S., *The Alloys of Iron and Carbon,* vol. 1 (New York 1936); Sauveur, A., *The Metallography and Heat Treatment of Iron and Steel* (Cambridge, Mass., 1936); Bullens, D. K., *Steel and Its Heat Treatment,* revised by Battelle Memorial Institute (New York 1938); Carpenter, H. C. H., and Robertson, J. M., *Metals* (New York 1939); Desch, C. H., *Metallography* (New York 1942); Dowdell, R. L., and others, *General Metallography* (New York 1943); Teichert, E. J., *Ferrous Metallurgy,* 3 vols. (New York 1944).

SAMUEL EPSTEIN,
Research Department, Bethlehem Steel Company.

12. IRON AND STEEL INDUSTRY IN THE UNITED STATES.

—The basic importance of the iron and steel industry in the economy and welfare of the United States may be glimpsed from three facts. Iron and steel are the most widely used of all the metallic materials and are also the most indispensable in modern civilization. From 1900 to 1938 the amount of steel in use in the United States increased 1,100 per cent while the population increased 70 per cent. Nearly 40 per cent of all the jobs in all the manufacturing industries of this country are created by the domestic manufacture and industrial uses of iron and steel.

This industry is so intimately associated with the economy of the country that it is very difficult to name one item of food, clothing, shelter, convenience, or luxury that does not contain iron or steel or is not made, transported, or consumed with the aid of iron or steel equipment. Consequently, the activity of this industry is a basic indicator of the economic health of the nation.

Despite its basic importance, this industry is essentially seasonal in operation. In addition, iron and steel, in the forms used by industry, are nearly always produced after orders are received; the requirements of many customers are so diversified and progressively changing that they cannot be anticipated in sufficient detail to warrant production for inventory.

During the spring months this industry produces the steel rails that are laid by the railroads during the spring and early summer. As rails are not laid in the winter, this highly seasonal business keeps rail mills operating at maximum capacity for only a few months of the year. The container industry which supplies the canners with steel containers for food packs similarly keeps the sheet and tin plate mills operating at capacity for a few months. Automobile companies order their steel requirements according to the model, as the model is in production. Agricultural implement manufacturers, machine tool builders, shipbuilders, bridge builders, and the host of manufacturers of the products of the retail stores likewise place orders seasonally for steel that is made after receipt of the orders.

This seasonal activity necessitates a capital investment of over 4 billion dollars, and demands at times extreme flexibility in manufacturing operations to make a wide variety of products that sell for a few cents a pound.

Centuries ago, the basic importance of iron to civilization was recognized. According to legend, when the temple of Jerusalem was completed, King Solomon gave a feast to the artificers employed in its construction. On unveiling the throne, it was found that a smith had usurped the seat of honor, at the right of the king's place, not yet awarded, whereupon the people clamored and the guard rushed to cut him down. "Hold, let him speak!" commanded Solomon. "Thou hast, O King, invited all craftsmen but me. Yet how could these builders have raised the temple without the tools I fashioned?" "True," decreed Solomon, "the seat is his of right. All honor to the iron worker."

Colonial Iron Industry.—A combination of unusual circumstances attended the founding of the iron and steel industry in the United States. Workable low-grade deposits of iron ore existed along the Atlantic seaboard in practically all of the colonies. Also abundant were virgin forests and easily dammed streams; the former furnished fuel for the furnaces, and the latter, the water power for the air blast and forge hammers. Slow communication with Europe and restrictive English laws and trade practices encouraged the colonists to work these deposits and to make iron products for local consumption.

The English Parliament might have severely handicapped the development of the colonial iron industry if timber had been plentiful in England or if iron smelting had been more advanced technically.

Wood in the form of charcoal was being consumed more rapidly than it could be grown in England. In the 17th century, charcoal was the only fuel used in blast furnaces and forges. The shortage of timber alarmed the English government, which was trying to maintain naval su-

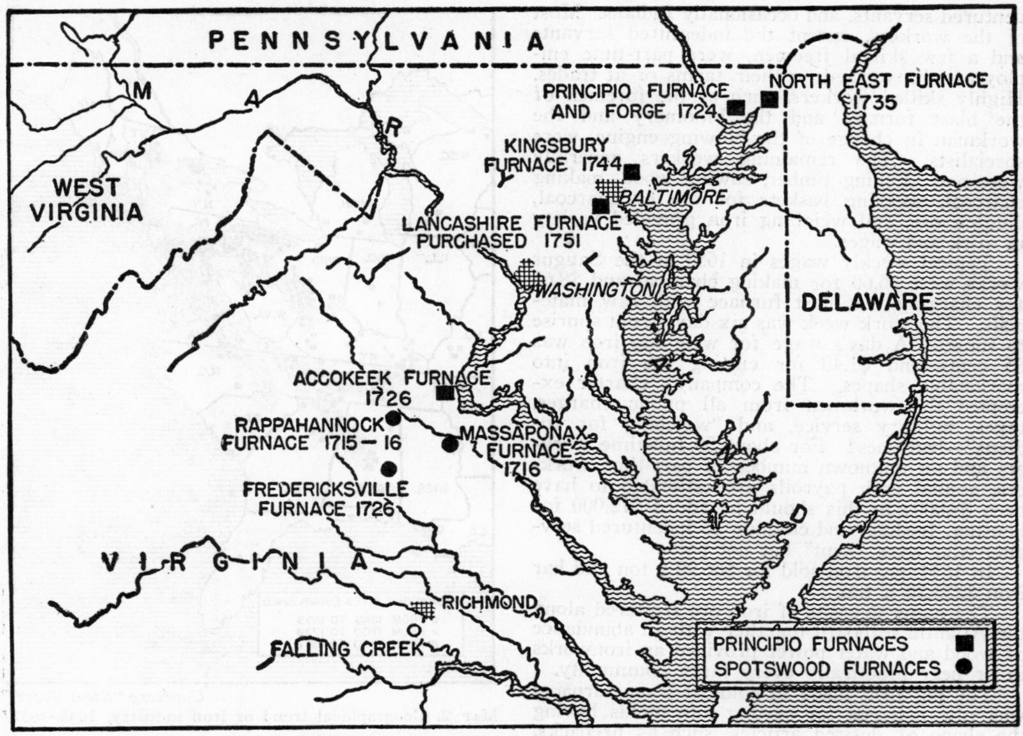

Map 1. Start of the Southern iron industry.

premacy and expand trade. Consequently, English ironworks were prohibited from using timber, suitable for shipbuilding, within 14 miles of the sea or any navigable river. England therefore became an importer as well as a producer of iron.

Had British ironworkers known that coal or coke could be used to smelt iron ore, the iron industry in colonial America might not have been established in the 17th century. English furnaces burned charcoal made from timber that grew near the furnaces; readily available deposits of coal were ignored.

As the English colonial trade policy was to import raw materials from the colonies and export finished products, it is very probable that English ironworks would have supplied the American colonies with iron and iron products during the 17th century, if English timber were plentiful or if the smelting of iron ore with coal or coke were known.

17th Century.—Although iron ore was discovered on an island off the shore of North Carolina in 1585, no colonial deposit was worked until 1608. Ore discovered in 1607 along the James River, Virginia was shipped by the East India Company to England in 1608. For the first shipment of 17 tons the colonists received £68.

By 1619, the Society of Southhampton Hundred (Southhampton Adventurers) planned to build three ironworks in Virginia, under patents granted by the Virginia Company, to smelt the ore that occurred in ponds and bogs. Falling Creek, 66 miles north of Jamestown, was the site of the first of these and the first American ironworks. (See Map No. 1.) On the day in 1622 when the equipment was scheduled to begin operation, Chief Opechancanough and his braves massacred the settlement of 348, save one—a boy who escaped to Jamestown. The society abandoned its plans to build the other ironworks. Little is known of the type of equipment at Falling Creek. From the length of time and number of workmen employed during the construction period, it is believed that the works included at least a blast furnace and possibly a forge Slag was found in the ruins, but no iron.

The first successful ironworks in America produced two grades of iron—cast iron and bar iron—and a few household articles such as hammer heads, pots, skillets, and scythes. It consisted of a blast furnace and forge or bloomery which were built in 1644 near Lynn, Massachusetts, in the village of Hammersmith on the banks of the Saugus River. It was also the first manufacturing establishment in the American colonies. Within three centuries, the industry established at Hammersmith spread throughout the country to supply the modern demand for iron and steel in 400 different chemical analyses and 200,000 kinds of products.

Although the Saugus ironworks was founded by The Company of Undertakers for the Iron Works under the leadership of John Winthrop, many colonial ironworks were established by individuals. The trend of the entrepreneur continued for two centuries. It persisted through the merging of iron and steel companies during the 19th and 20th centuries and is still evident in the leadership of the modern iron and steel producers.

The Saugus ironworks employed freemen, indentured servants, and occasionally Indians. Most of the workers, except the indentured servants and a few skilled freemen, were part-time employees who worked on their farms or at trades. Highly skilled workers, such as the foremen of the blast furnace and the bloomery and the workman in charge of the blowing engine, were specialists. The remaining workers generally were not. Felling timber, sawing wood, making charcoal, weaving baskets for ore or charcoal, digging ore, and weighing iron provided variety in work and wages.

Typical weekly wages in 1650 at the Saugus works were $6.60 for making charcoal and $8.65 for charging the blast furnace with raw materials. The work week was six days from sunrise to sunset. A day's wage for weighing iron was 85 cents and $1.40 for cutting the iron into marketable shapes. The company's charter exempted the workmen from all public charges, taxes, military service, and "watching for Indians"—bad ones! For about 50 full-time workers and an unknown number of part-time workers, annual cash payrolls are estimated to have been $8,000; to this should be added $12,000 for housing, feeding, and clothing 35 indentured servants who were "kept" but not paid.

In 1644, pig iron sold for $66.90 a ton and bar iron $223.20 a ton.

The many deposits of iron ore scattered along the Atlantic seaboard together with an abundance of wood and water power provided an ironworks in or near practically every large community.

The pig iron made in colonial blast furnaces was raw material for casting into molds having the shape of desired articles, such as firebacks, kettles, pots, salt pans, skillets, and stove parts; it was also raw material for the manufacture of one kind of "bar iron," the cast iron being refined on a hearth to remove excess carbon. The pig iron was usually cast into sand molds directly from the blast furnace. A cast-iron pot of about one-quart capacity, cast directly from the Saugus blast furnace, was the first product of colonial iron manufacture. The iron in the cast articles was known as cast iron. It contained too much carbon to be forged or hammered; hence it was cast.

The other type of colonial bar iron was obtained by heating iron ore with charcoal on a bloomery hearth without melting the extracted iron. This was a crude form of wrought iron. When carefully made, its content of carbon was sufficiently low so that the iron was malleable and ductile. (See article 5, *Wrought Iron.*) It was forged or hammered into bars, which in turn were reheated and hammered into axe heads and other tools, bolts, hinges, pot books, shutter hooks, agricultural implements, wagon tires, horseshoes and household articles.

During the third quarter of the 17th century, the colonial iron industry was concentrated in Massachusetts and Connecticut. During the last quarter, ironworks were established in northern New Jersey to smelt the magnetic iron ores that were richer than the New England bog and pond deposits.

18th Century.—In the first half of the 18th century, ironworks were built in New York, New Jersey, Pennsylvania, Delaware, Maryland, and Virginia. While Massachusetts and New Jersey were the leading iron producers during the last quarter of the 17th and first quarter of the 18th centuries, Pennsylvania rapidly challenged their lead. As in other colonies, lack of cheap transportation in Pennsylvania necessitated the location of ironworks near ore deposits, forests of oak, hickory, ash, chestnut or pine, water power, labor, food, and in many instances also near the market for cast iron and bar iron.

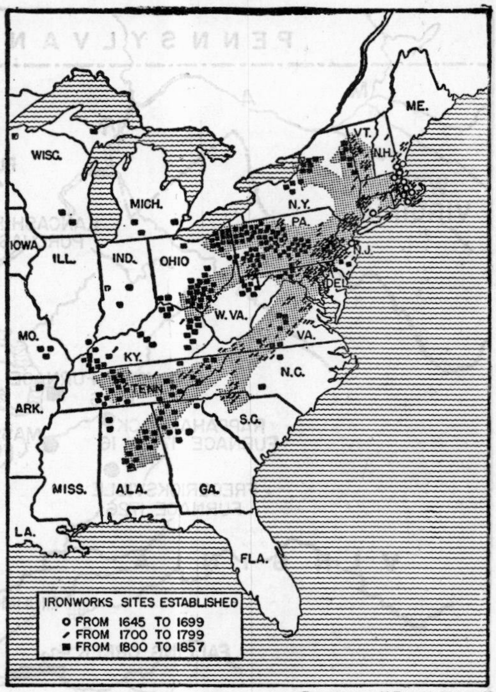

Courtesy "Steel Facts"

MAP 2. Geographical tren1 of iron industry, 1645–1857.

In the 18th century, the "iron plantation" flourished in Pennsylvania. An iron plantation was essentially a self-contained community, analogous to an Irish feudal barony. The proprietor of an ironworks in Pennsylvania, like the tobacco planter in Virginia, was in effect also the governor of the community that depended on him for its welfare as well as livelihood.

Some of the iron plantations embraced up to 10,000 acres. While none are now in operation, one has been restored by the National Park Service at Hopewell Village, six miles southeast of Birdsboro, Berks County, Pennsylvania.

Beginning with a bloomery forge in 1743, built by William Bird, the Hopewell Iron Plantation expanded until its population reached about 1,000. Also included in the plantation were an iron mine, about two miles from the center of the village, surrounding forests in which wood was cut and made into charcoal, charcoal storage houses, and an ore roaster. In addition, a dam with two head races and one tail race, a mill wheel, a blast furnace, a bridge over the west head race to the blast furnace, slag piles, a casting house, a blacksmith shop, a wheelwright shop, tenant houses, barns and farms, a spring house, a bake house, corn cribs, a combination office building and store, a carriage house, a schoolhouse and the proprietor's mansion were located there. The schoolhouse probably was also used as a church.

The products of the plantation were iron for industrial use and iron cast into stoves and hollow ware. Most of the products were shipped by boat or horseback to Philadelphia; the remainder were consumed on the plantation.

The geographical trend of the colonial iron industry to the west and south, as shown on Map No. 2, brought the first ironworks to Kentucky, Tennessee, and Georgia during the last quarter of the 18th century. While ironworks were in operation in both North Carolina and South Carolina prior to the Revolution, the date of erection of the first ironworks in North Carolina is not clearly established. (See Table 10.)

The westward and southward trend of the iron industry continued throughout the 19th century when ironworks were established in Alabama, Arkansas, California, Colorado, Illinois, Indiana, Iowa, Kansas, Michigan, Minnesota, Missouri, Ohio, Oregon, Texas, Utah, Washington, Wisconsin, and Wyoming.

Measurements of the ruins of colonial blast furnaces suggest that a typical furnace was a four-sided, hollow stone stack, about 20 feet high, from 20 to 24 feet square at the base and tapering to 16 to 20 feet square at the top. The interior egg-shaped cavity was lined with slate or other heat-resisting stone. The furnace was built against the side of a hill so that workmen could more easily charge it through the open top. They dumped in alternate layers of bog ore or magnetic ore, charcoal, and oyster shells or limestone. The lime in the shells or stone formed a slag with the unwanted materials in the ore.

Hot gases from the burning charcoal reduced the iron from the ore. Heat from the burning charcoal melted the metallic iron and fused the slag. As the charge of iron ore, charcoal, and flux (limestone or oyster shells) descended in the furnace, droplets of iron and slag collected in two layers in the hearth or bottom of the furnace, the lighter slag floating on the heavier iron. Periodically the slag and iron were drawn off through separate tap holes or "notches," the slag hole being at a higher level than the iron hole.

TABLE 1—SIGNIFICANT DEVELOPMENTS IN THE IRON AND STEEL INDUSTRY IN THE UNITED STATES, 1783–1864.

Date	Development
1783	Rolling mill built near Wilmington, Delaware, rolled Swedish and Russian iron to be made into cut-nails by a New York factory.
1787	Era Furnace, York County, South Carolina, built.
1788	Etna Furnace, York County, South Carolina, built.
1790	"Blue lump" iron ore discovered in Fayette County in western Pennsylvania by John Hayden of Haydentown.
1790	Tennessee's first ironworks, a bloomery, built at Embreville, Washington County.
1791	Kentucky's first blast furnace built on Slate Creek, Bath County, by Jacob Meyer; known as "Bourbon Furnace" or "Slate Furnace."
1794	Foundry cupola, a furnace for remelting pig iron to be cast into product form, patented by John Wilkinson and put in operation.
1800	Champlain iron mines opened in New York; provided ore for forges and furnaces erected later in Champlain district.
1801	Ironworks built at Willsborough Falls, Essex County, N. Y., by George Throop, Levi Highly, and Charles Kane, to make anchors, using Champlain iron ore.
1805	First successful foundry built in Pittsburgh, Pennsylvania, by Joseph McClurg, Joseph Smith, and John Gormley, later known as "McClurg's and McKnight's"; cast cannon, howitzers, balls and shells for Commodore Perry on Lake Erie and General Jackson at New Orleans, in War of 1812.
1806	Rolling mill built in Southfield, Delaware County, Pennsylvania.
1811	Pittsburgh Rolling Mill, Pittsburgh, Pennsylvania, first built in Pittsburgh.
1816	Wire fences made at White and Hazard Works, Chester County, Pennsylvania.
1816	First rolling mill to roll flat iron bars in United States erected in Plumstock, Pennsylvania, by Associate Judge Isaac Meason of Fayette County.
1818	Crucible steel plant built at Valley Forge, Chester County, Pennsylvania, by James Wood, John Parkins, and John Parkins, Jr. See entry opposite 1832.
1819	Bituminous coal first used in blast furnace experiment to make pig iron, at Bear Furnace, Armstrong County, Pennsylvania.
1819	Coke first used in blast furnace experiment to make pig iron, at Bear Furnace, Armstrong County, Pennsylvania; furnace built to use coke and cold blasts; steam driven blast too weak for successful operation. See entries opposite 1834 and 1835.
1819	Angle iron allegedly first rolled in United States by Samuel Leonard at Union Rolling Mill, Pittsburgh, Pennsylvania.
1820	Boiler plates first rolled by Dr. Charles Lukens at Brandywine Rolling Mill, Coatesville, Pennsylvania.
1826	"Malleable iron" made by Seth Boyden at Newark, New Jersey.
1826	Wire netting made by Charles Barnard at Norwich, Connecticut.
1827	Anthracite coal, mixed with charcoal or coke, experimentally used in blast furnace by Peter Ritmer in Perry County, Pennsylvania.
1827	Ohio's first blast furnace, Franklin Furnace, built in Green Township, Scioto County, 14 miles from Portsmouth, by Daniel Young, John Young, Jesse Y. Whitcomb, Josiah Merrill, John Hurd, and Martin Ruter, all from New Hampshire.
1828	Scioto Furnace built on Frederick Creek, 11 miles from Portsmouth, Ohio, by Gen. William Kendall; a blast furnace.
1830	Terne plate (iron coated with an alloy of lead and tin) allegedly made at Philadelphia, Pennsylvania. See Note 2 to this table.
1830	"Tee" or "T"-rail, for railroad tracks, invented by Robert L. Stevens, president of Camden and South Amboy Railroad, who also designed the hook-headed spike and other track accessories; first T-rails weighed 36 pounds per yard; 23 miles of railroad in operation in the United States.
1830	Furnace for welding pipe, first in United States, built in Philadelphia by Morris, Tasker & Morris.
1832	Crucible steel first made on a commercial

Date	Development
	scale in the United States at Cincinnati Steel Works, owned by Dr. William Garrard and brother; steel made from blister bar; product made into saws, axes, files, and blades of first McCormick reaper. Pin-making machine invented by John Ireland Howe of Derby, Conn.
1833	Anthracite coal in combination with "strong blast, preferably heated" patented by Dr. Frederick W. Geissenhainer, a New York City clergyman.
1834	Hot blast first "practical application" in a United States blast furnace, used in Oxford Furnace, New Jersey, by William Henry, manager.
1835	Coke first used successfully as a blast furnace fuel by William Firmstone in Mary Anne Furnace, Huntingdon County, Pennsylvania.
1835	Machine-made horseshoe patented by Henry Burden of Troy, New York.
1839	Anthracite coal used successfully in blast furnace by Benjamin Perry at Pioneer Furnace, Pottsville, Pennsylvania; and by David Thomas at Lehigh Crane Iron Company, Catasauqua, Pennsylvania.
1840	Wire rope first made in United States by John A. Roebling at Saxonburg, Butler County, Pennsylvania.
1840	Rotary squeezer to remove slag from "puddled iron" (wrought iron) invented and patented by Henry Burden of Troy, New York.
1842	Recovery of unburnt blast furnace gas for burning under steam boilers performed first at Greenwood Furnace, Orange County, New York, in accordance with method developed by Faber du Faur of Wasseralfingen, Germany.
1842	Connesville coke, made in western Pennsylvania, delivered by barge to foundries in Cincinnati.
1842–1845	Continuous rolling mill, first used to roll lead and copper pipe, rolled iron for first Morse telegraph wire installed between Baltimore and Washington.
1844	Lake Superior Iron Deposits first discovered by white men near eastern end of Teal Lake in northern Michigan by William A. Burt on September 16.
1844	Iron T-rails, 50 pounds per yard, made at Mount Savage Rolling Mill, Allegany County, Maryland.
1845	First wrought iron T-rail rolled in the United States at Montour Rolling Mill, Danville, Pennsylvania, in operation.
1845	Bituminous coal successfully used in blast furnace in Mercer County, Pennsylvania, and at Lowell, Mahoning County, Ohio.
1845	Railroad bridge of "Howe type truss," built by Richard B. Osborne at Manayunk, Pennsylvania, with cast iron top chord and web braces and wrought iron bottom chord and vertical web members.
1846	William Kelly at Suwanee Iron Works, Eddyville, Kentucky, observed that iron in a "finery" fire was heated by the blast of air without the aid of charcoal.
1847	Empire Furnace built in Vernon Township, Ohio, by Jefferson W. Glidden and Obadiah Glidden; a blast furnace.
1848	Andrew Carnegie, brother Thomas, and parents arrived in United States from Dunfermline, Scotland.
1852	Blowing engines built by David Thomas of Catasauqua, Pennsylvania, increased output of pig iron from blast furnaces.
1852	Lake Superior ore first used in a blast furnace at Sharpsville, Mercer County, Pennsylvania.
1855	Soo Canal, connecting Lake Superior and Lake Huron, built by Charles T. Harvey; of outstanding importance in developing the iron and steel industry in the United States.
1855	30-foot rails rolled at Cambria Iron Works, Johnstown, Pennsylvania.
1857	Converter process of steelmaking (known also as Bessemer process) patented by William Kelly of Eddyville, Kentucky.
1857[1]	Press first used to straighten rails.
1857	Continuous process of hardening and tempering music wire developed and patented by Ichabod Washburn of Worcester, Massachusetts.
1857	Chicago Rolling Mill, built to reroll iron rails, established in Chicago, Illinois, by Capt. E. B. Ward of Detroit.
1857	First Michigan iron ore railway, from deposits on Marquette range to Marquette on Lake Superior, completed.
1857	Three-high rolling mill invented by John Fritz, chief engineer and manager of the Cambria Iron Company's Johnstown works, Johnstown, Pennsylvania; one of the outstanding inventions of modern civilization.
1858–1859	Tin plate (iron coated with tin) made at Hussey's Copper Works, Pittsburgh, Pennsylvania. See note 2 to this table.
1859	Zinc made in experimental furnace by Joseph Wharton, manager of Lehigh Zinc Company, South Bethlehem, Pennsylvania; beginning of metallic zinc manufacture in the United States.
1859–1860	Cold rolling of iron and steel invented and patented by Bernard Lauth; an outstanding invention; Lauth was partner of B. F. Jones, founder of Jones & Laughlin Steel Corporation, Pittsburgh, Pennsylvania.
1861[1]	Continuous annealing, cleaning, and galvanizing of wire installed by Ichabod Washburn at Washburn and Moen Works, Worcester, Massachusetts; an English invention.
1862	Wrought iron and steel columns, used for bridges and other structures, invented by Samuel J. Reeves of Phoenix Iron Company, Phoenixville, Pennsylvania.
1864	Bessemer steel first made in the United States on a commercial scale by William F. Durfee, acting for the Kelly Pneumatic Process Company, at Wyandotte, Michigan.

The charcoal was burned by a blast of cold air which entered the furnace just above the hearth. A large pair of bellows, usually made of leather, was operated by a water driven wheel to supply the air or blast. Overshot water wheels in diameters up to 30 feet were used. A considerable area of land had to be flooded back of an iron-works dam, in some instances, to provide the volume of water and drop in height required for

[1] Approximate date.

[2] Terne plate and tin plate manufacture in the United States began on a large scale only after the McKinley Tariff Act became effective in July 1891.

water wheels. At the Saugus works, for example, about 1,000 acres were submerged. In northern colonies where freezing weather prevailed during the winter, ironworks were usually idle when the water wheel froze.

Several terms such as "bloomery," "forge," "finery," "refinery," "chafery," "ancony," "sowe iron," "pig iron," "bar iron," and "merchant bar" were in common use in the colonial iron industry. Some of these have persisted.

Bloomery, also spelled bloomary, has several distinct meanings. One type of furnace in which an iron "bloom" was made directly from iron ore was known as a bloomery or forge; it was also known as a block oven and block furnace. Bloomery also referred to an ironworks consisting of a forge, a hammer for working the bloom, and a blowing engine to supply air to the forge. Similarly, the term "forge" was used interchangeably with bloomery to include the equipment. Many ironworks had a heating furnace to reheat blooms as well as other iron products prior to pressing or squeezing under the hammer; bloomery as well as forge also included this furnace.

A refinery was a furnace, having a hearth similar to that in a bloomery furnace, in which pig iron from the blast furnace was placed in a charcoal fire to refine it into a malleable condition. In some refinery processes iron ore was also added to the hearth to assist in the refining. The main objective was to remove excess carbon which made the pig iron too brittle for working either hot or cold. The refinery was also called a charcoal finery or charcoal refinery. The product of a refinery was a chunk of plastic and nearly white-hot iron, called a half-bloom, which was placed on an iron anvil and pounded with an iron hammer to squeeze out the molten slag. The hammered half-bloom was reheated to a bright red color and rehammered to remove more slag. This operation yielded an "ancony," which was a thick bar, rectangular in cross-section, having a rough knob at each end. Ancony broadly applied to a bloom which had been partly worked under a hammer to the required width and thickness, except at the ends which were not hammered. It was an article of commerce.

If the ancony was further processed, it was placed in a chafery, a reheating hearth, and then hammered into bar iron, in dimensions up to 14 feet long, 2 inches wide, and ½ inch thick. When cut into convenient lengths, these bars were sold as merchant bars.

Although these bars were bought by blacksmiths, locksmiths, and even householders, they were frequently sold to peddlers and merchants. The term "merchant bar" was originally applied to a piece of iron that was sold from a peddler's wagon or over a merchant's counter. In the early part of the 18th century, an English pamphlet defined this term as "such shaped iron as is usually imported by the merchant, about inch and half or two inches broad and one-third thick, and squares of different sizes." The term later included bars of steel. During the 19th century, rolling mills were developed to roll iron into merchant bar sizes. When the larger mills were built to roll steel sections heavier than merchant bar sizes, the older mills continued to roll the smaller sizes of bars and were called merchant mills. Some sections of steel which are rolled today for general resale purposes are still known as merchant bars.

While the molten iron from many colonial blast furnaces was cast or run directly into molds having the form of hollow ware, a large amount of molten iron was also run into a main trough which led to smaller troughs. The solidified iron in the main trough was called sowe iron or sow iron, and that in the smaller troughs was known as pig iron, from the analogy of a sow with suckling pigs. Both sowe iron and pig iron were commercial products of the colonial blast furnace. The term "pig iron" has been retained to designate a class of iron made in the modern blast furnace.

Nail manufacture was extensively conducted in colonial homes, particularly in Massachusetts. In defiance of an English law which became effective in 1750, "slitting mills" were built in the American colonies to slit flat plates of iron into strips. These were made into nails in many colonial homes by adults and children during the winter and evenings, when little other work could be done, to augment the family income. The nails were made by inserting the iron strips into a vise or clamp and then shaping the head and point with blows from a hammer. Up to 2,000 small nails were made in a day by a skilled nailmaker. In some localities nails were so precious that colonial homes were burned to recover the nails when families were about to cross the Alleghenies in search of new farm lands or to join frontier settlements. Household nail manufacture continued until the invention of several nailmaking machines during the close of the 18th century. It is estimated that the machine invented by Jacon Perkins of Newburyport, Massachusetts, could produce 200,000 nails a day.

During the 131 years of the colonial iron industry, extending from 1644 to 1775, the principal consumers of iron and iron products were the householders, merchants, peddlers, ship chandlers, and metal craftsmen, such as gunsmiths, locksmiths and blacksmiths, in the vicinity of iron works. Lack of cheap transportation localized the iron industry.

There were no important colonial industrial consumers of iron although, when English laws and import taxes were favorable, considerable amounts of iron were exported to England. The first shipment of colonial bar iron to England was made in 1718 by the Principio Company from its works in Principio, Maryland. (See Map No. 1.) An import tax of two pounds, one shilling and six pence a ton was levied on the 3.5 tons in the shipment. This company was one of the main exporters of colonial iron. During 1750 it shipped 2,050 tons of iron to England. This amount represented two thirds of all colonial exports and one fifth of colonial iron production in that year.

The rapid growth of the colonial iron industry between 1715 and 1775 was not realized by the English Parliament, partly because reports from colonial governors were inadequate or incomplete and partly because the colonists did not publicize the nature and extent of their industry. Furthermore, England itself was divided on the desirability of expanding the colonial iron industry. English ironmasters, fearing competition, argued for a high tariff on pig iron and bar iron imported from the colonies. English manufacturers of iron wares, seeking cheap raw material, argued for colonial bar iron.

When Sweden fought Denmark, Hanover, Prussia, Russia, and Saxony in 1717, shipments of Swedish iron to England were suspended. In

1718, when shipments were resumed, English manufacturers sought another source of iron and looked to America. Their petitions to Parliament to increase the number of colonial ironworks started a long controversy that resulted in no parliamentary action until 1750.

In the meantime the depression of British industries in 1735 closed many factories. The contemporaneous arrival of bar iron from Maryland, Pennsylvania, and Virginia aggravated the controversy when it was found by English navy yard tests that the colonial iron was equal to the best grade of Swedish iron—the world's finest at that time. To complicate the controversy, the colonists were accused of depriving English industries of an important market in America because the colonists manufactured iron articles from their own iron!

After three decades of intermittent deliberation, the Parliament enacted a law which provided that after June 24, 1750 "no mill or other engine for slitting or rolling iron, or any plating forge to work with a trip hammer, or any furnace for making steel" should be built in the American colonies. Works of these types already built were permitted to continue in operation.

Enforcement of this law was the responsibility of colonial governors. They ordered the sheriffs to take a census in their respective counties to ascertain the status of the colonial industry. The census did not reveal the true status; the colonists did not cooperate, and the sheriffs were not sufficiently skilled in iron manufacture to identify what they saw in all cases. Census reports sent to the British Board of Trade indicated the following:

Connecticut—8 plating mills and 1 steel furnace;
Maryland—1 plating mill;
Massachusetts—2 slitting mills and 2 plating mills;
New Jersey—1 slitting mill, 1 plating mill, and 1 steel furnace;
New York—1 plating mill;
Pennsylvania—1 slitting mill, 1 plating mill, and 2 steel furnaces.

It is estimated that by 1775 the American iron industry had outstripped its British counterpart, as the colonists had an estimated 80 blast furnaces with an average capacity equal to or slightly larger than that of the 60 English blast furnaces, and an estimated 175 forges against a total of 135 in England and Wales.

The English parliamentary attempts to restrict the growth of the colonial iron industry were a minor but significant contributary cause of the War of Independence, as they united the majority of colonial ironworks owners and managers in support of the revolutionary movement.

The following signers of the Declaration of Independence were associated with the iron industry: as a lawyer, Charles Carroll of Carrollton was in close contact with Maryland's iron industry; Stephen Hopkins was part owner of the Hope Furnace, on the Pawtuxet River, Rhode Island, which made cannon and cannon balls during the Revolution; Philip Livingston was the son of the owner of a bloomery on Ancram Creek, Columbia County, New York; George Ross was a partner of Mark Bird in building the Mary Ann Furnace in West Manheim Township, York County, Pennsylvania, which cast shot and shell for the Continental Army; James Smith owned the Hellam Forge, later known as the Codorus Forge and Furnace, in York County, Pennsylvania; George Taylor worked in his youth as a "filler" at Durham Furnace, Bucks County, Pennsylvania, and later became sole lessee of this property; Durham Furnace was another outstanding supplier of iron for the Continental Army.

A score or more ironmasters and ironworkers, including Gen. Daniel Morgan, Gen. Nathanael Greene, and Col. Ethan Allen, served as officers under General Washington, whose father, Augustine Washington, was one of the owners of the Principio Company, the largest colonial iron producer.

While the estimated annual world output of iron climbed from 150,000 tons[1] in 1750 to 210,000 tons in 1775, the estimated annual output of colonial iron rose from 10,000 to 30,000 tons.

British regulation permitted shipment of iron from the American colonies only to Great Britain or its colonies until 1765, when shipments to Ireland were allowed. Nearly all of the American iron exported went to England; small amounts of pig iron and bar iron also went to Scotland.

Exports from the American colonies averaged 2,800 tons of pig iron and 570 tons of bar iron from 1730 to 1775. During this period the highest and lowest exports of pig iron were 5,303 tons in 1771 and 1,725 tons in 1730; bar iron exports were at a maximum of 2,222 tons in 1771 and at a minimum of 4 tons in 1748. Virginia and Maryland were important exporters of pig iron and Pennsylvania of bar iron; New England, New York, and the Carolinas also exported iron prior to the Revolution.

Colonial Steel Industry.—Very little steel was made in the colonial era of America; and until the Bessemer process was used in the 1860's only a small amount of steel in comparison with iron was made in the United States. The colonists relied mainly on England for steel.

It is believed that Samuel Higley made the first colonial steel at Simsbury, Connecticut, between 1725 and 1728; and that he used the cementation process.

The second steelworks appears to have been built in 1734 at Trenton, New Jersey, for the manufacture of edge tools. At least six steelworks had been built in Massachusetts, Connecticut, New Jersey, and Pennsylvania by 1750, the date beyond which the English parliamentary action prohibited the erection of new steelworks, slitting mills and plating mills in the American colonies. By 1776 steelworks had also been established in Rhode Island and New York. The product of the cementation process was not uniform in chemical composition or internal structure. Carbon was absorbed largely on the surface of the bar and only to a slight depth. The carbon content of the inner portion or "core" of the bar was much less than the maximum content of about 2 per cent carbon at the surface. The frequent presence of bands or threads of slag within the product also did not permit the steel to develop uniform properties. Blisters that formed on the surface gave this product its other name, "blister steel." In addition, it was expensive to make as it required considerable equipment and time for the relatively small output. Yet it served the demand for a material stronger and harder than iron which could be made into edge tools and firearms.

[1] Presumably long tons of 2,240 pounds each.

Iron and Steel Industry in the United States, 1783-1864.—*Iron.*—The westward and southward expansion of the iron industry from the northeastern and central seaboard states, which began in the latter part of the colonial era, continued throughout the 19th century. In 1800, ironworks were located in every one of the original 13 colonies and also in Maine, Vermont, Tennessee, Kentucky, and in that part of western Virginia which became West Virginia. (See Map No. 2.)

The arrival of the Industrial Revolution in America created new demands for iron in the manufacture of tools and machinery. The rapid rise of manufacturing in the northeastern part of the United States during the early 19th century was a major factor in the shift in economy of the country from agriculture to industry that persisted into the present century. Manufacturing in this area stimulated the expansion in capacity of existing ironworks and the erection of new works, particularly in Pennsylvania.

Lack of cheap transportation, however, continued to localize the making of iron largely in areas near markets for iron until the last half of the 19th century. Even in 1857, when several thousand miles of railroads were in operation, iron products were readily available only to the 500 communities in which ironworks were located. The majority of these communities were in Pennsylvania, Virginia, Ohio, Tennessee, New York, and Kentucky, in which 690 blast furnaces had been built; the remaining furnaces were in Maine, New Hampshire, Vermont, Massachusetts, Connecticut, New Jersey, Delaware, Maryland, North Carolina, South Carolina, Georgia, Alabama, Indiana, Illinois, Michigan, Wisconsin, and Missouri.

The iron industry during the first half of the 19th century was characterized more by expanded output than by improvements in technology, although many important technical advances were made as listed in Table 1. At the beginning of this era charcoal was the only fuel successfully used in American blast furnaces; at the end, charcoal, anthracite coal, bituminous coal and coke were employed.[1] Coke, hot blast and blowing engines were important technical advances in increasing the efficiency of blast furnaces and consequently the output of pig iron in this era. Rolling mills for bars, plates and rails, the process of cold rolling iron, the continuous annealing, cleaning and galvanizing of wire, and the making of wire rope were equally important developments in the manufacture of iron products. The first commercial manufacture of Bessemer steel in the United States during 1864 brought this era to a close.

The enormous increase in annual output of pig iron is the outstanding achievement of this era of the iron industry. The estimated production of pig iron and bar iron totaled 30,000 tons [2] in 1775 and 50,000 tons in 1800. Total production of pig iron alone in 1864 was 1,135,996 net tons (of 2,000 pounds each), of which 684,018 tons were made with anthracite coal, 241,853 tons with charcoal, and 210,125 tons with either bituminous coal or coke.

Two achievements in this era that made possible the industrial expansion of the last half of the 19th century and then its continuance through the first half of the 20th century were the discovery of the Lake Superior iron ore deposits and the building of the Soo (Sault Ste. Marie) Canal. A government surveyor, William A. Burt, discovered the first of the Lake Superior deposits in northern Michigan in 1844. A young scales salesman, Charles T. Harvey, envisioning Lake Superior ore in eastern furnaces, organized and managed the company which completed the 5,700-foot Soo Canal in 1855 to connect Lake Superior and Lake Huron. Without the rich ores of the Lake Superior district and without cheap transportation to utilize them, it is doubtful if the United States would have attained its present position as the leading industrial nation. A century after their discovery, the Lake Superior deposits are still among the richest and most extensive in the world; and through the Soo Canal more tonnage is annually transported than through any other.

Steel.—The manufacture of cemented steel which was practiced during the colonial era continued on a small scale during the first half of the 19th century. The output of cemented steel in 1810 was 917 long tons, as compared with 53,908 long tons of cast iron. By 1830, the annual capacity of the 14 steel furnaces in the United States totaled 1,600 tons. The introduction of the crucible process from England in 1832, as shown in Table 1, did not lead to any considerable increase in steel production. The Compromise Tariff of 1833 closed the first crucible steel plant in Cincinnati; and the tariffs of 1846 and 1857 gave no encouragement to this steelmaking method. The full development of this method occurred in the last half of the 19th century.

Neither the cementation process nor the crucible process could make steel cheaply or in large amounts. The small quantities of steel made by these processes were used mainly in tools, instruments, small arms, and machine parts. While many articles were made of cast iron, its use in structures and machinery was limited because it was brittle and weak in tension. The cast irons in modern use had not been developed. Consequently, the further industrial development of the United States awaited a steelmaking method that could satisfy the mounting demand for a cheap constructional material stronger than cast iron and bar iron.

The nearly simultaneous invention of the Bessemer process by Sir Henry Bessemer in England between 1854 and 1856 and of the Kelly pneumatic process by William Kelly in Kentucky between 1846 and 1857 provided a new and cheap steelmaking technique, now known as the Bessemer process. Each inventor blew air through molten pig iron to burn the excess carbon and other elements, the burning supplying the heat required to keep the metal molten. Each had to rely on others for technical improvements to make the process commercially workable. Each was an outstanding pioneer to whom the industry and mankind are indebted.

The Bessemer process provided the cheap, strong steel that made possible the great expansion in the building of railroads, bridges, new types of textile, printing, and other machinery, steel ships, telegraph lines, agricultural implements, pipelines, frameworks of buildings, and the infant, electrical industry. At the same time the widening demand for steel for small articles, ranging from bicycle spokes to safety pins, was supplied by Bessemer steel.

[1] Of the 243 modern blast furnaces in the United States on Jan. 1, 1946, 240 burned coke and 1 burned charcoal.

[2] Presumably long tons of 2,240 pounds each.

The flood of steel which poured from the converters in the last half of the 19th century began with the making of the first commercial heat of Bessemer steel in the United States by William F. Durfee at Wyandotte, Michigan. The Bessemer process has persisted as an important steelmaking method, despite the development of the open hearth process in the last half of the 19th century and the electric furnace process during the first decade of the 20th century.

Iron and Steel Industry in the United States, Since 1865.—While the technical advances in iron and steel manufacture were characteristic of American industry generally, they were overshadowed by the consolidation of iron and steel plants into combinations of companies during the last quarter of the 19th and first decade of the 20th centuries. Economies of operation resulting from consolidations generally resulted in lower prices of iron and steel.

The extensive development of transportation, by boat and rail, favored the consolidation of many of the existing companies into organizations that owned ore, coal, and limestone deposits, railroads and steamship companies, as well as completely integrated production units that controlled the quality of the product from the mine to the consumer.

Technological Progress.—The iron and steel industry in the United States grew rapidly after 1865 because it helped so many other industries to grow, a few of which are the railroad, petroleum, electrical, farm equipment, automobile, and machine tool industries. The development of each of these industries required more useful iron and steel products, new types of iron and steel, and lower costs of iron and steel.

Since 1865, new methods of working steel kept pace with new steelmaking methods. Technological development followed two paths, one mechanical and the other metallurgical. Methods of hot rolling steel into a variety of semifinished products, that in turn were rolled into rails, structural shapes and pipe, were put on an automatic basis. Knowledge acquired about the internal structure of steel permitted the development of continuous rolling mills to reduce steel to paper thickness. Hand methods of drawing wire were replaced by automatic processes that drew the many sizes and kinds of wire required by such diverse products as cables for suspension bridges and springs for typewriters. Methods of coating steel with cadmium, copper, lead, tin, and zinc were improved and mechanized, and the quality of the coatings was made more uniform. Development of methods of welding steel led to significant changes in design of many products in which steel assemblies were used.

The development of the open hearth and electric furnace for steelmaking required improved metallurgical and mechanical techniques. These in turn required better furnace refractories, more efficient methods of burning fuels, and sensitive and automatic devices for measuring temperature and controlling the chemical reactions in steelmaking and iron manufacture. The microscope opened the way to a better appreciation of the complex nature of commercial irons and steels; this resulted in the rapid development of methods of heat-treating iron and steel to enhance their properties. This line of investigation also led to the creation of a series of alloy steels and alloy irons containing elements added to obtain properties not present in conventional plain carbon steels or cast irons, such as extreme resistance to corrosion, elevated temperature, and repeated stressing.

One outstanding development problem concerned the beneficiation or enrichment of the lower grades of iron ore in the United States. The Lake Superior iron ore district, embracing the iron ranges in Minnesota, Wisconsin, and Michigan, produced 85 per cent of the ore consumed by the United States. The life of the high-grade deposits in these ranges was estimated in 1945 to be 20 years; and the known reserves, containing over 50 per cent metallic iron, were estimated at 500,000,000 gross tons.[1] From 1941 through 1945, the United States produced 482,055,313 gross tons of iron ore of which 409,834,624 gross tons came from the Lake Superior district. Tremendous deposits in the Lake Superior district, containing 30 to 50 per cent iron, were also worked. Ores from some of these deposits were blended with the high-grade ores, and others were beneficiated or concentrated by mechanical methods. But the cost of such beneficiation increased with the leanness of the ore. In 1945 there was also estimated to be 60 billion long tons of "taconite," a material containing from 20 to 35 per cent iron, in the Lake Superior district. Up to 1947 no commercially successful method had been developed to ultilize the taconite.

The estimated $9,200,000 research budget of the industry in 1936 was spent as follows: 40 per cent for improving the quality of steel; 20 per cent for developing new products; 18 per cent for reducing steelmaking costs; 12 per cent for finding new uses for steel; and 10 per cent for studying the markets for steel. The estimated 1935 budget of $8,100,000 represented 37 cents on every ton of finished products made by 42 steel companies having nearly 90 per cent of the steelmaking capacity. The 1929 estimated budget for research was $8,700,000. By 1939 the budget for research approximated $10,000,000.

The substantial annual expenditures for research on iron and steel are indirectly reflected in the $11,500 capital investment required to finance and maintain the average job for employees in 1936. For each employee the $4,700,000,000 total investment in the industry was represented as follows: raw material and manufacturing sites and equipment, $8,990; raw, semifinished, and finished materials and supplies, $1,580; other purposes, $930; or a total of $11,500.

Earnings and Net Income.—Earnings on capital invested in the iron and steel industry averaged 8 per cent from 1910 through 1919, 5.5 per cent in 1920–1929, and 1.8 per cent in 1930–1939. Earnings for the years 1941 through 1945 were 8.09, 5.63, 5.06, 4.70 and 4.89 per cent, respectively.

The annual net income of this industry during the ten-year period 1935 through 1944 averaged $179,317,281, which was 3.77 per cent of the average investment of $4,756,340,509. During the same period the sum of the federal, state, and local taxes annually averaged $326,487,114 or 6.87 per cent of the average investment.

Table 2 shows the investment, earnings, per cent earned on investment, net income, number of employees, wages and salaries, average hours worked per week, average earnings per hour of

[1] Of 2,240 pounds each.

employees, number of stockholders, cash dividends paid, and taxes for each year from 1936 through 1945, for this industry.

Wages.—The average hourly earnings of steelworkers in the United States were two to five times those of European steelworkers during 1937, according to International Labor Office data, as shown in Table 3.

TABLE 3—AVERAGE HOURLY EARNINGS OF STEELWORKERS DURING 1937

Country	Average hourly earnings
Belgium	$.17
England	.40
Germany	.345
France	.395
Italy	.20
Russia	.275
Sweden	.32
United States	.82

During 1944 the average hourly earnings in the iron and steel industry in the United States were $1.219, and in September 1945, they were $1.23. These figures do not include the earnings of salaried employees. A total of $2,282,371,932 in wages and salaries was paid to 773,419 employees in this industry during 1945. Average hourly earnings and total annual wages and salaries for the period 1936–1945 are shown in Table 2.

Safety.—The widespread application of science and technology to the iron and steel industry in the United States was accompanied by extensive programs of accident prevention. The continuous campaign against accidents, begun in 1905, made steel mills safer than the average home. National Safety Council records showed the steel industry in fourth place among the major industries in 1945. From 1908 to 1938 the frequency of steel mill accidents was reduced 90 per cent to 6.6 accidents per million man-hours worked; industrial plants generally averaged 13.9 accidents per million man-hours worked in 1938, in the United States.

About 22,000 manufacturing establishments, located in every state in the union, were direct customers of the iron and steel industry in 1938. They represented 13 per cent of the establishments reported by the *Census of Manufactures.* In addition, nearly 2,500 steel jobbers and warehouses were customers. The industry maintained about 1,200 district sales offices located in nearly 100 cities in 36 states during 1938.

Plant Obsolescence and Replacement.—The effect of science and technology on the iron and steel industry in the United States is evidenced by the abandonment or dismantling of 173 obsolete blast furnaces, 39 plants for producing steel ingots, and 144 plants for finishing iron and steel products between 1926 and 1938. In the same period the industry built 14 new blast furnaces, 12 steelworks, and 42 finishing plants, and also modernized remaining plants. The new blast furnaces averaged 2.5 times the capacity of abandoned furnaces and gave the industry an increased pig iron annual capacity of nearly 13,000,000 tons. At the end of 1938 there were a total of 222 blast furnaces. Their capacity was 37 per cent more than the furnaces existing in 1926. The 12 new steel ingot plants and the remaining modernized plants increased the ingot capacity over 19,400,000 tons a year. About 40 of the 144 discarded finishing plants were wrought iron plants, some as old as 50 years. One of the 42 new plants was a wrought iron plant. Annual capacity for finishing steel was increased by 15,000,000 tons in this period.

Prices of Iron and Steel.—The effect of science and technology is also evidenced by the lowering of prices and improvement in quality of iron and steel. Pig iron sold for $34 a gross ton[1] in 1839 and $21.49 in 1939. Hammered bar iron of 1839 (before tonnage steelmaking methods were developed) sold up to 4.5 cents a pound; stronger and more versatile steel bars sold up to 2.25 cents a pound in 1939. Steel rails in 1868, the second year of steel rail production in the United States, sold up to $174 a gross ton; in 1939 safer, stronger, and more durable rails sold at $40.00 a gross ton. Nails were cut from iron in 1839 and sold at $6.12 per keg of 100 pounds. Nails made from steel wire sold at $2.40 per keg of 100 pounds in 1939. Galvanized sheet iron sold up to 13 cents a pound in 1873; far superior galvanized sheet steel of 1939 sold for 3.5 cents a pound.

Average prices of a few important iron and steel products are shown in Table 4.

TABLE 4—AVERAGE ANNUAL PRICES OF IRON AND STEEL PRODUCTS

Product	1920	1930	1940	1944
Pig Iron, No. 2, Chicago, at furnace	$42.52	$18.47	$23.03	$24.00 (a)
Open Hearth Steel Rails, at mills in Pennsylvania	52.42	43.00	40.00	40.00 (a)
Open Hearth Steel Billets, at Pittsburgh	56.14	31.84	34.00	34.00 (a)
Wire Rods, at Pittsburgh	69.55	36.91	44.80	44.80 (a)
Tank Plates, at Pittsburgh	3.28	1.69	2.10	2.10 (b)
Structural Shapes, at Pittsburgh	2.95	1.69	2.10	2.10 (b)

(a) Per gross ton of 2,240 pounds. (b) Per 100 pounds.

Employment Created.—An analysis of employment created directly by iron and steel manufacture revealed an estimated total of 523,000 jobs in 1934, distributed as follows:

4,000 jobs in limestone quarrying
16,000 jobs in coke manufacture
33,000 jobs in ore mining
44,000 jobs in coal mining
83,000 jobs in rail and water transportation
343,000 jobs in iron and steel manufacture.

The estimated total number of jobs created directly by this industry in 1945 was 770,000. It was further estimated that this industry indirectly created 5,600,000 jobs in the plants of consumers of iron and steel.

Raw Materials for Iron and Steel Manufacture.—In 1940 this industry provided about 75 per cent of the total tonnage of raw materials it consumed annually, purchased nearly all of the remainder from domestic suppliers, and relied on foreign sources for less than 0.5 per cent. But

[1] Of 2,240 pounds.

TABLE 2—IRON AND STEEL INDUSTRY IN THE UNITED STATES INVESTMENT, INCOME, EMPLOYEES, PAYROLL, DIVIDENDS, ETC.

(Covering the consolidated organization results for all the affiliated interests comprehended within the parent companies rendering these reports)

	1945	1944	1943	1942	1941	1940	1939	1938	1937	1936
Total investment[1]	$4,416,651,055	$4,466,553,152	$4,502,759,774	$4,493,929,840	$4,405,263,785	$4,265,933,908	$4,192,352,268	$4,237,881,273	$4,281,264,890	$4,206,107,006
Total earnings before interest but after depreciation and depletion	216,167,415	210,040,232	227,942,774	253,099,280	356,366,357	321,222,100	184,163,631	20,109,275	264,383,189	190,770,303
Per cent earned on investment	4.89	4.70	5.06	5.63	8.09	7.53	4.39	0.47	6.18	4.54
Net income (after interest charges, depreciation and depletion)	179,653,823	179,834,150	200,754,185	221,229,926	327,328,012	281,227,778	147,467,945	14,879,461*	231,793,620	157,038,292
Number of employees (December)	773,419	869,000	958,284	937,968	868,351	719,902	659,194	529,364	613,747	625,936
Total wages and salaries for year	2,282,371,932	2,647,375,682	2,653,504,759	2,176,050,783	1,679,084,098	1,180,373,517	977,847,373	730,366,776	1,124,444,552	889,634,368
Average hours worked per week (all employees)[2]	44.2	46.3	42.8	39.2	38.8	36.7	35.6	29.1	37.3	41.6
Average earnings per hour (all employees)[2]	$1.295	$1.261	$1.181	$1.110	$1.016	$.915	$.908	$.914	$.877	$.784
Number of stockholders (December 31)	532,704	524,042	558,005	549,274	531,914	537,215	534,685	519,011	493,913	456,106
Cash dividends paid	137,796,931	139,013,769	148,749,156	152,715,862	166,747,989	137,868,878	72,380,910	48,951,644	151,144,769	109,240,183
Taxes										
Federal	246,565,588	447,560,831	488,021,875	654,382,330	470,245,993	127,275,756	53,703,391	22,601,720	80,812,509	40,685,219
State and local			129,097,262	121,721,855	120,684,504	98,047,198	89,248,904	76,004,677	88,273,501	65,163,866
Total	246,565,588	447,560,831	617,119,137	776,104,185	590,930,497	225,322,954	142,952,295	98,606,397	169,086,010	105,849,085
Per cent of industry represented by the companies reporting blast furnace capacity	89.8	90.8	93.3	93.4	94.2	94.2	94.7	94.0	92.6	93.6
Steelmaking capacity	87.9	89.0	91.6	92.1	92.5	92.5	92.7	92.6	92.9	94.1

[1] Average as of beginning and end of year.
[2] Covers only those employees who are directly engaged in the production and sale of iron and steel products.
* Deficit.
(*Annual Statistical Report, 1945.* American Iron and Steel Institute, copyright, 1946.)

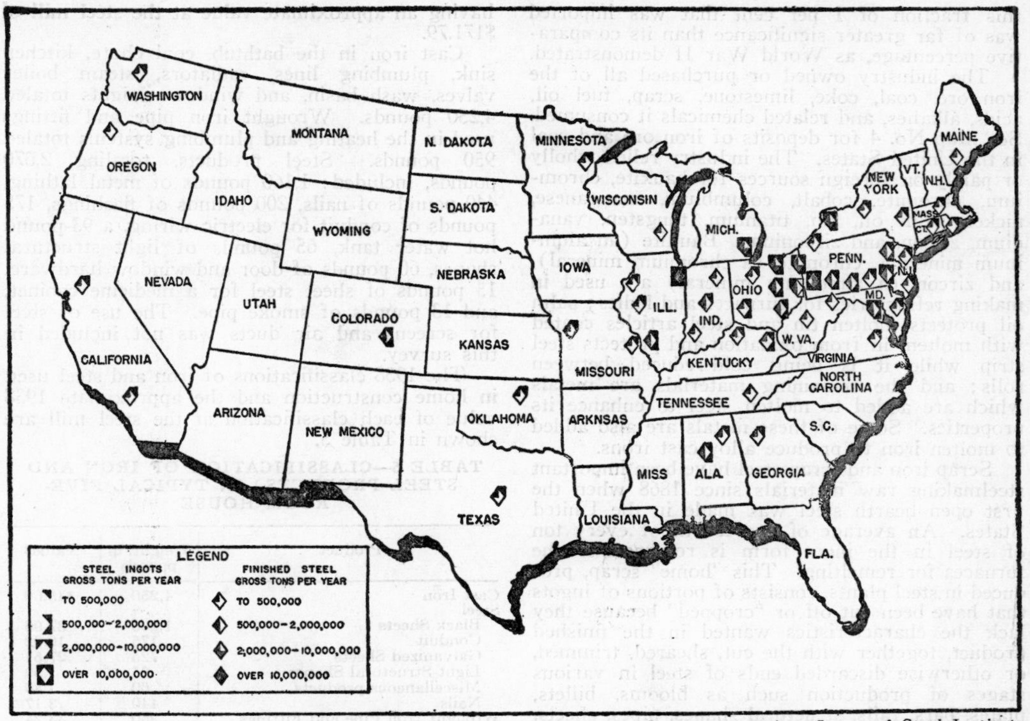

Courtesy American Iron and Steel Institute

MAP 3. Location of steel ingot and finished steel capacity in the United States as of 1937.

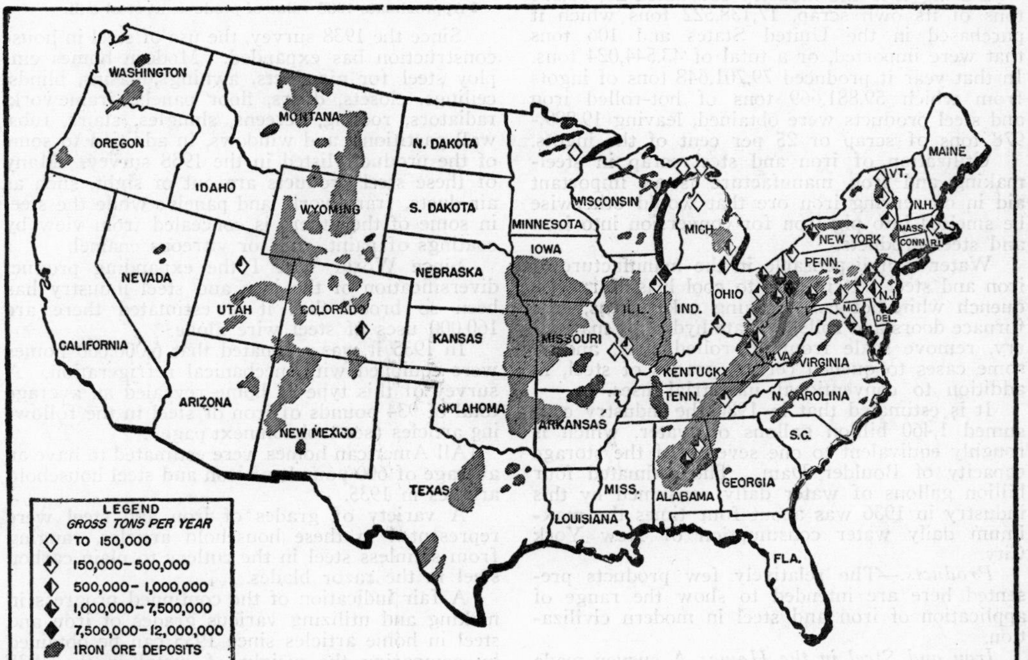

Courtesy American Iron and Steel Institute

MAP 4. Location of pig iron capacity and deposits of iron ore and coal in the United States as of 1937.

this fraction of 1 per cent that was imported was of far greater significance than its comparative percentage, as World War II demonstrated.

The industry owned or purchased all of the iron ore, coal, coke, limestone, scrap, fuel oil, acids, alkalies, and related chemicals it consumed. See Map No. 4 for deposits of iron ore and coal in the United States. The industry relied wholly or partly on foreign sources for bauxite, chromium, chromite, cobalt, columbium, manganese, nickel, palm oil, tin, titanium, tungsten, vanadium, zircon, and zirconium. Bauxite (an aluminum mineral), chromite (a chromium mineral), and zircon (a zirconium mineral) are used in making refractories for furnaces and ladles; palm oil protects molten tin and steel articles coated with molten tin from oxidation and protects steel strip while it is being cold-reduced between rolls; and the remaining materials are metals which are added to molten steel to enhance its properties. Some of these metals are also added to molten iron to produce alloy cast irons.

Scrap iron and scrap steel have been important steelmaking raw materials since 1868 when the first open hearth steel was made in the United States. An average of one fourth of every ton of steel in the ingot form is returned to the furnaces for remelting. This "home" scrap, produced in steel plants, consists of portions of ingots that have been cut off or "cropped" because they lack the characteristics wanted in the finished product, together with the cut, sheared, trimmed, or otherwise discarded ends of steel in various stages of production such as blooms, billets, plates, bars, rails, structural shapes, pipes, sheets, rods, and wire; and scrapped ingot molds and stools, open hearth doors and bottom plates, rails from the plant railroad, and discarded equipment.

During 1945 the industry consumed 26,405,396 tons of its own scrap, 17,138,522 tons which it purchased in the United States and 106 tons that were imported, or a total of 43,544,024 tons. In that year it produced 79,701,648 tons of ingots from which 59,881,669 tons of hot-rolled iron and steel products were obtained, leaving 19,889,-978 tons of scrap or 25 per cent of the ingots.

Utilization of iron and steel scrap in steelmaking and iron manufacture is an important aid in conserving iron ore that would otherwise be smelted into pig iron for conversion into iron and steel products.

Water is indispensable in the manufacture of iron and steel. It is used to cool blast furnaces, quench white-hot coke leaving coke ovens, cool furnace doors and rolls, operate hydraulic machinery, remove scale from hot-rolled steel, and in some cases to quench certain grades of steel, in addition to conventional industrial uses.

It is estimated that in 1936 the industry consumed 1,460 billion gallons of water, which is roughly equivalent to one seventh of the storage capacity of Boulder Dam. The estimated four billion gallons of water daily consumed by this industry in 1936 was about four times the maximum daily water consumption of New York City.

Products.—The relatively few products presented here are intended to show the range of application of iron and steel in modern civilization.

Iron and Steel in the Home: A survey made in 1938 of typical small homes indicated there were nearly four tons of cast iron and steel in a five-room house, exclusive of home furnishings, having an approximate value at the steel mill of $171.79.

Cast iron in the bathtub, coal chute, kitchen sink, plumbing lines, radiators, steam boiler valves, wash basin, and window weights totaled 4,250 pounds. Wrought iron pipe and fittings used in the heating and plumbing systems totaled 950 pounds. Steel products, totaling 2,670 pounds, included: 1,160 pounds of metal lathing, 440 pounds of nails, 200 pounds of flashings, 175 pounds of conduit for electric wiring, a 93-pound hot water tank, 65 pounds of light structural shapes, 60 pounds of door and window hardware, 15 pounds of sheet steel for a medicine cabinet, and 13 pounds of smoke pipe. The use of steel for screens and air ducts was not included in this survey.

The 1938 classifications of iron and steel used in home construction and the approximate 1938 value of each classification at the steel mill are shown in Table 5.

TABLE 5—CLASSIFICATION OF IRON AND STEEL PRODUCTS[1] IN TYPICAL FIVE-ROOM HOUSE

Product	Weight, in pounds	Value[2]
Cast Iron	4,250	$45.60
Steel		
Black Sheets	1,205	37.96
Conduit	175	10.92
Galvanized Sheets	725	27.51
Light Structural Shapes	65	1.59
Miscellaneous products	60	1.80
Nails	440	13.17
Wrought Iron Pipe and Fittings	950	33.24
Total	7,870	$171.79

1 Home furnishings excluded.
2 Approximate 1938 value of products at steel mill.

Since the 1938 survey, the use of steel in house construction has expanded. Modern homes employ steel for air ducts, awnings, basins, blinds, ceilings, closets, doors, floor panels, framework, radiators, roofing, screens, shingles, stairs, tubs, wall partitions, and windows, in addition to some of the products listed in the 1938 survey. Many of these steel products are out of sight, such as air ducts, framework, and panels; while the steel in some of the others is concealed from view by coatings of paint, zinc, or vitreous enamel.

Since World War I the expanding product diversification of the iron and steel industry has been so broad that it is estimated there are 160,000 uses of steel wire alone.

In 1935 it was estimated that 6,000,000 homes were equipped with mechanical refrigeration. A survey of this type of home revealed an average total of 934 pounds of iron or steel in the following articles (see table on next page).

All American homes were estimated to have an average of 600 pounds of iron and steel household articles in 1935.

A variety of grades of iron and steel were represented in these household articles, ranging from stainless steel in the cutlery to plain carbon steel in the razor blades.

A fair indication of the continued progress in making and utilizing various grades of iron and steel in home articles since 1935 can be obtained by comparing the weight of metal in the 1935 articles with the reduced weight of metal in the corresponding articles available in later years. Additional evidence of progress is the expanding

Article	Weight of iron or steel, in pounds
Stove	250
Mechanical refrigerator	190
Washing machine	150
Springs for 4 beds	109
Spring mattresses (4)	80
Steel bed	40
Bird cage and stand	25
Springs for upholstered chairs (4)	20
Bridge table	15
Davenport springs	15
Kitchen pans and utensils	10
Steel lamp	10
Electric iron	6
Garbage pail	5.5
Kitchen and table knives	2
Picture wire, ash trays, book ends, steel wool	2
Waste basket	2
Scissors (3 pairs)	1
Umbrellas (2)	1
Nail files, manicure sets, hairpins, needles, pins, compact, razor blades	0.5
Total	934

uses (now about 90) of various grades of steel in constructing and furnishing the homes built after World War II.

Tin plate: The quest for greater operating efficiency that characterized the iron and steel industry at the turn of the century led to the consolidation of 38 (a majority) of the tin plate plants and the consolidation of steel works and rolling mills during 1900 and 1901. In the first decade of the 20th century the manufacture of the sanitary tin coated container, or "tin can," was improved and can manufacture separated from food packing. A later consolidation of the major can companies increased the use of tin cans and the demand for tin plate correspondingly increased.

From the beginning of United States tin plate manufacture, important technical contributions were made by American technologists. The diameter and length of hot rolls were increased to obtain greater heat radiating efficiency and more pressure. In 1929 the cold reduction process of rolling steel into thin sheets was introduced. In 1939 about 75 per cent of the United States tin plate capacity was of this type, and by 1943 the entire production of tin plate was cold reduced. This method supplanted the older method of hot rolling.

Marked development of the electrolytic method of applying a very thin tin coating to steel occurred during World War II, following Japan's seizure of control of most of the world's tin supply. During 1942 and 1943 a total of 25 electrolytic tinning installations were built which resulted in lighter tin coatings on steel than could be applied by the conventional hot dipping method, and an appreciable saving of tin.

Another important technical advance was the development of methods of chemically treating the surface of sheet steel to improve the adhesion of organic enamels, lacquers, and paints. During 1942 and 1943, 18 units for producing chemically treated black plate were installed. This chemical treatment followed by an appropriate nonmetallic coating permitted the substitution of coated black plate for a limited number of parts of containers formerly made from tin plate.

Railroad Rails; Springs: Steel in the form of railroad rails is one of the highest quality because the service requirements are severe and the steel must be dependable. Yet steel in this form is sold on a tonnage basis at prices that average not over $50 a ton, or 2.5 cents a pound.

High quality steel in another type of product, such as some of the springs in watches and calculating machines, becomes extremely valuable in the form of the finished springs. When finished to such small sizes that they weigh only about twelve millionths of a pound each, these springs are worth about $100 a pound or $200,000 a ton.

Tubular Products: The production of coal gas for illumination in London during 1815 brought forth the first continuous iron or steel wrought or mechanically formed tubular product on record. Dissatisfied with the various kinds of cast iron, lead, bronze, and clay pipes then available, William Murdock threaded the ends of old musket barrels and screwed them together to form a pipeline for conveying coal gas.

The rapid rise of manufacturing and the equally rapid growth of public utility systems in the United States during the 19th century were heavily dependent on iron and steel tubular products that were butt-welded, lap-welded, or riveted. During the 20th century seamless tubing, and tubing formed by one of several methods of electric welding were developed. All of these types of steel tubing are currently made. Modern uses of steel tubing range from oil, gas, and water transmission lines up to two feet in diameter to hypodermic needles having an inside diameter approaching that of a human hair. Steel tubular products include circular, square, and rectangular cross sections.

A significant index of the importance of steel tubular products in this country during peacetime is the capacity of the iron and steel industry to make them. It was nearly 8,500,000 tons during 1936. Modern tubular products are made of various grades of iron and steel, including wrought iron and highly alloyed stainless steels, in the sizes and shapes required for pipes, tubes, tubing and casing that are used to convey gases, liquids, and solids and for a diversity of mechanical and structural purposes.

Steel in Use.—The oft-repeated claim that modern civilization in the United States rests on a base of steel is substantiated by the estimated 954 million tons of steel in use in this country in 1936. Calculations of the production and consumption of steel in the 70-year period ending 1935 indicate there were 17,000 pounds of steel in use in 1935 for every American. One of the heaviest concentrations of steel in 1936 was that on the island of Manhattan, a part of New York City, where the steel in buildings and transportation facilities was estimated at 27,000,000 tons. From 1900 to 1930 the amount of steel in use in the United States increased at an average rate of about 440 pounds a year, rising from 2,600 pounds per capita in 1900 to 15,940 pounds in 1930. Some of the steel produced before 1900 is still in use. The bulk of the 24,000 tons of steel in the Brooklyn Bridge was rolled in 1883; many steel-framed buildings constructed in the 19th century are still standing, and part of the 38,500,000 tons of steel rails in service in 1936 were laid prior to 1900.

Transportation.—One out of every five tons of freight hauled by American railroads in 1937 represented shipments of raw materials to plants of the iron and steel industry or shipments of finished products from these plants, which totaled

212,000,000 tons. Three million cars were required to transport nearly 162,000,000 tons of iron ore, coal, limestone, and steel scrap, the major raw materials consumed by the industry, to iron and steel plants. Shipments to customers of pig iron and finished steel products, totaling nearly 50,000,000 tons, represented 1,342,000 carloads.

Cooperative Research.—The joint cooperative efforts of the iron and steel industry and other industries to improve the quality of steel for specific purposes or to create new uses for steel are characterized by discoveries that often extend the usefulness of steel to many industries. Typical of such joint effort is the work of the iron and steel industry and the automobile industry, begun in 1920, in manufacturing sheet steel that can be severely deformed to take the shape and provide the smooth surface of mass-produced articles such as automobile bodies and fenders.

The creation of strong and ductile thin sheets of steel that could be shaped to exact and intricate contours without breaking, the preservation of the smooth surface of the steel after assuming the shape of the body or fender, and the uniformly high quality of the steel required for uninterrupted operation of the forming presses were three of several extremely difficult technical problems that demanded solutions.

Presses in automobile factories are designed to operate on precise clearances that necessitate extreme uniformity of deforming or "drawing" properties in the steel sheets. When a sheet is placed on the forming die and the press comes down with one blow, a perfect automobile body member is expected. Should a single sheet fail to shape properly, not only is the sheet ruined but the press is out of production until the sheet is removed and any resulting damage or readjustment of the press is repaired or made. This means loss of production of bodies, which if significant in amount would result in failure to meet assembly schedules.

Joint research and development work, going back to changes in steelmaking operations and forward to full-scale experiments on deforming sheets into body members, provided satisfactory steel for this use. This investigation also threw additional technical light on the manufacture and behavior of steel that extended its usefulness to deep-drawn or spun steel for vitreous porcelain enameled containers, steel that is drawn and porcelain enameled for stoves and refrigerators, and drawn steel products that are coated with zinc or tin.

Wrought Iron.—Modern wrought iron is iron of high purity containing many minute threads of iron silicate slag which give this grade of iron its characteristic fibrous appearance. (See WROUGHT IRON.)

While wrought iron was a forerunner of steel, having been used in Egyptian nails and hasps prior to 1600 B.C., it has not been completely replaced by steel or other metallic materials. The ductility corrosion resistance and resistance to repeated stresses are distinctive properties of wrought iron that provide markets for this metal in the form of bars, pipes, pipe fittings, plates, and sheets that are used in buildings, gas, oil and water lines, petroleum refineries, and transportation equipment.

The corrosion resistance of wrought iron is attributed to the barrier effect of the slag threads, which may amount to 250,000 threads per square inch of cross section; the resistance to repeated stresses is attributed to the homogeneity and ductility of the iron.

Production of wrought iron in the United States totaled 49,835 tons in 1942. Eight companies manufactured wrought iron in the United States in 1945.

Malleable Iron.—Malleable iron is an alloy consisting principally of iron and carbon, which is hard and brittle when cast but is made tough and ductile by heat treatment. Malleable iron resists heavy and repeated impacts and some types of corrosive conditions, is easy to machine, and can be made in a variety of product forms or "castings." (See article 6, *Malleable Iron.*)

Extensive research in the United States produced the modern grades of malleable iron which have many uses in the construction of machinery, railroad equipment, automobiles, agricultural implements, and anchor chain. There were 155 malleable iron foundries in operation during 1942 in the United States. The annual production of pig iron for conversion into malleable iron is shown in Table 6.

TABLE 6—PRODUCTION OF MALLEABLE PIG IRON, IN TONS

States	1945	1944	1943	1942	1941
Indiana, Illinois, Michigan, Minnesota	975,818	940,885	896,212	902,500	1,042,486
Ohio	842,957	919,164	930,850	942,915	890,304
Massachusetts, New York, Pennsylvania	531,301	634,610	566,179	554,105	484,347
Total	2,350,076	2,494,659	2,393,241	2,399,520	2,417,137

(*Annual Statistical Report, 1945*, American Iron and Steel Institute, 1946.)

Cast Iron.—Cast iron, which is mostly iron with a small amount of carbon and a few other elements, has been manufactured for approximately six centuries. It contains too much carbon to be worked by rolling or forging and hence must be cast into the form of the product. During the 20th century the manufacture of cast iron was so improved that it became widely used in a variety of chemical compositions and grain structures, both as plain cast iron and as alloy cast iron. Modern cast irons are extensively used in cylinder blocks for automobile engines, pipe for water and gas mains, foundations for machines, bath tubs, wash basins, radiators, toys, book ends, garden benches, lamp posts, fireplugs, stair treads and in other product forms for which it is technically and economically suitable. There were 3,337 iron foundries in the United States in 1942. The annual production of pig iron for remelting to produce iron castings is shown in Table 7. The annual output of iron castings, however, is over twice the tonnage shown in Table 7 because the great majority of the foundries in the United

TABLE 7—PRODUCTION OF FOUNDRY PIG IRON, IN TONS

States	1945	1944	1943	1942	1941
Maryland, Virginia, Kentucky, Tennessee, Alabama	1,156,756	1,076,370	958,509	1,297,393	1,409,334
Massachusetts, New York, Pennsylvania	585,431	565,603	599,066	770,792	702,391
Michigan, Minnesota, Indiana, Illinois, Colorado, Utah, California	368,537	383,309	370,440	322,776	466,972
Ohio	138,163	165,399	131,486	155,569	182,130
Total	2,248,887	2,190,681	2,059,501	2,546,530	2,760,827

(*Annual Statistical Report, 1945,* American Iron and Steel Institute, 1946.)

States remelt about seven tons of scrap for every three tons of pig iron.

Ferroalloys.—Ferroalloys is the term applied to an alloy of iron and some other element or elements (carbon excepted) when such an alloy is to be used as a raw material in the manufacture of ferrous materials such as irons and steels. Ferroalloys normally contain an amount of carbon equal to or greater than the carbon content of pig iron, but low-carbon ferroalloys are also commercially available. The part played by iron in a ferroalloy is a secondary one; it serves simply as a vehicle for carrying the desired alloying elements.

Modern ferroalloys include: ferrocolumbium, ferrochromium, ferromanganese, ferromolybdenum, ferrophosphorus, ferrosilicon, ferrotitanium, ferrotungsten, ferrovanadium, high-nitrogen ferrochromium, silicomanganese, spiegeleisen, and zirconium alloys. Some of these are made in the blast furnace, some in the electric furnace, and some are made by the thermit process. Those commonly made in the blast furnace are spiegeleisen, ferromanganese, ferrosilicon, and ferrophosphorus. As a class they are indispensable ingredients in the manufacture of modern irons and steels.

Some ferroalloys are used because they impart to steel specific properties when dissolved in the iron base of steel or when they combine with carbon wholly or in part to form carbides. Others are used because of their beneficial effects in ridding steel of impurities, or in rendering the impurities harmless. A third group is used to counteract harmful oxides or gases in steel. The elements of this latter group do not remain in the steel to any great extent after solidification, but are merely fluxes or scavengers of undesirable impurities. Some ferroalloys fall into more than one of the above groups. Similarly, ferroalloys are added to molten iron in the manufacture of plain cast iron, alloy cast iron, and malleable iron. In addition to the foregoing ferroalloys, other alloying and scavenging agents have been developed to perform similar functions.

Steel Castings.—Molten steel may be cast into molds to form ingots, which are rolled or forged into intermediate shapes and further worked into product forms; or it may be cast into molds having the shape of a particular article generally known as "steel castings." Some products of large size, shape or intricate design are made exclusively of steel castings; others are also made of cast iron or forged steel. Some steel castings are 30 to 40 feet long, several feet wide or high and weigh up to 125 tons; others weigh less than 100 pounds.

In some applications steel castings are now being replaced by steel plates which are automatically torch cut to shape and then welded to form the desired products. This is an important development because the cost of producing steel castings is relatively high in comparison with that of rolled steel.

TABLE 8—ANNUAL CAPACITY AND ANNUAL PRODUCTION OF STEEL FOR CASTINGS, IN THE UNITED STATES

Year, as of Jan. 1	Capacity, in tons	Production, in tons
1946	505,040	
1945	558,210	310,831
1944	567,190	399,585
1943	549,490	451,510
1942	570,630	485,755
1941	571,260	404,892
1940	668,595	332,822
1939	590,913	261,275
1938	592,234	155,848
1937	594,317	280,616

(*Annual Statistical Report, 1945,* American Iron and Steel Institute, 1946.)

There are about 325 foundries in the United States in which steel castings are made. Table 8 shows the annual capacity and annual production of steel for castings.

Byproducts.—Research uncovered markets for steelmaking slags once dumped on vacant land. Three types of blast furnace slags are now established byproducts. Crushed and screened slags are used as beds for oyster culture, concrete aggregate, covering material for roofs, filtering medium for sewage-treatment beds, and railroad ballast. Granulated slag, made by forcing water or steam against molten slag, is used in cement building blocks, filtration of water and gas, highway and railroad embankments, insulation for concrete highways, and as a soil corrective agent. "Mineral wool," made by blowing air into a stream of molten slag, is used as insulation against heat and cold in industrial and home construction. Slag from open hearth furnaces in the Southern states is a valuable conditioner for soils deficient in lime and phosphorus. A survey of these byproducts showed that 4,250,000 tons of the 15,000,000 tons of blast furnace slag produced in 1936 found byproduct applications; 2,000,000 tons were granulated, and of these 500,000 tons were used in cement manufacture. Of the smaller output of open hearth slag, 36,000 tons were used as soil conditioner.

Mothballs, sulfa drugs, and automobile tires are only three of a long list of household and industrial goods made wholly or in part from chemicals produced during the manufacture of coke used in the blast furnace. Gases and voltatile liquids driven from the coal during the "baking" of the coal in the coke ovens are recovered and refined, at least partially, at the coke plants. In most instances the partially refined chemicals are sold to chemical manufacturers for further processing, but some chemicals are produced in usable form by the steel industry.

During 1944, coal in coke ovens of the iron and steel industry yielded an estimated 551,000 tons of ammonium sulphate, an important source of nitrogen for commercial fertilizers, 127,000 gallons of benzol, 3,900,000 gallons of naphtha, 40,000 tons of naphthalene, and such other chemicals as pyridene, phenol, and toluol, as well as large quantities of tar and gas.

Benzol in various grades is used to produce varnishes, wood stains, and enamels; and waterproofing materials and solvents. In chemically pure form it is a base for such drugs as hydroquinon and acetanilid; it goes into dyestuffs like aniline and indigo and into the preparation of DDT.

Naphtha is a solvent in making rubber goods and an important dry cleaning agent. Naphthalene is the chief ingredient of mothballs; it is also used in insecticides and dyes. Pyridine is employed in preparing sulfa drugs, vitamins, and water repellents. Phenol is a raw material for one type of plastics and aspirin. Toluol enters into the manufacture of TNT, synthetic rubber, varnish removers, and aviation gasoline. Styrene, a derivative of benzene, is the base of the buna S type of synthetic rubber. Coke oven byproducts also aid in the making of vanilin, a synthetic flavoring, atabrine, saccharin, nylon, shoe polish, and some perfumes.

Geographical Center of Steel Capacity in the United States.—The geographical center of the industry's steel capacity in 1944 was about one mile south of the village of Dola (population 212) in Hardin County, Ohio. Dola has no steelmaking furnaces, the nearest being 60 miles eastward at Mansfield, Ohio. The closest industrial community is Lima, 22 miles west of Dola.

"Steel capacity" is the annual output in tons of steel ingots and steel for castings, assuming full operation of steelmaking equipment except when being periodically repaired. Actual production of ingots and steel for castings rarely equals the capacity during peacetime because some of the furnaces are idle for lack of orders. The ratio of steel production to steel capacity, expressed in per cent, is called the "operating rate." Even with full operation, the output of finished steel products does not average over 70 to 74 per cent of the ingot output, the remainder being removed during manufacture, as previously explained.

The geographical center is computed on the "tons times miles" basis. In this method of computation, a city within the United States is arbitrarily selected as a reference point. The north or south and the east or west distances of each steelmaking community from the reference point are determined. The capacity in tons of each community is multiplied by the appropriate north or south distance in miles, and a similar calculation is made for the east or west distance. After other calculations are made, the latitude of the geographical center is established so that the "tons times miles" of the communities to the north of the center equals the "tons times miles" of the communities to the south. Another group of calculations establishes the longitude of the geographical center. The intersection of the latitude and longitude determines the location of the center, which is also known as the "center of gravity" of the industry.

The westward and southward trend of the industry which began during the colonial period has continued, as shown on Maps Nos. 2 and 3. The migration of the geographical center of steel capacity accordingly shifted, as shown in Map No. 5. By 1874 the center was in Juniata County in central Pennsylvania. The expansion of the Pittsburgh steelmaking area and the development of the Chicago area were mainly responsible for

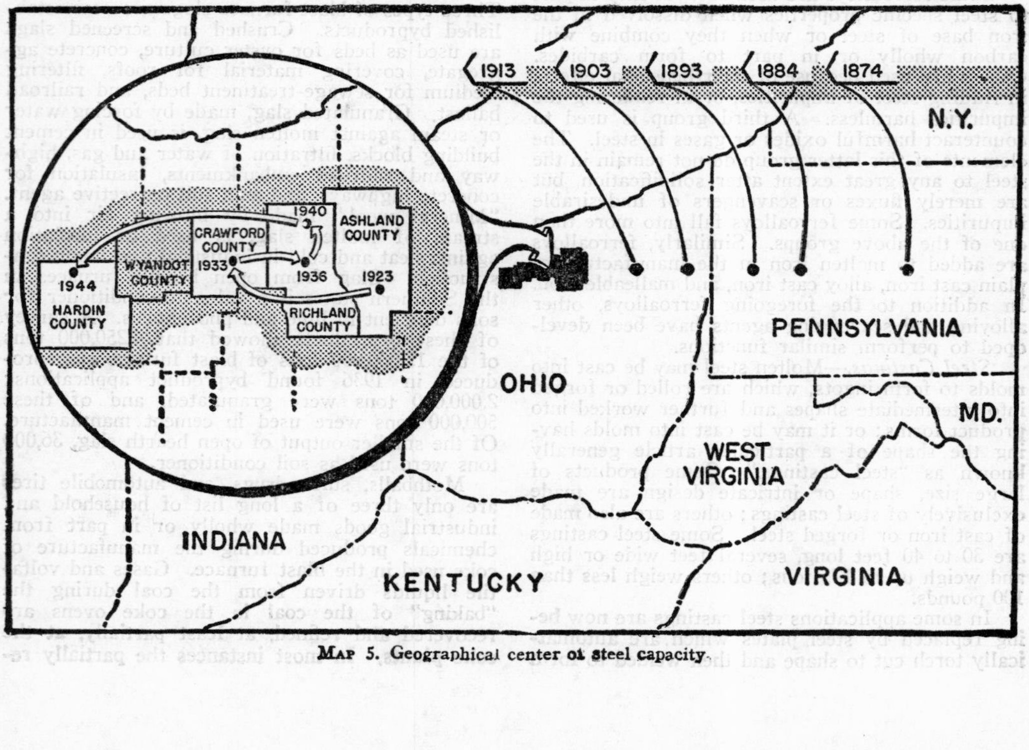

MAP 5. Geographical center of steel capacity.

the migration of the center in nearly a straight line westward.

From 1933 to 1940 the westward trend of the center was reversed, when additional steelmaking capacity was installed eastward of the center. The resumption of the westward trend from 1940 to 1944 resulted from the increase in capacity of plants in the western and Pacific Coast states during World War II.

In 1945 there were 36 companies having one or more blast furnaces and 83 companies having one or more steelmaking furnaces, not including subsidiary company units of the larger producers of iron and steel.

The location of the steel ingot and finished steel products capacities of the United States are shown on Map No. 3; the location of the pig iron capacity of the United States is shown on Map No. 4. See also Tables 9, 10, 11, and 12 for United States coke, pig iron and ferroalloys, ingots and steel for castings, and finished products capacities.

World War II.—After France succumbed to Germany in June 1940, the United States government began to plan the expansion of the iron and steel industry and other industries as a basic part of the defense program. As a "fighting" war became increasingly probable, the government accelerated its planning so that the major part of the plan for increasing the capacity of the iron and steel industry was completed by November 1941.

The magnitude of the wartime expansion of facilities for iron and steel manufacture between Jan. 1, 1940 and Jan. 1, 1945, may be seen from the figures in Table 13.

Nearly one billion dollars was spent by the industry in modernizing steelmaking facilities before Hitler invaded Poland. Had the demand existed, the industry could have produced over 80 million tons of steel in 1939, instead of the 52,800,000 tons actually made. At the request of the president, an additional 15 million tons of capacity were added in new facilities and exten-

TABLE 9—UNITED STATES IRON AND STEEL INDUSTRY—ANNUAL CAPACITY OF COKE OVENS, AS OF JAN. 1, 1945

Coke

	Beehive		Other		
	No. of ovens	Annual capacity (N. T.)	No. of ovens	Annual capacity (N. T.)	Total annual capacity (N. T.)
Companies:					
Alan Wood Steel Company			151	600,000	600,000
American Rolling Mill Company			85	516,000	516,000
Sheffield Steel of Texas			47	252,000	252,000
TOTAL			132	768,000	768,000
Bethlehem Steel Company			1,713	8,358,000	8,358,000
Colorado Fuel and Iron Corporation			192	675,000	675,000
Crucible Steel Company of America			100	474,000	474,000
Donner-Hanna Coke Corporation			216	1,200,000	1,200,000
Eastern Gas and Fuel Associates			204	1,112,000	1,112,000
Ford Motor Company			183	1,260,000	1,260,000
Geneva Steel Company	500	300,000	252	971,100	1,271,100
Inland Steel Company			419	2,143,400	2,143,400
Interlake Iron Corporation			437	1,564,500	1,564,500
International Harvester Company			133	600,000	600,000
Jones & Laughlin Steel Corporation	240	252,000	663	3,180,000	3,432,000
Kaiser Company, Inc.			90	340,000	340,000
Koppers Company, Inc.			49	435,000	435,000
Lone Star Steel Company			78	375,000	375,000
National Steel Corporation:					
Great Lakes Steel Corporation			130	996,600	996,600
Weirton Coal Company	136	120,000			120,000
Weirton Steel Company			156	920,000	920,000
TOTAL	136	120,000	286	1,916,600	2,036,600
Pittsburgh Coke & Chemical Company			70	500,000	500,000
Pittsburgh Steel Company	510	420,000	74	500,000	920,000
Republic Steel Corporation	296	215,000	961	4,863,000	5,078,000
Sloss-Sheffield Steel & Iron Company	94	60,600	120	678,000	738,600
Tennessee Products Corporation			44	268,000	268,000
United States Steel Corporation:					
American Steel & Wire Company			270	1,309,000	1,309,000
Carnegie-Illinois Steel Corporation			2,817	14,405,600	14,405,600
Columbia Steel Company			56	209,500	209,500
Frick Coke Company, H. C.	2,918	2,078,750			2,078,750
National Tube Company			208	1,050,000	1,050,000
Tennessee Coal, Iron & Railroad Company			509	2,809,500	2,809,500
TOTAL	2,918	2,078,750	3,860	19,783,600	21,862,350
Wheeling Steel Corporation			253	1,175,000	1,175,000
Woodward Iron Company			228	885,490	885,490
Youngstown Sheet and Tube Company			580	2,784,000	2,784,000
GRAND TOTAL	4,694	3,446,350	11,488	57,409,690	60,856,040

(*Directory of Iron and Steel Works of the United States and Canada*, American Iron and Steel Institute, 24th ed., 1945, page 496.)

sion of existing facilities. The 1945 steelmaking capacity of 95,500,000 tons was roughly four times that of the German prewar capacity and seven times that of Japan. United States capacity was expanded when the demand for steel was accelerating for war products and when the industry had to make steel to expand its own facilities. (To build a steel plant of one million tons annual capacity requires about 240,000 tons of steel!) It is estimateα that the maximum annual steelmaking capacity of Germany (including satellite and conquered countries) was 60 million tons, and that of Japan was 13 million tons.

World War II necessitated: the conversion of many existing rolling mills and units of heat treating and fabricating equipment to make war products; the building of new facilities to provide

TABLE 10—UNITED STATES IRON AND STEEL INDUSTRY—ANNUAL CAPACITY OF BLAST FURNACES, AS OF JAN. 1, 1945

Blast Furnaces

	Pig Iron		Ferroalloys		
	No. of stacks	Annual capacity (N. T.)	No. of stacks	Annual capacity (N. T.)	Total annual capacity (N. T.)
Companies (coke furnaces):					
Alan Wood Steel Company	2	454,800			454,800
American Rolling Mill Company	5	1,320,000			1,320,000
Sheffield Steel of Texas	1	274,000			274,000
TOTAL	6	1,594,000			1,594,000
Bethlehem Steel Company	29	9,474,000	2	180,000	9,654,000
Brooke Iron Company (E. & G.)	1	137,890			137,890
Colorado Fuel and Iron Corporation	(a) 4	798,000			798,000
Crucible Steel Company of America	2	532,000			532,000
Eastern Gas and Fuel Associates	1	176,400			176,400
Ford Motor Company	2	504,000			504,000
Geneva Steel Company	4	1,450,000			1,450,000
Globe Iron Company			1	84,000	84,000
Inland Steel Company	6	2,236,000			2,236,000
Interlake Iron Corporation	6	1,332,500			1,332,500
International Harvester Company	3	719,710			719,710
Jackson Iron & Steel Company			1	90,000	90,000
Jones & Laughlin Steel Corporation	13	4,080,000			4,080,000
Kaiser Company, Inc.	1	388,800			388,800
Koppers Company, Inc	2	465,000			465,000
Lavino & Company, E J			2	72,000	72,000
Lone Star Steel Company	1	399,850			399,850
National Steel Corporation:					
Great Lakes Steel Corporation	3	1,100,000			1,100,000
Hanna Furnace Corporation	3	594,180	1	120,000	714,180
Weirton Steel Company	3	1,200,000			1,200,000
TOTAL	9	2,894,180	1	120,000	3,014,180
New Jersey Zinc Company			2	134,400	134,400
Pittsburgh Coke & Chemical Company	1	291,600			291,600
Pittsburgh Ferromanganese Company	1	127,000			127,000
Pittsburgh Steel Company	2	554,000			554,000
Republic Steel Corporation	21	6,324,000			6,324,000
Sharon Steel Corporation	1	173,600			173,600
Shenango Furnace Company	2	417,300			417,300
Sloss-Sheffield Steel & Iron Company	3	386,470	1	36,800	423,270
Struthers Iron & Steel Company	1	181,440			181,440
Tennessee Products Corporation			(b) 3	21,900	21,900
Tonawanda Iron Corporation	1	171,000			171,000
United States Steel Corporation:					
American Steel & Wire Company	6	1,429,400			1,429,400
Carnegie-Illinois Steel Corporation	53	17,342,700	3	221,900	17,564,600
Columbia Steel Company	1	199,200			199,200
National Tube Company	9	3,042,400			3,042,400
Tennessee Coal, Iron & Railroad Company	9	2,332,400	(c)	31,600	2,364,000
TOTAL	78	24,346,100	3	253,500	24,599,600
Wheeling Steel Corporation	5	1,275,000			1,275,000
Wickwire Spencer Steel Company	2	390,000			390,000
Woodward Iron Company	3	526,170			526,170
Youngstown Sheet and Tube Company	12	3,456,000			3,456,000
TOTAL (coke furnaces)	225	66,256,810	16	992,600	67,249,410
Companies (charcoal furnaces):					
McCrossin Engineering Company	(d) 1	(d) 27,000			
Newberry Lumber & Chemical Company	1	32,000			32,000
Tennessee Products Corporation	1	32,480			32,480
TOTAL (charcoal furnaces)	2	64,480			64,480
GRAND TOTAL	227	66,321,290	16	992,600	67,313,890

(*Directory of Iron and Steel Works of the United States and Canada*, American Iron and Steel Institute, 24th ed., 1945, pages 502, 503.)

TABLE 11—UNITED STATES IRON AND STEEL INDUSTRY—ANNUAL CAPACITY FOR INGOTS AND STEEL FOR CASTINGS, AS OF JAN. 1, 1945

	Open Hearth		Bessemer		Electric and Crucible		
	No.	Annual capacity (N. T.)	No.	Annual capacity (N. T.)	No.	Annual capacity (N. T.)	Total annual capacity (N. T.)
Kinds:							
Open hearth—basic	940	82,611,730					82,611,730
Open hearth—acid	50	1,559,860					1,559,860
Bessemer			41	5,874,000			5,874,000
Electric					259	5,455,890	5,455,890
Crucible					3	3,800	3,800
TOTAL	990	84,171,590	41	5,874,000	262	5,459,690	95,505,280
Steel for castings included above		336,130				222,080	558,210
Companies:							
Alan Wood Steel Company	7	550,000					550,000
Allegheny Ludlum Steel Corporation	7	260,160			24	200,200	460,360
American Locomotive Company	6	181,000					181,000
American Rolling Mill Company	25	2,268,000			4	54,000	2,322,000
Sheffield Steel Corporation	6	480,000					480,000
Sheffield Steel of Texas	5	466,000					466,000
TOTAL	36	3,214,000			4	54,000	3,268,000
Andrews Steel Company	7	413,100					413,000
Atlantic Steel Company	3	154,000					154,000
Babcock & Wilcox Tube Company					2	50,400	50,400
Baldwin Locomotive Works	5	169,910			(a) 1	20	169,930
Barium Steel Corporation	3	50,000					50,000
Bethlehem Steel Company	133	12,242,000	6	500,000	9	158,000	12,900,000
Borg-Warner Corporation					3	24,000	24,000
Braeburn Alloy Steel Corporation					2	20,730	20,730
Byers Company, A. M.	2	75,000			2	75,000	150,000
Cabot Shops, Inc.					1	12,000	12,000
Carpenter Steel Company					6	74,880	74,880
Central Iron & Steel Company	6	336,000					336,000
Colonial Steel Company					1	7,020	7,020
Colorado Fuel and Iron Corporation	16	1,272,000					1,272,000
Columbia Tool Steel Company					2	6,600	6,600
Connors Steel Company					2	60,000	60,000
Continental Steel Corporation	5	364,000					364,000
Copperweld Steel Company					9	321,360	321,360
Crucible Steel Company of America	17	980,400			(b) 32	(b)527,280	1,507,680
Defense Plant Corporation					(c) 3	200,000	200,000
Disston & Sons Company, Henry					2	25,000	25,000
Edgwater Steel Company	4	140,170					140,170
Empire Steel Corporation	6	348,540					348,540
Erie-Forge Company	3	80,000					80,000
Erie Forge & Steel Company	2	128,950					128,950
Firth-Sterling Steel Company					5	17,540	17,540
Follansbee Steel Corporation	4	126,000					126,000
Ford Motor Company	10	770,100			31	197,320	967,420
Geneva Steel Company	9	1,283,400					1,283,400
Granite City Steel Company	13	703,200					703,200
Harrisburg Steel Corporation	3	100,750					100,750
Heppenstall Company	2	39,880			2	2,680	42,560
Hinderliter Tool Company					1	9,450	9,450
Inland Steel Company	36	3,400,000					3,400,000
International Harvester Company	11	900,000					900,000
Isaacson Iron Works					2	104,400	104,400
Jessop Steel Company					7	50,000	50,000
Jones & Laughlin Steel Corporation	40	4,098,000	5	918,000	2	8,400	5,024,400
Joslyn Manufacturing & Supply Company					3	37,500	37,500
Judson Steel Corporation	3	76,500					76,500
Kaiser Company, Inc.	6	720,000			1	30,000	750,000
Keystone Steel & Wire Company	3	302,400					302,400
Kilby Steel Company	2	54,000			2	20,400	74,400
Knoxville Iron Company					2	38,000	38,000
Laclede Steel Company	4	326,020					326,020
Latrobe Electric Steel Company					4	12,000	12,000
Lukens Steel Company	13	624,000					624,000
Mesta Machine Company	4	85,000			1	20,000	105,000
Midvale Company	8	430,830			6	88,540	519,370
National Forge & Ordnance Company					3	25,000	25,000
National Steel Corporation:							
Great Lakes Steel Corporation	16	2,050,000					2,050,000
Weirton Steel Company	12	1,850,000	(d) 2				1,850,000
TOTAL	28	3,900,000	(d) 2				3,900,000
National Supply Company					3	45,900	45,900
Newport News Shipbuilding & Dry Dock Co.					2	7,500	7,500

TABLE 11—UNITED STATES IRON AND STEEL INDUSTRY—ANNUAL CAPACITY FOR INGOTS AND STEEL FOR CASTINGS, AS OF JAN. 1, 1945—*Continued*

	Open Hearth		Bessemer		Electric and Crucible		Total annual capacity (N. T.)
	No.	Annual capacity (N. T.)	No.	Annual capacity (N. T.)	No.	Annual capacity (N. T.)	
Northwest Steel Rolling Mills	....	....	....	....	2	32,400	32,400
Northwestern Steel & Wire Company	....	....	....	....	3	321,000	321,000
Oregon Steel Mills	....	....	....	....	2	60,000	60,000
Pacific States Steel Corporation	....	....	....	....	5	88,820	88,820
Phoenix Iron Company	5	231,400	....	....	....	....	231,400
Pittsburgh Steel Company	12	1,072,000	....	....	....	....	1,072,000
Republic Steel Corporation	81	7,956,000	2	700,000	20	1,135,000	9,791,000
Roeblings Sons Company, J. A.	9	253,000	....	....	....	....	253,000
Rotary Electric Steel Company	....	....	....	....	2	170,000	170,000
Rustless Iron & Steel Corporation	....	....	....	....	6	114,000	114,000
Sharon Steel Corporation	6	600,000	....	....	1	36,000	636,000
Simonds Saw & Steel Company	....	....	....	....	3	21,600	21,600
Stanley Works	3	188,280	....	....	....	....	188,280
Texas Steel Company	....	....	....	....	2	22,320	22,320
Timken Roller Bearing Company	3	201,600	....	....	6	345,600	547,200
Union Electric Steel Corporation	....	....	....	....	2	25,200	25,200
United States Steel Corporation:							
American Steel & Wire Company	26	1,732,400	....	....	....	....	1,732,400
Carnegie-Illinois Steel Corporation	259	21,738,700	(e)12	1,956,000	14	448,300	24,143,000
Columbia Steel Company	13	594,900	....	....	3	32,700	627,600
National Tube Company	15	2,250,000	5	894,000	....	....	3,144,000
Tennessee Coal, Iron & Railroad Company	20	2,660,000	(d) 3	....	....	....	2,660,000
TOTAL	333	28,976,000	20	2,850,000	17	481,000	32,307,000
Universal-Cyclops Steel Corporation	....	....	....	....	4	54,120	54,120
Vanadium-Alloys Steel Company	....	....	....	....	3	11,910	11,910
Vulcan Crucible Steel Company	....	....	....	....	2	9,600	9,600
Washburn Wire Company	3	60,000	....	....	....	....	60,000
Wheeling Steel Corporation	21	1,624,000	2	336,000	....	....	1,960,000
Wickwire Brothers, Inc.	3	38,000	....	....	....	....	38,000
Wickwire Spencer Steel Company	4	180,000	....	....	....	....	180,000
Worth Steel Company	7	460,000	....	....	....	....	460,000
Youngstown Sheet and Tube Company	33	3,432,000	4	570,000	....	....	4,002,000
GRAND TOTAL	990	84,171,590	41	5,874,000	262	5,459,690	95,505,280

(a) Crucible furnace; (b) includes 2 crucible furnaces, one of which is idle, annual capacity 3,780 tons; (c) electric furnaces at South Chicago and East Chicago, Ind. (described under the respective plants of Republic Steel Corporation and Youngstown Sheet and Tube Company); (d) used in melting charge for open hearth furnaces; (e) includes 3 convertors used only in melting charge for open hearth furnaces.

(*Directory of Iron and Steel Works of the United States and Canada*, American Iron and Steel Institute, 24th ed., 1945, pages 509, 510, 511.)

the enormous tonnages of steels of many grades which went into plates for ships, barges, and tanks, armor plate, cast armor, guns, shells, tanks, trucks, and the specialized power plants that propelled the various types of fighting craft; and the production of structural steel, piping, and auxiliary products needed by plants constructed specifically for war purposes.

Mills that rolled the thin sheets for automobiles, refrigerators, and stoves were rapidly converted to roll plates of various thicknesses for the shipbuilding program and other urgent war programs. The quick conversion of these mills from sheet to plate assured the shipbuilding industry of an adequate supply of plates. There was no time to build conventional plate mills, or steel with which to construct them. In a single year, 1943, these mills delivered 12,967,000 tons of steel plates to the shipbuilders. This amounted to 19.3 per cent of all steel delivered to consumers in that year. The previous record on plates was established in another war year, 1918, when 5,734,000 tons were delivered.

Mills that drew wire for farm fence, coat hangers, and hairpins made barbed wire, communication wire, and wire for springs to control, guide, or operate nearly everything that moved in the war.

Alloying elements that went into flatirons, waffle irons, and toasters were switched to armor plate, truck axles and other war products. Stainless steels became surgical instruments and firewalls of airplanes, instead of cutlery and sinks. The great variety of steels that formerly supplied the automobile industry went into vehicles of all types to keep the armed forces on the move.

Steelmakers developed a steel containing specific amounts of and kinds of alloying elements, normally made in the electric furnace, that designers needed for crankshafts of powerful aircraft engines. This new aircraft-quality steel was the cleanest and soundest ever made—it had the smallest amounts of unwanted elements and compounds. It was what the designers wanted. Steelmakers also succeeded in making this steel in large tonnages in the op hearth furnace.

Early in World War II it was evident there was not enough of the alloying elements to make the many grades of conventional alloy steels. Japan had cut off the supply of tungsten from China. Tungsten was an important ingredient of armor piercing shot and of tools for machining steel and other metals. The metallurgists temporarily solved the tungsten shortage by using other alloying elements such as molybdenum and chromium, but a shortage developed in chromium also. The vicious circle that started with the shortage of chromium eventually affected nearly all of the alloying elements. The metallurgists had to develop new steels. Prewar research showed them how.

They did so by adding very small percentages

TABLE 12—UNITED STATES IRON AND STEEL INDUSTRY—ANNUAL CAPACITY FOR FINISHED PRODUCTS, AS OF JAN. 1, 1945

Total Finished Products

Products	Annual capacity (N. T.) Steel	Iron	Total
Structural shapes—Heavy	9,118,150	....	9,118,150
Steel piling—Rolled	436,400	....	436,400
Plates—Sheared	8,297,950	30,000	8,327,950
" —Universal	2,143,070	70,000	2,213,070
" —Strip mill	7,048,000	....	7,048,000
Rails—Standard (over 60 pounds)	3,684,000	....	3,684,000
" —All other	365,000	....	365,000
Splice bars and tie plates	1,857,960	....	1,857,960
Track spikes	353,000	12,000	365,000
Hot rolled bars other than tool steel bars	22,685,360	326,080	23,011,440
Concrete reinforcing bars included above	6,885,110	....	6,885,110
Tool steel bars—Rolled or forged	286,670	....	286,670
Cold finished bars	3,191,960	....	3,191,960
Skelp	5,968,800	310,000	6,278,800
Rounds for seamless tubes	4,869,300	....	4,869,300
Pipe and tubes—Butt weld	2,226,620	47,000	2,273,620
" " " —Lap weld	825,400	90,000	915,400
" " " —Electric weld	1,606,050	....	1,606,050
" " " —Spiral weld	88,000	....	88,000
" " " —Gas weld	17,000	....	17,000
" " " —Seamless	3,546,400	....	3,546,400
" " " —Conduit included above	183,000	....	183,000
" " " —Mechanical tubing included above	1,240,800	....	1,240,800
Wire rods	7,338,340	....	7,338,340
Wire—Plain	5,863,610	....	5,863,610
" —Galvanized	1,709,760	....	1,709,760
" —Nails and staples	1,266,870	....	1,266,870
" —Barbed	557,125	....	557,125
" —Woven fence	1,101,600	....	1,101,600
" —Bale ties	139,840	....	139,840
Black plate—Chemically treated	399,000	....	399,000
Tin and terne plate—Hot dipped	3,758,850	....	3,758,850
Tin plate—Electrolytic	2,231,850	....	2,231,850
Sheets—Hot rolled	17,434,820	....	17,434,820
" —Cold rolled	6,883,460	....	6,883,460
" —Galvanized	2,849,130	....	2,849,130
" —Long terne	319,400	....	319,400
Strip—Hot rolled	8,145,690	....	8,145,690
" —Cold rolled	3,736,310	....	3,736,310
" —Galvanized	127,000	....	127,000
Car wheels—Rolled steel	315,400	....	315,400
Axles	398,170	....	398,170
Bolts, nuts, rivets and washers	450,200	....	450,200

(*Directory of Iron and Steel Works of the United States and Canada*, American Iron and Steel Institute, 24th ed., 1945, page 521.)

of several alloying elements to produce many grades of steel formerly made of larger amounts of one or two alloying elements. These new steels were more sensitive to heat-treatment than the prewar alloy steels, but the products formed

TABLE 13—WORLD WAR II EXPANSION OF CAPACITY OF FACILITIES FOR PRODUCING COKE, PIG IRON, FERROALLOYS MADE IN BLAST FURNACE, STEEL INGOTS AND STEEL FOR CASTINGS, BETWEEN JAN. 1, 1940 AND JAN. 1, 1945

Capacity expanded	Capacity expansion, in net tons (2,000 pounds)	Per cent increase in capacity over Jan. 1, 1940	Per cent financed by: United States government	Industry
Coke	13,410,646	18.9[1]	37.3	62.7
Pig iron and ferroalloys made in blast furnace	15,412,064	27.7	45.1	54.9
Steel ingots and steel for castings	15,323,522	18.8	45.3	54.7

[1] Estimated.

from the new steels performed very satisfactorily in use. The new steels, which conserved critical alloying elements, were known as national emergency steels.

World War II consumed gigantic amounts of metals and alloys, particularly iron and steel, in the shape of products which are produced in relatively minute amounts during peacetime. Between the opening of the war with Japan on Dec. 7, 1941, and the surrender of Germany on May 8, 1945, the United States iron and steel industry consumed more raw materials than during eight years of peace, from 1932 through 1939. To keep the armed forces supplied and to provide essential civilian articles, 415 million tons of steel were made from 1940 through 1944.

World Trade in Iron and Steel.—During World War II the United States became the leading exporter of iron and steel because the demands of war far exceeded the capacities of all countries except the United States. Prior to this war the United States supplied only a small part of the iron and steel products that entered into world trade. Wages paid to workers in the iron and steel industries of European countries were appreciably lower than those paid to workers in the United States industry (see Table 3). Furthermore, government subsidizing of the iron and steel industries in European countries, together with subsidizing of transportation companies, en-

TABLE 14—EXPORTS OF IRON AND STEEL[1] FROM THE UNITED STATES, 1941–1945, CLASSIFIED ACCORDING TO PRODUCTS

Net tons[2]

	1945	1944	1943	1942	1941
Semi-Finished and Finished Products:					
Ingots, blooms, billets, slabs, sheet bars	203,745	1,107,450	2,065,054	2,196,423	2,314,559
Wire rods	109,334	123,837	176,140	145,251	187,326
Skelp	146,535	158,312	117,201	170,876	162,524
Iron bars	3,166	3,609	4,411	5,098	7,261
Concrete reinforcement bars	267,080	259,458	75,638	74,917	170,368
Steel bars, cold finished	65,783	140,782	223,501	153,008	90,750
Other steel bars (excluding alloy)	214,903	141,774	167,460	223,452	226,728
Alloy steel bars	51,769	113,051	165,534	180,382	92,186
Welding rods, electric	14,134	14,590	9,375	5,112	6,961
Boiler plate	25,543	24,107	45,090	38,818	26,998
Other plates, not fabricated	188,478	306,887	686,066	402,567	378,171
Plates, fabricated, punched or shaped	197,929	21,162	24,244	12,699	25,391
Iron sheets, black	12,835	19,125	4,709	14,941	24,553
Steel sheets, black	742,423	793,019	708,181	795,380	480,077
Galvanized sheets	174,746	97,120	73,168	100,411	118,987
Strip steel, cold rolled	57,761	88,551	98,452	129,168	71,618
Strip steel, hot rolled	84,667	128,565	105,972	92,854	107,322
Tin plate and tagger's tin	470,638	466,500	394,768	588,779	387,847
Terne plate (including long ternes)	57,050	43,014	69,851	76,607	9,685
Structural shapes, plain		165,971	184,750	191,127	295,023
Structural shapes, fabricated	343,790	55,222	46,721	33,236	56,818
Frames and sashes	24,511	466	1,613	960	2,185
Sheet piling		13,693	3,723	3,278	7,911
Rails, 60 pounds per yard and over		218,849	257,884	166,706	119,544
Rails, less than 60 pounds per yard	327,994	63,368	42,173	77,755	38,544
Rails, relaying		34,149	10,911	11,697	11,453
Splice bars and tie plates		77,014	57,730	30,997	19,423
Frogs and switches	129,570	36,715	20,979	13,297	2,334
Railroad spikes		17,827	14,443	6,854	7,724
Railroad bolts, nuts, and washers		4,811	5,350	3,751	2,481
Car wheels, tires and axles	83,956	84,196	109,050	56,526	40,793
Seamless black pipe	21,576	45,199	84,058	61,287	45,806
Seamless casing and oil line pipe	256,770	162,362	80,265	85,681	111,567
Seamless boiler tubes	52,728	73,272	53,851	28,266	50,780
Welded black pipe	64,326	63,731	93,550	115,274	86,246
Welded galvanized pipe	57,292	68,294	54,206	42,775	80,505
Welded casing and oil line pipe	*	36,672	33,657	51,145	30,381
Welded boiler tubes	*	6,182	3,752	2,054	2,738
Riveted pipe and fittings	61,793	115,050	133,192	116,588	34,884
Plain wire	59,620	72,144	92,410	69,172	79,740
Galvanized wire	61,929	70,357	72,318	79,988	63,649
Barbed wire	29,290	28,839	22,885	162,344	79,422
Woven wire fencing	5,879	4,199	3,365	2,224	5,537
Woven wire screen cloth	3,768	5,126	3,742	5,013	5,760
Wire rope and strand	31,607	43,274	42,157	37,061	22,595
Wire nails	31,263	45,585	43,985	23,907	56,808
Other wire and manufactures	22,203	31,543	26,661	22,615	20,468
Horseshoe nails		1,751	1,338	795	3,130
Tacks	11,079	2,218	1,955	487	1,561
Other nails, including staples		8,053	5,930	6,583	8,668
Bolts, nuts, rivets and washers, except railroad	41,805	59,234	57,407	33,646	49,720
Forgings	28,522	52,652	73,744	67,810	69,113
Horseshoes	1,681	319	163	71	851
TOTAL	4,841,471	5,819,250	6,954,733	7,017,713	6,403,474
Other Finished Products:					
Housing boilers	...	...	...	...	...
Tanks, complete and knocked down	33,371	44,696	29,987	27,945	21,775
Metal lath	†	642	537	1,156	3,282
Insulated wire and cable	†	...	...	...	...
Tin and galvanized hollow ware	†	2,134	1,006	1,618	3,007
Tin cans, finished or unfinished	†	7,325	9,588	10,278	14,581
Enameled household ware	...	...	...	...	...
Malleable iron screwed pipe fittings	3,681	4,861	6,195	5,024	5,707
Cast iron screwed pipe and fittings	938	814	2,151	1,430	1,344
Cast iron pressure pipe and fittings	65,649	34,192	18,849	16,008	43,638
Cast iron soil pipe and fittings	7,346	8,213	8,572	5,727	18,410
Iron castings	46,846	23,200	24,322	24,993	16,221
Steel castings	10,348	16,518	21,113	12,326	7,932
Sprocket and other power transmission chains	†	1,935	1,172	1,686	3,174
Other chains	†	16,370	20,223	21,035	20,914
TOTAL	168,179	160,900	143,715	129,226	159,985

***Included with seamless. †Not available**

Net tons—*Continued*

	1945	1944	1943	1942	1941
Pig iron	90,968	161,536	144,555	110,647	578,533
Ferromanganese and spiegel	3,231	821	13,073	7,223	5,155
Ferrotungsten, tungsten metal and wire. Other ferro-alloying ores and metals	5,380	8,481	35,008	14,638	18,908
TOTAL	99,579	170,838	192,636	132,508	602,596
GRAND TOTAL	5,109,229	6,150,988	7,291,074	7,279,447	7,166,055
Iron and steel scrap	95,734	95,857	55,041	141,736	904,249

[1] Exports of iron and steel not including scrap.
[2] 2,000-pound ton.
(*Annual Statistical Report, 1945*, American Iron and Steel Institute, 1944, copyright, 1946, by American Iron and Steel Institute; pages 74, 75.)

abled European countries to sell iron and steel in the world markets at prices with which the United States industry generally could not compete.

During 1935 a total of 405,221 gross tons[1] of iron and steel products were imported into the United States, a 49 per cent increase over 1934 imports of 272,369 gross tons. It is estimated that 13,414,000 man-hours of work, equivalent to 6,450 full-time jobs, would have been required if the iron and steel imported in 1935 had been made in the United States; and that wages thereby lost amounted to $9,500,000. During 1935 almost the entire tonnage of imported iron and steel products competed directly with products made in the United States. About 93 per cent of the 1,100,859 tons of iron and steel products exported from the United States in 1935 was bought by nations which either produced no iron or steel or were dependent on outside sources for a large part of their requirements.

In a typical peacetime year such as 1936, for example, United States exports amounted to only 8 per cent of the 16,600,000 tons of pig iron and rolled steel that constituted world exports of these products; and the United States ranked fifth behind Germany's exports of 4,000,000 tons, Belgium-Luxembourg's 3,300,000 tons, the United Kingdom's 2,300,000 tons, and France's 1,700,000 tons. See Map No. 6 for world trade in iron and steel products during 1936; and see Tables 14 and 15 for exports of iron and steel from the United States, and Tables 16 and 17 for imports of iron and steel into the United States for the periods 1940–1944 and 1941–1945.

Nearly half (8,200,000 tons) of the iron and steel in world trade during 1936 went into European countries, including the United Kingdom and Russia. Nearly 7,800,000 tons of pig iron and rolled steel products were shipped from one European country to another; this intra-European movement of iron and steel accounted for almost 47 per cent of the total world trade in these products during 1936. Most of this movement consisted of products made in one country and not in another. United States exports of about 238,000 tons of iron and steel to Europe in 1936 were only 17 per cent of total United States exports of these products.

Eastern Asia and the South Pacific countries constituted the second largest market for iron and steel in 1936, consuming about 3,200,000 tons. Japan imported 1,500,000 tons, China 700,000 tons, and the Netherlands Indies 200,000 tons. British Malaya and the Philippines each im-

[1] Of 2,240 pounds each.

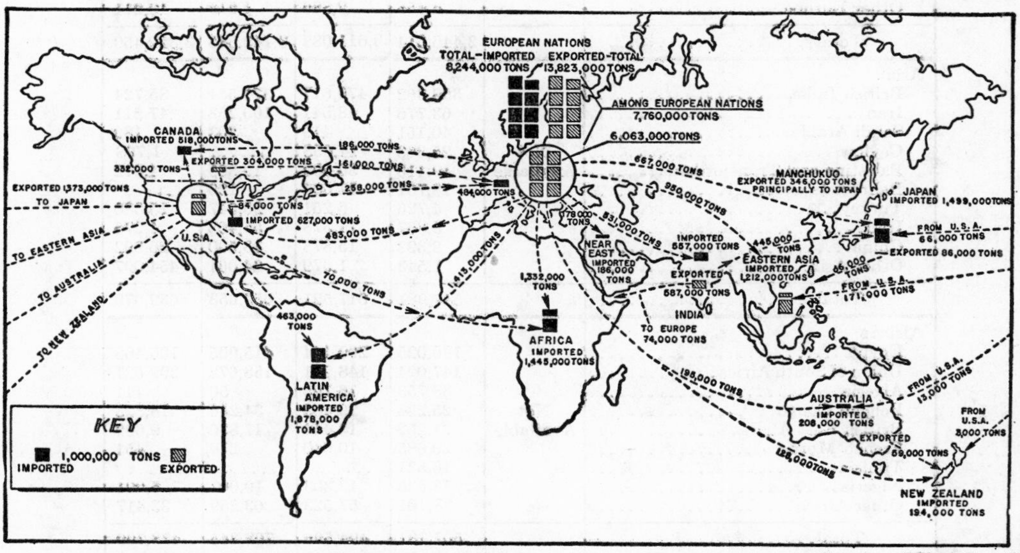

Courtesy "Steel Facts"

MAP 6. Major world trade in steel plant products in a typical pre-World War II year—1936.

TABLE 15—EXPORTS OF IRON AND STEEL * FROM THE UNITED STATES, 1941–1945, CLASSIFIED ACCORDING TO DESTINATION

Geographical Divisions	1945	1944	1943	1942	1941
North & Central America & West Indies:					
Canada		948,580	1,396,076	1,721,204	1,182,977
Mexico		293,425	151,391	82,534	115,693
Cuba		94,569	58,927	46,822	81,012
Netherlands W. Indies		17,800	22,733	34,632	8,987
Trinidad and Tobago		16,923	9,479	28,217	25,807
Guatemala		12,651	6,547	5,200	8,769
Jamaica	Not	10,718	2,762	3,665	1,479
Panama	Available	10,577	7,836	37,778	137,452
Dominican Republic		9,170	8,851	2,530	6,363
Honduras		8,181	2,864	3,376	11,944
Costa Rica		7,131	6,874	4,436	20,168
Iceland		6,729	15,993	13,114	6,498
El Salvador		5,180	5,678	972	4,367
Haiti		4,310	3,655	763	1,434
Other North & Central America & West Indies		17,579	13,034	10,711	15,658
Total		1,463,523	1,712,700	1,995,954	1,628,608
South America:					
Brazil		361,287	233,117	128,613	273,661
Venezuela		172,271	50,490	63,594	112,262
Chile		109,161	85,561	55,873	85,949
Colombia	Not	93,494	47,442	12,755	64,571
Peru	Available	69,139	44,986	25,402	47,285
Uruguay		54,105	50,215	29,272	43,059
Argentina		53,028	52,525	142,704	320,507
Ecuador		14,270	6,652	4,189	8,532
Bolivia		12,469	16,344	9,651	17,859
Other South America		11,505	16,333	12,979	18,542
Total		950,729	603,665	485,032	992,227
Australia & Oceania:					
Australia	Not	165,821	134,030	175,272	68,747
New Zealand	Available	62,812	114,618	120,153	38,962
Other Oceania		6,427	2,936	1,493	1,283
Total		235,060	251,584	296,918	108,992
Europe:					
United Kingdom		1,485,563	2,878,144	2,441,454	3,254,423
Russia (U.S.S.R.)	Not	898,377	702,514	688,278	18,670
Portugal	Available	36,359	26,264	6,902	23,868
Italy		19,021	......	......	......
Eire		2,736	1,200	4,296	6,287
Other Europe		4,458	2,886	1,615	19,211
Total		2,446,514	3,611,088	3,142,545	3,322,459
Asia:					
British India		368,362	470,617	371,531	85,724
Iran		63,776	48,541	100,263	47,511
Saudi Arabia		40,151	419	203	189
Ceylon	Not	25,363	14,653	......	1,798
Palestine and Transjordania	Available	19,110	36,602	19,865	4,012
Bahrein Islands		18,761	11,603	120	......
Turkey		4,726	6,251	25,647	15,380
Iraq		3,867	11,578	55,463	4,276
China		2,322	15,878	13,500	26,992
Other Asia		1,543	1,379	64,061	454,097
Total		547,981	617,521	650,653	639,979
Africa:					
Egypt		186,025	200,144	415,005	106,468
Union of South Africa		147,024	148,281	158,672	299,527
Algeria		38,753	16,795	50	111
Belgian Congo	Not	25,284	29,468	34,246	18,823
British East Africa	Available	21,252	13,442	17,836	9,002
French Morocco		20,685	10,640	270	451
Tunisia		16,521	......	......	......
Nigeria		13,536	18,303	19,007	5,991
Other Africa		38,101	57,523	63,259	33,417
Total		507,181	494,596	708,345	473,790
Total all countries	5,109,229	6,150,988	7,291,074	7,279,447	7,166,055

* Exports of iron and steel not including scrap.

ported a little more than 100,000 tons, and Australia and New Zealand about 200,000 tons each. This market was supplied chiefly by the following countries: United Kingdom, 555,000 tons; India, 454,000 tons (mostly pig iron to Japan); Germany, 418,000 tons; Russia, 408,000 tons (mostly pig iron to Japan); Japan (including Manchukuo), 402,000 tons; Belgium-Luxembourg, 291,000 tons; and the United States, 252,000 tons (largely to the Philippines and China).

Into Latin America, the third largest market for world exports of iron and steel in 1936, a total of nearly 1,900,000 tons was imported. The larger importers were: Argentina, 692,000 tons; Brazil, 370,000 tons; Mexico, 172,000 tons; and Chile, 123,000 tons. This market was supplied mainly by: Germany, with 588,000 tons; United States, with 463,000 tons; Belgium- Luxembourg, with 341,000 tons; United Kingdom, with 196,000 tons; and France, with 97,000 tons.

Africa imported nearly 1,500,000 tons of iron and steel in 1936, exclusive of shipments from the Union of South Africa to other parts of Africa. South Africa imported over 700,000 tons; Egypt, 200,000 tons; and Algeria, 174,000 tons. The United Kingdom supplied 493,000 tons; France, 322,000 tons (mostly to French colonies); Belgium, 295,000 tons; Germany, 174,000 tons; and the United States, 70,000 tons.

The United States imported nearly 627,000 tons

TABLE 16—IMPORTS OF IRON AND STEEL INTO THE UNITED STATES, 1940–1944, CLASSIFIED ACCORDING TO PRODUCTS

	1944	1943	1942	1941	1940
Semi-Finished and Finished Products:					
Steel ingots, blooms, etc.	81	3,897	319	4,294	501
Wire rods	2	32	58	121	4,372
Iron bars and slabs	1	3	1	17	222
Concrete reinforcement bars	....	....	11	6	9
Hollow bar and drill steel	18	9	5	249	976
Other steel bars	331	2,807	588	605	2,092
Boiler and other plate	5,903	397	226	64	17
Sheets, skelp, sawplates, n. e. s.	13	72	29	62	137
Tin plate, tagger's tin and terne plate	137	520	150	122	154
Other hoops and bands	....	2	1	....	705
Structural shapes and sheet piling	28,016	170	166	352	860
Rails and fastenings	9,893	7,397	14,435	7,672	1,780
Wheels and axles	49	59	60	92	110
Pipe and tubes	588	530	633	1,685	3,442
Round wire	2	105	91	38	995
Barbed wire	600	60	....	....	96
Flat wire and strip	16	189	275	2,609	2,481
Telegraph and telephone wire	161	621	52	27	1
Wire rope and strand	3,168	370	37	105	588
Other wire	7	5	2	1	1
Nails, tacks and staples	7	16	238	31	125
Bolts, nuts and rivets	88	60	64	55	147
Castings and forgings	7,212	1,041	446	383	685
Die blocks and blanks	229	413	53	19	16
Total	56,522	18,775	17,940	18,609	20,612
Other Finished Products:					
Cast iron pipe and fittings	102	25	....	....	469
Malleable iron pipe fittings	....	1	2	1	32
Enameled or glazed ware and utensils	1	2	....	1	27
Power trans. and other chains	416	853	30	35	39
Total	519	881	32	37	567
Pig iron	5,788	1,606	....	3,675	11,471
Sponge iron	....	....	....	....	683
Ferro-manganese (mang. content)	3,700	2,300	11,635	5,695	9,603
Spiegeleisen	3,761	3,254	1,782	4,794	17,522
Ferro-silicon (silicon content)	5,700	2,200	4,336	6,190	1,406
Ferro-chrome (chromium content)	100	400	582	88	1
Other alloys and metals	6,000	10,000	5,664	2,510	580
Total	25,049	19,760	23,999	22,952	41,266
Grand Total	82,090	39,416	41,971	41,598	62,445
Iron and steel scrap	111,060	147,206	82,240	71,978	2,285

TABLE 17—IMPORTS OF IRON AND STEEL[1] INTO THE UNITED STATES, 1940–1944, CLASSIFIED ACCORDING TO ORIGIN

IMPORTS OF IRON AND STEEL[1]

Net tons[2]

Countries	1944	1943	1942	1941	1940
North and Central America and West Indies:					
Canada	51,578	33,949	34,744	19,997	25,384
Mexico	282	4	32	9	102
Other	23	96	63		207
TOTAL	51,883	34,049	34,839	20,006	25,693
South America			29		
Europe:					
United Kingdom	28,185	1,433	6,848	12,181	1,223
Sweden	14	185	249	3,430	14,495
Norway				61	9,912
Belgium				2	2,262
Other Europe			2	29	1,006
TOTAL	28,199	1,618	7,099	15,703	28,898
Australia and New Zealand	600	784		3,367	1
Asia:					
British India	1,408	2,800			7,650
Burma				2,454	
Other Asia			4	68	203
TOTAL	1,408	2,800	4	2,522	7,853
Africa:					
French Morocco		165			
GRAND TOTAL	82,090	39,416	41,971	41,598	62,445

IMPORTS OF PIG IRON[2]

Net tons[2]

Countries	1944	1943	1942	1941	1940
Canada	5,788	45		308	3,826
United Kingdom		560			
British India		500			7,645
Australia		336		3,367	
French Morocco		165			
TOTAL	5,788	1,606		3,675	11,471

IMPORTS OF FERROALLOYS[3]

Net tons[2]

	1941	1940	1939	1938	1937
Ferromanganese:					
United Kingdom	4,481				143
Canada	1,202				3,791
Norway	12	9,564	21,929	11,813	19,564
Netherlands			8,931	6,544	316
France			971	1,274	851
Japan		39		345	809
Other countries			5,635	3,676	1,281
TOTAL	5,695	9,603	37,466	23,652	26,755
Spiegeleisen:					
Canada	4,740	17,455	41,967	18,797	17,322
Norway	49	45	840	448	1,540
Netherlands			49	73	
Other countries	5	22			
TOTAL	4,794	17,522	42,856	19,318	18,862
Ferrosilicon:					
Canada	6,190	1,238	1,160	701	1,716
Switzerland		168			
Other countries					552
TOTAL	6,190	1,406	1,160	701	2,268
Other Ferroalloys	2,510	581	1,251	1,726	4,581
GRAND TOTAL	19,189	29,112	82,733	45,397	52,466

NOTE.—Data for the years after 1941 are not available.

[1] Imports of iron and steel not including scrap.

[2] 2,000-pound ton.

[3] Includes ferromanganese (maganese content), spiegeleisen, ferrosilicon (silicon content), ferrochrome (chromium content), ferrophosphorus ferrotitanium, ferrozirconium and other alloys and metals used in the manufacture of steel.

(*Annual Statistical Report, 1944*, copyright, 1945, by American Iron and Steel Institute; pages 87. 88.)

TABLE 18—PRODUCTION OF IRON ORE BY COUNTRIES, 1925–1940

Net tons[1]

Years	(1) United States	(2) Canada[2]	(3) Newfoundland[2]	(4) Cuba[2]	(5) Chile	(6) United Kingdom	(7) Luxembourg	(8) Belgium	(9) France
1940	82,662.700	414,603	1,578,006	246,011	....	....	....	....	....
1939	57,939,538	123,598	1,572,480	302,250	....	....	....	....	....
1938	31,860,956	5,322	1,881,839	166,545	1,771,470	13,282,294	5,554,804	216,100	36,528,976
1937	80,744.774	6,197	1,799,954	494,480	1,686,207	15,920,794	8,561,225	259,276	41,724,604
1936	54,643.394	5,854	881,888	497,840	1,493,700	14,225,552	5,397,157	210,176	36,710,447
1935	34,205.082	2,288	741,890	247,531	936,305	12,202,831	4,556,954	181,356	35,326,189
1934	27,538 130	2,023	690,947	173.040	1,050,981	11,857,268	4,226,288	127,753	35,292,291
1933	19,659.571	....	254,383	308,662	622,834	8,357,126	3,714,807	117,071	33,340,747
1932	11.028.546	....	166,303	207,244	244,711	8,207,573	3,541,469	102,310	30,420,788
1931	34,867,282	1,509	789,897	250.236	817,556	8,540,963	5,252,675	138,700	42,505,984
1930	65,417,704	412	1,319,314	213,532	1,868,602	13,022,501	7,330,016	144,398	53,542,835
1929	81,791 046	2,453	1,699,039	751,878	1,997,858	14,800,736	8,346,211	171,605	55,923,937
1928	69,660 739	2,244	1,733,640	441,750	1,670,303	12,613,802	7,746,114	181,251	54,024,258
1927	69,150 032	2,029	1,495,679	464,628	1,671,666	12,551,393	8,010,037	199,406	50,075,972
1926	75,737,760	200	969,601	647,462	1,627,478	4,585,712	8,550,185	159,821	43,243,904
1925	69,336,957	3,978	1,267,851	625,147	1,470,869	11,363,880	7,355,062	182,606	39,081,881

Years	(10) Germany	(11) Austria	(12) Czechoslovakia	(13) Poland	(14) Hungary	(15) Yugoslavia	(16) Rumania	(17) Russia
1940	....	....	....	....	....	656,684	....	....
1939	....	....	....	....	....	735,078	145,418	....
1938	12,286,146	*	2,250,000	961,373	407,782	669,256	153,158	30,870,000
1937	9,394,616	2,077,953	2,002,560	855,434	319,156	681,808	142,265	30,866,080
1936	8,344,881	1,128,819	826,772	517,008	308,165	474,441	119,526	32,850,394
1935	6,662,677	854,756	805,890	366,323	212,090	241,733	102,968	29,832,126
1934	4,787,552	514,597	593,889	272,685	75,919	196,775	92,147	23,946,172
1933	2,857,327	293,228	472,662	177,107	55,141	51,427	15,247	16,052,819
1932	1,476,914	331,521	663,622	84,881	58,275	29,362	8,875	13,448,819
1931	2,889,622	564,349	1,361,503	313,790	92,635	147,069	68,219	11,698,268
1930	6,328,887	1,301,284	1,822,116	525,735	173,436	475,327	101,987	11,492,126
1929	7,026,100	2,084,986	1,992,700	726,685	277,477	471,752	99,228	7,727,559
1928	7,137,602	2,125,555	1,961,296	812,171	219,973	484,467	92,454	6,486,739
1927	7,303,741	1,762,205	1,753,336	594,952	214,300	370,503	107,081	5,295,167
1926	5,284,011	1,206,381	1,566,648	356,738	145,249	404,152	113,322	3,781,578
1925	6,529,180	1,124,832	1,355,855	232,331	78,138	153,380	118,376	2,452,158

Years	(18) Greece	(19) Italy	(20) Spain	(21) Norway	(22) Sweden	(23) Algeria	(24) Tunis	TOTAL (Columns 1 to 24, incl.)
1940	....	....	3,182,510	....	....	....	....	....
1939	....	1,137,350	3,527,360	....	....	....	....	....
1938	384,276	1,108,608	2,771,020	1,568,000	15,346,190	3,343,464	906,142	164,293,721
1937	331,258	1,120,245	1,092,148	1,111,377	16,483,125	2,575,119	1,054,960	221,305,615
1936	308,960	909,448	2,204,724	933,490	12,401,140	2,077,357	826,992	178,298,125
1935	225,043	627,244	2,902,519	843,474	8,744,878	1,846,049	555,834	143,224,030
1934	162,490	553,477	2,308,348	625,495	5,790,772	1,462,206	602,441	122,943,686
1933	93,944	579,396	2,001,321	522,369	2,975,000	841,102	320,787	93,684,078
1932	50,709	454,533	1,940,677	412,181	3,636,680	510,394	230,394	77,256,781
1931	260,121	618,264	3,516,760	633,734	7,794,658	993,228	487,244	124,604,266
1930	282,339	791,633	6,081,965	851,490	12,386,613	2,460,326	912,756	188,847,334
1929	278,927	788,377	7,216,777	822,485	12,641,395	2,420,988	1,077,008	211,137,207
1928	183,949	689,515	6,361,961	730,545	5,146,710	2,188,879	1,002,047	183,697,964
1927	136,544	554,808	5,468,151	528,399	10,649,896	2,209,342	1,008,662	181,577,929
1926	139,586	556,203	3,507,263	234,429	9,336,674	1,873,141	642,677	164,670,175
1925	98,105	546,666	4,897,655	468,971	9,005,980	1,985,547	797,008	160,532,413

* Included in Germany. [1] 2,000-pound ton. [2] Shipments from the mines.
(*Annual Statistical Report, 1944,* copyright, 1945, by American Iron and Steel Institute; pages 118-120.)

of iron and steel during 1936; Belgium-Luxembourg furnished 124,000 tons; Germany, 122,000 tons; Canada, 84,000 tons; and Sweden, 73,000 tons.

In 1936, Canada imported 518,000 tons of iron and steel; the United States shipped 332,000 tons; and the United Kingdom, 164,000 tons.

World Production of Iron Ore, Pig Iron and Ferroalloys, and Steel: The world production and the production by countries of iron ore, pig iron and ferroalloys are shown for the years 1925–1940, in Tables 18 and 19.

Bibliography.—Swank, J. M., *History of the Manufacture of Iron in all Ages* (Philadelphia 1892); Dunbar, D. E., *The Tin-plate Industry* (Boston 1915); Goodale, S. L., and Speer, J. R., *Chronology of Iron and Steel,* 2d ed. (Cleveland 1931); Tiemann, H. P., *Iron and Steel: A Pocket Encyclopedia* (New York 1933); Bining, A. C., *Pennsylvania Iron Manufacture in the Eighteenth Century* (Harrisburg, Pa., 1938); Rowe, F. H., *History of the Iron and Steel Industry in Scioto County, Ohio* (Columbus 1938); Holbrook, S. H., *Iron Brew: A Century of American Ore and Steel* (New York 1939); Camp, J. M., and Francis, C. B., *Making, Shaping and Treating of Steel* (Pittsburgh, 1940); United States Steel Corporation, *T. N. E. C. Papers,* papers sub-

TABLE 19—PRODUCTION OF PIG IRON AND FERROALLOYS BY COUNTRIES, 1925–1940

Net tons[1]

Years	(1) United States	(2) Canada	(3) United Kingdom	(4) Belgium	(5) Luxembourg	(6) France	(7) Netherlands	(8) Hungary
1940	47,398,529	1,447,703	9,300,000	2,450,000	1,180,000	5,100,000	305,000	510,000
1939	35,677,097	930,122	9,183,000	3,382,054	1,960,000	8,736,000	303,915	503,700
1938	21,460,164	848,968	7,574,224	2,717,323	1,709,436	6,668,189	330,709	369,291
1937	41,582,550	1,096,827	9,512,272	4,236,165	2,769,693	8,725,423	329,526	393,543
1936	34,752,689	836,895	8,647,968	3,484,942	2,186,016	6,867,456	319,770	337,323
1935	23,937,423	733,673	7,194,992	3,339,717	2,064,031	6,381,770	303,007	204,689
1934	18,075,202	487,127	6,685,392	3,204,886	2,155,403	6,780,630	284,235	154,312
1933	14,947,074	288,837	4,632,320	2,987,876	2,080,751	6,971,583	278,506	102,599
1932	9,835,227	179,526	4,002,880	3,030,107	2,160,840	6,104,232	260,627	73,064
1931	20,637,516	521,661	4,225,312	3,525,123	2,263,258	9,038,099	282,995	175,970
1930	35,562,429	909,587	6,935,488	3,709,723	2,726,041	11,062,313	300,615	283,556
1929	47,727,661	1,298,759	8,500,016	4,454,128	3,203,567	11,424,613	279,779	405,615
1928	42,734,400	1,212,915	7,403,312	4,251,800	3,053,611	11,002,553	284,630	314,919
1927	40,953,522	858,156	8,168,048	4,088,760	3,012,200	10,222,331	224,551	330,970
1926	44,097,456	890,704	2,753,184	3,713,138	2,821,111	10,397,047	157,087	207,038
1925	41,104,634	668,052	7,013,104	2,802,762	2,605,160	9,363,588	120,489	102,832

Years	(9) Germany	(10) Saar	(11) Austria	(12) Czechoslovakia	(13) Poland	(14) Yugoslavia	(15) Rumania
1940	23,100,000	*	*	*	*	92,453	150,000
1939	24,304,000	*	*	*	*	67,277	149,000
1938	20,407,490	*	*	1,360,315	1,067,087	65,328	143,300
1937	17,590,795	*	427,277	1,846,457	798,432	44,007	140,253
1936	16,868,872	*	273,514	1,256,976	644,199	47,522	106,828
1935	13,822,977	*	212,943	893,947	434,438	21,316	90,554
1934	9,636,477	2,012,544	147,240	661,774	421,102	36,114	63,380
1933	5,805,887	1,677,492	96,952	550,057	336,910	42,496	1,440
1932	4,335,052	1,487,630	104,135	496,180	219,011	10,993	9,751
1931	6,683,675	1,370,552	159,883	1,283,950	382,646	41,627	47,593
1930	10,686,861	2,108,206	316,379	1,584,193	526,871	38,595	75,890
1929	14,772,499	2,320,406	509,556	1,812,851	776,545	34,047	79,752
1928	13,012,647	2,134,376	504,784	1,729,897	753,748	32,303	77,301
1927	14,443,732	1,951,973	479,973	1,389,377	681,621	24,969	69,998
1926	10,630,651	1,805,726	366,935	1,199,352	361,290	20,689	69,425
1925	11,121,458	1,601,794	418,812	1,285,819	346,771	3,852	70,852

Years	(16) Russia	(17) Italy	(18) Spain	(19) Sweden	(20) Japan	TOTAL (Columns 1 to 20, incl.)
1940	17,100,000	980,000	575,000	640,000	3,300,000	113,628,685
1939	16,810,000	1,120,000	560,000	699,900	3,640,000	108,026,065
1938	16,526,614	1,014,173	484,903	786,623	3,362,000	86,896,137
1937	16,006,300	951,374	211,653	763,788	3,089,921	110,516,256
1936	15,783,712	888,504	309,764	696,401	3,162,677	97,472,028
1935	13,787,245	765,040	392,441	675,303	3,068,972	78,324,478
1934	11,508,441	641,120	410,482	615,261	2,710,717	66,691,839
1933	7,837,575	624,951	373,539	380,895	2,275,665	52,293,405
1932	7,022,047	545,876	331,400	311,045	1,727,179	42,246,802
1931	5,519,528	620,698	541,311	460,243	1,569,449	59,651,089
1930	5,492,189	663,518	685,549	547,224	1,860,159	86,075,386
1929	4,430,063	801,025	829,658	577,450	1,720,787	105,958,777
1928	3,617,927	610,833	620,433	482,297	1,697,638	95,532,324
1927	3,255,842	583,689	653,778	501,043	1,417,638	93,312,171
1926	2,444,966	615,720	538,720	551,938	1,251,181	84,893,358
1925	1,442,698	591,178	584,284	509,908	1,028,504	82,786,551

* Included in Germany.
[1] 2,000-pound ton.
(*Annual Statistical Report, 1944,* copyright, 1945, by American Iron and Steel Institute; pages 121-123.)

mitted to the Temporary National Economic Committee, vols. 1, 2, and 3 (New York 1940); Parker, C. M., *Steel in Action* (Lancaster, Pa., 1943); American Iron and Steel Institute, *Annual Statistical Report* (New York 1945); id., *Directory of Iron and Steel Works of the United States and Canada,* 24th ed. (New York 1945); id.; *Steel Facts,* No. 1, Oct., 1934, and No. 75, Dec., 1945; Hauck, W. A., *Steel Expansion for War* (Washington 1945); May, E. C., *Principio to Wheeling,* 1715–1945 (New York 1945).

JOHN W. W. SULLIVAN,
Metallurgist, American Iron and Steel Institute.

IRON AGE. See ARCHAEOLOGY.

IRON CROSS. See ORDERS AND DECORATIONS—*Belgium, Germany.*

IRON MOUNTAIN, city, Michigan, Dickinson County seat, altitude 1,142 feet, on the Chicago, Milwaukee and St. Paul; Wisconsin and Michigan; Chicago and Northwestern railroads, and on state and federal highways, 47 miles southwest of Marquette. It is the trade center for a large mining section in Michigan and a farming section in Wisconsin. Chief industrial products are lumber, chemicals, wood parts, and aluminum truck bodies, and lumber and iron ore are important to its industrial life. Iron Mountain has mayor-council government. Pop. (1950) 9,679.

IRON MOUNTAIN, peak, Missouri, the southern spur of the St. Francois Mountains, a low range in the eastern part of the state; altitude 1,077 feet. This mountain, which is really a hill or knob, is in St. Francois County, 38 miles west-southwest of St. Genevieve, the nearest point on the Mississippi River, on the Missouri Pacific Railroad. Its area is 500 acres.

Iron Mountain is famous for its remarkable deposit of hematite iron ore, the purest in the United States. Excavations were begun in 1845. An artesian well was sunk to the depth of 152 feet, with the result that the beds passed through from the surface were as follows: Iron ore mixed with clay, 16 feet; sandstone, 34 feet; magnesian limestone, 7½ inches; gray sandstone, 7½ inches; hard blue rock, 37 feet; pure iron ore, 5 feet; porphyritic rock, 7 feet; iron ore, 50 feet to the bottom. It would seem that nearly the whole mountain was a mass of magnetic iron ore. The adjacent valleys are underlaid with magnesian limestone in horizontal strata. Pilot Knob, about six miles south of Iron Mountain, also contained an extensive deposit of iron ore; Shepherd Mountain, a short distance southwest of Pilot Knob, is the largest of the iron mountains in the immediate vicinity. The Cerro del Mercado near Durango, Mexico, is another famous hill of iron.

IRON RIVER, city, Michigan; in Iron County, on the Upper Peninsula, 34 miles west-northwest of the city of Iron Mountain and 5 miles from the Wisconsin border; altitude 1,490 feet. It is a trading center for an iron-mining, lumbering, and agricultural region, and is served by the Chicago and North Western and the Chicago, Milwaukee, St. Paul and Pacific railroads. Settled about 1881, it was incorporated as a village in 1885 and as a city in 1926. Pop. (1950) 4,048.

IRONBARK, a name of several eucalyptus trees, the bark of which (except for *E. leucoxylon*) is persistent, rather than deciduous as with other eucalypti. In general the hardness of their wood makes the ironbarks highly prized for shipbuilding and underground construction. *Eucalyptus paniculata* (white or red ironbark), the hardest of the ironbarks, has grayish brown bark, and wood which is generally pale in hue; *E. melanophloia* (silver-leaved ironbark), is a small tree, with dark, furrowed bark; *E. siderophloia* (broad-leaved ironbark) is tall, and much planted in the San Joaquin Valley, California; *E. crebra* (narrow-leaved ironbark) has reddish wood, is frost-resistant, and is found in many parts of California. Other ironbarks are *E. leucoxylon* (white ironbark), bark deciduous; and *E. sideroxylon* (red ironbark). Originally Australasian, like other eucalypti the ironbarks have been spread to most of the warmer parts of the world.

IRONCLAD OATH, The, an act passed by the United States Congress, July 2, 1862, requiring every federal office holder, civil or military, to swear allegiance to the Constitution and declare that he had never voluntarily borne arms against the United States. It was used to debar Southerners from office.

IRONDEQUOIT, ȧ-rŏn-dĭ-kwoit′, town, New York; in Monroe County; bounded on the south by the city of Rochester. Chiefly a residential community and summer resort, it is situated on Irondequoit Bay and Lake Ontario.

In 1718 Jacques René de Denonville built the Fort des Sables on a sandbar in Irondequoit Bay, following visits by French explorers, notably Robert de La Salle in 1669 and 1678. First settled in 1791, Irondequoit was incorporated March 27, 1839. Government is by supervisor and council. Pop. (1950) 34,417.

IRONTON, ī′ẽrn-tŭn, city, Ohio; seat of Lawrence County; altitude 540 feet. It is situated on the Ohio River, 93 miles south-southeast of Columbus, and is served by the Detroit, Toledo and Ironton and the Norfolk and Western railroads. Industrial production includes malleable castings, coke, graphite products, portland cement, chemicals, construction steel, electrical equipment, automobile parts, dry pressed brick, quarry tile, and stoves. The city has considerable river commerce; a bridge over the Ohio enables shippers to connect with the Chesapeake and Ohio on the Kentucky side. It has an airport, with airline service. There are three hospitals, one of which is a county institution.

The wealth of iron ore in this part of Ohio began to be exploited in the 1820's. John Means, of Virginia, made pig iron, with a charcoal furnace, here in 1826. In 1834 John Campbell experimented with new methods, and was so successful that the industry became firmly established here. He founded Ironton; it was incorporated in 1849. But the iron and steel industry shifted to other regions, and the furnaces have been supplanted by factories. The city government is administered by a city manager and council. Pop. (1950) 16,333.

IRONWEED, in the United States the popular name for a genus, *Vernonia,* of tall, coarse, composite plants, several species of which grow abundantly in woods and along roadsides throughout the eastern and southern parts of the country as far west as Kansas and Texas. They bear heads of magenta-colored flowers somewhat like miniature thistles.

IRONWOOD, city, Michigan; in Gogebic County; altitude 1,505 feet. It is situated on the Upper Peninsula, on the Montreal River, opposite Hurley, Wis., and is served by the Chicago and North Western and the Soo Line railroads. It is the trading and shipping center of the Gogebic Range, rich in iron ore and timber. There is also dairying and truck farming in the area. The city has planing mills and manufactures of dairy and meat products. It is the seat of Gogebic Junior College (coeducational), a municipal institution founded in 1932.

Iron ore was discovered here by J. L. Norrie in 1884. The town was laid out and the railroad built to the site in the following year. Two years later it was incorporated as a village and received a city charter in 1889. Pop. (1950) 11,466.

IRONWOOD, a popular name for many trees whose timber is very hard and heavy. Probably the best known species in America is also known as leverwood, *Ostrya virginiana,* of the family Betulaceae, indigenous from Nova Scotia to Florida and westward to Minnesota and Texas. It is a medium sized tree with furrowed bark, birch-like foliage, pistillate flowers in catkins resembling the female flowers of hop, hence its popular name hop-hornbeam. The name ironwood is also sometimes applied to *Carpinus caroliniana,* of the same family. (See HORNBEAM). Among foreign «ironwoods,» perhaps the most widely known is *Mesua ferrea,* an East Indian tree planted around Buddhist temples for its fragrant flowers, which are used to decorate the images of Buddha. Another Asiatic species is *Metrosideros vera,* from which the Chinese and Japanese make rubbers. In Australia and South Africa various species of *Olea, Melaleuca, Sideroxylon, Notelaea,* and *Myrtus* are valued for their timber, locally called ironwood, employed where great toughness is desirable and weight no obstacle.

IRONY, a peculiar mode of thought and expression in which the meaning of the speaker is contrary to the literal sense. It is a form of covert sarcasm, mockery, or satire, perhaps the most crushing and irresistible figures of rhetoric. Instances are frequent in history and literature. One of the most celebrated is that recorded in Scripture, where Elijah taunts the discomfited priests of Baal on Mount Carmel. In philosophy the term has been used as a rule to characterize rather the Socratic attitude whereby the only criterion for the æsthetic worth is found in the consciousness of the artist himself.

IROQUOIAN FAMILY, a linguistic stock of North American Indians deriving their name from the form Iroquois (q.v.), the name given to the «Five Nations.» The Saint Lawrence River was probably their first habitat, and from there they gradually spread to the Great Lakes, primarily because of the hostility of the Algonquins. Cartier found, in 1535, a people living between Montreal and Quebec whose language showed them to be Wyandots, but 100 years later these had entirely disappeared and the Algonquins occupied their territory. The Iroquoian stock is divided into four groups: the northern — Wyandot, Tionontati, Wenrorono, Tohotænrat, Neuter, Hochelaga; the central — Mohawk, Oneida, Cayuga, Onondaga, Erie, Conestoga, Seneca; the southern — Tuscarora, Meherrin, Nottaway, Chowanoc, Coree; the Cherokee — Elati or Lower Cherokee, Middle Cherokee, and Atali or Upper Cherokee. The tribes of the Iroquoian stock were all agricultural, and were noted for their houses and fortifications. They have also made considerable advance in education. The whole population is about 46,000, of whom 12,000 are in Canada. The major portion of the population are Cherokee. See IROQUOIS; CHEROKEE; WYANDOT; SENECA and ONEIDA INDIANS.

Bibliography.—Bancroft, H. H., 'Native Races'; Berghaus, Heinrich, 'Physikalischer Atlas' (Gotha 1852); Gatschet, A. S., 'A Migration Legend of the Creek Indians' (Philadelphia 1884); Keane, A. H., 'Ethnography and Philology of America' (London 1878); Latham, R. G., 'Opuscula' (London 1860); 'Elements of Comparative Philology' (London 1862); Prichard, 'Physical History of Mankind' (1847); Schoolcraft, 'Indian Tribes.'

IROQUOIS, or **MATILDA,** Canada, port of entry in Dundas County, Ontario, on the Canadian National and the Saint Lawrence River, 20 miles southwest of Cornwall and 45 miles southeast of Ottawa. It is one of the termini of the Iroquois Canal. Pop. (1931) 936.

IROQUOIS (ĭr-ō-kwoi') **LEAGUE,** the name given by the French to the confederacy of North American Indians, called by the English the «Five,» and afterward the «Six Nations.» By the Delawares they were known as the Mingwe; by the Algonquins as Nadowa; by the Powhatan as Massawomekes. The Mohawks, Oneidas, Onondagas, Cayugas, Senecas, and Tuscaroras, after they were driven from their hunting-grounds in North Carolina in 1712, were the members of this confederacy. They called themselves Ongwanonsionni, «the people of the long house.» They formerly resided on the Mohawk River in New York State and on the lakes which still bear their names, and extended their conquests to the Mississippi and beyond the Saint Lawrence. Their valor and successes had procured them the name of the Romans of America. Their territory abounded with lakes well stored with fish; their forests were filled with game, and they had the advantage of a fertile soil. The sachems owed their authority to public opinion; the general affairs of the confederacy were managed by a great council, composed of the chiefs, which assembled annually at Onondaga. The history of the Iroquois dates back to 1535, when Cartier found the peoples who had settled along the shores of the Saint Lawrence River, from Quebec to Montreal, and who, judging from the similarity in languages were undoubtedly the ancestors of the later Iroquois. The Algonquins, who at this time were more powerful drove those people from their habitations and scattered them throughout the country, some, like the Hurons, traveling west, and the majority, among whom were the Iroquois, going south, settling mainly in North Carolina. Hiawatha, their leader, persuaded them to form a league or confederacy for their own protection. The league thus formed and afterwards known as the «Five Nations,» was based upon such sound and well-ordered plans that it is in existence at the present time. In 1712 they were driven from their territory in North Carolina and coming north again settled in Central and Western New York. Here they gathered other tribes and merged them into the confederacy. In 1715 they took in the Tuscaroras, after which the league was known as the «Six Nations.» They bought firearms and supplies from the Dutch and gradually strengthened themselves so that in 1630, they took the offensive in a long and bloody war against the Algonquins, first attacking the French missions among the Hurons in Canada and either slaying. capturing, or sending into exile all this tribe. They then rapidly subdued the Neutral Nation, the Erie, the Ottawa, and tribes of the Algonquin race; and conquered in quick succession the Conestogas in the south, those east of the Hudson, among whom were the Mohicans, and the Miami and Illinois tribes of the Middle West, the only tribes who successfully opposed them being the Ojibwas of the Northwest and the Cherokees of the South. In the long wars between the British and the French, which continued with some interruption for nearly a century, until 1763, they were, with a few exceptions in the British interest. These exceptions were notably the Cayugas and the Mohawks, over whom the French Jesuit missionaries exercised a great influence, and who later withdrew from the league and settled in the villages of Caughnawaga and Saint Regis. In the Revolution the Iroquois as a league were neutral, but the separate tribes took up the warfare generally in favor of the British, the Oneidas and some of the Tuscaroras being the only ones who sided with the Americans. Joseph Brant led the Mohawks and Cayugas into Canada, where, at the end of the war, the Canadian government gave them several reservations, and where a majority of them are at the present time. The reservations for the Iroquois in the United States are mostly in New York, where all now live except a part of the Oneidas, who in 1820 migrated to Wisconsin, and a small band of Senecas, who have a small reservation in Pennsylvania. According to the United States census, and a Canadian report, the total number of the Iroquois in 1902 was about 17,000, of whom about 8,000 were in the United States. Since then the Iroquois have increased somewhat. Numbers of them have left the reservations and gone out to take their place in the world. Those still classed as Iroquois are those at Gibson, Ontario, Canada; the Mohawks of the Bay of Quinte, Ontario, Canada; the Oneidas of the river Thames, Canada; the Grand River Six Nations, Ontario, Canada; those of Caughnawaga, Quebec, Canada; the Saint Regis Reservation; those of Two Mountains, Quebec, Canada; the New York reservations; the Oneidas of Wisconsin; and the Pennsylvania Senecas. See also SIX NATIONS; IROQUOIAN FAMILY.

Bibliography.—Morgan, L. H., *League of the Ho-de-no-sau-nee or Iroquois,* ed. by H. M. Lloyd (New York 1904); Beauchamp, W. M., *The Founders of the New York Iroquois League, and Its Probable Date* (Rochester, N. Y., 1921); Colden, Cadwallader, *History of the Five Indian Nations of Canada which are Dependent on the Province of New York,* 2 vols. (New York 1922); Devine, E. J., *Historic Caughnawaga* (Montreal 1922); Parker, A. C., *The Archaeological History of New York,* 2 vols. (Albany, N. Y. 1922); Hatzan, A. L., *The True Story of Hiawatha and History of the Six Nation Indians* (Toronto 1925); Seymour, F. W., *Lords of the Valley* (New York 1930); Powers, Mabel, *The Indian as Peacemaker* (New York 1932); Cornplanter, J. J., *Legends of the Longhouse* (Philadelphia 1938); Lydekker, J. W., *The Faithful Mohawks* (New York 1938); Hunt, G. T., *The Wars of the Iroquois* (Madison, Wis. 1940); Adams, S. L., *The Long House of the Iroquois* (Utica, N. Y., 1944).

IRRADIATION, *in physics,* an apparent enlargement of a bright body when seen against a background darker than itself. A simple method of observing this phenomenon is to view a bright sky through the spaces between a grating. If the breadth of the opening can be made equal to the breadth of the bars of the grating it will be seen that, when viewed from a little distance the bars look narrower than the spaces between them. This is obviously owing to the encroachment of the light upon the dark spaces around it. The first question to arise and one which was long discussed is whether the encroachment is due to an excitation of the nerves of the retina outside the limits on which the light falls upon the nerves, or whether it is necessary that the light should actually fall outside of its geometrical limits. The latter view is found to be the correct one, except in cases of extreme brilliancy of the light.

The phenomenon was explained by Plateau as due to the extension of the impression upon the nerves of the retina beyond the outlines of the image. Helmholtz, however, ascribed it to the want of a perfect accommodation in the eye, leading to the formation of a diffusion image about the proper image of a bright object, so that it encroaches upon the dark space about it, and hence appears larger than it really is. Still another explanation is offered: Irradiation is almost entirely in the nature of an optical defect or aberration of light. It begins with the atmosphere, which, when light passes through long stretches of it, slightly deflects the rays, so that a point is no longer seen as such, but as a small ill-defined waving surface. No lens ever brings the rays from a point to exactly the same focus. The lenses of the eye itself have defects which everyone who consults an oculist is acquainted with. The result of all these imperfections is to produce the enlargement we have described.

Irradiation is a notable subject in the history of astronomical observations. It was necessarily larger with the imperfect telescopes of former times than with the improved ones of our own period. Total eclipses of the sun, the transits of Venus and Mercury were especially productive of the phenomenon. The enlargement of the moon resulted in a star appearing as if within the bright disc of the moon, when its light was really only grazing the surface. The sharp points or horns of light formed by the limb of the sun during the transits of Venus and Mercury were rounded off, so as to present quite an illusory view of their form. Just at the beginning and end of total eclipses of the sun the phenomenon known as Bailey's beads, really enlargements of the last points of light from the sun's limb, which could be seen before the sun was quite covered, looked like a string of beads. Many learned memoirs have been written on the subject, but the consensus of opinion today is toward the simple and comprehensive theories above mentioned. "Irradiation" is also a name applied to the act of emitting beams of light, illumination, brightness emitted, and by extension, enlightenment.

IRRADIATION, *in physiological psychology,* a term borrowed from physics and extended to include cases of nerve stimuli, and the impulses of these stimuli from the normal path. As a word, "irradiation" is equivalent to the German word *Ausstrahlung,* the French term *irradiation,* the Italian, *irradiazione,* and the Spanish word, *irradiacion.* All these forms except the German were derived from the (quasi) Latin *irradiatio* (*n*), from Latin *irradiare,* meaning "to irradiate." More fully defined, irradiation is the lateral diffusion of nervous stimuli out of the path of normal nervous stimulated discharge, as a result of which the excitation of one peripheral end-organ may excite other central organs more than those directly correlated with it or anatomically related to it by direct nervous connections. Where it takes place is not yet certainly known. Dogiel has shown that in skin areas subject to great irradiation, the end organs of one order are connected by communicating rami, suggesting peripheral irradiation. There are also indications of excessive stimuli in the spinal cord. It has been suggested by Herrick that irradiation (or at least a very nearly similar and analogous process), is at the foundation of most pleasurable sensations. Consult Dogiel, A. S., "Die Nervenendigungen . . . des Menschen," *Archiv f. mikr. Anat.*, vol. 41, 1893; Herrick, C. L., "Modern Algedonic Ideas," *Journal of Comparative Neurology*, March 1895.

IRRATIONAL NUMBERS, those which are not integers or fractions; numbers which are incommensurable with unity. This $\sqrt{2}$ is an irrational number. The ratio π of the circumference of a circle to the radius is an irrational number — 3.1415. Incommensurable roots of numbers, like $\sqrt{2}$, are called surds. The irrational numbers are divided into algebraic, involving only extraction of roots, and transcendental, involving higher processes. Consult Dedekind, *Essays on Number* by Beman (Chicago 1901).

IRRAWADDY, ĭr ȧ-wŏd'ĭ, or **IRAWADI,** the chief river of Burma, flowing through the center of the province in a north to south direction with a westward deflection. It is formed by the confluence of the Mali and N'mai rivers in Upper Burma at 25° 45′ N. There are three rocky defiles in which its channel is suddenly contracted, the lowest near Mandalay; but from that point down to its delta it has generally a breadth of from 1 to 4 miles. About 140 miles from the bay of Bengal, which it enters by nine main channels on one of which Rangoon is situated, the delta commences. The Irrawaddy's chief affluent is the Chindwin which parallels its course to the west near the Assam frontier, joining the Irrawaddy below Mandalay. The Irrawaddy's current is generally slow—not more than two miles per hour even in its upper courses—except during inundations when the flow becomes so rapid as to make it unnavigable for sailing vessels but for the assistance of the southwest monsoon. Steamers of 5-foot draft voyage nearly 1,000 miles upstream to Bhamo all year round. A railway parallels the river from Rangoon to Bhamo, crossing it at Mandalay. Levees extending 100 miles protect the delta lands from floods.

IRREDENTISTS, an important modern Italian patriotic and political movement having for its avowed aims the "freeing" of alleged Italians and lands near Italy, and the incorporation of both within the Italian political dominion. The English word "Irredentists" is derived from an Italian name "Italia irredenta," or "unredeemed Italy" which natives apply to that territory and its inhabitants.

Irredentism, the principles, policies and the practice of Irredentists, gained an ascendency in Italian politics for the first time during the five or six years following 1878. Among its ardent disciples were members of the older Italian Radical and Republican parties, adherents whose main activities in support of Irredentism are confined, chronologically, within the last quarter of the 19th century. Having attained this temporary recognition, the forces behind Irredentism subsided, and after 1881 a long period of unruffled repose followed, save that manifest in specious oratory or political fanfaronade. Politicians from time to time circulated a resurrected form of Irredentism; but their procedure in these cases was based upon an affected fear of Austrian, French, or other aggression. The revival of present day Irredentism took place in 1908, during which year the ambitious ideal, "L'Idea Nazionale," first saw light. "L'Idea Nazionale" was the end toward which the new patriotic party of the Nationalists tended. The Irredentism of their fathers became an integral part of their program. After World War I, Benito Mussolini gave the nationalist movement a fatal impulse by embarking on the policy of territorial aggrandizement that culminated in the treacherous attack on France in June 1940.

Dante, pioneer of the Italian classical Renaissance, early treated his fellow countrymen to a magnificent vision of a united Italy. He helped to prepare their minds for the reception of Irredentism and L'Idea. After the Russo-Turkish War a conference of the powers was held at Berlin, and the award they made to Austria in 1877 disappointed Italy keenly. The vision of Dante was fresh in Italian memory: and in 1878 Irredentism appeared. Its adherents were to unite—they said—all portions of Italy, even all those parts which of old had passed beneath the sway of foreign power. In language they asserted they had found a touchstone which would reveal what belonged to Italy, what to a foreign power. Resting their claims upon this doubtful criterion, they suggested that France, Austria, Switzerland and England should surrender such territory to Italy. In this way they included all within the confines of Görz, South Tirol or Trentino, Istria, Trieste, Tessino, Nice, Corsica and Malta. Their test appears, however, to have been applied in an arbitrary manner and even in cases where it was not applicable. For the Italian language is not spoken universally in South Tirol, Görz and Istria; while Malta has its own dialect; and Dalmatia is non-Italian, although it once acknowledged the dominion of the old Venetian Republic.

Austria did not yield to the Irredentists, and retained Trieste and the Southern Tirol. In 1866 the great Italian general Giuseppe Garibaldi had temporarily conquered Trentino: and on this fact united with their linguistic principle they of Irredentist conviction found sufficient inducement to direct most of their operations against Austria. Over these territories both Italians and Austrians adopt the same opinion. Both with equal plausibility urge that the Trentino is a weak point in the armor of the owner, an "enclave," and a territory which each considers essential to its security; twice in the 20th century—at the peace settlements of World Wars I and II—it was subject to international adjudication.

When in 1881 France, to the chagrin of Italy, occupied Tunis, Italian operations against Austria subsided. Thereupon the Italian government entered into those relations with Austria and Germany which originated the Triple Alliance, and Irredentism entered upon a period of repose which lasted a generation.

The great European crisis of 1908 culminating in Austria's annexation of Bosnia-Hercegovina marks the awakening hour of "L'Idea Nazionale." "L'Idea" was the aspiration, really, of Imperialism. It engendered aggressive and expansionist ideas which Gabriele D'Annunzio glorified in his tragedy *La Nave* (1908) and actualized when he seized Fiume in 1919. During the three decades following the 1908 crisis Italian military victories and the Fascist policy after 1922 affected the substitution of "L'Idea Nazionale" for the older Irredentism.

Professor Sighele found reason to characterize the new spirit as a "voluptuousness of self-sacrifice," while another Nationalist eulogized his followers because: "L'Idea Nazionale" is a purely "realist and integral valuation of international relations in absolute antithesis to the sentimental tendencies of the old Radical and Republican Irredentism which looked to the abandonment of the Triplice and the rapprochement of Italy with the parliamentary powers of the west."

The above claim for the "National Idea," advanced by Signor Federzoni several years before Mussolini's advent to power, is indicative of the arrogant chauvinism which became a major tenet of the succeeding creed of fascism. Federzoni's boasted "realism" seems rather to have been a kind of somnambulism afflicting leading Italian Nationalists which was destined to make them docile followers of Mussolini. Indicative of the virtual identity of views of Irredentists and Nationalists in the first quarter of the 20th century is the statement of Professor Sighele recalling how the party to which he belonged welcomed the Nationalist ideal "vibrant with an enthusiasm at first judged ridiculous." No thoughtful independent observer could expect a realism, in any genuine sense of the term, to proceed from the cooperation merely of moods and emotions. Italy's misfortune was that the realism confidently proclaimed by her leading statesmen of both world wars more often reflected a combination of calculated cynicism with wishful thinking instead of a cool analysis of Italy's situation.

After the Tripolitan expedition in 1911, a congress of Nationalists gathered at Florence. Here they codified their characteristic doctrines, and in a sensational manifesto established their central organ, *L'Idea Nazionale.* Then they banded themselves together in a definite body, "L'Associazione Nazionalista." The outbreak of World War I in 1914 gave opportunity to propagate their traditionally anti-Austrian ideas. On May 10, 1915, a fortnight before Italy's declaration of war against the Germans and Austrians, *L'Idea Nazionale* declared: "Italy desires war in order to obtain Trent, Trieste and Dalmatia. The Nation desires it. A nation which has opportunity to free its lands should do so as a matter of imperative necessity." Here we see the identity of Irredentist and Nationalist aims.

During the span of over 20 years (1922–1943) when Italy was subject to the Fascist dictatorship, Irredentism became a cardinal tenet of the ruling party. The loss of European territory to France and Yugoslavia after World War II, and the possibly permanent loss of the Italian colonies have given fresh vitality to irredentism which has a dangerously explosive quality despite Italy's postwar prostration.

The term "Irredentist" is also applied to nationalist groups of other countries similarly seeking the incorporation within the national boundaries of adjacent territory occupied by racial kindred, or of lands that in some more or less distant past epoch had been a part of the national patrimony. In the latter case Irredentist claims are often based on dubious historical grounds. Thus, in 1946 Italian and Yugoslav Irredentists presented contradictory historical and ethnic evidence to support their claims for possession of Trieste. See also FIUME.

Bibliography.—Parato, A., *Storia Tempi Moderni,* vol. 3 of *Storia d'Italia* (New York 1909) ; Coolidge, A. C., *Origins of the Triple Alliance* (New York 1915) ; Powell, E. A., *Italy at War, and the Allies in the West* (New York 1918) ; Sforza, Carlo, *Contemporary Italy* (New York 1944).

IRRIGATION. Ancient Times.—From the beginning of recorded history, man in arid and semiarid parts of the world has been trying to increase agricultural production through irrigation—the artificial application of water to the land.

There are scriptural references to irrigation found in Genesis 2:10: "And a river went out of Eden to water the garden . . ." and again in II Kings 3:16-17:

"And he said, Thus saith the Lord, Make this valley full of ditches:

"For thus saith the Lord, Ye shall not see wind, neither shall ye see rain; yet that valley shall be filled with water, that ye may drink, both ye, and your cattle, and your beasts."

Still another clue to irrigation in antiquity is that of an inscription on the tomb of an Assyrian ruler, Queen Semiramis, who lived earlier than 2000 B.C. This was her proud statement: "I constrained the mighty river to flow according to my will and led its waters to fertilize lands that had before been barren and without inhabitants." Irrigation canals, supposed to have been built by orders of Queen Semiramis, are still delivering Nile River water to thirsty lands in Egypt.

River regulation was also practiced by the ancient Babylonians who controlled the Euphrates by means of depressions in the Arabian deserts. These man-made lakes, covering 650 square miles, were 25 feet deep when full of water. Modern engineers now mapping river basin developments are amazed to learn that the Babylonians not only controlled the large rivers, but they included tributaries like the Pallacopas in their water-conservation plans.

Another example of irrigation in ancient times is recounted in the story of Nimrod who barred the Tigris Valley by a massive earthen dam, raising the Tigris River some 40 feet. One of Nimrod's canals, 400 feet wide, 16 feet deep, and 250 feet long, existed for 3,000 years. Unfortunately, it was swept away in the time of the last feeble caliphs.

It was Amenemhet of the twelfth dynasty who put the whole Nile Valley under cultivation. He had his men create Lake Moeris as an escape, a reservoir for the longest river in the world. When flood waters were dangerously high on the Nile, they were diverted and stored in this depression, thus accomplishing two of the purposes of our modern-day developments, irrigation and flood control.

Interesting mechanical contrivances were devised by the ancients for bringing water from nearby rivers to their fields. They tired of bailing water by hand, so they invented the *shadoof,* as it was called in Egypt, and known as the *denkli* or *paecottah* in India. By this counterpoised sweep device, buckets were lifted from river to land. One *shadoof* can irrigate about 4 acres. The *sakia* in Egypt, which is the same as the *harat* or *Persian wheel* in northern India, used oxen for power. Another unusual method

FIG. 1. Shadoof

FIG. 3. Archimedes screw

for irrigation was the Archimedes screw (q.v.), invented by Archimedes of Syracuse about 200 B.C. It consisted of a tube bent spirally around an axis, or, of a broad-threaded screw incased by a hollow open cylinder. This apparatus was immersed in a slantwise direction and rotated. The water rose up through the internal screw and flowed on to the soil. All three of these ancient devices for irrigation are used in parts of the world today.

Reasons for Irrigation.—Many other examples could be given of water-resource developments in ancient times. To understand

FIG. 2. Sakia or Persian wheel

these, as well as modern instances, we must answer the question: Why irrigate when three fourths of the earth's surface is covered with water? It is true that there is plenty of water in the world; in some places there is too much Man, however, has learned that if he has sufficient food supplies he will also need to cultivate lands where rainfall is insufficient for crop production. Because he has found desert land very productive when water is applied to it, he has devised methods to make "rainfall" when and where he wants it.

Irrigation in the United States.—Irrigation in the United States has become an important factor in the agricultural and industrial development of the West. A glance at a weather map of the United States will show that a third of the land area in this country receives less than 20 inches of rain a year and part of it averages less than 10 inches a year. Thus, natural rainfall in these areas is insufficient for crop production. The United States Department of Agriculture states that the minimum amount of rainfall needed for ordinary farming under favorable seasonal distribution is usually about 15 inches in a cool climate where the summer temperature is about 65° F., and 20 to 25 inches in areas where the summer temperature rises to 75° and 80° F. In warmer climates much of the moisture is lost through evaporation from the soil.

West of the 100th meridian in the United States there are 740,000,000 acres that require irrigation to make them productive. About 21,000,000 acres are now irrigated, with some 25 per cent dependent for water on federal irrigation systems in whole or in part. It has been estimated that the water resources of this vast area are sufficient to irrigate 22,000,000 additional acres and to provide supplemental supplies for 11,000,000 acres now inadequately watered.

The first irrigation in this country was that of prehistoric Indians in the Southwest who dug ditches to bring water from the streams to their fields. Traces of these ditches can still be found within the boundaries of the Casa Grande National Monument of New Mexico. When the Spanish missionaries settled in what is now a part of California, Arizona, New Mexico, and Texas, they brought with them irrigation methods which they had practiced along the

IRRIGATION

Courtesy United States Department of the Interior

Roosevelt storage dam, Arizona.

Furrows.

Irrigating potatoes

Irrigating sugar beets.

IRRIGATION

Courtesy United States Department of the Interior

Granite Reef Diversion Dam, Salt River, Arizona.

Turning water from main canal to lateral.

Turning water from lateral to farm ditch.

Imperial Dam and desilting works.

Canal with irrigated land, right; desert, left.

Mediterranean shores of Spain and Egypt.

Modern irrigation in this country is said to date from the advent of the Mormons in Utah. Today this verdant valley is one of the best examples of the value of artificial watering of the land. Before westward migrations increased the population of the West, it was a simple matter for a farmer with a team of horses and ordinary tools to construct waterways to his fields by digging ditches from the creeks flowing out of the mountains. But the time came when the streams were fringed with farms, and it was impossible for new settlers to obtain the water they needed to grow crops. To transport water greater distances over the desert and to have sufficient amounts to last through long periods of drought in semiarid regions, Western leaders realized they must have large reservoirs and conserve the flood waters which often washed away their homes and crops. Skilled engineers and ample funds were required to build dams to back up the rivers into man-made lakes. The Western homemakers lacked the knowledge and money to build expensive irrigation projects. The country was aroused to their plight and in 1902 the Federal Reclamation Act was passed. (See IRRIGATION BILL.) Although this law was made to aid the Western states, it has proved to be a boon to the whole nation. Much of our country's prosperity and security has been built on Western expansion.

Under the Act of 1902, the Reclamation Service (later the Bureau of Reclamation) was established in the Department of the Interior. This federal agency has long been the leader in the field of irrigated agriculture and has irrigation responsibilities under the present law in 17 Western states. Repayments to the government for the construction costs come primarily from water users on the irrigation projects and from the sale of power generated by hydroelectric plants, operated in connection with some of the dams. Power development, although incidental to the bureau's major function of irrigation, is important as a means of reimbursing the United States for the cost of reclamation construction. (See RECLAMATION, UNITED STATES BUREAU OF.)

Irrigation Structures.—The key feature of most reclamation projects is the dam. Roosevelt Dam on the Salt River Project in Arizona, near Phoenix, was the first large storage dam constructed by the bureau. It was completed in 1911. Water is released for irrigation through spillways on either side of the dam or through outlet valves for use as needed downstream. Water impounded by the dam forms a beautiful lake where many people enjoy boating, fishing, swimming—unbelievable recreational opportunities in a desert land. Several miles below Roosevelt Dam is the Granite Reef Diversion Dam which diverts water from the Salt River into a canal system. Gates are raised on the dam, releasing water into the main canal which carries water to the irrigation districts.

Perhaps the best known of irrigation canals on reclamation projects is the All-American Canal (80 miles long) and its branch, the Coachella Canal (145 miles long) now under construction (1946). The All-American Canal, which taps the Colorado River at Imperial Dam downstream from Hoover Dam, serves approximately 500,000 acres of irrigable land in the Imperial Valley of California. The Coachella Canal will serve irrigation needs in the Coachella Valley. See also DAMS.

Another type of waterway used on irrigation projects is the aqueduct. Most famous is the Metropolitan Water Aqueduct (241 miles long) which delivers Colorado River water, regulated by the bureau's Hoover Dam and by the Parker Dam, to Los Angeles and 12 other California cities. (See AQUEDUCTS.)

Sometimes it is necessary to tunnel through a mountain to get water to the land. The 13-mile Alva B. Adams tunnel of the Colorado-Big Thompson Reclamation Project was holed through the Rocky Mountains under the Continental Divide. The longest irrigation tunnel in the world, it was designed to transport water from the western slope of the mountains to needy lands on the eastern slope.

After the water has been diverted into the main irrigation canals, it is released through headgates to a lateral canal which carries it to the farms. Check structures in the laterals are used to turn the water in to the farmer's ditch which runs along the head of his field. Thus, the irrigator has control over the flow of the water. A canvas dam or some other check in the farm ditch raises the level of the water to divert and spread it over the field. These canvas checks aid in rapid, even distribution of water.

For an equitable, economical distribution of water, fields to be irrigated should be leveled. Sometimes this is done by an inexpensive homemade leveler float, by a modern bulldozer, or by a land plane especially constructed for this type of leveling.

Irrigation Methods.—Methods of irrigation vary with the kind of soil and topography of the land. Veterans and others who are planning to settle on irrigated farms have been advised to consult with agricultural specialists on the best way to apply water to their fields. Irrigators have developed four good methods of controlled irrigation: the corrugation or furrow system, the border system, the ridge or bed system, and the contour flood system. The choice of method depends on the soil and contour of the field and the kind of crop to be grown on it.

The corrugation or furrow system is suitable for land too steep or too uneven for the border system and not level enough for the ridge system. It is used with either large or small streams of irrigating water, which can be run off in as few or as many corrugations or furrows as the farmer wishes, according to the size of the stream available. When he has only a limited stream of water, the corrugation system is particularly suitable.

The border system is fitted for fields that

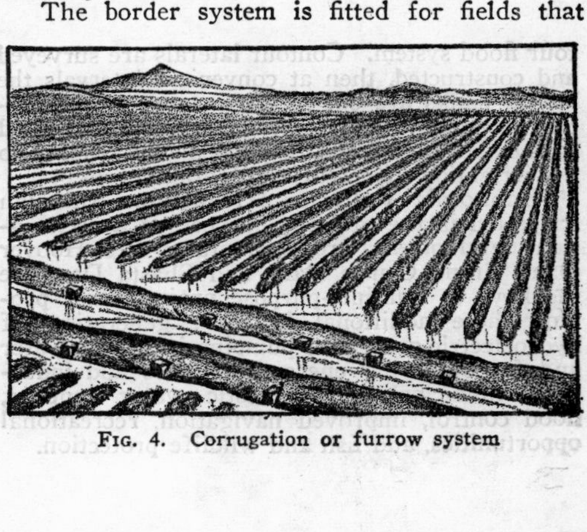

FIG. 4. Corrugation or furrow system

FIG. 5. Border system

have regular slopes in one direction. The slopes can be as flat as 1 inch in 200 feet or as steep as 1 foot in 100 feet. The border system is well adapted to alfalfa, clover, and other forage crops, and also to small grain, but it should never be used on level, heavy-type soils that do not release water readily.

The third method of irrigation, the ridge or bed system, is suitable where the ground is nearly level. Some of the most highly developed irrigated sections of this country, especially those on flat land, are using the ridge system. In regions where the spring is cold, the ridge system of irrigation permits the soil to warm more quickly and to bring about earlier seed germination.

The fourth method of irrigation, and one that is used most commonly on hilly lands and lands with sufficient surface drainage, is the contour flood system. Contour laterals are surveyed and constructed, then at convenient intervals the lateral banks are cut to allow an even distribution of water. This method is commonly used in the Northwest and is particularly adapted to the irrigation of cereals and forage crops.

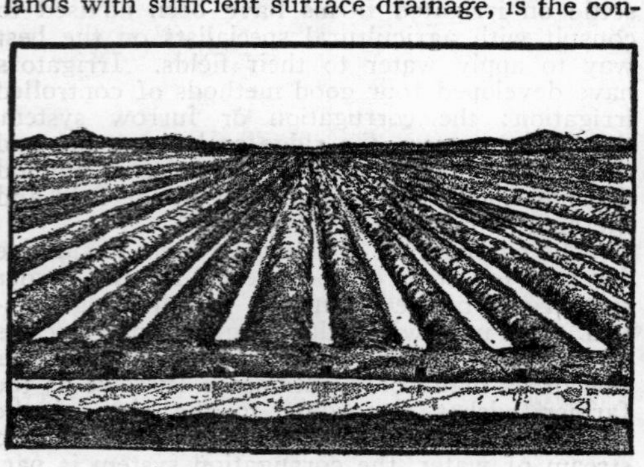

FIG. 6. Ridge or bed system

Economic Value of Irrigation.—Although irrigation is the primary purpose of a reclamation development, great structures like Hoover Dam, Grand Coulee Dam, and Shasta Dam are the keys to multiple-purpose projects that provide these additional benefits: generation of hydroelectric power for pumping irrigation water and for supplying energy to homes and industries, municipal and domestic water supplies, flood control, improved navigation, recreational opportunities, and fish and wildlife protection.

In 1945 the bureau had in operation, under construction, or authorized more than 100 projects, including 29 initial units of the Missouri River Basin Plan. Similar studies are being prepared for 14 other river basins in the West.

From the 4,000,000 acres now under irrigation by bureau facilities, the West and the nation have gained not only through increased production of essential foods, but also by greater purchasing power made possible by higher crop values. The gross value of food and forage crops on bureau projects totaled approximately $435,000,000 in 1945 which amounted to far more than the cost of building the irrigation systems. Farms on reclamation-served land produced almost 12,000,000 tons including feedstuffs that maintained meat and dairy production at a high level. Crops produced on irrigated lands are sugar beets, vegetables, fruits, and alfalfa. These crops are noncompetitive with those grown in other sections of the country. Many of the specialty vegetable and fruit crops are raised on Western irrigated farms in seasons of the year when Midwest and Eastern gardens are not producing.

FIG. 7. Contour flood system

Besides contributing to the agricultural supplies of the country, Bureau of Reclamation projects hold the record for the greatest power output of any single producer in the world. Hydroelectric plants on bureau projects in the fiscal year 1945 produced almost 14 billion kilowatt hours of electric energy. Water power has proved to be an important factor in stimulating the establishment of food processing plants and other industries in the West. Sale of excess power also helps to repay construction costs of an irrigation project. When the construction program now authorized is completed, the various services of the bureau, including irrigation, municipal water, and power will be extened to regions in which live more than 10,000,000 persons.

The federal government now has an investment of almost $1,000,000,000 in projects built and under construction by the bureau. The cost of building the irrigation features of the projects actually in operation was about $325,000,000 of which at the end of 1945 more than $75,000,000 had been repaid by water users under the reclamation law.

Since 1902, bureau engineers have designed 179 dams, some of which are the most famous in the world. Grand Coulee Dam, on the Columbia River and key to the development of more than a million acres in the state of Washington, is the largest concrete dam ever built. Shasta Dam, which regulates the Sacramento River for the multimillion acre Central Valley Reclamation Project in California, is the second largest, and Hoover Dam on the Colorado River is the highest dam in the world. (See DAMS.)

River Basin Plans.—Great river basin developments now planned by the bureau will make use of every drop of available water in the Columbia, the Colorado, and other western river basins. Small streams and tributaries will be brought into harness with the main rivers so that flood waters will not wreck homes and industries in their mad rush to the sea. And as Bureau of Reclamation engineers prepare to make the valleys full of ditches and "to constrain the mighty rivers to flow according to their will" people in other lands are looking to their rivers to increase food supplies and provide power for industrial advancement.

Modern methods of irrigation have gradually replaced ancient methods in many sections of the world. In Africa, Asia, Europe, and South America—wherever there are lands deficient in rainfall—irrigation through river regulation has become an important factor in economic development of the country. The most important irrigation projects in India and Australia, as well as in the United States, feature the construction of dams. The irrigation of the Nile Valley has been greatly extended by the controlling influence of the large dam at Assuan. Leaders in foreign lands who have long recognized the advancement of irrigation in this country are asking American engineers for help in solving some of their water-resource development problems. Aided by Bureau of Reclamation engineers, the government of China is planning the largest irrigation and hydroelectric power project the world has ever known. The key feature will be a huge dam in the gorge of the Yangtze River about 300 miles east of Chungking.

The Yangtze Gorge Dam, which will be 24 feet higher than Hoover Dam (726 feet) and contain 5 million more cubic yards of material than Grand Coulee Dam (10 million cubic yards), will impound the waters of the dragon's river to provide irrigation for 10 million acres of land and to protect the valley against floods. A 250-mile reservoir will store water for irrigation, for navigation, for flood control, and for power production. This reservoir will be 19 million acre-feet larger in capacity than Lake Mead (31,000,000 acre-feet), the famous reservoir created by Hoover Dam. Yangtze Gorge plans also call for construction of the world's largest hydroelectric plant with a generating capacity three times that of plants at Hoover, Grand Coulee, and Shasta combined. Preliminary overall designs for the Chinese project were prepared by John Lucian Savage, world-famous designer of the Bureau of Reclamation's greatest dams. Under an arrangement with, and financed by, the Natural Resources Commission of the Chinese government, the Bureau of Reclamation will assist in the preparation of final reports for the project. Chinese engineers and technicians paid by their own government are participating in this work in the Denver office of the bureau. The Yangtze Gorge Project marks an important scientific advancement from the simple irrigation systems built by ancient rulers.

Bibliography.—Willcocks, Sir William, *River Regulation and Control in Antiquity,* address delivered at National Drainage Congress, Savannah, Ga., April 24, 1914; United States Department of the Interior, Bureau of Reclamation, *Farmer's Irrigation Guide* (Washington 1939); id. *Reclamation Handbook,* Conservation Bulletin No. 32 (Washington 1942).

MICHAEL W. STRAUS,
Commissioner of United States Bureau of Reclamation.

IRRIGATION BILL or RECLAMATION ACT, a federal measure, approved June 17, 1902, for the reclamation by irrigation of arid and semiarid lands in Arizona, California, Colorado, Idaho, Kansas, Montana, Nebraska, Nevada, New Mexico, North Dakota, Oklahoma, Oregon, South Dakota, Utah, Washington, and Wyoming. On June 12, 1906, the Congress also extended the Act of 1902 to the State of Texas. Since the passage of the original act other reclamation laws have been added. Under the basic law to June 30, 1945, the Bureau of Reclamation had constructed, in addition to 179 dams, 15,495 miles of canals, 347 tunnels, 209,016 canal structures, 5,196 miles of waste-water ditches and drains, 13,676 bridges, 23,620 culverts, 6,318 flumes, and 331 pumping plants. It has excavated during construction of its projects 606,313,120 cubic yards of earth and rock, poured 33,671,861 cubic yards of concrete, and used 38,289,133 barrels of cement. The storage reservoirs behind its dams have a capacity of 66,558,840 acre-feet. Operating on its projects are 31 hydroelectric plants with an installed capacity of 2,439,300 kilowatts.

IRRITABILITY, in plants, term designating phenomena, very interesting and curious, but very little understood. Such are the phenomena of what is usually called the sleep of plants; the motion of the spores of many cryptogamic plants by means of cilia; the motions of *Oscillatoriae, Diatomaceae,* and others of the lowest Algae; the successive approaches of the stamens of *Parnassia* palustris to the pistil; the movements of the leaves of the moving plant of India; and those caused by agitation or by the touch of a foreign body in the leaves of sensitive plants of the *Dionaea muscipula* or Venus's-flytrap, etc., in the stamens of the barberry, shizanthus, etc., and in the stigmas of mimulus, etc. Many explanations have been proposed of these phenomena, but none satisfactory. Of the existence of anything analogous to the nervous system of animals, which has been imagined, there is not the slightest proof.

IRUN, Spain, town on the frontier, in the province of Guipúzcoa, on the Bidassoa, and on the Spanish Northern Railway, about five miles inland from the Bay of Biscay. It is a port of entry and has the largest customhouse in Spain for overland trade. It is served by several small mining railways and tramways which join it with the mines of Guipúzcoa and Navarre. It has also several medicinal springs and is a great clearing point for travelers. Its industrial establishments are numerous and thriving; they include iron foundries, tanneries, paper mills and potteries, brickyards, etc. Its most noteworthy buildings are the town hall and a parish church in the Renaissance style. Pop. (1940) 7,790.

IRUS, nickname of the beggar of Ithaca who served the suitors of Penelope as a messenger. His real name was Arnaeus. He was slain by Odysseus. Immortalized in the 18th book of Homer's 'Odyssey,' he becomes the typical beggar of later literature.

IRVINE, ėr'vĭn, **Frank,** American lawyer: b. Sharon, Pa., 15 Sept. 1858. After studying at Cornell University and at the National University at Washington he was admitted to the bar in 1883. For about one year he was assistant United States attorney. In 1884 he removed to Omaha, Neb., where he practised law and was appointed judge of the 4th district of Nebraska (1891–93) and Supreme Court commissioner (1893–99). In 1901 he became professor of pleading and practice in the Law College at Cornell, and dean of that faculty (1907–14). From 1914–21 he was a member of the Public Service Commission of the second district of New York. D. 1931.

IRVINE, William, American Revolutionary general: b. near Enniskillen, Ireland, 3 Nov. 1741; d. Philadelphia, 29 July 1804. Having graduated at Dublin University, he studied medicine and surgery, and was appointed surgeon on board a ship of war, serving during a part of the war of (1756–63) between Great Britain and France. On the declaration of peace he emigrated to America, and in 1764 settled in Carlisle, Pa. At the opening of the Revolution he took the part of the colonies, was a member of the provincial convention assembled in Philadelphia, 15 July 1774, until he was appointed by Congress, 9 Jan. 1776, colonel of the 6th battalion of the Pennsylvania line. He was sent with his command to Canada and in June 1776, was captured as the result of the disastrous engagement near Three Rivers. Exchanged 21 April 1778, he was promoted on 12 May 1779 to the rank of brigadier-general, and assigned to the command of the second brigade of the Pennsylvania line. In the autumn of 1781 he was ordered to Fort Pitt, to take command of the troops on the western frontier, and continued to fulfil the duties of this post, until after the war had closed. He was early in 1785 appointed by the State agent under an «act for directing the mode of distributing the donation lands promised to the troops of the commonwealth.» About this time he suggested to Pennsylvania the purchase from the United States of the tract of land known as «the triangle,» thus giving to the State an outlet upon Lake Erie. He was a member of Congress under the confederation (1787–88) and of the Third Federal Congress (1793–95). In 1794 he was assigned to the command of the Pennsylvania troops for the purpose of quelling the «whisky insurrection,» and in all the most important movements in connection with this subject took an active part. In 1797 he was one of the 13 presidential electors from Pennsylvania who elected John Adams President of the United States. In 1801, after Thomas Jefferson's election to the presidency, he was appointed intendant of military stores, having charge of arsenals, ordnance, army supplies and Indian affairs. He was president of the State society of the Cincinnati at the time of his death. Consult Butterfield, C. W., ed., 'Washington-Irvine Correspondence' (Madison 1881); Montgomery, T. L., ed., 'Pennsylvania Archives' (Series V, Vol. II, Harrisburg 1906).

IRVINE, er'vin, Scotland, royal, municipal, police burgh and seaport of Ayrshire, on the Irvine estuary, and on the Caledonian Railway, 30 miles southwest of Glasgow. Its public buildings include the town hall, academy, and fever hospital. It has also two old Norman castles. The chief industries are iron founding, shipbuilding, manufacture of machinery, soap, chemicals, bookcloth, etc. Coal, iron, and chemical products are exported. The harbor had become silted up by 1875, but has since been dredged and new wharves have been installed, and the volume of its sea trade has greatly increased. The water-supply system is the property of the burgh. Pop. 11,826.

IRVING, ėr'vĭng, **Edward,** Scottish preacher, founder of the religious sect known as Irvingites: b. Annan, Dumfriesshire, 4 Aug. 1792; d. Glasgow, December 1834. He was graduated at the University of Edinburgh in 1809, taught school for some eight years, meanwhile becoming, 1815, a licentiate of the Church of Scotland and, in 1819, Dr. Chalmer's assistant in Saint John's parish, Glasgow. During these years he formed an intimate friendship with Carlyle whom he introduced to his future wife, Jane Welsh. Irving himself had been in love with the latter, but, having become engaged some years before to a Miss Martin, finally married this lady. In 1822 he became minister of the Caledonian Asylum chapel in Cross Street, Hatton Garden, London. Here he soon attracted very large congregations by the force and eloquence of his discourses, and the singularity of his appearance and gesticulation. The greatest orators and statesmen of the day crowded with the wealthy and fashionable to hear him. The appearance of the preacher — tall, athletic, and sallow — displaying a profusion of jet-black glossy hair reaching to his shoulders, with a singular obliquity in one of his eyes, and a stern calm solemnity of aspect, enhanced the interest and excitement produced by his discourses. His phraseology was one of the peculiarities which gave him *éclat* with the public, for he expressed his ideas in the language of Milton, Hooker, and Jeremy Taylor. At London he began to publish books in which he broached novel theological views. 'Sermons, Lectures, and Occasional Discourses,' in which his theological divergences were first distinctly enunciated, were published in 1828. In the beginning of 1832 his inferences, especially in connection with the so-called «unknown tongues,» miraculous powers supposed to be owned by a Scotch girl, Mary Campbell, had appeared so extraordinary to his hearers, who in 1829 had erected for him a large church in Regent Square, that they preferred charges against their minister. On 2 May 1832 the London presbytery unanimously found him guilty of error. The consequence was that he was dismissed from his pulpit. In 1833 the presbytery of Annan, which had licensed him, deposed him from the ministry, on which occasion his defense of himself was a sublime effort of oratory. He retired to Scotland, broken in health and spirits, and was attacked with consumption. He also published 'Four Orations' (1823); 'For Judgment to Come' (1823); 'Babylon and Infidelity Foredoomed' (1826); 'Exposition of the Book of Revelation' (1831). A collection of his writings, edited by Gavin Carlyle, was published in 5 volumes

(1864–65). (See CATHOLIC APOSTOLIC CHURCH). Consult Anon., 'E. Irving and the Catholic Apostolic Church' (London 1856); Oliphant, Mrs., 'Life of E. Irving' (2 vols., London 1862); Wilks, W., 'E. Irving' (London 1854).

IRVING, Sir Henry (originally JOHN HENRY BRODRIBB), English actor: b. near Glastonbury, 6 Feb. 1838; d. Bradford, 13 Oct. 1905. He was a clerk in London, but adopted the theatrical profession, his first appearance being at Sunderland in 1856. He appeared first in London at the Princess' Theatre, in 1859; later went to Manchester and other provincial towns where he remained for five or six years, but returned to London in 1866, where his first marked success was as Digby Grant in Albery's 'Two Roses' (in 1870), which was followed by his powerful impersonation of Mathias in 'The Bells.' This began, in 1871, his long association with the Lyceum Theatre. His next noteworthy parts were Charles I, Eugene Aram, and Richelieu, in the plays so named. In 1874, at the Lyceum Theatre, he sustained the part of Hamlet so successfully as to raise himself to the first place among English actors. His chief Shakespearian parts were Macbeth, Othello, Shylock, and Richard III. In 1878 he leased the Lyceum Theatre for himself, and later put on the stage in excellent style 'Othello,' 'The Merchant of Venice,' 'Much Ado About Nothing,' 'Romeo and Juliet,' 'Twelfth Night,' 'Faust,' 'Macbeth,' 'Henry VIII,' 'King Lear,' etc., playing in them the principal character with Miss Ellen Terry as his leading lady. His appearances in the provinces were equally successful with those in London, and he met with like favor in his repeated visits to the United States. Of his last great rôles may be cited Becket in Tennyson's play of that name (1893), King Arthur in a play of that name (1895), Napoleon in 'Madame Sans-Gene' (1897), the title rôle in his son's play of 'Peter the Great' (1898), and Robespierre in a play of that name (1899), especially written for him by M. Victorien Sardou, and the title rôle in 'Dante' by the same author (1903). He was knighted in 1895, being the first actor to receive this honor, and the universities of Dublin, Glasgow and Cambridge conferred on him the honorary degree of LL.D. Although critics by no means agreed as to the merits of his acting, it must be admitted that he excelled in originality, versatility and intellectuality of his interpretations practically every actor of his times. His mannerisms of expression and deportment frequently lowered the value of his work, the sincerity of which, however, could not be decreased even by these handicaps. As a manager, too, he was a leading figure, both in respect to his elaborate productions and to the quality of his supporting companies. He was buried in Westminster Abbey. Some of his public addresses have been published, notably 'The Stage' (London 1878); 'The Stage as It Is' (London 1881); 'English Actors' (Oxford 1886); 'The Drama' (London 1893). Consult Archer, W., 'Henry Irving, Actor and Manager' (London 1883); Brereton, A., 'The Lyceum and Henry Irving' (London 1903); Id., 'Life of Henry Irving' (2 vols., London 1908); Child, H. H., 'Sir Henry Irving' (in 'Dictionary of National Biography,' 2d Supplement, Vol. II, London 1912); Drew, E., 'Henry Irving on and off the Stage' (London 1889); Fitzgerald, P., 'Sir Henry Irving' (London 1906); Forshaw, C. F., ed., 'Tributes to the Memory of the late Sir Henry Irving' (London 1905); Hiatt, C., 'Henry Irving' (London 1899); Marshall, F., 'Henry Irving, Actor and Manager' (London 1883); Menpes, M., 'Henry Irving' (London 1906); St. John, C., 'Henry Irving' (London 1906); Shaw, G. B., 'Dramatic Opinions and Essays' (London 1907); Stoker, Bram, 'Personal Reminiscences of Henry Irving (2 vols., London 1906); Terry, Ellen, 'The Story of My Life' (London 1908); Winter, W., 'Henry Irving' (New York 1855).

IRVING, Henry Brodribb, English actor-manager, son of Sir Henry Irving: b. London, 5 Aug. 1870; d. 17 Oct. 1919; educated at Marlborough College and New College Oxford. He appeared on the stage at the Garrick Theatre in 'School,' 1891; was called to the bar in 1894, but within a short time gave up the law for the stage. In 1895 he played at the Comedy with Comyns Carr and later in the same year toured the provinces with Ben Greet. The following year he appeared at the Saint James's. After 1900 he became one of the most successful London managers. In 1908 he became the lessee of the Shaftesbury Theatre and in 1909–11 was lessee of the Queen's. He toured America in 1906, Australia in 1911–12 and South Africa in 1912–13. From the latter year he was the lessee of the Savoy Theatre. He published 'The Life of Judge Jeffreys' (1898); 'French Criminals of the 19th Century' (1901); 'Occasional Papers' (1906); 'The Trial of Franz Müller' (1911); 'The Trial of Mrs. Maybrick' (1913).

IRVING, Isabel, American actress: b. Bridgeport, Conn., 28 Feb. 1871. In January 1887 she made her debut as Gwendolyn Hawkins in 'The Schoolmistress' with the Rosina Vokes Company. From 1888 to 1894 she was a member of Augustin Daly's company. Subsequently she was leading woman at the Lyceum Theatre, New York, and in John Drew's company for several years. Miss Irving has played leading rôles in England also; created the rôle of Lady Jocelyn Leigh in 'To Have and to Hold.' She starred under the management of James K. Hackett in 'The Crisis.' She played Louise in the all-star cast of 'The Two Orphans,' in 1905, under the management of Liebler and Company. She was engaged by Fitch to play in 'The Toast of the Town,' in 1906; in 'Susan in Search of a Husband,' and 'The Girl who Has Everything,' in 1907. In the following year Miss Irving created the title rôle in 'Mater' at the Savoy Theatre, New York. She played the leading woman's rôle in 'The Flag Lieutenant'; and leading rôle in 'The Commanding Officer' (1909). She also played the comedy rôle in 'Smith' with John Drew at the Empire Theatre, New York, and on tour in 1909–11. In 1913 she had the title rôle in the 'Mollusc,' with Kyrle Bellew, and later in the same year was leading woman with Leo Dietrichstein in 'The Concert' and 'The Temperamental Journey.' In 1914–15 she played the comedy rôle in 'Under Cover' in Chicago and San Francisco; in 1916–17, she played in 'The Merry Wives of Windsor'; in 1917 'Mistress Page'; in 1918–19 'She Walked in Her

Sleep'; in 1919–20 'Civilian Clothes'; in 1921 'A Bachelor's Night'; in 1922–23 'To the Ladies'; in 1924 'We Moderns'; in 1924 'The Bride'; in 1925–26 'A Lady's Venture.'

IRVING, John Duer, American geologist: b. Madison, Wis., 18 Aug. 1874; d. 27 July 1918. Graduated at Columbia University in 1896. He was geologic aid in 1899–1900; assistant geologist, in 1900–06; and geologist in 1906–07 of the United States Geological Survey. At the University of Wyoming in 1902–03, while on a special leave of absence he was acting professor of mining and geology and in 1906 was professor of geology at Lehigh University. From 1907–18 he was professor of economic geology at the Sheffield Scientific School of Yale. In 1907 he was employed as geologist by an Alaska syndicate. He was editor of *Economic Geology* and author of 'Economic Resources of the Northern Black Hills.'

IRVING, Lawrence (SYDNEY BRODRIBB), English actor, son of Sir Henry Irving: b. 1872; d. 31 May 1914. He received his education in Marlborough College, the Collège Rollin, Paris. He was intended for the diplomatic service and for three years studied in Russia. His theatrical debut took place at Dundee in 1893 in a Shakespearean rôle. From that time to 1900 he starred in provincial companies appearing in such plays as 'Trilby,' 'A Bunch of Violets,' and 'Under the Red Robe.' From 1900 to 1904 he was a member of his father's company. Soon after he appeared as Crawshay in 'Raffles.' In 1908–09 he visited America where he appeared in his own plays. In 1910 he produced 'The Unwritten Law' at the London Garrick. In 1912 he again appeared in a Shakespearean rôle — Iago in Tree's company at His Majesty's Theatre, Montreal. He lost his life on the *Empress of Ireland,* when that vessel was rammed and sunk by a collier in the Saint Lawrence. Irving wrote 'Peter the Great,' 'Bonnie Dundee,' 'Richard Lovelace,' 'The Typhoon,' and a translation of Gorky 'The Lower Depths' (1912).

IRVING, Washington, American author: b. New York, 3 April 1783; d. Tarrytown, N. Y., 28 Nov. 1859. His father, William Irving, merchant, came to New York from the Orkneys in 1763, having married Sarah Sanders, daughter of Cornish parents, two years before. Washington was the youngest of their 11 children. His school training was far from thorough, and was not directed toward academic culture — though two of his brothers had been sent to Columbia College — a decision of his father that he much regretted in maturer years. He made up for his lack of interest in school subjects by enthusiastic reading in English authors, particularly Chaucer and Spenser. At 16 he entered a law office, and in 1802 began authorship by contributing humorous sketches, over the name of «Jonathan Oldstyle,» to *The Morning Chronicle,* a daily edited by his brother Peter. Developing symptoms of consumption, he sailed in 1804 for France, and spent two years in travel, on the continent and in England, which restored his health. On return he was admitted to the bar, but instead of practice began, in 1807, with his brother William and James K. Paulding, the issue of 'Salmagundi,' the success of which determined his career, and the immediate character of his writing. At the close of the next year he set about reshaping the burlesque history of New York, which he had begun, with Peter Irving, some time before on a different plan. While in this work he met with the great affliction of his life, the loss of his betrothed, Matilda Hoffman, daughter of a prominent lawyer of the city, in whose office he had finished his legal studies. The completion of the book, 'Dietrich Knickerbocker's History of New York,' published in 1809, was the only solace that he permitted himself in the first months of seclusion and grief. In 1810 he wrote a short life of the poet Campbell, and was received into partnership by his brothers Peter and Ebenezer, who were founding an importing house, and wished to provide Washington the means, without contribution of time or labor to the business, of preparing himself more fully for his chosen work. In 1813 and 1814 he edited the *Analectic Magazine,* published in Philadelphia, and contributed biographical articles upon some of the naval commanders in the war then in progress with Great Britain. After the burning of our national capital in 1814 he offered his services to his native State, and was made aide-de-camp to Governor Tompkins, with the rank of colonel. At the close of the war he sailed for England, and was received with distinction by the American artists Allston and Leslie, and by Scott, Campbell, Moore and other literary men. In 1818 the firm of P. and E. Irving and Co. failed, and Washington's pleasant rambles in England and Scotland came to an end. He declined a post in the navy board, at home, and set himself at work in London with his pen. Early in the next year he sent over for publication in New York and Philadelphia the first number of the 'Sketch Book,' containing 'The Voyage,' 'Roscoe,' 'The Wife' and 'Rip Van Winkle.' Other numbers followed, the success was great, and in 1820 John Murray brought out an edition of the work in London. Its popularity with British readers was such that Murray became the first publisher of 'Bracebridge Hall' (1822), 'Tales of a Traveller' (1824), and other works. In 1826 Irving went to Madrid at the instance of his friend, Alexander H. Everett, American minister to Spain, who advised the translation of Naverreté's 'Voyages of Columbus,' then issuing in parts. Irving found the work impracticable to translate, being a collection of sources rather than a consistent narrative, and prepared instead the 'History of the Life and Voyages of Christopher Columbus,' finished in 1828. This first serious product of Irving's powers retained much of the ease and charm of 'The Sketch Book' and 'Tales of a Traveller,' and was eminently adapted to increase his fame. It was not especially successful, though Murray paid 3,000 guineas for the copyright; an abridgment of the work had a better sale. 'The Conquest of Granada' (1829), 'Companions of Columbus' (1831) and 'The Alhambra' (1832) were further fruits of his Spanish studies and travel. In the meantime he had been made secretary of legation (1829) in London, and received the medal of the Royal Society of Literature (1830), and the degree of LL.D. (1831) from Oxford. In 1832 he returned to America, but not to rest. He accompanied an Indian commission to Fort Gibson, on the Arkansas River, and wrote 'Tour on the Prairies,' published as the first volume of *The Crayon Miscellany,* in 1835. The second volume, *Abbotsford and Newstead Abbey,* and the third, *Legends of the Conquest of Spain,* followed in a few months. He now bought the little van Tassel farm at Tarrytown, and began to enlarge its Dutch cottage and improve the grounds. To this home, called "Sunnyside," he soon removed from the city, and eventually brought to it the brothers who had aided him in earlier years. In 1836 he finished *Astoria,* with the help of his nephew, Pierre M. Irving, from materials furnished by John Jacob Astor. The next year he published *The Adventures of Captain Bonneville, U.S.A.,* properly a continuation of the preceding. He then began a history of the conquest of Mexico, but on learning that W. H. Prescott was at work on the same subjects resigned the task to him. In 1839 he was engaged to write for the *Knickerbocker Magazine,* and furnished monthly articles for about two years. In 1842 he was appointed minister to Spain, and for the next four years wrote little. On his return he arranged with G. P. Putnam for a complete edition of his works, in 15 volumes, to which he added (1849) *Oliver Goldsmith,* and (1850) *Mahomet and his Successors.* The way was now open for the *Life of Washington,* which had long been contemplated. In 1855 appeared *Wolfert's Roost,* mainly a reprint of the Knickerbocker papers, and two volumes of the *Life.* The work told on his strength, and the fifth and last volume, finished in March 1859, left him a broken man. His death was from heart disease, in his 77th year. He was buried by the side of his mother, whose tastes he had inherited and whose sympathy and nurture had made him what he was. His authorship was the outcome of his personal character, and was little modified by the literatures of the world. With all his graces of expression he lacked the gift of deep insight, and failed to achieve much vigor of style. The best biography is still the *Life and Letters* by his nephew, Pierre M. Irving (1862–1864). (See also SKETCH BOOK, THE; KNICKERBOCKER HISTORY OF NEW YORK).

IRVINGTON, town, N. J., in Essex County; altitude 212 feet; which adjoins Newark on the southwest. It is a residential suburb with an industrial section where such varied products as chemicals, insulating material, toy trains, hosiery, cutlery, and metal castings and tools are made. Settled before 1700, it was called Camptown until 1852, when it was renamed in honor of Washington Irving. It was incorporated in 1898, and has commission government. Pop. (1940) 55,328; (1950) 59,201.

IRVINGTON, village, N. Y., in Westchester County; altitude 175 feet; on the Hudson River; on New York Central Railroad, 22 miles north of New York; immediately south of Tarrytown. A settlement made on the site about 1650 was called Dearman until 1854, when it was named for Washington Irving, who had bought 10 acres here called Wolfert's Roost. He renamed it Sunnyside and died there in 1859. In the 1880's many rich men lived here: Jay Gould, Cyrus W. Field, the Morgans, Fargos, and Harpers. The Jonathan Dell House (1693) was a Revolutionary War inn. Here are the Guiteau Public Library, a Children's Museum, and Irvington House for Cardiac Children. Although Irvington is mainly residential, it has several large industries, notably the manufacture of greenhouses and ventilating boilers. The village was incorporated in 1872. Pop. (1940) 3,272; (1950) 3,657.

IRWIN, May, American actress: b. Whitby, Ont., Canada, June 27, 1862; d. New York City, Oct. 22, 1938. She made her debut at the Adelphi Theater, Buffalo, in 1876 and the following year came to New York and joined Tony Pastor's company, where, in 1883, Augustin Daly discovered her. For the next four years she was a member of Daly's company, making her first success as a comedian and her London debut. Subsequently she appeared in *Junior Party, His Wedding Day, Poets and Puppets, A Straight Tip,* etc. Later she starred in *The Widow Jones.* This was one of her biggest hits and was followed by *The Swell Miss Fitzwell, Courted into Court, Kate Kip-Buyer, Sister Mary, Belle of Bridgeport, Mrs. Black is Back, Mrs. Peckham's Carouse, Getting a Polish, She Knows Better Now, Widow by Proxy, No. 33 Washington Square, On the Hiring Line.*

IRWIN, Wallace, American journalist and author: b. Oneida, N. Y., March 15, 1875. He was educated at Stanford University, and in 1900 became a special writer on the San Francisco *Examiner;* in 1902 he edited the *Overland Monthly Magazine;* in 1903, was a burlesque writer for the Republic Theater, San Francisco; in 1904–1905, he wrote topical verse for the New York *Globe;* and in 1906–1907 was on the staff of *Collier's Weekly.* In 1917–1919, he served as a member of the American Committee on Public Information. His numerous books include *Chinatown Ballads* (1905); *Letters of a Japanese Schoolboy* (1909); *Mr. Togo, Maid of All Work* (1913); *Venus in the East* (1918); *The Blooming Angel* (1919); *Mated* (1926); *Lew Tyler and the Ladies* (1928); *The Days of Her Life* (1931); *The Julius Caesar Murder Case* (1935); *Young Wife* (1936); *Yankee Doctor in Paradise,* with Dr. S. M. Lambert (1940–1941).

IRWIN, William Henry (WILL IRWIN), American journalist and author: b. Oneida, N. Y., Sept. 14, 1873; d. New York City, Feb. 24, 1948. He received an A. B. degree from Stanford University in 1899; entered journalism in San Francisco and was assistant editor in 1899, and editor in 1900 of the *Wave.* He joined the staff of the *Chronicle* in 1901, and was its Sunday editor in 1902–1904. He then went to New York and was a reporter on *The Sun,* 1904–1906. For it he wrote his journalistic classic—the story of the earthquake and fire which partly destroyed San Francisco; afterward published in book form under the title *The City That Was* (1907). He was managing editor of *McClure's Magazine,* 1906–1907; a writer on *Collier's Weekly,* 1907–1908, and thereafter devoted himself to general magazine writing. In 1914–1915, he was war correspondent for various American publications and also for the *London Daily Mail* with the German, Belgian and British armies. He was war correspondent for the *Saturday Evening Post,* 1916–1918, with the British, French, Italian and American armies, and in 1918 was also chief of foreign department of the American Committee on Public Information. He was a brother of Wallace Irwin (q.v.).

His published works include *Stanford Stories,* with C. K. Field (1900); *The Hamadryads* (verse, 1904); *Old Chinatown* (1908); *The Confessions of a Con Man* (1909); *The House of Mystery* (1910); *The Red Button* (1912); *Where the Heart Is* (1912); *Men, Women and War* (1915); *The Latin at War* (1916); *A Reporter in Armageddon* (1918); *The Thirteenth Chair*, play, with Bayard Veiler (1916); *The Next War* (1921); *Columbine Time* (1921); *Christ or Mars* (1923); *Youth Rides West* (1925); *How Red is America?* (1927); *Highlights of Manhattan* (1927); *Herbert Hoover—A Reminiscent Biography* (1929); *The House That Shadows Built* (1929); *Lute Song*, play with Sidney Howard (1930); *Propaganda and the News* (1936); *Spy and Counterspy*, with E. V. Voska (1940); *The Making of a Reporter* (1942); *Spies and Saboteurs*, with T. M. Johnson (1943).

ISAAC, ī'zȧk; ī'zĭk, Hebrew patriarch, son of Abraham and Sarah, the name signifying "laughter." According to the Biblical account given in Genesis 17, the birth of Isaac when Abraham was 100 years old and Sarah 90, was the guaranty of the existence of a covenant, in virtue of which, the descendants of Abraham would be a "chosen people" receiving special enlightenment. His life is highlighted in Scripture chiefly through the incidents of the dismissal of Hagar's son, whom Sarah had seen mocking Isaac (Genesis 21); the offering of Isaac as a sacrifice (Genesis 22) which was providentially averted, being only a test of faith and obedience; his marriage to Rebekah, the Aramean in his 40th year (Genesis 24); the birth of the twins Esau and Jacob after 20 years (Genesis 25), their later strife; Isaac's dream and God's promise to him of future enlargement (Genesis 26). The story of his old age is contained in the narration of the growing, open enmity between his two sons which had been foretold before their birth. In anticipation of his own death, Isaac bade Esau bring him some venison to receive his blessing; Jacob urged by Rebekah who had heard Isaac's request, appeared as Esau before the blind father to receive the blessing promised to his brother; and how Esau learned of Jacob's action and Jacob fled from Esau's wrath—are episodes that preserve after thousands of years their dramatic interest, while for the pulpit of all creeds they retain their power. All of the incidents of Isaac's life have become of great importance in metaphorical usage both in sacred and secular literature. At the age of 180 Isaac died at Hebron, cheered by the return of Jacob and his family from Mesopotamia, and was buried by both of his sons in the cave of Machpelah beside Abraham and Sarah (Genesis 35).

The early rabbis in the Midrash make frequent reference to Isaac. His name is made a compound of two Hebrew words denoting "Law was issued." In the Hebrew letters of his name allusion is found to the ten words (decalogue), and the respective ages of Sarah and Abraham at his birth. To silence evil tongues on the occasion of Isaac's weaning, Abraham's features were imprinted on his face, so that the likeness between father and son was very great. The sacrifice of Isaac furnishes a fertile field for Midrashic reflection and becomes a special feature of the Jewish liturgy. Christian interpretations sometimes regard it as a prefiguring of the crucifixion. Isaac is stated to have instituted the traditional afternoon prayer and to have had extraordinary attributes. In Mohammedan legend, Ishmael appears substituted for Isaac as offering and other points of similarity with the rabbinical Midrash are to be observed.

ISAAC I COMNENUS, Byzantine emperor: d. 1061. He was the son of Manuel Comnenus (q.v.) an eminent general under Basil II, emperor of Constantinople, and was the first of his family to assume the purple. He had distinguished himself as a soldier and commander in the wars against the Arabs, in Asia Minor and had married a captive Bulgarian princess. In 1057 he succeeded to the throne upon the deposition of the aged and incompetent Michael VI. During his short reign he made many reforms which are credited with prolonging the empire. His financial measures, though they improved conditions, were extremely unpopular. He also strengthened the empire by successfully repelling the Hungarians and Petchenegs who had been threatening the northern borders (1059). He abdicated in 1059 on account of sickness, appointing a relative, Constantine Ducas, as his successor. He spent the remainder of his life in the monastery at Studion where he had received his education as a youth. His interests were not purely military or political; he left a manuscript, still in existence, on Homer, entitled *Scholia*. He also wrote two other works on the same subject *Characteristics* and *On the Works of Homer*.

Consult Gibbon, E., *History of the Decline and Fall of the Roman Empire*, vol. 5 (London 1898); Finlay, G., *History of the Byzantine and Greek Empires, 1057–1453* (Edinburgh 1854); id., *History of Greece*, vols. 2, 3, 4 (Oxford 1877).

ISAAC II ANGELUS, Byzantine emperor: d. 1204. He became sovereign of the East as successor of Andronicus I in 1185, by a revolution, and reigned 10 years. During his rule the empire suffered several unsuccessful military campaigns and the excessive taxes caused the revolt of the Bulgarians and Vlachs (1186). After promising free passage through his empire to the crusaders under Frederic I Barbarossa (q.v.) of Germany, he treacherously formed an alliance against them with Saladin (q.v.) but was compelled to keep his promises through force of arms. Isaac was a vicious and weak prince. He was dethroned, blinded, and imprisoned by his brother Alexius in 1195. Eight years later he was restored to the throne, reigned for six months (1203–1204), was again dethroned and soon after died in prison.

Consult Gibbon, E., *History of the Decline and Fall of the Roman Empire*, vol. 5 (London 1898); Finlay, G., *History of the Byzantine and Greek Empires, 1057–1453* (Edinburgh 1854); id., *History of Greece*, vols. 3, 4 (Oxford 1877).

ISAAC, Heinrich, Flemish, composer: b. Brabant (East Flanders), c.1450; d. Florence, 1517. He arrived in Florence in 1484, married a rich butcher's daughter and was for years in Lorenzo de' Medici's service as organist. He set many of his patron's carnival songs to music and after Lorenzo's death (1492) took service with Emperor Maximilian. He was among the great musicians of his day, author of secular and sacred works.

ISAAC OF ANTIOCH, Syrian churchman and author: b. probably at Edessa, early in the 5th century. He removed to Antioch about 450 A.D. and for very many years was abbot of a monastery near that city. Many of his works are lost, but about 190 extant metrical homilies are attributed to him. Of these some most certainly are the work of another Isaac. (See SYRIAC LITERATURE). Consult Bedjan, 'Homiliæ S. Isaaci' (Paris 1903) and Brockelmann, 'Die Litteraturan des Ostens' (Vol. VII, Giessen 1907).

ISAACS, Rufus Daniel. See READING OF ERLEIGH.

ISAACS, Samuel Myer, Jewish editor: b. Leeuwarden, Holland, 4 Jan. 1804; d. New York, 19 May 1878. Coming to England in his early childhood, after work as educator in London, he was called to the ministry of the Elm Street synagogue in New York (1839). English sermons were then a novelty and his influence rapidly spread. In 1847 he was chosen minister of Wooster Street synagogue, with which he remained until his death. In the formative period of American Judaism, he was ceaseless in his activity — founding (1857) the *Jewish Messenger,* which he edited until the close of his life. His suggestions gave rise to many local and national institutions in education and charity; he was one of the founders and first vice-president of the Mount Sinai Hospital and universally esteemed for his genuine piety and usefulness.

ISAAKS, Jorge, HOR'HĀ ē'säks, Colombian novelist and poet b. Cali, State of Cauca, Colombia, 1843; d. 1895. He was the son of an English Jew who had married a Spanish woman and was taken to Bogotá in childhood, and ever after made it his home. He held various political offices, but is best known for his literary work. He published a volume of poems in 1864, and in 1867 his masterpiece, the novel, 'Maria,' a story of domestic life in Colombia, told with consummate skill and tender simplicity. An English translation of it was published by R. Ogden (New York 1890). He also wrote various other novels, none of which, however, achieved the fame of his first one.

ISABELA, ē-sä-bā'lä, Philippines, province of Luzon, on the northern Pacific Coast of the island with Cagayán on the north and Príncipe and Nueva Ecja on the south; length 118 miles; area, 5,395 square miles (including dependent islands), the largest province of Luzon. The Sierra Madre mountain range runs parallel to the coast, a short distance inland; the rest of the surface is broken by low hills; the Grande de Cagayán River traverses the entire length of the province; and the main highway from Aparri to Manila parallels this river. Rice, sugarcane, chocolate, coffee, corn and vegetables grow with little cultivation; tobacco is extensively raised and its growth and treatment is the most important industry. Cattle raising is also an important industry. Civil government was established in 1901. Pop. 76,431.

ISABELA, P. I., town in the province of Negros Occidental, Island of Negros, 35 miles south of Bacólod. Pop. (1940) 25,841.

ISABELLA, ISABEAU, or ELIZABETH OF BAVARIA, Queen of France: b. 1370; d. September 1435. In 1385 she was married to Charles VI of France, to whom she bore several children. She soon came under the influence of the dissolute court and when the king became insane in 1392 Isabella consorted with the king's brother, the Duke of Orleans. She was several times regent of the kingdom and on each occasion used her office to her own profit. After the assassination of the Duke of Orleans in 1407 she led a very scandalous life. She supported one political party after another and in 1417 was imprisoned. John the Fearless liberated her and in 1420, by the treaty of Troyes, Isabella surrendered the kingdom of France to the English. She gave her daughter in marriage to Henry V of England. After the Treaty of Troyes, Isabella was despised and hated by the French. She lived a lonely life of poverty in Paris. Consult Thibault, 'Isabeau de Bavière' (Paris 1903).

ISABELLA (ĭz-a-bel'a) **(I) OF CASTILE,** Queen of Spain, daughter of John II, King of Castile and Leon and his second wife Isabella of Portugal: b. Madrigal, 22 April 1451; d. Medina del Campo 26 Nov. 1504. She married, 19 Oct. 1469, Ferdinand V, King of Aragon (q.v.), surnamed «The Catholic.» After the death of her brother, Henry IV in 1474 she ascended the throne of Castile, to the exclusion of the latter's daughter, Joan, who was claimed to have been illegitimate. After the kingdoms of Aragon and Castile were thus once more united, Ferdinand and Isabella assumed the royal titles of Spain. She was always present at the transaction of state affairs and insisted that her name should be placed beside that of her husband in public ordinances. The conquest of Granada, after which the Moors were entirely expelled from Spain, was in a great degree her work; and the encouragement she gave Columbus, when everybody else doubted the feasibility of his plans, assisted him to the discovery of America. The broadness of her political vision and the strength of her character were chiefly responsible for the foundation of Spain's greatness. In all her undertakings Cardinal Ximenes was her assistant. In 1492 Pope Alexander VI confirmed to the royal pair the title of «Most Catholic,» already conferred on them by Innocent VIII. The zeal for the Roman Catholic religion, which procured them this title, unfortunately brought about the introduction of the Inquisition, which was instituted in Spain in 1480, at the suggestion of their confessor, Torquemada. (See FERDINAND V, XIMENES, SPAIN and COLUMBUS). Consult Clemencin, D., 'Précis Historique sur la Reine Catholique Doña Isabelle' (Paris 1847); George. A., 'Annals of the Queens of Spain, etc.' (2 vols., New York 1850); Hare, C., 'Queen of Queens and the Making of Spain' (New York 1906); Howard, O. O., 'Isabella of Castile' (New York 1894); Hume, M. A. S., 'Queens of Old Spain' (New York 1906); Lea, H. C., 'The Moriscos in Spain' (Philadelphia 1901); Id., 'History of the Inquisition of Spain' (4 vols., Philadelphia 1906–07); Mariejol, J. H., 'L'Espagne sous Ferdinand et Isabella' (Paris 1892); Nervo, G. D., 'Isabella, the Catholic' (trans. by T. Temple-West, London 1897); Prescott, W. H., 'History of the Reign of Ferdinand and Isabella, the Catholic' (3 vols., Philadelphia 1873); Sela, G., 'Politica Internacional de los Reyes Catolicos' (Madrid 1905).

ISABELLA II, ex-queen of Spain, daughter of Ferdinand VII and his fourth wife, Maria Christina of Naples: b. Madrid, 10 Oct. 1830; d. Paris, France, 9 April 1904. She succeeded her father in 1833, her mother, Queen Christine, acting as regent. The early years of her reign were disturbed by a rising in favor of her uncle, Don Carlos, who, if the Salic law had not been set aside, would have ascended the throne instead of her; but this was quelled in 1839. She was declared of age in 1843 and in 1846 she was married to her cousin, Don Francisco d'Assisi. She possessed few of the qualities that might have made her a successful ruler. She was bigoted, pleasure-loving, easily influenced and without political acumen. Her reign was so erratic and despotic that it resulted in many revolutions, the last of which, in 1868, finally drove her from the country. From then on she lived most of the time in or near Paris. She resigned her claims to the Crown in favor of her son Alfonso, who ascended the throne in 1875 as Alfonso XII (q.v.). Consult Abbott, J. S. C., 'Kings and Queens, Etc.' (New York 1848); Cambronero, C., 'Las Cortes de Isabel II' (in *España Moderna*, Vols. XXII–XXIII, Madrid 1910–11); Gribble, F. H., 'The Tragedy of Isabella II' (London 1913); Jarnar, A., ed., 'Les Rois Contemporains' (Bruxelles 1849); Molloy, J. F., 'The Romance of Royalty' (2 vols., New York 1904); Zöpfe, H., 'Historical Essay Upon the Spanish Succession' (London 1840). See SPAIN.

ISABELLA. 'Isabella, or the Pot of Basil,' written by John Keats in 1818 and published in the same volume with 'Lamia' and 'The Eve of Saint Agnes' in 1820, is a romantic tale in verse, founded on the fourth novel of the fifth day in Boccaccio's 'Decameron.' It tells of the love of the Florentine maiden Isabella for Lorenzo, a humble servitor in the establishment of her cruel and haughty brothers. Discovering her passion they treacherously murder her lover and bury his body in a forest. Lorenzo's spirit appears before the languishing Isabella and tells the story of his death. She, in her passion, digs up the body of the slain, cuts off the head and buries it in a garden pot, watering the basil plant which grows above it with her tears and dying of grief when it is stolen by her brothers. The revolting details of the story are not avoided by the author, but they are rendered tolerable by the rich poetic beauty with which they are invested. Love, which outlives death and can thrive on the «wormy circumstance» of dissolution, is the essential theme of the poem. The characteristic atmosphere of languishing beauty and decay is well rendered in Alexander's familiar painting, «Isabella.» The poem represents a considerable advance in art over Keats's earlier 'Endymion'; it is nevertheless inferior to his more mature and exquisite treatment of the theme of romantic love in 'The Eve of Saint Agnes.' For references consult article 'Ode on a Grecian Urn.'

JAMES H. HANFORD.

ISABELLITA. See BUTTERFLY-FISH.

ISABEY, e-za-ba', **Jean Baptiste,** French portrait painter: b. Nancy, 11 April 1767; d. 18 April 1855. He studied painting with David with the intention of applying himself to historical work, but began his art career with crayon portraits and achieved a wide renown as a miniature painter. His painting of Napoleon I reviewing his troops in the court of the Tuileries won the friendship of the Emperor and the appointment of court painter. The chief personages of Europe sat to him. His 'Napoleon at Malmaison' is considered the best portrait of that ruler. Besides a large number of portraits, he painted two notable historical and portrait-group works — the 'Tableau des Marechaux' (Napoleon and his principal generals), and the 'Conference at Vienna' after Napoleon's abdication. Consult Basili-Callemaki, 'J. B. Isabey' (Paris 1909).

ISABEY, Louis Gabriel Eugène, French painter: b. Paris, 1803; d. 1886. He received his artistic training from his father, Jean Baptiste Isabey, and in 1830 accompanied the Algerian expedition as painter. He exhibited regularly at the Salon until 1878. He excelled as a marine artist. His best known works are 'The Harbor of Honfleur' (1827); 'Battle of the Texel' (1839); 'View of Boulogne Harbor' (1843; not at Toulouse); 'Ceremony in the Church of Delft' (1847); 'Marriage of Henry IV' (1848); 'Embarkation of De Ruyter and De Witt' (1850); 'The Roadstead of Saint-Malo,' in the Luxembourg collection; 'The Banquet Hall,' in the Metropolitan Museum, New York.

ISAEUS: b. about 420 B.C.; d. about 350 B.C. one of the «Ten Attic Orators,» though probably a native of Chalcis, made his home in Athens, and there, in the first half of the 4th century B.C., we find him actively engaged in the profession of a speech-writer (logographer) for clients in the law courts. It is believed that he was a pupil of Isocrates (q.v.). In Attic oratory he represents the transitory period between Lysias (q.v.) and Demosthenes (q.v.). He seems also to have taught rhetoric, to Demosthenes among others, according to one tradition. We have from him a dozen orations dealing with inheritance cases, two of them in a fragmentary condition, although it is known that he wrote at least fifty. They are valuable not only as specimens of Attic Forensic style, but also as sources regarding early testamentary and private law and regarding the social life of ancient Greece. There are quite a number of manuscripts of his speeches, the best of which is known as 'Crippsianus A' in the British Museum. Of the many editions of his speeches the following should be mentioned: Aldus (Venice 1513); Bekker, I., (Oxford 1823); Dobson, W. S., (London 1828); Baiter, J. G., and Sauppe, H., (Zürich 1838–43); Schömann, G. F. (with commentary, Greifswalde 1831); Scheibe, C., (Leipzig 1860); Bürmann, H., (Berlin 1883); May, A., (Leipzig 1892); Wyse, W. (Cambridge 1904). The best edition is that of H. Buermann (Berlin 1883). There is an English translation by W. Jones, (London 1779); 'The Speeches of Isaeus'; a German translation by G. F. Schömann, 'Isäus der Redner' (2 vols., Stuttgart 1830); and a French translation by R. Dareste, 'Les Plaidoyers d'Isée (Paris 1898). Consult Baden, W. W., 'The Principal Figures of Language and Figures of Thought in Isaeus, Etc.' (Baltimore 1906); Belin de Balu, J. N., 'Histoire Critique de l'Éloquence chez les Grecs' (2 vols., Paris 1813); Blass, F., 'Attische Beredsamkeit' (2 vols., Leipzig 1887–93); Christ, W, von, 'Geschichte der Griechischen

Litteratur' (5th ed., 3 vols., Munich 1908–13); Hitzig, H., 'Studien zu Isaeus, Etc.' (Bern 1883); Jebb, R. C., 'Attic Orators from Antiphon to Isaeus' (2 vols., London 1876); Johnson, A. C., 'A Comparative Study in Selected Chapters in the Syntax of Isaeus, Isocrates, Etc.' (Athens 1911); Moy, L., 'Étude sur les Plaidoyers d'Isée' (Paris 1876); Roeder, W., 'Beiträge zur Erklärung und Kritik des Isaios' (Jena 1880); Volkmann, R., 'Rhetorik der Griechen und Römer' (Berlin 1872).

ISAIAH, ī-zā'yą or ī-zä'yą, one of the great Hebrew prophets. The name Isaiah, more exactly *Ye shă'ya* and *Ye shă'yāhû*, is derived from two Hebrew words and means «Jehovah saves.» It refers to the general burden of the prophet's message. The prophet, who was the son of Amoz (q.v.), a man otherwise unknown to us, was born probably at Jerusalem, and this place, the scene of his life work, and in his thought synonymous with his country, engrosses his attention. The year of his birth must have been about 760 B.C., his known activity begins in 739 and continues to 701 B.C., at least. He was married not far from the time of his call in 739, for in 735 a son of his, with a name symbolic of his prophetic message to Judah, *Shear-yashubh*, «a remnant shall turn» (i.e., to Jehovah), was of an age suitable to accompany his father in his walks. Another son, *Maher-shalal-hash-baz*, was born in 734, and his name also is symbolic of predicted events in the national history, namely, the fall of Damascus and Samaria, and means «hastening to booty, speeding to prey.»

It is to be remembered that Amos (750 B.C.), and Hosea (q.v.) (735 B.C.), are the only canonical prophets that preceded Isaiah and these had their work in the northern kingdom, though Micah (q.v.) prophesied in a country district of Judah during the middle and later periods of Isaiah's ministry. It is next to certain that Isaiah was of high rank, if not of the nobility in Judah, and at times might be as bold as he chose in his utterances to the court. We cannot be certain whether the Jewish traditions that he was the nephew of King Amaziah (Megilla, 10b), that he was slain by Manasseh (Jebamoth, 49b), and that he was sawn asunder ('The Ascension of Isaiah,' Ethiopic version; cf Justin Martyr, 'Dial. c. Trypho,' chap. cxx), have a basis in fact or not.

The principal crises of the country in Isaiah's time occurred in 735, 734 (during the reign of Ahaz), and in 701 (during Hezekiah's reign). The occasion of the first was the union of Damascus and north Israel against the Assyrian cver-lord, Tiglath-pileser III (745–727) and their attempt to overcome Judah. The occasion of the second crisis was the attempt of Judah and her neighbors to avoid tribute to Assyria and their alliance with Egypt against her. At this time Sennacherib was on the throne of Assyria (705–681). Besides these, there were moderate political disturbances in Judah during the reigns of Shalmanassar IV (727–722), and Sargon (722–705), for both of these warlike kings in these times were in the west country for conquest and subjugated north Israel, as well as the Philistine territory.

In meeting these crises, Isaiah showed himself the most consummate statesman and the most brilliant theological teacher in Israel in the times before Christ. His hold of truth was strong, his presentation of it was uncompromising, his oratory was superb, and the variety and finish of his discourses and the aptness of his illustrations, as well as the measured flow of his thought, were inimitable. It is of course true that in his teaching he built upon his predecessors, Amos and Hosea, but he put such a stamp of genius upon the ideas he cherished, that his influence has been the greatest of all the Hebrew prophets.

In general it may be said that Isaiah's messages had to do with the safety of the capital in the warlike times in which he lived, with the character of God in his sublime holiness and righteousness, and with the duty of his fellow-citizens to cultivate the righteous life, and, forsaking human political wisdom and alliances with the nations, to depend absolutely upon the Lord God. With him, religion and politics go hand in hand, and theological thinking is the kernel of his most practical and stirring addresses. Incidentally he has given us a view of the circumstances of his time, its social relations and habits, the fashions, the commotions and rumors, in times of peace and war, in seasons of prosperity and distress; in all showing himself the most vivid and powerful preacher of the olden time.

The convictions of Isaiah are due to his faith in God and arise out of the circumstances of the time. Jehovah is the Holy One of Israel, hence he must punish Jerusalem for her injustice to men and her falseness to God, and this he will do through the instrumentality of the most potent political powers of the age; but since Jerusalem is the throne of His glory, and the seat of true religion, however formal the people have made their worship, therefore, a portion of the Judeans will be spared, and the city will prove invincible. Indeed, his own beloved capital is destined to become the centre of religious truth for the nations, and is to have a new and perfect ruler, who will reign in wisdom and might, and will bring righteousness and peace to the people. See Isaiah, Book of.

Charles Rufus Brown,
Late Professor of Hebrew and Cognate Languages, The Newton Theological Institution, Newton, Mass.

ISAIAH, Book of. It must be premised that the old prophets of Israel, for the most part, gave themselves to oral utterance, and made little use of the written roll. In the case of some of them, the issue of written discourses was an after-thought, and the latter assumed forms revised to suit the practical needs of the readers, just as the first forms had been adapted to the needs of the audience that listened to the preacher's spoken words. This is undoubtedly true of the phophet Isaiah, who appears to have felt that by changes in phraseology he could the better meet the advancing needs of the men for whom he labored. In other words, the prophet's interest was not historical; he did not reproduce his sermons with the thought of preserving them for the world exactly as they were delivered, but he had the practical aim of moving a new circle of people to that faith in God which he had previously inculcated. This example was not lost upon the disciples and admirers of the prophets, and in the book of Isaiah the old messages have received modifications at different times to suit the conditions of successive generations. Indeed Isaiah in the pre-Christian centuries was held in such honor that authors added to his writings other discourses and historical material that were calculated to produce the results aimed at by our prophet, and in much of this material there is not even a kernel of Isaian authorship. It is true that such procedure is not in accord with modern ideas of literary ownership, but there is reason to suppose that in ancient times the name of the author of new material was of little consequence, and his work was often hidden in the product of some distinguished predecessor, the delivery of an exigent message being all important.

The book of Isaiah contains 66 chapters from various sources, being a combination of several collections of oracles, and divides itself naturally into seven grand divisions, viz.: chapters i–xii, xiii–xxvii, xxviii–xxxiii, xxxiv–xxxv, xxxvi–xxxix, xl–lv, lvi–lxvi.

1. Chapters i–xii contain several small sections or series of addresses, mostly by Isaiah himself. From the time of his call to the prophetic office in 739 B.C., he probably made notes of his discourses, and about 734, perhaps, he began to issue combinations of these, first for his disciples, and then doubtless for a larger circle of readers. Chapters vii, 1–ix, 7, composed of discourses delivered to Ahaz and the people of Judah in 735, 734, is probably the first of these combinations, and not long afterward this was increased by prefixing to it the inaugural vision, chap. vi, and by affixing ix, 8–x, 4 (with v, 25–30, now misplaced), the prophetic interpretation of north Israel's unhappy history and the application to Judah. Subsequently the prophet appears to have added the woe on Assyria, the instrument of Jehovah's anger against his people (x, 5–34), and a prophecy of the righteous king, to whom he had already referred, and of the restoration of Israel (chap. xi).

He, or some disciple of his, prefixed to the book ii, 1–iv, 1; chap. i; v, 1–24, series of discourses that present in most vivid manner the social conditions and the debased life of the age of Jotham and Ahaz, as well as the evil consequences to follow, ere the kingdom of God could be established. Chap. i, called by Ewald "The Great Arraignment, is a general introduction to this part, and was composed after 734, possibly several years afterward, chap. i:1, being an editorial note to introduce all the prophecies of Isaiah. Chap. iv, 2–6, chap. xii, are probably post-exilic additions to this division of Isaiah.

2. Chapters xiii–xxvii may be called the book of woes. The genuine Isaiah passages are in substance: xiv, 24–27, the removal of the Assyrian yoke, xiv, 28–32 woe on the Philistines, both delivered during the domination of Sargon or Sennacherib; xvi, 13–14, on Moab, delivered perhaps in 711; xvii, 1–11, the fall of Damascus, 735; xvii, 12–14, the repulse of Assyria, 701; chap. xviii, the message to Ethiopia concerning the disaster to Assyria, 701; chap. xx, on Egypt, 711; xxi, 11, 12, on Edom, and xxi, 13–17, on Arabia, of uncertain date, may have been readapted to the exilic situation in 545 B.C.; chap. xxii, against Jerusalem and one of its prominent statesmen, belongs to 702, 701; the substance of chap. xxiii (on Tyre), especially vss. 1–14, was given about 702 B.C. Upon these as a nucleus have been grafted oracles from various epochs and authors; namely xiii, 1–xiv, 23, the fall of Babylon, composed in Babylonia about 549 B.C.; xv, 1–xvi, 12, an old oracle quoted by Isaiah himself, possibly in 711; chap. xix, on Egypt, is a post-exilic oracle, but in vss. 1–15 there may be an Isaiah kernel, from 720, 711 or 702; xxi, 1–10, on Babylon, is exilic, dating from about 545 B.C.; chapters xxiv–xxvii form a long post-exilic apocalypse, concerning the judgment on the world and the future blessedness of Israel, and may be assigned with probability to the later Persian period.

3. Chapters xxviii–xxxiii are substantially from Isaiah's hand, and belong chiefly to the time of his later activity. In chap. xxviii, Isaiah's earlier message against Samaria (vss. 1–6, before 722) is reiterated with reasons, in or about 704. In chapters xxix–xxxii we have in several paragraphs a representation of the straits to which Jerusalem was put just before 701 B.C., the futility of reliance on Egypt for help, the weakness of the Judean politicians, the indifference of the women of the capital, the ultimate deliverance of the city, the fall of Assyria, and the coming of the Messianic age (the latter in three passages, xxx, 18–26; xxxii, 1–8, 15–20; chap. xxxiii) is supplementary to this, contains a woe upon some power hostile to Jerusalem, and the prediction of Judah's deliverance. This is probably a post-exilic expansion of Isaiah's utterances in 701 B.C. The sections xxix, 16–24; xxx, 18–26; chap. xxxii, have been assigned by some writers to exilic or post-exilic times, and they may contain some elements from these periods.

No further prophecies in the book can be assigned with probability to our prophet.

4. Chapters xxxiv–xxxv form a post-exilic prophecy of 450 B.C., or later, and treat of Israel's victory over Edom and of the joyful circumstances of Israel's restoration.

5. Chapters xxxvi–xxxix are historical chapters taken in large measure from 2 Kings. The Isaian passage omits 2 Kings–xviii, 14–16, and introduces the song of Hezekiah (Isa. xxxviii, 9–20) before 2 Kings xx, 12.

6. Chapters xl–lv are a long and developed prophecy, and comprise the great exilic prediction of about 540 B.C. concerning the return of Israel from Babylonia, through the instrumentality of Cyrus. Omitting subdivisions, of which there are many, Skinner and others divide about as follows:

Chapters xl–xlviii, the restoration: (1) xl, 1–11, the theme; (2) xl, 12–31, the infinity of God; (3) chap. xli, the historical situation, as it has been brought about by God for his servant Israel; (4) xlii, 1–xliii, 7, the work of Jehovah's ideal servant (xlii, 1–4) for Israel and the world, and the contrast with the servant Israel as he is; (5) xliii, 8–xliv, 5, the witness of Israel's history to the divinity of Jehovah, and the salvation of Israel and the nations through the divine interposition; (6) xliv, 6–23, the folly of idolatry; (7) xliv, 24–xlv, 25, the mission of Cyrus, the anointed of Jehovah, for Israel and for a world-wide religion; (8) chaps. xlvi, xlvii, the fall of Babylon; (9) chap. xlviii, the closing argument, and the joyful summons to Israel to depart from Babylon and to declare to the world their redemption by their God.

Chapters xlix–lv, the glorious future of Israel; (1) xlix, 1–13, the mission of the servant (vss. 1–6) to the world; (2) xlix, 14–l, 3, consolation for afflicted Zion; (3) l, 4–11, the perfection of the servant through suffering; (4) li, 1–lii, 12, the Israelites encouraged to accept the promises; (5) lii, 13–liii, 12, the servant's sacrificial work and his exaltation; (6) chaps. liv, lv, the felicity of Israel and the gracious call to accept the promised deliverance.

7. Chapters lvi–lxvi are probably for the most part of post-exilic origin, as they appear to contain detached messages of condemnation and promise to a people living in Palestine. Here there are details concerning the moral, social and religious duties of the people, and worship in the new temple appears to have been established. We divide: (1) lvi, 1–8, the admission of foreigners and eunuchs to the Israelitish community; (2) lvi, 9–lix, 21, a series of rebukes to several classes, interspersed with promises for fidelity; (3) chaps. lx-lxii, the new Jerusalem; (4) lxiii, 1–6, the divine hero in Edom; (5) lxiii, 7–lxiv, 12, confession of sin; (6) chaps. lxv–lxvi, the contrasted futures of true servants of God and apostates.

The principal idea of Isaiah, besides that of judgment, common to the prophets, was the deliverance from the foes of Jerusalem of the remnant of Israel, meditated by a righteous king. The principal ideas of Isaiah xl–lv are the deliverance of Israel from exile through Cyrus, and the deliverance of the people from sin and the impartation of spiritual graces through the suffering servant of Jehovah. Hope, therefore, is the keynote of this prophecy and comfort is the opening word. In connection with the theme, the prophet declares, in turn, after turn of speech, the reliability of God in bringing to pass his promises, the sublime grandeur of the Holy One, his creative power, the absurdity of idolatry. The writer makes it clear that the absolute and sole sovereign in the earth is Jehovah, the God of Israel. In Isaiah lvi–lxvi there is no advance upon these ideas, but many of them are reiterated there.

Bibliography.— Besides the appropriate sections in Encyclopedias, Old Testament Histories, Old Testament Introductions, Old Testament Theologies, works on Old Testament Prophecy and Messianic Prophecy, Dictionaries of the Bible, Histories of Assyria, Babylonia, Persia, Egypt and Syria, the following selected works may be consulted. For fuller lists the reader is referred to the articles in the Bible Dictionaries, and for the later books, to the lists of current literature in 'The Biblical World.' In the present list, works written in other languages and translated into English, are given in the translation only.

1. *Commentaries.*— Calvin (1850); Vitringa (1714–20, Latin); Lowth (1778); Gesenius (1821, German); Hitzig (1833, German); Ewald (1876–81); Henderson (1840); Umbreit (1846, German); Drechsler (1851–54, German); Alexander (1865); Delitzsch (1892); Reuss (1876, French); Nägelsbach in 'Lange' (1878); Birks (1878); Cheyne (1889); von Orelli (1889); G. A. Smith (1888, 1890); Duhm (1892, German); Skinner (1896, 1898); Guthe and Ryssel in 'Kautzsch' (1896, German); Mitchell (chaps. i–xii, 1897); Kittel's 'Knobel-Dillmann' (1898, German); Marti (1900, German); Whitehouse (1905).

2. *Other Works.*— Driver, 'Isaiah, His Life and Times' (1893); Davidson, 'Theology of Isaiah xl–lxvi' ('Expositor,' 1883–84); 'Theology of Isaiah' ('Expository Times' 1894); Guthe, 'Das Zukunftsbild des Jes' (1885); Giesebrecht, 'Beitrage zu Jes, Kritik' '1890); 'Der Knecht Jahves des Deuterojes' (1902); Hackmann, 'Die Zukunftserwartung des Jes' (1893); Cheyne, 'Introduction to Isaiah' (1895), Translation of Isaiah ii, 'Polychrome Bible' (1898); König, 'The Exiles' Book of Consolation' (1899); Davidson, 'The Servant of the Lord in Isaiah' (in *British and Foreign Evangelical Review,* 1872); Driver and Neubauer, 'The 53d of Isaiah according to Jewish Interpreters' (1876, 1877); Wright, 'Pre-Christian Jewish Interpretation of Isaiah LIII' (*Expositor,* May 1888); Lane, 'Die Ebed-Jahwe Lieder' (1898); Bertholet, 'Zu Jesaya LIII' (1899); Füllkrug, 'Das Gottesknecht des Deuterojes' (1900).

CHARLES RUFUS BROWN,
Late Professor of Hebrew and Cognate Languages, The Newton Theological Institution, Newton, Mass.

ISAR, or ISER, a river of Germany, rising in the Tyrol, north of Innsbruck, entering Bavaria, then flowing generally north and northeast, and joining the Danube at Deggendorf, after a course of about 180 miles. Munich and Landshut are on its banks. In the first part of its course, it is an impetuous mountain torrent; and even after it leaves the Alps, it has many rapids and islands, but for much of its course it is navigable for boats. Much wood is floated down the Isar from the mountains.

ISARD, or IZARD, the chamois of the Pyrenees. It is smaller and redder than its cousin of the Alps. See CHAMOIS.

ISAROG, a mountain peak of Luzon, P. I., in the Province of South Camarines. It is an extinct volcano and rises to a height of 6,450 feet from a base about 35 miles in circumference.

ISAURIA, in ancient geography, a district of Asia Minor, bounded north by Phrygia, east by Lycaonia, south by Cilicia, and comprising a barren upland plain with mountains in the south. The district is supposed to have contained but few towns, chief of which was Isaura, the capital, which was rebuilt by Amyutas. Extensive ruins, consisting of a massive wall with hexagonal towers, a triumphal arch, and tombs, are still seen near the town of Hajilar, 45 miles west of Karaman. The people believed to have been a daring lawless race, owing allegiance to either the Persian or Macedonian monarchy, appear in history as having been driven to their mountain strongholds and forced to submission by the pro-consul P. Servilius; as giving the Roman empire so much trouble that it was decided to leave them alone; as being a second time subjugated in the reign of Justinian; and as giving two occupants to the Byzantine throne, Zeno (474–495) and Leo III (717–41). Consult Ramsay, Sir W. M., 'Historical Geography of Asia Minor' (London 1890) and 'Nova Isauria' (in *Journal of Hellenic Studies,* ib., 1905).

ISCA DAMNONIORUM, the Roman name of the Celtic Caer-Isc, the modern Exeter, Devonshire (q.v.), England.

ISCHIA, ēs′kyä (the ancient *Aenaria*), Italy, an island between the Bay of Naples and the Bay of Gaeta, about 27 square miles in area and seven miles from the mainland. Ischia is a favorite summer resort, and is noted for the excellence of its mineral waters, great richness of soil, exquisite flavor of its fruits and wines, and enchanting scenery. Its highest point is the volcanic Monte Epomeo, 2,588 feet above sea level, of which the eruptions have been disastrous, especially that of 1302. The Lake of Ischia occupies an extinct crater of the volcano, and abounds in fish. The capital is Ischia, on the east coast, and other towns are Forio and Casamicciola; the last was nearly destroyed by earthquake in 1883. Pop. (1936) 29,550.

ISCHL, ĭsh′ĕl, Austria, market town and summer resort of Upper Austria, 55 miles southwest of Linz, at the confluence of the Ischl and Traun. It is picturesquely situated in the mountains about 1,500 feet above sea level. It contains a fine church built by Maria Theresa. There are a number of saline and sulphur springs, and also brine and brine vapor baths. Pop. (1939) 10,331.

ISEO, Lago d′, lä′gō-dē-zĕ′ō, a lake of northern Italy, northwest of Brescia and east of Bergamo, 24 miles wide and 17½ miles long. It is fed by the rivers Oglio and Borlazzo. The depth is nearly 1,000 feet. At the southern end of the lake is the town of Iseo.

ISERE, ē-zâr′, France, department of the southeast, part of the old province of Dauphiné, bounded north and west by the Rhone, east by Savoy, and south and southeast by Drome and Hautes Alpes. Its area is 3,178 square miles, about 50 per cent of which is arable and 20 per cent forest land. The surface is level in the north, but becomes very mountainous toward the south, where the scenery is magnificent. It is drained by the Rhone, and its tributary streams, the Isère, Drac, and Romanche. The department is rich in minerals. Coal, iron, lead, silver, gold, and marble are mined and the forest products are of importance. Gloves, paper, and silk are manufactured. Grenoble is the capital. Pop. (est. 1946) 574,019.

ISERE, ē-zâr′, a river of the southeast of France, which takes its rise in Savoy at the foot of Mount Iseran, flowing generally southwest through Savoy and through the departments of Isère and Drome, and joining the Rhone about six miles above Valence. Its entire length is about 190 miles, for the last 70 of which it is navigable.

ISERLOHN, ē-zĕr-lōn′, Germany, town in the province of Westphalia, on the Baar, 30 miles northeast of Barmen. It is a thriving manufacturing center, having numerous foundries, brass, iron, steel, and bronze mills, wire, needle, pins and hook works, silver and nickel ware factories, chemical works, and furniture and machine works. Mines beneath the town produce zinc and cadmium. The town has a technical school. Pop. (1939) 39,717.

ISERNIA, Italy, city in the province of Campobasso, 80 miles north of Naples. It contains several medicinal springs and is situated at an elevation of 1,495 feet. In the neighborhood are the ruins of the ancient Samnite town. Linen and pottery are the only manufactures of any consequence. Pop. (1939) 14,517.

ISEULT, ISOLD, ISOLDE, ISOND, ISOUD. See TRISTAN.

ISFAHAN, ĭs-fä-hän′, Iran, city 210 miles south of Tehran, former capital of the country. It is situated in the midst of an extensive plain watered by the Zaindeh Rud. At the heart of the city is a great square known as the Maiden-i-Shah, formerly encircled by a canal. Notable buildings still standing include a royal mosque built by Shah Abbas I, the royal palace, and a lofty archway which leads into magnificent gardens. The principal industries of the city include the manufacture of carpets, woolen and cloth textiles, and matches. There is also an extensive trade in leather goods, silver filagree work, and lacquered products. The city is the center of the activities of the Church Missionary Society (of the Anglican Church) and of Iranian adherents of the Roman Catholic Armenian rite.

Known to the ancients as *Aspadana,* the city reached its greatest prosperity under Shah Abbas I—early in the 17th century. Jean (later Sir John) Chardin (q.v.), who resided at Isfahan from 1664 to 1681, reported that the walls were 24 miles in circuit and contained 162 mosques, 48 colleges, 1,802 caravansaries, and 273 public baths. After the Afghans captured Isfahan in 1722 the capital was removed to Tehran; although soon retaken by Nadir Shah the city declined gradually in importance. During World War I, the Russians occupied it for a short period in 191‴–1916, then being replaced by a British force. Pop. (1942) 205,000. Consult Lockhart, L., *Famous Cities of Iran* (London 1939).

ISHAM, ī′shăm, **Samuel,** American painter and writer: b. New York City, May 12, 1855; d. Easthampton, N. Y., June 12, 1914. After graduating at Yale University in 1875 he studied law, but turned to painting after admission to the bar. He studied art in Paris and later in the United States, and in 1906 was made a National Academician. His fame rests, however, on his *History of American Painting* (1905), notable for its sympathetic and just appreciation.

ISHII, ē′shē-ē, VISCOUNT **Kikujiro,** Japanese diplomat: b. Chiba, 1866; d. Tokyo, May 25, 1945. Soon after taking a law degree at the University of Tokyo in 1890 he joined the staff of the Japanese legation in Paris, and from 1896 to 1900 he was consul in Chemulpo, Korea. In the latter year he was secretary of the legation in Peking (Peiping), during the siege by the Boxers (q.v.). He negotiated with the United States government in 1907 the agreement restricting emigration of Japanese to the United States, and the same year investigated the anti-Japanese riots in British Columbia. From 1912 to 1915 he was ambassador to France, then becoming minister of foreign affairs; in 1916 he received his viscountcy. In 1917 he went to Washington, D. C., as special envoy, there negotiating the Lansing-Ishii agreement with Robert Lansing, secretary of state, which recognized that Japan had special interests in China. Besides being versed in French, he was a fluent speaker and writer in English. From 1920 to 1927 he again served as Japanese ambassador in Paris. During this period he took an active part in the work of the League of Nations, becoming president of its council in 1923 and once more in 1926. He retired from public life in 1927. His death occurred in an air raid by United States planes during World War II.

ISHIM, ĭ-shĭm', Soviet Union. (1) Town of the Omsk Region, Russian Soviet Federated Socialist Republic, on the river of the same name, 180 miles northwest of Omsk. Founded in 1630, it is an agricultural center. Pop. 18,153. (2) River, rising in the north central area of the Kazak SSR and flowing northwest and north to join the Irtish after a course of 1,330 miles.

ISHMAEL, ĭsh'mā-ĕl, from Hebrew, signifying "God hears," was eldest son of Abraham and Hagar, his handmaid (Genesis 16:15, 16). Of him it was foretold (Genesis 17:18, 20) that he would beget 12 princes and become a great nation—a promise repeated (Genesis 21: 18) to his mother when, driven from home by Sarah's attitude, both she and the lad were wandering in the territory south of Beersheba and death by thirst was near. Later he became an archer, dwelling in the wilderness of Paran, where Hagar "took him a wife out of the land of Egypt" (Genesis 21:21). In a later chapter (Genesis 25:9-18) it is stated that he died at the age of 137, having had, like Jacob, 12 sons, progenitors of 12 tribes that dwelt from "Havilah unto Shur, that is before Egypt, as thou goest to Assyria." Apart from the Biblical record few of the names have historical associations. Among various identifications more or less plausible may be mentioned Nebaioth with the Nabataeans, Yetur with Ituraea, whose archers were early Roman mercenaries; Kedar with the Kidru of the Assyrian inscriptions.

In the Midrash, the rabbis show how Sarah's disposition to Hagar was at first kindly but that Hagar's actions compelled a change. Ishmael's intercourse with Isaac is told with considerable minuteness at times, as when he invites his five year old brother to a contest with the bow and arrow and aims at the child in his duplicity. When Ishmael was at the point of death, God heard his prayer and caused a well to bubble forth that later was to refresh the Israelites on their journey through the wilderness. In Arabic lore Ishmael is no less a picturesque figure, and the Koran adds to his importance for it calls him a prophet (Koran 19:55). His son Kedar is reported to have been an ancestor of Mohammed. It is characteristic of Mohammedan tradition that Ishmael should be offered as a sacrifice instead of Isaac. We cannot tell historically how far the descendants of Ishmael entered Arabia and settled there, with its mixed population of thousands of years. Possibly the Bedouins in the deserts between Sinai Peninsula and the Persian Gulf are more entitled to claims of Ishmaelitish origin with their primitive and patriarchal form of life and ancient traditions.

ISHMAELITES. See ISHMAEL.

ISHPEMING, ĭsh'pē-mĭng, city, Michigan, in Marquette County, 14 miles west of Marquette, served by the Duluth, South Shore, and Atlantic, the Lake Superior and Ishpeming, and the Chicago and Northwestern railroads. Machinery is manufactured for use in the neighboring great iron ore region. Settled about 1856, it received its first charter in 1857. Pop. (1940) 9,491; (1950) 8,962.

ISHTAR. See BABYLONIA.

ISIDORE OF SEVILLE, ĭz'ĭ-dōr sē-vĭl' (Lat. ISIDORUS HISPALENSIS), Spanish prelate and scholar: b. 560?; d. April 4, 636. In 600 he was appointed archbishop of Seville. A leading churchman of his day, he exerted a great influence upon the thought and literature of the whole Middle Ages. His *Originum seu Etymologiarum Libri XX* (known in English as *Etymologies*) was a great encyclopedic work. Consult Brihaut, E., *An Encyclopedist of the Dark Ages* (New York 1912).

ISINGLASS, ī'zĭng-glȧs, a form of gelatin (q.v.), whitish, firm in texture, and of great purity, prepared mainly from the sounds, or air bladders, of various species of fish, especially of the Russian sturgeon and, in the United States, of cod, sturgeon, and hake. In some cases the skins are also used for this purpose. Besides Russia, from which it had been principally obtained, the United States and Canada, Brazil, and the East Indies furnish considerable quantities. It is the basis of Russian glue, preferred to all other kinds for strength. It is used in making court plaster, cement, mock pearls, and many other articles; in clarifying fermented liquors for improving soups and jellies; and as sizing for linens, silk, gauzes, and other fabrics.

ISIS, ī'sĭs, the principal goddess of the Egyptians, the sister and wife of Osiris (q.v.), representing the moon, as Osiris did the sun. The Egyptians believed that Isis first taught them agriculture. She is represented in various forms. In one she has the form of a woman, with the horns of a cow, as the cow was sacred to her. She is also known by the attributes of the lotus on her head, and the sistrum in her hand, a musical instrument which the Egyptians used in the worship of the gods. She is often accompanied by her infant son Horus. In one celebrated Egyptian statue she was shown with her face veiled. It was she who, by wiles, learned the name of the great Ra (Re) which no one else knew. She is also represented in legends as mourning for Osiris with her sister Nephthys. Herodotus identifies her with the Greek Demeter. The same author states that the worship of Isis and Osiris was the only common ritual throughout Egypt. She was particularly worshipped in Memphis, but at a later period throughout all Egypt. From Egypt her worship passed over to Greece and Rome, in about the 3d century B.C.

ISIS AND SERAPIS, Temple of, a structure of ancient Rome, situated in the Campus Martius. It was erected from Egyptian materials and in Egyptian style, and the approach was lined with many monuments brought over from Egypt. Of these there remain in Rome three obelisks, and the Nile statuary group, the latter in the Vatican Museum. The Tiber statue has reposed in the Louvre since 1803. Various smaller pieces have been recovered.

ISKENDERUN, is-kĕn-dẽr-ōōn′, Turkey, seaport of the vilayet of Antakiya, in a gulf of the same name at the northeast extremity of the Mediterranean; formerly it was known as ALEXANDRETTE or ALEXANDRETTA. Much of the seaborne trade of northern Syria passes through the port, which has rail connection with the main Turkish system. Alexandrette formed part of the Ottoman Empire down to the close of World War I, when it was occupied by French troops. In 1920 the seaport was incorporated in the French mandate of Syria, and the sanjak (district) of which Alexandrette was the capital was granted considerable autonomy in 1937; in 1938 the name of the sanjak was changed to Hatay, and in 1939 Hatay was transferred to Turkish sovereignty. Hatay became part of the vilayet of Antakiya (Antioch), and Alexandrette resumed its earlier Turkish name of Iskenderun. Pop. (1940) 13,997.

ISLA, ēs′lä, **José Francisco de,** Spanish Jesuit preacher and satirist: b. Vidanes, province of Léon, April 24, 1703; d. Bolonia, Nov. 2, 1781. He entered the Jesuit order at the age of 16, and became a teacher of theology and philosophy in various Jesuit colleges. Best known of his writings was the picturesque novel entitled *Historia del Famoso Predicador Fray Gerundio de Campazas, alias Zotes* (1758), a witty satire on the extravagances of the preachers of his day. The ridicule cut so deep that it was never forgiven by some of his fellow preachers; and they raised up for him powerful enemies who, in 1760, succeeded in having the sale of *Fray Gerundio* prohibited. Among his most popular translations was *The Adventures of Gil Blas de Santillana,* the French work by Alain René Lesage (q.v.). Other works of Isla included *Triunfo del Amor y de la lealtad: Dia Grande de Navarra,* which satirized the accession ceremonies of Ferdinand VI; and the satire *Cartas de Juan de la Encina.* His *Sermones Morales,* published posthumously in 1792–1793, testifies to his excellence as a preacher.

ISLA DE PINOS. See ISLE OF PINES.

ISLAM is a system of belief and practice established by Mohammed (q.v.), the Arabian prophet. To the Westerners it is better known under the name Mohammedanism, to which its professors prefer the other term. They themselves would also rather be called Moslems than Mohammedans. Mohammed died in 632 A.D. in Medina. Today there are some 300 million followers of his, forming the bulk of the population of Northern Africa and Western Asia, and extending all the way through India into Malaya, the East Indies, and the Philippines. Every seventh man living today is a Moslem.

Religion of Surrender.—The word Islam (*islām*) means surrender, submission (to the will of God). It occurs several times in the Koran (q.v.) in its literal as well as technical meanings. The form is an infinitival noun from a stem used in the Koran in connection with the submission of Abraham and his son, at the attempted sacrifice by the father, to the Divine will (37:103). It is presumably this act that first prompted Mohammed to coin the new designation for his religion. "This day have I perfected your religion for you and completed My grace unto you; I have chosen for you as religion *al-Islām*" (5:5). "Verily the religion with God is *al-Islām*" (3:18).

Pervades all Domains of Life.—In the Western mind a clear distinction is normally drawn between two spheres of life: The spiritual, comprising religion; and the secular, comprising political, economic, social, and cultural activities. That is not the case with the Moslem. To him Islam embraces all departments of life, a kind of totalitarian system with control over all the varied domains of human activity. This is a unique feature of the Islamic religion. What Mohammed founded was not a religion only, but a society in which the religious, the political, and the social are inseparable.

Islam differs from Christianity in another important aspect. It has no ordained priesthood, no clerical hierarchy, and no mystic sacraments. It is a lay religion, a practical one, with no complicated theology and no unattainable ideals. As such, it has special appeal to the societies that are still on a low cultural level and makes progress where Christianity fails.

Viewed from our standpoint, the structure of Islam may be analyzed under three main headings: Religious, social, and political. The religious structure is composed of dogmas of belief and acts of worship.

Five Dogmas.—The first and most important article of Islamic faith relates to the oneness of God. It is expressed in the formula: *La ilāha illa-l-Lāh* (47:21), no god but Allah. This is one of the most often repeated formulas in the Arabic language. Its concept lies at the very foundation of the entire structure. Moslems pride themselves on being the only *muwaḥḥidūn,* unitarians. God is one, He is pre-existent, omnipotent, omniscient. He is the creator of all things. "He is God, the one; God the eternal. He begets not and is not begotten; nor is there like unto Him any one" (112).

In the Koran He is again and again described as "powerful over all things," "knowing all things." But He is also gracious, forgiving, merciful, and compassionate. As the ruler of all things He may do whatever seemeth good in His sight; yet He is a just God. He punishes only where punishment is due. Humble submission to His will has throughout the ages constituted the essence of Islamic piety.

Closely joined with this dogma is the second one, expressed in the formula *Muḥammadun rasūlu-l-Lāh,* Mohammed is the messenger of God. The two are usually repeated together. Mohammed, according to the learned system, was not divine. He was a messenger, a warner, and a prophet. As a prophet he was in the tradition of Noah, Abraham, Moses, and Christ. But he was "the seal of the prophets" (33:40), the last and therefore the greatest among them. He was the sole channel of revelation for his own time and generation, and the last apostle for all times and all generations. His dispensation supplements and, wherever necessary, supersedes all earlier ones. He performed no miracle unless it be that of the Koran. He was the means through which the Koran was revealed.

The third article of faith relates to the Koran. This book is the uncreated word of God. It was dictated piece by piece in Arabic through Gabriel. As such, it should be studied and recited in the original tongue. Only the Turks have recently violated this rule. When quoted, a koranic passage is introduced with "saith God." In its Arabic form, it is an exact replica of a divine book preserved in the seventh heaven, where it is well guarded. None therefore should touch it unless in a state of purity, which involves ablution (56:76-8; 80:13-15).

Then comes the belief in the angels, arranged in a hierarchy and headed by Gabriel, bearer of the revelation (2:91). Angels were created long before the world and are of finer material. They perform different functions. They intercede for man (42:3), act as guardians (13:12), and support the throne of God (69:17). The names of many of them, as recorded in the Koran and Moslem tradition, are of undoubted Hebrew origin.

Hell and Heaven.—The last fundamental article of faith is belief in a judgment day, immortality of the soul, reward for the righteous, and punishment for the wicked. "The last day," "the last hour," "the day of judgment" will be ushered in by certain extraordinary signs. On it, all actions shall be weighed in the scales. "Those whose scales are heavy are the successful ones; and those whose scales are light shall lose their souls and abide in hell forever" (23:104-5). The sin for which one is punished may be moral or ceremonial. One sin is unpardonable, that of *shirk,* associating other deities with the one God (4:51, 116). Later theologians distinguished between "little" sins, which are inherent in man's nature, and "great" sins, for which a Moslem, if he does not repent, will be consigned to hell-fire. Immediate expectation of a day of judgment and fear as a motive of piety were stressed before the time of Mohammed by Syrian Church fathers.

To Mohammed, as revealed in the Koran, the last day was not a hazy possibility in a remote future but an imminent certainty. On it, all the dead shall rise. Resurrection entails the body. Both reward and punishment are of the sensual type. Hell is portrayed as God's kindled fire, which shall verily rise above the wicked like a vault on outstretched columns (104:5-9). There the damned shall be "scorched by burning fire, made to drink from a boiling fountain. No food shall they have save the fruit of a bitter thorn, which doth not nourish nor appease their hunger" (88:4-7). Such passages provided material for the fertile imagination of Moslem commentators, who worked out elaborate and fantastic schemes of torment. They arranged hell in seven divisions, and consigned different evil doers into different divisions varying in the degree of torture.

Paradise is also painted in materialistic colors. In it the faithful is to enjoy all the delights and luxuries nearest to the heart of a denizen of the desert. The general picture is that of an oasis, a garden, with shady trees, running streams, and all facilities for rest, comfort, and enjoyment. Several passages in the Koran dilate on the scene: "He [God] hath awarded them [the believers], for all that they endured, with Paradise and silk attire, reclining therein upon couches. Naught shall they know of [hot] sun or bitter cold. Its shades shall close upon them, and low shall its fruits hang down. Vessels of silver are brought round for them, and goblets like flagons, flagons made of silver whose measure they themselves shall mete. There they are given to drink of a cup whereof the mixture is of ginger from the fount named *salsbīl.* There go round among them boys of everlasting youth whom, when thou seest, thou wouldst take for scattered pearls. And when thou lookest at this, thou wilt see bliss and high estate. Their raiment will be fine green silk and gold brocade. With silver bracelets they will be adorned, and their Lord will give them drink of a pure beverage" (76:12-12).

Belief in God's absolute decree is often treated as a sixth article of faith. The Koran is explicit in its teaching that everything that happens to man has already been fixed by God: "Naught befalleth us save that which God hath decreed for us" (9:51); "No soul can ever die except by Allah's leave, in accordance with what is written and determined" (3:139).

Five Religious Duties.—Islam is not only a system of faith but one of practice. It enjoins on its followers five acts of worship, religious duties, often termed the pillars of faith.

The first pillar involves a verbal profession of the unity of God and the prophethood of Mohammed. It is not enough for a Moslem to believe in God; he must declare his belief: No God but Allah; Mohammed is the messenger of Allah. This formula is of such importance that once a non-Moslem recites it, he is to all intents and purposes a believer. In order to be a good believer he should then proceed to the practice of the other acts.

The second act of worship is prayer. A good Moslem could informally commune with God any time of day or night, but he is obligated to practice five legally prescribed and defined prayers. This formal prayer is made with the utmost decorum. Preparatory to it the worshiper should go through certain ceremonies of purification and ablution (5:8-9). Every mosque is provided with facilities for such washings. Sand or dust would do in the absence of water. After going through the required ablutions the worshiper stands straight with his face toward Mecca, assumes a fixed position, recites certain formulas, and repeats a number of genuflections. The five times are early dawn, noon, mid-afternoon, sunset, and night. It is remarkable that in no single Koranic passage are the five periods mentioned. Even when added, the periods seem to be four. But all commentators agree that the *masā'* period includes two: sunset and evening (30:16-17).

The approach of each hour of prayer is heralded by the call to prayer, made by the muezzin (q.v.) from the minarets:

God is most great! (repeated four times)
I testify there is no god but Allah; (twice)
I testify Mohammed is the messenger of Allah. (twice)
Come to prayer; (twice)
Come to salvation. (twice)
God is most great! (twice)
There is no god but Allah.

Assuming a fixed posture while engaged in formal prayer, as well as bending the knees and prostrating oneself, were a well-known practice among monks and hermits of the Syrian Christian Church. An early Arabic poem refers to a monk's forehead as hard as a camel's knee on account of religious prostrations. Islam, however, regularized and popularized the practice. An orthodox Moslem is, as a rule, not ashamed of his God. He may be seen indulging in this devotional exercise in the bazaar, the field, or the modern street car.

Friday noon is the only prescribed congregational prayer. In it the members meet in mosques, devoid of pews and unornamented with pictures, arrange themselves in standing rows, and follow the leader (*imām*) in the conduct of the service. The leader delivers a sermon (*khuṭbah*) in which he invokes God's blessing for the success of Islam and the prosperity of the rulers and the caliph (in cases where there is one).

Almsgiving, the third duty of the believer, is often joined with prayer in the koranic injunctions. "Observe prayer, pay the alms, and kneel with those who kneel" (2:40; cf. 2:77, 9:5). In the early days of Islam alms were collected from believers by officials appointed for that purpose, and were used for building mosques, helping the needy, and in other ways promoting the cause of the religion. With the spread of Islam this procedure was necessarily abandoned; giving became a personal affair. The obligation to give is nevertheless universally recognized by Moslems. Even those among them who neglect other duties may not neglect this.

Fasting is the fourth religious duty prescribed by Islam. The month of Ramadan is devoted for this purpose. In it the faithful are supposed to abstain from food, drink, and other indulgences from dawn till sunset (2:183). Ramadan was chosen because it was the month in which the Koran was revealed. Being a lunar month it rotates around the year, and fasting in it becomes arduous when it falls in summer. Exemptions are made in favor of the feeble, the sick, and the traveler (2:181). To fast at other times is meritorious but not obligatory.

Both Christians and Jews practiced fasting before Islam. Besides regularizing and emphasizing it, Islam put a somewhat different interpretation on it. The object of Moslem fasting is not so much to mortify the body as to atone for evil deeds and to commune more intimately with God.

Pilgrimage.—The fifth requirement of practical religion is the pilgrimage to the holy places in Arabia. Once in a lifetime the Moslem, whether man or woman, is supposed to undertake the religious pilgrimage at a stated period: "It is a duty toward God, incumbent on those who are able, to visit this House" (3:91). Women with no male relatives to accompany them, lunatics, and those who cannot afford the trip are exempted. The time is fixed in the first half of the month of dhu-al-Ḥijjah. In that period the caravans from Syria, Egypt, Iraq, and other parts of the Moslem world converge on Mecca. In 1946 the estimated number of pilgrims was 50,000. Before World War II it rose as high as 250,000.

That pilgrimage to sanctuaries is an ancient Semitic rite is indicated by its prescription as an indispensable duty in the old part of the Pentateuch (Ex. 23:14). But, as in the case of other institutions borrowed by Islam, it was modified and crystallized. When the pilgrim approaches the sacred area around Mecca, he goes through the ablutions, puts on a special seamless garment, and proceeds with the other pilgrims. Guides instruct him as to the proper procedure. While in this state he cannot even trim his nails or kill a flea. First he must encircle the Kaaba (q.v.) seven times, kissing the Black Stone each time. This is a meteoric stone set in the southeast corner of the Kaaba and, like it, a relic of pre-Islamic heathenism. Moslem tradition says that it came down from Paradise, and that on the judgment day it will give evidence in favor of those who kissed it. Other prayers and ceremonies follow. Then the pilgrim must run seven times between two hills, al-Safa and al-Marwah, repeating certain formulas (2:153). Later he visits the Valley of Mina and Mount Arafat, where more prayers are recited and a sermon is preached. On the way to Mina each pilgrim casts stones at three pillars, seven stones at each. The stones are, according to Moslem explanation, really thrown at Satan, who appeared on this spot to Abraham. A sacrifice of a sheep or goat closes the performance. The rich may sacrifice a camel. It is considered meritorious to give the meat of the sacrificed animal to the poor. The day is celebrated throughout the world of Islam as 'Id al-Aḍḥa (the feast of sacrifice).

The pilgrim at last shaves, discards the special cloak, and reverts to the secular condition. While in Mecca he usually drinks from the water of Zamzam, the sacred well within the precincts of the mosque, supposed to be the one from which Hagar and Ishmael drank when lost in the wilderness. Before returning home the pilgrim should do homage at the tomb of Mohammed at Medina. He is entitled to the proud designation of *ḥājj* (pilgrim) before his name.

Holy War.—The obligation of waging holy war (*jihād*) has been raised to the dignity of a sixth religious duty by one of the Islamic sects. Moslem ideology divides the world into two zones: the abode of Islam, where peace prevails, and the abode of war, which includes all the non-Moslem domain. It is further considered obligatory on the Moslem to keep on pushing the wall that separates these two zones until all lands are brought under the banner of Islam. The ordinary greeting between one Moslem and another, no matter what their languages may be, is the Arabic *as-salāmu 'alaykum,* peace be to you!

The koranic passages in support of the holy war theory are not so explicit. This is one of the most elaborate among them: "Fight in the path of God against those who fight against you, but be not the aggressors; for verily God loveth not the aggressors. And slay them wherever ye find them, and drive them out of the places whence they drove you out, for persecution is worse than slaughter. But if they desist, then verily God is forgiving, merciful" (2:186-8).

Social Structure.—From analysis of the religious structure, we now proceed to that of the social structure of Islam.

Foremost in the koranic legislation on the social side is the consideration of all those within the fold of Islam as one brotherhood. "The believers are naught else but brothers" (49:10). The earliest biographer of Mohammed quotes from a sermon which the Prophet delivered at the last pilgrimage he made: "Know ye that every Moslem is a brother unto every other Moslem, and that ye are now one brotherhood." Until then blood relationship was the cohesive binding element in Arabian society. Now this is replaced by a new cementing element—faith. In its historic evolution the Moslem community fell short of this ideal, but Pan-Islam is still, until the present day, a conscious force in the lives of Moslems. It transcends race, color, or nationality. Perhaps more than any other religion, Islam has succeeded in breaking down ethnic and provincial barriers

Marital Laws.—Another important part of social legislation relates to marriage. Islamic marriage laws are quite liberal. "Marry of the women who seem good to you, two, or three, or four; and if ye fear that ye cannot be equitable, then only one, or what your right hands possess" (4:3). The last clause authorizes using female slaves as concubines. In this legislation Islam restricted polygamy rather than introduced it; but while restricting it, it put the religious label on it and froze it forever after. The modernized Moslem society has outgrown this legislation in favor of monogamy.

The believer is commanded to practice restraint and chastity and to treat his wives with kindness. Women are enjoined to be decent, to lower modestly their glances, and to display their charms only to their husbands and immediate relatives. This hardly involves the duty of veiling or confinement in a harem, both ancient Semitic institutions antedating Islam.

The statutes relating to divorce (2:226-38, 4:24) enable a husband to repudiate his wife without any misbehavior on her part, even without assigning a cause. Divorce is effective if expressed by one who is sound in mind and mature of age. But there are conditions to be fulfilled. The husband should wait for a prescribed time, to be sure that the wife is not pregnant, and should pay the fixed dowry. The period of waiting may be intended not only to remove all doubt about the real parenthood of a child, but to give the man an opportunity to change his mind in case of a hasty decision. The repeated admonitions to observe the divorce regulations indicate that the details were not previously known. Islam gives the wife the right of dissolving the marriage bond under certain conditions, a right she never enjoyed before.

The morality proclaimed by Mohammed is largely of social character. The koranic legislation in favor of the poor, the orphan, the sick, the stranger, and the destitute is copious and adequate. Here is a sample passage: "Unto your parents show kindness, and unto kindred and orphans and the needy, and unto the neighbor who is a kin and the neighbor who is a stranger, and unto the fellow traveler and the wayfarer, and whom your right hands possess" (4:40). The Prophet evidently never forgot that he himself was once an orphan, and was poor. Almsgiving, as noted above, was raised by Islam to a position of pre-eminence, along with prayer and fasting.

Slavery is authorized by Islam, as is evident from the last phrase in the passage quoted above, but humane treatment is enjoined throughout. Mohammed found slavery as an established institution in pre-Islamic heathenism, as well as in the Jewish communities, and recognized its legitimacy. Moslem men, as noted above, were authorized to use their female slaves as concubines. If one gave birth to a child, she usually became a freedwoman. Whenever a slave was in a position to redeem himself it was the duty of the Moslem master to grant emancipation (24:33). More than that, manumission has been treated throughout the Islamic age as something especially pleasing in the sight of God and regarded as an expiation for sin. Moslem history is rich in cases where masters sought God's favor through freeing slaves, sometimes going first through the trouble of purchasing them for the sake of enfranchising them. According to the strict law, no Moslem could enslave a fellow Moslem. If a slave adopts Islam, freeing him is meritorious but not obligatory.

Prohibition.—Other interesting parts of koranic legislation relate to drinking wine and to gambling. In one passage, the prohibition is explicit and absolute: "O ye who have believed, wine, games of chance, idols, and divining arrows are nothing but an infamy of Satan's handiwork. Avoid them so that ye may succeed" (5:92). In another passage, the prohibition is not so final: "They question thee concerning wine and games of chance. Answer: In both there is great sin, and also some utility for men; but their sinfulness is greater than their usefulness" (2:216).

Other Islamic prohibitions relate to food. Especially interesting among these is one involving pork (5:4), which should under no conditions be eaten. Any flesh that is eaten must come from an animal killed in a prescribed way.

Non-Koranic Sources.—For a full comprehension of Islamic religion in its varied aspects, and particularly in its social and political ones, a study should be made not only of the Koran but also of the practice and sayings of Mohammed as portrayed in the *Sunnah*. Basically, the term means "path," "way." First applied to the way Mohammed taught by word or deed, Sunnah was then stretched to include the way his immediate followers acted, and later to the way of life pursued by the Moslem community at large.

The Sunnah is recorded in books entitled *ḥadīth,* "communication," "narrative," "tradition." There are six authoritative collections of Moslem tradition. They constitute, next to the Koran, the most important source of Moslem religion, law, and practice. Then there is the established custom which conditioned the social and political development of Islam as it spread, and which contributed new elements to its social and political structure.

Certain universally accepted practices have no sanction in the Koran. The doctrine of the sinlessness of the prophets, including Mohammed, is not koranic but nevertheless is orthodox, as is the doctrine of his intercession on the day of judgment to the exclusion of all other prophets. The cult of the dead and the veneration of saints are contrary to the spirit of Islam, with its insistence on strict monotheism, but are practiced today all over Islam with the exception of its Wahhabi section. Circumcision is not even mentioned in the Koran, and yet it has been considered throughout all Moslem generations as the chief initiatory rite for converts, corresponding to Christian baptism. The custom is a very ancient one, and was practiced by Hebrews, Aramaeans, and other Semites.

Political Structure.—For our knowledge of the political structure of Islam we have to depend almost entirely upon non-koranic sources. The nearest approach in the Koran to what might be termed civic or state legislation is a general behest to the believers: "Obey God and obey the messenger and those of you who are in authority; and if ye have a dispute concerning any matter, refer to God and the messenger, if ye believe in God and the last day" (4:62). It was this command to obey "the messenger" that later sanctioned the use of the Sunnah as the second major source of authority in Islam

Caliphate.—The most important political institution is the caliphate, succession to Mohammed. On this the Koran is silent. For successor, Mohammed could have one who performed his functions only as a leader, ruler, judge, and commander in chief of the army, but not as a prophet; he, being the last of the prophets, could have no successor as such. As long as Mohammed lived, Islam was a theocracy, "a community of God," a state under the direct government of Allah through His Prophet. With his death, revelation forever ceased. In his prophetic function Mohammed, therefore, could have no substitute. Only the Fatimid caliphs of Egypt (909–1171), who were extreme Shi'ites, were considered by their followers as semidivine rulers of a theocratic state.

The unexpected death of Mohammed in 632 left the community in a state of confusion bordering on consternation. At his death, he had no living son. Even if he had, it would not have made much difference probably, as Arabian practice did not justify hereditary succession into positions of leadership, unless the son was the best qualified candidate. Nor did Mohammed designate a successor. The Shi'ites, however, maintain that he did, and that the designee was his son-in-law, Ali. But when the elders got together they elected the aged abu-Bakr, a kinsman and early believer, caliph. Abu-Bakr started the first series of caliphates, which was patriarchal in character, and used Medina as capital. In 661 the capital was shifted to Damascus and a new series, the Ommiad (Umayyad), was inaugurated. In 750 the Abbasid caliphate superseded the Ommiad; shortly after that, Baghdad replaced Damascus as the capital.

Caliphal Qualifications.—Moslem legists stipulate that the caliph should be a male, descended from Koreish, sound in body and mind, mature in age, learned in law and religion, and capable of defending Islam. In practice, however, little regard was paid to these stipulations. The last caliphate was that of the Ottoman Turks, who were not even Semites. This caliphate was abolished by the Kemalist Turks in 1924. Since then, several Pan-Islamic conferences have been held to revive this institution, but to no avail. Among the caliphal privileges is that of declaring a holy war, a privilege which was exercised by one of the last Ottoman sultans, Mohammed V, when Turkey entered World War I in 1914, but resulted in no action whatsoever.

Criminal Legislation.—The criminal legislation of the Koran, which is meager, follows ancient Semitic lines. It was revealed as different occasions arose, and constituted no organized comprehensive system. "We have prescribed for thee therein: A life for a life, an eye for an eye, a nose for a nose, an ear for an ear, and a tooth for a tooth, and for wounds, retaliation. But whoso forgoeth it, it shall be expiation for him" (5:49). "As for the thief, both male and female, cut off their hands. It is the reward of their own deeds, an exemplary punishment from God" (5:42). Only in Wahhabi Arabia is this stern legislation enforced. Moslem communities everywhere have adopted more liberal laws based on European practice. This is especially true of the modern Turks.

Local Institutions Adopted.—The tiny Medinese community of Mohammed's days expanded until it encompassed first the entire Arabian peninsula, then the Fertile Crescent to the north, and later adjacent lands in North Africa, Southeastern Europe, Western Asia, and Central Asia. It soon became apparent that the laws worked out for it did not suffice to meet the multitudinous and varied problems, political and economic, which confronted the far-flung caliphal state and its component parts. To supply the deficiency it was only natural for the new Moslem state to adopt much of the governmental organization of the conquered lands, together with the necessary local laws and methods of procedure.

When the seat of the caliphate was transferred to Syria, the ruling Moslems retained the native Christian staff, remnant of the Byzantine system, who continued for some time to keep their records in Greek. The provincial system of administration and taxation, somewhat modified, was continued. When a new caliphate arose in Iraq, the Persian system of rule through vizirs and provincial governors was appropriated. The Ottoman caliphs inherited Byzantine institutions, and followed Byzantine political patterns. What in the long run determined the governmental theories and administrative structures of the many successive and contemporaneous Moslem governments in Asia, Africa, and Europe was not so much the Koran and the Sunnah as the fresh heritage and the force of events in the new locales.

New Devices.—Meantime Moslem legists were exercising their ingenuity to provide new devices for meeting the new situations. In all the conquered territories Arab governors found themselves confronted with problems which had no exact counterparts in the limited Arabian experiences. The administrators in some such cases had to resort to their personal judgment and sense of equity (*ra'y*). This, then, became a secondary source of legislation. Under other circumstances it was found that for certain new cases parallels could be discovered in early Islamic experience, and judged accordingly. Reasoning by analogy (*qiyās*), analogy to a decision recorded in the Koran or tradition, thus became another new source of authority. Gradually a third doctrine was worked out, that of the consensus of opinion (*ijmā'*). According to this doctrine, all such practices or articles of belief as are general among Moslems are an acceptable part of religion. To bolster the theory behind this doctrine, Mohammed was quoted as having said: "My community shall not agree on an error."

Four Rites.—On the basis of these sources, four permanent schools of jurisprudence arose in Islam. The earliest and most liberal among them was that established by abu-Hanifah, who flourished in Iraq, where he died in 767. The school named after him, Hanafite, which emphasizes the principle of analogical deduction, today predominates in Turkey, Western and Central Asia, and India. A contemporary of abu-Hanifah, Malik ibn-Anas (d. 795), labored in Medina; he was naturally more conservative than his Iraqi colleague. Malik stressed the importance of the consensus of opinion as prevalent in Medina, and his school struck root in North Africa and Spain. The third school of jurisprudence, the Shafi'ite, occupies a medial position between the liberal Hanafite rite and the conservative Malikite. It still dominates

Lower Egypt, eastern Africa, Palestine and the East Indies. Al-Shafi'i, its founder, was born in Palestine but spent most of his life in Baghdad and Cairo, where he died in 819. His pupil, ibn-Hanbal of Baghdad (d. 855), insisted on uncompromising adherence to the Koran and tradition, and became the founder of the fourth and most conservative of the rites. The Hanbalite school declined after the 15th century but was revived by the Wahhabis, strict traditionalists, in the 18th. The ruling family of Saudi Arabia is Wahabi.

All four schools are orthodox. The Shi'ites, however, utterly reject consensus of opinion as a source of legislation, and follow a rite of their own. They maintain the absolute authority and judgment of the infallible imam, successor of Ali. The Shi'ites, moreover, hold that their own spokesmen are qualified to interpret the ideas of their imams; the Sunnites, on the other hand, maintain that the "door of interpretation has been closed forever."

Bibliography.—Macdonald, Duncan B., *Development of Muslim Theology, Jurisprudence, and Constitutional Theory* (New York 1903); Everyman's Library, *The Koran,* tr. by J. . Rodwell (London 1909); Macdonald, Duncan B., *Aspects of Islam* (New York 1911); Goldziher, Ignaz, *Die Religion des Islam,* 2d ed. (Berlin 1913); Hurgronje, Snouck C., *Mohammedanism* (New York 1916); Goldziher, Ignaz, *Le dogme et la loi de l'Islam* (Paris 1920); Roberts, Robert, *The Social Laws of the Qoran* (London 1925); Bell, Richard, *Origins of Islam in its Christian Enviroment* (New York 1926); Lammens, H., *Islam: Beliefs and Institutions,* tr. by E. Denison Ross (London 1929); Levy, Reuben, *An Introduction to the Sociology of Islam,* 2 vols. (London 1931); Wensinck, A., Jr., *The Muslim Creed* (Cambridge 1932); Torrey, Charles C., *The Jewish Foundation of Islam* (New York 1933); Hitti, Philip K., *History of the Arabs,* 4th ed. (London 1949); Gibb, H. A. R., *Mohammedanism* (Oxford 1949).

PHILIP K. HITTI,
Professor of Semitic Literature, Princeton University.

ISLAND, a body of land entirely surrounded by water. The *s* in island is due to a confusion with the Old French word *isle;* in fact, the word is compounded of the Anglo-Saxon word *ig,* meaning island, and land. Islands are usually classified as continental or oceanic. Continental islands consist of the same rocks as the neighboring mainland, are usually surrounded by shallow seas, the floor of which forms a continental shelf, and have similar flora and fauna to the mainland. Such islands belong to three groups: islets composed of resistant rocks, such as the Isles of Shoals (q.v.), the surrounding softer strata having been worn away; large islands, such as Great Britain and the islands of northern Canada, separated from the continent by comparatively narrow, shallow channels; and the festoons of islands, such as Japan, which are characteristic of the shorelands of the Pacific Ocean. Such islands may also be termed destructional, for they are the product of the destructive forces of erosion or earth movement.

Oceanic islands are usually far distant from the continental shores, surrounded by deep water, are generally coralline or volcanic, and have differing flora and fauna. They occur most frequently in the Pacific Ocean; the largest of them are in the Hawaiian, Fiji, New Hebrides, and Samoan groups. The coralline islands, in general, are based upon submerged mountain peaks or volcanoes. Islands of this class may also be termed constructional, as they have been built up in the development of the earth's existing superficial conformation. This term includes, in addition to the oceanic islands, those islands which occur along continental coasts either as developments from sandbanks or as temporary outlying portions of a growing delta. The Bermudas, the Florida Keys, and many West Indian islets are constructional; but the main West Indian islands are destructional

The largest island on the globe is Australia, but it is more generally regarded as the smallest continent; and is sometimes termed an island continent. Greenland, ranking next in size, is customarily considered to be the world's largest island.

ISLAND NUMBER 10, a former island in the Mississippi River, near the northwestern corner of Tennessee, and about 40 miles below Columbus, Ky. Since the American Civil War it has been washed away. It was the tenth in a succession of islands lying below Cairo, Ill. Early in 1862, having been fortified by the Confederate, Gen. Leonidas Polk, it was commanded by Gen. W. W. Mackall, who had about 7,000 troops of Gen. Pierre G. T de Beauregard's army. It was bombarded for three weeks by Commodore Andrew Hull Foote, commanding seven Federal gunboats, and surrendered April 7, 1862. The evacuation was forced by Polk with a large land force. He, under cover of a vigorous fire from two gunboats, which had run past the island by night, brought his men across the river in transports. The defenders of the batteries fled, and were pursued into the swamps. Over 6,000 prisoners were taken, together with an immense quantity of ammunition and supplies. The Federal forces lost only a few men.

ISLAY, ī'lā, an island on the west coast of Scotland, belonging to the group of the Inner Hebrides, and to the county of Argyll. It is west of the peninsula of Kintyre, about 15 miles southwest of Jura, from which it is divided by Islay Sound. It is 25 miles long, with an extreme width of 15 miles, and an area of 234 square miles. In the north the surface is hilly and the east is marked by a high ridge; while the central and western parts of the island are rolling or tableland. Great quantities of whisky are distilled.

ISLE LA MOTTE, Vt., in the northern part of Lake Champlain, the northern point about eight miles from Rouses Point, N. Y., on the Canadian border; the southern point about 15 miles north of Plattsburg, N. Y. It is about seven miles long and two miles wide. The island was a resort for the Algonquin and Iroquois Indians; at the south end was once an Indian village. It was discovered by Samuel de Champlain in July 1609, and was named after a French officer, Sieur La Mothe. In 1665 a wooden fort called Fort Sainte Anne was built on the south shore. The *Jesuit Relations* contain numerous references to Fort Sainte Anne, Isle La Motte, and the visits made to this island by the early missionaries. The chapel of Sainte Anne, erected near the ruins of Fort Sainte Anne, was consecrated July 16, 1893, by Bishop De Goesbriand of the diocese of Burlington, and it is now a place of pilgrimage. On Aug. 8, 1776, Benedict Arnold, after engaging the Indians in the British service on August 6, at the Bouquet River, fell back to Isle La Motte, where his fleet remained anchored until August 19, when he sailed south toward Cumberland Head. Isle La Motte was settled in 1785 by Ebenezer Hyde, Enoch Hall, and William Blanchard, and was organized as a town in 1790 The quarries of black marble on the island are the oldest in the United States.

ISLE OF MAN, Great Britain, an island in the Irish Sea, 16 miles south of Burrow Head, Wigtownshire, 221 square miles in area. It is 33 miles in length, and 12 miles in breadth at the widest point A range of mountains crosses the island from northeast to southwest, culminating in Snaefell, 2,034 feet in height. The coast is rugged and precipitous in the southwest. Granite, red sandstone, limestone, and slate are quarried for building purposes. The air is dry, clear, and bracing, and much southern vegetation grows freely here, owing to the warm currents of the Gulf Stream which envelop the shores. Agriculture is the main industry. There are also woolen mills where the famous "Manx homespun" is made; and woollen knitted goods are produced. Ruins of ancient churches and chapels, castles, and fortresses dating from the 5th century are found throughout the island Manx, the branch of Celtic formerly spoken by the people, is no longer in general use. The Isle of Man was subject to Scandinavian rulers from the 9th century until 1266, when it was ceded to Scotland. In 1399 it came into possession of the English crown. The legislature (Tynwald) consists of a Legislative Council and the House of Keys. The Council is composed of the lieutenant governor of the island, the bishop of Sodor and Man, 2 deemsters (judges), the attorney general, and 6 nominated members, of whom 2 are nominated by the lieutenant governor and 4 by the House of Keys; this latter body has 24 elected members. Douglas is the capital of the Isle of Man; and Castletown, Peel, and Ramsey are ports. Pop. (1931) 49,308; (1951) 55,213.

ISLE OF PINES (Span. Isla de Pinos, ēz'lä thā pē'nōs), a small island belonging to Cuba, 35 miles southeast of Pinar del Rio, 1,180 square miles in area. Nueva Gerona, the capital, is on the north coast. It is, in effect, two islands connected by a marsh, the one on the north being somewhat broken by hills and that on the south being low, flat, and sandy. The climate is healthful, and the fertile soil produces citrus fruits, pineapples, and potatoes. Mineral resources are extensive. Large marble quarries are worked. Cattle raising is the chief occupation of the people. For administrative purposes the island is a municipal district of the province of Havana The island was discovered by Columbus in 1494. The United States Supreme Court ruled in 1907 that the island was not United States territory; this was ratified by the United States Senate in 1925, thus recognizing that the Isle of Pines was part of Cuba. Pop. (1943) 9,812.

ISLE OF WIGHT, wīt, England, off the south coast, separated from Hampshire by the Solent and the Spithead. It is 23 miles from east to west, and 13 miles from north to south, the area being 147 square miles The island, the ancient Vectis, is rich in antiquities, having been inhabited in turn by the Romans, the Jutes, and the Danes. Cowes, the chief port, is the yachting center of England. Agriculture and fishing are of importance, and the island is a popular vacation resort. Pop. (1951) 95,594.

ISLE ROYALE, īl' roi'ăl (Fr. ēl' rwȧ-yȧl'), an island in Lake Superior, southeast of Port Royal, Canada, part of the State of Michigan. It is 44 miles long and 8 miles wide, and has an area of 229 square miles. Prehistoric copper mines have been found. In 1947 the island was dedicated as a national park.

ISLES OF SHOALS, New Hampshire, a group of eight barren islands in the Atlantic Ocean, 10 miles southeast of Portsmouth, N H., from which a daily steamer plies during the summer months. The three principal islands are Appledore (400 acres); Star (150 acres) and White (55 acres).

ISLES OF THE BLEST, or **FORTUNATE ISLANDS,** according to Greek mythology and legend an island group on the edge of the western ocean, where dwelt those fortunate beings on whom the gods bestowed immortality. Hesiod mentions the group, as do later authors. It is supposed that the idea of this paradise on an island group is due to the remembrance of an unrecorded voyage to Madeira and the Canary Islands, these being called Fortunate Islands in some medieval maps.

ISLETA, ēs-lā'tä, N. Mex., Indian pueblo in Bernalillo County, on the Rio Grande 10 miles south of Albuquerque, served by the Santa Fe Railroad. It is in the Isleta Reservation. Pop. (1948) 1,462.

ISLINGTON, ĭz'lĭng-tŏn, England, a metropolitan borough of London, 2 miles north of Saint Paul's. Within it are the Royal Agricultural Hall, Pentonville and Holloway prisons, and several hospitals and educational institutions. Pop. (1945) 195,770; (1951) 235,645.

ISLIP, ī'slĭp, town, New York, in Suffolk County, Long Island, on the shore of Great South Bay; it is served by the Long Island Railroad. Oyster fishing and agriculture are of importance, and the town is a popular summer resort. In the vicinity is a state hospital for the insane. The town is named for Islip, Oxfordshire, whence came the first English settlers in the 17th century. Villages within the town include Islip, East Islip, Central Islip, Sayville, Bay Shore Pop. (1940) 51,182; (1950) 71,465.

ISMAIL, ĭs-mä'ēl, 1 (Ismail Pasha), khedive of Egypt: b. Cairo, Dec. 31, 1830; d. near Constantinople (Istanbul), March 21, 1895. He was the son of Ibrahim Pasha (q v.) and nephew of Said Pasha (q.v.), and on the latter's death in 1863 he succeeded as Turkish viceroy in Egypt. By increasing the Egyptian tribute to Turkey and by aiding the sultan with his army in the Cretan insurrection of 1866, he secured from the sultan a change in the law of succession in Egypt to direct descent from father to son, and also in 1867, the titles of highness and khedive. He assumed jurisdiction over the Upper and White Nile, and sought to establish himself during 1868–1869 as an independent monarch.

However, he was forced to reduce his army, to cancel construction of warships, and to cease contracting loans in Europe. Subsequently he obtained concessions from the sultan which made him practically independent. He was one of the most zealous promoters of the Suez Canal, became very wealthy by growing cotton during the American Civil War, and improved Egypt vastly, but at a cost which destroyed the country's credit and brought about the intervention of England and France in Egyptian affairs. Ismail was deposed, June 26, 1879, and retired to a palace on the Bosporus where his remaining years were spent in virtual imprisonment.

ISMAIL, ĭz′mȧ-ĭl, or **IZMAIL**, Russ., ĭs-mŭ-ēl′, city, capital of Izmail Region (southern part of former Bessarabia), Ukrainian SSR, is located on the Kiliya branch of the Danube River on the north side of the Danube delta, about 45 miles from the Black Sea, and 120 miles southwest of Odessa.

Ismail is a rail terminus, and it is the commercial center for an agricultural and wine-growing area. Its industries include flour and lumber milling, tanning, the manufacture of vegetable oils, soap, and bricks; and it has naval repair yards. Since the 16th century the city has belonged successively to Turkey, Russia, Rumania, and the Union of Soviet Socialist Republics. Its cession to the USSR in 1940 was confirmed in 1947. Pop. (1941) 17,569.

ISMAILIA, ĭz-mȧ-ĭ-lē′ȧ, town, Egypt, on Lake Timsah, in the Canal Governorate, is the central station on the Suez Canal, 50 miles from the Mediterranean and 93 miles northeast of Cairo by rail. It dates from 1863 during the construction of the canal. It is well laid out and has wharves, warehouses, and factories producing confectioneries and electric light bulbs. Pop. (1947) 53,594; with suburbs, 68,338.

ISMAY OF WORMINGTON, 1st Baron (full name Hastings Lionel Ismay), British Army officer: b. Naini Tal, India, June 21, 1887. After attending the Royal Military College at Sandhurst, he was commissioned in the British Army in 1905, and between 1914 and 1920 fought in Somaliland, East Africa, where he led a camel corps column in 1920 against the "Mad Mullah," Mohammed ibn-Abdullah. He fulfilled assignments in India during the next few years and in the early 1930's, and served in London with the Committee of Imperial Defence as assistant secretary (1926–1930), deputy secretary (1936–1938), and secretary (1938).

At the outbreak of World War II he was appointed deputy secretary for the military to the war cabinet, and in 1940 he was also named chief of staff to the Ministry of Defence, headed by Prime Minister Churchill. Knighted in 1940 and promoted to full general in 1944, Sir Ismay accompanied Winston Churchill to all major war conferences of Allied leaders. He retired from the army in 1946, received a barony for his wartime services, and in 1947 went to India as chief of staff to Viceroy Earl Mountbatten.

In 1951 Lord Ismay was appointed secretary of commonwealth relations in Churchill's cabinet, and in January 1952 accompanied the prime minister to Washington for consultations with President Harry S Truman. On March 12, 1952, Lord Ismay was appointed to the newly created post of secretary general of the North Atlantic Treaty Organization and to the vice presidency of the North Atlantic Council.

ISOBAROMETRIC LINES, ī-sō-băr-ō-mĕt′rĭk linz, lines connecting on a map the places which exhibit the same mean difference between the monthly extremes of the barometer. These oscillations are greater in some countries, as Hindustan and Newfoundland, than in others, as western Europe and the Antilles.

ISOCLINES. See Folds.

ISOCRATES, ī-sŏk′rȧ-tēz, one of the 10 Attic orators: b. Athens, 436 B.C.; d. there, 338 B.C. His principal teachers were Tisias, Gorgias, Prodicus and Protagoras. On account of his weak voice and natural timidity he was reluctant to speak in public, but gave lessons in the art of eloquence, and composed orations for others. His school was opened about 392 B.C. and quickly gained a great reputation. People from many parts of Greece and even from Sicily and still more distant regions streamed to it. Isaeus, Ephorus, Lycurgus, Hyperides were among them. He was the first who saw the value of oratory in public life. By basing it on sound moral principles he rescued it from the abuses of the Sophists. He was distinguished for a polished style and a harmonious construction of his sentences. The composition, revision and repeated polishing of his speeches occupied so much time that he published little. His celebrated panegyric on Athens *Panathenaicus* employed him 10, or according to some, 15 years. As all his speeches were modeled after the same pattern, their sameness became wearisome, although his subjects were the most important points of morals and politics. During the rule of the Thirty Tyrants he lived at Chios. His patriotism was sincere, and his desire for the freedom of Greece so intense, that he starved himself to death in his ninety-eighth year from grief over the Battle of Chaeronea. The poet, John Milton, refers to this in his sonnet *To the Lady Margaret Ley:*

> as that dishonest victory
> at Chaeronea, fatal to liberty,
> Killed with report that old man eloquent.

Isocrates left an indelible impress on the cultural and political development, not only of Greece, but of the whole world through the purity of his style, the loftiness of his political ideas and ideals, and through the influence which he exerted over such men as Demosthenes and Cicero. In Plutarch's time 60 orations went under his name, not half of which were, however, deemed genuine. Twenty-one now remain, of which the principal are the *Panegyricus* (an oration intended to be read at the Olympic games of 380 B.C., in which he exhorts the Greeks to concord, and to war against the Persians); the *Panathenaicus* (in which he dilates on the services rendered by Athens to Greece); and the *Areopagiticus* (in which he advises the Athenians to return to the simplicity and purity of Solon's time). Plato spoke of him in laudatory terms in his *Phaedrus,* and so did Cicero in his *De Oratore.* There are many editions both of his complete works and of separate orations.

Consult Adams, C. D., *Recent Views of the Political Influence of Isocrates* (in *Classical Philology,* Vol. VII, p. 343, Chicago 1912); Hubbell, H. M., *The Influence of*

Isocrates on Cicero, Dionysius and Aristides (New Haven 1913); Loeb Classical Library, *Isocrates,* with English translation (Cambridge, Mass., 1951).

ISODIMORPHOUS SERIES. *See* Isomorphism.

ISODYNAMIC LINES, lines of equal force, equal inclination and equal declination; three systems of lines which being laid down on maps, represent the magnetism of the globe as exhibited at the earth's surface in three classes of phenomena, the varying intensity of the force, the varying dip or inclination of the needle, and its varying declination from the true meridian. See also Magnetism.

ISOETALES. See Ferns and Fern Allies.

ISOLA DEL LIRI, Italy, town of Lazio, in the Province of Frosinone, on the Rome-Naples Railroad, 5 miles northwest of Roccasecca, on the Liri. It has an interesting 12th century church and ample water power from the falls on the river. Manufactures are unimportant. Pop. (town) (1936) 980; (commune) (1936) 2,865.

ISOLA LUNGA, ē'zō-lä lōōng'gä, or **DUGI OTOK,** dōō'gē ō'tŏk, one of the many islands off the west coast of Dalmatia, Yugoslavia, in the Adriatic Sea. It extends between 43° 51′ and 44° 11′ north latitude. Its greatest length is 27 miles, greatest breadth, three miles. Figs, grapes and olives are produced and the fisheries are important. Sale is the chief town and port. Pop. (1948) about 4,000.

ISOLATION, applied in common parlance to the act of secluding, and of making "pure"; and also to the state of being alone, of being separate; to the states of exclusion, seclusion, or of insulation, and thus of being free from influences such as are incident to contact and conjunction,—in short, a state of "purity"—is a word which has several specific meanings.

A. *In philology.*—(1) To denote that process by which a word-form receives a character which distinguishes it as a compound from the parts of which it was composed, and also from any other group of words connected merely in some syntactical relation. Latin *māgnōpere,* for instance, was isolated from its component elements *māgnó* and *opere* by its vowel contraction, here the cause of the process. So also was the Homeric πἄν ἦμαρ or "all-day-long," *isolated* owing to the circumstance that the neuter when used independently takes a long "a" from πᾶς, πασα; (2) To denote the similar process by which verbal abstract nouns become infinitives, or supines. An infinitive may be said to be completely formed through isolation when the substantive denoting activity or a state, that is when a verbal abstract noun or *nomen actionis* is no longer regarded as a case form, and its construction no longer follows the analogy of its original use as a noun. This is true, for example, of the Greek δόμεναι δοῦναι and Latin *dare* at the earliest period of which Indo-European philology has any record. By this process of isolation, the infinitive word-form reached its most characteristic development in Latin and in Greek. For these are the only languages of the whole Indo-European group in which one finds a special expression for differences of voice. This kind of isolation seems to have had least influence in the Irish tongue, where the *nomina actionis* retains the construction of nouns. Even the ancient language of the Vedas is said to show in this respect a further degree of development than the so-called Irish infinitive; (3) To denote that characteristic device of juxtaposing words in a definite order in some languages (of the so-called isolating type) to express relational concepts, all words themselves remaining unchanged and unchangeable units, and thus receiving their various relational values, *not* from grammatical modifications, but from the position which they occupy in the sentence. Chinese affords a classical example of such a language. And it is a most interesting fact that English itself has ceased to be a clear example of the so-called inflective type, and may be said to be an example of an isolating language in the making. When comparative grammarians had succeeded in subjecting the entire content of mankind's linguistic power to careful scrutiny and critical examination, three main types of speech emerged. These groups were found to be co-ordinate; and tongues were thereafter distinguished as isolating, agglutinative, and as inflective for taxonomic reasons. This resulted when special regard was paid to the inner coherence of words, a characteristic produced in all tongues by the operation of various specific grammatical processes. In all such investigations attention was directed in particular to the relative degree of unity which the stem or unmodified word plus its various grammatical increments or modifications possesses, emphasis being always laid on the degree of unity which grammatical processes bring about between the stem and the increments which express relational concepts. On the basis of this formal criterion, emphasis being laid on the characters called inflection, agglutination, and isolation respectively, all the languages in the world can be classified into three main divisions or types, as inflectional, agglutinative and isolating types respectively.

B. *In chemistry,* isolation refers to the state of any substance when separated from all foreign elements; and also to the act or method of obtaining such a substance in a free state, or of rendering it pure.

C. *In physics* it has a similar meaning. It was in this sense that the classical experiments of R. A. Millikan, by which he succeeded in isolating an *ion,* were performed.

D. *In phylogeny* (theories of descent and *in ontogeny* (developmental history), isolation conveys in general the idea of freedom from crossing with the parent, or other, stocks, in the broader meaning which has been given to the term since the days of Charles Darwin. In this sense isolation is synonymous with biological and ecological separation; and also with habitudinal segregation. Isolation and all its synonyms, signify that the descendants of *one* ancestral form living amid a definite set of ecological, or environmental conditions, begin to adapt themselves to different sets of conditions, as a result of which, they become ecologically separated or segregated. Isolation with three other factors may enter into any process of speciation,—the latter name being applied by O. F. Cook to the process, the operation of which brings about the differentiation of one species into several coexisting species by the prevention of free crossing between groups

existing at the same time. It is above all the setting of individuals in groups, the members of each group intergenerating, and so securing *racial generalization,* or fundamental unity of inheritance, within each group, while between the groups there is prevention from free crossing. Reflexive selection, on the other hand, is applied to that kind of selection which may be described as depending on the relations of the members of a species to each other. Its most familiar forms are sexual selection and social selection. Now isolation is in its very nature the suspension not only of one form, but of all forms of reflexive selection between the separated portion of a species. Isolation as one of the four main factors of evolution, implies that the process of transformation is a very complex affair. We, on accepting isolation, recognize, by implication, in evolution the ultimate outcome of a number of factors, each of which has its own special efficacy, and each of which may also at times operate in a manner antagonistic to all of the others. This view, eclectic in its nature, is perhaps to be regarded as the most satisfactory explanation of the organic world and its upbuilding that has yet been put forward. But it must be repeated that it recognizes of the various factors thus engaged, the following four as the most potent and the most essential, and also as co-ordinate: The two Lamarckian factors, variation and inheritance, the Darwinian factor, natural selection, and the factor first postulated by Moritz Wagner, or isolation. Even Lamarck recognized that distinct organic types could not be maintained without some form of isolation, and such Neo-Lamarckians of to-day as Professor Packard have been even more emphatic in insisting on this principle as being among the essential conditions for any genuine divergent evolution. Charles Darwin used isolation as equivalent to geographical separation while later writers have come to use it as equivalent to independent generation. Isolation differs from selection in that the latter denotes the exclusion of certain kinds from opportunity to propagate, while the former denotes the division of those that propagate into classes that are prevented from intergenerating. Isolation, or the prevention of intergeneration, whether it be through separation or segregation is also called independent generation. Charles Darwin endeavored to explain the origin of species by the agency of natural selection plus the Lamarckian factors, variation and inheritance, and found in Wallace, Huxley and Haeckel, along with many other naturalists, ingenious supporters. On other sides, however, the specifically Darwinian explanation encountered vehement opposition. Moritz Wagner, for example, regarded free intercrossing as an insurmountable obstacle to the establishment of new modifications and contended very ably that the isolation of a few individuals, a condition which would occur most frequently during migrations, was a necessary postulate in accounting for the origin of each new variety or species. In these contentions Wagner showed the great value of migration and the intervention of geographical barriers in accounting for the process of speciation. The absence of interbreeding, as that resulting from geographical isolation,— what August Weisman calls *amixia,* **— is substantially the prevention of free intercrossing, and thus a form of isolation. And** Hugo de Vries, while his classical investigations resulted in the demonstration that it is possible to produce species, or true breeding forms, out of mutations by pedigree culture, still he failed to see that the essential factor is not the quality of the material he worked with (the mutations), but that it is the pedigree — culture, and that this corresponds to the well-known factors, selection and isolation. The importance of isolation as a co-ordinate factor with selection in the evolution of species is now gaining wide recognition. George J. Romanes insisted that «without isolation, or the prevention of free intercrossing, organic evolution is in no case possible.» And he even went so far as to urge that isolation «has been the exclusive means of modification, or more correctly, the universal condition of it.» But here it is to be remembered that Romanes failed to discriminate clearly between selection and isolation. It was the custom when he wrote to describe any influence that tends to transform species as a form of selection. For instance: Romanes says of infertility between varieties of the same species: «I will call this principle physiological selection or segregation of the fit.» Since 1886 when Romanes wrote, however, isolation has by general consent come to mean the prevention of free-crossing between groups existing at the same time. (Rev. John T. Gulick). And in accordance with this usage even Romanes later substituted physiological isolation for physiological selection, which Seebohm suggests, as does Gulick also, is a better term. But when Romanes defined isolation itself he extended its meaning so as to include the prevention of crossing between those members of the group who succeed in living and propagating and those who die without propagating; a definition of, isolation which makes it include natural selection as one of its many forms. Modern nomenclature would however restrict the term selection to the influences that determine the survival, or continued propagation, of the fit innate variations of any given group, and the elimination, that is, the disappearance of the unfit, thus preventing the crossing of fit with unfit. And naturalists would likewise restrict isolation to the prevention of free-crossing between groups existing at the same time. And present day naturalists are also gradually coming to the conclusion that if natural selection works without isolation, only monotypic evolution can result. It is even evident that variation, inheritance, plus natural selection, working together, do not suffice for the interpretation of the whole process of evolution. They fail to account for the fact that often two or more different forms have originated from a single ancestral type. They are capable at best of explaining the transformation of one existing form into one other form. So it came about that the principle of isolation has found recent and able supporters in Baur, Ortman, Gulick and many others.

The mode of operation and the forms assumed in the operation of the principle of isolation, have made a classification of the various forms in which it manifests itself essential; and most of the remaining portion of this article will devote itself to the definition of these various manifestations of this principle. Isolation itself has already been sufficiently defined. The principle immediately reveals two forms: (1) Autonomic isolation, which stands in contrast with heteronomic isolation, includes both endonomic isolation, produced by industrial, chronal and migrational isolation, and reflexive isolation, produced by sexual and social instincts, by impregnational incompatibilities, and by institutional requirements; (2) Heteronomic isolation, is that form of isolation determined by conditions outside of the organic group, for example, by geological subsidence, or other causes resulting in the transportation to an isolated position. In the four forms of environal isolation (see below), namely in transportational, geological, fertilizational and artificial isolation, heteronomic influences prevail. Treated from another point of view one may distinguish the following co-ordinate divisions of the principle of isolation: (a) Reflexive isolation, comprehending conjunctional, impregnational and institutional isolation (for which see below); (b) environal isolation, where the relations of the group and its environment are determined by conditions within the group. The importance of this form lies in the fact that it often opens the way for the entrance of more fundamental forms of segregation; (c) regressive isolation, or the amalgamation of races; (d) indiscriminate isolation, which results in the divergence in the aptitudes and innate characters of isolated groups, especially when at the time of the first setting apart, the group is represented by but one, or a few, individuals, and so producing initial racial segregation. It is usually attended with the loss of power to reproduce the average of the innate characters of the original stock.

Of the forms of reflexive isolation one may next distinguish: (1) Conjunctional isolation, which includes sexual and social isolation; (2) impregnational isolation due to the need of coordination between the size, structure, sexual elements and functions of each sex and the related characters of the other sex, in any intergenerating group; (3) institutional isolation, due to the differences of language, religion and education, a prevention to free association, will also prevent intermingling of races.

Of the forms of environal isolation may likewise be distinguished co-ordinate with the three foregoing: (1) Endonomic isolation, an example of which is presented, when varieties of the same species of plant occupying the same areas are prevented from crossing by flowering at different seasons, and among animals, when there occurs the cyclical isolation between the broods of the periodical cicada even when they succeed each other in the same district. And other forms of isolation so far as they are determined by the diversity of habits or instincts of the members of species, are forms of endonomic isolation; (2) herteronomic isolation, for which see above. It remains now to describe the following nearly to-ordinate sub-divisions of isolative influence.

The two forms of conjunctional isolation are (1) sexual isolation which arises between groups of the same species that have been separated by geographical barriers for several generations, and have in the meantime attained divergent forms of inherited characters by which they recognize each other, and also different methods of calling and winning each other; (2) social isolation which arises whenever two groups of a species have been separated by geography for many generations and in the meantime gain divergent social habits and instincts, rendering them unfit for being associated in one intergenerating group when brought together in one district. It is important to notice here that geographical isolation has ceased but the groups continue as separate groups through the influence of social isolation.

The eight forms of impregnational isolation are: (1) dimensional isolation, of which there is an example when local varieties of birds or of mammals that have become very divergent in size are brought together in the same district; (2) structural isolation, which arises when local varieties that have become so far divergent in structure as to be incompatible are brought together into the same district; (3) potential isolation, of which there are two forms: (a) Complete potential isolation which exists between types when their sexual elements are incapable of union in fertilized germs under any conditions; (b) Prepotential isolation which exists when cross-fertilization is possible if the alien fertilizing element has been applied sometime in advance; but which if the fertilizing element of the same species is applied at the same time, or in some cases, at any time during the several hours that follow, mixed fertilization is prevented by the prepotence of the pure fertilizing element; (4) segregate fecundity, the relation in which the species or the varieties stand to each other when intergeneration of members of the same species or varieties results in higher fertility than the crossing of different species or varieties; (5) segregate vigor, the relation in which species or varieties stand to each other when the intergeneration of members of the same species or variety produces offspring of more vigor than those produced by crossing with other species or varieties; (6) segregate adaptation, the relation in which species or varieties stand to each other when the intergeneration of individuals of the same species or variety produces offspring better adapted than the offspring produced by crossing with other species or varieties; (7) segregate freedom from competition, the segregate access to unused resources which results when the pure offspring have freer access to unused resources than do the cross-breeds or the original stock; (8) segregate escape from enemies arises whenever the pure offspring of a divergent variety are able to occupy a position freer from enemies than that occupied by the original stock.

The three forms of endonomic isolation are (1) industrial isolation, arising from the activities by which an organism protects itself against adverse influences in an environment, or by which it finds and then appropriates special resources in the environment; and having three forms: (a) Sustentational isolation, arising from the use of different methods of obtaining sustentation by members of the same species; (b) protectional isolation, or isolation from the use of different methods of protection against adverse influence in the environment; (c) nidificational isolation, the prevention of free interbreeding between the different sections of a species by diversity of industrial habits,— the separation of the individual from the mass of the same species by an industrial habit; (2) chronal isolation, isolation arising from the relations in which an organism stands to times and seasons; it is of two kinds: (a) Cyclical isolation, arising from the fact that the life-cycles of the different sections of a species do not mature simultaneously; (b) Seasonal isolation, produced whenever the season for reproduction in any section of the species is such that it can not interbreed with other sections of the species; (3) migrational isolation, caused by the powers of locomotion in an organism.

The four forms of heteronomic isolation are; (1) transportational isolation, caused by the activities in the environment that distribute the organisms in different districts; (2) geological isolation, caused by geological changes which divide the territory occupied by a species into sections; (3) fertilizational isolation, a segregative rather than a separative form, in that it perpetuates a segregation previously produced, depending on divergence of character already clearly established, and therefore on some form of isolation that has preceded. The forms of isolation that precede fertilizational isolation are in the majority of cases local, but may be chronal or impregnational; (4) artificial isolation arising from the relations in which the organism stands after an attempt has been made to rationalize its environment.

Attention having been given to other features other groupings of these various sorts of isolation is possible. Thus potential isolation, segregate vigor and segregate fecundity might be brought together as forms of physiological isolation, in the sense in which Romanes uses the term in his work 'Darwin and after Darwin.' And thus, too, all forms of environal and regressive isolation, including as environal isolation does, all forms of endonomic and heteronomic isolation,— might not unreasonably be brought under a single caption as forms of coincident isolation. All these forms of isolation are talked about by naturalists who saw a necessity to specify the modes of operation manifest in the behavior of bionomic isolation, which, with three other principles, already spoken of, serves to explain the process of organic evolution.

Through such isolation the swamping or leveling effects of free intercrossing, or mixing with allied varieties or incipient species, are prevented. As a consequence, variations or nascent species become fixed or localized, being prevented from spreading by some geographic or topographic barrier, with the result that there are many thousands of local races, varieties and species; indeed, probably over half of the number of known species are such forms. Not only species, but genera and higher groups are thus isolated. Thus the marsupials of Australia are, with one or two exceptions, confined to that continent, the connection once existing with Asia having been cut off.

Examples of Isolation.— These are found among cave animals (q.v.) where animals confined to the nether world, living in total darkness, are prevented from breeding with their ancestors of the upper world. The deep-sea fauna is another such assemblage, living in gloom and in water at the freezing point, although at the surface the winter temperature of the sea may be 80–85° F. Other examples of the result of isolation are the assemblage of animals peculiar to certain islands, to basins walled in by mountain chains, valleys, deserts and Alpine summits. Interesting cases of isolation on islands are the gigantic moa birds of New Zealand; the local species of birds confined to the different islands of the Galapagos archipelago, also the land shells living in the different valleys of Oahu, one of the Hawaiian Islands.

Consult: Bradley, J. H., 'Parade of the Living' (New York 1930); Butler, S., 'Luck or Cunning' (London 1922); Clark, A. H., 'The New Evolution: Zoögenesis' (Baltimore 1930); Cook, P., 'Instinct in the Cell and Organism' (Alhambra, Calif. 1926); Cutler, D. W., 'Evolution, Heredity and Variation' (London 1925); Fasten, N., 'Origin Through Evolution' (New York 1929); Gruenberg, B. C., 'The Story of Evolution' (New York 1929); Holmes, S. J., 'Life and Evolution' (New York 1926); Lull, R. S., 'Organic Evolution' (New York 1927).

ISOMERISM, ī'zō-măr'ĭzm (Gr., «having equal parts»). Chemists formerly assumed that two bodies must be identical in chemical nature, in all respects, provided they consist of the same elements, combined in the same proportions. This view was long ago found to be untenable, and many substances (mostly com pounds of carbon or nitrogen) are now known, which exhibit widely different properties, although possessing the same empirical formula. Bodies which possess this peculiarity are said to be «isomeric» with each other, and the property itself is called «isomerism.» In its broadest sense, isomerism may be regarded as embracing (1) polymerism; (2) metamerism; (3) isomerism in the narrower sense; and (4) geometrical isomerism.

Bodies are «polymeric» when they have the same percentage composition, but have different molecular weights. Acetic acid, $C_2H_4O_2$, and grape sugar, $C_6H_{12}O_6$, for example, are polymeric with each other, because they consist of the same elements, combined in the same proportions, and yet the molecular weight of grape sugar is three times as great as that of acetic acid. In this particular case there is no specially close relation between the polymeric substances, and the polymerism is therefore said to be «accidental.» When a close relation does exist between the bodies compared, the polymerism is said to be «generic.» Ordinary acetic aldehyde affords a good example of generic polymerism. Aldehyde has the formula C_2H_4O, but when treated with a mineral acid it becomes transformed into paraldehyde, which has the formula $C_6H_{12}O_3$; and the reverse transformation (of paraldehyde into aldehyde) may be effected by the application of heat.

Compounds are said to be «metameric» when they have the same empirical formula, but differ structurally by containing different radicals, joined by a polyvalent element such as oxygen, nitrogen, or sulphur. Ethyl ether and propylmethyl ether, for example, both have the empirical formula $C_4H_{10}O$; but ethyl ether contains two ethyl radicals, united by an oxygen atom, and propyl-methyl ether contains a propyl radical and a methyl radical united by oxygen in the same manner. Thus these two metameric bodies have the structural formulæ

$$\begin{matrix}C_2H_5\\C_2H_5\end{matrix}{>}O \text{ and } \begin{matrix}C_3H_7\\CH_3\end{matrix}{>}O, \text{ respectively.}$$

Metamerism is manifested, most commonly, by the ethers, esters and amines.

Isomerism in its narrower sense or "true isomerism," embraces those cases in which the bodies compared have the same empirical formulæ but have different structural formulæ and do not (like metameric bodies) consist of definite carbon radicals united by oxygen, sulphur, or nitrogen. True isomerism may be of two kinds: (1) "nucleus isomerism," and (2) "isomerism of position." The hydrocarbons afford good examples of both kinds of true isomerism. The paraffin known as propane, for example, has the empirical formula C_3H_8, and the structural formula $CH_3—CH_2—CH_3$. Propane may be converted into butane by replacing one of its hydrogen atoms by the methyl radical, CH_3; but the substitution may be made in two essentially different ways, according as the hydrogen that is replaced is attached to the interior carbon atom, or to one of the terminal ones. In the latter case the structural formula of the new substance is $CH_3—CH_2—CH_2—CH_3$, and the substance itself is known as "normal" butane. If the hydrogen that is replaced is attached to the interior carbon atom, a different substance known as "isobutane" and having different properties from normal butane, is formed; its structural formula being

$$\begin{array}{c}CH_3—CH—CH_3\\ |\\ CH_3\end{array}$$

These two substances,— normal butane and isobutane — are said to manifest «nucleus isomerism,» since they differ by the mode of arrangement of their fundamental carbon chains. As the number of carbon atoms in a compound increases, the possibilities of nucleus isomerism becomes enormous. Thus the general empirical formula of the saturated fatty hydrocarbons (or paraffins) is $CnH_2n + _2$. We have seen that in the case of butane (for which $n = 4$) two nuclear isomers are possible. If the same kind of reasoning is applied to the higher members of the series regarding each member as derived from the preceding one by the substitution of a methyl radical (CH_3) for a hydrogen atom, we shall find that there are 3 pentanes ($n = 5$) possible: 5 hexanes ($n = 6$); 9 heptanes ($n = 7$); 18 octanes ($n = 8$); 35 ennanes ($n = 9$); 75 decanes ($n = 10$); 159 hendecanes ($n = 11$); 355 dodecanes ($n = 12$); and no less than 802 tridecanes ($n = 13$).

In that kind of true isomerism which is called «isomerism of position,» the isomeric bodies contain substituted atoms or radicals, which occupy different positions in the main chain. Thus a paraffin may be converted into an alcohol by substituting a hydroxyl radical (OH) for one of the hydrogen atoms, and the resulting alcohol will have different properties according to the position of the hydrogen atom that was replaced. For example, four butane alcohols are possible. In normal butane, the **structural formula of which is given above, the hydroxyl radical may be substituted for one of the terminal hydrogen atoms, in which case an alcohol is obtained which has the structural formula**

$$CH_3—CH_2—CH_2—CH_2—OH$$

and is known as «normal primary butyl alcohol.» If the hydroxyl is substituted in the place of one of the interior hydrogen atoms, an alcohol is obtained which has the structural formula

$$\begin{array}{l}CH_3—CH—CH_2—CH_3\\ \quad\quad\;\, |\\ \quad\quad OH\end{array}$$

and is known as «secondary butyl alcohol.»

Proceeding, now to the consideration of isobutane, we note that two essentially different substitutions of the hydroxyl radical are here possible. We may replace a hydrogen atom in one of the three CH_3 groups, or we may replace the one in the CH group. In the first case the alcohol has the structural formula

$$\begin{array}{l}CH_3—CH—CH_2—OH\\ \quad\quad\;\, |\\ \quad\quad CH_3\end{array}$$

and is known as «isoprimary butyl alcohol»; and in the second case it has the structural formula

$$\begin{array}{c}OH\\ |\\ CH_3—C—CH_3\\ |\\ CH_3\end{array}$$

and is known as «tertiary butyl alcohol.» All of these four alcohols have been actually prepared. (For isomerism of position as manifested in the aromatic compounds, and for the nomenclature used in distinguishing the various isomers that those compounds can exhibit, see AROMATIC COMPOUNDS).

Certain compounds are known which possess not only the same empirical formula, but the same structural formula also, and yet manifest distinctly different properties either chemically or physically. Fumaric and maleic acids (see FUMARIC ACID) are examples of this. In such cases the provisional hypothesis is made, that the geometrical structures of the molecules of the two substances are related to one another in something like the same manner that the image of an object in a mirror is related to the object itself, and the isomerism is said to be «geometrical.» See STEREO-CHEMISTRY.

With reference to isomerism in general, consult Hjelt, 'Principles of General Organic Chemistry'; Lothar, Meyer, 'Modern Theories of Chemistry.'

ISOMETRIC PERSPECTIVE, in mechanical drawing, a species of mechanical drawing in which three sides of an object are shown. Most mechanical structures can be referred to an including parallelopipedon. If a point be taken at or near the centre of a sheet of paper and three lines be drawn radiating therefrom, one vertical and downward, and two upward and oblique, making angles of 120° with each other they may be taken as representing three edges of a parallelopipedon. The object to be drawn is referred to this. Its vertical dimensions are laid off on lines parallel to the front vertical. Its horizontal members on one side are laid off parallel to one of the oblique lines, and the corresponding members on the other **side parallel to the other oblique line. Thus**

three faces of the object are seen. All dimensions parallel to the directing lines are on a true scale. Of the two side faces, the horizontal and vertical dimensions are given on a true scale, the diagonal dimensions being incorrect. It is a kind of false perspective that is easily drawn, and that has the great advantage of permitting the use of a true scale on certain controlling parts.

ISOMORPHISM, ī'sō-môr'fĭzm, signifying a similarity in form between things, is a term employed in (1) Crystallography, Mineralogy and in Chemistry; (2) Biology; (3) Mathematics.

In *crystallography, mineralogy and in chemistry,* «isomorphism» is a similarity of crystalline form between substances of analogous composition or atomic proportions. Sometimes the term is extended to mean similarity of crystalline form between substances of unlike composition or atomic proportions; but this sort of similarity should more properly be designated homoeomorphism. Used, however, in a double sense isomorphism proper is distinguished as isomerous or isonomic isomorphism; while homoeomorphism is distinguished as heteromerous or heteronomic isomorphism. Isomorphism, as a word, originated from the Greek *isos* (ἴσος), equal, and morphe (μορφή), «form,» to which *ism* was suffixed according to laws of English analogy; thus iso[s]morph[e](-ous) + ism. In 1819 Eilhard Mitscherlich, a German investigator observed that compounds having the same number of atoms to the molecule are disposed to form the same angles of crystallization. This property he called isomorphism. This discovery of the coincidence of similarity in crystalline forms where the chemical-composition also is similar is a most important generalization for crystallography; in chemistry, it has been of essential service in facilitating the classification of compounds and in determining the combining numbers or atomic weights in elementary bodies. Carbonates, oxides, silicates, etc. all present close similarity in the arrangement of their molecules, a fact known from their crystallization, cleavage, and optic properties. And they all, likewise are so related by chemical composition as to form part of one and the same mineralogic division. Minerals so related form an isomorphous group; they illustrate isomorphism. The diamond, magnetic oxide of iron, and alum, all crystallize in octohedra; but there is no analogy in their chemical composition; thus they present only one of the conditions of chemical isomorphism. They are heteronomic; and illustrate homoeomorphism.

Mitscherlich long ago tried to show that crystalline form is independent of the chemical nature of the atoms, and that it is determined solely by their groupings and relative position; the same number of atoms combined in the same way always producing, he asserts, the same crystalline form.

Isomorphous bodies can form homogeneous mixed crystals; and each one is capable of growing in a saturated solution of the other, fresh crystals being gradually amassed around the original body as a nucleus. The presence of the same chemical elements of composition in substances does by no means imply isomorphism and substances of very varying components may yet be isomorphous. The isomorphous elements in isomorphous salts, as, for instance, the metals, are generally of the same or related groups of elements. In some instances a combination of elements occurs crystallized in two or more series of crystal forms which are notably separate and distinct and frequently present the symmetry of different systems. This gives rise to two (sometimes three) species of identical chemical composition and is known as dimorphism (or trimorphism where three species are concerned). Carbonate of calcium, which crystallizes in orthorhombic forms as the mineral aragonite and in the hexagonal system as the mineral calcite, presents an excellent example of dimorphism. Yet both aragonite and calcite stand at the head of isomorphous groups of carbonates, also. To illustrate this:

Carbonates of calcium, known as calcite, magnesite or magnesium, siderite or iron, rhodochrosite or manganese, smithsonite or zinc, respectively symbolized as $CaCO_3$, $MgCO_3$, $FeCO_3$, $MnCO_3$ and $ZnCO_3$, form together an isomorphous group. All crystallize in the rhombohedral system, and with nearly the same angles, — the angles of cleavage in rhombohedra, varying from 105 to 107½. Between the members of an isomorphous group «intermediate compounds» may occur, regarded as isomorphous mixtures of two unlike molecules. Thus dolomite, the carbonate of calcium, and magnesium may be considered as formed by the union of the calcium carbonate molecules with those of magnesium carbonate.

Isodimorphism is isomorphism between the two forms, severally, of two dimorphous substances. Isothrimorphism is isomorphism between the three forms, severally, of two isotrimorphous substances. (See CRYSTALLOGRAPHY). For further study consult Dana, J. D., ‹System of Minerology› (New Haven 1837 and later editions); Moh, F., ‹Grundriss der Mineralogie› (Dresden, n.d.); Naumann, C. F., ‹Lehrbach der Krystallographie› (Leipzig, n.d.); Goldschmidt, V., ‹Index der Krystallformen der Mineralien› (Berlin, n.d.); Whitlock, H. P., ‹Critical Discussion of the Crystal Forms of Calcite› (in Proceedings of the American Academy of Arts and Sciences, Vol. I, No. 12, August 1915).

Isomorphism in biology is a similarity in organisms of different ancestry. The similarity here results from convergence, or the development or possession of similar characters by animals or plants, explained as due to similarity in habits, or in environment. Consult Darwin, ‹Origin of Species,› on «convergence.»

Isomorphism in mathematics is the Theory of Groups, the quality of groups rendering them similar in form, or isomorphic.

ISOPODA, ī-sŏp'ō-da, an extensive and varied group of *Crustacea* (q.v.) usually ranked as a suborder of the *Arthrostraca* or sessile-eyed *Malacostraca.* The body is broad and flattened, and either short or elongated; the carapace is absent or little developed; the thorax long with seven free segments, each bearing a pair of walking limbs; the abdomen more or less shortened and bearing lamellar branchial appendages. The *Isopoda* are classified in several tribes and more than 30 families, embracing an enormous number of species. They vary greatly in form and mode of life but all are of relatively small size and retiring habits. The vast majority are marine, but a few are inhabitants of fresh water or terrestrial; the latter are familiar to everyone under the names wood-lice and pill-bugs. Most of the marine forms live a free life but conceal themselves in crevices or among sessile animals and plants, others bore into wood, some, as the gribble and its allies, being destructive to piling; many are commensal or parasitic, among the latter being the *Cymothoidæ*, which infest fishes and whales, and the greatly degenerated *Bopyridæ*, which live in the branchial chamber of prawns and similar crustaceans. Consult Packard, 'Zoology' (1887); Leichmann, Georg, 'Beiträge zur Naturgeschichte der Isopoden' (Cassel 1891); Richardson, H., 'Key to Isopods of North America' (in Proceedings United States National Museum, Vols. XXI and XXIII, 1899, 1901); Id., 'Isopods Collected at Hawaiian Islands by United States Steamer Albatross' (Washington 1903); id., 'Contribution to the Natural History of the Isopoda' (ib., 1904); id., 'Monograph on the Isopoda of North America' (ib., 1905); id., 'Isopods Collected in the Northwest Pacific' (ib., 1906).

ISOSPONDYLI, ī-sō-pŏn'dĭ-lī. See ICHTHYOLOGY.

ISOSTASY, ī-sŏs'tạ-sē, signifying «equal pressure,» is that condition of the Earth's crust compelled by the action of gravitation upon the various substances forming the crust— in proportion, of course, to their several densities. The idea was introduced by J. H. Pratt, an English geodesist, early in the 19th century as a result of his observations of the deflections of the plumbline in the vicinity of the Himalayas and upon the plains of India. Pratt's reasoning was based entirely upon the well established law of gravitation, namely, that the attraction between any two small portions of matter is proportional to the product of their masses and inversely proportional to the square of the distance between them. He computed roughly the attraction, due to the mass of the Himalayas, which would act upon a plumb bob hung at various points over the plains of India and computed the deflection of the plumb line which would be produced by this nearly horizontal attraction tending to pull the bob toward the mountains. The deflections of the plumb line as observed at these points by geodetic methods were much smaller than the deflections which Pratt thus computed. He offered the possible explanation that the material underlying the mountains is of smaller average density than that underlying the plains, or, in other words, that the excess of mass visible in the mountains is compensated by a defect of density, and therefore of mass, in the material below the mountains. This was the beginning of the idea now called isostasy.

Many years later various American geologists noted, as they believed, a prevailing tendency for large portions of the earth's crust to rise as load was removed from the surface by erosion, or to subside as load was added by deposition. They reasoned that such a sensitiveness to change of load indicates that there is a close approach to equality in the total load under the various equal areas of the earth's surface. Their idea may be roughly expressed by saying that the total weight of any conical mass of matter having the earth's centre for its apex, and any one square mile of the earth's surface as its base, is nearly the same as that of any other similar conical mass having some other square mile for its base.

Maj. C. E. Dutton, in an address before the Philosophical Society of Washington in 1889, coined the word isostasy, and then and there presented the idea which the word represents so clearly and marshalled the evidence in favor of the validity of the idea so skillfully as to attract general attention. From that day to the present the discussion of the idea and of its numerous important relations to geology and geodesy has been continuous and increasing in vigor.

From about 1898 to the present the geodetic evidence that the condition called isostasy exists has been steadily gathered in a continuous investigation by the United States Coast and Geodetic Survey,— an investigation which is more vigorous in this line than that carried on in any other country. Two methods are used in that organization. The first is a refinement and extension of the method used by Pratt which has already been mentioned. The other method of observation consists in measuring with great accuracy the acceleration due to gravity at various points on the earth's surface by swinging invariable pendulums. It is evident that if the material under the observing station is of very low density the gravitational force acting on the pendulum bob will be smaller, and it will swing slower, than it would if the material were of normal density. Similarly over material of high density the pendulum will swing faster than over material of normal density. By properly refined methods of observation and computation the pendulum serves to indicate variations in density of the material underlying the region of observation. Geodesists in various countries have been especially active since about 1906 in developing the evidence as to isostasy. It seems proven that the outermost seven-eighths of the earth is solid, with great rigidity, but elastic to an extent, and thus yielding somewhat under variations of stress.

If the earth were composed of homogeneous material, its figure of equilibrium, under the influence of gravity and its own rotation, would be an ellipsoid of revolution.

The earth is composed of heterogeneous material which varies considerably in density. If this heterogeneous material were so arranged that its density at any point depended simply upon the depth of that point below the surface, or, more accurately, if all the material lying at each equipotential surface (rotation considered) was of one density, a state of equilibrium would exist and there would be no tendency toward a rearrangement of masses. The figure of the earth in this case would be a very close approximation to an ellipsoid of revolution.

If the heterogeneous material composing the earth were not arranged in this manner at the outset, the stresses produced by gravity would tend to bring about such an arrangement. But as the material is not a perfect fluid, as it possesses considerable viscosity, at least near the surface, the rearrangement will be imperfect. In the partial rearrangement some stresses will still remain, different portions of the same horizontal stratum may have somewhat different densities, and the actual surface of the earth will be a slight departure from the ellipsoid of revolution in the sense that above each region of deficient density there will be a bulge or bump on the ellipsoid, and above each region of excessive density there will be a hollow, relatively speaking. The bumps on this supposed earth will be the mountains, the plateaus, the continents; and the hollows will be the ocean bed. However, it must not be assumed that mountains are formed by isostatic movements. Quite the contrary, the folding of strata into mountains is in direct opposition to the isostatic principle. The same is true of erosion. In consideration of these facts, the function of isostasy in restoring equilibrium should not be unduly exaggerated. It becomes more evident as observations multiply that more must be known before all facts can be reconciled.

The compensation of the excess of matter at the surface (continents) by the defect of density below, and of surface defect of matter (oceans) by excess of density below, may be called the isostatic compensation.

Let the depth within which the isostatic compensation is complete be called the depth of compensation. At and below this depth the condition as to stress of any element of mass is isostatic; that is, any element of mass is subject to equal pressures from all directions as if it were a portion of a perfect fluid. Above this depth, on the other hand, each element of mass is subject in general to different pressures in different directions — to stresses which tend to distort it and to move it.

In terms of masses, densities and volumes, the conditions above the depth of compensation may be expressed as follows: The mass in any prismatic column which has for its base a unit area of the horizontal surface which lies at the depth of compensation, for its edges vertical lines (lines of gravity) and for its upper limit the actual irregular surface of the earth (or the sea surface if the area in question is beneath the ocean) is the same as the mass in any other similar prismatic column having any other unit area of the same surface for its base. To make the illustration concrete, if the depth of compensation is 60 miles below sea level, any column extending down to this depth below sea level and having one square mile for its base has the same mass as any other such column. One such column, located under a mountainous region, may be two miles longer than another located under the seacoast. On the other hand, the solid portion of such a column under one of the deep parts of the ocean may be three miles shorter than the column at the coast. Yet, if isostatic compensation is complete at the depth of 60 miles, all three of these columns have the same mass. The water above the suboceanic column is understood to be included in this mass. The masses being equal and the lengths of the columns different, it follows that the mean density of the column beneath the mountainous region is two parts in 60 less than the mean density of the column under the seacoast. So, also, the mean density of the solid portion of the suboceanic column must be greater than the mean density of the seacoast column, the excess being somewhat less than three parts in 60 on account of the sea water being virtually a part of the column.

This relation of the masses in various columns, and consequently of the densities, follows from the requirement of the definition of the expression «depth of compensation» that, at that depth, each element of mass is subject to equal pressures from all directions. In order that this may be true the vertical pressures, due to gravity, on the various units of area at that depth must be the same

The geodetic evidence now available proves that the condition called isostasy exists in the earth. It is certain that there is isostatic compensation for continents as a whole, and for their larger features, and that the compensation is a fair approximation to being complete and perfect. In the same way there is isostatic compensation for the ocean basins. Elevation, however, is to some degree compensated by rock density. The high-standing portions of the lithosphere are, in general, underlaid by rock material of less density than are the low-standing areas. Again, the increased cubic compression occurring with increasing depth causes a strengthening of the rocks which, in turn, necessitates greater stress differences in order to cause deformation. So the outer figure of isostasy is very irregular, and only approximates a spherical surface. While it is decided that the densities above that outline vary considerably from place to place, it also becomes apparent that isostasy is a geometric idea—not geologic. In fact, very large parts of the mass of the Earth are supported by the strength of the material, aided beyond doubt by its elasticity. The effect of this latter property has been to transfer strains and practically dissipate them over very wide areas above the isostatic outline. To still further confuse the situation there are the myriads of intrusions of varying density cutting the Earth shell.

A fourth point of view, stated below, which may be called the engineering point of view, also leads inevitably to the conclusion that there must be some isostatic compensation beneath the earth's surface. Consider the continents and great mountain ranges to be loads on the earth's surface in the sense that a railroad embankment across a plain is an added load, and consider the great ocean basins to be excavations, or negative loads comparable to canals or railroad cuts. On this basis compute the strength which the material composing the earth must have in order that the irregular surface of the earth may be maintained unchanged. It then becomes evident that the necessary strength is far in excess of that possessed by the materials of which the earth is made. Under the condition stated, that is without isostatic compensation, even if the whole earth were made of the strongest granite known, the continents must necessarily slump down into the oceanic basins and partially fill them.

Bibliography.—Born, A., 'Isostasie und Schweremessung' (Berlin 1923); Bowie, W., 'Isostasy' (New York 1927); Joly, J., 'The Surface-History of the Earth' (Oxford, Eng. 1925); Lawson, A. C., 'The Cypress Plain' (Berkeley, Calif. 1925); Nansen, F., 'The Strandflat and Isostasy' (Olso, Norway 1922); United States

Coast and Geodetic Survey (Dept. of Commerce), *Isostatic Investigations* (Special Publication No. 99, 1924).

JOHN F. HAYFORD,
Late Director, College of Engineering, Northwestern University.

ISOTOPES, ī'sō-tōps. Atoms of the same atomic number or nuclear charge but of different masses. See also ATOMIC ENERGY; ATOMIC THEORY; CHEMISTRY; ELEMENT.

ISOUARD, ē-zwȧr', **Nicolas** (known professionally as NICCOLO), Franco-Italian pianist and composer: b. Malta, 1775; d. Paris, 1818. About 1800, after serving as chapel master to the Knights of Saint John of Malta, he went to Paris, where he became associated with the Opéra Comique. Best known of his 33 operas were *Le Médicin Turc* (1803); *L'Intrigue aux Fenêtres* (1805); *Le siège de Mezières* (1814). He also composed cantatas, masses, and motets.

ISPAHAN. See ISFAHAN.

ISRAEL.* An independent Jewish republic of the Middle East, proclaimed on May 14, 1948, on termination of the British Mandate over Palestine. The capital is the New City of Jerusalem. Hebrew is the official language. The national flag contains the six-pointed star of David set between two horizontal blue stripes on a white ground.

Israel lies at the western tip of the continent of Asia, on the eastern shore of the Mediterranean Sea, between latitudes 29° 30′ N. and 33° 15′ N., and longitudes 34° 17′ E. and 35° 41′ E. Israel's boundaries, based on the United Nations partition plan of 1947 and the 1949 armistice agreements with the neighboring Arab states, encompass 8,108 square miles, or about 78 per cent of the area of the former British mandate. Israel is bordered by Egypt on the south, Syria and the Hashemite Kingdom of the Jordan on the east, and Lebanon on the north. Off Israel's west coast lies the Mediterranean Sea; to the east lies the southern section of the Dead Sea; and at the extreme southeast, Israel touches the Gulf of Aqaba.

Mountain and plain, lake and seacoast, field and desert vary Israel's landscape. Newly productive soil adjoins barren stretches, sharpening the contrasts produced by the rapid reclamation of wasteland areas. From the coastal plain—warm and moist in summer, mild in winter—the land rises eastward to the Judean heights. then drops markedly to the hot and dry Jordan Valley. In the south lies the Negev desert—hot and dry in summer, cold and dry in winter—a frontier area in the process of settlement. In the north are the Galilee hills, cool and dry in summer, cold and rainy in winter; and the rich agricultural lands of the Jezreel Valley, reclaimed from once malarial swamps. Though not rich in natural resources, Israel profits from the abundant Dead Sea chemical deposits (magnesium bromide and the principal chlorides: potassium, sodium, magnesium, and calcium), and possesses ingredients for cement and other building materials, bituminous lime-slag, manganese, barite, feldspar, sulfur, peat, and papyrus. Copper lies in the hills north of Elath, at the site of King Solomon's ancient mines, while deposits of phosphates, kaolin, and iron have also been discovered in the Negev.

Population.—At the time of the proclamation of the state in May 1948, the Jewish population amounted to about 650,000. After four years of unprecedented immigration, the total population in May 1952 was approximately 1,600,000, of whom 1,426,000 were Jews and 174,000 were non-Jews, chiefly Arab Moslems, with some Christians and Druse. The major part of the Jewish population is concentrated near the Mediterranean coast and in the large towns. Despite the establishment of many new settlements in the first years of the new state, the increase in population was largely in existing communities, primarily the towns. At the end of 1951, Israel's 18 towns had nearly two thirds of the total population. The chief urban centers and their estimated populations in September 1951 were: Tel Aviv-Jaffa, 370,000; Greater Haifa, 190,000; and the New City of Jerusalem, 150,000.

Immigration.—Maintaining its policy to "welcome home every Jew who seeks entry," the new nation accepted some 700,000 immigrants in the first four years of its existence. The majority of the Jewish population under the mandate had come from the Jewish centers of eastern and central Europe during the waves of Zionist settlement between World Wars I and II. In the period 1948–1952, the greatest proportion of immigrants (44.3 per cent) also came from eastern Europe. An increasing number, however, came from Asia (34.5 per cent) and northern Africa (13.8 per cent), where the surge of Arab nationalism endangered many of the ancient Jewish communities . In the dramatic "Operation Magic Carpet" of late 1949 and early 1950, virtually the entire Jewish community of Yemen was transferred by air to Israel. In 1951, nearly 90,000 Jews of Iraq—the greater part of the Jewish community of that country—emigrated to the Jewish state.

JEWISH IMMIGRATION TO ISRAEL, 1948–1951

Year	Number of immigrants
1948	118,903
1949	239,141
1950	169,405
1951	174,014

The vast influx created a multitude of problems of adjustment and absorption. Among the newcomers were many sick and aged, incapable of self-support. Many former businessmen and professionals had to shed their former occupations and acquire new skills needed for the building of a nation. Within a few years, hundreds of thousands were settled in the towns and rural communities, and the hastily constructed immigrant camps gave way to the *ma'arbaroth,* or work camps, which afforded a better opportunity for productive work. By late 1951 the rate of influx appeared to have lessened, only 46,000 immigrants having arrived in the second half of the year, as compared with 128,000 in the first half. In 1952 an element of selectiveness in immigration was introduced, applying, however, only to those immigrants whose passage was paid

* For additional material on Israel, particularly the structure of the Jewish community, its historical background and relationship to the Zionist movement, see the sections *Jews in Modern Palestine,* and *Zionism,* in the series, JEWISH HISTORY AND SOCIETY, vol. 16.

ISRAEL

Top: **The inauguration of Chaim Weizmann (1874–1952) as the first president of Israel.**

Right: **Portrait sketching from life in a Jerusalem art class.**

Courtesy Israel Office of Information

Bottom: **Leonard Bernstein conducts the Israel Philharmonic in a Jerusalem concert. The soloist is Jascha Heifetz.**

ISRAEL

Left: Israeli workers in the diamond-cutting industry.

Center: The Bialik School, one of the many educational institutions in Israel which receives American financial support.

Bottom: Nahalal, northern Israel, six miles west of Nazareth. This modern village, founded in 1921, on reclaimed land, was the first smallholders' cooperative settlement in Palestine. Residents live in a circular formation and tend the land strips radiating from their circle frontages.

Courtesy (1) and (2) Palestine Foundation Fund; (3) Israel Office of Information

ISRAEL

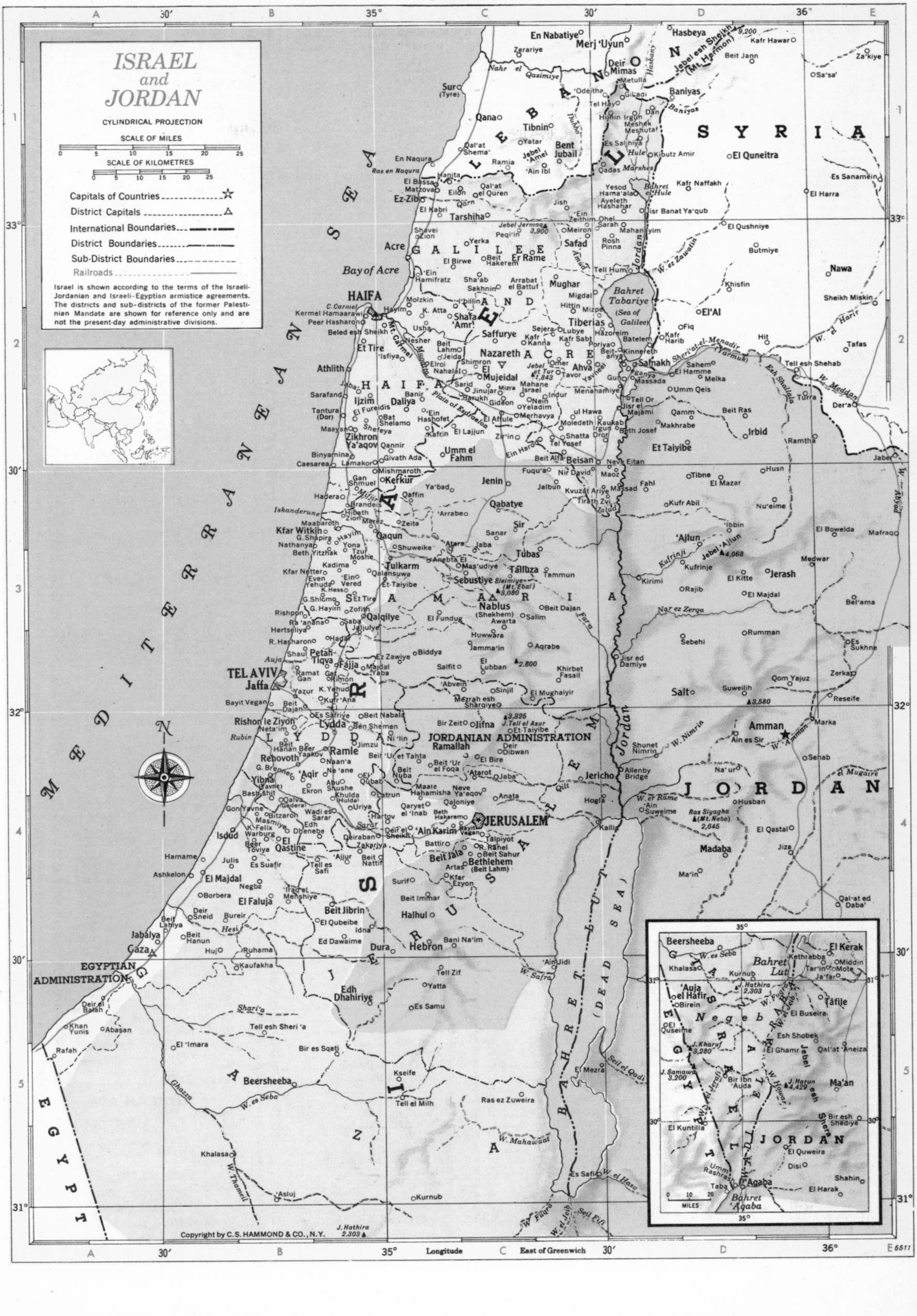

ISRAEL and JORDAN
CYLINDRICAL PROJECTION
SCALE OF MILES
0 5 10 15 20 25
SCALE OF KILOMETRES
0 5 10 15 20 25
Capitals of Countries
District Capitals
International Boundaries
District Boundaries
Sub-District Boundaries
Railroads
Israel is shown according to the terms of the Israeli-Jordanian and Israeli-Egyptian armistice agreements. The districts and sub-districts of the former Palestinian Mandate are shown for reference only and are not the present-day administrative divisions.
MEDITERRANEAN SEA
LEBANON
SYRIA
JORDAN
EGYPT
EGYPTIAN ADMINISTRATION
JORDANIAN ADMINISTRATION
GALILEE
ACRE
HAIFA
SAMARIA
LYDDA
JERUSALEM
GAZA
NEGEB
Bay of Acre
Bahret Tabariye (Sea of Galilee)
Bahret Lut (DEAD SEA)
Jordan
Yarmuk
TEL AVIV
Jaffa
HAIFA
JERUSALEM
Amman
Acre
Nazareth
Tiberias
Safad
Nablus (Shekhem)
Jenin
Tulkarm
Ramallah
Jericho
Bethlehem (Beit Lahm)
Hebron
Beersheba
Gaza
Khan Yunis
Rafah
Ashkelon
El Majdal
Ramle
Lydda
Rehovoth
Petah Tiqva
Natanya
Hadera
Salt
Irbid
Jerash
'Ajlun
Madaba
Es Salt
El Quneitra
Sur (Tyre)
Merj 'Uyun
Hasbeya
Baniyas
Beisan
Sebustiye
Qalqilye
Kafr Kanna
Shafa 'Amr
Athlith
Caesarea
Copyright by C. S. HAMMOND & CO., N. Y.
Longitude
East of Greenwich
35°
30′
36°
31°
32°
33°
A
B
C
D
E
1
2
3
4
5
Beersheba
El Kerak
Tafile
Ma'an
Aqaba
Bahret 'Aqaba
Bahret Lut
MILES

ISRAEL AND JORDAN

ISRAEL
Total Population 1,429,000

Acre, 12,200 C 2
Acre (bay) C 2
Affula (El Affule), 6,200 C 2
Ahva C 2
'Ain Jidi C 5
'Ain Karim, 1,700 C 4
'Ajjur, 729 B 4
'Aqir B 4
'Araba, El (dry riv.) D 5
Ashkelon B 4
'Asluj, 131 B 5
Athlith, 4,000 B 2
Ayeleth Hashahar, 547 D 1
Baniyas (river) D 1
Barukh, 189 C 2
Bash-shit B 4
Bat Shelamo, 178 C 2
Bayit Vegan, 5,460 B 3
Beer Toviya, 1,118 B 4
Beer Yaakov, 3,980 B 4
Beersheeba, 8,300 D 4
Beisan, 2,875 C 2
Beit Alfa, 655 C 2
Beit Dajan, 2,100 B 3
Beit Hakerem (Maj'd el Krum), 2,017 C 2
Beit Hanan, 531 B 4
Beit Jibrin, 43 B 4
Beit Lahm, 175 C 2
Beit Nabala, 211 C 4
Beit Nattif, 55 B 4
Beitanya, 135 D 2
Ben-Shemen, 483 B 4
Beth Josef, 152 D 2
Beth Yitzhak, 533 B 3
Binyamina, 3,269 B 2
Bitzaron, 409 B 4
Borbera, 158 B 4
Brandeis B 3
Caesarea, 387 B 2
Carmel, Mount C 2
Dan, 405 D 1
Dead (Lut) (sea) C 5
Deganya, 981 D 2
Deiraban B 4
Dor (Tantura), 180 B 2
Ed Dawaime B 4
Eilon, 460 C 1
'Ein Hamifratz, 506 C 2
'Ein Harod, 1,230 C 2
'Ein Hashofet, 568 C 2
'Ein Vered, 467 B 3
'Ein Zeithim, 84 C 1
Ekron, 305 B 4
El Affule, 6,200 C 2
El Bassa, 260 C 1
El Faluja B 4
El Fureidis, 891 B 2
El 'Imara, 58 B 5
El Kabri, 252 C 1
El Majdal, 5,100 B 4
El Mujeidal, 2,986 C 2
El Qastine, 666 B 4
El Qubab, 197 B 4
El Qubeibe, 434 B 4
Elroi, 427 C 2
Er Rame, 2,392 C 2
Es Safriye B 4
Es Salihiya D 1
Es Suafir, 278 B 4
Esdraelon (plain) C 2
Et Taiyibe, 5,108 C 3
Et Tire B 2
Et Tire, 5,255 B 3
Even Yehuda, 2,050 B 3
Ez-Zib, 188 C 1
Fuqra (dry riv.) D 5
Galilee (Tabariye) (sea) D 2
Gan-Hayim, 290 B 3
Gan-Shlomo, 340 B 3
Gan Shmuel, 549 B 3
Gat Rimon, 240 B 3
Gedera (Qalva), 2,530 B 4
Gideon, 191 C 2
Gil'adi, 854 D 1
Giv'at Brenner, 1,685 B 4
Givath Ada, 660 C 2
Gon Yavne, 1,350 B 4
Gun, 1,193 D 2
Hadar, 1,148 B 3
Hadera, 15,000 B 3
Haifa, 129,000 B 2
Hanita, 201 C 1
Hartov, 210 C 4
Hathira (mt.) D 5
Hayim, 1,193 B 3
Hayim, 11,000 C 2
Hazoreim, 2,106 D 2
Hertseliya, 12,200 B 3
Hesi (river) B 4
Hibath Zion, 332 B 3
Hulda (Khulda), 316 B 4
Hule (lake) D 1
I'Billin, 1,478 C 2
Ijzim, 344 B 2
Indur, 299 C 2
Iraq el Menshiye B 4
Irgun Meshek Meshutaf, 105 D 1
Isdud, 1,100 B 4
'Isfiya, 1,837 C 2
Iskanderune (river) B 3
Jaba', 327 B 2
Jaffa-Tel Aviv, 335,000 B 3
Jaljulye B 3
Jeib, el (dry riv.) C 6
'Jeida, 690 C 2
Jermaq (mt.) C 2
Jerusalem (New City) (cap.), 120,000 C 4
Jimzu, 100 B 4
Jinujar, 460 C 2
Jish, 1,304 C 1
Jisr Banat Ya'qub, 46 D 1
Jisr el Majami, 296 D 2
Julis, 1,019 B 4
Kadima, 1,309 B 3
Kafr Kanna, 2,478 C 2
Kafr Sabt, 632 C 2
Kaukab, 457 D 2
Kefar Atta, 5,700 C 2
Kefar Felix Warburg, 556 B 4
Kefar Hess, 443 B 3
Kefar Yehud, 3,100 B 3
Kerkur, 2,900 C 3
Kermel Hamaarawi B 2
Kfar Netter, 276 B 3
Kfar Witkin, 1,150 B 3
Khulda (Hulda), 316 B 4
Kinnereth, 909 D 2
Kufr 'Ana B 3
Kurnub D 5
Lubye, 201 C 2
Lut (Dead) (sea) C 5
Lydda, 12,150 B 4
Maabaroth, 632 B 3
Maale Hahamisha, 321 C 4
Maayan, 340 B 2
Mahanayim, 197 D 2
Mahane Israel, 5,474 C 2
Mahawuat (dry riv.) C 5
Maoz, 564 D 3
Masmiye, 733 B 4
Massad, 260 D 3
Massada, 330 D 2
Matzova, 252 C 1
Meiron, 129 C 2
Menahamiye, 200 D 2
Meona (Tarshiha), 639 C 1
Merhavya, 904 C 2
Metulla, 260 D 1
Migdal, 363 C 2
Mishmaroth, 236 C 3
Mizpe, 45 C 2
Mizra, 541 C 2
Moledeth, 251 C 2
Molzkin, 4,200 C 2
Mughar, 2,568 C 2
Muqatta (river) C 2
Naan'a 985 B 4
Nahalal, 1,060 C 2
Nathanya, 20,000 B 3
Nazareth, 23,000 C 2
Negba, 389 B 4
Negeb (Negev) (reg.) D 5
Nein, 254 C 2
Nesher, 1,750 C 2
Neta'im, 312 B 4
Neve Eitan, 273 D 2
Nir-David, 477 C 3
Omer, 62 C 5
Peqi'in, 1,086 C 2
Petah Tiqva, 31,500 B 3
Poriya, 300 D 2
Qalansuwa, 1,120 C 3
Qal'at el Quren, 540 C 1
Qalva (Gedera), 2,530 B 4
Qaqun, 85 C 3
Qarn (dry riv.) C 1
Qaryet el 'Inab, 326 C 4
Ra'anana, 7,800 B 3
Ramat Gan, 30,000 B 3
Ramath Hasharon, 2,780 B 3
Ramath Rahel, 163 C 4
Ramle, 12,580 B 4
Rehovoth, 18,200 B 4
Rishon le Ziyon, 18,000 B 4
Rishpon, 398 B 3
Rosh Pinna, 1,587 D 2
Ruhama, 409 B 4
Saba, 12,230 B 3
Safad, 5,500 C 2
Saffurye, 349 C 2
Sakhnin, 3,477 C 2
Samakh, 893 D 2
Samawa (mt.) D 5
Sarar (dry riv.) B 4
Sarid, 609 C 2
Sejera, 95 C 2
Shafa 'Amr, 3,905 C 2
Shari'a (river) B 5
Shatta, 907 C 2
Shaul, 236 B 3
Shavei Zion, 229 C 2
Shefeya, 503 B 2
Shimron, 81 C 2
Tabariye (Galilee) (sea) D 2
Tantura (Dor), 180 B 2
Tarshiha (Meona), 639 C 1
Tavor, 262 C 2
Tel Aviv-Jaffa, 335,000 B 3
Tel Yosef, 858 C 2
Tell es Safi B 4
Tell Hum D 2
Thameil (dry riv.) B 5
Tiberias, 12,200 C 2
Tirath Zvi, 367 C 3
Tur, et (mt.) C 2
Tzur Moshe, 421 B 3
'Umm el Fahm, 4,861 C 2
Uriya, 484 B 4
Usha, 301 C 2
Wadi es Sarar, 172 B 4
Yavne (Yibna), 1,540 B 4
Yavneel, 1,540 D 2
Yazur, 3,100 B 3
Yerka, 1,926 C 2
Yesod Hama'ala, 335 D 1
Yibna (Yavne), 1,540 B 4
Yona, 1,000 B 3
Zakariya, 138 B 4
Zikhron Ya'aqov, 3,000 B 2
Zir'in, 96 C 2
Zofith, 393 B 3

JORDAN
Total Population 1,250,000

Trans-Jordan (Jordan), 1,250,000 D 4
Abyad (dry riv.) E 3
Ain es Sir, 6,641 D 4
'Ain Suweime D 4
'Ajlun, 1,936 D 3
Ajlun (mt.) D 3
Amman (cap.), 90,000 D 4
Anata C 4
Aqaba, 931 D 5
Aqrabe C 3
'Arrabe C 3
Atara C 3
'Atarot C 4
Awarta C 3
Bani Na'im C 4
Battir C 4
Beit Dajan C 3
Beit Jala, 3,710 C 4
Beit Lahm (Bethlehem), 8,820 C 4
Beit Ras, 943 D 2
Beit Sahur C 4
Beit 'Ur el Foqa C 4
Beit 'Ur et Tahta C 4
Bel'ama, 3,326 E 3
Bethlehem (Beit Lahm), 8,820 C 4
Biddya C 3
Bir esh Shediye E 5
Bir Zeit C 4
Deir Dibwan C 4
Dura B 4
Ebal (Sleimiye) (mt.) C 3
Edh Dhahiriye B 5
El Bire C 4
El Boweida E 3
El Buseira, 1,700 D 5
El Fundug C 3
El Ghamr D 5
El Hamme D 2
El Kerak, 10,000 E 4
El Kitte, 939 D 3
El Lubban C 3
El Mas'udiye C 3
El Majdal, 340 D 3
El Mazar, 1,990 D 3
El Mezra, 5,000 C 5
El Mughaiyir C 3
El Qastal, 150 D 4
El Quweira D 5
Es Safi, 5,000 C 5
Es Samu C 5
Es Sukhne, 150 E 3
Esh Shobek, 3,000 D 5
Et Taiyibe, 2,213 D 2
Ez Zawiye C 3
Fahl, 94 D 3
Far'a (river) C 3
Fuqqu'a C 3
Halhul C 4
Hasa el (dry riv.) D 5
Hebron, 24,560 C 4
Husban D 4
Husn, 4,510 D 3
Huwwara C 3
Idna B 4
Irbid, 6,693 D 2
Jaba C 3
Jaber, 659 E 2
Ja'far, 50 E 5
Jalbun C 3
Jebel means mountain, *Arabic*
Jenin, 3,990 C 3
Jerash, 2,531 D 3
Jericho C 4
Jifna C 4
Jisr ed Damiye, 600 D 3
Jiza, 500 D 4
Jordan (river) D 4
Kfar Ezyon C 4
Kethrabba, 2,000 D 5
Kufr Abil, 1,021 D 3
Kufrinje, 3,674 D 3
Kufrinji (river) D 3
Latrun C 4
Ma'an, 8,629 E 5
Madaba, 5,000 D 4
Mafraq, 1,876 E 3
Ma'in, 1,000 D 4
Makhrabe, 296 D 2
Marka, 500 E 4
Medwar, 442 E 3
Melka, 1,923 D 2
Middin, 300 E 5
Mote, 1,500 E 5
Nablus (Shekhem), 23,250 C 3
Nar ez Zerqa (river) D 3
Na'ur, 4,650 D 4
Nebo (Siyagha) (mt.) D 4
Neve Ya'aqov C 4
Nimrin (dry riv.) D 4
Nu'eime, 2,097 D 3
Qabatye C 3
Qal'at 'Aneiza E 5
Qalqilye C 3
Qamm, 495 D 2
Qom Yajuz, 300 D 3
Rajib, 456 D 3
Ramallah, 5,080 C 4
Rame, er (dry riv.) D 4
Ramtha, 6,410 D 2
Reseife, 500 E 3
Rumman, 150 D 3
Safra (dry riv.) C 5
Sahem, 1,379 D 2
Salim C 3
Salt, 12,000 D 3
Sanar C 3
Sebehi, 520 D 3
Sebustiye C 3
Sehab, 6,050 D 4
Shekhem (Nablus), 23,250 C 3
Sheri'at-el-Menadir (Yarmuk) (river) D 2
Shunet Nimrin, 960 D 4
Sir C 3
Siyagha (Nebo) (mt.) D 4
Sleimiye (Ebal) (mt.) C 3
Suweilih, 5,070 D 3
Tafilah, 6,500 E 5
Talluza C 3
Tammun C 3
Tar'in, 1,000 D 5
Tell el Asur (mt.) C 4
Tell Or D 2
Tibne, 841 D 3
Tubas C 3
Tulkarm, 8,090 C 3
Turra, 1,689 D 2
Umm Qeis, 1,166 D 2
Wadi means dry river, *Arabic*
Yarmuk (Sheri'at-el-Menadir) (river) D 2
Yatta C 5
Zerka, 3,000 E 3

EGYPTIAN ADM.

Abasan A 5
Beit Hanun B 4
Beit Lahiya B 4
Gaza, 34,170 A 4
Jabalya A 4
Khan Yunis, 11,220 A 5
Rafah A 5

ISRAEL ADM.

'Auja el Hafir D 5
Birein D 5

for by Jewish Agency funds and who came from countries where there was no danger to the Jewish communities. Of this group, 80 per cent had to be under 35 years of age, have a useful skill or profession, or be willing to do agricultural work for two years. The citizenship and nationality law, effective on July 14, 1952, conferred Israeli citizenship on all Jews residing in Israel on that date, except those who officially declared their desire to retain their non-Israeli citizenship. Thenceforth, Jewish immigrants acquired citizenship on arrival. Arabs and other non-Jews could obtain citizenship upon meeting certain requirements.

Vital Statistics.—Because of Israel's widespread network of medical service and relatively high cultural level, vital statistics for the Jewish population compare favorably with those of most western European peoples. The average life expectancy at birth in 1949 was 65.0 years for males and 67.9 years for females. The crude birth rate in 1951 was 32.7; the crude death rate, 6.4. The infant mortality rate in 1951 was 39 deaths per 1,000 live births. The incidence of tuberculosis, one of Israel's most difficult medical problems, declined from seven per cent in 1949 to one per cent in 1951.

Public Health.—About 55 per cent of the population receives its medical services from Kupat Holim, the medical branch of Histadrut (General Federation of Labor). Also important in Israel's public health system are the government hospitals for new immigrants and those persons not eligible under other insurance programs; Hadassah, the women's Zionist organization; and Malben, a committee which cares for the chronically ill, the disabled, and the aged. In 1951 the country had 84 hospitals with a total of 8,379 hospital beds.

Government.—Israel has no written constitution. The duties of the president, the powers of government, the legislative authority, and certain other constitutional functions are laid down in a transition law adopted by the Knesset (Assembly) on Feb. 16, 1949. On June 13, 1950, the Knesset voted to legislate separately on basic matters within the next several years, these acts to be combined eventually into a fundamental code of laws. On Dec. 5, 1951, the Knesset passed a presidential tenure law providing for the election of the president of Israel by the Knesset for a five-year term. The Israeli presidency serves chiefly a symbolic function.

The Knesset, a unicameral, 120-member body, is elected by secret ballot and universal suffrage, through a system of proportional representation. The franchise is held by men and women over 18 years of age. The Knesset elects the president of Israel, who, after consultation with the chief parties represented in the Knesset, entrusts a member of the Knesset with the task of forming a cabinet. The cabinet, which is responsible to the Knesset, consists of a prime minister and a number of other ministers who may or may not be members of the Knesset. Dr. Chaim Weizmann, Israel's first president, died on Nov. 9, 1952, and Itzhak Ben-Zvi took office on December 10. David Ben-Gurion headed Israel's first cabinet, formed in March 1949, and continued as prime minister following the elections of July 30, 1951.

The judiciary of Israel consists of a Supreme Court which sits in Jerusalem, comprising a president and six judges; three district courts; 16 magistrate courts; and religious courts of the Jewish, Moslem, and Christian communities. Judges are appointed by the Israeli minister of justice, but the appointment of a Supreme Court judge must be confirmed by the Knesset.

Education and Culture.—The compulsory education law passed by the Knesset on Sept. 12, 1949, provides for free and compulsory education from the age of five to 13 years inclusive. The law specifically recognizes four established school trends: general schools, labor schools, Mizrachi schools, and Agudat Israel schools—the latter two being of the religious type. Schools of each trend are guided by supervisory committees composed of representatives of organizations and of parents belonging to the trend, with final supervision and control resting with the Ministry of Education and Culture. Elementary school consists of eight years of instruction; secondary school, four years. The language of instruction in the Jewish schools is Hebrew; in the government Arab schools, Arabic. Most schools are coeducational. Virtually all Jewish children of school age receive schooling. Many Arab children, especially girls, receive no schooling, although the number of Arab pupils has increased significantly since the passage of the education law.

In the 1950–1951 school year there were 703 elementary schools with 130,721 pupils; 113 secondary schools with 12,923 pupils; and 97 Arab schools with 24,240 pupils. In addition, there were 1,325 kindergartens with 51,485 children, a number of vocational and agricultural schools, evening classes for working youths, theological seminaries and schools for Torah study, schools for backward children, schools in immigrant and work camps, and intensive courses in Hebrew for immigrant adults. Higher education is provided at Hebrew University in Jerusalem, with faculties in the humanities, science, medicine, law, and a school of agriculture. University enrollment in 1950–1951 was 1,862. The Haifa Technicon (enrollment, 1,573) comprises a school of engineering, a technical high school, and a nautical school. The Weizmann Institute of Science at Rehovoth was staffed by some 55 research scientists and 60 laboratory assistants in 1951.

Cultural facilities in Israel include the art museums at Jerusalem, Tel Aviv, and Ain Harod, and several smaller historical, archaeological and natural history museums. Israel has several repertory theater companies, best-known of which is Habimah. In addition to the Israel Philharmonic Orchestra there are a number of other orchestras, conservatories of music, and ballet schools. Of Israel's 18 daily newspapers in 1951, 12 were in Hebrew; the others were in German, Arabic, English, and Hungarian. Numerous periodicals appear in several languages on various general, literary, and technical subjects. Israel, with one of the highest cinema attendance rates in the world, had 110 cinemas in 1951 with a seating capacity of about 70,000.

Religion.—A secular nationalism, rather than religion, is the predominant force in Israeli society. In the context of independent nationhood, many of the age-old Jewish holidays and observances have taken on a new applicability and significance. The holiday of *Shabuoth,* for example, has, on the farm settlements, become a true harvest festival; while the *Pesach* (Passover) holiday, commemorating the epochal exodus from Egypt—the greatest event in the development of the Jews as a people—has an almost contemporary relevancy to the struggle for the re-establishment of a Jewish nation in the 20th century. A relatively small proportion of the population—a fifth or less—embraces the full orthodox Jewish code and ritual. Though in the minority, the religious groups—chiefly Mizrachi (the religious wing of the Zionist movement), and the Agudat Israel (a non-Zionist group)—exert considerable influence in the life of the nation, particularly since the Mapai (Israel Labor Party) has depended on the religious parties for its parliamentary majority. The question of religious control in education and in matters of personal status (chiefly marriage, divorce, and inheritance), as well as official observation of kosher food laws and the recruitment of women for national service, are contested national issues. Personal status, as under the mandatory, continues to be exclusively within the jurisdiction of the ecclesiastical courts, with Moslem religious judges presiding over autonomous Moslem courts. Freedom of worship exists for the Moslem and Christian minorities in Israel.

Defense.—The Defense Service Law passed in 1949 and amended in 1952 provided for the creation of a regular army. Men aged 18 to 26 were made subject to a compulsory 30-month period of conscription; men aged 27 to 29 and unmarried women aged 18 to 26 had to serve two years. Part of the service period was devoted to agricultural training. Women were to be exempted from service in the armed forces if they had religious objections. All men aged 18 to 45, and childless women aged 18 to 34, were made liable for service in the reserves.

Finance.—Among the first acts of the provisional government in 1948 was the adoption of a national currency, the Israeli pound (I£), equal to U.S. $4.03 at the official rate. In the wave of international devaluations of September 1949, the Israeli pound was reduced to $2.80 at the official rate. Beginning Feb. 17, 1952, a threefold schedule of exchange rates came into effect. The former rate of $2.80 to the Israeli pound was retained as the basic official rate for government purposes, essential imports, and diamond exports. A rate of $1.40 was applied to incoming remittances of fund-raising institutions and proceeds of designated exports, as well as semiessential imports. A rate of $1 to the Israeli pound was applied to incoming remittances for investment purposes, to proceeds of exports not subject to either of the other rates, and (in October 1952) also to various tourist transactions.

In the first few years of the state, the Israeli budget consisted of three parts: an ordinary budget, covered mainly by direct and indirect taxes and customs duties; a development budget; and an undisclosed military budget. For the fiscal year ended March 31, 1951, the ordinary budget totaled I£59,465,000; and the development budget, I£65,000,000.

Economy.—Israel's economy is featured by an intensive agriculture and highly specialized light industries. Though cooperative and collective organizations are important, particularly in agriculture, private enterprise is predominant. Dependent upon imports for most of its raw materials and many of its manufactures and foodstuffs, the new nation has had to take heroic measures to sustain its growing population by developing its internal resources, expanding its industry and agriculture, and increasing its exports. Israel's national income of I£337.6 million in 1950 compared with I£250 million in 1949, and an estimated I£470 million in 1951. The 1950 national income originated as follows (in percentages): manufacturing and construction (including public utilities), 36.2; trade, 14.8; agriculture and fishing, 9.5; transport and communications (excluding postal services), 6.2; government, 14.8; all others, 18.5.

Industry.—Though lacking the resources for a large-scale heavy industry, Israel possesses important assets in its skilled labor force and abundant chemical deposits. Israel's largest industrial center is located in Tel Aviv and the surrounding area, where textiles and apparel, woodwork and furniture, chemical products, building materials, leather goods, pharmaceuticals, beverages, processed foods, and plastics are produced. Industries in the Haifa region include cement, oil refining, electrical and other machinery, chemicals, ceramics, glass, tools, and sanitary equipment. Handicrafts and printing are important in the Jerusalem area, while the diamond cutting and polishing industry is located in the Nathanya district on the coast. At the end of 1950 there were 90,000 wage earners in industry. From the founding of the state to the end of 1951, 2,250 industrial enterprises employing 15,400 workers were established. Outstanding among the new industries have been the small steel mill, automobile assembly plant, and tire and rubber plant in the Haifa area; the tire and rubber plant at Hadera; and the modern precision-tool factory at Tel Aviv. Electric power, supplied mainly by the large diesel-operated stations at Haifa and Tel Aviv, is available almost everywhere in the country.

Agriculture.—The backbone of Jewish land colonization prior to the establishment of the state was the collective farm, or *kibbutz*, which allowed for a sharing of hardships and risks and provided for a pooling of capital, skills, and defensive strength. Though still of central importance in agricultural production and land settlement, the *kibbutzim* have been supplemented by expanding newer forms of rural colonization, chief among which are the cooperative-type *moshvei ovdim*, and the *moshavot*, or ordinary rural villages based on private land ownership. Other types of organization, such as the *moshav shitufi*, combine various features of cooperative and private enterprise in production and marketing. The newer immigrants who have settled on the land have tended to favor the noncollective types. Nevertheless, in the 1949–1950 crop year about 70 per cent of the field crop area in Jewish farming was sown by the collective farms.

Area under cultivation in 1949–1950 totaled 2.5 million dunums, of which 330,000 dunums comprised irrigated land. (The dunum is equal to .22 acre.) Cultivated area in 1950–1951 was estimated at 3.5 million dunums, a 40 per cent increase over the 1949–1950 total. The value of agricultural output in 1949–1950 (excluding citrus fruits) was I£48.8 million, of which Jewish farming provided about 90 per cent. In addition to field crops, chief farm products are milk, eggs, vegetables and potatoes, cattle and poultry, fish, and green fodder. Fruits (other than citrus) include bananas, grapes, plums, apples, and figs. Israel's citrus fruits industry, in which private ownership is predominant, provides the nation's chief export. Production in the 1951–1952 season was an estimated 9 million boxes.

Agricultural expansion in Israel depends

chiefly upon the bringing of new land under cultivation through pioneering land settlement in the arid Negev region of the south, and the development of other areas, such as the northeast Lake Huleh district, where the fertile swampland must first be drained. Given sufficient capital and willing pioneers, the undeveloped Negev area offers vast possibilities for exploitation. In the period 1948–1951, the population of the Negev increased from 1,500 to 26,000, and the number of settlements also increased from 17 to 70.

Foreign Trade.—Conditions of internal expansion have produced an inevitable excess of imports over exports in Israel's foreign trade. This adverse balance on visible account has been met by private remittances from Jewish organizations, mainly American, and by various other forms of capital transfers, such as foreign investments in Israel, credits and grants from the United States, the liquidation of Israel's sterling balance in London, and income from the $500 million Israeli bond flotation launched in the United States in 1951.

Israel's imports in 1951 had a total value of I£122,592,848 (I£102,604,442 in 1950); while exports (including re-exports) amounted to I£16,720,065 (I£13,162,212 in 1950). Thus, Israel's adverse balance on visible trade in 1951 totaled I£105,872,783. The import total, however, included I£25,480,677 in imports for which no payment had to be made, such as gifts and personal effects of immigrants, thereby reducing the net adverse balance for 1951 to I£80,392,106 (I£71,156,711 in 1950).

Israel's imports cover a wide variety of foodstuffs, raw materials, and manufactured goods. Chief items are machinery, oilseeds, nuts, fats, grain, flour, iron and steel and manufactures thereof, aircraft, ships, vehicles, chemicals, and timber. Principal export products and values exported in 1951 were: citrus fruits, I£5,736,935; polished diamonds, I£4,167,574; textile manufactures, I£1,379,882; and fruit juices, I£1,135,154. Israel's main trading partners are the United States, chief market for Israel's diamond industry; and the United Kingdom, an important purchaser of Israel's citrus crops.

Transportation and Communications.—Expansion of transportation and communications facilities is an important part of Israel's program of development. Steps have been taken for the improvement of the Mediterranean ports of Haifa and Tel Aviv, and for the development of Elath, Israel's outlet on the Gulf of Aqaba. Vessels registered in Israel at the end of 1950 numbered 32, aggregating 90,000 gross tons. Israeli ships carried 12 per cent of Israel's cargo in 1950. At the end of 1951, 324 miles of railways (chiefly standard gauge) were in operation; while the length of paved roads totaled 1,526 miles. Registered motor vehicles in 1952 included 12,191 passenger cars and 14,223 trucks. City and interurban bus lines are operated by Histadrut, Israel's many-sided labor organization. Of Israel's two civil airfields, the main one is at Lod (formerly Lydda), the other at Haifa. Several European airlines and one American line regularly operate out of Lod. El Al, Israel's airline, maintains services to London, Paris, Rome, New York, and other world capitals. Kol Yisrael, Israel's radio network, is state-owned and consists of 4 transmitters. There were 177,428 licensed radio sets in 1951.

History.*—Following the proclamation of the state on May 14, 1948, by the Jewish National Council (Vaad Leumi), David Ben-Gurion was chosen prime minister, heading a provisional National Council. Dr. Chaim Weizmann, venerable leader of the world Zionist movement, was named president. The new nation held its first general election on Jan. 25, 1949. The Mapai, a moderate socialist party led by Ben-Gurion, obtained 35.7 per cent of the 440,095 Jewish and Arab votes cast, and 46 of the 120 seats in the Knesset (Assembly). The Mapam, a leftist labor group, emerged as the chief opposition, with 19 seats; the United Religious bloc obtained 16 seats; the rightist Herut, 14; and the General Zionists, 7. The newly elected Knesset was sworn in on February 14 in Jerusalem, and on February 17, by a vote of 83 to 15, elected Dr. Weizmann as president of Israel over Dr. Joseph Klausner, backed by the Herut. President Weizmann entrusted Ben-Gurion with the task of forming a government, and in early March the Mapai leader announced a coalition cabinet of the Mapai and the religious bloc. Envisioning a doubling of the population within four years, Prime Minister Ben-Gurion, on March 8, 1949, outlined an ambitious program to expand the nation's agriculture, industries, and communications, build up government services, and combat inflation by a system of rigid controls.

Despite the people's readiness to accept the hardships of building a new nation, and despite the generous aid of world Jewry, the floodtide of immigration produced an increasingly severe burden on the nation's economy. Although inflation had been held in check in 1949, by the late summer of 1950 the pressure of the expanding population, plus the rising cost of imports, produced an economic crisis involving a partial breakdown of the price control system, followed by a steady rise in price levels and a growing shortage of consumers goods. In October 1950, the government was forced to relax some controls on business and make other concessions to private enterprise, particularly in the export field.

Political repercussions of the economic difficulties were reflected in the cabinet crises of late 1950 and early 1951. Defeated in the Knesset on the question of the form of education for immigrant children, Prime Minister Ben-Gurion tendered his resignation on Feb. 14, 1951, but continued in office pending new elections. Israel's second national elections were held on July 30, 1951. The electorate, numbering close to 900,000, included 85,000 Arabs. As a result of the elections, the Mapai continued to be the largest party, although the 45 seats it obtained in the Knesset meant a loss of 1. The General Zionists, who opposed many features of the Mapai's policies of a planned economy, emerged as the chief opposition, increasing their seating to 20, a gain of 13. The leftist Mapam obtained 15 seats, a loss of 4; the religious bloc also obtained 15, a loss of 1; the Herut received 8, a loss of 6; and the Communists 5, a gain of 1. Failing to obtain the support of either the General Zionists or the Mapam, the Mapai renewed its coalition with the religious bloc by offering concessions in the issues of education and kosher food laws. The new cabinet, again headed by Ben-Gurion, took office in early

* For an account of the events leading up to the proclamation of the state, and of the warfare between Israel and the Arab states in 1948 and early 1949, see the sections *Jews in Modern Palestine*, and *Zionism*, in the series, JEWISH HISTORY AND SOCIETY, vol. 16.

October 1951. President Weizmann was re-elected by the Knesset on November 19.

To meet the continuing economic difficulties, Ben-Gurion, on Feb. 13, 1952, announced a new program of economic and fiscal reforms designed to encourage private enterprise, expand production, and combat inflation. A new system of exchange rates for the Israeli pound was introduced, offering advantages to the foreign investor and scaling import prices in a way to discourage nonessential imports. Government economies and an improved tax collection system were projected. The official pricing system was amended to restore competition in industry by eliminating the cost-plus system of prices which had kept inefficient firms in operation.

Foreign Relations.—International recognition of the State of Israel commenced with the *de facto* recognition granted by the United States and the full recognition by Soviet Russia almost immediately upon the proclamation of the new state. On Jan. 31, 1949, five days after Israel's first elections, the United States extended *de jure* recognition. Full recognition by Great Britain did not come until April 27, 1950, by which time most of the nations of the world, with the exception of the Arab states, had accorded recognition. Despite the opposition of the Arab nations, Israel was admitted as the 59th member of the United Nations by the General Assembly on May 11, 1949.

The armistice agreements concluded in 1949, with the aid of United Nations Mediator Ralph J. Bunche, between Israel and Egypt (February 24), Lebanon (March 23), Transjordan (April 3), and Syria (July 20), marked the end of open warfare between Israel and her Arab neighbors. A permanent peace settlement, however, did not emerge, despite the efforts of the U.N. Palestine Conciliation Commission, which, for a number of years, unsuccessfully sought to reconcile the opposing views of the two parties on the fate of the Arab refugees, the territorial boundaries of the Jewish state, and other matters involving the relations of Israel and the Arab states. Meanwhile, numerous small border clashes, road disputes, and other incidents took place, many of which were referred to the United Nations truce supervision staff in Palestine under Lieut. Gen. William E. Riley. About 200 Israeli troops and police, and 600 Arabs had been killed or wounded in skirmishes involving Arab infiltration across Israel's borders in 1951, according to an Israeli report. A brief flareup of fighting took place between Israeli and Syrian forces in April and May of 1951 over Syrian opposition to an Israeli reclamation project in the demilitarized zone of the Lake Huleh district. Both sides, however, accepted the U.N. Security Council's prompt request for a cease-fire. Further obstacles toward good relations were the economic boycott of Israel by the Arab states and the Egyptian harassment of Israeli-bound shipping in the Suez Canal.

Jerusalem, which the U.N. General Assembly on Dec. 9, 1949, declared to be an international area under the administration of the U.N. Trusteeship Council, remained divided between the Israeli-held New City and the Old City, held by the Hashemite Kingdom of the Jordan (formerly Transjordan). Both nations rejected the United Nations resolution on internationalization, and on June 14, 1950, the Trusteeship Council acknowledged the failure of the plan by referring the problem back to the General Assembly.

In the East-West cold war, Israel's position of neutrality—enunciated by Ben-Gurion on March 8, 1949—was altered in 1951 in the direction of closer ties to the West. On May 9, 1952, United States Ambassador Monnet B. Davis and Israeli Foreign Minister Moshe Sharett signed agreements in Tel Aviv completing a $64.3 million United States grant-in-aid to Israel for 1952 under the U.S. Mutual Security Program.

ISRAELITES. See Jewish History and Society.

ISRAELS, ĭz′rȧ-ĕls, **Jozef,** Dutch genre painter: b. Groningen, Jan. 27, 1824; d. The Hague, Aug. 12, 1911. He studied at Amsterdam and Paris, and in 1870 settled at The Hague. For the most part his subjects were fisher folk and the humbler classes, whose existence, particularly in its more serious or tragic phases, he depicted in a style likened to that of Frédéric Millet (q.v.). Perhaps his greatest work was *Toilers of the Sea.* Pictures by him in the Metropolitan Museum of Art, New York City, include *Expectation.* Other works include *A Frugal Meal; The Cradle; The Silent House; Alone in the World; David Singing before Saul; When We Grow Old; The Sacristan; The Zandvoort Fisherman; The Bric-à-brac Dealer.*

ISSACHAR, ĭs′ȧ-kär, the ninth son of Jacob, and the fifth by his mother Leah; also the name of the tribe of Israel descended from him. The tribal territory was south of that of Zebulun, Naphtali, Asher and Dan, in the plain of Esdraelon.

ISSOUDUN, ē-sōō-dûɴ′, France, town and capital of an arrondissement in the department of Indre, on the Théols, 20 miles southwest of Bourges. It contains a college, museum, and library, and manufactures include machinery, textiles, and parchment. Pop. (1946) 12,645.

ISSUE, *in law,* the descendants of a common ancestor, or in pleading, a point affirmed by one party in a suit and denied by the other. In the latter sense an *actual* issue is one formed in an action regularly brought to try a question of right; a *collateral* issue is one formed in a matter only indirectly in the line of the pleading; a *feigned* issue is one formed in a fictitious action, under authority of a court, to try a question of fact before a jury; a *formal* issue is one formed according to the rules required by law; a *general* issue denies the whole declaration in direct terms; an *immaterial* issue is formed on some nonessential matter which will not determine the merits of the cause; an *informal* issue arises when a material allegation is improperly traversed; a *material* issue determines the merits of the cause when decided; a *special* issue is a single point selected by the defendant on which he rests his whole cause; a *common* issue is one formed on the plea of *non est factum* to an action of covenant broken.

ISSY-LES-MOULINEAUX, ē-sē′lā-mōō-lē-nō′, or **ISSY,** France, a suburb of Paris, left of the Seine 2 miles above the city. Notable buildings include a castle, museum, and Sulpician seminary. Chemicals are manufactured.

ISTANBUL, ĭs-tăm-bōōl'; Turk. ê-stäm-bōōl', Turkey (corrupted from Gr. *eis tēn polin,* "to the city"); usual European form, STAMBOUL; formerly CONSTANTINOPLE (q.v.); anciently BYZANTIUM (q.v.). Principal city of the Republic of Turkey and capital of the vilayet (province) of Istanbul, it was previously capital of the Ottoman empire. The Ottoman Turkish names were Qostantiniyeh (city of Constantine) and Dersaadet (Abode of Felicity); the present name, informally used for more than a century, was officially adopted in 1930. The population (census of 1945) of the city proper is 860,558, and of the vilayet (provisional 1950), 1,179,666. The city, partly in Asia and partly in Europe, is built around the exit of the Bosporus into the Marmara (Marmora) Sea; latitude 41° 0′ 16″ N., longitude 28° 59′ 14″ E. The European portion is deeply indented by the Golden Horn (Turk. Haliç *; Gr. Keration), an inlet extending inland from the southern terminus of the Bosporus for some six miles, curving clockwise to the northwest and forming a remarkably secure and commodious harbor. On the shore of the Bosporus, north of the Golden Horn's entrance, are also deepwater docks, where the largest vessels can be berthed.

Istanbul comprises three principal divisions: (1) old Istanbul; (2) Galata-Beyoğlu; and (3) the quarters on the Asiatic shore. Each of these divisions is subdivided into numerous quarters, each with its distinctive name and many with distinctive populations, some largely Turkish, others largely Greek or Armenian or Jewish. In these, Istanbul, in contrast to the homogeneous nature of the rest of modern Turkey's population, continues to represent the heterogeneous population formerly characteristic of the Ottoman Empire, of which it was the capital until 1923.

Old Istanbul.—On the European shore between the Golden Horn and the Marmara lies Istanbul proper, in the limited sense of the name, the Turkish city converted after 1453 from the Greek Constantinople into which Constantine the Great had transformed in 330 the Roman-controlled Greek city-state of Byzantium. This is the area which in ancient and medieval times was surrounded by the walls whose famous remains—after 26 sieges and 44 earthquakes—are one of modern Istanbul's principal sights. The sea walls, which extended along the European coast of the Marmara from the fortress of Yedi Kule (Seven Towers, Byzantine Golden Gate) northeastward to Sarayburnu (Palace Point, Seraglio Point) and thence northwestward along the southern shore of the Golden Horn to Eyüp, are largely destroyed; but the land walls (Eyüp to Yedi Kule), which formed the third side of the triangle, are in a remarkable state of preservation.

Galata-Beyoğlu.—The regions on the European shores northeast of the Golden Horn form the second main division of the city. They include Galata, the quarter immediately skirting the shore, and above and behind it Beyoğlu (Gr. Pera) as well as many other built-up quarters along and above the Golden Horn and the Bosporus. Continuously from Byzantine times Galata-Beyoğlu have been cosmopolitan, polygot centers and have set the nonnational Levantine tone which travelers often wrongly regard as characteristic of the entire city. In fact, old Istanbul, the city's major division, is largely Turkish and was largely Greek until 1453. Cosmopolitan Galata-Beyoğlu include the most modern and westernized parts of the city. They contain the principal stores and hotels, and they form the commercial center of the entire city as well as the winter residential center of the modern city.

Asiatic Shore.—The third major division of modern Istanbul is the metropolitan area on the Asiatic shore, across from the mouth of the Golden Horn, and principally comprising the regions of Üsküdar (Scutari), Haydarpaşa (Haydar Pasha), and Kadıköy (Chalcedon).

Other Areas.—In addition to the three major areas there are many villages and towns, some quite sizable, which stretch in a virtually unbroken series along both shores of the Bosporus northward almost to the Black Sea, and also the increasingly important residential and industrial areas along the Marmara's European shore westward from Yedi Kule and along its Asiatic shore eastward from Kadıköy. Finally, opposite this Asiatic shore and some five miles into the Marmara from the center of the city (the mouth of the Golden Horn) are the idyllic Princes Islands, traditionally named from their role as a seat of exile for royalty in Byzantine times (395–1453). Of these islands (*adalar*), four today are inhabited in significant numbers. These range in size from Büyük Ada (Great Isle, Gr. Prinkipo), through Heybeli Ada and Burgaz Ada down to Kinalı Ada (Gr. Prōti). In addition to their permanent populations, the islands, as important resorts, attract numerous summer residents and visitors.

Topography, Communications, Climate.—Almost the entire metropolitan area, including suburbs, is extremely hilly. The attempt to demonstrate that old Constantinople, the "New Rome," was built like its prototype upon seven hills is not convincing, but there are few regions in the city where a commanding eminence does not offer a view over steep hills and shining waterways. The somber colors of unpainted wood houses and of coral tile roofs are everywhere broken by clumps of trees, the cypress being especially prevalent.

Communication and transportation between the several regions of Istanbul are complicated by the rugged terrain, the many waterways, and the fact that all except the few new or recently burned-over and rebuilt sections of the city are characterized by very narrow and crooked cobblestone streets. Two bridges span the Golden Horn. At its mouth is the Galata Bridge, a floating structure which can be opened to permit the passage of ships. This bridge carries from Galata to Yeni Cami (the New Mosque quarter of old Istanbul) all tram traffic crossing the Golden Horn. Further up that inlet is the newer Atatürk Bridge. Old Istanbul and Galata-Beyoğlu have adequate tram systems, the latter including a line along the European shore of the Bosporus past the village of Arnavutköy, location of the Istanbul American College for Girls, to Bebek, the seat of Robert College (q.v.), the American men's college. A tram system also operates in the Üsküdar-Kadiköy area. In addition, major streets have evolved into fair motor roads, and bus service greatly eases problems of communication. There is, however, no bridge across the Bosporus. Consequently ferries remain as indispensable as they are characteristic of Istanbul life. One line travels the Golden

* In Turkish, ç is pronounced *ch.* Where subsequently used in text, *c* is pronounced as *j,* and ş as *sh.*

Horn from the Galata Bridge to Eyüp. Others from the same terminus serve both shores of the Bosporus, and the Princes Islands. There are also motor vehicle ferries at main points and a railroad car ferry from the Sirkeci Station (in old Istanbul), terminus of the railroad from Edirne and European points, to Haydarpaşa, the railhead on the Asiatic shore of the Baghdad line. West of the walls at some distance along the Marmara shore is the Yeşilköy Airfield served regularly by several major international lines and one of the Middle East's principal landing fields. Here are also located large installations of the Turkish State Airways, which link Istanbul with the rest of the country.

The climate is temperate and continental. Summers are warm but dry and not excessively hot, the surrounding seas not only tempering the heat but also making much of the city itself a summer resort and bathing beach. Winters are cold and damp, December to February constituting the rainy season. Snows are not unusual, although they seldom last long. The beauty of Istanbul and its gardens in spring, summer, and fall has been celebrated by the many writers whom this cosmopolitan center between Europe and Asia has attracted over a period of centuries. Likewise well known are its excellent fruits and vegetables and the fish from the Bosporus fishing grounds.

Museums and Monuments.—Objects relating to the long and important past of Istanbul and of the provinces governed therefrom have been gathered into the city's uniquely rich museums. The most important are those comprised in the museum-complex of Top Kapu Sarayı (the Grand Seraglio, palace of the Ottoman sultans until the 19th century) on the point of land separating the Golden Horn from the Marmara. These include: (1) the archaeological museums and collections, rich in objects from Anatolia and Palestine-Syria, the great showpiece being the *Sarcophagus of Alexander;* and (2) the Islamic and particularly the Ottoman collections, most notable being the Ottoman rulers' vast living quarters (entirely restored and largely furnished with objects of the times), the Ottoman sultans' treasury and collection of Chinese ceramics, and an unrivaled collection of Moslem implements of war. In addition to the vast Top Kapu Sarayı collections, mention should be made also of the Evkaf Museum near the Süleymaniye Camii (Mosque of Sultan Süleyman the Magnificent) in old Istanbul, another collection of notable creations of Ottoman and Moslem art. St. Sophia (Aya Sofya; see SAINT SOPHIA), the last great gift of Greek genius, the most magnificent architectural monument of the Greek Orthodox world, and for centuries one of the chief mosques of Turkish Istanbul, has been converted by the Turkish Republic into a museum. Aside from the structure itself, it is particularly noteworthy for its Byzantine mosaics which, covered with plaster by the conquering Turks (1453), were uncovered and restored after the foundation of the Turkish Republic (1923).

Apart from Aya Sofya and the great walls, the other remaining Byzantine monuments of Istanbul are of importance chiefly to the specialist. Many were converted by the Ottomans to their own uses. Of those left unchanged the most spectacular are the vast underground cisterns, which still form part of Istanbul's water system. Modern Greek churches in the city are of no special architectural interest, and there are no outstanding Armenian or Jewish edifices. Nor are the monuments of Galata-Beyoğlu of great architectural interest, except possibly the Tower of Galata, dating from 474–491, which has been used in modern times as a fire lookout.

Ottoman monuments, many of them historically important, are numerous. Chief among them are the imperial mosques, erected by the principal sultans as burial places for themselves and their families. Of a distinctive style, their domes and minarets, crowning many of Istanbul's hills, give the city its renowned skyline. The principal Ottoman imperial mosques include those of Mehmed (Mohammed) II, the Conqueror; Bayezid (Bajazet) II; Süleyman (Suleiman) the Magnificent; Selim I; Ahmed I; and the Yeni Cami (New Mosque), each the center of a quarter bearing its name. Attached to the mosque-complexes are small and circular *turbehs,* in whose floors are the graves of the sultans, their families, and their close associates, while other graves are found around the mosques. Other famous men are buried near fountains, schools, libraries, or other foundations which they established as "good works," not infrequently along the public thoroughfares. This is particularly true of Divan Yolu (the Divan Street), which stretches from Aya Sofya to the Mosque of Bayezid II and which with Ankara Caddesi, formerly Bab-ı Ali Caddesi (Sublime Porte Street), now the principal book market of the city, forms the main artery of old Istanbul.

Other important Ottoman monuments include the twin fortresses of Anadolu Hisar (Castle of Asia) and Rumeli Hisar (Castle of Europe), built on the shores of the Bosporus near that strait's narrowest part. These were erected before the fall of the city proper into Turkish hands. Of 19th century royal palaces the most important are: (1) that of Dolmabahçe on the Bosporus shore at Beşiktaş, a principal landmark of the waterfront and frequently used as the residence of the Turkish president when he is in Istanbul; (2) Yıldız Sarayı, a palace-complex atop the hills farther up the Bosporus and well known as the home of the recluse Sultan, Abdül-Hamid II; and (3) Beylerbeyi on the Asiatic shore.

Quarters of the City.—No section of Istanbul is more famous than that of its bazaars, the great Kapali Çarşi (covered market) which stands on the slopes of old Istanbul looking down on the Golden Horn. Down from it stretches the principal open market of the city (the Mahmud Paşa Çarşısı). The covered bazaar includes miles of roofed and cobblestoned passages lined with tiny shops. The entire building can be locked at night. Its center is the Bedesten (Bezestan), or principal strong room and depot, formerly a depository of the most valuable wares. With the westernization of the city under the republic, the bazaars have lost some of their color, but their importance as the people's market place continues unabated.

At the head of the Golden Horn and beyond the city's mainland walls lies the quarter of Eyüp, in old-fashioned Moslem eyes the most sacred section of the city, owing to the location there of the mosque and supposed tomb of a companion of the Prophet Mohammed. It is held that the site of the tomb was miraculously revealed to the Ottomans during the siege of the city (1453). Since that date the site has been venerated, and until the 20th century it was closed to most Christians. It was the scene of ceremonies at the accession of a new sultan, and around it were created what are historically the most important cemeteries of the Ottoman capital. The vast burial grounds of Üsküdar are, however, far more picturesque. Early in the 20th century the importance of Eyüp began to decline, but it remains in many respects the most Ottoman and one of the most interesting quarters of Istanbul.

Libraries and Education.—During the centuries of Ottoman history, and especially as a result of conquests in Arab lands and in Persia (Iran), Istanbul gradually became and still remains the world's most important depository of Moslem manuscripts. These manuscripts, many of them unique and in a scientific sense priceless, were largely housed in small private libraries erected by individuals. Imperial collections also contained valuable items. The twin tasks of cataloguing and of providing centralized housing for this mass of material, as well as that of cataloguing and systematizing the great mass of official documents left from Ottoman times, have made increasing progress since about 1850, but still remain far from completed.

Centers of interest in the modern city include Istanbul University (q.v.), a large complex of buildings on the site of the Ottoman Ministry of War, housing Turkey's largest center of higher learning. A stately fire tower near the main building is the university's landmark. This tower, with its companion in Galata, remind one that fire, together with not infrequent earthquakes, is still the chief fear of the largely wooden-built city. Until the installation of motorized fire-fighting equipment, conflagrations frequently devastated large sections of the city. With the establishment of the republic (1923), however, the picturesque volunteer fire brigades disappeared as well as the once famous packs of street scavenger dogs, which formerly attracted the attention of all newcomers.

In addition to the university and the Superior Engineering School (near the newer Galata-Beyoğlu section), Istanbul contains numerous other institutions of higher learning, as well as adequate secondary and elementary schools, and is the center of education for the entire nation. In this respect Ankara has only partly supplanted the former capital.

Hospitals and Parks.—A number of good new hospitals, including the Admiral Bristol Hospital (an American Protestant Mission enterprise named for the American high commissioner to Turkey during the post-World War I years) also distinguish the city. Istanbul's several parks, many of them enclosing historic sites or designed to provide vistas leading to such sites, add to its attractiveness. The city also contains the modern Inönü Stadium, center of the football (soccer) matches which are Turkey's leading sports.

Industries.—Istanbul is not a large industrial center, but its tobacco processing plants, glass and shoe factories, gas and electric works, oil company installations, and the many and varied small industries and craftsmen's shops which it contains constitute an important component in Turkey's national economy. The city is the republic's major port of entry—that of export being Izmir (Smyrna)—and the customs houses and harbor works, as well as the shipyards, are vital in the city's and the nation's commerce. Istanbul is also Turkey's financial center.

With the creation of the Turkish Republic, many Stambulies (regular term for citizens of the city) felt that their city was being neglected in favor of the new construction undertaken at Ankara and elsewhere in Anatolia, that Istanbul was being heavily taxed—not in its own interest but to pay for developments in other regions of Turkey—and that it was not receiving a fair share of the new industrial plant which the republic, under its state socialist (*étatist*) program of westernization, was installing in the country. Subsequently these apprehensions were proved partly unjustified and much modernization was undertaken in the city. Nevertheless it remains true that in some respects Istanbul is as much a city of the past as of the present, that it continues more to typify the late Ottoman Empire than the modern Turkish Republic, and that the population of the city, or at least the non-Turkish sections of it, is not in wholehearted sympathy with all of the reforms characteristic of the new Turkey. On the other hand, it must be remembered also that in the late 19th and early 20th centuries Istanbul was the cradle and the principal center of nascent Turkish nationalism (see also TURKEY—*History*) and that it then was and subsequently has remained the center of the Turkish press (daily, periodical, and book), the professions, and the arts. Thus, on the basis of many considerations more important than its size (almost one in every 20 of Turkey's citizens lives in Istanbul), its influence over the rest of Turkey has persisted despite the shift of the capital to Ankara; and Istanbul is still unquestionably modern Turkey's most important city.

History.—Istanbul's uniquely strategic location gives it command of the Bosporus, a major link in the only sea route from the Black Sea to the Mediterranean. The narrowest point of the Bosporus, lying within the city limits, is little more than half a mile wide. At the same time, since Istanbul also stands at the easiest crossing between the land routes which descend through the Balkans from central and western Europe on the one hand, and those routes which come from Asia proper through Anatolia (Asia Minor, "Turkey in Asia") on the other hand, the city—together with the general straits area or Marmara region—is as strategically located with respect to land-borne travel and commerce as to that which goes by sea. In consequence Istanbul, which has been traditionally the center of government, commerce, finance, and intellectual activity for the entire Black Sea-Aegean-Balkan-Anatolian area, more than once and for long periods has vindicated her claims to be the naturally endowed seat of the capital of world empire.

The city's history falls into four periods:

(1) Ancient, classical, pre-Christian times—the period of old Byzantium (q.v.).

(2) Byzantine-Christian times, from the refoundation of the city by Constantine the Great (330) as Constantinople (q.v.) or "New Rome," capital henceforth of the Eastern Roman Empire which eventually became the Orthodox (Greek Christian) state and city and which survived despite all vicissitudes until its capture by the Ottomans in 1453.

(3) Ottoman-Turkish period (1453–1923), during which the city ceased to serve as Christendom's principal bulwark against Islam, but instead became the seat of the last great Moslem world state and the center of Islam's latest and greatest threat to European Christendom.

(4) The most recent period—that of the Turkish Republic (after 1923)—when the Turkish nation, no longer comprising any important non-Moslem or non-Turkish minorities, deliberately discarded much of its previously cherished Moslem tradition, as well as the Levantine type of government and life which had marked the later Ottoman period, and embarked on a course of nationalism and westernization which entailed the erection of new Ankara in the heart of Anatolia as the modern national capital of new Turkey. Under the republic Istanbul was reduced to the rank of a provincial capital still overshadowed by its own past glories and characterized, as the rest of new Turkey is not, by sizable non-Moslem and non-Turkish minorities who keep alive some measure of the elsewhere largely abandoned Ottoman past.

Bibliography.—Hammer-Purgstall, J. von, *Constantinopolis und der Bosphoros* (Pest 1822); Van Millingen, A., *Byzantine Constantinople* (London 1899); id., *Constantinople* (London 1906); id., *Byzantine Churches in Constantinople* (London 1912); Hutton, W. H., *Constantinople: The Story of the Old Capital of the Empire* (London 1900); Dwight, H. G., *Constantinople Old and New* (New York 1915); Pears, Sir E., *Forty Years in Constantinople* (New York 1916); Mamboury, E., *Constantinople: Tourists' Guide* (Constantinople 1922); Miller, B., *Beyond the Sublime Porte* (New Haven 1931); Penzer, N. J., *The Harem* (Philadelphia 1937); Webster, D. E., *The Turkey of Atatürk* (Philadelphia 1939); Birge, J. K., *A Guide to Turkish Area Study* (Washington 1949); Thornburg, M., *Turkey: An Economic Appraisal* (New York 1949).

LEWIS V. THOMAS,
Assistant Professor of Turkish Language and History, Princeton University.

ISTANBUL UNIVERSITY, Istanbul, Turkey, largest of Turkey's three universities, the others being the University of Ankara and the Technical University of Istanbul. The outgrowth of centuries of the episodic and abortive development of preceding institutions in Istanbul (Constantinople), the university was denied continuous existence by the effects of changing political and cultural conditions owing to differing Byzantine (Christian), Ottoman (Moslem), and ultimately Turkish Republican (secular) influences and controls. A parent institution named the University of Constantinople possibly existed at the time of the refoundation of Byzantium as Constantinople (330), but it is fairly certain that in 425, Emperor Theodosius II enlarged and reorganized an existing institution to which he appointed 31 state-paid professors. By the 6th century this university was ranked with others at Rome and Berytus (Beirut) as outstanding for its faculty of law; and in the latter half of the 9th century, the Constantinople University was a world center of humanistic and philosophical study. Under Constantine VII (905–959) special chairs of philosophy, geometry, astronomy, and rhetoric were created, and supplementary teaching in arithmetic, music, grammar, law, and medicine was provided. Then after a decline in the institution's fortunes, Constantine IX (1000?–1055) re-established the university with schools of law and philosophy. But by 1204 all that remained of the again declining university was moved to Nicaea. Michael VIII (1259–1282) restored the school of philosophy, and in 1300 a Constantinople university was being staffed by state-paid teachers, who were also regular government officials.

Immediately following the Mohammedan conquest of Constantinople (1453), the Turkish University of Constantinople was founded by Mehmed II (Mohammed the Conqueror) in a city quarter adjoining the mosques of Saint Sophia and Zeyrek, some lectures being given in the mosques. In 1470–1475 a university installation was completed in the Fatih section of the city, comprising 16 colleges and one clinic. Instruction was offered in theology, law, literature, science, and medicine; and the university, to which in 1555 Sultan Süleyman added new installations near the Süleymaniye Mosque, ranked among the largest and most advanced of its times.

In the 19th century the university deteriorated to an existence in name only, its fate paralleling the decline of the Ottoman Empire and accelerated by the university's undue emphasis on strictly theological training and by its failure to maintain contact with Western science and education. Selim III (1789–1807) attempted reforms, but was blocked by a conservative religious sect, although he succeeded in establishing an engineering school from which grew the existing Technical University of Istanbul. His successor, Mahmut II (1808–1838), founded a faculty of medicine in 1827. In 1844 plans for a modernized university were put into operation and new buildings were finally completed in 1863, but these were destroyed by fire. In 1870 a newly organized institution bearing the name Ottoman University of Istanbul was established on the model of contemporary European universities and included sections of law, philosophy, literature, natural science, and mathematics, the earlier surviving medical school remaining independent. In 1874 further reorganization produced an institution named Sultan's University, but this ceased in 1880, although both the medical and the law schools survived independently. In 1896 (considered the founding date of the modern university) under Abdül-Hamid II the institution was again reorganized, and between 1900 and 1903 it was once more placed in successful operation. The new establishment comprised sections in theology, mathematics, and literature, with the schools of law and medicine operating independently until 1908, when they were incorporated with the other faculties. Thus the institution, located principally in the former building of the Ottoman Ministry of War, became in a true sense a university. In 1924 the Turkish Republic placed the University of Constantinople under the jurisdiction of the Ministry of Education and transformed it to an institution of strictly nonreligious character. Between 1924 and 1933 the university was subjected to a final reorganization, given its present name, provided with an international faculty, and modernized with well-equipped institutes, laboratories, and improved library facilities. Eighteen new buildings were added to the educational plant.

In 1949 Istanbul University comprised faculties of arts or letters (founded 1863), economics (1936), law (1848), medicine (1827), science (1862), and forestry (1948), and enrolled 10,784 men and women students. Its faculty, in addition to administrators, numbered 150 professors, including almost 20 per cent foreign nationals, 385 lecturers, and 101 docents. The library contained 196,000 volumes, including 20,000 manuscripts in Turkish, Arabic, and Persian.

Loosely affiliated with Istanbul University and officially founded in 1883 is the Technical University of Istanbul, which offers study in architecture and civil, mechanical, and electrical engineering. In 1949 this institution's staff, in addition to administrators, numbered 47 professors, 20 supervisors, 110 assistants, and 7 lecturers, serving 1,600 students. The institution's library contained nearly 50,000 volumes.

ISTHMIAN GAMES, Panhellenic festival held near Corinth on the Isthmus of Corinth, in ancient Greece. Traceable back to at least the 6th century B.C., the Isthmian Games have been variously ascribed to Poseidon, in whose honor they were held, to Theseus, and to the mythological King Sisyphus of Corinth. Held in a stadium of white stone situated near a temple consecrated to Poseidon, the games usually occurred in the spring of the first and the summer of the third years of each Olympiad (four-year interval between the Olympic festivals; see GREEK FESTIVALS). They were celebrated with splendor comparable to that of the Olympian and other public Greek festivals. Featured contests included foot races, strength and endurance tests, four-horse chariot races, horse racing, wrestling, boxing, and quoit and javelin throwing. Victors at the game were adorned with crowns of fir, pine, ivy, parsley, or celery.

ISTHMUS, a narrow passage or neck of land connecting two larger land areas. First applied by the ancient Greeks to the Isthmus of Corinth, the term is universally used in designating such areas as the Isthmus of Suez, joining Asia and Africa, that of Panama, connecting Central and South America; the Isthmus of Perekop, joining the Russian land mass with the Crimea; and the Isthmus of Corinth connecting the Peloponnesus with the Greek mainland. Isthmuses of strategic and commercial importance are cut by canals such as the Panama and the Suez and the canal across the Isthmus of Corinth.

ISTLE, ĭs′tlē, **IXTLE,** ĭks′tlē, or **TAMPICO,** tăm-pē′kō, structural fiber produced from several species of small Mexican agaves, chiefly *Agave lecheguilla,* in combination with a few other plants. The agaves grow wild over a wide area extending from western Texas to New Mexico and southward. Fiber industry centers are located in the Mexican states of Coahuila, Nuevo León, San Luis Potosí, and Tamaulipas. In 1947 the United States imported from Mexico 15,270 long tons of unmanufactured istle (valued at $2,771,000) and 8,552,000 pounds of dressed istle ($2,011,000). Istle is used for rough cordage, saddle girths, and sacks. It is derived from the *cogollo,* or central spike of unopened leaves, the leaves of which are separated by hand and scraped on both sides with a dull-edged knife so as to release the fiber lying immediately under the epidermis. The removed yellowish white filament is harsh, stiff, but smooth.

ISTRIA, ĭs′trĭ-ȧ; Ital. ês′trê-ä, a peninsula largely under Yugoslav control, extending into the Adriatic Sea between the Gulf of Trieste and the Gulf of Veliki Kvarner (Ital. Quarnero). Principally inhabited by Slavs and Italians, it belonged to Italy after World War I and was ceded to Yugoslavia, except for the Free City of Trieste, after World War II. Possessing an area of about 1,545 square miles, its chief cities are Capodistria (11,995), Pazin (19,094), Poreč (12,036), Pulj (46,259), Rijeka (Rieka, 53,896), and Rovinj (10,082). First inhabited in the second century B.C., the peninsula was conquered by the Romans in 177 B.C. Although remaining under nominal Byzantine rule after the fall of the western Roman Empire, Istria was overrun by Lombards and Goths and in 788–789 annexed by the Franks as the Carolingian march of Istria. Subsequent overlords included the dukes of Carinthia and the patriarchs of Aquileia. In the 10th century Istria was united to the duchy of Bavaria; and by the 15th century Austria and Venice had respectively absorbed the northeastern and southwestern portions. The Treaty of Campo Formio (1797) and decisions of the Congress of Vienna (1815) added the Venetian portion to Austria. In 1915, according to the Treaty of London, Italy was promised Istria and other Austrian territory as a reward for her entrance into World War I on the side of the Allies. By the Treaty of Rapallo (1920) this promise was fulfilled, the bulk of Istria, not including Fiume (now Rijeka), being transferred to the Italian department of Venezia Giulia e Zara. In the summer of 1945, following the collapse of Germany in World War II, the peninsula was occupied by Yugoslav forces. It was later divided into a western zone (occupied by Anglo-American troops) and an eastern zone (occupied by the Yugoslavs). The Treaty of Paris (1947) gave most of the peninsula to Yugoslavia, while the northwestern sector became the Free City of Trieste (see TRIESTE).

Istria is chiefly an agricultural area in which approximately two thirds of the population are engaged in farming. Important products include cereals, fruits, lumber, and cattle, with olives, olive oil, and wines figuring prominently in the export trade. Extractive products include alum, bauxite, coal, marble, mercury, and salt. There is also considerable fishing along the Istrian coast, where summer resorts abound. Pulj is an important industrial and shipbuilding center as well as a naval base, and Rijeka is a valuable port.

ISVOLSKY, ĭs′vôl-skē, **Alexander Petrovitch,** Russian statesman: b. Moscow, March 18, 1856; d. Paris, France, Aug. 18, 1919. At the age of 22 he was sent on a mission to Pope Leo XIII, from which later resulted the re-establishment of Russian relations with the Vatican and his own appointment as Russian chargé d'affaires. After passing through a succession of minor offices he was appointed minister to Serbia (1897), Japan (1900), and Denmark (1902). In Tokyo he exerted himself to heal the grievance still rankling in Japan against Russia over the treaty of Shimonoseki. During Count Sergei Witte's tour of inspection over the Manchurian Railway in 1901, Isvolsky endeavored to induce him to make the short journey from Dalny (Dairen) and visit Japan. This Witte refused to do, notwithstanding that the Japanese government had decided to receive the Russian finance minister with the honors accorded to royal personages. Within less than three years Russia and Japan were at war. In May 1906 Isvolsky succeeded Count Vladimir Lamsdorf as foreign minister. The Austrian annexation of Bosnia-Hercegovina in 1908 aroused his strongest protests against the proceedings of Count von Aehrenthal (q.v.); in the diplomatic crisis that followed, the intervention of Germany in 1909 forced Isvolsky to withdraw from his position and accept the annexation of the provinces by Austria as a *fait accompli.* His prestige was seriously undermined;

he retired from the Foreign Office in September 1910 and in the following month succeeded M. Nelidoff as Ambassador to France. He resigned in June 1917 and settled in Biarritz. A brilliant scholar and linguist, he is described as a man of impetuous character with a fondness for unraveling complicated situations. To his credit must be placed the Anglo-Russian Agreement of 1907 and the Russo-Japanese Agreement of 1910.

ITACOLUMITE, ī-ta-kōl'ū-mīt, also known as flexible sandstone, is a mineral curiosity. It is a light colored, laminated-granular schistose quartzite containing besides quartz grains, mica, talc and chlorite. Usually thin bedded, pieces an inch thick or more have considerable flexibility. It derives its name from the Brazilian mountain Itacolumi. It is found in Brazil where it is usually associated with diamonds.

ITAGAKI, Taisuke, tī-soo'kā ē-tä-gä'kē, COUNT, Japanese statesman: b. Tosa province, Shikoku, 1837; d. 1920. He received a military education, and in the War of the Restoration (1868) was prominent in the imperial army. From 1871 until his resignation in 1873 he was a privy councillor to the emperor. He then became the centre of a movement for constitutional government which in 1877 addressed to the government a memorial asking for a representative assembly and broaching popular rights. Itagaki aimed at a system based on that of Great Britain or the United States, as opposed to the system based on that of Germany, drafted by the Marquis Ito and promulgated in 1890. But he would have been satisfied at first, it is said, with an assembly which quite excluded the popular element. He organized the *Jiyuto,* or Liberals, the first Japanese political party, which rapidly increased in numbers. In 1878 he became Minister of Public Works, in 1880 Minister of the Interior, and in 1898 the Liberals united with the Progressists, led by Count Okuma, to form the so-called Constitutional party, which had a large majority in the lower House of Parliament. At the Mikado's request Itagaki and Okuma formed a cabinet, with Itagaki as Minister of the Interior. The cabinet resigned after six months, and the Constitutional party was separated into its original parts. In 1887 he was made a count. Itagaki was not only the founder of the first political party in Japan, but the most steadfast propagandist for political freedom and a liberal constitutional government in Japan. In 1882 an unsuccessful attempt was made to assassinate him, and although severely wounded, his remark «Itagaki may die but liberty will live» became an inspiriting rallying cry. A bronze statue representing the count in modern attire was unveiled to his memory at Gifu in 1918. (See JAPAN). Consult Fitzgerald, W. G., 'Some Japanese Statesmen of To-day' (in *Putnam's Magazine,* Vol. III, p. 405, New York 1908).

ITALA, Latin versions of the Bible current in Italy previous to the Vulgate of Saint Jerome. (See BIBLE). Consult Schanz, 'Geschichte der römischen Litteratur' (2d ed., Munich 1905).

ITALIAN EAST AFRICA, name given to Italy's possessions in East Africa, consisting of Eritrea, Italian Somaliland, and Abyssinia (Ethiopia), which she invaded in October 1935 and conquered in early May 1936. The annexation of Ethiopia was decreed at Rome, 9 May 1936, and on the same day the King of Italy was proclaimed also Emperor of Ethiopia. The colony of Italian East Africa was established by Royal Decree, 1 June 1936. Following a campaign of many months British forces cleared the Italians out of Italian Somaliland and Eritrea early in 1941; invaded Ethiopia, took Addis Ababa in April and by 20 May 1941 when the Governor-General, the Duke d'Aosta, surrendered, had swept the Italians out of the country. The former emperor, Haile Selassie, was restored to his throne and capital, 5 May. See ABYSSINIA; ERITREA; ITALIAN SOMALILAND.

ITALIAN SOMALILAND, formerly a separate colony, since 1 June 1936 a province of Italian East Africa, extending along the coast of the Indian Ocean from the Gulf of Aden to Dik's Head, Kenya Colony. Its original area of 194,000 square miles, with a population in 1931 of 1,021,572, has been greatly increased by the addition to it of the former Ethiopian province of Ogaden. Mogadiscio (pop. 20,288) is the capital. It was taken by the British in 1941.

ITALIC LANGUAGES, a group of languages supposed to have been at an early date in their history, confined to Italy, and the group of languages developed out of these. It is usual to divide the Italic languages into two sub-groups, generally designated as the Latin-Faliscan and the Oscan-Umbrian, both of which belong to the Indo-European or Aryan (Indo-Germanic) family of languages. To a very considerable extent most of these tongues have acted and reacted upon one another in recent times, within the boundaries of their original habitat in the regions to which they were subsequently extended. The two great groups already mentioned seem also to have been influenced or modified by more aboriginal languages that preceded them in the Italian territory. There is very much uncertainty still existing with respect to this very early period of the Italic languages, which belongs to the years following the time when their possessors first made their way into the Italic peninsula. But though much relating to this early period is left in obscurity, yet enough has been drawn out of the shadow of the past to show the relationship of the various Italic dialects to one another.

Not only were the two great groups of Italic tongues apparently modified by the languages existing in the country when they first entered it, but they were again subject to modifications caused by influences exercised from without. So great was the introduction of Greek words at a certain period in the growth of the Italic languages that earlier philologists were led thereby to look upon Greek and Latin as very closely allied tongues, a conclusion not sustained by more recent investigations.

Throughout what is modern Italy there were, at the beginning of the earliest historical records of the country, various dialects. Two of these, approaching one another, formed the great Italic sub-division, Oscan-Umbrian. The Oscan tongue included the Samnite tribes, the Campania country and southern portion of the Italic peninsula, with the exception of the extreme south. The Umbrian tongue covered the greater part of the north and centre of Italy. The latter, though including a comparatively large extent of the isthmus, was much more homogeneous and much less dialectically inclined than the other local tongues of Italy. The Oscan-Umbrian group of Italic languages consisted of eight distinct dialects: the Oscan, Paelignian, Marrucinian, Marsian, Æquian, Sabine, Volscian and Umbrian in the 4th century B.C. All these dialects, though differing considerably from one another, differed still more notably from the tongue of Classical Latin, which gradually came to dominate, in the course of time, all the other tongues of central Italy, and extended its influence well toward the north and the south. The evidence, however, does not go to show that Classical Latin ever became the speech of the masses of the inhabitants of Italy to the south or the north though the literary tongue was everywhere the speech of the educated, especially when treating with the Roman officials or having intercourse with Roman society.

Latin-Faliscan.— This group of Italic languages is usually credited with being the mother of the Romance tongues. To a very great extent this is true yet there seems to be no doubt that all the dialects of Italy, every one of which furnished soldiers for the Roman army, contributed some part to the upbuilding of the Romance languages which became heirs to the Latin official tongue throughout the Roman Empire. Yet the influence of the Oscan-Umbrian dialects was probably greater on the popular speech of Italy in Roman days than upon the subsequent speech of any of the Roman provinces. In Italy, however, the result was quite different; for here the dialects remained the speech of the masses of the people long after Rome had become a great city and the centre of an extending empire; and so strong was their virility that they imposed many of their own tribal words on literary Latin, while hundreds of others passed current in the daily speech of the imperial city, where this vernacular became early known as Italian to distinguish it from Classical Latin. But to this popular tongue the dialects of Latin-Faliscan contributed very much more copiously than did those of the Oscan-Umbrian group. This was quite natural because the four sub-divisions of the Latin-Faliscan group (Latin, Lanuvian, Prænestine and Faliscan) were much more closely related to one another than to the Oscan-Umbrian dialects. Latin gradually absorbed the other three members of its own group, which may be said therefore to have dropped completely out of the linguistic theatre (except in so far as their influence on the popular Latin tongue is concerned) before the Romance languages began to differentiate themselves from Classical Latin, which had become the single representative of its group, and of Roman dominion, culture, organization and government. For this reason it has been called the mother of the Romance tongues, for out of it all of them have sprung. The Oscan-Umbrian group of Italic dialects, on the other hand, did not altogether disappear in many districts; and even to-day their influence is seen in numerous localities in the rural speech, more especially in the mountainous regions of the north. This influence extends very little beyond the borders of modern Italy, however, and that only in the one direction already indicated, the mountainous country to the north, and perhaps parts of eastern France and Spain.

Latin Tongues.— When the Roman Empire broke up it left its various domains in possession of the Latin tongue, modified greatly it is true, in the popular speech in different districts by all-compelling local conditions, yet still essentially Latin in its vocabulary, idiomatic expressions and grammatical structure. Out of this inheritance of the Latin language sprang a whole family of new tongues which are now known as the Romance languages. These differ very considerably from one another; yet their general Latin characteristics are so strong that the mastery of one Romance tongue is the key to the facile acquirement of all the others. The term Romance is expressive of the close relationship of these languages to one another. The Latin language was primarily the language of Rome. But, as we have seen, the language of the Roman Empire, in so far as the vast body of the people constituting its populace was concerned, had been enriched and materially strengthened by an extensive vocabulary borrowed from all the dialects of the Latin-Faliscan group of Italic languages. During the Middle Ages the name Romania was applied to the Roman Empire, and its speech was called the Roman tongue, a term used sometimes to designate Classical Latin, and, at others, to signify the more popular and somewhat corrupted speech of the Roman populace, more especially in Gaul. A knowledge, therefore, of the relation of the various members of the modern Latin or Romance group of languages to one another, demands complete familiarity with the origin, growth and external and internal influences brought to bear on each member of the group from the earliest days of the contact of Latin and aboriginal cultures in the region bounding each of the other members of this sub-group of closely related tongues. This Romanic tongue welded into a more or less homogeneous mass in the city of Rome itself, had become the speech of the masses of the Imperial city and gradually that of the Roman army and of the colonies. Thus there was, from the very beginning of the Roman colonial policy, some difference between Classical Latin and popular Latin. Already there had begun the disregard of unaccented syllables and the contraction of the longer and more sonorous words of the classical tongues. This process of contraction continued and extended to the inflection of Latin itself. The disappearance of most of the latter called for a pronounced analytical construction which found its most rigid form in French.

All these changes were encouraged, hastened and intensified by the influences brought to bear on the Roman or popular tongue after it began to extend from Italy into the surrounding country, with the success of Roman arms and the extension of the dominion of Rome. Even within the confines of Italy itself it was subject to similar influences, the effects of which are seen to-day in the dialectic and phonic difference existing between the spoken tongue of southern, central and northern Italy. These home changes were due to native dialects and Greek and Carthagenian influences at an early stage in the history of the peninsula and to

Germanic and other influences at a later period. But in the colonies still other influences were at work. Before noting these it is necessary to take a glance at the linguistic conditions produced by the dissolution of the Roman Empire. This event broke up the Latin or Roman tongue into nine or ten distinct languages generally designated as Rumanian, Rhæto-Romanic, Italian, Spanish, Portuguese, Catalán (Provençal), French, Dalmatian and Sardinian. Of these, Dalmatian disappeared at an early period in the history of these languages, owing to the fact that it had practically no native literature and that it was overrun by the Slavs, and the Roman tongue and culture were practically wiped out.

Southern Italy, under Greek influence, developed a distinct form of the Latin speech which was still further modified by other influences. The Rumanian tongue also strongly subjected to Greek influence, has developed along similar lines to that of southern Italy. France or Gaul, whose populace was principally Celtic, witnessed a terrific onslaught on the unaccented syllables of the Latin languages and a general shortening of the words of the vocabulary, coupled with a radical reconstruction of the construction of the Latin sentence, and the introduction into the common speech of many Celtic words. This was followed by a strong Germanic influence in the formation of the vocabulary of French in many of the offices of life.

Oscan-Umbrian.—The Umbrian tongue was spoken throughout central Italy; here too was the ancient habitat of the Picentes, Vestinians, Marrucinians, Paelignians Marsians, Sabines, Volscians and others, all with their own peculiar dialects, of which greater or less remains are extant in the form of inscriptions.

Umbrian.— Of the great Umbrian tongue there has come down to us more extensive remains than those of any other Italic tongue outside of Latin. The greater part of this body of linguistic remains is contained in the Iguvinian tablets, found at Gubbio, the ancient Iguvium, in the year 1444. The tablets average about 19 × 12 inches in size; they were originally nine in number, but in the 16th century two were lost while in transit to Venice and have since been lost to view. Seven of the tablets are inscribed on both sides, and the complete vocabulary has a range of almost 5,000 words. Two alphabets were employed: the Latin and the epichoric, a derivative of the Greek, through the medium of the Etruscan. The tablets very probably date back to the second century B.C. The contents consist of the acts of a certain guild or corporation, self-styled the Atiedian Brothers, and like the 'Acta Arvalium,' of a similar Roman brotherhood, the Fratres Arvales, made up of precepts for sacrifice, purification, taking of auspices, etc. The Umbrian dialect, while sharing in the special characteristics of the Oscan-Umbrian group, shows many secondary developments, some of which are paralleled by those witnessed in Latin within historical times. Such are the reduction of diphthongs to monophthongs and the loss of final *d*. Characteristic of Umbrian are further assibilation of *k* before light vowels as in fasia = Oscan, *fakiiad,* Latin *faciat;* the change of intervocalic *d* to a sound represented in Latin by *rs,* in the epichoric by a special sign transcribed *d* or *r,* as in *piri, pirsi* = *pid-i* (Latin quid + *i*).

Oscan.— The remains of this language are found throughout Samnium, Campania, Lucania, North Apulia and neighboring regions. These regions were the dwelling-place of the Samnitic stocks, and here we are evidently dealing with the cultured language of the Samnites. In calling this language Oscan rather than Samnitic we are following the usage of the great Latin writers, as when Livy relates how in one of the Samnite wars the Roman consul sent out spies who were acquainted with the Oscan language. This usage is to be attributed mainly to the fact that the Oscans of Campania were the first people speaking the language in question with whom the Romans came in contact. But aside from this, the Oscans were far more advanced in civilization than the Samnites of the mountains, and if, as would appear from the highly cultured aspect of the language, an Oscan literature once existed, it must have taken its rise and found its standard of expression in Campania. In this case the designation Oscan would have more than an incidental foundation. As the Samnite people was Rome's only contestant for the hegemony of Italy, so their language was at one time the most widely spoken of all the Italic dialects, and speculations as to the result of a Samnitic victory upon Italy and the world are scarcely less interesting from a linguistic than from an historical standpoint. The Romans knew more of Oscan than, for example, of Umbrian, and the well-known remark attributed to Ennius, himself a native of Calabria, that he had three souls since he could speak Greek, Oscan and Latin, seems to imply that Oscan was regarded as something more than a mere dialect or *patois.* The 200 odd inscriptions, which, together with the glosses of Roman grammarians and lexicographers, represent all that is left us of the Oscan dialect, range in date from the second half of the 4th century B.C. to the second half of the 1st century of our era. Three alphabets are in use: epichoric, Latin and Greek. Of the inscriptions four are of considerable length. These are: (1) the Cippus Abellanus, inscribed on both sides with the terms of an agreement between the two cities of Nola and Abella. The stone was found in 1685 and is now preserved at Nola; (2) the dedicatory inscription of Agnone, a bronze tablet found at Agnone and now in the British Museum; (3) the Curse of Vibia, a leaden roll found at Capua in 1876. This is an execration, such as are often found in graves where they have been placed in order to make the curse, or devotion to the avenging gods of the lower regions, more effective; (4) the Tabula Bantina, a fragment of a bronze tablet, found near the site of Bantia in 1793. The inscription, of which about one-sixth is preserved, consists of a decree in regard to municipal government. Next in importance to these four are a series of roadmakers' tablets and dedications found at Pompeii, and the so-called «jovilæ» inscriptions found at Capua. Coins with Oscan legends are numerous, and among them are the earliest remains of the language. Notwithstanding its inferiority to Umbrian in amount of extant material, Oscan is of all the Italic dialects the most important to the philologist. In relative antiquity it is to the Italic branch what Gothic is to Germanic and Old Bulgarian to Slavic. In conservatism and transparency its vowel system is rivaled only by Greek in the whole Indo-European field.

In Oscan, diphthongs are preserved intact in all positions: *deivinais* (Latin, *divinis;* divine); *ligatuis* (Latin, *legatis;* legate). The weakening of vowels in unaccented syllables is, with certain possible limitations, unknown, as also in Umbrian: *anterstatai* (Latin, *interstitae;* interstices). Finer nuances of pronunciation are expressed by a highly developed and consistently employed orthographic system. The qualitative difference between long and short vowels (except the *a* vowels)—a difference which the Romance languages show to have existed in Latin—is more marked in Oscan than elsewhere. Short *e* is denoted by the character *e,* but long *e* has become so close in pronunciation as to be represented by the character *í*: compare sounds of ε and η in modern Greek. So, too, long *o* is regularly denoted by *u,* not *o,* or by *ú.* Compare *estuch* (Latin, *esto;* be thou); *liqud* (Latin, *lēge;* by law); *púd* (Latin, *quod;* wherein, because).

Minor Languages of the Osco-Umbrian Group.—As we have said, there were in central Italy, between the Umbrians and the Samnites, the small groups of the Picenians, Vestinians, Marrucinians, Paelignians, Marsians, Sabines, Volscians, Aequians, and Hernici. The best known of their dialects is the Paelignian, which is represented by over 20 inscriptions. It shows a striking similarity to Oscan, even in cases where the point in question is a departure from, rather than a retention of, the original. But variations from the Oscan are not wanting. The dialect of the Marrucinians is represented by one well-preserved inscription and a fragment. This, too, is more closely related to Oscan than to any other dialect, but in the accusative plural *iaf* (Latin, *eas*) agrees with the Umbrian (*eaf*) rather than with the Oscan: compare *viass* = *vias* (Latin, ways). Volscian is known through only one inscription, the bronze of Velletri. It shows a number of secondary changes, such as the conversion from diphthongs into monophthongs, loss of final *d,* and assibilation of *k* before light vowels, which give it a stronger similarity to Umbrian than to Oscan. The Marsian and Vestinian dialects have also dispensed with diphthongs. See also ITALY—*Language.*

Bibliography.—Bréal, Michel, *Les tables Engubines* (Paris 1875); Zvetaieff, *Sylloge inscriptionum Oscarum* (Leipzig 1878); id., *Inscriptiones Italiae mediae dialecticae* (Leipzig 1884); Ascoli, G. I., *Italia dialettale* (Turin 1885); Zvetaieff, *Inscriptiones Italiae inferioris dialecticae* (Moscow 1886); Buck, C. D., *Vocalismus der Oskischen Sprache* (Leipzig 1892); Conway, R. S., *The Italic Dialects,* with texts, commentary, and vocabulary, 2 vols. (Cambridge 1897); Planta, R. von, *Grammatik der oskisch-umbrischen Dialekte,* 2 vols. (Strasbourg 1892–97); Buck, C. D., *Grammar of Oscan and Umbrian,* standard work by an eminent authority (Boston 1904); Gröber, G., *Grundriss der romanischen Philologie* (Strasbourg 1904); Ovidio, Francesco d', and Meyer-Lübke, Wilhelm, *Grammatica storica della lingua e dei dialetti d'Italia* (Milan Ernout, *Les éléments dialectaux du vocabulaire latin* (Paris 1909); Bertoni, Giulio, *L'Italia dialettale* (Milan 1916); Devoto, Giacomo, *Gli antichi italici* (Florence 1931); Conway, R. S., *The Prae-Italic Dialects of Italy,* 3 vols. (Cambridge, Mass., 1934); Hall, R. A., Jr., *Bibliography of Italian Linguistics* (Baltimore 1941).

ITALIOTES, ĭ-tăl'ĭ-ōtz, the Greek colonists in the southern part of the Italian peninsula, which was known in ancient times as Magna Graecia (q.v.). See ITALY—*History.*

ITALY, a republic of western Europe. By a plebiscite held June 2, 1946, the Italian people rejected the monarchy of Savoy by a vote of 12,717,932 to 10,719,284, in favor of a republican form of government. Following the peace treaty signed between the Allied and Associated Powers and Italy on Feb. 10, 1947, the area of the country was reduced to approximately 116,224 square miles, with a population estimated on Sept. 30, 1948, at 46,403,000. The capital, Rome, has a population estimated at 1,573,994 (July 1, 1947). From an administrative point of view, Italy is divided into 91 provinces grouped, according to the constitution which went into effect on Jan. 1, 1948, into the 19 following regions:

Regions	Regional Capitals
Piedmont (Piemonte)	Turin (Torino)
Valle d'Aosta	Aosta
Lombardy (Lombardia)	Milan (Milano)
Trentino-Alto Adige	Trento
Veneto	Venice (Venezia)
Friuli-Venezia Giulia	Udine
Liguria	Genoa (Genova)
Emilia-Romagna	Bologna
Tuscany (Toscana)	Florence (Firenze)
Umbria	Perugia
Marche	Ancona
Latium (Lazio)	Rome (Roma)
Abruzzi and Molise	L'Aquila
Campania	Naples (Napoli)
Apulia (Puglia)	Bari
Basilicata (Lucania)	Potenza
Calabria	Reggio di Calabria
Sicily (Sicilia)	Palermo
Sardinia (Sardegna)	Cagliari

The basic monetary unit is the lira, consisting of 100 centesimi. The metric system is used for all weights and measures.

The national flag of Italy is the former tricolor of white, red, and green, with the coat of arms of the Republic of Italy substituted for the crown and the cross of Savoy. Similarly, the royal anthem was replaced by the *Inno di Mameli* (*Hymn of Mameli*), a famous anthem of the Risorgimento.

The historical, social, and political development of Italy, its commerce and industry, arts and science, are treated under the following headings:

1. The Land
2. The People
3. History
4. Language
5. Literature
6. The Arts
7. Music
8. Science
9. Economic Structure and Problems
10. Political and Administrative Structure

1. THE LAND. Geographical Position.—Italy is the middle peninsula of the three which form the southern extension of Europe toward Africa and Asia. Its most important geographical features are its central position in the Mediterranean Sea, which bounds the peninsular portion of the country by three of its basins—namely, the Tyrrhenian Sea on the west, the Ionian Sea on the south, and the Adriatic Sea on the east—and the fact that the portion attached to the European continent is bounded by the great mountain chain of the Alps.

Italy extends between 47° 7′ and 36° 38′ north latitude, and between 6° 37′ and 18° 32′ east longitude. It is, therefore, at the same latitude as the United States from northern Maine to southern Virginia. The central parallel is 42°; at this latitude, the longest day has a duration of about 15¼ hours. The central meridian may be considered 12°, which crosses the central parallel at about 40 miles northwest of Rome.

Boundaries.—From a physical standpoint, Italy is very distinctly delimited by the Ligurian,

Tyrrhenian, Ionian, and Adriatic seas, and by the Alps, along which the physical boundary is marked, in accordance with a principle which goes back to ancient times, by the main watershed separating the rivers which empty into the Mediterranean Sea from the tributaries of the Rhone, the Rhine, and the Danube.

Considered as a natural region, Italy includes the three great islands of Sicily, Sardinia, and Corsica (or Corse, which belongs to France), as well as the minor archipelagoes of the Tyrrhenian Sea. On the northwest, between the Alps and the Ligurian Sea, the ancient historical boundary is marked by the Var River, now entirely French. The boundary is not so distinctly marked on the northeast, in the so-called Julian region, where the eastern Alps become gradually lower and slope to a succession of calcareous tablelands, such as the Selva di Ternova (Ternova Forest) and the Carso (Karst)—both now part of Yugoslavia—connected with the tablelands of Dalmatia and the neighboring regions of the Balkan Peninsula.

The political boundaries of Italy after the peace treaty of 1947 may be outlined as follows. On the west the frontier has been so established as to assign to France the upper valleys of the Vésubie, Tinée, and Roya rivers, including the villages of Briga (Brigue) and Tenda (Tende). France also received minor additions in the Mont Tabor (Thabor)-Chaberton and Mont Cenis areas, as well as Little St. Bernard Pass. But in general, the Franco-Italian frontier is marked, with little or no deviation, by the watershed of the western Alps. As for the boundary between Italy and Switzerland along the central Alps, the upper basin of the Ticino River (Canton Ticino or Tessin) belongs to Switzerland, together with a small portion of the upper river basin of the Adige (the Münster or Monastero Valley). The boundary with Austria is marked throughout by the watershed. Along the eastern boundary, a portion of the upper basin of the Isonzo River was assigned to Yugoslavia by the peace treaty; the boundary line runs very near Gorizia and reaches the Adriatic between Monfalcone and Duino. Trieste, with a small surrounding territory (about 277 square miles), was established as a free territory. All the remaining portion of the Istrian Peninsula with its adjacent islands was ceded to Yugoslavia. The island of Corsica has been part of France since 1768. Within these political boundaries, the area of Italy is approximately 116,224 square miles. Before World War II it was 119,764 square miles.

Relations.—The Italian peninsula extends into the Mediterranean from northwest to southeast like a huge boot more than 720 miles long and 80 to 150 miles wide. The distance across the Strait of Otranto, between the southeastern end of the peninsula and the Balkan Peninsula, is only 44 miles; the distance between Sicily and Africa is 90 miles. The Sicilian town of Messina is about midway between Gibraltar and the Suez Canal.

Because of this central location, Italy has always played a prominent role in the Mediterranean. Its ancient relations with other Mediterranean lands may be traced back to prehistory, while its relations with the other parts of continental Europe are much more recent. Italy shares with other Mediterranean countries some characteristics of climate and vegetation which affect human activities. But ever since the technical improvement of communications overcame the obstacle of the Alps, Italy's function has also become that of an intermediary between continental Europe and the countries of North Africa and the Middle East.

Sea Coast.—The length of the Italian coastline is about 4,971 miles, of which 2,237 belong to the mainland and 2,734 to the larger and smaller islands. The coast of the Ligurian Sea, high and steep because of the proximity of the mountains to the sea, bends to form the wide Gulf of Genoa, with the large port which is the outlet of the most important industrial districts of Italy. The Gulf of La Spezia, at the eastern end of the Riviera, is less wide but suitable for a naval base.

The coast of the Tyrrhenian Sea forms a series of sickle-shaped gulfs separated by high promontories; it is less favored in the northern portion, where many tracts were still marshy and unhealthy in the first decades of the 20th century. In the southern portion, the wide and splendid Bay of Naples, surrounded by an exceptionally fertile plain, attracts the greatest part of the maritime activity of southern Italy. The coast of Calabria is generally straight and lacking in good harbors. On the Ionian Sea is the Gulf of Taranto whose port is very well suited for a naval base.

The Adriatic coast is rather poor in harbors. Brindisi and Bari have acquired some importance only in the 20th century because of relations with the Middle East. Ancona, sheltered by Monte Conero, is the center of maritime relations between Italy and the Balkan Peninsula. In the extreme north, where the coast is low with many lagoons (Comacchio, Venice) and marshy tracts near the delta of the Po, are found the ports of Venice and Trieste, the importance of which was increased by the opening of the Suez Canal. In Sicily, the most favored coastline is found in the north (Palermo) and in the east (Catania and Siracusa, or Syracuse). The Sardinian coast has few good harbors except in the south (Gulf of Cagliari).

Geomorphology.—The Italian region is generally divided into three portions—continental, peninsular, and insular. The boundary between the first two portions is marked approximately by a line drawn from La Spezia on the Tyrrhenian Sea to Rimini on the Adriatic. This boundary runs mostly on the high ridge lines of the Apennines (Appennino), and it has always had a remarkable strategical importance in the history of Italy; it coincides roughly with the Gothic Line of World War II. But from a geomorphological point of view, the Italian region should be more exactly divided into four portions: (1) the internal or southern slopes of the Alps; (2) the plains of the Po and Venice; (3) the peninsula with Sicily; (4) Sardinia.

The Alps.—The Alps belong to the family of young Mediterranean chains (Alpids) in which folding continued during all the Tertiary. They are a series of big and often very irregular corrugations separated from each other by longitudinal valleys which form deep furrows. The highest tracts of the ridges are ordinarily found in the middle portion, where crystaline rocks (granite, gneiss, schists) predominate. In the western portion (Italo-French Alps) this higher ridge slopes precipitously toward the plain of the Po; but in the central portion (east of Lago di Como) and in the whole eastern portion the higher ridge is bordered by chains of a lesser altitude made up of sedimentary rocks with limestone predominating. These are the Outer Alps (Prealpi).

Along the French border are the chains of the Maritime, Cottian, and Graian Alps. Then, proceeding east along the Swiss and Austrian borders are the Pennine, Lepontine, and Rhaetian Alps, and then the Dolomites. To the east are the Carnic and Julian Alps, the latter largely Yugoslav. The highest peak is Mont Blanc (Monte Bianco), in France, which reaches 15,781 feet. All of the peaks over 13,000 feet are in the central Alps with the exception of the French Mont Pelvoux and the Italian Gran Paradiso, in the Graians, which is 13,323 feet high. In the Pennines are Monte Rosa (15,217 feet); the Matterhorn (Mont Cervin; Monte Cervino), Swiss and Italian, which is 14,780 feet high; and Dent d'Herens (Swiss and Italian, 13,690 feet). Monte Viso, in the Cottian Alps, is 12,601 feet high. The highest peak in the Dolomites is Marmolada (10,964 feet). These higher mountains, as well as many others attaining more than 10,000 feet, are covered with large glaciers, the limits of permanent snow being between 8,200 and 9,200 feet.

The Alps are indented by deep transverse valleys, situated in a normal or oblique direction to the geographical axis of the chains. These valleys (such as the Adige) reach the heart of the mountainous region and lead to passes which facilitate the crossing of the system. The passes become gradually lower from west to east; that is why the eastern portion of the Alps is generally more easy to cross than the western part.

The Plain of the Po.—At the foot of the Alps extends the largest Italian plain, formed by the hydrographic basin of the Po and of the Venetian rivers (Adige, Piave, Tagliamento). This plain covers about 17 per cent of Italy's total area, and from an agricultural and industrial standpoint, it is the most important region of Italy. The more elevated portion is devoted to grain and mulberry trees. In some of the drier parts agriculture must be assisted by irrigation. In the lower portion, in contrast, there are still some wet and marshy parts which require drainage. This portion is devoted to the two main agricultural products of Italy, rice and fodder grass. Cultivation of the latter results in a flourishing butter and cheese industry. Along the Adriatic coast there was in antiquity a succession of lagoons, but many of them were reclaimed beginning in the 16th century.

The Apennines.—The Apennines form, orographically but not geologically, the continuation of the Maritime Alps along the Gulf of Genoa, and they stretch down the whole peninsula to the Strait of Messina. The name Apennines applies, however, only to the middle chains, which, in the northern portion (Tuscan and Umbrian Apennines), are situated in succession from west to east like the wings on a stage, gradually approaching the Adriatic Sea. In the central and highest portion, within the limits of Abruzzo, the Apennines form two or three main ridges enclosing highlands and elevated basins. In the southern portion (Campania and Calabria) they divide into clusters and groups separated by low areas. The geological formation and external aspects of the Apennines are varied in the different portions. On the whole, however, the scenery of the Apennines is not so impressive and picturesque as the Alpine scenery, because of the lesser altitude, the lack of glaciers, and the smaller amount of water—the last due mainly to the fact that the mountains were, often long ago, deprived of their vegetation. The highest group of the Apennines is the Gran Sasso (Monte Corno, 9,560 feet). Other groups which attain a considerabe altitude are the Sibillini (Monte Vettore, 8,127 feet), Monti della Laga (Monte Gorzano, 8,055 feet), the Terminillo (7,261 feet), the Maiella (9,170 feet), the Velino (8,160 feet), and the Mèta (7,372 feet).

The passes from the Tyrrhenian toward the Adriatic slope are numerous but, especially in the central portion, they are at a great altitude and are therefore obstructed by snow in winter.

Some isolated elevations on the Tyrrhenian side form the so-called Antiapennines, of volcanic formation. On the peninsular portion of Italy only one active volcano is found, namely, Vesuvius (Vesuvio, 3,858 feet), but several other volcanoes, still active in the Quaternary period, have retained their characteristic aspect. Such are the Amiata, in southern Tuscany (5,689 feet), the groups of the Vulsini, Cimini, Sabatini, and Albani, in Latium; the volcano of Roccamonfina (3,291 feet), in Campania; the Campi Flegrei where, as recently as 1538, a volcanic eruption resulted in a new mountain called Monte Nuovo; the Epomeo (San Nicola, 2,589 feet), in the island of Ischia, still active in the 14th century; and Monte Vulture (4,357 feet), Basilicata. On the Adriatic side, isolated elevations are Monte Gargano, the spur of the boot of Italy (3,465 feet), and the plateau of the Murge, very poor in water.

The peninsula has but few and small plains. Along the Tyrrhenian Sea, the Maremma and the Pontine marshes have been both reclaimed in the 20th century. Farther south is the very fertile plain of Campania. Along the Adriatic Sea the Tavoliere of Apulia and the plains of Salento are found. In the inland portion some small plains amid the mountains were occupied by lakes in quite recent geological times. One of these lakes, Fucino, was drained only in the 19th century by means of an artificial effluent.

The mountains of northern Sicily are considered a continuation of the Apennines beyond the Strait of Messina. The highest group, called Le Madonie, is only 6,780 feet high. But Sicily has a thoroughly isolated and active volcano, Mount Etna (10,758 feet). South of this mountain extends the largest plain of the island, the Piana di Catania.

Sardinia.—Sardinia, with the French island of Corsica, forms a distinct portion, because it is probably the remains of a more ancient land (Tyrrhenys) which occupied a part of the Tyrrhenian Sea prior to the formation of the Italian peninsula. Ancient geological formations are therefore prevalent in Sardinia, where they form the framework of isolated mountain groups, the highest of which is Monti del Gennargentu (6,017 feet). Other fragments of ancient Tyrrhenys are the island of Elba and the elevations of southern Tuscany. Sardinia, Elba, and southern Tuscany are also the only really important regions from the viewpoint of mineral products. Useful minerals are scarce in Italy, where fossil fuels in the proper sense are lacking. In Sicily much sulphur is found; the Apuan Alps yield the well-known Carrara marble; the western Alps, a little iron; and the Trentine Alps, some metallic minerals.

Climate.—The complexity of the physical structure of Italy is increased by the remarkable climatic differences in the various regions, so that it is impossible to speak accurately of a "climate of Italy." The latitude range of 10°29′ between the extreme north and south would be sufficient in itself to cause considerable differences in temperature. But, in addition, the peninsula stretches far into the Mediterranean Sea, where seasonal alternations are felt only by a superficial layer of 1,000 feet, while all the remaining water down to the bottom has an almost constant temperature of 55°F. In winter, the Mediterranean is therefore a reservoir of warmth; in summer it is relatively cool. The influence of the Mediterranean thus accounts for mild winters and moderately hot summers. The farther a region is from the sea, the less this influence is felt, and in continental Italy the influence of the Mediterranean is almost negligible. However, the mountainous bulwark of the Alps protects this area against cold north winds and, in general, against the atmospheric influences of the north. The Alpine shelter is remarkably reduced in the eastern portion (the Venetian region and Istria), and here the northern influences are often felt in the severely cold and violent winds called bora. A climatic influence is also exerted by the Apennines. Because of this mountain system, the influence of the western winds from the Atlantic is limited to the Tyrrhenian side of the peninsula, and in the northern portion the favorable influence of the Tyrrhenian Sea is limited to the narrow southern slopes of the Ligurian Riviera.

With regard to temperature, Italy is broadly included between the annual isotherms of 52° and 66°F.; the coldest period occurs in December and January, the hottest in July and August. In the plain of the Po the average annual temperature is about 55°F.; in Sicily it is about 64°—a difference of 9° in relation to a distance of about 500 miles. The difference would certainly be greater but for the Alpine bulwark and the tempering action of the Mediterranean Sea. In continental Italy, the differences of temperature between summer and winter are very remarkable; in the central portion of the plain of the Po, differences of 36°–43°F. between average July and January temperatures are observed; in the inland portion of the peninsula also, in the mountainous regions of the Apennines—for instance, at L'Aquila—such differences exceed 36°F.

Even more remarkable are the differences in rainfall. In the Alpine region the rain is more and more copious as the altitude rises; in the eastern Alps and Outer Alps, as well as in the mountains between Lago Maggiore and Lago di Como, the annual precipitation exceeds 80 inches. The same amount is found also in some of the higher portions of the Apennines exposed to the western winds. The driest portions are the low areas far from mountainous elevations. In the eastern plain of the Po, a small area receives less than 24 inches, and rainfall is no greater in the Tuscan Maremma and the plains of Latium. (The general average in the north, however, is about 50 inches.) The Tavoliere of Apulia, the southeastern portion of Sicily, and the southern plains of Sardinia receive less than 20 inches.

No less important than the annual rainfall is the manner in which it is distributed in the various seasons. In the whole area of Italy south of the Tiber (Tevere) and Tronto rivers, including the larger islands, rain falls mostly in winter, and the summers are very dry. This phenomenon is typical of the Mediterranean climate. In Apulia, Sicily, and Sardinia there are three months with practically no rain at all. Such a long drought is likely to damage crops and pasture, and the need of water for agricultural purposes is keenly felt. In the center of the Alps, on the other hand, rainfall shows a tendency to concentrate in summer. During the winter there is a copious fall of snow which covers the ground for a long period. The same conditions are shared by the plain of the Po. The freezing of rivers, however, is almost unknown; even in the Venetian lagoon, freezing rarely occurs.

In some regions the climate is often modified by local conditions. Such is the case of the waters of the large subalpine lakes which exert a mitigating influence not unlike that of the Mediterranean. This is why, on Lago Maggiore and on Lago di Como and Lago di Garda, there are resorts with a Mediterranean climate. Again, in the center of the Alps, some well-sheltered valleys and some dells (such as the Merano dell) have a mild and dry climate. The mild climate of the Ligurian Riviera is celebrated; this region is encircled by the Apennines and opened southward to the favorable influence of the Tyrrhenian Sea.

Rivers.—The characteristics of the Italian rivers are determined by morphological and climatic conditions. The largest of them originated in the area bounded by the Alps and the Apennines, which was covered by the sea until the Quaternary period. The Po is the only river which crosses the whole plain from west to east; its course is about 420 miles long, with a drainage basin of some 29,000 square miles. The river is subject to two periods of high water. The principal one takes place around June; the lesser one in October. The low-water periods occur in January and August. Some of its Alpine tributaries, such as the Ticino, Adda, Oglio, and Mincio, have an ample, clear, and regular flow because they are fed by the Alpine glaciers and by many springs, and because they cross the large subalpine lakes, which act as regulators and clear their waters. On the other hand, the Apennine tributaries of the Po, such as the Tanaro, Trebbia, Taro, Secchia, and Panaro, are impetuous in the mountainous portion of their courses, irregular, and full of sediment. This is carried by the Po into the Adriatic, where the delta of the river, though subject to various alterations, is steadily increasing. It did not exist in the time of ancient Rome and was built up in the last 20 centuries. The importance of the different mouths has varied from time to time; the greatest volume of water is carried at present by the Po della Pila. The Po is subject to violent and disastrous floods; therefore, the entire lower course of the river, downstream from Cremona, has been securely dammed. As a waterway, the river has had little importance. Great works are in progress, however, with a view to opening a waterway from the Adriatic to Milan and Lago Maggiore.

The large northern plain is also crossed by the Adige and by some others of the longest Italian rivers, such as the Piave, the Tagliamento, and the Isonzo. In length, the Adige is third among the Italian rivers (220 miles). Its upper course is mountainous and often narrow and en-

Left: The interior of St. Peter's Basilica, Vatican City, with Pope Pius XII and his attendants officiating at the canonization of St. Frances Cabrini, July 7, 1946.

Center: The waterfront of Venice, dominated by the Campanile, overlooking the Piazza San Marco in the center. On the left is the Mint and on the extreme right is the Doges' Palace.

Bottom: The Ponte Vecchio, crossing the Arno River in Florence. On the left is the tower (308 feet) of the Palazzo Vecchio.

Photographs (1) © Triangle Photo Service; (2, 3) courtesy of Trans World Airline

ITALY

Right: An outdoor grocery store in Marino offering fruits, nutbread, candy, and, strung over the doorway, sausages and cheese.

Bottom left: The winter resort town of Positano, with the beach in the foreground. On extreme left is a Norman fort and watchtower built around 1000 to defend the coast against the Saracens.

Bottom right: The heights of Perugia, an important town in Italy as far back as 309 B.C.; and during the Renaissance, the seat of the Umbrian school of painting.

Photographs (1, 2) © Paul Pietzsch from Black Star; (3) courtesy Ivan Dmitri for American Export Lines

ITALY

Abruzzi e Molise (region), 1,600,631 D 3
Acireale, 36,871 E 6
Acqui, 18,336 B 2
Acri, 16,213 F 5
Adda (river) B 2
Adige (river) C 2
Adrano, 24,515 E 6
Adria, 37,762 D 2
Adriatic Sea E 3
Agira, 15,350 E 6
Agrigento, 32,951 D 6
Agrigento (province), 418,265 D 6
Alcamo, 38,396 D 6
Alessandria, 79,327 B 2
Alessandria (province), 493,698 B 2
Alghero, 15,998 B 4
Alicudi (island) E 5
Ancona, 89,198 D 3
Ancona (province), 372,229 D 3
Andria, 56,152 F 4
Anzio, 7,025 D 4
Aosta, 23,641 A 2
Aprilia (new town) E 7
Aragona, 14,839 D 6
Arborea B 5
Arezzo, 60,284 C 3
Arezzo (province), 316,380 C 3
Argenta, 28,032 C 2
Ariano Irpino, 24,357 E 4
Arno (river) C 3
Ascoli Piceno, 38,111 D 3
Ascoli Piceno (province), 303,869 D 3
Assisi, 22,514 D 3
Asti, 48,898 B 2
Asti (province), 245,764 B 2
Atessa, 10,596 E 3
Atri, 12,735 D 3
Augusta, 19,690 E 6
Avellino, 29,091 E 4
Avellino (province), 451,466 E 4
Aversa, 36,960 E 4
Avezzano, 16,866 D 3
Avigliano, 13,006 E 4
Avola, 21,883 E 6
Bagheria, 25,820 D 5
Barcellona Pozzo di Gotto, 27,134 E 5
Bari, 196,747 F 4
Bari (province), 1,010,907 F 4
Barletta, 52,386 F 4
Basilicata (region) F 4
Bassano del Grappa, 21,750 C 2
Belluno, 25,547 D 1
Belluno (province), 216,333 D 1
Benevento, 37,865 E 4
Benevento (province), 349,707 E 4
Bergamo, 86,043 B 2
Bergamo (province), 605,810 B 2
Bernina Pass C 1
Biancavilla, 16,644 E 6
Biella, 28,289 B 2
Bisceglie, 33,552 F 4
Bitonto, 30,622 F 4
Blanc, Mt. A 2
Bologna, 269,687 C 2
Bologna (province), 714,705 C 2
Bolsena, Lago di C 3
Bolzano, 45,505 C 1
Bolzano (province), 277,720 C 1
Bondeno, 27,192 C 2
Bonifacio, Strait of B 4
Bordighera, 7,334 A 3
Brenner Pass C 1
Brescia, 123,332 C 2
Brescia (province), 744,571 C 2
Bressanone, 9,503 C 1
Brindisi, 41,699 G 4
Brindisi (province), 254,062 G 4
Brisighella, 15,652 C 2
Bronte, 17,918 E 6
Budrio, 16,870 C 2
Busto Arsizio, 42,995 B 2
Cagli, 12,658 D 3
Cagliari, 106,649 B 5
Cagliari, Golfo di B 5
Cagliari (province), 507,201 B 5
Calabria (region), 1,771,651 F 5
Caltagirone, 39,349 E 6
Caltanisetta, 50,467 D 6
Caltanisetta (province), 256,687 D 6
Camaiore, 22,291 C 3
Camerino, 12,012 D 3
Camerota, 5,352 E 4
Campania (region), 3,698,695 E 4
Campiglia Marittima, 11,591 C 3
Campli, 11,109 D 3
Campobasso, 29,573 E 4
Campobasso (province), 399,095 E 4
Canicatti, 29,680 D 6
Canosa di Puglia, 28,377 E 4
Cantù, 18,517 B 2
Capraia (island) B 2
Capri (island) E 4
Capua, 14,183 E 4
Caravaggio, 10,691 B 2
Carbonara, Capo B 5
Carbonia (new town) B 5
Carini, 14,762 D 5
Carloforte, 8,030 B 5
Carmagnola, 12,737 A 2
Carnic Alps (mt. range) D 1
Carpi, 34,189 C 2
Casale Monferrato, 37,098 B 2
Casalmaggiore, 15,345 C 2
Cascina, 27,941 C 3
Caserta, 49,462 E 4
Cassano al Ionio, 11,428 F 5
Cassino, 20,064 D 4
Castelforte, 10,750 F 6
Castellammare di Stabia, 46,469 E 4
Castellammare, Golfo di D 5
Castel San Pietro, 15,263 C 2
Castelvetrano, 26,129 D 6
Castiglione del Lago, 16,828 C 3
Castiglione Fiorentino, 14,830 C 3
Castroreale, 12,240 E 5
Castrovillari, 11,943 F 5
Catania, 244,972 E 6
Catania (province), 713,160 E 6
Catanzaro, 45,400 F 5
Catanzaro (province), 606,364 F 5
Caulonia, 12,004 F 5
Cava de Tirreni, 33,051 E 4
Cavarzere, 25,199 D 2
Cecina, 10,527 C 3
Cefalù, 10,730 E 5
Ceglie Messapico, 20,764 F 4
Celano, 11,653 D 3
Cerignola, 39,540 E 4
Cesena, 61,314 D 2
Cesenatico, 11,646 D 2
Chiari, 13,880 C 2
Chiavari, 17,520 B 2
Chienti (river) D 3
Chieri, 13,736 A 2
Chieti, 30,266 E 3
Chieti (province), 374,727 E 3
Chioggia, 42,569 D 2
Cimone, Monte C 2
Circeo, Capo D 4
Circeo, Monte F 7
Cisterna di Littoria, 12,471 F 6
Cittadella, 12,966 C 2
Città di Castello, 32,658 D 3
Città del Vaticano (Vatican City), 1,025 D 4
Cittanova, 14,043 F 5
Cividale del Friuli, 10,424 D 1
Civitavecchia, 31,858 C 3
Como, 53,210 B 2
Como, Lago di B 2
Como (province), 501,752 B 2
Conegliano, 15,434 D 2
Conversano, 15,903 F 4
Corato, 44,661 F 4
Cori, 9,289 F 6
Corigliano, 16,285 F 5
Corleone, 14,725 D 6
Corno, Monte D 3
Correggio, 19,046 C 2
Cortina d'Ampezzo, 5,381 D 1
Cortona, 31,518 C 3
Cosenza, 40,032 F 5
Cosenza (province), 587,025 F 5
Crati (river) F 5
Crema, 25,163 B 2
Cremona ed Uniti, 64,019 B 2
Cremona (province), 369,483 B 2
Crotone, 21,496 F 5
Cuneo, 35,321 A 2
Cuneo (province), 608,912 A 2
Domodossola, 10,645 B 1
Dora Baltea (river) A 2
Dora Riparia (river) A 2
Dorgali, 6,140 B 4
Eboli, 14,727 E 4
Edolo, 5,474 C 1
Egadi (island group) C 6
Emilia-Romagna (region), 3,339,058 C 2
Empoli, 26,212 C 3
Enna, 23,817 E 6
Enna (province), 218,294 E 6
Erice, 32,933 D 5
Este, 14,438 C 2
Etna (volcano) E 6
Fabriano, 26,382 D 3
Faenza, 47,199 C 2
Fano, 31,617 D 3
Fasano, 21,923 F 4
Favara, 21,878 D 6
Favignana (island) D 6
Feltre, 17,777 C 1
Fermo, 25,203 D 3
Ferrara, 119,265 C 2
Ferrara (province), 381,299 C 2
Fertilia dei Giuliani B 4
Firenze (Florence), 322,535 C 3
Firenze (province), 853,032 C 3
Fiumini Manna (river) B 5
Fivizzano, 17,818 B 2
Florence (Firenze), 322,535 C 3
Floridia, 14,473 E 6
Foggia, 62,340 E 4
Foggia (province), 523,612 E 4
Foligno, 39,483 D 3
Fondi, 15,456 D 4
Forlì, 65,683 D 2
Forlì (province), 444,528 D 2
Formia, 16,905 D 4
Fossano, 19,627 A 2
Fossombrone, 10,650 D 3
Francavilla Fontana, 22,140 F 4
Frascati, 11,763 D 4
Frejus (pass) A 2
Friuli-Venezia Giulia (region) D 1
Frosinone, 18,447 D 4
Frosinone (province), 445,607 D 4
Gaeta, 18,332 D 4
Gaeta, Golfo di D 4
Galatina, 20,794 G 4
Galatone, 11,595 G 4
Gallarate, 24,505 B 2
Gallipoli, 13,048 F 4
Garda, Lago di C 2
Gargano, (peninsula) F 4
Gela, 32,885 E 6
Genova (Genoa), 634,646 B 2
Genova, Golfo di (Gulf of Genoa) B 2
Genova (Genoa, province), 867,162 B 2
Gorizia, 46,640 D 2
Gorizia (province) E 2
Graian Alps (mt. range) A 2
Gran Paradiso, Monte A 2
Gravina di Puglia, 23,208 F 4
Gt. St. Bernard Pass A 2
Grosseto, 26,428 C 3
Grosseto (province), 185,801 C 3
Grottaglie, 16,010 F 4
Guardiagrele, 12,243 E 3
Guastalla, 13,723 C 2
Gubbio, 33,727 D 3
Iesi, 29,587 D 3
Iglesias, 21,720 B 5
Imola, 41,525 C 2
Imperia, 28,540 B 2
Imperia (province), 158,565 A 3
Intra, 13,649 B 2
Ionio (province), 321,888 F 4
Ischia (island) D 4
Iseo, Lago d' C 2
Isernia, 14,517 E 4
Itri, 6,645 F 6
Ivrea, 14,473 A 2
Lagonegro, 5,099 E 4
La Maddalena, 10,968 B 4
L'Aquila degli Abruzzi, 54,722 D 3
L'Aquila degli Abruzzi (province), 365,716 D 3
La Spezia, 106,119 B 2
La Spezia (province), 222,080 B 2
Latina, 19,654 D 4
Latina (province), 227,218 F 6
Lauria, 11,097 E 4
Lavello, 11,453 E 4
Lazio (region), 2,647,088 D 4
Lecce, 49,261 G 4
Lecce (province), 526,553 G 4
Lecco, 36,973 B 2
Legnago, 21,771 C 2
Liguria (region), 1,466,915 B 2
Ligurian Sea B 3
Linosa (island) D 7
Lipari, 14,156 E 5
Lipari (island) E 5
Lipari, Isole (island group) E 5
Livorno (Leghorn), 124,963 C 3
Livorno (province), 249,468 C 3
Lodi, 30,636 B 2
Lombardia (region), 5,836,342 B 2
Lonigo, 12,393 C 2
Lucca, 82,300 C 3
Lucca (province), 352,205 C 3
Lucera, 18,447 E 4
Lugo, 30,125 D 2
Macerata, 26,708 D 3
Macerata (province), 290,057 D 3
Macomer, 5,588 B 4
Maddalena, La, 10,968 B 4
Maggiore, Lago B 1
Mantova (Mantua), 40,467 C 2
Mantova (province), 407,977 C 2
Marche (region), 1,278,071 D 3
Marettimo (island) C 6
Maritime Alps (mt. range) A 2
Marmolada, Monte C 1
Marsala, 62,171 D 6
Marsciano, 17,129 D 3

ITALY

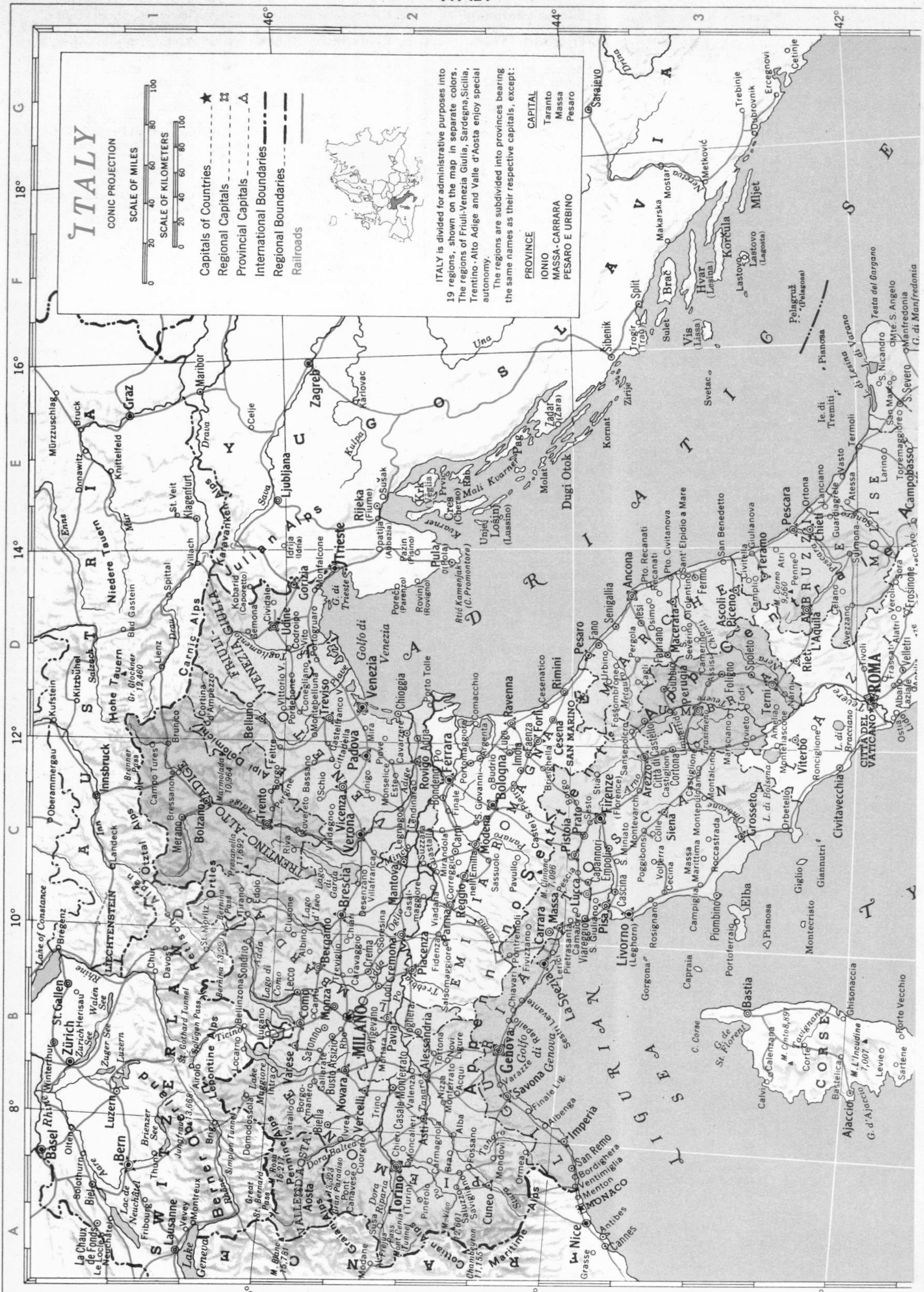
ITALY
CONIC PROJECTION
SCALE OF MILES
0 20 40 60 80 100
SCALE OF KILOMETERS
0 20 40 60 80 100
Capitals of Countries
Regional Capitals
Provincial Capitals
International Boundaries
Regional Boundaries
Railroads
ITALY is divided for administrative purposes into 19 regions, shown on the map in separate colors. The regions of Friuli-Venezia Giulia, Sardegna, Sicilia, Trentino-Alto Adige and Valle d'Aosta enjoy special autonomy.
The regions are subdivided into provinces bearing the same names as their respective capitals, except:
PROVINCE
CAPITAL
IONIO
Taranto
MASSA-CARRARA
Massa
PESARO E URBINO
Pesaro

ITALY

PROVINCIA DI LATINA
CITTÀ DEL VATICANO
TYRRHENIAN SEA
MEDITERRANEAN SEA
IONIAN SEA
Golfo di Taranto
Strait of Otranto
Malta Channel
Golfe de Hammamet
SARDEGNA
SICILIA
BASILICATA
CALABRIA
CAMPANIA
PUGLIA
TUNISIA
ISOLE LIPARI
ISOLE EGADI
ISOLE PONTINE
Napoli
Palermo
Messina
Catania
Siracusa
Reggio di Calabria
Bari
Brindisi
Lecce
Taranto
Cagliari
Sassari
Nuoro
Oristano
Salerno
Foggia
Potenza
Catanzaro
Cosenza
Trapani
Marsala
Agrigento
Caltanissetta
Enna
Ragusa
Malta (Br.)
Valletta
Tunis
Pantelleria
Lampedusa
Linosa
Ustica
Stromboli
Etna 10,741
Stretto di Messina
Golfo di Salerno
Golfo di Gaeta
Str. of Bonifacio
Longitude East of Greenwich
Copyright by C.S. HAMMOND & Co., N.Y.
45114

ITALY *Continued*

Martina Franca, 32,629 . . F 4
Massa, 106,378 . . . . C 2
Massa - Carrara (province), 196,716 . . . . C 2
Massafra, 13,388 . . . . F 4
Massa Marittima, 14,999 . C 3
Matera, 22,069 . . . . F 4
Matera (province), 166,776 . . . . F 4
Mazara del Vallo, 26,028 . D 6
Mazzarino, 17,715 . . . . E 6
Mediterranean Sea . . . . . . C 6
Melfi, 15,384 . . . . E 4
Merano, 25,902 . . . . C 1
Mesagne, 18,795 . . . . F 4
Messina, 192,051 . . . . E 5
Messina (province), 627,093 . . . . E 5
Messina, Stretto di . . . . . . E 6
Metauro (river) . . . . D 3
Milano, 1,115,848 . . . . B 2
Milano (province), 2,175,838 . . . . B 2
Milazzo, 19,800 . . . . E 5
Mincio (river) . . . . C 2
Minturno, 13,650 . . . . D 4
Mira, 21,130 . . . . D 2
Mirandola, 22,472 . . . . C 2
Mistretta, 11,546 . . . . E 6
Modena, 96,337 . . . . C 2
Modena (province), 467,555 . . . . C 2
Modica, 37,936 . . . . E 6
Mola di Bari, 19,831 . . . . F 4
Molfetta, 49,361 . . . . F 4
Moncalieri, 21,181 . . . . . . A 2
Mondovi, 19,621 . . . . A 2
Monfalcone, 19,634 . . . . . . D 2
Monopoli, 28,856 . . . . F 4
Monreale, 19,802 . . . . D 5
Monselice, 16,447 . . . . C 2
Montalcino, 10,216 . . . . C 3
Montalto Uffugo, 14,239 . E 5
Montebelluna, 18,412 . . . . D 2
Montecristo (island) . . . . C 3
Monte Sant' Angelo, 25,509 . . . . F 4
Montevarchi, 15,695 . . . . . C 3
Monza, 63,922 . . . . B 2
Mortara, 11,544 . . . . B 2
Napoli (Naples), 865,913 . E 4
Napoli (province), 2,192,245 . . . . E 4
Nocera, 29,347 . . . . E 4
Norma, 3,623 . . . . F 6
Noto, 29,992 . . . . E 6
Novara, 62,570 . . . . B 2
Novara (province), 395,730 . . . . B 2
Novi Ligure, 21,157 . . . . . B 2
Nuoro, 11,459 . . . . B 4
Nuoro (province), 224,643 . B 4
Ortona, 20,210 . . . . E 3
Orvieto, 21,461 . . . . D 3
Osimo, 21,182 . . . . D 3
Ostia . . . . D 4
Ostuni, 28,247 . . . . F 4
Pachino, 20,564 . . . . E 6
Padova (Padua), 138,709 . C 2
Padova (province), 668,025 . . . . C 2
Palazzolo, 11,584 . . . . E 6
Palermo, 411,879 . . . . D 5
Palermo (province), 890,752 . . . . D 5
Palma di Montechiaro, 15,615 . . . . D 6
Palmarola (island) . . . . . . D 4
Palmi, 18,179 . . . . E 5
Panarea (island) . . . . E 5
Panaro (river) . . . . C 2
Pantelleria, 9,806 . . . . C 6
Pantelleria (island) . . . . . D 6
Parma, 71,858 . . . . C 2
Parma (province), 381,771 . . . . C 2
Paterno, 32,179 . . . . E 6
Patti, 12,350 . . . . E 5
Pavia, 51,741 . . . . B 2
Pavia (province), 492,096 . B 2
Pavullo nel Frignano, 15,990 . . . . C 2

Penne, 12,784 . . . . D 3
Pennine Alps (mt. range) . A 2
Pergine Valsugana, 11,451 . . . . C 1
Pergola, 11,869 . . . . D 3
Perugia, 82,407 . . . . D 3
Perugia (province), 534,359 . . . . D 3
Pesaro, 44,589 . . . . D 3
Pesaro e Urbino (province), 311,916 . . . . D 3
Pescara, 51,808 . . . . E 3
Pescara (province), 211,561 . . . . E 3
Pescara (river) . . . . D 3
Pescia, 20,898 . . . . C 3
Piacenza, 64,210 . . . . B 2
Piacenza (province), 294,785 . . . . B 2
Pianosa (island) . . . . C 3
Piave (river) . . . . D 2
Piazza Armerina, 24,527 . . E 6
Piemonte (Piedmont, region), 3,506,134 . . . . A 2
Pietrasanta, 21,382 . . . . . . C 3
Pinerolo, 21,600 . . . . A 2
Piombino, 27,672 . . . . C 3
Piove di Sacco, 15,272 . . . C 2
Pisa, 72,468 . . . . C 3
Pisa (province), 341,428 . . C 3
Pisticci, 11,560 . . . . F 4
Pistoia, 72,212 . . . . C 3
Pistoia (province), 210,950 . . . . C 3
Po (river) . . . . C 2
Poggibonsi, 13,866 . . . . . . C 3
Pordenone, 22,174 . . . . D 2
Porto Civitanova, 10,560 . D 3
Porto Empedocle, 14,764 . D 6
Portoferraio, 11,650 . . . . . C 3
Portogruaro, 18,425 . . . . . D 2
Portomaggiore, 25,088 . . . C 2
Potenza, 25,103 . . . . E 4
Potenza (province), 376,486 . . . . E 4
Pozzallo, 10,090 . . . . E 6
Pozzuoli, 29,690 . . . . E 4
Prato, 70,206 . . . . C 3
Presanella (mt.) . . . . C 1
Priverno, 13,631 . . . . D 4
Puglia (region), 2,637,022 . . . . F 4
Putignano, 16,677 . . . . F 4
Quartu Sant'Elena, 12,201 . . . . B 5
Ragusa, 49,530 . . . . E 6
Ragusa (province), 223,086 . . . . E 6
Rapallo, 13,947 . . . . B 2
Ravenna, 81,086 . . . . D 2
Ravenna (province), 279,127 . . . . D 2
Recanati, 16,823 . . . . D 3
Reggio di Calabria, 119,804 . . . . E 5
Reggio di Calabria (province), 578,262 . . . . E 5
Reggio nell'Emilia, 93,913 . . . . C 2
Reggio nell'Emilia (province), 375,288 . . . . C 2
Rho, 19,823 . . . . B 2
Riesi, 19,709 . . . . E 6
Rieti, 34,769 . . . . D 3
Rieti (province), 174,961 . D 3
Rimini, 64,738 . . . . D 2
Rocca Massima, 1,602 . . . F 6
Roccastrada, 11,431 . . . . . C 3
Roma (Rome), 1,155,722 . D 4
Roma (province) 1,562,580 . . . . D 4
Ronciglione, 6,911 . . . . D 3
Rosignano Marittimo, 17,601 . . . . C 3
Rossano, 15,393 . . . . F 5
Rovereto, 20,758 . . . . C 2
Rovigo, 39,954 . . . . C 2
Rovigo (province), 336,807 . . . . C 2
Ruvo di Puglia, 25,452 . . . F 4
Sabaudia, 4,890 . . . . D 4

St. Bernard Pass, Gt. . . . . A 2
Sala Consilina, 9,020 . . . . E 4
Salemi, 17,308 . . . . D 6
Salerno, 67,009 . . . . E 4
Salerno, Golfo di . . . . E 4
Salerno (province), 705,277 . . . . E 4
Salina (island) . . . . E 5
Salsomaggiore, 15,259 . . . B 2
Saluzzo, 15,938 . . . . A 2
Sambiase, 16,062 . . . . F 5
San Antioco (island) . . . . . B 5
SanGiovanni in Persiceto, 20,859 . . . . C 2
San Giuliano, 22,204 . . . . C 3
Sangro (river) . . . . E 3
San Marco in Lamis, 19,608 . . . . E 4
San Miniato, 21,463 . . . . . C 3
San Remo, 31,769 . . . . A 3
Sansepolcro, 11,111 . . . . . . D 3
San Severino Marche, 16,141 . . . . D 3
San Severo, 37,702 . . . . . . E 4
Santa Maria Capua Vetere, 38,173 . . . . E 4
Santa Maria di Leuca, Capo . . . . G 5
Sant'Elpidio a Mare, 14,658 . . . . D 3
Santeramo in Colle, 17,069 . . . . F 4
Sant'Eufemia, Golfo di . . E 5
Sardegna (Sardinia, region), 1,034,206 . . . . . B 4
Saronno, 29,017 . . . . B 2
Sassari, 55,373 . . . . B 4
Sassari (province), 302,362 . . . . B 4
Sassuolo, 12,958 . . . . C 2
Savigliano, 17,511 . . . . A 2
Savona, 64,199 . . . . B 2
Savona (province), 219,108 . . . . B 2
Schio, 21,739 . . . . C 2
Sciacca, 22,713 . . . . D 6
Scicli, 21,827 . . . . E 6
Sele (river) . . . . E 4
Senigallia, 28,327 . . . . D 3
Sermoneta, 3,123 . . . . F 6
Sesto Fiorentino, 17,535 . . C 3
Sestri Levante, 16,237 . . . B 2
Sezze, 16,432 . . . . D 4
Sicilia (region), 4,000,078 . . . . E 6
Siderno, 14,497 . . . . F 5
Siena, 48,664 . . . . C 3
Siena (province), 268,459 . C 3
Sinnai, 10,412 . . . . B 5
Siracusa, 53,166 . . . . E 6
Siracusa (province), 277,572 . . . . E 6
Sondrio, 11,672 . . . . B 1
Sondrio (province), 142,919 . . . . B 1
Sonnino, 6,600 . . . . F 6
Sora, 20,841 . . . . D 4
Soresina, 11,314 . . . . B 2
Sorrento, 27,286 . . . . E 4
Sorso, 7,732 . . . . B 4
Spartivento, Capo . . . . B 5
Sperlonga, 2,647 . . . . F 6
Spezia, La, 106,119 . . . . . B 2
Spezia, La (province), 222,080 . . . . B 2
Spoleto, 32,341 . . . . D 3
Stromboli (island) . . . . E 5
Stura (river) . . . . A 2
Sulmona, 21,289 . . . . D 3
Susa, 4,952 . . . . A 2
Suzzara, 15,450 . . . . C 2
Tanaro (river) . . . . A 2
Taormina, 7,580 . . . . E 6
Taranto, 117,722 . . . . F 4
Taranto, Golfo di . . . . F 4
Taurianova, 18,710 . . . . . . E 5
Tempio Pausania, 15,752 . B 4
Teramo, 33,796 . . . . D 3
Teramo (province), 249,532 D 3
Termini Imerese, 20,845 . . D 6
Termoli, 8,755 . . . . E 3
Terni, 68,890 . . . . D 3

Terni (province), 191,559 . . . . D 3
Terracina, 23,559 . . . . D 4
Terralba, 11,767 . . . . B 5
Terranova Pausania, 10,157 . . . . B 4
Tevere (Tiber, river) . . . . D 3
Tirano, 6,772 . . . . C 1
Tirso (river) . . . . B 4
Tivoli, 20,875 . . . . D 4
Todi, 20,459 . . . . D 3
Tolentino, 14,356 . . . . D 3
Torino (Turin), 629,115 . . A 2
Torino (Turin, province) 1,168,384 . . . . A 2
Torre Annunziata, 72,935 . E 4
Torre d'Greco, 51,401 . . . E 4
Torremaggiore, 15,198 . . . E 4
Tortona, 20,361 . . . . B 2
Tortorici, 11,398 . . . . E 5
Toscana (Tuscany, region), 2,974,439 . . . . . C 3
Trani, 31,175 . . . . F 4
Trapani, 63,540 . . . . D 5
Trapani (province), 375,169 . . . . D 5
Trasimeno (lake) . . . . C 3
Trentino-Alto Adige (region) . . . . C 1
Trento, 56,017 . . . . C 1
Trento (province), 391,309 C 1
Treviglio, 19,164 . . . . B 2
Treviso, 53,886 . . . . D 2
Treviso (province), 570,580 . . . . D 2
Trieste, 248,379 . . . . D 2
Tyrrhenian Sea . . . . C 4
Udine, 63,098 . . . . D 1
Udine (province), 721,670 . D 1
Umbertide, 15,146 . . . . . . D 3
Umbria (region), 725,918 . . . . D 3
Urbino, 22,248 . . . . D 3
Ustica (island) . . . . D 5
Valdagno, 20,836 . . . . C 2
Valle d'Aosta (region) . . . . A 2
Varese, 44,832 . . . . B 2
Varese (province), 395,896 B 2
Vasto, 18,401 . . . . E 3
Vaticano, Città del . . . . . . D 4
Vaticano (cape) . . . . E 5
Velletri, 31,029 . . . . D 4
Venafro, 10,137 . . . . E 4
Veneto (region) . . . . C 2
Venezia (Venice), 264,027 D 2
Venezia (province), 629,123 . . . . D 2
Venezia, Golfo di (Gulf of Venice) . . . . D 2
Venosa, 11,045 . . . . E 4
Ventimiglia, 15,787 . . . . . . A 3
Ventotene (island) . . . . . . D 4
Vercelli, 38,956 . . . . B 2
Vercelli (province), 366,146 . . . . B 2
Veroli, 18,258 . . . . D 4
Verona, 153,708 . . . . C 2
Verona (province), 585,893 . . . . C 2
Vesuvio (volcano) . . . . E 4
Viadana, 18,165 . . . . C 2
Viareggio, 35,954 . . . . C 3
Vibo Valentia, 16,151 . . . . F 5
Vicenza, 69,379 . . . . C 2
Vicenza (province), 559,375 . . . . C 2
Vigevano, 38,039 . . . . B 2
Villacidro, 7,806 . . . . B 5
Villafranca di Verona, 14,479 . . . . C 2
Viso (monte) . . . . A 2
Viterbo, 36,123 . . . . C 3
Viterbo (province), 236,722 . . . . D 3
Vittoria, 37,575 . . . . E 6
Vittoria Veneto, 23,475 . . D 1
Vizzini, 14,706 . . . . E 6
Voghera, 30,180 . . . . B 2
Volterra, 20,638 . . . . C 3
Volturno (river) . . . . E 4
Vulcano (island) . . . . E 5

closed. After the gorge called Chiusa di Verona, famous in military history, the river enters the plain. In its lower course, the Adige has often shifted its bed; it is subject to violent floods and is navigable only by small craft.

The rivers of the peninsula portion of Italy are characterized by a considerable slope, especially in their upper courses, and by irregularity, with floods in spring and low water in summer. The rivers which empty in the Adriatic and Ionian seas flow in short transverse valleys; the longest of them are the Tronto, Pescara, and Ofanto. On the Tyrrhenian side more important rivers are found. The Tiber, which is a little longer than the Adige (244 miles), carries the waters of the principal mountainous groups of the central Apennines and has some notable tributaries, among them the Nera and the Aniene. Its lower course crosses the Roman Campagna. On its delta there was in antiquity the port of Rome, called Ostia, now filled with earth because of a very conspicuous alluvial process. Other notable rivers on the Tyrrhenian side are the Tuscan river Arno, north of the Tiber, and the Liri and Volturno south of the Tiber.

In Calabria and northeastern Sicily there are characteristic torrents, called *fiumare,* which are quite waterless during many months of the year and muddy and impetuous in the rainy season.

The Italian rivers are of little importance for navigation. However, the rivers of Alpine Italy are profitably used for irrigation, and above all for the production of electric power. For the same purpose, important plants have also been established on some rivers of the peninsula, such as the Aniene and the Nera, and on some rivers of Calabria, Sicily, and Sardinia.

Lakes.—The Italian lakes are divided into two main groups. The first includes the large subalpine lakes—Lago Maggiore or Verbano, Lago di Como or Lario, Lago d'Iseo or Sebino, and Lago di Garda or Benaco. They were all formed by ancient valleys once occupied by the extensive glaciers of the ice age, and are barred at the lower end by the terminal moraines of these glaciers. Their shores, favored with a mild climate, are thickly settled. The second group is in the Antiapennines and consists mostly of lakes which occupy the craters of ancient volcanoes. Such are the lakes of Bolsena, Vico, Bracciano, Albano, and Nemi. In contrast, Lago Trasimeno occupies a low area which is the remainder of a larger but very shallow basin. Other lakes, such as Fucino, have been drained.

Several small lakes are scattered along the coast of Latium, Campania, Apulia, and Sardinia; some have been reclaimed in the 20th century. There are also numerous artificial lakes or reservoirs for the production of electric power; some of the largest of these are found in the Venetian Alps, in Calabria, and Sardinia.

Plant and Animal Life.—In a country with such an ancient civilization as Italy has the natural landscape, as affected by the conditions of climate and soil, has been deeply modified by man. Mountain flora, with relics of the ice age, is found in the Alps above 6,500 feet, and in the Apennines above 7,200 to 7,900 feet. The belt of highest woods was originally, and is still partly, formed by conifers, but it was severely damaged by deforestation, which began in the Roman period and has been very actively pursued ever since with the exception of some pauses during the early Middle Ages. Below this altitude is a belt of such plants as beeches (still found in some regions of the eastern Alps and Outer Alps and of the Apennines), oaks, and chestnut trees. Oak woods, very widespread in antiquity, have suffered the heaviest damages from deforestation, particularly in the central and southern Apennines and in Sicily. Extensive oak woods still remain in Sardinia, however.

The plain of the Po has also thoroughly changed its original aspect. In the higher portion, which is very dry, there were once extensive areas with a scanty vegetation. These were later taken over for tillage by means of irrigation. Some small pieces of untilled territory, known variously as *brughiere, groane,* and *magredi,* still remain in Piedmont, Lombardy, and the Venetian region. In its lower portion, the plain was formerly covered with many marshy areas subject to floods, where poplars and willows thrived. But today the plain is almost entirely tilled, largely with cereal grains, rice, and hemp, or given over to pasture.

In the peninsula and in the larger islands, the hilly and level areas as well as the larger inland valleys were and still are the domain of Mediterranean vegetation. A natural formation was the *mácchia,* or bush, with evergreen trees and such shrubs as holm oak, cork trees, juniper, bramble, mastic, broom, laurel, myrtle, and dwarf palm. Since remote times man has eradicated this natural vegetation in extensive areas and replaced it with other growths, chiefly the olive tree, an appropriate emblem of the Mediterranean regions. Other cultivated plants are vines, and some fruit trees such as figs and almonds. Lemon and orange trees were imported in more recent times. Wheat thrives almost everywhere, but in the south and in Sicily it is often damaged because of the irregularity of rainfall. Among recent growths are sugar beets and tobacco. A typical feature of the Mediterranean landscape was the maritime or Italian cluster pine in the coastal areas, but there are few such pine groves left.

As for the animal kingdom, the primitive fauna has been thoroughly modified by man. The larger mammals are almost extinct. Bears are found very rarely in both the Alps and the Apennines, where they still live in a very small protected area. Wolves are still common in the peninsula but are no longer found either in the Alps or in Sicily. Wild stags and deer survive in Sardinia; chamois are still spread in the Alps. The large birds of prey are also disappearing; among the birds characteristic of Italy, ravens and swallows may be mentioned. In the peninsula and in the islands, countless lizards are found.

All the domestic animals have been present since the most remote times. Cattle and pigs are prevalent in continental Italy, whereas sheep prevail in southern Italy and in the islands, where pastures are poorer. In the same southern regions, there are also many donkeys and mules. Buffaloes were imported from Asia, and some semiwild herds of these mammals still survive in the coastal plains of southern Italy.

Roberto Almagià,
Professor of Geography, University of Rome.

2. THE PEOPLE. The Land and Its Earliest Inhabitants.

—Italy, in its present geographical structure, is of comparatively recent origin. The Alps and the Apennines, which form its skeleton, had already emerged from the Pliocene sea in the Tertiary period, together with the greater part of the continent of Europe, but the Po Valley and the plains to the east and west of the Apennine chain date from the Quaternary or, to be more exact, Lower Pleistocene period. This fact explains the scarcity of primitive peoples in Italy and the small quantity of Paleolithic (Old Stone Age) relics left behind them. Flint objects of the Pleistocene period, made in the Mousterian style, have been found, and from bones discovered in Rome and Latium between 1929 and 1939, we know that they were produced by a type of man living in the Riss-Würm interglacial stage about 50,000 years ago. This was Neanderthal man, thinly but widely distributed over many parts of Europe. His distinguishing marks were a long, narrow (dolichocephalic) skull, a low-swung face, a prominent occiput, a sloping forehead with a thick, bony visor just above the eyes, a wide nose, a receding chin, a strong, stocky body, and skin that may have been dark in color. He had a spoken language, made arms and tools, used fire both for heat and for cooking, and knew how to protect himself with what means he had against the cold and the wild animals around him. Later, other anthropological types made their appearance in Italy, including the Grimaldi who lived in Liguria, only to disappear, leaving no traces behind them. See also section on *History;* MAN, PREHISTORIC RACES OF; STONE AGE.

Pre-Roman and Latin Peoples.—The history of the human race in the second millennium before Christ is complex and for the most part little known. In northern Italy, peoples of pre-Indo-European stock, among whom we may single out the Ligurians, developed a Neolithic (New Stone Age) civilization. They buried their dead. Elsewhere in Italy, ancient groups of Sardinians, Corsicans, and Elymi, whose linguistic classification is still uncertain, were superseded by the first wave of Indo-European-speaking peoples, who eventually made up the Latinian and Sabellian branches of the Italic subfamily. In the north, around 2000 B.C., the first metals (copper, and then bronze) appeared, incineration was introduced, and dwellings were built on piles north of the Po, and, later, fortified villages of pile dwellings laid out in a geometrical plan on the dry land south of the river. This was the civilization known as terramara, related to the later (9th to 6th century B.C.) Villanova civilization which spread gradually over the central and southern parts of Italy. The Villanova civilization arose as a second wave of Indo-European-speaking peoples entered Italy, and from it came the third branch of the Italic subfamily, the Osco-Umbrian.

In the course of their expansion, these peoples discovered iron. From their contacts with the predecessors of the Etruscans, or, as some scholars think, with the Etruscans (who had migrated from Asia Minor between the 10th and 8th centuries B.C.), there arose along the northern part of the Tyrrhenian coast what we know as the Etruscan civilization.

This period marks the end of Italian prehistory. Peoples of Illyrian origin, Iapyges in the south and Veneti in the north, settled on the shores of the Adriatic, while Greeks colonized and civilized the coastal zones of the far south (Magna Graecia) and Sicily. Waves of barbarian invaders of Celtic stock, whom the Romans called Gauls, descended on northern Italy. They drove the older inhabitants toward the south and even ventured as far as the young city of Rome, from which they were driven back at the end of the 4th century B.C. It is impossible to determine what portion of the Ligurian, Etruscan, and Italic peoples stayed on in the northern plains after the Celtic invasions. There are, however, signs of a thorough anthropological mixture, particularly in the plains south of the Po.

The Romans were endowed with military prowess and with an incomparable talent for spreading civilization, and were thus able to carry out the task of unifying this heterogeneous aggregation of peoples, first imposing their political rule, and then their laws, culture, language, and thought. In the time of Augustus (r. 27 B.C.–4 A.D.), Italy was completely Romanized, although its regional division showed recognition of its varied origins. The unity created by the Romans did not give way before the barbarian invasions of the 5th and 6th centuries A.D., in which peoples of Germanic, Slavic, and even Mongol origin took part. It continued to develop until *latinitas* (Latinity) finally became the distinguishing characteristic of the Italian people. See also section on *History*.

Language and Dialects.—The language introduced into the provinces of the Roman Empire by Roman soldiers and civil authorities was not literary Latin but a popular speech which took root everywhere, absorbing local forms and customs, and evolving in different ways. Numerous Latin dialects developed, but the people who spoke them had to use a simplified and provincial form of standard Latin in official documents and in their communications with Rome and other parts of the empire. The passage of centuries brought with it the outgrowth from the various kinds of regional speech of the primitive Italian dialects, which are the prototypes of the dialects still spoken in modern Italy.

The replacement of local dialects by a standard literary language was a particularly slow process in Italy, because educated people were for a long time reluctant to give up Latin, which was still used in public papers and in the liturgy of the Roman Catholic Church. But the flowering at the beginning of the 12th century of Provençal poetry, whose widespread imitation stimulated literary exchanges among the various regions, led in the early 13th century to the predominance of the Tuscan dialect, generally considered the nearest to classical Latin. The position of Tuscan was strengthened by the tremendous influence of Dante Alighieri (1265–1321), followed by Petrarch (Francesco Petrarca, 1304–1374) and Giovanni Boccaccio (1313–1375). In this way, the Italian language came into being, and in the succeeding centuries other distinguished writers increased its importance as one of the world's great languages.

The general effect of linguistic unification was to reduce the number of differences among the various dialects. There are still fairly marked variations of vocabulary, accent, and pronunciation, but Italians of the upper and middle classes write and usually speak a standard language, which public education, the newspapers, the radio, motion pictures, and the development of communications and travel have brought into general use.

The linguistic unity of persons of Italian origin (among whom we must count the inhabitants of the Swiss canton of Ticino, of the cities of the Dalmatian coast of Yugoslovia, and of the island of Corsica) is shown by the very small number of Italian citizens who habitually use other languages or dialects (Slav, German, French, Albanian, Greek, Catalan). The majority of these foreign-language citizens live along the northern border. According to the 1921 census, there were 801,923 of them, or about 2.1 per cent of the general population, and about 45 per cent lived in the northeastern territories awarded to Italy after World War I and transferred in 1947 to Yugoslavia and the Free Territory of Trieste. The census of 1936 registered 109,000 persons of foreign nationality living on Italian soil. (See also sections on *Language* and *Literature*.)

Anthropology.—When we speak of the racial make-up of the Italian people, we do not refer to the three major groups (white, Mongoloid, and Negroid), since, with the exception of a few thousand Mongols who took part in the invasions of Attila (452 A.D.) and other barbarian leaders, the ancestors of the modern Italians were all of the white group. Rather, we refer to the various branches or subdivisions of the white group to which they belong.

The groups which over the centuries came to form the Italian people were themselves, to a certain extent, of varied origin, and some of these groups intermarried with other peoples. This explains the difficulties encountered by anthropologists in their attempts to classify the few skeletons which have come down from prehistoric times. It is important to note, however, that after the unification of the Roman Empire and the end of the period of the barbarian invasions there were no mass movements of population. The sporadic immigration of Germans, Normans, Arabs, Slavs, Catalonians, and Albanians had little influence on the make-up of the Italian people, and in any case their presence is recorded in history and we can take it into due account. Aside from the large cities, we may say that the anthropological composition of modern Italy is not very different from what it was in the time of Augustus. This simplifies many genealogical problems and permits us to concentrate on contemporary racial composition and distribution, which in turn shed light on the problems of the past.

In order to get our bearings, let us look at Table 1. In the first column are listed the regions of Italy prior to World War II; in the second, the average heights, in centimeters, of 20-year-old males from these regions who were born in 1908; in the third, the average head measurements (corrected), expressed in terms of the cephalic index (for definition, see ANTHROPOLOGY), of 20-year-old soldiers born between 1859 and 1863. The remaining columns give the frequency per 1,000 among these same soldiers of blond hair, blue eyes, and a fair complexion.

The greatest heights are found in Venezia Giulia (most of which is no longer part of Italy) and Veneto—168.28 centimeters (5 feet 6¼ inches) and 167.14 centimeters (5 feet 5¾ inches), respectively—and as we proceed west and south, the heights become progressively smaller. Throughout the north, however, they remain over an average of 166 centimeters (5 feet 5⅓ inches). In the heart of central Italy, the average is 163 centimeters (5 feet 4 inches); it decreases steadily thereafter, reaching its lowest point in the south and the islands. The absolute minimum, found in Sardinia, is 160.89 centimeters (5 feet 3⅓ inches). With regard to stature, therefore, we may divide Italy into three areas—the northeast, where the men are fairly tall; the northwest and center, where they are of medium height; and the south and the islands, where they are short.

Glancing again at Table 1, we find high cephalic indexes (indicative of brachycephalic, or short, wide heads) in the Veneto region and in Venezia Giulia. The very highest figure, however, occurs in Piedmont (84.9), in the extreme northwest, where heads are nearest to a round shape. Lower averages are found in Emilia, Lombardy, and possibly in Venezia Tridentina, and still lower ones in Tuscany, Marche, and Umbria. If we consider as fairly roundheaded all measurements over 82[1], then we may say that all of northern Italy (except Liguria) and the northern part of central Italy are definitely brachycephalic. Farther south, dolichocephalism (longheadedness) prevails increasingly. Sardinia again shows the lowest figure (76.5).

The data on pigmentation, in the last three columns of Table 1, follows that of head measurements, with high figures in Piedmont and Lombardy and low ones in Sardinia. In summary, we may say that in the brachycephalic regions there are fairly numerous examples of light hair, eyes, and complexion, but in the dolichocephalic regions these traits are rare and the population must be considered definitely dark in coloring.

Table 1—BASIC ANTHROPOLOGICAL TRAITS ADULT ITALIAN MALES

Region[1]	Average quantitative traits		Average qualitative traits (per 1,000)		
	Height (centimeters)[2]	Cephalic Index[3]	Blond hair[3]	Blue eyes[3]	Fair complexion[3]
Piedmont	166.39	84.9	124	136	488
Liguria	166.78	81.3	105	105	456
Lombardy	165.84	83.4	101	134	497
Venezia Tridentina	165.51	84.0?	?	?	?
Veneto	167.14	84.0	126	157	468
Venezia Giulia and Zara	168.28	84.2	?	?	?
Emilia	166.18	84.2	72	94	385
Tuscany	166.23	82.3	92	104	434
Marche	163.78	83.0	75	101	314
Umbria	163.97	83.1	90	117	415
Latium	164.53	80.0	64	83	353
Abruzzi and Molise	162.73	80.9	66	85	376
Campania	162.83	81.1	68	84	310
Apulia	162.33	78.8	57	76	303
Basilicata	160.94	79.8	48	67	311
Calabria	162.08	77.4	38	55	251
Sicily	162.54	78.6	50	77	283
Sardinia	160.89	76.5	17	40	183
All Italy	164.72	81.7	82	103	386

[1] Pre-World War II regional division.
[2] Based on corrected measurements of 20-year-old males, born 1908.
[3] Based on data on 20-year-old soldiers, born 1859–63.

Referring again to history, we may note the following allied facts:

(1) The northwest regions correspond in a general way to the territory invaded by the Celts, who dispossessed the former Ligurian, Etruscan, and Italic inhabitants. Indeed, the Romans called this region Cisalpine Gaul. Here we have found medium heights, brachycephalic heads, and predominantly dark coloring, with, however, a sizable number of blonds.

[1] Some authorities class all measurements between 80.1 and 83 as subbrachycephalic.

(2) The regions of Veneto and Venezia Giulia were invaded by the Illyrians, and Augustus called by the name of Venetia the whole northeastern section of Italy bordering on Illyrium. In this area are the greatest average heights in Italy, combined with brachycephalism and a high frequency of light coloring.

(3) Many of the central and southern regions bear the names of ethnic groups belonging to the great Italic-speaking subfamily which formerly occupied them, and some recall the era of Greek colonization. South of the 43d parallel (which runs about 70 miles north of Rome) begins the area of short stature, increasing dolichocephalism, and darker coloring.

(4) The middle ground between the 43d and 45th parallels includes Liguria and Tuscany on the west, which have medium heights and fairly small head measurements, and the regions of Emilia (where the terramara peoples lived), Marche, and Umbria, where there were frequent and sometimes violent contacts between the old Italic and Etruscan inhabitants and the later Celtic and Illyrian invaders.

Before passing from these notes to a fuller interpretation of the anthropological data at hand, we must take into consideration a number of points. First, other traits should be weighed. Of particular importance are the height of the cranium, the relative width of the nose, and the relationship between the length of the torso and that of the legs. In addition, we should eliminate from the averages given in Table 1 the influence of heterogeneous urban populations. Besides the averages, we should take into account the distribution of anthropological traits and the relationships among them. Moreover, we should consider the various ways in which hereditary traits are transmitted, and we must not forget the influence of geographical, social, and nutritional factors. Research has been done along these lines, but we must confine ourselves to remarking that all these points have their place in our discussion.

The average physical traits of the Piedmontese, and to a lesser degree of the Lombards and Tridentines, correspond to those usually attributed to peoples of Celtic stock. Actually the word Celtic is more properly applied in the field of linguistics, and the traits in question are not shared by all peoples of Celtic stock, nor are they the exclusive property of this stock. The modern term Alpine is preferable, describing as it does an abstract anthropological group of medium height and stocky physique, roundheaded and with prevalently dark coloring. The ways in which the traits of the Alpine people of Italy are transmitted by heredity, however, make us suspect numerous mixtures and amalgamations with people of very different physical characteristics, and the frequency in its most representative elements of numerous subjects of light coloring goes far to confirm this suspicion.

These Alpine peoples are bordered on the east by the Venetian and Julian Venetian descendants of ancient Illyrian invaders. Their fairly tall stature and brachycephalism, combined with dark coloring and other traits, roughly correspond to those of the so-called Dinaric type, which is found in all the Venetian regions as well as along the coast of Yugoslavia. This type, too, is racially mixed, for the cranial and pigmentary data is almost certainly hybrid, and the frequency of blonds is another index of irregularity. There is more consistency in the matter of height, a factor of great anthropological importance among these Adriatic peoples.

Let us look now at the south of Italy and the islands. Here the population is descended from many overlapping stocks—pre-Italic, Phoenician, Greek, and Italic. Under anthropological analysis, however, it is shown to be remarkably homogeneous, though not to such an extent, for example, as the Scandinavian population. For this reason, its most conspicuous traits—low stature, a long, narrow head, and dark complexion—are said to characterize a human type called Mediterranean. This type is widespread along the coasts of the Mediterranean Sea; it is most concentrated and uniform in Sardinia.

Are we to consider the modern Ligurians, with their head measurements approaching dolichocephalism, as representatives of the Mediterranean type? And the Tuscan descendants of the Etruscans, with measurements only slightly larger? We cannot exclude this possibility, although there is other contradictory data, based on the fact that Tuscany is part of the middle ground of central Italy, where there was such a great mixture of ethnic stocks. This mixture was especially pronounced in Emilia.

In conclusion, three of the major European racial types, in a more or less pure form, all of them with dark coloring, go to make up the population of Italy: the Alpine, the Dinaric, and the Mediterranean. There are, on the other hand, very few examples of the Nordic or East Baltic types.

Demography.—*Growth of Population.*—There is quite a difference between the few hundred men of the prehistoric era and the 1948 Italian population of 46,403,000. This population was not built up by immigration except during the pre-Roman and Roman periods and the 5th and 6th century barbarian invasions. Since then its growth has been due entirely to the predominance of births over deaths, and emigration has not altered the favorable balance. Since this growth has taken place over a period of 4,000 years, the average annual rate of increase has been slow: about 1 per 1,000. (Table 2 shows the population of Italy from the death of Augustus to 1948, with a forecast for the year 2050.)

Table 2—POPULATION OF ITALY

Year	No. Inhabitants
4 [1]	6,500,000
1500 [1]	11,600,000
1700 [1]	14,100,000
1800 [1]	18,124,000
1901 [2]	32,475,253
1911 [2]	34,671,377
1921 [2]	37,973,977
1931 [2]	41,176,671
1936 [2]	42,918,726
1946 [1]	44,994,000
1947 [1]	45,539,000
1948 [1]	46,403,000
2050 [3]	56,800,000

[1] Estimate. [2] Census. [3] Forecast.

Note: All figures are for area within political boundaries at the respective dates, and are not therefore entirely comparable.

According to calculations made by historians, the rate of increase was even lower in the period from the beginning of the Christian era to 1500, amounting to only about .4 per 1,000. After this time, however, under the influence of favorable European conditions and the Industrial Revolution, the population increased at a much faster rate, particularly during the 20th century. The maximum of 10.6 per 1,000 was reached in 1936–1941, after which the rate declined. If prophecies based on complex mathematical calculations are correct, there will be a decrease to less than 2 per 1,000 by the year 2050.

The density of population in 1948 was approximately 399 persons per square mile. It is true that other European countries—for example, Belgium, the Netherlands, and the United Kingdom —are more densely populated, but the Italian population problem is a serious one because of the mountainous nature of the terrain, the lack of mineral resources, and the poor condition of much of the soil, brought about by 3,000 years of unscientific agricultural practices.

Trades and Professions.—Occupational classifications may be made in various ways, two of which deserve mention here. The first and simpler way is to list all persons no longer infants according to their gainful activity. The Italian census of 1936 registered 33,728,406 persons over 10 years of age, of whom 18,345,432 exercised a trade or profession. Table 3 shows the division according to occupation of persons registered by the census. We note that 8,756,064 persons, or approximately 47.7 per cent of the total employed population, were engaged in agriculture.

Table 3—POPULATION OVER 10 YEARS OF AGE ENGAGED IN TRADES AND PROFESSIONS CENSUS OF 1936

Trades and professions	Number engaged		Number engaged per 1,000	
	Total	Males only	Total	Males only
Agriculture	8,756,064	6,328,531	477.3	483.1
Hunting and fishing	86,721	83,181	4.7	6.4
Industry and handicrafts	5,375,152	3,997,779	293.0	305.2
Transportation and communications	702,201	667,049	38.3	50.9
Commerce	1,504,820	1,068,285	82.0	81.6
Banking and insurance	100,543	88,242	5.5	6.7
Arts and letters	142,958	108,893	7.8	8.3
Public administration	808,866	575,938	44.1	44.0
Private administration	81,059	29,693	4.4	2.3
Religion	126,323	74,938	6.9	5.7
Domestic service	660,725	75,901	36.0	5.8
Total	18,345,432	13,098,430	1,000.0	1,000.0

The second method disregards age and divides the entire population into families, listing the trade or profession of the head of each family. According to this method of calculation, there were in Italy in 1936, 3,628,000 families whose head worked in agriculture (38 per cent of the total), and these families included 18,385,855 persons, or 42.8 per cent of the total population. This fact has particular social significance, because it shows that the members of many agricultural families have left the land and taken up other occupations.

All the major trades and professions except agriculture are concentrated in the large cities, and because of the enormous increase of industrial and commercial activity since the late 19th century, there has been a correspondingly heavy increase in the population of urban centers. In 1946, there were 70 cities with more than 50,000 inhabitants and a total population of approximately 12,400,000, or 27.5 per cent of the total; and 26 cities with over 100,000 inhabitants and a total population of 9,250,000, or 20.5 per cent of the total. The five cities with present populations of more than 500,000 increased as follows between 1901 and 1947: Rome, 462,783 to 1,573,994; Milan, 491,460 to 1,267,550; Naples, 563,540 to 977,946; Turin, 335,656 to 712,983; and Genoa, 234,710 to 649,367.

Religion.—The question asked by census takers in Italy concerning religion has, in recent years, been interpreted as having an official meaning. That is, it aims at establishing in which religion a person was born or reared rather than at ascertaining what his actual beliefs and church attendance are. This, then, is how we must interpret the figures of the 1931 census, which show that 99.6 per cent of those registered were Roman Catholics, .34 per cent belonged to other faiths, and only .06 per cent declared that they had no religion or were unwilling to make any statement. The small minority of 139,719 persons belonging to other than the Roman Catholic Church included 83,618 Protestants, 33,381 of whom were foreigners, and 47,825 Jews, of whom 8,713 were foreigners.

Vital Statistics.—The rapid increase in the Italian population in the 20th century, as shown in Table 2, is due to the fact that many more persons have been born than have either died or emigrated. The number of births hovers around 1,000,000 per year, while the number of deaths is about 500,000. (Birth, death, marriage, and emigration rates are given in Table 4.) As in most civilized countries, the birth rate has declined in Italy in the 20th century independently of the number of marriages. In 1948, the birth rate (21.5 per 1,000) was only about 56 per cent of what it had been in 1881–1885 (38.0 per 1,000). In the same period, the death rate declined from 27.3 to 10.6 per 1,000.

Table 4—MARRIAGE, BIRTH, DEATH, AND EMIGRATION RATES
(per 1,000 inhabitants)

Year	Marriages	Births	Deaths	Emigrants
1881–1885	8.1	38.0	27.3	5.36
1901–1905	7.4	32.7	22.0	16.82
1911–1915	7.4	31.5	19.1	15.46
1921–1925	8.4	29.5	17.3	7.87
1931–1935	6.8	23.8	14.1	2.19
1936–1940	7.6	23.2	13.8	1.11
1941	6.1	20.9	13.9	0.19
1942	6.4	20.5	14.3	0.18
1943	4.9	19.9	15.2	...
1944	5.0	19.2	15.9	...
1945	6.8	18.3	13.8	...
1946	7.6	22.8	12.3	1.17
1947	9.4	21.9	11.4	3.16
1948	8.3	21.5	10.6	2.93

The decline of the death rate is an important sign of civic progress in culture, public health, and material welfare. Evidence of this progress is shown in detailed fashion in Table 5, which compares the life spans of Italians in 1881 and 1941. From this table, we learn that whereas in 1881 only 788 of 1,000 males reached the age of 1 year, 592 reached 10 years, and 412 reached 50 years, in 1941 the corresponding figures were 908, 858, and 725, respectively. The death rate for males during the first year of life was 212.4 per 1,000 in 1881, but declined to 91.8 per 1,000 by 1941, a difference of 57 per cent. The difference for persons 10 years of age was 76 per cent; for those 50 years of age, 41 per cent. The life span of the average male increased from 35.2 years in

Table 5—LIFE SPAN OF THE ITALIAN PEOPLE, 1881 AND 1941
(per 1,000)

Age	Number reaching specified age				Death rate				Life expectancy (years)			
	1881		1941		1881		1941		1881		1941	
	Men	Women	Men	Women	Men	Women	Men	Women	Men	Women	Men	Women
0	1,000	1,000	1,000	1,000	212.4	191.3	91.8	75.1	35.2	35.7	57.6	60.9
1	788	809	908	925	109.2	108.2	30.3	25.8	43.5	43.0	62.4	64.8
2	702	721	881	901	53.3	53.6	8.1	7.9	47.8	47.1	63.3	65.5
3	664	683	874	894	33.1	33.6	5.5	5.1	49.4	48.8	62.8	65.0
4	642	660	869	889	23.9	24.0	3.4	3.3	50.1	49.4	62.2	64.3
5	627	644	866	886	17.9	18.7	2.6	2.5	50.3	49.6	61.4	63.6
10	592	606	858	878	5.9	6.5	1.4	1.3	48.2	47.6	56.9	59.1
15	578	589	852	872	5.0	6.1	1.6	1.6	44.3	43.9	52.2	54.2
20	561	569	841	862	8.2	7.9	3.2	3.0	40.6	40.4	47.9	50.2
30	514	520	817	837	7.9	9.8	3.2	3.1	33.8	33.7	39.1	41.9
40	471	468	781	806	10.6	10.9	6.3	4.2	26.4	26.9	30.7	32.9
50	412	415	725	765	17.4	14.6	10.2	7.4	19.5	19.6	22.6	24.4
60	326	337	628	690	31.7	30.1	21.7	16.0	13.2	12.9	15.3	16.4
70	200	207	450	525	74.0	79.7	50.6	45.0	8.2	7.8	9.2	9.8
80	67	63	186	241	145.2	151.3	136.8	122.7	5.0	4.9	4.9	5.2
90	8	7	20	30	248.6	246.5	285.4	275.9	3.1	3.2	2.7	2.7
100	....	....	....	....	365.6	347.4	449.2	462.5	2.1	2.3	1.7	1.6

1881 to 57.6 years in 1941, or 63 per cent. A similar though less marked increase took place in this period for all age groups up to 70.

Other signs of improved social conditions, and particularly of public health, are seen in the data concerning causes of death. Fig. 1 shows that from 1907 to 1939, except for the years of World War I, there were progressively fewer deaths from diseases of the heart, tuberculosis, and infectious diseases in general. There was a setback

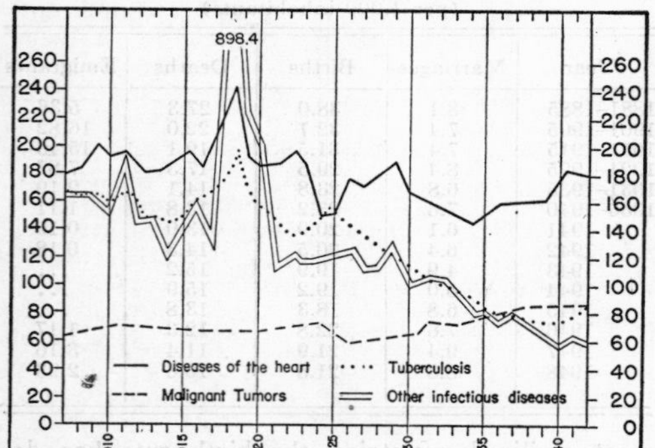

Fig. 1. Death rates from selected causes per 100,000 population in Italy, 1907 to 1942.

in 1941–1942, especially in the case of tuberculosis, as a result of World War II, during which the national income was reduced to 60 per cent of the prewar figure, and nutrition, which was based on carbohydrates and had lacked fats and proteins even in better times, declined to little more than 2,000 calories per day for an adult male.

In contrast to the general trend, we note an increase, dating from 1926, of deaths due to malignant tumors. This may be accounted for in part, however, by more accurate diagnoses than those made in the past.

Two characteristic diseases which had afflicted Italy for a long period seemed to have been almost entirely eliminated on the eve of World War II. These were pellagra and malaria. The first reappeared to a small extent as a result of malnutrition. and the second as a consequence of the destruction during the war of many reclamation projects and the movement of thousands of refugees. In general, however, there were no such epidemics as had occurred during World War I (cholera in the army, and influenza), and the few outbreaks of contagious diseases (smallpox, typhus) were quickly put down by an efficient public health organization, which provides the services of a doctor, midwife, and pharmacist in even the smallest villages.

Emigration.—Because of the density of the population and the poverty of the country, in past decades many Italians went abroad to make their livings. We note from Table 4 that during the first 15 years of the 20th century approximately 16 out of every 1,000 inhabitants emigrated each year. Some of the emigrants returned to Italy, but not in proportions to equal the number of those who left. During the period of heaviest emigration about 250,000 persons, mostly men and many of them skilled northern workers, went each year to other parts of Europe, while an additional 400,000, mostly peasants and day laborers from the south, went to the United States and South America. During World War I, the emigration rate was reduced to one seventh of its former level, but by 1920 substantial emigration had resumed. Later, restrictions on imigration imposed by various countries (such as the United States Immigration Act of 1924), and the economic and military policy of the Fascist government reduced emigration to negligible proportions. Among the policies of the new democratic postwar government has been the encouragement of emigration on a substantial scale, particularly to France and Argentina. Net emigration in 1946 amounted to about 53,000 persons; in 1947, to about 144,000; and in 1948 to about 136,000.

Many of those who emigrated at the beginning of the 20th century made their homes abroad and became citizens of their adopted countries. The United States census of 1940, for example, listed 1,561,100 persons of Italian birth. Italy has benefited from the emigration of the past, which relieved overpopulation and unemployment, and emigrant remittances helped to cover international financial commitments. Particular benefit accrued to the south, which centuries of bad government, poor soil, and difficulties in establishing modern industry had made into the least progressive part of Italy. The countries where the emigrants went were equally benefited. The emigrant is often more enterprising and hence more valuable economically than the man who stays at home. From a sociological point of view, we may note that the emigrant's ability to do hard work and his thrift have done much to dispel the mythical foreign conception of the Italian as lazy and pleasure loving, absorbed in *dolce far niente* (sweet idleness).

Culture.—Elementary schooling is free and compulsory in Italy. There were in 1946, 869,112 pupils attending the 10,599 *asili* (nursery schools or kindergartens), which had 20,552 teachers; and 4,357,137 pupils in the 35,252 public and private elementary schools, with 133,004 teachers. It was estimated that 90 per cent of the children in the age group between 6 and 14 were attending school. There were in the same year 675,732 students attending secondary schools, including art and technical schools. University students numbered 189,663.

These figures are of interest less for the present state of education than as an index of the future. If we speak of culture in the highest sense, we cannot properly measure it even from the data furnished by the 1936 census regarding the number of persons engaged in the most honored professions, shown in Table 6, for it omits

Table 6—PERSONS ENGAGED IN CULTURAL OR PROFESSIONAL ACTIVITIES, CENSUS OF 1936

Classification	Number engaged	Number per 100,000 population
Heads and teachers of secondary schools and colleges	188,736	439.7
Roman Catholic priests and ministers of other sects	150,234	350.0
Physicians and pharmacists	40,095	93.4
Lawyers, notaries, etc.	35,567	82.9
Prefects and other public and private officials	24,442	56.9
Engineers and architects	22,285	51.9
Painters, sculptors, and musicians	15,393	35.9
Chemists, physicists, and naturalists	5,425	12.6
Writers and editors	1,236	2.9
Diplomats	936	2.1
Total	484,349	1,128.3

many persons with university degrees, both publicly and privately employed. Only a relatively small number of the persons listed in the table make a direct contribution to Italian culture, but it is largely among the professional groups that we must look for those who before World War II produced the 25,000 books and 4,000 periodicals printed each year by Italian publishers, and the 1,000,000 readers at the public libraries, who borrowed more than 2,500,000 volumes. Here, too, we shall find those who visit art galleries, attend concerts and lectures, and support intellectual, artistic, and scientific development.

Way of Life.—There are great differences of outlook, customs, and living conditions among the Italian peasants, who make up the largest part of the population. There is the mountain dweller, who must break rocks in order to plant a small field; the prosperous farmer of the irrigated valleys of Lombardy; the tenant farmer who receives only a modest income in money or produce; his richer counterpart in Tuscany and Emilia; the shepherd of Abruzzi, the Maremma section, and Sardinia, who shares the solitary and nomadic life of his flocks.

Beside this varied rural way of life, there is another, thousand-year-old urban civilization. We must remember that as late as 1860 Italy was still divided into seven small, independent units, some of which had two capitals. There were, then, seven separate courts, each with its own ceremonies, nobility, clergy, bankers, and hangers-on of every kind, in addition to other, even more numerous, cultural and economic centers, some of which were the former capitals of vanished republics and principalities. This explains the wealth of monuments, art collections, archives, and historical libraries found throughout Italy, and the great number of bishoprics (282), universities and other institutions of higher learning (about 40), academies, and educational centers.

Apart from its position as the center of the Roman Catholic Church, Rome has none of the metropolitan character of Paris, London, and New York. Milan, Turin, and Genoa are greater industrial centers, as are many smaller cities and their suburbs. There are few great factories for the mass production of uniform goods; in fact, even such machine-made products as automobiles and watches are often turned out by skilled artisans whose talent and ingenuity make up for the lack of technical organization. The industrial census of 1937–1939 listed 217,893 manufacturing plants, of which only 87 employed more than 2,000 workers, and 804,646 handicraft industries, of which 786,000 employed fewer than 5 workers. Italian industry and handicrafts are known for the excellence and refinement of their production. Celebrated the world over for their quality are Florentine jewelry, Venetian lace and embroidery, Murano (Venetian) glass, leatherwork and gloves, faïence ware, the wooden statuary of the Italian Alps, the marble sculpture of Florence, and the corals of the coastal towns near Naples.

The cities, laden with memories and monuments of antiquity, and still holding out against the encroachment of heavy industry, are perhaps the most obvious demonstration of the Italian's strong attachment to tradition. Another aspect of this attachment is the retention of some very old legal and social institutions, such as the rural *mezzadria,* a medieval form of arrangement between landowners and their tenants whereby the former are paid by receiving exactly half the produce of their land.

The Protestant Reformation hardly touched Italy, and nearly the entire population belongs, at least in a formal sense, to the Roman Catholic Church. Religious faith is usually deep and sincere despite occasional manifestations of outworn custom and superstition. Religious beliefs, whether or not they are accompanied by church attendance, have a solidifying influence on family life. Divorce is prohibited. The infrequency of homicide (15 cases per 1,000,000 inhabitants in 1939), suicide (69 per 1,000,000), and death from chronic or acute alcoholism (10 per 1,000,000) bear witness to self-discipline and moral balance.

In a few districts the capital invested in industry or the natural fertility of the soil have produced good living conditions. On the whole, however, the poorer classes suffer much economic hardship.

The Italian character varies considerably from one part of the country to another. The Italian of the northwest is cold and reserved, accustomed by business dealings to concentration and prudence. The central Italian, particularly the Tuscan and the Umbrian, has a more open nature, and the southerner is highly imaginative and very much of an extrovert, witty and exuberant in words and gestures. It would be an error, however, to conclude that the southerner is a superficial wastrel. The people of the Naples area, for example, have to their credit the accomplishment of having turned a wasteland into a garden, bringing all the water from underground, and succeeding with great effort in raising five or six crops of fruit and vegetables a year.

There are many ancient holiday celebrations in Italy. These create local rivalry or bring the people together in a community effort which usually ends with banquets of regional food and wine. Among the more famous of these celebrations are the Palio delle Contrade, municipal races between the wards of Siena, held in July and August; the regattas of Venice; the *scoppio del carro,* a religious procession which takes place at Easter in Florence; the October wine festivals in the country around Rome; the Piedigrotta festival of Naples, with its song competitions (see section on *Music*); and the *ceri* (candlelight celebrations) of Catania. The night festivities of the Feast of the Redeemer (third Sunday in July) in Venice are particularly beautiful because of their illumination. The entire city is decked out with Japanese lanterns, and fireworks are mirrored in the lagoon. Good Friday is observed in Umbria and other places with a ghostly torchlight procession following an image of Christ's body.

To these popular celebrations must be added the biennial art exposition and the periodic motion-picture festival of Venice, the *Maggio musicale* of Florence, and the art competitions held every four years in Rome. In addition, sports are popular, and large crowds turn out for soccer and boxing matches and for automobile and bicycle races.

World War II changed many habits and had its effect on the spirit of the Italian people. Against the old individualistic and conservative background we see new currents and aspirations toward a more democratic form of government. Old Italy, which has often been called "the country with a thousand lives" may emerge from the troubled postwar period with a new aspect whose exact form we cannot as yet imagine, but whose success should be forwarded by a past history rich in experience and glories.

Italian Contributions to Modern Civilization.—The time is past when one could look at the history of one's native land with the same narrow pride which leads a father to consider his own child superior to all other children. The modern temper is practical and cosmopolitan, and its evaluations are made on an objective basis, taking into consideration only the fundamental contributions made by the various peoples of the world to present day civilization.

If we study Italy's more than 2,500 years of recorded history, we shall find a very large number of these contributions. We see first the spread of Roman civilization among the barbarians, which left behind it permanent traces. The Latin language was the vehicle of its transmission, and its chief expression was in the field of law, where it created the legal conceptions of private property and the family, and in a westernized form of Greek art and philosophy.

When the Roman Empire finally crumbled away, Italy again assumed leadership through the Roman Catholic Church, which extended to all men the religious and social principles of the Gospel, by means of a common liturgy and by its juridical and political structure. For several centuries, European culture was entirely a product of Catholicism, with St. Thomas Aquinas (1225?–1274) and Dante as its most representative figures.

Meanwhile, the geographical boundaries of the world were steadily enlarging. In the international rivalry for new routes and the discovery of new lands, a number of Italians, among them Christopher Columbus (1446?–1506) and Amerigo Vespucci (1451–1512), played a major role. As the known world grew larger, men strove to widen their intellectual horizons. This was the aim of humanism, which arose among a small group of Italian scholars, anxious to recover the classical values of Greek and Roman culture, and subsequently spread all over Europe. This movement had leaders in every country of western Europe, so that beside the Italian Count Giovanni Pico della Mirandola (1463–1494) we find the Dutch Desiderius Erasmus and the English Sir Thomas More. Humanist ideals were not confined to a small circle; rather, with the assistance of Renaissance art, as exemplified in such figures as Leonardo da Vinci (1452–1519), Michelangelo Buonarroti (1475–1564), Titian (Tiziano Vecelli or Vecellio, c.1480–1576), and Raphael (Raffaello Santi or Sanzio, 1483–1520), they penetrated every social level and left an abiding influence behind them.

Out of the Renaissance came the 17th century scientific development. No name is greater here than that of Galileo Galilei (1564–1642), who discovered planetary orbits, founded modern mechanics, and gallantly defended the Copernican system. Other great Italian scientists were Sanctorius (Santorio Santorio, 1561–1636), a professor of medicine who devised an apparatus for measuring the pulse and a clinical thermometer; Bonaventura Cavalieri (1598?–1647), mathematician who originated the method of indivisibles; Evangelista Torricelli (1608–1647), inventor of the barometer; Marcello Malpighi (1628–1694), founder of microscopic anatomy; and Giovanni Battista Morgagni (1682–1771), founder of pathological anatomy.

It has often been said that Italian culture declined after the 17th century. There is some truth in this statement, if we mean the relative decline brought about by the increase of intellectual effort the world over, and hence a lesser tendency toward monopoly of intellectual achievement on the part of a single nation. It is also true that since the mid-19th century a large portion of scholarly work has depended on collective study and modern apparatus, and so is more easily developed in wealthier countries than Italy. Nevertheless, Italians have made many and outstanding contributions to modern civilization. Italian writers scaled new intellectual heights with the profound philosophy of Benedetto Croce (1866–) and the literary relativism of Luigi Pirandello (1867–1936). Their accomplishments are matched in the field of science by the pioneer work in electricity of Luigi or Aloisio Galvani (1737–1798) and Count Alessandro Volta (1745-1827), inventor of the voltaic pile; by the application of electricity to power production of Antonio Pacinotti (1841–1912), inventor of the dynamo with ring winding, and Galileo Ferraris (1847–1897), who discovered the principle of the rotary magnetic field; by the development of wireless communications of Marchese Guglielmo Marconi (1874–1937); and by the work in atomic energy of Enrico Fermi (1901–). See also sections on *The Arts; Literature; Science.*

Bibliography.—Ripley, W. Z., *The Races of Europe* (New York 1899); Livi, Ridolfo, *Antropometria militare*, 2 vols. (Rome 1896–1905); De Sanctis, Gaetano, *Storia dei romani* (Turin 1907); Beloch, Giulio, *La popolazione del mondo greco-romano* (Milan 1909); Sergi, Giuseppe, *Italia, le origini* (Turin 1919); Pullé, F. L., *Italia, genti e favelle*, 3 vols. (Turin 1927); Ducati, Pericle, *Gli Etruschi* (Rome 1928); Croce, Benedetto, *Storia d'Italia dal 1871 al 1915* (Bari 1928); Volpe, Gioacchino, *L'Italia in cammino*, 2d ed. (Milan 1928); Devoto, Giacomo, *Gli antichi italici* (Florence 1931); Boldrini, Marcello, *Biometria e antropometria* (Milan 1934); Pullé, Giorgio, *Razze e nazioni* (Padova 1939–40); Biasutti, Renato, *Le razze e i popoli della terra* (Turin 1941); Boldrini, Marcello, *Demografia* (Milan 1946); Sforza, Carlo, *Italy and Italians* (New York 1949).

MARCELLO BOLDRINI,
Professor of Statistics, Catholic University of Milan; author, "Statistica, teoria e metodi."

3. HISTORY. The history of Italy extends over more than 2,500 years in an unbroken series of events. It is this continuity which is responsible for the development of one of the most clearly defined of nations. This is true despite the fact that people of diverse origins, belonging to different states, played prominent roles in that history. The Italian nation is thus very old—the oldest in Europe after Greece. As a modern state, however, it is very young, dating only from 1861. The Italian people appear, therefore, both new and ancient.

The complexity of Italian history and the slow development of the Italian nation are due not only to geographical diversity and the presence of a number of ethnic elements, but also to political and social trends. Perhaps no other European country has lived through so many events, been subjected to so much external pressure, suffered so many invasions. In no other country has the ecclesiastical element, ever since the early Middle Ages, assumed such dimensions and become so much a part of civil life. In no other land since antiquity do we find such disparity between cultural background and historical traditions on the one hand, and political efficiency and national independence on the other. The first element ranked high in Italy, sometimes very high, while the second was usually low or nonexistent.

Archaeology and Prehistory.—Traces of the Lower and Middle Paleolithic periods have been found in most parts of Italy except Sicily and Sardinia. The Upper Paleolithic period is represented in the northern, central, and southern parts of the peninsula, and in the islands as well. To this period belong the Grimaldi, Cro-Magnon, and Maiella types of man. The succeeding Neolithic period left evidence of great progress in both the peninsula and the islands. With it came the pastoral arts and the use of pottery. According to some authorities, pottery was introduced into Italy by foreign invaders; according to otners, it resulted from local evolution, possibly as a consequence of foreign influence.

We also find a variety of peoples in this period. Among the ancient Italian peoples of whom we have written evidence, the Ligurians may correspond to the Mediterranean people of the Neolithic period. They seem to have lived, in prehistoric times, in most parts of Italy. They were akin to the Siculi who inhabited Sicily at a later date. Soon, besides polished stone, copper utensils make their appearance, and we reach the Aëneolithic period, or Age of Copper. In addition to artifacts in stone, copper, and bone, this period produced painted pottery of definite artistic merit. Religious practices are further developed; the inhabitants of the peninsula foster trade and begin mining. The decorative arts make progress, and the plastic arts are introduced. Most archaeologists believe that the ethnic groups of the Neolithic period were still present. The well-known Italian historian Gaetano De Sanctis, on the other hand, assigns the beginning of the Aëneolithic period to the influx of an Indo-European-speaking people, the Italici. (See also ARCHAEOLOGY; MAN, PREHISTORIC RACES OF; NEOLITHIC PERIOD; PALEOLITHIC PERIOD; STONE AGE.)

During the Aëneolithic period, pile-built lake dwellings called palafitte appeared in northern Italy. They continued to be used through the Bronze Age, though in this period the analogous terramare (pile dwellings found in mounds of marl on swampy land) gained in importance. Although they are derived from the palafitte, they show far greater development and are found grouped in size and numbers which indicate embryonic cities. (See also BRONZE AGE; LAKE DWELLINGS.)

Palafitte and terramare dwellers practiced agriculture and molded new types of pottery. The terramare people cremated their dead instead of burying them as had the previous inhabitants. Both groups are generally identified with the Italici, but De Sanctis believes them Etruscans.

The Iron Age is represented in Italy by various groups of remains. Those of the Villanova civilization (named for a locality near Bologna where a typical burying vault was discovered) are particularly important. They are related to the Hallstatt civilization north of the Alps (see HALLSTATT EPOCH). Traces of the Villanova civilization are found in Emilia, Tuscany, and Umbria; they can be divided into four periods extending from around 1000 B.C. to 600 B.C., or into historic times. The Villanova people, as well as the other inhabitants of northern Italy, practiced cremation during the Iron Age; other groups south of the Piceno River buried their dead. According to general opinion, the Villanovans may have been the ancestors of the Umbrians and represented a second great invasion of Italic-speaking people from north of the Alps, but again De Sanctis dissents. He insists that the Villanovans, because of their affinity with the terramare dwellers, were Etruscans. According to the more generally accepted theory, however, the Etruscans came originally from Asia Minor and landed in small, warlike groups on the Tuscan coast between the 10th and 8th centuries B.C. They proceeded inland and gradually moved north. Greek colonization began in Sicily around the middle of the 8th century (the traditional date is 735 B.C.), displacing earlier Phoenician trading posts on the island. Other Greek colonies were established in southern Italy, which came to be called Magna Graecia (q.v.). Syracuse (modern Siracusa) in Sicily and Taranto in Apulia were the principal Greek cities. Phoenician traders reached Sardinia in the 8th century B.C., and the Phoenician colony of Carthage inherited their trading posts on the island. In the 6th century B.C., the Carthaginians gained possession of the south coast of Sicily. See also CARTHAGE; ETRURIA; PHOENICIA.

The Greek-Etruscan Age.—By the mid-7th century B.C., the ethnic pattern had achieved a certain stability. In the northwest (present day Piedmont, Liguria, and Tuscany north of the Arno) were the Ligures; in Venetia, the Veneti, an Illyrian people. Between the two groups were the Umbrians, representatives of the Osco-Umbrian branch of the Italic-speaking peoples; they extended from north of the Po River down to the Arno. The Etruscans lived between the Arno and the Tiber. East and south of the Tiber, we find first the Sabines, who spoke a language belonging to the Sabellian branch of the Italic subfamily, and then the Latins, chief representatives of the Latinian branch. Around the Apennine region of Abruzzi were other Sabellian peoples, among whom the Samnites played a leading role. From southern Latium to the end of the peninsula lived other Osco-Umbrian- and Sabellian-speaking peoples—Volsci, Aurunci, Campanians, Lucanians, and Bruttii. The Iapyges (Iapygii or Iapygians), another Illyrian people, inhabited southeastern Italy. The coasts of southern Italy and Sicily were populated by Greek colonies. The Phoenicians, and later the Carthaginians, had settled on the southwest coast of Sicily, while the aboriginal Sicani and the Siculi still held the central part of the island. (See also ITALIC LANGUAGES and separate articles on the various peoples.)

The predominant civilizations in the 7th century B.C. were Greek and Etruscan. The civilization of the Siceliots and Italiotes, as the descendants of the Greek colonizers in Sicily and Magna Graecia were called, was similar to that of Greece. The basic political unit was the polis, or city-state; when larger states were organized, they were always federations of cities. The Italiote and Siceliot city-states were established after the monarchial period of Greek history and never had kings. There was a landed aristocracy which generally remained in power until the mid-6th century B.C., when it was challenged by a plutocratic nobility. Sharply divided social classes developed, and commoners fought the aristocracy for legal equality and political influence. As in Greece itself, this struggle favored the rise of tyrants. Greek art, letters, philosophy, and science flourished almost as much among the Italiotes and Siceliots as they did in the homeland. Greek civilization spread to the Etruscans and the Italic-speaking peoples, though its influence was not fundamental. Both groups, and particularly the Etruscans, assimilated external and technical elements far more readily than they did spiritual elements.

In Etruria also the city was the basis of social life. Etruscan cities were governed by kings, appointed for a stated period or for life, and assisted by aristocratic chieftains called lucumones. The cities were grouped in federations, but the bond was a very loose one. The chief of these federations was the league of 12 cities of Etruria proper.

In the case of the Italici, political grouping into cities was far less frequent than among the Etruscans. Groups of villages and rural leagues predominated. In contrast to the Etruscans, businessmen and plain dwellers, the Italici were small farmers and mountaineers.

The Etruscans achieved a great commercial, colonial, maritime, and territorial expansion in the 7th century B.C. From the Po Valley, which they had colonized intensively, they reached down to Campania. Their expansion caused disagreements with both the Greeks and the Latins. The latter united to fight them, and between the end of the 6th century and the middle of the 5th century, Etruscan supremacy declined. The Italic-speaking peoples were able to take greater advantage of this circumstance than the Greeks, who were divided among themselves. Syracuse, which already dominated Sicily and aspired to a leading position in Magna Graecia, came into conflict with the Italiotes, and its tyrant, Dionysius the Elder (r. 405–367 B.C.), formed a temporary alliance with the Lucanians against them. The Campanians, Lucanians, and Bruttii were thus able to extend their territory in southern Italy at the expense of the Greeks. In the north, the Gauls descended from beyond the Alps in the 5th century, conquered the Etruscan cities in the Po Valley, and then penetrated central Italy. (See CELTIC PEOPLES; GAUL.) Toward the middle of the 4th century B.C., Rome began to predominate.

ROMAN ITALY

The Roman era of Italian history may be divided into four main periods: (1) the unification of the peninsula, ending in 272 B.C.; (2) expansion into the Mediterranean, up to the conquest of Greece (146 B.C.); the century of social and political crisis and civil war ending with the Battle of Actium (31 B.C.); the empire, to 476 A.D.

Unification Under Rome.—The pre-eminence of Rome was due to the continuity of a capable political class and to a geographical position which favored commercial expansion. From obscure beginnings, the city gradually increased its power and, during the 5th century B.C., became supreme in Latium. In 390, the Gauls attacked Rome and burned the city, but they were bought off and the raid proved to be only a momentary setback. A tenacious rival was the Samnite confederation, but because of superior political organization, Rome defeated it in a series of three wars (343–341, 326–304, and 298–290 B.C.), and also overcame the Etruscans, Latins, Umbrians, Campanians, and Gauls, who had failed to unite their forces against her. The subjection of the Italic peoples was followed by the defeat of the Italiotes in the Tarentine War (281–272 B.C.), despite the aid which they received from Pyrrhus, king of Epirus, and so the whole of peninsular Italy south of the Pisa-Rimini line was brought under Roman rule. (See also PYRRHUS; SAMNITES.)

Part of the conquered territory was organized into municipalities which retained a certain amount of administrative autonomy, or made into colonies—that is, given to Roman citizens who had settled there. (Some of these Romans kept their citizenship in their new homes; others retained only private rights.) Far wider was the territory of the so-called federated states, which renounced an independent foreign policy and bound themselves to fight for Rome by furnishing military contingents.

The Roman-Italic federation paved the way for Italian national unity. To the military and political bonds were added intermarriage, commerce, and the spread of the Latin language and Roman civilization, which in its turn had been influenced by that of Greece.

Mediterranean Expansion and Cultural Change.—The period of Italian unification was followed by a period of conquest in the Mediterranean, which began with the First Punic War (264–241 B.C.). In the course of this war, the greater part of Sicily was conquered and became, in 241, the first Roman province. Sardinia was acquired in 238, Corsica around 230, and the whole of Sicily in 211. (Meanwhile, in 222, the Gauls in northern Italy were decisively defeated, and Roman colonies were extended to the Alps. By 191, Cisalpine Gaul had become a Roman province.) By 201, the greater part of the Iberian peninsula had been conquered; it was organized into two provinces in 197. (All except the extreme northwest portion was acquired by 133 B.C.) Greece was acquired at the conclusion of the Macedonian Wars (215–205, 200–197, 171–168, and 149–146 B.C.). In 146, the year in which Greece was reduced to the status of a province, the Third Punic War was brought to a conclusion with the destruction of Carthage. The Mediterranean had become a Roman sea. (See also GREECE—*Ancient History and Culture;* PUNIC WARS.)

The initiative and political conduct of these wars were purely Roman; the other states and peoples merely contributed troops. Moreover, the provinces formed of the conquered territory belonged only to the Roman state. Yet the commercial and demographic expansion around the Mediterranean was an Italian as well as a Roman undertaking. The conquest of Cisalpine Gaul was accompanied by the declaration that all territory lying south of the Alps was *ager populi romani* (land of the Roman people). This was a fundamental step in the identification of geographical with political Italy. The transformation of Roman-Italian society accelerated the process of unification.

Until the period of expansion this society had consisted mainly of small farmers who lived a simple and traditional life. The neglect of agriculture during a period of continuous war and the competition of imports from the newly acquired provinces ruined the small owners of the peninsula, and their land was acquired by capitalists and war profiteers. Italian merchant fleets sailed east, competing with the Greek and Asiatic fleets. In agriculture, the transition from small to large ownership brought about the introduction of vineyards and olive groves beside the wheat fields. The economic and social transformation was accompanied by cultural changes. A Roman or Latin literature developed, influenced by Greek literature, but retaining its own character. The major writers were non-Romans from various parts of Italy. The development of Latin literature intensified the spread of Greek culture throughout Italy and helped create a new spiritual unity. Rationalism, individualism, and skepticism took hold of men's minds, undermining the strong but primitive Roman civic sense.

Social and Political Crisis and Civil War.—The agrarian problem which had developed during the period of expansion became acute toward the end of the 2d century B.C. The impoverished middle class demanded part of the public land that had been given to, or had been taken over by, the large landowners. The first effective agrarian laws were enacted. They were sponsored by two tribunes, the brothers Tiberius Sempronius and Gaius Sempronius Gracchus (q.v.), who served in 133 and 123–122 B.C., respectively. Both were defeated in armed strife with the nobility, but their program remained in part. Social problems were interwoven with the political claims of the Italians, who demanded Roman citizenship. The Italians of Osco-Sabellian descent broke their allegiance to Rome under the pressure of economic difficulties, organized an independent federal state, and set up a capital at Corfinium on the Pescara River. They were defeated in the Social War (90–88 B.C.), but Roman citizenship was then extended to all the Italic peoples, and later to all the inhabitants of Italy.

Nevertheless, Rome remained a city-state, not the capital of a national state. This structural defect was remedied in part by the municipalization of Italy, so that the Roman state came to consist of a network of city-states, locally autonomous but directed politically by the government in Rome.

The organization of Italy into municipalities coincided with the period of bitterest internal unrest, with rival groups fighting for power and for social and economic changes. The victorious faction would confiscate the land owned by the losers and distribute it among its own supporters, first choice being given to the soldiers. The army underwent a radical transformation. The earlier casual and unpaid assemblage of well-to-do citizens became a permanent and salaried force made up mostly of poor men, who were given grants of land upon their retirement. It was a potent instrument in the hands of leaders who had as their aim the end of the republic.

The civil wars aligned the *optimates* (the aristocratic-conservative faction) against the *populares* (the democratic-revolutionary party). The former were victorious with Lucius Cornelius Sulla against Gaius Marius and his son and namesake (88–81 B.C.); the latter, with Gaius Julius Caesar against Pompey (Gnaeus Pompeius Magnus) and his sons (49–45 B.C.). This second civil war established Caesar as dictator, at first for 10 years (46), and then for life (44). In March 44, however, he was assassinated, and a third civil war began between those responsible for his death (Decimus Junius Brutus, Marcus Junius Brutus, Gaius Longinus Cassius) and the heirs of his power and program: Mark Antony, Octavius (Caesar's adopted son), and Marcus Aemilius Lepidus, who formed a triumvirate in 43 B.C. In the following year, Mark Antony and Octavius defeated their opponents in the Battle of Philippi (q.v.), but were to fight each other in the fourth and last civil war, which ended with Octavius' victory in the Battle of Actium (q.v.), on Sept. 2, 31 B.C. This date marks the end of the republic and the beginning of the empire. Four years later, Octavius was given the title of Augustus by the Senate. See also biographies of the leading figures.

The Empire.—The advent of the empire made a national life for Italy impossible. From the city-state we pass to the universal state, governed formally by a diarchy (Senate and emperor), but substantially by an absolute monarchy. At its inception, the empire already extended from the Atlantic to the Rhine, and in Asia to the Euphrates, and included the greater part of the north coast of Africa. A provincial nobility grew in size and power beside the Italian nobility. After some resistance on the part of the Romans and Italians, Roman citizenship was extended to many classes of provincials, and in 212 A.D., all free inhabitants, with a few exceptions, were made citizens by the Emperor Caracalla. Italy's economic prosperity, which was at its height at the time of the death of Augustus (14 A.D.), began to decline at the end of the 1st century following the economic revival of the eastern provinces and the development of Gaul and Spain.

The concentration of landed property in the hands of a restricted class of agrarian nobles was accentuated during the 2d century A.D. to the detriment of small farmers and city dwellers. Under the Antonine emperors (Antoninus Pius, r. 138–161, and Marcus Aurelius Antoninus, r. 161–180), Italy's population had already decreased. Industry and commerce declined in Italy in the 2d century, while they flourished in the provinces. Italian merchants were no longer established in the East, while a rapidly growing number of Orientals were found in the West.

The economic depression brought about a decadence of municipal government in Italy. As early as the 2d century, interference by the central government had become more frequent and extensive. Even more rapid was the elimination of the Roman-Italian element from the army. During the 3d century, the soldiers—by then almost entirely provincials or barbarians—wielded all power and made up the greater part of the civil service. This meant that Italians had lost almost all influence in government. The growing despotism of the militaristic monarchy, and the anarchy caused by the competition of the aspirants to the throne put forth by the various armies, resulted in the disappearance of city autonomy. The empire, which had attained the height of its territorial extent and power under Trajan (r. 98–117) and Hadrian (r. 117–138), was diminished by barbarian encroachments.

The temporary restoration of imperial prestige and power which took place during the reigns of Diocletian (r. 284–305) and Constantine I (r. 306–337) represented the definitive tranformation of the imperial republic into an absolutistic, bureaucratic monarchy with a marked theocratic and Oriental character. Italy's distinctive personality within the empire vanished, and she became completely identified with the provinces.

The reign of Diocletian also saw the first division of the empire into eastern and western sections. Although Constantine reunited it in 330, it was again divided in 364, and after a temporary reunion (388–395 A.D.) under Theodosius I, it was permanently divided at his death into the Western Roman Empire and the Eastern Roman or Byzantine Empire with its capital at Constantinople.

In the 4th century the major part of surviving Roman vitality was found in the Catholic Church, which was granted legal status by Constantine's Edict of Milan in 313 A.D., and became the state church under Theodosius (r. 379–395). Bishops acquired great civic importance. The bishop of Rome not only claimed honorary primacy among them, but also effective supremacy in the direction of the church as the successor of St. Peter. Rome won in the religious sphere the importance which she was losing politically.

Early in the 5th century the barbarians, who had already invaded the provinces, attacked Italy. In 402, a Visigoth army led by Alaric was defeated at Pollentia, and in 405 or 406 an army of Alani and other tribes was beaten by Flavius Stilicho at Florence. In 408, Alaric again invaded Italy and two years later sacked Rome. Attila invaded northern Italy in 452, and, in 455, Rome was again sacked, this time by the Vandals under Genseric. In that year, Valentinian III, last of the Theodosian emperors to rule in the West, died. The last two decades of the Western Roman Empire present a rapid succession of impotent emperors (nine in all) dominated by barbarian generals, while some influence was exerted in Italy by the emperor in Constantinople. Finally, in 476 A.D., the barbarian soldiers stationed in Italy, in order to obtain land grants similar to those that had been given to soldiers outside the peninsula, deposed Romulus Augustulus, last Western emperor, and placed one of their own captains, Odoacer (Odovacar or Odovakar), on the throne. See also ALANI; ATTILA; GOTHS; OSTROGOTHS; ROME—*History;* VANDALS; VISIGOTHS.

THE EARLY MIDDLE AGES

With the disintegration of the Western Roman Empire, Italy gradually reassumed a distinctive character. By 476, the empire had been reduced to approximately the territory of Italy. As a result, the terms Roman and Italian were once more identical, as they had been in the late republican period. This did not mean, however, that the Romans had been absorbed by the Italians. Rather it meant that the Italians were Romans—that is, citizens of the empire, or the republic, as it was still called. Italy was still considered part of the empire, not only by the Romans, but also by the barbarian conquerors. Odoacer and his successor Theodoric were legally, and intended to remain, vicars of the Byzantine emperor in Constantinople. The secession which took place in Gaul and Spain, and which was followed by the fusion of the Roman population and the Germanic invaders, giving birth to new nations, did not occur in Italy.

Barbarian Rule and Byzantine Reconquest. —Odoacer was vanquished and killed (493) by Theodoric, king of the Ostrogoths, who were federated with the Eastern Roman Empire. Under both rulers, Roman civil administration remained untouched and was carried on by Romans, according to Roman law, with the participation, under Theodoric, of Gothic elements in both central and local government.

Among the Roman nobility (the large landowning class) a pro-Byzantine tendency persisted, partly because the Ostrogoths were Arians. (See ARIANISM.) It became more marked towards the end of Theodoric's reign (526). The Romans took sides with the empire when Justinian I (r. 527–565) undertook to reconquer Italy. The Gothic War (535–555), conducted by his generals Belisarius (to 548) and Narses, brought about the destruction of the Goths and the devastation of Italy, which thereafter became a Roman province governed from Constantinople.

Because of the state of war caused by the invasion of the Lombards (q.v.) in 568, executive power was vested in the commander in chief of the imperial armies, who served as exarch, or imperial vicar, and had his seat in Ravenna. He was assisted by duces, who held the command of troops in the various districts.

By this time the last remnants of municipal government had disappeared, with the exception of a few cities such as Ravenna and Naples, and city councils had been disbanded. The Roman Senate, which had already been decimated by the Goths during the Gothic War, now disappeared. Now more than ever the bishop became the most important citizen, especialy since the churches were among the largest landowners. In this period, large landownership was extremely important. As the cities declined, the courts within large estates became the centers of economic life.

The imperial reconquest tightened the bonds between Italy and Byzantium, particularly in the religious and cultural fields, spreading Byzantine art. The native element reacted by resisting Justinian's interference in ecclesiastical affairs in the Three Chapters schism (see VIGILIUS), and by organizing at the abbey of Monte Cassino, Benedictine monastic life, which differed widely from that of Eastern monasteries. The Benedictines gained more ground in other parts of western Europe, however, than they did in Italy.

Lombard Invasion and the Division of Italy.—The Byzantine Empire was unable to provide for the defense of Italy, which in 568 was invaded by the Lombards under Alboin. The Lombards did not succeed, despite repeated attempts, in conquering all of the peninsula, whose territorial and political organization was consequently split between a Lombard state ruled from Pavia and the Byzantine province with its capital at Ravenna. Neither state was clearly defined, and they were in turn divided into a great many fragments which were only weakly united. These conditions, and the weakness of the central power, contributed to the development of regionalism, which became characteristic of Italy into modern times.

The Lombard state was headed by a king elected by an assembly of freemen, which was identified with the army. The principle of dynastic continuity had a strong influence in the election. The assembly assisted the king in enacting laws and in making major decisions. Lombard territory was divided into duchies instead of provinces, and these in most cases were based on the administrative districts of the cities. Some border duchies, however, comprised entire provinces. The most important of these were Benevento (q.v.) and Spoleto. The duke was a state official, but he actually enjoyed considerable autonomy and in many cases the succession became hereditary. The weakness of royal power in dealing with the dukes was the principal cause of the fall of the Lombard kingdom. The duchies of Spoleto and Benevento, in particular, almost constituted independent states.

The Romans or Italians were treated at first as tribute-paying half-freemen. Their position gradually improved, however. They came closer to the Lombards, and a process of absorption began, especially after the conversion of the Arian or pagan Lombards to Catholicism. This took place in the late 7th century after a treaty based on the status quo had been negotiated between the Lombard kingdom and the Eastern Empire, in 681.

The division of Byzantine Italy favored the development of local autonomy under the direction of large landowners. The landowners headed local military organizations, which became very important. Among the chief causes of friction between the Roman-Italian people and the Byzantine conquerors were the repeated religious quarrels between Rome and Constantinople, brought about by the emperor's persistent interference in ecclesiastical affairs. The Italian population took the part of the bishop of Rome, or pope, as he had come to be called.

In Rome, the pope gained in power and political influence. Assisted by a number of ecclesiastical and lay councilors, he predominated not only through ecclesiastical primacy, but also through extensive landownership and religious ascendancy as the successor of St. Peter. The devotion to St. Peter, widespread among the peoples of western Europe, was a potent factor in increasing the pope's influence and in maintaining the universal importance of Rome.

A special and singularly fortunate instance of the development of local government under the suzerainty of the empire was the case of Venice —that is, of the inhabitants of Venetia who had fled from the mainland to the lagoon during the invasions and had succeeded in exploiting the natural resources of their new home by trading in fish and salt. In 697, they substituted a doge for the earlier government by tribunes.

Temporal Power and the Carolingian Empire.—A serious conflict between the papacy and the Italians on the one hand, and the Byzantine Empire on the other, developed in the first half of the 8th century. It came about partly because of political and economic factors, but more especially because Emperor Leo III (called the Isaurian, r. 717–741) had determined to abolish the worship of images (see ICONOCLASTS). There was a general rebellion in central Italy, and the Lombard king, Liutprand (r. 712–744), intervened with the intention of eliminating the empire and extending Lombard dominion in Italy. In 728, he captured Ravenna, and later defeated the dukes of Benevento and Spoleto. Pope Gregory II excommunicated the iconoclasts in 731.

With the iconoclastic threat removed, the popes turned to the Frankish kingdom for assistance against the Lombards, availing themselves of the great devotion to St. Peter existing among the Franks and the new Carolingian (Carlovingian) dynasty. The king of the Franks, Pepin (r. 751–768), invaded Italy and subdued the Lombard king Aistulf (r. 749–756), who was threatening Rome, and, in 755, compelled him to turn over the cities he had occupied to Pope Stephen II. The donation of Pepin, as the conquered territory was called, included the Roman duchy, the former Exarchate of Ravenna, and the Pentapolis (the Adriatic cities of Ancona, Fano, Pesaro, Rimini, and Senigallia). It formed the basis of the subsequent temporal power of the papacy. The pope made Pepin patrician of Rome. When King Desiderius (r. 756–774) threatened a new Lombard expansion, Pepin's son Charlemagne (Charles the Great, r. 768–814) invaded Italy, dispossessed the king, and appointed himself king of Lombardy, in 773. In the following year, Charlemagne confirmed Pepin's donation to the pope. The name Kingdom of Italy came into use, replacing that of Kingdom of Lombardy.

The Franks governed the conquered territory in collaboration with the Lombards. They replaced the dukes with counts and established margraves in the larger border states. Franks and Lombards continued to use their own laws, while the Italians and Roman followed Roman law. In central Italy, the Duchy of Spoleto continued to exist as part of the Italian kingdom. The papal domains were under the suzerainty of Charlemagne, who was, like his father, given the title of patrician of Rome. Meanwhile in southern Italy the dukes of Benevento took the title of princes of the Lombards and wavered between Frankish and Byzantine sovereignty. The principalities of Salerno and Capua later separated from Benevento, while the Duchy of Naples remained Byzantine but had an autonomous government. Sicily and Calabria were directly subject to Constantinople. The general picture shows an increase in the number of Italian subdivisions and local distinctions. After 827 the Saracens, who had settled in Sicily, extended their control in southern Italy, even, as in 846, attempting raids on Rome. (The Saracen conquest of Sicily was completed in 878.)

On Christmas Day in the year 800, on the initiative of Pope Leo III, Charlemagne was crowned emperor of the Romans in Rome. A dual conflict was to result, first between emperor and pope, then between Frankish and Byzantine empires. The Frankish empire itself was divided among Charlemagne's three grandsons in 843 by the Treaty of Verdun. (See also CARLOVINGIANS; CHARLES; CHURCH STATES; FRANCE—*History*.)

In the Carolingian period, the Kingdom of Italy was at times governed by a king as imperial vicar, and at times by a king-emperor. Royal-imperial authority was fairly effective until the death of Emperor Louis II (r. 855–875). The quarrels between the French and German Carolingians marked the beginning of the disintegration of imperial power, and the process was accelerated after the deposition of Emperor Charles III (called the Fat), in 887. In this period, feudalism reached its fullest development in Italy. Local lords became masters of their territory. Repeatedly the Italian crown became a bone of contention among warring pretenders who followed one another in rapid succession. In Rome, the local aristocracy gained control early in the 10th century. Power was concentrated in the hands of Theodora, wife of a senator, and her daughter Marozia, who married a Lombard adventurer, Alberic I. This period, called the pornocracy, or rule of profligate women, was brought to a close by Alberic II (r. 932–954), an able ruler who was made prince and senator of the Romans.

In the same period, we find another energetic sovereign in Hugh, count of Arles, who was king of Italy from 926 to 947, ruling jointly with his son, Lothair II, after 931. Hugh was defeated in 945 by Berengar II (r. 950–961), who, in his turn, was first made a vassal and then entirely dispossessed by Otto I, king of Germany (r. 936–973). In 962, Otto was crowned emperor in Rome.

FROM THE ESTABLISHMENT OF THE HOLY ROMAN EMPIRE TO THE COUNTER REFORMATION

The six centuries extending from the coronation of Otto to the Treaty of Cateau-Cambrésis may be divided into three major periods. The first, in which the German emperors, the popes, and the rising Italian cities vied for power, lasted until the early 14th century. It was followed by a 150-year period in which the various Italian principalities at first contended with each other and then reached a state of equilibrium. The third period extended from the French invasion in 1494 to the final establishment of Spanish hegemony in the peninsula in 1559.

The Holy Roman Empire.—The union of the crowns of Germany and Italy with the imperial crown in 962 marked the effective beginning of the Holy Roman Empire of the German Nation.* The elected king of Germany was at once king of Italy and emperor. Although the two kingdoms remained separate, northern and central Italy became an appendage of Germany, and Germans were added to the Lombards and Franks in the Italian governing nobility. In the south, however, an attempt made in 982 to expel the Saracens failed.

Under the first three emperors of the house of Saxony—Otto I (r. 962–973), Otto II (r. 973–983), and Otto III (r. 983–1002)—The Kingdom of Italy remained in quiet subjection to the empire. Rome, in contrast, showed repeated hostility to the emperors and the popes appointed by their orders. Under the last Saxon, Henry II (r. 1002–1024), an anti-German party gained ground in northern Italy as well, and proclaimed Ardoin (Arduin), marquis of Ivrea, king in 1002. His success was short-lived, however, and he was deposed by Henry in 1014.

The first two emperors of the Franconian or Salian dynasty, Conrad II (r. 1024–1039) and Henry III (r. 1039–1056), encountered far greater difficulty than had the Saxons in governing northern Italy. This was particularly true of Milan, where the middle-class citizens, at first in agreement with their bishop and later in opposition to him, showed an independent spirit. In the south, Norman chieftains, who had taken part in local quarrels between Lombard princes and citizens of Apulia and the Byzantine governors, gradually acquired power and defeated expeditions sent by the emperors against them.

In Rome, the papacy, which, after the reign of the Ottos, was once more controlled by the local aristocracy, had lost most of its prestige. In 1046, Emperor Henry III intervened and nominated Clement II, the first of a series of German popes. With Henry's support, Clement and his successors inaugurated reforms for which the religious orders and many leading persons had appealed. In particular, the reform movement fought simony and clerical marriage.

Under Henry IV (r. 1056–1106), the struggle against simony was transformed into a fight against the royal privilege of conferring investitures upon high church officials, a privilege which gave the emperor control over church affairs. In 1075, Pope Gregory VII (Hildebrand, r. 1073–1085) issued a decree against lay investitures. He excommunicated Henry, who, however, by presenting himself of Canossa, was absolved. In 1084, Henry deposed Gregory and was crowned by the antipope Clement III. The investiture question was finally settled in 1122 by the Concordat of Worms, concluded between Emperor Henry V (r. 1106–1125) and Pope Calixtus II (r. 1119–1124). The concordat was a compromise, providing for different methods of episcopal appointment in Germany and Italy. See also GERMANY—*History;* HOLY ROMAN EMPIRE.

The Two Sicilies and the Communes.—During the struggle between the empire and the

* Actually, the designation holy was not used until after 1155, when Frederick I was crowned emperor.

papacy, important changes were taking place in Italy. Southern Italy passed entirely under the domination of the Norman brothers, Robert Guiscard and Roger I of Hauteville. In 1059, the reformist papacy, in order to gain support against the Roman nobility and the emperor, recognized Robert Guiscard as duke of Apulia and Calabria. With the capture of Bari in 1071, he eliminated the last seat of Byzantine power in Italy. Meanwhile, the brothers had begun the conquest of Sicily from the Saracens, and, in 1071, Roger became count of the island. Count Roger II (r. 1105–1154) assumed the title of grand count, and, in 1130, having inherited the Duchy of Calabria and Apulia from his cousin William, united the Norman domains on both sides of the Strait of Messina and was crowned king of the Two Sicilies. In this way, the entire south was united into a single kingdom, which was subtracted from the Byzantine Empire and placed under the suzerainty of the papacy. (See also SICILIES, THE TWO.)

An entirely different development was occurring in northern Italy, with the growth of a number of separate republics, the communes. Despite the disappearance of the Roman municipalities in the 6th century, the cities had preserved an individual life and character, not only as centers of population, but also as episcopal sees and as administrative headquarters of dukes and counts. The development of courts on the estates had hurt them economically, and even more injurious was the growth of feudalism, which concentrated power in the hands of the lords, who lived on their estates, and so deprived the cities of political influence. The city dwellers became to a certain extent the vassals of the feudal lords. Nevertheless, the importance of city bishoprics remained and it grew with the extension of episcopal power, particularly under the Ottos. In greater or less degree, the sovereign privileges of the bishops placed them in charge of the actual government of their cities. Because of the press of ecclesiastical duties, they delegated a good deal of administrative power to lay citizens. After about 850, the cities of northern Italy began to display a certain independence of their bishops, as well as of the feudal lords.

The principal cause of the revival of communal spirit was the development of economic life, and particularly of trade, with a concomitant increase of urban population. Economic revival became general in the 11th century and was intensified in the 12th, partly as a result of the Crusades. Italy, particularly Venice and the Po Valley, became the clearinghouse for trade between the East and central Europe. Currency changed hands in unprecedented amounts, causing a decline in the value of landed property and also facilitating its exchange. Traders and artisans organized *arti*, or guilds, uniting the members of each profession within a city. They exercised a monopoly over the economic life of the cities, and also offered their members protection and social security. The associations of traders, organized in Italy before those of other European countries, became instruments for cooperative investment and the sharing of profits. Out of them developed a number of supplementary business enterprises, including storage facilities, banks, clearinghouses, commercial papers, and the establishment of branches. Together with the merchants and artisans, the small landowners gained in importance. Some were *secondi militi*, or minor nobles, who, while owning small landed estates, lived in town in order to take an active part in industry or commerce.

Out of the free association of these craft and trade guilds, at different times and in different ways, the communes came into being. The commune originated as a private organization, but gradually came to take over part of the administration of the city and so evolved into a public body. It did not at first try to supersede the authority of the bishops or feudal lords, but existed beside them and in active competition with them, limiting and combating their interference by organizing a growing number of individuals and public activities and by endeavoring to bring all the inhabitants of the city and its adjoining territories under its own leadership. In the commune, the Italian people acquired a distinctive and autonomous personality; after centuries they were once more a subject and not an object of history.

Although the communes upheld their authority against alleged ecclesiastical and feudal rights, they did not strive for complete autonomy, or for what we might term state sovereignty or independence from superior authority. The Italian communes recognized the sovereignty of the emperor and king of Italy. We might even say that the communes replaced the great feudal lords in their relationship with the sovereign. In fact, once they had reached maturity, the autonomy of the communes in ordinary times appears to have been complete.

In the first communes, a minority of citizens distinguished by birth, social position, or wealth took charge of the government. The *popolo grasso* (big people), as they came to be called, were mostly minor nobles and rich burghers who rapidly formed a new aristocracy which, besides possessing ready money, had acquired land, thus taking the place of the ancient nobility. Later, the minor artisans and dependents of the larger guilds—the so-called *popolo minuto* (little people)—grew in importance. The contest between the two groups for participation in city government took place through the guilds. Alongside the craft guilds or *arti* were the *societates armorum*, or armed companies, militia based mainly on the sectional divisions of the city, in each of which citizens were organized by a leader for the maintenance of public order and for defense against attack from outside the city.

The supreme governing body in the commune was the assembly of all citizens enjoying political rights: it was called *parlamento, concione*, or *arengo*. The assembly elected magistrates and passed on city bylaws, declarations of war, and peace treaties. More restricted bodies, such as the *consiglio di credenza* (fiduciary council), assisted the city magistrates in an advisory capacity. The magistrates were the administrative and judicial executives, and they commanded the city militia in time of war. In most cities they came to be called consuls, probably in reminiscence of Rome, because the memories of ancient Rome and the consciousness of being its descendants were characteristic elements of the renewed Italian national sense and of the civic pride of the communes. Consuls existed in Pavia in 1084, and in Milan in 1097.

Communal development in northern Italy generally preceded that in central and southern Italy.

Florence had its first consuls in 1138, while in Lucca they had appeared shortly after 1080. Development was even more precocious in the maritime cities of Pisa and Genoa (c. 1000). Venice continued her uninterrupted autonomous development without passing through a feudal period. The old real estate-owning aristocracy was gradually replaced by wealthy merchants. The head of the state was the doge, at first elected and later appointed for life. His power, however, was gradually superseded by the growing influence of the aristocracy.

The commercial expansion of Venice took place mainly in the eastern Mediterranean, through trade with the Byzantine Empire and the Moslems, and later with the Kingdom of Jerusalem and other states founded by the Crusaders. This expansion went hand in hand with the republic's growing naval power and territorial acquisitions. Venice endeavored to dominate the Adriatic and defend it against the Slavic people and the Saracens. To this end, she colonized the coasts of Istria and Dalmatia.

The maritime cities of Campania—Naples and Amalfi—had a similar development, though on a far smaller scale than that of Venice. However, they lost their autonomy after the Norman conquest, a fate which also befell other southern cities, particularly in Apulia, where communal organizations were already well under way. See also CRUSADES; GUILD; REPUBLICS, HISTORY OF; and articles on individual cities.

Conflict Between Communes and Empire; the House of Anjou.—Until the middle of the 12th century the communes encountered little opposition from the empire, which was occupied with dynastic struggles. They did not, therefore, feel the necessity of forming defensive leagues and concentrated on local expansion, which resulted in almost constant conflicts between one city and another. The cities formed counterbalancing alliances for war or for the maintenance of peace.

Emperor Frederick I (called Frederick Barbarossa, r. 1152–1190) of the house of Hohenstaufen or Swabia, having consolidated his power in Germany, resumed, in 1154, the program of the Ottos for the conquest of Italy. In all, he made six expeditions to the peninsula, coming into conflict with the communes in the north, with the papacy in the center, and with the Norman kings —William I (r. 1154–1166) and William II (r. 1166–1189)—in the south. In 1167, the communes formed the Lombard League, which entered into alliance with Pope Alexander III (r. 1159–1181) and William II. Frederick was defeated by the league's army at Legnano, on May 29, 1176. In the following year, he detached the pope from the league by the Treaty of Venice, and in 1183, came to an agreement with the communes at Konstanz (Constance), recognizing their right to local autonomy, but preserving imperial sovereignty. The league was dissolved and lost the opportunity of forming a permanent confederation, as the Swiss cantons were to do in 1291. In the south, the Hohenstaufen dynasty not only made peace but contracted a matrimonial alliance with the Normans. In 1186, Constance of Sicily, heiress of William II, married Frederick's son, Henry VI, who became emperor in 1190 and king of the Two Sicilies in 1194, after he had overcome the forces of King Tancred (r. 1190–1194).

After Henry's early death, in 1197, two contenders—Philip of Swabia (r. 1198–1208; never crowned), leader of the Waiblingen party, and Otto IV of Brunswick (r. 1198–1218; crowned 1209), leader of the Welfs—fought for the imperial crown, and the power of the empire consequently declined. The communes of central Italy were able to take advantage of this situation, and so was Pope Innocent III (r. 1198–1216), who began by favoring Otto and later negotiated with Philip. Innocent was an active politician who aspired to the temporal leadership of the Christian world. He recovered a certain amount of power in Rome, where a commune had been formed in 1143–1144, and renewed papal sovereignty over Umbria and Marche.

In 1210, Innocent excommunicated Otto IV, and in 1212 he secured the election of the son of Henry VI, Frederick II (r. 1212–1250), who had been king of the Two Sicilies since 1198. Exploiting the resources of Sicily, which was ruled by a centralized, despotic government, he attempted to dominate Italy, only to come into conflict with the papacy in 1227, when he was excommunicated. (He was excommunicated for a second time in 1239, and again in 1245.) The Italian cities took sides for or against the empire. The former were Ghibelline (Ital. *Ghibellino,* a corruption of the German Waiblingen); the latter, Guelph or Guelf (Ital. *Guelfo,* from the German Welf family). (See also GUELPHS AND GHIBELLINES.) The Guelphs, led first by Milan and then by Florence, gained supremacy. Frederick died excommunicate, without having triumphed over communal autonomy in northern and central Italy or over the papacy.

An illegitimate son of Frederick II, Manfred, became king of the Two Sicilies (r. 1258–1266) and leader of the Ghibellines. In the absence of imperial power, during the interregnum between Conrad IV (r. 1250–1254) and Rudolf I (r. 1273–1291), Italy's situation was in many ways reminiscent of that existing at the close of the Lombard period, and there was some possibility of finding a national solution. The popes, however, fearing Manfred's power, called Charles of Anjou, brother of King Louis IX of France, to Italy, and in 1266 he was crowned King Charles I of the Two Sicilies. Manfred was defeated and killed at Benevento in 1266, and his young nephew Conradin, the last Swabian, suffered a similar fate, at Tagliacozzo in 1268.

The dominion of the house of Anjou over the entire kingdom of the Two Sicilies was short-lived. Sicily, dissatisfied with the harsh rule of Charles I and with French customs, rebelled in the Sicilian Vespers (q.v.) in 1282, and called upon King Pedro III of Aragon for aid. The French were expelled from the island and the crown of Sicily was joined with that of Aragon. (In 1296, Frederick II, brother of James II of Aragon, became ruler of the separate Kingdom of Sicily.) The Angevins, who remained rulers of the Kingdom of Naples (in 1285, Charles was succeeded by his son Charles II, d. 1309), attempted to reunite the two Sicilies in a series of wars with the Aragonese, but were unsuccessful. (Angevin claims to Sicily were finally abandoned in 1373, by Queen Joanna I of Naples.) They had no greater success in their attempt to consolidate their dominion in Italy as leaders of the Guelphs. They played a major role, however, in thwarting the last imperial attempts to control Italy, undertaken by emperors Henry VII of Luxembourg (r. 1308–1313) and Louis IV of Bavaria (r. 1314–1347), but even in this respect the importance of Florence was greater than theirs. See also SICILIES, THE TWO; and separate biographies of important figures.

The Signories.—At the end of the 13th century, Italy consisted of several hundred states, which included the kingdoms of Naples and Sicily and the Papal States, these in turn being broken up into a number of communes. Tuscany and Lombardy were divided into a large number of communes and a few feudal domains. The leading commune in Tuscany was Florence, followed by Pisa, Siena, and Lucca. In Lombardy, Milan was outstanding, followed by Pavia, Alessandria, Brescia, and Verona. In the west, Piedmont contained a few important feudal domains, such as the Marquisate of Monferrato and the County of Savoy (Savoia; Savoie). The counts of Savoy (dukes after 1416), however, because of their origin and their possessions beyond the Alps, were Burgundians rather than Italians. (See SAVOY, HOUSE OF.) In the east, in Friuli, the patriarch of Aquileia was predominant. In Liguria, Genoa had extended her dominion along the eastern and western Riviera, while in Venetia, Venice had not as yet begun her territorial expansion.

In 1297, with the transformation of the Gran Consiglio (Great Council) into a restricted, hereditary body, Venice became an aristocratic oligarchy. Meanwhile, transformations had taken place in other Italian cities. Around 1200, the communes, which had originated as unions of citizens, tended to break up into opposing groups. The nobles, who had played a leading role in founding the communes, gained in strength as their ranks were increased by country nobles who had come to live in town by necessity or choice, and by the rich burgher families which had attained nobility. The middle class, with its growing prosperity, built up its own organizations (*societates mercatorum*) and demanded participation in city government with its own officials (*consules mercatorum*). There were, therefore, two classes, *milites* (nobles) and *pedites* (commons), which organized and formed two states within the commune. Later, the wealthy burghers (*popolo grasso*) were challenged by the artisans (*popolo minuto*).

The original commune had been governed by a *collegio*, or assembly, which provided a form of proportional representation for the various classes and parties. As the interests of the classes drew further apart, the *collegio* became unable to function. In order to resolve this impasse, an attempt was made to substitute a single executive for the governing body—a magistrate chosen outside and above the parties, the *podestà*. (Florence had its first *podestà* after 1202.) The growing strength of the *pedites* brought about the introduction of another magistrate, the *capitano del popolo*. The *capitano* presided over the *consiglio del popolo* (people's council); the *podestà*, over the *consiglio del commune* (city council). Finally, the leaders of the principal guilds (*priori*) became city magistrates, and in some cities, among them Florence, were the most important.

Local feuds between social groups and rival families were interwoven with quarrels between cities, exiles taking refuge in rival cities, and with the general conflict between papacy and empire. They were consequently classed as Guelph or Ghibelline. Alliances of the two parties formed chains through entire regions, and even from one region to another.

Neither the institution of the *podestà* nor the predominance of the people, which amounted to class dictatorship, sufficed to restore internal balance. A solution was sought through the *signoria*, or signory, which was a similar, but intensified and more permanent, form of government by *podestà*. Milan adopted this system in 1259. In the various cities, the *signore*, or lord, as he was called, became the head of the commune, following election by the popular assembly. Later, popular elections gave way to imperial or pontifical investiture. Republican institutions and magistrates survived for longer or shorter periods but lost both their significance and their autonomy.

The signory, in its fundamental character, in which mercenary armies played an essential part, and in its manner of functioning, was a monarchy. The people were excluded from the government and did not participate in political life. The process of development and political education which the communes had begun was destroyed for centuries to come. The monarchical character of the signory reached its full development when the office of *signore* became hereditary. Although political freedom was lost, the consolidation of the signory did insure order and impartial justice, respecting all parties and social classes. The institution of the signory hastened the grouping of minor cities around the larger centers, a process which had begun in the communal period. In this field also, the signory gave assurance of a greater degree of impartiality between the commune of the capital and those of the aggregated cities. The signory became an agglomeration of communes governed as a state by a single person. In time this personal unity evolved into a closer bond. Local autonomies were gradually replaced by uniform institutions and magistrates common to all, through which the *signore* governed and administered his state. The old elective magistrature was gradually replaced by a uniform and centralized bureaucracy. The signory, therefore, was the first step toward the development of the modern state, not only in the extension of its rule, but also in the organization of its government.

Italian Unity and Communal Civilization.—Progress in internal state unity was not accompanied by a trend toward complete external autonomy. Neither the signories nor the principalities which followed them claimed absolute independence of the empire, nor was any progress made toward national unity. The empire and the papacy were regarded as general directing principles, but they were at the same time too universal and too weak to bring about unity. Federalism, on the other hand, was not developed beyond brief, local enterprises. The number of Italian centers, the interlocking interests, and the physical nature of the country, unsuited as it was for cantonal demarcation, prevented the development of federalism and helped to maintain the fluidity of Italian political life. Italy was too uniform to permit rigid divisions, too varied to adopt a single constitution.

Nevertheless, an Italian national consciousness did exist. There was a historical unity which went beyond the specific internal problems of the various communes. There was also a unity of ethnic inheritance, of language, culture, and family life, and of economic, religious, and political affairs. A closely knit chain bound the life of each city or regional state with that of its neighbors.

This basic national unity became particularly apparent in the uniform and high civilization of communal Italy, especially during the period from the birth of St. Francis of Assisi (1182) to the death of Dante Alighieri (1321). Italy played a leading part, on a level with, or immediately after, that of France, in the revival of European civilization in the 11th century. A product and an instrument of this revival were the universities, with which Italy rivaled France. The University of Paris held first place in theology, the University of Bologna in law. In theology and scholastic philosophy, Italy was second only to France. She made an important contribution to the Western rediscovery of Aristotle (which became all important in medieval philosophy), with the translation from the Greek texts undertaken in Sicily, and the most imposing scholastic synthesis was the work of an Italian Dominican, St. Thomas Aquinas (1225?–1274). Italy accomplished, with Bologna as its center, the resurrection of Roman law through the contribution of a long series of famous scholars. Moreover, canon law, which had papal Rome as its cradle, was studied intensively.

The 12th century saw a new flowering of Latin literature, which no longer seemed the outworn repetition of ancient formulas or the medium of rough transcriptions compiled for immediate use, but the adequate expression of a new moral and intellectual life. It prospered particularly in the historical field. Besides universal chronicles, we find a number of analytical records describing the events in the communes and in contemporary Italy in general. In these works we frequently note a vivid and even politically partial interest in the recorded events. Sometimes they attained real art, revealing the personality of the observer and writer. A masterpiece of this kind is the *Cronica* (1168–1287), by the Franciscan friar Salimbene (Ognibene di Guido d'Adamo, 1221–?1289). In the field of pure literature, Italy was in the lead with the literary studies known as *ars dictandi* (art of composition).

During the first half of the 13th century—later than in other Latin countries because of the greater vitality of the Latin tradition in Italy—the vernacular literature began to appear. Through it the life of the people found direct expression, the obstacle of an erudite language having been removed. In the early days, Italian vernacular was largely a reflection of French models, as is evident in the Provençal-sounding lyrics of the Sicilian school which had been formed at the court of Emperor Frederick II. In Bologna and Tuscany, during the second half of the 13th century, an original lyric—the *dolce stil nuovo*—came to be used. It was finished and powerful, and was used even by the youthful Dante. The sacred *lauda* (hymn of praise) had a more popular character and was fostered by the contemporary religious movement. It gave birth to the dramatic *lauda* and to the religious drama in the vernacular.

After 1300, Italy made such rapid progress in the field of culture as to stand in the forefront of Europe during the late Middle Ages. Italian culture of the *trecento* (14th century), while still imbued with the medieval spirit, had a distinctly lay character, both in its content and in the men who created it. It was actually the first great lay culture since the decline of the Roman Empire. This aspect, as well as the renewed interest in classical culture, made the Italian *trecento* a forerunner of the Renaissance. Almost contemporaneously, Tuscany gave birth to three giants of the new European culture. Dante Alighieri (1265–1321) gave in the *Divina Commedia* the most powerful synthesis of the Middle Ages, at a stroke raising the level of the Italian vernacular to the height of classical Latin literature, and by far surpassing all contemporary Romance literature. Petrarch (Francesco Petrarca, 1304–1374) in *Il Canzoniere* transformed the Provençal lyric and the *dolce stil nuovo* into a fine and powerful instrument of psychological analysis and made it an expression of a very personal sensitivity. In his Latin works, by promoting classical culture, he originated a historical and aesthetic understanding of the age, which was no longer medieval but modern. Giovanni Boccaccio (1313–1375) in the 100 tales of the *Decameron* created an entire world observed in everyday life, and originated the classic-sounding Italian prose, with its involved but harmonious and majestic periods. (See also sections on *Language* and *Literature.*)

Romanesque art, which was one of the major manifestations of Europe's new spiritual life, had one of its creative centers in Italy around 1100, although there it was tempered by the persistent influence of antiquity. It flourished especially in northern Italy with the so-called Lombard architecture (Sant' Ambrogio in Milan, the cathedral in Modena), and in central and southern Italy (Cathedral of Pisa), where the basilica tradition was strongest. In Venice, St. Mark's combined Byzantine architecture with some Romanesque elements. At the end of the 12th century, lay architecture also flourished in portals, towers (as in Pisa), and communal halls.

From the second half of the 12th century to the first of the 13th century, Romanesque sculpture attained its greatest development in intimate relation with ecclesiastic and lay architecture. Around 1200 we meet the outstanding personality of Benedetto Antelami (fl. 1177–1233), in whose sculpture we find the contained and powerful expression of a profound religious and moral life. During the first half of the 13th century, painting also broke away from Byzantine influence and gave evidence of a fresh and robust expression analogous to contemporary sculpture.

In the middle of the 13th century, Gothic art reached Italy after having flourished for a century in France. In Italy, however, the distinctive character of the Gothic was far less evident. Romanesque structures persisted, and Gothic was used mainly as a decorative adjunct. Italian Romanesque-Gothic architecture, both civil and religious, produced its masterpieces, especially in Tuscany and Umbria. More properly Gothic, but belonging to a far later period, is the Cathedral of Milan. The Gothic style influenced sculpture much more decisively, with Nicola (or Niccolō) Pisano or d'Apulia and his son Giovanni Pisano, and painting with the Sienese school, while the Florentine painter Giotto di Bondone (1276?–?1337)—one of the most originally powerful personalities in all art history—stood apart as a precursor of the Renaissance. Dante and Giotto were the highest manifestations of Italian spiritual life, which had reached its full expansion. (See also section on *The Arts;* GOTHIC ARCHITECTURE; ROMANESQUE ARCHITECTURE.)

Characteristic of Italian art and literature at this period was their close relationship to the civil and religious life of the people. Italian religious life reached its greatest and most original intensity during the period from the 11th to the 14th centuries, in which the revival of lay culture and civilian life was closely associated with ecclesiastical life and tradition. This was true despite the conflicts caused by the schismatic and heretical movements of Arnold of Brescia (1100?–1155, q.v.); the Waldenses; the Cathari, who were akin to the Albigenses of France; and the Fraticelli (Little Brothers), an offshoot of the Franciscans; and the stern repression of these movements by the church in the Inquisition (founded by Pope Innocent III around 1203). The principal instruments of this spiritual unity were St. Francis of Assisi (1182–1226), a highly original religious personality whose European-wide influence lasted for centuries, and the Franciscan movement. This movement was regularized by Honorius III in 1223, through the founding of the Franciscan Order, which collaborated with the other mendicant order, the Dominicans or Preaching Friars, founded in 1215 by the Spaniard St. Dominic (1170–1221), and also widespread in Italy. The Franciscan Order was harassed for more than a century by internal quarrels between different tendencies, some of which—such as the Fraticelli movement—brought it into conflict with the church. See also ALBIGENSES; CATHARI; DOMINICANS; FRANCISCANS; WALDENSES.

The Principalities and the Equilibrium Policy.—Following the fruitless attempt, in 1327–1330, of Louis IV to control Italy, the emperors practically abandoned the country. (Frederick III [r. 1440–1493] was the last emperor to be crowned in Rome by the pope, in 1452.) The papacy continued to be active in Italian politics, but first the popes' absence from Rome during the Avignon period (the so-called Babylonian captivity) from 1309 to 1377, and then the Western Schism (1378–1417), which set up a pope in Avignon against the pope in Rome, deprived their actions of effectiveness. (See also PAPACY.) Moreover, the Kingdom of Naples, following the death of Robert of Anjou (r. 1309–1343), ceased to have any guiding influence, while the Kingdom of Sicily stood apart and, upon the death of Frederick III (r. 1355–1377), became a dependency of Aragon (in 1409 it was joined to that kingdom).

From the mid-14th century, therefore, local influences were predominant in Italy. Naples and Sicily fought one another and were torn by internal strife, and in the Papal States, despite temporary reforms, the anarchy of local communal and feudal governments persisted. Between 1347 and 1354, there was an unsuccessful revolution against aristocratic power in Rome, led by Cola di Rienzi, who was killed by his opponents. The Florentine commune dominated Tuscany, while in Lombardy the Visconti (q.v.), lords of Milan after 1311, were able, in 1387, to overthrow the Scaligeri (della Scala) family, which had ruled Verona from 1260. Coalitions were formed against the Visconti, in which Florence and the popes joined, but these did not succeed in shaking their supremacy. Gian Galeazzo Visconti (r. 1378–1402), who was appointed hereditary duke by Emperor Wenceslaus in 1395, extended his dominion from Piedmont to Venetia, from Bologna to Pisa, and aspired to the crown of Italy.

After the death of Gian Galeazzo, the Visconti dominion fell apart. In Venetia, their inheritance was taken over by Venice, which had become the most powerful state in the peninsula, constantly tending to increase its territory, though lacking a general Italian policy. The power of the Visconti was reconstructed by Filippo Maria (r. 1412–1447), who was opposed by an alliance of Venice and Florence. For three years after Filippo Maria's death, Milan was a republic and then passed into the hands of a new ducal dynasty headed by Francesco Sforza (r. 1450–1466), who had married Bianca Maria Visconti. (See also SFORZA.)

In the meantime, the power of the papacy was reconstituted by Martin V (r. 1417–1431), who brought to a close the Western Schism, and Naples and Sicily were reunited by Alfonso V of Aragon (Alfonso I of Naples, r. 1443–1458), who drove out the Neapolitan king, René I, duke of Anjou, in 1442. Florence, the most tenacious of the republics, was practically governed by the Medici (q.v.) after 1434, when Cosimo the Elder had with the support of the people defeated the oligarchy of the Albizzi family. Although a number of minor states continued to exist, these three principalities, with Venice and Milan, governed Italy.

During the second half of the 15th century, not without wars and disputes, a system of equilibrium was established among the five Italian powers under the patronage of Lorenzo de' Medici (r. 1469–1492). It was, however, an unstable equilibrium, deriving, as it did, not from a desire to enforce justice and peace, or even from the consciousness of political solidarity, but simply from mutual jealousy and suspicion. Temporary leagues were formed, but no stable and well-constituted federation was organized.

The independence of Italy was also imperfect and precarious. The emperor's nominal authority could always be re-established. Moreover, French control had been extended to Asti, and was often exercised in Genoa as a counterbalance to the domination of the Visconti. The Angevins, whose inheritance passed to the crown of France upon the death of Duke René in 1480, were perpetual pretenders to the Kingdom of Naples. Upon the death of Alfonso I, Naples and Sicily were again separated, Naples passing to his son Ferdinand I (r. 1458–1494), and Sicily being joined once more to Aragon. An Italian national consciousness, which might have opposed such foreign acquisitions, was lacking, particularly since the conquests seemed to have a personal character and the acquired states maintained their own individuality. The art of politics flourished in Italy, and Italian statesmen enjoyed a European reputation for ability and shrewdness. But their ability degenerated into virtuosity and intrigue, and they lacked vision or a direct and tenacious policy. For them, the pursuit of public affairs was a matter of personal interest, a problem of how to maintain and increase their power, and not a national service to be performed as a conscientious duty. Moreover, the various states (except, in part, Venice) were internally weak. They were still largely conglomerations of cities and territories—no longer city-states and not as yet unified modern states. The people, who no longer shared in public life, were estranged and passive.

The Renaissance.—The isolation of the governments from the people, which had developed during the 15th century, was accompanied by a detachment of cultural from social life. The traditional values of the Italian Middle Ages—religion and city—were shaken by the religious and political crisis. Beside these values, which were not forgotten but had lost their hold on popular feeling and were no longer so influential as they had been, we find in the higher levels of culture a development of the individual, freed from the bonds of tradition but indifferent to the life of the community, and a pursuit of letters and science for their own sake. This spirit of free inquiry produced the cultural and artistic splendors of the Renaissance, which made of Italy during a century the mistress of arts and civilization of Europe. The political indifference of the age, however, prevented the development of national unity and made it impossible for Italy to withstand renewed foreign aggression.

Besides this change of point of view, there was in the 15th century a notable increase in the study of the authors of classical antiquity, a movement that has properly been termed humanism (q.v.). It meant research into original texts, correction of translations, and critical editions. Extremely important was the revival of Greek studies brought about by learned Byzantines—such men as Manuel Chrysoloras (1355?–1415) and Johannes Argyropoulos (1416?–?1486)—who had settled in Italy, and by their pupils. Together with the study of the classics, an original humanist literature developed in which Latin was no longer the medieval tongue modified by the use of vernacular, but became an art Latin claiming to be the original tongue of classical antiquity.

Italian literature, neglected during the 15th century in favor of Latin, rose to new heights at the beginning of the 16th century. It attained European fame and influence with the chivalresque poem *Orlando Furioso* by Lodovico Ariosto (1474–1533), which was followed by the epic poem *Gerusalemme Liberata* by Torquato Tasso (1544–1595); with the Petrarchan lyric school of Pietro Bembo (1470–1547); with the new classical school of comedy and tragedy; with the prose featuring ample and harmonious periods in oratory; with didactic writing (*Il Cortegiano* by Baldassare Castiglione, 1478–1529); and with political history. (See also section on *Literature.*)

The splendor and European influence of the Renaissance in the field of arts was as great or greater than it was in letters, with the Florentine, Venetian, and Lombard-Roman schools of painting and sculpture; with the new architectural styles of Filippo Brunelleschi (1377?–1446), Bramante (real name Donato d'Agnolo, 1444–1514), and their successors, who ingeniously renewed the ancient forms; and with the great and many-sided personalities of Leonardo da Vinci (1452–1519), Raphael (Raffaello Santi or Sanzio, 1483–1520), and Michelangelo Buonarroti (1475–1564). The Italian Renaissance created modern art and transmitted it to the other countries of western Europe. (See also section on *The Arts.*)

Modern science also received its first impetus from the Renaissance. The direct study of classical texts and insatiable curiosity seeking new paths led thinkers to shake off in science, or in natural philosophy, as it was called, the Aristotelian yoke. Scholastic philosophy, which had placed ancient thought at the service of faith, was replaced by the direct study, as an end in itself, of ancient authors, especially Plato and Aristotle. The result was a far freer and more intrepid philosophical thought, nourished by rationalism, which often neglected dogma and sometimes questioned it. (See also section on *Science.*)

Modern political history was also born in Italy, with Niccolò Machiavelli (1469–1527), author of *Il Principe,* and Francesco Guicciardini (1483–1540), who wrote *Storia d'Italia.* Philology and erudition had their masters in the humanists Piero Vettori (1499–1583) and Carlo Sigonio (1524–1584).

The French and Spanish Invasions.—At the end of the 15th century, a divided Italy faced a united France and a united Spain, both of which wanted to increase their power by territorial acquisitions in the peninsula. The Italian principalities, instead of forming a union against foreign invasion, were drawn into the contest between France and Spain and sided with one or the other. France aspired to the Kingdom of Naples because of the Angevin inheritance, and to the Duchy of Milan because the duke of Orléans, the future King Louis XII (r. 1498–1515), was the grandson of Valentina Visconti, daughter of Duke Gian Galeazzo. Spain, already in possession of Sicily through the union of Aragon and Castile, opposed both French objectives.

The struggle began in 1494, with the invasion of the peninsula by King Charles VIII of France (r. 1483–1498), and ended with a Spanish triumph after Charles I, king of Spain (r. 1516–1556) and elected Holy Roman emperor as Charles V (r. 1519–1556), had defeated his rival Francis I, king of France (r. 1515–1547), and was crowned king of Italy by Pope Clement VII (Giulio de' Medici), in 1530. Empire and papacy were reconciled, after so many quarrels, over the body of Italian independence. The reconciliation was further confirmed by the final downfall of the Florentine republic (it had been restored in 1494, replaced by the Medici again in 1512, and renewed in 1527) in 1530, and the installation by the imperial armies of Alessandro de' Medici, a cousin of the pope, as duke in 1531. (His successor, Cosimo I [r. 1537–1574] was made grand duke of Tuscany in 1569.) The popes thereafter renounced the struggle for political supremacy in Italy, being satisfied with the Papal States, which the emperors, in their turn, fully recognized. The latter did not, however, exercise direct control over Italy, but renewed imperial sovereignty in the territory which had been the Kingdom of Italy. Empire and papacy, the supreme powers of the medieval world, which had lost all authority in the political field in matters which concerned western Europe, in Italy won out over local autonomies and the independent Italian states. With their victory, foreign domination was definitely established in the peninsula.

The two major contested principalities, the Kingdom of Naples and the Duchy of Milan, both passed to the king of Spain, who received the investiture for the first from the papacy, in 1504, and the second as a fief from the empire, in 1556. (Spain had controlled Milan since 1535, when Francesco II, the last Sforza duke, died.) Further French attempts against Spain by Francis and by Henry II (r. 1547–1559) failed. The Treaty of Cateau-Cambrésis (1559) sealed Spanish control of Italy. (In addition to the possessions already mentioned, Sardinia had been Aragonese since the end of the 13th century, and the State of the Presidii, an enclave in Tuscany, was now under Spanish control.) France abandoned all her Italian acquisitions. See also FRANCE—*History;* SPAIN—*History;* biographies of important figures.

FROM THE COUNTER REFORMATION TO THE FRENCH REVOLUTION

The Counter Reformation and the 17th Century.—The Italian states which came under Spanish control in the 16th century retained separate administrations, preserving a formal individuality and local institutions. None of them, however, constituted an organic whole with powers derived from the will of the people. In the main, they represented class interests in conflict with one another. For this reason, they tended to favor the supreme foreign authority, which was largely absolute and met with little or no opposition. Such revolts as that of Masaniello (properly Tommaso Aniello) in Naples in 1647, and others in Palermo and Messina (1670) were inconsequential episodes.

Spanish hegemony in the peninsula encountered very little opposition from the Republic of Venice, the Papal States, or the Grand Duchy of Tuscany, all of which followed a neutral policy. The Duchy of Savoy, however, reconstituted after Cateau-Cambrésis by Emmanuel Philibert (r. 1553–1580), pursued an active policy with both France and Spain, endeavoring to extend its domains in Monferrato, Lombardy, and Liguria, as well as in France and Switzerland. Its success for the moment was limited, but Savoy eventually became the major independent power in Italy. (See also SARDINIAN MONARCHY; SAVOY, HOUSE OF.)

In all of these states, the passage from feudal to absolute government was smoothly accomplished. The most perfect despotism was probably that of the Republic of Venice, in which the oligarchy became increasingly restricted and rigid (Council of Ten; state inquisitors). The weakest was the papal power.

Religious absolutism went hand in hand with political despotism. The ideas of the Protestant Reformation at first spread widely in Italy, but they were soon crushed by the papacy, supported by the various governments, with the Inquisition or Holy Office (made universal in 1542) as its principal instrument. In 1559, the Inquisition was supplemented by the first index of forbidden books. The Catholic Counter Reformation, codified during the Council of Trent (Trento, 1545–1563), had its headquarters in Italy, with the papacy, the Jesuit Order (founded in 1534), and other religious orders, and its religious and moral influence permeated the Italian people. (See also COUNTER REFORMATION; JESUITS; REFORMATION; TRENT, COUNCIL OF.)

With the end of the Renaissance and the progress of the Counter Reformation, Italian culture lost the predominant position which it had held in Europe for about 200 years. In the countries beyond the Alps, particularly those of western Europe, new national cultural strains, once they had felt the vivifying influence of the Renaissance, developed autonomously and vigorously. Little by little, with a reversal of roles, they acquired a preponderant influence on Italian culture. This autonomous foreign evolution was noticeable in every field—philosophy, philology, physical and mathematical sciences, natural sciences, letters, and art.

Foreign influence was more evident in Italy in the scientific than in the artistic and literary fields. In philosophy as well as in science, Italy held an important place until the first years of the 17th century, but in the course of that century she fell behind other western European countries. Post-Renaissance Italian literature commanded far less attention than science or philosophy, because there were no names which could compete with the great contemporary French, Spanish, and English writers. In art, on the other hand, Italy, and particularly Rome, was more than ever the land to which men turned for knowledge and inspiration. One and the other, however, were sought from the old masters, the landscape, and the classical ruins to a greater degree than from new artists. Italian painters and sculptors of European reputation became rare: a position of greater eminence was reserved to architecture, which spread widely outside of Italy with the baroque school. A great artist of European influence was the architect and sculptor Giovanni Lorenzo Bernini (1598–1680). (See also section on *The Arts*.)

During the first part of this period, Italy still enjoyed a leading place in scientific philosophy. She contributed to the definite advance from Aristotelian scholastic philosophy, with Bernardino Telesio (1509–1588), Tommaso Campanella (1568–1639), and especially Giordano Bruno (1548?–1600). An even greater impulse was given to modern science by Galileo Galilei (1564–1642), the great physicist and astronomer. But the imprisonment and exile of Campanella, the arrest of Bruno by the Inquisition and his death at the stake, and the retraction forced from Galileo concerning the Copernican system (1633), marked the extinction of independent thought in Italy. The country not only lost its intellectual primacy but dropped from the orbit of productive European culture, limiting itself to pure erudition and scholastic word battles. Modern thought lived and progressed outside of Italy. (See also section on *Science*.)

In the late 15th century, Italy had enjoyed an extraordinary economic prosperity, probably greater than that of any other part of Europe. This condition was altered simultaneously by political events and by geographical discoveries. The road to India, opened with the circumnavigation of Africa by Vasca da Gama, and the discovery of America by Christopher Columbus, transferred the center of world commerce from the Mediterranean to the Atlantic. This was a serious blow to Venice, Genoa, and all of Italy. In the Mediterranean, the predominant position of Venice was endangered and almost destroyed by the Ottoman Empire, which extended from Constantinople to Greece and Egypt. Isolated victories against the Turks, like the Battle of Lepanto (q.v.), in 1571, wrought no change in this situation until the end of the 17th century. The subsequent decadence of the Ottoman Empire was of advantage to Austria and Russia, not to Italy. Besides the Turkish menace, there were in this period raids of Moslem pirates from North Africa against the coasts of southern and central Italy.

18th Century Reformism.—The War of the Spanish Succession (1701–1714) brought to an end Spanish control of Italy. The treaties of Utrecht (1713) and Rastatt (1714) replaced Spain with Austria in Milan and Naples, a change which meant a better government in terms of order and administrative capacity. The duke of Savoy, Victor Amadeus II (r. 1675–1730), increased his territory in Lombardy with the acquisition of Alessandria and Monferrato and also received Sicily with the title of king. In 1720, however, he was forced to cede Sicily to Austria, receiving Sardinia in exchange. Thereafter, the territory of the house of Savoy was called the Kingdom of Sardinia. In 1748, by the Treaty of Aix-La-Chapelle (Aachen), at the close of the War of the Austrian Succession, the territory of the kingdom was extended to include that part of the Duchy of Milan west of the Ticino River. (See also SUCCESSION WARS; UTRECHT, PEACE OF.) Meanwhile, Tuscany passed, upon the extinction of the house of Medici, to Duke Francis of Lorraine (r. 1737–1745), who was married to Maria Theresa of Austria, and upon his death to their son, Leopold I (r. 1745–1790; later Emperor Leopold II). The advent of the house of Habsburg-Lorraine brought greater governmental efficiency to Tuscany. In 1734, the Kingdom of the Two Sicilies was freed from Austrian control and reconstituted as an independent state under a branch of the Spanish Bourbons. The first ruler, Charles IV (r. 1734–1759), upon his accession to the Spanish throne as Charles III, left the kingdom to his son, Ferdinand I (r. 1759–1806; 1815–1825).

These extensive territorial changes did not radically modify the condition of Italy, which remained divided under foreign control and impotent in international affairs. A far greater transformation took place in the internal policy of several of the Italian states. This was a period of governmental reform, led by Austrian Lombardy, Lorrainese Tuscany (with the great figure of Leopold I), and, at some distance, Bourbon Naples. Their reforms were characterized by antifeudalism; administrative and bureaucratic reorganization on a uniform and centralized basis replacing the chaos of legislation, institutions, and strata of customary privileges; anticlericalism, or rather anticurialism (that is, limitation of the power of the church and especially of the pope in favor of the state); religious tolerance and incipient lay policy; and humanitarianism, which was especially manifest in the revision of penal law and in Tuscany went as far as the abolition of capital punishment.

These reforms, like similar ones outside of Italy, were largely the result of the application of the principles of 18th century rationalism. The spread of these principles in Italy, with the consequent spiritual revival of the nation, is the most important trend in this period. It marked the beginning of the Risorgimento (the rebirth of Italy). With this movement, Italy returned to the great, European-wide tradition of the Renaissance.

Italian culture made notable contributions to rationalism in the fields of history (Lodovico Antonio Muratori, 1672–1750; Pietro Giannone, 1676–1748; Giovanni Battista Vico, 1668–1744) and of economics and political science (Cesare Bonesana, marchese di Beccaria, 1735?–?1794; Pietro Verri, 1728–1797; Antonio Genovesi, 1712–1769; Ferdinando Galiani, 1728–1787; Gaetano Filangieri, 1752–1788). As in the first *risorgimento* during the communal age, religious movements had a part in the second. Jansenism and Gallicanism (qq.v.), which were associated in France, by joining with the 17th century Augustinian movement in Italy, emphasized the latter's innate anti-Jesuit character (see AUGUSTINIANS). Gallicanism and Jansenism gave the state a theoretical basis and a moral impulse in jurisdictional discussions with the church. They encouraged hopes and fostered plans for ecclesiastical reforms of not merely political but moral value.

In the reforms undertaken by the governments and promoted by writers and thinkers there was a spirit both of civic progress and of moral and religious awakening. The reforms lacked popular appeal, however, and consequently had no wide national basis. The Italian thinkers of the 18th century reached a far more limited audience in Italy than would have been the case in either France or England. In general, the people remained indifferent and at times even hostile. Moreover, the rulers, who acquired added powers through the reforms, did not face the fundamental problems of which the best minds were already fully conscious—such problems as civil equality, civil and political liberty, constitutionalism, and popular control of, and participation in, government.

Far more effective than the action of the rulers, because of their moral and political inspiration, were the works of a number of Italian writers, particularly Giuseppe Parini (1729–1799) and Vittorio Alfieri (1749–1803). The former, by renewing Italian lyric poetry with his odes, became the interpreter and promoter of civil and moral ideals, and in his satirical poem *Il giorno,* by caricaturing the idle and pretentious nobility of the time, went beyond contemporary political reformism to develop a sense of social justice reflecting a philosophic and Christian consciousness. The latter, in his tragedies and other works, preached the hatred of all tyrannies, the love of liberty, and a sense of personal dignity.

FROM THE FRENCH REVOLUTION TO UNIFICATION

The Revolutionary-Napoleonic Period.— About 1790, the progressive reformism of the Italian governments was halted and there were signs of reaction. The events of the French Revolution, by frightening the rulers, caused the reactionary tendency to become permanent. At the same time, the new ideas influenced a restricted Italian circle, and Jacobin clubs were formed in a number of cities.

In 1792, Victor Amadeus III (r. 1773–1796), king of Sardinia, joined the First Coalition against revolutionary France and promptly lost Nice, Savoy, and part of Piedmont. Four years later, Napoleon Bonaparte, who commanded the French armies in Italy, defeated the Austrians at Millesimo, and the Piedmontese at Mondovi. Victor Amadeus was compelled to cede Savoy and Nice to France and to permit the establishment of French garrisons in the Piedmontese fortresses. Meanwhile, on May 10, 1796, Napoleon won the Battle of Lodi, and shortly thereafter controlled most of Lombardy. A strong movement for liberty, democracy, and unity developed in Lombardy and Emilia and spread to the rest of the peninsula. Under the protection of the French armies, a number of republics were formed—the Ligurian (1796); the Cisalpine (Lombardy and Emilia, 1797); the Roman (1798); and the Parthenopean (Naples, 1799). (See CISALPINE REPUBLIC; PARTHENOPEON REPUBLIC.) A minority of cultivated noblemen and, to a greater extent, the middle class took part in this movement, but the people remained passive, if not hostile. Venice, which had also been transformed into a democratic republic, in 1796, was ceded by France to Austria in exchange for

Lombardy and the Belgian provinces under the terms of the Treaty of Campoformio (1797). In 1799, the French occupied Florence and forced the grand duke of Tuscany, Ferdinand III (r. 1790–1799), to flee.

In 1799, the Austro-Russian armies of the Second Coalition drove the French from Italy. There was a popular as well as a clerical and reactionary movement against the French and the Jacobins, and the latter were massacred in both Piedmont and Naples. The former rulers returned to their thrones. Within two years, however, Napoleon, now first consul of France, was once more in control of the peninsula, and the Treaty of Campoformio was confirmed by the new Treaty of Lunéville (Feb. 9, 1801), which further provided that Tuscany be ceded to Parma. In 1802, Piedmont was annexed to France, and King Charles Emmanuel II (r. 1796–1802) abdicated in favor of his brother, Victor Emmanuel I (r. 1802–1821), whose kingdom was (1799) reduced to the island of Sardinia. (French acquisition of Piedmont was confirmed in 1805 by the Treaty of Pressburg, by which France also received Parma and Tuscany.) In 1802 the Cisalpine Republic was renamed the Italian Republic, and, in 1805, the Kingdom of Italy, comprising Lombardy, Venetia (ceded by Austria under the Treaty of Pressburg), Emilia, and part of central Italy. Napoleon, who had become emperor of France in 1804, was now crowned king of Italy, Eugène de Beauharnais serving as his viceroy. The Ligurian Republic was annexed to France (1805). In 1806, Ferdinand I was driven from Naples by Joseph Bonaparte, who ruled until 1808, when he was succeeded by Joachim Murat. (Sicily continued to be ruled by the Bourbons.) Pope Pius VII (r. 1800–1823), with whom the Italian Republic had concluded a concordat in 1803, was deported from Rome in 1809, and the Papal States (except Marche, which became part of the Kingdom of Italy) were incorporated in France.

The Napoleonic government was a police regime serving an enlightened despotism. Italy was completely dependent upon France and French interests. Representative bodies, where they existed, had a fictitious life; political liberties were nonexistent. The administration of government, however, was almost entirely in the hands of Italians, who accomplished with revolutionary methods what the reformist movement of the 18th century had begun: the disappearance of feudal and economic bonds and of church privileges (*manomorta*, mortmain); the creation of regular and centralized administrations; and the establishment of uniform weights and measures. In addition, public instruction and hygiene were given due attention. With the suppression of customs and tariff barriers, industry and commerce received a new impulse. Great roads were built, public works were fostered, cities were enlarged, and progress was noticeable in industry and agriculture. Of no small importance was the organization of an army of the Kingdom of Italy. Foreigners created the army and commanded it, and it fought almost always for foreign interests. The officers and men were Italian, however, and the army provided them with technical training and gave them a focus of national sentiment. The very name Kingdom of Italy kept this sentiment alive. Nevertheless, the Napoleonic period represented on the whole a spiritual and political retrogression when compared with the ideals of liberty, democracy, and unity of the brief revolutionary years.

Restoration and Risorgimento.—In 1815, after the fall of the Napoleonic empire and the conclusion of the Congress of Vienna, the political and territorial condition of Italy resembled that of 1748, following the Treaty of Aix-La-Chapelle, but it was even less favorable to internal progress or to the development of national independence. The independent republics of Venice and Genoa had disappeared, and the Republic of Lucca was made into a Bourbon duchy under María Luisa of Parma, who served as regent for her son Charles Louis. The other states were reconstituted, the Kingdom of Sardinia receiving Liguria. Lombardy and Venetia were under Austrian control, and Austria became the dominant power in the peninsula, which was regarded as her sphere of influence by the other states in the Holy Alliance. Austrian sovereigns ruled in the Grand Duchy of Tuscany (Ferdinand III, restored in 1814, was succeeded by his son Leopold II, r. 1824–1859); in the Duchy of Modena (Francis IV of Este-Lorraine, who was succeeded by his son Francis V, r. 1846–1859); and in the Duchy of Parma, which, with Piacenza and Guastalla, was given to Marie Louise, wife of Napoleon and daughter of Emperor Francis I of Austria. The Kingdom of the Two Sicilies (Ferdinand returned to Naples in 1815; he was succeeded by his son Francis I, r. 1825–1830), was bound by a treaty to Austria. In Piedmont, the restored Victor Emmanuel I and the ruling class regarded Austria with hostility, or at least with suspicion, but were bound to her in the common conservative interest of opposing liberal movements. This interest also made the other Italian sovereigns dependent upon Austria. The Papal States were reconstituted by Pius VII, who returned from exile. (See also VIENNA, CONGRESS OF; HOLY ALLIANCE.)

The restoration of the old order probably went further in Italy than in any other European country. This was particularly true of Piedmont under Victor Emmanuel I. The Austrian provinces, Tuscany, and Naples preserved to some extent the traditions of 18th century and Napoleonic reformism. In these states also, however, there was a marked retrogression from the Napoleonic period, which had taken Europe by storm, brought new energies to the fore and new classes into public life, and maintained the principle of popular sovereignty in place of divine right. Restoration Italy appears reactionary even in comparison with the period of 18th century reformism. The reforms which had taken place before and during the Napoleonic period were maintained, when they were maintained, only through fear of social disturbances or as instruments of absolutism and as a barrier against further innovations—that is, in a conservative and reactionary spirit.

In contrast to the situation in the 18th century, the distance between the governments and progressive public opinion in restoration Italy was very great. Classical and medieval memories, the tradition of local autonomy, the teachings and the reforms of the 18th century, the recent revolutionary experience, all fostered liberal ideas. National sentiment, pride in the Italian people, who had created ancient Rome, and the present foreign oppression, all helped to increase the desire for independence and to develop the idea of a *risorgimento*, or rebirth. This term had at first merely a literary and cultural significance, but later, after the writings of Vittorio Alfieri, assumed an ethical and political meaning. The conception of governmental unity, for which a united nation offered a solid basis, and to which the Napoleonic Kingdom of Italy had given an initial reality, was among the last to reappear. When it did reappear, it was rather timid and uncertain.

These ideas and sentiments were active in the minds of a chosen few. The nobility—with some exceptions in Lombardy—was largely uninterested, the clergy was almost entirely hostile, and the peasants knew nothing about them. National ideas found sympathy instead in the middle class, which was the most alert and most active part of the population, and which had suffered more than any other group from the reactionary ordinances of the restoration. The bureaucracy was in the hands of noblemen, church officials, and foreigners. Industry and commerce were hampered by customs barriers, weights and measures were no longer uniform, a suspicious vigilance was constantly exercised, and a number of aggravating rules were enforced. The administrative and judicial organizations were insufficient; cultural life was obstructed; and so was every form of activity with which the middle class, which had for some time grown and prospered in Italy, was concerned.

Although the Italian liberals and patriots constituted a minority, it was a larger and more varied one than is generally presumed. From the upper middle class, with a few noblemen, the movement extended rapidly to the artisans. The bravest and most impatient conspired through secret societies. Of the origins, bylaws, and programs of these societies, little is known with certainty. Probably they derived their common origin from Freemasonry, which in the revolutionary and Napoleonic period had spread widely in Italy. Chief among them was the Carbonari (q.v.), which seems to have absorbed others, such as the Guelfi (Guelphs) in Lombardy and Romagna, whose purpose was to promote Italian independence and to form a league among the various states, probably with the pope as president. The Carbonari advocated constitutional government and independence, but spoke neither of a republic nor of unity.

During the 15 years following the restoration, the Italian national movement was intimately connected with similar movements elsewhere in Europe, particularly in France. They all had common memories of the Revolutionary-Napoleonic period. Napoleon, deposed and exiled by the Holy Alliance, became a symbol of liberty. The armies were hotbeds of liberal movements. There was a common public opinion and state of mind in Europe, so that events in one country had immediate repercussions in others.

The revolution which broke out in Spain in January 1820 had its effect in Naples in July of the same year, with the insurrection of soldiers belonging to the Carbonari, led by Guglielmo Pepe, a former general in Murat's army. Ferdinand I granted a constitution, and a Parliament was assembled. Then the king, having left the country, accepted Austrian intervention, which the Congress of the Holy Alliance, meeting at Troppau and Laibach, had approved. Austrian troops easily scattered the constitutionalists (March 1821), and the absolute monarchy was restored.

As the revolution in Naples was ending, another one broke out in Piedmont. Here also the Carbonari had penetrated the army and had become a rallying point for all who were dissatisfied with the restoration. The movement supported the house of Savoy, but wanted Victor Emmanuel to establish a constitutional government and march against Austria, reviving the ancient Savoy aspiration for a union of Lombardy and Piedmont. Agreements had been made with the federalist Lombards and with the Carbonari in Romagna and Marche. The second in line to the throne, Prince Charles Albert of the Savoy-Carignan branch of the family, sympathized with the Carbonari and entered into negotiations with them. The revolution began on March 10. Victor Emmanuel abdicated in favor of his brother Charles Felix (r. 1821–1831). Charles Albert became regent and granted a constitution, but he was disavowed by the new king and left the country. The royal troops, with Austrian aid, defeated the constitutionalists near Novara, on April 8.

Neither the people nor the middle class took part in these revolutions, which were the work of officers and noblemen. Joint plans, organization, common sense, and constancy were lacking. The two movements had, however, demonstrated that ideas of liberty, independence, and even national unity were spreading without encountering great hostility among the majority of the population, and that the rulers alone, without Austrian support, were unable to prevent their success. Insurrections did not take place in Lombardy and Venetia, but the Carbonari conspired actively. Numerous arrests were made, and severe sentences of hard labor in the fortress of Spielberg in Brno (Brünn), Moravia, followed. The moral and material sufferings of the prisoners were revealed to Europe with the publication in 1832 of *Le mie prigioni* by Silvio Pellico; his simple and unembittered little book "was worse for Austria than a lost battle."

The Italian and French Carbonari were in touch with one another. When the latter shared in the successful revolution in Paris, in July 1830, and Louis Philippe had succeeded to the French throne, the Italian patriots, trusting in the principle of nonintervention which had been proclaimed by the new French government, revolted in Modena, Parma, and the Papal States (February 1831). In Bologna, an assembly declared the temporal power of the pope at an end, proclaimed the union of the liberated territory under the name United Italian Provinces, and drew up a provisional constitution. Austria, ignoring French opposition, intervened and reestablished the former governments in March. New revolts later in the year were put down in January 1832. Louis Philippe sent troops to occupy Ancona. (The foreign troops were finally withdrawn in 1838.)

The failure of the revolution in central Italy caused the decline of the Carbonari and its affiliated societies. They were replaced by another secret society, Giovane Italia (Young Italy, q.v.), which was of an entirely different character. It was founded in 1831 by a young Genoese and former member of the Carbonari, Giuseppe Mazzini. He gave the society as its aim an insurrection of all the people of Italy, and as a program the establishment of a united republic, which was to make Italy, in the name of God and the people, the leader of a European revolution for social, religious, and political reconstruction. The Young Europe movement was organized in 1834. The confederated nations of the movement were to serve a united and redeemed humanity, which was to progress toward a divine sublimation. The European importance of the Italian revolution and the unitarian idea, which were closely connected, found in Mazzini, for 40 years, an eloquent and tireless champion. By intimately associating the political program with moral renovation and the mission of serving all humanity, he brought the Italian Risorgimento to its greatest moral height and contributed more than anyone else to lending it universal significance.

Mazzini's propaganda was highly successful at first. Affiliated groups were organized all over Italy, particularly in the Kingdom of Sardinia. Charles Albert (r. 1831–1849), having discovered the diffusion of Giovane Italia in the ranks of the army, undertook very severe measures of repression in 1833. An attempt to invade Savoy from Switzerland, in February 1834, failed, and the movement declined for several years. Around 1840, Mazzini revived the work of Giovane Italia, this time from London, with a center of organization and propaganda in Paris. Other uprisings took place, particularly in Romagna and the Kingdom of the Two Sicilies. The expedition of Attilio and Emilio Bandiera in Calabria, in 1844, ended in their execution and that of their comrades.

The failure of these insurrections favored the development of a moderate liberal party which would endeavor to obtain from the existing governments political reforms and an Italian confederation. It was hoped that these reforms would be the first step toward Italian independence. The latter, the moderates thought, might be obtained at a later date, either through war with Austria, or through an agreement whereby Austria would renounce Lombardy and Venetia in exchange for territorial compensation in eastern Europe. One group of the moderate party, called the Neo-Guelphs, attributed great importance to an agreement with the pope, who they thought should be the head of the proposed confederation. Its most authoritative spokesman, Vincenzo Gioberti, demanded in *Del primato morale e civile degli italiani,* published in 1843, that the moral direction of the national movement be assumed by the papacy. Other distinguished writers among the moderates were Cesare Balbo (*Delle speranze d'Italia,* 1843); Massimo d'Azeglio (*Ultimi casi di Romagna,* 1846); and Niccolò Tommaseo.

The writings of these moderates are part of the general picture of Italian literature during the first half of the 19th century, all or mostly all of which had a patriotic, or at least a moral and civic, character. The romantic movement, which came to Italy by way of Germany and France—and of which the greatest Italian representative was Alessandro Manzoni (1785–1873), author of the *I promessi sposi*—made an essential contribution to patriotic writing. Other writers, democrats and republicans, played an important part in this civic literature. Besides Mazzini, there were Carlo Cattaneo (1801–1869) and Giuseppe Ferrari (1812–1876), who advocated radical liberalism and a federalist, republican organization of Italy. To the political writers and poets like Manzoni, Giovanni Berchet (1783–1851), and Giovanni Prati (1815–1884), we may add historians such as Balbo, Carlo Troya (1784–1858), and Michele Amari (1806–1889), all of whom fostered patriotism by recalling Italy's past. Reviews like *Il Conciliatore* and *Antologia* made use of literature for the same purpose.

This political, historical, and literary production lent to the political movement of the Risorgimento an idealistic foundation such as few political movements have ever had. Only the strength of these spiritual currents can explain the proportions which the Italian popular movement suddenly assumed in 1846–1848, and the fact that after an initial failure it began again and moved rapidly toward its final, overwhelming success. (See also section on *Literature.*)

The election of Pope Pius IX (r. 1846–1878) seemed to favor the success of the liberal-moderate program. The pope proclaimed a broad political amnesty and initiated reforms which were imitated first by Leopold II of Tuscany, and later by Charles Albert. These reforms—greater press freedom and the institution of a civil guard and of administrative and consultative bodies—were accompanied by popular manifestations of great enthusiasm, systematically organized. These manifestations were evidence of the return of the Italian people to public life, from which they had been excluded by centuries of servitude and passivity.

An anti-Bourbon revolution, victorious in Sicily in January 1848, created a strong liberal movement in Naples. On February 10, King Ferdinand II (r. 1830–1859) granted a constitution to his subjects. Similar constitutions were introduced by the rulers of Tuscany (February 17) and Sardinia (March 4), and by the pope (March 14). (In 1847, Tuscany had purchased Lucca from Charles Louis, who had succeeded to the throne of Parma as Duke Charles II upon the death of Marie Louise.) At the same time, the French revolution of February 1848, which replaced the house of Bourbon-Orléans with a republic, spread to Germany, Austria, and Italy. The people of Milan arose in the "five days" (March 18–22) and drove out the Austrians. Venice followed their example and proclaimed a republic on March 22. Charles Albert, on whom the Lombard moderates had called for aid, declared war on Austria on March 23 and adopted the three-colored flag inherited from the revolutionary movements of 1796–1797. Tuscan, Roman, and Neapolitan troops took the field against the Austrians. Lombardy and Venetia voted to unite with Piedmont and to recreate a kingdom of northern Italy.

After a few initial successes, Charles Albert was defeated by the Austrians in the Battle of Custoza (July 23-25), and was obliged to conclude, on August 9, the Armistice of Salasco and withdraw beyond the Ticino River. The other rulers abandoned the cause of national independence. Previously, on April 29, the pope had declared that he could not participate in the war because of his position as the head of all Roman Catholics. This statement pointed up the incompatibility between the positions of head of the church and national sovereign and meant the end of the Neo-Guelph movement. The democratic movement gained the ascendancy, particularly after Pope Pius and Leopold II had left their states (in November 1848 and February 1849, respectively). On Feb. 9, 1849, a constituent assembly proclaimed a republic in Rome, which Tuscany joined. Giuseppe Mazzini was placed at the head of a governing triumvirate, which also included Aurelio Saffi and Carlo Armellini. The Catholic powers—Naples, Spain, Austria, and France—intervened on behalf of the pope. A French army commanded by Gen. Nicolas Oudinot besieged Rome, which, after a heroic resistance led by Giuseppe Garibaldi, was forced to capitulate (June 30). The Austrians re-established papal sovereignty in the provinces of Bologna and Romagna, and in Marche and Umbria. An Austrian garrison was established in the legations, and a French garrison in Rome. On July 17, the pope revoked the constitution. Meanwhile, the dukes of Modena and Parma (Charles II, who had abdicated, was succeeded by Charles III, r. 1849–1854) were restored, and in May 1849, Leopold II was reinstated in Tuscany by the Austrians. (The Tuscan constitution was abolished in 1852.) Ferdinand II abolished the constitution of Naples in 1848, and, in May 1849, reconquered Sicily by bombardments which earned him the name King Bomba.

On March 12, 1849, Charles Albert again declared war on Austria, but was defeated at Novara on March 23 and immediately abdicated in favor of his son, Victor Emmanuel II. The new king made peace with Austria on August 9, but remained faithful to the constitution and to the national cause. Exiled patriots from every part of Italy made Turin, the capital of Piedmont, their meeting place. See also biographies of important figures.

The Unification of Italy.—The federalism of the moderates lost ground after the catastrophes of 1849, and the advocates of a united Italy gained support. Of the two principal groups of Italian patriots, the republican-Mazzinian and the Savoy-monarchist, the latter was less unitarian than the former and was prepared, if necessary, to accept a compromise between federalism and unity. Mazzini, although he did not reject the contribution of the house of Savoy, believed that the secret conspiracies and popular insurrections should be continued. From Lausanne and London he directed his followers in Italy, as in the abortive revolts of Mantova (Mantua) in 1852, and Milan in 1853. Although Mazzini's enterprises all failed, they were not useless to the national cause. They kept alive the spirit of resistance and hatred of Austria, which was aggravated by the repressive government of the Austrian officials, and by such actions as the execution, in 1853, of five patriots, called the martyrs of Belfiore. The Mazzinians also spread the idea of unity and counteracted the propaganda in southern Italy for a separate kingdom under Prince Napoléon Murat, son of Joachim, by means of the expedition of Carlo Pisacane to Sapri, Campania, in 1857. Finally, they offered an excellent means of presenting the national cause to the other countries of Europe.

From November 1852 to July 1859, Count Camillo Benso di Cavour was prime minister of the Kingdom of Sardinia. He believed that progress could be made by constitutional means and that groups of different political tendencies could work together in harmony. Himself the leader of the Right Center wing of the Piedmontese Liberal Party, he formed his government with the support of Urbano Rattazzi, leader of the Left Center. Cavour's was a career of manifold and indefatigable activity. His subtle and resourceful mind was always ready to make the best of every situation and to adapt itself to any circumstance. Before he took office, the ecclesiastical courts had been abolished, and the right of religious bodies to acquire real property had been restricted (April 1850); now, in 1855, all religious orders which were not engaged in preaching or educational and charitable activities were abolished—that is, deprived of their juridical personality. The conservative Catholic element was strongly opposed to these measures, and a conflict with the papacy ensued.

With regard to Italian aspirations, Cavour acted with prudence and adroitness. He made the liberals of the peninsula understand that they must rest their hopes in Piedmont. At the same time, he abstained from provoking Austria. He did, however, react to an Austrian provocation in 1853 by recalling the Piedmontese ambassador. It was Cavour's aim to place Piedmont at the head of the national movement which was endeavoring to form at least a kingdom of northern Italy. But he wanted the initiative to be taken by the government of Piedmont, and thereby assure the preservation of the monarchy and of bourgeois-liberal constitutionalism. He counted on the support of France and Great Britain, and particularly on Napoleon III's interest in Italy. (Mazzini, on the other hand, was bitterly opposed to an alliance with a foreign and illiberal monarch.) In the meantime, Cavour endeavored to take advantage of Piedmont's participation in the Crimean War on the side of the Western powers. Although the Congress of Paris at the close of the war (1856) did not bring Italy tangible results, Piedmontese prestige was increased, relations with France became more intimate, and Russia was approached at a moment in which she was hostile to Austria, which was also losing the support of Prussia.

At this time, a fusion of the monarchists with a majority of the republicans took place through the agency of the Società Nazionale, which was founded in 1857 by Daniele Manin (president of the Venetian Republic in 1848–1849), with the assistance of Giuseppe La Farina and Giorgio Guido Pallavicino-Trivulzio and the secret support of Cavour. The society accepted the house of Savoy on the condition that it favor Italian unity and independence. Garibaldi adhered to its program; Mazzini did not.

In July 1858, Napoleon III and Cavour made a secret agreement at Plombières, which was ratified by a formal treaty in January 1859. It provided that Napoleon would join Piedmont in a war against Austria, that an Upper Italian Kingdom would be formed, and that France would receive Nice and Savoy. War followed (April 29, 1859), and the Austrians were defeated at Magenta (June 4) and Solferino (June 24). In May, there were peaceful revolutions in Tuscany, Parma, and Modena, with the flight of their rulers (Leopold II; Robert, r. 1854–1860; and Francis V), and in June, there were revolts in the legations. Napoleon, frightened by these revolts and by the cost of the war, made a separate armistice with Emperor Francis Joseph of Austria on July 8. The two emperors met at Villafranca on July 11 and agreed that Austria should retain Venetia, but that Lombardy, with the exception of Mantova and Peschiera, should be ceded to France, which would turn it over to Piedmont. The rulers of Tuscany and Modena should return, but without external force. (These terms were confirmed by the Treaty of Zurich, on November 10.) Victor Emmanuel accepted the Austrian retention of Venetia, and Cavour resigned. Meanwhile, assemblies in the three duchies and Romagna had voted for union with Piedmont. Cavour, who returned to office in January, entered into diplomatic negotiations with Napoleon III, with a view to annexing this territory. In March, plebiscites were held in the four areas, all of which voted to join the Kingdom of Sardinia. By way of compensation, Sardinia ceded the provinces of Nice and Savoy to France (Treaty of Turin, March 24), subject to a referendum, which was held in April and resulted in approval of the acquisition of these two areas by France.

From this moment, the making of a united Italy progressed rapidly. The expedition of the One Thousand, headed by Garibaldi, overthrew the Bourbon government in Sicily (May 27, 1860) and Naples (September 7) with the program "Italy and Victor Emmanuel." King Francis II (r. 1859–1861) fled to Gaeta. In order to overcome the last Bourbon resistance, and assume once more the direction of the movement, the Piedmontese government occupied Marche and Umbria (September 1860), detaching them from the Papal States. Following favorable popular referendums in all these states (Naples and Sicily, October 1860; Marche and Umbria, November 1860), Victor Emmanuel II, on March 17, 1861, assumed the title of king of Italy by means of a law voted by the first national Italian Parliament, which met in Turin on February 18.

The collaboration between the Action Party (democratic-republican movement) and the liberal monarchist government of Piedmont was accepted by Mazzini, who set his republican program aside. He intended, however, that the Italian people should be consulted and allowed, freely, directly, and integrally, to choose their form of government; he demanded that a national covenant be drawn up by a constituent assembly. Moreover, the wing of the Action Party which did not follow Mazzini and was grouped around Garibaldi would not wait for the government to take the initiative in liberating Venetia and Rome, and repeatedly acted of its own accord. Out of this situation arose the Battle of Aspromonte (Aug. 29, 1862) between the royal troops and Garibaldi, who wanted to march on Rome. Garibaldi himself was taken prisoner, but was freed by an amnesty on October 5.

On March 27, 1861, Rome had been proclaimed the capital of Italy, on the initiative of Cavour, who also endeavored to have Pope Pius IX renounce temporal power in exchange for full liberty for the church in ecclesiastical affairs, according to the principle of a "free church in a free state," which Cavour believed would mean a renovation of the Catholic world. His efforts having failed, he entered into negotiations with France. Because of his early death (June 6, 1861), the negotiations were continued by others and resulted in the September Convention (Sept. 15, 1864), whereby Italy pledged herself not to attack, or to allow attacks on, the Papal States. France in exchange would withdraw her troops within two years from February 1865. Following the convention, the capital was moved from Turin to Florence (1865). Hopes centered on a Roman insurrection, once the French troops had departed (December 1866), but this did not occur, not even after Garibaldi had almost reached Rome with an army of volunteers in October 1867. Instead, Napoleon III sent back his troops, Garibaldi was defeated at Mentana (November 3), and the French once more garrisoned Rome.

In order to acquire Venetia, the Italian government, encouraged by Napoleon III, entered into an alliance with Prussia against Austria (April 8, 1866). The Austro-Prussian War, which began in June, was entirely successful for the Prussians, while the Italians were defeated by the Austrians on land at Custoza (June 24), and at sea near Lissa (July 20). They resumed the offensive with a considerable army, but were halted by a truce signed between Austria and Prussia (July 26). The Treaty of Vienna (Oct. 3, 1866) sanctioned the cession to Italy of Venetia, which Austria had ceded to France in July. However, the Italian claims to Trentino, Trieste, and Istria had to be abandoned. A plebiscite, held on October 21-22, approved the acquisition of Venetia by an overwhelming majority.

At the beginning of the Franco-Prussian War (July 1870), France began the withdrawal of her garrison from the Rome area, completing the removal of troops by August 19. Urged on by the Left-wing parliamentary parties, and by the Action Party, the Italian government sent an expedition which occupied Rome on September 20. After a plebiscite (overwhelmingly in favor of union with Italy), the annexation of Rome was effected on October 2, and the city became the capital of Italy. The pope's situation was regulated by the Law of Guarantees (May 13, 1871), which gave the pontiff sovereign honors, as well as extraterritorial privileges in the Vatican and Lateran and the summer residence of Castel Gondolfo. A yearly income was assigned to him, and he was to have complete liberty in the exercise of his spiritual ministry. The state renounced all interference in the life of the church, but maintained the exequatur and placet for the destination of ecclesiastical property and the provision of major and minor benefices. The pope did not accept the law, and, considering that he was "placed under hostile domination," shut himself in the Vatican. See also CHURCH STATES; FRANCE—*History;* PEACE TREATIES; biographies of important figures.

MODERN ITALY

The history of modern Italy may be divided into three major periods: the post-Risorgimento period (1870–1919), in which the country was a liberal monarchy; the period of the rise and fall of fascism and World War II (1919–1945); and the postwar period.

The Post-Risorgimento Period.—With the acquisition of Rome, a national and united Italian state had come into being for the first time in history. The new state was a constitutional monarchy. The king was empowered to nominate and remove his ministers, but it became constitutional practice for him to follow the wishes of Parliament in the choice of the prime minister, in the approval of the list of Cabinet ministers submitted by him, and in the retention or dismissal of the Cabinet. Notwithstanding the respect of the crown for parliamentary suggestions, however, Italy did not have a completely parliamentary government of the British type, with a regular two-party alternative, because parties and parliamentary groups in Italy were far more numerous and less clearly defined than in Great Britain. Therefore, the king had more initiative in the choice of a government.

In any case, during the first 10 years after the union of Rome with Italy, the division between Right and Left was in practice definite enough to make the formation of a government fairly simple. The Right was substantially a continuation of the government party created by Cavour. It favored restricted suffrage, with a certain tendency to oligarchy and a diffidence in regard to democracy and the popular masses. It believed in the idea of a strong state directing national political life, though respecting existing laws and individual liberty. The Left represented the fusion or mingling of the groups which had opposed Cavour and his successors. While it supported a constitutional monarchy, it had not lost contact with the extreme and tendentially republican elements and showed on the whole a more popular character and a more democratic tendency than the Right. The Left favored an extension of the suffrage and greater freedom in political manifestations. On the margin of this constitutional Left (led by Urbano Rattazzi from 1870 until his death in 1873, then by Agostino Depretis), more radical and republican elements found their place. The pure or Mazzinian republicans remained outside Parliament (Mazzini himself died in March 1872).

The organization of the new state from 1860 to 1873 was accomplished largely by the Right. In order to insure independence and unity, it favored centralization, excluding not only federalism, but also local autonomy. Municipal and provincial administrative elections were held (city mayors were for a long time appointed by the king), but the elected officials had limited powers, and were under the strict control of the prefects. Difficult and tremendous was the government's task in restoring state finances, developing railroads and other public works, and organizing the army and navy.

This program, whereby Italy with notable speed and efficiency approached the status of other major European states, was continued by the Left, which came into power in March 1876. In the 15-year period between 1876 and 1891, elementary education was made compulsory and free (1877); the suffrage was extended from 600,000 to about 3,000,000 persons; railway conventions were signed (1885); landed property was taxed according to its value; communal and provincial administration was reformed; a new penal code was published (1888); the number of army corps was increased from 10 to 12 (1882); and great battleships were built.

During the first years of the government of the Left, Humbert I succeeded Victor Emmanuel II (d. Jan. 9, 1878), and Pope Pius IX (d. Feb. 7, 1878) was followed by Leo XIII. The latter took a firm stand with regard to temporal power, but his language was more moderate than that of his predecessor and for some years he may even have thought of a reconciliation with the Italian government. In any event, Vatican policy was directed toward the restoration of temporal power, and the support first of Germany and then of France was vainly sought. The Leftists continued substantially the ecclesiastical policy of the Right respecting religious freedom and the pope's spiritual independence. At times, however, they displayed weakness in handling the outbursts of anticlericals, who in turn accused the clericals of provocation. Catholics, on orders from the Vatican, abstained from participation in the political life of Italy.

The Left broke up into various groups which had in part a personal rather than a political character. From 1876 to 1881, Depretis and Benedetto Cairoli governed successively and then formed a Cabinet together; from 1881 to 1887, Depretis remained alone at the head of the government. He introduced a policy known as transformism, which meant the contact and combination in parliamentary majorities and in the Cabinet of elements belonging to the two original parties, although the leadership and the majority of Cabinet appointments remained with the Left, while a section of the Left (especially the so-called Pentarchy, consisting of Cairoli, Giovanni Nicotera, Francesco Crispi, Giuseppe Zanardelli, and Alfredo Baccarini) went into opposition against their former leader.

From the death of Depretis in 1887 until 1896, Crispi was the leading political figure, serving as prime minister in 1887–1891 and 1893–1896, and he continued the policy of transformism. Besides fostering parliamentary expediency, transformism served to unite the conservative elements in defense of the monarchy, for which French influence and the propaganda of the Irredentists for the annexation of Trentino and Trieste (conducted mainly by republicans) were considered dangerous. Against the eventuality of a French attack, Italy concluded, on May 20, 1882, the Triple Alliance (q.v.) with the two authoritarian states of Austria-Hungary and Germany, allied since 1879. The alliance was motivated in part by the French occupation of Tunisia (May 1881), which had a large and prosperous Italian colony.

The alliance was renewed in 1887 (and again in 1891) with better terms for Italy, which received guarantees concerning an eventual French occupation of Tripoli and an Austrian advance in the Balkans. Crispi's foreign policy was pointedly pro-Triplicist, and resulted in tension between France and Italy accompanied by a tariff war. Crispi gave a vigorous impulse to Italian colonial settlement in Eritrea and Italian Somaliland, which were acquired between 1882 and 1890. This African expansion, for which an organic plan and sufficient means were lacking, brought about a conflict with Ethiopia. Italy's defeat at Adua (Adowa) caused Crispi's dismissal (March 1896). He had already been attacked because of his megalomania and his dictatorial and illiberal policy—he dissolved the Socialist Party in 1894—as well as for personal reasons. On Oct. 26, 1896, Italy recognized the independence of Ethiopia by the Treaty of Addis Ababa. (See also ETHIOPIA.)

Under Antonio Starrabba, marchese di Rudini (the leader of the Right, but supported by the Left), an uncertain period followed. It ended with the bread riots of May 1898, which were severely repressed, and in the reactionary policy attempted by the ministry of Luigi Pelloux (1898–1900). Pelloux met resistance from the Extreme Left, and also the Constitutional Left headed by Zanardelli and Giovanni Giolitti.

Following the death of King Humbert I, who was killed by an anarchist on July 29, 1900, the new king, Victor Emmanuel III, called Zanardelli to office (March 1901). This was the beginning of the kingdom's most prosperous period.

The new government adopted a liberal policy in domestic affairs and received extreme Leftist support in Parliament, especially in matters concerning labor organizations. These were allowed to organize and act freely within legal limits, while the government maintained an impartial stand in the conflict between capital and labor. The epidemic of strikes which followed (1901–1902) brought about a better standard of living for the working class, while it did not arrest the full development of Italian economy.

Agriculture flourished following vast land reclamations undertaken through private initiative, production increased, and specialized farming was developed. Income from agriculture advanced from around 3,000,000,000 gold lire in the first years of the kingdom to 8,000,000,000 lire after 1900. The metallurgical industries grew (they were, however, overprotected by tariffs, a matter of serious dispute in the economic field), as did the mechanical and rubber industries, silk production, textiles (from 27,000 looms in 1882 to 78,000 in 1902), sugar refineries, and the production of fertilizers. The electrification of industry made great strides. Joint stock company capital rose from 846,000,000 lire in 1898 to 1,500,000,000 lire in 1903. Foreign trade, which had increased from approximately 2,000,000,000 to 3,000,000,000 lire between 1890 and 1900, reached 5,326,000,000 in 1910. Although the trade balance showed a deficit, this was canceled by the 470,000,000 lire remitted by emigrants and the 450,000,000 lire brought in by foreign tourists (1910 figures). Emigration increased steadily, but a good portion of it was temporary, and the emigrants, in addition to remitting large sums of money, often, especially in the south, returned and invested their savings in land purchases. The budget of 1897–1898 showed the first of a series of surpluses which continued until 1911–1912. The quotations on the public debt rose above par, preparing for the conversion from 4 per cent to 3.75 per cent, which took place in 1906, and for the subsequent conversion to 3.5 per cent. Italian paper money sold at a premium over gold. (See also sections on *The People; Economic Structure and Problems.*)

Economic progress was accompanied by manifold cultural activities. During the second half of the 19th century, literary production was less forceful and original than in the first half, but showed greater variety and was more widely spread, bringing Italy into closer relation with the culture of other European countries. In narrative prose, Giovanni Verga (1840–1922), Antonio Fogazzaro (1842–1911), and Edmondo De Amicis (1846–1908) occupied distinguished places, but the forceful social organism represented by the French novel and even more by the French theater did not have its counterpart in Italy. On the other hand, Italy, as in the past, produced a great isolated personality in the poet Giosuè Carducci (1835–1907), who, besides inheriting the Italian literary tradition, was well versed in foreign philology. Classical in form and conception, his work echoed modern romanticism. Toward the end of the century, the leading place in Italian literature passed to Gabriele D'Annunzio (1863–1938), poet, novelist, and dramatist of European fame and influence. Second to him in influence was Giovanni Pascoli (1855–1912), a poet who, though imperfect in form, echoed new voices celebrating the love of nature and the human soul. The field of philosophical and historical writing was extremely active, capped by the intense and manifold work of Benedetto Croce (1866–). (See also section on *Literature.*)

In the political field, the beginning of the 20th century belonged to Giolitti: he was at the head of the government in 1903–1905, 1906–1909, and 1911–1914. The great majorities which he won in the elections of 1904 and 1909 included the votes of conservatives, liberals, and radicals, so that transformism was again a valid expedient. Giolitti's policy, with all its opportunism, was substantially liberal, but it did not further the formation of organic political parties. The Socialists generally supported his social policy, but declined to take part in the government and split into various factions, among them the revolutionary syndicalists. At the other extreme stood the new Nationalist Party, which was frankly antiliberal and imperialistic. In this period, for the first time, Catholics shared in the country's political life, supporting the moderates in the elections, and in 1909 a few of them entered Parliament. With the electoral reform of 1912, Giolitti introduced almost universal male suffrage, increasing the electorate from about 3,000,000 to more than 8,000,000.

In foreign policy, Italy steered a somewhat different course, beginning with the downfall of the Crispi ministry in 1896. The Triple Alliance was maintained—it was renewed twice, in 1902 and 1912—but merely as a defensive instrument (particularly with regard to Austria), and the friendship of France was sought. According to an agreement signed in December 1900, France renounced any interest in Tripoli, and Italy in turn held France free to act in Morocco. Later, in 1902, France and Italy reached an agreement whereby the two countries would maintain reciprocal neutrality in case of aggression. Meanwhile, Italy endeavored to halt Austrian expansion in the Balkans. Relations with Austria became strained, the Irredentist movement was once more active, and, in October 1909, the Racconigi agreement with Russia was signed (it provided that both countries would endeavor to maintain the status quo in the Balkans, and that Russia would not oppose Italy's attempt to acquire Tripoli). Through the Italo-Turkish War (1911–1912), Italy was able to annex Libya (Tripoli and Cyrenaica).

When World War I began in July 1914, Italy proclaimed her neutrality (August 3), stating that she was not bound by the Triple Alliance because Austria was an aggressor. She did, however, enter into negotiations with Austria in an attempt to obtain some compensation for Austrian acquisitions in the Balkans. When the Austrian concessions in this regard proved insufficient, Italy turned to the Allies and concluded with them the secret Treaty of London (April 26, 1915). On May 3, Italy denounced the Triple Alliance, and, after a crisis caused by the conflict between the supporters of neutrality (including Giolitti) and of intervention—the so-called *giornate di maggio* (May days)—declared war on Austria-Hungary (May 23, 1915). Later, on Aug. 27, 1916, she also declared war on Germany. (See also LONDON, TREATY OF [1915].)

Because of the strategically poor frontier she had inherited from the settlements of 1866, Italy entered the war under difficult conditions, and, in two years, her armies made a net advance of only 10 miles (11 battles of the Isonzo). The Italian Army ended as Russian resistance was collapsing, by sustaining the entire shock of the Austrian Army augmented by German divisions. Defeated at Caporetto (now Kobarid), on Oct. 24–Nov. 5, 1917, the Italians held firm on the Piave, repulsed a new offensive in June 1918, and finally won a substantial victory at Vittorio Veneto (Oct. 24–Nov. 4, 1918) while the Austro-Hungarian empire broke apart. (See also WAR, EUROPEAN—*Italian Campaign*.)

By the Treaty of Saint-Germain (Sept. 10, 1919), Trentino and Alto Adige (South Tirol) were ceded to Italy. Decisions concerning the frontier with the new state of Yugoslavia (then called the Kingdom of the Serbs, Croats, and Slovenes) were the occasion for bitter controversies concerning Istria, the port of Fiume (now Rijeka), and Dalmatia. The Treaty of Rapallo, concluded directly with Yugoslavia on Nov. 12, 1920, gave Italy all of Istria to the natural Alpine frontier, while Yugoslavia received all of Dalmatia except Zara (now Zadar). Fiume, which had been seized in September 1919 by Gabriele D'Annunzio, was made a free state, but on Jan. 27, 1924, by agreement with Yugoslavia, the city was annexed to Italy. In the general settlements decided at the peace conference in Paris, Italy had little influence, she did not receive any mandates over former German colonies, and only some years later received a modest enlargement of her African colonies (Somaliland, 1925; Libya, 1919 and 1935). See also WAR, EUROPEAN—*The Peace Conference of 1919; The Peace Treaties.*

The Rise and Fall of Fascism.—The crisis of May 1915 had put an end to Giolitti's policy of progressive transformism. The war and the disappointments of the peace settlements produced a dangerous state of unrest in Italy, which was aggravated by the propaganda of extremists. The elections of November 1919—the first held with universal male suffrage and proportional representation, and with the last papal ban on Catholic participation lifted—resulted in a victory for the Socialists (156 deputies) and the Populists (Christian Democrats, 101 deputies). The Socialists, who included a wide range of political opinion (the Communists broke away in 1921), supported a series of strikes which culminated in a temporary occupation of industrial plants by the workers (September 1920), and refused to take part in the government though they were the largest party. The Populists, who had attracted a large part of the liberal and conservative votes, followed a middle-of-the-road policy with scant success. New elections, held in May 1921, resulted in 157 seats for the Liberal Center, 108 for the Populists, 123 for the Socialists, 15 for the Communists, and 22 for the Fascists (actually elected in a joint list with the Liberals).

The Fascists, led by a former revolutionary Socialist, Benito Mussolini, found their support in groups without political consciousness, who lacked class feelng and belonged to no political party. They exploited a number of different sentiments and interests, especially the nationalism of the lower middle classes (misled by the nationalistic slogan of a "mutilated" or "betrayed" victory) and the fear of bolshevism on the part of the wealthy. Fascism, aided by the inertia or complicity of the leading classes, fought its opponents with the systematic violence of *squadrismo* (squadrism, or the use of armed groups to silence opponents), and in the end attempted to seize power by the march on Rome (Oct. 28, 1922). This gesture had little consistency and would have failed had not King Victor Emmanuel refused to proclaim martial law, and, on October 28, sent for Mussolini and commissioned him to form a government.

Mussolini at first maintained a show of constitutional government, although broad use was made of pressure, intimidation, and violence. He was granted dictatorial powers, and, in November 1923, forced a new electoral law through Parliament, providing that the party receiving the largest number of votes would be given two thirds of the seats, which the Fascists received after the election of April 1924. After the murder of Giacomo Matteotti secretary of the United Socialist Party and deputy (June 10, 1924), and the passive anti-Fascist reaction called the Aventine secession (whereby the majority of the non-Fascist third of Parliament abstained, protesting the illegality of the regime—their seats were finally declared vacant in 1926), the Fascists, by means of state and party power, broke the opposition of the remaining political parties and organized a totalitarian state. The Chamber of Deputies, which had first been rendered subservient to fascism, was later, in 1938, replaced by the Chamber of Fasci and Corporations, whose members were appointed by the council of the Fascist Party and the National Council of Corporations. Individual liberty was suppressed, justice was made dependent upon political power, party privilege replaced equal rights among citizens, and the national economy was exploited by profiteers. Italian culture was used for party purposes and vitiated by the spread of gross and inconsistent theories in marked contrast to the fundamental humanistic outlook of modern Italy.

The crown was a necessary accomplice in this work of destruction, because it gave fascism a free hand and repeatedly expressed spontaneous approval of Fascist policy. The upper middle class, especially the so-called plutocracy, also offered the regime its support. In addition, fascism was strengthened by the Lateran Treaty (Feb. 11, 1929), and the Concordat of 1929, by which Pope Pius XI and Mussolini settled the Roman question by creating Vatican City, and by the signing of a concordat favorable to the Holy See.

Fascist foreign policy encouraged nationalist and imperialist aspirations. It supported revision of peace treaties, showed hostility to France and to the League of Nations, and defied the latter by invading Ethiopia (Oct. 3, 1935). Sanctions imposed by the League were ineffectual, Ethiopia was conquered, and, on May 9, 1936, Victor Emmanuel assumed the title of emperor of Ethiopia. Following these events, Italy announced her withdrawal from the League of Nations, in December 1937. On April 7, 1939, Italy invaded Albania, which was rapidly conquered, and five days later, Victor Emmanuel became king of Albania. Mussolini had bound himself to Nazi Germany in October 1936 (Rome-Berlin Axis). He was supported by Adolf Hitler in his policy of intervention in support of Gen. Francisco Franco in the Spanish Civil War, and in his turn he supported Hitler in the German annexation of Austria (March 1938) and of the Sudetenland (September 1938), and in the occupation of Bohemia and Moravia (March 1939), and finally he concluded with Germany a defensive and offensive alliance (May 22, 1939).

At the outbreak of World War II, in September 1939, Mussolini proclaimed Italian nonbelligerence. Then, during the invasion of France, on June 10, 1940, he drew Italy into the war against France and Great Britain; on June 22, 1941, against Russia; and, finally, on Dec. 11, 1941, against the United States. After some initial successes in North and East Africa, Italy underwent a series of reverses, on land, with the loss of all her colonies; on the sea, with the destruction of most of her fleet; and in the air. The general discontent among the Italian people against war and fascism brought about a series of strikes and far-reaching conspiracies among old and new political parties, which formed a clandestine anti-Fascist alliance (committees of national liberation).

On July 25, 1943, the king dismissed Mussolini and formed a Cabinet of crown dictatorship led by Marshal Pietro Badoglio. An armistice was concluded with the Allies on September 3, but the Germans, who had been permitted to enter Italy in considerable numbers, took possession of northern and central Italy, and Mussolini organized the Republican Fascist Party (September 15) and proclaimed a "social republic" in the north.

Italy declared war on Germany on Oct. 13, 1943, and was recognized by the Allies as a cobelligerent. She took part in the war with regular armed forces, and, to an even greater extent, with partisan action behind the enemy lines. The fighting continued until April 1945, when the country was entirely liberated.

Postwar Italy.—In the political sphere, a beginning had been made to shift control from military to civilian authorities soon after the liberation of Rome (June 4, 1944). On June 9, Ivanoe Bonomi formed his first Cabinet, a coalition of anti-Fascist parties. Bonomi was replaced on June 17, 1945, by Ferruccio Parri, who resigned on Nov. 24, 1945, as the elections for the Constituent Assembly were approaching. The leader of the Christian Democratic Party, Alcide de Gasperi, then formed his first Cabinet on December 10. From then on, de Gasperi was prime minister as head of a changing team. The principal change occurred on May 31, 1947, when a government was formed without the Communists, who until then had always been represented in the Cabinet. After the elections of April 18, 1948, in which the Christian Democratic Party emerged in control of an absolute majority of the Chamber of Deputies, de Gasperi continued to insist upon a coalition government in which Right-wing Socialists, Liberals, and Republicans were also represented to a certain extent. As the result of a referendum held June 2, 1946, Italy had become a republic. Following the elections, Luigi Einaudi was chosen by Parliament on May 11, 1948, as the first constitutional president of the Italian Republic.

In the field of international relations, the main postwar problem of Italy was that of its adjustment to the conditions created by the peace treaty of Feb. 10, 1947. The treaty involved the surrender of Istria to Yugoslavia, the creation of the Free Territory of Trieste, a few boundary corrections in favor of France, the cession of the Dodecanese Islands to Greece, the renunciation of all titles to the African colonies, and reparation payments to the Soviet Union, Yugoslavia, Greece, Ethiopia, and Albania, totaling $360,000,000. Other clauses severely limited land, naval, and air forces. These provisions were substantially mitigated and in many ways obliterated by subsequent developments which led to Italy's participation in the Marshall Plan (July 1947), in the North Atlantic Pact (April 4, 1949), and the Council of Europe (statute signed May 5, 1949). Owing to the exercise of the veto power by the Soviet Union, Italy had not, by mid-1949, been admitted to the United Nations.

Bibliography.—Bibliographical Material: Two full and organic bibliographies of Italian history are those of Luigi Salvatorelli, *Sommario della storia d'Italia*, 5th ed. (Turin 1948); and the article on the history of Italy in the *Enciclopedia italiana* (Rome 1933). Bibliographies for special periods are found in the works of Pietro Egidi, *La storia medievale* (Rome 1922); Francesco Lemmi, *Il Risorgimento* (Rome 1926); Alberto Maria Ghisalberti, *Introduzione alla storia del Risorgimento* (Rome 1942). For more recent works, see *Rivista Storica Italiana* (Turin 1884–1947; Naples 1948–). For Italian works published since 1939, see *Bibliografia storica nazionale* (Rome, annually since 1942).

Source Material: Large collections of source material are found in Lodovico Antonio Muratori's *Rerum italicarum scriptores* (1723–51), of which a new and revised edition has been in process since 1900 (Città di Castello 1900–16; Bologna 1921–); *Monumenta Germaniae Historica* (Hanover 1826–1939); *Fonti della Storia d'Italia*, for the medieval period (Rome 1890–). Collections of documents for special periods include P. F. Kehr's edition of *Regesta Pontificum Romanorum: Italia Pontificia* (Berlin 1906–); *Relazioni degli ambasciatori veneti al Senato*, published for the 16th century by Eugenio Albèri (Venice 1839–63), and for the 17th century by Niccolò Barozzi and Guglielmo Berchet (Venice 1856–78); *Atti delle assemblee costituzionali italiane dal Medioevo al 1831* (Rome 1924–); *Le assemblee del risorgimento* (Rome 1911–); Giuseppe Mazzini, *Scritti editi ed inediti* (Imola 1906–); Camillo Benso di Cavour, *Carteggi* (Bologna 1926–).

General Works: Lodovico Antonio Muratori's *Annali d'Italia* (Milan 1744–49) was continued by Antonio Coppi for the period 1750–1861 (Rome 1848–67); Isaia Ghiron for the period 1861–70 (Milan 1888–90); and Pietro Vigo for the period 1870–98 (Milan 1908–15). The Milan publishing house of Francesco Vallardi published two general histories of Italy, composed of separate volumes of varying merit written by different authors, the first beginning in 1880 and the second after 1900; a third is in process. See also Luigi Salvatorelli's *Sommario della storia d'Italia*, 5th ed. (Turin 1948).

Prehistory, the Greek-Etruscan Age, and Roman Italy: Schiller, Hermann, *Geschichte der Römischen Kaiserzeit* (Gotha, 1883–87); De Sanctis, Gaetano, *Storia dei Romani*, 4 vols. (Turin 1907–23); Stein, Ernst, *Geschichte des Spätrömischen Reiches* (Vienna 1928); Devoto, Giacomo, *Gli antichi italici* (Florence 1931); Rostovtzeff, M. I., *Social and Economic History of the Roman Empire* (Oxford 1926); Ital. ed. (Florence 1933); Patroni, Giovanni, *La Preistoria*, 2 vols. (Milan 1937); Glotz, Gustave, ed., *Histoire romaine* in *Histoire générale* (Paris 1926–47).

The Early Middle Ages: Gregorovius, F. A., *Der Geschichte der Stadt Rom im Mittelalter* (Stuttgart 1859–72); Ficker, Julius, *Forschungen zur Reichs- und Rechtsgeschichte Italiens*, 4 vols. (Innsbruck 1868–74); Gay, Jules, *L'Italie méridionale et l'Empire byzantin, 867–1071* (Paris 1904); Hauck, Albert, *Kirchengeschichte Deutschlands*, vol. 3 (Leipzig 1906); Romano, Giacinto, *Le dominazioni barbariche in Italia* (Milan 1910); Duchesne, Louis, *Les premiers temps de l'état pontifical*, 3d ed. (Paris 1911); Hartmann, L. M., *Geschichte Italiens im Mittelalter*, 4 vols. (Gotha 1897–1915); 2d ed. in 1 vol. (Gotha 1923); Schipa, Michelangelo, *Il mezzogiorno d'Italia anteriormente alla monarchia* (Bari 1923); Caspar, Erich, *Geschichte des Papsttums*, 2 vols. (Tübingen 1930–33); Hampe, Karl, *Deutsche Kaisergeschichte in der Zeit der Salier und Staufer*, 7th ed. (Leipzig 1937); Salvatorelli, Luigi, *L'Italia medioevale, dalle invasioni barbariche agli inizi del secolo XI* (Milan 1938); Amari, Michele, *Storia dei Musulmani di Sicilia*, rev. ed., 3 vols. (Catania 1933–39); Holtzmann, Robert, *Geschichte der Sächsischen Kaiserzeit* (Munich 1941); Cessi, Roberto, *Storia della Repubblica di Venezia*, 2 vols. (Milan 1945–46).

The Late Middle Ages: Cipolla, Carlo, *Storia delle Signorie italiane dal 1313 al 1530* (Milan 1881); Amari, Michele, *Storia della guerra del Vespro Siciliano*, 9th ed., 3 vols. (Milan 1886); Carabellese, Francesco, *L'Apulia ed il suo comune nell'alto medioevo* (Bari 1905); Chalandon, Ferdinand, *Histoire de la domination normande en Italie et en Sicile*, 2 vols. (Paris 1907); Caggese, Romolo, *Firenze dalla decadenza di Roma al Risorgimento d'Italia*, 3 vols. (Florence 1912–21); Volpe, Gioacchino, *Medioevo italiano* (Florence 1923); Cohn, Willy, *Das Zeitalter der Hohenstaufen in Sizilien* (Breslau 1925); Ottokar, Nicola, *Il Comune di Firenze alla fine del Dugento* (Florence 1926); Bognetti, Gian Piero, *Sulle origini dei comuni rurali nel Medioevo* (Pavia 1927); Davidsohn, Robert, *Geschichte von Florenz*, 4 vols. (Berlin 1896–1927); Salvatorelli, Luigi, *Vita di San Francesco d'Assisi*, 2d ed. (Bari 1928); Caggese, Romolo, *Roberto d'Angiò*, 2 vols. (Florence 1922–30); Croce, Benedetto, *Storia del regno di Napoli*, 2d ed. (Bari 1931); *Il Regno normanno* (Messina 1932); Ottokar, Nicola, "I comuni," *Enciclopedia italiana*, vol. 11 (Rome 1933); Doren, Alfred, *Italienische Wirtschaftsgeschichte* (Jena 1934); Kretschmayr, Heinrich, *Geschichte von Venedig*, 3 vols. (Gotha 1905–34); Scarsella, A. R., *Il Comune dei Consoli*, vols. 2 and 3 of *Storia di Genova* (Genoa 1941–42); Morghen, Raffaello, *Osservazioni critiche sulle eresie medioevali*, Archivio della società romana di Storia patria Monograph No. 67 (Rome 1944); Cessi, Roberto, *Storia della Repubblica di Venezia*, 2 vols. (Milan 1945–46); Sapori, Armando, *Studi di storia economica medioevale*, 2d ed. (Florence 1946).

THE RENAISSANCE AND THE 17TH CENTURY: Galluzzi, J. R., *Istoria del granducato di Toscana sotto il governo della casa Medici*, 5 vols. (Florence 1781); Ricotti, Ercole, *Storia della monarchia piemontese*, 6 vols. (Florence 1861–69); Brosch, Moritz, *Geschichte des Kirchenstaates* (Gotha 1880); Leva, Giuseppe de, *Storia documentata di Carlo V in correlazione all'Italia*, 5 vols. (Venice and Padova 1863–94); Burckhardt, Jakob, *Die Kultur der Renaissance in Italien*, 12th ed., 2 vols. (Basel 1919); Fueter, Eduard, *Geschichte des Europäischen Staatensystems, 1492–1559* (Munich 1919); Pastor von Camperfelden, Ludwig von, *Geschichte der Päpste seit dem Ausgang des Mittelalters*, 16 vols. (Freiburg im Breisgau 1891–1933); Brandi, Karl, *Kaiser Karl V* (Munich 1937); Ettore Rota, ed., *Problemi storici e orientamenti storiografici*: Cantimori, Delio, *La Riforma in Italia;* Chabod, Federico, *Il Rinascimento* (Como 1942).

18TH CENTURY REFORMISM AND THE RISORGIMENTO: Zobi, Antonio, *Storia civile della Toscana, 1737–1848*, 5 vols. (Florence 1850–53); Bianchi, Nicomede, *Storia documentata della diplomazia europea in Italia, 1814–1861*, 8 vols. (Turin 1865–72); Tivaroni, G., *Storia critica del Risorgimento italiano*, 9 vols. (Turin 1888–97); Lemmi, Francesco, *Le origini del Risorgimento italiano, 1748–1815*, 2d ed. (Milan 1924); Salvatorelli, Luigi, *Pensiero e azione del Risorgimento*, 2d ed. (Turin 1944); Spellanzon, Cesare, *Storia del Risorgimento e dell'unità d'Italia*, 5 vols. (Milan 1933–45); Jemolo, A. C., *Chiesa e Stato in Italia negli ultimi cento anni* (Turin 1948).

MODERN ITALY: Croce, Benedetto, *Storia d'Italia, 1871–1915*, 3d ed. (Bari 1928); Salvatorelli, Luigi, *La Triplice Alleanza* (Milan 1939); Bonomi, Ivanoe, *La politica italiana da Porta Pia a Vittorio Veneto* (Turin 1944); Perticone, Giacomo, *La politica italiana nell'ultimo trentennio*, 3 vols. (Rome 1945–47); Barbagallo, Corrado, ed., *Cento anni di vita italiana, 1848–1948*, 2 vols. (Milan 1949).

LUIGI SALVATORELLI,
Author of "A Concise History of Italy."

4. LANGUAGE.

We shall discuss in this article two main questions: how the numerous dialects spoken in modern Italy grew out of Latin, and how the Tuscan dialect took precedence over the others and became the Italian language. First, however, we must set the linguistic boundaries of our inquiry and mention such peripheral variations as the Sardinian and Latin dialects.

Linguistic Boundaries.—The area in which Italian dialects are spoken and standard Italian is the accepted legal and literary language coincides for the most part with the territory of the Italian Republic. The following are the principal exceptions to this general rule.

Non-Italian Areas in Which Italian Dialects are Spoken.—The dialects of Corsica are of the Italian type, but the official language and that taught in the schools is French. The Ligurian dialect, strongly influenced by Provençal, is current in several French border villages and in the principality of Monaco.

In Switzerland, Lombard dialects are spoken, and standard Italian is the official language of the canton of Ticino and the valleys of Mesocco (Mesolcina), Bregaglia, and Poschiavo of the canton of Graubünden (Grisons).

The majority of the people of the Free Territory of Trieste are Italians. Italian dialects of the Venetian and **archaic** Istrian types are spoken in western Istria, which is part of Yugoslavia. Venetian dialects are also spoken by sizable minorities in the cities of Dalmatia and by a small group of Jews on the island of Corfu.

In the Republic of San Marino, dialects of Romagna are spoken, and Italian is of course the official language. Until 1934, Italian was used in the schools and courts of Malta on an equal footing with English, and about one sixth of the people on the island speak Italian. Finally, Italian is used extensively in the former Italian possessions in Africa and by Italian immigrants all over the world.

Italian Areas in Which Non-Italian Dialects Are Spoken.—There are in Italy a number of "peninsulas" (areas contiguous to foreign countries across the Alps) and "islands" where languages other than Italian are spoken. French dialects of the Franco-Provençal and Provençal groups (see PROVENÇAL LANGUAGE) are spoken in approximately 70 communes of Valle d'Aosta and in several valleys of western Piedmont where the Waldenses (q.v.) are established. Mid-14th century Waldensian migrations created two Franco-Provençal villages in the Province of Foggia, in Apulia, and one Provençal village in the Province of Cosenza, in Calabria.

German dialects are spoken by a majority of the people of the Alto Adige (South Tirol), but in some sections there are sizable Italian minorities, and in four valleys Ladin is spoken. Other small German-speaking groups, some of long standing, are scattered along the Alps from Monte Rosa in the west to the Carnic Alps in the east. They include in all no more than 9,000 persons.

There are a few Slovenes in the eastern part of Friuli, and a Croat "island" of three villages in the Province of Campobasso, in Molise. In southern Italy we find 47 Albanian-speaking villages, founded by Albanians who fled across the Adriatic during the wars of Scanderbeg (q.v.) against the Turks in the mid-15th century.

Greek is spoken in 13 villages grouped in two small areas at the extreme southern point of Calabria and near Lecce in Apulia. At Alghero, in Sardinia, the language is Catalan.

Inter-Italian Linguistic Migrations.—At Carloforte, on the tiny island of San Pietro west of Sardinia, a Ligurian dialect is spoken, and several villages in Sicily were founded by Lombards who came south from the valleys of Lago Maggiore between the 11th and 13th centuries.

Sardinian, Ladin, and Dalmatian.—There are two groups of dialects (the last trace of a third disappeared at the end of the 19th century), spoken along the borders of Italy, which without actually belonging to the Italian group are closer to it than they are to any of the other Romance languages.

Sardinian.—The dialects of Logudoro (north central Sardinia) and Campidano (southern Sardinia) have a conservative character all their own. In contrast to Italian, they retain the hard sound of the Latin *c* before *e* and *i*: Latin *decem*, Sardinian *deghe*, Italian *dieci* (ten); Latin *dulcis*, Sardinian *dulke*, Italian *dolce* (sweet). Final *s* is also retained: Latin *tres*, Sardinian *tres*, Italian *tre* (three); Latin *facis*, Sardinian *faghes* (you do or make). The definite article in Sardinian is *su, sa* (plural: *sos, sas*), derived from the Latin *ipse, ipsum* (self). All the other Romance languages except the Catalan spoken in the Balearic Islands have definite articles taken from the Latin *ille, illud* (that). Although Sardinian was formerly used in official papers and is a vehicle in folk literature, it has never been a literary language.

Ladin.—Three groups of Rhaeto-Romanic languages—the first in the Swiss canton of Graubünden; the second in several valleys of the Dolomites in Venezia Tridentina (Val Gardena, Val Badia e Marebbe, Val di Fassa, and Livinallongo); the third covering Friuli around Udine (and formerly Trieste)—were scientifically studied and first described as an independent linguistic unit under the name of Ladin by Graziadio Ascoli (q.v.) in 1873. (Strictly speaking, the name Ladin applies to only one of the Graubünden types.) Other scholars prefer the general term Rhaetian or Rhaeto-Romansh.

Even scholars who maintain that these dialects are a single unit consider their unity to be of a negative or passive kind. They are similar not in the active development of common characteristics, but in their retention of archaic traits and their refusal to accept innovations stemming from Italian dialects. The most widespread characteristic of the Ladin dialects is the palatalization of the *ca* group: as in Latin, *calida;* Ladin *ćauda, ćada, ćoda;* Italian *calda* (warm).

Friuli has a minor literary tradition, and the canton of Graubünden has produced a considerable body of verse and prose since the 16th century. In 1937, Romansh was recognized as a fourth national language by the Swiss Parliament, although it was not admitted to the official status of German, French, and Italian.

Dalmatian.—Dalmatian was spoken in the Middle Ages in the coastal cities of Dalmatia. It has been extinct for a fairly long time—in Dubrovnik (Ragusa), for example, since the end of the 15th century. Antonio Udina, the last man to speak Veglioto, the local Dalmatian dialect of Krk (Veglia), died in 1898.

Latin vowels change in Dalmatian to diphthongs—Latin and Italian *capra,* Veglioto, *kuobra* (goat)—but consonants have been retained. Here, as in Sardinian, *ce* is hard: Latin *cena* (supper), Italian *cena* (palatal), Veglioto *kaina.*

Italian Dialects.—Italian dialects differ more among themselves and from the standard language than those of any other country. So great are the differences that a Piedmontese and a Sicilian who knew only their own dialects would have great difficulty in understanding each other. Despite these differences between the dialects of one end of the peninsula and the other, however, there are very few cases of sharply drawn dividing lines between one dialect and another geographically adjacent to it. Different words and grammatical constructions cover areas which coincide only partially, if at all, with other factors. For these reasons, the classification of Italian dialects is in great part arbitrary and dependent upon nonlinguistic criteria. Keeping this point in mind, we may list the following groups.

Gallo-Italian Dialects.—This group includes dialects belonging to the following subdivisions: Piedmontese, Ligurian, Lombard, and Emilian. Each corresponds roughly to the region of the same name. We say roughly because Lombard, for example, not only includes the dialects of the Swiss canton of Ticino and the three Italian valleys of the canton of Graubünden, but is carried over into the dialects of western Trentino. Moreover, Voghera, Pavia, and Mantova, which belong administratively to Lombardy, have dialects of the Emilian type.

Generally speaking, the Gallo-Italian dialects closely resemble French dialects, particularly those of the Provençal group. Piedmontese, Ligurian, and Lombard have the mixed vowels *ü* and *ö,* while Emilian has only *ü.* They almost all drop final vowels, except for *a*: Latin *septe(m),* dialect *set,* Italian *sette* (seven); Latin *octo,* dialect *ot, vot, öt,* Italian *otto* (eight).

Venetian Dialects.—These dialects fall into three subdivisions: Venetian proper, Trentino, and Istrian. Their lack of mixed vowels and retention of final vowels brings them closer to Tuscan usage than to that of the Gallo-Italian group. On the other hand, Gallo-Italian affinities are seen in the substitution of the voiced for the voiceless stop—as in *séda,* Latin *seta,* Italian *seta* (silk)—in the reduction of a double to a single consonant—*sète,* Latin *septe(m)*; *òto,* Latin *octo*—and in vocabulary.

Tuscan Dialects.—This group has the greatest historical importance, since it became the basis of standard Italian. Cultivated Florentine speech is almost identical with the standard written language, although we may note the recent reduction of the diphthong *uo* to *o*—*bòno, còre,* instead of *buono* (good), *cuore* (heart)—and the aspirate pronunciation of guttural *c*—*amerihano* instead of *americano* (American). The latter does not occur, however, when *c* follows another consonant, as in *barca* (boat) and *panca* (bench). Vernacular Florentine speech has several characteristics of its own. There are also quite a few variations from cultivated Florentine in the popular spoken language of northwestern Tuscany (Lucca, Pisa) and southeastern Tuscany (Siena, Arezzo).

If we compare Tuscan with other Italian dialect groups in regard to its fidelity to Latin, we find it almost always more conservative. It has few peculiar deviations from Latin: let us look, for example, at the changes in the Latin ending *-ariu(m),* as in *Januariu(m)* and *librariu(m).* In northern and southern Italy, except for some later changes, it is pronounced *-aro;* only in Tuscany (and Umbria) do we find *-aio,* as in *gennaio* (January) and *librario* (bookseller).

As might be expected from its geographical position, Tuscan is often midway between northern and southern forms. The definite article, for example, in the north is usually of the *el* type, and in the south of the *lo* or *lu* type. In Tuscan both forms are used, depending upon the noun: *il libro* (the book); and *lo stato* (the state). In northern Italy the past indefinite (*ho fatto,* have done or made) is used rather than the past definite (*feci,* did or made) current in the south, while Tuscan assigns to each a separate use. Such compromises helped to bring about the adoption of Tuscan as the standard language.

Corsican Dialects.—In their modern form, Corsican dialects are very much like Tuscan, but beneath the surface there are traces of an archaic phase in which they must have resembled Sardinian. The dialects of northern Sardinia, both the Sassari type and that of Gallura, are closely akin to the Corsican.

Central Italian Dialects.—The dialects of northern Latium, Umbria, and Marche form a compact group in which characteristics of the south are visible. (This is particularly true of the central region around Ancona, since Pesaro is closer to the Emilian dialect, and Ascoli to the Abruzzan.) Over a wide area a distinction is made between Latin endings in *o* and *u*.

Southern Dialects.—These include the dialects of southern Latium, Abruzzi, Campania, Calabria, Apulia, and Sicily. Throughout this area and in part of central Italy, we find Latin *nd* changed into *nn* (Latin and Italian *quando,* dialect *quannë,* when) and *mb* into *mm* (Vulgar Latin *camba,* Italian *gamba,* dialect *gamma,* leg). Somewhat restricted to the south is the change of *pl* to *kj* (Latin *plus,* Italian *più,* dialect *kju,* more), and even more restricted (but interesting because it is found also in Corsica) is the change of *ll* to *ḍḍ,* a *d* sound pronounced with the tip of the tongue far back in the mouth (Latin and Italian *bella,* dialect *beḍḍa,* beautiful). In the far south (Calabria, southern Apulia, and Sicily) the accented Latin vowels *ĭ* and *ē* appear as *i* (Latin *pilu*[*m*], Italian *pelo,* dialect *pilu,* hair; Latin and Italian *tela,* dialect *tila,* cloth), and the vowels *ŭ* and *ō* as *u* (Latin *ingu*[*m*], Italian *giogo,* dialect *jugu,* yoke; Latin *spo*[*n*]*su*[*m*], Italian *sposo,* dialect, *spusu,* spouse).

Dialectal Diversity and Origins.—In order to give some idea of the complex differences among the Italian dialects, here are four versions of a passage from the *Decameron* (*First Day, Ninth Tale*), preceded by an English translation printed in 1620:

English Version: "Sir, I presume not into your presence, as hoping to have redresse by you, for divers dishonourable injuries done unto me; but, as full satisfaction for them, doe but teach me how you suffer such vile abuses, as daily are offered to your selfe. To the end, that being therein instructed by you, I may the more patiently beare mine owne."

Original Text, Florentine of the 14th Century: "Signor mio, io non vengo nella tua presenza per vendetta che io attenda della ingiuria che m'è stata fatta, ma, in sodisfacimento di quella, ti priego che tu m'insegni come tu sofferi quelle le quali intendo che ti son fatte, acciò che, da te apparando, io possa pazientemente la mia comportare."

Turin: Sgnor, i véno nen ant vostra presensa pĕrch'i spera d'otnine vendĕta dĕ l'ingiüria ca m'an fame; ma, pĕr chi pösa soportela, i v' prego de mostreme com i feve a tolerè cule ch'i sento ch'a fan a voi, pĕrchè, 'mparand da voi, i pösa soportè pasientement la mia."

Bologna: "Sgnôur mi en t' pinsar ch'at seppa vgnò dinanz perchè t'fagh el mi vendèt del'inzuri, ch'm'ein sta fatti da zert galiut, ma in scambi d' quèlli a pregh bèin ch' t' m'insègn almanch, cum t' fa a supurtar quèlli, cha intènd, ch' t' ein fatti da! zèint alti: aziò ch'a possa imparar d' guernarom, e d' supurtar anca me la mi cun pazenzia."

Palermo: "Maistà, iu nun vegnu a la tò prisenza pirchì m'aspettu giustizia di l'offisa ch'haju avuta fatta, ma pri prigàrivi di 'nsignàrimi comu suffriti tutti l'offisi chi iu haju 'ntisu diri chi vi fannu, acciucchì, 'mparannu da vui, putissi iu cu pacenza suppurtari la mia."

What are the reasons for such conspicuous differences? Linguists offer us three distinct explanations. According to the substratum theory, many differences are due to the fact that as the Latin language spread through Italy with the Roman conquests it was adopted by peoples of other stocks and languages, who pronounced it according to their own ways of talking and began to modify it. Changes would have taken place, then, either immediately, when the various peoples first learned Latin or later, when the decline of the Roman Empire and its cultural influences paved the way for mutations. The substrata which appear to have had the strongest influence were the Celtic (on the Gallo-Italian dialects) and the Osco-Umbrian (on the central and southern dialects). Tuscany, however, seems to have been practically immune to the influence of the Etruscan substratum.

According to the superstratum theory, much change is due to the Germanic invasions which brought about the fall of the Roman Empire. But while everyone recognizes a strong Germanic influence on the Italian vocabulary, phonetic and morphological influences are highly debatable.

The third theory is based on the development of local patriotism at the height of the Middle Ages, and particularly during the era of the Italian communes. This theory is substantiated by the fact that many of the differences found in modern Italy do not occur in the earliest texts and appear to have had a late origin.

There is no essential contradiction in these theories. We need only establish in what measure each of the three influences contributed to the changes that took place.

Standard Italian.—Latin remained the only written language for many centuries after it was no longer spoken and had been transformed in the former Roman provinces into a variety of dialects. Very gradually, in the countries which were to belong to the Romance language group, the spoken language crept into writing. The requirements of written language and the example of Latin prevented the development of writing in outright dialect form. On the contrary, there was an effort to eliminate terms that were too colloquial and to refine and broaden the dialect—in short, to make it into a language.

Except for a riddle written in Verona in the 9th century (which we cannot be sure the author intended to write in the vernacular rather than in Latin), the earliest examples of sentences written in the vernacular come from four documents written in the principality of Benevento between 960 and 963, referring to properties of monasteries connected with Monte Cassino. These sentences were prepared statements for witnesses on the stand. The first runs: *"Sao ko kelle terre, per kelle fini que ki contene, trenta anni le possette parte Sancti Benedicti."* ("I know that the land within the boundaries mentioned here has been for 30 years among the possessions of St. Benedict.")

There are few other examples of vernacular writing until the early part of the 13th century, when a courtly form of lyric derived from a Provençal model appeared at the court of King Frederick I of Sicily (Emperor Frederick II, q.v.). Though cold and conventional in feeling, this type of poetry is extremely important as the earliest example of Italian lyric verse. Unfortunately, we lack a thorough acquaintance with the language of the poets of the Sicilian school because their manuscripts were copied in Tuscany at the end of the 13th century and extensively altered. We can reconstruct the original Sicilian dialect to some degree only by studying the rhymes.

There was an attempt made in the 13th century to create a literary language in Bologna, seat of one of the most important medieval universities. During the second quarter of the century, Guido Fava (c.1190–c.1243) published *Gemma purpurea,* a collection of model letters written under various circumstances by imaginary characters. The purpose of the letters was practical, but their style aimed at a certain elegance. In the same period, Guido Guinizelli or Guinicelli (q.v.) wrote half-amorous, half-philosophical lyrics which are highly important in the development of the language, although here too the existing texts are none too exact. Guinizelli's example and the humble efforts of poets in Lucca, Pisa, and Arezzo came to a climax when Dante

Alighieri (q.v.) and his contemporaries created the *dolce stil nuovo* (sweet new style).

A number of circumstances combined to give Florence in the period from the end of the 13th century through the first half of the 14th century a privileged position among the cities of Tuscany, and indeed of all Italy. Speaking of its political influence, Giovanni Villani (1280?–1348) said that Florence, originally an offshoot of Rome, had begun at this time to rise while Rome was in decline. Other factors were the growth of commercial enterprises trading with all of western Europe, and the extraordinary flowering of the arts which accompanied the building of Santa Maria del Fiore (begun c. 1298) and the Palazzo Vecchio. Dante, who in the *Divina Commedia* sang of earthly passions and heavenly bliss, and in *Il Convivio* wedded prose to the subtleties of scholastic thought, won immortality for the language in which he wrote. The Florentine tongue, which in the 13th century had been the humble vehicle of commercial registers, chronicles, the rules of confraternities, and translations, was now the basis for literature of every kind. In the following generation, Petrarch (Ital. Francesco Petrarca) and Giovanni Boccaccio (qq.v.) continued the Florentine tradition. The subtle analysis and veiled melancholy of Petrarch's *Il Canzoniere* and the exuberant tribute to the man's ingeniousness of Boccaccio's *Decameron* made with the *Divina Commedia* a perfect three-sided picture. Different as the three writers were, their common greatness was such as to inspire a host of followers to use the Florentine vernacular and to withstand the humanist attempt in the 15th century to reinstate Latin as a literary language.

Books were printed in Italian for the first time in 1470. Within three years, along with the Bible and a very few other works, there were three editions of *Il Canzoniere,* three of the *Decameron,* and three of the *Divina Commedia.* The introduction of printing marks a decisive period in the history of the Italian language. Previously, in northern and southern Italy alike, each author had written as best he could, striving to dignify his native dialect with the aid of Latin and occasional reference to such Tuscan writings as might have come his way. Now the advent of printing made it plainly necessary for Italian, as well as Latin, to acquire uniformity. The printer's work reached readers in various parts of the peninsula, and he could not offend their taste with an excess of dialectal usages. Moreover in this same period national states were developing in other parts of Europe: in Spain with the union of Castile and Aragon (1479) and the expulsion of the Arabs (1492); in France with the triumph of Louis XI (r. 1461–1483) over feudal individualism and the annexation of Brittany (1491). In Italy the time was not yet ripe for political unification, but in the 16th century a considerable degree of linguistic unity was attained. This unity was accomplished by literary influences, that is, by imitation of the three great writers of the 14th century. Such imitation was recommended particularly by Pietro Bembo (q.v.), a Venetian who held undisputed sway over the fields of literature and linguistics in the early part of the 16th century. Tuscan as well as northern writers followed the rules which he laid down in 1525 in his *Prose della volgar lingua.* Writers of the south, too, tended to imitate the great 14th century models, as is shown in the work of Jacopo Sannazaro (q.v.), author of *Arcadia* (1504).

To what extent did the three great Tuscan writers influence the progress of linguistic unification? The following metaphor may give an idea. Imagine a forest where for several centuries hundreds of plants of the same species but of different varieties have reproduced themselves spontaneously without human interference. Then suppose that a horticulturist comes along, chooses the best variety, and grafts it on all the rest. If we compare the spontaneous growths to all the dialects of Latin origin, and Tuscan to the variety chosen for grafting upon the others, we shall see what happened in Italy in the 16th century.

A number of phonetic characteristics show that modern standard Italian grew out of the Tuscan, or rather the Florentine, dialect. We saw that in both northern and southern Italy the Latin ending *-ariu(m)* changed to *-aro,* while in Tuscany it became *-aio.* Moreover, closed *e* and *o* in certain positions (before palatal *gl* and *ng*) changed only in Florence and its immediate neighborhood to *i* and *u.* If dialects from various regions had combined to make Italian, or if another Tuscan type, such as the Sienese, had prevailed, then we should say *fameglia* instead of *famiglia* (Latin *familia,* family), and *longo* instead of *lungo* (Latin *longus,* long). Nevertheless, we must remember that in the 16th century the matter did not yet appear to be definitely settled, and innumerable disputes raged about what was called the *questione della lingua* (language question).

The position of Tuscan as a literary language was consolidated by an institution founded in 1582 which exercised for some time a considerable influence: the Accademia della Crusca (literally, Academy of the Bran, or Chaff). This name, originally somewhat of a joke, soon came to be considered symbolic of the academy's chief task, that of distinguishing between good language and bad, in the same way that wheat is separated from chaff. In 1612, the academy published the first great historical and grammatical dictionary of a modern language. This dictionary was imitated in other countries for two centuries thereafter.

The general trend of the 18th century dominated by Enlightenment and French influence, lessened the literary and linguistic sway of the classics. In the early 19th century writers wavered between a ponderous imitation of 14th or 16th century language and a loose style containing many Gallicisms. The two editions of Alessandro Manzoni's celebrated novel *I promessi sposi* (1825–1827 and 1840–1842) constitute what may be called a linguistic manifesto. (See BETROTHED, THE). The great Milanese romantic writer insisted on using a live, modern language patterned not on mere imitation of the past, but on the contemporary usage of the city of Florence. Thereafter, the course of the Italian language followed the political developments which led to the formation of the Italian nation and its life as a single political unit. Commercial and cultural exchanges increased, and the standard language became more uniform.

The formation of standard Italian took place in a different way from that of other major languages. Literature, as we have seen, was the chief factor in its evolution, rather than the extension of royal government, as was the case in France, or the translation of the Bible and the influence of the usage of the imperial chancery, as in Germany. This explains why it was so difficult for Italian to take definite shape. It achieved uniformity only after long struggles between various stylistic ideals, and this meant strong divergencies in both vocabulary and grammar. For this reason, modern Italian retains a number of legitimate variations of usage. We may say *danaro* or *denaro* (money); *obiettivo* or *obbiettivo* (objective); *patriota* or *patriotta* (patriot); and *soprintendere, sovrintendere, sopraintendere,* or *sovraintendere* (superintend). Many grammatical rules, too, are optional. We may use either *pomodori* or *pomidori* as the plural of *pomodoro* (tomato), and the forms *io ho visto i libri* and *io ho visti i libri* (I have seen the books) are both equally correct.

The struggles over usage, grouped together as the *questione della lingua,* were particularly sharp in the 16th and 19th centuries. First there was much discussion on what precisely the Italian language should be and whether the prevalent tongue should be called courtly or vernacular, Florentine, Tuscan, or Italian. In the first half of the 19th century controversy centered about the 14th century revival proclaimed by Father Antonio Cesari (1760–1828); in the second half about whether literary language should conform to the usages of the cultivated Florentine, as Alessandro Manzoni proposed. The constant patterning of the Italian language on literary models is due to the highly developed individuality of the Italian people and their strong aesthetic sense. Moreover, literary influence came to predominate on a large scale because, after the modest beginnings of its literary history, Italy produced three writers of the stature of Dante, Petrarch, and Boccaccio.

We must add a word about the stability of Italian grammatical forms. Italian never underwent changes so great as to upset its phonetic system; there was no mutation in vowel sounds such as took place in both French and English up to comparatively recent times. Here, then, we have the most striking characteristic of Italian as compared with other languages, its longevity. In France an understanding of the 11th century *Chanson de Roland* (q.v.) requires the study of what is almost a foreign language, and even writers of the 16th century use forms that are considered archaic today. The same is true of English, German, and Spanish. But the average modern Italian, although the meanings of some words and constructions may escape him, can still feel that his language is that of Dante.

Bibliography.—Bertoni, Giulio, *L'Italia dialettale* (Milan 1916); Grandgent, Charles H., *From Latin to Italian* (Cambridge, Mass., 1927); Wiese, Berthold, *Altitalienisches Elementarbuch,* 2d ed. (Heidelberg 1928); Hall, Robert A., Jr., *Bibliography of Italian Linguistics* (Baltimore 1941); Pei, Mario A., *The Italian Language* (New York 1941); Hall, Robert A., *The Italian Questione della Lingua* (Chapel Hill, N. C., 1942); Migliorini, Bruno, *Saggi sulla lingua del novecento,* 2d ed. (Florence 1942; id., *Lingua contemporanea,* 3d ed. (Florence 1943).

BRUNO MIGLIORINI,
Professor of History of the Italian Language, University of Florence.

5. LITERATURE. From the Earliest Times to Dante.—The writing that was done in Italy from the fall of the Western Roman Empire to the beginning of the 13th century was Latin; it belongs to a period of transition from Roman literature to Italian literature, and it was European rather than Italian in scope. Its chief subject was philosophy, especially scholastic philosophy, and such purely literary works as were written were of inferior caliber. A study known as *ars dictandi* (art of composition), which aimed at setting up standards in the literary field (more exactly, in letter writing), began at Monte Cassino in the 11th century and was elaborated in a number of treatises even beyond the 13th century. These treatises showed no trace of the classical spirit, which continued to be lacking until Dante revived it.

Among the literary documents of this period we may recall the *Chronicon Novaliciense* (first half of the 11th century), a crudely but vigorously told cycle of legends, and the 12th and 13th century verses of the wandering students or jesters known as the goliards, which broke out in every country of Europe (see GOLIARDERY). The tone of these verses was sensual and anticlerical, and they were written in rhythmical meter. The use of rhythmical meter and the development of the Italian language are milestones in the separation of Italian from Latin literature.

The first literary documents in popular Italian date from the 13th century; they consist largely of religious poetry and that of the so-called Sicilian school. Among the religious poems of the time are *De Jerusalem celesti* and *De Babilonia civitate infernali* by Giacomino da Verona (fl. second half of the 13th century); the *Libro delle tre scritture* of Bonvesin da la Riva (1240–1315), containing a vivid description of the torments of hell; *Il cantico del sole,* or *delle creature* (see CANTICLE OF THE SUN, THE), of St. Francis of Assisi (1182–1226), which set the tone of the tender and spontaneous ascetic prose of the 13th to the 15th century; and the *laudi* (hymns of praise) of the Franciscan monk Jacopone da Todi (c. 1230–1306), reputed author of the *Stabat Mater* (q.v.), which range from the heights of mystical ecstasy to the depths of despair and are, despite their faults, expressions of the most powerful Italian poetical genius before Dante. The Sicilian school, which centered about the court of King Frederick I of Sicily (Emperor Frederick II, q.v.) in the first half of the 13th century, was an offshoot of Provençal poetry and celebrated a somewhat conventional courtly love. The leaders of this school were Giacomo da Lentini or Lentino, Giacomino Pugliese, and Guido delle Colonne. Other poets were Rinaldo d'Aquino and Odo delle Colonne, who wrote two spontaneous popular poems. Also in the popular vein is *Rosa fresca aulentissima,* a sprightly tale of a lovers' quarrel by another Sicilian, Cielo d'Alcamo (fl. mid-13th century).

Epics wrought of Carolingian, Breton, and classical material in Franco-Venetian verse or Italian prose occupy a secondary place, together with such moral allegories as the *Fiore, Li Livres dou Trésor* (in French prose) of Brunetto Latini (1212?–?1294), and the same writer's *Il Tesoretto,* in seven-syllable verse (see TREASURY, THE LITTLE). Of distinct value is *Il Milione* (tr. in Eng. as *The Book of Marco Polo*), a fabulous narrative of Polo's travels through Asia as told to Rustichello da Pisa and written in a mingled French and Italian prose.

Several Tuscan poets of the transitional period stem from the Sicilian school, among them Guittone d'Arezzo (c. 1230–1294) and Chiaro Davanzati (fl. second half of the 13th century). Superior to them were the poets of the *dolce stil nuovo* (sweet new style). This school begins with Guido Guinizelli or Guinicelli (1240?–?1274). Its leaders were Dante Alighieri and Guido Cavalcanti (c. 1250–1300) of Florence, and a later follower of less importance was Cino da Pistoia (Guittoncino de' Sinibaldi, 1270–1336). Their poetry is idealistic with psychological overtones and is influenced by religion and philosophy. The chief subject is the angelic woman, described by Dante as *"venuta di cielo in terra a miracol mostrare."* Beside these idealistic lyrics are examples of realism and satire, best represented by Cecco Angiolieri (1250?–?1312) of Siena, the author of many sonnets, of which the most famous is a curse on the entire world, including his own father and mother.

The prose of this period is simple almost to the point of being elementary; translations from the Latin were only just beginning to nourish and invigorate its syntax and capacity for expression. It deals with the details of city life, adventures culled from the Breton cycle, and moral reflections. The best prose is found in *Il Novellino* (q.v.), a collection of biblical, classical, and medieval stories, told in short sentences and occasionally displaying real talent in pinning down the salient features of an event or a character. In the *Tavola ritonda* we find a more complex style and in certain passages a feeling of epic solemnity. Little originality is to be found in *Il libro dei Sette Savi, I conti di antichi cavalieri,* or *I fatti di Cesare.*

Dante.—With Dante a new spirit enters into the favorite themes of medieval literature and the echoes of classical antiquity. He was by nature vigorous and prone to synthesize; his art he learned from Vergil and his disciplined thinking from St. Thomas Aquinas. Dante Alighieri was born in Florence in May 1265. The most influential events of his life were his love for Beatrice (c. 1289) and the exile imposed upon him on Jan. 27, 1302, by the Neri (Black) faction of the Guelphs (q.v.), who, supported by Pope Boniface VIII, prevailed at this time over the Bianchi (Whites). After many wanderings the poet died in exile at Ravenna in 1321. Dante's love for Beatrice inspired *La Vita Nuova,* a youthful volume of poems and prose pieces whose heroine is celebrated in terms even more idealistic than those of the *dolce stil nuovo* and is promised the dedication of another and loftier work, the *Divina Commedia* (see DIVINE COMEDY, THE).

In the *Divina Commedia* the themes of love and politics are mingled. Beatrice saves Dante from a life of sin and leads him, first through the intermediary of Vergil and then herself in person, through hell, purgatory, and paradise to the contemplation of God, while at the same time we have projected into the three realms of the afterlife a picture of the spiritual and political life of the poet's time. The power of this masterpiece lies, then, in its depiction of Dante's own world as seen from beyond the grave. Other periods of history are involved, but only sporadically and as forerunners of the events of Dante's lifetime. Dante saw the world around him as ill governed because of the evil ways of the church and the abandonment of Italy by the Holy Roman Empire. It is plain in various parts of the poem that exile contributed to his pessimistic views and made him a scornful judge of his own times and a prophet of dire things to come.

This work, which he called simply the *Commedia* (the adjective *Divina* was added later) is, as we have seen. the story of Dante's spiritual purification in the course of an imaginary visit to the next world, accomplished through his contact with the inhabitants thereof, so that the poet is seen among the passions, struggles, and civilization of his age. The broad scope of the poem derives from its double meaning as an autobiography and the spiritual history of a period. Dante himself, who is vigorously portrayed, undergoes a change as he moves from region to region of the afterlife. In the *Inferno* he is an enemy of those whom he meets and an implacable judge. In the *Purgatorio* he turns inward and meditates as he walks in brotherly fashion beside the thoughtful souls who dwell there. In the *Paradiso* he rises above all earthly passions. Each region has an individual coloring, which is reflected in its physical background and the characters who people it, as well as in the frame of mind of the poet Quite naturally, then, the characters of the *Inferno* are the most powerfully drawn, attached as they still are to the sinful passions that brought about their damnation. The souls of the *Purgatorio,* torn between their earthly sins and their desire for expiation, nc longer live in mutual hate and enmity but are bound by a new feeling of brotherhood. In the *Paradiso* individuals lose their identity and are made one in a chorus of harmony and praise. The landscape of the *Inferno* is dark, rough, and fearsome; that of the *Purgatorio,* isolated in the ocean, is calm and invites to meditation; the *Paradiso* is laid among ever-widening and more luminous vistas of the heavens.

This is the general layout of the poem. If it had been rigidly maintained the result would have been methodical to the point of monotony, but, as it is, every now and then the pattern is broken. The damned are portrayed with sympathy, affection, and even admiration, for grave sins, after all, may be caused by humanly comprehensible motives; they may go hand in hand with great qualities or be essentially pitiful and tragic. Thus we have in the *Inferno* such figures as Francesca da Rimini, Brunetto Latini, Ulysses, and Ugolino della Gherardesca (qq.v.), and Farinata degli Uberti. The meditative pages of the *Purgatorio* are interrupted by the political invective of Canto VI and the reproaches and prophecies of Canto XIV. In like fashion, the bliss of the *Paradiso* is broken by the satire directed at degenerate religious orders and St. Peter's wrath at corrupt holders of the papacy. There is immense variety in Dante's poetry, especially in the *Inferno,* which is the richest of the three parts, while the *Purgatorio* is the smoothest, and the *Paradiso* most nearly touches the summits of sublimity. In its structure and balance the poem is a model of architectonic solidity; it is also one of the most imaginative and many-sided productions of world literature.

While he wrote the *Commedia,* Dante was working on *Il Convivio* (*The Banquet*), and some pages of the latter are permeated with the elevated and sorrowful feeling of the poem. *Il Convivio* is unfinished; it was intended to be a sort of encyclopedia of philosophy, a banquet of philosophical ideas served up to the unlearned. It is made up of four treatises—that is, an introduction and three commentaries, each accompanied by a poem—containing discussions of morals, politics, metaphysics, and astrology. Many passages are commentaries on the poetical interludes, and the style, which is far removed from the dreamy tone of *La Vita Nuova,* displays the manliness and maturity of the author of the *Commedia.*

Important for Dante's poetical theory and for the history of Italian literature, language, and versification is *De vulgari eloquentia,* a Latin work broken off at Chapter 14 of the second book. In the first book, Dante speaks of the origin and history of the Italian language; he derives Italian, French, and Provençal from a single source, thus anticipating the classification Neo-Latin or Romance later applied to them. He divides Italian dialects into 14 groups and tries to ascertain which is best suited to a tragic or lofty style, reaching the conclusion that none will suffice and that a new language must be formed by putting together the best elements that they have in common. In the second book he takes up the use of noble language in the loftiest form of poetry, which is to him the *canzone* or lyric, and studies the structure of this form.

The 13 Latin *Epistolae,* which are of considerable autobiographical interest, are close to the *De vulgari eloquentia;* they are practical demonstrations of the importance which Dante attached to painstaking study as the way to attain art. The *Epistolae* reflect many of the convictions we find in *De Monarchia,* a Latin work of a later date than *Il Convivio,* whose political views it amplifies and emends. In the three books of *De Monarchia,* Dante maintains that the world should be governed by one emperor, that this world empire is a prerogative of the Romans, and that emperor and pope are independent of one another, deriving their authority direct from God.

Among Dante's minor works we may note some of the *Rime pietrose* and the splendid political poem beginning: *"Tre donne intorno al cor mi son venute."*

Petrarch.—Politics did not play a major role in the life of Francesco Petrarca (1304–1374), known in English as Petrarch, whose chief themes are his love for Laura, his studies, and his soul. Petrarch's great love inspired *Il Canzoniere,* an idealized account of his sentiments from the first time he saw Laura until some time after her death. The prevailing feeling in *Il Canzoniere* is one of meditative sadness against a religious background that emerges more and more distinctly until the work ends with a hymn to the Virgin Mary. The originality of this book lies in the gentle contrast between love and religion, set forth in an intimate story whose bare facts count for less than their reflection in the thoughtful mind of the poet. *Il Canzoniere* set the style for lyric poetry for centuries thereafter and had a lasting influence on the love lyrics of every country of Europe. (See PETRARCH'S SONNETS.)

Petrarch also holds a prominent place in the history of the Renaissance, and may be called the first of the humanists. The Latin of the poem *Africa,* the *Epistolae metricae,* the prose letters, the moral and religious works, and *Secretum,* a book of confessions, is much closer to the classical model than that of Dante. Because of his mastery of Latin style, his deep study of the classics, and his search for lost ancient manuscripts, we may say that with Petrarch the history of humanism begins.

Boccaccio and the Lesser 14th Century Writers.—Giovanni Boccaccio (1313–1375) is less important than Petrarch in the history of humanism and linguistic development, but equally so with regard to the imprint he left on subsequent literature. His masterpiece. the *Decameron* (q.v.), was the only model followed by Italian short story writers up until the 18th century and has exercised a continuous influence on Italian prose. This work is made up of 100 tales told by seven young ladies and three young gentlemen who take refuge in the country near Florence during the plague of 1348. The subject matter comprises tragedy, burlesque, adventure, and love; the style is now slow and solemn, now rapid and vivacious. The whole makes up a many-sided picture of the life of the gentry, clergy, scholars, rascals, and common people of the time and has a greater variety of realistic characters than any Italian prose work before the 19th century *I promessi sposi.* There is promise of the masterpiece that was to follow in Boccaccio's youthful prose and poetry, particularly in *Il ninfale fiesolano,* an idyll rich in tender and dramatic scenes.

Franco Sacchetti (1335?–1400) is a talented writer of anecdotal short stories pitched in a minor key and concerned with middle-class and peasant life. Dino Compagni (1265?–1323) writes in a fast-moving and dramatic style of the Florence of the time of Dante. Religious writers of diverse temperaments include the anonymous author of the *Fioretti di San Francesco,* the simplest and most graphic biography of St. Francis of Assisi; Domenico Cavalca (c. 1270–1342), who adapted from the Latin the psychologically penetrating *Vite dei Santi Padri;* Jacopo Passavanti (c. 1300–1357), whose *Specchio di vera penitenza* contains some of the most effectively dramatic pages of medieval literature; and St. Catherine of Siena (1347–1380), whose letters are the most passionate expression of mysticism in Italian literature.

Humanism and the 15th Century.—The period from the age of Dante to the middle of the 16th century was one of deep transformation in Italian life and letters. The change came about slowly until halfway through the 15th century, when it consciously quickened its pace. By the second half of the century educational, literary, artistic, civic, and moral ideals were far removed from those of the 13th century and in some cases diametrically opposed to them. The ancients came to be considered masters of literature and the plastic arts and of the art of living as well. The rediscovery of Greek and Roman manuscripts and archaeological remains influenced art and letters, while at the same time the destiny of man and philosophical problems in general were seen in a new light and explained in a new manner. This period of change is called the Renaissance, and the philological inquiry which brought about the renewal of classical culture is known as humanism (q.v.), from *studia humanitatis* (studies aimed at perfecting the development of the human spirit by acquaintance with the grandeurs of the past).

Forerunners of humanism besides Petrarch were Albertino Mussato (1261–1329) and Lino Coluccio di Piero Salutati (1331–1406); its center was Florence; and the first great humanists to find and annotate ancient manuscripts were Giovanni Francesco Poggio Bracciolini (1380–1459) and Lorenzo Valla (1406–1457). Other centers were the academy at Rome headed by Giulio Pomponio Leto (1428–1498), and the Accademia Pontaniana at Naples, named after its most illustrious member, Giovanni Pontano (1426–1503). At this time the first great libraries were formed and culture was encouraged by the wealthy noblemen of Naples, Ferrara, Milan, and other cities as well as by the popes. Many authors wrote in Latin; Pontano, the greatest among them, while he imitated classical verse, also sounded a note of contemporary reality.

Colloquial Italian, submerged for a while in the humanist illusion that Latin could once more become a living language, was used in such works of a popular character as the *sacre rappresentazioni* (miracle plays) and love lyrics of Leonardo Giustiniani and the writings of other authors of various degrees of learning. Among them were Lorenzo de' Medici (1449–1492), who was prominent in the cultural life of Florence and wrote poems and songs for carnival celebrations, among them *Trionfo di Bacco e Arianna,* which is among the best lyrics of the century; Politian (Angelo Poliziano, real name Angelo Ambrogini, 1454–1494), author of *Orfeo* and *Stanze per la Giostra di Giuliano de' Medici,* an unfinished poem of incomparable polish and charm; and Luigi Pulci (1432–1484), whose poem *Il Morgante Maggiore* recalls in a style alternately tripping and stately the events of the Carolingian cycle and creates the new and immortal figure of the glutton Margutte. Away from Florence, in Ferrara, we have Matteo Maria Boiardo (1434–1494), author of *Orlando innamorato* (q.v.), wrought from material half Breton and half Carolingian in a preponderantly chivalrous, fairy-tale manner. The most notable prose writers are the architect Leon Battista Alberti (1404–1472), author of the treatise *Della Famiglia,* in dialogue form, of which certain pages are the best extant documentation of the humanistic ideals of wisdom and balance; Leonardo da Vinci (1452–1519), whose observations on life and nature show the religious element in the humanistic attitude toward the world; and Jacopo Sannazaro (1458–1530), author of *Arcadia* (q.v.), a pastoral and amorous romance which enjoyed extraordinary success all over Europe for several centuries.

First Half of the 16th Century; Ariosto and Machiavelli.—The exaggerated rhetoric and sensuality of much of 16th century literature have detracted from its reputation. There flourished during this period a literature serious in form and content and another that was frivolous in both. That is, there was a formal literary school and also a literary production that remained light and casual even when it was camouflaged by rhetorical devices derived from Latin writers and from Boccaccio. The literature of the first half of the century was based on Platonism (q.v.) and on classical wisdom and moderation. The moral aspirations and strength of the period turned toward the world and were bounded by a concern for man's position within its confines. In this sense, the 16th century grew out of the century that preceded it and is fittingly represented by Machiavelli and Ariosto.

Lodovico Ariosto (1474–1533) was for many years in the service of the Este family in Ferrara and the Garfagnana region. His *Satire* depict the worries and restrictions imposed upon him by his court duties in contrast to the poetical genius that drew him toward a quiet life where his imagination might find free rein. His poem *Orlando Furioso* (q.v.) portrays in a series of varied and skillfully arranged episodes his own half-dreaming, half-practical nature. His imagination is agile but never extravagant; it is restrained and colored by an intense feeling for reality which never fails to surprise us in this teller of extravagant tales. The plot, drawn from the Carolingian cycle, tells of the struggle between Christians and Saracens around Paris, where the scene of the poem is laid. But the real subject is Orlando's ill-fated love for Angelica, which eventually drives him mad. This madness dominates the greater part of the poem, but around it are built up any number of other love stories, intermittently connected with one another in an abrupt rhythm which is the poem's magical charm. The focus of the action is the palace of Atlante, where the knights wander about in a vain and illusory search for the image of their loved ones; another central episode is Astolfo's ascension to the moon. In this poem everything is at the same time concrete and elusive; the reader seems to be looking at a scene from real life when it melts away as if in a dream. Every sentiment appears and disappears again in an endless whirl of adventures; only Orlando's love for Angelica endures, in increasing tempestuousness. The style is the most natural and flowing ever to be achieved by a poet, and it has been imitated over and over again. We can see its influence in Francesco Berni and numerous poets of chivalry of the time, and it crops up continually in the mock-heroic verse of the 18th century, either alone or mingled with the heritage of Torquato Tasso and Giambattista Marini.

Niccolò Machiavelli (1469–1527), living in a period when Italian independence was disappearing, was the first prophet of its resurrection and the chief of its political thinkers. His two masterpieces are *Il Principe* (*The Prince,* q.v.), a political treatise, and a comedy entitled *La Mandragola* (*The Mandrake*).

Il Principe is based on a new and realistic political morality. The kingdom of this world is to the strong, and fortune smiles upon him. Amid a floating and spineless multitude we find a few men endowed with intelligence and will power. The heart has no place in Machiavelli's political system, and kindness is tolerated only when it does not sap a leader's energy and block the accomplishment of his plans. Machiavelli esteems strength of mind and purpose harnessed to a single goal, the highest good of the state. This treatise is a handbook for political leaders; it was written in order to instruct a prince how to take advantage of the fatal weakness of the multitude and turn it into the basis for a powerful and well-organized government. Machiavelli's philosophy is aristocratic as well as pessimistic to the point of cynicism; he has no love for the common people. It is significant that the characters of *La Mandragola,* which ranks with Carlo Goldoni's *I rusteghi* as a masterpiece of the Italian theater, should be people of humble estate whom the author treats with the utmost scorn. His attitude toward these characters is identical with the one that he recommends for a prince toward his subjects.

Machiavelli's political philosophy is inconceivable divorced from the idea of the people as passive and sheeplike masses; this is the core of his realism. No one has ever analyzed as thoroughly as Machiavelli did the temper of the leader and that of the crowd. Before his analysis political theorists had studied how man should behave rather than his actual behavior; they pursued Utopian ideals while he adheres to the "real truth." We must look for the cause of Machiavelli's attitude in the inert fatalism in which most Italians of his day had taken refuge when their country was in danger. His reaction was to call

for a prince or strong man able to stand up against fate.

The *Discorsi sulla prima deca di Tito Livio* and the series of dialogues called *Dell'arte della guerra* complete Machiavelli's political works. In these writings, Machiavelli reveals himself as a pupil of the ancient philosophers, not in regard to his style, whose terse, muscular, and trenchant quality is far from the prevailing classical model, but in his theories of life and government. The theme of *La Mandragola* is as indelicate and comic as that of a tale by Boccaccio and arouses a feeling of amusement tempered by severity. The atmosphere is cynical and sardonic from beginning to end, while the positive thought and lucid style remind us continually of *Il Principe*. In the *Storie fiorentine* we again meet the Machiavellian conception of history as the creation not of the people but of strong personalities.

Colder and more exact are the historical works of Francesco Guicciardini (1483–1540). His *Ricordi civili e politici* stems not from a desire to formulate general rules of human conduct, but from an attempt to describe the myriad variations of human behavior. His historical method is analytical, especially in the *Storia d'Italia*, where he demonstrates an unusual ability to weigh and coordinate the circumstances surrounding a given action and leaves with the reader an impression of wide-ranging vision.

Machiavelli and Guicciardini are both realists. Other writers have left us a more idealistic picture of the 16th century, among them Baldassare Castiglione (1478–1529), whose *Il Cortegiano* (q.v.) is an ample and artistic picture of court life; and Pietro Bembo (1470–1547), whose *Gli Asolani* is an exaltation of Platonic love. These moralists, too, show in their style and their balanced outlook on life the strong influence of the classics. Noteworthy for the same reason are *La prima veste dei discorsi degli animali* by Agnolo Firenzuola (1493–?1545), many pages of Anton Francesco Doni (1513?–1574), and *La Circe* by Giovanni Battista Gelli (1498–1563).

There is an abundance of Latin writing in the 16th century, but even more remarkable is *Baldus*, a poem by Teofilo Folengo (1496?–1544) written in macaronic or dog Latin, a parody of the classical tongue. (See MACARONIC VERSE.) This poem takes up the cudgels against the courtly and literary life; it embraces nature as opposed to refinement and represents a diametrically opposite view to that of *Il Cortegiano*. Without any intention of parody, Angelo Beolco (1502–1542), known as Il Ruzzante, makes use of the same realistic background in his brief dialect comedies of peasant life. Defiant of convention and often immoral are the copious writings of Pietro Aretino (1492–1556), who is a typical representative of the widespread degeneracy of the age, mirrored less in his comedies than in the huge bacchanalian work called *Ragionamenti*. Benvenuto Cellini (1500–1571) had the same impetuous temperament and left us in his *Vita* or *Autobiography* the liveliest and most complete picture of the boldness and vanity of a 16th century artist. (See CELLINI'S AUTOBIOGRAPHY.) The comic verses of Francesco Berni (1497–1536) have less intrinsic value, but his style influenced this form of writing for two centuries and we must grant him both cleverness and facility of expression.

Around these important authors is a galaxy of minor figures, chiefly writers of short stories and comedies. Such short story writers as Matteo Bandelo (1480?–1562) and Il Lasca (Antonio Francesco Grazzini, 1503–1584) are followers of Boccaccio; the comedians copy classical Latin models with the addition of contemporary material. *La Venexiana*, of unknown authorship, is by far the best comedy of the 16th century and, with *La Mandragola*, the only one which does not conform to a conventional pattern. Lyric poetry, except for Gaspara Stampa (1524?–?1554), Caleazzo di Tarsia (1520–1553), and Michelangelo, is still limited to the forms laid down by Petrarch.

The Age of Tasso.—Toward the middle of the 16th century conscience and taste underwent a revolution. The Counter Reformation called men back to forgotten duties, although men proceeded to perform them mechanically and without enthusiasm. Michelangelo Buonarroti (1475–1564) interpreted in painting the spiritual needs of the time, but no writer gave himself up wholeheartedly to the stern injunctions of the church in its attempt to recover the mastery of men's souls. The only important writers of this period, besides Tasso, were the physicist Giambattista della Porta (1538?–1615), who introduced elements of fancy and imagination into comedy; Giordano Bruno (1548?–1600), who in his philosophical works, particularly *Spaccio della bestia trionfante*, succeeded by means of a grandiose and baroque style in tracing a vast, powerful, and noble conception of the world; and Giovanni Battista Guarini (1538–1612), whose pastoral drama *Il pastor fido* (q.v.) did more than Tasso himself to transform poetry into a musical attenuation of reality.

Torquato Tasso was born at Sorrento in 1544 and lived for some time at the court of the Este family in Ferrara. He was driven to a wandering existence by a restlessness which for several years took the form of insanity, and died at the convent of Sant'Onofrio in Rome in 1595. His *Gerusalemme Liberata* (*Jerusalem Delivered*, q.v.) marks the beginning of a new period of Italian literature, which was to be strongly influenced until after the romantic period by his style and way of thinking and feeling.

Gerusalemme Liberata is a serious and melancholy poem in 20 cantos which portrays in the guise of history Tasso's own frame of mind. It relates, rather than the conquest of the Holy City, the passions of the two Christian heroes, Rinaldo and Tancredi (Tancred). The love story of Rinaldo and Armida occupies most of the poem from Canto IV to Canto XX, while the romantic adventures of Tancredi, which are first mentioned in Canto III, end only in Canto XIX. These two stories form the framework and plot of the poem. Beside the two heroes we have the feminine figures of Armida, Erminia, and Clorinda, who give rise to some of the most famous passages, including Erminia's flight among the shepherds, and Clorinda's death, brought about by a fatal error, at the hands of her lover. A dramatic fatality pervades the whole poem, and even the two pagan protagonists, Argante and Solimano (Suleiman), who do not enter into the sentimental episodes, are seen in a fundamentally melancholy light. There is in *Gerusalemme Liberata* a new feeling for life and nature, quite different from that of *Orlando Furioso* and its time, and expressed in a plaintive style in which words are valued less for their meaning than for their musical quality. The poem was immensely popular. It set the rhythm and style of the poetry of the century to follow, and for over 200 years was a source of romantic subtleties heretofore unknown in Italian literature.

Tasso's earlier pastoral drama, *Aminta* (q.v.), a finely balanced compromise between the traditional treatment of a conventional subject and the expression of a dreamy and meditative personality, met with less success. Here his poetic talent was muzzled by the requirements of dialogue, for which he had not yet found the form midway between the dramatic and the lyrical that he used in *Gerusalemme Liberata* for the expression in apparently objective terms of his innermost feelings.

The 17th Century.—In the 17th century poetry, uprooted from reality, became superficial and overrefined and ceased to interpret the life and spirit of the age. It was a mere tour de force, built on rhetorical figures of speech, particularly on complicated metaphors, and on alliteration and other devices related to the music of the period. Lyric poetry adopted new themes, but its departure from tradition was motivated merely by a frivolous desire for the strange and new. Sensuality was pronounced, and there was a taste for description, preferably of luxuriant scenic backgrounds. Religious themes were often marred by the poet's sensuality, yet there was in the 17th century a vein of sincere melancholy arising not only from the stern teachings of the Counter Reformation, but also from the contrasting pomp and theatricality of society and the fine arts. The writer most representative of this religious spirit was Federigo della Valle (1565–1628), whose tragedy *Judit* was the only great work of its kind before Vittorio Alfieri. Tommaso Campanella (1568–1639) was another poet of high moral standards, though more of a philosopher by vocation.

Perhaps the most typical 17th century writer was Giambattista Marini or Marino (1569–1625), who produced a number of poetical works, conspicuous among them *L'Adone,* made up of a plethora of incidents told in the exaggerated and disorderly manner characteristic of the time. Fulvio Testi (1593–1646), more oratorical than poetic, had ideas opposed to those of Marini, and so did Gabriello Chiabrera (1552–1637), a forerunner of the insipid airs and graces of the Arcadian school. A prose writer of the same verbosity as Marini but free of his metaphorical extravagance was Daniello Bartoli (1608–1685), author of *Storia della Compagnia di Gesù,* a long history of the Jesuit order. Giovanni Battista Basile, count of Morone (1575–1632), who wrote entertaining fables in Neapolitan dialect, obtained unusual artistic effects from the flowery imagery proper to the 17th century. Two poems unconnected with contemporary literary trends were the burlesque *La secchia rapita* of Alessandro Tassoni (1565–1635), containing characters and episodes of enduring liveliness; and the dithyrambic *Bacco in Toscana* of Francesco Redi (1626?–1697 or 1698), a lively story of the inebriation of Bacchus.

The more serious side of 17th century literature is represented by the profound and sometimes keen-witted scientific prose of Galileo Galilei (1564–1642), the great opponent of Aristotelian philosophy and the Ptolemaic system, author of *Dialogo dei due massimi sistemi del mondo* and *Il saggiatore,* and founder of a literary trend as well as a scientific school. Other serious writers were Paolo Sarpi (1552–1623), author of *Storia del Concilio di Trento;* and Traiano Boccalini (1556–1613), whose *Ragguagli di Parnaso* and *Pietra del paragone politico* were the best political essays of the time.

The 18th Century.—In 1690, there was founded in Rome the Arcadia, an academy whose purpose was to combat the bad taste of the 17th century. This academy held sway for the greater part of the 18th century, steering into oversimplification and impoverishment the idyllic and Anacreontic trend of the school it sought to supplant and accentuating its saccharine quality. The chief exponents of this academic effort were Paolo Rolli (1687–1765) and Carlo Innocenzo Frugoni (1692–1768); its only real poet was Metastasio (originally Pietro Trapassi, 1698–1782), who wrote two restrained and graceful songs and several dramas, including *Didone abbandonata, Olimpiade,* and *Demofoonte,* in which he endowed poetry with a new and melodramatic tone. Metastasio is the only poet in whom melodrama is not a fault but an original and genuine lyrical expression in which feeling is transformed into song, and melancholy, sorrow, regret, jealousy, and doubt no sooner appear than they vanish in melodious echoes.

There are traces of Metastasio's influence in Carlo Goldoni (1707–1793), the greatest Italian writer of comedy. His comedies are in appearance realistic depictions of the Venetian life of the age, but their realism is filtered through an optimistic and typically 18th century temperament and falls into cadences not far removed from those of Metastasio's melodrama. Goldoni continued Metastasio's gracefulness, enriching it and turning it away from the ancient heroic world toward the middle-class atmosphere of modern times. His plays impress us not as direct reflections of life, but as theatrical fictions based on lifelike models. The best of his comedies, which are written partly in Italian and partly in Venetian dialect, are *I rusteghi, La locandiera, Il ventaglio, Le baruffe chiozzotte,* and *La casa nuova.* Before Goldoni the Italian comic theater was the province of the *commedia dell'arte,* entrusted to the brilliant improvisation of great actors. (See DRAMA—*The Renaissance.*) The *commedia dell'arte* was famous throughout Europe and popularized such figures as Arlecchino (Harlequin), Pantalone (Pantaloon), and Brighella, but with the passage of time it degenerated into buffoonery. Goldoni opposed this tendency with his carefully thought-out comedies drawn from direct observation.

In the second half of the century the academic versification of Arcadia gave way to poetry of a more serious kind. Even Giovanni Meli (1740–1815), the great poet of Sicilian dialect, whose choice of subject matter and background recalls the Arcadian school, followed new and healthier ideals, as if he had been touched by the spirit of Jean Jacques Rousseau. The literature of this period stemmed from a general renewal of culture, as in the work of Giovanni Battista Vico (1668–1744) and Lodovico Antonio Muratori (1672–1750), who marked the revival of the traditional study of philosophy and history and paved the way, each in his own field, for the exact philological and critical scholarship of the 19th and 20th centuries. The decade of greatest interest falls later, from 1755 to 1765, the years dominated and epitomized by Giuseppe Parini.

Between Metastasio and Alfieri a large number of writers, both followers of the Arcadian school and independents—literary critics, moralists, and disseminators of ideas—contributed to a renewal of literature. Among them we may name Francesco Algarotti (1712–1764), Saverio Bettinelli (1718–1808), Gaspare Gozzi (1713–1786), and, most talented of all, Giuseppe Marc'Antonio Baretti (1719–1789), whose review *La frusta letteraria* opposed the lazy superficiality of Arcadia, and Ferdinando Galiani (1728–1787), the most biting critic of the abstract, antihistorical, and enclopedic mentality of his time. New ideas were spread by such periodicals as *La frusta letteraria,* Gozzi's *Osservatore veneziano,* and *Il Caffè,* published in Milan and written largely by Pietro Verri (1728–1797) and Cesare Bonesana, marchese di Beccaria (1735?–?1794), author of *Dei delitti e delle pene* (1764), which won fame throughout Europe in the field of penology.

Beccaria's influence extended to Giuseppe Parini (1729–1799), who wrote odes of public and personal interest (*Il bisogno, A Silvia, La caduta, Alla Musa, Il messaggio*) in a taut and finished style and on a more solid basis than the contemporary neoclassic poets, and a longer free verse poem, *Il giorno* (*The Day*). In this poem the writer pretends to be the mentor of a young man of fashion, and, while instructing him as to how he should pass the day, he satirizes his idle and vicious existence. The picture of society, narrow in the first section, *Il mattino,* is gradually enlarged in the *Mezzogiorno, Vespro,* and *Notte* until it comprises a wide variety of aristocratic types and foibles.

The decline of the Arcadian school was hastened by new romantic trends, particularly the melancholy vein of Thomas Gray, Edward Young, and the poems of Ossian (q.v.). The latter were introduced to Italy by the verse translation of Melchiorre Cesarotti (1730–1808).

This, then, was the background of Vittorio Alfieri (1749–1803), whose ideas and temperament, however, make him less a product of his century than a rebel against it, a forerunner of romanticism and the Risorgimento (q.v.) rather than an interpreter of the currents around him. Although Alfieri was brought up in Piedmont, a region where French culture prevailed, he became an enemy of the French; he despised the word philosophy, which was venerated by his contemporaries; he opposed the Enlightenment, and lived in a heroic world of his imagination. His principal works are his *Vita,* an autobiography, and his tragedies. Everything that Alfieri wrote is stripped down to essentials, which means that it is concerned with himself as protagonist, with his stubborn, reserved, and melancholy childhood, his youthful dissipations accompanied by an unconscious and desperate longing for a brilliant future, and the manhood out of which he created some masterpieces of despair: *Saul* (q.v.), *Mirra,* and *Filippo II.* The theme of Alfieri's tragedies is an iron will which is fed by an all-absorbing passion or struggles to escape from its bonds. Their noble tone derives from this element of will, which projects the emotions of a world vaster than our own. Several of the tragedies deal with the passion for freedom and influenced the period of the Risorgimento, but they are his best works from a literary point of view.

Foscolo, Leopardi, and Manzoni.—The preromantic themes which influenced Alfieri were enriched in the following years. On the other hand, the vogue of the classics, brought about by the studies of the great German archaeologist Johann Joachim Winckelmann, the ambitions of Napoleon, and the reaction against Arcadian superficiality, caused a recrudescence of classical forms. Vincenzo Monti (1754–1826), who lived during the zenith of the Arcadia, the influx of nocturnal and graveyard poetry inspired by Ossian, and the revival of classical style and taste (which was nevertheless open to new influences), is the poet most representative of his time. His translation of the *Iliad* is still known today.

The themes which are occasional and uncertain in Monti's poetry become strong and persistent in Ugo Foscolo (1778–1827). Love of country, which was superficial in Monti, is one of the prevailing themes of *Ultime lettere di Jacopo Ortis* (*Last Letters of Jacob Ortis,* q.v.) and *I Sepolcri;* the memory of past grandeur becomes a sacred tradition and the object of a cult; and classicism, which in Monti was mere ornamentation, means to Foscolo a purification of his romantic soul and a sublimation of his own melancholy and unrest in the sphere of an ideal world. Romanticism, which was only an external stimulus to Monti's poetry, takes on in Foscolo a note of profound pathos. Foscolo, the heir to Alfieri's patriotism and romantic feeling, the master of the Risorgimento and of the later poet Giosuè Carducci, and the forerunner of Giacomo Leopardi's pessimistic negation, is akin in his imaginative and melancholy spirit to the romantic poets north of the Alps, and his work forms an integral part of contemporary European literature. This work ranges from *Ultime lettere di Jacopo Ortis,* an early and unorganized but rich explosion of his romantic temperament, to *I Sepolcri,* in which romanticism and the discipline of classical training are perfectly balanced, and to the fragmentary *Grazie,* where classicism takes the upper hand, inspiring passages of exquisite poetry which lack, however, the passion that was the most fertile source of his inspiration. Closer in spirit to the *Grazie* are his two odes, and particularly delicate is the one *All'amica risanata.* Akin rather to *I Sepolcri* are his sonnets, among which *Alla sera* and *In morte del fratello Giovanni* give us a finished poetic portrayal of the writer.

While Monti is the decorative historian of the Napoleonic period and Foscolo its prophetic antagonist, a third poet, who wrote in Milanese dialect, Carlo Porta (1775-1821), is not the mere chronicler that he may appear at first glance, but a vivid painter of the age. He depicts life among the common people, nobility, and clergy and unobtrusively tells in verse of the repercussions of history upon the existence of the ordinary citizen. In the minor writers grouped around these great figures we see the continuation in both poetry and prose of the neoclassic tradition.

Though he belongs to the classical school, Giacomo Leopardi (1798–1837) stands in a category all his own. By virtue of his self-control, the chiseled lines of his poems, and the severity of his form, he is the most classical of Italian lyric poets; the atmosphere of his poems is as limpid and uncluttered as that of *I Sepolcri* is wavering and shadowy. But Leopardi is also influenced by the romantic tradition, whose despair, the *mal du siècle,* was anticipated in Foscolo's *Ultime lettere di Jacopo Ortis.* Leopardi does not belong to the age of Napoleon, but to the following period of depression and pessimism which set in as a reaction to its tumultuousness and was fertile soil for the growth of romanticism. He takes over many of Foscolo's most melancholy themes and early in his career shuts himself up in a state of grief which reflects not only the unhappiness of his own life but the mood prevalent in contemporary European literature. But Leopardi's despair is not morbid; it assumes well-defined contours and rises to a wider sphere where worldly troubles disappear and melancholy is the product not of human vicissitudes but of a deep feeling for man's inevitable fate. This is the meaning of such lyrics as *L'infinito, Canto notturno d'un pastore errante dell'Asia, Il sabato del villaggio,* and *La sera del dì di festa,* and the more subjective *A Silvia, Le ricordanze,* and *Alla sua donna.* It is, indeed, the significance of all his best poetry, which has as its point of departure the familiar scenes of his native town of Recanati but reaches out into the world. (See also ODES.) The prose *Operette morali* (*Dialogues of Leopardi,* q.v.) are thoughtful rather than sentimental. Their form is either narrative or dialogue, interspersed with imaginative passages which lend a gloomy majesty to the writer's conclusions. They are clear evidence of Leopardi's pessimism and serve as an introduction to his *Storia del genere umano*, a description of man's fatal satiety with the goods of this earth and his consequent state of ennui.

Alessandro Manzoni (1785–1873) is half classical, half romantic, although he is generally known as the leader of the Italian romantic school. An important factor not only in his private life but in his writing was the religious conversion he underwent in 1810. He had received his early philosophical education during the revolutionary period, that is, under the influence of clear, logical, and ironical French culture. His conversion took place at a time when mortal weariness and a wave of intellectual disillusionment were paving the way for the political, philosophical, and literary ideas of the period after Napoleon. The first fruits of his conversion were the *Inni sacri,* greatest among them *La Pentecoste,* and the *Osservazioni sulla morale cattolica.* There is religious feeling in his tragedies, *Il conte di Carmagnola* and the better written *Adelchi,* memorable for the choruses *Dagli atri muscosi* and *Morte d'Ermengarda.*

Manzoni's acknowledged masterpiece, *I promessi sposi* (*The Betrothed,* q.v.), which first appeared in 1825–1827, but is better read in the revised 1840–1842 edition, is based on a Christian concept of life. This novel is the love story of two young peasants whose marriage is opposed by an overbearing petty nobleman, abetted by the brutality and public disasters of the time. The action takes place around the Lago di Lecco and in Milan from 1628 to 1630. These scenes were dear to Manzoni and he displays his affection in mellow descriptions and a wealth of detail concerning everyday life. The period of the novel is made vivid to the reader not only by painstaking though not too obvious research, but also by the writer's extraordinary ability to infuse a rich, lifelike quality of thought and feeling into past events and to master and transfigure them with his own austere moral and religious ideas. Manzoni reconstructs and interprets this period with greater penetration than any of the others he studied. It lends itself to the display of the spiritual and artistic richness of his temperament and offers him numerous and skillfully woven themes illustrative of his irony and melancholy and a view of life which appears optimistic and pessimistic in turn and escapes categorical definition as either, because it has passed beyond sentimentality and prejudice and faces the complexities of real life.

Romanticism; De Sanctis.—Romanticism had only a limited influence on Italian literature: it never brought about the complete transformation that took place in other European countries. Italian romanticism restricted itself to a choice of certain themes and to a statement of theories of literature and nationality. In this respect, the most typical writer was Giovanni Berchet (1783–1851), a contributor to *Il Conciliatore,* author of the romantic manifesto *Lettera semiseria di Grisostomo,* and of the poetical works *Romanze* and *Fantasie.* A half patriotic and half satirical poet was Giuseppe Giusti (1809–1850), whose chief concern was with his native Tuscany, as that of the Roman dialect poet, Giuseppe Gioacchino Belli (1791–1863), was with Rome. Historical novels, notably those of Tommaso Grossi (1791–1853) and Massimo Taparelli, marchese d'Azeglio (1798–1866), flourished; they were modeled after Manzoni and had a patriotic and romantic tone. This same tone prevailed in autobiographies and autobiographical novels by such writers as Silvio Pellico (1788–1854), Luigi Settembrini (1813–1877), Giovanni Ruffini (1807–1881), and Ippolito Nievo (1831–1861). Nievo died very young, leaving an enormously promising book, *Confessioni di un ottuagenario.* The writers of the following generation—Giuseppe Mazzini (1805–1872), Francesco Domenico Guerrazzi (1804–1873), and Aleardo Aleardi (1812–1878), were deeply romantic. For some passages of excellent poetry we should mention Giovanni Prati (1815–1884). More complex are the later Lombard poets of an ultraromantic group known as the *scapigliati,* Emilio Praga (1839–1874) and Arrigo Boito (1842–1918). Giacomo Zanella (1820–1888), the meditative poet of *Sopra una conchiglia fossile nel mio studio,* and the series of sonnets, *L'Astichello,* and the poet-novelist Niccolò Tommaseo (1802–1874) hold a place of their own.

The greatest work of the Italian romantic period is that of Francesco De Sanctis (1817–1883), one of the major literary critics of any time and country. Living himself through the crucial period of the Risorgimento, he wrote the first real history of Italian literature.

From Carducci to the Mid-20th Century.—The dominant trend of the second half of the 19th century was a reaction to romanticism and a return to a healthier view of life. The lyric tone gave way to the study of contemporary backgrounds and the structure of modern society, and writers dealt with the people around them rather than with their own egos. The theater, in a first, moderate return to the portrayal of actual life, was dominated by Paolo Ferrari (1822–1889), Vittorio Bersezio (1830–1900), and Pietro Cossa (1830–1881). Later, with Giuseppe Giacosa (1847–1906), Giacinto Gallina (1852–1897), Gerolamo Rovetta (1851–1910), and Marco Praga (1863–1929), realism was accentuated into verism, though never exaggerated. In fiction, these tendencies appeared, at least in more important works, only in the verist period, with Luigi Capuana (1839–1915), Emilio De Marchi (1851–1901), and Matilde Serao (1856–1927).

Lyric poetry took an antiromantic and anticlassical turn about 1860, beginning with Vittorio Betteloni (1840–1910) and going on to Lorenzo Stecchetti (pseudonym of Olindo Guerrini, 1845–1916). Later it was absorbed by the *crepuscolare* (twilight) school and the futurists. Giosuè Carducci (1835–1907), a poet of aristocratic temperament remote from everyday life, was the most deliberate opponent of the false and unhealthy side of the romantic movement. His best work is in the two volumes *Rime nuove* and *Odi barbare*. Carducci took his material from history and his own surroundings and wove it into an expression of his balanced and straightforward personality. History, the classics, and his natural youthful exuberance combined to breathe a new spirit into the Italian lyric. He was inspired by the powerful spectacle of the glories of ancient Rome and the medieval Italian communes, by the strength and self-control of the classic writers, and by a vigorous and sympathetic outlook on the life around him. Carducci is the most concrete and nobly realistic of modern Italian poets. The fragrance of the woods and fields and the boundless silence of a southern landscape are all between the covers of his books. After Carducci studies of nature were complicated either by spiritual problems, as in Giovanni Pascoli, or by sensual violence as in Gabriele D'Annunzio.

Giovanni Verga (1840–1922) had a clear and manly view of life, but there was in him a strain of melancholy that Carducci never knew. His theme is the struggle of daily life, played against no majestic background and relieved by no unexpected adventures, but lived out in a mood of uninterrupted and taciturn sorrow. This is the subject of his best short stories—*Rosso Malpelo,* for instance—and his most successful novels, *I Malavoglia* and *Mastro don Gesualdo. I Malavoglia* is the story of a family that goes through endless trials with the weary and persistent hopefulness of the truly unfortunate. It is the first great example of the passage of the Italian novel from an epic to a lyric manner. *Mastro don Gesualdo,* less unified and more varied, tells of a man who rises by sheer tenacity from poverty to wealth, struggling against the envy, mistrust, and pride of both the aristocrats to whom he relates himself by marriage and the poor people with whom he grew up and whom he hopes to help. At the end of the book the hero is alone and forgotten. (See also CAVALLERIA RUSTICANA.)

Italian realism assumed a strictly regional character; it was Sicilian in Verga and Capuana, Tuscan in Renato Fucini (1843–1921), Neapolitan in Matilde Serao, and Sardinian in Grazia Deledda (1875–1936). Other regional works were the musical and melancholy poems in Neapolitan dialect of Salvatore di Giacomo (1862–1934) and the Roman poems of Cesare Pascarella (1858–1940).

Benedetto Croce (1866–   ) is an able critic of this period as well as a writer of clear and harmonious style. He is closer to Carducci and Verga than he is to the romantic soulfulness, mysticism, and decadent qualities of the writers making up the following Italian literary school: Antonio Fogazzaro, Arturo Graf, Giovanni Pascoli, and Gabriele D'Annunzio.

Antonio Fogazzaro (1842–1911) attempted to give spiritual guidance to those who were torn between science and religion, but he was not equal to this difficult task. He was sensitive, given to lofty feelings, and inclined to hear in nature the voice of a spirit mysteriously akin to that of man. This inclination is apparent to an overpowering degree in *Malombra,* an overly intricate and tempestuous novel which is an accurate reflection of Fogazzaro's own temperament. *Piccolo mondo antico* (*The Little Old World,* q.v.), in which his contradictory impulses are better balanced, is more clear-cut. The scene of this novel is laid in places which Fogazzaro remembered from his childhood, and the plot is concerned with incidents of the time of the Risorgimento of which he had heard at first hand during the youthful years he spent in Turin.

Arturo Graf (1848–1913), like Fogazzaro, belongs to the movement of reaction against realism. His poetry begins with the bewilderment of a lost soul and eventually rises to a tragically religious note.

Giovanni Pascoli (1855–1912) was another opponent of realism, dominated by a sense of the mystery that surrounds and governs human life. From this sense of mystery comes a resignation to evil which amounts to passivity and may perhaps be attributed to the influence of Leo Tolstoy, just as his perplexity in the face of the problem of evil seems to derive from Fëdor Dostoyevsky. Such an ethical stand on the part of a contemplative nature like that of Pascoli necessarily led to the solitary, meditative, and bewildered attitude which he assumed toward life. His inner confusion pours itself out most naturally in the silent countryside where it is easiest to hear the mysterious voice of nature. His best collections of verse are *Myricae, Canti di Castelvecchio, Primi poemetti,* and *Poemi conviviali.* In Fogazzaro and Pascoli alike there is something effete, a weak moral fiber, a surrender to the feeling of mystery, a submission to the irrational, and hence an increase in the musical quality of their poetry to the detriment of line and construction—all qualities characteristic of decadence.

This trend culminated in Gabriele D'Annunzio (1863–1938), in whom were inextricably mingled the temperament of a Renaissance nobleman and that of a modern decadent, avid for subtle new sensations and intent on grafting obscure and magical meanings onto the appearances and events of life. D'Annunzio was prey to a fundamental dualism, torn between heroism and decadence, epic violence and heedless frivolity. The essence of his poetry, in the lyrics of *Alcione,* the tragedy *La Figlia di Jorio,* and the best pages of his novels—*Il Piacere* (q.v.), *Il trionfo della morte,* and *Il fuoco*—is gloomy, nervous, and ultra-romantic. Although D'Annunzio is very often sensual to an extreme, we see him at his best carried away by music and suffering, lost in an ecstatic adoration of beauty, wondering at the discontent engendered by its enjoyment, and eager, all in vain, to penetrate its secret. (See also FRANCESCA DA RIMINI; LA CITTA MORTA; LA GIOCONDA.)

Italian poetry has remained more or less derivative from Pascoli and D'Annunzio. This is true of Guido Gozzano (1883–1916), whose illness and consequent scepticism toward heroic ideals made him the most notable representative of the *crepuscolare* school, and it is equally true of futurism and pure poetry. Strictly Italian influences have been tempered by those of Georges Rodenbach, Walt Whitman, Émile Verhaeren, Stéphane Mallarmé, Arthur Rimbaud, Paul Valéry, and others. Among living poets, Eugenio Montale (1896–   ) is worthy of mention, and the most profound of all is Umberto Saba (1883–   ).

Among modern prose writers, Aldo Palazzeschi (1885–   ), author of *Stampe dell'ottocento* and *Sorelle Materassi,* belongs in some ways to the *crepuscolare* group but has a vein of mingled pathos and comedy all his own. *Rubè,* a novel by Giuseppe Antonio Borgese (1882–), is typical of the disillusionment following World War I. Emilio Cecchi (1884–) is an ultraromantic who has written some of the most brilliant pages of Italian prose. Antonio Baldini (1889–) and Riccardo Bacchelli (1891–) belong to no particular school; the latter has a talent for the sensory and concrete. Important anti-Fascist writers are Gaetano Salvemini (1873–), historian, and Carlo Levi (1902–), author of *Cristo si è fermato ad Eboli* (*Christ Stopped at Eboli*), one of the most interesting of the post-World War II writers. Among the younger writers of note are Vitaliano Brancati (1907–), and Elio Vittorini (1908–), whose novels have appeared in English translation.

Perhaps the two best-known 20th century writers after D'Annunzio are Alfredo Panzini (1863–1939), whose prose contains varied and skillfully handled themes, half scholarly and half frivolous, as in *La Lanterna di Diogene;* and Luigi Pirandello (1867–1936), author of many short stories, one remarkable novel (*Il fu Mattia Pascal*), and a number of plays whose desperate and harrowing themes, well suited to the modern temper, have secured their performance all over the world. (See also separate biographies of important authors; NOVEL, THE MODERN; and DRAMA.)

Bibliography.—GENERAL: Gaspary, Adolfo, *Storia della letteratura italiana* (Turin 1887–1901); De Sanctis, Francesco, *Storia della letteratura italiana* (Bari 1912); *Storia letteraria d'Italia scritta da una società di professori* (Milan 1899–1913); Momigliano, Attilio, *Storia della letteratura italiana* (Milan 1945).

FROM THE EARLIEST TIMES TO DANTE: Monaci, Ernesto, *Crestomazia italiana dei primi secoli* (Città di Castello 1889–97); Satta, S., Egidi, P., and Festa, N., *Il libro de varie romanze volgare* (Rome 1902–06); Cesareo, G. A., *Le origini della poesia lirica e la poesia siciliana sotto gli Svevi,* 2d ed. (Palermo 1924); Rossi, Vittorio, *Il dolce stil nuovo* in *Scritti di critica letteraria* (Florence 1930); Manitius, Max, *Geschichte der lateinischen Literatur des Mittelalters,* 3 vols. (Munich 1911–31).

DANTE—*Collected Works: Opere di Dante,* critical text of the Società dantesca italiana (Florence 1921). *Commentaries:* Casini, T., and Barbi, S. A., *Divina Commedia* (Florence 1926); Momigliano, Attilio, *Divina Commedia* (Florence 1946–48). *Other Works on Dante:* Croce, Benedetto, *La poesia di Dante,* 2d ed. (Bari 1921); De Sanctis, Francesco, *Pagine dantesche* (Milan 1921); Parodi, E. G., *Poesia e storia nella Divina Commedia* (Naples 1921).

PETRARCH: Nolhac, Pierre de, *Pétrarque et l'humanisme* (Paris 1892); Petrarch, F., *Il Canzoniere,* with a commentary by Giosuè Carducci and Severino Ferrari (Florence 1908); De Sanctis, Francesco, *Saggio critico sul Petrarca* (Naples 1924).

BOCCACCIO AND THE LESSER 14TH CENTURY WRITERS: Hauvette, Henri, *Boccace* (Paris 1914); Croce, Benedetto, *Poesia popolare e poesia d'arte* (Bari 1946).

HUMANISM AND THE 15TH CENTURY: Monnier, Philippe, *Le Quattrocento* (Paris 1901); Gentile, Giovanni, *Giordano Bruno e il pensiero del Rinascimento* (Florence 1920); Burckhardt, Jakob, *The Civilization of the Renaissance in Italy,* tr. of 15th ed. (New York 1929).

FIRST HALF OF THE 16TH CENTURY; ARIOSTO AND MACHIAVELLI: Villari, Pasquale, *Niccolò Machiavelli e i suoi tempi,* 3 vols. (Milan 1895–96); Croce, Benedetto, *Ariosto, Shakespeare e Corneille* (Bari 1920); id., *Storia della storiografia italiana* (Bari 1921); Hauvette, Henri, *L'Arioste et la poésie chevaleresque à Ferrare* (Paris 1927); Russo, Luigi, *Machiavelli* (Rome 1943); Momigliano, Attilio, *Saggio sull'Orlando Furioso* (Bari 1945).

THE AGE OF TASSO: Donadoni, Eugenio, *Torquato Tasso,* 2 vols. (Florence 1921); Croce, Benedetto, *Storia dell'età barocca in Italia* (Bari 1929).

THE 17TH CENTURY: Maugain, Gabriel, *Étude sur l'évolution intellectuelle de l'Italie de 1657 à 1750 environ* (Paris 1909); Croce, Benedetto, *Lirici marinisti* (Bari 1910); id., *Saggi sulla letteratura italiana del Seicento* (Bari 1911).

THE 18TH CENTURY: Carducci, Giosuè, *Poeti erotici del secolo XVIII* (Florence 1868); id., *Studi su Giuseppe Parini,* vols. 13 and 14 of *Opere* (Bologna 1891–1908); Goldoni, Carlo, *Opere complete,* 20 vols. (Venice 1907–17); Hazard, Paul, *L'invasion des littératures du Nord dans l'Italie du XVIII siècle* in *Revue de littérature comparée* (Paris 1921); Petraccone, Enzo, *La commedia dell'arte* (Naples 1927); Lee, Vernon, *Il Settecento in Italia* (Naples 1932).

FOSCOLO, LEOPARDI, AND MANZONI: De Sanctis, Francesco, *Studio su G. Leopardi* (Naples 1885); Luchaire, Jean, *Essai sur l'évolution intellectuelle de l'Italie de 1815 à 1830* (Paris 1906); Hazard, Paul, *La révolution française et les lettres italiennes* (Paris 1910); De Sanctis, Francesco, *Manzoni, Studi e lezioni* (Bari 1922); Fubini, Mario, *Ugo Foscolo* (Turin 1928); Levi, G. A., *Giacomo Leopardi* (Messina 1931); Momigliano, Attilio, *Alessandro Manzoni* (Milan 1948).

ROMANTICISM; DE SANCTIS: De Sanctis, Francesco, *La letteratura italiana nel secolo XIX* (Naples 1898); Croce, Benedetto, *Gli scritti di F. De Sanctis e la loro varia fortuna* (Bari 1917); Borgese, G. A., *Storia della critica romantica in Italia* (Milan 1920); Nardi, Piero, *Scapigliatura* (Bologna 1924); Russo, Luigi, *F. De Sanctis e la cultura napoletana* (Florence 1928); Croce, Benedetto, *La letteratura della nuova Italia,* 3d ed., vol. 1 (Bari 1929).

FROM CARDUCCI TO THE MID-20TH CENTURY: Donadoni, Eugenio, *Antonio Fogazzaro* (Naples 1913); Russo, Luigi, *I narratori (1860–1922)* (Rome 1923); Flora, Francesco, *Dal romanticismo al futurismo,* 2d ed. (Milan 1925); Borgese, G. A., *Gabriele D'Annunzio,* 2d ed. (Milan 1932); Russo, Luigi, *Giovanni Verga* (Bari 1934); Binni, Walter, *La poetica del decadentismo* (Florence 1936); D'Amico, Silvio, *Il teatro italiano,* 2d ed. (Milan 1937); Croce, Benedetto, *La letteratura della nuova Italia,* 6 vols. (Bari 1914–40); Pancrazi, Pietro, *Scrittori d'oggi* (Bari 1942).

ATTILIO MOMIGLIANO,
Professor of Italian Literature, University of Florence.

6. THE ARTS.

The first Christian art in Italy resembled closely the contemporary late Roman work. Like the pagan pictures of the time, the paintings in the catacombs of Rome were done with a series of rapid strokes of the brush and very little shading against a light background. They were, however, distinguished by a new and largely symbolic iconography. Among the commonest of the symbols used were fish, ships, and vines. The sculpture of the period, consisting largely of bas-reliefs on sarcophagi, of which there are fine examples in the Lateran Museum, shows the same Roman Empire style.

EARLY CHRISTIAN AND BYZANTINE ART

After 313 A.D., when Constantine issued the Edict of Milan, granting legal status to the Catholic Church, architecture began to develop along new lines. This date marks the beginning of a new Christian art with forms of expression distinct from those of the ancient world.

Early Christian Churches.—In the fourth and fifth centuries, Rome was the chief artistic center of Italy. Among the great basilicas built in the city at this time were Old St. Peter's, which was later destroyed and rebuilt in the Renaissance; St. John Lateran, which we see today in baroque dress; Santa Maria Maggiore, the best preserved of all; St. Paul's Outside the Walls, which was rebuilt in the 19th century; and Santa Sabina, with its fine wooden doors. Circular buildings were also characteristic of the time: Mausoleum of Santa Costanza; Baptistery of the Lateran; Santo Stefano Rotondo. Mosaic decoration of interiors became common, and we have examples in Santa Pudenziana, Santa Maria Maggiore, Santi Cosma e Damiano, and Sant' Agnese.

The Byzantine Period.—The mosaics of Sant' Agnese in Rome date from the 7th century and show an increasing Byzantine influence. A new mystical spirit made for new forms of expression. Art abandoned the imitation of nature;

images lost their bodily mass, and colors were laid on a flat surface and were brightened in such a way that they gave an immaterial vision of light.

The chief monuments of the Byzantine period are at Ravenna, which was the capital of the Byzantine exarchate from the 6th to the 8th centuries (see section on *History*). Among them are the Mausoleum of Galla Placidia, the Baptistery of the Orthodox, Sant' Apollinare in Classe, Sant' Apollinare Nuovo, and San Vitale, all decorated inside with brilliant mosaics.

Sculpture veered away from prominent relief and effects of mass, and we see it flattened out on the sides of sarcophagi (many of which are found in Sant' Apollinare in Classe), or turned into the lacework of capitals and screens and the carving of pulpits and bishops' chairs. Other works of the Byzantine period survive in Naples and Milan.

THE ROMANESQUE PERIOD

The Romanesque period of Italian art lasted from the late 8th century to the early 13th century. The first part of this period, ending in approximately 1000 A.D., is known as early or pre-Romanesque.

Early Romanesque.—The monuments of this time are fewer in number than those of the Byzantine period, mixed in style, and imprecisely dated. Architecture and sculpture drew further away from the Byzantine tradition than did painting. The structures, scattered all over Italy, of the *maestri comacini,* who probably came from the Lago di Como region, derive many of their features from Byzantine architecture, but there is a changed relationship among them. They are heavier and thicker than the Byzantine churches, with brick walls that are interrupted by slit windows which admit little light. Churches of this type include San Pietro, Tuscania; San Salvatore, Brescia; the apse and presbytery of Sant' Ambrogio, Milan; and the baptisteries of Biella, Agliate, and Galliano. In Rome, on the other hand, the harmoniously proportioned basilicas of the 9th century—Santa Maria in Domnica and Santa Prassede, with its chapel of San Zenone, all decorated with mosaics, together with Santa Maria in Aracoeli—bear witness to the survival of a local architectural tradition of the early Christian period.

Since the churches are almost completely devoid of sculpture, we must look for the plastic arts of the time in carved capitals, baptismal fonts (Cathedral of Cividale, 8th century), ciboria (Sant' Apollinare, Ravenna), screens, and pulpits and above all in the work of goldsmiths, one of whose most notable examples is the altar by Vuolvinio (Vuolfvinus) in Sant' Ambrogio, Milan, reminiscent of the Carolingian style.

In the Eastern Roman Empire, Byzantine art still prevailed, conserving its almost religiously set color values, its technical sumptuosity and refinement, and a progressive rigidity of both iconographic and stylistic themes. But in western Europe—France, the Rhineland, Ireland, Spain, and northern Italy—a new form of art was born, rising out of the Byzantine tradition, but branching away from it by virtue of greater feeling and inventiveness, the absorption of barbarian decorative motifs, and a renewal of plastic values. Italian art of these centuries represents one phase of this international picture. This process developed in richness and multiplicity during the Romanesque period proper, which extended in Italy from about 1000 to 1200 and beyond.

Romanesque Art. — *Architecture.* — Romanesque architecture varies greatly from one part of Italy to another. Its style is most homogeneous in the Lombard sector, which covers Lombardy (Sant' Ambrogio, Milan; San Fedele, Como; San Michele, Pavia; and the Cathedral of Cremona); Piedmont (Monastery of San Michele, Val di Susa); Emilia (the cathedrals of Modena, an especially fine example; Parma, with its baptistery; Piacenza; Fidenza; Ferrara); and along the Adriatic coast. The architecture of this area is characterized by organic construction, vaulted ceilings, pilasters, arches, effects of mass and of light and shadow obtained by the use of bricks, deeply recessed portals, pillars standing in relief against the walls, blind arcades, porches, and rose windows. These characteristics are found with some local variations in churches of Marche (San Ciriaco Cathedral, Ancona); Umbria (San Rufino Cathedral, Assisi; San Pietro, Spoleto), where there are traces of influence from Latium; and Apulia (San Nicola, Bari; cathedrals of Trani, Troia, Bitonto, Barletta, and Altamura), where the Lombard style is mingled with Pisan, Norman, and Arab elements. In Rome and Latium, there prevailed the tradition of the Cosmati family, whose simple and serene churches remind us of early Roman forms, ornamented with a typical surface decoration of *tesserae* or plaques of colored marble in geometric patterns, as in the cloisters of St. John Lateran and St. Paul's Outside the Walls. In the Romanesque buildings of southern Italy, the mixture of Lombard, Norman, and Arab influences produced fanciful effects: cathedrals of Caserta Vecchia, Benevento (completely ruined in World War II), and Amalfi; and San Pantaleo, Ravello. Sicily was subject primarily to Arab influence, as is seen in the cathedrals of Cefalù and Monreale, with its magnificent cloister, and the Zisa of Palermo.

In western Venetia the Lombard influence was paramount (San Zeno and the Cathedral of Verona), but in the city of Venice the Byzantine tradition persisted in an elaborate and refined form: witness St. Mark's with its oriental cupolas, mosaics, and marble incrustations. In Tuscany the Florentine style was distinguished by a harmonious simplicity of structure and by the ornamentation of large surfaces with marble plaques in two colors and a geometric design: Baptistery of Florence; San Miniato al Monte, near Florence and the Abbey of Fiesole. In Pisa construction was more complex, and the most striking local characteristic is the superposition of external porches. The cathedral, begun in 1118, with its baptistery and bell tower, served as a model for many other churches outside the immediate region—San Martino, San Frediano, and San Michele, all in Lucca, where there was some infiltration from Lombardy—and for structures in Corsica, Sardinia, and even Apulia.

Sculpture.—Sculpture flowered along with architecture, and there was a rebirth of plastic feeling. It was sculpture that animated the façades, doors, and capitals of the churches, drawing inspiration from flowers and animals, but also emancipating itself from naturalism in order to create fantastic monsters and designs which blended with the architectural scheme. Plastic representations of the works and virtues of man, the months, planets, and signs of the zodiac—a whole illustrated encyclopedia was unfolded before the eyes of the faithful. Sculpture is most abundant where architectural forms are most complex and massive, and less evident where flat surfaces and marble incrustations prevail, as they do in Florence, Rome, and Latium.

The first identifiable Romanesque sculptors are Viligelmo, who created the bas-relief stories from Genesis on the façade of the Cathedral of Modena (beginning of the 12th century); Niccolò, who decorated the façade of the Cathedral of Ferrara in 1135; and Benedetto Antelami (fl. 1177–1233), greatest of the three, who carved the *Deposition* in the Cathedral of Parma (1178) and the decorations of its baptistery (1196). The figures of prophets on the outside of the Cathedral of Fidenza are close to Antelami, if not by him. There are also many anonymous sculptures of high quality in the Cathedral of Modena; San Michele, Pavia; the Cathedral of Cremona; and San Zeno, Verona, with its 12th century bronze door.

In Tuscany much activity centered around the atelier of the Cathedral of Pisa. Maestro Guglielmo (William of Innsbruck), its chief artisan, did the old pulpit, which is now at Cagliari, in 1159. There is a notable stylistic resemblance between him and his Lombard and Provençal contemporaries, and he was the originator of a trend that held the field for over 100 years in Tuscany, with Gruamonte, Biduino, and Guido da Como.

In Pisa, after Maestro Guglielmo, Bonanno (Bonannus) held sway. His style was more decorative and nearer to the Byzantine model, as is seen in the bronze doors of the cathedrals of Pisa and Monreale (1186). There is an even stronger Byzantine influence in the reliefs on the main portal of the Baptistery of Pisa. In Lucca sculpture had a more Lombard Romanesque character, as in Guidetto's sculpture on the façades of San Martino (1204) and San Michele, and the scenes from the lives of St. Martin and St. Regulus under the portico of the cathedral. In Tuscany and Latium there was considerable sculpture in wood: Depositions (Tivoli, Pescia, and Volterra); crucifixes (Petrognano); and groups of the Virgin and Child. In the south sculpture flowered along with architecture, exhibiting a mixture of varied elements, particularly imagination: the portals at Troia and Trani; the bronze doors at Trani (by Barisano da Trani), and at Benevento (destroyed in World War II); the pulpits at Ravello, Salerno, and Sessa Aurunca; and everywhere carved capitals (notably beautiful in the cloisters of Cefalù and Monreale), friezes, doorposts, and bishops' chairs. Perhaps it was in the south, where Emperor Frederick II favored everything classical, that Italian Romanesque sculpture had its last resurgence before the advent of the Gothic, and that Nicola Pisano found his models.

Painting.—There are fewer examples left of Romanesque painting, but we can see that in this branch of art the Byzantine tradition lasted longer, especially in Venetia (mosaics of St. Mark's and the Cathedral of Torcello) and Sicily, where it is mingled with Arab themes (mosaics of the cathedrals of Cefalù and Monreale, and the Palatine Chapel in Palermo). In Latium we can still see numerous frescoes of the 11th and 12th centuries: Lower Church of San Clemente, Rome; Sant' Elia, near Nepi; Monastery of Grottaferrata; and San Silvestro, Tivoli. Even more impressive are those of Sant' Angelo, Formia (11th century). There are scattered Romanesque frescoes in all parts of northern Italy: crypt of the Cathedral of Aquileia; San Pietro, Civate; San Michele, Oleggio; Baptistery of Parma. The mosaics in the Baptistery of Florence are of a later date, having been begun in 1225. The newest accent in the language of Romanesque painting is found in miniatures. Among paintings on wood there are numerous crucifixes, one of the finest of which is in the Cathedral of Sarzana. In Sant' Agata, Cremona, there is a fine but almost unknown painting of St. Agatha.

At the beginning of the 13th century we can begin to distinguish the first Tuscan painters: Berlinghiero Berlinghieri, first mentioned in 1228, and Bonaventura Berlinghieri (1235), of Lucca, Giunta Pisano (fl. 1229–1254), Margheritone di Arezzo (mentioned in 1262), and Coppo di Marcovaldo, who worked in Florence from 1260 to 1271.

GOTHIC ART

Architecture.—Gothic architecture, which originated north of the Alps, began to penetrate Italy at the beginning of the 13th century. The first Italian Gothic buildings were Cistercian abbey churches: Fossanova (1208) and Casamari (1217), in Latium; San Galgano (begun in 1227), near Siena; Chiaravalle, near Milan; and Sant' Andrea, Vercelli. The principles of Gothic construction spread rapidly in Italy, but proportions differed from those of northern Europe, and there was not the same predominance of vertical lines. Italian builders preferred a more serene harmony between height and width and never attained the prodigious lacework of the northern Gothic cathedrals and their miracles of stained glass. The only exception is the Cathedral of Milan, which was begun very late, in 1386, with the aid of architects from beyond the Alps.

The rise during the 13th century of two religious orders, the Franciscans and Dominicans, stimulated the building of churches all over Italy, most of them in the Gothic style. Among them are San Francesco of Assisi (1228–1253); San Francesco (partly ruined in World War II) and San Domenico, Bologna; San Francesco of Arezzo; Santa Maria Novella (apparently begun in 1278) and Santa Croce (1294), Florence; and Santa Maria sopra Minerva, Rome. Three large cathedrals were also constructed in Gothic style: Siena, which went over into the following century; Santa Maria del Fiore, Florence, which was begun by Arnolfo di Cambio, probably the same as Arnolfo da Firenze (1232?–1302), in 1296; and Orvieto, begun around 1285.

Many nonecclesiastical buildings date from this same period. Their style is massive and closed in Florence (Palazzo Vecchio and various houses [many destroyed] and towers), winged and lacy in Venice (Ducal Palace). Almost every Italian city built a town hall at this time, and that at Piacenza is one of the most beautiful.

Early Gothic Sculpture.—Sculpture, too, took on new forms. After the middle of the 13th century the striking personality of Nicola (or Niccolò) Pisano or d'Apulia, who was both architect and sculptor, the master and teacher of the Pisan school, came into view. It is uncertain whether he received his early training in Tuscany or in southern Italy. There are many Tuscan elements in his style, but he must have been acquainted with the art that flourished at the court of Frederick II in Palermo, the most cultivated in Italy. The head formerly on a gate and now in the Museum of Capua, the heads on the keystones of Castel del Monte near Adria, and the pulpit of Ravello appear to antedate but foreshadow Nicola's style. The first work that can be definitely attributed to him is the pulpit in the Baptistery of Pisa (1260), a massive, hexagonal piece supported by strong columns and arches and covered with sculpture. On its five panels is portrayed the cycle of the Redemption, from the Nativity to the Crucifixion and Last Judgment. The numerous figures stand out in powerful relief among deep shadows, with the folds of their garments as taut as nervures. There is growing pathos and an expansion of thick and heavy forms from Nativity to Crucifixion, and this is the subsequent direction taken by Nicola's style, as we see it in the pulpit of the Cathedral of Siena (1265–1268). Here he worked with his son Giovanni Pisano and with his pupils, Arnolfo di Cambio, Lapo, and Donato di Ricevuto. But the master's imprint is the strong unifying force, even if we see distinct traces of his assistants, especially Giovanni and Arnolfo, in some bas-reliefs. Another joint effort of the Pisan school is the tomb of St. Dominic in Bologna (c. 1264–1267), where Arnolfo's personality is more easily recognizable than in Siena.

After Siena, Arnolfo left Nicola's workshop, while Nicola and Giovanni went on working together and jointly signed the splendid Fountain of Perugia (1278). From 1284 to 1299, Giovanni worked at the Cathedral of Siena, and in particular on the lower part of the façade, with its three portals and the large statues on the cornice, which make of it the first Italian cathedral as peopled with sculptured figures as the French churches, but whose sculpture is more independent of the architectural framework. Between 1294 and 1299, Giovanni divided his time between the Cathedral of Siena and the Baptistery of Pisa, on which he had already collaborated with his father. These works were followed by the pulpit of Sant' Andrea (1301), Pistoia; that of the Cathedral of Pisa (1302–1310); and the tomb of Margaret of Luxembourg (1313), now in a fragmentary state in the Museum of Genoa. Nor must we forget the splendid groups of the Virgin and Child which we see in the Campo Santo and in Baptistery of Pisa, in the Scrovegni or Arena Chapel at Padova (Padua), and in the Cathedral of Prato (c.1317). Giovanni was as great an artist as his father was, but in an entirely different manner, more rapid and abrupt, more Gothic. He abbreviated forms by summarizing them in a single gesture and accentuated their expressiveness by the deeply cut outlines made by his chisel, creating a tense and dramatic effect.

We find the third master of the Pisan school, Arnolfo di Cambio, 10 years after his collaboration on the Cathedral of Siena, working in 1277 in the service of Charles I, king of the Two Sicilies, at Rome. Until 1295 he stayed on for the most part in Rome, where his works include the tomb of Cardinal Annibaldi in St. John Lateran, the crib of Santa Maria Maggiore, the tomb of Boniface VIII, the ciboria of St. Paul's Outside the Walls (1283), and Santa Cecilia in Trastevere (1295). In 1277 and in 1281 he was apparently in Perugia (there are fragments of a fountain and the headless statue of a scribe in the museum there) and Orvieto, where he did the tomb of Cardinal de Braye in the Church of San Domenico. From 1296 until his death in 1302 he worked on the Cathedral of Florence, particularly the sculpture on its façade. Where Giovanni was nervous, dramatic, and immediate, Arnolfo was crystal clear and almost architectural in his forms. Modern art criticism has stressed the relationship between Arnolfo and the painter Giotto in values of volume and space.

Early Gothic Painting.—A new style was inaugurated in painting after the first great cycle of Pisan sculpture was over. The Florentine Giovanni Cimabue (properly Cenni di Pepo, fl. 1272–1302) and the Sienese Duccio di Buoninsegna (fl. 1278–1319), great masters as they are, were still linked to the Byzantine tradition. Cimabue's painting is more gaunt and severe with traces of the Romanesque, while Duccio is richer in color and ornamentation, with wavy lines reminiscent of the Gothic. Cimabue's main works are the grandiose frescoes of San Francesco of Assisi; the crucifixes of San Domenico, Arezzo, and Santa Croce, Florence; and the *Madonna Enthroned* of the Uffizi Gallery, Florence. Those considered Duccio's are the *Rucellai Madonna* in Santa Maria Novella, Florence, and the small *Virgin of the Franciscans* in the Siena Gallery. His only authenticated work, however, is the *Maestà* (*Madonna in Majesty*) of the museum of the Cathedral of Siena, dated 1308, with the life of Christ on the back, many pieces of which are scattered in foreign museums. Between these two masters we must mention an anonymous painter of Pisa, who did the fine *Madonna Enthroned and St. Martin* of the Pisa Civic Museum. In Rome, Pietro Cavallini, the painter to whom we owe mosaics of Santa Maria in Trastevere (1291) and the frescoes of Santa Cecilia (c.1295), left the Byzantine tradition behind him and achieved powerful chiaroscuro effects and majestic poses reminiscent of ancient art.

Giotto di Bondone (1276?–?1337), of Florence, transformed the style of painting "from Greek to Latin"—that is, into something truly Western. His contemporaries were quick to acclaim his greatness. Giotto was concise and intense; he was concerned with the human body in action, and he built basic forms of clearly defined volume with expressive gestures and positions, relinquishing the splendor of Byzantine colors in order to secure the dominance of chiaroscuro masses, and limiting his backgrounds to a few synthetic and unadorned elements. His chief works are the St. Francis cycle in the Upper Church of San Francesco of Assisi; the fine painting *Madonna Enthroned,* which is now in the Uffizi Gallery; the frescoes of the Scrovegni Chapel in Padova (c.1303–1305); the crucifix, in Santa Maria Novella, Florence; and the frescoes in the Bardi and Peruzzi chapels in Santa Croce, Florence. The last two were painted about 1320, and his outlook is more peaceful and there is a greater impression of space. Giotto worked also in Rome (mosaic, *La Navicella,* or *St. Peter's Ship,* in the entrance of Old St. Peter's, of which only fragments remain), and in Milan, Rimini, and Naples, leaving a strong influence behind him in each city. In his later years he was an architect. He began the campanile of Florence Cathedral in 1334 and raised it as high as the second story.

Giotto's followers were Taddeo Gaddi (fl. 1322–

1366); Bernardo Daddi (d. 1348); the great Maso di Banco (mentioned 1341–1350), who did the frescoes portraying St. Sylvester, notable for their limpidity, in Santa Croce; and Giottino (mentioned 1368–1369). In the latter 14th century the most important Florentine painters were Andrea Orcagna (real name Andrea di Cione, 1308?–?1368), and his brother Nardo (d. 1365 or 1366). A noteworthy monument of 14th century Florence is the fresco decoration of the Cappellone degli Spagnuoli by Andrea da Firenze (fl. 1343–1377).

At this time, Siena was the center of another important school of painting, richer in color and ornamentation than that of Florence. Simone Martini or di Martino (1283?–1344), a pupil of Duccio, painted in bright colors against a gold background and drew figures whose bodily form is barely indicated by a slender chiaroscuro under draperies that flow in delicate linear arabesques. His chief works are the *Maestà* (1315) and the portrait of Guidoriccio da Fogliano, in the Palazzo Pubblico of Siena; *Louis of Toulouse Crowning His Brother Robert of Naples,* in the Naples Gallery (1317); the Sant' Ansano *Annunciation* in the Uffizi Gallery (1333); and the frescoes portraying St. Martin, in the Lower Church of San Francesco of Assisi. After 1339 he was at Avignon, and the work he did there, which is largely lost, had great influence in France and laid some of the groundwork for the so-called international Gothic style.

The brothers Pietro Lorenzetti (also called Pietro Laurati or Laurati da Siena, first dated work 1315-d.–?1348) and Ambrogio Lorenzetti (Ambrogio di Lorenzo, mentioned 1332-d.–?1348) are more plastic than Simone but more ornate than Giotto. They drew lines around their figures to bring out their depth, and both of the brothers, but especially Ambrogio, had splendid rhythms. Many of their paintings are to be seen in the churches and galleries of Siena, Florence, Vico l'Abate, and other cities. Pietro did frescoes in the Lower Church of San Francesco of Assisi, and Ambrogio in the Palazzo Pubblico of Siena (allegory of *Good and Bad Government*).

Northern Italy, too, had important though lesser known schools of painting in the 14th century. Giotto's influence was felt, but it was transformed by a more empirical, intimate, and narrative local tradition. Among the fine frescoes extant in Lombardy are those at Viboldone, Solaro, Chiaravalle, Vertemate, and Mocchirolo. A leading artist of Lombardy was Giovanni da Milano (fl. 1350–1369), who came there after his Florentine period (1350–1366), during which he had painted the frescoes of the Rinuccini Chapel in Santa Croce.

In 14th century Padova there was a lively and original group of artists, including Guariento, a pupil of Giotto; Giusto di Giovanni di Menabuoi of Florence (d. before 1393), author of the series of frescoes in the baptistery and of those, unfortunately now destroyed, of the Palazzo del Podestà and the Eremitani, with their strictly theological themes; and, a little later, Altichiero or Aldighero da Zevio (1330?–?1400) from Verona together with his assistant, Jacopo Avanzo, who collaborated on the frescoes of Sant' Antonio and the oratory of San Giorgio (after 1377). Giotto's stay in Rimini gave rise to a local school of painting, which in its turn influenced a school of Bologna, whose major exponent was the sensitive and clever Vitale Cavalli (mentioned 1334–1359). Tommaso da Modena (c.1329–1379) had some stylistic resemblance to Vitale, but a different personality, for he was gifted in characterization rather than imagination. He did the frescoes of *Dominican Monks* in the chapter house of San Niccolò at Treviso and the stories of St. Ursula in the museum of the same city. Meanwhile in Venice the Byzantine tradition still prevailed, exemplified by Maestro Paolo and Lorenzo Veneziano (fl. 1356–1379).

Later Gothic Sculpture.—The Pisan school of sculpture continued in the first half of the 14th century. In Naples its tradition was carried on by Tino di Camaino (fl. 1312–1337) of Siena, a pupil of Giovanni Pisano, who was active in Pisa, Siena, and Florence. His Neapolitan works (1325–1337) are the Anjou tombs in Santa Chiara and Santa Maria Donna Regina. In Milan Giovanni di Balduccio of Pisa was author of the tomb of St. Peter Martyr, in Sant' Eustergio (1339). Of a style akin to that of the Pisan school are many early 14th century sculptures in Umbria, among which the most splendid are those on the façade of the Cathedral of Orvieto, attributed to Lorenzo Maitani, who was the superintendent from 1310 to 1330, and those at Ramo di Paganello.

We may relate to these sculptures the obscure origins of Andrea Pisano (also called Andrea da Pontedera, died in 1348), whom we find for the first time in his maturity at Florence in 1330, charged with the execution of the bronze doors of the baptistery, where he carved the story of St. John the Baptist and the cardinal virtues. Andrea shows keen awareness of linear rhythm in his flowing robes, but the most conspicuous parts of his bodies are carved in a refined, synthetic archaic style. Andrea was certainly acquainted with the French art of his time, but he must also have learned from Giotto a new kind of composition and space relationship, which he softened in adapting it to his own talents. The work of these two artists crossed in the campanile of Florence Cathedral, where Andrea Pisano succeeded Giotto as superintendent and, with some assistance, carved most of the bas-reliefs of the lower part of the tower, which represent the story of Genesis and the mechanical arts. According to tradition, these were first sketched by Giotto, who is supposed to have carried some of them out, but this is a controversial and unsupported claim. The bas-reliefs of *Weaving, Horseback Riding, Hercules and Cacus, Navigation,* and *Agriculture* are among the finest ever produced in Italy. In 1347–1348, Andrea was in charge of the Cathedral of Orvieto. He was succeeded there by his son Nino (died in 1368), a graceful but somewhat artificial sculptor (*Madonna* in Santa Maria Novella, Florence; Cornaro tomb in Santi Giovanni e Paolo, Venice).

After Andrea Pisano, the leading place in the field of Florentine sculpture passed to Andrea Orcagna, who carved the tabernacle at Or San Michele (1358–1360). In Pavia, Milan, and Verona (della Scala or Scaligeri tombs), we find the Maestri Campionesi; in Venice, the brothers Jacobello (mentioned to 1409) and Pier Paolo (d. 1403) dalle Masegne (statues of the rood screen of St. Mark's, c.1394), which are in the most ornate Gothic style.

Later Gothic Painting.—The ornate Gothic style, called international because of the common characteristics it had in various parts of Europe, was marked by a progressive diminution of plastic forms and an overabundant development of rhythmically flowing draperies. This style is considered predominantly northern, but the two greatest painters are the Italians Gentile da Fabriano and Pisanello.

Gentile da Fabriano (real name Gentile Massi, died in 1427) came from Marche, where the Gothic style had been made widely known. He worked all over Italy, but particularly in Venice and Rome. Unfortunately, neither his frescoes in the Ducal Palace nor those in St. John Lateran have survived. Such of his paintings as do remain prove him to have been a master of the delicate touch: *Adoration of the Magi* (Uffizi Gallery), and Madonnas of Orvieto, Milan, and the National Gallery, London.

Antonio or Vittore Pisano (il Pisanello, b. before 1395-d. 1455), was trained in the school of Verona (of which the chief figure was Stefano da Zevio, c.1374–1451), which was characterized, like all Lombard painting of the first half of the 15th century (for example, Giovannino de' Grassi, died in 1398; the brothers Zavattari; Bonifazio Bembo; Michelino da Besozzo), by an ornate Gothic style, but he was also inspired by Gentile da Fabriano. The works of Pisanello still preserved include the frescoes of San Fermo (*Annunciation*) and Sant' Anastasia (*St. George and the Princess*), Verona, *Portrait of a Princess* in the Louvre, Paris, *Lionello d'Este* in the Accademia Carrara at Bergamo, and a considerable number of fine drawings. Pisanello was also an excellent engraver and coined medals and medallions for all the princes of Italy.

In Venice, too, painting continued to be in an ornate Gothic style despite a few hesitant foreshadowings of the Renaissance. The greatest masters were Antonio Vivarini (Antonio da Murano, died 1476–1486), who painted the *Madonna Enthroned* (1446) in the Venice Academy in collaboration with Giovanni d'Alemagna (fl. 1440–1447), a triptych at San Zaccaria, and various Madonnas; and Iacopo Bellini (c.1400–c.1470), who is represented by Madonnas in the Louvre, the Venice Academy, and the Uffizi Gallery, and by sketchbooks in the Louvre and the British Museum. Vivarini and Bellini were the respective heads of two families that divided the field of Venetian painting between them.

Even in Florence, both Lorenzo Monaco (called Don Lorenzo, c.1370–1425) and Masolino da Panicale (1383?–?1447), who has been identified with Tommaso di Cristoforo Fini, were essentially Gothic. But here it was, while the rest of Italy continued for a number of years to follow the late Gothic style, that at the beginning of the 15th century three major artists—Filippo Brunelleschi, Donatello, and Masaccio—brought about a revolution in style that developed into the Renaissance.

THE RENAISSANCE

The Renaissance period of Italian art extended from the early part of the 15th century to the latter part of the 16th century. In the early Renaissance, Florence was the leading artistic center of Italy. Later, Rome was pre-eminent, and then, Venice.

Early Florentine Architecture.—Filippo Brunelleschi or Brunellesco (1377?–1446) was not only the greatest Italian architect of the 15th century, but also the first to establish the scientific theory of perspective, which, when applied to the arts, became the basis of Renaissance style. All during the 14th century a feeling for space had been notable in the Florentine school, but this was largely a matter of intuition. Through the use of perspective, spaces could be constructed geometrically, with harmoniously proportioned partitions. Brunelleschi's buildings are the most enlightening example of this development. From the outside they show a clear outline of volumes, while within a large, unencumbered space gradually unfolds before the eye in the rhythm of various planes and a succession of pauses. Together with this impression of space, Brunelleschi's buildings retain the almost elastic tension of the Gothic style and the slenderness and movement of its forms. At one time, Brunelleschi's style was attributed to the study of classical models, but in recent years it is more frequently considered close to the Romanesque—for example, to the Baptistery of Florence and San Miniato—or to the Gothic architect Arnolfo di Cambio. Brunelleschi's chief works are the dome of Florence Cathedral; the Church of San Lorenzo with the old sacristry; the Pazzi Chapel, in the cloister of Santa Croce, an architectural jewel which is entirely his own; the Church of Santo Spirito; and the Pitti Palace, which underwent many changes in the 16th century.

Brunelleschi influenced all the other Florentine architects of his time. They include Michelozzo or Michelozzi di Bartolommeo (1396–1472), who designed the Careggi Villa and the Medici-Riccardi Palace in Florence; Giuliano da Maiano (1432–1490); Benedetto da Maiano (1442–1497), known for Santa Maria delle Grazie at Arezzo and the Strozzi Palace in Florence; Giuliano da Sangallo (1445–1516), builder of Santa Maria delle Carceri at Prato and the sacristry of Santo Spirito in Florence; Simone Pollaiuolo, known as il Cronaca (1454?–?1508), author of the Church of the Saviour at San Miniato.

Architects who broke away from the Brunelleschi tradition were Leon Battista Alberti (1404–1472), who had a more classical and solemn style, which we see in the façade of Santa Maria Novella and the Ruccellai Palace in Florence, the Church of San Francesco (Malatesta Temple), partly destroyed in World War II, at Rimini, and Sant' Andrea at Mantova. Alberti wrote three treatises: *De pictura* (1436), *Della statua,* and *De architettura.* One of his followers was Bernardo Rossellino or Rossellini (1409–1464), who designed the Palazzo Pubblico, Piccolomini Palace, and Cathedral of Pienza, and there are traces of Alberti's style in Luciano da Laurana (fl. 1468–1482), who reveals, however, a personality of his own in the purity of the Ducal Palace of Urbino.

Early Florentine Sculpture.—Donatello (real name Donato di Niccolò di Betto Bardi, 1386?–1466), the great innovator in the field of Florentine sculpture, was one of Brunelleschi's closest friends. His contemporary, Lorenzo Ghiberti (originally Lorenzo di Cione di Ser Buonaccorso, 1378–1455), continued with an older style, extremely delicate and sensitive to decorative, linear rhythms. Ghiberti's chief works are the two gold-covered bronze doors of the Baptistery of Florence, 1403–1424 and 1425–1452), executed with all the delicacy of a goldsmith, which was his real trade. The first door is close to the plans of Andrea Pisano, the second definitely more Renaissance in feeling.

Donatello emerged from the group of late Gothic sculptors working on the Florence cathedral—Nammi d'Antonio di Banco (1374–?1420) among them—and based his sculpture on opposition to the refined elegance of the Gothic tradition. Donatello emphasized the plastic element in his art. He favored realistic forms and brusque motions. In a clear manner Donatello applied Brunelleschi's principles of perspective to the bas-relief, causing his forms to melt into space by telescoping one plane into another and modeling with a rapid, impressionistic, and lively touch. His main works are the *St. George* (1416) now in the Bargello; the statues on the campanile of the cathedral, the *Annunciation* in Santa Croce; the *cantoria,* or singers' gallery, of the cathedral; the ceiling medallions and bronze doors of the old sacristy of San Lorenzo, all in Florence; the statue of Erasmo da Narni, called Gattamelata, in Padova, where he worked from 1443 to 1453, exercising a notable influence on local art, especially that of Mantegna; and the late pulpits of San Lorenzo (in Florence again).

Donatello's influence was supreme among 15th century Florentine sculptors—such men as Michelozzo, who was one of his collaborators; Bernardo Rossellino (tomb of Leonardo Bruni in Santa Croce); Desiderio da Settignano (1428–1464), the most sensitive of the group, author of many *putti* and groups of the Virgin and Child; Mino da Fiesole (1431?–?1481); Antonio Rossellino (1427–?1479); and Benedetto da Maiano. A sculptor who remained aloof from the Donatello tradition was Luca della Robbia (1400?–1482); he discovered the possibilities of glazed terra cotta, which became a specialty of his family.

Another celebrated member of the generation of Ghiberti and Donatello was Jacopo della Quercia (1378?–1438), a Sienese, equally great in spite of the fact that he attracted a lesser following. He worked at first in the late Gothic style, but soon added to it a plastic strength that swelled his forms with power, while still preserving their flowing sinuosity. In Siena, della Quercia did the Fonte Gaia as well as a bas-relief on the baptismal font of the cathedral. He also did the tomb of Ilaria del Carretto in the Cathedral of Lucca (1406) and the famous portal of San Petronio in Bologna.

Early Florentine Painting.—Masaccio (real name Tommaso Guidi, 1401–1428), a contemporary of Brunelleschi and Donatello, achieved something profoundly new in the field of painting. He was a spiritual descendant of Giotto, favoring forms stripped to their essentials, strong chiaroscuro effects, and a muted intensity of gestures and motions. He took over Brunelleschi's discovery of perspective and laid out his spaces and the figures peopling them in such a way as to focus attention on the center of action. The frescoes of the Brancacci Chapel in Santa Maria del Carmine in Florence are his greatest achievement. Here he had Masolino da Panicale as a collaborator, but his own influence was far stronger than that of the older man. His scenes include the *Expulsion from the Garden,* the *Tribute Money, St. Peter Healing the Sick,* and *St. Peter Distributing Alms.* Other of Masaccio's works are the painting of *St. Anne* in the Uffizi Gallery; the altarpiece originally in the Carmine Church at Pisa, now scattered among galleries in Pisa, London, Naples, and other cities; the fresco of the *Trinity* in Santa Maria Novella; part of the Crucifixion in San Clemente in Rome; and a few others.

Up to the time of Michelangelo all the Florentine painters studied the Brancacci frescoes, among them Fra Giovanni da Fiesole, known as Fra Angelico (1387–1455), usually praised for his religious feeling but not sufficiently valued for his great artistic importance. He probably began as a miniaturist, in a manner akin to that of Lorenzo Monaco, but soon developed a radiant style of painting where enamel-like colors are combined with bright spaces, and planes are made to stand out by means of the light falling upon them, and delicately drawn figures are caught in postures of exceeding grace. Fra Angelico worked at Fiesole, Cortona, Florence (whose Convent of San Marco, where he left frescoes in every cell, has been turned into a personal museum), Orvieto, and Rome (frescoes of the Chapel of Nicholas V in the Vatican).

Fra Filippo (or Lippo) Lippi (1406?–1469) is generally associated with Fra Angelico, although he was equally subject to the influence of Masaccio (*Coronation of the Virgin* in the Uffizi Gallery and frescoes in the Cathedral of Prato). Other prominent 15th century Florentine painters were Paolo Uccello (real name Paolo di Dono, 1397–1475), a master of perspective and author of battle scenes in the Uffizi Gallery, Louvre, and the National Gallery of London, as well as the frescoes in the Green Cloister of Santa Maria Novella; Andrea del Castagno (1423–1457), who had a rough but clear-cut style and painted frescoes in Sant' Apollonia, the Villa Pandolfini (now at Sant' Apollonia), and in S. Annunziata; and Domenico Veneziano (c.1400–1461), noted for his powerful drawing and luminous colors (*Santa Lucia* altarpiece in the Uffizi Gallery).

Piero della Francesca (real name Piero dei Franceschi, 1420?–1492) became an apprentice of Domenico Veneziano and achieved a "synthesis of perspective, form, and color" to be seen in his frescoes of the *Story of the True Cross* in San Francesco, Arezzo; the *Baptism of Christ,* National Gallery, London; the altarpiece at his birthplace, Borgo San Sepolcro; the *Flagellation* in the Ducal Palace of Urbino; and the portraits of Federigo da Montefeltro and Battista Sforza in the Uffizi Gallery. Piero, in his turn, influenced Alessio Baldovinetti of Florence (1425?–1499); Melozzo da Forlì (1438–?1495), who painted frescoes in Loreto and Rome; Il Perugino (real name Pietro Vannucci, also called Pier della Pieve, 1446–1523); and Luca d'Egidio di Ventura de' Signorelli (also called Luca da Cortona, 1441–1523), who owes some of his dynamic movement and anatomical knowledge to Antonio Pollaiuolo, and is known for his frescoes in the Cathedral of Orvieto.

Toward 1460 two Florentine masters stood out above the rest: Antonio Pollaiuolo (1429–1498) and Andrea del Verrocchio or Verocchio (real name Andrea di Michele Cione, 1435–1488), both of whom combined painting and sculpture. Pollaiuolo's preferred theme was the nude in motion, sketched in strong and incisive outlines. Among his paintings are the *Hercules and Antaeus* and *Hercules and the Hydra* in the Uffizi Gallery, the *Martyrdom of St. Sebastian* in the National Gallery, London, and *Tobias and the Archangel* in the Turin Gallery. His sculptures include the *Hercules and Antaeus* of the Bargello, Florence, and the tomb of Sixtus IV in the Vatican, Rome. Verrocchio, too, in contrast to the preceding generation, stressed an anatomical treatment of the body and dealt with it in hard outlines, but with less tension than did Pollaiuolo. On the other hand, he lingered more over detail, displayed greater psychological insight and deeper study of chiaroscuro. Among his sculptured works are the sarcophagus of Giovanni and Piero de'Medici in San Lorenzo, the bronze *David* and marble *Bust of a Woman* in the Bargello, the Fountain of the Palazzo Vecchio, and *Christ* and *St. Thomas* on the outside of Or San Michele (all in Florence), and the monument to Bartolomeo Colleoni in Venice. Among his paintings are the *Baptism of Christ* (done with Leonardo) in the Uffizi Gallery, the *Madonna and Child* in the Museum of Berlin, and an altarpiece in the Cathedral of Pistoia.

Sandro Botticelli (originally Alessandro di Mariano dei Filipepi, 1444?–1510) came under the influence of Pollaiuolo and Verrocchio and was a pupil of Filippo Lippi. His lines are poetic and graceful with fine decorative rhythm and he conveys a feeling of melancholy and meditation: Madonnas, portraits, *La Primavera* (*Spring*), and *Birth of Venus,* in the Uffizi Gallery. There was an almost endless number of painters in Florence in the 15th century; let us note further Domenico di Tommaso Bigordi, known as Ghirlandajo (1449–1498), who painted portraits and frescoes in Santa Maria Novella and Santa Trinità; Filippino Lippi (1457?–1504), who was the son of Filippo and a bizarre and unequal painter; and Piero di Cosimo, or di Lorenzo (1462–1521), who had an even more lively style, influenced by that of Leonardo.

Early Non-Florentine Art.—Away from Florence the arts also flourished, but not always in so continuous and coherent a fashion. The Sienese painters favored extremely delicate but more traditional forms, as in the work of Stefano di Giovanni, called Il Sassetta (1392–1450), Giovanni di Paolo (1403?–c.1482), and Neroccio di Bartolommeo di Benedetto de' Landi (1447–1500). Domenico di Bartolo (c.1400–?1447) and Matteo di Giovanni di Bartolo (1434–1495) came under the spell of the Florentine school, and in sculpture Lorenzo di Pietro, known as Vecchietta (c.1412–1480), and Francesco di Giorgio (in full Francesco Maurizio di Giorgio Martini, or di Martino, Pollaiuolo 1439–1502), who in addition did architectural work at the court of Urbino, were influenced by Donatello.

In northern Italy, Gothic forms continued side by side with Renaissance encroachments. In Venice, for instance, at the beginning of the 15th century architecture still had a completely Gothic character, as in the Cà d'Oro and the Cà Foscari. It was considerably later in the century that Antonio Rizzo (or Rizzi or Rizo, 1430?–?1498) and Pietro Lombardo or Lombardi (real name Solaro, c.1435–1515), aided by his sons Antonio (c.1458–?1516) and Tullio (c.1455–1532), introduced the Renaissance style, which we see in the Foscari Arch and the Giants' Staircase in the Ducal Palace (Rizzo) and Santa Maria dei Miracoli (Lombardi). These men were also responsible for a new trend in Venetian sculpture. This had hitherto been dominated by the elaborate late Gothic style, as represented by the sculptors from other regions who worked on St. Mark's and the Ducal Palace, and also by a native Venetian Bartolomeo Buon or Buono (also Bon or Bono, d. ?1464), who carved the *Four Virtues* of the Porta della Carta. Pietro Lombardi is chiefly remembered for the tomb of Pietro Mocenigo (1476) in Santi Giovanni e Paolo, and Rizzo for the monument to the doge Niccolò Tron in Santa Maria dei Frari (1473), completed by others, and the splendid *Adam and Eve* of the Foscari Arch of the Ducal Palace.

In Lombardy, Tuscan architects undertook much work in the 15th century: Ospedale Maggiore of Milan (seriously damaged in World War II) by Filarete (real name Antonio di Pietro Averlino or Averulino, 1400?–?1470), and the Portinari Chapel in Sant' Eustorgio, also in Milan, by Michelozzo. Giovanni Antonio Amadeo or Omodeo (1447?–1522), architect and sculptor, was the chief Lombard artist, designer of the Colleoni Chapel at Bergamo and the façade of the Certosa (Carthusian Monastery) of Pavia, both extremely ornate. In the latter half of the century, the chief influence on Lombard architecture was that of Bramante.

As the Renaissance slowly made itself felt in Lombard painting, this took on an empirical naturalism and love of detail, together with a strong leaning for effects obtained from outlines of light. Vincenzo Foppa (c.1427–1515) was the leader of the Lombard school. Other painters were Bernardino Zenale (1436–1526) and Bernardino Butinone (1436–1507), authors of the altarpiece in San Martino, Treviglio; Ambrogio da Fossano, known as Bergognone or Borgognone (c.1450–1523), who was very active at the Certosa of Pavia; Gian Martino Spanzotti (mentioned 1480–1524), founder of the school of Vercelli; and Gaudenzio Ferrari (1484?–1546), who painted the frescoes of the Sacro Monte of Varallo and worked at San Cristoforo, Vercelli, and the Sanctuary of the Beata Vergine at Saronno, in addition to executing several altarpieces in churches and galleries of Lombardy and Piedmont.

In Padova, the school that came into being after the sojourn of Donatello was dominated by Andrea Mantegna (1431–1506), who had a conscious enthusiasm for classical antiquity and interpreted it in a style still marked by a certain Gothic crudity, with clear-cut, writhing, and violently foreshortened figures, monumental antique backgrounds, and architectural frameworks. Mantegna is known for the frescoes of the Eremitani of Padova, destroyed during World War II, and the bridal chamber of the Ducal Palace of Mantova. There are links with the school of Padova in the style of the Venetian painter Carlo Crivelli (1430?–?1494), long active in Marche and author of many valuable Madonnas, and in Cosmè Tura (1430?–1495), the earliest of the masters of Ferrara, who was followed by Francesco del Cossa (1438?–1480) and Ercole de' Roberti (c.1456–1496). In Venice, Mantegna had a deep influence on Bartolommeo Vivarini, originally da Murano (1432?–?1491), brother of Antonio (1415?–?1470) and uncle of Alvise Vivarini (1446?–?1503), and on the two sons of Jacopo Bellini. Gentile Bellini (1429?–1507) retained in his style an archaic element of distant Byzantine origin (organ doors in the Opera di San Marco), and later revealed a narrative vein akin to that of his pupil, Carpaccio, painting cycles of holidays, miracles, and processions: canvases formerly in the Scuola di San Giovanni Evangelista and now in the Venice Academy. His brother, the great Giovanni Bellini (c.1431–1516), in the course of his long career, moved away from the influence of Mantegna.

Leonardo, Michelangelo, and Raphael.—Toward the end of the 15th century the marked differences among the local schools began to diminish. Increasing exchanges between northern and central Italy, the prevalence of the same artistic problems among all artists, and, above all, the dominance of several outstanding personalities made for greater unity and easier communication among the various regions. In this way Italian art acquired a national character and served as a guide and model to the rest of Europe.

This second stage of the Renaissance was opened by Leonardo da Vinci (1452-1519), a pupil of Verrocchio, who displayed in his very first works a magical use of chiaroscuro, an originality, loftiness, and graceful expression of ideas that set him at once head and shoulders above his fellow pupils, chief among whom was Lorenzo di Credi (1459–1537): *Annunciation* and *Adoration of the Shepherds* (Uffizi Gallery), a *Madonna* (Leningrad), and a *Portrait of a Lady* (Liechtenstein Gallery of Vienna). Leonardo spent the years from 1482 to 1499 in Milan in the service of Lodovico Sforza. He was a painter (*Madonna of the Rocks,* now in the Louvre, with another version in the National Gallery of London; *Last Supper,* which has worn badly, in Santa Maria delle Grazie, in Milan); sculptor (monument to Francesco Sforza, of which he did only a clay horse, which was, unfortunately, shortly destroyed by the French invaders); musician; organizer of parties and masquerades; mathematician; and architect and engineer. In every field to which he turned his hand he had no rival. When Lodovico was driven out by the French, Leonardo returned via Mantova and Venice to Florence. Here, in 1503, he was asked by the Signoria to compete with Michelangelo for a painting in the Palazzo Vecchio: Battle of Anghiari. He made a sketch but never did the mural. From this same period date the *Cartoon of St. Anne,* now in the Royal Academy of London (the Louvre painting—*Madonna with Christ Child in the Lap of St. Anne*—came later), and the famous *La Gioconda,* or *Mona Lisa,* in the Louvre.

Leonardo went further and further into study and research, with the result that he has left us a number of wonderful drawings (Uffizi Gallery, Louvre, British Museum, Windsor Castle, and other museums) and manuscripts, rediscovered and published in the 20th century, which furnish a mine of ideas, experiments, inventions, and prophecies in every field of science: *Codice Atlantico* (*Codex Atlanticus*) in the Ambrosian Library of Milan, manuscripts at the Institut de France, *Codice del Volo degli Uccelli* (*Treatise on the Flight of Birds*) in Turin, notebooks on anatomy at the Royal Library of Windsor.

Leonardo returned to Milan in the service of King Louis XII of France and stayed there from 1506 to 1513, except for the year 1507–1508, which he spent in Florence. After this he went to Rome, and in 1516 to France, where he died. In his art Leonardo went beyond the carefully drawn and circumscribed forms of the Florentine tradition. His edges were less clearly defined, while his atmosphere was enveloping, and deep shadows made the figures emerge in a mysterious way and seem possessed of a new spiritual complexity. His interest extended not only to man but to the whole universe as well.

Michelangelo Buonarroti (1475–1564), on the other hand, raised man, particularly in the representation of the nude, to new heights. He, too, was at once painter, sculptor, and architect. As a very young man he frequented the Medici Garden with its collection of antique sculpture, and his very first work, the *Battle of the Centaurs,* contained the essence of his whole vision: a group of nude figures in combat with taut muscles standing out in relief. There followed the *Madonna of the Steps* in the Casa Buonarroti in Florence, the *Kneeling Angel* and *St. Proculus* and *St. Petronius* for the tomb of St. Dominic in Bologna, the *Bacchus* (Bargello), the *Pietà* in St. Peter's, the *David* (Bargello), the round bas-reliefs of the Royal Academy of London and the Bargello and the round painting of the Uffizi Gallery of Florence, and the unfinished *St. Matthew* of the Florence Academy.

In 1505, Michelangelo was called to Rome to build the tomb of Pope Julius II. He drew up a grandiose plan for a miniature temple under the roof of St. Peter's but eventually had to reduce it to the architectural structure dominated by the figure of Moses which was placed in San Pietro in Vincoli in 1546. The two figures of slaves now in the Louvre were intended to go on this tomb, as were the four unfinished slaves of the Florence Academy. Julius II himself made it difficult for Michelangelo to complete this work by assigning him soon afterwards the decoration of the ceiling of the Sistine Chapel (1508–1512). This gigantic work tells the story of Genesis, framed by magnificent nude festoon bearers and great figures of sibyls and prophets, which had a revolutionary influence on painting. The unveiling of the ceiling was witnessed by everyone of importance in Rome and its influence spread at once all over Italy. Later Michelangelo painted the *Last Judgment* on the altar wall of the chapel and the *Martyrdom of Peter* and *Conversion of Paul* in the Pauline Chapel (1542–1550), but these did not add any new element to his fame or touch the heights that he had reached earlier. Michelangelo at this point went back to sculpture and architecture.

Raphael (Raffaello Santi or Sanzio, 1483–1520) came in between the two great figures of Leonardo and Michelangelo. He was born in Urbino, an important artistic center of the 15th century, known for the work of Piero della Francesa, Melozzo da Forlì, Luciano da Laurana, Francesco da Laurana (c. 1425–1502), Francesco di Giorgio Martini, and others. He was a pupil of Perugino, and between 1500 and 1504 he painted in a style very much like that of his master, but radiant with youthful freshness and incomparable virtuosity (*Marriage of the Virgin* in the Brera Gallery at Milan, *Coronation of the Virgin* in the Vatican Gallery).

In 1504, Raphael went to Florence, where both Leonardo and Michelangelo were then active. He was quick to appreciate the quality and newness of their styles and to modify his own, which he modeled upon that of Leonardo. During the next years he painted a series of Madonnas—the *Madonna del Granduca* (Pitti Palace), the *Madonna del Cardellino* (Uffizi Gallery), *Madonna of the Meadow* (Vienna), *Madonna and Child with the Little St. John* (Berlin; see color plate), and *La Belle Jardinière* (Louvre)—and the portraits of Angelo and Maddalena Doni (Pitti Palace) and of Tommaso Inghirami (Gardner Coll., Boston). In 1508, he was called to Rome by Pope Julius II to paint frescoes in the Vatican: Stanza della Segnatura (1509–1511), Stanza d'Eliodoro (1511–1514), Stanza dell' Incendio di Borgo (1514–1517), Sala di Costantino (1517–1524, executed by his pupils). His style at this point attained the solemn proportions of the portrayals of the *School of Athens, Expulsion of Heliodorus from the Temple*, and the *Mass of Bolsena*. Here he seems to have drawn upon Venetian coloring, which he may have learned from Lorenzo Lotto (a collaborator in the Stanza della Segnatura) even before the arrival in Rome about 1509–1511 of Sebastiano del Piombo, a pupil of Giorgione. At a later period the attempt to imitate Michelangelo caused a certain strain to appear in Raphael's style (Stanza dell' Incendio del Borgo and the *Transfiguration* in the Vatican Gallery). As a whole, however, his work is a monument of harmony and balance, intellect and culture.

Raphael's portraits are also remarkable: *Cardinal* (Prado Museum, Madrid), *Baldassare Castiglione* (Louvre), *Donna Velata* and *Leo X* (Pitti Palace). Another excellent portraitist was Sebastiano del Piombo (real name Sebastiano Luciani, 1485?–1547), who worked at the Villa Farnesina in Rome in 1512–1514, at the same time as Raphael, but in style came closer to Michelangelo: *Flagellation* in San Pietro in Montorio, *Deposition* in the Viterbo Museum. Raphael had several direct pupils—Giulio Romano (real name Giulio Pippi de' Giannuzzi, 1499–1546), who went to Mantova in 1524 and was very active there as both architect and painter; Gianfrancesco Penni, known as Il Fattore (1488?–?1528); and Perino del Vaga (real name Pietro Buonaccorsi, 1501–1547), and his influence was felt all over Italy to an extent surpassed only by that of Michelangelo.

Later Florentine and Northern Italian Painting.—While the greatest artists were flocking to Rome, Florence was falling from the position of capital of Italian art which it had acquired in the 15th century. It could still boast such masters as Fra Bartolommeo della Porta (Bartolommeo di Pagolo de Fattorino, 1475–1517) and Andrea del Sarto (real name Andrea Domenico d'Angnolo di Francesca, 1486–1531), who tried each in his own way to blend Leonardo's chiaroscuro with the form of Michelangelo, but in general Florentine art had taken on a provincial tone.

After 1512 there came a sort of crisis, in the form of mannerism, which spread throughout Italy as more and more people came to know the ceiling of the Sistine Chapel. Jacopo da Pontormo (real name Jacopo Carrucci, 1494–1557), a pupil of Andrea del Sarto, was led by natural sensibility and dissatisfaction with the naturalistic and chiaroscuro effects of the traditional Florentine manner to adopt a certain stylistic exasperation, but at the same time he displayed a new and untrammeled imagination. Among his works are the *Deposition* in the Church of Santa Felicità in Florence, frescoes at Poggio a Caiano and the Certosa, and many portraits. Il Rosso or Il Rosso Fiorentino (real name Giovanni Battista de' Rossi, 1494–1540) had some points in common with Pontormo, but his chief successor in the field of portraiture was his pupil Il Bronzino (real name Agnolo or Angiolo di Cosimo, 1502–1572), who painted in a more formal vein. Other members of the mannerist school were Domenico Beccafumi (originally Domenico di Pace, 1486–1551) of Siena, called Il Meccherino, and Il Parmigianino or Parmigiano (real name Girolamo Francesco Maria Mazzuoli or Mazzola, 1503–1540), an extremely graceful artist who painted the frescoes in the Castle of Fontanellato and the Church of the Steccata in Parma, and various portraits.

Parmigianino was a pupil of Correggio and came from northern Italy, where, toward the end of the 15th century, artistic trends as important as those at Rome developed. Correggio (Antonio Allegri da Correggio, 1494–1534) was trained in the school of Ferrara but was largely influenced by Mantegna and the delicate chiaroscuro of Leonardo, as is seen in the *Campori Madonna* in the Modena Gallery, the *Zingarella* in the Naples Gallery, and *Madonna Blessing St. Francis* at Dresden. Later he felt the influence of Rome and his style developed with the frescoes on the ceiling of the Convent of San Paolo in Parma (1518), those of the cupola of San Giovanni, Parma (1520–1523), and of the Cathedral of Parma (1526–1530), where the vault gives the illusion of breaking through and opening on figures daringly projected into space and foreshortened in order to achieve perspective. This original concept had an enormous influence in the following years. Here we may see the beginning of the fluttering veils and draperies and the glimpses of sky with which the baroque painters decorated domes and ceilings.

In his later period, Correggio did a great many altar panels—*Madonna della Scodella* and *Madonna with St. Jerome* in the Parma Gallery, *Madonna and St. George* and the *Holy Night* or *Nativity* of Dresden—and a number of mythological compositions—*Ganymede* and *Io and Jupiter* (Vienna), and *Danaë* (Borghese Gallery in Rome), a gay and voluptuous vision, softened by the marvelous flexibility of the figures and the delicate use of chiaroscuro.

Venetian Painting.—In Venice during the last quarter of the 15th century there came into being a school which by its unity and originality was equal to the earlier school of Florence. This Venetian movement was still in full flower when the group in Rome had passed its prime. The Venetian painters of the Renaissance obtained effects of depth through the use of colors rather than line, blending them in aerial perspective and creating a new relationship between light and shadow. Their figures were wrapped in an enveloping atmosphere and stood out without rigid outlines. The effect was intimate and natural rather than abstract and rational as had been true of the Florentines. Landscape also assumed a new importance.

The painter who began this movement was Giovanni Bellini. Around 1475, after the altarpiece *Coronation of the Virgin* at Pesaro, he drew away from the influence of Mantegna and achieved more open spaces with softer and more sculptured forms. This change of style is generally attributed to the influence of Antonello da Messina (1430?–1479), who had become acquainted in Naples with Flemish painting and doubtless also knew the work of Piero della Francesca. After working for a time in the south (*Annunciation* and *Madonna with Saints Gregory and Benedict* in the Museum of Messina), Antonello came to Venice (1475–1476), where his lost altarpiece of San Cassiano served as a model for Venetian painters for the next 20 years. Antonello was also a first-rate portraitist, witness the examples in the Louvre, the Castle of Milan and the Civic Museum of Turin.

It is equally probable, however, that the modification of Bellini's style was coincidental rather than derived. This phase of Bellini inspired the rustic and serene Giovanni Battista Cima, called Cima da Conegliano (c.1459–1517 or 1518), and Bartolommeo Montagna of Vicenza (1450?–1523). During his next period (San Giobbe altarpiece, Santa Maria dei Frari triptych of 1488, the *Baptism* in Santa Corona at Vicenza of 1502, and the altarpiece of San Zaccaria of 1505), he influenced Giorgione and Titian and in his turn, was influenced by them (*Lady at Her Toilet* in Vienna and *Feast of the Gods* in the Widener Collection, Philadelphia). Bellini painted an enormous number of pictures, which are scattered in museums on both sides of the Atlantic. His contemporary, Vittore Carpaccio (b. before 1460–d. before 1526), painted in a vein of story and fable, immersing his narratives in an atmosphere of life and light (*History of St. Ursula* in Venice Academy, 1490–1500; scenes of St. George and St. Jerome, San Giorgio degli Schiavoni).

Il Giorgione or Giorgione da Castelfranco (originally Giorgio Barbarelli, c.1478–1510) is generally considered the creator of tonal painting, but this innovation was previously evident in the late Bellini and Carpaccio. Giorgione accentuated atmospheric effects and a blending of colors harmonized in one dominant tone in such a way as to express a dreamlike and poetic vision. He originated and developed a taste for nonreligious themes, rich in allusions and naturalistic touches, and for pictures of small size which were acquired by individual collectors. His larger paintings include the altarpiece *Enthroned Madonna* at Castelfranco, the *Judith* in Leningrad, *The Storm* in the Giovanelli Gallery, Venice, *The Three Philosophers* in Vienna, the *Portrait of a Young Man* in Berlin, the *Fête Champêtre* of the Louvre, and the *Venus* of Dresden. These last two works are often attributed to Tiziano Vecelli or Vecellio, known as Titian, who is the author of *The Concert* in the Pitti Palace, formerly credited to Giorgione.

In Titian's long career (he was born about 1480 and died in 1576), there was a period in which he painted somewhat like Giorgione (*The Concert,* Prado *Madonna*), which ended with the frescoes *Miracles of St. Anthony of Padua* in the Scuola del Santo of Padova (1511). After this his forms were enlarged, his luminous colors spread out over wide areas, and he created images of Olympian beauty: *Sacred and Profane Love* (Borghese Gallery), *Flora* (Uffizi Gallery), the series of pictures painted for Alfonso d'Este, the *Bacchanals* of the Prado, the portraits *Alfonso d'Este* and *Laura Dianti* (Louvre), and a series of sacred conversation groups. In the Frari *Assumption of the Virgin* (1518), there appeared a new rush of movement, which was characteristic of the next 20 years: *Bacchus and Ariadne* in the National Gallery of London, the altarpiece *Resurrection* of Santi Nazzaro e Celso at Brescia (dated 1522), the *Madonna Pesaro* altarpiece at the Frari, the *Deposition* now at the Louvre, and others.

Titian's fame was immense, and after the dukes of Ferrara his patrons included the dukes of Mantova: Emperor Charles V, of whom he did some famous portraits; the dukes of Urbino (the *Venus of Urbino,* the portrait of *Francesco Maria della Rovere, duke of Urbino,* now in the Uffizi Gallery, and *La Bella* in the Pitti Palace); Francis I; Pope Paul III (portraits in the Naples Gallery); and Philip II of Spain. His style continued to develop, characterized by a remarkable quality of painting and a gift for psychological interpretation most evident in his portraits. In the years 1535–1550 his compositions revealed a plastic element undoubtedly inspired by Michelangelo. This phase was followed by an increasingly immaterial vision of life. His human figures were enveloped and almost absorbed by a dense atmosphere, and the play of light and shadow made for fantastic transmutations in which they seemed to be only concrete embodiments of the surrounding air. From this final period date the *Martyrdom of St. Lawrence,* the *Annunciation* in San Salvatore, Venice, and the unfinished *Pietà* of the Venice Academy.

All the Venetian painters of Titian's time were drawn into his orbit: Jacopo Palma, called Palma Vecchio, or Il Vecchio (1480?–1528), who did the *St. Barbara Between St. Anthony and St. Sebastian* in Santa Maria Formosa, Venice); Giovanni Antonio da Pordenone (real name Giovanni Antonio de' Sacchi, 1483–1539); Bonifazio Veronese or Veneziano (properly Bonifazio dei Pitati, 1487–1553); Paris Bordone (1500–1571); and others.

Lorenzo Lotto (c.1480–c.1556) had a restless and imaginative spirit, and great originality, as well as a sense of form less regular and humanistic than that of Titian, and a more incisive use of light. He went from Venice to Marche and then to Rome (1509–1512); to Bergamo (1513–1527), where he influenced the local school of painting and that of Brescia, represented by Giovanni Girolamo Savoldo (c.1480–c.1548), Il Romanino (real name Girolamo Romani, 1485–1566), and Il Moretto (real name Alessandro Bonvicino or Buonvicino, 1498–1554); and to Loreto, where he died. He was receptive to every influence—Raphael, the German and Lombard schools—and although he sometimes appears rudderless, he maintains a uniformly high level. Among his works are the *St. Jerome* in the Louvre (1500); the altarpiece of Santa Cristina, Tiverone, and those of Asolo (1506), Recanati (1508), and Bergamo—San Bartolommeo in 1516, and San Bernardino and Santo Spirito in 1521—the frescoes at Trescorre; the altarpieces of the Carmine (1529), and of Santi Giovanni e Paolo (1542) in Venice, and those at Jesi, Cingoli, and Macerata; many fine portraits and smaller pictures; and his last work at Loreto, which has the beauty of the older Titian with an added note of intimate trepidation.

Il Tintoretto (real name Jacopo Robusti, 1518–1594) marks the beginning of a more spectacular type of painting. He matured at the time when Titian was laboring under the spell of Michelangelo and adopted mannerist forms, which were transfigured by fantastic effects of light and shadow, which grew more and more accentuated. Tintoretto's compositions are full of motion and drama, painted with a rapid touch, with strong light effects standing out against shadow. His production was enormous. It consisted mostly of sets of large pictures such as those of the Scuola di San Marco, now divided between the Venice Academy and the Brera Gallery, including the *Miracle of St. Mark* (which first brought him fame in 1548), the *Transportation of the Body of St. Mark,* and *St. Mark Rescuing a Shipwrecked Saracen;* and the immense cycle of mural paintings of the Scuola di San Rocco, on which he worked at three different periods between 1560 and 1587. Other works are the canvases in Santa Maria dell' Orto (*Presentation of the Virgin in the Temple*), the Ducal Palace (*Marriage of Bacchus and Ariadne* and *Paradise*), and San Giorgio Maggiore (*Last Supper*).

Paolo Veronese (real name Paolo Cagliari or Caliari, 1528–1588) painted in a very different style. After studying with Antonio Badile (1518–1560) in Verona, he was attracted to Michele Sanmicheli, who gave him a classical grandiosity, and came to Venice with a style all his own and a range of deep, bright colors set against the light and carried over into large and serene forms, together with a remarkable sense of intervals and harmony. The Venetian tendency was to melt colors into one another and make shadow predominant, whereas Veronese lightened the shadows, played on contrasting colors, and created a world more luminous than that of reality, suffused with an atmosphere of joy and festivity. He, too, painted large pictures and decorative cycles: ceilings of the council room and the college of the Ducal Palace (*Venice Enthroned*), from 1572 to 1575; the ceilings, altarpieces, and frescoes of San Sebastiano, Venice; the frescoes of the Villa Barbaro at Masèr; and a series of biblical banquets now in the Turin Gallery, the Louvre (*Christ at Emmaus*), and the Venice Academy, besides many other altarpieces, portraits, and mythological compositions.

Jacopo, or Giacomo, da Bassano (originally Ponte, 1510–1592) was closer to Tintoretto than to Veronese. Though living in the atmosphere of 16th century humanism, he preferred to depict peasants, animals, and market places, and is sometimes called the forerunner of genre painting.

16th Century Architecture.—*Rome.*—The transition from 15th to 16th century architecture is typified by Bramante (real name Donato d'Agnolo or d'Angelo, 1444–1514). About the years 1477–1479, at about the same time as Leonardo, Bramante was active in Lombardy: Santa Maria presso San Satiro and the apse and doorway of Santa Maria delle Grazie, both of which are in Milan. In 1499, he transferred his activities to Rome, where the circular temple (Il Tempietto) of San Pietro in Montorio and the cloisters of Santa Maria della Pace led up to his major works: the court of the Belvedere in the Vatican and the project for rebuilding St. Peter's with a central plan and a dome. A grandiose conception of space and a strengthening of the architectural masses in such a way as to intensify the effects of light and shadow and chiaroscuro are characteristics of his style, which inspired all those who followed him, including his successors at St. Peter's: Fra Giovanni Giocondo (1433–1515); Giuliano da Sangallo (originally Giuliano Giamberti, 1445–1516); Raphael, whose genius for painting has overshadowed his harmonious achievements in building; Baldassare Peruzzi of Siena (1481–1536), close to Raphael and designer of the Villa Farnesina; and, greatest of all, Antonio da Sangallo il Giovane (originally Antonio Cordiani, 1483?–1546), who during the pontificates of Leo X (r. 1513–1521), Adrian VI (r. 1522–1523), Clement VII (r. 1523–1534), and Paul III (r. 1534–1549) dominated the Roman scene, with his work at St. Peter's and the Farnese Palace in Rome, and military constructions at Orvieto, Civitavecchia, and Perugia (this last, a citadel demolished in 1860).

Antonio da Sangallo was for a long time a rival of Michelangelo, who was turning more and more to architecture. The latter's first assignments were given to him by Leo X and Clement VII in Florence—the façade of San Lorenzo (which he never carried out), the Laurentian Library and the new sacristy (Medici Chapel) in San Lorenzo, with the tombs of Giuliano and Lorenzo de' Medici, ornamented with the famous statues, *Day* and *Night, Twilight* and *Dawn.* The model for the chapel was Brunelleschi, but we can see that a powerful breath of something new has blown through his designs: the space seems more grandiose, and the framework more robust, the pediments are broken, and niches are placed where Brunelleschi had planned flat surfaces.

Michelangelo continued to work after his return to Rome, with no less fire but with still more grandiose movement. He had more to do after the death of Antonio da Sangallo, whom he succeeded at the Farnese Palace (cornice and central window) and at the architectural workshop of St. Peter's, which he directed from 1547 until his death. He changed Sangallo's plan to one "of lesser size but greater majesty," and built both the apse and dome. In 1546 he began to draw up a project for the arrangement of the Piazza del Campidoglio (Capitoline Place); under Julius III (r. 1550–1555), he worked on San Pietro in Montorio and San Giovanni dei Fiorentini; while under Pius IV (r. 1559–1565), he supplied plans for the Porta Pia (1561) and transformed the Baths of Diocletian into the Church of Santa Maria degli Angeli (1561–1563). While most of his efforts were devoted to bringing about revolutionary changes in building methods, the old Michelangelo went off by himself to sculpture and because his thoughts turned continually to death he did three *Pietà,* one for his own tomb, which is in Florence Cathedral, the Palestrina *Pietà* now in the Strozzi Palace of Florence, and the *Pietà* now in the courtyard of the Rondanini Palace in Rome. Each has outlines more worn out than the last, and their unfinished quality is the most perfect expression of a vision more and more immaterial.

Architecture continued to develop vigorously in Rome after Michelangelo's death. Architects thronged to the city from all over, and particularly from northern Italy, bringing with them tastes and training alien to the Florentine tradition and, in general, a trend toward more irregular and ornate forms. Giacomo da Vignola (real name Giacomo or Barozzi, 1507–1573) stands out above the rest of these architects. He was Michelangelo's successor at St. Peter's, and with the Villa Farnese at Caprarola, and Il Gesù, or the Church of the Jesuits, in Rome, which he was commissioned to do in 1568, he created types which were to serve as models to all his successors. Vignola's most immediate follower was Giacomo della Porta (1541–1604), who did the façade of Il Gesù. Another important architect of late 16th century Rome, in the footsteps of Michelangelo and Vignola, was Domenico Fontana (1543–1607) who came from Lago di Como and worked on St. Peter's under Pope Sixtus V (r. 1585–1590).

Venice.—In architecture as in painting, the other pole of Italian art at this period was Venice and its vicinity. The chief architects were Jacopo Sansovino, Michele Sanmicheli, and Andrea Palladio.

Jacopo Sansovino (real name Jacopo Tatti, 1486–1570) was educated in Florence and Rome,

ITALY

© N.G.S. Reproduced by Special Permission from National Geographic Magazine

Raphael Santi (1483–1520)—"Madonna and Child With the Little Saint John."
Under the brushes of the painters of the mature Italian Renaissance, who were influenced by the rediscovered art of the Hellenic World, religious figures which had previously been stiff and stylized became warm and human, as is demonstrated in this painting, often called the Terranuova Madonna, which Raphael executed at Florence.

The Louvre, Paris, reproduction courtesy The Metropolitan Museum of Art

LEONARDO DA VINCI (1452–1519)—"MONA LISA" OR "LA GIOCONDA."

but only in Venice, where he settled after 1527, did he create a style of his own, in which he brilliantly combined the monumental grandeur of structure characteristic of central Italy with the animated and airy pictorial effects of the north. The arcades and large windows of his buildings provide a background of shadow against which the well-modeled framework is projected into the light. Among his works are the old library of St. Mark, the Zecca (mint), the Scuola della Misericordia, and the Cornaro Palace. Sansovino brought Tuscan Renaissance forms to Venice and fused them with the dominant features of local architecture.

Michele Sanmicheli (1484–1559) of Verona was trained at Rome in the Bramante tradition and served as an assistant to Antonio da Sangallo in the latter's military constructions. After the sack of Rome in 1527, Sanmicheli returned to the north and worked at Venice, Verona, and other inland cities. His style is more massive and robust than that of Sansovino, but also his constructions blend together monumental structure with intense effects of light and shadow, obtained by deep openings and the alternation of recesses and projections in the body of his buildings, among them the Malfatti and Bevilacqua palaces, the Porta Nuova, and Porta Pallio at Verona, and the Grimani Palace at Venice.

Andrea Palladio of Vicenza (1508–1580) has always been considered the most classical of 16th century Italian architects. Modern critics stress the fact that his feeling for wide space is allied to contrasts of shading, which are accentuated by the antithesis between stretches of solid wall and deep doorways, together with luminous colonnades standing out against an empty background. Palladio left a vast number of works behind him, reflective of a wealth of ideas and highly original architectural devices: the Basilica (damaged in World War II) and Loggia del Capitano, the Chiericati and Valmarana (partly destroyed) palaces, and the Teatro Olimpico at Vicenza; San Giorgio Maggiore and the Church of Il Redentore at Venice; and a series of wonderful country houses in the surrounding region—Villa Godi-Porto at Lonedo, Villa Barbaro at Masèr, Villa Foscari at Malcontenta, and Villa Rotonda or Capra near Vicenza. Palladio's followers—the closest among them was Vincenzo Scamozzi (1552–1616)—interpreted his style in a cold, academic, and colorless manner. This was even more true of the neoclassical architects who throughout Europe took him as a model.

Florence.—The monumental architecture of 16th century Florence took on a more severe character. Giorgio Vasari (1511–1574) of Arezzo, who shone as an architect rather than a painter, built the Uffizi Palace in Florence, the headquarters of the Order of St. Stephen at Pisa, and the Logge at Arezzo. Bartolommeo Ammanati (1511–1592), who was also a sculptor, designed the handsome Santa Trinita Bridge in Florence, which was unfortunately destroyed during World War II, and Bernardo Buontalenti (1530–1608), the Casino Mediceo. In Milan and Genoa, Pellegrino Tibaldi (1527–1596) and Galeazzo Alessi (1512–1572), both very active, obtained pictorial effects in their styles.

16th Century Sculpture.—Some of the great architects whom we have mentioned above were, like Michelangelo, first-rate sculptors as well. Jacopo Sansovino adapted the refined plastic forms of the prevailing Florentine style to softer and more pictorial effects in both fields. The *Bacchus* in the Bargello is one of his youthful accomplishments, but he is better represented by his Venetian works: the *Madonna dell' Arsenale,* the statues of the loggia of the Campanile, the bas-reliefs of the bronze door leading to the sacristy of St. Mark's. Under his influence, the Venetian sculptors used animated surface movements subject to the play of light and shadow. The greatest of them, Alessandro Vittoria (1524–1608), did remarkable portrait busts fashioned with a quick, easy touch.

In 16th century Florence all the sculptors imitated Michelangelo, but with varying shades of interpretation. Baccio or Bartolommeo Bandinelli (1493–1560), who did the monument to Giovanni de' Medici (Giovanni dalle Bande Nere), copied him in a smooth but coldly academic style, while Bartolommeo Ammanati and Benvenuto Cellini (1500–1571) adapted his mannerist side to decorative purposes and drew from it greater flexibility of form and elegance of rhythm. Ammanati's masterpiece is the Fountain of Neptune in the Piazza della Signoria, and Cellini's the *Perseus* in the Loggia dei Lanzi. Cellini was also famous as a goldsmith and worked for a long time in France. Il Tribolo (Niccolò di Raffaello de' Pericoli, 1500–1550) revealed a vein of fresh rustic poetry in the fountains of Petraia and Castello.

In Lombardy, Giovanni Antonio Amadeo was a leading sculptor as well as an architect. After the activity of Gian Cristoforo Romano (1470–1512), Cristoforo Solari or Solario, known as Il Gobbo (1450?–1527), Benedetto Briosco, Agostino Busti, known as Il Bambaja (1483–1548), and the many other comparatively little-known sculptors who did the mass of statues in the Cathedral of Milan, Leone Leoni, known as Il Cavaliere Aretino (1509–1590), suddenly introduced into Lombardy the mannerist style (tomb of the marquis of Marignano in the cathedral). In Rome, on the other hand, a Lombard, Fra Guglielmo della Porta (died in 1577), with his tomb of Pope Paul III in the choir of St. Peter's introduced into the mannerist Roman style an accent of greater truth and directness and a robust plasticity. This was one of the ways in which the 16th century moved toward the baroque. Another move in the same direction can be seen in the work of Jean Boulogne, who was known as Giambologna (1529?–1608), a sculptor from Douai who came to Italy around 1551 and settled first in Rome and then in Florence. After studying the work of Ammanati, Tribolo, and Cellini, he created an increasingly complex type of composition, where the figures are in elaborate counterposition, presenting their surfaces in the round and requiring the spectator to look at them not from one but from many points of view. This process was a development of the serpentine line enunciated by Giovanni Lomazzo. Giambologna's most famous works are the *Neptune* in the principal fountain of Bologna, the *Rape of the Sabines* in the Loggia dei Lanzi in Florence, the *Hope* of the University of Genoa, numerous small bronzes such as the *Apollo* in the small study of the Palazzo Vecchio, the *Mercury* and *Bathing Venus* of the Bargello, the *Apennine Fountain* at Pratolino, and the *Venus* in a grotto of the Boboli Gardens.

17TH AND 18TH CENTURY ART

The chief elements of the baroque period of Italian art (which characterized the 17th century, and a good part of the 18th century before being superseded by the rococo and the neoclassical styles) are the Accademia degli Incamminati of the Carracci family at Bologna; the architectonic creations of Giovanni Lorenzo Bernini and Francesco Borromini in Rome, along with the architectural works that accompanied them; Caravaggio; the development of the Roman style into Piedmontese baroque, which was really due to Guarino Guarini of Modena and the Sicilian Filippo Iuvara, both of whom were trained in Rome; Bernini's sculpture; and the formation of an international school of art in Rome, where artists came to study and work from all parts of Europe.

Painting.—The Carracci or Caracci—Lodovico (1555–1619), Agostino (1557–1602), and Annibale (1560–1609)—founded an academy for the purpose of combating the caprices and exaggerations of the mannerists. They preached the study of the 16th century masters and held that a combination of the best features of each one—the plastic quality of Michelangelo, the chiaroscuro of Leonardo and Correggio, and the color of Titian—would produce an ideal eclectic style. For this theoretical aberration modern critics have unmercifully condemned them. In reality, among a host of merely clever and calculated academic compositions, they succeeded in some of their best works, especially those of Lodovico and Annibale, in attaining a mixture of realism and allusive feeling that was a new contribution to the art of the time and brought them a following throughout the continent. Such works include the *Annunciation, Madonna and Saints, Madonna of the Rosary,* and *Madonna degli Scalzi,* all in the Bologna Gallery, by Lodovico; and the *Baptism of Christ* in San Gregorio, Bologna, landscapes in the Doria Gallery, and frescoes of the Farnese Palace, Rome, by Annibale.

A host of painters flourished in the wake of the Carracci at Bologna. Outstanding among them was Guido Reni (1575–1642), who like most members of the school worked chiefly in Rome, painting an enormous number of portraits, altarpieces, and mythological compositions: *Atalanta* (Naples Gallery); *Aurora* or *Triumph of Phoebus* (Casino Rospigliosi), *Concert of Angels* (San Gregorio Magno, Rome). Among other followers of the Carracci, we may mention Francesco Albani or Albano (1578–1660) and Il Domenichino (real name Domenico Zampieri, 1581–1641).

Michelangelo da Caravaggio (real name Michelangelo Merisi, or Merisio, 1577–1610) rebelled against this exceedingly cultured circle. Coming to Rome from his native Lombardy around 1585, he soon found himself in open personal and artistic conflict with the painters of the day: hence a series of quarrels, prison sentences, and escapes, and creation of a kind of painting directly opposed to both mannerism and the eclecticism of the Carracci school. Caravaggio turned his back on tradition and effected a great simplification. He treated sacred themes in a manner which his contemporaries branded as brutally realistic, stripping them of their conventional idealization and interpreting them as scenes of everyday life, peopled by figures drawn from the lower classes. People were shocked to see him portray St. Matthew as a rough fisherman, with bare feet and widespread legs, and to take as a model for the Madonna on her deathbed a poor girl who had drowned in the Tiber. What Caravaggio was really doing was to refresh his spirit with elemental truths, which he then presented in a powerful and compelling manner. He painted not only human figures but also objects (his *Fruit Basket* in the Ambrosian Library of Milan is the first Italian still life) emerging from a shadowy background, in all their bodily solidity, giving them the illusion of reality without excessive detail so that they stand out like glimpses of nature struck by a ray of light. His was a naturalism that was not rational, but he had a feeling for direct lighting which he drew from the tradition of Lombardy, where all the great masters from Foppa to the school of Brescia (Lorenzo Lotto and Giovanni Girolamo Savoldo) had worked along the same line.

After a series of half figures with still lifes, the *Magdalen* and *Flight into Egypt* of the Doria Gallery, Caravaggio's first monumental work was the St. Matthew cycle in San Luigi dei Francesci (French Church of St. Louis) in Rome. There followed the *Virgin and Pilgrims* in Sant' Agostino (1597), the *Fall of St. Paul* and *Crucifixion of St. Peter* in Santa Maria del Popolo (1600–1601), the *Entombment of Christ* in the Vatican Gallery (1602), the *Death of Mary* in the Louvre (1605–1606), and the *Madonna dei Palafrenieri* in the Borghese Gallery. In 1607, Caravaggio fled from Rome to Naples, where he executed the *Madonna of the Rosary,* now in Vienna, and the paintings in the Church of the Misericordia; thence to Malta (1608), where he did work for the church of La Valletta and the portrait of Alof di Vignacourt (*Grand Master of the Knights of Malta*) now in the Louvre; and finally to Sicily (*Burial of St. Lucy* at Siracusa and *Nativities* at Palermo and Messina). He died a fugitive on the beach of Porto Ercole.

Caravaggio's revolutionary, antiacademic, and luminous vision influenced all of European art from the Flemish school to Diego Velázquez. He had many followers in Rome, among them Orazio Gentileschi (1563–1647), a Tuscan who was greatly influenced by the style of the youthful work of Caravaggio, migrating from Rome to Marche, and then to Genoa, Turin, Paris, and London; Carlo Saraceni (1585–1625); Bartolomeo Manfredi (1572–1605); the Roman Orazio Borgianni (1578–1616); the French Jean de Boulogne, known as Le Valentin (1600–1634); and a group of Flemings that included Gerard van Honthorst. In Italy, he chiefly influenced the 17th century Neapolitan school: Battista Caracciolo, known as Battistello (c.1570–1637); José or Giuseppe Ribera, known as Lo Spagnoletto (1588–1652), Mattia Preti, known as Il Cavaliere Calabrese or Il Calabrese (1613–1699), and Bernardo Cavallino (1622–1654). But his influence extended also to Genoa, Lombardy (Antonio d'Enrico, known as Tanzio da Varallo, c.1574–1644), and even to Bologna, still the domain of the Carracci (Guido Reni, sporadically, and, more, Guercino, real name Giovanni Francesco Barbieri, 1591–1666).

The Carracci school inspired the lively group of baroque decorators who, as the 17th century progressed, complicated their compositions with more and more illusory and scenic effects and intensified the restlessness of their movement. Among them were Pietro da Cortona (originally Pietro Berrettini, 1596–1669); Il Baciccio (real name Giovanni Battista Gaulli, 1639–1709) of Genoa (the frescoes in the church Il Gesù); and Andrea dal Pozzo (1642–1709) of Trento, who did the frescoes in Sant' Ignazio, Rome. In Naples the influence of both Carracci and Caravaggio was reflected in the numerous paintings of Luca Giordano (1632–1705), who worked all over Italy; Salvator Rosa, also called Salvatoriello (1615–1673); the still-life painters such as Giovanni Battista Ruoppolo (1620–1683); and, in the 18th century, in Francesco Solimena (1657–1743), Francesco de Mura (1696–1782), and Corrado Giaquinto (1699–1765). In Genoa the influence of Peter Paul Rubens and Sir Anthony Vandyke made itself felt alongside those of Caravaggio and the Roman baroque school, with the work of Orazio de' Ferrari (1605–1657) and his son Giovanni Andrea (d. 1657), Gioacchino Assereto (1600–1649), Giovanni Andrea Ansaldo (1584–1638), Valerio Castello (1625–1659), Giovanni Benedetto Castiglione, called Il Grechetto (1616–1670), and Bernardo Strozzi, a Genoese (1581–1644). The 17th century Lombard school was close to that of Genoa, with an added vein of pathos and piety designed to appeal to the religious feelings of the beholder: Pier Francesco Mazzucchelli, known as Il Morazzone (1571–1626); Giovanni Battista Crespi, known as Il Cerano (1576–1633), and his nephew Daniele Crespi (c.1590–1630). In Venice, 17th century painting was dominated by outsiders: Domenico Fetti or Feti (1589–1624) from Rome, Giovanni Lys (c.1600–c.1630) from Oldenburg, and Bernardo Strozzi from Genoa. Francesco Maffei (c.1625–1660) of Vicenza was the only heir to the local 16th century tradition.

The line of 18th century baroque decorators culminated in Giovanni Battista Tiepolo (1696–1770). To find his origins we must go back to Sebastiano Ricci (1660–1734), who after the long period of stagnation that followed the death of the 16th century Venetian masters was the first to re-establish contact with the new movements in Italian art in which the Venetians had no part. He went to Bologna, Rome, Milan, and Florence and acquired a free, mobile style, with a facility for light and vivacious decoration. Another forerunner of Tiepolo was Giovanni Battista Piazzetta (1682–1754), who studied with Giuseppe Maria Crespi, known as Lo Spagnuolo (1665–1747), the most intelligent painter of his time at Bologna. Tiepolo also drew upon Paolo Veronese, whose range of colors was lighter and brighter than that of the baroque decorative school. He soon abandoned the theatrical elements of this school's ornamentation, reduced to a minimum the use of architectural framework, thinned out his masses, and launched his figures into luminous open skies. In his work the theatrical quality of the baroque is lighter and more imaginative, and its melodramatic accents give way to an airiness of tones that lends his composition genuine decorative value.

Tiepolo painted a number of altarpieces, but for the most part he decorated walls and ceilings —frescoes of the cathedral (1726) and bishop's palace at Udine; frescoes of the Colleoni Chapel at Bergamo and the Villa Valmarana near Vicenza (destroyed); Gesuati ceiling in Venice, Clerici (destroyed) and Dugnani palaces in Milan (all of these between 1730 and 1740); then the ceiling of the Scuola del Carmine (1740–1744) and the drawingroom of the Palazzo Labia in Venice (1757); the stairway of the partially destroyed archbishop's palace of Würzburg (1751–1753); and the ceiling of the Scalzi at Venice (destroyed), until his late works in the royal palace of Madrid, where the artist went in 1763.

By this time there was a neoclassical reaction to the liberties and caprices of the 18th century. With Tiepolo we may say that the great Italian tradition came to a close. Eighteenth century Venice did, however, produce several landscape painters who were to attain fame abroad. Francesco Guardi (1712–1793) made fantastic transformations of landscape in a shifting atmosphere where architecture and figures alike lost all consistency. The two Canalettos—Antonio Canaletto (originally Canale or Canal, 1697–1768) and Bernardo Belotto or Bellotto (1720–1780), his nephew—painted their landscapes as views. Their conscientiously faithful interpretations are distinguished by a marvelous unity of tone and perspective. Antonio worked for some years in London, and Bernardo Canaletto at Dresden, Vienna, and Warsaw. Eighteenth century Venice dissolved in caprice and the melancholy of Francesco Guardi bore traces of the approach to landscape painting that marked the two Canalettos. So-called 18th century frivolity found a last interesting artistic expression in the pastel portraits of Rosalba Carriera (1675–1757), which were known over most of Europe, and the genre paintings of Pietro Longhi (originally Pietro Falca, 1702–1785).

Architecture and Sculpture.—Architecture and sculpture in the 17th and 18th centuries developed along the same lines as painting. Architecture began by breaking down the unified, enclosed spaces of the Renaissance, while keeping and indeed accentuating monumental mass effects and vigorous contrasts. Then gradually it grew lighter in weight and even in color, for with a decrease in the contrast between recesses and protuberances the shadows thrown on the body of the buildings were less deep and glided almost luminously over the vast extents of flat surface. The same thing was reflected in the delicate modeling of sculpture.

Giovanni Lorenzo Bernini (1598–1680) was the great artist who transformed the mannerist style into baroque. The multiple trends of 16th and 17th century Rome, all the attempts to achieve effects of motion and open, pictorial space, were blended by his genius into an integral new vision. Internally, the irregularity of his ground plans, the chapels and galleries which interrupt the periphera walls, give an effect of illusory and indefinite space much greater than that of reality. And the outside of his buildings, too, broken by lively bas-reliefs, offers a new prospect with every change in the onlooker's point of view, drawing the surrounding space into the general artistic effect. Bernini's constructions cannot be detached from the places where they have been erected, for he designed them in such a way that they should be seen from a particular standpoint and among definite local atmospheric effects, including in the effect what already existed around the building. Typical is the grandiose colonnade of St. Peter's (1656–1663), which opens up like the two arms of an immense ellipse. The broad, low façade of the church, which was designed by Carlo Maderna or Maderno (1556–1629) and was bitterly criticized for destroying the effect of the dome, is cleverly incorporated into the colonnade, with its heavy horizontal lines displayed to advantage above the pillars. Others architectural works of Bernini in Rome are the Barberini Palace, which he completed, and Sant' Andrea al Quirinale (1678).

Bernini worked with equal freedom in the field of sculpture. Here, too, we have no cohesion of plastic masses, but a central force that projects the shape of the figures into space, accompanied by a continuous vibration of light and shadow. As the surrounding space is drawn into the architectonic effect, so the figures direct their gestures and motions into the air around them and belong in a compellingly natural manner to the real world. The first work that bears witness to these qualities is the *David* (1619) of the Borghese Gallery; then come the *Apollo and Daphne* and the *Rape of Proserpine* in the same place, the *Santa Bibiana* in the church of the same name (1626), the *San Longino* in St. Peter's (1638), the famous *St. Teresa* in Santa Maria della Vittoria (1644), the *Beata Lonovica Albertoni* in the Church of San Francesco at Ripa, and the tombs of popes Urban VIII (1647) and Alexander VII in St. Peter's, not far from his bronze altar canopy and *cathedra Petri,* or throne of St. Peter. There are also a number of splendid portrait busts (*Cardinal Scipione Borghese, Francis I d'Este, Costanza Bonarelli*) and fountains (the Four Rivers in Piazza Navona and the Triton in Piazza Barberini).

Bernini's production was enormous. He held a position of supreme prominence in the papal court, and his fame spread throughout Europe. Only two of his Roman contemporaries can be mentioned in the same breath: the architect Francesco Borromini and the sculptor Alessandro Algardi. Borromini (1599–1667), born in Canton Ticino, then Italian, was a very great and original artist, worthy of comparison to Bernini, whose glory overshadowed his except for a brief period of fame under Pope Innocent X (r. 1644–1655). His imagination was more sinuous, lighter, and more bizarre, and he made daring architectonic solutions: elliptic ground plans, undulating walls, interrupted entablatures, and towers that narrow into spires and pinnacles. He was imitated more in the later rococo period than in his own. His chief works are the churches of San Carlo alle Quattro Fontane, Sant' Agnese in Piazza Navona, Sant' Ivo alla Sapienza, the Collegio di Propaganda Fide, and the Filippini Oratory. Other important Roman architects of the 17th century were Pietro da Cortona (more sober in architecture than in painting), Carlo Rainaldi (1611–1691) and Carlo Fontana (1634–1714).

Outside of Rome, in Florence, which was still closely bound to the Renaissance tradition, and in Venice, the baroque style never acquired deep roots. One talented piece of work in Venice dating from this period is the church of Santa Maria della Salute by Baldassare Longhena (1604–1682), who also built the Pesaro Palace, The city of Turin, which had no architecture worthy of mention during the Renaissance, acquired one of considerable importance in the 17th and 18th centuries through the work of Guarino Guarini and Filippo Iuvara.

Guarino Guarini (1624–1683) brought to Turin a complex style formed by the influence of Borromini in Rome and travels in Emilia, Sicily, and France. He showed himself a daring builder in the high domes of Santissima Sindone and San Lorenzo, where he topped the churches below with a system of ribs and slender intersecting arches, functionally essential but possessing at the same time a decorative value of lines and perforations. His chief other works are the church of La Beata Vergina della Consolata, and the Carignano Palace and the Academy of Sciences, with their handsome brick walls. Guarini gave new architectural ideas not only to Piedmont but to the rest of Italy as well, and his work marked the transition from baroque to rococo.

Guarini's work was continued on an even greater scale by Filippo Iuvara or Juvara (1676?–1736), who had also studied in Rome. His style was more luminous, harmonious, and serene, and the buildings he left behind him are familiar landmarks in the modern city of Turin: the new façade and the double staircase of the Madama Palace, the splendid Basilica of Superga on top of the hill of that name, the church of the Castle of Venaria and the Church of the Carmine in the city (both of these last damaged during World War II), the façade of Santa Cristina, and the grandiose hunting lodge at Stupinigi, with wings radiating out of a central body. He also worked outside Italy, building the royal palace in Lisbon and drawing up plans for that in Madrid, which was actually constructed by Giovanni Battista Sacchetti, his pupil.

Luigi Vanvitelli (1700–1773) was connected in his beginnings with Iuvara, and accomplished much work of similar style and equal importance at the court of the Neapolitan Bourbons. His greatest single building is the royal palace at Caserta, a sort of Italian Versailles, with wonderful perspectives of gardens and fountains. Notable 18th century architects in Rome included Alessandro Galilei (1691–1737) and Ferdinando Fuga (1699–1780). After this time the greatest Italian architects went to work abroad. Francesco (or Bartolomeo) Rastrelli (1700–1771) built the Winter Palace and the Peterhof in Leningrad, and the palace at Detskoe (Tsarskoe) Selo, preceding Jacomo Quarenghi (1744–1817), who worked for many years at the court of Catherine II and was followed in his turn by Carlo Rossi (1775–1849).

Although Bernini's sculpture exercised a wide influence in the 17th century, its essential values were not properly understood even by his collaborators. He had as a rival in papal favor the architect-sculptor, Alessandro Algardi (1602–1654) of Bologna, who was in favor during a brief eclipse suffered by Bernini under the pontificate of Innocent X. He opposed to Bernini's animated and pictorial style a sterner and more static concept, which is expressed not so much in an academic work such as the marble altarpiece depicting the *Retreat of Attila from Rome* in St. Peter's as in his smaller figures and portrait busts, where he made strong characterizations: statue of *Innocent X* on the Campidoglio, bust of *Donna Olimpia Pamphili* in the Doria Gallery.

Other notable 17th century sculptors in Rome were François Duquesnoy, known as François Flamand (1594–1643), and Francesco Mochi (1580–1654), a native of Montevarchi, who first studied in Florence and carved the fine equestrian statues of Alessandro and Ranuccio Farnese in Piacenza. At the turn of the century we find the Lombard Camillo Rusconi (1658–1728); the Italianized Frenchman

Pierre Legros (1666–1718); the Roman Pietro Bracci (1700–1773), perhaps the freest and most vivacious of all, who directed the decoration of the Trevi Fountain; and Filippo della Valle (1697–1768), a Florentine whose work had clear, almost academic outlines. After him art passed over into the neoclassical style. Outside Rome, we must recall Gian Maria Morlaiter (1699–1781) of Venice, who left roughed-out pieces in the Correr Museum and also worked in Saxony and Russia, and Giacomo Serpotta (1656–1732) of Palermo, an original worker in plaster, who produced partitions, garlands, draperies, feminine figures, and *Putti* applied to the decoration of the oratory of San Lorenzo and the churches of Santa Cita and the Rosario.

International Influences.—In the course of the 17th and 18th centuries, Rome became a center of attraction for all Europe. As early as the 16th century Italian artists had worked in other countries. Leonardo died in France. Andrea del Sarto went there in 1518, followed by Sebastiano Serlio (1475–1554), Francesco Primaticcio (Le Primatice, 1504–1570), Niccolò dell' Abbate (also Abate or Abati, 1512?–1571), Il Rosso, and Benvenuto Cellini. Such were, indeed, the origins of the school of Fontainebleau. Titian worked for Francis I, Charles V, and Philip II, and Leone Leoni and his son Pompeo (d. 1608) were active for a long time in Spain. In the 17th and 18th centuries, we recall that Tiepolo died in Spain, the Canalettos worked in England, Saxony and Poland, and various architects and portrait painters were scattered about the courts of Europe.

An opposite movement also developed in the 16th century and grew in the two centuries that followed—namely, the migration to Italy of foreign artists, attracted by the flowering of the Renaissance. First came the Flemings of Rome, then Rubens, Vandyke, the Dutch followers of Caravaggio, and finally the French: Le Valentin, Simon Vouet, Nicolas Poussin, Claude Lorrain, and the rest. It became the custom for artists of every country to make a trip to Italy, and more particularly to Rome, the seat of many academies and a truly international center. There came a time when the leading artists and critics of Rome were none of them Italian. This fact was most apparent during the neoclassical movement, which had scholarly and archaeological origins, contemporaneous with the excavations of Herculaneum, Pompeii, the Palatine Hill, and Hadrian's villa at Tivoli. Little by little, archaeological interest developed into an aesthetic theory, and the brilliant light touch of the 18th century was judged to be frivolous in comparison with a revived ideal of classical grandeur and severity. Two Germans living in Rome, Johann Joachim Winckelmann (1717–1768) and Anton Raphael Mengs (1728–1779), established the canons of the new theory.

Among the Italian neoclassical artists only one, Antonio Canova (1757–1822), won European fame. Canova was trained in Venice, and his early works reflected the grace of the 18th century (*Apollo* and *Daedalus and Icarus* in the Venice Academy). Coming in 1779 to Rome, he executed the monuments to Pope Clement XIII in St. Peter's and Clement XIV in the Santi Apostoli, in which his style was abstract and academic, displaying great virtuosity of detail. His fame grew, and his sculptures of members of the Bonaparte family—the famous *Pauline (Venus Borghese)* in the Borghese Gallery, Napoleon's mother, and Napoleon himself—his *Venus* in the Pitti Palace, and his *Hebe Pouring Nectar* (Berlin), and *Cupid and Psyche* (Louvre), together with many highly stylized busts, were generally considered to be perfect expressions of the taste of the times.

An active neoclassic artistic center grew up in Milan. Here we find Andrea Appiani (1754–1817), inheritor of some 18th century qualities, more praiseworthy for his portraits than for his official panegyrics of Napoleon (frescoes of the Royal Palace of Milan, which were completely ruined in World War II); and the architects Giuseppe Piermarini (1734–1808), a well-balanced pupil of Vanvitelli, builder of the façade of the Belgioioso Palace and La Scala Theater; Leopoldo Pollack (1751–1806); Simone Cantoni (1736–1818), and Marchese Luigi Cagnola (1762–1833), all of whom endowed the city with a distinguished and coherent architectural style. In general, however, Italian art was becoming provincial—the real center was now elsewhere. This condition held true throughout the 19th century.

19TH AND 20TH CENTURIES

Art of the 19th Century.—Italy had its romantic trend, but it made very little impression upon the academic style. Francesco Hayez (1791–1882), who taught at the Brera Academy of Milan, substituted medieval themes for those of classical antiquity, while the so-called Nazarenes in Rome and the purist groups of Rome and Florence substituted religious themes and looked to painters before Raphael rather than to either classical or Renaissance art but remained essentially academic and did not create a new style.

After 1850 groups in several Italian cities tried to combat the prevailing academic trend. Domenico Morelli (1826–1901), Filippo Palizzi (1818–1899), and Gioachino Toma (1836–1891) worked in this direction in Naples; Federico Faruffini (1831–1869) and the *scapigliati* (wild-haired ones), including Tranquillo Cremona (1837–1878) and Daniele Ranzoni (1843–1889), in Milan; and above all, the groups called the *macchiaioli*, in Florence: Giovanni Fattori (1825–1908), Silvestro Lega (1826–1895), Telemaco Signorini (1835–1901), Vito d'Ancona (1825–1884), Odoardo Borrani (1834–1905), and Adriano Cecioni (1836–1886), the sculptor. Giovanni Boldini (1845–1931) went to Paris and became a fashionable portrait painter. Giuseppe de Nittis (1846–1884) was another who won fame in Paris. Worthy of note were the Piedmontese artists Antonio Fontanesi (1818–1882), Enrico Reycend (1855–1928), and Lorenzo Delleani (1840–1908).

For the most part 19th century sculpture was insignificant, but Medardo Rosso (1858–1927), originally one of the *scapigliati* of Milan, was a sensible artist. His heads of laughing women and sick children reach the extreme limit of plastic disintegration, and the extremely light touch of his modeling pulverizes the light over his sculptured surfaces.

If the activity in building was uncommonly great during all the 19th century, architecture, in the chaotic imitation of all manners of styles, never reached so low a level of incoherence as then.

20th Century Trends.—In the 20th century, a new culture gradually formed in art, based on greater consciousness of the real problems of artistic form and vision. One painter, Amedeo Modigliani (1884–1920), who worked entirely in Paris, stands by himself. The futurist movement (1910–1914) was noisily pugnacious but exercised a rousing influence on Italian art. Many of the most intelligent artists were futurists, at least for a time: Umberto Boccioni, (1882–1916), the painter, and Antonio Sant' Elia (1888–1916), the architect, both of whom died in World War I, as well as Carlo Carrà (1881–), who did not remain long in the movement but was stimulated by it to define his style more rigorously. Carrà, along with Giorgio di Chirico (1888–), had a later surrealist period, in which he lost his dogmatism and became one of the leaders of 20th century Italian art. Di Chirico went farther in the surrealist direction, and his evocative themes made him well known in Paris and other foreign cities.

Among living Italian painters, two are especially worthy of note—Giorgio Morandi (1890–), and Filippo de Pisis (1896–). Morandi is from Bologna, a painter of landscapes and still lifes with a thoroughly thought-out sobriety of style. De Pisis, who lived for many years in Paris, is still bound up with the last phase of impressionism, plus some surrealist traces. A talented and productive painter, he calls up with a light touch and precision and beauty of tone the fleeting aspects of life around him. The best modern sculptors are the late Arturo Martini (1889–1947); Marino Marini (1901–), whose style is more stylized and archaic; and Giacomo Manzù (1908–), who expresses psychological values with greater emotion. There is general admiration among young artists for Pablo Picasso, and abstract art is the subject of furious debate.

Bibliography.—General: Crowe, Joseph A., and Cavalcaselle, G. B., *A History of Painting in North Italy,* 3 vols. (New York 1912); id., *A History of Painting in Italy,* 6 vols. (London 1903–14); Toesca, Pietro, *Storia dell'arte italiana: Il medioevo* (Turin 1927); Berenson, Bernhard, *The Italian Painters of the Renaissance* (Oxford 1930); id., *Italian Pictures of the Renaissance* (Oxford 1932); Schlosser, Julius, *La letteratura artistica* (Florence 1935); Venturi, Lionello, *History of Art Criticism* (New York 1936); Marle, Raimond van, *The Development of the Italian Schools of Painting,* 19 vols. (The Hague 1923–38); Venturi, Adolfo, *Storia dell'arte italiana,* 10 vols. (Milan 1901–40).

Special: Muratoff, Paul, *La pittura bizantina* (Rome n.d.); Richter, Jean P., ed., *The Literary Works of Leonardo da Vinci,* 2 vols. (London 1883); Kristeller, Paul, *Andrea Mantegna* (Berlin 1902); Wilpert, Josef, *Roma sotterranea: Le pitture delle catacombe romane* (Rome 1903); Bertaux, Émile, *L'Art dans l'Italie Méridionale* (Paris 1904); Venturi, Lionello, *Le origini della pittura veneziana* (Venice 1907); Ffoulkes, Constance, and Maiocchi, R., *Vincenzo Foppa* (London 1909); Sack, Eduard, *Giambattista und Domenico Tiepolo* (Hamburg 1910); Hind, Arthur M., *A Short History of Engraving and Etching* (London 1911); Thode, Henry, *Michelangelo und das Ende der Renaissance,* 3 vols. (Berlin 1902–12); Toesca, Pietro, *La pittura e la miniatura nella Lombardia* (Milan 1912); Venturi, Lionello, *Giorgione e il Giorgionismo* (Milan 1913); Folnesics, Hans, *Brunelleschi* (Vienna 1915); Wilpert, Josef, *Die Römische Mosaiken und Malereien der Kirchlichen Bauten vom IV. bis XIII. Jahrhundert,* 4 vols. (Freiburg 1916); Porter, Arthur K., *Lombard Architecture,* 4 vols. (New Haven 1915–17); Venturi, Lionello, *La critica e l'arte di Leonardo da Vinci* (Bologna 1919); Hetzer, Theodor, *Die frühen Gemälde des Tizians* (Basel 1920); Voss, Hermann, *Die Malerei der Spätrenaissance in Rom und Florenz,* 2 vols. (Berlin 1920); Froehlich-Bum, Lili, *Parmigianino und der Manierismus* (Vienna 1921); Derschau, Joachim von, *Sebastiano Ricci* (Heidelberg 1922); Fiocco, Giuseppe, *Francesco Guardi* (Florence 1923); Porter, Arthur K., *Romanesque Sculpture of the Pilgrimage Roads,* 10 vols. (Boston 1923); Riegl, Alois, *Die Entstehung der Barockkunst in Rom,* 2 vols. (Vienna 1923); Suida, Wilhelm, *Leonardo und sein Kreis* (Munich 1923); Frey, Dagobert, *Architettura della Rinascenza* (Rome 1924); Hempel, Eberhard, *Francesco Borromini* (Vienna 1924); Voss, Hermann, *Die Malerei des Barock in Rom* (Berlin 1924); Ancona, Paolo d', *La Miniature italienne du Xe au XVIe siècle* (Paris 1925); Fischel, Oskar, *Tizian* (Stuttgart 1925); Pittaluga, Mary, *Il Tintoretto* (Bologna 1925); Cecchi, Emilio, *Pittura italiana dell'Ottocento* (Rome 1926); Diehl, Charles, *Manuel d'art byzantin,* 2 vols. (Paris 1925–26); Salmi, Mario, *L'architettura romanica in Toscana* (Milan 1927); Frey, Dagobert, *Architettura barocca* (Milan 1928); Longhi, Roberto, "Quesiti Caravaggeschi," *Pinacotheca* (Rome 1928); id., "Frammenti di Giusto da Padova," *Pinacotheca,* p. 137, Sept.–Oct. 1928; Salmi, Mario, *Romanesque Sculpture in Tuscany* (Florence 1928); Somaré, Enrico, *Storia dei pittori italiani dell'Ottocento,* 2 vols. (Milan 1928); Fiocco, Giuseppe, *Venetian Painting of the Seicento and the Settecento* (New York 1929); Sedlmayr, Hans, *Die Architektur Borrominis* (Munich 1929); Toesca, Pietro, *Florentine Painting of the Trecento* (New York 1929); Yashiro, Yukio, *Sandro Botticelli* (London 1929); Delogu, Giuseppe, *Pittori veneti minori del Settecento* (Venice 1930); Galassi, Giuseppe, *Roma o Bisanzio?* (Rome 1930); Gronau, Georg, *Giovanni Bellini* (Stuttgart 1930); Arslan, Wart, *I Bassano* (Bologna 1931); Brinckmann, A. E., *Theatrum Novum Pedemonti* (Düsseldorf 1931); Cecchi, Emilio, *The Sienese Painters of the Trecento* (London 1931); Delogu, Giuseppe, *Pittori minori liguri, lombardi, piemontesi del Seicento e Settecento* (Venice 1931); Fiocco, Giuseppe, *Carpaccio* (Rome 1931); Venturi, Adolfo, *North Italian Painting of the Quattrocento* (New York 1931); id., *North Italian Painting of the Quattrocento: Emilia* (New York 1931); Verga, Ettore, *Bibliografia Vinciana,* 2 vols. (Bologna 1931); Coletti, Luigi, *Tommaso da Modena* (Bologna 1933); Marucchi, Orazio, *Manuale di archeologia cristiana* (Rome 1933); Rivoira, G. T., *Lombardic Architecture, Its Origin, Development, and Derivatives,* 2 vols. (Oxford 1933); Fiocco, Giuseppe, *Paolo Veronese* (Rome 1934); Longhi, Roberto, *Officina ferrarese* (Rome 1934); Nicco, Giusta, *Jacopo della Quercia* (Florence 1934); Pallucchini, Rodolfo, *L'arte di G. B. Piazzetta* (Bologna 1934); Vitali, Lamberto, *L'incisione italiana moderna* (Milan 1934); Vito Battaglia, S. de, *Correggio: Bibliografia* (Rome 1934); Giovannoni, Gustavo, *Saggi sull'architettura del Rinascimento* (Milan 1935); Tietze, Hans, *Tizian,* 2 vols. (Vienna 1936); Venturi, Adolfo, *Raffaello* (Milan 1936); id., *Correggio* (Milan 1936); Cecchi, Emilio, *Giotto* (Milan 1937); Fiocco, Giuseppe, *Mantegna* (Milan 1937); Paatz, Walter, *Werden und Wesen der Trecento Architektur in Toskana* (Burg, Germany, 1937); Fokker, Timon, *Roman Baroque Art,* 2 vols. (Oxford 1938); Salmi, Mario, *Masaccio, Paolo Uccello, Domenico Veneziano* (Rome 1938); Planiscig, Leo, *Donatello* (Vienna 1939); Kriegbaum, Friedrich, *Michelangelo: Die Bildwerke* (Berlin 1940); Longhi, Roberto, *Ampliamenti nell' Officina ferrarese* (Florence 1940); id., "Fatti di Masolino e Masaccio," *La Critica d'Arte* (Florence 1940); Baroni, Costantino, *Bramante* (Bergamo 1941); Bercken, Erich von der, *Tintoretto* (Munich 1941); Fasola, G. Nicco, *Nicola Pisano* (Rome 1941); Fiocco, Giuseppe, *Giorgione* (Bergamo 1941); Marquand, Allan, *Luca della Robbia* (Princeton 1941); Planiscig, Leo, *Andrea del Verrocchio* (Vienna 1941); Reale Commissione Vinciana, *I manoscritti e i disegni di Leonardo da Vinci,* 12 vols. (Rome 1923–41); Sanpaolesi, Piero, *La cupola di S. Maria del Fiore* (Rome 1941); Schlosser, Julius, *Lorenzo Ghiberti* (Basel 1941); Toesca, Pietro, *Giotto* (Turin 1941); Brizio, Anna M., *La pittura in Piemonte* (Turin 1942); Ortolani, Sergio, *Raffaello* (Bergamo 1942); Planiscig, Leo, *Desiderio da Settignano* (Vienna 1942); Longhi, Roberto, "Ultimi studi sul Caravaggio e la sua cerchia," *Proporzioni,* vol. 1 (Florence 1943); Morassi, Antonio, *Tiepolo* (Bergamo 1943); Sinibaldi, Giulia, and Brunetti, G., *Pittura italiana del Duecento e Trecento* (Florence 1943); Bettini, Sergio, *Giusto de' Menabuoi* (Padova 1944); Pallucchini, Rodolfo, *Sebastian Viniziano* (Milan 1944); Sabatini, Attilio, *Antonio e Piero del Pollaiuolo* (Florence 1944); Bertini, Aldo, *Michelangelo fino alla Sistina* (Turin 1945); Briganti, Giuliano, *Il manierismo e Pellegrino Tibaldi* (Rome 1945); Brizio, Anna M., *Ottocento e Novecento* (Turin 1945); Degenhart, Bernhard, *Pisanello* (Turin 1945); Longhi, Roberto, *Piero della Francesca* (Florence 1946); id., *Viatico per cinque secoli di pittura veneziana* (Florence 1946); Offner, Richard, *A Critical and Historical Corpus of Florentine Painting,* 5 vols. (New York 1930–47); Pane, Roberto, *Palladio* (Turin 1947); De Tolnay, Charles, *Michelangelo,* 3 vols. (Princeton 1943–48); Gnudi, C., *Nicola, Arnolfo, Lapo* (Florence 1948); Longhi, Roberto, "Giudizio sul Duecento," *Proporzioni,* vol. 2 (Florence 1948); Wittgens, Fernando, *Foppa* (Milan 1948).

Anna Maria Brizio,
Author of "La pittura in Piemonte"; "Ottocento e Novecento."

7. MUSIC. The genesis of Italian music is in the language of Italy itself. Before the middle of the 13th century, the founding of the Italian *dolce stil nuovo* (sweet new style), and, later, the work of Dante Alighieri (1265–1321), the language of the literature of Italy had been Latin, quasi-Provençal, and French. The Latin literature of the Middle Ages began about the 7th century. It contained chronicles and hymns, such as the *Dies Irae* (later incorporated in the service of the Roman Catholic Church) and the *Veni Sancte Spiritus.* It included poems, often satirical, and treatises on natural history and theology, together with religious and secular legends, both old and new. This Latin, however, was not the tongue of classical purity, for after the coming of the northern invaders in the 5th and 6th centuries, the language, even as used in writing, lost its ancient character, while in verbal use it altered constantly until it evolved into the various dialects of the land. These dialects possessed simple grammatical structure as a common characteristic, though in vocabulary some remained nearer to their source than others. (See also sections on *Language* and *Literature.*)

The oldest musical examples set to Italian texts are to be found in the *laudi spirituali,* or sacred songs, many of which are preserved in a manuscript in the Magliabechiana Library of Florence. The composers, known as *laudisti,* were found principally among Franciscan monks, the most famous of whom was Jacopone da Todi (c. 1230–1306). The *laudi* represent an extention of the ecclesiastical spirit into the vernacular.

Early *laudi spirituali* were monodic in character, and were sung by fraternities of penitents who practiced flagellation as a means of atonement. In traveling from place to place, they were met by local religious groups who joined in the singing of these sacred folk songs. The penitential practice spread into Germany, where the participants were known as *Geissler* (flagellants). The movement reached its height about 1348–1349, during the Black Death. The melodic schemata of the *Geisslerlied* anticipated the Lutheran chorale, which played such an important part in the work of Johann Sebastian Bach. Papal disapproval hastened the end of this movement, especially in Italy, although bands of *laudisti* remained until the 16th century and exerted an influence upon Palestrina and the oratorio form.

The *laudi* belong to the genre of folk creation closely allied to the *ballata*—the Italian equivalent of the French *virelai* (virelay), with its *ripresa* (refrain), stanza (a middle section), and a repetition of the *ripresa.* The *ballata,* of which the popular *Donna Lombarda* is a favorite of the Piedmontese, was originally a song sung while dancing, and is not unlike the English ballad. Other species of popular *canzoni* (songs) are the *zingaresca,* the *frottola,* the *stornello* and *rispetto* (both beloved of the Tuscans), the *mattinata,* sung at the break of day, and the *vicariola,* a type of song indigenous to Sicily and named after a prison in Palermo. The *stornello* is variously known as *ritondelle, ritornelle, ritornello, fiore,* or *fioretto.* Authorities differ as to its origin, but the accepted explanation is that it was derived from the practice of singing *storno,* that is, one singer singing against another antiphonally.

In examining the regional differences in folk song, we find that Sicily is considered to be the source and parent through which all poetry, both popular and cultivated, passed to the rest of Italy. In the songs of the Piedmont, Liguria, Lombardy, and Venice, we find many legends, but none records such historical traditions as are to be found in those of Sicily. Tuscany, Umbria, Romagna, Marche, and even Calabria record little of the historical data found in the Sicilian ballads. The saga of that island is set forth in its lyrical folk literature. The Greek, Saracen, Norman, French, and Spanish occupations are all recorded in song. So, too, are the revolutions of 1820, 1848, and 1860, and the sanguinary revolt of 1866. Many of these songs have been transcribed for modern concert use by Geni Sadero (1891–).

In contrast to the Sicilian songs, the Tuscan folk airs are tempered by the kindness and gentleness of the northern disposition and invested with a quiet dignity and delicate charm. Some of these poetic fragments were translated by the German poet Paul Heyse, making them available for musical settings by Hugo Wolf. Central Italy focuses its attention on the Neapolitan Piedigrotta, a festival held yearly in honor of the Madonna in August and in which many songs receive their initial hearing. Such tunes as *Funiculi, funicula,* a modern song par excellence, written to celebrate the opening of the funicular railway up Mt. Vesuvius, *Torna a Sorrento, Addio a Napoli* (a favorite of Enrico Caruso, 1873–1921), and many others, find their way into the folk literature of the people, although strictly speaking they are not of the folk genre. It is interesting to note that the exceedingly popular tune *I zampognari* (*The Bagpipers*), a Christmas melody, was the source of George Frederick Handel's Pastoral Symphony and aria *He shall feed His flock* in *The Messiah,* while many a composer has delicately lifted other lyrical folk segments and incorporated them into his own larger musical forms.

The most important species of folk poetry is the madrigal. It is the only species that became the property of the cultivated poet, and it subsequently led to the formation and development of the great polyphonic school of writing. This form was enthusiastically adopted by the Flemish school of composers who found themselves in Italy as *maestri di cappella* (choirmasters). The word madrigal is derived from a song sung by shepherds (*mandriano*) while taking their flocks (*mandria*) to pasture. Some authorities trace the word to the Italian *madre* (mother), signifying a poem addressed to the Madonna, while others conceive it as a corruption of the Spanish *madrugada* (dawn), equivalent to the Italian *mattinata.*

Rome and Venice cultivated the madrigal with great success. In Florence it attained tremendous popularity, appearing initially in the form of the *frottola.* In Naples it took firm root and flourished as the villanella. Transplanted to England, the madrigal found a freedom of harmonic treatment which it did not possess under the quasi-ecclesiastical guidance of the Roman and Venetian schools. The Italian text was soon supplanted by the English. Although this deprived the madrigal of its original flavor, the lack was compensated by the enthusiasm the new form found in its adopted country. Subsequently, it was neglected by both the Flemings and the Italians, and it gradually evolved into a species of chamber music with instrumental accompaniment. In England, it merged into the glee, a form of composition cultivated in no other country. Some English authorities regard the glee as aesthetically superior to its German complement, the part song. By achieving a harmonic elasticity and substituting the modern tonalities for the ecclesiastical modes, the madrigal form opened an avenue for further progress in part writing, directly influencing the great Germanic school, which was to bloom and flower with the chorale. Thus, the madrigal, a product of Italian poetic thought, profoundly influenced the whole course of music composition of its day.

The golden period of the Italian madrigal reached its apex in the works of Giovanni Giacomo Gastoldi (c. 1556–1619), Baldassare Donato or Donati (c. 1530–1603), and Luca Marenzio (c. 1553–1599), who was called *il piú dolce cigno* (the sweetest swan) and was doubtless the leading madrigalist of his time. At the beginning of the 17th century, the madrigal was invested with a new dramatic element. We see it influence the chromaticism of the coming opera and oratorio, and a new lyrical trinity is found in the brilliant works of Carlo Gesualdo, prince of Venosa (c. 1560–c. 1614), Orazio Vecchi (1550?–1605), and the great Claudio Monteverdi (1567–1643). In his *L'amfiparnasso,* Vecchi touches upon the novel idea of madrigal-comedy and choral forms for the stage, intermediaries between the madrigalian formalism and the coming experimentalism of the Florentine Camerata. Gesualdo and his bold chromatic progressions were strangely prophetic of the Wagnerianism to come almost 300 years later. The introduction of the unique tremolo effects in the violin, first found in his *Il combattimento di Tancredi e Clorinda,* together with the use of massive harmonies and expert treatment of dissonances, stamps Monteverdi as one of the bold geniuses of musical history.

It is in the transitional decades linking the 16th and 17th centuries that we find the development of new forms on which modern music relies: opera, oratorio, and accompanied solo song. Imbued with a desire to revive the Greek classical ideals, a group of Florentine nobles, poets, and musicians banded together. Known as the Camerata (sometimes as Bardists), they met at the palace of Giovanni Bardi, conte del Vernio (1534?–?1612) and at the home of Jacopo Corsi (1560–1604) to discuss plans for the revival of the tonal art of classical antiquity. The first practical experiment of this group, undertaken by Vincenzo Galilei (c. 1533–1591), father of the famous astronomer, was a musical setting of Count Ugolino's lament from Dante's *Divina Commedia.* Galilei was the most prominent figure in the work of the Camerata, and his interest in art prompted him to write *Il Fronimo,* a literary dialogue in which he explained the method of tuning, then in vogue by Italian lutanists. His theoretical studies in tuning were in juxtaposition to those of his teacher, Gioseffo Zarlino (1517–1590), who believed that the octave should be divided into 12 equal semitones, whereas Galilei, in his blind adherence to Greek ideals, insisted upon the Pythagorean immutable system.

Zarlino and his contemporary, Lodovico Zacconi (born Giulio Cesare Zacconi, 1555–1627), constituted a formidable brace of theorists of the late 16th century. Zacconi's fame rests on his valuable *Prattica di musica,* a series of four books published in Venice between 1592 and 1622, which, in conjunction with the *Dodecachordon* of the Swiss Henricus Glareanus (real name Heinrich Loris), and the *Musicae activae micrologus* of the German Andreas Ornithoparcus (real name Vogelsang or Vogelgesang), comprise the only clear works explaining the musical practices of the day. An earlier and more celebrated treatise similarly entitled *Micrologus,* now in the library of the Vatican, was compiled by Guido d'Arezzo (995?–?1050) about 1025, and printed in 1784 by Martin Gerbert von Hornau in his *Scriptores ecclesiastici de musica.*

In addition to his advocacy of equal temperament for keyed instruments, a practice which was adopted by Bach 100 years later and completely realized only in comparatively recent years, Zarlino assured his place in music history by his three tracts entitled: *Istitutioni armoniche* (1558), *Dimostrationi armoniche* (1571), and *Sopplimenti musicali* (1588). His triple literary effort clearly paved the way for the major and descending minor scales of modern music. One of Zarlino's considerations takes us to the human pulse as a unit of music measurement. This same human measuring device was used by Galileo Galilei (1564–1642) in determining the theory of isochronous vibration, when he timed the oscillations of a swinging lamp in the Cathedral of Pisa by means of pulse beats and found that amplitude of oscillation did not affect the isochronism of a swinging pendulum. This proved conclusively that frequency, not amplitude, of oscillation affects the pitch of a vibrating body.

The work of the Camerata gained impetus with *Dafne* (*Daphne*), a dramatic poem (1594) of Ottavio Rinuccini (1562–1621), set to music by Jacopo Peri (1561–1633). This early effort was received with such acclaim that for three years it was repeatedly performed during the carnival season. The actual history of opera, however, may be said to commence with *Euridice* (*Eurydice*), a *dramma per musica* written by Rinuccini at the behest of Grand Duke Ferdinand I, with musical settings by both Peri and Giulio Caccini (c. 1550–1618). This opera was performed as part of the festivities in honor of the wedding of Henry IV of France and Marie de Médicis in the Pitti Palace on Oct. 6, 1600. At this performance part of Peri's and part of Caccini's music was performed. It included a few choruses in madrigal style with dialogue carried on in the *stile rappresentativo.* This *stile rappresentativo* was nothing more than the subjugation of melody to fit the natural emotional surge of the text. It later gave rise to the recitative and the aria as we know them today. The music contained many vocal flourishes. This was especially true of Caccini's work. These flourishes proved to be the contributing factors to the decline of opera before the advent of Verdi, Puccini, and the moderns of the operatic school in Italy.

It was left to the genius of Monteverdi to reveal the possibilities of this new form. In his *Orfeo,* we find a tremendous advance over the simple music dramas of the Florentines, and in his pupil Francesco Cavalli (originally Pietro Francesco Cavalli-Bruni, 1602?–1676), we discern an improvement in the recitative and discover the use of male sopranos (castrati) for the first time. Cavalli foreshadowed the *aria da capo,* which was to become so prominent a feature of opera for the Italians.

At the beginning of the 17th century some comedy was being injected into an otherwise classic and formal music drama. It was, at first, considered out of place and relegated to the entr'acte. These comedies were called intermezzi or *opera buffa* and formed a distinct part of *opera seria*. Fittingly enough, they were developed in Naples, which wrested the operatic leadership from Florence and Venice. The Neapolitan pre-eminence is due principally to Alessandro Scarlatti (1659–1725), a musician of natural gifts and one of the most indefatigable workers of his time—his operas alone numbered over 108. Under his guidance, the recitative took three distinct forms—the *recitativo secco* (unaccompanied), the *recitativo strumentato* (used in moments of intensity with orchestral accompaniment), and the aria (for impassioned vocal soliloquy).

By this time the opera had become more and more a vehicle for vocal display. The chorus faded in importance, and the librettos gradually assumed the melodramatic form of love intrigue, leaving the classic Greek drama behind. By 1725, the singing virtuosos had attained such influence over the operatic composers that they actually dictated their demands. Their insistence on vocal display rapidly led composers to a kind of formality that contained the seeds of decadence and artistic sterility. The golden age of *bel canto* had descended upon Italy, but, blinded by sheer virtuosity and vocal beauty, together with a degeneration of literary taste, opera was brought to a temporary decline.

In Domenico Cimarosa (1749–1801) we have a culminating point of both *opera buffa* and *opera seria*. A contemporary of Wolfgang Amadeus Mozart, Cimarosa had a much simpler and less varied style than his younger rival of Salzburg. His great success was achieved with *Il matrimonio segreto* (first produced in 1792), a work heard to this day. In *opera seria* he contributed *Gli Orazii e Curiazii* (1794), one of the strongest heroic pieces of its time. Cimarosa is important chiefly as a type of his era; he bridges the gap between the early classical opera and the period of romanticism.

If the Italian composers did not take kindly to the spirit of romanticism that spread throughout Europe, they could not evade it completely. Gioacchino Rossini (1792–1868) was among the first to revise his design and adjust his methods to fit the new lyrical attitudes. He headed a group of writers who assumed the responsibility of salvaging the opera from an ever-widening pit of decadence. A thorough technical mastery in treating the human voice, however, was the only compensation for the general musical impoverishment that prevailed. But Italy's operatic conquest of the world was by this time complete.

It is in this generation that we glimpse an incipient schism between the Italian and German styles. One path led to mythological figuration and metaphysical speculation, while the other clung desperately to living human characterization that mirrored the soul of the auditor himself. The northern temperament plunged into a sea of ponderous musical dialectics, while the southerner cast deep beams of illumination on the operatic horizon, returning with characteristic Latin candor and simplicity to limn human emotion on a stage peopled with human beings.

Rossini, Gaetano Donizetti (1797–1848), and the Sicilian Vincenzo Bellini (1801–1835)—the three giants of the period—while retaining the Italian love for lyricism, at the same time effected certain reforms and brought about many improvements upon which the moderns were destined to build. That the works of these men are heard today is eloquent proof of their excellence and intrinsic worth. Despite the sparkle and musical wit of his *Il Barbiere di Siviglia* (*The Barber of Seville*), Rossini's sincerest work was *Guillaume Tell* (*William Tell*). Here he shows a strength of orchestral technique which greatly influenced the French operatic writers of his time. The simplicity and dignity vested in the work prove that he could set aside the flimsy and conventional and attack the subject of Tell with seriousness and reserve.

Although Donizetti and Rossini worked equally well in *opera seria* and *opera buffa*, the young Bellini was successful only in the serious vein. Both his *Norma* and *La Sonnambula* (*The Sleepwalker*) show a delicacy and sensitivity that surpassed even the great Rossini himself. For mastery of melodic power, Bellini has no peer. Despite a certain naive quality and a strain of effeminate sentiment, he rises at times to a grandeur which is not often found in Donizetti. Although the latter did not possess the melodic gift of Bellini, yet there is ample compensation for it in his characterizations, such as that of Naffeo Orsini in *Lucrezia Borgia*, which, for brilliancy and fierce dramatic power, were not equaled during his period. Both composers sustained the Italian love for lyricism so well that Wagner, years later, fairly shouted his praise of them. Both were alive to the necessity for reforms in their day. Neither could stem the Rossinian popularity, nor could they cope with the popularity of the *fioriture* (vocal flourish) and flowing cadences so dear to the heart of the singer. On the whole, opera at this period was a sickeningly sweet (although beautifully melodious), ear-tickling, sensuous form which lacked virility. Opera awaited the coming of Giuseppe Verdi for definitive reforms.

When the most delicate taste had tired of the Donizetti-Bellini *dolcezza*, Giuseppe Verdi (1813–1901) breathed new life and hope into this moribund institution of the Camerata. He brought to bear the earthiness, the refreshing virility, and the savage strength it needed. His genius ran the gamut from vulgar depths to soaring heights. A fearless, sincere, and genuine artist, he had as his most noteworthy trait the ability to grow artistically to the very end of his life. In his early operas—*Oberto, Nabucco* (*Nabucodonosor*), *I Lombardi, Ernani*—he showed stiffness and a groping for freedom. It is in his *Rigoletto* (1851), that he first revealed a freer and more original style. His development through *Il Trovatore, La Forza del Destino, Aïda, Otello,* and *Falstaff* shows a steady, methodical, and inexorable climb to the pinnacle of operatic fame. Mention must be made of his contemporary, Arrigo Boito (1842–1918), librettist and composer in his own right, without whose encouragement the world would probably never have heard *Otello* or *Falstaff*.

With the close of the 19th century, Italy saw a movement by her younger composers toward operatic story dealing with folklore and the everyday, prosaic existence in the provinces. In this group were Pietro Mascagni (1863–1945) and Ruggiero Leoncavallo (1858–1919), whose programmatic use of thematic material gave rise to the school of *verismo* (verism or realism). Both *I Pagliacci* of Leoncavallo and *Cavalleria*

Rusticana of Mascagni were products of this period. Both operas were built on popular folk legends; both were brilliantly orchestrated and achieved great popularity.

Out of the school of *verismo* came Giacomo Puccini (1858–1924), whose works have attained a great vogue. He was a sensitive artist with an active imagination, but his predilection for an expansive melodic phrase, extending even to those textual passages not warranting such treatment, has been criticized. Subsequent operatic successes were realized by a group of composers including Alfredo Catalani (1854–1893), Alberto Franchetti (1860–), Francesco Cilea (1866–1950), Riccardo Zandonai (1883–1944), Franco Alfano (1876–), the well-known Italo Montemezzi (1875–1952), who wrote *L'amore dei tre re* (*The Love of Three Kings*); Amilcare Ponchielli (1834–1886), author of *La Gioconda* and teacher of Mascagni; Umberto Giordano (1867–1948) with his *Andrea Chénier;* and Ermanno Wolf-Ferrari (1876–1948), whose *I gioielli della Madonna* (*The Jewels of the Madonna*) and *Il segreto di Susanna* (*The Secret of Susanne*) are very popular in the United States.

The popular view that Italian music concerns itself with problems of the theater only, has obscured the fact that Italy has given birth to many instrumental and dance forms. A cursory glance at the 16th and 17th century musical files reveals a wealth of material conclusively dispelling this misconception. No doubt, this mistaken belief was fortified by the fact that Italians have been purveyors of opera to the entire world. The overwhelming successes of the 18th and 19th century Italian theatrical enterprises, which influenced the entire Continent and had subsequent repercussions in England and the United States, contributed further to this warped viewpoint. The complete acceptance of operatic art by the musical world was inevitable, since it dealt with fundamental elements of human expression in its use of voice and gesture. Their coordinated use, joined with the power of sound, make for simple understanding as contrasted with symphonic complexities, which too often are poverty stricken in meaning. The psychology of sound is such that it comes closest to comprehension when it attains some kinship with the emotional tensions and releases of everyday experiences. It is precisely in this field that the Italian excels.

Italian melodic ingenuity gained impetus in the Middle Ages, when Gregorian art predominated. The subsequent unfolding of the Italian *Ars nova* (14th century music) reveals the acquisition of thirds and sixths as an advance over the simple organum of the Middle Ages. In Gioseffo Zarlino's *Istitutione armoniche,* we find mention of the untutored singers, who invariably sing the major third and sixth, at that time considered dissonant. Often the compositions of the *Ars nova* were aided by instruments reinforcing the voices which they accompanied.

While the Flemish group of composers in Italy relied heavily upon instruments, the Italians developed a purely vocal style that stands to this day as a supreme example of beautiful writing. This style was perfected by Giovanni Pierluigi (called da Palestrina, 1525?–1594), who stripped all artifice from his work to the end that exquisite melody and skillful use of declamation be happily united. In Palestrina we see the seed of a harmonic sense in the modern manner. The Roman Palestrinian orbit must include his pupil Giovanni Maria Nanini or Nanino (1545?–1607), well known through his motet *Hodie Christus Natus Est;* Marco Antonio Ingegneri (1545?–1592), whose *Responsoria Hebdomodae Sanctae* (*Responses for Holy Week*) were at one time considered a work of Palestrina; Felice Anerio (1560?–1614), whose *Adoramus Te, Christe,* has erroneously been attributed also to Palestrina; and Gregorio Allegri (1582?–1652), known principally for his world-famous *Miserere.*

While the Roman school was occupied with compositions for church use, the northern school of the Venetians was founding an independent form of organ and orchestral composition. Andrea Gabrieli or Gabrielli (c. 1510–1586), through his *Agnus Dei* for five voices, was achieving antiphonal effects with double choirs at St. Mark's, while his nephew Giovanni Gabrieli (1557–1612), with his *Sonata Pian e Forte* and the instrumental *Canzone* for two violins, two cornets, and two trombones, was a pioneer in instrumental forms. Simultaneously these Venetians were perfecting the *ricercare,* precursor of the fugue; and Claudio Merulo (real surname Merlotti, 1533–1604), predecessor to Giovanni Gabrieli as first organist at St. Mark's, was developing an improvisational form in his toccatas. These *canzoni, ricercari,* and toccatas represent the transitional polyphonic forms linking the purely vocal art with early orchestral composition.

The first formal sonata imprint is to be found several generations later in Arcangelo Corelli (1653–1713), who established the four-part, slow-fast alternation that was to prevail up to the middle of the 18th century, when it evolved into the threefold fast-slow-fast conception. There were two types of sonatas in Corelli's day: the *sonata da camera* (chamber sonata) and the *sonata da chiesa* (church sonata). Continuing the work of the Venetians in establishing free forms in organ music, the Roman Girolamo Frescobaldi (1583–1643), sometimes known as the Italian Bach, extended, elaborated, and perfected all the accepted ideas which were to form the basis for the contrapuntal art of his northern musical brothers. A little later, we see a new type of instrumental music in the form of concerto where the solos and tuttis were, at first, known as *concerto grosso,* and several soloists were employed in opposition to the *tutti* effects. The sinfonia (symphony) appears as a later development through the genius of Alessandro Scarlatti, in the form of an orchestral introduction to opera. Here is the birth of the overture consisting of three movements: an allegro, then an adagio or andante, followed by an allegro, usually in dance form. The sonata and concerto adopted this structure, while the symphony divorced itself from the opera and became the pedestal for all instrumental music to this day.

A prolific writer, Scarlatti penned over 108 operas, perhaps 200 masses (though only 10 are extant), and approximately 700 cantatas and oratorios. He stands at the head of the Neapolitan school. Another specialist in church music of this period was Francesco Durante (1684–1755), with his masses, psalms, motets, and hymns. Antonio Lotti (1667–1740) stands high in the esteem of the church for his *Crucifixus* for six voices, in addition to his numerous masses, while Benedetto Marcello (1686–1739) is remembered for his keenly biting work *Il teatro alla moda,* directed at operatic abuses then in vogue, together with his famous settings for the first 50 psalms.

Giovanni Battista Pergolesi or Pergolese (1710–1736) and his *Stabat Mater* are products of this period. Lesser representatives of church art include Giovanni Battista (known as Padre) Martini (1706–1784) of Bologna and Antonio Caldara (1670–1736). In recent times the great *Manzoni Requiem* of Verdi stands supreme, while the works of Lorenzo Perosi (1872–) attempt to recapture the ecclesiastical traditions of Palestrina.

The development of instrumental forms was matched by the instrumentalists and instrument makers, who were quick to seize upon new ideas and adapt them for their own use. In the field of violin makers were Andrea Amati (1530?–?1611), Gasparo da Salò (real name Bertolotti, c. 1542–1609), and Antonio Stradivari (1644–1737), who improved the acoustical quality of the instrument. The Guarnieri or Guarnerius family of Cremona (latter half of the 17th century) was interested mainly in strength of tone. In the field of the solo violin concerto, we find the names of Antonio Vivaldi (1678?–1741), Giuseppe Tartini (1692–1770), Gaetano Pugnani (1731–1798), and Pietro Antonio Locatelli (1693–1764), while the romantic figure of Nicolò Paganini (1782–1840) conjures up visions of demoniacal techniques that have never been surpassed. The development of the piano by Bartolommeo Cristofori (1665–1731) to an instrument to be played *pian e forte* (soft and loud), whence it receives its name, opened vistas in composition for that instrument.

The heroic march of Italian music is one vast accumulation of tonal art through the centuries. Since the early 18th century, the Latin temperament has shown a marked preference for music of the theater, and the world has gratefully accepted the fruits of Italian lyrical genius. There is, however, another and very different Italy immeasurably removed from the spell of *verismo* and the lovelier terrain of Giovanni Sgambati (1841–1914), Giuseppe Martucci (1856–1909), Marco Enrico Bossi (1861–1925), and Leone Sinigaglia (1868–). The neoclassicism of the 20th century has its roots in Italy, and its initial efforts were given impetus by the gigantic musical intellect of Ferrucio Busoni (1866–1924). This movement marked the revolt against the romantic and postromantic subjectivism of the 19th century. The modern harmonic fabric enlists the creative power of Ildebrando Pizzetti (1880–), Riccardo Pick-Mangiagalli (1882–), and Francesco Malipiero (1882–). Mario Castelnuovo-Tedesco (1895–) and Vincenzo Tommasini (1880–) still cling to romantic remnants, although Tommasini's later works are neoclassic in style, while Ottorino Respighi (1879–1936) harks back to classical sources for his *Antiche danze e arie per liuto* (*Old Airs and Dances for Lute*). A prolific composer in all forms, Respighi will be remembered chiefly for his handling of orchestral techniques, although his operas, *Maria Egiziaca* (*Mary of Egypt*), *Belfagor*, and *La Campana sommersa* (*The Sunken Bell*) have weathered the test of frequent performances. Vittorio Rieti (1898–) and Ruggero Vené (1898–) carry on their master's orchestral traditions. Rieti has achieved his greatest successes with the ballets *Noah's Ark* and *Barabau*, produced by Sergei Diaghilev. Lodovico Rocca (1895–) stands somewhat alone with his programmatic music, although one of his five operas, *Il dibuk* (*The Dybbuk*), based on a Hebrew legend, was produced at La Scala with great success in 1934.

Further revulsion against romantic sentimentalism and the pastel colorations of impressionism led to a mercifully short-lived movement representing extremely radical methods in all the arts in the cult of *futurismo* (futurism). Its musical tenets were, in part, outlined by Francesco Pratella (1880–) in his *Musica futurista* (1912). Futuristic music embodying new musical resources of nonperiodical vibrations was written by Luigi Russolo (1885–), who constructed noise instruments (*intonarumori*). Though unsuccessful, this movement spread to France, where *bruitisme*, as the French called it, may be tersely summarized by Jean Cocteau's observation on impressionism: "After the music of the silk brush, the music with the axe."

In the vanguard of young and extremely active composers delving into Arnold Schönberg's twelve-tone mechanisms is Luigi Dallapiccola (1904–), whose *Volo di notte* (*Night Flight*), based on an excerpt from a book by Antoine de Saint-Exupéry, uses a twelve-tone (called dodecachordal by Italians) melodic series. An integral application of the dodecachordal technique is found in his *Greek Lyrics*. Ennio Porrino (1910–), Antonio Veretti (1900–), Virgilio Mortari (1902–), Nino Rota (1911–), Riccardo Nielsen (1908–), and Giorgio Federico Ghedini (1892–) are members of this school. Luigi Cortese (1899–), a polytonalist, is known principally for his *Prometheus Bound*, while Adone Zecchi (1904–) applied his twelve-tone technique to his *Requiem for Men's Voices and Orchestra* (1943) and his *Invectives* for the same combination. Goffredo Petrassi (1904–), a neoclassicist who occasionally ventures into quartal harmony, achieved a degree of fame beyond Italian borders with his *Partita for Orchestra* (1933), while Renzo Rossellini (1908–), a neoimpressionist occupied principally with music for films, was introduced to New York audiences in 1946 through his *Canto de Palude* (1938).

At least three Italian Americans occupy a prominent place in the musical scene of the United States. Gian-Carlo Menotti (1911–) is justly famous for his operas *Amelia Goes to the Ball* (1937) and *The Island God* (Metropolitan Opera House, 1942); his charming radio opera *The Old Maid and the Thief* (1939); and his more recent works, *The Medium* (1946) and *The Telephone* (1947). Walter Piston, born in Maine in 1894, leaped to fame with his ballet *The Incredible Flutist* (1938), while Paul Creston, born in New York in 1906, is known principally for music in the symphonic medium.

The Italian directorial genius is a recognized commodity and precludes extended comment. Besides Arturo Toscanini (1867–), its stellar light, it includes Bernardino Molinari (1880–), Victor de Sabata (1892–), whose compositions have been heard in the United States, Gino Marinuzzi (1882–1945), Antonio Guarnieri (1883–), Leopoldo Mugnone (1858–1940), Verdi's favorite conductor, and Sergio Failoni (1890–1947).

The tremendous national interest in music and its makers keeps over 30 publications busy chronicling the musical events in the peninsula. Among the leading contributors in the field of musicology are Guido M. Gatti (1892– , *La Rassegna musicale*), Fausto Acanfora di Torrefranca (1883– , *Revista musicale italiana*), Fernando Liuzzi (1884–1940), Andrea della Corte (1883–), and Guido Pannain (1891–). Over 400 societies devote themselves exclusively to chamber music.

The Società del Quintetto has toured the Continent as well as Italy, while the Venetian Quartet and the Trio Italiano have toured as far afield as South America. The Gruppi Universitari Musicali—comprising students from 18 universities, with its Poltronieri Quartet—and the Corporazione delle Nuove Musiche concern themselves with ancient and new music in Rome, Milan, and Palermo. The ladies' lyceum clubs display a keen interest in new music.

Modern Italian music, endeavoring to revive symphonic forms of native caliber, spells grandeur, austerity, robustness, and conciseness—traits ordinarily associated with such old composers as Corelli, Monteverdi, and Scarlatti. Despite slight influences of French impressionism, Stravinskian primitivity, and Schönbergian complexities, its chief characteristic remains an Italianate lyricism. The postwar endeavors to settle regional differences should restore Italy to her historic position as chief purveyor of music to the world. See also separate biographies of the major composers.

Bibliography.—Frojo, Giovanni, *Saggio storico-critico intorno alla musica indiana-egiziana-greca e principalmente italiana* (Cantanzaro 1873); Florimo, Francesco, *La scuola musicale di Napoli,* 4 vols. (Naples 1880–84); Pasquetti, Guido, *L'Oratorio musicale in Italia* (Florence 1906); Harcourt, Eugène d', *La Musique actuelle en Italie* (Paris 1907); Alaleona, Domenico, *Studii sulla storia del Oratorio musicale in Italia* (Turin 1908); Warrack, Grace, ed., *Florilegio di canti toscani: Folk Songs of the Tuscan Hills* (London 1914); *Raccolta nazionale delle musiche italiana* (Milan 1919); Melchiorre, Nicola, *Saggi di critica musicale* (Abruzzi 1925); Schinelli, Achille, ed., *L'anima musicale della patria (Il Risorgimento italiano nella sua espressione musicale, 1796–1922)* (Milan 1928–29); Acanfora di Torrefranca, Fausto, *Le origini italiane del romanticismo musicale: i primitivi della sonata moderna* (Turin 1930); Toye, Francis, *Giuseppe Verdi, His Life and Works* (New York 1931); Benvenuti, Giacomo, ed., *Istituzioni e monumenti dell' arte musicale italiana,* 2 vols. (Milan 1932); Gatti, Guido Maria, *Musicisti moderni d'Italia e di fuori* (Bologna 1925); tr. as *Modern Italian Composers* (New York 1932); Dent, E. J., *Music of the Renaissance in Italy* (London 1933); *Grove's Dictionary of Music and Musicians,* 3d ed. (New York 1935); Liuzzi, Fernando, *La Lauda e i primordi della melodia italiana,* 2 vols. (Rome 1935); Della Corte, Andrea, *Le relazioni storiche della poesia e della musica italiana* (Turin 1936); Sachs, Curt, *World History of the Dance* (New York 1937); Della Corte, Andrea, *Tre secoli di opera italiana* (Turin 1938); Leichtentritt, Hugo, *Music, History, and Ideas* (Cambridge, Mass., 1938); Reese, Gustave, *Music in the Middle Ages* (New York 1940); Lang, P. H., *Music in Western Civilization* (New York 1941).

GIOVANNI CAMAJANI, PH.D.,
Fellow, Trinity College, London.

8. SCIENCE. We cannot give an account of the progress of the experimental sciences in Italy from the beginning of the 17th century to the mid-20th century—from Galileo Galilei to Enrico Fermi—without reference to the political history of that period. There is a relationship of cause and effect between political and economic conditions and the material possibilities of carrying out research and experiment. The 17th century was a golden age for science in Italy and elsewhere. Probably even without Galileo, Sir Isaac Newton (1642–1727) would have made a contribution to physics as great as that of his Italian predecessor. But apart from the time lag between the two physicists, we must not overlook one striking and entirely original element in Galileo's work—namely, his break with Aristotelian tradition as revived by the Roman Catholic Church. It was this break that permitted not only the creation of a new science, but also the rise of a whole new spirit of inquiry, embodied in what we now call experimental research. Galileo lived at a particularly happy period for the Italian universities, when born Padova and Pisa were in a position to subsidize scientific laboratories. Of course, any visitor to Pisa is impressed by the primitive equipment of the places where Galileo carried on his famous experiments with falling bodies, but they involved what were, for his times, considerable expenditures, certainly no less than those made for similar purposes by other European universities. This availability of funds accounts in part for the rapid growth of experimental science in the 17th century. Another factor of importance was the incipient conflict between the rising middle class and the old aristocracy.

The following period presents us with an entirely different set of conditions; indeed, in Italy the late 17th and the 18th centuries were times of political decadence. There was a shattering of the ideal of unity spread through the peninsula by the Renaissance and even a decay of the wealthy middle class. The discoveries of Marcello Malpighi (1628–1694), Luigi or Aloisio Galvani (1737–1798) and Alessandro Volta (1745–1827) would surely have led to further theoretical development and practical application within Italy had they found a more propitious political and economic environment. As it was, the voltaic pile attained recognition under the more favorable circumstances enjoyed by Sir Humphry Davy in England. It is no wonder, then, that experimental science declined in 18th century Italy, and that such first-rate talents as there were in this field did not assert themselves as they should, because a proper background was lacking.

The 19th century completes the picture we have sketched in above. Political and social conditions in Italy up to 1870 and unification did not favor the efficient organization of the universities or their laboratories. But with political unity and Italy's entrance into the ranks of industrial nations, there came a renewed impulse, made possible by grants of funds, toward activities in the field of science. From 1880 to 1914, Italy made scientific progress of a truly remarkable kind. Had it not been for the political degeneration of the Fascist period, this progress would have continued and been proportionate to the important role traditionally played by Italians among the civilized peoples of the world. In Fascist Italy a man like Fermi could not find scope for developing his creative genius, whereas under a democratic government he could have carried out his work in line with the great Italian contributions to progress and civilization.

The Age of Galileo.—We cannot understand the 19th century development of experimental science in the Galilean tradition unless we take into account the cultural and technical conditions prevailing in Italy since the Renaissance. "The appearance of a Leonardo or a Galileo is comprehensible only if we connect it with Italian industry," writes Harald Höffding in his *Den nyere Filosofis Historie* (*History of Modern Philosophy,* 1894), and as Gabriel Séailles, the art historian, said in his *Léonard de Vinci: l'artiste et le savant* (1892): "A hundred years before Galilei there was in Italy a small group of free men whose minds were not cluttered up with excessive erudition. . . . They observed the sky and the earth, the life of plants and animals. . . . They made experiments, they went in for empirical and mathematical thinking, because they refused to accept anything as true that could not pass the test of demonstration and be proved by the evidence of their own senses. They were aware that science represents a collective, social effort, that one man cannot build it up in a hurry, because it does not spring fully formed from his mind. For this reason, they met together, questioned one another, and exchanged news of their studies and discoveries. We may say that in the 15th century a group of artists, travelers, doctors, engineers, and gentlemen were the leaders of modern science."

Another valuable source of information about social and cultural conditions in Italy at this time is Jakob Burckhardt's classic work, *Die Kultur der Renaissance in Italien* (*The Civilization of the Renaissance in Italy,* 1860). Galileo Galilei (1564–1642) himself, at the beginning of his *Discorsi e dimostrazioni matematiche intorno a due nuove scienze* (*Dialogues Concerning Two New Sciences,* 1638) said: "The constant activity which you Venetians display in your arsenal suggests to the studious mind a large field for endeavor, especially that part of the work which involves mechanics." The rise of experimental science in 17th century Italy is an example of the interaction of technology and scientific development.

Although we are not chiefly concerned with Galileo's contributions to astronomy, we must note the influence of his *Sidereus nuncius* (1610) and *Istoria e dimostrazioni intorno alle macchie solari* (*Letters on the Solar Spots,* 1613), his development of the refracting telescope, and his discovery of the satellites of Jupiter, sunspots, the phases of Venus, the first traces of the ring around Saturn, and planetary orbits. His two principal scientific achievements, however, may be summarized as follows:

(1) *Experimental method,* of which he must be considered the founder, although nowhere in his writings has he given a detailed description of methodology or naturalistic logic. It would require considerable effort to coordinate the analyses of his sensations and experiments which we find scattered through *Il saggiatore* (1623), the *Dialogo dei due massimi sistemi del mondo* (1632), and the *Discorsi e dimostrazioni matematiche intorno a due nuove scienze.* Connected with his use of the experimental method are his study of the resistance of various materials, particularly cylindrical and prismatic rods fixed at one or both ends; his calculations for the first rangefinding tables, based on his study of the motion of projectiles; and his study of the speed of light.

(2) *Foundation of dynamics and of experimental physics.* Galileo gives us in the *Discorsi* the theory of inertia and the laws that govern the motion of bodies falling through air or on an inclined plane, particularly the law that relates time and distance in uniformly accelerated motion, and the law governing the fall of bodies in a vacuum. (Although the laws of motion were conceived by Galileo, however, they were not definitely formulated until Newton.) Galileo did not use formulas in his work, but he did employ geometrical methods of demonstration. Closely allied to the foregoing is his discovery of the isochronism of the pendulum, found in the *Dialogo* along with the idea of the inertia frame of reference, a conception also called Galilean relativity. Besides demonstrating these laws and principles, Galileo based his work on axioms and postulates that were in direct contradiction to Aristotelian physics and have survived as classics of mechanics. He also made various technical inventions of great importance to scientific progress, such as the development of the telescope, the pendulum equipped with a counter, which may be considered a predecessor of the pendulum clock made quite independently by the Dutch scientist, Christian Huygens or Huyghens, in 1656, and the geometric and military compass (1597).

Galileo created a school of scientists, some of whom left their mark in the history of science. The greatest of his pupils was Evangelista Torricelli (1608–1647). Out of Torricelli's experiments on the rise of water in pumps, which he attributed to external pressure, came the invention of the barometer (1643). He also made discoveries in the field of geometry (*Opera geometrica; De motu gravium*) which drew the attention of René Descartes and Huygens and paved the way for the later discoveries of Blaise Pascal and Newton.

Other scientists in the orbit of the school of Galileo were the mathematician Bonaventura Cavalieri (1598–1647), who created the method of indivisibles, and Giovanni Alfonso Borelli (1608–1679), one of the most renowned members of the Accademia del Cimento and founder of a school of iatromechanics. His most significant work is *De motu animalium* (1680–1681), in which he sought to apply mechanical principles to animal movements. It is within the tradition of Galileo that we must also mention Domenico Guglielmini (1655–1710), whose *Riflessioni filosofiche dedotte dalle figure dei sali* (*Philosophical Reflections Based on the Configurations of Salt,* 1705) was a fundamental step in the development of crystallography.

The conditions that favored the rapid development of experimental science as conducted by Galileo and his pupils were equally favorable to chemistry, as is shown by the publication of the treatises *De la pirotechnia* (1540), by Vannoccio Biringuccio (1480–1539); *I tre libri dell'arte del vasaio* (*Three Books on the Art of Pottery,* 1548), by Cipriano Piccolpasso (1524–1579); Rosetti's *Plicto de l'arte dei tentori* (*The Art of Dyers,* 1540); *Magia naturalis* (*Natural Magic,* 1558) by Giambattista della Porta (1538?–1615); and *De arte vitraria* (*The Art of Glassmaking,* 1612) by Antonio Neri (d. 1614). We must also call attention to the earlier physician and botanist, Andrea Cesalpino (1519–1603), who was influenced by the same environment that paved the way for Galileo and his school.

In the second half of the 17th century and during the greater part of the 18th century, Italy, unlike England and France, fell into a period of political and social decay. In order to find a real sequel to the Galilean tradition, we must pass on to the three great scientists of the end of the 18th century: Galvani, Volta, and Spallanzani.

Early Nineteenth Century.—Luigi or Aloisio Galvani, student of Jacopo Bartolomeo Beccari (1682–1766), with his *De viribus electricitatis in motu musculari commentarius* (1791), was a pioneer in the study of the physiological action of electricity. He observed that when the ends of a metal strip were placed against the lumbar nerves and muscles of a frog a spark was produced. This electricity he attributed to the frog, thus entering into controversy with Count Alessandro Volta, who, as a result, made a further study of the phenomena. This led in turn to the discovery of the voltaic pile (1800), a landmark in the development of electricity and hence of modern civilization. Volta also studied the composition of marsh gas, perfected the udometer, and expounded the law governing the expansion of air at high temperatures. Lazzaro Spallanzani (1729–1799), who taught at the University of Pavia, made experiments in fertilization, disproving the theory of spontaneous generation, and wrote an account of his travels which was a considerable contribution to natural science.

During the first half of the 19th century, Italy's political condition, particularly the fact that the peninsula was split up into a number of small states, served to retard its technical progress in comparison with that of other European nations. It is not surprising, therefore, that scientific research should have fallen behind. Nevertheless some great things were accomplished, so that the Italian contribution to science continued to be of primary importance. The most distinguished Italian scientist of the period was Count Amedeo Avogadro (1776–1856), professor of physics at the University of Turin. His truly great scientific accomplishment was the formulation of the molecular theory, which developed the atomic discoveries previously made by John Dalton. Avogadro stated that there are particles known as molecules (compound molecules), which are made up of two or more atoms and may be broken down by a chemical reaction into their component atoms, or simple molecules. "On the basis of this hypothesis," Avogadro said, "we have a fairly easy means of determining the relative masses of molecules of bodies in a gaseous state and the relative number of these molecules in combinations, because the relations among the masses of molecules correspond to those of the densities of the various gases at the same pressure and temperature, and the relative number of molecules in any combination is obtained from the relationship among the volumes of gas of which it is made up." He is stating in this hypothesis, which is based on Joseph Louis Gay-Lussac's law of volumes, that there is no difference between volume and molecular mass—that the weight of the molecules is proportionate to their density, so that if we know the density then we know the molecular weight as well.

Avogadro elaborated his hypothesis in several fundamental studies, among them the *Trattato della costituzione generale dei corpi* (*Treatise on the General Constitution of Bodies,* 1837–1841), but his ideas failed at first to interest chemists, in part because he had not proved them experimentally. They found full acceptance only after his death, but his work became the basis of Cannizzaro's improvement upon Dalton's statement of the atomic theory.

Stanislao Cannizzaro (1826–1910), a student of Raffaele Piria, in his *Sunto di un corso di filosofia chimica* (*Short Course of Chemical Philosophy,* 1858), laid the experimental basis of modern atomic theory. Cannizzaro worked on already familiar ground to accomplish a necessary coordination of the theories of Avogadro with the results of another 50 years' experimentation. He gathered together the conclusions reached by Dalton, Avogadro, André Ampère, Marc Antoine Gaudin, and the later Jean Baptiste Dumas, Jöns Jakob Berzelius, Charles Frédéric Gerhardt, and Auguste Laurent, and established a clear distinction between molecular and atomic weights. He stated that the various quantities of the same element contained in different molecules are all whole multiples of one quantity, which, because it always forms a single unit, properly deserves the name of atom. The value of this law transcends that of Avogadro's hypothesis because it gives a rigorous interpretation of the facts. Cannizzaro's clarification of the concept of atomic weight also went far toward the establishment of the theory of valence. Another of his contributions was the impulse he gave to scientific research by the setting up of well-equipped laboratories in both Palermo and Rome. Italian chemistry of the second half of the 19th century bears a strong imprint of the work of this great scientist, who also played an important role in the political life of his time.

Exchanges with other countries, particularly France and Germany, gave still more Italians a chance to make themselves known. Faustino Malaguti (1802–1878), a political exile who lived in France, was only one of the many notable chemists to emerge in the early part of the century. Ascanio Sobrero (1812–1888), a pupil of Théophile Pelouze and Justus von Liebig, discovered nitroglycerin. In 1852, Luigi Chiozza (1828–1889), a professor in Milan and a participant in Gerhardt's classic research in the field of the anhydrides of organic acids, discovered and made a synthesis of carbostyril and studied the effects of alkalis on unsaturated acids. Raffaele Piria (1814–1865), who taught at Pisa and Turin, introduced new methods of synthesis, did fundamental research on salicin, populin, tyrosine, and aspartic acid and, in 1838, discovered salicylic acid. Cesare Bertagnini (1827–1857), a pupil of Piria and professor at Pisa, obtained a synthesis of cinnamic acid and did research on oxamide, phillyrin, and the alterations undergone by certain organic acids in animal organisms.

Physics shared the position of chemistry in the mid-19th century, and had its share of distinguished practitioners. Ottorino Fabrizio Mossotti (1791–1863), whose reputation extended beyond the borders of Italy, did painstaking research in molecular physics and was a pioneer of mathematical physics in Italy. Macedonio Melloni (1798–1854), a Neapolitan liberal forced to leave his professorship in Parma after the insurrections of 1831, did much of his work in exile, in Geneva and Paris. Later, after he had returned to Naples, he founded Vesuvius Observatory (1847), did research in the fields of electricity and optics, with special attention to radiant energy, and established the identity of the energies of light and heat. He studied the thermal absorption of bodies, which he termed diathermancy, and discovered the spectrum of various kinds of heat emission. Carlo Matteucci (1811–1868), a friend of Piria who also took an interest in politics, investigated the physiological effects of electricity and worked to spread acceptance of atomic theory. He deserves further praise for having contributed, along with Piria, Pacinotti, and others, to the foundation in 1855, of the famous journal of physics, *Il Nuovo Cimento*.

Astronomy, geology, and mineralogy also produced scholars worthy of note in the first half of the 19th century. Father Pietro Angelo Secchi (1818–1878) directed the astronomical observatory of the Roman College and studied the spectrum of the fixed stars. Giovanni Virginio Schiaparelli (1835–1910), director of the Brera Observatory in Milan, is remembered for his important studies of the planet Mars and of comets. Annibale Riccò (1844–1919), geophysicist and astronomer, studied Mount Etna, and also the relation between sunspots and protuberances. Among vulcanologists and seismologists the best known is Father Antonio Stoppani (1824–1891), who created a school of geology. Besides going in very actively for research, he wrote with great facility and his books spread the love of nature among the general public.

The Modern Period.—Italy's slow development of a national character, achieved only with the accomplishment of political unity, is reflected in the field of scientific research. Many scientists had only the scantiest means to enable them to pursue their studies, not a few of them took part in the political struggles of the time, and some were forced into exile. All this was tragic for science. After 1870, through the efforts of Quintino Sella (1827–1884), a man of modest scientific accomplishments, but a first-rate statesman, Italian universities were endowed with well-equipped laboratories, which soon stimulated scientific research. The period from 1870 to 1914, that is from the achievement of national unity to World War I, is of capital importance for scientific progress in Italy. This period deserves more detailed study, which should be linked with the history of Italian industry. Another very important factor in experimental science was the rapid development of mathematics.

Mathematics.—The mathematical tradition of the Italian Renaissance was revived in the late 19th century by a number of outstanding figures. They included Enrico Betti (1823–1892), who taught physics and mathematics at Pisa and was a pioneer topologist; Francesco Brioschi (1824–1897), a professor at Milan and a politician, who studied the theory of invariants, equations, and elliptic functions; Eugenio Beltrami (1835–1900), who took up non-Euclidean geometry and laid the foundation of mechanics in curved spaces; Luigi Cremona (1830–1903), who studied graphical statics and projective and algebraic geometry; Ulisse Dini (1845–1918), who taught at Pisa and made a profound study of the basis of the theory of the functions of real variables; and Luigi Bianchi (1856–1928), who left behind him important work in differential geometry. Giuseppe Peano (1856–1932), a professor at the University of Turin and a student of symbolic logic, indicated in his *Principi di geometria logicamente esposti* (*A Logical Exposition of the Principles of Geometry,* 1889), every logical proposition with symbols and developed the fundamentals of arithmetic and geometry in a rigidly rational but simple and intuitive manner.

Among other mathematicians were Giuseppe Veronese (1854–1917), who studied the geometry of hyperspaces; Corrado Segrè (1863–1924), a professor at the University of Turin and a distinguished scholar in the field of algebraic and projective geometry; and Vito Volterra (1860–1940), of the University of Rome, who investigated analytic functions, hyperbolic and integral equations, and functional calculus. Tullio Levi-Civita (1873–1942), a professor at the universities of Padova and Rome, achieved far-reaching results in calculus, was a forerunner of the theory of relativity, and in 1918 introduced the notion of parallelism in curved spaces. Finally, Federico Enriques (1871–1946), a professor at the universities of Bologna and Rome and a positivist philosopher, is known for his book *Problemi della scienza* (*Problems of Science,* 1906), containing studies in arithmetic and analytic geometry.

Chemistry. — The mathematical discoveries formed the basis for chemical research in Italy. Its organization was due in large part to Cannizzaro, who, aside from his atomic studies, was a great organic chemist. The Cannizzaro reaction, which bears his name, led to the discovery of benzyl alcohol (1853), and to his research on santonin and its derivatives. He created a school of original research scientists whose leaders in turn enriched the various branches of chemistry. The most important of them were Emanuele Paternò, marchese di Sessa (1847–1935), Giacomo Luigi Ciamician (1857–1922), and Raffaello Nasini (1854–1931).

Paternò taught at the universities of Palermo and Rome and was also vice president of the Italian Senate. Soon after François Marie Raoult's work on cryoscopy, he investigated the molecular weight of dissolved substances (1886), and did research in the field of photochemistry, and on phosgene, polysulphides of hydrogen, and fluorides. Along with Cannizzaro, Ugo Schiff (1830–1915), and others, Paternò founded *La gazzetta chimica italiana* (1871), Italy's foremost chemical journal.

Ciamician was a professor at the universities of Padova and Bologna, chiefly known for his studies of the chemistry of pyrrole, the chemical action of light, and the behavior of alkaloids in plants. Nasini taught at the universities of Padova and Pisa. He popularized the electrolytic dissociation theory, worked on the refractivity of organic compounds in relation to their chemical composition, and studied the natural gases of Italy, the boracic exhalations of Tuscany, and the chemistry of many natural mineral waters.

Among Cannizzaro's students we must not forget Amerigo Andreocci (1863–1899), professor of pharmaceutical chemistry at the University of Catania, who is known for his studies of pyrodiazole, santonin, and triboluminescence. An illustrious contemporary of Cannizzaro was Francesco Selmi (1817–1881), professor of pharmaceutical chemistry at the University of Bologna, who distinguished the ptomaines and did research, which preceded that of Thomas Graham, on the colloids.

We find few great names at this time in the field of inorganic chemistry, if we except that of Augusto Piccini (1854–1905). But organic chemists in great numbers have left their names attached to some discovery or a new line of research in their field. Angelo Angeli (1864–1931), a student of Ciamician and professor at Florence and Palermo, discovered in 1896 nitrohydroxylamine and made a noteworthy contribution to the knowledge of pyrrole derivatives and of nitrous compounds. Giorgio Errera (1860–1933), a professor at Palermo and Pavia who gave up his teaching rather than take the Fascist oath of allegiance, studied the chemistry of terpenes. Icilio Guareschi (1847–1928), of the University of Turin, worked chiefly in organic chemistry, toxicology, and chemical history, and conducted experiments with asparagine, urea, and naphthalene derivatives. He made a significant contribution to the chemistry of the ptomaines and the synthesis of hydropyridic compounds. Bernardo Oddo (1882–1941), a professor at the University of Pavia, was one of the most distinguished organic chemists of the early 20th century. Among his researches was a study of the reductive action of ethylaniline on Grignard's reagent. At the same time, he enriched the chemistry of the pyrrole and indole group with the preparation of derivatives of these two compounds.

Physical chemistry came to be the object of special study in Italy after the diffusion of Svante Arrhenius' theory of electrolytic dissociation. One of the pioneers in this field was Raffaello Nasini, at the end of the 19th century. The Gibbs-Roozeboom theory of phase rule opened wide possibilities of research in the field of metallography, in which we must count among the most important scholars Federico Giolitti (1880–1946), professor at the Polytechnic Institute of Turin and later an industrial consultant.

Industrial chemistry has a more modest history because up to the beginning of the 20th century there was no real chemical industry in Italy except in perphosphates and mineral acids. Luigi Gabba (1841–1916) of the Polytechnic Institute of Milan was a pioneer of teaching in this field, and his successor, Ettore Molinari (1867–1926), studied the action of ozone on unsaturated compounds, particularly oleic acid. Luigi Casale (1882–1927) introduced into Italy the process of synthesis of ammonia under high pressure, a method which has been applied in other countries, including the United States. In connection with the synthesis of ammonia we must mention Giacomo Fauser (1892–), engineer and director of the Montecatini Company, who obtained the synthesis under medium pressure. Fauser, the best trained technical chemist of modern Italy, brought about certain modifications of the technique of hydrogenation or cracking of the petroleum found in Albania. The economic self-sufficiency and isolation aimed at by the Fascist regime had very bad effects on the Italian chemical industry. Industrial chemistry depends on scientific research, which was retarded by World War II and by the deficiencies of many young teachers whose jobs had been secured by political influence rather than scholarly merit.

Biochemistry dates from Baron Justus von Liebig's *Die Chemie in ihre Anwendung auf Agrikultur und Physiologie* (1840), and Italy has had three great practitioners in this field. Gino Galeotti (1867–1921) was one of the first in Italy to apply the methods of physical chemistry to the study of physiological processes. Filippo Bottazzi (1867–1941) created a school for the study of biochemistry at the University of Naples, where he taught for a long time, and his *Trattato di chimica fisiologica* (*Treatise of Physiological Chemistry,* 1898–1899) had for 30 years a great influence in this field. Luigi Sabbatani (1863–1928) is responsible for the physico-chemical interpretation of many toxic processes.

Other chemists and physiologists contributed to biochemical studies. Among the glucosides we have Piria's studies of salicin (1838), and Bertagnini's of phillyrin (1854). When Piria submitted salicin to the action of warm, dilute acids and to that of emulsin, he discovered its glucosidic character and cleared up the nature of saligenin. In 1855, he proved that populin, discovered by Henri Braconnot in 1830, was a derivative of benzoylsalicin. Bertagnini observed that phillyrin is a glucoside, and when heated with dilute acids it breaks up into glucose and phillygenin. The group of proteides has not received much study, but we must mention Malaguti's observation of the presence of sulphur in cystine (1837), and Piria's observation of the deamination of amino acids under the action of nitrous acid (1846). Also worthy of note is the research on the ptomaines, which are produced by the putrefaction of proteid substances. Selmi, in 1872, was the first to enter this field, which received further study from the physiologist Angelo Mosso (1846–1910). Nor must we forget the work done by various scientists on hormones and melanin.

Biology and Zoology.—There are both importance and originality in the work of Giuseppe Levi (1872–), a teacher of anatomy at the University of Turin who has done research in cytology and histology. In 1933, Levi observed that, in cultures of the rhombencephalon of advanced embryos, after a few passages of a certain regularity in the wide space between the smear and the edge of the retracted coagulum, there appears a membrane made up of flattened epithelial cells and nerve cells, some of which maintain their atypical character and put forth multiple anastomosed feelers among themselves. This research on the part of Levi and his students was made possible by the Rockefeller Institute.

In the field of zoology, one of the pioneers of transformist theories was Filippo de Filippi (1814–1867), a professor at the University of Turin. During the first half of the 19th century systematic zoology flourished in Naples through the work of Gabriele Costa (1787–1867), who left behind him various works on the fauna of the region. His successor, Michele Lessona (1823–1894), a strong supporter of Charles Darwin, worked on the fauna of the Piedmont region. In 1872, Anton Dohrn (1806–1892) set up the Zoological Station of Naples, which was frequented by many scientists from abroad. Enrico Giglioli (1845–1909), a professor at the University of Florence, also contributed greatly to zoology with his monumental work, *Avifauna italica.*

Later came Carlo Emery (1848–1925) and Giovanni Battista Grassi (1854–1925). Emery was a student of Paolo Panceri (1833–1877), and was among the first Italians to base zoological research on new histological and anatomical techniques. He made a fundamental morphological chart of tetrapod mammals and accomplished a very interesting study of ants. Grassi, a professor at the University of Rome, took up Nematoda, leptocephalous Cestoda, and Phylloxera. He came to the conclusion that malaria is spread among human beings solely by the Anopheles mosquito, in which a life cycle of the malaria parasite takes place. In his work entitled *Studi di uno zoologo sulla malaria* (*A Zoologist Looks at Malaria*), he gave a biological description of the various forms of Plasmodia. This work and the method prescribed therein powerfully influenced all research on malaria for almost a half century afterwards. Among students of parasitology, we must mention Edoardo Perroncito (1847–1922), a professor at the University of Turin, known for his work on intestinal worms, and Corrado Parona (1848–1922), author of an important volume, *Elmintologia italiana* (*Italian Helminthology*).

Anatomy.—Several anatomists are worthy of note. Bartolomeo Panizza (1785–1867), a professor at the University of Pavia, is celebrated for his doctrines of cerebral localization and radicular ataxia. Filippo Pacini (1812–1883) was a pioneer in biological and histological research. Giulio Bizzozzero (1846–1907), a professor at the University of Turin, did inspiring work in histology and general pathology; he discovered plastins and demonstrated the hematopoietic function of bone marrow. Camillo Golgi (1844–1926), a professor at the University of Pavia, was one of the most eminent scientists of the second half of the 19th century. His name is linked to the study of the structure of the nervous system and the Golgi reaction. Giuseppe Levi is the author of *Trattato di istologia* (*Treatise of Histology,* 1928), which has been translated into various languages. Besides making the cultures of tissues on slides described above, he discovered new details in the nuclei of nerve cells.

Botany.—Botany has been practiced as an experimental science in Italy since 1860, when the first institutes of research along this line were set up in the universities. Two schools of botany held sway during the following years, one Italian and the other German. The outstanding figure in the Italian school was Federico Delpino (1833–1905), who did fundamental work in plant biology. Meanwhile, the German school influenced the work of another Italian, Giuseppe Gibelli (1831–1898), and he had two able followers, Pietro Pirotta (1853–1936) and Oreste Mattirolo (1856–1947), who taught in the universities of Rome and Turin, respectively. Pier Andrea Saccardo (1845–1920), noted for his fungological research, left a monumental work entitled *Sylloge fungorum omnium,* while his pupil, Giovanni Battista de Toni (1864–1924), worked on the algae. Among the cytologists we must recall Luigi Buscaglioni (1863–), who worked on histological technique for plants, and Sergio Tonzig (1905–), who did interesting work on the structure of protoplasm. Gabriele Luigi Montemartini (1869–) studied the fixation of atmospheric nitrogen on the part of certain saprophyte fungi with fallen leaves, while Gino Luigi Pollacci (1872–) covered the same process on the part of higher plants.

Physics.—Physics has always been brilliantly represented in Italy, even if an Alessandro Volta is not born every day. In the second half of the 19th century both teaching and laboratory research were on a high level. One of the most renowned physicists of the century was Augusto Righi (1850–1920), who made memorable experiments on electromagnetism, Hertzian waves, X-rays, and optics. His work on Hertzian waves was an incentive to Marchese Guglielmo Marconi (1874–1937) in his discovery of wireless telegraphy, one of the leading technical conquests of modern times.

The universities of Rome, Pisa, Bologna, and Florence, all of them endowed with up-to-date institutes of physics, furnished large numbers of teachers and research scientists to other universities and technical schools. Two names stand out in the second half of the 19th century: Antonio Pacinotti (1841–1912) and Galileo Ferraris (1847–1897). The former—son of Luigi Pacinotti (1810–1881), who taught experimental physics at the University of Pisa—was director of a modest laboratory of technical physics at the Normal School of Pisa. In 1858, he invented the Pacinotti ring, and in 1860, the "little machine," or forerunner of the dynamo, which was imitated by Zénobe Théophile Gramme in 1872. Galileo Ferraris, a professor at the Museum of Industry and the Polytechnic Institute of Turin, was an eminent physicist and electrical engineer who discovered the rotary magnetic field. In his electrical studies, Ferraris upheld the importance of vectorial methods and demonstrated their usefulness in the exploration and representation of physical phenomena.

After the beginning of World War I, experimental physics entered a period of decay, due in part to the lack of adequate laboratories, and also to the small interest shown by students in the traditional subjects of research, most of which had already been undertaken in wealthier countries. The main fields seemed to have been thoroughly explored and all that was left to do, on condition of finding financial support, was to carry systematic research in them a little further. A new and fruitful period was opened, however, by a talented young scholar, Enrico Fermi (1901–), who developed a flourishing school in atomic physics. This school was broken up by the racial laws of 1938, which drove Fermi and some of his most gifted students into exile.

Fermi is internationally famous for his studies of the quantum theory and his pioneer research in molecular physics. In 1926, Fermi founded the statistical tables that bear his name, based on the study of the behavior of gases at a low temperature. He found a solution to his problem by applying to gases Pauli's exclusion principle, originally applied to internal quantum conditions.

After the discovery by Walther Bothe and H. Becker (1930) and Irène and Frédéric Joliot-Curie (1932) of artificial radioactivity, Fermi began research in Rome aimed at ascertaining whether a bombardment of neutrons would produce the same phenomena of radioactivity as those discovered by Joliot-Curie. Experiments carried out in collaboration with Franco Rasetti (1901–), Edoardo Amaldi (1908–), Oscar D'Agostino, Emilio Segrè (1905–), and B. Pontecorvo led in 1934 to the activation of some 40 heavy elements out of the more than 60 which were tested. Fermi and his collaborators discovered the slowing up of neutrons by means of paraffin, a phenomenon which is due to the presence of hydrogen. After the neutrons have for some time bombarded the nuclei of hydrogen, they give up their own vital force and move at a velocity the same as that of thermal agitation. By bombarding uranium with slow neutrons, Fermi obtained the two transuranium elements whose atomic numbers are 93 and 94, respectively. Further research on artificial radioactivity was done in 1936–1938 by M. Ageno, Gilberto Bernardini (1906–), D. Bocciarelli, Z. Ollano, G. P. Occhialini, C. Perrier, N. B. Cacciapuoti, and others, who made it possible to obtain radioactive isotopes of various elements. It is fitting to recall at this point the studies of cosmic rays begun in 1930 by Bruno Rossi (1905–) of the University of Padova, who eventually left Italy for racial reasons and taught at Cornell University.

The forced departure of Fermi, Rasetti, and others, as well as the growing attraction exercised on younger scholars by the immense possibilities of work in the United States, posed problems of great importance in the postwar period.

Michele Giua,
Member of the Italian Senate; Professor of Industrial Organic Chemistry, University of Turin.

9. ECONOMIC STRUCTURE AND PROBLEMS. The traveler in Italy, who is generally attracted by its natural and artistic beauties, historic places, and mild climate, seldom forms a clear picture of economic conditions. Moreover, the main arteries of communication take him through the most active and prosperous sections of the country. He is therefore inclined to adopt the romantic and literary view, which only the vicissitudes of World War II to some degree corrected, that Italy, in spite of the burden of its history, is so favored by nature as to reap easily the benefits of modern technical progress. In reality, conditions vary so greatly even within a single region that highly contradictory conclusions may be formed. Striking contrasts may be found by anyone who travels from the orange-laden Conca d'Oro (Golden Bowl) surrounding Palermo to the nearby Sicilian hinterland; from the fertile Campanian country just back of Naples to Gaeta, in Latium; from the plains of Lombardy to the overhanging Alpine valleys; and from Genoa, Bologna, or Florence across the rugged Apennines. There are numerous other examples available to the conscientious observer of the Italian countryside, one of whose charms is its variety.

GENERAL FEATURES OF THE ITALIAN ECONOMY

Natural Resources.—The variety of the Italian economy stems first of all from environmental conditions. The climate, for instance, is characterized by unfavorable distribution and great irregularity of rainfall. Particularly in the south vegetation suffers from excessive rains in autumn and winter and drought during the balance of the year. This fact, coupled with a lack of irrigation, is an obstacle to intensive cultivation. Other limitations are caused by geological conformation: more than 40 per cent of the land is mountainous; only 20 per cent, plain. Moreover, the plains of the peninsula are crossed by narrow streams which are not generally useful for irrigation. The only exception is the Po River valley, one of the most productive sections of the country, which owes its development to hundreds of years of efforts to perfect irrigation and farming. Even here, however, the highest part of the valley and the Venetian plain which continues it have comparatively poor soil. The mountainous areas in many places allow for intensive cultivation of grapevines and olive and fruit trees, but the type of soil (generally sandy, clayey, or stony) does not facilitate agricultural development. (See also section on *The Land*.)

Another grave obstacle to a strong economy is the lack of minerals. In 1948, for example, Italian mines produced 974,000 metric tons of coal and 901,200 metric tons of lignite, while 8,302,291 tons of coal were imported. In 1938, 11,921,747 tons were imported. (During World War II, a maximum annual production of 2,305,200 tons of lignite and 2,520,000 tons of coal was achieved.) Lead and zinc are mined, particularly in Sardinia, as well as iron, iron pyrites, and mercury. Copper and other metals exist only in negligible quantities. Sulphur is abundant, but the mines operate under difficulties.

The Italian economy is also hampered by a lack of easy means of communication, particularly by river, and by the fact that the country is not situated on the main world trade routes. Finally, the country lacks the major raw materials essential to an industrial economy: rubber, cotton, wool, timber, cellulose, and oil. (There is, however, some natural gas, of which 108,200,000 cubic meters were produced in 1948. Promising discoveries were made near Piacenza in June 1949.) These factors have restricted Italy in large part to agriculture, despite the unfavorable conditions of the terrain for intensive cultivation.

Population and Employment.—The scarcity of natural resources is accompanied by a very dense population, which increased from 23,617,153 in 1848 to an estimated 46,403,000 in 1948, or to an average of 399 persons per square mile. This is a high figure in an absolute sense, and it is even higher when we consider the available agricultural and forest land, of which only 52 per cent can be used for intensive cultivation. In a prevailingly agricultural country, this density of population retards the modernization of farming techniques and prevents the absorption on the land of a constantly increasing population. As a result, few more people were engaged in agriculture in 1949 than there had been 70 years before.

Of the 42,918,726 persons listed in the census of 1936, 18,345,432, or 42.7 per cent, were gainfully employed. The proportional distribution of the working population in 1936, as shown in Table 1, remained substantially the same in the period following World War II.

Table 1—EMPLOYMENT IN ITALY, 1936

Field	Number employed	Percentage of total	Percentage of independent workers in field
Agriculture, hunting, fishing	8,842,785	48.2	72.0
Industry, transportation	6,077,353	33.2	22.7
Commerce, banking, insurance	1,605,363	8.7	63.8
Professions and fine arts	142,958	.8	78.4
Public administration	808,866	4.4	...
Other	868,107	4.7	.1
Total	18,345,432	100.0	48.5

Italy's poverty in natural resources, a scarcity of savings available for capital investment, and the growing population are responsible for a sizable permanent unemployment. World War II aggravated this problem by causing extensive damage to plants and equipment and by increasing the number of women in factory employment. As of April 1949, there were 1,753,600 unemployed persons in Italy. (The number of persons on state and town relief rolls as of June 30, 1949, was 3,564,142.) In order to absorb all of them into the national economy, a capital investment of 4,000 billion lire[1] would be required. Moreover, it would be necessary for the world market to accept the resulting increased production, the greater part of which would have to be exported in order to pay for the required raw material imports. After World War II the Italian government endeavored, with United States aid, to alleviate the unemployment situation. The problem cannot be solved, however, without sizable emigration. (See section on *The People*.) There is also some hope of relieving the pressure of excess population by an international program of employment for Italian labor, and we must also note that the excess has been caused largely by a decline in the death rate (from an average of 19.1 per 1,000 in 1911–1915 to 10.6 per 1,000 in 1948). Moreover, in the same period the birth rate declined from an average of 31.5 per 1,000 to 21.5 per 1,000.

[1] In June 1949, 1 lira = 0.1739 cents in U.S. money; in November 1949, 0.1601 cents.

Development of the Italian Economy Since 1870.—Political factors have alternately arrested, stimulated, and altered the trend of production in Italy. The country did not attain final unity and political independence until 1870, and then only after a long and painful struggle against foreign and domestic enemies. Following unification, consolidation of the new government took precedence over economic development.

In 1870 the economy of Italy was overwhelmingly agricultural, and the scarcity of natural resources, lack of capital, high taxes, poverty of the great mass of the peasant class, lack (except in a few northern cities) of a commercial middle class prepared to organize bold new enterprises, and the inheritance of an antiquated social system from the various states into which the country had been divided, all these factors were responsible for a lag in industrial and general economic progress which required long years and much sacrifice to overcome. The critical circumstances under which the Italian nation was born are reflected in the lack of increase in agricultural production, in spite of an increase of population, and in emigration on a scale so large as to take on the character of an exodus, comparable only with that from Ireland (see Table 2).

Table 2—AGRICULTURAL PRODUCTION AND EMIGRATION, 1876–1905

Years	Agricultural products per inhabitant [1]	Average annual emigration [2]
1876–1880	...	108,600
1881–1885	100	153,400
1886–1890	93	221,600
1891–1895	89	256,400
1896–1900	91	310,400
1901–1905	111	553,200

[1] Index: 1881–85 = 100.
[2] Temporary and permanent.

This initial crisis, superimposed on adverse circumstances, greatly retarded industrial development. Domestic purchasing power was low, and the free-trade policy in force until 1887 opened the doors to long-established foreign products with which Italian handicraft enterprises and newly established factories could not hope to compete. The risks encountered by any new enterprise were great. Moreover, the abolition of internal customs duties among the former states of the peninsula had destroyed industries which had depended upon them for protection.

Nevertheless, the general political upheaval, the increase of travel and trade from one region of the country to another, the growth of population, and the greater frequency of contacts with other countries paved the way for an industrial development which culminated in the years immediately preceding World War I. By 1898 production in all fields was increasing, and between 1898 and 1913 imports of raw materials increased by 70 per cent. The index of economic activity prepared by the economist Giorgio Mortara shows an equivalent rise for this period.

The economic trend from 1871 to 1913 is reflected in the changing character of Italian foreign trade, as shown in Table 3. By 1911–1913 imported foodstuffs and manufactured goods were proportionately in lesser demand than raw materials, and the export of manufactured products had taken precedence over that of food. In the same period, Italy's international exchange picture was transformed in another way. Until the end of the 19th century, Italy had an unfavorable balance of international payments, but thereafter tourist expenditures and emigrant remittances helped substantially to make up the deficit.

World War I and the ensuing political unrest had an important influence on the Italian economy. The harmonious development of the first decade of the 20th century was arrested, and only in 1923–1924 did national income regain the level of 1909–1913. Important changes took place in the industrial field. Before the war the textile industry (according to the census of 1911) employed a third of the country's industrial workers. As a result of the wartime demand for armaments, the group of industries in the mechanical field (machinery, motor vehicles, ships, aircraft, tools, motors, engines) took first place, and there was a corresponding increase in the industrial application of power. Between 1911 and 1927, the installed horsepower of nonelectric primary motors increased from 1,620,404 to 5,468,588; and that of electric motors in industry, from 586,161 to 2,642,860. The number of corporations increased from 2,189 in 1914 to over 4,000 in 1921, and between 1911 and 1921 the number of industrial workers went from 3,600,000 to more than 4,000,000. Unrest and the collapse of some insecure war industries lowered production in the immediate postwar period, but industrial development resumed thereafter, and by 1927 there were approximately 8,000 corporations with a capital investment (in lire at their 1913 value) twice as large as that of prewar corporate investment.

The economic crisis of 1929 had its effect on the Italian economy, which was further altered, particularly after the outbreak of the Italo-Ethiopian War in 1935, by the Fascist policy of autarchy, or economic self-sufficiency. This policy made free trade impossible and caused the emergence of new industries which could not have existed without government protection, thus stimulating an additional, though artificial, growth of industrialization. The deficit in the interna-

Table 3—DISTRIBUTION OF ITALIAN IMPORTS AND EXPORTS, 1871–73 AND 1911–13

Type of goods	Percentage of imports		Percentage of exports		Index of shipments, 1911–13 *	
	1871–73	1911–13	1871–73	1911–13	Imports	Exports
Foodstuffs	26	20	44.0	30.3	329	184
Raw materials	30	38	17.5	14.5	557	222
Half-processed raw materials	14	19	26.5	24.1	580	244
Manufactured products	30	23	12.0	31.1	335	700
Total	100	100	100.0	100.0	433	268

* 1871–73 = 100.

tional balance of payments, which amounted to about 6 or 7 billion lire annually from 1922 to 1929, declined in the 1930's to approximately 3 billion lire annually (exclusive of colonial trade, which was distinctly favorable to metropolitan Italy). Imports of raw materials increased, both absolutely and relatively, compared with those of manufactured products, and there was a corresponding increase in the export of manufactured products. By 1938, the index of industrial production had risen to 243 (1922, the most inactive year of the immediate postwar period, = 100).

The direction of Italian industrial development from 1900 to 1939 is illustrated by Table 4,

Table 4—INDEX OF AVAILABLE INDUSTRIAL POWER
(Base, 1905–09 = 100)

1900–04	69
1905–09	100
1910–14	124
1915–19	116
1920–24	155
1925–29	201
1930–34	210
1935–39	260

which gives the index of available power, from all sources, for this period. This remarkable industrial progress was not matched by agricultural production, nor by the income of the average Italian, which is indicated by the average per capita daily consumption of calories (see Table 5).

Table 5—AGRICULTURAL PRODUCTION AND FOOD CONSUMPTION

Years	Average daily calories per capita	Agricultural production index *
1911–15	2,568	100
1916–20	2,596	101
1921–25	2,780	108
1926–30	2,883	112
1931–35	2,619	102
1936–40	2,652	103

* Base, 1911–15 = 100.

The damage inflicted by World War II on the Italian economy was enormous. Agricultural production in 1945 was only 60 per cent of that of 1938, and industrial production, which in 1945 was almost completely paralyzed, had in 1946 reached a level of only 65 per cent of that of 1938. The number of livestock had been reduced by 30 per cent, the railways were running at only 60 per cent efficiency, and only 15 per cent of the merchant marine had escape destruction. Buildings, both public and private, were extensively damaged. (Approximately 2,625,000 rooms were either destroyed or so badly damaged as to require rebuilding, and an additional 3,300,000 rooms suffered repairable damage.) Besides material losses and a consequent social upheaval, prices rose to more than 50 times their average prewar value (see Table 7, below), the tax system was disrupted, there was a large defiicit in the national budget (in 1945–1946, this amounted to 357 billion lire), and there was an equally serious deficit in the balance of payments. It was very difficult to maintain even the minimum amount of food provided for in the rationing system, and the lack of raw materials forced many industries to dismiss their employees. This postwar crisis was overcome in large part by aid from the United States. Before the end of the war, the Allied armies had given various forms of aid. This was succeeded by the work of the Allied Control Commission and, from March 1945, by that of the United Nations Relief and Rehabilitation Administration (UNRRA). By means of an aid agreement signed July 4, 1947, the United States distributed $121,000,000 worth of supplies, and by the interim aid agreement of Jan. 3, 1948, an additional $200,000,000. In all, from the beginning of 1947 to March 31, 1948, which marked the beginning of the European Recovery Program (ERP), $820,000,000 worth of goods was given to Italy. To foodstuffs were added raw materials, thus enabling industry to resume production.

Meanwhile, the Italian government took an active part in the restoration of public services. Of the 22,955 kilometers of railways in service in 1939, 21,013 kilometers were in operation by 1948. By Jan. 1, 1949, the merchant marine totaled 2,275,272 tons, or about 67 per cent of the prewar figure. The roads, of which about 15,000 kilometers had been damaged, were restored to good condition, with the building of 3,300 bridges (of which 1,500 have a span greater than 10 meters), as well as tunnels, embankments, and repair shops. (Italy has a highway system totaling about 109,000 miles, including national, provincial, and local roads.) About 55 kilometers of harbor works were repaired, and 7,000 hospital rooms, 2,500 school rooms, and numerous other public buildings were rebuilt.

The arrest of Italian production, the exhaustion of reserves, and the necessity of importing large quantities of food created problems whose gravity is apparent from the figures, as estimated by the Bank of Italy, on the international balance of payments, which are shown in Table 6. The

Table 6—INTERNATIONAL BALANCE OF PAYMENTS, 1947 AND 1948
(active balance +; passive balance —)

Category	1947	1948
Goods (F.O.B.)	−$661,300,000*	−$320,400,000
Tourist trade	+ 6,400,000	+ 23,900,000
Freight and insurance	− 161,000,000	− 107,500,000
Income and investments	− 4,900,000	− 12,300,000
Government transactions	− 3,300,000	− 3,300,000
Emigrant remittances	+ 34,100,000	+ 84,900,000
Miscellaneous	+ 1,200,000	+ 62,000,000
Total deficit	−$788,800,000	−$272,700,000

* Including $62,000,000 worth of surplus property sold in Italy.

deficits given for 1947 and 1948 may be compared with that of $38,000,000 for 1938. This situation was met without a disastrous reduction of imports through United States aid. In 1948, exports amounted to $1,067,600,000, and imports to $1,388,000,000, exclusive of freight and insurance charges. Under ERP, designed to restore economic activity and to stimulate international trade, assignments to Italy through May 31, 1949, amounted to $668,000,000, and paid exports to $397,900,000. In the period from June 1948 to June 1949, ERP imports represented more than 25 per cent of the total of imported goods. The most important items were cereal products (more than 50 per cent of those imported), coal (50 per cent), petroleum products (62 per cent), and cotton (51 per cent). In addition, the United States lent Italy $67,000,000. The counterpart fund built up in lire from the sale of ERP goods permitted Italy to undertake an extensive public works program. including railroads, public buildings, shipping, and irrigation and reclamation projects, especially in the south.

Financial Factors.—In 1937, the lira was valued officially at 19 to the U.S. dollar; in 1943, the official exchange rate was set at 100 lire to the dollar. As inflation increased, the rate was raised, first to 225 (January 1946), and then to 350 (August 1947). Finally, in November 1947, the government exchange bureau was authorized to acquire 50 per cent of the foreign money derived from exports on the basis of the free market rate of the preceding month. The difference between the free and official rates declined, and in 1948 the exchange rate was stabilized at 575 lire to the U.S. dollar. Following the devaluation of the pound sterling in September 1949, the value of the lira declined; in November 1949 the rate was 624.5 to the dollar. For a comparison of monetary circulation, wholesale prices, and the cost of living in 1938, 1946, 1947, and 1948, see Table 7.

Table 7—MONETARY CIRCULATION, WHOLESALE PRICE INDEX, AND COST OF LIVING INDEX, 1938–48

Year	Circulation of lire (in billions) at year's end	Monetary circulation index	Wholesale price index	Cost of living index
1938.......	22.5	100	100	100
1946.......	512.7	2278	2884	2823
1947.......	795.0	3533	5159	4575
1948.......	970.0	4310	5443	4844

By 1949 the rise in prices had been checked. Imports and the gradual increase of domestic factory production enabled the Italian government to pursue a firm stabilization policy. Rationing was almost entirely eliminated, and the black market in commodities disappeared. The deficit in the national budget was reduced from 787 billion lire for the fiscal year 1947–1948 to 481 billion lire for 1948–1949, with an estimated deficit of 174 billion lire for 1949–1950. In spite of the high level of government expenditures (1,548 billion lire in 1947–1948, and an estimated 1,252 billion lire in 1948–1949) compared with a national income of approximately 5,400 billion lire (1948), there is a gradual but steady increase of government income. In 1947–1949, the monthly tax revenue rose from 50 billion lire to 80 billion lire. The government's stabilization policy also had the effect of increasing the proportion of the national income devoted to new savings and investments, which in 1948–1949 amounted to about 13 per cent, compared with about 10 per cent before World War II. Because of the low average income,[2] however, the volume of savings in Italy has never been large, but monetary stabilization was a strong incentive for the rebuilding of savings lost during the war.

In 1948, real national income was approximately 90 per cent of its 1938 level (84 per cent if allowance is made for the increase of population during the decade). In its report for 1947–1948, the Bank of Italy estimated the national income, in 1948 lire, at 6,000 billion lire in 1938, 5,050 billion lire in 1947, and 5,400 billion lire in 1948. The value of available goods and services for 1948 is shown in Table 8, and their distribution in Table 9. The distribution of the 1,310,000,000,000 lire devoted to investment and amortization in 1948 is given in Table 10.

[2] Colin Clark in *The Economics of 1960* (New York 1942) gave the average annual income of an employed person in 1935–1938 as $410 in Italy, $804 in France, $1,206 in the United Kingdom, and $1,389 in the United States.

Table 8—VALUE OF AVAILABLE GOODS AND SERVICES, 1948

Category	Amount (in lire)
Net national income	5,400,000,000,000
Direct taxation	640,000,000,000
Amortization and maintenance	560,000,000,000
Imports	852,000,000,000
Total	7,452,000,000,000

Table 9—DISTRIBUTION OF AVAILABLE GOODS AND SERVICES, 1948

Category	Amount (in lire)
Internal consumption	5,525,000,000,000
Exports	617,000,000,000
Net investments	750,000,000,000
Amortization	560,000,000,000
Total	7,452,000,000,000

Table 10—DISTRIBUTION OF GROSS INVESTMENTS, 1948

Field	Amount (in lire)
Agriculture	160,000,000,000
Industry	460,000,000,000
Railroads	140,000,000,000
Communications	30,000,000,000
Motor vehicles	50,000,000,000
Merchant marine	60,000,000,000
Public works	260,000,000,000
Miscellaneous	50,000,000,000
Reserve	100,000,000,000
Total	1,310,000,000,000

INDUSTRY

Italian industry is characterized by a large number of small enterprises, sizable government participation, and great concentration in a number of important sectors.

General Features.—According to the 1937–1939 census of Italian industry, there were 1,022,539 active businesses with 4,373,652 employees, or an average of 4.2 per business. Of the total, however, 804,646 businesses were handicraft enterprises, and only 217,893 were industries in the technical sense of the word. The latter employed 3,154,394 persons (or an average of 14.5), of whom 2,809,730 were factory workers. Distribution of employees in the various fields of production is shown in Table 11. The difference between the totals given in the table and those of the 1936 census (see Table 1 and section on *The People*) is accounted for by the fact that

Table 11—INDUSTRIAL CENSUS, 1937–39

Industry	Employees (in thousands)	Factory workers (in thousands)	Added value of production (billions of lire)*	Horsepower (in thousands)
Mechanical.......	846.7	676.9	8.4	1,202.0
Textiles.........	628.5	573.7	4.9	869.2
Foodstuffs........	574.5	361.7	5.2	948.2
Construction......	558.5	480.6	2.4	159.1
Metallic minerals..	206.8	175.9	1.0	389.0
Lumber, etc.......	283.6	130.9	1.0	210.0
Mining and quarrying..........	137.4	120.7	1.0	200.3
Chemicals........	127.9	107.7	3.6	548.3
Clothing.........	308.7	105.1	0.9	30.3
Paper and printing.	126.3	105.7	0.6	261.8
Metallurgical.....	103.6	94.3	2.1	984.0
Leather..........	215.5	77.2	0.9	66.1
Services and other.	351.5	246.0	1.8	406.2
Total.......	4,469.5	3,256.4	33.8	6,274.5

* 1938 value.

the census included domestic workers, workers in military service (of whom there were large numbers in 1936), and unemployed.

Excluding handicraft industries, 85.9 per cent of the business enterprises in the 1937–1939 census had less than 10 employees (14.4 per cent of the total number of employees); 10 per cent had from 11 to 50 employees (17.5 per cent of the total); 2 per cent had from 51 to 100 employees (11 per cent of the total); 1.8 per cent had from 101 to 500 employees (27.2 per cent of the total); 0.2 per cent had from 501 to 1,000 employees (11 per cent of the total); 0.1 per cent had 1,001 to 2,000 employees (9.6 per cent of the total); and only 87 enterprises had more than 2,000 employees (9.3 per cent of the total). Small and medium-sized enterprises prevail except in metallurgy, the production of electric power, and a few chemical products.

The prewar capital investment in industry was estimated at 110 billion lire (1938 value), of which two thirds was in corporations. In 1938 only nine corporations had a capital of more than 500,000,000 lire; they accounted for 21.6 per cent of all capital invested in corporations. In contrast, 96 per cent of the corporations had a capital of less than 10,000,000 lire; these comprised 20.75 per cent of the total corporate capital. Up to 1914 foreign capital was heavily invested in Italian industry. The amount of this capital declined after World War I, particularly after the Fascist government inaugurated its policy of autarchy, and just before World War II it amounted to 12 per cent of the corporate capital.

The Role of the Government.—The direct participation of the government and of governmental agencies in Italian industry is relatively large. The government began to play an important role at the time of the economic crisis of 1929, and its intervention in industry increased for political reasons in the period 1935–1940. This participation assumes four principal forms.

Government Administration.—The Italian government directly administers arms and munitions factories, naval shipyards, some chemical laboratories and mechanical enterprises, the mint, various mineral bath establishments, public works projects, and a few specialized plants, such as those devoted to the restoration of national monuments and to engraving.

Government Enterprises.—There are various autonomous agencies of the government, of which the chief is the Italian State Railways, controlling 73 per cent of the total railway mileage and large repair shops, and employing 200,000 persons. The next largest is the state monopoly of tobacco, salt, and quinine, with its farms, refineries, and laboratories. In addition, part of the telephone system is run by the government.

Government Ownership.—The role of the Italian government as a stockholder was developed during the Fascist regime. In this period the government acquired all or part of the stock of a number of companies which maintain a legal status of private ownership. Apart from the Istituto per la Ricostruzione Industriale (Institute for Industrial Reconstruction, IRI), there are 30 such companies with a capital of 2,600 million lire (1938 value) and 30,000 employees. They include the Cogne Corporation, which is engaged in the mining of iron and coal and the production of iron and steel and employs 5,400 persons; the Azienda Generale Italiana Petroli (Italian General Oil Corporation, AGIP), which refines, produces, and distributes petroleum and petroleum products; and the Azienda Nazionale Idrogenazione Combustibili (ANIC), owned by the government and the Montecatini Company, which produces gasoline and lubriating oils. AGIP and ANIC together have 7,000 employees. These two companies were instruments of the Fascist policy of autarchy in the field of fuel.

Public Corporations.—In addition to the foregoing, there are the semigovernmental enterprises, which, though publicly managed, are not part of the government proper. Chief among them is IRI, which owes its creation to a law of Jan. 23, 1933, designed to aid three large banks which had been affected by the depression of 1929. In 1949, the enterprises controlled by IRI had 234,900 employees and constituted the most important group of Italian industries. The distribution of this group among various fields of production is shown in Table 12.

Table 12—ISTITUTO PER LA RICOSTRUZIONE INDUSTRIALE

Field	Principal enterprises	Number of employees
Shipping	Finmare, a financial group controlling the four main Italian steamship companies	18,200
Mechanical	Shipyards (Ansaldo, Adriatico, OTO, Navalmeccanica) and others (Alfa Romeo, San Giorgio)	101,200
Iron and steel	Ilva, Terni, Siac, Dalmine	70,600
Electricity	SIP, SME, UNES, Terni	7,400
Telephone	All lines in northern Italy	8,500
Mineral	Monte Amiata	6,600
Chemical	Cellulose, synthetic rubber	3,000
Land reclamation and other projects	Sardinian, Maccarese, and Italstrade projects	19,400
Total		234,900

Scope of Government Intervention.—Government-controlled companies produce 85 per cent of Italian anthracite coal, 80 per cent of lignite, 65 per cent of mercury, 30 per cent of zinc, 15 per cent of lead, 80 per cent of pig iron, 65 per cent of steel, 80 per cent of ship construction, and 24 per cent of electric power. They manage 80 per cent of the telephone service, 40 per cent of all water transportation, and 73 per cent of the railway mileage.

Industrial Concentration.—Another aspect of the Italian industrial picture requires clarification if data on the prevalence of small and medium-sized enterprises is not to be subject to misinterpretation. This is the concentration of industry,

Table 13—CONCENTRATION OF ITALIAN INDUSTRY

Field	Number of large companies	Percentage of production controlled
Lead and zinc	6	92
Aluminum	3	95
Mercury	1	70
Coal	3	86
Pig iron and steel	6	84
Shipbuilding	3	97
Rubber	4	82
Caustic soda	4	90
Synthetic ammonia	2	86
Artificial textile fibers	2	90
Automobiles	2	84
Ball bearings	1	90
Matches	1	81

from both a technical and a financial standpoint, in a very few hands. Technical concentration is particularly pronounced in the mineral, iron and steel, electrical, and rubber industries, in shipbuilding, and in certain mechanical and chemical enterprises. The major examples of this concentration are shown in Table 13. Equally worthy of note is the concentration in the sugar, gas, and paper industries.

From a financial standpoint, besides the IRI group, described above, there is great concentration of capital in the production of electricity, the four major groups, which control 76.5 per cent of production, being connected with two large financial groups; and in the telephone service, largely controlled by IRI and two large private groups. Four industrial groups deserve special mention: (1) in chemicals, controlling 67 per cent of total production; (2) in the automotive industry, controlling 80 per cent; (3) in rubber, controlling about 70 per cent; and (4) in rayon, controlling 65 per cent. There are other large groups in the gas, coke, sugar, paper, and cement industries. In the textile industry there is far less concentration.

The total nominal capital of the enterprises listed above is about 200 billion lire (1949 value), compared with a nominal value of 337.8 billion lire for the 123 corporations listed by the Milan Stock Exchange.

In addition, there is a network of trusts, some of which were established by private interests and others through government action, all of them favored by protective tariffs. The most important are in the iron and steel and other metal industries.

After 1935, and to an even greater extent during World War II, many new organizations were created for the purpose of importing and distributing raw materials. The most important dealt with fuel. These excrescences, which may have been justified by an abnormal domestic market but which hindered healthy commercial development, were being abolished, slowly and with difficulty, after the war.

In general, although the larger groups have made sizable contributions to the development and renewal of productive equipment, the excessive concentration in the major sectors of Italian industry has had an unfavorable effect on the economy of the country.

Raw Materials.—We have seen that a scarcity of raw materials is a major characteristic of the Italian economy. Moreover, lack of capital and restriction of foreign trade have prevented the growth of plants processing imported supplies, such as are found in other countries equally poor in raw materials. One of Italian industry's most difficult problems has always been that of supply. The scope of this problem is shown by the following statistics for fuel, textile, metal, and other raw materials.

Fuel.—In Table 14 are given comparative figures of the amount of foreign and domestic coal, electric power, and petroleum consumed in Italy in 1926–1930, the period of maximum productive activity between World Wars I and II, and in 1936–1938, when the policy of autarchy prevailed. It is evident that in the second period a tremendous effort was made to achieve a certain independence from imported sources of power, but it is equally obvious that, despite drastic government intervention, this effort was not successful. After World War II, production of electric power increased; in 1948, it amounted to approximately 22,692,000,000 kilowatt hours.

Table 14—SOURCES OF POWER, 1926–30 AND 1936–38

Source	1926–30		1936–38	
	Quantity*	Percentage of total calories	Quantity*	Percentage of total calories
Foreign coal	13,310	84.3	11,441	71.1
Domestic coal	1,031	4.3	1,991	8.2
Electric power	8,503	6.2	14,628	10.4
Petroleum, gasoline and naphtha	609	5.2	1,258	10.3

* Coal and petroleum in thousands of metric tons; electric power in millions of kilowatt hours.

Textiles.—Cotton imports reached a high point of 220,000 metric tons in the period 1926–1930. The development of the manufacture of artificial textiles and limitations imposed upon the use of cotton reduced cotton imports to an average of 140,000 metric tons in the period 1935–1938. In 1948, 138,889 metric tons were imported. The reduction of cotton imports was made up by large imports of cellulose for the production of artificial fibers; these amounted to 145,429 metric tons in 1938, and 35,305 metric tons in 1948.

Wool, too, must be almost entirely imported. Italy received 60,763 metric tons of foreign wool in 1948. Among the less important textile fabrics, hemp is grown in sufficient quantity in Italy, but jute is almost entirely imported (25,427 metric tons in 1948). Domestic flax meets part of Italian requirements.

Metals.—In 1938, Italy imported 621,327 metric tons of iron and steel scrap, 69,878 metric tons of pig iron, and 184,268 metric tons of iron and steel products. Corresponding figures for 1948 were 122,722, 132,387, and 241,617 metric tons, respectively. Despite an increase in aluminum, lead, and zinc production in the decade before World War II, and measures taken by the government to limit the consumption of copper, this last especially has been imported in large quantities, amounting in 1938 to 80,612 metric tons (copper and copper alloys), and in 1948 to 70,874 metric tons. Nickel, tin, and antimony are also imported.

Other Raw Materials.—Other imported raw materials particularly necessary to Italian industry are rubber, wood, pulp, oilseeds, and phosphate rock.

Industrial Production.—By 1949 the industrial production index had recovered to approximately 95 per cent of the 1938 level. Production in the major fields of Italian industry is described below.

Metallurgy.—The iron and steel industry had before World War II reached a stage of development in keeping with domestic requirements, with a productive capacity of about 3,000,000 metric tons of steel and 1,500,000 metric tons of pig iron per year. In 1938, there were 19 blast furnaces, 5 of which were electric; 110 open-hearth furnaces; and 126 electric furnaces. About 84 per cent of production was concentrated in the plants of large combines. Many of the problems of a modern iron and steel industry have not been met; among other things, there is need for a reorganization of the plants producing steel plate.

In 1938, 928,800 metric tons of pig iron and ferroalloys and 2,328,000 metric tons of steel ingots and castings were produced. Corresponding figures for 1948 were 525,600 and 2,124,000 metric tons, respectively.

The manufacture of wire and nails is divided among a number of small companies. The same is true of secondary smelting plants, of which there are about 300, with 25,000 employees.

The aluminum industry, which grew considerably after World War I, is concentrated in four plants which process domestic bauxite and together have a capacity of 60,000 metric tons per year. From a maximum production of 48,195 metric tons in 1941, there was a decline to about 4,200 metric tons in 1945 and a rise to 33,000 metric tons in 1948. Increasing production depends upon the availability of cheap electric power.

The old-established lead and zinc industries, supplied from Sardinian mines, were extensively developed in the decade before World War II. There are three primary lead-smelting plants, with a capacity of 100,000 metric tons a year. In 1938, they produced 44,040 metric tons, and in 1948, 26,400 metric tons. The four Italian zinc plants have a capacity of 45,000 metric tons. Their maximum production (1940) was 39,360 metric tons; that of 1948, 26,630 metric tons.

Other branches of the metallurgical industry are unimportant if we except a few plants for the fabrication of imported copper and the production of mercury. In 1938, 2,027 metric tons of mercury were produced; in 1947, 1,861 metric tons.

The mining industry, except for the mines supplying the plants described above, was passing through a crisis after World War II, partly because its earlier prosperity had been bound up with the Fascist policy of autarchy. This was particularly true of coal, but applies equally to crude sulphur (380,345 metric tons in 1938, and 147,329 in 1947) and marble blocks (323,089 metric tons in 1938, and 263,646 in 1947). Production of iron ore amounted to 989,793 metric tons in 1938, and 454,300 in 1948; that of iron pyrites, to 930,312 metric tons in 1938, and 629,750 in 1947.

Industries in the Mechanical Field.—Together, the mechanical industries occupy first place in the Italian industrial picture, and chief among them is the manufacture of motor vehicles. In 1938, Italy produced about 52,000 passenger cars and 10,000 trucks; in 1948, 44,425 cars and 15,548 trucks and buses. In addition to the large automobile plants, there is a flourishing group of smaller body manufacturers whose craftmanship is highly regarded in foreign countries. The production of bicycles and motorcycles increased after World War II, reaching 120 per cent of the 1938 level in 1947.

The manufacture of aircraft, which grew during the war until it numbered 150,000 employees, was in a process of reconversion after the war. In 1947, only 125 planes were produced.

There are 160 privately owned shipyards with 50,000 employees and a capacity (exclusive of wood bottoms) of about 200,000 gross tons per year. Even before World War II, their capacity was never fully exploited despite government subsidies. The four largest manufacturers of ship engines have a combined capacity of 500,000 horsepower-years in turbines and 300,000 horsepower-years in motors.

After World War II, the Italian railway machine shops were very busy replacing lost equipment. These shops, which are perhaps overly subdivided (there are 93, with 20,000 employees), have a combined capacity greater than that normally required by the Italian railways. Before the war they suffered from periodic difficulties, in which plants were shut down and the largest shops combined in order to secure export outlets.

The electromechanical industry is an active one, represented by four major firms, special departments in other mechanical industries, and numerous small and medium-sized plants. In all, they employ 70,000 workers. Widespread electrification has made for a large production of generators, transformers, motors, and all the equipment necessary to the production, distribution, and use of electric power. There has been an equal growth in the production of cables and conductors (17 plants with more than 5,000 employees), batteries, light bulbs (60,000,000 produced annually), and telephone material. The manufacture of precision tools also is prosperous.

Textiles.—The second largest Italian industry is that of textiles, with 6,000 factories and 600,000 employees, in addition to numerous small handicraft units. Textiles have been since the Middle Ages an Italian specialty, with silk enjoying a particularly long tradition. The chief textile centers are Prato, in Tuscany, and the regions around Milan, Biella, and Vicenza.

Silk manufacture is the most important and is supplied by the domestic output of cocoons, of which an estimated 9,000,000 were produced in 1948. Unfortunately, this industry declined noticeably after 1930. Many spinning establishments located near the mulberry groves closed down, but some plants specializing in the later processes of manufacture were modernized.

As silk declined, there was an increase in the manufacture of cotton cloth. Despite the destruction caused by World War II there were at the end of 1947, 5,301,663 spindles and 138,276 looms. The industry employs some 200,000 workers. The production of both yarn (200,000 metric tons) and cloth (in the best years, 900,000,000 meters) is larger than the domestic market can absorb. Both silk and cotton goods require an export market.

In spite of war damage the 1949 capacity of the wool industry was on a par with that of 1939. As of 1939, there were 1,162,244 spindles and 19,455 power looms. There are about 70,000 employees, of whom 20,000 produce yarn, 5,000 work in combing, 40,000 in weaving, and the remainder in various allied lines. Plant capacity totals 30,000 metric tons of yarn, 20,000 metric tons of combed wool, and 40,000 metric tons of cloth. In 1947, the mills produced 40,000 metric tons of wool tops, 32,000 metric tons of worsted yarns, 50,000 metric tons of woolen yarns, and 50,000 metric tons of wool fabrics. The spinning and combing plants are concentrated in a few hands, but the weaving industry is more generally divided except for the large combines in Valdagno and Schio, near Vicenza. The plants around Biella are medium to large in size, and those at Prato small to medium. The wool industry also exports a large part of its output, particularly finished goods.

The newer rayon industry grew rapidly during the period of autarchy. As of 1949, it had 36,000 employees, who worked in 80 plants, of which 30 produced fiber. There are 130,000 spinnerette machines and 736,000 twisting spindles. A maximum production of 200,000 metric tons was attained in 1941. Production in 1949 was only 50 per cent of capacity.

The less important manufactures of hemp, flax, and jute together employ 40,000 workers.

Clothing is not big business in Italy. Of the 308,723 persons listed in the industrial census of 1937–1939, only 105,100 were factory workers. There are, however, some large establishments producing carpets, hats, elastic fabrics, underwear, and stockings.

Chemicals.—While the textile industry has been stabilized since 1930, the chemical industry has grown rapidly. As of 1949, it had 150,000 employees. Typical is the increase in the production of sulphuric acid, which went from 660,000 metric tons in 1914 to 777,000 in 1922, 1,127,000 in 1928, and 1,889,000 in 1938. A similar advance took place between 1928 and 1938 in almost all branches of the chemical industry. Production recovered rapidly after World War II, and by May 1949 it had reached 99 per cent of the 1938 level.

Foodstuffs.—The production of food is an important branch of Italian industry. According to the industrial census of 1937–1939, it employed 574,473 persons, of whom 361,700 were factory workers, the balance working in numerous small units. The census of 1937–1939 listed 292,906 individual plants, far more than the 168,451 in clothing. There are, however, some large firms. Among them are the 54 sugar refiners with 43,000 employees and a daily capacity of 7,000 metric tons. These were hard hit by World War II but by 1949 had regained their prewar level of more than 300,000 metric tons of sugar a year. There are also sizable firms producing candy, preserves, cheese, wine, beer, and spaghetti.

Lumber.—The lumber industry is divided among 123,162 units, and although some of them (such as the factories producing furniture and plywood) attain considerable size, most are classified as handicrafts. In 1947, Italy produced 3,693,110 cubic meters of timber.

Leather.—Of the 123,804 units listed by the industrial census of 1937–1939 for the tanning and leatherwork industry, only about 700 can be classified as industrial. Italian leather goods, noted for their high quality, supply the entire domestic market and are also exported.

Rubber.—Rubber is a large-scale industry in Italy. There are 269 producing units with approximately 40,000 employees. In 1948, 31,841 metric tons of crude rubber were imported. In addition, there is some production of synthetic rubber. Consumption has been increasing, and the industry recovered rapidly after World War II, reaching 120 per cent of 1938 production by May 1949.

Paper.—There is an old tradition of papermaking in Italy. According to the industrial census of 1937–1939, there were 1,992 producers with 56,127 employees. Newsprint is produced in a few large establishments. The production of paper increased from 350,000 metric tons in 1929 to 470,000 metric tons in 1938. Production in 1947 amounted to about two thirds of the prewar level. In general, the industry is hampered by high prices and a scarcity of pulp.

Construction.—Although the building trades occupied 558,544 persons according to the 1937–1939 industrial census, there are few large companies. In the postwar period, high costs and rent controls combined to produce a crisis in the building industry despite government intervention to stimulate the repair of war damage and the undertaking of public housing projects. All necessary building materials are produced domestically. The production of building stone and brick is divided among a large number of companies, but the cement industry is concentrated in a few hands. Cement capacity, which totals 7,000,000 metric tons a year, is utilized only in part. In 1947, 2,943,000 metric tons were produced; in 1948, approximately 5,000,000 metric tons.

Electric Power.—There are 320 electric power companies and 1,091 central power plants belonging to the 11 major groups which control 85 per cent of the total installed power capacity. About 90 per cent of the plants are hydroelectric, and two thirds of them use water from the Alps. There are about 100 reservoirs and artificial lakes with a combined capacity of almost 2,000,000,000 cubic meters of water. By 1949, all the damage caused by World War II, which was particularly heavy in central and southern Italy, had been repaired and new facilities were under construction. The 1948 production of 22,692,000,000 kilowatt hours of electricity exceeded the previous maximum of 20,760,000,000 kilowatt hours attained in 1941. It was twice that of 1929, and considerably above the 15,800,000,000 kilowatt hours produced in 1938. Nevertheless, the supply of electric power has been unable to keep pace with the demands of Italian industry. Plans were under way in 1949 to increase facilities so as to produce 30,000,000,000 kilowatt hours of electricity annually by 1954.

AGRICULTURE

Crop Distribution.—Because local conditions are so varied in Italy, existing agricultural statistics cannot be classified so as to present a thorough conception of crop distribution. By resorting to extreme simplification, however, it is possible to give an approximate idea of land uses in the mountain, hill, and plain regions, as shown in Table 15. The percentages in this table are based on the pre-World War II total of agricultural and forest land, which amounted to approximately 28,500,000 hectares, or about 70,500,000 acres. (According to the 1947–1948 report of

Table 15—PERCENTAGE DISTRIBUTION OF AGRICULTURAL AND FOREST LAND

Land Use	Mountainous	Hilly	Plain	All Italy
Cultivated	26	49	70	45
Orchards and olive groves	4	12	7	8
Permanent meadows	5	2	6	4
Total cultivated area	35	63	83	57
Permanent meadows and grazing land (rotating)	2	1	1	1
Permanent grazing land	22	15	7	16
Forests and chestnut groves	32	15	5	19
Uncultivated but productive	9	6	4	7
Total, uncultivated area	65	37	17	43
Total	100	100	100	100

the National Institute of Agrarian Economy, the total area of agricultural and forest land is 68,730,291 acres.) This roughly indicated division must be supplemented by a description of local conditions.

First, we must distinguish between the Po Valley and the peninsula proper. In the great plain of the Po, agriculture is very different from what it is beyond the Apennines, in central and southern Italy—the characteristically Mediterranean region from Emilia to Sicily. Northern Italy produces large quantities of grain (wheat, corn, rice, rye, oats, barley), industrial plants (sugar beets, hemp, tomatoes), and fodder (irrigated single-crop meadowland or meadowland rotated with different kinds of clover). Central Italy and most of the south are characterized by grapes, almonds, citrus fruits, green vegetables, and large quantities of olives. Everywhere wheat is the largest crop, since it furnishes the bread and spaghetti which, with olive oil, form the staple diet of the rural Mediterranean population. Some wheat is grown on almost every Italian farm. In the north it is a soft wheat from which bread flour is ground; in the south it is hard wheat with a high gluten content that is particularly adapted to the production of the various kinds of spaghetti. This hard wheat is an invaluable source of protein for people who do not eat much meat. The widespread cultivation of wheat, then, is due in large part to the nourishment it guarantees a peasant family. Aside from this general north-south division, the chief agricultural zones of Italy are indicated in Table 16. The divisions are based on the total prewar area of Italy (76,649,080 acres).

Table 16—PRINCIPAL ITALIAN AGRICULTURAL ZONES

Zone	Approximate area in hectares
Mountains (Alps and Apennines)	11,000,000
Outer Alps and plateaus	3,100,000
Po Valley, irrigated	1,000,000
Po Valley, nonirrigated	2,000,000
Central Italy	4,500,000
Southern Italy and Sicily	6,800,000
Sardinia	2,400,000
Total	30,800,000

Mountains.—The Alpine portion of the mountainous zone is composed of forest and grazing land. The land under cultivation amounts to no more than 7 per cent of the total and is divided among a number of small farms. The forests and pastures are usually owned collectively or by municipalities. The typical mountain dweller lives in a house in a village (which is located as often as not in a valley) only during the winter months. The rest of the year he spends in the upland pastures. Stock raising is his chief means of livelihood, and his modest crop of wheat, rye, and potatoes does not supply all of his family's needs. The living standard is low, and the population is sparse.

The mountainous area of the Apennines, on the other hand, is cultivated. Here a typical agricultural economy prevails. A denser population and the nature of the terrain have overstimulated cultivation. Livestock consists of sheep rather than cattle, and in some areas the flocks are moved back and forth from winter to summer pastures.

The mountains of Italy have long since lost their original forest covering. Most of the existing forests are grown for periodic cutting, and only a third of the forest area consists of tall trees. The most favored sections of the mountainous zone permit the cultivation of fruit, and there are many chestnut groves.

Outer Alps and Plateaus.—In this zone we find small farm units consisting of patches of cultivated land, pasture, an orchard or vineyard, and a small tract of woods. The fields of grain are planted with mulberry trees, which formerly stimulated the cultivation of silkworms. These farms produce comparatively little, and few head of livestock are raised.

In a category by themselves are the hilly regions of Langhe and Monferrato, where fruit trees and grapes are cultivated intensively in a fourth of the area.

Po Valley, Irrigated.—The irrigated portion of the Po Valley, by virtue of the terrain, water supply, large-scale irrigation projects, and intensive cultivation, makes up the richest agricultural zone of Italy. Here we find grains cultivated in rotation with meadowland, and in some places permanent meadows. Livestock is raised on a large scale, and some areas specialize in a single crop, notably rice. Individual returns are high, and considerable sums of money are invested in this zone.

Po Valley, Nonirrigated.—The nonirrigated portion of the Po Valley is somewhat less fertile than the irrigated portion, but it is still intensively cultivated. Industrial crops (hemp, sugar beets, tomatoes), together with orchards and vineyards, prevail. In some reclaimed areas there are large commercial farms. Here there is a serious labor problem because the employment of farm workers is seasonal.

Central Italy.—Agriculture in central Italy is characterized by the system of *mezzadria,* or cropping on half shares. The crops vary from one area to another. Olives prevail in one section; grapes (Chianti, Orvieto, Val di Pesa), in another. In addition, fruit, grain, and vegetables are cultivated, and there are areas of forest or fallow land. The coastal plains of Tuscany and Latium have benefited from reclamation projects and raise grain on a large scale.

Southern Italy and Sicily.—This agricultural zone is greatly handicapped by a scarcity of water. Olives, grain, and grapes prevail in various districts.

Along the coastal plains of Sicily and the Adriatic and Ionian seas, as well as in some dry sections of the interior, there are latifundia, or large private estates, which are devoted to the cultivation of grain and the raising of livestock. Around the towns, on the other hand, landholding is on a tiny scale. Neither extreme is very profitable. Only in some irrigated coastal areas is there intensive cultivation of citrus and other fruits, vegetables, and some industrial crops, such as hemp, tomatoes, and tobacco. Wherever the land is least fertile, we find olives and grapes.

Sardinia.—Sardinia is in a category of its own because so much of it consists of poor pasture, scrub forest, and fallow land. The population is not dense, and ownership of what little land can be intensively cultivated is widely distributed. Investments are small. In the more favored areas we find crops similar to those of the southern part of the peninsula, with grapes and olives predominating.

Production.—The principal agricultural products of Italy are shown in Table 17, which compares the output of 1936–1939 with that of 1948. It should be noted that the harvest of 1948 was

Table 17—PRINCIPAL ITALIAN AGRICULTURAL PRODUCTS, 1936–39 AND 1948

Principal crops	Average 1936–39 (metric tons)	1948 (metric tons)
Wheat	7,550,800	6,136,000
Corn	2,960,100	2,254,000
Rice	776,000	618,700
Oats	560,000	229,500
Potatoes	2,716,500	3,014,500
Tomatoes	952,200	962,600
Other vegetables	1,710,800	2,157,800
Sugar beets	3,271,500	3,408,500
Hemp fiber	109,700	76,800
Forage crops	30,447,700	29,833,500
Grapes	6,158,600	5,786,200
Olives	1,426,200	635,700
Oranges	325,500	352,900
Lemons	326,900	254,600
Other citrus fruit	85,100	84,400
Other fruit	1,567,800	1,573,200

distinctly better than those of 1945–1947. The olive crop, however, was exceptionally poor because of adverse weather conditions. Normal oil production is more than 200,000 metric tons; that of 1947 was 258,000 metric tons. In the same year, 31,858,000 hectoliters of wine were produced. These and all other items vary considerably from year to year, depending on climatic conditions. The average wheat production is 1.5 metric tons per hectare for the entire country, with a maximum of 2.5 to 3 metric tons in Lombardy and a minimum of less than 1 ton in Latium, the south, and the islands. More than half the grain produced in Italy comes from the Po Valley and Sicily.

In 1939, Italy had approximately 7,879,000 cattle, 3,303,000 swine, 9,875,000 sheep, and 1,867,000 goats. Livestock numbers were cut greatly during World War II, but these losses were largely replaced, and as of 1949 it was estimated that there were 7,500,000 cattle, 3,800,000 swine, 10,000,000 sheep and goats, 700,000 horses, and 700,000 donkeys and mules. The last two are found particularly in the south, while most of the other stocks are in the Po Valley.

Compared with its population, Italy's livestock resources are very small. In 1947, Italy had 161 head of cattle to every 1,000 inhabitants, in contrast to 371 for France, 217 for Germany (Bizone), and 552 for the United States. If the numbers of Italian livestock could be substantially increased, both the standard of living and agricultural exports could be raised, thereby providing funds for badly needed imports. In 1938, food products, particularly grain and fats, made up 14.1 per cent of total imports by value; and 35.5 per cent of total exports (citrus fruit, other fruit, vegetables, and wine). Corresponding figures for 1948 were 46.4 per cent and 20.4 per cent, respectively. It is essential that Italy increase its agricultural production and find additional foreign outlets for fruit and vegetables.

Land Distribution.—Approximately 40 per cent of the productive land of Italy is occupied by small one-family farms, far from any market, which produce only enough to meet the family needs. Even within this category, however, there are marked differences that require further explanation if we are to see how the land is actually distributed and how the farms are run. In the period following World War II, the distribution of the population engaged in agriculture remained approximately the same as it was at the time of the 1936 census (see Table 18).

Table 18—DISTRIBUTION OF POPULATION ENGAGED IN AGRICULTURE, 1936

Classification	Number	Percentage of total
Farmers cultivating their own land	2,872,648	32.8
Lessees	788,340	9.0
Other types of farmers	74,766	0.8
Farmers with title to more than one farm	709,939	8.1
Sharecroppers	1,787,601	20.4
Persons who are both farmers and laborers	138,877	1.6
Managers	17,388	0.2
Day laborers	1,817,283	20.8
Laborers on yearly contracts	381,785	4.4
Cosharers and others	167,437	1.9
Total	8,756,064	100.0

Around the villages of the Alpine valleys there are small farms, composed of patches of fields, meadows, vineyards, and woodlands, whose owners have a communal arrangement for sharing grazing land and forests in the mountains. The same sort of farm, of more recent origin, is characteristic of the Outer Alps and plateau zone. It is very often run by its owner, but is sometimes leased or farmed on shares. This condition also prevails among the Piedmont hills.

The farms of the Po Valley are frequently run by a lessee who hires the necessary labor. Where the land is rich, the workers receive regular wages and a percentage of the produce. In the nonirrigated or recently reclaimed areas, the work is done by seasonally recruited day laborers. In the Lombard plain a large number of the workers are migrants who come for the season, particularly to the rice fields. The condition of the day laborers is unfavorable because of the seasonal character of their employment with long intervening periods of unemployment, and because of their enforced absence from their homes while they are working. Large and medium-sized properties are the rule, although some small farms are found on the edges of the Po plain.

In central Italy, where the system of *mezzadria* prevails, the farm unit is called the *podere* and usually has an area of 20 to 50 acres, or enough to be worked by one peasant family. Larger properties, especially in Umbria and Tuscany, consist of 5 to 20 *poderi* grouped together in one *fattoria*, which is under the direction of either the landowner or his manager. This system is adapted to the terrain, which is often unsuited to the use of agricultural machinery, and to the fact that a constant investment of money is necessary in order to show a profit. Except in some small mountain areas large and medium-sized properties prevail in central Italy.

From the Maremma southward to the end of the peninsula, large-scale properties are more numerous, particularly where grain or livestock is the major interest. Where cultivation is more intensive, properties are likely to be smaller, and even in the south there are small farms, particularly in the mountains. In the far south and Sicily farms are not laid out in single units; instead, pieces of land are leased and subleased to the peasants. Large tracts are often leased to a wealthy operator who hires the necessary day labor for longer or shorter periods. The limited arable area of Sardinia, on the other hand, is broken up into small, poor units.

According to the report of the National Institute of Agrarian Economy given in Table 19, 77.5 per cent of the agricultural and forest land is the property of individuals. The land owned by the various private and public bodies has an economic value below what might be expected from its size, representing 10 per cent of taxable farm income as against 22.5 per cent of the agricultural and forest land area. Of the 9,512,242 individually owned holdings, 53.96 per cent have a size of half a hectare (1.235 acres) or less (see Table 20). About 74.1 per cent of the area individually owned is in units of less than 100 hectares (247.1 acres), and 4.1 per cent in units of over 1,000 hectares (2,471 acres). On the other hand, of the land owned by private and public bodies, holdings of less than 100 hectares account for only 13.8 per cent of the total area of such land. Individual holdings of agricultural and forest land are distributed as shown in Table 20. These figures, which apply to Italy as a whole, are supplemented by statistics on taxable income divided by major agricultural regions (Table 21). Because of great variations in land productivity, taxable income is a more meaningful criterion of land distribution than area is. We learn from this data that the least valuable properties are found in greatest numbers in the mountains and in Liguria, the small- to medium-value properties in the northern hills and in Sardinia, the medium-value ones in the center and south and in Sicily, and the medium- to large-value ones in the Po Valley.

Table 19—OWNERSHIP OF AGRICULTURAL AND FOREST LAND, REPORT OF THE NATIONAL INSTITUTE OF AGRARIAN ECONOMY, 1947–48

Class of ownership	Number of holdings	Area (in acres)
Individual	9,512,242	53,285,188.97
National government	3,000*	1,304,184.70
Provincial government	3,955	35,671.74
Municipal	23,869	8,661,489.72
Roman Catholic Church and other religious bodies	66,489	1,148,137.51
Commercial corporations	30,651	1,476,696.91
Welfare agencies	14,018	676,327.99
Peasant associations and other groups	23,990	2,142,594.09
Total	9,678,214	68,730,291.63

* Estimate.

Table 20—DISTRIBUTION OF INDIVIDUALLY OWNED AGRCULTURAL AND FOREST LAND, 1947–48

Classification by hectares	Number of holdings	Percentage of total	Area (in hectares)	Percentage of total area
Up to 0.5	5,132,851	53.96	875,000	4.1
0.5–2	2,795,122	29.38	2,883,000	13.4
2–5	950,070	9.99	2,943,300	13.6
5–10	330,733	3.48	2,289,700	10.6
10–25	192,815	2.03	2,945,500	13.6
25–50	60,874	0.64	2,104,400	9.7
50–100	28,381	9.29	1,956,400	9.1
100–200	12,918	0.14	1,782,100	8.3
200–500	6,536	0.07	1,946,600	9.0
500–1,000	1.440	0.02	971,200	4.5
Over 1,000	502	0.00	875,700	4.1
Total	9,512,242	100.00	21,572,900	100.0

With regard to the land owned by public and private bodies, as shown in Table 19, 56.1 per cent of the total of such land belongs to municipalities, 9.6 per cent to commercial corporations, 8.7 per cent to the national and provincial governments, 7.4 per cent to the Roman Catholic Church and other religious bodies, 4.4 per cent to welfare organizations, and the balance (13.8 per cent) to peasant associations and other groups. Commercial ownership is found especially in the plains; communal ownership, in the mountains. Organizational ownership is most important in Trento, Latium, Umbria, Lombardy, and Tuscany.

Table 21—PERCENTAGE DISTRIBUTION OF TAXABLE INCOME, AGRICULTURAL AND FOREST LANDS, 1947–48

Zone	Taxable income, based on assessments as of Jan. 1, 1943, in lire at their 1938 value			
	To 1,000	1,000–10,000	10,000–100,000	Over 100,000
Alps	63.2	31.1	5.6	0.1
Liguria	57.7	36.9	5.4	0.0
Northern hills	27.9	47.1	21.8	3.2
Po Valley	6.7	28.9	47.5	16.9
Central	13.9	36.9	36.6	12.6
Apennines	39.7	39.0	17.7	3.6
Southern	28.6	36.2	26.5	8.7
Sicily	25.3	36.3	28.7	9.7
Sardinia	38.9	47.7	13.1	0.3
Total	22.0	36.2	31.8	10.0

Agricultural Problems.—The major problem of Italian agriculture after World War II was the return to normal production. Although this goal was well on the way to realization by 1949, there remained the problem of raising production above prewar levels in order to take care of the increased population and improve the average standard of food consumption.

A second group of problems is related to the necessity of adapting production to market conditions. During the Fascist regime, Italian agriculture aimed at national self-sufficiency and the extension of the acreage devoted to the cultivation of grain. Some of the circumstances that determined this policy—the difficulty of securing certain foreign supplies and of exporting fresh fruit, vegetables, and wine—still obtained after the war. Nevertheless, for Italian agriculture to prosper there must be freedom to concentrate on improving and increasing those types of cultivation to which soil and terrain are best suited, and to place the products of this cultivation on a free world market.

The large number of small holdings, the existence of a large class of farm laborers, and lack of capital make technical improvement difficult. There is much to be done in the development of professional instruction, in the provision of easier farm credit, and, eventually, in organizing cooperatives for the use of agricultural machinery and the processing and sale of farm products.

In addition to these technical problems, there are two social problems: overpopulation in certain areas, and the existence of approximately 2,000,000 farm laborers who have no economic security. The first, as explained above, is a general problem of the Italian economy, and its solution would require a number of long-range measures, such as greater emigration, emphasis on different types of crops, and further industrial development supported by new capital.

The problem of the *bracciante*, or laborer, is closely connected with overpopulation and with land distribution and farming methods. The term *bracciante* includes both those whose work is seasonal and those whose wages are uncertain. There are, however, many different types of laborer. There is, for example, a tremendous difference between the employees of a large commercial farm of the Po Valley and the peasants of a large southern estate. In both cases, however, it is not sufficient to increase the amount of goods that the laborer can acquire with his wages. There is need also for some form of contract, whether tenancy or *mezzadria,* by virtue of which the farm worker can feel some ownership or at least participation, and also certainty of employment. For large masses of the rural population, that is the only way to achieve a better life. As conditions have existed, the peasant in some areas is caught in a vicious circle of poverty. The laborer in Apulia, for instance, has no share in what he produces and does his work slackly and reluctantly. Much energy is wasted because of the lack of incentive or any real connection with the land. Such conditions were responsible, for example, for the strike of about 1,000,000 farmhands in the Po Valley and central Italy in the spring of 1949.

Even when a peasant has saved enough money to buy his own farm, in those regions where large holdings prevail there has been no land on the market for him to purchase. For this reason, proposals for agrarian reform have long been made. As a matter of fact, agrarian reform has been under way for centuries, with the steady increase of small holdings and intensive cultivation. There are two chief aspects to the problem. First, there must be a change from extensive to intensive cultivation in certain areas, and, second, in areas where large holdings monopolize the land they must be broken up. In addition, the efficiency of the smallest type of landholding must be increased, and fairer leasing and sharecropping arrangements must be made where a further increase in the number of holdings is impractical.

Only in a part of central and southern Italy is there need for forced redistribution of the land. In many areas such parceling would reduce productivity. In a proposal made by the Italian government in April 1949, it was suggested that the excess land of extensively cultivated properties yielding a taxable income of more than 40,000 or 50,000 lire (1938 value), and intensively cultivated properties yielding more than 60,000 lire, based on assessments as of Jan. 1, 1943, be sold for redistribution over a specified period. Any such land remaining unsold would then be expropriated, its owners receiving compensation. It was expected that this plan would make available a minimum of 3,000,000 acres for redistribution.

Bibliography.—GENERAL FEATURES OF THE ITALIAN ECONOMY: Sensini, Guido, *Le variazioni dello stato economico dell'Italia nell'ultimo trentennio del secolo XIX* (Rome 1904); *Cinquant'anni di storia italiana,* Vol. 3 (Milan 1911); Banca Commerciale Italiana, *Progresso economico dell'Italia nel ventennio 1893–1912* (Milan 1913); Bachi, Riccardo, *L'Italia economica* (Turin 1909–21); La Cassa di risparmio delle provincie lombarde, *La Cassa di risparmio delle provincie lombarde nella evoluzione economica della regione, 1823–1923* (Milan 1923); Porri, V., *L'evoluzione economica italiana dell'ultimo cinquantennio* (Turin 1926); Istituto di Statistica della Università di Roma, *Indici del movimento economico italiano* (Rome 1926–30); *Annali di statistica,* 6th series, Vol. 20 (Rome 1931); Banca Commerciale Italiana, *Movimento economico dell'Italia,* 21 vols. (Milan 1911–32); Corbino, Epicarmo, *Annali dell'economia italiana, 1861–1900* (Città di Castello 1931–33); Einaudi, Luigi, *La condotta economica e gli effetti sociali della guerra italiana* (Bari 1933); Mortara, Giorgio, *Prospettive economiche* (1921–37); Istituto Centrale di Statistica, *VIII censimento generale della popolazione, 1936,* Vols. 1 and 4 (Rome 1937–39); Istituto di Statistica della Università di Roma, *La vita economica italiana* (Rome 1931–39); *Compendio statistico italiano* (Rome 1946); Saraceno, Pasquale, *Elementi per un piano di sviluppo dell'economia italiana* (Rome 1948); *Bollettino dei prezzi* (Rome, monthly); Comitato Interministeriale per la Ricostruzione ERP, *Relazioni* (Rome, quarterly).

INDUSTRY: Istituto Centrale di Statistica, *Censimento commerciale e industriale, 1927,* Vol. 8 (Rome 1929–32); id., *Censimento commerciale e industriale, 1937–39* (Rome 1939); Ministero per la Costituente, *Rapporto della Commissione Economica: Industria,* 2 vols. (Rome 1947); Confederazione Generale dell'Industria Italiana, *Annuario* (Rome 1948); Istituto Nazionale di Statistica, *Annuario Statistico, 1944–48* (Rome 1949).

AGRICULTURE: Coletti, Francesco, *La popolazione rurale in Italia* (Piacenza 1925); Serpieri, Arrigo, *La guerra e le classi rurali italiane* (Bari 1930); Istituto Nazionale di Economia Agraria, *Inchiesta sullo spopolamento montano in Italia* (Rome 1932–38); id., *Rapporti tra proprietà, impresa e mano d'opera nell'agricoltura italiana* (Rome 1932–38); Lorenzoni, Giovanni, *Inchiesta sulla piccola proprietà coltivatrice formatesi nel dopo guerra* (Rome 1928–38); Medici, Giuseppe, *L'agricoltura e la riforma agraria* (Milan 1946); Ministero per la Costituente, *Rapporto della Commissione Economica: Agricoltura* (Rome 1946); Ministero dell'Agricoltura, *Programma delle irrigazioni italiane* (Rome 1947); Medici, Giuseppe, *La distribuzione della proprietà fondiaria in Italia* (Rome 1948).

SILVIO GOLZIO,
Professor, University of Turin.

10. POLITICAL AND ADMINISTRATIVE STRUCTURE.

The study of Italian political problems and the description of Italy's constitutional and administrative structure fall properly into three main chronological subdivisions: (1) Italy under the Constitution of 1848, and until 1922, when the Fascists seized power; (2) the Fascist interlude, from 1922 to 1943; and (3) the period from the downfall of fascism in 1943 to the establishment of the Italian Republic in 1946 and the framing of a new constitution in 1947.

LIBERAL ITALY UNDER THE CONSTITUTION OF 1848

The Constitution of 1848, granted originally to the people of the Kingdom of Sardinia by Charles Albert (q.v.), became the constitution of the Kingdom of Italy upon its formation in March 1861, and was later extended to the entire peninsula as the process of unification proceeded. While the framers of the constitution had in mind the creation of a system of government in which the powers of the king would be quite broad and independent of Parliament, custom and the influence of the English system gradually led to the development of a parliamentary regime. The shift in emphasis from king to Parliament was achieved rather early. Indeed, the principle of the supremacy of Parliament, and of the primary responsibility of the government to Parliament, was already firmly established by the time of the death of the great builder of Italian unity, Camillo Benso di Cavour (q.v.), in June 1861.

Considering, then, the Italian system of government from 1861 to 1922 as a parliamentary monarchy, we can observe the following fundamental characteristics:

The Monarchy.—In general, the three rulers of this period—Victor Emmanuel II, Humbert I, and, until October 1922, Victor Emmanuel III (qq.v.)—behaved as expected of constitutional monarchs. Their task was to reign and not to rule, to keep wholly outside of politics, and to accept as mandatory whatever political move was dictated by the parliamentary majority of the moment.

Parliament.—Two houses existed throughout this period—a lower house, the Chamber of Deputies, and an upper house, the Senate. The suffrage was not extended to all adult males (with the exception of illiterates under 30 years of age) until 1912, so that for the first half century the Chamber of Deputies was elected on a relatively narrow, though constantly widening, basis. (All literacy requirements for voting were finally abolished in 1919.) Senators were appointed for life by the king, upon recommendation of the prime minister. Effective political power belonged to the Chamber of Deputies; all cabinets had to seek its confidence and could be overthrown by it. The Senate's role was one of advice and, presumably, of debate of fundamental issues on a higher level.

Until 1919 the electoral laws were based on single-deputy constituencies. This meant the establishment of strong personal relationships between political candidates and the electors. The local ties, the family background, the personal views of a deputy mattered a good deal more than his membership in one or another political party. Italian political life at this period thus bears a strong resemblance to that of France, personal issues and attitudes being more significant than any steady attachment to rigid political programs. This was the era of transformism (see section on *History*), and to some critics of Italian politics the word bears vituperative connotations. It was, to be sure, a system which made for blurred party lines, and for insecure governments, because no government could count on the allegiance of well-disciplined ranks of supporting parties. Nevertheless, the system brought into political life a human touch and a sense of political realities which are missing when Parliament is rigidly aligned among great parties whose members have been reduced to the status of robots. The parliamentary history of this period, therefore, is known not through the vicissitudes of political parties but through those of political leaders, as they succeeded or failed in retaining a following sufficient to keep them in power. This is especially true of the period after 1876, when the Right was driven from office. The outstanding name of this period is that of Giovanni Giolitti, who served five terms of office as prime minister and knew better than anyone else how to manipulate parliamentary majorities with a cleverness which, while not contributing to the raising of the level of political morality, helped to maintain effective government.

After 1919, the political scene changed. The major cause was the war; the contributing cause, the revision of the electoral machinery. In Italy, as in most countries, World War I precipitated political developments whose formation would otherwise have proceeded at a much slower pace. Two of these developments were of major proportions, and such as to change the complexion of Parliament. The first was the birth of a full-fledged Christian Democratic movement; the second, the great increase in strength of the Socialist Party.

The appearance of Christian democracy, if sudden and dramatic, was not unforeseen. For several decades, the political, economic, and organizing activities of groups calling themselves Christian Democrats had been increasing. By the end of World War I it was apparent that the only factor withholding this movement from a public appearance on the political stage was the Vatican's veto against the participation of Catholics in the political life of the country. This veto had gradually been softened to permit participation in local politics, but up to 1919 no national Catholic party could have been organized. When, during the war, the pope made it clear that the church, far from desiring the political destruction of Italy, favored the strengthening of the country and implied that the Roman question (see section on *History*) no longer had any real significance from a territorial point of view, the end was in sight. The dam was broken when the pope let it be known that he would not object to Catholics standing for office. In January 1919, the Italian Popular Party was formed. It won 101 seats in the election of 1919 and 108 in the election of 1921, becoming the second most important political party in the Chamber of Deputies.

The strongest was the Socialist Party. As a party it was committed to a revolutionary program and could, therefore, admit no compromise that entailed any degree of collaboration with the existing political regime, constitutionally a monarchy and politically bourgeois. The revolutionary climax seemed at hand in September 1920, when, under Socialist leadership, workers occupied the largest industrial factories. There was no resistance, and the bourgeois state seemed to be collapsing. As the barricades were being manned, the Socialist leaders suddenly discovered that there was no Lenin or Trotsky among them and that they had retained bourgeois ideas under their revolutionary appearance. The call to the barricades was off, the factories were surrendered, and the revolution was postponed indefinitely.

This was the essence of the crisis which weakened postwar Italian socialism: an official revolutionary attitude coupled with an innate incapacity for revolution. In 1919, and again in 1921, the Socialists, as the largest political group, could have formed a Cabinet, but they took the position that they could never participate in any government. This position, logical if we consider the revolutionary premises of the party, became political suicide for a party incapable of revolution and led to a serious weakening of parliamentary government.

The changed political outlook was accompanied by a change in the electoral machinery, from a single constituency system to proportional representation applied within fairly large constituencies. The chief consequence of this development was the strengthening of organized political party life—a good thing in itself, provided normal relationships could be established among the parties. As it was, the Socialists cut themselves off as a result of their rigid and preconceived position, the Christian Democrats were viewed with suspicion by the liberal and democratic groups imbued with the old lay tradition, while these groups were themselves incapable of providing strong government and of renovating their outworn political leadership.

Administrative System.—The general pattern consistently followed by Italy since her unification has been one of centralization based largely on the Napoleonic system. As Piedmont gradually extended its control over the whole country, it imposed a uniform system of administration which failed to take into account the regional differences of the past. The country was ruled from the center and divided into provinces, each headed by a prefect appointed by the central government. There is nothing wrong with a centralized administrative system in so small a country as Italy, provided certain limitations are recognized beyond which the power of the central government generally does not extend. In Italy these limitations were not recognized, and the development of democratic institutions at the periphery was thwarted. Nevertheless, Italian bureaucracy, though all-embracing and rigid and not very up to date in its methods, developed into a good administative machine with high standards of honesty and devotion to the ideals of public service. Only fascism succeeded in corrupting it. Similar limitations hampered the judiciary, which had to move within the stiff framework provided by a system of codified law, with no room for imagination and feeling for social change on the part of the judges.

Local governments were independent in name. Each province had an elective provincial council with limited jurisdiction. Each commune, or town, was governed by an elective municipal council. But over them all hovered the omnipotent figure of the prefect. Stifled and controlled at every turn, local administrators could hardly be expected to develop independent plans and the proud spirit which has made of the institution of local self-government a pillar of strength of democratic traditions in Anglo-Saxon countries. But the power of control was not the only one which the central government could exercise through the prefects. It could, and repeatedly did, dissolve popularly elected municipal councils and replace elected mayors with central government commissioners. Such drastic moves had to be justified by a substantial degree of administrative malfeasance on the part of the local bodies. While malfeasance existed in some instances, it was invented in others, when the primary purpose was the removal of recalcitrant local political leaders whose activities were deemed a nuisance to the political groups in power in Rome. It is important to establish as a historical fact that even before 1922 the weakening of local democratic institutions had begun as the result of a belief in the superiority of a centralized administrative system.

Political Freedoms.—Notwithstanding these shortcomings, the historical balance must weigh heavily in favor of the conclusion that, in the period under consideration, personal and political liberties were greatly strengthened. The citizen remained secure in his fundamental rights, even though suffering at times from an excess of police zeal in the maintenance of law and order; and voting could be freely exercised by all except in some areas of southern Italy where ignorance and political pressure combined to produce unsatisfactory results. Above all, that fundamental and first of political freedoms, freedom of the press, was in full bloom and vivified political life with its presence.

It has become increasingly difficult to define the conditions which are required for the existence of a free press. For our purposes, it is perhaps enough to say that freedom of the press exists in any country which has a certain minimum number of independent newspapers. An independent newspaper is one whose policies are established by a board of editors which is free of ties with any political party, group, or particular economic interest, and is entirely devoted to the promotion of the public welfare. Such a newspaper must have achieved, because of its independent criticism of policies and of views, because of its full and objective coverage of news as distinguished from opinion, because of the good quality of its writing, a wide circulation and must be available to all throughout the country. A country which is blessed by two or three newspapers of this type has come as near to the ideal of freedom of the press as it is human to expect. Italy, together with a very few other countries, found herself in this condition during the first quarter of the 20th century. An informed public opinion, educated by a strong press, was one of the greatest obstacles fascism had to surmount before it could achieve its dictatorial goal. This was attainable only after the use of violence, legal or otherwise, had allowed fascism to gain complete physical control of the Italian press.

Economic Policies.—This period was one of great economic development. Old industries, such as the manufacture of textiles, expanded, while new industries, such as iron, steel, and engineering, were created. Not all of this growth was achieved without government intervention and protection, including the use of subsidies and protective tariffs. Such aid brought about the rise to influence of a group of industrialists who could not justify their existence except as representatives of the state, and the development of labor groups which considered it logical to thrive on government privileges. This artificial economic structure helped to aggravate the 1919 crisis and led some industrial leaders to consider the state as their own preserve, which they could use for the satisfaction of their private interests.

THE FASCIST CRISIS

Many reasons have been given to explain the development of a strong Fascist movement in Italy after the autumn of 1920, and the seizure of power by that movement on Oct. 28, 1922. The least valid of the explanations seems to be the purely Marxist one, which sees everything in terms of a struggle between a declining but aggressive capitalist system and the proletariat, with the triumphant capitalists establishing a dictatorship to keep the working class under their control. The reality is far more complex. Sentimental and entirely uneconomic nationalistic feelings played a major role. Traditions which made the maintenance of law and order appear desirable as a matter of principle have also to be taken into account. From our point of view, however, it is sufficient to point out the failure of the political system, and specifically of Parliament, to function in times of crisis. Any inquiry into historical might-have-beens is usually unrewarding. The fact is that among the elder statesmen who in 1922 held the balance of power there was a widespread sentiment of resignation and of self-admitted failure. Under the circumstances, they reasoned, the only way out of the political crisis was to let the new Fascist movement assume the responsibility of government and show what it could do. The twin hope was never abandoned that, on the one hand, once in power fascism would become a normal and constitutional political movement and that, on the other, it would gradually decline and allow the older political groups to return to office. Both hopes were inevitably destined to be disappointed, and fascism developed as a ruthless totalitarian dictatorship, unconstitutional by definition, which completely abolished all non-Fascist political leadership.

Fascism and Government.—The apex of the Fascist system was the dictator, who enjoyed all the extraordinary legal powers granted to him by special laws and the even wider sphere of illegal and personal powers possessed by the leader in any dictatorial system. Benito Mussolini's power remained quite strong almost to the end. His influence reached down into the administrative sphere, and no policies could be adopted without his sanction. His influence was also used to symbolize the new Italy fascism was said to be developing and to create that leader-and-follower complex which is the essence of such a system. To him was attributed an all-encompassing wisdom and knowledge, and an attempt was made to train the people to accept all his decisions as indisputably right.

Next to the dictator was the Gran Consiglio del Fascismo (Fascist Grand Council), which was made an organ of the state in 1928. It was the highest assembly in which the top leadership of the Fascist Party could act as a corporate body. What the actual accomplishments of this agency were in terms of establishing general policy directives is difficult to say in the absence of any exhaustive published record of its activities. Great mystery surrounded its meetings, which were usually held late at night. It is likely, however, that within it the various currents of fascism found expression and tried to gain ascendency by influencing Mussolini. This was a fruitless process, since he was easily accessible to successive and contradictory views. By 1943, fierce conflicts had arisen within the council, with a large group revolting against the leadership of the dictator.

Next in order, but actually at the bottom of the scale in point of influence, came Parliament in the various stages of its transformation under fascism. As a result of the elections of 1924, a Fascist-dominated Chamber of Deputies came into existence, bearing, however, some outward resemblance to the chambers of the past, owing to the existence of an effective opposition, whose chief leader was the United Socialist deputy Giacomo Matteotti. Matteotti's murder on June 10, 1924, marks the beginning of a complete totalitarian regime. The Chamber of 1929 was the first elected by plebiscite (from an official slate by a sharply reduced electorate), and was composed solely of Fascists. The Chamber of 1935 represented the first fruit of the corporative phase of fascism, for all its members were representatives of organized economic groups. In 1938, the Chamber of Deputies was abolished and replaced by the Chamber of Fasces and Corporations.

Throughout these vicissitudes the organization of the Senate remained unchanged. Its members continued to be appointed by the king, though of course from among deserving Fascists recommended by the government. To the end, however, a small group of pre-Fascist senators continued to exercise their functions. In the last decade of fascism, they remained silent of necessity, but a few black balls continued to mar the principle of unanimity deemed so important by the official doctrine. As parliamentary bodies, both Chamber and Senate were reduced to the task of recording decisions taken by the higher party hierarchy.

Fascism and Administration.—In its attitude toward the civil service, fascism followed a policy of expediency, compounded of cynicism and the realization that it needed the daily support of hundreds of thousands of public employees working at routine tasks. A few were discharged. The majority seized upon the first suitable occasion to join the Fascist Party. Among the higher ranks of civil servants, judges, and university professors, those who refused to join the party were more numerous. In 1931, all civil servants were required to take an oath of allegiance to the regime, which most of them did take after Benedetto Croce pointed out the invalidity of such an oath. Those who refused to take the oath were dismissed, but party membership was not made compulsory on civil servants who had acquired permanent tenure. Naturally, promotions and transfers to more desirable jobs and locations were out of the question for nonmembers. As the years of Fascist rule wore on, a new generation of younger and Fascist appointees occupied a majority of the administrative posts, while at the same time the functions of government were greatly expanded. As a whole, the competence and the high regard for the public weal which had obtained in the past were seriously weakened.

In the field of local administration, fascism developed logically its premise that authority flows from above, and that elections of all kinds should be abolished, by eliminating all traces of self-government and replacing local elective mayors with centrally appointed officials.

Fascism and Political Freedom.—The basic element of political freedom, the possibility for the citizen to choose between different courses of action, disappeared. A monopoly of political power was in the hands of the Fascist Party. Within this framework, all other freedoms disappeared. Freedom of association was suppressed. All groups had to receive the government's stamp of approval. Freedom of assembly and freedom of speech were similarly limited. Freedom of the press continued to exist only within the framework of the interests of the ruling ideology. The courageous resistance of the great majority of non-Fascist papers was finally overcome in 1925. In that year, a law was passed which required each newspaper to accept a government-appointed director. Thereafter, only Fascist papers existed, distinguished among themselves only by the degree of virulence in their vocabulary and by the degree of proximity to the treasury of the Fascist Party (some of them had to be financed outright by the party, while others bearing old and famous names continued to be financially self-supporting). Their make-up, headlines, and general distribution of contents were regulated by a central propaganda office in Rome. There was no old-fashioned censorship: no modern dictator could stand the sight of newspapers appearing with large blank spaces on the front page. By far the most effective method was that of decreeing every day what the papers should print.

Fascism and Economic Life.—Having destroyed civil liberties, fascism could not maintain freedom in the economic sphere. The system of regulation which began in 1926 with the establishment of syndicates, as the monopolistic Fascist trade unions were called, was extended gradually to all spheres of economic life. The Fascist economic controls sprang both from a desire for regulating people's lives and from the logic of a political system which very soon made war its final goal. When, during the depression of the early 1930's, fascism gained control of a sizable portion of the industry and the banking structure of Italy, the element of chance was still very great. After 1935, however, the extension of government controls became a deliberate policy. These were the years when the corporative system was put into effect and was hailed by Fascist apologists as an epoch-making discovery, giving economic life its due in a world accustomed for too long to recognize the primacy of political values. But the corporative system was nothing but a screen hiding the much simpler reality of mobilization for aggressive war.

Fascism and the People.—There were three major phases in the relation of the Italian people to fascism. The first was the long and generally unrecognized period of resistance which extended from 1920 to 1926. This was a time of warfare in which substantial numbers of people actively participated. The costly fight was unavailing. The second phase lasted from 1926 to 1936. It was a period of resignation and of open allegiance on the part of many who were satisfied by the limited economic improvement which then took place. This was a time when opposition to fascism seemed the attitude of Utopian dreamers who failed to notice the worldwide chorus of approval for the system. The third phase extended from 1936 to 1943. The Ethiopian War (1935–1936) brought home to many the realization of what fascism meant. Extensive underground activities began, and free Italy matched the Fascist intervention in Spain in support of Gen. Francisco Franco with an anti-Fascist intervention of thousands of courageous fighters in defense of democratic institutions. The name of Carlo Rosselli, publisher of an anti-Fascist Italian weekly in France, should be remembered at this point. It was because he symbolized the new Italy which was being born that Mussolini had him murdered in France in 1937 together with his brother Nello. With the beginning of World War II, anti-Fascist activities became more intense and new and old party lines began to be drawn. In the spring of 1943, strikes and other openly rebellious movements took place, and, under the joint impact of British and American invasion and popular revolt, fascism quickly disintegrated. It was obvious that it had long since ceased to command the allegiance of the great majority of the Italian people, who were slowly and confusedly groping their way toward some new kind of political organization. This is not to say that 21 years of Fascist rule could go by without leaving profound consequences. The old cynicism of a very old people had increased. The lack of morality in public life which had characterized fascism was not entirely remedied, and new generations wholly innocent of democratic processes still found it easier to accept slogans and goals which were only thinly separated from Fascist ideology. The recovery of the mind was going to be a slower process than the recovery of the body. (See also FASCISM.)

THE TRANSITIONAL PERIOD: 1943–1946

With the Allied invasion of Italy, beginning in July 1943, Allied Military Government (AMG) was imposed on the areas freed from German occupation. The existence of AMG did not mean that the Italian state had ceased to exist. A government recognized by the Allied powers was at all times in existence after the downfall of the Fascist regime on July 25, 1943. There was thus no break in the continuity of the Italian state such as occurred in the case of Germany. In practice, the functions of the Italian government were suspended for a time and then gradually restored as the military front advanced toward the north. By the end of 1945 the Italian government had reacquired substantial jurisdiction over the entire national territory with the exception of the colonies and certain border areas. To a far greater degree than in any other former enemy territory, the functions of AMG were limited to zones of immediate military significance and to a generic and limited task of control of the activities of the committees of national liberation and of the Italian government itself. This limited control points up the fact that in Italy far more than Germany the hold of the Fascist dictatorship was a superficial one, and one quickly eliminated by the unfolding of historical events.

The Forty-five Days.—From July 25 to Sept. 8, 1943, Italy underwent a strange experience. Seeking peace, yet still appearing to fight on the side of Germany, the country got rid of its Fascist government and made a hopeful beginning toward the reassertion of democratic liberties. In this period, Germany refrained from open intervention and occupation of the territory of its ally. Political parties emerged from hiding, and a free press, subject only to normal military censorship, began to appear. In these weeks government was headed by Marshal Pietro Badoglio, whose authority extended throughout the peninsula. The machinery of the state seemed intact, and many Italians hoped that the change from war to peace could be achieved without destructive consequences.

Occupation and Liberation.—The scene changed overnight after the announcement, on September 8, of the armistice concluded with the Allies. Acting swiftly, Germany occupied all of northern and central Italy. (After the fall of Naples, on October 1, the battleline was stabilized north of that city.) The Allied inability to make landings to the north meant the beginning of a long military struggle which ended only in April 1945. As an effective administrative machinery the Italian government disappeared in northern Italy, where a rump Fascist republic was organized under German control in September 1943. Until the occupation of Rome (June 4, 1944), the Badoglio government continued in office. This was the period when the government of Italy was effectively in the hands of AMG. After the liberation of Rome, the first political government was formed under Ivanoe Bonomi, on June 9. Finally, with the liberation of the north, a new government, deemed representative of the new Italian political forces, was formed under the underground leader Ferruccio Parri, on June 17, 1945. The old Italy was fading away, and new political figures were asserting themselves. The Parri government lasted until Nov. 24, 1945. Shortly thereafter, on December 10, the first Alcide de Gasperi government was formed on the assumption that political responsibility should belong primarily to the largest organized political party, the Christian Democrats.

The Republic.—Throughout this period the monarchy survived, if not unchallenged, at least undisturbed. A violent debate raged among the advocates of immediate elimination of the monarchy, of abdication of the king, and of the status quo. It was finally decided to submit the issue to a popular referendum to be held on June 2, 1946, together with elections for a constituent assembly. Shortly before the date fixed for the referendum, on May 9, Victor Emmanuel III abdicated in favor of his son, who ascended the throne as Humbert II. This move was interpreted as an attempt to improve the chances of the monarchy by eliminating from the debate the person judged by most to bear a heavy responsibility for fascism.

The results of the referendum went against the monarchy by a fairly small margin (12,717,932 to 10,719,284), with the north voting overwhelmingly in favor of the republic and the south overwhelmingly in favor of the monarchy. The new king accepted the results of the referendum after some hesitation and left with his family for Portugal on June 13. With the proclamation of the Italian Republic on June 10, the 9-century rule of the house of Savoy came to an end.

THE POSTWAR POLITICAL LANDSCAPE

The accompanying table compares the results of the last Italian elections before fascism and of the two general elections of 1946 and 1948. The figures show that the Right and Liberal Center suffered major defeats in the 1946 and 1948 elections, with many of their followers voting in 1948 for the Christian Democratic Party because of its strong anti-Communist position. The Christian Democrats gained ground steadily since 1921, with a remarkable upswing in the 1948 elections. Their parliamentary majority after 1948 had no precedent in the history of Italy since 1876. The percentage strength of the Marxist parties remained substantially the same in 1946 and 1948. Since 1921, however, the Communists gained much more than the Socialists. In the elections of 1948 the Christian Democrats improved their position throughout the country, while the Communists, defeated in their strongholds in the industrial north, made up for the loss by gaining among the peasants of the south.

From the point of view of ideology, the Christian Democratic Party, which bore the main burden of governmental responsibilities following the 1948 elections, occupied a difficult middle position between the old individualistic approach to economic and political problems and the new collectivistic concepts. If, on the one hand, it was anxious to maintain the value and the function of the individual citizen in a political sense and to build a constitutional system in which individual freedoms would be strongly guaranteed, on the other, it stressed the need for collective intervention and planning in the economic sphere. Here, again, however, the importance attached to the methods to be followed and to the choice to be made between different solutions stood out in contrast to the simplified centralizing solutions of the Marxist parties. With regard to the equally important question of limits to state intervention, the Christian Democrats proposed that private activities should have full room for development and that state intervention should not extend to more than a part of the economic activity of the country.

To the Communists, questions of limits, procedures, and alternatives had a more limited appeal, since they did not occupy a middle position on the political stage, but wholeheartedly favored a given type of political and economic solution based theoretically on Marxism, but practically on the interpretation which Soviet Russia has given of Marxism. As such, they were the bearers of a specific set of economic and political solutions which they claimed to be the true solutions from which no deviation was possible. They had before them the concrete example of the Soviet Union and did not intend to deviate in any substantial respect from the general structure established there. The compromises which the Italian Communists appeared in 1948 to be willing to accept, such as the right of the individual peasant to own his own land, did not have a persuasive quality and were not believed to have any chance of survival in an economy as fully collectivized as that envisaged by the Communists. Their view of government appeared to be one in which there would be no room for the peaceful rotation in office of different political parties. It is true that in 1945 a leading Italian Communist said that he saw the possibility of normal competition between two fundamental political currents, the bourgeois or conservative one on the one hand, and the popular or progressive one on the other. But more and more thereafter the Communist tendency was to identify as democratic forces only those whose political activities could be tolerated from the Communist point of view or, at any rate, not to consider any government democratic in which the Communists did not participate.

ELECTIONS TO THE ITALIAN CHAMBER OF DEPUTIES
VOTES AND SEATS: 1921, 1946, AND 1948
(Votes in thousands)

Parties	1921			1946 [1]			1948 [2]		
	Votes	Per cent of total	Seats	Votes	Per cent of total	Seats	Votes	Per cent of total	Seats
Right	1,290	19.6	107	2,626	11.4	66	1,934	7.4	32
Liberal Center	1,712	25.9	157	2,287	10.0	55	1,215	4.6	19
Christian Democrats	1,347	20.4	108	8,083	35.2	207	12,752	48.7	307
Socialists	1,631	24.7	123	4,745	20.7	115	4,739	18.4	81
Communists	305	4.7	15	4,343	18.9	104	4,886	18.5	132
Others	323	4.7	25	869	3.8	9	638	2.4	3
Total	6,608	100.0	535	22,953	100.0	556	26,164	100.0	574

[1] Constituent Assembly.
[2] Figures rearranged to make them comparable with previous returns.

After World War II, the Socialists in the main tended to go along with the general attitudes and policies of the Communists, and it soon became clear that the party leadership aimed at an eventual fusion of the two parties. To the old-line Socialists, brought up in the humanitarian and free traditions of the British Labour Party, the possibility of adhering entirely to Communist theories and practices did not look attractive. When all efforts failed to maintain the Socialists as an autonomous party, the anti-Communist Socialists split from the main body of the party in January 1947, and two Socialist parties resulted. Thereafter, the larger of the two pursued a policy of close alliance with the Communists over what appeared by 1949 increasing internal opposition. The other tried to maintain itself as an independent workers' movement inspired by Marxism but modeling its political activities on the pattern established by the Socialist parties of western Europe. In the elections of 1948 this group won over to its side the allegiance of some middle-class groups which had hitherto been frightened by the Communist leanings of socialism.

THE CONSTITUTION OF 1948

The Italian Constitution is the result of a year-and-a-half's work by the Constituent Assembly elected in June 1946. The final text, approved by the assembly in December 1947, and put into effect on Jan. 1, 1948, without need for popular referendum, reflects on the whole, and to a greater extent than had the original draft, the numerical superiority of the Christian Democrats over the Marxist parties. It retains, in less ambiguous terms and with greater attention to the demands of common sense, the major solutions which had asserted themselves since the opening of the debate:

(1) A bill of rights which, in its political aspects, is inspired essentially by the individualistic tradition of human rights.

(2) A bill of economic rights and duties incorporating the contemporary version of the duties of the community and of the state toward the individual, and of the duties of the individual toward the state, such as his duty to work. There is no specific mandate to nationalize basic industries.

(3) A central administrative system which has yielded some of its powers in favor of regionalism. Nevertheless, sufficient power is vested in the central government to make the reality or ultimate success of the regional experiment a matter of doubt.

(4) A parliamentary system of government in which a balance of power between the executive and legislative branches is envisaged. Two equally powerful legislative bodies, a Chamber of Deputies and a Senate, are provided for.

(5) A Constitutional Court. For the first time in Italian history, an attempt has been made to imitate the American tradition of a court with power to declare laws unconstitutional.

The Bill of Rights.—The constitution vests sovereignty in the people and declares Italy to be a democratic republic based on labor. The initial attempt to declare that political rights are dependent upon the fulfillment of some activity or function contributing to the material or spiritual development of society was abandoned, as were several other Communist-inspired imitations of phraseology borrowed from the Eastern European "people's democracies." With certain limitations, all fundamental personal and political freedoms are recognized. Two of these limitations deserve mention. First, all secret associations are forbidden, as are groups which pursue political aims through military means. The revival of Fascist societies is prohibited. Second, in guaranteeing freedom of the press and of other means of communication of thought. the constitution declares that violation of press laws may justify government seizure in cases of extreme urgency and in cases where judicial intervention cannot be obtained in time to prevent publication of the offending material. Judicial support must, however, be procured within 48 hours in order to validate such action.

Trade unions must be organized democratically and must obtain recognition by the state. Thereafter, unions may negotiate collective contracts binding upon all workers affected by the contract, whether they are union members or not. The right to strike may be exercised only within the limits of the laws regulating it.

Both private and public property are recognized. The former is guaranteed by law, although limits may be set to its accumulation and use in order to make it accessible to all and to establish equitable social relationships. For the sake of the general welfare, the state may transfer to itself or to workers' or consumers' cooperatives enterprises in the fields of public service and power, and monopolies. By recognizing the general principle that certain fields of economic activity may come under state supervision, while private property and the right of private economic initiative survive, the constitution makes possible an experimental approach to the problems of the future.

Church and State.—The problem of the relationship of the Italian state to the Roman Catholic Church had finally been settled by the Lateran Treaty and the Concordat of 1929. The Lateran Treaty resolved the question of the pope's temporal possessions in Italy. On the one hand, papal sovereignty over the state of Vatican City was recognized; on the other, the pope gave belated official acknowledgment of the unity of the Italian people by recognizing the Kingdom of Italy as then constituted. In the concordat, the wholly different matter of the relationship between church and state in Italy was settled. Roman Catholicism was recognized as the state religion, and the right of the Italian government to approve the appointment of bishops was admitted, while the requirements of religious teachings and the legal validity of religious marriage were recognized.

After the end of fascism, no responsible voice was raised to maintain that the Lateran Treaty should be abrogated. The territorial and political settlement contained in that treaty still appeared the best solution of a difficult problem. But the concordat was viewed in a different light. Disregarding the privileges which had been granted to the Italian government, which permitted it to control to a large extent the life of the church in Italy, the critics of the concordat objected to the provisions which gave the Roman Catholic religion a position which formally could not be equaled by other religious confessions. The proposals advanced varied from outright repeal to substantial modifications, particularly in the direction of ending the recognition of Roman Catholicism as the state religion. Against these proposals the Christian Democratic Party waged a successful fight. Article 7 of the constitution, voted with full Communist support, reads: "The state and Catholic Church are, within their respective spheres, independent and sovereign. Their relationships are regulated by the Lateran treaties." This makes the Concordat of 1929 a part of the constitution. The unbalance created by this inclusion, deprecated by some as unwise, is redressed, however, by a further provision passed by all other parties over Christian Democratic opposition, which makes future negotiated changes possible without the need for amending the constitution, as well as by Article 8, which declares all religious faiths equally free before the law and recognizes their right to organize themselves freely.

Regionalism.—The attempt made, principally by the Christian Democrats, to decentralize the traditionally highly centralized administration of Italy was a reaction against the Fascist regime's intensification of controls from the center, as well as an endeavor to embody in the constitution the Christian Democratic belief that the region is a natural body which cannot be suppressed. The constitution represents a compromise between the Christian Democratic position and the Communists' insistence that a strong central government would be necessary for postwar economic reconstruction.

The two main traditional units of local government had been the commune (municipality) and the province, the latter being the chief subdivision through which the central government exercised its control over local affairs. Under the Constitution of 1948, an entirely new entity—the region—was created. The boundaries of the regions generally follow the historical boundaries which separated the various states before the unification of Italy. Nineteen autonomous regions are recognized, while special privileged positions are given to the islands of Sicily and Sardinia and to the three frontier regions of Friuli-Venezia Giulia (bordering on Yugoslavia), Trentino-Alto Adige (bordering on Austria), and Valle d'Aosta (bordering on France and Switzerland).

The constitution embodies the following principles:

(1) Each region is governed by a popularly elected regional council, which in turn chooses the regional executive, the president.

(2) Subject to the general principles established by national laws, and provided the national interest and the interests of other regions are safeguarded, the region may issue legislative norms in the fields of local administration and police, local markets and public works, public welfare and health, professional schools, local transportation, agriculture, forestry, and town planning.

(3) In order to carry out its functions, each region is to have financial autonomy within the limits established by national laws. Regions may acquire funds either through their own taxation or through receipt of parts of the revenue of the central government.

(4) The central government maintains powers of control over the regions in several significant ways:

(a) Regional councils can be dissolved for acts contrary to national unity, serious violation of national laws, failure to remove the regional president after the central government has asked for his removal for similar acts, reasons of national safety, or inability of a council to function. This power of dissolution is exercised by the president of the republic after he has heard a joint parliamentary committee on regional questions. The control thus given to the central government is sufficient to indicate that regions are far from autonomous.

(b) The government maintains continuous control over the legislative enactments of the regions. Laws approved by a regional council must be transmitted to a representative of the national government resident in the regional capital. The government can return them to the council because they exceed regional jurisdiction or conflict with the interests of the nation or of other regions, or can challenge their constitutionality.

(c) Each region is to have a constitution or statute of its own. First approved by the regional council, the statute must also be embodied in a law of the republic. Presumably, it would not be approved if it contained anything considered to conflict with the national constitution.

In summary, it may be said that useful tasks of a local nature are given to the regions, and opportunity is afforded for training in citizenship, administration, and independent thinking. This is a positive gain over the old system. Nevertheless, this attempt to combine strong central administration with quasi federalism leaves a sufficient preponderance of power in the national government to indicate that regions are not to play as significant a role as the Christian Democrats had hoped.

Legislative Power.—Defeating all Communist proposals in favor of a single legislative assembly, the Constituent Assembly organized the legislative system as follows:

(1) Legislative powers are divided equally between a Chamber of Deputies and a Senate. Each has jurisdiction and powers equal to the other. The two chambers are brought together as a National Assembly in cases prescribed by the constitution.

(2) The Chamber of Deputies is elected for a term of five years by universal suffrage. The system of election, not provided for in the constitution, is that of proportional representation with preferential voting. The number of deputies is 574.

(3) The Senate is elected on a regional basis with each region except Valle d'Aosta sending at least six senators. There is one senator for every 200,000 inhabitants. Senators hold office for six years and are elected under a hybrid system combining features of both majority and proportional representation. Total normal elective membership of the Senate is 237. In addition, but for the period 1948–1954 only, there are a number of senators of right. (In 1948, there were in all 344 senators.)

(4) Since the two chambers have equal legislative powers, unresolved conflicts would presumably lead to dissolution by the president of one or both of the chambers. The constitution itself is silent on this point.

(5) The limited use of popular referendum and initiative is admitted.

The President of the Republic and the Cabinet.—Both the initial draft and the final text show a strong effort to create a relationship between executive and legislature similar to the British one. The final text, overcoming Communist-Socialist opposition, provides for greater executive powers than even the draft had allowed.

The president of the republic is elected for seven years by the two chambers meeting in joint session, and by three representatives from each regional council except that of Valle d'Aosta, which sends one representative. His foremost power is that of dissolution of the chambers at any time except during his last six months in office. He can send back to the chambers, within the time limit allowed for promulgation, and with a message stating his reason for such action, any bill of which he disapproves. Presidential promulgation must follow if the bill is again approved by the chambers. He can also send general messages to the chambers, and he must authorize the presentation of government bills. In addition to the powers already mentioned, the president, as chief of state and symbol of national unity, receives and accredits diplomatic representatives, ratifies treaties, commands the armed forces, and declares war upon decision of Parliament.

The prime minister and, upon his advice, the members of the Cabinet are appointed by the president. The Cabinet as a whole must seek the confidence of Parliament within 10 days of its appointment and must continue to enjoy that confidence if it is to remain in office. A vote of nonconfidence by one house is sufficient to overthrow a Cabinet, but three days must elapse before a vote on a motion of nonconfidence may be taken.

The prime minister is responsible for the direction of the general policies of the government and for the maintenance of unified political and administrative action among the ministries. Executive decree laws are legitimized, though only in extraordinary cases of necessity and urgency, and under rigid conditions.

The Constitutional Court.—The strongest pressure in favor of a Constitutional Court came from the Christian Democrats.

The court is composed of 15 justices nominated for terms of 12 years, one third by the president, one third by Parliament, and one third by the highest ordinary and administrative courts. It has jurisdiction over the constitutionality of both national and regional laws, conflicts between regions and the national government, and the impeachment of the president and Cabinet members. The question of constitutionality may be raised by the bench or by either party to a judicial action. Decisions of the court are final, and laws declared unconstitutional cease to have effect one day after publication of the court's decision. There is no time limit on the testing of a law's constitutionality.

Bibliography.—Sturzo, Luigi, *Italy and Fascism* (New York 1927); Croce, Benedetto, *A History of Italy, 1871–1914* (Oxford 1929); Salvemini, Gaetano, *Under the Axe of Fascism* (New York 1936); Borgese, G. A., *Goliath, The March of Fascism* (New York 1937); Binchy, D. A., *Church and State in Fascist Italy* (New York 1941); Matthews, H. L., *The Fruits of Fascism* (New York 1943); Sprigge, C. J. S., *The Development of Modern Italy* (New Haven 1944); Sturzo, Luigi, *Italy and the Coming World* (New York 1945).

MARIO EINAUDI,
Professor of Government, Cornell University.

NOTE: The foregoing 10 articles on Italy were prepared under the joint direction of the editor of the Encyclopedia Americana and Dr. Mario Einaudi, professor of government at Cornell University.

ITALY, Free Church in, the Evangelical Italian Church, a reformed religious sect founded in 1870 by Alessandro Gavazzi (q.v.). In 1874, a confession of faith was formulated, an ecclesiastical constitution framed under a general assembly, and the title "Free Church in Italy" assumed. The confession resembles that of other Protestant churches, and the constitution is based on a government by elders, like that of the Presbyterians, although the several congregations are practically uncentralized. In 1891, by royal decree, the title "Chiesa Evangelica Italiana" was given to this body. Elementary and Sunday schools are maintained. The schools of the church in Florence are partially supported by the state, and a gift bought and presented by British friends is the old church of San Jacopo, Florence.

ITASCA, ī-tăs'kȧ, **Lake,** farthest source of the Mississippi, in Clearwater County, northwestern Minnesota. It is located at about 47°13'10"N., and 95°12'W., at an altitude of 1,457 feet above sea level. It was first definitely proved to be the source of the Mississippi by Henry Rowe Schoolcraft (q.v.) in 1832, as a result of a journey of exploration undertaken under the auspices of the United States government. At the same time it received its name by a fanciful combination of the last four letters of the Latin word *veritas* (truth) and the first syllable of *caput* (head). The ground has a substratum of sand and gravel, mingled with large boulders, and the surface is swampy. The basin has been made into a state park of 30.78 square miles. In the center, fed by springs so permanent and with a flood plain so small that it has actually risen in dry seasons, is the lake, which has an area of only 1¾ square miles. It consists of a center running east and west for about a mile, with two arms in the south, each about 1½ miles long, and another in the north about 1 mile long. The shoreline extends more than 13 miles; the average depth is 20 to 35 feet. The Mississippi flows from the north arm. See also MISSISSIPPI RIVER. Consult Clarke, H., *The Source of the Mississippi* (New York 1886); Winchell, N. H., "The Source of the Mississippi," *Collections,* Minnesota Historical Society, vol. 8, p. 226 (St. Paul 1898); Brower, J. V., *Itasca State Park* (St. Paul 1904).

ITATA CASE, 1891, the cause of differences between Chile and the United States, resulting from the revolt against President José Manuel Balmaceda (q.v.) by the Congressional Party. The latter through an agent had bought a quantity of arms and ammunition in New York, which were shipped to San Francisco and then sent by schooner down the coast, where the cargo was transferred to the insurgents' vessel, the *Itata.* The attorney general issued a writ of detention on the ground that the *Itata* was violating United States neutrality laws. The ship set sail, however, and the U.S.S. *Charleston* was sent in pursuit, overhauled and captured her, and placed her on trial in the United States district court in San Diego. The court discharged the vessel as not having been guilty of violation, but its detention angered the Congressionalists, who had meanwhile been successful in overthrowing Balmaceda. Consult Godkin, E. L., "Itata Case," *The Nation,* 52:416 (1891).

ITCH, a contagious eruption of the skin caused by its invasion by the itch mite (q.v.). See also SCABIES.

ITCH MITE (*Sarcoptes scabiei*), a parasitic mite which enters the skin and multiplies, causing itch or scabies. The female itch mite, which is longer than the male, is about one fifth of an inch in length and is visible to the naked eye. In order to penetrate the horny layer of the epidermis, the mite assumes a nearly perpendicular position; and to avoid as much trouble as possible, it usually selects such spots as give least resistance, such as the space between the fingers, the inside of the wrists, or the groin. Once fairly buried it does not again come out but burrows, and forms tortuous galleries within the skin. These galleries resemble the mark which is formed when a pen is drawn lightly over the skin without causing a scratch. At certain intervals the galleries are pierced by small openings for the admission of air. The vesicles characteristic of the itch disease are attributed to a poison ejected by the mite.

For treatment soften the affected area by massaging it with green soap and warm water, then apply a sulphur ointment. All clothing that has come in contact with the infection should be boiled.

ITHACA, city, New York, and seat of Tompkins County, at an altitude of 389 feet, situated at the southern end of Cayuga Lake, 29 miles northeast of Elmira, and served by the Lehigh Valley and the Delaware, Lackawanna and Western railroads and state highways. Its industrial products include power drive chains, adding machines, shotguns, salt, cement, ladies' underwear, electric clocks, fertilizers, clay products, leather goods, paper, technical apparatus, and shirts. Through Cayuga Lake, the city has shipping access to the New York State Barge Canal System, and it also has a municipal airport, one mile outside the city, with a scheduled airline service.

One of the major educational centers in the state of New York, Ithaca is the seat of Cornell University (q.v.), the state colleges of Veterinary Medicine (founded 1894), Agriculture (founded 1904) and Home Economics (founded 1925), all located on the Cornell University campus, and Ithaca College, founded in 1892, with over 1,300 students (1951). The city's library has some 48,000 volumes, the Cornell University library more than 1,500,000 volumes. The historical society maintains a museum, and there are several special museums at Cornell.

The city has three general hospitals and one state hospital. There are three state parks nearby and Stewart Park, at the head of the lake, is the city's principal place of outdoor recreation. It has as notable and distinctive features the Renwick Bird Sanctuary and the Fuertes Wildfowl Sanctuary. These refuges are maintained by the city in cooperation with the ornithology department of the university. There is a memorial gateway with a tablet commemorating Louis Agassiz Fuertes, who was born at Ithaca and painted many of his famous bird pictures there.

First settled in 1788, Ithaca was named by Simeon De Witt, surveyor general of New York State, in 1806, following a military survey of central New York. It was during that time, the first decade of the 19th century, that many towns received names of ancient Greek and Roman origin. It was incorporated as a city in 1888 and is governed by a mayor and council. Pop. (1950) 29,257.

ITHACA, ĭth'ȧ-kȧ (Gr. ITHÁKĒ, ē-thä'kyē), one of the Ionian Islands, Greece, and the smallest except Paxos, 17 miles northwest of the mainland of Greece and two miles northeast of Cephalonia, with which it forms Cephalonia Department. The surface is divided into two mountainous masses, with a narrow isthmus between, but there are many pleasant valleys. The chief products are wine, currants, and olive oil. The island has an area of 36 square miles and was celebrated among the ancients as the home of Odysseus (Ulysses). Vathy (or Ithaca) is the capital. Pop. (1951) 7,083.

ITINERANCY, ī-tĭn'ẽr-ȧn-sĭ, a passing from place to place. In ecclesiastical usage, the Methodist system of limited pastorates instituted by John Wesley. In the American Methodist Episcopal Church no time limit has been placed on pastorates since 1900, although the bishop appoints preachers from year to year. See also METHODISM.

ITINERARY or ITINERARIUM, the schedule of a route or table of the stages between two places of importance with the distances from one to another. Much of our knowledge of ancient geography is due to the itineraries issued by ancient peoples. Of these the best known are *Itinararium Antonini,* a sketch of the stations and distances along various Roman roads; *Itinerarium maritimum,* giving the distances from Corinth to Sicily and Carthage, made during the reign of Antoninus Pius; and *Itinerarium Hierosolymitanum,* made by a Christian pilgrim in 333 A.D. The first mentioned itinerary contains the *Itinerarium Proviniarum Anto(ni)ni Augusti,* further accounts of distances and stations in the Roman provinces.

ITIUS PORTUS, the port on the French coast, nearly opposite Dover, from which Julius Caesar sailed on his second expedition to Britain in 54 B.C. Its position has been a matter of much controversy, but the majority of geographers identify it with Wissant, a village nine miles west-southwest of Calais.

ITO, ē-tō, MARQUIS **Hirobumi,** Japanese statesman: b. Choshu, Sept. 2, 1841; d. Harbin, Manchuria, Oct. 26, 1909. His father was a samurai retainer of the daimio of Choshu, with whom the youth became a trusted agent in his opposition to the shogunate. While at Yedo in the interests of his chief, Ito became acquainted with western methods of warfare, consequent on the visit of Commodore Matthew C. Perry in 1854, and determining to study these in their native countries, with four comrades, including Kaoru Inouye, left Japan secretly, and eventually arrived in London. Diplomatic complications arising, owing to his daimio ignoring the right conferred by the shogun on European powers to navigate the Inland Sea, Ito hastened home before two years had elapsed, but was unsuccessful in his efforts to persuade the daimio of Choshu from opposing the European fleets assembled at Shimonoseki. The daimio defeated, Japan awakened to the power of the West, and Ito became the impelling factor in its reorganization on models more in accord with the leading powers of the world. He took an active part in the overthrow of the shogunate and the restoration of the imperial power in the person of the emperor or mikado; in 1868 was appointed governor of Hiogo, and in 1869 vice minister of finance. He then became prominent as an advocate of uniform coinage. In this connection he visited the United States and after studying the financial system of that country returned to Japan with the recommendation that the decimal system of money be adopted, which was done, and a mint established at Osaka. In 1871–1873 he made a tour of the world, as a member of Prince Tomomi Iwakura's embassy, for the purpose of revising or modifying the treaties then in force. In 1872 he became minister of public works in which office he established a college of engineering and secured the building of the railway from Yokohama to Tokyo. In 1876 he again visited Europe to study the constitutions of the various countries for the purpose of remodelling that of Japan. On his return he inaugurated a radical plan for changing social customs. Having become minister president of state he started these reforms in the government offices, eliminating men of the old schools and substituting men of modern training and thought. He also reconstructed the laws and codes according to the ideas of western countries and carried out many reforms in economy. In 1882, the emperor, desirous of adopting the constitutional form of government, commissioned Ito to proceed to Europe and America in order to investigate the governmental systems of the two continents. While in Europe he attended the coronation ceremony of Czar Alexander III, as a representative of Japan, and returning in the following year, he began the work of drafting the constitution of the Empire. One year later Ito was appointed minister of the imperial household and created count.

As premier for four various periods between 1886 and 1901, he successfully saw the constitution that he and Kimmochi Saionji had so laboriously worked on proclaimed in 1889, was appointed president of the House of Peers when the Japanese Imperial Diet first convened, and concluded with China the Shimonoseki Treaty after the Chinese-Japanese War of 1894–1895 (for which he was created marquis in 1895). He resigned his fourth premiership in June 1901 and was later appointed president of the privy council. He failed to reach an understanding with Russia and at once opened negotiations which resulted in the Anglo-Japanese alliance of 1902. During the war with Russia (1904–1905) Marquis Ito, as one of the "elder statesmen" was the most trusted counsellor of the emperor. After the conclusion of peace which he did much to bring about, he was twice dispatched to Korea, these visits resulting in the Japan-Korea Treaty, declaring the Japanese protectorate over the peninsula. The marquis was ultimately appointed resident general of Korea, which high office he held until 1909 when he retired to become president of the privy council. He was assassinated by a Korean while visiting Manchuria.

Bibliography.—Kuramata, K., *A Maker of New Japan: Marquis Ito's Experience* (London 1904); Ladd, G. T., *In Korea with Marquis Ito* (New York 1908); Nakamura, K., *Prince Ito, the Man and Statesman* (New York 1910).

ITRI, town, Italy, in Rome Province, Latium, six miles north-northwest of Gaeta. It contains many ancient remains and has many houses erected from stone taken from the Via Appia, which runs past the town. Itri, with its cork industry, was heavily damaged during World War II. Pop. (1936) 6,219.

ITURBI, ē-tōōr′bē, **José,** Spanish-American conductor and pianist: b. Valencia, Spain, Nov. 28, 1895. One of the finest of concert pianists in contemporary America, Iturbi has given more concerts in the United States than any other pianist, with the exception of Ignace Jan Paderewski, and has broken box office records wherever he appeared.

He studied piano at the Valencia Conservatory (1908) and the Paris Conservatory, graduating with highest honors in 1912. After playing a short while in a fashionable café in Zurich, he became head of the pianoforte department of the Geneva Conservatory (1919–1923), leaving to devote himself to concert recitals. He was an immediate success, touring all of Europe, South America, and, from 1928, the United States with constant acclaim.

In one year alone (1930) he played 77 concerts in America, and during his tours averaged 100 concerts a year. In 1933 he turned his attention to conducting, directing 15 concerts at Mexico City and later that year appearing as a conductor at the Lewisohn Stadium, New York City. He appeared in 1934 as guest conductor of the Philadelphia Orchestra and since then he has continued to conduct major orchestras throughout the United States, being appointed permanent director of the Rochester Philharmonic Orchestra in 1936.

In 1938 he toured South America as conductor and pianist, and in 1941 took out citizenship papers in the United States. He has appeared in several motion pictures, among them *As Thousands Cheer* (1944), *Anchors Aweigh* (1945), and *Three Daring Daughters* (1948).

ITURBIDE, ē-tōōr-bē′thä, **Agustín de,** emperor of Mexico: b. Valladolid (now Morelia), Mexico, Sept. 27, 1783; d. Padilla, State of Tamaulipas, Mexico, July 19, 1824. In 1810 he was lieutenant in the provincial regiment of his native city, but on the breaking out of the troubles in Mexico joined the royalist party, and in this cause displayed such valor and ability that in 1816 he rose to the command of what was called the Northern Army, which occupied the provinces of Guanajuato and Michoacán. In 1820 the imprudent acts of the Spanish Cortes produced so much exasperation among the clergy and the partisans of absolutism in Mexico that these persons united to effect the independence of their country, selecting Iturbide as their agent and appointing him commander of the army in the south. He issued with Vicente Guerrero the Plan of Iguala for the unification of Mexico in February 1821, and other revolutionary forces quickly joined him. He quickly bore down all opposition, forced the signing of the Treaty of Córdoba in August 1821 acknowledging Mexico's independence, and was proclaimed emperor of Mexico in May 1822 under the name of Agustín I.

His troubled reign, during which he showed great arrogance, disregard of all constitutional restraints, and cruelty toward his opponents, came to an end in less than a year, by his abdication in March 1823, after Santa Anna's pronouncement against him. He went with his family to Leghorn, Italy, where he resided for a year until he was induced to make an attempt to recover his lost crown. He first went to London where he published his famous *Statement of Some of the Principal Events in the Public Life of Agustín de Iturbide* (translated into English in 1824) and sailed for Mexico, May 11, 1824. He landed with but a single attendant at Soto la Marina on July 15, 1824, but immediately was arrested and four days later was shot by order of the state of Tamaulipas without even being given a chance to appeal to Congress. His remains were, in 1838, brought to Mexico City and repose in its cathedral. At the same time he was officially invested with the title "Liberator." See also MEXICO—*History*.

Bibliography.—Bustamante, C. M. de, *Historia del Emperador Agustín de Iturbide* (Mexico 1846); Navarro y Rodrigo, Carlos, *Agustín de Iturbide* (Mexico 1906); Bulnes, Francisco, *La Guerra de Independencia, Hidalgo-Iturbide* (Mexico 1910).

ITURAEA or **ITUREA**, ĭt-ū-rē′ȧ, Biblical country, Palestine, the historical name of the district now in the province of Damascus, Syria, south of Mount Hermon and northeast of the Sea of Galilee. The Ituraeans were seminomadic Arabs, supposed to have been descendents of Jetur, a son of Ishmael, who had migrated northwards from Medina. In the 2d century B.C. they were subjugated by Aristobulus I (Judah), "the friend of the Greeks" and king of Judaea, who added their land to his kingdom and compelled them to accept Judaism. In 20 B.C. the district came under the rule of Herod the Great and at his death (4 B.C.) fell to his son Philip the Tetrarch, who is mentioned by Luke 3:1 as tetrarch of the Iturean and Trachonitic region. In 44 A.D. the district became part of the Roman province of Syria, and many of the inhabitants became soldiers in the Roman legions. They were celebrated as archers, brave and fearless, often mentioned by Julius Caesar, Strabo, and Flavius Josephus. Marc Antony is accused of attempting to intimidate the Roman Senate with his Ituraean guards by Cicero in his *Philippics*.

ITZA, ēt′sä, a Mayan people of northern Guatemala. They came thither from Yucatán in the 15th century after the fall of the Maya Empire and settled on the shores of Lake Petén. Hernando Cortes saw them in 1525 but the Spaniards did not subdue them until 1697 when their city was taken and pillaged. The records of this people date back to the 4th century and references to them are frequent in all Maya chronicles. Many of their records were destroyed by the Spaniards at the time of the conquest.

ITZCOATL, ĭsh-kō′ä-t′l, or **IZCOHUATL**, first Aztec emperor: b. 1360?; d. ?1440. His reign began in 1427. With his tribe of Tenochas he formed a confederacy with the rulers of Texcoco and Tlacopan against Maxtla of Tepanec, whom they captured after a short campaign and sacrificed to their gods. Itzcoatl instituted many reforms and greatly improved the state of his realm, making Tenochtitlán (Mexico City) a great power and cultural center.

Consult Bancroft, H. H., *Native Races*, vol. 5 (San Francisco 1882).

ITZEHOE, ĭt′sĕ-hō, town, Germany, in Schleswig-Holstein, on the Stor River, 33 miles northwest of Hamburg. It has cement factories, carpet mills, sugar mills, and shipyards, and manufactures soap, chemicals, cigars, nets, wallpaper, machinery, and pumps. It carries on a considerable trade in cattle, grain, lumber, and wine. Among its ancient buildings are the 12th century church of St. Laurence and a convent, now Protestant, founded in 1256. It grew around a castle erected here in 809 and is consequently the oldest town in Holstein, receiving municipal rights in 1238. Pop. (1950) 34,182.

IUKA, ī-ū′kȧ, town, Mississippi, seat of Tishomingo County, 20 miles east-southeast of Corinth, served by the Southern Railroad, in the extreme northeast part of the state. It has manufactures of brick, tile, and crossties, and there are limestone, sandstone, and clay deposits and a mineral spring nearby.

The town was the scene of a severe engagement during the Civil War. Early in September, 1862, it was occupied by a small Union regiment as an outpost. On the morning of September 13, Gen. Sterling Price, moving north from Tupelo with a force of 14,000 men, drove the Union regiment from the village and occupied it. Gen. Ulysses S. Grant had been closely watching the movements of Price and when he heard that he had occupied Iuka he determined to attack. Gen. William S. Rosecrans, who was near Corinth with 9,000 men, was ordered to move south to Rienzi and Jacinto, then eastward and, marching on the roads from Jacinto and Fulton, to attack Iuka from the south. Gen. Edward O. C. Ord, with 6,000 men, was to move along the Memphis and Charleston Railroad to Burnsville, thence by roads north of the railroad, and to attack on the north and west of Iuka.

General Rosecrans made first contact with the enemy on September 19, but due to a confusion of orders, General Ord failed to thrust down at the same time, allowing the Confederate forces to escape from the trap after a severe fight. General Price retreated southward and reached Baldwyn on September 23d. Rosecrans and Ord returned to Corinth. Rosecrans reported a loss of 141 killed, 513 wounded, and 36 missing; Price reported a loss of 86 killed and 408 wounded, although Union estimates placed it much higher.

The town was incorporated in 1857. Pop. (1950) 1,527.

IVAN I, ī-văn′ (called IVAN KALITA, *Moneybags*), prince of Vladimir and grand duke of Moscow: d. 1341. As the prince of Vladimir he was made collector of taxes by the Tatar khan, and by following the policy of rigorously enforcing the payment of tribute to the Tatars, he was able in a short while to dominate Moscow and Tver and also assure his realms of privacy from Tatar intervention. He became grand duke of Moscow in 1328 and vastly extended the dominions of his empire, annexing Rostov in 1330 and Smolensk in 1340. He worked ceaselessly for the unification of his realm, overseeing monetary matters even to the smallest amounts (hence his nickname, Moneybags) and causing the metropolitan see to be transferred to Moscow, thus increasing immensely the importance of the Muscovite kingdom.

Bibliography.—Soloviëv, S. M., *Istoriya Rossii*, vol. 3 (Moscow 1851–59); Presnjakov, A. E., *Obrazovanye velikorusskovo gosudarstva* (Petrograd 1918); Vernadsky, G., *Ancient Russia* (New Haven, Conn. 1943).

IVAN II (called IVAN KRASNY, *the Red*), grand duke of Moscow: b. 1326; d. 1359. The younger son of Ivan I, he became grand duke of Moscow in 1353. Novgorod and several other principalities refused to recognize his title and waged war with him until 1354. His rule was generally weak and colorless, with most of his principalities vowing allegiance but privately going their separate ways. He was the father of Demetrius Donskoi, who built the Kremlin and fought against the Tatars, and by his will divided his dominions among his children, thus increasing the internal discord. For bibliography see IVAN I.

IVAN V, Romanov czar of Russia: b. Aug. 27, 1666; d. Jan. 29, 1696. The son of Czar Alexis I and the half brother of Peter I, with whom he shared the throne, he was a physically and mentally weak ruler, leaving the management of his affairs entirely to his half sister, Sophia, who attempted through various ruses to dethrone Peter and have herself proclaimed empress. Meanwhile Ivan gave himself entirely to religious devotions, and when Sophia was overthrown in 1669 he was deposed. One of his five daughters, Anna Ivanovna, later ascended the throne as empress (r. 1730–1740).

Bibliography.—Soloviëv, S. M., *Istoriya Rossii*, vols. 13 and 14 (Moscow 1851–59); Schliemann, T., *Russland, Polen, und Livland bis ins 17 Jahrhundert*, 2 vols. (Berlin 1886); Bain, R. N., *The First Romanovs* (London 1905).

IVAN VI, Russian czar: b. Aug. 24, 1740; d. Dec. 5, 1764. He was the son of Princess Anna Leopoldovna and Prince Anthony Ulrich of Brunswick-Bevern and the great-grandson of Ivan V. He was named successor to the Russian throne by Anna Ivanovna and on her death in 1740 was proclaimed czar at the age of eight weeks, under the regency of Ernst Johann Biron, duke of Kurland. The latter was overthrown by Ivan VI's mother who assumed the regency, and in December 1741 Elizabeth, the younger daughter of Peter the Great, through a coup d'état, became empress. The infant czar was thrown into prison where he was destined to spend the rest of his days. In the fortress of Schlüsselburg, after 22 years of solitary confinement which had succeeded in deranging his mind, he was murdered by some officers in whose charge he was put to forestall an effort to liberate him.

Bibliography.—Manvillon, E. de, *Histoire de la vie d'Iwan VI* (Paris 1766); Stählin, K., *War der 1764 getotete Gefangene von Schüsselburg der russische Exkaiser Iwan VI?* (Berlin 1927); id., *Geschichte Russlands*, vol. 2 (Berlin 1930).

IVAN III VASILIEVICH (called IVAN THE GREAT), grand duke of Moscow: b. Jan. 22, 1440; d. Oct. 27, 1505. He succeeded his father, Basil II, as grand duke of Moscow in 1462 and continued energetically to strengthen the leadership of Moscow. From 1471 to 1478 he waged two wars on Novgorod, the strongest principality next to Moscow in Russia, and finally conquered and annexed it to the Muscovite kingdom. To further unification, he refused to recognize his brothers' claims to continue lineal inheritance of their principalities and by threat or actual war annexed the principalities of Yarslavl (1463), Rostov (1474), and Tver (1485).

In 1480 he refused to pay the onerous tribute to the Tatar khan and successfully threw off the yoke of Tatar rule in spite of attempts by the latter to regain sovereignty by threat of arms. To gain access to the sea, he twice invaded Lithuania (1492 and 1501), finally acquiring in 1503 a part of it by treaty.

As a result of his second marriage in 1472 to Sophia (Zoë), daughter of Thomas Palaeologus, brother of the last Byzantine emperor, autocratic forms of government and court ceremonies gradually developed at Moscow. This marriage was also important in establishing the claim of Moscow as the protector of Orthodox Christianity. As a further symbol of his identity with the Byzantine Empire and Orthodox Christianity he adopted the Byzantine double-headed eagle into the Muscovite coat of arms. Ivan did much to introduce western civilization into his domains and was also responsible for the compilation of the first Russian law code. The boyars or nobles fell from their high position as advisors to the duke and became mere fiefs of the sovereign. By his last will, leaving all his dominions to the next reigning grand duke rather than dividing them customarily among his children, he established Muscovy as a permanently unified realm.

Bibliography.—Soloviëv, S. M., *Istoriya Rossii*, vol. 5 (Moscow 1851–59); Pierling, P., *La Russie et L'Orient* (Paris 1891); id., *La Russie et le Saint-Siège*, vol. 1 (Paris 1896); Ilovajskij, D. I., *Istoriya Rossii*, vol. 2 (Moscow 1898).

IVAN IV VASILIEVICH (called IVAN THE TERRIBLE), Russian ruler: b. Aug. 25, 1530; d. March 17, 1584. The son of Basil III and grandson of Ivan III, he was proclaimed ruler of Muscovy at the age of three, ruling under the regency of his mother until 1538 and under the regency of the boyars from 1538 to 1544, when at the age of 14 he assumed control of the kingdom himself. On Jan. 16, 1547 he had himself crowned czar of Russia, the first ruler to dare do so, and immediately began forming his government. Having formed a lasting hatred of the power-conniving boyars, he completely broke with them and surrounded himself with able men of humble origin whose interests were primarily for the good of Russia and not themselves.

In 1550 he held the first meeting of the national assembly (Zemski Sobor) and in 1551 he even went so far as to submit a hundred questions to a gathering of prelates concerning the betterment of the government. Constantly seeking ways to enlarge his kingdom, he conquered the khanates of Kazan in 1552 and Astrakhan in 1554. His efforts to acquire additional territory in Livonia and Estonia, though carried on with large forces from 1557 to 1582 almost without intermission, failed as a result of the stout resistance of Poland and Sweden. It was during his reign that the conquest of Siberia was completed by Cossack forces under Ermak Timofeev.

Ivan IV was a peculiar mixture of political sagacity and admiration of western civilization and eastern barbarity. He was an indefatigable worker, comparatively well educated, but possessed such a strong strain of cruelty and immorality that it amounted at times almost to madness, especially after a series of events, including the death of his wife and son, turned him against the world and made him suspect all of attempting to harm him. Amongst his many barbarous deeds was the almost complete destruction of Novgorod and the slaughter of thousands of its inhabitants as punishment for an unproven attempt at revolution (1570). Another deed of similar nature was the killing of his beloved son Ivan by a blow, given in a moment of uncontrollable fury. Twice during his rule (1564 and 1580) he publicly expressed a desire to abdicate, but was persuaded to continue on the throne.

Bibliography.—Pierling, P., *Rome et Moscou, 1547–79* (Paris 1883); id., *Un arbitrage pontifical au XVIe siècle entre la Pologne et la Russie* (Brussels 1890); Pember, A., *Ivan the Terrible* (London 1895); Brückner, A., *Geschichte Russlands bis zum Ende des 18ten Jahrhunderts* (Gotha 1896); Pierling, P., *La Russie et le Saint-Siège*, vol. 2 (Paris 1896); Waliszewski, K., *Ivan le Terrible* (Paris 1904; tr. into English by M. Lloyd, Philadelphia 1904); Bain, R. N., *Slavonic Europe; a Political History of Poland and Russia from 1447 to 1796* (Cambridge 1907); Stählin, K., *Der Briefwechsel Iwans des Schrecklichen mit dem Fürsten Kurbskij* (Leipzig 1921); Platonov, S. F., *Ivan Groznyj* (Saint Petersburg 1923); Graham, S., *Ivan the Terrible* (New Haven, Conn. 1933).

IVANHOE, ī'văn-hō. *Ivanhoe,* written by Sir Walter Scott and published anonymously in 1819, is a story of love and adventure in the days of chivalry. Following his usual practice in the historical novels of interweaving a fictitious romance with actual events, and coloring the whole with the manners of the time, Scott has in *Ivanhoe* produced a picture of the chivalric age which, besides being full of entertainment, serves more effectively than any merely literal history to make the Middle Ages a vivid reality to the imagination. The work is, especially for young students, an excellent introduction to the study of the feudal period in England, and it contributes much toward laying a foundation for the appreciation of romantic literature. Hence its almost universal use as a textbook in the English courses in high schools of the United States.

The period which Scott has chosen is the late 12th century, when the two elements of English society have not united in a common national life. The Saxons, dispossessed of their old inheritance but still constituting the sturdy body of the English people, are set against the Norman conquerors, brilliant feudal lords, endowed with all the knightly graces but haughty and tyrannical. Of each of the two contrasting groups Scott has given a memorable picture. The scene changes from the patriarchal home of Cedric the Saxon, with its rough hospitality and homespun comforts, in which master and serf live on terms of kindly familiarity, to the Norman castle, with its courtly life of hall and bower and the dark mysteries of its gloomy dungeons, then again to the leafy forest, where Robin Hood and his merry men lead the lawless but honorable life of the greenwood. The chief historical event involved in the story is the return of the heroic Richard the Lion-Hearted to England. By seizing the throne from his unpopular brother John, Richard restores justice to the realm and wins the loyalty even of his Saxon subjects.

The fiction of which Ivanhoe is the hero is less interesting than the historical setting and atmosphere which envelop it. The knight, Ivanhoe, son of Cedric, has been disinherited by his father because of his love for the noble Saxon heiress Rowena, whom Cedric hopes to marry to Athelstane, a descendant of Edward the Confessor, thereby uniting the Saxon factions and restoring the ancient monarchy. At the opening of the story Ivanhoe has returned to England from Palestine, where he has won the favor of Richard, disguised as a palmer. Furnished with a suit of armor by the much persecuted Jew, Isaac of York, he appears at the tournament at Ashby, where, after being wounded and forced to reveal himself, he is crowned victor by Rowena. On their return from the tournament the whole party of Cedric is captured and imprisoned in the castle of Torquilstone by a band of Norman nobles led by Maurice de Bracy, who attempts to force Rowena to marry him by threatening the life of Ivanhoe. At the same time the Templar, Brian de Bois Guilbert, seizes Rebecca, daughter of Isaac, and tries in vain to make her his mistress. Meanwhile the castle is attacked by Robin Hood, who, under the name of Locksley, has won the prize for archery at the tournament. Rebecca, who loves Ivanhoe and is nursing him to health by her oriental arts, describes to him from a window the progress of the siege. At length the castle is set on fire by Ulrica, a half crazed Saxon hag, seeking vengeance on the Normans. The Templar flees with Rebecca to the Preceptory of Templestowe. The Jewess is there condemned to death for sorcery and De Bois Guilbert is commanded to appear in the lists against her. He offers to save her if she will accept him, but she refuses and is about to be burned at the stake when suddenly Ivanhoe, still weak from his wounds, appears dramatically as her champion. De Guilbert falls dead at the first encounter and Rebecca is released. Meanwhile John has received word that Richard is in England. The king had in fact been present at the tournament and performed remarkable deeds of valor disguised as The Black Sluggard. Barely escaping by the intervention of the outlaws from a plot of John's to assassinate him, he now reveals himself, resumes his authority, and punishes the traitorous adherents of Prince John. Cedric, whose hope of restoring the Saxon dynasty has fallen with the return of the popular Richard, at last consents to the marriage of Ivanhoe and Rowena.

The story is rich in incident and full of stirring adventure. If the hero and the heroine are somewhat insipid, the other figures, whom Scott sees chiefly in their historical and typical aspects, are vividly portrayed and thoroughly interesting.

JAMES H. HANFORD,
Professor of English, Western Reserve University.

IVANOVO, ĭ-vä'nŭ-vŭ (formerly IVANOVO VOZNESENSK), city, European Union of Soviet Socialist Republics, the capital of the Ivanovo Oblast, south of the Volga River, about 145 miles northeast of Moscow on the unnavigable Klyazma River. It has railways to Moscow, the Urals, and Archangel. The city was founded in the 17th century, and is now often called the "Soviet Manchester," as it is the largest center for cotton cloth manufacture in the USSR. There are also machine building factories and other heavy industries. Most of the city's colleges and research institutes specialize in textile and chemical studies. The city was formed in 1871 by the merging of two towns. The large worker population took an active part in the Revolution of 1917–1918 and the town was made temporary capital of the revolutionary government in 1918. Pop. (1939) 285,069.

IVANOVO OBLAST, district, European Union of Soviet Socialist Republics, in the Central Industrial Region, a wooded steppe area with a moist climate and an area of 24,472 square miles. The region has large cotton cloth and chemical industries, and mines peat extensively. There are textile centers at Ivanovo, Rodniki, Furmanov, Kokhma, and Teykovo, and linen mills at Privolzhsk and Puchezh. Agriculture is important, the main farm products being flax, milk, butter, cheese, potatoes, grain, meat, and vegetables. The region was formerly part of Ivanovo Industrial Area but was recognized as a separate region in 1936. Pop. (1946 est.) 1,500,000.

IVEAGH, 1st Earl of. See GUINNESS, EDWARD CECIL.

IVES, īvz, **Charles Edward,** American composer: b. Danbury, Conn., Oct. 20, 1874. A composer whose works came into prominence some three decades after they were written, Ives is credited with being the pioneer of atonality, first developing such devices as major and minor seconds, quarter tones, polyrhythms, and polyharmonies that Igor F. Stravinsky and Arnold Schönberg were to use with such success later.

His father was a bandmaster and he imparted to his son his experimental work in atonality and acoustics, as well as teaching him harmony, counterpoint, instrumentation, and sight reading. He later studied organ under Dudley Buck and while at Yale University studied with Horatio W. Parker. On his graduation from Yale in 1898 he became a clerk in an insurance firm, opening his own insurance offices in 1906 and continuing active in them until his retirement in 1930.

He wrote most of his important music between 1906 and 1916, composing his pieces after his daily work at the insurance office. His Piano Concerto No. 2 (1911–1915), subtitled *Concord, Mass.*, and divided into the four movements Emerson, Hawthorne, The Alcotts, and Thoreau, was first performed in 1939 and is considered by most critics to be his best piece, wherein the composer attempted to give his "impression of the spirit of the literature, the philosophy, and the men of Concord, Mass."

Another work worth mentioning is his Third Symphony (1911) which was first performed in 1946 by the New York Little Symphony Orchestra, and the following year won for Ives the Pulitzer Prize for music. Ives wrote four symphonies in all, each of which has been called a masterpiece of inventiveness and originality.

Other compositions include chamber music pieces, nearly 150 songs, a series of works celebrating national holidays (1912–1913), and several unique pieces, among them *The Unanswered Question—a Cosmic Landscape* (1908) for orchestra; *Quarter-tone Music* (1913) for chamber orchestra; and *General Booth's Entrance into Heaven* (1914) for chorus and orchestra.

IVES, Frederic Eugene, American inventor: b. Litchfield, Conn., Feb. 17, 1856; d. Philadelphia, Pa., May 27, 1937. He received a public school education and became director of the first photographic laboratory at Cornell University in 1874–1878, later lecturing with distinction before scientific societies in this country and in England.

Among his many important inventions may be mentioned the process of half-tone photoengraving now generally in use (1886), the three color half-tone printing process in the typographic press that is still basically used (1881), and the patented processes of color photography known as Kromskop, Tripak, Hicrom, and Polychrome. He also produced the first trichromatic camera in 1891 and invented a process for making moving pictures in color. Other inventions include a half-tone photogravure process that was a forerunner of the rotogravure process, a short-tube binocular microscope, and a photochromoscope. He was awarded many medals and citations by scientific societies for his inventions.

IVINHEIMA, ē-vē-nyā'mä, river, Brazil, in Mato Grosso state. It is 200 miles long, and flows southeast into the Paraná River.

IVIZA, ē-vē'thä (Span. IBIZA, ē-vē'thä; anc. EBUSUS, ĕb'ū-sŭs), island, the third largest of the Balearic Islands, Spain, in Baleares Province, situated in the Mediterranean Sea, 55 miles southwest of Majorca and about 80 miles east of the coast of Spain. The island, with an area of 230 square miles, is about 25 miles long and 12-13 miles wide, and reaches a maximum altitude of 1,558 feet. The terrain is fertile and, on the hills, heavily wooded. The principal agricultural crops include carobs, figs, almonds, olives, and grapes, and there is extensive raising of hogs. However, the salt works on the southern side of the island and the fisheries form the principal means of income, and charcoal and lead are also exported.

The principal town and the capital is the seaport of Iviza, with a population (1940) of 9,644. It exports figs, raisins, salt, and pine lumber and is a tourist resort. The picturesque surroundings also attract many artists. Several Roman and Phoenician necropolises provide interesting archaeological remains.

The island was early occupied by Nationalist forces during the Spanish Civil War (1936–1939), although it was held for some time against them by Loyalist forces. Pop. (1940) 33,961. See also BALEARIC ISLANDS.

IVORIES. On account of the fineness of its grain, warm tone, the polish it easily acquires, its adaptability to carving, and its incorruptibility, ivory has been a favored medium for plastic art work from the very earliest times. In ancient Egyptian and Assyrian reliefs we see representations of conquered Ethiopians bringing elephant tusks as tribute. In Egypt and Mesopotamia have been found ivory carvings of idols and utensils. But the oldest graphic work on ivory extant is prehistoric and derived from the cave-dwellers when elephants inhabited Europe. Such pieces have been discovered in caves in the Dordogne (France), others in Switzerland. Incised on these pieces of tusk are outlines of reindeer and mammoths. In the Grotte du Pape (France) was found the carved torso of a woman; and so on. In the museums at London, Paris, and Cairo are goodly collections of ivory work done in the early Dynasties of the Egyptians. Two specimens in the Louvre are supposed to be a pair of clappers or castanets; one has rudely incised outlines of figures; the other has a head carved in relief and its extremity is carved in the shape of a beautifully formed hand. The British Museum has two daggers ornamented and inlaid with ivory dating back to the Pharaoh of the Exodus; in the Louvre are a small vase, spoons, and toilet boxes.

Next in date are pieces from Assyria, of which 50 remarkable pieces of ivory from Nineveh are in the British Museum; they were taken from the ruins of the Palace of Nimrod and have evidently suffered badly from fire. In the collection are fragments of winged sphinxes, plaques from a throne or couch, probably; a lion's head, portions of bulls' bodies, and human heads, hands, and legs. Other museums have daggers, sword handles, sceptres, and musical instruments. The ancient Greeks used ivory on their large statues putting gold on the marble form for clothing and ivory for the flesh parts —they called the work "chryselephantine"; nothing is extant but the records. The Roman consular diptychs are the earliest refined ivory carving existing, with few exceptions. Probably of the 3d century A.D. is the beautiful statuette of Penthea in Cluny Museum; it is 15 inches high. The ancient head of a woman in the Vienna Museum is of fine workmanship, nearly half natural size. Found in Etruscan tombs (Chiusi and Calvi) are a few ivory examples dating, probably, back to the 4th century B.C., such as a Gorgon head with eyes of gold inlaid, horses' heads, lions, parts of mirrors and caskets, a large bust of a woman, all in the style of Greek art. And the Greeks used ivory, for Homer, in his Odyssey, speaks of the artisan Icmalios, goldsmith of Ithaca, making a chair of ivory and silver on which Penelope sat. Solomon's throne appears to have been of ivory. The Roman curulean chairs were frequently of ivory. Most noted of the early Roman carved ivories are the «diptychs» or writing tablets; they consisted of two tablets folding over one another and fastened together loosely on one side. Their carved external sides give a representation of a consul, scenes of public games, fights, etc., the inner side being plain and covered with wax on which to write notes with the *style*; they measured about 12 inches by 5 or 6, and were strong and thick. The most important, perhaps, of the early diptychs extant is that in the Liverpool Mayer Museum; its lower bas-relief depicts men fighting stags in the arena, above are three persons in a gallery. It has been attributed to the 3d century. Another early diptych (the other may not have been *consular*) extant is that dedicated to Marcus Aurelius Romulus Cæsar (308 A.D.), in the British Museum; it represents a funeral procession and above is the apotheosis of the consul driven in a four-horse chariot to Heaven. Altogether about 50 diptychs dedicated to consuls are extant. Some are to the following: Consul Rufus Probianus (322 A.D.), typically seated with scribes attendant; Amicius Probus (406); Flavius Felix (428 A.D.); respectively in Berlin, Aosta and Paris. Of the consul Areobindus (506) no less than eight diptychs are extant. A number of existing diptychs were carved for private individuals, and these are often superior, as works of art, to those carved for consular adulation. Three lovely early diptych specimens are known as the Bellerophon, Aesculapius and Hygeia, and the Bacchantes, in the museum at Kensington and that of Liverpool. They are of beautiful workmanship, and belong to those usually designated as «classical diptychs.» An ivory curule chair and ivory sceptre were frequently given by the Roman Senate to tributary sovereigns.

Early Christian and Byzantine Ivories.— The first ivory carvings of the Christians were, of course, «transitional,» showing many of the former pagan features as well as copying the style, as they are contemporaneous till we come to the developed Byzantine style. Early Christian diptychs gave the names of those baptized, some gave the names of bishops and benefactors, martyrs, saints, others recorded the names of the dead. Several cylindrical pyxes (caskets), made from a section of elephant tusk, exist that are beautifully carved; one in the Berlin Museum has reliefs of the Saviour enthroned, Saint Peter and Saint Paul on curule chairs, other apostles standing around, etc. Four small ivory plaques of great interest are in the British Museum and contain carvings that depict events in the history of Christ (Crucifixion, etc.); they date somewhere between the 5th and 8th century. The leaf from the diptych of Rambona in the Vatican is a 9th century production and shows a bust of the Saviour with hand in act of benediction, an allegorical sun and moon holds a torch each, and, strangely, below is a wolf suckling two children with the inscription «Romulus and Remus nourished by a wolf,» in Latin. These plaques are frequently used as book-covers (a 9th century example is in the Bodleian Library, Oxford; a 14th century one in the British Museum is perhaps the most beautiful). The «Nativity» was one of the favorite subjects with ivory carvers; one, a plaque of Rhenish execution, in the Cologne Museum dates from the 11th century. Of Byzantine ivories there are few after the 10th century, then come several of Russian origin. We cannot fail to note that the religious stiffness and conventionalism of Byzantine works, are little present in the ivory reliefs; there is a freedom of action and resemblance to nature quite remarkable and different from art expressed in other mediums. In the British Museum is, perhaps, the most noted of these carvings; it represents an archangel holding an orb in one hand and a long rod in the other. This is one of the largest known (16¼ inches by 5½) and dates about the 4th century; it doubtless is part of a writing tablet, as the Greek inscription reads «Accept this gift, and having learned the cause,» proving that another plaque is missing, which contained the rest of the sentence. The noted Brescia casket in the Quiriniana Library, Brescia, is a 5th or 6th century work; it has an overelaborated top and sides, but in classic style. Busts range round the upper part, two scenes of Jonah and the whale, the Saviour, Magdalen, Good Shepherd and sheep, story of Susannah, all in bewildering closeness. The Episcopal chair of Maximianus (546) at Ravenna from Assyrian workers, apparently) is of ivory with beautifully carved panels. A superb archangel Saint Michael in the British Museum is attributed to Antioch artists. In Byzantine style is the Carlovingian 9th century ivory bookcover in the Victoria and Albert Museum (London). The centre panel displays a Virgin and Child and a figure on each side, architectural columns are the frame, beautiful figures of angels float on the top panel. The Vatican owns a bookcover very similar but claimed as three centuries earlier. The 11th century Byzantine triptych in the Paris Cabinet de Médailles is claimed to be the most beautiful specimen of extant Byzantine art. The central division has a Crucifixion with the Virgin Mary and Saint John on either side, all of the characteristic «elongated» anatomy and straight close folds of drapery; Constantine and Empress Helen are in diminutive size below. The statuettes in the Byzantine shrine from the Soltikoff collection are some of walrus tusk and some of elephantine ivory. The Russian Church would be expected to furnish numerous specimens of Byzantine ivory carving; it affords however, only a few heads of pastoral staffs, plaques and other liturgical accessories. A 16th century *panagia* (a flat locket-shaped receptacle to hold the consecrated bread) of ivory in the Vatican has 10 scenes from the New Testament carved in the minutest form with great skill and producing facial expressions clearly. These surround a larger central circle containing three angels sitting at meat with Abraham. Two thrones in the Kremlin at Moscow are of ivory. One, attributed to Constantinople (1472), is the

IVORIES

Right: **This is one of India's artists in ivory carving at work on an intricate object.**

Lower left: **Ornate cup carved by the Flemish 17th-century artist, Lucas Faydherbe.**

Lower right: **Ivory Chinese puzzle ball, consisting of nine open working balls one within the other.**

(1) © Photo by Deane Dickason, from Ewing Galloway; courtesy (2) The Metropolitan Museum of Art, and (3) American Museum of Natural History

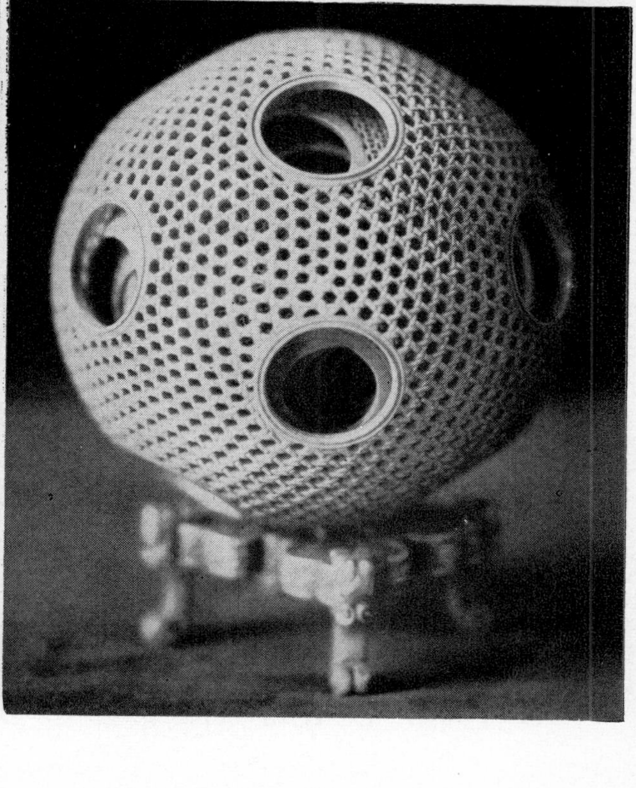

IVORIES

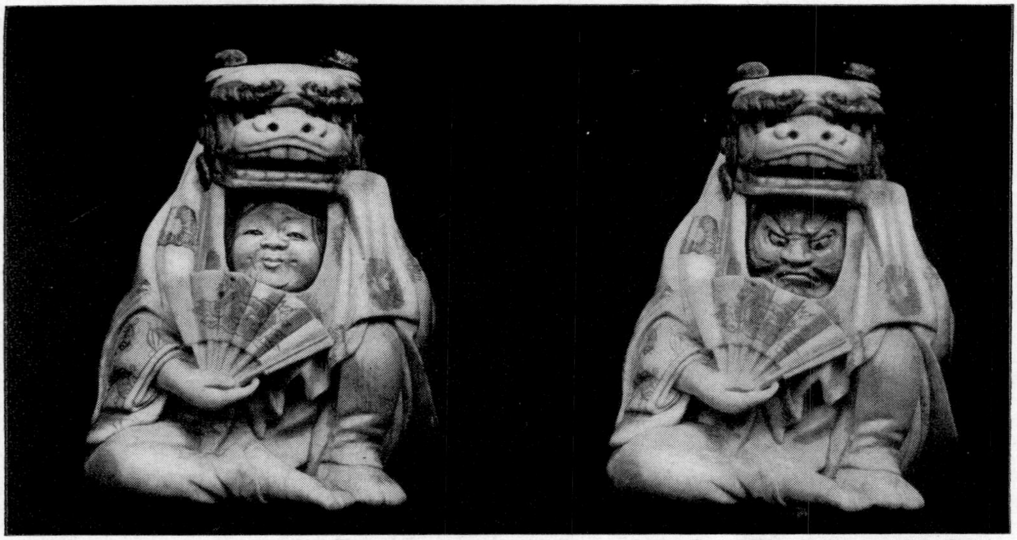

Courtesy American Museum of Natural History

Ivory Japanese *netsuké* with movable face (two views), one pleasant and one grotesque, representing Shishimai, a performing street beggar.

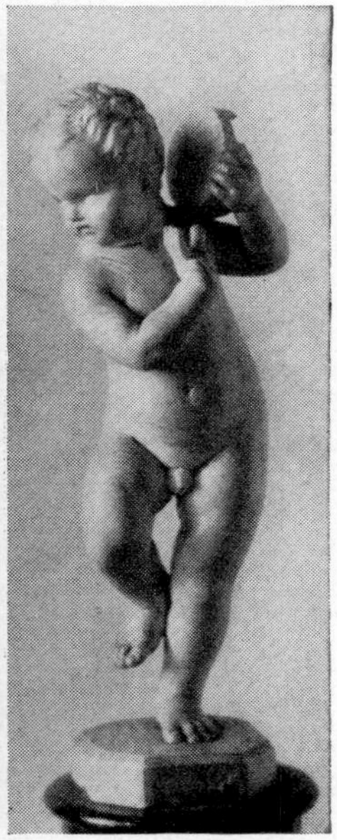

Left: **An example of Austrian 17th-century ivory carving. This is the "Assumption" by Adam Lenckhardt.**

Left above: **French ivory statuette of Virgin and Child, 15th or 16th century.**

Right above: **A child with a musical instrument is the subject of this 17th-century French or Flemish ivory.**

Courtesy The Metropolitan Museum of Art

Ivan III throne; its plaques were added and dated 16th to 17th century. The other probably comes from Persia and is covered with ornaments of gold and gem stones. Plaques of ivory of Hindu workmanship are on front and sides, picturing an elephant hunt amongst open interlaced work. Saint Peter's ivory chair is in the Basilica (Rome). It is a massive square structure, the low back supporting a triangular pediment. Square ivory plaques covering the surface depict the labors of Hercules and six constellations.

Ecclesiastical Diptychs.— It is to the custom, which dates back to very early times of the Church, of using ivory plaques (both «consular» and «classical») for liturgical decoration that so many have survived; later, when no longer used, fortunately, these works of art were carefully preserved in the treasuries of the churches. But diptychs have *palimpsests* just as do manuscripts (see MANUSCRIPTS) and sepulchral brasses (see BRASSES). In these certain parts of a carved diptych that are not desired are planed down and other work substituted. An example in the Victoria and Albert Museum, London, has all its original reliefs erased but traces remain of a consul's figure; a figure of the Saviour in 13th century Russo-Byzantine is carved on the back. Another such in the Liverpool Museum has the original substituted by an inscription to Bishop Baldricus (10th century). The cathedral at Monza has two leaves of another.

Gothic Ivories.— In the 13th, 14th and 15th centuries we come across Gothic architectural effects in the carving. For liturgical purposes we meet with ivory in diptychs, triptychs, retables or altar-pieces, pastoral staffs or croziers, shrines, statuettes, caskets, bookcovers, liturgical combs, portable altars, holy-water buckets (*situlæ*), flabelli (fans), rosary beads, etc. The quality of the workmanship varies considerably, the French being best. In France, the Revolution destroyed most pieces; in England, the Reformation. Noted extant pieces of this period are the cylindrical pyx in Saint Gereon treasury, Cologne; a 13th century casket, in the museum at Kensington, of wood overlaid with ivory plaques painted and gilt, showing Saint Felix enthroned, etc.; two fine caskets (in the latter museum), one with the figures of Christ, Saint Peter and Saint Paul in richly carved canopies («tabernacles») of Gothic architecture. There are also *polyptyches* (with more than three leaves) which often form a recess in which is a statuette or group; these are termed «shrines.» Germany and Italy did splendid work in such pieces. Nothing of great art value in diptychs or shrines later than the 14th century has come down to us. Charming statuettes exist of the Gothic period as found in the museums of Paris and London. The Virgin and Child is a favored subject for ivory statuettes, the Virgin is frequently standing and has a tendency to lean over above, utilizing to the full the curve in the tusk; some are seated. Some of these are colored, even gilded. The «Vierge de Bourbon» (Louvre) is very noted, it is a «Vierge ouvrante,» a style in which the figure can be opened in the centre producing two doors and disclosing groups carved in the interior. The Saint George and dragon group was another favorite with ivory carvers; this is usually thus divided: there is a hillock with castles above, lower we find the kneeling princess praying for delivery and at base Saint George is slaying the dragon, all in full relief. The Wallace Museum, London, has one of these of the 15th century, the Salting Collection had a smaller one. The Coronation of the Virgin (Louvre) from the Soltikoff Collection is very noted, the Christ figure is said to be a portrait of Philip III, and the Virgin a likeness of Mary, daughter of Henry III. A number of «Deposition from the Cross» groups in ivory are in existence, in Byzantine and Western style, in panels as well as diptychs, triptychs and caskets.

Secular Art in Ivory.— Caskets for secular use from the 13th century with carved panels and borders exist; they are frequently carved with classic subjects, as the stories of Europa, Orpheus, Pegasus, with figures of centaurs and other monsters. Noted secular caskets are in the Brussels Museum, British Museum (the «Franks» casket) and that in the Brunswick Museum, with their inscription in Runic and interlaced work. In the 14th century we come to the decoration depicting the era of classic romance, such as the story of King Arthur and his knights of the Round Table, and we get portrayals of the Quest of the Sangreal, Queen Guinevere, Tristan and Yseult, etc., also Chaucer's Romance of the Rose, tournaments, knights before the Castle of Love, etc. All these are reproduced in the carved ivories of this period. In the museum at Kensington is a casket with 13 panels of classic and romantic subjects such as Castle of Love, Cupid shooting, romance of Lancelot, story of Tristan as a beggar, Fountain of Youth, etc. Numerous 15th century Italian marriage coffers (*cassone*) of bone are in the museums. Mirrors and hair combs extant show quite elaborate scenic carving. Olifants, too, belong to this period, some from the 12th century. They retained the horn shape and were used for hunting horns and often for drinking from; they show profuse carving at times.

Noted Ivory Sculptors.— François Girardon (17th century) is supposed to have created the famous crucifix in the archiepiscopal palace at Troyes; a replica or the original is in Sens Cathedral. Joseph Villerme (d. 1720) of Saint Claude carved crucifixes exclusively and his work is extant in a number of churches in France. Other noted crucifixes are: one in Calvet Museum, Avignon, by J. B. Guillermin; high altar at the Sorbonne, Paris, by F. Anguier; in Saint Germain-des-Près Hospital, Paris, by Simon Jaillot. Famous German crucifix carvers were: Andreas Feistenberger (created beautiful crucifix of the archbishop of Tours); his work is supposed to be the greatly admired crucifix in the Benedictine abbey church at Downside, near Bath (19 inches high); another was Georg Petel (example in Imperial Vienna Museum); Melchior Barthel (in Florence Museum); Balthasar Permoser (Brunswick Museum); Bernhard Bendel (Frankenkirche, Munich). The «Flagellation» scene was a chosen subject for ivory carvers.

Post-Renaissance Ivories.— In the 17th century we get the strong Italian influence bearing on all Christian art, the religious intensity in art is now displaced by appeal to the eye more than the mind. The nude enters largely into the treatment of figure work. But the art of ivory carving enters its decline to become decadent by the 18th century (rococo and baroque). In the 17th century we have a series of antique subjects, gods and goddesses, bacchanals, satyrs, mostly of inferior talent but frequently of fine execution and some pieces of remarkable art value and originality. Examples are plentiful, for they had a popular demand. And ivory found its uses not only in statuettes and groups but for furniture decoration and inlays, for tankards and ewers, for busts, portrait medallions, caskets, chessmen and draughtsmen, handles for arms, turnery, etc. The wealthy German princes encouraged the art, some even took ivory artists into their court retinue. Of such were Augustus the Pious, Elector of Saxony, founder of the Dresden «Green Vaults»; Maximilian, Elector of Bavaria; the princely family of Fuggers; Ferdinand of Bavaria; Elector Georg Wilhelm of Brandenburg. Augsburg, Munich, Nuremberg became centres for ivory work, also Geislingen, Ulm, Stuttgart and Gmünd. France had as centres Dieppe, Saint Claude, Rouen. A few works worth citing are: the allegorical group of Christoph Maucher (Vienna) showing princes in wigs alongside holy persons, cherubs, scrolls, garlands, angels blowing trumpets; the Louis XIII sceptre (Londesborough Collection), an elegantly formed hand; a German 16th century dagger; a Nuremberg cup held up by a mermaid, some horns. In the museums of Nuremberg, Cassel, Gotha, Brunswick, Carlsruhe, Vienna, are good collections, also in Dresden, Berlin and Munich are fine pieces. Of Flemish work we have 16th century pieces of François Duquesnoy (called Il Fiamingo), six are in the Museum at Kensington, his favorite subject was youthful satyrs and naked children playing; his Diana and her nymphs bathing is very beautiful. Lucas Fayd'herbe, another Fleming, is supposed to have executed the piping Pan group in the Madrid Prado Museum, but his best work is in tankards and standing cups with satyr processions and dances in the museum at Kensington and other museums. Gerhard van Opstal (d. 1698), also Flemish, worked in Paris; his bacchanal figures, amorini and Venuses, etc., are full of charm. Other clever and noted carvers are François van Bossuit (Dutch), and the Germans, Christoph Angermair (with his wonderful cabinets, called *Kunstschränke*), Georg Petel, Leonhard Kern, Bernhard Strauss, Balthasar Permoser, Ignaz Elhafen, etc. Lathe or turned work in ivory shows considerable skill in technique in this period; noted workers were: the Zick family, Lorenz and his sons, Martin Teuber, Fil. Senger, etc. Their extant examples show tours-de-force aided by rose-engine lathes, ellipse chucks, and other mechanical means. With the Spanish, ivory has not been a favorite medium for art work. The Moors, however, with the conquest brought the technique, as we see in openwork boxes, in which Oriental or Mohammedan treatment is evident, as well as the Cufic inscriptions.

Oriental Ivories.— India, as the home of the elephant, was naturally fond of using ivory in decoration. As with all other civilized nations, India's arts are bound up with her creed; as the Christian carvers depicted Bible scenes, so the Indians found motifs in Buddhas, Krishnas, Vishnus, Ramas and other monster gods and goddesses of Hindu mythology. On account of their monotonous frequency and absolute similarity of expression, Indian art does not appeal to all western minds as does their own much variegated, historical field of pictorial work. Again, in its purely ornamental work its *repeat* treatment tends to soon pall on the untrained western eye. The barbaric profusion of detail covering the entire surface, also, is against Occidental tenets. And, perhaps above all, the ivory medium does not afford the tonic effect produced by the polychromes seen and enjoyed in the Indian textiles, enamels, lacquers, etc., in their gorgeous splendor. The Indian Museum at Kensington affords examples covering the entire field of Hindu art in ivory and other mediums. Reliefs show lions and elephants surrounded and enmeshed with scroll foliage done in intricate, minute open-work. Benares, Bombay, Delhi, Travancore, etc., are centres for the finer work. Persia appears to have done very little in ivory carving worth notice; her sword handles show, invariably, careful work, almost always in walrus tusk, however. Arab usage of ivory or bone is largely one of inlays, and the Saracenic type of geometrical motifs is displayed on door-panels and furniture to good effect. In combination with ebony and other dark woods very clever effects are seen in arabesque interlacing lines. Coptic screens, the pulpit (nimbar), etc., at Kensington afford us beautiful examples of this work in perfection, the former having carved relief panels of ivory.

China and Japan.—Practically all the carved ivory emanating from China consists of objects prepared specially for the Western markets. Her native «puzzle» balls, which are so carved that a series of different size balls, one within the other, and made of a single piece of ivory (seamless), are familiar objects and proof of skill and patience. Models of ships (*sampans*), dwellings, gardens, seen in museums, are of delicate minute construction. China's Buddhist gods, of course, appear in ivory. While the work of the Celestials in ivory is cold and appeals little to the westerner, Japanese ivories keenly interest us. In her *netsukés* we find a fund of pictorial art, diminutive nature in every detail, idealistic and grotesque, all in perfection though of microscopic proportion. These intricate pictures in relief in buttons are the surprise and admiration of all art students, and their scope in depiction and classification take pages to describe. The Japanese *inros* (medicine or candy boxes) with their tiny drawers, so full of artistry in decoration, displayed in the museums with the netsukés (to which they belong) always attract admiring attention. Japanese figurines and groups (*okimono*), their shrines, screens, sword-scabbards, etc., all show the perfection born only with the enthusiasm of an artist, and the names of these clever carvers have survived in honor in their land.

Recent Work.— The uses of ivory in strictly modern days have been chiefly confined to brush-backs, billiard balls, paper cutters, etc., but good art work still is done in Europe in this medium in such centres as Dieppe and Paris. And, in the quiet of the studio a number of artists of this and last century have done fine art work in ivory, some allied to the gold and silversmiths. Moreau-Vauthier trained a number of pupils in this art; the shops of François Froment-Meurice and Joseph L. Falize (Paris) created talented ivory work. Among artists of genius in this line figure such names as Jean François Soitoux, Meugniot, James Pradier, Descrieux, Baron Henri Triqueti (high-altar at the Invalides), Joseph Rosset du Pont, all in France. In Italy, Constantin Meunier, Giuseppe Bonzanigo (1740–1820) trained pupils. Pierre Simart's design for the reproduction of the Minerva of the ancient Greek sculptor Phidias was carried out (reduced) in chryselephantine work (gold and ivory) by Froment-Meurice for the 1857 Paris Exposition. Other ivory sculptors of note are the Belgians, Julien Dillens, Charles van der Stappen, Phillippe Wolfers, Charles Samuel, Alphonse van Beurden (worked in England) and others.

Bibliography.—Montfaucon, B. de., *L'Antiquité expliquée et representée en figures* (Paris 1719–1724); Didron, A. N., *Manual d'iconographie chrétienne, grecque et latine* (Paris 1845); Labarte, C. J., *Histoire des arts industriels au moyen âge et à l'epoque de la Renaissance* (Paris 1864–1866); Maze-Sancier, *Le libre des collectionneurs* (Paris 1885); Linas, C. de, *Ivoires et emaux* (Bruges 1886); Molinier, C. L., *Catalogue des ivoires, Louvre* (Paris 1895–1896); Scherer, C., *Studien zur Elfeinbeinplastik seit der Renaissance* (Leipzig 1903); Masell, A., *Ivoires* (London 1905); Cust, A., *The Ivory Workers of the Middle Ages* (London 1906); Dalton, O. M., *Catalogue of the Ivory Carvings of the Christian Era in the British Museum* (London 1909); id., *Byzantine Art and Archaeology* (Oxford 1911); Kunz, G. F., *Ivory and the Elephant* (Garden City, N. Y., 1916); Pelha, O., *Elfenbein* (Berlin 1920); Laufer, B., *Ivory in China* (Chicago 1925); Williamson, G. C., *Book of Ivory* (London 1938).

CLEMENT W. COUMBE.

IVORY, SIR **James,** Scottish mathematician: b. Dundee, 1765; d. London, Sept. 21, 1842. He was educated at the University of Saint Andrews. From 1804 until 1819 he served as professor of mathematics at the Royal Military College, Marlow (later removed to Sandhurst). In 1809 he published in the *Philosophical Transactions* a notable paper on the attraction of ellipsoids. He contributed others on the attraction of sphereoids and the theory of the figure of the earth, and he investigated the possible equilibrium of a spheroid with three unequal axes. His *Theory of Astronomical Refractions* (1839) was of special interest to mathematicians. He received a knighthood in 1831.

IVORY, properly the substance of which the tusks of the elephant consist, though the similar substance constituting the tusks of the hippopotamus and the horn of the narwhal is also so called. There is also a wholly different substance known as vegetable ivory (q.v.). Ivory is prized for its beautiful color, the fineness of its grain and the high polish it is capable of receiving. That of the African elephant is most esteemed by the manufacturer for its density and whiteness. It is used as a material for knife handles, piano keys, combs, the back of brushes, billiard balls, chess men, carved figures, and various ornamental articles. The ivory of the hippopotamus is preferred by the dentist. The shavings and sawdust of ivory, by burning in a crucible, are converted into a black powder, from which is prepared a pigment known as ivory black. Ivory may be stained or dyed. The use of ivory was well known in very early ages. The ancients were acquainted with the art of sculpturing in ivory, of dyeing and inlaying it, and they often employed it in statuary. Some of the most famous Grecian statues were chryselephantine, that is, were overlaid with plates of gold and ivory in conjunction. The medium weight of a tusk is about 60 pounds, but some weigh as much as 170 pounds. See also IVORIES.

IVORY-BILL, the great black and white, scarlet-crested woodpecker (*Campephilus principalis*), formerly numerous and greatly admired throughout the southern United States, but now surviving only in a few of the most secluded cypress swamps of the Florida coast. Its extermination was begun by the Indians, who valued its splendid head feathers as an ornament for warriors, and was completed by sportsmen and plume-hunters.

IVORY CARVING. See IVORIES.

IVORY COAST (French COTE D'IVOIRE, kōt dē-vwär'), a territory, French West Africa, on the coast of the Atlantic Ocean west of the Gold Coast and east of Liberia; it has common frontiers with French Guinea, French Sudan, and Upper Volta. Some districts of Upper Volta were merged in the Ivory Coast during 1933–1947. The Ivory Coast has an area of 123,359 square miles, and population (est. 1948) of 2,065,000. Along the coast are numerous lagoons, and from about 40 miles inland the surface of the territory rises gradually to a plateau. There are hills and mountains in the west and northwest. Among the rivers flowing into the Atlantic are the Sassandra and the Bandama, both of them navigable for only a short distance from the sea. In the northern part of the territory are tributaries of the Niger. Abidjan, a town on one of the coastal lagoons, is the capital; its port is Port Bouet, across the lagoon. Other ports, all difficult of access because of sand bars and heavy surf, include Grand Bassam, Assinie, Grand Lahou, Sassandra, and Tabou (Tabu). Bingerville, a coastal town, was formerly the capital. On the railroad from Abidjan to Bobo-Dioulasso (in Upper Volta), is the considerable commercial town of Bouaké (Bwake), 180 miles north-northwest from the capital. The forests are worked for mahogany and products of the palm tree, and cacao, coffee, and cotton are cultivated. Other crops include peanuts, corn, rice, millet, manioc, yam, and tropical fruits. In the northern grazing lands are large herds of cattle and flocks of sheep and goats. Gold is produced in several places, and manganese has been located.

French trading posts were established along the coast early in the 18th century, and in 1842 France secured formal cessions of territory at Assinie and Grand Bassam. The whole area between the coast and the Niger was visited during 1887–1889 by Louis Gustave Binger (for whom Bingerville was named), and treaties with native chiefs, which he made at that period and subsequently, enabled France to establish a protectorate. The Ivory Coast was constituted a colony in 1893, and two years later this was included in the newly organized French West Africa. With formation of the French Union (q.v.) in 1946, the colony of the Ivory Coast became a territory.

IVORY PALM, a South American palm tree yielding corozo nuts—large white seeds called vegetable ivory (q.v.).

IVREA, ē-vrâ'ä, town, Italy, in Aosta Province, Piedmont, 32 miles east-southeast of Aosta. Parts of the existing cathedral were constructed in the 10th century. On the hill dominating the town is the 14th-century Castello delle Quattro Torri. Known to the ancients as *Eporedia,* from the earliest times Ivrea has been prominent in Italian history. It was a military station of the Salassi prior to 100 B.C., when Romans were settled there. During the Middle Ages it was successively the capital of a Lombard duchy and of a marquisate, and in the 14th century it passed to the house of Savoy. The town was the scene of military operations during Napoleon's Italian campaign of 1800. Pop. (1936) 14,473.

IVRY-LA-BATAILLE, ē-vrē' lȧ bȧ-tä'y', village, France, in the Eure Department, on the Eure River 40 miles west of Paris. There, on March 14, 1590, the Huguenots, led by Henry IV, scored a notable victory over the forces of the Catholic League commanded by the duke of Mayenne.

IVRY-SUR-SEINE, ē-vrē' sür sân', town, France, in the Seine Department, on the left bank of the Seine just below Paris, of which it is a suburb. There are manufactures of chemicals, metal products, and tiles. It is a river port. Pop. (1936) 44,859.

IVY, a popular name for various climbing, creeping, and drooping herbs and shrubs, the most widely known of which are the following: common or English ivy (*Hedera helix*) is a tall climbing evergreen shrub of the family Araliaceae, widely planted in Europe (where, as in northern Africa and eastern Asia, it is native), and in the warmer parts of the United States, its ornamental, abundant foliage being highly valued for covering walls, rocks, and trellises. Its small and inconspicous greenish, perfect flowers appear late in the autumn, and the small black fruits (three to five-seeded berries) ripen the succeeding year. The fruits, which are devoured by birds, are bitter and pungent and were formerly in medicinal repute. The gummy juice obtained from the stem, as also from the fruit, contains the bitter principle hederin and the hederic acid characteristic of the plant. It has been used in making varnish. Contrary to popular opinion, ivy is not parasitic upon such trees as support it. It merely clings to them by its numerous holdfast roots produced along the entire length of its stems. Such trees as it injures are killed by constriction. The other popular notion that it makes the walls and houses upon which it climbs damp and unhealthy is also erroneous; in reality it dries them, the roots abstracting such water as reaches the wall through the dense foliage; yet exceptional cases of damage occur. It has numerous horticultural varieties which differ mainly in the form, color, and markings of the leaves. These succeed best in rather moist, rich soils and shady positions, and are not usually found to be hardy much farther north than New York unless well protected from the winter sun, as upon the north side of buildings. As a greenhouse and a house plant it is very popular. Ivy leaves and ivy berries were formerly used for various medicinal purposes, but this has been discontinued. The leaf and habit of the common ivy are so characteristic that reference is often made to them in the specific names of other plants, "ivy-leaved" being common as a designation.

Japanese or Boston ivy (*Parthenocissus tricuspidata*) and its near relative Virginia creeper (*P. quinquefolia*) of the family Vitaceae, are probably the next best known species to which this name is applied. The former is the more graceful, and is gradually gaining in general favor over the latter, which demands more attention to keep it looking presentable. Both climb by means of tendrils, but the Boston ivy clings better to walls. It has three-lobed leaves; its rival, a compound leaf of five leaflets.

Among the herbaceous ivies Kenilworth ivy (*Linaria cymbalaria*), German ivy (*Senecio mikanioides*), and ground ivy (*Glecoma hederacea*) are best known in North America. They are all popular greenhouse plants and are frequently planted in hanging baskets because of their graceful habits. Poison ivy or poison oak is a climbing sumach whose leaflets somewhat resemble those of Virginia creeper, but are in threes instead of fives. See also POISON IVY.

IVY GERANIUM (*Pelargonium peltatum*), a commonly cultivated trailing South African plant with ivylike leaves.

IVY POISONING, a skin disease or dermatitis characterized by erythema, wheals, papules, vesicles, pustules, bullae, or a combination of two or more of them, with an addition of crusting and excoriations. It is caused by *Rhus toxicodendron* (poison ivy), a climbing plant and a small tree or shrub (poison oak) are the most common causes in the eastern part of the United States, and also in the West. In the Middle states the poison sumach seems to be the more commonly poisonous one *Rhus venenata* (poison dogwood, sumach elder). The nettle commonly seen in the woods and unkept meadows, the primrose (*Primula obconica*), the oleander (*Nerium oleander*), the rue (*Ruta*), the smartweed (*Persicaria hydroppier*) are the most common ones known, but there are many others.

The inflammatory reaction produced by *Rhus toxicodendron* is quite typical and so commonly seen in the springtime and summer that even the ordinary person may make an accurate diagnosis. The disease starts primarily upon the exposed parts. The hands and wrists or forearms are the first members attacked, then the face, the genitalia, and anal regions; barefooted children also are great sufferers. It is said that toxicodendric acid, a volatile substance, is the cause, although it has not been specifically proved. Many persons who at one time or another have had severe attacks, have found that in passing through the woods, or anywhere in the proximity of the plant, they may have a recurrence of the attack, even though the plant is not touched. As the years pass and there has been no contact made with the ivy, this peculiar susceptibility to the air-laden poison becomes almost nil. There is a belief that after one attack of some severity there is a recurrence at the same time the following year, regardless of any proximity to plants. Probably these are really cases of vesicular eczema. There is a serious tendency in some instances of ivy poisoning to a persistency toward a chronic condition, which, according to our present knowledge of eczema, may be classed as such.

Persons prone to attacks of eczema are very susceptible to the poison. There are individuals, too, who from childhood have never been subject to plant poisoning, but with change of climate or methods of living, suddenly are rendered susceptible.

The poison ivy is a shrub which usually climbs by means of rootlets over rocks, walls, and trees, sometimes low and erect. Leaves are divided into three somewhat four-sided pointed leaflets. This much dreaded plant is often confused with the beautiful Virginia creeper; the two can be distinguished by the three-divided leaves of the ivy and the usually five-divided leaves of the creeper. A more or less mild attack may be ushered in by a burning or itching of the skin. Within a few hours up to 24 or 48, an erythema may appear, followed by swelling, with vesicles, or the vesicles may arise with little areola. The vesicles may be few in number, or clustered in great multitudes on the affected parts. At first they may be tense, but often rapidly become flaccid, rupturing easily. The yellowish serum in the vesicles doubtless carries the poison, as it seems to inoculate nearby previously unaffected areas, spreading the disease. The lesions often develop in streaks or stellate patches slightly raised, surmounted by vesicles. The parts may swell to enormous proportions. The face becomes quite distorted, the eyelids suffer, and conjunctivitis is not uncommon. The suffering from the itching and burning is intolerable. The dermatitis usually progresses to a certain point before regression takes place. Some abortive cases clear up rapidly. After the vesicles rupture and dry the erythema and swelling slowly disappear. The disease may last but a few days or remain from several weeks to several months. Its common duration is from 10 days to three weeks. It often leaves in its wake a mass of freckles or pigmentation such as often follows a sunburn.

A homely but very efficacious remedy is bathing the poisoned parts (not the eyes, however) with a strong solution of laundry soap in water as hot as can be borne. This gives instant relief from the itching and reduces the swelling. If the itching returns repeat the hot soapy bath, three or four times if necessary. A standard lotion is a compound resorcin, one containing boric acid and resorcin, ā ā ʒ i; pulv. zinci oxidi, ʒ i; aq. calcis q.s. ad ℥ viii. In mild cases healing may be obtained by a simple astringent ointment such as unguentum, zinci oxidi, but ointments as a rule are not so pleasant as lotions.

IWAKURA, ē-wä-kōō-rä, Prince **Tomomi,** Japanese statesman: b. Kyoto, 1835; d. Tokyo, July 20, 1883. He was one of the *kuge* (court nobility) and became chamberlain of the imperial household. At first opposing the opening of the ports to foreign trade, he later joined the progressives and in 1868 helped to restore the authority of the emperor. In 1870, as envoy of the emperor to the recalcitrant Satsuma leaders, he led the movement to abolish feudalism; and during 1871–1873 he headed missions to Europe and the United States which vainly sought revision of unfavorable treaties. Appointed foreign minister on his return to Japan, he successfully opposed the plan for war upon Korea. Until his death he continued to be one of the emperor's most influential advisers. He escaped numerous attempts to assassinate him, notably that carried out by nine men in 1873.

IWASA or **IWASA MATABEI,** ē-wä-sä mä-tä-bā, Japanese landscape and genre painter: b. 1577?; d. 1650. He originated the Ukiyoye school of painting, departing from the old traditions exemplified in the Tosa and Kano schools and portraying everyday scenes. The method was later adapted to the wood block technique and became a truly popular art.

IWASAKI, ē-wä-sä-kē, **Koyata,** 2d Baron, Japanese banker and philanthropist: b. 1879. He was the nephew of Yataro Iwasaki (1834–1885), founder of the great Mitsubishi banking, shipping, and insurance company, and in 1909 succeeded his father, Yanosuke Iwasuki, in the barony. Educated at the Imperial University, Tokyo, and Cambridge University, England, he became president of the banking department of the Mitsubishi company and acquired great wealth.

IWO JIMA, ē'wō yē'mȧ, a Western Pacific island, one of the Volcano Islands (q.v.) annexed by Japan in 1891, 760 miles south of Tokyo. It is 5 miles long and 2 miles wide, the area being 8 square miles; the population normally numbers about 1,000. During World War II it was captured by United States forces after heavy fighting. Marines landed on Feb. 19, 1945, attacked Mount Suribachi, a volcano on the south, and raised the American flag on its summit on February 23. Conquest of Iwo Jima was completed by March 16. Marine casualties totaled 19,938, of whom 4,189 were killed; and Japanese dead were estimated to number 21,000. After the war the United States retained control of the island for security purposes.

IXION, ĭk-sī'ŏn, in Greek mythology, king of the Lapithae, in Thessaly, son of Phlegyas. He married Dia, daughter of Deioneus. He murdered his father-in-law, and as punishment, became insane until Zeus cured him and permitted him to reside in Olympus. He became enamored of Hera, and attempted to seduce her. Zeus made a cloud in the shape of Hera, and carried it to the place where Ixion had appointed to meet her. Ixion was caught in the snare, and from his embrace with the cloud were born the Centaurs (q.v.). Zeus banished him from heaven; struck him with his thunder, and ordered him tied to a winged or fiery wheel which was to revolve eternally, according to some in the air, and to others in the underworld.

IXTLILXOCHITL, ĭsh-tlĭl-shō'chĭt-l, **Fernando de Alva Cortes,** Mexican historian: b. Texcoco, 1568?; d. ?1648 Through his mother, he was descended from the ancient kings of Texcoco, and in 1602 became heir to the family's titles and possessions. The Spanish viceroy, for whom he was interpreter, commissioned him to write histories of the ancient Mexican peoples, of whom he possessed great knowledge. His works remained unknown until their importance was revealed by Francisco Javier Clavijero (Clavigero), and afterward by Baron Alexander von Humboldt. They were deposited in the library of the Jesuits in Mexico. The series of histories consisted of 13 books or relations, many of which were repetitions of the former relations, and covered the period from the most ancient times to the destruction of the Mexican Empire. His *Histoire des Chichimecas* was published in Paris (1840); and a two-volume edition in Mexico City (1891–92).

IYAR, the eighth month of the Jewish civil year, and the second month of the sacred year, corresponding, at the earliest, with April; but it may be as late as June; it has always only 29 days.

IYEYASU, ē'yä-yä'sōō, Japanese statesman, founder of the Tokugawa shogunate: b. Okasaki, Mikawa, 1542; d. 1616. He served under Nobunaga and Hideyoshi, and at the latter's death in 1598 promised to look after his son, Hideyori. Becoming one of four regents for Hideyori, he defeated his rivals at the battle of Sekigahara (15 Oct. 1600) and made himself master of Japan. The emperor commissioned him as shogun (1603), and he established his capital at Yedo (later Tokyo). His dynasty of the Tokugawas endured until 1868. Although he nominally abdicated in 1605 in favor of his son, Hidetada, he retained complete control of the country. He was buried at Nikko, and was deified under the posthumous name of Gongen-Sama.

IZABAL, a Guatemalan department, and its capital (pop. 5,000), situated on a lake (30 miles long) of the same name. The lake, known also as *Golfo Dulce* («Freshwater Lake»), is connected with the Caribbean Sea by the *Golfete Dulce* («Little Freshwater Lake»). The commercial importance of the town is slight.

IZARD, George, American general: b. Richmond, Surrey, England, 21 Oct. 1776; d. Little Rock, Ark., 25 Jan. 1828. He was a son of Ralph Izard (q.v.). He was graduated from the College of Pennsylvania in 1792, and after a tour in Europe, and study in private military schools in England, Germany and France, he was appointed in 1794 a lieutenant in the regiment of artillerists and engineers in the United States Army. He did not return to the United States until 1797, then held various commands, but resigned in 1803. Upon the breaking out of the War of 1812 with Great Britain he served as colonel of the 2d artillery, and was successively promoted to be brigadier general in 1813 and major general in 1814. At one period of the war he held chief command of the northwest frontier. In defense of his actions in this command, attacked by anonymously published pamphlets, he published *Official Correspondence with the Department of War Relative to the Military Operations of the American Army under the Command of Major General Izard on the Northern Frontier of the United States, 1814–15* (Philadelphia 1816). In 1825 he became governor of Arkansas Territory, in which office he died.

IZARD, Ralph, American statesman: b. near Charleston, S.C., 1742; d. South Bay, near Charleston, 30 May 1804. He was educated at Christ's College, Cambridge, England, and, inheriting an ample fortune, establishing himself in 1771 with his family in London, whence the troubled condition of American politics induced him in 1774 to retire to the Continent where he traveled extensively. He subsequently endeavored to impress upon the British ministry the ill-advised nature of the course they were pursuing, but without effect. Although appointed in 1776 by the Continental Congress, United States Commissioner at the court of the grand duke of Tuscany, he continued to reside in Paris and played a prominent part in the differences existing between the American commissioners in France. In 1780 he returned to the United States, and found occasion to serve the country in various ways, having been instrumental in procuring the appointment of General Greene to the command of the southern army, and having once pledged his whole estate as security for funds needed in the purchase of ships of war in Europe. In 1782 he entered the Continental Congress, of which he remained a member until the peace; and upon the adoption of the federal constitution he was elected a United States senator from South Carolina, serving until 1795. As a legislator he was able, but not particularly eloquent and in the Senate possessed the confidence of all parties. The *Correspondence of Ralph Izard from 1774 to 1804, with a Short Memoir,* was published by his daughter (New York 1844).

IZARD, the chamois (q.v.); so called in the Pyrenees.

IZMIR, ĭz-mĭr', a Turkish vilayet (pop. 597,812) and its seaport capital (184,362), the latter formerly known as Smyrna. The city is situated on the west coast of Anatolia, at the head of the Gulf of Izmir. Large quantities of tobacco are grown in the vilayet, as well as figs and grapes. The seaport was one of the most important of Asia Minor since Ionian times, carrying on the largest share of the trade of the Levant. Earthquakes and fire have frequently devastated the city. The climate is variable, and fever (usually of a mild type) is prevalent. About 688 B.C. the city fell into the hands of the Ionians of Colophon. This earliest city, called by the Greeks Old Smyrna, was situated on the banks of the Meles, on the northeast side of the Hermaean Gulf (now the Gulf of Smyrna). It laid claim to the honor of being the birthplace of Homer, and its coins bore his image. This old city was abandoned and was succeeded by a new town on the southeast side of the gulf (the present site), which was said to have been built by Antigonus, and enlarged and embellished by Lysimachus, both generals of Alexander the Great. It was laid out with great magnificence, and adorned with several splendid buildings, among which was the Homereum, where the poet was honored as a god. It soon became one of the greatest and most prosperous cities in the world. It was especially favored by the Romans on account of the aid it lent them in the Syrian and Mithridatic wars. In the civil wars it was taken and partly destroyed by Dolabella, but it soon recovered. It is one of the two among the seven churches in Asia which Saint John addresses without rebuke, and it was the scene of the labors and martyrdom of Polycarp. In the 13th century only the ruins of its former splendor were left; but after the Turks became masters of the country it began to revive until it became the most flourishing city of Asia Minor. In May 1919, as an outcome of the defeat of Turkey in the First World War, the city was occupied by Greek forces. The Treaty of Lausanne restored the city to the Turks 9 Sept. 1922, and a most destructive fire which occurred three days later cost 1,000 lives.

J the tenth letter of the English alphabet, was unknown to the ancient Latins and Greeks as an alphabetic character and representative of a vocal sound.

Till the 16th century the Latin and other alphabets of western Europe had only the letter *i* to represent both the vowel sound *i* and the consonant sound now represented by *j*: at least in fonts of type of that century, and till the end of that century or later, the character *i* served to represent both the vowel and the consonant, though a distinction was made between them in manuscripts of the previous century by continuing the stroke of the *i* a little below the line when it stood for the consonant. This letter *j* from the first represented in English the sound of *dzh,* in French that of *zh*; in German and other languages its value is that of the consonant *y*; for example, Julius, pronounced yulius, jacio, pronounced yacio.

For speakers of the modern European languages the *j* in Latin has usually the same value as in their native tongues. But though for Spaniards *j* in Latin is equal to *y,* in their own speech *j* is a strong guttural aspirate that might be represented in English by *kh.* The sound of *j* in English is always represented in Italian by *g,* invariably followed by *e* or *i*; the French and English "journal" is in Italian *giornale;* the Latin *judex,* English "judge" is in Italian *giudice.*

The sound of *dzh* is represented in English not only by its proper letter *j,* but also by *g* and by *dg*: jest, gem, edge. In the word "hallelujah" the *j* retains its early consonantal value of *i* or *y.*

JABALPUR. See JUBBULPORE.

JABBOK, jăb′ŏk (Arabic WADI ZERQA), a river in Jordan (Transjordan), about 100 miles in length, traversing the northwestern part of the kingdom in a westerly direction and emptying into the River Jordan about 20 miles north of the Dead Sea. In ancient Palestine, it was a boundary line between the ancient kingdoms of the Amorites and the land of Bashan. It was also a boundary between the Jewish tribe of Reuben and the half tribe of Manasseh. In the time of Origen, he says it was known as the Jambice. The night struggle of Jacob with his visitor occurred on the south bank of the river (Genesis 32:22-32).

JABESH-GILEAD, jā′bĕsh-gĭl′ē-ăd, town of the land of Gilead, in ancient Palestine, in the valley of the Jordan, east of that river, about 20 miles south of the Sea of Galilee. The place is mentioned several times in the Old Testament. It was captured and destroyed by the Israelites, and 400 of its virgins taken as wives by the Benjamites (Judges 21:8-15). Later the city was attacked by Nahash, leader of the Amorites. The city appealed to Saul, king of Israel, for succor; he came to their rescue and routed the Amorites. They never forgot this service and after the fatal battle of Mount Gilboa the citizens of Jabesh-gilead recovered the bodies of Saul and his sons and gave them burial with honors (I Samuel 31). David commended the men of Jabesh-gilead (II Samuel 12:4). Later the bones of Saul and his sons were buried in the territory of Benjamin (II Samuel 21:12-14).

JABIRU, jăb′ĭ-rōō, a large species of stork (*Mycteria americana*), somewhat resembling the adjutant, found mostly throughout South America and northward into Mexico and Texas. It is about five feet high, with stilt-like legs, and massive, slightly upcurved beak; the plumage is white and the naked head and neck black. In habits it resembles the other storks (q.v.). Storks of Africa, the East Indies, and Australia have received the same name.

JABLONEC, yä′blô-nĕts (German GABLONZ), city, Czechoslovakia, 95 miles northeast of Prague (Praha). Glass beads and ornaments are manufactured. There are also woolen and cotton factories. Pop. (1947) 23,112.

JABORANDI, jăb-ō-răn′dĭ, a Brazilian shrub (*Pilocarpus pennatifolius*) of the order Rutaceae, which yields a volatile oil from which is derived a principle (pilocarpine) in the form of an amorphous white powder having properties similar to atropine. It is the basis of the drug jaborandi, which is diaphoretic and sialagogic in its effects.

JACA, hä′kä, town, Spain, in Huesca Province 114 miles northwest of Saragossa (Zaragoza). It contains a fine Gothic cathedral of the 11th century or earlier. Chocolate and cement are manufactured. Pop. (1936) 7,056.

JACAMAR, jăk′ȧ-mär, a group of small, gaudy, South American birds of the family Galbulidae, and related to the puffbirds and woodpeckers. Their plumage is highly colored, red and bronze-green and blue predominating. They live mostly along the outskirts of forests, and feed upon large insects caught in flight.

JAÇANA, zhä-sȧ-nä′, a group of birds (Parridae) related to the rails, and remarkable for the extraordinary length of the toes, which are further extended, especially the hallux, by long, slender claws. There are four genera and about a dozen species, most of which inhabit the Old World—Africa, India, and Australia. The genus *Parra* is American, and one Mexican species (*Parra spinosa*) enters Texas. The beak is plover-like and the bend of the wing bears a stout and acute horny spur; the plumage is of a rich purplish brown with the wings green and black. The great spread of the toes enables these birds to walk with ease on the floating leaves of water-lilies and similar plants, otherwise their habits are much like those of rails (q.v.).

JACARANDA, jăk-ȧ-răn′dȧ, a genus of tropical American trees of the Bignoniaceae family. One (*B. brasiliana*) yields the wood called jacaranda wood, or blue ebony, which is very hard and capable of receiving a fine polish. The name is carelessly applied to several other South American woods used in cabinetwork. See also BIGNONIA.

JACARE, jăk′ȧ-rā, Pg. zhä-kȧ-rā′, a South American name for an alligator of the genus *Caiman,* of which the large black species (*C. niger*) reaches a length of 20 feet and is called on the upper Amazon *jacaré nassu,* while the *jacaré tinga* (*C. trigonatus*) is only six feet long, and has a slender muzzle and black-banded tail. See also CAYMAN.

JACCOUD, zhȧ-kōō′, **François Sigismond,** French physician: b. Geneva, Nov. 20, 1830; d. Paris, April 27, 1913. He was educated in Geneva and Paris; became professor of pathology in Paris in 1876 and professor of clinical medicine there in 1883. In 1877 he was elected member of the Academy of Medicine and became perpetual secretary thereof. He made investigations of the causes of albuminuria; described prominence of the aorta in the region of the suprasternal notch as symptomatic of aortic dilatation; and was also known for his description of a type of fever in tuberculous meningitis, with irregular, slow pulse, called Jaccoud's dissociated fever. He wrote *De l'organisation des facultés de médicine en Allemagne* (1864); *Leçons de clinique médicale* (1867–1888); *Traité de pathologie interne,* 7th ed. (1883); and *Du froid comme cause de pneumonie* (1887). He was editor of *Nouveau dictionnaire de médicine et de chirurgie* (1864–1886).

JACHYMOV, yä′kĭ-môf (Ger. JOACHIMSTHAL), commune, Czechoslovakia, in the Erz Gebirge, 12 miles north of Karlovy Vary (Carlsbad). Pitchblende is mined here as well as lead, silver, radium, and uranium. Pop. (1946) 7,320.

JACK, an apparatus for raising heavy bodies and for moving machinery. The moving parts consist sometimes of a simple screw moving within a nut fixed in the shell of the instrument, and turned by a long handle or a system of gearing; sometimes of a hydraulic press of compact form, small size, and high power; and occasionally of combinations of levers and gearing. The first of these forms of the tool is called a jackscrew; the second is usually termed an hydraulic jack; the last a geared jack. The jackscrew is most commonly used for moderate weights, as a few hundred pounds, or perhaps a ton; the others are used up to 10 or 20 tons, or even more, but finally merge into the hydraulic press, as they lose portability, which is an essential characteristic of the jack. The machine is always compact, as light as is consistent with proper strength and safety in operation, simple in design, and of the best material and workmanship, to insure the desired combination of strength and lightness. Its exterior is commonly a plain cylinder, mounted upon a properly formed foot and having concentric with it another cylinder, moving snugly within or outside it. The introduction of the automobile has made everybody familiar with a compact type of gear jack.

JACK, JACA, or **JACK TREE** (native name *Jaca*), a tree (*Artocarpus integra*), related to the breadfruit, a native of the East Indian archipelago and southeastern Asia, often planted for ornament and for its fruit which grows to a larger size than the breadfruit of the southern Pacific Islands. Specimens often weigh more than 30 pounds, and contain from 200 to 300 seeds, each of them four times as large as an almond. The seeds or nuts are eaten after being roasted or boiled, and the sweet fleshy pulp of the fruit is also eaten by coolies and natives but is less palatable than breadfruit. When the tree is young the fruit grows from the twigs; in middle age it grows from the trunk; and when the tree gets old, from the roots. The yellowish timber is used for almost any purpose. It yields a yellow dye. To succeed in growing the tree, hot moist atmosphere, ample water, and perfect drainage are essential.

JACK AND JILL, the first words of an old nursery rhyme, of considerable folklore interest. Jill is a corruption of the French Julienne, once common in England under the form Gillian. It also appears in the legend of Saint Kilian (Cilian), where Geilana vindictively causes the good bishop's death. This incident of Jack and Jill is probably based on one of the moon myths of Scandinavia. The Norse peasant sees in the spots on the moon the two children rescued by the moon from their father, who had forced them to draw water all the day.

JACK AND THE BEANSTALK, an English nursery tale relating to the heroism of a boy. Its analogue occurs in many national folklore legends. It is supposed to represent in a figure the restoration to the earth of those fertilizing and elemental activities, which are necessary to human life. The harp is the wind, which drives the ships and turns the mills to grind the wheat. The bags of treasure are the raindrops that scatter wealth and plenty. The red hen is the sun that brings life to birth by its fostering heat.

JACK HORNER, the first words of an old nursery rhyme. The rhyme is said to be based on a historic fact. Horner was the messenger whom the abbot of Glastonbury sent to Henry VIII with the deeds of certain manors involved in the dissolution of monasteries. Horner obsequiously handed the parcel to the royal spoliator, but first of all managed to abstract the deeds of the manor of Wells, a "plum" indeed, and the abbot was afterward punished on the charge that he had withheld them.

JACK-IN-THE-PULPIT, or **INDIAN TURNIP,** a perennial herb (*Arisaema triphyllum*) of the arum family (see ARACEAE), so called from its spadix, which is upright, with the spathe surrounding and arching over it, suggesting a preacher in an old-fashioned pulpit with a sounding board. It is common in the United States, east of the great plains, in damp shady woods, and is easily grown in moist garden soil. The spathe falls away in early summer. By late summer the berries which form a dense ovoid head become a brilliant, waxy scarlet. Its acrid tuber or corm is valued for its medicinal properties.

JACK RABBIT. See Hares.

JACK THE GIANT KILLER, the hero of an English nursery story, which reflects triumph of skill over strength and bulk such as makes the point of the story in David and Goliath, or Ulysses (Odysseus) and Polyphemus. The English form is based upon the legend that Saint Michael's Mount, in Cornwall, was once the fortress or castle of a giant, who was dislodged by the valor of an English knight. In adapting the story so as to claim the sympathies of children, the knight is made to take the shape of a child.

JACKAL, a small active wild dog or wolf of the warmer regions of the Old World, found in southeast Europe, Africa, Syria and southern Asia. The common jackal averages about 2 or 2½ feet in length and about 14 inches in height, with a bushy tail about 8 inches long. The eyes are small and the pupil is round. The general color of the body is a dirty yellow or brown, lighter on the throat and belly. Jackals inhabit holes and burrows whence they come forth in the evening to hunt in packs. Their cry consists of a series of prolonged howls, followed by shorter yelps, much like that of the American coyote. The jackal subsists largely upon carrion, often that left after the repast of the fiercer and larger Carnivora; but it also kills prey for itself, a pack hunting down antelopes, deer or other animals, besides getting much small fare, as mice, lizards, insects, and the like. They also eat certain kinds of vegetable food, and sometimes they do considerable damage to sugar and other plantations. The jackal is susceptible of being tamed, but its odor makes it by no means a desirable domestic animal. It is believed to be exceedingly cunning, and in many Eastern tales, especially among the people of India, plays exactly the same part as the fox does in those of Europe. It is probable that jackals have contributed frequently to the commingled stock represented in our domestic dogs, some of which betray very jackal-like points. They interbreed with domestic races.

The common jackal (*Canis aureus*) is the most widely distributed species; but another species, found mostly in eastern southern Africa, is the blackbacked jackal (*C. mesomelas*). This latter form has the back and end of the tail black, the other parts mostly red or yellowish-red. A third species of jackal found in South Africa is the canduc (*C. adustus*), marked by a light stripe on the sides.

JACKASS KINGFISHER, or LAUGHING JACKASS, the name of a large inland kingfisher (*Dacelo gigas*) of Australia, given by the colonists in allusion to its loud, hoarse cry. It is about 17 inches long, brown in general color, does not frequent water or catch fish, but lives on insects, small reptiles, etc., and lays its eggs in a hole in a tree.

JACKDAW, a small, black European crow (*Corvus monedula*), with black legs and feet and grayish neck. They inhabit towers, spires and like elevated situations, and even in towns and populous cities are present and breed freely. The nests and eggs are like those of other crows (q.v.) which they resemble in general habits.

JACKS, jăks, **Lawrence Pearsall,** English educator and editor: b. Nottingham 1860; d. Feb. 23, 1949. He was educated at University School, Nottingham, University of London, Manchester College, Oxford, Göttingen University, and Harvard University. He was professor of philosophy in Manchester College, Oxford, dean of the college and warden of residence, 1903–1915, and principal, 1915–1931. He was editor of the *Hibbert Journal* from its foundation in 1902 until he retired in 1947. He is the author of *Mad Shepherds and other Human Studies* (1910); *From the Human End* (1916); *Philosophers in Trouble* (1916); *Life and Letters of Stopford Brooke,* 2 vols. (1917); *Heroes of Smokeover* (1926); *Constructive Citizenship* (1927); *My Neighbour the Universe* (1928); *The Inner Sentinel* (1930); *The Education of the Whole Man* (1931); *Education through Recreation* (1932); *My American Friends* (1933); *Elemental Religion* (1934); *Revolt against Mechanism* (1934); *Co-operation or Coercion* (1938); *The Stolen Sword* (1938); *The Last Legend of Smokeover* (1939); *Construction Now* (1940); and *The Confession of an Octogenarian* (1942).

JACKSNIPE, also called grass or meadow snipe, which is in reality a sandpiper, named in books the pectoral sandpiper (*Tringa maculata*). The perversion of names is due to its somewhat gamelike habits of lying to a dog and flushing correctly from the grass, like a true snipe which render it an attractive object of pursuit; besides which, in the fall it becomes very fat, and it is then excellent eating.

The English jacksnipe is a true snipe (*Limnocryptes gallinula*) of very small size, and therefore also known as "half-snipe." See also Sandpipers.

JACKSON, Abraham Valentine Williams, American Indo-Iranian scholar: b. New York, Feb. 9, 1862; d. there, Aug. 8, 1937. Graduated from Columbia in 1883, he was fellow in letters there (1883–1886), and, after study at Halle (1887–1889), instructor in Anglo-Saxon and the Iranian languages (1889–1891), and adjunct professor of English language and literature (1891–1895). From 1895–1935 he was professor of Indo-Iranian languages and public lecturer at Columbia. By way of recognition of the instruction given by him in their ancient books, the Parsees made to the Columbia library the gift of an important manuscript collection of Zoroastrian works. He appeared also as a public lecturer, became one of the directors of the American Oriental Society, and in addition to numerous contributions to the *Journal* of that society and other learned periodicals, wrote *A Hymn of Zoroaster, Yasna XXXI* (1888); *An Avestan Grammar* (1892); *An Avestan Reader* (1893); *Zoroaster, the Prophet of Ancient Iran* (1899); *Persia, Past and Present* (1906); *From Constantinople to the Home of Omar Khayyam* (1911); with A. Yohannan the *Descriptive Cat-*

alogue of the Persian MSS. in the Metropolitan Museum of Art' (1913).

JACKSON, Alexander Young, Canadian painter: b. Montreal, P. Q., 3 Oct. 1882. He received his education in the Montreal public schools; worked for a time in the lithographic business, and then studied art in Montreal, Chicago, and at the Julian Academy in Paris. He is noted for his landscapes of Canada. In the First World War he served in France with the Canadian infantry. He is represented in the National Gallery of British Art, the National Gallery of Canada, and the art galleries of Montreal, Toronto, and other Canadian cities.

JACKSON, Andrew, seventh President of the United States: b. in the Waxhaw settlement near the border line between North and South Carolina, 15 March 1767; d. at his home, «The Hermitage,» near Nashville, Tenn., 8 June 1845. It is a matter of dispute to which of these States the honor of his birth belongs, but the evidence is in favor of South Carolina. Andrew Jackson, his father, emigrated from Carrickfergus, County Antrim, in the north of Ireland, in 1765, and died a few days before the birth of his famous son. The early environment of the future President was extremely unpropitious. He lived in a rough frontier region, with little opportunity for education or other form of culture. In fact, Jackson received very little «schooling,» and was never able to write correct English. Little is known of his early life beyond the fact that he was a headstrong, pugnacious boy. During the Revolutionary War the Waxhaw district was invaded by the British who took Jackson prisoner, then a boy of 13, illtreated him and carried him to Camden for imprisonment. His two brothers lost their lives in the war and his mother died as a result of hardships incurred on a journey to Charleston to help care for prisoners there. These early incidents account for his antipathy toward England, and doubtless stimulated him at the battle of New Orleans, where he evened up old scores.

At the age of 17 he entered a law office at Salisbury, N. C. Traditions exist of what would now be considered a wild life, and it is likely that they are true, for frontier societies, such as he lived in, took delight in gambling, horse-racing, cock fighting, dueling and similar pastimes. Jackson was admitted to the bar in November 1787. In the spring of 1788 he started for Tennessee, and in the fall established himself at Nashville as a practising lawyer. In 1789 he was given the solicitorship, with a salary of 40 pounds, for a Superior Court district comprising three counties in Tennessee. The region where Jackson was to take up his duties as public prosecutor was wilder than the Waxhaw Settlement. It was a real frontier filled with persons who were individualists, who believed in the personality of law, and who were unwilling to submit to any form of restraint. Here was the home of quarrels and feuds, a harvest for the young lawyer, but he must needs be a brave man, better versed in human nature than in precise knowledge of the law, to succeed in such an environment. Jackson had exactly these characteristics, with others, which made him the ideal man for such a position. Himself a product of the frontier, and chafing under the restraint of law, yet he instinctively was somewhat of a despot, a master of men, and quite as determined to make others obey the law, as he himself was often determined to break it. Jackson's main business from 1789 was to introduce law and order into a community that did not care for it. He found plenty to do, and it is on record that in the April term, 1790, out of 192 cases on the docket of the County Court at Nashville, Jackson was employed as counsel in 42 of them; in the year 1794, out of 397 cases he acted as counsel in 228. Besides devoting his energies to putting down lawlessness among the whites, he found time to look after the Indians, who committed numerous murders in the district in this period. He thus acquired a taste for Indian fighting, which greatly influenced his subsequent career.

He married a Rachael Robards in Natchez, Miss., in the summer of 1791, believing that the legislature of Virginia had granted her husband a divorce, instead of, as was the case, a mere permission to bring suit for divorce. The suit was not brought until 1793 and the divorce was granted, because technically Robards' wife was unlawfully living with Jackson as his wife. Jackson immediately procured another license and had another ceremony performed in 1794. There is no good evidence that Jackson's wife was unfaithful, or that Jackson was not acting in good faith and in the honest belief that a divorce had been granted. Nevertheless, as a lawyer, he should have known that the Virginia legislature did not grant divorces at this time, but only gave permission for a suit to be brought in the proper court. The incident was used mercilessly by the partisan press in the campaign of 1828, but it is evident that those who knew Jackson believed in his honesty.

Jackson was a member of the convention which drafted the first constitution of Tennessee, and in 1796 was chosen representative in Congress from this State. The next summer, 1797, he was chosen senator to fill a vacancy, but resigned in 1798 to become a judge of the Supreme Court of Tennessee, a position which he held until 1804. While in Congress he did not distinguish himself particularly, but showed even so early his opposition to the United States Bank and to federalist doctrines. Little is known of his work as a judge of the Supreme Court, since few decisions were recorded, and not one of them was Jackson's. It is generally agreed that his knowledge of the law was extremely meagre and that he decided cases on the principles of common sense, modified, however, by his own personal feelings and prejudices.

From 1804 to 1811 he was engaged as a planter, trader and merchant. He ran a general country store in partnership with others. As a trader he was successful, but as a retail merchant he was nearly a failure, and was glad to sell out at almost a total loss. This was the period of one of his famous duels, that with Charles Dickinson, and of numerous quarrels. Though without previous military experience to speak of, he was elected major-general of militia for the western district of Tennessee in 1802. When war was declared against England in 1812, Jackson offered his services with 2,500 volunteers, and in the autumn was ordered

to proceed to New Orleans. In March 1813 he was at Natchez, Miss., when orders came from the Secretary of War to dismiss his troops. He refused and marched them back home 500 miles on his own responsibility and partly at his own expense, though later he was reimbursed by the government. In the fall of 1813 and spring of 1814 he was engaged in an expedition against the Creek Indians, who had massacred the garrison and refugees at Fort Mims, Ala., 30 Aug. 1813. He finally overwhelmed them at Tohopeka or Horseshoe Bend, Ala., 27 March 1814. This Indian war was outside the Federal operations and was carried on by the States of Tennessee, Georgia, Louisiana and Mississippi, but it had an important bearing on the whole campaign. For with the destruction of the Indian power in this region there could be a concentration of military power at any point where it was needed in the Southwest, and this really made possible the victory at New Orleans.

On 31 May 1814, Jackson was appointed major-general in the Regular Army and given command of the Department of the South. His headquarters were established at Mobile, then in dispute between Spain and the United States. On 6 November, without waiting for orders from Washington, he attacked the English, who had occupied Pensacola, apparently without objections from Spain, and drove them out of Florida. This left him free for the defense of New Orleans, where he arrived 2 Dec. 1814. He declared martial law, impressed soldiers and sailors, and inspired his army of about 6,000 men with his own courage and determination to resist attack at any cost. The English had about 12,000 veteran troops under General Pakenham. In the main attack 8 Jan. 1815, he defeated the British, who lost over 2,000 in killed, wounded and captured, while Jackson lost the astonishingly small number of only seven killed and six wounded. This victory, won when there was great discouragement over the progress of the war, made him a national military hero, and paved the way for his political career. Although the battle occurred after peace had been concluded, this did not affect Jackson's popularity. He became especially popular in the West, for this section felt that he had ended for all time the danger of the control of the Mississippi Valley by a foreign power.

Florida next demanded Jackson's attention. There was great disorder in this Spanish territory because the coasts were a haunt for privateers and filibusters. It was believed that the Indians got aid and encouragement from the Spanish and that British agents were stirring them up to wage a frontier war on the United States. Massacres of whites occurred and Spain took no vigorous measures to preserve order. In December 1817 Jackson was ordered to the Florida frontier to prepare for a possible invasion of the territory. Without waiting for direct orders, but understanding from the letter of a friend in Congress that President Monroe had approved his plan for the conquest of Florida, Jackson, who had raised troops in Tennessee and neighboring States, advanced through Georgia. He captured Saint Marks, Florida, in March 1818, and within three months **had overthrown the Seminole Indians, arrested two British subjects, Arbuthnot and Ambrister,** had them tried by court martial for inciting the Indians to war and for spying, and, on insufficient evidence, had them executed. This raised delicate diplomatic questions and led to a proposal by Calhoun, then Secretary of War, that Jackson should be censured for his conduct. When Jackson found this out, during his first term as President, he vowed vengeance on Calhoun, and this incident was one of the causes of the break between the two men and the ousting of Calhoun's friends from the Cabinet.

After the acquisition of Florida by purchase in 1819, Jackson was appointed its territorial governor (1821). According to the testimony of Parton, his biographer, he governed badly and his conduct while governor was «arrogant and disgraceful.» On 20 July 1822, the legislature of Tennessee nominated him for President. In 1823 he was chosen senator from Tennessee for the second time. In the election of 1824–25 Jackson received 99 of the electoral votes to 84 for John Quincy Adams, 41 for Henry Clay and 37 for William H. Crawford. No candidate receiving a majority, the election was thrown into the House of Representatives, with the result, due to Clay's support of Adams, that Jackson was defeated. When Clay was immediately appointed Secretary of State, the cry of «corrupt bargain» was raised, though there is no evidence that Adams promised this office in return for Clay's support. Nevertheless Jackson believed the story, and his political managers made as much capital as possible out of it in the next campaign for the presidency, which in fact started at once. It was also maintained that Jackson had been cheated out of the presidency because he had the largest number of electoral votes, and hence should have been chosen President by the House of Representatives rather than Adams. This, however, was another party war cry to gain votes for Jackson.

The election of 1828 was a great victory for Jackson, as he received 178 electoral votes to 83 for Adams. The result was a great surprise to many, especially to the conservative North Atlantic States. While many voted for Jackson for personal reasons, because he was a military hero or because of a belief that he was unjustly deprived of the presidency in 1824–25, and others as a protest against alleged misgovernment by Adams, or personal antagonism to him, yet the real causes of Jackson's extraordinary success lie deeper. His election was the result of a protest against what many considered too much centralization of power in the national government, and a tendency to interpret the Constitution too broadly. This was shown in decisions of the Supreme Court in several well-known and important cases, as well as in acts of Congress providing for internal improvements at national expense, chartering the Second United States Bank, upholding the principle of a high protective tariff and refusing to distribute the public lands in a manner satisfactory to the West. These measures were looked upon as on the whole favoring the interests and power of the manufacturing, commercial and financial classes of the Northeast rather than the great agricultural **classes of the South and West who composed** the mass of the people. This combination of the South and West to gain their special interests, a low tariff for the South and cheap lands for the West, was the greatest force in the election of Jackson.

The election also turned on the question of what type of man should administer the government and make the laws. The Federalist, Jeffersonian-Republican and National-Republican parties had never represented the great mass of the people, and this largely because of the belief that the government should be run by carefully selected educated leaders. Jackson represented the great new West and its democracy. The notion, «He is one of us» appealed very strongly to common men, and the election of Jackson was the answer to the question whether a class could be safely entrusted with the power to act wisely for the whole people. Jackson's real views on some of the important public questions were unknown, such as his attitude on the tariff, internal improvements, public lands and National vs. State rights. On the other hand, he was known to favor slavery, the removal of the Indians from lands coveted by the white man, the interests of the common people, and hence to be opposed to all forms of special privilege, monopolies and the centring of power in the hands of a favored class. It was thought probable also that he would favor a lower tariff and laws pleasing to the West on the question of the distribution of the public lands, since he was a western man. It was known also that Jackson was a master of men, almost despotic by nature, in spite of his humble origin and his interest in the common man; that his military career had taught him the necessity of obedience to law, at least by those subject to his orders, and that he was not likely to allow his authority to be questioned as President, or in the enforcement of the law as he understood it.

These views help to explain the principal events and policies of Jackson's two administrations. His democracy, expressed by a phrase, «Let the people rule,» accounts in part for his approval of the spoils system, whereby some 2,000 were removed from office in the first year of his administration to make room for his friends, «the people.» His frontier life and experience developed the peculiar personal character of his administration, as shown by his «kitchen cabinet.» Jackson's military and political successes were due largely to his ability to inspire the fealty of those associated with him. Like the leaders of primitive societies, he depended on the unswerving loyalty of personal intimate friends. It was natural, then, that he should treat his regular cabinet officers as clerks, heads of departments, as was apparently intended by the Constitution, and that his real advisors should be those more intimate friends whom he knew well and could depend upon. His secretaries were chosen with this end in view, and they were in fact not much above the capacity of clerks. The principal members of his «kitchen cabinet» were William B. Lewis, his party manager; Duff Green, the editor of *The Telegraph* at Washington, a partisan newspaper; and Amos Kendall, a politician with brains, the chief advisor of Jackson on all important state questions. This personal character of his administration was also prominent in the relations of the executive to the legislative and judicial departments. Jackson greatly enlarged the importance and influence of the President in his contests with Congress and the Supreme Court.

His war on the United States Bank to prevent its securing a second charter was due primarily to his distrust of anything savoring of monopoly or special privilege. He gave notice in his first annual message of his doubts about the Bank, and vetoed the bill introduced by Clay for a new charter on 10 July 1832. This became the principal issue in the election of 1832 between Jackson and his opponent Clay. With his re-election by a large majority he was convinced that he had received a mandate from the people approving his attitude towards the Bank. In his second annual message he questioned its solvency, without warrant, and then made plans to destroy it. He ordered two successive Secretaries of the Treasury to remove the government deposits, and after both refused, appointed a third, Roger B. Taney, who, in September 1833, ordered government money to be deposited in sundry State banks, «pet banks,» after 1 Oct. 1833. As money was withdrawn from the United States Bank to pay government expenses, its resources decreased. Jackson's avowed purpose was to prevent the Bank from buying up members of Congress in order to secure another charter. There followed the resolution of the Senate 28 March 1834, originally introduced bv Clay, to censure Jackson on the ground that he had usurped powers not conferred upon him by the Constitution. Later, in 1837, Jackson had the satisfaction of having this resolution expunged from the records. Growing out of the activity of the State banks in making loans of public funds, and through the issuing of large quantities of paper money by other State banks, with little or no specie as a reserve, there arose a fever of speculation, especially in western lands which were paid for in paper money. Jackson called in a part of the government funds and issued his famous specie circular 11 July 1836, to the effect that only gold and silver would be received in payment for public lands. These incidents contributed largely to the panic of 1837.

Jackson reversed the policy of Adams in upholding the right of the Indians of Georgia to own lands, as guaranteed by treaties with the United States. He upheld Georgia in its refusal to obey decrees of the Supreme Court, and himself refused to execute them. He withdrew Federal troops from the Cherokee country, and allowed the State to assume jurisdiction over the Indian lands. This attitude was due partly to his hatred of the Indians, partly to the fact that he did not look upon the attitude of Georgia as one of defiance to the National government, but considered her as acting wholly within her rights. This was not understood thoroughly at the time, and misled the leaders of nullification in South Carolina, who supposed that Jackson had conclusively proved himself to be a states' rights man, and could be depended on to support their theories.

The first hint of trouble with Jackson in the nullification controversy came at a dinner in honor to Jefferson held at Washington 13 April 1830. Jackson proposed a toast in reply to several in favor of nullification, «Our Federal Union: it must be preserved,» in contrast with one proposed by Calhoun, in effect, «Liberty dearer than Union.» The question arose because of the opposition of South Carolina to the high tariff of 1828, «the tariff of abominations.» This was believed to be unconstitutional and peculiarly unjust to the South. A convention held 19 Nov. 1832, declared the tariffs of 1828 and 1832 null and void in South Carolina, to go into effect 1 Feb. 1833, and threatened secession if the federal government attempted to collect duties. Jackson ordered General Scott to Charleston, and sent two war vessels to the same port. He instructed the collector of the port to collect duties by force. He issued a proclamation 10 December telling the people of South Carolina that disunion by force was armed treason, and said, «I consider the power to annul a law of the United States, assumed by one State, incompatible with the existence of the Union, contradicted expressly by the letter of the Constitution, unauthorized by its spirit, inconsistent with every principle on which it was founded, and destructive of the great object for which it was formed.» This made Jackson almost as popular a civil as a military hero. The controversy ended in Jackson's favor, as the ordinance was never enforced, though the tariff was reduced by the Act of 1833.

Jackson's constitutional views as illustrated by his attitude on the Bank, Indian and nullification questions, are difficult to comprehend unless one thoroughly understands his view of the final source of authority in our governmental system, and the agency for executing it. According to Jackson, final power was the will of the people. A popular mandate was superior to acts of Congress or even to a decision of the Supreme Court. The President was the interpreter of just what the will of the people was, and must execute it independently of and without interference from Congress or the Supreme Court. The chief results of Jackson's two administrations were a reduction of the tariff, the preservation of national authority as against the states, a check on tendencies toward monopoly and privilege, the enhancing of the power of the executive, the introduction of the spoils system, the destruction of the United States Bank, encouragement of speculation and inflation, and the extension of a vicious banking system.

Jackson's character and policies affected people differently and opinions vary even to this day. His nature was so positive that his traits stand out boldly, whether good or bad. His was an untrained mind, but one of great natural power, and he would have made his mark in any society or environment. Lacking the discipline which comes from close association with trained minds and from study, he was incapable of weighing evidence and deciding questions on the basis of the facts. Rather he formed his opinions and made his decisions intuitively, or in accordance with his feelings. He made fewer mistakes than many men highly trained, because of his honesty of purpose, and his determination to carry out a policy once he had made up his mind. His ideas were original and grew out of his experience. They were seldom directly borrowed from other men, either the dead or the living. He was a typical son of the unadulterated frontier, and truly represented the mass mind of the frontier, and that meant at this period the greater portion of the American people. His most striking traits were those of the frontier — provincialism, self-confidence, energy, persistency, belligerency, insubordination, individualism, honesty, simplicity, ignorance of books, loyalty to friends, and hatred of enemies. He was the idol of the mass of the people — of the common man. To the more cultured portions of American society he was an uncouth, illiterate backwoodsman. Though Harvard University conferred on him the degree of doctor of laws, the comment of John Quincy Adams doubtless represented the attitude of many of the educated class towards Jackson. Adams said, «As myself an affectionate child of our *Alma Mater*, I would not be present to witness her disgrace in conferring her highest literary honors upon a barbarian who could not write a sentence of grammar and hardly could spell his own name.» The language is exaggerated, but the spirit of the remark was the sentiment of many, who could not divorce from their minds the notion that government must be administered only by trained, educated men.

Bibliography.—Biographies of Jackson include M. James' ‹Andrew Jackson, Portrait of a President› (1937) and ‹Andrew Jackson, the Border Captain› (1933). Earlier biographies are those by John Spencer Bassett (2 vols., Garden City, New York 1911); William G. Sumner (Boston 1882); James Parton (3 vols., New York, 1861); W. G. Brown (Boston 1900); John H. Eaton (Philadelphia 1817); Amos Kendall (New York 1843). For important phases of Jackson's career as President consult Catterall, R. C. H., ‹The Second Bank of the United States› (Chicago 1903); Boucher, Chauncey Samuel, ‹The Nullification Controversy in South Carolina› (Chicago 1916). For extended bibliographies on all phases of Jackson's life, consult Edward Channing, Albert Bushnell Hart and Frederick Jackson Turner, ‹Guide to the Study and Reading of American History› (pp. 412–420, Boston 1912).

MARCUS W. JERNEGAN,
Former Professor of History, Univ. of Chicago.

JACKSON, Benjamin Daydon, English botanist: b. London, 3 April 1846. He was educated in private schools, was secretary of the Linnean Society, 1880–1902; general secretary, 1902–26; curator of Linnean collection after 1926. In 1900–01 he was secretary to the departmental committee of the Treasury on botanical work. He published ‹Life of Gerard› (1877); ‹Life of Dr. William Turner› (1878); ‹Guide to the Literature of Botany› (1881); ‹Vegetable Technology› (1882); ‹Pryor's Flora of Herts› (1887); ‹Index Kewensis› (engaged nearly 14 years on its preparation, 1893–95); ‹Supplement to Index Kewensis,› with Th. Durand (1901–06); ‹Glossary of Botanic Terms› (1900; 3d ed., 1916); ‹Life of George Bentham› (1906); editor of ‹New Genera and Species of Cyperaceæ,› by the late C. B. Clarke (1908); ‹Darwiniana› (1910); ‹Index to the Linnean Herbarium› (1912); ‹Catalogue of Linnean Specimens of Zoology› (1913); ‹Linnaeus; Story of His Life› (1923), and many shorter articles on botany, botanic history and bibliography. He died in London, October 1927.

JACKSON, Charles, American jurist: b. Newburyport, Mass., 1775; d. 1855. In 1793 he was graduated at Harvard; entered on the study of law in the office of Chief Justice Theophilus Parsons. In 1796 he began the practice of his profession in his native Newburyport, remaining there for seven years, when he removed to Boston. In the latter city he became a partner of Judge Hubbard, and the firm was soon the most prosperous in Massachusetts. From 1813 to 1824 Mr. Jackson was justice of the Supreme Court of Massachusetts; served as delegate to the State Constitutional Convention of 1820, and in 1833 was appointed member of the commission charged with the revision of the state laws. Justice Jackson is the author of the important work, *Treatise on the Pleadings and Practice in Real Actions* (1828).

JACKSON, Charles Loring, American chemist: b. Boston, Mass., April 4, 1847; d. Boston 1935. He was graduated at Harvard in 1867, and subsequently studied at Heidelberg and Berlin. In 1868 he was appointed assistant in chemistry at Harvard, in 1881 full professor, and in 1911 he became professor emeritus. He discovered a new method of preparing borneol from camphor in 1883–1884. He published *Lecture Notes in Chemistry* (1878) and numerous papers on organic chemistry in *Proceedings of the American Academy* and in the *American Journal of Science.*

JACKSON, Charles Thomas, American scientist: b. Plymouth, Mass., June 21, 1805; d. Somerville, Mass., Aug. 28, 1880. He was graduated at Harvard Medical College in 1829. He assisted in a geological and mineralogical survey of Nova Scotia, publishing his results in *Memoirs of the American Academy of Arts and Science.* He went to Europe in 1829, spending his time in Germany, Italy, and Paris. On his return he began practicing at Boston, but abandoned this for the study of the sciences. In 1836 he became state geologist of Maine, and later held the same post in Rhode Island 1839 and in New Hampshire 1840. He claimed to have been the first to indicate, in 1832, the applicability of electricity to telegraphic use, and also claimed, in 1842, to have been the discoverer of the anesthetic effects of the inhalation of ether. He received the Montyon Prize of 2,500 francs from the French Academy of Sciences in 1852. He published a *Manual of Etherization, with a History of Its Discovery* (1861).

JACKSON, Chevalier L., American laryngologist: b. Pittsburgh, Pa., Nov. 4, 1865. He studied at Western University of Pennsylvania (now University of Pittsburgh), 1879–1883; took his M.D. at Jefferson Medical College, Philadelphia, 1886, and for a number of years was professor of laryngology in the University of Pittsburgh. In 1916 he became professor of laryngology in Jefferson Medical College, and also was professor of bronchoscopy and esophagoscopy in the University of Pennsylvania. Later he transferred to Temple University. Generally conceded to be the foremost bronchoscopist in the United States, he developed the method of removing foreign bodies from the lungs by the insertion of tubes through the mouth. Honors conferred upon him include honorary fellow of the Royal Society of Medicine, and of the Scottish, French, Italian, Polish and Rumanian otolaryngological societies; Officer, Legion of Honor, France; Chevalier, Order of Leopold, Belgium. He is a member of numerous American medical societies, and published *Peroral Endoscopy and Laryngeal Surgery; Bronchoscopy and Esophagoscopy.*

JACKSON, Dugald Caleb, American electrical engineer: b. Kennett Square, Pa., Feb. 13, 1865; d. Cambridge, Mass., July 1, 1951. In 1885 he was graduated at the Pennsylvania State College, and took a postgraduate course in electrical engineering at Cornell in 1885–1887. For the next two years he was vice president and engineer of the Western Engineering Company at Lincoln, Nebr. Subsequently he was assistant chief engineer of the Sprague Electric Railway and Motor Company and chief engineer of the central district of the Edison General Electric Company. From 1907 until his retirement in 1935 Dr. Jackson was head of the Department of Engineering at Massachusetts Institute of Technology. He published *A Textbook on Electricity and Magnetism and the Construction of Dynamos* (1893); *Electricity and Magnetism* (1895); *Alternating Currents and Alternating Current Machinery* (1896; new ed., 1913); *An Elementary Book on Electricity and Magnetism and Their Applications* (1902; rewritten 1919); *Engineering's Part in the Development of Civilization* (1939); *Present Status and Trends of Engineering Education in the United States.*

JACKSON, Edward Payson, American author: b. Erzerum, Turkey, March 15, 1840; d. 1905. He was educated at Amherst College; served in the Union Army during the Civil War as private of the 45th and lieutenant of the 5th Massachusetts; was principal and superintendent of various educational institutions, and in 1877 was appointed master in the Boston Latin School.
His works include *Mathematical Geography* (1873); *A Demigod* (1886), a story published anonymously, and at first attributed to various well-known authors; *The Earth in Space* (1889); and *Character Building* (1892), to which was awarded a prize of $1,000, offered by the American Secular Union, jointly with N. P. Gilman's *The Laws of Daily Conduct,* with which it was published in the volume, *Conduct as a Fine Art* (1894). He also became the editor of *The Bohemian,* a Boston magazine of short fiction.

JACKSON, Frederick George, English Arctic explorer: b. Alcester, Warwickshire, 1860; d. London, March 13, 1938. He was educated at Denstone College and the University of Edinburgh, made journeys across the Australian deserts and the Great Tundra of Siberia, in 1894–1897 was leader of the Jackson-Harmsworth expedition to Franz Josef Land, and during the second Boer War was in command of a company of mounted infantry; mapped Franz Josef Land, which he proved to be a collection of islands, and made valuable magnetic and meteorological observations; awarded gold medal, Paris Geographical Society in 1899. His publications include: *The Great Frozen Land* (1895); *A Thousand Days in the Arctic* (1899); *The Lure of the Unknown Lands* (1935). He was awarded the Victory Medal in World War I.

JACKSON, Gabrielle Emilie Snow, American writer for young people: b. New York, Oct. 13, 1861. She is the author of *Denise and Ted Toodles* (1897); *Pretty Polly*

Perkins' (1900); 'Laddie and Lassie' (1900); 'Caps and Capers' (1901); 'Three Graces' (1903); 'Three Graces at College' (1904); 'Mother and Daughter' (1904); 'Little Miss Cricket Series' (1905); 'Wee Winkles and Wideawake' series (1906); 'Ned Toodles the Second' (1906); 'A Blue Grass Beauty' (1907); 'Joy of Piney Hill' (1907); 'Sunlight and Shadow' (1907); 'The Dawn of Womanhood' (1907); 'Three Little Women' series (1908); 'A Maid of Middies' Haven' (1909); 'Captain Polly of Annapolis' series (1910-11); 'Peggy Stewart' series (1911-12); 'Peterkin' (1914); 'Silverheels' (1916).

JACKSON, George, English and Canadian clergyman and educator: b. 15 Oct. 1864. Educated at Collegiate School, Grimsby, Wesleyan Methodist College, Richmond and London University. In 1880 he entered the Wesleyan Methodist ministry and was in charge of the Clitheroe circuit. Superintendent of the Wesleyan Methodist Mission, Edinburgh, 1889-1906; pastor of Sherbourne Street Methodist Church, Toronto, 1906-09; professor of the English Bible, Victoria College, Toronto University, 1909-13; resident tutor, Didsbury College, Manchester, 1913-16; Brixton Hill, London, 1916-19; since 1919, professor of English language, literature and Bible, Didsbury College. He is author of 'First Things First' (1894); 'The Table Talk of Jesus' (1896); 'Judgment, Human and Divine' (1897); 'The Ten Commandments' (1898); 'A Young Man's Bookshelf' (1898); 'A Young Man's Religion' (1900); 'The Teaching of Jesus' (1903); 'The Old Testament and the New' (1903); 'Studies in the Old Testament' (1909); 'The Preacher and the Modern Mind' (1912); 'In a Preacher's Study' (1914); 'Leaves of Healing' (1916); 'Reasonable Religion' (1922); 'Collier of Manchester' (1923).

JACKSON, George Anson, American Congregational clergyman: b. North Adams, Mass., 17 March 1846; d. Swampscott, Mass., 8 May 1907. He was graduated from Yale in 1868, from the Andover Theological Seminary in 1871; was ordained to the Congregational ministry, and in 1872-97 held pastorates successively at Leavenworth, Kan., Southbridge, Mass., and Swampscott, Mass. In 1897 he became librarian of the General Theological Library of Boston, serving till his death. He wrote 'The Apostolic Fathers' (1879); 'Fathers of the Third Century' (1881); 'Post-Nicene Greek Fathers' (1883); 'Post-Nicene Latin Fathers' (1883); 'The Son of a Prophet' (1894), a historical novel.

JACKSON, George Thomas, American dermatologist: b. New York, 19 Dec. 1852; d. 3 Jan. 1916. He received his education at the College of the City of New York and at the universities of Berlin, Vienna and Strassburg. In 1878 he was graduated in medicine at Columbia University and for the next six years was engaged in general practice. He finally gave special attention to dermatology, in which he lectured at the New York Woman's Medical College from 1890 to 1899, and also at the University of Vermont and at Columbia. His published works are 'Diseases of the Hair and Scalp' (1887, 1893); 'The Ready Reference Handbook of Diseases of the Skin' (1893; 7th ed., 1914); 'Treatise on the Diseases of the Hair,' with C. W. McMurtry (1912).

JACKSON, Helen Maria Fiske Hunt, «H. H.,» American novelist and poet: b. Amherst, Mass., 18 Oct. 1831; d. San Francisco, 12 Aug. 1885. At 21 she married Capt. Edward Hunt (d. 1863) of the United States army, and began the wandering existence of an army officer's wife. From 1867 to her death, 16 years later, her pen hardly rested. She wrote verses, sketches of travel, essays, children's stories, novels and tracts for the time, generally over the pen-name «H. H.» Her life in the West after her marriage to W. S. Jackson, a banker of Colorado Springs, revealed to her the wrongs of the Indian, which she set herself at once to redress. Newspaper letters, appeals to government officialism, and finally her 'Century of Dishonor' (1881), a sharp arraignment of the nation for perfidy and cruelty toward its helpless wards, were her service to this cause. Her most popular story, 'Ramona,' (1884), a romance whose protagonists are of Indian blood, was also an appeal for justice. This book, however, rose far above its polemic intention; the beauty of its descriptions, its dramatic movement, its admirable characterization, and its imaginative insight entitling it to high rank. Two novels in the 'No Name Series' — 'Mercy Philbrick's Choice' (1876) and 'Hetty's Strange History' (1877) — show the qualities that infuse her prose: color, brilliancy of touch, grace of form, certainty of intuition and occasional admirable humor. She had not the gift of construction and lacked the power of self-criticism; so that she is singularly uneven. It is no doubt chiefly her poems which have gained for «H. H.» a place in literature. They reveal genuine lyrical power, although at times marred by defective technique. Among books of hers not already named are 'Bits of Travel' (1873); 'Glimpses of Three Coasts'; 'Sonnets and Lyrics' (1886). To her have often been attributed the noted 'Saxe Holm' stories. Consult Higginson, T. W., 'Contemporaries' (Boston 1900). See RAMONA.

JACKSON, Henry Rootes, American diplomat and soldier: b. Athens, Ga., 24 June 1820; d. Savannah, Ga., 23 May 1898. He was graduated at Yale in 1839, admitted to the bar in Georgia and for several years was district attorney. He served in the Mexican War, became judge of the Superior Court, and in 1853 went to Vienna as chargé d'affaires, and the following year was made Minister resident there resigning in 1858. Before the outbreak of the Civil War he seceded from the Charleston Convention and, when his State seceded, commanded the State troops. He eventually resigned and joined the Confederate forces. Near the close of the war he was made a brigadier-general in Hood's army and was captured with his whole command at Nashville after the battle of Franklin. In 1885 he was appointed United States Minister to Mexico, but resigned in the following year, because of a disagreement with government authorities over the ruling in the case of the American schooner *Rebecca,* which had been seized by the Mexicans on the charge of smuggling. He was the author of 'Tallulah, and Other Poems' (1850).

JACKSON, Howell Edmunds, American jurist: b. Paris, Tenn., 8 April 1832; d. West Meade, Tenn., 8 Aug. 1895. He was graduated from the University of Virginia in 1854, from the law department of Cumberland University in 1856, began practice in Jackson and later in Memphis, and upon the organization of the Confederate government became receiver for property in West Tennessee confiscated to the purposes of the Confederacy. Subsequent to the war he became a member of the Court of Referees of Tennessee, a tribunal which acted as a provisional Supreme Court in the hearing of cases that had arisen during the war period. Elected to the State legislature in 1880, he took his seat in the United States Senate in 1881, afterward left the Senate to become United States Circuit Court judge for the West Tennessee district, and in 1893 was appointed an associate justice in the United States Supreme Court.

JACKSON, James, American soldier and statesman: b. Moreton Hampstead, Devonshire, England, 21 Sept. 1757; d. Washington, D. C., 19 March 1806. He emigrated to America with his father in 1772 and studied law in Savannah. In March 1776 he aided in repelling a British attack upon that town, was appointed member of the first constitutional convention of Georgia in 1777 and subsequently was appointed brigade major of the Georgia militia. In 1781 he aided in the capture of the fort at Augusta, and was left in command of the place and upon the evacuation of Savannah by the British in 1782 was appointed by General Wayne to receive the keys of the town. In 1789 he was chosen a representative in Congress, and from 1792 to 1795 was a member of the United States Senate. He had the principal share in the framing of the Georgia constitution of 1798 and upon its adoption was elected governor of the State and held that office until his re-election in 1801 to the United States Senate. He was a Jeffersonian in his political views.

JACKSON, James, American physician, brother of Charles Jackson (q.v.): b. Newburyport, Mass., 3 Oct. 1777; d. 1867. He was graduated at Harvard College in 1796; studied medicine in London and on his return to Boston in 1800 commenced practice there, devoting himself entirely to medical practice, to the exclusion of surgery and other branches. In 1803 he became a member of the Massachusetts Medical Society, of which he later became president. In 1810, with Dr. John C. Warren, he brought before the community a proposition for establishing a hospital in the city of Boston. The first result of this was the organization of the asylum for the insane at Somerville, then included in Charlestown, and afterward of the Massachusetts General Hospital in Boston. Dr. Jackson was the first physician, and Dr. Warren the first surgeon to this institution. In 1810 he was chosen professor of clinical medicine in Harvard, and in 1812 professor of theory and practice, becoming professor emeritus in 1835. His principal publications were 'On the Brunonian System' (1809); 'Remarks on the Medical Effects of Dentition'; 'Letters to a Young Physician' (1855). Of the last work several editions were printed. Consult Putnam, 'Memoir of Dr. James Jackson' (Boston 1905).

JACKSON, John Adams, American sculptor: b. Bath, Me., 5 Nov. 1825; d. Pracchia, Tuscany, 30 Aug. 1879. He was apprenticed to a machinist in Boston, where he gave evidence of talent by modeling a bust of Thomas Buchanan Read. He studied linear and geometrical drawing in Boston, gave much time to crayon portraits and then went to Paris, where he studied under Suisse. In 1858 he went to New York and remained there until 1860, when he returned to Florence, which was afterward his home. His portrait busts include those of Daniel Webster (1851), Adelaide Phillips (1853) and Wendell Phillips (1854). His ideal productions are noted for their anatomical accuracy and graceful treatment. These include 'Eve and the Dead Abel' (1862); 'Autumn,; 'Cupid Stringing his Bow'; 'Titania and Nick Bottom'; 'The Culprit Fay'; 'Dawn'; 'Peace'; 'Cupid on a Swan'; 'The Morning Glory'; 'Reading-Girl'; 'Musidora' (1873); 'Hylas' (1875) and 'Il Pastorello.' He designed a statue of Dr. Elisha K. Kane, the Arctic explorer, in 1860; a group for the southern gatehouse of the reservoir in Central Park, N. Y. (1867) and the soldiers' monument at Lynn, Mass. (1874).

JACKSON, Mercy Bisbee, American physician: b. Hardwick, Mass., 17 Sept. 1802; d. Boston, 13 Dec. 1877. She was graduated at the New England Female Medical College in 1860, having previously practised medicine in Plymouth, Mass., for 20 years and in Boston for 15 years. She was the first woman that was admitted to the American Institute of Homœopathy in Philadelphia, in June 1871, became a member of the Massachusetts Homœopathic Society and of the Boston Homœopathic Society in 1873, and in that year was made professor of diseases of children in the Boston University School of Medicine, which office she held until her death. She was twice married, her first husband being the Rev. John Bisbee, and her second, Capt. Daniel Jackson, of Plymouth. She was an active worker for the cause of temperance and woman suffrage, addressed large audiences and contributed frequently to the *Woman's Journal,* published in Boston.

JACKSON, Patrick Tracy, American merchant brother of Charles Jackson (q.v.): b. Newburyport, Mass., 14 Aug. 1780; d. Beverly, Mass., 12 Sept. 1847. At the age of 15 he was apprenticed to a merchant of Newburyport and subsequently established himself in Boston in the India trade, in which he acquired a handsome fortune. In 1812, at the invitation of his brother-in-law, Francis C. Lowell, who had recently examined the process of the cotton manufacture in England, he engaged in a project to introduce the power loom, then newly invented, and the mode of constructing which was kept secret, into the United States. After repeated failures they succeeded in 1812 in producing a model from which a machine was subsequently constructed by Paul Moody. In 1813 they built their first mill at Waltham, near Boston, the first in the world that combined all the operations for converting the raw cotton into finished cloth. In 1821 Jackson made large purchases of land on the Merrimack River near the Pawtucket canal, on which a number of mills were constructed by the Merrimack Manufacturing Company, a corporation organized under his auspices. This settlement formed the germ of the present city of Lowell. He procured in 1830 a charter for a railroad between Lowell and Boston and directed its construction until completion.

JACKSON, Robert Houghwout, American jurist: b. Spring Creek, Pa., Feb. 13, 1892; d. Washington, D. C., Oct. 9, 1954. After attending the Albany Law School he returned to his home in Jamestown, N. Y., was admitted to the bar (1913), and within a few years became corporation counsel of Jamestown and general counsel for several local public service corporations. Appointed general counsel of the Internal Revenue Bureau in 1934, he sucessfully prosecuted on a tax evasion charge former Secretary of the Treasury Andrew D. Mellon, compelling him to pay $750,000 of unpaid taxes. Appointed solicitor general in 1938, of the 44 cases which he argued for the government he lost only six. Attorney general in 1940, during his brief tenure he was active in prosecuting fifth-columnists, while safeguarding civil liberties. Appointed by President Roosevelt to the Supreme Court, he took his seat on Oct. 6, 1941. In May 1945 President Truman appointed him chief of counsel for the United States in prosecuting the leading Axis war criminals. When the International Military Tribunal before which the culprits were tried was established Justice Jackson was chief prosecutor for his country. So well did he and his English, French, and Russian colleagues conduct the prosecutions that 12 of the 22 defendants were given the death penalty. A radical New Dealer who had supported Roosevelt's attempt to pack the Supreme Court, he moved to a "middle-of-the-road" position in his later years.

JACKSON, Sheldon, American educator: b. Minaville, N. Y., May 18, 1834; d. 1909. He was graduated at Union College in 1855, at Princeton Theological Seminary in 1858; was ordained to the ministry of the Presbyterian Church in the latter year; and was missionary to western Wisconsin and southern Minnesota in 1859–69. In 1869–82 he was superintendent of Presbyterian missions in western Iowa, Nebraska, the Rocky Mountain territories, Wyoming, Colorado, New Mexico, Arizona, Utah, and Montana, and from 1877 in Alaska. In 1885 he became United States general agent of education in Alaska, and in 1887 organized the Alaskan society of natural history and ethnology at Sitka. He aided in founding a missionary college in Utah in 1896, was moderator of the Presbyterian General Assembly in 1897, and wrote *Alaska and Missions on the North Pacific Coast* (1880); *Education in Alaska* (1881). Consult Stewart, R. L., *Sheldon Jackson* (New York 1908).

JACKSON, Stonewall. See JACKSON, THOMAS JONATHAN.

JACKSON, Thomas, English Wesleyan clergyman, educator and editor: b. Sancton, Yorkshire, Dec. 12, 1783; d. Shepherd's Bush, London, March 10, 1873. He was largely a self-made man. He was editor of *The Wesleyan Methodist Magazine* and also of *The Youth's Instructor and Guardian,* 1824–42; professor of divinity in the Richmond Theological College, 1842–61. He edited a new edition of *John Wesley's Christian Library* (30 vols.). He also edited *The Works of John Wesley* (14 vols., 1829–31; *A Library of Christian Biography* (12 vols., 1837–40); *The Lives of the Early Methodist Preachers* (3 vols., 1837–38; 3d ed., 6 vols., 1865–66); *Anthony Farindon's Sermons* (4 vols., 1849). He was the author of many volumes and pamphlets. The most important are *The Life of John Goodwin* (1822); *Memoirs of the Life and Writings of Rev. Richard Watson* (1834); *The Centenary of Wesleyan Methodism* (1839); *The Life of Rev. Charles Wesley* (2 vols., 1841). Consult also Dunn, Samuel, *Recollections of Thomas Jackson and His Acts* (1873). His large library is now the property of Garrett Biblical Institute, Evanston, Ill.

JACKSON, Sir Thomas Graham, English architect: b. Hampstead, Dec. 21, 1835; d. London, Nov. 7, 1924. He was educated at Oxford University; was a pupil of Sir George Gilbert Scott (q.v.) (1858–61), specializing in Gothic style; was made baronet in 1913; designed many of the new buildings in Oxford, Cambridge, Eton, Westminster School, Rugby, Harrow, etc., and has restored Great Malvern Priory, Bath Abbey and Winchester Cathedral, besides building many new Gothic churches. He has written *Modern Gothic Architecture* (1873); *Wadham College, Oxford; Its History and Buildings* (1893); *The Church of Saint Mary the Virgin, Oxford: Reasons in Architecture* (1906); *Byzantine and Romanesque Architecture* (1913); *Gothic Architecture in France, England and Italy* (1915); *A Holiday in Umbria* (1917); *Renaissance of Roman Architecture* (1921–22); *Memories of Travel* (1923).

JACKSON, Thomas Jonathan, commonly called "STONEWALL JACKSON," American general: b. Clarksburg, Harrison County, W. Va., Jan. 21, 1824; d. near Chancellorsville, Va., May 10, 1863. Lieutenant General Thomas Jonathan Jackson was one of the most unique, romantic characters of the War between the States, and crowded into the two years in which he served brilliant achievements which won him wider fame than any other soldier on either side. Descended from Scotch-Irish stock and inheriting many of the qualities of his ancestry, he was left a penniless orphan when three years old, and soon showed "the stuff of which heroes are made," in his manly self-reliant efforts to support himself. Learning of a vacancy from his Congressional district in the military academy at West Point, he determined to make the journey to Washington and seek the appointment, and set out at once — traveling a part of the way on foot — appearing before the member of Congress from his district in his suit of homespun, and with his leather saddlebags over his shoulders. The congressman presented him to the secretary of war, who was so much pleased with the youth's determination that he at once made out his appointment to West Point. He was very badly prepared to enter the academy and barely "squeezed through" on his entrance examination, but by persevering work he gradually rose in his grade until in July 1846 he was graduated No. 17 in a brilliant class containing such men as McClellan, Foster, Reno, Stoneman, Couch, Gibbon, A. P. Hill, Pickett, Maury, D. R. Jones, Wilcox and others; and one who knew him intimately expressed the confident belief that if the course had been longer "Old Jack" would have graduated at the head of his class. He immediately reported for duty in Mexico, and serving in the artillery won distinction on every field, always seeking the post of danger, being made first lieutenant at the siege of Vera Cruz, brevetted captain at Contreras and Churbusco, and major at Chapultepec, rising to this rank in seven months, and being promoted more rapidly than any other officer of his grade in the Mexican War. He was frequently and honorably mentioned in the official reports, and John B. Magruder, his immediate superior, wrote of him: «If devotion, industry, talent and gallantry are the highest qualities of a soldier, then he is entitled to the distinction which their possession confers.»

On the recommendation of his old comrade, D. H. Hill, whose brother-in-law he afterward became, Jackson was elected, in 1851, professor of natural science and instructor of military tactics in the Virginia Military Institute, Lexington, Va., being elected over McClellan, Reno, Rosecrans and G. W. Smith, whose names were submitted by the faculty at West Point. He made little reputation as a professor, and the cadets were always playing pranks upon him, and laughing at his eccentricities. From his habit of instructing his own servants in Scripture lessons every Sunday afternoon grew his famous negro Sunday school to which he devoted so much time and thought to which he contributed so liberally of his moderate means, — sending his pastor checks for it in the midst of his most active campaigns,— and which made such an impress upon the negroes and gave Jackson so warm a place in their affections that the first contribution to his monument was made in 1887 by the negro Baptist Church of Lexington. Jackson was a Union man, opposed to secession as a remedy for Southern wrongs, though thoroughly believing in the abstract right of a State to secede, and greatly deprecated the war which he predicted would follow; but when the news reached the quiet little town of Lexington that Mr. Lincoln had called for 75,000 troops to coerce sovereign States, and that the Union Convention of Virginia had passed an ordinance of secession, Jackson said in a speech before a public meeting: «I have longed to preserve the Union and would have been willing to sacrifice much to that end. But now that the North has chosen to inaugurate war against us, I am in favor of meeting her by drawing the sword and throwing away the scabbard.» Governor Letcher, his old neighbor and friend, who had a high estimate of his abilities, commissioned him colonel in the Virginia forces; but his brilliant record in Mexico had been forgotten — he was only thought of as the quiet, eccentric professor, and when his name was presented to the Virginia convention, a prominent member arose and asked: «Who is this Major Jackson, anyway?» and it required all the eloquence of the Rockbridge delegates to secure his confirmation.

Marching the corps of cadets to Richmond where he remained for a brief season assisting in organizing and drilling the raw recruits in the «Camp of Instruction,» he was ordered to Harper's Ferry on 3 May, where he bent his energies toward reducing the high-spirited rabble who had rushed to the front at the first sound of the bugle to the respectable Army of the Shenandoah, which he turned over to the command of General J. E. Johnston 23 May. Placed in command of the Virginia brigade which afterward became so famous, he met the advance of General Patterson at Falling Waters on 2 July, gave them a decided check, and captured a number of prisoners. Soon after he received his commission as brigadier-general in the following characteristic letter from General Lee:

RICHMOND, 3rd July, 1861,

MY DEAR GENERAL:— I have the pleasure of sending you a commission of brigadier-general in the Provisional Army; and to feel you merit it. May your advancement increase your usefulness to the State.

Very truly,

R. E. LEE.

But it was in the battle of first Manassas (Bull Run) that Jackson won his new name and fame, and the ringing words of the gallant Bee: «There stands Jackson like a stone wall,» changed the name of «Thomas Jonathan» into the immortal «Stonewall» Jackson. He was wounded in the hand but refused to leave the field, and while the surgeons were dressing his wounds President Davis rode on the field, and Jackson, pushing aside the surgeons, tossed his cadet cap in the air and exclaimed: «Hurrah for the President. Give me ten thousand men and I will be in Washington to-night!» In September he was made major-general, and was sent on 4 October to command the «Valley District» and enter in the early part of 1862 on that famous «Valley Campaign,» which is now studied in military academies in Europe as illustrative of able strategy, rapid movements, and heroic fighting. In March he fell back before Banks' army of 35,000 men, and Banks reported him «in full retreat from the valley» and started a column to cross the mountains and attack Johnston in flank as he was falling back from Manassas, when Jackson suddenly turned, marched 18 miles in the morning, and with 2,700 men fought at Kernstown, near Winchester, 8,000 of the enemy, and though sustaining the only defeat that ever befell him he accomplished his purpose in recalling the column which was moving on Johnston's flank, quietly moved up the valley and took a strong position in Swift Run Gap from which he could easily defend himself or strike the enemy if he attempted to move on Staunton. Ewell's division coming to take his place, he left this grim soldier to watch Banks, and moved so secretly that neither friend nor foe had divined his plans until he thrilled the Confederacy and sent terror to the North by the following laconic and characteristic dispatch:

Valley District, May 9th, 1862.

GEN. S. COOPER:— God blessed our arms with victory at McDowell yesterday.

T. J. JACKSON, Major-General.

He had defeated the advance of Fremont under Milroy and driven it back in great confusion. Then followed in rapid succession the uniting of Ewell's division with his at Luray, the driving in of Banks' flank at Front Royal, the cutting of his retreating column at Middletown, and on 25 May the rout of Banks' army from the heights of Winchester, and driving him pellmell across the Potomac. He was about to cross the Potomac into Maryland in pursuit of Banks when he learned that Fremont from the west, and Shields, the head of McDowell's column, from the east, were marching to form a junction in his rear at Strasburg. He at once put his army in motion and by forced marches (one of his brigades marched 52 miles in one day) he reached the point of danger in time to hold Fremont in check with one hand and Shields with the other until his whole army, prisoners and immense wagon trains loaded with captured stores passed on in safety. He then moved leisurely up the valley, burning the bridges over the Shenandoah to prevent a juncture between Fremont and Shields — his rear being protected by that chivalrous knight and brave soldier, Gen. Turner Ashby, who filled the valley with the fame of his brilliant achievements, and whose fall in a severe fight near Harrisonburg on 6 June was sadly lamented as a great calamity to the Confederate cause. On 7 June, at Cross Keys, Ewell badly defeated Fremont, and on 8 June, at Port Republic, on the opposite side of the river, Jackson routed Shields, and the armies sent to «crush» him were soon rapidly retreating down the valley, while «Stonewall» — that name will cling to him, but «Thunderbolt,» «Tornado,» or «Hurricane,» would be more expressive of his character, — remained master of the situation. This campaign may be thus summarized: In 32 days Jackson and his «foot cavalry» had marched nearly 400 miles, skirmishing almost daily, fought five battles, defeated three armies, two of which were completely routed, captured 20 pieces of artillery, 4,000 prisoners, and immense quantities of stores of all kinds, and had done all this with a loss of fewer than 1,000 men killed, wounded and missing, and with a force of only 15,000 men, while there were at least 60,000 men opposed to him. He had spread consternation throughout the North and had neutralized McDowell's 40,000 men at Fredericksburg, who were about to march to the aid of McClellan in investing Richmond. Jackson now rested for a brief season, was reinforced from Lee's army, made the impression on the enemy that he would advance down the valley again, and managed matters so secretly that Banks at Strasburg was busily engaged in fortifying against an expected attack from him at the very time he was thundering on McClellan's flank at Richmond over 200 miles away. The part he bore in the Seven Days around Richmond, the second Manassas campaign, and the Maryland campaign was so conspicuous and so important that it would be, indeed, to write the history of the army to give it in detail. His skill and daring in the Seven Days battle, his defeat of Pope's advance under Banks at Cedar Run, his flank march to Pope's rear, and the pertinacity with which he held him at bay along the Warrenton road until Lee could come up with Longstreet and drive him into the fortifications around Washington, his capture of Harper's Ferry with 11,000 prisoners, 13,000 stand of small arms, 73 pieces of artillery, and large quantities of provisions and stores of every description, and his conduct on the field of Sharpsburg, all added greatly to the fame of Stonewall Jackson and his grand old corps of «Foot Cavalry.» It was the privilege of the writer of this sketch to have been under Jackson during the whole of his brilliant career, and it may not be amiss to describe him as he appeared at the head of his victorious legions; about 37 years old, six feet tall, medium build, gray-blue eyes, light brown hair, set jaw and wide nostrils. He wore a plain gray uniform which soon became faded and soiled, cavalry boots and an old gray cadet cap with its rim tilting on his nose. He rode a raw-boned sorrel horse which the men said «could not run except toward the enemy,» but whenever he appeared among the troops they would begin to give the Confederate yell, and he would take off his cap, put spurs to «Little Sorrel» and gallop away from them as rapidly as possible. On 10 Oct. 1862 he was made lieutenant-general, and his corps made to consist of his old division, under W. B. Taliaferro, Early's division, A. P. Hill's division, and D. H. Hill's division, Colonel Brown's regiment of artillery, and numerous light batteries. At Fredericksburg, 13 Dec. 1862, he held the extreme right of Lee's army, and defeated with great slaughter Franklin's attack upon him. The following winter and spring Jackson spent in improving the organization, discipline and efficiency of his corps, and as, in his judgment, a most important means of accomplishing this, he labored to have chaplains in every regiment and missionaries to visit the army, and did everything in his power to promote the religious welfare of his soldiers. It was largely through his influence that a chaplains' association was formed, and he had regular prayer-meetings at his headquarters during the weeks and preaching on Sundays. But the end hastened on, General Hooker threw Sedgwick across the river below Fredericksburg the latter days of April 1863, crossed the bulk of his army above and strongly fortified his lines at Chancellorsville in the confident hope that Lee would either retreat on Richmond, or attack him in his strong position, where a crushing defeat would await him. But instead of doing either of these things Lee left Early to watch Sedgwick, moved up to Hooker's front, and sent Jackson with 22,000 men to make a march to Hooker's flank and rear. This was brilliantly executed and Jackson routed that flank of Hooker's army, and was proceeding to cut him off from his line of retreat and take a position where Hooker would have been compelled to attack him, when in returning from one of those bold reconnoissances which he so frequently made, his party was mistaken for the enemy and fired on by his own men and he was very severely wounded. His left arm was amputated, his other wounds dressed, and he was doing well and gave every promise of recovery, when pneumonia, brought on by exposure before the battle, set in and he died at a quarter past three P.M., Sunday, 10 May 1863.

The great soldier had fought his last battle, won his last victory, and gone to wear his glittering «crown of rejoicing.» He was buried as he had requested in «Lexington in the valley of Virginia.» A beautiful bronze statue marks his grave; on the hill at the Virginia Military Institute has been reared the stately «Jackson Memorial Hall,» and in the capitol square of his native State stands the noble bronze statue, the gift of English admirers. Lee spoke his fittest eulogy when he wrote him after hearing that he was wounded: «Could I have dictated events I should have chosen for the good of the country to have been disabled in your stead.» Consult Cooke, J. E., 'Stonewall Jackson: A Military Biography' (New York 1876);

Jackson, M. A. M., *Memoirs* (Louisville 1895); Henderson, *Stonewall Jackson and the Civil War* 2 vols. (New York 1902).

JACKSON, William, American soldier and secretary of the Constitutional Convention: b. Cumberland, England, Mar. 9, 1759; d. Philadelphia, Pa., Dec. 18, 1828. He was brought to South Carolina and educated there by his guardian, Robert Owens. Commissioned lieutenant at the outbreak of the American Revolution, he participated in the 1778 expedition against St. Augustine, Fla. Accompanying John Laurens to France as his secretary in the mission of 1781, Jackson supervised the shipments of supplies from France to the Continental Army. After returning to the United States in February 1782, he was assistant secretary of war for two years, resigning to engage in a mercantile venture. When the Constitutional Convention met in Philadelphia, he appealed to Washington for the post of secretary to the convention, and on Hamilton's nomination received the appointment. By orders of the convention its records were burned, except the journal of proceedings and the yea and nay votes; these in Jackson's hand are the only surviving convention records. Admitted to the Pennsylvania bar in 1788, the following year President Washington appointed him one of his personal secretaries. In 1792, a year after he had resigned his secretaryship, the president tendered him the post of adjutant general of the army; but Jackson declined, preferring a business partnership with William Bingham. One of Washington's last official acts made him surveyor of customs at Philadelphia, a post he lost when Jefferson ejected all Federalists.

JACKSON, city, Michigan, and Jackson County seat; altitude 995 feet; on the Grand River, which runs through the business section; 37 miles south of Lansing; on the Toledo Division, New York Central; Michigan Central; Cleveland, Cincinnati, Chicago and St Louis; and Grand Trunk railroads. A railroad division point, Jackson has extensive shops for construction and repair of rolling stock. A network of highways, both state and federal highways serve the city and supply adequate facilities for truck transportation. There is a municipal airport. The surrounding area is agricultural, producing fruits, grains, and vegetables. The city is a variously productive industrial center, its manufactures including rubber tires; radios; automobile, airplane, and radio parts and accessories; corsets, electric refrigerators, grinding wheels, machine tools, forgings, and castings. Jackson is an important trade center and distributing point. Several car-making companies built plants and began operating here, but as the industry concentrated at other points, Jackson adjusted itself to a new schedule of industrial activities. Educational, cultural, and civic facilities are excellent. The first permanent settlement on the site of the present city was made in 1829; in 1830 the place was called Jacksonburg, in honor of President Andrew Jackson. In 1831 the township of Jacksonburg was formed. Finally, in 1838 the name was officially changed to Jackson. Incorporation as a village was effected in 1843; as a city, in 1857. The city's government is administered by a commission, with a city manager. This form of government was installed in 1915. The water supply system is municipally owned; power and light systems are privately owned and operated. Pop. (1940) 49,656; (1950) 50,904.

JACKSON, city, Mississippi, state capital and seat of Hinds County, is located in the southwest central part of the state, by air 195 miles south of Memphis and 165 miles north of New Orleans. The eastern boundary is the Pearl River; and the city, situated on the river bluffs at an altitude of 296 feet, spreads over an area of 27.2 square miles. The annual mean temperature is 65.6°F. (range of monthly means from 45.8°F. in January to 82.2°F. in July), and the average annual precipitation is 52.7 inches. Jackson has a commission form of government. Its water supply, drawn from Pearl River, is under municipal ownership.

Transportation.—The city is served by the Illinois Central and the Gulf, Mobile and Ohio railroads, and is an intersection point of three federal highways. Bus and trucking companies maintain daily schedules from the city in all directions. Near the city's outskirts is the municipally owned Hawkins Airport with scheduled airline service, and within a radius of about 20 miles are several other airfields.

Industries.—Jackson is an industrial city and an important wholesale trade center. In the surrounding counties, more than 40 oil and gas fields had been developed by 1951, and the city was a headquarters for oil exploration companies. As of January 1951, Jackson had 192 manufacturing plants, the most important manufactures being lumber products, meat and poultry products, asphalt tile, brick, cosmetics, dirt-moving equipment, fluorescent lamps, cotton clothing, cottonseed oil, and glass bottles.

Education.—In addition to its public schools for white and for Negro youth, Jackson's educational facilities include Belhaven College (Presbyterian, for women), Millsaps College (Methodist, coeducational), and two colleges for Negroes—Jackson College (state) and Campbell College (African Methodist Episcopal Church). Five miles northeast of Jackson is Tougaloo College (American Missionary Association), also for Negroes, as is Mississippi College in Clinton (q.v.).

Cultural Activities.—The city's library facilities include the Jackson Public Library, the college libraries, and large collections in the state library. In the War Memorial Building there is a state historical museum and a collection of portraits of Mississippians who have played important parts in state history. The Municipal Art Gallery houses paintings principally by Mississippi artists. Jackson has its own symphony orchestra, and local concert managers and the Jackson Music Association annually sponsor appearances of internationally famous music organizations and artists. Jackson has 121 churches, or about one to every 700 in the population. The city has two newspapers with morning, evening, and Sunday editions; and five radio stations, the largest number of any city in the state.

Points of Interest.—More than 7,000 crape myrtle bushes have been planted in the city's streets and parks, and the masses of purplish bloom on these tall bushes in the spring are the city's outstanding natural beauty. Jackson has 12 city parks, totaling 720 acres, with facilities for such sports as swimming, tennis, and golf. Livingston Park contains a zoo, and Battlefield

Park contains the remains of trenches and several cannon used by Confederate troops. The Hinds County Stadium and the state fairgrounds are also located in Jackson. Among the city's buildings of special historic interest are the beautiful Old Capitol (Greek Revival in style) and the Governor's Mansion, both completed in 1842. A few of the dwellings built before the Civil War still stand. One of them is the Manship Home, a frame building with gallery and balustrade, built in 1857, in front of which is now displayed the only bell in Jackson that was not melted down to make cannon balls during the Civil War.

History.—The site on which Jackson stands was part of a large tract of land purchased by the United States from the Choctaws in 1820. On a bluff near the river, Louis Le Fleur, a French Canadian, had established a trading post in the 1790's, which had come to be known as Le Fleur's Bluff; but the land around it was still wilderness in 1820, and Natchez was Mississippi's capital. In 1821, the legislature, having decided to locate the capital close to the center of the state, chose Le Fleur's Bluff as the new site. Before the end of 1822 the capital was platted, lots were offered for sale, a two-story, brick capitol was erected, and Le Fleur's Bluff was renamed Jackson in honor of Andrew Jackson, hero of the Battle of New Orleans and soon to be the nation's seventh president.

The location of the new capital was not acceptable to everyone, and until 1832 there was agitation for its removal. Then the state constitution provided it should remain the capital until 1850. By that time, the question was an academic one. Railroads had reached Jackson, incorporation had been effected, the Governor's Mansion and the City Hall had been erected, a fine large Capitol had replaced the small brick building, and the city had a population of 1,881, exclusive of slaves. It was attractively laid out, with squares for building alternating with squares reserved as "commons" or parks, in accordance with the original plan. (The evidence of this plan can still be seen today.)

By 1860 Jackson's population had reached 3,191. It was there, on Jan. 9, 1861, that the legislature made Mississippi the second state in the Confederacy. As the state capital and a railroad center, Jackson was an important strategic point during the Civil War; but in 1863, under the threat of siege, the capital was moved, and after the city's capture by General Sherman's troops, it was gutted by fire. (See JACKSON [MISS.], BATTLE OF; JACKSON, SIEGE OF.) Jackson became the seat of state government again in 1865, and the scene of bitter conflict in the legislature for several years thereafter. Slowly the city began to be rebuilt, but not until about 1900 did rapid expansion take place, as its industrial possibilities were recognized.

Population.—The population of this capital city has grown rapidly during the 1900's, as the following figures indicate: (1900) 7,816; (1920) 22,817; (1930) 48,282; (1940) 62,107; (1950) 97,674. About a third of the population are Negroes, among whom many are professional or skilled workers.

JACKSON, city, Ohio, Jackson County seat; altitude 670 feet; on the Baltimore and Ohio, the Chesapeake and Ohio, and the Detroit, Toledo and Ironton railroads, 38 miles northeast of Portsmouth. While a considerable amount of farming is done in the vicinity, the region is one of coal and iron mining. There are deposits of sand and clay, quartz, shales, and natural gas. Jackson is an industrial city, with railroad shops, blast furnaces, and a soil pipe foundry. The city has good schools and churches, and a public library. Pop. (1940) 6,295; (1950) 6,508.

JACKSON, city, Tennessee, Madison County seat; altitude 450 feet; in the valley of Forked Deer River; and on the Illinois Central; the Nashville, Chattanooga and St. Louis; the Gulf, Mobile and Ohio railroads; 85 miles northeast of Memphis. It has a municipal airport, four miles out of town. Located in an agricultural district, Jackson is an important trading and shipping center. Railroad shops employ many of the city's workers, and its industrial plants produce cotton bagging, store fixtures, furniture, handles, articles of hardwood and clay, aluminum foil, clothing, and batteries.

Union University, Lambuth College, and Lane College are here; they all have four-year courses, and are coeducational. Lane College is for Negro students; it was established in 1880 by the Colored Methodist Episcopal Church of America. The Carnegie library has a museum with collections of geological specimens; of fish and birds, and of Indian curios.

First settled about 1820 by families moving in from North Carolina, Jackson was incorporated as a town in 1823, and made county seat. Incorporation as a city occurred in 1845. On June 7, 1862 the city was taken by Union forces. In December of that year Gen. Nathan Bedford Forrest raided the region, and in 1863, the city was occupied by a Confederate garrison, which held it until July 1863 when the Confederates through lack of ammunition were defeated by a Union force under Col. Edward Hatch with 1,500 men of the 2d Iowa Cavalry. John Luther Jones, railroad engineer, of the "Casey Jones" ballad fame is buried in the Catholic cemetery.

Jackson has the commission form of government. Its water supply system is municipally owned, and draws from artesian wells. Tennessee Valley Authority power is used by the city, under its own operating system. Pop. (1940) 24,332; (1950) 30,098.

JACKSON (Miss.), Battle of, a battle of the American Civil War. After the battle of Raymond (q.v.) May 12, 1863, General Grant assigned McPherson's and Sherman's corps, and part of McClernand's, to the task of capturing Jackson, the state capital, 12 miles northeast of Raymond. The Confederate Gen. J. E. Johnston, defending the city, on May 14 ordered the brigades of Gregg and Walker (6,000 men) to delay the Union advance while records and other public property were being removed. However, McPherson and Sherman fought their way into the city that afternoon, and Sherman stayed for a time to complete destruction of railroads, bridges, factories and arsenals.

JACKSON (Miss.), Siege of. Hearing that Vicksburg had fallen, Gen. J. E. Johnston fell back on Jackson (evacuated by the Union forces after their capture of it in May) and occupied a line of works with flanks on the Pearl River. On July 11, 1863, General Sherman began shelling the city; 100 guns dropped shells on every part of town. The siege was prosecuted night and day, and on the morning of July 17, Jackson was found evacuated, General Johnston having retreated. General Sherman remained five days at Jackson, destroying much property, and then returned to Vicksburg. The Union loss at Jackson from July 11 to 16 was 129 killed, 762 wounded, and 231 missing or captured. The Confederate loss from July 5 to 25 was 71 killed, 504 wounded, and 764 captured or missing.

JACKSONVILLE, city, Alabama, in Calhoun County; altitude 720 feet; on the Southern Railroad, 18 miles southeast of Gadsden. Situated in a cotton and dairying region, the city's chief industries are the manufacture of cotton fabrics and yarn. A state teachers college is located here. The town was settled in 1822. Pop. (1950) 4,751.

JACKSONVILLE, city and port of entry, Florida, seat of Duval County, in the northeastern corner of the state, on the west bank of the St. Johns River, 20 miles from the ocean by water and 14 miles by land; altitude 20 feet. It is an important trading port and one of the leading railroad, air, and motor freight centers in the South. It is 138 miles south of Savannah, 212 north of Tampa, 165 east of Tallahassee, and about 1,000 miles from New York. It is served by the Seaboard Air Line, the Atlantic Coast Line, the Florida East Coast, and the Southern Railway System.

The port enjoys a strategic geographical position with respect to ocean routes to South America, Panama, and the Far East, and is usually the last port of call for vessels bound to those countries from ports northward on the Atlantic Coast. It has an excellent harbor on the Saint Johns River, sheltered from all storms and open to navigation throughout the year. The mean tide range is about 13 inches, with tidal currents not of sufficient strength to affect shipping adversely. The control of the port is vested in the City of Jacksonville, a commission of five men having supervision and control of the municipal terminals with power to extend and improve them, as well as to fix the rates and charges for their use. In 1950 there were 81 piers, wharves, and terminals at the port of Jacksonville, of which 65 were owned and operated by private interests. These provide more than 8 miles of vessel berthing space with water depths alongside up to 34 feet at mean low water, which is the channel depth. In 1950 work was begun on the Dames Point-Fulton Cut-off Channel which would materially shorten the distance from the ocean to the harbor.

Commerce and Industry.—Jacksonville's industrial activities show remarkable expansion since 1940. Wood and metal-working plants produce lumber, furniture, millwork, boxes, paper, and machinery. Other manufactures include naval stores, cigars, concrete blocks, glassware, fertilizers, and feeds. The processing of citrus fruits and meat products, and boat building and fishing are also important occupations. The growing tourist trade provides one of the city's major sources of income, and the selection of Jacksonville as the site of a large naval training station in 1940 has added further to city development.

Cultural Facilities.—In addition to primary, secondary, parochial, and private schools, Jacksonville has a junior college and a college of music, the latter offering a four-year course. Other cultural advantages include a public library; a Little Theater group; the Children's Theatre, known as Teen Town, and the Children's Museum; the Art Center, the Garden Center, and the Symphony Society.

Places of Interest.—The Jacksonville Recreation Department has jurisdiction over a large number of widely scattered city areas which provide organized recreation facilities for the city's population. These include tennis courts, soft ball diamonds, swimming pools, and golf courses. The excellent freshwater and saltwater fishing attracts both residents and visitors. The city has an annual $10,000 fishing tournament open to all comers. There is a free zoo overlooking Trout River, and two dog-racing tracks provide entertainment. The enormous Gator Bowl is the scene of the New Year's Day football game.

Government and History.—The city's government is a combination of the mayor-council and the commission types. The early history of Jacksonville is the story of the river on whose banks the city stands. The French naval officer Capt. Jean Ribaut placed a stone column beside the mouth of the river in 1562. In 1564 a Huguenot colony built Fort Caroline at St. Johns Bluff, a few miles upriver. The next year the Spanish mariner Pedro Menendez de Avilés, then adelantado of Florida, destroyed the little French colony. During the 18th century the English slave hunters were raiding the Florida missions repeatedly and by 1763 they had become masters of Florida.

The first settlement on the present city site was made by Lewis G. Hogan in 1816, whence Hogan's Creek, dividing the city, is named. In 1822 the town was laid out and named in honor of Andrew Jackson, the first territorial governor of Florida. It was incorporated in 1833.

Population.—The Seminole War (q.v.) greatly retarded the development of Jacksonville, but at conclusion of hostilities in 1842 a steady growth took place. The population in 1910 numbered 57,699; in 1930 (including South Jacksonville), 135,146; and in 1950, 204,517.

JACKSONVILLE, city, Illinois, seat of Morgan County; altitude about 600 feet; on the Burlington, the Wabash, and the Gulf, Mobile, and Ohio railroads; 34 miles southwest of Springfield. The principal crops of the county are corn, wheat, oats, soybeans, and hay. The city's principal industries are the manufacture of textile goods, Ferris wheels, electric appliances, food products, and steel bridges; also book binding. Jacksonville has a public library, two college libraries, and an art museum. It is the home of Illinois College, founded in 1829, and of MacMurray College for Women. When established in 1846, MacMurray College was known as the Illinois Conference Female Academy and was sponsored by the Methodist Episcopal Church. It has ceased to be denominational. Courses are offered in music, fine arts, and home economics, in addition to the ordinary academic subjects. The city is also the seat of state schools for the blind and the deaf, and a state mental hospital.

Jacksonville played a prominent part in the development of culture in Illinois as well as in the state's political history, and it was one of the first communities in Illinois to enjoy the advantages of railroad transportation. Here Stephen A. Douglas and William Jennings Bryan began their careers in the practice of law; the site of Bryan's home is marked. Duncan Park is named in honor of Gov. Joseph Duncan, head of the state government from 1834 to 1838; he moved to Jacksonville in 1830, and died there. The site of another home, that of Col. John J. Hardin, is marked as the birthplace of Col. Hardin's daughter, Ellen Hardin Walworth (q.v.), who was one of the three founders of the Daughters of the American Revolution. An interesting point in Jacksonville is the Corner of the Four Churches, a street intersection with a church at each corner. Notable buildings are the courthouse, the federal building, the city hall, the American Legion Memorial Home, the Masonic Temple, and the state institutional buildings. The origin of the city's name is somewhat obscure, but the most probable tradition seems to be that it was selected in honor of Andrew Jackson. First settled about 1818, the city was platted in 1825, and incorporated in 1830. In 1837 it contended for the honor of selection as capital of the state. Before the Civil War it was a station on the Underground Railroad. The city's government is administered by mayor and council. The water, power, and lighting systems are under municipal ownership. Pop. (1950) 20,387.

JACKSONVILLE, town, North Carolina, Onslow County seat, on the New River, 36 miles south of Kinston. It is a popular resort, with fishing. Camp Lejuene, the United States Marine base, is 10 miles southeast of the town. Pop. (1950) 3,960.

JACKSONVILLE, city, Texas, in Cherokee County; altitude 515 feet; served by the Missouri Pacific, the St. Louis Southwestern, and the Southern Pacific railroads; about 120 miles southeast of Dallas. Situated in a productive agricultural area, the town is a trading and shipping center. The principal crop of the area is tomatoes which are shipped to markets in the United States and Canada. Industries include basket, box, and garment factories, canneries, and cotton presses. Lon Morris College and Jacksonville College are situated here. The city also has a public library and several parks. First settled on the present site about 1872, Jacksonville was incorporated as a city in 1930. It has commission government with a city manager. The water supply system is publicly owned. Pop. (1950) 8,607.

JACKSONVILLE BEACH, city, Florida, in Duval County; on the Atlantic Ocean, 15 miles east of Jacksonville. It is noted as a beach resort; there is also a concrete industry. The city was incorporated in 1907. Pop. (1950) 6,430.

JACMEL, zhäk-mĕl′, seaport, Haiti, in the Ouest Department, on the south coast of the republic, on Jacmel Bay, about 25 miles southwest of Port-au-Prince. Vessels anchor offshore. There is regular steamer communication with American and English ports. A commercial center, it ships bananas, coffee, and other products of this fertile agricultural region. There are manganese deposits near by. Pop. (1950) 8,545.

JACOB, from Hebrew word *Ya-aqob*, literally "to seize the heel," or "supplant," also called Israel, third patriarch and son of Isaac and Rebekah. The story of his life as told in Genesis has many dramatic incidents. The struggle before birth between the two brothers, their antagonism due to the episode of the birthright and later to the subterfuge whereby Jacob secured his father's blessing, Esau's deadly hatred, the wanderer's dream and Jacob's fleeing to safety, his marriage with Laban's daughters, how his quiet life was disturbed and again he became a pilgrim; the vision of the wrestling angel, his reconciliation with Esau and subsequent arrival at Hebron, where his parents lived, with his twelve sons, fathers of the ten tribes of Israel—all these events can be read and read again without losing their interest. The resemblances throughout the careers of the patriarchs—brotherly strife, parental overfondness and the rest, only emphasize the human quality of the narrative.

After ten years, as the closing chapters of Genesis inform the reader, Jacob's favorite son, Joseph, became leading actor in the drama. In their anger at his airs of superiority, his brothers sell him to a band of Ismaelites, telling Jacob that a wild beast had devoured him. Later, as Canaan was visited by a severe famine, the sons were sent to Egypt to buy corn, Benjamin being retained at home, but Jacob was obliged to let him go with the rest, as Joseph had refused otherwise to release Simeon held as hostage. How Jacob heard on the second return of his sons from Egypt that Joseph was ruler, how he set out to meet him, with a retinue of 66 persons, 11 sons and their children, and how Joseph met him at Goshen, to be received later by Pharaoh and assigned a residence "in the best part of the land, in the land of Rameses," complete a thrilling narrative. At that time, Jacob was 130 years of age. His death was the next great episode, but before his passing he made Joseph swear not to bury him in Egypt, but in the family sepulchre in Canaan. Then adopting Joseph's two sons, he blessed all his sons in solemn assembly, giving Joseph's younger son precedence over the elder and assigning to Joseph a portion more than his brothers. He was 147 at his death, his body being embalmed in Egyptian fashion. It was accompanied back to Canaan by an immense retinue including all the servants of Pharaoh and all the elders of Egypt and was laid at rest in the cave of Machpelah at Hebron.

The story of Jacob, as can be said of the other patriarchs, has been attacked as unhistorical, a charge easily made, if not substantiated. It is, however, a source-book of evidence on marriage customs, pastoral occupation, belief and traditions of the people, which must have had a basis of fact to be related with such naturalness and simplicity. The olden rabbis in their popular expositions of the Bible or "midrashim" realize their value for character building. Jacob is a favorite theme, and the homilies, however apparently trivial at times, had their significance in keeping alive the study of Scripture. Much that seems obscure and of doubtful worth in the text receives fresh meaning. Take the story of the birthright, for example. Esau was fresh from the slaying of Nimrod and two of his companions, when he sold the birthright. In desiring it, Jacob wished chiefly its spiritual prerogatives. It is another opinion that Jacob wanted the birthright, because the first born was forerunner of the priest who offered the family sacrifices and he felt that Esau was not fit to bring offerings to God. How the Midrash enlarges upon Scripture is illustrated by the statement that Jacob gave three injunctions to his sons before his death. They should not worship idols, nor blaspheme the name of God, nor permit a pagan to touch his corpse. On each side of his coffin, three of his sons were to be stationed, just as the tribes were later gathered in the wilderness. Joseph's order to have Jacob's body embalmed was not regarded with favor; it seemed to indicate a limitation of divine power.

ABRAM S. ISAACS.

JACOB, John, British soldier and colonial administrator: b. Woolavington, Somerset, Jan. 11, 1812; d. Jacobabad, India, Dec. 5, 1858. Commissioned in the East India Company's service in 1828, he participated in the Afghan War of 1838 and many Indian frontier operations. Political superintendent and commandant of the frontier of Upper Sind in 1843, he suppressed marauding tribesmen. A brilliant cavalry leader, he invented an improved rifle, to be used with an explosive bullet, also of his invention. The year of his death he was authorized to raise two infantry regiments to be called "Jacob's Rifles" and to be armed with the weapon he invented. Among General Jacob's publications are *Large map of Cutchee and the north-west frontier of Scinde* (London 1848); *Record Book of the Scinde Irregular Horse,* 2 vols. (London 1853, 1856); *Tracts on the Native Army of India, its Organisation and Discipline* (London 1857).

JACOB, Joshua, Irish founder of the "White Quakers": b. Clonmel, County Tipperary, c.1805; d. Wales, Feb. 15, 1877. By birth a Quaker, he was disowned by the Society of Friends in 1838. He then formed a religious society of his own which, commencing in 1843, held a yearly meeting in Dublin. Because of their practice of wearing only undyed garments they were called "White Quakers." The sect condemned the use of clocks, watches, bells, and newspapers. Accused of misappropriating the property of orphans of whom he was guardian to use for the furtherance of his religious experiments, Jacob was sued in chancery court for recovery of the funds and received a prison sentence of two years for contempt of court. About 1849 he established a community at Newlands, near Dublin. The members made bruised grain their staple diet and abstained from flesh foods. On the death of his wife, from whom he was separated, he married a Roman Catholic and reared a large family in that faith.

JACOB BEN CHAYYIM BEN-ISAAC IBN-ADONIA, Jewish author: b. Tunis about 1470; d. Venice about the middle of the 16th century. Soon after the year 1500 the Jews of Tunis were severely persecuted. He fled to Italy and lived in Rome, Florence and Venice. At Venice he found employment as proofreader on the Bamberg edition of the Rabbinic Bible which was prepared under the direction of Felix Pratensis. The second edition (4 vols., Venice 1524–1525) was prepared by Jacob ben Chayyim. It is noted for the amount of erudition displayed, especially in connection with the Masorah. It contains the text, with the Masorah, the Targums, the Commentaries of many Jewish scholars including his own.

JACOBA or **JACQUELINE, OF BAVARIA** or **OF HOLLAND,** countess of Holland, Zeeland and Hainault: b. July 25, 1401; d. Teilingen castle, near Sassenheim, South Holland, Oct. 6, 1436. The only child and heiress of William IV, duke of Bavaria and count of Holland, Zeeland, and Hainault, she was married as a child to John of Touraine, second son of King Charles VI of France, who became dauphin on the death of his older brother Louis. The death of John in April 1417, and of Jacoba's father two months later, left the young widow an heiress of vast estates. Her uncle John the Fearless, duke of Burgundy, married her to her cousin John IV, duke of Brabant in 1418. However, another uncle, her father's brother John of Bavaria, bishop of Liége, contested her inheritance. In 1419, through the mediation of John the Fearless, a treaty of partition was made between the rapacious prelate and his niece. But this did not satisfy the uncle who, on April 21, 1420, extorted from her weak husband possession of Holland and Zeeland.

Later that year Jacoba took refuge in England where she was granted a court pension and was one of the godmothers of Henry VI. Pedro de Luna, the Spanish antipope who maintained his title of Benedict XIII, annulled her marriage with Brabant, and in the autumn of 1422 she married, as third husband, Humphrey, duke of Gloucester (1391–1447). Politically the marriage was very injurious to English ambitions for hegemony in the Netherlands, since it placed Gloucester in opposition to Philip, duke of Burgundy, who had succeeded his murdered father in 1419 and the following year had concluded an alliance, the Treaty of Troyes, with Henry V of England. The Anglo-Burgundian alliance against France was thus imperiled. Gloucester and his older brother John, duke of Bedford, now endeavored to obtain from Pope Martin V a legitimization of the marriage; but before any papal decision had been reached Gloucester and Jacoba crossed to Calais in October 1424, with 5,000 troops, bent on reconquering Hainault (the modern Belgian province of Hainaut and French Department of Nord). Marching through Burgundian territories unopposed, they took peaceable possession and, on December 4, the estates of Hainault recognized Gloucester as their count.

Philip at once concluded a truce with France and challenged Gloucester to a duel. On the pretext of preparing for it Humphrey returned to England with Eleanor Cobham, his latest mistress, leaving Jacqueline to be captured on June 25, 1425 when Philip overran Hainault. In September Jacqueline escaped to Holland which she defended with the support of the Hoek faction. Humphrey sent her a reinforcement of 500 English, but lost interest in her fortunes after Philip had defeated her at Brouwershaven in June 1426. The pope annulled her marriage with Humphrey in January 1428. In July she was forced to sign the Treaty of Delft with Philip which authorized him to administer Holland, Zeeland, and Hainault, declared him her heir should she die childless, and allowed her only her title of countess. She also promised never to marry without Philip's consent.

In need of funds, Philip in 1430 mortgaged Holland and Zeeland to the Borsselen family. In a final effort to recover her lost inheritance Jacqueline early in 1432 secretly married its head, Frans van Borsselen, and initiated a rising in Holland against the Burgundians. Philip immediately invaded the country, captured her husband and demanded as a condition of his liberation that she abdicate her three countships, retaining only her title of duchess of Bavaria. She submitted in April 1432 and two and a half years later died on her husband's estate, childless. Duke Philip of Burgundy, her heir, thus became lord of the Netherlands.

JACOBEAN FURNITURE. See FURNITURE.

JACOBI, jȧ-kō'bĭ, **Abraham,** German-American physician: b. Hartum, Westphalia, May 6, 1830; d. Lake George, N. Y., July 10, 1919. He studied at Greifswald, Göttingen and Bonn, and graduated M.D. at Bonn University in 1851. Those were years of revolutionary ferment in Germany and Jacobi, becoming identified with the movement, was imprisoned for "high treason" at Berlin and Cologne (1851–1853). In 1853 he settled in practice in New York, where his abilities soon brought him into notice. He was appointed professor of diseases of children at the New York Medical College (1860–1865) and held a similar chair in the medical department of the University of the City of New York (1865–1870). Some years later he became professor of the diseases of children at the College of Physicians and Surgeons. He held many important appointments, and was president of the New York State Medical Society (1882); of the New York Academy of Medicine (1885–1889); in 1896 was president of the Association of American Physicians, and in 1912 president of the American Medical Association. In 1900 his 70th birthday was the occasion of a public demonstration in his honor.

Among his works are *Dentition and its Derangements* (1862); *Infant Hygiene* (1873); *Diphtheria* (1880); *Therapeutics of Infancy and Childhood* (1895); *Aufsätze, Vorträge, und Reden* (1893); *Collectanea Jacobi,* 8 vols. (1909).

JACOBI, yä-kō'bē, **Friedrich Heinrich,** German philosopher and writer: b. Düsseldorf, Jan. 25, 1743; d. Munich, March 10, 1819. He was educated at the University of Geneva, and in 1764 entered upon a commercial career in his native town; after a few years he retired from business, and in 1770 became a member of the councils for the duchies of Juliers and Berg. From his university days he was actively interested in literature and philosophy, and with Wieland started a journal in which some of his own writings were first published. In 1779 he went to Munich for a short time; and in 1793 left Düsseldorf and settled in Holstein. In 1804 he was called to Munich as a member of the Academy of Sciences then newly established; from 1807 to 1812 he was president of the academy; and in 1812 retired to prepare a collected edition of his works, which, however, was not finished before his death.

His writings include two philosophical romances, *Allwills Brief-Sammlung* (1774) and *Woldemar* (1779); and the more important philosophical treatises, *Briefe über die Lehre Spinozas* (1785); *David Hume über den Glauben oder Idealismus und Realismus* (1785); *Von den Göttlichen Dingen* (1811). In these treatises he defines his theory that man's thought—or reason—is by its nature partial and limited, and can only connect facts, not explain their existence; and that the higher truths must be understood through another different faculty which he calls "faith" or "belief" ("Glaube"); he does not, therefore, seek to establish a systematic philosophy. His theories involved him in considerable controversy, especially with the adherents of the critical philosophy. His collected works were published at Leipzig, 6 vols. (1812–1824).

JACOBI, Hermann Georg, German Sanskrit scholar: b. Cologne, Feb. 11, 1850; d. Bonn, Oct. 19, 1937. He was educated at Cologne Gymnasium, and later took up a course of studies in Sanskrit and allied languages at the universities of Bonn and Berlin. After spending a year (1872–1873) in the India office in London on the old Sanskrit manuscripts, he went to India, making a tour of Rajputana. In 1875 he became a docent in Sanskrit at Bonn; from 1876–1885 was professor extraordinarius of Sankrit and Comparative Philology at Münster, Westphalia; in 1885 was made professor ordinarius of Sankrit at Kiel; and in 1889 was appointed professor of Sankrit at Bonn. He made a special study of Jainism and Prâkrit grammar, writing exhaustively on those subjects as well as on the Sanskrit poetical languages. Among the most important of his works are *The Indian Antiquary* and the *Epigraphia Indica,* published in 1892, in which he gives two sets of tables showing the Hindu dates in inscriptions.

His other works include *De Astrologiae Indicae, Horâ appellatae originibus* (1872); *The Kalpasûtra of Bhadrabâhu* (1879); *The Ayaramgo Sutta of the Cvetāmbra Jains* (1882); *Gaina Sûtras* (1884); *Ausgewählte Erzählungen in Mâhârâshtri. Zur Einführung in das Studium des Prâhrit* (1886); *The Porisishtaparvan by Hemachandra* (1891); *Sthavirâvali Charita* (1891); *Das Râmâyana Geschichte und Inhalt, nebst Concordanz der gedruckten Recensionen* (1893); *Kompositum und Nebensatz* (1897); *Bhasa's Svapnavasayadatta* (1913); *Die Entwicklung der Gottesidee bei den Indern und deren Beweisse für das Dasein Gottes* (1923).

JACOBI, Karl Gustav Jakob, German mathematician: b. Potsdam, Dec. 10, 1804; d. Berlin, Feb. 18, 1851. He obtained his education at the University of Berlin, where he studied especially mathematics and philosophy, later in 1824 becoming a privat-docent there. In 1825 he became assistant professor of mathematics at Königsberg and in 1827 was appointed professor. He was appointed a member of the Prussian Academy of Sciences in 1836 and from 1842 till his death in 1851 lectured at the University of Berlin. His most important work was on the theory of elliptic functions, but he also made some valuable contributions to the theory of numbers and determinants.

Only a small portion of his writings and lectures were published during his lifetime and the greater part of these were published in the *Crelles Journal.* Among these are *Fundamenta Nova Theoriae Functionum Ellipticarum* (1829); *Canon Arithmeticus* (1839); *De Formatione et Proprietatibus Determinantium* (1841); *Mathematische Werke* (1846–1871). A complete edition of his works, *Gesammelte Werke,* was published in seven volumes by the Berlin Academy of Sciences (1881–1891). His *Vorlesungen über Dynamik* did not appear until 1866, long after his death, and later in 1895, his essay, *Über die vierfach periodischen Functionen*

Zweier Variabeln,' was published in Latin.

JACOBI, Mary Putnam (MRS. ABRAHAM JACOBI), American physician: b. London, England, 31 Aug. 1842; d. New York City, 10 June 1906. Graduated from the Woman's Medical College of Philadelphia, 1864, from Ecole de Médecine, Paris, 1871. She practiced in New York, and in 1881 became clinical professor of diseases of children, New York Post-Graduate Medical School. In 1874 she established an association for the promotion of the medical education of women, and became its president. She published 'The Question of Rest for Women during Menstruation' (1877); 'Acute Fatty Degeneration of New Born' (1878); 'Cold Pack and Anæmia' (1880); 'The Prophylaxis of Insanity' (1881).

JACOBI, Victor, Hungarian composer: b. Budapest, 1885; d. New York City, 10 Dec. 1922. His works were chiefly light operas. The first work to be presented in the United States was 'The Marriage Market' (1914). His greatest success was 'Sybil' (1916), afterward played in London. He collaborated with Fritz Kreisler in 'Apple Blossoms,' 'The Love Letter'; his latest work is founded on Molnar's play 'The Wolf.'

JACOBINS, jăk'ō-bĭnz, the most famous of the clubs of the first French Revolution. When the States-General assembled at Versailles in 1789 it was formed and called the Club Bréton. On the removal of the court and national assembly to Paris it acquired importance and rapidly increased. It adopted the name of Société des Amis de la Constitution, but as it met in a hall of the former Jacobin (Dominican) convent in Paris it was called the Jacobin Club. After the fall of the monarchy, in September 1792, it called itself Société des Jacobins, Amis de la liberté et de l'egalité. It gradually became the controlling power of the Revolution (see FRENCH REVOLUTION) and spread its influence over France, 1,200 branch societies being established before 1791, and obeying orders from the headquarters in Paris. Originally it was not particularly radical, either in its membership or in its political views. The former consisted chiefly of professional men of liberal ideas, some few liberal aristocrats like Louis Philippe, duc de Chartres, the duc d'Aiguillon, the prince de Broglie, the vicomte de Noailles, etc. Its large mass was made up of the *bourgeois.* Amongst its best known members were Mirabeau, Robespierre, David, Barnave, Pere Gerard, Abbé Grégoire, the two Lamells, etc. In the provinces the membership was much more democratic. Gradually its political tendencies became more and more radical and its more moderate members either resigned or were expelled, in many instances to form new political clubs, such as the Club of 1789, the Feuillants, etc. In the beginning the sessions of the Jacobins were secret, but in October 1791 they were thrown open to the public. For a while the Jacobins ruled supreme, and the Convention itself was but their tool. Robespierre (q.v.) was their most influential member; they ruled through him during the Reign of Terror, and were overthrown after his downfall in 1794. In that year the Convention forbade the affiliation of societies; the Jacobin Club was suspended and its hall was closed. Two or three attempts were made later, especially in the provinces, to revive the club, but they had only passing success. The term Jacobin is now often used to designate anyone holding extreme revolutionary views in politics. Numberless pamphlets were then published in regard to the Jacobins, the most noted being 'La Jacobinade,' 'Le secret des Jacobins' and 'Les crimes des Jacobins.' There is a very extensive literature on the Jacobins. Its proceedings were published as 'Journal des Amis de la Constitution' (4 vols., Paris 1793–95). The most authoritative work on the Jacobins is Aulard, F. A., 'La Société des Jacobins' (6 vols., Paris 1889–97), containing a very full bibliography. Consult Barrnel, A. de, 'Memoirs, Illustrating the History of Jacobinism' (4 vols., Hartford 1799); Dufay, P., 'Les Société Populaires et l'Armée, 1791–94' (Paris 1913); Farmer, J. E., 'Essays on French History' (New York 1897); Fribourg, A., 'Le Club des Jacobins en 1790' (in 'Revolution Française,' Vol. LVIII, p. 507, Paris 1910); Gros, J., 'Le Comité de Salut Public' (Paris 1893); Kuhlmann, C., 'On the Conflict of Parties in the Jacobine Club' (in *University of Nebraska Studies,* Vol. V, No. 3, p. 229, Lincoln 1905); id., 'The Relation of the Jacobines to the Army, the National Guard, and Lafayette' (ib. Vol. VI, No. 2, p. 153, Lincoln 1906); Mallet, G., 'La Politique Financière des Jacobins' (Paris 1913); Mortimer-Ternaux, M., 'Histoire de la Terreur d'apres des Documents Authentiques et Inédits' (8 vols., Paris 1862–81); Playfair, W., 'The History of Jacobinism, etc.' (2 vols., Philadelphia 1796); Schmidt, A., 'Tableaux de la Revolution Française, etc.' (3 vols., Leipzig 1867–69); Taine, H. A., 'The Jacobine Conquest' (in 'The French Revolution,' translated by J. Durand, New York 1881); Wallon, H., 'Histoire du Tribunal Revolutionair de Paris' (5 vols., Paris 1880); Zinkeisen, J. W., 'Der Jakobinerklub' (2 vols., Berlin 1852–53).

JACOBITE CHRISTIANS, a subdivision of the sect of the Monophysites (q.v.) comprising those who dwelt in Syria, Mesopotamia and Babylonia, organized by a certain Jacobus Baradæus, in the reign of Justinian, somewhat later than the middle of the 6th century. Jacobus had been a monk whose poverty-stricken asceticism gained for him the title of Jacobus Baradæus (Ragged James). He had been appointed bishop of Edessa in 541, and from that year to 578 he traveled round gathering the members of his heretical sect, until they formed a compactly ordered body which has survived to the present time. They now number about 80,000 and are governed by a Patriarch of "Antioch and all the East." Under him is the Maphrian, seven metropolitans and three bishops. There are many monks, from whose number the bishops are chosen. Consult Adeney, W. F., 'The Greek and Eastern Churches' (New York 1908); Assemani, 'Bibliotheca Orientalis' (Vol. II, Rome 1719); Bliss, F. J., 'The Religions of Modern Syria and Palestine' (New York 1912); Duval, R., 'La Litérature Syriaque' (Paris 1899); Kleyn, M., 'Jacobus Baradeus' (Leyden 1882); Krüger, G., 'Monophysitsche Streitigkeiten' (Jena 1884); Silbernagel, N., 'Verfassung der Kirchen des Orients' (Landshut 1865); Wright, G., 'History of Syriac Literature' (London 1894).

JACOBITES, a party in Great Britain (so styled from Lat. *Jacobus,* James), who after the revolution in 1688 continued to be the adherents of the dethroned King James II, his descendants and, after the death of the last male representative (Cardinal York) in 1807 of the descendants of Charles I. Its members were chiefly, though not exclusively, Roman Catholics, its strongholds were Northumberland, North Wales and the Scottish Highlands. In Ireland they were soon put down by conquest. In England the revolution was accomplished with the apparent consent of all parties; but in a year or two the Jacobite party gained considerable influence and continued to disturb the government of William throughout his reign. After the accession of Anne and the death of James their efforts slackened for a time; but toward the close of her reign they revived. Bolingbroke and Oxford, with others of the Tory ministers of Anne, were in treaty with the son of James II, and either really or pretendedly negotiated for a restoration. On the arrival of George I in 1715 a rebellion broke out in Scotland, supported by a more insignificant rising in the north of England. The failure of both these movements dampened the enthusiasm of the English Jacobites, but in Scotland the party maintained its influence until the unsuccessful rebellion of 1745 put an end to its political importance, though some ultra-Jacobites did not think themselves justified in transferring their allegiance to the house of Brunswick till the death of Cardinal York in 1807. Even after that date sentimental Jacobitism had a certain amount of hold on a small group of people. It found expression in the formation of Jacobite societies, such as the «Cycle of the White Rose» in Wales, «John Shaw's Club» in Manchester and the «Order of the White Rose» with branches in England and the United States, the «Legitimist Jacobite League of Great Britain and Ireland,» the «Thames Valley Legitimist Club,» etc. Members of these associations consider the present British dynasty as usurpers and claim that the rightful occupants of the British throne is Ruprecht, ex-crown prince of Bavaria, whose mother was Marie Therese of Modena, great-great-great-great-great-granddaughter of Henrietta of Orleans, daughter of Charles I. Henrietta married Philip I, Duke of Orleans. Her daughter, Anne Marie (b. 1669; d. 1728), was joined in marriage to Victor Amadeus II, Duke of Savoy and later king of Sardinia. Of this union was born the future King Charles Emmanuel III, whose son was known as Victor Amadeus III. The latter's son, Victor Emmanuel I, left no sons, but his eldest daughter, Marie Beatrice, became the wife of Francis IV, Duke of Modena. Their son, Ferdinand (d. 1849), left one daughter, Marie Thérèse (d. 1919). The latter married Louis III of Bavaria, and in the eyes of the legitimists, her son is the rightful sovereign of Great Britain. The hopes and wishes of the Scottish Jacobites found expression in many beautiful songs, which form an interesting feature of the national literature. These may be found in the following collections: Grosart, A. B., ed., ‹English Jacobite Ballads› (Manchester 1877); Hogg, J., ed., ‹The Jacobite Relics of Scotland› (Paisley 1874); Mackey, C., ed., ‹Jacobite Songs and Ballads, etc.› (London 1861); Macquoid, G. S., ed., ‹Jacobite Songs and Ballads› (London 1887). Many incidents in the history of the Jacobite party form the background of historical novels. The most important of these are Scott, Sir Walter, ‹Waverley› (1814); id., ‹The Black Dwarf› (1816); id., ‹Rob Roy› (1817); Stevenson, R. L., ‹David Balfour› (2 vols., 1886–92); id., ‹The Master of Ballantrae› (1889); Thackeray, W. M., ‹The History of Henry Esmond› (1852). An exhaustive list of the fictional treatment of Jacobitism will be found in Baker, A. E., ‹A Guide to Historical Fiction› (London 1914). There is a vast literature on the subject which includes the large numbers of histories of famous Scottish families. Of other works on the subject consult Allardyce, J., ed., ‹Historical Papers Relating to the Jacobite Period, 1690–1750› (Aberdeen 1895–96); Beamont, W., ‹Jacobite Trials at Manchester in 1694› (in *Chetham Society*, Vol. XXVIII, Manchester 1854); Blaikie, W. B., ‹An Itinerary of Prince Charles Edward Stuart› (Edinburgh 1897); id., ‹Origins of the '45, etc.› (Edinburgh 1916); Carmichael, A., ‹Some Unrecorded Incidents of the Jacobite Risings› (in *Celtic Review*, Vol. VI, pp. 278, 334, Edinburgh 1910); Forbes, J. M., ‹Jacobite Gleanings› (Edinburgh 1903); Francillon, R. E., ‹Underground Jacobitism› (in *Monthly Review*, London 1905); Gilbert, J. T., ed., ‹Jacobite Narrative of the War in Ireland, 1688–91› (Dublin 1892); Grew, E. S. and M. S., ‹The English Court in Exile› (London 1911); Hadden, J. C., ‹Prince Charles Edward› (London 1913); Hale, E., ‹James Francis Stuart, the Old Chevalier› (London 1907); Head, F. W., ‹The Fallen Stuarts› (Cambridge 1901); Jesse, J. H., ‹Memoirs of the Pretenders and their Adherents› (2 vols., London 1845); Klose, C. L., ‹Memoir of Prince Charles Stuart, etc.› (2 vols., London 1845); Lang, A., ‹Pickle the Spy, or the Incognito of Prince Charles› (London 1897); Mahon, Lord, ‹The Forty-Five› (London 1852); Murdoch, W. G. B., ‹The Spirit of Jacobite Loyalty› (Edinburgh 1907); Power, W., ‹Prince Charlie› (London 1912); Ray, J., ‹A Compleat History of the Rebellion› (York 1749); Rose, D. M., ed., ‹Prince Charlie's Friends, or Jacobite Indictments› (Aberdeen 1896); Ruvigny, Marquis de, ‹The Jacobite Peerage, etc.› (Edinburgh 1904); Terry, C. S., ‹The Rising of 1745› (London 1900); id., ed., ‹The Chevalier de Saint George and the Jacobite Movements in his Favour, 1701–20› (London 1915); Thomson, Mrs., ‹Memoirs of the Jacobites of 1715 and 1745› (3 vols., London 1845–46); Thomson, J. P., ‹The Jacobite Rebellions 1689–1746› (London 1914); Tulloch, A. B., ‹The Forty-Five› (Inverness 1896); Vaughan, H. M., ‹The Last of the Royal Stuarts› (London 1906); White, S. D., ‹Revival of Jacobitism› (in *Westminster Review*, Vol. CXLVI, p. 417, London 1896).

JACOBS, Henry Eyster, American Lutheran clergyman and theologian: b. Gettysburg, Pa. 10 Nov. 1844. He was graduated from Pennsylvania College (Gettysburg) in 1862, from the Lutheran Theological Seminary at Gettysburg in 1865, was professor of Latin and history in Pennsylvania College in 1870–80, of ancient languages in 1880–81 and of Greek in 1881–83. He was professor of systematic theology, Lutheran Theological Seminary, after 1883; dean, 1894–1920; president, 1920–27; emeritus thereafter until his death, 7 July 1932. He was president of the Board of Foreign Missions of the General Council of the Lutheran

Church (1901–07); president of the American Society of Church History' (1910–11); and president of the Pennsylvania German Society (1911–12). Besides writing several Bible commentaries, contributing to encyclopædias, translating and writing various German theological works, his publications include 'The Lutheran Movement in England' (1891); a 'History of the Lutheran Church in America' (1893); 'Elements of Religion' (1894); 'Life of Martin Luther' (1898); 'The German Emigration to America, 1709–40'; 'Summary of the Christian Faith' (1906); 'Lincoln's Gettysburg World-Message' (1920).

JACOBS, Joseph, Anglo-American author and journalist: b. Sydney, New South Wales, 29 Aug. 1854; d. 30 Jan. 1916. He was graduated from Saint John's College, Cambridge, traveled in Spain in 1888 and in the United States in 1896, was at various times editor of 'Folk Lore,' the 'Literary Year-Book' and the 'Jewish Year-Book,' was elected president of the Jewish Historical Society and became literary editor of the 'Jewish Encyclopædia' in New York in 1906. His publications include, besides translations and editions of English classics, 'Celtic Fairy Tales' (1891); 'Indian Fairy Tales' (1892); 'The Jews of Angevin England' (1893); 'Studies in Biblical Archæology' (1894); 'Literary Studies' (1895); and 'Jewish Ideals' (1896).

JACOBS, Michael, American Lutheran clergyman: b. near Waynesboro, Franklin County, Pa., 1808; d. 1871. He was graduated, in 1828, at Jefferson College, Canonsburg, and in the following year was appointed instructor at the Gettysburg Gymnasium. After 1832 he served as professor there and retired in 1865. In 1832 he entered the Lutheran ministry. He was a very versatile man; invented a method of preserving fruit and was a meteorologist of note. He published 'The Rebel Invasion of Maryland and Pennsylvania' (1863).

JACOBS, William Wymark, English novelist: b. London, 8 Sept. 1863. He was educated privately and at the age of 20 entered the civil service, Savings Bank Department, where he remained until 1899. His works deal mostly with the lives and passion of those who toil on the sea, they include 'Many Cargoes' (1896); 'The Skipper's Wooing' (1897); 'Sea Urchins' (1898); 'A Master of Craft' (1900); 'Light Freights' (1901); 'At Sunwich Port' (1902); 'The Lady of the Barge' (1902); 'Odd Craft' (1903); 'Dialstone Lane' (1904); 'Captains All' (1905); 'Short Cruises' (1907); 'Salthaven' (1908); 'Sailors' Knots' (1909); 'Ship's Company' (1911); 'Night Watches' (1914); 'The Castaways' (1916); 'Sea Whispers' (1926). He also wrote several one-act plays. Died, London, 1 Sept. 1943.

JACOB'S CAVERN, a remarkable natural cavern near Pineville, McDonald County, Mo. It was discovered by E. H. Jacobs, and was named in his honor. The opening to the cavern is about 68 feet long and 45 feet deep. The height of the cavern varies from four feet to eight and one-half feet. The rock formation is stratified and is of limestone of the Subcarboniferous era. The floor is covered with a deep crust of ashes, in which were found flint knives, bone awls, hammer stones, human skeletons, and animal bones. Many of these relics are now in the Museum of Phillips Academy, Andover, Mass. Consult Gould, C. N. (in *Science,* 31 July 1903) and Peabody (in *American Anthropologist,* Sept. 1903).

JACOB'S WELL is situated near the ancient Sychar or Samaria, about two miles from the modern Nablus. It is not mentioned in the Old Testament, but is mentioned in the Gospel of John (iv, 6). The traditions of Moslems, Jews and Christians identify it with Bir Yakub or Jacob's Well. Here it was that Jesus had his remarkable conversation with the woman of Samaria. It is about seven feet six inches in diameter with a narrow mouth. Its depth has been variously estimated. Arculfus (A.D. 670) estimated it at 240 feet. Major Anderson measured it in 1866 and found it to be 75 feet. It is now the property of the Greek Church of Nablus and a hut has been built over the well and the surroundings improved. It is the site of several churches. The Crusaders built a church there which was destroyed soon after 1187.

JACOBSEN, Johan Adrian, Norwegian ethnologist and explorer: b. Risö, 1853. For seven years after 1867 he was member of a whaling crew on the Spitzbergen and Murman coasts. He traveled along the west coast of South America in 1876–77 and subsequently visited the Arctic regions, bringing back hundreds of ethnographical specimens. In 1881 he was engaged by the Berlin Museum für Völkerkunde to gather ethnographical and other specimens on the west coast of North America, also Korea, Japan, Siberia, the South Sea Islands, etc. He spent seven years in this work, collecting in all over 18,000 specimens. Subsequently he made collections in Germany and Norway. At the Columbian Exposition of 1893 he exhibited a marvelous ethnographical collection from 25 non-European peoples. These formed the nucleus around which has grown the Field Columbian Museum of Chicago. He has published 'Reise an der nordwestküste Amerikas' (1884); 'Eventyrlige farter' (1894); 'Reise in der inselwelt des Banda-Meeres' (1896).

JACOBUS, Melancthon Williams, American Presbyterian clergyman and educator: b. Allegheny, Pa., 15 Dec. 1855. He was graduated from Princeton, 1877; from Princeton Theological Seminary, 1881, and after studying at Göttingen and Berlin (1881–84), was pastor, Presbyterian Church, Oxford, Pa. (1884–91); became professor of New Testament exegesis and criticism, Hartford (Conn.) Theological Seminary in 1891; acting president (1902–03); dean of faculty from 1903. He received the degree of D.D. Lafayette College (1892); and Yale University (1910). He did editorial work on numerous theological standard texts and wrote 'A Problem in New Testament Criticism' (1900). He was chairman of the editorial board 'Standard Bible Dictionary.' D. 31 Oct. 1937.

JACOBUS BARADÆUS. See JACOBITES.

JACOBY, Harold, American astronomer: b. New York, 4 March 1865. On his graduation from Columbia University in 1885, he applied himself to astronomical research, and was appointed assistant astronomer United States eclipse expedition to West Africa (1889–90). He became professor of astronomy at Columbia in 1894 and an active member of the leading astronomical and scientific societies at home and abroad. His writings include numerous technical monographs in astronomical photography, stellar parallax and star clusters which have been published by French, English and Russian societies, frequent contributions to the periodical press on popular astronomy, and standard textbooks ‘Practical Talks by an Astronomer’ (1891); ‘Astronomy, a popular handbook’; ‘Navigation’. D. 20 July 1932.

JACOPONE DA TODI, Italian monk and poet: b. Todi, Umbria, about 1230; d. 1306. He took up the profession of the law and became a successful practitioner. His wife died in 1268 and immediately afterward he abandoned his profession, gave his property to the poor, and took up a life of penance, attacking from time to time the licentiousness of the age. In 1278 he became a lay brother of the Order of Saint Francis. He was one of the opponents of Boniface VIII, and when taken captive at Palestine in 1298, was thrown into prison, where he remained until the death of Boniface in 1303. Jacopone wrote several hymns, including the immortal ‘Stabat Mater Dolorosa.’ Consult Bruguali ‘Fra Jacopone da Todi’ (Assisi 1907); Macdonnell, ‘Sons of Francis’ (London 1902); Sorio, ‘Poesie scelte di Fra Jacopone da Todi’ (Verona 1859).

JACOTOT, Jean Joseph, zhŏn zhō-zĕf zhä-kō-tō, French educator: b. Dijon, 4 March 1770; d. Paris, 30 July 1840. He studied at the University of Dijon, became professor of Latin, then studied law and during the revolution was successively soldier, secretary to the minister of war, and deputy-director of the Polytechnic School, where he was also professor of mathematics. He was elected to the chamber of deputies in 1815, but was forced, after the second restoration, to leave France. He went to Brussels, in 1818 was appointed lecturer on the French language in the University of Louvain, and in 1827 director of the Military Normal School. He returned to France after the revolution of 1830. The fundamental principle upon which his system of education rests is that every person is able to educate himself, provided he is once started in the right way. Knowledge should first be acquired through instinctive experience, or by the memory. For example, in imparting a knowledge of a language, Jacotot began by making the pupil commit to memory a single passage; he then encouraged him to study for himself, first the separate words, then the letters, then the grammar, and lastly the full meaning and import. His steps were learn, repeat, reflect and verify. He expounded his views in ‘Enseignement Universel’ (Louvain and Dijon 1822) which has been translated into various other languages. It consists of five parts: ‘Langue Maternelle’; ‘Langue Etrangère’; ‘Messigue, Dessin et Peinture’; ‘Droit et Philosophie’; ‘Mathematiques.’ Consult Cornelius, B., ‘An Account of M. Jacotot's Method of Universal Instruction’ (London 1830); Guillard, A., ‘Biographie de J. Jacotot’ (Paris 1860); Kenaston, G. F., ‘Educational Doctrines of J. J. Jacotot’ (in *Education,* Vol. II, pp. 446, 564, Boston 1882); Payne, J., ‘Lectures on the History of Education’ (London 1892); Quick, R. H., ‘Essays on Educational Reformers’ (New York 1907); Seltzsam, C., ‘Beiträge zur Würdigung der Jacototischen Methode’ (Breslau 1848); Wurm, C. F., ‘Hamilton und Jacotot’ (Hamburg 1831).

JACQUARD, Joseph Marie, zhō-zĕf mä-rē zhä-kär, French inventor: b. Lyons, 7 July 1752; d. Oullins, near Lyons, 7 Aug. 1834. His parents were silk weavers, and he learned the same trade. After a long period of hardship, during which he shared in some of the campaigns of the Revolution, he made his name famous by the invention of his new loom, which was publicly exhibited at Paris in 1801 and patented 23 December of the same year. During the final work on his loom he enjoyed the support of Napoleon who had become interested in his inventive genius. He endeavored to introduce it into general use in Lyons, but was mobbed, and all but lost his life while his loom was ordered to be burned. Ultimately, however, his invention gained extensive use, he was granted a small pension by the French government, and was able to spend the latter part of his life in comfortable independence. In 1819 he was made a chevalier of the Legion of Honor. The subsequent prosperity of Lyons is largely attributable to his invention, and a more enlightened generation erected a statue to him in 1840 on the very spot where his loom was publicly destroyed. (See LOOM). Consult Bell, T. F., ‘Jacquard Weaving and Designing’ (London 1895); Donat, F., ‘Technologie der Jacquard-Weberei’ (Vienna 1902); Du Saussois, A., ‘Galerie des Hommes Utiles’ (Paris 1875); Grandsard, A., ‘Jacquard, sa Vie, etc.’ (Paris 1869); Humphries, S., ‘Oriental Carpets, etc.’ (London 1910); Kohl, F., ‘Geschichte der Jacquard Machine’ (Berlin 1872); Lamartine, A. de, ‘Memoirs of Celebrated Characters’ (Vol. II, New York 1854); id., ‘Jacquard-Gutenberg’ (Paris 1864); Posselt, E. A., ‘The Jacquard Machine Analized and Explained’ (Philadelphia 1893).

JACQUARD MACHINE. See DAMASK.

JACQUE, Charles Emile, French painter: b. Paris, 1813; d. 1894. He gave his attention to wood-engraving and about 1846 turned his attention to genre painting. He excelled in depicting rural and family life, domestic animals, flocks and herds, etc. There remain from his hand a great number of vignettes engraved on wood and copper. Among his best-known canvasses are ‘Basse-cour’; ‘La sortie du troupeau’; ‘Un Intérieur’; ‘Poulailler’ (1861); ‘Un clos à Barbizon’ (1863); ‘Grand troupeau au pâturage’; ‘L'Abreuvoir’; ‘Le clair de lune’ (1888). He was awarded a gold medal at the exposition of 1889. He was the last survivor of the great Barbizon school. He published ‘Le poulailler, monographic des poules indigènes et exotiques’ (1869).

JACQUEMART, Jules Ferdinand, French etcher: b. Paris, 1837; d. Nice, 1880. He studied painting and more particularly etching and exhibited for the first time at the Salon of 1861. Besides the remarkable series representing the works of Rembrandt, Franz Hals, Meissonier, etc., he also illustrated his father's ‘Histoire de la porcelaine’ and ‘Histoire de la céramique’; also Barbet de Jouy's ‘Gemmes et joyaux de la couronne,’ and several portraits. At the exposition of 1878 he received the Grand Médaille for etching. He also executed over 100 watercolors, three of which are in the Metropolitan Museum, New York.

JACQUERIE, zhäk-ē-rē', the name given to the rising of the French peasantry in the 14th century after the battle of Poitiers. They committed great devastations and outrages — burning castles, murdering men and violating women — particularly in the northeast of France. They were at length quelled by the Captal de Buch and Gaston Phébus, count of Foix, who slaughtered 7,000 of them near Meaux. The term *Jacquerie* is derived from *Jacques Bonhomme,* a familiar epithet for a peasant. Consult Luce, 'Histoire de la Jacquerie' (Paris 1895).

JACTITATION. (1) An action to enjoin a false statement by the respondent that he or she is married to the petitioner. (2) An untrue statement which injures another. In both senses, the offense is punishable in English law by the high court of justice and by the ecclesiastical courts. In sense 1, it is often called «jactitation of marriage.» (3) In Louisiana, an action for damages for slander of title brought by one in possession.

JADE, ya'de, or **JAHDE,** a bay of the North Sea on the coast of Oldenburg. It is about 70 square miles in extent and is very shallow. It was formed mostly by storm-floods from the 13th to the 16th century. The inlet is about 1½ miles wide and admits the largest vessels. On the west side of the inlet is the naval base of Wilhelmshaven.

JADE, a remarkably tough, compact, ornamental stone, of green to white color and vitreous lustre, used by the prehistoric peoples of Switzerland, Mexico, Alaska and other countries for axes, utensils and carvings. It is still highly prized in the East, especially in China and New Zealand. Jade is a general term including two distinct minerals, jadeite and the more common nephrite. Jadeite belongs to the pyroxene group and chemically is a soda-spodumene, easily fusible (at 2.5) and having a specific gravity of 3.3 to 3.35. Nephrite is a variety of amphibole identical with tremolite when of white color, or with actinolite when green, fusing much less easily (at 4) and with specific gravity of 2.95 to 3.0. Much information as to jade and implements made from it may be found in the publications of the Smithsonian Institution, especially a paper by S. Blondel, 'A Historical, Archæological and Literary Study of Jade,' in the annual report for 1876.

JADLOWKER, Herman, Russian tenor: b. Riga, 1879. His father destined him for a commercial career but in order to avoid it the youth fled to Vienna in 1894. Here he studied under Gänsbacher and in 1899 made his début in Kreutzer's 'Nachtlager von Granada' at Cologne. Subsequently he appeared at Stettin and Karlsruhe. The late Emperor, William II, offered him a five-year contract at the Berlin Opera House. He next appeared in Vienna and in 1910 appeared at the Metropolitan Opera House, New York. He returned to Berlin in 1912.

JADWIN, Edgar, American military engineer: b. Honesdale, Pa., 7 Aug. 1865. He studied at Lafayette College, was graduated from West Point in 1890, was an assistant in government engineering in 1890–91; in the Spanish-American War was major and lieutenant-colonel 3d United States Volunteer Engineers and commanded a battalion of this regiment in the sanitation of Matanzas, Cuba. Promoted captain in the corps of engineers, U. S. A. (1900); organized and commanded 15th U. S. Engineers in 1917; served with A. E. F. in France; directed work of 160,000 men engaged in general construction program—dredging, building barracks, etc.; appointed assistant to chief of engineers with rank of brigadier-general, 1924; served as chief of engineers, U. S. A., with rank of major-general, 1926–29, when he was retired. Died 2 March 1931.

JAEGER, yā'gėr. See GULL; SKUA.

JAEGERS, Albert, American sculptor: b. Elberfeld, Germany, 28 March 1868; d. Suffern, N.Y., 22 July 1925. Self-taught in art he began as a sculptor in 1890. He carved statuary for the Buffalo and Saint Louis expositions; the Fine Arts Building, Saint Louis; the new customhouse, New York; also private monuments, busts and tablets in marble and bronze. He was commissioned by the United States government to erect the Baron von Steuben Statue for Washington; of which a replica was ordered and presented by Congress to William II, then Emperor of Germany, from whom Jaegers received a decoration. One of the sculptor's last commissions was the execution of the Germantown monument. He was a member of the National Sculpture Society and of the National Institute of Arts and Letters.

JAEL, the wife of Heber the Kenite of Ancient Israel. The kings of Canaan under the leadership of Sisera oppressed Israel. Deborah and Barak were then judges. They rallied their hosts to throw off the oppressive yoke. The Canaanites were defeated in a pitched battle «in Toanach by the waters of Megiddo.» Sisera escaped and in his flight asked hospitality from Jael. She gave him food and drink. Then she took a nail and a workman's hammer and after piercing his head through the temples, cut it off. Deborah in her song celebrating the victory commends Jael as «blessed above women.»

JAÉN, Spain, capital of the province of the same name, on the slopes of the Jabalcuz Mountains, 40 miles southeast of Cordoba, on the Linares-Puente Genil Railway. The streets are narrow and irregular and it is surrounded by ancient Moorish fortifications all crowned by a Moorish citadel. It contains several fine old churches, and several palaces, art galleries and a library. Leather, soap, alcohol and linen are manufactured. Pop. 34,994.

JAÉN, Spain, a province in the southern part of the kingdom, bounded on the north by Cindad Real, east by Albacete, south and southeast by Granada, and west by Cordoba. Its surface is broken by the ranges of the Sierra Morena, the Sierra de Segura and the Sierra Cazoola. It is watered by the Guadilquivir and its affluents the Guadalimar, the Guadianamen and the Jaén. Copper, lead, iron, zinc and salt are found in considerable quantities. Lead is mined to the extent of 85,000 tons annually, much of the ore containing silver. The mountain regions are barren but the Guadalquivir valley is very fertile and produces cereals and olives. Jaén was a Moorish kingdom for a short time after the Moorish conquest, but the kingdom was ended by Ferdinand III in 1246 after which it remained part of Castile. Pop. 565,000.

JAFFA, jăf′fȧ or yäf′fä (ancient JOPPA; Ar. *Yafa;* Heb. *Yapho,* beauty), an ancient city in the western part of Palestine on the Mediterranean Sea, about 35 miles from Jerusalem. Jaffa is an old Phœnician town mentioned in several places in the Bible. It was the port of entry for Jerusalem and for several of the interior cities of Palestine. Here the cedars from Lebanon were landed and then carried overland for the building of the Temple in Jerusalem. The house where Simon the tanner lived, and where Saint Peter lodged, is still pointed out. In 1187 it was taken by Saladin, in 1191 by Richard I. In 1799 it was captured by Napoleon, who here put to death 1,200 Turkish prisoners. The remains of Roman fortifications and dwellings are near by. A railway built in 1892 connects the city with Jerusalem (54 miles). Jaffa is one of the two chief ports of Palestine. It has a branch of Barclay's Bank, two magistrates' courts, and it is the seat of one of the four District courts of Palestine. In the year ended 30 September 1929, 438 steamers and 683 sailing vessels in the foreign trade, with a total tonnage of 1,137,767 entered the port. The coasting trade in the same period brought 185 steamers and 105 vessels of 478,262 tons in all, into Jaffa. The old road to Jerusalem is very interesting. The chief exports are: oranges (of world-wide fame), almonds, cereals, chocolate, honey, soap, wine, wool, and cigarettes. The imports include: amber, coal, drugs, petroleum, textiles, leather, clothing, machinery, and leaf tobacco. The city has a population of about 50,000, one-third of whom are Jewish farmers mainly from Russia, and maintained, some by various Zionist societies and others by the Jewish Colonization Association (founded by Baron E. de Rothschild). The colony maintains Hebrew schools, agricultural schools and experiment stations. There are also four German agricultural colonies in the Jaffa region. In the European War the British took Jaffa on 18 Nov. 1917. See WAR, EUROPEAN — TURKISH CAMPAIGN.

JAFFNA, Ceylon, town at the north end of the island. It contains an old Dutch church and an ancient Portuguese fort. It has a large important export trade; the imports are cotton, rice, sugar, petroleum, tobacco and lumber, the exports fruits, wine, oils, sesame and soap, oranges, etc. It is the seat of a government agent and district judge. In 204 B.C. it was taken by the Tamils whose rajahs held it till 1617, when they were ousted by the Portuguese. The latter were displaced by the Dutch in 1658. Pop. 42,439, mostly Mohammedans together with 8,000 Jews.

JAGANNATH, or JUGGERNAUT (Sanskrit, *Jagannâtha,* lord of the world, one of the names of Vishnu), called by the natives Puri, a town and celebrated temple of Hindustan, in the presidency of Bengal, province of Orissa, on the Bay of Bengal, 48 miles south of Kattack. The town derives all its importance from the temple. This, the most celebrated shrine in Hindustan, was completed in the 12th century, at an enormous expense. The worship of Jagannath, the God of the people, aims at a catholicity with every form of Indian devotion and at the incorporation therein of every Indian conception of God. The main street of the city, at the extremity of which the temple stands, consists entirely of religious structures built of stone. The gardens here produce the finest fruits in the province. The temple stands near the shore, in a waste, sandy tract, and appears like a shapeless mass of stone. The idol is a carved block of wood, with a hideous face, painted black, and a distended blood-red mouth, and is magnificently dressed. On festival days the throne of the image is placed on a high tower moving on wheels. Long ropes are attached to the tower, by which the people draw it along. The belief that devotees used to cast themselves headlong in front of this car to be crushed to death probably grew out of the accidental fatalities sometimes occurring. Every year pilgrims flock in crowds to the temple.

JAGELLONS. See POLAND, *History.*

JAGERNDORF, Germany, town of Silesia on the Oppa, 15 miles northwest of Troppau. It contains a castle of the Liechtenstein family, a church and technical schools. It carries on an active trade and has manufactures of cloth, woolens, linen and machinery. The town suffered severely during the Thirty Years' War and more than once witnessed conflicts between Prussia and Austria. Pop. 15,000, mostly Germans.

JAGERSFONTEIN (yä′gėrz-fŏn-tīn) **EXCELSIOR**, The, a name given the largest known diamond; found in the mine of the Jagersfontein Company, Orange Free State, South Africa, in 1893; weight, 971 carats, color, blue white.

JAGGARD, William, British bibliophile: b. 1568; d. 1623. He began as a bookseller in London about 1592, as a printer about 1604, was appointed Printer to the City of London in 1610, and although stricken blind about 1612, prospered. He published in 1599 an anthology, 'The Passionate Pilgrime' as by Shakespeare, though five of the poems only were his, and in 1612 offended Shakespeare by issuing an enlarged edition. In 1619 he printed surreptitiously ten plays, some by Shakespeare, some falsely ascribed to him. In 1621, he began printing for Shakespeare's actor-friends his collected plays, a financially hazardous venture. Interrupted to permit completion of a controversial work, Vincent's 'Discoverie of Errours', the First Folio of Shakespeare which preserves the previously unpublished half of Shakespeare's plays and in its Droeshout engraving records Shakespeare's likeness, was finally issued in 1623, shortly after Jaggard's death. Consult E. E. Willoughby, 'A Printer of Shakespeare' (1934); 'The Printing of the First Folio of Shakespeare' (1932); 'Coronet' I (1937) 179–180.

EDWIN ELIOTT WILLOUGHBY,
Folger Shakespeare Library.

JAGGERY, a coarse brown sugar made in the East Indies by the evaporation of the juice of several species of palms, chemically the same as cane-sugar. The sap which yields jaggery becomes by fermentation palm-wine, and from it arrack (q.v.) is distilled. Jaggery is consumed at home, little or none of it entering commerce. See PALM.

JAGIC, ya'gich, **Vatroslav,** Croatian philologist: b. Warasdin, 1838; d. there, 5 Aug. 1923. He was educated at the university of Vienna; taught for a time at Agram and in 1870 was appointed professor of comparative philology at Odessa. Four years later he became professor of Slavic philology at Berlin and in 1875 founded there the *Archiv für Slavische Philologie.* He removed to Saint Petersburg in 1880, succeeding Sresnevski at the university there and in 1886 to Vienna as professor of Slavonic philology.

JAGOW, Gottlieb von, German Secretary of State for Foreign Affairs: b. 26 June 1863. Educated at the University of Bonn, he entered the diplomatic service in 1895. He first made his mark as private secretary to Prince Bülow, former Imperial Chancellor. He became Minister to Rome in 1907 and Ambassador in 1908. During the Turco-Italian war he conducted important negotiations with the Italian government and, it is said, prevented a war between Austria and Italy at the time. He was recalled to Berlin and appointed foreign secretary on the death of Kiderlen-Waechter (q.v.) in 1913. A quiet, retiring and scholarly man, he was one of the worst speakers in the Reichstag. He retired in 1916. He wrote 'Ursachen und Ausbruch des Weltkrieges' (1919); 'England und der Kriegsausbruch' (1925). D. Berlin, 12 Jan. 1935.

JAGUAR, jăg'ū-är or jăg'wär, a great American spotted cat (*Felis onca*), once numerous as far north and east as Arkansas, but since the early part of the 19th century rare even in Mexico. It resembles the leopard, but is more robust (exceeding the cougar in weight), has a rounder head, relatively shorter legs and a shorter, thicker tail. The tawny yellow hide is spotted with black, the spots larger than those of the leopard, and inclined to form broken rings with a spot in the centre. Jaguars abound in the tropical forests, especially along the great rivers, where they find most prey. They subsist largely on capybaras, agoutis, etc., but frequently pounce upon deer when they come down to drink. They seem to be more arboreal than most large cats, and a favorite method of obtaining their food is to lie along a tree-limb in some favorable spot and leap down upon the victim. But jaguars also abound in the treeless morasses of the Gran Chaco, and even on the dry uplands of Paraguay and Argentina, where their food and habits are entirely different from those that dwell in the forests. In view of the great extent of country and variety of circumstances in which this animal lives, formal statements as to its habits are full of error and superstition. It has the manners and disposition of other great cats, changing with environment, season and circumstances. It hates captivity and gives reluctant submission to circus training like other great cats. In some regions it is greatly feared by the people, while in other places it is regarded as little to be feared. Its greatest pecularity, perhaps, is the tendency to terrific roars and cries, more loud and continuous than those of cougars or leopards. Consult the works of South American travelers and naturalists, especially Humboldt, Azara and Walterton. Their accounts are well summarized by Porter in 'Wild Beasts' (New York 1894). Consult also Bates, H. W., 'The Naturalist on the Amazon' (7th ed., London 1895); Hudson, W. H., 'The Naturalist in La Plata' (4th ed., ib. 1903); Wallace, A. R., 'Travels on the Amazon' (ib. 1889).

JAGUARONDI, jăg-wa-rŏn'dĭ, or **YAGUARONDI,** a slender, long-tailed, unspotted, blackish-gray wildcat (*Felis jaguarondi*) of tropical America. It is not common, and is little known. It measures about 30 inches from snout to tail, and the tail is 25 inches long; and the sides of its nose are curiously pinched in.

JAHDE. See JADE.

JAHN, Friedrich Ludwig, German patriot: b. Lanz, 11 Aug. 1778; d. Freyburg, 15 Oct. 1852. He was educated at Halle, Göttingen and Greifswald, paying special attention to theology and philology. He served for a time in the Prussian army and in 1809 removed to Berlin, where he became a teacher. To restore the morale of his young countrymen, then at its lowest ebb after the Napoleonic conquest, he hit upon the idea of practising gymnastics. The result was the first *Turnplatz,* opened in 1811, and which was soon attended by 1,000 of the youth of the German capital. Branches were soon formed in other cities, but the reactionary policy of the rulers in that day soon put an end to the movement, it being feared that it had a political or revolutionary significance. Jahn was arrested in 1819 and the *Turnplatz* suppressed. He was liberated in 1825, but was never after fully free and his remaining years were spent in comparative obscurity. The Turnvereine of present-day Germany is modeled closely on the designs of Jahn. In 1859 a monument was erected to his memory at Freyburg.

JAHN, Otto, German philologist: b. Kiel, 16 June 1813; d. Göttingen, 9 Sept. 1869. He was educated at Kiel, Leipzig and Berlin and subsequently traveled for three years in France and Italy. In 1839 he was appointed privatdocent at Kiel, and in 1842 removed to Griefswald as professor extraordinary of archæology and philology, becoming ordinary professor in 1845. He was called to Leipzig in 1847 to the chair of archæology but four years later he was deprived of his chair for having participated in the revolutionary movement of 1848–49. In 1855 he was called to the chair of the science of antiquity and to the directorship of the academical art museum of Bonn. He was called to succeed Gerhard at Berlin, but died before his installation there. His services to classical philology were immense as also in the field of classical archæology. His principal works are 'Palamides' (1836); 'Telephos and Troilos' (1841); 'Die Gemälde des Polygnot' (1841); 'Pentheus und die Mänaden' (1841); 'Paris und Oinone' (1844); 'Die hellenische Kunst' (1846); 'Peitho, die Göttin der Überredung' (1847); 'Ueber einige Darstellungen des Paris-Urteils' (1849); 'Die Ficoronische Cista' (1852); 'Pausaniæ descriptio arcis Athenarum' (3d ed., 1901); 'Darstellungen griechischer Dichter auf Vasenbildern' (1861). His critical editions of the classics include Juvenal, Persius and Sulpicia' (3d ed., 1893); 'Censorinus' (1845); 'Florus' (1852); Cicero's 'Brutus' (4th ed., 1877); Livy's 'Periochæ' (1853); Spuleius' 'Psyche et Cupids' (5th ed., 1905). Other works are 'Biographie Mozarts' (3d ed. by H. Disters, 1891; English trans., by P. D. Townsend, 1891); 'Ludwig Uhland' (1863);

Gesammelte Aufsätze über Musik (1866); *Biographische Aufsätze* (1866); *Griechische Bilderchroniken* (1871).

JAI ALAI. See PELOTA.

JAINISM, jĭn′ĭz'm, is one of the many religions of India, followed by only about one million people, mostly in the northwest region. It closely resembles Buddhism, being a reaction contemporary with it in the 6th century B.C., from the precedent Brahmanism. These revolts arose from several causes: (1) the Kshatriya (warrior caste) sought release from the religious domination of the Brahman (priest caste); (2) Kshatriya philosophy rejected the Vedic deities; (3) the doctrine of noninjury. This last item gave to Jainism its outstanding trait. Softened by a tropical climate, humanized by a settled life in place of the old nomadic one, and driven by economy to abandon animal food, Indians had become increasingly reluctant to kill animals, except that the Brahmans naturally still demanded them for sacrifice. This practice was condemned by the Jains, who then proceeded with that extravagance characteristic of every Indian activity to spare all animal life whatsoever, even when noxious. To that end, the Jaina monk is equipped with a broom to sweep insects from his path, and a veil to sift them from his mouth, besides the inevitable almsbowl. Nor may he kill or disturb insects feeding upon his body. Moreover, Jains support beast-hospitals in many cities of western India, where old or lame buffaloes, cows, goats, sheep, fowl, and hordes of vermin are housed and fed.

Jainism was founded in the 6th century B.C., by Nataputta, entitled by his followers Mahavira (Great Hero) and Jina (Conqueror). The son of a chieftain, he led a worldly life until at 30, upon the death of his beloved parents, he was so agitated by the seriousness of life that he left his wife and relatives and wandered naked as a homeless ascetic. For 12 years he practiced the severest austerities with deep meditation, and was never moved to anger, though beaten by sinful men. Thus did he become the Jina (Conqueror) and Kevalin (Perfect Sage).

The Jaina monk attains deliverance for his spirit from the bonds of flesh by following the triratna (three jewels): knowledge, faith, and virtue.

This knowledge teaches that the world consists of eternal spirits and eternal atoms, without any supreme being. Eight re-births, after becoming a Jaina monk will secure the spirit's release from matter; not for absorption into the absolute —as Brahmanism taught—nor for annihilation in Nirvana—as Buddhism taught—but for something beyond human speculation; so that the Jaina was termed "the may-be philosopher." Such agnosticism has never flourished among the credulous, imaginative Indians, who, moreover, lack the mental discipline afforded by science. The second jewel is faith which reposes in the word of their master, Mahavira, and the declarations of their scriptures, the Agamas. Virtue, the third jewel, consists of the five-fold conduct that results from such knowledge and such faith, namely: (1) to kill nothing whatever; (2) not to lie; (3) not to steal; (4) to abstain from sexual pleasures; (5) to renounce all the attachments of the senses. "What is discontent and what is pleasure? One should live subject to neither. Giving up all gaiety, circumspect, restrained, one should lead a religious life. Man! Thou art thine own friend; why lookest thou for a friend beyond thyself?"

Seven sects are classed as Svetambara (white-attire) in contrast with the Digambara (sky-attire) who migrated to the South where a more equable climate allowed them to make compulsory that nakedness which had been only recommended in the earlier texts. These may be the gymnosophists mentioned by Greek historians, but nowadays they merely doff their upper garments during meals. There are other Indian ascetics, however, who still discard clothing, and are generally countenanced.

This monk-regimen was much tempered for the Jains laity, who in fact, were mostly prosperous tradespeople, farming being prohibited by the non-injury doctrine. But, furthermore, this extension of Jainism to include laity introduced two important changes in the religion. First, to meet the religious needs of common folk, a worship of the founder, Jina, was instituted with temples, idols, festivals, and offerings of flowers and incense. Second, the monks were compelled to abandon their homeless wanderings, in order to care for the souls of their resident laity. This, in turn, led to the erection of temples, the most costly and delicately beautiful in all India, as at Mount Abu, and the erection of cloisters where the leisured monks produced a varied literature. Thus does Nature, though expelled with a pitchfork, return in the end. Unlike Buddhists, the Jains maintain caste, some of them being even Brahmans.

EDMUND BUCKLEY.

JAIPUR, jī′po͝or, or **JEYPORE,** city, Union of India, capital of the state of Rajasthan, 140 miles west of Agra. It is the only city in India laid out in rectangular blocks. The city contains the palace of the maharaja of the former state of Jaipur, several colleges, and a notable open-air observatory. Manufactures include silk and cotton textiles, pottery, and brass and lacquer work. The city was founded in 1728 by Maharaja Jai Singh II to supplant Amber, 5 miles to the north as capital of the state; the state came under British protection in 1818. Pop. (1941) 175,810.

JAIR, the name of several men mentioned in the Old Testament. The most important of that name judged Israel 22 years. He is said to have had 30 sons who rode on 30 ass colts. Considerable discussion has arisen among commentators because of the attempt made to distinguish the Jair mentioned in the Hexateuch from the Jair of the book of Judges.

JAIRUS, jā′ĭ-rŭs, in the New Testament the name of a certain ruler of a synagogue whose home was not far from Capernaum. He had a daughter 12 years old who became critically ill, lying at the point of death. He sought Jesus in order that he might exercise his healing power. Jesus at once accompanied the anxious father. Before the home was reached, a messenger met them announcing the child's death. When they arrived at the home, Jesus said, "She is not dead but sleepeth." The professional mourners were sent from the room after ridiculing the statement. The parents and three disciples were detained. He then went to the bed, took the child by the hand and pronounced two Aramaic words *Talitha Cumi* or "daughter arise," and "she arose and walked" (Mark 5:22-43; Luke 8:41-56).

JAISALMER, jī′säl-mĕr, town, Union of India, in Rajasthan 140 miles west-northwest of Jodhpur. It was formerly the capital of the Indian state of Jaisalmer. The state, 15,980 square miles in area, lay within the great Indian desert. Lack of rainfall and permanent streams makes agriculture almost impossible, the inhabitants depending mainly on livestock for their sustenance. In 1156 a Rajput ruler built the fort around which grew the town of Jaisalmer. Pop. (1941) 7,120.

JAJCE, yī′tsĕ, town, Yugoslavia, 62 miles by rail southeast of Šarajevo, occupying a hill overlooking the picturesque Pliva River where it falls 100 feet into the Vrbas River. A series of small lakes and cascades along the course of the Pliva through miniature gorges and tree-clad mountains, with the main fall at Jajce, are utilized for industrial purposes without detracting from the natural scenic beauties of the neighborhood. The "Lake Fort" or Turkish Djöl Hissar, at Jezero, lies five miles west of Jajce. A 14th century fortress crowns Jajce hill. The 15th century church of Saint Luke with a fine Italian campanile is said to cover the traditional grave of the evangelist. In the church are preserved and exhibited the casket and skeleton of the last king of independent Bosnia, Stefan Tomasevic, who was flayed alive by the Turks and beheaded in Kraljeva Polje, the "King's Field" just outside the walls. During the Moslem invasion of Europe in the 15th century, the districts of Jajce and Srebenica, organized as the banate or kingdom of Bosnia, and garrisoned by Hungarians, fiercely opposed the Turks as the outpost of Christendom. In 1528, two years after the defeat of the Hungarians at Mohacs, Jajce surrendered to the Turks, who held it until the annexation of Bosnia and Herzegovina by Austria in 1908. Pop. (1931) 7,515.

JAKARTA. See DJAKARTA.

JAKOBSHAVN, yȧ-kôps-houn′, Danish settlement on the west coast of Greenland, situated on an inlet of Disko Bay. Established in 1741, it was named for Jakob Severin, a leading trader in Greenland. Fishing is the principal means of livelihood for the inhabitants. Pop. 681.

JALAL-AD-DIN or JELAL AD-DIN, jă-lä′lo͞od-dēn′, shah of Khwarazm: d. 1231. In 1220 he succeeded his father, Ala-ad-Din Mohammed, who had overrun most of Persia before coming into conflict with the forces of Genghis Khan. Jalal-ad-Din, forced to flee from Persia, sought refuge in India and was brought to battle on the banks of the Indus. Once more defeated there by Genghis Khan, he fled to Delhi and for a time was safe. He regained some portions of his khanate but again the Mongols defeated him, and his life was terminated by assassination.

JALAL-UD-DIN MUHAMMAD. See AKBAR.

JALAL-UD-DIN RUMI, jă-lä′lo͞od-dēn′-ro͞o′mē, Persian philosopher: b. Balkh, Khorasan, 1207; d. 1273. His father was a scholar and carefully educated the son, who also was educated at Aleppo and Damascus. In 1231 he was made director of a college at Konieh in Asia Minor. He gradually developed into a mystic. He founded an order of dervishes in 1247 for whom he wrote a collection of rules entitled *Mathnawi.* The *Diwan* is a lyrical collection of great poetic merit. This philosopher was the first to teach the transmigration doctrine.

Consult Browne, Edward G., *Literary History of Persia* (New York 1906), and Davis, *The Persian Mystics* (New York 1908).

JALALABAD or JELALABAD, jȧ-läl′ȧ-băd, town, Afghanistan, on the Kabul River 70 miles east of Kabul and 80 miles west of Peshawar. Situated west of the Khyber Pass and commanding the valley of the Kunar northward to Kabul, it is of considerable strategic importance. Baber, the Mogul emperor, chose the site as a defensive point, but it was not until 1560 that the town was built by Akbar, his grandson. During the First Afghan War (1841–1842) Jalalabad was captured by the British, whose troops, under Sir Robert Sale, withstood a determined siege which lasted from November 1841 to April 1842. Pop. (1948) 14,756.

JALAP, the tuberous root of *Exogonium* (*Ipomoea*) *purga,* or the plant bearing those roots, or the powdered drug derived therefrom. *Exogonium purga,* in the morning-glory family, Convolvulaceae, is suggestive of the cultivated morning-glory. It has twining stems—in cultivation grown on poles—alternate, entire, pointed, cordate leaves, and trumpet-shaped, rose-purple flowers, 2 to 3 inches long, with slightly exserted anthers. Some of the roots on the underground stems become enlarged and tuberous, like the related sweet potato. Native of Mexico, the plants grow in mountainous regions at altitudes of five to eight thousand feet, in rich, moist soil, near the city of Jalapa—hence the name jalap. Propagation is often by young roots. The older ones, which yield the drug, are thick, brownish, furrowed, bearing cork and lenticels. They are commonly dried in nets over fires, thus acquiring a smoky odor. They are also sometimes sun-dried, the resulting root-slices being lighter in color. Jalap has also been grown in cultivation in Jamaica, South America, India, Ceylon, and to some extent in Europe. The roots can be harvested in about three years. It was formerly used more generally than at present, although over 50,000 pounds are annually imported into the United States. The purgative principle is apparently in the resinous material of the root. It is glycosidic in nature, and has been designated as convolvulin and/or jalapin. It is sometimes considered a mixture, although there is disagreement concerning its components. Insects feeding on jalap seem to avoid the resinous material, and as a result the "worm-eaten" remains are more potent than the original. A number of other plants in the morning-glory family and their roots are also called jalap; some have properties similar to those of jalap in varying degrees. Among them are: Tampico jalap, *Ipomoea simulans* (Mexico); male or Orizaba jalap, also called Mexican scammony—not true scammony —*Ipomoea orizabensis* (Mexico); wild jalap, *Ipomoea pandurata* (United States and Canada); Indian jalap or turpeth root, *Ipomoea turpethum* (India, Malaya and Australia); and Brazilian jalap, *Piptostegia pisonis.*

EDWIN B. MATZKE.

JALAPA, *hä-lä′pä* (older **XALAPA;** in full JALAPA ENRÍQUEZ), city, Mexico; capital of the

State of Veracruz. It is situated at an altitude of some 4,500 feet, on the southern slope of Macuiltépetl, one of the mountains of the Sierra Madre Oriental. The city attracts numerous people because of the fine climate, being both warmer in winter than the cities of the lofty central plateau and cooler in summer than the port of Veracruz on the coast. The streets, generally cobbled, are narrow and winding due to the broken ground on which the city is built. It is constructed in the Spanish style and has many fine plazas filled with brilliantly colored flowers. Jalapa was a sizeable Indian town, and its situation on the main route between Mexico City and Veracruz gave it a continued importance after the Spanish conquest. It is the center of an agricultural region which is particularly known for its coffee, tobacco, and fruit wines. There is a large cigar industry in the city, as well as cotton mills and tanneries. Pop. (1940) 39,530.

JALGAON, jäl′goun, town, Union of India, in the state of Bombay 235 miles northeast of the city of Bombay. Under the former British administration it was the headquarters of a district of the Bombay presidency. Pop. (1941) 34,375.

JALISCO, hä-lēs′kô, **state, Mexico; on the** central Pacific coast. The Sierra Madre Occidental, known locally as the Sierre de Jalisco, separates a narrow zone, which is tropical in climate and which follows the coast, from the more moderate plateau area to the east which comprises by far the greater part of the state. The southeastern region is volcanic and the Volcano of Colima, 12,792 feet high, is located along the border with the State of Colima. Cereals are the chief agricultural products of the uplands, while cotton, sugarcane, rice, and tobacco are grown near the coast. Silver, gold, cinnabar and bismuth are the chief mineral products. The most famous products of the state are its pottery and its tequila. The latter, an alcoholic beverage made from the juice of the maguey cactus, is produced largely in the town of Tequila, 40 miles northwest of Guadalajara, the state capital. The beautiful Lake of Chapala, from which a delicious white fish is obtained, is located in the eastern part of the state along the border with Michoacán, and is the largest lake in Mexico. Railroads and highways run inland from both north and south along the coast to meet in Guadalajara, thence running eastward toward Mexico City. The area of the state is 31,149 square miles. Pop. (1940) 1,744,700.

JALPAIGURI, jŭl′pī-gŏŏ′rê, **town, Union of** India, located in West Bengal on the right bank of the Tista River, 50 miles southeast of Darjeeling. Under the former British administration, it was the capital of the Jalpaiguri district of the Bengal province; in 1947 the district, 3,050 square miles in area, was divided, one fifth of the area and a quarter of the population being assigned to Pakistan and the remainder going to the Union of India. Tea is grown extensively; other crops include rice, jute, and tobacco. Pop. (1940) 18,962.

JALUIT, jăl′ŏŏ-ĭt, **largest of the Marshall** Islands, in the western Pacific Ocean; it is in the Ralik Chain. The atoll is 38 miles long and 21 miles in breadth. There are some 50 islets. At Jabor, an inlet on the southeast side of the atoll, is a safe harbor and the administrative headquarters.

JAM, a food consisting of fruit boiled down with sugar to the consistency of paste. The proportion of sugar varies according to the taste and the particular kind of fruit, but roughly there should be from 12 ounces to 16 ounces of sugar to every pound of fruit. The best results are obtained with dry, sound fruit and white sugar of good quality. As the mixture is cooked and the fruit breaks up, the sugar dissolves in the juices of the fruit. The fruit itself is preserved and the cane sugar, which many find indigestible, is changed by the action of the fruit acids into invert sugar, a far more digestible form.

Homemade jam, being boiled much longer than the commercial product, contains a larger quantity of invert sugar than manufactured jam; the proportion of invert to cane sugar varies in jams made from different fruits, and experiments have shown that while in strawberry jam two fifths of the cane sugar is inverted, in plum jam the proportion is six sevenths.

To keep the jam for any length of time in good condition, it is essential that the jars into which it is poured when hot, and the place in which it is stored when cold, should be perfectly dry.

JAMAICA, jȧ-mā′kȧ, **largest island of the** British West Indies, is 95 miles south of the southeastern end of Cuba. The island occupies a central position in the Antillean region. Its length is about 145 miles, and the maximum breadth is 45 miles. The area is 4,411 square miles. The Cayman Islands and the Turks and Caicos Islands (qq.v.) are administered as dependencies of the colony of Jamaica. By an agreement signed in January 1952 between the United States and Great Britain, the Bahamas proving ground for guided missiles was extended to include the Turks and Caicos Islands. Kingston, on the southwest coast of the island, is the capital of Jamaica and a commercial seaport. Spanish Town, 20 miles southwest of Kingston, was the capital prior to 1870. Other seaport towns include Montego Bay, on the northwest coast, and Port Antonio, 26 miles northeast of Kingston. By an agreement signed between the United States and Britain in 1941, certain areas in and around the island were leased to the United States for 99 years for use as a defense base. These areas comprise a fleet anchorage in Portland Bight and 2 square miles of adjacent land, the 45-acre Pigeon Island, and 4 tracts of land aggregating 278 square miles.

Topography.—The eastern part of the island has, as its most commanding feature, the Blue Mountain range (highest peak 7,388 feet). The center and west, an elevated plateau of later geologic formation, show the characteristic Antillean limestone and, more perfectly here than elsewhere in the West Indies, the extraordinary results of exposure of that soluble material to the tropical rainfall. This upland plain, by the action of the elements, has been carved into hills, basins, called "cockpits," 500 feet or more in depth, and much larger and deeper valleys, in which the plantations are situated, and from which the numerous streams often find their way to the sea by underground passages. One of these depressions, the Clarendon Valley (drained through a cañon), is 25 miles wide and 50 miles long; another, Saint-Thomas-in-the-Vale, is circular in form, with a diameter of about 10 miles. Throughout the western half of the island such valleys occur, some with, others without, apparent drainage outlets. Coastal plains are most extensive on the south side, where the largest, the plain of Liguanea, has an area of 200 square miles. There are no navigable rivers, but a great number of small streams, pools, and thermal springs. In the limestone region there are many caverns, interesting on account of their size and beauty, relics of the old Indian population. The mean temperature at the coast is very little more than 78°F.; that of the larger part of the habitable regions (1,000 to 3,000 feet above sea-level) is about 73°F.; and at the altitude of 5,500 feet it is 60°F. On the plateau the annual variation is scarcely 9°; for example, at Saint Elizabeth the maximum is 75°F. and the minimum 67°F. The average rainfall is 66 inches, the extremes being 100 inches on the high mountains and 44 inches at Kingston. The death rate is 16.29 in 1,000; but this favorable showing, as compared with the other islands of the Antilles, is due much less to natural advantages than to the strict enforcement of local sanitary and quarantine regulations.

Fauna and Flora.—Jamaica has no distinctively native mammals. There are many species of lizards, including the large iguana, a few harmless snakes, and the slightly poisonous centipede and scorpion. In the lowlands mosquitoes, ants, sandflies, butterflies, fireflies and beetles, parrots, pigeons, waterfowls, and 20 different kinds of songbirds are common. Edible marine fish are seldom caught near the island, but the streams contain a few fresh-water species. The flora is distinguished from that of the other Antillean regions by the total absence of the royal palm, and by the abundance of pimentos, or allspice trees, which are rarely found elsewhere. Common trees are the ceiba, mango, wild orange, plantain, fustic, logwood, coconut palm, and cedar. Begonias, orchids, ferus, and grasses abound, except on the southern coast, which has a flora of the arid type, including the cactus, thorny acacias, and similar plants.

Government.—A governor (who bears the old Spanish title of captain general) appointed by Britain is assisted by a Privy Council (4 exofficio and 2 nominated nonofficial members) and an Executive Council (4 exofficio, 2 nominated nonofficial, and 5 elected members—the last being elected from amongst the members of the House of Representatives). The bicameral legislature comprises the Legislative Council (3 exofficio, 2 nominated official, and 10 nominated unofficial members) and the House of Representatives (32 members elected for a term of 5 years on a basis of universal adult suffrage). Under a ministerial system of government, committees of the House of Representatives supervise departments of the administration. Kingston has a town council consisting of a mayor, 8 exofficio members of the House of Representatives, 8 elected members, and 2 coopted members.

The government conducts a large number of elementary, vocational, and teacher training schools, and gives financial aid to secondary and high schools operated by religious bodies. The University College of the West Indies, which serves all British colonies in the Caribbean area, is located at Mona, St. Andrews; it was opened in 1948.

Economy.—Sugarcane is the major economic crop, and rum is manufactured. Coffee, cocoa, coconuts, citrus fruits, and tomatoes are cultivated on an extensive scale for the export market. Other exports include ginger, bananas, limejuice, tamarinds, nutmegs, and a number of dyewoods and cabinet woods. Jamaica has extensive deposits of beauxite, production of which commenced in 1952.

Railways aggregate 245 miles, and there are 6,992 miles of highways which are for the most part usable in all weather. The island's tramway system has been abandoned. The government operates Palisadoes Airport, near Kingston, and Montego Bay Airport. The colony is served by British West Indian Airways and several foreign airlines.

History.—Jamaica was discovered on May 3, 1494, by Christopher Columbus, who named it Saint Iago. The island was a Spanish colony from 1509 until 1655. Saint Iago de la Vega, the first capital, which was founded between 1520 and 1526, subsequently was known as Spanish Town; it remained the capital until 1870. The Arawaks, the original inhabitants, were virtually exterminated by the Spaniards, who were compelled to import Negro slaves to work their plantations. However, the total population, white and black, numbered only 3,000 in 1655, when the island was captured by an English force commanded by Sir William Penn (father of the founder of Pennsylvania). Within three years the Spaniards were expelled and the Negroes fled to the mountains; the latter, known as Maroons, struggled for more than a century to preserve their independence. The island was quickly colonized by English settlers, many of them disbanded soldiers from the parliamentary army. Jamaica was under military jurisdiction until 1661 when, following the Restoration, a constitution was adopted and a legislative assembly established. The Treaty of Madrid of 1670 confirmed English possession of the island. Negroes were once more imported, and Port Royal became a center of the slave trade with neighboring islands and the mainland of America. An earthquake engulfed most of Port Royal in 1692; cyclones devastated it in 1712 and 1722; and a fire in 1815 completed its destruction. By the end of the 18th century the island was highly productive, but the abolition of slavery in 1833 was a great blow to its prosperity. A hurricane in 1903 caused enormous damage in the island; and an earthquake in 1907 shattered Kingston, involving the loss of 800 lives. Pop. (1951) 1,442,699.

Consult Gardner, W. J., *History of Jamaica,* 2d ed. (London 1909); Olivier, Lord, *Jamaica, The Blessed Island* (London 1936); *Handbook of Jamaica* (London, annually).

JAMAICA, jȧ-mā'kȧ, New York, industrial center, has been a part of the borough of Queens in the City of New York since January 1898. The seat of Queens County, it is located in the southeast section of New York City on Long Island. It is a subway terminus and an important junction on the Long Island Rail Road. In 1656 Governor Peter Stuyvesant gave permission for settlement of the town and in 1660 he granted it a charter. The early name of Rustdorp was soon changed to Jamaica, a name derived from the local Jameco Indian tribe. During the Revolutionary War the Battle of Long Island was fought within the limits of Jamaica. Among the

Straw articles for the tourist trade, Kingston, Jamaica.

Kingston's municipal market never fails to supply travelers with scenes of color and interest.

JAMAICA

© Screen Traveler, from Gendreau

Rodney Monument, Spanish Town, Jamaica, B.W.I.

© Screen Traveler, from Gendreau

Workers leaving the banana fields in evening. Note the cut trees across the road, uncut ones line fence at right.

several well-preserved pre-Revolutionary houses is King's Mansion which once belonged to Rufus King, a signer of the Constitution and an early minister to England. The population is over 200,000 (1952).

JAMAICA BAY, bay, New York, is an inlet of the Atlantic Ocean which indents the southwest corner of Long Island in the boroughs of Brooklyn and Queens in New York City. Elliptical in shape and slightly less than 20 square miles in area, it contains many marshy islands. It is separated from the ocean for nearly its whole extent by the peninsula of Rockaway Beach. Coney Island is near the entrance channel. Floyd Bennett Field is located on the southwest shore while the New York International Airport is situated on the northwest shore at Idlewild.

JAMBLICHUS, another spelling of Iamblichus (q.v.).

JAMDINA or **JAMDENA,** yäm-dā′nä, island, Indonesia, largest of the Tanimbar group, in the Moluccas 300 miles southeast of Ambon (Amboina). It is 70 miles long and 28 miles wide, the area being 1,100 square miles. Saumlakki, the chief village, is at the southern end of the island.

JAMES, Saint (often known as SAINT JAMES THE GREATER), the son of Zebedee. He was called to be an apostle together with his brother St. John, as they were mending their nets with their father Zebedee, who was a fisherman. They then followed Christ, were witnesses with St. Peter of the transfiguration, and accompanied Christ in the garden of Gethsemane. In the lists of the apostles given in the synoptic Gospels and in the Acts the names of Peter, Andrew, James and John stand first; and it is plain that these four were at the head of the 12 throughout. After the ascension St. James persevered in prayer with the other apostles and the women and the Lord's brethren. Nothing further is certainly known of him until the Passover of 44, when, being in Jerusalem, the Jews stirred up Herod Agrippa I against him, and he was put to a cruel death. Thus St. James was the first of the apostles who suffered martyrdom. There is a legend that he went to Spain, and that his bones, said to be in the foundation of the Cathedral of Santiago-de-Compostella in Coruña, lent miraculous aid to the Spaniards against the Saracens.

JAMES, Saint (called THE LESS), an apostle, was the son of Alphaeus. Little is known of him, though legend has it that he was active in Palestine and Egypt and finally was crucified in lower Egypt.

JAMES (called THE JUST), a brother or cousin of Jesus, became head of the Christian religious community of Jerusalem. At first skeptical of Jesus, he later became a convert after being favored by an appearance of the risen Christ. Free from strictly legalistic views, he nevertheless felt that Gentile Christians ought to respect observances of laws by Jewish Christians. The Epistle of James is generally ascribed to him.

JAMES I, king of England and, as James VI, also of Scotland: b. Edinburgh, June 19, 1566; d. Theobalds, Hertfordshire, March 27, 1625. He was the son of Mary, Queen of Scots, and Henry, Lord Darnley, and great-great-grandson of Henry VII of England. With the forced abdication of his mother in 1567 he was proclaimed king of Scotland, and during his minority the country was governed by a succession of regents—the earls of Moray, Lennox, Mar, and Morton. During most of this period he was under the tuition of the notable George Buchanan. From the first he seems to have imbibed those exalted notions of the royal authority and divine right which proved so injurious to his posterity. But James soon found it advisable to ally himself with Queen Elizabeth and to accept a pension from her. When, however, it became apparent that the life of his mother was in danger from the sentence of an English judicature, James sent representatives to England to intercede with Elizabeth; but his whole procedure in the matter shows a singular callousness. As a matter of form he ordered the clergy to pray for his mother, but when the news of Mary's execution in 1587 arrived James was not much moved, though he attempted to make a show of indignation by condemning one of the commissioners to death, a sentence which, however, he commuted to banishment. On Nov. 23, 1589 James married Anne, daughter of Frederick II, king of Denmark. On his return home, after passing the winter in festivities at Copenhagen, he was in some danger from the unruliness of the nobles; and for several succeeding years of his reign the history of Scotland displays much turbulence and party contest, but the supremacy of the crown was finally vindicated. In 1603 James succeeded to the crown of England, on the death of Elizabeth, and proceeded amidst the acclamations of his new subjects to London. One of his first acts was to bestow a profusion of honors and titles on the inhabitants of both countries. At a conference held at Hampton Court between the divines of the Established Church and the Puritans, James exhibited the ill will he bore to popular schemes of church government. The meeting of Parliament also enabled him to assert those principles of absolute power in the crown which he could never practically maintain, but the theoretical claim of which provided the increasing spirit of freedom in the House of Commons with constant matter of alarm and contention. Although James had behaved with great lenity to the Catholics in Scotland, those in England were so disappointed in their expectations of favor that the famous gunpowder plot was concerted in 1605, the object of which was to blow up the king and Parliament. (See GUNPOWDER PLOT; GREAT BRITAIN—*History—House of Stuart.*

In 1612 he lost his eldest son Henry, a prince of great promise, then 19; and in the following year the eventful marriage of his daughter Elizabeth with the Elector Palatine took place. No circumstance in the reign of James was more unpopular than his treatment of the celebrated Sir Walter Raleigh (q.v.). James had set his heart on marrying his son Charles to a Spanish princess, but the negotiations failed through the overbearing temper of Buckingham (George Villiers), the royal favorite, who quarreled with the grandees of the Spanish court. The close of the life of James was marked by violent contests with his Parliament. He was also much disquieted by the misfortune of his son-in-law, the Elector Palatine, who, having been induced to accept the crown of Bohemia, and to head the Protestant interest in Germany, was stripped of all his dominions by the emperor. Urged by national feelings for the Protestant cause, he was at length (10 March 1624) induced to declare war against Spain and the emperor; and troops were sent to Holland to act in conjunction with Prince Maurice. James was not destitute of abilities nor of good intentions, but the former were not those of a ruler, and he was neither beloved at home nor esteemed abroad. He received during his lifetime a great deal of adulation on the score of his literary abilities, and to him the authorized version of the Bible (1611) is inscribed. He was aptly described by Sully as «the wisest fool in Christendom.» Consult Aikin, 'Memoirs of the Court of King James the First' (1822); Burton, 'History of Scotland' (1873); Macaulay, 'History of England' (1858); Gardiner, S. R., 'History of England' from the Accession of James I to the Spanish Marriage' (1863–69); id., 'The First Two Stuarts' (1876); Henderson, T. F., 'James I and VI' (1904); and 'Cambridge Modern History' (Vol. III, 1910).

JAMES II, king of England, second son of Charles I and of Henrietta of France: b. London, 15 Oct. 1633; d. Saint Germain, France, 16 Sept. 1701. He was at once declared Duke of York, though only formally raised to that dignity in 1643. At the Restoration in 1660 he took the command of the fleet as lord high-admiral, and was also made warden of the Cinque Ports. He had previously married Anne, daughter of Chancellor Hyde, afterward Lord Clarendon (q.v.). In March 1671 the Duchess of York died. Before her death she declared herself a convert to the Roman Catholic faith, which had been secretly that of the duke for many years, and was now openly avowed by him. This declaration laid the foundation of the opposition which finally drove him from the throne. A test act being soon after passed, to prevent Roman Catholics from holding public employments, the duke was obliged to resign his command. On 21 Nov. 1671 he married Mary Beatrice of Este, daughter of the Duke of Modena, and in 1677 his eldest daughter, Mary, was united to William, Prince of Orange.

On the death of Charles II, 6 Feb. 1685, the duke succeeded, under the title of James II, and from the time of his ascending the throne seems to have acted with a steady determination to render himself absolute and to restore the Roman Catholic religion. At variance with his Parliament, he was under the necessity of accepting a pension from Louis XIV. He sent an agent to Rome to pave the way for a solemn readmission of England into the bosom of that Church, conduct which encouraged the rebellion of the Duke of Monmouth (1685). The unrelenting temper of James was again exhibited in the executions on this account. The legal proceedings under Jeffreys were brutal in the extreme; and no fewer than 320 persons were hanged on the western circuit alone, which attained an unenviable notoriety as the Bloody Assize. The New Netherlands (which included the city of New York) had been granted to him by Charles II, and his subserviency to the French King was seen in the Treaty of Neutrality agreed on in 1686 governing the relations of their American colonies. James gradually proceeded to a direct attack on the Established Church by the formation of an ecclesiastical commission, which cited before it all clergymen who had done anything to displease the court. Apparently to conciliate the Puritans a declaration of indulgence in matters of religion was ordered to be read by the clergy in all the churches of the kingdom, but its real object, however, was to favor the Roman Catholic element. Seven bishops met and drew up a loyal and humble petition against this ordinance, and for this act they were sent to the Tower, on a charge of seditious libel. On 29 June 1688, not many days after the birth of his son, the Old Pretender, they were acquitted amid the most enthusiastic rejoicings of the populace. The innovations, in regard both to the religion and government, gradually united opposing interests, and a large body of nobility and gentry concurred in an application to the Prince of Orange, signed by seven of the most prominent and influential political leaders, to occupy the throne. James, who was long kept in ignorance of these transactions, when informed of them by his minister at The Hague, was struck with terror equal to his former infatuation, and immediately repealing all his obnoxious acts, practised every method to gain popularity. All confidence was, however, destroyed between the king and the people. William arrived with his fleet in Torbay 5 Nov. 1688, and landed his forces, amounting to 14,000 men. Several men of rank went over to William, and the royal army began to desert by entire regiments. Incapable of any vigorous resolution, and finding his overtures of accommodation disregarded, James resolved to quit the country. He repaired to Saint Germain, where he was received with great kindness and hospitality by Louis XIV. In the meantime the throne of Great Britain was declared abdicated, and was occupied, with the national and parliamentary consent, by his eldest daughter, Mary, and her husband, William, conjointly; Anne, who had equally with her sister been educated a strict Protestant, being declared next in succession, to the exclusion of her infant brother, known in history as the Pretender, who had been born on 10 June of that year. Assisted by Louis XIV, James was enabled, in March 1689, to make an attempt for the recovery of Ireland. The result of the battle of the Boyne, fought 1 July 1690, compelled him to return to France. All succeeding projects for his restoration proved equally abortive. Before his death he underwent a spiritual transformation, and died in the odor of sanctity. Consult Acton, 'Lectures on Modern History' (1906); Burnet, 'History of the Reign of King James the Second'; Cavelli, 'Les derniers Stuarts à Saint Germain-en-Laye' (1871); Fea, 'James II and his Wives' (1908); Klopp, 'Der Fall des Hauses Stuart' (1875–88), and 'Cambridge Modern History' (Vol. IV, 1911).

JAMES I, king of Scotland, of the house of Stuart: b. Dunfermline, 1394; d. Perth, 21 Feb. 1437. He was the son of Robert III. In

1406, while on his way to France, he was taken by the English and carried to the Tower of London. For the next 18 years he remained a prisoner in England, being confined during part of his captivity in Nottingham Castle, Evesham, and Windsor Castle, where he wrote the 'King's Quhair' and other poems. Robert III died very shortly after learning of his son's captivity, and James was proclaimed king; but during the remainder of the reign of Henry IV and the whole of that of Henry V, he was detained in England, with a view to prevent the alliance of Scotland with France. In 1424, under the regency of the Duke of Bedford, he was restored to his kingdom, at which time he was in his 30th year. Previous to his departure he married Jane or Joanna Beaufort, daughter of the Earl of Somerset, a lady of the blood royal of England, who is the fair dame alluded to in his poem 'The King's Quhair.' On his return to Scotland he restored Scotland to some degree of order, but so severe was his treatment of his turbulent nobles that he was at last murdered by their emissaries at Perth in the 13th year of his reign. His works, edited by Skeat, were published by the Scottish Text Society (1884).

JAMES II, king of Scotland, son of James I: b. 16 Oct. 1430; d. Roxburgh, Scotland, 3 Aug. 1460. During the minority his kingdom was distracted by struggles for power between his tutors Livingston and Crichton and the great house of Douglas. In 1449 he assumed the government and married Mary of Guelderland. He had latterly allied himself with the Douglases, but being deprived of all real power, he resolved to free himself from their yoke. This he did in 1452 by inducing the Earl of Douglas to come to Stirling Castle, where he stabbed him with his own hand. He then quelled a powerful insurrection headed by the next earl, whose lands were confiscated. In 1460 he infringed a truce with Henry VI of England by besieging the castle of Roxburgh, and was killed by the bursting of a cannon in the 29th year of his age.

JAMES III, king of Scotland, son of James II: b. 10 July 1451; d. 11 June 1488. He was crowned at Kelso on his father's death, but in 1465 came under the influence of Bishop Kennedy and the Boyd family, one of the latter espousing the king's sister in 1467. James married Margaret of Denmark in 1469, and dismissed the Boyds from favor only to advance other favorites. Prominent among these was Cochrane, through whom one brother of James was obliged to flee the kingdom, and another was put to death. The nobles seized Cochrane and five others and hanged them. Subsequently a plot was formed to dethrone the king, and though many peers remained loyal to him the royal army was defeated at Sauchieburn near Stirling. James escaped from the field, but was murdered during his flight.

JAMES IV, king of Scotland: b. 17 March 1473; d. Flodden, 9 Sept. 1513. He was the son of James III. He commanded the nobles who vanquished and killed his father at Sauchieburn, and was crowned at Scone in June 1488. He married Margaret, the daughter of Henry VII of England, but taking umbrage at the hostile attitude of his brother-in-law, Henry VIII, allied himself with France. He was defeated and slain at the battle of Flodden (q.v.) during an invasion of England.

JAMES V, king of Scotland, son of James IV: b. Linlithgow, Scotland, 10 April 1512; d. Falkland Palace, 14 Dec. 1542. He came to the throne under the regency of his mother in 1513 and assumed the reins of government in 1528. He married Madeleine of France in 1537, and on her death married the daughter of the Duke of Guise, Mary of Lorraine, in 1538. He ruled with much vigor and decision, and on account of his mingling freely with his people was called «the king of the commons.» Becoming entangled in war with England in 1542, he was defeated at the battle of Solway Moss and died a month later. He was succeeded by his daughter, Mary, Queen of Scots, who was but seven days old at his death.

JAMES (JAMES FRANCIS EDWARD STUART), Prince of Wales, styled James III by the Jacobites and the Old Pretender by the Hanoverian party, and son of James II, king of England. See STUART, JAMES FRANCIS EDWARD.

JAMES, Bushrod Washington, American oculist: b. Philadelphia, 25 Aug. 1836; d. 1903. Graduated from the Homœopathic Medical College of Pennsylvania in 1857, he became well known as a practitioner; he was elected president of the Pennsylvania Homœopathic Medical Society in 1873, of the American Institute of Homœopathy in 1883, and in 1896 was vice-president of the Homœopathic Medical Congress held at London, England. His publications include 'American Climates and Resorts' (1889), a manual of climatology (1889); 'Alaskana' (1892); 'Echoes of Battle' (1895), and 'Alaska: Its Neglected Past and its Brilliant Future' (1897; rev. ed. 1901).

JAMES, Daniel Willis, American merchant and philanthropist: b. Liverpool, England, 1832; d. 1907. He came to America in early life and engaged in commercial life with the firm of Phelps, Dodge & Co., of New York. He amassed a huge fortune which he distributed to a great number of public institutions and seats of learning. Among the institutions which benefited from his philanthropy were Union Theological Seminary, $1,000,000; Amherst and Oberlin colleges, Columbia University, Cathedral of Saint John, New York, and the Hartford Theological Seminary. Under the terms of his will $100,000 was left to each of the following: Columbia, Yale, Union Theological Seminary, Cooper Union, Amherst College, American Board for Foreign Missions, Children's Aid Society, Cathedral of Saint John, New York, Presbyterian Hospital, New York. To Madison, N. J., he gave a library, assembly hall and public park.

JAMES, Edmund Janes, American educator and author: b. Jacksonville, Ill., 21 May 1855; d. Covina, Calif., 20 June 1925. He was educated at Illinois State Normal School, at Northwestern and Harvard universities; received the degrees of A.M., Ph.D., University of Halle, 1877; LL.D., Cornell College, Iowa, 1902; Wesleyan, 1903; Queen's College, 1903; Harvard, 1909; Michigan, 1914; Northwestern 1914. After scholastic positions at Evanston and Normal, at the universities of Pennsylvania and of Chicago, instructing in political and social science, he was president of Northwestern University, 1902–04; president of University of Illinois, 1904–20, and emeritus till his death. He was a member of numerous learned societies; author of a great number of miscellaneous articles in scientific journals; a founder and president (1889–1901) Amer. Acad. of Polit. and Soc. Sciences and editor of its *Annals*. He wrote: 'Relation of the Modern Municipality to the Gas Supply' (1886); 'The Canal and the Railway' (1890); 'Federal Constitution of Germany' (1890); 'Federal Constitution of Switzerland' (1890); 'Legal Tender Decisions' (1887); 'Charters of City of Chicago' (1900); 'Growth of Great Cities in Area and Population' (1900); 'Government of a Typical German City—Halle' (1900); 'The Immigrating Jew in America' (1907); 'Sixteen Years as President of the University of Illinois' (1920).

JAMES, Florence, «FLORENCE WARDEN,» English novelist: b. Hanworth, Middlesex, 16 May 1857; d. 11 Mar. 1929. She was a governess, 1875–80, and an actress, 1880–85. Her novels many of which are strongly sensational in character, have been very popular in this country as well as in England. They are published under the pseudonym of «Florence Warden,» and among them are 'At the World's Mercy'; 'The House on the Marsh,; which established her reputation; 'A Prince of Darkness'; 'Those Westerton Girls'; 'A Passage Through Bohemia'; 'The Inn by the Shore'; 'Mad Sir Geoffrey'; 'The Man with the Amber Eyes'; 'The Grey Moth' (1920); 'Lilith' (1923), etc.

JAMES, George Payne Rainsford, English novelist and historian: b. London, 9 Aug. 1799; d. Venice, 9 June 1860. As a young man he traveled widely on the Continent. He began his writing under the influence of Scott's novels, and wrote in all over 100 novels; he was also known as the author of popular historical books, and in 1839 was appointed historiographer royal, in this capacity writing 'History of the United States Boundary Question' and 'The Corn Laws.' In 1850 he was British consul in Massachusetts, two years later was transferred to Norfolk, Va., and in 1856 became consul general at Venice. His novels include 'Richelieu' (written 1825, published 1829); 'Darnley' (1829); 'DeLorme' (1830); 'Philip Augustus' (1831); 'Henry Masterton' (1832); 'The Gypsy' (1835); 'Attila' (1837); 'The Man-at-Arms' (1848); 'King's Highway' (1840); 'Agincourt' (1844); 'The Smuggler' (1845); 'Ticonderoga' (1854). His historical works include 'Memoirs of Great Commanders' (1832); 'Life of the Black Prince' (1836); 'Life of Richard I' (1842–49). James' novels were very popular when first written, and a new edition appeared in 1903.

JAMES, George Wharton, American explorer: b. Gainsborough, Lincolnshire, England, 27 Sept. 1858; d. St. Helena, Calif., 8 Nov. 1923. He spent many years in making geological and other researches in California and elsewhere in the southwestern United States, was a member of various learned societies in this country and England; was associate editor *The Craftsman,* 1904–05; editor *Out-West,* 1912–14, and lecturer at the Panama-Pacific and Panama-California expositions, 1915–16. He published 'The Lick Observatory' (1888); 'Nature Sermons'; 'Picturesque Southern California'; 'Missions and Mission Indians of California'; 'From Alpine Snow to Semi-Tropical Sea'; 'In and Around the Grand Canyon' (1900); 'Indian Basketry' (1900); 'The Indians of the Painted Desert Region' (1903); 'How to Make Indian and other Baskets' (1903); 'Travelers' Handbook to Southern Californa'; 'In and Out of the Old Missions of California' (1905); 'The Story of Scraggles'; 'The Wonders of the Colorado Desert' (1906); 'What the White Race May Learn from the Indian'; 'Through Ramona's Country' (1907); 'The Grand Canyon of Arizona' (1909); 'The Hero of California' (1910); 'Indian Blankets and their Makers'; 'California, Romantic and Beautiful' (1914); 'The Lake of the Sky, Lake Tahoe'; 'Our American Wonderlands' (1915); 'Living the Radiant Life'; 'Quit Your Worrying'; 'Arizona, the Wonderland'; 'Reclaiming the Arid West' (1916); 'Exposition Memories' (1917); 'House Blessing and Guest Book' (1918).

JAMES, Henry, American Swedenborgian theologian: b. Albany, N. Y., 3 June 1811; d. Cambridge, Mass., 18 Dec. 1882. He was educated at Union College and Princeton Theological Seminary, traveled abroad and became a Sandemanian and later a Swedenborgian. He subsequently lived in New York, Newport, R. I., and lastly at Cambridge. Among the most noted of his works on morals and religion are 'What is the State?' (1845); 'Moralism and Christianity' (1852); 'Lectures and Miscellanies' (1852); 'The Nature of Evil' (1855); 'Christianity the Logic of Creation' (1857); 'Substance and Shadow' (1863); 'The Secret of Swedenborg' (1869). His 'Literary Remains,' edited by William James, appeared in 1885. He was the father of William and Henry James (qq.v.).

JAMES, Henry, American novelist and essayist: b. New York, 15 April 1843; d. London, 28 Feb. 1916. He was the son of a clergyman, Henry James (q.v.), who gained fame as a writer on philosophico-theological subjects, first from the Sandemanian and afterward from the Swedenborgian standpoint. The novelist, known until his father's death as Henry James, Junior, was educated under his father's guidance in New York, Geneva, Paris and Boulogne. He lived in Europe with his parents during the years 1855–59, and after his return to the United States studied in the Harvard Law School in 1862. He began his literary career about 1865 as a contributor to American magazines, and soon afterward published 'The Story of a Year, a tale of the American Civil War.' In 1869 he took up his residence in Europe, and resided chiefly in England and Italy. In 1915, the year before his death, he became a naturalized British subject and on 2 Jan. 1916 was decorated by King George V with the Order of Merit. 'Roderick Hudson' (1875) was his first long novel. His subsequent novels include 'Watch and Ward' (1878), originally published in 1871, in the *Atlantic Monthly*; 'The American' (1877), by some regarded as his best; 'Daisy Miller' (1878); 'The Europeans: a Sketch' (1878); 'Confidence' (1880); 'Washington Square' (1880); 'A Bundle of Letters' (1880); 'Diary of a Man of Fifty' (1880); 'The Portrait of a Lady' (1881); 'The Bostonians' (1886); 'Princess Casamassima'

(1886); 'The Tragic Muse' (1892); 'The Other House' (1896); 'The Spoils of Poynton' (1897); 'What Maisie Knew' (1897); 'The Awkward Age' (1899); 'The Sacred Fount' (1901); 'The Wings of a Dove' (1902); 'The Better Sort' (1903). He has also written a great many short stories, among which are 'A Passionate Pilgrim, and other Tales' (1875); 'Pension Beaurepas' (1878); 'An International Episode' (1879); 'The Madonna of the Future, and Other Tales' (1879); 'The Siege of London' (1883); 'The Point of View' (1883); 'Tales of Three Cities' (1884); 'The Author of Beltraffio, and other Stories' (1885); 'Stories Revived' (1885); 'The Aspern Papers, and other Stories' (1888); 'The Reverberator' (1888); 'A London Life, and other Stories' (1889); 'The Lesson of the Master, and other Stories' (1892); 'The Real Thing, and other Tales' (1893); 'Picture and Text' (1893); 'The Private Life' (1893), a collection of stories; 'The Album' (1894); 'The Reprobate' (1894); 'Tenants' (1894); 'Disengaged' (1894); 'Terminations, and other Stories' (1896); 'In a Cage' (1898); 'The Two Magics' (1898), consisting of two stories; 'The Soft Side' (1900), a series of stories; 'Question of our Speech; The Lesson of Balzac' (1905); 'American Scene' (1906); 'Italian Hours' (1909); 'Julia Bride' (1909); 'Finer Grain' (1910); 'The Outcry' (1911); 'Small Boys and Others' (1913). After his death, his incomplete novel, 'The Sense of the Past,' was published, in 1917; and a compilation of notes and papers under the title 'Travelling Companions,' appeared in 1919. A 'Bibliography' of his writings, by LeRoy Phillips was published in 1930. Though prolific, he was never careless. His style was felicitous, and in substantiality of work he ranks as the subtlest of American novelists. A dramatic version of 'The American' was produced in London in 1891, but neither it nor his subsequent play 'Guy Domville' (1895) was successful. He turned his intimate knowledge of modern French literature to good account in his volume of essays entitled 'French Poets and Novelists' (1878). Other works of a similar kind are 'Transatlantic Sketches' (1875); 'Portraits of Places' (1884); 'A Little Tour in France' (1884; new ed., 1900); 'Partial Portraits' (1888); 'Essays in London and Elsewhere' (1893). He also contributed the volume on 'Hawthorne' (1879) in the 'English Men of Letters' series, and in 1903 published 'William Wetmore Story and his Friends,' a notable biography. A revised definitive edition was issued of his 'Novels and Tales' (24 vols., 1909). See AMBASSADORS, THE; DAISY MILLER.

JAMES, James Alton, American educator: b. Hazel Green, Wis., 17 Sept. 1864. He is a graduate of the State Normal School, Platteville, Wis., and the University of Wisconsin 1888, receiving his Ph.D. from Johns Hopkins University in 1893. He was superintendent of schools in Darlington, Wis., 1888–90; professor of history in Cornell College, Iowa, 1893–97. Since 1897 he has occupied the chair of history in Northwestern University as head of the department, and is also the chairman of the graduate student work of the university. He is a member of several educational and historical societies. He is the author of (with Allen Hart Stanford) 'Government in State and Nation' (1901); 'Our Government' (1903); 'American History' (1909); 'George Rogers Clark Papers, Vol. I' (1912); 'Readings in American History' (1914); 'George Rogers Clark Papers, Vol. II' (1926); 'Life of George Rogers Clark' (1928). He edited Charles Seignobos's 'History of Contemporary Civilization.'

JAMES, Jesse W., American outlaw: b. Clay County, Mo., 1847; shot to death, Saint Joseph, Mo., 3 April 1882. During the Civil War the family, sympathizing with the cause of the South, suffered greatly at the hands of their neighbors who favored the Union side. Jesse became a member of the guerilla band led by Quantrell and soon established a reputation for courage and daring second to none. At the end of the war he surrendered and returned to his home. In the following year, however, enemies of his family managed to have him declared an outlaw, and thereafter for 16 years he was hunted throughout the land, a price upon his head. His name became a household word throughout America during this long struggle with the authorities. Many romantic adventures and not a few crimes were ascribed to him. He was invariably successful in the exploits he undertook to replenish his stores of ammunition or food, usually effected by train or bank robberies. A reward of $10.000 for his capture dead or alive was offered by the Governor of Missouri, and James was betrayed by the Ford brothers, members of his own gang. Charles and Robert Ford surrendered themselves after shooting James, received the reward, and, strange to relate, were placed on trial and sentenced to death for murder. They were pardoned by the governor. Later in the same year another member of James' band, his brother Frank, surrendered, was in jail awaiting trial for over a year and finally released. He subsequently occupied a farm in the vicinity of Excelsior Springs, Mo., where he died, 18 Feb. 1915. It has been asserted that Jesse James desired to surrender if he could be given a fair trial. Jesse was far from the criminal desperado many have represented him to be. He was chivalrous to women, and during the long years of his struggle with the law committed no crime with the primary intention of taking human life, but was solely actuated by the motive of maintaining his status as a free man. Consult James, Jesse, Jr., 'Jesse James, My Father' (Independence, Mo., 1899).

JAMES, John Angell, English Congregational clergyman: b. Blandford, Dorsetshire, 6 June 1785; d. Birmingham, 1 Oct. 1859. He was educated at the denominational college at Gosport. He entered the ministry when 17 years old and before he was 20 was settled as pastor of the Carr's Lane Parish, Birmingham, where he served until his death. He was one of the most noted preachers of his time. He was the author of 'The Anxious Inquirer' (1849, many other eds.); 'Christian Charity Explained' (6th ed., 1850); 'Christian Father's Present' (13th ed., 1841); 'Christian Fellowship' (11th ed., 1855); 'Christian Professor Addressed' (5th ed., 1852); 'Christian Progress' (1853); 'Church in Earnest' (4th ed., 1851); 'Course of Faith' (1852); 'Earnest Ministry, the Want of the Times' (6th ed.,

1855); 'Elizabeth Bates' (1845); 'Family Monitor' (9th ed., 1848); 'Female Piety' (4th ed., 1855); 'Sunday School Teachers' Guide' (17th ed., 1845), and ma. v other minor works. His works were collected and published in 17 vols. (1860–64). The last volume contains his autobiography. Consult also Dale, R. W., 'Life and Letters of John Angell James' (1861).

JAMES, Louis, American actor: b. Tremont, Ill., 3 Oct. 1842; d. 1910. His first appearance on the stage was at Louisville, Ky., in 1864. From 1865 to 1870 he was a member of the company organized by Mrs. John Drew, and from 1871 to 1875 was a member of the famous company of Augustin Daly, New York. After 1875 he appeared with Lawrence Barrett and Joseph Jefferson. From 1892 to 1895 he starred in a series of classical revivals. His most successful Shakespearean rôles were Autolycus, Nick Bottom and Cardinal Wolsey. Consult Clapp and Edgett, 'Players of the Present' (New York 1900).

JAMES, Ollie M., American legislator: b. Crittenden County, Ky., 27 July 1871; d. 28 Aug. 1918. He received an academic education and in 1887 was appointed page of the Kentucky legislature. He made his law studies under his father and in 1891 was admitted to the Kentucky bar. In the contest for the governorship of Kentucky Mr. James was one of the attorneys for the late Governor Goebel. In 1896 he was a delegate to the Democratic National Convention; was delegate-at-large in 1904 and in 1908. In the convention of 1908 he seconded the nomination of William J. Bryan for the Presidency. He was chairman of the Kentucky State Democratic Convention of 1900 and from 1903 to 1913 was a member of Congress from the First Kentucky District. On 10 Jan. 1912 he was elected United States Senator for the term 1913–19. In 1912 he was chairman of the Democratic National Convention, which nominated Woodrow Wilson for the Presidency.

JAMES, Thomas Lemuel, American banker and Postmaster-General of the United States: b. Utica, N. Y., 29 March 1831; d. New York, 11 Sept. 1916. He early learned the printer's business and bought out a weekly Whig paper, the *Madison County Journal,* at Hamilton; and in 1856 changed its name to the *Democrat-Republican,* which was for 10 years the most powerful Republican organ in Madison County. He was collector of canal tolls at Hamilton 1854–73; was appointed inspector of customs in New York 1861; weigher in 1864; and in 1870 was promoted to be deputy collector in charge of the bonded warehouse, which department he immediately proceeded to arrange according to a new system. In 1873 President Grant appointed him postmaster of New York, and he was reappointed by President Hayes in 1877. He filled this office with signal success and originated improvements in the delivery system, involving the whole postal methods of the United States. President Garfield in 1881 gave him the portfolio of Postmaster-General, and his chief important service was his initiation of inquiries which led to the investigation of the Star Route frauds, the saving of over $2,000,000 a year to the department, and a recommendation for a reduction of letter postage from three cents to two cents which was soon adopted. He received the degree of A.M. from Hamilton College in 1863 and that of LL.D. from Madison University 1883, Saint John's College 1884 and Saint Francis Xavier's College 1886. From 1882 he was president of the new Lincoln National Bank of New York city, which brought him into intimate relations with some of the most powerful financiers of the metropolis and the nation. In 1895 he was elected mayor of Tenafly, N. J.

JAMES, Thomas Potts, American botanist: b. Radnor, Pa., 1803; d. 1882. He acquired an interest in a wholesale drug firm in Philadelphia, in which city he lived nearly all his life. Removing to Cambridge, Mass., in 1867, he began extensive researches in botany. Many of his papers appeared in 'Proceedings of the Philadelphia Academy of Natural Sciences' and in 'Proceedings of the American Academy of Arts and Sciences.' He wrote the article «Musci» in King's 'Exploration of the 40th Parallel' and collaborated with Lesquereux in 'Manual of American Mosses' (1884).

JAMES, William, English naval historian: d. London, 28 May 1827. The date of his birth is unknown. In 1801–13 he practised as a proctor in the Jamaica Admiralty Court. He was interned in the United States when war broke out with Britain in 1812, but he effected his escape and reached Halifax. In the *Naval Chronicle* he published a number of articles which he signed «Boxer.» In 1816 appeared his 'Inquiry into the Merits of the Principal Naval Actions between Great Britain and the United States,' which in the following year appeared in an enlarged edition. This work was very partisan, James being violently anti-American. Cooper wrote a refutation in 1839, but erred on the other side. Roosevelt's 'Naval War of 1812' (1882) was the first fair presentation of the subject. James' fame rests, however, on his great 'Naval History of Great Britain,' begun in 1819, which appeared in five volumes (1822–24) and reprinted (6 vols., 1826). Editions appeared in 1837 and in 1886, and an epitome by R. O'Beirne appeared in 1888. In 1895 an 'Index' was issued by the Naval Records Society.

JAMES, William, American psychologist and philosopher: b. New York, 11 Jan. 1842; d. Chocorua, N. H., 26 Aug. 1910. He was the son of Henry James, theologian, and brother of Henry James, novelist. He was educated in New York and abroad, studied in 1861–63 at the Lawrence Scientific School of Harvard University, accompanied the Thayer expedition to Brazil in 1864–65, was graduated from the Harvard Medical School in 1870, in 1872 was appointed instructor in anatomy and physiology at the school, and in 1876 assistant professor of physiology. In 1885 he was appointed assistant professor of philosophy in the university, in 1889 professor of psychology, and subsequently professor of philosophy. He was Gifford lecturer on natural religion in the University of Edinburgh (1899–1901); Lowell Institute lecturer (1906); and Hibbert lecturer on the modern status of philosophy at Manchester College, Oxford (1909). His best-known work was done in the domain of analytical psychology, in which he won European recognition. His works are marked by a most readable style and skilful exposition of different topics, notably radical empiricism and pragmatism.

James was a founder of the American Society for Psychological Research, in 1884, and published *Principles of Psychology* (1890), and *Psychology, Briefer Course* (1892), both popular textbooks; *The Will to Believe* (1897); *Human Immortality* (1898); *Talks to Teachers on Psychology* (1899); *The Varieties of Religious Experience* (1902); *Pragmatism* (1907); *a Pluralistic Universe* (1909); *The Meaning of Truth* (1909); *Memories and Studies* (1911); *Some Problems of Philosophy* (1911); *Essays in Radical Empiricism* (1912).

Bibliography.—Knox, H. V., *The Philosophy of William James* (London 1914); Flournoy, T., *The Philosophy of William James*, tr. by E. B. Holt and W. James, Jr. (New York 1917); Kallen, H. M., ed., *The Philosophy of William James* (New York 1925); Grattan, C. H., *The Three Jameses* (New York 1932); Perry, R. B., *The Thought and Character of William James*, 2 vols. (Boston 1935); id., *In the Spirit of William James* (New Haven 1938); Matthiessen, H. O., *The James Family* (New York 1947).

JAMES, river, North Dakota and South Dakota. See DAKOTA, river.

JAMES, river, Virginia, the largest in the state. It rises in the western part of Virginia in the Allegheny Mountains, the headwaters being the Jackson and Cowpasture rivers which unite at Iron Gate in Virginia. The James flows southeast to Buchanan, in Botetourt County, then northeast to Balcony Fall, where it breaks through the Blue Ridge Mountains, again southeast to Lynchburg, then northeast to Scottsville, from which point the general course is southeast to the Chesapeake Bay. Its length is about 340 miles.

At the Rocketts, just below Richmond, where the river becomes a tidal stream, is the head of navigation, about 150 miles from the mouth. Ocean steamers come up the river as far as City Point, at the mouth of the Appomattox River. From City Point to the mouth, 66 miles, the stream is really a broad, deep estuary with Hampton Roads at its entrance to the Chesapeake. The falls in the river at Richmond, about 100 feet in six miles, furnish a large amount of water power. From Richmond to Buchanan, a distance of nearly 200 miles, the Kanawha Canal follows the course of the river and utilizes extensive reaches of slack water navigation.

The chief tributaries of the James are the Chickahominy from the north, and the Appomattox from the south. The broad body of water at the entrance into Chesapeake was early explored by European navigators, and Jamestown, the first permanent English settlement, was located on this river.

JAMES, Epistle of, one of the seven New Testament epistles called catholic and general, because addressed, unlike Paul's writings, to no specific group or individual, but "to the twelve tribes of the Dispersion," the latter term being given no such local limitation as is attached to it in I Peter 1:1. Though lacking the customary thanksgiving, prayer and concluding salutations or benediction, the conventional epistolary tokens appear in the introductory signature, address and formula of greeting, followed by some 60 hortatory imperatives. The readers addressed as "the twelve tribes," like those who in I Peter 1:1 and Galatians 6:16 are styled "the elect" and "the Israel of God" are Christian believers. (Compare Galatians 3:29 and Philippians 3:3.)

The writer has added to his name "James" no further clue to his identity, such as Paul and Peter's designation of themselves as "apostles," or the words "the brother of James," attached to the name of Jude (verse 1). The assumption that the author was "James, the Lord's brother" (Galatians 1:19; 2:9, 12) has made from the time of Origen (230 A.D.) an inevitable and fascinating appeal to the imagination. The adamantine obstacle, however, to the theory of a pre-Pauline date and authorship lies in the drastic polemic of 2:14-26 against such an antinomian abuse of his distinctive doctrine of saving faith as he foreshadowed and reprobated in Philippians 3:18 ff. A Hebrew Christian, familiar with Old Testament characters, the Septuagint version and the Wisdom books, he shows no trace of the mysticism of Paul and John, making no single allusion to Christ's incarnation, death, resurrection, or to forgiveness in His name. Twice only does he mention Jesus' name (1:1; 2:1), though no whit behind Paul in reproducing the ethical lucidity and rigor of his divine Master.

His literary form is that of the Greek diatribe, the traditional style of the street-preacher of philosophic morals, shaped to arrest and hold the attention of passers-by (Acts 17:17 ff.). It is "wisdom crying aloud in the street" (Proverbs 1:20) with bold challenges, pointed questions, imaginary interruptions from objectors, striking metaphors, cogent similes and abrupt transitions and repetition of topics. His method is not the systematic development of argument, but that of antiphonal contrast, as found in the Proverbs and the Sermon on the Mount. Thus the double meaning of the Greek word πειρασμός suggests in 1:2-11 the mutual aspects of prayerful fortitude in trials from without, and in 1:12-18 the tragic issues of temptation from within. Similarly the ethics of word and deed are treated in recurrent refrains. Tongue religion and heart religion are contrasted in 1:19-26, reckless and conceited censoriousness with the spirit of peacemaking in 3:1-18, the thoughtless boasting of future plans with trust in Providence in 4:13-17, and the Oriental habit of profane swearing with simplicity of utterance in 5:12. So in 1:27-2:26 the caricature of a dead faith that courts the rich and feeds the poor with pious platitudes is opposed to a living faith of deeds; and in 5:1-6 and 4:1-12 the spirit of worldly greed and pride is set over against a humble walk with God. In 5:7-11, 13-20, as before in 1:5, prayer for patience and intercession are commended.

Though authorship and date must remain uncertain, as in the case of Job and Hebrews, yet none the less aptly do the words of the Pastoral Epistle apply to this Scripture as "profitable for teaching, for reproof, for correction, for instruction which is in righteousness." (II Timothy 3:16.)

Bibliography.—Discussion of authorship, date, style, vocabulary may be found in New Testament introductions: T. Zahn (Eng. trans., 1909); J. Moffatt (1911); B. Weiss (1897); H. J. Holtzmann (1892); A. Juelicher (1904); A. S. Peak (1910); and detailed exegesis in commentaries; J. B. Mayor (3d ed., 1910); W. Beyschlag's Meyer (3d ed., 1897); H. von Soden in Holtzmann's *Hand-Commentar* (3d ed., 1899); Oesterley in *Expositor's Greek Testament* (1910); E. H. Plumptre in *Cambridge Bible* (1884); F. J. A. Hort (1909); R. J. Knowling in *Westminster New Testament* (1904); J. H. Ropes (1916).

MARCUS D. BUELL,
Late Professor of New Testament Greek and Exegesis, Boston University School of Theology.

JAMES BAY, Canada, an inlet of Hudson Bay, in the southern part, named in honor of Capt. Thomas James, an English navigator, who explored this body of water in 1631–1633. The bay is about 280 miles long and from 140 to 160 miles wide. It contains a number of islands, the largest, Akimiski, being about 60 miles in length. Several large rivers flow into James Bay. The largest of these are the Moose, which is the estuary of the Abitibi, Mattagami, Missinaibi and other rivers; and the Albany, Nottaway, and Eastmain rivers. Moose Factory, at the mouth of the Moose River, on the southern shore adjacent to Moosonee, is the most important Canadian trading station, next to York Factory, of the Hudson's Bay Company.

JAMES ISLAND, one of the Sea Islands, South Carolina, forming part of the southwest side of Charleston harbor. It is about nine miles long, and is famous for its sea-island cotton. James Island is separated from the city of Charleston by the Ashley River and the South Channel of the harbor, here a little over a mile wide. On the northeast coast of the island is Fort Johnson and nearby a former quarantine station. Just northeast of the island is Fort Sumter (q.v.). The Battle of Secessionville (see SECESSIONVILLE, BATTLE OF), fought on June 16, 1862, and several other engagements of the Civil War, took place on this island. Pop. of township (1950) 6,024.

JAMES MILLIKIN UNIVERSITY, Decatur, Ill., a coeducational, liberal arts institution. It was chartered in 1901 and opened in 1903, and is controlled by the Presbyterian Church. It has about 1,000 students.

JAMES OF COMPOSTELA or **COMPOSTELLA.** See COMPOSTELLA, ORDER OF SAINT JAMES OF; JAMES, SAINT (the "Greater").

JAMESON, jām's'n, **Anna Brownell Murphy,** Irish author and art critic: b. Dublin, May 17, 1794; d. Ealing, Middlesex, England, March 17, 1860. In 1827 she was married to Robert Jameson, afterward speaker of the house of assembly of Upper Canada, and attorney general, but the union proved unhappy. She made her first appearance as an author with the publication of *The Diary of an Ennuyée* (1826), which was very favorably received. Her *Loves of the Poets* appeared (1829), and was succeeded by *Celebrated Female Sovereigns* (1831) and *Characteristics of Women* (1832; on Shakespeare's heroines). In 1836 Mrs. Jameson visited her husband in Canada and published *Winter Studies and Summer Rambles in Canada* (1838). Later works of hers include *Companion to the Public Picture Galleries of London* (1842); *Memoirs of the Early Italian Painters* (1845); and her chief work, *Sacred and Legendary Art,* consisting of *Legends of the Saints* (1848), *Legends of the Monastic Orders* (1850), *Legends of the Madonna* (1852), and *The History of Our Lord* (1864; completed by Elizabeth Eastlake). In these the author has given admirable expositions of the works of the old masters and the religious bearings of medieval art.

JAMESON, John Franklin, American historian: b. Somerville, Mass., Sept. 19, 1859; d. Washington, D.C., Sept. 28, 1937. He was graduated from Amherst College in 1879; Ph.D. from Johns Hopkins in 1882. Jameson was professor of history at Brown University, 1888–1901; at the University of Chicago, 1901–1905; and in the latter year became director of historical research of the Carnegie Institution, Washington, D.C., leaving this post in 1928 to become chief of the division of manuscripts of the Library of Congress, which he remained until his death.

One of the founders of the American Historical Association, Jameson was managing editor of the *American Historical Review,* 1897–1901 and 1905–1928. He was the author of *History of Historical Writing in America* (1891); *Dictionary of United States History* (1894; rev. ed. 1931); and *The American Revolution Considered as a Social Movement* (1926). He edited *Original Narratives of Early American History* (19 vols.; 1906–1917), and was chairman of the committee of management for the monumental *Dictionary of American History* (20 vols.; 1928–1936).

JAMESON, SIR **Leander Starr** (known as DOCTOR JAMESON), South African statesman: b. Edinburgh, Scotland, Feb. 9, 1853; d. London, Nov. 26, 1917. He was gaining a reputation as a skillful young physician when he went to South Africa in 1878 and met Cecil Rhodes in Kimberley. Rhodes, then forming the British South Africa Company as part of his plan to expand British rule north of the Transvaal, in 1889 sent Jameson as envoy to negotiate with the Matabele chief Lobengula. Jameson's tact and medical skill overcame the chieftain's objections to Rhodes' expedition, which set out in 1890. Jameson accompanied this expedition into Mashonaland and in 1891 was appointed administrator of what became the nucleus of Rhodesia. In the Matabele rising of 1893 he accompanied the column to Bulawayo, where he remained after the flight of Lobengula, to establish another British administration over Matabeleland. These British acquisitions caused great resentment in the Transvaal (South African Republic), as they limited Boer expansion to the north.

The internal struggle in the Transvaal between the government of President Paulus Kruger and the *Uitlander* (mainly British settlers) striving for government reform led to the belief that a rising among the latter was imminent. In December 1895 Jameson, at the head of a small force of the British South Africa Company's police and volunteers, stood waiting on the Bechuanaland border for the signal. On account of disagreement, however, the revolt in Johannesburg was postponed, and Jameson, with or without the orders of Rhodes, forced the hands of the conspirators by invading the Transvaal with 500 men and three field guns on Dec. 29, 1895, thus beginning the famous Jameson Raid. On Jan. 2, 1896 they were surrounded by the Boers near Doornkop, where they were compelled to surrender. The British government repudiated Jameson's action and entirely disowned him. He was brought back to England, tried and sentenced in 1896 to fifteen months' imprisonment, but was released after four months on account of sickness.

The ill-starred raid produced untold trouble in South Africa, whither Jameson returned to the assistance of Rhodes. He was elected to the Parliament of Cape Colony in 1900. He had a burdensome "past" to live down, but by 1904, following the death of Rhodes in 1902, he became the recognized leader of the Progressive Party.

In that year he became prime minister of Cape Colony, holding that office until 1908. His administration was marked by economy, internal reforms and a sincere desire to reconcile the conflicting elements of Boer and Briton. Rhodes' great dream of union in South Africa was unswervingly pursued by Jameson, and it was in a large measure due to his efforts that that ideal was realized in 1909. The policy which he stamped upon the Unionist Party at the Bloemfontein Conference in 1910 has been maintained to the present day. From 1908 to 1912 he sat in the opposition; in the latter year illness compelled him to resign and return to England. He was created a baronet in 1911. In 1913 he was elected president of the British South Africa Company, of which he had been a director since 1902.

Jameson is buried next to Rhodes in the Matopo Hills, near Bulawayo, Southern Rhodesia.

JAMESON, Robert, Scottish mineralogist: b. Leith, July 11, 1774; d. Edinburgh, April 19, 1854. In 1800 he went to Freiberg, Saxony, to study natural history under Abraham Gottlob Werner, and in 1804 was appointed to the professorship of natural history in the University of Edinburgh. In 1809 he published *Elements of Geognosy*, in which he gave a comprehensive exposition of the neptunian theory as modified by Werner. In 1819, with Sir David Brewster, he founded the *Edinburgh Philosophical Journal*, of which he became editor. Others of his principal works are *System of Mineralogy* (1804–1808); *Manual of Minerals and Mountain Rocks* (1821); *Elements of Mineralogy* (1840). He was a fellow of almost all the learned societies of Europe.

JAMESON RAID. See Jameson, Sir Leander Starr.

JAMESONITE, jām'sŭn-īt, a sulphide of lead and antimony, $Pb_2Sb_2S_5$. Known as feather ore and a minor source of lead in various mines in Arizona, California, Nevada, South Dakota and Utah. It is named for Robert Jameson (1774–1854).

JAMESTOWN, jāmz'toun, city, New York; in Chautauqua County; altitude 1,315 feet. It is situated at the southern end of Chautauqua Lake, 57 miles south-southwest of Buffalo, and is served by the Erie and the New York Central railroads; it has regular air service. The region surrounding this industrial city is agricultural, with truck and dairy farms, orchards, and vineyards.

Jamestown is one of the leading cities in the United States in the manufacture of furniture. In its early days woodworkers in the settlement made wooden furniture for their pioneer neighbors, and this activity developed into an important industry. Leading manufacturers of metal furniture are also located here. In addition to furniture, both of wood and of metal, Jamestown factories produce filing cabinets and other metal articles of office equipment, voting machines, washing machines, metal doors and window frames, textiles, mattresses, mirrors, kitchen cabinets, and sinks, ball bearings, toys, and automobile parts.

The city has a public library, the James Prendergast Free Library, named after the founder of the town, for whom the city itself was named. It was Prendergast who bought here 1,000 acres of land, originally purchased by his brother from the Holland Land Company at $2 an acre. Jamestown has a business college and a community college, a music association, a civic forum, and a Little Theater. The proximity of the famous Chautauqua Institution brings many visitors here annually. Jamestown was the home of Senator Reuben E. Fenton; his memory is honored in a memorial park, in which are his old home and a bronze statue of him.

The first permanent settlement at the outlet of Chautauqua Lake was made about 1806. The site proved attractive and in 1849 Swedish immigrants settled here. After the Civil War others came, most of whom were cabinet makers, drawn here by the furniture industry. The population of Jamestown became largely Swedish. It was incorporated as a village in 1827, and as a city in 1886.

Jamestown is governed by a mayor and council. The water supply system is municipally owned, the water coming from artesian wells. The city also owns and operates the system of generating and distributing current for light and power. Pop. (1950) 43,354.

JAMESTOWN, city, North Dakota; seat of Stutsman County; altitude 1,410 feet. It is situated on the Dakota (James) River, 95 miles west of Fargo, and is served by the Northern Pacific and the Midland Continental railroads. There is an airline service. The surrounding region is agricultural, in which wheat growing and the raising of livestock are important activities. The city manufactures flour, cereal foods, and dairy products, and has bottling works. There are a public library, a radio station, two general hospitals, a state hospital for the insane, and the North Dakota School for Crippled Children. The site of Fort William H. Seward, abandoned in 1877, is on the outskirts of Jamestown. The city is the seat of Jamestown College (coeducational), and of a business college. Jamestown was settled in 1871; incorporated in 1896. Government is by mayor and council. Pop. (1950) 10,697.

JAMESTOWN, town, St. Helena, South Atlantic Ocean; port and capital of that British island. It was formerly a naval coaling station of great importance, but this activity declined following the opening of the Suez Canal. It has an observatory. Nearby is the tomb in which the body of Napoleon lay until it was transported to Paris in 1840. Pop. (1942) 2,381.

JAMESTOWN, former village, Virginia; in what is now James City County; site of the first permanent English settlement in the United States, and capital of Virginia, 1607–1699. It was founded May 13, 1607 by the Virginia Company of London, on what was then a marshy peninsula (now Jamestown Island) of the James River, about 32 miles from its mouth. The settlement originally consisted of a triangular blockhouse and several huts; these were destroyed by fire in 1608, but soon rebuilt. By 1609 there were some 50 wooden structures, a chapel, and a storehouse, all surrounded by a palisade with a fort at the neck. During the winter of 1609–1610, the settlement was almost wiped out by famine, and the survivors abandoned the site June 7, 1610. Already embarked on ships for the return to England, they met Thomas West, baron De La Warr (Lord Delaware) at the mouth of the James.

De La Warr brought with him supplies and additional colonists; the settlers turned back and reoccupied the village.

By 1619 the colony had attained some degree of stability; tobacco cultivation was introduced, and plantations established to the east and west, along the river. Peaceful relations with the Indians contributed to this period of comparative prosperity. In this year, the first legislative body to meet in the United States convened at Jamestown; 1619 also marked the bringing of the first Negro slaves to Virginia. In the great Indian massacre of 1622, Jamestown suffered less than the surrounding plantations, having been warned before the Indians struck. During Bacon's Rebellion (q.v.) in 1676, the village was again burned and rebuilt; and in the last decade of the century, fire swept it once more. This final disaster, coupled with the removal of the capital to the Middle Plantation (now Williamsburg) in 1699, depopulated the village, and it fell into decay.

The peninsula on which Jamestown was built had become an island by the middle of the 19th century. It was not until 1893, when the Association for the Preservation of Virginia Antiquities began its work, that an effort was made to retrieve what remained of the site. In 1900 the association induced the federal government to build a sea wall to prevent further erosion of the island. About 23 acres on the upper end of the island are owned by the association; the remainder is part of the Colonial National Historical Park, established as the Colonial National Monument, Dec. 30, 1930.

Jamestown is visited by more than 100,000 persons each year. Points of interest on the site include the old church tower, dating from the middle of the 17th century; foundations of the state houses; the Robert Hunt Memorial Shrine, erected in honor of the man who conducted the first Anglican communion in America, in 1607; the statues of Pocahontas and John Smith; and the federal monument, built in 1907, commemorating the 300th anniversary of the founding of the colony, which was the occasion of the Jamestown Tercentennial Exposition, held April 26 to Nov. 30, 1907. Significant work is being done here in the Jamestown Archaeological Laboratory which contains many 17th-century relics unearthed during excavations by the National Forest Service. The colonial park area includes also parts of the city of Williamsburg, the Yorktown Battlefield, and the Cape Henry Memorial at Cape Henry.

JAMESTOWN COLLEGE, Jamestown, N. Dak., a coeducational, liberal arts institution. It was founded in 1883 by the Presbyterian Church and was the first institution in the state to offer normal school training for teachers. The financial panic of 1893 closed its doors temporarily, but it reopened in 1909. There are about 350 students.

JAMI, jä′mĭ (so called from his birthplace; in Persian Nur ud-din 'Abd-ur-Raḥman ibn Aḥmad), Persian poet and mystic: b. Jam, Khurasan, 1414; d. Herat, Nov. 9, 1492. He received an excellent education as is evident from his polished style. Jami was the last great classic poet of Persia and was deeply versed in philosophy. In three *Diwans,* appearing from 1479 to 1491, are his odes and lyrical poems. His principal prose work is the *Baharistan* (1847), a collection of short didactic tales. Other works are in the collection *Haft Aurang* (*Seven Thrones*). The *Baharistan* has been translated into English several times. Edward Fitzgerald translated *Salaman wa Absul* from the *Haft Aurang* collection, in 1856, and *Yusuf wa Zalikha,* a version of the story of Joseph and Potiphar's wife, was translated by R. T. H. Griffith in 1882.

JAMIESON, jā′mĭ-s′n, **John,** Scottish lexicographer: b. Glasgow, March 3, 1759; d. Edinburgh, July 12, 1838. He was educated at the University of Glasgow and also studied for a short time in Edinburgh. In 1781 he was licensed to preach and became pastor of an Antiburgher congregation at Farfar; in 1797 he accepted a call to the Nicholson Street Antiburgher Church of Edinburgh. Jamieson's reputation as a man of letters rests on his *Etymological Dictionary of the Scottish Language* (1808; supplements in 1825). It is a work of great industry and considerable value as a collection of Scottish words, phrases, and customs, but as first published had little critical or philological merit, according to modern standards. The philological department was greatly strengthened in the edition of 1879–1887 by David Donaldson and John Longmuir. Jamieson also published *Ancient Culdees of Iona* (1811); *Hermes Scythicus, or the Radical Affinities of the Greek and Latin Languages to the Gothic* (1814).

JAMMU, jŭm′ōō, **town, India; in Kashmir;** chief town of the region of the same name. It is situated on the river Tawi, a tributary of the Chanab, 85 miles north-northeast of Lahore. Extensive ruins attest the former splendor of the town. Jammu, which is the winter capital of Kashmir, is the terminus of a railroad linking it with the Indian railroad system. Coal mines are operated in the vicinity. The region of Jammu, formerly an independent kingdom, was conquered in 1820 by Gulab Singh (d. 1857); he joined Kashmir to it in 1846. Pop. (1941; including cantonment) 58,847.

JAMNITZER, yäm′nĭt-sẽr, or **JAMITZER,** yä′mĭt-sẽr, **Wenzel,** German goldsmith: b. Vienna, 1508; d. Nürnberg, Dec. 19, 1585. Early in life he went with his family to Nürnberg, and in 1534 was admitted to the guild of master craftsmen. Subsequently he was appointed goldsmith to the court, serving successively the emperors Charles V, Ferdinand I, Maximilian II and Rudolph II. Specimens of his handiwork include a jewel box in the collection of the Dresden Palace, a gilt silver table piece in the Rothschild collection, Paris, statuettes in the treasury of Vienna, a jewel box in the Munich Treasury, and a cup which belonged to William II of Germany.

Wenzel's brother, Albrecht, worked with him until 1550. Wenzel's grandson Christoph (1563–1618) was a designer of ornamental works and an engraver. His *Groteskenbuch* (1610) contains 63 fantastic engravings.

JAMSHEDPUR, jäm′shĕd-pŏŏr, **city, India;** in southern Bihar. It is situated at the confluence of the Subarnarekha and Karkhai rivers, 140 miles west of Calcutta. The city was founded in 1909 as the headquarters of the Tata Iron and Steel Company, the largest concern of its kind in India, and was named for Jamsetji Tata, who first advocated the exploitation of the iron and coal deposits. The center of the Indian iron and steel industry, Jamshedpur has large iron and steel works, railroad shops, and machine factories. Pop. (1941) 148,711.

JAN MAYEN, yän mī′ĕn, island, Arctic Ocean, belonging to Norway. It is 360 miles north-northeast of Iceland; area 144 square miles. The island is volcanic, with an irregular surface, mountainous near the extinct volcano, Beerenberg, 8,347 feet high. One of the active volcanoes is about 1,500 feet high. There are some large glaciers on the island, one near Beerenberg. The island was named after Jan Mayen, a Dutch navigator, who visited it in 1611. Later is was ascertained that Henry Hudson had discovered it earlier, in 1607. It was frequently visited later by sealers, whalers, and scientists, and in 1921 a Norwegian observatory was established on the island. On May 8, 1929 Norway annexed Jan Mayen, and that country's sovereignty was subsequently recognized by other powers.

JANACEK, yȧ′nä-chĕk, **Leoš,** Czech composer: b. Hukvaldy, Moravia, July 3, 1854; d. Ostrau, Czechoslovakia, Aug. 12, 1928. In 1865 he became a chorister in the Augustinian monastery at Brno (Brünn), where he studied under the Moravian nationalist composer Paval Křížhovský. Janáček later studied at Prague, Leipzig, and Vienna. In 1881 he founded the Organ School at Brno, where he taught until 1920, then becoming professor at the conservatory in Prague.

Due to the veneration in which musical circles in his own country held the tradition of Bedřich Smetana (1824–1884), Janáček received little recognition until 1916, when his opera *Její Pastorkyna* (*Her Foster Daughter*), which had been performed at Brno in 1904, was presented at the Vienna Court Opera in a German version, as *Jenufa.* The melody of his national speech, which he studied in great detail, is the basis of his music, and translations of his vocal works are notoriously difficult due to the intimate relationship of speech tone and melody.

Among his more important other works, with dates of composition are the operas *Šárka* (1887), *Výlety Páně Broučkovy* (*The Exclusions of Mr. Broucek,* 1914), *Kat'a Kabanova* (1919–1921), *Lyška Bystrouška* (*The Cunning Little Vixen,* 1921–1923), *Več Makropulos* (*The Makropulos Affair,* 1923–1924), and *Aus einem Totenhaus* (*From a House of the Dead,* performed 1930); many choral works, including *Zápisn k Zmizeleho* (*The Day-Book of One Who Vanished,* 1916); orchestral works; chamber music; and songs.

JANAUSCHEK, yä′nou-shĕk, **Fanny** (in full Franziska Magdalena Romance), Bohemian actress: b. Prague, July 20, 1830; d. Amityville, N. Y., Nov. 28, 1904. She first appeared on the stage at Cologne, playing in that city and also in Frankfurt am Main, 1848–1860, and subsequently in Dresden and the principal cities of Germany, becoming a leading tragedienne. She made her first tour of the United States in 1863, playing in the German language and receiving most favorable notices. She later studied English and after 1869 played the most exacting Shakespearean roles in that language. After further tours of Europe and the United States, she made the latter country her home in 1880. Fanny Janauschek was best known for such roles as Lady Macbeth; Medea; Mary, queen of Scots; and Meg Merrilies. Changing styles of drama, however, gradually deprived her of her audiences.

JANE, jān, **Frederick T.,** English naval author: b. Aug. 6, 1870; d. Southsea, Hampshire, March 8, 1916. He was educated at Exeter School, invented the naval war game, and was naval correspondent of the *Engineer,* the *Scientific American,* and the *Daily Chronicle.* A prolific writer on naval affairs, he published many books on the subject, and in 1897 founded, and became first editor of the authoritative annual *Jane's Fighting Ships.* In 1909 he founded a companion work entitled *Jane's All the World's Aircraft.*

JANE EYRE, a novel by Charlotte Brontë, published under the pseudonym "Currer Bell" in 1847. For its day, it was a most unconventional novel. It came in the wake of sentimental novels in which the heroines were perfect and lifeless beings, and the heroes were all handsome and correct in their conduct. Against this unreality *Jane Eyre* was a protest, highly emotional, not to say hysterical. The author, the daughter of a Yorkshire clergyman, had grown up amid the hard surroundings of a bleak parish on the moors, and of boarding schools where the children were ill treated and ill fed. At the age of 30 she decided to put her own rebellious spirit into a novel, which should also follow in some degree the details of her own life.

Instead of being rich and beautiful, Jane Eyre is a poor and obscure girl, very small and plain in stature, with pale cheeks and green eyes. But she has a keen intelligence, and is thoroughly honest, outspoken and brave. In this heroine of a new type, Charlotte Brontë sought to depict a young woman who should be true to her opinions, true to herself, under all circumstances, whatever might be the consequence to herself or to others. Likewise the hero, Edward Rochester, was of a kind new to fiction. He was unshapely, his features were large and distorted and he had had an unsavory past. Nevertheless Jane Eyre fell in love with him, to the consternation of readers. There had never been in fiction any proposal of marriage like Rochester's, nor any acceptance like Jane Eyre's, on that moonlit night which ended in thunder and lightning and a deluge of rain.

Though the novelty of *Jane Eyre* has partially worn away, it still remains a most interesting story. It was admired by Thackeray, to whom the second edition was dedicated; and Trollope praised its just balance between the ordinary incidents of real life and extraordinary occurrences, such as an interrupted marriage, strange premonitions, dreams and a spectre. *Jane Eyre* was a sincere book, written by the sincerest of women.

Wilbur L. Cross.

JANESVILLE, jānz′vĭl, city, Wisconsin; seat of Rock County; altitude 800 feet. It is located on both banks of the Rock River, 32 miles southeast of Madison, and is served by the Chicago and North Western, and the Chicago, Milwaukee, St. Paul and Pacific railroads. It has regular air service. A center of trade for a region of dairy farming and the growing of grains and tobacco, Janesville has diversified industries, the products of which include automobiles, automobile bodies, fountain pens, woolens, cotton goods, thread, shades and awnings, and metal fencing. The educational, civic, and cultural resources of the city include good schools, a public library, hospital, civic music association, Little Theater, and service and social clubs. Janesville has the lowest illiteracy percentage among Wisconsin cities. Its public park system is recognized as one of the best in the state. The Wisconsin State School for the Blind is located here. This school, established as a private enterprise, was acquired by the state in 1850, and ranks as the oldest among Wisconsin's welfare institutions.

Janesville is one of the oldest cities of the state. It was first settled in 1835. Incorporation was effected in 1853, and the city became the county seat in 1859. Local points of interest include a soldier's monument; the birthplace of Carrie Jacobs Bond, composer of popular songs; and the one-room schoolhouse where Frances E. Willard taught. The city was named in honor of Henry F. Janes, an early settler. It has the council-manager form of government. Pop. (1950) 24,899.

JANET, zhȧ-nĕ', **Pierre Marie Félix,** French psychologist and neurologist: b. Paris, May 30, 1859; d. there, Feb. 24, 1947. He was educated at the École Normale Supérieure and the École de Médecine, Paris. After teaching at several lycées, he was director of the laboratory of pathological psychology at the hospital of La Salpêtrière in Paris, 1889–1898; lecturer at the Sorbonne, 1898–1902; and professor of psychology at the Collège de France from 1902. He is known especially for his researches in mental pathology and his investigations of hysteria by the use of hypnosis.

Janet laid the foundation of automatic psychology in his *L'automatisme psychologique* (1889), and was the first to describe psychasthenia (*Les obsessions et la psychasthénie;* 1903). His other works include *L'état mental des hystériques* (1893); *Névroses et idées fixes* (1898); *The Major Symptoms of Hysteria* (1908; consisting of a series of lectures delivered at Harvard University); *Les méditations psychologiques* (1920); *De l'angoisse à l'extase* (1926, 1928); and *Cours sur l'amour et la haine* (1933).

JANEWAY, jăn'wā, **Edward Gamaliel,** American physician: b. New Brunswick, N. J., Aug. 31, 1841; d. Summit, N. J., Feb. 10, 1911. In 1860 he was graduated from Rutgers College, and four years later from the College of Physicians and Surgeons in New York. He was professor of pathology and practical anatomy at Bellevue Medical College, 1872–1879; professor of diseases of the mind and nervous system, 1881–1886; professor of medicine, 1886–1892; and dean 1898–1905. He was also commissioner of health of New York City from 1875 to 1881, and president of the New York Academy of Medicine, 1897–1898. Janeway was one of the most eminent medical diagnosticians and consultants of his day in the United States.

Janeway's nodes, which he described, are small hemorrhagic lesions, generally on the palms and soles, resulting from bacterial endocarditis.

JANEWAY, Theodore Caldwell, American physician: b. New York, N. Y., Nov. 2, 1872; d. Baltimore, Md., Dec. 27, 1917. The son of Edward Gamaliel Janeway, he was graduated from Yale in 1892 and from the College of Physicians and Surgeons, New York City in 1895. He immediately entered his father's office, serving at the same time as instructor in bacteriology at his alma mater. In 1898 he became instructor and later lecturer at Bellevue Hospital Medical College. He resigned in 1907 to become associate professor of clinical medicine at the College of Physicians and Surgeons and became Bard Professor of Medicine two years later. He was largely responsible for the merger of the Presbyterian Hospital with the College of Physicians and Surgeons, thus forming the nucleus of the medical center on Washington Heights, New York City. In 1907 he became secretary of the Russell Sage Pathological Institute and in 1911 a scientific director of the Rockefeller Institute for Medical Research. He was called to Johns Hopkins Hospital in 1914 to become professor of medicine and head of the hospital. He helped establish a post graduate school for the study of tuberculosis at Saranac Lake. When the United States entered World War I he took charge of the section of cardiovascular diseases of the Division of Internal Medicine. The heavy work thus put upon him led to his early death.

His chief published work was *The Clinical Study of Blood Pressure* (1904). He was perhaps the first to make routine use of this resource in the clinic and introduced the first practicable apparatus for this purpose, called for him Janeway's sphygomanometer.

JANICULUM, jȧ-nĭk'ū-lŭm, or **MONS AUREUS,** mŏnz ô'rē-ŭs (modern MONTE GIANICOLO), a ridge a little more than three miles long on the west bank of the Tiber, opposite ancient Rome. It rises to a height of 300 feet above sea level and affords a fine view of the modern city, being immediately southeast of Vatican City. It was fortified as a defensive outpost at an early date. The Janiculum was first connected with Rome by the Sublician Bridge; the Aemilius Pons was added in 181 B.C.; the Pons Valentinianus in 366 A.D. It was included in the city limits by Augustus, becoming the 14th Ward (or Region) as Trans Tiberim (modern Trastavera), and was enclosed by a salient of the Wall of Aurelian (built 271–275 A.D.). Through the Porta Aurelia (modern Porta San Pancrazio) in the point of this salient, the Via Aurelia left the city. The Trans Tiberim was chiefly an industrial section, with water power supplied by the Aqua Traiana. The aqueduct of the Aqua Traiana was built by Trajan in 109 A.D. and restored in 1611 by Pope Paul V, hence the modern name of Acqua Paola.

JANIN, zhȧ-năɴ, **Jules Gabriel,** French critic: b. St. Étienne, Department of the Loire, Feb. 16, 1804; d. Paris, June 20, 1874. He was educated at Saint Étienne and at the Collège Louis-le-Grand; studied law and became a private tutor in the Latin quarter of Paris; and then turned to literature, becoming editor, novelist, journalist and critic. He soon became a contributor to several papers, notably the Liberal opposition paper *Le Figaro* and the government paper *Quotidienne,* and in 1836 became connected as dramatic critic with the *Journal des Débats,* in the columns of which he wrote for nearly 40 years. He possessed a wonderful piquancy of style and an airy grace of sentiment and wit, which made him a delightful retailer of small talk; as a critic, however, he was utterly inconsistent through lack of any general principles of judgment, and said the first thing that entered his mind, though fortunately his lack of judgment was linked with amiability. He was an indefatigable worker and was in constant demand by the publishers of Paris to review books, write prefaces, and do other literary work. Of his published works, one or two of which are remarkable both in substance and style, the following are noteworthy: *L'ane Mort et la Femme Guillotinée* (1829), which went through several edition; *Histoire de la littérature dramatique en France,* 6 vols. (1858), a selection of his weekly *feuilletons,* altered and remodeled so as to present a sketch of the history of the French stage and dramatic artists during nearly a quarter of a century; *Rachel et la tragédie,* a biographical and critical work upon that great tragic artist, with photographic illustrations (1859), and a translation of *Horace* into French, 6th ed. (1885). His *Oeuvres diverses,* 12 vols. (1876–1878), and *Correspondence* (1877) appeared after his death.

JANIN, jăn'ĭn, **Louis,** American mining engineer: b. New Orleans, La., Nov. 7, 1837; d. Santa Barbara, Calif., March 6, 1914. He did much to further the development of western mining. He was educated at Yale university, at the mining academy in Freiberg, Saxony, and at the school of mines in Paris. After practicing mining engineering in California, he turned his attention to the treatment of silver ores, especially on the Comstock lode in Nevada, and worked out a system to overcome the costly waste in extracting the metal from the ores. For a year during the 1870's he was adviser to the Japanese government about the development of the country's gold, silver and copper mines. Among the many young American engineers who received their early training with him were Herbert Hoover and John Hays Hammond.

JANINA or **JANNINA.** See IOANNINA.

JANIS, jăn'ĭs, **Elsie** (ELSIE JANIS BIERBOWER), American actress: b. Columbus, Ohio, March 16, 1889. She was educated privately; first appeared on the stage as Cain in *The Charity Ball* (1897). She played in vaudeville in 1898–1903; starred in *The Belle of New York* (1904); appeared in *The Fortune Teller* and *The Vanderbilt Cup* (1905–1907); under the management of C. B. Dillingham in *The Hoyden, The Fair Co-ed* (1908–1909); and *Slim Princess* (1910–1911). In 1911 she appeared in her own play *A Star for a Night* and in 1913 in *The Lady of the Slipper* and (1919) *Elsie Janis and Her Gang,* a vaudeville production. She has written *Love Letters of an Actress* (1913); *The Big Show; If I Know What I Mean* (1925).

JANITSCHEK, yä'nē-chĕk, **Hubert,** Austrian art historian: b. Troppau, Silesia, Oct. 30, 1846; d. Leipzig, June 21, 1893. He was educated at the university at Gratz 1868–1873, and from the latter year until 1877 pursued the study of art history in Italy. From 1877–1879 he was custodian of the Austrian Museum of Art and Industry in Vienna, and was subsequently professor in the universities of Prague (1879), Strasbourg (1881) and Leipzig (1891). He was the author of the following biographies in Robert Dohme's *Kunst und Künstler* collection: Andrea del Sarto, Bellini, Paolo Veronese, Il Tintoretto, and others, and also wrote *Die Gesellschaft der Renaissance in Italien und die Kunst* (1879); *Zwei Studien zur Geschichte der karolingischen Malerei* (1885); *Geschichte der deutschen Malerei* (1890); *Dantes Kunstlehre und Giottos Kunst.*

His wife, MARIE (b. Vienna, July 23, 1859) became known as a poet and novelist, her principal works being *Legenden und Geschichten* (1885); *Im Kampf um die Zukunft,* an epic poem (1887); *Gesammelte Gedichte,* 2 vols. (1892); *Aus Alten Zeiten* (1900); the novels *Aus der Schmeide des Lebens* (1890); *Lichthungrige Leute* (1891); *Atlas* (1893); *Gott hat es gewollt* (1895); *Frauenkraft* (1900); *Harter Sieg* (1901), etc.

JANIUAY, hä-nē-wī, **municipality, Philippine Islands,** of the Province of Iloílo, Panay, situated 19 miles northwest of the city of Iloílo, near the Jalaur River. It lies in a hilly country raising rice and sugar cane, and petroleum has been reported in the vicinity. Pop. (1948) 44,348.

JANIZARIES, jăn'ĭ-zĕr-ēz (Turkish *jenitcheri,* new soldiers), an infantry force of Turkey, first organized by the Sultan Orkhan about 1330, and in 1362 increased to about 10,000 by Amurath (Murad) I, who gave them considerable importance by bestowing on them special privileges. The janizaries thus became a class of warriors so deeply imbued with the military spirit that they proved in many instances a means of salvation to the empire. It was their boast that they had never fled in battle, and they were the nerve and sinew of the Ottoman Army. The regular troops of janizaries at one time numbered 60,000 or more, but they were afterward reduced to 25,000. They were kept in barracks in Constantinople and a few other cities. The irregular troops amounted to 300,000 or 400,000, and were scattered among all the cities of the empire, in time of peace performing police duties. The janizaries who constituted the sultan's bodyguard became in time so dangerous and their insurrections so frequent that several unsuccessful attempts were made to reform or disband them. In 1826 they rebelled on account of a proposal to form a new militia, when the sultan, Mahmud II, having displayed the flag of the Prophet, and being supported by their commander in chief, defeated the rebels and burned their barracks, and many of them perished in the flames. A royal proclamation abolished the corps. As many as 15,000 were executed, and 20,000 banished.

JANK, yängk, **Angelo,** German artist: b. Munich, Oct. 30, 1868. He was educated at the Munich Academy under Paul Höcker and Ludwig von Löfftz and in 1907 he was appointed to a chair there. He is best known for his execution of hunting scenes. In 1909 his *The Hunt* and *The Horsewoman* were exhibited at the Metropolitan Museum, New York. In addition to these he has executed *Mailed Defense; The Hurdle Race,* in the Elberfeld Museum; equestrian portrait of the duke of Saxe-Coburg-Gotha; *Princess and Swineherd,* in Munich. His colored lithographs are also well known.

JANKO, yŏn'kō, **Paul von,** Hungarian pianist and inventor: b. Totis, Hungary, June 2, 1856; d. Constantinople, March 17, 1919. He made his musical studies at the Conservatory of Vienna and in Berlin under Ehrlich. His execution on the piano was hampered through not being able to reach an octave. He therefore invented (1882) the keyboard known by his name and made several tours in 1886–90 to show its practicability first in London and later in New York. A Janko Society was founded in Vienna in 1905. He removed to Constantinople in 1892. The keyboard has six rows of keys placed fanwise in a semi-circle, with three keys to each note, one below the other, and is sometimes called the chromatic keyboard. It is claimed that fingering is much easier and simpler by this method, which despite its undoubted merit has not taken popular hold. The keyboard can be attached to any pianoforte, grand, upright or square.

JANNARIS, Anthony, Greek educator: b. Lakkoi, a village in Kydonia, southwest of Canea, island of Crete, 25 Aug. 1852; d. at sea, 26 April 1909. He was educated at Canea, Athens and Marburg; was Foreign Secretary to the Cretan government 1882–84; headmaster of the public gymnasium there 1883–85; head clerk to the British consulate in Crete 1884–88; and lecturer on Greek literature at Athens University in 1889. He took a prominent part in the Cretan insurrection of 1889–90, and was proscribed by the sultan; and subsequently went to England, where for six years he studied in the British Museum investigating the history of the Greek language. Upon his return to Crete he was elected a member of the Assembly, and during the troubles of 1897 acted as correspondent for the *Times*. From 1896 to 1904 he was lecturer on post-classical and modern Greek at Saint Andrews University and was afterward Inspector-General of Education in Crete. He was a prolific writer on Greek grammar and philology.

JANNES AND JAMBRES. When Moses wrought his wondrous magic before Pharaoh he was opposed by two Egyptian magicians — Jannes and Jambres. They were so much impressed that they became proselytes and accompanied the Children of Israel on their march to the promised land. According to the Talmud, the golden calf was made by Aaron at their instigation. They are mentioned in several apocryphal writings and in 2 Tim. iii, 8. Pliny and Apuleius mention Moses and Jannes as the names of ancient magicians. Eusebius quotes Numenius, a Greek philosopher of the 2d century, as representing Jannes and Jambres as Egyptians.

JANNET, Claudio, French economist: b. Paris, 22 March 1844; d. there, 21 Nov. 1894. He was educated as an advocate and became professor of political economy at the Catholic University of Paris. His work was largely influenced by P. G. F. LePlay (1802–82). Author of ‹Etude sur la Voconia› (1867); ‹De l'Etat présent et de l'avenir des associations coopératives› (1867); ‹L'internationale et la question sociale› (1871); ‹Les résultats du partage forcé des successions en Provence› (1871); ‹Les Etats-Unis contemporains› (1875; 4th ed., 1888); ‹Les sociétés secrètes› (1876); ‹Le crédit populaire et les banques en Italie› (1885); ‹Le Socialisme d'Etat et la réforme sociale› (1889); ‹Le capital, la spéculation et la finance au XIXe siècle› (1892); ‹Les ouvriers des deux mondes› (1893), etc.

JANOW, jä'nôv, **Matthias von, theologian** and reformer, considered the Wiclif of the Bohemian Church: date of birth unknown, though he was probably born in Prague; d. there, 30 Nov. 1394. Very little concerning his early life is known, except that he was descended from a noble Bohemian family, studied theology at the University of Prague and later spent about six years at the University of Paris. He then went to Rome, in 1381 was appointed canon of the cathedral of Saint Vitus in Prague and confessor to Charles II, and continued in that office until his death. He had no oratorical ability, but through his writings exercised a remarkable influence on the religious thought of his time. His writings were collected in a work entitled ‹De Regulæ Veteris et Novi Testamenti› (1392). In this book he denounced the corruption and evil that existed in the Church, alleged gross misconduct of bishops and priests and urged that all human additions to Christianity, both doctrinal and ceremonial, be eliminated, and that the Church return to its original beliefs and doctrines. The Pope declared these writings heretical, and 16 years after his death they were publicly burned with those of Wiclif. Consult Lützow, ‹Life of John Hus› (New York 1909).

JANS, Anneke, än'nä-kė yäns (or ANNETJE), Dutch colonist in America: d. Albany, N. Y., 1663. She came from Holland to New Netherland in 1630 with Roeloff Jansen, her husband, who secured in 1636 a grant of a tract of land containing 62 acres and reaching from the Hudson to the present Broadway and from a point near Desbrosses street to Warren street. In 1654, Anneke, upon the death of her second husband, Evarardus Bogardus (q.v.), obtained in her name a patent-right to the tract. In 1671 the land was sold by the heirs to the English Governor Lovelace. Three of the heirs, however, did not sign the document. Subsequently the property was confiscated by the English government and deeded to Trinity Church corporation (1705). From 1749 the possession of the property has been the subject of numerous suits by the heirs, based chiefly on the omitted signatures, and all decided for the defendants.

JANS, Jansen Enikel, or **Enenkel,** Austrian historian and poet: 13th century. He is notable as the author of ‹Weltchronik,› a narrative of little historical worth but valuable from a literary standpoint. It was edited by Strauch in ‹Monumenta Germaniæ Historica› (Vol. II, Part I, 1891). He also wrote a ‹Fürstenbuch,› which deals with the Austrian dukes Leopold VII and Frederick the Quarrelsome, and while historically inaccurate is noteworthy because of the personal anecdotes it contains. It was edited by Rauch in ‹Scriptores Rerum Austriacarum› (Vol. I, 1790).

JANSEN, yän'sĕn, or jăn'sĕn, **Cornelius,** Dutch theologian: b. near Leerdam, Holland, 28 Oct. 1585; d. Ypres, Belgium, 6 May 1638. From his 17th year he applied himself to the study of theology and first came into notice while professor of theology at Louvain (1630), as a teacher of the most rigid Augustinianism, especially in connection with the doctrine of free will and divine mercy. This brought him into conflict with the Jesuits. He was appointed (1636) bishop of Ypres, where he completed his famous work, on which he had labored for 22 years, under the title 'Augustinus, seu Doctrina Sti. Augustini de humanæ naturæ sanitate, ægritudine, medicina.' In this he declared philosophy, especially that of the Aristotelians, to be the source of Pelagian error, and in accordance with rigid Augustinianism, maintained the utter corruption of human nature and the extinction of free will, together with predestination. The school of thought he thus founded is now known as Jansenism (q.v.).

JANSEN, Olaus, Swedish naturalist: b. Christianstadt, 1714; d. Copenhagen, Denmark, 1778. He was educated in Germany; was a professor in the University of Tübingen for several years; was then appointed to a professorship in the University of Copenhagen, of which he was rector in 1761; and was elected a member of the Academy of Sciences in 1762. In 1764 he was sent by the Danish government to study the natural resources of the South American countries, but during his travels he reached as far north as Central America, Louisiana and Florida. In 1772 he visited Boston. His chief publications are 'Den Geist in den Naturvidenskaben og naturens almindelige laere' (1773); 'Neue Reisen durch Brazilien und Peru' (1775); 'Neue Reisen durch Louisiana und Neuva España' (1776); 'Anmarkningar till Historia Naturalis och climatet i Nye England och Nye Spanien' (1778), etc.

JANSENISM, strictly speaking, denotes both a theological system in the matter of grace and free will, and the Christian sect that has arisen from that system. In a loose sense, Jansenism is the rigid, straightlaced severity of the Jansenists in the application of the principles of morality,— especially in the almost impracticable dispositions they required for Holy Communion. This article confines itself to the strict sense of the word Jansenism; and presents a brief survey of the origin and evolution of both the doctrine and the sect.

I. Origin of Jansenism.— Imbued with the principles of Baius,— Michel de Bay, former professor of scripture at the University of Louvain,— Cornelius Jansenius, bishop of Ypres, wrote his 'Augustinus' to set forth what he deemed to be the teaching of Saint Augustine in the matter of grace and free will. After his death the work was published, A.D. 1640, under the auspices of the University of Louvain. It was prohibited by the papal internuncio, condemned by a decree and by briefs of Pope Urban VIII, denounced and vigorously attacked by the Jesuits; and yet gained rapid vogue. The following year, 1641, a second edition was published at Paris with the approbation of the Sorbonne. A papal commission was then appointed to examine the 'Augustinus'; and it was condemned, 19 June 1643, by Urban VIII in the bull 'in eminenti,' because of its defense of the condemned propositions of Baius.

The complete title of this epoch-making folio is 'Augustinus, seu doctrina Sancti Augustini de humanæ naturæ sanitate, ægritudine, medicina, adversus Pelagianos et Massilienses, tribus tomis comprehensa.' The first part expounds Pelagianism in such wise as to identify therewith the teaching of the Jesuits on grace. The second part treats of Saint Augustine's three states of human nature: the state of innocence before the fall of Adam, that of corruption after the fall, and the hypothetical state of human nature that is neither elevated by grace nor degraded by sin. Herein the teaching of Baius is closely followed. The third part is on grace and predestination.

To make the condemnation of the 'Augustinus' more specific, a new papal commission (1651) selected therefrom five propositions, which are here subjoined and referred to their respective parts in the volume:

1°. Some of God's precepts are impossible to the just, even though they desire and try to observe such, with the strength that they at present have; nor have they the grace by which such precepts might be possible. (Pt. III, Bk. ii, Ch. 13).

2°. In the state of fallen nature, one never resists interior grace. (Pt. III, Bk. ii, Ch. 24).

3°. For merit or blame, in the state of fallen nature, freedom from all internal determining force (*libertas a necessitate*) is not necessary; but freedom from all external determining force (*libertas a coactione*) is enough. (Pt. III, Bk. vi, Ch. 38).

4°. The Semi-Pelagians admitted the necessity of an interior grace, that should precede each act,— even the beginning of the act of faith; and they were heretics in that they taught this grace to be such as man's will might resist or obey. (Pt. I, Bk. viii, Ch. 6).

5°. It is Semi-Pelagian to say that Christ died or shed his blood for all men without exception. (Pt. III, Bk. iii, Ch. 21).

These propositions were condemned as heretical, by Innocent X, in the Constitution 'Cum occasione' (1653); by Alexander VII, in the Constitution 'Ad sanctam B. Petri Sedem,' (1656), and in the Constitution 'Regiminis Apostolici' (1664); by Clement XI, in the Constitution 'Vineam Domini' (1705).

II. The Question of Right.— Before the condemnation by Innocent X, the Jansenists admitted that the five mooted propositions were representative of the theological system of Jansenius. Fundamental to this system is the Baian theory of a never rejected grace (*gratia victrix*). Without this *great grace,* man by the necessity of fallen nature yields to desire (*voluptas*); against this grace, man is not free to follow desire. The elect are predestined to victorious grace and to glory, and that previous to God's foreknowledge of their future merit; only the elect does God sincerely will to save, for them alone did Christ pray and give up his life. The reprobate are absolutely predestined to be deprived of this never failing grace, and that previous to God's foreknowledge of their future blame; and so God does not sincerely will to save the reprobate, nor did Christ die for them. That the condemned propositions of the 'Augustinus' were a nucleus of this theory of morally necessitating grace, and of morally necessitated will, was at first admitted by the Jansenists. Their defense was that the five propositions correctly set forth Saint Augustine's doctrine on nature and grace; and that they had not been rightly condemned.

III. The Question of Fact.— Once the condemnation of Innocent X was published, the Jansenists shifted ground; and undertook their famous evasion by the question of fact. They rejected the five propositions as rightly condemned; but clung to the 'Augustinus.' They denied the fact that the propositions were contained in the 'Augustinus' in the meaning that had been censured as heretical; and insisted that the infallibility of the Church had nothing to do with such facts as the meaning intended by Jansenius and set forth in the 'Augustinus.' Antoine Arnauld was the mightiest champion of this evasion between 1653 and 1655. The bishops met in Paris, 28 March 1654, and declared that the Pope had condemned the meaning intended by Jansenius; their declaration was approved by Innocent X the following September. The Sorbonne respectfully submitted in 1656. It was then that Pascal stepped into the arena. His ‹Lettres Provinciales,› 23 Jan. 1656 to 24 March 1657, poked fun at the Sorbonne for discussing the statements of Arnauld, reveled in raillery about the condemnation and sparkled with witty banter of the Jesuits and their casuistry. Indeed, most of the ‹Provinciales› are occupied with villifying the Jesuits, because of the fact that from start to finish they were the chief opponents to Jansenism. At the height of these controversies, the Assembly of the French clergy published its decision, that the infallibility of the Church extended to dogmatic facts, — that is, to facts connected with the deposit of faith,— and therefore to the fact that the meaning of Jansenius, set forth in the ‹Augustinus,› was that which had been condemned by the branding of the five propositions as heretical. This decision was confirmed by Alexander VII, 1656, who decided the fact of the heresy of the ‹Augustinus.›

Still the Jansenists went on without submission, either in a negative attitude of «respectful silence» or in such positive opposition to the papal decrees as was evidenced by Quesnel in ‹Réflexions Morales.› That book reproduced the theory of Jansenius on grace and free will, and was approved by de Noailles, bishop of Châlons, later cardinal and archbishop of Paris. A new papal condemnation was needed. It came in the bull ‹Unigenitus,› 1713, whereby Clement XI condemned 101 propositions of ‹Réflexions Morales.› Jansenism now reached its strongest and stormiest epoch. The universities of Paris, Rheims and Nantes rejected the bull. Four bishops appealed to a future general council against the ‹Unigenitus,› 1717. They were joined by other bishops and many priests. Cardinal de Noailles appealed «from the Pope ill informed to the Pope better informed.» Clement XI, by the bull ‹Pastoralis officii,› 1718, excommunicated the recalcitrants. The Jansenists and recalcitrants, including Cardinal de Noailles, appealed from the bull ‹Pastoralis officii› to a general council. For a while the Church in France was rent with the schism. On the side of the Jansenists were a cardinal, 18 bishops and about 3,000 priests; on the side of the Pope were four cardinals, at least an hundred bishops, and more than an hundred thousand clerics. The schism lasted some 10 years. De Noailles submitted in 1728, and Jansenism gradually died out in France. Not so in the Netherlands. Here the vicars apostolic, who governed the small body of Catholics, were tainted with the ideas of the ‹Augustinus› on grace; and gave a refuge to Arnauld, Quesnel and many priests and nuns who refused to submit to the papal decrees against Jansenism. The result was a sect that to-day has dwindled down to about 6,000 members. They keep up the succession of bishops at Utrecht. The Pope is notified of the election and consecration of each new bishop. Rome straightway nullifies the election, and excommunicates the new bishop together with his followers.

Bibliography.— Rapin, ‹Histoire du Jansénisme› (1861); Dumas, H., ‹Histoire des cinq propositions de Jansénius› (1699); Maynard, ‹Les Provinciales et leur réfutation› (1851); Lafitau, ‹Histoire de la Constitution Unigenitus› (1737); Le Roy, ‹La France et Rome de 1700 à 1715› (1892); Saint Dechamps, ‹De hæresi janseniana ab Apostolica Sede merito proscripta› (1654).

WALTER DRUM, S.J.,
Late Professor of Scripture, Woodstock College.

JANSON, zhän-sŏn, **Kristofer Nagel,** Norwegian novelist and educator: b. Bergen, 5 May 1841. He was educated for the ministry at the University of Christiana, later interested himself in the movement for popular education and established a «Popular High School,» first in Sel, a district of Gudbrandsdalen, Norway, and afterward in Gausdal. Subsequently he traveled in Italy, in 1879 lectured in the United States, and from 1882 until 1892 was pastor of a Unitarian church in Minneapolis, where he had settled. He also became editor of a Unitarian paper, *Saamanden* («The Sower»), published in the Norwegian language at Minneapolis. He returned to Norway in 1893. For several years the Norwegian Storthing granted him a poet's pension. Among his published works, of which his earlier novels are written in the so-called *Landsmaal,* are ‹Fra Bygdom› (‹From the Up-Country Districts,› 1866); ‹Norske Dikt,› poetry (1867); ‹Jon Arason› (1867), a drama portraying the fate of the last Roman Catholic bishop of Iceland; ‹Marit Skjölte› (1868); ‹Han og ho› (‹He and She,› 1872); ‹Torgrim› (1872); ‹Sigmund Bresteson› (1872); ‹Fraa Dansketidi› (‹From the Times of Danish Rule,› 1875); ‹Den Bergtekne› (‹The Spell-Bound Fiddler,› 1876); ‹Vore Bedsteforældre› (‹Our Grandparents›); ‹Paa begge Sider Havet› (‹On Both Sides of the Ocean›); ‹Præriens Saga› (‹The Tale of the Prairie,› 1885); ‹Sara› (1891); ‹Jesus Sangene,› a collection of religious songs (1893), ‹Hvad jèg har oplevet› (1913); ‹Aspasia› (1914); ‹Mangeslags kjaerlighed› (1923).

JANSON, Paul, Belgian advocate and politician: b. Herstal, 11 April 1840. He became well known for his speeches on social reform, was elected to Parliament in 1877 and in 1878 became a member of the Liberal Cabinet. His activities in behalf of universal suffrage caused a split in the Liberal party and in 1884 Janson lost his seat in Parliament. The party was reunited and Janson returned to Parliament in 1889. He revived the question of universal suffrage and secured its adoption 18 April 1893, but lost his seat in the following year. He was re-elected in 1900, became an active worker for equal suffrage and was prominent in the parliamentary discussion of the Kongo investigations in 1906. He was appointed State Minister in 1912.

JANSSEN, Cornelius (also **JANSEN** or **JOHNSON**), English portrait painter: b. London, 1593; d. 1664. After earnest effort for many years he was rewarded in 1618 by being made the fashionable painter at the court. He maintained his pre-eminence until Van Dyck came to England. Janssen went to Holland during the troubled years of the wars between Charles I and the Parliament. His work is of a refined order, finished with infinite care and all portray his powers as colorist. His scheme of throwing features into high relief by providing a dark background has never been excelled. His best portraits are those of Charles I, the Duke of Buckingham, John Milton as a boy, and 'The Magistrates.' Janssen is represented in many private collections and also in the collections of Rotterdam, Lille, Dresden and Brunswick.

JANSSEN, yän'sĕn, **Johannes**, German Roman Catholic historian: b. Xanten, Rhenish Prussia, 10 April 1829; d. Frankfort-on-the Main, 24 Dec. 1891. He was educated at the universities of Louvain, Bonn (1851–53) and Berlin, was professor of history in the Gymnasium at Frankfort-on-the-Main in 1854, became a priest in 1860 and domestic prelate to the Pope in 1880. He is chiefly known by a work in six volumes, published in 1876, and which subsequently went through 14 editions, entitled 'Geschichte des deutschen Volkes seit dem Ausgang des Mittelalters' ('History of the German People from the Close of the Middle Ages to the Beginning of the Thirty Years' War 1618'). This work attained instant and great popularity among the German people, yet though its learning and thoroughness were not questioned, it was severely attacked by Baumgarten, Ebrard, Schweizer and others as being partial and unfair. A French translation of the first two volumes was published in Paris in 1887–88. Janssen's other works include 'Wibald von Stahlo und Corven' (1854); 'Frankreichs Rheingelüste und deutschfeindliche Politik in frühern Jahrhunderten' (2d ed., 1883); 'Schiller als Historiker' (2d ed., 1879); 'Zur Genesis der ersten Teilung Polens' (1865); 'Gustav Adolph in Deutschland' (1865); 'Frankfurts Reichskorrespondenz von 1376–1519' (1875; 4th ed., 1889); 'Friedrich Leopold, Graf zu Stolberg' (2d ed., 1882); 'An meine Kritiker' (1882); 'Ein zweites Wort an meine Kritiker' (1883), etc.

JANSSEN, Peter, German painter: b. Düsseldorf, 12 Dec. 1844; d. Berlin, 19 Feb. 1908. His father was J. Theodor J. Janssen, a noted engraver, and from him he obtained his early education; in his 16th year he entered the Academy at Düsseldorf and became a pupil of Bendemanns and Sohn. In 1877 he was appointed a professor in the Düsseldorf Academy, in 1895 its director, and in 1885 was elected a member of the Berlin Academy. In 1868 he painted his first great work, 'The Denial of Peter,' in the Academy at Philadelphia. In the same year he obtained first prize in a contest for decorating the walls of the Rathaussaal in Krefeld and completed this work in 1873. In the summer of 1872 he completed the colossal wall painting in the Bremen Exchange, 'The Colonization of the Baltic Coast.' In 1874 he decorated the walls of one of the rooms of the National Gallery in Berlin in wax colors, the painting taken from 12 subjects being entitled 'The Myth of Prometheus.' During 1880–82 he decorated the walls of the town hall at Erfurt with six large and three small paintings in wax colors entitled 'Momentous Episodes in the History of Erfurt.' These are noted for their brilliant color scheme and dramatic development. Other paintings by him are 'The Infancy of Bacchus' (1883), exhibited at the International Exhibition in Munich; 'Walther Dodde and the Peasants of Berg before the Battle of Worringen, 1288,' in the Düsseldorf Gallery, a picture that was awarded a gold medal at Berlin in 1893: 'The Battle at Fehrbellin' (1884); 'Nature,' 'Beauty,' 'Human Life' and 'Imagination' in the Aula of the Academy at Düsseldorf.

JANSSEN, Pierre Jules Cesar, French astronomer: b. Paris, 22 Feb. 1824; d. Meudon, 23 Dec. 1907. He was graduated in 1852 as licentiate in the mathematical sciences, and in 1860 as doctor of physical sciences, his graduating thesis, 'L'absorption de la chaleur rayonnante obscure dans les milieux de l'œil,' creating widespread discussion. In 1853 he became temporary professor in the Lycée Charlemagne, and from 1865 to 1871 was professor of general physics in the Special School of Architecture. In 1857 he went to Peru to fix the location of the magnetic equator; from 1861 to 1864 was in Italy observing the solar spectrum; and from the latter year until 1867 was in the Azores with Saint Claire Deville. In 1867 he went to Trani and in 1868 to Guntoor, India, to observe the total eclipse of the sun, making special spectroscopic observations on the protuberances. In 1870 he escaped in a balloon from Paris, then in a state of siege, in order that he might witness the Algerian obscuration; in 1874 watched the transit of Venus in Japan; in 1875 went as astronomer with the English expedition to Siam; and in the latter year was appointed director of the astrophysical observatory at Meudon, near Paris. In 1883 he was in the Caroline Islands. In 1891 he began his ascensions of Mont Blanc, and in 1892–93 founded an observatory there.

JANSSENS VAN NUYSSEN, zhän'sän, **Abraham**, Flemish painter: b. Antwerp, 1575; d. there, 1632. In early youth he showed remarkable aptitude for painting, and when 18 years of age became the pupil of Jan Snellinck. In 1601 he was admitted as a master into the guild of Saint Luke of which he was dean 1606–07; he then visited Italy. As a colorist he ranks next to Rubens among the Flemish painters of the 17th century; in correctness of drawing he excelled him, in treatment of the nude and in bold composition he equaled him, but in general freedom of disposition and touch and in faculty of color he fell far short. The most important of his paintings, which include biblical, allegorical and mythological subjects, are 'Madonna with Saints' and 'Entombment,' in the Carmelite church at Antwerp; 'Ecce Homo' and 'Descent from the Cross,' in the cathedral of Saint Bavon at Ghent; 'The Resurrection of Lazarus,' in the Elector Palatine's Gallery; 'Madonna,' 'Adoration of the Magi' and 'Scaldis,' in the Antwerp Museum; 'Venus and Adonis' and 'Day and Night,' in the Vienna Museum; 'Old Age Resting on Faith and Hope,' in the Brussels Museum; 'Meleager and Atalanta' and 'Vertumnus and Pomona,' in the Berlin Museum; 'Diana and Nymphs Watched by Satyrs,' in the Cassel Gallery, etc.

JANUARIUS, jăn-ū-ā'rĭ-ŭs, **Saint**: b. Naples or Benevento, Italy, 21 April 272; d. Pozzuoli, Italy, 19 Sept. 305. He became bishop of Benevento in 303 and at the time of the persecution of the Christians by Diocletian was beheaded. He is the patron saint of Naples. His body lies in the crypt of the cathedral at Naples; and two phials of his blood which a pious matron caught, according to tradition, at his execution, are preserved in a chapel in the south aisle. It is asserted that the blood liquefies on being brought near the head of the saint. A trial is made on three festivals of each year, the chief of which is the anniversary of the martyrdom, and also when public danger or calamity exists or is impending. It is believed that the patron saint is particularly propitious if the blood moves briskly in the phials and appears of a clear red, while the opposite is regarded as presaging some ill to the country.

JANUARY, the first month of the year, was by the Romans held sacred to Janus, from whom the name was derived. The Roman year originally began with March and consisted of only 10 months. Numa is said to have added January and February to the calendar; but although the Romans as early as 251 B.C. accepted January as the first month of the year, the nations of Europe did not universally adopt it as such till the 18th century. Wulfmonath was the Anglo-Saxon name for the first month. The 25th of March was the beginning of the ancient Jewish year, and that day, instead of 1 January, long held a legal position in Christian countries as the opening of the new year.

JANUS, jā′nŭs, an ancient Latin divinity, after whom the first month of the year was named. He was sometimes represented as a porter or keeper with a sceptre in the right hand and a key in the left, seated on a glittering throne; but was most commonly represented on the Roman *as* of the early coinage as having one head with two bearded faces, one looking forward and the other backward, and this latter image was set up under the arch in the Forum. Janus was called «father,» his name was first invoked at the beginning of all solemn sacrifices and he was worshipped as the god of gods, the sovereign disposer of war and peace and the dispenser of the fortunes of mankind. By some he was regarded as the god of light and heaven — the sun-god, the supreme janitor in heaven and on earth, identical with Jupiter (q.v.) — who opened the gates of heaven to let out the day and closed them again upon the return of evening. Others held that all doors (*janua*) and all passages (*janus*) were under his care. The commencement of both the year, month and day were regarded as sacred to Janus. The temple of Janus, standing on the north side of the Forum near the curia, was in reality only two parallel arches facing east and west, connected by side walls and furnished with gates. According to an ordinance of Numa Pompilius these gates were to be opened at the beginning of every war and remain open until peace was established in every country subject to Rome, but during the long space of 700 years the gates were closed only three times. Consult Fowler, 'The Roman Festivals' (1899); Toutain, 'Etudes de Mythologie' (1909).

JANVIER, jăn′vĭ-ā, **Catharine Ann,** American painter and author: b. Philadelphia, Pa. She was the widow of T. A. Janvier (q.v.), whom she married 26 Sept. 1878. Her paintings include 'Geoffrey Rudel and the Countess of Tripoli'; 'The Princess Badroulbadour'; 'The Guitar Player'; 'Daniel at Prayer'; 'The Violinist,' etc. She published 'Keramics for Students' (1880); 'London News' (1904); and translated (from the Provencal of Félix Gras) 'The Reds of the Midi' (1896); 'The Terror' (1898); and 'The White Terror' (1900). Died 17 July 1923.

JANVIER, Margaret Thomson, American author, sister of T. A. Janvier: b. New Orleans 1844; d. February 1913. Under the pen-name «MARGARET VANDEGRIFT» she wrote many juvenile stories and verses, including 'Under the Dog-Star' (1881); 'Clover Beach'; 'Little Helpers'; 'The Absent-Minded Fairy, and Other Verses' (1883); 'The Dead Doll, and Other Verses' (1888); 'The Queen's Body-Guard'; 'Doris and Theodora'; 'Rose Raymond's Wards'; 'Ways and Means'; 'Holidays at Home'; 'Little Bell, and Other Stories'; 'Umbrellas to Mend,' etc.

JANVIER, Thomas Allibone, American author: b. Philadelphia, Pa., 16 July 1849; d. 18 June 1913. He received a common school education; was an editorial writer for the Philadelphia *Press, Bulletin* and *Times* in 1870–81; married and passed some time in Colorado, New Mexico and Mexico; lived in New York during most of the period 1884–94, and then made his residence in France and England. Among his works are 'Color Studies' (1885); 'The Mexican Guide' (1887); 'The Aztec Treasure House' (1890); 'Stories of Old New Spain' (1891); 'The Uncle of an Angel and Other Stories' (1891); 'An Embassy to Provençe' (1893), the chronicle of a European journey; 'In Old New York' (1894), popular historical sketches; 'In the Sargasso Sea' (1898); 'The Passing of Thomas, and Other Stories' (1900); 'In Great Waters' (1901); 'The Christmas Kalends of Provençe' (1902); 'The Dutch Founding of New York' (1903); 'Legends of the City of Mexico' (1910); 'From the South of France' (1912); 'At the Casa Napoleon,' with 'Memoir' by Hitchcock, R. (1914).

JAOK, a large sculpin, *Myoxocephalus jaok,* of the Bering Sea, used locally as a food fish. It is from 12 to 18 inches long, olive grayish above and white below, common in shallow waters along the Bering Sea coasts and into the Arctic. «Jaok» is the Kamchatka name for the fish. The «cottus jaok» of the Kamchatkas in these waters is also used as a food fish, and is known by various names, the Koriahs calling it «i laal,» the Russian Kamchatkas «ramscha,» the Kouriles «susiatki.» It is reddish above and white below, about two feet in length and is said to live for two days out of water.

JAORA, India, a native state in the Malwa agency, Central India, comprising two separate tracts lying between Neemuch and Ratlam. The total area, which includes also the dependencies of Piplanda and Pant Piplanda, is 568 square miles. The head of the state is styled nawab, is of Afghan descent and of Mohammedan faith. In 1818 the native state was guaranteed its independence by the British under the Treaty of Mandsaur. The region is fertile and produces cotton, Indian corn, opium and several kinds of millet. The Malwa opium of commerce is largely produced in Jaora. The annual revenue is about $285,000, of which about $45,000 is paid as tribute. Pop. (1921) 85,578.

JAORA, India, town and capital of the native state of the same name, situated on the Rajputana-Malwa Railway, about 20 miles north of Ratlam. The town is regularly laid out and has several substantial buildings of modern construction. There are also a dispensary and a high school. The Zenana dispensary dates from the jubilee year of 1897. Pop. 17,151.

JAPAN (Jap. NIHON or NIPPON), island empire of eastern Asia. Including the Amami Islands, restored to Japanese sovereignty in 1953, it has an area of 142,798 square miles; its population was estimated at 88,000,000 on June 1, 1954. The capital, Tokyo, has a population (1950 census) of 5,385,071. For administrative purposes, Japan is divided into 46 prefectures.

The basic monetary unit is the yen, divided into 100 sen; in 1949 its value was set officially at 360 to the U.S. dollar. The metric system is used for weights and measures. The national flag is white, with a red sun in the center.

The historical, social, and political development of Japan, its economy, religion, literature, arts, and science, are treated under the following headings:

1. The Land	13. Religion
2. Political Divisions and Population	14. Cultural Life
3. The People	15. Scientific Research
4. Natural Resources	16. The Fine Arts
5. Agriculture	17. Architecture
6. Industrial Development	18. Language
7. Trade	19. Literature
8. Labor Relations	20. History: From the Earliest Times to 1853
9. Transportation and Communications	21. Development of the Modern State (1850–1945)
10. Financial Development	22. Foreign Relations (1931–1945)
11. Government	23. Occupation and Foreign Relations (1945–1954)
12. Changing Cultural Patterns	

1. THE LAND. Japan is an insular mountainous land lying between the gigantic mass of the Asiatic continent and the profound oceanic depths of the Pacific Basin. The bulk of its area is included in the four main islands of Honshu, Shikoku, Kyushu, and Hokkaido, but there are many smaller islands adjacent to the larger ones. Between the Japanese islands and the eastern shore of the Asiatic continent lie the relatively deep Sea of Japan, whose maximum depth is 12,178 feet, and the very shallow East China Sea, which, for the most part, overlies the continental shelf. In sharp contrast, the mighty Tuscarora Deep, which occurs just off the eastern or Pacific shores of the Japanese islands, reaches a maximum depth of 30,659 feet.

Japan, without its pre-World War II possessions, is a small country in terms of land area, which totals only 142,798 square miles. The area of the more important islands follows, in square miles:

Honshu	88,031	Amakusa-shimo	220
Hokkaido	30,077	Yaku	193
Kyushu	13,768	Tane	173
Shikoku	6,857	Tsushima-shimo	168
Amami-O-shima	333	Fukae (Goto group)	126
Sado	331	Tsushima-kami	95
Awaji	228	Dogo (Oki group)	95

Topography.—The islands of Japan, without exception, are but a part of the insular arcs of the Western Pacific, which have been formed by the intensive orogenic processes of recent geologic time. Largely in consequence of this, they are composed primarily of high and rugged mountains and contain many volcanoes. These mountain-forming processes are still vigorously active, as is witnessed by the frequency of destructive earthquakes and of violent volcanic eruptions.

The arrangement of mountain ranges and depressed lowlands and the distribution of volcanoes indicate that the form and the major surface features of the Japanese islands are dominated by six main mountain systems. From northeast to southwest these are: (1) the mountain arc accounting for the Kuril or Chishima Islands and continuing into Hokkaido from the northeast; (2) the mountains of Sakhalin or Karafuto entering Hokkaido at its northwest corner; (3) the Tohoku, or northeastern, range dominating the northern half of Honshu and the southern peninsula of Hokkaido; (4) the Seinan, or southwestern, system extending southwestward from central Honshu to form the backbone of the Chugoku Peninsula and to reach its greatest dimensions in the mountains of Shikoku; (5) the Shichito-Mariana chain reaching northward across central Honshu through the Pacific island groups from which its name is derived; and (6) the Ryukyu arc curving northward from Formosa to penetrate Kyushu. Where two or more of these mountain systems join, there occur high mountain masses or knots, extensive plains, and profuse groupings of volcanoes. In the central part of Honshu the Seinan and Shichito-Mariana arcs meet, and here are found the highest mountain lands of nonvolcanic origin in Japan. Here too occurs the Fuji volcanic group, with Mounts Fuji, Akaishi, and Hida (Ontake), whose summits reach 12,395, 10,456, and 10,444 feet, respectively. Also at this juncture of the two great arcs lies the greatest of Japan's lowlands, the Kanto plain. In Hokkaido, where the Tohoku, Kuril, and Sakhalin arcs join, is found the so-called Roof of Hokkaido, with complex clusters of mighty volcanoes. Another highland mass, with groups of volcanoes, is found in Kyushu where the Seinan and Ryukyu arcs meet. The axis lines of these great arcs are marked by mountain masses and extensive plateaus, which are often accompanied by extensive adjoining lowlands. In crossing Hokkaido, the two separated mountain ranges of Sakhalin give rise to the Kitami and Hidaka mountain lands in the eastern part of the island and to the Teshio and Yubari Mountains in the western part. Between them are extensive lowlands. The southwestward extension of the Kuril arc into Hokkaido is expressed in several separated volcanic groups, which reach their highest elevation in Taisetsu-zan (Asahi-dake) at 7,513 feet in central Hokkaido. Japan's second largest lowland, the Tokachi plain, in the western part of Hokkaido, lies just south of and adjacent to the juncture of the Kuril and Sakhalin arcs.

The Tohoku mountain system comprises the southwestern peninsula of Hokkaido and extends southward to the central part of Honshu. Here both the three mountain chains and the bordering and intervening lowlands run quite exactly parallel to the axis of the Tohoku arc. This is especially pronounced in the central and western portion of northern Honshu. The central range is the highest and forms the backbone of the area. It is surmounted by many towering volcanoes. The Dewa range in the west is much lower and in parts is hardly more than hill country. Between these two ranges is the Median Groove, an intermittent chain of down-faulted basins whose floors afford fertile plains. These three terrain elements—the two mountain ranges and the intervening lowlands—extend northward to form the southwestern peninsula of Hokkaido. The island of Hokkaido, then, is divided into two quite distinct parts in terms of terrain features. Separating these two sharply contrasting divisions is the wide and uninterrupted Ishikari-Yufutsu lowland, which runs north and south between the two bays whose names are combined to identify the plain. A genetic continuation of this lowland extends southward between the central and eastern ranges of Tohoku. In the far north of Honshu it accounts for the elevated Sambongi-hara or Mutsu plain. Just southward and terminating with the Gulf of Sendai is the Kitakami lowland, which southward from the Gulf of Sendai continues as the Abukuma lowland, including the Fukushima and Koriyama basins. The southernmost extension of this intermontane line of lowlands accounts for the great Kanto plain and the depression occupied by Tokyo Bay. The eastern of the three ranges of Tohoku borders the Pacific shore. It is broken in two by the Gulf of Sendai. The northern half is known as the Kitakami, and the southern is called the Abukuma. Peneplain remnants characterize both of the mountain lands, and both lie somewhat oblique to the general trend of the major arc.

The Shichito-Mariana arc is of tremendous topographic importance to Japan. It is associated with the mighty transverse tectonic depression of the Fossa Magna, which cuts north and south through the center of the main island of Honshu; with the famous and beautiful Fuji-Hakone-Amagi volcanic mountains; and with the high intermontane basins of central Honshu, including Matsumoto, Suwa, Kofu, Zenkoji, and Saku. The high, bordering mountain lands of Akaishi, Kiso, and Hida, though belonging to the Seinan system, seem to have been effected by the same orogenic forces and so trend in the same direction as the Shichito-Mariana arc. As the Shichito-Mariana arc approaches Japan from the Pacific, it gives rise to the spectacular Seven Isles of Izu (Izu Shichito), which are volcanic islands resting upon a submarine range. It then continues northward to form the massive and jumbled volcanic Izu Peninsula, with its famed hot springs and coastal resorts. This volcanic land continues northward and includes the great dissected volcano of Hakone, with beautiful Lake Ashi lying within its large crater. Nearby towers Japan's highest and most beloved mountain, Fuji-san, or Fujiyama, a majestic and nearly perfect conical volcanic cone, rising from sea level to 12,395 feet.

The Fuji volcanic chain continues northward through the Fossa Magna, and the western margin of this great transversal depression is marked by a tremendous and spectacular fault scarp. The eastern margin is also scarp bound, but is much less impressive. Between these scarps and the included volcanic lands of the Fuji chain occur the intermontane basins mentioned above.

The Seinan, or southwest, arc trends nearly due east and west and is divided into three parallel topographic zones. The northernmost lies within the inner zone of Japan and includes from west to east: the Chugoku range, which forms the backbone of the Chugoku Peninsula; the Tamba Plateau, lying just west of Lake Biwa; and the high nonvolcanic lands of Kiso and Hida. Elevations in this zone increase from west to east. Except for the two volcanic peaks of Daisen (5,620 feet) and Hyo-no-sen (4,954 feet) and the monadnock, Kanmuri (Kamori) -yama (4,393 feet), the highest peaks of the Chugoku range barely exceed 3,900 feet, while Hotaka-dake, at the eastern end of the zone and towering above the Fossa Magna, reaches a height of 10,138 feet.

The southernmost portion of the Seinan system bears the general name of the Kuma-kii mountain land. It belongs to the outer zone of Japan and is broken into four segments by three water channels—Bungo Strait, Kii Channel, and Ise Bay. The four mountain sections thus separated are uniformly characterized by very rugged terrain features, with sharp ridges and deep V-shaped valleys. From east to west these four areas are known as the Kyushu, Shikoku, Kii, and Akaishi mountain lands. General elevations also increase from west to east, terminating in the Akaishi, the highest nonvolcanic mountains in Japan, where Mount Kita reaches 10,456 feet.

The third and middle portion of the Seinan system is the great depression occupied by the Setonaikai, or Inland Sea. This beautiful body of water presents two contrasting seascapes—the Seto and Nada. The former are stretches of island-studded water and the latter are spacious areas of open sea. The major island groupings from east to west are those of Awaji, Bisan, Geiyo, and Hoyo, which separate the open seas: Izumi-nada, Osaka-wan, Harima-nada, Bingo-nada, Hiuchi-nada, Aki-nada, Iyo-nada, and Suwo-nada. The great depression which holds the Inland Sea is continued genetically northeastward to account for the down-faulted basins and block mountains of Kinai. The more important of these rich and anciently settled basins of Kinai are the Yamato (Nara), the Yamashiro (Kyoto), the Omi (Biwa), and the Osaka (Settsu). A western extension of the Inland Sea depression also accounts for the down-faulted basins and block mountains of northern Kyushu. These basin plains, like those of Kinai, are rich, long settled, and densely populated. The Chikugo and Chikuzen plains are among these. The southern portion of the depression in Kyushu is largely buried by volcanoes. Here are the famous hot springs of Beppu, the summer resort of Mount Unzen, and the gigantic caldera of Aso, whose floor supports a dense agricultural population as well as a central cluster of new volcanoes, one or more of which are almost constantly active. Still farther west the depression continues to give again the characteristic scenery of the Inland Sea in the Amakusa Islands and Yatsushiro Bay.

The influence of the Ryukyu arc is most marked in the extensive volcanic region of southern Kyushu and in the smaller islands of Japan just south of it. It is probable too that the southward trend of the central Kyushu mountain land results from the orogenic forces of Ryukyu. In the Japanese islands just south of Kyushu three zones are found. Tanegashima, in the east, is a low, flat island of young Tertiary rock. Yakushima, in the center, is a spectacularly mountainous island of much older rock. On this small, circular-shaped island, which is but 16 miles in diameter, the highest peak of Kyushu, Yae-san, reaches 6,348 feet above the sea. The third, or western, zone is composed of a series of volcanic islands which belong to the Tokara volcanic chain and which are genetically continuous with the volcanic lands of southern Kyushu.

Lakes.—Though not particularly numerous and generally not of large size, Japan's lakes fall into three main types. Lake Biwa (Biwa-ko), which is the country's largest lake (278.37 square miles), occupies the western half of the tectonic depression known as the Omi Basin. Of this same type is Suwa-ko, occupying a tectonic basin of the same name. A second type is the lake of volcanic origin. The great majority of these are caldera lakes. These are quite numerous in northeastern Japan and in Hokkaido. Ashi-no-ko in the Hakone caldera is the most famous lake of this type. Other well-known examples are Tazawa-ko in northern Honshu and Toya-ko, Shikotsu-ko, Akan-ko, and Kutcharo-ko in Hokkaido. Chuzenji-ko, in Nikko and well known to tourists, is also a caldera lake, but has been modified by later down faulting. A third type results from the blocking off of former estuaries by sand bars. Important examples of these are Hamana-ko in the middle Tokai region, Ogara-numa and Hachiro-gata in Tohoku, and Saroma-ko and Abashiri-ko behind the Sea of Okhotsk shore of Hokkaido.

In addition to these three main types, a number of small lakes have resulted from the damming of valleys by volcanic action or other cause, and there are also a sizable number of crater lakes. The five famous lakes lying just north of Mount Fuji are the result of volcanic damming. Unagi-ike and Kagami-ike (Mirror Lake) in the far south of Kyushu are the best known of the crater lakes. The almost complete absence of glacial lakes reflects the fact that even the high mountains of Japan were scarcely affected during the glacial period—a marked disadvantage in the development of hydroelectricity.

Rivers.—The extremely mountainous character of Japan, the abundant precipitation, and the fact that no drainage divide is far from the sea have resulted in many short, small, and torrential rivers. Only 10 of Japan's rivers have lengths of as much as 125 miles. They are all subject to sudden and violent flood, and flood damage over the years is much heavier than that caused by volcanic action and earthquakes. They are everywhere shallow and, except as they flow over the limited areas of plain, have extremely steep gradients. They are therefore of very limited value for transport, except for the floating of logs in the high-water period. Short and narrow valleys, allowing but limited storage capacity, combined with sudden and sharp alterations in the regimen of river flow, seriously handicap the development of hydroelectric power. The narrow mountain valleys permit only slight development of flood plains, and these are usually subject to inundation. Most such valleys have multiple river terraces, which afford safer sites for settlement and trajectories for communication routes than the present flood plains. As these swift and torrential streams leave the mountains and pass over the littoral plains or through intermontane basins, their flow is rapidly checked and heavy deposition takes place. Nearest the base of the mountains they deposit their coarsest materials and build steeply inclined alluvial fans. Farther on, the depositional materials tend to become finer, and the stream channels markedly broader. The characteristic streambed on the larger plains is very broad and in the dry season carries a braided stream. Deposition continues to be heavy, and with a strong seasonal differentation of flow the river channels tend to build higher than the surrounding plain. In extreme cases roads and even railroads follow tunnels under the riverbeds. These elevated rivers make irrigation easy, but greatly increase flood damage if the levees give way in times of high water.

Japan's greatest debt to its rivers lies in the fact that virtually all its plains have surfaces of river deposition. This has given Japan its best agricultural land and the great bulk of all its rice land. The same rivers have remained to supply water for irrigation. There is a close correlation between the size of the river and the size of the alluvial plain with which it is associated. The Tone-gawa, Japan's second largest river, accounts for most of the alluvial surface of the Kanto plain. The Shinanogawa, Japan's longest river, has built and waters the great alluvial plain of Echigo on the Sea of Japan. The three large rivers—the Kiso, the Nagara, and the Ibi—have built the largest continuous area of alluvium, the Nobi or Nagoya plain. The Yodo-gawa crosses the Osaka plain, the Kitakami-gawa built the Sendai plain, and the Chikugo-gawa waters the Tsukushi plain in northwest Kyushu. The Tokachi and Ishikari rivers are associated with Hokkaido's two largest plains, which bear the same names.

Shorelines.—Japan has an exceptionally long shoreline. The roughly 17,000 miles of coast gives to Japan one linear mile of shoreline to each 8.4 square miles of area. This shoreline is not only highly irregular, but also is exceedingly rich in variety and complex in origin. Many types of coastline can be encountered within relatively short distances, and much of Japan's justly famous scenery is found along its coast. If, for example, one follows the Tokaido Railway southwestward from Tokyo for the 77 miles to Numazu, one finds a rich variety of shorelines. First, there is the flattish, muddy deltaic shore of Tokyo Bay. This has been largely reclaimed and is used as sites for industrial plants. Then, along the eastern part of the head of Sagami Bay, extensive stretches of smooth sandy beach are encountered, but the western part is very rocky with narrow coastal terraces inland. Next, narrow sand dunes stretch along the shore of the Sakawa plain. Just southwestward is the Izu Peninsula, where deeply eroded volcanoes reach the sea. As Numazu is approached, a deeply indentured coast, formed by the drowning of the margin of a maturely dissected mountain land, occurs. This short stretch of coast from Tokyo to Numazu is not exceptional in its variety, although the Pacific shore is more rugged and varied than that of the Sea of Japan.

In general, the shorelines of Japan fall into two types, sandy and rocky, each of which can be divided into several subtypes. The sandy shoreline occurs where plains, large and small, reach the sea. These characteristically consist of a smooth and sandy beach with a beach ridge in the rear. The shoreline of some sheltered deltaic plains, where wave action is at a minimum, are backed by extensive shore flats. The head of Tokyo Bay, at the mouths of the Sumida and Edo (Yedo) rivers, and the head of Ariake Bay, where the Chikugo River debouches, are of this subtype. The rocky shoreline is found where mountain slopes descend directly into the sea. Where submergence has taken place, the sea's invasion of the erosion valleys results in a highly indentured coastline. The best examples of this subtype are found along the coast of the Kii Peninsula facing the Sea of Kumano and along the coast of the southeastern part of the Kitakami mountain land. Another rather common subtype is found where uplift has resulted in a series of coastal terraces backing the present sea cliff. These are commonly associated with the ends of rocky peninsulas, such as the southern parts of the Boso and Kii peninsulas. Much of the Hokkaido coast presents such shorelines, with Cape Erimo as the most spectacular. Cape Muroto in southeast Shikoku is another fine example, as is the Ajigasawa district on the Sea of Japan coast of northernmost Honshu. The fault-line shore, displaying the present sea cliff without backing terraces, is well represented by the coast running northeastward from Tsuruga. Still another rocky subtype, of which western Kyushu is an example, occurs where uplifted and down-faulted blocks alternate. The former account for peninsulas and island groups, and the latter for bays and inlets. A modification of the rocky shoreline types is found where there is an active development of sand bars producing land-tied islands and bay-mouth bars. Shio-no-misaki at the end of Kii Peninsula is an example of the first, and Cape Miho at the head of Suruga Bay exemplifies the second.

ROBERT BURNETT HALL,
Professor of Geography, Director of the Center for Japanese Studies, University of Michigan.

2. POLITICAL DIVISIONS AND POPULATION. For purposes of local administration, Japan is divided into 46 primary units, each having considerable autonomy. Most of these units are called ken, which is usually translated as prefecture, but there are three kinds of exceptions. The unit which contains the capital and metropolis is known in Japanese as Tōkyō-to, usually translated as Tokyo Capital Prefecture. (For Tokyo's special status see section on *Government.*) The entire island of Hokkaido constitutes one unit known as do (Jap. *dō*). The large cities of Osaka and Kyoto are in units known as fu, which is usually translated as city prefecture. This system is referred to as *to-dō-fu-ken,* stated in the order of rank and importance. Table 1 lists the 46 primary political divisions of Japan, their area in square miles, their population as of the census of Oct. 1, 1950, and their capital cities.

The system of ken or prefectures was adopted in 1871 to replace the system of feudal fiefs. At first Japan was divided into 302 ken, but in the same year amalgamation began and the number was reduced to 3 fu and 72 ken. This trend continued until by 1876 the total stood at 3 fu and 35 ken. The following years saw considerable readjustment, which resulted in the creation of some new ken. By 1888 the present (1954) number of divisions (46) and their boundaries were established, except for the western part of what is now Tokyo Fu, which was not annexed until 1892. The aims of the ken system, in addition to facilitating local administration, were at least twofold. The first was to break down the spirit of sectionalism, which had developed under the feudal and earlier *kuni,* or provincial, system. The second was to create political divisions with approximately equal resources. The first aim was, on the whole, successfully achieved, although people still like to refer to themselves as residents of an old *kuni* or *daimiate.* The second aim was defeated by the rise of industry, which gave great advantage to some areas and little or none to others. The names of most ken were derived from that of their largest city, which became the ken capital, such as Kyoto, Osaka, Kagoshima, and Hiroshima. Some ken, on the other hand, took their names from that of their most important county, such as Miyagi, Hyogo, and Ishikawa. There were other exceptions as well; Kanagawa took its name from one of the 53 stages of the Tōkaidō (Eastern Sea Road).

Until 1948 the ken were administered by governors appointed by the central government in Tokyo, but since that year the ken governors must stand for popular election.

Table 1—THE PREFECTURES OF JAPAN

Prefecture	Area	Population	Capital
Hokkaido (do)	30,332	4,295,567	Sapporo
Aomori	3,719	1,282,867	Aomori
Iwate	5,882	1,346,728	Morioka
Miyagi	2,808	1,663,442	Sendai
Akita	4,503	1,309,031	Akita
Yamagata	3,602	1,357,347	Yamagata
Fukushima	5,321	2,062,394	Fukushima
Ibaraki	2,352	2,039,418	Mito
Tochigi	2,485	1,550,462	Utsunomiya
Gumma	2,446	1,601,380	Maebashi
Saitama	1,468	2,146,445	Urawa
Chiba	1,954	2,139,037	Chiba
Tokyo (*to*)	789	6,277,500	Tokyo
Kanagawa	912	2,487,665	Yokohama
Niigata	4,856	2,460,997	Niigata
Toyama	1,644	1,008,790	Toyama
Ishikawa	1,619	957,279	Kanazawa
Fukui	1,646	752,374	Fukui
Yamanashi	1,725	811,369	Kofu
Nagano	5,261	2,060,831	Nagano
Gifu	4,052	1,544,538	Gifu
Shizuoka	2,999	2,471,472	Shizuoka
Aichi	1,963	3,390,585	Nagoya
Mie	2,226	1,461,197	Tsu
Shiga	1,564	861,180	Otsu
Kyoto (fu)	1,784	1,832,934	Kyoto
Osaka (fu)	700	3,857,047	Osaka
Hyogo	3,214	3,309,935	Kobe
Nara	1,426	763,883	Nara
Wakayama	1,822	982,113	Wakayama
Tottori	1,347	600,177	Tottori
Shimane	2,558	912,551	Matsue
Okayama	2,720	1,661,099	Okayama
Hiroshima	3,258	2,081,967	Hiroshima
Yamaguchi	2,349	1,540,882	Yamaguchi
Tokushima	1,600	878,511	Tokushima
Kagawa	717	946,022	Takamatsu
Ehime	2,188	1,521,878	Matsuyama
Kochi	2,743	873,874	Kochi
Fukuoka	1,909	3,530,169	Fukuoka
Saga	946	945,082	Saga
Nagasaki	1,574	1,645,492	Nagasaki
Kumamoto	2,870	1,827,582	Kumamoto
Oita	2,446	1,252,999	Oita
Miyazaki	2,988	1,091,427	Miyazaki
Kagoshima	3,013 [1]	1,804,118	Kagoshima
Total	142,300 [1]	83,199,637	

[1] With the restoration of the Amami Islands in 1953, the area of Kagoshima was increased to 3,511 square miles, and that of Japan to 142,798 square miles.

The ken are divided into secondary political units of three types: (1) *shi,* or city; (2) machi (*chō*), or town; (3) mura (*son*), or (as generally translated) village. This system is known as *shi-chō-son,* stated in order of rank. These units consistently have had a considerable degree of autonomy. Until 1926 the *gun,* or county, was an intermediate division, but it functioned rather as a detached branch of the ken government than as an autonomous unit. Although the *gun* was officially abolished, some offices continued to function under the *gun* name, such as certain agricultural experiment stations. In fact, after considerable inconvenience had been experienced, an office known as the *chihō-jimusho* (local administrative office) was created to perform the functions of the *gun* office for one or more of the old *gun* areas. Both the *shi* and the machi involve sizable settlements which have urban functions, but they usually also include country areas of rural settlement. The *shi* is the more important urban settlement and by law must contain 30,000 or more people. It also has much more autonomy than the machi.

On Sept. 1, 1952, there were 280 *shi,* including Tokyo-to. Their combined population was estimated at 32,326,000, or 37.8 per cent of that of the nation. Although many of the *shi* embrace extensive and well-populated rural areas, if this population were subtracted from the inclusive figures, it would make no important difference in the ratio given above. There are 27 *shi* with populations of over 200,000, and 6 with over 600,000. The latter are Tokyo, Osaka, Kyoto, Nagoya, Yokohama, and Kobe, stated in order of size. The population of Tokyo, which was 6,778,804 in 1940, probably approximated 8,000,000 in the early part of World War II and decreased to probably 2,500,000 after bombing had been intensified, but rose to 4,556,000 by August 1949. It was estimated to have reached 6,704,000 by Sept. 1, 1952. The seventh largest city is Fukuoka, with 425,000 people, leaving a gap of some 460,000 between it and Kobe as of Sept. 1, 1952.

The more important of Japan's cities, with 1950 census populations, appear in Table 2.

The distribution of Japan's cities reflects the overall distribution of population as well as that of manufacturing and related industries. Where cities are numerous, the surrounding rural population is dense and, conversely, in regions of low rural densities cities are both scarce and small. Japan's phenomenal industrial growth has accrued primarily to a narrow east-west belt extending from Tokyo through the Tokai, Kinki, and Setouchi regions into northern Kyushu. Here Japan's seven largest cities and a considerable number of its smaller ones are found. It is into

Table 2—POPULATION OF PRINCIPAL JAPANESE CITIES

City	Population	City	Population
Tokyo	5,385,071	Kumamoto	267,506
Osaka	1,956,136	Kanazawa	252,017
Kyoto	1,101,854	Yokosuka	250,533
Nagoya	1,030,635	Nagasaki	241,805
Yokohama	951,189	Shizuoka	238,629
Kobe	765,435	Kagoshima	229,462
Fukuoka	392,649	Hakodate	228,994
Sendai	341,685	Niigata	220,901
Kawasaki	319,226	Sakai	213,688
Sapporo	313,850	Himeji	212,100
Hiroshima	285,712	Gifu	211,845
Amagasaki	279,264	Yawata	210,051

these cities that Japan's equally phenomenal population growth has been largely absorbed.

Population.—The problem of population and food supply in Japan has long been chronic. The nation's loss of empire and markets and its strong upsurge in population made the problem more than ever one of stark reality after World War II. During 1949 the increase in population was 1,773,476, the largest of any year in Japanese history. The number of births was 2,724,206, or 33.1 per 1,000; the number of deaths, 950,730, or 11.6 per 1,000. The birth rate, then, was that of the Orient and the death rate approached that of western Europe. Total population on Dec. 1, 1953, was officially estimated at 87,200,000.

During the latter half of the Tokugawa period (1603–1867) the population of Japan seems to have remained stationary, probably at about 30,000,000. The estimated figures of the time ranged from 25,000,000 to 27,000,000, but admittedly omitted samurai and outcasts, who together probably totaled 3,000,000. In any event, the first comprehensive estimate, made in 1872 after the Meiji Restoration, indicated a population something in excess of 33,000,000. From that date there was a steady increase, supported by an improved agriculture and absorbed largely into agriculture, until the end of the Sino-Japanese War in 1895. The population in 1897 was estimated at 42,400,000. Especially noteworthy was the growth of population in the semifrontier lands of Tohoku and southern Kyushu and on the actual frontier of Hokkaido. This was also a period of rapid land reclamation, and there was a healthy, but not spectacular, increase in urban population. After the Sino-Japanese War came the manufacturing industries and a greatly increased production. There was a steady increase in light industrial production until World War I. Particularly pronounced was the increase in urban population and in that of coal mining and sericultural districts. In the older, overcrowded agricultural districts the rural population actually showed some decline, but continued to increase where new opportunities were available. The 50,000,000 mark was exceeded in 1909, and the population reached 54,134,000 by 1917. Following World War I there was a period of industrial vicissitudes lasting for about a decade. Then began a new era of industrial activity, both light and heavy, and a most rapid increase in the size of cities. Rural populations everywhere showed a relative decline and in many areas an absolute loss. By 1927 a total of 61,317,000 was reached; in 1937 the population was 71,253,000, representing an average annual increase for the decade of approximately 1,000,000 people. The rate of increase then began to show a slight decline. The figure for 1940, just before Japan's entry into World War II, was 73,114,000. Between 1937 and 1945, Japan lost about 1,200,000 army and navy personnel, as well as nearly 250,000 civilians by bombing. The figure of 83,199,637 in 1950 represented a rapid increase. In part this was due to the return of Japanese from abroad, but still more to a rising birth rate. The rise after the war was certainly due in large part to the return of millions of young male Japanese to Japan. In 1950, however, the birth rate dropped to 28.2 and in 1951 to 25.6. Estimates for 1952 and 1953 indicate a reduction to 23.4 and 21.5, respectively. It should be noted that the death rate also dropped, to 10.9 in 1950, 10.0 in 1951, and 8.9 in 1952 and 1953.

ROBERT BURNETT HALL,
Professor of Geography, Director of the Center for Japanese Studies, University of Michigan.

3. THE PEOPLE. This section treats Japanese racial and cultural origins, the family, the life cycle, special groups, and cultural patterns.

Racial and Cultural Origins.—The people of contemporary Japan consist of the predominant Japanese and some 15,000 or so Ainu, a people of Caucasoid affiliations found chiefly in northern Japan. Modern Japanese, while basically of Mongoloid stock, are of mixed racial background. The basic Mongoloid traits include black hair and dark brown eyes, tan skin, the Mongoloid spot on infants, and a common occurrence of the epicanthic eye fold (slanting eyes). In addition, Japanese have relatively short legs, giving an average stature of 1.65 meters (five feet five inches) for men and somewhat less for women. They are distinctly roundheaded (cephalic index of 80 and over). The Ainu genetic strain, however, gives many Japanese more body and facial hair than is characteristic of the true Mongol, and another, southern, genetic strain frequently gives wavy hair. This waviness was once a source of misfortune to such Japanese women as were born with it, because the social ideal used to be straight black hair. For a similar reason the occasional Japanese born with a brownish hair tinge may employ dye rinses to achieve an ideal black.

The origin of the Ainu and of the Japanese people themselves has been the object of considerable archaeological research and is also the subject of Japanese mythology. The full story of the Shintō myth of origin may be found in the *Kojiki,* written in 712 A.D. by imperial order, and in the *Nihon Shoki* (*Nihongi*), written in 720. The myth of origin told in these books retraces the ancestry of the Japanese people to a primeval divine pair, Izanami and Izanagi, who first inhabited the islands which they had formed out of drops of mud from Izanagi's honorable spear. As the original pair, Izanami and Izanagi were at first not certain how to go about getting married and having offspring. When this problem had been settled, numerous offspring were produced, the last being a deity of fire. In giving birth to this being, Izanami was fatally burned and she went to a nether world of death. Izanagi, distraught, sought to follow her, but she warned him not to look upon her in her unclean state of death. He did so nevertheless, and in shame and anger his late spouse sent the old woman of the underworld to chase him. As he fled, Izanagi cast behind him his headdress, which turned to grapes; these the old woman paused to eat. Next he discarded his comb, which turned into bamboo sprouts; these the old woman lingered to uproot and to eat. By such means Izanagi eventually succeeded in escaping. Then when he stopped at a stream to wash away the uncleanness of his contact with death, Amaterasu-ōmikami was born of his left eye. This deity, the Sun Goddess, became the divine ancestress of the Japanese imperial line. Her spirit is honored to this day at the great Shintō shrine at Ise in Mie Prefecture.

This tale of the origins of the Japanese is of interest not only for its importance in Japanese religion, but also because some of the content of the myth indicates affiliation with the east Asian mainland and with the Malayan culture of Formosa and of other Malayan peoples to the south. The account of the first conversations of Izanami and Izanagi and the problem of marriage, for example, is paralleled in the mythology of Formosa and of the islands farther south. The incident in which Izanagi flees from the old woman of the underworld is similar to "magic flight" stories of the Asian mainland and northwestern North America. The evidence of folklore thus indicates two outside cultural influences in early Japan: one from mainland Asia and another from the southern islands.

Archaeological evidence also indicates early cultural influences from more than one area. Prehistoric pit dwellings which have been excavated resemble those of historic tribes in northeast Asia. The contemporary rural dwellings of Japan have a strong architectural resemblance to Malaysian forms, being raised from the ground on piles and having a thatch roof and relatively open sides. These are quite different from the tile-roofed and earthbound dwellings of China. Early pottery types are of forms similar to Korean types. Some of the early jewelry, such as the claw-shaped *magatama,* is made of stones, such as nephrite, not found in Japan.

Not only are the early cultural forms of diverse origin, but the physical types of the Japanese also indicate mixed origins. No Paleolithic finds of man or his culture have been positively identified in Japan, but early Neolithic finds indicate that one of the most widespread early inhabitants of the islands was a kind of man similar to the Ainu. This type seems to have existed as far south as the Ryukyus. The notable hairiness of the face and body of men of the Ainu type has led many anthropologists to conclude that they are part of an early east Asiatic Caucasoid stock which was later overwhelmed by Mongoloid types. In Japan the latter seem to have come largely via Korea and to have spread gradually northward and southward from Kyushu and western Honshu. Today the Ainu type is found in scattered individuals on Okinawa and as a distinct ethnic group with much of its own culture in Hokkaido. Notable older traits of Ainu culture include a bear festival and sacrifice, tattooing of the lips of women, and garments bearing characteristic broad white line designs on a blue background.

Another early type in parts of Japan was probably of Malayan affiliation. The wavy hair and facial features of many Japanese have parallels among some of the peoples of the Philippines and Indonesia. Some cultural traits of Malayan origin found in traditional Japan included the blackening of teeth as a mark of beauty, the characteristic Japanese house, and the marriage ritual. It is probable that the Malayan traits of the Japanese and their culture and those of the southern regions were diffused from some common area in Southeast Asia rather than that these came to Japan from Indonesia.

In historic times the strongest outside cultural influence has been the Chinese. Certain governmental forms, Confucian philosophy, and Buddhism, as well as the arts of painting and sculpture associated with Buddhism, are notable influences.

While the Japanese are thus of mixed racial background and their cultural origins come from diverse mainland sources, they have developed, like the British, as an insular nation and have created their own characteristic culture. Nor is Japanese culture restricted to combinations of borrowed elements. Some distinctive Japanese cultural inventions include the deep hot bath and the whole complex of behavior surrounding it, the characteristic alternating 5-7-7 syllable, nonrhyming lines of the Japanese poetic form, and the delicate light paper used for multitudinous purposes long before the people of the West had heard of Kleenex. Japan has also contributed her share in religious development, Shinshū and Nichiren being distinctive Japanese sects of Buddhism, and the characteristic forms and deities of Shintō being peculiar to Japan. (See section on *Religion.*)

Family and Household.—The primary social unit of Japanese society is the household consisting of a family, an occasional other relative, and, if the family is well to do, one or more servants. The size of a community is usually calculated not in individuals but in households, and many local civic duties are reckoned in terms of days' work per household rather than per individual.

The basic kinship group in Japanese society, as in all societies, is the family. It differs, however, from the family in the United States in composition and in the social roles of its constituent members. Members of a Japanese family include the head of the house and his wife, the eldest son (by birth or adoption) and any of his children, and any unmarried children of the

Photograph © Philip Gendreau, N. Y.

JAPAN: A department store window in the shopping center of Tokyo, showing traditional Japanese kimonos.

Photographs © (left) Philip Gendreau, N. Y.; (right) T. M. McKeon from Black Star

Left: A couple enjoying an outdoor picnic near Kobe. They are seated in the accepted eating positions. *Right:* Small boys bearing a miniature Shinto shrine through the streets of Tokyo during the Omikoshi Happiness Festival.

Photographs (1) © D. L. Burkett from Black Star; (2) © C. Hogenbirk, Triangle Photo Service; (3) courtesy American President Lines

Left: A Japanese "sandwich man," walking on huge wooden clogs and wearing a red paper skirt. *Center:* A small Yokohama apprentice shoe cobbler reading his comic book while waiting for business. *Right:* Cooking sukiyaki (beef and soy sauce) at the table over an earthenware brazier.

Photographs (1, 3, 4) © Horace Bristol from Black Star, (2) courtesy of American President Lines

JAPAN: *Top:* Japanese laborers weeding rice plants in water-covered paddies. *Center left:* Geisha girls performing a traditional dance. *Center right:* Girls forming cups in a pottery factory. *Bottom:* Harvesting tea leaves on the terraces near the city of Shizuoka.

JAPAN: The waterfront of Osaka, Honshu Island, looking up the Yodo River, coming from Osaka Bay. Osaka is the second largest city in Japan.

Left: The great bronze Buddha, Daibutsu, in the city of Kamakura. Cast in 1252, it is 50 feet high and 96 feet in circumference. *Right:* Two girls in native dress standing under the elaborate Karamon, gateway to Toshogu Shrine in the village of Nikko. *Below:* The Diet Building, Tokyo, the Japanese capitol, where all legislation takes place.

Photographs courtesy of (top, right, left) American President Lines, (bottom) © Philip Gendreau, N. Y.

Photograph courtesy American President Lines

JAPAN: Mount Fuji, the Japanese sacred mountain, as seen from Lake Kawaguchi. This mountain, a quiescent volcano, is 12,395 feet high, topped with a perfect cone nearly 2,000 feet in diameter.

Photographs © (left) Philip Gendreau, N. Y., (right) T. M. McKeon from Black Star

Left: A modern moving picture theater in Tokyo. The coolie with the two-wheeled cart and the automobile and bus emphasize the tremendous gap between modern and ancient that exists in Japan. *Right:* The Himeji Castle in the city of Himeji, Honshu Island. It was used as palace and fortress by feudal lords over 500 years ago.

Photograph © J. Sennewitz from Black Star

A view across the Emperor's Moat of the Imperial Theater (left) and U.N. headquarters in the Daiichi Building, Tokyo.

JAPAN AND KOREA

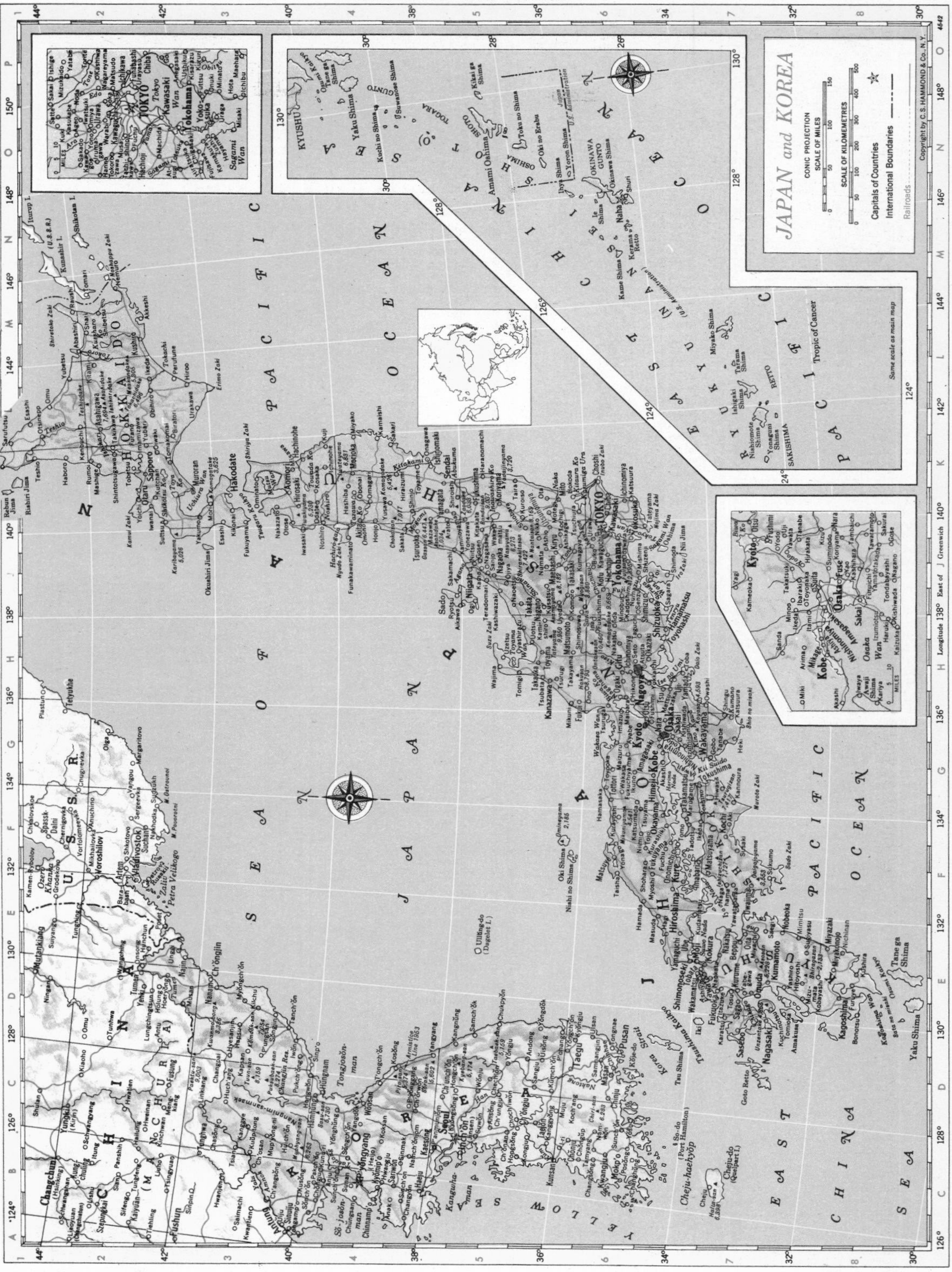

JAPAN AND KOREA

Abashiri, 39,218 M 1
Aikawa, 8,509 H 4
Akashi, 65,642 G 6
Aki, 12,452 F 7
Akita, 126,074 J 4
Amagasaki, 279,264 G 6
Amakusa (island) D 7
Amami (isl.), 105,534 N 5
Aomori, 106,417 K 3
Arato, 6,039 J 4
Asahigawa, 123,238 L 2
Ashikaga, 52,810 J 5
Ashio, 18,994 J 5
Atsuta, 61,592 H 6
Awaji (island) G 6
Ayabe, 33,573 G 6
Beppu, 93,033 E 7
Biratori, 12,358 L 2
Chiba, 133,844 K 6
Chichibu, 31,510 J 6
Chosi, 73,512 K 6
Esashi, 9,862 J 3
Esashi, 10,518 L 1
Fuchu (Hiroshima) 14,178 F 6
Fujisan (mt.) J 6
Fukuchiyama, 45,085 G 6
Fukui, 100,691 G 5
Fukuoka, 392,649 D 7
Fukushima (Fukushima), 93,435 K 5
Fukushima (Nagano), 9,087 H 6
Fukuyama (Hiroshima), 67,063 F 6
Fukuyama (Hokkaido) J 3
Funakawaminato, 16,865 J 4
Furano, 20,345 L 2
Fushimi, 105,437 H 6
Gifu, 211,845 H 6
Gobo, 16,074 G 7
Gosen, 18,748 J 5
Goto (islands) D 7
Haboro, 17,664 K 1
Hachinohe, 104,335 K 3
Hachioji, 82,539 J 6
Hagi, 41,613 E 6
Hakodate, 228,994 K 3
Hamada, 40,440 E 6
Hamamatsu, 152,028 H 6
Hamasaka, 7,501 G 6
Haranomachi, 17,404 K 5
Heki, 5,433 G 7
Hikone, 49,207 H 6
Himeji, 212,100 G 6
Hiraizumi, 6,838 K 4
Hiroo, 9,909 L 2
Hirosaki, 65,597 K 3
Hiroshima, 285,712 E 6
Hitoyoshi, 45,169 E 7
Hiwasa, 5,929 G 7
Hokkaido K 2
Hokoda, 6,285 K 5
Honjo, 19,143 J 4
Honshu F 6
Ichinohe, 5,570 K 3
Ichinomiya (Aichi), 71,431 H 6
Ichinomiya (Chiba), 6,646 K 6
Iida, 32,684 H 6
Ikeda (Hokkaido), 15,696 L 2
Ikeda (Osaka), 45,177 H 7
Iki (island) D 7
Ikuno, 9,489 G 6
Imabari, 60,191 F 6
Imamizawa, 47,951 L 2
Imazu, 5,913 G 6
Ina, 23,273 H 6
Ishinomaki, 52,351 K 4
Itazuke E 7
Iwanai, 23,319 K 2
Iwasaki, 5,516 J 3
Izumiotsu, 33,341 H 8
Izumisano, 32,153 G 6
Kagoshima, 229,462 E 8
Kamaishi, 35,231 L 4
Kaminoyama, 16,222 J 4
Kamishiro, 3,170 H 5
Kamisuwa (Suwa), 35,480 H 6
Kamo, 27,741 J 5
Kanazawa, 252,017 H 5
Kannoura, 4,034 G 7
Karatsu, 51,820 D 7
Kashiwazaki, 38,142 J 5
Katsumada, 4,770 F 6
Katsuura (Chiba), 15,115 K 6
Katsuura (Wakayama), 5,519 H 7
Kawagoe, 52,820 J 5
Kawaguchi, 124,783 J 6
Kawasaki, 319,226 O 2
Kenbuchi, 9,283 L 1
Kikonai, 12,434 K 3
Kiryu, 95,533 J 5
Kishiwada, 98,821 G 6
Kitakata, 17,767 J 5
Kitami, 45,952 L 2
Kobayashi, 41,410 E 8
Kobe, 765,435 G 6
Kochi, 161,640 F 7
Kofu, 121,645 J 6
Kokura, 199,397 E 7
Komoro, 17,039 J 5
Koriyama (Fukushima), 70,866 K 5
Kuchinotsu, 10,614 D 7
Kudamatsu, 39,923 E 6
Kuji, 10,315 K 3
Kumagaya, 65,487 J 5
Kumamoto, 267,506 E 7
Kurashiki, 53,301 F 6
Kurayoshi, 20,568 F 6
Kure, 187,775 F 6
Kuroiso, 10,952 K 5
Kurume, 100,997 E 7
Kusatsu, 7,178 J 5
Kushira, 18,390 E 8
Kushiro, 93,357 M 2
Kutchan, 15,975 K 2
Kyoto, 1,101,854 G 6
Kyushu E 8
Maebashi, 97,394 J 5
Maibara, 7,434 H 6
Maizuru, 91,914 G 6
Marugame, 37,312 G 6
Mashige, 16,552 K 2
Masuda, 22,059 E 6
Matsumoto, 86,005 H 5
Matsuyama, 163,859 F 7
Matsuye, 74,018 F 6
Matsuzaka, 48,743 H 6
Mikuni, 10,531 G 5
Mimitsu, 4,574 E 7
Minobu, 5,096 J 6
Mishima, 47,333 J 6
Mito, 67,163 K 5
Miyachi, 6,046 E 7
Miyako, 39,255 L 4
Miyakonojo, 75,114 E 8
Miyazaki, 103,443 E 8
Mizumata, 43,661 E 7
Moji, 124,399 E 7
Mori, 24,294 K 2
Morioka, 117,578 K 4
Motegi, 11,098 K 5
Muroran, 110,443 K 2
Myoshi, 9,579 F 6
Nagahama (Ehime), 7,301 F 7
Nagahama (Shiga), 46,722 H 6
Nagano, 101,426 J 5
Nagaoka, 66,818 J 5
Nagasaki, 241,805 D 7
Nagasawa, 6,606 J 5
Nagoya, 1,030,635 H 6
Nakatsu (Gifu), 23,451 H 6
Nakatsu (Oita), 51,410 E 7
Nakazato, 5,695 K 3
Naoetsu, 18,712 J 5
Naokata, 53,638 E 7
Nara, 77,866 G 6
Nemuro, 20,222 M 2
Nichinan, 41,432 E 8
Nii (island), 5,012 J 6
Niigata, 220,901 J 5
Niimi, 7,596 F 6
Niitsu, 37,370 J 5
Nikko, 29,363 J 5
Nishi no (island) F 5
Nishinomiya, 126,783 H 8
Nobeoka, 88,117 E 7
Noshiro, 49,027 J 3
Numata, 20,623 J 5
Numazu, 101,976 J 6
Obihiro, 51,794 L 2
Obonai, 6,394 K 4
Odate, 23,444 K 3
Odawara, 75,334 J 6
Ogaki, 74,811 H 6
Ogi, 6,521 J 5
Oita, 94,455 E 7
Ojiya, 25,724 J 5
Okayama, 162,904 F 6
Okazaki, 96,030 H 6
Oki (island) F 5
Okushiri (island) J 2
Omagari, 15,325 K 4
Ominato, 14,424 K 3
Omu, 8,427 L 1
Omuda, 191,978 E 7
Onagawa, 16,475 K 4
Ono, 17,711 H 6
Onomichi, 61,411 F 6
Osaka, 1,956,136 G 6
Oshima (island) J 6
Oshima (isls.), 214,086 N 5
Ota, 11,155 K 5
Otaru, 178,330 K 2
Otose, 6,896 J 3
Otsu, 85,251 H 6
Owashi, 19,075 H 6
Raushi, 3,686 M 1
Rishiri (island) K 1
Rumoi, 32,513 K 2
Ryotsu, 9,402 J 4
Sado (island), 125,597 J 4
Saegi, 39,776 E 7
Saga, 66,807 E 7
Sagara, 15,001 J 6
Sakai, 213,688 J 8
Sakari, 4,478 K 4
Sakata, 54,291 J 4
Sanjo, 46,646 J 5
Sapporo, 313,850 K 2
Sarufutsu, 7,429 L 1
Sasebo, 194,493 D 7
Sendai, 341,685 K 4
Seto, 45,752 H 6
Shari, 15,346 M 2
Shibetsu, 7,253 M 2
Shikoku F 7
Shimizu, 88,472 J 6
Shimoda, 8,865 J 6
Shimonoseki, 193,572 E 6
Shimosuwa, 18,798 H 5
Shingu, 33,827 H 7
Shinjo, 31,140 K 4
Shintotsugawa, 15,766 K 2
Shiobara, 4,854 K 5
Shiroishi, 17,792 K 4
Shizuoka, 238,692 H 6
Shohara, 9,206 F 6
Shuzenji, 7,746 J 6
Sukumo, 14,286 F 7
Susaki, 16,180 F 7
Suttsu, 5,573 J 2
Suwa, 35,480 H 6
Suwa (Kamisuwa), 35,480 H 6
Tadotsu, 13,240 F 6
Taguchi, 5,261 H 6
Taira, 42,891 K 5
Taisha, 10,737 F 6
Takamatsu, 124,545 G 6
Takaoka, 142,046 H 5
Takasaki, 92,964 J 5
Takata, 36,255 J 5
Takayama, 42,823 H 5
Takikawa, 27,844 L 2
Tanabe (Wakayama), 37,602 G 7
Tateyama, 37,291 J 6
Teradomari, 12,819 J 5
Teshio, 9,091 K 1
Toba, 11,117 H 6
Tobata, 87,885 E 6
Tobetsu, 17,686 K 2
Tochigi, 42,248 K 5
Toi, 7,769 J 6
Tojo, 7,518 F 6
Tokushima, 121,416 G 7
Tokyo (capital), 5,385,071 K 6
Tomakomai, 39,226 L 2
Tomigi, 3,626 H 5
Tomioka, 4,059 D 7
Tomo, 18,013 F 6
Tosu, 16,567 E 7
Tottori, 61,721 G 6
Toyama, 154,484 H 5
Toyohashi, 145,855 H 6
Toyooka, 31,677 G 6
Tsu, 76,077 H 6
Tsubata, 4,444 H 5
Tsuchiura, 62,246 J 5
Tsuruga, 31,092 G 6
Tsurugi, 5,810 H 5
Tsuruoka, 44,019 J 4
Tsuyama, 51,645 F 6
Ube, 128,569 E 6
Uji-Yamada, 69,489 H 6
Uotsu, 15,548 H 5
Urakawa, 13,994 L 2
Urawa, 115,019 J 6
Utsunomiya, 107,210 K 5
Uwajima, 56,570 F 7
Uyeda, 42,778 J 5
Wajima, 15,604 H 5
Wakamatsu (Fukuoka), 89,574 E 7
Wakamatsu (Fukushima), 60,034 J 5
Wakasa, 7,132 G 6
Wakayama, 191,337 G 6
Wakkanai, 34,529 K 1
Yabe, 6,251 E 7
Yakumo, 20,525 J 2
Yamagata, 104,891 K 4
Yamaguchi, 77,759 E 6
Yashiro, 47,658 E 7
Yawata, 210,251 E 7
Yawatahama, 39,932 F 7
Yoichi, 26,396 K 2
Yokkaichi, 123,870 H 6
Yokohama, 951,189 O 3
Yokosuka, 250,533 O 3
Yonago, 58,661 F 6
Yonezawa, 55,008 J 5
Yubari, 99,530 L 2
Yubetsu, 1,833 L 1
Yusawa, 17,465 K 4

KOREA

Amnok (river) B 3
Andong, 35,275 D 5
Ansŏng, 17,740 C 5
Changjin (res.) C 3
Changsŏng, 21,767 C 6
Chech'ŏn D 5
Cheju, 57,573 C 7
Cheju (Quelpart) (isl.) C 7
Cheju-haehyŏp (str.) C 7
Chinhae, 36,449 D 6
Chinju, 77,473 D 6
Chinnamp'o, 82,162 B 4
Chiri (mt.) C 6
Choch'iwŏn, 16,109 C 5
Ch'ŏnan, 22,661 C 5
Ch'ŏngjin, 184,301 E 3
Chŏngju, 18,633 B 4
Ch'ŏngju, 51,522 C 5
Chŏnju, 100,624 C 6
Ch'unch'ŏn, 54,539 D 5
Ch'ungju, 64,571 C 5
Dagelet (Ullŭng) (isl.) E 5
Fusan (Pusan), 473,619 D 6
Haeju, 82,135 B 4
Halla (mt.) C 7
Hamhŭng, 112,184 C 4
Han (riv.) C 5
Hongsŏng, 15,718 C 5
Hongwŏn, 25,663 C 3
Hŭngnam, 143,600 C 4
Hwangju, 16,993 C 4
I-ri, 46,674 C 6
Inch'ŏn (Jinsen), 265,767 C 5
Jinsen (Inch'ŏn), 265,767 C 5
Kaesŏng, 88,708 C 5
Kanggye, 30,013 C 3
Kanggyŏng, 20,327 C 5
Kangnŭng, 31,820 D 5
Kangwha (bay) B 5
Kapsan, 58,077 C 3
Kŏje (isl.) D 6
Kongju, 20,394 C 5
Korea (str.) D 6
Kŭm (riv.) C 5
Kunsan, 74,447 C 6
Kwangju, 138,883 C 6
Kwanmo (mt.) D 3
Kyŏmip'o, 53,035 C 4
Kyŏngju, 33,260 D 6
Kyŏngsong (Seoul) (cap.) 1,446,019 C 5
Masan, 91,291 D 6
Mokp'o (Moppo), 111,128 C 6
Myohyang (mt.) C 3
Najin, 34,338 E 2
Naktong (riv.) D 6
Namwŏn, 23,002 C 6
Nanam, 20,936 D 3
Nangnim (mt. range) C 3
Paektu (mt.) C 3
Pakch'ŏn, 17,184 B 4
P'anmunjŏm C 5
P'ohang, 45,147 D 5
Port Hamilton (So) (isl.) C 6
Pukch'ŏng, 30,709 C 3
Puksubaek (mt.) C 3
Pusan, 473,619 D 6
P'yŏngyang (cap.), 342,551 C 4
Quelpart (Cheju) (isl.) C 7
Samch'ŏk, 28,117 D 5
Sangju, 41,983 D 5
Sariwŏn, 42,957 C 4
Sasu (mt.) C 4
Seoul (cap.), 1,446,019 C 5
Sinuiju, 118,414 B 3
So (Port Hamilton) (isl.) C 6
Sŏ-josŏn (bay) B 4
Sŏnch'on, 22,725 B 4
Sŏngjin, 67,778 D 3
Sŏrak (mt.) D 4
Suwŏn, 42,173 C 5
Taebaek (mt.) D 5
Taedong (riv.) C 4
Taegu, 313,705 D 6
Taejŏn, 126,704 C 5
Tongjosŏn (bay) D 4
Tumen (riv.) D 2
Tuun (mt.) C 3
Ullŭng (Dagelet) (isl.) E 5
Wŏnju, 20,429 D 5
Wŏnsan, 112,952 C 4
Yellow (sea) B 6
Yŏngch'ŏn, 25,487 D 6
Yongju, 21,056 D 5

RYUKYU ISLANDS

Ie (isl.), 6,530 N 6
Ihya (isl.), 3,569 N 5
Ishigaki (isl.), 27,907 L 7
Kame (isl.), 16,086 M 6
Kerama (isls.), 3,556 M 6
Miyako (isl.), 56,416 L 7
Naha (cap.), 44,779 N 6
Nishiomote (isl.), 3,705 K 7
Okinawa (arch.), 579,791 N 6
Okinawa (isl.), 517,634 N 6
Sakishima (isls.), 43,973 K 7
Shuri, 20,006 N 6

master and his wife. The family thus can comprise two marriage units or elementary families. This kin group lives together in a single household. Sometimes there are also living as part of the family a grandfather and grandmother who have retired. This means that the old man has surrendered to his son the headship of the family and the responsibility for household affairs.

A larger kinship unit is also recognized in the form of the extended family, comprising not only the brothers and sisters of the male side of the immediate family, but also any of the master's children who may have married or have been adopted by others or have established branch families. This extended family comes together for weddings and funerals. They help one another in certain agricultural work, and the older members form a family council for reaching important decisions concerning the family welfare, such as buying or selling land or arranging a marriage. In family dwellings servants also form part of the household. The manservant or maidservant in the house usually comes from one of the less well-to-do families in rural areas and may even be a nephew or niece of the master or his wife. Servants are usually hired by the year and are treated as part of the family in work and at meals.

The social position of the master of the house is reflected in the fact that he takes the first bath, receives the first food, and is responsible for taking care of the income of the family. At the same time he is responsible for the family welfare. He represents the family in its dealings with the government and with other external institutions. While the head has ultimate financial responsibility, the wife generally manages the internal economy of the household, covering such matters as the purchase of food and of clothes for the family and for the servants. Japanese women by tradition also play an important part in family affairs. For example, the older women make most of the preliminary family arrangements leading to a marriage and conduct the necessary preparations for funeral and memorial services. Informal education of the children also in large part falls to the mother.

The custom of adoption is widespread in Japan. One of its important social functions is that of preserving the continuity of the family and of the family name when there is no heir. Japanese also have a great fondness for children, and a childless couple is likely to adopt a child quite apart from the consideration of the family name. There are a number of forms of adoption, including adopting a son if one has no children, adopting a husband for one's daughter if one has no son, and adopting a younger brother as a son. Adoptions, like marriages, must be recorded and also can be legally dissolved. In general, an adopted son has both the rights and the duties of a real son.

The Japanese place considerable emphasis on age status. This is reflected in the fact that in Japanese one refers to "older sister" or "younger sister," not just "sister" or "brother." Similarly, the oldest son has more privileges and also more responsibilities than a second or third son (it is usually second or third sons who are adopted by other families, whereas a first son is expected to continue the family line). A corollary of this emphasis on relative age is the closeness of coeval neighbors or classmates.

Life Cycle.—In the course of the lifetime of a Japanese, a number of important events mark changes in his social status in his family and community. These include the rites of passage related to birth, marriage, and death common to so many societies.

Birth.—In most of Japan midwives rather than physicians assist the mother. A few days after the birth there is a naming ceremony, to which are invited the midwife and a few relatives and close friends, all of whom bring gifts for the new baby. Special birth ceremony cakes are served at this time. The details of the naming ceremony vary from region to region, but the essential gathering which serves to introduce the newborn child to the immediate family and to the neighborhood group is universal. Since the child is small and may die before reaching adulthood, he has as yet little social personality, a fact which is reflected in the smallness of the gathering at a naming ceremony.

Hiaki.—At 31 days after birth if a boy or 33 if a girl, *hiaki* is observed. The child is taken to visit the deities at the village Shintō shrine, where a brief ritual is performed by the priest. This serves to introduce the child to the village gods and marks the end of an initial stage in the child's life. At this time the mother is also relieved of a number of restrictions concerning food and now may cross water and may resume ordinary house or farm work. *Hiaki* marks the end of a period of anxiety and uncertainty as to the survival of the child.

Early Training.—A Japanese child is usually nursed until another is born. It is taught early to value cleanliness. The young child, especially if a boy, is a favored person and is rarely subjected to physical punishment. With the birth of the next child, the erstwhile youngest loses the center of attention and is put in care of a less attentive brother or sister or nurse. He soon adjusts to his new position and joins the young age group of two and three year olds of his neighborhood.

Children learn both the physical and the social differentiation between boys and girls early in life. In general, in teaching the young child proper behavior the sanctions of praise and ridicule are strongest and resort to physical punishment is not ordinarily made.

The earliest and closest ties of a child are with his mother, who feeds and bathes him and sleeps next to him at night. Thus is formed between child and mother a strong sentimental bond which may persist through life despite the many traditional restrictions placed upon it in Japanese society. Even an adult man may heed an old mother's advice.

Marriage.—Traditionally marriages in Japan are matters of arrangement between two families of similar social class. The first step is for a "chance" meeting to be arranged between the two principals. After such a meeting their feelings are sounded and, if there are no serious objections, further negotiations may be undertaken. One aim of such an early casual meeting is that, in the event that either side objects to the proceedings, the engagement may be canceled before it becomes public knowledge and neither family need lose face.

After these preliminaries a family friend, who is chosen partly for his social standing, will be invited to act as go-between. Since marriage arrangements involve investigations of delicate matters in family history, such as leprosy, tuberculosis, and police records, it is easy to see the need for an intermediary in order to avoid direct face-to-face embarrassment between the families concerned.

If all goes well, the next step may be a formal betrothal exchange (*yuinō*) between the two families, but this is not typical of the average farm family. When the marriage date has been set, partly on the basis of astrology and partly on general convenience (it usually takes place in the fall), the groom's family prepares the house to receive the bride, installing new screens, refurbishing the kitchen, and the like, while the family of the bride prepares the wedding clothes and purchases such wedding gifts as a chest of drawers.

On the day of the wedding the bride, accompanied by her relatives, goes to the groom's home, where the ceremony of *sansan-kudo* is held. This is a formal exchange of sake (rice wine) between the immediate relatives, the marriage broker and his wife, and the bride and groom. Then the wedding banquet takes place, after the bride's relatives, seated on one side of the room, have been introduced to the groom's relatives, seated on the other. On the second day there is another banquet given by the groom's family to introduce the bride to the important people of the community, such as the mayor or the village headman and the schoolmaster; and on the third day there is a lesser, but nonetheless gay, party to introduce the bride to the women of her neighborhood. A wedding is usually a high point in the life of a household and may involve considerable expense.

The marriage often is not formally registered until some time after the social event. If the marriage should prove unsuccessful during this intermediate period and the principals separate, there is thus no record whatsoever that a marriage has taken place. In general, if a child is expected, the marriage will be registered to ensure its legitimacy. The birth of a child tends to consolidate a marriage and improve the social position of the wife in her new family.

A few days after the ceremony the bride and groom make a ceremonial visit, bearing gifts, to the go-between. He continues his responsibilities for the marriage and may be consulted in the event of marital disagreements and invited to any important events in the family, such as naming ceremonies and funerals.

Since World War II there has been some increase in the number of marriages which result from free choice on the part of the individuals concerned, but even under these conditions a go-between is often used for form's sake and to arrange the actual marriage ceremony.

Retirement.—When a person reaches the age of 60, he is likely to retire, surrendering the responsibilities of family and household to his eldest son. There is sometimes a small party of a few relatives and friends to celebrate a man's attaining this age. In a sense he has achieved a second childhood and again may wear red underclothes and may speak freely without being called to account. In rural Japanese society it is the young ladies who are prim and proper and the old women who may do and say what they please.

Death.—The final event of the life cycle is death. The neighbors come together to console the bereaved and to assist in funeral preparations, while the relatives meet to mourn. The funeral itself, however, does not mark the end of a man's social life, inasmuch as it is followed by a series of memorial services, which begin the day after death. In Japan the death day of a famous man is as likely to be celebrated as his birthday and he is also likely to be known by a posthumous name, as are the Emperor Jimmu and the great Buddhist leader and scholar Kōbō Daishi.

There are seven memorial services marking the first seven weeks following death. The last of the seven (on the 49th day) is *hiaki* and represents the end of the heavy mourning period, after which a number of mourning taboos may be lifted. (This is similar to *hiaki* following birth.) There are then yearly memorial services at traditional intervals for 100 years. Most ordinary families rarely observe these memorial services beyond the 50th year, and for women and children the last memorial service may fall considerably short of this interval. Traditionally, Japanese funeral and memorial services are performed by Buddhist priests.

It may be noted that in all the celebrations associated with birth, marriage, and death there is an intermediary present—the midwife, the go-between, the priest—and that he sits in the place of honor at the banquet. It also may be noted that there is a banquet for kin associated with these events and that the size of the social gathering varies in accordance with the social importance of the event or of the person for whom the ceremony is held.

Special Groups.—In Japan there are several special categories or groups of people whose status, until comparatively recent years, was defined by law and who, even today, continue to occupy a special position by force of custom and public opinion.

Eta.—In pre-Meiji Japan, the eta, or pariah class, ranked below the social classes of warrior, farmer, artisan, and merchant. The eta performed tasks considered menial and unclean, such as those of slaughterers, tanners, and executioners. Although these distinctions were legally abolished during the Meiji period (1868–1912), the traditional prejudices against the million or more people descended from this class persist to this day. The term eta is not a polite one and today the term *suiheisha* (water level, that is, equal) is preferred. Other Japanese ordinarily will not intermarry with *suiheisha,* and they frown upon the rise of people of this origin in the social or political hierarchy. Their economic position has not changed greatly, and many remain as tanners, shoemakers, butchers, tenant farmers, peddlers, and day laborers. The people organized themselves into the Suiheisha Undō (Water-Level, or Equalization, Movement) for their social betterment in the 1920's and succeeded in forcing greater recognition of their civil rights. The organization aroused such hostile public sentiment by its militant and terrorist tactics that during the crisis of World War II the movement was largely suppressed.

Geisha.—The geisha are entertainment girls, who dance, serve drinks, and provide light company at a banquet in the tradition of the court ladies of old Japan. The geisha undergoes an apprenticeship and is licensed by the police. Strictly speaking, she is not a prostitute (*jorō*). The geisha's entertainment is by no means innocent, however, and her jokes often carry double meanings. The geisha provides glamorous sex appeal, which middle- and upper-class Japanese men do not expect from their wives. Since World War II the careful training of the geisha in the art of song and dance has declined and some of her traditional functions have been assumed by cabaret girls and others.

Women.—Traditionally the Japanese woman was supposed to be the loving and respectful servant first of her father, then of her husband, and finally of her son. Until the Allied occupation of Japan the principle of the inequality of the sexes was also embodied in the civil code, in such matters as property, inheritance, and divorce. The culture demanded that the woman be dutiful, patient, and good natured. The career woman was rare.

In actual fact, however, the Japanese woman did not occupy so inferior a position as was generally believed. A distinction must be drawn between women in the upper and middle classes and women of the farming and poorer classes. Among the latter, numerically more significant than the former, the woman was in many ways the social equal of the man, partly due to the greater economic interdependence of the sexes and partly due to the fact that the Confucian traditions of woman's inferior status were less firmly entrenched among them. Lower-class women are much freer in speech and gesture than their middle- or upper-class sisters. Even the higher-class woman had certain advantages of social and psychological security. She could be reasonably sure that her husband's affair with a geisha would not interfere with his family obligations and thus break up the home. In the event of widowhood her husband's family would look after her.

Since the Allied occupation a number of legal changes, giving women the vote and greater rights in initiating a divorce, have been made. It is doubtful, however, if the actual social changes are as great as the legal changes indicate, partly because women in Japan have never been so unimportant in the family as many foreigners have thought and partly because social changes are rarely so dramatic as legal changes.

Cultural Patterns.—A cultural pattern is a traditional mode of behavior characteristic of the members of a particular society. Every society is characterized by its own peculiar texture of such patterns of behavior on the part of its constituent members. In Japan, for instance, when greeting one another people bow, whereas in the United States they shake hands. This reflects a general Oriental pattern of culture whereby bodily contact between the sexes in public is bad form. In this subsection six predominant cultural patterns of Japanese society are outlined:

(1) The pattern of group action and group responsibility rather than individual action and individual responsibility.

(2) The pattern of avoidance of face-to-face relations of embarrassment.

(3) The pattern of loyalty and group solidarity.

(4) The pattern of self-discipline and the attainment of success against great odds.

(5) The pattern of ritual cleanliness.

(6) The pattern of ceremonial suicide.

Group Action and Group Responsibility.—Throughout Japanese society from the central government to village communities stress is laid on the group rather than on the individual.

Although the Japanese Cabinet, including the prime minister, reaches its decisions as a result of discussion and compromise, the final decision is published as unanimous. No vote is taken on an issue, and no majority and minority reports are made. It is considered more important to achieve a unanimous decision by compromise; if this cannot be done, dissenting members may resign.

In rural areas the village councils, when discussing policy with the village headman, come to a group decision in the same manner. A headman or mayor would never think of pursuing any policy without the agreement of his council.

Associated with group responsibility is a pattern of rotating responsibility. In village affairs the hamlet head changes annually, and a local god house (*dō*) is tended by a different group of neighbors (*kumi*) each year. In the national government no one man is prominent as the responsible leader for a long time—different leaders appear as prime minister, but none becomes a permanent officeholder.

Avoidance of Face-to-Face Relations of Embarrassment.—This involves the concept of face—personal self-respect and prestige—so important in the Orient. To disagree point-blank with a person over a cup of tea would be rude in the highest degree—hence the tendency for polite agreement with most comments even though they be inconsistent one with another. On more important matters, such as marriage or a business deal, where some disagreement is inevitable, embarrassing face-to-face relations are avoided by means of a third party or go-between.

A marriage, which is primarily a social and economic relationship between two families, involves, as already shown, much careful investigation of familial backgrounds, and such investigations, if made directly, easily could lead to embarrassment and loss of face by one or another of the families concerned. This is avoided by a go-between, who serves to maintain relations between the families during the critical period.

Since in business dealings direct bargaining would be unseemly, Japanese prefer to employ the services of a broker or business go-between, who may receive a commission from both parties for his services—from the one for getting a high price, from the other for reducing the price.

In the employment of servants it is usually best to work through an intermediary in Japan. And a servant is likely to resign on a moment's notice if his employer causes him to lose face by openly accusing him of some error before other persons. For a servant to tell his master that he is resigning because he does not like the work or because he has an offer of a better job elsewhere, would be to cause loss of face to his employer. So he may give illness as the cause of his no longer working. The wise employer will understand and either will search for another servant or will offer to raise the wages.

Group Solidarity and Loyalty.—The Japanese emphasis on group solidarity involves the duty of loyalty to one's group, so that the individual will traditionally defend the interests of his employer, of his family, and of any other group of which he is an active member. The Japanese government and army of prior days, for example, stressed loyalty to the nation through personal loyalty to the emperor as the supreme duty of all Japanese citizens. The most famous of Japanese historical dramas, *The Forty-seven Rōnin,* is a tale of great personal loyalty to the memory of a feudal lord.

A corollary to these two traditional behavior patterns in Japanese society—group responsibility and face saving—is that an individualist is regarded as selfish and antisocial. The democracy of the United States was regarded before World War II by many Japanese as a society full of stress and strain because of its many members who—to the Japanese way of thinking—regarded their own individual welfare to be more important than that of their family or of their country.

These concepts of loyalty, group action, and avoidance of face-to-face embarrassment have developed in Japan as a result of two factors: (1) a long national history, especially the 250-year period of feudalism and peace which ended in the 19th century; and (2) the influence of Confucian ethics on Japanese thought.

The concept of rugged individualism found in the United States comes from the frontier and pioneer tradition of a newly settled nation. Japan, by way of contrast, has a long cultural history during which traditional patterns of social relations became stabilized. In such a society an individualist or a man who acts in an unexpected manner is criticized as upsetting social equilibrium.

Self-Discipline and Attainment of Success Against Great Odds.—Every year on May 5 there is a special festival in Japan to honor boys, at which time large paper carps are flown from poles. The carp, a fish which swims upstream and which does not wriggle when laid on the chopping block, is the traditional ideal of Japanese manhood.

In this ideal the societies of Japan and the United States come somewhat closer than in the first three national traditions. The Japanese schoolboy, for instance, is taught the story of how Abraham Lincoln rose to greatness from humble beginnings and how he walked for miles to borrow a book. Many Japanese heroes are men who rose to greatness by hard work and from humble beginnings.

Associated with the ideal of achieving great ends by overcoming handicaps is the Japanese ideal of frugality and self-discipline. This is perhaps a reflection of the frugality of Japanese daily life in homes with little in the way of material comforts. Zen Buddhism, popular in Japan, stresses mental discipline. In the Japanese Army, which was Spartan in all its phases, the conscript was soon taught the virtues of an even greater self-discipline and frugality than he had experienced in his civilian life.

Ritual Cleanliness.—When arriving at a Japanese inn or home, the guest must remove his shoes before entering and soon after arrival is expected to bathe. Almost everyone in Japan—even a poor worker or a rural peasant—takes a daily bath. The deep Japanese bath, incidentally, is a purely Japanese development different from anything in the rest of Asia or the West.

A small infant soon learns to respect cleanliness and to avoid dirt, so that all a mother need say to her child to make him drop something is that it is dirty.

The ritual aspect of this Japanese emphasis on cleanliness is seen in the sharp contrast between custom in regard to a Japanese house or temple and that in regard to Western-style buildings in Japan. In a Japanese home or inn or temple, where one removes footgear, the interiors are spotless; but in a train or a railway station, where one does not remove one's footgear, the floor may be littered with trash.

The whole basis of Shintō ritual is one of cleansing one's self—body and soul. Before entering a Shintō shrine one must wash one's hands and rinse one's mouth. Before the priestly ceremony begins, each participant presents a sacred branch at the altar as a symbol of a pure and sincere soul.

Ceremonial Suicide.—In Japan there is no religious sanction against suicide, which is not considered a sign of moral weakness or degradation. On the contrary, there are circumstances under which the courage to take one's own life is essential to the honor of the family name. In feudal times a sentence of self-destruction (*seppuku,* or harakiri) was considered more honorable than that of death at the hands of an executioner. Wives of samurai (gentry or lesser nobility of military vocation in the former feudal system) had as part of their dress a short dagger with which they could commit suicide in the event of a threat of personal dishonor. As is well known, Japanese soldiers were told that the only honorable course in the face of defeat and capture was suicide.

A man who regards himself as responsible for some tragic error may commit suicide. There have been cases of police officials who have committed suicide as the result of a relatively minor confusion in regard to arrangements for the emperor's progress through the area of their jurisdiction.

Another motive for suicide is that of protest. A man who feels some act to be very wrong, but who sees no way of changing it, may commit suicide at the doorstep of the man whom he holds responsible, that he may draw attention to the wrong. Such a suicide occurred before the American Embassy in Tokyo when the Immigration Act of 1924, which excluded Japanese, was passed by the United States Congress. This type of suicide is intended to embarrass the person against whom the protest is made.

Still another form of suicide is the rather mystical one involving a desire to follow in death some beloved leader. The most famous modern example of this was when General Maresuke Nogi and his wife took their lives after the death of Emperor Meiji in 1912.

In all these types of suicide it is clear that the individual must have considerable will power and be in a state of high rather than low morale. These are not the acts of men at the end of a downward moral course. In peacetime, however, none of these forms of suicide is common. Most suicides in Japan are prosaic self-dispatching as the result of poverty or of some social or moral impasse, such as the joint suicide of a young couple whose parents will not countenance their marriage. The suicide rate for Japan in the 1930's was just a little above that of the United States and below that of France.

In the physical or material culture of the Japanese there are also a number of characteristic patterns. For example, in the domestic architecture the low, horizontal line is stressed, giving to the interior of a Japanese-style house or inn a restful, aesthetic effect. Smallness of art objects is another characteristic trait. Japanese craftsmen have elaborated on small and carefully worked objects such as the netsuke. These matters are discussed in more detail in the sections on *The Fine Arts* and *Architecture.*

Bibliography.—Hearn, Lafcadio, *Japan, An Attempt at an Interpretation* (New York 1904); Embree, J. F., *Suye Mura, A Japanese Village* (Chicago 1939); Sansom, G. B., *Japan, A Short Cultural History,* rev. ed., chap. 1 (New York 1943); Embree, J. F., *The Japanese Nation*

(New York 1945); Benedict, Ruth, *The Chrysanthemum and the Sword* (New York 1946).

JOHN F. EMBREE,
Late Director, Southeast Asia Studies, Yale University.

4. NATURAL RESOURCES. In this section are discussed the following resources: food, forest, mineral, fiber, fuel and power. That each of these overlaps with the others illustrates the complexity of the use of natural resources in all save the most primitive societies.

Japan proper—the islands of Honshu, Hokkaido, Kyushu, and Shikoku, together with nearby islands and the Ryukyus north of latitude of 27° N. —covers an area of 142,798 square miles. The estimated population of the country on Dec. 1, 1953 was 87,200,000. The pre-World War II area and population of Japan were much greater, since Formosa (Taiwan), the Kwantung Leased Territory, Korea, Karafuto (southern Sakhalin Island), the Kuril Islands, Okinawa, and the former mandated islands of the Western Pacific were then included. Although the empire, including Manchuria as well as the above-named territories, was far from being self-sufficient, it was relatively so at least in terms of food, and many strategic raw materials also were supplied in large quantities.

Japan is poorly endowed with natural resources from any standpoint, but it is unwise to attempt an analysis of her resource position without taking into account the markedly lower Japanese living standards as compared with United States standards. The following evaluation of resources is geared to Japanese standards.

Food Resources.—The qualities of the land and of the seas immediately adjacent to the land determine in large part the nature and quantity of food domestically available to any country. Topographically, Japan is a land of steep slopes and mountains with relatively small lowlands interrupting the dominant mountain structures. Furthermore, considerable areas of lowland are not cultivable for reasons of poor drainage or competing land uses. Thus, of the 91.4 million acres of land surface in Japan, only some 16 per cent is arable. Most of this land is in the lowland areas, of which the largest is the Kanto plain on the middle east coast of Honshu (3.2 million acres). Other major lowlands are the Ishikari plain in Hokkaido (.5 million acres), the Echigo in northwestern Honshu (.45 million acres), the Nobi on Honshu near Nagoya (.45 million acres), the Sendai along the northeastern Honshu coast (.37 million acres), the Settsu near Osaka (.31 million acres), and the Tsukushi in northern Kyushu (.30 million acres). All these lowlands are along the coast, and each contains a major urban center or centers. In addition, there are numerous smaller mountain basins on each of the major islands.

Climatically, Japan is better favored. No portion of the country can be said to be deficient in rainfall, although seasonal droughts occur, especially in the Inland Sea area, which with 40 inches of rainfall is the driest region. Japan's position on the eastern margin of Asia places it well within the monsoon realm, and the summer monsoon, the season of maximum rainfall, coincides with the growing season. At the same time, some areas (especially on the Japan Sea coast) suffer from excessive winter rainfall, and floods are not uncommon. In terms of climate in general and temperature in particular, Japan proper, stretching from 27° to 45° 50′ north latitude, resembles the southern and eastern coasts of the United States. Temperatures permit two crops a year in much of the country south of 37°, and the arable land surface can be increased substantially by this means. Indeed, 30 per cent of the cultivated land in Japan is double cropped. In Hokkaido, however, the climate resembles that of New England; severe winters and a relatively short growing season prohibit double cropping.

Japanese soils may be divided into two types: the irrigated and the dry. By and large, the irrigated soils are alluvial in origin, and alluvium accounts for about 15 per cent of Japan's surface area. Yet, not all alluvial soils are capable of agricultural use for reasons of drainage, slope (on terrace margins), or alternative uses chiefly in connection with urban occupancy. The irrigated soils are compact, uniform, and deep, but centuries of intensive use and monocultural practices have reduced their fertility to a point where constant fertilizing is necessary. Excess water percolating below the surface and constant puddling have led to a leaching of the upper horizon (essentially only one rather than several horizons as in nonirrigated soils) and to the formation of an impervious hardpan below the surface which further impedes drainage on level land. The dry soils are chiefly mountain and hill soils, thin and relatively infertile, though formed from a variety of parent materials. In the far north are found true podsols or forest soils; farther south these tend to become gray and brown podsolics; and in the south red and yellow podsolics with lateritic qualities predominant. Also common are the so-called *ando* soils, found only in Japan, which generally have developed over acid volcanic materials and are infertile. Some of the dry soils, however, are in the lowlands on terraces or gentle slopes. These are alluvial in origin and generally quite fertile, having been improved somewhat, as compared with most Japanese soils, over their natural state.

Associated with soils is the problem of drainage. The generally abundant rainfall characteristic of Japan is conducive to rapid soil erosion on cultivated or cleared slopes. Irrigated land, though little disturbed by erosion, is subject to frequent flash floods and to almost universal poor drainage. It is estimated that 40 per cent of the land under irrigation cannot grow a second crop, even when climatically feasible, because of inadequate drainage. Along the coasts land reclaimed from the sea and former lagoons is subject to flooding during storms and periods of strong onshore winds.

In the light of this complex of natural conditions, it is not strange that Japanese agriculture, the basis of livelihood for almost half of the population, is compressed into valleys and lowlands, where high production is maintained by an unparalleled expenditure of human effort and by the liberal application of fertilizers. Where level land has not been available, there has been either an upsurge along the slopes of valleys and lowlands and the laborious creation of artificial terraces, or the clearance of forest slopes where soils are thin and easily eroded. Farm units are small, averaging 2.5 acres in 1954, but two thirds are even smaller. Holdings are scattered, and plots are separated from each other by ridges which serve both as property boundaries and as dikes to hold the irrigation water.

Agricultural patterns and production vary with climatic, topographic, and edaphic conditions. The characteristic pattern, however, is one of paddy cultivation on flats and level terraces, with other grains, tubers, and vegetables on the higher ground where water for irrigation is not available. Rice is grown throughout Japan, but in lesser quantities in Hokkaido and northern Honshu, where the growing season is short. In these areas wheat, oats, millet, buckwheat, and corn predominate, and pasture land, which is of negligible importance in central and southern Japan, becomes of some significance. Livestock raising is of small importance except in Hokkaido, where pasture is available, and animal products are of minor importance in the food consumption patterns of Japan as a whole. A corollary of this condition is a general shortage of hides and skins for use as leather.

The possibilities for enlarging the cultivated area appear to be few. In 1948, 3.8 million acres were considered capable of reclamation for agriculture. At the end of 1951 over 1 million acres had been reclaimed, chiefly former military lands and airfields. The remainder is submarginal land which may be too costly to reclaim—undrained lakes, marshes, and coastal lagoons, gentle slopes now in brush, fuel-wood scrub in cultivated areas, and grazing land. On the other hand, improvements in drainage of paddy fields could add another 15 per cent to the producing acreage, while the consolidation of field plots through the rearrangement of property holdings might also contribute substantial acreages.

The waters surrounding Japan are a rich source of sea food, the chief domestic source of protein in the Japanese diet. Almost the entire coast is dotted with small fishing villages, and the fishing industry employs close to a million men. The warm Japan Current (Kuroshio), which sweeps northeastward along the southeastern coasts of the country, has temperatures ranging from 68°F. in late winter to 80.1°F. in late summer, and in its waters are found an abundance of fish—sardines (most important of Japan's marine products in volume), mackerel, tuna, bonito, skipjack, albacore, and sea breams. Where the Japan Current meets the cold Okhotsk or Kuril Current (Oyashio) off the northeastern coast of Honshu, there is a zone of mixing, in which both cold- and warm-water fish are found. The waters of the Okhotsk Current, which seldom exceed 64.9°F., harbor herring, salmon, cod, and crab. Both the warm and cold waters also produce large quantities of edible seaweed.

It is estimated that in the period 1935–1940 over 75 per cent of Japan's sea food landings came from waters within 20 miles of Japan proper, exclusive of the colonial sources of supply. Before World War II, Japanese fishermen operated also in far distant waters. In all, over 7 million tons of fish and other sea food were harvested annually. After the war, however, Japan's fishing activities were restricted by Allied agreement to an area bounded on the east by the 165th meridian of east longitude (extended in 1949 to the international date line); on the south by the Tropic of Capricorn; on the north by a line which separates Hokkaido from Sakhalin and the Kurils; and on the west by a line which divides the Sea of Japan in two, cuts through Korea Strait and the East China Sea, and separates the Ryukyus from Formosa. Fish landings primarily from this area, but including special whaling expeditions to Antarctic waters, totaled 4.2 million short tons in 1951. In 1952, however, the areal restrictions were removed, and fish landings totaled 5.2 million tons.

The possibilities for expanding the annual production of sea foods, both animal and plant, in the postwar period are few. There is evidence that since 1920 overfishing has resulted in a gradual depletion of fisheries resources. As a corollary, fish formerly used for fertilizer are being used for food. As a result of the war, Japan lost the right to fish in northern waters from which much of her highest-quality sea food came—crab, salmon, agar-agar. These were important prewar export products.

Despite the intense utilization of the resources of domestic agriculture and fisheries the Japanese are unable to provide food in sufficient quantity to maintain health. Japan in 1953 produced enough food for only 80 per cent of her population at a standard of 2,250 calories and 70 grams of protein daily. Even if some future increases in the production of food are registered, it is expected that they will be countered by increases in population. See also section on *Agriculture*.

Forest Resources.—More than one half of Japan is forested: 55 million acres of a total of 91.4 million. Of these 55 million acres, 50 per cent are in broad-leaved forest, 29 per cent in conifers, and 21 per cent in mixed forest. Less than 0.5 per cent is in bamboo, a giant grass growing in groves much like tree forest. In addition there are about 6 million acres of brush (*gen-ya*). There are three general forest zones: (1) the boreal zone in northern and eastern Hokkaido and on elevation outliers in Honshu, which is composed of spruce, fir, larch, and birch; (2) the great mixed forest zones, which cover much of Honshu to points south of the latitude of Tokyo and contain both deciduous broad-leaved species—beech, ash, chestnut, poplar, and oak—and natural and planted stands of conifers—chiefly pines, cryptomeria, firs, and cedar; and (3) the southern forests of broad-leaved evergreens and deciduous trees, of which oaks are most important. About 60 per cent of the mixed forests are coppice and fuel-wood stands unsuitable for the production of construction timber. Furthermore, about 6 million acres of forest were still inaccessible in 1954 because of lack of transportation. In 1952 production of wood totaled 1,829 million cubic feet, or slightly below the prewar average and well below the record production of 3,300 million cubic feet set in 1943. Fuel wood accounts for half of the total; before the war, however, it accounted for closer to two thirds of all production.

The importance of wood and wood products in Japan cannot be minimized. With the exception of public buildings and the homes of the wealthy, most of the buildings in Japan are made of wood. Wooden utensils are used wherever possible instead of metal implements. Wood cellulose is used, of course, for the manufacture of paper and rayon, and Japan was sixth among the nations of the world before World War II in the production of wood pulp. Furthermore, the Japanese rely heavily on wood rather than coal for fuel; charcoal is the common heating and cooking fuel in the Japanese household, and charcoal gas provides fuel for a substantial percentage of the motor vehicles. On the other hand, the importance of forests to the stabilization of soils and water resources is immeasurable, and care must be taken to avoid overcutting and the resultant economic penalties of erosion and floods, which already have been evidenced.

The estimated needs for wood of all kinds—lumber, pulp, fuel, and general manufacturing—at the 1930–1934 level of consumption come to 2.6 billion cubic feet a year of which 1.6 billion cubic feet is for fuel. The growth rate for accessible forests, however, is estimated at some 1.68 billion cubic feet annually, leaving a deficit of around 900 million cubic feet. Before the war Japan, an exporter of both timber and pulp products, imported almost one third of her pulp and a substantial percentage of her lumber from Karafuto. Tropical hardwoods came from Southeast Asia, and some 10 per cent of her softwood production and 30 per cent of the pulp consumed were imported from western North America and the Scandinavian countries. Without these outside sources of supply, Japan cannot be expected to supply her domestic timber needs, let alone exports for markets abroad, without depleting her forest resources.

At the same time, some possibilities exist for the increased and economical exploitation of forest resources. Tapping of existing "inaccessible" forests would make available 146 million cubic feet of wood a year. The placing of marginal agricultural lands into productive forests is a long-range possibility, as are improvements in, and expansion of, reforestation in cutover areas. In addition, more selective cutting practices at less frequent intervals would eventually provide larger timbers and help prevent the serious soil erosion which is encouraged by present clean-cutting practices. On the debit side, however, is the probability that demand will increase far above 1930–1934 levels as population increases and industrialization continues.

Mineral Resources.—The Japanese islands possess a great variety of mineral resources, few of which, unfortunately, are in sufficient quantity to supply Japan's normal peacetime needs.

Metals.—The variety of metals is especially extensive. Of the 33 metallic minerals used in industry, Japan is supplied to some extent with 22, but only 6—chromite, copper, gold, magnesium, silver, and zinc—are present in sufficient quantity to meet minimum domestic requirements. The possibilities for new discoveries in the postwar period were slight, but not without foundation, since thorough geological exploration had never been accomplished in full. Magnesium is considered to be in unlimited quantity, since it can be extracted from seawater, but commercial production from that source has yet to begin.

Iron ore is present in only small quantities. The major deposit is near Kamaishi in northeastern Honshu, where reserves amount to some 35 million tons of magnetite averaging 60 per cent iron. Lesser deposits, chiefly bog ore, are found in Hokkaido; also, extensive deposits of iron-bearing sands of 30 per cent iron, as yet unexploitable economically, are found in northeastern Honshu. Domestic sources supplied only 12 per cent of Japan's needs before World War II, and, as they become depleted, will remain inadequate to satisfy more than a small percentage of requirements. Imports of at least 2.2 million tons of ore a year will be required; more will be needed as domestic supplies dwindle and industrial expansion develops. In 1952, Japanese iron ore production totaled 1,135,000 short tons of ore, averaging 50 per cent of metal content.

Deposits of low-grade manganese ore are found scattered throughout the islands, but are inadequate for more than a small percentage of requirements. Nickel deposits are even more deficient, and resources of tungsten, molybdenum, vanadium, cobalt, and titanium are meager and inadequate. Tin and antimony deposits also are small and cannot be expected to supply more than 15 per cent of domestic requirements—and then for a short time only. Lead reserves are estimated at 11 million tons of ore containing some 130,000 tons of metal. Annual production is approximately 14,000 tons of metal, about one fifth of the anticipated demand. As for aluminum, there are no bauxite deposits of consequence in Japan, no known aluminum shales, and only small quantities of alunite. Prewar production of aluminum was based on imports of bauxite from eastern Asia and the Western Pacific and of alunite from Korea. Extensive deposits of high-alumina clays are scattered over the islands, but an economical process for their utilization has not been developed.

Gold and silver are found in much of Japan proper, in sufficient quantity to supply anticipated domestic needs. Platinum, however, is available only in minute quantities. Chromite deposits apparently are extensive enough to meet domestic requirements for some years, an estimated maximum of 800,000 tons of ore being in reserve. The chief mines are in southern Hokkaido and in the Okayama-Tottori area of south central Honshu. Production in 1951 reached 15,800 short tons of chrome oxide from ores grossing about 40,000 tons.

Until 1935 Japan produced domestically almost all of the copper she consumed, but thereafter imports rose to meet increased industrial and military demands. Annual production (estimated at 77,000 short tons in 1939 and 59,000 tons of metal in 1952) is sufficient to supply ordinary peacetime needs, although most of the Japanese copper mines have been worked for many years and the best ores have been consumed. The chief exploited deposits are in Akita, Ibaraki, and Tochigi prefectures in central and northern Honshu, and in Ehime Prefecture in western Shikoku. Zinc deposits, estimated at 2 million tons of metal, also should be sufficient to meet annual needs. Production in 1952 was 96,000 short tons of metal. The chief mines are in Gifu, Iwate, and Miyagi prefectures in Honshu, several of which are also major lead producers. Although Japan had been a major importer of zinc since 1900, increased domestic output after 1940 practically eliminated imports.

Coal.—The most important and valuable of the minerals in Japan is coal, whose value amounted to more than half of all the minerals produced in Japan in 1936. Proved, probable, and possible reserves are estimated at 18 billion metric tons, of which almost half is in Hokkaido and 38 per cent is in Kyushu. More than three fourths of Japanese coal is a low-grade bituminous; only 4 per cent is believed to be anthracite; and the remainder is sub-bituminous. Production is costly because of fragmentary, thin, and crooked coal seams; large amounts of ground water in the mines; and the limited use of mechanized equipment. Per ton costs before World War II were almost twice those in the United States; and in 1936 the output per underground worker in Japan was 318 tons, as compared with 1,010 tons in the United

States in the same year. Furthermore, Japanese coal is not only ashy and high in volatile matter, but its calorific value averages between 11,000 and 13,000 British thermal units (Btu.), as compared with a typical United States figure of over 14,000 Btu.

Despite the primary position occupied by coal in Japan's mineral resources, the per capita reserves amount to only 220 metric tons, as compared with the United States figure of 27,000 metric tons and the United Kingdom's 4,200 metric tons. Japan's coal deposits, though by far the most fully exploited in the Far East, are still small in comparison with those of the world's major coal-producing areas.

Coal production during the war averaged close to 60 million short tons annually, as compared with 40 to 50 million tons in the immediate prewar period. By 1947 production had declined to 32 million tons; by 1952 it had risen to 49 million tons, at which figure reserves should last some 200 years. The estimated needs are approximately 50 million tons annually, and production should meet almost all of that demand. Unfortunately, the high-volatile Japanese coals are unsuitable for coking purposes. Formerly coking coal was imported from north China, Manchuria, and Korea. A minimum of 1 million tons of this higher-quality coal must be imported, at least until such time as technological advances make it possible to convert economically Japanese coals to coke.

In addition to the coal reserves there are extensive lignite deposits which are variously estimated at 500 to 2,200 million tons. Most of them, however, are relatively small, scattered, impure, and underground; therefore, technical production problems of size exist. Until 1940 very little lignite was mined (less than 300,000 metric tons a year), but by 1947, 3,250,000 short tons were produced. With increased coal production, however, lignite output fell to 1,700,000 tons in 1952. Although useful primarily as a heating fuel, the 5 to 10 million tons of lignite produceable annually would do much to alleviate the fuel shortage in Japan.

Although Hokkaido contains more than half of the total Japanese coal reserves, it produces less than one third of the coal mined and until the outbreak of the Sino-Japanese War in 1937 produced less than one quarter. The greatest output has come from the coalfields of northern and western Kyushu: about 57 per cent in the period 1935–1945. The prospects for future development in Hokkaido, however, are better than in Kyushu, since many of the best seams in the latter island already have been exploited. There are several smaller deposits in Honshu, the chief of which is the Joban field in Fukushima Prefecture, which supplies much of the fuel coal for the Kanto area, and the deposits in western Yamaguchi Prefecture, largely subanthracite, which are ancillary to the northern Kyushu fields. Numerous other deposits exist and are mined in small quantities for local consumption, but Shikoku is said to be without any coal at all.

Petroleum.—Reserves of petroleum were estimated in 1951 to be about 26 million barrels, a negligible quantity for any modern industrialized country. It was possible that this estimate was too low; geological surveys indicate the possibility of additional reserves, but at most Japan will be able to supply only a small percentage (10 to 15 per cent) of her petroleum needs, and then only for a limited time. Before World War II, Japan imported almost 90 per cent of her petroleum and petroleum products, and a similar percentage of imports was required in the postwar period. In 1952, Japanese production totaled 2,100,000 barrels, less than 10 per cent of total consumption. The main Japanese oilfields are in Akita and Niigata prefectures in northwestern Japan; secondary pools are found in western Hokkaido; and all belong to the same geological formations.

Minerals Used in the Chemical Industry.—Of these, eight may be considered basic: coal, copper, nitrates, limestone, and sulphur, all of which are produced in sufficient supply in Japan; and salt, phosphates, and potash.

Coal and copper are in adequate, though not in generous, supply. Nitrates, essential for the manufacture of agricultural fertilizers, can be produced artificially by the nitrogen-fixation process. Both high- and low-grade limestone is abundant in Japan and quarries are located on every island. Recorded production, concentrated largely in northern Kyushu, in 1939 was 813 million tons and actual production is believed to have been 20 per cent greater. Reserves are sufficient for at least 200 years and considerable exports are possible. Sulphur likewise is sufficient for anticipated needs. Reserves of close to 60 million tons are known, including 20 million tons of native sulphur and nearly 40 million tons of sulphur content in pyrite deposits. Production in 1952 reached 1,344,000 short tons, a quantity which slightly exceeded domestic demands and which could be produced without strain for another half century. Refined sulphur constituted 156,000 tons of production, the balance coming from pyrites which are used primarily for the production of sulphuric acid.

The lack of adequate supplies of salt in Japan may seem strange in view of the insular nature of the country, despite the absence of deposits of rock salt. The coasts of Japan are dotted with small salt factories engaged in the evaporation of seawater and the extraction of salt. Climatically, however, there are few areas where rainfall is consistently light enough to permit solar evaporation of seawater. Even in the Inland Sea area, where the bulk of Japan's salt is manufactured, the rainfall is close to 40 inches and is spread fairly evenly over the year. Thus, final evaporation is effected in pans over fires of wood, charcoal, and coal or by electrical means (12 per cent before World War II). In 1936, 590,000 tons of salt were produced, while requirements amounted to more than 2.2 million tons. In 1952 production was only 497,000 tons, or about 20 per cent of consumption.

Both phosphates and potash are necessary for the fertilizing of infertile and overused Japanese soils. About 75 per cent of Japan's prewar potash needs and about 40 per cent of her phosphate needs were supplied domestically. Both these materials are derived largely from waste products: night soil, farm manures, bone meal, and fish meal. Some small percentages come from domestically produced bean and seed cake. It was expected that almost 1 million tons of phosphate rock and potassium salts would have to be imported by 1960 to maintain the productivity of cultivable land.

Lesser Minerals and Mineral Products.—Of these, Japan possesses adequate supplies of arsenic, bismuth, bromine, cadmium, garnet, iodine, mercury, clays, gypsum, sands and gravels, and building stones. Higher-quality building materials, however, are lacking, and the fine china clays for Japan's china export industry, as well as refractory clays, kaolin, and fine glass sands, are imported. Asbestos, fluorspar, mica, and graphite also must be imported.

Fiber Resources.—It is questionable to what extent Japan is deficient in the domestic production of fibers. She has a supply of wood fibers from her forests and an almost unlimited supply of straw from her grain fields. But in the competition with food crops for agricultural acreage, textile fiber crops have done poorly, especially since 1940. The approximate annual production of hard, chiefly textile, fibers in Japan is 77 million pounds. About one third of this quantity is silk; another third, hemp; and the remainder, flax, jute, ramie, and cotton. The 77 million pounds produced can be compared with the 872 million pounds of fibers necessary for a population of 87,200,000 at a per capita quota of 10 pounds. Furthermore, no wool to speak of is produced in Japan, very little leather relative to the demand, and no rubber. The deficit conceivably could be balanced by the use of wood pulp for rayon, but only at the expense of other wood uses. Since in the postwar period there was a deficit anticipated for some years in wood production, the complete elimination of fiber shortages through the use of wood products seemed hardly probable, though in the long run possible.

Japanese farmers produce an estimated 42 billion pounds of straw fiber each year. About 10 billion pounds is available for fiber uses, hats, mats, raincoats, sandals, rope, packing, wallboard, paper, and padding. Another 13 billion pounds is used for fodder, compost, thatch, and fuel, the remainder being unused or unusable.

Silk has long been the great textile fiber of Japan and was the leading item in its export trade to the West for decades. Most production is conducted as a cash-crop auxiliary to agricultural activity. Silk is far from being a cheap fiber, however, even in Japan, and the costs of producing mulberry leaves, necessary for the raising of cocoons, are maintained at a high level by the pressure on arable land for food-raising purposes. This pressure, as well as the loss of much of the United States market for Japanese silk, was reflected in the diminution of mulberry acreage from 1.45 million acres in the 1931–1940 period to 428,000 acres in 1952. Production likewise has declined, from 95 million pounds in the prewar period to 33 million in 1952. It appears, therefore, that increases in silk production would help counteract part of the deficit in hard fibers, but only at a relatively high price and at the expense of some food production.

Among other possibilities for expanding fiber production was the increased use of inner bark from the silkworm mulberry varieties and related species. In addition, the utilization of synthetic fibers other than rayon (nylon and the like) was anticipated, but no production in quantity had taken place by 1952.

If Japan were to regain an export trade at all similar to that preceding World War II, it would be necessary for her to import vast quantities of raw cotton and wool as well as wood pulp, abaca, jute, ramie, kapok, and flax. Therefore, although by the judicious utilization of wood pulp and straw Japan might counter certain of her fiber deficiencies on a domestic basis, for the re-establishment of overseas trade she would continue to be a fiber-deficit country. See also section on *Agriculture*.

Power and Fuel Resources.—Japan is fortunate in having a relatively high hydroelectric power potential due to the ample precipitation throughout most of the country and to a mountainous topography laced with short, swift-flowing streams. On the basis of a six-month flow, the potential waterpower available is estimated at 10.9 million kilowatts. At the beginning of 1951, Japan had 1,424 hydroelectric plants in operation with an installed capacity of 6.56 million kilowatts. Several plants were under construction, and were expected by late 1953 to bring the total hydroelectric capacity to 6.94 million kilowatts. Most of the plants are small. In 1951, 88 per cent of them had installed capacities of less than 10,000 kilowatts. Of the 51.6 billion kilowatt-hours produced in Japan in 1952, 78 per cent were of hydroelectric origin.

On the other hand, hydroelectric power plants operated at an average of only 66 per cent of theoretical capacity in 1950. The reasons for this seeming insufficiency are two: (1) the irregularity of rainfall and runoff, which has prevented the even distribution of power production over the months; (2) the scarcity of storage dams and reservoirs, the means for equalizing water resources over the year. Only an estimated 1.2 billion kilowatt-hours, or 3 per cent of total annual production, are available from existing storage facilities. Hydroelectric plants are scattered throughout Japan, but are concentrated in greater numbers in certain areas. In terms of percentage of national hydroelectric capacity in 1951, the plants were distributed as follows: in Kanto, 23.7 per cent; in Kansai or Kinki, 19.1 per cent; in Tohoku, 16.2 per cent; in Chubu, 12.8 per cent, and in Kyushu, 9.5 per cent; the balance was spread in other areas.

As a supplementary source of power there were at the beginning of 1951, 273 thermoelectric plants in Japan with an authorized capacity of 3.99 million kilowatts. These, combined with the hydroelectric plants, gave Japan a total electric power capacity of 10.55 million kilowatts, roughly equal to that in the states of Illinois and Michigan combined. This figure is misleading, however, since neither the hydroelectric nor the thermoelectric plants operated at full capacity. The actual production from public utility thermoelectric plants in 1949 was estimated at about 40 per cent of the installed capacity, and at no time has the actual output amounted to more than 75 per cent of capacity even under the press of wartime conditions. Although thermal plants are distributed widely, there are major concentrations in the Kansai or Kinki region (32.2 per cent at the beginning of 1951), in Kyushu (22.5 per cent), in the Kanto region (12.5 per cent), and in Chugoku (11.2 per cent). The largest thermoelectric plants are in Osaka-Kobe, Tokyo-Yokohama, and Nagoya. Since the monthly variations in hydroelectric output may amount to some 1.1 billion kilowatt-hours, 40 per cent or more of the thermal plants are necessary for standby and auxiliary purposes. The remainder are necessary where hydroelectric power is inadequately supplied, as in the largest cities.

When reduced to equivalent heat units, all

domestic sources of fuel and power can supply 90 million Japanese annually with 16.9 million Btu. per capita. About 75 per cent comes from coal and lignite, 9 per cent from hydroelectricity, and 12 per cent from fuel wood. If total mechanical power is considered, however, it is estimated that there will be an equivalent of 1,353 kilowatt-hours per capita available. Of this energy, 56 per cent is from coal and 33 per cent from hydroelectricity, with coal increasing somewhat in importance in relation to hydroelectricity. This compares favorably with the per capita consumption in 1930–1934, but falls far short of the consumption after 1936; it is equivalent, however, to only about 10 per cent of the per capita electrical equivalents available in the United States in 1945.

Bibliography.—Trewartha, G. T., *Japan: A Physical, Cultural, and Regional Geography* (Madison, Wis., 1945); General Headquarters, Supreme Commander for the Allied Powers, Natural Resources Section, *Technical Reports* (Tokyo 1946–52); Ackerman, E. A., *Japan's Natural Resources and Their Relation to Japan's Economic Future* (Chicago 1953).

NORTON S. GINSBURG,
Assistant Professor, Department of Geography, University of Chicago.

5. AGRICULTURE. Agriculture is the backbone of Japan's economic life. The unprecedented progress of industrialization in Japan before World War II tended to obscure this fact, but in reality the importance of agriculture was very great even then. The war saw the destruction of much of Japan's industrial fabric and the loss of many of her foreign markets. Agriculture was the only segment of Japanese economy that survived the defeat of the country in relatively good condition. In 1952 the rural population accounted for almost 43 per cent of Japan's 86,000,000 people and provided from 80 to 85 per cent of the food consumed by the Japanese. In terms of capital invested and net value of output, agriculture is by far the country's leading industry. And all this agricultural structure rests on only 15 million acres of cultivated land, made up of minute, well-tilled farms and gardens.

Roughly 75 per cent of the area of Japan is hilly or mountainous, with slopes usually too steep, and soils too thin, for ordinary cultivation. With a few notable exceptions, the typical Japanese plains consist mainly of narrow coastal lowlands; they are found also along the banks of some of the larger rivers or along the bottoms of narrow, steep-sided valleys. This preponderance of highlands with steep slopes and rock wastes sets definite and striking limits to the cultivated area and explains why only some 16 per cent of the total estimated land area of Japan is cultivated. Compared with that of other countries, the ratio is small; before World War II, Italy cultivated 41 per cent, Germany 40 per cent, France 39 per cent, and Great Britain 22 per cent, of the total land area. Even in the continental United States, 18 per cent of the total area is under cultivation. See also section on *Natural Resources*.

Climate.—In northern Japan, where snowfall is heavy, a second crop on rice fields is very difficult, if not impossible; where it is practiced, damages are extensive. Somewhat the same is true of frost in the north and in some other regions of the country. The typhoon, too, contributes its share of damage. It is almost a yearly occurrence, usually taking place in August and September. The typhoons are accompanied by severe rainstorms that bring in their wake floods and damage to crops.

From the point of view of utilizing fully the available soil resources, Japan enjoys ample precipitation. Rainfall for the entire country ranges between 40 and 100 inches annually. From north to south, and through the entire north and some of central Japan, precipitation varies from 40 to 60 inches. The heavier rainfall occurs west and south of this belt. The seasonal rains in June and July, together with the fairly dry weather in August, are peculiarly suited to the growing of irrigated rice. On the whole, precipitation is sufficient to meet the needs of Japanese agriculture, and normally almost no region suffers from a shortage of water for crops. Occasionally rains result in devastating floods; for example, in 1953 they caused considerable loss of life in Kyushu as well as property damage estimated at $100 million.

Soils.—There are many kinds of soil in Japan, but for purposes of description, three main groups may be defined: (1) the podsolic soils of a large part of Hokkaido and of the highlands of Honshu; (2) the brown soils of southwestern Hokkaido and the northern and central parts of Honshu; and (3) the yellow and red soils of the remaining part of Honshu, together with all of Shikoku and Kyushu.

Japanese soils are not naturally very fertile. The greater part appear to be inferior in this respect, and high yields seem to have been obtained in most cases only by careful attention to the needs of each particular soil situation. In upland and paddy soils, where a legume is grown as a winter crop, lime must be applied to make up the deficiency of calcium. The application of phosphorus is often found profitable, and in certain cases potash is necessary. Nearly all the soils are strongly deficient in nitrogen. A painstaking effort to meet the needs of these soils is the chief reason for the success Japanese farmers have had in securing high levels of production.

Farm Population.—In the mid-19th century, when Japan came into contact with the West, almost 80 per cent of the people were classed as farmers. The proportion of farmers in the total population decreased to 48 per cent by 1930, and to 40 per cent by 1939. This decline in ratio was due not to a decrease in the farming class but to an increase in the nonfarm population. There was, in fact, an increase in the total number of agricultural families, which reached a prewar maximum of 5,642,500 in 1932, compared with 5,518,000 in 1886. The number of farm families in 1947 was 5,900,000, and in 1952 it was estimated at 6,200,000. The rise in the number of farm families was attested by the general rise in farm population. After World War II the total farm population increased to a point where it constituted almost half the total population in 1949. This was in no way a reflection of any improvement, or greater absorptive capacity, of Japanese agriculture. On the contrary, it reflected the immediate postwar industrial and commercial dislocation of Japan, the country's slow economic recovery, and, by the same token, the steady movement of expatriates and unemployed from the cities to the villages, where they hoped to eke out a living from the farms of their relatives. Economic recovery thereafter served to reduce the ratio of farm population to the total.

Land Utilization.—The land of Japan falls into four groups: cultivated, forest, pasture, and wasteland (*gen-ya*) and land under various other uses. In 1939, cultivated land represented 16 per cent of the total area; forest land, 55 per cent; pasture, 8 per cent; and land in other uses, 21 per cent. This relationship had not changed to any material degree by 1954.

Forested hills and mountains, which account for 55 per cent of the country's surface, are the basic limiting factor in the expansion of the cultivated acreage. The forests are primarily mountain forest and generally of poor quality. Nearly half of them consist of dwarf woods fit only for fuel. The grasses of the pasture land are of poor quality, and the limited attempts to improve them have not been successful.

Cultivated land is scarce in relation to the rapidly growing population as a whole as well as to the farm population. The Japanese government has been well aware of this fact, which explains to a degree not only the development of industry and foreign trade, but, above all, the official policy of attempting to increase crop acreage and the productive capacity of the land.

By the time of the Meiji Restoration of 1868 most of the level land had already been taken up by the farmers. To increase their acreage they had to turn, and successfully, to the remaining lowlands, the mountain slopes, and the hillsides in spite of heavy expenditures and other unfavorable conditions. The cultivated area between 1880 and 1921 increased 36 per cent, from 10.5 million to about 15 million acres. Since 1921 the cultivated acreage has remained almost unchanged. In fact, due to acquisition for military purposes, the cultivated area actually decreased by about 500,000 acres between 1937 and 1945.

The effort to expand the land under cultivation gained momentum early in the Allied occupation of Japan following World War II. Former military land and other readily available tracts were promptly made available for cultivation. The Japanese government estimated that nearly 4 million acres were still reclaimable as crop land. In the main, this was a rather optimistic estimate. Since most of the desirable land was already in use, the greater part of the reclaimable land left was inferior to the land in cultivation. The cost of reclamation on some land was prohibitive, and land which was not suitable for reclamation was included in the program.

In 1954 the total arable land was estimated at 15.5 million acres. The acreage would have been larger but for the fact that a good deal of land had shifted to nonagricultural purposes. A total of 880,000 acres of uncultivated land had been reclaimed from September 1945 to July 1, 1949, providing new farms for 172,000 settlers and additional cultivated land for 500,000 local farmers. By the end of 1951 a total of over 1,000,000 acres had been reclaimed. It should be noted, however, that this was land that lent itself to reclamation very easily and at relatively little expense.

Farming Practices.—*Intensive Cultivation.*—Since the pressure on the land is so great, the fields of Japan are cultivated intensively; they are treated much more carefully than many a garden in other parts of the world. The rice fields are graded to level, and each is surrounded by dikes. Many of the upland fields are also leveled and made secure by terracing. Leveling not only facilitates working, but enables the land to retain all natural or artificial fertilizers, making possible the continuous growing of such heavy-yielding crops as irrigated rice, as well as multiple crops on the upland. All this calls for an immense amount of labor. Careful cultivation, constant weeding, repeated applications of fertilizers, painstaking watering of crops where irrigation is lacking, multiple cropping—all these are indicative of the intensive cultivation of the fields.

Multiple Cropping.—A characteristic feature of Japanese agriculture is that two successive crops are grown each year on a large part of the land. Two crops of rice are rare, but from 30 to 40 per cent of the irrigated rice land, except where the climate is least favorable on account of severe winters, is replanted to winter crops, such as wheat and barley. On the upland fields (unirrigated cropped land) also, the same unit of land produces more than one crop each year, farmers commonly having three or more crops growing at the same time in different stages of maturity. Because of the practice of double and multiple cropping, there is a distinction in Japan between cultivated and harvested area. For instance, in 1939 Japan's harvested area amounted to 20 million acres, or one third more than the land reported as cultivated. Practically the same was true in 1952.

Fertilizing.—Fertilizers are of unusual importance in a country like Japan, where the system of agriculture is very intensive and a scarcity of agricultural land makes it important to secure high yields from every field. Understanding the necessity to fertilize, Japanese farmers for many years have fully utilized materials locally available—mainly compost, night soil, green manure, and wood ashes. Bean cake and fish fertilizers were added to this list following a development of the soybean industry in Manchuria and of the fish-packing industry in Japan. More recently, large quantities of chemical fertilizers, particularly ammonium sulphate and superphosphate, have also been employed.

It is a common practice of farmers in Japan to dump fertilizers of various kinds into a shallow cement storage cistern to which water is added. The manure is allowed to decompose, and when field applications are to be made, the liquid fertilizer is ladled out of the cistern and carried to the field in large wooden buckets. The Japanese farmer does not spread the fertilizer over his field, but applies it directly to the growing plant. It is poured over the plant so that only the soil next to the crop is fertilized.

Despite the great importance of chemical fertilizers in Japanese agriculture, the role of farmyard manures is undiminished. It is estimated that during 1936–1940 the percentage of the total quantities of fertilizer nutrients supplied by farm manures was as follows: nitrogen (N), 48 per cent; phosphoric acid (P_2O_5), 35 per cent; potash (K_2O), 74 per cent. In 1946 total consumption of farm manures (compost, night soil, green manures, and others) on a fertilizer-equivalent basis was 4.5 million tons.

In 1935–1937, it was estimated that in terms of pounds per acre of arable land, Japan was third among the nations of the world in the total amount of nitrogen derived from organic and inorganic fertilizers, with 37 pounds per acre of arable land; fifth in phosphoric acid, with 34 pounds; and fifth in the amount of potash, with 15 pounds. During the same period, Japan was the world's largest user of ammonium sulphate.

In the 1920's and 1930's, Japan built up a large fertilizer industry. Peak production of commercial organic and inorganic nitrogenous fertilizers occurred during 1936–1940, when an average of 1,800,000 metric tons of ammonium sulphate equivalents was produced annually. Production of such fertilizers declined rapidly after 1941, and by 1945 it amounted to only 335,000 metric tons. The period 1936–1940 was also the peak period of production of inorganic and organic forms of commercial phosphatic and potassic fertilizers. The yearly average was 1,900,000 metric tons of superphosphate equivalents and 20,000 metric tons of potassium sulphate equivalents. In this instance, too, by the end of the war production was at its lowest level.

In consequence of a major effort on the part of the Allied occupation authorities and the Japanese government, the fertilizer industry made very rapid recovery after the war, but fertilizer availability was still far from prewar levels; in 1949 commercial organic and inorganic fertilizers accounted for only 64 per cent of the 1936–1940 average. In 1952, however, the fertilizer industry not only provided for the country's needs, but was in a position to export fertilizer products. In that year, Japan produced nearly 2,000,000 tons of ammonium sulphate equivalents (20 per cent N), 1,400,000 tons of superphosphate equivalents (16 per cent P_2O_5), 530,000 tons of potash (40 per cent K_2O), and a not insignificant quantity of other chemical fertilizers. The total volume of chemical fertilizers was in excess of 3,900,000 tons.

Use of Labor and Equipment.—The intensive work performed on Japanese farms from planting to harvesting is carried on almost exclusively by hand. With some minor exceptions, motor-driven machines are scarcely ever used in seeding, fertilizing, and harvesting, although animal power often is used in plowing. Even in Hokkaido, which is best suited to mechanization, animal-drawn farm implements have been in use for generations and no need has been felt for replacing them with modern equipment.

The farm equipment used in field work is light and of the simplest construction. The dikes and ditches could not stand heavy equipment and in the tiny fields too much maneuvering of the machinery would destroy the crop. Aside from physical factors, mechanization has been retarded for economic reasons. Human labor is abundant, and this fact in itself tends to preclude the use of laborsaving devices.

To assume, however, that mechanization is an unknown quantity in Japanese agriculture would be erroneous. Japanese farmers employ some mechanical equipment adjustable to the size of the farm, but it is employed to process agricultural products and no mechanical equipment is used directly in raising crops. Before World War II, for example, one electric motor was used per 107 farm families, and one gasoline engine per 22 farm families. The electric motors averaged not more than 1.5 horsepower; the gasoline engines, 3 horsepower. After the war there was a sharp increase in the utilization of farm equipment, some motorized. Between 1937 and early 1952 the number of threshers (129,000) and hullers (192,000) increased threefold; that of mechanical pumps (44,000) more than threefold, and that of electric and gasoline engines from 188,000 to nearly 650,000. Considering the number of farm households, the use of such equipment was far from widespread, but progress was undeniable.

Livestock.—Japanese agriculture has only a limited livestock industry despite the preponderance of highlands. There are two principal reasons for this: (1) There is a lack of good natural pasture land, because the native wild grass is coarse and unnutritious and generally crowds out the valuable forage grasses. (2) Farming is limited to the cultivation of the soil for the produce derived directly from it, because in a densely populated country with limited food resources the food value produced from an acre under grains is 6 to 7 times larger than the food value of the meat or milk that can be obtained by feeding the grain to livestock.

Cattle and horses are raised chiefly for draft purposes and for stable manure. The total number of cattle prior to World War II averaged 1,800,000 and reached a peak of 2,300,000 in 1945. In the immediate postwar period the number was considerably reduced, but it was estimated that in 1949 it attained the 1945 level. Horses in 1949 were estimated at 1.1 million, or about one fifth less than in 1930–1934. Hogs play a particularly small role in the farm economy of the average farmer, and at no time has their number exceeded 1,000,000. They declined sharply in the war and postwar years, and in 1949 there were only about 500,000 hogs in Japan. By 1953 the livestock industry was above prewar levels in virtually every category; the most notable gains were in cattle, horses, sheep, and poultry. Yet numbers were still small in relation to the number of farm households. In 1952 the number of cattle per farm household averaged .4; that of horses, .3; that of hogs, .2. Japan has considerable possibilities of increasing and improving its livestock industry, but in order to do that it must concentrate on the formidable task of improving its pasture and grazing lands.

Agricultural Production.—The cultivated land of Japan falls into two main groups: (1) rice fields (irrigated land), and (2) upland farms (unirrigated land) that produce other crops. Many of the cultivated crops in the uplands are also grown on rice fields as winter crops.

A distinguishing feature of Japanese agriculture is the preponderance of food crops, of which rice is the most outstanding. The emphasis upon rice is probably no accident, because the type of agriculture developed has been influenced largely by the amount of cultivable land available in relation to the population. With relatively little land suitable for cultivation, with a rapidly growing population demanding larger supplies of food, and with a fixed government policy to encourage self-sufficiency in food, the concentration upon food crops was natural. Rice became the dominant food crop because under Japanese conditions it yields more calories per unit of land than any other cereal. Individually, other food crops are not so important to Japan as rice, but taken together they utilize over 40 per cent of the harvested area. All food crops together account for four fifths of the land under crops.

During World War II and immediately thereafter agricultural production in Japan declined, but thereafter considerable recovery took place. This was particularly true of food crops. Just before the war the harvested acreage under food crops was slightly over 14 million acres, or only 150,000 acres more than the area under the same crops in 1948. The general trend of acreage,

Table 1—ACREAGE, YIELD, AND PRODUCTION[1] OF THE MAJOR CROPS OF JAPAN
Averages, 1935–1939 and 1940–1944; specified years, 1945 through 1952

Period	Rice[2] Planted area (1,000 acres)	Rice[2] Yield (bushels per acre)	Rice[2] Production (1,000 bushels)	Wheat Planted area (1,000 acres)	Wheat Yield (bushels per acre)	Wheat Production (1,000 bushels)	Barley Planted area (1,000 acres)	Barley Yield (bushels per acre)	Barley Production (1,000 bushels)
1935–39	7,862	76	595,845	1,735	29	49,954	844	41	34,559
1940–44	7,659	73	556,057	2,044	26	52,228	933	36	33,170
1945	7,089	64	456,667	1,789	19	34,660	990	25	24,587
1946	6,871	82	560,660	1,562	15	22,613	910	21	19,160
1949	7,377	78	571,147	1,680	23	39,279	961	37	36,054
1950	7,441	79	587,629	1,888	26	49,180	1,060	39	41,175
1952	7,436	81	604,188	1,782	32	56,480	1,008	49	49,512
	Naked barley			Sweet potatoes			White potatoes		
1935–39	1,044	30	30,842	618	203	125,620	385	166	64,101
1940–44	1,164	28	32,113	697	201	140,308	467	152	70,817
1945	1,180	22	26,471	988	158	156,209	527	124	65,094
1946	1,101	15	16,565	921	240	221,047	477	136	64,678
1949	1,275	25	32,187	1,038	204	211,441	544	142	77,161
1950	1,460	27	39,032	983	265	260,150	475	189	89,729
1952	1,290	38	49,604	932	267	248,702	489	189	92,409
	Mulberry[3]			Tea[3]			Millets		
1935–39	1,308[4]	574[4]	750,814[4]	96	1,192	114,451	306	25	7,636
1940–44	1,014	502	508,695	89	1,410	125,456	247	21	5,219
1945	526	354	186,210	65	802	52,150	236	13	3,034
1946	400	295	117,919	60	787	47,219	242	20	4,849
1949	457	301	136,244	67	1,119	74,970	261	20	5,099
1950	450	346	155,865	67	1,372	91,932	309	23	7,029
1952	428	532	227,730	74	1,728	127,867	275	25	6,914

[1] The weights of the various bushels are as indicated: rice (rough), 45 pounds; wheat, 60 pounds; barley, 48 pounds; naked barley, 61 pounds; sweet potatoes, 55 pounds; white potatoes, 60 pounds. The data on millets include foxtail, barnyard, and proso millet, which weigh, respectively, 56, 33, and 49 pounds per bushel.

[2] The prewar and 1940–44 averages are not comparable with the yearly averages because the Japanese Ministry of Agriculture and Forestry has since improved its methods of crop estimating.

[3] For tea and mulberries, production is expressed in thousands of pounds, and yield in pounds per acre.

[4] 1939 only.

Source: Foreign Agricultural Service, United States Department of Agriculture.

production, and yields before and after World War II are shown in Table 1. With the exception of the wheat acreage and that under mulberry and tea, the recovery was very marked, and it should be noted that the decline in the acreage planted to tea and mulberry was due to a sharp decline in foreign demand for tea and silk.

In 1952, as in the past, rice dominated Japanese agricultural economy. Fully 55 per cent of the cereal acreage was under rice. Rice is used at practically every meal; although other grains are consumed, they supplement rather than replace rice. Efforts to increase the yield of rice have been most successful and Japanese yields are the highest in Asia. In comparison with other principal rice-producing countries, such as Indochina, the Philippines, Thailand, Burma, and India, the Japanese yields are from two to three times larger. This success was achieved through ample use of manpower, improved rice varieties, abundant use of fertilizers, and improved agricultural practices. In Japan, 96 per cent of the rice acreage is irrigated; the remaining upland rice area is without irrigation. The cereal is planted in May and June and harvested from August to November.

Despite the high yields of agricultural products, however, the total output is not sufficient to provide the country's basic food requirements. Before the war Japan had to import approximately 15 per cent of the food it consumed. The annual production of staple crops (rice, wheat, barleys, sweet and white potatoes) in terms of brown rice equivalents reached a prewar peak of 14,615,000 metric tons in 1939. During the war years, production held up well until 1945, when fertilizer shortages and unfavorable weather caused short crops. In 1948, total production of staples was 13,927,000 metric tons, or 6 per cent more than the average annual production of these crops during the period 1931–1940, but still 5 per cent less than in 1939. In the meantime the total population of the country had increased by more than 10 million and the food shortage in terms of prewar consumption was greater than ever before. The estimated deficit in terms of staple food requirements for the year 1952 was nearly 4 million metric tons. Japan's chances of becoming self-sufficient in food in the foreseeable future were rather poor. Any success in such an attempt would depend upon one or more of the following factors: (1) expansion of arable acreage, (2) higher yields, (3) additional labor for the cultivated acreage, and (4) the effect of agrarian reform upon the food supply. An examination of the likely trends in the development of these factors indicated, however, that Japanese agriculture would not be in a position to satisfy the basic food requirements of the growing population. On the contrary, Japan's dependence upon imported foodstuffs would continue to grow.

Social Factors in Japanese Agriculture and Postwar Changes.—The fact that more than 6 million farm families cultivate 15 million acres of land indicates that the size of the farm units is quite small, averaging about 2.5 acres. In southwest Japan, farm units are generally under 2 acres in size, with some of the holdings along the Inland Sea averaging 1.5 acres. In northern Honshu this figure increases to 3.5 acres, and only in the northernmost, sparsely populated island of Hokkaido do the farms average 12.5 acres. The size of holdings actually cultivated shows that approximately one third of all households cultivate less than 1.2 acres each; 33 per cent, from 1.2 to 2.4 acres; and only about 10 per cent, more than 5 acres. Moreover, the 15 million acres of cultivated land are divided into approximately 100 million plots, which means that most Japanese farmers work on small plots, often resembling gardens rather than fields.

Before the Allied occupation of Japan in 1945 one of the characteristic features of the Japanese land system was the striking concentration of land ownership. About 50 per cent of all the farm households owned only 9 per cent of all the land, whereas 7.5 per cent of the households owned 50 per cent of the land. The corollary of this situation was that the holdings cultivated by a Japanese farmer did not correspond with the amount of land owned by him. This inequality in landownership was expressed in terms of owners, part owners and part tenants, and tenants. Until the end of 1947 about 31 per cent were independent farm owners; 42 per cent, part tenants and part owners; 27 per cent, tenants who owned no land at all.

The small acreage cultivated by the average farmer was in itself an explanation of his poverty, but the situation was made worse by widespread tenancy and by the conditions under which the tenants worked the land. Land hunger and the intensity of competition for land ownership and cultivation rights preserved land values and rental rates far above a level justifiable by the productivity of the soil. Rentals of 50 per cent of the rice crop and only slightly less of other crops were customary. In addition, the tenant had to meet a number of other assessments and dues, buy his own expensive fertilizer, and provide the farmhouse, farm buildings, implements, and seed. The share from which he drew his living frequently represented not more than 30 per cent of the crop. Under these conditions the life of an average Japanese tenant prior to World War II conformed to the feudal adage that "farmers should neither live nor die."

The lot of the small owner-cultivator was better only by comparison. Until the more prosperous war and postwar years the standard of living of the vast majority of the Japanese farmers was very low. And it is precisely the marginal existence of the small Japanese owner-cultivator and tenant that explains, but only in part, why Japan's 15 million acres of cultivated land can support more than 6 million farm families. The results of numerous studies carried out by the Ministry of Agriculture before the war indicate that the average peasant generally could not make ends meet solely by farming. Even the peasant proprietor had practically no surplus at the end of the year. Naturally, the status of the tenants was considerably worse. Subsidary occupations, therefore, have always played an important role in the life and work of the Japanese farmer. It has been estimated that the income from such sources ranged from one fifth to nearly one third of the total income before the war.

That agriculture was not a sufficiently profitable enterprise for most Japanese farmers, especially for tenants and part tenants, is further indicated by the fact that a Japanese farmer could count upon a surplus only when his holding was about 4.5 acres, or nearly twice the theoretical acreage he cultivated. Even the industry and thrift of the farmer cannot obviate the fact that the income of a farm family is the product not only of output per acre, but of the number of acres as well. In Japan the output per acre is large compared to that of most Western countries, but the acreage per farm is so small that the total income per family is only a fraction of that in the West.

Farm living conditions improved during and immediately after the war in consequence of great food shortages, inflationary conditions, high prices, and black marketing. It was clear, however, that this essentially paper-money prosperity was not going to last very long and that the basic economic and social problems of the Japanese countryside would reassert themselves unless drastic changes were affected in the existing land ownership pattern, in the cooperative movement, and in the services rendered by agricultural research and science. With that view in mind, a strong effort to improve the conditions of the majority of the Japanese farmers and to give rural Japan a greater measure of economic, political, and social stability was made under the direction of the Allied powers after their occupation of Japan.

Land Reform.—On Dec. 9, 1945, Gen. Douglas MacArthur, the supreme commander for the Allied powers (SCAP), issued a directive to the Japanese government that it "take measures to insure that those who till the soil of Japan shall have a more equal opportunity to enjoy the fruits of their labor." As a result of this directive, the Japanese government enacted, on Oct. 21, 1946, the Special Measure for the Establishment of Owner-Farmers (Land Reform Law) and Agricultural Land Adjustment Law of 1946. This legislation provided the legal basis for land reform. It had two main objectives: (1) transfer of land ownership to farmers who actually till the soil and (2) improvement of farm tenancy practices for those who continue as tenants. The underlying principle of the legislation was private rather than state, and individual rather than collective, ownership of the land.

In accordance with the main provisions of the legislation, all the land of absentee owners is made subject to sale. Resident landlords may retain 2.5 acres of tenant-cultivated land, except in Hokkaido, where they are permitted 10 acres. The size of holdings of owner-cultivators is also subject to limitations in order to place the ownership of the maximum amount of land in the hands of as many former tenants as possible. The government purchases the land at an average price of 3,000 yen per acre for rice land, and 1,860 yen per acre of dry or upland fields. In addition, the owners receive a government subsidy of 880 yen per acre for paddy fields, and 520 yen per acre for uplands. This subsidy, however, is not paid on more than 7.5 acres per individual seller in Honshu, Kyushu, and Shikoku, and on more than 30 acres in Hokkaido. The government pays the landlords in 24-year annuity bonds bearing interest at the rate of 3.65 per cent per year. A tenant may discharge his obligation in one payment or in several (not exceeding 30 annual installments), at an annual interest rate of 3.2 per cent.

Another basic provision of the land reform is the reduction in rents and the elimination of rent payments in kind at a fixed proportion of the crop. Rents must be made in cash at a stated amount, which may not exceed 25 per cent of the value of the rice crop and 15 per cent of the value of other crops. The land reform also outlaws a long-standing grievance of the tenants—the custom of renting by a verbal agreement which landowners might terminate on short notice. A written contract specifying the rent, the period of tenure, and other terms of the agreement is registered in the village office. It conforms to a model contract prescribed by the Japanese Ministry of Agriculture and Forestry.

By 1950 approximately 2.7 million cultivators —tenants or part tenants—had acquired in ownership 27 million separate tracts of land with a total area of approximately 4.5 million acres. The cultivated land area operated by tenants before the reform had been reduced from 6,300,000 acres to approximately 1,670,000 acres. Through these changes the lot of the average Japanese tenant had been measurably improved. They had finally achieved what every farmer the world over strives for—individual ownership of land. In achieving that they also secured a stake in the society in which they live, thus bringing Japan closer to the creation of a stable, middle-of-the-road agricultural society. Such an accomplishment marked a peaceful revolution in the social and economic pattern of Japanese agriculture and weakened measurably the tie that had bound the Japanese peasantry to forces of militant reaction and equally militant nationalism.

Cooperatives.—The brighter side of Japan's agricultural economy has been the widespread development of the cooperative movement, which has become the mainstay of the country's agriculture since 1900. The Japanese government and the farmers have understood that the extremely small size of the holdings makes it essential that farmers pool their efforts and resources through cooperatives. The main functions of the cooperatives are confined to the provision of credit, the making of sales and purchases, and the joint utilization of warehouses, milling establishments, and farm equipment. Between 1900 and 1939 the number of cooperatives increased from 21 to over 15,000 with a membership of nearly 7 million. Approximately 70 per cent of the membership was represented by farmers.

The Japanese agricultural cooperative movement was from its inception primarily a government-sponsored movement. During the war cooperatives became mere instruments for carrying out the aims of the military as they affected agriculture. They served to control agricultural prices and production, to handle collections and rationing, and to siphon rural capital for the war effort.

During the Allied occupation the cooperatives underwent certain changes designed to free them from undue domination by the government and to make certain that they were dedicated to the economic and cultural advancement of the Japanese farmers. In accordance with Law 132, which became effective on Dec. 15, 1947, the cooperatives were authorized to perform practically any economic service which contributes to the advancement of farm communities. Fifteen or more farmers may organize a cooperative. Membership is voluntary, and each farmer member has one vote. Persons residing within the business area of the organization may be associate members with all privileges except voting. Two or more cooperatives may organize a federation of agricultural cooperatives; such federations may perform any activity which the local cooperatives are authorized to perform, except that if a federation is engaged in making loans and receiving deposits, it is prohibited from performing additional functions not connected with these activities. A cooperative may be organized as a capital stock or a nonstock association, but no nonstock association may carry on both the functions of making loans and of receiving deposits. Liability for a share is limited to the amount of the share or, in the case of a nonstock organization, to the amount of the authorized fee. The primary responsibility for carrying out the agricultural cooperative program is vested in the Ministry of Agriculture and Forestry. As of June 30, 1949, a total of 33,000 new cooperative associations and federations were approved under the new law. The volume of business recorded for the year 1948 shows that the cooperatives handled 36 per cent of all farm purchases, 61 per cent of all farmer sales, 64 per cent of financial deposits, and 71 per cent of loans to farmers.

Cooperatives are undoubtedly of great benefit to the farm community. In the past they alleviated many financial burdens, although they could not cure the problems of indebtedness, usurious interest rates, taxation burdens, and the unfavorable relationship between prices farmers received for their products and those they had to pay for the commodities they purchased. In 1954 it was safe to assume that, whatever the difficulties under which Japanese agriculture must operate in the future, the work of the cooperatives would undoubtedly serve to mitigate them.

Agricultural Research and Science.—One of the principal agricultural policies of Japan has been to increase production so as to make the country as nearly self-sufficient in food supplies as possible. Considering the agricultural resources of Japan, this policy has been successful. As early as 1879 the government launched a program of agricultural experiment work. It established and financed experiment stations where improvements in fertilizing, selection of seed, and development of new varieties first took place. These were subsequently applied by the farmers with telling results. In the words of a student of Japan's agricultural economy, the program was "a chemical and botanical revolution" fostered by the government. By the end of World War II, Japan had 386 national and prefectural agricultural experiment stations, 164 sericultural stations, 139 livestock breeding or animal hygiene stations, and 9 tobacco stations. In addition, there were 83 agricultural educational institutions, 20 miscellaneous government institutes, and 91 private institutions devoting at least part of their time to agricultural research.

The entire work of research and science in agriculture was decentralized, uncoordinated, and, in many instances, overlapping. The agricultural experts attached to SCAP recognized the notable results achieved by the Japanese in this field, but they also were aware that the existing agricultural experiment station system was not conducive to efficiency and coordination of research. In many instances individual stations did not have sufficient financial support to attract highly trained personnel, to buy modern equipment, and to deal successfully with the practical problems confronting the farmers. The advice given to the Japanese government by United States specialists was embodied in the Law for Improvement and Promotion of Agriculture, enacted on July 5, 1948. The Agricultural Improvement Bureau, dealing with research, extension, and statistics, was established in the Ministry of Agriculture and Forestry in August 1948, to administer the new law. Research requirements were consolidated by 7 regions in order to determine the stations that could best serve the needs of the nation as a whole. The program provided that 135 stations be closed, 53 stations be combined, and 191 stations be continued. Funds, essential projects, and the best-trained personnel were to be transferred to the remaining stations. Prefectual agricultural experiment stations and their branches would be administered by a single staff in each prefecture. The National Agricultural Experiment Station and its regional stations would each have a separate administration, but the work of the branches would be directed by the national station.

Along with improvement in agricultural research and science, measures were taken to improve the means of transmitting technical knowledge to farmers. Since 1899, Japan has had an agricultural extension system under which the government provided each village with one or more agricultural technicians who worked with farmers in improving their agricultural practices. In addition, many of the agricultural cooperatives employed technicians to advise farmer members on production problems. This technical guidance and advisory service was effective, and it was a primary factor in the record increases in the yields of many crops in Japan prior to 1940.

Much of this extension work had fallen into disuse during the war years, and after the war an agricultural extension system was being developed under the provisions of the Law for Improvement and Promotion of Agriculture. More than 6,000 farm advisers were selected from lists of qualified candidates and assigned to duties as extension workers in the rural villages of Japan. The goal of the program was the assignment of an adviser for each of Japan's 10,500 villages. Of the 46 prefectures, 39 have from 2 to 13 home advisers engaged in field work, and more than 3,300 rural youth project clubs have been organized in farm communities.

Agricultural Prospects.—Even the most thorough agrarian improvements, economic and social, will not solve all the problems of rural Japan. There is simply not enough arable land in Japan to give the enormous farm population the reasonable assurance of a decent standard of living. If all the cultivated land in the country were to be equally distributed, the average holding would amount to only 2.5 acres, or nearly 2 acres less than the amount estimated as necessary to make farming in Japan profitable. Since the rural areas contribute the larger part of the annual increase in the Japanese population—at present (1954) somewhat more than 1,000,000—agricultural congestion is expected to be aggravated. Under the circumstances, the amelioration of the lot of the farm population, rather than an ultimate solution of the agrarian problem, is all that can be hoped for. Lasting answers to the problems which are inherent in an agricultural economy of "too many people on too little land" can come only through expanded industrialization and commerce, which decrease Japan's dependence on home-grown food and absorb the surplus rural population, and eventually from a falling birth rate.

Bibliography.—Nasu, Shiroshi, *Aspects of Japanese Agriculture* (New York 1941); Embree, J. F., *Suye Mura, A Japanese Village*, 3d ed. (Chicago 1944); General Headquarters, Supreme Commander for the Allied Powers, Natural Resources Section, *Fertilizers in Japan*, Report No. 55 (Tokyo 1946); id., *Farm Tenancy in Japan*, Report No. 79 (Tokyo 1947); Gilmartin, W. M., and Ladejinsky, W. I., "The Promise of Agrarian Reform in Japan," *Foreign Affairs*, January 1948; Leonard, W. H., "Rice As a Crop in Japan," *Journal of the American Society of Agronomy*, July 1948; "Prospects for Japanese Agriculture," *Foreign Agriculture*, November 1948; General Headquarters, Supreme Commander for the Allied Powers, Natural Resources Section, *Japanese Agriculture; Programs Under the Occupation* (Tokyo 1949); Hewes, L. I., Jr., "On the Current Readjustment of Land Tenure in Japan," *Land Economics*, August 1949; Japan, Ministry of Agriculture and Forestry, *An Analytical Study of the Present Status of Agriculture in Japan* (Tokyo 1949); General Headquarters, Supreme Commander for the Allied Powers, Natural Resources Section, *Weekly Summary*, a very good source of information on Japanese agriculture (Tokyo, weekly to 1952).

W. I. Ladejinsky,
Agricultural Attaché,
United States Embassy,
Tokyo, Japan.

6. INDUSTRIAL DEVELOPMENT.

The tempo of industrialization in modern Japan sustained over half a century has rarely been equaled in the Western World. When Commodore Matthew C. Perry visited the Japanese islands in 1853, he found a nation of approximately 30 million people living in a stage of economic development no more advanced than that of 15th century Europe. Most of them were unfree, impoverished peasants cultivating their tiny farms with primitive methods handed down from their ancestors. A meager development of internal trade and handicrafts supported the limited population of castle towns and cities. The latter found employment mainly in serving the needs of an aristocratic ruling class who lived off the proceeds of feudal rice revenues extracted from the farmers. By 1940 Japan had transformed herself into a front-rank industrial power. She now supported a population of 73 million people at a standard of living well above anything their grandfathers had known. A quarter of her working population was engaged in industrial pursuits, which had come to furnish 40 per cent or more of her greatly expanded national income. When this industrial potential was mobilized for total war after 1941, Japan quickly overran the entire Far East. She was only brought to her knees when the world's greatest industrial nation was free to project an overwhelming power across the Pacific and to strike against the shipping lanes and inflammable cities which were the arteries and heart of her modern industrial system.

Foundations of Modern Industry, 1868–1893.—The foundations of industrial Japan were laid in the first quarter century after the Meiji Restoration of 1868. With feverish energy the young clan bureaucrats who had risen to national power around the emperor set to work to destroy the crumbling edifice of feudalism and build the new nation-state. Machine industry, mining, and commerce were among their most urgent concerns, for these could supply the economic sinews of national power. Students were sent abroad to learn the new Western technology; foreign experts were invited to Japan; machinery and equipment were imported in increasing amounts;

and state funds were applied to the founding of pilot factories, mines, and technical schools.

By 1893 industrial capitalism in Japan had passed through its early formative stage and was preparing for rapid expansion in subsequent decades. Here, as in other aspects of modernization, the Japanese responded eagerly to the quickening ideas and ambitions imbibed from the West. The speed and momentum of development, however, reflected a growing spirit of commercial and industrial enterprise long latent in Japan and now released from the stifling restrictions of the *ancien régime*. Other favorable factors of social tradition, geography, and historical circumstance also helped to produce aggressive leadership in forging a united nation able to seize upon the opportunities now afforded by entry upon the world stage.

Given Japan's tradition of mercantilism and feudal clan monopoly, it was natural that the new Meiji government should lead in industrial pioneering, in close association with influential commercial and industrial magnates. Moreover, only the state was able at this time to mobilize the necessary capital, to provide official protection, and to assume the inevitable risks. Railways, shipping, arsenals, foundries, silk filatures, cement and glass factories, coal and copper mines—almost every new industry—developed initially under government patronage if not under government ownership.

Even more important for industrial progress was the abolition by the state of feudal barriers to freedom of occupation and movement; the encouragement of foreign trade and contacts, and the creation of a national framework of government, finance, and communications. These architectural reforms provided a framework and a climate conducive to the growth of capitalist enterprise both large and small. Foreign markets bulked large, especially in the case of the rising silk industry, but the chief stimulus to manufacturing production came from the growing internal market, reinforced in the heavy industries by the building of the new army and navy.

After 1880 the industrial properties of the state were transferred largely to private ownership. Often this was done at bargain prices which laid the foundation for some of the great industrial fortunes of later decades. Thereafter the state retained close control over such strategic industries as iron and shipbuilding. More indirectly it guided general economic development through subsidies, tariffs, government banks, and close personal affiliations between the bureaucracy and the *zaibatsu* (the great financial combines). After 1890, however, Japanese industry developed primarily under private ownership and initiative within the general framework of national policy. With due allowance for state intervention and controls and for the pervasive influence of the family system, Japan adhered to private capitalism until the eve of World War II.

War and Industrial Development, 1893–1913.—Between 1893 and 1913 a marked impetus to industrial expansion was afforded by two wars, both of them limited in duration and crowned with victory (see Table 1).

The conflict with China (1894–1895) produced an inflationary boom in Japanese war industries, which carried over into later years under the stimulus of continuing arms expenditures. It also gave Japan the power and prestige to regain her tariff independence (new treaties were negotiated with the Western powers, which rid her of the former 5 per cent limitation on her tariff) and won her an indemnity of £38,000,000 from China. Customs autonomy made possible more effective protection of her new industries; the Chinese indemnity provided her with a gold and sterling reserve with which she adopted the gold standard in 1897. Her public credit now solidly established, Japan proceeded to borrow heavily abroad during the next decade. The proceeds were used mainly to purchase arms, industrial equipment, and materials for further industrial and military expansion, which in turn carried her successfully through the war with Russia in 1904–1905.

Table 1[1]—GROWTH OF PRIVATE FACTORY INDUSTRY IN JAPAN PROPER, 1884–1914

Year	Factory operatives[2] (in 1,000's)	Factory consumption of coal[2] (1,000's of metric tons)	Output of raw silk (1,000's of kilograms)	Output of cotton yarn (1,000's of 400-pound bales)	Net supply of pig iron[3] (1,000's of metric tons)
1884......	—	147[4]	2,697	13	18
1894......	381	1,093	5,218	292	55
1904......	526	3,705	7,488	695	133
1914......	854	8,359	14,084	1,666	474

[1] Source: Japan, Department of Agriculture and Commerce, *Statistical Reports* (annual); Asahi Shimbun-sha, *Nippon Keizai Tōkei Sōkan*, pp. 1213-22 (Tokyo 1930).
[2] Before 1909, plants employing 10 or more operatives; thereafter, plants employing 10 or more workers of all types.
[3] Production plus imports minus exports.
[4] 1886.

Japanese industry now began to assume the basic patterns which were to characterize it for the next 25 years. One branch comprised the metallurgical, engineering, and other heavy industries. These were the industries essential to military strength. Yet they were especially difficult to establish in Japan because of their heavy capital requirements and advanced technology. Here the state assiduously fostered development, itself, for example, launching the big Yawata Iron Works in 1901. Government subsidies also built up the ship construction industry to the point where Japanese yards could turn out 60,000 to 70,000 tons of steam vessels per year after the Russo-Japanese War. In such fields, however, Japan's technical capabilities remained decidedly limited. All except the simplest types of machinery and equipment still had to be imported from abroad. Her deficiency in mineral resources also restricted the mining industry to small proportions except for the production of coal and copper. The output of pig iron reached 243,000 tons, and that of steel 255,000 tons, in 1913. But Japan still imported half of her requirements of the former, and two thirds of the latter.

It was not these protected, high-cost industries which accounted for the substantial growth in Japanese national income and wealth through these decades. This growth came about, first of all, through the expansion and technical improvement of agriculture, which still occupied over half of the working population. Food production, for example, probably increased as much as 40 per cent from 1894 to 1914. In addition, there was a rapid development of numerous industries producing textiles, foodstuffs, pottery, paper, and other wares for the foreign and domestic market. With this growth and specialization of commodity production came a corresponding increase in the demand for transportation, trade, banking, and professional services. These, too, afforded added employment opportunities for Japan's expanding population.

Unlike the strategic industries, other manufacturing trades mushroomed with little direct assistance from the state. Some were factory industries like cotton spinning, glass, cement, and beer, organized on a fairly large scale with modern equipment and corporate finance. Others were small-scale trades producing textile fabrics, foodstuffs, pottery, wood products, and miscellaneous consumer goods. Many of the latter remained largely on a workshop basis, perhaps with the introduction of some modern equipment —for example, the power loom in weaving. In a number of fields the small plant was linked with a steadily widening market through merchant capitalists, banks, and factories. They supplied materials and credit, and outlets for the finished product. The strength and resilience of Japan's developing industrial system owed much to these myriads of small establishments, coordinated and controlled through a superstructure of large-scale trade and finance. By 1913, Japan boasted nearly 2,000,000 workers in manufacturing. More than half of them were in establishments with less than 10 employees. Over 40 per cent of them were in the textile industries alone.

Textiles thus were the pioneer in the industrial system of Japan, as they had been elsewhere. In this field machine techniques were readily assimilated, capital requirements were small, and at hand were a large market and a reservoir of traditional skills. Raw silk production nearly tripled from 1894 to 1914, as steady improvements in quality enlarged the demand for Japanese silk abroad. Cocoon raising now afforded supplementary employment to one in every three farm families. The cotton industry also increased tremendously after 1890. By 1914 Japanese spinners were equipped with 2,400,000 spindles, and yarn output had reached 1,700,000 bales. Already monopolizing the domestic market, Japanese cotton goods were now spreading steadily through the Far East. As in other countries beginning to be industrialized, in Japan the cotton industry first established its independence in coarse yarns and woven goods. Only later could it enter world competition in the market for finer yarns and fabrics.

Labor conditions in Japanese mining and manufacturing reproduced all the raw evils which had characterized the early stages of the Industrial Revolution in the West. Over half of all factory workers in 1913 were women, many of them young peasant girls from the farms. There were neither factory laws nor trade unions. Hours ran to 10 or 12 or more; accidents and disease took a heavy toll; and the slums and sweatshops of Osaka and Tokyo rivaled those of any city in the world. So high was the turnover of labor that employers had to resort to extensive recruiting in the countryside. Many factory workers, especially women, were housed in dormitories which afforded food, lodging, and a considerable measure of employer control. Despite lack of economic opportunity in Japan's overcrowded agriculture, labor entered the factory only with reluctance.

Industry's Coming of Age, 1914–1929.— Through the decade before World War I armament and war expenditure imposed a heavy strain on Japan's financial capacity. Large-scale foreign borrowing fostered military and industrial development, but it also burdened the country with increasing debt obligations abroad, which brought growing difficulties in balancing international accounts.

Just as Japan seemed headed for a serious financial crisis, war broke out in Europe. Almost immediately a limitless opportunity developed for exports of Japanese manufactures. War orders poured in, European competitors disappeared from Far Eastern markets, and the merchant marine inherited a large share of the world's carrying trade. Exports built up large foreign credit balances, which were used to sustain a rapid inflation of credit and prices at home. Japanese manufacturing thus embarked on a period of unprecedented prosperity (see Table 2). Factory production increased fourfold in value from 1914 to 1919, while the paid-up capital and reserves of all industrial companies jumped from 944 to 3,264 million yen.

Table 2[1]—GROWTH OF FACTORY INDUSTRY IN JAPAN PROPER, 1909–1938[2]

Year	Factories	Installed electric motors (horsepower in 1,000's)	Employees (1,000's)	Gross production (millions of current yen)
1909	32,390	—	1,102	781
1919	44,087	992	2,025	6,738
1929	60,275	2,600[3]	2,384	7,994
1938	113,205	6,290[4]	3,718	20,101

[1] Source: Ministry (Department) of Commerce and Industry, *Kōjō Tōkeihyō* and *Statistics of the Department of Commerce and Industry;* other official sources. [2] Includes private and public plants employing 5 or more operatives. Statistics of electric motors exclude electric and gas industries; gross production values exclude publicly owned plants. [3] Estimated. [4] 1937.

This war boom had two consequences for Japanese industry. The first was a rapid growth in capacity, diversity, and technical maturity. Factories doubled both their employment and their motive capacity from 1914 to 1919. New engineering and chemical industries grew to substantial proportions for the first time. The cotton industry increased its power looms from 55,000 to 110,000, as it expanded the volume and range of fabrics produced for foreign consumption. Steel production passed the 500,000-ton mark; coal consumption rose by 35 per cent.

In 1919 came the postwar financial crisis, with its ensuing fall in prices and stagnation of trade. Now the second and less fortunate aspect of war inflation began to show itself. Many industries and banks found themselves with inflated capital values which could not be supported with the return to more normal conditions. To make matters worse, the authorities attempted to maintain an artificial structure of prices and exchange rates by liberal credit policies and by the use of foreign balances accumulated abroad during the wartime boom. To these circumstances was added the shattering earthquake of 1923. Through most of the postwar decade Japanese industry struggled against deflationary pressures and financial disorders, which culminated in a serious bank crisis in 1927. As a result, this period saw the disappearance of many small banks and industrial firms unable to weather the strain. It brought a pronounced trend toward combination and cartelization, which strengthened the position of the *zaibatsu*, the great trusts which led the movement. The decade of the 1920's was also the high point of liberal, parliamentary government in prewar Japan. Social issues, including the long-neglected problems of industrial labor, came to the fore. Trade unions began for the first time to assert their power in industries where they could gain a foothold. The first significant reforms were undertaken in the field of factory legislation. (See also sections on *Labor Relations; Development of the Modern State.*)

Despite the financial difficulties plaguing many Japanese industries—perhaps because of them—this was also a period of marked technological advance. While agriculture had now virtually ceased to grow, the manufacturing trades moved steadily ahead. Raw silk and cotton goods were still the mainstay of the export trade, and they also provided the major share of industrial employment and income. Raw silk output reached 42,300,000 kilograms in 1929, or three times the 1914 level. Japan now stood second only to the United States and Great Britain as a consumer of raw cotton, with 6,500,000 spindles and a yarn output of 2,800,000 bales.

More significant for the future of Japan was the growth in range and maturity of other, newer industries. The production of electric power and cement, for example, tripled from 1919 to 1929. Steel output had advanced to 2,000,000 tons; coal production was running over 30,000,000 tons a year. Manufacturing output as a whole nearly doubled in the course of the decade (see Table 3). The more advanced types of machinery and equipment still had to be imported, but Japan could now meet her own needs in a wide range of electrical products, industrial machinery, and vehicles.

at the same time increasing the urbanization of the population. Yet in many ways industry remained closely linked with the countryside. It drew its low-wage labor from the nation's overcrowded farms, and its whole structure bore the stamp of the traditional modes of social organization still deeply rooted in rural Japan.

Industries like steel, shipbuilding, and paper developed as highly mechanized, large-scale establishments affiliated with big banks and trading houses. Here modern technology dictated the large plant. In addition, the absence of a broad middle class with capital to invest favored a concentration of control in the hands of great trusts like Mitsui, Mitsubishi, and Sumitomo. Elsewhere the shortage of industrial capital, the lack of advanced skills, and the localized or diversified character of markets encouraged the survival of more than 1,000,000 small plants. Many of these were rural trades offering byemployment to hard-pressed peasant families. Others crowded the growing industrial cities. In 1930 establishments of less than five workers still provided one third of Japan's total manufacturing output and accounted for over half of all persons chiefly engaged in manufacturing activity.

No country has exhibited wider contrasts between large capitalistic enterprise on the one hand, and myriads of tiny workshops still operating largely on the traditional handicraft pattern on the other. Nor has industrialism anywhere produced wider disparities between the immense fortunes piled up by big industrial magnates and the meager living of the masses of workers, small entrepreneurs, and farmers.

Trade, Armament, and Industrial Expansion, 1930–1940.—The great depression of 1929–1932 fell with crushing impact on Japan. The drop in farm prices spread bankruptcy through

Table 3[1]—PHYSICAL VOLUME OF OUTPUT IN MAJOR INDUSTRIES OF JAPAN PROPER, 1895–1938
(indices, 1910–1914 = 100)

Year	Manufacturing industries					Mining
	Total	Textiles	Metals and machinery	Chemicals and ceramics	Food products	
1895–99	37	41	25		80	28
1905–09	69	70	61	53	85	68
1915–19	160	152	162	186	123	138
1925–29	313	270	355	453	193	157
1935–38	582	466	950	835	189	227

[1] Source: For the years 1895–1930, indices prepared at Nagoya Commercial College and published in *Hompō Seisan Sūryō Shisū Sōran, 1894–1931* (Nagoya 1933). Here these indices are shifted from a 1919 to a 1910–14 base and projected roughly to 1935–38 by means of the indices of the *Oriental Economist.*

By 1930 Japan stood at a midpoint in her transition to an industrial economy. National income and wealth had increased manyfold, far outdistancing the growth of population. This had come about through the rapid accumulation of capital and technology, together with the steady redirection of labor and capital toward manufacturing and the services. Agriculture still provided the chief occupation of half of Japan's 29,600,000 workers. Farming and fishing, however, now contributed no more than 20 per cent of the national income, as compared with 35 per cent provided by industry and the balance by the service trades (transport, commerce, the professions, and others).

Japanese industry was thus moving toward a predominant place in the national economy and

the countryside, and the collapse of the United States silk market produced a crisis in the Japanese balance of payments. Deflationary pressures forced the depreciation of the yen in 1931, just as the Japanese Army struck in Manchuria. These two latter events set in motion a train of forces which were to dominate the ensuing decade and culminate in Japan's entrance into World War II.

The depreciation of the yen gave a sharp impetus to Japanese exports, especially exports of cotton and rayon textiles and other cheap consumer goods. Japan's total exports, which now consisted mostly of industrial products, increased tremendously, doubling in quantity from 1930 to 1936. In part, however, the gains from this trade boom were more specious than real, for the lowered value of the yen required that Japan ship a larger quantity of goods abroad to purchase a given amount of food, raw materials, or machinery. The volume of imports from foreign countries and colonies increased only 38 per cent. With the notable exception of silk, however, the export industries grew rapidly in capacity and output. They also improved greatly the range and variety of goods shipped abroad. (See also section on *Trade.*)

The second stimulus to industrial recovery after 1931 came from the policy of internal reflation pursued by Japan's skillful finance minister, Korekiyo Takahashi. Government spending chiefly took the form of rising expenditures for war, armament, and Manchurian development; it was facilitated by low interest rates and by heavy borrowing from financial institutions. From 1930 to 1936 national expenditures rose from 1,558 to 2,282 million yen, nearly doubling the national debt in the meantime.

Deficit financing thus reinforced the stimulus afforded by the export boom, and Japanese industry forged rapidly ahead. Mining output increased 30 per cent from 1930 to 1936; manufacturing output, 63 per cent. Wage rates recovered only slowly from depression levels because of the pressure on the labor market exerted by the stagnation of Japanese agriculture and the mechanization of many industries. Business profits reached boom levels, however, and provided huge sums for the expansion and re-equipment of Japan's major industries.

The progress of different sectors of Japanese industry was nevertheless uneven. The textile trades, as well as other industries producing consumer goods for foreign or domestic markets, made substantial gains in their scale of production, equipment, and organization. For example, the adoption of high-draft ring spinning and of automatic power looms in the cotton industry increased output per worker severalfold in the decade before 1936. Especially noteworthy was the sudden growth of the rayon industry, in which production jumped from 16,662 tons in 1930 to 125,420 tons in 1936. The woolen industry likewise won a substantial foothold in foreign markets.

It was chiefly the machinery, metallurgical, and chemical industries, however, which grew rapidly under the stimulus of armament spending and industrial construction in Japan and the overseas territories. While consumer goods production rose 33 per cent from 1930 to 1936, the output of producer goods jumped 83 per cent.

The metallurgical industries all expanded rapidly, in the process adopting new methods which raised output per worker by about 25 per cent. Steel ingot production increased from 2,300,000 tons in 1930 to 5,200,000 tons in 1936. In the machinery trades, whose output was valued at 1,609 million yen in the latter year, imports were now confined to advanced and specialized types. In fact, a flourishing export market was beginning to develop with the aid of capital investments in Manchuria and north China. Production of coal, cement, glass, and electricity reflected similar gains. The output of soda ash, caustic soda, dyestuffs, and other basic chemicals increased twofold and threefold, or even more. Throughout manufacturing there took place a general growth in the scale of industrial organization and also in the preponderance of the great firms and holding companies which had always dominated heavy industry.

The relative importance of factory industries (including all private plants of five or more workers) in 1936 is shown in Table 4. Metallurgy, machinery, and chemicals now accounted for 1,122,000 of Japan's 2,876,000 factory workers. They furnished as much as 2,202 million of the 3,633 million yen of net product (value added by manufacture).

While the armament business, government tariffs, and subsidies had contributed heavily to the large output and high prices which now characterized these industries, their new importance reflected a trend toward industrial diversification long evident in Japan. This trend doubtless represented the natural course of Japan's economic development, now reinforced by the stagnation of agriculture and by the increasing resistance to Japanese textile exports abroad. In the 1930's, however, it was greatly accelerated, and twisted toward the military ends of armament and empire building. As a result, Japan's industrial capacity and her capacity for waging war were enlarged. The flush of industrial prosperity, however, brought comparatively little gain in the Japanese standard of living. The consumption of civilian goods just about kept pace with the growth of population.

By 1937 Japan had reached virtual full employment. A brake had to be applied unless serious financial difficulties were to be invited. Military expansion, once begun, however, was not to be stopped. The outbreak of war in China was the signal for increased armament and military expenditure.

Table 4[1]—EMPLOYMENT AND NET PRODUCT IN PRIVATE FACTORY INDUSTRY OF JAPAN PROPER, 1936

Industries	Number of workers		Net product value	
	in 1,000's	Per cent	Million yen	Per cent
Textiles	1,089	37.8	521	14.3
Machinery, vehicles, etc.	525	18.3	822	22.6
Chemicals	318	11.1	911	25.1
Metals	279	9.7	469	12.9
Foodstuffs	192	6.7	247	6.8
Ceramics	113	3.9	201	5.5
Wood products	105	3.7	74	2.0
Printing and binding	70	2.4	86	2.4
Other	184	6.4	302	8.3
Total, all private factories	2,876	100.0	3,633	100.0

[1] Source: Basic data from Japan, Ministry of Commerce and Industry, *Kōjō Tōkeihyō*, 1936.

Immediately two difficulties began to appear. Continuing imports of war materials on a large scale weakened the yen. This led to the imposition of drastic exchange controls which seriously impaired the textile and other civilian industries requiring materials from abroad. In the domestic field as well, the acceleration of war preparations began to cut into the requirements of the civilian economy. The government was thus forced to spread a network of controls over investment, the allocation of materials, wages, and prices. By 1940, Japan was already devoting 17 per cent of her gross national product to war purposes. When the Japanese Navy struck at Pearl Harbor, the groundwork had been laid for full-scale industrial mobilization.

Japanese Industry at War, 1941–1945.—Japan entered World War II with an impressive record of industrial preparation. During the previous decade she had created virtually from nothing her aircraft, motor vehicle, tank, aluminum, and machine tool industries. By 1941 she was producing annually 5,000 aircraft, 48,000 motor vehicles, and nearly 500,000 tons of steel shipping. Steel ingot production was running at 6,800,000 tons; coal at 55,600,000 tons. Electric generating capacity had doubled since 1931. Immense stockpiles of equipment and raw materials, including a two-year reserve of oil, had been accumulated. Feeding the home industries of the Japanese islands were the controlled resources of Manchuria and north China. These were now developed to the point where they furnished a major part of Japan's requirements of iron, coking coal, salt, and certain other minerals.

With all these gains Japan still possessed hardly 10 per cent of the industrial potential of the United States. Moreover, she remained basically dependent on overseas supplies of oil, rubber, iron, bauxite, tin, and other strategic metals. The decision to strike at Pearl Harbor was therefore a desperate gamble on a war of limited liabilities. By seizing the rich regions of Southeast Asia and by establishing a defensive perimeter, Japan's military leaders hoped to win the resources with which to hold out until war weariness in the United States or a favorable turn in the international situation should enable her to retain significant gains.

This Japanese war plan may explain the lack of decisive measures to increase industrial capacity and production during the first year of hostilities. Not until the military reverses of late 1942 was industrial mobilization placed in high gear. Emergency controls were tightened under a Munitions Ministry established in 1943. Key industries—aircraft, shipping, coal, and metals—were singled out for concentrated effort. Direct outlays on war and munitions, which stood at only 31 per cent of the gross national product in 1942, were raised to 52 per cent in 1944. Some 9,500,000 persons were now engaged in factory industry and construction. This was 30 per cent of the nation's entire civilian labor force.

In the technical realm the war effort at its peak was impressive, especially in view of Japan's late entry into the industrial field. In 1944 aircraft production was raised to 26,364 planes, and over 2,000,000 tons of warships and steel merchant vessels were launched. Steel capacity was enlarged to 14,000,000 tons. Japanese fighter planes and other equipment proved the equal of those of any other country in many aspects of design and performance.

As early as 1943, however, the inherent weaknesses of Japan's industrial war effort were becoming evident. Its scale was necessarily limited by the meager Japanese standard of living, which could not be sharply reduced without impairing civilian efficiency and morale. Yet consumer expenditures in 1944 dropped 30 per cent from the 1940 level. Meanwhile, the lack of a large reserve of skilled workers created acute bottlenecks in essential industries. Overhead direction of industrial mobilization was crippled throughout the war by diffusion of responsibility. Sharp conflicts prevailed among separate ministries and between the government and business interests. Most importantly, Japan's basic vulnerability to sea blockade began to manifest itself in 1943, as Allied attacks on Japanese shipping began to cut off the inflow of strategic materials.

Peak production of finished military products was not reached until late in 1944. Already, however, the basic industries had begun to decline. Supplies of oil, aluminum, iron, and coal dwindled as submarine and air blockade progressively closed off the southern regions, and then even north China and Manchuria. Both imports and stocks of crude oil were virtually eliminated by the last quarter of 1944. Finished steel production had dropped 50 per cent. In short, Japan's war economy was crumbling at its foundations.

In the spring of 1945 came devastating air attacks on the home islands. These destroyed 40 per cent of the area of 66 cities, making 30 per cent of the urban population homeless. By July 1945, industrial output had declined to 40 per cent of the 1944 peak, and the Japanese will to continue resistance was broken. The atomic bomb and the Soviet Union's entry into the war were the *coups de grâce* which brought surrender.

Postwar Industrial Recovery and Reform.—With the war ended, Japan faced formidable tasks of industrial reconstruction. Great industrial areas lay in ruins. Foreign trade was at a standstill. The colonies were gone. The merchant marine lay at the bottom of the ocean.

Still more serious was the cumulative effect of Japan's war effort in dislocating the structure of peacetime industry and trade. The defeated nation now found itself with a surplus of idle war plants. But its cotton textile industry—to cite one civilian industry—was reduced to 2,150,000 spindles. The remaining 10,000,000 spindles of its 1937 plant had been scrapped, damaged, or converted to war uses. Raw materials and food were urgently needed from abroad. Yet Japan had nothing with which to pay for them. To add to the demoralization, the country's finances were in a chaotic state. As a result of deficit spending by the government and other inflationary stimuli, wholesale prices rose tenfold during 1946 and 1947. Especially acute was the shortage of food in the cities. Operating at only 31 per cent of its 1934–1936 level in 1946, Japanese industry faced a painful uphill struggle (see Table 5).

The Allied authorities, during the first two years of the occupation, were more concerned with Japan's disarmament and democratic reform than with industrial recovery. An interim reparations program was drawn up and approved by the Far Eastern Commission in 1946. It called for the removal from Japan of industrial plant capacity in excess of the nation's peacetime needs,

Table 5 [1]—INDUSTRIAL PRODUCTION IN JAPAN, 1944–1952
(1934–1936 = 100)

Year	Total	Manufacturing		Mining
		Durable	Nondurable	
1944.........	179	320	51	139
1946.........	31	37	22	52
1948.........	59	79	36	83
1950.........	94	119	69	102
1952.........	136	174	103	120

[1] Source: Economic Counsel Board, *Japanese Economic Statistics*, July-August 1953.

and its distribution among the Allies as compensation for war damage. Meanwhile, two principal steps were taken by the supreme commander for the Allied powers to democratize the control and operation of Japanese industry: the government was directed to legalize and encourage trade unions and collective bargaining (see section on *Labor Relations*), and a determined attack was launched on the monopolistic structures of the great *zaibatsu* combines. This latter undertaking was to achieve only limited results, owing to its inherent complexity and the lack of positive support in Japan. The leading *zaibatsu* families were largely shorn of their wealth and power; many nuclear companies at the center of the combines were dissolved or deconcentrated; and lateral ties among the remainder were weakened by the temporary purge of business executives and by restrictions on intercorporate shareholdings and interlocking management. By 1951, however, new business blocs were beginning to re-form around the big banks. An antimonopoly law, patterned on United States antitrust laws and forced through the Diet in 1947, was emasculated by amendments in 1949 and 1953.

Industrial recovery proceeded only slowly through the early occupation years. Except for emergency imports of food and essential materials, the Allied authorities placed responsibility for economic rehabilitation mainly on the Japanese government. But successive Cabinets proved themselves weak and dilatory in acting to restore the economy to solvency. By 1948 exports were still hardly 10 per cent of their prewar volume. Now the argument for more decisive stabilization measures was reinforced by growing international tension in the Far East, which highlighted Japan's weakness. Accordingly, the United States government took the lead in re-examining the reparations issue, and removals of industrial equipment for this purpose were discontinued in 1949, before they had gone beyond the token stage. At the same time, the Japanese government was required to balance its budget, and to tighten controls over prices, credit, and wages. With inflation stopped, the economy quickly began to show greater strength and stability. The outbreak of the Korean War in June 1950 gave a new stimulus to industrial production. Again, however, powerful inflationary pressures were revived, and soon created fresh difficulties in the export field.

By 1953 Japanese industry was producing 50 per cent more than in 1934–1936. On the surface this was an impressive gain. Yet the prospect was clouded by one grave weakness—the lagging recovery of exports. Industrial revival (see Table 5) had been built on a level of imports which far outran exports and were financed only by huge expenditures of United States government funds in Japan (see section on *Trade*). Some of Japan's export difficulties lay abroad beyond her control. But her export industries were also handicapped at home by ineffectual controls over inflation, which raised costs and diverted resources to other uses. Although capital investment was at high levels, too little was going into the replacement of inefficient, obsolete equipment in export trades whose competitive strength in world markets was still weak.

As the postwar decade drew to a close, it appeared that Japan had yet to resolve the basic issue of how she was to prosper in the changed postwar world. With her population approaching 90 million, she depended more than ever on her industrial economy. A people of such enterprise and skills might be expected to resume the search for economic opportunity through building on a still larger scale one of the great workshops of the world. How well they would succeed depended on whether they could gain ever wider access to overseas materials and markets.

Bibliography.—Schumpeter, E. B., ed., *The Industrialization of Japan and Manchukuo, 1930–1940* (New York 1940); Allen, G. C. *A Short Economic History of Modern Japan, 1867–1937* (London 1946); U.S. Strategic Bombing Survey, *The Effects of Strategic Bombing on Japan's War Economy* (Washington 1946); Cohen, J. B., *Japan's Economy in War and Reconstruction* (Minneapolis 1949); Japan, Prime Minister's Office, Statistics Bureau, *Japan Statistical Year Book* (Tokyo 1949–); Bisson, T. A., *Zaibatsu Dissolution in Japan* (Berkeley, Calif., 1954); Borton, Hugh, Elisséeff, Serge, Lockwood, W. W., and Pelzel, J. C., *A Selected List of Books and Articles on Japan in English, French and German*, rev. and enl. ed. (Cambridge,, Mass., 1954); Lockwood, W. W., *The Economic Development of Japan* (Princeton 1954).

WILLIAM W. LOCKWOOD,
Assistant Director, Woodrow Wilson School of Public and International Affairs, Princeton University.

7. TRADE. This section treats the trade of Japan as it developed in (1) the domestic market, (2) the foreign market before World War II, and (3) in war and defeat.

Growth of the Japanese Market.—Japan's economic development in modern times illustrates Adam Smith's famous dictum that division of labor, the key to industrialization, is limited by the extent of the market.

During the Tokugawa shogunate (1603–1867), Japan's once flourishing maritime trade in the China seas was interdicted by the country's military dictatorship. For more than 200 years the nation was walled off from all but the most meager contacts with the outside world. In 1637 the authorities decreed that no Japanese might leave the country and return on pain of death. Seclusion was reinforced by a ban on the building of any ship with a capacity of more than 50 tons.

Internal commerce was also cramped and confined by political regulations, lack of transport, and the general self-sufficiency of preindustrial, peasant life. As late as 1868 there were virtually no highways in Japan worthy of the name. Nor were there even many wheeled vehicles of any description. The cost of transporting rice by land doubled its price in 10 to 20 miles or less. Bulk cargoes went chiefly by sea, but the 600-mile passage by junk from Tokyo to Kyushu was a hazardous one consuming a month or more. Trade was further limited by many toll barriers and by various restrictions on occupation, residence, dress, and the like.

In the latter half of the Tokugawa period

there appeared, it is true, a quickening of commercial activity and a rise of specialized handicraft production for local or interregional exchange. This growth of merchant capitalism, indeed, had much to do with the decay of the old semifeudal regime and its overthrow in the 19th century. Only with the reorganization of political power and the abolition of multifarious restraints on trade could the new forces of capitalism and nationalism find full expression.

The Meiji Restoration in 1868 ushered in a period of intensive modernization under the new national government. The remnants of feudal political organization with its semiautonomous territorial clans were abolished in favor of a centralized nation-state. The country was thrown open to a flood of Western influences. Within Japan the new government proceeded to establish a national system of taxation, banking, and currency; the beginnings of universal, primary education; a modern code of commercial law; new warehouses and commodity exchanges facilitating trade; a national network of posts and telegraphs; and, not least in importance, an expanding system of railways, shipping, and trunk highways.

One contribution of the state to economic modernization was its early encouragement of foreign trade, especially imports of machinery and equipment. Its most signal contribution, however, was to create and maintain a framework for a unified national market through such measures as those indicated above. Together these developments afforded the basis for a rapid expansion of Japan's productive power in subsequent decades and for a corresponding growth of commerce.

This structural framework for national economic development was not, of course, built overnight. By the turn of the century, however, the foundations had been laid. Between 1897 and 1927 railway freight traffic rose from 8,600,000 to 101,000,000 tons; shipping cargoes entered and cleared in coastwise trade reached 93,000,000 tons; and the number of animal-drawn carts licensed to haul goods multiplied fourfold. The index of the physical volume of imports from foreign countries (1913=100) meanwhile advanced from 45 to 200; the export index, from 32 to 175. These figures point to a tremendous increase in the exchange of goods and services produced for the market.

The expansion of Japanese commercial activity had two aspects. First, it reflected, and made possible, a steady growth in per capita production of agricultural and industrial products and services. This resulted from the introduction of capitalistic forms of production, especially in nonagricultural pursuits. Substantial gains in output per worker came about through the application of science, machinery, and modern business forms. At the same time population increased rapidly, rising from 38,000,000 to 69,000,000 between 1885 and 1935.

To what extent population growth actually expanded the national market is conjectural. It enlarged the demand for basic necessities like rice and cotton clothing, but it also restricted the market for other imported and domestic manufactures by limiting the advance of per capita output and levels of living. By any Western standard the Japanese internal market remained strikingly poor, mainly because of the severe pressure of population, accentuated by large expenditures on armament, colonies, and strategic industries. Nevertheless, from available evidence it would appear that Japan's total national income and production at least quadrupled from 1885 to 1935.

In the second place, as an essential condition of this economic growth, production was increasingly commercialized for sale in the market. The old localized household and village economy of traditional Japan lingered on, especially in the more remote countryside. More and more, however, it gave way to a complex specialization of occupations, of regions, and of production processes, all tied together in expanding circuits of exchange. Some of these circuits represented primarily the exchange of goods and services in the domestic market; others involved wholly or in part the import of materials and equipment from abroad, paid for through exports.

The result was a pervasive spread of a money economy. The population of Japan's swarming cities naturally supplied most of their requirements through purchasing goods and services on the market. And by 1935 one in every three Japanese lived in a city of 30,000 or more. Even the Japanese farmer had come by this time to provide for two thirds of his family consumption of goods by purchasing them with cash income. The creation of capital goods, now a significant share of the national product, also meant production for the market, except as the farmer, the petty merchant, or the industrialist used his own labor to improve his land, buildings, and tools.

Both the specialization and expansion of production, then—two interlocking processes—steadily enlarged the sphere of market organization and the volume of exchange transactions in modern Japan.

While this widening of markets is commonly recognized as a necessary feature of Japanese industrialization during the past century, it is often thought of primarily in terms of overseas trade. Attention is centered on the rapid growth of the foreign market for Japan's major industries, with the implication that the home market failed to develop *pari passu*—indeed, was of little significance in industrialization. This is a gross misinterpretation of the historical facts, which fails entirely to account for the substance and momentum of Japan's economic modernization.

It is true that foreign trade has played a peculiarly important role in Japanese development since 1868. No country has been more suddenly transformed through contact with the outside world, or has built up a large complex of industry more dependent on those contacts. The nature of this dependence and its extent are examined below.

Before turning to foreign trade, however, it is important to place it in its proper perspective in Japanese economic life. Throughout the modern period the commerce of Japan has been predominantly the exchange of goods and services *within* the country. The home market has far outweighed the foreign market.

Except for shipping and certain financial operations, this is necessarily true of most services produced in any economy—the movement of goods and people and various private and public professional services, which are by nature nonexportable. Together they accounted in Japan for 20 to 30 per cent of all gainful employment and 50 per cent or more of all income produced between World Wars I and II. The production of farm commodities, which probably doubled in the half century ending in 1935, was likewise geared almost wholly to the domestic market, with the conspicuous exception of sericulture. Certain sectors of Japanese industry were heavily oriented toward foreign trade; others, not at all. Japanese manufacturing as a whole (eliminating double counting of items) disposed of no less than 65 to 75 per cent of its product at home toward the end of this period.

The relative magnitude of Japan's foreign and domestic market is best expressed for the entire economy by the ratio between (1) the value of merchandise exports to foreign countries and colonies and (2) the total value of all goods and services produced in Japan. Throughout most of the period 1914–1938 this ratio averaged about 20 per cent. The relationship fluctuated from year to year; in 1930, for example, total exports (including those to Korea and Formosa) came to 1,828 million yen, while the national product was valued at about 10 billion yen. Over the 25-year period, however, both series appear to have maintained a fairly consistent ratio of 1:5. Nor would the inclusion of certain exported services materially alter the conclusion. Evidently the prewar Japanese economy as a whole expanded more or less in proportion to the growth of foreign trade after 1914.

Thus the spectacular rise of foreign trade described below should not be allowed to obscure the fact that it was part of a more general process of expansion characterizing all parts of the Japanese economy in varying degrees. Indeed, foreign trade could not have increased so rapidly without a concurrent growth of domestic production and purchasing power. Some imports were purchased every year to supply such export industries as cotton goods with raw materials and equipment. In effect they were re-exported. But the bulk of the imports of food, raw materials, and manufactures went into home consumption. In 1936, for example, total imports from foreign countries, Korea, and Formosa were valued at 3,599 million yen. Offsetting these imports were exports of similar types, or imported materials embodied in export manufactures, amounting to about 1,100 million yen. The balance of imports, 70 per cent of the total, may be said to have been retained (net) for domestic use.

Foreign Trade of Prewar Japan.—While the growth of Japan's foreign commerce after 1868 was only one phase of her general development, it played a peculiarly strategic role. In a real sense, the whole increase of Japanese national income and wealth in modern times was founded upon expanding contacts with the outside world. Equally, the extension of her political empire in Asia (and its collapse in World War II) was closely associated with the growth of foreign trade, the ambitions which it fostered, and the dependence which it created.

During the early decades of the Meiji period (1868–1912), Japan's foreign commerce was significant chiefly as a newly opened highway of communication over which all sorts of new stimuli and new knowledge flowed from the West into the once isolated country. Foreign trade and foreign traders brought in industrial machinery and equipment, ships and munitions, and Western textiles and other consumer goods, as well as new techniques of industrial and financial organization. Through this channel, as well as through foreign travel and study, the Japanese began to import and to assimilate the industrial arts which were to revolutionize a large part of their traditional economic life in the next 75 years.

Soon the second potentiality of foreign trade for Japan commenced to assume growing proportions. Most of the basic natural resources necessary for modern industry were lacking in Japan—notably, iron ore, coking coal, petroleum, and other essential minerals. In addition, as her population grew, her agriculture was increasingly unable to provide food, cotton, and other agricultural raw materials to sustain her growing industries. With the steady progress of industrialization, Japan soon reached a degree of national dependence on overseas materials that was exceeded by few nations. By 1930 net imports (imports minus exports) from foreign countries, Korea, and Formosa furnished the following percentages of Japanese consumption: cereals, beans, potatoes (grain equivalent), 13 per cent; fats and oils, 41 per cent; nitrogen fertilizer materials, 20 per cent; hides and skins, 75 per cent; petroleum products, 79 per cent; iron and steel (iron content), 85 per cent; lead, zinc, tin, and aluminum, 70-100 per cent; cotton, wool, rayon pulp, and rubber, 100 per cent. With a few exceptions like raw cotton, these imports did not so much replace as supplement the growing output of Japan's own farms, forests, and mines.

Table 1 summarizes the growth and changing character of Japan's international trade (excluding trade with her colonies) over three decades. Several broad characteristics may be noted.

Imports and exports, valued at only 11 and 16 million yen, respectively, in 1868, both passed the 100-million yen mark on the eve of the Sino-Japanese War (1894–1895). During the next 20 years they increased threefold and fourfold. World War I brought further gains, which were carried over through the postwar decade. (See also section on *Industrial Development*.)

A fresh impetus was given by the depreciation of the yen in 1931. In the ensuing trade boom, between 1930 and 1936, exports advanced from 1,470 to 2,693 million yen; imports, from 1,546 to 2,764 million yen. Import prices rose more rapidly than export prices, so that the terms of exchange moved against Japan. By 1936, however, Japan was importing more than twice as much as in 1913 and exporting three to four times as much. Except in the years 1915–1918, imports exceeded exports in value throughout this period. The trade deficit was offset by net earnings on shipping and foreign investments, by capital and gold movements, and by other invisible items in the balance of payments.

The figures in Table 1 refer only to trade with foreign countries. In addition, Japan built up a large source of food supplies in Korea and Formosa, paying for them with manufactures sold in these protected empire markets. If this colonial exchange is included, total Japanese imports from overseas amounted to 3,599 million yen in 1936, and exports to 3,508 million yen.

The changing composition of Japan's exports over these decades reflected the world economy of the times and the growing capabilities of her industries. For 50 years raw silk (classified as a semimanufacture in Table 1) held the lead. Japanese silk early won a preponderant place in

Table 1[1]—FOREIGN TRADE OF JAPAN PROPER, 1893–1936

Total Trade	Exports			Imports		
	1893	1913	1936	1893	1913	1936
Value in yen (millions)	90	632	2,693	88	729	2,764
Index of physical quantity (1913 = 100)	21	100	356	24	100	226
Distribution by Classes[2]			Percentages			
Food and tobacco	20	10	8	23	17	8
Raw materials	10	8	5	22	48	63
Semimanufactures	41	52	27	20	17	17
Manufactures	25	29	58	33	17	11
Distribution by Regions; Exports to and imports from:						
North and South America	34	30	27	7	17	38
United States	31	29	22	7	17	31
Asia	30	43	51	42	48	38
China[3]	26	30	27	30	13	14
Europe	32	23	11	47	30	12
United Kingdom	6	5	5	32	17	3
Other Regions	3	3	11	4	5	12

[1] Source: Basic data from Japan, Department of Finance, *Annual Returns of the Foreign Trade of Japan.*
[2] Omitting "miscellaneous."
[3] Including Hong Kong, Kwantung Leased Territory, and (in 1936) Manchukuo.

the great American silk market. From 1920 to 1930 this single item furnished 36 per cent of Japan's total export trade. Its contribution toward payment of foreign products consumed in Japan was even more important than this figure would indicate, for, unlike cotton goods exports, no part of the proceeds of silk sales had to be used to recover the cost of imported materials used in the export industry.

When silk prices collapsed in 1930–1931 the yen fell drastically in value—from \$.49 in U.S. currency in 1930 to \$.28 in 1932. This gave a sharp stimulus to exports of cotton textiles, which had been expanding steadily since 1900 in Far Eastern markets. Aided by technical improvements, and by currency depreciation unmatched by corresponding increases in wages and other costs, Japanese cotton goods and other cheap manufactures spread rapidly through world markets. By 1936 Japan had become the world's premier exporter of cotton piece goods, with shipments of 2,710,000,000 square yards valued at 473 million yen. Other leading exports were as follows (in millions of yen); raw silk, 393; rayon piece goods, 149; machinery, 139; pottery and glass, 74; canned foodstuffs, 71; and a wide variety of other textiles, toys, chemicals, metal wares, and wood products.

Industrialization brought equally striking changes in Japan's import trade. During the early decades her purchases abroad were distributed over a wide range of foodstuffs, industrial materials, machinery, and other Western manufactures. Increasingly, however, as Japanese industry gained in capacity and maturity, it ousted foreign manufactures from the domestic market. Imports of consumer manufactures were restricted by high Japanese tariffs: machinery imports became confined more and more to advanced and specialized types still purchased more cheaply in the West. By 1913 cotton, metals, and other raw materials already constituted one half of Japan's total imports (see Table 1). Thereafter the principal growth took place in imports of these industrial materials, together with rice, sugar, and other foodstuffs secured from colonies and foreign countries. In 1936, at the peak of Japan's prewar trade boom, her chief purchases from foreign countries were as follows (in millions of yen): raw cotton, 850; iron and steel, 231; wool, 201; petroleum products, 183; machinery, automotive vehicles, and instruments, 156; fertilizer materials, 145; nonferrous metals, 141; wood and wood products, 122; and rubber, 73.

These changes in the composition of Japanese foreign trade resulted in corresponding shifts in its distribution among the principal regions of the world, as shown in Table 1. Throughout the prewar period this trade preserved a dual character. On the one hand, Japan sold to the West (mainly to the United States) one major industrial material, raw silk, together with a variety of simple manufactures like pottery and toys. The latter, however, were heavily restricted by high tariffs which tended to rise as Japanese competition became more severe. In Asiatic markets, meanwhile, Japan came to occupy increasingly the typical position of the industrial supplier, selling cheap cotton and rayon goods, metal wares, and other manufactures in exchange for rice, beans, coal, oil, rubber, and numerous other raw materials. By 1936 half of her exports to foreign countries were being marketed in Asia—as much as 63 per cent, if exports to Korea and Formosa are included.

Nevertheless, Japan remained heavily dependent upon the West for some of her most vital imports and for markets where she could earn the foreign exchange to pay for them. Here she continued to purchase essential machinery and vehicles, as well as large amounts of cotton, wool, oil, steel, and other basic materials. The United States, in particular, still played a major role in Japanese trade, taking more than one fifth of her exports and supplying nearly one third of her imports. Japan's trade and armament boom from 1931 to 1936 so swelled her purchases of American materials and equipment that by 1936 she was absorbing half of all United States exports to Asia—more than were sold in all of Latin America.

Japan's Trade in War and Defeat.—From the foregoing survey it is apparent that foreign trade played an indispensable role in Japan's rise as an industrial power. No country derived greater benefit from the fortunate circumstance that the world economy of 1880–1935 was an expanding economy organized on a fairly free and competitive basis. Especially important for Japan was the system of multilateral trading relations in which a nation could buy and sell according to its economic advantage, settling its credits in one region against its debits in another.

The spread of trade and exchange restrictions in the 1930's, and especially the sharp increase in tariffs and quotas directed specifically against Japanese goods, was an ominous portent of the future. In part, however, Japan could only blame herself if a sudden, sharp influx of her cheap manufactures into the national or colonial markets of industrial nations struggling with depression provoked defensive measures. In any case, these measures failed to prevent a great expansion of Japanese trade, which contrasted favorably with the relative stagnation of economic activity elsewhere.

Japan thus had a special stake in preserving a free world economy. As she became a great trading power, however, she was exposed to the insecurities of this world economy, with its booms, depressions, and currency disorders. More important in the eyes of her military leaders, she found herself heavily dependent on markets and materials controlled by the other great powers, particularly the United States and the British Commonwealth. This was unacceptable to the militarists. Their dreams of Japanese hegemony in the Western Pacific required for their fulfillment the creation of a great east Asian bloc securely under Japan's domination and capable of satisfying her economic requirements, at least insofar as the sinews of war were concerned. With the seizure of Manchuria in 1931, national policy was directed increasingly toward the realization of this aim.

From 1931 to 1936 Japan found it possible to expand her armaments and extend her conquest of China while simultaneously enjoying a boom in foreign trade throughout the world. The latter fed the former, as evidenced in the huge import of war materials from the United States. After 1936, however, Japanese resources were fully employed (see section on *Industrial Development*). Continued deficit financing of war industry and colonial development brought rising inflation and progressive dislocation of civilian production and trade. Total imports and exports continued at a high level from 1936 to 1939. The trade with occupied China, Formosa, and Korea even registered large increases. But trade with countries outside this yen bloc began to dwindle in the face of growing exchange difficulties. Imports were diverted sharply to oil, steel, and other strategic materials, in which the yen bloc remained seriously deficient. By 1940 food purchases from all overseas sources had fallen by one quarter, and shipments of raw cotton and wool by one half. The crisis came the following year, when the United States, Great Britain, and the Netherlands, aroused by Japan's aggressive military actions, at last embargoed all trade with her, pending a political settlement.

In World War I, Japan remained a neutral in all but name, reaping large profits from the trading opportunities it afforded. In World War II she cast the die in favor of a desperate bid for empire in east Asia. The result in the end was to destroy the whole structure of foreign trade upon which she had built her economic life, and to leave her a defeated and impoverished nation surrounded by neighbors similarly impoverished by her gamble.

Japan's war economy possessed hardly 10 per cent of the potential of her principal antagonist, the United States. And it was fatally dependent on overseas shipments of critical war materials.

Manchuria and north China had been developed to supply an important part of the Japanese deficit in coking coal, iron, salt, and foodstuffs. But oil, bauxite, rubber, manganese, chrome, nickel, and a dozen other strategic items had still to be brought in from the distant southern regions now overrun by the Japanese armies. Almost immediately these exposed sea lanes to the south came under attack from Allied submarines and aircraft. As the attack gathered weight and momentum through 1942 and 1943, the Japanese merchant fleet began to suffer relentless attrition.

As early as 1943 the peak output of basic materials in Japan was passed, and thereafter production and stocks steadily dwindled. By the second half of 1944, imports of four essentials had declined to the following percentages of 1943 shipments: coking coal, 35 per cent; iron ore, 28 per cent; bauxite, 17 per cent; crude oil, 9 per cent. Imports of rice, sugar, and textile fibers also approached the vanishing point. Half of all military supplies shipped from Japan to armies in the field were lost at sea during 1945. By the end of the war only 1,400,000 gross tons remained of the 6,000,000 tons of steel ships of 100 gross tons and over with which Japan had entered the war, despite the construction of 4,100,000 tons in the meantime. The United States Strategic Bombing Survey concluded that by August 1945 the interdiction of overseas materials alone would have reduced war production in Japan to 50 or 60 per cent of the 1944 level, even without air attack directly on the home islands. The latter largely destroyed Japan's war economy twice over and finally demoralized the nation to the point of surrender.

The early postwar years witnessed the slow and painful rehabilitation of the Japanese economy (see section on *Industrial Development*). The Allied occupation authorities faced the immediate necessity of importing large quantities of food to meet the critical shortage in the cities, as well as raw materials to restock the empty pipelines of industry. Beyond this it was evident that no long-term reconstruction of a politically stable and economically viable Japan could take place without restoring her access to world markets and supplies. Yet her ability to pay for imports was virtually nonexistent as the occupation began. Her export industries were greatly impaired in capacity and efficiency. Her sheltered colonial market had disappeared. And elsewhere her structure of prewar trading relationships lay in ruins.

The revival of Japanese industry was closely correlated with the revival of the import trade which furnished its principal materials. By 1948 imports still totaled only 18 per cent of their 1934–1936 volume. Thereafter they rose year by year, reaching 48 per cent in 1951 and about 75 per cent in 1953. Half of their total value in 1953 was divided about equally between textile fibers (mainly cotton) and foodstuffs. The remainder consisted of machinery, fertilizers, coal, oil, and other industrial materials. The United States and Asia each supplied about one third of the total.

The crucial weakness of Japan's postwar recovery was the fact that even at this reduced level of imports she was living well beyond her means. United States government funds paid for 62 per cent of Japanese imports from September 1945 to June 1950. Some $1,800 million was devoted to the purpose. Thereafter such aid was rapidly tapered off, and it ended in 1952. This was possible, without economic collapse, only because the Korean War brought a stream of dollars to Japan in the form of procurement contracts and troop spending. Meanwhile, commercial exports continued to lag far behind imports. While they rose steeply in 1949 and 1950, they were still only 35 per cent of their 1934–1936 volume in 1953. In that year they amounted to only $1,275 million, as against imports of $2,410 million. This huge gap was largely covered by $809 million of United States offshore procurement payments and troop spending in Japan. Even then the remaining deficit reduced foreign exchange reserves to dangerously low levels.

These subsidies and windfall gains could not be expected to continue. The Japanese thus faced the necessity in 1954 of finding new export outlets on a large scale or of drastically reducing their standard of living. The silk trade, so long the mainstay of the economy, had now almost disappeared. Although Japan led the world in cotton goods exports in 1953, her shipments ran to only 914,000,000 square yards, as compared with 2,710,000,000 square yards in 1936. Exports to Asia nearly balanced imports and, as in 1936, comprised half the total. In volume, however, they were much reduced, especially because of the decline in sales to Korea and Formosa, and the virtual disappearance of the mainland China trade. The general imbalance in the commodity accounts was especially acute in trade with the United States and other dollar areas. Here receipts fell short of payments by $538 million in 1953.

Japan's unsolved trade problem was twofold. In the sharpening competition for world markets she could hardly hope to meet her needs unless she cut her nonessential imports to the bone, curbed inflationary tendencies at home, and increased the efficiency of her export industries. Even this would be inadequate, however, unless progress could be made in stabilizing the Far East and in restoring a freer structure of world trade. Though loyally abiding by the United Nations embargo on shipping strategic materials to Communist China, many Japanese felt that their future was hopeless without access to Chinese markets and raw materials. Moreover, the opportunities required by Japan if she was again to prosper depended on the reconstruction of an international economy based on a durable peace.

Bibliography.—Oriental Economist, *The Foreign Trade of Japan: A Statistical Survey* (Tokyo 1935); U.S. Department of State, *The Place of Foreign Trade in the Japanese Economy* (Washington 1946); Cohen, J. B., *Economic Problems of Free Japan* (Princeton 1952); titles listed in bibliography of section on *Industrial Development.*

WILLIAM W. LOCKWOOD,
Assistant Director, Woodrow Wilson School of Public and International Affairs, Princeton University.

8. LABOR RELATIONS. Although the Japanese labor movement dates back to the 19th century, it did not become a strong force in Japanese society until after Japan's surrender to the Allied powers in 1945. The postwar labor movement was nevertheless conditioned by its past.

During the late 19th and early 20th centuries Japan was rapidly industrialized under the aegis of a government modern in form but still largely feudal in spirit. In this process a large industrial proletariat was created. By 1930, 36 per cent of the gainfully occupied population was engaged in commerce and industry as against 51 per cent in agriculture and fisheries. Before World War II, however, the industrial working class, despite its large numbers, played on the whole a passive role in the economic, social, and political life of the nation.

There were several reasons for this situation, one basic reason being economic. Owing to the rapid increase in population and the limited supply of arable land, Japanese industry, despite its steady expansion, was never able to absorb all the surplus labor of the countryside. Since the supply of labor always exceeded the demand, labor's economic bargaining power was weak. This condition, which is paralleled in other Asiatic countries and which still exists, helps to explain why Japanese labor has sought to improve its status through political as well as through economic action. The structure of Japanese industry also militated against successful efforts at labor organization. A few huge, semimonopolistic family concerns (the *zaibatsu*) dominated industry and trade, while at the other end of the scale were thousands of tiny workshops employing less than five workers; medium-sized enterprises were relatively few in number. Hence labor unions found that most employing establishments were either too big to challenge with success, or too small to organize effectively. Wages remained low, and although the 20th century saw a gradual increase in real wages and in workers' living standards, this was not commensurate with the increase in national income.

Another reason for labor's passivity was social. Habits of thought and action derived from the feudal period, when carried over into modern industry, resulted in a high degree of paternalism. According to prevailing concepts, the proper relationship between employer and employee was one of mutual loyalty resembling the relationship between a feudal lord and his faithful retainers. The employee was expected to obey his employer dutifully and to accept his guidance not only on the job, but also in moral and political affairs; in return, the employer accepted an obligation to provide for the welfare of his employees. While this ideal pattern was not always realized in practice, it did something to mitigate the social evils which usually accompany the growth of industrialism. It also discouraged individual initiative on the part of employees and the formation of group loyalties conflicting with the older concept of loyalty to persons. The strongly entrenched family system played a similar role as a focus for loyalties which in a more individualistic society might have attached themselves to trade unions or to the working class as a whole, and as a cushion against the evils of industrialism. A man who lost his job, or who could not live on his earnings in the city, could usually return to his native village and eke out a living with the aid of his relatives. Thus for many workers the family system provided a refuge which, however unsatisfactory, was safer and surer than the problematical gains of organizing to better their condition.

The principal obstacle to the growth of labor organization, however, was the attitude of the government, a narrowly based oligarchy essentially authoritarian in character. Aiming at national greatness rather than at national welfare, Japan's rulers sought to indoctrinate the masses with unquestioning loyalty to the state and sternly discouraged all movements of a popular or democratic nature. Trade unions were regarded as suspicious, if not subversive, and attempts to organize a union were made punishable by imprisonment under a law enacted in 1900. While this law was not always strictly enforced in later years, other laws, notably the Peace Preservation Law of 1925, rigidly circumscribed labor's activities and conferred broad powers on the police. Trade unions were kept under close surveillance; many strikes were broken by police action, unions were dissolved, and labor leaders were imprisoned. During the 1920's some attempts were made to set up impartial machinery for adjusting labor disputes, but they were not very successful and jurisdiction over labor affairs remained largely in the hands of the police.

This state of affairs led many labor leaders to conclude that improvement of the condition of labor required political action. Some thought in terms of democratic reforms which would make it possible to mobilize the voting strength of the masses by constitutional means. Others, who believed that a regime founded on force could be moved only by force, advocated direct action for revolutionary goals. Still others felt that labor could gain most by accepting the existing regime and cooperating with the authorities. Western social philosophies, such as social democracy, syndicalism, and communism, as well as the official doctrines of nationalism and the "way of the emperor," competed for allegiance among the intellectuals who provided most of the leadership for labor organizations. As a result, constant factional conflict seriously weakened the labor movement.

Development of the Labor Movement to 1945.—Feudal Japan had developed a number of craft guilds of skilled artisans, but these gradually disappeared with the growth of factory industry. As in other countries, the modern labor movement in Japan began with spontaneous demonstrations by small groups of workers in protest against specific grievances, with little thought of permanent organization. Such small-scale protests are recorded as early as the 1870's. Perhaps the first large dispute occurred in 1883, when the ricksha men of Tokyo went on strike in protest against the introduction of streetcars. Their organization was short lived, as were others formed in the next few years in other trades. In 1897 a Society for the Formation of Trade Unions (Rodo-kumiai Kisei-kai) was organized by several Japanese who had lived in the United States and had studied the operations of the American Federation of Labor. Some progress was made among ironworkers, printers, lithographers, carpenters, dollmakers, and other groups, notably locomotive engineers, who conducted a well-organized and successful strike in 1898, led by the well-known Socialist, Sen Katayama (who later became a Communist). Following the Public Peace Police Law of 1900, however, these unions were stamped out, and no further attempts at open and systematic labor organization occurred until 1912. Nevertheless, several large strikes took place, notably those at the Ashio copper and Besshio silver mines in 1907, which were suppressed by military force.

In 1912, Bunji Suzuki founded the Yuai-kai (Friendly Love Society), whose purpose was to advance the interests of workingmen by moderate and lawful methods of education, mutual aid, and cooperation between labor and management. This movement was tolerated by the authorities and made some headway, but was soon caught up in the wave of labor unrest during and immediately after World War I. This was a period of great industrial expansion which provided relatively favorable conditions for trade union growth. Business prospered, but labor often suffered when wages failed to keep pace with the rising cost of living. Many strikes occurred, reaching a peak in 1919, with 497 strikes involving 63,000 workers. One dispute alone, at the Kawasaki dockyards, involved 15,000 employees and was successful in winning an eight hour day. The great rice riots of 1918 also testified to a rising tide of discontent among urban workers. The cautious moderation of the Yuai-kai was challenged by other organizations with a more militant program, and in 1921 the Yuai-kai reorganized on modern trade union lines, taking the name of Nippon Rodo Sodomei (Japanese Federation of Labor).

The 1920's were a relatively liberal period in Japan, during which military influence was subordinated to civilian, and progress was made toward the development of true parliamentary government. Japan cooperated with the League of Nations and the International Labor Organization (ILO) and was on the whole receptive to currents of Western liberal thought. The appointment in 1924 of Bunji Suzuki, a trade union nominee, as the Japanese workers' representative to the ILO amounted to recognition by the government of labor unions as legitimate organizations. They were still viewed with suspicion, however, and militant action or radical views were sternly dealt with. Under the Peace Preservation Law of 1925 thousands of labor leaders, including a few Communists, were arrested. After the invasion of Manchuria in 1931 military control over the government grew steadily stronger and the nation moved toward a war footing, with almost complete regimentation of economic and political life. Repression of labor activities became increasingly severe, culminating in 1940 with the extinction of independent trade unionism.

Many labor disputes occurred in this period, their number fluctuating with changing economic and political conditions. From a low point during the postwar depression the number of disputes rose to a peak of 2,456 in 1931, when they involved 154,000 workers, according to official figures. Of these, 998 disputes, involving 64,000 workers, were accompanied by a strike or other interruption of production. Following the Manchurian crisis the number of disputes declined, then rose to 2,126, involving 213,000 workers, in 1937. After the outbreak of the Sino-Japanese War in 1937, labor disputes decreased rapidly; only 330 occurred in 1941. Many of these disputes were small affairs, precipitated by local grievances, sometimes without previous union organization. Large, organized strikes were comparatively rare, although some occurred, notably the great seamen's strike of 1928, which won Japan's first minimum wage agreement, and the strike which broke out in 1930 in the Kanegafuchi cotton mills despite highly paternalistic conditions. In these conflicts with management, labor's objectives were almost entirely economic, wages being the principal issue. Labor lost more strikes than it won, although many disputes were settled by compromise. Collective bargaining, as the term is understood in Western countries, hardly existed except in the strongly organized shipping industry.

Although labor victories were few, trade union membership increased steadily from 103,000 in 1921 to 420,000 in 1936, but this peak figure represented only 6.9 per cent of all nonagricultural workers. Seamen were the most highly organized group (about 90 per cent), followed by municipal transit workers. In factory industry labor organization was weak except in certain sectors of metals, machinery, chemicals, and communications. Japan's leading industry, textiles, where much of the labor force consisted of young girls living in company dormitories, remained almost entirely unorganized.

Owing to conflicting views on ideology and tactics and to changing circumstances, labor organizations in this period appeared and disappeared, split and recombined, with great frequency. The principal Right-wing group was the Japanese Federation of Labor (JFL), which, after a short period of militancy under radical leadership in the early 1920's, pursued cautious and moderate policies, seeking gradual improvement of labor's condition by legal and orderly methods. Like other national federations, the JFL was rather loosely organized, with local affiliates enjoying considerable autonomy and often seceding from the parent body. Nevertheless, the JFL preserved its identity throughout the period as the leading Japanese labor organization. Even stronger in its own field was the Japan Seamen's Union (Nippon Kaiin-kumiai), a highly conservative group which enjoyed the patronage of both the shipowners and the government. In the 1930's these and other Right-wing groups were loosely linked in the Japanese Trade Union Congress (Nippon Rodo-kumiai Kaigi), which served chiefly as a vehicle for consultation on matters of general policy. On the extreme Right, the 1930's saw the emergence of a fascist labor group, the National Convention of Patriotic Labor Unions (Aikoku Rodo-kumiai Zenkoku Konwa-kai).

During World War I, Japanese Left-wing thought was influenced chiefly by anarchosyndicalism. Later, socialism of various brands gained ascendancy, while after the Russian Revolution communism won converts on the extreme Left. In 1925 a Leftist group seceded from the JFL and formed the Council of Japanese Labor Unions (Nippon Rodo-kumiai Hyogi-kai), which, after leading a number of strikes, was dissolved by the government in 1928. Its successor, the National Congress of Japanese Labor Unions (Nippon Rodo-kumiai Zenkoku Kyogi-kai), reputedly under Communist influence, continued to carry on some underground activity. Another group, which held radical views, but sought to operate within the law—the so-called legal Left—was organized in 1930, and in 1934 took the name of National Council of Japanese Labor Unions (Nippon Rodo-kumiai Zenkoku Hyogi-kai). This body was dissolved by the government in December 1937, and its leaders were arrested.

In addition, there were a number of small centrist organizations, notably the National League of Labor Unions (Zenkoku Rodo-kumiai Domei), formed in 1930 by several groups which had split off from the JFL. Inclining more to the Right than to the Left, the center groups made several unsuccessful attempts to bring about some measure of unity in the labor movement.

Prior to 1925 it was hardly possible for ordinary citizens to exert any political influence except by humble appeals to the authorities or by direct action. The introduction of universal manhood suffrage in 1925 provided an impetus for the formation of farmer-labor parties, usually sponsored by existing labor and peasant unions; leadership of parties and unions was largely interchangeable. The Left-wing parties suffered from the same schismatic tendencies as the labor unions, as well as from the attentions of the police. Nevertheless, the proletarian parties made considerable progress in the decade preceding the Sino-Japanese War, though they did not seriously challenge the electoral supremacy of the two older conservative parties, the Seiyukai and the Minseito.

A Social Democratic Party had been founded as early as 1901 by Isoo Abe, Sen Katayama, and others, but it was immediately suppressed, as was a Socialist League formed in 1920. A Communist Party was organized in 1922, but by 1929 most of its members were in jail.

The first Farmer-Labor Party (Nomin Rodoto) was organized in 1925 by the Japan Farmers' Union (Nippon Nomin-kumiai) and certain centrist trade unions, but it was immediately dissolved by the government. By 1928, however, when the first election with full suffrage was held, there were four proletarian parties, which polled 489,000 votes and elected 8 members to the lower house of the Diet (total membership, 466). The strongest of these, the Labor-Farmer Party (Rodo Nominto), was dissolved by the government after the election for alleged radical tendencies. In the ensuing decade the principal proletarian group was the Social Democratic Party (Shakai Minshuto), organized in 1926 by Bunji Suzuki, Isoo Abe, and others of moderate Socialist views; in 1932 it merged with other organizations to form the Social Mass Party (Shakai Taishuto). Both of these parties were closely linked to the JFL and the Japan Farmers' Union. In general they advocated mild reforms designed to introduce greater democracy in government and to improve the condition of peasants and industrial workers, such as reducing the powers of the House of Peers, the reduction of farm rents, and unemployment insurance. There were in addition various smaller parties linked with Left-wing farmer and labor organizations and having somewhat more radical programs. In the election of April 1937, a few months before the outbreak of war with China, the proletarian parties polled nearly 1,000,000 votes (10 per cent of the total) and elected 37 candidates, doubling their Diet membership.

This increase in the Left-wing vote indicated a significant degree of popular dissatisfaction with the growing militarization of the Japanese government, which laid heavy burdens on the masses and restricted their freedom of action. Labor and farmer unions and parties, weak as they were, represented a divisive force in a Japan which, especially after passage of the National Mobilization Law of 1938, was moving ever closer to total regimentation for total war. Japan's leaders therefore sought to win over some of the mass organizations and suppress the rest. Appeals to patriotic sentiment were effectively used to combat unrest among the masses. After the Manchurian incident of 1931, and even more after the beginning of war with China in 1937, many Right-wing labor leaders espoused the doctrines of ultranationalism, whether from conviction or from expediency. Leaders who had earlier opposed imperialistic adventures, at least in principle, were now forced to change their views, keep silent, or go to jail.

Employers, in contrast to labor, were strongly organized in numerous trade associations, chambers of commerce, and local groups, which were concerned among other things with securing legislation favorable to employers' interests and with measures to combat the growth of trade unionism. Outstanding among the groups primarily concerned with labor relations were the Japan Industrial Club (Nippon Kogyo Kurabu) of Tokyo and the Osaka Industrial Society (Osaka Kogyo-kai). The first national employers' association was the National Federation of Industrial Organizations (Zenkoku Sangyo Dantai Rengokai), a powerful body formed in 1931 to oppose a pending trade union law. Employers sought to counteract labor unrest by fostering the spirit of paternalism in industry, and to head off the growth of independent trade unionism by organizing welfare associations or company unions among their own employees. In 1936 the company unions counted 1,347,000 members, or three times as many as the independent unions.

Somewhat similar in purpose was the Harmonization Society, organized in 1919 to promote harmony between capital and labor, and backed by the government and by representatives of big business. Early in the Sino-Japanese War, in 1938, this society launched the Industrial Patriotic League (Sangyo Hokoku Renmei) with the object of promoting cooperation between labor and capital to advance Japan's national aims. In 1940 this movement was taken over by the government, which formed the Industrial Patriotic Association (Sangyo Hokoku-kai, commonly abbreviated as Sampo). The Left-wing unions had been dissolved in 1937, and the remaining unions, voluntarily or otherwise, were absorbed into Sampo. In 1940 also, the Social Mass Party, along with all other political parties, voluntarily disbanded and merged into the Imperial Rule Assistance Association, Japan's state-sponsored totalitarian party, which worked closely with Sampo.

The purpose and functions of Sampo were roughly similar to those of the Nazi Labor Front in Germany. Branches were organized in every industrial establishment having 50 or more workers. All employees were expected to join, and the owner or factory manager was usually the head of the association. By 1943, Sampo had 86,000 branches and approximately 6,000,000 members. It carried on intensive patriotic propaganda, organized various projects to aid the war effort and to promote industrial efficiency, and conducted certain welfare activities. As World War II progressed, more forceful measures were found necessary. Labor conscription was introduced in 1942, and in 1944 military discipline was applied to workers in war plants and mines. Meanwhile, the conditions of labor steadily deteriorated as a result of inflation, shortages of food and other commodities, longer working hours, and the bombing of Japanese cities. While labor unrest was kept well under control, several hundred small strikes were recorded during the war years.

Labor After World War II.—The years immediately following World War II provided, for the first time in Japanese history, a favorable climate for the growth of labor organization. Released from former restraints and aided by Allied occupation policies, the labor movement quickly revived and, for a time, made rapid progress. As before the war, its objectives were political as well as economic, and it was in constant factional turmoil. As time went on, the opposition stiffened, and various legal limitations were imposed on labor action.

In line with their policy of encouraging democratic tendencies in Japan, the Allied occupation authorities proclaimed, within broad limits, freedom of speech, press, and organization. Sampo was dissolved, old laws restricting labor activity were abrogated, the powers of the police were curbed, and political prisoners were released. On Oct. 11, 1945, Gen. Douglas MacArthur, supreme commander for the Allied powers (SCAP), publicly called on the Japanese government to encourage the unionization of labor. This policy was based on the belief that industrial labor could, with proper guidance, become a powerful force for democracy and a bulwark against political reaction. The occupation authorities sought to introduce into Japan a system of labor relations based, so far as possible, on the best United States practice. A new Trade Union law (1945) guaranteed the right of organization and collective bargaining, and a Labor Relations Adjustment Law (1946) set up machinery for peaceful settlement of labor disputes through conciliation, mediation, or arbitration by impartial committees (both laws were revised in 1949 to impose certain restrictions on unions). A Labor Standards Law (1947) and related legislation sought to fix minimum legal standards for wages and conditions of employment. A Labor Ministry was established in 1947.

Having set up this machinery, SCAP intended to let the Japanese operate it with a minimum of interference, but the inexperience of Japanese labor, employers, and government officials made it necessary for SCAP to give strong, though usually informal, guidance to all parties in important labor disputes. On several occasions, SCAP intervened openly to prohibit strikes which, it was feared, would disrupt the national economy. This reflected not only the gradual shift of emphasis in occupation policy from political reform to economic recovery, but also its opposition to communism. for Communists had been active in organizing strikes. Similar motives lay behind SCAP's recommendations of July 1948, which resulted in revision of the civil service law to cancel or limit the rights of collective bargaining previously enjoyed by government employees.

The postwar labor movement was conditioned not only by occupation policies, but also by the economic and political situation in Japan. In the first postwar years production was stagnant; food, clothing, and other necessities were in extremely short supply; and prices mounted rapidly on a wave of inflation. To urban labor, which had suffered severe privations during the war, peace brought no improvement. Unemployment was widespread, although the paternalistic tradition against discharging workers counteracted in part the effects of business depression. Under such circumstances labor unrest was inevitable, and occupation policies gave it the opportunity of expression.

Labor's demands were addressed to the government as well as to employers. Many of the workers' early grievances—for example, an inefficient rationing system and inequitable income taxes—could be corrected only by government action. About one fourth of the nonagricultural labor force was employed directly by the government, which owned most of the railways, the communications systems, and several state monopolies. Other major industries were regulated or subsidized by the government, which could in effect determine their wage policies. In any case, it was obvious that no substantial improvement in labor's condition could be expected except through an overall program of national economic reconstruction, which the government was slow to undertake. Beyond this, democratization was the watchword of the day, and most labor leaders were dissatisfied with the rate of progress. The conservative parties, which largely dominated successive Cabinets, were reincarnations of prewar parties which had represented big business interests and were unsympathetic, if not hostile, to the claims of labor. Although many wage earners voted for conservative candidates, most leaders of organized labor rejected them, dividing their support among the parties of the Left or taking an independent Left-wing stand.

The young postwar unions suffered from a lack of experienced leaders, which often led to ill-considered or irresponsible tactics. The millions of workers who swarmed into the unions, some with enthusiasm and some from the habit of conformity, had little knowledge of trade union methods or of elementary democratic procedures. Accustomed to submitting to superior authority, they tended to follow their leaders blindly, and the leaders in turn tended to expect unquestioning loyalty and obedience from their followers. On the other hand, competition within the leader group led to heated and sometimes violent debates, which made it difficult for any small group at the top to impose its views. Nevertheless, dictatorial control by political fanatics or ambitious careerists was a constant danger. Another danger was that of falling under the control of employers. "Puppet" or company unions, well known in prewar Japan, were a favorite tactic of employers in combating independent trade unionism.

Organization was strongest in the large-scale industries, leaving Japan's many small-scale industries almost untouched. Most unions were organized on a plant or company basis, embracing both white-collar and manual workers. Such units tended to be oriented toward their own individual enterprises, which often had a divisive effect upon the labor movement as a whole. Nevertheless, many of the local units soon combined to form national industrial unions and then federations. Two national federations were organized in 1946: on the Right the Japanese Federation of Labor (known as Sodomei; later called the General Federation of Japanese Trade Unions), a revival of the prewar organization of the same name; and on the Left the new National Congress of Industrial Unions (known as Sanbetsu). There were also a smaller centrist federation, numerous independent national unions, many smaller groupings set up on a local, company-wide, or other basis, and many unaffiliated local unions.

Social Democrats (Socialists) and Communists, competing keenly for labor support, took an active part in organizing the new unions. The Social Democrats, who sought to gain political power by constitutional means, tended to counsel moderate and legal tactics, while the Communists advocated more aggressive and militant methods, including use of the strike as a political weapon. Sodomei was controlled largely by the Social Democrats. When, in 1950, the party split into Left and Right wings, the Right wing retained control of the labor federation, but several unions later seceded. Sanbetsu was originally somewhat larger than Sodomei and much more loosely organized. The Communists made strenuous and partially successful efforts to bring it under their control; they played a dominant role in determining the policies of the national headquarters, but often failed to impose centralized control on the various affiliated unions.

In many labor disputes it was difficult to disentangle economic from political motives. The peak of direct action by labor came in January 1947, when a threatened strike of government employees in support of legitimate wage demands mushroomed until it approached the proportions of a general strike to force the resignation of Shigeru Yoshida's first Cabinet. This mass movement, which was partly but not wholly of Communist inspiration, reflected a protest against economic hardship and also a confused desire for political change, vaguely defined as "a Cabinet based on the Social Democratic Party." At the 11th hour the proposed strike was banned by order of SCAP. Later, the wage demands of the government employees were met in part, and a new election was held, which resulted in the formation of a coalition Cabinet headed by a Social Democrat. After this episode labor did not lose interest in politics, but shifted its efforts toward normal political channels. Many unions took an active part in election campaigns, generally supporting Social Democratic candidates. On various occasions, however, brief but widespread strikes were called in protest against legislation regarded as prejudicial to labor.

After the abortive strike in January 1947 factional struggles became more intense within Sanbetsu and many independent unions. These frequently took the form of a three-way conflict among Communist sympathizers, conservatives, and a third group which was militant but anti-Communist. In 1947–1948, with SCAP encouragement, democratization leagues were organized within many unions to combat Communist influence, and by 1949 Sanbetsu had lost more than half of its membership. The decline of Communist influence was due partly to a revulsion against Communist tactics, partly to anti-Communist measures taken by SCAP and the Japanese government, and partly to the discharge by government and private employers, in 1949, of many known or suspected Communists. The outbreak of war in Korea in June 1950 led to intensified action by SCAP and the government to curb Communist activity. By the end of 1950, Sanbetsu had practically disappeared, and the newly formed General Council of Japanese Trade Unions (Sohyo), under anti-Communist (chiefly Left Socialist) leadership, had assumed the leading position in the labor movement. The Communists, now forced to operate largely underground, made vigorous efforts to recoup their losses, and by 1953 were said to have gained considerable influence in Sohyo. As a result several unions seceded from Sohyo and, in 1954, combined with Sodomei to form a new anti-Communist federation, Zenro.

Union membership reached its peak in March 1949, with 6,896,000 organized workers, of whom about one fourth were women. The total dropped in the next two years, then turned upward; in June 1953, it was 5,851,000, representing about 40 per cent of all nonagricultural labor. In 1953 Sohyo had 3,273,000 members (56 per cent of all organized labor), Sodomei 240,000, Sanbetsu 13,000, and Shinsanbetsu (an anti-Communist splinter group) 39,000. Zenro, formed in 1954, claimed 800,000 members including several former Sohyo unions. Among the major unions affiliated with Sohyo in 1954, with approximate membership, were the teachers (535,000), government railway workers (370,000), coal miners (270,000), local government employees (200,000), postal employees (160,000), iron and steel workers (125,000), private railway workers (120,000), telephone and telegraph workers (105,000), and United States garrison force employees (100,000). Zenro included, besides Sodomei, the textile workers (360,000) and seamen (100,000). There were also in 1953 about 30 independent national unions with 796,000 members; 856,000 in unions affiliated with local or minor groups; and 695,000 in unaffiliated locals.[1] Government and government enterprise employees were strongly organized with their own liaison council.

In the economic field, labor's principal demands were for higher wages and security of employment. Demands for wage increases were insistent, especially in 1946–1949, when prices were rising rapidly. Mass discharge of workers by government or private employers, in the interests of economy and rationalization, met with strong protests from organized labor. A demand often heard in the early postwar years was for democratization of management, an ill-defined term which sometimes meant union participation in determining company policies. In the first year or two after the war labor's claims met with little opposition, Later, the opposing forces recovered their self-confidence; employers offered stiff resistance to union demands, and the police took a stronger hand in labor affairs.

Although thousands and, at some periods, millions of workers were involved in labor disputes, the amount of time lost through strikes was not large; many disputes were settled peacefully, and most strikes were short. Figures on work stoppages in 1946–1953 are as follows:

	Number of stoppages	Number of workers involved	Man-days lost	
			Number	Per cent of total worked
1946	702	517,415	6,266,255	.253
1947	464	218,832	6,035,783	.142
1948	744	2,304,492	6,995,332	.197
1949	554	1,122,123	4,320,688	.172
1950	584	763,453	5,486,059	.158
1951	576	1,162,585	6,014,512	.132
1952	590	1,623,610	15,075,269	.432
1953	585	1,173,958	4,222,026	.116

Nevertheless, strikes in key industries sometimes had adverse effects on the entire economy, which led to stronger regulatory legislation. Since SCAP discouraged large strikes as harmful to economic recovery, and strikes by government employees were eventually banned, many alternative methods of protest were devised, such as demonstrations, slowdowns, absenteeism, and brief walkouts. The machinery of peaceful settlement by impartial committees, backed at first by strong SCAP support and guidance, played a major role in the settlement of many disputes. Some progress was made in developing written contracts and other instruments of collective bargaining on Western models. Occasional violence appeared on the part of labor, and employers, but serious incidents were rare.

After Japan resumed full sovereignty on April 28, 1952, the government took a stronger line toward labor. Various regulatory laws were passed, and it was hard to draw a line between suppression of subversive activity, necessary regulation of labor affairs, and repression of legitimate union action. Employers also became more active in combating labor tendencies of which they disapproved. The labor unions were financially weak and were rent by factional and ideological strife, and Communist influence was by no means dead. By 1954 it could be said that, by comparison with prewar years, organized labor had achieved a position of considerable strength and standing in Japan, where it represented a substantial political minority group. Yet because of its own organizational weaknesses, together with the persistence of prewar social and economic patterns, the future of the labor movement was far from clear.

Bibliography.—Harada, Shuichi, *Labor Conditions in Japan* (New York 1928); International Labor Office, *Industrial Labour in Japan* (London 1933); Foreign Economic Administration, Enemy Branch, *Trade Unions and Collective Bargaining in Japan* (Washington 1945); Farley, M. S., *Aspects of Japan's Labor Problems* (New York 1950); Japan Ministry of Labor, *Analysis of Labor Economy in Japan in 1950* (Tokyo 1950); Ayusawa, Iwao, *Post-war Developments in Organized Labor* (Tokyo 1953); *Oriental Economist* (Tokyo, monthly).

MIRIAM S. FARLEY,
Research Associate, Institute of Pacific Relations.

9. TRANSPORTATION AND COMMUNICATIONS. The development of transportation and communications systems in Japan has been conditioned by two basic factors. First, the fact that Japan is an insular country with a mountainous terrain and with most of its leading cities situated along the coasts has made coastal shipping important, has shaped the pattern of the railroads, and has retarded the development of highways. Second, the Japanese government has played a significant role in developing, supervis-

[1] These figures include some overlapping.

ing, and controlling virtually all means of transportation and communications. All forms of communications have always been operated either directly by the Japanese government or through government-controlled corporations; all forms of transportation have been regulated by the government, which has also operated directly most of the railroads and, since 1941, most domestic shipping. These two factors can be traced in the following sections, which discuss the development of Japanese railroads, domestic shipping, highways, air transportation, telephone and telegraph services, international communications, radio and television, and postal services.

TRANSPORTATION

Railroads.—Shortly after the Meiji Restoration of 1868, the government began to draw up plans for the building of a railroad to connect Tokyo with other Japanese cities. In 1869 plans were completed for a railroad linking Shimbashi in Tokyo with Yokohama, Kyoto, Kobe, and Tsuruga (Fukui Prefecture). Authorization was granted to construct the first part of the line between Tokyo and Yokohama, a distance of 18 miles; the cost of this project was estimated at about 500,000 yen. The Japanese government, however, was unable to raise this amount from domestic sources, and it therefore accepted the offer of H. N. Lay, an Englishman, to finance the project. A Japanese government loan of £913,000 was then floated in London. This financing not only represented Japan's first foreign loan, but also resulted in the initial use of British engineers and British railroad equipment in building Japanese railroads.

The line between Tokyo and Yokohama was completed in September 1872; it was followed in 1874 by a line between Kobe and Osaka (a distance of 20 miles), which was extended three years later to Kyoto. By 1889, two decades after the first plans for railroad construction had been made, the Japanese government had completed the Tokaido line between Tokyo and Kobe (a distance of 380 miles), and had virtually completed a branch line connecting Tsuruga with the Tokaido line in order to connect the Japan Sea with the Pacific Ocean by rail. In addition to these lines, 55 miles of railroad had been completed in Hokkaido to aid in the colonization of that island. Some private railroads were also built during this period with the aid of government subsidies.

Railroad development in Japan, however, did not advance as rapidly as the government thought necessary in the light of the development of other sectors of the country's economy, as well as of the strategic importance of an adequate railroad network. As a result, in 1892 the Diet passed the Railway Construction Law, which established a comprehensive railroad building program for 149 lines with a total length of 6,350 miles. The law also recommended that the government consolidate all rail lines into a unified state-owned system by purchasing private lines. The government embarked on its construction program, but it was not until 1907, after it had experienced difficulty in controlling the private lines during the Russo-Japanese War, that nationalization of the railroads took place. Of the 36 private lines with a total mileage of 3,248 miles then in existence, the government purchased the 17 most important lines, with a total mileage of 2,823 miles, leaving only minor local lines in private hands.

The government's railroad building program advanced steadily after 1907, and even private local railroad building increased. By 1953 the total length of main track in Japan amounted to 17,200 miles, of which 12,400 miles were government owned. Over 10 per cent of the electrified trackage in operation in 1953 had been built since 1945. The total mileage of Japanese railroads compared with the approximately 223,000 miles of first main track in the United States in 1953. It should be noted, however, that Japan had more trackage per unit-area than the United States, though less than England, France, or Germany.

Japan's railroad system closely reflects the shape and terrain of the country. Because the interior of the country is mountainous, the main lines generally follow the coasts, while the secondary lines cross the mountain chains to connect the east and west coast main lines. Since the most important Japanese cities are located on or near the coasts, they are directly connected by the main routes.

Only a few lines are of major importance. The oldest and most important is the Tokaido line between Tokyo and Kobe. The Sanyo line, which is a continuation of the Tokaido, connects Kobe with Shimonoseki at the western tip of Honshu. At Shimonoseki an undersea railroad tunnel to Moji connects the Sanyo line with the Kagoshima and Nippo lines, which run, respectively, along the west and east coasts of Kyushu. North of Tokyo the Tohoku and Ou lines connect the capital with Aomori in the northern part of Honshu. A railroad ferry connects the Tohoku and Ou lines with Hokkaido's Hakodate main line. The latter connects Hakodate with Asahigawa, which in turn is connected with Wakkanai at the northern tip of Hokkaido by the Soya line. Other important lines are the Sanin line between Kyoto and Shimonoseki along the northern coast of Honshu; the Chuo line, which connects Tokyo with Nagoya through the interior of Honshu; and the Takasaki, Joetsu, and Shinetsu lines, which connect Tokyo with Naoetsu and Niigata on the Japan Sea coast.

The nature of the Japanese terrain necessitated the construction of many tunnels, curves, bridges, retaining walls, and steep grades. In order to economize in the building of a railroad system that required these features, a narrow gauge of 3 feet 6 inches (1.067 meters) was adopted as the standard, compared with a railroad gauge of 4 feet 8½ inches in most other countries of the world. Because of the use of a narrow gauge, Japanese trains are slower and have a smaller carrying capacity than those of the United States and of most European countries. The rolling stock is small and light weight, and the trains have relatively few cars.

About 28 per cent of the railroad system was electrified by mid-1953; over three fourths of the electrified mileage was privately owned, being similar to suburban electrified passenger lines in the United States. Most of the mileage of Japanese railroads is single track. In mid-1953 the government-owned railroads had 5,066 steam and 402 electric locomotives, 11,625 passenger cars, 106,626 freight cars, and 2,710 electric cars. Employees on government and private railroads totaled 573,000, or 33.3 per mile, compared with 5.7 employees per mile in the United States. The number of employees on Japanese railroads in 1953, however, represented a significant reduction from the 753,000, or 40.5 per mile, at the beginning of 1948.

Before World War II the Japanese railroads carried only about 30 per cent of the tonnage of the country's domestic trade. Little of the rail tonnage required long hauls, and most of it moved between local ports and their hinterlands, longer shipments being made by coastwise shipping. Unlike the case with railroad systems in other countries, revenue from passenger traffic and passenger train mileage consistently exceeded revenue from freight and freight train mileage respectively.

During World War II the amount of freight carried on Japanese railroads increased significantly as ships that had been engaged in coastal trade were diverted to other routes, and gasoline, tires, and other automotive essentials were diverted from civilian to military needs. By 1943 the railroads reached their peak operations. In that year freight tonnage totaled 214,400,000 metric tons, and freight train kilometers totaled 42.1 billion. Passenger traffic amounted to 4.6 billion, and passenger train kilometers totaled 93 billion.

The heavy volume of wartime freight, the Allied bombings, and a lack of repair parts resulted in a marked deterioration of the Japanese railroad system by the end of the war, and the economic chaos that prevailed in Japan in the first two years after the surrender in 1945 prevented the early rehabilitation of the railroads. Despite a great decrease in the number of trains that could be operated, there was a significant increase in passenger travel as the Japanese people went into the country in search of food. Although there was a sharp decrease in freight movements, the railroads continued to carry a larger portion of the country's freight than did coastal shipping. It was not until 1950, when the Japanese economy entered a period of increasing activity because of the Korean War, that the Japanese railroad system began to make some progress toward rehabilitation. By 1952 the national railways carried more freight than at any time previously except for the war years, and a new record was set for the number of passengers carried. The proportion of the total freight carried by rail, however, remained about the same as before the war. Freight carried in 1952 by both national and private railroads aggregated 172,600,000 metric tons. In the same year these railroads carried 5.7 billion passengers, and the street railways carried 2.9 billion. The big problem facing Japanese railroads was the transportation of commuters, especially in the Tokyo area. Although by 1952 the national railways had doubled their electric railway capacity over prewar (1936) levels, passenger traffic had increased more than threefold.

Until 1908 government railroads had been administered first by the Home Ministry and later by the Communications Ministry. In December of that year they were placed under the newly created Railway Board, which was directly responsible to the Japanese Cabinet. In May 1920, the board was converted into the Ministry of Railways as an independent department of the government. This organization operated until 1943, when wartime conditions led to the creation of the Ministry of Transportation and Communications, which united the administration of railroads, highways, waterways, aviation, telephone, telegraph, radio, and postal services under a single control. In 1945 the ministry was dissolved into two separate organizations, one for transportation and the other for communications. In December 1948, the Diet passed a law establishing the Japanese National Railways as a government corporation empowered to carry on all activities involved in the operation of the government-owned railroads. The Ministry of Transportation was given responsibility for supervision of the corporation, but the latter was made largely autonomous in its operations. The minister of transportation has the power to approve or disapprove new railroad construction, the taking over of other transportation enterprises, the supervision or cessation of any working line, and the inauguration of ferry service or motor transportation related to the railroads. He also supervises private rail lines.

Domestic Shipping.—Until its entrance into World War II, Japan probably moved a larger share of its domestic traffic by water than did any other country. In the prewar period the value of Japan's domestic waterborne commerce was twice that of its foreign commerce; only four ports in 1936 handled foreign trade with value exceeding that of their domestic trade.

The prewar importance of coastal shipping was due to a number of factors. Japan has a long coastline and numerous good harbors. The quiet waters of the Inland Sea make it possible for very small vessels to ply between the ports of Kobe and Osaka at its eastern end and Moji and Shimonoseki at its western end. Most of Japan's population and industrial centers are located on or near the coasts. The rugged terrain of the country has made railroad and highway development difficult and expensive. Lastly, before World War II water freight rates were as little as one third of the rail freight rates.

With World War I as an impetus, the Japanese merchant marine increased steadily until during the 1930's it ranked third in size behind the British and United States merchant marines. In 1940, Japan had a total of about 6,900,000 gross tons of all types of shipping, of which about 6,000,000 tons consisted of steel ships of 100 gross tons and over; 15 to 20 per cent of the total tonnage was engaged in coastal shipping.

The effect of World War II on Japanese coastal shipping was to shift many of these vessels to ocean shipping and thereby to place a greater emphasis on rail transportation for domestic freight movements. As a result of Allied sea and air operations, the Japanese merchant marine lost 8,900,000 gross tons of shipping. By the end of the war, therefore, despite wartime construction there were only about 4,000,000 gross tons of all types of shipping afloat, of which only 1,400,000 gross tons represented steel ships of over 100 gross tons in size. Moreover, a large part of this tonnage was unserviceable.

By 1953 coastal shipping had not been able to regain its prewar position in freight movements, although the Korean War had resulted in substantially increased coastwise traffic, and the Japanese merchant marine had increased the tonnage of its steel ships of over 100 gross tons in size to a total of 2,900,000 gross tons. In October 1945, only about 750,000 metric tons were moved in coastal trade in all types of vessels; in 1950 these shipments averaged 3,725,000 tons monthly; in May 1951, a postwar peak of 6,160,000 tons was reached. Whereas in 1936 coastal vessels had moved 18 per cent of Japan's total freight, in 1952 coastal vessels moved only 9 per cent of the total. Important factors in the poor postwar position of coastal shipping were artificially low railroad and truck rates and significant increases in the costs of building and maintaining ships.

Until 1937, Japanese shipping was in private hands and free from government control, although it had been subsidized by the government for many years. In that year, however, the Japanese government passed legislation which gave the Ministry of Communications (and later its wartime successor, the Ministry of Transportation and Communications) authority over civilian merchant shipping, including ship transfers, prices, construction, routes, and rates. Although the ministry relied at first on voluntary controls, by the outbreak of the Pacific war Japanese shipping was subject to full control by the ministry. In March 1942, the Japanese government seized all civilian-operated merchant shipping and paid the owners charter fees. The ships were then turned over to a newly created Shipping Control Association for operation. The control exercised by the association was terminated at the end of the war. The United States Naval Shipping Control Authority for Japan ((SCAJAP) was then established by the occupation authorities to supervise the control and operation of all Japanese merchant steel vessels of 100 gross tons and over. These controls were terminated with the end of the occupation in 1952, and the Ministry of Transportation exercised supervision over the merchant marine thereafter.

Highways.—Besides being the oldest means of transportation in Japan, highway transportation is the starting point of much other transportation. The existence of a large number of industrial facilities off the railroad lines makes it necessary for vehicles, under motor, animal, or human power, to haul freight to rail lines and to dockside.

The first systematic development of roads in Japan occurred during the Tokugawa era (1603–1867), when the shoguns laid out five trunk highways. These were (1) the Tōkaidō, connecting Tokyo with Kyoto along the coast, a distance of 310 miles; (2) the Nakasendō, connecting Tokyo with Kyoto through the interior, a distance of 324 miles; (3) the Nikkōkaidō, connecting Tokyo with Nikko (Tochigi Prefecture), a distance of 89 miles; (4) the Ushūkaidō, connecting Tokyo with Aomori, a distance of 465 miles; and (5) the Koshūkaidō, connecting Tokyo with Shimosuwa (Nagano Prefecture), a distance of 132 miles. After the Meiji Restoration, these highways became the basis for Japan's modern transportation system, with railroads as well as highways following the routes of the old trunk roads.

Because of the rugged nature of the terrain, the concentration of the population along the coast, and the intensive development of railroads, highway development was neglected. This situation continued even after the introduction of motor vehicles, although the earthquake of 1923 caused the rebuilding of many highways and the building of additional roads to accommodate increased traffic. The industrial development and military preparations of the latter 1930's saw further development of Japanese highways. Yet in 1939 the length of national roads amounted to 5,350 miles, or only a slight increase over the mileage that had existed several decades before.

Although highway development did not keep pace with Japan's industrial development, motor trucks carried the major portion of the freight that was moved before World War II. In 1936 motor trucks transported almost 20,000,000 metric tons a month, or 55 per cent of the total freight moved in Japan.

The highway system suffered during the war from failure to keep up maintenance and from Allied military operations. Shortages of road-building materials continued into the postwar period, and, except for highways of strategic importance to the Allied occupation, little was done in the early postwar years to repair Japanese roads. The possibility that deteriorating roads might present an obstacle to Japan's economic recovery led the supreme commander for the Allied powers (SCAP), on Nov. 27, 1948, to issue a directive to the Japanese government to develop a comprehensive five-year public works program for the repair, maintenance, and extension of roads throughout the country. The United States continued to supply Japan with surplus army road-building machinery and with certain materials, especially asphalt. The Ministry of Construction, established on July 10, 1948, replaced the Ministry of Home Affairs (abolished Dec. 31, 1947) as the ministry responsible for Japanese road construction and maintenance.

There are four classes of roads in Japan—national (*kokudō*), prefectural (*fūkendō*), municipal (*shidō*), and town and village (*chōsondō*). National roads were built originally to connect Tokyo with the headquarters of army divisions and naval bases, with the Ise Shrine, and with prefectural capitals. The minimum width of these roads is 24 feet. The full cost of military national roads and one half of the cost of other national roads were borne by the national government. Prefectural roads connect the prefectural capital with important places within the prefecture. Their minimum width is 18 feet, and one third of their cost is paid by the national government. Important city roads have a minimum width of 18 feet, and all other roads must be at least 12 feet wide.

In 1950 there were 515,000 miles of all types of roads, of which 6,000 miles were national roads, 72,000 miles were prefectural roads, 54,000 miles were city roads and streets, and the remaining 383,000 miles were town and village roads. Of the total mileage, only about 1.5 per cent represented paved roads; by types, 19 per cent of the national roads, 4 per cent of the prefectural roads, 7 per cent of the city roads, and 0.1 per cent of the town and village roads were paved.

It took five years after the end of World War II for highway transportation to recover fully from the effects of the war. The increased economic activity resulting from the Korean War was primarily responsible for an increase in the motor transport of freight to a level exceeding the prewar peak. A monthly average of over 29,000,000 tons of freight was moved in 1952, and in March 1953 a record of over 32,000,000 tons was reached. Trucks increased their share of freight moved to about 60 per cent of the total in 1952. Bus travel also increased, to a monthly average of 169,000,000 passengers in 1952.

The late and limited development of a motor vehicle industry in Japan was both a contributing factor and an effect of the retarded status of the highways. Until the mid-1930's, Japan was dependent on imported vehicles for most of its cars and trucks; in 1938, Japanese motor vehicle production exceeded imports for the first time. Production generally increased until a peak output of about 48,000 motor vehicles of all types was reached in 1941. In March of that year there were 204,000 motor vehicles registered in Japan, including 120,000 trucks of various sizes. Production declined during the war and immediate postwar years, but began to rise again in 1947. By 1952 output had increased to an all-time peak of 177,000 vehicles. In February 1953, there were 732,000 vehicles registered in Japan (as compared with 53,294,493 registered in the United States in 1952), of which 415,000 were trucks; 273,000, passenger cars; 25,000, buses; and 19,000, special vehicles such as fire and police trucks and ambulances.

Air Transportation.—In 1910 the first airplane flight in Japan was made. World War I gave an impetus to the development of aviation in Japan, as it did in many other countries. Japanese military airplanes took part in combat for the first time in 1914, in the Tsingtao campaign against German forces. The first regular civil air service was inaugurated in 1922, when hydroplanes began to fly between Sakai, near Osaka, and the island of Shikoku. In January 1923, the newspaper Osaka *Asahi Shimbun* started regular service between Tokyo and Osaka. In July of the same year the Japan Aerial Navigation Company opened regular service between Osaka and Beppu. Airmail service was inaugurated in April 1925 between Tokyo and Osaka. With the formation of the Japan Air Transportation Company (Nippon Koku Yuso Kabushiki-kaisha) in 1929, Japanese civil air transportation began to develop on an extensive route basis. Regular flights were made between Tokyo, Osaka, and Fukuoka, and were later extended to Korea, Manchuria, Formosa, and the mandated islands. By 1938 the lines of this company extended over a distance of 9,575 miles, and it controlled virtually all of the commercial air routes in Japan.

As the Japanese government extended its control over all means of transportation and communications, the Japanese Ministry of Communications fostered the merger in 1938 and 1939 of all airlines into a new company, the Japan Airways Company (Dai Nippon Koku Kabushiki-kaisha). This company was a semi-governmental concern, with a monopoly over all Japanese civil air transportation. It was subsidized by the Japanese government, which also contributed one half of the company's capitalization of 100 million yen. At the end of 1939 the company was operating almost 12,000 miles of air routes. In the same year, Japan had about 120 civil aircraft, of which 85 were scheduled air carriers. About 4,800 airplanes were produced in Japan in that year, but almost all were allocated for military use. In 1939 the Japan Airways Company carried 69,268 passengers, 298 metric tons of freight, and 819 metric tons of mail.

After 1939 considerable expansion took place in the air routes of the Japan Airways Company. With the outbreak of the Pacific war two years later, civil aviation was placed under military control and the civil air routes were used to support military operations. At the end of the war all flying by Japanese was prohibited by the Allied occupation authorities. In November 1945, the Japan Airways Company was dissolved and all aeronautic research institutes and aviation schools were ordered closed by a SCAP directive.

In 1950, SCAP permitted Japanese corporations to inaugurate air transport service, the actual operation of aircraft to be undertaken by foreign airlines. The first Japanese airline company to be established was the Japan Air Lines Company (Nippon Koku Kabushiki-kaisha), organized in August 1951. In October of that year, Japan Air Lines inaugurated in cooperation with Northwest Airlines the first postwar regular civilian air route, connecting Tokyo, Osaka, Sapporo, and Fukuoka. With the end of the occupation restrictions on Japanese aviation were removed, and in October 1952, Japan Air Lines undertook independent domestic operations. By the end of 1953 at least 11 other airlines were organized to conduct domestic service. In October 1953, a semigovernmental airline was created for international operations. The new company, also called Japan Air Lines, was established through an investment of 2 billion yen, one half by the original Japan Air Lines and the remainder by the Japanese government. It began overseas service to the United States in February 1954. In addition, 11 foreign airlines were engaged in air transportation with Japan at the end of 1953.

COMMUNICATIONS

Telephone and Telegraph.—Telephone service in Japan was first opened for public use in and between Tokyo and Yokohama, in December 1890. Long-distance service was not inaugurated until 1897, when Tokyo and Osaka were connected. The telephone service has usually been regarded as the least efficient communication system in Japan. Although Japanese telephone equipment is considered to be good, ever since telephone service was inaugurated there have been inadequate facilities to meet public demand. In 1940 there were about 1,000,000 telephone subscribers with about 1,500,000 telephones.

During World War II the telephone system suffered heavy damage from aerial bombing. About one fourth of the wire system and half of the telephone instruments were destroyed. Since then much rehabilitation has taken place. From a low of about 800,000 in 1945, the number of telephones increased to 2,400,000 by March 1953. In 1953 there were about 28 telephones in service for every 1,000 Japanese, compared with 310 telephones for every 1,000 persons in the United States. The number of telephone calls grew steadily in the postwar period, reaching over 200,000,000 monthly at the beginning of 1953, compared with a monthly average of 35,000,000 in 1941. Telephone routes cover about 50,000 miles and reach over 6,0000 telephone exchanges.

Telegraph service, which was started between Tokyo and Yokohama in 1869, has become the most important means of telecommunications in Japan. In 1939 the number of telegrams sent in Japan exceeded the figure for any other country except the United States. In that year land telegraph lines covered 31,000 miles and connected over 13,000 telegraph offices. Since the end of the war there has been much rehabilitation of the war-damaged telegraph system. The previous peak of 7,000,000 telegrams per month reached in 1943 was surpassed in 1951, and in December 1952 an all-time peak of 9,200,000 telegrams was reached.

Telephone and telegraph services in Japan have always been a government monopoly under the direct control of the Ministry of Communications and of its wartime successor, the Ministry of Transportation and Communications. Telephone and telegraph services were placed under the Ministry of Electrical Communications in 1949, when the Ministry of Communications was split into two separate organizations for electrical communications and for postal services. On Aug. 1, 1952, the Ministry of Electrical Communications was abolished, and most of its functions were transferred to the Ministry of Postal Affairs. At the same time, there was created under the latter the Japan Telegraph and Telephone Public Corporation to operate Japan's telephone and telegraph facilities. For administrative purposes, the country is divided into 10 telephone and telegraph zones with regional bureaus in the following cities: Tokyo, Osaka, Nagoya, Nagano, Kanazawa, Hiroshima, Matsuyama, Kumamoto, Sendai, and Sapporo.

International Communications.—Japan's international communications facilities include radiotelegraph (wireless telegraph), radiotelephone (wireless telephone), and submarine cable.

Although Japan had radiotelegraph facilities in operation as early as 1908, these facilities were used until 1915 for domestic communications and for contact between Japanese ships and land. In that year the first overseas radiotelegraph message took place between Ochiishi in Hokkaido and Petropavlovsk (now Petropavlovsk-Kamchatski) in Kamchatka. Overseas radiotelegraph communications increased over the succeeding years, and direct circuits were established with the leading cities of the world. In 1925 the Japanese government established the Japan Wireless Telegraph Company (Nippon Musen Tsushin Kabushiki-kaisha), to which the government turned over its radiotelegraph facilities. In 1938 the government merged all international communications in a new company, the International Telecommunications Company (Kokusai Denki Tsushin Kabushiki-kaisha). Half of the stock of the company was owned by the government, and the election of its officers and directors, as well as the company's actions, was subject to the approval of the Ministry of Communications.

The first radiotelephone experiments in Japan were made in 1911, but it was not until 1923 that the service was opened to the public. At first radiotelephone communication was limited to service between ships in Japanese harbors and land. In 1932 the government decided to extend the service, and the International Telephone Company (Kokusai Denwa Kabushiki-kaisha) was formed. Soon radiotelephone service was extended to ships at sea, to Japanese colonies, and, between 1934 and 1937, to most parts of the world. In 1938 the International Telephone Company was also taken over by the International Telecommunications Company.

The International Telecommunications Company continued to operate for almost two years after V-J Day. On March 25, 1947, however, SCAP issued a directive to the Japanese government, ordering it to liquidate the company, and to take over the operation of international telecommunications directly. An International Telecommunications Division in the Ministry of Electrical Communications, created in 1949 as a result of the division of the Ministry of Communications, became the successor to the liquidated company. This function was transferred to the Ministry of Postal Affairs when the Ministry of Electrical Communications was abolished in 1952. Local administrative bureaus for international telecommunications are located in the same cities as those for telephone and telegraph services.

Japan's international telecommunications transmitting and receiving facilities are handled by two systems: the Eastern Japan Radio Central at Tokyo and the Middle Japan Radio Central at Osaka. The principal transmitting station for radiotelephone communications is at Nazaki in Ibaraki Prefecture, and the principal receiving station is at Komuro in Saitama Prefecture. Radiotelegraph communications are handled through transmitting stations at Oyama in Tochigi Prefecture and Yosami in Aichi Prefecture and through receiving stations at Fukuoka in Saitama Prefecture, Yokkaichi in Mie Prefecture, and Ono in Hyogo Prefecture. In March 1953, there were 14,700 radiotelephone calls and 326,300 radiotelegraph messages. These figures represented approximately a fivefold increase and more than a threefold increase, respectively, over the 1949 monthly averages.

Before World War II, Japan had an extensive network of submarine cables connecting the various islands of Japan proper as well as connecting Japan with its colonies and with foreign countries. The principal overseas cables connected Nagasaki in Kyushu with Shanghai and Vladivostok (owned by the Great Northern Telegraph Company, Ltd., a Danish company), and Kamakura (near Yokohama) with Guam (owned by the Commercial Pacific Cable Company, a United States concern). Cables to Europe went through Vladivostok, while cables to the United States went through Guam.

Since the end of the war only the cables connecting the islands of Japan have been in full operation. In view of the development of radiotelegraph and radiotelephone facilities, it was believed that extensive use of submarine cables would probably not develop in Japan.

Radio and Television.—Japan's first radio program was presented over station JOAK in Tokyo on March 22, 1925. Within a few months stations were built in Osaka and Nagoya to meet a growing public demand for radio broadcasts. Before the end of the year the three stations were merged and the Broadcasting Corporation of Japan (Nippon Hoso Kyokai) was formed with the approval of the Ministry of Communications. The corporation was given a monopoly over all radio broadcasting in Japan. Until 1935 the corporation enjoyed considerable independence in its operations; beginning in that year, however, the approval of the Communications Ministry was required for virtually all actions.

When the war ended, the Allied occupation authorities directed the Japanese government to reorganize the Broadcasting Corporation of Japan and to eliminate the control over the corporation that the Communications Ministry enjoyed. When the Ministry of Communications was split in 1949, a Radio Regulatory Agency was created in the Ministry of Electrical Communications. This agency's major function was "to insure that the radio spectrum is employed expressly for the public interest, convenience or necessity in a fair and efficient manner in compliance with international and regional radio conventions, regulations, and agreements. . . ." Regional radio regulatory offices are located in the same cities as the regional telephone and telegraph bureaus.

Although the administration of broadcasting is centered in Tokyo, the actual operation of local stations is under the control of so-called central stations in eight major cities: Tokyo, Osaka, Nagoya, Hiroshima, Sendai, Kumamoto, Sapporo, and Matsuyama. Two radio networks link these cities with each other and with the local stations. As of May 30, 1953, the Broadcasting Corporation of Japan operated 39 local broadcasting stations and 38 rebroadcasting stations in addition to the 8 central stations. Revenue for the support of the corporation, which excludes advertising, is derived from a license fee of 50 yen per month for each radio receiving set. Overseas broadcasting, which had been suspended since the end of World War II, was resumed by the corporation in February 1952.

Commercial radio broadcasting was initiated in April 1951 with the issuance by the Radio Regulatory Commission (successor to the Radio Regulatory Agency) of licenses to 16 commercial radio stations. As of July 31, 1953, there were 33 commercial stations in operation, supported by paid advertising. The commercial stations organized the National Association of Broadcasters in Japan (Nippon Minkan Hoso Renmei) in 1951 to enforce an ethical code of broadcasting.

Television began in Japan in February 1953 with a telecast from Tokyo by the Broadcasting Corporation of Japan. Subsequently stations were opened in Osaka and Nagoya, and a five-year program called for the completion of 29 other television stations by the corporation by the end of 1956. A monthly fee of 200 yen is charged per set to support the corporation's television operations. Commercial television also got under way in 1953 with the organization of the Japan Television Network Corporation.

Postal Services.—Japan's postal system began in 1871, when service was inaugurated between Tokyo and Osaka. In that year post offices were opened in five other cities and service began between Tokyo and Nagasaki, delivery between the two cities taking from 7 to 8 days. In the following year post offices were opened in all other important cities and towns. There was a steady development thereafter, and within 10 years there were 5,500 post offices.

Foreign mail service was established in 1872 with the creation of British, United States, and French post offices in Yokohama, Kobe, and Nagasaki. The United States post offices were withdrawn in 1873, and the French and British post offices were withdrawn after Japan signed the International Postal Convention in 1877.

Postal savings and postal money order services were started in 1875, parcel post service in 1892, and airmail service in 1925. Other services include an extremely rapid special delivery, registered mail, postal life insurance, the receiving of taxes for the government, the payment of government pensions, and the sale of government bonds. Many local post offices are also telegraph and telephone offices.

The postal system was originally operated by the Ministry of Communications and its wartime successor, the Ministry of Transportation and Communications. In 1949, when the Ministry of Communications was split up, an independent Ministry of Postal Affairs was created. Ten regional postal bureaus were established in the same cities as the regional telephone and telegraph bureaus. Local post offices were originally divided into five and then into three classes depending upon the size of the city or town in which they were located. In 1941 this classification was dropped and two groups, ordinary post offices (formerly 1st and 2d class) and special post offices (formerly 3d class), were created. In July 1953, there were 678 ordinary and 13,514 special post offices. At the same time there were 177.5 million postal savings accounts with total deposits amounting to about 294 billion yen, and postal life insurance policies with a total face value of about 752 billion yen.

Bibliography.—Supreme Commander for the Allied Powers, *Civil Transportation in Japan* (Tokyo 1947); U.S. Strategic Bombing Survey, *The War Against Japanese Transportation, 1941–1945* (Washington 1947); Supreme Commander for the Allied Powers, *Summation of Non-Military Activities in Japan*, nos. 1-35, September-October 1945–August 1948; Japanese National Railways, *A Yearbook of JNR Information* (Tokyo 1952); Japan. Economic Counsel Board, *Economic Survey of Japan, 1952–53* (Tokyo 1953); id. *Japanese Economic Statistics* (Tokyo 1953); Japan, Ministry of Postal Affairs, *Yūkei Tōkei Geppō (Postal Services Statistical Monthly)*, October 1953; Japan, Ministry of Transportation, *Unyu Yōran (Transport Statistical Series)* (Tokyo 1953).

STANLEY NEHMER,
Office of International Materials Policy, Department of State; Lecturer, American University.

10. FINANCIAL DEVELOPMENT. The old Japanese merchant houses which developed in the feudal period, mainly in Osaka, carried on a limited, rudimentary type of banking operation. They acted as financial agents for the daimyō, selling their rice in the few commercial centers and transmitting funds to the various localities. In times of crop failure they granted loans to the feudal lords. As in Great Britain, many of the leading modern banks in Japan can trace their origins to old merchant bankers, houses such as Mitsui, Iwasaki, and Konoike. It was these *chōnin* (townsmen, or merchants)—especially of Osaka, where 70 per cent of Japan's wealth was concentrated—who provided the financial support which made possible the overthrow of the Bakufu. And it was their financial support, by means of contributions and loans (*goyōkin*), which enabled the new regime to establish itself. The Japanese economic historian Eijiro Honjo states that in the very earliest days of its existence, in December 1867, the Revenue Office (Kinkokusuitosho) of the new government issued an urgent plea to Mitsui-gumi for financial aid.

The confused and disorderly state of the currency at the time of the Meiji Restoration of 1868, brought about largely by the varying coinage and paper money emissions of the daimyō and the continued debasing of the coinage by the shogunate government, was increased by the paper money issues of the new government. These issues were necessary because during the early years the new government was unable to balance its budget. The cost of suppressing the hostile clans resulted in 25 million yen of expenditure in 1868, while government revenues plus loans from the merchant bankers or exchange houses amounted to only 9 million yen, leaving a deficit of 16 million yen to be covered by paper money issues. In the following year expenditures totaled 20.8 million yen, while revenues, including *goyōkin*, were only 10.5 million. After the clans were put down and the han (feudal district governments) were abolished, other expenses developed. The note issues of the han governments were assumed by the state, which also took over the debts of the daimyō and had to provide indemnities for the Buddhist sects on their disestablishment. As a result, in 1872 expenditures totaled 58 million yen but revenues amounted to only 33 million yen. The expedition to Formosa and the Saga Rebellion in 1874 and the very serious Satsuma Rebellion of 1877 added to the burden of expenditure. The voluntary privilege given to the upper feudal classes in 1873 to capitalize and exchange their annual hereditary pensions for government bonds was made compulsory in 1876; this added 190 million yen to the public debt.

As E. Herbert Norman, chief of the postwar Canadian mission in Japan, states, "In Japan the feudal lord ceased to be a *territorial* magnate drawing his income from the peasant and became instead, by virtue of the commutation of his pension, a *financial* magnate investing his freshly capitalized wealth in banks, stocks, industries, or landed estates, and so joined the small financial oligarchy." The holders of pension bonds found banking an attractive field as a result of the liberalization of the national bank regulations in 1876. Consequently, between 1876 and 1880, 148 new national banks, all authorized to issue inconvertible paper money, were established.

In 1871, Assistant Secretary of Finance Hirobumi Ito (later Prince Ito), had been sent to the United States to study banking and financial institutions. As a result of his suggestions, and over the objections of the advocates of a European-style central bank, the Japanese National Bank Law, closely patterned after the United States National Bank Act, had been passed in 1872, mainly to unify the country's currency and to replace the inconvertible paper money with national bank notes redeemable in gold and silver. Until 1876 only four banks were established under this law, the most important being the First National Bank (Dai Ichi Kokuritsu Ginko), founded jointly by the Mitsui and Ono houses. (National banks took as trade names their Ministry of Finance registration number.) Specie holdings of the banks were required to amount to two thirds of their note issue, which was to be convertible. Since government inconvertible paper money emissions continued, specie began to command a premium and the national bank notes were immediately presented for redemption. As a result of this development, and to maintain the value of the bonds issued to the daimyō as a lump sum settlement for their hereditary pensions, the bank law revision of 1876 made it possible for the pensioned daimyō to use their government bonds to finance banking activities and suspended the specie convertibility requirement. The largest of the new banks, which sprang up in the banking boom which the new revision made possible, was the Fifteenth (Jugo) Bank, established in 1877 by a group of nobles, with a capital of 18 million yen. The new banks added 34 million yen to the inconvertible paper currency total, which by 1879 reached 170 million yen, while the total government debt rose to 254 million yen.

As a result of the steady increase in paper money and in government debt a violent inflation developed. The price of rice, by far the most important commodity, doubled between 1877 and 1880. Specie began to flow out of the country in large amounts. Anxious to adopt modern forms, the new government had established a gold standard in 1871. Patterned on the United States coinage law, the gold yen was defined as containing 25.72 grains of gold, 9/10 fine. At the same time a 1 yen silver coin containing 416 grains of silver, 9/10 fine, was issued to be used exclusively at the treaty ports. (The silver yen was equivalent in metallic content to the Mexican silver dollar, then widely used in trade in the Orient.) The constant emissions of paper money and its depreciation, however, soon led to the disappearance of gold, and in 1878 the bimetallic standard was adopted, the government allowing the use of 1 yen silver pieces as legal tender throughout the country. In effect, however, the country was on a *de facto* silver standard. As the inflation developed, the paper money depreciated in terms of silver until by 1881, 1 yen of silver was equivalent to 1 yen 80 sen of paper. In October of that year, Count (later Prince) Masayoshi Matsukata was transferred from the position of minister of home affairs to that of minister of finance and financial conditions were taken in hand.

A New Foundation and Stability, 1881–1913.—Matsukata's first efforts were directed toward building up a specie reserve so that government paper money might either be made convertible or be retired. In 1880 the Yokohama Specie Bank (Yokohama Shokin Ginko), the first of a long line of special banks, had been established for the purpose of discounting foreign bills of exchange on the security of exported goods. The main object was, on the one hand, to encourage the direct export trade; on the other, to secure specie. The system worked poorly at first, but a revision in the bank's practices and procedures, instigated by Matsukata and made effective in March 1882, resulted in very considerable improvement, with the result that the government's specie reserve rose from 8 million yen in 1881 to more than 42 million yen at the end of 1885 and continued to grow thereafter. The government used its specie reserve gradually to retire its inconvertible paper money.

The next step was the establishment of a central bank, the Bank of Japan (Nippon Ginko), in October 1882. The bank's charter ran for an original term of 30 years; half of its 10 million yen capital was supplied by the government. Modeled after the National Bank of Belgium, the new bank issued convertible bank notes, held specie reserves of the national banks, acted as fiscal agent for the government, discounted the Yokohama Specie Bank's foreign bills, granted loans to subsequent special banks, and absorbed government bonds. It failed to act as a bankers' bank in the fashion of European central banks, nor did it exercise any extensive control over the money market, since its discount rate and open market policies were the result of treasury requirements more than of its own policies.

With the establishment of the central bank the task of retiring the national bank notes was begun. In 1883 the national bank law was amended to provide that the charters of national banks (originally issued for 20 years) should not be renewed, and that national bank notes were to be redeemed gradually with Bank of Japan convertible notes. National banks were gradually converted into ordinary banks, and 1899 saw the end of the last national bank. There followed the rapid growth in the number of ordinary banks (which did not have the note issue privilege, this now being confined to the Bank of Japan), and the increase in their importance resulted in regulatory statutes being promulgated in 1890 and put into force in 1893. Under the Ordinary Bank Law, all banking institutions were placed under the control of the Ministry of Finance, which licensed new banks, controlled mergers, and generally supervised the conduct of banking business. The years 1893–1901 witnessed the greatest growth of Japanese banking. The number of banking institutions of all types increased from 703 in 1893 to 2,359 in 1901. In the latter year a panic occurred, causing a number of bank failures, especially among the small banks. As a result, the banking law was amended to provide that joint stock banks should have a capital of at least 500,000 yen, and private banks a capital of 250,000 yen. This measure encouraged bank consolidations, and by the end of 1913 the number of banks had declined to 2,156.

Matsukata's currency reform plans halted the inflation of the late 1870's, and the money contraction led to a severe depression, in 1883–1884. The price of rice fell sharply and farm discontent grew, but the government, despite protests, refused to be diverted from its task—to place Japan on a sound, convertible money basis. The redemption of the inconvertible notes continued steadily. The deflationary policy was mitigated somewhat by the concomitant depreciation of silver in terms of both gold and commodities. This continued decline of silver led to a rise in the price level, particularly in the early 1890's, and, since by that time Japan was conducting two thirds of her trade with gold standard countries, with the result that exchange rates were highly unstable, a commission was appointed in 1893 to study the problem. The commission recommended that the money base be changed and advocated a gold standard. In March 1895, Matsukata returned to the post of finance minister. In the following month Japan concluded with China the Treaty of Shimonoseki, which provided that China pay Japan a war indemnity amounting to 200,000,000 taels or £38,000,000 (360 million yen). This fortuitous windfall was utilized to enable Japan to adopt a gold standard. Arrangements were made to have this indemnity paid in sterling instead of in taels; part of the sum was brought back to Japan in gold and part was maintained in Britain as a foreign exchange reserve. By the Gold Standard Law of 1897, the unit of value, the yen, was fixed at 11.574074 grains of pure gold, equivalent to $.49845 (pre-1934 dollar). By the end of the 19th century, therefore, Japan had stabilized her money structure by the adoption of the gold standard and by the retirement of practically all the government paper money and national bank notes.

Matsukata's view that the peculiar conditions of Japanese development required banks of a specialized nature in addition to the ordinary banks led to the establishment of the Hypothec Bank (Nippon Kwangyo Ginko) in 1897, the Bank of Formosa (Taiwan Ginko) and the Hokkaido Colonial Bank (Hokkaido Takushoku Ginko) in 1899, the Industrial Bank (Nippon Kogyo Ginko) in 1900, and the Bank of Korea (Chosen Ginko) in 1909–1911.

The Hypothec Bank, modeled upon the Crédit Foncier of France and capitalized at 10 million yen, was authorized to make loans having a maturity of up to 50 years on the security of such immovable property as paddy and upland fields, forests, and fishing rights. In addition, it might make loans to public authorities, cooperative societies, and agricultural and fishing associations and issue debentures up to 10 times (this was later increased) its paid-up capital. Such deposits as it accepted had to be invested in government bonds and bills of exchange. Simultaneously, 46 agricultural and industrial banks were established, one in each prefecture; they functioned as local subsidiaries of the Hypothec Bank. The bank is still in operation.

The Industrial Bank of Japan, modeled upon the French Crédit Mobilier, was established to carry out the government's policy of developing such new industries as the political and economic realities of the time required. As a result, it granted loans to the shipbuilding, public utility, iron and steel, chemical, and other heavy industries. As in the case of the Hypothec Bank, its loan funds were obtained by the sale of debentures, which were at first limited to 10 times its paid-up capital. Through the years the bank has served as an organ of state policy and has from time to time made loans considered to be in the strategic interest of the nation.

Another important financial agency, developed in the early days of the restoration and continuing to play an important role, is the Deposit Bureau of the Ministry of Finance, established in 1877 after the pattern of the British post office savings system. The bureau is entrusted with the very considerable postal savings and postal insurance funds of the Japanese people. The popularity of this method of saving among the large number of small depositors is seen by the fact that the system grew from about 300,000 depositors with 9 million yen of deposits in 1885 to 12 million depositors with 189 million yen of deposits in 1914. The Deposit Bureau gains its importance from the fact that it serves to funnel the mass savings of the whole people into investment channels favored by the state. The bureau invests its funds in government securities and in the debentures of the special banks. It has made loans to national policy companies, essential government-sponsored enterprises, and government-approved colonial projects.

In the field of public finance the national debt, which had risen sharply during the early unsettled years of the restoration and had reached 240 million yen by 1877, remained stable until the advent of the Sino-Japanese War of 1894–1895. The debt, which stood at 234 million yen in 1894, rose by 117 million yen as a result of the war and by 1903 reached 539 million yen (including about 100 million yen for the building of the national railways), of which 98 million yen had been borrowed abroad. The war against Russia (1904–1905) cost Japan about 1.5 billion yen, of which 1.2 billion yen was borrowed abroad. The alliance with Britain in January 1902 gave Japan greater access to the British capital market, and with Japanese military successes against Russia the borrowing rate in London fell from 6 per cent in 1904 to 4½ per cent in 1905. By 1907 the total Japanese national external and internal debt stood at 2.2 billion yen. Thus, as a result of two wars between 1894 and 1905, the national debt had increased tenfold. By 1914 it stood at 2.5 billion yen.

To meet growing central government expenditures, which rose elevenfold between 1869 and 1899 and by 1914 were three times the 1899 level, taxes were raised steadily. Under the shogunate revenues had come chiefly from the land tax, which was arbitrary in amount and payable in rice. During the 1870's land tax reform was undertaken. A capital value was fixed for each piece of land by capitalizing, at rates varying from 6 to 7 per cent, the net average produce of the unit over a five-year period, valued at then current prices. On such valuations a tax of 2½ per cent was levied. Some 1,500 nuisance taxes were abolished, and by 1879–1880 four fifths of the whole tax revenue came from the land tax. Although the tax rate was raised to 5 per cent in 1899 and to as much as 11½ per cent after the Russo-Japanese War, the growth of other taxes, mainly indirect, such as the liquor excises, the tobacco monopoly revenues, the customs, and stamp duties, brought the land tax receipts down to only one fifth of total ordinary receipts just prior to World War I.

World War I, 1914–1920.—Whereas in the years immediately prior to the war Japan had had an excess of imports and had experienced international financial difficulties and strains, the unparalleled wartime demand for her goods and services led to a sharp reversal of the trade balance. As a result, Japan's net credits on international account from trade and services aggregated over 3 billion yen between 1914 and 1919, or about 1 billion yen more than her total foreign indebtedness in 1913. She did not, however, use these foreign earnings primarily to repay debts owed abroad. Instead, she used them to make foreign investments, mainly short term, and to increase the combined gold reserves of the Bank of Japan and the Japanese government. These rose from 342 million yen at the end of 1914 to 2.1 billion yen at the end of 1920. Despite this rise in gold reserves, Japan in 1917 placed an embargo on gold exports, which was not lifted until January 1930. When the United States embargoed gold in September 1917, Japan was unable to convert her foreign credits into gold imports and the Japanese exchange bankers, principally the Yokohama Specie Bank, encountered great difficulties. Their advances to exporters were offset only by frozen credits overseas. As a result, they were forced to borrow from the central bank and sell their foreign holdings to it. The central bank's loans to the exchange banks grew from 44 million yen in December 1913 to 444 million yen at the end of 1918. As was to be expected, the note issue also rose sharply, from 385 million yen in December 1914 to 1.5 billion yen in December 1919. As Japan changed from debtor to creditor, prices climbed rapidly, industrial activity grew, real wages fell, and rice riots developed. Due to the war Japanese banks almost entirely took over the financing of Japanese foreign trade. Whereas in 1913 the Yokohama Specie Bank and the Bank of Formosa together financed 50 per cent of Japan's imports and 59 per cent of her exports, in 1918 they financed 95 per cent of the imports and 83 per cent of the exports.

As banking resources mounted during the war, a bank consolidation movement developed. Banks with a capital of less than 500,000 yen fell in numbers from 1,755 at the end of 1913 to 1,054 at the end of 1920, while those with a capital of 10 million yen and over rose from 15 to 46. Both the larger private banks and several of the special banks undertook operations in China during the war. The boom reached a peak in 1919, and as the year advanced a tightening in money conditions became apparent. Finally, in March 1920, the bubble burst and the stock market crashed, the index number of 120 leading securities falling from 250 in January to 165 in April. Commodity prices dropped and banks began to face runs and to fail. The Bank of Japan was forced to intervene and to grant liberal aid to distressed financial institutions, while the government aided basic industry by substantial advances from the Industrial Bank of Japan.

The Difficult Interwar Period, 1920–1931.—Two additional serious banking crises and an attempt to strengthen the banking system by requiring more adequate minimum capitalizations led to a series of consolidations and mergers which, coupled with numerous bank failures, reduced the total number of banks from 2,285 in 1918 to 913 in 1930. A severe crisis developed with the occurrence of the earthquake of Sept. 1, 1923. Again the intervention of the Bank of Japan and of the government itself held the number of bank failures to a minimum and shortened the length of the moratorium, despite the fact that 76 of the 84 clearing banks of Tokyo lost their main offices in the earthquake. The goverment agreed to reimburse the Bank of Japan to a maximum of 100 million yen for any losses incurred in the discount of bills in the stricken area. As a result, the Bank of Japan extended credit to banks on far more liberal terms than usual and discounted large amounts of what were called "earthquake bills." Loans and discounts of the Bank of Japan rose from 580 million yen at the end of 1922 to 862 million yen at the end of 1923. The next, and most severe, crisis came in April 1927. On April 28, the Fifteenth or Peers Bank, one of the five largest, failed and some 36 large banks and many smaller ones immediately followed suit. A special session of the Diet authorized the Bank of Japan again to come to the assistance of the banks and provided government indemnification for any losses the bank might sustain.

The bank failures were due in part to the nature of the banking operations in which the Japanese ordinary private banks, especially the country banks, were engaged. Their assets consisted mainly of promissory notes backed by collateral not easily liquidated because it represented long-term loans to industry and agriculture, particularly advances on mortgages of land and buildings. Entry into this hazardous type of banking business was partly due to failure to develop the bankers' acceptance and a discount market. Also responsible was the shortage of high-grade stocks or bonds, which resulted from the fact that so many of the great business undertakings were in the hands of the *zaibatsu,* which seldom resorted to the securities market. There was no popular tradition in Japan of security ownership, only a rudimentary capital market, and almost no investment banking mechanism in the Western sense.

The banking law was amended in 1927 to double the minimum capital requirements of banks. Banks in Tokyo and Osaka had to have a minimum of 2 million yen capital; other banks, 1 million yen. Government powers of bank inspection were strengthened. The crisis and the higher capital requirements stimulated the bank consolidation movement. In the 18 months following the April 1927 banking crisis, 328 banks were absorbed by consolidations. By the end of 1928 the "big five" banks (Mitsui, Mitsubishi, Dai Ichi, Sumitomo, and Yasuda) held 34 per cent of the deposits of all ordinary banks in Japan.

Japan's desire to return to the gold standard after World War I was thwarted and delayed by losses of gold reserves, by an excess of imports over exports, and by the fact that she once more became a borrowing country. From 1920 to 1929 Japan paid out the balances accumulated abroad during the war and sold her bonds abroad. The specie holdings of the government and of the Bank of Japan fell from 2 billion yen at the end of 1919 to 1.1 billion yen in March 1929. In the summer of 1929 the Minseito Party assumed power with Junnosuke Inouye as finance minister. Minister Inouye, who had long advocated classical financial principles, announced his intention of removing the gold export embargo and of restoring the gold standard. On Jan. 11, 1930, the gold embargo was removed, officially re-establishing the old prewar gold parity of $.49845 per yen. The timing of the attempted return to the gold standard was unfortunate, and it was followed by an extremely severe deflation, the Bank of Japan's index of wholesale prices falling from 155 in December 1929 to 110 by the end of October 1931. The gold reserves of the Bank of Japan fell from 1,072.3 million yen at the end of 1929 to 469.5 million yen at the end of 1931. Inouye persisted in attempting to balance the budget, even to the extent of reducing military and naval expenditures. Agrarian and military discontent grew, and the government fell in December 1931. Two months later, Inouye was murdered by "patriotic elements."

War Economy, 1931–1945.—The new government of the Seiyukai Party immediately reimposed the gold embargo and introduced control over international capital transfers and foreign exchange transactions by means of the Capital Flight Prevention Law of July 1, 1932 and the Foreign Exchange Control Law of May 1, 1933, later revised several times. The new finance minister, Korekiyo Takahashi (who served from May 26, 1932 to Feb. 26, 1936), initiated a reflation policy whereby mild deficits were incurred to stimulate the economy. The sharp growth in military expenditures provided an inflationary fillip. The total army and navy budget rose from 434 million yen in 1931 to 7,266 million yen in 1940. The military budget, which represented 29 per cent of total expenditures in 1931, rose to 75 per cent of total expenditures in 1938. Naturally, military expenditures on this scale could not be financed out of current tax revenues. Deficit financing caused the total national debt outstanding to rise from 6.8 billion yen on March 31, 1931 to 31.1 billion yen on March 31, 1941. The necessity of absorbing this expansion of the public debt, as well as of meeting the capital demands of the expanding munitions industries, led to a material increase in the expansion of bank credit despite a sharp decrease in the number of banks. While the number of ordinary commercial banks declined from 782 to 186 between Dec. 31, 1930 and Dec. 31, 1941, deposits rose from 8.7 billion yen to 29.8 billion.

Early in 1936, Takahashi announced that recovery had been achieved and that the time had come to call a halt to inflation. He was assassinated shortly thereafter and his successor proved more amenable to theories of military economics. Takahashi had kept the budget within 1.9 to 2.2 billion yen. After his murder it was doubled and then rose even more sharply to 18.7 billion yen in 1941–1942. He had considered 600 million yen a safe limit for government deficits, but the deficit was increased to 1.5 billion yen in 1937–1938 and to 6.9 billion yen in 1941–1942. He had believed that the inflationary influence of government deficits could be minimized if banks and investment institutions invested the liquid funds they created in government bonds. This "capital circuit," he believed, would result in easy money and declining interest rates but would check an increase in the Bank of Japan note issue. During the new era in Japanese fiscal policy, which his murder inaugurated, the note issue of the Bank of Japan rose from 1.7 billion yen (Dec. 31, 1935) to 5.9 billion yen (Dec. 31, 1941).

The beginning of the active war against China in 1937 saw a sharp intensification of government control over the financial apparatus. A variety of measures were adopted, beginning with the Temporary Funds Adjustment Law of September 1937, to direct capital and credit into the war industries and to dry up the flow to the nonessential industries. Toward this end, effective use was made of the special banks, particularly the Industrial Bank of Japan, whose borrowing power was expanded to make possible extensive financing of government-sponsored munitions and overseas projects and national policy companies. Financial institutions and security underwriters were required to obtain permission from the Ministry of Finance either when making long-term loans or when subscribing to or underwriting securities. In August 1941 a munitions bill acceptance system was established.

In the 55 years of its existence prior to 1937, the Bank of Japan had adhered to what was considered relatively orthodox central banking practice. In the ensuing 5 years, culminating in the new Bank of Japan Act of 1942, every orthodox tenet of central banking was violated, and the bank took on every conceivable financial task, including long-term industrial financing. By the end of 1941 total assets of the bank, which had stood at 2.4 billion yen on June 30, 1937, reached a new high of 7.7 billion. This expansion was attributable for the most part to the growth in government bond holdings, which rose over the same period from 880 million yen to 5.3 billion yen, an increase of 507 per cent. By the end of 1941 the bank had been almost completely converted into a tool for government war finance.

Government control over the financial system was tightened greatly after Japan's entrance into World War II. The charter of the Bank of Japan, which had been renewed for an additional 30 years in 1912, expired early in 1942 and the government took the opportunity, in the act renewing the charter indefinitely, to place the bank completely under the control of the minister of finance. It also increased the bank's lending power by removing most of the remaining provisions regarding necessary kinds of security. The National Financial Control Association (Zenkoku Kinyu Tosei Kai) and a number of subsidiary control associations were established in 1942. The association acted as a central advisory and coordinating organization between the minister of finance and the various financial institutions. Its principal function was participation in the formulation and application of the government's yearly financial plans for (1) the collection of savings, (2) the issuance of corporate debentures, and (3) the absorption of government bonds. These plans were the main basis for government wartime financial programming. They set savings goals, allocated savings quotas, and established government bond absorption targets. The National Financial Control Association was entrusted by the Finance Ministry with the task of carrying out the Ordinance for the Consolidation of Financial Institutions of 1942, which gave the finance minister broad powers to bring about amalgamations of banks, trust companies, and other financial institutions. Under this program consolidation was carried forward vigorously, and by Aug. 31, 1945 the number of ordinary banks had been reduced to 61 (from 186 at the end of 1941) and the number of savings banks to just 5 (from 69 at the end of 1941).

A variety of new financial institutions were established to assist in various phases of war finance. The most important was the Wartime Finance Bank (Senji Kinyu Ginko), which, capitalized at 300 million yen, was patterned after the Industrial Bank of Japan and performed somewhat similar, though (perhaps) what at the time appeared to be more speculative, functions. The formation of the Munitions Ministry in 1943 led, in 1944, to the establishment of the munitions company financing system, under which companies performing basic war production functions were assigned to designated banks, which were then responsible for meeting their financial needs. These loans were in turn guaranteed by the government.

Despite a basic tax revision in 1940, which attempted to give central importance to the income tax as the chief revenue producer, Japan, in contrast to Great Britain and the United States, made no serious attempt to finance the war by any appreciable degree of taxation. The proportion of Japanese government revenues to expenditures, which stood at 74 per cent in 1936–1937, declined to 24 per cent in the fiscal year 1944–1945—a clear indication of the increasing degree of Japan's dependence on deficit financing. The resultant growth of the national debt carried it by the end of the war to 177 billion yen, or 17 times greater than the prewar (1936) figure of 10.3 billion yen. The absorption of so large a deficit year after year expanded the credit base and brought on some degree of inflation, particularly in the last year of the war. Money in circulation in Japan rose 785 per cent between 1940 and 1945, in contrast to the 240 per cent increase in the United States. The ballooning of the whole financial system in Japan is seen in the growth of the total assets of all ordinary banks. These increased by 27.5 billion yen during the Sino-Japanese War period and by approximately 100 billion yen during the World War II period.

Finances in Defeat and Reconstruction, 1945–1954.—The pent-up inflationary pressures, which had been partly restrained and repressed during the war, broke loose with the collapse of Japanese governmental authority. Partly because of uncontrolled disbursements in the months immediately after surrender, the note issue doubled between August 1945 and February 1946, and prices rose 295 per cent. As a result, occupation authorities formulated a control program, which included a currency conversion program, the freezing of deposits, 100 per cent taxation of war indemnities, a capital levy, and the establishment of an economic stabilization board.

The currency conversion plan carried out in March 1946 temporarily reduced the currency in circulation from 62 billion yen in late February 1946 to 15.2 billion yen on March 12, 1946, but it had no lasting influence. By September 1946 the volume of new note issue had reached 64 billion yen, surpassing the preconversion peak. As a result of the conversion, some 45 billion yen were frozen in old yen blocked accounts in the banks.[1] Since individuals were permitted to convert only 100 yen per person, all additional yen had to be deposited in the blocked accounts. Withdrawals from these old yen blocked accounts were limited by the Ministry of Finance, although no restrictions were placed upon the deposit or withdrawal of new yen. In August 1946 the old yen blocked deposits were divided into first and second blocked accounts, because with the cancellation of war indemnities many of the corporations had become technically insolvent and could not repay their wartime loans, nor was the government permitted to make good its guaranty of these loans, thus rendering the majority of banks technically insolvent. Under a series of emergency financial laws steps were outlined under which both banks and corporations were to reorganize, write off their unrealizable wartime assets and liabilities, increase their capitalizations, and begin anew. In the case of the banks, losses were written off by canceling the bulk of the second blocked deposits. This reorganization process was completed by mid-1948, at which time all restrictions were removed from the first blocked deposits and from such part of the second blocked deposits as were not needed to offset losses. Most of the banks were recapitalized at this time, and the formerly *zaibatsu*-named and -controlled banks changed their names, although the original names were restored shortly after the end of the occupation in 1952.

A new financial institution, the Reconstruction Finance Bank (RFB), was established in October 1946; it began operations in January 1947. While its original purpose had been defined as the financing of Japanese industry's requirements for new and replacement capital goods, its funds were used more and more to meet the ever-increasing working capital needs of Japanese business, as operating deficits grew larger and larger with the inflationary distortion of costs. The outstanding loans of the bank rose from 4.1 billion yen in January 1947 to a peak of 132 billion yen in March 1949, at which point its activities were curtailed, for it had become a prime vehicle of inflation, and its outstanding loans were a kind of side-pocket government deficit.

The mounting inflation which characterized the first few years of the postwar period caused growing concern among Allied occupation authorities. By May 1949 the price level was some 200 times the prewar 1934–1936 base. Note issue of the Bank of Japan had risen twelvefold since the surrender. Budget deficits grew. National debt rose from 128 billion yen at the end of 1944 to 575 billion yen at the end of 1949. Despite an occupation-sponsored capital levy, a 100 per cent tax on war indemnities, and reform of the income, capital gains, estate, and gift taxes, in 1946–1947

[1] On Jan. 21, 1946, the government froze all bank deposits of business corporations.

tax revenues failed completely to keep pace with mounting expenditures.

Alarmed at this prospect, the United States Departments of State and of the Army publicly directed the supreme commander for the Allied powers (SCAP) to order the Japanese government to "carry out an effective economic stabilization program calculated to achieve fiscal, monetary, price and wage stability in Japan as rapidly as possible." Accordingly, a nine-point economic stabilization program was adopted in late 1948 and, in early 1949, Joseph M. Dodge, former president of the American Bankers Association and president of the Detroit Bank, was sent to Japan, with the rank of minister, to see that the financial rehabilitation program was developed effectively.

The achievements of the first Dodge mission may be summarized as follows: (1) It ended deficit financing and produced a balanced budget for the first time since 1930. (2) A single foreign exchange rate was set at 360 yen to the U.S. dollar. In the mid-1930's the yen had been worth about 28 cents and immediately after the surrender a military conversion rate of 15 yen to $1 had been established. This was raised to 50 to 1 the following year, and in mid-1948, with the advance of inflation, to 270 to 1. For the conduct of foreign trade a complex multiple exchange rate structure had been in effect. (3) The deficit loans and enormous credit expansion activities of the RFB were halted. It was required that all RFB debentures be retired by the end of the 1949–1950 fiscal year and that new loans by the RFB be permitted only to the extent of repayment of outstanding loans. (4) Stock markets in the principal cities, which had been closed since the end of the war, were reopened in order to stimulate the flow of capital into industry and to maximize security investment. (5) The control and management of the Bank of Japan was reorganized. A policy board of seven members, modeled after the board of governors of the United States Federal Reserve System, was established. The purpose was to free the bank from domination by the Ministry of Finance. The functions of the board include the determining of policies of basic credit control, open market, discount rate, loans, and other matters, which the bank then carries out.

Shortly after Dodge left in April 1949, a tax mission, headed by Professor Carl S. Shoup of Columbia University, arrived in Japan. Its recommendations, contained in an exhaustive four-volume report, increased the emphasis upon the income tax as the main source of Japanese national government revenues, reorganized the tax on corporate profits, and gave the local governments independent tax sources of their own, principally a revised real property tax. Dodge returned to Japan in November 1949 to ensure that the budget for the fiscal year 1950–1951 remained balanced.

Until the outbreak of the Korean War in June 1950, Dodge's program halted the inflationary spiral From this point on, however, prices began moving upward again. The budget became unbalanced once more, but taxes continued to be reduced. The banks overextended themselves by making illiquid long-term capital loans to industry. Bank of Japan note issues soared again, and by 1954 wholesale prices were more than 50 per cent above June 1950 levels. As a result, the government in 1954, undertook a new program of fiscal restraint, designed to balance the budget, limit government capital outlays, and lower prices.

Bibliography.—Tsuchiya, Takao, and Ouchi, Hyoye, *Meiji Zenki Zaisei Keizai Shiryo Shusei (Collection of Historical Material on Finance and Economy in the Early Years of the Meiji Era)*, 20 vols. (Tokyo 1931); Andréadès, André, *Les Finances de l'Empire Japonais et leur Évolution* (Paris 1932); Norman, E. H., *Japan's Emergence as a Modern State* (New York 1940); General Headquarters, Supreme Commander for the Allied Powers, *Report on Japanese Taxation by the Shoup Mission*, 4 vols. (Tokyo 1949); Cohen, J. B., "Fiscal Policy in Japan," *Journal of Finance*, March 1950.

JEROME B. COHEN,
Associate Professor of Economics, School of Business, College of the City of New York.

11. GOVERNMENT. Japan passed through a period of political experimentation unprecedented in history in the nearly seven years of military occupation following the close of World War II in 1945. Whatever the lasting effects of this interesting experiment may be, they can be viewed in proper perspective and evaluated accurately only after a considerable passage of time.

The national program of westernization adopted in the 19th century never had the opportunity to achieve full and natural development, since it was at best a superficial adoption of the organization and structure of European and American institutions. This resulted in façades which concealed traditional concepts and attitudes that were much too deeply rooted to be easily superseded by alien ideas and ways of doing things.

While the Japanese governmental structure before World War II was as Western and modern as any in Europe or America, the concepts and attitudes which constituted the mainsprings of government and politics bore little if any resemblance to those of the West. Nor could the behavior and actions of the leaders or the people be judged in terms of Western patterns or standards of value. Needless to say, the inception of the modern Japanese political system was impelled more by external pressures than by internal needs to establish a Western type of constitution and a parliamentary government. In the carefully planned and executed modernization of the nation's administrative machinery, the primary objective was the achievement of such overall organization as would ensure a high degree of efficiency and a rapid development of industrial and military power. Inevitably emphasis fell on organizational modernization, which influenced only very slightly traditional ideas.

It was natural that the Meiji Constitution of 1889, which clothed Japanese government in Western garb, should have been not an instrument designed primarily to secure the inalienable rights of the individual, but rather a means of achieving national strength and international recognition. Western concepts of liberty and popular rights which were then espoused had been acquired largely out of context and without the benefit of the necessary environment which only working institutions and practices could render meaningful. Traditional ideas and attitudes continued to dominate political thought, unaffected by the remarkable scientific and technological advances which had been attained in the meantime. In fact, old ideas were refurbished to serve the needs of the nation, especially in molding a new nationalism adequate to cope with the rising tide of nationalism of the 19th century world.

See also section on *Development of the Modern State.*

Constitution of 1947.—The Japanese Constitution which went into effect on May 3, 1947 charts in broad outline a democratic political system. As an incorporation of the principles and objectives of the Potsdam Declaration of July 26, 1945, its goal is a peaceful and democratic nation, a political system based on the freely expressed will of the people. Sovereignty is vested in the people: this is a complete reversal of the monarchical principle of the Meiji Constitution and a negation of the traditional theory which held that sovereignty resided irrevocably and permanently in the emperor. The affairs of the imperial household are under the control of the national Diet. The bureaucratically operated authoritarian political system, which was not responsible to the people, has disappeared and the peerage has given way to a system of equality in which no special privileges are permitted. Respect for the dignity of the individual is firmly established in a Bill of Rights which is very specific in its provisions.

With the adoption of legislative supremacy as a basic principle, the Diet has been made the highest organ of the state. Separation of power has been established in substance, while a system of checks and balances has been introduced for the first time, together with such democratic devices as the referendum and recall. The doctrine of judicial review is an integral part of the system in which the independence of the judiciary exists in fact.

In establishing the principle of the supremacy of law, the Constitution of 1947 places legal control over administrative acts through the exercise of judicial power. Formerly the executive branch transcended judicial control and was not subject to any check over its administrative acts. Sanctity of laws has superseded the idea of the practically omnipotent ruler, giving to the Japanese for the first time the principle of "government of laws" instead of the "government of men" which had been their tradition.

Undoubtedly the most unique feature of the Constitution is the provision completely renouncing war as an instrument of national policy. This unprecedented step attracted worldwide attention and has been characterized by some as utterly unrealistic and utopian and hailed by others as a beacon light to the troubled world.

The new constitution of 103 articles is only slightly longer than the old, but, despite the insistence of some Japanese that it is a mere revision, it represents a radical change in substance. The preamble is reminiscent of the Declaration of Independence, the Preamble to the Constitution of the United States, Lincoln's Gettysburg Address, and the Atlantic Charter, all of which inspired those who drafted the constitution. Highly significant is the use of the simple colloquial style of Japanese. The abandonment of the stilted and difficult court style formerly used for decrees and proclamations represents another definite step toward democratization.

National Diet.—As the highest organ of national power, the legislative branch is supreme over the executive. The Diet has become the sole lawmaking organ of the state, stripping the executive of the emergency ordinance powers which it used extensively under the old constitution to the detriment of the legislative branch. Sovereignty used to be vested exclusively in the emperor, who was the source of executive, legislative, and judicial power; the Diet could not legislate without imperial approval, and the initiative in lawmaking rested with the executive branch.

Under the Constitution of 1947 the Diet not only legislates, but also designates the prime minister from among its own membership and possesses exclusive initiative in proposing constitutional amendments. Fiscal powers, including the power to tax, belong to the lower house, whose approval is necessary for emergency appropriations. Control of foreign relations is also vested in the Diet, and its approval is necessary for the ratification of treaties. Through the exercise of investigative power, control over imperial household property, and the power to impeach judges, the Diet's position is greatly strengthened.

As is customary on the national level, a bicameral legislature is provided, but the upper chamber, the House of Councilors, has become entirely elective. The two houses, however, do not have equal powers. Formerly the appointive House of Peers could obstruct the enactment into law of any bill passed by the elected House of Representatives. Now the lower chamber has superiority over the upper chamber in appropriations and fiscal matters, in foreign relations, and in the selection of the prime minister, and may easily override the actions of the latter. The House of Councilors has no power to do anything about a bill which has been defeated by the House of Representatives. If the House of Councilors should either fail to pass or attempt to modify a bill already passed by the House of Representatives, however, the latter can enact it into law by a two-thirds vote.

Despite the strong powers it possesses, the House of Representatives is subject to dissolution by the Cabinet, while the House of Councilors is not. This provision gives the latter both stability and continuity and, in spite of its relatively weaker powers, it has attracted to its membership persons of experience and prominence largely because of its prestige, which is at least partly a carry-over from the old House of Peers. Of the 250 members of the House of Councilors, 100 represent the nation at large, while the remaining 150 represent the prefectures, each of which has two to eight seats. Councilors are elected for a term of six years, one half of the membership being chosen every three years. The membership of the House of Representatives remains at 466, as formerly, and the members all represent the prefectures, which are divided into one to five election districts, except for Tokyo, which has seven. The term of office is four years, and the entire membership stands election simultaneously.

One regular session of 150 days must be held every year. It usually opens in early December and may be extended whenever necessary beyond the five-month period. Extraordinary sessions are called as needed, the duration being decided each time by both chambers. As a rule, sessions and even committee meetings are open to the public except when secrecy is decided upon by a two-thirds vote. Decision is by simple majority. The lawmaking procedure in the Diet is very similar to that of the United States Congress, as are its rules of procedure.

Executive.—In the administrative branch simplification has been achieved through the reconstitution of executive organs. Gone are the Privy Council, the lord keeper of the privy seal, and the minister of imperial household, all of whom exerted powerful influence on national policy making as well as on the management of state affairs. As "the symbol of the State and of the unity of the people," the emperor has no powers related to the government and performs only ceremonial functions. The only important executive organ now is the Cabinet, headed by the prime minister, who is chosen by the Diet from its own membership. The premier is required to select at least half of his Cabinet from the Diet. The Cabinet, which is collectively responsible to the Diet, enjoys greater powers than it ever did before. Furthermore, the constitution clearly defines its functions, powers, and responsibilities, which include administration of laws, conduct of state affairs, management of foreign affairs, preparation of the budget, issuance of Cabinet orders, and decisions on amnesties, commutations of punishment, reprieves, and the restoration of rights.

As head of the government and representative of the Cabinet, the premier submits bills and the budget and reports on the state of the nation and foreign relations to the Diet; exercises control over the administrative departments, determines their jurisdiction and powers, and sets aside their acts and orders; acts for his ministers during their absence or holds portfolios concurrently; issues Cabinet orders; and has exclusive control of the office of the prime minister. He is thus the actual head of the Cabinet and not merely a moderator-coordinator.

Several important changes have been effected in the component executive departments of the government since 1945. In late August, immediately following the surrender, the Munitions and Greater East Asia ministries were abolished. The first postwar innovation was the creation, on Sept. 1, 1947, of the Ministry of Labor, designed to achieve the stabilization of national livelihood and social security through labor administration. The most significant of all the organizational changes was the liquidation, on Dec. 31, 1947, of the Ministry of Home Affairs, which had, through extensive appointive and police power and control over prefectural assemblies, imposed the will of the national government upon local political entities and left little room for actual self-government. The abolition of the Home Ministry removed the stronghold of bureaucracy and nerve center of highly authoritarian national government and prepared the ground for popularly based and democratically managed local government. This action was followed by the creation, on Feb. 15, 1948, of the Office of the Attorney General, which superseded the Ministry of Justice. The change effected the complete separation of investigative and judicial functions and a more logical allocation, as well as an expansion, of functions.

The Ministry of Construction was established on July 10, 1948 to take over such functions of the Home Ministry as those pertaining to rivers, public works, city planning, buildings, and construction, particular emphasis being given to the reconstruction of war-damaged areas. On May 25, 1949 the Ministry of International Trade and Industry superseded the Ministry of Commerce and Industry, effectuating a shift in policy from the emphasis on general production to concentrated efforts on the promotion of international trade and, particularly, the production of foreign trade commodities. Last in the series of changes was the splitting, on June 1, 1949, of the Communications Ministry into two departments: Postal Affairs and Electrical Communications. The Cabinet then comprised the following ministries: Foreign Affairs, Office of the Attorney General, Finance, Education, Welfare, Agriculture and Forestry, International Trade and Industry, Transportation, Postal Affairs, Electrical Communications, Labor, and Construction. In 1952 the Office of the Attorney General resumed the name of Ministry of Justice, and the Ministry of Electrical Communications was abolished, most of its functions being transferred to the Ministry of Postal Affairs.

Executive power, formerly supreme, now is not only subordinated to the legislative, but is also subject to judicial review. The police is no longer the strong arm of the executive branch. Nor is executive power bolstered by a special court to handle administrative disputes and render decisions favorable to it, for the Court of Administrative Litigation has been abolished. The power to determine the organization of the executive branch has been transferred to the Diet from the emperor, whose exclusive prerogative it had been. Government officials are no longer the officials of the emperor, to whom alone they were responsible and loyal; they are public servants answerable for their actions to the people through the Diet.

The civil service has been removed from the direct control of the Cabinet and placed in the hands of the National Personnel Authority to insure greater rationality, efficiency, and economy as well as to preclude any sort of spoils system. Grades are based on functions rather than on personal status and rank, and the principle of equal pay for the same work has been adopted. Appointments and promotions are based on competitive examinations. In spite of these organizational changes designed to bring about a democratically controlled administrative machinery, however, bureaucratic-feudalistic attitudes and practices still persist as serious obstacles to the democratization of the political system. The tendency to judge individuals on the basis of former court ranks, service grades, decorations, and the like is still apparent. So are the ideas and attitudes of a considerable segment of the bureaucracy, which reflect their unwillingness or inability to grasp or even to tolerate democratic ideas and processes, their negation or denial of political parties, their persistence in the mystical concept of the state, which they try to impose on the public, and their reluctance to give up the theory of absolute monarchy.

Although the Diet is the sole lawmaking organ, initiative in national policy making is held by the Cabinet, which enjoys the legal right to draft and submit bills to the Diet. The Cabinet has consistently played a dominant role in the constitutional and legal changes effected in the period since the surrender, while the Diet has not asserted by anything approaching vigorous action its right to formulate policies through the lawmaking process. On the contrary, the lawmakers have deferred their prerogative to the Cabinet by default rather than by delegation of powers.

Judiciary.—There has been a radical change in the administration of justice both in concept and in procedure. Previously resort to law courts was regarded as disgraceful and was scrupulously avoided by the public. Because of traditional biases, the natural inclination of an individual was to avoid altogether the use of the judicial machinery and to settle disputes out of court. Law courts were seldom if ever regarded as courts of justice. Under the new system the independence of the judiciary has been firmly established, and there no longer exists administrative or executive control of the courts. Furthermore, the democratization of courts and trials which has been undertaken increases respect for individual rights and dignity.

In recognition of the new status of the judiciary, the chief justice of the Supreme Court has been accorded a rank equivalent to that of the prime minister. The doctrine of judicial review gives the court the power to declare laws unconstitutional, making it the guardian of the constitution. An innovation of note in the judicial system is the device of referendum employed in determining the fitness of the judges of the Supreme Court. On the theory that the judges of the highest tribunal must reflect the collective will of the people, the constitution provides that they shall be reviewed "by the people at the first general election of the members of the House of Representatives following their appointment, and shall be reviewed again at the first general election of the House of Representatives after a lapse of 10 years and in the same manner thereafter." If the dismissal of a judge is favored by the majority of voters, the popular mandate must be carried out. In addition, impeachment is provided against judges as well as against all officials.

Of the 15 judges of the Supreme Court, 10 must be legal experts of at least 20 years' professional standing, but the remaining 5 may be learned persons of experience, though not necessarily in the field of law; this permits a democratic representation of expertness. Below the Supreme Court are the eight higher courts, which are regional courts of appeal, and below them are the 48 district courts—1 in each of the 46 prefectures except Hokkaido, which has 3 in order to cover its large area. At the lowest level are the 600 newly created summary courts, with jurisdiction in cases involving not over 5,000 yen. They are designed to simplify legal procedure and to overcome the public dislike of courts as well as the stigma attached to litigation itself.

A distinct innovation is the court of family relations, which was set up on Jan. 1, 1948 to maintain harmony within the family as an institution. The new arrangement is designed to help advance both the dignity of the individual and the equality of the sexes. Matters handled by the 276 courts of family affairs include divorce, breach of promise, alimony, mutual support, guardianship, adoption, property settlement, and the like. After the establishment of these courts, the number of cases brought by women increased greatly.

For the first time a complete separation of criminal investigation and judicial functions has been achieved in Japan. Under the old system the procurators were attached to and subservient to the courts, but now investigations are conducted independently of the courts. Summary punishments, which used to be administered by the chief of a police station and which gave rise to numerous and serious abuses, have been abolished. Both the preliminary investigations and the forced confessions, which were conspicuous features of the old system, are gone. The legal validity of confessions has been greatly reduced, while habeas corpus as well as the double jeopardy clause have been accepted as an integral part of the judicial procedure.

Local Government.—Local government formerly was no more than an administrative adjunct of the central government. Since the old constitution neither denied nor guaranteed local autonomy, and since it was subject to the vicissitudes of shifting political fortunes, government at the prefectural level suffered from a lack of stability. Moreover, local government was controlled at will by the bureaucracy. The authorities discouraged, if they did not forbid, party politics from the prefectural level downward in order to keep a firm grip on local governmental activities. Consequently, popular participation seldom, if ever, went beyond periodic casting of votes in the national, prefectural, and local elections. Once this was done, local self-government was managed by elected assemblies which were controlled by prefectural governors, who executed orders and instructions emanating from the Ministry of Home Affairs.

It had been the practice for prefectural governors appointed by the Home Ministry to be transferred with each change of government and with only incidental regard for the well-being and interests of the people. Governorships were at best steppingstones for ambitious bureaucrats. Their attitude of superiority, if not of condescension, was reflected in their officiousness and contempt for the people, who knew only the form and not the substance of local government. Moreover, what little semblance of local autonomy there existed was taken away beginning in 1943 by a reorganization which made local entities an integral part of the central government. This was done in the name of all-out prosecution of the war. The central government thereafter became supreme in the sphere of local government, and any pretense of local autonomy was dropped completely.

It was to correct these conditions and to permit greater and direct participation in self-government that the Local Self-Government Law was enacted by the Diet in March 1947. It was clear that the effective democratization of the nation must begin at the grass-roots level. Every possible means had to be utilized to encourage the people to participate in politics by arousing them from political apathy, and to insure a broader base for local government and politics. Decentralization of administration was a necessary prerequisite to the growth of self-government.

The local government system adopted in 1947 provides for the direct election of governors and of mayors of wards, municipalities, towns, and townships. Local government has lawmaking powers, police powers, financial powers (including the power to make public levies in emergencies), and control over education through local commissions elected directly by the people. Twenty-one enumerated categories of powers are exercised by local government, while only eight are reserved exclusively for the central government. Residual legislative powers accrue to the local government. Yet the fact that the drafting of the Local Self-Government Law enacted by the Diet was left almost completely in the hands of the Home Ministry virtually on the eve of its demise, with only a perfunctory, ineffective participation by the Diet, left much to be desired.

Direct measures such as the initiative, referendum, and recall make possible a much greater participation on the part of the people. The electorate can also demand the dissolution of local assemblies and the examination of records and the auditing of books. In order to broaden the political base the voting age was lowered from 25 to 20 years, women were given equal voting rights, the residence requirement was reduced to six months, and bankrupt and financially dependent persons and charity cases were given the right to vote. By these changes the number of voters was trebled.

Local legislative bodies are unicameral and members are elected for four-year terms. Prefectural assemblies have from 40 to 100 members, depending on the population. The metropolis of Tokyo has a distinctive metropolitan government which is a combination of municipal and prefectural types. The city of Tokyo itself does not have the ordinary type of municipal government; it and the rest of what was formerly Tokyo Prefecture are under a single metropolitan government.

Police System.—The old police system was employed as an effective instrument by the military as well as by the bureaucracy, since the Meiji Constitution enabled the government to exercise police power with great flexibility over all areas of the life of the people. It was for the protection of the interests of the state, and at the expense of individual rights, life, and property, and social security that this power was extensively used, contributing directly to the strengthening and expansion of the authority of the central government. The constitutional rights given to the people could be restricted or nullified by legislation. Freedom of speech, assembly, and association was restricted by police power through the various thought-control laws, of which the best known was the Peace Preservation Law of 1925, aimed at Leftist movements in general and communism in particular. Laws enacted before and during World War II served to tighten further already existing controls over freedom of speech, the press, assembly, and association.

One of the initial acts of the supreme commander for the Allied powers (SCAP) was the abolition, in October 1945, of the special higher police of the Home Ministry, which had been in charge of thought control. Political offenders were released immediately, and the notorious Peace Preservation Law and all other restrictive laws were abolished. This series of measures was climaxed by the abolition of the Home Ministry, bringing the police state to an end.

Police power has been reduced to normal proportions by the delimitation of its scope to the prevention, search, and suppression of crime, and to the protection of life and property. As a result, the police relinquished administrative jurisdiction over matters relating to labor, health, social insurance, and the control of economic matters, all of which were transferred to appropriate administrative departments. Police power has been made subject to the close scrutiny of the regularly constituted courts of law and must be exercised within the specific limits set by law. In keeping with the principle and spirit of local autonomy, as well as with the realization of the highest degree of the dignity of the individual, decentralization of the police has been effected.

Beginning in March 1948, each city or urban section of a town or township with 5,000 or more inhabitants was authorized to maintain a local autonomous police force under the supervision of a local public safety commission. By 1953, of the 2,303 towns and townships, only 206 still had their local police forces. Of the 276 municipalities, nearly one fifth were leaning toward abandoning their own police forces and coming under the protection of the national rural police, which is under the overall supervision of the National Public Safety Commission, appointed by the premier with the advice and consent of the Diet. In 1952 the premier was given the power to control the nation's entire police force in the event of an emergency. Two years later, on June 7, 1954, the Diet passed a bill abolishing the autonomous police forces and renationalizing all police powers.

Abuses of police power under the new system have been made difficult by the provisions that no one may be detained longer than 72 hours, that the reason for detention must be given, and that the opportunity to secure counsel must be offered. Through the constitutional prohibition of the use of the third degree, police brutality has become illegal. An interesting change has been the appointment of women police officers for the first time in Japanese history, and with satisfactory results.

National Defense.—Demilitarization, which was one of the conditions of surrender in the Potsdam Declaration, had been initiated by the Japanese themselves even before the Allied initial postsurrender policy was effectuated. On Aug. 22, 1945 the Supreme Council for the Direction of War was abolished, and a few days later the Munitions Ministry was also abolished. On September 2—the day of the formal signing of the Instrument of Surrender—SCAP ordered the disbanding of the armed forces by General Orders No. 1. Within a fortnight the Imperial Headquarters was liquidated. Demobilization of troops in Japan proper was completed by mid-October and was followed shortly by the abolition of the army and navy general staffs. The military conscription system came to an end on November 17, and the War and Navy ministries were abolished on November 30. Within three months, complete demobilization and demilitarization had been successfully achieved.

Undoubtedly the most conspicuous feature of the new constitution is the absolute and unconditional renunciation of war as a sovereign right of a nation, thereby outlawing the use of threat as well as of force itself as a means of settling international disputes. The requirement that the prime minister and all Cabinet ministers must be civilians excludes the military from participation in the government. For the first time in Japan's constitutional history, the influence of the military has been removed completely from government.

In spite of the complete demilitarization of the nation provided in the constitution, the right of national self-preservation has been explicitly conceded to Japan. On Jan. 1, 1950, Gen. Douglas MacArthur stated that Japan has "the inalienable right of self-defense against unprovoked attack." In July of that year, following the outbreak of the Korean War, a police reserve was created, and on Oct. 15, 1952, this became the National Security Corps. Chapter 3 of the Japanese Peace Treaty recognizes Japan's right of self-defense, as well as her right to enter into collective security arrangements. On the same day that the treaty was signed, Sept. 8, 1951,

Japan and the United States signed a security treaty. On March 8, 1954, the United States and Japan signed a mutual defense assistance agreement. Three months later, on June 2, the Diet passed bills creating, as of July 1, a new army, navy, and air force. See also section on *Occupation and Foreign Relations (1945–1954)*.

Social Security and Welfare.—The traditional family system, which placed the burden of social and economic welfare of its members on the family, stifled, if it did not prevent, the development of the responsibilities and functions of the state in social security and welfare. As a result, social welfare had come to be regarded as the special province of private charity. The system of social security and welfare provided by the Constitution of 1947, however, guarantees the people "the right to maintain the minimum standard of wholesome and cultural living" by "the promotion and extension of social welfare and security and of public health." Necessary legislation and the organizational framework have been provided to carry out an integrated and coordinated program of public health, public welfare, and social security. An entirely new concept was introduced not only in social welfare, but in civic responsibility as well, when the first community chest campaign was conducted with marked success throughout the nation in the fall of 1947.

Public assistance is now available to those involuntarily in need. Unemployment insurance, health insurance, and welfare annuity insurance help to offset insecurity, while child welfare legislation gives protection to children. The National Disaster Law enacted in October 1947 places the financial responsibility for the relief work necessary in times of natural disaster on both the prefectural and the national governments. Great progress has been achieved in the field of public health, which had lagged far behind the systems of the progressive nations of the West. A systematic and effective program of public education, together with the reorganization of medical education and health facilities, has been instituted. Programs instituted under SCAP supervision for the control of communicable diseases were so successful that the overall death rate for 1948 showed a 53 per cent drop over that of 1945.

Political Parties.—Revival of political parties followed the surrender of Japan by a few weeks. The SCAP directive of Oct. 4, 1945, abrogating and suspending all laws, orders, and regulations restricting freedom of thought, religion, assembly, association, speech, and the press, was the signal for the resumption of political activities, which had been virtually banned during the war. First to reappear was the Social Democratic Party, which was formed on November 2; it was followed by the Communist Party and the Liberal Party within a week, the Progressive Party in mid-November, and the Peoples' Cooperative Party in late December.

The labels of the new parties were of little value in identifying them. These parties actually constituted a revival of old political forces, alignments, and personalities. To be sure, they emerged in seemingly new garb, but old political ties and personal relationships were unmistakably there. The Liberal Party showed a number of familiar faces from the Seiyukai; the Progressive Party drew its membership largely from the Minseito and the Seiyukai. The Social Democratic Party included the Socialists from the old Social Mass Party and other groups ranging from the extreme Left to the extreme Right. Somewhat new in appearance was the Peoples' Cooperative Party, drawing conservative support from middle-and small-scale business and industrial elements as well as from the landowners. Its goal has been a working compromise through cooperation between capitalism and socialism. The Japanese Communist Party has been by far the most vociferous and militant political party. It is the only party which derives its policies, inspiration, and support from external, non-Japanese sources and employs tactics abhorrent to the majority of the electorate. However, in the general election of January 1949, it won 35 seats in the House of Representatives by polling close to 3,000,000 votes and also succeeded in placing six members in the House of Councilors. After reaching its peak of power in late 1948 and early 1949, the Communist Party began to show signs of decline largely through the alienation of voters, the public, and even the labor unions. In 1954, however, it still remained a force to be reckoned with, especially since it could become an effective fifth column for the cause of communism.

Postwar governments have all been formed through coalitions of some kind, involving all sorts of political deals. The possible exceptions—if they were really such—were the third and fourth governments of Prime Minister Shigeru Yoshida, which were formed in 1949 and 1952, respectively.

As in the past, political parties are still plagued by internal disunion, resulting in splitting and fragmentation. These parties all suffer in various degrees from inexperience and lack of proper leadership as well as of new blood. Old party men accustomed to old ways of thinking and doing things and bureaucratically trained men with bureaucratic ideas, attitudes, and techniques of handling men and problems occupy positions of party leadership. Political deals are still consummated behind the scenes in the customary manner. Corruption has not disappeared, nor has bossism been removed from every level of politics. Naturally public distrust of political parties is still strong. Political parties which still lack a popular base concern themselves primarily, though not exclusively, with a relentless pursuit for power, constantly maneuvering to gain control of the government. Personalities more than principles influence their decisions and actions. Parties and their leadcrs must demonstrate their firm grasp of the meaning of democracy, not merely in the abstract but as an attitude of mind as well as a process in the context of Japanese politics, if they are to become an effective force in building a democratic system of government.

Bibliography.—Kanamori, Tokujirō, *Nihon Kempō Minshuka no Shōten* (Tokyo 1946); id., *Kokkai Ron* (Tokyo 1947); Kokka Gakkai, *Shin Kempō no Kenkyū* (Tokyo 1947); Minobe, Tatsukichi, *Shin Kempō no Kihon Genri* (Tokyo 1947); Ōdaka, Tomoo, *Kokumin Shuken to Tennōsei* (Tokyo 1947); Hayashi, Keizō, *Chihō Jichi Kōwa* (Tokyo 1949); Nakamura, Akira, *Shin Kempō Nōto* (Tokyo 1949); Sasaki, Sōichi, *Nihonkoku, Kempō Ron* (Tokyo 1949); Yokota, Kisaburō, *Tennōsei* (Tokyo 1949).

CHITOSHI YANAGA,
Associate Professor of Political Science, Yale University.

12. CHANGING CULTURAL PATTERNS.

The broad outlines of Japanese society, as described in the section on *The People*, have persisted for centuries. The rapid changes since the 1930's, however, invite more detailed description, both of persisting features and of innovations.

Homogeneity.—The striking cultural homogeneity of the Japanese people is no innovation enforced by an adventitious dictator. The stern sumptuary laws of the Tokugawa period (1603–1867) laid the basis of a conformity that still persists. By the 17th century samurai were authorized to behead any civilian whose conduct was "other than expected," and until 1945 police supervision continued to ensure high uniformity in conduct. Japan's geographical insularity has been abetted by these controls, by a written language that minimizes international communication, and by indoctrination in the public schools. Despite obvious individual differences, every Japanese has resembled every other Japanese much more closely than American or European individuals have resembled their compatriots. Although the stress on democracy after World War II fostered individual differences, Japan's population continues to be less diversified than Occidental populations.

Superficially the smooth channels of etiquette and custom have confined behavior within accepted limits, but the consequent efforts to ensure that everyone conforms to expected conduct have betrayed deep insecurities in personal relations. The pressure to conform has appeared in numberless small items of behavior; common folk formerly bowed abjectly before their superiors and still do so. Even in feudal days, when oppression called forth peasant revolts, no one proposed the abolition of the upper classes, and there was general acceptance of the savage penalties visited on leaders of a revolt. After World War II the people relaxed visibly when police supervision diminished. Were this situation to continue for a generation, Japan's cultural homogeneity could give way to considerable diversity in behavior and personality.

The persisting cultural homogeneity of Japan has been evident in features that have outlived the centuries and that change in form but continue in essence. These include the idea that government is a magical ritual to ensure national welfare—an idea sorely battered by the facts of World War II and thereafter competing with the concept of government as the business of the people; high regard for learning and respect for teachers; glorification of frugality and renunciation of wealth as a criterion of status; family-like guilds of craftsmen and specialists; men's associations, often secret and sometimes actively violent in politics; subordination of females ever since the Buddhist ascendancy of the 9th and 10th centuries; stress on formal etiquette as the technique of social intercourse; emotional tautness that appears both as alertness and as hypersensitivity to insult; freedom from prudery and unemotional acceptance of nudity when dictated by convenience; cultivated aesthetic sensitivity and delicately disciplined manual dexterity; adoration of the scenic beauty of "the land of the gods"; distaste for animal husbandry; seasonal festivals that regulate the peasant's calendar, perpetuate ritual, and afford recreation; houses built on posts with clear space beneath the floor, paper-covered doors, and a place of honor in a guest room; exaltation of the warrior as the social cynosure, and reckless devotion in battle to the overlord—a tradition vociferously repudiated since World War II; and profound insecurity when confronted by situations not provided for by rule and custom—a corollary to the stress on conformity.

The conservatism inherent in the family organization has preserved these and many other time-honored cultural traits. Although the family organization and its attendant customs have decayed rapidly since the United States occupation, it is too soon to conclude that this trend is irreversible. A characteristic aspect of Japanese cultural homogeneity has been the unanimous and rapid swings of fashion and of political and general opinion from one extreme to another, and this trait may easily reverse many current trends.

Cultural Receptivity.—In contrast with the urge toward conformity, and often in sharp conflict with it, established tradition assumes that desirable ideas and contrivances may be obtained from abroad. Eager borrowing of Chinese cultural patterns from the 7th to the 10th centuries foreshadowed the intensive quest for Euro-American learning and technology in the 19th and 20th centuries. Such avid pursuit of alien culture is unique in history. Wholesale adoption of foreign practices often engenders feelings of inferiority, however, and repeatedly the Japanese have overcompensated for these feelings by feverish attempts to "improve" borrowed ideas and devices and by recurrent waves of hatred of foreigners. Nevertheless, the tradition of selective adoption of exotic ideas has constituted Japan's major cultural asset. It effected a remarkable flowering of civilization that transformed a minor cultural satellite of China into a progressive nation that barely missed the hegemony of Asia.

The traditional openness toward foreign institutions facilitated acceptance of numerous reforms introduced by the postwar occupation, but the usual reaction against an overdose of new practices was gaining headway in the 1950's. The same cultural receptivity also favored rapid expansion of communism; in Japanese eyes, any foreign ideology deserves investigation, even though a period of trial may lead to vigorous repudiation. Both American democratic practices and Communist-Marxist ideology are candidates for this mass acceptance and subsequent rejection. Ultimately such ideological turmoil results in assimilation of some of the foreign ideas and techniques, and Japanese culture manages to preserve its distinctive aspect.

The occupation was unique in Japan's history—not primarily for its military implications, but because it brought large numbers of Japanese into personal contact with foreigners. The social and cultural consequences of this contact are not readily ascertainable as yet, but certain apparently minor cultural innovations, such as the relaxation of formality in social contacts and the establishment of new forms of recreation, may outlast the formal institutional changes that were supported by military fiat.

Simultaneously, the Communists demonstrated that Japanese could challenge the sanctity of their emperor. In practical consequences, this breach with the past may outweigh the military defeat that made it possible. The Communists have busily fomented anti-Americanism, and the effect on cultural innovations attributed to the United States is unpredictable. One clear effect of the war and of Japanese cultural receptivity is the enhanced prestige of American technology and standards of living.

The Family as Model.—The traditional pattern of family organization reappears in larger associations and in the nation itself. Pertinent aspects of family custom include the orientation of loyalty upward toward seniors, parents, and ancestors rather than toward spouses, juniors, or collateral relatives. Transmission of lineage from eldest son to eldest son enhances the status of the first-born male and depreciates that of junior siblings and females. By law and custom ties of descent outweigh the bonds of matrimony. Formerly marriage contracts were entered into by the house, not by individuals, and a son's wife was called the bride of the house. Younger sons normally have left the house to seek independent careers. In theory they still support the house financially and submit to the family council, and in illness or hardship they may receive succor. This displacement of junior sons—and, in modern times, of unwed daughters—combined with the transfer of married daughters to other households, underlies many unique aspects of Japanese society.

Family interests appear also in the pervasive etiquette of face—that is, protection of family status and dignity against a hostile world. Although emphasis on face has declined, especially in the rearing of children, a child still knows that his misconduct may lose face for the house. Before World War II scarcely a year passed without newspaper reports of suicide by a small child after a reprimand at school. Teachers often said that it was better to promote all pupils in a class than to risk face for some family. Etiquette supports polite fictions (*yūmei mujitsu*) that protect families from public exposure of their weaknesses.

In feudal times social organization was patterned strictly after the extended family. Even in the modern period it has been customary for travelers who hail from one's ancestral *kuni* or ancient province to expect and receive the hospitality accorded to relatives. Political alliances and rivalries often have stemmed from loyalty to the old-time *kuni*. Organs of local government, committees, industrial combines, professional associations, and, in theory, the nation acknowledge the familial pattern of human organization and determine their policies much as family councils arrive at decisions.

Typical of the infusion of family concepts throughout Japanese social organization is the institution called *oyabun-kobun*. This is a ritual pseudo kinship that appears in labor groups, craft associations, political parties, professions, and racketeering. An occupational or other group centering in a vested interest sanctioned by custom often assumes the form of an extended family. Members, not blood kin, nevertheless assume ties that bear kinship designations, and within the framework of the association treat each other as kindred. The head of the organization is addressed as *oyabun; oya* means "parent," and the suffix *-bun* (sometimes *-kata*) distinguishes these terms of pseudo kinship from the otherwise identical terms of family affiliation. Protégés and subordinate members of the pseudo kindred are addressed as *kobun; ko* means "child." There may be a ritual grandfather, uncles, elder and younger brothers, and grandchildren—all addressing each other by the appropriate kinship terms carrying the suffix *-bun*.

The initial organization of an *oyabun-kobun* group includes a ceremony in which the members pledge filial and fraternal loyalty by drinking sake to which salt and a bit of fish have been added to symbolize blood. Usually the group assumes a "family" name, and *kobun* may wear jackets bearing this ritual name. The *oyabun* obligates himself to aid his *kobun* in obtaining vocational training and in finding employment, and provides loans when needed and care in illness. In turn, the *kobun* are expected to aid the *oyabun* in retirement and to provide for his funeral.

Family solidarity and social stability formerly centered in the ownership of real estate and other property by the house; the current head served as a sort of trustee. Normally he retired sometime after reaching the age of 50 in favor of his eldest son or heir. A last will and testament was superfluous, and the death of a retired head rarely occasioned redistribution of property. If the heir was a minor, the family council appointed an acting head. Consequently, testamentary problems received slight attention in Japanese law; the durable issues centered in problems of inclusion in, or exclusion from, membership in a house, and in succession.

All this was upset by new inheritance laws promoted by the postwar occupation. American concepts of individual ownership and disposal of property by a will were embodied in laws working to disrupt the traditional family organization. Brothers and sisters now inherited equally, and family property thus became subject to dispersal whenever the head of a family died. In litigation the emphasis shifted to problems of inheritance and allotment of individual shares in property formerly held by a family. If these laws continued in force, radical changes in the family system would be inevitable, and Japanese social organization might adopt new patterns and shift away from the *oyabun-kobun* model.

Country and City.—In the 20th century divergence of urban and rural populations has threatened the homogeneity of Japanese society. In earlier times Japan was notable for its simple feudal dichotomy of helpless peasants and military overlords. As elsewhere in southern and eastern Asia, the peasant who raised wet rice was tied to his paddy and hamlet. He lacked the means of broadening his horizon and resignedly accepted the inscrutable vagaries of flood, drought, typhoon, earthquake, civil war, and government. Over tangible issues such as land rent and water rights he flared into violence, but the hills that furnished his precious water circumscribed his imagination.

Urban life, however, was no novelty in Japan. There have been cities for a dozen centuries. Their luxuries were formerly obtained at the peasant's expense, but modern industrial urbanization has achieved a measure of independence from the local agrarian economy. In the late 1930's frenzied preparations for war accelerated the concentration of industry, and the cities grew explosively. From the 1880's to the 1930's the rural-farm population continued stable at 35 to 40 millions, the farms were saturated, and the population increase was accommodated in the cities. World War II drove many city dwellers back to the farms, however, while other urbanites moved to suburban fringes away from the bombed-out centers and thereby seriously reduced the effective area of cropland.

Meanwhile, a startling agricultural revolution, based on the intensive education of farmers in scientific agriculture, gained momentum beginning in the late 1920's. Scientific techniques thus diffused among farmers include precise knowledge of fertilizers—animal, chemical, and vegetable; knowledge of the uses of hybrid seeds; pest control; minute attention to soil chemistry; control of plant diseases; and ingenious mechanization of many farm operations. Threshing, formerly done by flails, is performed by footpower machines of Japanese invention; the laborious hand manufacture of the indispensable straw rope has been replaced by a footpower machine that turns out better rope in a fraction of the former time; and rice is ground or hulled in power mills. Electricity has become available in most rural districts, and many farmers own small internal combustion power units. Since the mid-1930's increased productivity of cropland has permitted farm population to increase, even as rural standards of living have risen. Land tenure reforms initiated by the occupation, abetted by inflation and black markets for farm produce, have cut sharply into farm tenancy and farmers' debts.

Consequently, by the mid-1950's the farmers in many parts of Japan had begun to approach urban standards of living. Their diets had expanded to include canned foods, bread, candy, and other luxuries. Universal schooling had equipped farm people to acquire scientific knowledge, to read newspapers and magazines, and to take advantage of the general availability of radio sets to keep in touch with the outer world—especially to keep posted on markets. Small factories close to farm villages offered part-time employment to members of rural households and provided many families with cash.

Since urban populations have been recruited from junior sons and daughters whom rural homes could not accommodate, the cities include millions of individuals whose old family ties are tenuous and whose outlook is congenial to innovation. Urban workers, however, often maintain one tie to their rural kindred: during the economic stringency of the 1930's unemployed workers returned to the ancestral villages to share the meager fare of their country cousins. Similarly, during World War II urban refugees dispersed to live with rural kinsmen until cities once more became habitable. Such emergencies impose a heavy burden on the peasants' straitened resources—a burden mitigated in postwar years by black-market prices for foodstuffs that brought cash to the farms. Given a stable economy free of depressions and wars, however, the gap between peasant and city dweller might continue to widen along lines evident before 1930.

The widespread Asian tradition that land is the safest investment persists despite the development of a capitalist economy. In an overpopulated country this kind of investment quickly forces land prices far above the level of profitable farming. Peasants fall into debt, good land is concentrated in the hands of landlords who do not understand farming, and the wastes and human misery of tenancy multiply. A further threat to Japan's rural population inheres in the failure to divide the tax load equitably between industry and agriculture. Prior to World War II, Japan's entire economy involved hidden dependence of "modernization" upon the farmers and fisherfolk. Tax-subsidized heavy industry, plus governmental bureaucracy, plus armament costs imposed a crushing burden on the farmers. Some redistribution of the tax load occurred during the occupation, but fundamental reforms have continued to be postponed, and farmers speak of the future with deep misgivings.

City and country alike manifest certain far-reaching social changes in the status and behavior of women. The woman's movement, which had its roots in the democratic enthusiasms of the early 1920's, was carried far toward fruition by the postwar reforms of the 1940's and early 1950's. Women's societies are universal. During World War II they were drawn into the net of governmental organization in patriotic endeavor. Since the war they have followed the lines of development familiar to Americans and to many north Europeans. Women speak out in political matters as never before, and a notable increase in educational facilities for women contributes richly to the new public spirit.

The new outlook of women has been accompanied by a whole series of innovations in infant care and child-rearing practices. Improved access to physicians and the scientific training of midwives have combined with the wide reading of baby-care books to revolutionize the early months of life for millions of Japanese. As these babies mature and assume responsibility, their generation may conceivably accept goals and values that have not been congenial to their forebears. The numerous inexpensive magazines for women exert great influence, continually diffusing new methods of homemaking, cooking of novel dishes, child psychology, Occidental fashions, and diverse points of view concerning women's status, sex, politics, and the technology of domestic life.

Sheer physical changes in Japanese cities facilitate changes in living habits. Playgrounds, parks, and public recreation facilities; public water supplies, gas, electricity, and cheap rapid transportation; and, above all, the endless variety of goods on display in both old-style shops and luxurious modern department stores—all these combine to render impossible the return to ancient patterns of living. Japan's cities, prior to World War II, had approximated the appearance and the animation of Occidental cities. The devastation that razed much of their area during the war proved a boon from one point of view; it suddenly became possible to substitute wide, straight boulevards for narrow, winding streets, to make room for parks, and to improve transportation. On the whole, most cities took full advantage of these opportunities, and the new physical aspect of urban Japan carries few hints of the ancient Orient. People who ride in subways, live to the blare of radio and television, read books of every country in translation, grow up on paved streets and find their pleasure in theater, dance hall, night club, ball park, or race track can reconstitute the social forms of the past only in sentimental pretense, never in reality.

So, like all great cities, those of modern Japan provide advantages for their denizens and also expose them to specific dangers. Ancient customs lose prestige, and demagogues can sweep urban crowds into fantastic hysterias. On the other hand, the Japanese have learned that in modern war cities are fatally vulnerable, and that even in peacetime employment may be irregular and security precarious. Stable marriage and parent-child relationships are undermined by a bewildering variety of superficial secondary contacts, with a consequent increase in divorces, suicides, and crimes. Through mass-communication media foreign customs and ideologies are adopted overnight, and are as speedily forgotten.

Ever since the opening of the 17th century, Japanese society has been tightly organized on a class pattern, and even after the restoration of 1868, four distinct classes—nobility, gentry, commoners, and "new commoners"—were recognized and everyone had to state his class when he filled out legal documents, police records, school certificates, or similar formal papers. This simple scheme has not survived the changing needs of an increasingly industrialized, bureaucratically ruled society in an urban setting. The formal abolition of class distinctions occurred in the 1930's in the course of the egalitarian movement incidental to the prewar totalitarian, militarist enthusiasms. The obsolescence of formal social classes occurred not through democratic, but through antidemocratic, influences. Nevertheless, the success of this attempt to fit the nation into the egalitarian formula of totalitarianism was possible because economic status, skill, occupation, learning, military rank, civil service grades, and differences in income already had reduced the four-class system to a meaningless rubric. Sensitivity to differences in social status, and to the differences embodied in the obsolete class system, however, persists rather conspicuously in the social behavior of most individuals.

Etiquette and Morals.—The entrenched regard for social class attained explicit formulation in the language and etiquette of Japan, and despite a notable relaxation of the rules of etiquette and a corresponding simplification of language after World War II, the traditional patterns have not vanished. The phenomenon of a divine upper class which must be addressed in special words is found again and again in southern and eastern Asia, and perhaps the closest parallel to the traditional Japanese usages occurred in Polynesia. The Japanese language comprised several languages in one, each adapted to addressing persons of social status above or below that of the speaker.

This linguistic etiquette symbolized the entire pattern of social relations. Quite in the Confucian mood, one has needed to know one's own position in relation to the status of everyone encountered, and has governed social contacts in accordance with the rigid patterns thus indicated. Traditionally, introductions are performed only if both individuals desire to meet, and the ritual of presentation amounts to self-introduction. The nearest equivalent to the Occidental handshake is the deep bow from the hips; this gesture of courtesy upon meeting is not optional, as is the handshake, but marks every meeting, parting, or expression of courtesy.

The assumption of humility toward equals or superiors is fundamental, together with a degree of arrogance, however restrained, toward inferiors. One's own family and possessions are deprecated, while the use of honorific linguistic forms indicates the person or possessions of another. One compliments another person by calling at his home, but in the mood of humility refrains from inviting others to one's "mean abode."

In the mood of the basic Confucian relationships, most Japanese are involved in complex patron-protégé situations. In social or business contacts one normally relies on a guarantor (*hoshōnin*) who prepares introductions and negotiations in advance and mediates divers transactions. For example, in filling an important post an employer deals with a trusted acquaintance who proposes and vouches for a prospective employee. The latter would not dream of any breach of trust that would lose face for his sponsor.

Etiquette merges indistinguishably with moral standards. It was taught of old—and indeed until 1945—that the ordinary Japanese owed his very existence to ineffably glorious, supernaturally endowed overlords, even as he owed his bodily form to his parents. Thus he was born under obligations that could be acknowledged but never could be repaid. One receives *on*—the beneficence of emperor, parent, overlord, teacher, or patron—and owes *gimu,* an obligation or liability that under the old code must be kept constantly in mind. It was taught that the *gimu* of loyalty due the emperor could not be repaid, not a ten-thousandth part of it, even by death in battle. *Giri,* on the other hand, denotes the obligations that one incurs and repays in the normal reciprocities of living. *Giri* is the sense of propriety that prompts one to offer a return gift, to work for a neighbor who has rendered assistance, to avenge an insult, or to perform duties to relatives. Maintenance of face depends on sensitive awareness of *on, gimu,* and *giri;* the comment *giri wo shiranu* (he does not know *giri*) may imply moral deficiency as well as ignorance of manners. Benefaction, loyalty, reciprocity, duty —a household is judged and accorded neighborhood status in these terms. But the old traditions lose force in the cities, and many young people ignore them.

Integral in the patterns of etiquette and morals are aesthetic ideals such as the goal of sophisticated simplicity in the arts. The relative absence of furniture in a typical Japanese home exemplifies this ideal. A guest kneels on the thick straw floor mats and sits back on his crossed feet; politely he defers acceptance of a proffered cushion and resists the host's urging to move toward the place of honor. Meals are served with due regard to aesthetics; the little dining tables are about a foot high, while the lacquered bowls and porcelain dishes are arranged tastefully on lacquered trays to display the colors and textures of the foods. Rooms are not adorned with pictures or bric-a-brac; usually a single long scroll painting graces the place of honor, and this probably has been changed just before the arrival of an expected guest. If the guest is skilled in the social graces, he will notice the picture, interpret the literary or other symbolic allusion, and thereby compliment his host. Such complex rituals of etiquette as the famed tea ceremony are charged with moral, aesthetic, and religious significance. On the whole, the urban younger generation exhibits considerable ignorance respecting traditional etiquette, aesthetics, rituals, and folklore.

Obsolescence of Handicrafts.—The displacement of handicraft production by factory-centered technology, well under way in the 1920's, was accelerated tremendously by World War II. Formerly every locality proudly displayed and sold its *meibutsu* or local product, and most goods used domestically came from handicraft technology. Many craftsmen were organized into guilds that maintained unity by rituals and rules enforced on members. Quite generally the technique of production was dramatized and kept uniform by chanted rituals that sometimes required the specialized knowledge of a Shintō ritualist. The war changed all this. Craftsmen were drafted into factories in which their special skills supposedly would count, tools were remelted, and other equipment was dismantled. Very few of the traditional handicrafts remained by the 1950's.

Recreation.—The idea of regular vacation periods was adopted into Japanese culture from Euro-American sources in the 1920's. Previously rest days had been limited to the 15th and final days of each month, to seasonal festivals like the cherry-blossom holidays in spring, the New Year, and celebrations at shrines and temples. Pilgrimages, nominally religious, were prolonged picnics at holy places, shrines, and spots renowned for natural beauty. Recognized vacation areas other than hot springs came into vogue in the 20th century, and national parks were established after 1930.

The ancient nobles enjoyed trials of skill such as archery, a form of football, and military exercises, as well as aesthetic rituals like the tea ceremony and incense-smelling contests. Modern popular sports incline to mass spectatorship at baseball games, all sorts of track races, *sumō* (a kind of wrestling between specially nurtured giants), sword or fencing practice called *kendō,* and *jūdō* or *jūjitsu.* *Kendō* and *jūdō* differ in psychology from Occidental sports; their exponents regard them as preparation for deadly combat without quarter. Prior to and during World War II all Occidental sports were discouraged, and some of them prohibited, on the ground that they did not prepare men for victory in combat. Since the war all of the banned sports have been resumed enthusiastically.

Many Japanese devote time to a decorative garden, the care of dwarf trees, and the making of tray gardens, or to more active pastimes such as hiking and mountain climbing. Women practice flower arrangement. Such activities include religious and aesthetic values in addition to recreational aspects. Calligraphy, the composition of tiny poems, the mastery of an ancient dance or song, and the practice of a skilled craft combine hobby, recreation, and art in a uniquely Japanese fashion. Among hobbies borrowed from the Occident, photography probably occupies first place; ham radio, philately, numismatics, and the collection of books, antiques, and phonograph records all claim devotees.

Japan's assimilation of Occidental music constitutes a striking cultural transformation, for Occidental music and Japan's traditional music are almost totally incommensurable. The ancient types of music survive, but much folk music follows Western patterns. The people sing folk songs of every nation, dance tunes, opera arias, and the latest jazz. When a symphony concert is broadcast, it is an unusual group of listeners that does not include someone who can identify Occidental works by name and composer.

The cinema appeared in Japan almost as soon as it spread in the Occident. Foreign films are popular, and Japanese producers turn out films that win audiences abroad despite the handicap of language.

Bibliography.—Mitford, A. B. (1st Baron Redesdale), *Tales of Old Japan* (London 1871); Sugimoto, E. I., *A Daughter of the Samurai* (Garden City 1925); Chamberlain, B. H., *Things Japanese,* 5th ed. (Kobe 1905; reprinted 1927); Taut, Bruno, *Houses and People of Japan* (Tokyo 1937); Embree, J. F., *Suye Mura, A Japanese Village* (Chicago 1939); Lamott, W. C., *Nippon: The Crime and Punishment of Japan* (New York 1944); Benedict, R. F., *The Chrysanthemum and the Sword* (Boston 1946); Haring, D. G., ed., *Japan's Prospect* (Cambridge, Mass., 1946); Hulse, F. S., "A Sketch of Japanese Society," *Journal of the American Oriental Society,* July-September 1946; Braibanti, R. J. D., "Neighborhood Associations in Japan," *Far Eastern Quarterly,* February 1948; Linton, Ralph, ed., *Most of the World,* pp. 814-75 (New York 1949); Reischauer, E. O., *The United States and Japan* (Cambridge, Mass., 1950); Sansom, G. B., *The Western World and Japan* (New York 1950); Haring, D. G., "Japanese National Character," *Yale Review,* spring 1953; Ishino, Iwao, "The *Oyabun-Kobun,*" *American Anthropologist,* December 1953; Norbeck, Edw., *Takashima, a Japanese Fishing Community* (Salt Lake City 1954).

DOUGLAS G. HARING,
Professor of Anthropology, Syracuse University.

13. RELIGION.

Religion in Japan today means primarily the three recognized religions—Shintō, Buddhism, and Christianity. Prior to about 1900, Confucianism was the third religion, instead of Christianity. The role these religions have played in the life of the Japanese is seen best when presented historically. Japan's religious history may be divided into seven periods:

(1) Prehistoric and semihistoric, ending in the 6th century A.D.

(2) Early Buddhist, 6th to 8th century, in which Buddhism was introduced and was accepted primarily as the vehicle of the higher Chinese civilization.

(3) Heian Buddhist, 9th to 12th century, when Buddhism, together with other elements of Chinese civilization, became an integral part of the religious and cultural life of the upper classes, while Shintō remained predominantly the religion of the masses.

(4) Indigenous Buddhist, 12th to 16th century, when Buddhism with marked changes became the dominant religion of all classes.

(5) Period of the regimentation of all life, including religion, in the interest of a police state, 16th century to 1868. Buddhism remained the dominant religion but lost ground to neo-Confucianism and renascent Shintō. Christianity flourished for a short time, only to be rigorously suppressed.

(6) Period in which religion was an instrument of an expanding state (1868–1945). Shintō, Buddhism, and Christianity were regarded in varying ways as of possible service to the state but were circumscribed in their activities, while State Shintō was sponsored as a cult of patriotism superior to all religion.

(7) Post-World War II.

Prehistoric and Semihistoric Period.—The religion of the early Japanese was primarily a naive nature worship to which was added, possibly under Chinese influence, a form of ancestor worship. The objects worshiped were designated by the term *kami,* meaning "above" or "superior." Any object or natural phenomenon giving rise to a feeling of wonder, awe, or fear was regarded as a *kami.* The most widely worshiped *kami* were the sun, moon, mountain peaks, streams, waterfalls, and devastating storms, but innumerable other objects such as large trees, stones of peculiar shape, certain animals, and even insects were worshiped.

The *kami* concept naturally underwent some changes in meaning as the Japanese gradually emerged from their primitive state. We can distinguish roughly three levels in this early period. There is first the preanimistic conception by which the natural object or phenomenon is worshiped as such without the worshiper formulating any definite idea about it. This holds true especially for such awe-inspiring objects as the sun, majestic mountain peaks, or the terrible storms. The second level is typical animism, in which certain objects or natural phenomena are seen as controlled by some indwelling spirit, good or evil, which must be worshiped or propitiated. On the third level the innumerable nature spirits are made over more and more into the image of man himself, and thus we get the familiar gods and goddesses of polytheistic Shintō with its growing mythology. On this third level of Japan's early religion appears a form of ancestor worship—that is, the deification of clan chieftains, heroic warriors, benefactors, and ancestors. The two lines—the nature spirits and the deified humans—were then more or less merged, and we see the picture of early Shintō's *yao-yorozu-no-kami* (800 myriads of gods).

This development of the *kami* concept took place apparently before the early Japanese came consciously under the influence of the more mature religions of China. Japan's oldest literary records, the *Kojiki* (712 A.D.) and *Nihon Shoki* (720), reflect this type of religion. At the same time, however, they show how the unorganized and primitive nature and ancestor worship was being more or less organized into a system called Shintō, a Chinese term meaning "way of the gods." In these records we find a crude theogony and cosmology. There are two major groupings of deities: the seven generations of celestial deities, and the subsequent terrestrial deities. Prominent in the first group are deities representing creative or productive powers such as the high-producing or the divine-producing deity. The last pair of the celestial deities, Izanagi and Izanami, produce the Japanese archipelago and various lesser objects of nature. Izanagi alone begets Amaterasu-ōmikami, the Heaven-Shining Great Deity, and Susa-no-wo, the Swift-Impetuous Deity, or Storm God, the former standing increasingly for enlightenment and all that is good, and the latter for the forces of violence and evil. This nascent dualism was never developed, probably because of the overpowering influences of Chinese civilization in the subsequent period.

The Sun Goddess, Amaterasu, originally a major nature deity worshiped by all the clans, was recast at the dawn of history as the divine progenitor of the ruling family. Each clan had its own clan deity, *uji-gami* with the clan chieftain, *uji-no-gami,* serving as high priest, and, as such, regarded as semidivine.

The shrines of early Japanese religion were at first objects and places which called forth a feeling of awe and wonder. Then, simple structures of wood or stone were erected to house the object in which the spirit was believed to dwell. Such objects were called *shintai* (god body). The most famous of them were the three insignia of imperial authority: the sacred mirror, the curved jewel, and the sword.

The good-life ideal was conceived largely in terms of the physical. The gods received in sacrifice the kind of things the pious devotee expected of them in return. Ethical and spiritual elements were present only in a rudimentary form. There is also very little regarding man's ultimate destiny. The early records speak of a realm of gloom, and the gods are pictured as descending from the heavenly realm, but there is little in the way of giving man hope in a life after death. Possibly, however, there was more than appears in the records, and it was forgotten as the early Japanese turned to Buddhist teachings about the individual's destiny.

Early Buddhist Period (6th to 8th Century). —Buddhism reached Japan first by way of Korea in 552 A.D. To gain help against his rivals, the king of Paekche sent to the Japanese court a mission which included Buddhist monks. Among the gifts they brought were Buddhist scriptures, a Buddhist statue, and various ceremonial objects. An accompanying letter recommended Buddhism as "the most excellent of all teachings," and explained that it was generally accepted in all countries from Korea to India.

A great controversy soon developed, some Japanese advocating acceptance of the new religion, while others bitterly opposed it. Within a few decades, however, Buddhism gained a real foothold, and when the prince regent, the famous Shōtoku Taishi (r. 593–621/622) began sponsoring the new faith its future was assured. In an edict he urged his people to "sincerely reverence the Three Treasures (Buddha, the doctrine, and the order)," for these "are the refuge of the four classes of living things and are in all countries the supreme object of faith." In thus sponsoring Buddhism, Shōtoku Taishi set an example which subsequent Japanese sovereigns usually followed. The prince himself was well versed in Buddhist lore and gave lectures on certain Buddhist texts. Of greater consequence, however, was his establishment of direct connection with T'ang China in order to learn more about the new religion and the higher Chinese civilization. In fact, Buddhism gained its first ascendancy in Japanese life because of what it brought in its train as the vehicle of Chinese civilization. Buddhist monks transmitted in ever-increasing volume much of Chinese literature, art, architecture, medical lore, and various crafts. Great temples, monasteries, hospitals, and asylums were established. The Buddhist ideal of the unity of all life was a factor in the Taikwa (Great Reform) of 646 which reshaped Japan's political structure on the Chinese administrative pattern. Even those loyal to the native faith showed the influence of Buddhism in their organization of the innumerable local cults into a sort of system, with the Sun Goddess given greater prominence as the divine ancestress of the ruling family. The naive legends and mythologies were arranged into a kind of history by following the Chinese model.

The influence of Buddhism is perhaps best seen in connection with Japan's first real capital city, Nara, which was patterned after the Chinese capital, Changan. With its great temples and monasteries it grew into a city of real magnificence. The gigantic bronze statue dedicated to the Buddha Vairochana (Vairocana), known in Japanese as Dainichi (Great Illuminator) and declared to be one with the Sun Goddess, prepared the way for reconciling the claims of the two religions. To be sure, the vast majority of the people continued to worship their local Shintō deities, but many, especially in the capital and in some of the provincial centers where Buddhist temples were being built, came increasingly under the sway of Buddhist teachings.

Six different schools of Chinese Buddhism found their way into Japan during this period. In varying ways they accustomed the Japanese to think in terms of universal concepts. The Buddhist conception of the divine, of man as a citizen of eternity, the ministry of mercy as expressed in the Bodhisattva ideal, and the general ethical teachings of Buddhism were all of them far more satisfying than what the old faith had to say on such matters.

Heian Buddhism (800–1200).—The removal of the capital in 794 to Heian, later called Kyoto, marked a change in the religious situation. The very word *heian,* which means "peace and tranquility," expresses the Buddhist ideal of life. Whereas in the preceding period Buddhism had been propagated largely by foreign missionaries, now the work was done almost wholly by Japanese who had studied at Buddhist centers in China or at great centers of Japanese Buddhism as these developed, especially at the Tendai establishment on Hieizan, near Kyoto. Two monks in particular helped to usher in this new period: Saichō (767–822), better known by his posthumous name of Dengyō Daishi; and Kūkai (774–835), the famous Kōbō Daishi. In 804 they had as young monks accompanied a government mission to China, and after a few years' study on the mainland, they returned to Japan bringing with them new forms of Buddhism.

Dengyō Daishi studied at the great center of T'ien-t'ai Buddhism, a type most comprehensive in its teachings, and he founded in Japan the Tendai sect, which subsequently played an important role both as one of the two major sects during this period, and later as the source of new sects. Dengyō was faithful in transmitting to Japan the all-inclusive Tendai type of Buddhism, which tries to find room for all the varied teachings of the voluminous Buddhist canon. Nevertheless, he felt that the great essentials of faith were best formulated in the famous Lotus Sutra (*Saddharmapuṇḍarīkasūtra;* in Japanese, *Myōhōrengekyō*), which glorifies the historic Buddha Śākyamuni as the eternal Buddha. In this view, although the eternal Buddha as absolute being transcends man's comprehension, for practical purposes a religious man may think of Buddha in terms of ideal personality. The eternal reveals itself on different levels and thus fills the needs of finite man. This conception made room for whatever truth there was in other religions, even for the crudities of Shintō. In Dengyō's Buddhism there is also a place for different ways by which man can be saved—the hard way of moral discipline, in which man works out his own salvation; the way of philosophic insight into the truth; and the way of faith and simple trust in the mercy and grace of the eternal Buddha.

Kōbō Daishi, trained for an official career, had studied Confucianism. He also investigated Taoism, but was finally converted to Buddhism. Truth was to him a matter of varying degrees and so he arranged what he had found in his studies in an ascending scale with Buddhism at the top, and with a particular form of Buddhism found in the Chinese Chên-yen school as the most excellent of all. This type he introduced into Japan under the name of Shingon (true word) or Himitsukyō (secret teaching). Kōbō, like Dengyō, had much to say about the eternal Buddha, especially Dainichi Nyorai, the Great Illuminator, but less about the divine as personal. According to Shingon, Dainichi Nyorai is the central sun from which all truth radiates. The many rays are the fragmentary truths seen by different finite minds. Just as these rays radiate in various and even opposite directions, so man's half truths and even contradictory views may each have its place and meaning. Not only is there room for the wide variety of partial truths found in Buddhism, but also for the naive views of Shintō. It was Kōbō's system which more than any other supported that syncretism of the two faiths which prevailed down to modern times.

The eternal Buddha is also represented as the source from which all things emanate so that "in every particle of dust" may be found the nature of Buddha. How much more, then, is man in his inmost nature an offspring of the eternal. He therefore can become one again with the eternal in spite of all his frailties and evil. Sometimes this view of man's nature and his possible destiny found worthy expressions in Kōbō's system, but frequently there is reflected too much of the degenerate type of Indian Tantric Buddhism which makes room in religion for anything man desires. Very little of the moral seriousness of original Buddhism remains and Shingon (true word) becomes the "magic word" which combines a fantastic idealism with the grossest form of materialism.

In one form or another, Buddhism became dominant in the life of the upper classes. Japanese sovereigns continued to support the imported faith, and some of them became monks themselves upon abdicating, taking the title Hō-Ō, or king of the law (of Buddha). Such abdications were often forced, but nevertheless the step taken was represented as honorable. The elaborate Buddhist ceremonials invaded the court ceremonies and added to their splendor, and Kyoto became a city of great magnificence with numerous temples and religious institutions, many of them examples of the best in architecture and filled with fine paintings and sculpture. Serious literature was almost wholly Buddhist, and even such as dealt with secular subjects reflected the Buddhist view of life. In spite of this outward splendor, however, the inner life was not correspondingly rich. In fact, there was often an emptiness stemming from an awareness of the fleeting character of all earthly things, without the real assurance that mortal man could become a citizen of eternity, a conception which Buddhism was supposed to stress. Moreover, the all too facile compromises with Shintō and the religion of the masses left many Buddhists religiously illiterate.

There were, nevertheless, minor movements preparing the way for a type of Buddhism which had real vitality and meaning for the common man. This was especially true of the *Ōjōyōshū* (*Essays on Birth into Paradise*) of Genshin (Eshin, 942–1017), and the preaching of a few others about the eternal Buddha Amida and the way of salvation through faith in his mercy and grace. This teaching was not wholly unknown in Tendai Buddhism, but Genshin lifted it above the many other teachings and gave it prominence. Its real significance appeared with the rise of the great Amida sects in the following period.

Indigenous Buddhism (1200–1600).—The tremendous changes in the political life of Japan during the latter half of the 12th century affected the religious situation and opened the way for new and more popular forms of Buddhism. Three new types developed and became more or less dominant throughout the land.

First in time and in its continuing influence is Amida Buddhism with its two major sects, Jōdoshu and Jōdo Shinshu, founded respectively by Genkū, known as Hōnen Shōnin (1133–1212), in 1175, and Shinran (1173–1262), in 1224. Hōnen had been a studious monk of the Tendai sect, poring over the voluminous canonical scriptures without finding actual peace of mind until he read Genshin's *Ōjōyōshū*. Then he saw that the heart of Buddhism was the prayer *Namu Amida Butsu* ("I worship thee, Amida Buddha"). "When we invoke Buddha and say '*Namu Amida Butsu*' with the firm belief that we shall be born in Buddha's paradise, we shall surely be born there." To his friends, who were perplexed by a profound scholar's giving such a simple interpretation of the essentials of Buddhism, he replied that if he knew anything more profound and withheld it from others he would be forsaken by the "two lords"—the eternal Buddha Amida and the historic Buddha Śākyamuni, regarded as the one who taught about Amida.

Hōnen's simple gospel was heard with joy by all classes of society. Court circles and upper classes whose world was crashing with the decline of imperial power found hope in his message. Military classes, sickened by the horrors of civil war, longed for the peace of Amida's paradise. The common people, so little touched by the older forms of Buddhism, felt that this was a message for them.

Among Hōnen's numerous disciples was Shinran, who, with all his admiration for his teacher, felt that there was still too much emphasis on the old "save thyself" doctrine in the endless repetition of Hōnen's simple prayer. He also felt that religion should be less confined to temples or monasteries, and instead should express itself in the normal life of man. In place of celibacy and the ideal of the monk, he advocated marriage and family life. Thus Buddhism, which had usually been otherworldly in emphasis, became in Shinran's 13th century Japan a religion for citizens of both this and the next world. Although Shinran and his followers were accused of making salvation a bit too easy and the religious life altogether too normal, his Buddhism not only won a great following in his day, but has held its own and still shows great vitality.

Differing greatly from Amida Buddhism is Zen Buddhism, introduced from China by two Japanese monks who had studied at Chinese centers of the Ch'an sect. In 1191 Eisai (1141–1215) introduced the Rinzai sect, and about 1244 Dōgen (1200–1253) introduced the Sōtō sect, of Zen. Zen (Sanskrit *dhyāna*) means "meditation," and it is through deep meditation that man is to realize his essential identity with ultimate reality. The multiplicity of the phenomenal world with all its distracting details, when illumined by the light of the eternal, takes on new meaning. What man obtains through an intuitive insight into truth and the real nature of things cannot be expressed in intellectual concepts, for the deepest truth is "the white silence of truth." Where Eisai stressed the mystical experience and intuitive insight into inner reality, Dōgen placed greater emphasis on what is ordinarily regarded as practical and made more room for thought. Both types of Zen appealed peculiarly to the soldier class, probably because they found in Zen primarily a method of self-discipline and self-assurance, so important in meeting fearlessly the vicissitudes of the battlefield. The characteristics of Zen discipline are the quiet retreat, proper bodily posture, correct breathing, concentration of thought on a given problem expressed often in paradoxes, the intuitive grasp of the truth, momentary ecstasy, and the sense of oneness with the ultimately real.

The third type of Buddhism appearing in 13th century Japan was the Nichiren sect, taking its name from its founder Nichiren (1222–1282). Nichiren had been a monk of the Tendai sect, and he felt that it was time to protest against the Amida and Zen teachings. He sought to restore the pure teachings of Dengyō Daishi, based on the great Lotus Sutra. Japan was then threatened by the Mongols and to meet this danger the country must be united in religion. Unity in religion to him meant loyalty to the historic Buddha glorified as the eternal Buddha in the Lotus Sutra. This loyalty was being undermined, he insisted, by the new sects which talked so much about Amida Buddha and by the vagaries of Zen mysticism. Thus, in Nichiren Buddhism religion and loyalty to one's country had become one. This is a major reason why it made its appeal to Japanese. Nichiren's belligerent spirit, which brought him into conflict with the authorities, seemed contrary to the spirit of true Buddhism which he claimed to champion. And certainly many of his fanatical followers, with their blind worship of the Lotus Sutra while ignorant of its content can hardly be regarded as true representatives of traditional Buddhism, which has usually stressed enlightenment and intellectual tolerance.

All three types of Buddhism flourished during this period. Amida Buddhism with its heavenly paradise presented its message through art and a literature that made its appeal to all classes. The gigantic bronze statue dedicated to Amida at Kamakura about 1252 was a vivid reminder of the Buddhist ideal of calm and eternal peace. This message became all the more meaningful during the incessant civil wars which lasted from about 1330 to 1600. Zen Buddhism likewise won a great following both for its spiritual discipline and essential message and for other aspects of Chinese civilization which it introduced. Sung painting, landscape gardening, flower arrangement, and the tea ceremony, all became truly Japanese. Nichiren Buddhism won many adherents by its very intensity of spirit and also because of its identification of religion with the spirit of loyalty to one's country. One major reason why Buddhism in its various forms now became truly indigenous was that its message was couched in the language of the people instead of the Chinese canonical scriptures and it was made a real part of the common man's life.

In some ways Buddhism during the latter part of this period became too much like the world it was supposed to save. Some of the great temples and monasteries came to resemble feudal states, with many of the monks engaged less in spiritual warfare than in fighting with real swords in defense of their worldly possessions.

With Buddhism becoming thoroughly indigenous, men like Ichijō Kanera (1402–1481) attempted to harmonize it more completely with Shintō, even to the extent of reinterpreting the symbolism of the imperial regalia, giving these a cosmological and ethical connotation. Thus the mirror represented the sun and stood for intelligence and sagacity, the jewel symbolized the moon and the moral qualities of mercy and benevolence, and the flashing sword stood for the stars and signified strength and courage. Ancestor worship was revived and combined with Buddhist philosophical concepts. On the other hand, men like Yoshida Kanetomo (1435–1511) attempted to give the Shintō elements in the religious syncretism greater prominence. In their

Ryobu Shintō, or dual Shintō, they claimed that the Shintō deities were the originals and the Buddhas and Bodhisattvas mere pale Indian reflections of them.

At the end of this period, in 1549, Christianity was introduced with amazing success by Jesuit fathers, led by St. Francis Xavier. Some Japanese saw in it another form of the comprehensive Buddhism. Certain military leaders welcomed the foreigners because of the firearms which the European traders accompanying the missionaries introduced. Oda Nobunaga (1534–1582), the first of the great trio of military leaders who unified Japan, welcomed them for the use he could make of them. His successor, Hideyoshi Toyotomi (1536–1598) was friendly at first but later became convinced that the missionaries were the advance agents of European powers bent on conquest. He therefore adopted a policy of banishing all missionaries and suppressing their converts. Many, under cruel pressure, recanted their faith, but thousands chose martyrdom. By 1638 the last stronghold of the Christians who had risen in revolt was destroyed, and what remained of Christianity was driven underground.

Regimentation of Life and Religion (1600–1868).—With the subjugation of the various feudal states under the Tokugawa shogunate, Japan had peace, but it was more the peace of a police state than that of a free country. In religion the government sought to maintain the status quo. Buddhism was recognized as the dominant religion and was allowed to regulate its own affairs within fixed limits and with the responsibility of keeping a strict religious census to guard against the reappearance of Christianity. The different sects worked out their dogmatic systems and published numerous works. Some monks continued teaching, but the more significant educational work was carried on by the so-called mental culture movement, which was more Confucian than Buddhist. As the guardian of man's ultimate destiny, Buddhism continued to play its accustomed role, but it was less of a factor in this-worldly affairs.

The Tokugawa shogunate turned primarily to Confucianism for support in stabilizing the social structure, because central to Confucianism is the ideal of a well-regulated state whose citizens are indoctrinated with the spirit of obedience. Faithfulness to duty, self-discipline, or stern justice constitute the core of morality for all who exercise authority in the state, the community, or the family. It was especially the neo-Confucianism of the Chinese philosopher Chu Hsi (1130–1200) which was favored, though other forms also flourished, sometimes manifesting such a high degree of independence of thought that the government found it necessary to restrict their freedom. Names of such Confucianists as Fujiwara Seikwa (1561–1619), Hayashi Razan (1583–1657), Nakae Tōjū (1608–1648), Hayashi Shunsai (1618–1680), Itō Jinsai (1627–1705), Kaibara Ekken (1630–1714), Arai Hakuseki (1656-1726), and Muro Kyūsō (1658–1734) indicate that the intellectual leadership had passed from the Buddhists who had held it so long. Another marked change was that, whereas Buddhists, especially Zen scholars, had formerly been friendly toward Confucianism, in this period antagonism developed between the two religions. Not only were the neo-Confucianists anti-Buddhist, but many were virtually antireligious or indifferent to religion, their major interest being political philosophy or humanistic ethical teachings. Nominally they and their families continued some connection with Buddhism, and when a death occurred last rites were performed by Buddhist clerics, but beyond this they had little interest in religion.

One school of Confucian scholars not satisfied with the neo-Confucianism of the Shushi (Chu Hsi) or the Ō-Yōmei (Wang Yang-ming) schools turned its attention to the older Confucianism. This in turn led to an interest in Japan's own older literature and religion, including ancestor worship and the Shintō doctrine of the descent of the imperial family from the divine ancestress Amaterasu. As good Confucianists, they stressed loyalty to the feudal lord, but some began to see that the Tokugawa shoguns who had so zealously sponsored neo-Confucianism in the interest of their own regime were really usurpers.

A parallel movement begun by the Buddhist monk Keichū (1640–1701) put in vogue the study of national antiquities, which was later brought to fruition by such Shintō scholars as Kamo Mabuchi (1697–1769), Motoori Norinaga (1730–1801), and Hirata Atsutane (1776–1843). From their studies arose a pride in Japan's ancient faith as opposed to the imported Buddhism and Confucianism. This in turn became one of the major factors in restoring the imperial authority in 1868. It also resulted in the appearance of new Shintō sects which gradually severed their connection with Buddhism in the interest of a pure national faith. It was, of course, impossible for them to divest themselves of the age-long Buddhist and Confucian influences, and hence these Shintō sects were really syncretistic in their teachings. Some of them were fairly faithful to the typical Shintō emphasis on loyalty to the heaven-descended ruler, but even these showed the influence of Japan's Buddhist and Confucian heritage. Other sects were virtually Confucian in temper and motivating ideals. And still others stressed not only decidedly Buddhist elements, but also, in their later developments, showed the influence of Christianity, especially in their monotheistic trends. One and all of these Shintō sects had moved far from the sort of religion we find in the early Shintō documents.

What made all of these movements really significant beyond their religious aspects was the part they played in the political developments leading to and following the restoration of the emperor to his rightful place in 1868.

Religion As an Instrument of an Expanding State (1868–1945).—With the restoration of 1868 a new situation was created for religion. Shintoists and Confucian samurai who had taken the lead in the restoration undertook the establishing of a national religion subservient to their interests. The age-long Shintō-Buddhist amalgamation was dissolved. Buddhist priests were ejected from Shintō shrines, Buddhist scriptures and ceremonial objects were burned, and much temple property was confiscated. In short, Buddhism, which for centuries had had a privileged position, was deposed.

These severe measures, however, proved unpopular, and in 1872 an arrangement was made which allowed both Buddhists and Shintoists to manage their own internal affairs with the understanding that they would serve the interests of the state by sponsoring "patriotic and humanitarian principles." The young samurai leaders who had led the restoration movement were little interested in religion as such. Their major concern was a strong state which could hold its own against the aggression of Western powers. To achieve this objective they were ready to learn from these powers and to take whatever measures were necessary to avoid any conflict with them while Japan was weak. That is one reason why in 1873 the edicts against Christianity were removed from the public notice boards and this religion, which had been feared and suppressed for some 250 years, was at last permitted to carry on its work.

In the charter oath taken by Emperor Meiji in 1868, the 5th article stated that "knowledge shall be sought for throughout the world. . . ." Thus when Christian missions established their schools and churches in various cities ambitious young men, including many from the samurai class, were eager to learn from these representatives of the Western World. Christianity became quite popular, probably more for what it brought in its train than for its own essential religious message, though a growing number of Japanese become real converts. In fact, during the 1880's, Christianity was making such an impression on Japan that some officials proposed recognizing it as the national religion. Even some missionaries, believing that their work was no longer seriously needed, returned to their homelands.

It was perhaps natural that this wave of enthusiasm for things Western should be followed in the 1890's by a reaction. Some of the more conservative Buddhists took the lead in anti-Christian movements. They were joined by Shintoists and Confucianists, who were ready to forget their past differences, in forming an organization sometimes called the Great Way Uniting the Three Religions. Some of the leaders were familiar with writings of Western philosophers critical of Christianity, and so they attacked Japanese Christianity as being both anti-Japanese and outmoded in the Western World. This anti-Christian movement, however, was soon overshadowed by the war with China (1894–1895) and the Russo-Japanese War (1904–1905), which tended to unite all Japanese in an ardent nationalism irrespective of religious differences. Japan was well launched on her career as an expanding military state, in which religion often became little more than an instrument of the government instead of preserving its own sovereign rights.

Accompanying this nationalistic spirit was a strong trend toward secularism and indifference to religion. This secularism had its most far-reaching effect through Japan's rapidly developing educational system, which borrowed much from the Western World in the field of the natural sciences and all that makes for industrial progress and military power, but little in things of the spirit. That area of life was supposedly provided for in the Imperial Rescript on Education of 1890. This rescript, largely Confucian in content insofar as it dealt with moral ideals, was proclaimed as representing "the teachings of the Imperial Forefathers," and its aim was the unification of national morality. It soon became a sacred text from which teachers were supposed to derive all that was needed for moral training. Religion as such had no place in public schools and only a very restricted place in private ones. This was not so much separation of church and state as the ignoring of religion and the substitution of the all-sufficient "religion of patriotism" zealously fostered through so-called State Shintō.

State Shintō was called into being during the 1880's after an earlier attempt to make traditional Shintō the state religion had failed. The government by decree divided Shintō into two divisions: State or Shrine Shintō, and Sectarian Shintō. State Shintō, the government leaders explained, was not a religion but a cult of patriotism in which all loyal Japanese could participate irrespective of the religious views they might hold privately. Sectarian Shintō, on the other hand, was to be regarded as a religion and as such equal before the law with Buddhism and Christianity. In the Japanese Constitution of 1889 all recognized religions were given a certain degree of freedom to manage their own affairs and to propagate their faiths. The government exercised control but gave them little encouragement, while at the same time it fostered State Shintō with increasing zeal as Japan advanced steadily toward world power. The restrictions placed upon the recognized religions, though real, were not fatal, and so each of the three religions—Shintō, Buddhism, and Christianity—made fairly substantial headway during most of this period.

Buddhism, which had lost much property, made up for this loss by greater activity in educational, literary, and social service fields. By 1940 the 56 sects and subsects maintained more than 70,000 temples in good repair. Adherents numbered about 45,000,000, though many of these were nominal only. Some sects, particularly Jōdo Shinshu, followed Japanese citizens beyond the borders of the empire and in other ways adapted their work to meet the needs of modern life.

Sectarian Shintō, with its 13 sects, claimed about 17,000,000 adherents. Some of these, especially Tenrikyō, manifested a marked missionary zeal both at home and abroad. In several there was a notable doctrinal restatement by which the myriads of gods of the old Shintō records were replaced by a monotheistic faith. The characteristic Shintō emphasis on loyalty to the ruler was maintained by most of these sects, though there were trends among minor Shintō groups not recognized by the government which seemed subversive and so were suppressed.

Christianity showed a slow but steady advance. Adherents numbered upwards of 300,000, with approximately two thirds Protestants and one third Roman and Orthodox Catholics. Probably 1,000,000 or more could be regarded as affiliated with Christianity. Moreover, Christian influence was considerably greater than the number of professed adherents would indicate.

From time to time the government, concerned about evidences of corruption in society, called together representatives of the three religions, urging them to do more in the way of moral instruction and guidance. After World War I, when Communist influences began to manifest themselves, some officials looked especially to Christianity to combat them. These friendly gestures by officialdom were not taken too seriously, however, since those who made the gestures did not take religion very seriously themselves and at best looked upon it as an instrument of state.

This attitude became increasingly evident through the way in which State Shintō was fostered after the mid-1920's. The wave of internationalism which spread over Japan for a few years after World War I began to ebb, and the nation came more and more under the dominance of military leaders whose religion was an intense nationalism. The cult of State Shintō assumed menacing proportions. The Imperial Rescript on

Education and the imperial pictures became more and more sacred. They were often housed in special sanctuaries in schools, and when brought forth on stated occasions they were handled with reverent care. While the pictures were unveiled and the rescript read, the assembled faculty and student body bowed low. The reader's voice trembled in fear lest he mispronounce some word and so be eternally disgraced. Some school principals actually committed suicide in expiation for such an error.

Compulsory attendance at ceremonies conducted at State Shintō shrines was another way in which this religion of patriotism made its demands. These ceremonies contained elements of traditional Shintō, and so Christians and some Buddhists found it difficult to conform. Some of the State Shintō shrines had for centuries been sanctuaries where the *kami* were worshiped and in the eyes of the public continued to be regarded as religious shrines. Therefore participation in the ceremonies was interpreted as a religious act and not simply an expression of loyalty to the throne. Nevertheless, under pressure and with the repeated official affirmation that participation did not compromise non-Shintoists, most of the Christian and Buddhist schools conformed. In Christian schools it was customary to hold a Christian service at which it was explained carefully that Christians worship God alone and that they attend the State Shintō ceremonies only as an expression of patriotism and loyalty to country and ruler. While this could be done with a clear conscience in Japan proper, in annexed territories, such as Korea, the problem was more difficult for the reason that military officials often stressed the religious meaning, including the old Shintō doctrine of the divinity of the emperor.

In short, the whole trend at the end of this period was to subordinate all areas of life, including the individual's soul, to what the military leaders regarded as the highest interest of an expanding military state, a state which had as its foundations the Shintō myth about the divine descent of the Japanese emperor who, as they boastfully proclaimed, was destined to rule over all of eastern Asia, if not the whole world.

Postwar Religion.—Japan's defeat in 1945 had a decided effect on religion. State Shintō, with its tax-supported shrines and compulsory attendance at stated ceremonies, has been abolished. (Certain historic shrines like Ise continue, however, as ceremonial places for the imperial family and high public officials.) Sectarian Shintō, like other religions, enjoys complete freedom. This freedom, however, has resulted in the proliferation of "new religions," most of which are registered as Voluntary Shintō. Buddhism participates in the new freedom but has been faced with financial difficulties in rebuilding its war losses, and this has led in some cases to strife and divisions. Japanese Christianity has not only shared in the new freedom, but has also enjoyed great support from abroad. Roman Catholicism has shown a new vigor and a corresponding increase in membership. In Protestantism the United Church, embracing about two thirds of all Protestants in Japan, has increased substantially in membership and influence. The new freedom and unprecedented opportunities, coupled with the closing of the doors of Communist China, also have resulted in the influx of many new American sects.

All in all, religion faced a new challenge in postwar Japan.

Bibliography.—Cary, Otis, *A History of Christianity in Japan* (Chicago 1909); Reischauer, A. K., *Studies in Japanese Buddhism*, rev. ed. (New York 1925); Kato, Genchi, *A Study of Shintō* (Tokyo 1926); Anesaki, Masaharu, *History of Japanese Religion* (London 1930); Eliot, C. N. E., *Japanese Buddhism* (New York 1935); Holtom, D. C., *The National Faith of Japan* (New York 1938); *The Japan Christian Year Book*, formerly *The Christian Movement* (1903–1941); Takakusu, Junjiro, *The Essentials of Buddhist Philosophy* (Honolulu 1947); Spae, J. J., *Itô Jinsai, A Philosopher, Educator, and Sinologist of the Tokugawa Period* (Peiping 1948).

A. K. Reischauer,
Lecturer, History of Religion, Union Theological Seminary.

14. CULTURAL LIFE. In considering Japanese cultural life, primary emphasis will be placed on present day education, with lesser attention being devoted to other aspects of culture, such as exchange of persons, youth organizations, literacy, libraries, institutes, learned societies, and museums.

EDUCATION

Education in Japan before the nation's surrender to the Allied powers in 1945 was highly centralized and thoroughly nationalistic in its organization and aims. Great emphasis was placed on rote learning and very little original thinking was allowed. Textbooks and teachers' manuals were prepared by the Ministry of Education and contained much factual information, but they were not designed to encourage free and unfettered thought on the part of either students or teachers. Entrance to higher schools and assignments to better positions were achieved on the basis of competitive examinations, with often the candidate who could accumulate the greatest amount of facts and write the fastest being given the promotion. The relationship between teacher and student was thoroughly feudalistic, the former showing a paternal concern for the well-being of the latter, and the latter giving unquestioning belief in, and obedience to, the former. As a government official and representative of the emperor, the teacher's word was law.

War Damage.—Great was the damage done by World War II to education in Japan. Four thousand school buildings and 80 per cent of the textbooks and equipment were completely destroyed by bombing. Far greater, however, was the damage done to the minds and spirits of students, teachers, and people in general. The war resulted in thousands of minds being warped by fear, hatred, pride, greed, uncertainty, and hopelessness. The Japanese people felt that they had been tricked and deceived by their leaders. They had lost face before Asia and the world. Students were cold, hungry, tired, and despondent. Teachers were ragged, undernourished, overworked, and dispirited, those who were not killed having been forced to leave their schools because of lack of food, shelter, and adequate salary. To heal the wounded spirits of the people of Japan and to develop a new outlook on life would entail a long period of wise, sympathetic, and thoroughgoing re-education.

Education Under Allied Occupation.—*The Task.*—To reform and regenerate education in Japan was one of the most important tasks of the supreme commander for the Allied powers (SCAP). The Education Division of SCAP was given responsibility for (1) the removal of all ultranationalism and militarism from the school system, and (2) the complete reorganization of education so as to insure the training of administrators, teachers, and students for a democratic Japan. Directives were issued by the supreme commander to the Japanese government, which passed laws, ordinances, and instructions to implement them.

United States Education Mission.—In March 1946, the United States Education Mission to Japan, composed of distinguished educators, arrived in Tokyo on the invitation of Gen. Douglas MacArthur and for four weeks conferred with Japanese educational leaders and inspected school plants and equipment. The mission then submitted to the supreme commander a comprehensive report which in brief recommended the decentralization of the educational system through prefectural and local administration of primary and secondary schools; the revision of the morals, history, and geography textbooks; a broad health program with increased emphasis on vocational training at all levels of education; the formation of a language commission to effectuate drastic reform in both the written and spoken languages; the extension of compulsory education for nine years or until the student reached the age of 16; the establishment of tax-supported, tuition-free, coeducational schools on the basis of six years' elementary, three years' lower secondary, and three years' higher secondary education, leading to higher education; the modification of teaching methods so as to eliminate memorization and to encourage independent thinking; the re-education of teachers, school administrators, and supervisors; the encouragement of adult education, and the establishment of parent-teacher activities, extension classes, and libraries; the liberalization of the curriculums of junior colleges; the establishment of more and better universities; and complete freedom from government control of all institutions of higher learning.

Japanese Educational Reform Council.—This council, composed of 49 members distinguished in the fields of education, religion, culture, business, politics, and economy, was established on the Cabinet level by imperial ordinance on Aug. 10, 1946. Yoshishige Abe, former minister of education, was made chairman, and Shigeru Nambara, president of Tokyo University (formerly Tokyo Imperial University), was chosen vice chairman. Although it operates autonomously, the council has maintained close liaison with the Japanese Ministry of Education. In general, the council expressed approval of the recommendations of the United States Education Mission. It also made broad and extensive recommendations on the elimination of bureaucracy, equality of opportunity in education, decentralization of educational administration, the establishment of research institutes and postgraduate courses in universities, the improvement of the status of teachers, and the reform of the entire educational system.

Far Eastern Commission.—Another group that contributed no little to the postwar reform of education in Japan was the Far Eastern Commission (FEC). That body, meeting in Washington, D.C., sent in April 1947, as a directive to SCAP, a short but comprehensive statement entitled "Policy for the Revision of the Japanese Educational System." This directive emphasized that education should prepare all Japanese for life in a democratic nation, enabling them to exercise the political and social responsibilities which freedom entails. To accomplish this aim it was necessary to reform the training, recruitment, and treatment of teachers; to make drastic changes in textbooks, curriculums, and teaching methods; to develop adult and vocational education; to decentralize Japanese education; to provide equal opportunity for both sexes at all levels of education; to forbid discrimination against graduates of private schools in civil service appointments; and to encourage the formation and reorientation of parent-teacher and educational associations to consider practical problems of education. The Ministry of Education and the Japanese Educational Reform Council have undertaken measures for carrying out most of these recommendations.

Kindergartens.—The lowest institutions in the educational ladder are the kindergartens, ministering to children 3, 4, and 5 years of age. Enrollment is entirely voluntary, and a small tuition fee is generally charged. In 1938 there were more than 2,000 kindergartens, of which two thirds were privately operated, with a total enrollment of 270,000 children. During the war almost all kindergartens were closed, but after the surrender many were reopened, and by April 1949, 1,785 were listed, with 8,438 teachers and 228,628 children. At these institutions the following subjects are used or taught: music, stories, painting, construction, nature studies, drama, social studies, health education, rhythms, rest, free play, and excursions.

Elementary and Secondary Schools.—Compulsory and tax-free education begins with the elementary or primary school. Though first established in 1872 as required schooling, elementary education has, since the surrender, been completely reorganized in administration, curriculum, textbooks, teaching methods, and aims. The old educational system was strictly regimented and highly centralized. The bureaucratic spirit was widespread from the official in the Ministry of Education down to the elementary school teacher. The principal ruled his faculty and students with an iron hand, demanding unquestioning obedience, but in turn gave the same obedience to the inspectors and supervisors sent down from the capital. From the beginning of the occupation bureaucrats fought stubbornly against decentralization, which they knew would destroy their power, but in spite of their determined opposition new basic laws of education were promulgated.

Fundamental Law of Education.—This law, which came into force on March 29, 1947, states: "Education shall aim at the full development of personality, striving for the rearing of people, sound in mind and body, who shall love truth and justice, esteem individual value, respect labor and have a deep sense of responsibility, and shall be imbued with the independent spirit, as builders of the peaceful state and society." It also provides for equal opportunity in education, without discrimination on account of race, sex, social status, economic position, or family origin, and for coeducation, home education, and education carried out in places of work. It recognizes the value of politics and religion in life, but directs that schools established by state and local bodies refrain from teaching these subjects.

School Education Law.—This law, effective April 1, 1947, provides for the establishment of sufficient primary or elementary and secondary schools to accommodate school-age children in each city, town, or village. When necessary, however, a group of communities may organize school unions. It directs that prefectural authorities shall have jurisdiction over public and private schools from kindergartens through high or secondary schools. The minister of education has jurisdiction over public and private universities.

Administration.—Boards of education, elected by the people, were functioning by 1950 in all the prefectures, the larger cities, and to some extent in the towns, and were soon to be extended to all local communities. The administration of elementary and secondary schools was entrusted to these boards, whose autonomy over the nature of the school program was increasing. In April 1949 there were 20,952 elementary schools, with 10,989,069 students and 304,207 teachers. Although a few new school buildings had been erected by 1950, budgetary difficulties and the scarcity of building materials prevented the carrying out of the program for the repair of war-damaged schools and delayed new construction to provide 14,000 additional classrooms. The resulting cramped conditions necessitated two-shift and sometimes three-shift class instruction in many schools. Numerous elementary schools damaged by bombing suffered complete or partial loss of classroom and teaching equipment. Some of this equipment had been replaced by 1950, but in urban centers, where the war damage was greatest, school furnishings were still deficient.

Elementary Teaching and Curriculum.—The school year in elementary schools commences on April 1 and closes the following March 31, but national holidays, Sundays, spring, summer, and winter vacations, and special holidays authorized by prefectural boards of education cut the teaching days to some 235 per school year. In many schools instruction is given six days a week, but an increasing number of prefectures have adopted the five-day week. Class size is limited by law to 50 pupils, but the shortage of classrooms has frequently necessitated crowding 60 or more children into one room. An increasing number of schools are using progressive teaching methods, the main emphasis being placed on social studies. The following subjects are taught in the regular six-year elementary school: national language (reading and writing), social studies, arithmetic, science, music, drawing, handicrafts, practical art, and physical education.

Textbooks.—The elimination of militaristic and ultranationalistic ideas from education and the need for developing a progressive and democratic curriculum in the schools resulted in the revision of nearly all the textbooks of the nation after the surrender. Scores of educators and others interested in writing textbooks daily visit the 13 textbook and curriculum centers scattered over Japan, where they may read hundreds of modern United States textbooks and professional books on education. In spite of the very critical shortage of paper over 200,000,000 textbooks were produced during the school year which began April 1949. In January 1948, the Textbooks Commission of the Education Ministry recommended that beginning with the 1950 school year all textbooks, which had previously been compiled by the government, be replaced gradually by textbooks compiled by private authors, provided such texts met certain approved standards.

Lower Secondary Schools.—The lower secondary school, or junior high school, includes grades 7 to 9. In enforcing the nine-year minimum of compulsory education, the government allotted the buildings of the former youth schools and higher elementary schools to the new secondary schools, but there still remained a considerable shortage of buildings. Budgetary difficulties prevented the construction of needed classrooms. This necessitated, as in the case of many elementary schools, two-shift and sometimes three-shift class instruction. In April 1949 there were 12,415 public and private lower secondary schools, with 195,383 teachers and 5,177,455 students. Each city, town, and village is normally required to provide, free of charge, educational opportunities for the entire school population in grades 7 to 9. It was expected that when the system reached full operation, cities would have several lower secondary schools, each large town or village would have at least one, and smaller villages might join other small communities in supporting a consolidated school. In 1950 many of the schools already established were still sadly deficient in classroom facilities and equipment.

The curriculum of the lower secondary schools lays particular emphasis on the development of the pupil's personality and individuality and on the ability to participate effectively in community life. It also provides vocational guidance and some vocational training.

Private Secondary Schools.—Upon completion of the six years of elementary work the pupil is automatically promoted to the lower secondary school, thus eliminating entrance examinations in public schools. The number of applicants for private secondary schools, both lower and higher, far exceeds the available openings, and students are selected on the basis of reports from elementary schools, physical examination, and personal interviews. Thus these private schools have been able to maintain their school traditions and have held to a higher standard of education than most public lower secondary schools. Private schools also do not have to adopt coeducation. Many conservative parents prefer to send their children, especially their daughters, to a private secondary school which is not coeducational. Private secondary schools are generally not so crowded as the public schools, which permits more individual attention to be given to the student.

Upper Secondary Schools.—Upper secondary schools, or senior high schools, are the connecting link between the lower secondary schools and the universities. In April 1949 there were 2,935 such schools, with 95,489 teachers and 1,624,384 students. There are two types of upper secondary schools: those offering full-time courses either during the day or at night or both; and part-time schools for working students and those in farming and fishing areas, who can pursue their subjects only during certain seasons of the year. Most secondary schools also give specialized courses in agricultural, technical, industrial, commercial, and other vocational fields. Because of the limited capacities of upper secondary schools students were in 1950 selected on the basis of competitive examinations covering the Japanese language, the social sciences, and mathematics, but considerable attention also was paid to reports from the lower secondary schools on achievement tests, physical examination, and personality. Like the lower secondary schools, the upper secondary schools are under the control and administration of the prefectures. Coeducation is encouraged but is not mandatory, and a relatively small tuition fee is charged. In 1950 it was expected that these schools would eventually be free, and that there would be enough of them to take care of all graduates of the lower secondary schools who desired to continue their education.

There are a number of elective courses in the curriculum of the upper secondary school. In addition to the required subjects of Japanese language, social studies, mathematics, natural science, and physical education, the student may select from a comparatively wide range of electives the special subjects which interest him and may be of use in his chosen profession. Upon graduation the student may sit for the entrance examination of any university. Eventually upper secondary schools were to be well-equipped, well-housed, and adequately staffed institutions, but in 1950 they were still greatly handicapped by economic obstacles and shortages.

Vocational Training.—In view of the urgent need for trained personnel to aid Japan in her economic recovery, many courses are given in upper secondary schools, colleges, and universities which "are designed to provide students with the technical knowledge and skill necessary to qualify them for successful employment in specialized occupations on the vocational level." Vocational education is also provided for public service occupations such as the fire and police systems and the civil service. Modern programs of education and rehabilitation are provided in prisons and reformatories. Vocational and special educational activities are carried on for blind, deaf, crippled, or otherwise handicapped persons.

Teacher Training.—*Reorientation.*—In the reorganization and reformation of Japanese education great stress was laid upon the proper training and reorientation of teachers. An early SCAP directive called for the elimination from the educational system of all persons known to be ultranationalistic, militaristic, or antagonistic to the objectives and policies of the Allied occupation. Steps were also taken for the reinstatement of properly qualified teachers and educational officials who had been purged by the Japanese militarists since July 7, 1937. Committees were set up to investigate and screen all educational personnel, and to certify all who were found to be properly qualified. Of the approximately 600,000 teachers in Japanese elementary and secondary schools, about 120,000 resigned or were purged between August 1945 and April 1947. The teachers who survived the purge and those who were newly appointed were sent to teacher training institutes, vacation schools, and refresher courses for reorientation. For the re-education of teachers, the Ministry of Education prepared courses of study to cover the various subjects taught in the schools. Teachers were learning to think for themselves. A new generation of Japanese was being trained to act and speak as independent individuals. Emphasis was placed on personality and character development as well as on intellectual training, not on regimentation and subordination to the state, as was the case before the surrender.

Organizations and Training.—Teachers' associations of all kinds including teachers' unions have been organized. The aim of the latter is to improve the economic condition of teachers, for as a profession they are grossly underpaid. Each year teachers hold many conferences for the exchange of information and the consideration of practical problems of education. Normal school courses have been modernized, and universities are offering courses in education, psychology, teaching methods, school administration, educational research, and other subjects. Books, pamphlets, and magazines for the teaching profession have appeared in increasing numbers.

Adult Education.—For the prewar adult education, which was completely under government control, there have been substituted various educational programs for training in citizenship and in the development of leadership. Parent-teacher associations have rapidly grown in influence and number and have increasingly accepted new and larger responsibilities. Citizens' public halls have been established in local communities. The halls are managed by local boards and provide opportunities for the townspeople to practice democratic procedures. In many communities books, radios, motion picture projectors, and athletic equipment have been purchased for use in the halls, thus making them the cultural and social centers of the district, town, or village. Correspondence and extension courses have been established, with a full-time teacher for each 100 correspondents. Leading private universities, such as Keio, Waseda, and Hosei, offer correspondence courses for in-service training of elementary and secondary school teachers. To preserve the old arts and to promote new cultural forms, various essay, drama, music, and art contests are sponsored throughout the country.

Audio-Visual Education.—In the program for reorientating Japanese education, audio-visual media have been used very effectively. In nearly all institutions of learning, motion pictures, film strips, and phonograph records have provided supplementary teaching material which has been integrated into the courses of study. The Educational Film Exchange, operated by SCAP, has provided a large number of Allied educational and documentary films, to which sound tracks in Japanese have been added. Radio broadcasts to and from schools have proved to be very effective media for democratic education.

Higher Education.—Before the surrender, Japanese institutions of higher education, like the primary and secondary schools, were under government domination. The prestige of the six imperial universities was so great that 40 per cent of the graduates went into government service. Graduates of private universities were greatly handicapped in securing positions either in government service or in private business organizations. Only a few women were admitted to the universities. Competition among men applicants was so keen that selection was made through an examination system which stressed rote memory to the exclusion of many other important qualifications of a good student.

After 1946 many important changes were made in higher education. The three-year universities were changed to four-year institutions, and by improving the curriculums and standards of other colleges many new four-year universities were added. The University Accreditation Association, an autonomous body independent of governmental control, was established to evaluate university work in terms of credit and to make certain that minimum standards of curriculums, instruction, and equipment were met. Accredited universities enjoy privileges of transfer of students from one institution to another without loss of credit. The University Chartering Committee was established on Jan. 15, 1948, under the supervision of the minister of education, to "make inquiries and deliberate on matters concerning approval of the establishment of universities as well as the doctorate and other academic degrees. . . ." Plans were also made to establish graduate schools in certain qualified universities. The new universities, which presumably would have full administrative autonomy, were placing special emphasis on general education as a preparation for later professional training.

The physical plants of many colleges and universities in the large cities were severely damaged by bombing. Because of the lack of building materials and economic resources, only relatively few of the damaged buildings had been repaired or rebuilt by 1950. Nonetheless, on April 1, 1950, there were 197 fully accredited four-year universities, of which 68 were national, 25 public, and 104 private. In addition, there were 150 two-year junior colleges. Over 500,000 students were enrolled in these institutions of higher learning. Many of the universities were coeducational, women being admitted on the same basis as men. Students are selected on the basis of achievement tests, scholastic aptitude tests, physical examinations, and reports from schools. Graduates of private universities may now enter government service on the same competitive basis as the graduates of national and public universities.

EXCHANGE OF PERSONS

Before World War II, a great many Japanese students and scholars went abroad for further study, training, and scientific investigation. For nearly 10 years Japan was cut off from cultural contacts with the West, contacts which had proved mutually beneficial. Recognizing the importance to Japanese cultural leaders, teachers, and students of visits to the United States for purposes of reorientation, special funds were appropriated by the United States Congress in 1949 for this purpose. Japanese leaders who have made such visits are contributing to the growth of Japan as a democratic nation. In addition, many United States specialists in all fields of culture and science were brought by SCAP to Japan to advise and assist leaders there. Since 1947 a number of private social, cultural, and educational organizations in the United States have supported financially Japanese students and cultural leaders in their visits abroad. In addition, in 1951 an educational exchange program was inaugurated under the provisions of the Fulbright Act.

YOUTH ORGANIZATIONS

The economic and social disruption of the war and postwar periods resulted in extreme confusion among Japanese youth. Militaristic and ultranationalistic youth leaders were purged, and it was difficult to find qualified, democratically inclined leaders to take their places. By 1950, however, youth organizations were beginning to participate in programs for rebuilding Japan into a democratic nation. Among the most important of these organizations are the Nippon Seinen Kan (Japan Young Men's Hostels), Nippon no Seinen Kai (Japanese Youth Associations), the Boy Scouts, the Girl Scouts, the Junior Red Cross Society, and the Young Men's and Young Women's Christian Associations. The two last-named organizations are actively engaged in leadership programs along spiritual, moral, and social lines, with special emphasis upon the importance of international relations.

LITERACY

The question of literacy in Japan is intimately connected with the problem of language reform. If by literate we mean the ability to read kana (Japanese phonetic symbols), it would be safe to say that nearly all Japanese from the age of 6 upward are literate; but if the criterion of literacy is the ability to read and understand completely the newspapers, which are printed in an admixture of Chinese ideographs and Japanese phonetic symbols, it is doubtful whether 60 per cent of the population can be considered literate. The United States Education Mission to Japan recognized that the intricacy of the Japanese language is a great obstacle to the democratic development of the people. Consequently, it recommended that steps be taken to simplify and romanize the written language. While that recommendation has not been fully adopted, Japanese leaders recognize the need for language simplification, and are endeavoring to solve the problem by teaching Romaji (Jap. *rōmaji,* or Roman letters) in elementary schools, by reducing the number of Chinese ideographs to be taught in elementary schools, by encouraging newspapers and periodicals to stay within that prescribed number, and by promoting the use of simple language in both writing and speaking.

LIBRARIES

The Ministry of Education, reporting on the condition of libraries in Japan on May 1, 1946, listed 3,398 libraries, of which only 874 contained 3,000 or more volumes. Most of the largest Japanese libraries are in urban areas where they suffered heavy loss from bombing, and consequently were still in a state of confusion in 1950. For example, the Tokyo Metropolitan Library with its 27 branches lost, during the incendiary bombing, one third of its collection of 700,000 volumes, while the Nagoya Municipal Library lost 93,000 volumes out of a total of 160,000. Statistics indicate that 138 libraries were heavily damaged or entirely demolished. It was recognized that there was great need for revising and reforming the whole library system. This was being accomplished by giving libraries greater financial support from government and private sources, by improving the training and raising the professional standing of librarians, by making libraries more accessible and attractive to the public, by establishing in each prefecture and large city at least one good free public library, and by improving school and university libraries. The Japanese government has made appropriations for expanding and improving the Diet Library, and two prominent United States librarians have assisted in studying and solving the problems connected with this institution.

Information Centers.—In the forefront of the battle for more and better libraries were the 17 information centers conducted by the Civil Information Section of SCAP, which were located in the major cities and four main islands of Japan. These served as small but well-staffed and carefully equipped models for Japanese libraries. Each center contained at least 6,000 books, 400 periodicals, and several thousand pamphlets and documents, all in English (which many Japanese can read), and covering all fields of knowledge. They were easily accessible to the public and free of charge. Not only the general public, but hundreds of Japanese government officials, political and labor leaders, industrialists, physicians, research workers, teachers, and students availed themselves of the excellent facilities of the information centers, where they received the latest and most authoritative information in international affairs, research, technology, World War II, and "the policies and activities of the United States as they develop from American customs, institutions and government." At each center films were shown, United States music was played, English language classes and discussion groups were held, and numerous other activities took place. Many of these centers extended their usefulness by depositing United States books, magazines, films, and records in adjacent Japanese schools and public libraries.

INSTITUTES AND LEARNED SOCIETIES

Some professional and learned societies have training and research institutes, but the Institute for Educational Leadership, which was sponsored jointly by the Japanese Ministry of Education and the Education Division, Civil Information and Education Section of SCAP, has been outstanding in meeting a real need in the field of Japanese education. The institute, with 21 United States and 26 Japanese specialists on its staff, conducted courses in 1948 and 1949 for the training of elementary school consultants, secondary school consultants, superintendents and professors of education, youth leaders, university administrators, and student guidance personnel. A total of 3,700 persons completed the training and returned to their communities to assume active leadership in guiding and educating youth in all parts of Japan. In March 1948 there were 253 Japanese learned and professional societies in 60 different fields of science and culture.

MUSEUMS

As depositories of culture, both ancient and modern, museums have an important place in Japanese education. Many of the fine collections, especially those in urban areas, were badly damaged by bombing, and those that remained were greatly disorganized. The Religions and Cultural Resources Division, Civil Information Section of SCAP, greatly assisted the Japanese government with advice and recommendations regarding the financing and management of many projects for the preservation, protection, restitution, and restoration of antiquities, archives, cultural treasures, art collections, and museums. In spite of the financial limitations of individuals as well as public organizations, by 1950 much had been done along these lines.

Bibliography.—General Headquarters, Supreme Commander for the Allied Powers, Civil Information and Education Section, Education Division, *Education in Japan* (Tokyo 1946); Ministry of Education, *Guide to New Education in Japan* (Tokyo 1946); Stoddard, G. D., *Report of the United States Education Mission to Japan* (Washington 1946); Department of State, *Activities of the Far Eastern Commission* (Washington 1947); id., *The Program for Re-education in Japan: A Survey of Policy*, Documents and State Papers, vol. 1, no. 1 (Washington 1948); General Headquarters, Supreme Commander for the Allied Powers, Civil Information and Education Section, Education Division, *Education in the New Japan*, vols. 1, 2 (Tokyo 1948); Hall, R. K., *Education for a New Japan* (New Haven 1949); Ohta, Kaneo, and Taketa, Ichiro, *School Education in New Japan* (Tokyo 1949); Russell, J. D., and others, *Report of the Education Survey to the Supreme Commander for the Allied Powers* (Tokyo 1949); Taylor, P. H., "The Administration of Occupied Japan," *The Annals of the American Academy of Political and Social Science*, January 1950.

DANIEL CRUMP BUCHANAN,
Foreign Affairs Officer, Bureau of Far Eastern Affairs, United States Department of State.

15. SCIENTIFIC RESEARCH.

Although science as understood in the Occident developed in Japan after the Meiji Restoration of 1868, the Portuguese had introduced certain aspects of Western science, such as medicine, navigation, cartography, and gunnery, in the 16th century. This section emphasizes the relation of scientific research to the development of modern Japan, with minimum attention being given to individual achievements in specific fields.

Pre-Meiji Science.—For the greater part of the three centuries prior to the Meiji Restoration the Tokugawa shoguns had forbidden all Japanese to leave the country and had prohibited the entry of foreigners, excepting only the annual Dutch factory at Nagasaki. Hence ambitious youths thirsting for the arts and sciences of the West surreptitiously made their way to Nagasaki. By 1774 this group of so-called Dutch scholars was able to translate and publish a Dutch work on anatomy, the first European work to be printed in Japan. And by the end of the 18th century translations of standard European works on astronomy, mathematics, medicine, and botany had been published. In appraising their work, the difficulties met by these scholars must not be forgotten. Foreign books, virtually banned by the government in its enforcement of the seclusion policy, had to be obtained, and the more formidable problem of learning the Dutch language and of coining appropriate Japanese terminology had to be overcome. In 1823, Philip Franz von Siebold, a German physician in Dutch employ, arrived in Nagasaki and initiated lectures on clinical medicine; later he opened a school where young Japanese who braved the difficulties of learning the Dutch language might study medicine and botany. Tacitly conceding the value of medical knowledge, the shoguns winked at these illegal activities. Thus, knowledge of Western medicine continued to grow. In time the Japanese turned from the translation of Dutch works to British and United States treatises. On the eve of the restoration the Japanese were not only studying the medical science of Great Britain and the United States, but were also using the personal services of doctors from these countries.

Meanwhile, the Japanese were investigating the intricacies of other sciences. Gennai Hiraga, for example, had acquired some knowledge of electricity while visiting Nagasaki. He returned to Edo (now Tokyo), built an electrostatic machine, and demonstrated it publicly. The shogun, however, deemed Western learning politically dangerous, and Hiraga was punished severely for "misleading the public with Western magic."

It should be noted that during this period certain advances independent of Western influence had been made in some aspects of science. In mathematics the numerical solution of equations of higher degree had been mastered by the Japanese without the assistance of the West, and Kowa Seki had conceived and utilized the idea of determinants in his calculations. In surveying and cartography, Ino Chukei had accomplished the feat of surveying and mapping the shoreline of Hokkaido a few years before von Siebold's arrival in Japan. Astronomy also had long been a subject of interest to the Japanese because of its importance to navigation and calendar making. Careful records of astronomical phenomena had been kept and preserved for centuries. In descriptive biology some notable catalogues had been compiled. But even with these sciences it remained for Western science, with its methodology and experience, to provide the stimulus and guidance for their further development.

From the Meiji Restoration to World War I.—The Meiji Restoration repudiated the isolation policy of the Tokugawas and actively fostered the introduction of Occidental knowledge. Science, however, requires a foundation of mass education; although the Meiji government established a compulsory educational system, some 20 years elapsed before Tokyo Imperial University (founded in 1877) could assume the form of a truly modern institution. Its early faculty included such distinguished Westerners as Sir James A. Ewing of Great Britain (physics), R. W. Atkinson and S. Divers of Great Britain (chemistry), and Edward S. Morse of the United States (zoology). Until 1900 most of the medical chairs were occupied by Germans, to whom the Japanese had turned upon learning that German medicine was then far in advance of that of other countries. Among them, E. O. E. von Baelz was outstanding. Japanese scholars, trained abroad at government expense, returned home to lead in education and research. Notable among these scientists were Dairoku Kikuchi, in mathematics; Kenjiro Yamakawa, in physics; Naokichi Matsui and Joji Sakurai, in chemistry; Kiyokage Sekiya, in seismology; and Ryokichi Yetabe and Masakazu Toyama, in botany. As additional imperial universities were established and private institutions took shape, science developed apace.

By 1900, European scientific journals were carrying reports of research by Japanese scientists. Perhaps the first Japanese achievement to draw international attention was the discovery of the so-called Z-term by Sakac Kimura, professor at Tokyo Imperial University. At an international scientific conference on the variations in position of the earth's axis, Mizusawa in northern Japan was selected as one of many scattered observation points. Professor Kimura offered to conduct the observations. At a subsequent conference, the results of observations in various countries, except for Kimura's data, conformed consistently to a simple mathematical formula. The discrepancy was explained away on the basis of inferior technique, but Kimura remained unconvinced and stood by his data despite the censure of his Japanese colleagues. He then returned to his observatory and analyzed his data mathematically. He discovered that by correcting the formula by the addition of what he called the Z-term his conclusions could be aptly expressed. European scientists tested his revision of their formula and vindicated his observations. The Japanese public heralded this incident as proof that Japan's science now equaled that of the West—a conclusion congenial to the intense nationalism that followed the Russo-Japanese War. The Imperial Academy of Japan established the Academy Prize, and Kimura was the first Japanese scientist to be thus honored.

Japanese scientists themselves disliked such publicity, for they were quite aware of the fact that the level of science in Japan averaged below Occidental standards. Gradually, however, research in other fields began to draw attention from scientists in Europe and the United States. Hantaro Nagaoka of Tokyo Imperial University developed a theory of atomic structure; at the same institution, in 1910, Umetaro Suzuki discovered vitamins, and Kikunae Ikeda discovered *aji-no-moto* (essence of taste), a discovery in which United States scientists showed interest after World War II.

Professor Nagaoka's model of the atom—as electrons revolving about a positively charged heavy particle—anticipated the discovery of the atomic nucleus by the 1st Baron Rutherford of Nelson; Niels Bohr used a similar model in his quantum theory. In older discussions, this model was termed the Nagaoka-Rutherford-Bohr model.

Professor Suzuki's independent discovery of vitamins generally had not been accorded priority over the discoveries of Occidental scientists. At that time the authenticity of Japanese scientific journals was not accepted, and Suzuki lost the opportunity to assert prior discovery. To correct this situation the Imperial Academy decided to publish monthly periodicals in English and other foreign languages. In due season these journals achieved international acceptance.

Professor Ikeda's discovery of *aji-no-moto* has been important in applied science. The product has enjoyed worldwide sale as a means of intensifying the flavor of foods to which it is added.

Meanwhile, the science of seismology was making phenomenal progress. Within a few years after its introduction in the 1870's, the Japanese, through Kiyokage Sekiya and Fusakichi Omori, gained international renown. Among the achievements of this group of scientists was the perfection by Aikitsu Tanakadate of the parallel-motion seismograph and of the spiral seismograph for recording vertical motion.

In geology and mineralogy the Japanese had taken over the teaching of these sciences at Tokyo Imperial University from their Western tutors by the late 1880's. And by 1896 Japanese botanists had made a notable contribution to the science of plant morphology by their discovery of spermatozoids in the pollen tubes of the gingko and cycad.

In technology, the Japanese had been almost wholly dependent on the West. In the early decades of the Meiji era (1868–1912) importations of Western technology had gone on at a feverish pace. One notable Japanese contribution, however, was the invention of the automatic power loom by Sakichi Toyoda (1895). This machine revolutionized the Japanese textile industry.

Developments from 1914 to 1941.—World War I and the immediate postwar period constituted a very important era for modern Japan. National economic potential and living standards increased rapidly; scientific research expanded, and projects multiplied, with notable increases in the number of universities and laboratories. Outstanding, perhaps, was the work of Kotaro Honda, professor at Tohoku Imperial University and president of its metallurgical institute, who pioneered in the investigation of the magnetic properties of ferromagnetic metals and alloys. His K.S. magnet exhibited the highest permanent magnetism then known and was used widely in industry.

From its inception, however, Japanese research showed an almost fatal weakness: the lack of close coordination between science and industry. In Great Britain, for example, rapid development of science had accompanied the Industrial Revolution; the industrial development of the steam engine was inseparable from the theory of heat and thermal properties of matter. As an integral part of human civilization, science must find its *raison d'être* in its utility for better living. Japan imported science from the Occident without maintaining its connection with the industry that also was being imported from the West. While government-aided scientists were striving vigorously for world recognition, Japanese industrialists were importing both machines and engineers from Europe and the United States, oblivious of the inevitable liaison between science and industry. Neither group should be blamed; the borrowing of an alien culture is a herculean task, and Japan had no precedent to guide her. The industrialists had to achieve a return on invested capital and the surest and shortest way was direct reliance on ready-made, well-tested products from the West.

Understandably, if unwisely, the scientists reacted by taking refuge in an ivory tower of academic isolationism and by looking down upon industrialists as mere money grubbers. This deeply rooted attitude of Japanese scientists has blocked progress. Professor Honda's work with magnetism was one of the happy exceptions: the institute over which he presided was a gift from the industrialist Kichizaemon Sumitomo. Many of the findings of research at this institute were developed commercially on a large scale by the Sumitomo Manufacturing Company. Honda's use of the initials K.S. to denote his new magnet was a tribute to his industrial backer. Nevertheless, it remained for European and American industrialists to apply this discovery extensively.

The Japanese government took cognizance of the separation of science and industry and, as a possible bridge over the gap, established the Institute of Physical and Chemical Research (IPCR) in Tokyo in 1916. Leading industrialists contributed large sums, laboratories were built and equipped, and noted scientists were invited to join the staff. Among them were Hantaro Nagaoka, Kotaro Honda, and Umetaro Suzuki. The plan was to support the institute from patent royalties, and the government granted a 10-year subsidy to tide it over until such support materialized.

The IPCR soon produced important inventions and became a major shareholder in numerous companies that were established to manufacture the new inventions. Among these products were synthetic sake (rice wine), different kinds of vitamins, scientific precision instruments, and piston rings. Profits from the synthetic sake and vitamins enabled the institute to attain self-support. With the general economic expansion of the 1930's and the early 1940's, the concerns affiliated with IPCR expanded rapidly and became important industrial forces.

A special feature of the IPCR was its conduct of extensive research in pure science without detracting from its industrial program. This the institute continued to do until it had to change its organization in 1945. It had maintained one of the most active research centers in Japan; its laboratories were better equipped and maintained than those of the universities, and they were staffed by capable young workers. In 1937 a very large cyclotron was begun under the direction of the distinguished physicist Yoshio Nishina; this enterprise resulted in important contributions to nuclear physics. Under IPCR auspices, Umetaro Suzuki pursued his investigations of the chemistry of vitamins in relation to nutrition. Shoje Nishikawa's study of crystal structures by X-rays and cathode rays were highly fruitful; under his direction Seishi Kikuchi investigated the diffraction of cathode rays by crystals, which attracted attention in 1927.

The IPCR undoubtedly pioneered in the integration of Japanese science and industry. It has been criticized on the ground that it competed with other industries instead of preserving a neutral position and extending to all industries the benefits of its discoveries. Masatoshi Okochi, president of the institute from about 1930 to 1945, seemed to feel differently. If he admitted the truth of this criticism in principle, on the basis of experience he doubted whether capitalists motivated by a desire for profits would return in contributions any fair proportion of the profits they obtained from IPCR achievements. Okochi encouraged every kind of research undertaken by institute scientists; and, research being expensive, this policy entailed considerable reduction in the profits of the companies under IPCR control.

Objectively considered, it is reasonable to doubt whether a problem so large as the effective coordination of science and industry could have been solved so quickly by a single organization. As it happened, the economic improvement of the 1930's generally increased incomes in Japan, and wealthy industrialists donated large sums to universities to aid scientific research. At the same time, the Japanese Army and Navy began to support research directly and indirectly. Unhappy encounters with Soviet mechanized troops along the Manchurian border in 1938 (see section on *Foreign Relations* [*1931–1945*]) had convinced the army command of the need for the promotion of scientific research in collaboration with industry. The result was an appropriation by the Diet of an annual budget for research.

Simultaneously, the Japan Association for the Promotion of Science and Industry was instituted and granted government subsidies. This organization selected for investigation the most urgent problems from various scientific and industrial fields and assigned each problem to a special committee of engineers and scientists. Some of the projects, such as nuclear physics, were in pure science; others, such as synthetic oil, synthetic rubber, and improved carbon brushes for motors, were industrial. The committees encountered problems of practical psychology; engineers affiliated with competing industrial organizations were loath to pool their special techniques and secret discoveries. Furthermore, the army and navy, for reasons of security, kept their findings secret. Nevertheless, Japanese scientists were working more directly with practical problems than they had before.

All these circumstances stimulated and expanded the scope of research in Japan in the 1930's. It was then that Hideki Yukawa evolved the meson theory for which he was awarded a Nobel Prize in 1949. Two cyclotrons were operating by 1938, one at the IPCR and the other at Osaka Imperial University. While we have stressed the field of physics, analogous situations existed in other branches of science.

Science in World War II.—In 1941, when Japan became an active belligerent in World War II, Japanese science and industry lost contact with their Occidental counterparts. The test was severe; after 80 years of struggle, would they be strong enough to proceed alone?

In the field of pure science, the theoretical physicists, headed by Hideki Yukawa, continued research on the meson. Shinichiro Tomonaga contributed to a new formulation of quantum electrodynamics; Shoichi Sakata contributed to the two meson theory and the neutral meson theory, and these played an important part in postwar theoretical physics. In general, however, the results were disheartening. Progress ceased completely in experimental nuclear physics, although at the beginning of the war nuclear physicists had urged research into atomic energy. The army and navy, acting separately, surveyed the sources of uranium-bearing minerals and soon discovered that almost no sources of uranium were within reach. Previously all uranium products had been imported; hence there were no factories for refining such minerals and the technology was almost unknown. A group of nuclear physicists tried in 1942 to obtain uranium, but got only a few pounds of uranium oxide and uranium nitrate that had been imported from Germany before the war. It was thus impossible to conduct even the fundamental studies that might have ascertained the probability of a chain reaction of nuclear fission. Hence most of the nuclear physicists turned to other projects. Even in applied science fields that were vital to the conduct of the war, activity was limited severely by the lack of an administrative policy for research and by shortages of every kind of raw material. In fact, the overcoming of these shortages was an immediate and primary concern of Japanese science after 1941. In this connection, some results were obtained in the production of methane gas from sewage and garbage, of lubrication oil from animal matter, of wool from whale collagen and fish refuse, and of synthetic fibers from an ever-increasing number of fibrous materials. Attempts were also made to supplement the power shortage by utilizing subterranean heat and water from hot springs. These developments, however, with the exception of synthetic fiber, were on an extremely small scale. Thus, except for theoretical physics, almost no progress was made during the war. There were too many handicaps; the test was too severe.

Postwar Scientific Research.—With the collapse of Japan in August 1945, the background for scientific research seemed entirely lost. The industrialists were helpless; their factories had been destroyed, and there was no capital and no means of buying machinery from abroad. The scientists were similarly helpless. Laboratories and facilities had been destroyed or neglected. The Tokyo Astronomical Observatory, which had been able to maintain contact with the Copenhagen Astronomical Observatory for a year after the start of hostilities, was damaged and a section of its library was destroyed by fire. Seismology, a science not directly useful to the prosecution of the war, lost valuable ground. In December 1943, when a severe earthquake shook the area between Aichi and Wakayama prefectures, the routine seismological check-ups could not be conducted because of the deterioration of instruments and the lack of competent personnel. Geology also suffered, though not for the same reasons: since 1937 there had been a gradual exodus of trained geologists to the conquered areas of eastern and southeastern Asia to make surveys and studies of mineral resources. The suspension of the compilation of pre-Meiji scientific source materials, a project begun during the war under the auspices of the Imperial Academy, was a severe blow to students of the history of Japanese science.

Early in the postwar period, however, the urgency of effecting industrial recovery began to stimulate a revival of the work of Japanese scientists. The IPCR, which had partially lost its identity, began afresh as the Science Institute, headed by Yoshio Nishina. Under the joint supervision of former nuclear physicists and its own staff chemists, the institute initiated, and took the lead in, the production of penicillin. Every field of science and industry saw similar developments; the ivory tower had been destroyed. The problem of cooperation between science and industry seemed to be finding its own solution.

After the war there was considerable reflection and discussion on the role of science in Japan's future. Scientists and technicians clamored for a reorganization of the structure of Japanese science. The result was the creation of the Japan Council of Science in 1948 by an act of the national Diet. Its establishment was preceded by a survey of the state of Japanese science by an advisory group of eminent scientists from the United States, and by a series of studies and deliberations by a committee of 108 Japanese scientists. Through the council the government aimed to democratize science by making its membership of 210 scientists and technicians (30 in each of seven departments, of which four are in the sciences and three in the humanities and social sciences) elective for three-year terms, and by empowering it to advise the government on all matters pertaining to science and to make recommendations for the disbursement of government subsidies for research. In the first election, which was held in December 1948, 35,354 qualified scientists and technicians cast their votes to select 210 council members from among 945 candidates. With the creation of the council, the Imperial Academy was dissolved and replaced by the Japan Academy to serve under the direction of the council. The new academy's function is to accord due recognition through annual prizes to outstanding Japanese scientists by appraising their findings, treatises, and works.

The subject of science education in the schools also received much attention after the war. In the reorganization of the Ministry of Education in 1946 a new Bureau of Scientific Education was created. It was charged with some of the functions of the former Bureau of Vocational Education, but was concerned essentially with scientific education.

The award of a Nobel Prize in 1949 to Hideki Yukawa for his theory of mesons was an outstanding event in postwar Japan. It should be remembered, however, that his research was accomplished before the war under conditions more favorable to science. While postwar conditions were far from ideal for the promotion and development of science, there were nevertheless isolated but significant signs of recovery by 1950. For example, at the 8th International Genetics Conference in Stockholm in 1948, Hitoshi Kihara of Kyoto University, the first Japanese scientist to attend a postwar international scientific meeting, read his paper on the synthetization of bread wheat, a method he had developed after his discovery of one of the basic components of bread wheat in 1944. Also in 1948, the results of experiments and research on as many as 770 subjects were announced at the general meeting of the Japan Chemical Association. On the subject of vitamins, in which the Japanese had made notable contributions in the past, Kazuo Nakahara of Tokyo University (formerly Tokyo Imperial University) isolated an important factor from the vitamin B group which he named vitamin L. This factor, which controls the mammary secretions of rats and mice, consists of L_1 (anthranilic acid) and L_2 (adenylthiomethylpentose). In the sericultural and agricultural laboratories experiments were being made to improve the cocoon and grain seeds, while the industrial laboratories were concerned with the improvement of textile machines, mining instruments, and other equipment.

In medicine the paramount trend after the war was toward preventive medicine, as was to be expected by the nature of its most urgent problems: malnutrition, public health, and sanitation. In the early months of 1946 epidemics of typhus and smallpox were brought under control with the cooperation of the Allied occupation authorities. There was also a noticeable reduction in the high death rate from tuberculosis, mainly through the intracutaneous administration of BCG (Bacillus of Calmette and Guérin) vaccine. Among other studies being made in the clinical laboratories of Japan were ones on the effects of exposure to radioactive rays, on the relation of viruses to cancerous growth, and on the removal of pain through simple operations on minute nerves.

An event which foretold closer cooperation of Japanese and Western scientists was the observation of the annular solar eclipse of May 8-9, 1948, conducted under the joint auspices of the supreme commander for the Allied powers, the American Geographical Society, and the Tokyo Astronomical Society. Another indication of closer international cooperation was the growing number of Japanese scientists going abroad, especially to the United States, for research. It was hoped thereby that scientific research would recover its former position and that Japanese scientists would have opportunities to serve mankind.

Bibliography.—IN JAPANESE: Heibon-sha, *Dai Hyakka Jiten* (Tokyo 1931–1935); Minshu-shugi Kagakusha Kyōkai, *Kagaku Nenkan, 1947* (Tokyo 1947); Jiji Tsūshin-sha, *Jiji Nenkan* (Tokyo 1947–1950); Mainichi Shimbun-sha, *Mainichi Nenkan* (Osaka 1947–1950).

IN ENGLISH: Third Pan Pacific Science Congress, *Scientific Japan, Past and Present* (Tokyo 1926); Nitobe, I. O., and others, *Western Influences in Modern Japan* (Chicago 1931); Otani, Ryōichi, *Tadataka Ino, the Japanese Land-surveyor* (Tokyo 1932); Foreign Affairs Association of Japan, *Japan Yearbook* (Tokyo 1939–1940; 1943–1944); Stoddard, G. D., *Report of the United States Education Mission to Japan* (Washington 1946); Hall, R. K., *Education for a New Japan* (New Haven 1949); Yanaga, Chitoshi, *Japan Since Perry* (New York 1949); Mainichi Publishing Company, *New Japan* (Osaka): vol. 2 (1949); vol. 3 (1950); Sansom, G. B., *The Western World and Japan* (New York 1950).

SEISHI KIKUCHI,
Laboratory of Nuclear Physics, Cornell University.

16. THE FINE ARTS.

Much of the history of Japanese art is concerned with the importation of foreign art forms and their subsequent development into forms which bear the unmistakable stamp of Japanese characteristics. It is therefore of interest to study the art forms existing in Japan before the first great wave of foreign influence, which came with the introduction of Buddhism in the 6th century A.D.

Most of the objects still extant naturally fall under the heading of applied arts—that is, they are objects made primarily for practical use. They include weapons, pottery, mirrors, horse trappings, and the like. Those which can be traced with considerable sureness to the ancestors of the present Japanese people (as distinguished from the Ainu aborigines) show in their form and decoration considerable likeness to contemporary foreign objects, mostly Korean and Chinese.

Fortunately, however, for our present purpose (which is concerned only with the fine arts of painting and sculpture) the earliest Japanese sculpture shows little if any trace of outside influence. These sculptures are grave figures (*haniwa*) made of hollow baked clay; they represent not only human beings, but also a variety of animals. They were made to be buried around the tombs of chieftains and other high personages, and therefore the lower halves of many of them were simple cylinders. Nevertheless, they show simplicity and directness in both apprehension and representation. This may be regarded as fundamental. The animal figures, especially, show a sympathy with nature which also seems a general characteristic of Japanese art. No painting of this period has survived. If we may judge by the few pictorial designs found on bronze mirrors and bells (*dōtaku*), it was probably quite primitive.

Suikō (Asuka) Period (c.570–650).[1]—Japanese records indicate that the indigenous production of Buddhist images had begun during the 6th century, but these seem to have been for the most part made of wood and none of the very early ones has survived. The oldest extant definitely dated statue which gives a clear idea of the style is a bronze figure of a seated Yakushi (Buddha of Healing) of the year 607. Both this and other figures which date from the first quarter of the 7th century are so like the Wei type of Chinese sculpture that it has been suggested that they were made by Chinese artists. Yet we have documentary proof to the contrary. Shiba Tori, the most famous sculptor of the period, was the son of Shiba Tasuna, an artist recorded as working in 585, and a grandson of Shiba Tattō, who was the original immigrant of the family. Then there is the question of dates. One of Tori's "Wei" statues is dated 623, at which time the Wei style had long been outmoded in China. The probability is very strong that early Japanese artists simply copied the images brought over when Buddhism was introduced. These were indubitably of the then contemporary Wei type.

It should be noted that, although the Wei type is primarily adapted to a stone technique, all the Japanese early work seems to have been either wood or bronze. There is no work in stone, apparently because Japan is of volcanic origin and there was no marble or other fine-grained stone available. Nevertheless much of it is artistically highly admirable, and at least one piece, the so-called Yumedono Kwannon at Hōryūji, near Nara, is rated among the great statues of the world. During the second quarter of the century, apparently with the help of Korean artists, the old style was modified to fit a wood technique, resulting in several marvelous statues—such as the Kudara Kwannon and the Maitreya or Miroku at Chūgūji—which differ considerably from their Chinese prototypes.

[1] The dates given to art periods in this section do not correspond exactly with those of the historical periods of the same name. They are necessarily arbitrary divisions, since uniformity among specialists has not been reached.

The only extant painting of the period, that on the Tamamushi Shrine, is obviously foreign. The well-known portrait of Shōtoku Taishi and his sons, though apparently a later copy, illustrates the contemporary style.

Hakuhō Period (650–710).—This is a transition period. In its early stages native artists were apparently bewildered by a variety of Chinese styles, mainly Sui and early T'ang, which had been brought in from the latter part of Suikō onward. In an attempt to supply the constantly growing needs for Buddhist images, they produced many statues not wholly artistically integrated. In the middle Hakuhō period a very successful synthesis was obtained in such works as the small bronze triad in the Tachibana Shrine (now at Hōryūji), but this style was soon superseded by a new one, that of the middle T'ang.

The government was at this time trying to reform itself along Chinese lines and was looking forward to its first capital, Nara, which itself was being laid out on a Chinese model. In pursuit of this objective it brought over Chinese artists, who, among other things, produced the great Yakushi trinity at the Yakushiji. These magnificent bronzes, well over life size, represent T'ang sculpture at its height, and are particularly important because no large Chinese bronzes of this type have come down to us.

All extant painting of the period is also Chinese in type. The most important examples are the murals on the walls of the Buddha, or Golden, Hall (Kondō) of the Hōryūji. Their exact date is questionable, but it cannot be far from the turn of the 8th century. There seem to have been several artists employed, certainly not all Chinese, but there is no indication that any were natives of Japan.

Nara (Tempyō) Period (710–800).—Conditions in this period, especially during its first 50 years, were especially favorable for Japanese artists. The new capital was filled with temples, and under government direction Buddhism was spreading rapidly throughout the country. Great numbers of Buddhist images were needed, and needed in a hurry. To supplement the works in bronze and wood, new media, such as clay (built up around a wooden framework) and hollow dry lacquer (used especially for large statues to be carried in processions) came into fashion, and in these the native artists soon became masters.

The earliest clay images are almost pure T'ang, and the earliest known hollow dry lacquer was almost surely of Korean workmanship, but from about 730 to 750 a definitely Japanese style developed. It is marked by a tautness, a sense of power held in leash, which has often been compared to that of a coiled steel spring. It is especially evident in images of the more active minor divinities, such as Vajrāpaṇi and the so-called Four Guardian Kings, and is so widespread that it must reflect a general ideal of the time. In the quieter divinities, it sometimes takes a form that is extraordinarily reminiscent of the Greek.

There seems to have been comparatively little work in wood, at least in the capital itself, and almost none in bronze. This last was presumably due to the scarcity of copper, enhanced by the determination of the emperors to build one gigantic central image of the Buddha Vairochana (Roshana), which took some 10 years to make and was finally unveiled in 752. This immense seated statue, called the Daibutsu (Great Buddha) of Nara, had to be cast in sections, as it was some 53 feet high, and its making taxed the resources of the country. It has been so much damaged and repaired that little of the original remains save one knee and part of its lotus pedestal, but it was presumably T'ang in style. The incised engravings of Buddha groups and other figures on the pedestal are definitely T'ang. Japanese adaptations of T'ang are evident, however, on the bas-relief panels of a 15-foot bronze lantern standing outside the temple of the Daibutsu (Tōdaiji).

In 754 the arrival of the Chinese priest Ganjin (Chien-chên, d. 763) with many attendants, including sculptors and artisans, brought with it a new style, known as that of the Tōshōdaiji, the temple in which Ganjin was established. This style was marked by a continental massiveness and grandeur which greatly influenced the Japanese but was never thoroughly assimilated by them.

Painting of the period seems to have followed continental models, although it is not fair to judge it solely from the extraordinary collection of objects preserved in the Shōsōin (the repository of the Tōdaiji), as most of these had belonged to the Emperor Shōmu (r. 724–749) and include a disproportionately large number of imported articles. That there was at least some adaptation of foreign styles can be seen, for example, in the well-known late Nara portrait of Kichijōten (Śrī), who resembles a fairy princess in comparison with the ample proportions then in vogue for T'ang female figures.

Early Heian Period (c.800–c.980).—After the foundation of the new capital of Heian (Kyoto) in 794, there was a long period in which art, especially religious art, was rather stagnant. The revenues of the Nara temples were drastically reduced, and the great period of production for them was over. In Kyoto, in the early years of the 9th century, some statues were made which were rather curiously Bourbon and baroque, and the introduction of the esoteric sects (Tendai in 805, and Shingon in 807) demanded images of a new type. In the main, however, there was little native development of Chinese prototypes, and most of the remaining examples seem ponderous and uninspired.

Buddhist statues, now mostly of lacquered wood, often have a sensuous surface, but they tend toward obesity. Many have well-developed rolls of flesh around their waists. In many paintings, too, fatness seems almost an ideal. And it is significant that there is very little difference between the murals in the Daigōji pagoda (951) and those in the Murōji, painted almost exactly 100 years before.

There was apparently some development in secular painting, but none of it remains. Wonderful stories are told of such artists as Kose Kanaoka (fl. 850–880) and Kudara Kawanari. Artistic criticism, however, was apparently not very highly developed at the time, since one of the tales is that the artist was actually able to sketch a recognizable portrait of a man whose name he did not know. Extant portraits of monks do not differ much in style from the beginning to the end of the period.

Two peculiar developments should be noted. One was an attempt to reproduce (at Katada) the cave sculptures of the continent. Several caves were hollowed out of a mountainside, and many stone statues were made. But the material was unsuitable. Today the caves are no more than hollow niches, and most of the statues are in ruins. The other development was the production of Shintō statues. The earliest extant (probably about 890) are excellent examples of the cult of obesity, and the portrait of the war god Hachiman in the robes of a Buddhist monk is entirely Buddhist in style.

Later Heian (Fujiwara, c.980–c.1170).—The proper dates for this, as an art period, are debatable. It is probable that a secular art first developed in the confines of the highly cultured court circles, and that this then affected the religious art. It reached its highest expression in the 11th and early 12th centuries, and is marked by an extraordinary delicacy and refinement. Its ideal seems to be that of an otherworldly, unreal fairyland, and it is perhaps noteworthy that it seems to express itself better in two dimensions than in three. Even its best statues, lovely as some of them are, seem somehow reminiscent of paintings.

From the few examples of secular art still extant it can be seen that the characteristically Japanese style of painting known as Yamato-e developed in this period. It is based on color mass and outline and is splendidly exemplified in the illustrations for *The Tale of Genji* (c.1120), attributed to the artist Fujiwara no Takayoshi.

Religious art was greatly influenced by the rise of the Jōdo (Pure Land) or Amida sects, with their comparatively simple tenets. It becomes gentler and more human than in the previous period. Perhaps the most important single example is the Hōōdō (Phoenix Hall) at Uji (1053). Here a large central Amida is surrounded by masses of angels on clouds carved in high relief and set against the walls, while on the inner sides of the great wooden doors are paintings representing the coming of the Buddha and his attendants to the deaths of the nine classes of believers. There is considerable landscape which may be regarded as secular painting; much of it is very charming. This is definitely Yamato-e, uninfluenced by contemporary Chinese painting (Sung), but it is of interest that the wood carving, especially that of the angels and the halos, is extraordinarily like that of the stone carving then being done in Manchuria under the Liao. There is some suggestion of Liao technique in religious painting also, especially in the color and the profuse use of cut gold leaf (*kirigane*) in addition to the painted gold, but there is no doubt that the mass of Fujiwara painting was an indigenous development.

In the latter part of the Fujiwara period art seems to reflect the unsettled conditions of the country. In sculpture inspiration seems to fail, and there are indications of the coming of a new and more robust ideal, as yet imperfectly assimilated. A more active style of painting appeared, exemplified in such magnificent scrolls as those attributed to Toba Sōjō (1053–1140), where emphasis is placed on brushwork and strength of line. But the old ideals were by no means wholly suspended. The epitome of Fujiwara gorgeousness—though not, indeed, of its delicacy—comes in its last days, in the scrolls of the Lotus Sutra made by the Taira family about 1164.

Kamakura (c.1170–1350).—This was a time of robustness, vigor, and concern with mundane affairs. As an art period it extends about 17 years beyond the historical Kamakura period.

In sculpture a realistic, fully three-dimensional style was introduced by Kōkei and further developed by a number of talented successors, chief among them being his son Unkei (d. 1223), Japan's greatest sculptor. His work shows the influence of Nara rather than of Heian, but has an added realism, force, and activity. He is most successful in his carving of human figures and the semihuman guardian divinities, less so in the necessarily more conventional Buddhas. His school continued with only gradually decreasing vigor until about the middle of the 13th century, after which it rapidly declined. Most of the statues made at this time were of wood. The most important bronze was the Great Buddha at Kamakura, some 35 feet high (1252).

In secular painting there was some magnificent portraiture, and a new type of narrative scroll was introduced by Mitsunaga (c.1173). These were practically books, with little or no writing, which told a story in one continuous picture, in fully developed Yamato-e style. The type was soon adopted for religious purposes also, and was produced in great numbers by many excellent artists throughout the period. Conventional book illustrating was of course not abandoned, but it, too, took on new qualities of vigor and realism.

Although there was a certain hang-over of Fujiwara ideals, especially in the capital city of Kyoto, even the more conservative religious painting soon developed new ideals. Amida begins to come to the deathbeds of the faithful not softly, but on great whirling clouds, and new subjects become popular, such as the great Yamagoshi Buddhas rising from behind the mountains, and paintings of the Bodhisattva Monju (Mañjuśrī) crossing the sea bringing wisdom to Japan. Shintō painting, in a rather curious combination of Buddhist and secular styles, also became more common.

The beginnings of a new Chinese (Sung) inflence on painting is discernible as early as 1192. It gradually increased but did not become dominant until the Ashikaga period. In general the unrest brought on by the attempts of Kublai Khan to invade Japan did not affect painting as much as they did sculpture, but it, too, gradually lost its vigor. Toward the end both seem to reflect the national weariness with war, to become meticulous and tangled in detail.

Ashikaga (1350–1570).—From the point of view of the history of art the most important happening in the Ashikaga period was an enormous increase in the popularity of Zen Buddhism. The traditional types of Buddhist art were still used by other sects but they became formalized and repetitive. Life went out of them. The traditional secular art was also affected, increasing in quantity, but gradually decreasing in quality.

In sculpture the only advance was a type originated to portray Zen abbots, and the first exponents of a new style of painting were all Zen monks. Many of these monks journeyed to China and brought back with them Chinese paintings, both religious and secular. Zen religious painting was wholly different from the previous types and was not primarily concerned with Buddhas. It might show arhats (rakan), or sages, but tried above all else to suggest the unity of all things, animate and inanimate, and it tended to do the suggesting in the simplest possible way. Hence most Zen paintings have little color and much blank space, and many of the finest are simple ink line and wash (*suiboku*).

The preferred Chinese paintings were those of the Sung period, not contemporary, and these were collected not only in monasteries but also by the nobility. The Japanese at first tended to copy these, or at least their type. There were many famous artists of this time painting these "Chinese" pictures (Kanga), but unquestionably the greatest was Sesshū (1420–1506). Though inspired by China, he was in no sense a copyist, and he exerted an immense influence on subsequent painting in Japan.

Sesshū had few direct pupils and at his death several secular schools claimed to be his legitimate successors. Of these the most permanent was the Kanō, whose name has come to be almost synonymous with Kanga. The first artist of this school was Kanō Masanobu (1434–1530), but its real founder and the artist who gave it its distinguishing Japanese characteristics, was his son Motonobu (1476–1559). Motonobu had married into the Tosa family, the foremost exponents of Yamato-e, his wife being the daughter or, as some say, the granddaughter of Tosa Mitsunobu (1434–1525), the last great Yamato-e painter of the period. He himself sometimes painted in the "Japanese" style. His pictures, even those done in strictly "Chinese" technique, are not primarily religious in feeling, but are rather decorative, the product of an artist reveling in his medium and delighting in the natural scenery of his own country.

Momoyama (1570-c.1630).—This was the age of the warrior barons who had helped to unify Japan under Nobunaga, Hideyoshi, and Ieyasu, and who wished to enjoy the fruits of victory. The art they wanted and obtained reflected their desire for gorgeousness and was often barely saved from vulgarity by its vigor and ebullience. They could turn even the tea ceremony, with its canons of simplicity and refinement, into an occasion for ostentation, and though comparatively few in numbers, they provided work for many artists.

Momoyama was a time when great six-fold screens, often with gold-leaf backgrounds, might be ordered by the hundred pair; in general the objective of Momoyama art was that of sweeping decoration. Black-and-white painting was not neglected, and indeed could often be a most effective foil to the almost overpowering glitter of gold. The Kanō school continued dominant under the leadership of Eitoku (1543–1590) and his adopted son Sanraku (d. 1635), but there was room for other schools as well, such as the Unkoku and the Hasegawa, which claimed to be the artistic heirs of Sesshū, and the newer Soga and Kaihō, which also were developments of "Chinese" painting. In addition, there were, of course, fine artists who belonged to no school, such as Niten (1584–1645) and Shōkadō (1584–1639).

The history of Yamato-e from the end of Ashikaga through Momoyama is very complicated. Its great champion, the Tosa school, had gone into an eclipse, but its spirit had great influence on most of the contemporary schools. The fortunes of Tosa had been bound up with those of the aristocrats of Kyoto, and with the coming of peace it began to revive. This revival started with Tosa Mitsuyoshi (1539–1613) and continued with his successors. One important development of Yamato-e was the work of two outstanding artists, Tawaraya Sōtatsu (d. ?1643) and Honami Kōetsu (1558–1637). Their art was decorative rather than profound, and their styles were too individual to allow them to found a school. Their work, however, has greatly influenced all Japanese decorative art down to the present day.

Sculpture had a certain renaissance, chiefly as an adjunct to architecture, in *ramma* (ventilation panels) and other decoration. The best-known artist was Hidari Jingorō (1584?–1634), who did much of the wood carving for the Tōshōgū, the famous memorial to Ieyasu at Nikko.

Foreigners had reached Japan in 1542, and European art was brought in by traders and missionaries. A number of Japanese became fairly skillful in the techniques of oil painting, but most of their work was destroyed in the 17th century anti-Christian persecutions, and had little effect on Japanese art as a whole.

Tokugawa (Edo) Period (1630–1870).—The Momoyama type of art continued with gradually decreasing exuberance up to "gorgeous Genroku" (1688–1703). The shogun encouraged his vassals in nonmilitary spending, and it was a good time for artists. The Kanō school split into three slightly differing branches under Eitoku's grandsons, Tanyū (1602–1674), Naonobu (1607–1650), and Yasunobu (1613–1685). The Tosa school had an outstanding artist in Mitsuoki (1617–1691), and the decorative style of Sōtatsu was revived and extended by Ogata Kōrin (1658–1716).

A new non-Tosa Yamato-e, exemplified by the Sumiyoshi school, depicted scenes of the contemporary life of the people, usually at the orders of the shogun and other feudal lords. This was the forerunner, and may have been the origin, of the Ukiyo-e, a school primarily of, by, and for the common people, but in which a number of artists of samurai origin also played a part. The townspeople of the rapidly growing cities, particularly Edo (Tokyo), were enjoying more and more leisure and liked a pictorial record of their pleasures. As the demand grew, mass production became a necessity, and the work of the artists was printed, first in books and then in separate prints. The pioneer in this field was Hishikawa Moronobu (d. c.1694). About 1695, Torii Kiyonobu (1664–1729) began to make prints of actors, and his family, which had long been connected with the theater, soon became dominant in this field. These prints were in black and white, sometimes colored by hand.

Early in the 18th century the Kanō and Tosa schools declined, at least partially because many of the nobles and samurai, their principal patrons, were in great financial difficulties. They continued, however, to paint in the classical style, with great emphasis on technique, and many of the best subsequent artists were trained in their ateliers. Some of these artists, like Morikage (fl. c.1700) and Watanabe Shikō (1683–1755), developed their own styles but clung to more or less classical subjects; others, like Hanabusa Itchō (1652–1724) and Miyagawa Chōshun (1682–1752), tended to turn to genre.

There were other revolts against tradition, such as the so-called Nagasaki school, inspired by the work of contemporary Chinese artists, but the most important was the development of the *bunjinga* (literary man's painting). This was hardly a school, but rather a movement among poets, mostly of the samurai class, amateurs who drew their inspiration chiefly from Yüan China and placed their emphasis on emotion and spirituality rather than on technique. Its founder is usually considered to be Gion Nankai (1677–1751). It is the most difficult of all Japanese painting for foreigners to understand, but it has had a great influence in Japan itself. Ukiyo-e printing—the antithesis of *bunjinga*—made considerable technical advances, and with the invention of color printing (about 1741) entered a new phase.

The latter half of the 18th century produced many important artists, chief among them being Maruyama Ōkyo (1733–1795), who started a new realistic school influenced by the works of contemporary Chinese and European artists which he had studied at Nagasaki. An offshoot of the Maruyama school (the Shijō) was founded in Kyoto by Matsumura Goshun (1752–1811), who also had studied under Yosano Buson (1716–1783), one of the finest of the poet-painters. Its combination of realism and spirituality was very popular and had much influence on Japanese painting in the 19th century. The Tosa and Kanō schools, though still alive, were dormant, but the Kōrin type of painting had an excellent exemplar in Sakai Hōitsu (1761–1828), and there were some very fine painters of *bunjinga*. European painting (*yōga*) was also attempted, based mostly on illustrations in books imported from the Netherlands. No great works resulted, but European perspective became more familiar to Japan.

This was the great period for Ukiyo-e color prints. The technique of full-color printing was first employed for calendar prints of 1765, and a succession of great artists designed figure prints. Suzuki Harunobu (1724–1770), Katsukawa Shunshō (1726–1792), Torii Kiyonaga (1752–1815), Kitagawa Utamaro (1754?–1806), Tōshūsai Sharaku (fl. 1794–1795)—they are known in the West as well if not better than in Japan. By 1800, however, the great day of the figure prints was over. After that time most of the work of Utagawa Toyokuni (1769–1825) and his followers shows garish color and confused design. In the 19th century there were two outstanding artists, Hokusai and Hiroshige, but most of their work was landscape, and out of the Ukiyo-e tradition. Katsushika Hokusai (1760–1849) was the great eclectic; Andō Hiroshige (1797–1858) was greatly influenced by the Shijō school, especially in his *kachō* (bird-and-flower designs).

The 19th century produced a welter of different styles, too many to mention in detail. There was a revival of "Japanese" painting (*fukko* Yamato-e); some excellent painters were developed in the Kanō school; the Shijō school continued with gradually decreasing popularity under Matsumura Keibun (1779–1843) and Okamoto Toyohiko (1773–1843) and their followers; Tani Bunchō (1764–1841), in his time considered the greatest painter in Edo, worked in many styles; and of the *bunjinga* painters, many, like Tanomura Chikuden (1777–1835), took their inspiration from China, while others, like Watanabe Kazan (1793–1841), were at least partially influenced by European art. The world of art reflected the confusion and lack of unity then more or less general throughout the country.

Modern Period (Since 1870).—Immediately after the Meiji Restoration there was great enthusiasm for foreign techniques, which were at first copied without complete understanding, and of course many excellent artists such as Shibata Zeshin (1807–1891) continued to paint in the traditional manner. Other outstanding artists were Kanō Hōgai (1828–1888), Hashimoto Gahō (1835–1908), and Kawabata Gyokushō (1842–1913), all of whom were trained by Kanō masters and later developed their own styles. Hishida Shunsō (1874–1907), an artist of extraordinary promise who unfortunately died young, was somewhat more influenced by the West.

In the mid-20th century the art world was divided between Western- and Japanese-style artists, and at least the beginnings of a fusion were discernible, though it had not progressed to anything like a full synthesis. Most famous among the more modern Japanese-style artists have been Takeuchi Seihō (1865–1944) in Kyoto and Yokoyama Taikan (1868–) in Tokyo. It is difficult, and perhaps out of place here, to evaluate the living Western-style artists, especially since a number of the best known in the Occident, like Yasuo Kuniyoshi (1893–1953), received their artistic training outside Japan. It should also be noted that there has been a revival of color printing, some of which is very successful. See also sections on *Architecture; Religion;* article on CHINA—*Art*.

Bibliography.—Fenollosa, E. F., *Epochs of Chinese and Japanese Art: An Outline History of East Asiatic Design,* 2 vols. (London 1912); Binyon, Laurence, and Sexton, J. J. O., *Japanese Colour Prints* (New York 1923); Warner, Langdon, *Japanese Sculpture of the Suiko Period* (New Haven 1923); Minamoto, Hoshu, *An Illustrated History of Japanese Art,* tr. by H. G. Henderson (Kyoto 1935); Toda, Kenji, *Japanese Scroll Painting* (Chicago 1935); Tsuda, Noritake, *Handbook of Japanese Art* (Tokyo 1935).

HAROLD G. HENDERSON,
Assistant Professor of Japanese, Columbia University.

17. ARCHITECTURE. All Far Eastern architecture is based on the structural use of wood. The Chinese have exploited this material to achieve an ideal of discipline and clarity. Their grand plans face to the south, and are symmetrical about a central axis. The wooden framework is painted with formal designs in strong colors. Other materials heighten the impression of artifice: brilliantly glazed tile roofs, stone platforms and balustrades. Where the purpose is purely monumental, as in a pagoda, the design may depend entirely on masonry, or metal, or even porcelain. The Japanese, although they have been strongly influenced by the Chinese ideal, have steadfastly kept a preference for opposite effects of irregularity and naturalness. Their deepest instinct has been to make a building at home in its natural environment, and to give it a kind of homeliness for human occupancy. When the instinct has been allowed full expression, this has resulted in an architecture that in farmhouse, mansion, temple, or palace has made an almost exclusive use of vegetable materials left in their natural colors: wood posts and planks, straw matting, bamboo, rice paper. Where tradition or aesthetic preference has outweighed the desire for fireproofing, the roof as well has been covered with thatch or shingles.

The history of Japanese architecture prior to 19th century westernization may be divided into three broad periods corresponding to the degrees in which native preferences have dominated. The first, down to around 600 A.D., was an age of slow advance from the primitive, stimulated toward the end by sporadic contacts with the mainland. The second, covering about three centuries, brought an amalgamation of Japan into the cultural orbit of China, and a resolute attempt to make over

Japanese architecture, like every other side of civilized life, on the Chinese model. The third has been a long backwash, in which the Chinese forms have been assimilated or abandoned, and a truly national style of high sophistication has been developed.

Early Native Architecture (to c.600 A.D.).—No buildings remain from the first period, but it is possible to gain a fairly clear idea of their characteristics from secondary evidence. The earliest inhabitants of Japan whose way of life can be reconstructed, perhaps the Stone Age ancestors of the historic Ainu, have left in their settlements the traces of pit houses. In plan these are circular or squarish with rounded corners, around 15 feet across; the most pretentious have a rough stone paving around the central hearth. Post holes suggest a tent-shaped roof of thatch. That the ancestors of the Japanese preferred instead a building with a floor raised on posts (uncomfortable in winter, but preferable in humid summer) is attested by a variety of evidence. What seem to be farm dwellings and storehouses are represented in art toward the latter part of this early period, in line relief on bronzes and as three-dimensional pottery miniatures. Plans are now simple oblongs, with an entrance and windows on the long side. The most elaborate dwellings, with their platforms reached by ladders, and steep thatched roofs flaring widely at the gable peak, have a flavor of the Southwest Pacific that has encouraged theories linking the proto-Japanese to the tropics (see section on *The People*).

The look of these early representations recurs in the modern Shintō sanctuaries that more or less faithfully follow an ancient model. Of a half dozen, the most famous are those at Izumo and Ise, the latter having been identically rebuilt (at least in principle) every 20 years since its cult was standardized in 686. The series seems to show a gradual advance in design. The Izumo sanctuary is a big gabled box on a platform, entered from the end to one side of the ridge pillar, and with a pillar at the middle inside. Its form is only a stage beyond the tent-like bamboo shelters still used by harvesters. Intermediate sanctuary types gain formality by shifting the supports so a door may be centered. With the Ise Shrine (which may have taken form in the 3rd century) the building has been turned around so as to be entered at the middle of the long side, like the Chinese or Korean hall type that may have distantly suggested it. The Ise sanctuary shows most fully a complex of details that recur in part in the rest, and that testify to the preservation of primitive building techniques as a mark of holy antiquity. Most noticeable are the 10 heavy billets set crosswise on the ridge (originally to help weigh down the thatch, as may still be seen in back-country farmhouses); and the prolongation of the bargeboards as a fork high above each end of the roof.

In addition, the earliest Japanese histories contain scattered information on palace buildings. In the age of myth the marriage hut of the primal deities Izanami and Izanagi had a central pillar like the Izumo Shrine. In the last centuries of the period, when cultural infiltration from Korea had become a factor, the palaces are described with a new complication of plan, and with new features like towers. Throughout, the palace and the capital around it were lightly built for temporary use, since the death of the ruler would require (at least in theory) a move to a new site.

Period of Dominant Chinese Influence (c.600–900 A.D.).—The opening of Japan to close contact with the brilliant civilization of T'ang dynasty China brought two new major architectural problems, the Buddhist temple and the formal, permanent palace-and-capital complex. The two varied only in dimensions and details, using almost identical building types and the same sort of symmetrical grand plan, laid out facing the south in enclosed courtyards, approached through monumental gateways. Building now became vastly more expensive, and served as the prime symbol of a new formality imposed on the life of the ruling class. The permanence required, and obtained by the use of stone-faced platforms, tile roofs, and much heavier timbers protected from weathering by paint, has incidentally resulted in the preservation of many buildings from this period, as well as the layout of two capital cities, Nara and Kyoto (then called Heian), and the group plans of a large number of Buddhist monasteries, followed throughout later rebuilding or still traceable on the sites. Most are in Nara or its environs. One monastery complex there, Hōryūji, still retains its major structures of the 7th century.

The Sinophile period of about three centuries, marked by an admiration that sometimes became a desperate race with T'ang achievement, reached its climax about 725–825. Beginning in 794, Kyoto was built as the last and most ambitious of a series of capitals on the Chinese model, with a regular checkerboard of streets and a central avenue leading from the palace compound on axis at the north. The essentials of the design are still visible in modern Kyoto, though human needs ran counter to symmetry in the city's later growth. The 8th century at Nara saw the number and size of Buddhist monasteries increase steadily, to a climax around 750–759 with the building of Tōdaiji: a huge central hall housing a colossal bronze Buddha, at the center of an *enceinte* as spacious as the imperial palace. The nation emerged from this fever almost bankrupt, fearful of the power wielded by the big metropolitan temples, and already half surfeited with Chinese ways. Even at the climax of the imported fashion native taste was still stubborn. Below the top level, building in the old style continued; even the emperor, though he held court in Chinese robes in a T'ang hall of state, preferred living quarters of a more comfortable homeliness. At Kyoto there were no temples as oppressively grand as Tōdaiji; and Chinese influence ebbed there until around 900 a native reaction was unmistakable.

Surviving monuments show a progression from a 7th century style quite out of date by Chinese standards, to a full T'ang modernity reached by 750. Hōryūji derives through Korea from a north Chinese architecture of the 6th century. Its details show an archaic flatness and a liveliness of line that are the architectural counterpart of Northern Wei dynasty Buddhist sculpture. All architecture of Chinese inspiration uses regularly spaced wood columns in the plane of the wall, with some kind of bracketing above each column to support the heavy roof overhang. At Hōryūji this bracketing consists of only a single transverse beam, reaching out to support the purlin running along the eaves, and braced by a planklike corbel in the same plane, cut out with the fluid irregularity of a cloud pattern. In the plane of the wall, on the other hand, and on the interior, the bracketing unit is quite different. The column, which in the 7th century has a fine entasis, is capped by a simple square capital. Into the top is let a sturdy bracketing arm, which runs out on either side to end in a subtly drawn curve. There are three bearing blocks like small capitals, one at each end of the arm and one at the middle. These carry the beam above, part of the upper wall system, or in the interior the support for a ceiling. In the mature T'ang style followed in the 8th century, the bracketing over the column becomes a complex built out in three dimensions for maximum structural and visual effectiveness. The irrelevant cloud corbel is abandoned; and on the basis of an architectonic unit like the Hōryūji bracketing arm, the complex is constructed in orderly steps outward and sideways. At this stage the only intercolumnar support provided in the wall plane is a simple strut between two beams, or a bifurcated brace that the Japanese call *kaerumata* (frog's legs).

The original 7th century buildings at Hōryūji include: a pagoda; the Buddha Hall or Kondō (literally, Golden Hall); veranda corridors enclosing three sides of the courtyard; and a gateway on axis at the south. All rise from stone platforms and show similar details. Kondō and gateway are two storied (though the upper is not used), with a penthouse roof skirting the first floor and the whole crowned by the roof form called *irimoya,* which rises halfway as a hip and then becomes a gable. The pagoda is made up of five standard stories, square in plan, separated by the same skirting roofs, and diminishing as they rise. At the top is a typical spire, a mast fitted with superimposed metal disks and crowned by an openwork finial. In plan the only real problem is that of the Kondō, to provide a room for images and worship. At Hōryūji the solution is simple. The hall is five bays wide by four deep. Inside is a surrounding aisle under the skirting roof; in the remaining space, three bays by two, the other columns are omitted to make room for a platform, covered with images, and dignified above by a coved ceiling. The stage of development of the Buddha Hall is still so early here that a memory is preserved of ancient worship in India, where the focus of adoration was not an oblong altar with statues but a round stupa mound enclosed by a processional path. Thus the Kondō images face outward in all directions, only the principal Buddhas being oriented toward the south. It was natural in the Far East, however, that Buddhist worship should be modified by a secular ceremonial that insisted on a southward orientation. By the middle of the 8th century the Hokkedō (Lotus Hall) chapel at Tōdaiji has its altar platform closed by a partition at the back, and its images all face to the south.

The group planning of the monastery is seen earliest at Shitennōji (begun in 593), in Osaka. There the main axis enclosed by the courtyard and corridors holds first the gateway; then the pagoda; then the Buddha Hall; and finally, closing the rear, the Lecture Hall (Kōdō). The trend thereafter being toward a gradual reduction of the pagoda to secondary importance, its first demotion is to be removed from the axis. Hōryūji shows a unique variant in placing it and the Kondō to left and right respectively. Under the Chinese code of symmetry, however, a nonaxial element must normally be doubled. That next stage may still be traced at Yakushiji (718) outside Nara, where a pagoda was set in each front corner of the courtyard. In the extravagant climax at Tōdaiji, the two pagodas were brought outside to balance on east and west, and were given their own small courtyard complexes. See also CHINA—*Art.*

Development of a National Style (from c.900 A.D.).—The indigenous reaction during the remainder of the period of Kyoto rule, under the Fujiwara clan down to 1184, took several forms. Though there were still large city temples, the greatest influence was exerted from the mountain headquarters of the new esoteric Buddhist sects, Hieizan and Kōyasan. In their surroundings irregularity of grouping and orientation was natural. There was a general drift away from mandarin formality toward greater comfort and intimacy. The mansions that in the Sinophile design called *shinden-zukuri* had been almost as strictly laid out as city temples lost their tight symmetry and began to ramble. Details were increasingly influenced by the instincts that had never entirely been suppressed. The first natural substitution was a wood platform floor in place of the tile or stone pavement. Construction became lighter; the bracketing was simplified. Buildings were often left unpainted, and were shingled more often than tiled. In this way palaces, temples, and mansions gradually took on a common character of domestic informality.

The most notable development in plan was the creation of a different Buddha hall type, under the pressure of new needs. The T'ang formula of altar platform and surrounding aisle had been adapted neither to elaborate ritual nor to a large lay audience. Both of these factors had a much greater importance during the Fujiwara period, particularly because the new esoteric worship insisted that ritual be performed unseen. The solution reached by about 1200 was a much more elaborate plan, with ample room for the laity in front in a spacious forechamber often the full width of the building, the so-called *raidō.* This public area was divided by a partition with doors or grillwork from the chancel beyond. In the latter a large floor area was left for ritual performances. Across the rear would run a shallow platform, with the main images often enclosed in cabinet shrines. Such a building, completed by a service room at the back, might be deeper than it was wide, in marked distinction to Chinese proportions. Where the 8th century hall had been symmetrical on both axes, this would remain so only in a left and right sense.

Under the military regime at Kamakura (1185–1333) two crosscurrents opposed the long ebb of the Chinese ideal. One, seen around Nara in the restoration of old monasteries, was a deliberate attempt to recreate the 8th century. The other, stronger and more widely felt, was a new stream of Chinese influence. Into Kamakura architecture were injected two alien styles from different regions of South China, inaccurately called "Indian" and "Chinese." The first featured a curiously graceless, powerful technique of bracketing, and was in general so unlike the taste of the time that its popularity was brief. Its most impressive surviving monument is the Great South Gate of Tōdaiji. The other, actually the imperial style of the Southern Sung dynasty, was a more complex and delicate version of the T'ang manner. Frankly ingenious in balancing the weights of interior framing by a system of levers, it was characterized outside by one obvious change. The bracketing complex no longer rose only from the column top, but was repeated once or twice between with only a wall beam as support, thus transforming the under-eaves zone into a kind of continuous half-structural frieze. The "Chinese" style was an importation of the newly popular Zen Buddhist sect, and later kept much of its original purity in Zen monastic building, together with a standard Chinese group plan. Elsewhere both it and the "Indian" style soon lost identity, and in the end merely contributed a few new terms to the growing eclecticism of architectural decoration.

Post-Kamakura architecture has developed the trends already perceptible around 1200, without radical change. A huge popular place of worship of the 18th century, like the main halls of the Honganji in Kyoto, is hardly more than an enlargement of the mature Kamakura design. The whole temple compound will usually show the free placing made respectable by the old mountain monasteries. The principal novelty will be a great richness of sculptural decoration. Development in this last direction reached its extreme in the parvenu splendors of the 17th century Tokugawa tomb shrines at Nikko; while for more sophisticated patrons it provoked a reaction toward the equally exaggerated austerity seen in the rooms used for the cult of ceremonial tea.

The final flowering of Japanese taste has come with the type of house perfected in recent centuries. The building and its garden are drawn closely together by irregular planning and an absence of strict boundaries; sliding screens permit the rooms to be thrown together and interior to merge with exterior. All is light, and finely worked but simple in design; almost every surface is of vegetable origin, in its natural color. The pleasure taken in such an environment is so great that its charm has been borrowed for every other traditional building type. So completely has it satisfied the aesthetic sense that the Japanese have been willing to overlook its vulnerability to the annual problem of cold, and the periodic catastrophes of earthquake and fire.

Bibliography.—Morse, E. S., *Japanese Houses and Their Surroundings* (Boston 1886); *Japanese Temples and Their Treasures* (Tokyo 1915); Cram, R. A., *Impressions of Japanese Architecture and the Allied Arts* (Boston 1930); Taut, Bruno, *Houses and People of Japan* (Tokyo 1937); Soper, A. C., *The Evolution of Buddhist Architecture in Japan* (Princeton 1942).

ALEXANDER C. SOPER,
Department of the History of Art, Bryn Mawr College.

18. LANGUAGE. The language spoken by the middle and upper classes in Tokyo is regarded as the standard language of Japan. It is universally taught in the schools, and is understood, even if it is not completely controlled, by most provincial speakers. This standard language has five vowels, with the qualities in *a*mah, machine, *u*hlan, b*e*ta, and n*o*te. The vowels may be lengthened or may be paired in diphthongs. In rapid speech, *i* and *u* tend to disappear when they occur between voiceless consonants. The consonants are: *p, b, m, t* (*ts* before *u*), *d, n, ñ* (syllabic), *k, g* (nasalized when in the middle of a word), *s, sh, z, j, ch, h* (bilabial *f* when found before *u;* like the German *ch* in *ich* when found before *i* or *y*), *y, w, r* (flapped), and *v* (found in a few words borrowed from foreign languages). Consonants may be palatalized—that is, followed by *y.* The consonants *p, t, k, s,* and *n* may be doubled.

The accent is musical: a difference in pitch rather than stress is often distinguished between adjacent syllables of a word. Three levels of pitch are heard: low, middle, and high, with the intervals approximating that between one note on the piano and that which is two above it. Different pitch schemes distinguish words that are otherwise pronounced alike: *sakè,* with the first syllable pronounced at low pitch and the second at middle, means "rice wine," whereas *sáke,* with the first syllable taking high pitch and the second middle, means "salmon."

Grammatical categories fall into two groups. inflected and uninflected. The first group includes verbs, copulas, adjectives, and suffixes; the second, nouns, adverbs, and particles. There are four conjugations of verbs, two of which consist of one verb only: *kuru* (to come) and *suru* (to do). Two kinds of copula are found: one abrupt in connotation (*da*), and the other polite (*desu*). The forms of the adjective that may terminate a sentence end in *-ai, -oi, -ui,* or *-ii.* The word order is subject, object (if any), verb; subject, adjective; or subject, predicate noun, copula. Qualifying words and phrases precede the words they qualify. Particles follow the words, phrases, clauses, and sentences they govern. There are various levels of politeness, depending on the relative social standing of the speaker, the person spoken to, and the persons or things spoken of.

The characters used in writing the Japanese language are of three types: the kanji, which are the more complicated characters borrowed from China (see CHINA—*Language*); the katakana, which are syllabic characters that are angular in shape; and the hiragana, which are syllabic characters that are cursive in shape. The katakana and the hiragana each number 48; there is a one-for-one correspondence between the two types. The kanji are used to express the chief meaningful elements, such as nouns and the basic root ideas of verbs and adjectives. The katakana and hiragana are phonetic and are used to express the categories whose chief function is grammatical—that is, the syllables which comprise the particles and suffixes. In a typical text only kanji and hiragana are used; katakana are employed to represent foreign words borrowed into Japanese. In most texts these characters are arranged in vertical columns and read from top to bottom, right to left. In a few reference works and scientific texts, however, the arrangement is horizontal, as in English, and the characters are read from left to right, top to bottom; this method permits the inclusion of Roman letters, Arabic numerals, mathematical and chemical formulas, and the like. When written with brush or pen. characters may take the following forms: *kaisho,* or angular writing; *gyōsho,* a somewhat cursive form; and *sōsho,* the most abbreviated and cursive form.

The written language of the earliest times probably closely represented the colloquial. By the 9th or 10th century, however, the spoken and written languages began to separate. The spoken form changed rapidly; the written form was much more conservative. Hence, until the end of World War II, most materials intended for adult reading contained sizable numbers of linguistic forms that had long since been lost in speech. An example is the use of *yukan to su* (to try to go) instead of the colloquial *ikō to suru.* The use of such constructions peculiar to classical grammar, the large number of arbitrary spellings that had developed in the supposedly phonetic kana, and the need of knowing a great many kanji—perhaps 2,000 to 2,500 before fluent reading could be achieved—meant that the load on the reader's memory was particularly burdensome. Various reforms have thus been suggested. These look forward to the colloquialization of the written language, reduction in number of kanji, the use of phonetic spellings in kana in place of the older historical spellings, and greater use of romanization.

Bibliography of Works in English.—Sansom, G. B., *An Historical Grammar of Japanese* (Oxford 1928); Yamagiwa, J. K., *Introduction to Japanese Writing* (Ann Arbor, Mich., 1942); id., *Modern Conversational Japanese* (New York and London 1942); Henderson, H. G., *Handbook of Japanese Grammar* (Boston 1943); Elisséeff, Serge, Reischauer, E. O., and Yoshihashi, T., *Elementary Japanese for College Students,* 3 vols. (Cambridge, Mass., 1944); Yamagiwa, J. K., *The Modern Japanese Written Language* (Ann Arbor, Mich., 1945); Bloch, Bernard, and Jorden, E. H., *Spoken Japanese,* 2 vols. (New York 1945–1946).

JOSEPH K. YAMAGIWA,
Department of Far Eastern Languages and Literatures, University of Michigan.

19. LITERATURE. This section traces the development of Japanese fiction, drama, and poetry from their beginnings to the mid-20th century.

Fiction.—The earliest extant Japanese narrative materials are found in the *fudoki,* or provincial records, which were compiled in the early 8th century; and in the chronicle entitled *Kojiki* (*A Record of Ancient Matters*), traditionally dated in the year 712. These texts record with great simplicity the legends and traditions that had been handed down orally from generation to generation. In the *Taketori Monogatari* (*Tale of the Bamboo Hewer,* 9th century) a superlatively beautiful heavenly girl is found between the nodes of a bamboo stem. When she grows up, five suitors seek her hand, and each is sent forth on an impossible quest. The *Utsubo Monogatari* (end of the 10th century) also uses fabulous material. A more realistic approach is taken in the *Ochikubo Monogatari* (written before 999), in which a beautiful girl is harassed by a wicked stepmother. Meanwhile, the *Ise Monogatari* (c.877) and the *Yamato Monogatari* (c.950) reflected the great vogue of poetry, telling a series of amorous incidents, each centered around an example of the tanka, or 31-syllable poem. Anecdotal and poetic materials were also used in the *Tosa Nikki* (*Tosa Diary*), written about 935 by Ki no Tsurayuki; in the diaries of Murasaki Shikibu, Izumi Shikibu, and the author of the *Sarashina Nikki,* all court ladies of the late 10th and early 11th centuries; and in the miscellany entitled *Makura no Sōshi* (*Pillow Book*), written by another court lady, Sei Shōnagon.

The realistic and lyric strands were finally joined, with a heightened sense of psychological and narrative values, in the great story of courtly life, *Genji Monogatari* (*The Tale of Genji*), which was written by Murasaki Shikibu early in the 11th century. *The Tale of Genji* stands at the apex of the fiction of Heian times (784–1184). In this novel is told the early love life of the hero, Prince Genji, his exile to Suma and Akashi, subsequent recall, rise to the highest political offices of the kingdom, and solicitude over all the women with whom he has been involved. As Genji grows older, and especially after his death, when the scene shifts from the capital at Heian (now Kyoto) to the hamlet of Uji a dozen miles away, the story becomes much more somber.

The tales and diaries of Heian times were for the most part written by women. Using the easily written hiragana (see section on *Language*), and enjoying considerable freedom of observation and experience in a highly literary and artistic atmosphere, the women of the court virtually monopolized the writing of fiction.

Later writers failed to match the special genius of these women. The collection of 10 short stories known as the *Tsutsumi Chūnagon Monogatari* (*Tales of the Middle Councilor of the Embankment*) was probably written between 1050 and 1250, most of the stories dating from the 11th century. They are distinguished by their comic, satiric, and ironic effects. The *Konjaku Monogatari* (*Tales Modern and Ancient*) is a collection of 1,200 stories, many of them having a Buddhistic flavor. Another fresh departure was the *rekishi monogatari,* or historical tale, of which the outstanding examples are the *Eiga Monogatari* (*Tales of Glory*) and the *Ōkagami* (*Great Mirror*), both dating from the end of the 11th century and telling of the pomp and circumstance surrounding the greatest family of Heian times, the Fujiwara, especially as represented by its most eminent member, Michinaga (966–1028).

Literature decayed in the Kamakura age (1185–1333), which was ushered in by civil war between the Taira and Minamoto clans. The warrior on horseback and the fighting monk now took the center of the stage. Literature became sober and depressing, instructive and moralizing. Typical of the age were various polemical essays written by such religious leaders as Nichiren (1222–1282). Of greater literary interest is the *Hōjōki* (*Ten Foot Square Hut*), written in the year 1212 by Kamo no Chōmei (1153–1216), who records his life as a recluse, and the *Tsurezuregusa* (*Idle Jottings*) of Yoshida Kenkō (1283–1350), who gives his impressions of men, writings, and nature, with many nostalgic references to the life of Heian times. In this period the blending of Chinese and Buddhist words with the native vocabulary added a new vigor to the language, and the warring times gave to a new narrative type, the *gunki monogatari,* or war tale, its quality of strength and freshness. The best of these war tales was the *Heike Monogatari* (*Tales of the Heike*), written for the most part in the first two decades of the 13th century. Sentimental, high flown, and extremely rhetorical, these texts were intended, not to be read, but to be heard to the accompaniment of the *biwa,* or four-stringed lute, played by the *biwa hōshi* (*biwa* priests), who roamed the country and held their audiences in rapt attention as they chanted the fall of men in battle, thus in their way helping to crystallize and to idealize the code of the samurai-warrior.

The next great development in narrative writing came in the Tokugawa era (1603–1867). In the 17th century a peaceful rule, greater literacy among the middle and lower classes, the growth of a class of independent and professional writers, the development of the art of printing, and better facilities for transportation helped to spread fiction throughout the country. Edo (now Tokyo), the seat of the shogunate, began to rival

Kyoto and Osaka as a literary and cultural center. The writing was essentially in kana. The first works, reaching as far back as the end of the 14th century, were the *otogizōshi,* or elementary stories intended to amuse the uneducated. These developed into the *kusazōshi* (grass books) of the middle of the 18th century. Moral, romantic, filled with characters, and containing many twists of plot, they took such names as *akahon* (red books), *kibyōshi* (yellow covers), and *gōkan* (bound books), depending on the color and nature of their bindings. Branching out from this development were the *kanazōshi,* or writings in the syllabic script, and the *yomihon,* or reading books, both didactic types depending largely on Buddhist and Chinese ideas. The *yomihon* were distinguished by their use of ghosts and fabulous creatures. Kyokutei Bakin (1767–1848) was the greatest writer of this genre; his most famous work was the *Satomi Hakkenden.*

From about 1680 a worldly-minded genre known as the *ukiyozōshi,* or tales of the floating world, began to achieve great popularity. Ibara Saikaku (1642–1693) was the leading author; with great realism and in plain words he pictured the effect on family life of affairs in the demimonde. In the 1750's the *sharehon* (wit book) continued the vogue of erotic writing; in this form the plots were for the most part developed by means of conversations. Another development was the *kokkeibon* (comic book), represented by the *Dōchū Hizakurige* (*Shank's Mare over a Road*), a story by Jippensha Ikku (1765–1831) in which two roisterers of Edo, Yajirobei and Kitahachi, travel down the Tōkaidō (Eastern Sea Road) to Kyoto and become involved in all manner of comic misadventures. The love affairs of the sons and daughters of the merchant class are told in the *ninjōbon* (books of human feeling).

The lighter fiction of Tokugawa times lingered on into the period after the Meiji Restoration (1868), but with the impact of Western literature various new types began to flourish. Kanagaki Robun (1829–1894) and Yano Ryūkei (1850–1931) took Western political ideas as the themes of their novels. In the 1870's and 1880's the historical novels of the 1st Baron Lytton and the scientific novels of Victor Hugo were translated into Japanese and enjoyed great popularity. A major event in the history of the novel took place in 1885–1886 when Tsubouchi Shōyō (1859–1935) published his famous *Shōsetsu Shinzui* (*Essence of a Novel*). In this work, Shōyō struck a blow against the didacticism of earlier writers like Bakin and demanded clear objectivity in the description of human life. Shōyō's precepts were followed by Hasegawa Shinnosuke (1864–1909), who wrote under the pen name Futabatei Shimei ("Die and be done with you"). Mori Ōgai (1862–1922), a student of Goethe and inclined to follow a more subjective and deductive line of reasoning, also emancipated himself from traditional points of view.

The subsequent history of the novel is marked by the rise of many schools and writers ranging from realism to idealism. An early realist was Ozaki Kōyō (1867–1903). Among his successors were a group of naturalistic writers including Tayama Katai (1871–1930), Masamune Hakuchō (1879–), and Shimazaki Tōson (1872–1943) for a part of his work; and such modern realists as Kikuchi Kan (1888–1948), Akutagawa Ryūnosuke (1892–1927), and Yamamoto Yūzō (1887–). Among idealists may be mentioned Kōda Rohan (1867–1947), Higuchi Ichiyō (1872–1896), Tokutomi Roka (1868–1927), and Kunikida Doppo (1871–1908), the Mita school headed by Mori Ōgai and Nagai Kafū (1879–), the Yoyū (leisure) school of Natsume Sōseki (1867–1916), the Shirakaba (white birch) school of Mushanokōji Saneatsu (1885–) and Arishima Takeo (1878–1923), and Tanizaki Jun'ichirō (1886–), an extraordinary exponent of art for art's sake. Christianity, proletarianism, and various other ways of thought and life were espoused by many writers.

Drama.—Examples of Japanese religious drama are the *kagura* and *saibara,* both of which date from the early Heian age and are still performed at Shintō shrines. The *kagura* (literally, "pleasing the deities") is a dance or musical performance that in some forms is purely religious and intended to supplicate the gods; in other forms it is partly ritualistic and partly intended for entertainment. The *saibara* (literally, "get-ready-horse music") is a less polished form presented after the *kagura* has been performed.

Early in the 7th century a religious dance using masks arrived from Korea. This was the *gigaku* (skillful music), which was meant both to add dignity to Buddhist ceremonies and to serve as entertainment. The *gigaku* was performed only until the 10th century. In the 8th century a continental form known as *bugaku* (dance music) had reached Japan. This was an elegant mask dance accompanied by many instruments. More methodical and better arranged than the *gigaku,* it is still performed under the name *gagaku* (refined music). Another development connected with Buddhism is the *ennen-no-mai* (dance of longevity), which is recorded from about the year 1000. It first consisted of a shapeless performance of dances and stunts presented by priests. Soon, however, it began to include Chinese verse, Buddhist stories, and Buddhist poems, called *imayō,* which were made up of 8 or 12 lines consisting alternately of 7 and 5 syllables. The *ennen-no-mai* finally developed a chorus and parts in dialogue. It has persisted to the present day.

Popular drama also had religious beginnings in performances involving supplications for success in farming, fishing, and marriage. The *demmai* (paddy field dance) and the *denka* (paddy field song) evolved into the *dengaku* (paddy field music), which was intended partly as a prayer for a plentiful harvest and partly as amusement for the farmers as they went about their planting. Later, acrobatic stunts were added. The *dengaku* lasted until the 19th century under the name of *dengaku no nō* (accomplishment in paddy field music).

In the 9th century a comic dance incorporating folk music was introduced from India by way of China. This importation was the sangaku, or scattered music. Performed at Shintō shrines, it was at first a combination of music, antics, and joking. As sarugaku (monkey music), it came to include singing and recitation; later it took the name *sarugaku no nō* (accomplishment in monkey music), and finally it became the major ingredient of the no (Jap. *nō*) drama. This drama of "accomplishment" took its present shape in the 14th and 15th centuries. It owes its development also to various elements derived from the *ennen-no-mai;* from the singing and dancing known as *shirabyōshi* (literally, "white rhythm"), which took its name from certain professional dancing girls; and from various dances associated with particular shrines and festivals.

The sarugaku was the source of the type of chanting employed by the *biwa* priests who recited the more stirring portions of the war romances. It also helped to develop the *kyōgen* (crazy words) that became the comic complement of the no drama. The *sarugaku no nō* and the chanting of the *biwa* priests contributed to the eventual development of the *jōruri,* or marionette drama, in the 16th century. The *kyōgen* was a source of the popular dramatic form *kabuki,* whose literal meaning is "eccentricity," "impudence," or "abnormality."

The two major figures associated with the early history of the no drama are Kannami (1333–1384) and Zeami (1363–1444). The latter in particular rejected the lighter elements of the sarugaku, and he is held to be the father of the no. He was the ancestor of the Kanze school (the other major no schools are the Komparu, Hōshō, Kita, and Kongō). Elegant and slow moving, the no appeals primarily to the initiate. In a typical plot a traveling priest is met by a person at the scene of a famous action. As the two talk, the latter suddenly confesses that he is a spirit in disguise and leaves. When he reappears, he is found to be the hero or major figure who has made the place famous. He sings and dances the role he played in life in making the place a historic spot. A prayer by the priest finally sets the spirit to rest, freed at last from the *shūshin* (heart attachment) which had made him return. The elements of the no drama are contrary to realism. Its poetic qualities are enhanced by the dancing and singing of the chorus, and by a kind of aesthetic frenzy that seems to grip both performers and audience.

The *kyōgen,* in contrast, is a comic form depending on unexpected actions in more or less absurd situations. It is given as comic relief in a no program; its satire attacks both foolish masters and ignorant priests.

The *jōruri* has only one real home in Japan, the Osaka theater called the Bunrakuza. The *kabuki,* however, is popular everywhere. It is extravagantly produced and is spectacular to eye and ear. Living actors, all men, take the place of the dolls of the marionette drama, the acting is exaggerated, and the language relatively simple; the chorus and musical accompaniment add to the color and excitement. The plots take four typical forms: the *jidaimono,* or historical drama; the *sewamono,* or domestic drama; the *aragoto,* or rough mime; and the *shosagoto,* or more elegant dramatic dance. A principal motif of the *jidaimono* is loyalty to one's master; the most famous example is the *Chūshingura* (*Treasury of Loyalty,* or *The Forty-seven Rōnin*), which tells of the vengeance of the 47 samurai whose lord had been forced to commit harakiri. The drama in the *sewamono* arises from the fact that a love affair between hero and heroine is opposed by the parents of one of them. The clash between love and filial duty is most frequently resolved by double suicide, the lovers dying in the belief, fostered by Buddhism, that they will meet in the next existence. The acknowledged master writer of both the *kabuki* and *jōruri* is Chikamatsu Monzaemon (1653–1724).

In the 19th century, Kawatake Mokuami (1816–1893) preserved most of the traditions of the *kabuki.* Toward the end of the century the *shinkabuki* (new *kabuki*) attempted to free the older style from its conventionalized subject matter, style, and acting. This new type was followed in turn by the dramas of the *shimpa* (new school), which took its subjects from daily life, used the spoken language in place of the older literary idiom, allowed for freedom in style of acting, and permitted actresses to appear on the stage. The modern theater was at last born in the first decade of the 20th century. Tsubouchi Shōyō, in his *Shingakugekiron* (*Argument for a New Drama,* 1905), fought against the sensationalism of the older theater and demanded sound characterization and coherent plots. He was soon followed by a naturalistic school, an idealistic school whose principal representatives were Mushanokōji Saneatsu and Arishima Takeo, a neorealist school made up of writers like Kikuchi Kan and Yamamoto Yūzō, a neoromantic school, and others. The result of these divergent trends is that the modern Japanese theatergoer may see a variety of types of drama—no, *kabuki, shimpa* plays, and the modern play, in all their forms. In addition, motion pictures have a popular following, especially in the principal cities.

Poetry.—Japanese poetry is characterized by the alternation of lines of 5 and 7 syllables and the terminating of each poem with a final 7-syllable line. The poetic effects depend on the combination of sounds, the musical accents of the words, and the flow of intonation, punctuated by pauses, from line to line, as well as on the handling of the images. The most popular poetic form, found from the earliest times, is the tanka (short poem) of 31 syllables, with five lines running 5-7-5-7-7 syllables. Longer than the tanka is the *chōka* (long poem), a general name for all poems containing more than five lines. A special form is the *sedōka* (literally, head-turning poem), a six-line poem with the syllables running 5-7-7-5-7-7. One half of a *sedōka,* running 5-7-7, is the *katauta* (half poem). In the 8th century a comic variety of tanka, the *haikai-uta,* arose; known as *kyōka* (crazy poem), it has persisted to modern times. A popular diversion of the Kamakura period was the joint composition by many poets of the *renga* (linked poem). Each *renga* was composed by a group of poets alternately contributing lines of 5-7-5 and 7-7 syllables. The first three lines—the initial contribution of the leading poet—began to achieve independent status in the 16th century. Known as the *hokku,* or *haiku,* it is the 17-syllable poem which, next to the tanka, is the most popular Japanese poetic form. In the 17th and 18th centuries a comic variety of the 17-syllable poem found its acknowledged master in Senryū (1718–1790), who gave his name to this form.

Japanese poetry is unusually elliptical. Among the special poetic devices is the *makura-kotoba* (pillow word), a stock epithet, consisting usually of five syllables, which qualifies particular nouns. *Ashibiki no* (foot-dragging), for example, is applied to mountains. The significance of many pillow words, however, has been lost. The *jo* (introduction) is a long decorative phrase placed before a word; unlike the pillow word, it is not fixed in form, and it may run over many lines. Fortunately it died with the earliest long poems. The *kakekotoba* (pivot word), punningly used both at the end of one phrase and at the beginning of the next, frequently plagued the poetry of the late Heian era and after. An even more pervasive device is the *engo* (associative word), which is used in one part of a poem with a specific meaning, but carries overtones of a second or third meaning because of its common association with words used in other parts of the poem.

The earliest poetry, still preserved in the chronicles of the 8th century, possesses the exuberant quality of speech. The earliest anthology is the *Man'yōshū* (*Collection of Ten Thousand Leaves*), compiled mainly in and after the year 759. Consisting of 20 scrolls and 4,516 poems which were written by poets in all walks of life, from emperors to farmers and guardsmen in the provinces, the *Man'yōshū* achieved early lyrical heights. Its spirit is characterized by great freshness, simplicity, and directness. The *Man'yōshū* poet was optimistic; he rejoiced in the colors and scents of nature and enjoyed the present moment. His favorite theme was love, but he also wrote many elegies, poems expressing homesickness, and nature poems, as well as poems of a humorous and even derisive cast; poems with a patriotic coloration; buoyant banqueting, drinking, and hunting songs; and poems inspired by various legends. The finest poets of the *Man'yōshū* are Kakinomoto no Hitomaro (662–c.710), a court poet best remembered for his lengthy elegies; Yamabe no Akahito (d. c.736), a superlative nature poet; Yamanoe no Okura (660–733), a Confucianist; and Ōtomo no Tabito (664–731), a poet known for the depth of his human sympathies.

The second great anthology was the *Kokinshū* (*Collection Ancient and Modern,* c.922). Its principal compiler was Ki no Tsurayuki (d. 946). Like the *Man'yōshū,* this collection is divided into 20 scrolls. The total number of poems, however, is only 1,111. Whereas the *Man'yōshū* contains 262 *nagauta* and 61 *sedōka,* the *Kokinshū* includes only 5 of the former and 4 of the latter. The tanka has thus become the predominant form. Of the 20 scrolls, 6 are devoted to nature poetry, and 5 to love poetry. There is a considerable loss in vigor. The poet is more reflective and pessimistic, more Buddhistic. In addition to Tsurayuki, who provided a preface which is the earliest extended treatise on native poetry, the priest Henjō (815–890), Ariwara no Narihira (825–880), and Ono no Komachi (d. c.890) are the leading poets.

The *Kokinshū* was the first of 21 anthologies whose compilation was decreed by various emperors. The last in the series was compiled in 1438. Each collection consists of 20 scrolls; the average number of poems is 1,600. Of all the 20 collections which followed the *Kokinshū,* however, only the *Shinkokinshū* (*New Collection Ancient and Modern,* 1205) achieved a degree of poetic excellence. The *Shin'yōshū* (*Collection of New Leaves,* 1381), was a private collection and not compiled by imperial command. It, too, contained poetry of excellent quality. A few major poets like the priest Saigyō (1118–1190) and Fujiwara no Toshinari (1114–1204) appeared, but the old flair was gone; poetry became the property of masters who professed to know its secrets but were completely obsessed by rules; the subjects became conventionalized, and, as in the case of the *renga,* poetry became a pastime rather than an art.

Signs of revival in the tanka form came in the 17th century, when the first great scholars of earlier literature began to imitate the poetry of Nara and Heian times. Toda Mosui (1629–1706), the priest Keichū (1640–1701), and Shimokawabe Chōryū (1624–1686) imitated, not too consciously, the poetry of the *Kokinshū* and *Shinkokinshū.* Kamo Mabuchi (1697–1769), on the other hand, deliberately went back to the *Man'yōshū.* Motoori Norinaga (1730–1801) favored the style of the *Shinkokinshū.* Others, like Tachibana Chikage (1735–1808) and Kagawa Kageki (1768–1843), imitated the *Kokinshū.*

The greatest poets of the time wrote *haiku.* The finest writer in this medium was Matsuo Bashō (1644–1694), who recorded impressionistically and thoughtfully his reactions to nature. Gentle and wise, he gathered a host of disciples. Taniguchi or Yosano Buson (1716–1783) was a painter-poet. His *haiku* dealt realistically with human affairs as well as with nature. Kobayashi Issa (1763–1827) is known for his humanity and pathetic quality. A sarcastic strain is found in some of his poems, but his sympathy for living things extended even to the fleas that infested his cottage.

The tanka and the *haiku* retained their popularity in modern times. A few of the tanka poets, notably those connected with the Outadokoro (Imperial Palace Poetry Bureau), worked along traditional lines. But the greater majority tried to renovate the tanka, joining various schools and publishing their poems in the magazines supported by these schools. The Asakasha (light fragrance school) was founded by Ochiai Naobumi (1861–1903), who was rooted in the classics but is also known for his romantic tone. Among his followers were Yosano Tekkan (1873–1935), known for his masculine vigor, Onoe Shibafune (1876–), known for his intellectual scepticism, and Sasaki Nobutsuna (1872–), known for his easy and graceful style and for his reflective nature poetry. Yosano Tekkan soon dissented from this group. Seeking for poetry the right to describe human life in all its emotional turmoil, seeking, moreover, the right to use a wide-ranging vocabulary, he headed the naturalists of the Shinshisha (new poetry school). In the magazine *Myōjō,* founded in 1900, he produced poetry of extreme emotionalism, glorifying love. Belonging to his school were his wife Akiko (1878–1942); Ishikawa Takuboku (1885–1912), in his earlier work; and Horiguchi Daigaku (1892–). A reaction set in with the Negishi school, founded by Masaoka Shiki (1867–1902) and named for the section in Tokyo in which he lived. Shiki was a superlative poet who preached reserve and decorum, realism and objectivity. He took the rhythms of the poetry of the *Man'yōshū* for his model; his leading followers are Shimaki Akahiko (1876–1925), Saitō Mokichi (1882–1953), Itō Sachio (1864–1913), and Nagatsuka Takashi (1879–1915). Their work is found in the newspaper *Nihon* and in the magazines *Ashibi* (1903–1908), *Akane* (1908–1909), *Araragi* (1908—), and *Nikkō* (1924–1927).

The *haiku,* too, had its adherents who were unable to strike out along original lines. Imitating Bashō and Issa, men like Setchūan Jakushi (1848–1908) were known as "masters of the commonplace." It was Masaoka Shiki who preached the renovation of the *haiku* as he did of the tanka. He called upon each poet to control his emotions, which were to be suggested rather than openly displayed. Using Buson as his model, Shiki strove for a sober and concrete notation. Shiki's principles were not completely accepted. Some felt that his emphasis on sobriety and technique could lead only to the impoverishment of the *haiku;* they therefore espoused complete liberty of theme and technique. Also opposed to Shiki were certain poets who were academic in their leanings and tended to rely on studious research rather than on a creative spirit. Shiki's principles gained widespread acceptance with the publication of the journal *Hototogisu* (1897—), first edited by him and then by Takahama Kyoshi (1874–), but the Shinkeikō (new tendencies school), which was led by one of Shiki's former disciples, Kawahigashi Hekigodō (1873–1936), claimed for the *haiku* the suppression of all traditional ideas, even of the 5-7-5 line scheme, and other writers also claimed independence from Shiki's tenets.

One of the most important developments in the field of poetry came with the revival of the long poem. In the 1880's the first translations into Japanese of Occidental, especially of English, poetry suggested the creation of a poetic form of unlimited length. The resulting *shintaishi* (new-form poetry) appeared in the collection known as the *Shintaishishō* (1882), which was fathered by three men: Toyama Shōichi (1848–1900), Yatabe Ryōkichi (1852–1899), and Inoue Tetsujirō (1855–1944). Fourteen of the works in this collection were translations from English, American, and French poetry, but five were original. The alternation of lines of 7 and 5 syllables reverses the usual 5-7 alternation; other poems were written with each of the lines containing 5 syllables or 7, and alternations of 8-6 and 7-4 syllables were also attempted. Each of the three translators provided a preface. Both by precept and by example the three men called for freedom in the choice of poetic subjects; in length, form, and scope; in the use of the modern colloquial idiom; and in the adoption of foreign models. The *Shintaishika* (1882) and *Shintaishisen* (1886) followed shortly thereafter. The last dozen years of the 19th century were a period of great activity, with the poets aligning themselves in such groups as the Bungakukai (Literary Club), the Kokumin no Tomo (Friends of the People), the Akamonha (Red Gate School, consisting mainly of poets connected with Tokyo Imperial University), and the Wasedaha (composed of poets connected with Waseda University). Other schools rose with the dawn of the 20th century, so that the picture from about 1920 on is one of great confusion, with Whitmanesque, sentimental, symbolist, impressionist, and other schools vying with each other, and with the composition of popular poetry and of children's songs in form longer than the tanka.

Bibliography of Works in Western Languages.—

GENERAL: Florenz, Karl, *Geschichte der Japanischen Litteratur* (Leipzig 1905); Revon, Michel, *Anthologie de la Littérature Japonaise des Origines au XXe Siècle,* 3d ed. (Paris 1918); Kokusai Bunka Shinkōkai, *Introduction to Classic Japanese Literature* (Tokyo 1948).

PROSE: Aston, W. G., tr., *Nihongi, Chronicles of Japan from the Earliest Times to A.D. 697,* 2 vols. (London 1896); Ballard, S., "Some Tales from the Ujishui Monogatari," *Transactions,* Asiatic Society of Japan, 28:31-45 (1900); Parlett, Harold, tr., "Sumiyoshi Monogatari," *Transactions,* Asiatic Society of Japan, 29:43-123 (1901); Sansom, G. B., tr., "The Tsuredzure Gusa of Yoshida no Kaneyoshi," *Transactions,* Asiatic Society of Japan, vol. 39 (1911); Porter, W. N., tr., *The Tosa Diary* (London 1912); Futabatei, Shimei, *An Adopted Husband (Sono Omokage),* tr. by Buhachiro Mitsui and G. M. Sinclair (New York 1919); Elisséeff, Serge, tr., *Neuf Nouvelles Japonaises* (Paris 1924); Natsume, Soseki, *Botchan (Master Darling),* tr. by Y. Mori (Tokyo 1924); Futabatei, Shimei, *Mediocrity,* tr. by G. W. Shaw (Tokyo 1927); Sadler, A. L., tr., *The Ten Foot Square Hut and Tales of the Heike* (Sydney, Australia, 1928); Jippensha, Ikku, *Hizakurige (Tōkaidō Circuit),* tr. by T. Satchell (Kobe 1929); Sei Shōnagon, *Pillow-book,* tr. by Arthur Waley (Boston 1929); Akutagawa, Ryūnosuke, *Tales Grotesque and Curious,* tr. by G. W. Shaw (Tokyo 1930); Chamberlain, B. H., tr., *"Ko-ji-ki" . . . or "Records of Ancient Matters,"* 2d ed. (Kobe 1932); Ibara, Saikaku, "Life of a Voluptuous Woman," Book 2, tr. by Johannes Rahder, *Acta Orientalia,* 13:292-318 (1934); Kikuchi, Kan, *Victory or Defeat* (*Shōhai*), tr. by Kiichi Nishi (Tokyo 1934); Whitehouse, Wilfrid, tr. *Ochikubo Monogatari* (Kobe and London 1934); Omori, A. S., and Doi, Kochi, tr., *Diaries of Court Ladies of Old Japan* (Tokyo 1935); Waley, Arthur, tr., *The Tale of Genji,* 2 vols. (Boston 1935); Tanizaki, Jun'ichirō, *Ashikari and the Story of Shunkin,* tr. by Roy Humpherson and Hajime Okita (Tokyo 1936); Kokusai Bunka Shinkōkai, *Introduction to Contemporary Japanese Literature* (Tokyo 1939); Reischauer, E. O., and Yamagiwa, J. K., trs., *Translations from Early Japanese Literature* (Cambridge, Mass., 1951).

DRAMA: Waley, Arthur, tr., *The Nō Plays of Japan* (London 1921); Kikuchi, Kan, *Tōjūrō's Love and Four Other Plays,* tr. by G. W. Shaw (Tokyo 1925); Kincaid, Zoë, *Kabuki, the Popular Stage of Japan* (London 1925); Lombard, F. A., *An Outline History of the Japanese Drama* (London 1928); Iacovleff, A. Y., and Elisséeff, Serge, *Le Théâtre Japonais* (Paris 1933); Sadler, A. L., tr., *Japanese Plays: Nō-Kyōgen-Kabuki* (Sydney, Australia, 1934); Yamamoto, Yūzō, *Three Plays,* tr. by G. W. Shaw (Tokyo 1935); Sakanishi, Shio, tr., *Kyôgen: Comic Interludes of Japan* (Boston 1938); Peri, Noël, *Le Nô* (Tokyo 1944); Chikamatsu, Monzaemon, *The Battles of Coxinga,* tr. by D. Keene (Cambridge, England, 1951); Shively, D. H., ed. and tr., *The Love Suicide at Amijima* (Cambridge, Mass., 1953).

POETRY: Waley, Arthur, tr., *Japanese Poetry: the "Uta"* (Oxford 1919); Page, C. H., *Japanese Poetry* (Boston and New York 1923); Miyamori, Asatarō, tr., *An Anthology of Haiku, Ancient and Modern* (Tokyo 1932); Henderson, H. G., *The Bamboo Broom* (Boston 1934); Sakanishi, Shio, tr., *A Handful of Sand; from the Works of Takuboku Ishikawa* (Boston 1934); Bonneau, G., tr., *Anthologie de la Poésie Japonaise* (Paris 1935); Sakanishi, Shio, tr., *Tangled Hair; from the Works of the Poet Akiko Yosano* (Boston 1935); Miyamori, Asatarō, tr. and ed., *Masterpieces of Japanese Poetry, Ancient and Modern,* 2 vols. (Tokyo 1936); Sakanishi, Shio, tr., *Songs of a Cowherd; from the Works of Sachio Itō* (Boston 1936); Nippon Gakujutsu Shinkōkai, *The Manyōshū: One Thousand Poems* (Tokyo 1940); Blyth, R. H., tr., *Senryu: Japanese Satirical Verses* (Tokyo 1949).

JOSEPH K. YAMAGIWA,
Department of Far Eastern Languages and Literatures, University of Michigan.

20. HISTORY: FROM THE EARLIEST TIMES TO 1853. This section discusses the history of Japan to the final and permanent opening of the country to Occidental influence in 1853 by Commodore Matthew C. Perry (q.v.).

Prehistoric Japan.—Little is known for certain about the origins of the Japanese people. No Paleolithic remains have been discovered but there is good evidence to show that in prehistoric times the country was peopled by immigrants from several parts of eastern Asia, mostly of Tungusic origin, but some from southern regions. Neolithic remains show that prior to these migrations Japan was sparsely inhabited by ancestors of the people now known as Ainu, who are thought to be of proto-Caucasic origin. By the beginning of the Christian era the later migrants had reached a fair degree of ethnic fusion and had acquired from China and Korea the rudiments of a metal culture. The Ainu were gradually pushed northward. See also section on *The People.*

Early History to About 400 A.D.—Archaeological evidence and Chinese records provide a picture of Japan in the first four or five centuries of our era. It shows a number of tribal communities competing with one another for influence or military strength. Those native chieftains who made the best use of new techniques acquired from Korean teachers were able in the course of time to outstrip their rivals; and before long certain tribes or clans had achieved over others a measure of dominance which by the beginning of the 5th century had brought a group known as the Yamato people to a position of supremacy in central Japan. In the eventual recognition of the leader of one clan as the sovereign of the Yamato people we see the beginnings of the tradition of imperial rule in Japan. But despite the obedience nominally due to the head of the imperial clan the other clans claimed such a virtual independence that the history of Japan for many succeeding centuries is a record, on the one hand, of attempts by powerful clan leaders to supersede or to dominate the imperial clan and, on the other hand, of efforts by the imperial clan to form a centralized, monarchical state. Unity was not easy to achieve, since each separate clan was a self-contained patriarchal unit, composed of households of the same ancestry, all under the leadership of a hereditary chieftain. Its members tended to place loyalty to clan before the common interest of all clans, for family feeling was strong and it was reinforced by the worship of a tutelary deity, from whom the leader of the clan claimed descent.

A trend toward cohesion among the clans, however, was created by the need for unity in war, especially in campaigns on the Korean peninsula. There had been close and constant intercourse between western Japan and Korea since the 1st century A.D., and by the end of the 4th century Japanese armies were taking part in struggles between Korean kingdoms. These kingdoms were under strong Chinese influence, and by about 400 A.D., the Japanese, learning from Korean tutors, began to use the Chinese script. This was a turning point in the history of Japan, since it enabled the Japanese to adopt important features of Chinese culture which depended upon written documents.

Adoption of Buddhism.—Probably the most important borrowing to follow the adoption of a script was the introduction (about 552) of Buddhism, which was flourishing in China at that time and lately had been accepted in Korea. Besides being a strong civilizing influence, fostering the arts and promoting both religious and secular learning, Buddhism hastened political development by intensifying the conflict between conservative forces, which stood for the old tribal institutions, and progressive forces working for a centralized government. A struggle for power between contending clans turned upon the question of religion, and in 587, after a short and bloody civil war, the party which favored Buddhism gained the upper hand. When the reigning emperor had been murdered, the Empress Suikō was recognized in his place, in 593. During most of her reign, which lasted to 628, affairs of state were conducted by a regent, Crown Prince Shōtoku (d. 621 or 622), one of the greater figures in Japanese history. He promoted the cause of Buddhism and worked hard for political reform. In 604 he issued his "constitution" of 17 articles, a set of moral injunctions addressed to the clans. These contain a new view of the state, for they dwell upon duties as well as rights and enunciate clearly the ideal of a centralized state in which the great nobles exercise authority as servants of the throne. But the power of the emperor was not yet so firmly established as his prestige; and it was not until 646 that a further necessary step was taken by the issue of the Taikwa (Great Reform) edict, which introduced a new system of central and local government, land tenure, and taxation designed to deprive the clans of their autonomy. Throughout the 7th century Japanese envoys, monks, and scholars visited China and returned with impressive accounts of that country under the Sui and T'ang dynasties. The fact that reforms were based on their reports enhanced in Japan the prestige of all branches of Chinese learning.

The Nara Period (710–784).—By 710 the first permanent capital of Japan was built at Nara, a beautiful city on the model of the Chinese capital at Changan (Sian), with palaces, official mansions, great monasteries, and pagodas filled with treasures of sacred art. (See sections on *The Fine Arts; Architcture.*) Here the emperors reigned and exercised a growing authority, though already one of the great clans, the Fujiwara, had made itself a power behind the throne. In the capital the arts and learning flourished as never before. Religion flourished too: the Buddhist church grew to such heights of influence as to threaten secular authority. It was largely to escape this danger that the court was moved from Nara to Nagaoka in 784, and then to a new capital, on the site of the modern Kyoto, in 794.

The Heian Period (784–1184).—This period takes its name from that of the new capital, which was called Heian-jō (Citadel of Peace). In these four centuries a new Japanese culture was formed by the incorporation of Korean and Chinese elements into Japanese life. After Japanese tradition had begun to reassert itself, the resultant product was something Chinese in form but Japanese in essence. As Buddhism grew in strength, a certain reaction in favor of the indigenous cult made itself felt. This cult was a simple pantheism, in which an essence of divinity was perceived in all natural objects as well as in the tribal ancestors. Japan was thought to have been founded by the Sun Goddess, Amaterasu-ōmikami, and the emperors were regarded as her descendants, while other clans traced their ancestry to other *kami,* or gods. The nature religion, called Shintō (the way of the gods) to distinguish it from *Butsudō* (the way of the buddhas), was the expression of deeply rooted sentiments. By the end of the Nara period a compromise had been found by regarding both gods and buddhas as manifestations of one truth. (See section on *Religion.*) This characteristic fusion of native and borrowed elements is exhibited in the institutional history of the Heian period. At the height of Chinese influence administrative systems closely following Chinese models had been introduced in the Taihō Code of 702 and the Yōrō Code of 757. But since the schematic methods of the Chinese did not suit Japanese tradition and temperament, the organs of central and provincial government gradually came under the control of the leading clans. The carefully devised systems of land tenure and taxation were weakened by the fiscal immunities which great nobles and monasteries acquired. Thus during the Heian period the institutions created by the Taikwa reforms were so changed in character that they retained only their names and little of their original substance. The clan spirit—the native tradition—had reasserted itself.

A similar trend is visible in literature and the arts. At first the native language was contemned, but Japanese poetry and prose came into fashion by 1000, and such works as the famous *Genji Monogatari* (*The Tale of Genji*) represent the high-water mark of pure Japanese literature. Religious developments also, particularly toward the close of the Heian period, testify to a growing national pride and to a desire to stamp with a Japanese imprint the foreign doctrines which hitherto had dominated intellectual life. This is particularly true of the sects devoted to the worship of Amida, which, arising from a need for simple doctrine to replace the abstruse teaching of the older sects, had acquired by the end of the Heian period a distinctive Japanese character; and it is true in varying degree of all subsequent versions of Buddhism in Japan.

The last, and perhaps the most important departure from the Chinese pattern, is visible in the political history of the late Heian era. Strife between factions for the control of the emperor, beginning with palace intrigues, broadened into civil war, in which first the Fujiwara lost their power and then the two great clans of Taira and Minamoto clashed until they met in a decisive struggle. The Chinese system of government collapsed, and the ancient rivalry of the clans was resumed. Both Taira and Minamoto were clans composed of fighting men who had established themselves in the provinces, acquiring and holding their land by armed strength. In the course of the 12th century they formed a class of warriors owing allegiance to their clan leaders rather than to the throne, and by 1185, after the final defeat of the Taira, the Minamoto house was supreme in Japan. Its chieftain Yoritomo (1147–1199) established his headquarters—the Bakufu (seat of military government)—at Kamakura, so as to be remote from court influence and to live among his important vassals, who were established in eastern Japan. Here began the final phase of Japanese history, which in one form or another lasted until 1868.

The Kamakura Period (1185–1333).—By the defeat of his enemies Yoritomo acquired in most parts of Japan great estates, which he distributed among his supporters as a reward for services in battle. In the course of his campaigns he had obtained from the emperor a commission to chastise the "rebels" and eventually was nominated (1192) Sei-i Tai-Shōgun (barbarian-quelling generalissimo), a title which first had been conferred upon the leader of an expedition against the Ainu in 794 and which gave its holder the command of all military forces in the empire. Like all his successors in this office, Yoritomo did not pretend to sovereign powers. He always observed forms of reverence to the emperor; and he was flattered by the grant of high court rank. He was careful to obtain the reluctant consent of the court to the appointment of constables and stewards throughout Japan. Yoritomo himself became constable general and steward general of the realm, thus gaining control of police affairs in each province and power to levy taxes upon all cultivated land, whether in public or private domains.

The creation of these new offices was the first phase in a long process by which the old bureaucratic system was replaced by an organized feudalism. To bring it to perfection time was needed. The first half century or more of the Kamakura regime was devoted to legislation devised to strengthen the ties of allegiance between the Minamoto house and its vassals by dispensing justice in disputes as to their rights and duties and by creating a strong feudal hierarchy dependent upon a rigid code of loyalty. It was in this period that the code of military virtue—*Bushidō* (the way of the warrior)—became a coherent doctrine, embodied in the oaths and charters which defined the relationships between overlord and vassal, landowner and tenant, master and man. Among the fundamental documents of Japanese feudalism is the *Jōei Shikimoku* (*Formulary of Jōei*) of 1232, a set of rules and maxims which embodied the results of half a century's working of the feudal system. This was not presented as a national law, but only as the house law of the Minamoto family to be observed by its vassals. In effect, however, it displaced the old Taihō and Yōrō codes and in substance became the common law of Japan.

For nearly a century after 1185 the Kamakura regime continued peaceful and stable. After Yoritomo's death the Kamakura government was carefully administered by regents of the family of Hōjō Tokimasa (1138–1215), Yoritomo's father-in-law and one of his trusted allies. The Hōjō controlled the shogun just as Fujiwara nobles had controlled the emperors. But signs of discontent among the landed gentry were already visible in the early history of the Kamakura shogunate. The amount of land available was not enough to satisfy their growing families and the court was always ready to plot with disaffected feudal lords against the Bakufu. In 1274 the Mongol emperor of China, Kublai Khan, sent a great expedition to invade Japan. This was repulsed, as was a second attack in 1281; but the cost of defensive measures and the strain upon the resources of the vassals who had borne the burden of the attack were so great that the Bakufu, itself in financial straits, could not recompense its own supporters. Its authority diminished, and by 1333, under color of disputes as to succession to the throne, the capture and destruction of Kamakura brought the Hōjō regency to an end.

A new emperor, Daigo II (Go-Daigo, r. 1318–1339), occupied the throne and Kyoto was once more the seat of government. But he depended upon the support of a feudal lord named Ashikaga Takauji (1305–1358), who was made shogun in 1338. The Ashikaga family, after some 50 years of dynastic struggles, gained the upper hand over their feudal rivals and enjoyed a checkered and uneasy supremacy until about 1500, when sporadic feudal conflicts merged into a civil war which spread over the entire country.

Ashikaga Shogunate (1338–1573).—This period may be briefly dismissed as one of civil war, in which the remnants of the centralized rule exercised by the early Kamakura shoguns were discarded, and power was divided among a number of great barons over whom the Ashikaga shoguns held only a shadowy authority. Warfare was almost continuous, yet in the 14th and 15th centuries progress was made in many fields of endeavor. The movement of troops and supplies about the country improved communications and developed domestic trade; the shifting of allegiances, the collapse of old institutions, the use of new men dissolved the rigidity of the old social order and brought about a violent rearrangement of classes. It was an age of turmoil and of destruction, but not of decay.

Perhaps its most remarkable feature was the progress of the arts. The upstart feudal leaders used their newly gained wealth to patronize artists and men of letters. Two of the Ashikaga shoguns in particular—Yoshimitsu (r. 1367–1395) and Yoshimasa (r. 1447–1474)—are celebrated as leaders of aesthetic coteries which displayed a great connoisseurship in the arts and developed an aesthetic tradition which has been a strong influence in Japanese life. (See section on *The Fine Arts.*)

It should be added that in this age there was close contact between Japan and China which, besides bringing to Japan many valuable examples of Chinese art, enlarged trade between the two countries. Ventures were undertaken by the shoguns, by great monasteries, and by feudal magnates, especially those in coastal provinces. There were also frequent voyages, many of which were piratical, to the Philippines, Indonesia, Siam, and Malacca. Japanese maritime enterprise grew steadily, and Japanese traders or adventurers were familiar with most Far Eastern ports by the end of the 15th century. The chief ports, notably Sakai, gained considerable autonomy and resembled in some ways the free cities of medieval Europe. What might have led to a great expansion of foreign trade and to the growth of a politically influential mercantile class was interrupted, however, by the course of political events at home, for by the year 1500 fighting between contending feudal powers, hitherto intermittent and local, had spread over all Japan.

The Warring Provinces.—The 16th century brought the final struggle for the redistribution of feudal power. Fierce, widespread, and protracted as it was, it must be regarded as a progress toward unity and order. Three great men were the successive architects of the centralized state which was to emerge in the 17th century.

The first was Oda Nobunaga (1534–1582), a small landholder who by skillful strategy was able to consolidate a strong position in the central provinces, to occupy the capital, and by 1568 to become the *de facto* shogun, though the Ashikaga were titular shoguns until 1597. Thereafter he, with his two celebrated lieutenants, Hashiba (later Toyotomi) Hideyoshi (1536–1598) and Tokugawa Ieyasu (1542–1616), set about subduing hostile barons east and west of the territory which he held. By 1582, when Nobunaga was murdered, they had between them overcome most of their enemies, who included not only feudal lords but also powerful Buddhist sects, whose monasteries had great military strength. It was in the extreme west of Japan, in the island of Kyushu, and across the straits on the mainland that some of his most stubborn rivals had their domains. To these regions there came about 1542 the first Europeans to see Japan—a few Portuguese, driven to shore in the province of Satsuma by stress of weather. They soon were followed by other Portuguese—traders and then Jesuit missionaries under the leadership of St. Francis Xavier.

Christian evangelization in Japan had a remarkable success, which was due largely to the untiring devotion of the Jesuit fathers. They were favored by contemporary political conditions, for the feudal barons soon perceived that Portuguese traders would come where missionaries were well treated and that the traders could furnish them with arms, ammunition, and other supplies, which would increase their military strength and give them commercial profit. Most of these rulers therefore treated the Jesuits well, and some went so far as to order the people in their domains to accept the Christian faith. Moreover, many genuine conversions occurred, since the missionaries offered both spiritual and material comforts to the common people, whose condition in those times of civil war was wretched. Within 20 years of Xavier's arrival they had succeeded in making converts among the upper classes in central Japan, and in 1568 they were received by Nobunaga, who showed them some favors. His patronage, which owed something to his hatred of the insubordinate Buddhist sects, was of such value to them that by 1582 they claimed 150,000 converts.

Nobunaga was succeeded by Hideyoshi, who with Ieyasu's military aid continued the work of unification. Hideyoshi was now master of more than half of the Japanese provinces. He next reduced to such submission those great barons who still opposed him that by 1590 Japan was at peace for the first time in more than a century. Hideyoshi was a great man whose ambition was unbounded. Since he was of humble origin and could not aspire to the title of shogun, he was appointed to the ancient office of *kwambaku* (regent) and was in effect the ruler of the land. During his lifetime Hideyoshi laid the foundation of the new feudal edifice which was to be erected by his successor, Ieyasu. He put an end to the relatively free movement between classes which had developed under the Ashikaga shoguns (and to which he himself had owed his rise) by decreeing in 1586 that every man should remain in his own calling, whether peasant or tradesman or soldier. In 1587 he confiscated all weapons in the hands of peasants, thus emphasizing the distinction between the military caste and all others and making the sword a badge of rank. In general Hideyoshi legislated to preserve the balanced system of feudal power which he had erected. All his undertakings—his fortresses, his palaces, his entertainments—were on a grand scale. The Momoyama period (named after his palace at Momoyama in Kyoto, built in 1594) is distinguished for bold design and lavish execution, which reflect a certain heroic quality in the society of his day.

Hideyoshi treated the foreign missionaries well for some years. For a long time he had planned a war against China and he thought that the Portuguese might supply him with ships and guns. Although some of his ablest generals were converts to Christianity, Hideyoshi presently began to suspect that the missionaries were forerunners of armed aggression by Spain or Portugal and in 1587 without warning he issued an edict banishing them from Japan. This was not seriously enforced until after his expedition against China, which took the form of an invasion of Korea in 1592. After some preliminary successes this venture failed and the Japanese withdrew before a large Chinese army in 1593. A second attempt, made in 1597, was inconclusive and was abandoned on the death of Hideyoshi in 1598. It was in 1597 that persecution of Christians began at the order of Hideyoshi, who by then had judged from the behavior of Spanish Franciscans that Spain had designs upon Japan. Even so, after the first outburst, the anti-Christian edicts were not strictly enforced and the missionaries continued their work. By 1600 the number of converts had reached 300,000 and promised further increase.

Tokugawa Shogunate (1603–1867).—Ieyasu followed Hideyoshi in 1598, making his capital at Edo (Yedo), the modern Tokyo. His family, named Tokugawa, was of Minamoto descent. He was appointed shogun in 1603, after he had defeated at the Battle of Sekigahara (1600) a hostile combination of feudal lords who, though subdued by Hideyoshi, had never been reconciled to his supremacy. Ieyasu then redistributed the fiefs to ensure against further rebellion and by 1615 he disposed of the last of his enemies. Ieyasu died in June 1616, but he had already won for the Tokugawa family a dominance over Japan which was to last for more than 250 years.

Ieyasu at first showed no animosity toward the missionaries. He planned to encourage the growth of Japan's merchant marine and the expansion of her foreign trade. He went so far as to offer open ports in eastern Japan to Spanish vessels, and he made it clear that he would not enforce the anti-Christian edicts. But before long, growing suspicious of Christians in general and Spaniards in particular, he sought other channels of foreign trade. Having learned of the enmity between Catholic and Protestant states, Ieyasu gave trading privileges to the Dutch and the English and he began to turn against the Jesuits and the Franciscans. Some perfunctory bans against them were issued by him as early as 1606, but in 1615 severe persecution commenced. It was directed mainly against Japanese converts, and during Ieyasu's lifetime no foreigner was executed.

After his death his son Hidetada, the second shogun (r. 1616–1623), continued his father's policy of building a system of checks and balances which would make it difficult for the unreconciled barons to rebel against the shogunate. Since he saw that this system might collapse if those barons, some of whom favored Christianity, could obtain arms and ships and perhaps military aid from the foreigners, Hidetada accordingly ordered all foreign priests without exception to leave the country and ruthlessly persecuted all Japanese Christians. In 1624 under Iemitsu, the third shogun (r. 1623–1651), all Spaniards were deported. In 1637 a rebellion, in which Japanese Christians were implicated, began at Shimabara in western Japan, but was savagely repressed in 1638. Thereafter all Japanese were forbidden to travel abroad, all Portuguese were expelled, and other foreigners (Dutch and Chinese) were confined to a small area in Nagasaki where (and nowhere else) a very limited foreign trade was permitted. By 1640 Japan was virtually isolated from the outside world and Christianity was eradicated.

In this seclusion the Tokugawa rulers endeavored to fix society in one unchangeable pattern. They established in their own domains a strict official hierarchy and, though they left a measure of autonomy to the great feudal lords, they kept them under close watch, intervening when they thought it necessary. All vassals were obliged to subscribe to an oath of allegiance renewed with each change of shogun, and all were compelled to attend regularly at the shogun's court, leaving their families in Edo as hostages when they returned to their fiefs. The duties, privileges, and emoluments of each grade of the military class were minutely regulated, from the daimyō (daimio, or great feudal lord) down to the simple samurai (soldier). Below these ranked the farmer, the artisan, the merchant, and, last of all, the outcasts, actors, butchers, and other workers in defiling trades; and legally it was not possible to move from one class to another.

These conditions persisted for a century or more after 1600. There were peace and order and firm, if harsh, government. The growth of great cities, like Edo and Osaka, and of a number of castle towns led to an increased demand for commodities and to the development of a more complex urban life than had been known. The townspeople developed a lively society of their own, which was devoted to good living and fostered popular arts: the theater, the novel, and the color print. Population continued to increase, reaching perhaps 29 million in the first quarter of the 18th century, but thereafter remained stationary, pressing upon the limits of subsistence and occasionally diminishing as a result of famine or pestilence, which occurred at frequent intervals until well into the 19th century. These economic disasters combined with other causes to weaken the system of government, which the Tokugawa rulers had endeavored to preserve unchanged. Contradictions inherent in that system were revealed with the passage of years. It proved increasingly difficult to maintain the prestige of a military class which was superfluous in time of peace, for the duties of most of the samurai were little more than nominal and their emoluments were a drain upon the national economy. Not only had the growth of urban life brought into prominence a class of merchants and bankers who throve at the expense of their feudal masters, but also the penetration of a money economy tended to destroy the rice economy upon which the feudal system was based. To bolster its public finance the Bakufu resorted to depreciation of the coinage and forced loans, policies which in the long run increased the distress of the samurai. The peasants were overtaxed and agrarian risings were frequent. The merchants resented the levies by the authorities and their interference with trade. The intellectuals chafed under the restraints of orthodoxy.

Under Yoshimune, the eighth shogun (r. 1716–1745), these disruptive tendencies were checked for a while by measures of economy. Yoshimune relaxed the interdicts on Western learning which were part of the anti-Christian policy of the Bakufu, thereby unwittingly encouraging studies which led to discontent. Scholars began to learn Dutch and so to gain some knowledge of Western science. Samurai with active minds began to resent the strict class system, which denied them full use of their abilities, and to question the official school of Confucianism. Economists, dismayed by recurring famines and wild fluctuations in price, began to suspect that there was some fundamental weakness in the Tokugawa government. From this it was a short step to questioning the legitimacy of Tokugawa rule. All these currents of subversive thought were swollen toward the end of the 18th century by the arrival of Russian and American vessels off the shores of Japan. The Bakufu refused their requests for trading facilities and reissued the decrees against the entry of foreign vessels. An American vessel, the *Morrison,* was repulsed by gunfire in 1837. But foreign vessels continued to arrive, and the Bakufu, financially embarrassed and aware of the superior military strength of the Western powers, began to doubt whether the policy of seclusion could be maintained. In the clans and even among Bakufu officials there was a growing opinion in favor of opening the country, based on the conviction that Japan was weak and might renew her strength by the application of Western scientific methods to her military and economic problems. The Bakufu vacillated for a time and refused an invitation to open trade relations carried by United States warships in 1846. But when in 1853 Commodore Matthew C. Perry with a strong squadron arrived in Tokyo Bay and repeated the invitation, saying that he would come for an answer next year, it was clear that there could be no refusal.

Bibliography.—Murdoch, James, *A History of Japan,* 3 vols. (Kobe and London 1903–1926); Brinkley, Frank, *A History of the Japanese People* (New York 1915); Sansom, G. B., *Japan: A Short Cultural History,* rev. ed. (New York 1943); Reischauer, E. O., *Japan Past and Present* (New York 1946); Sansom, G. B., *The Western World and Japan* (New York 1950).

G. B. Sansom,
Formerly Visiting Lecturer of Japanese History and Director of East Asian Institute, Columbia University.

21. DEVELOPMENT OF THE MODERN STATE (1850–1945). This section traces Japan's evolution from the decline of the Tokugawa shogunate, through the restoration of imperial authority and the adoption of Western institutions, to the totalitarian state of the mid-20th century.

Formation of a Constitutional Monarchy, 1850–1890.—Since 1850, Japan has undergone a complete cycle in its history. Both internal and external forces during the turbulent years of the mid-19th century resulted in the overthrow of the military dictatorship of the Tokugawa family, which had effectively forced its policies on the country for 250 years. New forms of a modern state, a centralized government, with a new constitution, universal education, a conscript army, modern systems of communications and transportation under governmental ownership, and a modern industrialized economy were substituted for basically feudal institutions and customs. A strong, closely knit empire slowly evolved to include the rich island of Formosa in the south and the Kwantung Leased Territory, the South Manchurian Railway zone, and the Korean peninsula on the Asiatic continent. Through conquest and the establishment of puppet governments direct Japanese control extended from the southern frontiers of the Asiatic continent to Kamchatka in the north. After the invasion of Manchuria in 1931, this new empire again fell into the hands of a military dictatorship, not of a single individual or of a single family but of an elite and powerful group of leaders from the army and navy supported by civilian industrialists and politicians. By Sept. 1, 1945, Japan had been completely defeated, its military machine smashed, its economy thoroughly dislocated and temporarily reduced to impotency, and its emperor and government made subservient to the authority of Gen. Douglas MacArthur as supreme commander for the Allied powers. Finally, its territory was reduced to that of the mid-19th century: the four main home islands of Hokkaido, Honshu, Shikoku, and Kyushu, and innumerable smaller islands lying within the traditional territorial waters of Japan.

In 1850 the traditional policy and strict enforcement of exclusion of Japan from the outside world, except for a few Dutch and Chinese traders, the continued concentration of political power in the hands of a small group of warriors, the stratification of society, the inability to inaugurate basic economic reforms which would relieve the peasantry of the onerous task of being the main productive class, and the weaknesses inherent in a military dictatorship were ample cause for the collapse of the central government. Added to these factors were the requests of the Western powers (especially the Netherlands, the United States, and Russia), with their superior technical knowledge and their higher standard of living, that Japan sign treaties of peace and friendship. Nowhere is the inherent weakness of the Tokugawa government better revealed than by its action in 1853 following the demand of the United States, delivered by Commodore Matthew C. Perry and supported by a strong naval squadron which was to return the next year, that Japan be opened to American trade and that foreigners be allowed to reside there. The military dictator —the Tokugawa shogun (then Ieyoshi, succeeded that year by Iesada)—was unwilling and unable to decide the question alone and sought the opinion of all the feudal barons (daimyō), his allies and enemies alike. As less than a third of the barons opposed the American demands, as the Russians were simultaneously pressing for a treaty of peace and friendship, as Japan was impotent militarily and wished to avoid the semicolonial status which the Western powers had forced on China, the first foreign treaty was signed with the United States at Kanagawa in 1854.

Many of the young warriors of this period had been influenced by nationalist scholars whose studies clearly showed that the real ruler of Japan should be the emperor. Those who lived in western Japan in the feudal domains of Satsuma, Choshu, Tosa, and Hizen (usually referred to collectively as Satcho Dohi) were particularly sensitive to such teachings, because their masters, though kept in unwilling obedience, had been the traditional enemies of the Tokugawa rulers. These men, who were to be the real leaders of the new Japan, had been exposed to the even more drastic teachings of nationalists such as Shoin Yoshida and Sanai Hashimoto. The former advocated military preparedness not only to expel the foreigners, but also to permit Japanese colonization of the surrounding islands and of Korea, Manchuria, and Formosa. The latter proposed a military alliance with Russia to safeguard Japan's position. Furthermore, such industrialization as then existed in Japan was largely concentrated in those same western domains of Satcho Dohi. Small iron foundries, reverberatory furnaces for the manufacture of guns, industries making silk, paper, sugar, glazed porcelain, and other products, and even the construction of a small steamboat gave the future national leaders the training which they needed for modernizing Japan.

The presence of the foreigners as a result of the treaties with the Western powers irked the nationalist-minded and arrogant Satcho Dohi warriors. They increased the antiforeign sentiment in Japan by their attack on the consulates and on individual foreigners without fear of retaliation from the tottering Tokugawa dictatorship. The foreigners refused to be intimidated, however, and undertook the chastisement of the culprits by naval bombardments of their fiefs. Finally, in 1867, combining the rapidly growing movement for the "expulsion of the foreign barbarians (Americans and Europeans)" with that of the "veneration of the emperor," the Satcho Dohi warriors allied themselves with the emperor and forced the capitulation of the Tokugawa dictatorship. Emperor Mutsuhito (better known by his reign name of Meiji) was restored in 1868 as the actual ruler of Japan; minor military resistance to the Meiji Restoration, as it was called, was soon suppressed.

The first task of the new leaders was the abolition of the outward vestiges of feudalism and the establishment of a central government deriving its power from the emperor. Consequently they persuaded the feudal barons to surrender to the emperor the titles to their fiefs and to ask him to issue such decrees as were necessary to place the lands and people of the four Satcho Dohi clans directly under his authority. After many other feudal barons had followed their example, all the fiefs were formally abolished in 1871. In the next few years the support of the feudal barons and the warriors, whose annual income heretofore had been measured in terms of rice, was assured for the new government by the liquidation of their rice incomes, which were converted into government bonds. Meanwhile, the new government sent technical missions abroad to study European technology and institutions. Universal conscription and a modern army and navy, a uniform national tax on the value, not the produce, of the land, a national currency, railroads, the telegraph, a postal system, public utilities, universal education, and similar accouterments of a modern state were inaugurated. The government either constructed at its own expense or subsidized those heavy industries necessary to develop a modern army and navy. The chief positions in the central government were filled by a few persons who formed a closely knit oligarchy that rotated from one position to another. Thus Gen. Prince Aritomo Yamagata first organized the army while war minister and then became home minister and premier (1889–1891; 1898); and Prince Hirobumi Ito first concentrated on finances and public works, then supervised the drafting of the constitution, and was premier four times in the period 1885–1901.

When the practical problems confronting the new state had largely been solved, the next basic problem confronting the oligarchs was the formation of a constitutional government which would preserve the rights and powers of the emperor as an absolute monarch and also would satisfy the people's ever-increasing demands for a representative legislature. The prestige of the government and of the ruling oligarchs had been greatly enhanced by their ability to suppress a movement for the annexation of Korea and to substitute for it a relatively minor expedition against the Formosan aborigines. Furthermore, the new conscript army subjugated the formidable revolt of Takamori Saigo and his followers in southern Kyushu in 1877.

Ito, the leader of the conservative oligarchs, advocated a constitutional monarchy with absolute powers. The greatest challenge to this concept came from the leaders of two new political factions: the Liberals and the Reformers (Progressives). They urged a parliamentary form of government with a maximum of power concentrated in the hands of the people's elected representatives. This threat to autocratic control was met by the emperor's promise to establish a parliament by 1890, by the promulgation of stringent laws to control the press and public meetings, and by the dispatch of a mission abroad under Ito's leadership to study foreign forms of government. He found the Prussian Constitution the best model to follow for the preservation of the throne's special characteristics and powers. Consequently Ito prevented public interference with his plans by drafting the constitution under the protection of the emperor through the Imperial Household Ministry. As president of the Privy Council, the highest body of advisers to the throne, he obtained approval for a constitution which placed absolute power in the emperor. It was promulgated to the people on Feb. 11, 1889. Furthermore, General Yamagata, who was minister of home affairs during this critical period, freely used the national police to suppress any signs of opposition by the people.

Henceforth, under the provisions of the constitution, which was never amended and was replaced only in 1947, the emperor was virtually the state. The military could circumvent the Cabinet by appealing directly to the throne, but the political parties in the lower house of Parliament could not insist on the premier being selected from the majority party, since Parliament did not have full budgetary powers and because individual liberties were greatly restricted. See also section on *Government*.

Emergence of Japan as a Modern Power (1890–1920).—With the completion of a political structure which assured the continued ascendancy of the clan oligarchs who had shaped the constitutional monarchy, the first 30 years of parliamentary government saw a vain attempt on the part of the representatives of the political parties in the lower house of the Diet to win control. The prime minister was chosen invariably from among the leaders of the Satsuma or Choshu (Satcho) clans and any obstreperous move by Parliament was countered by proroguing or adjourning it. Japan's position in the Korean peninsula, which had been steadily strengthened by intrigues with the opposing political factions within Korea, was challenged in 1894 by China, which refused to relinquish its long dominance over Korean affairs, and the oligarchs at home found the opposition to their rule rapidly increasing in Parliament. Furthermore, the military leaders were anxious to test the strength of their new army, and a new spirit of nationalism was engendered by a chauvinistic press and by an educational system which emphasized the subservience of the individual to the good of the state. As a result of the Sino-Japanese War of 1894–1895, Japan not only replaced China in the control of Korean internal affairs, but also secured the first of its overseas territories, the island of Formosa, and exacted from China an indemnity to cover most of the expenses of the war, which had been fought outside Japan.

Nationalism was stimulated further by Japan's experience with power politics as practiced by European states. China had awarded the Liaotung Peninsula to Japan at the Treaty of Shimonoseki in 1895. Fearful lest Japan usurp its position on the Asiatic continent, Russia persuaded France and Germany to join it in forcing Japan to relinquish this territory. After this bitter experience the nation as a whole was convinced that its new position as a world power could be maintained and strengthened only by the development of an armament sufficiently powerful to challenge any potential or real enemy or group of enemies.

It likewise saw the Western powers acquire leaseholds and military bases in China, and the United States develop into a colonial power through the acquisition of the Hawaiian Islands and the Philippines in 1898.

No objection was raised by the political parties to these wars. Moreover, no one challenged the assignment of a military officer as governor of Formosa or the fact that regulations were promulgated to restrict to the highest-ranking generals and admirals on the active list those eligible to serve as ministers of war or navy. This ordinance, which was rescinded only to be reissued, gave the military actual control over the Cabinet. When any Cabinet refused to obey their wishes, the military could order their representatives in the Cabinet to resign, thus causing its downfall. Likewise they could prevent formation of a Cabinet when the premier designate was unacceptable to them. Thus, when Prince Ito had formed a powerful political party, which gave him strong support in the lower house of Parliament, General Yamagata, who was the leader of the military group, feared that his powers might be checked. In 1901, after forcing Ito to resign as premier, Yamagata maneuvered the appointment of one of his protégés, Prince Taro Katsura, as the next prime minister. Even though Ito's party (the Seiyukai) won a majority in the next election (1903), Ito did not return to power.

This impotency on the part of Parliament and its lack of interest in opposing expansionism and Japanese designs on Korea led inevitably to the Russo-Japanese War (1904–1905). As in the previous conflict, the fighting was outside Japan. Southern Sakhalin (Karafuto) became an integral part of the empire and Japan replaced Russia in Manchuria. Meanwhile, through the Anglo-Japanese Alliance (1902), Japan had obtained an ally in the West. Through the formal annexation of Korea (1910), Japan secured its flank from attack, added roughly one third to both the area and the population of the empire, and acquired a colony with great economic potentialities.

Economically, the years following the Sino-Japanese War were a period of encouragement and growth of industry as a whole. The war indemnity reduced the need for foreign borrowing and made capital available for investment in new industries. Markets were extended and a general capitalistic expansion increased the concentration of wealth in the hands of a small privileged class. After 1905 domestic products were protected by tariffs and Japanese industries stood on an equal footing with their foreign rivals. Strategic industries were expanded, as evidenced by the growth of the Japan Steel Works and 35 other factories manufacturing arms, and all the important railroads were nationalized. Consumer goods, particularly textiles, appeared on the foreign market, so that the new industrial structure with its resultant products for export was to become a cause rather than an effect of war.

World War I afforded Japan another unique opportunity to increase its position as a world power. Militarily, Japan defeated the German forces in the Shantung Peninsula in China, and in the Pacific islands north of the equator. Politically, Japan assured confirmation of these conquests in the Treaty of Versailles through secret agreements with European powers. Despite the fact that the prime minister, Marquis Shigenobu Okuma, had been the leader of the movement for a representative form of government, Japan consolidated its special economic and political position in China through the Twenty-one Demands in 1915 and later strengthened its strategic position by sending an expedition to Soviet Siberia. Economically, the war likewise provided Japan with an unprecedented opportunity. Its limited military responsibilities permitted the concentration of national energies on industrial production and expansion. During the war years new markets were acquired in Asia, Africa, Australia, and the South Seas. The production of silk trebled; the number of workers in factories employing over five persons doubled to more than 2,000,000. A prewar unfavorable trade balance was rapidly eradicated and Japan emerged from the war with a net credit on its international account of approximately 3,000,000,000 yen.

Rise of Nationalism and Defeat (1920–1945).—Immediately following World War I, Japan entered a period during which it was to have at least a minimum of experience with party governments. The first commoner to become prime minister, Takashi Hara, president of the Seiyukai, had come into power in 1918 on a wave of popular discontent with the high cost of living and of general disapproval of the oligarchs' policies. In the first postwar election his party received an absolute majority in the House of Representatives (283 seats to 176), and he confidently announced that militarism had been defeated.

Internationally, Japan appeared to have abandoned its aggressive intentions. It welcomed membership in the League of Nations. At the Washington Conference (1921–1922) it agreed to cancel the Anglo-Japanese Alliance, to withdraw from Shantung, to abandon its occupation of Siberia and northern Sakhalin, and to reduce its naval armaments. It acquiesced in the principles of no further fortifications in the Pacific and of equal opportunity in and respect for the territorial integrity of China.

Yet normal parliamentary government was to be hampered greatly by one of the most important, but unpredictable, characteristics of modern Japan—direct action by recalcitrant and disgruntled elements. Premier Hara was murdered on Nov. 4, 1921 by a railway employee who hoped by his action to attract attention to the corruption and degeneracy of the government leaders. His death was the signal for disintegration within the Seiyukai, so that the Cabinet was forced to resign in June 1922. The conservative advisers to the emperor disregarded the leaders of the political parties and selected the next three premiers from among the military. Simultaneously the Japanese were shocked by the passage of the Immigration Act of 1924, which excluded Orientals from the United States. A temporary collapse of the silk market and the overvaluation of the yen caused the rapid exhaustion of Japan's foreign credit accumulated during the war. Unrest among labor groups, "dangerous thought" among the students, and the fear of the results of universal manhood suffrage resulted in the passage of the Peace Preservation Law of 1925, which gave the police wide powers. Violent outbreaks in the lower house were commonplace; opportunism, not political principles, guided its members in their voting. Each of the two largest business combines allied themselves with one of the leading political parties.

Such was the generally unstable atmosphere existing in 1924, when the Seiyukai and the Minseito, the two principal parties, took turns in running the government for the next eight years. Even during this period only two premiers had a majority in the lower house. Premier Yuko Hamaguchi (1929–1931) obtained an absolute majority for his party (the Minseito) in the elections of February 1930. He openly challenged the military by insisting that the London Naval Treaty (1930) be ratified despite strenuous opposition from the Navy General Staff. Unfortunately for him and for liberalism in Japan, however, he came to power just when the world depression struck Japan. The loss of the silk market in the United States, the shrinkage of other foreign trade, and the government's policy of retrenchment and of return to the gold standard intensified the situation and created an atmosphere favorable to the growth of ultranationalism.

The cry of the militarists that Japan's economic ills could be cured only by direct action in China and by the exploitation of Manchuria fell on sympathetic ears. The wounding of Hamaguchi a few months later greatly simplified the task of the military in regaining control from the political parties. The constitutional provisions which gave them direct access to the throne and the lack of any provision for joint Cabinet responsibility to the Diet strengthened their position. Furthermore, developments in China played into their hands. Japan's monopoly of railway traffic in Manchuria through the Japanese-owned South Manchurian Railway was threatened by a complicated network of new Chinese lines. The Japanese guards along the zone of the railroad claimed that they were threatened constantly by Chinese bandits and that Japanese agents had been killed in the hinterland. Chinese unification was extending north of the Great Wall to such a degree that Chang Hsueh-liang, the Manchurian war lord, refused to make local agreements with the Japanese. Plans were carefully made and a simulated bombing of the South Manchurian Railway on Sept. 18, 1931 was the signal for the rapid and effective occupation of Manchuria by the Japanese Army. The organizers of this policy of direct action came to be known as the Manchurian clique in the army. Thus began the period of dual diplomacy: the Foreign Office placating the Western powers by statements which disclaimed any aggressive intentions of Japan in Asia; the military, largely guided by the Manchurian clique, slowly expanding their control through intrigue and by military campaigns.

The second prime minister during this short period of party governments to obtain an overwhelming majority in the Diet was Ki Tsuyoshi Inukai (1931–1932). His party (the Seiyukai) won the elections of February 1932, but the army already controlled Manchuria. Direct action at home also had its effects on the parties. In the same month Junnosuke Inouye, the campaign manager of the opposition party (the Minseito), was murdered by members of an ultranationalist group. Three months later Prime Minister Inukai was assassinated in an abortive coup d'état by another group determined to destroy the existing political parties, which it labeled as the enemies of the nation. His was the last party Cabinet, and Parliament became increasingly impotent and unwilling to check the spread of militarism. In 1940 the political parties voted themselves out of existence and were replaced by the government-sponsored Imperial Rule Assistance Association, which assured the election of only those supporting national policy.

Moreover, whenever there was the slightest threat to the control by the military, direct action at home effectively eliminated the opposition or further expansion abroad placed Japan in an international position from which it became increasingly difficult to withdraw. The most violent of all the attempted coups d'état in those years occurred in February 1936. The ultranationalists had just received a thorough defeat at the polls. A moderate element within the army had attempted to remove some of the Manchurian clique from key positions. A group of young army extremists, aided by some of their superiors, decided that the time had come to seize the government by force. The result of this uprising was the murder of three senior statesmen who had opposed ultranationalist policies, and the wounding of others. Furthermore, the emperor's personal advisers and any other leaders holding moderate views realized that their lives were in danger if they opposed the extremists.

Meanwhile, the army and navy leaders lost no opportunity to convert all elements within Japan to their cause. They bombarded the conscript troops from the impoverished rural areas with pamphlets which extolled patriotism and sacrifice for the state and which insisted that Japan was destined to bring order and peace to the continent of Asia. It was argued that Japan must protect herself from within against the enemies of communism and capitalism by developing a powerful nationalistic government and must prepare for attack from without by relentlessly perfecting her military machine. The educational system was geared to this new concept of nationalism; the history texts concentrated on the divine origin of the emperor and of the empire; courses in "ethics" taught that the highest life for the Japanese subject was one in which he offered himself in perfect loyalty to the throne; teachers and professors who deviated from this line were summarily dismissed. Already in existence were laws which made it easy to control recalcitrant writers or any subversive elements. The government-owned radio also lent its aid. The labor movement, which never had been strong in Japan before World War II, became a willing supporter of the nationalist program. Agrarian unrest, which had been increasing during the depression years, was checked by promises that the expansion in Manchuria and in China would solve the problem of rural indebtedness and by the placing of local government officials in charge of farmers' cooperatives. In view of Japan's military tradition and heritage, it was comparatively easy to condition the people for a totalitarian state.

Several obstacles, however, still prevented the immediate formation of a completely totalitarian military state. First, the Manchurian clique lacked practical experience in organizing and operating a military state and were not yet in complete control of the army. Second, they had not convinced the conservative financial and industrial leaders (*zaibatsu*), that they would profit from expansion. Finally, the bureaucrats were still trying to sabotage the plans of the extremists.

The puppet government of Manchukuo (first

organized in 1932) gave the new leaders an opportunity to apply their most radical concepts of state control of industry. Here was a testing ground for a planned wartime economy, where they developed a plan for the expansion of strategic industries under governmental supervision and control and for the formation of semiofficial companies. The economy of Manchukuo was closely linked with the overall Japanese armament program. Its success contributed not only to the growth of a new group of industrialists dedicated to ultranationalism, but also to the prestige of the Manchurian clique within the army. Consequently the architects of Manchukuo later became the planners of Japan's wartime structure. Such opposition to the expansionists as had existed among the *zaibatsu* was silenced by the profits which they were making from the enormous expansion of heavy industries and from the insatiable demands of the army and navy for more goods. Furthermore, the *zaibatsu* saw their special position challenged by the new industrialists who had invested in Manchuria and in north China, and by the huge government-sponsored development corporations for each of the conquered areas. Consequently many of them accepted appointments to the nationalist Cabinets as ministers of finance, ministers of commerce and industry, or governors of the Bank of Japan. The managers of their leading subsidiaries were made presidents of the new control associations in their respective industries. Another potential source of danger to military rule had capitulated. Finally, the jurisdiction over all affairs on the Asiatic continent was wrested from the Foreign Office and was placed under the direct control of the military. Even the bureaucrats were powerless to object effectively to expansionism. Thus it was possible for Japan to develop into a military state within the framework of the constitution during the decade before Pearl Harbor. Elections were held, prime ministers were appointed by the emperor's advisers, and Parliament continued in session, but the dictatorship which finally emerged under Gen. Hideki Tojo as premier was complete.

On the international front the military leaders did not have matters so completely under control. They had underestimated the difficulty of conquering China, but used that as the excuse for the passage of the National Mobilization Law (1938). In the hope that a close alliance would develop between Japan and China, a Chinese puppet government was inaugurated (1940). To bolster this movement both at home and abroad, the prime minister expounded on the virtues of a new order for East Asia and a Greater East Asia Co-Prosperity Sphere under the aegis of Japan. After the outbreak of World War II in 1939, Germany and Italy put constant pressure on Japan to join the Axis. On the other hand, Germany and Soviet Russia had signed a nonaggression pact and Japan was reluctant to take any steps which would involve her in a war against the Soviet Union, especially after the sobering experiences of the battles on the Korean and Mongolian borders. Moreover, the subjugation of China was not complete and the new puppet regime at Nanking was not winning the support of influential Chinese. In July 1939, the United States had given six months' notice of its intention to abrogate its commercial treaty with Japan, which was a clear indication that it expected to embargo the shipment of war materials, including oil. To the army's desire to expand on the continent of Asia was added the navy's compulsion to conquer the rich oilfields in Southeast Asia.

It was no surprise, therefore, that Japan capitalized on the downfall of France by obtaining privileges in French Indochina from the Vichy government and by establishing military and air bases there (September 1940). In the Tripartite Pact concluded in the same month with Germany and Italy, Japan obtained from her Axis partners recognition of the new order in Greater East Asia under Japanese leadership and the promise of assistance in the event of war with the United States. Despite these developments, Japan still hoped for the impossible—namely, the capitulation of Generalissimo Chiang Kai-shek, the continued neutrality of the United States, and the promotion of economic cooperation between Japan and the United States. Consequently the ubiquitous Yosuke Matsuoka, who had led the Japanese delegation out of the League of Nations, had been president of the South Manchurian Railway Company and a staunch supporter of an aggressive policy in Asia, and had become foreign minister, attempted the unbelievable task of maintaining the Tripartite Pact and of reaching a settlement with China, the United States, and the Soviet Union. Friendly relations with the Soviet Union, which had been exemplified by the Soviet-Japanese Nonaggression Pact of April 1941, were strained by Germany's attack on Russian two months later.

Negotiations between Japan and the United States were begun, but it was soon clear that Japan was unwilling to abandon its expansionist policy. As the American proposals, which were based on the principle of respect for the territorial integrity of other states, were counter to all the basic moves taken by the Japanese military leaders since the invasion of Manchuria, it was impossible for them to reverse their position and still to remain in power. When an attempt by Prime Minister Prince Fumimaro Konoye to arrange a meeting with President Franklin D. Roosevelt in the summer of 1941 had failed, the final phase of the struggle within Japan between the military extremists and the moderates for the control of Japan's destinies was reached. On Oct. 18, 1941, Gen. Hideki Tojo became prime minister and appointed to his Cabinet those men who favored a totalitarian military state. Japan again had fallen under the complete domination of a military dictatorship. Plans already made for war against the Allies were then put into effect.

In less than two months Pearl Harbor and Manila were attacked and the United States entered the war against the Axis. Through unbelievably speedy military advances in the entire Pacific, the rapid amalgamation of the industries and resources of the conquered territories into Japan's war economy, and the complete control of the government over all phases of life at home, Japan threw the Allies off balance. But Japan could not withstand the slow, yet steady, pressure exerted against it on the sea and in the air by the Allies, principally by the United States, and finally agreed to accept the Allied terms in August 1945. When the Japanese representatives signed the Instrument of Surrender on the U.S.S. *Missouri* on Sept. 2, 1945, Japan admitted complete defeat, promised to abide by whatever orders Gen. Douglas MacArthur, the supreme commander for the Allied powers, might issue, and agreed to the dismemberment of its empire and to the return to its boundaries of a century earlier. See also section on *Foreign Relations (1931–1945)*; CHINA—*History*; KOREA—*History*; WORLD WAR II—*Japan's Pattern for Conquest*; biographies of major figures.

Bibliography.—Takeuchi, Tatsuji, *War and Diplomacy in the Japanese Empire* (Chicago 1935); Reischauer, R. K., *Japan, Government-Politics* (New York 1939); Borton, Hugh, *Japan Since 1931, Its Political and Social Developments* (New York 1940); Yanaga, Chitoshi, *Japan Since Perry* (New York 1949); Sansom, G. B., *The Western World and Japan* (New York 1950).

HUGH BORTON,
Professor of Japanese and Director of East Asian Institute, Columbia University.

22. FOREIGN RELATIONS (1931–1945).

—In 1931, Japan came to an irrevocable turning point in foreign policy. Late in 1929 the New York silk market had collapsed, bringing acute distress to the Japanese countryside, which depended heavily upon cocoons as a cash crop. The military leaders became concerned lest the economic crisis cause disaffection in the army, whose composition and outlook were largely agrarian. The situation also presented them with an opportunity to gain a political dominance which they long had sought and to discredit the civilian moderates, during whose brief ascendancy Japan had subscribed, in the treaties concluded at the Washington Conference (1921–1922) and the London Naval Conference (1930), to policies of self-restraint toward China and to limiting naval armaments. Military propagandists denounced the parliamentary parties and big business for allegedly exploiting the masses and betraying national interests, assailed the United States for discriminatory treatment of Japanese and for erecting tariff walls against Japanese manufactured goods, declared that Japan as a have-not nation must expand in order to survive, and proposed a program of social and economic reconstruction, of reactionary nationalism, and of a strong and independent foreign policy. The ascendancy attained by the army in the government was the key to Japan's international relations during the following decade.

Conquest of Manchuria.—In Manchuria stiffening Chinese resistance to further Japanese penetration led to incidents and an accumulation of unsettled cases. Japanese military extremists agitated to have the army take the Manchuria question out of the hands of the Foreign Office. On Sept. 18, 1931 elements in the Kwantung Army (as the Japanese garrisons in Manchuria were designated), using a manufactured incident near Mukden (Shenyang) as a pretext, struck suddenly and proceeded to overrun and to subjugate southern Manchuria and some months later the entire territory. Popular feeling against Japan rose throughout China as a result of this so-called Mukden incident. In Shanghai a boycott against Japanese goods and a clash between Chinese and Japanese residents in January 1932 became enlarged until more than three Japanese army divisions and 3,000 marines were fighting the Chinese Nineteenth Route Army. In pursuance of a truce reached on May 5 through the intercession of the United States and other powers, the Chinese forces retired from the Shanghai area, after which the Japanese forces were withdrawn.

In Manchuria, however, Japan was not to be deterred from her course of conquest. A League of Nations commission, headed by the 2d Earl of Lytton, visited the Far East to make a firsthand study and report. The Japanese government, though it accorded the commission adequate facilities for investigation, did not await its findings to execute Japanese plans. A puppet regime was created in Manchuria under the name of Manchukuo, which was given recognition on March 15, 1932 in a protocol defining Japan's special relation to the regime. The Lytton Commission's report, which appeared two weeks later, evoked bitter criticism in Japan, especially the report's denial of the plea that Japan had acted in self-defense, the finding that the creation of Manchukuo was contrived by the connivance of the Japanese Army, and the recommendations, implementation of which would have involved undoing the creation of Manchukuo. When the League of Nations Assembly adopted the recommendations (February 1933), Japan announced (May 27, 1933) her withdrawal from the League, effective at the expiration of the necessary two-year period. The League members and the United States withheld recognition from Manchukuo.

Sino-Japanese Relations, 1933–1937.—Between 1933 and 1937 the Japanese extended their aggressions from Manchuria farther into China. In January 1933 they occupied Shanhaikwan (Linyu) within the Great Wall. In rapid succession they conquered Jehol Province, which was annexed to Manchukuo, overran the eastern part of Hopeh Province, and forced upon the Chinese at Tangku a truce establishing eastern Hopeh as a demilitarized zone. In 1935, Gen. Yoshijiro Umezu exacted from Gen. Ho Ying-chin an agreement providing for the exclusion of the Chinese central government's troops from Hopeh and Chahar provinces, where a semiautonomous Hopeh-Chahar Political Council was constituted. Autonomous regimes were established under Japan's aegis in Inner Mongolia and East Hopeh, the latter becoming a base for smuggling Japanese goods into north China.

While Japanese military diplomacy, which was conducted independently of the Foreign Office, was thus active in north China, the imperial government had itself been moving toward a stronger foreign policy. On April 18, 1934, Foreign Office spokesman Eiji Amau emitted an official statement, known as the "hands-off China" statement, announcing that Japan would oppose certain types of third-power activities in China, such as political loans, military instruction, and joint projects of financial and technical assistance to China. Thereupon the United States reminded Japan that there were involved in the situation in China both American and international rights and obligations under international law and existing treaties. On December 29, Japan gave formal notice of her intention to withdraw at the end of 1936 from the Naval Limitation Treaty of 1922. After the lapse of that treaty Japan actively resumed the construction of capital ships to augment an expansion of armaments which had been under way for some time.

By 1936 mounting resentment in China against Japanese aggression resulted in growing Chinese unity and also in several incidents involving the killing or the injuring of Japanese subjects. When the Japanese ambassador in China sought, in conjunction with negotiating a settlement of the incidents, to dispose of "fundamental issues," the Chinese government refused even to discuss the questions of fiscal and administrative autonomy for the five northern provinces (in two of which, Hopeh and Chahar, this had been achieved in fact), and of "joint Sino-Japanese defense against communism," a formula affording Japan a basis for asserting military control in north China. The Chinese in turn presented counterproposals, which included cancellation of the Tangku truce and of the Ho-Umezu Agreement, dissolution of the East Hopeh regime, and cessation of Japanese smuggling. The negotiations ended in a deadlock. In December the National government and the Chinese Communists agreed to form a common front to resist Japan.

Sino-Japanese War.—A minor clash on July 7, 1937 between Chinese and Japanese soldiers at the Marco Polo Bridge near Peiping (Peking) brought the relations of their two countries rapidly to a crisis after the Chinese had refused to yield to Japanese demands for a local settlement which would confirm Japan's influence in north China. The Japanese made preparations to resort to force and the Chinese to resist. The Japanese government was unresponsive to an offer of good offices by the United States and sent heavy reinforcements to China. Soon hostilities became general and there ensued a conflict which influenced developments in Europe and four years later merged with World War II.

Japanese public opinion strongly supported its government, which remained united on objectives in China to the end of the war. On Sept. 5, 1937 the prime minister, Prince Fumimaro Konoye, informed the Diet that Japan's purpose was to force China to accept a basic readjustment of its relations with Japan, to which end the sole means then open to Japan was "to administer a thoroughgoing blow to the Chinese Army so that it will completely lose its will to fight."

The League of Nations Assembly's First Report on the conflict in the Far East, adopted Oct. 6, 1937, expressed the conclusion that Japan's military operations against China were out of all proportion to the incident which had occasioned these; that such action could not facilitate the friendly cooperation between the two nations which Japanese statesmen had affirmed was their aim; that Japan's action could be justified neither under existing legal instruments nor under the right of self-defense; and that it contravened Japan's obligations under the Nine-Power Treaty of 1922 and the Pact of Paris of 1928. The United States expressed its general concurrence with the conclusions of the League's Assembly. Nineteen nations in November 1937 participated at Brussels in a conference, held in accordance with a provision of the Nine-Power Treaty, to "study peaceful means of hastening the end of the regrettable conflict which prevails" in the Far East. The Japanese government's refusal to send delegates to the conference defeated the purpose to bring the conflict to an end through mediation and conciliation.

Japanese Rule in Occupied China.—In the areas of China which came under their military occupation the Japanese created regimes having a façade of Chinese control, but with real authority exercised by Japanese officials. The system offered a convenient subterfuge for disclaiming Japanese responsibility for infringement of the rights of third powers and for denying that Japanese assurances that they had no territorial ambitions had been violated. The Japanese government was thus also able to satisfy its own public that it had no enmity toward the Chinese people, but was combating only an anti-Japanese military leadership in the Chinese National government.

Japan's economic policy in occupied China early tended to establish such a general preference for Japanese interests as to deprive third-power nationals of equality of opportunity. Tariffs were lowered on Japan's staple imports, and discrimination in favor of Japanese enterprise was effected by the regulation, taxing, or prohibition of trade, by the imposition of exchange controls, and by the establishment of special Japanese-controlled companies, which were granted preferred status or monopolistic rights. As the Japanese armies advanced, they took possession of practically all publicly owned Chinese enterprise, such as railways, electric power companies, salt fields, waterworks, navigation facilities, and certain iron and coal mines, as well as industries which in large part were privately owned.

On Nov. 3, 1938, after the capture of Hankow and Canton, Japan announced that the Chinese National government had been reduced to a local regime and that it was Japan's aim to establish, in cooperation with China and Manchukuo, a new order in East Asia. On December 22, Prince Konoye announced Japan's peace terms, which were that China was: (1) to recognize Manchukuo; (2) to adhere to the Anti-Comintern Pact; (3) to accord Japan the right to station troops in areas to be stipulated by Japan (Inner Mongolia being designated as a "special anti-Communist area"); and (4) to agree to economic cooperation with Japan and to the extension of facilities for the Japanese development of natural resources (especially in Inner Mongolia and north China). This announcement was made by prearrangement with Wang Ching-wei, vice president of the Kuomintang, who had deserted the National government and was then in Indochina. On December 27, Wang declared that Konoye's terms were consistent with the principles of peace and proposed that the National government negotiate with Japan. As was expected, the National government ignored his appeal. Japan thus had prepared the ground for instituting on March 30, 1940 a Chinese regime in central China subservient to Japan, with Wang as its head. The Wang regime was recognized by Japan on Nov. 30, 1940 as the national government of the Republic of China in a "treaty" containing provisions substantially similar to the Konoye peace terms of Dec. 22, 1938.

Relations with Great Britain and the United States.—From the outset of the hostilities the rights and interests of third powers in China suffered from Japanese acts. British property interests in China were greater than those of any other power, but Great Britain was largely preoccupied with the crisis and the subsequent war in Europe. Consequently it was chiefly the United States that led in efforts to restrain Japan. On Dec. 12, 1937, Japanese aircraft bombed and sank the U.S.S. *Panay* in the Yangtze River under circumstances which pointed to either a deliberate disregard of consequences or negligence by some responsible person. The Japanese government called the act unintentional and made a prompt settlement, consisting of an expression of regret, assurances that measures would be taken against infringement of the rights and interference with the interests of the United States and other third powers, disciplinary action against the responsible commanders, and indemnification amounting to $2,214,007.

The Japanese failure to keep the assurances given in connection with the *Panay* settlement and the vain efforts by the United States to obtain the discontinuance of and redress for Japanese violations of American rights and the cessation of indiscriminate bombings from the air, which had caused the death of many thousands of the Chinese civil population and were jeopardizing the lives of third-power nationals, induced eventually, on July 1, 1938, the United States to place a moral embargo upon the export of aircraft and aircraft equipment to Japan. On October 6, in consequence of the Japanese government's continued failure to fulfill its repeated assurances to observe the principle of equality of commercial opportunity, the United States addressed to the Japanese government a comprehensive note on its discriminatory practices and interference with American rights and asked that these be discontinued promptly. The Japanese government's reply, on November 19, was an open challenge to the Western powers in the assertion of Japan's pretensions to the domination of China and it constituted a repudiation of the treaties concerning China. The note stated in part that Japan was devoting her energy to the establishment of a new order based on international justice throughout east Asia, the attainment of which end was indispensable to the very existence of Japan and was the foundation of the enduring peace and stability of that region. The conviction was expressed that in the new situation fast developing in east Asia an attempt to apply inapplicable ideas and principles of the past neither would contribute to the establishment of a real peace in east Asia nor would solve the immediate issues.

Since the Japanese note contained no satisfactory assurances for an amelioration of the situation, the United States on December 31 delivered to the Japanese government another note expounding more fully the American position. No reply to that note was made. On July 26, 1939 the United States notified Japan of its desire to terminate the Treaty of Commerce and Navigation of 1911. The United States reasoned that the treaty was not affording adequate protection to American commerce either in Japan or in Japanese-occupied portions of China, while at the same time the operation of the most-favored-nation clause of the treaty was a bar to the adoption of retaliatory measures against Japanese commerce. This notification came at a juncture when Great Britain was being subjected to pressure, through a partial blockade by Japan of the British and French concessions at Tientsin to surrender to a local Japanese-controlled court four Chinese whom the Japanese had accused of complicity in the murder of a puppet Chinese official. On August 18, however, the British ambassador informed the Japanese government that Britain would be unable to consider in a conference with Japan alone problems affecting the interests of third powers. It was not until a year later that the blockade at Tientsin was lifted, after the British had made substantial concessions to Japan. In July 1940 the British, under pressure of intense Japanese military activity near Hong Kong, agreed to stop the movement of military supplies from Hong Kong to Chinese territory and to close the Burma Road for the transit of certain war material for three months, on the understanding that during this period the Japanese would make a special effort to conclude a peace with China. On October 17 the Burma Road was reopened, since in the meantime Japan had made no serious diplomatic effort to come to an agreement with China.

Relations with the Soviet Union and Germany.—While Japan thus had been taking the offensive in China against the Western powers, she had been essentially on the defensive against the Soviet Union, at least after 1935, when Japanese pressure had effected the sale of the Russian interests in the Chinese Eastern Railway to Manchukuo. After the outbreak of the Sino-Japanese conflict, the Soviet Union, which viewed with concern the prospects of Japan's absorption of China, gave the Chinese government extensive aid in the form of military supplies and technical advice and by her military dispositions along the border immobilized in Manchuria a considerable part of Japan's best troops. An armed clash in July 1938 between Soviet and Japanese forces at Changkufeng Hill led to 10 days' fighting, and another clash in 1939 along the Mongolian border inaugurated extensive hostilities lasting from May until September. As a means of checking the Soviet Union, the Japanese Army, after the outbreak of the conflict with China, worked actively for a closer tie with Germany than that afforded by the Anti-Comintern Pact concluded in November 1936. Germany, which had extensive commercial interests in China, was none too pleased with Japan's program there and was willing to consider an alliance only if it assured Germany of Japan's support against Britain and France. Japan's civilian and naval leaders, however, opposed making commitments which might involve it in a European war. In May 1939, Baron Kiichiro Hiranuma, who in January had succeeded Konoye as premier, undertook a fresh initiative toward an alliance. Suddenly, on August 23, the conclusion of the German-Soviet Nonaggression Pact was announced. Germany's action without giving prior notice to Japan and the fact that the plea for an alliance had rested on its expected value against Russia resulted in the discrediting of the pro-German policies of the Hiranuma Cabinet and forced it to resign.

Expansion to the South.—The next Cabinet, under Gen. Nobuyuki Abe, sought a reorientation of policy toward the Anglo-Saxon powers, but this aim was foredoomed to failure, because Japan's "immutable" policy in China stood in the way of harmonious relations with them. After the outbreak of war in Europe on Sept. 1, 1939 the unconcealed eagerness in Japan to seize the opportunity thereby presented for the extension of empire southward was also an obstacle to good relations with the Western powers. The fall of France and the Netherlands in the spring of 1940 gave an additional impetus in Japan to the movement for southward expansion. As Britain and the United States stood in the way, they replaced Russia as the principal enemy in Japanese eyes. Moreover, as Germany now indicated that she no longer needed Japanese help in Europe, but wanted Japan to divert American attention from the Atlantic to the Pacific, the principal obstacles to an alliance were removed. Upon Konoye's resumption of the premiership in July, final negotiations ended in the signing of the Tripartite Pact on Sept. 27, 1940. Japan obligated itself thereunder to come to the aid of any of the parties thereto, if attacked by a power not at the time in the European war or in the Sino-Japanese conflict, other than the Soviet Union, which was expressly excepted.

Meanwhile, Japan had been pressing forward

in Indochina. On Aug. 30, 1940, a preliminary agreement was reached with France as a foundation for subsequent discussions. On September 22, three days after the issuance of a Japanese ultimatum, the French colonial authorities agreed to the Japanese use of three airports in Indochina and to the transit of Japanese forces for operations in China. Acting independently of the negotiators of the agreement, the Japanese Army in south China invaded Tonkin on the same day and five days of bloody fighting ensued.

After Germany's invasion of the Netherlands in May 1940, Britain, France, and the United States declared that they would respect the neutrality of the Netherlands East Indies. Japan gave similar assurances. Japan obtained from Germany assurances interpreted by Japan as giving her a free hand in the islands. In September a Japanese mission arrived in Batavia and demanded guarantees of delivery to Japan of 3,150,000 tons of petroleum products annually, an amount six times as large as the normal export to Japan, and extensive rights to exploit oil resources. The Dutch demurred and made a counteroffer beyond which they would not yield. Since the Japanese were not satisfied, the negotiations were suspended. Japan then sent to Batavia ex-Foreign Minister Kenkichi Yoshizawa, who in January 1941 presented far-reaching demands for special rights, which, if they had been accepted, would have placed the Indies under virtual Japanese economic control. When the negotiations reached an impasse, Yoshizawa returned in June to Japan empty-handed.

Japan's freedom of action for the southern enterprise was hampered by the undeclared and still unsettled war in China. China was receiving American, British, and Soviet aid. In July 1940, the United States had begun to deny licenses for the export of an expanding list of strategic commodities, including scrap iron, to Japan. Foreign Minister Yosuke Matsuoka made clear in the Japanese Diet on Jan. 21, 1941 that he would seek from the United States recognition of the vital concern to Japan of the establishment of the Greater East Asia Co-Prosperity Sphere, assent to Japan's supremacy in the Western Pacific, and cessation of economic restrictions upon Japan.

Japanese-United States Negotiations, 1941. —A new Japanese ambassador, Admiral Kichisaburo Nomura discussed in March and April 1941 with President Franklin D. Roosevelt and with Secretary of State Cordell Hull means of improving Japanese-American relations. He suggested the conclusion of a new agreement. Secretary Hull informed Admiral Nomura that the United States would consider any Japanese proposal for an agreement whose terms would be consistent with peaceful principles and purposes and that he would ask for assurances that the Japanese government had the willingness and the power to adopt those principles and to abandon its course of conquest. (During those two months Foreign Minister Matsuoka visited Berlin and Rome for the purpose of strengthening relations with the Axis. On his way home he stopped at Moscow, where on April 13 a neutrality pact between Japan and the Soviet Union was concluded.) Ambassador Nomura presented to Secretary Hull on May 12 a proposal for a general settlement, which was taken as a starting point for exploratory conversations, which were continued until December 1941. What the Japanese sought as disclosed in that proposal and in subsequent formulations and clarification, was that the United States should stop interference, by its aid to the Chinese government, with Japan's efforts to impose a peace settlement on China on terms which had not changed substantially since 1936 and whose acceptance would have meant China's surrender of military and economic control of north China and of Inner Mongolia to Japan. Japan asked that normal Japanese-American trade relations be resumed and that the United States assist Japan to acquire rights to exploit natural resources in the Southwest Pacific. The United States made clear from the outset its unwillingness to discontinue aid to China and to be a party to a settlement between Japan and China which the latter could not accept freely by amicable negotiation. The United States expressed its readiness to offer its good offices for a settlement between China and Japan, to resume normal trade relations with Japan, and to assist Japan in endeavoring to obtain nondiscriminatory commercial access to raw materials in the Pacific area, provided that Japan abandon its policy of aggression, agree to respect in China the principle of nondiscriminatory treatment in international commercial intercourse, and make it clear that it was not under obligations under the Tripartite Pact to take action against the United States if the latter should be drawn by self-defense into the European war.

Germany's attack on Russia on June 22 precipitated an acute issue in the Japanese government on whether Japan should join the attack on Russia or complete the plan for southward expansion. The latter course was chosen at an imperial conference on July 2. Military preparations on a vast scale were launched, and soon a military movement into southern Indochina, which threatened the security of American, British, and Dutch possessions and vital trade routes south of China was begun. Secretary Hull suspended the exploratory conversations at Washington. On July 24, President Roosevelt proposed to Japan the neutralization of Indochina, but Japan was unresponsive to the proposal. On July 26, the United States froze Japanese assets in American territory, causing a virtual cessation of trade between the two countries. The British and the Dutch followed suit.

In August, following an initiative by Japan, the exploratory conversations at Washington were resumed and continued through the autumn. To a Japanese proposal for a meeting in the Pacific between the responsible heads of the two governments as a means of resolving the issues between them, the United States suggested that such a meeting should await agreement on essential principles and on their practical application. On November 20, Japan made what proved to be her final proposal. In it were repeated in blunt terms the essence of the demands from which Japan had never receded and there was no suggestion of any concession to the American views. The United States, after consulting with the British, the Australians, the Dutch, and the Chinese, answered Japan on November 26. The reply revealed the unacceptability of the Japanese proposal and contained what was essentially a summation of the American position which had been demonstrated fully. There was offered "for the consideration of the Japanese government a plan of a broad but simple settlement covering the entire Pacific area." On December 7, Ambassador Nomura delivered to Secretary Hull a communication containing an abusive tirade against the United States and announcing that Japan considered it impossible to reach an agreement through further negotiations. More than an hour before the delivery of this communication, Japanese armed forces had struck without warning at Pearl Harbor and had invaded British Malaya.

World War II.—Japanese armies proceeded rapidly to invade and to occupy American, British, and Dutch possessions in southeastern Asia and swarmed into Thailand, with whose government an alliance was concluded. Hong Kong fell on December 25, Singapore on Feb. 15, 1942, Batavia on March 5, Mandalay on May 1, and Corregidor on May 6. In the new acquisitions to the Co-Prosperity Sphere, much the same patterns were followed as had been adopted in China. In 1943, Burma and the Philippines were given "independence," but it was not until late in the war that independence movements were supported in Indochina and Indonesia.

After the loss of Saipan in June 1944 conviction of the inevitability of defeat began to grow in Japan, but the army had no plan except to fight to the bitter end. By the spring of 1945 leading statesmen reached the conclusion that in order to escape national annihilation peace must be obtained. In July the Soviet government was approached with a view to its mediation with the Allies for a peace short of unconditional surrender, but the Soviet government rebuffed the approach on the ground that the basis proposed for peace was too indefinite. On July 26, the Allied powers issued at Potsdam a declaration outlining their terms of surrender to Japan. A few days later the Soviet government entered the war against Japan and adhered to the Potsdam Declaration. The declaration called for the limitation of Japanese sovereignty to Japan's four main islands and such minor islands as the Allies might determine; the disarming of Japan's military forces; the punishment of Japanese war criminals; the military occupation of Japan; and the eventual formation of a democratic government in Japan. Japan announced on August 10 its acceptance of these terms subject to the qualification that the emperor's prerogatives as sovereign would not be prejudiced. The Allies replied that the emperor's authority and that of the Japanese government would be "subject to the Supreme Commander of the Allied Powers, who will take such steps as he deems proper to effectuate the surrender terms." Japan accepted this answer, and on Sept. 2, 1945, Japanese representatives signed, on board the U.S.S. *Missouri* in Tokyo Bay, the Instrument of Surrender.

Bibliography.—Stimson, H. L., *Far Eastern Crisis* (New York 1936); Hornbeck, S. K., *The United States and the Far East: Certain Fundamentals of Policy* (Boston 1942); Department of State, *Foreign Relations of the United States: Japan, 1931–1941* (Washington 1943); Grew, J. C., *Ten Years in Japan* (New York 1944); Ballantine, J. W., "Mukden to Pearl Harbor," *Foreign Affairs,* July 1949.

JOSEPH W. BALLANTINE,
United States Foreign Service, 1909–1947.

23. OCCUPATION AND FOREIGN RELATIONS (1945–1954). An Allied military occupation of Japan was established after Japan had accepted the Allied terms of surrender on Aug. 14, 1945. In contrast with the occupation of Germany, where the four major European Allies divided the country into national zones and originally shared equally in the formulation of the overall policy of occupation, in Japan the United States assumed the dominant role in the formulation and execution of occupation policies. Participation of the other powers in the formulation of these policies was not effectively provided until the creation of the Far Eastern Commission (FEC) on Dec. 27, 1945, and even under the terms of reference of the FEC the primary interests of the United States were recognized. Furthermore, the occupation forces were predominantly American. Only the countries of the British Commonwealth responded to the United States invitation to send troops, but these forces had no jurisdiction over military government in their area.

Allied Policy Formulation.—In the interim between Japan's surrender and the actual organization of the FEC on Feb. 26, 1946, the United States assumed sole responsibility for the formulation and the implementation of the policy of occupation within the general context of the Potsdam Declaration. The policies enunciated by the United States in this initial period were to a large extent incorporated in the FEC's subsequent decisions of policy.

Since the United States had borne the brunt of the war against Japan, the United States expected and the other powers, with the exception of the USSR, agreed that the United States should assume this primary responsibility for the direction of the occupation. The United States, for its part, was also anxious that all the principal powers at war with Japan participate, at least in an advisory capacity, in the formulation of occupation policy. At the same time the United States was determined to avoid a repetition of the disagreements and delays already encountered in the German occupation, where agreement of the four principal powers was a prerequisite to the formulation and implementation of policy. In view of these considerations the United States had proposed on Aug. 21, 1945, the creation of a Far Eastern Advisory Commission (FEAC), composed of the representatives of the United States, the United Kingdom, the USSR, China, France, the Netherlands, India, Australia, New Zealand, Canada, and the Philippines, to make recommendations on the formulation of occupation policies to their respective governments. The USSR declined to participate in the FEAC because of the limited powers of the commission and favored instead the creation of an Allied control commission similar in powers and composition to the Allied Control Commission for Germany. The other powers, however, joined with the United States in organizing the FEAC, which held its first meeting in Washington on October 30. In December 1945, the foreign ministers of the United States, the United Kingdom, and the USSR met in Moscow and reopened negotiations on the question of the nature of Allied participation in the occupation of Japan. On December 27, with the concurrence of China, the foreign ministers announced the creation of a Far Eastern Commission (FEC) to supersede the FEAC. The terms of reference of the FEC represented a compromise between the United States and USSR positions. Furthermore, the FEC met the desire of the other principal powers at war with Japan for a greater voice in the determination of occupation policies than was provided within the limited framework of the FEAC.

The FEC was composed originally of one representative each from the United States, the United Kingdom, the USSR, China, Australia, New Zealand, India, Canada, the Netherlands, France, and the Philippines. Burma and Pakistan were later admitted to membership. All decisions of the commission on substantive, as opposed to procedural, matters required the concurrence of a majority of the members including the United States, the United Kingdom, the USSR, and China. The FEC was empowered (1) to formulate policies under which Japan could fulfill the terms of surrender; (2) to review, on the request of any member, any directive issued to SCAP or any action taken by him, which involved policy decisions within the commission's jurisdiction; and (3) to consider any other matter assigned to it by agreement among the member governments. The conduct of military operations and territorial questions were excepted specifically from the commission's jurisdiction. The commission was obligated to respect the existing control machinery in Japan, including the chain of command between SCAP and the United States government. All the FEC's decisions of policy were transmitted to SCAP through the United States government in the form of directives to SCAP from the United States Joint Chiefs of Staff.

The effectiveness of the veto power in the FEC was limited by the fact that the terms of reference to the commission also gave to the United States broad authority to act in the event that the FEC failed to agree on decisions of policy. The United States was empowered to issue interim directives to SCAP on matters not already covered by the FEC's decisions of policy, except in the case of directives concerned with "fundamental changes in the Japanese constitutional structure or in the regime of control, or dealing with a change in the Japanese Government as a whole," in which the FEC had prior jurisdiction. These so-called reserved subjects constituted the only limitation on United States power to issue interim directives. Within the scope of the reserved subjects the United States, through its veto power, could prevent the FEC's adoption of decisions contrary to United States policies, although the United States was prevented from taking unilateral action in the absence of the FEC's agreement. All United States interim directives had to be submitted to the FEC for review after issuance, but the directives remained in force unless the FEC disapproved them—which, of course, it could not do without United States concurrence.

The Moscow agreement also provided for an Allied Council for Japan to be established in Tokyo. The council was composed of the supreme commander or his deputy, who was chairman and United States member; one member each from the USSR and China; and one member representing jointly the United Kingdom, Australia, New Zealand, and India. The purpose of this council was to consult with and advise the supreme commander in regard to the implementation of the terms of surrender, the occupation and control of Japan, and directives supplementary thereto. The supreme commander was not obligated either to consult with the council or to accept its advice. It was only in relation to SCAP's implementation of the FEC's decisions of policy on fundamental changes in the Japanese constitutional structure or in the regime of control or to his dealing with changes in the Japanese government that the Allied Council could effectively intervene. If the council or any member thereof disagreed with the supreme commander's implementation of the FEC's decisions of policy on these reserved subjects, the supreme commander had to refrain from taking action until the FEC reviewed the matter and rendered a decision. This power of the council was modified to some extent by the provision that in case of necessity the supreme commander "might take decisions concerning the change in individual Ministers of the Japanese Government . . . after appropriate preliminary consultation with the representatives of the other Allied Powers on the Allied Council."

Objectives of the Occupation.—The objectives of the Allied occupation were stated in the Potsdam Declaration and in the FEC Basic Post-Surrender Policy for Japan, approved by the FEC on June 19, 1947. The primary objectives of the occupation were: (1) to ensure that Japan never again would menace world peace and security, and (2) to effect the establishment of a democratic and peaceful government in Japan, in accordance with the freely expressed will of the Japanese people. More specifically, the Allied powers promulgated a series of subordinate objectives or means by which the primary objectives would be achieved. These subordinate objectives were (1) demobilization and demilitarization of Japan, (2) punishment of war criminals, (3) elimination of those who led Japan to war from positions of influence, (4) elimination of war industries, (5) payment of reparations, (6) restitution of looted property, and (7) limitation of Japanese territory to the four main islands and to such minor islands as the Allies subsequently might determine. These essentially punitive or negative objectives were counterbalanced by positive or constructive objectives in accord with the general Allied position that it was not their intention to enslave the Japanese people or to destroy the Japanese nation. The positive objectives were: (1) repatriation of Japanese armed forces and their demobilization in Japan; (2) removal of all obstacles to revival and confirmation of democratic tendencies and to establishment of freedom of speech, religion, thought, and respect for human rights; and (3) permission for Japan to maintain such industries as would sustain its economy and to participate eventually in world trade. The Allies further committed themselves to withdraw the occupation after all these objectives had been achieved.

Powers of the Supreme Commander for the Allied Powers.—Gen. Douglas MacArthur was appointed supreme commander for the Allied powers (SCAP) by the president of the United States in August 1945.[1] Subsequent decisions of the Allied powers stated that the supreme commander was to be designated by the United States; there was no provision that the other powers had to concur in this appointment. The Instrument of Surrender gave the supreme commander full powers to effectuate the terms of surrender and to implement the Potsdam Declaration. Occupation policies were formulated by either the FEC or the United States government, but SCAP was the sole executive authority for the Allied powers in Japan and was responsible for the implementation of all Allied or United States

[1] He was succeeded by Gen. Matthew B. Ridgway in 1951.

decisions of policy. SCAP's powers in the field of implementation were defined broadly, and the United States resisted any attempts by the FEC to encroach on what the United States considered to be SCAP's field of responsibility. While the Allied Council for Japan could question, in relation to the reserved subjects, SCAP's implementations of the FEC's decisions of policy, it never did this.

SCAP was directed by the United States to operate through the existing Japanese governmental machinery and agencies, including the emperor, rather than by direct military government. This policy neither committed SCAP to support the existing form of government in Japan nor excluded SCAP's taking direct action if the necessity for such action arose. All directives and orders to the Japanese government were issued by SCAP, and neither the United States government nor the FEC nor the Allied Council was competent to deal directly with the Japanese government. Foreign missions accredited either to SCAP or, in the case of the USSR mission, to the Allied Council, could deal with the Japanese authorities only through the agency of SCAP.

Organization of SCAP Headquarters and Its Relations with the Japanese Government.—The dual nature of General MacArthur's position, as supreme commander for the Allied powers and as commander in chief of United States forces in the Far East, resulted in the establishment of two separate headquarters to discharge the responsibilities arising from these positions. On the one hand, there was the general headquarters of SCAP, which was responsible for implementation of the political and economic phases of the occupation's program, and, on the other hand, there was the general headquarters of the Far East Command, which was responsible for the occupation forces. In the highest echelons the personnel of these two headquarters were the same. Below this level the personnel and organizational structure were distinct, reflecting differences in functions and responsibilities. Special staff sections were added to the military organization. These were responsible for formulation and implementation of operational policies and programs and for direction and supervision of the Japanese government in its implementation of SCAP's orders and directives.

In the initial period of the occupation (from mid-1945 until mid-1947) written directives were the primary means by which SCAP instructed the Japanese government. During this period intervention by the staff sections in day-to-day operations of the Japanese government was necessary to ensure Japanese understanding of, and prompt compliance with, occupation directives. At this time the occupation's program was in its formative stage: on the negative side it was concerned with destroying the Japanese military potential, eliminating wartime leaders from public office, and rescinding repressive legislation; on the positive side it was concerned with drastic revisions in the legal basis and organizational structure of the government.

In mid-1947 the occupation shifted its attentions to the problems arising from the operation of the newly established governmental system which in turn produced a change in the method of dealing with the Japanese government. The formal written directive, while still utilized occasionally, yielded for the most part to informal memorandums and particularly to verbal instructions. This alteration in the method of operation caused a marked increase in daily contacts between the personnel of the special staff sections and their Japanese counterparts. On the whole, these personal relations were good, and both sides derived considerable benefit in terms of a greater understanding of the problems involved and of more practical solutions. At the same time, this method of operation encouraged the Japanese officials to avoid responsibility for day-to-day decisions by taking both major and minor problems to SCAP officials for advice and instructions.

To encourage Japanese initiative, General MacArthur, characterizing the future role of the occupation as that of friendly guidance, directed his headquarters staff in July 1949 to permit and to encourage the Japanese government and its agencies to assume the normal powers of government in matters of domestic administration.

There was one outstanding exception to this policy of permitting the Japanese government to assume primary responsibility for the country's domestic affairs. On Dec. 10, 1948, the United States issued an interim directive to SCAP instructing him to direct the Japanese government to undertake a specific program for the stabilization of the Japanese economy. This directive reflected a shift, which began early in 1948, in the focus of United States attention from the original economic objectives of the occupation to the problem of Japanese economic recovery. The United States considered economic recovery essential to the achievement of the occupation's objective of establishing a peaceful and stable Japanese government. Furthermore, the United States had been appropriating funds to be used in Japan to prevent disease and unrest, which, if permitted to develop, would endanger the security of the occupation forces. To relieve itself of this continuing financial burden the United States decided early in 1948 that it would be more economical in the long run if the United States appropriated funds to promote Japanese economic recovery rather than to continue what was essentially a dole. By the end of 1948, however, it became apparent that to obtain the maximum benefits from the money appropriated for Japanese economic recovery it would first be necessary to stabilize the Japanese economy. Accordingly the United States interim directive was issued, and SCAP in turn, on Dec. 18, 1948, issued a directive to the Japanese government outlining the stabilization measures required. To ensure that the Japanese would execute this program it again became necessary for the occupation to give close attention to such aspects of the Japanese economy as related to the program of economic stabilization.

The occupation of Japan was prolonged beyond the period of two to three years originally envisaged and for which its program had been devised. The occupation was extended, not because its basic program had not been accomplished, but essentially because the international situation delayed the conclusion of a treaty of peace.

Accomplishments of the Occupation.—The FEC adopted over 60 policy decisions concerned with all aspects of the occupation, including, in addition to the Basic Post-Surrender Policy, specific policies on such subjects as war crimes, restitution of looted property, the constitution, education, trade unions, farmers' organizations, level of economic activity, interim reparations, and imports and exports. There were some conspicuous gaps in the FEC's policies, notably in respect to reparations, where the FEC could not agree on the division of reparations shares.

Throughout its existence the effectiveness of the FEC was limited by the fact that the occupation did not have to wait for the FEC to direct its activities or to provide policy guidance. Thus, when the FEC finally adopted its Basic Post-Surrender Policy for Japan in June 1947, much of the policy stated therein had been implemented by SCAP. It was, however, the original intention of the United States not to permit the occupation of Japan to be handicapped by the failure of the Allied powers to agree on policies of occupation.

The contribution of the FEC to formulation of Allied policy declined markedly in 1948 and 1949, during which years the commission adopted only 17 policy decisions. This was due in part to the facts that the commission in its first two years largely had exhausted the field of activity and that in the few important remaining fields it could not reach agreement. Another factor in the decline of the FEC's activity and influence was the growth of tension between the USSR and the Western powers, although this tension did not affect the activities of the FEC to the same extent as it did those of other international bodies. Moreover, the United States attention since 1948 was focused primarily on problems relating to Japanese economic recovery in order to minimize the financial burdens of the occupation. These factors led the United States to resort increasingly to the use of interim directives as a means of directing policies of occupation.

The Allied Council for Japan was not an effective instrument of Allied policy. In the first place, its meetings were, unlike those of the FEC, open to the public, which obviated its being consulted by the supreme commander for advice prior to the issuance of directives to the Japanese government. Moreover, while the FEC was directed in its terms of reference to proceed in its activities from the fact that there was an Allied Council for Japan, there was no exchange of views or consultation between the two bodies. The Allied Council never utilized its power to hinder SCAP's implementation of the FEC's decisions of policy on the reserved subjects by referring SCAP's actions to the FEC for review.

The objectives of the occupation, as expounded in the decisions of policy of the United States and the FEC, had been largely accomplished by 1950. Demilitarization and demobilization, except for the military personnel who remained to be repatriated from the USSR was completed by the end of 1947. The Class A war crimes trials ended in November 1948; Class B and C trials were, with few exceptions, completed by October 1949. All told, some 4,200 Japanese were convicted of war crimes. Identifiable looted property was returned to the original owners. Reparations in the form of capital equipment from certain government arsenals were divided and distributed among certain of the Allied powers in accordance with a United States interim directive. Certain small Japanese naval vessels were also transferred as reparations. This equipment was only a small part of the total goods designated by the FEC as available for reparations. In the absence of the FEC's agreement on reparations shares, the United States, by an interim directive in May 1949, halted all additional reparations as contrary to the interests of the program of Japanese economic recovery.

A Japanese Constitution was drafted in conformity with the FEC's policies and became effective on May 3, 1947. This new constitution provided for the establishment of a representative government based on universal adult suffrage, an executive responsible to the legislature, an independent judiciary, guarantees of fundamental civil rights, and popularly elected local government. The constitution also renounced both war as a sovereign right of the nation and the threat or use of force as a means of settling international disputes, and it stated that military forces would not be maintained for these purposes. Legislation implementing this constitution and including revised criminal and civil codes was enacted. Elections in April 1947 for both houses of the Diet and for local executives and legislatures complied with the occupation objective, which called for the establishment of a democratic government in accordance with the freely expressed will of the Japanese people. Extensive land reform was made; the development of democratic and free trade unions to protect the interests of labor was encouraged; the educational system was reorganized; the police system was decentralized; and the wartime leaders were removed and excluded from public office. On the economic side there was an extensive reorganization of the economic system through means such as the dissolution of *zaibatsu* (family holding company) control and the adoption of legislation designed to permit development of the economic system along free competitive lines.

In the summer of 1947 the United States attempted to negotiate a Japanese peace treaty by inviting the other 10 FEC nations to a preliminary conference on treaty procedures at which decisions would be reached by majority vote. The USSR declined the invitation on the ground that preliminary treaty discussions should be confined to the United States, the United Kingdom, China, and the USSR. China proposed that the conference voting procedure should be the same as in the FEC, where the above-mentioned four powers had a veto. While the other powers accepted the United States proposals, the conference was not held.

It was not until 1950 that the United States formally renewed its efforts to negotiate a peace treaty, and on September 8 of that year, President Harry S. Truman appointed John Foster Dulles as the principal United States negotiator. Mr. Dulles began the negotiations with bilateral discussions with each of the FEC powers and with Indonesia, Ceylon, and the Republic of Korea. Japanese leaders also were consulted. From the outset the United States opposed a punitive treaty and sought instead a treaty of reconciliation. This view was shared by some of the powers, but there was a reluctance on the part of the Philippines, Australia, and New Zealand particularly to conclude a treaty which did not contain guarantees against Japanese rearmament. To meet this point of view the United States concluded treaties of mutual security and defense with these powers.

The Japanese Peace Treaty was signed by 48 Allied nations and Japan in San Francisco on Sept. 8, 1951. The USSR, Poland, and Czechoslovakia attended the conference but did not sign the treaty; Burma, India, and Yugoslavia declined to attend the conference; and China was not represented because the Allies could not agree on whether the Nationalist government or the Communist regime should represent China. The United States and Japan also signed, on September 8, a security treaty by which the United States agreed to station forces in Japan until such time as both nations agreed that Japan's security was assured by other means. On April 28, 1952, the peace treaty was brought into force between Japan and the powers which had ratified it. The occupation of Japan ended, and the regime of control, including SCAP, the FEC, and the Allied Council for Japan, was terminated.

Summary of the Treaty.—The Japanese Peace Treaty was signed by Japan and the following 48 countries: Argentina, Australia, Belgium, Bolivia, Brazil, Cambodia, Canada, Ceylon, Chile, Colombia, Costa Rica, Cuba, Dominican Republic, Ecuador, Egypt, El Salvador, Ethiopia, France, Greece, Guatemala, Haiti, Honduras, Indonesia, Iran, Iraq, Laos, Lebanon, Liberia, Luxembourg, Mexico, Netherlands, New Zealand, Nicaragua, Norway, Pakistan, Panama, Paraguay, Peru, Philippines, Saudi Arabia, Syria, Turkey, Union of South Africa, United Kingdom, United States, Uruguay, Venezuela, Viet Nam. The treaty contains a preamble and 7 chapters, subdivided into 27 articles. Major provisions are as follows:

Chapter 1.—The state of war is terminated, and Japanese sovereignty over Japan and its territorial waters is recognized.

Chapter 2.—Japan recognizes the independence of Korea; renounces claims to Formosa, Pescadores, Kurils, Southern Sakhalin and adjacent islands, any part of Antarctica, and Spratly and Paracel Islands; renounces claims in connection with the League of Nations mandates system and accepts the United Nations ruling extending the trusteeship system to Pacific Islands formerly under her mandate; and agrees to any United States proposal to place under the United Nations trusteeship system, with the United States as sole administering authority, the Ryukyus south of latitude 29°N., the Nanpo Shoto south of Sofu Gan, and Parece Vela and Marcus Island.

Chapter 3.—Japan accepts obligations of Article 2 of the United Nations Charter. The Allied powers recognize Japan's right of self-defense and right to enter into collective security arrangements. Occupation forces shall be withdrawn within 90 days after the treaty goes into effect, but this provision shall not prevent retention of foreign armed forces as result of other agreements.

Chapter 4.—Within one year after treaty has come into force between it and Japan, each of the Allied powers will notify Japan which of its prewar treaties it wishes kept in force. Japan renounces all special rights and interests in China. She agrees to enter promptly into negotiations with the Allied powers for the conclusion of fishing agreements and for agreements relating to international civil air transport. Japan accepts the judgments of the International Military Tribunal for the Far East and other Allied war crimes courts and will carry out sentences imposed on those Japanese nationals imprisoned in Japan. She declares her readiness to enter promptly into negotiations with each of the Allied powers to place commercial relations on a stable basis, meanwhile according them most-favored-nation treatment.

Chapter 5.—The treaty recognizes Japan's lack of capacity to make complete reparations for damages and still maintain a viable economy, but provides that Japan shall enter promptly into negotiations with a view to assisting to compensate the countries she occupied during the war by making available the services of the Japanese people. Japan must return all Allied property held in Japan during the war; transfer assets held in neutral countries during the war to members of the Allied armed forces who suffered undue hardships while prisoners of war of Japan; and reaffirm liability for prewar external debt.

Chapter 6.—Disputes arising concerning the treaty that are not otherwise settled shall be referred to the International Court of Justice.

Chapter 7.—The treaty will come into force for all states that have ratified it when it has been ratified by Japan and a majority, including the United States, of the following powers: Australia, Canada, Ceylon, France, Indonesia, the Netherlands, New Zealand, Pakistan, the Philippines, and the United Kingdom. No benefits, with certain exceptions, shall be conferred on any state not signing the treaty. Japan will be prepared to make a separate peace treaty with any state that signed or adhered to the United Nations Declaration of Jan. 1, 1942, and is still in a state of war with her and has not signed this treaty, but this obligation on the part of Japan expires within three years after this treaty comes into force.

Foreign Relations (1952–1954).—Japan's foreign relations following the restoration of her sovereignty has been dominated by problems arising from her special relation to the United States and the absence of normal relations with many of her Asian neighbors. Basic to these problems is the struggle between the Communist and non-Communist powers, in which Japan is aligned on the side of the latter. In this situation, Japan has sought to adjust, but not substantially to alter, her special relation to the United States in order to permit her to assume the position of a major power in Asia.

Relations with the United States.—The United States has continued to exert a predominant influence on Japanese affairs in the post treaty period. Japan is dependent on the United States for defense against external aggression, on a high level of United States expenditures in Japan to support her economy, and on United States support of her efforts to gain admittance to international organizations and acceptance in the counsels of the major powers.

The United States-Japan Security Treaty of 1951 provides that United States forces will remain in Japan until it is mutually agreed that United Nations or other regional security arrangements provide for Japan's defense. The security treaty is not only a United States guarantee to defend Japan, but is considered by many Asian countries as a guarantee against a renewal of Japanese aggression. Aside from the National Security Corps of less than 150,000 men, Japan had no armed forces until 1954. There was much debate over whether the constitution of 1947 permitted Japan to have military forces and much discussion over whether Japan's already weak economy could support such forces. At the same time, many elements in Japan realized that the nation must prepare to defend itself, and believed that the continued presence of United States forces limited Japan's freedom of action. On its part, the United States was anxious that Japan build up adequate defense forces so that United States forces could be withdrawn. To this end negotiations for United States aid under a mutual defense assistance agreement began in the summer of 1953. An agreement was signed by the two countries on March 8, 1954, and on June 2 the Diet passed bills creating a limited army, navy, and air force as of July 1, 1954.

The high level of United States expenditures in Japan is expected to decline in proportion to the decrease in United States forces in both Korea and Japan. Japan must therefore renew her efforts to find new outlets for her production and cheaper sources for her raw materials if she is to attain a volume of foreign trade necessary to support a viable economy.

While Japan realizes that self-interest dictates a continuance of her dependence on the United States for some time, she also seeks to achieve at least as much freedom of action and equality of treatment in her relations with the United States as the nations of western Europe have maintained. Thus, after the United States and the other members of the North Atlantic Treaty Organization (NATO) agreed that national rather than United States courts would have jurisdiction in crimes committed by United States military personnel and civilian employees off duty and their dependents stationed in NATO countries, Japan sought and obtained a similar agreement on Sept. 28, 1953. Since the restoration of her sovereignty, Japan has cooperated in maintaining controls over her trade with Communist China, and in fact has maintained stricter controls than any other major trading nation except the United States and Canada. In view of Japan's commercial trade deficit, which amounted to $1,134,804,000 in 1953, however, the Japanese government has been under increasing economic and political pressure to relax its controls down to the multilaterally agreed level.

The peace treaty stripped Japan of her overseas territories, but in the case of the Ryukyu Islands permitted Japan to retain residual sovereignty, at the same time making it possible for the United States as administering authority to place these islands under a United Nations trusteeship system. On Dec. 24, 1953, the United States returned to Japan the Amami-gunto (Amami Islands), part of the Ryukyu group lying between Japan and Okinawa.

Relations with Other Asian Countries.—The Japanese Peace Treaty was ratified by the United States, the powers of western Europe, a number of Latin American countries, and in Asia by Pakistan, the Associated States of Indochina, and Ceylon. Nationalist China and India signed bilateral peace treaties with Japan in 1952. The other Asian nations either did not sign the Japanese Peace Treaty or have failed to ratify it. In Asia, Japan has been concerned with establishing normal relations with the Philippines, Indonesia, Burma, and South Korea. She has also been concerned with working out a *modus vivendi* with Communist China and the USSR that would at least permit expanded trade relations.

A major obstacle to Japan's renewal of relations with the Philippines, Indonesia, and Burma is the amount and type of Japan's reparations payments. Article 14 of the peace treaty recognizes that Japan's resources are not sufficient to make complete reparation possible, but Japan does agree to enter into negotiations to assist in compensating for the damage done "by making available the services of the Japanese people in production, salvaging and other work. . . ." In negotiations with these countries, Japan has maintained the position that her economy will support only modest payments and that these payments should be made in services rather than by goods. The Philippines and Indonesia particularly have insisted on reparations in excess of the amount which the Japanese economy can afford and have preferred that these payments be made in goods rather than services. It was not until 1954 that Japan indicated that it might be possible to make payments in goods as well as services. Although the gulf between the reparations offered and reparations demanded narrowed somewhat and a tentative agreement was reached with the Philippines in April 1954, subsequent negotations with that country were deadlocked, and talks with Indonesia were halted.

Negotiations for the establishment of normal relations between Japan and South Korea began in October 1951, but by mid-1954 the two powers were still far from agreement. The principal issues are fishing rights, property claims, and the status of Koreans in Japan. On Jan. 18, 1952, the Republic of Korea proclaimed the Rhee Line, which coincided roughly with that part of the MacArthur Line between Japan and the Asian mainland which SCAP had drawn around the Japanese home islands early in the occupation to restrict Japanese movements. The South Korean government announced that no Japanese vessels could cross to the mainland side of the line, which at some points was over 100 miles from the Korean coast. The Japanese fishing fleet was thus cut off from some of its most important fishing areas. Furthermore, South Korean naval vessels seized Japanese vessels and cargoes and tried the crews in Korean courts. Japan demanded the elimination of these restrictions, while South Korea insisted that they were needed to protect the area's marine resources.

Property claims of both sides are also unresolved. South Korea demands the return of all assets in Japan alleged to be of Korean origin, while Japan demands compensation for private Japanese property seized in Korea. The Republic of Korea maintains that Koreans residing in Japan who obtained Japanese citizenship before the war can renounce it and obtain Korean citizenship, but that if they elect to reside in Japan they are entitled to all the privileges accorded to Japanese citizens plus the immunities accorded to foreign nationals. Japan is willing to guarantee equal treatment to Japanese citizens of Korean origin, but contends that citizens of the Republic of Korea who reside in Japan should be treated the same as other foreign nationals.

The USSR, which did not sign the Japanese Peace Treaty, has not re-established normal relations with Japan. In order to undermine the firm anti-Soviet policies of the Japanese government, however, it has made such overtures as returning additional Japanese prisoners and offering limited trade opportunities to private Japanese groups. A small barter trade has been carried on, and there have been discussions between Soviet representatives and private Japanese fishing interests on fishing in northern waters.

The long history of intercourse between Japan and the Chinese mainland, the potential markets for Japanese goods, and the proximity of cheap raw materials exert constant pressure on the Japanese government to develop a *modus vivendi* with the Chinese Communists. Private barter agreements were negotiated in 1952 and 1953, but the volume of this trade has been insignificant and restricted in scope by both governments. Japan has reduced the list of items embargoed in her trade with Communist China, but this has not appreciably increased the volume of the trade. The Chinese Communists have maintained a prospect of unlimited trading opportunities before the Japanese while setting up conditions which the Japanese cannot meet. Specifically, they demand that Japan withdraw recognition from Nationalist China, lift the trade embargo against Communist China, and discontinue building up its military forces with United States aid. Japanese hopes for normal relations have been fanned by the small increase in trade between the two countries, by the repatriation of some Japanese long detained in China, and by permission for a few private groups to travel in China.

Bibliography.—Department of State, *Activities of the Far Eastern Commission*, report by the secretary general (Washington 1947); Martin, E. M., *The Allied Occupation of Japan* (New York 1948); Department of State, *Activities of the Far Eastern Commission*, second report by the secretary general (Washington 1949); id., *Occupation of Japan: Policy and Progress* (Washington 1949); General Headquarters, Supreme Commander for the Allied Powers, Government Section, *Political Reorientation of Japan, September 1945–September 1948* (Washington 1950); Fearey, R. A., *The Occupation of Japan; Second Phase: 1948–50* (New York 1950).

JANE M. ALDEN,
Foreign Affairs Analyst, United States Department of State.

NOTE: The foregoing 23 articles on Japan were prepared under the joint direction of the editors of THE ENCYCLOPEDIA AMERICANA and Dr. Hugh Borton, professor of Japanese and director of the East Asian Institute, Columbia University.

JAPAN, Bank of. See JAPAN—*Financial Development.*

JAPAN CURRENT. See KUROSHIO; JAPAN—*Natural Resources.*

JAPAN LILY, the name given to several lilies, including *Lilium auratum,* which has white flowers with crimson spots; *Lilium japonicum,* which has rose or light pink flowers; and *Lilium speciosum,* a white, rose-tinted variety with rose-red spots.

JAPAN WAX. See WAX.

JAPANESE AND ORIENTAL ARMS AND ARMOR. Nippon's upper classes have, from the very distant past, shown a depth of study and reverence for the fashioning of arms and armor, including a complex etiquette, that amounts to a military cult. Their Samurai were fighting nobles devoted to military achievement as a career. Their warriors (*bushi*) lived in religious devotion to their martial ethics—termed *bushido.*

Armor (*Yoroi*).—The earliest armor was of sheepskin or oxhide, later (before the 7th century) it was of leather. By the 7th century iron armor was in use; this was a corselet of iron plates riveted together, a flaring skirt of metal, leather guards for shoulders and the upper arm and a conical helmet. By the 16th century guns were introduced, but the ethics of warriors upheld the use of their revered longbow and arrows (so inseparable was the bow and arrow in their ideals that *yumi-ya* is synonym of both), and their religiously reverenced sword (*katana*). And the light and loose-hanging armor continued in constant use, conservatively retaining the same parts though subject to changes in fashion. The headpiece (*kabuto*) consists of three parts: the *hachi* or skull, the *shikoro* or articulated neck protector, and the *maye-zashi* or peak. At the sides are curved wing-pieces (*fuki-gayeshi*), sometimes part of the *shikoro.* Varieties of the *hachi* are: *dzu nari* and *saku nari* (shaped like the crown of the head), *mono nari* (peach shaped), *tokamuri* (form of the *kamuri* ceremonial hat), *kimen* (demon's head), *shii nari* (nut shaped), *toppai* (tall conical form flattened at sides). The bowl (*hachi*) is of iron or hard-lacquered leather in a single piece or of riveted strips. The *tatami kabuto* (folding helmet) is constructed of loosely joined articulate circlets capable of closing up more or less flat. The ordinary *hachi's* outer surface is composed of numerous elongated triangular ribs running from the lower rim to the socket surrounding the opening in the apex. The outer rim of this socket is termed *hachiman-za,* and is sacred to the god of war and used for occult decoration, often an embossed or engraved conventional chrysanthemum (*kikumon*), when it is called *kiku-za.* A silk cloth sometimes closed this opening against the weather and was fastened by strings to four metal knobs called *shi-tenbiyo* (four Dêva knobs). For higher ranks are added quarterings in gold and silver in bands extending from the *hachimanza* to the back and front, sometimes also to the sides, thus dividing the helmet ornamentally into two, four or eight parts (termed respectively *kata-jiro, shiho-jiro, happo-jiro*). Small holes on four sides allow thin leather strips to connect with the inside cap. The *shikoro* (neck defense) consists of either three, five, six or seven laminated metal plates or stiff leather of a curved form fastened together with silk cords. In some examples the laminations consist of small metal scales (*kozane*), 100 to 136 in a row. The inner side of the *shikoro* is usually coated with bright red lacquer (said to reflect fierce color on the warrior's face). The before-mentioned *fuki-gayeshi* (curved wing pieces) at the sides are generally fastened to the edge of the *shakoro* plates and curl round projecting at the sides. They are generally covered with ornamented leather and a decorated border, the center having the metal crest of the wearer. The right side piece is sometimes hinged to be movable when the bow is in action. The peaks or frontlets (*maye-hashi*) are inside of gilt, red lacquer, or lined with red leather, usually with a metal border. Each has a three-branched metal socket (*harai-date*); in the center is a dragon or crest form (*mayedate*), and on either side are placed curved hornlike metal branches (*tsunamoto*), broad and thin with foliated ends. Behind the *hachi* is a decorated brass ring from which to hang a thick tasseled silk cord (*kasajirushi no kuwan*) hanging in bow form behind, used sometimes for attaching the *kasajirushi,* a white cloth badge worn as distinguishing mark in battle. In some helmets is another similar ring above this one for attaching the *horo,* a large bag, filled with cotton or stretched on wicker-work frame, hung at the back for the protection of cavalry from arrow-shots. Besides crests (*mayedate*) other badges (*wakidate* and *ushiro-date*) are sometimes worn on the sides or back. The face is protected by a visor (*menko* or *saku-bo*) separate from the helmet and attached by strings; it is a metal mask covering the whole features (then termed *mempo*) with eye and nostril perforations, or only covering the cheeks and portion below the nose (then termed *ho-ate*). The masks are named according to the character of the features, as: *tsubame-bo* (swallow-face), *suru-bo* (monkey-face), *okina-men* (old-man's face), *shiwadzura* (wrinkled face), *waradzura* (young boy's face), etc. The *menko* is generally made of one piece, except the nose and upper lip covering which is generally detachable for eating and drinking. Two small holes with metal tubes near the bottom of the mask give egress for perspiration. Hair of the wild boar, horse or deer are furnished for the upper lip, chin and cheeks, usually, but they are sometimes painted. Deep wrinkles appear, sometimes, on the cheeks to prevent a weapon slipping over the smooth surface into the eyehole. Knobs afford hold for the fastening cords. A kind of gorgette (*yodare-gane* or *yodare-kake* or *yen-u*) hangs from the bottom of the *menko* made of either laminated plates, leather, or chain mail and widening gradually toward the bottom. The Japanese had a half-helmet (*han buri*) or skull cap of leather or metal worn instead of the *kabuto,* some reaching to the temples, some only covering the crown. The former consisted of several hinged plates, and had ear-holes and a hole on top for the tuft of hair, and was covered with leather, the ends being used for tying beneath the chin. The Japanese term *do* takes in trunk armor and leg as well as posterior protective parts. The *do-maru* was a corselet opening at the side, the *hotoke-do* was of a single piece of metal wrought into the form of a naked torso. Such pieces are usually black, some covered with shark-skin are termed *same-tsudzumi;* when covered with tortoiseshell, velvet, silk, etc., they are called, respectively, *bekko-tsudzumi, birodo-tsudzumi, moji-tsudzumi,* etc., while those covered with leather (*kawa-tsudzuma*) were given also names according to the styles of leather used such as gilt, blue, lacquered, diapered, etc. Polished brass, iron inlaid with colored or precious metals, were the material of some *do-maru.* Folding corselets (*tatami-do*) had two or four plates (*shinai-kane-no do* and *ni-mai-kane-no do*) hinged at the sides and fastening with clasps and strings. The *hato-mune do* ("pigeon-breasted") corresponded to the bulging "peas-cod" European cuirass. The *oke-gawa do* was a *do-maru* composed of metal or hard leather scales overlapping. The skirt-pieces (*kusadzuri*) depending from the corselet, taking the place of European "taces," in old armor were each in a continuous piece lengthening toward the bottom considerably, the lower part having a central slit to facilitate the movement of the legs. In later armor the *kusadzuri* consisted of a number of taces hanging quite loosely and overlapping; the front portion was divided into three, the back three or four, and one piece at each side. They were laminated plates or scales hung by a row of silk cords. Pieces corresponding to the European "l'palettes" were the *sendan-no-ita,* for the right side, and the *hato-wo-no-ita,* for the left side, protecting the front of the armpits. They are only on old and perfect specimens. Right and left had different shapes, hence different names. The former was a narrow board (3 inches by 9 inches) composed of three plates or rows of scales connected by cords and lined with leather; the *hato-no-wo-ita,* smaller than the other, is an oblong piece of metal or thick lacquered leather having a kind of dove-tailed projection above. Both are suspended from the *wata-gami* (shoulder braces). The *sode* (*epauliè re* in European armor) protected the shoulder and upper arm; it consisted of a broad, slightly convex, piece made of laminated steel plates or imbricated scales and lined with leather, and was suspended from the *wata-gami* by cords of leather. There were several varieties of *sode* such as the *kawara-sode, namban-sode, maru-sode, ha-sode, hiyotan-sode, ki-no-ha-sode,* named according to their make up and shape. The *kote,* in some respects, answers to the European *avant-bras* and *brassart,* being a tight defensive sleeve protecting the entire arm. It was of padded cloth, leather or silk, widening at the mouth, where it fits the shoulder, and was tied by strings round the chest. The *kote* is covered in part by mail with additional metal plates and terminates in a metal hand-guard or semi-gauntlet called *tetsu-gai.* They only cover the front of the arm and are laced behind. The top plate (*kamuri-ita*) covers the shoulder; below is a large metal plate (*gaku-no-ita*) or scales connected by mail to protect the muscles of the upper arm. A circular plate (*hiji-gane*) protects the elbow point. The lower part of the fore arm has long parallel splint-like strips of metal connected by chain mail (the *ikada*) or a single piece of pierced and embossed metal. Attached to this, at bottom, is usually a second plate (*tetsugai*) rounded to fit the shape of the back of the hand above the knuckles. Gloves also were worn. *Kote* varieties: *tsutsu-gote* mail covered and reinforced with plates; *tsugi-gote* shaped more like the *sode,* but smaller. Protecting the thighs, as do European *"cuissards,"* was the *hai-date* hanging loose like a double apron, which was made in different styles known as *ita-hai-date, oboshi-hai-date,* etc. The Japanese defenses for the lower part of the legs (called *sune-ate*) are mostly curved plates formed to the calf and fastened by clasps or strings, like the Greek and Roman greaves. Varieties are *bishamon-sune-ate* made of three continuous metal plates reaching above the knee; *shimotate-sune-ate* made of plates and strips of chain mail alternating; *tsutsu-sune-ate, nivo-sune-ate, kiyahan-sune-ate,* etc. The feet were clad with shoes (*kutsu*) having pointed curved toes for riding or ceremonies, but straw sandals were preferred for marching and fighting. Soles were of stiff leather, uppers of bear's skin. The *jim-bauri* was a kind of tabard or surcoat worn by Japanese warriors over the armor for display.

Arms.—The sword was the Samurai's most valued possession; he called it his "soul." But the longbow and the arrow were always a chief weapon. The long sword (*katana*) was preserved with religious care, wrapped in the finest silks and enclosed, often in the costliest of lacquered and inlaid caskets. Allowing a view of its sheath and blade (Japanese blades are of great perfection and superior to the Western) to a foreigner is a mark of intimate friendship. The short sword (*wakizashi*) and the *katana* were so closely associated as to be considered a "pair" and termed *daisho,* and both had similar mountings and were stuck in the same sheath. A dagger-sword (*tanto*) was also carried. Great artistic talent was expended on the Japanese warrior's sword "furniture": sword-guards (*tsuba*), ferrule-like pommels (*kashiri*), ring-bands (*fuchi*), decorative peg-heads (*me-nuki*), to attach blade to the grip. So lovely is the workmanship of the *tsuba,* depicting life and scenery in marvelous metallic delicacy, that these miniatures in metal (the wealthy carried actual "stocks" for frequent changes of display) are greatly prized by museums and Western connoisseurs, who have numerous large collections. A peculiar instrument was the small knife (*ko-zuka*) with its flat ornamented handle; it was used with remarkable precision for throwing. Skewers (*kogai*) were in the same sheath with the *kozuka,* used for hairpins, also to "tag" the dead victim with the victor's identity. *Pole arms* —The spear was a favorite weapon with the Japanese, who were very skillful in its use, the higher classes having many racks full. One old form was the *hoko,* a guard's spear with six-foot pole and eight-inch blade either leaf-shape or waved (like the Malay *kris*); a sickle-shaped horn projected on one or both sides at the joint of blade. A lance (*yari*) was used by the 14th century with "hog-backed" blade five inches long. The *nagi-nata* had a three-foot long scimiter blade fixed on a slightly longer haft. It was a weapon favored by female warriors. They had halberds also. Spear heads were of beautiful construction. While the Japanese in their feudal warfare did not make much use of firearms they had guns, pistols and cannon, mostly imported by 16th century Portuguese traders. Little development occurred in these arms, and from 1853 when Commodore Perry opened up their ports, they copied European types (revolvers, etc.).

EAST INDIAN

Armor.—Helmet, *top*. Gorget or neckpiece, *kant'hah sobha*. Cuirass, *char-aina* ("four mirrors"), *Peti*. Coat with gorget attached, *bhanju*. Coat of mail, *zirih* or *zirah*. Coat of mail having head and body in single piece, *g'hug'hwah*. Coat worn over the armor (surcoat), *angirk'hah*. Armguard *dastana*. *Horse armor*. *Quashpah*, horse's headpiece.

Arms.—Shields: Ordinary shield, *dhal, maru;* shield made of cane, *udanal*. Spears, pointed at both ends, *tschehontah; sangu, bhala*. Boomarangs, *katariya*. Battleaxes, *tarangaleh* (common axe), *tabar-zaghnol* (pointed, crowbill), *tabar-zaghnol* (double-axe), *shushpar* (globular head), *buckie*. Swords. Scimiter, *baneh, bhelhetah, ayda-katti, khanda, pattisa, pata* (guauntlet sword), *dha* (short sword), *abbasi, gupti* (swordstick — concealed). Sabres: *Talwar, tegha*. Daggers: *Katar* (short dagger), *jamdhar* (ordinary dagger), *jamdhar doulicaneh* (dagger ending in two points), *jamdhar sehlicaneh* (ending in three points), *jambiyah, bank, pichangatti, gupti kard* (long dagger). Bows: *Maktah* (simple bow), *raman* (composite bow), *tarkash, gulel* (pellet bow). Arrows: *Tir* (iron-tipped), *bitla* (hardwood-tipped). Maces. *Gargaz* or *garz*. "Tigerclaw" knuckles, *bag'hnak*. Guns. *Toradar* (matchlocks).

SIAMESE

Arms. — Single-bow, *kasun*. Cross-bow, *thami*. Spear, *hak* (plain spear), *hak sat* (seven feet long, thrown by the foot). Lance or javelin, *khoum* (seven feet long). Swords. *Dass* (long curved sword), *ngao* (curved knife or sword 18 inches long with 6 foot pole). Shields. Oblong, *dang;* round, *lo*.

Malays use a *kris* (undulating dagger or sword) and straight sword.

Persia, Kashmir, Afghanistan, etc. Saber, *samsher*. Sword, *salawar yataghan*. Battleaxe, *tabar*. Daggers, cuirass same as India.

Chinese.—Armor and arms of the Chinese are of little interest. They have had no military caste for many centuries and the little inconsequential armor found is of a "parade" or "costume" form, consisting chiefly of rich vestments with some splints or other reinforcements beneath of little practical defensive value. They used bows and arrows, swords, daggers, maces, etc.

Arab Arms.—The *jambiya* was the characteristic dagger. The sword was termed *khanjar;* shields were circular and oblong, of hippopotamus hide. Maces were of ebony. Guns and pistols are generally decorated (some very beautifully) with arabesque ornament.

See also PLATE ARMOR.

Bibliography.—Conder, J., "The History of Japanese Armor," in Asiatic Society of Japan *Transactions* (Yokohama 1881); Ogawa, K., *Military Costume in Old Japan* (Tokyo 1893); Church, A. H., "The Furniture of the Sword," in Burlington Fine Arts Club *Catalogue* (London 1894); Egerton, W., *A Description of Indian and Oriental Armour* (London 1896); Dean, B., *Catalogue* of Loan Collection of Japanese Armor, in Metropolitan Museum of Art (New York 1903); Hawkshaw, J. C., *Japanese Sword-Mounts* (London 1910); Garbutt, M., "Japanese Armour from the Inside," in Japan Society of London *Transactions* (London 1912–13); Laking, Sir G. F., *Catalogue*, Wallace Collection of Oriental Arms and Armour (London 1914); Boots, J. L., *Korean Weapons and Armor*, Royal Asiatic Society of Great Britain and Ireland (Seoul, Korea, 1934); Stone, G., *Glossary of the Construction, Decoration and Use of Arms and Armor in all Countries and in all Times* (Portland, Maine 1934); Yamagami, H., *Japan's Ancient Armour* (Pasadena, Calif., 1941).

JAPANESE BEETLE (*Popillia japonica* Newm.), an insect native to Japan, which was accidentally introduced into the United States some time prior to 1916, when it was first found by Harry B. Weiss, as a very small infestation near Riverton, New Jersey. Since that time it has continued to spread at a fairly rapid rate and it is now found in most of the northeast states and in isolated infestations east of the Mississippi. The adult beetle is about one-half inch long, about one-fourth inch wide, broadly oval, and shining metallic green. The hard outer wings are coppery brown. There are two small tufts of white hairs just behind the wing covers and five patches along each side of the body. The eggs are elliptical, translucent, one-sixteenth inch to one-eighth inch in diameter, and white or cream colored. The newly hatched larva, or grub, is about one-sixteenth inch in length, has three pairs of legs, and has the general shape of a blunt-ended crescent. When fully grown it is about an inch long. The pupa, or the stage in which the grub transforms to the adult beetle, has a pale-cream to tan color and is about one-half inch long and one-fourth inch wide. The life cycle of this beetle normally requires one year. The larval stage continues from the time the eggs hatch in the summer through the fall and winter and until the latter part of May or early in June of the following year. During the summer and early fall the larvae are mostly in the upper three inches of soil, feeding on plant roots; as winter approaches they go down to a depth of 4 to 8 inches, moving nearer to the surface the following spring.

In the latitude of Philadelphia the first Japanese beetles usually begin to emerge from the soil between June 10 and 20, and in an average season they are present in considerable numbers by July 5. The peak of the feeding season usually occurs the last of July or the early part of August. The normal life of a beetle is from 30 to 45 days, but since all do not emerge at one time, a few may be found as late as October. On warm, sunny days the beetles fly about actively and feed, going from one plant to another. They tend to feed in groups and to feed on certain plants, leaving others untouched. For laying their eggs the beetles prefer medium-moist loamy soil with closely cropped grass, such as is found in lawns, pastures and golf greens and fairways. After burrowing to a depth of two to four inches, the female beetle deposits from one to three or four eggs at one time, usually at night. She then emerges, and after spending several days in feeding, returns to the soil to deposit another lot of eggs. This procedure goes on until a total of from 40 to 60 eggs have been laid.

The injury caused by the feeding of the adult beetle on foliage and fruit is conspicuous. Feeding is confined chiefly to the foliage on the upper and outer parts of plants and trees exposed to bright sunlight and takes place during the warmer part of the day. On cloudy or cool days there is almost no feeding. The beetles consume the tissue between the veins of the leaves, causing the leaves to become wholly or partly skeletonized. As a result preferred food plants in heavily infested areas are often entirely stripped of their foliage. The beetle is also a pest of considerable importance on early-ripening fruits, especially apples, peaches and plums. The feeding on such fruits is often very severe. Beetles also cause much injury to field and sweet corn by feeding on the silk as it grows out from the husk, before pollination takes place. The beetle is known to feed on more than 260 different plants, but most of the injury is confined to a limited number of the more favored species. Favorites are grape leaves, raspberry, both foliage and fruit, apple, cherry, sweet corn, field corn, soybean, rose, foliage, buds and flowers, Virginia creeper, dahlia, hollyhock, marshmallow, zinnia, elm, horsechestnut, linden, Lombardy poplar, Norway maple, willow, and a number of weed and noneconomic plants. The grubs, too, cause frequently severe damage to turf in lawns, parks and pastures. They cut and feed on plant roots causing the grass to die out in patches.

Attempts have been made to introduce natural enemies from the Orient. Among those which have become definitely established and which are important in control are two species of *Tiphia* (parasitic wasps) one of which, from Korea, attacks the grubs in the spring; the other is from Japan and attacks the grubs in the fall. The *Centeter* fly, from Japan, belonging to the family Tachinidae, is parasitic on the adult beetles. It deposits its eggs while the beetles are in flight. Types of bacteria causing "milky disease" of the larvae were discovered in New Jersey and have been extensively cultured. Cultures are available for seeding: bacteria are planted at intervals in heavily infested sod and in some cases the results have been excellent. The European starling feeds on the grubs in spring and autumn and the English sparrow feeds on the adults when they are available. Other birds attacking the pest are grackles, the cardinal, meadowlark and robin. Moles, skunks and pine mice feed on the grubs. Chemical control of the grubs consist of treating sod with arsenate of lead, DDT, chlordane and other chemicals. Traps baited with geraniol and eugenol are used to capture the adults. Spraying of foliage is employed to kill adults.

Consult "The Japanese Beetle and Its Control," United States Farmers Bulletin 1856 (Washington, D.C.).

CHARLES HOWARD CURRAN,
Curator, Department of Insects and Spiders, The American Museum of Natural History.

JAPANESE CERAMICS, the skill of the Japanese as ceramicists has been known to the Occidental world since shortly after 1542 when a Portuguese ship went ashore at Tanegashima, the southernmost point of the Nippon "home islands." This accidental landing brought the first Europeans to Japan. Fairly soon thereafter, western trading ships began calling at Nagasaki and taking back to Europe various Japanese products, including ceramics. Portugal was the first, with Spain and the Netherlands close seconds. For nearly 80 years, under the earlier Tokugawa shoguns, all were welcome. During this period strife developed among these western foreigners which resulted in the Spaniards being expelled in 1624, and the Portuguese in 1638. The Dutch were permitted to stay but were obliged to trade under the most restricted conditions. They were allowed one trading post or factory which was located on Deshima, a small island in the harbor of Nagasaki. Further, the number of trading vessels were rigidly limited. But though the conditions were humiliating, and the men stationed there were virtual prisoners, the Dutch found this trading monopoly very profitable.

The situation continued for over 200 years, or until Commodore Perry's visit in 1853 reopened Japan to foreign trade. During these two centuries of self-imposed isolation, a considerable amount of Japanese ceramics arrived in Europe through the medium of the single Dutch trading post where these wares had a marked influence on Occidental potteries and porcelains. In Holland, examples in underglaze blue were copied by the potters of Delft. At the Meissen porcelain factory the finely decorated pieces done by Kakiyemon were studied and carefully copied, resulting in the Kakiyemon decorations for which Meissen was famous. These in turn were copied by contemporary French factories as well as by Chelsea and other English porcelain producers.

Another Japanese porcelain, made solely for export, was of great influence, especially on Worcester and Derby china. Known as the Imari or Japanese pattern, many handsome dinner services were produced by both factories during the late 18th and early 19th centuries. This Japanese Imari porcelain was also the inspiration for the Staffordshire "gaudy Dutch." But though their ceramics and the artistry with which they were decorated had a powerful impact on European porcelains and earthenwares, practically nothing was known about how or where they were made until the Paris Exhibition of 1867. At this, the Japanese display included fine examples of antique earthenwares and porcelains. They attracted attention and since then have been studied extensively. As the result, it is now known that there were potteries making earthenware in at least 24 provinces and that the production of porcelains was carried on in some six different provinces. Not any of these, previous to the industrialization of Japan in the second half of the 19th century, were extensive establishments, like that at Ching-te-Chen (Fowliang since 1931) in China. They were small ventures, built around the accomplishments of some master of the potting arts or some gifted amateur and made possible by the patronage of an important feudal lord.

In some instances, like the pottery at Seto in the old province of Owari, the venture was continued by gifted descendants of the founder for generations and each one was known by the same name, as Toshire I, Toshire II, Toshire III, etc. In others, as happened at the Karatsu pottery in Hizen Province, the nucleus might consist of a group of Korean potters brought back to Japan by officers in the army of the great conqueror Toyotomi Hideyoshi (1536–1598).

As far as the Japanese were concerned, porcelains ranked a poor second to the finest of their earthenwares as works of art. As with the Imari, their porcelains were often made for export and shaping and decoration were studied attempts to approximate what Japanese potters and decorators thought were the European tastes. In fact, after the western industrialization of Japan was firmly established and large ceramic factories built in the larger cities, such as Kobe, Tokyo, and Osaka, quantities of earthenwares and porcelains were produced in the Japanese manner but adapted for foreign trade.

Although the Japanese are considered by many Occidentals as one of the most gifted pottery-making people in the world, their actual accomplishments in that art were all based on borrowings from, and copying of, the achievements of Asiatic mainland neighbors, the Chinese and Koreans. Further, the special provenance or origin of a given piece of Japanese earthenware or porcelain is by no means easy to determine. From about 1250 on and especially during the 18th and 19th centuries, the various Japanese potteries continuously copied each others' wares and decorative designs. In addition, some of the highly regarded wares of previous generations were reproduced at other places and so cleverly done that today experts are sometimes at a loss as to whether a specific example was made at the place where it originated or is a later revival, made elsewhere by a master potter who was an admirer of the older ware.

Then too, with the introduction of porcelain making about 1650, some of the better-known potteries produced both earthenware and the newer porcelain. Those in or near Kyoto, especially, made stonewares and porcelains in considerable variation. A large proportion of collectible antique wares were marked but the copying habit was present even here. Not only were the marks of potteries and master potters copied by others but even some of the master potters at times marked their pieces with Ming and other established Chinese marks. Therefore a Japanese ceramic mark is not always reliable proof of origin. Also, the identities of some of the best Japanese ceramic craftsmen are obscured because of their custom of using either their family name or totally different art names. An example is the Taizan family, long active in potting at Kyoto. Beginning about 1680, they used the art name of *Yohei* and later, during the 18th century, changed to *Baikei*. Finally, not all of the wares were always decorated at the pottery where they were made. Some were sent as blanks to such cities as Tokyo where there were large decorating shops, similar to those of Canton where so much of the Chinese porcelains intended for exportation was decorated.

Unlike the Chinese, the Japanese were not established workers in ceramics before the start of their recorded history. Nevertheless, there are evidences that some Nipponese pottery was made as early as the 1st century B.C. and continued for some five or six centuries. These earliest examples were small unglazed figures of horses, boats, men in armor and the like. Their discovery occurred in the course of excavating grave sites that antedate 700 A.D. These rude and crude burial pieces are considered by experts to show strong Chinese or Siberian influences. They are the first indication that the art of pottery making reached Japan from the Asiatic mainland and was not indigenous to the home islands of Honshu, Shikoku, Kyushu, and Hokkaido.

After 700 A.D., broadly taken as the beginning of recorded pottery making in Japan, some useful earthenware pieces were made in Nippon potteries located here and there. Judging from the limited number of examples still extant, these closely resembled Chinese pottery of the T'ang period and undoubtedly at first were the work of Chinese craftsmen. During the 8th and 9th centuries, there were sizeable migrations from China to Japan of potters as well as Buddhist priests. During this two-century span the Japanese liberally adopted Chinese culture, customs and literature. As a result, the earthenware with mottled glaze then made in Japan closely resembled, if it did not copy, that made in China.

Following this, there were no outstanding developments in Japanese pottery throughout the Early Heian (784–897) and the Late Heian (897–1184) periods save that the Nipponese potters made their wares with a marked ornateness and elaboration and began to use some gilding. Buddhist religious figures with multiple pairs of arms and ornate decoration characterized Japanese pottery and native artistic restraint so apparent in later ceramics was completely lacking.

With the Kamakura period, which lasted for close to two centuries (1185–1333), the culture of the Sung dynasty that ruled China from 960 to 1279 A.D. became manifest in Japanese ceramics and continued to make its influence felt for close to another century. This was the time of Kato Shirazaemon, first outstanding native potter. About 1223 a priest named Doyen is believed to have taken him to China to study the work of potters of the Sung period, then more popular in Japan than they were at home. In time this student potter returned, became known as Toshiro I and began to put in practice what he had learned. He established a pottery in Owari Province. Here, working with a purplish clay brought from China, he produced thin walled pieces that were turned on a wheel and finished first with an even brown glaze and then so covered by a black glossy one as to show streaks and spots. Later, Toshiro I had a pottery at Seto in the same province where he used native gray clay and finished the pieces with a reddish-brown underglaze and a brilliant black overglaze.

Such pieces are called Old Seto. The town itself was the first important pottery center. Here flourished his successors, Toshiro II and Toshiro III, who made the Old Seto ware, chiefly known from later pieces similar to it. They were followed by other masters who worked in Seto and nearby towns until the end of the 19th century. One of the towns was Nagoya, best-known for the work of the 19th century potter Oki Toyosuke. He originated an earthenware with a white opaque crackled glaze decorated with green spots.

Toward the close of this period or early in the Askikaga (1338–1573) the tea ceremony became an established part of Japanese life. This too was of Chinese origin as the ancient tea testing competition in which individual tea bowls were wagered as to which dried first or remained moist longest after the tea in them had been drunk simultaneously by the owners. The Japanese changed this wagering contest into a formal ceremony, governed by strict rules of behavior, which is still a vital part of their social life. The host generally does not invite more than four guests. The ceremony is conducted in a small room about nine feet square, entered not from the house but from the garden. The door is so low that one enters on hands and knees. The tea ceremony equipment is always austerely simple for the idea is to show the best of taste by using inexpensive materials. The individual parts may be of great age. All follow the designs established before the 16th century. Aside from the iron kettle in which the tea water is boiled, the iron chopsticks for handling the charcoal and the bamboo dipper for the hot water, the pieces are of stoneware. They consist of the brazier or *hure* over which the water is heated, a small jar for the powdered green tea, called a *chaire,* an incense box or *kogo,* a tray or *sara,* a water jar or *takatori,* and tea bowls, called *chawan.* The host serves each guest separately. A small amount of the powdered tea is put directly into the tea bowl and hot water added. The contents are then stirred with a bamboo splint until it froths and the guest drinks his bowl of tea in three and a half sips, sucking it audibly to show keen enjoyment as well as showing the proper expression of delight. Throughout the ceremony, the water in the kettle is kept simmering to give the illusion of wind blowing through pine trees. There are no decorative accessories in the room other than a small tea screen, painted with a stylized landscape, and a few flowers arranged in a vase or single art object. The flower arrangement is placed on a little platform or *takanoma,* standing about six inches from the floor. Tea ceremony flower arrangements are designed to be used only once and young Japanese women spend a major part of their lives learning how to do them.

During the Momoyama period (1574–1602) came the Korean potters. Under the conquering general Hideyoshi, who rose from a humble groom to be Japan's military hero, Korea was subjugated and on their return a number of his generals brought with them trained Korean potters. These were settled under their patronage in various of the leading pottery towns. Here they soon introduced pottery shapes and wares that had been made for many years in their native land. Karatsu in Hizen Province was one of the important places where these Koreans were located. At first their pieces were probably pure Korean, including the *mishima* or inlayed type which the Japanese named *Oku-Korai* or Old Korean. Later, at the same place, these captive potters or their descendants developed several special wares known as *Chosen Karatsu.* One was made of blue-black clay and had a glaze resembling cast iron. Another with a green, black or brown glaze was streaked with an overglaze of olive green or white. There was also the painted Karatsu where the glaze was swiftly and crudely touched with strokes of brown or black overglaze.

Finally, there was a finer but similar ware produced for the princes of Hizen as presentation pieces. It was made of a fine yellow or brown clay, finished with a transparent crackle glaze combined with mishima inlay and called *Kenjo-Karatsu.* Other Korean potters were settled in Chikuzen Province. They made tea ceremony stoneware pieces with a dull brown, yellow or black spotted glaze and another ware having a golden brown glaze that was largely used for making ceremony tea jars. Still other Korean potters worked at Kyoto. One of them, Ameya, had a son named Chojiro who before his death, about 1610, was presented with a golden seal by the conqueror Hideyoshi. It was cut with the character *raku* meaning contentment. Chojiro developed his raku ware of a coarse, lightly fired clay shaped by hand into thick-walled bowls with carved or scraped surfaces. This ware was first glazed in black, then red or green and, finally, a straw yellow or even white. It was especially used for making tea bowls since it did not transmit heat readily. Many copies have been and still are being made of the raku ware. Members of the family are reported to be even now making it and marking it with the same presentation seal.

Satsuma, best-known of all the earthenwares, was also originated by a Korean working in Japan. The Prince of Satsuma (Saigo Takamori) was the patron of the pottery of the same name, located on the Island of Kyushu where Koreans had worked from sometime in the 15th century. Toward the end of the 16th century, the then ruling Prince of Satsuma induced 17 more Koreans to come to work in his pottery. They soon scattered but not before one of them named Boku Heii discovered nearby deposits of a fine white clay. From it he made a finely crackled cream ware. Then, working with another potter, named Kanyu, from about 1640, the first white Satsuma resulted. It was a fine ware without decoration but covered with an ivory colored, very finely crackled glaze.

Most of this new ware was made at the nearby pottery at Tadeno in the same province and was also controlled by the prince whose name the ware has borne ever since. As these Korean workers left the Satsuma pottery, they took with them knowledge of how to make this special ware and in time it was produced in a number of different potteries, such as Chosa, Awata, and Ota. Old Satsuma stands foremost and surpassed all the other earthenwares. The pieces are small and the modeling fine. The color ranges from cream to old ivory but the glaze always has a very fine crackle. Later some of the pieces were decorated with raised ornaments and overglaze enamel colors. Brocaded Satsuma, so-called because the decoration simulates the design of a fine piece of silk brocade, was first made at the pottery in Chosa.

Other variations of Satsuma had the same crackled glaze but occurred in such colors as apple-green, straw-yellow, a pure black and sometimes black dusted with gold. In the 19th century, especially the latter half, examples of Satsuma or imitations of it were made for export. Artistically they rank very low since such ornaments as dragons, peacocks, the phoenix and human figures were added. These examples were largely produced in factories located chiefly in Osaka, Tokyo, and Kobe.

Besides the Korean craftsmen, there were a number of outstanding potters of native Japanese stock during the 17th century. The two who are best-known worked in Kyoto. Ogata Kenzan who lived from 1663 to 1743 was a potter, a poet, painter and master of the Tea Ceremony. He decorated his wares with flowers, landscapes, birds, trees and occasionally figures. His decorations were rendered with the fewest possible brush strokes and in a few simple colors. He was constantly varying his style and had many followers. The Japanese have always revered his work. Today there are collectors of Kenzan examples in all parts of the world though some of their pieces are "in the style of Kenzan" rather than genuine examples. The other great ceramic artist was Ninsei who worked about ten years some time before 1640. An artist and amateur potter, it is said that he could make any type of pottery though he is best known for his yellow or gray crackle glazed pieces with a circular mesh on which he painted flowers or ornamental patterns in red, silver, gold and other enamel colors, always simply done. Some pieces bearing his mark are still extant and are among the most costly of all Japanese ceramics.

In the 18th century the artistic quality of Japanese earthenwares began to deteriorate. Possibly this was because the best artists were modeling and decorating porcelains and those of artisan grade concerned themselves chiefly with making copies of the work of earlier masters. Consequently many 18th century earthenware pieces and most of those produced in the 19th century fall far short of the artistic standards that had prevailed earlier and are generally ignored by well-informed collectors and museum curators.

JAPANESE PORCELAINS

Porcelains were not made in Japan until the beginning of the 16th century. The first Japanese potter to work in this ware was Gorodayu go Shonzui who lived in Hizen Province. It is stated that he went to China and worked for five years in the potteries at Ching-te-Chen. Having learned all he could he returned home, bringing with him specimens of Chinese blue and white porcelain and a supply of the necessary kaolin and petuntse. On reaching home he produced a limited quantity of porcelain which closely resembled the Chinese but when his supplies were exhausted he had to stop work. Nothing further was accomplished until the opening years of the 17th century when a Korean potter named Risampei who was settled in Hizen Province discovered deposits of kaolin and petuntse near Arita, another potting center in the same province.

Porcelain kilns were then established about 1610. First located at Hyakken, they were later moved to Arita to be near the source of supplies. It is believed that a limited amount of blue and white porcelain was made here but not until nearly 40 years later was porcelain making undertaken seriously, as the result of the initiative of Kakiyemon, great Japanese maker and decorator of porcelain mentioned earlier, and his companion Tokuemon. They intended to go to China to learn the secrets of enamel colors but in Nagasaki the captain of a Chinese junk gave them the information and they returned to Arita. Kakiyemon soon perfected the beautiful type of decorating that is still known by his name and his porcelains not only became well-known in Japan but were used as models at Meissen and other European factories.

After this success at Arita other works were established at Nabeshima and Mikawachi, also in Hizen Province, which were under the control of such powerful feudal lords as the Prince of Nabeshima. At all three places a sizeable amount of fine porcelains were produced in a comparatively short time. Other porcelain factories sprang up in the provinces of Kyoto, Owari, and Kaga. They all tried to duplicate the porcelains of Hizen Province. Prince Maeda who controlled the pottery at Enuma in Kaga Province sent one of his master workmen, Goto Saijiro, to Arita to learn their secrets of porcelain making and decorating. He came back with the desired information and porcelains were made at Enuma from the latter part of the 17th century until about 1750. These are now called Kutani.

Early Japanese porcelains varied somewhat in the quality of body and glaze but modeling was always done with restraint and decorations were either delicately drawn designs done underglaze in blue or with overglaze enamels handled in excellent good taste. Since the Japanese greatly admired the Chinese celadon wares, these were often used as models for porcelain shapes.

The dominant characteristic of Japanese porcelain was its reticence of coloring and design. The composition of decoration always had high artistic merit and was kept well within bounds. Consequently decorative exuberance was virtually unknown except for the Imari ware which was made for export. With this the decoration was planned and executed to adhere to the suggestions of Dutch traders. Popularity of Imari pieces when they reached Europe indicates that these traders knew the European taste of the time better than some present-day experts who have little good to say about Imari ware.

In general all Japanese porcelains of the 17th, 18th and early part of the 19th centuries were of a very hard paste. The glaze had a slightly bluish tint and decorations were striking and effective in color and design. Figures and landscapes were seldom used; those often employed were the crane, symbol of prosperity, the tortoise for longevity, the lion for valor and other animals, birds and fish, all were delineated with great simplicity. Flowers and trees were frequently used as decorations carefully posed and executed. In addition to blue used for underglaze decoration, the chief colors of overglaze enamels were a thick opaque Indian red, a light tone of yellow, sometimes with a grayish tinge and a green that tends to have a bluish cast. Another distinguishing mark whereby Japanese antique porcelains can be recognized are the three slightly rough spur marks found on the underside of each piece. These were caused by the spurs or thin rods of clay on which the pieces rested during firing.

Besides the usual porcelain, Japanese factories also produced very thin eggshell porcelain. It was first made at Mikochi in Hizen Province where it was decorated with underglaze blue. It was later made elsewhere and in the 19th century was decorated with figures of women and warriors done usually in gold, red and blue. These figures are sometimes covered by a very fine network.

The artistic quality of porcelains was maintained throughout the 18th and well into the 19th centuries. Among the outstanding artists who decorated porcelains after 1800 were Rokubei, father and son of Kyoto; Zengoro, also of Kyoto, whose reputation rests on his gold brocade and gold pattern on red ground, considered in Japan as among the most precious; Tamikichi of Seto in Owari Province who was backed by the Prince of Owari and had a number of fine decorators working under him. Also there was the important factory at Enuma in Kaga Province which suspended in 1868 but reopened and by 1885 employed some 2,700 workers. Of the well-known factories, that at Arita is reported to have resumed operation under the United States occupation of Japan and is again making fine quality porcelain, more for export than for home consumption.

Bibliography.—Audsley, G. A., and Bowes, J. L., *Keramic Art of Japan* (London 1881); Eberlein, H. D., and Ramsdell, R. W., *The Practical Book of Chinaware* (Philadelphia 1925); Cox, W. E., *The Book of Pottery and Porcelain* (New York 1944); Honey, W. B., *Dresden China* (London 1934); Bond, H. L., *An Encyclopedia of Antiques* (Boston 1937).

JAPANNING, the art of giving a brilliant finish to a surface by applying several coats of varnish, dried and hardened so as to be fixed. The article to be japanned is first brushed over with two or three coats of priming. It is then covered with varnish, previously mixed with a pigment of the tint desired. This is called the ground color; and if the subject is to exhibit a design, the objects are painted upon it in colors mixed with varnish, and used in the same manner as for oil-painting. The whole is then covered with additional coats of transparent varnish, dried or baked on and polished. The process is subject to considerable variations, being a combination of painting and partial enameling. See LACQUERS, INDUSTRIAL; VARNISH.

JAPHETH, jā'fĕth, a son of Noah and progenitor of the branch of the human race called Japhetic, born when his father had attained his 500th year (Genesis 5:32). For his act of filial respect to his father (Genesis 9:23-27) he received the latter's blessing and promise of future enlargement, when his descendants would extend over the world, and Canaan to be his as well as Shem's servant. Married before the Flood, he and his wife were saved in the ark. The birth of his seven sons occurred after the Deluge (Genesis 10:1). The name has been variously explained. According to Genesis 9:27, it is derived from an Aramaic root, signifying "to expand," in allusion to the wide expansion of Japheth's descendants in the west of Europe, and the north of Asia, including Armenians, Medes, Greeks, Thracians, and so forth. Others trace it to the root "fair," in reference to the light complexion of his posterity. The former derivation has most in his favor. Arab legend invests Japheth with wondrous powers, and mentions 11 of his sons as founders of as many Asiatic nations. But the gift of imagination was not given to rabbinical and Mohammedan writers alone. Some more modern authors seek to identify Japheth with the Iapetus (q.v.) of Greek fable (Margoliouth, G., in Hasting's *Dictionary of the Bible*), whose wife, Asia, bore Prometheus, civilization's founder. The word, too, has been loosely employed by some philologists in the term Japhetic or Indo-European languages, in contradistinction to Semitic and Hamitic. The homiletical tendencies of the rabbis are exemplified in the Midrashic comment on Genesis 9:1, when God blessed Noah and his sons. In blessing Japheth He promised that all his sons should be white and gave as their portion deserts and fields.

JAPIKS, jä'pĭks, **Gijsbert**, Frisian poet: b. Bolsward, 1603; d. 1666. He was carefully educated and became a schoolmaster at Bolsward. He made translations from French verse and also wrote a number of versions of the Psalms. His original verse was exceptionally meritorious and did much to restore the Frisian dialect to its place in literature. His *Friesche Rymlerye* (1668), was edited by Epkema (Leeuwarden 1821; with vocabulary and grammar, 1825).

Consult Halbertsma, Joost and Eeltje, *Hulde aan Gijsbert Japiks* (Bolsward 1824; Leeuwarden 1827).

JARARACA, zhä-rȧ-rä'kȧ, venomous South American serpent of the crotaloid family, classified as *Lachesis jararaca, Bothrops jararaca,* and also as *Trimeresurus jararaca,* a closely allied species being the labaria, *Trimeresurus atrox,* from which it is almost indistinguishable. The jararaca ranges from the Amazon regions southward to São Paulo and westward to Peru and Ecuador. The color is grayish brown, splotched with darker brown above and gray beneath with longitudinal rows of whitish or yellowish spots. The bite is generally fatal.

JARDIN D'ACCLIMATATION, zhär-dăɴ dä'klē-mä-tä-syoɴ', Paris, a plot of 50 acres in the northwest angle of the Bois de Boulogne devoted to the acclimatization of foreign plants and animals. It was founded in 1860, and contains more animals, except beasts of prey, than the Jardin des Plantes. It has also a permanent exhibition of the processes and equipment of a dairy, aviary, greenhouses, poultry and carrier pigeon raising and gardening, and there is a winter garden and an aquarium. It forms a popular resort for pleasure and information.

JARDIN DES PLANTES, zhär'dăɴ dā plänt, Paris, a plot of 74 acres originally known as the Jardin du Roi, founded by Gui de La Brosse, physician to Louis XIII in 1635 as a garden for medicinal herbs. After the appointment of Georges Louis Leclerc, comte de Buffon as director, in 1739, the menagerie, galleries of collections, libraries, laboratories and lecture-rooms were established there and since 1794 it has been known as the Museum d'Histoire Naturelle.

JARDIN MABILLE, zhär'dăɴ mä'bēl', Paris, a popular resort of the demimonde founded by a dancer, Mabille, in 1840 and continuing one of the showplaces of the city until its close in 1875. It was celebrated for its beautiful fittings and for its originations in dancing.

JARDINE, jär'dĭn, **William M.**, American agronomist: b. Oneida County, Idaho, Jan. 16, 1879. In 1904 he was graduated at the Agricultural College of Utah and subsequently studied at the Graduate School of the University of Illinois. Until his 20th year he lived and worked on ranches in Idaho and Montana; in 1904 was made assistant in the department of agronomy, instructor in 1905, and professor in 1906 at the Agricultural College of Utah. From 1907 to 1910 he was engaged as assistant United States cerealist in charge of dry land grain investigations. In 1910 he was appointed agronomist of the Kansas State Agricultural College and Experiment Station; from 1913 to 1918 he served as director, when he became president, acting until 1925. Mr. Jardine is the author of numerous papers and bulletins on dry farming and crop production. In 1915–1916 he was president of the International Dry Farming Congress and Soil Products Exposition. He is a member of the American Society of Agronomy, of which he was president in 1916–1917, and fellow of the American Association for the Advancement of Science. On March 14, 1925 he became secretary of agriculture of the United States, serving until 1929. He was minister to Egypt 1930–1933; president of Wichita Municipal University since 1934. His work in agriculture is of recognized worth.

JARNAC, zhȧr-näk', France, town in the department of Charente, on the river Charente, 18 miles west of Angoulême. It has a large trade in brandy and wine and manufactures wine casks. It was the scene, March 13, 1569, of the defeat of the Huguenot forces under Louis, Prince of Condé and Gaspard de Coligny by the Catholics under Francois, Duke of Anjou. Pop. (1946) 4,075.

JARNEFELT, yăr'nĕ-fĕlt, **(Edvard) Armas**, Finnish composer: b. Viborg, Aug. 14, 1869. He studied under Martin Wegelius and Ferruccio Busoni at the Conservatory at Helsingfors, under Jules Massenet at Paris and A. Becker at Berlin. He became conductor of the theater at Magdeburg in 1897, at Düsseldorf in 1898, and principal conductor of the Royal Opera at Stockholm in 1907. He succeeded Wegelius as director of the Helsingfors Conservatory in 1906. In the year 1907 he became conductor of the Royal Opera, Stockholm; in 1911 Hofkapellmästare, Stockholm. He is author of overtures, suites for orchestra, choral work with orchestra, male choruses, piano pieces, serenades, six fantasies and a symphonic poem.

JARO, hä'rō, Philippine Islands, name of two towns: (1) In the northern part of Leyte Island, 15 miles southwest of Tacloban, in a mountainous district. Pop. about 17,514. (2) In the province of Iloilo, Panay, on the Jaro River, two miles northwest of the capital city, Iloilo. It was founded by the Spanish in 1584, and in 1903–08 it was a part of the municipality of Iloilo, but resumed its separate identity. It is situated in a rich agricultural district producing sugar, and manufactures silk, cotton and pina tissues. Pop. 24,572.

JAROSITE. A mineral consisting of a hydrous potassium ferric sulphate, $K_2O\ 3Fe_2O_3\ 4SO_3.6H_2O$. It is common in many mines of Utah but of no economic value.

JAROSLAU, yä'rō-slou', Poland, town in Galicia, 17 miles northwest of Przemysl, on the river San, and on the railroad between Lemberg and Cracow. It is a garrison town, has manufactures of textiles, pottery and brandy, and is an active trading centre. In the European War the town was twice taken by the Russians in the operations around Przemysl. Pop. 24,974.

JARRATT, Devereux, American colonial clergyman: b. New Kent County, Va., 6 Jan. (O.S.) 1732–33; d. Bath, Va., 29 Jan. 1801. He was largely a self-educated man. In 1762 he went to England in order to enter the ministry of the Established Church and receive orders. On his return he began his long service of nearly 30 years at Bath, Va. In the beginning of the Methodist movement in America he was very friendly with the leaders, especially Bishop Asbury, who makes frequent mention of him in his 'Journal.' He published 'Sermons on various and important subjects in practical Divinity' (3 vols., 1795). His 'Autobiography' appeared in 1806.

JARRIC, zhär'rēk, **Louis Etienne**, CHEVALIER DE, West Indian revolutionist: b. Aux Cayes, Haiti, 1757; d. there, 21 Feb. 1791. He was a mulatto, the natural son of a wealthy creole nobleman and had no claim to the title he assumed, but was well educated and possessed of means. He served as a captain in the French Revolution and was member of the Assembly in 1789. He organized a society «Amis des Noirs» (Friends of the Blacks) with the purpose of securing equal recognition with the whites. Failing to gain his purpose he engaged with Oge in an armed revolution in San Domingo in October 1790, their forces were defeated and Jarric was captured and put to death by torture.

JARROW-ON-TYNE, England, municipal borough in Durham, on the estuary of the Tyne, about six miles east of Newcastle, and on a branch of the Northeastern Railway. The parish church of Saint Paul was built in 685 and still shows much pre-Norman work, although the tower is Norman. The Benedictine monastery was founded in 681 and was the abode of the Venerable Bede. The town was of little commercial importance until the establishment there of large shipbuilding yards and marine-engine works. There are also iron foundries, gun factories, chemical works and paper mills, and there are large exports of coal. The town was incorporated in 1875. Pop. 35,576.

JARVES, jär'vēs, **James Jackson**, American art writer: b. Boston, Mass., 20 Aug. 1818; d. Tarasp, Switzerland, 28 June 1888. In 1838, he sailed for the Sandwich Islands and resided for several years in Honolulu where he published the first newspaper ever printed there, the *Polynesian.* Before returning to the United States he traveled in California, Mexico and Central America, and subsequently published a 'History of the Hawaiian or Sandwich Islands' (1843); 'Scenes and Scenery of the Sandwich Islands' (1844), and 'Scenes and Scenery in California' (1844). He afterward resided in Europe, was United States vice-consul at Florence 1879–82, and engaged in making a collection of old masters the largest part of which, consisting of early Italian masters, eventually became the property of Yale University. Another collection, of Venetian glass, is now at the Metropolitan Museum, New York. For his services to Italian art he was made a chevalier of the Crown of Italy. His later works include 'Art Studies: The Old Masters of Italy' (1861); 'Glimpses at the Art of Japan' (1876); 'Italian Rambles' (1884).

JARVIS, a small, isolated island in the Pacific Ocean south of the Hawaiian group, containing approximately 1,000 acres. It was claimed independently for both the United States and Great Britain by ship commanders; the priority of the former was established in 1936, and Jarvis was placed under the jurisdiction of the Department of the Interior in the same year. Jarvis has an air base. The island is economically unimportant except for its guano industry.

JARVIS, Edward, American physician: b. Concord, Mass., 9 Jan. 1803; d. Dorchester, Mass., 31 Oct. 1884. He was graduated at Harvard in 1826 and at the Harvard Medical School in 1830. He engaged in practice at Northfield and Concord, Mass., Louisville, Ky., and after 1842 at Dorchester, Mass. He made a sanitary survey of Massachusetts under orders of the government in 1855, and in 1860 was appointed by the Secretary of the Interior to tabulate the mortality statistics of the United States census of that year. He was president of the American Statistical Association from 1852 until his death. Author of numerous medical reports and 'Practical Physiology' (1848); 'Primary Physiology for the Schools' (1849).

JARVIS, John Wesley, American portrait painter: b. South Shields, England, 1780; d. New York, 1834. He was a nephew of the great John Wesley and was sent to Philadelphia at the age of five. He was principally self-taught, and settled in New York where his portrait work early gained recognition. He studied anatomy and phrenology in their relation to art, and he was especially successful in securing a characteristic likeness. His sitters included Gen. Andrew Jackson, Gov. Dewitt Clinton, Fitz-Greene Halleck, Bishop Benjamin Moore, John Randolph and many other prominent persons. He was a man of erratic temperament and convivial habits and his mode of life eventually injured his work. His wit and eccentricities were famous and his popularity enabled him to live extravagantly for a time, but he eventually died in poverty. Two of his portraits are in the Metropolitan Museum, New York, and others are in the city hall and in the collection of the New York Historical Society. Both Sully and Inman studied under him.

JARVIS, Samuel Farmer, American Protestant Episcopal clergyman: b. Middletown, Conn., 20 Jan. 1786; d. there, 26 March 1851. He was graduated at Yale in 1805, ordained in 1811, and was appointed rector of Saint Michael's Church, Bloomingdale, N. Y. In 1813 he became rector of Saint James' Church, New York and retained both charges until 1819 when he became professor of biblical learning at the General Theological Seminary. In 1820–26 he was rector of Saint Paul's, Boston, and afterward spent nine years in Europe in the study of church history. He was professor of Oriental literature at Washington (now Trinity) College, in 1835–37, and in 1837–42 he was rector of Christ Church, Middletown, Conn. He was appointed historiographer of the Episcopal Church of America in 1838, and after 1842 devoted himself to literature. He was one of the editors of the *Gospel Advocate* in 1821–26. Author of ‹A Discourse on the Religion of the Indian Tribes of North America› (1820); ‹A Chronological Introduction to the History of the Church› (1844); ‹The Church of the Redeemer› (Vol. I, 1850), etc.

JASHER, jā'sher, **Book of,** a lost book of the Hebrew Scriptures, twice mentioned in the Bible (Josh. x, 13, and 2 Sam. i, 18), and about which various conjectures have been made. It was most probably a national song book of post-Solomonic age whose concerts were partly secular, partly religious. From the mention of the book in Joshua and 2 Samuel it has been inferred that the book of Jasher could not have been written before the time of David's lamentation. But this assumes that the book of Jasher was all written at once, an assumption which in our ignorance regarding it we are not at liberty to make; for the book of Jasher may have been written at different times. The theory of Dr. Donaldson as to its scope and contents, in conformity with which he proceeded to reconstruct it from the fragments which he thought he could trace throughout the several books of the Old Testament, has met with little favor either from English or Continental scholars. Consult Donaldson, ‹Fragmenta Archetypa Carminum Hebraicorum in Masorethico Veteris Testamenti Textu passim tessellata.›

JASMIN, zhäs'măn', **Jacques Boé,** Provençal poet: b. 6 March 1798; d. 4 Oct. 1864. Of humble parentage, he became a wig-maker; but devoted all his leisure to reading and study. From his father he inherited a talent for the composition of poems and songs in the Provençal tongue. His local poems, especially those composed for the carnival and the country fairs, became quite popular. In 1825 he published ‹Lou Chalibary,› a mock-heroic poem which found readers throughout the langue d'oc country. ‹Lou Tres de May› (1830), an ode of great power and beauty, made him famous throughout France and Provençal Spain. Then followed poems relating to the humble life from which he had sprung and filled with remembrances of the joys and sorrows of his childhood days, and like the minstrels of olden time he went about from village and town to village and town reciting his poems. ‹Las Papillotos› (1835) contained the best of his poems up to that date. Other collections followed in 1842, 1851 and 1863. He was hailed by the Paris critics as a great poet. Of his longer poems, the best known, most popular and of greatest merit is ‹Françounetto› (1842), a dramatic and touching story of thwarted love, in which village superstitions and prejudices are painted in a most vivid and realistic manner. Literary honors were showered upon him not only in the Provençal country but throughout France. Among those who publicly recognized his genius were Louis-Philippe and the Duchesse d'Orléans. His poetical recitations brought out more people than the theatres and he was in demand everywhere for the inauguration of societies, the consecration of churches and similar functions; and always the funds taken in at these functions were devoted to charitable purposes.

JASMINE, or **JESSAMINE,** a genus (*Jasminum*) of beautiful plants of the olive family, including many cultivated species and varieties. Most of these are shrubs with long slender branches bearing usually compound leaves and panicles of fragrant white or yellow flowers. They are natives principally of the East Indies. The common jasmine (*J. officinale*) has become naturalized in the south of Europe, where it grows 8 or 10 feet tall, and is practically an evergreen. The oil of jasmine is obtained from *J. officinale* and *J. grandiflorum,* but it is usually imitated or adulterated. *J. sambac* also furnishes an oil in the East. A very common greenhouse species is *J. humile.*

Several shrubs are called jasmines which are not closely related to the true jasmine. Thus the red jasmine of the West Indies (*Plumeria rubra*), the source of the perfume frangipanni, is of the oleander family; the Chile jasmine (*Mandevillea suavolens*), is another fragrant species of the same family, widely cultivated, and others might be mentioned. Two of these outside «jasmines» are familiar in the United States, one of which is a native. The Cape jasmine (*Gardenia florida*) is a Chinese shrub of the madder family, which found its way to England and America about the middle of the 18th century; a double-flowered variety is sometimes grown in greenhouses and it grows out of doors along the southern seaboard, it being the special pride of Charleston, S. C., after one of whose citizens the genus *Gardenia* was named by Linnæus.

The native species is the Carolina or yellow jasmine (*Gelsemium sempervirens*), an exceedingly odorous climbing plant of the family *Loganiaceæ,* common throughout the South Atlantic States. It is a vine, whose blossoms grow in axillary racemes of from one to six vivid yellow tubular flowers; and «evening trumpet-flower» is a common name. «Early laden, indeed, is the warm air of spring with its delicious perfume. . . . Through woods and thickets it wends its way vigorously and gleams as brightly as does later the Cherokee rose. It is one of the joys of the season."

JASON, jā′s'n, a Jewish high priest in 174–171 B.C. He was the second son of Simon II and a brother of Onias III, whom he succeeded in the high priesthood. He is stated by Flavius Josephus (*Antiquities of the Jews,* vol. 12, chap. 5) to have changed his name to Jason from Jesus, and he is said to have paid a large sum for his appointment as high priest. While Onias was answering the charges of the Hellenists, Jason is supposed to have joined forces with them. He secured permission to build at Jerusalem a gymnasium and an ephebum, and by payment of a further sum gained for the people of Jerusalem the title and privileges of citizens of Antioch. He furthered by all means in his power the spread of Hellenism and sent competitors, and a large sum of money for a sacrifice to Hercules, to the Olympian games at Tyre. He was succeeded by Menelaus in 171 B.C., but in the absence of Antiochus Epiphanes in a campaign against Egypt in 170 B.C., he rallied the people to his aid and forced Menelaus to take refuge in a fortress. His seizure of power was soon followed by the return of Antiochus who took the city, and Jason was expelled. He took refuge with the Ammonites and finally with the Lacedaemonians, among whom he died.

Bibliography.—2 Maccabees 4:7-26, *Douay Version;* Josephus, Flavius, *Antiquitates Judaicae,* chap. 12; Stanley, Arthur P., *The History of the Jewish Church,* vol. 3 (New York 1879); Wellhausen, Julius, *Israelitische und jüdische Geschichte,* 2d ed. (Berlin 1895).

JASON, *in Greek legend,* the son of Aeson, king of Iolcus in Thessaly, a hero of ancient Greece, celebrated for his share in the Argonautic expedition, before which he had distinguished himself in the Calydonian hunt. He belonged to the family of the Aeolidae at Iolcus, and his instructor was the centaur Chiron, who educated most of the heroes of that time. (For his adventures in the Argonautic expedition see ARGONAUTS). On his return to Iolcus with Medea as his wife he avenged the murder of his parents and his brother by putting Pelias to death. But he was unable to retain possession of the throne, and was obliged to resign it to Acastus, son of Pelias, and flee with his wife to Corinth. Here they passed 10 years, until Jason, wearied of Medea, fell in love with Glauce (Creusa, according to some accounts), daughter of Creon, king of Corinth, married her and put away Medea and her children. Medea, having revenged herself on her hated rival, fled from the wrath of Jason in her car drawn by winged dragons, the gift of Helios, to Aegeus, king of Athens, after she had put to death Mermerus and Pheres, her sons by Jason. According to some Jason killed himself from grief; but others relate that, after passing a miserable wandering life, he came to his death by accident when, while sleeping in the shade of his old ship *Argo,* part of the stern fell on him.

JASON OF CYRENE, a Hellenistic Jew who flourished about 100 B.C. and whose history of the times of the Maccabees, written originally in five books now lost, is embodied in 2 Maccabees, reference to the original historian being made in 2 Maccabees 2:19-32. Nothing is known of Jason except the references to him in 2 Maccabees.

JASONVILLE, city, Indiana, in Greene County; on the Chicago, Milwaukee, St. Paul and Pacific Railroad; 23 miles south-southeast of Terre Haute. It is in a coal mining region and has mayor and council government. Pop. (1950) 2,937.

JASPER, jăs′pẽr, city, Alabama, and Walker County seat; altitude 307 feet; 38 miles northwest of Birmingham; on the Illinois Central, the St. Louis-San Francisco, the Alabama Central, and the Southern railroads. Industrially, the city is chiefly concerned with coal mining, lumbering, tanning, and the growing and processing of cotton. It was settled in 1815 and is governed by council-manager. Pop. (1950) 8,589.

JASPER, unincorporated community, Province of Alberta, Canada, gateway to and administrative center of the Jasper National Park which is the largest (4,200 square miles) of all the reservations set aside by the Canadian government as a national playground and wild life preserve and which is unsurpassed for grandeur and diversification as well as extent of mountain, glacier, lake, and river scenery. On the eastern slope of the Rocky Mountains, here broken into ranges, adjoining Banff and Yoho National parks on the south, the park takes its name from Jasper House, a post of the North West Company established in 1813 on the historic Athabaska Trail. The town is on the Athabaska River at the junction of the Miette, at an altitude of 3,472 feet, and is reached by highway and by the Canadian National Railway, 236 miles west of Edmonton. It has 3 churches, public and high schools, and a hospital. Pop. (1951) 1,899.

JASPER, city, Indiana, and Dubois County seat; on the Patoka River, and the Southern Railway; 54 miles northeast of Evansville. Jasper, founded in 1818, is situated in an agricultural, timber and coal mining region, for which it serves as a shopping center. The principal crops are wheat, corn and strawberries; and manufactures include office furniture, plywood, gloves, veneer, and food products. Pop. (1950) 5,215.

JASPER, an impure quartz, less hard than flint or even than common quartz, but which gives fire with steel. It is entirely opaque, or sometimes feebly translucent at the edges, and presents almost every variety of color. It is found in metamorphic rocks and often occurs in very large masses. It admits of an elegant polish and is used for vases, seals, and paperweights. There are several varieties, as red, brown, blackish, bluish, Egyptian. Ribbon or agate jasper is jasper in layers.

JASPER NATIONAL PARK. See CANADA—28. *National Parks.*

JASPER PLACE, city, Alberta, Canada, immediately adjacent to Edmonton of which it is largely a residential suburb. Pop. (1951) 9,114.

JASPER WARE, a white terra cotta or porcelain bisque invented by Josiah Wedgwood and used for the delicate reliefs in his cameo ware. It is also used for jewelry settings and statuettes. See also WEDGWOOD WARE.

JASPILITE, a compact siliceous rock similar to jasper in appearance. Its occurrence in the Lake Superior region is of economic importance as it appears invariably above the ore-bearing formation.

JASSY, yäs'sē, Rumania, the former capital of Moldavia, on the Bahluiu River. There is a university with 900 students; the industrial enterprises are few; but the commerce is extensive and important. The chief exports are petroleum, grain, meat and salt; the chief imports are coal and clothing. A treaty between Russia and Turkey was concluded here in 1792. It was in Jassy, in 1821 that Alexander Ypsilanti really began the work for Greek independence. About one half the population are Jews. Pop. 104,471.

JASTROW, yäs'trō, **Ignaz,** German economist and historian: b. Nakel, 13 Sept. 1856. He was educated at Breslau, Berlin and Göttingen, and in 1885 was appointed privat-docent of social economy at the University of Berlin. He visited the United States in 1904 and since 1905 has been professor of administrative science at Berlin. He edited the *Jahresberichte der Geschichtswissenschaft* in 1888–91; the *Sociale Praxis* in 1895–97; since 1896 he has edited *Das Gewerbegericht,* and since 1897 *Der Arbeitsmarkt.* Author of *Geschichte des deutschen Einheitstraumes und seiner Erfüllung* (1884; 4th ed., 1891); *Die Volkszahl Deutscher Städte am Ende des Mittelalters und zu Beginn der Neuzeit* (1886); *Das interesse des Kaufmannsstandes am Bürgerlichen Gesetzbuch* (1890); *Bürgertum und Staatsverwaltung* (1907); *Cedächtnisrede auf Dunker* (1911); *Arbeiterschutz* (1912); *Geld und Kredit* (1914), etc.

JASTROW, jăs'trō, **Joseph,** American psychologist: b. Warsaw, Poland, 30 Jan. 1863; d. Stockbridge, Mass., 8 Jan. 1944. The son of Rabbi Jastrow (q.v.), he was graduated from the University of Pennsylvania in 1882 and in 1888 was appointed professor of psychology at the University of Wisconsin. He became president of the American Psychological Association in 1900. In 1893 he was head of the psychological section at the World's Columbian Exposition. He was associate editor of the *Psychological Review;* editor of *The Conduct of Mind Series,* and author of *Time Relations of Mental Phenomena* (1890); *Epitomes of Three Sciences* (1890); *Fact and Fable in Psychology* (1900); *The Subconscious* (1906); *The Qualities of Men* (1910); *Character and Temperament* (1915); *Psychology of Conviction* (1918); *Keeping Mentally Fit* (1928).

JASTROW, Marcus M., American rabbi and lexicographer: b. Rogasen, Posen, 1829; d. Germantown, Pa., 13 Oct. 1903. After the usual rabbinic and academic studies he was graduated from the University of Halle in 1854, became a barber in Berlin and then rabbi at Warsaw. After five years he was obliged to leave by reason of his political opinions, after being subjected to arrest. He was rabbi in Baden 1859–63, at Worms 1863–66, whence he was called to the Congregation Rodef Sholen, Philadelphia, with which he was connected until his death, but in later years (1892–1903) as rabbi emeritus. Besides some monographs and contributions to the press, he is best known for his *Dictionary of the Targumim, the Talmud Babli and Yerushalmi, and the Midrashic Literature* (16 parts, 1904), a monument of untiring erudition and broad scholarship. He edited the Talmudic department of the *Jewish Encyclopaedia.*

JASTROW, Morris, Jr., American Orientalist: b. Warsaw, Poland, 13 Aug. 1861; d. Jenkintown, Pa., 22 June 1921. Coming to Philadelphia with his parents in early childhood (1866), he was trained in the schools of that city, was graduated from the University of Pennsylvania in 1881, and from the University of Leipzig 1884, receiving the degree of Ph.D., after which he spent another year in the study of Semitic languages at the Sorbonne, the Collège de France and the École des Langues Orientales Levant Vivantes. He had intended to devote himself to the Jewish ministry, carrying on for this purpose theological studies at the Jewish Seminary of Breslau (Germany) while pursuing the study of Semitic languages at German universities. On his return to the United States in 1885 he was appointed assistant to his father in Philadelphia, which position he voluntarily resigned after one year, in order to devote himself entirely to linguistic and archaeological studies. He gradually extended his field to include the history of religions. He was connected with the University of Pennsylvania after 1885, first as instructor in Semitic languages and afterward, in 1891, appointed to the chair of Semitic languages which position he held till his death. In 1888 he was made assistant librarian of the university, and in 1898 librarian-in-chief. His published works are *Religion of the Assyrians and Babylonians* (1898); *Two Grammatical Treatises of Abu Zakariyya Hayyug* (1897); *A Fragment of the Babylonian Dibbarra Epic* (1891); *The Study of Religion* (1901); *Aspects of Religious Practice and Belief among the Babylonians and Assyrians* (1911); *Die Religion Babyloniens und Assyriens* (3 vols., 1905–12), an enlarged and entirely rewritten German edition of the English work above, together with a separate volume of illustrations bearing on the religion of the Babylonians and Assyrians; *Bildermappe zur Religion Babyloniens und Assyriens* (1912); *Hebrew and Babylonian Traditions* (1914); *Babylonian-Assyrian Birth Omens and Their Cultural Significance* (1914); and *The Civilization of Babylonia and Assyria* (1915). In collaboration with his wife (Helen Bachman Jastrow) he edited an English translation of *Selected Essays of James Darmesteter* (1895), the translation from the French being made by Mrs. Jastrow, and he adding a memoir of Darmesteter. In addition to the above he published a large number of papers on Assyriological, biblical and Hebrew topics, as well as articles dealing with the history of religions and with archaeological problems in the periodicals of learned societies of America and Europe and in technical periodicals of various parts of the world. He was also a contributor to various Bible dictionaries, to the *Jewish Encyclopaedia, Encyclopaedia Britannica, International Encyclopaedia,* to *Webster's Dictionary,* etc. A bibliography of his books, monographs and papers, covering the years 1885–1916, was compiled and published (for private circulation) by Profs. A. T. Clay and J. A. Montgomery.

JÁSZBERÉNY, yäs-bĕ-rān-y, Hungary, town of the District of Jász-Nagykun Szolnok, on the Zagyva, 40 miles east of Budapest. It is situated in an agricultural district and has a trade in grain and livestock. There is an agricultural school, a museum and an interesting Franciscan cloister. Pop. 29,675.

JATAKA, jä'tạ-kạ, a collection of 547 stories of the different births of Buddha, known to have been in existence as early as 380 B.C. The book is written in the Pali language and forms a part of the Buddhist sacred canon. It is evident that the identification of Buddha with the heroes of the fables and stories current in India began soon after his death. The leading character in each fable was made a Bodhisatta, one who is destined through rebirths to become a Buddha, and the stories deal with the "ten perfections," generosity, goodness, renunciation, wisdom, energy, patience, truthfulness, resolution, kindness and equanimity. The existence of the Jataka stories in the original Pali text forms a valuable contribution to the knowledge of folklore, as its antiquity insures its freedom from Western influences or coloring. On the other hand, various versions found their way through Sanskrit and Old Persian into European literature and form the basis of many Western fairy tales and fables, among them those of Æsop. Bas-reliefs illustrating the Jatakas were in existence as early as the middle of the 3d century B.C. The Jataka was translated into English under the direction of E. B. Cowell assisted by Chalmers, Rouse, Francis and Neil (7 vols., Cambridge 1895–1913). An earlier edition of the Jataka in the Pali text was edited by Fausböll (7 vols., London 1879–97). The introduction to the old Jataka book in the original Pali gives a life of Buddha which was translated into English by T. W. Rhys Davids (London 1880). Consult Kern, H., 'Jātaka-māla,' Sanskrit text (Cambridge, Mass., 1891; Eng. trans., Speyer, J. S., Oxford, 1895); 'Buddhist India' (chap. XI, London 1903); Kuhn, E., 'Barlaam und Joasaph' (Munich 1893); Cunningham, A., 'The Stipa of Barhut' (London 1879).

JATROPHA, jăt'rō-fa, a genus of euphorbiaceous plants of the tribe *Crotoneæ,* tropical and chiefly American. They are of interest principally for their medicinal properties, which reside mostly in the seeds. These, in the case of *Jatropha curcas,* are called Barbados or physic nuts,— the last in allusion to their purgative power. The so-called jathropha-oil is extracted from the seeds of the coral-plant (*J. multifida*) and of the East Indian *J. glauca,* and is used externally as a stimulant. A common species in the southern United States is the spurge-nettle or tread-softly (*J. stimulosa*). See MANIHOT.

JATS, jâts, the most numerous of the agricultural population of the Punjab, India, numbering about four and a half millions. They are by many identified with the *Getæ;* and some of the best authorities accept the theory that they are descended from Scythian invaders of India in prehistoric times. Some scholars believe them cognate with the Gypsies (q.v.). Their religion is Mohammedan. They are tall, light brown in coloring, with long faces, high forehead and clean-cut features. Consult Risley, H., 'The People of India' (Calcutta 1908).

JAUNDICE, jän'- or jân'dĭs, a morbid condition arising from the circulation of bile in the blood, with consequent staining of the tissues and a peculiar train of symptoms resulting from the poisoning. The tint of the skin and certain mucous membranes varies from a light yellow to a brownish or saffron hue. Staining of the conjunctiva is first observed, and is most intense. Jaundice, with reference to its origin, may be either obstructive or toxic. The term obstructive means causing a hindrance to the outflow of the bile from the gall-ducts into the intestine, with its consequent absorption into the hepatic vein and general circulation. Not only is the skin stained, but all the secretions as well, the urine becoming dark brown. As no bile is thrown into the intestine, the stools become clay-colored and usually hard. There is frequently distressing cutaneous itching, and other skin-maladies are not uncommon. The blood partially loses its power of coagulation, and the vessels are apt to allow the escape of blood into the tissues, giving rise to purpuric spots. The pulse is usually slow, and the patient somewhat melancholic. In bad cases death may follow a period of convulsions, delirium or coma. The cause of this obstruction may be anything occluding the lumen of the ducts from within as catarrh of the membrane of the intestine, where the bile-ducts open, or catarrh anywhere along the course of the ducts; stones or thickened bile may block up some part of the tubes, or they may be occluded from pressure on the outside by tumors, constricting bands or shrinking of the liver-substance. (See LIVER, DISEASES OF THE). The toxic form of jaundice is due to the circulation of poisons in the blood which break down the red cells or, more rarely, destroy the liver cells. The jaundice in this form is not so intense, and the other symptoms caused by the poison are of more importance. Many of the infectious diseases, such as influenza, typhoid fever, yellow fever, pneumonia, pyæmia and acute atrophy of the liver, cause this form. Mineral poisons, particularly phosphorus, act in the same way. Jaundice in the new-born is so common as to be considered a natural condition, and usually lasts but a few days. It is evident from the many conditions that may give rise to jaundice that it must be considered as a symptom, and treatment should be directed to aiding the bodily functions until the exact cause can be determined.

JAUNPUR, jown-poor, British India, city in the district of the same name in the Benares division, on the river Gumti, 34 miles by rail northwest of Benares. It is a city of great antiquity and was formerly the capital of a Mohammedan kingdom extending from Budaun and Etawah to Behar. It has many fine architectural monuments, among them a gateway of the 16th century, a mosque dating from 1376, the baths of Ibrahim Shah, the bridge over the Gumti, built in 1569–73, and other splendid remains. The city was a centre of revolt during the Indian mutiny in 1857. While it is famous for its perfumes it is no longer commercially important. Pop. 32,771.

JAUREQUI Y AGUILAR, hou'rạ-gē ē ä'gē-lär, **Juan Martínez de,** Spanish poet: baptized Seville, 24 Nov. 1583; d. Madrid, 11 Jan. 1641. He studied at Rome and in 1610 is known to have been in Spain with a reputation as both painter and poet. He is supposed to have painted the portrait of Miguel de Cervantes Saavedra mentioned in the prologue to *Noveles Ejemplares*, which is believed to be the one now in the possession of the Real Academia Española; and his translation of Tasso's *Aminto* (Rome 1607) is praised in the second volume of *Don Quixote*. His *Rimas* (1618) comprised a collection of charming lyrics, and in its preface the poet severely scored the affectations of the school of Luis de Góngora y Argote.

JAURES, zhô-râs', **Jean Léon,** French socialist and politician: b. Castres, Sept. 3, 1859; d. Paris, July 31, 1914. He taught in Albi and Toulouse, and in 1885 entered politics and was elected to the Chamber of Deputies from Tarn; at this time he was a moderate Republican. In 1889 he failed of re-election, and returned to Toulouse, where he was active in the establishing of a college of medicine. Becoming a Socialist, Jaurès defended the strikers at Carmaux, and in 1893 was again elected to the Chamber, where he became one of the leaders of the Socialists. He failed of re-election in 1898, but was again elected in 1902. When the Socialist Alexandre Millerand accepted a position in the cabinet, Jaurès defended his action, thus opposing Jules Guesde and the *Parti Ouvrier*, but sought at the same time to reconcile the factions. He also took an important part in obtaining a revision of the Alfred Dreyfus case. He stood out as a champion of the workmen in the great strike of 1910. At a Socialist conference in Brussels in the summer of 1914 he made a strong attack on militarism, and declared himself in favor of an international strike for the prevention of war—an attitude which subjected him to severe criticism, and was directly the cause of his assassination by shooting at the hands of a half-demented man outside a café in Paris at outbreak of World War I. He was one of the greatest leaders of French Socialism, and probably the greatest orator in the Chamber of Deputies. He founded *L'Humanité* in 1904, and contributed six of the 12 volumes of the *Histoire Socialiste* (1904–1908).

JAVA, jä'vȧ, **island of Indonesia, fifth largest** and most important of the islands of the Malay Archipelago, is bounded on the north by the Java Sea, on the east by Bali Strait, on the south by the Indian Ocean, and on the west by Sunda (Soenda) Strait. Across the 16-mile-wide Sunda Strait lies the great island of Sumatra; and only one mile across Bali Strait, at its narrowest point, is the island of Bali. Madura (Madoera) Island is close to the northeast coast of Java and is considered almost a part of it. Java has a length, from east to west, of 600 miles, and at its widest part it has a width of 125 miles. The area is 48,830 square miles. With a population of 52,756,000 (1952), Java is the most densely populated of the islands of Indonesia.

Djakarta (Jakarta), the capital of the republic and known as Batavia under the former Dutch administration, lies on the northwest coast of Java at the mouth of the Tjiliwung (Tjiliwong) River; it has a population of 2,800,000 (1952). Tandjong Priok (Tandjoengpriok), the port of Djakarta, is six miles to the eastward. The second largest city and port in Indonesia is Surabaja (Surabaya), at the mouth of the Kali Mas River opposite Madura; the population totals 800,000. Semarang (pop. 250,000) is a port on the north central coast; and Tjilatjap (30,000) is the only safe harbor on the island's south coast. Djokjakarta (Jogjakarta), a city (1,500,000) in central Java, is mainly a spiritual and cultural center; from 1946 to 1950 it was the capital of the republic. Other inland cities include Bandung (750,000), a holiday and tourist resort on the high plateau in the northwest; Surakarta (500,000), 35 miles northeast of Djokjakarta and likewise a center of Hindu-Javanese culture; Bogor (124,000), a scientific center 35 miles south of Djakarta; and Magelang (60,000), site of the immense 9th-century temple of Borobudur (q.v.).

Geology.—Java is formed mainly of tertiary, though partly of post-tertiary strata; but by volcanic action the arrangement has been much disturbed. Rocks containing fossil invertebrates are common, and the fossils of vertebrates have also been discovered. Lignite is found in various parts of the island, and coal is mined in Djokjakarta and Bantam. There are petroleum deposits near Rembang and Surabaja, and also on the island of Madura. Tin is mined, and other minerals include sulphur, asphalt, salt, and manganese. Limestone and marble are plentiful in the southern part of the island.

Topography.—The Indian Ocean, which beats with great force along the south coast, has prevented the formation, on that side, of such alluvial plains as extend along the north coast. From the same cause the south coast is generally unsafe for shipping, while the north affords excellent anchorage at almost all times and places. The south presents a continuous front of crags and rocks, forming the outer edge of an extremely mountainous country. The north is flat and low, and covered in many places with mangrove swamps. Mountains in the wide western section of Java lie, for the most part, close to the southern coast, the land sloping abruptly to the Indian Ocean and, on the north, descending gently across rich agricultural country to the Java Sea. In the center of the island, the mountains are situated roughly midway between the north and south coasts and virtually constitute a range. The mountains and lowlands are irregularly intermixed in the eastern section of the island.

The whole configuration of Java has been transformed by volcanic action. There are 20 or more mountain peaks with elevations exceeding 8,000 feet, and more than 100 volcanoes, of which 13 are still active. Semeroe (Semeru), 12,060 feet in height, is an active volcano and the highest mountain in Java; it is in the eastern part of the island, southeast of Malang, and joins with the Tengger Mountains, to the northward. Salak (7,254 feet), in western Java, had severe eruptions in 1669 and 1699 but is now extinct; Gede (9,705 feet), 45 miles southeast of Djakarta, has had many eruptions since 1832; Papandayan (8,744 feet), 12 miles southwest of Garut (Garoet), western Java, erupted violently in August 1772, destroying some 3,000 persons; Galunggung (7,221 feet), 10 miles east of Garut, had a destructive eruption in 1822; Tjikoeraj (9,255 feet) is the highest extinct volcano in the mountain groups around Garut; and Slamet (11,247 feet), in west central Java, is also inactive. The eruption of Krakatoa (q.v.), the volcanic island in Sunda Strait, in August 1883 was the most tremendous of modern times; it killed 36,000 people in western Java. The island is subject to earthquakes, though as a rule they are not severe. Three earthquakes are known to have preceded and 19 accompanied volcanic eruptions. A most destructive earthquake occurred in 1867.

Rivers flowing into the Indian Ocean, to the south, are short and rapid; while those flowing northward, into the Java Sea, are longer and more suitable for navigation. The longest river is the Solo (335 miles in length), which empties into the Java Sea opposite the west end of the island of Madura; in its lower course it is known as the Bengawan. The Brantas (195 miles) also known as Kediri, flows into Madura Strait in two branches, on one of which (named Kali Mas) stands Surabaja; it is navigable as far as Kediri. The capital city of Djakarta stands at the mouth of the Tjiliwung (50 miles), which rises on the northern slopes of Mount Pangerango.

Climate.—During the day the temperature of the plains and valleys ranges from 85°F. to 94°; and during the night from 73° to 80°. The mean temperature at Djakarta is 78.69°F. At an elevation of 6,000 feet the thermometer descends to 60°, while the tops of the highest peaks are often covered with ice, but no snow falls. The breezes from the sea modify the temperature. There are two seasons: the dry from April to October, and the rainy season from November to March. During the rainy season there is an almost continuous rainfall except for a short time in the morning. The annual rainfall is about 80 inches. The island is not subject to storms which injure life or property, but near the high mountains there are frequent thunderstorms.

Fauna.—Including domestic and marine animals, at least 100 kinds of mammalia inhabit Java. In the western area the one-horned rhinoceros is not uncommon; and in the higher elevations the royal tiger, panther, and wild cat keep the inhabitants in constant alarm by their depredations. Wild pigs of two different species are most destructive of crops. There are only two species of the ape kind, but they people the forest in countless numbers. Two kinds of lemurs inspire the inhabitants with superstitious fear by their mysterious nocturnal habits; and this island may be esteemed the native seat of the largest bats, some of which measure five feet across the wings. They may be seen suspended from the branches in hundreds during the day, and at night they devastate the orchards and gardens. Two civets are common and supply a perfume of which the Javanese are passionately fond; the wild ox abounds in the woods; and the buffalo is the only animal used in agricultural labor. The horses are small, but vigorous, and, as in India, are not used for agricultural purposes. Two species of wild dogs and six species of deer are found here. Among the domestic animals are the buffalo, ox, horse, goat, and sheep. The ornithology of Java is rich and varied, both in genera and in species. About 300 species of land birds have been found on the island, among them the peacock, partridge, quail, 10 different species of pigeon, 11 species of heron, two of cuckoo, the woodpeckers, the black and crimson oriole, the hornbill, eagle, owl, the brilliant looking and appropriately named minaret flycatcher, and the "swift" (q.v.); and the mino bird, so apt in learning to mimic human speech, is common. Almost all the known generic groups of rapacious birds are found here in great numbers, and gallinaceous fowls are plentiful. A variety of reptiles are found on the island, among them the python. Insects cover the grounds and plants in countless numbers; but few are distinguished for brilliancy or variety of color, or are remarkable in form. Fish are plentiful in the rivers and along the coast; but those of the rivers are of inferior quality for food. Excellent oysters are abundant on the north coast, and prawns, from which a condiment called trasi is prepared, are considered delicious by the natives. Crocodiles from 20 to 30 feet in length inhabit the watercourses.

Flora.—With a temperature ranging from 94°F. to the freezing-point, a volcanic soil plenteously watered naturally and artificially, it is not surprising that Java should be of astonishing fertility; the range of its vegetation naturally follows that of its temperature, from the palms of the tropics to the mosses of the temperate zone. Mangrove swamps fringe most of the coast line, and a short distance inland occur the coconut, nipa, and other palms. Low hills are covered with alang-alang grass, 3 to 4 feet high, wild sugar cane, acacia, and bamboo—the last frequently of immense size. Most of the cultivated crops, particularly rice and sugar, grow at elevations below 2,000 feet. The vast forests cover a very extensive surface. In the rain forests are magnolias, a great variety of vines, rattans, and at least 80 species of fig trees, which are remarkable for their great height and vigorous growth. The dense forests of central Java contain the valuable teak tree (which sheds its leaves in June and buds again in October), mahogany, camphor, and many other forms of vegetation. These are followed still higher up by the plane-like liquidambars, with their erect stems covered with parasites, and *Rubiaceae,* the latter of numerous species; some of them exhaling a very fetid odor. Along the upper limits of the liquidambars, about 4,000 feet above sea level, lofty trees are still plentiful. Here may be seen *Podocarpus cupressus,* with its lofty straight stem, a tree allied to the yew and furnishing the best timber in Java. There are also the dammar pine, rhododendrons, laurels of numerous species, chestnuts, oaks, magnolias, myrtles, and other vegetation common to the temperate zones. About an elevation of 7,000 feet the vegetation changes its aspect. Mosses appear, and these, with heaths, are the principal plants found on the loftier peaks.

The People.—Although Java comprises only seven per cent of the land area of Indonesia, it supports two thirds of the archipelago's people, and is one of the most densely populated islands of the world. The three main ethnic groups are people of the Deutero-Malay race. The whole of central Java is occupied by the Javanese, who comprise about three quarters of the population; they are also found on the north coast to the westward and on the south coast eastward. The Sundanese, who form about 15 per cent of the population, live at the western end of the island at the higher elevations; and the Madurese, about 10 per cent of the population, are found in eastern Java as well as on the neighboring island of Madura. All three races are shorter than Mongolians and Caucasions. The shortest and the most sturdy are the Sundanese, and their eyes are more slanted than those of the Javanese and Madurese. In general, it may be said that all three races are light brown in color, and the hair of the head is black, thick, lank, and harsh; a few, short straggling hairs compose the beard, and on other parts of the body hair is either scanty or altogether wanting. The people are patient and enduring, but they are most susceptible to affronts, which they are not slow to avenge with the kris—a dagger having a serpentine blade. All the people, without distinction, are passionately fond of gaming, more especially of cockfighting. Most of the people, being agriculturists, live in small villages. Their houses are light structures of bamboo, built upon the ground except in the case of the Sundanese, who raise them on piles several feet above the ground. Leaves of the nipa palm or alang-alang grass are used for thatching the roofs of the houses, and bamboo, split and flattened, provides the walling; the floors are of pounded earth.

Religion.—The advent of Indians in the 11th century brought Buddhism to Java. This was largely displaced in the 15th century, however, when Arab conquerors arrived and influenced Javanese life with Moslem culture. Islam was eventually embraced by 90 per cent of the people of Java. There still remain some primitive Animists, and Christianity has some 2,000,000 adherents. The polygamy permitted by Islam continues to be practiced by wealthier Javanese, but most of the people are monogamous.

Language.—It is not certain whether the name of Java be connected with the Sanskrit Javanna and Yavana, both of which, besides being related to Ἰωνία as names of Greece, also signify (especially the latter) Bactria, Arabia, and other foreign countries, and, moreover, swift, horse, etc.; or whether its etymon be of a different origin. The Javanese is the most cultivated of all Polynesian languages, owing to the very early intercourse of the island with the continent of India, whose Aryan as well as Dravidan influence is attested by the presence of Malabaric words along with those from the Sanskrit, not only in Javanese, but also in the idioms of Sumatra, Madagascar, and other islands. Both religious and political revolutions have served to modify the condition of the languages.

There are four dialects on the three islands which form the linguistic group in question, namely: (1) the tongue of the mountaineers of Sunda, in the western part of Java, east of Tagal, probably vernacular through this whole region before the introduction of Islam, now spoken by about one tenth of the population of the island; it contains many Malay and some Sanskrit words, stands in the same relation to the principal language as the Welsh does to the English, and is best spoken at Bantam, sluggishly at Bogor and Chianjore and verging to the Javanese at Cheribon. (2) The Javanese proper, east of the last-named city, extending through the rest of the island, especially along its north shore; its words are long at Tagal, shorter at Samarang, full, short and strong at the courts of Surakarta in the center and Djokjakarta in the south; it approaches the Madurese at Surabaja and the Balian at Banyuwangi. (3) The dialect of Madura and Sumanap, which has many Sunda words, with more of Malay, and with peculiar endings. (4) That of Bali, little different from the general Javanese. This island preserves the ancient letters as well as Brahminism, both expelled from Java in the 15th century. A sort of jargon, analogous to the *lingua franca,* is spoken at Djakarta, being a medley of Dutch, Portuguese, Javanese, and Malay.

Along with the preceding there are also peculiar styles or idioms of speech, varying in accordance with social position and age, as the *madhjo* (intermediate), between equals; the *bása* or *bohoso-ngoko* (language popular), to inferiors; the *bása-kramo* (language superior), urbane, court idiom, about three fourths of it Sanskrit, used by poets as the speech of gods, heroes, and ghosts. As to locality, there are also two vernacular idioms, namely, the *bása-dalam* of the interior and the *bása-luar,* spoken along the shores. The Kavi (learned, wise, poet) is the ancient sacred language of Java and consists of about six parts of Sanskrit, less altered than in the Pali, to four of Javano-Malay. It owes its origin to Brahminic immigration, about the beginning of our era. It is to the Javanese what Sanskrit is to the Hindostani, and Pali to the Indo-Chinese languages. Declining in the 14th century, it took refuge in Bali and was imperfectly known by the Panambahan at Sumanap at the time when Sir Stamford Raffles (q.v.) was in Java. Passages in the Kavi are sometimes quoted on peculiar occasions, as for instance in fables and dramas; the term itself is employed as a title of works, etc., such as *Sekar-kavi,* flowers of poetry, whence *Sekarini,* a Kavi meter; *Rama-kavi,* the Javanese Ramayana; *Kavindhra,* principal singer or poet (named *ma-kathā,* narrator, in Tagala). A few specimens of words may show the relation of the Javanese to the common Malay, where the difference, if not specially noted, is sometimes more in the accent than otherwise: *langit,* heaven; *tanah,* earth (Mal. also *benua,* region); *ayer* (Jav. also *banyu*), water; *laut* (Jav. *lahut*), sea; *dhina* (Mal. *hāri*), day; *bengi* (Mal. *mālam*), night; *vūlan* (Mal. *būlan*), moon; *terang* (Mal. *trang*), light; *mati,* to die; *lulat* (Mal. *kāsih*), to love; *dara,* virgin; *dhēva* (Mal. *tuhan*), god, lord; *mangan* (Mal. *mākan, santap*), to eat; *bāpa,* pak (Mal. *pā,* politely *ayah*), father; *ma, bok* (Mal. *mā, amā,* politely *ibu, bonda*), mother, etc. Compounds and derivatives abound, but the latter are more frequently formed by suffixes than by prefixes, in which the Tagala is very rich. There are many contractions into *tr, ngl, ngr,* with the dropping of short vowels, together with the alteration of the initial sound (similar to the Celtic), and other variations which obscure the etymic origin, thus: Sans. *nātha,* master, lord, becomes *tata,* order, to reign; Jav. *neda,* to eat, *teda,* food; *nulis,* to write, *tulis,* scripture; *nitik,* to prove, *titik,* proof. The prefix *n* denotes verbs, *t* substantives; other changes are: *nyatur,* to tell, *chatur,* tale; *nyerrat,* to write, *serrat,* writing, etc. The doubling of the first syllable makes verbs, as *tutulung,* to help, from *tulung,* aid; *gagriya,* to dwell, from *griya,* house. The insertion of *in* is the sign of the passive voice. Substantives are also made by prefixing *pem* (*pen, pe*), denoting an agent; thus: *pem-pekto,* carrier, from *pekto,* to carry; *pen-dahar,* eater, etc.; by prefixing *ka,* a sign of the past participle; *ka-bekto,* Lat. *allatum;* by suffixing *n* (*en, an*): *bakt-en,* the carrying, *dahar-an,* Lat. *cibus;* and by both prefix and suffix: *ka-da-har-an,* an eatable. Articles, gender, and the dual number are wanting. In the plural, cases are denoted by particles, and also by reduplication, as in Japanese. The genitive relation is shown by the precedence of the noun or by inserting *ing.* The other relations of case are indicated by means of verbs. The adjective is unchanged after the substantive. Pronominal forms are fewer than in Malay: *kita,* we in Malay, means I in Javanese.

Literature.—The literature, which is in Kavi, dates from about the commencement of our era, and is rich, especially in legends concerning cosmogony. The subjects of the works are mostly either of a mythical or ethical character. Prominent among the former are the *Kānda* (Sans. *Khandata,* fragment, section), *Pepakem* (book), or *Sejarah* (history); *Manek-Maya,* a mythical genesis, in which Buddhism predominates; *Vivaha-Kavi* (matrimonial poem), about a *Rasaksa* (evil spirit) who courts a *Vidaduri* (nymph); *Rama-Kavi,* the Javanese *Ramayana; Parikespit,* "Arjuna's Grandson"; *Mintaraga,* a poem on Arjuna in the Indra mountain. This kind of composition comes down to the time of Aji Saya Baya. Of the ethical order are the *Niti Sastra Kavi,* in the purest style, of about the 13th century; and *Srūti,* which already alludes to Islam. But the *Brata Yudha* ("Holly War") is an epos mostly on the deeds of Arjuna; being an episode of the Mahabharata, in 712 stanzas, with varying rhymes. The *Sastra Menava* is a Javanese imitation of the ordinances of the Indian Menu. Indeed, most of the Kavi works are such imitations. Whether mere versions of Sanskrit works have been made or still exist is not precisely known; but there are many Javanese versions from the Kavi. Javanese literature abounds in romantic compositions, mostly of elegiac form. Among these, the adventures of the popular hero Pandji are most prominent. Dramas, and especially puppet shows, called *wayang* (shadows), and with figures of either leather or wood personating heroes, are popular.

Production.—The vast majority of the people of Java are engaged in agriculture, despite the fact that the great cities are of major industrial and commercial importance. There is a small class of fishermen on the sea coasts and an increasing number of urban residents are skilled artisans, but most Javanese live directly or indirectly by the cultivation of the land. Rubber, sugar, coffee, tea, and cocoa, the principal economic crops, have long been cultivated on immense foreign-owned plantations, and since establishment of the republic following World War II an increasing number of these products have been grown by small farmers. The island also produces some 90 per cent of the cinchona bark from which quinine, the specific for malaria, is manufactured; and other products which are exported include copra (the dried meat of the coconut), palm oil, kapok (a silky fiber used to fill mattresses), and sisal hemp. Rice, the staple foodstuff in Java, is produced on a great scale; with the aid of irrigation two crops can be raised each year. Sugarcane and tobacco are also cultivated, and other crops include corn, cassava, peanuts, soya beans, and capsicum.

The forests yield teak and other valuable woods, many of them exported, while coal is mined and petroleum is produced in several parts of the island. The Javanese practice about 30 crafts, some of them of considerable antiquity and of high artistic standard. They excel all others in the archipelago in the working of metals, being especially skillful in the manufacture of the kris—the dagger customarily worn by every man and boy above 14 years of age; the kris is also worn by many ladies of high rank. Excellent gongs and other musical instruments of brass are also made; there is a ready market for them in neighboring countries. Silverwork is also a highly developed craft. The only textile material woven by the Javanese is cotton, of which they make only a stout durable calico; this is purely a domestic manufacture, carried on exclusively by the women. Women also weave a coarse cloth from raw silk imported from China. The Javanese are widely known for the process of dyeing cloth known as *batik,* in which wax is applied to those parts of the cloth not to be dyed; the threads are dyed before weaving in a more complicated textile process known as *ikat.* Textiles of both *batik* and *ikat,* of great artistic merit, are worn by men and women alike. Paper of the nature of the ancient papyrus is a manufacture peculiar to the Javanese.

History.—Between the 1st century A.D. and 700 A.D. Java was overrun by Hindu princes from India, who introduced Buddhism. Javanese history at this period is written in the still existing magnificent remains of temples and other public buildings, which are plentifully scattered over the island. Near Prambanan (Brambanan) are the ruins of many Hindu temples, one of them dating from the 9th century, which are eloquent of the magnificence of the period in Java. At Borobudur (q.v.), near Magelang, is probably the largest Buddhist temple in the world; perched on the summit of a hill, above which it towers to a height of 120 feet, it is adorned with 998 bas-reliefs illustrating the life of Buddha. These and similar remains attest that the worship of Brahma and Buddha once prevailed in the island. Between 1335 and 1380 the state of Majapahit, in eastern Java, conquered the Sriwidjaja empire of Sumatra (which had had its beginnings in the 7th century) and extended its influence to include almost the whole of the Malay Archipelago. In turn, the Moslems had seized most of the colonies of Majapahit by about 1478, after a period of internecine strife, and by 1518 Majapahit itself had been totally destroyed. Bantam and Mataram were the most powerful Moslem states in 1511, when the Portuguese, the first of a succession of European traders, arrived. The Portuguese were followed in 1595 by the Dutch, who soon eclipsed them. In 1619 the Dutch established their capital on Java at Batavia, a town built on the site of Djakarta (Jakarta), chief port for the Sundanese kingdom of Padjadjaran, and from that point gradually extended their influence through most of the island. Java was occupied by the British from 1811 until 1816. In 1825 the Dutch authorities were confronted with a large-scale revolt which was not put down until 1830. The Dutch decreed abolition of slavery in Java on Sept. 20, 1859. The Javanese had never had slaves, and there were but a few thousand on the island. During World War II Java, together with all the Malay Archipelago, was occupied by Japanese forces. With Japan's surrender the Dutch attempted to reestablish their authority in Java, but were compelled to acquiesce in creating the independent Republic of Indonesia. Batavia, resuming its ancient name of Djakarta, became the capital of the republic in 1950. See also INDONESIA, REPUBLIC OF.

Bibliography.—Nyessen, D. J. H., *The Races of Java* (Batavia 1929); Ponder, H. W., *Javanese Panorama* (London 1942); Daniel, Hawthorne, *Islands of the East Indies* (New York 1944); Vandenbosch, Amry, *The Dutch East Indies* (Berkeley 1944); Flekke, B. H. M., *Nusantara* (Cambridge, Mass. 1945); Talbot, Phillips, *South Asia in the World Today* (Chicago 1950).

WHEELER B. PRESTON.

JAVA, The. See CONSTITUTION.

JAVA SEA, a body of water which is a part of the Pacific Ocean north of Java, south of Borneo, and east and south of Sumatra. It borders on a number of other islands, all small. It is about 200 miles wide and 600 miles long, but is very shallow, with a maximum depth of 300 feet. During World War II a battle between the Japanese Fleet and the Allied Nations was fought there, the Japanese being victorious.

JAVA SPARROW, a species of Oriental weaverbird (*Munia cryzivora*), called rice bird or paddy bird by the British in India and China, where it has become naturalized from its original home in Java. It has a poor song, but is kept in cages for its beauty and liveliness, and is sold by bird dealers all over the world. Its colors are slate blue and black, with conspicuous white cheeks and a swollen rosy bill. It is about seven inches from beak to tip of tail. The female is lighter in color. Fanciers have produced a pure white cage variety.

JAVAN JUNGLEFOWL. See POULTRY.

JAVARI, zhȧ-vȧ-rē′, or **YACARANA,** yȧ-kȧ-răʹnȧ, a river which has its rise on the Peru-Brazilian border, opposite Aguas Termales, Peru, in about latitude 6°S., flows northwest, then north and northeast into the Amazon River. The greater part of its course of 650 miles forms the boundary line between Brazil and Peru. It is navigable from the south to the Anahuacas Mountains.

JAVELIN, jăvʹlĭn, a short and light spear thrown from the hand and in ancient warfare used by both horse and foot soldiers. The *pilum* of the Romans was a weapon of this description and was used either to throw or to thrust with. The shaft was four and one-half feet long and the barbed iron head was of equal length, but as it extended half way up the shaft, the whole length of the weapon was nearly seven feet. The small spears of many savage tribes have been known by this name. The throwing of javelins was one of the contests in the Olympic games (q.v.).

JAVELLE WATER or **JAVEL WATER,** zhȧ-vĕlʹ, originally a solution containing potassium hypochlorite, obtained by mixing potassium carbonate, bleaching powder, and water. The liquid is employed as a disinfectant, as a bleaching agent, and in photography. The solution is now sodium hypochlorite. See also EAU—*Eau de Javelle;* HYPOCHLOROUS ACID.

JAWS, Anatomy of the. The upper jaw is formed by the union of the two superior maxillae; these bones each form part of the cheek, the outer wall of the nasal cavity, the hard palate and the lower part of the eye-socket. The lower jaw is formed of one bone, the inferior maxilla, which presents a horseshoe-shaped body, and vertical plates of bone ascending from the body posteriorly. The top of these vertical plates is widened into a knoblike end for articulation with the skull.

Dislocation of the jaw may take place during excessive laughter or yawning. The articular knob slips forward and the jaw is held open. Reposition is accomplished by placing the thumbs on the back teeth and making forcible downward and slightly backward pressure until the bone is felt to snap into place. Fracture of the upper jaw is uncommon except when the face is crushed in. Usually it is the body of the lower jaw near the front that is broken.

JAY, SIR James, American physician, brother of John Jay (q.v.): b. New York, Oct. 27, 1732; d. Springfield, N. J., Oct. 20, 1815. He received his medical degree from the University of Edinburgh in 1753, began practice in New York, became dissatisfied and went to London, where in 1762 he agreed to undertake to raise funds for King's College, now Columbia University. Rev. William Smith was there on a similar mission for what is now the University of Pennsylvania. Together they raised about £10,000 for each of the institutions. George III knighted him in 1763. After the outbreak of the Revolution, Jay, apparently sympathizing with the American cause, invented an ink which he used in communicating to the colonies military information obtained in England. He returned to America in 1778; was a member of the New York Senate, 1778–1782; and aided John Morin in bringing about the passage of the Act of Attainder (1779), confiscating the property of prominent New York Loyalists. In April 1782 he was captured by the British, but was released by Sir Guy Carleton, and allowed to go to England. Thereafter even his brother John doubted his patriotism. After practicing for a time in England and on the Continent, he returned to America. He was a trustee of the College of Physicians and Surgeons (New York), 1807–1811, and his name appeared in the charter of the college in 1791.

JAY, John, American statesman and jurist: b. New York, Dec. 12, 1745; d. Bedford, Westchester County, N. Y., May 17, 1829. His father was a wealthy merchant of Huguenot stock, and his mother a daughter of Jacobus Van Cortlandt. His father—early discovering, to use his own words, that Jay was of "a very grave disposition, and took to learning exceedingly well"—sent him to a school in New Rochelle similar to Dotheboys Hall in *Nicholas Nickleby.* Three years at school were followed by study under a tutor until he entered King's College at 14. He was graduated in 1764, the subject of his oration being the blessings of peace, of which he was to have still keener appreciation. Two weeks later, on payment of £200, he entered the office of Benjamin Kissam, a prominent lawyer of New York, as an apprentice bound to serve five years, the last two years to be devoted to the study of the law. Admitted to the bar in 1768, he soon attained prominence in the profession, forming a partnership with Robert R. Livingston, afterward chancellor of the state, and secretary of foreign affairs. In 1773 he began his public career, as secretary to the Royal Commission to determine the boundary between New York and Canada; and for the following 28 years his public services were constant, varied and of supreme importance to the country so fortunate in being his birthplace.

Bound by no ancestral ties to England, and having married in 1774 a daughter of the famous Whig and Revolutionary governor of New Jersey, William Livingston, many would suppose that in the conflict impending between the colonies and mother country, Jay's voice, like those of James Otis and Samuel Adams, would have been from the first «still for war.» But he was constitutionally so calm and conservative that he was unwilling to be too precipitate in determining upon a change in the mode of government. When, however, the colonists decided that their only safety lay in separation, Jay was found to be as staunch and aggressive a patriot as any, and represented the citizens of New York on the committee to settle the question arising out of the Boston Port Bill. Jay drafted the suggestion of that committee that «a Congress of Deputies from the Colonies in general» be convoked — in fact, the convocation of the Continental Congress. He was a member of that Congress, and met with it in Philadelphia on 5 Sept. 1774. Congress at once appointed a committee to «state the rights of the colonies in general,» of which Jay was made a member. This committee designated him to draft an address to the people of Great Britain, which was so satisfactory that it was at once reported to Congress, and adopted by it. Jefferson, without knowing who was the author, pronounced it «a production certainly of the finest pen in America.»

Jay was also sent to the 2d Continental Congress, but in the interim devoted himself to shaping the public mind in the direction of obedience to Congress and in hostility to enforcement of Parliamentary taxation. When the 2d Congress convened, the signal shot — «heard round the world» — had been fired at Lexington, and Congress, realizing that a condition of war existed, deputed Jay to draft an address to the people of Canada, which was prepared and adopted, and circulated in that country. He also wrote an address to the people of Jamaica and Ireland by request of Congress, but the second petition to the king that he prevailed upon Congress to make was written by Dickinson. Other important and effective work by him in that general direction might be cited, but I shall be content with the assertion I deem supported by the facts, that as a creator and molder of public opinion at that particular juncture Jay stands unrivaled; and all this was in the main accomplished through the wise use of his pen, the efficacy of which was strongly presented by John Adams when he wrote regarding it to Jefferson, «I never bestowed much attention to any of those addresses, which were all but repetitions of the same things; the same facts and arguments; dress and ornaments rather than body, soul or substance. I was in great error, no doubt, and am ashamed to confess it, for these things were necessary to give popularity to the cause, both at home and abroad.» Jay's contribution to the debates in Congress, like all his public work, showed that he followed in all things and upon all questions the path illuminated by the light of his well-balanced judgment, and his conscience, thinking not of personal popularity, but simply of the right. He served actively upon the committee that carried on negotiations with foreign powers friendly to America and inimical to England. Indeed, during the year 1775 he was a member of so many committees, each having different and important objects, that it is difficult to understand how he was able to accomplish so much important and laborious work.

If it be asked why so good a patriot as Jay was not a signer of the Declaration of Independence, the answer is, that in 1776, while a member of the Continental Congress, Jay was also elected to the New York Provincial Congress, and the Continental Congress having directed the colonies to each adopt a government, Jay, on the call of his colony, proceeded to New York to take part in the formation of the local government, where he was forced to remain while the Declaration of Independence was being signed. During 1777, and while the war was going on in the vicinity of New York, the Provincial Congress, then styled the Convention of the Representatives of the State of New York, was laboring with exceeding difficulty, the members, as is recorded, performing «all the various and arduous duties of legislators, soldiers, negotiators, committees of safety and ways and means, judges, juries, fathers and guardians of their own families, flying before the enemy, and then protectors of a beloved commonwealth.» Yet amid all this turmoil and unrest a constitution was drafted by Jay which was, in the main, adopted as drafted, and was published upon 22 April 1777, by being read in front of the courthouse in Kingston. A committee was at once appointed, Jay being a member, to organize a new government; and a council of safety was created to act until the legislature should meet. Robert R. Livingston was appointed chancellor and Jay chief justice, and the judicial department of government was temporarily organized.

Jay was urged to be a candidate for governor at the first election under the constitution, but declined. General Clinton was elected over his opponent, General Schuyler, and took the oath of office, it is said, while «clothed in the uniform of the service, standing on the top of a barrel in front of the Court-House in Kingston.» On 9 September following, Chief Justice Jay delivered an address to the grand jury at Kingston, which is to be found in the first volume of his correspondence and public papers. The address is a much prized document of Revolutionary times, and was, undoubtedly, intended to reach and affect a much larger constituency than the grand jury to whom it was delivered. Of course, in those unsettled days, with the struggle between the old and the new countries raging, but little litigation of importance came before the Supreme Court, so that during Jay's chief justiceship the work of the court was mainly confined to criminal trials, and the court never sat in banc. During 1778 he was active in the Council of Revision, of which he was a member ex-officio. The legislature in 1779 appointed Jay to Congress without requiring him to vacate the office of chief justice, it being resolved that owing to serious questions between certain States «a special case» obtained under the constitution. Shortly afterward Congress elected him its president. Later in the year, however, he resigned the office of chief justice, designing, he said, to recoup his failing fortunes. But his desires in that direction were not to be gratified. More than 20 years elapsed before the public he had served so well would submit to be deprived of his services.

In October, 1779, Jay resigned the presidency of Congress to accept the office of Minister to Spain. His instructions in part were to secure if possible a commercial treaty with Spain similar to that existing with France, to acquire a port in Spanish dominion on the Mississippi, and to negotiate a loan of $5,000,000. That his mission was not entirely successful, and was personally disagreeable, was due to the fact that Spain disliked the new nation because it occupied lands formerly held by Spain, and it was apprehended that with increasing strength it might reach out and take more — fears that we know now were not groundless. While Minister to Spain, Jay was appointed, with Franklin, Jefferson, Adams and Laurens, commissioner for a general peace. Their instructions rested on the mistaken theory that France would aid in procuring for us the best possible terms. In June 1782, Jay joined Franklin, then Minister to France, in Paris, and promptly but cautiously entered upon an investigation which disclosed that France had other interests to serve than those of the United States. Possessed of the situation, he boldly entered upon negotiations with England's representative without even consulting his only colleague in Paris, whom he regarded as necessarily embarrassed by his position as Minister to France, and his instructions. With firmness, and yet with great tact, he conducted the negotiations alone until joined by Adams, who enthusiastically approved of his action, and so advised Mr. Franklin, who, after consultation, agreed that the negotiations should be concluded without consulting the French court. The result of these most interesting negotiations with England was a treaty by which the United States gained more than Congress had ever ventured to propose. And Jay's part in this great triumph of diplomacy is well summed up in a letter written by his fellow commissioner John Adams to Jonathan Jackson, «a man and his office were never better united than Mr. Jay and the commission for peace. Had he been detained at Madrid, as I was in Holland, and all left to Franklin, as was wished, all would have been lost.» He was appointed by Congress Secretary of Foreign Affairs. This office he filled with his usual ability, settling international questions, and advocating the building of a navy, and the organization of a Federal government under a constitution. His papers in the *Federalist* evidence both his activity and forcefulness in this direction; and his influence contributed in no small degree in bringing New York to the support of the Federal Constitution.

It is said that after the first election of Washington to the presidency he offered Jay the choice of any office in the government, and that he chose that of chief justice of the Supreme Court of the United States, which he justly regarded as the most exalted position next to the presidency; but be that as it may, Washington appointed him to that position, and in his letter to Jay, advising him of the nomination, said, «I not only acted in conformity with my best judgment, but I trust I did a grateful thing to the good citizens of these United States.» His term of office was effective in shaping the foreign policy of the United States as well as in establishing the dignity and independence of the Federal judiciary. He resigned in 1795; but in the meantime and in 1792 the Federalists supported him unsuccessfully against Governor Clinton for the governorship of New York. In 1794 President Washington urged him to go to Great Britain as special envoy to settle differences growing out of the failure of that country to keep the obligations of the Treaty of 1784,— differences which had aroused a strong war spirit all over the land. It was easy for Jay to foresee that the outcome of the situation would in all probability be unpopular with the people, but he did not hesitate to meet the responsibility that Washington believed he could meet better than any other man, partly because of the reputation he had established in England while negotiating the Treaty of Peace of 1784. A treaty resulted, known on this side of the ocean as «Jay's Treaty,» which settled the eastern boundary of Maine; recovered for illegal captures by British cruisers $10,000,000; secured the surrender of the Western forts still garrisoned by the British, and came to a point of agreement about the West India trade. With the exception of the latter article the treaty was approved by the President and ratified by the Senate. But many were not satisfied, and they denounced him with tongue and pen, and even burned him in effigy in Boston, Philadelphia and at his own home, New York.

He found on his return that he had been elected governor of New York — before the public had knowledge of the terms of the treaty, of course. Before the close of that term, and in April 1799 he was re-elected by a majority so large as to constitute a personal triumph. During this term the statute was passed providing for the gradual emancipation of slaves within the State, then numbering about 22,000. The six years of his incumbency of the office of governor were crowded with interesting legislative and executive events in which he performed his part with that staunch devotion to the public interests which ever characterized his efforts throughout his career as a servant of the public, as is well illustrated by his refusal to be a party to the scheme of certain leaders of the Federalists to secure the electoral vote of New York for the ensuing election. The unexpected result of the spring elections of 1800 assured the Republicans of a substantial working majority on joint ballot, and hence of the Presidential electors under the law as it then stood. It was generally conceded that New York would determine the choice of the next President. Although the Federalists had, in March prior to the elections, defeated the attempt of the Republicans to redistrict the State, and had insisted that it was necessary that the State should act as a unit in the choice of Presidential electors, the leaders changed their position after the election had gone against them and insisted that the electors should be chosen by districts. Alexander Hamilton wrote Governor Jay on 7 May advising that he call an extra session of the legislature to enact such a statute before July first, the end of the legislative year. Philip Schuyler also wrote a letter strongly urging that such a course furnished the only means of saving the «nation from more disasters.» But Jay, although a staunch Federalist, who had received the votes of New Jersey and Delaware, five votes from Connecticut and one from Rhode Island for the Presidency in the preceding electoral college, refused to take such action, and endorsed on Hamilton's letter these words: «Proposing a measure for party purposes which I think it would not become me to adopt.» He refused a renomination for the office of governor on the ground that he now intended to retire from public life, and his purpose was unshaken by President Adams announcing to him his nomination and confirmation a second time as chief justice of the United States. This office he held until 1801 when he retired from public life.

Bibliography.—Jay, W., *Life of John Jay, with Selections from His Correspondence and Miscellaneous Papers* (New York 1833); Whitelocke, W., *Life and Times of John Jay* (New York 1887); Johnston, J. P., ed., *Correspondence and Public Papers of John Jay* (New York 1890–93).

ALTON B. PARKER,
Late Chief Judge of the Court of Appeals of the State of New York.

JAY, John, American diplomatist: b. New York, June 23, 1817; d. there, May 5, 1894. He was the son of William Jay, American jurist (q.v.). He was graduated from Columbia in 1836, studied law in New York, was admitted to the bar in 1839, became a prominent opponent of slavery, was secretary of the Irish Relief Committee in 1847, and was counsel for several fugitive slaves. He organized the meetings at the Broadway Tabernacle, New York, in 1854, and took a leading part in the organization of the Republican Party at Syracuse, Sept. 27, 1855. From 1869 until his resignation in 1874 he was United States minister to Austria, in 1877 was appointed chairman of the so-called Jay Commission for the investigation of the New York customhouse administration, and in 1884 was appointed the Republican member of the New York State Civil Service Commission. He was long corresponding secretary of the New York Historical Society and was one of the charter members of the Huguenot Society of America. In 1890 he became president of the American Historical Association.

JAY, William, American jurist: b. New York, June 16, 1789; d. Bedford, New York, Oct. 14, 1858. He was the son of John Jay, and after graduating from Yale in 1808, studied law with J. B. Henry at Albany. He was obliged by defective eyesight to withdraw from the profession, and became interested in various philanthropic movements, including the antislavery cause. He was a founder of the American Bible Society (1816) which he greatly promoted and long defended against attacks by Bishop John H. Hobart. From 1818 to 1843, with one small interruption, he was judge of the court of Westchester County, and he served as corresponding foreign secretary of the American Anti-Slavery Society from 1835–1837. He wrote much on antislavery, and was recognized as a leader of the more conservative of the abolitionists. Among his publications were *Life of John Jay,* 2 vols. (1833); *An Inquiry into the Character and Tendency of the American Colonization and American Anti-Slavery Societies* (1835); *War and Peace: The Evils of the First and a Plan for Preserving the Last* (1842); *Miscellaneous Writings on Slavery* (1853).

JAY, William, English Congregational clergyman and writer: b. Tisbury, Wiltshire, May 8, 1769; d. Bath, Dec. 27, 1853. After studying for the Congregational ministry, he officiated at Hope Chapel, near Bristol, and became pastor in 1791 of Argyle Chapel, Bath, where he remained until 1853. As a preacher he not only enjoyed a high celebrity in his own denomination, but won the applause of fastidious critics like John Foster, Richard B. Sheridan, and William Beckford. His sermons are esteemed as well for their catholic spirit as their practical earnestness and simplicity of style. His collected works were published in 12 volumes, 1842–1848; and his autobiography in 1854.

JAY, town, Maine, in Franklin County, situated on the Androscoggin River, 28 miles north of Lewiston, and served by the Maine Central Railroad. There are white granite quarries and large paper and pulp mills within the town limits. Pop. (1950) 3,102.

JAYADEVA, jŭ'yȧ-dā'vȧ, Hindu poet and dramatist: flourished about 1200 A.D. The time and details of his life are unknown, but his *Gītagōvinda,* the "Song of the Cowherd," is the only known example of the religious drama in Sanskrit. The drama is a lyric poem, divided into 12 short cantos, with the text providing for musical accompaniment, and is usually given a mystical interpretation. It delineates the love of Krishna, as a cowherd, for Radha, the milkmaid, his faithlessness and subsequent return to her, and is taken as symbolical of the human soul's straying from its true allegiance but returning at length to the God which created it. The work is of great poetic beauty and is remarkable for its melodious and truthful mirroring of passionate emotions. A native edition is that of Ishwar C. Vidyasagara (Calcutta 1882), and English translations are those of Sir William Jones (London 1799) and Sir Edwin Arnold, *The Indian Song of Songs* (London 1875).

JAYHAWKER, a name originating in Kansas during the slavery and antislavery warfare. It was applied to a few Free State men who organized a system of retaliation against proslavery outrages. Gov. James H. Lane of Kansas declared, in 1861, that "the people of Kansas were neither thieves, plunderers, nor jayhawkers."

JAYNE, Horace Fort, American biologist: b. Philadelphia, March 5, 1859; d. Wallingford, Pa., July 8, 1913. He was graduated at the University of Pennsylvania in 1879, received his M.D. there in 1882, and later studied at the University of Leipzig and under Ernst Haeckel at Jena. He became professor of biology at the University of Pennsylvania in 1884, and in 1896–1904 was professor of zoology there, as well as being director of the Wistar Institute of Anatomy and Biology (1894–1904). He was secretary of the biological faculty at the University of Pennsylvania in 1884–1889, and dean of the collegiate faculty in 1889–1894, when he resigned to accept an appointment as one of the trustees at Drexel Institute. Author of many scientific papers, he published "Descriptions of Some Monstrosities Observed in North American Coleoptera," *Transactions of the American Entomological Society,* vol. 8 (1880).

JAYS, jāz, a group of birds forming with the magpies a subfamily (Garrulinae) of the family Corvidae. They are readily distinguished from the true crows (Corvinae) by their relatively short wings, long conspicuous tails, and usually showy plumage, in which blue colors are prominent. They are generally smaller than the crows, have weaker and smaller bills, and feet better adapted to the more completely arboreal life which they lead. Jays are found throughout the greater part of the world, but America leads in number and variety of species. North America has four genera and 10 species with many additional local varieties. A familiar representative is the blue jay (*Cyanocitta cristata*), which is numerous throughout the eastern half of the United States and Canada. It is about one foot long, of which the tail is nearly half; the head conspicuously crested; purplish-blue above with a slight tinge of the same color on the generally gray underparts; the wings and tail are a nearly saturated blue in the males, duller in the females, cross-barred with black and with white markings especially conspicuous on the end of the tail; a rich black collar encircles the neck. The blue jay eats all kinds of nuts, fruits, large insects, and at times the eggs and young of other birds; it seldom leaves the trees in search of food, and when on the ground hops instead of walking like the crow. Except in Canada it is resident, and it breeds throughout its entire range. The nest, a large structure of twigs, grass and leaves, is built in trees, bushes or old buildings. Five is the usual number of eggs. Like the magpie, this jay is known to collect and hoard various glittering or brightly colored objects, but is chiefly noteworthy on account of the variety and quality of its notes which range from the harshest cries to full flutelike tones. On the Pacific Coast this species is replaced by the darker and duller Steller's jay (*C. stelleri*). The Canada jay, or whisky jack (*Perisoreus canadensis*) is, as its name indicates, a Northern bird, found within the United States only along the northern border, and occasionally breeding in northern Maine. This is a dull-colored gray bird, without a crest, and with soft, lax plumage. It is well known to hunters and lumbermen whose camps it haunts with great boldness; and in manners and voice resembles the blue jay. It nests very early in the spring. Related species are the Oregon jay (*P. obscurus*) and the Siberian jay (*P. infaustus*) of boreal Eurasia. Several species of crestless deep-blue "Florida" jays (*Aphelocoma*) inhabit Florida and the West and the Southwest. The brilliant green jay (*Xanthura luxuriosa*) is an example of the gorgeous tropical jays which just enter the United States in Texas. Consult the works of Wilson, Audubon, Nuttall and American ornithologists generally; for Western species in particular, Coues, Elliott, *Birds of the Northwest* (Washington 1874), *Birds of the Colorado Valley* (1878); Dresser, *Birds of Europe* (London 1879); Dawson and Bowles, *The Birds of Washington* (Seattle 1909); Keyser, L. S., *Birds of the Rockies* (Chicago 1902); Newton, William, *Dictionary of Birds* (London and New York 1893–96).

JAY'S TREATY, 1794. The Articles of Confederation provided that the states might nullify at will any provisions of whatever commercial treaty Congress might negotiate; of course, therefore, no nation with much commerce to be disturbed by our competition would make such treaties with us. Our chief commerce was with Great Britain; and that country would make no commercial treaty whatever with us, even for years after the Constitution had given Congress power to enforce its treaties. There were two main reasons for this: first, that Great Britain had valuable commercial monopolies (especially in the West Indies) for which she thought we could return no equivalent; second, she was angry over the *sequelae* of the Peace of 1783. She had agreed to surrender the border forts on the Great Lakes, the Saint Lawrence and Lake Champlain, and carry off no Negroes, on condition that Congress "recommend" to the states to restore confiscated Tory property, and agree to confiscate no more. Congress did so twice emphatically, but the states paid no attention to it; the British government, though it knew very well how much the recommendation meant, made this an excuse to retain the forts and refuse payment for 3,000 Negroes carried off; this in turn hardened the states to refuse compliance with the treaty, and the forts being made a basis for Indian outrages winked at by the British commandants enraged the country still more. The Republicans, who sympathized with the new French republic and hated Great Britain, held the House; the Federalists, whose sympathies were exactly opposite, the Senate by a small majority. On Dec. 16, 1793, Jefferson made a famous report on a House resolution, recommending retaliatory duties; and after an acrid debate the Republicans pushed through a nonintercourse resolution, only defeated even in the Senate by Vice President Adams' casting vote. But Washington threw his weight into the scale of peace, and nominated Chief Justice John Jay as envoy extraordinary to negotiate a commercial treaty. With Lord Granville he drew up one on Nov. 19, 1794, which removed the chief American grievance by surrendering the forts, but refused compensation for the Negroes and referred all other claims to commissioners; and as to commerce, allowed direct but not coasting trade between the United States and the British East and West Indies (the latter in vessels of not over 70 tons), but denied the United States the right to export sugar, molasses, coffee, cocoa or cotton to Europe—in other words, to become an intermediary for the British colonies to evade the British commercial monopoly; and limited even this provision to two years after peace with the powers then at war with Great Britain. There were also clauses which impliedly recognized British right of search and impressment, and power to make anything contraband. The treaty was ratified by the Senate in secret session (June 8, 1795), but when published excited an uproar of public indignation; Jay was burned in effigy, and even Washington vilified incredibly. The Virginia legislature and the Federal House practically passed votes of censure; but the people gradually came to recognize that it was the best thing to be had, hard as were the terms; the commercial bodies in the states openly commended it; Hamilton wrote his *Camillus* letters in its favor; and after a bitter struggle for many weeks in the House to refuse compliance with the Senate action, the treaty won by 51 to 48.

JAZZ, a type of popular American music closely associated with dancing and characterized in general by catchy melodies, complex rhythms, and varied orchestration. The etymology of the word is uncertain, and its source disputed, although a fairly credible origin for the term was supplied by Lafcadio Hearn, who found it in the Creole patois of New Orleans about 1880. It was his opinion that the Creoles had obtained it from the Negroes, and that it meant "to speed things up" as applied to music of a syncopated nature.

One of the two immediate ancestors of jazz was ragtime, which, in turn, drew upon such earlier minstrel show sources as the buck and wing, cakewalk, and jig. The majority of rags had no text, and were more instrumental than vocal in character. The basic rhythmic forms of ragtime were Negroid, and may be divided into two principal types known as primary and secondary rag. A common type of primary rag calls for an unaccented note in what is normally a position of stress in the measure, an accented note in what is normally an unstressed position. This is a typical device of syncopation, which is essentially a deliberate shifting or displacement of normal metrical accent. Primary rag likewise suppresses accents proper to the established rhythmic pulse and, by various means, anticipates and postpones them.

Secondary rag goes farther in that it sets up two independent rhythmic patterns whereby the melody may be in triple, while the accompaniment is in double time. Thus groups of three or six notes in the treble are played against an established 2/4 or 4/4 meter in the bass. Extended over several measures, secondary rag is considered to exceed the limits of syncopation, and to become what is defined in serious music as polyrhythm.

The second immediate ancestor of jazz was the "blues," a type of vocal music developed by the Southern Negro from his plantation work songs and spirituals. The blues took their name from the so-called "blue" (slightly flatted) notes characteristic of their melodies when sung. These flatted notes, falling as they did on the third and seventh degrees of the scale, gave a mournful, minor mode cast to the major tonality in which they were customarily established. Unlike ragtime, the blues usually had a text, the bittersweet nature of which dictated a declamatory style of rendering, an appropriately smooth rhythm, and a tempo slower than that of ragtime. The blues also made use of "barbershop" harmonies (highly chromatic chordal progressions) and an additional feature that later became a prominent jazz device—the "break." In its early form, the break was a brief, improvised instrumental cadenza containing much syncopation.

Jazz emerged as a synthesis of the more promising elements of ragtime and the blues. It seized upon ragtime's rhythmic patterns, particularly secondary rag, while from the blues, it acquired melodic and harmonic resources which were wanting in the somewhat bleak themes and limited harmony of typical ragtime. From the blues, jazz also assimilated a moderate tempo, a supple meter, and the potentialities for freedom and variety afforded by the improvised break.

Early jazz was "hot" jazz, which emphasized spontaneity, intensity, percussiveness, and dissonance. A pioneer jazz band, which might consist of clarinet, saxophone, trombone, banjo, piano, and drums, would select a tune, announce it once in order to establish a point of departure, and then proceed to develop it freely under the inspiration of the moment. The development was of at least two kinds, a free-for-all in which each instrument went its own way in melodic, harmonic, and rhythmic competition with the others, or a take-your-turn scheme by which each instrument took a solo in rotation, the others supplying a subdued background. This kind of music-making came to be known as a "jam session."

A reaction to hot jazz set in with the appearance of "sweet" jazz. This type sacrificed spontaneity and intensity in favor of softer, more conventional blandishments. Where the hot band played without written parts, beyond a mere sketch for the piano, the sweet band employed a full score, the players sticking to their parts as written and rehearsed. Suavity, languor, close coordination, and much prettiness, the product of dulcet harmonies and pleasant instrumental combinations, were the inevitable result. The sweet band also introduced a number of relatively mild instruments, such as the violin, double-bass, harp, chimes, and celeste, to offset the dominant brass and percussion of the traditional hot jazz combination, and certain sweet bands were ultimately expanded to a point where they approached the symphony orchestra in numbers and musical discipline.

Meanwhile, sweet jazz adopted the portamento style characteristic of the blues when sung, exaggerating it into the perpetually sliding manner of the crooner. Sweet jazz likewise reached out to various non-Negroid features of contemporary music: for example, melodic material of the sentimental ballad, or Viennese light opera species, and harmonic devices adapted from 19th century romanticism and 20th century impressionism. The jazz idiom was thus carried so far afield that it remained jazz only by virtue of the fact that it preserved the duple time of the fox trot which, during World War I, superseded the one-step and two-step. In the course of time, the fox trot became a general term that embraced such passing fancies as the Shimmy, the Charleston, and the Black Bottom, but it has never come to include the tango, rumba, or conga, although these dances have been incorporated gradually into the body of jazz in its widest application.

A reaction to the temporary predominance of sweet jazz came in the form of swing. Swing, apart from the possible innovation of a faintly rubato style in the playing of jazz, and such novelty as is involved in the swinging of the classics, is a re-emphasis of the freedom, intensity, and dissonance of hot jazz, but it includes an increased self-consciousness and professionalism. A by-product of this return to the past is boogie-woogie, which was heard at private Negro gatherings more than a decade prior to its public appearance in the mid-1930's. Boogie-woogie is a type of piano blues that consists of a fixed rhythmic figure in the left hand, above which the right hand improvises freely.

The history of ragtime is not too well documented, yet there are a few landmarks of tolerable accuracy. Making its appearance near the close of the last century with such an early example (1895) as *Harlem Rag,* by the pianist, T. M. Turpin, ragtime was featured by the pioneering band of Buddy King Bolden, at New Orleans, from about 1895 onwards, and by another pianist, Ben Harney, who began a series of New York appearances at Tony Pastor's in 1897. The first New York stage presentation of ragtime is said to have taken place at Proctor's Theatre in 1905, when William Marion Cook's Memphis Students played a number of rags.

The recorded history of the blues is introduced by the now famous *Memphis Blues,* composed by the cornetist and band leader, W. C. Handy. This piece was published in 1912, although it had been written three years earlier. Handy's equally well-known *St. Louis Blues* dates from 1914. Intended, at the outset, to be sung, the blues had a great exponent in Bessie Smith, and they remained essentially vocal until the advent of exclusively instrumental blues such as Duke Ellington's *Blue Light.*

Although the word "jazz" is considered to have first appeared in print during the year 1916, the musical form it represents can be traced to examples predating World War I. Transitional types, falling between ragtime and the blues, on the one hand, and true jazz on the other, are credited to the pianist-composer, Ferdinand "Jelly Roll" Morton, whose *King Porter Stomp* and *Tiger Rag* pointed the way for many successors in the hot jazz manner. From about 1912, jazz (hot) began to migrate from its birthplace in the red-light district of New Orleans, and was carried northward to Chicago by Brown's Band from Dixieland; eastward to New York by the same band, and also by the orchestras of Jim Europe; and westward to San Francisco by Art Hickman, whose white musicians introduced a somewhat sweetened variety at the St. Francis Hotel during 1914.

Sweet jazz owes much to Paul Whiteman, who is credited with the first playing of jazz from fully scored parts at Los Angeles, in 1920. Whiteman's pianist and arranger, Ferde Grofé, became widely known for his effective scoring of jazz music, through which jazz reached semi-symphonic proportions. Whiteman toured the United States and Europe with great success, particularly during the 1920's, establishing a landmark by his jazz concerts, first in Aeolian Hall, then in the much larger Carnegie Hall, New York. The Aeolian performance, which took place on Feb. 12, 1924, and was attended by the first-string music critics of the metropolitan newspapers, was the first jazz concert ever given. The program was high-lighted by the debut performance of George Gershwin's *Rhapsody in Blue,* a brilliantly impressionistic work for piano and orchestra in the jazz idiom.

Continuing his interest in symphonic jazz, Gershwin followed his *Rhapsody in Blue* with a Concerto for Piano and Orchestra; the tone-poem, *An American in Paris;* a Second Rhapsody; a set of Preludes for Piano (later scored for orchestra); and a Negro folk-opera, *Porgy and Bess* (1935), which was revived for a long run on Broadway in 1942. By means of their freshness and originality, these works made Gershwin the first prominent composer to win simultaneous recognition both in Tin Pan Alley and the concert room without undue concession to either. A vein of true creativeness bridged the supposedly impassable gulf between the two worlds.

Although preoccupation on the part of serious composers with jazz music and jazz performers may be said to have reached a peak both in America and Europe about the middle of the 1920's, ragtime and jazz influences can be found in their output as far back as 1908, the publication year of *The Golliwog's Cake Walk* from *The Children's Hour* by Achille Claude Debussy. Three additional early contributions were made by Igor Stravinsky with his *Piano Rag-Music, Ragtime* (for eleven instruments), and the *Story of a Soldier* (1918).

Apart from Gershwin, and by way of supplement to the contributions to jazz music by Stravinsky and Debussy mentioned above, the following representative list of European and American composers and their compositions which employ ragtime and jazz will serve to indicate the extent to which these musical forms invaded the art music of the 20th century: John Alden Carpenter, Concertino for Piano and Orchestra featuring ragtime (1915); also Carpenter's ballet, *Krazy Kat,* containing sections labelled *Fox Trot* and *Blues* (1922); likewise the same composer's ballet entitled *Skyscrapers,* using fox trot rhythms and blues melodies (1926); Aaron Copland, Concerto for Piano and Orchestra, which employes Charleston rhythms and special jazz mutes for trombone (1926); Morton Gould, *Chorale and Fugue in Jazz* (1936); Louis Gruenberg, *The Daniel Jazz,* scored for small ensemble and solo voice, text by the American poet, Vachel Lindsay (1924); Paul Hindemith, *1922,* a suite for piano, with movements designated "Shimmy" and "Ragtime" (1922); Arthur Honegger, Concertino for Piano and Orchestra, in jazz rhythms (1925); Ernest Krenek, *Jonny Spielt Auf,* known in English as *Johnny Strikes Up the Band,* an opera having a Negro band leader as hero and sections marked "Shimmy," "Blues," and "Spiritual" (1925); Constant Lambert, *Rio Grande,* a composition for voices and orchestra containing jazz rhythms (1918); Darius Milhaud, *Le Boef sur le Toit,* known in English as *The Nothing-doing Bar,* a ballet with jazz rhythms, and the same composer's *La Création du Monde* (*The Creation of the World*), a ballet based on a scenario by Blaise Cendrars, treating of the creation of the world according to African Negro legends, and including a fugue on a jazz subject, a blues section, and an extended melodic passage with a barbershop harmonic accompaniment (1923); Maurice Ravel, Sonata for Violin and Piano, of which the second movement is a blues (1927); and Erik Satie, *Parade,* a ballet written for the Russian impresario, Sergei P. Diaghilev, and carrying the sub-title, *Ragtime du Paquebot* (1917).

Serious composers have been attracted to jazz by its rhythmic possibilities, by the uncommon tonal qualities to be had from special jazz handling of familiar instruments, and, above all, by a spirit of freedom and crisp candor rarely absent from genuine hot jazz and its performers. Composers have been less interested in the emotional gamut of jazz because it tends to generate only two fundamental moods—the melancholy of the blues and the abandoned exhilaration of jive. The commercial moonlight and roses of *My Blue Heaven* or *I'll Buy That Dream* stem rather from the sentimental ballad (Jerome Kern, Sigmund Romberg) than from jazz.

The interest of Tin Pan Alley in so-called classical music has likewise been conspicuous and persistent. Early borrowings, such as a theme from Frédéric F. Chopin's *Fantasie-Impromptu* as the melodic basis of *I'm Always Chasing Rainbows,* and the considerable thematic assistance rendered to *Yes, We Have No Bananas* by the *Hallelujah Chorus* in George Frederick Handel's oratorio, *Messiah,* have sired a numerous progeny. Various classics have been swung, from time to time, prominent examples including a theme from a Mozart piano sonata, which was turned into a fox trot and renamed *In An Eighteenth Century Drawing Room;* Ignace Paderewski's *Minuet à L'Antique;* and Franz Liszt's *Liebestraum.*

Other standard instrumental works have been dealt with more radically, emerging from the musical sausage factory as popular songs. Among these may be cited the transformation of the opening theme of Peter Ilich Tschaikovsky's Piano Concerto in B Flat Minor into *Tonight We Love,* and the yet more drastic metamorphosis of one of Chopin's most virile polonaises into the sentimental ballad (sweet jazz type) *Till the End of Time.* The last is an example of the way in which commercial ballyhoo can disseminate false impressions, in this instance to the effect that there is such a thing as a one and only polonaise by Chopin; that his music is all sweet tea and ladyfingers; and that the greatest of composers for the piano was capable of a creation full of national pride and fiery rebelliousness which could, nevertheless, be appropriately set to maudlin words and fittingly scored for crooner and orchestra. It is the false-to-fact and false-to-probability aspect of this particular brand of musical popularization that is more harmful to the national culture than mere false-to-art tinkering with master works for unearned profit.

The renascence of hot jazz in the form of swing has acquired great momentum through the playing, and the recordings, of highly expert jazz bands under the leadership of such men as Louis Armstrong, Duke Ellington, the Dorsey brothers (Tommy and Jimmy), and Benny Goodman, to name only a representative few. Further, this leadership has proved genuinely creative to the extent that it has reaffirmed the importance to any art form of innovation, imagination, and a high order of technical skill, not to mention wide popular acceptance. Swing at its best has likewise helped to keep alive the practice of musical improvisation, which reached its zenith in Beethoven's time but suffered a gradual decline in Western music until a fresh impetus was supplied by early ragtime and jazz performers. Enthusiasts rightly place emphasis upon the extempore element in hot jazz, and are justified in regarding it as the hallmark of the gifted swing musician.

Throughout its history, religion and education have tended to look askance at the influence of jazz on American life exerted through its undoubted hold upon youth. Its dubious origins, its relentless ding-dong between the exaggerated self-pity of the blues and the frenzy of jive, both pervaded by a more or less obvious eroticism, have been widely deplored, while its exploitation of imported dances like the tango and the rumba have been vigorously protested. The advent of the tango in particular, based as it is upon the suggestive patterns of the Spanish habanera, provoked the churches to open denunciation, and efforts were made to supplant it by more conservative dances of a similar type.

A more effective, because less repressive, countermeasure to the alleged excesses of hot jazz is sweet jazz. Typically less headlong in tempo, and of a romantic rather than frenetic character, it evokes the comparatively decorous responses of the traditional fox trot. Moreover, it may be contended that even the hottest jazz affords the jitterbug a least a quasi-therapeutic release of surplus energy that otherwise might be yet more antisocially directed, jazz thus approaching the status of a sport and as such affording its devotees the customary benefits of any vigorous, cheerful, and unreflective activity.

That jazz will one day emerge as the American art music of the future remains, everything considered, problematical. Although it is undeniably interesting to the analytic mind, and stimulating to the creative spirit, and is, at the same time, inseparable from so deeply intrenched a form of popular recreation as dancing, jazz as music has as yet made but a narrow appeal to the emotive life of man, whereby enduring art has thus far been nourished and sustained.

Bibliography.—Osgood, H. O., *So This is Jazz* (Boston 1926); Whiteman, P., *Jazz* (New York 1926); Armstrong, L., *Swing That Music* (New York 1936); Panassié, H., *Hot Jazz* (London 1936); Scholes, P. A., *Oxford Companion to Music* (London, New York, 1938); Ramsay, F., and Smith, C. E., *Jazzmen* (New York 1939); Goodman, B., and Kolodin, I., *The Kingdom of Swing* (Harrisburg, Pa., 1939); Hobson, W., *American Jazz Music* (New York 1939); Miller, P. E., ed., *Down Beat's Yearbook of Swing* (Chicago 1939); Thompson, O., ed., *Cyclopedia of Music and Musicians* (New York 1939); *Grove's Dictionary of Music and Musicians,* supplementary volume (New York 1940); Delaunay, C., *Hot Discography* (Paris 1941); Handy, W. C., *Father of the Blues, an Autobiography* (New York 1941); Howard, J. T., *This Modern Music* (New York 1942); Panassié, H., *The Real Jazz* (New York 1942); *Harvard Dictionary of Music* (Cambridge 1944).

Markham Harris,
Formerly of the Department of English, Williams College; Student of Piano and Theory of Music.

JEAFFRESON, John Cordy, English author: b. Framlingham, Suffolk, Jan. 14, 1831; d. London, Feb. 2, 1901. His first novel *Crewe Rise* (1854) was followed by a lengthy series in the three-volume type then popular, among them *Live it Down* (1863) and *Not Dead Yet* (1864), which were moderately successful. He was appointed inspector of documents for the Historical Manuscript Commission in 1874, and from 1858 until his death he was a contributor to the *Athenaeum.* He wrote five popular works of two volumes each, of anecdotal social history *A Book about Doctors* (1860); *A Book about Lawyers* (1866); *A Book about the Clergy* (1870); *Brides and Bridals* (1872); *A Book about the Table* (1874). His duties as inspector of documents gave him access to manuscript collections which resulted in his publication of *The Real Lord Byron,* 2 vols. (1883); *The Real Shelley,* 2 vols. (1885); *Lady Hamilton and Lord Nelson,* 2 vols. (1888); *The Queen of Naples and Lord Nelson,* 2 vols. (1889; new ed., 1897).

JEAN CHRISTOPHE, zhăṅ krĭs'tŏf, by Romain Rolland. One of the most noteworthy novels to appear in France, from the death of Zola to the opening of World War I, was the *Jean Christophe* of Romain Rolland. Its importance lies partly in the novelty of its informal manner and partly in the range and importance of its theme. With regard to manner, Rolland has put away rhetoric and eloquence, climax, dramatic effect and all the traditional methods of the novelist, to tell his story in the simple language of conversation and to follow in his meandering and now and then clogged and almost tedious narrative, the slow moving processes of life. With regard to his theme, he had set himself the task of studying the unfolding of a musical genius, tracing him from infancy through childhood and adolescence in Germany, to full maturity in Paris, at a time of unsettled, shifting, and conflicting ideals. This gradual unfolding of the temperament of Jean Christophe provides the principle of unity which links the 10 small volumes of the French edition. But the analysis of Jean Christophe's psychology is but one element of interest; for the larger aspects of the theme imposed themselves upon the author as he proceeded and as he brings his hero into contact with the ruling classes in Germany, with newfound French friends and with the world of music and letters. His minute study of a single great man thus widens, until it becomes a dispassionate yet keen survey of the national ideals of leading European peoples in the somber twilight that marked the closing of the 19th century. Teacher and critic rather than great creative artist, Rolland had been moved to write the history of the inner life of the generation that came to maturity before World War I and to present its account to posterity.

The task was a large one and the results were uneven. The earlier volumes, especially the first, dealing with the childhood of Jean Christophe in the old-fashioned south German town, have the clearness, quaintness and charm of old engravings and are artistically the most perfect. As he proceeds and his subject broadens, the author loses himself in disquisitions on art and politics, but especially on music, which even when correct in substance are out of focus. The later volumes therefore give an impression of diffuseness and lack of artistic mastery and are marked by the touch of resentment of one who had struggled long and bitterly for recognition. No author of the time, however, had shown greater penetration, and the contrast between Teuton and Latin character and civilizations was clearly and truthfully drawn. Rolland knew the hidden springs from which France drew her strength and was conscious of the coming "revival" of the spirit of France. He foresaw also the rapidly approaching era of force and war, and his later volumes read like a prophecy of the coming cataclysm which he deplored. This is a testimony to the truth of his diagnosis. When, however, after the outbreak of the war he pleaded in *Above the Conflict,* as he had done in his novel, for mutual understanding, he was disowned by the generation which had earlier acclaimed him as its spokesman.

When all is said, in spite of the touches of sourness, of inconsistencies, tiresome disquisitions, and occasionally grotesque psychology, Rolland's scope and range, his earnestness, sincerity and vision mark his work as one of the truly important achievements in French prose fiction of the early 20th century.

CHRISTIAN GAUSS,
Late Dean of the College, Princeton University.

JEAN DE MEUNG, zhän′ dẽ mün′ (real name JEAN or JEHAN CLOPINEL or CHOPINEL), French poet: b. Meung-sur-Loire, France, ?1240; d. ?1305. According to tradition, he studied at the University of Paris. His literary fame rests on his authorship of the greater part of the *Roman de la Rose* (q.v.), the most famous French poem of the 13th century, of which Geoffrey Chaucer was to make good use in *The Canterbury Tales.* The first part of the *Roman* consisting of 4,669 lines was the work of Guillaume de Lorris who died some time before 1240. Internal evidence indicates that the additional 18,000 lines were composed by Jean de Meung some time between 1268 and 1285. It is by far the more important section of the poem. In theme and spirit the two authors are in striking contrast: de Lorris began the work as an allegory to teach the art of love to courtiers and their ladies; de Meung, with an immense scientific and literary learning, continued it as a satire on the social system of his day, his shafts striking all the vested interests with perfect impartiality. The poem entitles Jean de Meung to rank as the greatest of French medieval poets; its skeptical, mocking spirit is echoed down the centuries in the writings of prose writers as well as poets. Other works of de Meung include a translation of the *De re militari* of Vegetius, appearing as *Le Livre de Vegèce de l'art de chevalerie* (1284); the first French version of the letters of Abélard and Héloïse; a translation of Boethius' *De consolatione philosophiae.* Toward the end of his life appeared his *Testament* in which, while praising sincere piety, he poured his scorn on the monastic orders.

Consult: Paris, Paulin, "Jean de Meung," vol. 28 in *Histoire littéraire de la France* (Paris 1840); Langlois, C. V., introduction to his 1914 ed. of *Roman de la Rose.*

JEAN PAUL. See RICHTER, JEAN PAUL FRIEDRICH.

JEANERETTE, jĕn-ĕr-ĕt′, town, Louisiana, in Iberia Parish, 32 miles east of Lafayette, situated on the Bayou Teche, and served by the Missouri Pacific and Southern Pacific railroads and state highways. Located in a rich agricultural section producing pecans, rice, and sugar cane, it has six sugar refineries, a cane cutter factory, and a boiler works. Other manufactures include agricultural machinery, boats, wood and machine shop products, and mattresses. The town has a library and a municipal airport. Nearby is a federal livestock experimental station. Pop. (1950) 4,692.

JEANES, jēnz, **Anna T.,** American Quaker philanthropist: b. Philadelphia, April 7, 1822; d. Germantown, Pa., Sept. 24, 1907. She was deeply interested in charitable and educational institutions and gave freely to their support, as well as to projects for the elevation of the Negro race in the United States. By her will she disposed of her estate, worth over $5,000,000, among 30 charitable institutions, also giving $200,000 to the Friends Boarding Home, Germantown, Pa., to which she retired in her last years. She also gave $1,000,000 as a "Fund for Rudimentary Schools for Southern Negroes," known as the Anna T. Jeanes Foundation (q.v.).

JEANES (Anna T.) FOUNDATION, a fund of $1,000,000 placed under the trusteeship of Booker T. Washington and Hollis B. Frissell, April 1907, by Anna T. Jeanes, for the purpose of "assisting in the southern United States community, country and rural schools for the great class of Negroes to whom the small rural and community schools are alone available." The work of the foundation is closely allied with that of the General Education Board. It concerns itself chiefly with industrial education, extension work, and the improvement of educational and home conditions.

JEANNE D'ARC. See Joan of Arc.

JEANNETTE, jĕ-nĕt', city, Pennsylvania, in Westmoreland County, located 22 miles east-southeast of Pittsburgh. Jeannette is in an agricultural and coal mining region, and has plentiful natural gas. The city has several industries. Manufactures include window glass and pressed glassware of many varieties, rubber tires and tubes, turbines, condensers, and electrical equipment. Settled in 1888 and incorporated in 1889, Jeannette is called the "Glass City" from having grown up around glass works founded in 1889 by a group including H. Sellers McKee, for whose wife it was named. Pop. (1940) 16,220; (1950) 16,172.

JEANNETTE EXPEDITION, an enterprise projected in 1879 by James Gordon Bennett, Jr., of the New York *Herald,* who sent out an Arctic expedition for exploration by way of the Bering Strait in the *Jeannette,* under the command of George Washington De Long, United States Navy. Sailing from San Francisco, Calif., the *Jeannette* was early caught in the ice pack, drifted for nearly two years, and never escaped from its grip. After the *Jeannette* sank on June 13, 1881, the crew attempted to reach Siberia in three open boats. One boat disappeared, and that of chief engineer George Wallace Melville reached an eastern mouth of the River Lena; De Long, with 14 companions, reached the main mouth of the Lena but died shortly afterward from exposure. Melville recovered his body and brought it to New York City, which he reached in May 1882. In June 1938 a Russian party found De Long's indecipherable diary in an improperly sealed copper cylinder on Henrietta Island, which the explorer had named.

Consult Ellsberg, E., *Hell on Ice* (New York 1938); De Long, E. W., *Explorer's Wife* (New York 1939).

JEANS, Sir **James Hopwood,** English physicist, astronomer, and author: b. London, Sept. 11, 1877; d. Dorking, Surrey, Sept. 16, 1946. He graduated at Trinity College, Cambridge University, with high distinction in mathematics in 1898, and in 1904 was appointed university lecturer in mathematics. From 1905 to 1909 he was professor of applied mathematics at Princeton University, and during 1910–1912 he was Stokes lecturer in applied mathematics at Cambridge. In 1919 he was appointed secretary of the Royal Society, a post he continued to occupy until 1929; he was also professor of astronomy in the Royal Institution during 1924–1929, and again from 1934. From 1923 to 1944 he was research associate of Mount Wilson Observatory, in California. As a physicist, he devoted much attention to the kinetic theory of gases and aspects of radiation; and as an astronomer, he was concerned with mathematical analysis of problems in the field of cosmogony. He propounded theories of the effect of gravitational motion on the motion of stars, and of the nature and formation of binary stars, spiral nebulae, giant and dwarf stars, and gaseous stars. His numerous works, some of them popularizing science, included *A Dynamical Theory of Gases* (1904); *Theoretical Mechanics* (1906); *The Mathematical Theory of Electricity and Magnetism* (1908); *Radiation and the Quantum-Theory* (1914); *Problems of Cosmogony and Stellar Dynamics* (1919); *Atomicity and Quanta* (1926); *Astronomy and Cosmogony* (1928); *The Universe Around Us* (1929); *The Mysterious Universe* (1930); *The Stars in Their Courses* (1931); *Through Space and Time* (1934); *Science and Music* (1937); *An Introduction to the Kinetic Theory of Gases* (1940); *Physics and Philosophy* (1942).

JEBB, Sir **(Hubert Miles) Gladwyn,** British diplomat: b. Rotherham, Yorkshire, April 25, 1900. From Eton, he went to Magdalen College, Oxford University, where he graduated with honors in history in 1922. Entering the diplomatic service, he served in Teheran (Tehran) and Rome, and at the Foreign Office in London. During the early years of World War II he was attached to the Ministry of Economic Warfare, and in 1942 he returned to the Foreign Office to head its reconstruction department, concerned with postwar problems. In March 1943 he visited Washington, D.C., in company with Foreign Secretary Anthony Eden to discuss prospects for a United Nations organization, and he subsequently went to the Dumbarton Oaks Conference, in Washington, and to the conference at Yalta where President Franklin D. Roosevelt and Winston Churchill met with Marshal Stalin. He was a leading British delegate to the San Francisco Conference in the spring of 1945 when the United Nations Charter was signed, and in August of that year he became executive secretary of the United Nations Preparatory Commission—which worked out detailed plans for the organization. In 1946 he deputized for Foreign Secretary Ernest Bevin at the Paris Conference which evolved the Italian peace treaty, and in 1948, with the personal rank of ambassador, he was British representative on the Brussels Treaty Permanent Commission. He was knighted in 1949. In March 1950 he succeeded Sir Alexander Cadogan as Great Britain's permanent representative to the United Nations.

JEBB, Sir **Richard Claverhouse,** Scottish Greek scholar: b. Dundee, Aug. 27, 1841; d. Cambridge, Dec. 9, 1905. He was educated at the Charterhouse, London, and at Trinity College, Cambridge University. From 1875 until 1889 he was professor of Greek at the University of Glasgow, and thereafter he occupied a like chair at Cambridge until his death. From 1891 he was also member of Parliament for Cambridge University. In 1874 he married the widow of Gen. Adam J. Slemmer, American army officer, and he paid several visits to the United States. He published translations, with notes, of several of the Greek writers; his greatest work was his edition of Sophocles, which was regarded as the most completely satisfactory commentary on a classical author that has been written in the English language. He was knighted in 1900, and received the Order of Merit in 1905.

JEDBURGH, jĕd'bŭ-rŭ, burgh, Scotland, county town of Roxburgh, located on the Jed, a tributary of the Teviot, 56 miles southeast of Edinburgh. Here is a stately ruined abbey founded as a priory for the Augustinian monks in 1118 or 1138 and erected into an abbey by David I in 1147. The castle, erected by David in 1174 and occupied by William the Lion and other Scottish kings, was leveled by the townspeople in 1409. The site was occupied by a prison in 1823, but the building fell into disuse and is now known as the castle. There are standing houses in which Mary Queen of Scots lived in 1566, and where Prince Charles Edward resided in 1745. The town was sacked and burned many times during the Border strife. The modern town has an excellent grammar school, fine county buildings, library, public hall and two public parks. Industries include the manufacture of woolen blankets and hosiery, breweries, tanneries, iron foundries, and the town is noted for its pears and garden produce. Pop. police borough 4,270.

JEDDAH, Arabia, (Arabic, *Juddah*), the chief trading port on the Red Sea, 60 miles west of Mecca, in the kingdom of Saudi Arabia. It is a walled city containing many fine buildings and wide streets. The custom house and the mosques are the chief structures. The city is very prosperous but is handicapped by a bad water supply and an exceedingly sultry climate, the latter very trying to Europeans. In early times Jeddah was about the only point of commercial contact between Asia and Africa, and its commerce frequently reached the great sum of $4,500,000 annually. In late years this commerce has declined to about $1,000,000. The city is the centre of the trade in pearls, mother-of-pearl, coral, balsam, coffee, aromatic herbs, horses, Oriental rugs and carpets, etc. Thousands of pilgrims to Mecca pass through the city annually, and catering to their needs is an important source of income to the inhabitants. There are two lines of steamers to Suez and other lines touch here. The tomb of Eve, one of the holy places of Islam, is just without the city. Jeddah was long in the hands of the Egyptians; fell to Turkey in 1840 and in 1858 was the scene of the murder of Christian missionaries. In the July following, an English war vessel besieged the city for three days. During the World War it was included in the new kingdom of Hedjaz, and on the fall of the latter was included in Saudi Arabia. Pop. about 20,000.

JEDIDAH, wife of Amon, king of Judah, the daughter of Adaiah of Bozkath, and mother of Josiah, one of the most enlightened of the kings of Judah.

JEFFERIES, Richard, English author and naturalist: b. near Swindon, 6 Nov. 1848; d. Goring, 14 Aug. 1887. He was practically self-educated, but inherited from his father, a small farmer, a love for the beauties of the country and strongly developed powers of observation. His early literary efforts, including the writing and publishing of several novels, bore scanty fruits, and his first literary production of importance was 'The Wiltshire Labourer,' published in the *Times* in 1872. In 1873 he began writing for *Fraser's Magazine* on 'Farms and Farming,' and in 1877 he achieved a considerable success by his publication in the *Pall Mall Gazette* of his series 'The Gamekeeper at Home.' His work combined beauty of expression amounting at times to prose poetry, with the acute observation of a naturalist, and his succeeding productions found an appreciative circle of admirers. His health began to break in 1881, and for the last two years of his life his work was dictated to his wife. He wrote 'The Gamekeeper at Home' (1878); 'Wild Life in a Southern County' (1879); 'Bevis' (1882); 'The Story of My Heart' (1883); 'Life of the Fields,' containing the remarkable paper, 'The Pageant of Summer' (1884); 'After London' (1885); 'Amaryllis at the Fair' (1887), etc. Too proud to make known the straightened circumstances occasioned by his many illnesses, Jefferies died harassed by poverty, but the sympathy aroused at his death caused the grant of a pension to his wife. Consult Besant, Sir W., 'Eulogy of Richard Jefferies' (1888); Salt, H. S., 'Richard Jefferies, a Study' (1894); Thomas, E., 'Richard Jefferies, His Life and Work' (1909).

JEFFERS, Wellington, Canadian clergyman: b. Cork, Ireland, 1814; d. 1896. While Wellington was still a youth he removed with his parents to Kingston, Ontario. After making his preparatory theological studies and the regular theological course he was ordained in 1841 to the ministry of the Wesleyan Methodist Church. From 1841 to 1884 he held several important pastorates within the boundaries of Ontario. He served also as district chairman for several years, was secretary of the conference in 1853, was appointed co-delegate in 1866 and in 1879 was president of the conference. He retired from active duty in 1884. From 1860 to 1869 Mr. Jeffers was editor of the official organ of his church—the *Christian Guardian*. As a pulpit orator he had few peers in Canada and was famous as an extempore speaker. In theological matters Jeffers belonged to the conservative, traditional group of his church among the members of which he wielded a powerful influence. Victoria University gave him the honorary degree of D.D. in 1863.

ELLESMERE I.
Arctic
Baffin Bay
GREENLAND
WRANGEL I.
VICTORIA I.
BAFFIN I.
Godthaab
ALASKA
Nome
Hudson Bay
Bering Sea
Juneau
North
KAMCHATKA PENIN.
CANADA
ALEUTIAN IS.
Vancouver
Montreal
Quebec
Ottawa
Toronto
St. John's
North Pacific
Chicago
Atlantic
New York
UNITED STATES
San Francisco
Denver
Washington
AZORES
Ocean
Los Angeles
New Orleans
Houston
BERMUDA
Ocean
Gulf of Mexico
MIDWAY IS.
MEXICO
Havana
BAHAMAS
Honolulu
HAWAIIAN IS.
CUBA
HAITI
WAKE
Mexico City
BR. HON.
VIRGIN IS.
DOM. REP.
PUERTO RICO
GUATEMALA
HON.
Caribbean Sea
CAPE VERDE IS.
NIC.
EL SALVADOR
Caracas
MARSHALL IS.
CLIPPERTON
COSTA RICA
VENEZUELA
BIKINI
PANAMA
GILBERT IS.
COLOMBIA
Bogotá
GUIANAS
EQUATOR
GALÁPAGOS IS.
Quito
ECUADOR
SOLOMON IS.
ELLICE IS.
MARQUESAS IS.
PERU
BRAZIL
SAMOA
Lima
NEW HEBRIDES
TUAMOTU ARCH.
La Paz
FIJI IS.
BOLIVIA
Rio de Janeiro
NEW CALEDONIA
SOCIETY IS.
Sucre
PARAGUAY
Asunción
São Paulo
PITCAIRN IS.
South Pacific
CHILE
URUGUAY
Santiago
Buenos Aires
Montevideo
Tasman Sea
NEW ZEALAND
Wellington
ARGENTINA
Ocean
FALKLAND IS.
N
TIERRA del FUEGO
S. GEORGIA
S. ORKNEYS
S. SHETLAND IS.
PALMER PENINSULA
ANTARCTICA